The ENCY
Of SI

Fifth Re

The Encyclopedia of

SPORTS

5th Revised Edition

FRANK G. MENKE

Revisions by

SUZANNE TREAT

South Brunswick and New York: A.S. Barnes and Company
London: Thomas Yoseloff Ltd

© 1944, 1947, 1953, 1960, 1963, 1969, and 1975
by A.S. Barnes and Co., Inc.

A.S. Barnes and Co., Inc.
Cranbury, New Jersey 08512

Thomas Yoseloff Ltd
108 New Bond Street
London W1Y OQX, England

Library of Congress Catalogue Card Number: 73-10529

ISBN 0-498-01440-1

Printed in the United States of America

CONTENTS

FOREWORD

The Encyclopedia of Sports, conceived as a paperback pamphlet many years ago by the late Frank G. Menke, is now an impressive book of more than 1000 pages.

In it, the reader may find the complete history of nearly 80 sports which range from the violent world of pro football to the more gentle shuffleboard.

The athletic life stories of thousands of men and women who have flashed through the headline sky ever since sports history was first recorded are in these pages. Both the casual reader and the more serious researcher will find herein thousands of items which will bring memories of the thrilling history of any recognized sport he cares to recall.

This revision is the result of several factors: first, the dedication of the athletes themselves who wrote these pages with their feet and hands and brains and their determination to be the best; second, the co-operation of several dozens of information directors of the associations, foundations and other groups which control and supervise the sports. They are all noted individually throughout the book.

ROGER L. TREAT
Editor

The ENCYCLOPEDIA
Of SPORTS

Fifth Revised Edition

AMATEUR ATHLETE

What is the definition of an amateur? That question has occupied the leaders of sports for some time. Many answers have been devised as applied to a specific sport but no all-inclusive definition has been arrived at. No doubt the question—and definition—will continue to perplex sports authorities for many years to come.

The first time the amateur question was raised in the United States was in 1872, prior to the staging of a rowing regatta on the Schuylkill River, near Philadelphia, under the auspices of an organization then known as the "Schuylkill Navy."

In 1872 the number of sports in which men indulged as competitors almost could be counted on ten fingers. Since the lines between the amateurs and the professionals seemed so clearly drawn, and the distinction so definitely established, the rowing legions were tossed into a turmoil by the ruling of the Nominating Committee of the "Schuylkill Navy."

About four years earlier—Nov. 11, 1868—the newly formed New York Athletic Club put on the pioneer indoor track and field meet. Subsequently, members congratulated themselves on the fact that the "contests were strictly among amateurs." It was not made clear then, nor since, just how amateurs were separated from the professionals, who, in that era, were dominant in foot racing, jumping, weight tossing, etc.

The club members may have limited competition to members, and have gone along on the assumption that since none was a known professional, he must be an amateur. At any rate, there was no forcing an athlete to prove he was an amateur, and there was no committee delegated to make the ultimate decision.

What had been the rule for that athletic meet was, generally, the rule concerning sports of that distant era. The professionals were an established group, publicly known as such, and if one was not a professional, competing for wages or for cash prizes, the conclusion was that he must be a non-professional and deserved recognition as such.

Jockeys who rode running horses and reinsmen who piloted harness horses and took fees for their services, naturally, were professionals. Pugilists, who split the money put up by the spectators, were professionals. Since almost all the human sprinters were rewarded with part of the funds put up by owners of picnic and amusement resorts, they, too, were part of the professional group. Baseball players who worked for salaries were professionals; others were not.

Participants in sailing, lawn bowling, croquet, rowing, rifle shooting, and other sports on the programs of the generation were supposed to be amateurs, since none was paid for any muscular effort involved. In fact, most of the competitors not only did not receive cash, but few received trophies of any sort. Contests, generally, were "for the fun of it."

The word "amateur" rarely was used in this country at the time. Many folks were unaware as to its exact meaning. The men who competed for fees or shared in purses were professionals. The others were simply "non professionals." Therefore, when the "Schuylkill Navy" stated that the races were open to "amateurs only," all the oarsmen filled out nominating blanks and assumed that they were eligible.

The Committee on Nominations for the "Schuylkill Navy" was almost ruthless in its rejection of applicants. It ruled out about half the men who had entered for the different events. When explanations were demanded, the committee was tactful. It did not declare that the men were professionals; it merely insisted they were "not amateurs." And so the boat races of 1872 were run off with half the oarsmen in the Philadelphia area, who had wanted to compete, sitting on the river banks.

After the regatta was concluded, the barred oarsmen again uttered demands for classification. The "Navy" stated that, first of all, a man was a professional, who took money for athletic endeavors. When the oarsmen insisted they never had been paid, the committee rebutted with the statement that a man was not an amateur who "benefited financially through rowing." It was aiming at the practice, rather common then, of oarsmen betting among themselves on the outcome of the water duels and competing for cash prizes.

Quite a few of the oarsmen uttered even louder protests, when such a decision was made known, pointing out that while they may have bet on themselves to win a race, they not only lost the race, but also their money. So how could they have benefited financially through the sport of rowing? The committee answered that by saying that they had hoped to make money, and thus their amateur status was destroyed.

The controversy wasn't making much sense to a lot of people, so the "Navy" officials appointed William B. Curtis of New York, later called the "Father of Amateur Rowing," and James Watson, a Philadelphia newspaper man, to study the subject. The gentlemen finished up by preparing two small booklets: (1) "What is an Amateur?" and (2) "Who is an Amateur?"

Simmered to substance, an amateur was one who rowed only for sport's sake; a professional was one who competed with the hope of a cash reward. The definition was accepted in 1873 at a general meeting of rowing clubs, at which time the National Association of Amateur Oarsmen took over control of the sport, supplanting the Schuylkill Navy. There hasn't been material change in the ruling since that time, although organizations, in different sports, have looked at the standards with differing viewpoints.

The punsters, in the years since, have declared that "an amateur is an athlete who won't take checks and demands cash." But, in truth, the American amateur is a sports competitor who does not, as player or teacher, try to commercialize on his prowess as an athlete. If you play the game for the sake of the sport and make no cash profit, you are an amateur in the strictest sense. If you gain cash because of athletic fame, even if it comes from recommending somebody's soap or somebody else's muscle tonic, it violates the strict rules of amateurism and puts you in the professional class.

However, the various sports bodies in the United States interpret the rule differently. The Amateur Athletic Union, which has supervision of a vast number of sports, holds rigidly to the idea that one is a professional who gains cash for performance, by teaching effort or "sideline" performance. The United States Lawn Tennis Association is even stricter. It takes the position that an amateur becomes tainted who engages in a contest with a professional, even if for only the fun in such competition. A relaxing of this attitude is being sought in tennis circles. A proposal for an "open" tournament, involving professional and amateur players, is undergoing study by a U.S.L.T.A. committee.

In collegiate football, a player may compete against the "pros" without losing his amateur standing. The same is true in baseball and other games. In the early days of ski jumping, many contestants took cash. It was ruled they could regain their amateur rating, if they remained aloof from the cashier's payoff window for a year. The United States Golf Association also takes a liberal view. It has on occasions restored amateur ranking to those who turned pro, became penitent and requested re-rating as amateurs. The late Mrs. Mildred (Babe) Didrikson Zaharias is an example.

Throughout foreign countries, the definition of an amateur differs from the American idea. In Australia, for instance, if a cricket team goes on a tour in quest of international honors, the players are paid a sum about equal to what they might have earned if they had remained at home in some gainful occupation—about $2,400 per annum, as an average. Such an act would make them "pros," in an American sense. But they continue amateurs in Australia.

The same is true in Australian Rules football in Australia. Players get paid, but do not lose their amateur status.

What is true in Australia is equally so elsewhere. If a man is asked to quit doing his regular work and participate in some championship play, he is paid the exact amount he loses by taking such a vacation and remains an amateur. The whole system is based on the assumption that man should not be denied his wage if he is asked, because of his skill, to quit work for a while to indulge in athletics.

In fact, when plans were discussed for the Olympic Games of 1948, 1952 and 1956, there were tart exchanges of views between the Americans and the English, on one side, and representatives from other countries on the question of amateurism. Some foreign delegations felt that payments to athletes, while they were away from their work and performing in Olympic Games, should be permitted. This is called "broken-time" payment. The matter has not yet been resolved.

Therefore, who is an amateur and who is not depends upon which game one plays and where one plays it. But, regardless of the different rules in the different nations, the whole matter boils down to the fact that an amateur is someone who does not profit financially from his greatness as an athlete; he is one who plays the game because of his love for it, prompted by an eager desire to convert his skill into bringing glory of some kind to the team he plays with or the nation under whose flag he goes into competition.

The word *amateur* is one of the most important and frequently used in the world of sport. But in its application, it can have—and does have—some distinctly different meanings.

It is used to describe a novice, or a beginner, whether in sport or some other activity. It also is applied, usually sarcastically, to anyone engaged in any endeavor whose performance is indifferent, crude or far below standard.

Amateur is derived from the Latin, *amator*, which means lover. Quite likely it was used soon after the dawn of the Christian Era, to distinguish between the Olympic Games champions who refused to capitalize on their fame and those who went on tours and displayed their prowess for a price.

After the Olympiads were abandoned in 392 A.D., as a result of jealousies and bickerings, which led to many acts of violence between the Greek and Roman athletes and their followers, the word, so far as sport is concerned, was in disuse for about 1,400 years. It probably was revived in 1788, in England, and given its present Anglo-Saxon spelling, to separate "Gentleman Jack" Jackson, aristocrat, collegian and boxer, from the heavyweight bare-knuckle fighters of his time, who fought for side bets or small purses put up by somebody in funds, who wanted to see a battle, the fighters splitting the money.

Jackson would not make any side bets, nor

would he share in any of the collected money. By the strictest standards of today, he was 100 percent amateur.

It was pointed out by Jackson's legion of admirers, which included the Prince of Wales and Lord Byron, the man of letters who named Jackson the "Emperor of Pugilism," that Jackson was an amator (amateur) of boxing; that he battled professionals only because they had taunted him and belittled the boxing skill he had acquired during college years.

Jackson had enough fistic ability to batter one of England's great heavyweights into submission and, later, in 1795, he won the championship of the world—the first and only amateur to hold that title—by knocking out Daniel Mendoza, a professional of renown.

Years before the birth of Jackson there was horse racing in England, and there were amateur and professional riders. It is probable that the word "professional," as applied to participation in sports, was originated in those early years.

Some men made it a practice to ride the horses of other men for a fee, and riding became known as their profession. Thus, they were classified as "professionals."

Other men rode their own horses, never made side bets and would not accept money for prizes. This, naturally, made them amateurs. But they were not called such. They were distinguished from the professional by being referred to as "Gentleman Rider," while the professional was a "Jockey."

In all other forms of sports, the word "gentleman" is not in general use. A man is an amateur or he is a professional. The amateur receives nothing but plaudits, or medals or some trophy. The professional gets a salary, a fee of some sort, a percentage of the gate receipts or part of a donated purse.

With few exceptions, an American athlete who once turns professional is a professional forever. There is no return for him into the ranks of the amateurs.

ANGLING

To the average person angling and fishing are synonymous. However, though the sports are related, there is a difference. Fishing is catching fish without regard to method. Angling requires special tactics.

The angler rates classification as an artist for his handling of the frail rod, the casting of his line and the special technique in the operation of his reel, whereas the ordinary fisherman is concerned only in acquiring something, and a lot of it, for the frying pan.

The scientific angler is one who can make a cast from any designated spot, and hit a designated spot 125 to 350 or 375 feet away, depending upon the weight of his lead sinker. Furthermore, the high class angler uses nothing but artificial bait, whereas the fisherman calls on anything that will lure fish to strike.

Beyond all that, the angler can find a great deal of sport in merely making casts in competition, whereas the fisherman gains joy only through catching fish. In fact, in the earliest days of angling contests, the outstanding casters were just as likely to use an elaborate lawn or a barren field to determine championships, as to seek water, while the fisherman had to have water to achieve his ends.

No historian knows the identity of the first fisherman. But it is established that fish first were caught with bare hands, and that Persia was the pioneer nation to add fish to the national diet.

In the dim ages, floods swept many lands, as they sometimes do now. When the waters receded, fish were left stranded on beaches or in holes. The "fishermen" needed merely to make a

snatch to gain a fish, but "fishing" in that age before fish were known to be food was only "for the fun of it."

The next method was "tickling"—a rare sport, indeed. "Tickling" involved leaning over a pool in a stream, where fish swam lazily. The "fisherman" slipped his hand under the belly of the fish and proceeded to tickle it. While the fish was enjoying such attention, the sly human carefully would open his fingers, spread them around the fish, make a sudden grab and the fish and the water parted company.

Acquiring fish by "tickling" still is done in many countries. In the Rocky Mountain region of the United States it is quite popular, especially during droughts. When the streams are almost dry and the only water of consequence is in the pools, trout loiter there in sluggish condition. They won't dart away at the intrusion of a hand—because there is nowhere to dart. Thus the trout fall easy victims to the "ticklers."

The third form of fishing brought the spear into action. That was long before the Christian Era. Inasmuch as harpooning fish involved possible loss of the spear by poor marksmen, it would seem that the spearing wasn't for the sport of the thing; that men caught fish for use as food. Spears were treasured; their loss was not to be risked in "fishing." Therefore, the spearmen may be regarded as the first to know that fish was food for humans.

The next method was a crude form of modern line fishing, originated by the Egyptians. They used a stout vine to which a burr was attached. The burr was swished around in the waters to attract the fish, the fish struck and swallowed the burr. The smaller fish then were hauled in; the larger ones, which might disgorge the burr or break the vine, were pulled in as close to shore as possible, and then dispatched with a sharp blow of a club.

The resourceful Egyptians, realizing the weakness of the vine in struggles with large fish, devised a fishing line made of animal hair, which they braided. They manufactured lines of unlimited length and attached them to thornwood branches, which enabled them to cast well out from shore. The new lines held the fish, but the burrs did not function satisfactorily with big fish, which disgorged them. Therefore, the Egyptians invented crude hooks—made of bone—with one end sharpened, and, as time went on, people of other nations substituted ivory for bone, then bronze hooks, iron hooks and steel hooks.

The reverse barb on fishhooks, to prevent the fish from slipping off, is of modern creation.

The Persians started eating fish about 3000 B.C. The food value of fish was their secret for hundreds of years, until the Assyrians learned about it and, in time, fish became one of the principal food items of ancient nations. The Chinese did not take up fishing until about 900 B.C. They were line fishermen at first, using braided silk, but since then the Chinese have devised more ways of catching fish than any other nation. India learned about fish as food about 800 B.C., using lines, but depending chiefly on spears. The spears had long, stout vines attached. Hit or miss, the fisherman could haul the spear back.

The Jews started fishing about 500 B.C. and were quick to realize the folly of catching one fish at a time. They introduced the woven net, which was the start of wholesale fishing and the beginning of a new enterprise. Until the Jews perfected their nets and were able to capture vast quantities of fish in a short time, fish were caught singly. The Jews made such huge hauls with their nets that not only did they have enough for themselves, but they also could sell or trade the excess.

For many centuries it was assumed that the early Egyptians had used a fishing rod with a reel attached. This belief was created by Plaque 141 found in the tomb of King Pi, which showed a man with a plain fish pole in one hand and, to quote a historian, "with another pole in the other hand, to which pole, it appears, a reel-like device was attached." This idea existed until a curious and sharp-eyed gentleman made a careful study of the Plaque and discovered that while one pole undeniably was a fish pole, the other was much stouter, had a knob on its end and undoubtedly was a club used to subdue the larger, stronger fish.

It has not been established when the sport of fly-casting originated or where. This method was a departure from the old way, since it called for substitution of an artificial bait for the live lure. The original artificial bait was an imitation of a fly, which insect usually fell onto the surface of lakes and streams and was eagerly gulped by the fish.

Aelian, an Italian (170–230 A.D.), is credited with being first to write on fly-casting. His works are known as "Natural History," sometimes referred to as "Natural History Recordings." However, William Radcliffe of Baliol College, Oxford, England, who wrote "Fishing From the Earliest Times," generally regarded as the most elaborate volume on the angling subject, concluded that Martial was the first author to write about fly-casting—between 10 B.C. and 20 A.D. He quotes this Latin sentence from Martial:

"Namque quis nescit avidum vrata decipiscarum musca."

Translated, it means:
"Who has not seen the scarus rise,
"Decoyed and killed by fraudful flies."

The "scarus" is a species of fish.

Radcliffe made another surprising statement when he declared that "The Booke of St. Albans," regarded for many centuries as the first volume on fishing printed in Western Europe, was preceded many centuries by a book which had 26 short chapters, published in Antwerp. Despite Radcliffe's apparently indisputable proof, "The Booke of St. Albans" continues to be regarded in England as the first on the subject, perhaps because it was the first to be written in English.

In 1651, Barker, an Englishman, wrote "The Art of Angling," and not only described the reel and its use, but also included in his book a drawing made in 1647 of a reel. Barker referred to the reel as a "wind" and stated that it was created "about 1496 A.D." He supplied no further data. Other historians agree that a crude reel existed in the 15th Century.

Izaak Walton, patron saint of anglers, doesn't promenade into the picture until 1653, when he was acclaimed as an author on the art of fishing. That was two years after Barker had handled the subject rather painstakingly. Perhaps Walton lives so heroically in memory and Barker practically is forgotten because Walton was tremendously popular and a thorough sportsman, whereas Barker, a man with many enemies, was referred to in his day as the "Father of Salmon Poaching." His ambition was to catch fish—many, many fish—and he never observed laws, ethics or another man's rights. Walton was the exact opposite.

Barker usually fished alone, ignoring the rights of others to waters. Walton, on the other hand, always observed the laws. He was a born organizer and was happiest when conducting parties of friends to the best possible fishing spots. He was an angling missionary and made many converts to the rod and reel.

Although the first reels were called "winds" or "winches," Walton wrote of them as "wheeles." Later this was changed to "reel," appearing to be more appropriate.

Within 100 years after Walton's death, angling had gained so much popularity that fly-casting contests were put on in various parts of England to settle disputes as to who was the champion in his district. Informal angling clubs soon resulted and, going into the 19th Century, real English sportsmen spurned every method other than fly-casting to catch fish.

In 1732 the first fishing club on the North American continent was formed. It was called the Schuylkill Fishing Company, with head-quarters at Philadelphia. The organization still functions in an obscure way, and, thus, is probably the oldest sports body—of any type—on the continent in the matter of continuous existence. It now is known as the Fish House Club with headquarters in Andalusia, Pa. Membership is limited to 30 and annual meetings are held, at which a toast is made to George Washington, who was an early day guest.

The American Rod and Reel Association was founded in the United States over 100 years ago, with all members pledged to fish only by fly-casting. The activities of this organization were limited and no national impetus was given the sport until the formation in 1893 of the Chicago Fly-Casting Club, which seized upon the World's Fair of that year as a medium of exploitation by staging the first United States national tourna-ment. The events were accuracy, accuracy fly, delicacy fly, long-distance bait and long-distance fly. The distances were 75, 80 and 85 feet. All casts were made on a lawn because methods for

measuring casts on water had not been perfected.

Although the records of the early activities of the fly-casters, prior to 1893, are vague, there is a memorandum that "a national tournament first was arranged in 1861," and the supposition is that others followed periodically. But the 1893 event is the first which is replete with details.

In 1897 the Chicago Fly-Casting Club held the second National tournament. The third was in 1903 and the fourth in 1905. At the fifth tourna-ment, at Kalamazoo, Mich., in 1906, the idea of a permanent organization took shape and evolved into the National Association of Scientific Angling Clubs, at Racine, Wis., where the sixth tournament, the first under the auspices of the N.A.S.A.C., was held in 1907.

This permanent organization was made up of nine pioneer clubs—Chicago, Cincinnati, Fox River Valley, Grand Rapids, Kalamazoo, Kansas City, Racine, San Francisco and Illinois. Other clubs since have become part of the Association, which, until 1972, was strictly amateur and governs the fly-casting sport.

In 1969, several events were changed, dropped, or added: the Wet Fly Accuracy was dropped, the 3/8 Oz. Distance (Revolving Spool Reel) was also dropped, the Trout Fly Distance was renamed "1-Hand Fly Distance," the Salmon Fly Distance was renamed "2-Hand Fly Distance"; added, were 1 Oz. Plug Distance (Fixed Spool), 3/8 Oz. Distance (Fixed Spool Reel), Trout Fly Accuracy, Bass Bug Accuracy, and 1/4 Oz. Plug Accuracy.

The official name of the governing body of fly-casting was changed to American Casting Association in January, 1961. Before that it had been called the National Association of Angling and Casting Clubs.

Famous Fly Casters

Men

Among the American fly-casters who have been champions or record-makers are:

Call J. McCarthy, A.D. Whitby, Dr. R. Johnson, George G. Chatt, W.C. Luebbert, Jack Schwinn, Fred N. Peet, W.P. Arend, Walter Willman, A. (Tony) Accetta, William Stanley, Edwin F. Sutter, D.F. Beatty, L.E. DeGarmo, C.E. Edwards, Howard Chatt, Otto H. Peters, Ernest Liotta Sr., Walter Buckwalter, Marvin K. Hedge, R.E. Lyttaker, E.A. MacFarland, W.C. Newcomb, E.E. Cavanaugh, Allen E. Fogle, C.E. Braddon, Frank R. Steele, Richard Fujita, Fred Arbogast, F.S. Leach, H. Carl Hittenberger, Dick Miller, William Lovely, Harold H. Smedley, Clyde

Marshall, George Hess, Richard Wilkey, Jack Sparks, Henry Fujita Jr., Ernest Liotta Jr., Clarence Anthes, J.A. Halbleib, Charles Schall, Walter Willman, Ben Rice, Len Williams, Charles Sutphin, Lee Sens, Earl Osten, Jimmy Green, Marion Garber, Jack Crossfield, Jon Tarantino, Myron C. Gregory and Richard R. Ward.

Women

Mrs. Jack Lewis, Mrs. Ernest Liotta, Mrs. Otto Reisman, Mrs. A. McDonald, Mrs. U.J. Bauer, Aunalee Crusey, Mrs. Clarence Anthes, Carol Steel, Joan Salvato, Margaret Weaver, Mary Reisman, Dorothy Vogel, Mrs. Harry Sutphin, Bonnie Glatz, Mel Gavin and Kay Brodney.

U.S. Fly and Bait Casting Champions

CURRENT CHAMPIONSHIPS

(Courtesy of Paul N. Jones, American Casting Association, P.O. Box 51, Nashville, Tenn., 37202)

Men

All Around

1959—Marion Garber
1960-61—Jon Tarantino
1962—Jon Tarantino, Terry Schneider (tie)
1963—Jon Tarantino
1964—Zack Willson, Jr.
1965—Casper Rigamer
1966-68—Zack Willson, Jr.
1969—Ed Lanser
1970-71—Zack Willson, Jr.
1972—Steve Rajeff

Anglers All-Around

1970-72—Steve Rajeff

All Distance

1959—Marion Garber
1960-62—Jon Tarantino
1963—Terry Schneider
1964—Zack Willson, Jr.
1965—Casper Rigamer
1966-68—Zack Willson, Jr.
1969—Ed Lanser
1970—Zack Willson, Jr.
1971—B.L. Farley
1972—Zack Willson, Jr.

All Accuracy

1959—William Peters
1960—Jon Tarantino
1961—Steve Aleshi
1962—Thomas Sibila
1963—Jon Tarantino
1964—Casper Rigamer
1965—Casper Rigamer, Zack Willson, Jr. (tie)
1966—Eugene Lentz, Tom Sibila (tie)
1967-68—Zack Willson, Jr.
1969—Ed Lanser
1970-72—Steve Rajeff

Women

All Accuracy

1959-61—Mel Gavin
1962—Mollie Schneider
1963-64—Mel Gavin
1965—Dawn Holiday
1966-67—Mel Gavin
1968—Donna Monty
1969—Cheryl Engle
1970-71—Mollie Schneider
1972—Ann Strobel

Men

1-Hand Fly Distance (Trout Fly Distance)

1909-10—Fred N. Peet
1911—No competition
1912—Call J. McCarthy
1913—Fred N. Peet
1914—Call J. McCarthy
1915—H.C. Golcher
1916—George G. Chatt
1917—No competition
1918—Fred N. Peet
1919—David R. Linder
1920—Call J. McCarthy
1921—B.B. Farr
1922-26—George G. Chatt
1927—William Behnen
1928—George G. Chatt
1929—Wade Shrumm
1930-31—Jules P. Cuenin
1932—Otto H. Peters
1933—A. Accetta
1934—Marvin K. Hedge
1935—Ernest Liotta Jr.
1936—G.L. McLeod
1937—Dick Miller
1938—Ernest Liotta Jr.
1939—Ernest Liotta Jr., W.H. Loskot (tie)
1940—Jack Sparks
1941—Eugene Anderegg
1942-43—Dick Miller
1944-45—Marvin K. Hedge
1946—James Green
1947—Marvin K. Hedge
1948—Dick Miller
1949—Joseph Masa
1950—Phil Miravalle
1951—Myron C. Gregory
1954—Jack Crossfield
1955—Jon Tarantino
1956—Jack Crossfield
1957—Myron C. Gregory
1958—Richard R. Ward
1959-62—Jon Tarantino
1963—R.L. Hetzel
1964—Dave Cohen
1965—Ben Fontaine
1966—Zack Willson, Jr.
1967—Dave Cohen
1968-69—Dick Ward
1970—Ed Lanser
1971-72—Steve Rajeff

Record: Steve Rajeff, 191-1/3' Avg.

2-Hand Fly Distance (Salmon Fly Distance)

1871—James Meyer Jr.
1872-78—No record

1879—John J. Meldram
1880—No record
1881—James Meyer Jr.
1882—Hiram Hawes
1883—R.C. Leonard
1884—Hiram Hawes
1885—R.C. Leonard
1886—No record
1887—R.C. Leonard
1888—Hiram Hawes
1889—R.C. Leonard
1890-93—No record
1894—Al M. Cummings
1895-1904—No record
1905—R.C. Leonard
1906—Edward J. Mills
1907—Fred N. Peet
1908-09—John Waddell
1910—William Ball
1911—No record
1912—Call J. McCarthy
1913—Fred N. Peet
1914—C.E. Lingenfelter
1915—Fred N. Peet
1916—George G. Chatt
1917—No competition
1918—George G. Chatt
1919—Call J. McCarthy
1920—C.C. Lucke
1921—No competition
1922—George G. Chatt
1923—William C. Luebbert
1924—George G. Chatt
1925—Jack Schwinn
1926—C.C. Lucke
1927-28—C.E. Braddon
1929—Leo Connelly
1930—Jules P. Cuenin
1931—Leo Connelly
1932—Otto H. Peters
1933—G.F. Ericson, C.E. Braddon (tie)
1934—No competition
1935—C.E. Braddon
1936—E.E. Cavanaugh, C.E. Braddon (tie)
1937—Dick Miller
1938—H.C. Hittenberger
1939—Dick Miller
1940—Dick Miller, Jack Sparks (tie)
1941-43—Dick Miller
1944—Robert Piros Sr.
1945-46—Dick Miller
1947—Jimmy Green
1948—Dick Miller
1949—Earl Osten
1950-51—Myron C. Gregory
1952—Jack Crossfield
1953—Jon Tarantino
1954-55—Myron C. Gregory
1956—Jon Tarantino
1957—Billy Peters
1958—Marion Garber
1959—Jon Tarantino

1960—Robert Budd
1961—R.L. Hetzel
1962—R.L. Hetzel, Robert Budd (tie)
1963—Terry Schneider
1964—Robert Budd
1965—R.L. Hetzel
1966—Zack Willson, Jr.
1967—Bob Budd
1968-69—William Peters
1970-71—Bob Budd
1972—Zack Willson, Jr.

Record: Bob Budd, 216 2/3' Avg.

Dry Fly Accuracy (unknown distances)

1916—Lou S. Darling
1917—No competition
1918—Fred N. Peet
1919—William F. Backus
1920—No competition
1921—Webb L. Kinzer
1922—No competition
1923—W.P. Arend
1924—No competition
1925—W.P. Arend
1926—Lew Morrison
1927—Otto H. Peters
1928—R.P. Merrill
1929—Frank R. Steel
1930—Jules P. Cuenin
1931—Lou Guerin
1932—Frank R. Steel
1933—Eddie Davis
1934—E.E. Cavanaugh
1935—R.E. Lyttaker
1936—Henry Fujita
1937—Otto H. Peters
1938—Henry Fujita
1939—Ralph Keating
1940—Charles Schall
1941—James Price
1942-44—Harold H. Smedley
1945-46—Henry Fujita
1947—Jim Corbell
1948—Ed Tassi
1949—Lee Slaughter Jr.
1950—Allan Childers
1951—Lee Slaughter Jr.
1952—Steve Aleshi
1953—Richard R. Ward
1954—D. Myer
1955—Frank J. Nulty
1956—Myron C. Gregory
1957—George Applegren
1958—Charles Sutphin
1959—Baldi Darnay
1960—Jon Tarantino
1961—Steve Aleshi
1962—Marion Garber
1963—Jon Tarantino
1964—Gary Martin

1965—B.L. Farley, Casper Rigamer (tie)
1966—Casper Rigamer, William Peters (tie)
1967—Doug Holiday
1968—George Applegren
1969-70—Ed Lanser
1971—Ed Thomas
1972—Steve Rajeff

Record: Average—19 casters tied, 100

3/8 Oz. Plug Accuracy

1930—Jay Packard
1931—Charles Edwards
1932—A. Accetta
1933—Leonard Allen
1934—Ben Robison
1935—Howard Chatt
1936—E.H. Burlinggame
1937—Everett J. Gibbons
1938—James H. Wine
1939—Ernest Liotta Jr.
1940—James Price
1941—H.C. Hittenberger
1942—Dick Wilkey
1943—William Lovely
1944—Earl Osten
1945—S.G. Dennis
1946-48—Charles Sutphin
1949—Marvin Allen
1950—Marion Garber
1951—James H. Wine
1952—Bryant Black
1953—Marvin Allen
1954—Marion Garber
1955—Bobby Spear
1956—Billy Peters
1957—Bobby Spear
1958—Billy Peters
1959—Charles Sutphin
1960-61—William True
1962—Don Dortolson
1963—Charles Sutphin
1964—Steve Jures
1965—Casper Rigamer
1966—Eugene Lentz, Bob Budd, Bill Drown (tie)
1967-68—Zack Willson, Jr.
1969—B.L. Farley
1970—Zack Willson, Jr.
1971—Gary Martin
1972—Tom Sibila

Record: Charles Sutphin, Bill True, 100 points.

3/8 Oz. Plug Distance (Fixed Spool)

1970—B.L. Farley
1971—Steve Aleshi
1972—B.L. Farley

Record: Steve Aleshi, 293 1/3' Avg.; Aleshi,
          299' Long Cast.

5/8 Oz. Plug Accuracy

1921—E.A. Mac Farland
1922—Walter Willman
1923—Andrew Trimble
1924—Allen E. Fogle
1925—Otto H. Peters
1926—Howard Chatt
1927—Frank Leach
1928-29—Otto H. Peters
1930—Robert Clarkson
1931—Edwin F. Sutter
1932—Charles Edwards
1933—Robert Clarkson
1934—Charles Ward
1935—C.E. Braddon
1936—Ernest Liotta Jr.
1937—A. Sunn
1938—H.C. Hittenberger
1939—William C. Block
1940—E.E. Cavanaugh
1941—E.R. Broeker
1942—George Hess
1943—Edward J. Olson
1944—Richard Fujita
1945—Ernest Liotta Jr.
1946—J.A. Halbleib
1947—Earl Osten
1948—Charles Sutphin
1949—Wilbur Brooks
1950—Marion Garber
1951—Len Williams
1952—Frank Halper
1953—W. Wernet
1954—W. Rector
1955—Don Allen
1956-57—Casper Rigamer
1958—Marion Garber
1959—James Kangas
1960—Jon Tarantino
1961—Charles Sutphin
1962—Thomas Sibila
1963—Eugene Lentz
1964—Casper Rigamer
1965—Clarence Anthes, Eugene Lentz (tie)
1966—Chuck Reilly
1967—Eugene Lentz
1968—Zack Willson, Jr.
1969—William Peters
1970—Charles Phillips
1971—B.L. Farley
1972—William Peters

Record: 100 points, 7 men.

5/8 Oz. Plug Distance

1920—F. Kleinfeldt
1921—William Stanley
1922—George G. Chatt
1923—No competition
1924—Fred Arbogast

1925-26—George G. Chatt
1927—Lou Hurst
1928—Andrew Trimble
1929—C.E. Braddon
1930—Walter C. Newcombe, Leo Connelly (tie)
1931—Jules P. Cuenin, Karl Kinnear (tie)
1932—Robert Clarkson, A. Accetta (tie)
1933—Robert Clarkson, Al Foss (tie)
1934—A. Accetta, Walter Buckwalter (tie)
1935-36—Joseph Weber
1937—Walter Willman
1938—Lee Sens
1939—Lee Sens, H.C. Hittenberger (tie)
1940-41—Clyde Marshall
1942—John Kiedaisch
1943—Dick Miller
1944-45—Charles Schall
1946—Ernest Liotta Jr.
1947—Ben Rice
1948—Earl Osten
1949—Wilbur Brooks
1950—Doug Merrick
1951—Phil L. Varney
1952—Charles Schall
1953—William Lovely
1954—Richard R. Ward
1955-57—William Lovely
1958—Jon Tarantino
1959—Ernest Liotta, Jr.
1960-61—Edward Lanser
1962—Jon Tarantino
1963—Terry Schneider
1964-68—Zack Willson, Jr.
1969—72—Ed Lanser

World records: Average—Zack Willson, Jr., 474 feet. Long cast—Z. Willson, Jr., 483 feet.

1/4 Oz. Plug Accuracy

1970—B.L. Farley
1971—Zack Willson, Jr.
1972—B.L. Farley

Record: B.L. Farley, 97 points.

1 Oz. Plug Distance (Fixed Spool)

1970-71—Zack Willson, Jr.
1972—Steve Rajeff

Record: Steve Rajeff, 489 1/3' Avg.,
        Rajeff, 497' Long Cast.

Trout Fly Accuracy

1970-71—Steve Rajeff
1972—Zack Willson, Jr.

Record: S. Rajeff, Z. Willson, 100 points.

Bass Bug Accuracy

1970—Steve Rajeff
1971—Steve Rajeff, Steve Aleshi (tie)
1972—Zack Willson, Jr.

Record: S. Rajeff, S. Aleshi, Z.
        Willson, 97 points.

Women

Dry Fly Accuracy

1943-46—Joan Salvato
1947-50—Dorothy Vogel
1951—Joan Salvato
1952—Zelma Stevenson
1953—Zelma Stevenson
1954—Kay Brodney
1955—Mel Gavin
1956—Kay Brodney
1957-58—Mel Gavin
1959-61—Mel Gavin
1962—Grace Perkins
1963-64—Mel Gavin
1965—Mollie Schneider
1966-67—Mel Gavin
1968—Elsie Seiffert
1969—Cherly Engle
1970—Mollie Schneider
1971—Eleanor Turner
1972—Cheryl Engle

3/8 Oz. Plug Accuracy

1940-41—Aunalee Crusey
1942-44—Adelea McDonald
1945—Dorothy Vogel
1946—Mrs. Harry Sutphin
1947—Dorothy Hunt
1948—Adelea McDonald
1949—Dorothy Vogel
1950—Joan Salvato
1951—Bonnie Glatz
1952—Doris Bright
1953—Dawn M. Strover
1954—Mildred Wolfe
1955—Mel Gavin
1956—Beverly Allen
1957-58—Mel Gavin
1959—Edna Mae Wilson
1960-61—Mel Gavin
1962—Dawn Holiday
1963—Verdna Mae Strebeck
1964—Mel Gavin
1965—Dawn Holiday
1966—Mel Gavin
1967—Mollie Schneider, Mel Gavin (tie)
1968—Donna Monty
1969—Evelyn Klenk
1970-71—Verdna Strebeck
1972—Cheryl Engle

5/8 Oz. Plug Accuracy

1923—Mrs. Louis J. Hurst
1924—Mrs. V. Dean Reese
1925—Mrs. Louis J. Hurst
1926—Mrs. William Candless
1927-28—Mrs. Louis J. Hurst
1929—Mrs. Ed Thomas
1930—Mrs. John Casey
1931-32—Mrs. Louis J. Hurst
1933—Mrs. Al Simms
1934—Mrs. Hazel Mewes
1935—Mrs. Ernest Liotta
1936—Mrs. Helen Sulzer
1937—Mrs. Walter Willman
1938—Mrs. James Scafidi
1939—Patricia Krause
1940—Mrs. Clyde Marshall
1941—Aunalee Crusey
1942—Mrs. Jack Lewis
1943—Dorothy Vogel
1944—Mrs. Otto Reisman
1945—Mrs. C. Liotta
1946—Margaret Weaver
1947—Adelea McDonald
1948—Dorothy Vogel
1949—Adelea McDonald
1950—Dorothy Vogel
1951—Bonnie Glatz
1952—Dawn Strover
1953—Ronnie Miller
1954—Mildred Wolfe
1955—Mel Gavin
1956—Mildred Wolfe
1957-58—Mel Gavin
1959—Norma Collins
1960—Dawn Holiday
1961—Mel Gavin
1962—Mollie Schneider
1963-64—Mel Gavin
1965—Dawn Holiday
1966—Mel Gavin
1967—Mel Gavin, Mollie Schneider (tie)
1968—Donna Monty
1969—Cheryl Engle
1970-71—Verdna Strebeck
1972—Betty Chadwick

Trout Fly Accuracy

1970—Cheryl Engle
1971—Barbara Rohrer
1972—Mollie Schneider

Record: Barbara Rohrer, 94 points

Bass Bug Accuracy

1970—Verdna Strebeck
1971—Pauline Cathcart
1972—Ann Strobel

1/4 oz. Plug Accuracy

1970-71—Mollie Schneider
1972—Ann Strobel

DISCONTINUED CHAMPIONSHIPS

Men

Trout Fly Distance (heavy tackle)

1861—George Linnebacker
1862-63—Seth Green
1864—Robert B. Roosevelt
1865—No record
1866—Seth Green
1867—H.H. Morse
1868—Robert B. Roosevelt
1869—Seth Green
1870—L.A. Pratt
1871—Charles H. Wells
1872—Seth Green
1873-76—Reuben Wood
1877—A.H. Fowler
1878—Seth Green
1879—John J. Meldram
1880—Ira Wood
1881—Reuben Wood
1882—Harry Pritchard
1883-93—R.C. Leonard
1894—R.R. Flint
1895-96—No record
1897—W.D. Mansfield
1898—I.H. Bellows
1899—No record
1900—A.E. Lovett
1901—No record
1902—W.D. Mansfield
1903-04—No record
1905—Edward J. Mills
1906—R.C. Leonard
1907—H.G. Hascall
1908—Fred N. Peet
1909—Perry D. Frazer
1910—Fred N. Peet
1911—No competition
1912—Call J. McCarthy
1913—No competition
1914—Call J. McCarthy
1915—W.D. Mansfield
1916—Call J. McCarthy
1917—No competition
1918—George G. Chatt

Trout Fly Distance (4 3/4 oz. rod)

1882—Hiram W. Hawes
1883—Thomas Pritchard
1884—Hiram W. Hawes
1885-86—No competition
1887-89—R.C. Leonard
1890-1918—No competition
1919-20—Call J. McCarthy
1921-22—George G. Chatt

Wet Fly Accuracy

1915—C.G. Young
1916—Call J. McCarthy
1917—No competition
1918—George G. Chatt
1919-20—William C. Luebbert
1921—William Stanley
1922-23—George G. Chatt
1924—C.E. Braddon
1925—William Stanley
1926-27—John S. Schwinn
1928—R.P. Merrill
1929—Walter Willman
1930—G.F. Ericson
1931—C.E. Braddon
1932—A. Accetta
1933—Ralph E. Lyttaker
1934—A. Accetta
1935—Howard Chatt
1936—Jay Packard
1937—C.E. Braddon
1938—C. Johnston
1939—M.L. Sulser
1940—C.E. Braddon
1941—Clyde Marshall
1942—Harold H. Smedley
1943—Roscoe Reamer
1944—William Morris
1945—Ernest Liotta Jr.
1946—A. Accetta
1947—Jimmy Green
1948—Archie Vogel
1949—Herman Deiser
1950—C.F. Forcade
1951—Sam Thompson
1952—Roy Mabee
1953—Casper Rigamer
1954—Jon Tarantino
1955—George Applegren
1956—C.F. Forcade
1957—Steve Aleshi
1958—George Applegren
1959—Clem Forcado
1960—Marion Garber
1961—Edward Thomas
1962—Thomas Sibila
1963—Charles Sutphin
1964—Zack Willson, Jr.
1965—David Cohen
1966—(6-way tie)—William Peters, Tom Sibila, Zack Willson, Jr., Mike Steller, Marion Garber, Dick Fujita
1967—Eugene Lentz
1968—Jim Green
1969—Zack Willson, Jr.

World record: Held by 72 casters, with 100 points.

Dry Fly Accuracy (fixed distances)

1893—W.H. Babcock
1894—A.M. Cummings
1895-96—No record
1897—W.D. Mansfield
1898—I.H. Bellows
1899—No record
1900—I.H. Bellows
1901—Fred N. Peet
1902—W.D. Mansfield
1903-04—No record
1905-07—Fred N. Peet
1908—I.H. Bellows
1909-10—L.E. DeGarmo
1911—No competition
1912—I.H. Bellows
1913—Call J. McCarthy
1914—F. Kleinfeldt
1915—P.W. Shattuck
1916—R.C. Jenkins
1917—No competition
1918—William Stanley
1919—George G. Chatt
1920—William C. Luebbert
1921—Fred W. Kuesel
1922—K.Y. James
1923-24—William Stanley
1925—George G. Chatt
1926—C.E. Braddon
1927-28—John S. Schwinn
1929—Arthur J. Neu

Accuracy Fly (heavy tackle)

1893—R.C. Leonard
1894—H.E. Skinner
1895-96—No record
1897—H.A. Newkirk
1898—B.W. Goodsell
1899—No record
1900—A.E. Lovett
1901—I.H. Bellows
1902—J.B. Kenniff
1903-04—No record
1905—H.G. Hascall
1906—R.C. Leonard
1907—I.H. Bellows
1908—L.E. DeGarmo
1909—I.H. Bellows
1910—F.A. Forsythe
1911—No competition
1912—I.H. Bellows
1913—J.W. Bramhall
1914—C.E. Lingenfelter
1915—C.H. Gardner

3/8 Oz. Plug Distance (Revolving Reel)

1930—Leo Connelly
1931—A. Accetta, F.N. White (tie)
1932—A. Accetta
1933—W. Buckwalter, Howard Chatt (tie)
1934—No competition
1935—C.E. Braddon
1936—C.E. Braddon, Ernest Liotta Jr. (tie)

1937—Lee Sens
1938—H.C. Hittenberger
1939—Walter Willman
1940—Dick Miller
1941—Clyde Marshall
1942—Clarence Anthes
1943—Everett J. Gibbons
1944—A. Accetta
1945-46—William Lovely
1947—John Kiedaisch
1948—William Lovely
1949—Jack Moore
1950—Ben Rice
1951—William Lovely
1952—C.F. Forcade
1953—William Lovely
1954—Jon Tarantino
1955—Richard R. Ward
1956—Robert Budd
1957—William Lovely
1958—Jon Tarantino
1959—Marion Garber
1960—Edward Lanser
1961-62—Jon Tarantino
1963-64—Zack Willson, Jr.
1965—Casper Rigamer
1966—Robert Budd
1967—Zack Willson, Jr.
1968—Ed Lanser
1969—B.L. Farley

World records: Average—Casper Rigamer, 386 1/3 feet. Long cast—Zack Willson, Jr., 395 feet.

1/4 Oz. Bait Accuracy

1905—H.G. Hascall
1906-07—William Stanley
1908-09—Daniel F. Beatty
1910—William H. Ball
1911—No competition
1912—David R. Linder
1913—E.K. Pierson
1914—William Stanley
1915—Oscar Lane
1916—William Stanley
1917—No competition
1918—George G. Chatt
1919—William Stanley
1920—Rodney D. Heetfield
1921—LeRoy S. Jeffers
1922—F.J. Atwood
1923—William C. Luebbert
1924—William Stanley
1925—Vernon D. Reese
1926—Fred Arbogast
1927-28—C.E. Braddon
1929—Edwin F. Sutter

1/4 Oz. Bait Distance

1909—A.D. Whitby, R.J. Held (tie)
1910—B.F. Flegel

1911—No competition
1912—C.E. Lingenfelter
1913—No competition
1914—B.F. Flegel
1915—Stanley Forbes
1916—E.M. Town, George G. Chatt (tie)
1917—No competition
1918—William Stanley, George G. Chatt (tie)
1919—William Stanley, C.E. Lingenfelter (tie)
1920—A.E. Fogle, Edwin F. Sutter (tie)
1921—Rodney D. Heetfield
1922-23—Fred Arbogast
1924—William Stanley, Fred Arbogast (tie)
1925—Fred Arbogast
1926—Fred Arbogast, Walter C. Newcomb (tie)
1927—Walter C. Newcomb
1928—Otto H. Peters, George G. Chatt (tie)
1929—George G. Chatt

1/2 Oz. Bait Accuracy

1884—Alfred M. Mayer
1885—A.F. Dresel
1886—No record
1887-89—A.F. Dresel
1890-96—No record
1897—Fred N. Peet
1898—B.W. Goodsell
1899—No record
1900—A.C. Smith
1901—No record
1902—I.H. Bellows
1903-04—No record
1905—E.R. Letterman
1906—E.R. Owens
1907—E.R. Letterman
1908—L.E. DeGarmo
1909—A.Jay Marsh
1910—Daniel F. Beatty
1911—No competition
1912—R.C. Nicholsson
1913—E.K. Pierson
1914—George G. Chatt
1915—W.D. Mansfield
1916—Call J. McCarthy
1917—No competition
1918—F.A. Smitley
1919-20—William Stanley
1921—Call J. McCarthy
1922—A.E. Fogel
1923-24—William Stanley
1925—Andrew A. Trimble
1926—E.G. Delaunty
1927—C.E. Braddon
1928—Arthur J. Neu
1929—Eddie Davis

1/2 Oz. Bait Distance

1884—Alfred M. Mayer
1885—A.F. Dresel
1886—No record
1887-89—A.F. Dresel

1890-92—No record
1893—E.E. Wilkinson, F.B. Davidson (tie)
1894—A.D. Ayers
1895-96—No record
1897—F.B. Davidson
1898-99—No record
1900—George Salter, A.E. Lovett (tie)
1901—No record
1902—Ernest Bartholamew
1903—No record
1904—Lloyd J. Tooley
1905—Ernest Bartholamew, Lloyd J. Tooley (tie)
1906—Abe Rabers
1907—Ray Lum, E.R. Letterman (tie)
1908—R. Johnson Held, Ray Lum (tie)
1909—R. Johnson Held
1910—B.F. Flegel
1911—No competition
1912—B.F. Flegel, C.E. Lingenfelter (tie)
1913—Call J. McCarthy, C.E. Lingenfelter (tie)
1914—B.F. Flegel
1915—Oscar Lane, B.F. Flegel (tie)
1916—George G. Chatt, A. Jay Marsh (tie)
1917—No competition
1918—William J. Jamison, George G. Chatt (tie)
1919—George G. Chatt, C.E. Lingenfelter (tie)
1920—Allen E. Gogle
1921—William Stanley
1922-24—Fred Arbogast
1925-26—Walter C. Newcomb
1927—Fred White, Walter C. Newcomb (tie)
1928—Fred White, George G. Chatt (tie)
1929—C.E. Braddon
1930-42—No competition
1943—William Lovely

Women

1/2 Oz. Bait Accuracy

1923—Billie Brown
1924—No competition
1925—Mrs. Louis J. Hurst, Mrs. Walter Willman
(tie)
1926—Mrs. Walter Willman
1927—Marjorie Mathie

Wet Fly Accuracy

1923—J.F. Atwood
1924-39—No competition
1940—Mrs. Clarence Anthes
1941-42—Mrs. Otto Reisman
1943—Dorothy Vogel
1944—Carol Steel
1945—Joan Salvato
1946—Mary Reisman
1947—Dorothy Vogel
1948—Joan Salvato
1949-50—Dorothy Vogel
1951—Joan Salvato
1952—Kay Brodney
1953—Ronnie Miller

1954—Mildred Wolfe
1955—Mel Gavin
1956—Roma Saunders
1957—Ann Strobel
1958—Mel Gavin
1959—Janice Specht
1960—Norma Collins
1961—Mel Gavin
1962—Grace Perkins
1963—Mel Gavin
1964-65—Ronnie Miller
1966-67—Mel Gavin
1968—Elsie Seiffert
1969—Cheryl Engle

FLY-CASTING TECHNIQUE

In fly-casting tournaments, the target usually is a rubber circle, much like a bicycle tire, about 30 inches in diameter. When accuracy tests are made, five rings are placed about 5 feet apart, and the caster tries for a bullseye in each, being permitted two casts at each circle. All the casts must be completed within a specified period of time, generally about 8 minutes.

In tests for distance, the target is placed at ordinary range, and then moved farther and farther out as one caster or another exceeds the distance.

FISHING TOURNAMENTS

In recent years fishing tournaments have sprung up from Nova Scotia to Western Mexico. One of the best known is the annual international tuna team series for the Alton B. Sharp Trophy, held off Wedgeport, Nova Scotia.

Other well-known contests include the Metropolitan Miami (Fla.) Tournament; West Flagler Kennel Club White Marlin Trophy (Miami); Florida Keys Award (South Florida); Rod and Gun Club, Miami; Sportsmen's Club, Miami; Fishing Club, Miami; Florida Tackle and Gun Club, Jacksonville; Field and Stream Magazine Contest; George Ruppert Sailfish Contest; Carrier Rod and Gun Club, Syracuse, N.Y.; Collins Sport Shop, Jamestown, N.Y.; Free Press, Detroit, Mich., and Muskegon Sportsman, Muskegon, Mich. Also, New Jersey Governor's Tournament; Denver Post (Dave Cook) Contest, Denver, Colo.; Corral, Great Falls, Mont.; Madison's Sporting Goods Co., Brainerd, Minn.; Tarpon Rodeo, New Orleans, La.; Evans Sporting Goods, Shreveport, La.; Aransas Pass, Tex.; Usher's Annual Fishing Guide, Dallas, Tex.; Ben Paris Recreation, Seattle, Wash.; Poggy Club, Portland, Ore.; Tyee Club, Victoria, B.C.; Tarpon Rodeo, Tampico, Mexico; Acapulco Sailfish Rodeo, Acapulco, Mexico (for tuna); United States Atlantic Tuna tournament and many others.

WORLD FISHING RECORDS

(Courtesy International Game Fish Association, 3000 E. Las Olas Boulevard, Fort Lauderdale, Florida, 33316)

CAUGHT WITH ROD AND REEL IN SALT WATER
All-Tackle
Men and Women
Asterisk (*) indicates line not tested.

Species	Lbs. – oz.	Length	Girth	Place	Date	Angler	Line
Albacore	69 lbs. 2 oz.	3'10"	32"	Montauk, N.Y.	August 21, 1964	Larry R. Kranz	80
Albacore	69 lbs. 1 oz.	4'¼"	33¼"	Hudson Canyon, N.J.	Oct. 8, 1961	Walter C. Timm	50
Albacore	69 lbs.	3'6"	32½"	Helena, At'tic Ocn.	April 7, 1956	P. Allen	130
Amberjack	149 lbs.	5'11"	41¾"	Bermuda	June 21, 1964	Peter Simons	30
Barracuda	83 lbs.	6'¼"	29"	Lagos, Nigeria	Jan. 13, 1952	K.J.W. Hackett	50
Calif. Black Sea Bass	563 lbs. 8 oz.	7'5"	72"	Anacapa Island, Cal.	Aug. 20, 1968	James D. McAdam, Jr.	80
Calif. White Sea Bass	83 lbs. 12 oz.	5'5½"	34"	San Felipe, Mexico	Mar. 31, 1953	L.C. Baumgardner	30
Channel Bass	83 lbs.	4'4"	29"	Cape Charles, Va.	Aug. 5, 1949	Zack Waters, Jr.	50
Giant Sea Bass	680 lbs.	7'1½"	66"	Fernandina Beach, Fla.	May 20, 1961	Lynn Joyner	80
Sea Bass	8 lbs.	1'10"	19"	Nantucket Sound, Mass.	May 13, 1951	H.R. Rider	50
Striped Bass	72 lbs.	4'6½"	31"	Cuttyhunk, Mass.	Oct. 10, 1969	Edward J. Kirker	50
Blackfish or Tautog	21 lbs. 6 oz.	2'7½"	23½"	Cape May, N.J.	June 12, 1954	R.N. Sheafer	30
Bluefish	31 lbs. 12 oz.	3'11"	23"	Hatteras Inlet, N.C.	Jan. 30, 1972	James M. Hussey	50
Bonefish	19 lbs.	3'3 5/8"	17"	Zululand, S. Africa	May 26, 1962	Brian W. Batchelor	30
Oceanic Bonito	39 lbs. 15 oz.	3'3"	28"	Walker Cay, Bahamas	Jan. 21, 1952	F. Drowley	50
Oceanic Bonito	40 lbs.	3'2¾"	27½"	Baie du Tambeau, Mauritius	April 19, 1971	Joseph R.P. Caboche, Jr.	50
Cobia	110 lbs. 5 oz.	5'3"	34"	Mombasa, Kenya	Sept. 8, 1964	Eric Tinworth	50
Cod	98 lbs. 12 oz.	5'3"	41"	Isle of Shoals, Mass.	June 8, 1969	Alphonse J. Bielevich	20
Dolphin	85 lbs.	5'9"	37½"	Spanish Wells, Bahamas	May 29, 1968	Richard Seymour	50
Black Drum	98 lbs. 8 oz.	4'5"	40"	Willis Wharf, Va.	June 12, 1967	Gary Hilton Kelley	50
Flounder	30 lbs. 12 oz.	3'2½"	30½"	Vina del Mar, Chile	Nov. 1, 1971	Augusto Nunez Moreno	20
Kingfisher	78 lbs. 12 oz.	5'5½"	30"	La Romana, Dom. Rep.	Nov. 26, 1971	Fernando Viyella	50
Black Marlin	1560 lbs.	14'6"	81"	Cabo Blanco, Peru	Aug. 4, 1953	Alfred C. Glassell, Jr.	130
Atlantic Blue Marlin	845 lbs.	13'1"	71"	St. Thomas, Virgin Is.	July 4, 1968	Elliot J. Fishman	80
Pacific Blue Marlin	1153 lbs.	14'8"	73"	Ritidian Point, Guam	Aug. 21, 1969	Greg D. Perez	180
Striped Marlin	415 lbs.	11'	52"	Cape Brett, New Zealand	Mar. 31, 1964	B.C. Bain	80
White Marlin	159 lbs. 8 oz.	9'	36"	Pompano Beach, Fla.	April 25, 1953	W.E. Johnson	50
Permit	50 lbs. 8 oz.	3'8¾"	33¾"	Key West, Fla.	March 15, 1971	Marshal E. Earnest	20
Pollack	43 lbs.	4'	29"	Brielle, New Jersey	Oct. 21, 1964	Philip Barlow	50
Rainbow Runner	30 lbs. 15 oz.	3'11"	22"	Kauai, Hawaii	Apr. 27, 1963	Holbrook Goodale	130
Roosterfish	114 lbs.	5'4"	33"	La Paz, Mexico	June 1, 1960	Abe Sackheim	30
Atlantic Sailfish	141 lbs. 1 oz.	8'5"		Ivory Coast, Africa	Jan. 26, 1961	Tony Burnand	130
Pacific Sailfish	221 lbs.	10'9"		Santa Cruz Is., Galapagos Is.	Feb. 12, 1947	C.W. Stewart	130
Blue Shark	410 lbs.	11'6"	52"	Rockport, Mass.	Sept. 1, 1960	Richard C. Webster	80
Blue Shark	410 lbs.	11'2"	52½"	Rockport, Mass.	Aug. 17, 1967	Martha C. Webster	80
Mako Shark	1061 lbs.	12'2"	79½"	Mayor Island, N. Zealand	Feb. 17, 1970	James B. Penwarden	130
Man-Eater or White Shark	2664 lbs.	16'10"	114"	Ceduna, So. Australia	Apr. 21, 1959	Alfred Dean	130
Porbeagle Shark	430 lbs.	8'	63"	Channel Islands, England	June 29, 1969	Desmond Bougourd	80
Thresher Shark	729 lbs.	8'5"	61"	Mayor Island, N. Zealand	June 3, 1959	Mrs. V. Brown	130
Tiger Shark	1780 lbs.	13'10½"	103"	Cherry Grove, S. C.	June 14, 1964	Walter Maxwell	130
Snook or Robalo	52 lbs. 6 oz.	4'1½"	26"	La Paz, Mexico	Jan. 9, 1963	Jane Haywood	30
Swordfish	1182 lbs.	14'11¼"	78"	Iquique, Chile	May 7, 1953	L. Marron	130
Tanguigue	81 lbs.	5'11½"	29¼"	Karachi, Pakistan	Aug. 27, 1960	George E. Rusinak	80
Tarpon	283 lbs.	7'2 3/5"		Lake Maracaibo, Venezuela	Mar. 19, 1956	M. Salazar	30
Allison or Yellowfin Tuna	296 lbs.	6'9"	56"	San Benedicto Is., Mex.	March 7, 1971	Edward C. Malnar	80
Atlantic Big-eyed Tuna	295 lbs.	6'6½"	40"	San Miguel, Azores, Port.	July 8, 1960	Dr. Arsenio Cordeiro	130
Pacific Big-eyed Tuna	435 lbs.	7'9"	63½"	Cabo Blanco, Peru	Apr. 17, 1957	Dr. Russel V.A. Lee	130
Blackfin Tuna	38 lbs.	3'3¼"	28¾"	Bermuda	June 26, 1970	Archie L. Dickens	30
Bluefin Tuna	1065 lbs.	10'3"	96"	Cape Breton, Nova Scotia	Nov. 19, 1970	Robert Glen Gibson	130
Wahoo	149 lbs.	6'7¾"	37½"	Cat Cay, Bahamas	June 15, 1962	John Pirovano	\130
Weakfish	19 lbs. 8 oz.	3'1"	23¾"	Trinidad, W. Indies	April 13, 1962	Dennis B. Hall	80
Spotted Weakfish	15 lbs. 3 oz.	2'10½"	20½"	Ft. Pierce, Fla.	Jan. 13, 1949	C.W. Hubbard	50
Spotted Weakfish	15 lbs. 6 oz.	2'9"	23¾"	St. Lucie River, Fla.	May 4, 1969	Michael J. Foremny	30
Yellowtail	111 lbs.	5'2"	38"	Bay of Islands, N. Zeal.	Jun. 11, 1961	A.F. Plim	50

Women

Women's Records

Species	Lbs–oz.	Length	Girth	Place	Date	Angler	Line
Albacore	59-8	3'9½"	29½"	Montauk, N.Y.	Aug. 14, 1971	Eileen B. Merten	30
Amberjack	108-0	5'9"	36"	Palm Beach, Fla.	Dec. 30, 1967	Peggy Kester Luke	50
Barracuda	66-4	5'10"	25 1/5"	Cape Lopez, Gabon, Africa	July 17, 1955	Mme. M. Halley	80
Bass (Calif. Black Sea)	452-0	7'2¼"	64¼"	Coronado Is., Calif.	Oct. 8, 1960	Lorene Wheeler	80
Bass (Calif. White Sea)	62-0	4'9"	28"	Malibu, Calif.	Dec. 6, 1951	Mrs. D.W. Jackson	20
Bass (Channel)	69-8	4'3½"	33¼"	Cape Hatteras, N.C.	Nov. 16, 1958	Jean Browning	30
Bass (Sea)	5-2	1'1"	15"	Virginia Beach, Va.	May 17, 1971	Mrs. Charlotte J. Wright	20
Bass (Giant Sea)	366-0	7'4½"	68"	Guayabo, Panama	Feb. 8, 1965	Betsy B. Walker	80
Bass (Striped)	64-8	4'6"	30"	North Truro, Mass.	Aug. 14, 1960	Rosa O. Webb	30
Blackfish or Tautog	17-6	2'3½"	23¼"	Virginia Beach, Va.	May 5, 1971	Lillian T. Barrett	50
Bluefish	24-8			North Carolina	Nov. 12, 1971	Rita Mizelle	20
Bonefish	15-0	2'8½"	18½"	Bimini, Bahamas	Mar. 20, 1961	Andrea Tose	12
Bonito (Oceanic) (tie)	31-0	2'11"	24¾"	Nassau, Bahamas	Jan. 25, 1956	Mrs. Barbara Wallach	80
Bonito (Oceanic) (tie)	31-0	2'11"	24"	Kona, Hawaii	June 16, 1963	Anne H. Bosworth	130
Bonito (Oceanic) (tie)	31-0	2'10½"	24½"	San Juan, P.R.	Dec. 26, 1954	Gloria de Marques	50
Cobia	97-0	5'6½"	33"	Oregon Inlet, N.C.	June 4, 1952	Mary W. Black	80
Cod	81-12	4'11¾"	39"	Middlebank, Mass.	Sept. 24, 1970	Mrs. Sophie Karwa	80
Dolphin	73-11	4'11½"	43½"	Baja Calif., Mex.	July 12, 1962	Barbara Kibbee Jayne	30
Drum (Black)	93-0	4'2½"	42"	Fernandina Beach, Fla.	Mar. 28, 1957	Mrs. Stella Moore	50
Flounder	20-7	3'1"	29½"	Long Island, N.Y.	July 8, 1957	Mrs. M. Fredriksen	50
Kingfish (Tanguigue)	78-0	5'6½"	28½"	Guayanilla, P.R.	May 25, 1963	Ruth M. Coon	50
Marlin (Blue)	723-0	13'2"	68"	Bimini, Bahamas	Aug. 10, 1967	Mrs. J.M. Hollobaugh, Jr.	130
Marlin (Black)	1525-0	14'4"	80"	Cabo Blanco, Peru	Apr. 22, 1954	Kimberly Wiss	130
Marlin (Striped)	401-0	9'2"	50½"	Cavalli Is., New Zealand	Feb. 24, 1970	Mrs. Margaret Williams	50
Marlin (White)	142-0	8'2"	34"	Ft. Lauderdale, Fla.	Mar. 14, 1959	Marie Beneventi	80
Marlin (Pacific Blue)	623-0			Prince Edward Isl.	Oct. 15, 1971	Gertrude Collings	130
Permit	.39	3'5"	30"	Islamorada, Fla.	Apr. 2, 1966	Shelagh B. Richards	50
Pollack	38-0			Nova Scotia	Aug. 30, 1971	Ruth G. Verber	20
Rainbow Runner	23-0	3'6"	19½"	Oahu, Hawaiian Isl.	May 9, 1961	Lila M. Neuenfelt	50
Roosterfish	99-0	4'11½"	34½"	La Paz, Mex.	Nov. 30, 1964	Lilly Call	30
Sailfish (Atlantic)	108-4	8'9½"	34"	Luanda, Angola	Mar. 30, 1971	Mrs. Ellen Botha	50
Sailfish (Pacific)	199-0	10'	42"	Pinas Bay, Panama	Jan. 17, 1968	Carolyn B. Brinkman	80
Shark (Blue)	410-0	11'2"	52½"	Rockport, Mass.	Aug. 17, 1967	Martha C. Webster	80
Shark (Mako)	911-12	11'2"	70"	Palm Beach, Fla.	Apr. 9, 1962	Audrey Cohen	130
Shark (Maneater or White)	1052-0	13'10"	72½"	Cape Moreton, Australia	June 27, 1954	Mrs. Bob Dyer	130
Shark (Porbeagle)	369-0	8'6"	48"	Looe, Cornwall, Eng.	July 20, 1970	Mrs. Patricia W. Smith	130
Shark (Thresher)	729-0	8'5"	61"	Mayor Is., New Zealand	June 3, 1959	Mrs. V. Brown	130
Shark (Tiger)	1314-0	13'9"	89"	Cape Moreton, Australia	July 27, 1953	Mrs. Bob Dyer	130
Snook (or Robalo)	52-6	4'1½"	26"	La Paz, Mexico	Jan. 9, 1963	Jane Haywood	30
Swordfish	772-0	12'10"	70"	Iquique, Chile	June 7, 1954	Mrs. L. Marron	80
Tanguigue	68-0	5'8"	26"	Hayman Is., Australia	May 19, 1969	Lady Joan Ansett	30
Tarpon	203-0	7'11"	44"	Marathon, Fla.	May 19, 1961	June Jordan	80
Tuna (Allison or Yellowfin)	254-0	6'3"	52"	Kona, Hawaii	Aug. 19, 1954	Jean Carlisle	130
Tuna (Atlantic Bigeyed)	182-0	5'8"	56"	Cat Cay, Bahamas	June 2, 1958	Mrs. Matilde Catta	130
Tuna (Pacific Bigeyed)	336-0	7'3"	56½"	Cabo Blanco, Peru	Jan. 16, 1957	Mrs. Seymour Knox III	130
Tuna (Blackfin)	32-2	3'2"	26¾"	Bermuda	Oct. 23, 1968	Mrs. Herbert N. Arnold	20
Tuna (Bluefin)	886-0			Prince Edward Isl.	Oct. 15, 1971	Gertrude Collings	130
Wahoo	113-0	6'2"	33¼"	Yanuca, Fiji	June 30, 1967	Jan K. Bates	50
Weakfish	11-12	2'7¾"	18"	Newport, R., N.C.	Oct. 29, 1950	Mrs. L.A. Denning	50
Weakfish (Spotted)	14-0	2'9"	18"	Stuart, Fla.	Apr. 25, 1970	Marilyn C. Albright	30
Yellowfish (tie)	81-0	4'9½"	32½"	Cape Brett, New Zealand	May 18, 1960	Kora Beale	80
Yellowfish (tie)	81-0	4'11½"	32½"	Mayor Isl., New Zealand	Apr. 8, 1966	Patricia E. Jack	130

CAUGHT WITH ROD AND REEL IN FRESH WATER

Source: Field & Stream Magazine, 383 Madison Avenue, New York N.Y., 10017

Species	Lbs.–Oz.	Length	Girth	Place	Date	Angler
Bass, Largemouth	22-4	32½"	28½"	Montgomery Lake, Ga.	June 2, 1932	George A. Perry
Bass, Redeye	6-½	20½"	15 4/5"	Hallawakee Creek, Ala.	Mar. 24, 1967	Thomas L. Sharpe
Bass, Rock	2-2	13"	14"	Mille Coquin Lake, Mich.	Aug. 13, 1971	Richard M. Barta
Bass, Smallmouth	11-15	27"	21 2/3"	Dale Hollow Lake, Ky.	July 9, 1955	David H. Hayes
Bass, Spotted	8-0	24"	18¼"	Smith Lake, Ala.	Mar. 7, 1966	Bob Hamilton
Bass, White	5-5	19½"		Ferguson Lake, Calif.	Mar. 8, 1972	Norman W. Mize
Bass, Yellow	2-2	14"	13"	Lake Monoma, Wis.	Jan. 18, 1972	James Thrun
Bluegill Sunfish	4-12	15"	18¼"	Ketona Lake, Ala.	Apr. 9, 1950	T.S. Hudson
Bowfin	17	34"	21¾"	Barnett Reservoir, Miss.	May 10, 1972	Oliver Leonard
Bullhead, Black	8	24"	17¾"	Lake Waccabuc, N.Y.	Aug. 1, 1951	Kani Evans
Carp	55-5	42"	31"	Clearwater Lake, Minn.	July 10, 1952	Frank J. Ledwein
Catfish, Blue	97-0	57"	37"	Missouri River, S.D.	Sept. 16, 1959	Edward B. Elliott
Catfish, Channel	58-0	47¼"	28 1/8"	Santee-Cooper Res., S.C.	July 7, 1964	W.B. Whaley

Catfish, Flathead 76	53"	32"	Piedmont Lake, Ohio ....July 12, 1972	Dale C. Yoho
Char, Arctic 29-11	39¾"	26"	Arctic River, N.W.T. ..... Aug. 21, 1968	Jeanne P. Branson
Crappie, Black 5	19¼"	18 5/8"	Santee Cooper Reserv., S.C. ..Mar. 15, 1957	Paul E. Foust
Crappie, White 5-3	21"	19"	Enid Dam, Miss. ....July 31, 1957	Fred L. Bright
Dolly Varden 32	40½"	29¾"	Pend Oreille Lake, Ida. .....Oct. 27, 1949	N.L. Higgins
Drum, Freshwater 54-8	31½"	29"	Nickajack Dam, Tenn. .....Apr. 20, 1972	Benny E. Hull
Gar, Alligator 279	93"		Rio Grande River, Tex. ......Dec. 2, 1951	G. Valverde
Gar, Longnose 50-5	72¼"	22¼"	Trinity River, Tex. ....July 30, 1954	Townsend Miller
Grayling, Arctic 5-15	29 7/8"	15 1/8"	Katseyedie River, N.W.T. .... Aug. 16, 1967	Jeanne P. Branson
Muskellunge 69-15	64½"	31¾"	St. Lawrence River, N.Y. ... Sept. 22, 1957	Arthur Lawton
Perch, White 4-12	19½"	13"	Messalonskee Lake, Me. ..... June 4, 1949	Mrs. Earl Small
Perch, Yellow 4-3½			Bordentown, N.J. ....May 1865	Dr. C.C. Abbot
Pickerel, Chain 9-6	31"	14"	Homerville, Ga. ....Feb. 17, 1961	Baxley McQuaig, Jr.
Pike, Northern 46-2	52½"	25"	Sacandaga Reservoir, N.Y. ... Sept. 15, 1940	Peter Dubuc
Salmon, Atlantic 79-2			Tanaelv, Norway 1928	Henrik Henriksen
Salmon, Chinook 92	58½"	36"	Skeena River, B.C. ....July 19, 1959	Heinz Wickmann
Salmon, Landlocked 22-8	36"		Sebago Lake, Me. .... Aug. 1, 1907	Edward Blakely
Salmon, Silver 31			Cowichan Bay, B.C. ....Oct. 11, 1947	Mrs. Lee Hallberg
Sauger 8-12	28"	15"	Lake Sakakawea, N.D. ......Oct. 6, 1971	Mike Fischer
Sturgeon, White 360-0	111"	86"	Snake River, Ida. ....April 24, 1956	Willard Cravens
Sunfish, Redear 4-8	16¼"	17¾"	Chase City, Va. .... June 19, 1970	Maurice E. Ball
Trout, Brook 14-8	31½"	11½"	Nipigon River, Ont. ....July 1916	Dr. W.J. Cook
Trout, Brown 39-8			Loch Awe, Scotland 1866	W. Muir
Trout, Cut-Throat 41	39"		Pyramid Lake, Nev. ....Dec. 1925	John Skimmerhorn
Trout, Golden 11	28"	16"	Cook's Lake, Wyo. .... Aug. 5, 1948	Chas. S. Reed
Trout, Lake 65	52"	38"	Great Bear Lake, N.W.T. .... Aug. 8, 1970	Larry Daunis
Trout, Rainbow				
(Kamloops & Steelhead) 42-2	43"	23½"	Bell Isl., Alaska ...... June 22, 1970	David Robert White
Trout, Sunapee 11-8	33"	17¼"	Lake Sunapee, N.H. .... Aug. 1, 1954	Ernest Theoharis
Walleye 25	41"	29"	Old Hickory Lake, Tenn. .... Aug. 1, 1960	Mabry Harper
Warmouth 1-13	10¾"	12¼"	Cumberland County, Ill. ....May 22, 1971	Wesley Mills
Whitefish, Mountain 5	19"	14"	Athabasca R., Alberta ...... June 3, 1963	Orville Welch

OTHER FRESH-WATER RECORDS
(Caught by any method)

If no species is listed, the above records stand.

Carp—83 lbs., 8 oz., caught at Pretoria, South Africa

Catfish, Blue—117 lbs., Osage River, Mo.

Muskellunge—102 lbs., Minocqua Lake, Wis.

Salmon, Atlantic—103 lbs., 2 oz., River Devon, Scotland

Salmon, Chinook—126 lbs., 8 oz., Petersburg, Alaska

Salmon, Landlocked—35 lbs., Crooked River, Me.

Trout, Brown—40 lbs., Great Lake, Tasmania

Trout, Lake—102 lbs., Lake Athabasca, Sask.

ARCHERY

(Courtesy Dr. Grace Frye Amborski, President, National Archery Association, 2833 Lincoln Highway, East, Ronks, Pennsylvania 17572

Archery is making tremendous strides in popularity. Whereas once it was a means of livelihood and defense, archery today in the civilized world is pursued as a sport. Increasing numbers are turning to it, and many persons are using it as a means of hunting—a method that makes the acquisition of game, especially deer, more difficult and more fascinating than by means of firearms. In some states, special deer seasons are allocated to archers. Where game is not involved targets are used.

Perhaps the most remarkable sport in the world is archery, partly because of its antiquity, but chiefly because this gentle form of modern diversion once was used as the means to kill in warfare.

Arrows now are shot away from bows—by refined, civilized people—only at a target with a variety of circles, the one driving closest to the inner circle with a specific number of arrows being acclaimed the champion. It was this principle of shooting—but with humans as targets—that devastated the world for thirty centuries—until gunfire became the more effective weapon, about 300 years ago.

No historian has been able to establish exactly which people were first to use the bow and arrow. Inasmuch as archery equipment of ancient kind has been found on all the continents, the conclusion is that the principle of archery was hit upon by the different nations, or tribes, without foreign prompting.

Most writers on archery have held that Australia was the one continent where the bow and arrow were unknown in more ancient times. This is disputed by Dr. Robert P. Elmer, many times United States archery champion, in his book "Archery," who stated that arrows about one foot in length, the size usually used when the tips are treated with poison, have been found in Australia and belonged to tribes long since vanished from earth.

Dr. Elmer's search caused him to offer the thought that perhaps the Aurignacians, a race which existed about 15,000 years ago, might have been first to use the bow and arrow. The bow and arrow next are discovered in Egypt, and the time is fixed by Dr. Elmer as about seventy centuries ago. Other authorities place archery's extreme age at 5,000 to 6,000 years. Since the Hebrew Chronology, compiled carefully through many centuries, fixes the creation of Adam, the first man, as less than 6,000 years ago, the reader is left to create his own conclusions as to the age of archery.

The bow and arrow were used first for hunting, but the war-like Egyptians, in the time of the earliest Pharaohs, discovering that the arrow could outrange both the sling-shot, man's first weapon in warfare, and the spear, which was the next weapon, took speedy advantage of that knowledge. Inasmuch as the sling-shot had a shooting range of only 140 feet and the javelin a maximum throwing range around 175 feet, the Egyptians secretly equipped their troops with bows and arrows and caused them to practice marksmanship. The arrow could be shot up to 300 feet.

A short time later, Egypt went to war with Persia, then a mighty power, and the Persian warriors, using only sling-shots and javelins, were almost annihilated by the arrows fired by the Egyptians from distances where they were safe from the javelins of the Persians. Egypt quickly conquered Persia and immediately warred successfully on other nations before any of them could train troops in archery. The bow and arrow made Egypt a victorious nation after years of being Persia's puppet.

Very quickly thereafter other nations discarded the sling-shot and javelin and developed their own archers, and the bow and arrow was the major weapon in warfare for centuries before the dawn of the Christian Era and for approximately 1,600 years thereafter.

If an arrow did not immediately kill its victim through those 3,000 odd years of countless battles, it usually meant death if the warrior were struck in the upper body or head. Surgery was practically unknown, and even if it had been developed to the high science of today, the life of the stricken man hardly could have been saved because modern surgeons regard the extraction of an arrow from a human body as an almost fatal operation.

It was the custom, when an army had been victorious, for the able warriors to move over the battlefield and—as an act of mercy—to slit the throats of comrades whose bodies had been pierced by an arrow. The stricken soldiers of the defeated army usually were left where they fell to die slowly from loss of blood, from thirst or from gangrene.

The original Egyptian bow was from 4½ to 5 feet tall, and the arrows were from 24 to 32 inches in length, tipped with bronze. In countries where bronze was not available, stone, or flint, was used, while in others the wooden tip was sharpened to a fine point. Some authorities credit the Greeks with using a bow made of a composition of wood, horn and sinew. When unstrung, it took the form of a letter "C." It was a bow of this type that Ulysses, the jealous one, used to shoot his wife's admirers.

Frederick W. Kasch, former Director of Physical Education at the University of Illinois, offered the conclusion, based on research, that the Turks, not the Greeks, pioneered the use of the "C" bow, which bow was very short.

Experiments developed that the longer the bow, the greater the firing range, and as time went on the standard bow became 6 feet in height. The cross-bow, a devastating weapon, followed, and its greatest success was in the various wars that rent Europe for hundreds of years.

The Turks, according to some historians, used a bow about 6 feet long as well as the short "C" bow. African bows of the dim years were straight and about 5 feet tall. The Pygmies called on a 3-foot bow. The South American bow was between 6 and 7 feet high, while that of the North American Indian was rather short and generally made of hickory.

Just which European country was first to adopt archery is still a matter in dispute. The Genoese are known to have been experts with the bow since shortly after the dawn of the Christian Era. Drawings uncovered a few years ago in caverns in Southwestern France and Spain, which are regarded as at least 2,000 years old, show archers with bows in their hands and stricken animals with arrows in their bodies. Archery equipment, with age estimated at between 1,500 and 2,000 years, has been uncovered in Northern Europe.

So far as can be established, the English, up to about 1,200 years ago, used a bow of from 4½ to 5 feet. Soon afterward, that nation, destined to become the most expert and successful in all Europe in the use of the bow, was using one about 6 feet tall. The change is said to have been influenced by the successes of the Norsemen, who invaded England, won many victories and, from 850 A.D. until almost 1050 A.D. controlled more of England than did the English.

Early in the 14th Century, the English Army, which had used the bow only in limited fashion up to that time, having depended mainly on mounted lancers, decided that archery was something really worth while in warfare, and thereafter its kings made practice at archery compulsory. As a consequence, England developed the best bowmen in Europe. The entire history of Europe might have been radically different if England had not gone in for expertness at archery exactly when she did. Otherwise she might have been conquered—and perhaps absorbed—by France during the war that started in 1340 and lasted for 100 years.

France had its crack archers massed for attack on English troops. Its warriors outnumbered those of England. But the English had been drilled in marksmanship, and it was because of this that they won important victories at Crécy, Poitiers and Agincourt.

In 1360, the English leaders, who previously had kept the bowmen on the ground, mounted a few as a test, and the result was an increase in shooting range from a maximum of 400 feet up to 650 and 700 feet. In the next battle, England flung its mounted bowmen against the French and the result was a catastrophe for France, which lost 11 princes, 1,200 knights and about 15,000 soldiers, whereas the English loss was fewer than 50.

England, however, was not the first to mount its archers. Genghis Khan, the mighty Mongol, used mounted troops in his battles that started about 1200 A.D. He allotted his cavalrymen two and sometimes three horses, and history records that almost all of his soldiers were mounted. The Khan's mounted archers could outrange the foot enemy, and, because this was so, his warriors could—and did—keep out of danger, while his cavalry bowmen dealt out death and devastation to all enemies.

The invasion by the Spanish Armada, in 1588, marked the end of the bow as a weapon of first importance. The Spanish, as usual, called on the bow and arrow. The English equipped 10,000 of their troops with firearms, as an experiment, and their success against the Spaniards relegated archery into a secondary position as a factor in warfare.

In 1644 the Royalists used the bow in Scotland against the Covenanters, and the final appearance of the bow for warfare in the British Isles was in 1888, during the brief clash between the clans of MacDonald and MacIntosh. France discarded the bow after some internal conflicts in 1630. The last time the bow was used in a major battle was by the Chinese in 1860 at Taku, although, of course, American Indians used them for many years later, and savage tribes in Africa and elsewhere still fight with bow and poison-tipped arrow.

Japan, during the 16th and 17th Centuries, used the biggest bows known to history. They were from 7 feet 6 inches to beyond 8 feet in height. Occasional tournaments were staged in the royal halls of Kioto and Tokyo, where the marked-off shooting range was 384 feet. It is recorded that Wada Daihachi, in the 17th Century, shot 8,133 arrows down the hall in a 24-hour endurance contest—a rate of 5 shots per minute.

In England in 1673 a small group of enthusiasts in Yorkshire created the "Ancient Scorton Arrow" contest and awarded a small silver bow to the winner. This organization still functions and the "Arrow" is the oldest continuous archery tournament.

Archery was fostered as a sport in 1676 by King Charles II of England. Queen Catherine of Braganza, an enthusiast, advocated the formation of clubs and awarded a silver shield, on which was inscribed "Marshal of the Fraternity of Archery" to those who won championships. Other European nations gave hearty approval and the sport flourished through the 17th, 18th, 19th and into this century.

The "Society Royal Toxophilite" was formed in England about 1790 for the purpose of advancing archery as a sport. In 1844 the Grand National came into existence and now is the ruling group in Great Britain. It arranged the first championship for the year 1844.

Archery was introduced into the United States as a sport in the 17th Century, but made little progress during the next 150 years. In 1828 a group was organized as the "United Bowmen of Philadelphia" and then discovered that it had no equipment. In this emergency, a committee visited a museum in Philadelphia, where sketches were made of the bows and arrows there. The bowmen then fashioned their own equipment, which served them until the following year, when they imported standard bows and arrows from England.

The club disbanded in 1859.

A revival in archery in the United States occurred in 1878 and led to the formation, in 1879, of the National Archery Association, now the governing body of the sport. The organization had its headquarters in Boston for nearly thirty years, with Louis C. Smith serving as secretary-treasurer during that period. His daughter, Mrs. Dorothy Smith Cummings, won the national championship seven times and the Eastern title eleven. Smith's son-in-law, Henry S.C. Cummings, was chairman of the Board of Governors of the N.A.A. for eight years and succeeded Smith as secretary-treasurer.

As the years went by interest in archery has continued to grow. In the 1940's quite a few states legalized hunting with bow and arrow and opened up a complete new phase of archery to thousands of hunters. These hunters were not interested in formal target archery. Archery hunters, or field archers, had revised the old British sport of Rovers to give them sufficient practice for hunting. Like the English, however, they found that they needed a competitive round to enjoy to the maximum the skills that they had acquired in shooting the bow. A group of these field archers formed the National Field Archery Association.

Before 1930 the sport of archery attained considerable growth not only in the United States but in many other countries throughout the world. An international organization was formed and was officially titled, Federation Internationale de Tir a l'Arc (FITA). FITA shot its first World Championship Tournament in 1931 in Poland. At first FITA held annual tournaments; however, travel costs and time involved were so great that the tournaments were finally held every two years.

Although archery had been included in the 1908 and 1920 Olympic Games, it was not until 1958 that it was again included as an optional sport. In 1965, it was announced that the International Olympic Committee had accepted archery on the program of the 1972 Olympics. With this recognition the N.A.A. had to make new rulings regarding the amateur standing of competitors. Up to the 1960's, the N.A.A. had made no differential between the amateur archer and the professional. If the United States hoped to field a team in the Olympics, more stringent rules had to be made.

The Professional Archers Organization (P.A.A.) was organized in 1961 for archers who wished to engage in phases of the sport that would disqualify them as amateur archers. The P.A.A. has an annual championship competition with cash prizes for the winners.

One of the modern contributions to archery is the establishment of indoor ranges. The use of these ranges, fully automated, is growing in popularity all over the country.

Many classes of competition (rounds) have been developed in American Archery. The York Round, used in men's contests from 1879 through 1910 to determine the national champion of the N.A.A., requires the shooting of 72 arrows at a 100-yard range, 48 at 80 yards and 24 at 60. In 1911, the American Round calling for 30 shots at 60 yards, 30 at 50 and 30 at 40 was introduced and from then until 1914 champions were decided in both categories. Since 1915 the United States champion has been the one with the highest aggregate score of both rounds.

The International Round (FITA Round) which which is shot in World Championship competition is now included in the N.A.A. Championship Tournament. In this round 36 arrows are shot at 90 meters, 36 at 70 meters, 36 at 50 meters and 36 at 30 meters.

There also are several rounds for women. From 1879 through 1909, the National Round, 48 shots at 60 yards and 24 at 50, determined the United States champion. The Columbia, 24 shots at 50 yards, 24 at 40 and 24 at 30, was

introduced in 1910 and through 1914 had a separate champion. In 1915 both rounds were combined to decide the titleholder on the basis of aggregate score. In addition, women now shoot an American Round as well as a FITA Round in N.A.A. championship competition. The women's FITA Round is similar to the men's except the distances are 70, 60, 50 and 30 meters.

With the development of automated archery ranges, indoor shooting, particularly in the winter time, had become very popular. One of the oldest indoor rounds is the Chicago Round consisting of 96 arrows shot at 20 yards on a 16 inch target face. The indoor P.A.A. Round and the 300 Round consist of 60 arrows at 20 yards.

The professional archers have designed an Outdoor Round called the P.A.A. Round which is ideal for their purpose. They use short shooting distances and a large high-scoring area on the target face.

The National Field Archery Association (N.F.AAA) has three main tournament rounds; the Field Round, the Hunter's Round, and the Animal Round. In the Field Round the target distances vary from 15 to 80 yards, and in the Hunter's Round the distances average roughly one-third less. The Animal Round distances are even shorter and the target faces are drawings or cutouts of animals.

The N.A.A. has been trying for years to get field archery accepted by FITA for international competition. FITA has now specified regulations for an International Field Round. These standards vary only slightly from the N.F.A.A. Field Round. One of the greatest difficulties in getting Field Archery accepted in International Competition has been the great amount of space required for the rounds. Some countries already shoot field and are quite enthusiastic about it. However, many of the smaller European and Asiatic countries have such a large population that they do not have 20 acres or more of land free for a field archery course.

FAMOUS AMERICAN ARCHERS

Men

The first of the great bowmen developed in this country was Will H. Thompson, winner of the pioneer national tournament at Chicago in 1879, who repeated as champion in 1884, 1888, 1901 and in 1908, which was 29 years after he won his first title.

L.W. Maxson was another star in the early years. He won championships in 1889, 1890, 1891, 1892, 1893, 1894 and 1898. Dr. Elmer, not only a great bowman but also an authority on the history of archery, won the American Round in 1911 and 1913 and won both the American and York rounds in 1914, 1915, 1916,

1919, 1920 and 1922. Russ Hoogerhyde, one of the brightest stars, captured titles in 1930, 1931, 1932, 1934, 1937 and 1940.

Other outstanding bowmen of earlier years were R. Williams Jr., W.A. Clark, G.P. Bryant, W.H. Palmer Jr. and P.W. Crouch. Included among the moderns who have gained a great measure of fame are Carl Oelschleger, Larry Hughes, Curtis L. Hill, Homer Prouty, G. Wayne Thompson, Herbert Henderson, Russ Reynolds, Stan Overby, Jack Wilson, Paul Berry, Charles Pierson, Jack Stewart, Irving H. Baker, Robert Larsen, Joe Fries, Bill Glackin, Robert Rhode, Bill Bednar, Charles Sandlin, and David Keaggy, Jr.

Women

The most remarkable woman archer in the history of the sport in America was Mrs. M.C. Howell. She gained her first United States title in 1883. She also won the national championship in 1885, 1886, 1890, 1891, 1892, 1893, 1895, 1896, 1898, 1899, 1900, 1902, 1903, 1904, 1905 and 1907—seventeen times a champion over a span of a little more than two decades.

Mrs. A.H. Gibbs twice was a national champion; Mrs. A.M. Phillips won the title three times—1887, 1888, 1889—in the era when Mrs. Howell was at her peak. Cynthia Weston won the national crown three times—1915, 1916 and 1920. Dorothy Smith, later Mrs. Cummings, flashed into national prominence for the first time in 1919 by winning the championship. She repeated in 1921, 1922, 1924, 1925, 1926 and 1931, to make her runner-up to Mrs. Howell in the ownership of titles.

Jean Lee of Springfield, Mass., and Mrs. Ann Weber Corby of Boonton, N.J., also have a high rating in this group. Both women have won the United States championship four times, Miss Lee in successive years starting in 1948 and Mrs. Corby in 1940, 1946, 1947 and 1952. In 1952, Miss Lee also won the world title for the second year in a row.

Other fine performers in the more modern era include Mrs. Rea Dillinger Dietrich, Mrs. Eloise Ruby, Sharlene Skanes, Mrs. Jean Richards, Artie Palkowski, Mrs. Olive Crouch, Carole Meinhart, Ann Clark, Margaret Tillbury, Nancy Vonderheide Kleinman, Victoria Cook, Doreen Wilbur, and John Williams.

WORLD ARCHERY CHAMPIONS

Men	Points
1931—M. Sawicki, Poland	478
1932—L. Reith, Belgium	456
1933—D. Mackenzie, United States	1,126
1934—H. Kjellson, Sweden	1,225
1935—A. van Kohlen, Belgium	422
1936—E. Heilborn, Sweden	1,870
1937—G. de Rons, Belgium	2,072
1938—F. Hadas, Czechoslovakia	2,305
1939—R. Beday, France	2,407
1940-45—No competition	
1946—E. Tang-Holbek, Denmark	2,577
1947—H. Deutgen, Sweden	2,953
1948—H. Deutgen, Sweden	2,963
1949—H. Deutgen, Sweden	2,949
1950—H. Deutgen, Sweden	3,141
1951—No competition	
1952—S. Andersson, Sweden	3,151
1953—B. Lundgren, Sweden	3,205
1954—No competition	
1955—N. Andersson, Sweden	3,020
1957—O.K. Smathers, United States	2,231
1958—S. Thysell, Sweden	2,101
1959—James Casper, United States	—
1961—Joseph Thornton, United States	—
1963—C.T. Sandlin, United States	—
1965—M. Haikonen, Finland	—
1967—Ray Rogers, United States	2,298
1969—Hardy Ward, United States	2,423
1970—Stephen Lieberman, United States	—
1971—John Williams, United States	2,445
1972—John Williams, United States	1,068

(Competition held every 2 years from 1959 to 1969.)

Women	
1933—J. Kurkowska, Poland	942
1934—J. Kurkowska, Poland	867
1935—I. Catani, Swedden	332
1936—J. Kurkowska, Poland	1,875
1937—Mrs. Simons, England	1,776
1938—Mrs. Weston-Martyr, England	1,973
1939—J. Kurkowska, Poland	2,087
1940-45—No competition	
1946—P. Burr, England	1,922
1947—J. Kurkowska, Poland	2,321
1948—P. Burr, England	2,506
1949—Miss Waterhouse, England	2,605
1950—J. Lee, United States	3,254
1951—No competition	
1952—J. Lee, United States	3,185
1953—J. Richards, United States	3,056
1954—No competition	
1955—K. Wisniowska, Poland	3,033
1957—C. Meinhart, United States	2,120
1958—S. Johansson, Sweden	2,053
1959—Mrs. Ann Weber Corby, United States	—
1961—Nancy Vonderheide, United States	—
1963—V. Cook, United States	—
1965—M. Lindholm, Finland	—
1967—Maria Maczynska, Poland	2,240
1969—Dorothy Lidstone, British Columbia	2,361
1970—Eunice Schewe, United States	—
1971—Emma Gapchenko, Russia	2,380
1972—Maureen Bechdoldt, United States	921

(Competition held every 2 years from 1959 to 1969.)

Men's Team

1931—France	1,277
1932—Poland	1,190
1933—Belgium	2,428
1934—Sweden	3,361
1935—Belgium	1,151
1936—Czechoslovakia	5,093
1937—Poland	5,809
1938—Czechoslovakia	6,154
1939—France	6,745
1940-45—No competition	
1946—Denmark	7,300
1947—Czechoslovakia	7,637
1948—Sweden	8,087
1949—Czechoslovakia	8,370
1950—Denmark	2,391
1951—No competition	
1952—Sweden	2,493
1953—Sweden	9,355
1954—No competition	
1955—Sweden	8,697
1957—United States	6,591
1958—Finland	5,936
1959—United States	—
1961—United States	—
1963—United States	—
1965—United States	—
1967—United States	6,816
1969—United States	7,194
1971—United States	7,050

(Competition held every 2 years since 1959.)

Women's Team

1933—Poland	2,627
1934—Poland	2,265
1935—England	753
1936—Poland	5,239
1937—England	4,879
1938—Poland	5,754
1939—Poland	5,605
1940-45—No competition	
1946—England	5,021
1947—Denmark	5,647
1948—Czechoslovakia	6,535
1949—England	7,622
1950—Finland	2,417
1951—No competition	
1952—United States	2,675
1953—Finland	7,681
1954—No competition	
1955—England	8,679
1957-59—United States	—
1961—United States	—
1963—United States	—
1965—United States	—
1967—Poland	6,686
1969—Russia	6,897
1971—Poland	6,907

(Competition held every 2 years since 1959.)

UNITED STATES ARCHERY CHAMPIONS

Men

(York Round only from 1879–1910; separate champions listed for American Round, 1911–1914; thereafter highest aggregate scorer in both rounds became champion.)

1879—Will H. Thompson
1880—L.L. Peddinghaus
1881—F.H. Walworth
1882—H.S. Taylor
1883—R. Williams Jr.
1884—Will H. Thompson
1885—R. Williams Jr.
1886-87—W.A. Clark
1888—Will H. Thompson
1889-94—L.W. Maxson
1895—No record
1896—D.F. McGowan
1897—W.A. Clark
1898—L.W. Maxson
1899—M.C. Howell
1900—A.R. Clark
1901—Will H. Thompson
1902—R. Williams Jr.
1903—W. Bryant
1904-05—G.P. Bryant
1906—No record
1907—H.B. Richardson
1908—Will H. Thompson
1909—G.P. Bryant
1910—H.B. Richardson
1911—G.P. Bryant (York)
1911—Robert P. Elmer (American)
1912—G.P. Bryant (York and American)
1913—J.W. Doughty (York)
1913—Robert P. Elmer (American)
1914—Robert P. Elmer (York and American)
1915-16—Robert P. Elmer
1917-18—No competition
1919-20—Robert P. Elmer
1921—J.S. Jiles
1922—Robert P. Elmer
1923—W.H. Palmer Jr.
1924—J.S. Jiles
1925—P.W. Crouch
1926—S.F. Spencer
1927—P.W. Crouch
1928—W.H. Palmer Jr.
1929—E.H. Roberts
1930-32—Russ Hoogerhyde
1933—R. Miller
1934—Russ Hoogerhyde
1935-36—Gilman Keasey
1937—Russ Hoogerhyde
1938-39—Pat Chambers
1940—Russ Hoogerhyde
1941—Larry Hughes
1942-45—No competition
1946—G. Wayne Thompson
1947—Jack Wilson
1948—Larry Hughes

1949—Russ Reynolds
1950—Stan Overby
1951—Russ Reynolds
1952—Robert Larsen
1953—Bill Glackin
1954—Robert J. Rhode
1955-57—Joe Fries
1958—Robert Bitner
1959 Bert Vetrovsky
1960—Robert Kadlec
1961—Clayton Sherman
1962—Charles Sandlin
1963—James Yoakum
1964—David Keaggy, Jr.
1965—George Slinzer
1966—Lester Gervais
1967—Ray Rogers
1968—Hardy Ward
1969—Ray Rogers
1970—Joe Thornton
1971-72—John Williams

Women

(From 1879 through 1909, the winner of the National Round was the champion; from 1910 through 1914, a Columbia Round champion also was determined; thereafter the highest aggregate scorer in both rounds was declared the title-holder.)

1879—Mrs. S. Brown
1880—Mrs. T. Davis
1881-82—Mrs. A.H. Gibbs
1883—Mrs. M.C. Howell
1884—Mrs. G.S. Hall
1885-86—Mrs. M.C. Howell
1887-89—Mrs. A.M. Phillips
1890-93—Mrs. M.C. Howell
1894—Mrs. A.S. Kern
1895-96—Mrs. M.C. Howell
1897—Mrs. J.S. Barker
1898-1900—Mrs. M.C. Howell
1901—Mrs. C.E. Woodruff
1902-05—Mrs. M.C. Howell
1906—E.C. Cooke
1907—Mrs. M.C. Howell
1908-09—H. Case
1910—J.V. Sullivan (National)
1910—L.M. Witwer (Columbia)
1911—Mrs. J.H. Taylor (National and Columbia)
1912—Mrs. W. Tayler (National and Columbia)
1913—Mrs. P.S. Fletcher (National)
1913—Mrs. L.C. Smith (Columbia)
1914—Mrs. B.P. Gray (National and Columbia)
1915-16—Cynthia Weston
1917-18—No competition
1919—Dorothy Smith
1920—Cynthia Weston
1921-22—Dorothy Smith
1923—N. Peirce
1924-26—Dorothy Smith
1927—Mrs. R. Johnson
1928—Mrs. B. Hodgson

1929-30—Mrs. A. Grubbs
1931—Mrs. Dorothy Smith Cummings
1932—Ilda Hanchett
1933—Mildred Taylor
1934—Mrs. G.D. Mudd
1935—Mrs. Ruth Hodgert
1936—Mrs. Gladys Hammer
1937-38—Jean A. Tenney
1939—Mrs. Belvia Carter
1940—Ann Weber
1941—Mrs. Rea Dillinger Dietrich
1942-45—No competition
1946-47—Ann Weber
1948-51—Jean Lee
1952-53—Mrs. Ann Weber Corby
1954—Laurette Young
1955—Mrs. Ann Clark
1956-59—Carol Meinhart
1960—Ann Clark
1961—Victoria Cook
1962—Nancy Vonderheide
1963—Jewel Hamilton
1964—Victoria Cook
1965—Nancy Pfeifer
1966—Evelyn Goodrich
1967—Ardelle Mills
1968—Victoria Cook
1969—Doreen Wilber
1970—Nancy Myrick
1971—Doreen Wilber
1972—Janet Craig

(For Olympic Archery champions, see section on Olympic Games.)

FLIGHT SHOOTING

In addition to shooting at fixed targets, the archers also indulge in variations called "flight shooting" and "free style shooting," both being for distance, and not accuracy.

In "flight shooting" the archer stands erect, holding the arrow in one hand, the bow in the other—the same position as when shooting at a target. But in "free style shooting" the archer lies on his back, with the bow strapped to his feet, and draws the bowstring with both hands. The pull on the bow in regular flight shooting scales from 45 to 85 pounds, but in free flight shooting, the pull is about 150 pounds.

Flight shooting records have skyrocketed in recent years. In 1928 the best the men could do in the unlimited division (regular style) was 300 yards 9 inches. The record in 1958 was 705 yards 2 feet. The free-style mark, 518 yards in 1933, was boosted to 790 yards in 1958. Women also have made long strides in the flight field. Their unlimited record in 1928 was 259 yards. This was almost doubled when the measuring rod showed 505 yards in 1950. The women's free-style mark has jumped from 406 yards 1 foot 10 inches in 1937 to 575 yards 2 feet.

FIELD ARCHERY

Field Archery is so named because it is the style of archery used for thousands of years by our ancestors, when efficient use of the bow spelled the difference between life and death, both in hunt and warfare.

After the invention of gunpowder, archery, in civilized lands, was pretty well forgotten, only to be revived in England in the middle of the 19th Century in an entirely different and rather artificial form, advises John L. Yount, secretary of the National Field Archery Association. Where the bow originally had belonged to the rough and ready peasants, it now was used in a gentlemanly target archery contest by the aristocracy.

This game of target archery continued to be the only archery game until about 1935, when a small group in Redlands, Calif., started experimenting with games that called for the kind of shooting that the peasants had done in the old days when the chips were down and good shooting meant survival. That is, shooting without sight or point of aim at targets which have been placed at various distances in natural surroundings.

Even though the first field courses were crude affairs, it didn't take long to find that here was a game that would popularize the bow with a whole new section of the American public. It was a carefree game that required a great deal of skill, but it was a game, and not a contest. The targets were small and hard to hit, so a miss was no disgrace. Everybody missed, and a hit was a thrill! Furthermore, when you had learned to shoot a fair score on a course you could go hunting and expect to get your share of the game.

In 1939 the popularity of this new sport led to the formation of a National Association. The first president was A.J. Michelson of Flint, Mich. The first annual Field Archery championship was held at Allegan, Mich., in 1946.

The organization has grown from a half dozen clubs scattered through three or four states to one of over 800 clubs and 10,000 members, representing every state of the union and 17 foreign countries.

ARCHERY RULES AND EQUIPMENT

Yew is the traditional wood for making bows. It now is somewhat scarce. As a result, manufac-

turers in the United States have been using lemon wood in general. Some also use orange and hickory.

The bow string is made of flax, which is waxed. From 30 to 60 strands of flax are used, according to size of bow and the strength needed in the string.

The outside of the bow is called the "back"; the inside is the "belly." A bow that is made of one piece of wood is a "self bow"; if of two pieces glued together, it is known as a "backed bow."

Men usually use a 6-foot bow; women 5½. The bows are of different strength. The average man's bow requires a pull of about 45 pounds to take the string back the length of the arrow; the required pull for a woman's bow is about 30 pounds. In technical language, the pull is called "the weight of the bow."

Arrows generally are made of pine, birch or yew dowels. The spine of the wood must have both resiliency and stiffness. The feathers used chiefly are those from turkeys or geese. The shafts of the arrows are highly painted so that, if shot into brush, they can be easily located.

The men's arrows average 28 inches long; the women's 25 inches. However, the length of the arrow is optional with the archer. Those with short arms use a shorter arrow than the average; those with long arms use some somewhat larger.

Quite a few bowmen make a hobby of fashioning their own bows and arrows. The pioneer American "hobbyist" was Maurice Thompson, who, in 1879, using bows and arrows of his own creation, conducted numerous experiments and wrote at length on the sport.

The target is made usually with straw as the basic material, over which is stretched an oilcloth or canvas covering. On this covering is a series of concentric rings. The inner ring, or the bullseye, has a diameter of 9.6 inches; the four other circles all are a trifle less than 5 inches in diameter.

The center ring is painted gold. Receding from it, in succession, are red, blue, black and white. The archer scores 9 points for hitting the gold, 7 for red, 5 for blue, 3 for black, and 1 for white. The target is placed on an easel, with the exact center being 48 inches from the ground.

ASSOCIATIONS
Amateur Athletic Union

For some time in the latter half of the 19th Century, corrupt promoters flourished in the United States and amateurism in athletics appeared doomed. Young athletes were in the grasp of unscrupulous persons, who had no concern for clean, healthful and honorable sportsmanship. These were black times, indeed, for simon-pure sports. Into the breach stepped the

Amateur Athletic Union of the United States.

The basic thought of the creators of the A.A.U. was to preserve amateurism, or sport for sport's sake, in this nation. But the A.A.U. soon developed, through its creed, into the most potent factor in the advancement of sports throughout the world.

The A.A.U. helped spread the gospel of amateurism into every city, town and village in this country; it has carried its preachments into every civilized country on earth. Within a few years, it had set up such a high standard that it furnished the pattern that served the founders when the Olympic Games were revived in 1896 at Athens, Greece.

The organization not merely has been a mighty power in the upsurge of amateur sports, but it also has helped the professional games tremendously. This is so because it has brought about, within its ranks, the advancement of many athletes to such high degree of capability that there were no more amateur fields for them to conquer, and they graduated into such professional sports as basketball, boxing, wrestling, ice hockey and swimming.

The A.A.U. was formed in the muddled year of 1888 when amateur athletics, beyond the colleges, were chiefly controlled by unscrupulous promoters. It was a case of redemption of the sport—speedy and thorough—by the new organization, or chaos, and perhaps extinction, for many amateur games.

Prior to the creation of the A.A.U., almost no lines separated the amateur from the professional in track and field athletics. In instances where an amateur competed in professional games and also wished to continue to strive for prizes in amateur fields, he simply changed his name, or the geographical location of his next athletic effort.

Some promoters of the 1880's were on the fly-by-night order. They announced prizes of substantial kind, to attract the outstanding athletes, but when the games were done, the winners discovered that the promoter had departed—and so had the prizes.

Other promoters, advertising a "strictly amateur" meet, would donate a trophy to the winner in full view of the spectators, after which promoter and victorious athlete would meet in some sheltered spot. The winner would give back the trophy and get cash, and the promoter would start shining the trophy to award to some other "amateur" at a later promotion.

Those meets were almost the only outlets for college athletes after graduation. The Intercollegiate Association of Amateur Athletes of America (I.C.A.A.A.A.), made up chiefly of colleges on the Atlantic Seaboard, held its track and field meets annually, starting with 1876. But when the athletes finished school, there were few responsible organizations sponsoring contests where such ex-collegians, as well as the non-scholastic amateurs, could compete.

The New York Athletic Club was almost alone in arranging strictly amateur track and field meets in the 1870's and 1880's, beyond those at colleges.

The A.A.U. changed all that in 1888—the first year of its existence.

The original plans of the founders of the A.A.U. called for an organization of individual clubs. But during the first year, the overwhelming number of applications for A.A.U. membership convinced its first president—Harry McMillan, of Philadelphia—and his associates that to go on with this plan would create an unwieldly organization, which could not administer competently.

In 1889, a "Reorganization Plan," drawn up by A.G. Mills, of New York, was tried. This called for dividing the United States into a number of districts. All clubs in the same district formed an association, representing their district, each association becoming a separate unit in the A.A.U. The plan worked so well from the start that it was adopted in 1890, since which time the A.A.U. has not been an organization of individual clubs; it is one composed of associations representing the clubs, colleges, schools and other athletic groups in its district.

The A.A.U., starting off with a membership, which, through its associations, included only 2,500 or 3,000 athletes, and supervising chiefly those sports which make up a track and field program, now supervises the activities of several million amateur athletes, and has jurisdiction over 19 sports, including basketball, bobsledding, boxing, codeball, gymnastics, handball, horseshoe pitching, ice hockey, swimming, toboganning, track and field, tug of war, volleyball, water polo (hard ball), water polo (soft ball), wrestling (catch-as-catch-can), wrestling (Greco-Roman). It is the officially recognized member of 11 international sports federations, including the International Amateur Athletic Federation, the International Body Controlling Track and Field; The Internation Amateur Swimming Federation (FINA), The International Body Controlling Aquatic Sports; and the International Basketball Association.

In 1895 and going into 1896, when the Europeans responsible for the revival of the Olympic Games sought an athletic program, they decided it should be modeled after that of the A.A.U. rather than after those in ancient days of Greece and Rome. And so it has been through all the Olympiads ever since—the A.A.U. furnishing the pattern.

The immortal figure in A.A.U. history is James E. Sullivan of New York. He became its secretary-treasurer soon after the organization was formed, and was elected president in 1906, serving three consecutive terms. In 1909 he was re-elected as secretary-treasurer and served until his death in 1914. During the years Sullivan was identified with the A.A.U., his was the brain that conceived many of its progressive policies, and his was the will that carried them through to magnificent completion.

Sullivan had few equals as an organizer and promoter. He spread the doctrine of amateurism throughout the land, and then journeyed to far distant climes to make converts. The A.A.U. had a healthy growth in the time before Sullivan became its chief executive, but he piloted it to high places during his busy years as president, and gave it the momentum which it has known since his passing.

Indianapolis became the new home for the A.A.U. in 1970, featuring mementos from A.A.U. competitions throughout the world, including Olympic games dating back to 1896. The central feature in the trophy area is a replica of A.A.U.'s highest tribute, the Sullivan Award. Building is located at 3400 West 86th Street.

SULLIVAN AWARD WINNERS

In 1930 the A.A.U. put up the James E. Sullivan Memorial Trophy to go to the "amateur athlete who, by performance, example and good influence did the most to advance the cause of good sportsmanship during the year." An athlete does not have to participate in a sport under A.A.U. domination to win the award. Selections are made on votes cast by the outstanding sports authorities in a nation-wide poll.

SULLIVAN AWARD WINNERS

1930—Robert T. Jones Jr. . . . . Golfer
1931—Bernard E. Berlinger . . . . Decathlon
1932—James A. Bausch . . . . Decathlon
1933—Glenn Cunningham . . . . Middle Distance Runner
1934—William R. Bonthron . . . . Middle Distance Runner
1935—W. Lawson Little Jr. . . . . Golfer
1936—Glenn Morris . . . . Decathlon
1937—J. Donald Budge . . . . Tennis Player
1938—Donald R. Lash . . . . Distance Runner
1939—Joseph W. Burk . . . . Oarsman
1940—J. Gregory Rice . . . . Distance Runner
1941—T. Leslie MacMitchell . . . . Middle Distance Runner
1942—Cornelius Warmerdam . . . . Pole Vaulter
1943—Gilbert Dodds . . . . Distance Runner
1944—Ann Curtis . . . . Swimmer
1945—Felix Blanchard . . . . Football Player and Shot-putter
1946—Y. Arnold Tucker . . . . Football, Basketball, Track
1947—John B. Kelly Jr. . . . . Oarsman
1948—Robert B. Mathias . . . . Decathlon
1949—Richard T. Button . . . . Figure Skater
1950—Fred Wilt . . . . Distance Runner
1951—Robert E. Richards . . . . Pole Vaulter
1952—Horace Ashenfelter . . . . Distance Runner
1953—Major Sammy Lee . . . . Diver
1954—Malvin Whitfield . . . . Middle Distance Runner
1955—Harrison Dillard . . . . Sprinter
1956—Mrs. Patricia K. McCormick . . . . Diver
1957—Bobby Joe Morrow . . . . Sprinter
1958—Glenn Davis . . . . Middle Distance Runner and Hurdler
1959—Parry O'Brien . . . . Shot Putter
1960—Rafer Johnson . . . . Decathlon
1961—Wilma Rudolph . . . . Sprinter
1962—James Beatty . . . . Middle Distance Runner
1963—John Pennel . . . . Track
1964—Don Schollander . . . . Swimming
1965—Bill Bradley . . . . Basketball
1966—James Ryun . . . . Track
1967—Randy Matson . . . . Shot Putter
1968—Debbie Meyer . . . . Swimming
1969—Bill Toomey . . . . Decathlon
1970—John Kinsella . . . . Swimming
1971—Mark Spitz . . . . Swimming

ATHLETIC AGES

The age of peak efficiency of an athlete is a frequent topic of discussion and conjecture. Generally, most persons believe it to be in the twenties, but frequently there are exceptions.

A scientist at Ohio University, Professor Harvey C. Lehman, sought the answers on a scientific basis.

Athletes, as a group, are at their best between the ages of 27 and 29, inclusive, according to Professor Lehman, who has devoted years to research.

Professor Lehman, in establishing the exact years when persons in the different arts and professions are at their peak, arrived at his conclusions concerning athletes by getting the birth dates of almost 10,000 sports performers and then checking laboriously through their records to find when they were at their peaks.

In his article, "The Most Proficient Years at Sports and Games," in the October, 1938, issue of *Research Quarterly,* Professor Lehman gave some very interesting details about athletes, how they move along gradually to their finest year and eventually are forced into decline.

Dealing with baseball players, Professor Lehman split them into two groups: pitchers and non-pitchers. He compared the birth dates of 1,666 major league pitchers, past and present, with their best years, and found that the thrower is keenest at 27, that he then can count on 4.39 good years, after which he slips. Studying 3,126 major leaguers, other than pitchers, Professor Lehman found them sharpest at 28, with a peak spread of 4.04 years.

On Nov. 9, 1946, Professor Lehman wrote:

"Approximately 68% of major league pitching service is rendered between ages 25.11 and 33.89 These two latter numerals are obtained by subtracting 4.39 from 29.50 and adding 4.39 to 29.50. This means, of course, that about 16% of such service occurs prior to age 25.11 and about 16% subsequent to age 33.89."

After completing his first article, Professor Lehman went more deeply into baseball, which resulted in his writings concerning "The Geographic Origin of Professional Ballplayers." He learned that the players are born more frequently in the southern part of the United States.

Professor Lehman in his original article compared both men and women duck-pin bowlers and found that whereas women reach championship crest at 25 and carry on until 29, men do not achieve titles until 30, continuing until 34.

Here are Professor Lehman's findings:

Sport	Peak Age	Span	Gen. Av.
AUTO RACING (Professional)	27—30	4.50	28.81
BASEBALL			
Non-pitchers	28	4.04	29.07
Pitchers	27	4.39	29.50
Batting champions ...	26—29	3.46	29.16
Pitching champions ..	26—31	3.72	28.18
Base stealing champions	25—29	3.46	27.96
BILLIARDS			
Record makers	30-34	5.83	35.67
Champions	25—29	8.75	34.35
BOWLING			
Individuals	30—34	7.56	32.78
As teams	27—37	7.83	33.38
Duck Pins—Men	30—34	4.36	32.19
Duck Pins—Women ..	25—29	3.47	28.13
BOXERS	25—26	3.98	26.98
Bantamweights	——	–	24.83
Heavyweights	——	–	29.29
FOOTBALL (Professional)	24	2.33	25.72
GOLF (U.S. and English)			
Amateur champions .	25—29	7.66	29.88
Open champions	25—34	6.37	31.01
Professional champions	30—34	6.49	32.33
HOCKEY (Professional)	24—25	4.00	27.56
RIFLE AND PISTOL SHOOTING	27	8.13	32.05
TENNIS (U.S., English, French)	25—27	5.25	27.63

Professor Lehman did not offer any conclusion as to what causes an athlete to slip from prime.

The generally accepted idea is that when age proceeds to manifest itself in an athlete, the attack is upon the legs. But this was disputed by a member of the Coroner's staff in New York City, who stated:

"In performing more than 4,500 autopsies, I never found a body beyond 30 years of age which did not show a deterioration in the lungs. It is this, I am sure, which explains why athletes begin to slow up after reaching 30. The idea that they are slowed by lessening power of the leg muscles appears to be wrong.

"Their lungs do not function as they did in youth. Therefore, after muscular effort, which calls for a high turn of speed, or some special effort that strains at the muscles, their lungs falter. Consequently, they cannot get the full amount of oxygen they need, and it is this which causes them to slow down in their pace—not a faltering of the leg muscles.

"It is to be observed that when athletes have amazing lungs, they can carry on as champions not merely until they are 30, but far into the thirties, and in some rare instances, until they are beyond the 40-year mark, thus disproving the theory that legs fail an athlete after 30."

AUTOMOBILE RACING

Thrilling and dangerous sports always attract spectators. One of the leading crowd-pleasing sports is automobile racing. A prime example is the annual Memorial Day 500-mile race at Indianapolis Speedway, which draws almost 300,000 fans. Thousands of races are held throughout the country on a weekly, sometimes twice-weekly basis. The crowds are big, as are the purses for the successful drivers. Races for big cars, midgets, stock, sports, and drag have brought drivers from all over the world, either amateur or pro, into their particular classification.

Although the automobile is a modern invention and came into existence after the practice of keeping records, was adopted there is a controversy, and always will be, as to who created the first vehicle that actually could travel under its own power.

England, France, Italy and the United States present claims, whereas Germany, which never aspired to credit, certainly seems entitled to the honor of perfecting the first device that could operate, both on land and water, under its own means of propulsion.

The claim of France is centered in something put together by M. Cugat about 1769. Cugat had the idea for a vehicle that was to be steam-driven. What he put together is not fully established, but there is no evidence that Cugat built anything that was practical, or could move along through its own power.

The English award the invention prize to Robert Treverthick and attempt to bolster it with untenable claims. Treverthick is given the distinction of building a steam-driven automobile. He is supposed to have put it into operation in 1824, at which time it is reported to have "hauled 3 or 4 cars from Gloucester to Cheltenham (England) at the rate of 14 miles an hour." The time that is quoted provokes the challenge, since it was not until more than 70 years after Treverthick's machine that an automobile, blessed by internal combustion, which was unknown to Treverthick, traveling alone, and at limited speed, and for merely one mile, moved at 39.24 miles per hour.

The Italians had in the Industrial Museum, Torino, Italy, a strange contraption created in 1837 by General Bordio, who also was an engineer, which they claimed was the "first automobile." The operating principle was steam. However, there is nothing to indicate that the Bordio vehicle ever moved an inch under its own power. It was something Bordio thought might travel by its own power, not something that actually did travel by itself.

Until Gottlieb Daimler perfected internal combustion in 1885 using petroleum spirits, which actually meant kerosene, the men striving

to create an automobile worked on the idea that it must be steam-propelled. To create steam, an enormous tank of water was necessary, plus a gigantic furnace, since wood then was used as fuel. The steam-driven theory appeared to be impractical because the required boiler and water tank were too large.

Daimler, a German, tinkered with the internal combustion idea through the early 1880's. In 1885 he attached his engine to an ordinary bicycle, with chains operating off the engine onto the wheels. He succeeded, by using "petroleum spirits," in driving the bicycle forward. In 1887 he attached his motor to a rowboat on the River Seine and the experiment was successful. Thus, the motorcycle and the motorboat, which were supposed to have followed the automobile, actually preceded it.

Levassor, a Frenchman, improved on the Daimler idea by building an automobile body, into which he placed an engine. This was in 1887 or 1888. Therefore, while Daimler originated internal combustion, making the automobile possible, Levassor was the actual creator of the automobile as we know it today, since Daimler perfected only the motorcycle and motorboat.

There was considerable commotion over automobile building in the United States before the turn of the 20th Century. It was created by George Selden of Rochester, N.Y. Selden claimed he had constructed a self-propelling machine in the 1880's. He asked for patents at the time, but could not get them since his vehicles did not move under their own power. In November, 1895, after other Americans had put automobiles on the market, Selden renewed his request for a patent, insisting that the working model he had for display then was the same one he had perfected in the 1880's and that he was entitled to patent rights dating from the 1880's.

Selden sought recourse at law. The suit was bitterly contested, the defense being that his machines, prior to 1895, would not work and that, therefore, no one manufacturing an automobile before that time was infringing on Selden's rights. Selden lost the suit, during the progress of which considerable "evidence" was produced by amateur historians that automobiles had been made and put into use in ancient times. Some of the more fantastic and facetious "historians" almost planted an automobile in the Garden of Eden.

While Selden was making claims to perfecting the first automobile, the Duryea brothers— Charles and Frank—of Philadelphia declared they had pioneered in the field. They manufactured cars over 50 years ago, and the speed of their machines gave considerable fame to the Duryea name as automobile builders. In fact, the Duryea was perhaps the best known of the early automobiles in the United States. However, the field quickly became filled with rivals, and most of them prospered for a while despite the fact that Selden was carrying on his court battle.

Arthur Pound, in his book "The Turning Wheel," gave credit to the Duryeas for building the "first successfully operated American automobile," fixing 1892 as the year and Springfield, Mass., as the place. When the argument as to who was the creator of the automobile in the United States was resumed some years ago, after *The New York Times* had printed a picture of the Selden car, classifying it as "the pioneer vehicle," Pound wrote to *The Times:*

"The Selden picture is not truthful. The vehicle shown was Selden's first, but it was not made until 1905–6. It was (intent) to prove that the famous Selden patent, issued in November, 1895, described an operative thing. Many attempts to run it (the Selden car of 1895) were made before court witnesses, and the longest run of all was about one-fourth of a mile. The court ruled that 'to say Selden solved a great problem, and is entitled to the status of a pioneer, is without foundation.'

"The automobile idea was well described by Homer in the Iliad, Book XVIII. F. Verbiest, a Belgian missionary in China, built the first-known self-propeller in 1665 and ran it. Oliver Evans seems to have been the first to sell his product. He ran it on Philadelphia streets in 1805. Samuel Morey of Oxford, N.H., was first to make a real liquid-fuel engine. He drove a boat with it and wrote of his intent to fit it to a carriage.

"Drake, who built a liquid-fuel engine as early as 1842 and showed one in New York in 1855, advocated them for 'locomotive use.' W.M. Storm in 1851 so fully set forth the facts about such engines that he surely must have had experience before getting his patent. Brayton began work on such engines in 1852 and continued for forty years. He continually advocated such engines for road vehicles and licensed Joshua Rose and A.R. Shattuck in January, 1876, to use them on road vehicles. That year Selden saw Brayton's engines at the Centennial and doubtless talked with Brayton. He tried to improve, but failed. He applied for a patent in 1879 and kept it alive until late in 1895.

"A Duryea patent was issued nearly five months earlier and America's first automobile race was won by a Duryea vehicle in 1895."

Complicating the situation a trifle more, *The Times* printed a letter from Elisha Flagg of New York City at the same time it reproduced Pound's communication, in which Flagg stated:

"It was in the year of 1864 that a friend of my mother, who was living with her family at Auburndale, a suburb of Boston, drove a horseless carriage from Boston, a matter of 14 miles as I recall the distance, to our home in the former

place. I was then a lad of 9 years, yet I distinctly remember his arrival, his coming up the road, seeing little puffs of steam vapor jetting out from the back of a regular carriage, called a box buggy.

"When he came to a stop I was simply astonished to see no horse. The shafts had been removed and there did not seem to be much mechanism. No doubt there was a tank for water, with the addition of what was needed in automotive mechanism. I, however, recall the whip socket—no whip but in its place a bunch of flowers!

"Every one familiar with the history of the automobile knows that horseless carriages were developed as far back as 1760 or '80. One American, named James, produced a workable one with a tubular boiler for steam propulsion; all of which helps to confirm my contention that Selden was far from being the first to drive a horseless carriage."

"Dudgeon's Steam Wagon," better known as the "Red Devil" because it frightened horses, and sketches of which were generally distributed throughout the United States, is another contraption that enters into the confusing situation.

Richard Dudgeon built this steam-driven vehicle in 1865 and it is reported to have appeared on the streets of New York in 1866. It also was driven over Long Island roads. Wood was used to provide the fires that created the steam. In appearance, the car looked much like a tractor of today—except it had a sizable smokestack. It could seat 12 persons. It had a publicized speed of 30 miles an hour, but when tested in 1903 it could do only 10, which might have been its maximum in the 1860's.

The road races on Long Island, originated about 1904, became increasingly dangerous. Cars often went out of control and killed or injured not merely the drivers, but also many of the onlookers. There was a violent protest against the continuation of such races, and they were abandoned about 1908. Since some drivers still had a craving for speed and thousands of Americans found a great thrill in watching the contests, work was started in 1909 on the first of America's speedways—and the greatest—which is the Indianapolis Speedway of today.

For a few years the European drivers, working for the different manufacturers who regarded high speed as the best form of publicity for their product, held a monopoly on the mile record. But, soon, the Americans, driving cars made in this country, entered the competition and took turns with the Europeans in lowering the record.

The first mile marks were made on roads. The action later was transferred to speedways. It then was found that the straight-away along the packed sand on the beach at Daytona, Fla., permitted faster speed. Still later, Ted E. Allen of the Contest Board of the American Automobile Association, who had supervised speed tests for many years, discovered that an even faster strip was the hard-salt surface at Bonneville, Utah, which has been the testing ground for all high speed performers in recent years.

Regardless of who built the first self-propelled car and what was used to start it and keep it in motion, the French were first to take wholesale advantage of the Levassor idea. They built automobiles, each operated by "petroleum spirits," later known as gasoline, and each manufacturer made speed his particular object. Since arguments developed early in 1894 as to who was putting together the most durable and fastest car in France, an automobile race—the first in history—was arranged for June 22, 1894, the route to be from Paris to Rouen.

Perhaps the original program was Paris to Rouen and return, but there exists no detailed account of the race, the only memo being that the distance between the towns was 78 miles. It is quite likely that some cars did get to Rouen, while others failed, and that none was able to make the return trip until some extensive repairs had been completed.

However, in 1895 a "reliability run" was proposed. This resulted in a race from Paris to Bordeaux and return, a matter of 544 miles, beginning July 13. Beyond the statement that the better cars involved in the "run" averaged 15 miles an hour, details also are unknown. But the fact that cars could make such a long trip and hold together encouraged the automobile manufacturers and confounded the skeptics, who had declared a car could travel no more than a limited distance.

The success of the "run" in France resulted in the arrangements for a "run" of shorter duration in the United States, to test both the speed and the stamina of American-made cars. It was held on Nov. 28, 1895, under the auspices of the *Chicago Times Herald,* a newspaper. The route was from the heart of Chicago to one of the suburbs and return. The distance was 54.36 measured miles. The contest was won by J. Frank Duryea, in a Duryea car, and his speed average was 7½ miles per hour.

In 1898, when there was debate as to how fast a car could travel if the route were limited to exactly one mile, Chasseloup-Laubat of France agreed to engage in the "dangerous experiment." The test drew a considerable crowd, impelled there by the morbid idea that a car, pressed to its limit, might explode into fragments during some part of the journey. However, the car held together, and Chasseloup-Laubat became the world's first "speed demon" with an average of 39.24 miles per hour.

Automobile races and tours in Europe were infrequent until 1902, when James Gordon Bennett, an American who spent a great deal of his time in France, put up a trophy for a race to be run from Paris to Vienna and return. The winner was S.F. Edge, but the time is not a matter of record. The contest was continued for several years, Bennett always awarding the prize.

Because cars of European manufacture were heavier and rated as faster than those built in the United States, most of the early cars operated on American soil were of foreign make. Since they were costly, only persons with a good deal of money could afford them. Most of the owners liked speed and frequently raced against each other whenever they could find level stretches of road. These eventually led to the Vanderbilt (William K.) Cup races on Long Island over routes mapped out by the Cup Committee, with Vanderbilt donating the trophy.

The first Vanderbilt Cup race was on Oct. 8, 1904, and the winner was A.L. Campbell in a foreign-built Mercedes. The course measured 28.4 miles; the race called for 10 laps. There were 18 starters in that free-for-all and about 25,000 to 30,000 spectators. The cup was over 30 inches high and weighed about 500 pounds.

The time average of early cup races was about 30 m.p.h. and the carnage created by reckless drivers was too much for Vanderbilt. However, the entries increased and so did the onlookers. As improvements were made in cars the speed moved up to 70 and 80 miles an hour despite the deeply rutted and bumpy roads.

Because there were so many deaths and accidents during the cup races and because foreign cars did most of the winning, Vanderbilt withdrew the cup about 1908 and gave it to the American Automobile Association. It is now housed in the Washington office of that organization. However, so great an enthusiasm had been developed over auto racing in the United States that, since racing was no more, a group built an oval track at Indianapolis to feature such contests.

Meanwhile, Charles Glidden of Boston decided that the way to bring American cars to perfection was to put them to long and severe tests. In 1905 he originated the tours which bore his name. Any American, with any sort of car, was permitted to take part in such tours, which were continued for almost a decade, by which time American cars had reached such a high standard of performance, both as to speed and durability, it was not necessary to put them to further tests to find out what was wrong with them.

Since 1911 the 500-mile race held at the Indianapolis Speedway each Memorial Day has been the annual highlight of auto racing. The track is 2½ miles in circumference. The prize money to winning drivers has increased rapidly through the years until it is now well over $100,000 for each race. Speed records climbed, too.

Other speed records have been set on the hard sand of Daytona Beach and Bonneville, where the packed salt-bed was found to be ideal for velocity. The world record of 394.2 m.p.h. for a straightaway measured mile was set at Bonneville by John R. Cobb of England in September, 1947. Cobb was killed in Scotland while driving a jet-propelled speedboat at more than 200 m.p.h. in 1952.

Cobb, in his record run at Bonneville, also gained the distinction of being the first person to travel more than 400 m.p.h. on land. The Englishman drove at the rate of 385.645 m.p.h. for the mile and 388.019 for the kilometer on the southward journey. He increased his pace to 403.135 m.p.h. for the mile and 399.808 for the kilometer on the northward trip, the best times ever recorded in either category. Out of the two runs came new world records for the mile and the kilometer, the latter mark being raised to 393.8 m.p.h.

In the early years of the automobile in the United States, as well as Europe, the best possible advertising as to the merits of a car was to win some sort of race—speed, or reliability or endurance run—with a stock model. Thus, over a period of many years, most of the cars used in contests were stock models. However, when the demand came for speed and still more speed in road races and in the later-day speedway contests, the stock cars were no longer used. Special types, suitable only for racing, were constructed, although a few retained some of the best features of the standard makes of cars.

INDIANAPOLIS 500-MILE RACE

The most famous automobile race in the United States is the annual International 500-mile classic at the Indianapolis Motor Speedway. It is run on a two-and-a-half-mile rectangular course, built originally in 1909 as a proving ground for the rapidly growing automotive industry.

Carl G. Fisher, James A. Allison, Arthur C. Newby, and Frank H. Wheeler—the Speedway's four founders—all had benefited materially from their early association with the industry, and they operated the track successfully until the summer of 1927.

Edward V. Rickenbacker, former race driver and World War I flying ace, purchased the facilities at that time and guided the event through the economic "depression" of the 1930s before selling the track in 1945 to Indiana sportsman and businessman Anton Hulman, Jr.

The facilities were modernized and enlarged steadily under Mr. Hulman's guidance, and the race now attracts almost 300,000 spectators who watch the world's outstanding drivers compete in championship cars for prize money of more than $1,000,000 annually. The management never has revealed exact attendance figures, but more than 230,000 reserved seats are available and many fans watch the event from the unreserved infield area.

The original course was built of crushed stone and tar, but it disentegrated rapidly during the first series of races beginning August 19, 1909; and it was resurfaced with paving brick (3,200,000 of them) in time for another speed program three months later. Three week-ends of racing also were presented during 1910, with events ranging in distance from five to 300 miles, before the management adopted the policy of one race per year over the 500-mile distance.

Ray Harroun won that inaugural "500" on May 30, 1911, in a six-cylinder Marmon Wasp at an average speed of 74.59 miles an hour; and since then it has been run annually on Memorial Day (or the Saturday or Sunday of the Memorial Day weekend) except during the years of World War I and World War II. Portions of the track were resurfaced with asphalt in 1937 and the course was made into an all-asphalt surface after the 1961 event, except for a traditional 36-inch strip of brick at the start-finish line.

The present race record of 3:04:05.54 (162.962 mph) was set by Mark Donohue in 1972, and his share of the $1,011,845.94 purse amounted to $218,767.90.

Although the race now is regarded primarily as one of the world's great sports spectacles, it also has been an important factor in the development of such passenger car features as high compression engines, hydraulic shock absorbers and four-wheel brakes, torsion bars, tires, and lubricants.

STOCK CAR RACING

The history of stock car racing is, in a sense, the history of the automobile. The first recognized race in the United States between stock production models generally is considered to have been the match contest between automobile manufacturers Henry Ford and Alexander Winton in Detroit. This historic event was held in either 1899 or 1900. Ford won.

Many early stock automobiles were raced against one another and against time on the sands of Daytona Beach in the early 1900's. Among the most highly regarded performances in those days were the achievements of the Buick and the Packard. Many of the cars, of course, were constructed with special bodies, but were considered stock cars none the less.

The Vanderbilt Cup races and Elgin Road races were actually the earliest events in which large numbers of stock cars participated. The sport was short-lived, however, for shortly before World War I American plants concentrated on mass production and no longer had the time, inclination or enthusiasm to devote to racing machines.

Following the First World War, stock car racing was sporadic at best. There was limited activity on the West Coast, to this day one of the hotbeds of automotive enthusiasm. This extended through the 1930's and into the 1940's, when enterprising groups—particularly in the South and West—began a series of what we now call "pasture races." A plot of ground would be cleaned and neighborhood stock cars would compete, more for the sport than for financial gain.

The National Association for Stock Car Auto Racing was formed in 1947 by Bill France and William R. Tuthill, both of Daytona Beach. France is the president of the National Stock Car Racing Commission and E.G. (Cannonball) Baker of Indianapolis is the national commissioner.

The group has grown steadily in recent years. In 1949, NASCAR sanctioned 87 races on 25 tracks, with a purse total of $181,289. By 1951 the figures were 585 race meets on 91 tracks and the purse offerings reached nearly $800,000. These figures were improved upon in 1952. Membership soared from 875 in 1949 to more than 4,500 three years later. The number of races and value of purses continue to show annual increases. Every year NASCAR stages a two-week racing program at Daytona Beach. All top manufacturers are represented. Thereafter drivers race weekly in various categories for national championship points.

More than 1,000 events were conducted, in 1971, under the NASCAR Banner with prizes in all divisions totaling more than $5 million. For 1972, a new Grand National Racing Division was formed, while the Winston Cup Grand National Division was streamlined to 32 major events.

The American Automobile Association reported that its stock car program produced the greatest gain in public acceptance recorded by any division of A.A.A. racing for 1952. The 14 championship races run was an increase of 11 over the preceding year. New track, purse and attendance marks were set everywhere, in spite of the fact the actual competition was dominated by one make of car and 3 drivers.

For the first time stock cars in the A.A.A. raced on half-mile tracks. As an experiment a sprint type program was scheduled at some places and found great favor. All A.A.A. stock car events are classed as championship races with points awarded being determined by the length of the feature event. The A.A.A. has since dropped out of the racing field and its role has been taken over by the United States Auto Club. There also are a number of independent stock car race promoters.

MIDGET CAR RACING

In the early 1940's auto racing enthusiasts, unable to afford costly cars required for "big time" speedway racing, started building midget cars. Many types of engines, such as motorcycle, motorboat and discarded automobile power plants—were put into skeletonized bodies and pepped up with special fuel. Thus midget auto racing was born.

The sport gained in favor rapidly. So many races are held that the better drivers devote full time to it.

In the early years of midget racing, the contests were on dirt tracks at fair grounds. Since then hundreds of special midget tracks have been built. The distances for the races vary, but 25 miles is considered a long race. The top prizes also vary. Most midget races are on the basis of a minimum purse guarantee, with an option of a percentage of the gate. Purses at some of the tracks scale up to $3,500 for a race.

At least a part of the success of midget racing is due to the circuit plan of operation. This means a series of races that enable the drivers to see action often. The arrangement not only keeps them busy, but also affords reasonable weekly earnings. In the East, one circuit includes tracks in New England, New York, New Jersey and Pennsylvania. There are many circuits in the Middle West, the South Central area, Texas and the Pacific Coast.

The cars, depending upon the motors, the daring of the drivers, the strength of the tires and the fuel, can make from 60 to 85 miles an hour on a straightaway stretch.

One rule specifies that cars using valve-in-block engines are limited to a maximum displacement of 140 cubic inches, whereas 105 cubic inches is the maximum displacement for engines employing overhead valves. The wheelbase is restricted to a maximum of 76 and a minimum of 66 inches, and the tread width is restricted to a maximum of 46 and a minimum of 42 inches.

Regardless of how little or how much has gone into the midget construction, the cars rigidly comply with specifications drawn by some of the most experienced men in racing. Particular attention is paid to the use of special hats and other safety measures for protection of the drivers and the spectators.

SPORTS CAR RACING

While in Europe during World War II, American military men developed a fondness for the small sports car, and when the war was over many, on their return home to civilian life, acquired these cars. As the number of sports cars grew, there naturally developed a desire to race them. Informal tests became commonplace and soon racing was held on an organized basis.

Sports car racing in this country is conducted under the international formula and rules for that type of event in Europe. The one exception is that no competition is permitted on a course in which public highways must be utilized. This exception does not apply to rallies, which use public roads.

So rapid has been the growth of sports car racing that where once all cars raced in one division there now are several classes according to piston displacement. As interest increased so did the ability of the drivers. The United States now boasts of drivers, such as Carroll Shelby, Paul O'Shea, Phil Hill and Masten Gregory, who can hold their own with their European rivals. The leading driver in the world without doubt has been Juan Manuel Fangio of Argentina, who retired in 1958.

The Sports Car Club of America with more than 8,000 members is the largest of its type in this country. It has about 1,000 competitive drivers, all amateurs, as are the members. Another large one is the California S.C.C. There probably were 100 clubs in existence in 1957. Some of the top races are held at Bridgehampton and Watkins Glen in New York, Thompson and Lime Rock in Connecticut, Elkhart Lake in Wisconsin and Sebring in Florida. The Sebring race is the only one in the United States in which a driver can earn points toward the world title.

Foreign races that count toward the world championship include the Argentine Grand Prix, Monte Carlo Rally and races in Belgium, the Netherlands, England, France, Sweden, Italy and Germany. There also is a world title competed for by manufacturers of sports cars. They enter their cars at Sebring, in the Mille Miglia (Italy), the Le Mans (France) 24-hour endurance event and other tests.

The foreign races are held on public roads and sometimes accidents have taken high tolls of lives of drivers and spectators. As a result, there have been many demands to eliminate this type of racing.

In May, 1958, the United States Auto Club announced the formation of a professional sports car racing division. Plans were set up to hold professional races at courses in Danville, Va.; Marlboro, Md.; Riverside, Calif., and Lime Rock, Conn. Operators, who invested $250,000 to $1,500,000 in building courses, petitioned the U.S.A.C. for this new division because they felt professional drivers would attract larger crowds.

DRAG RACING

The National Hot Rod Association (NHRA), formed in the 1950s using dry lake beds or abandoned air strips, has more than 160 sanctioned drag strips in North America, with well over 3,000 drag racing events, eight of them major National Championship meets. NHRA has been a member of the Automobile Competition Committee for the U.S. since 1965, along with NASCAR, SCCA, and USAC.

With over 100 different classes of vehicles taking part in NHRA racing, it is sometimes difficult to identify one group from another, but classification is determined by car weight divided

by advertised horsepower. "Hot" or competition cars are classed by a weight to cubic-inch ratio.

A drag race is a descriptive title for an acceleration contest involving two vehicles in a standing-start race over a closed and measured quarter-mile course.

World Grand Prix Drivers

1950—Giuseppe Farina, Italy
1951—Juan Manuel Fangio, Argentina
1952-53—Alberto Ascari, Italy
1954-57—Juan Manuel Fangio, Argentina
1958—Mike Hawthorn
1959-60—Jack Brabham, Australia
1961—Philip Hill, U.S.A.
1962—Graham Hill, England
1963—Jimmy Clark, Scotland
1964—John Surtees, England
1965—Jimmy Clark, Scotland
1966—Jack Brabham, Australia
1967—Denis Hulme, New Zealand
1968—Graham Hill, England
1969—Jackie Stewart, Scotland
1970—Jochen Rindt, Austria
1971—Jackie Stewart, Scotland
1972—Emerson Fittipaldt, Brazil

UNITED SAVINGS – HELMS HALL

Racing Hall of Fame

Tony Bettenhausen	Rex Mays
Jimmy Bryan	Louis Meyer
Bob Burman	Tommy Milton
Floyd Clymer	Ralph Mulford
Harvey Firestone	Jimmie Murphy
Henry Ford	T.E. (Pop) Myers
Earl Cooper	Barney Oldfield
Bill Cummings	John Parsons
Ralph De Palma	Eddie Rickenbacker
Peter De Paolo	Mauri Rose
Dan Gurney	Wilbur Shaw
Sam Hanks	William K. Vanderbilt
Harry Hartz	Bill Vukovich
Eddie Hearne	Rodger Ward
Ted Horn	
Anton Hulman, Jr.	

HOW WORLD RECORDS ARE CAUGHT

At Daytona Beach, Fla., which was the automobile speed proving ground from 1927 to 1935, with some racing and tests there prior to 1927, and Bonneville, Utah, the present high speed center, the method of scoring records is the same. The driver must make a 1-mile run in both directions, usually within an hour, the average time for both tests to be his speed for the mile. The racing strip at Daytona was 10 miles; at Bonneville, where the surface is hard-packed salt, it is 13 miles. The actual testing mile at Daytona was between Posts 4 and 5; at Bonneville, it is between Posts 6 and 7. The drivers use the preceding miles to gain speed, the subsequent miles to slow down.

At both places a steel timing wire was placed between the posts which marked the actual mile for high speed. As the car passed over the first wire, it registered as the exact starting second; as it passed over the wire at the other end, it showed when the run had been completed. The electric eye now is used in Utah.

CHAMPIONS AND LEADERS
(Courtesy Al Bloemker, Indianapolis Motor Speedway, Speedway, Ind.)
Indianapolis Speedway 500-Mile Race

Year	Winner	Car	Time	Average m.p.h.
1911—Ray Harroun	Marmon	6:42:08	74.59
1912—Joe Dawson	National	6:21:06*	78.72 *
1913—Jules Goux	Peugeot	5:35:05	75.93
1914—Rene Thomas	Delage	6:03:45*	82.47 *
1915—Ralph De Palma	Mercedes	5:33:55.51*	89.84 *
1916—Davis Resta	Peugeot	3:34:17†	84.00
1917-18—No competition			
1919—Howard Wilcox	Peugeot	5:40:42.87	88.05
1920—Gaston Chevrolet	Monroe	5:38:32.00	88.62
1921—Tommy Milton	Frontenac	5:34:44.65	89.62
1922—Jimmy Murphy	Murphy Special	5:17:30.79*	94.48 *
1923—Tommy Milton	H.C.S. Special	5:29:50.17	90.95
1924—L.L. Corum and Joe Boyer	Duesenberg Special	5:05:23.51*	98.23
1925—Peter De Paolo	Duesenberg Special	4:56:39.46*	101.13 *
1926—Frank Lockhart	Miller Special	4:10:14.95‡	95.90
1927—George Souders	Duesenberg	5:07:33.08	97.54
1928—Louis Meyer	Miller Special	5:01:33.75	99.48
1929—Ray Keech	Simplex Special	5:07:25.42	97.58
1930—Billy Arnold	Hartz-Miller	4:58:39.72	100.44
1931—Louis Schneider	Bowes Special	5:10:27.93	96.62
1932—Fred Frame	Miller Special	4:48:03.79*	104.14 *
1933—Louis Meyer	Miller Special	4:48:00.75*	104.16 *
1934—Bill Cummings	Miller Special	4:46:05.20*	104.86 *
1935—Kelly Petillo	Gilmore Special	4:42:22.71*	106.24 *
1936—Louis Meyer	Ring Free Special	4:35:03.39*	109.06 *
1937—Wilbur Shaw	Shaw-Gilmore Special	4:24:07.80*	113.58 *
1938—Floyd Roberts	Burd Piston Reg. Special	4:15:58.40*	117.20 *
1939—Wilbur Shaw	Boyle Special	4:20:47.39	115.03
1940—Wilbur Shaw	Boyle Special	4:22:31.17	114.27
1941—Mauri Rose and Floyd Davis	Noc-Out Hose Clamp Special	4:20:36.24	115.11
1942-45—No competition			
1946—George Robson	Thorne Eng. Special	4:21:26.70	114.82
1947—Mauri Rose	Blue Crown Special	4:17:52.17	116.33
1948—Mauri Rose	Blue Crown Special	4:10:23.33*	119.81 *
1949—Bill Holland	Blue Crown Special	4:07:15.97*	121.32
1950—Johnny Parsons	Wynn's Special	2:46:55.97‡	124.00
1951—Lee Wallard	Belanger Special	3:57:38.95*	126.24*
1952—Troy Ruttman	Agajanian Special	3:52:41.88*	128.92*
1953—Bill Vukovich	Fuel Injection Special	3:53:01.69	128.74
1954—Bill Vukovich	Fuel Injection Special	3:49:17.27*	130.840 *
1955—Bob Sweikert	John Zink Special	3:53:59.13	128.209
1956—Pat Flaherty	John Zink Special	3:53:28.84	128.490
1957—Sam Hanks	Belond Exhaust Special	3:41:14.25*	135.601 *
1958—Jimmy Bryan	Belond AP Special	3:44:13.80	133.791
1959—Rodger Ward	Leader Card 500	3:40:49.20*	135.857*
1960—Jim Rathman	Ken-Paul Special	3:36:11.36*	138.767*
1961—A.J. Foyt	Bowes Seal Special	3:35:37.49*	139.130*
1962—Rodger Ward	Leader Card 500	3:33:50.33*	140.293*

1963—Parnelli Jones	Agajanian-Willard Special	3:29:35.40*	..143.137*
1964—A.J. Foyt	Sheraton-Thompson Special ...	3:23:35.83*	..147.350*
1965—Jim Clark	Lotus powered by Ford	3:19:05.34*	..150.686*
1966—Graham Hill	American Red Ball Special	3:27:52.53	..144.317
1967—A.J. Foyt	Sheraton-Thompson Special ...	3:18:24.22*	..151.207*
1968—Bobby Unser	Rislone Special	3:16:13.76*	..152.882*
1969—Mario Andretti	STP Oil Treatment Special	3:11:14.71*	..156.867*
1970—Al Unser	Johnny Lightning Special	3:12:37.04	..155.749
1971—Al Unser	Johnny Lightning Special	3:10:11.56*	..157.725*
1972—Mark Donohue	Sunoco McLaren	3:04:05.54*	..162.962*

*Record at the time.   †300 miles.   ‡400 miles.   ‡ 345 miles.

National Champions
A.A.A.——U.S.A.C.

Year

1909—George Robertson	1928—Lou Meyer	1950—Henry Banks
1910—Ray Harroun	1929—Lou Meyer	1951—Tony Bettenhausen
1911—Ralph Mulford	1930—Billy Arnold	1952—Charles Stevenson
1912—Ralph De Palma	1931—Lou Schneider	1953—Sam Hanks
1913—Earl Cooper	1932—Bob Carey	1954—Jimmy Bryan
1914—Ralph De Palma	1933—Lou Meyer	1955—Bob Sweikert
1915—Earl Cooper	1934—Bill Cummings	1956—Jimmy Bryan
1916—Dario Resta	1935—Kelly Petillo	1957—Jimmy Bryan
1917—Earl Cooper	1936—Mauri Rose	1958—Tony Bettenhausen
1918—Ralph Mulford	1937—Wilbur Shaw	1959—Rodger Ward
1919—Howard Wilcox	1938—Floyd Roberts	1960-61—A.J. Foyt
1920—Tommy Milton	1939—Wilbur Shaw	1962—Rodger Ward
1921—Tommy Milton	1940—Rex Mays	1963-64—A.J. Foyt
1922—Jimmy Murphy	1941—Rex Mays	1965-66—Mario Andretti
1923—Eddie Hearne	1942-45—No competition	1967—A.J. Foyt
1924—Jimmy Murphy	1946—Ted Horn	1968—Bobby Unser
1925—Pete De Paolo	1947—Ted Horn	1969—Mario Andretti
1926—Harry Hartz	1948—Ted Horn	1970—Al Unser
1927—Pete De Paolo	1949—Johnny Parsons	1971-72—Joe Leonard

(NASCAR)

(Courtesy National Association for Stock Car Auto Racing, Inc.)

GRAND NATIONAL

1948-49—Red Byron, Atlanta, Ga. ....
1950—Bill Rexford, Conewango
  Valley, N.Y. 1,959
1951—Herb Thomas, Sanford, N.C. .. 4,208.45
1952—Tim Flock, Atlanta, Ga. 6,858.5
1953—Herb Thomas, Sanford, N.C. .. 8,460
1954—Lee Petty, Randleman, N.C. .. 8,649
1955—Tim Flock, Atlanta, Ga. 9,596
1956—Elzie (Buck) Baker,
  Spartanburg, S.C. 9.272
1957—Elzie (Buck) Baker,
  Spartanburg, S.C. 10,716
1958—Lee Petty, Randleman, N.C. . 12,232
1959—Lee Petty, Randleman, N.C. . 11,792
1960—Rex White, Spartanburg, S.C. 21,164
1961—Ned Jarrett, Conover, N.C. .. 27,272
1962—Joe Weatherly, Norfolk, Va. . 30,836
1963—Joe Weatherly, Norfolk, Va. . 33,398

1964—Richard Petty, Randleman, N.C. .40,252
1965—Ned Jarrett, Camden, S.C. 38,824
1966—David Pearson, Charlotte, N.C. ...35,638
1967—Richard Petty, Randleman, N.C. .42,472
1968—David Pearson, Spartanburg, S.C. . 3,499
1969—David Pearson, Spartanburg, S.C. . 4,170
1970—Bobby Isaac, Catawba, N.C. 3,911
1971—Richard Petty, Randleman, N.C. . 4,435
1972—Bobby Allison, Hueytown, Ala. ... ——

NATIONAL MODIFIED

1949—Fonty Flock, Atlanta, Ga. 1,943.5
1950—Charley Dyer, North Bergen, N.J. 1,008.75
1951—Wally Campbell, Trenton, N.J. .. 2,356.25
1952—Frank Schneider, Sandbrook, N.J. 5,164
1953—Joe Weatherly, Norfolk, Va. 6,466
1954—Jack Choquette, West Palm Beach,
  Fla. 5,402
1955—Bill Widenhouse, Midland, N.C. .. 3,086
1956—Charles (Red) Farmer, Hialeah,
  Fla. 3,382
1957—Ken (Bones) Marriott, Palm
  Harbor, Fla. 3,324

1958—Budd Olsen, Paulsboro, N.J. 3,510
1959—Glenn Guthrie,
       Washington, D.C. 2,120
1960—Johnny Roberts,
       Brooklyn, Md. 4,514
1961—Johnny Roberts,
       Brooklyn, Md. 5,752
1962—Edward Crouse, Glen Allen, Va. . . 5,044
1963—Eddie Crouse, Glen Allen, Va. 5,930
1964—Bobby Allison, Hueytown, Ala. . . 5,756
1965—Bobby Allison, Hueytown, Ala. . . 6,324
1966—Ernie Gahan, Dover, N.H. 6,560
1967—Bugs Stevens, Rehoboth, Mass. . 8,207
1968—Bugs Stevens, Rehoboth, Mass. . 6,452
1969—Bugs Stevens, Rehoboth, Mass. . 7,634
1970—Fred DeSarro, Hope Valley, R.I. . 7,721
1971—Jerry Cook, Rome, N.Y. 5,488

SPORTSMAN NATIONAL

1950—Mike Klapak, Warren, O. 3,815.75
1951—Mike Klapak, Warren, O. 4,218.5
1952—Mike Klapak, Warren, O. 7,280
1953—Johnny Roberts, Brooklyn, Md. . . 5,692
1954—Danny Graves, Gardena, Calif. . . . 5,992
1955—Billy Myers, Germanton, N.C. 4,810
1956—Ralph Earnhardt, Kannapolis, Md. 4,272
1957—Ned Jarrett, Newton, N.C. 3,916
1958—Ned Jarrett, Newton, N.C. 4,494
1959—Rick Henderson,
       Petaluma, Calif. 4,136
1960—Bill Wimble, Lisbon, N.Y. 5,680
1961—Dick Nephew
       Mooers Falls, N.Y. 5,578
       Bill Wimble, Lisbon, N.Y. 5,578
1962—Rene Charland,
       Agawam, Mass. 5,708
1963—Rene Charland, Agawam, Mass. . . 6,622
1964—Rene Charland, Agawam, Mass. . . 6,236
1965—Rene Charland, Agawam, Mass. . . 5,614
1966—Don MacTavish, Dover, Mass. . . . 8,964
1967—Pete Hamilton, Dedham, Mass. . . 8,183
1968—Joe Thurman, Rocky Mount, Va. . 4,608
1969—Red Farmer, Hueytown, Ala. 8,276
1970—Red Farmer, Hueytown, Ala. 5,516
1971—Red Farmer, Hueytown, Ala. 9,688

Sebring Sports Car Race

The leading sports car event in this country is the Sebring (Florida) 12-hour endurance test. The first race, held in 1950, was a 6-hour grind, all others have been of 12-hours duration. The race is patterned after the Le Mans, France, 24-hour event. At the start, the drivers race on foot to their cars. The world's leading drivers participate.

Year	Car and drivers	Miles
1950—Crosley, Fred Koster-Bob Deshon		288.3
1951—No competition		
1952—Frazier Nash, Harry Grey-Larry Kulok		754
1953—Cunningham, John Fitch-Phil Walters		899.6
1954—Osca, Stirling Moss-Bill Lloyd		883.6
1955—Jaguar D, Mike Hawthorn-Phil Walters		946.4
1956—Ferrari, Juan Manuel Fangio-Eugenio Castellotti		1,008.8
1957—Maserati, Juan Manuel Fangio-Jean Behra		1,024.4
1958—Ferrari, Phil Hill-Peter Collins		1,040
1959—Farrari, Phil Hill, Olivier Gendebien		977.6
1960—Porsche, Olivier Gendebien-Hans Hermann		1,019.2
1961—Ferrari, Phil Hill-Olivier Gendebien		1,092
1962—Ferrari, Phil Hill-Olivier Gendebien		1,071
1963—Ferrari, John Surtees, Lodovico		1,086.8
1964—Ferrari, Mike Parkes, Umberto Maglioli		1,112.8
1965—Chaparral, Jim Hall, Hap Sharp		1,019.2
1966—Ford Roadster XL, Ken Miles, Lloyd Ruby		
1967—Ford Mark IV, M. Andretti, B. McLaren		
1968—Porsche, Jo Siffert, Hans Herrmann		
1969—Ford GT, J. Ickx, J. Oliver		1,242.8
1970—Ferrari, I. Giunti, N. Vaccarella, M. Andretti		1,289.6
1971—Porsche, V. Elford, G. Larousse		260 laps
1972—Ferrari, M. Andretti, J. Ickx		1,347

Land Speed Records

The Contest Board of the American Automobile Association kept and recognized track records for more than 50 years. In 1955, the A.A.A. withdrew from the automobile racing field and many of its functions, including sanctioning of speed record attempts, were taken over by the United States Auto Club.

In 1956, its first year of operation, the U.S.A.C. purchased a $15,000 machine for timing record runs. The instrument has been established as the most accurate of its kind in the world, according to the U.S.A.C.

All claims for world and international class records must be submitted to the F.I.A., and all American claims must first have U.S.A.C. approval as national records.

BADMINTON

Badminton is a fascinating game for the players and spectators. It has wide appeal as an organized and as an informal form of sport. The ranking players engaged in organized competition possess speed, dexterity and endurance. On the other hand, a court can be set up easily in the back yard and members of the family, young and adult, can enjoyably engage in the pursuit of the erratic shuttlecock—at small expense. To the spectator the high-speed action of this volleying-only game is intriguing.

The devotees of court games who have played all or most incline to the belief that badminton is the fastest. The game originated in India many centuries ago and was transported to England, whence it spread throughout the world, having its greatest popularity in the English-speaking countries.

In India, it was known as "Poona." It was adopted by English army officers in the 1860's and some equipment was conveyed to England in 1871 or 1872. The army men introduced the game to friends, but the new sport was definitely launched there at a party given in 1873 by the Duke of Beaufort at his country place, "Badminton," in Gloucestershire. At the time, the game had no name, but it was referred to as "the game at Badminton," and, therefore, badminton became its official name.

Until 1887 the sport was played in England under the rules that prevailed in India. They were, from the English viewpoint, somewhat contradictory and confusing. Since a small army of badminton players had been recruited, a group formed itself into the Bath Badminton Club, standardized the rules, made the game applicable to English ideas and the basic regulations, drawn up in 1887, still guide the sport. In 1895, the Badminton Association (of England) was formed to take over the authority of the Bath Club, and the new group made rules which now govern the game throughout the world.

Badminton quickly spread from England to the United States, Canada and Australasia (Australia and New Zealand), and made big strides in Europe. Although it first was played by men, women became enthusiastic about it, and interest now is about equally divided.

The first All-England championships for men were held in 1899 and in 1900 the pioneer tournament for women was arranged. These, however, were regarded as "unofficial" and 1904 marked the beginning of the official All-England matches. The growth of badminton's popularity in the British Isles is evidenced by the fact that in 1910 there were 300 badminton clubs in England, about 500 in 1930, and over 9,000 in the British Isles soon after World War II. In recent years badminton has made even more gigantic strides in popularity, gaining many recruits from tennis players, who seem to regard badminton as something of a post-graduate course.

The first organized badminton club established in the United States is the Badminton Club of the City of New York, which was established in 1878 and has been in existence continuously since that date. This club holds the distinction of being the oldest existing badminton club in the world.

An international team championship was envisioned about a decade after the successful launching of the Davis Cup tennis matches in 1900, but it was not until the 1930's that the game became organized in a sufficient number of countries to make the dream feasible. During this period no fewer than 9 countries—Australia, Denmark, India, Malaya, Norway, Sweden, the United States, Mexico and the Netherlands—organized national championships. Later, South Africa and New Zealand entered the fold and by 1940 badminton was on an organized scale in more than 16 countries. Today there are 49 member nations affiliated with the I.B.F.

The International Badminton Federation decided in March, 1939, that the time had arrived for the inauguration of international competition. Its president, Sir George A. Thomas, Baronet, offered a trophy for the winning team. The war and post-war shortages of shuttlecocks delayed the first Thomas Cup matches until the 1948—49 season.

The preliminary rounds for the Thomas Cup are played in four zones—American, Asian, Australasian, and European. The Asian Zone is subdivided into two sections—eastern and western. In 1967, the challenge tie was abolished and the champion nation now enters the competition in the semi-final round of its respective geographical division. The site of the final round (inter-zone semi-final and final ties) is determined by the International Badminton Federation.

In June 1970, Indonesia regained the Thomas Cup, defeating defending champion Malaysia at Kuala Lumpur, Malaysia, 7-2. Each of these two nations has won the Thomas Cup four times. Next competition will take place in 1973.

The idea of a women's international team badminton championship along the lines of the Thomas Cup was broached in 1950. It was turned down then because of financial problems. The topic continued to be brought up and eventually it was decided to establish the tournament on a triennial basis. Mrs. H.S. Uber of England donated the trophy, which is called the Uber Cup. The first tournament was held during the 1956-57 season. The United States team, captained by Margaret Varner, won the cup by defeating Denmark, 6 to 1, in England in March, 1957.

The United States successfully defended the Uber Cup in 1960, defeating Denmark at Philadelphia, 5-2, and again in 1963, beating England at Wilmington, Delaware, 4-3. However, in 1966 at Wellington, New Zealand, Japan succeeded in wresting the cup from the U.S., 5-2. Japan successfully defended the Uber Cup in 1969 and again in 1972, both times defeating Indonesia at Tokyo by scores of 6-1.

Badminton can be played both indoors and outdoors, but finds its greatest vogue in the open air. For that reason, while it is played chiefly in the summer time in most of America, it is a year-round game in California, which has produced the outstanding players. The game not only intrigues the contestants, but is also a dazzling exhibition from the spectator's viewpoint. It calls for terrific volleying of an eccentric shuttlecock, which the players bat over a net. The flights of the shuttlecock and its sudden, unanticipated descents demand the utmost in speed and dexterity, calling for far more endurance than is demanded of a lawn tennis player.

In badminton, during a volley, the competing players are almost in perpetual motion, and the smallest fraction of a second not only may decide a point but also may determine a championship.

FAMOUS PLAYERS

Rube Samuelson, former sports editor of the *Pasadena* (Calif.) *Star-News* and an authority on the game, stated:

"The greatest American player ever developed is David G. Freeman of Pasadena, Calif. From 1939, until the national championships were abandoned after 1942 because of the war, he dominated the sport. Fantastic stories are told about Freeman's skill, one being that, in the midst of any volley, he can drive the shuttlecock at any designated spot and make a 'bullseye.' Freeman has the speed of a projectile, when in action, and accuracy of placement beyond that of any amateur performer in the history of the sport. He also is the greatest retriever badminton has produced."

Other great American men players have been Walter R. Kramer, Chester Goss, Donald Eversoll, Hamilton Law, Richard Yeager, William Markham, Carl Loveday, Donald Richardson, Phillip Richardson, LeRoy Erikson, Reaford Haney, William Faversham, Wayne Schell, C. Raynor Hutchinson, Clinton Stephens, Richard Mitchell, Barney McCay, Webb Kimball, Roy Lockwood, Wynn Robers, Marten Mendez, Joseph Alston, Dr. Jim Poole, Dr. Don Paup, Dr. Stanton Hales, and Chris Kinard.

The great English badminton men players through the last 40 years have included F. Chesterton, G.A. Sautter, H.N. Marrett, Sir George A. Thomas, G.B.S. Mack, J.F. Devlin, F. Hodge, E. Hawthorn, D.C. Hume, H.G. Uber, A.K. Jones, R.C.F. Nichols, R.M. White and Ken Davidson (later of the United States).

The Canadian men stars were Col. A.E. Snell, McTaggart Cowan, Dr. H.T. Douglas, C.W. Aikmen, Jack Underhill, Jack Purcell, J.W. Taylor, Douglass Grant, Rod Phelan, Jack G. Muir, Noel Radford, George Goodwin Jr., James Forsythe, J.E. Sibbald, Reginald Hill, D.W.R. McKean, Grant Henry, John Samis, James Snyder, Paul Snyder, Richard Birch, Len Schlemm, Allan France, H.K. Pollock, H.E. Porter, Gordon Simpson, Don Smythe, Daryl Thompson, Alan Williams, Dave McTaggart, Wayne MacDonnell, Jamie Paulson, Bruce Rollick, and Yves Pare.

Malaya has produced such stellar stars as Wong Peng Soon, Eddy B. Choong, Ooi Teik Hock, Punch Gunalan, Ng Boon Bee, Ong Poh Lim, and Tan Aik Huang. Denmark has contributed Finn Kobbero, Jorgen Hammergaard-Hansen, Erland Kops, Svend Pri, and Henning Borch.

Mexican Athletes are Ernesto Villareal, Dr. Antonio Rangel, Roy Diaz Gonzalez, and Victor Jaramillo, Jr. Indonesian outstanding players include Rudy Hartono, Tan Joe Hok, Ferry Sonneville, Muljadi, and Indra Gunawan.

The outstanding women players of the United States, with Mrs. Judy Devlin Hashman considered by most experts to be the greatest woman player of all time, have included Mrs. Del Barkhuff, Mary E. Whittemore, Mrs. Evelyn Boldrick Howard, Mrs. Roy C. Bergman, Helen Gibson, Mrs. Zoe Smith Yeager, Mrs. Thelma Scovil (who was England's champion as Thelma Kingsbury), Janet Wright, Elizabeth Anselm, Mrs. Helen Zabriski Ough, Shirley Stuebgen, Ethel Marshall, Margaret Varner, Sue Devlin, Thelma Welcome and Lois Alston.

Also, Patricia Donovan, Sally L. Williams, Mrs. Huelet (Loma Moulton) Smith, Mary Hagan, Mrs. Ray Casey, Mrs. George Wightman, Mrs. Charles (Helen Noble) Tibbetts, Connie Horner, Marianna Gott, Dorothy Hann, Shirley Blanchett, Mrs. Bert (Tody Rahmn) Rhine, Mrs. M.B. Reel, Patsy Starrett, Barbara Templeton, Beatrice Massman, Mrs. Virginia Hill, Tyna Barinaga, Mrs. Diane Hales, and Pam Stockton.

The brilliant English women players were Miss M. Lucas, Mrs. R.C. Tragett, Miss Gowenlock, Miss Cundall, Miss Hogarth, Miss Bateman, Miss E.G. Peterson, Miss L.C. Radeglia, Mrs. Kathleen McKane Godfree, Mrs. A.D. Stocks, Mrs. M. Barrett, Miss L.M. Kingsbury, Miss M. McKane, Miss V. Elton, Mrs. H.S. Uber, Miss A. Woodruff, Thelma Kingsbury, Miss D.M.C. Young, Mrs. Margaret Barrand, Mrs. Ursula Smith Oakley, Mrs. Angela Bairstow Palmer, Mrs. Heather Ward Nielsen, Mrs. Iris Cooley Rogers, and Mrs. Gillian Perrian Gilks.

Outstanding Canadian women were Mrs. G.A. Boone, Mrs. M. Brunet, Mrs. E.F. Coke, Mrs. W.R. Walton Jr., Miss E. George, Mrs. John Porteous, Ruth Robertson, Mrs. Anna Kier Patrick, Margaret Taylor, Miss J. Woodman, Miss M. Barron, Mrs. M. DeLage, Mrs, E.W. Whittington, Nancy Bonnar, Marjorie Mapp, Lois Reid, Mrs. Clare Lovett, Marjory Shedd, Dorothy

Tinline, and Sharon Whittaker.

Other outstanding women players are Mrs. Norika Takagi Nakayama, Hiroe Yuki, and Etsuko Takenaka of Japan; Mrs. Eva Twedberg of Sweden; Miss Minarni and Miss Retno Koestijah of Indonesia; Mrs. Imre Rietveld Nielsen (formerly of the Netherlands, now player for Denmark), also Mrs. Karin Jorgensen and Mrs. Ulla Strand of Denmark, as well as Miss Carolina Allier of Mexico.

CHAMPIONS

(Courtesy Jack H. van Praag, Chairman National Badminton News Committee, American Badminton Assoc., 380 South Euclid Ave., Apt. 207, Pasadena, Calif., 91101)

All-England

Men's Singles

1899–No competition
1900–S.H. Smith
1901–Capt. H.W. Davies
1902–03–Ralph Watling
1904–05–H.N. Marrett
1906–07–N. Wood
1908–H.N. Marrett
1909–10–F. Chesterton
1911–G.A. Sautter
1912–F. Chesterton
1913–14–G.A. Sautter
1915–19–No competition
1920–23–Sir George A. Thomas
1924–G.S.B. Mack
1925–29–J.F. Devlin
1930–D.C. Hume
1931–J.F. Devlin
1932–R.C.F. Nichols
1933–R.M. White
1934–R.C.F. Nichols
1935–R.M. White
1936–38–R.C.F. Nichols
1939–Tage Madsen
1940–46–No competition
1947–Conny Jepsen
1948–Jorn Skaarup
1949–David G. Freeman
1950–52–Wong Peng Soon
1953–54–Eddy B. Choong

1955–Wong Peng Soon
1956–Eddy B. Choong
1957–Eddy B. Choong
1958–Erland Kops
1959–Tan Joe Hok
1960–62–Erland Kops
1963*–Erland Kops
1964*–K.A. Neilsen
1965*–Erland Kops
1966*–Tan Aik Huang
1967–Erland Kops
1968–72–Rudy Hartono
*Unofficial World Championships.

Women's Singles

1899–No competition
1900–01–E. Thomson
1902–M. Lucas
1903–04–E. Thomson
1905–M. Lucas
1906–E. Thomson
1907–10–M. Lucas
1911–M. Lamine
1912–Mrs. R.C. Tragett
1913–14–L.C. Radeglia
1915–19–No competition
1920–22–Kathleen McKane
1923–L.C. Radeglia
1924–Kathleen McKane
1925–Mrs. A.D. Stocks

1926–31–Mrs. F.G. Barrett
1932–L.M. Kingsbury
1933–A. Woodrofe
1934–L.M. Kingsbury
1935–Mrs. H.S. Uber
1936–37–Thelma Kingsbury
1938–D.M.C. Young
1939–Mrs. W.R. Walton Jr.
1940–46–No competition
1947–Marie Ussing
1948–Kirsten Thorndahl
1949–Aase Schiott Jacober
1950–Mrs. G. (Tonny) Ahm
1951–Aase Jacobsen
1952–Mrs. G. (Tonny) Ahm
1953–Miss M. Ussing
1954–Judith Devlin
1955–56–Margaret Varner
1957–58–Judith Devlin
1959–Miss H.M. Ward
1960–Judith Devlin
1961–62–Judith Devlin Hashman
1963*-64*–Judy Devlin Hashman
1965*–Ursula Smith
1966*-67–Judy Devlin Hashman
1968–Mrs. Eva Twedberg
1969–Hiroe Yuki
1970–Etsujo Takenaka
1971–Mrs. Eva Twedberg
1972–Mrs. Norika Nakayama
*Unofficial World Championships

Men's Doubles

1899–D. Oakes–S.M. Massey
1900–02–H.L. Mellersh–F.S. Collier
1903–S.M. Massey–E.L. Huston
1904–A.D. Prebble–H.N. Marrett
1905–C.T.J. Barnes–S.M. Massey
1906–H.N. Marrett–G.A. Thomas
1907–08–A.D. Prebble–H.N. Marrett
1909–F. Chestron–A.D. Prebble
1910–H.N. Marrett–G.A. Thomas
1911–P.D. Fitton–E. Hawthorn
1912–H.N. Marrett–G.A. Thomas
1913–14–F. Chestron–G.A. Thomas
1915–19–No competition
1920–A.F. Englebach–R. du Roveray
1921–Sir G.A. Thomas–F. Hodge
1922–G.A. Sautter–J.F. Devlin

1923–J.F. Devlin–G.S.B. Mack
1924–Sir G.A. Thomas–F. Hodge
1925–H.S. Uber–A.K. Jones
1926–27–J.F. Devlin–G.S.B. Mack
1928–Sir G.A. Thomas–F. Hodge
1929–31–J.F. Devlin–G.S.B. Mack
1932–35–D.C. Hume–R.M. White
1936–38–L. Nichols–R.C.F. Nichols
1939–T.H. Boyle–J.L. Rankin
1940–46–No competition
1947–Tage Madsen–Poul Holm
1948–Preben Dabelsteen–Borge Frederiksen
1949–Ooi Teik Hock–Teoh Seng Khoon
1950–Jorn Skaarup–Preben Dabelsteen
1951–53–Eddie and David Choong
1954–Ooi Teik Hock–Ong Poh Lim
1955–Finn Kobbero–J. Hammergaard-Hansen

1956—Finn Kobbero—J. Hammergaard-Hansen
1957—Joe Alston—H.A. Heah
1958—Erland Kops—P.E. Nielsen
1959—Lim Say Hup—Teh Kew San
1960—Finn Kobbero—P.E. Nielsen
1961—62—J. Hammergaard Hansen—Finn Kobbero
1963*-64*—Finn Dobbero—Jorgen Hammergaard-
Hansen
1965*-66*—Ng Boon Bee—Tan Yee Khan
1967—69—Henning Borch—Erland Kops
1970—Tom Bacher—Paul Petersen
1971—Ng Boon Bee—Punch Gunalan
1972—Christian Chandra—Ade Chandra
*Unofficial World Championships.

Women's Doubles

1899—1900—M. Lucas—Miss Graeme
1901—Miss St. John—E.M. Moseley
1902—M. Lucas—E. Thomson
1903—M. Hardy—D.K. Douglass
1904—06—M. Lucas—E. Thomson
1907—09—M. Lucas—G.L. Murray
1910—M.K. Bateman—M. Lucas
1911—12—A. Gowenlock—D. Cundall
1913—H. Hobarth—M.K. Bateman
1914—Mrs. R.C. Tragett—E.G. Peterson
1915—19—No competition
1920—L.C. Radeglia—V. Elton
1921—K. McKane—M. McKane
1922—23—R.C. Tragett—H. Hogarth
1924—Mrs. A.D. Stock—K. McKane
1925—Mrs. R.C. Tragett—H. Hogarth
1926—Mrs. A.M. Head—V. Elton
1927—Mrs. R.C. Tragett—H. Hogarth
1928—30—Mrs. F.G. Barrett—V. Elton
1931—Mrs. H.S. Uber—Mrs. R.J. Horsley
1932—Mrs. F.G. Barrett—L.M. Kingsbury
1933—T. Kingsbury—M. Bell
1934—36—T. Kingsbury—Mrs. M. Henderson
1937—38—Mrs. H.S. Uber—D. Doveton
1939—Mrs. R. Dalsgard—T. Olsen
1940—46—No competition
1947—48—Mrs. G. (Tonny) Ahm—Kirsten
Thorndahl
1949—Mrs. H.S. Uber—Q.M. Allen
1950—51—Mrs. G. (Tonny) Ahm—Kirsten
Thorndahl
1952—Mrs. G. (Tonny) Ahm—Aase Jacobsen
1953—Iris L. Cooley—June R. White
1954—Judith and Susan Devlin
1955—Iris L. Cooley—June R. White
1956—Judith and Susan Devlin
1957—Mrs. K. Grandlund—Mrs. A. Hammergaard
1958—Margaret Varner—Heather Ward
1959—Mrs. W.C.E. Rogers—Mrs. E.J. Timperly
1960—Judith and Susan Devlin
1961—Judith Devlin Hashman—Mrs. F.W. Peard
1962—Judith Devlin Hashman—Mrs. T. Holst-
Christensen
1963*—Judith Devlin Hashman—Sue Peard
1964*—Karen Jorgensen—U. Rasmussen
1965*—Karen Jorgensen—Ulla Strand

1966*—Judith Devlin Hashman—Sue Peard
1967—Imre Rietveld—Ulla Strand
1968—Miss Minarni—Retno Koestijah
1969—70—Margaret Boxall—Mrs. Susan Whetnall
1971—Noriko Takagi—Hiroe Yuki
1972—Machiko Aizawa—Etsuko Takenaka
*Unofficial World Championships.

Mixed Doubles

1935—36—D.C. Hume—Mrs. H.S. Uber
1937—I. Maconache—Thelma Kingsbury
1938—R.M. White—Mrs. H.S. Uber
1939—R.C.F. Nichols—Miss B.M. Staples
1940—46—No competition
1947—Poul Holm—Mrs. G. (Tonny) Ahm
1948—Jorn Skaarup—Kirsten Thorndahl
1949—Clinton Stephens and Mrs. Stephens
1950—52—Poul Holm—Mrs. G. (Tonny) Ahm
1953—Eddy B. Choong—June R. White
1954—J.R. Best—Iris L. Cooley
1955—Finn Kobbero—Kirsten Thorndahl
1956—A.D. Jordan—E.J. Timperley
1957—Finn Kobbero—Mrs. K. Grandlund
1958—June Timperley—A.D. Jordan
1959—P.E. Nielsen—Mrs. I.B. Hansen
1960—61—Finn Kobbero—Kirsten Thorndahl
1962—Finn Kobbero—Miss U. Rasmussen
1963*—Finn Kobbero—Ulla Rasmussen
1964*—Tony Jordan—Jennifer Prichard
1965*-66*—Finn Kobbero—Ulla Strand
1967—Svend Andersen—Ulla Strand
1968—A.D. Jordan—Susan Pound
1969—R.J. Mills—Gillian Perrin
1970—P. Walsoe—Pernille Molgaard-Hansen
1971—72—Svend Pri—Ulla Strand
*Unofficial World Championships.

United States – Open
(Open since 1954)

Men's Singles

1937—38—Walter R. Kramer
1939—42—David G. Freeman
1943—46—No competition
1947—48—David G. Freeman
1949—50—Marten Mendez
1951—Joseph Alston
1952—Marten Mendez
1953—David G. Freeman
1954—Eddy B. Choong
1955—Joseph Alston
1956—57—Finn Kobbero
1958—Jim Poole
1959—60—Tan Joe Hok
1961—Jim Poole
1962—Ferry Sonneville
1963—Erland Kops
1964—Chanarong Ratana-Saeng-Suang
1965—Erland Kops
1966—Tan Aik Huang
1967—Erland Kops
1968—Channarong Ratana Saeng-Suang
1969—Rudy Hartono

1970—Junji Honma
1971—Muljadi
1972—Sture Johnsson

Women's Singles

1937—38—Mrs. Del Barkhuff
1939—Mary E. Whittemore
1940—Evelyn Boldrick
1941—Thelma Kingsbury
1942—Evelyn Boldrick
1943—46—No competition
1947—53—Ethel Marshall
1954—Judith Devlin
1955—Margaret Varner
1956—60—Judith Devlin
1961—62—Judith Devlin Hashman
1963—Judith Devlin Hashman
1964—Dorothy O'Neill
1965—67—Judith Devlin Hashman
1968—Tyna Barinaga
1969—Miss Minarni
1970—Ersuko Takenaka
1971—Noriko Takagi
1972—Mrs. Eva Twedberg

Men's Doubles

1937—Chester Goss—Donald Eversoll
1938—39—Hamilton Law—Richard Yeager
1940—42—Chester Goss—David G. Freeman
1943—46—No competition
1947—David G. Freeman—Webster Kimball
1948—David G. Freeman—Wynn Rogers
1949—50—Wynn Rogers—Barney McCay
1951—53—Wynn Rogers—Joseph Alston
1954—Ooi Teik Hock—Ong Poh Lim
1955—Wynn Rogers—Joseph Alston
1956—Finn Kobbero—J. Hammergaard
1957—58—Finn Kobbero—J. Hammergaard
1959—Lim Say Hup—Teh Kew San
1960—Finn Kobbero—Charoen Watansin
1961—62—Wynn Rogers—Joe Alston
1963—Erland Kops—Robert McCoig
1964—Joe Alston—Wynn Rogers
1965—Robert McCoig—Tony Jordan
1966—Ng Boon Bee—Tan Yee Khan
1967—Joe Alston—Erland Kops
1968—Jim Poole—Don Paup
1969—Ng Boon Bee—Punch Gunalan
1970—Ippei Kojima—Junji Honma
1971—Ng Boon Bee—Punch Gunalan
1972—Elliott Stuart—Derek Talbot

Women's Doubles

1937—Mrs. Del Barkhuff—Zoe G. Smith
1938—Mrs. Roy C. Bergman—Helen Gibson
1939—Mrs. Del Barkhuff—Zoe G. Smith
1940—Elizabeth Anselm—Helen Zabriskie
1941—Thelma Kingsbury—Janet Wright
1942—Evelyn Boldrick—Janet Wright
1943—46—No competition

1947—50—Mrs. Thelma Kingsbury Scovil—Janet
         Wright
1951—Dorothy Hann—Mrs. Loma Moulton Smith
1952—Ethel Marshall—Beatrice Massman
1953—55—Judith and Susan Devlin
1956—Ethel Marshall—Beatrice Massman
1957—60—Judith and Susan Devlin
1961—Judith Devlin Hashman—Mrs. F.W. Peard
1962—Judith Devlin Hashman—Pat Stephens
1963—Judith Devlin Hashman—Susan Devlin
         Peard
1964—Tyna Barinaga—Caroline Jensen
1965—Margaret Barrand—Jennifer Pritchard
1966—Judith Devlin Hashman—Susan Devlin
         Peard
1967—Judith Devlin Hashman—Rosine Jones
1968—Tyna Barinaga—Mrs. Helen Tibbetts
1969—Miss Minarni—Retno Koestijah
1970—Etsuko Takenaka—Machiko Aizawa
1971—Hiroe Yuki—Noriko Takagi
1972—Anne Berglund—Mrs. Pernille Kaagaard

Mixed Doubles

1937—38—Hamilton Law—Mrs. Del Barkhuff
1939—Richard Yeager—Zoe G. Smith
1940—42—David G. Freeman—Sally L. Williams
1943—46—No competition
1947—Wynn Rogers—Mrs. Virginia Hill
1948—Clinton Stephens and Mrs. Stephens
1949—51—Wynn Rogers—Mrs. Loma Moulton Smith
1952—Wynn Rogers—Helen Tibbitts
1953—54—Joseph and Lois Alston
1955—Wynn Rogers—Dorothy Hann
1956—58—Finn Kobbero—Judith Devlin
1959—Michael Roche—Judith Devlin
1960—Finn Kobbero—Judith Devlin
1961—62—Wynn Rogers—Judith Devlin Hashman
1963—Sancob Rattanusorn—Margaret Barrand
1964—Chanarong Ratana-Saeng-Suang—
         Margaret Barrand
1965—Robert McCoig—Margaret Barrand
1966—Wayne MacDonnell—Tyna Barinaga
1967—J.R. Sydie—Judith Devlin Hashman
1968—Larry Saben—Mrs. Carlene Starkey
1969—Erland Kops—Pernille Molgaard-Hansen
1970—Paul Whetnall—Margaret Boxall
1971—Jim Poole—Maryann Breckell
1972—Fleming Delfs—Mrs. Pernille Kaagaard

Senior Men's Singles (Veterans)

1965—66—Charles Thomas
1967—James Butler
1968—Dick Mitchell
1969—John Leib
1970—71—Ted Moehlmann
1972—Jim Poole

Senior Men's Doubles (Veterans)

1938—Herbert Hendriques—George McCook
1939—C.R. Hutchinson—Lealand Gustavson
1940—T.M. Royce—George McCook

1941—C.R. Hutchinson—Lealand Gustavson
1942—Lealand Gustavson—Frank N. Hinds
1943—46—No Competition
1947—Lewis Rulison—Hulet Smith
1948—Frank N. Hinds—Fred Fullin
1949—50—Wayne Schell—Robert Wright
1951—52—Howard Holman—Fred Fullin
1953—54—Wayne Schell—Robert Wright
1955—Roy Lockwood—Dick Fleming
1956—Rupert Mee—Robert Traquiar
1957—George Lane—Carl Anderson
1958—Wayne Schell—Robert Wright
1959—Robert Traquiar—Ray Young
1960—Wayne Schell—Harold Seavey
1961—Wynn Rogers—Dick Mitchell
1962—Wynn Rogers—Waldo Lyon
1963—Bart Harvey—Charles Randolph
1964—65—Waldo Lyon—Wynn Rogers
1966—William Anderson—Robert Traquair
1967—Charles Randolph—Edward Spruill
1968—Waldo Lyon—Wynn Rogers
1969—Wynn Rogers—Bob Gerzine
1970—72—Ted Moehlmann—Jim McQuie

Senior Ladies' Doubles

1958—Thelma Welcome—Louise Kirby
1959—Mary Connor—Mildred Sirwaitis
1960—Thelma Burdick—Eleanor Coambs
1961—62—Lois Kirby—Charlotte Decker
1963—Thelma Burdick—Eleanor Coambs
1964—Lois Kirby—Jeanne Pons
1965—Ethel Marshall—Beatrice Massman
1966—Helen Tibbetts—Jeanne Pons
1967—70—Ethel Marshall—Bea Massman
1971—Mrs. Lois Alston—Mrs. Beulah Armendariz
1972—Ethel Marshall—Bea Massman

Senior Mixed Doubles

1964—Larry Calvert—Jeanne Pons
1965—Robert Love—Mrs. Virginia Andersen
1966—Waldo Lyon—Mrs. Helen Tibbetts
1967—Robert Traquair—Ethel Marshall
1968—Wynn Rogers—Mrs. Helen Tibbetts
1969—Wynn Rogers—Ethel Marshall
1970—71—Ted Moehlmann—Ethel Marshall
1972—Jim Poole—Maryann Breckell

United States — Closed
(Restricted to U.S. players)

Men's Singles

1970—71—Stan Hales
1972—Chris Kinard

Men's Doubles

1970—72—Jim Poole—Don Paup

Women's Singles

1970—Tina Baringa
1971—Diane Hales
1972—Pam Stockton

Women's Doubles

1970—Tina Baringa—Carolyn Hein

1971—Carolyn Hein—Carlene Starkey
1972—Polly Bretzke—Pam Stockton

Mixed Doubles

1970—Jim Poole—Tina Baringa
1971—Don Paup—Helen Tibbetts
1972—Tom Carmichael—Pam Stockton

BASIC RULES

Badminton is played with a shuttlecock (usually called a bird or shuttle) which has a half-ball cork head 1 to 1 1/8 inches in diameter and contains 14 to 16 feathers, each 2½ inches long, imbedded in the flat cork face and rising like a crown with a 2½-inch spread at the top. The shuttlecock weighs 73 to 85 grains and is of correct pace if, when a player of average strength strikes it with a full underhand stroke from one back-court boundary, it falls not less than 1 foot nor more than 2 feet 6 inches short of the other back boundary.

The singles court is 17 x 44 feet. For doubles the width is increased to 20 feet. The top of the net bisecting the court is 5 feet high. The racquet—or "bat"—is lighter and slightly larger than that used in squash. The "bird" must be hit on the volley. Scoring is possible only while serving. Failure to return the bird over the net results in loss of service or scores a point. The men's game ends at 15 points and the women's singles at 11.

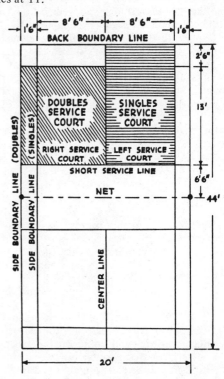

Badminton Court. (Taken from Sports for Recreation, *edited by E.D. Mitchell, A.S. Barnes and Company, New York.)*

BASEBALL
Major League

Baseball is called the national pastime in this country, and it has earned and deserves the title. Rare is the boy who has not played the game. In season or out, baseball is a topic of discussion and debate. Though television has cut attendance at games, it has increased, rather than diminished, interest in the game. Where formerly major league baseball was limited to those who could attend games, today it is available throughout the country by way of the video screen.

After the majors became established around the turn of the century, they went along without change for fifty years. In that time they prospered generally and had smooth sailing except for a futile challenge by the Federal League in 1914-15 and the "Black Sox" scandal involving Chicago White Sox players who conspired to "throw" the 1919 world series to Cincinnati. Then the year 1953 saw the start of a change in the leagues' set-ups. The Boston Braves moved to Milwaukee. The next year the St. Louis Browns shifted to Baltimore. The Athletics' franchise was transferred from Philadelphia to Kansas City. In 1958, the West Coast at last got big league ball as the New York Giants shifted to San Francisco and the Brooklyn Dodgers moved to Los Angeles.

The American League expanded to ten teams in 1960 with the formation of new teams in Los Angeles and Washington, the Angels and the Senators. The old Senators moved to Minneapolis-St. Paul and took the name Minnesota Twins. The National League followed suit in 1961 with two new teams, the Houston Colt .45s and the New York Mets. The two new A.L. teams started play in 1961, the N.L. teams in 1962.

Those who acclaim Abner Doubleday as originator of the game of baseball, those who fix 1839 as the year of its beginning and honor Cooperstown, N.Y., as the birthplace are wrong on all counts.

Doubleday probably never played baseball. The game was an established sport long before 1839, and the chances are that the villagers of Cooperstown never knew what a baseball looked like until the Civil War, or afterward.

The erroneous tributes came about in this fashion:

About 1934 or 1935 interest in baseball was sagging. The outlook was none too cheerful. It was deemed fitting and proper by the executives, who were interested financially in the game, that something be done to stimulate conditions. The prime mover in the gesture to continue baseball in the spotlight was Kenesaw Mountain Landis, the commissioner.

While all the executives were busy groping for something that would act like a shot of digitalis, one discovered a report about the origin of the game that had been made in 1907 by A. G. Mills. It was covered with dust and cobwebs and was an almost forgotten document, but they read it, and a few shrieked "Eureka!" since the report was like a heaven-sent gift.

The report gave the baseball folks the chance to chant about how the game originated and, best of all, it gave them an opportunity to bang the cymbals in prolonged harmony. The report, fixing 1839 as the founding year, afforded them, prior to 1939, an opportunity to prepare items about a forthcoming centennial and to get a lot of space in newspapers about the game of baseball.

Funds were appropriated to build a shrine at Cooperstown. There was a great deal of ballyhoo about a Hall of Fame. The baseball writers, loyal to Landis & Company, went to work industriously toward pepping up things for the sport in their columns. Each week the newspapers were full of pictures and stories concerning the plans and the program for the centennial.

If anyone took time out to study the Mills report or to analyze circumstances concerning it, such person adroitly kept from mentioning it. The stress was on popularizing the Doubleday–1839–Cooperstown trinity, not on actual facts or historical data, which liken the Mills report to gibberish.

After the turn of the 20th Century, A. G. Spalding, who had been a titan in the early days of baseball, became curious as to the origin of the game. The editor of Spalding's "Baseball Guide," Henry Chadwick, had told him it was nothing other than the American adaptation of the English game of "rounders." Since Chadwick was of English birth, had been a cricketer and a rounders player and thought all things with an English background were superlative, Spalding disputed the Chadwick version as biased. A series of friendly arguments resulted.

As time went on, Chadwick, writing in Spalding's "Baseball Guide," took matters into his own hands by composing an article for 1903 printing, which read, in part:

"THE ORIGIN OF BASE BALL"

"Over seventy years ago (1833), when I was a schoolboy in England, my favorite field sport was the old English game of Rounders. This was played with an ordinary ball, and with stout round sticks as bats. After schooltime, we boys would proceed to the nearest field, select a smooth portion of it, and lay out the ground for a contest. This was easily done by placing four stones, or posts, in position as base stations, and by digging a hole in the ground where the batsman had to stand. We then tossed up for sides and innings, and started the game. Custom made the rules of play, as there was no written code to govern the game.

"The evolution of Base Ball from the early period of its old Rounders form of the Town Ball of New England, which was played in the 1830's, to that of the Americanized form which marked the 'New York Game' of the '40s, was a matter of slow progress. In fact, the game may be said to have grown by decades. For instance, it was in 1831 that the 'Town Ball' was first introduced into Pennsylvania, and the Olympic Town Ball Club was organized in Philadelphia in 1833. But it was not until 1842 that the 'New York Game' began to be played in New York, and it was in 1845 that the first regular Base Ball club was organized in that city. The 'Town Ball' form of the game had two conspicuous features of Rounders in its rules, viz., the four post base stations and the putting out of base runners by throwing the ball at them.

"The change made in the rules by the old Knickerbocker club, which gave the method of playing it the distinctive title of the 'New York Game,' was that of reducing the number of bases from five to four, and altering the form of the infield from an oblong square to a diamond square. The 'New York Game' had three base bags with an iron plate for its base stations, the latter being at the home base. The Town Ball game had a post at each of the corners of its oblong square, with a base for the batsman between the first and fourth post, the base runner completing his round of the bases when he touched the fourth post. In the 'New York Game,' however, the runner scored his run when he touched the home base at the batsman's position.

"The way the change was brought about from using the diamond square in the place of the oblong square was this: The New York players found that in playing Town Ball they had difficulty, after making a home-run hit, in turning the corners of the posts of the square, whereas by using the diamond square they could almost run the bases in a circle. This was the first innovation in the transformation from Town Ball to Base Ball."

Spalding made a vigorous retort to the Chadwick assertions in the 1905 issue of the "Baseball Guide." Among other things, Spalding wrote:

"Having read. .the writings of Mr. Chadwick that our American game of Base Ball originated from rounders, and having been taunted with this statement around the world, generally spoken in derision of our game, I am now convinced that Base Ball did not originate from rounders, any more than Cricket originated from that asinine pastime."

Chadwick had some snappy answers for Spalding's assertion, and whenever the gentlemen met, the verbal battle was resumed. Chadwick held steadfastly to rounders as the basis for baseball. Although Spalding did not know the source, he was more and more certain that it was not rounders. People of English origin, who were drawn into the debate, backed up Chadwick, if for no other than "patriotic reason," while Spalding's group sneered at the idea of rounders being worthy of adoption by anybody, anywhere. The controversy boiled, not only along the Atlantic Seaboard, but also spread to all the places where baseball was well established.

Chadwick was known as the "Father of Baseball" because he was the original scorer for the game and the pioneer writer, his first view of the sport going back to the late 1840's. Spalding, on the other hand, had been one of the greatest pitchers and all-around players, and he took the position that he should know a little more about the sport than was credited to him by Chadwick, who extracted delight in "sizzling" Spalding with his claims about rounders.

When half the baseball legions either had been drawn into the whirlpool of discussion or sat on the sidelines watching for the next move by the opposing "armies," Spalding offered the suggestion that a committee be appointed to search every nook and cranny to determine the place where the game originated, how it originated, when it originated and who was responsible. He promised he would abide by the ruling of such a commission. The rounders group also agreed to accept the findings, and, early in 1907, a committee was named, made up as follows:

A. G. Mills of New York, who had been third president of the National League and who was named committee chairman.

Morgan G. Bulkeley of Hartford, Conn., who had been first president of the National League, later Governor and then United States Senator for Connecticut.

Arthur P. Gorman of Maryland, a player in the 1850's and 1860's, who later had been a United States Senator.

Nicholas E. Young of Washington, D.C., who had been a player in his youth and later served as both president and secretary of the National League.

Al Reach of Philadelphia, an early-day ball player and later a manufacturer of sports goods.

George Wright, once a cricket player and later a star at baseball.

James E. Sullivan, president of the Amateur Athletic Union of the United States.

The parties interested in the findings of the commission began to get a little restless as time marched on and there was no report. The pressure was applied to Mills, since he was chairman. As far as can be established, Mills was the only one of the entire committee who felt a sense of responsibility in the matter. The others regarded the affair as merely a long-standing dispute between Spalding and Chadwick, and, being busy with other things, they did not join the hunt for historical facts.

Mills was prodded more and still more, and answered with his report, submitted Dec. 30, 1907, which was in the nature of a personal document not a committee conclusion. It bore only the signature of Mills. The others dodged approving, in writing, the document prepared by Mills.

The Mills report follows:

"As I have stated, my belief has been that our National Game of Baseball originated with the Knickerbocker club, organized in New York in 1845, and which club publicized certain elementary rules in that year; but, in the interesting and pertinent testimony, for which we are indebted to Mr. A. G. Spalding, appears a circumstantial statement by a reputable gentleman, according to which the first known diagram of the diamond, indicating positions for the players, was drawn by Abner Doubleday in Cooperstown, N.Y., in 1839.

"Abner Doubleday subsequently graduated from West Point and entered the regular army, where, as Captain of Artillery, he sighted the first gun fired on the Union side (at Fort Sumter) in the Civil War. Later still, as Major General, he was in command of the Union army at the close of the first day's fight in the battle of Gettysburg, and he died full of honors at Mendham, N.J., in 1893.

"It happened that he and I were members of the same veteran military organization—the crack Grand Army Post (Lafayette)—and the duty devolved upon me, as Commander of that organization, to have charge of his obsequies, and to command the veteran military escort which served as guard of honor when his body lay in state, January 30, 1893, in the New York City Hall, prior to his interment in Arlington.

"In the days when Abner Doubleday attended school in Cooperstown, it was a common thing for two dozen or more of schoolboys to join in a game of ball. Doubtless, as in my later experience, collisions between players in attempting to catch the batted ball were frequent, and injury due to this cause, or to the practice of putting out the runner by hitting him with the ball, often occurred.

"I can well understand how the orderly mind of the embryo West Pointer would devise a scheme for limiting the contestants on each side and allotting them to field positions, each with a certain amount of territory; also substituting the existing method of putting out the base runner for the old one of plugging him with the ball.

"True, it appears from the statement that Doubleday provided for eleven men on a side instead of nine, stationing the two extra men between first and second, and second and third bases, but this is a minor detail, and, indeed, I have played, and doubtless other old players have, repeatedly with eleven on a side, placed almost identically in the manner indicated by Doubleday's diagram, although it is true that we so played, after the number on each side had been fixed at nine, simply to admit to the game an additional number of those who wished to take part in it.

"I am also much interested in the statement made by Mr. Curry, of the pioneer Knickerbocker club, and confirmed by Mr. Tassie, of the famous old Atlantic club of Brooklyn, that a diagram, showing the ball field laid out substantially as it is today, was brought to the field one afternoon by a Mr. Wadsworth. Mr. Curry says 'the plan caused a great deal of talk, but, finally, we agreed to try it.' While he is not quoted as adding that they did both try and adopt it, it is apparent that such was the fact; as, from that day to this, the scheme of the game described by Mr. Curry has been continued with only slight variations in detail. It should be borne in mind that Mr. Curry was the first president of the old Knickerbocker club, and participated in drafting the first published rules of the game.

"It is possible that a connection more or less direct can be traced between the diagram drawn by Doubleday in 1839, and that presented to the Knickerbocker club by Wadsworth in 1845, or thereabouts, and I wrote several days ago for certain data bearing on this point, but as it has not yet come to hand I have decided to delay no longer sending in the kind of paper your letter calls for, promising to furnish you the indicated data when I obtain it, whatever it may be.

A. G. Mills."

Some persons contend that Mills was a relative of Doubleday and performed a classical "brother-in-law" act. Others, regarding Mills and Doubleday merely as intimate friends for about 30 years before Doubleday's death, took the attitude that Mills, in his report, paid a final tribute, regardless of whether it was deserved, to a friend whose memory he cherished. Still more paid little attention to the Mills report, since very few persons beyond Spalding were interested in what Mills had to say on the subject of baseball's invention.

Spalding's comment on the Mills document, which he had been so hopeful would convey definite and authentic data, is not a matter of public record. If he became speechless, there was reason. For the report, instead of being the work of a committee, was the writing of one man; instead —it became, in a major way, a tribute of one man to his soldier friend, tribute extending to the point where it honored him for originating the game of baseball without evidence, tangible or otherwise, to support him.

Mills' statement that "in the interesting and pertinent testimony, for which we are indebted to Mr. A. G. Spalding, appears a *circumstantial statement* by a *reputable gentleman,* according to which the first known diagram of the diamond was drawn by Abner Doubleday, in Cooperstown, N.Y., in 1839," was heatedly disputed by Spalding. He declared that he never had given any testimony to Mills, directly or indirectly, and had never known of any information from "a reputable gentleman."

Any analysis of the Mills report finds it on the fantastic side. Mills based his entire gesture in creating the "Doubleday—1839—Cooperstown" trinity upon a "statement" by "an unidentified person." The strange conclusion Mills reached is complicated further by the fact that although Doubleday was his companion for something like 30 years and Doubleday knew Mills as a baseball executive, not a word is quoted by Mills concerning anything Doubleday might have said about baseball.

Doubleday, after retiring from the Army in 1873, took up writing and contributed articles to many magazines. He chose his own subjects as an author, at a time when baseball was moving from infancy to robust manhood. If Doubleday had anything at all to do with the origin of baseball or knew anything about the game's beginning, it is logical to assume he would have written an article or two on the subject to clear up the muddled situation. But Doubleday never wrote a line about baseball. Nor is there mention anywhere, beyond the Mills report, that Doubleday ever had anything whatsoever to do with baseball. The known facts about baseball shatter practically every conclusion of Mills.

The baseball diagram was made by Alexander Cartwright in 1845 and first was used in a game at Hoboken, N.J., in 1846. The practice of "plugging" in the early games, which Mills stated Doubleday had abolished in 1839, continued as a feature of play long after that year.

Although Mills credited Doubleday with making a diagram and outlining rules for baseball play at Cooperstown in 1839, neither a copy of the diagram nor a copy of the rules exists anywhere. Cooperstown, incidentally, was unaware until 1907 that anybody named Doubleday ever was supposed to have played baseball on the village terrain.

Mills in his report pictured Doubleday in 1839 as "a schoolboy in Cooperstown" and refers to him as an "embryo West Pointer." Doubleday in 1839 was about 20 years of age and, instead of being an "embryo West Pointer," had been a student at the military academy for 2 years. Doubleday devoted 1836, 1837 and 1838 to work as a surveyor, not as a Cooperstown ball-playing youth. His job took him to places far beyond any possible baseball field in Cooperstown. Those were years when any male aged 20 was a man, not a boy.

The Mills report was received by Spalding as it was submitted and carefully stored away. But not before Spalding had made a copy of it for his book, "The National Game," published in 1910. This copy fell into the hands of Landis & Company in the 1930's and promptly was used to do a lot of preliminary hurrahing about the coming of baseball's 100th birthday and to make plans for the celebration, accompanied by a lot of publicity, which the game sorely needed.

Spalding, in his book, did not take direct exception to the Mills report, because of his pledge, but in commenting on the report stated:

"I have no intention in this work of reopening a discussion which waxed so warm a short time ago, as to the origin of the game. It would be an act of disloyalty to the Commission, that was appointed at my suggestion in 1907, with instruction to consider all available evidence and decide the case upon its merits, were I ever again to enter upon details of that vexed controversy."

At the time the Mills report was submitted, the two men in America who had more fundamental knowledge about baseball than anyone else were Chadwick, who was born in 1824 and had been a student of baseball from about 1848 until his death, April 20, 1908, and Spalding, born Sept. 2, 1850, who started playing the game in the 1860's and was one of its devotees until his death, Sept. 9, 1915. Neither Chadwick nor Spalding ever had heard about Doubleday, the 1839 origination or Cooperstown, prior to Mills' mention. There was nothing about the trinity created by Mills in any of the vast number of scrapbooks about baseball that Chadwick had collected through nearly 60 years and which he bequeathed to Spalding, who willed them to the New York Public Library.

No one was more concerned than A. G. Spalding about tracing the source of baseball. He failed. So have others. The story of the real beginning of the sport has been—perhaps always will be— shrouded in impenetrable mists.

Baseball may have been evolved from a combination of rounders and cricket, with cricket the more fruitful source. So much of early-day baseball called for cricket terms, with some cricket equipment in use, that, regardless of Chadwick's teasing assertion (when with Spalding) that rounders was the pattern, baseball may have begun as a modified form of cricket.

Cricket was introduced to what now is the United States about 1751. There was little play, since the time was limited for settlers from England. Homes had to be built, farm lands had to be hewed out of forests. Pioneers in the cities were busy with affairs of the community, and the hours for indulgence in sport were few. But the cricketers found a few intervals for play at the game, using equipment they had brought from England.

There is nothing in the story of early America to indicate when rounders was first played on this soil. While cricket was a game for adults, rounders appears to have been a boys' game in England, and the newcomers to the American shores, at least until well into the 19th Century, failed to import paraphernalia to fashion the rounders pastime for the boys.

The boys, no doubt, saw their elders playing at cricket. They, too, wanted to indulge. But cricket balls were few; so were bats and wickets. The parents perhaps passed along well-battered balls and derelict bats to the youngsters, but wickets were something they preserved. Therefore, since the boys had balls and bats, they perhaps devised their own game, free of wickets, and this was the beginning of baseball in crude form.

First of all, there must have been a boy with a bat, another with a ball. They took turns at pitching and throwing. Other boys wanted to get into the game, and those youngsters, not having wickets toward which the cricket batter runs, drove a wooden stake into the ground and made such stakes substitute for a wicket. As more and more boys wanted to get into the game, and few, if any, had a ball or a bat, more players were added to a team and more stakes were driven into the ground to provide for enlarged play.

One of the early rules of the game permitted "plugging." That meant a batter was out if hit by a thrown ball while running from one stake to another. Since some boys were injured by being hit with balls thrown from a short distance, the "plugging" feature became objectionable and was ruled out of the game in the 1840's in most places, although it was continued elsewhere— Boston, for instance— for some years.

As time went on, the boys wore out baseballs quicker than they could get replacements and hopelessly broke more bats than inherited gifts could replace. The resourceful youngsters then began to make their own balls by using something for a center—purhaps bunched-up rags— wrapping the whole with string until it had become sizable enough to serve as a ball. The pioneer bats were replaced by sticks made frc.n cord wood or tree branches.

Naturally, as the game increased in popularity, there had to be some improved playing rules and some outline of the "running area" for the batsmen. Since boys stumbled over stakes and were injured, stakes were ruled out and were replaced by flat stones at designated spots, although the original cry of "Run to your stake" was continued.

There was, at the outset, just one stake, at a point back of the pitcher, just as there is one wicket back of a cricket bowler. The next stake was about where first base now is placed, while the original stake, which was back of the pitcher, was moved to what now is third base. A boy ran from home to first, across the field, back of the pitcher, to what now is third and then home. The infield, thus, was a triangle. The distance between the stakes was a matter left to the captains. It could be 20 paces (60 feet) up to 25 paces (75 feet).

The progressively popular game was known by many different names. It was "Town Ball" in Philadelphia and "Town Ball" in Boston. In New York, it was "One Old Cat" and "Two Old Cat," or anything else by which the players cared to designate it, eventually becoming the "New York Game." But wherever it was played, the scoring terms were those that had been used in cricket, and the other references were similar to those involved in cricket. Obviously, the boys had taken cricket as the pattern and woven a game to fit their limited equipment, and their youthful ideas of what would provide the fastest and best form of contest.

The rules of the earliest game are not of record. It is known that a team could be made up of as many players, providing the sides were equal, as was decided by the captain. As a result, some teams had as many as 20 players. The scoring rules that guided the sport in the late 18th Century and going into the 19th are unknown. Many other points are obscure, largely for the reason that it was decidedly a boys' game and nobody paid attention to historical details. Therefore, there are no documents that convey information of what was happening in baseball 150 years ago.

It never has been absolutely established when the game was given the name of "Base Ball." It came in an era long after the stakes had been abandoned for flat rocks. Since the object for a base-runner's anchorage no longer could be called a "stake," and it is unlikely that boys would cry "Run to your rock," then they may have substituted "base" to mean station, and in time the process of running to a "base" during the progress of play, which featured a ball, resulted in "base ball."

Spalding could not find anything, nor did Chadwick produce anything, that linked the name with any specific date. However, Spalding did succeed in getting a copy of a letter written in 1910 by a man who was born in 1827 and who reported that as a boy he had played baseball. The letter, which appeared in the Erie (Pa.) *Tribune*, April 9, 1910, while the controversy over baseball and its origin still raged, was signed by Andrew H. Caughey, and read:

"To the Editor of 'The Tribune':
"Sir: I find this morning in 'The Tribune' an article on the 'Origin of Base Ball' quoted from another periodical. In this article it is said that

Base Ball probably grew out of the English game of 'rounders.'

"I am in my eighty-third year, and I know that seventy years ago, while a boy at school in a country school district in Erie County, Pa., I played Base Ball with my schoolmates; and I know it was a common game long before my time. It had just the same form as the Base Ball of today, and the rules of the game were nearly the same as they are now.

"One bad feature of the old game, I am glad to say, is not now permitted. The catchers, the one behind the batter and those on the field, could throw the ball and hit the runner between the bases with all the swiftness he could put into it—'burn him,' as it was called. That cruel part of the game has been abolished; the ball is now thrown to the base before the runner reaches it, if possible, and this puts him out.

"I never heard of the game called 'rounders.' 'One old cat' or 'two old cat' was played then as now; but it was nothing like the Base Ball of my boyhood days. Real Base Ball, with some slight variation of the rules, as it has come down to the present day must be at least a hundred years old. Erie, Pa., April 8, 1910.   Andrew H. Caughey."

Spalding in "The National Game" also quoted the following from a pamphlet—"Base Ball"—prepared by John Montgomery Ward, one of the great players of an early day and later a New York attorney:

"Col. James Lee, elected an honorary member of the Knickerbocker Club in 1846, said that he had often played the game when a boy, and at that time he was a man of sixty or more years.

"Dr. Oliver Wendell Holmes said to the reporter of a Boston paper that Base Ball was one of the sports of his college days at Harvard, and Dr. Holmes graduated in 1829.

"Mr. Charles DeBost, the catcher and captain of the old Knickerbockers, played Base Ball on Long Island fifty years ago, and it was the same game which the Knickerbockers afterward played."

Although the game was played in quite a few cities along the Atlantic Seaboard in the 1820's and 1830's, the rules were different, and there was no intercity play. The boys of one town learned how the boys in others were playing the new games from men who travelled from one city to another and always were sources of general information wherever they arrived.

The "home-made" bats generally were fashioned like cricket bats, with a flat surface for hitting. In some games, play terminated when one team had made a certain number of scores. In others, the playing periods were agreed upon in advance, and the team that had done the most scoring during those periods was the winner. The bases continued to be as many, and as far apart,

as the captains agreed upon. But the tendency had been to cut down on the membership of each team, since the batters, who still were subjected to "plugging," rarely could escape, because the field was full of fielders, ready to grab anything that was hit at them, for the fun of making a "plugging" throw at the runner.

Historians have found that while the youths in the New York area patterned their game much after cricket, those in Boston, where a sort of standardized game started in 1830, and in Philadelphia, which became an organized center in about 1833, used some of the basic principles of rounders in playing their "Town Ball."

The New Yorkers decided about 1841 that there should be more and better rules to govern their game, and this led to the sketching of the first "Base Ball Diagram," which came into use beginning in 1842. What is home plate of today then was "the striker's box." The batsman ran from there to first base, which meant 48 feet. His next trip was to second base, 60 feet away. The distance between second and third was 72 feet. The distance from third to the fourth base—which was somewhat to the left of "the striker's box"—was 72 feet. Thus the runner did not return to the original starting point to make a score.

The drafting of the diagram of 1842 meant that a change had come in baseball play. It had ceased to be a game only for teen-age boys. The young men, who had watched its progress, saw in it the possibilities for a stirring kind of sport. They began to play at baseball in the late 1830's and continued into the 1840's, with a revolutionary procedure coming about in 1845, with the formation of the Knickerbocker Baseball Club of New York, the first organization of its kind in history.

Clubs of an earlier era in America, which had been formed for the purpose of sport and recreation among adults or near adults, were those which featured play at cricket. The Knickerbockers, however, were not concerned with cricket, even though most members of the Knickerbocker Club had been cricket players.

The Knickerbockers were organized on Sept. 13, 1845, and the officers elected were: D.F. Curry, president; W.H. Wheaton, vice president; W.H. Tucker, secretary and treasurer.

The assemblage, having decided that baseball was to be the game, was aware that the sport always had been played under haphazard rules on fields of any choosing by the captains, and that the infield was not suitable for good play. The result was the naming of a committee headed by the youthful Alexander Cartwright, who was a draftsman and surveyor. The committee's job was to formulate some standard rules for baseball play. Cartwright studied the diagram which was introduced in New York in 1842, found it faulty and also discarded the "baseball square" which had been guiding "Town Ball" in Boston.

As the result of work performed during the winter of 1845—46, Cartwright designed his "baseball square," which, with a few exceptions as regards positions for players, is the baseball diamond of today. Cartwright's associates worked out details for a regulation game. The first standard rules which were to govern the game, submitted to the club early in 1846, were:

Section 1—The bases shall be from "home" to second base, 42 paces; from first to third base 42 paces—Equidistant.

Section 2—The game to consist of 21 counts, or aces, but at the conclusion an equal number of hands must be played.

Section 3—The ball must be pitched and not thrown for the bat.

Section 4—A ball knocked outside the range of the first or third base is foul.

Section 5—Three balls being struck at and missed, and the last one caught is a hand out; if not caught, it is considered fair, the striker bound to run.

Section 6—A ball being struck, or tipped, and caught either flying or on the first bound is a hand out.

Section 7—A player, running the bases, shall be out if the ball is in the hands of an adversary on the base, or the runner is touched by it before he makes his base; it being understood, however, that in no instance is a ball to be thrown at him. (An early change in this rule stated that only the first baseman could put a player out by holding the ball on the base before the striker reached it.)

Section 8—A player running, who shall prevent an adversary from catching or getting the ball before making his base, is a hand out.

Section 9—If two hands are already out, a player running home at the time a ball is struck cannot make an ace if the striker is caught out.

Section 10—Three hands out, all out.

Section 11—Players must take their strike in regular turn.

Section 12—No ace, or base, can be made on a foul strike.

Section 13—A runner cannot be put out in making one base when a balk is made by the pitcher.

Section 14—But one base allowed when the ball bounds out of the field when struck.

The Knickerbockers in the spring of 1846 announced they had organized "for play at baseball" and were willing to meet any club under the "Knickerbocker Rules of Baseball." A challenge came from a group which called itself the "New York Team." However, when those men learned that, under the new rules, a team was limited to 9 players, they changed the name to the "New York Nine."

As time neared to select a field for play, none on Manhattan Island was found suitable. It was learned that there was an old cricket ground in Elysian Fields, a summer resort in Hoboken, N.J., and this was found ideal for Cartwright's "baseball square." But in doing the plotting out, there was some blundering. The marked-off pitching distance was 45 feet—not 46 as Cartwright had outlined. But there was no argument about the difference of 1 foot, and so 45 feet became the standard and remained so until a change was made to 50 feet in 1881, later changed to the present 60 feet 6 inches.

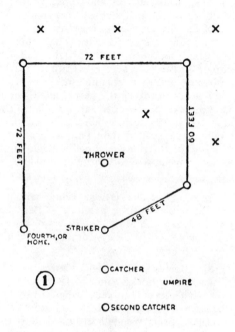

No. 1—This diagram of a baseball playing field made its appearance in and around New York City in 1842, two years after bases had replaced stakes and the game had gained its name of "Base Ball." It provided for 12 players: two catchers, one pitcher, four basemen, three regular outfielders, a roving infielder and also a roving outfielder. This diagram remained in use until after Alexander Cartwright's "Base Ball Square" was adopted in 1846.

No. 2—Diagram showing playing field for game of "town ball." This seems to have appeared in 1845 in Boston, and continued to be the standard for "town ball" as long as the game existed, which was into the 1860's. One feature of this game was that it had no harsh rules limiting the number of players. Usually there were 11 or 12 on a side, but sometimes 15 to 16.

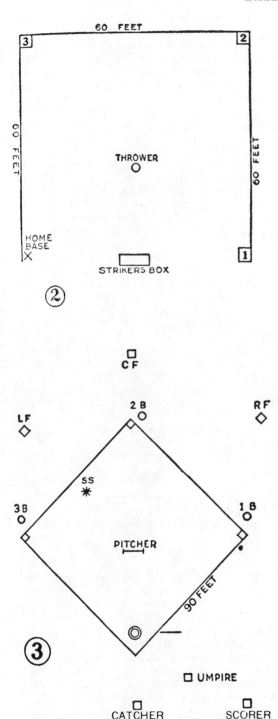

60 FEET

60 FEET

60 FEET

3

2

THROWER
○

HOME
BASE
X

STRIKERS BOX

1

②

CF
□

2B
○

LF
◇

RF
◇

SS
✳

3B
○

1B
○

PITCHER
⊢—

90 FEET

◎

③

□ UMPIRE

□
CATCHER

□
SCORER

No. 3—Diagram made by Alexander Cartwright of New York City late in 1845 and introduced for practice sessions in spring of 1846 by Knickerbocker Baseball Club, New York, of which Cartwright was a member. Players voted in favor of it, and playing field for first game

between organized clubs was marked off according to this diagram, with the pitching distance 45 feet. The game was played June 19, 1846, in Hoboken, N.J., and the New York Nine defeated the Knickerbockers, 23 to 1, in four innings. Since then the only changes in arrangement by Cartwright are that shortstop now plays back of the baseline, catcher plays closer to the plate, positions of umpire and scorer have shifted, and plate has been moved back into the corner of the triangle.

The Knickerbockers who took the field against the "New York Nine" in the first real ball game under organized rules on June 19, 1846, were: D. Anthony, H. Anthony, Tyron, Adams, W.H. Tucker, Birney, Turney, Pauling and Avery. The "New York Nine" line-up was: Davis, Winslow, Lalor, Thompson, Case, Trenchard, Murphy, Ransom and Johnson. Cartwright, a leading player for the Knickerbockers, chose to umpire this historic game instead, and fined Davis of the New York Nine "six cents for swearing."

The "New York Nine" defeated the Knickerbockers, 23 to 1, in four innings. Immediately afterward they disbanded and their individual exploits thereafter are unknown. The unexpected defeat suffered by the Knickerbockers somewhat depressed the athletes, and there was no further interclub baseball by the Knickerbockers until 1851. But through the years between 1846 and 1851 they chose sides and played among themselves. Those were regarded as practice games, each practice presumably developing the Knickerbocker regulars in expertness.

For a practice game of baseball in 1849, the regular team of Knickerbockers appeared in what was the first baseball uniform. Since the equipment was almost identical with the cricket uniforms that were used elsewhere, there exists belief that those baseball uniforms simply were those which the Knickerbockers had used in cricket matches. The color scheme was blue and white.

On March 1, 1849, Cartwright, hearing of the discovery of gold in California, left New York to join the rush to the Pacific Slope. He traveled overland by way of Independence, Mo., and arrived in California in July, 1849, having with him the baseball used in the first game of 1846.

Cartwright soon decided he wished no further part in the gold stampede and in August determined to return to New York. He took passage on the Peruvian bark "Pacifico," which was going back by way of China.

Cartwright became ill between San Francisco and the Sandwich Islands, as Hawaii then was known, and was put ashore at Honolulu, Aug.

28, 1849. After recovering, he determined to make his home in Honolulu. In 1851 his family arrived—a wife and 3 children.

Cartwright died in Honolulu, July 13, 1892. He left a diary dealing with his transcontinental trip, and among the interesting items was this:

"1849—April 23—Monday—Independence, Mo.:—During the past week we have passed the time in fixing wagon-covers, stowing property, etc., varied by hunting and fishing and playing baseball. It is comical to see the mountain men and Indians playing the new game. I have the ball with me that we used back home (New York). Our party consists of 32 wagons and 119 men."

In 1938—when there was so much tumult and shouting by Landis and his group over the centennial of 1939, which was to honor Doubleday, Cooperstown and the mythical baseball square credited to Doubleday in the Mills report—Bruce Cartwright went into action. He lived in Honolulu and was a grandson of Alexander Cartwright. He had old clippings, the diary of his grandfather and much else to prove that Alexander Cartwright, not Doubleday, was the real founder of modern baseball.

The baseball folks were caught squarely in the middle by Bruce Cartwright's claims, but it did not alter their plans to celebrate the anniversary of the game in 1939, and to glorify both Cooperstown and Doubleday. They had gone too far and spent too much money to change the program to conform with facts that Bruce Cartwright was willing to place at their disposal. They met the situation by announcing that there would be an "Alexander Cartwright Day" during the festival—which honored the wrong man and the wrong town and fixed the wrong date.

Baseball, which had been launched so gaily by the Knickerbockers of 1846, was in a comatose condition until 1851. Then the Knickerbockers, concluding they had learned the game via 5 years of practice, went into "big time" action again and took on the "Washington Baseball Club of "New York" on June 3, 1851, in the second contest of definite record. They met on the "Red House Grounds," 106th Street and Second Avenue, in New York City. The Knickerbockers won, 21–11, in 8 innings. In a return match, 2 weeks later at Hoboken, the teams went 10 innings before the Knickerbockers won again, 22–20. The Washingtons changed their name to "Gothams" and played the Knickerbockers 5 more times in the next 3 years.

In April, 1853, the first story about a baseball game appeared in a newspaper. It spoke of an impending contest between the Knickerbockers and Gothams, and was written by Senator William Cauldwell for the New York *Sunday Mercury,* of which he was editor and owner. Frequently thereafter, Cauldwell contributed articles about the game.

The contest mentioned by the Senator wasn't played until 1854. Two things about it are important, from the historical standpoint. It resulted in the first tie, and the game was the first wherein a count was kept of the score by innings. It was played in New York City, Oct. 26, 1854, and was called at the end of the 12th, when autumnal darkness made further action impossible. The final score was 12–12.

Until the Gothams tied the Knickerbockers in 1854, there wasn't a collection of players who thought they had much chance against the Knickerbockers or their rivals. They contented themselves by playing on the "choose-up-sides" basis. But that tie brought about a revolution. Teams came into existence throughout what is now the Greater New York district.

Through 1855 and 1856 the teams in and around New York played what was called "The New York Game," which meant under the Knickerbocker rules of 1845. Late in 1856, when one of the New York teams was matched to play a New England club, the game was under compromised rules, part "Town Ball," part "Knickerbocker Club." At its conclusion, the rival captains proceeded to agitate for a meeting where rules would be made standard for all cities. However, the Knickerbocker Club continued to maintain the attitude that baseball was its game and had to be played under its rules, which hardly had been changed since 1846.

When the Knickerbocker Club refused to call a meeting for proposed rule changes in late 1856, the captains of rival teams resolved to hold one of their own, make new rules and create a new governing organization. The Knickerbockers, under this threat, agreed to a meeting for May, 1857, packed the convention with their own delegates, squelched all reform movements and conceded to only one change—that a game was to be 9 innings, and not 21 aces (runs).

In late 1857, with new players wanting a modernization of the rules, and with the Knickerbockers standing pat, the cry arose "Unshackle baseball from Knickerbocker control!" The independents called a meeting for March 10, 1858, "open to all baseball clubs." The Knickerbockers sent a large delegation, hoping it would be able to control the convention, but the Knickerbockers were told that each club was limited to 3 delegates. The 3 finally selected to represent the Knickerbocker Baseball Club were shouted down every time they tried to speak.

Twenty-five clubs were represented at that important meeting. The game was taken completely from control of the Knickerbockers, with the formation of the National Association of Baseball Players—the first body duly appointed to govern baseball. Evidence of how decidedly the Knickerbockers had been thrust into the background is shown by the fact that not one of its members was among the officers of the new association. The officials elected were: William H. Van Cott (Gothams), president; L.B. Jones (Excelsiors), first vice president; Thomas S. Dakin (Putnams), second vice president; J.R. Postley (Metropolitans), recording secretary; Theodore F. Jackson (Putnams), corresponding secretary, and E.H. Brown (Metropolitans), treasurer.

The clubs of importance that became affiliated with the new association, with the date of their formation in parentheses, follow:

Knickerbockers (Sept., 1845), New York
Gothams (April, 1852), New York
Eagles (April, 1854), New York
Empires (Oct., 1854), New York
Excelsiors (Dec., 1854), South Brooklyn
Putnams (May, 1855), Williamsburg, Brooklyn
Newarks (June, 1855), Newark, N.J.
Baltics (June, 1855), New York
Eckfords (June, 1855), Greenpoint, Brooklyn
Unions (July, 1855), Morrisania, Bronx
Atlantics (Aug., 1855), Williamsburg
Continentals (Oct., 1855), Williamsburg
Atlantics (Aug., 1855), Jamaica, L.I., N.Y.
Harlems (March, 1856), New York
Enterprise (June, 1856), Williamsburg
Actives (Oct., 1856), Hoboken
Stars (Oct. 1856), South Brooklyn
Independents (Jan., 1857), New York
Libertys (March, 1857), N. Brunswick, N.J.
Metropolitans (March, 1857), New York
Champions (March, 1857), New York
Hamiltons (March, 1857), Brooklyn
St. Nicholas (April, 1857), Hoboken
Mutuals (June, 1857), Williamsburg

Chadwick, early disciple and observer of the game in the late 1840's, wrote an article for "Johnson's Revised Universal Encyclopedia" in 1888, stating that baseball did not begin until it was pioneered by a group called the National Association of Baseball Players in 1857, which is almost 10 years after he stated in another article he had seen baseballers in action.

Chadwick might have meant it did not start as an organized game, to the best of his knowledge, until 1857, when the association was formed. Chadwick, by a variety of admissions, conceded that the game had been in existence for years before being put under supervised control in 1858.

All players were amateurs and, until July 20, 1858, no admission was charged to games. The competing clubs paid all incidental expenses. On that date, however, a star team of New Yorkers played the first game of a best 2-of-3 series "for the championship" against a star team of Brooklynites at the Fashion race track in Long Island. Because a rental had to be paid for the track, and the clubs encountered other expenses, an admission fee of 50 cents was fixed. The paid

attendance was 1,500 and the gate was $750, which meant a nice profit for the first professionally promoted game.

The New York All-Stars won the first game (July 20, 1858), 22–18; the second (Aug. 19, 1858) was won by Brooklyn, and the third (Sept. 10, 1858) was taken by the New Yorkers, 29–18.

The Brooklyn-New York series, which attracted interest throughout the baseball centers along the Atlantic seaboard, had a stimulating effect upon the sport. More and more clubs were organized, the popularity of baseball gradually extended to the Middle West, and baseball definitely came into its own as a major recreation in the United States.

In 1860 the Excelsiors (Brooklyn) made the pioneer baseball tour. They played their first game in Albany, N.Y., on June 30 and won, 24 to 6. They went to Troy, winning by 13 to 7, after which they journeyed to Buffalo, defeating the Niagaras, 50 to 19. Returning, they beat the "Rochester Flour Cities," 21 to 1, the "Rochester Live Oaks," 27 to 9, and the Newburgs, 59 to 14. In July the Excelsiors started on a new tour, going to Pennsylvania, Delaware and Maryland and repeating their successes. Upon returning to Brooklyn, they agreed to a game with their old rivals—the Atlantics (Brooklyn).

With James Creighton, a recruit who became one of baseball's immortals, pitching for them, the Excelsiors defeated the Atlantics, 23 to 4. Later the Atlantics won, 15 to 14, breaking the great winning streak of the Excelsiors, who in 1860 were rated as the most powerful team in America. This provoked the third and deciding contest—with a strange finale.

The clubs met in the third game on Aug. 23, 1860, on the new grounds built by the Putnam Club, before a crowd that was immense for that era, some estimates fixing it at 2,500. The bitter rivalry between the teams was shared by the crowd and during the course of play there were many free-for-all fights between fans. At the end of the sixth inning the Excelsiors led, 8 to 6. The toughs backing the Atlantics made things so difficult that further play by the Excelsiors became impossible. J.B. Leggett, captain of the Excelsiors, ordered his team to leave the field, there being nothing else to do. As the Excelsiors were climbing into a coach, Leggett tossed the ball to O'Brien, captain of the Atlantics, and, in acknowledgment of forfeiture of the game said: "Your ball, O'Brien. Keep it."

In those years, as in football today, the winning team was entitled to the ball as a trophy. O'Brien, who had tried vainly to halt the rowdyism of the Atlantics' rooters, replied: "Leggett, will you call it a draw?" Leggett answered, "As you wish." The clubs never met again.

The outbreak of the Civil War in 1861 halted

the progress of baseball, but many games were played in Northern army camps. Southerners, held prisoners by the Yankees, were treated to their first sight of the game. They found it interesting to watch and when the conflict was over they carried the idea back to Dixie, and that was the start of baseball there.

At the convention of the National Association of Baseball Players in 1865 (when the Civil War was over) there were 91 clubs represented, as compared with 34 in 1861. St. Louis, Louisville (Ky.), Leavenworth (Kan.) and Portland (Me.) were among the newcomers that had delegates at the meeting. In 1866 the presentation went beyond 100, and in 1867 there were 237 clubs answering the roll call. The remarkable growth of the game was shown further by the fact that while New York, the state where modern baseball was born, was represented by only 24 clubs in 1867, Illinois had 56, Ohio had 42, Pennsylvania 27, Wisconsin 25, Indiana 21, Maryland 20 and Connecticut 22.

The National Association of Baseball Players had ceased to be powerful in 1869. It was pledged to perpetuate the game as purely amateur. Also, it was supposed to supervise the sport, crowd out the increasing horde of gamblers and keep the game clean and honorable. It succeeded in none of those purposes. Charges of "sell-outs" became rife. Fans lost interest in baseball. Attendance dwindled. The increase in the number of teams around the country halted. Many disbanded. Evil days had come for amateurism in baseball, while professionalism was rated as sordid.

Betting on games in that era was as great, in ratio, as it is on horse racing today. The spectators were intrigued by skillful play, but basically were concerned about winning their wagers.

In 1869 the Cincinnati Red Stockings, organized as an amateur team in 1866, went radical. Becoming disgusted with the floundering rulership of the National Association, the Red Stockings announced that its team henceforth would operate as an out-and-out professional group and end hypocrisy. It made deals with players, agreeing to pay each a certain sum for a season of play, increased the general admission fee of 25 cents to 50 cents, and the leaders of the club pledged that if the income did not meet the salary obligations and all other expenses, they would draw, pro rata, on private funds to make up the deficit.

Gasps came from all parts of the land over the Cincinnati act. Some, who felt that "baseball should not be prostituted by salary payments," registered furious objections. The more tolerant classified it as a "daring experiment that might be futile but deserves a fair trial." The players who had taken money in secret, while posing as amateurs, watched the progress of the tour with eager attention. Success meant that they, too,

could get jobs as professionals and be paid outright for having their fun in exciting struggle in the great outdoors.

The president of the Cincinnati club, and the most vociferous advocate of salaries for players, was A.B. Champion, a Cincinnati lawyer. The manager of the team was the great Harry Wright, amateur baseball player and cricketer. The players were pitcher, Brainard; catcher, Allison; first base, Gould; second base, Sweasy; shortstop, George Wright; third base, Waterman; right field, McVey; center field, Harry Wright; left field, Leonard. Harry Wright, as manager, received a salary of $1,200 for the season, $200 less than his brother George, who was the captain and great star. The salaries of the other players scaled from $600, paid to a utility player, to about $1,000, the season lasting 8 months.

The tour started March 15 and ended Nov. 15. The Red Stockings first journeyed East, returned for a home stand, then invaded the Middle West. Going East once more, they met all the outstanding teams, revisited the Middle West and finally trouped to the Pacific Coast, defeating 3 strong clubs there. They won 39 straight, before being held to a 17-17 tie by the Haymakers of Troy, N.Y., and finished the season with 65 victories and 1 tie. They scored 2,395 runs, against 574 by their opponents, and made 169 homers. George Wright, playing in 52 of the 56 games, scored 339 runs and hit 59 homers. He had a batting mark of .518. The Red Stockings traveled 12,000 miles that year, played to 200,000 paid admissions, and their share of the receipts wrote a page in black ink.

The tour was resumed in 1870, and the winning streak of the Red Stockings was halted on June 14 by the Brooklyn Atlantics in the 11th inning, after Cincinnati had run its string to 92 victories and 1 tie in 93 starts. This is how defeat came to them:

The score at the end of the 9th was 5 to 5. The Atlantics began picking up their bats indicating they were about to leave the field because the contest had ended in a draw. Harry Wright rushed to the Atlantics and pointed out that the new rules provided that a game tied in the 9th must be continued until a victor was determined. The Brooklyn captain argued to the contrary. The umpire suggested that decision be left to Chadwick, the official scorer. Chadwick supported Wright, whereupon the field was cleared and the game resumed.

The Red Stockings failed to score in the 10th. The Atlantics put on a rally in their part of the inning, but George Wright, at shortstop, halted the rally by using the "hidden ball" trick—the first time it was ever seen—converting it into baseball's first recorded double play. Cincinnati went into the lead in the 11th by scoring 2 runs. The Atlantics then went to bat.

Smith, the first batter, singled and went to

third on a wild pitch. He scored on Start's triple into the outfield crowd. Ferguson singled, scoring Start with the tying run. Zettlein grounded to Gould, who fumbled, and then tossed wild to second, trying to catch Ferguson. The ball rolled into the outfield and Ferguson coasted home, the game ending Brooklyn Atlantics 8, Cincinnati Red Stockings 7.

The greatest winning streak in all baseball history was broken.

The tremendous success of the Red Stockings' tour sounded the death-knell of the long ailing National Association of Baseball Players. The annual convention at the end of the 1870 season was a farce, because fewer than 12 clubs sent delegates. The association attempted to function for a while in 1871, was almost entirely ignored and ceased to exist as any factor in the game before that season ended.

Before the actual demise of the amateur organization, the players who had quit that league met on March 4, 1871, and formed the National Association of Professional Base-Ball Players, with teams representing the following cities: New York, Brooklyn, Boston and Philadelphia in the East; Cleveland, Chicago, Fort Wayne (Ind.) and Rockford (Ill.) in the West. J.W. Kerns of Troy, N.Y., was elected president. Other clubs joined later, and all players were paid salaries.

Nine teams entered for play during the 1871 season. Eight finished, in this order: Athletics (Philadelphia), Boston, White Stockings (Chicago), Haymakers (Troy), Mutuals (New York), Forest Citys (Cleveland), Nationals (Washington), Forest Citys (Rockford). The Kekiongas (Fort Wayne) disbanded during the season.

The champion Athletics of 1871 were made up of the following players: McBride (pitcher), Malone (catcher), Fisler (1B), Al Reach (2B), Radcliff (ss), Meyerle (3B), Bechtel (RF), Sensenderfer (CF), Cuthbert (LF) and Heuble, utility.

The success of professional baseball through 1871 sounded the death-knell of the sport as an amateur game of importance. Every player with ability wanted to become a "pro," and the annual convention of 1872, held in Cleveland, found the professionals in high spirits. They envisioned increasing popularity for the sport, greater gate receipts and the opportunity to attract the topflight amateurs with liberal offers.

Up to then, some great players who had been with the amateurs refused to join the "pros," but in 1872 many changed attitude and joined when offered important salaries. Baseball very decidedly had become a sport for professionals, and the amateur association, which had dominated the sport, passed into history.

The 1872 convention of the "pros" elected Bob Ferguson president, and re-elected him in 1873. He has the distinction of being the only regular player lofted to the presidency of a major baseball circuit.

There were 11 "pro" clubs at the start of the 1872 season, but 4 folded during the season, on account of poor patronage. The circuit of 1873 was reduced to 9 teams, and, after the season was over, there was the usual annual convention, at which some radical rules were adopted.

It was decided that a team was to be made up of 10 men, instead of 9, the extra man to hold a roving position. A legal game was to be 10 innings instead of 9, but these two changes were soon rescinded. It was also determined that the circuit was to be limited to 8 clubs in 1874. The program that was worked out made Chicago the only Western entry. The other teams were: Mutuals (New York), Boston, Atlantics (Brooklyn), Hartford (Conn.), Marylands (Baltimore), while Philadelphia was permitted 2 clubs—the Philadelphias and the Athletics.

The professional league executives met in conclave, after the 1874 season, which hadn't been one of great prosperity, and resolved that an 8-club league was not sufficient. All applicants for league play in 1875 received recognition and, as a consequence, the National Association of Professional Base-Ball Players went into 1875 with 13 clubs. No one had taken measures to prevent conflicting schedules, which was bad enough, but the players began to grumble they weren't being paid well enough and sought to increase their regular income by making deals with wagering cliques.

There was a great deal of betting on the outcome of the contests. Since all this became public knowledge, the fans proceeded to question the honesty of the contests. The failure of players to hit in pinches and the making of errors when such blunders meant runs for the opposition hurt the sport. The 1875 season ended with the game in disrepute and its future clouded by charges of dishonesty and corruption. In such a dismal hour, the National League succeeded the floundering professional organization and salvaged the sport.

But the establishment of the National League was not in the role of savior. The National League emerged to dominance because of some ethical conniving by men who assumed the National Association of Professional Base-Ball Players would carry on into 1876. But a whimsical Fate blotted out the National Association and ushered the National League into control.

In June, 1875, William A. Hulbert, who had assumed the presidency of the Chicago club of the National Association only a few months earlier, decided to build a great club in Chicago in 1876. Hulbert went to Boston and secretly signed, for his club, beginning with the 1876 season, the following stars who constituted "Boston's Big Four": Al G. Spalding, pitcher; Cal McVey, catcher; Ross Barnes, second base, and

James (Deacon) White, a catcher with all-round ability.

That was an era when players signed a contract for only one season and there was no reserve clause. Each player was free to choose his club for the next year, but there was a sort of unwritten agreement among the owners that none would try to influence the star of another team to jump to his club. Hulbert, a newcomer to the game, wanted no part of that agreement, and the fact that Hulbert had secretly signed the "Big Four" to play for him in 1876 leaked out late in 1875.

There was a terrific commotion in Boston, led by the truculent N.T. Appolonio, owner of the Boston club. Predictions were made throughout the circuit that Hulbert's Chicago club would be expelled from the National Association of Professional Base-Ball Players for violating the "gentleman's agreement," and there was great tumult within association councils.

Hulbert talked matters over with Spalding and determined to form a league to rival the National Association. Hulbert held a secret meeting, with St. Louis, Cincinnati and Louisville represented—in addition to Chicago. Those cities made up the Western flank of the National Association. At the meeting were Hulbert, Spalding, John J. Joyce, Thomas Shiley, Charles E. Chase, Charles A. Fowle and W.N. Haldeman. They met in Louisville. Hulbert pointed out that the National Association had lost control of the game. Secondly, he stated that if the association excommunicated Chicago, that would demoralize the circuit in the West. He proposed a rival league to oppose the National Association of Professional Base-Ball Players and suggested "National League of Professional Baseball Clubs" as the name. This was agreed upon. The next move was to draft a constitution which, as it worked out, regulated baseball for almost 4 decades. Judge Orrick C. Bishop of St. Louis drew it up. He also prepared the first standard contract for players.

With power of attorney to act for St. Louis, Cincinnati and Louisville, Hulbert went to New York and extended an invitation to the 4 Eastern magnates to meet with him in the Grand Central Hotel, Feb. 2, 1876. A hostile group faced Hulbert. It consisted of Appolonio; W.H. Cammeyer, president of the New York Mutuals; M.G. Bulkeley, president of the Hartfords, and G.W. Thompson, president of the Philadelphia Athletics. Hulbert's eloquence and logic finally swung the meeting in his favor. It was decided that the National Association could flounder to its finish, and that the new ruling body to dominate play, with the beginning of the 1876 season, was to be known as the National League of Professional Baseball Clubs.

Appolonio, still smouldering over the loss of his "Big Four," made every effort to get them returned to him, but failed. He had expected to gain sympathy and help from associate magnates in the East, but when they learned that Hulbert represented 4 clubs in the West and that resistance to him would provoke a rupture, they swung to Hulbert, and Appolonio was left to comfort himself.

Hulbert nominated Bulkeley to become first president of the National League, and Bulkeley was elected. Nicholas E. Young was made secretary. And so the present National League came into existence for competition beginning in 1876 and the writing of the modern history of baseball dates from that year. With the creation of the National League, the National Association ceased to exist.

Prior to 1879, it had been the custom of the rival captains to agree mutually upon the umpire. But in that year, the league made up a list of 19 names and ruled that the games were to be umpired only by one or another of the specified group. The first official umpires of 1879 were G.W. Bredburg, T.H. Brunton, J.A. Cross, Charles Daniels, J. Dunn, F.W. Feber, E.G. Fountain, W.E. Furlong, W.H. Geer, T. Gillian, A.D. Hodges, W. McLean, George Seward, C.G. Stambaugh, James Summer, Mike Walsh, C.E. Wilbur, J.A. Williams and J. Young.

Until 1882, umpires not seeing a play and thus unable to decide could get testimony from the players or spectators. Beginning in 1882, the umpire was required to depend on his own judgment, and in that year it was ruled that no player other than the captain could talk to an umpire.

Up to 1882, all umpires served without salary. That year, the American Association inaugurated a paid staff of umpires, and the next year the National League followed suit. In 1883, the National League appointed 4 regular umpires, who drew fixed salaries, and operated in the cities where the league games were played. The original staff was made up of S.M. Decker, Bradford, Pa.; A.F. Odlin, Lancaster, N.H.; Frank Lane, Norwalk, Ohio, and W.E. Furlong, Kansas City, Mo. The reason for naming umpires in cities where the league was without representation was so that none would show any partisanship in his decisions.

The National League has weathered the storms of 5 baseball wars. The first thrust made at it was in 1882, with the formation of the American Association. The Association signed some of the National's surplus players and raided the Northwestern League, a minor circuit.

The American Association enjoyed popularity and was a success for quite a few years because it operated in cities where Sunday baseball was permitted—the National cities didn't—and the Association, unlike the National, wasn't fussy on the liquor question and permitted the sale of beer in its important parks.

The National League and the American Association went along happily and prosperously until they encountered rather feeble but annoying opposition in key cities from the Union Association, organized in 1884. However, the Union circuit was poorly bankrolled and folded at the end of 1884.

No further ripples disturbed the tranquillity of the National League and the American Association for 5 years.

Before the end of 1889, players in both organizations decided they weren't being recompensed adequately. Their demands for salary increases were rejected. Therefore many of the hot-headed players decided they could make more money playing for themselves and dividing profits on a pro rata system. Many quit the National League and also the American Association through the winter of 1889–1890, split themselves into what looked like evenly balanced teams and took the field for 1890 play as the Players (or Brotherhood) League. Since the standard wage in the American Association had been lower than that of the National, players deserted the American Association in droves. The teams which the American Association clubs sent into action in 1890 contained only a few Association veterans, assisted by "sandlotters."

The National League went through the 1890 season with luck and a prayer. It played a total of 540 games, and the attendance was only 813,678. It lost heavily on the season's operations. Fortunately, however, its club owners had some reserve capital. The Players League, staging 532 games, outdrew the National with 980,887, but the backers lost heavily. The American Association was hardest hit of the trio, but it floundered through the season.

The Nationals resumed operations in 1891. So did the groggy Association, its club owners obtaining cash from outside sources to continue operations. The Players League disbanded before 1891 began, and the major league field was left again to the Nationals and the American Association. The Nationals were financial losers during the 1891 operations, but still had enough cash to make plans for 1892—and carry them out. The Association, however, finished 1891 in wreckage and went out of business, leaving the major field the exclusive property, once again, of the National League.

The Nationals were blended into a 12-club circuit for 1892 and had things completely in hand until Ban Johnson came along in 1900 and asked for recognition of his new American League, nee the Western League, as a major circuit. Up to the end of 1899, the Western League had been ranked as a minor outfit, subject to the whims and caprices of the National and forced to genuflect to the National. Johnson determined to end all that.

He disbanded the Western League at the end of 1899 and early in 1900, choosing most of the same cities that had made up the Western, declared his new circuit was the American League and asked the Nationals to classify it as a major circuit.

Johnson's request was scorned even though he had advised the Nationals that his major league gesture was, first of all, one of "self-preservation, secondly, a protection for the National against entrance into action of some unfriendly group, and that the American wished to act wholly in concert with the Nationals and on absolutely friendly terms."

The National League ignored Johnson and in left-handed fashion served notice that his league was still regarded as minor by having Secretary Nick Young write to Johnson asking that the league send in its fees for continuation of the National Agreement, the customary thing for minors. Johnson wrote to Young explaining that no fee was being sent because the American was a major league candidate. He also advised Young that the American expected to expand into Eastern territory in 1901 and hoped that this could be done amicably. Young never replied. Instead, there was considerable scoffing by the Nationals, concerning Johnson's league, and a belittling of Johnson, whereupon Johnson and his associates served notice:

"We will become a major league, whether the Nationals wish it so, or not."

The American League, unofficial "major" circuit, played in 1900 with these teams: Chicago, Detroit, Minneapolis, Kansas City, Milwaukee, Cleveland and Indianapolis in the West, with Buffalo the only Eastern member.

After the close of 1900, with the Nationals still sneering at the American League pretensions, Johnson appointed a "circuit committee," consisting of himself, Charles Comiskey, owner of the Chicago club, and Charles Somers of Cleveland. The committee was delegated to look over various cities in the East for possible baseball grounds.

Meanwhile, Connie Mack acquired backing for an American League club in Philadelphia. James Manning, owner of the 1900 Milwaukee club, agreed to back its transfer to Washington, and John McGraw and Wilbert Robinson agreed to sponsor a club in Baltimore. There was a group in Boston that declared it would finance a team in 1901.

Johnson knew Boston was sacred National territory. Not wishing to antagonize the Nationals too much at the time, Johnson asked permission to discuss matters with the National magnates at their meeting in December, 1900. The Nationals told Johnson they would see him, and Johnson waited outside the door of the conference to be summoned. The Nationals concluded their session, slipped quietly out of a side door and Johnson sat for hours. When he finally was made aware of the trick, he became infuriated and announced a war "to the finish."

The Nationals retaliated by advising the press they would operate a new minor league in the Middle West in 1901 and would include Kansas City and Minneapolis in the circuit—cities where they would conflict with the American League. Johnson went white with anger when the news was imparted to him, and he declared:

"Well, if they want a real war, they can have war."

Johnson went to Boston and made arrangements to place a team there for 1901 play. It was financed by Somers. Not knowing whether the Nationals meant business or merely were bluffing about a new minor league, Johnson took no chances for 1901 and abandoned both Kansas City and Minneapolis.

The 1901 make-up of the American League was: Chicago, Detroit, Milwaukee and Cleveland in the West; Boston, Baltimore, Washington and Philadelphia in the East.

The American League decided to strengthen its clubs by the process of enticing stars of the National with larger salary offerings. In some instances they more than doubled the players' wages and gave most of them long-term contracts. At the outset of the raiding, A.G. Spalding, acting for the Nationals, asked for a truce, and the American League granted it—for 30 days. Spalding attempted to make the Nationals see the folly of war. Some magnates agreed with Spalding; the majority, headed by Andrew Freedman of New York, demanded continuation of the battle.

The Spalding truce ended in the middle of 1901 and then the real cannonading started. The beneficiaries were the players. The Nationals bid up, to try to hold the men to their contracts, but most of the time they did not bid high enough. Johnson was topping the Nationals almost every time he started angling for a player of skill and reputation.

In the winter of 1901-02 Spalding made new efforts to bring about some compromise. The group of Nationals, headed by Freedman, insisted the fight must be to the finish. Johnson and his men resumed signing more players from the National League and switched the Milwaukee franchise to St. Louis—the only change in the circuit of 1902, as compared with 1901.

When players Lajoie, Bernhard and Fraser "jumped" their reserve clause contract with the Philadelphia Nationals in 1901 to join the Americans, the Nationals went to court to test the validity of the reserve clause. A lower court ruled that the reserve clause was not legal. The Nationals went to the Supreme Court of Pennsylvania, which reversed the ruling. That was a victory for the Nationals, but it was short-lived because a Missouri court ruled that the reserve clause was not legal, and a New York court arrived at a similar decision.

Lajoie, an infielder, and Bernhard and Fraser, pitchers, were ordered by the Pennsylvania court to return to the Philadelphia Nationals. They had been with the Athletics since jumping in 1901. Fraser did return to the Nationals and resumed mound duties for the Phillies in 1902. Lajoie and Bernhard could not reach terms with their old club and signed with the Cleveland Americans for 1902, violating the Pennsylvania court order. For some years thereafter, neither entered the state of Pennsylvania, fearing arrest, and on trips they made long detours to avoid entering the state.

On July 8, 1902, John McGraw, manager of the Baltimores, who had exchanged his interest in a Baltimore saloon for the stock owned by Wilbert Robinson, resigned as American League manager and jumped to the New York Nationals. McGraw sold his stock to John J. Mahon, then president of the Baltimores, and a partner of Mahon's named Kelly. About a week later, Mahon sold that stock, together with his own holdings, to John T. Brush, chairman of the National League Executive Committee, for $15,000, each National club being assessed pro-rata. Therefore, Johnson was faced with the extraordinary situation of having the National League as majority owner of one of the franchises in his own league. It was a situation without parallel. Johnson and the American League seemed trapped by the trickery of McGraw.

Strangely enough, the Nationals themselves rescued the Americans from this predicament by a weird blunder.

The Nationals, as owners of the Baltimore Americans, immediately notified players McGinnity, Cronin, Bresnahan and McGann that they were released, and should report to the New York Nationals. They sent Seymour and Kelley to Cincinnati. Because of injuries to a few other players, incapacitating them for play, the Baltimore club could not summon enough able men to take the field as a team against St. Louis on July 17, 1902, thus forfeiting the game.

In accordance with American League rules, the Baltimore franchise automatically was cancelled by failure to put a team on the field and the club again became the property of the American League—with Brush holding $15,000 worth of stock that meant nothing at all. The Americans at once reorganized the Baltimore club, other teams lending needed players, and finished the season.

Early in December, 1902, the Nationals in session in New York appointed a committee to meet with the Americans, the committee consisting of owners James Hart of Chicago, Frank DeHaas Robinson of St. Louis and Garry Herrmann of Cincinnati. The Americans on Dec. 22, 1902, in Chicago agreed to a meeting and named Johnson, Somers and John F. Kilfoyl of Cleveland. The first session was on Jan. 5, 1903, with Harry Pulliam, president of the National League, added to the Nationals' committee. The Nationals proposed a consolidation making just one league of 12 clubs. The Americans refused, and that ended the conference with the Americans walking out.

The Nationals asked for another meeting, and it took place in the Grand Hotel, New York, Jan. 9, 1903. The Nationals asked if the Americans intended, if war were continued, to invade Pittsburgh. Johnson replied that he was satisfied with the circuit as it was: Detroit, Chicago, Cleveland, St. Louis, Philadelphia, Washington, Boston and New York (to succeed Baltimore in 1903).

The Nationals then declared in favor of separate leagues, as the Americans had demanded. Territory rights were arranged, agreement was reached over some disputed players which the Americans had taken and the following men were returned to the Nationals by the Americans: Mertes, Hulswitt, Mathewson, Bowerman, Leach, Willis and Harry Smith. Thus the war ended.

The American had won on all counts. It was recognized as a major circuit. It had picked up $500,000 worth of the Nationals' baseball talent, without the payment of a dollar. Lajoie was the grand prize, since he was a flawless fielder and a superlative batter. The Americans came out of the conflict more richly endowed than when they had entered it, and the Nationals counted their losses in high figures.

There has been but one flareup between the 2 leagues since then. It happened in 1904 and was precipitated by the sarcastic John McGraw. As manager of the pennant-winning New York Giants in 1904, he refused to meet the flag-winning Boston Americans in a post-season duel, classifying the Americans as a "minor league." Johnson exploded and made preparations for another war, but National League leaders apologized for McGraw and the incident ended harmoniously.

The Nationals and Americans knew no further trouble until 1914, when the men guiding the United States League in 1913 renamed it the Federal League for 1914 play and demanded recognition as a third big league. When it was denied, they declared war on the National and American Leagues.

James A. Gilmore, president of the 1914 and 1915 Federals, enlisted as magnates such wealthy men as Charles Weeghman of Chicago, Phil Ball of St. Louis, Harry Sinclair, multi-millionaire oil man, the Ward family, controlling one of the biggest baking establishments in the world, and several others. Repeating the American League tactics of 1901-02, the Federals proceeded to raid, and lured away more than 50 shining stars of the National and American Leagues. The older circuits had to bid up to "ruinous amounts" to retain other stars.

The Federals operated optimistically through 1914 and went into 1915 with a buoyant feeling. But they soon discovered that fans would not support 3 teams in some cities and 2 in others, and the attendance dwindled alarmingly. At the close of the 1915 season the Federal magnates took stock, discovered they had lost enormously and sought the easiest way out.

"If we could win this fight with another $5,000,000 or $20,000,000 it wouldn't bother us," said Sinclair. "We have unlimited funds. But I am convinced there isn't room for a third league. So why go on?"

Peace was made in Cincinnati late in 1915, the Federals accepting the best possible terms for their playing fields and players that they had developed or raided from the National and the American. Then they disbanded and vanished into history.

CHRONOLOGICAL HISTORY
OF BASEBALL

1800—Boys, using cricket balls and discarding cricket bats, playing game which later became baseball.

1820—Teams in New York City area playing game which was making ever closer approach to baseball game as defined by Knickerbocker Baseball Club in 1845.

1830—Several teams in Boston started playing what was called "Town Ball." It had no real relation to baseball, but was copied to an extent from English game of rounders.

1833—Olympic Club of Philadelphia organized 2 teams from among its members and played "Town Ball," but this game varied somewhat from the Boston game because it included some features of the game played around New York, which was called "New York Game." The club's regular team was known as the "Town Ball Club" and it played games every year from 1833 until 1860 under altered "Town Ball" rules. In 1860 it shifted to baseball "of modern kind," because all other clubs in the vicinity had ceased playing "Town Ball."

1835-1840—Because so many players were injured by collision with them, the 4-foot high stakes were discarded and flat stones were substituted at the stations. Expression "run to your stake" was abandoned for "run to your base." Stones soon were found impracticable for bases because many boys stumbled over them, and this brought sacks filled with sand into existence. These were referred to as "bases," and the game came to be known, for the first time, as "baseball." Teams were of different sizes, ranging from 11 to 15 players, and in some instances up to 20.

1841—To circumvent base guardians who had a trick of kicking the base as far away from the runner as possible, it was ruled that all bases must be staked down. This was accomplished by driving a small stake in the ground and attaching the base to it with a piece of rope.

1842—Baseball until this time was played under haphazard rules and on any type of field that satisfied the home team. In an effort to end arguments, a diagram was drawn which sketched out the playing field. This appears to have been the first sketch of any kind outlining a baseball infield. Diagram placed the "thrower's (pitcher's)" box 35 feet from the "striker's box." There were 4 bases: 1, 2, 3 and 4. The fourth base, which a runner had to cross to score, was at a point well to the left of what is called home plate now. The plate was used only as the "striker's (batter's) box." A team was 12 players; the thrower, the catcher and an assistant who played well back of him; 4 regular infielders, an infield "rover," 3 regular outfielders and an outfield "rover." Players were called "scouts."

1845—First baseball organization was formed in New York. Called itself Knickerbocker Baseball Club. Committee appointed to draft rules for standardized play in 1846. These limited a team to 9 players. Alexander Cartwright was detailed to sketch new playing field. He drew what is the baseball "diamond" of today, then known as a "square." ... Boston decided it needed a diagram for its game, too. Bostonians sketched their diagram for a "Town Ball" game, which was the only form of game played in New England until 1858. It differed from the Cartwright design.

1846—Knickerbocker Committee offered its draft of new rules. Cartwright presented his "baseball square." Knickerbockers decided upon Elysian Fields, a summer picnic and former cricket grounds in Hoboken, N.J., as the first baseball field. Knickerbockers were challenged by the newly organized "New York Nine." They met in Hoboken, June 19, 1846, the "New York Nine" defeating the Knickerbockers 23 to 1, in 4 hands (innings). Rules then provided that game would end when a team scored 21 aces (runs), each side having equal turns at bat. The ball weighed 3 ounces. Home plate was to cover a space equal to 1 square foot and was made of iron, flat and circular. Pitching distance fixed at 45 feet, with 90 feet between bases.

1848—The rule that a runner between bases could be retired by tagging any base, before he reached it, was amended so he could be retired this way only at first base.

1849—Knickerbockers first appeared in uniform, blue and white, during practice. The uniforms were identical with those used by cricket players. They perhaps were old cricket uniforms put to a new use.

1851—Knickerbockers beat Washington of New York, June 3, score 21 to 14, in 8 hands (innings) at Red House Grounds, New York City.

1853—The first story on the subject of baseball appeared in the New York "Mercury" in April, with Senator William Cauldwell, owner and editor of the paper, as the author.

1854—New rule provided ball weigh from 5½ to 6 ounces and be 2¾ to 3½ inches in diameter.

1856—Chicago Unions organized, being the first ball club in that city.

1857—Rule adopted that every game of championship variety had to begin at least 2 hours before sunset.

1857—First baseball association was formed, and rules made that game was to be decided by 9 innings of play instead of on basis of first to score 21 runs. Organization was called National Association of Base-Ball Players, strictly amateur.

1858—"Called" strike rule written into records. ... Rule abolished whereby batter was out if fielder caught ball on first bounce. Thereafter outs were scored only when ball was caught on fly. New rule first applied in game between New York Knickerbockers and Brooklyn Excelsiors. ...Baseball clubs, in convention in March, decided that umpire, chosen by home team, alone should rule game. Previously there had been 2 umpires and a referee, 1 umpire being chosen by each club. Referee usually had to cast deciding vote on close plays because umpires always favored their own club. ... New England devotees of "Town Ball" met in Dedham, Mass., and a group attempted to bring about adoption of "Knickerbocker game." It failed. Boston continued to play "Town Ball." ... (July 20)—First time admission was charged, Brooklyn vs. "New York Stars," at Fashion Race Course, Long Island. Admission 50 cents; 1,500 spectators paid.

1859—At meeting in New York, March 9, rule adopted that bat was not to exceed 2½ inches in diameter. This was done to aid pitchers who were complaining because batters were using sticks of immense size. Many had the flat paddle-like face of a cricket bat, about 4 inches wide. ... Adoption of rule whereby players were barred from receiving money for services. ... First intercollegiate game was played July 1 between Williams and Amherst Colleges in Pittsfield, Mass. Each side had 13 players. Rules of game provided man could be retired only on caught fly ball. Sixty-five runs was to constitute game. Play lasted 26 "rounds." Amherst won, 66 to 32.

1860—First organized game played in San Francisco, Feb. 22. ... The Philadelphia Athletics, organized May 31, 1859, for purpose of playing "Town Ball" and playing on the grounds of the St. George Cricket Club, shifted and played its first game of baseball on April 7. ... Baseball introduced to Cincinnati, original playing field becoming site many years later of Cincinnati Hospital. ... First tour by baseball club was started by Brooklyn Excelsiors, visiting several cities in New York state, Pennsylvania and Maryland.

1860-61—So many arguments as to whether ball was fair or foul that whitewash was used to mark the dividing line.... First trophy ever offered for a baseball championship was put up by newspaper, "New York Clipper," of which Henry Chadwick was baseball editor for almost 40 years.

1862—First baseball enclosure (Union Grounds, Brooklyn) opened May 15. New rule required that bat must be of wood, round, and could not exceed 2½ inches in thickest part, but there was no restriction as to length.

1864—Al Reach, playing with Brooklyn Atlantics, was offered money if he would "jump" to the Philadelphia Athletics. Reach accepted and became the first paid ball player, starting with the Athletics in June. In 1866, 2 others became "pros" when Pike and Dockney demanded—and received—salaries from the Athletics.... New rule required runner to touch each base in making circuit.... William A. (Candy) Cummings, pitching for Brooklyn Stars against Brooklyn Atlantics, was credited with throwing a ball which curved on its way to plate. Scientists declared this was impossible; that it was an "optical illusion." Cummings never put on a public demonstration.

1865—Eddie Cuthbert of Philadelphia Keystones credited with being the first player to attempt a steal of base, climaxing it with slide, against Brooklyn Atlantics.

1866—Dickey Pearce of Brooklyn Atlantics credited with laying down first deliberate bunt.

1867—Washington Nationals (amateurs) on tour defeated Buckeyes (Cincinnati), 88-12, Louisville, 82-21, Western Indianapolis, 106 to 21. Fox and Studley each made 14 runs in latter game.

1868—Cincinnati Red Stockings, then still an amateur club, introduced uniforms featuring short (knickerbocker) pants. Laughed at originally, but became standard baseball regalia.

1869—Cincinnati Red Stockings turned professional—first salaried team in game's history. George Wright, captain and shortstop, was guaranteed $1,400 for season which began March 15, ended Nov. 15. Other salaries scaled from $1,200 for Harry Wright, manager and centerfielder, down to $600 for utility player Richard Hurley. Asa Brainard, the pitcher, was paid $1,100. Team played 66 games, won 65, tied 1. After winning 39 in row, Cincinnati was tied, 17-17, by Haymakers of Troy, N.Y.

1870— Cincinnati Red Stockings suffered first defeat since turning professional, on June 14 at hands of Brooklyn Atlantics, 8 to 7, in 11 innings. Red Stockings 2-year record was: 92 victories and 1 tie in 93 starts, losing the 94th. In the losing game of 1870, George Wright, shortstop for Cincinnati, was credited with making the first double play by using hidden ball trick in 10th inning. It halted Brooklyn rally....

Rockford (Ill.) club started on tour of East, the first Western team to make invasion. The old rule which barred batter from over-running first base was eliminated. At meeting in New York, Nov. 30, a rule was passed giving batter right to call for high or low ball. Abolished in 1887.... On Aug. 16, Fred Goldsmith put on public exhibition of curve ball pitching which was reported by Henry Chadwick in the "Brooklyn Eagle," as follows:

"Yesterday, at the Capitoline grounds, a large crowd assembled, and cheered lustily, as a youth from New Haven, Conn., Fred Goldsmith, demonstrated to the satisfaction of all that a baseball could be so manipulated and controlled by throwing it from one given point to another, as to make a pronounced arc in space.

"The test was made by drawing a chalkline on the ground a distance of 45 feet from one extremity to the other. An eight-foot pole was driven in an upright position at one end. Another pole was driven in the same manner half-way between the two end poles, planted directly on the line. Now, everything was set for the test.

"Goldsmith was placed on the left side of the chalkline near the end pole facing the pole at the other end. The purpose of this was that the ball delivered from the thrower's hand was to cross the line, circle the center pole and return to the same side of the line from which it was thrown, before reaching the far pole. This feat was successfully accomplished six or eight times and that which up to this point seemed an optical illusion and against all rules of physics was now an established fact."

1871—First professional baseball association, known as National Association of Professional Base-Ball Players, was organized. The National Association of Base-Ball Players, an amateur group controlling game since 1858, collapsed.

1872—On Oct. 15, on Union Baseball Grounds, Brooklyn, John Hatfield threw a baseball 400 feet, 7½ inches, which remained the record for 38 years. (It was broken Oct. 9, 1910, during a field meet on the Cincinnati ball field, by Sheldon Lejeune, who had a trial with Cleveland, but then was with Evansville, Ind. Lejeune's throw was 426 feet, 9½ inches.) ... New rule specified that ball weigh not less than 5 nor more than 5¼ ounces, and measure not less than 9 nor more than 9¼ inches in circumference. No change since then.

1873—Boston reported gross receipts for the season of $13,990 and a profit of $767.93. It also reported that A. G. Spalding, pitcher, was paid the top salary of $1,800 for the season; James (Deacon) White, a catcher, $1,500; Harry Wright, $1,200, and James O'Rourke, the next high salaried man, $800.

1874—Boston reported receipts of $19,995 for the year, which produced an operating profit of $833.13.... (Feb. 27)—Baseball first played in England, at Lord's Cricket Grounds. Teams made up of English cricket and football players and a few American baseball players. A. G. Spalding of the United States pitched for one team. Charles E. Alcock, English cricket bowler, pitched for the other, while player named Briggs, of Detroit, caught Alcock. The Alcock-Briggs team defeated Spalding's 17 to 5, in 6 innings. Later in year, 2 teams of ball players, representing Boston and Philadelphia, toured England, Boston winning 8, losing 6. After baseball tour was completed, the 18 Americans (as a team) played cricket against England, whose team was limited to regulation number of 11 players. With their 18 players, Americans won 6 games, while seventh was unfinished.

1875—Unpadded catching glove introduced by Charles G. Waite. . . . Mask invented by Fred W. Thayer was first used by James Tyng of Harvard. A mask used in fencing served as the model. Thayer started work on his mask in 1873, but the professional catchers would not try it at the time. . . . The Boston club, winner of championship of National Association, reported the following for the 1875 season: Receipts, $37,767.06; expenses, $35,505.99; balance (profit), $2,261.07. Boston played 79 games that year, winning 71, losing 8, for a percentage of .899. Game receipts of the champions averaged around $475. . . . First recorded 1-0 game in professional baseball achieved May 12 when Chicago defeated St. Louis.

1876—National League came into playing existence and National Association of Professional Base-Ball Players folded. National League constitution drawn up by Judge Orrick C. Bishop of St. Louis and remains almost unchanged. He also drew up first player contracts. National League rule required that no city could be represented with a club that had less than 75,000 population. Cost of franchise was $100 as compared with $10 in National Association. National League was composed of following clubs in 1876: Boston, Hartford (Conn.), New York Mutuals, Philadelphia Athletics in East, Cincinnati, Louisville, Chicago and St. Louis in West. . . . National League ruled bat must not exceed 42 inches in length.

1877—Rules required canvas-covered bases, 15 inches square. Two minor leagues came into existence—International Association (created Feb. 20) and League Alliance. . . . Professional catchers began adopting the mask, which fans called "a bird cage". A Hartford man perfected a crude chest protector for catchers, who often were knocked out by stopping foul tips with their chests, but the protector was scoffed at for some time. . . . Players Hall, Craver, Devlin and Nichols, members of Louisville club, expelled from baseball, Oct. 30, for "crooked play." Evidence indicated they had "thrown" games to oblige clique of gamblers that had bet on out-

come. . . . Home plate was moved from its position, just back of the edge of the diamond, to a spot exactly within the diamond—or square—where it now is. . . . Rule adopted by National League that club owners could deduct $30 of a player's annual salary toward expense of uniform.

1878—Turnstiles introduced for first time. . . . Rule adopted by National League whereby visiting team was allowed 15 cents per paid admission. The home team was required to pay the umpire, the wages then being $5 per game. Players on tour were assessed 50 cents per day toward cost of meals.

1879—Northwestern League, a minor organization, created at meeting in Rockford, Ill., Jan. 2. . . . National League named 20 men as "fit" to be umpires. They were Mike Walsh, James Summer, C. E. Wilbur, Charles Daniels, W. McLean, W. E. Furlong, A. D. Hodges, J. A. Cross, R. Wheeler, J. A. Williams, W. H. Geer, George Seward, J. Dunn, G. W. Bredburg, T. H. Brunton, T. Gilliam, J. Young, E. G. Fountain, F. W. Feber and C. G. Stambaugh. These men lived in—or near—cities where league had clubs and home captain made his choice. This rule remained in force until 1883 when the league appointed 4 salaried men, each from a city not represented in the league, to insure impartial verdicts. . . . Rule adopted that runner was out if hit by a batted ball. That was to curb baserunners of the practice of running into it to prevent infielders from making play. . . . Reserve clause made its first appearance in baseball contracts. This was decided upon by National League at secret meeting, Sept. 30, 1879, in Buffalo. Prior to then players had privilege of joining any team they chose at end of each playing season. Under the new rule, each club was permitted to reserve 5 players, the other clubs pledging they would not sign such players. . . . Until this year 9 balls gave batter first base. Change was made in 1880 to 8, 1881 to 7, 1884 to 6, 1887 to 7, 1887 to 5, 1889 to present rule of 4 balls.

1881—Pitching distance lengthened to 50 feet. . . . Perhaps smallest paid attendance at any contest in National League history was 12, when Chicago and Troy played final game of season, Sept. 27, in blinding rain storm.

1882—American Association formed as rival of National and decided that percentage system be used to determine pennant winners. It was baseball innovation then, now in universal use. . . . National League decreed that teams no longer could use any uniforms they chose, and specified the hues, which were as follows: Boston, red; Cleveland, navy blue; Chicago, white; Buffalo, gray; Troy (N.Y.), green; Detroit, old gold; Worcester (Mass.), brown; Providence (R.I.), light blue. Those 8 clubs made up the circuit that year. . . . American Association introduced regular salaried umpires. . . . Only team captains were permitted to address umpire. In this year it was ruled that henceforth umpire must depend upon his own judgment in rendering decision. Previously, on disputed plays, umpires often took testimony from players or spectators before making ruling . . . . . Baseball magnates voided rule which had been in force up to this year, whereby players were assessed 50 cents per day toward the cost of meals while on the road.

1883—National League and American Association agreed that each club could reserve 11 specified players who were not to be tampered with by other clubs. Changed to 12 players in 1884 and 14 in 1887. . . . First game under electric lights, June 2, in Fort Wayne, Ind. Fort Wayne beat Quincy, Ill., 19-11, in 7 innings . . . . The National League's first staff of salaried umpires was made up of W. E. Furlong, Kansas City, Mo.; S. M. Decker, Bradford, Pa.; Frank Lane, Norwalk, Ohio, and A. F. Odlin, Lancaster, N.H. . . . Color regulations for clubs in National League made to apply only to stockings, and not to entire uniform. . . . Charles (Old Hoss) Radbourn pitched 72 games for Providence Nationals, winning 44.

1884—Nationals followed American Association in determining pennant winner on percentage basis. Union Association appeared as rival of National and American Association; disbanded at end of disastrous season. . . . Almost all restrictions on pitcher removed, and he was allowed to throw ball with any motion he chose, but was forced to face batter at moment of windup. . . . Charles Radbourn pitched 72 games for Providence and won 60. . . . Moses Fleetwood (Fleet) Walker of Toledo (American Association) first Negro to play in a major league. He was a catcher, played in 41 games, hit .251. His brother, Welday Wilberforce Walker, also played for Toledo in 1884. He was an outfielder and appeared in only 6 games.

1885—Chest protectors for catchers introduced. . . . Detroit Club, in National League, failing to get acceptance of its various offers for the "Big Four of Baseball"—Richardson, Brouthers, White and Rowe—purchased the entire Buffalo club, which owned the quartet.

1886—National League and American Association formed working agreement. . . . Captain of home team was permitted to decide which team would go to bat first. . . . Rule adopted that when ball was lost, umpire immediately substituted new one. Prior to this year rule provided that if a ball was lost during course of game umpire was to allow players 5 minutes to search for it before tossing a new one into play.

1887—Batter allowed 4 strikes. Bases on balls counted as hits. Both rules abolished at end of season. Batter allowed to take first when hit by pitched ball. Rule still in force. Double umpire

system introduced in post-season games—National League vs. American Association. John Gaffney and John Kelley officiated. Mike Kelly was sold by Chicago to Boston for $10,000 and became "$10,000 beauty." His 1888 salary was $4,200. . . . Minor leagues were: International, Northwestern, Western, Southern, New England, Ohio State, Eastern, Pennsylvania, California.

1888—In a throwing contest, Ed Williamson of Chicago won with 399 feet 11 inches, which was short of Hatfield's 1872 record. De Wolf Hopper first recited "Casey at the Bat" on American stage. . . . Batsman credited with base hit when his batted ball hit runner. . . . Two clubs, under auspices of A. G. Spalding, made foreign tour, visiting Hawaii, Australia, Ceylon, Egypt, Italy, France, England and Ireland.

1890—National League sponsored the publication of baseball paper devoted to its interests—"Sporting Times"—with O. P. Caylor as editor. . . .Players (Brotherhood) League proceeded to function with 8 clubs: Pittsburgh, Chicago, Cleveland, Buffalo, New York, Philadelphia, Boston and Brooklyn. League was started in protest against low salaries paid by National League and American Association. New league had losing season, disbanded at end of year. Players League was accused of having "enlivened" the ball to produce more hits. The 1890 attendance totals were: Players League, 980,887 for 532 games; National League, 813,678 for 540 games. American Association estimated at 500,000. . . . Uniforms worn by Boston Nationals reported to have cost $56 each. A "census" of the Boston team was issued. This was the first time any club had issued data as to birth dates, places, etc., concerning players. The oldest Boston player was 35, youngest 22, average 28. . . . Amos Rusie, pitching for New York Nationals, struck out 345 batters but established an all-time record of 276 passes.

1891—Players substitution allowed any time during game. Heavily padded gloves for catchers introduced. No restriction as to size or padding. American Association had bad season; disbanded at close.

1892—National League increased from 8- to 12-club league and had bad season. Total attendance was only 1,700,000. League lost about $125,000. Players' salaries were cut and there were threats of their forming a new Players League. National League played only split season in its history. Makeup of league that year was: Boston, New York, Philadelphia, Baltimore, Brooklyn and Washington in East; Chicago, St. Louis, Cincinnati, Cleveland, Pittsburgh and Louisville in West.

1893—In effort to get publicity for game, Nationals conducted "popularity contest," which ended in tie—Buck Ewing, Ed Williamson, Mike Kelly and Adrian Anson. Pitching distance increased from 50 feet to 60 feet 6 inches. Plan was 60 feet; diagram read 60'0", but surveyor mistook it for 60'6". Batter who made sacrifice was exempted from time at bat. Washington and St. Louis played 12-inning scoreless tie, Aug. 27, and both went scoreless for 14 innings, Aug. 28—total 26—for two successive days. Washington won the second game in 15th inning.

1894—Efforts to revive American Association failed. Attempted bunts that rolled foul ruled as strikes. League had first profitable season in many years.

1895—Umpire Hank O'Day ruled Connie Mack, who protested play, out of game. Mack was fined $100. Infield fly rule adopted. A caught foul-tip was ruled a strike.

1896—Ed Delahanty hit 4 home runs in a game and received four boxes of chewing gum as a prize.

1897—Honus Wagner signed by Ed Barrow to play for Paterson, N.J. Willie Keeler hit safely in 44 consecutive games. Australian baseball team made first tour of United States. Played and won 10 games.

1898—League scheduled 154 games for first time. Regular season usually had been 140.

1899—Bank rule adopted. Cleveland Nationals lost 134 games.

1900—Old Western League regrouped as American League at meeting in Chicago, Jan. 29. Americans demanded recognition as major circuit. Nationals refused. Brooklyn and Pittsburgh played post-season series. Effort to revive American Association failed. Nationals reduced circuit to 8 clubs. Present-day 5-sided home plate introduced.

(All attendance figures which follow are from "Sporting News," St. Louis.)

1901—Nationals and Americans at war. National attendance, 1,920,031; American, 1,683,584. Nationals adopted foul strike rule; Americans balked at it. The National Association of Minor Leagues was organized. New major rule prohibited catcher from catching first two strikes on bounce; he was required to remain directly behind plate at all times.

1902—Nationals and Americans still at war. Americans drew 2,206,457; Nationals, 1,688,012. Harry O'Hagen of Rochester, against Jersey City (minors), made first triple play unassisted. Paul Hines, originally credited with first unassisted triple play for Providence, against Boston, May 8, 1878, but final version of this play still disputed.

1903—At end of 1902, Nationals made peace overtures, which were accepted early in 1903. Americans gained recognition as major circuit. Nationals, Americans and the minor league group banded into "Organized Baseball," to be ruled by National Commission. Americans, during 1903 playing season, adopted foul strike rule. Attendance in 1903: Nationals, 2,390,362; Americans, 2,345,888. Boston Americans and Pittsburgh

Nationals, rival pennant winners, engaged in post-season play-off, but not under league supervision.

1904—American League attendance, 3,024,028; National, 2,666,271. Foul strike rule adopted by minor leagues. Rube Waddell of Philadelphia Athletics fanned 343,347, or 349 batsmen, total since being in dispute because of faulty scoring system.

1905—American League drew 3,120,752; National, 2,734,310. Modern World Series, under National Commission, started, New York Nationals vs. Philadelphia Americans, New York winning.

1906—American League attendance, 2,938,076; National, 2,781,213.

1907—American League attendance, 3,398.764; National, 2,737,793.

1908—A record was established June 9 by the Cleveland Americans against Boston. In the fifth inning, every one of the 9 Cleveland players made a hit, and each scored a run. American League season attendance, 3,611,366; National, 3,634,988. Chicago led the American with 636,906; New York led National with 910,000, for a home game average of 13,000. . . . Shin guards introduced by Roger Bresnahan, New York Nationals. Later, Charles Dooin, Philadelphia Nationals, claimed he had introduced them a year or so earlier. Pitchers prohibited from soiling or scuffing new ball. . . . (Sept. 23)—Fred Merkle of New York Giants pulled his famous "boner" by failing to touch second base and thus preventing the scoring of the winning run against Chicago Cubs. As a result of the 1-1 tie, the teams finished even at the end of the regular season and played an extra game to determine the pennant winner. Chicago won, 4-2.

1909—Cork-center ball introduced for occasional play.

1910—American League drew 3,692,260; Nationals, 3,586,737. Cork-center ball put into regular play. . . . Sheldon Lejeune, with Evansville, Ind., made record baseball throw, 426 feet 9½ inches, in exhibition at Cincinnati.

1911—Philadelphia Americans won 11 of 18 double-headers. William Harridge took job as secretary to Ban Johnson, president of American League. Harridge later became league president.

1914—Organization known as United States League, in 1913, changed name to Federal League, demanded major status, began raiding American and National for players.

1915—At end of season, Federal League disbanded.

1916—New York Giants created modern record, winning 26 straight, Sept. 7 to Sept. 30, losing second game of Sept. 30 double-header.

1918—Because of war, major league season ended Sept. 1. Players asked guarantee of $1,800 minimum for World Series winning players, $1,200 minimum for losers. Request denied.

Miller Huggins became New York Yankees manager.

1919—Major leagues adopted 140-game schedule. World Series changed from 4-of-7 to best 5-of-9 basis, in this year. Continued rule in 1920 and 1921, changed back to 4-of-7 in 1922. Babe Ruth hit 29 homers for new record.

1920—Major league schedule resumed at 154 games. It was established that 1919 World Series was crooked, 8 Chicago Americans having conspired to "throw" victory to Cincinnati Nationals. As result, the following Chicago players barred from baseball: Joe Jackson, Eddie Cicotte, Chick Gandil, Lefty Williams, Swede Risberg, Buck Weaver, Happy Felsch and Fred McMullin. . . . Rule adopted barring use of "spitball" by pitchers. A limited few pitchers, long addicted to "spitter," exempted from rule. . . . (May 1)—Brooklyn and Boston (N.L.) played longest game in major history, at Boston. Ended 1-1 tie in 26 innings. Time 3 hours 50 minutes. Cadore of Brooklyn and Oeschger of Boston, rival pitchers, went entire route. . . . "Lively ball" made appearance in American League by accident. Manufacturer shifted to use of Australian yarn, which was stronger and stouter than American yarn. This made it possible to wind balls tighter, producing harder, "bouncier" ball. Babe Ruth hit 54 homers. . . . In fifth game of World Series between Cleveland (A.L.) and Brooklyn, Bill Wambsganss, Cleveland second baseman, made the first unassisted triple play in the history of the classic, and Elmer Smith, Cleveland outfielder, hit the first home run with bases filled.

1921—Kenesaw M. Landis elected as commissioner of baseball, 7-year contract, $50,000 annually. National Commission was abolished, Landis becoming supreme ruler of game. Babe Ruth hit 59 homers.

1922—World Series restored to best 4-of-7 basis, which has been rule since then. Morgan G. Bulkeley, first president of National League, died.

1923—For second time in its history (other time 1916), Philadelphia Americans lost 20 games in row, tying record made by Boston Nationals in 1906. Yankee Stadium was opened. Willie Keeler died.

1924—Jimmy O'Connell, outfielder and Cozy Dolan, coach, New York Nationals, barred from baseball because of charge they requested Heinie Sand, Philadelphia (N.L.), not to "bear down" too hard on New York.

1925—Christy Mathewson died, as did Charles Ebbets, owner of Brooklyn club.

1926—Cushioned cork-center baseball introduced.

1927—Babe Ruth made modern record, hitting 60 homers for New York Yankees.

1931—Sacrifice fly ruled out.

1932—Evar Swanson of Columbus (American Association) circled bases in 13.3 seconds—still the record. In 1929, while with Cincinnati, he was timed in 13.4 seconds.

1933—All-Star series originated. Played in Chicago, Americans winning, 4-2.

1935 (May 23)—Night baseball introduced into majors by Cincinnati vs. Philadelphia; attendance 20,422.

1938—Bob Feller of Cleveland Indians (A.L.) established modern major league strikeout record of 18 for one 9-inning game.

1941—Joe DiMaggio made major league record, hitting safely in 56 consecutive games, May 15 through July 16, with 91 hits for .408 average. Streak halted at Cleveland, July 17, in night game.

1943—Because of restricted railroad travel as a result of war traffic, major league teams trained in North for first time in modern baseball history. Minor leagues badly hurt by travel restrictions, only 9 leagues completing season.

1944—Teams again trained North. Number of night ball games greatly increased. Because draft and enlistments took so many regular players from the diamonds and because of dearth of youthful talent, many players who either had gone to minors or were in retirement returned to active big league play. Only 10 minor leagues were in operation. . . . (Nov. 25) —Landis died.

1945—A.B. Chandler, United States Senator from Kentucky, succeeded Landis; 7-year contract, $50,000 annually.

1946 (Aug. 9)—For first time in major league history, all 8 games were played at night. Total attendance 205,980. . . . Decision made to increase Advisory Council, which once was dominated by Landis, to 7 members: Chandler, both major league presidents, one club president each league, one player each league. . . . Bob Feller of Cleveland Indians (A.L.) established modern major league strikeout record of 348 for one season. . . . Jackie Robinson, second baseman for Montreal (International League), becomes first Negro player in modern minor league history. . . . National League race ended in its first tie, between Brooklyn and St. Louis, each winning 96, losing 58. In play-off, best 2-of-3, St. Louis won both games, 4-2 and 8-4. . . . Many major league players "jumped" to the Mexican League, outside organized baseball, despite the threat of a 5-year ban.

1947—Major leagues adopted annuity plan, starting April 1, for players, coaches and trainers. Players' contributions range from $45.45 to $545.75 per season, or part of season, depending upon length of major service. The players are insured from $5,300 to $10,600 while they are owned by major club. Annuities range from $50 to $100 per month, and retirement age is 50, annuities continuing for life. . . . Jackie Robinson of Brooklyn Dodgers became first Negro player in National League in modern history of majors.

Later in same season, American League used Negro players for first time. . . . Commissioner Chandler suspended Brooklyn manager, Leo Durocher, for one year. . . . Bonus rule adopted, forcing a major league team to keep, or else submit to waivers, any player signed for a bonus of more than $6,000. (Eliminated at end of 1950 season, restored for 1953.) . . . Floyd (Bill) Bevens of New York (A.L.) pitched 8 2/3-inning no-hitter, but lost World Series game to Brooklyn, 3-2. Bevens allowed only one hit, but walked 10.

1948–(Aug. 16)–Babe Ruth died of cancer, age 53. . . . American League drew record season attendance of 11,150,099; Cleveland set all-time gate record for a club, 2,620,627; majors had record 20,920,842. . . . First-place tie for first time in American League history necessitated single-game play-off, with Cleveland beating Boston, 8-3.

1949–Minor leagues set attendance record for fourth consecutive year: 41,982,335. . . . Chandler declared amnesty for all players who had jumped to Mexican League, including 18 ex-major leaguers. Danny Gardella, ex-New York Giant, sued for $300,000 damages, challenging validity of reserve clause, and won out-of-court settlement. . . . Organized baseball reached all-time high of two major and 59 minor leagues. . . . Baseball playing rules recodified, Dec. 21.

1950 (Oct. 18)–Connie Mack retired after 50 seasons as manager of Philadelphia Athletics. . . . Major leagues' meetings in December failed to renew Commissioner Chandler's contract, due to expire in April, 1952. . . . Majors signed 6-year $6,000,000 contract for television rights in World Series, with all the money to be used for players' pension fund.

1951–Ford C. Frick elected baseball commissioner, Warren C. Giles new president of National League. Frick received 7-year contract at $65,000 per year. . . . Overcoming 13½-game deficit in August, New York Giants tied Brooklyn Dodgers for National League pennant, then won 2 of 3 play-off games, 3-1, 0-10, 5-4. Bobby Thomson won last of these with a 3-run homer in the ninth inning. . . . Pacific Coast League became first to gain "open classification," allowing it freedom from annual player draft by majors.

1952–Manager Casey Stengel led New York Yankees to record-tying fourth straight pennant and world championship. . . . Mrs. Eleanor Engle became first woman to sign modern-day playing contract in organized baseball, but minor league commissioner George Trautman (with approval of Commissioner Frick) voided her contract with Harrisburg (Pa.) Senators of Interstate League. . . . The long-distance throwing record of 426 feet 9½ inches, set by Sheldon Lejeune in 1910, was broken by Don Grate, an outfielder with Chattanooga of the Southern Association.

Grate made his record-breaking toss of 434 feet 1 inch at Engel Stadium, Chattanooga, on Sept. 7.

1953–Special major league meetings held in April to vote on change in franchises. American League vetoed Bill Veeck's plan to switch St. Louis Browns to Baltimore, but a few days later National League club owners sanctioned Lou Perini's transfer of his Braves from Boston to Milwaukee, former American Association franchise. This was first change in N.L. set-up in 20th Century. Braves responded by finishing second in the league race and setting a league home attendance record of 1,826,397. The Yankees, under Manager Stengel, set records by winning their fifth straight pennant and their fifth straight world series. At the close of the season, a syndicate headed by Clarence W. Miles purchased the St. Louis Browns and transferred the franchise to Baltimore for the 1954 season. Team took nickname of Orioles. . . . U.S. Supreme Court granted writ of certiorari to hear case charging organized baseball with operating illegally in interstate commerce. Later the Court reaffirmed the 1922 opinion delivered by Associate Justice Oliver Wendell Holmes that baseball is a sport rather than interstate business within the meaning of the Federal antitrust laws. The vote was 7 to 2.

1954–Sacrifice fly not counted as time at bat when run was driven in. . . . Syndicate headed by Arnold Johnson of Chicago purchased Philadelphia Athletics and transferred club to Kansas City for 1955 season.

1954–Joe Bauman of the Roswell Club in the Class C. Longhorn League hit 72 homers, an all-time record for organized ball. . . . Cleveland Indians ended Yankees' string of pennant successes at 5, rolling up 111 victories, a record high. Indians set record attendance for one day when 86,563 jammed Municipal Stadium on Sept. 12 to see Indians beat Yankees in a double-header.

1955–Commissioner Frick fines Milwaukee club and 14 Braves' players for violating March 1 spring training deadline. . . . Richie Ashburn misses Phillies' opener and his consecutive game streak ends at 731. . . . Dodgers set major league record by winning first ten games in row. . . . Dodgers clinch pennant on Sept. 8, earliest date in N.L. history. . . . Dodgers win world series first time, beating Yankees, who resumed their winning ways in the American League. Athletics drew 1,393,054 in their first season at Kansas City. . . . Don Larsen of Yankees pitches perfect game in world series, against Dodgers in fifth game—no hits, no runs, no walks and no opponent reached first base. It was first no-hitter in world series history, and only seventh perfect game in major league history. . . . Ted Williams of Red Sox fined $5,000 for spitting at fans. . . . Dodgers play seven "home" games in Jersey City, N.J.

1957–Traded to Giants after 1956 season,

Jackie Robinson decides to retire from baseball. . . . N.L. club owners approve relocation of Dodgers from Brooklyn to Los Angeles and of Giants from New York to San Francisco. . . . Stan Musial of Cardinals breaks Gus Suhr's N.L. consecutive-game record by playing in 823d straight game. Stan runs streak to 862 when he is forced out by shoulder injury but this break in his streak is not counted because the July 21 game was suspended and he appeared as a pinch runner in the completion of the suspended game and thus ran his string to 895 games, which is officially considered as the N.L. record. , . . Ford Frick elected to another 7-year term as commissioner. . . . Braves set N.L. season attendance record of 2,215,104. . . . Majors voted to scrap bonus rule, which called for major clubs that signed players for bonuses over $4,000 retaining those players on their rosters, thus preventing the development of these bonus players in the minors. Four-year draft rule was adopted.

1958—Dodgers attract 78,672 to their first game in Los Angeles Coliseum, setting N.L. record. Their season total was 1,845,556, second to that of the Braves in the majors. . . . Yanks win twenty-fourth pennant and eighteenth world series. . . . Stan Musial becomes eighth player in history to reach 3,000-hit total. . . . Unrestricted draft rule on first-year players adopted, that is, players signed as free agents who are not brought up to the major league parent roster after their first year in the minors will be subject to unrestricted draft. The rule was passed on an experimental basis, to be in effect for one year. Waiver rule dropped for a limited period in fall to permit free interleague trading. . . . Will Harridge resigns as president of American League, ending an association that started in 1911. Joe Cronin named to succeed Harridge. . . . Leon Cadore, Mort Cooper, Wade Killefer, Chuck Klein, Mel Ott and Tris Speaker died.

1959—The Los Angeles Dodgers brought the West Coast its first Major League pennant when they defeated Milwaukee, 2 games to 0 in a play-off for the National League championship. The Dodgers downed the Chicago White Sox, 4-2, in the World Series. The Oct. 6 Series game in Los Angeles Coliseum drew a crowd of 92,706, most ever in the post-season classic.

1960—Pittsburgh (N.L.) defeated New York, 4-3, in the World Series, although the Yankees batted a record .338 and scored more runs, 82, and made more hits, 151, than any team in Series history. The American League decided to expand to 10 teams to start play in 1961, with new franchises in Los Angeles and Washington. The old Washington team moved to Minneapolis-St. Paul. The new teams were stocked largely from players made available — at $75,000 each — by existing League teams. Ted Williams, most recent .400 hitter, retired.

1961—With an expanded American League schedule, 162 games compared to the old 154, Roger Maris of the New York Yankees broke Babe Ruth's most famous record by hitting 61 home runs. Through 154 games, Maris hit 59. The Yankees defeated Cincinnati, 4-1, in the World Series. The National League decided to expand to 10 teams in 1962, with new franchises in Houston and New York.

1962—The San Francisco Giants won the National League pennant in a 3-game playoff with Los Angeles and New York won the World Series in seven games. The New York Mets bowed into the N.L. with 120 defeats in 160 games. In the expanded schedule, Maury Wills of Los Angeles cracked Ty Cobb's base stealing record with 104 thefts.

1963—The Los Angeles Dodgers (A.L.) won four straight games over the New York Yankees (N.L.) with fine pitching talent, in the World Series. Stan Musial of the St. Louis Cardinals retired at the end of the season with several N.L. records in batting. The Baseball Rules Committee enlarged the strike zone above home plate to reduce the number of bases on balls.

1964—The St. Louis Cardinals (N.L.) won the World Series, 4-3, over the New York Yankees (A.L.). The next day, Johnny Keane resigned as manager of the Cardinals and Yogi Berra was dismissed as manager of the Yankees. The Columbia Broadcasting System purchased the New York Yankees. Manager Fred Hutchinson of the Cincinnati Reds died. Organized Baseball adopted a "free agent draft" and "unrestricted draft" package. Under new regulations, professional teams will "draft" rights to negotiate with high school, college and other amateur players.

1965—William D. Eckert succeeded Ford Frick as Commissioner. Houston commenced play in the "Astrodome," the first domed stadium. The Los Angeles Dodgers (N.L.) won a four-to-three game World Series over the Minnesota Twins (A.L.). Casey Stengel of the New York Mets ended his 55-year baseball career at 75. New attendance records were made in the National League.

1966—The Baltimore Orioles (A.L.) won their first pennant and a four-game sweep over the Los Angeles Dodgers (N.L.) in the World Series. Sandy Koufax of the Dodgers retired due to arthritis. Frank Robinson of the Baltimore Orioles, after being traded by the Cincinnati Reds, became the tenth player to win the batting triple crown. He also was elected the most valuable player in his new league and became the first player to win the award in both major leagues. The Milwaukee Braves moved to Atlanta.

1967—This was considered the Year of the Yaz—Carl Yastrzemski of the Boston Red Sox led the ninth place Red Sox to the pennant before losing to the St. Louis Cardinals (N.L.) in the World Series, 4-3. Whitey Ford of the New York Yankees retired. Mickey Mantle switched to first baseman. Kansas City moved to Oakland.

1968—Detroit (A.L.) overcame St. Louis' 3-1 edge in games to take its first World Series since 1945. Pitchers dominated hitters. Players threatened to strike over contract issues after banding together in a professional union. Franchises of teams and cities were switched. Six managers fell by the wayside with the biggest vacancy of all right at the top, Commissioner of Baseball.

1969—Four teams were added—Montreal and San Diego in the National League, Seattle and Kansas City in the American. Denny McLain, Detroit Tigers' pitcher, won pitching honors for the second straight year. The New York Mets (N.L.) won four consecutive games after losing the opener to Baltimore in the World Series.

1970—The Seattle Pilots, running into financial difficulties and low game attendance, were forced to give up their franchise. Milwaukee gained the defunct Pilots for a reported $10.8 million. The Baltimore Orioles (A.L.) took the World Series, 4 games to 1, from injury-plagued Cincinnati.

1971—Washington franchise shifted at end of season to Dallas-Fort Worth, playing field at Arlington, Tex. The World Series featured one night game which was an instant success with the viewers. Pittsburgh took the Series, 4 games to 3, over A.L. Baltimore.

1972—The Major League Baseball Players Assoc. staged a 13-day strike that delayed the opening of the season by 10 days, cancelling 86-regular season games. Willie Mays traded to New York Mets. Ten managers were either fired or resigned. The baseball world was saddened at the tragic death of Pittsburgh's Roberto Clemente while on a mercy mission for earthquake victims in Managua.

1973—New hitter rule to be adopted by American League for 1973 season: A hitter may be designated to bat for the starting pitcher and all subsequent pitchers in any game without otherwise affecting the status of the pitcher(s) in the game. A designated hitter for the pitcher must be selected prior to the game and must be included in the lineup card presented to the umpire in chief.

EXECUTIVE HISTORY OF ORGANIZED BASEBALL

The National League was organized late in 1875, for play in 1876. It succeeded the National Association of Professional Base-Ball Clubs. The National was alone in the major field until 1882, when the American Association was formed. The AA demanded—and received—recognition as a major group. The Union Association was formed in 1884, operated through that year at a loss, and then disbanded.

In 1890, some players, dissatisfied with salary arrangements, formed their own organization, known as the Players (or Brotherhood) League. It played through 1890, and then disbanded, because of losses. The American Association, hurt by opposition of the Players League, played through 1891 and then disbanded, the Nationals again being alone in major play.

Ban Johnson disbanded the Western Association at the end of 1899. It had been a minor group. He immediately organized, with teams in most of the cities that had made up the Western, and called his new organization the American League. Johnson asked the Nationals for recognition as a major group. When the Nationals refused, Johnson declared war and started to raid the Nationals for players. After 2 years of a losing battle, the Nationals acceded. But the American League was a full-fledged major league starting in 1901.

In 1903 the Nationals and Americans, at a meeting with the minor leagues, decided to band together in what since has been called Organized Baseball. It was decreed that the game should be supervised by the National Commission, of which Garry Herrmann, owner of the Cincinnati (N.L.) club, was to be chairman; the other two members were to be presidents of the National and American Leagues.

In 1921 the National Commission was dissolved, to be succeeded by the Advisory Council, of which Kenesaw M. Landis was the supreme ruler. The league presidents were, at times, consulted, but Landis always had the final say. This condition continued until Landis died on Nov. 25, 1944.

Leslie M. O'Connor was elected secretary of the Advisory Council in 1921 and later became treasurer. O'Connor served in the dual capacity until some months after the passing of Landis, and then resigned to take an executive position with the Chicago (A.L.) club.

Landis, at the outset, received a 7-year contract at $50,000 annually. Before its expiration, he received a new 7-year contract at $65,000. During the depression years of 1933 and 1934, that yearly pay was reduced to $50,000. Later the salary, under another contract, was raised again to $65,000. Shortly before the death of Landis, he signed a new contract, which was to expire Jan. 12, 1946. The salary of O'Connor was $12,500.

A.B. Chandler, United States Senator from Kentucky, succeeded Landis as commissioner in 1945, receiving a 7-year contract, calling for $50,000. When O'Connor resigned, Herold Ruel replaced him, but in the capacity of contact man between the commissioner's office and the players. Ruel resigned late in 1946 to take over management of the St. Louis (A.L.) club. Meanwhile, Walter Mulbry, who had been personal secretary for Chandler, was secretary for Chandler in the commissioner's office.

At the major league meetings of December,

1950, Chandler failed to rally the three-quarters majority necessary to renew the option of his contract, which didn't expire till April 30, 1952. At first he announced he would resign, but then decided to stay on to the end of his term. Notified he would be reimbursed on the rest of his contract and further indemnified against any suits pending against him as baseball commissioner, Chandler resigned July 15, 1951.

After a lengthy meeting in Chicago, the majors elected the National League president, Ford C. Frick, as the new commissioner. He signed a 7-year, $65,000-a-year contract. His assistant, Charles M. Segar, was named secretary-treasurer. Soon afterward, the Cincinnati general manager, Warren C. Giles, himself a candidate for commissioner, was made president of the National League.

Frick retired after the 1965 season and William D. Eckert, a retired Air Force Lieutenant General, was named to succeed him. Three years afterward, Eckert was forced out with Bowie Kuhn, a New York attorney, becoming Interim Commissioner for one year in Feb. 1969. His appointment was made permanent with a seven-year contract in Aug., 1969.

National Commission Members

August Herrmann—1903—1920.
Ban Johnson—1903—1921.
Harry C. Pulliam—1903—1909.
John A. Heydler—Part of 1909.
Thomas A. Lynch—1910—1913.
John K. Tener—1913—1918.
John A. Heydler—1918—1921.

Advisory Council

Organized 1921. Kenesaw M. Landis, commissioner. Leslie M. O'Connor, secretary and later secretary-treasurer. Landis died Nov. 25, 1944. Albert B. Chandler succeeded him as commissioner. Rule adopted August, 1946, made Advisory Council a 7-man board, now called the Executive Council.

National League Executives

Presidents

1876—Morgan G. Bulkeley, Hartford, Conn.
1877—82—William H. Hulbert, Chicago.
1883—84—A.G. Mills, New York.
1885—1902—Nicholas E. Young, Washington.
1903—09—Harry C. Pulliam, New York.
1909—John A. Heydler, Washington.
1910—13—Thomas J. Lynch, New Britain, Conn.
1913—18—John K. Tener, Pennsylvania.
1919—34—John A. Heydler.
1934—51—Ford C. Frick, New York.
1951—1969—Warren C. Giles, Cincinnati
1970— —Charles S. Feeney

Vice Presidents

1929—32—Barney Dreyfuss
1933—36—Charles A. Stoneham
1936—47—Sam Breadon
1948—65—Philip K. Wrigley
1966—68—Horace Stoneham
1969—John J. McHale

Secretaries and Treasurers

1876—1902—Nicholas E. Young
1906—07—Harry E. Pulliam
1907—34—John A. Heydler
1934—38—Harvey Traband
1938—51—Ford C. Frick
1951 to date—Fred G. Fleig

American League Executives

Presidents

1901—27—Ban Johnson, Chicago (Frank J. Navin of Detroit served as acting president while Johnson was absent because of illness during part of 1927).
1927—31—Ernest S. Barnard, Cleveland.
1931—Navin was acting president for 2 months following Barnard's death.
1931—58—William Harridge, Chicago
1959——Joe Cronin, Boston.

Secretaries and Treasurers

1901—27—Ban Johnson
1927—58—William Harridge
1960 to date—Joseph E. Cronin

Vice Presidents

1901—16—Charles W. Somers
1917—19—Charles A. Comiskey
1921—35—Frank J. Navin
1935—39—Jacob Ruppert
1939—55—Clark Griffith
1946—55—Connie Mach (joint holder of office with Griffith)
1956——Thomas A. Yawkey

NATIONAL LEAGUE TEAMS—SINCE 1876

The complete roster of clubs in the National League since the circuit was organized in 1876 follows:

Chicago, since 1876; Boston, 1876—1952; Mutuals (New York), 1876 only; Athletics (Philadelphia), 1876 only; Hartford (Conn.), 1876—1877; St. Louis, 1876—1877, when temporarily resigned; Cincinnati, 1876 until 1880, when expelled; Louisville, 1876—1877, when resigned; Indianapolis,. 1878, when temporarily resigned; Milwaukee, 1878; Providence, 1878—1885; Buffalo, 1879—1885; Cleveland, 1879—1884; Syracuse, 1879 only; Troy, 1879—1882; Worcester, 1880—1882; Philadelphia, since 1883; Detroit,

1881–1888; New York, 1883–1957; St. Louis, 1885–1886, when temporarily resigned; Washington, 1886–1889; Kansas City, 1886 only; Pittsburgh since 1887; Indianapolis 1887–1889; Cleveland, 1889–1899; Brooklyn, 1890–1957; Cincinnati, since 1890. St. Louis, since 1892; Baltimore, 1892–1899; Louisville, 1892–1899; Washington, 1892–1899; Milwaukee, 1953–1965; Los Angeles since 1958; San Francisco, since 1958; Houston, since 1962; New York, since 1962; Atlanta, since 1966; San Diego, since 1969.

AMERICAN LEAGUE TEAMS– SINCE 1901

The complete roster of clubs in the American League since the circuit gained major recognition in 1901 follows:

Chicago, since 1901; Milwaukee, 1901 only; Cleveland, since 1901; Detroit, since 1901; Washington, 1901–71; Philadelphia, 1901–54; Boston, since 1901; Baltimore, 1901–02; St. Louis, 1902–53; New York, since 1903; Baltimore, since 1954; Kansas City, since 1955; California, since 1961; Minnesota, since 1961; Oakland, since 1968; Seattle, 1969 only; Milwaukee, since 1970; Texas, since 1972.

OTHER LEAGUES OF MAJOR PRETENSIONS

Pennant Winners

NATIONAL ASSOCIATION
(First of professional leagues)

1871–Philadelphia
1972–75–Boston

UNION ASSOCIATION

1884–St. Louis

AMERICAN ASSOCIATION

1882–Cincinnati
1883–Philadelphia
1884–New York Metropolitans
1885–88–St. Louis
1889–Brooklyn
1890–Louisville
1891–Boston

PLAYERS (BROTHERHOOD) LEAGUE

1890–Boston

FEDERAL LEAGUE

1914–Indianapolis
1915–Chicago

ALL-TIME BATTING LEADERS
Ten or more seasons through 1972

	Years	G	AB	R	H	Avg.
Ty Cobb	24	3,033	11,429	2,244	4,191	.367
Rogers Hornsby	23	2,259	8,173	1,579	2,930	.358
Joe Jackson	13	1,330	4,981	873	1,772	.356
Roger Browning	13	1,180	4,839	867	1,716	.355
Frank O'Doul	11	970	3,264	624	1,140	.349
Dennis Brouthers	19	1,665	6,737	1,523	2,347	.348
Ed Delahanty	16	1,825	7,493	1,596	2,591	.346
Willie Keeler	19	2,124	8,564	1,720	2,955	.345
Tris Speaker	22	2,789	10,208	1,881	3,515	.344
Ted Williams	19	2,292	7,706	1,798	2,654	.344
William Hamilton	14	1,578	6,262	1,694	2,157	.344
Babe Ruth	22	2,503	8,389	2,174	2,873	.342
Jesse Burkett	16	2,063	8,389	1,708	2,872	.342
Harry Heilmann	18	2,146	7,787	1,291	2,660	.342
Bill Terry	14	1,721	6,428	1,120	2,193	.341
George Sisler	15	2,055	8,267	1,284	2,812	.340
Lou Gehrig	17	2,164	8,001	1,888	2,721	.340
Napoleon Lajoie	21	2,475	9,589	1,503	3,251	.339
Adrian Anson*	22	2,253	9,084	1,712	3,081	.339

*Does not include Anson's National Association career, 1871–75.

.400 HITTERS–SINCE 1901
(100 or more games.)

	Avg.
1901–Nap Lajoie, Philadelphia (AL)	.422
1911–Ty Cobb, Detroit (AL)	.420
1911–Joe Jackson, Cleveland (AL)	.408
1912–Ty Cobb, Detroit (AL)	.410
1920–George Sisler, St. Louis (AL)	.407
1922–George Sisler, St. Louis (AL)	.420
1922–Ty Cobb, Detroit (AL)	.401
1922–Rogers Hornsby, St. Louis (NL)	.401
1923–Harry Heilmann, Detroit (AL)	.403
1924–Rogers Hornsby, St. Louis (NL)	.424
1925–Rogers Hornsby, St. Louis (NL)	.403
1930–Bill Terry, New York (NL)	.401
1941–Ted Williams, Boston (AL)	.406

3,000 OR MORE HITS

Ty Cobb	4,191
Stanley Musial	3,630
Tris Speaker	3,515
Hans Wagner	3,430
Hank Aaron*	3,391
Eddie Collins	3,311
Napoleon Lajoie	3,251
Willie Mays	3,239
Paul Waner	3,152
Adrian Anson	3,081
Roberto Clemente	3,000

* Still active

BATTING CHAMPIONS

(Figure in parentheses indicates the number of times the player has won the title to that point.)

National League

Year Player and Club	Games	Hits	Avg.
1876–Roscoe C. Barnes, Chicago (1)	66	138	.404
1877–James L. White, Boston (1)	48	82	.385
1878–Abner F. Dalrymple, Milwaukee (1)	60	95	.356
1879–Adrian C. Anson, Chicago (1)	49	90	.407
1880–George F. Gore, Chicago (1)	75	114	.365
1881–Adrian C. Anson, Chicago (2)	84	137	.399
1882–Dennis Brouthers, Buffalo (1)	84	129	.367
1883–Dennis Brouthers, Buffalo (2)	97	156	.371
1884–James H. O'Rourke, Buffalo (1)	104	157	.350
1885–Roger Connor, New York (1)	110	169	.371
1886–Michael J. Kelly, Chicago (1)	118	175	.388
1887–*Adrian C. Anson, Chicago (3)	122	224	.421
1888–Adrian C. Anson, Chicago (4)	134	177	.343

1889—Dennis Brouthers, Boston (3) . . . . . 126 181 .373
1890—John W. Glasscock, New York (1) . . 124 172 .336
1891—William R. Hamilton, Philadelphia (1) 133 179 .338
1892—Dennis Brouthers, Brooklyn (4) . . . . 152 197 .335
  —Clarence A. Childs, Cleveland (1) . . . 144 185 .335
1893—Hugh Duffy, Boston (1) . . . . 131 203 .378
1894—Hugh Duffy, Boston (2) . . . . 124 236 .438
1895—Jesse C. Burkett, Cleveland (1) . . . . . 132 235 .423
1896—Jesse C. Burkett, Cleveland (2) . . . . . 133 240 .410
1897—William H. Keeler, Baltimore (1) . . . 128 243 .432
1898—William H. Keeler, Baltimore (2) . . . 128 214 .379
1899—Edward J. Delahanty, Philadelphia (1) 145 234 .408
1900—John P. Wagner, Pittsburgh (1) . . . . . 134 201 .381
1901—Jesse C. Burkett, St. Louis (3) . . . . . 142 228 .382
1902—Clarence H. Beaumont, Pittsburgh (1) 131 194 .357
1903—John P. Wagner, Pittsburgh (2) . . . . . 129 182 .355
1904—John P. Wagner, Pittsburgh (3) . . . . . 132 171 .349
1905—John B. Seymour, Cincinnati (1) . . . . 149 219 .377
1906—John P. Wagner, Pittsburgh (4) . . . . . 140 175 .339
1907—John P. Wagner, Pittsburgh (5) . . . . . 142 180 .350
1908—John P. Wagner, Pittsburgh (6) . . . . . 151 201 .354
1909—John P. Wagner, Pittsburgh (7) . . . . . 137 168 .339
1910—Sherwood R. Magee, Philadelphia (1) . 154 172 .331
1911—John P. Wagner, Pittsburgh (8) . . . . . 130 158 .334
1912—Henry Zimmerman, Chicago (1) . . . . 145 207 .372
1913—Jacob E. Daubert, Brooklyn (1) . . . . 139 178 .350
1914—Jacob E. Daubert, Brooklyn (2) . . . . 126 156 .329
1915—Lawrence V. Doyle, New York (1) . . . 150 189 .320
1916—Harold H. Chase, Cincinnati (1) . . . . 142 184 .339
1917—Edd J. Roush, Cincinnati (1) . . . . . . 136 178 .341
1918—Zachary D. Wheat, Brooklyn (1) . . . 105 137 .335
1919—Edd J. Roush, Cincinnati (2) . . . . . . 133 162 .321
1920—Rogers Hornsby, St. Louis (1) . . . . . 149 218 .370
1921—Rogers Hornsby, St. Louis (2) . . . . . 154 235 .397
1922—Rogers Hornsby, St. Louis (3) . . . . . 154 250 .401
1923—Rogers Hornsby, St. Louis (4) . . . . . 107 163 .384
1924—Rogers Hornsby, St. Louis (5) . . . . . 143 227 .424
1925—Rogers Hornsby, St. Louis (6) . . . . . 138 203 .403
1926—Eugene F. Hargrave, Cincinnati (1) . . 105 115 .353
1927—Paul G. Waner, Pittsburgh (1) . . . . . 155 237 .380
1928—Rogers Hornsby, Boston (7) . . . . 140 188 .387
1929—Frank J. O'Doul, Philadelphia (1) . . . 154 254 .398
1930—William H. Terry, New York (1) . . . . 154 254 .401
1931—Charles J. Hafey, St. Louis (1) . . . . . 122 157 .349
1932—Francis J. O'Doul, Brooklyn (2) . . . . 148 219 .368
1933—Charles H. Klein, Philadelphia (1) . . . 152 223 .368
1934—Paul G. Waner, Pittsburgh (2) . . . . . . 146 217 .362
1935—J. Floyd Vaughan, Pittsburgh (1) . . . 137 192 .385
1936—Paul G. Waner, Pittsburgh (3) . . . . . . 148 218 .373
1937—Joseph M. Medwick, St. Louis (1) . 156 237 .374
1938—Ernest N. Lombardi, Cincinnati (1) . 129 167 .342
1939—John R. Mize, St. Louis (1) . . . . 153 197 .349
1940—Debs C. Garms, Pittsburgh (1) . . . . . 103 127 .355
1941—Harold P. Reiser, Brooklyn (1) . . . . . 137 184 .343
1942—Ernest N. Lombardi, Boston (2) . . . 105 102 .330
1943—Stanley F. Musial, St. Louis (1) . . . . 157 220 .357
1944—Fred Walker, Brooklyn (1) . . . . 147 191 .357
1945—Philip J. Cavarretta, Chicago (1) . . . . 132 177 .355
1946—Stanley F. Musial, St. Louis (2) . . . . 156 228 .365
1947—Harry W. Walker, St. Louis-Phila. (1) 140 186 .363
1948—Stanley F. Musial, St. Louis (3) . . . . 155 230 .376
1949—Jack R. Robinson, Brooklyn (1) . . . . 156 203 .342
1950—Stanley F. Musial, St. Louis (4) . . . . 146 192 .346
1951—Stanley F. Musial, St. Louis (5) . . . . 152 205 .355
1952—Stanley F. Musial, St. Louis (6) . . . . 154 194 .336
1953—Carl A. Furillo, Brooklyn (1) . . . . . . 132 165 .344
1954—Willie Mays, New York (1) . . . . 151 195 .345
1955—Richie Ashburn, Philadelphia (1) . . . 140 180 .338
1956—Henry Aaron, Milwaukee (1) . . . . . . 153 200 .328
1957—Stanley F. Musial, St. Louis (7) . . . . 143 176 .351
1958—Richie Ashburn, Philadelphia (2) . . . 152 215 .350
1959—Henry Aaron, Milwaukee (2) . . . . . . 154 223 .355
1960—Richard Groat, Pittsburgh (1) . . . . . . 138 186 .325
1961—Roberto Clemente, Pittsburgh (1) . . 146 201 .351
1962—Tommy Davis, Los Angeles (1) . . . . . 163 230 .346
1963—Tommy Davis, Los Angeles (2) . . . . . 146 181 .326
1964—Roberto Clemente, Pittsburgh (2) . . 155 211 .339

1965—Roberto Clemente, Pittsburgh (3) . . . 152 194 .329
1966—Mateo Alou, Pittsburgh (1) . . . . 141 183 .342
1967—Roberto Clemente, Pittsburgh (4) . . . 147 209 .357
1968—Peter Rose, Cincinnati (1) . . . . 149 210 .335
1969—Peter Rose, Cincinnati (2) . . . . 156 218 .348
1970—Ricardo Carty, Atlanta (1) . . . . 136 175 .366
1971—Joseph Torre, St. Louis (1) . . . . 161 230 .363
1972—Billy L. Williams, Chicago (1) . . . . . . 150 191 .333

* Bases on balls counted as hits in 1887.

American League

Year	Player and Club	Games	Hits	Avg.
1901—Napoleon Lajoie, Philadelphia (1)	. . .	131	220	.405
1902—Edward J. Delahanty, Washington (1)		123	178	.376
1903—Napoleon Lajoie, Cleveland (2)	. . . . .	126	173	.355
1904—Napoleon Lajoie, Cleveland (3)	. . . .	140	211	.381
1905—Elmer H. Flick, Cleveland (1)	. . . . . .	131	152	.306
1906—George R. Stone, St. Louis (1)	. . . . . .	154	208	.358
1907—Tyrus R. Cobb, Detroit (1)	. . . .	150	212	.350
1908—Tyrus R. Cobb, Detroit (2)	. . . .	150	188	.324
1909—Tyrus R. Cobb, Detroit (3)	. . . .	156	216	.377
1910—Tyrus R. Cobb, Detroit (4)	. . . .	140	196	.385
1911—Tyrus R. Cobb, Detroit (5)	. . . .	146	248	.420
1912—Tyrus R. Cobb, Detroit (6)	. . . .	140	227	.410
1913—Tyrus R. Cobb, Detroit (7)	. . . .	122	167	.390
1914—Tyrus R. Cobb, Detroit (8)	. . . .	97	127	.368
1915—Tyrus R. Cobb, Detroit (9)	. . . .	156	208	.369
1916—Tristram E. Speaker, Cleveland (1)	. . .	151	211	.386
1917—Tyrus R. Cobb, Detroit (10)	. . . . . .	152	225	.383
1918—Tyrus R. Cobb, Detroit (11)	. . . . . .	111	161	.382
1919—Tyrus R. Cobb, Detroit (12)	. . . . . .	124	191	.384
1920—George H. Sisler, St. Louis (1)	. . . . . .	154	257	.407
1921—Harry E. Heilmann, Detroit (1)	. . . . .	149	237	.394
1922—George H. Sisler, St. Louis (2)	. . . . . .	142	246	.420
1923—Harry E. Heilmann, Detroit (2)	. . . . .	144	211	.403
1924—George H. Ruth, New York (1)	. . . . .	153	200	.378
1925—Harry E. Heilmann, Detroit (3)	. . . . .	150	225	.393
1926—Henry E. Manush, Detroit (1)	. . . . . .	136	188	.378
1927—Harry E. Heilmann, Detroit (4)	. . . . .	141	201	.398
1928—Leon A. Goslin, Washington (1)	. . . . .	135	173	.379
1929—Lewis A. Fonseca, Cleveland (1)	. . . .	148	209	.369
1930—Aloysius H. Simmons, Philadelphia (1)	138	211	.381
1931—Aloysius H. Simmons, Philadelphia (2)	128	200	.390
1932—David Dale Alexander, Det.-Boston (1)	124	144	.367
1933—James E. Foxx, Philadelphia (1)	. . . . .	149	204	.356
1934—Henry Louis Gehrig, New York (1)	. . .	154	210	.363
1935—Charles S. Myer, Washington (1)	. . .	151	215	.349
1936—Lucius B. Appling, Chicago (1)	. . . . .	138	204	.388
1937—Charles L. Gehringer, Detroit (1)	. . .	144	209	.371
1938—James E. Foxx, Boston (2)	. . . .	149	197	.349
1939—Joseph P. DiMaggio, New York (1)	. . .	120	176	.381
1940—Joseph P. DiMaggio, New York (2)	. . .	132	179	.352
1941—Theodore S. Williams, Boston (1)	. . .	143	185	.406
1942—Theodore S. Williams, Boston (2)	. . .	150	186	.356
1943—Lucius B. Appling, Chicago (2)	. . . . .	155	192	.328
1944—Louis Boudreau, Cleveland (1)	. . . . . .	150	191	.327
1945—George H. Stirnweiss, New York (1)	. .	152	195	.309
1946—James B. Vernon, Washington (1)	. . .	148	207	.353
1947—Theodore S. Williams, Boston (3)	. . .	156	181	.343
1948—Theodore S. Williams, Boston (4)	. . .	137	188	.369
1949—George C. Kell, Detroit (1)	. . . .	134	179	.343
1950—William D. Goodman, Boston (1)	. . . .	110	150	.354
1951—Ferris R. Fain, Philadelphia (1)	. . . .	117	146	.344
1952—Ferris R. Fain, Philadelphia (2)	. . . . .	145	176	.327
1953—James B. Vernon, Washington (2)	. . .	152	205	.337
1954—Robert F. Avila, Cleveland (1)	. . . . . .	143	189	.341
1955—Al Kaline, Detroit (1)	. . . .	152	200	.340
1956—Mickey Mantle, New York (1)	. . . . . .	150	188	.353
1957—Theodore S. Williams, Boston (5)	. . .	132	163	.388
1958—Theodore S. Williams, Boston (6)	. . .	129	135	.328
1959—Harvey Kuenn, Detroit (1)	. . . .	139	198	.353
1960—James (Pete) Runnels, Boston (1)	. . .	143	169	.320
1961—Norman Cash, Detroit, (1)	. . . .	159	193	.361
1962—James (Pete) Runnels, Boston (2)	. . .	152	183	.326
1963—Carl Yastrzemski, Boston (1)	. . . . . .	151	183	.321

1964—Tony Oliva, Minnesota (1) 161	217	.323
1965—Tony Oliva, Minnesota (2) 149	185	.321
1966—Frank Robinson, Baltimore (1) ..155	182	.316
1967—Carl Yastrzemski, Boston (2) 161	189	.326
1968—Carl Yastrzemski, Boston (3) 157	162	.301
1969—Rodney Carew, Minnesota (1) ...123	152	.332
1970—Alexander Johnson, California (1) 156	202	.329
1971—Pedro (Tony) Oliva, Minnesota (3) 126	164	.337
1972—Rodney Carew, Minnesota (2) ...142	170	.318

TOP ALL-TIME HOME-RUN HITTERS

(Through 1972)   Total

Babe Ruth	.714
Hank Aaron*	.673
Willie Mays*	.654
Harmon Killebrew*	.541
Mickey Mantle	.536
Jimmy Foxx	.534
Frank Robinson*	.522
Ted Williams	.521
Eddie Mathews	.512
Ernie Banks	.512
Mel Ott	.511
Lou Gehrig	.493
Stan Musial	.475
Duke Snider	.407
Willie McCovey*	.384
Al Kaline*	.376
Rocky Colavito	.374
Gil Hodges	.370
Ralph Kiner	.369
Joe DiMaggio	.361

*Still active

HOME RUN CHAMPIONS

National League

1876—George Hall, Philadelphia Athletics .	5
1877—George Shaffer, Louisville	3
1878—Paul A. Hines, Providence	4
1879—Charles W. Jones, Boston	9
1880—James H. O'Rourke, Boston	6
—Harry D. Stovey, Worcester	6
1881—Dennis Brouthers, Buffalo	8
1882—George A. Wood, Detroit	7
1883—William Ewing, New York	10
1884—Edward N. Williamson, Chicago	27
1885—Abner F. Dalrymple, Chicago	11
1886—Arthur H. Richardson, Detroit	11
1887—Roger Connor, New York	17
—William S. O'Brien, Washington	17
1888—Roger Connor, New York	14
1889—Samuel L. Thompson, Philadelphia .	20
1890—Thomas P. Burns, Brooklyn	13
—Michael J. Tiernan, New York	13
1891—Harry D. Stovey, Boston	16
—Michael J. Tiernan, New York	16
1892—James W. Holliday, Cincinnati	13
1893—Edward J. Delahanty, Philadelphia .	19
1894—Hugh Duffy, Boston	18
—Robert L. Lowe, Boston	18
1895—William M. Joyce, Washington	17

1896—Edward J. Delahanty, Philadelphia .	13
—Samuel L. Thompson, Philadelphia .	13
1897—Napoleon Lajoie, Philadelphia	10
1898—James J. Collins, Boston	14
1899—John F. Freeman, Washington	25
1900—Herman C. Long, Boston	12
1901—Samuel E. Crawford, Cincinnati ...	16
1902—Thomas W. Leach, Pittsburgh	6
1903—S. James Sheckard, Brooklyn	9
1904—Harry G. Lumley, Brooklyn	9
1905—Fred W. Odwell, Cincinnati	9
1906—Timothy J. Jordan, Brooklyn	12
1907—David L. Brain, Boston	10
1908—Timothy J. Jordan, Brooklyn	12
1909—John J. Murray, New York	7
1910—Fred T. Beck, Boston	10
—Frank Schulte, Chicago	10
1911—Frank Schulte, Chicago	21
1912—Henry Zimmerman, Chicago	14
1913—Clifford C. Cravath, Philadelphia ...	19
1914—Clifford C. Cravath, Philadelphia ...	19
1915—Clifford c. Cravath, Philadelphia ...	24
1916—Davis A. Robertson, New York	12
—Frederick Williams, Chicago	12
1917—Davis A. Robertson, New York	12
—Clifford C. Cravath, Philadelphia ..	12
1918—Clifford C. Cravath, Philadelphia ..	8
1919—Clifford C. Cravath, Philadelphia ..	12
1920—Frederick Williams, Philadelphia ...	15
1921—George L. Kelly, New York	23
1922—Rogers Hornsby, St. Louis	42
1923—Frederick Williams, Philadelphia ...	41
1924—Jacques F. Fournier, Brooklyn	27
1925—Rogers Hornsby, St. Louis	39
1926—Lewis R. Wilson, Chicago	21
1927—Lewis R. Wilson, Chicago	30
—Frederick Williams, Philadelphia ...	30
1928—Lewis R. Wilson, Chicago	31
—James L. Bottomley, St. Louis	31
1929—Charles H. Klein, Philadelphia	43
1930—Lewis R. Wilson, Chicago	56
1931—Charles H. Klein, Philadelphia	31
1932—Charles H. Klein, Philadelphia	38
—Melvin T. Ott, New York	38
1933—Charles H. Klein, Philadelphia	28
1934—Melvin T. Ott, New York	35
—James A. Collins, St. Louis	35
1935—Walter A. Berger, Boston	34
1936—Melvin T. Ott, New York	33
1937—Melvin T. Ott, New York	31
—Joseph M. Medwick, St. Louis	31
1938—Melvin T. Ott, New York	36
1939—John R. Mize, St. Louis	28
1940—John R. Mize, St. Louis	43
1941—Adolph L. Camilli, Brooklyn	34
1942—Melvin T. Ott, New York	30
1943—William B. Nicholson, Chicago	29
1944—William B. Nicholson, Chicago	33
1945—Thomas F. Holmes, Boston	28
1946—Ralph M. Kiner, Pittsburgh	23
1947—Ralph M. Kiner, Pittsburgh	51
—John R. Mize, New York	51

1948—Ralph M. Kiner, Pittsburgh 40
   —John R. Mize, New York 40
1949—Ralph M. Kiner, Pittsburgh 54
1950—Ralph M. Kiner, Pittsburgh 47
1951—Ralph M. Kiner, Pittsburgh 42
1952—Ralph M. Kiner, Pittsburgh 37
   —Henry J. Sauer, Chicago 37
1953—Ed Mathews, Milwaukee 47
1954—Ted Kluszewski, Cincinnati 49
1955—Willie Mays, New York 51
1956—Duke Snider, Brooklyn 43
1957—Henry Aaron, Milwaukee 44
1958—Ernie Banks, Chicago 47
1959—Ed Mathews, Milwaukee 46
1960—Ernie Banks, Chicago 41
1961—Orlando Cepeda, San Francisco 46
1962—Willie Mays, San Francisco 49
1963—Henry Aaron, Milwaukee 44
   —Willie McCovey, San Francisco 44
1964—Willie Mays, San Francisco 47
1965—Willie Mays, San Francisco 52
1966—Henry Aaron, Atlanta 44
1967—Henry Aaron, Atlanta 39
1968—Willie McCovey, San Francisco 36
1969—Willie McCovey, San Francisco 45
1970—Johnny Bench, Cincinnati 45
1971—Wilver Stargell, Pittsburgh 48
1972—Johnny Bench, Cincinnati 40

American League

1901—Napoleon Lajoie, Philadelphia 13
1902—Ralph O. Seybold, Philadelphia 16
1903—John F. Freeman, Boston 13
1904—Harry H. Davis, Philadelphia 10
1905—Harry H. Davis, Philadelphia 8
1906—Harry H. Davis, Philadelphia 12
1907—Harry H. Davis, Philadelphia 8
1908—Samuel E. Crawford, Detroit 7
1909—Tyrus R. Cobb, Detroit 9
1910—J. Garland Stahl, Boston 10
1911—J. Franklin Baker, Philadelphia 9
1912—J. Franklin Baker, Philadelphia 10
1913—J. Franklin Baker, Philadelphia 12
1914—J. Franklin Baker, Philadelphia 8
   —Samuel E. Crawford, Detroit 8
1915—Robert F. Roth, Chicago-Cleveland . 7
1916—Walter C. Pipp, New York 12
1917—Walter C. Pipp, New York 9
1918—George H. Ruth, Boston 11
   —Clarence W. Walker, Philadelphia . . . 11
1919—George H. Ruth, Boston 29
1920—George H. Ruth, New York 54
1921—George H. Ruth, New York 59
1922—Kenneth R. Williams, St. Louis 39
1923—George H. Ruth, New York 41
1924—George H. Ruth, New York 46
1925—Robert W. Meusel, New York 33
1926—George H. Ruth, New York 47
1927—George H. Ruth, New York 60
1928—George H. Ruth, New York 54
1929—George H. Ruth, New York 46

1930—George H. Ruth, New York 49
1931—George H. Ruth, New York 46
   —Henry Louis Gehrig, New York 46
1932—James E. Foxx, Philadelphia 58
1933—James E. Foxx, Philadelphia 48
1934—Henry Louis Gehrig, New York 49
1935—James E. Foxx, Philadelphia 36
   —Henry B. Greenberg, Detroit 36
1936—Henry Louis Gehrig, New York 49
1937—Joseph P. DiMaggio, New York 46
1938—Henry B. Greenberg, Detroit 58
1939—James E. Foxx, Philadelphia 35
1940—Henry B. Greenberg, Detroit 41
1941—Theodore S. Williams, Boston 37
1942—Theodore S. Williams, Boston 36
1943—Rudolph P. York, Detroit 34
1944—Nicholas R.T. Etten, New York 22
1945—Vernon D. Stephens, St. Louis 24
1946—Henry B. Greenberg, Detroit 44
1947—Theodore S. Williams, Boston 32
1948—Joseph P. DiMaggio, New York 39
1949—Theodore S. Williams, Boston 43
1950—Albert L. Rosen, Cleveland 37
1951—Gus E. Zernial, Philadelphia 33
1952—Lawrence E. Doby, Cleveland 32
1953—Albert L. Rosen, Cleveland 43
1954—Lawrence E. Doby, Cleveland 32
1955—Mickey Mantle, New York 37
1956—Mickey Mantle, New York 52
1957—Roy Sievers, Washington 42
1958—Mickey Mantle, New York 42
1959—Rocky Colavito, Cleveland 42
   —Harmon Killebrew, Washington 42
1960—Mickey Mantle, New York 40
1961—Roger Maris, New York 61
1962—Harmon Killebrew, Minnesota 48
1963—Harmon Killebrew, Minnesota 45
1964—Harmon Killebrew, Minnesota 49
1965—Anthony Conigliaro, Boston 32
1966—Frank Robinson, Baltimore 49
1967—Harmon Killebrew, Minnesota 44
   —Carl Yastrzemski, Boston 44
1968—Frank Howard, Washington 44
1969—Harmon Killebrew, Minnesota 49
1970—Frank Howard, Washington 44
1971—William E. Melton, Chicago 33
1972—Richard Allen, Chicago 37

TY COBB AND BABE RUTH—
A COMPARISON

When it comes to the selection of baseball's greatest players, the names of Ty Cobb and Babe Ruth usually land on top, not necessarily in that order.

Cobb, on offense, depended on speed and strategy. Ruth relied on power. Both were extremely successful. Cobb was an outfielder. Ruth was a star pitcher before he was converted into an outfielder and became the greatest slugger the game has known.

As a World Series pitcher for the Boston Americans, Ruth was unbeaten. He won 3 games in 3 starts (1 in 1916 and 2 in 1918). On Oct. 9, 1916, he defeated Brooklyn, 2–1, in a 14-inning game, the longest in the history of the classic. He pitched 13 scoreless innings that day and in 1918 he hurled 16 runless frames to establish a series record of 29 consecutive scoreless innings.

Cobb, born in 1886, became a big leaguer in 1905. He played in 41 games that year and had a batting average of .240. That was the first and only time he dipped under the .300 mark in his 24-year career with Detroit and Philadelphia of the American League. Cobb, who managed Detroit from 1920 through 1926, left the game in 1928 after two seasons with Philadelphia.

Ruth, born in 1895, became a pitcher for the Boston Americans in 1914 and remained with that club until the end of 1919, when he was sold to the New York Yankees. It was while he was with the Yankees (1920–34) that he set slugging records that may never be equaled. Ruth died on Aug. 16, 1948.

Comparative Records

TY COBB

Yrs.	Games	At Bat	Runs	Hits	2B	3B	HR	Total Bases	SB	Bat. Avg.
24	3,033	11,429	2,244	4,191	724	297	118	5,863	892	.367

BABE RUTH

Yrs.	Games	At Bat	Runs	Hits	2B	3B	HR	Total Bases	SB	Bat. Avg.
22	2,502	8,389	2,174	2,873	506	136	714	5,793	123	.342

Cobb's Career Records

Most years played as regular	23
Most games	3,033
Most times at bat	11,429
Most runs	2,244
Most hits	4,191
Most total bases	5,863
Most stolen bases	96
Highest lifetime batting average	.367
Most years batting champion	12
Most successive years batting champion	9
Highest American League batting average (tied with George Sisler)	.420
Most times batting over .400 (tie)	3
Most years hit over .300	23
Most years more than 200 hits	9
Most years base-hit leader	8
Most years 5 hits in 1 game	14
Most years leading in singles	6
Most singles	3,052
Most triples	297
Most total bases, 1 game	*16

*On May 5, 1925, Cobb made 6 hits, including 3 homers and a double, in 6 trips to the plate.

Ruth's Regular-Season Records

Most homers	714
Most homers, season (151 games in 1927)	60
Most years leading league in homers	12
Most years 50 or more homers	4
Most years 40 or more homers	11
Most years 30 or more homers	13
Most homers, bases filled	15
Most times hitting 2 homers, 1 game	72
Most homers, Consecutive games (July 11, 12 (2), 13, 14, 15, 16, 1924)	7
Most runs, season	177
Most long hits, season	119
Most bases on balls	2,056
Most bases on balls, season	170
Most strikeouts	1,330

Ruth's Lifetime Home-Run Record

Regular Season

1914—Boston (A)	0
1915—Boston (A)	4
1916—Boston (A)	3
1917—Boston (A)	2
1918—Boston (A)	11
1919—Boston (A)	29
1920—New York (A)	54
1921—New York (A)	59
1922—New York (A)	35
1923—New York (A)	41
1924—New York (A)	46
1925—New York (A)	25
1926—New York (A)	47
1927—New York (A)	60
1928—New York (A)	54
1929—New York (A)	46
1930—New York (A)	49
1931—New York (A)	46
1932—New York (A)	41
1933—New York (A)	34
1934—New York (A)	22
1935—Boston (N)	6
Total	714

World Series

1915—Boston (A)	0
1916—Boston (A)	0
1918—Boston (A)	0
1921—New York (A)	1
1922—New York (A)	0
1923—New York (A)	3
1926—New York (A)	4
1927—New York (A)	2
1928—New York (A)	3
1932—New York (A)	2
Total	15

All-Star Game

1933—American League	1
1934—American League	0
Total	1
Grand total	730

Ruth's Earnings

1914—Baltimore (IL)	$	600
1914—Providence (IL), Boston (AL)		1,300
1915—Boston (AL)		3,500
1916—Boston (AL)		3,500
1917—Boston (AL)		5,000
1918—Boston (AL)		7,000
1919—Boston (AL)		10,000
1920—New York (AL)		20,000
1921—New York (AL)		30,000
1922—New York (AL)		52,000
1923—New York (AL)		52,000
1924—New York (AL)		52,000
1925—New York (AL)		52,000
1926—New York (AL)		52,000
1927—New York (AL)		70,000
1928—New York (AL)		70,000
1929—New York (AL)		70,000
1930—New York (AL)		80,000
1931—New York (AL)		80,000
1932—New York (AL)		75,000
1933—New York (AL)		52,000
1934—New York (AL)		35,000
1935—Boston (NL)		8,000
1938—Brooklyn (coach)		15,000
Exhibitions		150,000
Total		$1,045,900
10 World Series		42,477
"Series place" money		3,100
Total		$1,091,477

Record of Ruth's 60 Home Runs in 1927

(R)—Right-handed pitcher. (L)—Left-handed pitcher.

No.	Game	Date	Opposing pitcher and club	Where made
1.	4	April 15	Howard Ehmke (R), Philadelphia	Yankee Stadium, New York
2.	11	April 23	Rube Walberg (L), Philadelphia	Shibe Park, Philadelphia
3.	12	April 24	Hollis Thurston (R), Washington	Griffith Stadium, Washington
4.	14	April 29	Slim Harriss (R), Boston	Fenway Park, Boston
5.	16	May 1	Jack Quinn (R), Philadelphia	Yankee Stadium, New York
6.	16	May 1	Rube Walberg (L), Philadelphia	Yankee Stadium, New York
7.	24	May 10	Milton Gaston (R), St. Louis	Sportsman's Park, St. Louis
8.	25	May 11	Ernie Nevers (R), St. Louis	Sportsman's Park, St. Louis
9.	29	May 17	Rip Collins (R), Detroit	Navin Field, Detroit
10.	33	May 22	Benny Karr (R), Cleveland	League Park, Cleveland
11.	34	May 23	Hollis Thurston (R), Washington	Griffith Stadium, Washington
12.	37	May 28	Hollis Thurston (R), Washington	Yankee Stadium, New York
13.	39	May 29	Danny MacFayden (R), Boston	Yankee Stadium, New York
14.	41	May 30	Rube Walberg (L), Philadelphia	Shibe Park, Philadelphia
15.	42	May 31	Jack Quinn (R), Philadelphia	Shibe Park, Philadelphia
16.	43	May 31	Howard Ehmke (R), Philadelphia	Shibe Park, Philadelphia
17.	47	June 5	Earl Whitehill (L), Detroit	Yankee Stadium, New York
18.	48	June 7	Tommy Thomas (R), Chicago	Yankee Stadium, New York
19.	52	June 11	Garland Buckeye (L), Cleveland	Yankee Stadium, New York
20.	52	June 11	Garland Buckeye (L), Cleveland	Yankee Stadium, New York
21.	53	June 12	George Uhle (R), Cleveland	Yankee Stadium, New York
22.	55	June 16	Tom Zachary (L), St. Louis	Yankee Stadium, New York
23.	60	June 22	Harold Wiltse (L), Boston	Fenway Park, Boston
24.	60	June 22	Harold Wiltse (L), Boston	Fenway Park, Boston
25.	70	June 30	Slim Harriss (R), Boston	Yankee Stadium, New York
26.	73	July 3	Horace Lisenbee (R), Washington	Griffith Stadium, Washington
27.	78	July 8	Earl Whitehill (L), Detroit	Navin Field, Detroit
28.	79	July 9	Ken Holloway (R), Detroit	Navin Field, Detroit
29.	79	July 9	Ken Holloway (R), Detroit	Navin Field, Detroit
30.	83	July 12	Joe Shaute (L), Cleveland	League Park, Cleveland
31.	94	July 24	Tommy Thomas (R), Chicago	Comiskey Park, Chicago
32.	95	July 26	Milton Gaston (R), St. Louis	Yankee Stadium, New York
33.	95	July 26	Milton Gaston (R), St. Louis	Yankee Stadium, New York
34.	98	July 28	Walter Stewart (L), St. Louis	Yankee Stadium, New York
35.	106	Aug. 5	George Smith (R), Detroit	Yankee Stadium, New York

No.	Game	Date	Opposing pitcher and club	Where made
36.	110	Aug. 10	Tom Zachary (L), Washington	Griffith Stadium, Washington
37.	114	Aug. 16	Tommy Thomas (R), Chicago	Comiskey Park, Chicago
38.	115	Aug. 17	Sarge Connally (R), Chicago	Comiskey Park, Chicago
39.	118	Aug. 20	Walter Miller (L), Cleveland	League Park, Cleveland
40.	120	Aug. 22	Joe Shaute (L), Cleveland	League Park, Cleveland
41.	124	Aug. 27	Ernie Nevers (R), St. Louis	Sportsman's Park, St. Louis
42.	125	Aug. 28	Ernie Wingard (L), St. Louis	Sportsman's Park, St. Louis
43.	127	Aug. 31	Anton Welzer (R), Boston	Yankee Stadium, New York
44.	128	Sept. 2	Rube Walberg (L), Philadelphia	Shibe Park, Philadelphia
45.	132	Sept. 6	Anton Welzer (R), Boston	Fenway Park, Boston
46.	132	Sept. 6	Anton Welzer (R), Boston	Fenway Park, Boston
47.	133	Sept. 6	Jack Russell (R), Boston	Fenway Park, Boston
48.	134	Sept. 7	Danny MacFayden (R), Boston	Fenway Park, Boston
49.	134	Sept. 7	Slim Harriss (R), Boston	Fenway Park, Boston
50.	138	Sept. 11	Milton Gaston (R), St. Louis	Yankee Stadium, New York
51.	139	Sept. 13	Willis Hudlin (R), Cleveland	Yankee Stadium, New York
52.	140	Sept. 13	Joe Shaute (L), Cleveland	Yankee Stadium, New York
53.	143	Sept. 16	Ted Blankenship (R), Chicago	Yankee Stadium, New York
54.	147	Sept. 18	Ted Lyons (R), Chicago	Yankee Stadium, New York
55.	148	Sept. 21	Sam Gibson (R), Detroit	Yankee Stadium, New York
56.	149	Sept. 22	Ken Holloway (R), Detroit	Yankee Stadium, New York
57.	152	Sept. 27	Lefty Grove (L), Philadelphia	Yankee Stadium, New York
58.	153	Sept. 29	Horace Lisenbee (R), Washington	Yankee Stadium, New York
59.	153	Sept. 29	Paul Hopkins (R), Washington	Yankee Stadium, New York
60.	154	Sept. 30	Tom Zachary (L), Washington	Yankee Stadium, New York

BASE STEALING CHAMPIONS

National League

1886—George Andrews, Philadelphia	56
1887—John M. Ward, New York	111
1888—William Hoy, Washington	82
1889—James Fogarty, Philadelphia	99
1890—Billy Hamilton, Philadelphia	102
1891—Billy Hamilton, Philadelphia	115
1892—John M. Ward, Brooklyn	94
1893—John M. Ward, New York	72
1894—Billy Hamilton, Philadelphia	99
1895—Billy Hamilton, Philadelphia	95
1896—Bill Lange, Chicago	100
1897—Bill Lange, Chicago	83
1898—Fred Clarke, Louisville	66
1899—Jimmy Sheckard, Baltimore	76
1900—James Barrett, Cincinnati	46
1901—Honus Wagner, Pittsburgh	48
1902—Honus Wagner, Pittsburgh	43
1903—Frank Chance, Chicago	67
—Jimmy Sheckard, Brooklyn	67
1904—Honus Wagner, Pittsburgh	53
1905—Arthur Devlin, New York	59
—Bill Maloney, Chicago	59
1906—Frank Chance, Chicago	57
1907—Honus Wagner, Pittsburgh	61
1908—Honus Wagner, Pittsburgh	53
1909—Bob Bescher, Cincinnati	54
1910—Bob Bescher, Cincinnati	70
1911—Bob Bescher, Cincinnati	80
1912—Bob Bescher, Cincinnati	67
1913—Max Carey, Pittsburgh	61
1914—George Burns, New York	62
1915—Max Carey, Pittsburgh	36
1916—Max Carey, Pittsburgh	63
1917—Max Carey, Pittsburgh	46
1918—Max Carey, Pittsburgh	58
1919—George Burns, New York	40
1920—Max Carey, Pittsburgh	52
1921—Frank Frisch, New York	49
1922—Max Carey, Pittsburgh	51
1923—Max Carey, Pittsburgh	51
1924—Max Carey, Pittsburgh	49
1925—Max Carey, Pittsburgh	46
1926—Kiki Cuyler, Pittsburgh	35
1927—Frank Frisch, St. Louis	48
1928—Kiki Cuyler, Chicago	37
1929—Kiki Cuyler, Chicago	43
1930—Kiki Cuyler, Chicago	37
1931—Frank Frisch, St. Louis	28
1932—Chuck Klein, Philadelphia	20
1933—Pepper Martin, St. Louis	36
1934—Pepper Martin, St. Louis	33
1935—Augie Galan, Chicago	22
1936—Pepper Martin, St. Louis	23
1937—Augie Galan, Chicago	23
1938—Stan Hack, Chicago	16
1939—Lee Handley, Pittsburgh	17
—Stan Hack, Chicago	17
1940—Lonny Frey, Cincinnati	22
1941—Danny Murtaugh, Philadelphia	18
1942—Pete Reiser, Brooklyn	20
1943—Arky Vaughan, Brooklyn	20
1944—John Barrett, Pittsburgh	28
1945—Red Schoendienst, St. Louis	26

1946—Pete Reiser, Brooklyn 34
1947—Jackie Robinson, Brooklyn 29
1948—Richie Ashburn, Philadelphia 32
1949—Jackie Robinson, Brooklyn 37
1950—Sam Jethroe, Boston 35
1951—Sam Jethroe, Boston 35
1952—Peewee Reese, Brooklyn 30
1953—William Bruton, Milwaukee 26
1954—William Bruton, Milwaukee 34
1955—William Bruton, Milwaukee 25
1956—Willie Mays, New York 40
1957—Willie Mays, New York 38
1958—Willie Mays, San Francisco 31
1959—Willie Mays, San Francisco 27
1960—Maurice Wills, Los Angeles 50
1961—Maurice Wills, Los Angeles 35
1962—Maurice Wills, Los Angeles 104
1963—Maurice Wills, Los Angeles 40
1964—Maurice Wills, Los Angeles 53
1965—Maurice Wills, Los Angeles 94
1966—Louis Brock, St. Louis 74
1967—Louis Brock, St. Louis 52
1968—Louis Brock, St. Louis 62
1969—Louis Brock, St. Louis 53
1970—Robert Tolan, Cincinnati 57
1971—Louis Brock, St. Louis 64
1972—Louis Brock, St. Louis 63

American League

1901—Frank Isbell, Chicago 48
1902—Topsy Hartsel, Philadelphia 54
1903—Harry Bay, Cleveland 46
1904—Elmer Flick, Cleveland 42
1905—Danny Hoffman, Philadelphia 46
1906—Elmer Flick, Cleveland 39
    —John Anderson, Washington 39
1907—Ty Cobb, Detroit 49
1908—Pat Dougherty, Chicago 47
1909—Ty Cobb, Detroit 76
1910—Eddie Collins, Philadelphia 81
1911—Ty Cobb, Detroit 83
1912—Clyde Milan, Washington 88
1913—Clyde Milan, Washington 74
1914—Fritz Maisel, New York 74
1915—Ty Cobb, Detroit 96
1916—Ty Cobb, Detroit 68
1917—Ty Cobb, Detroit 55
1918—George Sisler, St. Louis 45
1919—Eddie Collins, Chicago 33
1920—Sam Rice, Washington 62
1921—George Sisler, St. Louis 35
1922—George Sisler, St. Louis 51
1923—Eddie Collins, Chicago 49
1924—Eddie Collins, Chicago 42
1925—Johnny Mostil, Chicago 43
1926—Johnny Mostil, Chicago 35
1927—George Sisler, St. Louis 27
1928—Buddy Myer, Boston 30
1929—Charles Gehringer, Detroit 27
1930—Marty McManus, Detroit 23
1931—Ben Chapman, New York 61

1932—Ben Chapman, New York 38
1933—Ben Chapman, New York 27
1934—Billy Werber, Boston 40
1935—Billy Werber, Boston 29
1936—Lyn Lary, St. Louis 37
1937—Ben Chapman, Wash.-Bos. 35
    —Billy Werber, Philadelphia 35
1938—Frank Crosetti, New York 27
1939—George Case, Washington 51
1940—George Case, Washington 35
1941—George Case, Washington 33
1942—George Case, Washington 44
1943—George Case, Washington 61
1944—George Stirnweiss, New York 55
1945—George Stirnweiss, New York 33
1946—George Case, Cleveland 28
1947—Bob Dillinger, St. Louis 34
1948—Bob Dillinger, St. Louis 28
1949—Bob Dillinger, St. Louis 20
1950—Dom DiMaggio, Boston 15
1951—Minnie Minoso, Chicago 31
1952—Minnie Minoso, Chicago 22
1953—Minnie Minoso, Chicago 25
1954—Jack Jensen, Boston 22
1955—Jim Rivera, Chicago 25
1956—Luis Aparicio, Chicago 21
1957—Luis Aparicio, Chicago 28
1958—Luis Aparicio, Chicago 29
1959—Luis Aparicio, Chicago 56
1960—Luis Aparicio, Chicago 51
1961—Luis Aparicio, Chicago 53
1962—Luis Aparicio, Chicago 31
1963—Luis Aparicio, Baltimore 40
1964—Luis Aparicio, Baltimore 57
1965—Dagoberto Campaneris, Kansas City 51
1966—Dagoberto Campaneris, Kansas City 52
1967—Dagoberto Campaneris, Kansas City 55
1968—Dagoberto Campaneris, Oakland .. 62
1969—Tommy Harper, Seattle 73
1970—Dagoberto Campaneris, Oakland .. 42
1971—Amos Otis, Kansas City 52
1972—Dagoberto Campaneris, Oakland .. 52

PITCHING CHAMPIONS

National League

1876—A.G. Spalding, Chi. 47   14   .770
1877—Thomas Bond, Bost.....31   17   .646
1878—Thomas Bond, Bost. 40   19   .678
1879—John M. Ward, Prov.....44   18   .710
1880—Fred Goldsmith, Chi. ...22   3   .880
1881—Larry Corcoran, Chi. ...31   14   .689
1882—Larry Corcoran, Chi. ...27   13   .675
1883—Jim McCormick, Cleve. ..27   13   .675
1884—Charles Radbourne, Prov. 60 12   .833
1885—John Clarkson, Chi......52   16   .765
1886—John Flynn, Chi. 24   6   .800
1887—Charles Getzein, Detroit .29 13   .690
1888—Tim Keefe, N.Y. 35   12   .745
1889—John Clarkson, Bost.....48   19   .716
1890—Tom Lovett, Bklyn. 32   11   .744
1891—John Ewing, N.Y. 22   8   .733

PITCHING CHAMPIONS

NATIONAL LEAGUE - Continued

	W.	L.	Pct.
1892—Cy Young, Cleve.	36	10	.783
1893—Henry Gastright, Bost.	15	5	.750
1894—Jouett Meekin, N.Y.	35	11	.761
1895—Willie Hoffer, Balt.	31	7	.816
1896—Willie Hoffer, Balt.	26	7	.788
1897—Amos Rusie, N.Y.	28	8	.778
1898—Ed Lewis, Bost.	25	8	.758
1899—Jay Hughes, Bklyn.	25	5	.833
1900—Joe McGinnity, Bklyn.	20	6	.769
1901—Sam Leever, Pitt.	19	5	.737
1902—Jack Chesbro, Pitt.	28	6	.824
1903—Sam Leever, Pitt.	25	7	.781
1904—Joe McGinnity, N.Y.	35	8	.814
1905—Sam Leever, Pitt.	20	5	.800
1906—Ed Ruelbach, Chi.	19	4	.826
1907—Ed Ruelbach, Chi.	17	4	.810
1908—Ed Reulbach, Chi.	24	7	.774
1909— S.H. Camnitz, Pitt.	25	6	.806
C. Mathewson, N.Y.	25	6	.806
1910—Deacon Phillippe, Pitt.	14	2	.875
1911—Rube Marquard, N.Y.	24	7	.744
1912—C.R. Hendrix, Pitt.	24	9	.774
1913—Grover Alexander, Phila.	22	8	.733
1914—Bill James, Bost.	26	7	.788
1915—Grover Alexander, Phila.	31	10	.756
1916—Grover Alexander, Phila.	33	12	.733
1917—Ferdie Schupp, N.Y.	21	7	.750
1918—C.R. Hendrix, Chi.	20	7	.741
1919—Dutch Ruether, Cinc.	19	6	.760
1920—Burleigh Grimes, Bklyn.	23	11	.676
1921—Art Nehf, N.Y.	20	10	.667
1922—Pete Donohue, Cinc.	18	9	.667
1923—Adolfo Luque, Cinc.	27	8	.771
1924—Arthur Vance, Bklyn.	28	6	.824
1925—Arthur Vance, Bklyn.	22	9	.710
1926—Ray Kremer, Pitt.	20	6	.769
1927—Jesse Haines, St. L.	24	10	.706
1928—Larry Benton, N.Y.	25	9	.735
1929—Charles Root, Chi.	19	6	.760
1930—Fred Fitzsimmons, N.Y.	19	7	.731
1931—Paul Derringer, St. L.	18	8	.692
1932—Lon Warneke, Chi.	22	6	.786
1933—Lyle Tinning, Chi.	13	6	.684
1934—Dizzy Dean, St. L.	30	7	.811
1935—Bill Lee, Chi.	20	6	.769
1936—Carl Hubbell, N.Y.	26	6	.813
1937—Carl Hubbell, N.Y.	22	8	.733
1938—Bill Lee, Chi.	22	9	.710
1939—Paul Derringer, Cinc.	25	7	.781
1940—Fred Fitzsimmons, Bklyn.	16	2	.889
1941—Elmer Riddle, Cinc.	19	4	.826
1942—John Beazley, St. L.	21	6	.778
1943—Mort Cooper, St. L.	21	8	.724
1944—Ted Wilks, St. L.	17	4	.810
1945—Harry Brecheen, St. L.	15	4	.789
1946—Howie Pollet, St. L.	21	10	.677
1947—Larry Jansen, N.Y.	21	5	.808
1948—Harry Brecheen, St. L.	20	7	.741
1949—Preacher Roe, Bklyn.	15	6	.714
1950—Sal Maglie, N.Y.	18	4	.818
1951—Preacher Roe, Bklyn.	22	3	.880
1952—Hoyt Wilhelm, N.Y.	15	3	.833
1953—Carl Erskine, Brooklyn	20	6	.769
1954—John Antonelli, New York	21	7	.750
1955—Don Newcombe, Brooklyn	20	5	.800
1956—Don Newcombe, Brooklyn	27	7	.794
1957—Robert Buhl, Milwaukee	18	7	.720
1958—Warren Spahn, Milwaukee	22	11	.667
—Lew Burdette, Milwaukee	20	10	.667
1959—Elroy Face, Pitt.	18	1	.947
1960—Ernest Broglio, St. L.	21	9	.700
1961—John Podres, L.A.	18	5	.783
1962—Robert Purkey, Cinc.	23	5	.821
1963—Ronald Perranoski, L.A.	16	3	.842
1964—Sanford Koufax, L.A.	19	5	.792
1965—Sanford Koufax, L.A.	26	8	.765
1966—Juan Marichal, S.F.	25	6	.806
1967—Richard Hughes, St. L.	16	6	.727
1968—Stephen R. Blass, Pitts.	18	6	.750
1969—G. Thomas Seaver, N.Y.	25	7	.781
1970—Robert Gibson, St. Louis	23	7	.767
1971—Donald E. Gullett, Cinc.	16	6	.727
1972—Gary L. Nolan, Cincinnati	15	5	.750

American League

	W.	L.	Pct.
1901—Clark Griffith, Chi.	24	7	.774
1902—Rube Waddell, Phila.	23	7	.767
1903—Earl L. Moore, Cleve.	22	7	.759
1904—Jack Chesbro, N.Y.	41	13	.759
1905—Rube Waddell, Phila.	27	10	.730
1906—Eddie Plank, Phila.	19	6	.760
1907—Bill Donovan, Det.	25	4	.862
1908—Ed Walsh, Chi.	40	15	.727
1909—George Mullin, Det.	29	8	.784
1910—Chief Bender, Phila.	23	5	.821
1911—S.A. Gregg, Cleve.	23	7	.767
1912—Joe Wood, Bost.	34	5	.872
1913—Walter Johnson, Wash.	36	7	.837
1914—Chief Bender, Phila.	17	3	.850
1915—E.G. Shore, Bost.	19	7	.731
1916—Harry Coveleskie, Det.	23	10	.697
1917—Carl Mays, Bost.	22	9	.710
1918—Walter Johnson, Wash.	23	13	.639
1919—Ed Cicotte, Chi.	29	7	.806
1920—Jim Bagby, Cleve.	31	12	.721
1921—Carl Mays, N.Y.	27	9	.750
1922—Joe Bush, N.Y.	26	7	.788
1923—Herb Pennock, N.Y.	19	6	.760
1924—Walter Johnson, Wash.	23	7	.767
1925—Stan Coveleskie, Wash.	20	5	.800
1926—George Uhle, Cleve.	27	11	.711
1927—Waite Hoyt, N.Y.	22	7	.759
1928—Alvin Crowder, St. L.	21	5	.808
1929— Lefty Grove, Phila.	20	6	.769
Tom Zachary, N.Y.	12	0	1.000
1930—Lefty Grove, Phila.	28	5	.848
1931—Lefty Grove, Phila.	31	4	.886
1932—John Allen, N.Y.	17	4	.810
1933—Lefty Grove, Phila.	24	8	.750

1934—Vernon Gomez, N.Y. ...26	5	.839	1954—Sandalio Consuegra, Chic. 16	3	.842
1935—Eldon Auker, Det......18	7	.720	1955—Thomas Byrne, New York 16	5	.762
1936—Monte Pearson, N.Y. 19	7	.731	1956—Whitey Ford, New York .19	6	.760
1937—John Allen, Cleve......15	1	.938	1957—Thomas Sturdivant, N.Y. ..16	6	.727
1938—Charles Ruffing, N.Y. ...21	7	.750	—Richard Donovan, Chic ..16	6	.727
1939—Lefty Grove, Bost. 15	4	.789	1958—Bob Turley, New York ..21	7	.750
1940—Lyn Rowe, Det. 16	3	.842	1959—Robert Shaw, Chicago...18	6	.750
1941—Vernon Gomez, N.Y. ...15	5	.870	1960—James Coates, New York .13	3	.813
1942—Ernie Bonham, N.Y. ...21	5	.808	1961—Whitey Ford, New York .25	4	.862
1943—Spud Chandler, N.Y....20	4	.833	1962—Ray Herbert, Chicago ...20	9	.690
1944—Cecil Hughson, Bost.....18	5	.783	1963—Whitey Ford, New York .24	7	.774
1945—Hal Newhouser, Det.....25	9	.735	1964—Wallace Bunker, Baltimore 19	5	.792
1946—Dave Ferriss, Bost. 25	6	.806	1965—James Grant, Minnesota .21	7	.750
1947—Allie Reynolds, N.Y.....19	8	.704	1966—Wilfred Siebert, Cleveland 16	8	.667
1948—Jack Kramer, Bost. 18	5	.783	1967—Joel E. Horlen, Chicago ..19	7	.731
1949—Ellis Kinder, Bost......23	6	.793	1968—Dennis McLain, Detroit ..31	6	.838
1950—Vic Raschi, N.Y. 21	8	.724	1969—James Palmer, Baltimore .16	4	.800
1951—Bob Feller, Cleve......22	8	.733	1970—Miguel Cuellar, Baltimore 24	8	.750
1952—Bob Shantz, Phila......24	7	.774	1971—David McNally, Baltimore 21	5	.808
1953—Ed Lopat, New York 16	4	.800	1972—James A. Hunter, Oakland 21	7	.750

EARNED RUN LEADERS

NATIONAL LEAGUE	Inn. pitched	E.R. avg.	AMERICAN LEAGUE	Inn. pitched	E.R. avg.
1912—C. Tesreau, N.Y............	243	1.96	Not tabulated		
1913—C. Mathewson, N.Y........	306	2.06	W.P. Johnson, Wash..............	346	1.09
1914—W.L. Doak, St. L.........	256	1.72	H.B. Leonard, Bos..............	222	1.01
1915—G.C. Alexander, Phila.	376	1.22	*W.P. Johnson, Wash..........	337	1.55
1916—*G.C. Alexander, Phila.	389	1.55	G.H. Ruth, Bos.	324	1.75
1917—G.C. Alexander, Phila.	388	1.85	E.V. Cicotte, Chi..............	346	1.53
1918—J.L. Vaughn, Chi.........	290	1.74	W.P. Johnson, Wash..........	325	1.28
1919—G.C. Alexander, Chi.	235	1.72	W.P. Johnson, Wash..........	290	1.49
1920—G.C. Alexander, Chi.	363	1.91	J.R. Shawkey, N.Y..........	267	2.46
1921—W.L. Doak, St. L.	209	2.58	U.C. Faber, Chi..............	331	2.48
1922—W.D. Ryan, N.Y.	192	3.00	U.C. Faber, Chi..............	353	2.81
1923—A. Luque, Cinc.	322	1.93	S. Coveleskie, Cleve.,.........	228	2.76
1924—A.C. Vance, Bklyn.	309	2.16	W.P. Johnson, Wash..........	278	2.72
1925—A. Luque, Cinc.........	291	2.63	S. Coveleskie, Wash..........	241	2.84
1926—Ray Kremer, Pitts.	231	2.61	R.M. Grove, Phila............	258	2.51
1927—Ray Kremer, Pitts.	226	2.47	W. Wilcy Moore, N.Y.........	213	2.28
1928—A.C. Vance, Bklyn.	280	2.09	E.G. Braxton, Wash..........	218	2.52
1929—Wm. Walker, N.Y.	178	3.08	*R.M. Grove, Phila...........	275	2.82
1930—A.C. Vance, Bklyn.	259	2.61	R.M. Grove, Phila............	291	3.00
1931—Wm. Walker, N.Y.	239	2.26	R.M. Grove, Phila............	289	2.05
1932—L. Warneke, Chi.	277	2.37	R.M. Grove, Phila............	292	2.84
1933—C.O. Hubbell, N.Y.........	309	1.66	*M.L. Harder, Cleve...........	253	2.95
1934—C.O. Hubbell, N.Y.........	313	2.30	V. Gomez, N.Y.	282	2.33
1935—D.E. Blanton, Pitts.	254	2.59	R.M. Grove, Bos.............	273	2.70
1936—C.O. Hubbell, N.Y.........	303	2.31	R.M. Grove, Bos.............	253	2.81
1937—J.R. Turner, Bos.	257	2.38	V. Gomez, N.Y.	278	2.33
1938—W.C. Lee, Chi.	291	2.66	R.M. Grove, Bos.............	164	3.07
1939—W.H. Walters, Cinc.	319	2.29	R.M. Grove, Bos.............	191	2.54
1940—W.H. Walters, Cinc.	305	2.48	R.W. Feller, Cleve............	320	2.62
1941—E.R. Riddle, Cinc.	217	2.24	T.S. Lee, Chi.	300	2.37
1942—M.C. Cooper, St. L.	279	1.77	T.A. Lyons, Chi.	180	2.10
1943—H.J. Pollet, St. L.	118	1.75	S.F. Chandler, N.Y............	253	1.64
1944—E.B. Heusser, Cinc.	193	2.38	P.H. Trout, Det.	352	2.12
1945—H.L. Borowy, Chi.	122	2.14	H. Newhouser, Det.	313	1.81
1946—H.J. Pollet, St. L.	266	2.10	H. Newhouser, Det.	293	1.94
1947—W.E. Spahn, Bos.	290	2.33	S.F. Chandler, N.Y.	128	2.46

EARNED RUN LEADERS — Continued

NATIONAL LEAGUE	Inn. pitched	E.R. avg.	AMERICAN LEAGUE	Inn. pitched	E.R. avg.
1948—H.D. Brecheen, St. L.	233	2.24	H.E. Bearden, Cleve.	230	2.43
1949—G.B. Koslo, N.Y.	212	2.50	M.L. Parnell, Bos.	295	2.78
1950—J.T. Hearn, St. L.-N.Y.	134	2.49	E. Wynn, Cleve.	214	3.20
1951—C. Nichols, Bos.	156	2.88	S. Rogovin, Det.-Chi.	217	2.78
1952—J.H. Wilhelm, N.Y.	159	2.43	A.P. Reynolds, N.Y.	244	2.07
1953—W.E. Spahn, Milw.	266	2.10	E.W. Lopat, N.Y.	178	2.43
1954—J.A. Antonelli, N.Y.	259	2.29	E.M. Garcia, Cleve.	259	2.64
1955—R.B. Friend, Pitts.	200	2.84	W.W. Pierce, Chi.	206	1.57
1956—L. Burdette, Milw.	256	2.71	E. Ford, N.Y.	226	2.47
1957—J. Podres, Bklyn.	196	2.66	R. Shantz, N.Y.	173	2.45
1958—S. Miller, San Francisco	182	2.47	E. Ford, N.Y.	219	2.01
1959—S. Jones, San Francisco	271	2.82	H. Wilhelm, Baltimore	226	2.19
1960—M. McCormick, San Francisco	253	2.70	Frank Bauman, Chi.	185	2.68
1961—W.E. Spahn, Milw.	263	3.01	R. Donovan, Wash.	169	2.40
1962—S. Koufax, Los Angeles	184	2.54	H. Aguirre, Det.	216	2.21
1963—S. Koufax, Los Angeles	311	1.88	G. Peters, Chi.	243	2.33
1964—S. Koufax, Los Angeles	223	1.74	D. Chance, L.A.	278	1.65
1965—S. Koufax, Los Angeles	336	2.04	S. McDowell, Cleve.	273	2.18
1966—S. Koufax, Los Angeles	323	1.73	G. Peters, Chi.	205	1.98
1967—P. Niekro, Atlanta	207	1.87	J. Horlen, Chi.	258	2.06
1968—R. Gibson, St. Louis	305	1.12	L. Tiant, Cleve.	258	1.60
1969—J. Marichal, S.F.	300	2.10	R. Bosman, Wash.	193	2.19
1970—T. Seaver, New York	291	2.81	D. Segui, Oakland	162	2.56
1971—T. Seaver, New York	286	1.76	V. Blue, Oakland	312	1.82
1972—S. Carlton, Phil.	346	1.98	L. Tiant, Boston	179	1.91

*The nominal leaders were: 1915—J. Wood, Boston AL, 157 inn., 1.49 average; 1916—F. Schupp, New York NL, 140 inn., 0.90; 1929—J.T. Zachary, New York AL, 120 inn., 247; 1933—M.M. Pearson, Cleveland AL, 135 inn., 2.33.

WINNERS OF 300 OR MORE GAMES

	Years	Games	W	L	Pct.
Denton (Cy) Young	22	874	511	315	.619
Grover Alexander	20	696	373	208	.642
*John W. Clarkson	11	509	328	176	.651
*James F. Galvin	14	663	355	308	.535
Robert M. Grove	17	616	300	141	.680
Walter P. Johnson	21	802	414	276	.600
*Tim Keefe	14	587	345	228	.602
Christy Mathewson	17	634	373	189	.664
Charles Nichols	15	586	360	202	.641
Edward Plank	17	620	324	190	.630
*Charles Radbourne	11	517	310	191	.619
Warren Spahn	21	750	363	245	.597
*Mickey Welch	13	540	316	214	.596
Early Wynn	23	691	300	244	.551

*Pitched in era when distance to plate was 50 feet. Distance changed to 60½ feet in 1893. Nichols' career began 1890, ended 1906. Young's career began in 1890, ended 1911.

NO-HIT GAMES SINCE 1900

(9 innings or more.)

The dream of every pitcher is to hurl a game in which he holds the opposition to no hits and no runs and does not permit a man to reach first base—in short, a perfect game.

Only five major leaguers since the turn of the century have pitched perfect games. Denton (Cy) Young, then with the Boston Americans, became the first of the quintet when he performed the feat against Philadelphia on May 5, 1904.

The others in the select group are Addie Joss, Cleveland Americans, who turned back Chicago, Oct. 2, 1908; Ernie Shore, Boston Americans, who beat Washington, June 23, 1917; Charley Robertson, Chicago Americans, who blanked Detroit, April 30, 1922, and Don Larsen of the New York Americans, who beat the Brooklyn Nationals in the fifth game of the world series on Oct. 8, 1956. It was the first world series no-hitter.

In Shore's game, Babe Ruth was the starting pitcher. After passing Morgan, the first batter, Ruth was replaced by Shore. Morgan, attempting to steal, was put out. No one else reached first base.

The list of no-hitters since 1901:

1901—Christopher Mathewson, New York, vs. St. Louis NL, July 15	5—0
Earl L. Moore, Cleveland, vs. Chicago AL, May 9. Moore pitched 9 innings, Chicago not making a hit in that time, but Cleveland lost in the 10th	2—4
1902—James J. Callahan, Chicago, vs. Detroit AL, Sept. 20 (1st game)	3—0
1903—Charles Fraser, Philadelphia, vs. Chicago NL, Sept. 18	10—0
1904—Denton T. Young, Boston, vs. Philadelphia AL, May 5	3—0

Jesse N. Tannehill, Boston, vs. Chicago AL, August 17 6–0

Robert K. Wicker, Chicago, vs. New York NL, June 11, 12 innings; Mertes, NY, made a single in the 10th 1–0

1905—Christopher Mathewson, New York, vs. Chicago NL, June 13 1–0

Weldon Henley, Philadelphia, vs. St. Louis AL, July 22 (1st game) 6–0

William H. Dinneen, Boston, vs. Chicago AL, Sept. 27 (1st game) 2–0

Frank E. Smith, Chicago, vs. Detroit AL, Sept. 6 (2d game) 15–0

1906—John C. Lush, Philadelphia, vs. Brooklyn NL, May 1 1–0

Malcolm W. Eason, Brooklyn, vs. St. Louis NL, July 20 2–0

1907—Frank X. Pfeffer, Boston, vs. Cincinnati NL, May 8 6–0

Nicholas Maddox, Pittsburgh, vs. Brooklyn NL, Sept. 20 2–1

1908—Denton T. Young, Boston, vs. New York AL, June 30 8–0

George N. Rucker, Brooklyn, vs. Boston NL, Sept. 5 (2d game) 6–0

Robert S. Rhoades, Cleveland, vs. Boston AL, Sept. 18 2–0

Frank E. Smith, Chicago, vs. Philadelphia AL, Sept. 20 1–0

Adrian C. Joss, Cleveland, vs. Chicago AL, Oct. 2 1–0

1909—Leon K. Ames, New York, vs. Brooklyn NL, April 15. Ames pitched 9 innings, Brooklyn not making a hit in that time, but New York lost in the 13th 0–3

1910—Adrian C. Joss, Cleveland, vs. Chicago AL, April 20 1–0

Charles A. Bender, Philadelphia, vs. Cleveland AL, May 12 4–0

Thomas J. Hughes, New York, vs. Cleveland AL, Aug. 30. Hughes pitched 9 innings, Cleveland not making a hit in that time. Cleveland made its first hit in the 10th and won in the 11th 0–5

1911—Joseph Wood, Boston, vs. St. Louis AL, July 29, (1st game) 5–0

Edward A. Walsh, Chicago, vs. Boston AL, Aug. 27 5–0

1912—George E. Mullin, Detroit, vs. St. Louis AL, July 4 (P.M.) 7–0

Earl Hamilton, St. Louis, vs. Detroit AL, Aug. 30 5–1

Charles M. Tesreau, New York, vs. Philadelphia NL, Sept. 6 (1st game) 3–0

1914—James Scott, Chicago, vs. Washington AL, May 14. Washington scored in the 10th . . . 0–1

Joseph D. Benz, Chicago, vs. Cleveland AL, May 31 6–1

George A. Davis, Boston, vs. Philadelphia NL, Sept. 9 (2d game) 7–0

Edward F. LaFitte, Brooklyn, vs. Kansas City FL, Sept. 19 (1st game) 6–2

1915—Richard W. Marquard, New York, vs. Brooklyn NL, April 15 2–0

James S. Lavender, Chicago, vs. New York NL, Aug. 31 (1st game) 2–0

Claude R. Hendrix, Chicago, vs. Pittsburgh FL, May 15 10–0

Frank L. Allen, Pittsburgh, vs. St. Louis FL, April 24 2–0

Miles G. Main, Kansas City, vs. Buffalo FL, August 16 5–0

Arthur D. Davenport, St. Louis, vs. Chicago FL, Sept. 7 (1st game) 3–0

1916—Thomas J. Hughes, Boston, vs. Pittsburgh NL, June 16 2–0

George Foster, Boston, vs. New York AL, June 21 2–0

Joseph L. Bush, Philadelphia, vs. Cleveland AL, August 26 5–0

Hubert B. Leonard, Boston, vs. St. Louis AL, August 30 4–0

1917—Edward V. Cicotte, Chicago, vs. St. Louis AL, April 14 11–0

George Mogridge, New York, vs. Boston AL, April 24 2–1

James L. Vaughn, Chicago, vs. Cincinnati NL, May 2. (Toney, Cincinnati, pitched 10 no-hit innings in the same game) 0–1

Ernest Koob, St. Louis, vs. Chicago AL, May 5 1–0

Robert Groom, St. Louis, vs. Chicago AL, May 6 (2d game) 3–0

Ernest Shore, Boston, vs. Washington AL, June 23 (1st game) 4–0

1918—Hubert B. Leonard, Boston, vs. Detroit AL, June 3 5–0

1919—Horace O. Eller, Cincinnati, vs. St. Louis NL, May 11 6–0

Raymond Caldwell, Cleveland, vs. New York AL, Sept. 10 (1st game) 3–0

1920—Walter P. Johnson, Washington, vs. Boston AL, July 1 1–0

1922—Charles C. Robertson, Chicago, vs. Detroit AL, April 30 2–0

Jesse Barnes, New York, vs. Philadelphia NL, May 7 6–0

1923—Samuel Jones, New York, vs. Philadelphia AL, Sept. 4 2–0

Howard Ehmke, Boston, vs. Philadelphia AL, Sept. 7 4–0

1924—Jesse J. Haines, St. Louis, vs. Boston NL, July 17 5–0

1925—Arthur C. Vance, Brooklyn, vs. Philadelphia NL, Sept. 13 (1st game) . . . 10–1

1926—Theodore A. Lyons, Chicago, vs. Boston AL, Aug. 21 6–0

1929—Carl O. Hubbell, New York, vs. Pittsburgh NL, May 8 11–0

1931—Wesley C. Ferrell, Cleveland, vs. St. Louis AL, April 29 9–0

Robert J. Burke, Washington, vs. Boston AL, August 8 5–0

1934—Louis N. Newsom, St. Louis, vs. Boston AL, Sept. 18 (pitched 9 hitless innings, allowed 1 hit in 10th). 1–2

Paul Dean, St. Louis, vs. Brooklyn NL, Sept. 21 (2d game) 3–0

1935—Vernon Kennedy, Chicago, vs. Cleveland AL, Aug. 31 5–0

1937—William Dietrich, Chicago, vs. St. Louis AL, June 1 8–0

1938—John Vander Meer, Cincinnati, vs. Boston NL, June 11 3–0

John Vander Meer, Cincinnati, vs. Brooklyn NL, June 15 (night) 6–0

M. Monte Pearson, New York, vs. Cleveland AL, Aug. 27 (2d game) 13–0

1940—Robert W. Feller, Cleveland, vs. Chicago AL, April 16 (opening day) 1–0

James O. Carleton, Brooklyn, vs. Cincinnati NL, April 30 3–0

1941—Lonnie Warneke, St. Louis, vs. Cincinnati NL, Aug. 30 2–0

1944—James A. Tobin, Boston, vs. Brooklyn NL, April 27 2–0

Clyde M. Shoun, Cincinnati, vs. Boston NL, May 15 1–0

1945—Richard J. Fowler, Philadelphia, vs. St. Louis AL, Sept. 9 (2d game) 1–0

1946—Edward M. Head, Brooklyn, vs. Boston NL, April 23 5–0

Robert W.A. Feller, Cleveland, vs. New York AL, April 30 1–0

1947—Ewell Blackwell, Cincinnati, vs. Boston NL, June 18 (night) 6–0
Donald P. Black, Cleveland, vs. Philadelphia AL, July 10 (1st game) 3–0
William McCahan, Philadelphia, vs. Washington AL, Sept. 3 3–0

1948—Robert G. Lemon, Cleveland, vs. Detroit AL, June 30 (night) 2–0
Rex E. Barney, Brooklyn, vs. New York NL, Sept. 9 (night) 2–0

1950—Vernon E. Bickford, Boston, vs. Brooklyn NL, Aug. 11 (night) 7–0

1951—Clifford D. Chambers, Pittsburgh, vs. Boston NL, May 6 (2d game) 3–0
Robert W. Feller, Cleveland, vs. Detroit AL, July 1 (1st game) 2–1
Allie P. Reynolds, New York, vs. Cleveland AL, July 12 (night) 1–0
Allie P. Reynolds, New York, vs. Boston AL, Sept. 28 (1st game) 8–0

1952—Carl D. Erskine, Brooklyn, vs. Chicago NL, June 19 5–0
Virgil O. Trucks, Detroit, vs. Washington AL, May 15 1–0
Virgil O. Trucks, Detroit, vs. New York AL, Aug. 25 1–0

1953—Alva L. Holloman, St. Louis, vs. Philadelphia AL, May 6 (night) 6–0

1954—James A. Wilson, Milwaukee, vs. Philadelphia NL, June 12 2–0

1955—Samuel Jones, Chicago, vs. Pittsburgh NL, May 12 4–0

1956—Carl Erskine, Brooklyn, vs. New York NL, May 12 3–0
Mel Parnell, Boston, vs. Chicago AL, July 14 4–0
Sal Maglie, Brooklyn, vs. Philadelphia NL, Sept. 25 (night) 5–0
Don Larsen, New York AL, vs. Brooklyn NL, Oct. 8 (world series) 2–0

1957—Bob Keegan, Chicago, vs. Washington AL, Aug. 20 6–0

1958—Jim Bunning, Detroit, vs. Boston AL, July 20 3–0
Hoyt Wilhelm, Baltimore, vs. New York AL, Sept. 20 1–0

1959—Harvey Haddix, Pittsburgh, vs. Milwaukee NL, May 26 (night) 0–1*

1960—Donald Cardwell, Chicago, vs. St. Louis, NL, May 15 4–0
S. Lewis Burdette, Milwaukee vs. Phila., NL, Aug. 18 (night) 1–0
Warren Spahn, Milwaukee vs. Phila., Sept. 16 (night) 4–0

1961—Warren Spahn, Milwaukee vs. San Francisco, April 28 (night) 1–0

1962—Bo Belinsky, Los Angeles AL vs. Baltimore, May 5 2–0
Earl Wilson, Boston, vs. Los Angeles, June 26 2–0
Bill Monbouquette, Boston vs. Chicago, Aug. 1 ... .s.... 1–0
Jack Kralick, Minnesota vs. Kansas City, Aug. 26 1–0
Sandy Koufax, Los Angeles NL vs. New York, June 30 5–0

1963—Sandy Koufax, Los Angeles NL vs. San Francisco, May 11 (night) 8–0
Don Nottebart, Houston NL vs. Philadelphia, May 17 (night) 4–1
Juan Marichal, San Francisco vs. Houston NL, June 15 1–0

1964—Ken Johnson, Houston vs. Cincinnati NL, April 23 0–1
Sandy Koufax, Los Angeles vs.

Philadelphia NL, June 4 3–0
Jim Bunning, Philadelphia vs. New York NL, June 21 6–0

1965—Jim Maloney, Cincinnati vs. New York NL, June 14 (night) 0–1
Jim Maloney, Cincinnati vs. Chicago NL, (1st game) August 19 1–0
Sandy Koufax, Los Angeles vs. Chicago NL, Sept. 9 1–0
Dave Morehead, Boston vs. Cleveland AL, Sept. 16 2–0

1966—Sonny Siebert, Cleveland vs. Washington AL, June 10 (night) 2–0

1967—S. Barber, Stu Miller, Baltimore vs. Detroit AL, April 30 .... 0–2**
Don Wilson, Houston vs. Atlanta NL, June 18 2–0
Dean Chance, Minnesota vs. Cleveland AL, Aug. 25 2–1
Joe Horlen, Chicago vs. Detroit AL, Sept. 10 4–0

1968—James Hunter, Oakland vs. Minnesota AL (night) May 8 4–0
George Culver, Cincinnati vs. Philadelphia NL (2nd game, night) July 29 6–1
Gaylord Perry, San Francisco vs. St. Louis NL (night) Sept. 17 1–0
Ray Washburn, St. Louis vs. San Francisco NL, Sept. 18 2–0

1969—William Stoneman, Montreal vs. Philadelphia NL (night) April 17 7–0
James Maloney, Cincinnati vs. Houston NL (night) April 30 10–0
Donald Wilson, Houston vs. Cincinnati NL (night) May 1 4–0
James Palmer, Baltimore vs. Oakland AL (night) Aug. 13 8–0
Kenneth Holtzman, Chicago vs. Atlanta NL, August 19 3–0
Robert Moose, Pittsburgh vs. New York NL, Sept. 20 4–0

1970—Dock Ellis, Pittsburgh vs. San Diego NL (1st game) June 12 2–0
Clyde Wright, California vs. Oakland AL, July 3 4–0
William Singer, Los Angeles vs. Philadelphia NL, July 20 5–0
Vida Blue, Oakland vs. Minnesota AL, Sept. 21 6–0

1971—Kenneth Holtzman, Chicago vs. Cincinnati NL (night) June 3 1–0
Richard Wise, Philadelphia vs. Cincinnati NL, June 23 4–0
Robert Gibson, St. Louis vs. Pittsburgh NL (night) Aug. 14 11–0

1972—Burt Hooten, Chicago vs. Philadelphia NL, April 16 4–0
Milt Pappas, Chicago vs. San Diego NL, Sept. 2 8–0
William Stoneman, Montreal vs. New York NL, October 2 7–0

*Haddix pitched perfect game for 12 innings, retiring 36 batters in row, the first pitcher to perform the feat, but lost the game in the 13th inning.

**Barber pitched 8 2/3 innings, Miller 1/3 of an inning.

PITCHING RECORDS

Most Games—906, Denton (Cy) Young, Cleveland (NL), 1890–98; St. Louis (NL), 1899–1900; Boston (AL), 1901–08; Cleveland (AL), 1909–11 (part); Boston (NL), 1911.

Most Games Won—511, Cy Young (291 in National League, 220 in American League).

Games Won, Season—60, Charles Radbourne, Providence (NL), 1884. *Modern record*—41, Jack Chesbro, New York (AL), 1904.

Most Consecutive Games Won, Season—19, Rube Marquard, New York (NL), 1912.

Most Games, Season—75 (tie), William White, Cincinnati (NL), 1879, and James McCormick, Cleveland (NL), 1880. *Modern record*—84, Ted Abernathy, Chicago (NL), 1965.

Most Innings, Season (since 1901)—464 (equals 51 full games and 5 innings), Ed Walsh, Chicago (AL), 1908.

Most Strikeouts—3,508, Walter Johnson, Washington (AL), 1907-27.

Most Strikeouts, Season—382, Sanford Koufax, Los Angeles (NL), 1965.

Most Strikeouts, 9-Inning Day Game—19, Tom Seaver, New York (NL), vs. San Diego, Apr. 22, 1970.

Most Strikeouts, 9-Inning Night Game—19, Steve Carlton, St. Louis (NL), vs. New York, Sept. 15, 1969

Most Strikeouts, Extra-Inning Game—21, Thomas Cheney, Washington (AL) vs. Baltimore, Sept. 12, 1962 (night), 16 innings.

Most Shut-Outs—113, Walter Johnson, Washington (AL), 1907—27.

Most Shut-Outs, Season—16, Grover Alexander, Philadelphia (NL), 1916.

Most Consecutive Shut-Out Innings—58, Don Drysdale, Los Angeles (NL), 1968.

Lowest Earned-Run Average, Season—0.90, Ferdie Schupp, New York (NL), 1916.

Fewest Hits in 2 Consecutive Games—0, Johnny Vander Meer, Cincinnati (NL), 1938 (both no-hitters).

MARQUARD'S WINNING STREAK

Rube Marquard of the New York Giants set a pitching record when he won 19 straight games in 1912. Under modern scoring rules the left-hander actually won 20 in succession.

Marquard's streak started on opening day, April 11, with an 18—3 victory over the Brooklyn Dodgers. He remained unbeaten until July 8, the Chicago Cubs ending the string with a 7—2 triumph.

The following was the situation in the disputed game in the Marquard skein:

Jeff Tesreau pitched 8 full innings against the Dodgers and the Giants held a 2—0 lead. In the ninth Tesreau filled the bases without retiring a man. Marquard replaced him. The 3 runners scored, putting the Dodgers ahead, 3—2. The Giants, behind by 1 run, won the game when Art Wilson hit a homer with one on.

Modern scoring would have given that victory to Marquard. However, the National League rules then required it be credited to Tesreau because "Tesreau had pitched more innings."

Marquard's streak, which consisted of 11 victories on alien soil and only 8 at New York, follows:

Date	Opponent	Score	Losing Pitcher
April 11	Brooklyn(a)	18—3	Rucker
April 16	Boston	8—2	Tyler
April 24	Philadelphia (b) ..	11—4	Alexander
May 1	Philadelphia	11—4	Seaton
May 7	St. Louis	6—2	Steele
May 11	Chicago	10—3	Richie
May 16	Pittsburgh	4—1	O'Toole
May 20	Cincinnati	3—0	Fromme
May 24	Brooklyn	6—3	Ragan
May 30	Philadelphia	7—1	Seaton
June 3	St. Louis	8—3	Sallee
June 8	Cincinnati	6—2	Benton
June 12	Chicago	3—2	Richie
June 17	Pittsburgh	*5—4	O'Toole
June 19	Boston	†6—5	Hess
June 21	Boston	5—2	Perdue
June 25	Philadelphia	2—1	Alexander
June 29	Boston	8—6	Brown
July 3	Brooklyn	2—1	Rucker

(a) Retired after 6 innings. (b) Retired after 7 innings. *11 innings. † 10 innings. May 11—Relieved by Drucke; June 12—removed for Shafer, a pinch-hitter; June 19—relieved by Ames, with score 5—5.

HUBBELL'S 24 STRAIGHT

Carl Hubbell of the New York Giants, also a southpaw pitcher, holds the modern consecutive unbeaten record for more than one season. He won 24 straight in 2 years, taking his last 16 games in 1936 and the first 8 in 1937.

KOUFAX' FOUR NO-HITTERS

Sandy Koufax, brilliant lefthander of the Los Angeles Nationals, set an all-time pitching record when he hurled his fourth no-hitter in 1965. The only pitchers in major league history with 3 no-hitters to their credit are Larry Corcoran of the Chicago Nationals (in 1880, 1882, 1884), Denton (Cy) Young of the Cleveland Nationals (1897) and the Boston Americans (1904, 1908), and Bob Feller of the Cleveland Americans (1940, 1946, 1951).

Statistics on Koufax follow:

No-Hit Games (4)

Date	Opponent	Score	SO	BB
June 30, 1962	..New York	5-0	13	5
May 11, 1963	...San Francisco ...	8-0	4	2
June 4, 1964	..Philadelphia	3-0	12	1
Sept. 9, 1965	..Chicago	1-0*	14	0

*Perfect game.

Single-Season Record

Statistics on Feller follow:

(Made in 1965)

Opponent	Games	Strikeouts
Houston	5	51
Cincinnati	5	48
New York	5	48
Pittsburgh	4	44
St. Louis	6	44
San Francisco	5	44
Chicago	5	38
Philadelphia	5	37
Milwaukee	3	28
Totals	43	382

FELLER'S PITCHING MASTERPIECES

Although Bob Feller's record of three no-hitters has been broken, his record of low-hit games hasn't. The Cleveland righthander threw a major league high of 12 one-hitters in addition to his three no-hitters. Koufax, by comparison, has only two one-hitters.

PENNANT WINNERS

Figures in parentheses after club names indicate in each instance the number of the pennant for that club. The same system is applied to the managers, some of whom won with different clubs.

No-Hit Games (3)

Date	Opponent	Score	SO	BB
April 16, 1940 .. Chicago	1–0	8	5
April 30, 1946 .. New York ...	1–0	11	5
July 1, 1951 ... Detroit	2–1	5	3

One-Hit Games (12)

Date	Opponent	Score	SO	BB
April 20, 1938 .. St. Louis	9–0	6	6
May 25, 1939 ... Boston	11–0	10	5
June 27, 1939 .. Detroit	5–0	13	6
July 12, 1940 ... Philadelphia .	1–0	13	2
Sept. 26, 1941 .. St. Louis	3–2	6	7
Sept. 19, 1945 .. Detroit	2–0	7	4
July 31, 1946 ... Boston	4–1	9	9
Aug. 8, 1946 .. Chicago	5–0	5	3
April 22, 1947 .. St. Louis	5–0	10	1
May 2, 1947 ... Boston	2–0	10	6
April 23, 1952 .. St. Louis	0–1	5	2
May 1, 1955 ... Boston	2–0	2	1

In 1969, with the expansion of teams, the American and National Leagues split their teams into Eastern and Western Divisions. A league playoff series determined who went to The World Series.

National League

Year	Club	Manager	Won	Lost	Pct.
1876—Chicago (1st)	Albert G. Spalding (1st)	52	14	.788
1877—Boston (1st)	Harry Wright (1st)	31	17	.646
1878—Boston (2d)	Harry Wright (2d)	41	19	.683
1879—Providence (1st)	George Wright (1st)	55	23	.705
1880—Chicago (2d)	Adrian C. Anson (1st)	67	17	.798
1881—Chicago (3d)	Adrian C. Anson (2d)	56	28	.667
1882—Chicago (4th)	Adrian C. Anson (3d)	55	29	.655
1883—Boston (3d)	John F. Morrill (1st)	63	35	.643
1884—Providence (2d)	Frank C. Bancroft (1st)	84	28	.750
1885—Chicago (5th)	Adrian C. Anson (4th)	87	25	.777
1886—Chicago (6th)	Adrian C. Anson (5th)	90	34	.726
1887—Detroit (1st)	William H. Watkins (1st)	79	45	.637
1888—New York (1st)	James Mutrie (1st)	84	47	.641
1889—New York (2d)	James Mutrie (2d)	83	43	.659
1890—Brooklyn (1st)	William McGunnigle (1st)	86	43	.667
1891—Boston (4th)	Frank Selee (1st)	87	51	.630
1892—Boston (5th)	Frank Selee (2d)	102	48	.680
1893—Boston (6th)	Frank Selee (3d)	86	44	.662
1894—Baltimore (1st)	Edward H. Hanlon (1st)	89	39	.695
1895—Baltimore (2d)	Edward H. Hanlon (2d)	87	43	.669
1896—Baltimore (3d)	Edward H. Hanlon (3d)	90	39	.698
1897—Boston (7th)	Frank Selee (4th)	93	39	.705
1898—Boston (8th)	Frank Selee (5th)	102	47	.685
1899—Brooklyn (2d)	Edward H. Hanlon (4th)	88	42	.677
1900—Brooklyn (3d)	Edward H. Hanlon (5th)	82	54	.603
1901—Pittsburgh (1st)	Frederick C. Clarke (1st)	90	49	.647
1902—Pittsburgh (2d)	Frederick C. Clarke (2d)	103	36	.741

National League — Continued

Year Club	Manager	Won	Lost	Pct.
1903—Pittsburgh (3d)	Frederick C. Clarke (3d)	91	49	.650
1904—New York (3d)	John J. McGraw (1st)	106	47	.693
1905—New York (4th)	John J. McGraw (2d)	105	48	.686
1906—Chicago (7th)	Frank L. Chance (1st)	116	36	.763
1907—Chicago (8th)	Frank L. Chance (2d)	107	45	.704
1908—Chicago (9th)	Frank L. Chance (3d)	99	55	.643
1909—Pittsburgh (4th)	Frederick C. Clarke (4th)	110	42	.724
1910—Chicago (10th)	Frank L. Chance (4th)	104	50	.675
1911—New York (5th)	John J. McGraw (3d)	99	54	.647
1912—New York (6th)	John J. McGraw (4th)	103	48	.682
1913—New York (7th)	John J. McGraw (5th)	101	51	.664
1914—Boston (9th)	George T. Stallings (1st)	94	59	.614
1915—Philadelphia (1st)	Patrick J. Moran (1st)	90	62	.592
1916—Brooklyn (4th)	Wilbert Robinson (1st)	94	60	.610
1917—New York (8th)	John J. McGraw (6th)	98	56	.636
1918—Chicago (11th)	Frederick F. Mitchell (1st)	84	45	.651
1919—Cincinnati (1st)	Patrick J. Moran (2d)	96	44	.686
1920—Brooklyn (5th)	Wilbert Robinson (2d)	93	61	.604
1921—New York (9th)	John J. McGraw (7th)	94	59	.614
1922—New York (10th)	John J. McGraw (8th)	93	61	.604
1923—New York (11th)	John J. McGraw (9th)	95	58	.621
1924—New York (12th)	John J. McGraw (10th)	93	60	.608
1925—Pittsburgh (5th)	William B. McKechnie (1st)	95	58	.621
1926—St. Louis (1st)	Rogers Hornsby (1st)	89	65	.578
1927—Pittsburgh (6th)	Owen J. Bush (1st)	94	60	.610
1928—St. Louis (2d)	William B. McKechnie (2d)	95	59	.617
1929—Chicago (12th)	Joseph V. McCarthy (1st)	98	54	.645
1930—St. Louis (3d)	Charles E. Street (1st)	92	62	.597
1931—St. Louis (4th)	Charles E. Street (2d)	101	53	.656
1932—Chicago (13th)	Charles J. Grimm (1st)	90	64	.584
1933—New York (13th)	William H. Terry (1st)	91	61	.599
1934—St. Louis (5th)	Frank F. Frisch (1st)	95	58	.621
1935—Chicago (14th)	Charles J. Grimm (2d)	100	54	.649
1936—New York (14th)	William H. Terry (2d)	92	62	.597
1937—New York (15th)	William H. Terry (3d)	95	57	.625
1938—Chicago (15th)	Charles L. Hartnett (1st)	89	63	.586
1939—Cincinnati (2d)	William B. McKechnie (3d)	97	57	.630
1940—Cincinnati (3d)	William B. McKechnie (4th)	100	53	.654
1941—Brooklyn (6th)	Leo E. Durocher (1st)	100	54	.649
1942—St. Louis (6th)	William H. Southworth (1st)	106	48	.688
1943—St. Louis (7th)	William H. Southworth (2d)	105	49	.682
1944—St. Louis (8th)	William H. Southworth (3d)	105	49	.682
1945—Chicago (16th)	Charles J. Grimm (3d)	98	56	.636
1946—St. Louis (9th)	Edwin H. Dyer (1st)	98	58	.628
1947—Brooklyn (7th)	Burton E. Shotton (1st)	94	60	.610
1948—Boston (10th)	William H. Southworth (4th)	91	62	.595
1949—Brooklyn (8th)	Burton E. Shotton (2d)	97	57	.630
1950—Philadelphia (2d)	Edwin M. Sawyer (1st)	91	63	.591
1951—New York (16th)	Leo E. Durocher (2d)	98	59	.624
1952—Brooklyn (9th)	Charles W. Dressen (1st)	96	57	.627
1953—Brooklyn (10th)	Charles W. Dressen (2d)	105	49	.682
1954—New York (17th)	Leo E. Durocher (3d)	97	57	.630
1955—Brooklyn (11th)	Walter Alston (1st)	98	55	.641
1956—Brooklyn (12th)	Walter Alston (2d)	93	61	.604
1957—Milwaukee (1st)	Fred Haney (1st)	95	59	.617
1958—Milwaukee (2d)	Fred Haney (2d)	92	62	.597
1959—Los Angeles (1st)	Walter Alston (3d)	88	68	.564
1960—Pittsburgh (7th)	Dan Murtagh (1st)	95	59	.617

National League — Continued

Year Club	Manager	Won	Lost	Pct.
1961—Cincinnati (4th)	Fred Hutchinson (1st)	93	61	.604
1962—San Francisco (1st)	Alvin Dark (1st)	103	62	.641
1963—Los Angeles (2d)	Walter Alston (4th)	99	63	.611
1964—St. Louis (10th)	John Keane (1st)	93	69	.574
1965—Los Angeles (3d)	Walter Alston (5th)	97	65	.599
1966—Los Angeles (4th)	Walter Alston (6th)	95	67	.586
1967—St. Louis (11th)	Albert Schoendienst (1st)	101	60	.627
1968—St. Louis (12th)	Albert Schoendienst (2d)	97	65	.599
1969—*New York (E.)	Gil Hodges	100	62	.617
Atlanta (W)	Luman Harris	93	69	.574
1970—Pittsburgh (E)	Danny Murtagh	89	73	.549
*Cincinnati (W)	George Anderson	102	60	.630
1971—*Pittsburgh (E)	Danny Murtagh	97	65	.599
San Francisco (W)	Charlie Fox	90	72	.556
1972—Pittsburgh (E)	Bill Virdon	96	59	.619
*Cincinnati (W)	George Anderson	95	59	.617

*Playoff Winner

LEAGUE PLAYOFF SERIES

Best-of-five series between Eastern and Western Division leaders to determine Pennant winner.

1969 — New York (East) beat Atlanta (West), 3 games to 0.

1970 — Cincinnati (West) beat Pittsburgh (East), 3 games to 0.

1971 — Pittsburgh (East) beat San Francisco (West), 3 games to 1.

1972 — Cincinnati (West) beat Pittsburgh (East), 3 games to 2.

American League

Year Club	Manager	Won	Lost	Pct.
1901—Chicago (1st)	Clark C. Griffith (1st)	83	53	.610
1902—Philadelphia (1st)	Connie Mack (1st)	83	53	.610
1903—Boston (1st)	James J. Collins (1st)	91	47	.659
1904—Boston (2d)	James J. Collins (2d)	95	59	.617
1905—Philadelphia (2d)	Connie Mack (2d)	92	56	.622
1906—Chicago (2d)	Fielder A. Jones (1st)	93	58	.616
1907—Detroit (1st)	Hugh A. Jennings (1st)	92	58	.613
1908—Detroit (2d)	Hugh A. Jennings (2d)	90	63	.588
1909—Detroit (3d)	Hugh A. Jennings (3d)	98	54	.645
1910—Philadelphia (3d)	Connie Mack (3d)	102	48	.680
1911—Philadelphia (4th)	Connie Mack (4th)	101	50	.669
1912—Boston (3d)	J. Garland Stahl (1st)	105	47	.691
1913—Philadelphia (5th)	Connie Mack (5th)	96	57	.627
1914—Philadelphia (6th)	Connie Mack (6th)	99	53	.651
1915—Boston (4th)	William F. Carrigan (1st)	101	50	.669
1916—Boston (5th)	William F. Carrigan (2d)	91	63	.591
1917—Chicago (3d)	Clarence H. Rowland (1st)	100	54	.649
1918—Boston (6th)	Edward G. Barrow (1st)	75	51	.595
1919—Chicago (4th)	William J. Gleason (1st)	88	52	.629
1920—Cleveland (1st) ....:...	Tristram E. Speaker (1st)	98	56	.636
1921—New York (1st)	Miller J. Huggins (1st)	98	55	.641
1922—New York (2d)	Miller J. Huggins (2d)	94	60	.610
1923—New York (3d)	Miller J. Huggins (3d)	98	54	.645
1924—Washington (1st)	Stanley R. Harris (1st)	92	62	.597
1925—Washington (2d)	Stanley R. Harris (2d)	96	55	.636
1926—New York (4th)	Miller J. Huggins (4th)	91	63	.591
1927—New York (5th)	Miller J. Huggins (5th)	110	44	.714
1928—New York (6th)	Miller J. Huggins (6th)	101	53	.656
1929—Philadelphia (7th)	Connie Mack (7th)	104	46	.693

American League —Continued

Year	Club	Manager	Won	Lost	Pct.
1930—Philadelphia (8th)	Connie Mack (8th)	102	52	.662
1931—Philadelphia (9th)	Connie Mack (9th)	107	45	.704
1932—New York (7th)	Joseph V. McCarthy (1st)	107	47	.695
1933—Washington (3d)	Joseph E. Cronin (1st)	99	53	.651
1934—Detroit (4th)	Gordon S. Cochrane (1st)	101	53	.656
1935—Detroit (5th)	Gordon S. Cochrane (2d)	93	58	.616
1936—New York (8th)	*Joseph V. McCarthy (2d)	102	51	.667
1937—New York (9th)	Joseph V. McCarthy (3d)	102	52	.662
1938—New York (10th)	Joseph V. McCarthy (4th)	99	53	.651
1939—New York (11th)	Joseph V. McCarthy (5th)	106	45	.702
1940—Detroit (6th)	Delmar D. Baker (1st)	90	64	.584
1941—New York (12th)	Joseph V. McCarthy (6th)	101	53	.656
1942—New York (13th)	Joseph V. McCarthy (7th)	103	51	.669
1943—New York (14th)	Joseph V. McCarthy (8th)	98	56	.636
1944—St. Louis (1st)	Luke Sewell (1st)	89	65	.578
1945—Detroit (7th)	Stephen F. O'Neill (1st)	88	65	.575
1946—Boston (7th)	Joseph E. Cronin (2d)	104	50	.675
1947—New York (15th)	Stanley R. Harris (3d)	97	57	.630
1948—Cleveland (2d)	Louis Boudreau (1st)	97	58	.626
1949—New York (16th)	Charles D. Stengel (1st)	97	57	.630
1950—New York (17th)	Charles D. Stengel (2d)	98	56	.636
1951—New York (18th)	Charles D. Stengel (3d)	98	56	.636
1952—New York (19th)	Charles D. Stengel (4th)	95	59	.617
1953—New York (20th)	Charles D. Stengel (5th)	99	52	.656
1954—Cleveland (3d)	Al Lopez (1st)	111	43	.721
1955—New York (21st)	Charles D. Stengel (6th)	96	58	.623
1956—New York (22d)	Charles D. Stengel (7th)	97	57	.630
1957—New York (23d)	Charles D. Stengel (8th)	98	56	.636
1958—New York (24th)	Charles D. Stengel (9th)	92	62	.597
1959—Chicago (5th)	Al Lopez (2d)	94	60	.610
1960—New York (25th)	Charles D. Stengel (10th)	97	57	.630
1961—New York (26th)	Ralph G. Houk (1st)	109	53	.673
1962—New York (27th)	Ralph G. Houk (2nd)	96	66	.593
1963—New York (28th)	Ralph Houk (3d)	104	57	.646
1964—New York (29th)	Yogi Berra (1st)	99	63	.611
1965—Minnesota (1st)	Sabath Mele (1st)	102	60	.630
1966—Baltimore (1st)	Henry Bauer (1st)	97	63	.606
1967—Boston (8th)	Richard H. Williams (1st)	92	70	.568
1968—Detroit (8th)	Edward Smith (1st)	103	59	.636
1969—*Baltimore (E)	Earl Weaver	109	53	.673
Minnesota (W)	Alfred Martin	97	65	.599
1970—*Baltimore (E)	Earl Weaver	108	54	.667
Minnesota (W)	Bill Rigney	98	64	.605
1971—*Baltimore (E)	Earl Weaver	101	57	.639
Oakland (W)	Dick Williams	101	60	.627
1972—Detroit (E)	Alfred Martin	86	70	.551
*Oakland (W)	Dick Williams	93	72	.600

*Won Playoff

* McCarthy won one pennant (1929) in the National League.

LEAGUE PLAYOFF SERIES

Best-of-five series between Eastern and Western Division leaders to determine Pennant winner.

1969 — Baltimore (East) beat Minnesota (West), 3 games to 0.

1970 — Baltimore (East) beat Minnesota (West), 3 games to 0.

1971 — Baltimore (East) beat Oakland (West), 3 games to 0.

1972 — Oakland (West) beat Detroit (East), 3 games to 2.

TEAM AND INDIVIDUAL RECORDS

In 1969, National and American Leagues split their teams into Eastern (E) Division and Western (W) Division:

National League

Atlanta Braves

WON–LOST RECORD
(Franchise transferred from Boston in 1953. Transferred to Atlanta, starting season in 1966.)

Year	Fin-ish	Won	Lost	Pct.	Manager
1900	4	66	72	.478	Frank Selee
1901	5	69	69	.500	Frank Selee
1902	3	73	64	.533	Al Buckenberger
1903	6	58	80	.420	Al Buckenberger
1904	7	55	98	.359	Al Buckenberger
1905	7	51	103	.331	Fred Tenney
1906	8	49	102	.325	Fred Tenney
1907	7	58	90	.392	Fred Tenney
1908	6	63	91	.409	Joseph J. Kelley
1909	8	45	108	.294	Frank Bowerman, Harry Smith
1910	8	53	100	.346	Fred Lake
1911	8	44	107	.291	Fred Tenney
1912	8	52	101	.340	John Kling
1913	5	69	82	.457	George T. Stallings
1914	1*	94	59	.614	George T. Stallings
1915	2	83	69	.546	George T. Stallings
1916	3	89	63	.586	George T. Stallings
1917	6	72	81	.471	George T. Stallings
1918	7	53	71	.427	George T. Stallings
1919	6	57	82	.410	George T. Stallings
1920	7	62	90	.408	George T. Stallings
1921	4	79	74	.516	Fred Mitchell
1922	8	53	100	.346	Fred Mitchell
1923	7	54	100	.351	Fred Mitchell
1924	8	53	100	.346	Dave Bancroft
1925	5	70	83	.458	Dave Bancroft
1926	7	66	86	.434	Dave Bancroft
1927	7	60	94	.390	Dave Bancroft
1928	7	50	103	.327	Jack Slattery, Rogers Hornsby
1929	8	56	98	.364	Emil Fuchs, Walter Maranville
1930	6	70	84	.455	Bill McKechnie
1931	7	64	90	.416	Bill McKechnie
1932	5	77	77	.500	Bill McKechnie
1933	4	83	71	.539	Bill McKechnie
1934	4	78	73	.517	Bill McKechnie
1935	8	38	115	.248	Bill McKechnie
1936	6	71	83	.461	Bill McKechnie
1937	5	79	73	.520	Bill McKechnie
1938	5	77	75	.507	Charles D. Stengel
1939	7	63	88	.417	Charles D. Stengel
1940	7	65	87	.428	Charles D. Stengel
1941	7	62	92	.403	Charles D. Stengel
1942	7	59	89	.399	Charles D. Stengel
1943	6	68	85	.444	Charles D. Stengel
1944	6	65	89	.422	Bob Coleman
1945	6	67	85	.441	Coleman, Del Bissonette
1946	4	81	72	.529	Billy Southworth
1947	3	86	68	.558	Billy Southworth
1948	1	91	62	.595	Billy Southworth
1949	4	75	79	.487	Billy Southworth
1950	4	83	71	.539	Billy Southworth
1951	4	76	78	.494	Southworth, Tommy Holmes
1952	7	64	89	.418	Holmes, Charlie Grimm
1953	2	92	62	.597	Charlie Grimm
1954	3	89	65	.578	Charlie Grimm
1955	2	85	69	.552	Charlie Grimm
1956	2	92	62	.597	Grimm, Fred Haney
1957	1*	95	59	.617	Fred Haney
1958	1	92	62	.597	Fred Haney
1959	2†	86	70	.551	Fred Haney
1960	2	88	66	.571	Charlie Dressen
1961	4	83	71	.539	Dressen, B. Tebbetts
1962	5	86	76	.531	Birdie Tebbetts
1963	6	84	78	.519	Bobby Bragan
1964	5	88	74	.543	Bobby Bragan
1965	5	86	76	.531	Bobby Bragan
1966	5	85	77	.525	B. Bragan, Billy Hitchcock
1967	7	77	85	.475	B. Hitchcock, Ken Silvestri
1968	5	81	80	.500	Luman Harris
1969	1W†	93	69	.574	Luman Harris
1970	5W	76	86	.469	Luman Harris
1971	3W	82	80	.506	Luman Harris
1972	4W	70	84	.455	Harris, Eddie Mathews
Total		5208	5946	.467	

*Won World Series   †Lost Playoff

TOP MARKS
(1900-72)

Batting—Rogers Hornsby, 1928	.387
Hitting Streak—Tommy Holmes, 1945 . .	37
Home Runs—Eddie Mathews, 1953	47
Hank Aaron, 1971	47
Runs Batted In—Eddie Mathews, 1953. . .	135
Hits—Tommy Holmes, 1945.	224
Runs—Hank Aaron, 1962	127
Extra Base Hits—Hank Aaron, 1959	92
One Base Hits—Ralph Carr, 1971	180
Two Base Hits—Tommy Holmes, 1945 . .	47
Three Base Hits—Ray Powell, 1921	18
Total Bases—Hank Aaron, 1959	400
Stolen Bases—Ralph Meyers, 1913	57
At Bats—Felipe Alou, 1966	666
Bases on Balls—Bob Elliott, 1948	131
Strikeouts (most)—Vince DiMaggio, 1938	134
Strikeouts (fewest)—Tommy Holmes, 1945	9
Games—Felix Millan, 1969	162
Grounded into Double Plays (most)—Sid Gordon, 1951	28
Grounded into Double Plays (fewest)—Bill Bruton, 1955	2

Pitching

Percentage—Tom Hughes, 1916, 16-3 842
Games (Appearances)—Clay Carroll, 1966 73
Complete Games—Vic Willis, 1902 45
Innings Pitched—Vic Willis, 1902 402
Games Won—Vic Willis, 1902; Chas. Pittenger,
    1902; Dick Rudolph, 1914 (tie) 27
Games Lost—Vic Willis, 1905 29
Games Started—Vic Willis, 1902 45
Games Finished—Don McMahon, 1959 . . 49
Bases on Balls—Charles Fraser, 1905 149
Strikeouts—Vic Willis, 1902 221
Shutouts—Pittenger, 1902; Young, 1905; and
    Spahn, 1947, 1951, 1963 (tie) 7

Chicago Cubs

WON—LOST RECORD

Year	Fin-ish	Won	Lost	Pct.	Manager
1900	5	65	75	.464	Tom Loftus
1901	6	53	86	.381	Tom Loftus
1902	5	68	69	.496	Frank Selee
1903	3	82	56	.594	Frank Selee
1904	2	93	60	.608	Frank Selee
1905	3	92	61	.601	Selee, Frank Chance
1906	1	116	36	.763	Frank Chance
1907	1*	107	45	.704	Frank Chance
1908	1*	99	55	.643	Frank Chance
1909	2	104	49	.680	Frank Chance
1910	1	104	50	.675	Frank Chance
1911	2	92	62	.597	Frank Chance
1912	3	91	59	.607	Frank Chance
1913	3	88	65	.575	John Evers
1914	4	78	76	.506	Hank O'Day
1915	4	73	80	.477	Roger Bresnahan
1916	5	67	86	.438	Joe Tinker
1917	5	74	80	.481	Fred Mitchell
1918	1	84	45	.651	Fred Mitchell
1919	3	75	65	.536	Fred Mitchell
1920	5	74	79	.487	Fred Mitchell
1921	7	64	89	.418	Evers, Bill Killefer
1922	5	80	74	.519	Bill Killefer
1923	4	83	71	.539	Bill Killefer
1924	5	81	72	.529	Bill Killefer
1925	8	68	86	.442	Killefer, Walter Maranville, George Gibson
1926	4	82	72	.532	Joseph V. McCarthy
1927	4	85	68	.556	Joseph V. McCarthy
1928	3	91	63	.591	Joseph V. McCarthy
1929	1	98	54	.645	Joseph V. McCarthy
1930	2	90	64	.584	McCarthy, Rogers Hornsby
1931	3	84	70	.545	Rogers Hornsby
1932	1	90	64	.584	Hornsby, Charlie Grimm
1933	3	86	68	.558	Charlie Grimm
1934	3	86	65	.570	Charlie Grimm
1935	1	100	54	.649	Charlie Grimm
1936	2	87	67	.565	Charlie Grimm
1937	2	93	61	.604	Charlie Grimm
1938	1	89	63	.586	Grimm, Charles Hartnett
1939	4	84	70	.545	Charles Hartnett
1940	5	75	79	.487	Charles Hartnett
1941	6	70	84	.455	Jimmy Wilson
1942	6	68	86	.442	Jimmy Wilson
1943	5	74	79	.484	Jimmy Wilson
1944	4	75	79	.487	Wilson, Charlie Grimm
1945	1	98	56	.636	Charlie Grimm
1946	3	82	71	.536	Charlie Grimm
1947	6	69	85	.448	Charlie Grimm
1948	8	64	90	.416	Charlie Grimm
1949	8	61	93	.396	Grimm, Frank Frisch
1950	7	64	89	.418	Frank Frisch
1951	8	62	92	.403	Frisch, Phil Cavarretta
1952	5	77	77	.500	Phil Cavarretta
1953	7	65	89	.442	Phil Cavarretta
1954	7	64	90	.416	Stan Hack
1955	6	72	81	.471	Stan Hack
1956	8	60	94	.390	Stan Hack
1957	7	62	92	.403	Bob Scheffing
1958	5	72	82	.468	Bob Scheffing
1959	5	74	80	.481	Bob Scheffing
1960	7	60	94	.390	Charlie Grimm Lou Boudreau
1961	7	64	90	.416	coaches
1962	9	59	103	.364	coaches
1963	7	82	80	.506	coaches
1964	8	76	86	.469	coaches
1965	8	72	90	.444	coaches
1966	10	59	103	.364	Leo Durocher
1967	3	87	74	.540	Leo Durocher
1968	3	84	78	.519	Leo Durocher
1969	2E	92	70	.568	Leo Durocher
1970	2E	84	78	.519	Leo Durocher
1971	3E	83	79	.512	Leo Durocher
1972	2E	85	70	.548	Durocher, Whitey Lockman
Total		5796	5397	.518	

*Won World Series.

TOP MARKS
(1900-72)

Batting—Rogers Hornsby, 1929 380
Hitting Streak—Ron Santo, 1966 28
Home Runs—Hack Wilson, 1930 56
Runs Batted In—Hack Wilson, 1930 190
Hits—Rogers Hornsby, 1929 229
Runs—Rogers Hornsby, 1929 156
Extra Base Hits—Hack Wilson, 1930 97
One Base Hits—Earl Adams, 1927 165
Two Base Hits—Billy Herman, 1935, 1937 57
Three Base Hits—Frank Schulte, 1911; Victor
    Saier, 1913 (tie) 21
Total Bases—Hack Wilson, 1930 423
Stolen Bases—Frank Chance, 1903 67
At Bats—Billy Herman, 1935 666
Bases on Balls—Jimmy Sheckard, 1911 . . 147
Strikeouts (most)—Byron Browne, 1966 . . 143
Strikeouts (fewest)—Charles Hollocher, 1922 5

Games—Ron Santo, 1965; Billy
  Williams, 1965 164
Grounded into Double Play (most)—Ron
  Santo, 1961 25
Grounded into Double Play (fewest)—Augie
  Galan, 1935 0

Pitching

Percentage—Len Cole, 1910, 20-4 ...... .833
Games (Appearances)—Ted Abernathy,
  1965 84
Complete Games—John Taylor, 1903;
  Grover Alexander, 1920 (tie) 33
Innings Pitched—Grover Alexander, 1920 363
Games Won—Mordecai Brown, 1908 29
Games Lost—Tom Hughes, 1901; Dick
  Ellsworth, 1966 (tie) 22
Games Started—Fergie Jenkins, 1969 ... 42
Games Finished—Ted Abernathy, 1965 .. 62
Bases on Balls—Sam Jones, 1955 185
Strikeouts—Fergie Jenkins, 1970 274
Shutouts—Brown (1906, 1908), Overall
  (1907, 1909), Alexander (1919),
  Lee (1938) 9

Cincinnati Reds

WON—LOST RECORD

Year	Fin-ish	Won	Lost	Pct.	Manager
1900	7	62	77	.446	Robert Allen
1901	8	52	87	.374	John McPhee
1902	4	70	70	.500	McPhee, Frank C. Bancroft, Joseph J. Kelley
1903	4	74	65	.532	Joseph J. Kelley
1904	3	88	65	.575	Joseph J. Kelley
1905	5	79	74	.516	Joseph J. Kelley
1906	6	64	87	.424	Ned Hanlon
1907	6	66	87	.431	Ned Hanlon
1908	5	73	81	.474	John Ganzel
1909	4	77	76	.503	Clark Griffith
1910	5	75	79	.487	Clark Griffith
1911	6	70	83	.458	Clark Griffith
1912	4	75	78	.490	Hank O'Day
1913	7	64	89	.418	Joe Tinker
1914	8	60	94	.390	Buck Herzog
1915	7	71	83	.461	Buck Herzog
1916	7	60	93	.392	Herzog, Christy Mathewson
1917	4	78	76	.506	Christy Mathewson
1918	3	68	60	.531	Mathewson, Heinie Groh
1919	1*	96	44	.686	Pat Moran
1920	3	82	71	.536	Pat Moran
1921	6	70	83	.458	Pat Moran
1922	2	86	68	.558	Pat Moran
1923	2	91	63	.591	Pat Moran
1924	4	83	70	.542	Jack Hendricks
1925	3	80	73	.523	Jack Hendricks
1926	2	87	67	.565	Jack Hendricks
1927	5	75	78	.490	Jack Hendricks
1928	5	78	74	.513	Jack Hendricks
1929	7	66	68	.429	Jack Hendricks
1930	7	59	95	.383	Dan Howley
1931	8	58	96	.377	Dan Howley
1932	8	60	94	.390	Dan Howley
1933	8	58	94	.382	Donie Bush
1934	8	52	99	.344	Bob O'Farrell, Charles Dressen
1935	6	68	85	.444	Charles Dressen
1936	5	74	80	.481	Charles Dressen
1937	8	56	98	.364	Dressen, Bobby Wallace
1938	4	82	68	.547	Bill McKechnie
1939	1	97	57	.630	Bill McKechnie
1940	1*	100	53	.654	Bill McKechnie
1941	3	88	66	.571	Bill McKechnie
1942	4	76	76	.500	Bill McKechnie
1943	2	87	67	.565	Bill McKechnie
1944	3	89	65	.578	Bill McKechnie
1945	7	61	93	.396	Bill McKechnie
1946	6	67	87	.435	Bill McKechnie
1947	5	73	81	.474	John Neun
1948	7	64	89	.418	Neun, William (Bucky) Walters
1949	7	62	92	.403	William Walters
1950	6	66	87	.431	Luke Sewell
1951	6	68	86	.442	Luke Sewell
1952	6	69	85	.448	Sewell, Rogers Hornsby
1953	6	68	86	.442	Rogers Hornsby
1954	5	74	80	.481	Birdie Tebbetts
1955	5	75	79	.487	Birdie Tebbetts
1956	3	91	63	.591	Birdie Tebbetts
1957	4	80	74	.519	Birdie Tebbetts
1958	4	76	78	.494	Birdie Tebbetts, Jimmy Dykes
1959	5	74	80	.481	Mayo Smith Fred Hutchinson
1960	6	67	87	.435	Fred Hutchinson
1961	1	93	61	.604	Fred Hutchinson
1962	3	98	64	.605	Fred Hutchinson
1963	5	86	76	.531	Fred Hutchinson
1964	2†	92	70	.568	Fred Hutchinson
1965	4	89	73	.549	Dick Sisler
1966	7	76	84	.475	Don Heffner, Dave Bristol
1967	4	87	75	.537	Dave Bristol
1968	4	83	79	.512	Dave Bristol
1969	3W	89	73	.549	Dave Bristol
1970	1W‡	102	60	.630	George "Sparky" Anderson
1971	4W†	79	83	.488	Sparky Anderson
1972	1W‡	95	59	.617	Sparky Anderson
Total		5528	5660	.494	

*Won World Series.
†Tie for place.
‡ Won Playoff.

TOP MARKS
(1900-72)

Batting—Cy Seymour, 1905 .... .377

Hitting Streak—Edd Roush, 1920, 1924;
  Vada Pinson, 1965 (tie)   27
Home Runs—Ted Kluszewski, 1954   49
Runs Batted In—Johnny Bench, 1970 . . .   148
Hits—Cy Seymour, 1905   219
Runs—Frank Robinson, 1962   134
Extra Base Hits—Frank Robinson, 1962 .   92
One Base Hits—Frank McCormick, 1938 .   160
Two Base Hits—Frank Robinson, 1962 . .   51
Three Base Hits—Sam Crawford, 1902 . . .   23
Total Bases—Frank Robinson, 1962   380
Stolen Bases—Bob Bescher, 1911   80
At Bats—Pete Rose, 1965   670
Bases on Balls—Joe Morgan, 1972   115
Strikeouts (most)—Lee May, 1969   142
Strikeouts (fewest)—Frank McCormick, 1941   13
Games—Leo Cardenas, 1964   163
Grounded Into Double Plays (most)—Ernie
  Lombardi, 1938   30
Grounded Into Double Plays (fewest)—
  Lonnie Frey, 1938   1

Pitching

Percentage—Elmer Riddle, 1941, 19-4 826
Games (appearances)—Wayne Granger,
  1969   90
Complete Games—Noodles Hahn, 1901 . .   41
Innings Pitched—Noodles Hahn, 1901 . . .   375
Games Won—Adolfo Luque, 1923; Bucky
  Walters, 1939 (tie)   27
Games Lost—Paul Derringer, 1933   25
Games Started—Noodles Hahn, 1901   42
Games Finished—Ted Abernathy, 1967 . .   61
Bases On Balls—John VanderMeer, 1943 .   162
Strikeouts—Jim Maloney, 1963   265
Shutouts—Jake Weimer, 1906; Fred Toney,
  1917; and Hod Eller, 1919   7

Houston Astros

(Started league play in 1962)

WON—LOST RECORD

Year	Fin-ish	Won	Lost	Pct.	Manager
1962	8	64	96	.400	Harry Craft
1963	9	66	96	.407	Harry Craft
1964	9	66	96	.407	H. Craft, Lum Harris
1965	9	65	97	.401	Lum Harris
1966	8	72	90	.444	Grady Hatton
1967	9	69	93	.426	Grady Hatton
1968	10	72	90	.444	Hatton, Harry Walker
1969	5W	81	81	.500	Harry Walker
1970	4W†	79	83	.488	Harry Walker
1971	4W	79	83	.488	Harry Walker
1972	2W	84	69	.549	Walker, Leo Durocher
Total		797	974	.450	

† Tie For Place

TOP MARKS
(1962-72)

Batting—Rusty Staub, 1967 333
Hitting Streak—Rusty Staub, 1967   20
Runs Batted In—Jim Wynn, 1967   107
Home Runs—Jim Wynn, 1967   37
Hits—Rusty Staub, 1967   182
Runs—Jim Wynn, 1972   117
Extra Base Hits—Jim Wynn, 1967   69
One Base Hits—Sonny Jackson, 1966 . . .   160
Two Base Hits—Rusty Staub, 1967   44
Three Base Hits—Joe Morgan, 1965   12
Total Bases—Cesar Cedeno, 1972   300
Stolen Bases—Cesar Cedeno, 1972   55
At Bats—Roger Metzger, 1972   641
Bases On Balls—Jim Wynn, 1969   148
Strikeouts (most)—Lee May, 1972   145
Strikeouts (fewest)—Nellie Fox, 1964 . . .   13
Games—Rusty Staub, 1968; Cesar
  Cedeno, 1971   161
Grounded Into Double Play (most)—
  Doug Rader, 1970   23
Grounded Into Double Play (fewest)—
  Joe Morgan, 1966, 1967   2

Pitching

Percentage—Larry Dierker, 1971, 12-6 . .   .667
Games (appearances)—Fred Gladding, 1970   63
Complete Games—Larry Dierker, 1969 . .   20
Innings Pitched—Larry Dierker, 1969 . . .   305
Games Won—Larry Dierker, 1969   20
Games Lost—Dick Farrell, 1962   20
Games Started—Larry Dierker, 1969;
  Denny Lemaster, 1969   37
Games Finished—Hal Woodeshick, 1964 .   48
Bases on Balls—Don Wilson, 1969   97
Strikeouts—Don Wilson, 1969   235
Shutouts—Larry Dierker, 1972   5

Los Angeles Dodgers

(Franchise shifted from Brooklyn in 1957,
with first season at Los Angeles in 1958)

WON—LOST RECORD

Year	Fin-ish	Won	Lost	Pct.	Manager
1900	1	82	54	.603	Ned Hanlon
1901	3	79	57	.581	Ned Hanlon
1902	2	75	63	.543	Ned Hanlon
1903	5	70	66	.515	Ned Hanlon
1904	6	56	97	.366	Ned Hanlon
1905	8	48	104	.316	Ned Hanlon
1906	5	66	86	.434	Patsy Donovan
1907	5	65	83	.439	Patsy Donovan
1908	7	53	101	.344	Patsy Donovan
1909	6	55	98	.359	Harry Lumley
1910	6	64	90	.416	Bill Dahlen

Year	Fin-ish	Won	Lost	Pct.	Manager
1911	7	64	86	.427	Bill Dahlen
1912	7	58	95	.379	Bill Dahlen
1913	6	65	84	.436	Bill Dahlen
1914	5	75	79	.487	Wilbert Robinson
1915	3	80	72	.526	Wilbert Robinson
1916	1	94	60	.610	Wilbert Robinson
1917	7	70	81	.464	Wilbert Robinson
1918	5	57	69	.452	Wilbert Robinson
1919	5	69	71	.493	Wilbert Robinson
1920	1	93	61	.604	Wilbert Robinson
1921	5	77	75	.507	Wilbert Robinson
1922	6	76	78	.494	Wilbert Robinson
1923	6	76	78	.494	Wilbert Robinson
1924	2	92	62	.597	Wilbert Robinson
1925	6	68	85	.444	Wilbert Robinson
1926	6	71	82	.464	Wilbert Robinson
1927	6	65	88	.425	Wilbert Robinson
1928	6	77	76	.503	Wilbert Robinson
1929	6	70	83	.458	Wilbert Robinson
1930	4	86	68	.558	Wilbert Robinson
1931	4	79	73	.520	Wilbert Robinson
1932	3	81	73	.526	Max Carey
1933	6	65	88	.425	Max Carey
1934	6	71	81	.467	Charles D. Stengel
1935	5	70	83	.458	Charles D. Stengel
1936	7	67	87	.435	Charles D. Stengel
1937	6	62	91	.405	Burleigh Grimes
1938	7	69	80	.463	Burleigh Grimes
1939	3	84	69	.549	Leo Durocher
1940	2	88	65	.575	Leo Durocher
1941	1	100	54	.649	Leo Durocher
1942	2	104	50	.675	Leo Durocher
1943	3	81	72	.529	Leo Durocher
1944	7	63	91	.409	Leo Durocher
1945	3	87	67	.565	Leo Durocher
1946	2†	96	60	.615	Leo Durocher
1947	1	94	60	.610	Burt Shotton
1948	3	84	70	.545	Durocher, Shotton
1949	1	97	57	.630	Burt Shotton
1950	2	89	65	.578	Burt Shotton
1951	2†	97	60	.618	Charles Dressen
1952	1	96	57	.627	Charles Dressen
1953	1	105	49	.682	Charles Dressen
1954	2	92	62	.597	Walter Alston
1955	1*	98	55	.641	Walter Alston
1956	1	93	61	.604	Walter Alston
1957	3	84	70	.545	Walter Alston
1958	7	71	83	.461	Walter Alston
1959	1*	8	68	.564	Walter Alston
1960	4	82	72	.532	Walter Alston
1961	2	89	65	.578	Walter Alston
1962	2†	102	63	.618	Walter Alston
1963	1*	99	63	.611	Walter Alston
1964	6**	80	82	.494	Walter Alston
1965	1*	97	65	.599	Walter Alston
1966	1	95	67	.586	Walter Alston
1967	8	73	89	.451	Walter Alston
1968	7**	76	86	.469	Walter Alston
1969	4W	85	77	.525	Walter Alston
1970	2W	87	74	.540	Walter Alston
1971	2W	89	73	.549	Walter Alston
1972	3W	85	70	.548	Walter Alston
Total		5790	5379	.518	

*Won World Series after winning playoff.
†Lost playoff.
**Tie for place.

TOP MARKS
(1900-72)

Batting—Babe Herman, 1930 .... .393
Hitting Streak—Willie Davis, 1969 31
Home Runs—Duke Snider, 1956 43
Runs Batted In—Tommy Davis, 1962 ... 153
Hits—Babe Herman, 1930 241
Runs—Babe Herman, 1930 143
Extra Base Hits—Babe Herman, 1930 ... 94
One Base Hits—Willie Keeler, 1900; Maury
   Wills, 1962 179
Two Base Hits—John Frederick, 1929 ... 52
Three Base Hits—Harry "Hi" Myers, 1920 22
Total Bases—Babe Herman, 1930 416
Stolen Bases—Maury Wills, 1962 104
At Bats—Maury Wills, 1962 695
Bases on Balls—Eddie Stanky, 1945 148
Strikeouts (most)—Billy Grabarkewitz, 1970 149
Strikeouts (fewest)—James Johnston, 1923 15
Games—Maury Wills, 1962 165
Grounded into Double Play (most)—Carl
   Furillo, 1956 27
Grounded into Double Play (fewest)—John
   Roseboro, 1961 1

Pitching

Percentage—Phil Regan, 1966, 14-1 ..... .933
Games (Appearances)—Bob Miller, 1964 . 74
Complete Games—Oscar Jones, 1904 38
Innings Pitched—Oscar Jones, 1904 378
Games Won—Joe McGinnity, 1900 29
Games Lost—George Bell, 1910 27
Games Started—Don Drysdale, 1963, 1965 42
Games Finished—Ron Perranoski, 1964 .. 52
Bases on Balls—Bill Donovan, 1901 151
Strikeouts—Sandy Koufax, 1965 382
Shutouts—Sandy Koufax, 1963 11

Montreal Expos
(Started league play in 1969)

WON—LOST RECORD

Year	Fin-ish	Won	Lost	Pct.	Manager
1969	6E	52	110	.321	Gene Mauch
1970	6E	73	89	.451	Gene Mauch
1971	5E	71	90	.441	Gene Mauch
1972	5E	70	86	.449	Gene Mauch
Total		266	375	.415	

TOP MARKS
(1969-72)

Batting—Rusty Staub, 1971	.311
Hitting Streak—Rusty Staub, 1971	16
Home Runs—Rusty Staub, 1970	30
Runs Batted In—Rusty Staub, 1971	97
Hits—Rusty Staub, 1971	186
Runs—Rusty Staub, 1970	98
Extra Base Hits—Rusty Staub, 1969, 1970	60
One Base Hits—Rusty Staub, 1971	127
Two Base Hits—Rusty Staub, 1971	34
Three Base Hits—Rusty Staub, 1970	7
Total Bases—Rusty Staub, 1969, 1971 . .	289
Stolen Bases—Maury Wills, 1969	15
At Bats—Rusty Staub, 1971	599
Bases on Balls—Rusty Staub, 1970	112
Strikeouts (most)—Bob Bailey, 1972	112
Strikeouts (fewest)—Ron Hunt, 1972 . . .	29
Games—Rusty Staub, 1971	162
Grounded into Double Play (most)—John Bateman, 1971	27
Grounded into Double Play (fewest)—Ron Hunt, 1971	1

Pitching

Percentage—Mike Marshall, 1972, 14-8 . .	.636
Games (appearances)—Dan McGinn, 1969	74
Complete Games—Bill Stoneman, 1971 . .	20
Innings Pitched—Bill Stoneman, 1971 . . .	295
Games Won—Carl Morton, 1970	18
Games Lost—Bill Stoneman, 1969	19
Games Started—Bill Stoneman, 1971	39
Games Finished—Mike Marshall, 1972 . . .	56
Bases on Balls—Bill Stoneman, 1971	146
Strikeouts—Bill Stoneman, 1971	251
Shutouts—Bill Stoneman, 1969	5

New York Mets

(Started league play in 1962)

WON—LOST RECORD

Year	Fin-ish	Won	Lost	Pct.	Manager
1962	10	40	120	.250	Casey Stengel
1963	10	51	111	.315	Casey Stengel
1964	10	53	109	.327	Casey Stengel
1965	10	50	112	.309	C. Stengel, Wes Westrum
1966	9	66	95	.410	Wes Westrum
1967	10	61	101	.377	W. Westrum, Salty Parker
1968	9	73	89	.451	Gil Hodges
1969	1E*	100	62	.617	Gil Hodges
1970	3E	83	79	.512	Gil Hodges
1971	4E	83	79	.512	Gil Hodges
1972	3E	83	73	.532	Yogi Berra
Total		743	1030	.419	

*Won World Series

TOP MARKS
(1962-72)

Batting—Cleon Jones, 1969	.340
Hitting Streak—Cleon Jones, 1970	23
Home Runs—Frank Thomas, 1962	34
Runs Batted In—Donn Clendenon, 1970 .	97
Hits—Tommie Agee, 1970	182
Runs—Tommie Agee, 1970	107
Extra Base Hits—Tommie Agee, 1970 . . .	61
One Base Hits—Tommy Davis, 1967	126
Two Base Hits—Tommy Davis, 1967	32
Three Base Hits—Charlie Neal, 1962	9
Total Bases—Tommie Agee, 1970	298
Stolen Bases—Tommie Agee, 1970	31
At Bats—Tommie Agee, 1970	636
Bases on Balls—Bud Harrelson, 1970	95
Strikeouts (most)—Tommie Agee, 1970 .	156
Strikeouts (fewest)—Ron Hunt, 1964 . . .	30
Games—Roy McMillan, 1965; Bud Harrelson, 1970	157
Grounded into Double Play (most)—Cleon Jones, 1970	26
Grounded into Double Play—Kranepool, 1966; Bud Harrelson, 1967, 1969; Tommie Agee, 1969; Wayne Garrett, 1969	5

Pitching

Percentage—Tom Seaver, 1969, 25-7	.781
Games (appearances)—Bill Wakefield, 1964	62
Complete Games—Tom Seaver, 1971	21
Innings Pitched—Tom Seaver, 1970	291
Games Won—Tom Seaver, 1969	25
Games Lost—Roger Craig, 1962; Jack Fisher, 1965	24
Games Started—Jack Fisher, 1965; Tom Seaver, 1970	36
Games Finished—Tug McGraw, 1972	47
Bases on Balls—Nolan Ryan, 1971	116
Strikeouts—Tom Seaver, 1971	289
Shutouts—Jerry Koosman, 1968	7

Philadelphia Phillies

WON—LOST RECORD

Year	Fin-ish	Won	Lost	Pct.	Manager
1900	3	75	63	.543	Bill Shettsline
1901	2	83	57	.593	Bill Shettsline
1902	7	56	81	.409	Bill Shettsline
1903	7	49	86	.363	Chief Zimmer
1904	8	52	100	.342	Hugh Duffy
1905	4	83	69	.546	Hugh Duffy
1906	4	71	82	.464	Hugh Duffy
1907	3	83	64	.565	Bill Murray
1908	4	83	71	.539	Bill Murray
1909	5	74	79	.484	Bill Murray
1910	4	78	75	.510	Charles Dooin
1911	4	79	73	.520	Charles Dooin

Year	Fin-ish	Won	Lost	Pct.	Manager
1912	5	73	79	.480	Charles Dooin
1913	2	88	63	.583	Charles Dooin
1914	6	74	80	.481	Charles Dooin
1915	1	90	62	.592	Pat Moran
1916	2	91	62	.595	Pat Moran
1917	2	87	65	.572	Pat Moran
1918	6	55	68	.447	Pat Moran
1919	8	47	90	.343	Jack Coombs, Gavvy Cravath
1920	8	62	91	.405	Gavvy Cravath
1921	8	51	103	.331	Bill Donovan, Irvin Wilhelm
1922	7	57	96	.373	Irvin Wilhelm
1923	8	50	104	.325	Art Fletcher
1924	7	55	96	.364	Art Fletcher
1925	6	68	85	.444	Art Fletcher
1926	8	58	93	.384	Art Fletcher
1927	8	51	103	.331	Stuffy McInnis
1928	8	43	109	.283	Burt Shotton
1929	5	71	82	.464	Burt Shotton
1930	8	52	102	.338	Burt Shotton
1931	6	66	88	.429	Burt Shotton
1932	4	78	76	.506	Burt Shotton
1933	7	60	92	.395	Burt Shotton
1934	7	56	93	.376	Jimmy Wilson
1935	7	64	89	.418	Jimmy Wilson
1936	8	54	100	.351	Jimmy Wilson
1937	7	61	92	.399	Jimmy Wilson
1938	8	45	105	.300	Wilson, Hans Lobert
1939	8	45	106	.298	Doc Prothro
1940	8	50	103	.327	Doc Prothro
1941	8	43	111	.279	Doc Prothro
1942	8	42	109	.278	Hans Lobert
1943	7	64	90	.416	Stanley R. Harris, Fred Fitzsimmons
1944	8	61	92	.399	Fred Fitzsimmons
1945	8	46	108	.299	Fitzsimmons, Ben Chapman
1946	5	69	85	.448	Ben Chapman
1947	7	62	92	.403	Ben Chapman
1948	6	66	88	.429	Chapman, Eddie Sawyer
1949	3	81	73	.526	Eddie Sawyer
1950	1	91	63	.591	Eddie Sawyer
1951	5	73	81	.474	Eddie Sawyer
1952	4	87	67	.565	Sawyer, Steve O'Neill
1953	3	83	71	.539	Steve O'Neill
1954	4	75	79	.487	Steve O'Neill
1955	4	77	77	.500	Mayo Smith
1956	5	71	83	.461	Mayo Smith
1957	5	77	77	.500	Mayo Smith
1958	8	69	85	.448	Smith, Eddie Sawyer
1959	8	64	90	.416	Eddie Sawyer
1960	8	59	95	.383	Sawyer, Gene Mauch
1961	8	47	107	.305	Gene Mauch
1962	7	81	80	.503	Gene Mauch
1963	4	87	75	.537	Gene Mauch
1964	2†	92	70	.568	Gene Mauch
1965	6	85	76	.528	Gene Mauch
1966	4	87	75	.537	Gene Mauch
1967	5	82	80	.506	Gene Mauch
1968	7†	76	86	.469	Mauch, Bob Skinner
1969	5E	63	99	.389	Skinner, George Myatt
1970	5E	73	88	.453	Frank Lucchesi
1971	6E	67	95	.414	Frank Lucchesi
1972	6E	59	97	.378	Lucchesi, Paul Owens
Total		4927	6221	.442	

†Tie for place.

TOP MARKS
(1900-72)

Batting—Frank O'Doul, 1929 .... .398
Hitting Streak—Chuck Klein, 1930 (twice) 26
Home Runs—Chuck Klein, 1929 43
Runs Batted In—Chuck Klein, 1930 170
Hits—Frank O'Doul, 1929 254
Runs—Chuck Klein, 1930 158
Extra Base Hits—Chuck Klein, 1930 107
One Base Hits—Frank O'Doul, 1929; Richie Ashburn, 1951 (tie) 181
Two Base Hits—Chuck Klein, 1930 59
Three Base Hits—Elmer Flick, 1901; Sherry Magee, 1905, 1910 17
Total Bases—Chuck Klein, 1930 445
Stolen Bases—Sherry Magee, 1906 55
At Bats—Richie Ashburn, 1949; Granny Hamner, 1949 662
Bases on Balls—Richie Ashburn, 1954 ... 125
Strikeouts (most)—Richie Allen, 1968 ... 161
Strikeouts (fewest)—Emil Verban (1947) 8
Games—Richie Allen, 1964; John Callison, 1964 162
Grounded into Double Play (most)—Del Ennis, 1950 25
Grounded into Double Play (fewest)—Richie Ashburn, 1948 1

Pitching

Percentage—Robin Roberts, 1952, 28-7 .. .800
Games (Appearances)—Jim Konstanty, 1950 74
Complete Games—Grover Alexander, 1916 38
Innings Pitched—Grover Alexander, 1916 389
Games Won—Grover Alexander, 1916 ... 33
Games Lost—Charles Fraser, 1904 24
Games Started—Grover Alexander, 1916 . 45
Games Finished—Jim Konstanty, 1950 .. 62
Bases on Balls—Earl Moore, 1911 164
Strikeouts—Steve Carlton, 1972 310
Shutouts—Grover Alexander, 1916 16

Pittsburgh Pirates

WON—LOST RECORD

Year	Fin-ish	Won	Lost	Pct.	Manager
1900	2	79	60	.568	Fred Clarke
1901	1	90	49	.647	Fred Clarke
1902	1	103	36	.741	Fred Clarke
1903	1	91	49	.650	Fred Clarke

1904 4	87	66	.569	Fred Clarke
1905 2	96	57	.627	Fred Clarke
1906 3	93	60	.608	Fred Clarke
1907 2	91	63	.591	Fred Clarke
1908 2	98	56	.636	Fred Clarke
1909 1*	110	42	.724	Fred Clarke
1910 3	86	67	.562	Fred Clarke
1911 3	85	69	.552	Fred Clarke
1912 2	93	58	.616	Fred Clarke
1913 4	78	71	.523	Fred Clarke
1914 7	69	85	.448	Fred Clarke
1915 5	73	81	.474	Fred Clarke
1916 6	65	89	.422	Jimmy Callahan
1917 8	51	103	.331	Callahan, Hans Wagner, Hugo Bezdek
1918 4	65	60	.520	Hugo Bezdek
1919 4	71	68	.511	Hugo Bezdek
1920 4	79	75	.513	George Gibson
1921 2	90	63	.588	George Gibson
1922 3	85	69	.552	Gibson, Bill McKechnie
1923 3	87	67	.565	Bill McKechnie
1924 3	90	63	.588	Bill McKechnie
1925 1*	95	58	.621	Bill McKechnie
1926 3	84	69	.549	Bill McKechnie
1927 1	94	60	.610	Donie Bush
1928 4	85	67	.559	Donie Bush
1929 2	88	65	.575	Bush, Jewel Ens
1930 5	80	74	.519	Jewel Ens
1931 5	75	79	.487	Jewel Ens
1932 2	86	68	.558	George Gibson
1933 2	87	67	.565	George Gibson
1934 5	74	76	.493	Gibson, Harold Traynor
1935 4	86	67	.562	Harold Traynor
1936 4	84	70	.545	Harold Traynor
1937 3	86	68	.558	Harold Traynor
1938 2	86	64	.573	Harold Traynor
1939 6	68	85	.444	Harold Traynor
1940 4	78	76	.506	Frank Frisch
1941 4	81	73	.526	Frank Frisch
1942 5	66	81	.449	Frank Frisch
1943 4	80	74	.519	Frank Frisch
1944 2	90	63	.588	Frank Frisch
1945 4	82	72	.532	Frank Frisch
1946 7	63	91	.409	Frank Frisch
1947 7	62	92	.403	Billy Herman
1948 4	83	71	.539	Bill Meyer
1949 6	71	83	.461	Bill Meyer
1950 8	57	96	.373	Bill Meyer
1951 7	64	90	.416	Bill Meyer
1952 8	42	112	.273	Bill Meyer
1953 8	50	104	.325	Fred Haney
1954 8	53	101	.344	Fred Haney
1955 8	60	94	.390	Fred Haney
1956 7	66	88	.429	Bobby Bragan
1957 8	62	92	.403	Bragan, Danny Murtaugh
1958 2	84	70	.545	Danny Murtaugh
1959 4	78	76	.506	Danny Murtaugh
1960 1*	95	59	.617	Danny Murtaugh
1961 6	75	79	.487	Danny Murtaugh
1962 4	93	68	.578	Danny Murtaugh
1963 8	74	88	.457	Danny Murtaugh
1964 6†	80	82	.494	Danny Murtaugh
1965 3	90	72	.556	Harry Walker
1966 3	92	70	.568	Harry Walker
1967 6	81	81	.500	H. Walker, Danny Murtaugh
1968 6	80	82	.494	Larry Shepard
1969 3E	88	74	.543	Larry Shepard
1970 1E‡	89	73	.549	Danny Murtaugh
1971 1E*	97	65	.599	Danny Murtaugh
1972 1E‡	96	59	.619	Bill Virdon
Total	5865	5314	.525	

†Tie for place. ‡Lost playoff. *Won World Series.

TOP MARKS
(1900-72)

Batting—Arky Vaughan, 1935 .... .385
Hitting Streak—Danny O'Connell, 1953 . 26
Home Runs—Ralph Kiner, 1949 54
Runs Batted In—Paul Waner, 1927 131
Hits—Paul Waner, 1927 237
Runs—Kiki Cuyler, 1925 144
Extra Base Hits—Kiki Cuyler, 1925 86
One Base Hits—Lloyd Waner, 1927 198
Two Base Hits—Paul Waner, 1933 62
Three Base Hits—J. Owen Wilson, 1912 .. 36
Total Bases—Kiki Cuyler, 1925 366
Stolen Bases—Max Carey, 1916 63
At Bats—Matty Alou, 1969 698
Bases on Balls—Ralph Kiner, 1951 137
Strikeouts (most)—Donn Clendenon, 1968 163
Strikeouts (fewest)—Pie Traynor, 1929 .. 7
Games—Bill Mazeroski, 1967 163
Grounded into Double Play (most)—Al Todd, 1938 25
Grounded into Double Play (fewest)—Matty Alou, 1966, 1967 3

Pitching

Percentage—ElRoy Face, 1959, 18-1 .... .947
Games (Appearances)—Pete Mikkelsen, 1966 71
Complete Games—Vic Willis, 1906 32
Innings Pitched—Burleigh Grimes, 1928 . 331
Games Won—Jack Chesbro, 1902 28
Games Lost—Murry Dickson, 1952 21
Games Started—Bob Friend, 1956 42
Games Finished—ElRoy Face, 1960 61
Bases on Balls—Marty O'Toole, 1912 159
Strikeouts—Bob Veale, 1965 276
Shutouts—Jack Chesbro, 1902; Al Leifield, 1906; Al Mamaux, 1915 and Charles Adams, 1920 (tie) 8

St. Louis Cardinals

WON—LOST RECORD

Year	Fin-ish	Won	Lost	Pct.	Manager
1900	5	65	75	.464	Oliver Tebeau, Lewis Heilbroner

Year	Fin-ish	Won	Lost	Pct.	Manager
1901	4	76	64	.543	Patsy Donovan
1902	6	56	78	.418	Patsy Donovan
1903	8	43	94	.314	Patsy Donovan
1904	5	75	79	.487	Charles (Kid) Nichols
1905	6	58	96	.377	Nichols, Jimmy Burke, Matthew Robison
1906	7	52	98	.347	John J. McCloskey
1907	8	52	101	.340	John J. McCloskey
1908	8	49	105	.318	John J. McCloskey
1909	7	54	98	.355	Roger Bresnahan
1910	7	63	90	.412	Roger Bresnahan
1911	5	75	74	.503	Roger Bresnahan
1912	6	63	90	.412	Roger Bresnahan
1913	8	51	99	.340	Miller J. Huggins
1914	3	81	72	.529	Miller J. Huggins
1915	6	72	81	.471	Miller J. Huggins
1916	7	60	93	.392	Miller J. Huggins
1917	3	82	70	.539	Miller J. Huggins
1918	8	51	78	.395	Jack Hendricks
1919	7	54	83	.394	Branch Rickey
1920	5	75	79	.487	Branch Rickey
1921	3	87	66	.569	Branch Rickey
1922	3	85	69	.552	Branch Rickey
1923	5	79	74	.516	Branch Rickey
1924	6	65	89	.422	Branch Rickey
1925	4	77	76	.503	Rickey, Rogers Hornsby
1926	1*	89	65	.578	Rogers Hornsby
1927	2	92	61	.601	Bob O'Farrell
1928	1	95	59	.617	Bill McKechnie
1929	4	78	74	.513	McKechnie, Billy Southworth
1930	1	92	62	.597	Charles Street
1931	1*	101	53	.656	Charles Street
1932	6	72	82	.468	Charles Street
1933	5	82	71	.536	Street, Frank Frisch
1934	1*	95	58	.621	Frank Frisch
1935	2	96	58	.623	Frank Frisch
1936	2	87	67	.565	Frank Frisch
1937	4	81	73	.526	Frank Frisch
1938	6	71	80	.470	Frisch, Mike Gonzales
1939	2	92	61	.601	Ray Blades
1940	3	84	69	.549	Blades, Gonzales, Billy Southworth
1941	2	97	56	.634	Billy Southworth
1942	1*	106	48	.688	Billy Southworth
1943	1	105	49	.682	Billy Southworth
1944	1*	105	49	.682	Billy Southworth
1945	2	95	59	.617	Billy Southworth
1946	1*†	98	58	.628	Eddie Dyer
1947	2	89	65	.578	Eddie Dyer
1948	2	85	69	.552	Eddie Dyer
1949	2	96	58	.623	Eddie Dyer
1950	5	78	75	.510	Eddie Dyer
1951	3	81	73	.526	Marty Marion
1952	3	88	66	.571	Eddie Stanky
1953	3	83	71	.539	Eddie Stanky
1954	6	72	82	.468	Eddie Stanky
1955	7	68	86	.442	Stanky, Harry Walker
1956	4	76	78	.494	Fred Hutchinson
1957	2	87	67	.565	Fred Hutchinson
1958	5	72	82	.468	Hutchinson, Stanley
1959	7	71	83	.461	Solly Hemus
1960	3	86	68	.558	Solly Hemus
1961	5	80	74	.519	Hemus, Johnny Keane
1962	6	84	78	.519	Johnny Keane
1963	2	93	69	.574	Johnny Keane
1964	1*	93	69	.574	Johnny Keane
1965	7	80	81	.497	Red Schoendienst
1966	6	83	79	.512	Red Schoendienst
1967	1*	101	60	.627	Red Schoendienst
1968	1‡	97	65	.599	Red Schoendienst
1969	4E	87	75	.537	Red Schoendienst
1970	4E	76	86	.469	Red Schoendienst
1971	2E	90	72	.556	Red Schoendienst
1972	4E	75	81	.481	Red Schoendienst
Total		5784	5395	.517	

*Won World Series.   †Won play-off for first.

‡ Won playoff.

TOP MARKS
(1900-72)

Batting—Rogers Hornsby, 1924 424
Hitting Streak—Rogers Hornsby, 1922 . . 33
Home Runs—Johnny Mize, 1940 43
Runs Batted In—Joe Medwick, 1937 154
Hits—Rogers Hornsby, 1922 250
Runs—Rogers Hornsby, 1922 141
Extra Base Hits—Stan Musial, 1948 103
One Base Hits—Jesse Burkett, 1901 180
Two Base Hits—Joe Medwick, 1936 64
Three Base Hits—Tom Long, 1915 25
Total Bases—Rogers Hornsby, 1922 450
Stolen Bases—Lou Brock, 1966 74
At Bats—Lou Brock, 1967 689
Bases on Balls—Miller Huggins, 1910 116
Strikeouts (most)—Lou Brock, 1966 134
Strikeouts (fewest)—Frank Frisch (1927)   10
Games—Bill White, 1963; Ken Boyer,
   1964; Curt Flood, 1964 162
Grounded into Double Play (most)—
   Nippy Jones, 1948 25
Grounded into Double Play (fewest)—
   Lou Brock, 1965, 1969 2

Pitching

Percentage—Howie Krist, 1942, 13-3 813
Games (Appearances)—Lindy McDaniel, 1960;
   Ron Willis, 1967 (tie) 65
Complete Games—John Taylor, 1904 . . . 39
Innings Pitched—Grant McGlynn, 1907 . . 352
Games Won—Dizzy Dean, 1934 30
Games Lost—Grant McGlynn, 1907; Arthur
   Raymond, 1908 (tie) 25
Games Started—John Taylor, 1904 39
Games Finished—Lindy McDaniel, 1959-60 47
Bases on Balls—Bob Harmon, 1911 181
Strikeouts—Bob Gibson, 1970 274
Shutouts—Bob Gibson, 1968 13

San Diego Padres
(Joined league in 1969)

WON–LOST RECORD

Year	Fin-ish	Won	Lost	Pct.	Manager
1969	6W	52	110	.321	Preston Gomez
1970	6W	63	99	.389	Preston Gomez
1971	6W	61	100	.379	Preston Gomez
1972	6W	58	95	.379	Gomez, Don Zimmer
Total		234	404	.367	

TOP MARKS
(1969-72)

Batting—Clarence Gaston, 1970 318
Hitting Streak—Ivan Murrell, 1969; Nate
   Colbert, 1972; Clarence Gaston, 1972   15
Home Runs—Nate Colbert, 1970, 1972 . .   38
Runs Batted In—Nate Colbert, 1972   111
Hits—Clarence Gaston, 1970   186
Runs—Clarence Gaston, 1970   92
Extra Base Hits—Nate Colbert, 1972   67
One Base Hits—Clarence Gaston, 1970 . .   122
Two Base Hits—Ollie Brown, 1970   34
Three Base Hits—Nate Colbert, 1969;
   Clarence Gaston, 1970, 1971   9
Total Bases—Clarence Gaston, 1970   317
Stolen Bases—Enzo Hernandez, 1972 . . .   24
At Bats—Clarence Gaston, 1970   584
Bases on Balls—Nate Colbert, 1972   70
Strikeouts (most)—Nate Colbert, 1970 . .   150
Strikeouts (fewest)—Enzo Hernandez, 1971   34
Games—Nate Colbert, 1970, 1971   156
Grounded into Double Play (most)—
   Nate Colbert, 1971   17
Grounded into Double Play (fewest)—
   David A. Roberts, 1972   5

Pitching

Percentage—Clay Kirby, 1971, 15-13 536
Games (appearances)—Frank Reberger, 1969   67
Complete Games—Dave Roberts, 1971 . .   14
Innings Pitched—Dave Roberts, 1971 . . .   270
Games Won—Clay Kirby, 1971   15
Games Lost—Steve Arlin, 1972   21
Games Started—Steve Arlin, 1972   37
Games Finished—Bill McCool, 1969;
   Frank Reberger, 1969   35
Bases on Balls—Steve Arlin, 1972   122
Strikeouts—Clay Kirby, 1971   231
Shutouts—Fred Norman, 1972   6

San Francisco Giants

(Franchise shifted from New York in 1957, with first season at Los Angeles in 1958)

WON–LOST RECORD

Year	Fin-ish	Won	Lost	Pct.	Manager
1900	8	60	78	.435	Buck Ewing, George Davis
1901	7	52	85	.380	George Davis
1902	8	48	88	.353	Horace Fogel, George Smith, John J. McGraw
1903	2	84	55	.604	John J. McGraw
1904	1	106	47	.693	John J. McGraw
1905	1*	105	48	.686	John J. McGraw
1906	2	96	56	.632	John J. McGraw
1907	4	82	71	.536	John J. McGraw
1908	2	98	56	.636	John J. McGraw
1909	3	92	61	.601	John J. McGraw
1910	2	91	63	.591	John J. McGraw
1911	1	99	54	.647	John J. McGraw
1912	1	103	48	.682	John J. McGraw
1913	1	101	51	.664	John J. McGraw
1914	2	84	70	.545	John J. McGraw
1915	8	69	83	.454	John J. McGraw
1916	4	86	66	.566	John J. McGraw
1917	1	98	56	.636	John J. McGraw
1918	2	71	53	.573	John J. McGraw
1919	2	87	53	.621	John J. McGraw
1920	2	86	68	.558	John J. McGraw
1921	1*	94	59	.614	John J. McGraw
1922	1*	93	61	.604	John J. McGraw
1923	1	95	58	.621	John J. McGraw
1924	1	93	60	.608	John J. McGraw
1925	2	86	66	.566	John J. McGraw
1926	5	74	77	.490	John J. McGraw
1927	3	92	62	.597	John J. McGraw
1928	2	93	61	.604	John J. McGraw
1929	3	84	67	.556	John J. McGraw
1930	3	87	67	.565	John J. McGraw
1931	2	87	65	.572	John J. McGraw
1932	6	72	82	.468	McGraw, Bill Terry
1933	1*	91	61	.599	Bill Terry
1934	2	93	60	.608	Bill Terry
1935	3	91	62	.595	Bill Terry
1936	1	92	62	.597	Bill Terry
1937	1	95	57	.625	Bill Terry
1938	3	83	67	.553	Bill Terry
1939	5	77	74	.510	Bill Terry
1940	6	72	80	.474	Bill Terry
1941	5	74	79	.484	Bill Terry
1942	3	85	67	.559	Mel Ott
1943	8	55	98	.359	Mel Ott
1944	5	67	87	.435	Mel Ott
1945	5	78	74	.513	Mel Ott
1946	8	61	93	.396	Mel Ott
1947	4	81	73	.526	Mel Ott
1948	5	78	76	.506	Ott, Leo Durocher
1949	5	73	81	.474	Leo Durocher
1950	3	86	68	.558	Leo Durocher
1951	1†	98	59	.624	Leo Durocher
1952	2	92	62	.597	Leo Durocher
1953	5	70	84	.455	Leo Durocher
1954	1*	97	57	.630	Leo Durocher
1955	3	80	74	.519	Leo Durocher
1956	6	67	87	.435	Bill Rigney
1957	6	69	85	.448	Bill Rigney
1958	3	80	74	.519	Bill Rigney
1959	3	83	71	.539	Bill Rigney

Year	Fin-ish	Won	Lost	Pct.	Manager
1960	5	79	75	.513	Rigney, Tom Sheehan
1961	3	85	69	.552	Alvin Dark
1962	1	103	62	.624	Alvin Dark
1963	3	88	74	.543	Alvin Dark
1964	4	90	72	.556	Alvin Dark
1965	2	95	67	.586	Herman Franks
1966	2	93	68	.578	Herman Franks
1967	2	91	71	.562	Herman Franks
1968	2	88	74	.543	Herman Franks
1969	2W	90	72	.556	Clyde King
1970	3W	86	76	.531	King, Charlie Fox
1971	1W‡	90	72	.556	Charlie Fox
1972	5W	69	86	.445	Charlie Fox
Total		6163	5005	.552	

*Won World Series.
†Won play-off for first.
‡Lost playoff.

TOP MARKS
(1900-72)

Batting—Bill Terry, 1930 401
Hitting Streak—Fred Lindstrom, 1930; Don
   Mueller, 1955; Willie McCovey, 1963 (tie) 24
Home Runs—Willie Mays, 1965 52
Runs Batted In—Mel Ott, 1929 151
Hits—Bill Terry, 1930 254
Runs—Bill Terry, 1930 139
Extra Base Hits—Willie Mays, 1962 90
One Base Hits—Bill Terry, 1930 177
Two Base Hits—Bill Terry, 1931; Willie
   Mays, 1959 43
Three Base Hits—Larry Doyle, 1911 25
Total Bases—Bill Terry, 1930 392
Stolen Bases—George Burns, 1914 62
At Bats—Joe Moore, 1935 681
Bases on Balls—Eddie Stanky, 1950 144
Strikeouts (most)—Bobby Bonds, 1970 . . 189
Strikeouts (fewest)—Don Mueller, 1956 . 7
Games—Jose Pagan, 1962 164
Grounded into Double Play (most)—Billy Jur-
   gess, 1939; Sid Gordon, 1943 (tie) . . . 26
Grounded into Double Play (fewest)—Joe
   Moore, 1936; Whitey Lockman, 1954, 1957;
   Tom Haller, 1967, 1967 (tie) 3

Pitching

Percentage—Hoyt Wilhelm, 1952, 15-3 . . .833
Games (Appearances)—Hoyt Wilhelm, 1952 71
Complete Games—Joe McGinnity, 1903 . 44
Innings Pitched—Joe McGinnity, 1903 . . 434
Games Won—Christy Mathewson, 1908 . . 37
Games Lost—Luther Taylor, 1901 27
Games Started—Joe McGinnity, 1903 . . . 48
Games Finished—Ace Adams, 1943 52
Bases on Balls—Jeff Tesreau, 1914 128
Strikeouts—Christy Mathewson, 1903 . . . 267
Shutouts—Christy Mathewson, 1908 12

AMERICAN LEAGUE

Baltimore Orioles

(Left American League after 1902 season; then St. Louis Browns franchise was shifted to Baltimore in 1953, with first season in 1954)

WON—LOST RECORD

Year	Fin-ish	Won	Lost	Pct.	Manager
1901	5	68	65	.511	John McGraw
1902	8	50	88	.369	McGraw, Wilbert Robinson
1954	7	54	100	.351	Jimmy Dykes
1955	7	57	97	.370	Paul Richards
1956	6	69	85	.448	Paul Richards
1957	5	76	76	.500	Paul Richards
1958	6	74	79	.484	Paul Richards
1959	6	78	80	.481	Paul Richards
1960	2	89	65	.578	Paul Richards
1961	3	95	67	.586	Richards, L. Harris
1963	4	86	76	.531	Bill Hitchcock
1964	3	97	65	.599	Henry Bauer
1965	3	94	68	.580	Henry Bauer
1966	1	97	63	.606	Henry Bauer
1967	6	76	85	.472	Henry Bauer
1968	2	91	71	.562	Bauer, Earl Weaver
1969	1E†	109	53	.673	Earl Weaver
1970	1E*	108	54	.667	Earl Weaver
1971	1E†	101	57	.639	Earl Weaver
1972	3E	80	74	.519	Earl Weaver
Total		1604	1400	.503	

†Won Playoff Series.
*Won World Series.

TOP MARKS
(1954-72)

Batting—Bob Nieman, 1956 320
Hitting Streak—R. Nieman, 1956 20
Home Runs—Frank Robinson, 1966 49
Runs Batted In—Jim Gentile, 1961 141
Hits—Brooks Robinson, 1964 194
Two Base Hits—Brooks Robinson, 1961 . 38
Three Base Hits—Paul Blair, 1967 12
Runs—J. Williams, 1901 114
Bases on Balls—Don Buford, 1970 109
Strikeouts (most)—Boog Powell, 1966 . . . 125
Strikeouts (fewest)—Clint Courtney, 1954 7
Stolen Bases—Luis Aparicio, 1964 57

Pitching

Games Won—Mike Cuellar, 1970; Dave
   McNally, 1970 (tie) 24
Games Lost—McGinnity, H. Howell, 1901;
   D. Larsen, 1954 (tie) 21
Games—Stu Miller, 1963 71
Games Started—Dave McNally, 1969-70;
   Mike Cuellar, 1970 40
Games Finished—Stu Miller, 1963 59

Complete Games—Mike Cuellar, 1970-71   21
Innings Pitched—Jim Palmer, 1970   305
Bases on Balls—Robert Turley, 1954   181
Strikeouts—Dave McNally, 1968   202
Shutouts—Steve Barber, 1961   8
Home Runs Allowed—Robin Roberts, 1963   35

St. Louis Browns
WON—LOST RECORD

Year	Fin-ish	Won	Lost	Pct.	Manager
1902	2	78	58	.574	James R. McAleer
1903	6	65	74	.468	James R. McAleer
1904	6	65	87	.428	James R. McAleer
1905	8	54	99	.354	James R. McAleer
1906	5	76	73	.510	James R. McAleer
1907	6	69	83	.454	James R. McAleer
1908	4	83	69	.546	James R. McAleer
1909	7	61	89	.407	James R. McAleer
1910	8	47	107	.305	John O'Connor
1911	8	45	107	.296	Rhoderick Wallace
1912	7	53	101	.344	Wallace, George Stovall
1913	8	57	96	.373	Stovall, Branch Rickey
1914	5	71	82	.464	Branch Rickey
1915	6	63	91	.409	Branch Rickey
1916	5	79	75	.513	Fielder Jones
1917	7	57	97	.370	Fielder Jones
1918	5	60	64	.484	Jones, James Burke
1919	5	67	72	.482	James Burke
1920	4	76	77	.497	James Burke
1921	3	81	73	.526	Lee A. Fohl
1922	2	93	61	.604	Lee A. Fohl
1923	5	74	78	.487	Fohl, James Austin
1924	4	74	78	.487	George Sisler
1925	3	82	71	.536	George Sisler
1926	7	62	92	.403	George Sisler
1927	7	59	94	.386	Dan P. Howley
1928	3	82	72	.532	Dan P. Howley
1929	4	79	73	.520	Dan P. Howley
1930	6	64	90	.416	William Killefer
1931	5	63	91	.409	William Killefer
1932	6	63	91	.409	William Killefer
1933	8	55	96	.364	Killefer, Rogers Hornsby
1934	6	67	85	.441	Rogers Hornsby
1935	7	65	87	.428	Rogers Hornsby
1936	7	57	95	.375	Rogers Hornsby
1937	8	46	108	.299	Hornsby, James Bottomley
1938	7	55	97	.362	Charles Street
1939	8	43	111	.279	Fred Haney
1940	6	67	87	.435	Fred Haney
1941	6	70	84	.455	Fred Haney, Luke Sewell
1942	3	82	69	.543	Luke Sewell
1943	6	72	80	.474	Luke Sewell
1944	1	89	65	.578	Luke Sewell
1945	3	81	70	.536	Luke Sewell
1946	7	66	88	.429	Luke Sewell, Zack Taylor
1947	8	59	95	.383	Herold Ruel
1948	6	59	94	.386	Zach Taylor
1949	7	53	101	.344	Zach Taylor
1950	7	58	96	.377	Zach Taylor
1951	8	52	102	.338	Zach Taylor
1952	7	64	90	.416	Rogers Hornsby, Marty Marion
1953	8	54	100	.351	Marty Marion
Total		3416	4465	.433	
Overall Total		4651	5902	.439	

TOP ST. LOUIS BROWNS MARKS

Batting—George Sisler, 1922 .... .420
Hitting Streak—George Sisler, 1922 41
Home Runs—Ken Williams, 1922 39
Runs Batted In—Ken Williams, 1922 155
Hits—George Sisler, 1920 257
Runs—Harlond Clift, 1936 145
Two Base Hits—Roy Bell, 1937 51
Three Base Hits—Henry Manush, 1928 .. 20
Stolen Bases—George Sisler, 1922 51
Bases on Balls—Lu Blue, 1929 126
Strikeouts (most)—Gus Williams, 1914 .. 120
Strikeouts (fewest)—John Tobin, 1923 .. 13
Games (Appearances)—Arthur Davenport, 1916 59
Games Started—Buck Newsom, 1938 ... 40
Games Finished—Leroy Paige, 1952 35
Complete Games—John Powell, 1902 ... 36
Innings Pitched—Urban Shocker, 1922 .. 348
Games Won—Urban Shocker, 1921 27
Games Lost—Fred Glade, 1905 25
Bases on Balls—Buck Newsom, 1938 192
Strikeouts—George Waddell, 1908 232
Shutouts—Fred Glade, 1904; Henry Howell, 1906 (tie) 6

Boston Red Sox
WON—LOST RECORD

Year	Fin-ish	Won	Lost	Pct.	Manager
1901	2	79	57	.581	James J. Collins
1902	3	77	60	.562	James J. Collins
1903	1*	91	47	.659	James J. Collins
1904	1	95	59	.617	James J. Collins
1905	4	78	74	.513	James J. Collins
1906	8	49	105	.318	Collins, Charles Stahl
1907	7	59	90	.396	George Huff, Robert Unglaub, James McGuire
1908	5	74	79	.484	McGuire, Fred Lake
1909	3	88	63	.583	Fred Lake
1910	4	81	72	.529	Pat Donovan
1911	5	78	75	.510	Pat Donovan
1912	1*	105	47	.691	J. Garland Stahl
1913	4	79	71	.527	Stahl, William Carrigan
1914	2	91	62	.595	William Carrigan
1915	1*	101	50	.669	William Carrigan

Year	Fin-ish	Won	Lost	Pct.	Manager
1916	1*	91	63	.591	William Carrigan
1917	2	90	62	.592	John J. Barry
1918	1*	75	51	.595	Edward G. Barrow
1919	6	66	71	.482	Edward G. Barrow
1920	5	72	81	.471	Edward G. Barrow
1921	5	75	79	.487	Hugh Duffy
1922	8	61	93	.396	Hugh Duffy
1923	8	61	91	.401	Frank Chance
1924	7	67	87	.435	Lee A. Fohl
1925	8	47	105	.309	Lee A. Fohl
1926	8	46	107	.301	Lee A. Fohl
1927	8	51	103	.331	William Carrigan
1928	8	57	96	.373	William Carrigan
1929	8	58	96	.377	William Carrigan
1930	8	52	102	.338	Charles Wagner
1931	6	62	90	.408	John F. Collins
1932	8	43	111	.279	Collins, Martin J. McManus
1933	7	63	86	.423	Martin J. McManus
1934	4	76	76	.500	Stanley R. Harris
1935	4	78	75	.510	Joseph E. Cronin
1936	6	74	80	.481	Joseph E. Cronin
1937	5	80	72	.526	Joseph E. Cronin
1938	2	88	61	.591	Joseph E. Cronin
1939	2	89	62	.589	Joseph E. Cronin
1940	4	82	72	.532	Joseph E. Cronin
1941	2	84	70	.545	Joseph E. Cronin
1942	2	93	59	.612	Joseph E. Cronin
1943	7	68	84	.447	Joseph E. Cronin
1944	4	77	77	.500	Joseph E. Cronin
1945	7	71	83	.461	Joseph E. Cronin
1946	1	104	50	.675	Joseph E. Cronin
1947	3	83	71	.539	Joseph E. Cronin
1948	2	96	59	.619	Joseph V. McCarthy
1949	2	96	58	.623	Joseph V. McCarthy
1950	3	94	60	.610	McCarthy, Steve O'Neill
1951	3	87	67	.565	Steve O'Neill
1952	6	76	78	.494	Lou Boudreau
1953	4	84	69	.549	Lou Boudreau
1954	4	69	85	.448	Lou Boudreau
1955	4	84	70	.545	Mike Higgins
1956	4	84	70	.545	Mike Higgins
1957	3	82	72	.532	Mike Higgins
1958	3	79	75	.513	Mike Higgins
1959	5	75	79	.487	Higgins, Bill Jurges
1960	7	65	89	.422	Jurges, Mike Higgins
1961	6	76	,86	.469	Mike Higgins
1962	8	76	84	.475	Mike Higgins
1963	7	76	85	.472	John Pesky
1964	8	72	90	.444	J. Pesky, William J. Herman
1965	9	62	100	.383	William Herman
1966	9	72	90	.444	W. Herman, James Edward Runnels
1967	1	92	70	.568	Richard H. Williams
1968	4	86	76	.531	Richard H. Williams
1969	3E	87	75	.537	Williams, Edward Popowski
1970	3E	87	75	.537	Edward Kasko
1971	3E	85	77	.525	Edward Kasko
1972	2E	85	70	.548	Edward Kasko
Total		5536	5486	.502	

*Won World Series

TOP MARKS
(1900-72)

Batting—Ted Williams, 1941	.406
Hitting Streak—D. DiMaggio, 1949	34
Home Runs—Jimmy Foxx, 1938	50
Runs Batted In—Foxx, 1938	175
Hits—Tris Speaker, 1912	222
Runs—Ted Williams, 1949	150
Two Base Hits—Earl Webb, 1931	67
Three Base Hits—Charles Stahl, 1904; Speaker, 1913 (tie)	22
Stolen Bases—Speaker, 1912	52
Bases on Balls—Ted Williams, 1947-1949 .	162
Strikeouts (most)—George Scott, 1966 ..	152
Strikeouts (fewest)—John McInnis, 1921 .	9

Pitching

Games Won—Joe Wood, 1912	34
Games Lost—Charley Ruffing, 1928	25
Games (Appearances)—Dick Radatz, 1964	79
Games Started—Cy Young, 1902	43
Games Finished—Dick Radatz, 1964	67
Complete Games—Cy Young, 1902	41
Innings Pitched—Cy Young, 1902	386
Bases on Balls—Mel Parnell, 1949	134
Strikeouts—Joe Wood, 1912	258
Shutouts—Young, 1904; Wood, 1912 (tie)	10
Home Runs Allowed—Earl Wilson, 1964 .	37

California Angels
WON—LOST RECORD

Year	Fin-ish	Won	Lost	Pct.	Manager
1961	8	70	91	.434	Bill Rigney
1962	3	86	76	.530	Bill Rigney
1963	9	70	91	.435	Bill Rigney
1964	5	82	80	.506	Bill Rigney
1965	7	75	87	.463	Bill Rigney
1966	6	80	82	.494	Bill Rigney
1967	5	84	77	.522	Bill Rigney
1968	8†	67	95	.414	Bill Rigney
1969	3W	71	91	.438	Rigney, Harold Phillips
1970	3W	86	76	.531	Harold Phillips
1971	4W	76	86	.469	Harold Phillips
1972	5W	75	80	.484	Del Rice
Total		922	1012	.477	

†Tied for Position.

TOP MARKS
(1961-72)

Batting Average—Alex Johnson, 1970 ...	.329
Hitting Streak—Sandy Alomar, 1970	22
Home Runs—Leon Wagner, 1962	37
Runs Batted In—Leon Wagner, 1962	107

Runs—Albie Pearson, 1962	115
Hits—Alex Johnson, 1970	202
Two Base Hits—Bob Rodgers, 1962	34
Three Bases—Jim Fregosi, 1968	13
Stolen Bases—Sandy Alomar, 1971	39
Bases on Balls—Albie Pearson, 1961	96
Strikeouts (most)—Bobby Knoop, 1966 .	144
Strikeouts (fewest)—Albie Pearson, 1965	17

Pitching

Games Won—Clyde Wright, 1970	22
Games Lost—George Brunet, 1967	19
Games (appearances)—Minervino Rojas, 1967	72
Games Started—Clyde Wright, 1970; Nolan Ryan, 1972 (tie)	39
Games Finished—Minervino Rojas, 1967 .	53
Completed Games—Nolan Ryan, 1972 ..	20
Innings Pitched—Nolan Ryan, 1972	284
Bases on Balls—Nolan Ryan, 1972	157
Strikeouts—Nolan Ryan, 1972	329
Shutouts—Dean Chance, 1964	11
Home Runs Allowed—Tom Murphy, 1970	32

Chicago White Sox

WON—LOST RECORD

Year	Fin-ish	Won	Lost	Pct.	Manager
1901	1	83	53	.610	Clark C. Griffith
1902	4	74	60	.552	Clark C. Griffith
1903	7	60	77	.438	James J. Callahan
1904	3	89	65	.578	Callahan, Fielder Jones
1905	2	92	60	.605	Fielder Jones
1906	1*	93	58	.616	Fielder Jones
1907	3	87	64	.576	Fielder Jones
1908	3	88	64	.579	Fielder Jones
1909	4	78	74	.513	William J. Sullivan
1910	6	68	85	.444	Hugh Duffy
1911	4	77	74	.510	Hugh Duffy
1912	4	78	76	.506	James J. Callahan
1913	5	78	74	.513	James J. Callahan
1914	6	70	84	.455	James J. Callahan
1915	3	93	61	.604	Clarence H. Rowland
1916	2	89	65	.578	Clarence H. Rowland
1917	1*	100	54	.649	Clarence H. Rowland
1918	6	57	67	.460	Clarence H. Rowland
1919	1	88	52	.629	William Gleason
1920	2	96	58	.623	William Gleason
1921	7	62	92	.403	William Gleason
1922	5	77	77	.500	William Gleason
1923	7	69	85	.448	William Gleason
1924	8	66	87	.431	Frank Chance, John J. Evers
1925	5	79	75	.513	Edward T. Collins
1926	5	81	72	.529	Edward T. Collins
1927	5	70	83	.458	Ray W. Schalk
1928	5	72	82	.468	Schalk, Russell Blackburne
1929	7	59	93	.388	Russell Blackburne
1930	7	62	92	.403	Owen J. Bush
1931	8	56	97	.366	Owen J. Bush
1932	7	49	102	.325	Lewis A. Fonseca
1933	6	67	83	.447	Lewis A. Fonseca
1934	8	53	99	.349	Fonseca, James J. Dykes
1935	5	74	78	.487	James J. Dykes
1936	3	81	70	.536	James J. Dykes
1937	3	86	68	.558	James J. Dykes
1938	6	65	83	.439	James J. Dykes
1939	4	85	69	.552	James J. Dykes
1940	4	82	72	.532	James J. Dykes
1941	3	77	77	.500	James J. Dykes
1942	6	66	82	.446	James J. Dykes
1943	4	82	72	.532	James J. Dykes
1944	7	71	83	.461	James J. Dykes
1945	6	71	78	.477	James J. Dykes
1946	5	74	80	.481	Dykes, Ted Lyons
1947	6	70	84	.455	Ted Lyons
1948	8	51	101	.336	Ted Lyons
1949	6	63	91	.409	Jack Onslow
1950	6	60	94	.390	Onslow, John Corriden
1951	4	81	73	.526	Paul Richards
1952	3	81	73	.526	Paul Richards
1953	3	89	65	.578	Paul Richards
1954	3	94	60	.610	Paul Richards
1955	3	91	63	.591	Marty Marion
1956	3	85	69	.552	Marty Marion
1957	2	90	64	.584	Al Lopez
1958	2	82	72	.532	Al Lopez
1959	1	94	60	.610	Al Lopez
1960	3	87	67	.565	Al Lopez
1961	4	86	76	.531	Al Lopez
1962	5	85	77	.525	Al Lopez
1963	2	94	68	.580	Al Lopez
1964	2	98	64	.605	Al Lopez
1965	2	95	67	.586	Al Lopez
1966	4	83	79	.512	Edward Stanky
1967	4	89	73	.549	Edward Stanky
1968	8†	67	95	.414	Stanky, Al Lopez
1969	5W	68	94	.420	Lopez, Donald Gutteridge
1970	6W	56	106	.346	Gutteridge, Marion Adair
1971	3W	79	83	.488	Charles Tanner
1972	2W	87	67	.565	Charles Tanner
Total		5579	5441	.506	

*Won World Series.   †Tied for position.

TOP MARKS
(1900-72)

Batting—Luke Appling, 1936	.388
Hitting Streak—Appling, 1936	27
Home Runs—Dick Allen, 1972	37
Runs Batted In—Zeke Bonura, 1936	138
Hits—Eddie Collins, 1920	222
Runs—Johnny Mostil, 1925	135
Two Base Hits—Floyd Robinson, 1962 ..	45
Three Base Hits—Joe Jackson, 1916	21
Stolen Bases—Wally Moses, 1943; Luis Aparicio, 1959	56
Bases on Balls—Lu Blue, 1931	127
Strikeouts (most)—Dave Nicholson, 1963	175
Strikeouts (fewest)—Nelson Fox, 1951, 1958	11

Pitching

Games Won—Ed Walsh, 1908	40
Games Lost—Pat Flaherty, 1903	25
Games (Appearances)—Wilbur Wood, 1968	88
Games Started—Ed Walsh, 1908; Wilbur Wood, 1972 (tie)	49
Games Finished—Wilbur Wood, 1970 . . .	62
Complete Games—Ed Walsh, 1908	42
Innings Pitched—Ed Walsh, 1908	464
Bases on Balls—Vern Kennedy, 1936	147
Strikeouts—Ed Walsh, 1908	269
Shutouts, Ed Walsh, 1908	12
Home Runs Allowed—W. Pierce, 1958 . . .	33

Cleveland Indians

WON—LOST RECORD

Year	Fin-ish	Won	Lost	Pct.	Manager
1901	7	54	82	.397	James R. McAleer
1902	5	69	67	.507	William R. Armour
1903	3	77	63	.550	William R. Armour
1904	4	86	65	.570	William R. Armour
1905	5	76	78	.494	Napoleon Lajoie
1906	3	89	64	.582	Napoleon Lajoie
1907	4	85	67	.559	Napoleon Lajoie
1908	2	90	64	.584	Napoleon Lajoie
1909	6	71	82	.464	Lajoie, James McGuire
1910	5	71	81	.467	James McGuire
1911	3	80	73	.523	McGuire, George Stovall
1912	5	75	78	.490	Harry Davis, J.L. Birmingham
1913	3	86	66	.566	J.L. Birmingham
1914	8	51	102	.333	J.L. Birmingham
1915	7	57	95	.375	Birmingham, Lee A. Fohl
1916	6	77	77	.500	Lee A. Fohl
1917	3	88	66	.571	Lee A. Fohl
1918	2	73	56	.566	Lee A. Fohl
1919	2	84	55	.604	Fohl, Tris Speaker
1920	1*	98	56	.636	Tris Speaker
1921	2	94	60	.610	Tris Speaker
1922	4	78	76	.507	Tris Speaker
1923	3	82	71	.536	Tris Speaker
1924	6	67	86	.438	Tris Speaker
1925	6	70	84	.455	Tris Speaker
1926	2	88	66	.571	Tris Speaker
1927	6	66	87	.431	Jack McAllister
1928	7	62	92	.403	Roger Peckinpaugh
1929	3	81	71	.533	Roger Peckinpaugh
1930	4	81	73	.526	Roger Peckinpaugh
1931	4	78	76	.506	Roger Peckinpaugh
1932	4	87	65	.572	Roger Peckinpaugh
1933	4	75	76	.497	Peckinpaugh, Walter P. Johnson
1934	3	85	69	.552	Walter P. Johnson
1935	3	82	71	.536	Johnson, Steve O'Neill
1936	5	80	74	.519	Steve O'Neill
1937	4	83	71	.539	Steve O'Neill
1938	3	86	66	.566	Oscar Vitt
1939	3	87	67	.565	Oscar Vitt
1940	2	89	65	.578	Oscar Vitt
1941	4	75	79	.487	Roger Peckinpaugh
1942	4	75	79	.487	Lou Boudreau
1943	3	82	71	.536	Lou Boudreau
1944	5	72	82	.468	Lou Boudreau
1945	5	73	72	.503	Lou Boudreau
1946	6	68	86	.442	Lou Boudreau
1947	4	80	74	.519	Lou Boudreau
1948	1*	97	58	.626	Lou Boudreau
1949	3	89	65	.578	Lou Boudreau
1950	4	92	62	.597	Lou Boudreau
1951	2	93	61	.604	Al Lopez
1952	2	93	61	.604	Al Lopez
1953	2	92	62	.597	Al Lopez
1954	1	111	43	.721	Al Lopez
1955	2	93	61	.604	Al Lopez
1956	2	88	66	.571	Al Lopez
1957	6	76	77	.497	Kerby Farrell
1958	4	77	76	.503	Bobby Bragan, Joe Gordon
1959	2	89	65	.578	Joe Gordon
1960	4	76	78	.494	Gordon, Jimmy Dykes
1961	5	78	83	.484	Jimmy Dykes
1962	6	80	82	.494	Mel McGaha
1963	5	79	83	.488	George Tebbetts
1964	6	79	83	.488	George Tebbetts
1965	5	87	75	.537	George Tebbetts
1966	5	81	81	.500	G. Tebbetts, George Strickland
1967	8	75	87	.463	Joseph Adcock
1968	3	86	75	.534	Alvin Dark
1969	6E	62	99	.385	Alvin Dark
1970	5E	76	86	.469	Alvin Dark
1971	6E	60	102	.370	Dark, John Lipton
1972	5E	72	84	.462	Ken Aspromonte
Total		5744	5301	.520	

*Won World Series.

TOP MARKS
(1901-72)

Batting—Joe Jackson, 1911	.408
Hitting Streak—Joe Jackson, 1911; Hal Trosky, 1936 (tie)	28
Home Runs—Al Rosen, 1953	43
Runs Batted In—Hal Trosky, 1936	162
Hits—Joe Jackson, 1911	233
Runs—Earl Averill, 1931	140
Two Base Hits—Geo. Burns, 1926	64
Three Base Hits—Joe Jackson, 1912	26
Stolen Bases—Ray Chapman, 1917	52
Bases on Balls—Les Fleming, 1942	106
Strikeouts (most)—Larry Doby, 1953; Leon Wagner, 1964; Max Alvis, 1965 (tie) . .	121
Strikeouts (fewest)—Joe Sewell, 1925-29	4

Pitching

Games Won—Jim Bagby, 1920	31
Games Lost—Pete Dowling, 1901; Luis Tiant, 1969 (tie)	20

Games (Appearances)—Don McMahon,
   1964 70
Games Started—George Uhle, 1923 43
Games Finished—Frank Funk, 1961 43
Complete Games—Bob Feller, 1946 36
Innings Pitched—Bob Feller, 1946 371
Bases on Balls—Bob Feller, 1938 208
Strikeouts—Bob Feller, 1946 348
Shutouts—Feller, 1946; Bob Lemon,
   1948 (tie) 10
Home Runs Allowed—Luis Tiant, 1969 . . 37

Detroit Tigers

WON—LOST RECORD

Year	Fin-ish	Won	Lost	Pct.	Manager
1901	3	74	61	.548	George T. Stallings
1902	7	52	83	.385	Frank Dwyer
1903	5	65	71	.478	Edward G. Barrow
1904	7	62	90	.408	Barrow, Robert Lowe
1905	3	79	74	.516	William R. Armour
1906	6	71	78	.477	William R. Armour
1907	1	92	58	.613	Hugh Jennings
1908	1	90	63	.588	Hugh Jennings
1909	1	98	54	.645	Hugh Jennings
1910	3	86	68	.558	Hugh Jennings
1911	2	89	65	.578	Hugh Jennings
1912	6	69	84	.451	Hugh Jennings
1913	6	66	87	.431	Hugh Jennings
1914	4	80	73	.523	Hugh Jennings
1915	2	100	54	.649	Hugh Jennings
1916	3	87	67	.565	Hugh Jennings
1917	4	78	75	.510	Hugh Jennings
1918	7	55	71	.437	Hugh Jennings
1919	4	80	60	.571	Hugh Jennings
1920	7	61	93	.396	Hugh Jennings
1921	6	71	82	.464	Tyrus Cobb
1922	3	79	75	.513	Tyrus Cobb
1923	2	83	71	.539	Tyrus Cobb
1924	3	86	68	.558	Tyrus Cobb
1925	4	81	73	.526	Tyrus Cobb
1926	6	79	75	.513	Tyrus Cobb
1927	4	82	71	.536	George Moriarty
1928	6	68	86	.442	George Moriarty
1929	6	70	84	.455	Stanley R. Harris
1930	5	75	79	.487	Stanley R. Harris
1931	7	61	93	.396	Stanley R. Harris
1932	5	76	75	.503	Stanley R. Harris
1933	5	75	79	.487	Stanley R. Harris
1934	1	101	53	.656	Gordon S. Cochrane
1935	1*	93	58	.616	Gordon S. Cochrane
1936	2	83	71	.539	Gordon S. Cochrane
1937	2	89	65	.578	Gordon S. Cochrane
1938	4	84	70	.545	Cochrane, Delmar Baker
1939	5	81	73	.526	Delmar Baker
1940	1	90	64	.584	Delmar Baker
1941	4	75	79	.487	Delmar Baker
1942	5	73	81	.474	Delmar Baker
1943	5	78	76	.506	Steve O'Neill
1944	2	88	66	.571	Steve O'Neill
1945	1*	88	65	.575	Steve O'Neill
1946	2	92	62	.597	Steve O'Neill
1947	2	85	69	.552	Steve O'Neill
1948	5	78	76	.506	Steve O'Neill
1949	4	87	67	.565	Robert A. Rolfe
1950	2	95	59	.617	Robert A. Rolfe
1951	5	73	81	.474	Robert A. Rolfe
1952	8	50	104	.325	Rolfe, Fred Hutchinson
1953	6	60	94	.390	Fred Hutchinson
1954	5	68	86	.442	Fred Hutchinson
1955	5	79	75	.513	Bucky Harris
1956	5	82	72	.532	Bucky Harris
1957	4	78	76	.506	Jack Tighe
1958	5	77	77	.500	Tighe, Bill Norman
1959	4	76	78	.494	Norman, Jimmy Dykes
1960	6	71	83	.461	Dykes, Joe Gordon
1961	2	101	61	.623	Robert Sheffing
1962	4	85	76	.528	Robert Sheffing
1963	5	79	83	.488	R. Sheffing, Charles Dressan
1964	4	85	77	.525	Charles Dressan
1965	4	89	73	.549	Charles Dressan
1966	3	88	74	.543	C. Dressan, Robert Swift, Francis Skaff
1967	2	91	71	.562	Edward Mayo Smith
1968	1*	103	59	.636	Edward Mayo Smith
1969	2E	90	72	.556	Edward Mayo Smith
1970	4E	79	83	.488	Edward Mayo Smith
1971	2E	91	71	.562	Alfred Martin
1972	1E†	86	70	.551	Alfred Martin
Total		5761	5290	.521	

*Won World Series.
†Lost in playoff series.

TOP MARKS
(1900-72)

Batting—Ty Cobb, 1911 420
Hitting Streak—Cobb, 1911 40
Home Runs—Hank Greenberg, 1937 58
Runs Batted In—Hank Greenberg, 1937 . 183
Hits—Ty Cobb, 1911 248
Runs—Ty Cobb, 1911 147
Two Base Hits—Hank Greenberg, 1934 . . 63
Three Base Hits—Sam Crawford, 1914 . . . 26
Stolen Bases—Ty Cobb, 1915 96
Bases on Balls—Roy Cullenbine, 1947 . . . 137
Strikeouts (most)—Jake Wood, 1961 141
Strikeouts (fewest)—Chas. Gehringer, 1936;
   Harvey Kuenn, 1954 (tie) 13

Pitching

Games Won—Denny McLain, 1968 31
Games Lost—Mullin, 1904 23
Games (Appearances)—Fred Scherman,
   1971 69
Games Started—Mickey Lolich, 1971 . . . 45
Games Finished—Tom Timmerman, 1970 43
Complete Games—Mullin, 1904 42
Innings Pitched—George Mullin, 1904 . . . 382
Bases on Balls—Paul Foytack, 1956 142
Strikeouts (most)—Mickey Lolich, 1971 . 308

Shutouts—Denny McLain, 1969   9
Most Home Runs Allowed—Denny McLain,
   1966   42

Kansas City Royals
WON—LOST RECORD

Year	Fin-ish	Won	Lost	Pct.	Manager
1969	4W	69	93	.426	Joseph L. Gordon
1970	4W†	65	97	.401	Charles Metro, Robert Lemon
1971	3W	85	76	.528	Robert Lemon
1972	4W	76	78	.494	Robert Lemon
Total		295	344	.462	

†Tied for position

TOP MARKS
(1969-72)

Batting Average—Lou Piniella, 1972 312
Hitting Streak—Lou Piniella, 1971   18
Home Runs—Bob Oliver, 1970   27
Runs Batted In—John Mayberry, 1972 . .   100
Runs—Amos Otis, 1970   91
Hits—Lou Piniella, 1972   179
Two Base Hits—Amos Otis, 1970   36
Three Base Hits—Fred Patek, 1971   11
Stolen Bases—Amos Otis, 1971   52
Bases on Balls—Paul Schaal, 1971   103
Strikeouts (most)—Bob Oliver, 1970   126
Strikeouts (fewest)—Cookie Rojas,
   1971–72   35

Pitching

Games Won—Dick Drago, 1971   17
Games Lost—Dick Drago, 1972   17
Games (Appearances)—Tom Burgmeier,
   1971   67
Games Started—Dick Drago, 1970-71 . . .   34
Games Finished—Ted Abernathy, 1971 . .   46
Complete Games—Dick Drago, 1971   15
Innings Pitched—Dick Drago, 1971   241
Bases on Balls—Jim Rooker, 1970   102
Strikeouts—Bob Johnson, 1970   206
Shutouts—Bill Butler, 1969; Dick
   Drago, 1971 (tie)   4
Home Runs Allowed—Wally Bunker, 1969   29

Milwaukee Brewers
(Franchise transferred from Seattle in 1970)
WON—LOST RECORD

Year	Fin-ish	Won	Lost	Pct.	Manager
1969	6W	64	98	.395	Joseph Schultz
1970	4W†	65	97	.401	James David Bristol
1971	6W	69	92	.429	James David Bristol
1972	6E	65	91	.417	Bristol, Delmar Wesley Crandall
Total		263	378	.410	

†Tied for position

TOP MARKS
(1969-72)

Batting Average—Tommy Harper, 1970 . .   .296
Hitting Streak—Tommy Davis, 1969   18
Home Runs—Tommy Harper, 1970   31
Runs Batted In—George Scott, 1972   88
Runs—Tommy Harper, 1970   104
Hits—Tommy Harper, 1970   179
Two Base Hits—Tommy Harper, 1970 . . .   35
Three Base Hits—Jim Hegan, 1969;
   Ted Kubiak, 1970 (tie)   6
Stolen Bases—Tommy Harper, 1969   73
Bases on Balls—Tommy Harper, 1969 . . .   95
Strikeouts (most)—George Scott, 1972 . .   130
Strikeouts (fewest)—Roberto Pena, 1970   45

Pitching

Games Won—Marty Pattin, 1970-71; Jim
   Lonborg (tie)   14
Games Lost—Lew Krausse, 1970   18
Games (Appearances)—Ken Sanders, 1971   83
Games Started—Marty Pattin, 1971   36
Games Finished—Ken Sanders, 1971   77
Complete Games—Bill Parsons, 1971   12
Innings Pitched—Marty Pattin, 1971   265
Bases on Balls—Gene Brabender, 1969 . . .   103
Strikeouts—Marty Pattin, 1971   169
Shutouts—Marty Pattin, 1971   5
Home Runs Allowed—Lew Krausse, 1970   33

Minnesota Twins
(Franchise transferred from Washington, D.C., in 1961)

WON—LOST RECORD

Year	Fin-ish	Won	Lost	Pct.	Manager
1961	7	70	90	.438	Harry Lavagetto, Sam Mele
1962	2	91	71	.562	Sam Mele
1963	3	91	70	.565	Sam Mele
1964	6	79	83	.488	Sam Mele
1965	1	102	60	.630	Sam Mele
1966	2	89	73	.549	Sam Mele
1967	2	91	71	.562	S. Mele, Calvin Ermer
1968	7	79	83	.488	Calvin Ermer
1969	1W†	97	65	.599	Alfred Martin
1970	1W†	98	64	.605	William Rigney
1971	5W	74	86	.463	William Rigney
1972	3W	77	77	.500	Rigney, Frank Quilici
Total		1038	893	.538	

†Lost in playoff series.

TOP MARKS
(1961-72)

Batting Average—Tony Oliva, 1971 337
Hitting Streak—Lennie Green, 1961   24
Home Runs—Harmon Killebrew, 1964,
   1969   49
Runs Batted In—Harmon Killebrew, 1969   140
Runs—Zoilo Versalles, 1965   126

Hits—Tony Oliva, 1964	217
Two Base Hits—Zoilo Versalles, 1965 . . .	45
Three Base Hits—Zoilo Versalles, 1963;	
Cesar Tovar, 1970 (tie)	13
Stolen Bases—Cesar Tovar, 1969	45
Bases on Balls—Harmon Killebrew, 1969 .	145
Strikeouts (most)—Bob Darwin, 1972 . . .	145
Strikeouts (fewest)—Vic Power, 1963 . . .	24

Pitching

Games Won—Jim Kaat, 1966	25
Games Lost—Pedro Ramos, 1961	20
Games (Appearances)—Ron Perranoski,	
1969	75
Games Started—Jim Kaat, 1965	42
Games Finished—Ron Perranoski, 1969 . .	52
Complete Games—Jim Kaat, 1966	19
Innings Pitched—Jim Kaat, 1966	305
Bases on Balls—Dave Boswell, 1967	107
Strikeouts—Dean Chance, 1968	234
Shutouts—Camilo Pascual, 1961	8
Home Runs Allowed—Pedro Ramos, 1961;	
Jim Perry (tie)	39

New York Yankees

WON—LOST RECORD

Year	Fin-ish	Won	Lost	Pct.	Manager
1903	4	72	62	.537	Clark C. Griffith
1904	2	92	59	.609	Clark C. Griffith
1905	6	71	78	.477	Clark C. Griffith
1906	2	90	61	.596	Clark C. Griffith
1907	5	70	78	.473	Clark C. Griffith
1908	8	51	103	.331	Griffith, Norman Elberfeld
1909	5	74	77	.490	George T. Stallings
1910	2	88	63	.583	Stallings, Hal Chase
1911	6	76	76	.500	Hal Chase
1912	8	50	102	.329	Harry Wolverton
1913	7	57	94	.377	Frank Chance
1914	6	70	84	.455	Chance, Roger Peckinpaugh
1915	5	69	83	.454	William E. Donovan
1916	4	80	74	.519	William E. Donovan
1917	6	71	82	.464	William E. Donovan
1918	4	60	63	.488	Miller J. Huggins
1919	3	80	59	.576	Miller J. Huggins
1920	3	95	59	.617	Miller J. Huggins
1921	1	98	55	.641	Miller J. Huggins
1922	1	94	60	.610	Miller J. Huggins
1923	1*	98	54	.645	Miller J. Huggins
1924	2	89	63	.586	Miller J. Huggins
1925	7	69	85	.448	Miller J. Huggins
1926	1	91	63	.591	Miller J. Huggins
1927	1*	110	44	.714	Miller J. Huggins
1928	1*	101	53	.656	Miller J. Huggins
1929	2	88	66	.571	Miller J. Huggins
1930	3	86	68	.558	Robert Shawkey
1931	2	94	59	.614	Joseph V. McCarthy
1932	1*	107	47	.695	Joseph V. McCarthy
1933	2	91	59	.607	Joseph V. McCarthy
1934	2	94	60	.610	Joseph V. McCarthy
1935	2	89	60	.597	Joseph V. McCarthy
1936	1*	102	51	.667	Joseph V. McCarthy
1937	1*	102	52	.662	Joseph V. McCarthy
1938	1*	99	53	.651	Joseph V. McCarthy
1939	1*	106	45	.702	Joseph V. McCarthy
1940	3	88	66	.571	Joseph V. McCarthy
1941	1*	101	53	.656	Joseph V. McCarthy
1942	1	103	51	.669	Joseph V. McCarthy
1943	1*	98	56	.636	Joseph V. McCarthy
1944	3	83	71	.539	Joseph V. McCarthy
1945	4	81	71	.533	Joseph V. McCarthy
1946	3	87	67	.565	McCarthy, William Dickey, John Neun
1947	1*	97	57	.630	Stanley R. Harris
1948	3	94	60	.610	Stanley R. Harris
1949	1*	97	57	.630	Charles D. Stengel
1950	1*	98	56	.636	Charles D. Stengel
1951	1*	98	56	.636	Charles D. Stengel
1952	1*	95	59	.617	Charles D. Stengel
1953	1*	99	52	.652	Charles D. Stengel
1954	2	103	51	.669	Charles D. Stengel
1955	1	96	58	.623	Charles D. Stengel
1956	1*	97	57	.630	Charles D. Stengel
1957	1	98	56	.636	Charles D. Stengel
1958	1*	92	62	.597	Charles D. Stengel
1959	3	79	75	.513	Charles D. Stengel
1960	1	97	57	.630	Charles D. Stengel
1961	1*	109	53	.673	Ralph Houk
1962	1*	96	66	.593	Ralph Houk
1963	1	104	57	.646	Ralph Houk
1964	1	99	63	.611	Yogi Berra
1965	6	77	85	.475	Johnny Keane
1966	10	70	89	.440	Johnny Keane, R. Houk
1967	9	72	90	.444	Ralph Houk
1968	5	83	79	.512	Ralph Houk
1969	5E	80	81	.497	Ralph Houk
1970	2E	93	69	.574	Ralph Houk
1971	4E	82	.80	.506	Ralph Houk
1972	4E	79	76	.510	Ralph Houk
Total		6149	4590	.573	

*Won World Series.

TOP MARKS
(1903-72)

Batting—Babe Ruth, 1923	.393
Hitting Streak—Joe DiMaggio, 1941	56
Home Runs—Babe Ruth, 1927	60
Home Runs—Roger Maris, 1961	61
Runs Batted In—Lou Gehrig, 1931	184
Hits—Earl Combs, 1927	231
Runs—Babe Ruth, 1921	177
Two Base Hits—Lou Gehrig, 1927	52
Three Base Hits—Earl Combs, 1927	23
Stolen Bases—Fred Maisel, 1914	74
Bases on Balls—Babe Ruth, 1923	170
Strikeouts (most)—Mickey Mantle, 1959 .	126
Strikeouts (fewest)—Yogi Berra, 1950 . . .	12

Pitching

Games Won—Jack Chesbro, 1904	41

Games Lost—A. Orth, 1907; J. Lake, 1908;
  R. Ford, 1912; S. Jones, 1925 (tie) . . .   21
Games (Appearances)—Luis Arroyo, 1961;
  Pedro Ramos, 1965; Dooley Womack, 1967
  (tie)   65
Games Started—Jack Chesbro, 1904   51
Games Finished—Sparky Lyle, 1972   56
Complete Games—Jack Chesbro, 1904 . .   48
Innings Pitched—Jack Chesbro, 1904 454
Bases on Balls—Tommy Byrne, 1949 179
Strikeouts (most)—Jack Chesbro, 1904 . . 240
Shutouts—Russell Ford, 1910; Whitey Ford,
  1964 (tie)   8
Home Runs Allowed—Ralph Terry, 1962   40

Oakland Athletics

(Franchise transferred from Philadelphia in 1954, with first season at Kansas City in 1955; franchise transferred from Kansas City in 1967, first season played in 1968.)

WON—LOST RECORD

Year	Fin-ish	Won	Lost	Pct.	Manager
1901	4	74	62	.544	Connie Mack
1902	1	83	53	.610	Connie Mack
1903	2	75	60	.556	Connie Mack
1904	5	81	70	.536	Connie Mack
1905	1	92	56	.621	Connie Mack
1906	4	78	67	.538	Connie Mack
1907	2	88	57	.607	Connie Mack
1908	6	68	85	.444	Connie Mack
1909	2	95	58	.621	Connie Mack
1910	1*	102	48	.680	Connie Mack
1911	1*	101	50	.669	Connie Mack
1912	3	90	62	.592	Connie Mack
1913	1*	96	57	.627	Connie Mack
1914	1	99	53	.651	Connie Mack
1915	8	43	109	.283	Connie Mack
1916	8	36	117	.235	Connie Mack
1917	8	55	98	.359	Connie Mack
1918	8	52	76	.402	Connie Mack
1919	8	36	104	.257	Connie Mack
1920	8	48	106	.312	Connie Mack
1921	8	53	100	.346	Connie Mack
1922	7	65	89	.422	Connie Mack
1923	6	69	83	.454	Connie Mack
1924	5	71	81	.467	Connie Mack
1925	2	88	64	.579	Connie Mack
1926	3	83	67	.553	Connie Mack
1927	2	91	63	.591	Connie Mack
1928	2	98	55	.641	Connie Mack
1929	1*	104	46	.693	Connie Mack
1930	1*	102	52	.662	Connie Mack
1931	1	107	45	.704	Connie Mack
1932	2	94	60	.610	Connie Mack
1933	3	79	72	.523	Connie Mack
1934	5	68	82	.453	Connie Mack
1935	8	58	91	.389	Connie Mack
1936	8	53	100	.346	Connie Mack
1937	7	54	97	.358	Connie Mack
1938	8	53	99	.349	Connie Mack
1939	7	55	97	.362	Connie Mack
1940	8	54	100	.351	Connie Mack
1941	8	64	90	.416	Connie Mack
1942	8	55	99	.357	Connie Mack
1943	8	49	105	.318	Connie Mack
1944	5	72	82	.468	Connie Mack
1945	8	52	98	.347	Connie Mack
1946	8	49	105	.318	Connie Mack
1947	5	78	76	.506	Connie Mack
1948	4	84	70	.545	Connie Mack
1949	5	81	73	.526	Connie Mack
1950	8	52	102	.338	Connie Mack
1951	6	70	84	.455	James J. Dykes
1952	4	79	75	.513	James J. Dykes
1953	7	59	95	.383	Jimmy Dykes
1954	8	51	103	.331	Eddie Joost
1955	6	63	91	.409	Lou Boudreau
1956	8	52	102	.338	Lou Boudreau
1957	7	59	94	.386	Boudreau, Harry Craft
1958	7	73	81	.474	Harry Craft
1959	7	66	88	.429	Harry Craft
1960	8	58	96	.377	Robert Elliott
1961	9	61	100	.379	Joe Gordon, H. Bauer
1962	9	72	90	.444	Henry Bauer
1963	8	73	89	.451	Edmund Lopat
1964	10	57	105	.352	E. Lopat, F. Melvin McGaha
1965	10	59	103	.364	F.M. McGaha, Haywood Sullivan
1966	7	74	86	.463	Alvin Dark
1967	10	62	99	.385	A. Dark, Lucius Appling
1968	6	82	80	.506	Robert Kennedy
1969	2W	88	74	.543	Henry Bauer, John McNamara
1970	2W	89	73	.549	John McNamara
1971	1W†	101	60	.627	Richard H. Williams
1972	1W*	93	62	.600	Richard H. Williams
Total		5415	6198	.466	

*Won World Series.
†Lost in playoff series

TOP MARKS
(1901-72)

Batting—Nap Lajoie, 1901 422
Hitting Streak—Bill Lamar, 1925   29
Home Runs—Jimmy Foxx, 1932   58
Runs Batted In—Jimmy Foxx, 1932 169
Hits—Al Simmons, 1925 253
Runs—Al Simmons, 1930 152
Two Base Hits—Al Simmons, 1926   53
Three Base Hits—Frank Baker, 1912   21
Stolen Bases—Eddie Collins, 1910   81
Bases on Balls—Eddie Joost, 1949 149
Strikeouts (most)—Reggie Jackson, 1968 171
Strikeouts (fewest)—Dick Siebert, 1942   17

Pitching

Games Won—Jack Coombs, 1910; Bob Grove,
  1931 (tie)   31
Games Lost—Scott Perry, 1920   25

Games (Appearances)—John Wyatt, 1964   81
Games Started—George Waddell, 1904 ..   46
Games Finished—John Wyatt, 1964; Jack
   Aker, 1966 (tie)   57
Complete Games—George Waddell, 1904 .   36
Innings Pitched—George Waddell, 1904 .. 384
Bases on Balls—Elmer Myers, 1916   168
Strikeouts—George Waddell, 1904   349
Shutouts—Jack Coombs, 1910   13
Most Home Runs Allowed—Orlando
   Pena, 1964   41

Texas Rangers
(Formerly Washington Senators, franchise moved
in 1972)

WON—LOST RECORD

Year	Fin- ish	Won	Lost	Pct.	Manager
1901	6	61	72	.459	James H. Manning
1902	6	61	75	.449	Thomas J. Loftus
1903	8	43	94	.314	Thomas J. Loftus
1904	8	38	113	.251	P.J. Donovan
1905	7	64	87	.421	J. Garland Stahl
1906	7	55	95	.367	J. Garland Stahl
1907	8	49	102	.325	Joseph Cantillon
1908	7	67	85	.441	Joseph Cantillon
1909	8	42	110	.276	Joseph Cantillon
1910	7	66	85	.437	James R. McAleer
1911	7	64	90	.416	James R. McAleer
1912	2	91	61	.599	Clark C. Griffith
1913	2	90	64	.584	Clark C. Griffith
1914	3	81	73	.526	Clark C. Griffith
1915	4	85	68	.556	Clark C. Griffith
1916	7	76	77	.497	Clark C. Griffith
1917	5	74	79	.484	Clark C. Griffith
1918	3	72	56	.563	Clark C. Griffith
1919	7	56	84	.400	Clark C. Griffith
1920	6	68	84	.447	Clark C. Griffith
1921	4	80	73	.523	George F. McBride
1922	6	69	85	.448	Clyde Milan
1923	4	75	78	.490	Owen J. Bush
1924	1*	92	62	.597	Stanley R. Harris
1925	1	96	55	.636	Stanley R. Harris
1926	4	81	69	.540	Stanley R. Harris
1927	3	85	69	.552	Stanley R. Harris
1928	4	75	79	.487	Stanley R. Harris
1929	5	71	81	.467	Walter P. Johnson
1930	2	94	60	.610	Walter P. Johnson
1931	3	92	62	.597	Walter P. Johnson
1932	3	93	61	.604	Walter P. Johnson
1933	1	99	53	.651	Joseph E. Cronin
1934	7	66	86	.434	Joseph E. Cronin
1935	6	67	86	.438	Stanley R. Harris
1936	4	82	71	.536	Stanley R. Harris
1937	6	73	80	.477	Stanley R. Harris
1938	5	75	76	.497	Stanley R. Harris
1939	6	65	87	.428	Stanley R. Harris
1940	7	64	90	.416	Stanley R. Harris
1941	6	70	84	.455	Stanley R. Harris
1942	7	62	89	.357	Stanley R. Harris
1943	2	84	69	.549	Oswald Bluege
1944	8	64	90	.416	Oswald Bluege
1945	2	87	67	.565	Oswald Bluege
1946	4	76	78	.494	Oswald Bluege
1947	7	64	90	.416	Oswald Bluege
1948	7	56	97	.366	Joseph Kuhel
1949	8	50	104	.325	Joseph Kuhel
1950	5	67	87	.435	Stanley R. Harris
1951	7	62	92	.403	Stanley R. Harris
1952	5	78	76	.506	Stanley R. Harris
1953	5	76	76	.500	Bucky Harris
1954	6	66	88	.429	Bucky Harris
1955	8	53	101	.344	Charles Dressen
1956	7	59	95	.383	Charles Dressen
1957	8	55	99	.357	Charles Dressen, Harry Lavagetto
1958	8	61	93	.396	Harry Lavagetto
1959	8	63	91	.409	Harry Lavagetto
1960	5	73	81	.474	Harry Lavagetto
1961	9	61	100	.379	Mickey Vernon
1962	10	60	101	.373	Mickey Vernon
1963	10	56	106	.346	M. Vernon, Gilbert Hodges
1964	9	62	100	.383	Gilbert Hodges
1965	8	70	92	.432	Gilbert Hodges
1966	8	71	88	.447	Gilbert Hodges
1967	6	76	85	.472	Gilbert Hodges
1968	10	65	96	.404	James Lemon
1969	4E	86	76	.531	Theodore Williams
1970	3E	70	92	.432	Theodore Williams
1971	5E	63	96	.396	Theodore Williams
1972	6W	54	100	.351	Theodore Williams
Total		5017	5996	.456	

*Won World Series.

TOP MARKS
(1901-72)

Batting—Goose Goslin, 1928 .... .379
Hitting Streak—Heinie Manush, 1933 ...   33
Home Runs—Frank Howard, 1969   48
Runs Batted In—Goose Goslin, 1924 129
Runs—Joe Cronin, 1930   127
Hits—Edgar "Sam" Rice, 1925 227
Two Base Hits—Mickey Vernon, 1946 ...   51
Three Base Hits—Goose Goslin, 1925 ...   20
Stolen Bases—Clyde Milan, 1912   88
Bases on Balls—Eddie Yost, 1956 151
Strikeouts (most)—Frank Howard, 1967 . 155
Strikeouts (fewest)—Sam Rice, 1929   9

Pitching

Games Won—Walter Johnson, 1913   36
Games Lost—J. Townsend, 1904; Robert B.
   Groom, 1909 (tie)   26
Games (Appearances)—Ron Kline, 1965 .   74
Games Started—Walter Johnson, 1910 ...   42
Games Finished—Ron Kline, 1965   58
Complete Games—Walter Johnson, 1910 .   38
Innings Pitched—Walter Johnson, 1910 .. 374
Bases on Balls—Buck Newsom, 1936 146
Strikeouts—Walter Johnson, 1910 313
Shutouts—Walter Johnson, 1913   12
Home Runs Allowed—Pete Ramos, 1957 .   43

Top Team Records
(Since 1901)

Batting—.319, New York Nationals, 1930; American League—.316, Detroit, 1921.

Runs—1,067, New York Americans, 155 games, 1931; National League—1,004, St. Louis, 154 games, 1930.

Runs Batted In—995, New York Americans, 155 games, 1936; National League—942, St. Louis, 154 games, 1930.

Hits—1,783, Philadelphia Nationals, 156 games, 1930; American League—1,724, Detroit, 154 games, 1921.

Two-Base Hits—373, St. Louis Nationals, 154 games, 1930; American League—358, Cleveland, 154 games, 1930.

Three-Base Hits—129, Pittsburgh Nationals, 152 games, 1912; American League—112 (tie), Baltimore, 134 games, 1901, and Boston, 141 games, 1903.

Home Runs—240, New York (AL) 1961, 162 games; National League—221, New York, 1947, and Cincinnati, 1956, 154 games; American League—193, New York, 1960, 154 games.

Total Bases—2,703, New York Americans, 155 games, 1936; National League—2,684, Chicago, 156 games, 1930.

Stolen Bases—347, New York Nationals, 154 games, 1911; American League—288, Washington, 155 games, 1913.

Longest Winning Streak—26 games, New York Nationals, Sept. 7 to Sept. 30, 1916. Streak ended when the Giants were beaten by the Boston Braves, 8–3, in the second game of a double-header. The American League record for consecutive victories is 19, set by Chicago in 1906 and tied by New York in 1947.

Longest Losing Streak—20 games (tie), by Boston Americans, 1906, and Philadelphia Americans, 1916, 1943. National League—19 games (tie) Cincinnati, 1914, and Boston, 1906.

Longest Game in the Majors

Box Score of Boston-Brooklyn
26-Inning Game
(At Braves Field, Boston, May 1, 1920.)

BROOKLYN (N)

	ab	r	h	po	a	e
Olson, 2b	10	0	1	5	8	1
Neis, rf	10	0	1	9	0	0
Johnston, 3b	10	0	2	3	1	0
Wheat, lf	9	0	2	3	0	0
Myers, cf	2	0	1	2	0	0
Hood, cf	6	0	1	9	1	0
Konetchy, 1b	9	0	1	30	0	0
Ward, ss	10	0	0	5	3	1
Krueger, c	2	1	0	4	3	0
Elliott, c	7	0	0	7	3	0
Cadore, p	10	0	0	1	12	0
Total	85	1	9	78	31	2

BOSTON (N)

	ab	r	h	po	a	e
Powell, cf	7	0	1	8	0	0
Pick, 2b	11	0	0	6	11	2
Mann, lf	10	0	2	6	0	0
Cruise, rf	9	1	1	4	0	0
Holke, 1b	10	0	2	42	1	0
Boeckel, 3b	11	0	3	1	7	0
Maranville, ss	10	0	3	1	9	0
O'Neil, c	2	0	0	4	1	0
a Christenbury	1	0	1	0	0	0
Gowdy, c	6	0	1	6	1	0
Oeschger, p	9	0	1	0	11	0
Total	86	1	15	78	41	2

a Batted for O'Neil in the ninth.

```
Brooklyn... 0 0 0 0 1 0 0 0 0 0 0 0 0
            0 0 0 0 0 0 0 0 0 0 0 0 0–1

Boston..... 0 0 0 0 0 1 0 0 0 0 0 0 0
            0 0 0 0 0 0 0 0 0 0 0 0 0–1
```

(Called, darkness)

Runs batted in—Olson, Boeckel.

Two-base hits—Maranville, Oeschger. Three-base hit—Cruise. Stolen bases—Myers, Hood. Sacrifices—Hood, Powell, Cruise, Holke, O'Neil, Oeschger. Double plays—Olson and Konetchy; Oeschger, Holke and Gowdy. Left on bases—Boston 16, Brooklyn 11. Earned runs—Boston 1, Brooklyn 1. Struck out—by Cadore 7 (Pick, Mann, Cruise, Gowdy, Oeschger 3), Oeschger 7 (Olson, Neis 2, Johnston, Hood, Elliott, Cadore). Bases on balls—Off Cadore 5 (Powell 3, Mann, Cruise), Oeschger 4 (Wheat, Hood, Konetchy, Krueger). Wild pitch—Oeschger. Umpires—McCormick and Hart. Time—3:50. Attendance—2,000.

ATTENDANCE RECORDS

National League

Club	Grounds	Record Crowd	Visiting Club	Date	Record season attendance
Atlanta	Atlanta Stadium	52,270	Los Angeles (N)	Aug. 9, 1966	1,539,801 (1966)
Chicago	Wrigley Field	46,965	Pittsburgh (2)	May 31, 1948	1,674,993 (1969)
Cincinnati	Riverfront Stadium	52,116	Chicago (2)	July 9, 1972	1,803,568 (1970)
Houston	Astrodome	50,908	Los Angeles (N)	June 22, 1966	2,151,470 (1965)
Los Angeles	Dodgers Stadium	*78,672	San Francisco	April 18, 1958	2,755,184 (1962)
Montreal	Jarry Park	31,004	New York	May 18, 1970	1,424,683 (1970)
N.Y. (Mets)	Shea Stadium	57,175	Los Angeles (2)	June 13, 1965	2,697,479 (1970)
Philadelphia	Veterans Stadium	57,267	New York	May 21, 1972	1,511,223 (1971)
Pittsburgh	Three Rivers Stadium	50,469	New York	Sept. 27, 1970	1,705,828 (1960)
St. Louis	Busch Stadium	49,743	Atlanta (2)	June 23, 1968	2,090,145 (1967)
San Diego	San Diego Stadium	40,189	Los Angeles (N)	July 3, 1971	644,273 (1972)
San Francisco	Candlestick Park	42,894	Milwaukee	April 14, 1964	1,795,356 (1960)

*Crowd record set in Coliseum.

American League

Club	Grounds	Record Crowd	Visiting Club	Date	Record season attendance
Baltimore	Memorial Stadium	47,987	New York (N)	Aug. 15, 1964	1,203,366 (1966)
Boston	Fenway Park	41,766	New York (2)	Aug. 12, 1934	1,940,788 (1968)
California	Anaheim Stadium	53,591	New York (N)	July 13, 1962	1,400,321 (1966)
Chicago	Comiskey Park	54,215	New York (2)	July 19, 1953	1,644,460 (1960)
Cleveland	Municipal Stadium	84,587	New York (2)	Sept. 12, 1954	2,620,627 (1948)
Detroit	Briggs Stadium	58,369	New York (2)	July 20, 1947	2,031,847 (1968)
Kansas City	Royals Stadium	35,623	Oakland (2)	Aug. 3, 1971	910,784 (1971)
Milwaukee	County Stadium	44,387	Cleveland	Aug. 16, 1970	933,690 (1970)
Minnesota	Metropolitan Stadium	44,184	Chicago	May 4, 1969	1,483,547 (1967)
New York	Yankee Stadium	81,841	Boston (2)	May 30, 1938	2,373,901 (1948)
Oakland	Oakland Coliseum	48,758	Detroit	June 6, 1970	921,323 (1972)
Texas	Arlington Stadium	24,222	Detroit (N)	July 21, 1972	662,974 (1972)

Top Individual Records

Batting, Season—.424, Roger Hornsby, St. Louis Nationals, 143 games, 1924; American League—.420 (tie), Ty Cobb, Detroit, 146 games, 1911, and George Sisler, St. Louis, 142 games, 1922. (Hugh Duffy, Boston Nationals, hit .438, the all-time high, in 1894.)

Batting (10 or more seasons)—.367, Ty Cobb, Detroit and Philadelphia Americans, 1905—28.

Most Years Batting Over .300—23, Ty Cobb.

Most Hits, Lifetime—4,191, Ty Cobb.

Most Hits, Season—257, George Sisler, St. Louis Americans, 631 times at bat, 143 games, 1920; National League—254 (tie), Lefty O'Doul, Philadelphia, 638 times at bat, 154 games, 1929, and Bill Terry, New York, 633 times at bat, 154 games, 1930.

Long Hits—1,356, Babe Ruth, Boston and New York Americans and Boston Nationals, 1914—35 (506 doubles, 136 triples, 714 home runs).

Total Bases, Lifetime—6,134, Stan Musial.

Total Bases, Season—457, Babe Ruth, New York Americans, 1921; National League—450, Rogers Hornsby, St. Louis, 1922.

Total Bases, Game—18, Joe Adcock, Milwaukee Nationals, 1954 (4 home runs, 1 double).

Home Runs, Lifetime—714, Babe Ruth; National League and American Leagues—673 Hank Aaron, Milwaukee and Atlanta (NL), 654 Willie Mays, New York and San Francisco (NL)

Home Runs, Season—61, Roger Maris, New York (AL), 1961; 60, Babe Ruth, New York (AL), (1927); National League, 56, Hack Wilson, Chicago, 1930.

Home Runs, Game—4 (tie), Lou Gehrig, New York Americans, 1932; Chuck Klein, Philadelphia Nationals, 1936 (10 innings); Pat Seerey, Chicago Americans, 1948 (11 innings); Gil Hodges, Brooklyn National, 1950; Joe Adcock, Milwaukee Nationals, 1954.

3-Base Hits, Lifetime—312, Sam Crawford, Cincinnati Nationals and Detroit Americans, 1899–1917.

3-Base Hits, Season—36, J. Owen Wilson, Pittsburgh Nationals, 1912; American League—26 (tie), Joe Jackson, Cleveland, 1912, and Sam Crawford, Detroit, 1914.

2-Base Hits, Lifetime—793, Tris Speaker, Boston, Cleveland, Washington and Philadelphia Americans, 1907–28.

2-Base Hits, Season—67, Earl Webb, Boston Americans, 1931; National League—64, Joe Medwick, St. Louis, 1936.

Singles, Lifetime—3,052, Ty Cobb.

Singles, Season—198, Lloyd Waner, Pittsburgh Nationals, 1927; American League—182, Sam Rice, Washington, 1925.

Runs, Lifetime—2,244, Ty Cobb (AL); 2,011, Willie Mays (NL)

Runs, Season—177, Babe Ruth, New York Americans, 152 games, 1921; National League—158, Chuck Klein, 158 games, 1930.

Runs Batted In, Lifetime—2,209 Babe Ruth (AL & NL), 2037, Hank Aaron (NL)

Runs Batted In, Season—190, Hack Wilson, Chicago Nationals, 1930; American League—184, Lou Gehrig, New York, 1931.

Runs Batted In, Game—12, Jim Bottomley, St. Louis Nationals, vs. Brooklyn, Sept. 16, 1924; American League—11 (tie), Tony Lazzeri, New York, 1936, and Rudy York, Boston, 1946.

Stolen Bases, Lifetime—892, Ty Cobb.

Stolen Bases, Season—104, Maury Wills, Los Angeles (NL), 1962 (162 games); American League—96, Ty Cobb, Detroit, 1915 (154 games); National League—80, Bob Bescher, Cincinnati, 1911 (154 games)

Bases on Balls, Lifetime—2,056, Babe Ruth.

Bases on Balls, Season—170, Babe Ruth, New York Americans, 1923; National League—148, Eddie Stanky, Brooklyn, 1945 and Jim Wynn, Houston, 1969 (tie)

Bases on Balls, Game—6, Jimmy Foxx, Boston Americans, 1938; National League—5, by a number of players.

Consecutive Games Batted Safely—56, Joe DiMaggio, New York Americans, 1941; National League—37, Tommy Holmes, Boston, 1945.

Successive Hits—12 (tie), Frank Higgins, Boston Americans, 1938, and Walt Dropo, Detroit Americans, 1952; National League record of 10 is held by 7 players.

Fewest Strikeouts, Season (150 or more games)—4, Joe Sewell, Cleveland Americans, 1925 and 1929.

Consecutive Games Played—2,130, Lou Gehrig, New York Americans (streak started June 1, 1925, and stopped May 2, 1939); National League—1,117 Billy Williams, Chicago (streak started Sept. 22, 1963 and ended Sept. 2, 1970)

NOTE—Wilbert Robinson of the Baltimore Nationals in 1892 made 7 consecutive hits in one game, a record never equaled. The modern mark is 6, held by a number of players. Bobby Lowe, Boston Nationals (1894), and Ed Delahanty, Philadelphia Nationals (1896), are the others credited with hitting 4 home runs in one game. Willie Keeler of Baltimore hit safely in 44 straight games in 1897 to set an all-time National League record.

Joe DiMaggio's Consecutive-Game Hitting Record

(56 in 1941.)

Game	Date and opponent	ab	r	h	2b	3b	hr
1.	May 15—Chicago	4	0	1	0	0	0
2.	May 16—Chicago	4	2	2	0	1	1
3.	May 17—Chicago	3	1	1	0	0	0
4.	May 18—St. Louis	3	3	3	1	0	0
5.	May 19—St. Louis	3	0	1	1	0	0
6.	May 20—St. Louis	5	1	1	0	0	0
7.	May 21—Detroit	5	0	2	0	0	0
8.	May 22—Detroit	4	0	1	0	0	0
9.	May 23—Boston	5	0	1	0	0	0
10.	May 24—Boston	4	2	1	0	0	0
11.	May 25—Boston	4	0	1	0	0	0
12.	May 27—Washington	5	3	4	0	0	1
13.	May 28—Washington	4	1	1	0	1	0
14.	May 29—Washington	3	1	1	0	0	0
15.	May 30—Boston	2	1	1	0	0	0
16.	May 30—Boston	3	0	1	1	0	0
17.	June 1—Cleveland	4	1	1	0	0	0
18.	June 1—Cleveland	4	0	1	0	0	0
19.	June 2—Cleveland	4	2	2	1	0	0
20.	June 3—Detroit	4	1	1	0	0	1
21.	June 5—Detroit	5	1	1	0	1	0
22.	June 7—St. Louis	5	2	3	0	0	0
23.	June 8—St. Louis	4	3	2	0	0	2
24.	June 8—St. Louis	4	1	2	1	0	1
25.	June 10—Chicago	5	1	1	0	0	0
26.	June 12—Chicago	4	1	2	0	0	1
27.	June 14—Cleveland	2	0	1	1	0	0
28.	June 15—Cleveland	3	1	1	0	0	1
29.	June 16—Cleveland	5	0	1	1	0	0
30.	June 17—Chicago	4	1	1	0	0	0
31.	June 18—Chicago	3	0	1	0	0	0
32.	June 19—Chicago	3	2	3	0	0	1
33.	June 20—Detroit	5	3	4	1	0	0
34.	June 21—Detroit	4	0	1	0	0	0
35.	June 22—Detroit	5	1	2	1	0	1
36.	June 24—St. Louis	4	1	1	0	0	0
37.	June 25—St. Louis	4	1	1	0	0	1
38.	June 26—St. Louis	4	0	1	1	0	0
39.	June 27—Philadelphia	3	1	2	0	0	1
40.	June 28—Philadelphia	5	1	2	1	0	0
41.	June 29—Washington	4	1	1	1	0	0
42.	June 29—Washington	5	1	1	0	0	0
43.	July 1—Boston	4	0	2	0	0	0
44.	July 1—Boston	3	1	1	0	0	0
45.	July 2—Boston	5	1	1	0	0	1

46. July 5—Philadelphia	4	2	1	0	0	1
47. July 6—Philadelphia	5	2	4	1	0	0
48. July 6—Philadelphia	4	0	2	0	1	0
49. July 10—St. Louis	2	0	1	0	0	0
50. July 11—St. Louis	5	1	4	0	0	1
51. July 12—St. Louis	5	1	2	0	0	0
52. July 13—Chicago	4	2	3	0	0	0
53. July 13—Chicago	4	0	1	0	0	0
54. July 14—Chicago	3	0	1	0	0	0
55. July 15—Chicago	4	1	2	1	0	0
56. July 16—Cleveland	4	3	3	1	0	0
Totals	223	56	91	16	4	15

DiMaggio was stopped by Pitchers Al Smith and Jim Bagby Jr. in 3 official times at bat in a night game at Cleveland on July 17. He grounded to third twice and drew a pass against Smith and hit into a double play against Bagby.

BASEBALL'S HALL OF FAME

When baseball's leaders made plans to build a shrine in Cooperstown, N.Y., it was decided that there should be a Hall of Fame for the immortals of the game.

The Centennial Committee,which consisted of Judge Kenesaw M. Landis, Commissioner of Baseball; William Harridge, president of the American League; Ford C. Frick, president of the National League; John A. Heydler, chairman of the board of the National League; Clark C. Griffith of the Washington club, Edward G. Barrow of the New York Americans and Connie Mack of the Philadelphia Americans, chose the old-time group of notables. The modern players were selected by a 75 per cent vote of the Baseball Writers' Association.

The Centennial Committee, functioning through 1936 and 1937, named the following:

Abner Doubleday.

Alexander Cartwright, designer of the baseball diamond and framer of the first definite rules.

Morgan G. Bulkeley, first president of the National League.

Henry Chadwick, called the "Father of Baseball."

Ban Johnson, first president of the American League.

A.G. Spalding, pitcher and later baseball executive.

George Wright, of Cincinnati Red Stockings, the first professional team.

Connie Mack, player and later manager of the Philadelphia Americans.

Charles A. Comiskey, player and later owner of the Chicago Americans.

John J. McGraw, player and later manager of the New York Nationals.

Charles (Old Hoss) Radbourne, most famous pitcher of his time.

William (Buck) Ewing, one of the greatest of catchers.

William (Candy) Cummings, pitcher, credited with originating curve ball in 1864.

In 1936, the baseball writers chose these five players:

Ty Cobb, outfielder and champion batsman.

John (Honus) Wagner, shortstop and champion batsman.

George H. (Babe) Ruth, pitcher, outfielder and "Home Run King."

Christy Mathewson, pitcher.

Walter P. Johnson, pitcher.

Later selections by the writers were:

1937—Denton T. (Cy) Young, pitcher, who pitched in the most games and won the greatest number.

Tris Speaker, outfielder and batting champion.

Napoleon Lajoie, second baseman and batting champion.

1938—Grover Alexander, pitcher.

1939—George H. Sisler, pitcher, first baseman and batting champion.

Eddie T. Collins, second baseman, batting and base running star.

Willie Keeler, third baseman-outfielder and batting champion.

Lou Gehrig, durable first baseman and powerful batsman.

1942—Rogers Hornsby, infielder and batting champion.

1943—Judge Kenesaw Mountain Landis, baseball's first commissioner.

1945—Wilbert Robinson, James Collins, Hugh Jennings, Fred Clarke, Hugh Duffy, Roger Bresnahan, Dan Brouthers, Ed Delahanty, James O'Rourke, Mike Kelly.

1946—Jesse Burkett, Frank Chance, Johnny Evers, Clark Griffith, Tom McCarthy, Joe McGinnity, Eddie. Plank, Joe Tinker, Rube Waddell, Ed Walsh, Jack Chesbro.

1947—Carl Hubbell, Robert M. (Lefty) Grove, Gordon (Mickey) Cochrane, Frank Frisch.

1948—Harold (Pie) Traynor, Herb Pennock.

1949—Mordecai (Three-Finger) Brown, Charles Gehringer, Charles (Kid) Nichols.

1951—Mel Ott, Jimmy Foxx.

1952—Harry Heilmann, Paul Waner.

1953—Al Simmons, Jerome (Dizzy) Dean.

1954—Walter (Rabbit) Moranville, Bill Dickey and Bill Terry.

1955—Joe DiMaggio, Ted Lyons, Arthur (Dazzy) Vance and Charles (Gabby) Hartnett.

1956—Hank Greenberg and Joe Cronin.

1957—Joe McCarthy and Sam Crawford.

1959—Zach Wheat.

1961—Max Carey, William Hamilton

1962—Robert Feller, Jackie Robinson, Edd Roush, Bill McKechnie.

1963—Eppa Rixey, Edgar (Sam) Rice, Elmer Flick, John Clarkson.

1964—Luke Appling, Urban (Red) Faber,

Burleigh Grimes, Tim Keefe, Heinie Manush, Miller Huggins, John Montgomery Ward.

1965—James (Pud) Galvin.

1966—Ted Williams, Casey Stengel.

1967—Charles (Red) Ruffing, Branch Rickey, Lloyd Waner.

1968—Hazen (Kiki) Cuyler, Leon (Goose) Goslin, Joe (Ducky) Medwick.

1969—Stan (The Man) Musial, Roy Campanella, Stan Coveleski, Waite Hoyt.

1970—Lou Boudreau, Earle Combs, Jesse Haines, Ford Frick.

1971—Chick Hafey, Rube Marquard, Joe Kelley, Dave Bancroft, Harry Hooper, Jake Beckley, George Weiss, Satchel Paige.

1972—Sandy Koufax, Yogi Berra, Early Wynn, Lefty Gomez, Will Harridge, Ross Youngs, Josh Gibson, Walter (Buck) Leonard.

HONOR ROLL OF BASEBALL

(Created in 1946 by Old-Timers Committee: Paul Kerr, Edward G. Barrow, Connie Mack, Robert Quinn, Melville Webb.)

Writers—Walter Barnes and Tim Murnane, Boston; Harry Cross, William Hanna, Sid Mercer, William Slocum, George Tidden and Joe Vila, New York; Frank Hough and Frank Richter, Philadelphia; Si Sanborn, Chicago; John B. Sheridan, St. Louis.

Umpires—Tom Connolly, William Dinneen, Robert Emslie, Billy Evans, John Gaffney, Tim Hurst, William Klem, John Kelly, Tom Lynch, Silk O'Loughlin, Jack Sheridan.

Managers—William Carrigan, Ed Hanlon, Miller Huggins, Frank Selee, John M. Ward.

Executives—Ernest S. Barnard, Edward G. Barrow, John E. Bruce, John T. Brush, Barney Dreyfuss, Charles Ebbets, August Herrmann, John A. Heydler, Bob Quinn, Art Soden, Nicholas Young.

MOST VALUABLE PLAYER SELECTIONS

Chalmers Award
(Discontinued after 1914.)

National League

1911—Frank Schulte, Chicago
1912—Lawrence Doyle, New York
1913—Jacob Daubert, Brooklyn
1914—John J. Evers, Boston

American League

1911—Tyrus Cobb, Detroit
1912—Tris Speaker, Boston
1913—Walter Johnson, Washington
1914—Edward Collins, Philadelphia

League Awards

National League
(Selections discontinued after 1929.)

1924—Arthur Vance, Brooklyn

1925—Rogers Hornsby, St. Louis
1926—Robert O'Farrell, St. Louis
1927—Paul Waner, Pittsburgh
1928—Jim Bottomley, St. Louis
1929—Rogers Hornsby, Chicago

American League
(Selections discontinued after 1928.)

1922—George Sisler, St. Louis
1923—George Ruth, New York
1924—Walter Johnson, Washington
1925—Roger Peckinpaugh, Washington
1926—George Burns, Cleveland
1927—Lou Gehrig, New York
1928—Gordon Cochrane, Philadelphia

Sporting News
(Selections discontinued after 1945.)

National League

1930—William Terry, New York
1931—Charles Klein, Philadelphia
1932—Charles Klein, Philadelphia
1933—Carl Hubbell, New York
1934—Jerome Dean, St. Louis
1935—Floyd Vaughan, Pittsburgh
1936—Carl Hubbell, New York
1937—Joseph Medwick, St. Louis
1938—Ernest Lombardi, Cincinnati
1939—William Walters, Cincinnati
1940—Frank McCormick, Cincinnati
1941—Adolph Camilli, Brooklyn
1942—Morton Cooper, St. Louis
1943—Stanley Musial, St. Louis
1944—Martin Marion, St. Louis
1945—Thomas Holmes, Boston

American League

1929—Al Simmons, Philadelphia
1930—Joseph Cronin, Washington
1931—Lou Gehrig, New York
1932—James Foxx, Philadelphia
1933—James Foxx, Philadelphia
1934—Lou Gehrig, New York
1935—Henry Greenberg, Detroit
1936—Lou Gehrig, New York
1937—Charles Gehringer, Detroit
1938—James Foxx, Boston
1939—Joe DiMaggio, New York
1940—Henry Greenberg, Detroit
1941—Joe DiMaggio, New York
1942—Joe Gordon, New York
1943—Spurgeon Chandler, New York
1944—Robert Doerr, Boston
1945—Harold Newhouser, Detroit

Baseball Writers' Association

National League

1931—Frank Frisch, St. Louis
1932—Charles Klein, Philadelphia
1933—Carl Hubbell, New York
1934—Jerome Dean, St. Louis

1935—Charles Hartnett, Chicago
1936—Carl Hubbell, New York
1937—Joseph Medwick, St. Louis
1938—Ernest Lombardi, Cincinnati
1939—William Walters, Cincinnati
1940—Frank McCormick, Cincinnati
1941—Adolph Camilli, Brooklyn
1942—Morton Cooper, St. Louis
1943—Stanley Musial, St. Louis
1944—Martin Marion, St. Louis
1945—Phil Cavaretta, Chicago
1946—Stanley Musial, St. Louis
1947—Robert Elliott, Boston
1948—Stanley Musial, St. Louis
1949—Jackie Robinson, Brooklyn
1950—Jim Konstanty, Philadelphia
1951—Roy Campanella, Brooklyn
1952—Henry Sauer, Chicago
1953—Roy Campanella, Brooklyn
1954—Willie Mays, New York
1955—Roy Campanella, Brooklyn
1956—Don Newcombe, Brooklyn
1957—Henry Aaron, Milwaukee
1958—Ernie Banks, Chicago
1959—Ernie Banks, Chicago
1960—Richard, Groat, Pittsburgh
1961—Frank Robinson, Cincinnati
1962—Maury Wills, Los Angeles
1963—Sandy Koufax, Los Angeles
1964—Kenton Boyer, St. Louis
1965—Willie Mays, San Francisco
1966—Roberto Clemente, Pittsburgh
1967—Orlando Cepeda, St. Louis
1968—Robert Gibson, St. Louis
1969—Willie McCovey, San Francisco
1970—Johnny Bench, Cincinnati
1971—Joseph Torre, St. Louis
1972—Johnny Bench, Cincinnati

American League

1931—Robert Grove, Philadelphia
1932—James Foxx, Philadelphia
1933—James Foxx, Philadelphia
1934—Gordon Cochrane, Detroit
1935—Henry Greenberg, Detroit
1936—Lou Gehrig, New York
1937—Charles Gehringer, Detroit
1938—James Foxx, Boston
1939—Joe DiMaggio, New York
1940—Henry Greenberg, Detroit
1941—Joe DiMaggio, New York
1942—Joe Gordon, New York
1943—Spurgeon Chandler, New York
1944—Harold Newhouser, Detroit
1945—Harold Newhouser, Detroit
1946—Ted Williams, Boston
1947—Joe DiMaggio, New York
1948—Lou Boudreau, Cleveland
1949—Ted Williams, Boston
1950—Phil Rizzuto, New York
1951—Lawrence Berra, New York

1952—Bobby Shantz, Philadelphia
1953—Al Rosen, Cleveland
1954—Lawrence Berra, New York
1955—Lawrence Berra, New York
1956—Mickey Mantle, New York
1957—Mickey Mantle, New York
1958—Jackie Jensen, Boston
1959—J. Nelson Fox, Chicago
1960—Roger E. Maris, New York
1961—Roger E. Maris, New York
1962—Mickey Mantle, New York
1963—Elston Howard, New York
1964—Brooks Robinson, Baltimore
1965—Zoilo Versalles, Minnesota
1966—Frank Robinson, Baltimore
1967—Carl Yastrzemski, Boston
1968—Dennis McLain, Detroit
1969—Harmon Killebrew, Minnesota
1970—John (Boog) Powell, Baltimore
1971—Vida Blue, Oakland
1972—Dick Allen, Chicago

Cy Young Award

Because few pitchers, regardless of their records, had a chance to win the most valuable player awards, it was decided in 1956 to honor them separately. The Cy Young Award is now presented annually to the player selected as the pitcher of the year in the major leagues.

The winners:

1956—Don Newcombe, Brooklyn, National
1957—Warren Spahn, Milwaukee, National
1958—Bob Turley, New York, American
1959—Early Wynn, Chicago AL
1960—Vernon Law, Pittsburgh NL
1961—Edward C. Ford, New York AL
1962—Don Drysdale, Los Angeles NL
1963—Sandy Koufax, Los Angeles NL
1964—Dean Chance, Los Angeles AL
1965—Sandy Koufax, Los Angeles NL
1966—Sandy Koufax, Los Angeles NL
1967—Jim Lonborg, Boston AL; Mike McCormick, San Francisco NL
1968—Dennis McLain, Detroit AL; Robert Gibson, St. Louis NL
1969—Dennis McLain, Detroit AL; Mike Cuellar, Baltimore AL (tie); Tom Seaver, New York NL
1970—Jim Perry, Minnesota AL; Bob Gibson, St. Louis, NL
1971—Vida Blue, Oakland AL; Ferguson Jenkins, Chicago NL
1972—Gaylord Perry, Cleveland AL; Steve Carlton, Philadelphia NL

ALL-STAR GAMES

The All-Star game was originated in 1933 by Arch Ward, the late sports editor of *The Chicago Tribune*. There was no game in 1945 because of wartime curtailment of travel. Two All-Star games were played each year from 1959 through

1962 and the Majors returned to a single game in 1963.

The contest brings together the stars of the American and National Leagues. At the beginning, selections were made by the votes of fans, but this system was abandoned later and the choices made by league executives and managers. Voting by fans was resumed in 1947 but later this method was abandoned again and the players, coaches and managers became the selectors. Of the net receipts, including television and radio income, 75 per cent goes into the players' pension fund.

Balloting of players was again given to the fans in 1970, after 13 years.

Record of The Games

Winning and losing pitchers in capital letters.

1st game, at Chicago (AL), July 6, 1933

```
                                R.  H.  E.
National .......000 002 000 --   2   8   0
American .......012 001 00x --   4   9   1
```

Pitchers—HALLAHAN, Warneke (3), Hubbell (7) vs. GOMEZ, Crowder (4), Grove (7). Homers—Ruth (AL), Frisch (NL). Managers—John McGraw (NL); Connie Mack (AL). Attendance—49,200. Receipts—$56,378.50.

2d game, at New York (NL), July 10, 1934

```
American .......000 261 000 --   9  14   1
National .......103 030 000 --   7   8   1
```

Pitchers—Gomez, Ruffing (4), HARDER (5) vs. Hubbell, Warneke (4), MUNGO (5), J. Dean (6), Frankhouse (9). Homers—Frisch (NL), Medwick (NL). Managers—Joe Cronin (AL); Bill Terry (NL). Attendance—48,363. Receipts—$52,982.

3d game, at Cleveland (AL), July 8, 1935

```
National .......000 100 000 --   1   4   1
American .......210 010 00x --   4   8   0
```

Pitchers—WALKER, Schumacher (3), Derringer (7), J. Dean (8) vs. GOMEZ, Harder (7). Homer—Foxx (AL). Managers—Frankie Frisch (NL); Mickey Cochrane (AL). Attendance—69,812. Receipts—$82,179.12.

4th game, at Boston (NL), July 7, 1936

```
American .......000 000 300 --   3   7   1
National .......020 020 00x --   4   9   0
```

Pitchers—GROVE, Rowe (4), Harder (7) vs. J. DEAN, Hubbell (4), C. Davis (7), Warneke (7). Homers—Gehrig (AL), Galan (NL). Managers—Joe McCarthy (AL); Charlie Grimm (NL). Attendance—25,534. Receipts—$24,588.80.

5th game, at Washington (AL), July 7, 1937

```
National .......000 111 000 --   3  13   0
American .......002 312 00x --   8  13   2
```

Pitchers—J. DEAN, Hubbell (4), Blanton (4),

Grissom (5), Mungo (6), Walters (8) vs. GOMEZ, Bridges (4), Harder (7). Homer—Gehrig (AL). Managers—Bill Terry (NL); Joe McCarthy (AL). Attendance—31,391. Receipts—$28,475.18.

6th game, at Cincinnati (NL), July 6, 1938

```
American .......000 000 001 --   1   7   4
National .......100 100 20x --   4   8   0
```

Pitchers—GOMEZ, Allen (4), Grove (7) vs. VANDER MEER, Lee (4), Brown (7). Homers—None. Managers—Joe McCarthy (AL); Bill Terry (NL). Attendance—27,607. Receipts—$38,469.05.

7th game, at New York (AL), July 11, 1939

```
National .......001 000 000 --   1   7   1
American .......000 210 00x --   3   6   1
```

Pitchers—Derringer, LEE (4), Fette (7) vs. Ruffing, BRIDGES (4), Feller (6). Homer—J. DiMaggio (AL). Managers—Gabby Hartnett (NL); Joe McCarthy (AL). Attendance—62,892. Receipts—$75,701.

8th game, at St. Louis (NL), July 9, 1940

```
American .......000 000 000 --   0   3   1
National .......300 000 01x --   4   7   0
```

Pitchers—RUFFING, Newsom (4), Feller (7) vs. DERRINGER, Walters (3), Wyatt (5), French (7), Hubbell (9). Homer—West (NL). Managers—Joe Cronin (AL); Bill McKechnie (NL). Attendance—32,373. Receipts—$36,723.03.

9th game, at Detroit (AL), July 8, 1941

```
National .......000 001 220 --   5  10   2
American .......000 101 014 --   7  11   3
```

Pitchers—Wyatt, Derringer (3), Walters (5), PASSEAU (7) vs. Feller, Lee (4), Hudson (7), SMITH (8). Homers—Vaughan (NL) 2, Williams (AL). Managers—Bill McKechnie (NL); Del Baker (AL). Attendance—54,675. Receipts—$63,267.08.

10th game, at New York (NL), July 6, 1942

```
American .......300 000 000 --   3   7   0
National .......000 000 010 --   1   6   1
```

Pitchers—CHANDLER, Benton (5) vs. M. COOPER, Vander Meer (4), Passeau (7), Walters (9). Homers—Boudreau (AL), York (AL), Owen (NL). Managers—Joe McCarthy (AL); Leo Durocher (NL). Attendance—33,694. Receipts—$86,102.98.

11th game, at Phila. (AL), July 13, 1943

```
National .......100 000 101 --   3  10   1
American .......031 010 00x --   5   8   2
```

Pitchers—M. COOPER, Vander Meer (3), Sewell (6), Javery (7) vs. LEONARD, Newhouser (4), Hughson (7). Homers—Doerr (AL), V. DiMaggio (NL). Managers—Billy Southworth (NL); Joe McCarthy (AL). Attendance—31,938. Receipts—$65,674.

12th game, at Pittsburgh (NL), July 11, 1944

American . . . . 010 000 000 –– 1 6 3
National . . . . 000 040 21x –– 7 12 1
Pitchers–Borowy, HUGHSON (4), Muncrief (5), Newhouser (7), Newsom (8) vs. Walters, RAFFENSBERGER (4), Sewell (6), Tobin (9). Homers–None. Managers–Joe McCarthy (AL); Billy Southworth (NL). Attendance–29,589. Receipts–$81,275.

(NO GAME IN 1945)

13th game, at Boston (AL), July 9, 1946

National . . . . 000 000 000 –– 0 3 0
American . . . . 200 130 24x –– 12 14 1
Pitchers–PASSEAU, Higbe (4), Blackwell (5), Sewell (8) vs. FELLER, Newhouser (4), Kramer (7). Homers–Williams (AL) 2, Keller (AL). Managers–Charlie Grimm (NL); Steve O'Neill (AL). Attendance–34,906. Receipts–$89,071.

14th game, at Chicago (NL), July 8, 1947

American . . . . 000 001 100 –– 2 8 0
National . . . . 000 100 000 –– 1 5 1
Pitchers–Newhouser, SHEA (4), Masterson (7), Page (8) vs. Blackwell, Brecheen (4), SAIN (7), Spahn (8). Homer–Mize (NL). Managers–Joe Cronin (AL); Eddie Dyer (NL). Attendance–41,123. Receipts–$105,314.90.

15th game, at St. Louis (AL), July 13, 1948

National . . . . 200 000 000 –– 2 8 0
American . . . . 011 300 00x –– 5 6 0
Pitchers–Branca, SCHMITZ (4), Sain (4), Blackwell (6) vs. Masterson, RASCHI (4), Coleman (7). Homers–Musial (NL), Evers (AL). Managers–Leo Durocher (NL); Bucky Harris (AL). Attendance–34,009. Receipts–$93,447.07.

16th game, at Brooklyn (NL), July 12, 1949

American . . . . 400 202 300 –– 11 13 1
National . . . . 212 002 000 –– 7 12 5
Pitchers–Parnell, TRUCKS (2), Brissie (4), Raschi (7) vs. Spahn, NEWCOMBE (2), Munger (5), Bickford (6), Pollet (7), Blackwell (8), Roe (9). Homers–Musial (NL), Kiner (NL). Managers–Lou Boudreau (AL); Billy Southworth (NL). Attendance–32,577. Receipts–$79,225.02.

17th game, at Chicago (AL), July 11, 1950

National . . 020 000 001 000 01 –– 4 10 0
American . . 001 020 000 000 00 –– 3 8 1
Pitchers–Roberts, Newcombe (4), Konstanty (6), Jansen (7), BLACKWELL (12) vs. Raschi, Lemon (4), Houtteman (7), Reynolds (10), GRAY (13), Feller (14). Homers–Kiner (NL), Schoendienst (NL). Managers–Burt Shotton (NL); Casey Stengel (AL). Attendance–46,127. Receipts–$126,179.51.

18th game, at Detroit (AL), July 10, 1951

National . . . . 100 302 110 –– 8 12 1
American . . . . 010 110 000 –– 3 10 2
Pitchers–Roberts, MAGLIE (3), Newcombe (6), Blackwell (9) vs. Garver, LOPAT (4), Hutchinson (5), Parnell (8), Lemon (9). Homers–Musial (NL), Elliott (NL), Hodges (NL), Kiner (NL), Wertz (AL), Kell (AL). Managers–Eddie Sawyer (NL); Casey Stengel (AL). Attendance–52,075. Receipts–$124,294.07.

19th game, at Philadelphia (NL), July 8, 1952

American . . . . 000 20 –– 2 5 0
National . . . . 100 20 –– 3 3 0
Called, rain.
Pitchers–Raschi, LEMON (3), Shantz (5) vs. Simmons, RUSH (4). Homers–J. Robinson (NL), Sauer (NL). Managers–Casey Stengel (AL); Leo Durocher (NL). Attendance–32,785. Receipts–$108,762.

20th game, at Cincinnati (NL), July 14, 1953

American . . . . 000 000 001 –– 1 5 0
National . . . . 000 020 12x –– 5 10 0
Pitchers–Pierce, REYNOLDS (4), Garcia (6), Paige (8) vs. Roberts, SPAHN (4), Simmons (6), Dickson (8). Homers–None. Managers–Casey Stengel (AL); Charles Dressen (NL). Attendance–30,846. Receipts–$155,654.

21st game, at Cleveland (AL), July 13, 1954

National . . . . 000 520 020 –– 9 14 0
American . . . . 004 121 03x –– 11 17 1
Pitchers–Roberts, Antonelli (4), Spahn (6), Grissom (6), CONLEY (8), Erskine (8) vs. Ford, Consuegra (4), Lemon (4), Porterfield (5), Keegan (8), STONE (8), Trucks (9). Homers–Rosen (AL) 2, Boone (AL), Kluszewski (NL), Bell (NL). Attendance–68,751. Receipts–$292,678.

22nd game, at Milwaukee (NL), July 12, 1955

American . . . 400 001 000 000 –– 5 10 2
National . . . 000 000 230 001 –– 6 13 1
Pitchers–Pierce, Wynn (4), Ford (7), SULLIVAN (8) vs. Roberts, Haddix (4), Newcombe (7), Jones (8), Nuxhall (8), CONLEY (12). Homers–Mantle (AL), Musial (NL). Attendance–45,314. Receipts–$179,545.50.

23rd game, at Washington (AL), July 10, 1956

National . . . . 001 211 200 –– 7 11 0
American . . . . 000 003 000 –– 3 11 0
Pitchers–FRIEND, Spahn (4), Antonelli (6) vs. PIERCE, Ford (4), Wilson (5), Brewer (6), Score (8), Wynn (9). Homers–Mays (NL), Musial (NL), Williams (AL), Mantle (AL). Attendance–28,843. Receipts–$105,982.50.

24th game, at St. Louis (NL), July 9, 1957

American . . . . 020 001 003 --   6 11   0
National . . . . 000 000 203 --   5   9   1

Pitchers—BUNNING, Loes (4), Wynn (7), Pierce (7), Mossi (9), Grim (9) vs. SIMMONS, Burdette (2), Sanford (6), Jackson (7), Labine (9). Attendance—30,693. Receipts—$122,027.

25th game, at Baltimore (AL), July 8, 1958

National . . . . 210 000 000 --   3   4   2
American . . . . 110 011 00x --   4   9   2

Pitchers—Spahn, FRIEND (4), Jackson (6), Farrell (7), vs. Turley, Narleski (2), WYNN (6), Odell (7). Attendance—48,829. Receipts—$202,494.

26th game, at Pittsburgh (NL), July 7, 1959

American . . . . 000 100 030 --   4   8   0
National . . . . 100 000 22x --   5   9   1

Pitchers—Drysdale, Burdette (4), Face (7), ANTONELLI (8), Elston (9) vs. Wynn, Duren (4), Bunning (7), FORD (8), Daley (8). Homers—Mathews (NL), Kaline (AL). Attendance 35,277. Receipts—$194,303.

27th game, at Los Angeles (NL), Aug. 3, 1959

American . . . . 012 000 110 --   5   6   0
National . . . . 100 010 100 --   3   6   3

Pitchers—WALKER, Wynn (4), Wilhelm (6), O'Dell (7), McLish (8) vs. DRYSDALE, Conley (4), Jones (6), Face (8). Homers—Malzone, Berra, Colavito (AL), Robinson, Gilliam (NL). Attendance—54,982.

28th game, at Kansas City (AL), July 11, 1960

National . . . . 311 000 000 --   5 12   4
American . . . . 000 001 020 --   3   6   1

Pitchers—FRIEND, McCormick (4), Face (6), Buhl (8), Law (9) vs. MONBOUQUETTE, Estrada (3), Coates (4), Bell (6), Lary (8), Daley (9). Homers—Banks, Crandall, Kaline. Attendance—30,619.

29th game, at New York (AL), July 13, 1960

National . . . . 021 000 102 --   6 10   0
American . . . . 000 000 000 --   0 18   0

Pitchers—LAW, Podres (3), Williams (5), Jackson (7), Henry (8), McDaniel (9) vs. FORD, Wynn (4), Staley (6), Lary (8), Bell (9). Homers—Mathews, Mays, Musial, Boyer. Attendance—38,362.

30th game, at San Francisco (NL), July 11, 1961

National . . . . . 010 100 010 2 --   5 11   5
American . . . . . 000 001 002 1 --   4   4   2

Pitchers—Spahn, Purkey (4), McCormick (6), Face (9), Koufax (9), MILLER (9) vs. Ford, Lary (4), Donovan (4), Bunning (6), Fornieles (8),

WILHELM (8). Homers—Killebrew, Altman. Attendance—31,851.

31st game at Boston (AL), July 31, 1961

National . . . . 000 001 000 --   1   5   1
American . . . . 100 000 000 --   1   4   0

Pitchers—Purkey, Mahaffey (3), Koufax (5), Miller (7) vs. Bunning, Schwall (4), Pascual (7). Attendance—31,851.

32nd game, at Washington (AL), July 10, 1962

National . . . . 000 002 010 --   3   8   0
American . . . . 000 001 000 --   1   4   0

Pitchers—Drysdale, MARICHAL (4), Purkey (6), Shaw (8) vs. Bunning, Pascual (4), Donovan (7), Pappas. Attendance—45,480.

33rd game, at Chicago (NL), July 30, 1962

American . . . . 001 201 302 --   9 10   0
National . . . . 010 000 111 --   4 10   4

Pitchers—Stenhouse, HERBERT (3), Aguirre (6), Pappas (9) vs. Podres, MAHAFFEY (3), Gibson (5), Farrell (7), Marichal (8). Attendance—38,359. Homers—Runnels, Wagner, Colavito, Roseboro.

34th game, at Cleveland (AL), July 9, 1963

National . . . . 012 010 010 --   5   6   0
American . . . . 012 000 000 --   3 11   1

Pitchers—O'Toole, JACKSON (3), Culp (5), Woodeshick (6), Drysdale (8) vs. McBride, BUNNING (4), Bouton (6), Pizarro (7), Radatz (8). Attendance—44,160.

35th game, at New York (NL), July 7, 1964

National . . . . 000 210 004 --   7   8   0
American . . . . 100 002 100 --   4   9   1

Pitchers—Drysdale (3), Bunning (4), Short, Farrell, MARICHAL vs. Chance (2), PASCUAL. Attendance—50,850. Homers—Williams, Boyer, Callison.

36th game, at Minnesota (AL), July 13, 1965

National . . . . 320 000 100 --   6 11   0
American . . . . 000 140 000 --   5   8   0

Pitchers—Marichal, Maloney (4), Drysdale (5), KOUFAX (6), Farrell (7), Gibson (8) vs. Pappas, Grant (2), Richert (4), McDOWELL (6), Fisher (8). Attendance—46,706. Homers—Mays, Torre, Stargell, McAuliffe, Killebrew.

37th game, at St. Louis (NL), July 12, 1966

National . . . . . 000 100 000 1 --   2   6   0
American . . . . . 010 000 000 0 --   1   6   0

Pitchers—Koufax (1), Bunning (2), Marichal (2), PERRY vs. McLain (3), Kaat, Siebert, RICHERT. Attendance—49,936.

38th game, at Anaheim (AL), July 11, 1967

National .010 000 000 000 001 —— 2 9 0
American .000 001 000 000 000 —— 1 8 0
  Pitchers—Marichal (3), Jenkins (6), Gibson (2), Short, Cuellar (2), DRYSDALE (2), Seaver vs. Chance, McGlothlin (2), Peters (4), Downing (2), HUNTER (4). Attendance—46,309. Homers—Allen, B. Robinson, Perez.

39th game, at Houston (NL), July 9, 1968
American . . . . . . .000 000 000 —— 0 3 1
National . . . . . . .100 000 00x —— 1 5 0
  Pitchers—TIANT, Odom (3), McLain (5), McDowell (7), Stottlemyre (8), John (8) vs. DRYSDALE, Marichal (4), Carlton (6), Seaver (7), Reed (9), Koosman (9). Attendance—48,321.

40th game, at Washington (AL), July 23, 1969
National . . . . . . .125 100 000 —— 9 11 0
American . . . . . . .011 100 000 —— 3 6 2
  Pitchers—CARLTON, Gibson (4), Singer (5), Koosman (7), Dierker (8), P. Niekro (9) vs. STOTTLEMYRE, Odom (3), Knowles (3), Mc-Lain (4) McNally (5), McDowell (7), Culp (9). Attendance—45,259. Homers—Bench (NL), Howard (AL), McCovey 2 (NL), Freehan (AL).

41st game, at Cincinnati (NL), July 14, 1970
American . . .000 001 120 000 —— 4 12 0
National . . .000 000 103 001 —— 5 10 0
  Pitchers—Palmer, McDowell (4), J. Perry (7), Hunter (9), Peterson (9), Stottlemyre (9), WRIGHT (11) vs. Seaver, Merritt (4), G. Perry (6), Gibson (8), OSTEEN (10). Attendance—51,838. Homer—Dietz (NL).

42nd game, at Detroit (AL), July 13, 1971
National . . . . . . .021 000 010 —— 4 5 0
American . . . . . . .004 002 00x —— 6 7 0
  Pitchers—ELLIS, Marichal (4), Jenkins (6), Wilson (7) vs. BLUE, Palmer (4), Cuellar (6), Lolich (8). Attendance—53,559. Homers—Bench (NL), Aaron (NL), Jackson (AL), F. Robinson (AL), Killebrew (AL), Clemente (NL).

43rd game, at Atlanta (NL), July 25, 1972
American . . . . .001 000 020 0 —— 3 6 0
National . . . .000 002 001 1 —— 4 8 0
  Pitchers—Palmer, Lolich (4), Perry (6), Wood (8), McNALLY (10) vs. Gibson, Blass (3), Sutton (4), Carlton (6), Stoneman (7), McGRAW (9). Attendance—53,107. Homers—Aaron (NL), Rojas (AL).

RECAPITULATION

1908 NEW YORK-CHICAGO "PLAY-OFF"

The most famous play-off game in baseball history was that between the New York and Chicago Nationals, on Oct. 8, 1908, which was won, 4—2, by Chicago.

Somewhat earlier, Fred Merkle of New York had made the celebrated "boner" of not touching second base. He was on first, started for second when a single was made against a Chicago pitcher. When Merkle saw a Giant crossing the plate with what would have been a game-winning run, he quit running for second and ran into the clubhouse.

The Cubs, noting that Merkle had not touched second, regained the ball, after a wild scramble with the Giants and the crowd. John Evers touched second, and Umpire Henry O'Day ruled that Merkle was out, the side was out, that the run did not count, and the score was tied.

The league president ruled that the game must be replayed, if it might be a factor in deciding the pennant.

New York and Chicago ended the season in a tie—98 won, 55 lost. Had Merkle touched second, New York would have been winner, by a game margin.

In the play-off, Christy Mathewson pitched for New York. Jack Pfeister started for Chicago and was replaced by Mordecai Brown. The Giants scored a run in the first inning, Chicago tallied 4 in the fourth, a double by Frank Chance and a triple by Joe Tinker being mighty factors in the rally. The New Yorkers scored a run in the seventh—and that ended the scoring. Chicago—4 runs, 8 hits, 0 errors; New York—2 runs, 5 hits, 1 error.

OTHER POST-SEASON PLAY-OFFS

The 1908 affair was really a replay of a regular-season game rather than a bona fide play-off following a first-place tie after playing the full season's schedule. The first full-fledged play-off occurred when the Brooklyn Dodgers and the St. Louis Cardinals tied for the National League flag in 1946. Pitted in a best-2-of-3 series, the Cards beat the Dodgers twice in a row, 4—2 and 8—4.

The only pennant deadlock in American League history occurred in 1948, necessitating a play-off between the Cleveland Indians and the Boston Red Sox. Since the American League ruled a single-game play-off, Cleveland gained the pennant with an 8—3 triumph, with shortstop-manager Lou Boudreau as the batting hero.

Brooklyn made history in reverse in 1951. Squandering a 13½-game lead they were enjoying in August, the Dodgers finished September in a dead heat with the Giants. The teams engaged in 3 torrid play-off battles. Jim Hearn's pitching brought the Giants the opener, 3—1. Rookie Clem Labine tamed the Giants in the next one,

10—0. With Brooklyn enjoying a 4—2 lead in the last of the ninth inning of the deciding game, Bobby Thomson hit a home run with one out and two aboard for a 5—4 victory that sent the Giants soaring into the World Series.

The Los Angeles Dodgers defeated Milwaukee in a 1959 National League playoff but dropped two of three to the San Francisco Giants in a 1962 playoff. The Giants scored four runs in the ninth inning of the third game to win.

RESERVE CLAUSE

One of the most important parts of the contract between a player and a club is the reserve clause, which binds the player to the club so long as the club desires to retain his services. This means that a player may not of his own accord leave one team to join another in organized baseball.

The reserve clause has been a matter of dispute through the years. Opponents of the covenant have fought it in the courts, charging that baseball was interstate commerce and that the clause violated the anti-trust laws of this country. Early in the 1920's the Supreme Court of the United States upheld the clause. Since that time the opinion of Justice Oliver Wendell Holmes has been held as a precedent.

The development of radio and television broadcasts recently have inspired the resumption of attacks on the clause. Congress took cognizance of the controversy by forming a House of Representatives Judiciary Subcommittee to inquire into baseball and the monopoly charges against it.

The reserve clause reads as follows:

"On or before February 1st (or if a Sunday, then the next preceding business day) of the year next following the last playing season covered by this contract, the club may tender to the player a contract for the term of that year by mailing the same to the player at his address following his signature hereto, or if none be given, then at his last address or record with the club. If prior to the March 1 next succeeding said February 1, the player and the club have not agreed upon the terms of such contract, then on or before 10 days after said March 1, the club shall have the right by written notice to the player at said address to renew this contract for the period of 1 year on the same terms, except that the amount payable to the player shall be such as the club shall fix in said notice; provided, however, that said amount, if fixed by a major league club, shall be an amount payable at a rate not less than 75 per cent of the rate stipulated for the preceding year."

FAMOUS UMPIRES

Umpires play a mighty part in the affairs of baseball, and down through the years some have come along who, because of their ability or their picturesque ways, have joined the unforgettables of the sport.

Included are Tim Hurst, baseball umpire, prize fight referee and master of repartee in an earlier era in baseball; Henry (Hank) O'Day, who quit umpiring to manage a ball club, and then quit that job to go back to umpiring; Bill Dinneen, a former big league pitcher; Charlie Rigler (Rigler the Great); Bob Emslie, who umpired from 1891 to 1929 in the National League—38 years—and Tom Connolly, who umpired about 35 years in the American.

A thousand and one tales have been written about Bill Klem, of the sharp and ready tongue, who became a big league umpire soon after the end of the Spanish-American war and ceased field duty in the late 1940's.

Billy Evans, a Cornell graduate, took up umpiring many years ago and revolutionized the profession. He was young and vigorous, and it was his custom to run with the play, whenever possible, and make his decision at the point where the play was made, in contrast with the old method of calling decisions on bases from a rigid position. Evans quit the field to take up club general management.

A.D. (Dolly) Stark, in and out of the National League, also was a youngster when he broke in and carried on the tradition of Evans, with a few inventions of his own, and managed to be on top of the plays when they happened.

Also there have been George Moriarty, once a third baseman, who wrote poetry; George Hildebrand; Charlie Moran, who taught football when not umpiring; John (Beans) Reardon; Ernie Quigley, and Cal Hubbard, who was a football star.

Jack Sheridan was one of the great umpires of an earlier day; so was the picturesque "Silk" O'Loughlin. Bill Byron was known as the "Humming Bird" because he would break into song when players protested decisions. W.A. McGowan, Roy Van Graflan, R.F. Nallin, R.A. (Babe) Pinelli, E.T. (Red) Ormsby and Harry Geisel are others of enduring fame.

John K. Tener, who later became National League president, Governor of Pennsylvania and a United States Senator, also served a stint as a big league umpire.

BAT WEIGHTS

About 12 per cent of the major leaguers use 36-inch bats, according to Hillerich and Bradsby, bat manufacturers. Bats 35 inches in length are the most popular, the percentage being 56. The 34-inch size is used by 26 per cent and 6 per cent use the 33. The maximum bat length is 42 inches. Willie Keeler used a 31½-inch bat in the majors, the shortest on record. The weight ranges from 30 ounces up. In recent years batters have had a tendency to select a slim, whippy type of club.

RADIO AND TELEVISION

Perhaps the most important single development in baseball over the past decade has been the rise of radio and television. These media have brought the national pastime its largest following of all time. More than a thousand radio stations throughout the nation daily broadcast play-by-play of games in organized baseball. It is estimated that some 80,000,000 persons follow the World Series via radio and television.

No less phenomenal is the revenue realized from radio and TV, comprising a major share of the profits of every club. The Gillette Safety Razor Company sponsors the World Series telecasts and broadcasts and pays millions of dollars for the privilege. Each club keeps all the proceeds for regular season broadcasts from its home park. Radio and TV revenue realized from the All-Star Game and World Series go into a fund underwriting the Players' Pension Fund.

Graham McNamee broadcast the first baseball game, directly from the Polo Grounds at the 1921 World Series. Hal Totten was the first to broadcast daily games from the ballpark, over WMAQ, Chicago, in 1924. The first ball game to be telecast (though a limited number of sets were in use) was the Brooklyn-Cincinnati doubleheader at Ebbets Field, August 26, 1939, with Walter L. (Red) Barber as announcer, over W2XBS, New York.

BASEBALL'S FAMOUS POEM

The most famous poem ever written about baseball is "Casey at the Bat," penned about 70 years ago by a former Harvard student, Ernest Thayer of Worcester, Mass. He wrote it in San Francisco. The poem was recited on the stage thousands of times by De Wolf Hopper. It was not written about any particular player or situation. It simply was the result of Thayer's imagination working on a mythical ball game.

The pitcher who fanned Casey is baseball's "Unknown Man."

The poem follows:

"Casey at the Bat"

The outlook wasn't brilliant for the Mudville
    nine that day;
The score stood four to two with but one inning
    more to play.
And then when Cooney died at first, and
    Barrows did the same,
A sickly silence fell upon the patrons of the
    game.

A straggling few got up to go in deep despair.
    The rest

Clung to that hope which springs eternal in the
    human breast;
They thought if only Casey could get a whack at
    that—
We'd put up even money now with Casey at the
    bat.
But Flynn preceded Casey, as did also Jimmy
    Blake,
And the former was a lulu and the latter was a
    cake;
So upon the stricken multitude grim melancholy
    sat,
For there seemed but little chance of Casey's
    getting to the bat.

But Flynn let drive a single, to the wonderment
    of all,
And Blake, the much despised, tore the cover off
    the ball;
And when the dust had lifted and the men saw
    what had occurred,
There was Johnnie safe at second and Flynn
    a-hugging third.

Then from 5,000 throats and more there rose a
    lusty yell;
It rambled through the valley, it rattled in the
    dell;
It knocked upon the mountain and recoiled upon
    the flat,
For Casey, mighty Casey, was advancing to the
    bat.

There was ease in Casey's manner as he stepped
    into his place;
There was pride in Casey's bearing and a smile on
    Casey's face.
And when, responding to the cheers, he lightly
    doffed his hat,
No stranger in the crowd could doubt 'twas
    Casey at the bat.

Ten thousand eyes were on him as he rubbed his
    hands with dirt;
Five thousand tongues applauded when he wiped
    them on his shirt.
Then while the writhing pitcher ground the ball
    into his hip,
Defiance gleamed in Casey's eye, a sneer curled
    Casey's lip.

And now the leather-covered sphere came
    hurtling through the air,
And Casey stood a-watching it in haughty
    grandeur there.
Close by the sturdy batsman the ball unheeded
    sped—
"That ain't my style," said Casey. "Strike one,"
    the umpire said.

From the benches, black with people, there went
    up a muffled roar,

Like the beating of the storm waves on a stern
    and distant shore.
"Kill him! Kill the umpire!" shouted some one in
    the stand;
And it's likely they'd have killed him had not
    Casey raised his hand.

With a smile of Christian charity great Casey's
    visage shone;
He stilled the rising tumult; he bade the game go
    on;
He signalled to the pitcher, and once more the
    spheroid flew;
But Casey still ignored it, and the umpire said,
    "Strike two."

"Fraud!" cried the maddened thousands, and the
    echo answered "fraud!"
But one scornful look from Casey and the
    audience was awed.
They saw his face grow stern and cold, they saw
    his muscles strain,
And they knew that Casey wouldn't let that ball
    go by again.

The sneer is gone from Casey's lip, his teeth are
    clenched in hate;
He pounds with cruel violence his bat upon the
    plate.
And now the pitcher holds the ball, and now he
    lets it go,
And now the air is shattered by the force of
    Casey's blow.

Oh! somewhere in this favored land the sun is
    shining bright;
The band is playing somewhere, and somewhere
    hearts are light.
And somewhere men are laughing, and
    somewhere children shout;
But there is no joy in Mudville—mighty Casey has
    struck out.

World Series

The first of the post-season duels to determine
which rival league had the better collection of
ball players was fought in 1882. Cincinnati
(A.A.) played 2 games against Chicago (N.L.),
which they split. Executive objections canceled
the rest of the series, and there was no series the
following year.

In 1884 the National League permitted its
pennant winner—the Providence club, headed by
Charles Radbourne, the phenomenal pitcher—to
meet the Metropolitans of New York, who had
won the American Association flag that year.

Providence won 3 straight in a best 3-of-5
series, and had the comfort of knowing it had
put the "upstart" Association in its proper place.
There was another post-season play-off after

the 1885 season between the Chicago Nationals
and St. Louis (A.A.) club. Each team won 3
games and the moguls were content to let it end
there, rather than go on to the deciding contest.
In 1886 the St. Louis outfit of the American
Association, spark-plugged by its eccentric
owner, Chris Von der Ahe, won the play-offs,
4–2, and that gave the Association the prestige it
sought.

The play-offs in 1887 consisted of 15 games,
the Detroit Nationals winning 10, the Browns of
St. Louis, 5. The general idea wasn't to play a
specified series to determine who was champion.
It was a barnstorming trip, with the athletes
appearing for battle in practically every city of
both circuits. The total attendance for the 15
games was 51,455 and the total receipts only
$41,050. Even the customers were worn out
before that prolonged duel had run its course.

In 1888, the chieftains felt 10 games were
enough. The New York Nationals won, 6 games
to 4, again defeating the St. Louis Browns in a
series that was featured by Von der Ahe hiring a
special train for his team and his guests. There
was so much celebrating by the entire party,
including the St. Louis players, that the East-
erners found it easy to subdue the hilarious
Browns, who, on the "mornings after," were in
no condition for play. The "party" tossed by
Von der Ahe cost him thousands of dollars. He
topped his liberality as host by letting all the
players, as well as the special guests, each order a
suit of clothes, for which he paid. There never
was a post-season conflict quite so elaborate as
that of 1888, and although it cost Von der Ahe
around $50,000 and his team was beaten, he con-
sidered it "lots of fun and a good investment."

The 1889 series, between New York Nationals
and the Brooklyn Associations, was sedate, and
New York won, 6 to 3. Brooklyn was in again in
1890, representing the NL this time against
Louisville (AA). After each team had won 3, the
Louisville players declared they were all
"tuckered out," and the seventh game was
canceled.

The Association had a bad season in 1891,
went on the rocks at the conclusion of the year
and that ended the National-American Association play-offs. The Nationals decided something
had to be done in 1892 about a post-season
combat and ordered a split season for its newly
formed 12-club circuit. Boston and Cleveland
won in the split sections and met in a play-off of
9 games, best 5-of-9. The first game ended in a
0–0 tie. Boston won the next 5 and the championship. However, the plan wasn't popular and
the split season was abandoned after its 1892
experiment, although 2 National League clubs—
Brooklyn and Pittsburgh played a few post-
season games in 1900.

In 1894, William Chase Temple, owner of the
Pittsburgh Nationals, felt that a play-off was an

interesting procedure and donated what became known as the "Temple Cup," to be contested for by the first and second clubs in the National. The early combats, featuring the pugnacious Baltimore Orioles and the fight-loving Cleveland Spiders, became an umpire's nightmare. The 1897 battle between Boston and Baltimore provided little excitement. Since the play-offs decided nothing of consequence, the plan was abandoned after 1897 and the Temple Cup games became merely a bit of history.

Here are the results of the National-American Association play-offs, the 1892 split season and the Temple Cup results:

NATIONAL LEAGUE–AMERICAN ASSOCIATION SERIES

1882–Chicago (N.L.) won 1 game, Cincinnati won 1.

1884 (3 of 5)–Providence (N.L.) 3 games, Metropolitans 0.

1885 (4 of 7)–Chicago (N.L.) 3 games, St. Louis 3; 1 tie, no play-off.

1886 (4 of 7)–St. Louis (A.A.) 4 games, Chicago 2.

1887–15 games played, clubs barnstorming. Final result: Detroit (N.L.) 10 games, St. Louis 5.

1888–10 games played (4 in New York, 4 in St. Louis, 1 in Brooklyn, 1 in Philadelphia). New York (N.L.) 6 games, St. Louis 4.

1889–9 games played (5 in New York, 4 in Brooklyn). New York (N.L.) 6, Brooklyn 3.

1890 (7 games)–Brooklyn (N.L.) 3, Louisville 3; 1 tie, no play-off.

1891–No series. Association disbanded at end of season.

SPLIT SEASON

In 1892 the National League played a split season. Boston won the first half, winning 52 games and losing 22; Cleveland triumphed in the second half, 53 victories against 23 defeats.

Play-off was on the basis of best 5 of 9. The first game, played in Cleveland, Oct. 17, 1892, ended 0–0, being called at the end of the 11th inning on account of darkness. Boston won the next five, 4–3, 3–2, 4–0, 12–7, 8–3.

TEMPLE CUP SERIES

In 1894, William Chase Temple of Pittsburgh donated a cup to be fought for at the end of the National League season (there was only 1 major circuit then) between first and second teams. Play continued from 1894 to 1897, inclusive, on basis of best 4-of-7, with the following results:

1894–New York beat Baltimore, 4 to 0.
1895–Cleveland beat Baltimore, 4 to 1.
1896–Baltimore beat Cleveland, 4 to 0.
1897–Baltimore beat Boston, 4 to 1.

MODERN WORLD SERIES

In 1900, 1901 and 1902, the American and National Leagues were at war. The hostilities ended after 1902 and conditions were amicable in 1903. Therefore, when Boston won the American League pennant of 1903 and Pittsburgh gained the National, the rival managers exchanged challenges. This resulted in the first of the modern World Series games. It was on the best 5-of-9 basis, but went only 8 games, with Boston winning, 5 games to 3. The teams agreed in advance how the money was to be split, the contest not being under supervision of Organized Baseball's National Commission.

The series attracted little attention, as is shown by the fact that the gross attendance for the 8 games was only a trifle more than 100,000, while the total receipts were only about $50,000. The winning Boston players received $1,182 each, while the losing Pirates were enriched $1,316.50 apiece. Barney Dreyfuss, Pittsburgh owner, gave the club's share of the receipts to his players.

Since annual baseball salaries in that era were around $5,000 for the top-notch performers, the Boston Americans, having repeated their pennant conquest in 1904 and being eager for additional funds, fired a challenge at the New York Giants, headed by John McGraw, who won the National flag in 1904. The sarcastic reaction of McGraw nearly brought about a resumption of the war that had lasted over 2 years and had cost the Nationals millions of dollars.

McGraw had been a player for the original Baltimore Americans in 1901 and 1902. When he "jumped" the club to join the Giants for 1903 play and made himself part of the deal that sold an American League franchise–Baltimore–to the Nationals, Ban Johnson, president of the Americans, was violent in his denunciation of McGraw. The latter, smoldering under the whip-lash of Johnson through 1903, sought to get "square" and found an opportunity when Boston challenged him for a post-season series in 1904.

McGraw declared that he would not "demean" his Giants by letting them meet "a minor league aggregation" in post-season competition. Johnson went into a new rage. He sharpened his tools for resumption of battle with the Nationals, whom he had brutally whipped in the 1901-1902 conflict. A war was something the still groggy Nationals certainly did not want, and they proceeded to put out the fire McGraw had started.

Although McGraw, a stubborn man, would neither retract nor apologize, the outstanding executives of the National made verbal amends for him. Since it was then too late for a 1904 series, the Nationals pledged that their pennant winner of 1905, which happened to be managed by the same McGraw, certainly would meet the American flag winner after regular play of 1905 was done.

And so it came to pass.

When the Nationals in 1904 pledged themselves to a world series in 1905, it was only to placate Johnson. No one, with the 1903 statistics before him, felt that the series ever would amount to anything financially. In that, all conclusions were in gross error. The series conflicts, beginning in 1905, and continuing as an annual classic, have proved to be a gold mine. They have grossed more than $50,000,000, which has been split among the contesting players, the players of the second, third and fourth place teams, the participating leagues and the competing clubs and has provided funds to carry on the operations first of the National Commission, the office of the Baseball Commissioner, Advisory Council and Players' Pension Fund.

The series has resulted in a bonanza, in which the major leagues and a great number of players have shared, and some of the performers have earned more money from series competition than they were paid for an entire season. At the same time, many clubs that ended a baseball year in the red, or on the borderline, have been able to show a profit from the income derived from post-season play, which was agreed upon merely as a temporary sop.

It is almost fantastic to realize that the 1905 series, arranged to make amends for McGraw's tactless comment, by its continuance, has enabled some clubs—the St. Louis Cardinals, for one—to profit more than they would have through regular-season operations.

Any moderately detailed story of the modern World Series, beginning in 1903, lapsing in 1904, resuming in 1905 and continuing uninterrupted to the present, demands a book of its own. It has had its heroes—by the scores and by the hundreds; it has known the wonder-players who failed when the big test came, and the mediocre who, inspired, played more spectacularly than ever before or ever afterward.

Because the style of play changed considerably between 1903 and 1958, because pitching tricks of the earlier years were legislated out later, because the "bounce" in the ball has been augmented since 1905, there is little basis for comparison of the games of a distant past and those of the present.

The spitball, the emery ball and other altered baseballs were hurled by old-time pitchers—with an advantage to them. What those men might have accomplished without such aids or what modern pitchers could have done if permitted such trickery constitute questions that cannot be answered.

Along in 1920, Australian yarn was substituted for American in the making of the ball. The Australian yarn was much stouter, permitting tighter winding and creating a harder, faster

ball. So the "rabbit ball" came into existence and made a tremendous change. Prior to that era, any player who hit a home run during a series was something of a hero. When Frank Baker, operating for the Philadelphia Athletics against the New York Giants in 1911, batted a homer on 2 successive days he was hailed as a wonder-man. But in modern years, benefited by the "lively ball," Lou Gehrig amassed 4 home runs in a 4-game series; Babe Ruth gathered 4 in a 7-game series, and the Babe made 3 homers in 1 game in 1926 and repeated in the 1928 series.

Of all the stars that ever gleamed in World Series play, Ruth was the most brilliant. He was the owner of a vast array of records compiled during 10 series years—1915, 1916 and 1918 with the Boston Americans, and 1921, 1922, 1923, 1926, 1927, 1928 and 1932 with the New York Americans. He hit the most home runs—15; hit for the greatest number of total bases in one game—12—in both 1926 and 1928. He scored the most runs—37.

In the 4-game series of 1928, by making 10 hits in 16 trips to the plate, he chalked up the record batting average for any series—.625. He had a 10-series batting average of .333.

Ruth struck out oftener than any other series player—30 times until Duke Snider of Brooklyn fanned 33 times in 5 series against New York, 1949 (8), 1952 (5), 1953 (6), 1955 (6) and 1956 (8). Babe collected more bases on ball—33. He was passed 11 times in the 7-game series against the New York Nationals in 1926—a record—and is tied with three others in getting 4 passes in a single game.

An almost forgotten fact is that Ruth was a southpaw pitcher for the Boston Americans before he was purchased by the Yankees and was detailed to outfielding, but his name appears as holder of one of the great pitching feats in World Series play. In the 1916 series against Brooklyn, Ruth pitched 13 scoreless innings and ran his string to the record of 29 by keeping the Chicago Nationals runless for 16 innings in 1918. That record stood until 1961 when it was broken by Edward (Whitey) Ford of the New York Yankees against the Cincinnati Reds.

The most audacious act in Ruth's spectacular career was in the last series in which he figured—1932—Yankees vs. Chicago Nationals, and won by the Yankees in 4 straight. Ruth failed to hit a homer in the first 2 games played in New York. The scene shifted to Chicago. During practice for the opening game there, Oct. 1, the fans taunted Ruth. He answered by hitting a homer on his first trip to the plate, driving 2 runs in ahead of him and giving the Yankees a lead they never surrendered.

Ruth accomplished nothing on his next turn at bat. Coming up in the 5th, he was greeted by a wild chorus of "boos." The Babe looked around the stands, then, with his bat, pointed to the fence in center field—400 feet away—and indicated by his gesture that he would drive the ball over that spot. And that is exactly what he did. Other accounts of this feat have Ruth in a running feud with the Cub bench, dramatically quelling their taunts by raising one finger (either to point out a spot in the distant bleachers or to indicate he still had "one" strike coming to him)—and then, the colossal clout!

Perhaps the greatest single-series performance by any pitcher was that of Christy Mathewson of the New York Nationals, opposed to Philadelphia in 1905. He met them 3 times—and shut them out 3 times, a feat no other World Series pitcher has approached.

Fans waited until 1956 for the first World Series no-hit game. When it finally came it was with a flourish. On Oct. 8, in the 5th game of the autumn classic, Don Larsen of the New York Americans pitched a perfect game against the Brooklyn Nationals, winning by 2—0. Larsen did not yield a hit, a run or pass a batsman. No Brooklyn player reached first base.

Ed Reulbach, pitching for the Chicago Nationals against the Chicago White Sox on Oct. 10, 1906, was credited with a one-hit game—long since disputed. The opponents claimed 2 hits, insisting that one hit was overlooked by the scorekeeper.

However, on Oct. 5, 1945, Claude Passeau of the Chicago Nationals shut out Detroit with 1 hit. The score was 3—0. On Oct. 3, 1947, Floyd (Bill) Bevens of the New York Americans allowed Brooklyn only 1 hit, but lost the game, 3—2.

The "Iron Man" pitcher in World Series history was Deacon Phillippe of the Pittsburgh Nationals. He appeared in 5 of the 8 games of 1903, against the Boston Red Sox—a total of 44 innings.

A series is decided on the best 4-of-7 games basis, although some years—1903, 1919, 1920 and 1921—it was 5-of-9. Four series have gone 8 games—1903, 1912, 1919 and 1921. Seven series have ended in 4 straight, the Yankees accomplishing the feat 6 times—1927, 1928, 1932, 1938, 1939 and 1950—with the 1914 Braves the other club to conclude a series in record time.

Modern World Series Record

National League (NL) vs. American League (AL)

(Managers in parentheses; winning and losing pitchers in capitals.)

1903 Final Standing

	W.	L.
Boston AL (James J. Collins)	5	3
Pittsburgh NL (Fred C. Clarke)	3	5

1st Game, at Boston, Oct. 1   R. H. E.

Pittsburgh (NL) .. 401 100 100 ——	7 12	2
Boston (AL) .... 000 000 201 ——	3 6	4

Pitchers—PHILLIPPE vs. YOUNG. Homer—Sebring (Pitt.) Attendance—16,242.

2nd Game, at Boston, Oct. 2

Pittsburgh (NL) .. 000 000 000 ——	0 3	2
Boston (AL) .... 200 001 00x ——	3 9	0

Pitchers—LEEVER, Vail (2) vs. DINEEN. Homers—Dougherty (Bost.) 2. Attendance—9,415.

3d Game, at Boston, Oct. 3

Pittsburgh (NL) .. 012 000 010 ——	4 7	0
Boston (AL) .... 000 100 010 ——	2 4	2

Pitchers—PHILLIPPE vs. HUGHES, Young (3). Attendance—18,801.

4th Game, at Pittsburgh, Oct. 6

Boston (AL) .... 000 010 003 ——	4 9	1
Pittsburgh (NL) .. 100 010 30x ——	5 12	1

Pitchers—DINNEEN vs. PHILLIPPE. Attendance—7,600.

5th Game, at Pittsburgh, Oct. 7

Boston (AL) .... 000 006 410 ——	11 14	2
Pittsburgh (NL) .. 000 000 020 ——	2 6	4

Pitchers—YOUNG vs. KENNEDY, Thompson (8). Attendance—12,322.

6th Game, at Pittsburgh, Oct. 8

Boston (AL) .... 003 020 100 ——	6 10	1
Pittsburgh (NL) .. 000 000 300 ——	3 10	3

Pitchers—DINNEEN vs. LEEVER. Attendance—11,556.

7th Game, at Pittsburgh, Oct. 10

Boston (AL) .... 200 202 010 ——	7 11	4
Pittsburgh (NL) .. 000 101 001 ——	3 10	3

Pitchers—YOUNG vs. PHILLIPPE. Attendance—17,038.

8th Game, at Boston, Oct. 13

Pittsburgh (NL) .. 000 000 000 ——	0 4	3
Boston (AL) .... 000 201 00x ——	3 8	0

Pitchers—PHILLIPPE vs. DINNEEN. Attendance—7,455.

Total attendance—100,429. Receipts—$55,500. Winning player's share—$1,316.50. Losing player's share—$1,182.

1904—No Series

Owner John T. Brush and Manager John J. McGraw of the New York Giants felt such personal bitterness toward the "upstart" American League that they refused to let their 1904 National League champions meet Boston's repeating American League winners. Giant players petitioned in vain to have the series played. However, fans and writers criticized Brush so severely that he later drew up the Brush Rules to govern annual post-season play-offs. These regulations are the same ones that are used today, with few exceptions.

1905 Final Standing

	W.	L.
New York NL (John J. McGraw)	4	1
Philadelphia AL (Connie Mack)	1	4

1st Game, at Philadelphia, Oct. 9   R. H. E.
New York (NL) ..000 020 001 −−   3 10 1
Philadelphia (AL) 000 000 000 −−   0 4 0
    Pitchers−MATHEWSON vs. PLANK. Attendance−17,955.

2nd Game, at New York, Oct. 10
Philadelphia (AL) 001 000 020 −−   3 6 2
New York (NL) ..000 000 000 −−   0 4 2
    Pitchers−BENDER vs. McGINNITY, Ames (9). Attendance−24,922.

3d Game, at Philadelphia, Oct. 12
New York (NL) ..200 050 002 −−   9 9 1
Philadelphia (AL) 000 000 000 −−   0 4 5
    Pitchers−MATHEWSON vs. COAKLEY. Attendance−10,991.

4th Game, at New York, Oct. 13
Philadelphia (AL) 000 000 000 −−   0 5 2
New York (NL) ..000 100 00x −−   1 4 1
    Pitchers−PLANK vs. McGINNITY. Attendance−13,598.

5th Game, at New York, Oct. 14
Philadelphia (AL) 000 000 000 −−   0 6 0
New York (NL) ..000 010 01x −−   2 5 1
    Pitchers−BENDER vs. MATHEWSON. Attendance−24,187.

    Total attendance−91,723. Receipts−$68,437. Winning player's share−$1,142. Losing player's share−$833.75.

1906 Final Standing

	W.	L
Chicago AL (Fielder A. Jones)	4	1
Chicago NL (Frank L. Chance)	1	4

1st Game, at West Side Park, Chi., Oct. 9
                           R. H. E.
Chicago (AL) ....000 011 000 −−   2 4 1
Chicago (NL) ....000 001 000 −−   1 4 2
    Pitchers−ALTROCK vs. BROWN. Attendance−12,693.

2d Game, at Comiskey Park, Chi., Oct. 10
Chicago (NL) ....031 001 020 −−   7 10 2
Chicago (AL) ....000 010 000 −−   1 1 2
    Pitchers−REULBACH vs. WHITE, Owen.

Attendance−12,595.

3d Game, at West Side Park, Chi., Oct. 11
Chicago (AL) ....000 003 000 −−   3 4 1
Chicago (NL) ....000 000 000 −−   0 2 2
    Pitchers−WALSH vs. PFEISTER. Attendance−13,750.

4th Game, at Comiskey Park, Chi., Oct. 12
Chicago (NL) ....000 000 100 −−   1 7 1
Chicago (AL) ....000 000 000 −−   0 2 1
    Pitchers−BROWN vs. ALTROCK. Attendance−18,385.

5th Game, at West Side Park, Chi., Oct. 13
Chicago (AL) ....102 401 000 −−   8 12 6
Chicago (NL) ....300 102 000 −−   6 6 0
    Pitchers−WALSH, White (7) vs. Reulbach, PFEISTER (3), Overall (4). Attendance−23,257.

6th Game, at Comiskey Park, Chi., Oct. 14
Chicago (NL) ....100 010 001 −−   3 7 0
Chicago (AL) ....340 000 01x −−   8 14 3
    Pitchers−BROWN, Overall (2) vs. WHITE. Attendance−19,249.

    Total attendance−99,845. Receipts−$106,550. Winning player's share−$1,874.63. Losing player's share−$439.50.

1907 Final Standing

	W.	L.	T.
Chicago NL (Frank L. Chance) ..	4	0	1
Detroit AL (Hugh Jennings)	0	4	1

1st Game, at Chicago, Oct. 8   R. H. E.
Detroit (AL) 000 000 030 000 −−   3 9 3
Chicago (NL) 000 100 002 000 −−   3 10 5
       (called, end of 12th; darkness)

    Pitchers−Donovan vs. Overall, Reulbach (10). Attendance−24,377.

2d Game, at Chicago, Oct. 9
Detroit (AL) ....010 000 000 −−   1 9 1
Chicago (NL) ....010 200 00x −−   3 9 1
    Pitchers−MULLIN vs. PFEISTER. Attendance−21,901.

3d Game, at Chicago, Oct. 10
Detroit (AL) ....000 001 000 −−   1 6 1
Chicago (NL) ....010 310 00x −−   5 10 1
    Pitchers−SIEVER, Killian (5) vs. REULBACH. Attendance−13,114.

4th Game, at Detroit, Oct. 11
Chicago (NL) ....000 020 301 −−   6 7 2
Detroit (AL) ....000 100 000 −−   1 5 2
    Pitchers−OVERALL vs. DONOVAN. Attendance−11,306.

5th Game, at Detroit, Oct. 12
Chicago (NL) . . . . 110 000 000 — — 2 7 1
Detroit (AL) . . . . 000 000 000 — — 0 7 2
   Pitchers—BROWN vs. MULLIN. Attendance—7,370.

Total attendance—78,068. Receipts—$101,728.50. Winning player's share—$2,142.85. Losing player's share—$1,945.96.

1908 Final Standing

	W.	L.
Chicago NL (Frank L. Chance)	4	1
Detroit AL (Hugh Jennings)	1	4

1st Game, at Detroit, Oct. 10

               R. H. E.
Chicago (NL) . . . . 004 000 105 — — 10 14 2
Detroit (AL) . . . . 100 000 320 — — 6 10 4
   Pitchers—Reulbach, Overall (7), BROWN (8) vs. Killian, SUMMERS (3). Attendance—10,812.

2d Game, at Chicago, Oct. 11
Detroit (AL) . . . . 000 000 001 — — 1 4 1
Chicago (NL) . . . . 000 000 06x — — 6 7 1
   Pitchers—DONOVAN vs. OVERALL. Homer—Tinker (Chi.). Attendance—17,760.

3d Game, at Chicago, Oct. 12
Detroit (AL) . . . . 100 005 020 — — 8 11 4
Chicago (NL) . . . . 000 300 000 — — 3 7 2
   Pitchers—MULLIN vs. PFEISTER, Reulbach (9). Attendance—14,543.

4th Game, at Detroit, Oct. 13
Chicago (NL) . . . . 002 000 001 — — 3 10 0
Detroit (AL) . . . . 000 000 000 — — 0 4 1
   Pitchers—BROWN vs. SUMMERS, Winter (9). Attendance—12,907.

5th Game, at Detroit, Oct. 14
Chicago (NL) . . . . 100 010 000 — — 2 10 0
Detroit (AL) . . . . 000 000 000 — — 0 3 0
   Pitchers—OVERALL vs. DONOVAN. Attendance—6,210.

Total attendance—62,232. Receipts—$94,975.50. Winning player's share—$1,317.58. Losing player's share—$870.

1909 Final Standing

	W.	L.
Pittsburgh NL (Fred C. Clarke)	4	3
Detroit AL (Hugh Jennings)	3	4

1st Game, at Pittsburgh, Oct. 8

               R. H. E.
Detroit (AL) . . . . 100 000 000 — — 1 6 4
Pittsburgh (NL) . . 000 121 00x — — 4 5 0
   Pitchers—MULLIN vs. ADAMS. Homer—Clarke (Pitt.) Attendance—29,264.

2d Game, at Pittsburgh, Oct. 9

Detroit (AL) . . . . 023 020 000 — — 7 9 3
Pittsburgh (NL) . . 200 000 000 — — 2 5 1
   Pitchers—DONOVAN vs. CAMNITZ, Willis (3). Attendance—30,915.

3d Game, at Detroit, Oct. 11
Pittsburgh (NL) . . 510 000 002 — — 8 10 3
Detroit (AL) . . . . 000 000 402 — — 6 10 5
   Pitchers—MADDOX vs. SUMMERS, Willett (1), Works (8). Attendance—18,277.

4th Game, at Detroit, Oct. 12
Pittsburgh (NL) . . 000 000 000 — — 0 5 6
Detroit (AL) . . . . 020 300 00x — — 5 8 0
   Pitchers—LEIFIELD, Phillippe (5) vs. MULLIN. Attendance—17,036.

5th Game, at Pittsburgh, Oct. 13
Detroit (AL) . . . . 100 002 010 — — 4 6 1
Pittsburgh (NL) . . 111 000 41x — — 8 10 2
   Pitchers—SUMMERS, Willett (8) vs. ADAMS. Homers—D. Jones (Det.), Crawford (Det.), Clarke (Pitts.). Attendance—21,706.

6th Game, at Detroit, Oct. 14
Pittsburgh (NL) . . 300 000 001 — — 4 7 3
Detroit (AL) . . . . 100 211 00x — — 5 10 3
   Pitchers—WILLIS, Camnitz (6), Phillippe (7) vs. MULLIN. Attendance—10,535.

7th Game, at Detroit, Oct. 16
Pittsburgh (NL) . . 020 203 010 — — 8 7 0
Detroit (AL) . . . . 000 000 000 — — 0 6 3
   Pitchers—ADAMS vs. DONOVAN, Mullin (4). Attendance—17,562.

Total attendance—145,295. Receipts—$188,302.50. Winning player's share—$1,825.22. Losing player's share—$1,274.76.

1910 Final Standing

	W.	L.
Philadelphia AL (Connie Mack)	4	1
Chicago NL (Frank L. Chance)	1	4

1st Game, at Philadelphia, Oct. 17

               R. H. E.
Chicago (NL) . . . . 000 000 001 — — 1 3 1
Philadelphia (AL) 021 000 01x — — 4 7 2
   Pitchers—OVERALL, McIntire (4) vs. BENDER. Attendance—26,891.

2d Game, at Philadelphia, Oct. 18
Chicago (NL) . . . . 100 000 101 — — 3 8 3
Philadelphia (AL) 002 010 60x — — 9 14 4
   Pitchers—BROWN, Richie (8) vs. COOMBS. Attendance—24,597.

3d Game, at Chicago, Oct. 20
Philadelphia (AL) 125 000 400 — — 12 15 1
Chicago (NL) . . . . 120 000 020 — — 5 6 5
   Pitchers—COOMBS vs. Reulbach, McINTIRE

(3), Pfeister (3). Homer—Murphy (Phila.). Attendance—26,210.

4th Game, at Chicago, Oct. 22
Philadelphia (AL) .001 200 000 0 — 3 11 3
Chicago (NL) . . . . . 100 100 001 1 — 4 9 1
    Pitchers—BENDER vs. Cole, BROWN (9). Attendance—19,150.

5th Game, at Chicago, Oct. 23
Philadelphia (AL) 100 010 050 —— 7 9 1
Chicago (NL) . . . . 010 000 010 —— 2 9 2
    Pitchers—COOMBS vs. BROWN. Attendance—27,374.

    Total attendance—124,222. Receipts—$173,980. Winning player's share—$2,062.79. Losing player's share—$1,375.16.

1911 Final Standing

	W.	L.
Philadelphia AL (Connie Mack)	4	2
New York NL (John J. McGraw)	2	4

1st Game, at New York, Oct. 14   R. H. E.
Philadelphia (AL) 010 000 000 —— 1 6 2
New York (NL) . .000 100 10x —— 2 5 0
    Pitchers—BENDER vs. MATHEWSON. Attendance—38, 281.

2d Game, at Philadelphia, Oct. 16
New York (NL) . .010 000 000 —— 1 5 3
Philadelphia (AL) 100 002 00x —— 3 4 0
    Pitchers—MARQUARD, Crandall (8) vs. PLANK. Homer—Baker (Phila.). Attendance—26,286.

3d Game, at New York, Oct. 17
Philadelphia (AL) 000 000 001 02 — 3 9 2
New York (NL) . .001 000 000 01 — 2 3 5
    Pitchers—COOMBS vs. MATHEWSON. Homer—Baker (Phila.). Attendance—37,216.

4th Game, at Philadelphia, Oct. 24
New York (NL) . .200 000 000 —— 2 7 3
Philadelphia (AL) 000 310 00x —— 4 11 1
    Pitchers—MATHEWSON, Wiltse (8) vs. BENDER. Attendance—24,355.

5th Game, at New York, Oct. 25
Philadelphia (AL) 003 000 000 0 — 3 7 1
New York (NL) . 000 000 102 1 — 4 9 2
    Pitchers—Coombs, PLANK (10) vs. Marquard, Ames (4), CRANDALL (8). Homer—Oldring (Phila.) Attendance—33,228.

6th Game, at Philadelphia, Oct. 26
New York (NL) . .100 000 001 —— 2 4 3
Philadelphia (AL) 001 401 70x —— 13 13 5
    Pitchers—AMES, Wiltse (5), Marquard (7) vs. BENDER. Attendance—20,485.

    Total attendance—179,851. Receipts—$342,164.50. Winning player's share—$3,654.58. Losing player's share—$2,436.39.

1912 Final Standing

	W.	L.	T.
Boston AL (J. Garland Stahl) . .	4	3	1
New York NL (John J. McGraw)	3	4	1

1st Game, at New York, Oct. 8   R. H. E.
Boston (AL) . . . .000 001 300 —— 4 6 1
New York (NL) . .002 000 001 —— 3 8 1
    Pitchers—WOOD vs. TESREAU, Crandall (8). Attendance—35,730.

2d Game, at Boston, Oct. 9
New York (NL) . .010 100 030 10 — 6 11 5
Boston (AL) . . . . .300 010 010 10 — 6 10 1
    (called, end of 11th; darkness)
    Pitchers—Mathewson vs. Collins, Hall (8), Bedient (11). Attendance—30,148.

3d Game, at Boston, Oct. 10
New York (NL) . .010 010 000 —— 2 7 1
Boston (AL) . . . .000 000 001 —— 1 7 0
    Pitchers—MARQUARD vs. O'Brien, Bedient (9). Attendance—36,624.

4th Game, at New York, Oct. 11
Boston (AL) . . . .010 100 001 —— 3 8 1
New York (NL) . .000 000 100 —— 1 9 1
    Pitchers—WOOD vs. TESREAU, Ames (8). Attendance—36,502.

5th Game, at Boston, Oct. 12
New York (NL) . .000 000 100 —— 1 3 1
Boston (AL) . . . .002 000 00x —— 2 5 1
    Pitchers—MATHEWSON vs. BEDIENT. Attendance—34,683.

6th Game, at New York, Oct. 14
Boston (AL) . . . .020 000 000 —— 2 7 2
New York (NL) . .500 000 00x —— 5 11 2
    Pitchers—O'BRIEN, Collins (2) vs. MARQUARD. Attendance—30,622.

7th Game, at Boston, Oct. 15
New York (NL) . .610 002 101 —— 11 16 4
Boston (AL) . . . .010 000 210 —— 4 9 3
    Pitchers—TESREAU vs. WOOD, Hall (2). Homers—Doyle (N.Y.), Gardner (Bost.). Attendance—32.694.

8th Game, at Boston, Oct. 16
New York (NL) 001 000 000 1 —— 2 9 2
Boston (AL) . .000 000 100 2 —— 3 8 5
    Pitchers—MATHEWSON vs. Bedient, WOOD (8). Attendance—17,034.

    Total attendance—252,037. Receipts—$490,449. Winning player's share—$4,024.68.

Losing player's share—$2,566.47.

1913 Final Standing

	W.	L.
Philadelphia AL (Connie Mack)	4	1
New York NL (John J. McGraw)	1	4

1st Game, at New York, Oct. 7   R. H. E.

Philadelphia (AL) 000 320 010 ——   6 11   1
New York (NL) ..001 030 000 ——   4 11   0
    Pitchers—BENDER vs. MARQUARD, Crandall (6), Tesreau (8). Homer—Baker (Phila.). Attendance—36,291.

2d Game, at Philadelphia, Oct. 8

New York (NL) . 000 000 000 3 –   3   7   2
Philadelphia (AL) 000 000 000 0 –   0   8   2
    Pitchers—MATHEWSON vs. PLANK. Attendance—20,563.

3d Game, at New York, Oct. 9

Philadelphia (AL) 320 000 210 ——   8 12   1
New York (NL) ..000 010 100 ——   2   5   1
    Pitchers—BUSH vs. TESREAU, Crandall (7). Homer—Schang (Phila.). Attendance—36,896.

4th Game, at Philadelphia, Oct. 10

New York (NL) ..000 000 320 ——   5   8   2
Philadelphia (AL) 010 320 00x ——   6   9   0
    Pitchers—MARQUARD vs. BENDER. Homer—Merkle (N.Y.). Attendance—20,568.

5th Game, at New York, Oct. 11

Philadelphia (AL) 102 000 000 ——   3   6   1
New York (NL) ..000 010 000 ——   1   2   2
    Pitchers—PLANK vs. MATHEWSON. Attendance—36,682.

Total attendance—151,000. Receipts—$324,980. Winning player's share—$3,246.36. Losing player's share—$2,164.22.

1914 Final Standing

	W.	L.
Boston NL (George T. Stallings)	4	0
Philadelphia AL (Connie Mack)	0	4

1st Game, at Philadelphia, Oct. 9   R. H. E.

Boston (NL) ....020 013 010 ——   7 11   2
Philadelphia (AL) 010 000 000 ——   1   5   0
    Pitchers—RUDOLPH vs. BENDER, Wyckoff (6). Attendance—20,562.

2d Game, at Philadelphia, Oct. 10

Boston (NL) ....000 000 001 ——   1   7   1
Philadelphia (AL) 000 000 000 ——   0   2   1
    Pitchers—JAMES vs. PLANK. Attendance—20,562.

3d Game, at Boston, Oct. 12

Philadelphia (AL) 100 100 000 200 –   4   8   2
Boston (NL) ... 010 100 000 201 –   5   9   1

Pitchers—BUSH vs. Tyler, JAMES (11). Homer—Gowdy (Bost.). Attendance—35,520.

4th Game, at Boston, Oct. 13

Philadelphia (AL) 000 010 000 ——   1   7   0
Boston (NL) ....000 120 00x ——   3   6   0
    Pitchers—SHAWKEY, Pennock (6) vs. RUDOLPH. Attendance—34,365.

Total attendance—111,009. Receipts—$225,739. Winning Player's share—$2,812.28. Losing player's share—$2,031.65.

1915 Final Standing

	W.	L.
Boston AL (William F. Carrigan)	4	1
Philadelphia NL (Patrick J. Moran) ...	1	4

1st Game, at Philadelphia, Oct. 8   R. H. E.

Boston (AL) ....000 000 010 ——   1   8   1
Philadelphia (NL) 000 100 02x ——   3   5   1
    Pitchers—SHORE vs. ALEXANDER. Attendance—19,343.

2d Game, at Philadelphia, Oct. 9

Boston (AL) ....100 000 001 ——   2 10   0
Philadelphia (NL) 000 010 000 ——   1   3   1
    Pitchers—FOSTER vs. MAYER. Attendance—20,306.

3d Game, at Boston, Oct. 11

Philadelphia (NL) 001 000 000 ——   1   3   0
Boston (AL) ....000 100 001 ——   2   6   1
    Pitchers—ALEXANDER vs. LEONARD. Attendance—42,300.

4th Game, at Boston, Oct. 12

Philadelphia (NL) 000 000 010 ——   1   7   0
Boston (AL) ....001 001 00x ——   2   8   1
    Pitchers—CHALMERS vs. SHORE. Attendance—41,096.

5th Game, at Philadelphia, Oct. 13

Boston (AL) ....011 000 021 ——   5 10   1
Philadelphia (NL) 200 200 000 ——   4   9   1
    Pitchers—FOSTER vs. Mayer, RIXEY (3). Homers—Hooper (Bost.) 2, Lewis (Bost.), Luderus (Phil.). Attendance—20,306.

Total attendance—143,351. Receipts—$320,361.50. Winning player's share—$3,780.25. Losing player's share—$2,520.17.

1916 Final Standing

	W.	L.
Boston AL (William F. Carrigan)	4	1
Brooklyn NL (Wilbert Robinson)	1	4

1st Game, at Boston, Oct. 7   R. H. E.

Brooklyn (NL) ..000 100 004 ——   5 10   4
Boston (AL) ....001 010 31x ——   6   8   1

Pitchers—MARQUARD, Pfeffer (8) vs. SHORE, Mays (9). Attendance—36,117.

2d Game, at Boston, Oct. 9
Brooklyn (NL)100 000 000 000 00 — 1 6 2
Boston (AL) .001 000 000 000 01 — 2 7 1
   Pitchers—SMITH vs. RUTH. Homer—H. Myers (Brook.). Attendance—41,373.

3d Game, at Brooklyn, Oct. 10
Boston (AL) .... 000 002 100 — — 3 7 1
Brooklyn (NL) .. 001 120 00x — — 4 10 0
   Pitchers—MAYS, Foster (6) vs. COOMBS, Pfeffer (7). Homer—Gardner (Bost.). Attendance—21,087.

4th Game, at Brooklyn, Oct. 11
Boston (AL) .... 030 110 000 — — 6 10 1
Brooklyn (NL) .. 200 000 000 — — 2 5 4
   Pitchers—LEONARD vs. MARQUARD, Cheney (5), Rucker (8). Homer—Gardner (Bost.). Attendance—21,662.

5th Game, at Boston, Oct. 12
Brooklyn (NL) .. 010 000 000 — — 1 3 3
Boston (AL) .... 012 010 00x — — 4 7 2
   Pitchers—PFEFFER, Dell (8) vs. SHORE. Attendance—42,620.

Total attendance—162,859. Receipts—$385,590.50. Winning player's share—$3,910.26. Losing player's share—$2,834.82.

1917 Final Standing

	W.	L.
Chicago AL (Clarence H. Rowland) ..	4	2
New York NL (John J. McGraw)	2	4

1st Game, at Chicago, Oct. 6   R. H. E.
New York (NL) .. 000 010 000 — — 1 7 1
Chicago (AL) .... 001 100 00x — — 2 7 1
   Pitchers—SALLEE vs. CICOTTE. Homer—Felsch (Chi). Attendance—32,000.

2d Game, at Chicago, Oct. 7
New York (NL) .. 020 000 000 — — 2 8 1
Chicago (AL) .... 020 500 00x — — 7 14 1
   Pitchers—Schupp, ANDERSON (2), Perritt (4), Tesreau (8) vs. FABER. Attendance—32,000.

3d Game, at New York, Oct. 10
Chicago (AL) .... 000 000 000 — — 0 5 3
New York (NL) .. 000 200 00x — — 2 8 2
   Pitchers—CICOTTE vs. BENTON. Attendance—33,616.

4th Game, at New York, Oct. 11
Chicago (AL) .... 000 000 000 — — 0 7 0
New York (NL) .. 000 110 12x — — 5 10 1
   Pitchers—FABER, Danforth (8) vs. SCHUPP.

Homers—Kauff (N.Y.) 2. Attendance—27,746.

5th Game, at Chicago, Oct. 13
New York (NL) .. 200 200 100 — — 5 12 3
Chicago (AL) .... 001 001 33x — — 8 14 6
   Pitchers—SALLEE, Perritt (8) vs. Russell, Cicotte (1), Williams (7), FABER (8). Attendance—27,323.

6th Game, at New York, Oct. 15
Chicago (AL) .... 000 300 001 — — 4 7 1
New York (NL) .. 000 020 000 — — 2 6 3
   Pitchers—FABER vs. BENTON, Perritt (6). Attendance—33,969.

Total attendance—186,654. Receipts—$425,878. Winning player's share—$3,669.32. Losing player's share—$2,442.21.

1918 Final Standing

	W.	L.
Boston AL (Edward G. Barrow)	4	2
Chicago NL (Fred L. Mitchell)	2	4

1st Game, at Chicago, Sept. 5   R. H. E.
Boston (AL) .... 000 100 000 — — 1 5 0
Chicago (NL) .... 000 000 000 — — 0 6 0
   Pitchers—RUTH vs. VAUGHN. Attendance—19,274.

2d Game, at Chicago, Sept. 6
Boston (AL) .... 000 000 001 — — 1 6 1
Chicago (NL) .... 030 000 00x — — 3 7 1
   Pitchers—BUSH vs. TYLER. Attendance—20,040.

3d Game, at Chicago, Sept. 7
Boston (AL) .... 000 200 000 — — 2 7 0
Chicago (NL) .... 000 010 000 — — 1 7 1
   Pitchers—MAYS vs. VAUGHN. Attendance—27,054.

4th Game, at Boston, Sept. 9
Chicago (NL) .... 000 000 020 — — 2 7 1
Boston (AL) .... 000 200 01x — — 3 4 0
   Pitchers—Tyler, DOUGLASS (8) vs. RUTH, Bush (9). Attendance—22,183.

5th Game, at Boston, Sept. 10
Chicago (NL) .... 001 000 002 — — 3 7 0
Boston (AL) .... 000 000 000 — — 0 5 0
   Pitchers—VAUGHN vs. JONES. Attendance—24,694.

6th Game, at Boston, Sept. 11
Chicago (NL) .... 000 100 000 — — 1 3 2
Boston (AL) .... 002 000 00x — — 2 5 0
   Pitchers—TYLER, Hendrix (8) vs. MAYS. Attendance—15,238.

Total attendance—128,483. Receipts—

$179,619. Winning player's share—$1,102.51. Losing player's share—$671.09.

1919 Final Standing

	W.	L.
Cincinnati NL (Patrick J. Moran)	5	3
Chicago AL (William Gleason)	3	5

1st Game, at Cincinnati, Oct. 1   R. H. E.

Chicago (AL) .... 010 000 000 — 1 6 1
Cincinnati (NL) .. 100 500 21x — 9 14 1
    Pitchers—CICOTTE, Wilkinson (4), Lowdermilk (8) vs. RUETHER. Attendance—30,511.

2d Game, at Cincinnati, Oct. 2

Chicago (AL) .... 000 000 200 — 2 10 1
Cincinnati (NL) .. 000 301 00x — 4 4 2
    Pitchers—WILLIAMS vs. SALLEE. Attendance—29,690.

3d Game, at Chicago, Oct. 3

Cincinnati (NL) .. 000 000 000 — 0 3 1
Chicago (AL) .... 020 100 00x — 3 7 0
    Pitchers—FISHER, Luque (8) vs. KERR. Attendance—29,126.

4th Game, at Chicago, Oct. 4

Cincinnati (NL) .. 000 020 000 — 2 5 2
Chicago (AL) .... 000 000 000 — 0 3 2
    Pitchers—RING vs. CICOTTE. Attendance—34,363.

5th Game, at Chicago, Oct. 6

Cincinnati (NL) .. 000 004 001 — 5 4 0
Chicago (AL) .... 000 000 000 — 0 3 3
    Pitchers—ELLER vs. WILLIAMS, Mayer (9). Attendance—34,379.

6th Game, at Cincinnati, Oct. 7

Chicago (AL) .. 000 013 000 1 — 5 10 3
Cincinnati (NL) 002 200 000 0 — 4 11 0
    Pitchers—KERR vs. Ruether, RING (6). Attendance—32,006.

7th Game, Cincinnati, Oct. 8

Chicago (AL) .... 101 020 000 — 4 10 1
Cincinnati (NL) .. 000 001 000 — 1 7 4
    Pitchers—CICOTTE vs. SALLEE, Fisher (5), Luque (6). Attendance—13,923.

8th Game, at Chicago, Oct. 9

Cincinnati (NL) .. 410 013 010 — 10 16 2
Chicago (AL) .... 001 000 040 — 5 10 1
    Pitchers—ELLER vs. WILLIAMS, James (1), Wilkinson (6). Homer—Jackson (Chi.). Attendance—$32,930.

Total attendance—236,928. Receipts—$722,414. Winning player's share—$5,207.01. Losing player's share—$3,254.36.

1920 Final Standing

	W.	L.
Cleveland AL (Tristram E. Speaker) ..	5	2
Brooklyn NL (Wilbert Robinson)	2	5

1st Game, at Brooklyn, Oct. 5   R. H. E.

Cleveland (AL) .. 020 100 000 — 3 5 0
Brooklyn (NL) .. 000 000 100 — 1 5 1
    Pitchers—COVELESKIE vs. MARQUARD, Mamaux (7), Cadore (9). Attendance—23,573.

2d Game, at Brooklyn, Oct. 6

Cleveland (AL) .. 000 000 000 — 0 7 1
Brooklyn (NL) .. 101 010 00x — 3 7 0
    Pitchers—BAGBY, Uhle (7) vs. GRIMES. Attendance—22,559.

3d Game, at Brooklyn, Oct. 7

Cleveland (AL) .. 000 100 000 — 1 3 1
Brooklyn (NL) .. 200 000 00x — 2 6 1
    Pitchers—CALDWELL, Mails (1), Uhle (8) vs. SMITH. Attendance—25,088.

4th Game, at Cleveland, Oct. 9

Brooklyn (NL) .. 000 100 000 — 1 5 1
Cleveland (AL) .. 202 001 00x — 5 12 2
    Pitchers—CADORE, Mamaux (2), Marquard (3), Pfeffer (6) vs. COVELESKIE. Attendance—25,734.

5th Game, at Cleveland, Oct. 10

Brooklyn (NL) .. 000 000 001 — 1 13 1
Cleveland (AL) .. 400 301 00x — 8 12 2
    Pitchers—GRIMES, Mitchell (4) vs. BAGBY. Homers—E. Smith (Cle.), Bagby (Cle.). Attendance—26,884.

6th Game, at Cleveland, Oct. 11

Brooklyn (NL) .. 000 000 000 — 0 3 0
Cleveland (AL) .. 000 001 00x — 1 7 3
    Pitchers—SMITH vs. MAILS. Attendance—27,194.

7th Game, at Cleveland, Oct. 12

Brooklyn (NL) .. 000 000 000 — 0 5 2
Cleveland (AL) .. 000 110 10x — 3 7 3
    Pitchers—GRIMES, Mamaux (8) vs. COVELESKIE. Attendance—27,525.

Total attendance—187,737. Receipts—$564,800. Winning player's share—$4,168. Losing player's share—$2,419.60.

1921 Final Standing

	W.	L.
New York NL (John J. McGraw)	5	3
New York AL (Miller J. Huggins)	3	5

1st Game, at Polo Grounds, N.Y., Oct. 5
R. H. E.
New York (AL) . . 100 011 000 —— 3 7 0
New York (NL) . . 000 000 000 —— 0 5 0
Pitchers—MAYS vs. DOUGLAS, Barnes (9). Attendance—30,202.

2d Game, at Polo Grounds, N.Y., Oct. 6
New York (NL) . . 000 000 000 —— 0 2 3
New York (AL) . . 000 100 02x —— 3 3 0
Pitchers—NEHF vs. HOYT. Attendance—34,929.

3d Game, at Polo Grounds, N.Y., Oct. 7
New York (AL) . . 004 000 010 —— 5 8 0
New York (NL) . . 004 000 81x —— 13 20 0
Pitchers—Shawkey, QUINN (3), Collins (7), Rogers (8) vs. Toney, BARNES (3). Attendance—36,509.

4th Game, at Polo Grounds, N.Y., Oct. 9
New York (NL) . . 000 000 031 —— 4 9 1
New York (AL) . . 000 010 001 —— 2 7 1
Pitchers—DOUGLAS vs. MAYS. Homer—Ruth (AL). Attendance—36,372.

5th Game, at Polo Grounds, N.Y., Oct. 10
New York (AL) . . 001 200 000 —— 3 6 1
New York (NL) . . 100 000 000 —— 1 10 1
Pitchers—HOYT vs. NEHF. Attendance—35,758.

6th Game, at Polo Grounds, N.Y., Oct. 11
New York (NL) . . 030 401 000 —— 8 13 0
New York (AL) . . 320 000 000 —— 5 7 2
Pitchers—Toney, BARNES (1) vs. Harper, SHAWKEY (2), Piercy (9). Homers—E. Meusel (NL), Snyder (NL), Fewster (AL). Attendance—34,283.

7th Game, at Polo Grounds, N.Y., Oct. 12
New York (AL) . . 010 000 000 —— 1 8 1
New York (NL) . . 000 100 10x —— 2 6 0
Pitchers—MAYS vs. DOUGLAS. Attendance—36,503.

8th Game, at Polo Grounds, N.Y., Oct. 13
New York (NL) . . 100 000 000 —— 1 6 0
New York (AL) . . 000 000 000 —— 0 4 1
Pitchers—NEHF vs. HOYT. Attendance—25,410.

Total attendance—269,976. Receipts—$900,233. Winning player's share—$5,265. Losing player's share—$3,510.

1922 Final Standing

	W.	L.	T.
New York NL (John J. McGraw)	4	0	1
New York AL (Miller J. Huggins)	0	4	1

1st Game, at Polo Grounds, N.Y., Oct. 4
R. H. E.
New York (AL) . . 000 001 100 —— 2 7 0
New York (NL) . . 000 000 03x —— 3 11 3
Pitchers—BUSH, Hoyt (8) vs. Nehf, RYAN (8). Attendance—36,514.

2d Game, at Polo Grounds, N.Y., Oct. 5
New York (NL) 300 000 000 0 —— 3 8 1
New York (AL) 100 100 010 0 —— 3 8 0
(called, end of 10th: darkness)
Pitchers—Barnes vs. Shawkey. Homers—E. Meusel (NL), Ward (AL). Attendance—37,020.

3d Game, at Polo Grounds, N.Y., Oct. 6
New York (AL) . . 000 000 000 —— 0 4 1
New York (NL) . . 002 000 10x —— 3 12 1
Pitchers—HOYT, Jones (8) vs. J. Scott. Attendance—37,620.

4th Game, at Polo Grounds, N.Y., Oct. 7
New York (NL) . . 000 040 000 —— 4 9 1
New York (AL) . . 200 000 100 —— 3 8 0
Pitchers—McQUILLAN vs. MAYS, Jones (9). Homer—Ward (AL). Attendance—36,242.

5th Game, at Polo Grounds, N.Y., Oct. 8
New York (AL) . . 100 010 100 —— 3 5 0
New York (NL) . . 020 000 03x —— 5 10 0
Pitchers—BUSH vs. NEHF. Attendance—38,551.

Total attendance—185,947. Receipts—$605,475. Winning player's share—$4,470. Losing player's share—$3,225.

1923 Final Standing

	W.	L.
New York AL (Miller J. Huggins)	4	2
New York NL (John J. McGraw)	2	4

1st Game, at Yankee Stadium, N.Y., Oct. 10
R. H. E.
New York (NL) . . 004 000 001 —— 5 8 0
New York (AL) . . 120 000 100 —— 4 12 1
Pitchers—Watson, RYAN (3) vs. Hoyt, BUSH (3). Homer—Stengel (NL). Attendance—55,307.

2d Game, at Polo Grounds, N.Y., Oct. 11
New York (AL) . . 010 210 000 —— 4 10 0
New York (NL) . . 010 001 000 —— 2 9 2
Pitchers—PENNOCK vs. McQUILLAN, Bentley (4). Homers—Ward (AL), E. Meusel (NL), Ruth (AL)2. Attendance—40,402.

3d Game, at Yankee Stadium, N.Y., Oct. 12
New York (NL) . . 000 000 100 —— 1 4 0
New York (AL) . . 000 000 000 —— 0 6 1
Pitchers—NEHF vs. JONES, Bush (8). Homer—Stengel (NL). Attendance—62,430.

4th Game, at Polo Grounds, N.Y., Oct. 13
New York (AL) ..061 100 000 —— 8 13 1
New York (NL) ..000 000 031 —— 4 13 1
Pitchers—SHAWKEY, Pennock (8) vs. J. SCOTT, Ryan (2), McQuillan (3), Jonnard (8), Barnes (9). Homer—Youngs (NL). Attendance—46,302.

5th Game, at Yankee Stadium, N.Y., Oct. 14
New York (NL) ..010 000 000 —— 1 3 2
New York (AL) ..340 100 00x —— 8 14 0
Pitchers—BENTLEY, J. Scott (2), Barnes (4), Jonnard (8) vs. BUSH. Homer—Dugan (AL). Attendance—62,817.

6th Game, at Polo Grounds, N.Y., Oct. 15
New York (AL) ..100 000 050 —— 6 5 0
New York (NL) ..100 111 000 —— 4 10 1
Pitchers—PENNOCK, Jones (8) vs. NEHF, Ryan (8). Homers—Ruth (AL), Snyder (NL). Attendance—34,172.

Total attendance—301,430. Receipts—$1,063,815. Winning Player's share—$6,143.49. Losing player's share—$4,112.89.

1924 Final Standing

	W.	L.
Washington AL (Stanley R. Harris) . . .	4	3
New York NL (John J. McGraw)	3	4

1st Game, at Washington, Oct. 4   R. H. E.
New York (NL) . 010 100 000 002 — 4 14 1
Washington (AL) 000 001 001 001 — 3 10 1
Pitchers—NEHF vs. JOHNSON. Homers—Kelly (N.Y.). Attendance—35,760.

2d Game, at Washington, Oct. 5
New York (NL) ..000 000 102 —— 3 6 0
Washington (AL) .200 010 001 —— 4 6 1
Pitchers—BENTLEY vs. ZACHARY, Marberry (9). Homers—Goslin (Wash.), Harris (Wash.). Attendance—35,922.

3d Game, at New York, Oct. 6
Washington (AL) .000 200 011 —— 4 9 2
New York (NL) ..021 101 01x —— 6 12 0
Pitchers—MARBERRY, Russell (4), Martina (7), Speece (8) vs. McQUILLAN, Ryan (4), Jonnard (9), Watson (9). Homer—Ryan (N.Y.). Attendance—47,608.

4th Game, at New York, Oct. 7
Washington (AL) .003 020 020 —— 7 13 3
New York (NL) ..100 001 011 —— 4 6 1
Pitchers—MOGRIDGE, Marberry (8) vs. BARNES, Baldwin (6), Dean (8). Homer—Goslin (Wash.). Attendance—49,243.

5th Game, at New York, Oct. 8
Washington (AL) .000 100 010 —— 2 9 1
New York (NL) ..001 020 03x —— 6 13 0

Pitchers—JOHNSON vs. BENTLEY, McQuillan (8). Homers—Bentley (N.Y.), Goslin (Wash.). Attendance—49,211.

6th Game, at Washington, Oct. 9
New York (NL) ..100 000 000 —— 1 7 1
Washington (AL) .000 020 00x —— 2 4 0
Pitchers—NEHF, Ryan (8) vs. ZACHARY. Attendance—34,254.

7th Game, at Washington, Oct. 10
New York (NL) . 000 003 000 000 — 3 8 3
Washington (AL) 000 100 020 001 — 4 10 4
Pitchers—Barnes, McQuillan (8), Nehf (10), BENTLEY (11) vs. Ogden, Mogridge (1), Marberry (6), JOHNSON (9). Homer—Harris (Wash.). Attendance—31,667.

Total attendance—283,665. Receipts—$1,093,104. Winning player's share—$5,969.64. Losing player's share—$3,820.29.

1925 Final Standing

	W.	L.
Pittsburgh NL (William B. McKechnie)	4	3
Washington AL (Stanley R. Harris) . . .	3	4

1st Game, at Pittsburgh, Oct. 7   R. H. E.
Washington (AL) .010 020 001 —— 4 8 1
Pittsburgh (NL) ..000 010 000 —— 1 5 0
Pitchers—JOHNSON vs. MEADOWS, Morrison (9). Homers—J. Harris (Wash.), Traynor (Pitt.). Attendance—41,723.

2d Game, at Pittsburgh, Oct. 8
Washington (AL) .010 000 001 —— 2 8 2
Pittsburgh (NL) ..000 100 02x —— 3 7 0
Pitchers—COVELESKIE vs. ALDRIDGE. Homers—Judge (Wash.), Wright (Pitt.), Cuyler (Pitt.). Attendance—43,364.

3d Game, at Washington, Oct. 10
Pittsburgh (NL) ..010 101 000 —— 3 8 3
Washington (AL) .001 001 20x —— 4 10 1
Pitchers—KREMER vs. FERGUSON, Marberry (8). Homer—Goslin (Wash.). Attendance—36,495.

4th Game, at Washington, Oct. 11
Pittsburgh (NL) ..000 000 000 —— 0 6 1
Washington (AL) .004 000 00x —— 4 12 0
Pitchers—Morrison, YDE (5), Adams (*) vs. JOHNSON. Homers—Goslin (Wash.), J. Harris (Wash.). Attendance—38,701.

5th Game, at Washington, Oct. 12
Pittsburgh (NL) ..002 000 211 —— 6 13 0
Washington (AL) .100 100 100 —— 3 8 1
Pitchers—ALDRIDGE vs. COVELESKIE, Ballou (7), Zachary (8), Marberry (9). Homer—J. Harris (Wash.). Attendance—35,899.

6th Game, at Pittsburgh, Oct. 13
Washington (AL) . 110 000 000 —— 2 6 2
Pittsburgh (NL) . . 002 010 00x —— 3 7 1
    Pitchers—FERGUSON, Ballou (8) vs.
KREMER. Homers—Goslin (Wash.), Moore
(Pitt.). Attendance—43,810.

7th Game, at Pittsburgh, Oct. 15
Washington (AL) . 400 200 010 —— 7 7 2
Pittsburgh (NL) . . 003 010 23x —— 9 15 2
    Pitchers—JOHNSON vs. Aldridge, Morrison
(1), KREMER (5), Oldham (9). Homer—Peckinpaugh (Wash.). Attendance—42,856.

    Total attendance—282,848. Receipts—
$1,182,854. Winning player's share—$5,332.72.
Losing player's share—$3,734.60.

1926 Final Standing

	W.	L.
St. Louis NL (Rogers Hornsby)	4	3
New York AL (Miller J. Huggins)	3	4

1st Game, at New York, Oct. 2   R. H. E.
St. Louis (NL) . . . 100 000 000 —— 1 3 1
New York (AL) . . 100 001 00x —— 2 6 0
    Pitchers—SHERDEL, Haines (8) vs. PEN-
NOCK. Attendance—61,658.

2d Game, at New York, Oct. 3
St. Louis (NL) . . . 002 000 301 —— 6 12 1
New York (AL) . . 020 000 000 —— 2 4 0
    Pitchers—ALEXANDER vs. SHOCKER,
Shawkey (8), Jones (9). Homers—Southworth
(St. L.), Thevenow (St. L.). Attendance—63,600.

3d Game, at St. Louis, Oct. 5
New York (AL) . . 000 000 000 —— 0 5 1
St. Louis (NL) . . . 000 310 00x —— 4 8 0
    Pitchers—RUETHER, Shawkey (5), Thomas
(8) vs. HAINES. Homer—Haines (St. L.). Attendance—37,708.

4th Game, at St. Louis, Oct. 6
New York (AL) . . 101 142 100 —— 10 14 1
St. Louis (NL) . . . 100 300 001 —— 5 14 0
    Pitchers—HOYT vs. Rhem, REINHART (5),
H. Bell (5), Hallahan (7), Keen (9). Homers—
Ruth (N.Y.) 3. Attendance—38,825.

5th Game, at St. Louis, Oct. 7
New York (AL) 000 001 001 1 —— 3 9 1
St. Louis (NL) .000 100 100 0 —— 2 7 1
    Pitchers—PENNOCK vs. SHERDEL. Attend-
ance—39,552.

6th Game, at New York, Oct. 9
St. Louis (NL) . . . 300 010 501 —— 10 13 2
New York (AL) . . 000 100 100 —— 2 8 1
    Pitchers—ALEXANDER vs. SHAWKEY,

Shocker (7), Thomas (8). Homer—L. Bell (St.
L.). Attendance—48,615.

7th Game, at New York, Oct. 10
St. Louis (NL) . . . 000 300 000 —— 3 8 0
New York (AL) . . 001 001 000 —— 2 8 3
    Pitchers—HAINES, Alexander (7) vs. HOYT,
Pennock (7). Homer—Ruth (N.Y.). Attendance—
38,093.

    Total attendance—328,051. Receipts—
$1,207.864. Winning player's share—$5,584.51.
Losing player's share—$3,417.75.

1927 Final Standing

	W.	L.
New York AL (Miller J. Huggins)	4	0
Pittsburgh NL (Owen Bush)	0	4

1st Game, at Pittsburgh, Oct. 5   R. H. E.
New York (AL) . . 103 010 000 —— 5 6 1
Pittsburgh (NL) . . 101 010 010 —— 4 9 2
    Pitchers—HOYT, Moore (8) vs. KREMER,
Milijus (6). Attendance—41,567.

2d Game, at Pittsburgh, Oct. 6
New York (AL) . . 003 000 030 —— 6 11 0
Pittsburgh (NL) . . 100 000 010 —— 2 7 2
    Pitchers—PIPGRAS vs. ALDRIDGE, Cvengros
(8), Dawson (9). Attendance—41,634.

3d Game, at New York, Oct. 7
Pittsburgh (NL) . . 000 000 010 —— 1 3 1
New York (AL) . . 200 000 60x —— 8 9 0
    Pitchers—MEADOWS, Cvengros (7) vs.
PENNOCK. Homer—Ruth (N.Y.). Attendance—
60,695.

4th Game, at New York, Oct. 8
Pittsburgh (NL) . . 100 000 200 —— 3 10 1
New York (AL) . . 100 020 001 —— 4 12 2
    Pitchers—Hill, MILJUS (7) vs. MOORE.
Homer—Ruth (N.Y.). Attendance—57,909.

    Total attendance—201,705. Receipts—
$783,217. Winning player's share—$5,592.17.
Losing player's share—$3,728.10.

1928 Final Standing

	W.	L.
New York AL (Miller J. Huggins)	4	0
St. Louis NL (William B. McKechnie)	0	4

1st Game, at New York, Oct. 4   R. H. E.
St. Louis (NL) . . . 000 000 100 —— 1 3 1
New York (AL) . . 100 200 01x —— 4 7 0
    Pitchers—SHERDEL, Johnson (8) vs. HOYT.
Homers—Meusel (N.Y.), Bottomley (St. L.).
Attendance—61,425.

2d Game, at New York, Oct. 5

St. Louis (NL) ...030 000 000 –– 3 4 1
New York (AL) ..314 000 10x –– 9 8 2
   Pitchers–ALEXANDER, Mitchell (3) vs. PIPGRAS. Homer–Gehrig (N.Y.). Attendance–60,714.

3d Game, at St. Louis, Oct. 7

New York (AL) ..010 203 100 –– 7 7 2
St. Louis (NL) ...200 010 000 –– 3 9 3
   Pitchers–ZACHARY vs. HAINES, Johnson (7), Rhem (8). Homers–Gehrig (N.Y.) 2. Attendance–39,602.

4th Game, at St. Louis, Oct. 9

New York (AL) ..000 100 420 –– 7 15 2
St. Louis (NL) ...001 100 001 –– 3 11 0
   Pitchers–HOYT vs. SHERDEL, Alexander (7). Homers–Ruth (N.Y.) 3, Durst (N.Y.), Gehrig (N.Y.). Attendance–37,331.

Total attendance–199,072. Receipts–$777,290. Winning player's share–$5,531.91. Losing player's share–$4,197.37.

1929 Final Standing

	W.	I
Philadelphia AL (Connie Mack)	4	1
Chicago NL (Joseph V. McCarthy) ...	1	4

1st Game, at Chicago, Oct. 8   R. H. E.
Philadelphia (AL) 000 000 102 –– 3 6 1
Chicago (NL) ....000 000 001 –– 1 8 2
   Pitchers–EHMKE vs. ROOT, Bush (8). Homer–Foxx (Phila.). Attendance–50,740.

2d Game, at Chicago, Oct. 9
Philadelphia (AL) 003 300 120 –– 9 12 0
Chicago (NL) ....000 030 000 –– 3 11 1
   Pitchers–EARNSHAW, Grove (5) vs. MALONE, Blake (4), Carlson (6), Nehf (9). Homers–Simmons (Phila.), Foxx (Phila.). Attendance–49,987.

3d Game, at Philadelphia, Oct. 11
Chicago (NL) ....000 003 000 –– 3 6 1
Philadelphia (AL) 000 010 000 –– 1 9 1
   Pitchers–BUSH vs. EARNSHAW. Attendance–29,991.

4th Game, at Philadelphia, Oct. 12
Chicago (NL) ....000 205 100 – 8 10 2
Philadelphia (AL) 000 000 (10)0x – 10 15 2
   Pitchers–Root, Nehf (7), BLAKE (7), Malone (7), Carlson (8) vs. Quinn, Walberg (6), ROMMEL (7), Grove (8). Homers–Grimm (Chi.), Haas (Phila.), Simmons (Phila.). Attendance–29,991.

5th Game, at Philadelphia, Oct. 14
Chicago (NL) ....002 000 000 –– 2 8 1
Philadelphia (AL) 000 000 003 –– 3 6 0

Pitchers–MALONE vs. Ehmke, WALBERG (4). Homer–Haas (Phila.). Attendance–29,991.

Total attendance–190,490. Receipts–$859,494. Winning player's share–$5,620,57. Losing player's share–$3,782.01.

1930 Final Standing

	W.	L.
Philadelphia AL (Connie Mack)	4	2
St. Louis NL (Charles E. Street)	2	4

1st Game, at Philadelphia, Oct. 1   R. H. E.
St. Louis (NL) ...002 000 000 –– 2 9 0
Philadelphia (AL) 010 101 11x –– 5 5 0
   Pitchers–GRIMES vs. GROVE. Homers–Cochrane (Phila.), Simmons (Phila.). Attendance–32,295.

2d Game, at Philadelphia, Oct. 2
St. Louis (NL) ...010 000 000 –– 1 6 2
Philadelphia (AL) 202 200 00x –– 6 7 2
   Pitchers–RHEM, Lindsey (4), Johnson (7) vs. EARNSHAW. Homers–Cochrane (Phila.), Watkins (St. L.). Attendance–32,295.

3d Game, at St. Louis, Oct. 4
Philadelphia (AL) 000 000 000 –– 0 7 0
St. Louis (NL) ...000 110 21x –– 5 10 0
   Pitchers–WALBERG, Shores (5), Quinn (7) vs. HALLAHAN. Homer–Douthit (St. L.). Attendance–36,944.

4th Game, at St. Louis, Oct. 5
Philadelphia (AL) 100 000 000 –– 1 4 1
St. Louis (NL) ...001 200 00x –– 3 5 1
   Pitchers–GROVE vs. HAINES. Attendance–39,946.

5th Game, at St. Louis, Oct. 6
Philadelphia (AL) 000 000 002 –– 2 5 0
St. Louis (NL) ...000 000 000 –– 0 3 1
   Pitchers–Earnshaw, GROVE (8) vs. GRIMES. Homer–Foxx (Phila.). Attendance–38,844.

6th Game, at Philadelphia, Oct. 8
St. Louis (NL) ...000 000 001 –– 1 5 1
Philadelphia (AL) 201 211 00x –– 7 7 0
   Pitchers–HALLAHAN, Johnson (3), Lindsey (6), Bell (8) vs. EARNSHAW. Homers–Dykes (Phila.), Simmons (Phila.). Attendance–32,295.

Total attendance–212,619. Receipts–$953,772. Winning player's share–$5,785. Losing player's share–$3,875.

1931 Final Standing

	W.	L.
St. Louis NL (Charles E. Street)	4	3
Philadelphia AL (Connie Mack)	3	4

1st Game, at St. Louis, Oct. 1   R. H. E.

Philadelphia (AL) 004 000 200 –– 6 11 0
St. Louis (NL) . . . 200 000 000 –– 2 12 0
 Pitchers–GROVE vs. DERRINGER, Johnson (8). Homer–Simmons (Phila.). Attendance–38,529.

2d Game at St. Louis, Oct. 2

Philadelphia (AL) 000 000 000 –– 0 3 0
St. Louis (NL) . . . 010 000 10x –– 2 6 1
 Pitchers–EARNSHAW vs. HALLAHAN. Attendance–35,947.

3d Game, at Philadelphia, Oct. 5

St. Louis (NL) . . . 020 200 001 –– 5 12 0
Philadelphia (AL) 000 000 002 –– 2 2 0
 Pitchers–GRIMES vs. GROVE, Mahaffey (9). Homer–Simmons (Phila.). Attendance–32,295.

4th Game, at Philadelphia, Oct. 6

St. Louis (NL) . . . 000 000 000 –– 0 2 1
Philadelphia (AL) 100 002 00x –– 3 10 0
 Pitchers–JOHNSON, Lindsey (6) vs. EARNSHAW. Homer–Foxx (Phila.). Attendance–32,295.

5th Game, at Philadelphia, Oct. 7

St. Louis (NL) . . . 100 002 011 –– 5 12 0
Philadelphia (AL) 000 000 100 –– 1 9 0
 Pitchers–HALLAHAN vs. HOYT, Walberg (7), Rommel (9). Homer–Martin (St. L.). Attendance–32,295.

6th Game, at St. Louis, Oct. 9

Philadelphia (AL) 000 040 400 –– 8 8 1
St. Louis (NL) . . . 000 001 000 –– 1 5 2
 Pitchers–GROVE vs. DERRINGER, Johnson (5), Lindsey (7), Rhem (9). Attendance–39,401.

7th Game, at St. Louis, Oct. 10

Philadelphia (AL) 000 000 002 –– 2 7 1
St. Louis (NL) . . . 202 000 00x –– 4 5 0
 Pitchers–EARNSHAW, Walberg (8) vs. GRIMES, Hallahan (9). Attendance–20,805.

 Total attendance–231,567. Receipts–$1,030,723. Winning player's share–$4,467.59. Losing player's share–$3,023.09.

1932 Final Standing

	W.	L.
New York AL (Joseph V. McCarthy) .	4	0
Chicago NL (Charles J. Grimm)	0	4

1st Game, at New York, Sept. 28   R. H. E.

Chicago (NL) . . . . 200 000 220 –– 6 10 1
New York (AL) . . 000 305 31x –– 12 8 2
 Pitchers–BUSH, Grimes (6), Smith (8) vs. RUFFING. Homer–Gehrig (N.Y.). Attendance–41,459.

2d Game, at New York, Sept. 29

Chicago (NL) . . . . 101 000 000 –– 2 9 0
New York (AL) . . 202 010 00x –– 5 10 1
 Pitchers–WARNEKE vs. GOMEZ. Attendance–50,709.

3d Game, at Chicago, Oct. 1

New York (AL) . . 301 020 001 –– 7 8 1
Chicago (NL) . . . . 102 100 001 –– 5 9 4
 Pitchers–PIPGRAS, Pennock (9) vs. ROOT, Malone (5), May (7), Tinning (9). Homers–Ruth (N.Y.) 2, Gehrig (N.Y.) 2, Cuyler (Chi.), Hartnett (Chi.). Attendance–49,986.

4th Game, at Chicago, Oct. 2

New York (AL) . . 102 002 404 –– 13 19 4
Chicago (NL) . . . . 400 001 001 –– 6 9 1
 Pitchers–Allen, MOORE (1), Pennock (7) vs. Bush, Warneke (1), MAY (4), Tinning (7), Grimes (9). Homers–Demaree (Chi.), Lazzeri (N.Y.) 2, Combs (N.Y.). Attendance–49,844.

 Total attendance–191,998. Receipts–$713,377. Winning player's share–$5,231.77. Losing player's share–$4,244.60.

1933 Final Standing

	W.	L.
New York NL (William H. Terry)	4	1
Washington AL (Joseph E. Cronin) . . .	1	4

1st Game, at New York, Oct. 3   R. H. E.

Washington (AL) . 000 100 001 –– 2 5 3
New York (NL) . . 202 000 00x –– 4 10 2
 Pitchers–STEWART, Russell (3), Thomas (8) vs. HUBBELL. Homer–Ott (N.Y.). Attendance–46,672.

2d Game, at New York, Oct. 4

Washington (AL) . 001 000 000 –– 1 5 0
New York (NL) . . 000 006 00x –– 6 10 0
 Pitchers–CROWDER, Thomas (6), McColl (7) vs. SCHUMACHER. Homer–Goslin (Wash.). Attendance–35,461.

3d Game, at Washington, Oct. 5

New York (NL) . . 000 000 000 –– 0 5 0
Washington (AL) . 210 000 10x –– 4 9 1
 Pitchers–FITZSIMMONS, Bell (8) vs. WHITEHILL. Attendance–25,727.

4th Game, at Washington, Oct. 6

New York (NL) . . 000 100 000 01 – 2 11 1
Washington (AL) . 000 000 100 00 – 1 3 0
 Pitchers–HUBBELL vs. WEAVER, Russell (11). Homer–Terry (N.Y.). Attendance–27,762.

5th Game, at Washington, Oct. 7

New York (NL) . 020 001 000 1 – 4 11 1
Washington (AL) 000 003 000 0 – 3 10 0

Pitchers—Schumacher, LUQUE (6) vs. Crowder, RUSSELL (6). Homers—Schulte (Wash.), Ott (N.Y.). Attendance—28,454.

Total attendance—163,076. Receipts—$679,365. Winning player's share—$4,256.72. Losing player's share—$3,019.86.

1934 Final Standing

	W.	L.
St. Louis NL (Frank F. Frisch)	4	3
Detroit AL (Gordon S. Cochrane)	3	4

1st Game, at Detroit, Oct. 3

	R.	H.	E.
St. Louis (NL) ...021 014 000 ——	8	13	2
Detroit (AL) ....001 001 010 ——	3	8	5

Pitchers—J. DEAN vs. CROWDER, Marberry (6) Hogsett (6). Homers—Medwick (St. L.), Greenberg (Det.). Attendance—42,505.

2d Game, at Detroit, Oct. 4

St. Louis (NL) 011 000 000 000 –	2	7	3
Detroit (AL) . 000 100 001 001 –	3	7	0

Pitchers—Hallahan, W. WALKER (9) vs. ROWE. Attendance—43,451.

3d Game, at St. Louis, Oct. 5

Detroit (AL) ....000 000 001 ——	1	8	2
St. Louis (NL) ...110 020 00x ——	4	9	1

Pitchers—BRIDGES, Hogsett (5) vs. P. DEAN. Attendance—34,073.

4th Game, at St. Louis, Oct. 6

Detroit (AL) ....003 100 150 ——	10	13	1
St. Louis (NL) ...011 200 000 ——	4	10	5

Pitchers—AUKER vs. Carleton, Vance (3), W. WALKER (5), Haines (8), Mooney (9). Attendance—37,492.

5th Game, at St. Louis, Oct. 7

Detroit (AL) ....010 002 000 ——	3	7	0
St. Louis (NL) ...000 000 100 ——	1	7	1

Pitchers—BRIDGES vs. J. DEAN, Carleton (9). Homers—Gehringer (Det.), DeLancy (St. L.). Attendance—38,536.

6th Game, at Detroit, Oct. 8

St. Louis (NL) ...100 020 100 ——	4	10	2
Detroit (AL) ....001 002 000 ——	3	7	1

Pitchers—P. DEAN vs. ROWE. Attendance—44,551.

7th Game, at Detroit, Oct. 9

St. Louis (NL) ...007 002 200 ——	11	17	1
Detroit (AL) ....000 000 000 ——	0	6	3

Pitchers—J. DEAN vs. AUKER, Rowe (3), Hogsett (3), Bridges (4), Marberry (8), Crowder (9). Attendance—40,902.

Total attendance—281,510. Receipts—$1,128,995.27 (including $100,000 for radio rights). Winning player's share—$5,389.57. Losing player's share—$3,354.57.

1935 Final Standing

	W.	L.
Detroit AL (Gordon S. Cochrane)	4	2
Chicago NL (Charles J. Grimm)	2	4

1st Game, at Detroit, Oct. 2

	R.	H.	E.
Chicago (NL) .... 200 000 001 ——	3	7	0
Detroit (AL) ....000 000 000 ——	0	4	3

Pitchers—WARNEKE vs. ROWE. Homer—Demaree (Chi.) Attendance—47,391.

2d Game, at Detroit, Oct. 3

Chicago (NL) ....000 010 200 ——	3	6	1
Detroit (AL) ....400 300 10x ——	8	9	2

Pitchers—ROOT, Henshaw (1) Kowalik (4) vs. BRIDGES. Homer—Greenberg (Det.). Attendance—46,742.

3d Game, at Chicago, Oct. 4

Detroit (AL) . 000 001 040 01 ——	6	12	2
Chicago (NL) . 020 010 002 00 ——	5	10	3

Pitchers—Auker, Hogsett (7), ROWE (8) vs. Lee, Warneke (8), FRENCH (10). Homer—Demaree (Chi.). Attendance—45,532.

4th Game, at Chicago, Oct. 5

Detroit (AL) ....001 001 000 ——	2	7	0
Chicago (NL) ....010 000 000 ——	1	5	2

Pitchers—CROWDER vs. CARLETON, Root (8). Homer—Hartnett (Chi.). Attendance—49,350.

5th Game, at Chicago, Oct. 6

Detroit (AL) ....000 000 001 ——	1	7	1
Chicago (NL) ....002 000 10x ——	3	8	0

Pitchers—ROWE vs. WARNEKE, Lee (7). Homer—Klein (Chi.). Attendance—49,237.

6th Game, at Detroit, Oct. 7

Chicago (NL) ....001 020 000 ——	3	12	0
Detroit (AL) ....100 101 001 ——	4	12	1

Pitchers—FRENCH vs. BRIDGES. Homer—Herman (Chi.). Attendance—48,420.

Total attendance—286,672. Receipts—$1,173,794 (including $100,000 for radio rights). Winning player's share—$6,544.76. Losing player's share—$4,198.53.

1936 Final Standing

	W.	L.
New York AL (Joseph V. McCarthy) .	4	2
New York NL (William H. Terry)	2	4

1st Game, at Polo Grounds, N.Y., Sept. 30

	R.	H.	E.
New York (AL) ..001 001 000 ——	1	7	2
New York (NL) ..000 011 04x ——	6	9	1

Pitchers—RUFFING vs. HUBBELL. Homers—Bartell (NL), Selkirk (AL). Attendance—39,419.

2d Game, at Polo Grounds, N.Y., Oct. 2
New York (AL) . . 207 001 206 — — 18 17 0
New York (NL) . . 010 300 000 — — 4 6 1
Pitchers—GOMEZ vs. SCHUMACHER, Smith (3), Coffman (3), Gabler (5), Gumbert (9). Homers—Dickey (AL), Lazzeri (AL). Attendance—43,543.

3d Game, at Yankee Stadium, N.Y., Oct. 3
New York (NL) . . 000 010 000 — — 1 11 0
New York (AL) . . 010 000 01x — — 2 4 0
Pitchers—FITZSIMMONS vs. HADLEY, Malone (9). Homers—Gehrig (AL), Ripple (NL). Attendance—64,842.

4th Game, at Yankee Stadium, N.Y., Oct. 4
New York (NL) . . 000 100 010 — — 2 7 1
New York (AL) . . 013 000 01x — — 5 10 1
Pitchers—HUBBELL, Gabler (8) vs. PEARSON. Homer—Gehrig (AL). Attendance—66,669.

5th Game, at Yankee Stadium, N.Y., Oct. 5
New York (NL) 300 001 000 1 — — 5 8 3
New York (AL) 011 002 000 0 — — 4 10 1
Pitchers—SCHUMACHER vs. Ruffing, MALONE (7). Homer—Selkirk (AL). Attendance—50,024.

6th Game, at Polo Grounds, N.Y., Oct. 6
New York (AL) . . 021 200 017 — — 13 17 2
New York (NL) . . 200 010 110 — — 5 9 1
Pitchers—GOMEZ, Murphy (7) vs. FITZSIMMONS, Castleman (4), Coffman (9), Gumbert (9). Homers—Moore (NL), Ott (NL), Powell (AL). Attendance—38,427.

Total attendance—302,924. Receipts—$1,304.399 (including $100,000 for radio rights). Winning player's share—$6,430.55. Losing player's share—$4,655.58.

1937 Final Standing

	W.	L.
New York AL (Joseph V. McCarthy) . .	4	1
New York NL (William H. Terry)	1	4

1st Game, at Yankee Stadium, N.Y., Oct. 6
R. H. E.
New York (NL) . . 000 010 000 — — 1 6 2
New York (AL) . . 000 007 01x — — 8 7 0
Pitchers—HUBBELL, Gumbert (6), Coffman (6), Smith (8) vs. GOMEZ. Homer—Lazzeri (AL). Attendance—60,573.

2d Game, at Yankee Stadium, N.Y., Oct. 7
New York (NL) . . 100 000 000 — — 1 7 0
New York (AL) . . 000 024 20x — — 8 12 0
Pitchers—MELTON, Gumbert (5), Coffman

(6) vs. RUFFING. Attendance—57,675.

3d Game, at Polo Grounds, N.Y., Oct. 8
New York (AL) . . 012 110 000 — — 5 9 0
New York (NL) . . 000 000 100 — — 1 5 4
Pitchers—PEARSON, Murphy (9) vs. SCHUMACHER, Melton (7), Brennan (9). Attendance—37,385.

4th Game, at Polo Grounds, N.Y., Oct. 9
New York (AL) . . 101 000 001 — — 3 6 0
New York (NL) . . 060 000 10x — — 7 12 3
Pitchers—HADLEY, Andrews (2), Wicker (8) vs. HUBBELL. Homer—Gehrig (AL). Attendance—44,293.

5th Game, at Polo Grounds, N.Y., Oct. 10
New York (AL) . . 011 020 000 — — 4 8 0
New York (NL) . . 002 000 000 — — 2 10 0
Pitchers—GOMEZ vs. MELTON, Smith (6), Brennan (8). Homers—DiMaggio (AL), Loag (AL), Ott (NL). Attendance—38,216.

Total attendance—238,142. Receipts—$1,085,994 (including $100,000 for radio rights). Winning player's share—$6,471.10. Losing player's share—$4,489.05.

1938 Final Standing

	W.	L.
New York AL (Joseph V. McCarthy) .	4	0
Chicago NL (Charles L. Hartnett)	0	4

1st Game, at Chicago, Oct. 5
R. H. E.
New York (AL) . . 020 000 100 — — 3 12 1
Chicago (NL) . . . . 001 000 000 — — 1 9 1
Pitchers—RUFFING vs. LEE, Russell (9). Attendance—43,642.

2d Game, at Chicago, Oct. 6
New York (AL) . . 020 000 022 — — 6 7 2
Chicago (NL) . . . . 102 000 000 — — 3 11 0
Pitchers—GOMEZ, Murphy (8) vs. J. DEAN, French (9). Homers—Crosetti (N.Y.), DiMaggio (N.Y.). Attendance—42,108.

3d Game, at New York, Oct. 8
Chicago (NL) . . . . 000 010 010 — — 2 5 1
New York (AL) . . 000 022 01x — — 5 7 2
Pitchers—BRYANT, Russell (6), French (7) vs. PEARSON. Homers—Dickey (N.Y.), Gordon (N.Y.), Marty (Chi.). Attendance—55,236.

4th Game, at New York, Oct. 9
Chicago (NL) . . . . 000 100 020 — — 3 8 1
New York (AL) . . 030 001 04x — — 8 11 1
Pitchers—LEE, Root (4), Page (7), French (8), Carleton (8), Dean (8) vs. RUFFING. Homers—Henrich (N.Y.), O'Dea (Chi.). Attendance—59,847.

Total attendance—200,833. Receipts—$851,166. Winning player's share—$5,782.76. Losing player's share—$4,674.87.

1939 Final Standing

	W.	L.
New York AL (Joseph V. McCarthy) .	4	0
Cincinnati NL (William B. McKechnie)	0	4

1st Game, at New York, Oct. 4

		R.	H.	E.
Cincinnati (NL) . .	000 100 000 ——	1	4	0
New York (AL) . .	000 010 001 ——	2	6	0

Pitchers—DERRINGER vs. RUFFING. Attendance—58,541.

2d Game, at New York, Oct. 5

Cincinnati (NL) . .	000 000 000 ——	0	2	0
New York (AL) . .	003 100 00x ——	4	9	0

Pitchers—WALTERS vs. PEARSON. Homer—Dahlgren (N.Y.). Attendance—59,791.

3d Game, at Cincinnati, Oct. 7

New York (AL) . .	202 030 000 ——	7	5	1
Cincinnati (NL) . .	120 000 000 ——	3	10	0

Pitchers—Gomez, HADLEY (2) vs. THOMPSON, Grissom (5), Moore (7). Homers—Keller (N.Y.) 2, DiMaggio (N.Y.), Dickey (N.Y.). Attendance—32,723.

4th Game, at Cincinnati, Oct. 8

New York (AL)	000 000 202 3 ——	7	7	1
Cincinnati (NL)	000 000 310 0 ——	4	11	4

Pitchers—Hildebrand, Sundra (5), MURPHY (7) vs. Derringer, WALTERS (8). Homers—Keller (N.Y.), Dickey (N.Y.). Attendance—32,794.

Total attendance—183,849. Receipts—$845,329 (including $100,000 for radio rights). Winning player's share—$5,614.26. Losing player's share—$4,282.58.

1940 Final Standing

	W.	L.
Cincinnati NL (William B. McKechnie)	4	3
Detroit AL (Delmar D. Baker)	3	4

1st Game, at Cincinnati, Oct. 2

		R.	H.	E.
Detroit (AL)	050 020 000 ——	7	10	1
Cincinnati (NL) . .	000 100 010 ——	2	8	3

Pitchers—NEWSOM vs. DERRINGER, Moore (2), Riddle (9). Homer—Campbell (Det.). Attendance—31,793.

2d Game, at Cincinnati, Oct. 3

Detroit (AL)	200 001 000 ——	3	3	1
Cincinnati (NL) . .	022 100 00x ——	5	9	0

Pitchers—ROWE, Gorsica (4) vs. WALTERS. Homer—Ripple (Cin.). Attendance—30,640.

3d Game, at Detroit, Oct. 4

Cincinnati (NL) . .	100 000 012 ——	4	10	1
Detroit (AL)	000 100 42x ——	7	13	1

Pitchers—TURNER, Moore (7), Beggs (8) vs. BRIDGES. Homers—York (Det.), Higgins (Det.). Attendance—52,877.

4th Game, at Detroit, Oct. 5

Cincinnati (NL) . .	201 100 010 ——	5	11	1
Detroit (AL)	001 001 000 ——	2	5	1

Pitchers—DERRINGER vs. TROUT, Smith (3), McKain (7). Attendance—54,093.

5th Game, at Detroit, Oct. 6

Cincinnati (NL) . .	000 000 000 ——	0	3	0
Detroit (AL)	003 400 01x ——	8	13	0

Pitchers—THOMPSON, Moore (4), Vander Meer (5), Hutchings (8), vs. NEWSOM. Homer—Greenberg (Det.). Attendance—55,189.

6th Game, at Cincinnati, Oct. 7

Detroit (AL)	000 000 000 ——	0	5	0
Cincinnati (NL) . .	200 001 01x ——	4	10	2

Pitchers—ROWE, Gorsica (1), Hutchinson (8) vs. WALTERS. Homer—Walters (Cin.). Attendance—30,481.

7th Game, at Cincinnati, Oct. 8

Detroit (AL)	001 000 000 ——	1	7	0
Cincinnati (NL) . .	000 000 20x ——	2	7	1

Pitchers—NEWSOM vs. DERRINGER. Attendance—26,854.

Total attendance—281,927. Receipts—$1,322,328.21 (including $100,000 for radio rights). Winning player's share—$5,803.62. Losing player's share—$3,531.81.

1941 Final Standing

	W.	L.
New York AL (Joseph V. McCarthy) .	4	1
Brooklyn NL (Leo E. Durocher)	1	4

1st Game, at New York, Oct. 1

		R.	H.	E.
Brooklyn (NL) . .	000 010 100 ——	2	6	0
New York (AL) . .	010 101 00x ——	3	6	1

Pitchers—DAVIS, Casey (6), Allen (7) vs. RUFFING. Homer—Gordon (N.Y.). Attendance—68,540.

2d Game, at New York, Oct. 2

Brooklyn (NL) . .	000 021 000 ——	3	6	2
New York (AL) . .	011 000 000 ——	2	9	1

Pitchers—WYATT vs. CHANDLER, Murphy (6). Attendance—66,248.

3d Game, at Brooklyn, Oct. 4

New York (AL) . .	000 000 020 ——	2	8	0
Brooklyn (NL) . .	000 000 010 ——	1	4	0

Pitchers—RUSSO vs. Fitzsimmons, CASEY (8), French (8), Allen (9). Attendance—33,100.

4th Game, at Brooklyn, Oct. 5

New York (AL) . .	100 200 004 ——	7	12	0
Brooklyn (NL) . .	000 220 000 ——	4	9	1

Pitchers—Donald, Breuer (5), MURPHY (8) vs. Higbe, French (4), Allen (5), CASEY (5). Homer—Reiser (Brook.). Attendance—33,813.

5th Game, Brooklyn, Oct. 6

New York (AL) . . 020 010 000 — — 3 6 0
Brooklyn (NL) . . 001 000 000 — — 1 4 1
    Pitchers—BONHAM vs. WYATT. Homer—Henrich (N.Y.). Attendance—34,072.

Total attendance—235,773. Receipts—$1,107,762 (including $100,000 for radio rights). Winning player's share—$5,943.31. Losing player's share—$4,829.40.

1942 Final Standing

	W.	L.
St. Louis NL (William H. Southworth)	4	1
New York AL (Joseph V. McCarthy) .	1	4

1st Game, at St. Louis, Sept. 30   R. H. E.

New York (AL) . . 000 110 032 — — 7 11 0
St. Louis (NL) . . . 000 000 004 — — 4 7 4
    Pitchers—RUFFING, Chandler (9) vs. M. COOPER, Gumbert (8), Lanier (9). Attendance—34,385.

2d Game, at St. Louis, Oct. 1

New York (AL) . . 000 000 030 — — 3 10 2
St. Louis (NL) . . . 200 000 110 — — 4 6 0
    Pitchers—BONHAM vs. BEAZLEY. Homer—Keller (N.Y.). Attendance—34,255.

3d Game, at New York, Oct. 2

St. Louis (NL) . . . 001 000 001 — — 2 5 1
New York (AL) . . 000 000 000 — — 0 6 1
    Pitchers—WHITE vs. CHANDLER, Breuer (9), Turner (9). Attendance—69,123.

4th Game, at New York, Oct. 4

St. Louis (NL) . . . 000 600 201 — — 9 12 1
New York (AL) . . 100 005 000 — — 6 10 1
    Pitchers—M. Cooper, Gumbert (6), Pollet (6), LANIER (7) vs. Borowy, DONALD (4), Bonham (7). Homer—Keller (N.Y.). Attendance—69,902.

5th Game, at New York, Oct. 5

St. Louis (NL) . . . 000 101 002 — — 4 9 4
New York (AL) . . 100 100 000 — — 2 7 1
    Pitchers—BEAZLEY vs. RUFFING. Homers—Rizzuto (N.Y.), Slaughter (St. L.), Kurowski (St. L.). Attendance—69,052.

Total attendance—277,101. Receipts—$1,205,249 (including $100,000 for radio rights). Winning player's share—$5,573.78. Losing player's share—$3,018.77.

1943 Final Standing

	W.	L.
New York AL (Joseph V. McCarthy)	4	1
St. Louis NL (William H. Southworth)	1	4

1st Game, at New York, Oct. 5   R. H. E.

St. Louis (NL) . . . 010 010 000 — — 2 7 2
New York (AL) . . 000 202 00x — — 4 8 2
    Pitchers—LANIER vs. CHANDLER. Homer—Gordon (N.Y.). Attendance—68,676.

2d Game, at New York, Oct. 6

St. Louis (NL) . . . 001 300 000 — — 4 7 2
New York (AL) . . 000 100 002 — — 3 6 0
    Pitchers—M. COOPER vs. BONHAM, Murphy (9). Homers—Marion (St. L.), Sanders (St. L.). Attendance—68,578.

3d Game, at New York, Oct. 7

St. Louis (NL) . . . 000 200 000 — — 2 6 4
New York (AL) . . 000 001 05x — — 6 8 0
    Pitchers—BRAZLE, Krist (8), Brecheen (8) vs. BOROWY, Murphy (9). Attendance—69,990.

4th Game, at St. Louis, Oct. 10

New York (AL) . . 000 100 010 — — 2 6 2
St. Louis (NL) . . . 000 000 100 — — 1 7 1
    Pitchers—RUSSO vs. Lanier, BRECHEEN (8). Attendance—36,196.

5th Game, at St. Louis, Oct. 11

New York (AL) . . 000 002 000 — — 2 7 1
St. Louis (NL) . . . 000 000 000 — — 0 10 1
    Pitchers—CHANDLER vs. M. COOPER, Lanier (8), Dickson (9). Homer—Dickey (N.Y.). Attendance—33,872.

Total attendance—277,312. Receipts—$1,205,784 (including $100,000 for radio rights). Winning player's share—$6,139.46. Losing player's share—$4,321.96.

1944 Final Standing

	W.	L.
St. Louis NL (William H. Southworth)	4	2
St. Louis AL (James Luther Sewell) . .	2	4

1st Game, at Sportsman's Park, Oct. 4 R. H. E.

St. Louis (AL) . . . 000 200 000 — — 2 2 0
St. Louis (NL) . . . 000 000 001 — — 1 7 0
    Pitchers—GALEHOUSE vs. M. COOPER, Donnelly (8). Homer—McQuinn (AL). Attendance—33,242.

2d Game, at Sportsman's Park, Oct. 5

St. Louis (AL) . 000 002 000 0 — — 2 7 4
St. Louis (NL) . 001 100 000 1 — — 3 7 0
    Pitchers—Potter, MUNCRIEF (7) vs. Lanier, DONNELLY (8). Attendance—35,076.

3d Game, at Sportsman's Park, Oct. 6

St. Louis (NL) . . . 100 000 100 — — 2 7 0
St. Louis (AL) . . . 004 000 20x — — 6 8 2
    Pitchers—WILKS, Schmidt (3), Jurisich (7), Byerly (7) vs. KRAMER. Attendance—34,737.

4th Game, at Sportsman's Park, Oct. 7
St. Louis (NL) ... 202 001 000 –– 5 12 0
St. Louis (AL) ... 000 000 010 –– 1 9 1
   Pitchers–BRECHEEN vs. JAKUCKI, Hollings-
worth (4), Shirley (8). Homer–Musial (NL).
Attendance–35,455.

5th Game, at Sportsman's Park, Oct. 8
St. Louis (NL) ... 000 001 010 –– 2 6 1
St. Louis (AL) ... 000 000 000 –– 0 7 1
   Pitchers–M. COOPER vs. GALEHOUSE,
Homers–Sanders (NL), Litwhiler (NL). Attend-
ance–36,568.

6th Game, at Sportsman's Park, Oct. 9
St. Louis (AL) ... 010 000 000 –– 1 3 2
St. Louis (NL) ... 000 300 00x –– 3 10 0
   Pitchers–POTTER, Muncrief (4), Kramer (7)
vs. LANIER, Wilks (6), Attendance–31,630.

   Total attendance–206,708. Receipts–
$1,006,122 (including $100,000 for radio
rights). Winning player's share–$4,626.01.
Losing player's share–$2,743.79.

1945 Final Standing

	W.	L.
Detroit AL (Stephen F. O'Neill)	4	3
Chicago NL (Charles J. Grimm)	3	4

1st Game, at Detroit, Oct. 3   R. H. E.
Chicago (NL) .... 403 000 200 –– 9 13 0
Detroit (AL) .... 000 000 000 –– 0 6 0
   Pitchers–BOROWY vs. NEWHOUSER,
Benton (3), Tobin (5), Mueller (8). Homer–
Cavaretta (Chi.). Attendance–54,637.

2d Game, at Detroit, Oct. 4
Chicago (NL) .... 000 100 000 –– 1 7 0
Detroit (AL) .... 000 040 00x –– 4 7 0
   Pitchers–WYSE, Erickson (7) vs. TRUCKS.
Homer–Greenberg (Det.). Attendance–53,636.

3d Game, at Detroit, Oct. 5
Chicago (NL) .... 000 200 100 –– 3 8 0
Detroit (AL) .... 000 000 000 –– 0 1 2
   Pitchers–PASSEAU vs. OVERMIRE, Benton
(7). Attendance–55,500.

4th Game, at Chicago, Oct. 6
Detroit (AL) .... 000 400 000 –– 4 7 1
Chicago (NL) .... 000 001 000 –– 1 5 1
   Pitchers–TROUT vs. PRIM, Derringer (4),
Vandenberg (6), Erickson (8). Attendance–
42,923.

5th Game, at Chicago, Oct. 7
Detroit (AL) .... 001 004 102 –– 8 11 0
Chicago (NL) .... 001 100 201 –– 4 7 2
   Pitchers–NEWHOUSER vs. BOROWY,
Vandenberg (6), Chipman (6), Derringer (7),

Erickson (9). Attendance–43,463.

6th Game, at Chicago, Oct. 8
Detroit (AL) 010 000 240 000 –– 7 13 1
Chicago (NL) 000 041 200 001 –– 8 15 3
   Pitchers–Trucks, Caster (5), Bridges (6),
Benton (7), TROUT (8) vs. Passeau, Wyse (7),
Prim (8), BOROWY (9). Homer–Greenberg
(Det.). Attendance–41,708.

7th Game, at Chicago, Oct. 10
Detroit (AL) .... 510 000 120 –– 9 9 1
Chicago (NL) .... 100 100 010 –– 3 10 0
   Pitchers–NEWHOUSER vs. BOROWY, Der-
ringer (1), Vandenberg (2), Erickson (6), Passeau
(8), Wyse (9). Attendance–41,590.

   Total attendance–333,457. Receipts–
$1,592,454 (including $100,000 for radio
rights). Winning player's share–$6,443.34.
Losing player's share–$3,930.22.

1946 Final Standing

	W.	L.
St. Louis NL (Edwin H. Dyer)	4	3
Boston AL (Joseph E. Cronin)	3	4

1st Game, at St. Louis, Oct. 6   R. H. E.
Boston (AL) .. 010 000 001 1 –– 3 9 2
St. Louis (NL) . 000 001 010 0 –– 2 7 0
   Pitchers–Hughson, JOHNSON (9), vs.
POLLET. Homer–York (Bost.). Attendance–
36,218.

2d Game, at St. Louis, Oct. 7
Boston (AL) .... 000 000 000 –– 0 4 1
St. Louis (NL) ... 001 020 00x –– 3 6 0
   Pitchers–HARRIS, Dobson (8) vs.
BRECHEEN. Attendance–35,815.

3d Game, at Boston, Oct. 9
St. Louis (NL) ... 000 000 000 –– 0 6 1
Boston (AL) .... 300 000 01x –– 4 8 0
   Pitchers–DICKSON, Wilks (8) vs. FERRISS.
Homer–York (Bost.). Attendance–34,500.

4th Game, at Boston, Oct. 10
St. Louis (NL) ... 033 010 104 –– 12 20 1
Boston (AL) .... 000 100 020 –– 3 9 4
   Pitchers–MUNGER vs. HUGHSON, Bagby
(3), Zuber (6), Brown (8), Ryba (9), Dreisewerd
(9). Homers–Slaughter (St. L.), Doerr (Bost.).
Attendance–35,645.

5th Game, at Boston, Oct. 11
St. Louis (NL) ... 010 000 002 –– 3 4 1
Boston (AL) .... 110 001 30x –– 6 11 3
   Pitchers–Pollet, BRAZLE (1), Beazley (8) vs.
DOBSON. Homer–Culberson (Bost.). Attend-
ance–35,982.

6th Game, at St. Louis, Oct. 13

```
Boston (AL) .... 000 000 100 ——   1   7   0
St. Louis (NL) ... 003 000 01x ——   4   8   0
```
   Pitchers—HARRIS, Hughson (3), Johnson (8) vs. BRECHEEN. Attendance—35,768.

7th Game, at St. Louis, Oct. 15

```
Boston (AL) .... 100 000 020 ——   3   8   0
St. Louis (NL) ... 010 020 01x ——   4   9   1
```
   Pitchers—Ferriss, Dobson (5), KLINGER (8), Johnson (8) vs. Dickson, BRECHEEN (8). Attendance—36,143.

Total attendance—250,071. Receipts—$1,202,900 (including $150,000 for radio rights). Winning player's share—$3,742.34. Losing player's share—$2,140.89.

1947 Final Standing

	W.	L.
New York AL (Stanley R. Harris)	4	3
Brooklyn NL (Burton E. Shotton) ...	3	4

1st Game, at New York, Sept. 30   R. H. E.

```
Brooklyn (NL) .. 100 001 100 ——   3   6   0
New York (AL) .. 000 050 00x ——   5   4   0
```
   Pitchers—BRANCA, Behrman (5), Casey (7) vs. SHEA, Page (6). Attendance—73,365.

2d Game, at New York, Oct. 1

```
Brooklyn (NL) .. 001 100 001 ——    3   9   2
New York (AL) .. 101 121 40x ——   10  15   1
```
   Pitchers—LOMBARDI, Gregg (5), Behrman (7), Barney (7) vs. REYNOLDS. Homers—Walker (Brook.), Henrich (N.Y.). Attendance—69,865.

3d Game, at Brooklyn, Oct. 2

```
New York (AL) .. 002 221 100 ——   8  13   0
Brooklyn (NL) .. 061 200 00x ——   9  13   1
```
   Pitchers—NEWSOM, Raschi (2), Drews (3), Chandler (4), Page (6), vs. Hatten, Branca (5), CASEY (7). Homers—DiMaggio (N.Y.), Berra (N.Y.). Attendance—33,098.

4th Game, at Brooklyn, Oct. 3

```
New York (AL) .. 100 100 000 ——   2   8   1
Brooklyn (NL) .. 000 010 002 ——   3   1   3
```
   Pitchers—BEVENS vs. Taylor, Gregg (1), Behrman (8), CASEY (9). Attendance—33,443.

5th Game, at Brooklyn, Oct. 4

```
New York (AL) .. 000 110 000 ——   2   5   0
Brooklyn (NL) .. 000 001 000 ——   1   4   1
```
   Pitchers—SHEA vs. BARNEY, Hatten (5), Behrman (7), Casey (8). Homer—DiMaggio (N.Y.). Attendance—34,379.

6th Game, at New York, Oct. 5

```
Brooklyn (NL) .. 202 004 000 ——   8  12   1
New York (AL) .. 004 100 001 ——   6  15   2
```
   Pitchers—Lombardi, BRANCA (3), Hatten

(6), Casey (9) vs. Reynolds, Drews (3), PAGE (5), Newsom (6), Raschi (7), Wensloff (8). Attendance—74,065.

7th Game, at New York, Oct. 6

```
Brooklyn (NL) .. 020 000 000 ——   2   7   0
New York (AL) .. 010 201 01x ——   5   7   0
```
   Pitchers—GREGG, Behrman (4), Hatten (6), Barney (6), Casey (7) vs. Shea, Bevens (2), PAGE (5). Attendance—71,548.

Total attendance—389,763. Receipts—$2,021,348.92 (including $175,000 for radio rights and $65,000 for television rights). Winning player's share—$5,830.03. Losing player's share—$4,081.19.

1948 Final Standing

	W.	L.
Cleveland AL (Louis Boudreau)	4	2
Boston NL (William H. Southworth) ..	2	4

1st Game, at Boston, Oct. 6   R. H. E.

```
Cleveland (AL) .. 000 000 000 ——   0   4   0
Boston (NL) .... 000 000 01x ——   1   2   2
```
   Pitchers—FELLER vs. SAIN. Attendance—40,135.

2d Game, at Boston, Oct. 7

```
Cleveland (AL) .. 000 210 001 ——   4   8   1
Boston (NL) .... 100 000 000 ——   1   8   3
```
   Pitchers—LEMON vs. SPAHN, Barrett (5), Potter (8). Attendance—39,633.

3d Game, at Cleveland, Oct. 8

```
Boston (NL) .... 000 000 000 ——   0   5   1
Cleveland (AL) .. 001 100 00x ——   2   5   0
```
   Pitchers—BICKFORD, Voiselle (4), Barrett (8) vs. BEARDEN. Attendance—70,306.

4th Game, at Cleveland, Oct. 9

```
Boston (NL) .... 000 000 100 ——   1   7   0
Cleveland (AL) .. 101 000 00x ——   2   5   0
```
   Pitchers—SAIN vs. GROMEK. Homers—Doby (Cle.), Rickert (Bost.). Attendance—81,897.

5th Game, at Cleveland, Oct. 10

```
Boston (NL) .... 301 001 600 ——   11  12   0
Cleveland (AL) .. 100 400 000 ——    5   6   2
```
   Pitchers—Potter, SPAHN (4) vs. FELLER, Klieman (7), Christopher (7), Paige (7), Muncrief (8). Homers—Elliott (Bost.) 2, Mitchell (Cle.), Hegan (Cle.), Salkeld (Bost.). Attendance—86,288.

6th Game, at Boston, Oct. 11

```
Cleveland (AL) .. 001 002 010 ——   4  10   0
Boston (NL) .... 000 100 020 ——   3   9   0
```
   Pitchers—LEMON, Bearden (8) vs. VOISELLE, Spahn (8), Homer—Gordon (Cle.). Attendance—40,103.

Total attendance—358,362. Receipts—$1,923,685.56 (including $150,000 for radio rights and $140,000 for television rights). Winning player's share—$6,772.05. Losing player's share—$4,651.51.

1949 Final Standing

	W.	L.
New York AL (Charles D. Stengel) ...	4	1
Brooklyn NL (Burton E. Shotton) ...	1	4

1st Game, at New York, Oct. 5   R. H. E.

		R	H	E
Brooklyn (NL)	..000 000 000 ——	0	2	0
New York (AL)	..000 000 001 ——	1	5	1

Pitchers—NEWCOMBE vs. REYNOLDS. Homer—Henrich (N.Y.). Attendance—66,224.

2d Game, at New York, Oct. 6

		R	H	E
Brooklyn (NL)	..010 000 000 ——	1	7	2
New York (AL)	..000 000 000 ——	0	6	1

Pitchers—ROE vs. RASCHI. Attendance—70,053.

3d Game, at Brooklyn, Oct. 7

		R	H	E
New York (AL)	..001 000 003 ——	4	5	0
Brooklyn (NL)	..000 100 002 ——	3	5	0

Pitchers—Byrne, PAGE (4) vs. BRANCA, Banta (9). Homers—Reese (Brook.), Olmo (Brook.), Campanella (Brook.). Attendance—32,788.

4th Game, at Brooklyn, Oct. 8

		R	H	E
New York (AL)	..000 330 000 ——	6	10	0
Brooklyn (NL)	..000 004 000 ——	4	9	1

Pitchers—LOPAT, Reynolds (6) vs. NEW-COMBE, Hatten (4), Erskine (6), Banta (7). Attendance—33,934.

5th Game, at Brooklyn, Oct. 9

		R	H	E
New York (AL)	..203 113 000 ——	10	11	1
Brooklyn (NL)	..001 001 400 ——	6	11	2

Pitchers—RASCHI, Page (7) vs. BARNEY, Banta (3), Erskine (6), Hatten (6), Palica (7), Minner (9). Homers—DiMaggio (N.Y.), Hodges (Brook.). Attendance—33,711.

Total attendance—236,710. Receipts—$1,511,527.82 (including $150,000 for radio rights, $200,000 for television rights and $31,900 for movie-TV rights). Winning player's share—$5,665.54. Losing player's share—$4,272.73.

1950 Final Standing

	W.	L.
New York AL (Charles D. Stengel) ...	4	0
Philadelphia NL (Edwin M. Sawyer) ..	0	4

1st Game, at Philadelphia, Oct. 4   R. H. E.

		R	H	E
New York (AL)	.000 100 000 ——	1	5	0
Philadelphia (NL)	000 000 000 ——	0	2	1

Pitchers—RASCHI vs. KONSTANTY, Meyer (9). Attendance—30,746.

2d Game, at Philadelphia, Oct. 5

		R	H	E
New York (AL)	... 010 000 000 1 –	2	10	0
Philadelphia (NL)	. 000 010 000 0 –	1	7	0

Pitchers—REYNOLDS vs. ROBERTS. Homer—DiMaggio (N.Y.). Attendance—32,660.

3d Game, at New York, Oct. 6

		R	H	E
Philadelphia (NL)	000 001 100 ——	2	10	2
New York (AL)	..001 000 011 ——	3	7	0

Pitchers—Heintzelman, Konstanty (8), MEYER (9) vs. Lopat, FERRICK (9). Attendance—64,505.

4th Game, at New York, Oct. 7

		R	H	E
Philadelphia (NL)	000 000 002 ——	2	7	1
New York (AL)	..200 003 00x ——	5	8	2

Pitchers—MILLER, Konstanty (1), Roberts (8) vs. FORD, Reynolds (9). Homer—Berra (N.Y.). Attendance—68,098.

Total attendance—196,009. Receipts—$1,928,669.03 (including $175,000 for radio rights and $800,000 for television rights). Winning player's share—$5,737.95. Losing player's share—$4,081.34.

1951 Final Standing

	W.	L.
New York AL (Charles D. Stengel) ...	4	2
New York NL (Leo E. Durocher)	2	4

1st Game, at Yankee Stadium, Oct. 4   R. H. E.

		R	H	E
New York (NL)	..200 003 000 ——	5	10	1
New York (AL)	..010 000 000 ——	1	7	1

Pitchers—KOSLO vs. REYNOLDS, Hogue (7), Morgan (8). Homer—Dark (NL). Attendance—65,673.

2d Game, at Yankee Stadium, Oct. 5

		R	H	E
New York (NL)	..000 000 100 ——	1	5	1
New York (AL)	..110 000 01x ——	3	6	0

Pitchers—JANSEN, Spencer (7) vs. LOPAT. Homer—Collins (AL). Attendance—66,018.

3d Game, at Polo Grounds, Oct. 6

		R	H	E
New York (AL)	..000 000 011 ——	2	5	2
New York (NL)	..010 050 00x ——	6	7	2

Pitchers—RASHCI, Hogue (5), Ostrowski (7) vs. HEARN, Jones (8). Homers—Woodling (AL), Lockman (NL). Attendance—52,035.

4th Game, at Polo Grounds, Oct. 8

		R	H	E
New York (AL)	..010 120 200 ——	6	12	0
New York (NL)	..100 000 001 ——	2	8	2

Pitchers—REYNOLDS vs. MAGLIE, Jones (6), Kennedy (9). Homer—DiMaggio (AL). Attendance—49,010.

5th Game, at Polo Grounds, Oct. 9

New York (AL) ..005 202 400 –– 13 12 1
New York (NL) ..100 000 000 –– 1 5 3
　　Pitchers–LOPAT vs. Jansen, Kennedy (4), Spencer (6), Corwin (7), Konikowski (9). Homers–McDougald (AL) Rizzuto (AL). Attendance–47,530.

6th Game, at Yankee Stadium, Oct. 10

New York (NL) ..000 010 002 –– 3 11 1
New York (AL) ..100 003 00x –– 4 7 0
　　Pitchers–KOSLO, Hearn (7), Jansen (8) vs. RASCHI, Sain (7), Kuzava (9). Attendance–61,711.

Total attendance–341,977. Receipts–2,708,457.47 (including $150,000 for radio and $925,000 for television). Winning player's share–$6,446.09. Losing player's share–$4,951.03.

1952 Final Standing

	W.	L.
New York AL (Charles D. Stengel) ...	4	3
Brooklyn NL (Charles W. Dressen) ...	3	4

1st Game, at Brooklyn, Oct. 1　　R. H. E.

New York (AL) ..001 000 010 –– 2 6 2
Brooklyn (NL) ..010 002 01x –– 4 6 0
　　Pitchers–REYNOLDS, Scarborough (8) vs. BLACK. Homers–Robinson (B'klyn), Snider (B'klyn), Reese (B'klyn), McDougald (N.Y.). Attendance–34,861.

2d Game, at Brooklyn, Oct. 2

New York (AL) ..000 115 000 –– 7 10 0
Brooklyn (NL) ..001 000 000 –– 1 3 1
　　Pitchers–RASCHI vs. ERSKINE, Loes (6), Lehman (8). Homer–Martin (N.Y.). Attendance–33,792.

3d Game, at New York, Oct. 3

Brooklyn (NL) ..001 010 012 –– 5 11 0
New York (AL) ..010 000 011 –– 3 6 2
　　Pitchers–ROE vs. LOPAT, Gorman (9). Homers–Berra (N.Y.), Mize (N.Y.). Attendance–66,698.

4th Game, at New York, Oct. 4

Brooklyn (NL) ..000 000 000 –– 0 4 1
New York (NL) ..000 100 01x –– 2 4 1
　　Pitchers–BLACK, Rutherford (8) vs. REYNOLDS. Homer–Mize (N.Y.). Attendance–71,787.

5th Game, at New York, Oct. 5

Brooklyn (NL) .. 010 030 100 01 – 6 10 0
New York (AL) .. 000 050 000 00 – 5 5 1
　　Pitchers–ERSKINE vs. Blackwell, SAIN (6). Homers–Snider (B'klyn), Mize (N.Y.). Attendance–70,536.

6th Game, at Brooklyn, Oct. 6

New York (AL) ..000 000 210 –– 3 9 0
Brooklyn (NL) ..000 001 010 –– 2 8 1
　　Pitchers–RASCHI, Reynolds (8) vs. LOES, Roe (9). Homers–Snider (B'klyn) 2, Berra (N.Y.), Mantle (N.Y.). Attendance–30,037.

7th Game, at Brooklyn, Oct. 7

New York (AL) ..000 111 100 –– 4 10 4
Brooklyn (NL) ..000 110 000 –– 2 8 1
　　Pitchers–Lopat, REYNOLDS (4), Raschi (7), Kuzava (7) vs. BLACK, Roe (6), Erskine (8). Homers–Woodling (N.Y.), Mantle (N.Y.). Attendance–33,195.

Total attendance–340,906. Receipts–$2,747,753.01 (including $200,000 for radio and $925,000 for television). Winning player's share–$5,982.65. Losing player's share–$4,200.64.

1953 Final Standing

	W.	L.
New York AL (Charles D. Stengel) ...	4	2
Brooklyn NL (Charles W. Dressen) ...	2	4

1st Game, at New York, Sept. 30　　R. H. E.

Brooklyn (NL) ..000 013 100 –– 5 12 2
New York (AL) ..400 010 13x –– 9 12 0
　　Pitchers–Erskine, Hughes (2), LABINE (6) Wade (8) vs. Reynolds, SAIN (6). Homers–Gilliam (B'klyn.), Hodges (B'klyn.), Shuba (B'klyn.), Berra (N.Y.), Collins (N.Y.). Attendance–69,374.

2nd Game, at New York, Oct. 1

Brooklyn (NL) ..000 200 000 –– 2 9 1
New York (AL) ..100 000 12x –– 4 5 0
　　Pitchers–ROE vs. LOPAT, Homers–Martin (N.Y.), Mantle (N.Y.). Attendance–66,786.

3rd Game, at Brooklyn, Oct. 2

New York (AL) ..000 010 010 –– 2 6 0
Brooklyn (NL) ..000 011 01x –– 3 9 0
　　Pitchers–RASCHI vs. ERSKINE. Homer–Campanella (Bklyn.). Attendance–35,270.

4th Game, at Brooklyn, Oct. 3

New York (AL) ..000 020 001 –– 3 9 0
Brooklyn (NL) ..300 102 10x –– 7 12 0
　　Pitchers–FORD, Gorman (2), Sain (5), Schallock (7) vs. LOES, Labine (9). Homers–McDougald (N.Y.), Snider (Bklyn.). Attendance–36,775.

5th Game, at Brooklyn, Oct. 4

New York (AL) ..105 000 002 –– 3 8 3
Brooklyn (NL) ..010 010 041 –– 7 14 1
　　Pitchers–MCDONALD, Kuzava (8), Reynolds (9) vs. PODRES, Meyer (3), Wade (8), Black (9). Homers–Woodling (N.Y.), Mantle (N.Y.), Martin

(N.Y.), McDougald (N.Y.), Cox (Bklyn.), Gilliam (Bklyn.). Attendance—36,665.

6th Game, at New York, Oct. 5
Brooklyn (NL) ..000 001 002 —— 3 8 3
New York (AL) ..210 000 001 —— 4 13 0
    Pitchers—Erskine, Milliken (5), LABINE (7), vs. Ford, REYNOLDS (8). Homer—Furillo (Bklyn.). Attendance—62,370.

Total attendance—307,350. Receipts—$2,979.269.44 (including $175,000 for radio and $1,025,000 for television). Winning player's share—$8,280.68. Losing Player's share—$6,178.42.

1954 Final Standing

	W.	L.
New York NL (Leo E. Durocher)	4	0
Cleveland AL (Alfonso R. Lopez)	0	4

1st Game, at New York, Sept. 29   R. H. E.

Cleveland (AL) 200 000 000 0 —— 2 8 0
New York (NL) 002 000 000 3 —— 5 9 0
    Pitchers—LEMON vs. Maglie, Liddle (8), GRISSOM (8). Homer—Rhodes (N.Y.). Attendance—52,751.

2nd Game, at New York, Sept. 30
Cleveland (AL) ..100 000 000 —— 1 8 0
New York (NL) ..000 020 10x —— 3 4 0
    Pitchers—WYNN, Mossi (8) vs. ANTONELLI. Homers—Smith (Cleve). Rhodes (N.Y.). Attendance—49,099.

3rd Game, at Cleveland, Oct. 1
New York (NL) ..103 011 000 —— 6 10 1
Cleveland (AL) ..000 000 110 —— 2 4 2
    Pitchers—GOMEZ, Wilhelm (7) vs. GARCIA, Houtteman (4), Narleski (6), Mossi (9). Homer—Wertz (Cleve). Attendance—71,555.

4th Game, at Cleveland, Oct. 2
New York (NL) ..021 040 000 —— 7 10 3
Cleveland (AL) ..000 030 100 —— 4 6 2
    Pitchers—LIDDLE, Wilhelm (7), Antonelli (8). Homer—Majeski (Cleve.). Attendance—78,102.

Total attendance—251,507. Receipts—$2,741,203.38 (including $150,000 for radio and $1,025.000 for television). Winning player's share—$11,147.90. Losing player's share—$6,712.50.

1955 Final Standing

	W.	L.
Brooklyn NL (Walter E. Alston)	4	3
New York AL (Charles D. Stengel) ...	3	4

1st Game, at New York, Sept. 28   R. H. E.
Brooklyn (NL) ..021 000 020 —— 5 10 0
New York (AL) ..021 102 00x —— 6 9 1
    Pitchers—NEWCOMBE, Bessent (6), Labine (8) vs. FORD, Grim (9). Homers—Furillo (Bklyn), Snider (Bklyn), Howard (N.Y.), Collins (N.Y.) 2. Attendance—63,869.

2nd Game, at New York, Sept. 29
Brooklyn (NL) ..000 110 000 —— 2 5 2
New York (AL) ..000 400 00x —— 4 8 0
    Pitchers—LOES, Bessent (4), Spooner (5), Labine (8) vs. BYRNE. Attendance—64,707.

3rd Game, at Brooklyn, Sept. 30
New York (AL) ..020 000 100 —— 3 7 0
Brooklyn (NL) ..220 200 20x —— 8 11 1
    Pitchers—TURLEY, Morgan (2), Kucks (5), Sturdivant (7) vs. PODRES. Homers—Campanella (Bklyn), Mantle (N.Y.). Attendance—34,209.

4th Game, at Brooklyn, Oct. 1
New York (AL) ..110 102 000 —— 5 9 0
Brooklyn (NL) ..001 330 10x —— 8 14 0
    Pitchers—LARSEN, Kucks (5), R. Coleman (6), Morgan (7), Sturdivant (8) vs. Erskine, Bessent (4), LABINE (5). Homers—McDougald (N.Y.), Campanella (Bklyn), Hodges (Bklyn), Snider (Bklyn). Attendance—36,242.

5th Game, at Brooklyn, Oct. 2
New York (AL) ..000 100 110 —— 3 6 0
Brooklyn (NL) ..021 010 01x —— 5 9 2
    Pitchers—GRIM, Turley (7) vs. CRAIG, Labine (7). Homers—Cerv (N.Y.), Berra (N.Y.), Amoros (Bklyn), Snider (Bklyn) 2. Attendance—36,796.

6th Game, at New York, Oct. 3
Brooklyn (NL) ..000 100 000 —— 1 4 1
New York (AL) ..500 000 00x —— 5 8 0
    Pitchers—SPOONER, Meyer (1), Roebuck (7) vs. FORD. Homer—Skowron (N.Y.). Attendance—64,022.

7th Game, at New York, Oct. 4
Brooklyn (NL) ..000 101 000 —— 2 5 0
New York (AL) ..000 000 000 —— 0 8 1
    Pitchers—PODRES vs. BYRNE, Grim (6), Turley (8). Attendance—62,465.

Total attendance—362,310. Receipts—$3,512,515.34 (including $50,000 for radio and $1,125.000 for television). Winning player's share—$9,768. Losing player's share-$5,598.

1956 Final Standing

	W.	L.
New York AL (Charles D. Stengel) ...	4	3
Brooklyn (Walter E. Alston)	3	4

1st Game, at Brooklyn, Oct. 3   R. H. E.

New York (AL) ..200 100 000 —— 3 9 1
Brooklyn (NL) ..023 100 00x —— 6 9 0
  Pitchers—FORD, Kucks (4), Morgan (6),
Turley (8) vs. MAGLIE. Homers—Mantle (N.Y.),
Robinson (Bklyn), Hodges (Bklyn), Martin
(N.Y.). Attendance—34,479.

2nd Game, at Brooklyn, Oct. 5
New York (AL) ..150 100 001 —— 8 12 2
Brooklyn (NL) ..061 220 02x —— 13 12 0
  Pitchers—Larsen, Kucks (2), Byrne (2), Sturdi-
vant (3), MORGAN (3), Turley (5), McDermott
(6) vs. Newcombe, Roebuck (2), BESSENT (3).
Homers—Berra (N.Y.),· Snider (Bklyn). Attend-
ance—36,217.

3rd Game, at New York, Oct. 6
Brooklyn (NL) ..010 001 100 —— 3 8 1
New York (AL) ..010 003 01x —— 5 8 1
  Pitchers—CRAIG, Labine (7) vs. FORD.
Homers—Martin (N.Y.) Slaughter (N.Y.). Attend-
ance—73,977.

4th Game, at New York, Oct. 7
Brooklyn (NL) ..000 100 001 —— 2 6 0
New York (AL) ..100 210 20x —— 6 7 2
  Pitchers—ERSKINE, Roebuck (5), Drysdale
(7) vs. STURDIVANT. Homers—Mantle (N.Y.),
Bauer (N.Y.). Attendance—69,705.

5th Game, at New York, Oct. 8
Brooklyn (NL) ..000 000 000 —— 0 0 0
New York (AL) ..000 101 00x —— 2 5 0
  Pitchers—MAGLIE vs. LARSEN. Homer—
Mantle (N.Y.). Attendance—64,519.

6th Game, at Brooklyn, Oct. 9
New York (AL) 000 000 000 0 —— 0 7 0
Brooklyn (NL) 000 000 000 1 —— 1 4 0
  Pitchers—TURLEY vs. LABINE. Attend-
ance—33,224.

7th Game, at Brooklyn, Oct. 10
New York (AL) ..202 100 400 —— 9 10 0
Brooklyn (NL) ..000 000 000 —— 0 3 1
  Pitchers—KUCKS vs. NEWCOMBE, Bessent
(4), Craig (7), Roebuck (7), Erskine (9).
Homers—Berra (N.Y.) 2, Howard (N.Y.),
Skowron (N.Y.). Attendance—33,782.

Total attendance—345,903. Receipts—
$3,333,254.59 (including $125,000 for radio and
$1,025,000 for television). Winning player's
share—$8,714. Losing player's share—$6,934.

1st Game, at New York, Oct. 2   R. H. E.

Milwaukee (NL) .000 000 100 —— 1 5 0
New York (AL) ..000 012 00x —— 3 9 1
  Pitchers—SPAHN, Johnson (6), McMahon (7)
vs. FORD. Attendance—69,476.

2nd Game, at New York, Oct. 3
Milwaukee (NL) .001 200 000 —— 4 8 0
New York (AL) ..011 000 000 —— 2 7 2
  Pitchers—BURDETTE vs. SHANTZ, Ditmar
(4), Grim (8). Homers—Logan (Mil.), Bauer
(N.Y.). Attendance—65,202.

3rd Game, at Milwaukee, Oct. 5
New York (AL) ..302 200 500 —— 12 9 0
Milwaukee (NL) .010 020 000 —— 3 8 1
  Pitchers—Turley, LARSEN (2) vs. BUHL,
Pizzaro (1), Conley (3), Johnson (5), Trowbridge
(7), McMahon (8). Homers—Kubek (N.Y.) 2,
Mantle (N.Y.), Aaron (Mil.). Attendance—
45,804.

4th Game, at Milwaukee, Oct. 6
New York (AL) 100 000 003 1 —— 5 11 0
Milwaukee (NL) 000 400 000 3 —— 7 7 0
  Pitchers—Sturdivant, Shantz (5), Kucks (8),
Byrne (8), GRIM (10) vs. SPAHN. Homers—
Aaron (Mil.), Torre (Mil.), Howard (N.Y.),
Mathews (Mil.). Attendance—45,804.

5th Game, at Milwaukee, Oct. 7
New York (AL) ..000 000 000 —— 0 7 0
Milwaukee (NL) .000 001 00x —— 1 6 1
  Pitchers—FORD, Turley (8) vs. BURDETTE.
Attendance—45,811.

6th Game, at New York, Oct. 9
Milwaukee (NL) .000 010 100 —— 2 4 0
New York (AL) ..002 000 10x —— 3 7 0
  Pitchers—Buhl, E. JOHNSON (3), McMahon
vs. TURLEY. Homers—Berra (N.Y.), Torre
(Mil.), Aaron (Mil.), Bauer (N.Y.). Attendance—
61,408.

7th Game, at New York, Oct. 10
Milwaukee (NL) .004 000 010 —— 5 9 1
New York (AL) ..000 000 000 —— 0 7 3
  Pitchers—BURDETTE vs. LARSEN, Shantz
(3), Ditmar (4), Sturdivant (6), Byrne (8).
Homer—Crandall (Mil.). Attendance—61,207.

Total attendance—394,712. Receipts—
$5,475,978.94 (including $3,000,000 for television). Winning player's share—$8,924. Losing
player's share—$5,606.

1957 Final Standing

	W.	L.
Milwaukee NL (Fred Haney)	4	3
New York AL (Charles D. Stengel)	3	4

1958 Final Standing

	W.	L.
New York AL (Charles D. Stengel)	4	3
Milwaukee NL (Fred Haney)	3	4

1st Game, at Milwaukee, Oct. 1   R. H. E.
New York (AL) 000 120 000 0 ––   3   8   1
Milwaukee (NL)000 200 010 1 ––   4 10   0
    Pitchers–Ford, DUREN (8) vs. SPAHN.
Homers–Skowron (N.Y.), Bauer (N.Y.). Attendance–46,367.

2nd Game, at Milwaukee, Oct. 2
New York (AL) .. 100 100 003 ––   5   7   0
Milwaukee (NL) . 710 000 23x –– 13 15   1
    Pitchers–TURLEY, Maas (1), Kucks (1),
Dickson (5), Monroe (8) vs. BURDETTE.
Homers–Bruton (Mil.), Burdette (Mil.), Mantle
(N.Y.) 2, Bauer (N.Y.). Attendance–46,367.

3rd Game, at New York, Oct. 4
Milwaukee (NL) .000 000 000 ––   0   6   0
New York (AL) .. 000 020 20x ––   4   4   0
    Pitchers–RUSH, McMahon (7) vs. LARSEN,
Duren (8). Attendance–71,599.

4th Game, at New York, Oct. 5
Milwaukee (NL) .000 001 110 ––   3   9   0
New York (AL) .. 000 000 000 ––   0   2   1
    Pitchers–FORD, Kucks (8), Dickson (9) vs.
SPAHN. Attendance–71,563.

5th Game, at New York, Oct. 6
Milwaukee (NL) .000 000 000 ––   0   5   0
New York (AL) .. 001 006 00x ––   7 10   0
    Pitchers–BURDETTE, Pizarro (6), Willey (8)
vs TURLEY, Homer– McDougald (N.Y.).
Attendance–65,279.

6th Game, at Milwaukee, Oct. 8
New York (AL) 100 001 000 2 ––   4 10   1
Milwaukee (NL)110 000 000 1 ––   3 10   4
    Pitchers–Ford, Ditmar (2), DUREN (5),
Turley (10) vs SPAHN, McMahon (10). Homers
–Bauer (N.Y.), McDougald (N.Y.). Attendance–
46,376.

7th Game, at Milwaukee, Oct. 9
New York (AL) .. 020 000 040 ––   6   8   0
Milwaukee (NL) . 100 001 000 ––   2   5   2
    Pitchers–Larsen, TURLEY (3) vs.
BURDETTE, McMahon (9). Homers–Crandall
(Mil.), Skowron (N.Y.). Attendance 46,367.

    Total attendance–393,889. Receipts–
$5,397,223.03 (including $3,000,000 for radio
and television). Winning player's share–$8,759.
Losing player's share–$5,896.

1959 Final Standing

	W.	L.
Los Angeles NL (Walter Alston)	4	2
Chicago AL (Al Lopez)	2	3

1st Game, at Chicago, Oct. 1   R. H. E.
Los Angeles (NL) 000 000 000 ––   0   8   3
Chicago (AL) .... 207 200 00x –– 11 11   0
    Pitchers–CRAIG, Churn (3), Labine (4),
Koufax (5), Klippstein (7) vs. WYNN, Staley (8).
Attendance–48,013.

2nd Game, at Chicago, Oct. 2
Los Angeles (NL) 000 010 300 ––   4   9   1
Chicago (AL) .... 200 000 010 ––   3   8   0
    Pitchers–PODRES, Sherry (7) vs. SHAW,
Lown (7). Attendance–47,368.

3rd Game, at Los Angeles, Oct. 4
Chicago (AL) .... 000 000 010 ––   1 12   0
Los Angeles (NL) 000 000 21x ––   3   5   0
    Pitchers–DONOVAN, Staley (7) vs.
DRYSDALE, Sherry (8). Attendance–92,294.

4th Game, at Los Angeles, Oct. 5
Chicago (AL) .... 000 000 400 ––   4 10   3
Los Angeles (NL) 004 000 01x ––   5   9   0
    Pitchers–Wynn, Lown (3), Pierce (4),
STALEY (7) vs. Craig, SHERRY (8). Attendance–92,550.

5th Game, at Los Angeles, Oct. 6
Chicago (AL) .... 000 100 000 ––   1   5   0
Los Angeles (NL) 000 000 000 ––   0   9   0
    Pitchers–SHAW, Pierce (8), Donovan (8) vs.
KOUFAX, Williams (8). Attendance–92,706.

6th Game, at Chicago, Oct. 8
Los Angeles (NL) 002 600 001 ––   9 13   0
Chicago (AL) .... 000 300 000 ––   3   6   1
    Pitchers–Podres, SHERRY (4) vs. WYNN,
Donovan (4), Lown (4), Staley (5), Pierce (8),
Moore (9). Attendance–47,653.

    Total attendance–420,784. Receipts–
$2,626,973.44 (not including radio and television fees). Winning player's share–$11,231.18.
Losing player's share–$7,275.17.

1960 Final Standing

	W.	L.
Pittsburgh NL (Danny Murtaugh)	4	3
New York AL (Casey Stengel)	3	4

1st Game, at Pittsburgh, Oct. 5   R. H. E.
New York (AL) .. 100 100 002 ––   4 13   2
Pittsburgh (NL) .. 300 201 00x ––   6   8   0
    Pitchers–DITMAR, Coates (1), Maas (5),
Duren (7) vs. LAW, Face (8). Attendance–
26,076.

2nd Game, at Pittsburgh, Oct. 6
New York (AL) .. 002 127 301 –– 16 19   1
Pittsburgh (NL) .. 000 100 002 ––   3 13   1
    Pitchers–TURLEY, Shantz (9) vs. FRIEND,
Green (5), Labine (6), Witt (6), Gibbon (7),

Cheney (9). Attendance—37,308.

3rd Game, at New York, Oct. 8
Pittsburgh (NL) . . 000 000 000 — — 0 4 0
New York (AL) . . 600 400 00x — — 10 16 1
   Pitchers—MIZELL, Labine (1), Green (1), Witt (4), Cheney (6), Gibbon (8) vs. FORD. Attendance—70,001.

4th Game, at New York, Oct. 9
Pittsburgh (NL) . . 000 030 000 — — 3 7 0
New York (AL) . . 000 100 100 — — 2 8 0
   Pitchers—LAW, Face (7), vs. TERRY, Shantz (7), Coates (8). Attendance—67,812.

5th Game, at New York, Oct. 10
Pittsburgh (NL) . . 031 000 001 — — 5 10 2
New York (AL) . . 011 000 000 — — 2 5 2
   Pitchers—HADDIX, Face (7), vs. DITMAR, Arroyo (2), Stafford (3), Duren (8). Attendance—62,753.

6th Game, at Pittsburgh, Oct. 12
New York (AL) . . 015 002 220 — — 12 17 1
Pittsburgh (NL) . . 000 000 000 — — 0 7 1
   Pitchers—FORD vs. FRIEND, Cheney (3), Mizell (4), Green (6), Labine (6), Witt (9). Attendance—38,580.

7th Game, at Pittsburgh, Oct. 13
New York (AL) . . 000 014 022 — — 9 13 1
Pittsburgh (NL) . . 220 000 051 — — 10 11 0
   Pitchers—Turley, Stafford (2), Shantz (3), Coates (8), TERRY (9) vs. Law, Face (6), Friend (9), HADDIX (9). Attendance—36,683.

   Total attendance—341,213. Receipts $2,230,627.88. Winners' share—$8,417.94. Losers' share—$5,214.64.

1961 Final Standing

	W.	L.
New York AL (Ralph Houk)	4	1
Cincinnati NL (Fred Hutchinson)	1	4

1st Game, at New York, Oct. 4   R. H. E.
Cincinnati (NL) . . 000 000 000 — — 0 2 0
New York (AL) . . 000 101 00x — — 2 6 0
   Pitchers—O'TOOLE, Brosnan (8) vs. FORD. Attendance—62,397.

2nd Game, at New York, Oct. 5
Cincinnati (NL) . . 000 211 020 — — 6 9 0
New York (AL) . . 000 200 000 — — 2 4 3
   Pitchers—JAY vs. TERRY, Arroyo (8). Attendance—63,083.

3rd Game, at Cincinnati, Oct. 7
New York (AL) . . 000 000 111 — — 3 6 1
Cincinnati (NL) . . 001 000 100 — — 2 8 0
   Pitchers—Stafford, Daley (7), ARROYO (8)

vs. PURKEY. Attendance—32,589.

4th Game, at Cincinnati, Oct. 7
New York (AL) . . 000 112 300 — — 7 11 1
Cincinnati (NL) . . 000 000 000 — — 0 5 0
   Pitchers—FORD, Coates (6) vs. O'TOOLE, Brosnan (6), Henry (9). Attendance—32,589.

5th Game, at Cincinnati, Oct. 9
New York (AL) . . 501 502 000 — — 13 15 1
Cincinnati (NL) . . 003 020 000 — — 5 11 3
   Pitchers—Terry, DALEY (3) vs. JAY, Maloney (1), Johnson (2), Henry (3), Jones (4), Purkey (5), Bronsnan (7), Hunt (9). Attendance—32,589.

   Total Attendance—223,247. Receipts—$1,480,059.95. Winners' share—$7,389.13. Losers' share—$5,356.37.

1962 Final Standing

	W.	L.
New York AL (Ralph Houk)	4	3
San Francisco NL (Alvin Dark)	3	4

1st Game, at San Francisco, Oct. 4   R. H. E.
New York (AL) . . . 200 000 121 — 6 11 0
San Francisco (NL) 011 000 000 — 2 10 0
   Pitchers—FORD vs. O'DELL, Larsen (8), Miller (9).

2nd Game, at San Francisco, Oct. 5
New York (AL) . . . 000 000 000 — 0 3 1
San Francisco (NL) 100 000 10x — 2 6 0
   Pitchers—TERRY, Daley (8) vs. SANFORD.

3rd Game, at New York, Oct. 7
San Francisco (NL) 000 000 002 — 2 4 3
New York (AL) . . . 000 000 30x — 3 5 1
   Pitchers—PIERCE' Larsen (7), Bolin (8) vs. STAFFORD.

4th Game, at New York, Oct. 8
San Francisco (NL) 020 000 401 — 7 9 1
New York (AL) . . . 000 002 001 — 3 9 1
   Pitchers—Marichal, Bolin (5), LARSEN (6), O'Dell (7) vs. Ford, COATES (7), Bridges (7).

5th Game, at New York, Oct. 10
San Francisco (NL) 001 010 001 — 3 8 2
New York (AL) . . . 000 101 03x — 5 6 0
   Pitchers—SANFORD, Miller (8) vs. TERRY.

6th Game, at San Francisco, Oct. 15
New York (AL) . . . 000 010 010 — 2 3 2
San Francisco (NL) 000 320 00x — 5 10 1
   Pitchers—FORD, Coates (5), Bridges (8) vs. PIERCE.

7th Game, at San Francisco, Oct. 16
New York (AL) . . . 000 010 000 — 1 7 0
San Francisco (NL) 000 000 000 — 0 4 1

Pitchers—TERRY vs. SANFORD, O'Dell (8).

Total attendance—376,864. Receipts—$2,878,891.22. Winning player's share—$9,882.74. Losing player's share $7,291.49.

1963 Final Standing

	W.	L.
Los Angeles NL (Walt Alston)	4	0
New York AL (Ralph Houk)	0	4

1st Game, at New York, Oct. 2

		R.	H.	E.
Los Angeles (NL)	041 000 000 ——	5	9	0
New York (AL)	..000 000 020 ——	2	6	0

Pitchers—KOUFAX vs. FORD, Williams (5), Hamilton.

2nd Game, at New York, Oct. 3

Los Angeles (NL)	200 100 010 ——	4	10	1
New York (AL)	..000 000 001 ——	1	7	0

Pitchers—PODRES, Perranoski vs. DOWNING, Reniff.

3rd Game, at Los Angeles, Oct. 5

New York (AL)	..000 000 000 ——	0	3	0
Los Angeles (NL)	100 000 00x ——	1	4	1

Pitchers—BOUTON, Reniff vs. DRYSDALE.

4th Game, at Los Angeles, Oct. 6

New York (AL)	..000 000 100 ——	1	6	1
Los Angeles (NL)	000 010 10x ——	2	2	1

Pitchers—FORD, Reniff vs. KOUFAX.

Total attendance—247,279. Receipts—$5,495,189.09*. Winning player's share—$12,794.00. Losing player's share—$7,874.32.
*Includes $3,500,000 radio-television receipts.

1964 Final Standing

	W.	L.
St. Louis NL (John Keane)	4	3
New York AL (Yogi Berra)	3	4

1st Game, at St. Louis, Oct. 7

		R.	H.	E.
New York (AL)	..030 010 010 ——	5	12	2
St. Louis (NL)	...110 004 03x ——	9	12	0

Pitchers—FORD, Downing vs. SADECKI, Schultz.

2nd Game, at St. Louis, Oct. 8

New York (AL)	..000 101 204 ——	8	12	0
St. Louis (NL)	...001 000 011 ——	3	7	0

Ptichers—STOTTLEMYRE vs. GIBSON (9), Craig.

3rd Game, at New York, Oct. 10

St. Louis (NL)	...000 010 000 ——	1	6	0
New York (AL)	..101 000 001 ——	2	5	2

Pitchers—Simmons (2), SCHULTZ vs. BOUTON.

4th Game, at New York, Oct. 11

St. Louis (NL)	...000 004 000 ——	4	6	1
New York (AL)	..300 000 000 ——	3	6	1

Pitchers—CRAIG (8), Taylor (2) vs. DOWNING (4), Mikkelsen, Terry (3).

5th Game, at New York, Oct. 12

St. Louis (NL)	.000 020 000 3 ——	5	10	1
New York (AL)	000 000 002 0 ——	2	6	2

Pitchers—GIBSON vs. Stottlemyre (6), MIKKELSEN (3).

6th Game, at St. Louis, Oct. 14

New York (AL)	..000 012 050 ——	8	10	0
St. Louis (NL)	...100 000 011 ——	3	10	1

Pitchers—BOUTON vs. SIMMONS (6), Humphreys.

7th Game, at St. Louis, Oct. 15

New York (AL)	..000 003 002 ——	5	9	2
St. Louis (NL)	...000 330 10x ——	7	10	1

Pitchers—STOTTLEMYRE (2), Sheldon (2), Hamilton (2) vs. GIBSON.

Total attendance—321,807. Receipts—$5,743,187.96*. Winning player's share—$8,622.19. Losing player's share—$5,309.29.
*Includes $3,500,000 radio-television receipts.

1965 Final Standing

	W.	L.
Los Angeles NL (Walter Alston)	4	3
Minnesota AL (Sam Mele)	3	4

1st Game, Minnesota, Oct. 6

		R.	H.	E.
Los Angeles (NL)	010 000 001 ——	2	10	1
Minnesota (AL)	..016 001 00x ——	8	10	0

Pitchers—DRYSDALE (4), Reed, Brewer, vs. GRANT.

2nd Game, at Minnesota, Oct. 7

Los Angeles (NL)	000 000 100 ——	1	7	3
Minnesota (AL)	..000 002 12x ——	5	9	0

Pitchers—KOUFAX (9), Perranoski vs. KAAT (3).

3rd Game, at Los Angeles, Oct. 9

Minnesota (AL)	..000 000 000 ——	0	5	0
Los Angeles (NL)	000 211 00x ——	4	10	1

Pitchers—PASCUAL, Klippstein vs. OSTEEN (2).

4th Game, at Los Angeles, Oct. 10

Minnesota (AL)	..000 101 000 ——	2	5	2
Los Angeles (NL)	110 103 01x ——	7	10	0

Pitchers—GRANT (2), Worthington (2) vs. DRYSDALE (11).

5th Game, at Los Angeles, Oct. 11

Minnesota (AL)	..000 000 000 ——	0	4	1
Los Angeles (NL)	202 100 20x ——	7	14	0

Pitchers—KAAT, Boswell (3), Perry (3) vs. KOUFAX (10).

6th Game, at Minnesota, Oct. 13
Los Angeles (NL) 000 000 100 —— 1 6 1
Minnesota (AL) ..000 203 00x —— 5 6 1
    Pitchers—OSTEEN (2), Reed (3) vs. GRANT (5).

7th Game, at Minnesota, Oct. 14
Los Angeles (NL) 000 200 000 —— 2 7 0
Minnesota (AL) ..000 000 000 —— 0 3 1
    Pitchers—KOUFAX (10) vs. KAAT (2), Klippstein (2), Merritt, Perry.

    Total attendance—364,326. Receipts—$6,475,041.60*. Winning player's share—$10,297.43. Losing player's share—$6,634.36.
*Includes $3,500,000 radio-television receipts.

1966 Final Standing

	W.	L.
Baltimore AL (Hank Bauer)	4	0
Los Angeles NL (Walt Alston)	0	4

1st Game, at Los Angeles, Oct. 5   R. H. E.
Baltimore (AL) ..310 100 000 —— 5 9 0
Los Angeles (NL) 011 000 000 —— 2 3 0
    Pitchers—McNally, DRABOWSKY (11) vs. DRYSDALE, R. Miller, Perranoski.

2nd Game, at Los Angeles, Oct. 6
Baltimore (AL) ..000 031 020 —— 6 8 0
Los Angeles (NL) 000 000 000 —— 0 4 6
    Pitchers—PALMER (6) vs. KOUFAX (2), Perranoski, Regan, Brewer.

3rd Game, at Baltimore, Oct. 8
Los Angeles (NL) 000 000 000 —— 0 6 0
Baltimore (AL) ..000 010 00x —— 1 3 0
    Pitchers—OSTEEN (3), Regan vs. BUNKER (6).

4th Game, at Baltimore, Oct. 9
Los Angeles (NL) 000 000 000 —— 0 4 0
Baltimore (AL) ..000 100 00x —— 1 4 0
    Pitchers—DRYSDALE (5) vs. McNally (4).

    Total attendance—220,791. Receipts—$5,547,142.46*. Winning players share—$11,683.04. Losing player's share—$8,189.36.
*Includes $3,500,000 radio-television receipts.

1967 Final Standing

	W.	L.
St. Louis NL (Red Schoendienst)	4	3
Boston AL (Dick Williams)	3	4

1st Game, at Boston, Oct. 4   R. H. E.
St. Louis (NL) ...001 000 100 —— 2 10 0
Boston (AL) ....001 000 000 —— 1 6 0

Pitchers—Ro. GIBSON (10) vs. SANTIAGO (5), Wyatt.

2nd Game, at Boston, Oct. 5
St. Louis (NL) ...000 000 000 —— 0 1 1
Boston (AL) ....000 101 30x —— 5 9 0
    Pitchers—HUGHES (5), Willis, Lamabe (2) vs. LONBORG (4).

3rd Game, at St. Louis, Oct. 7
Boston (AL) ....000 001 100 —— 2 7 1
St. Louis (NL) ...120 001 01x —— 5 10 0
    Pitchers—BELL, Waslewski (3) vs. BRILES (4).

4th Game, at St. Louis, Oct. 8
Boston (AL) ....000 000 000 —— 0 5 0
St. Louis (NL) ...402 000 00x —— 6 9 0
    Pitchers—Morehead (2), Brett, SANTIAGO vs. GIBSON (6).

5th Game, at St. Louis, Oct. 9
Boston (AL) ....001 000 002 —— 3 6 1
St. Louis (NL) ...000 000 001 —— 1 3 2
    Pitchers—LONBORG (4) vs. CARLTON (5), Washburn (2), Lamabe (2).

6th Game, at Boston, Oct. 11
St. Louis (NL) ...002 000 200 —— 4 8 0
Boston (AL) ....010 300 40x —— 8 12 1
    Pitchers—Hughes (2), LAMABE vs. Waslewski (4), WYATT.

7th Game, at Boston, Oct. 12
St. Louis (NL) ...002 023 000 —— 7 10 1
Boston (AL) ....000 010 010 —— 2 3 1
    Pitchers—R. GIBSON (10) vs. LONBORG (3), Santiago, Morehead.

    Total attendance—304,085. Receipts—$8,044,607 10*. Winning player's share—$8,314.81. Losing player's share—$5,115.23.
*Includes $5,694,000 radio-television receipts.

1968 Final Standing

	W.	L.
Detroit AL (Mayo Smith)	4	3
St. Louis NL (Red Schoendienst)	3	4

1st Game, at St. Louis, Oct. 2   R. H. E.
Detroit (AL) .... 000 000 000 — 0 5 3
St. Louis (NL) ... 000 300 10x — 4 6 0
    Pitchers—McLAIN, Dobson (6), McMahon (8) vs. GIBSON.

2nd Game, at St. Louis, Oct. 3
Detroit (AL) ....011 003 102 —— 8 13 1
St. Louis (NL) ...000 001 000 —— 1 6 1
    Pitchers—LOLICH vs. BRILES, Carlton (6), Willis (7), Hoerner (9).

3rd Game, at Detroit, Oct. 5

St. Louis (NL) ...000 040 300 –– 7 13 0
Detroit (AL) ....002 010 000 –– 3 4 0
 Pitchers–WASHBURN, Hoerner (6) vs. WILSON, Dobson (5), McMahon (6), Patterson (7), Hiller (8).

4th Game, at Detroit, Oct. 6

St. Louis (NL) ...202 200 040 –– 10 13 0
Detroit (AL) ....000 100 000 –– 1 5 4
 Pitchers–GIBSON vs. McLAIN, Sparma (3), Patterson (4), Lasher (6), Hiller (8), Dobson (8).

5th Game, at Detroit, Oct. 7

St. Louis (NL) ...300 000 000 –– 3 9 0
Detroit (AL) ....000 200 30x –– 5 9 1
 Pitchers–Briles, HOERNER (7), Willis (7) vs. LOLICH.

6th Game, at St. Louis, Oct. 9

Detroit (AL) .. 0210 010 000 –– 13 12 1
St. Louis (NL) . 00 0 000 001 –– 1 9 1
 Pitchers–McLAIN vs. WASHBURN, Jaster (3), Willis (3), Hughes (3), Carlton (4), Granger (7), Nelson (9).

7th Game, at St. Louis, Oct. 10

Detroit (AL) ....000 000 301 –– 4 8 1
St. Louis (NL) ...000 000 001 –– 1 5 0
 Pitchers–LOLICH vs. GIBSON.

Total attendance–379,670. Gate receipts–$3,018,113.40. Winning player's share–$10,936.66. Losing player's share–$7,078.71.

1969 Final Standing

	W.	L.
New York NL (Gil Hodges)	4	1
Baltimore AL (Earl Weaver)	1	4

1st Game, at Baltimore, Oct. 11   R. H. E.
New York (NL) ..000 000 100 –– 1 6 1
Baltimore (AL) ..100 300 00x –– 4 6 0
 Pitchers–SEAVER, Cardwell (6), Taylor (7), vs. CUELLAR.

2nd Game, at Baltimore, Oct. 12

New York (NL) ..000 100 001 –– 2 6 0
Baltimore (AL) ..000 000 100 –– 1 2 0
 Pitchers–Koosman, Taylor (9) vs. McNALLY.

3rd Game, at New York, Oct. 14

Baltimore (AL) ..000 000 000 –– 0 4 1
New York (NL) ..120 001 01x –– 5 6 0
 Pitchers–PALMER, Leonhard (7) vs. GENTRY, Ryan (7).

4th Game, at New York, Oct. 15

Baltimore (AL) 000 000 001 0 –– 1 6 1
New York (NL) 010 000 000 1 –– 2 10 1
 Pitchers–Cuellar, Watt (8), HALL (10) vs.

RICHERT.

5th Game, at New York, Oct. 16

Baltimore (AL) ..003 000 000 –– 3 5 2
New York (NL) ..000 002 12x –– 5 7 0
 Pitchers–NcNally, WATT (8) vs. KOOSMAN.

Total attendance–272,378. Gate receipts–$2,857,782.78. Winning player's share–$18,338.18*. Losing player's share–$14,904.21*.

*Total combined figures for World Series & League Championship Series.

1970 Final Standing

	W.	L.
Baltimore AL (Earl Weaver)	4	1
Cincinnati NL (Sparky Anderson)	1	4

1st Game, at Cincinnati, Oct. 10   R. H. E.
Baltimore (AL) ..000 210 100 –– 4 7 2
Cincinnati (NL) ..102 000 000 –– 3 5 0
 Pitchers–PALMER, Richert (9) vs. NOLAN, Carroll (7).

2nd Game, at Cincinnati, Oct. 11

Baltimore (AL) ..000 150 000 –– 6 10 2
Cincinati (NL) ...301 001 000 –– 5 7 0
 Pitchers–Cuellar, PHOEBUS (3), Drabowsky (5), Lopez (7), Hall (7) vs. McGlothlin, WILCOX (5), Carroll (5), Gullett (8).

3rd Game, at Baltimore, Oct. 13

Cincinnati (NL) ..010 000 200 –– 3 9 0
Baltimore (AL) ..201 014 10x –– 9 10 1
 Pitchers–CLONINGER, Granger (6), Gullett (7) vs. McNALLY.

4th Game, at Baltimore, Oct. 14

Cincinnati (NL) ..011 010 030 –– 6 8 3
Baltimore (AL) ..013 001 000 –– 5 8 0
 Pitchers–Nolan, Gullett (3), CARROLL (6) vs. Palmer, WATT (8), Drabowsky (9).

5th Game, at Baltimore, Oct. 15

Cincinnati (NL) ..300 000 000 –– 3 6 0
Baltimore (AL) ..222 010 02x –– 9 15 0
 Pitchers–MERRITT, Granger (2), Wilcox (3), Cloninger (5), Washburn (7), Carroll (8) vs. CUELLAR.

Total attendance–253,183. Gate receipts–$2,599,170.26. Winning player's share–$18,215.78*. Losing player's share–$13,687.59*.

*Total combined figures for World Series & League Championship Series.

1971 Final Standing

	W.	L.
Pittsburgh NL (Danny Murtaugh)	4	3
Baltimore AL (Earl Weaver)	3	4

1st Game, at Baltimore, Oct 9   R. H. E.
Pittsburgh (NL) ..030 000 000 —— 3 3 0
Baltimore (AL) ..013 010 00x —— 5 10 3
  Pitchers—ELLIS, Moose (3), Miller (7) vs.
McNALLY.

2nd Game, at Baltimore, Oct. 11
Pittsburgh (NL) ..000 000 030 —— 3 8 1
Baltimore (AL) ..010 361 00x —— 11 14 1
  Pitchers—R. JOHNSON, Kison (4), Moose (5),
Veale (6), Miller (7), Giusti (9) vs. PALMER,
Hall (9).

3rd Game, at Pittsburgh, Oct. 12
Baltimore (AL) ..000 000 100 —— 1 3 3
Pittsburgh (NL) ..100 001 30x —— 5 7 0
  Pitchers—CUELLAR, Dukes (7), Watt (8) vs.
BLASS.

4th Game, at Pittsburgh, Oct. 13
Baltimore (AL) ..300 000 000 —— 3 4 1
Pittsburgh (NL) ..201 000 10x —— 4 14 0
  Pitchers—Dobson, Jackson (6), WATT (7),
Richert (8) vs. Walker, KISON (1), Giusti (8).

5th Game, at Pittsburgh, Oct. 14
Baltimore (AL) ..000 000 000 —— 0 2 1
Pittsburgh (NL) ..021 010 00x —— 4 9 0
  Pitchers—McNALLY, Leonard (5), Dukes (6),
vs. BRILES.

6th Game, at Baltimore, Oct. 16
Pittsburgh (NL) 011 000 000 0 —— 2 9 1
Baltimore (AL) 000 001 100 1 —— 3 8 0
  Pitchers—Moose, R. Johnson (6), Giusti (7),
MILLER (10) vs. Palmer, Dobson (10), Mc-
NALLY (10).

7th Game, at Baltimore, Oct. 17
Pittsburgh (NL) ..000 100 010 —— 2 6 1
Baltimore (AL) ..000 000 010 —— 1 4 0
  Pitchers—BLASS vs. CUELLAR, Dobson (9),
McNally (9).

Total attendance—351,091. Gate receipts—
$3,049,803.46. Winning player's share—
$18,164.58*. Losing player's share—
$13,906.46*.

*Total combined figures for World Series &
League Championship Series.

1972 Final Standing

	W.	L.
Oakland AL (Dick Williams)	4	3
Cincinnati NL (Sparky Anderson)	3	4

1st Game, at Cincinnati, Oct. 14   R. H. E.
Oakland (AL) ...020 010 000 —— 3 4 0
Cincinnati (NL) ..010 100 000 —— 2 7 0
  Pitchers—HOLTZMAN, Fingers (6), Blue (7),
vs. NOLAN, Borbon (7), Carroll (8).

2nd Game, at Cincinnati, Oct. 15
Oakland (AL) ...011 000 000 —— 2 9 2
Cincinnati (NL) ..000 000 001 —— 1 6 0
  Pitchers—HUNTER, Fingers (9) vs.
GRIMSLEY, Borbon (6), Hall (8).

3rd Game, at Oakland, Oct. 18
Cincinnati (NL) ..000 000 100 —— 1 4 2
Oakland (AL) ...000 000 000 —— 0 3 2
  Pitchers—BILLINGHAM, Carroll (9), vs.
ODOM, Blue (8), Fingers (8).

4th Game, at Oakland, Oct. 19
Cincinnati (NL) ..000 000 020 —— 2 7 1
Oakland (AL) ...000 010 002 —— 3 10 1
  Pitchers—Gullett, Borbon (8), CARROLL (9),
vs. Holtzman, Blue (8), FINGERS (9).

5th Game, at Oakland, Oct. 20
Cincinnati (NL) ..100 110 011 —— 5 8 0
Oakland (AL) ...030 100 000 —— 4 7 2
  Pitchers—McGlothlin, Borbon (4), Hall (5),
Carroll (7), GRIMSLEY (8), Billingham (9) vs.
Hunter, FINGERS (5), Hamilton (9).

6th Game, at Cincinnati, Oct. 21
Oakland (AL) ...000 010 000 —— 1 7 1
Cincinnati (NL) ..000 111 50x —— 8 10 0
  Pitchers—BLUE, Locker (6), Hamilton (7),
Horlen (7) vs. Nolan, GRIMSLEY (5), Borbon
(6), Hall (7).

7th Game, at Cincinnati, Oct. 22
Oakland (AL) ...100 002 000 —— 3 6 1
Cincinnati (NL) ..000 010 010 —— 2 4 2
  Pitchers—Odom, HUNTER (5), Holtzman (8),
Fingers (8) vs. Billingham, BORBON (6), Carroll
(6), Grimsley (7), Hall (8).

Total attendance—363,149. Gate receipts—
$3,954,542.99. Winning player's share—
$20,705.01*. Losing player's share—
$15,080.25*.

*Total combined figures for World Series and
League Championship Series.

Club Standing

	Series	Won	Lost	Pct.
Baltimore (A)	4	2	2	.500
St. Louis (A)	1	0	1	.000
Los Angeles (N)	4	3	1	.750
Brooklyn (N)	9	1	8	.111
St. Louis (N)	12	8	4	.667
Boston (A)	7	5	2	.714
New York (A)	29	20	9	.690

Cleveland (A) 3	2	1	.667
Philadelphia (A) 8	5	3	.625
Cincinnati (N) 6	2	4	.334
Boston (N) 2	1	1	.500
Milwaukee (N) 2	1	1	.500
Chicago (A) 4	2	2	.500
New York Giants (N) 14	5	9	.357
San Francisco (N) 1	0	1	.000
Washington (A) 3	1	2	.333
Minnesota (A) 1	0	1	.000
Detroit (A) 8	3	5	.375
Chicago (N) 10	2	8	.200
Philadelphia (N) 2	0	2	.000
Pittsburgh (N) 6	4	2	.667
New York Mets (N) 1	1	0	1.000
Oakland (A) 1	1	0	1.000

HOW PLAYERS SHARE IN POOL

Sixty per cent of the money taken in for the first 4 games of a World Series goes into what is known as the players' pool. The other 40 per cent of the receipts of the first 4 games is divided among the Commissioner's office, the rival leagues, rival clubs, and other clubs—second, third and fourth-place finishers—in each league. Since the players do not participate in any receipts after 4 games, all revenue from games thereafter is split among the Commissioner's office, rival leagues and participating clubs. Radio and television receipts, which used to be included in the pool, now are deposited in a central fund that underwrites the players' pension fund.

Of the players' pool, 70 per cent is set aside for division among the competing players. The winning team gets 60 per cent of that sum, the losers 40. Prior to the series, players of the competing teams decide into how many shares they will divide their money. The manager, coaches and regular players get a full share; the newly recruited players, bat boys, club (road) secretary, etc., are cut in for a fraction of a share.

Naturally, if a team votes to distribute 30 full shares, the value per share will be greater than if there is a division into 32, 35, or 40 shares. That accounts for the fact that in some instances, where the pool is greater than in others, the per-share value is less.

After the competing players take their 70 per cent of the players' pool, the remaining 30 per cent is divided among the players of the second, third and fourth-place clubs in each league.

WORLD SERIES RECORDS

Individual

Most Series as Player—14, Yogi Berra, New York (AL); 1947, 1949-53, 1955-58, 1960-63.

Most Series Played, One Club—Lawrence (Yogi) Berra, 1947, 1949, 1950, 1951, 1952, 1953, 1955, 1956, 1957, 1958, 1960-63 with New York (AL).

Played in Most Games—75, Yogi Berra.

Best Lifetime Batting Average—.391, Lou Brock, St. Louis (NL), 3 series, 87 at bats, 34 hits.

Best Batting Average, Single Series—.625, Babe Ruth, New York (AL), 4 games, 1928, 16 at bats, 10 hits.

Most Series Batting Over .300—6, Babe Ruth.

Most Runs, Lifetime—42, Mickey Mantle, New York (AL).

Most Runs, One Game—4 (tie), Babe Ruth, Oct. 6, 1926; Earle Combs, New York (AL), Oct. 2, 1932; Frank Crosetti, New York (AL), Oct. 2, 1936; Enos Slaughter, St. Louis (NL), Oct. 10, 1946.

Most Times at Bat, Lifetime—259, Yogi Berra.

Most Runs Batted in, Lifetime—40, Mickey Mantle New York (AL).

Most Hits, Lifetime—71, Yogi Berra.

Most Hits, Single Series—13, Robert C. Richardson, New York (AL), 1964, in 7-game series; Lou Brock, St. Louis (NL), 1968, in 7-game series.

Most Singles, Lifetime—49, Yogi Berra.

Most Doubles, Lifetime—10, Frank Frisch, Pittsburgh (NL); Yogi Berra.

Most Triples, Lifetime—4 (tie), Tommy Leach, (NL); Tris Speaker (AL); and Billy Johnson (AL).

Most Home Runs, Lifetime—18, Mickey Mantle.

Most Home Runs, Single Series—4 (tie), Lou Gehrig, 4-game series, 1928; Babe Ruth, 7-game series, 1926; Duke Snider, 7 game series, 1952 and 1955; Hank Bauer, 1958; Gene Tenace, 1972.

Most Home Runs, One Game—3, Babe Ruth (twice), Oct. 6, 1926, and Oct. 9, 1928.

Most Total Bases, Lifetime—123, Mickey Mantle.

Most Extra Bases, Lifetime—64, Mickey Mantle.

Most Bases on Balls—43, Mickey Mantle.

Most Strikeouts, Lifetime—54, Mickey Mantle.

Pitching

Pitching in Most Series—11, Whitey Ford, New York (AL), 1950, 53, 55-58, 60-64.

Most Victories, Lifetime—10, Whitey Ford.

3-Game Winners, One Series—Bill Dinneen, Boston (AL), 1903 (8-game series); Deacon Phillippe, Pittsburgh (NL), 1903 (8-game series); Christy Mathewson, New York (NL), 1905 (all Mathewson's victories in the 5-game series were shut-outs); Charles (Babe) Adams, Pittsburgh (NL), 1909 (7-game series); Jack Coombs, Philadelphia (AL), 1910 (5-game series); Joe Wood, Boston (AL), 1912 (8-game series); Urban Faber, Chicago (AL), 1917 (6-game series); Stanley Coveleskie, Cleveland (AL), 1920 (7-game series); Harry Brecheen (only left-hander), St. Louis (NL), 1946; Lewis Burdette, Milwaukee, 1957; Robert Gibson, St. Louis (NL), 1967 (7-game series); Mickey Lolich, Detroit (AL), 1968 (7-game series).

Most Shut-Out Games—4, Christy Mathewson (3 in 1905, 1 in 1913).

Most Games, One Series—6, Hugh Casey, Brooklyn (NL), 1947 (7-game series); Pedro Borbon, Cincinnati, (NL) 1972; Rollie Fingers, Oakland (AL), 1972.

Most Innings, Lifetime—146, Whitey Ford.

Consecutive Shut-Out Innings, One Series—27, Christy Mathewson, 1905.

Consecutive Shutout Innings, Lifetime—33 2/3, Whitey Ford.

Most Strikeouts, One Game—17, Bob Gibson, St. Louis (NL), Oct. 2, 1968.

Most Strikeouts, Lifetime—94, Whitey Ford.

Most Bases on Balls, One Game—10, Floyd (Bill) Bevens, New York (AL) vs. Brooklyn, Oct. 3, 1947. (Bevens pitched a 1-hitter, but lost, 3 to 2.)

Most Bases on Balls, Lifetime—34, Whitey Ford in 11 series, 22 games.

Most Home Runs Off Pitcher, One Game—4, Charlie Root, Chicago (NL), Oct. 1, 1932; Eugene E. Thompson, Jr., Cincinnati (NL), Oct. 7, 1939; Richard Hughes, St. Louis (NL), Oct. 11, 1967.

Most Home Runs Off Pitcher, Lifetime—8 (tie), Burleigh Grimes, Charlie Root, Allie Reynolds, Donald Newcombe, Whitey Ford, Don Drysdale.

Most Pitchers Used, One Game—11, by St. Louis (NL), 8, and Boston (AL), 3, Oct. 11, 1967. Boston won, 8 to 4.

Winning Pitcher, Longest Game—Babe Ruth, Boston Americans, beat Brooklyn, 2 to 1, in 14-inning game at Boston, Oct. 9, 1916.

Team

Most Series Won—20, New York (AL), 1923, 27, 28, 32, 36-39, 41, 43, 47, 49-53, 56, 58, 61, 62. (Lost in 1921, 22, 26, 42, 55, 57, 60).

Most Series Lost—10, New York-San Francisco (NL), 1911-13, 17, 23, 24, 36, 37, 51, 62. (Won in 1905, 21, 22, 33, 54).

Club Batting, One Series—.338, New York (AL), 1960, (7 games).

Most Runs, One Game, One Club—18, New York (AL), Oct. 2, 1936.

Most Runs, One Game, Both Clubs—22, New York (AL) 18 vs. New York (NL) 4, Oct. 2, 1936.

Most Runs, One Series, Both Clubs—82, New York (AL), 55 vs. Pittsburgh (NL), 27, 1960, (7 games).

Most Runs, 4-Game Series, Both Clubs—56, New York (AL) 37 vs. Chicago 19, in 1932.

Most Runs, One Inning, One Club—10, Philadelphia (AL), Oct. 12, 1929, 7th Inning; Detroit (AL), Oct. 9, 1968, 3rd inning.

Most Hits, One Game, One Club—20 (tie), New York (NL) vs. New York (AL), Oct. 7, 1921,

and St. Louis (NL) vs. Boston, Oct. 10, 1946.

Most Hits, One Game, Both Clubs—32, New York (AL) 19 vs. Pittsburgh (NL) 13, Oct. 6, 1960.

Most Hits, One Series, Both Clubs—151, New York (AL), 64, vs. Pittsburgh (NL), 60, 1960 (7 games).

Most Doubles, One Series, Both Clubs—30, Philadelphia (AL) 19 vs. Chicago, 11, in 1910 (5 games).

Most Doubles, One Series, One Club—19 (tie), Philadelphia (AL), 1910; St. Louis (NL), 1946.

Most Triples, One Series, Both Clubs—25, Boston (AL) 16 vs. Pittsburgh 9, in 1903 (8 games).

Home Runs—One game, both clubs, 6, New York AL (4) vs. Chicago (2), Oct. 1, 1932, and New York AL (4) vs. Brooklyn NL (2), Oct. 4, 1953; one game, one club, 5, New York AL (Ruth 3, Durst, Gehrig) vs. St. Louis, Oct. 9, 1928; one inning; both clubs, 3, second inning, New York AL (2) vs. New York NL (1), Oct. 11, 1921; Boston (AL) 3, vs. St. Louis (NL) 0, Oct. 11, 1967, fourth inning.

Longest Game—14 innings, Boston (AL) 2, Brooklyn 1, Oct. 9, 1916.

Longest Game (by Time)—3 hours 28 minutes, Detroit (AL) vs. Chicago, Oct. 8, 1945 (12 innings). Chicago won, 8-7.

Shortest Game (by Time)—1 hour 25 minutes, Chicago (NL) vs. Detroit, Oct. 14, 1908. Chicago won, 2-0.

General

Most Receipts, One Series—$8,044,607.10, St. Louis NL vs. Boston AL, 1967, 7 games. (Includes $5,694,000 radio and television receipts.)

Most Receipts, One Game—$557,384.00, Baltimore (AL) at Los Angeles (NL), Oct. 6, 1966.

Highest Attendance, One Game—92,706, Chicago (AL) at Los Angeles (NL), Oct. 6, 1959.

Highest Attendance, One Series—Los Angeles (NL) vs. Chicago (AL), 1959 (6 games), 420,784.

Lowest Receipts, One Series—$50,000, Boston (AL) vs. Pittsburgh, 1903 (8 games).

Lowest Receipts, One Game—$8,348, Philadelphia (AL) vs. New York at Philadelphia, Oct. 12, 1905.

Lowest Attendance, One Series—62,232, Chicago (NL) vs. Detroit, 1908 (5 games).

Lowest Attendance, One Game—6,210, Detroit (AL) vs. Chicago, Oct. 14, 1908.

Highest Pool for Players—$1,044,042.65, Los Angeles (NL) vs. Baltimore (AL), 1966 (4 games).

Highest Pay-Off per Share to Winning Players—$20,705.01, to Oakland (AL), 1972 (includes League Championship share).

Lowest Pay-Off per Share to Winning Players—$1,102.51, to Boston (AL), 1918 (war year).

Highest Pay-Off per Share to Losing Players—
$15,080.25, to Cincinnati (NL), 1972
(includes League Championship share).
Lowest Pay-Off per Share to Losing Players—
$439.50, to Chicago (NL), 1906.

WORLD SERIES UMPIRING

Only 2 umpires officiated in a World Series
from 1903 to 1908. Then 2 more were added to
the staff. Now 6 take the field for each game.
Each of the officiating umpires (4) is paid $3,000
for the series. The 2 "emergency" umpires, who
serve near the foul poles, receive $1,500 a piece.

The late Bill Klem, for many years a National
League umpire, holds the record for the classic.
He appeared in 18 series—1908, 1909, 1911,
1912, 1913, 1914, 1915, 1917, 1918, 1920,
1922, 1924, 1926, 1929, 1931, 1932, 1934 and
1940. Charles Rigler and Henry (Hank) O'Day,
also National Leaguers, appeared in 10 series.
Tommy Connolly, Bill McGowan and Bill
Dinneen each officiated in 8 series, the high for
American League umpires.

Minor League

Before the advent of radio and television,
especially the latter, minor league baseball teams
prospered throughout the country, even in cities
and towns fairly near cities that had major league
teams. This was true until 1950. Broadcasting by
radio of major league games had some effect on
minor league game attendance but as matters
turned out it was not serious. The introduction
of televised major league games was a severe blow
to minors. As the number of network radio and
television broadcasts of major league games increased, minor leagues began to fold, for fans
preferred to stay at home to listen to or watch
the major league teams. From a high of 59 in
1949, the number of minor leagues has been
declining steadily, so that in 1958 there were
only 24 minor loops in operation. Unless the
major leagues take some strong measures of
assistance, the future of the minors will be bleak,
indeed. Whereas, in the early days ownership was
largely on an independent basis, currently the
minors to a great extent depend on the majors
for players and financial assistance, either
through direct ownership or by working agreements.

The first minor leagues were the International
Association and the League Alliance. Both
started play in 1877, willing to act in a minor
role, while the National League operated as the
major organization. Both circuits made themselves subject to the dictates of the National.

The League Alliance disbanded after the end
of the 1877 season and no history exists. The
International operated through 1878. During the
1878–79 winter it was reorganized and took the
name of the National Association, but then it
folded.

The International of 1877 was made up as
follows: Alleghenys (Pittsburgh), Live Oaks
(Lynn, Mass.), Buckeyes (Columbus, Ohio), Man-
chesters (N.H.), Rochesters (Rochester, N.Y.),
Maple Leafs (Guelph, Ont.) and Tecumsehs
(London, Ont.). The pennant was won by the
London Tecumsehs.

In 1878 the International make-up was

Alleghenys (Pittsburgh); Buffalo; Hartford,
Conn.; Manchester; Hornellville, N.Y.; Rochester;
Springfield, Ill.; Syracuse, N.Y.; Utica, N.Y., and
the London (Ont.) Tecumsehs. Buffalo won the
pennant.

The Northwestern League came into existence
in 1879. It was a 4-club group—Omaha, Neb.;
Dubuque, Iowa; Rockford, Ill., and Davenport,
Iowa. Its operations through that season and in
1880, 1881 and 1882 are not detailed in the
history books, but it must have grown to importance. For, late in 1881, when the gentlemen
who decided upon an American Association as a
rival of the National needed players, they made
wholesale raids on the Northwestern.

The American Association tapped the Northwestern for Charles Radbourne, Charles A.
Comiskey, Billy Gleason and Jack Gleason, while
the Nationals, having been raided by the American Association, also took players from the
Northwestern. However, as fast as the American
Association and National League lured seasoned
performers from the Northwestern, that minor
circuit signed up youngsters to replace them, and
it became a testing ground for youthful talent.

The Northwestern survived the storm of 1882,
and when the Nationals and American Association gained major status, the Northwestern asked
protection from future raids. This resulted in the
"Triparty Agreement," the first of its kind in
baseball annals. It served as a model for baseball
through other wars. It pledged the majors not to
raid the minors and provided a purchase agreement.

The Northwestern played an important role in
baseball's history. It remained as the Northwestern until the end of 1887. In 1888 and until
1891, inclusive, it was the Western Association.
In 1892 and until the end of the 1899 season, it
was known as the Western League. When the
1899 season closed, Ban Johnson, its president,
disbanded it as a minor league. Then, taking
practically all the cities that had been in the
1899 Western League, he organized them into
the American League, which became a major

organization starting in 1901, and is the American of today.

The minors gained momentum through the 1880's and the records of the "Sporting News" of St. Louis show that at the end of the 1887 season the minor leagues included: North-western, International, Western, Southern, New England, Ohio State, Pennsylvania, Eastern and California. All were bound to the National League and American Association by the "Triparty Agreement," which permitted the drafting of a certain number of players each year by the majors. In 1888, the minors consisted of International, the Western (which was a merger of the old Western and the Northwestern), the Central League, Southern, New England, Texas, California, and the Tri-State, which had been the Ohio League.

After the American Association had dis-banded at the end of 1891, a new agreement between the major National League group and the minors was drawn to substitute for the "Triparty Agreement." The pact was observed until about Sept. 1, 1901, when the Nationals, desperate for ball players to replace those taken by the warring Americans, notified the minors, through its representatives, James A. Hart of the Chicago Nationals and John T. Brush of the New York Nationals, that the terms of the agreement would be ignored and that the Nationals would raid as they chose.

The Nationals at once proceeded with their raids.

Confronted by the likelihood of their players being taken in wholesale numbers by the majors if war were prolonged, the leaders among the minors resolved to form an organization for their own protection and met for that purpose in Chicago on Sept. 5, 1901. There they called themselves the "National Association of Profes-sional Baseball Leagues" (suggested by Pat Powers). Present at that session were Mike H. Sexton (Three Eye League—Illinois, Indiana, Iowa); Powers (Eastern League); John H. Farrell (New York State League); Thomas J. Hickey (Western League); William Meyers Jr. (Western Association, which had taken up where the old Western League had left off); W.H. Lucas (Pacific Northwestern), and Tim H. Murnane (New England League). Powers was elected president and Farrell, secretary.

At a later meeting in New York—Oct. 24, 1901—Powers refused to take any salary as presi-dent. Farrell was voted $1,200 a year remunera-tion for his work. Applications from other minor leagues for admittance to the association were granted. The association decided that the leagues should be grouped into classes, according to population of the cities they represented. Class A was tops, then—not "Class AAA," as at present. The fee for admission into the association was: Class A clubs, $50; Class B clubs, $30; Class C clubs, $20; Class D clubs, $10.

Monthly salaries for clubs during 1902 were limited as follows: Class A, $2,000; Class B, $1,200; Class C, $1,000; Class D, $900, these sums representing salary payment for the entire team.

The Class A Clubs received permission to make their own deals with majors as regards dis-posal of players. The draft prices for other leagues were: Class B, $600; Class C, $400; Class D, $300. A Board of Arbitration was appointed. Its members were Hickey, Sexton, Meyer, Lucas and Murnane.

The original association was made up of the following classes and leagues:

Class A—Eastern League; Western League.

Class B—Southern Association; Western Asso-ciation; New York State League; Three Eye League.

Class C—Pacific Northwestern; Connecticut League (later New England).

No clubs were graded into Class D at that Oct. 1901 meeting.

Before the start of the 1902 season—the first under the association's domination—the Missouri Valley, Texas, North Carolina, Cotton States and Pennsylvania State League joined the Associa-tion. Thus, 13 minor leagues went into action under the association standard in 1902. All except Pennsylvania played out the schedule.

The war between the majors ended after the 1902 season, and, in 1903, a total of 19 minor leagues was in action. An agreement had been reached, early in 1903, whereby the majors were to respect the rights of all the minors, and all leagues, major and minor, were grouped into "Organized Baseball." A new agreement was made, whereby the majors had to pay certain fixed sums when drafting minor league players. The minors, to protect themselves from competi-tion with each other via fancy salaries, agreed to certain maximum limits, beginning in 1904, which were:

Class A Leagues—Not to pay more than $2,400 monthly in salaries. Class B—Limit, $1,800; Class C—Limit, $1,000; Class D—Limit, $800.

In 1914 and 1915 the higher class minors suffered a financial setback when the "outlaw" Federal League, reaching out for players, took star athletes from the minors without payment. The Federal League war ended at the conclusion of 1915 without much damage to the minors. The minors had a good year in 1916, but in 1917 and 1918, with the United States involved in World War I, chaos prevailed. Many teams lost outstanding players, because of enlistments or the draft, attendance dwindled, and red ink was splashed everywhere.

In 1917 twenty leagues started, but only 12 completed the schedule, and only 2 showed a profit. In 1918 the 9 leagues decided to play a short season. Only the International completed the schedule, and it, too, was a financial loser.

In 1921 another baseball war, instead of creating the usual havoc among the minors, actually brought them benefit and put them in a powerful position. Three clubs in the American League (New York, Boston, Chicago) deserted Ban Johnson, its president, and joined with the Nationals in an effort to curb Johnson's power and to put Kenesaw M. Landis in office as the Commissioner. Johnson wanted the support of the minors, as did the rival group. Each faction bid high in promises, and the minors practically dictated their own terms for allegiance to the anti-Johnson group, which included the 8 National and the 3 rebel American League clubs.

When Landis became commissioner in 1921, a new agreement was made with the minors—one that was tremendously favorable to them. Wholesale drafting ceased, draft prices were increased throughout the entire minor league classification and boom days were ahead for the minors.

John Farrell, formerly secretary of the minor league group, declared that during one season "there must have been at least 43 or 45 minor leagues in operation," but the exact year and other details, were not made available. However, the association records showed that in 1939 there were 41 minor leagues, with a paid attendance of 18,500,000. In 1940, a then record number of 44 leagues started the season and 43 finished, but the attendance record of 1939 was not broken.

When the United States entered World War II, the minors again took a severe beating. Since most of their players were young, the minors lost many through drafts and enlistments, beginning in 1942 and continuing throughout the war.

After the war in 1946, a total of 43 minor leagues took the field for action, of which 42 finished, the Mexican League dropping out.

Prior to the beginning of the 1946 season, it was decided to reclassify the minors. Under the old system the top leagues—International, American Association and Pacific Coast—were graded AA. They were advanced to grade AAA, while the Southern and Texas, previously A, were advanced to AA. The classification of leagues was based on total population of all the cities in each circuit. In 1951, the Pacific Coast League finally obtained "Open" classification, which restricted the majors' draft power as regards the P.C.L. player personnel. This was granted as a step toward eventual major status for the P.C.L. But with the transfer of the Brooklyn Dodgers to Los Angeles and the New York Giants to San Francisco, the Pacific coast lost two of its strongest franchises and reverted to the AAA classification in 1958.

The fortunes of the National Association of Professional Baseball Leagues have ebbed and flowed through the last decade or so, as shown by the following membership list of minor leagues as originally prepared by L.H. Addington of Durham, N.C., former publicity director of the organization, and Carl Lundquist, its current director of public relations:

Year	Minor Leagues
1933	14
1934	19
1935	21
1936	26
1937	37
1938	37
1939	41
1940	44
1941	41
1942	31
1943	16
1944	10
1945	12
1946	43
1947	52
1948	58
1949	59
1950	58
1951	50
1952	43
1953	38
1954	36
1955	33
1956	28
1957	28
1958	24
1959	21
1960	22
1961	22
1962	20
1963	20
1964	20
1965	20
1966	19
1967	19
1968	19
1969	21
1970	21
1971	20
1972	19

CLASSIFYING MINOR LEAGUES

Class	Population
AAA	3,000,000
AA	1,750,000
A1 (none in operation)	1,450,000
A	1,000,000
B	250,000
C	150,000
D	Up to 150,000

Further, for a league to obtain "Open" classification, it must have an aggregate population of 10,000,000. No open league is in operation.

Prices Paid by Majors When Drafting

All minor league players are still subject to draft by the majors. Until the 1957 winter meeting of the major and minor leagues, a graduated scale of prices was in effect. Thus, the major leagues paid $15,000 for a player drafted from a team in the Open classification, $10,000 for one from Class AAA, $7,500 from Class AA, $6,000 for Class A1 and Class A, $4,000 from Class B, $2,500 from Class C, $2,000 from Class D.

This was changed at the 1957 winter meeting. The new rule provides for a $25,000 draft price for any player selected by a major league club regardless of classification. Minor league clubs of one classification may draft players from lower leagues as follows: $12,000 for a player selected by an AAA club, $7,500 for one selected by an AA club, $4,000 by an A club, $2,000 by a B club and $1,000 by a C club.

At the 1958 winter meeting, an experimental rule was adopted in relation to first-year players in the minors. This amendment, in effect one year, provided for unrestricted draft of first-year players. Players signed as free agents who were not brought up to the major league parent roster were subject to unrestricted draft at the 1959 winter meeting. If selected by a major league club from any classification, the price was $15,000; if selected by an AAA club $7,500; by an AA club $6,000; by an A club $4,000; by a B or C club $3,000. The amendment was enacted in an effort to cut down the wave of bonus payments by major league clubs to untried athletes.

The drafting of players to the major league in the sixties and seventies brought price tags of $25,000. First-year playres brought payments of $8,000 to $12,000.

SALARY AND PLAYER LIMITS

Clubs in Classes AAA and AA set their own amounts as to salary payments. One big reason for this is that they often have to take players on option from major league clubs and pay major league salaries. The salary and player limits for the various classifications follow:

Class AAA—No set salary figure. A club may have 38 players under control at any time but this total must be reduced to 24 after the first 30 days of the season.

Class AA—Nor set salary figure. A club may be 37 players under control but this total must be reduced to 23 after the first 30 days of the season.

Class A—Salary limit is $5,700 per team per month. Club may control 32 players but this total must be reduced to 21 after the first 30 days of the season.

Class B—Salary limit is $4,800 per team per month. Club may control 28 players but this total must be reduced to 18 after the first 30 days of the season.

Class C—Salary limit is $4,200 per team per month. Club may control 25 players but this total must be reduced to 17 after first 30 days of the season.

Class D—Salary limit is $3,400 per team per month. Club may control 22 players but this total must be reduced to 16 after first 30 days of the season.

EXECUTIVE HISTORY OF MINORS

Pat Powers, the first president of the minors, was elected in 1901 and resigned in 1909. He was succeeded by Mike Sexton, who was elected on Nov. 10, 1909. Sexton remained in office until December, 1932.

William G. Bramham became the next head of the organization, serving until December, 1946. Then followed George M. Trautman, who received a 5-year contract at $25,000 a year. Trautman's pact was renewed when it expired. When Bramham first took the position the salary was $6,000 a year. Later it was increased to $8,500 and then to $25,000. Trautman has continued as president.

John Farrell was named secretary and treasurer in 1901 and retained both offices until 1933, when the title of secretary was abolished. Farrell was the association's treasurer until he retired in 1937 and Bramham took over his office. The work is now handled by Trautman.

The Board of Arbitrations, created in 1901, existed until November, 1933. Its successor was a Board of Appeals, made up, usually, of the presidents of 3 minor leagues. The Board of Appeals later was replaced by the Executive Committee.

CHAMPIONS

Over the years the various minor leagues have had their own systems of determining championships. In the Pacific Coast League the custom was to play a split season, with the two winners meeting in a series to determine the over-all championship. The pennant winners in the other two top circuits—the American Association and the International League—met in what is known as the "Junior World Series."

Beginning in 1932 the American Association and the International League, after completing their regular play, held what is called the "Shaughnessy Play-Offs" among the first 4 clubs to determine each league's representative in the Junior World Series. In 1936 the Pacific Coast League started a similar post-season play-off program and called it the President's Cup series. The name was changed to Governor's Cup in 1943.

The basic Shaughnessy play-off method, first put into effect in ice hockey, works about as follows:

At the end of the regular season the clubs finishing first and third meet in a best 2-of-3, 3-of-5 or 4-of-7-game series, while the second and fourth-place clubs meet in a similar set. The winners then play a best 4-of-7 series for post season honors.

The Pacific Coast League was divided into Northern, Southern Divisions in 1936, 1969-71; into Eastern, Western Divisions from 1964-68.

Pacific Coast League (AAA)

Los Angeles—1903, 1905, 1907, 1908, 1916, 1921, 1926, 1933, 1934, 1938, 1943, 1944, 1947, 1956.
Tacoma—1904, 1961, 1969.
Portland—1906, 1910, 1911, 1913, 1914, 1932, 1936, 1945.
San Francisco—1909, 1915, 1917, 1922, 1923, 1925, 1928, 1931, 1935, 1946, 1957.
Oakland—1912, 1927, 1948, 1950.
Vernon—1918, 1919, 1920.
Seattle—1924, 1939, 1940, 1941, 1951, 1955, 1966.
Hollywood—1929, 1930, 1949, 1952, 1953.
Sacramento—1937, 1942.
San Diego—1954, 1962, 1964, 1967.
Phoenix—1958.
Oklahoma City—1963, 1965.
Salt Lake City—1959, 1971.
Spokane—1960, 1970
Tulsa—1968.
Albuquerque—1972.

International League (AAA)

Trenton—1884.
Syracuse—1885, 1888, 1897, 1969, 1970.
Utica—1886.
Toronto—1887, 1902, 1907, 1912, 1917, 1918, 1926, 1943, 1954, 1956, 1957, 1960, 1965, 1966.
Detroit—1889, 1890.
Buffalo—1891, 1904, 1906, 1915, 1916, 1927, 1936, 1949, 1959, 1961.
Providence—1892, 1894, 1896, 1900, 1905, 1914.
Binghamton—1892.
Erie—1893.
Springfield (Mass.)—1895.
Montreal—1898, 1935, 1945, 1946, 1948, 1951, 1952, 1955, 1958.
Rochester—1899, 1901, 1909, 1910, 1911, 1928, 1929, 1930, 1931, 1940, 1950, 1953, 1964, 1971.
Jersey City—1903, 1939, 1947.
Baltimore—1908, 1919, 1920, 1921, 1922, 1923, 1924, 1925, 1944.
Newark—1913, 1932, 1933, 1934, 1937, 1938, 1941, 1942.

Atlanta—1962.
Indianapolis—1963.
Toledo—1967.
Jacksonville—1968.
Tidewater—1972.

American Association (AAA)

(Did not operate 1963-68.)

Indianapolis—1902, 1908, 1917, 1928, 1948, 1954, 1956.
St. Paul—1903, 1904, 1919, 1920, 1922, 1924, 1931, 1938, 1949.
Columbus—1905, 1906, 1907, 1933, 1934, 1937, 1941, 1950.
Louisville—1909, 1916, 1921, 1925, 1926, 1930, 1946, 1959, 1960, 1961, 1962.
Minneapolis—1910, 1911, 1912, 1915, 1932, 1935, 1955.
Milwaukee—1913, 1914, 1936, 1943, 1944, 1945, 1951, 1952.
Kansas City—1918, 1923, 1929, 1939, 1940, 1942, 1947.
Toledo—1927, 1953.
Wichita—1957.
Charleston—1958.
Omaha—1969, 1970.
Denver—1971.
Evansville—1972.

Mexican League (AAA)

Mexico City Tigers—1955, 1960, 1965, 1966.
Mexico City Reds—1956, 1957, 1959, 1964, 1968.
Nuevo Laredo—1958.
Veracruz—1961.
Monterrey—1962.
Puebla—1963.
Jalisco—1967, 1971.
Reynosa—1969.
Aguila—1970.
Cordoba—1972.

Southern Association (AA)

(disbanded 1962)

Augusta—1893 (1st half), 1898.
Macon—1893 (2d half).
Nashville—1901, 1902, 1908, 1916, 1940, 1943, 1944, 1948, 1949.
Memphis—1894, 1903, 1904, 1921, 1924, 1930, 1953, 1955.
New Orleans—1887, 1889, 1896, 1905, 1910, 1911, 1915, 1918, 1923, 1926, 1927, 1933, 1934.
Birmingham—1888, 1892 (2d half), 1906, 1912, 1914, 1928, 1929, 1931, 1958.
Atlanta—1885, 1886, 1895, 1907, 1909, 1913, 1917, 1919, 1925, 1935, 1936, 1938, 1941, 1945, 1946, 1950, 1954, 1956, 1957.
Little Rock—1920, 1937, 1942, 1951, 1960.
Mobile—1899, 1922, 1947, 1959.

Chattanooga—1892 (1st half), 1932, 1939, 1952, 1961.

Eastern League (AA)

(New York-Pennsylvania League prior to 1958)

Williamsport—1923, 1924, 1934, 1960*.
York—1925, 1969.
Scranton—1926, 1936, 1939, 1942, 1946, 1948, 1951.
Harrisburg—1927, 1928, 1931.
Binghamton—1929, 1933, 1935, 1940, 1944, 1949, 1952, 1953, 1958, 1967.
Wilkes-Barre—1930, 1932, 1950.
Elmira—1937, 1938, 1943, 1941, 1962, 1964, 1966, 1971.
Albany—1945, 1954.
Utica—1947.
Allentown—1955.
Schenectady—1956.
Reading—1957, 1968.
Springfield—1959, 1960*, 1961.
Charleston—1963.
Pittsfield—1965.
Waterbury—1970.
West Haven—1972.
*Co-champions.

Southern League (AA)

(Did not operate in 1918, 1931 through 1935, 1943 through 1945. In 1971, clubs were members of Dixie Assoc.)

Macon—1904, 1905, 1938, 1942, 1949, 1950, 1958, 1962.
Savannah—1906, 1913, 1914, 1937, 1947, 1953, 1954, 1960.
Charleston—1907, 1922.
Jacksonville—1908, 1912, 1956.
Chattanooga—1909.
Columbus—1910, 1911, 1915, 1936, 1940, 1965, 1970.
Augusta—1916, 1924, 1939, 1946, 1955, 1963.
Columbia—1917, 1919, 1920, 1921, 1941.

Charlotte—1923, 1957, 1969.
Spartanburg—1925.
Greenville—1926, 1927, 1930, 1948.
Asheville—1928, 1961, 1968.
Knoxville—1929.
Montgomery—1951, 1952, 1972.
Gastonia—1959.
Lynchburg—1964.
Mobile—1966.
Birmingham—1967.

Texas League (AA)

Dallas—1888, 1898 (league disbanded, with Dallas in lead), 1903, 1910 (tied with Houston; no play-off), 1917, 1918, 1926, 1929, 1941, 1946, 1952, 1953.
Houston—1889, 1891, 1892, 1896, 1909, 1910 (tied with Dallas; no play-off), 1912, 1913, 1914 (tied with Waco; no play-off), 1928, 1931, 1939, 1940, 1947, 1951, 1954, 1956, 1957.
Galveston—1890, 1897 (tied with San Antonio; no play-off), 1899, 1934.
Fort Worth—1895, 1905, 1920, 1921, 1922, 1923, 1924, 1925, 1930, 1937, 1939, 1946, 1948.
San Antonio—1897 (tied with Galveston; no play-off), 1908, 1933, 1950, 1961, 1964.
Corsicana—1902, 1904.
Cleburne—1896 (tied with Fort Worth; won title by default).
Austin—1907, 1911, 1959.
Waco—1914 (tied with Houston; split-season; no play-off), 1915, 1916.
Shreveport—1919, 1942, 1954.
Beaumont—1932, 1938, 1942, 1950.
Oklahoma City—1935, 1937.
Tulsa—1936, 1949, 1960, 1962, 1963.
Corpus Christi—1958.
Albuquerque—1965, 1967, 1970.
Arkansas—1966.
El Paso—1968, 1972.
Memphis—1969.
League did not operate in 1943 through 1945. In 1971, club was a member of Dixie Assoc.

JUNIOR WORLD SERIES

(Source: Information Please Almanac.)
International League (1) vs. American Association (AA)
No series in 1905, 1908 to 1916, inclusive; 1918, 1919 and 1935.

Year and Winner	Manager	Games Won	Loser	Manager	Games Won
1904—Buffalo (1)	George Stallings	2	St. Paul	Mike Kelley	1
1906—Buffalo (1)	George Stallings	3	Columbus	Bill Clymer	2
1907—Toronto (1)	Joe Kelley	4	Columbus	Bill Clymer	1
1917—Indianapolis (AA)	Jack Hendricks	4	Toronto	Nap Lajoie	1
1920—Baltimore (1)	Jack Dunn	5	St. Paul	Mike Kelley	1
1921—Louisville (AA)	Joe McCarthy	5	Baltimore	Jack Dunn	3
1922—Baltimore (1)	Jack Dunn	5	St. Paul	Mike Kelley	2
1923—Kansas City (AA)	Wilbur Good	5	Baltimore	Jack Dunn	4
1924—St. Paul (AA)	Nick Allen	5	Baltimore	Jack Dunn	4

1925—Baltimore (1)	Jack Dunn	5	Louisville	Joe McCarthy . . .	3
1926—Toronto (1)	Dan Howley	5	Louisville	Bill Meyer	0
1927—Toledo (AA)	Casey Stengel	5	Buffalo	Bill Clymer	1
1928—Indianapolis (AA) .	Bruno Betzel	5	Rochester	Billy Southworth	1
1929—Kansas City (AA) . .	Dutch Zwilling	5	Rochester	Billy Southworth	4
1930—Rochester (1)	Billy Southworth	5	Louisville	Al Sothoron	3
1931—Rochester (1)	Billy Southworth	5	St. Paul	Al Leifield	3
1932—Newark (1)	Al Mamaux	4	Minneapolis	Donie Bush	2
1933—Columbus (AA) . . .	Ray Blades	5	Buffalo	Ray Schalk	3
1934—Columbus (AA) . . .	Ray Blades	5	Toronto	Ike Boone	4
1936—Milwaukee (AA) . .	Al Sothoron	4	Buffalo	Ray Schalk	1
1937—Newark (1)	Oscar Vitt	4	Columbus	Burt Shotton . . .	3
1938—Kansas City (AA) . .	Bill Meyer	4	Newark	Johnny Neun . . .	3
1939—Louisville (AA) . . .	Bill Burwell	4	Rochester	Billy Southworth	3
1940—Newark (1)	Johnny Neun	4	Louisville	Bill Burwell	2
1941—Columbus (AA) . . .	Burt Shotton	4	Montreal	Clyde Sukeforth .	2
1942—Columbus (AA) . . .	Eddie Dyer	4	Syracuse	Jewel Ens	1
1943—Columbus (AA) . . .	Nick Cullop	4	Syracuse	Jewel Ens	1
1944—Baltimore (1)	Tommy Thomas	4	Louisville	Harry Leibold . . .	2
1945—Louisville (AA) . . .	Harry Leibold	4	Newark	Bill Meyer	2
1946—Montreal (1)	Clay Hopper	4	Louisville	Harry Leibold . . .	2
1947—Milwaukee (AA) . . .	Nick Cullop	4	Syracuse	Jewel Ens	3
1948—Montreal (1)	Clay Hopper	4	St. Paul	Walter E. Alston .	1
1949—Indianapolis (AA) .	Al Lopez	4	Montreal	Clay Hopper	2
1950—Columbus (AA) . . .	Rollie Hemsley	4	Baltimore	Nick Cullop	1
1951—Milwaukee (AA) . .	Charlie Grimm	4	Montreal	Walter Alston . . .	2
1952—Rochester (1)	Harry Walker	4	Kansas City	George Selkirk . .	3
1953—Montreal (I)	Walter Alston	4	Kansas City	Harry Craft	1
1954—Louisville (AA) . . .	Pinky Higgins	4	Syracuse	Lamar Newsome .	2
1955—Minneapolis (AA) .	Bill Rigney	4	Rochester	Dixie Walker	3
1956—Indianapolis (AA) .	Kerby Farrell	4	Rochester	Dixie Walker	0
1957—Denver (AA)	Ralph Houk	4	Buffalo	Phil Cavarretta . .	1
1958—Minneapolis (AA) .	Gene Mauch	4	Montreal	Clay Bryant	0
1959—Havana (1)	Preston Gomez	4	Minneapolis	Gene Mauch	3
1960—Louisville (AA) . . .	Bill Adair	4	Toronto	Mel McGaha	2
1961—Buffalo (1)	Kerby Farrell	4	Louisville	Ben Geraghty . . .	0
1962—Atlanta (1)	Joe Schultz	4	Louisville	Jack Tighe	3
1963-69—No competition					
1970—Syracuse (IL)	Frank Verdi	4	Omaha (AA)	Jack McKeon . . .	1
1971—Rochester (IL)	———	4	Denver (AA)	———	3
1972*Caribbean All Stars	———	6	Albuquerque Dukes	———	2

*World baseball classic, Round Robin, elimination tournament consisting of postseason playoff winners from The American Assoc., (AA), International (IL) and Pacific Coast Leagues (PC), and an all-star team of Latin players who participate regularly in the Caribbean winter leagues, plus a team from the host site.

Tie games in 1906, 1924, 1928.

DIXIE SERIES

Southern Association (SA) vs.
   Texas League (TL)

1920—Fort Worth (TL) beat Little Rock, 4 games to 2.
1921—Fort Worth (TL) beat Memphis, 4—2.
1922—Mobile (SA) beat Fort Worth, 4—2.
1923—Fort Worth (TL) beat New Orleans 4—2.
1924—Fort Worth (TL) beat Memphis, 4—3.
1923—Fort Worth (TL) beat New Orleans 4—2.
1924—Fort Worth (TL) beat Memphis, 4—3.
1925—Fort Worth (TL) beat Atlanta, 4—2.

1926—Dallas (TL) beat New Orleans, 4—2.
1927—Wichita Falls (TL) beat New Orleans, 4—0.
1928—Houston (TL) beat Birmingham, 4—2.
1929—Birmingham (SA) beat Dallas, 4—2.
1930—Fort Worth (TL) beat Memphis, 4—1.
1931—Birmingham (SA) beat Houston, 4—3.
1932—Chattanooga (SA) beat Beaumont, 4—1.
1933—New Orleans (SA) beat San Antonio, 4—2.
1934—New Orleans (SA) beat Galveston, 4—2.
1935—Oklahoma City (TL) beat Atlanta, 4—2.
1936—Tulsa (TL) beat Birmingham, 4—0.
1937—Fort Worth (TL) beat Little Rock, 4—1.

1938–Atlanta (SA) beat Beaumont, 4–0.
1939–Fort Worth (TL) beat Nashville, 4–3.
1940–Nashville (SA) beat Houston, 4–1.
1941–Nashville (SA) beat Dallas, 4–0.
1942–Nashville (SA) beat Shreveport, 4–2.
1943-45–No competition.
1946–Dallas (TL) beat Atlanta, 4–0.
1947–Houston (TL) beat Mobile, 4–2.
1948–Birmingham (SA) beat Fort Worth, 4–1.
1949–Nashville (SA) beat Tulsa, 4–3.
1950–San Antonio (TL) beat Nashville, 4–3.
1951–Birmingham (SA) beat Houston, 4–2.
1952–Memphis (SA) beat Shreveport, 4–2.
1953–Dallas (TL) beat Nashville, 4–2.

1954–Atlanta (SA) beat Houston, 4–3.
1955–Mobile (SA) beat Shreveport, 4–0.
1956–Houston (TL) beat Atlanta, 4–2.
1957–Houston (TL) beat Atlanta, 4–2.
1958–Birmingham (SA) beat Corpus Christi, 4–2.
1959-66–Discontinued.
1967–Birmingham (SL) beat Albuquerque (TL),
    4-2.
1968-72–Discontinued

SL–Southern League.

Tie games in 1920, 1922, 1923, 1924, 1926,
    1938.

Special

NATIONAL BASEBALL CONGRESS OF AMERICA

(Semi-pro.)

Raymond Dumont of Wichita, Kan., conceived the idea of a state-wide non-professional tournament to increase interest in baseball. So successful was the first Kansas State tournament that by 1934 the event had drawn 50,000 fans, paid $5,000 in total prize money to teams and resulted in hundreds of clubs organizing for the purpose of seeking state championships. In 1936, the plan was applied to a national program comprised of 48 state tournaments with championship teams advancing further in competition leading to the national finals at Wichita.

Every succeeding year the program has gained momentum and now it includes a National Association with leagues affiliated throughout the world, a National Association of Umpires and Scorers, Old-Timers Groups, and a world-wide system of tournaments.

Any team not in organized professional baseball in the United States or classified as a barnstorming group is eligible to participate in the program.

The process is:

In the United States, affiliated N.B.C. league leaders as of the July 1 and district champions advance to the state tournaments. State titlists meet in bi-state play-offs to reduce the field to the 32-team national brackets. The National tournament is a double-elimination event.

According to zoning plans, 9 states qualify championship teams directly to the National. They are California, Kansas, Texas, Oklahoma, Pennsylvania, Minnesota, Wisconsin, Alaska and Florida. The other states are zoned together with adjacent state champions meeting each other in bi-state play-offs and the winners advancing to the National tournament. Others qualifying for the National include the defending national champions and runners-up and Southern States Negro champions from a series below the Mason-Dixon line.

District tournaments to qualify for the state tournaments are held in June and early July, with state events taking place in middle and late July and early August.

District and state tournaments are played either on single or double elimination systems, with two finalists playing for the respective championships.

To the United States champions an annual $10,000 first-place purse is awarded plus mileage allowances. The National tournament is staged annually in Wichita, Kan.

All tournaments are operated uniformly under N.B.C. system through franchises issued to district and state commissioners. The teams share in fifty per cent gross gate receipts in the form of prize money and mileage allowances. The top teams share in prize money and all teams share in mileage allowances, pro-rated according to distances travelled to respective tournament sites.

The annual champions:

1935–Bismarck, N.D.
1936–Duncan, Okla.
1937–Enid, Okla.
1938–Buford, Ga.
1939–Duncan, Okla.
1940-41–Enid, Okla.
1942–Wichita, Kan.
1943–Camp Wheeler, Ga.
1944–Sherman Field, Kan.
1945–Enid, Okla.
1946–St. Joseph, Mich.
1947-50–Fort Wayne, Ind.
1951–Sinton, Tex.
1952–Fort Myer, Va.
1953–Fort Leonard Wood, Mo.
1954-55–Wichita, Kan.
1956–Fort Wayne, Ind.
1957–Sinton, Tex.
1958–Drain, Ore.
1959–Houston, Tex.
1960–Grand Rapids, Mich.
1961–Ponchatoula, La.
1962–Wichita, Kan.

1963-68—No record
1969—Anchorage, Alaska
1970—Grand Rapids, Mich.
1971—Anchorage, Alaska
1972—Fairbanks, Alaska

NATIONAL COLLEGIATE CHAMPIONS

The East-West Collegiate All-Star Game, arranged by the American Association of College Baseball Coaches in 1946, found 40 players from 33 colleges competing at Fenway Park, Boston. Out of this came the annual "College World Series" under the sponsorship of the National Collegiate Athletic Association. The series is conducted on the same 8-district play-off plan that the N.C.A.A. uses in its other sports.

1947—California
1948—Southern California
1949-50—Texas
1951—Oklahoma
1952—Holy Cross
1953—Michigan
1954—Missouri
1955—Wake Forest
1956—Minnesota
1957—California
1958—Southern California
1959—Oklahoma State
1960—Minnesota
1961—Southern California
1962-65—Wichita, Kan.
1966-67—Boulder, Colo.
1963—Southern California
1964—Minnesota
1965—Arizona State
1966—Ohio State
1967—Arizona State
1968—Southern California
1969—Arizona State
1970-73—Southern California

BASIC RULES

Baseball is played on a field made up of 2 parts: an infield and an outfield. The infield is square and erroneously referred to as a "diamond." The distance from "home plate," which is between the left and the right-handed batters' boxes, to first base is 90 feet. The distance between first base and second base, between second base and third base, and between third base and the home plate also is 90 feet. The pitcher's "box," from which he makes delivery of the ball, is 60 feet 6 inches from home plate.

The outfield area has no maximum or minimum limit. However, when a ball field is laid out in an enclosed area, the farthest limit of the outfield is fixed by stands or fences. In areas not enclosed, the outfield is that part of the playing area back of the infield, regardless of size.

The game is played with a ball and bat, and the players wear leather gloves. The ones used by the catcher and first baseman are thicker than those used by the other players and are called mitts.

The ball has a cork and rubber core, wound with yarn and has a leather cover, which is stitched on. The ball must not weigh less than 5 ounces nor more than 5¼, and must not be less than 9 nor more than 9¼ inches in circumference. The bat must be round, not over 2¾ inches in diameter at the thickest part nor longer than 42 inches, and must be made entirely of wood. There is no limitation as to weight.

Nine players make up a team: catcher, pitcher, first baseman, second baseman, third baseman, shortstop, right fielder, center fielder, left fielder. A substitution may be made at any time, but the retired player may not re-enter the game.

The game is ruled by an umpire or umpires. There can be as many as 4 umpires: 1 to judge balls and strikes back of the plate, one to make decisions at first base, another at second base, another at third base. Two extra umpires man the foul lines near the foul poles in crucial games, as in the World Series.

A game consists of 9 innings, with each team having equal turns at bat. If the score is tied at the completion of 9 innings, game continues until the tie is broken. If weather, visibility or any other condition makes continuation impossible, the plate umpire may call a halt.

The visiting team takes the first turn at bat. It continues at bat until the defending team has put out 3 of the visiting players, after which the home team bats until 3 of its men have been put out. That completes an official inning.

A player may be put out in various ways. If he hits a fly ball that is caught before it touches the ground he is out. If he hits a ground ball and the ball is scooped up and thrown to first base, arriving there before he does, he is out. Base runners can be forced out. For instance, if a runner is on first base and his team-mate hits a ground ball, the runner must vacate first base so as to make room for the hitter, and must try to advance to second. If the ball reaches that base before the runner arrives, he is out. Runners can be forced at any of the bases and also at home plate.

Of course, to make the putout, the infielder must be touching the base when the ball is caught.

If a base runner is tagged with the ball during time in at a moment when he is not standing on the base, he is out. A runner also is out if hit by a ball batted by a team-mate.

A player can be "struck out." If 3 strikes are called against him before he has received 4 bad pitches, called "balls," he is a "strikeout" victim. The first 2 foul balls hit by a batsman count as strikes against him. If a pitch to the batter has been over the plate, anywhere between the height of his knees and armpits, and the batsman did not strike at it, the umpire calls a strike on the batter. It also is a strike if he swings at a pitch and misses.

The batter is out if the umpire declares an infield fly. That is, if, before 2 men are out, while first and second, or first, second and third bases are occupied, the batter hits a fair fly ball other than a line drive that can be handled by an infielder. This is declared an infield fly. However, the base runners may be off their bases or advance at the risk of the ball being caught, the same as any other fly ball. A bunt that results in a fair fly is not regarded as an infield fly.

Those are the major methods by which a batsman, or base runner, may be put out.

A batsman may get on base in various ways. If he is hit by a pitched ball, he automatically goes to first base. If the pitcher throws 4 balls that are judged as "bad" by the umpire, before the pitcher has thrown 3 strikes, that gives the batter a pass to first base. He also is passed to first if the opposing catcher interferes with the swing of his bat.

If the batter makes a clean hit, he may advance along the bases as far as possible. If he hits just far enough to get to first base, that is called a single; if he gets to second base, it is a double; if to third, it is a triple; if he knocks the ball into fair territory in the stands or knocks it over the fence inside the foul line, he gets 4 bases, called a home run. It also is a home run if he hits to the far outfield and beats the ball back to the plate.

A runner may also advance by stealing the next base. He may be advanced by hits made by succeeding batters or by a sacrifice hit—meaning when a team-mate deliberately makes an out in such a way that the base runner has the opportunity to advance to the next base. Of course, runners also are permitted to advance on errors made by the defensive team.

The object of the game is to score runs. It is counted as a run when a player has advanced from home plate all the way around to home plate again. The team scoring the most runs wins the game. In cases where games are forfeited by action of the umpire, the official score is 9 to 0 in favor of the non-violating team.

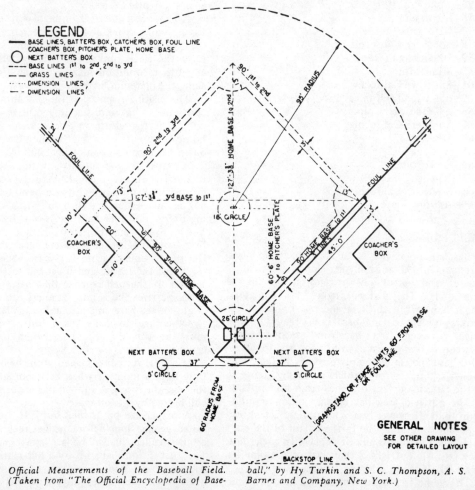

Official Measurements of the Baseball Field. (Taken from "The Official Encyclopedia of Base-ball," by Hy Turkin and S. C. Thompson, A. S. Barnes and Company, New York.)

BASKETBALL

There is no mystery about the origin of basketball. The game is an American invention. It has achieved great success as an attraction, drawing more and more spectators as it has developed. Today it attracts as many, perhaps more, fans as any sport in existence. Rules changes that led to increased scoring and intensified activity on the court can be credited for the game's rise in popularity. From America the game has spread to many parts of the world.

Two peach baskets fastened to a gymnasium balcony in the winter of 1891 provided the start for the game. The peach baskets gave the game its name—basketball. Its inventor was the late Dr. James Naismith, an instructor at the International Y.M.C.A. Training School at Springfield, Mass., now Springfield College.

Twelve of the 13 rules that Dr. Naismith laid down still are basic, although the game itself has changed vastly. The peach baskets were displaced quickly by metal ones and, in 1906, by open hoops of the kind used today. Backboards were introduced to keep overzealous spectators from interfering with the ball. Backboards first were of wire mesh, then of wood, and now are often of glass so spectators behind them can see.

Basketball is a lot faster than it used to be even a few years back and it has come a long way from the days when it was chiefly a Y.M.C.A. sport played in bandbox gymnasiums. The speed has been brought about by rule changes, including the elimination of the center jump after each foul. The rule tinkering continues, but basketball remains a game in which teamwork, agility and speed rather than strength, fast passing and accurate shooting are fundamental. The ball hasn't changed much in many years, nor has the number of players to a side—5—although larger numbers have been used.

Like almost any new organism, basketball has been afflicted with growing pains, partly because the rules were not standardized until 1934. It has been tainted by outright corruption, too, as reflected by the college "fixing" scandals of 1951 and 1952, but the gambling evil has touched only a minute fraction of the players and many thousands continue to find the game a wholesome recreation.

There were times when as many as 5 sets of rules, not counting those for women, were in effect and there were many variations, besides, to fit local conditions. To add further confusion, there was no uniformity of interpretation, so that basketball was a wrangling game, accompanied by charges that referees were biased.

The Springfield Y.M.C.A. was the chief arbiter of the rules for the game's first 2 years. Then the Y.M.C.A. was joined by the Amateur Athletic Union. The colleges weren't satisfied and in 1908 the National Collegiate Athletic Association assumed charge of the college rules. The N.C.A.A. and the A.A.U. formed the Joint Basketball Rules Committee in 1915. There still remained numerous variations in the country, however, until 1934, when the rules were standardized.

Basketball is the only game devised in the United States with no roots in the sports of other nations. It has fought for and has won the right to be designated a major sport.

In the years before basketball was originated, gymnasiums were not popular places. Members were bored by calisthenics and other non-competitive gymnasium activities. Weight lifting, Indian club twirling and bar chinning were held dull and routine and gymnasium memberships began to decline. There was a need for a game that could be played indoors under artificial light, would not be too difficult and would be interesting.

Dr. Naismith set to work to create such a game, lived to see it burgeon to the point where it became one of the greatest of sports, with spectators for big events numbering in the thousands. Basketball wasn't merely a dream come true; it was a miracle wrought when it was felt that all sports miracles belonged to history.

The extraordinary popularity of the game is reflected not only by the great crowds that watch, but also by the fact that before World War II there were between 18,000,000 and 20,000,000 players throughout the world. The rules had been translated into some 30 languages.

Basketball reached its present eminence in the United States partly through the efforts of Ned Irish, now a top executive of Madison Square Garden, New York. As a sports writer he had watched college gymnasiums filled to capacity and large overflow crowds turned away. There were big attendances in those years, but truly intersectional games were rare.

In 1934, Irish persuaded the officers of Madison Square Garden to schedule a double-header in which the main game was between Notre Dame and New York University. The other was between St. John's University and Westminster. The venture was successful. Basketball became one of the great attractions of the winter in the New York arena, with teams from all over the country competing. The national character of the sport in the Garden was pointed up when the National Invitation and the N.C.A.A. tournaments were scheduled. Tickets were at a premium.

The game's popularity in New York was dimmed after District Attorney Frank S. Hogan revealed that college players had accepted bribes from professional gamblers to win games by less than the "quoted points." Basketball wagering was of runaway proportion and the gamblers handicapped games by a "point system." The players who accepted bribes did so on the premise that their team would win by less than the "point line." The scandals touched players only in the New York schools at first—C.C.N.Y., Long Island University, N.Y.U. and Manhattan. Then players from Bradley, Kentucky and Toledo were implicated. Altogether there were over 30 arrests in 1951 and attendance for the Garden double-headers fell off sharply.

The cry to clean up the corruption and clean out the gamblers was echoed around the country and de-emphasis began. Coaches were dismissed and some institutions barred their teams from playing in large arenas, returning the sport to the campus.

College basketball survived in the Garden, however, while the professional variety, under the aegis of the National Basketball Association, boomed.

When the Grand Jury ended its task on April 29, 1953, Hogan said that the inquiry had uncovered 49 fixed games in 23 cities in 17 states. "There have been hopeful signs which indicate that colleges which have commercialized their athletic programs have taken to heart some of the hard lessons taught by this investigation," he said.

Basketball, designed as an indoor game, is played outdoors as well, but chiefly it is an indoor game. In other countries it is indoors and outdoors as the climate dictates.

Basketball originally was played with 7 men on a side, then 9, then 8. Now it is 5. At one time the game consisted of 3 periods of 20 minutes each. Now amateurs play four 10-minute quarters, and the professionals four 12-minute sessions. At one time 3 penalties constituted a point. Goals from field, which now count 2 points, once counted 3. In other days, when a foul was committed, the injured team called upon a specialist foul shooter. Under those rules a specialist at Fordham once shot 28 goals. Now the man fouled must make the throw and scores 1 point for his team if he cages the ball.

The sport, popular from the time it was introduced, was played in more than 75 countries before the outbreak of World War II. The extent of basketball's popularity in foreign climes is shown by the fact that a 3-night tournament in Peiping, China, in 1931 attracted over 70,000 customers.

But it remained for an American team, under the direction of Abe Saperstein and called the Harlem Globetrotters, to spread the gospel in foreign countries in a way that never has been equaled. Saperstein and his group of all-Negro players virtually have "covered the world" in more than 25 years, and in 1951 they played before 75,000 fans, the largest gathering in the history of the sport, in the Olympic Stadium at Berlin, Germany.

Basketball became so much the game of games in Puerto Rico that in 1938 they had a national celebration for three weeks because that year marked the 25th anniversary of the introduction of the sport to the island.

The sport gained national impetus at the turn of the century when it was adopted by Eastern universities, with Yale and Pennsylvania among the pioneers. Other Eastern colleges took up the game. The Eastern Intercollegiate League was formed in 1902. Then the Western Conference swung into action, and soon the popularity of the sport rolled it along from the Atlantic Ocean to the Pacific, from the Gulf of Mexico to the Canadian border—and then throughout the world.

Prep schools, high schools, and grammar schools are represented by thousands of teams, both boys and girls. There are from 1 to 4 teams for almost each gymnasium in the land, playing on alternate nights, or participating in double-headers. Villages and towns have their teams. The Amateur Athletic Union sponsors a National tournament. Industrial organizations have teams in organized leagues.

Every county of practically every state has a legion of teams. They strive for titles ranging from county to national level in various categories, i.e., high school, college, A.A.U., Y.M.C.A., etc.

Here is Dr. Naismith's story about the origin of basketball, written in 1937, while he was a professor at the University of Kansas, in Lawrence:

"In the fall of '91, the physical directors of the country had come to the conclusion that maybe neither the German, Swedish or French system gave us the kind of work that would hold our membership in the Y's.

"We decided that there should be a game that could be played indoors in the evening and during the winter seasons. Dr. Gulick assigned me the task of inventing a game to fill this particular part of our work. He was led to assign this work to me because of a couple of statements I had made that it was possible to invent such a game and that mature individuals did not desire physical development but some enjoyable form of recreation.

"I first tried to modify some of the existing games so that they would meet the requirements, but failed to make any game suitable for indoor work. I then left out the idea of any individual game and began to think of the fundamental principles of all games. I discovered that in all team games some kind of a ball was used.

"The next step was to appreciate the fact that football was rough because you had to allow the defense to tackle because the offense ran with the ball. Accordingly, if the offense didn't have an opportunity to run with the ball, there would be no necessity for tackling and we would thus eliminate roughness.

"This is the fundamental principle of basketball.

"The next step was to secure some kind of a goal through which the ball could be passed. In thinking of upright goals, the fact was brought out that the more force that was put on the ball, the more likelihood there was of having it pass through the goal. It then occurred that if the ball be thrown in a curve it would not be necessary nor advisable to put too much force on the ball.

"I decided that by making the goal horizontal the ball would have to be thrown in a curve, minimizing the severe driving of a ball. In order to avoid having the defense congregate around the goal, it was placed above their heads, so that once the ball left the individual's hands, it was not likely to be interfered with.

"Then rules were made to eliminate roughness such as shouldering, pushing, kicking, etc. The ball was to be handled with the hands only. It could not be drawn into the body and thus encourage roughness.

"The manner of putting the ball into play was then considered. Two individuals were selected and took their stations in the middle of the floor. The ball was thrown up so as to land between them, giving as nearly equal chance as possible. The nearest approach to the ball needed was the soccer ball, which we selected.

"To get goals, we used a couple of old peach baskets, hanging one at each end of the gym. From this basketball developed.

"In my estimation, there are four fundamental principles in basketball:

"(1) That the player in possession of the ball must not make progress while it is in his possession.

"(2) The goal is horizontal and above the heads of the players.

"(3) Roughness is eliminated so far as possible by making it a no-contact contest.

"(4) The ball belongs to the player at any time that he can get it without making personal contact.

"These four I consider fundamental and a necessary part of basketball. They persisted from 1891 to 1937. There has been a tendency of late to modify the last of these principles to develop a stronger offense, somewhat at the expense of the defense.

"It is rather interesting that 12 of the original 13 rules were, in 1937, still in the game. I am enclosing a copy of the first rules which were posted on the bulletin board in the gym at Springfield before the game was actually played."

Original Rules of Basketball

1. The ball may be thrown in any direction with one or both hands.
2. The ball may be batted in any direction with one or both hands (never with the fist).
3. A player cannot run with the ball. The player must throw it from the spot on which he catches it, allowance to be made for a man who catches the ball when running if he tries to stop.
4. The ball must be held by the hands; the arms or body must not be used for holding it.
5. No shouldering, holding, pushing, tripping, or striking in any way the person of an opponent shall be allowed; the first infringement of this rule by any player shall count as a foul, the second shall disqualify him until the next goal is made, or, if there was evident intent to injure the person, for the whole of the game, no substitute allowed.
6. A foul is striking at the ball with the fist, violation of Rules 3, 4 and such as described in Rule 5.
7. If either side makes three consecutive fouls it shall count a goal for the opponents (consecutive means without the opponents in the meantime making a foul).
8. A goal shall be made when the ball is thrown or batted *from the grounds* into the basket and stays there, provided those defending the goal do not touch or disturb the goal. If the ball rests on the edges, and the opponent moves the basket, it shall count as a goal.
9. When the ball goes out of bounds it shall be thrown into the field of play by the person first touching it. He has a right to hold it unmolested for five seconds. In case of a dispute the umpire shall throw it straight into the field. The thrower-in is allowed five seconds; if he holds it longer, it shall go to the opponent. If any side persists in delaying the game the umpire shall call a foul on that side.
10. The umpire shall be judge of the men and shall note the fouls and notify the referee when three consecutive fouls have been made. He shall have power to disqualify men according to Rule 5.
11. The referee shall be judge of the ball and shall decide when the ball is in play, in bounds, to which side it belongs, and shall keep the time. He shall decide when a goal has been made, and keep account of the goals, with any other duties that are usually performed by a referee.
12. The time shall be two fifteen-minute halves, with five minutes' rest between.
13. The side making the most goals in that time shall be declared the winner. In case of a draw the game may, by agreement of

the captains, be continued until another goal is made.

So rapid was the growth of basketball that gymnasiums in different parts of the country merely adopted the basic principles of the game, and never waited to get the detailed rules from Dr. Naismith. This eventually led to confusion in intersectional play, because colleges had one set of rules, high schools had others, and the same was true of Y.M.C.A. and A.A.U. branches throughout the country.

Professional Basketball

Professional basketball, on an organized basis, was launched in 1898. The group was called the National Basketball League, with teams in Philadelphia, New York City, Brooklyn and Southern New Jersey. The circuit lasted 2 seasons.

In 1898 the New England League was formed, with players being paid from $150 to $225 a month. This circuit had a brief career. It was followed by others in the early years of the sport, but they, too, were unable to survive.

In the 1920's the professional sport showed signs of coming to life, thanks to the activities of a team called the Original Celtics, which started as a semi-pro team in 1915. It dominated the American Basketball League, formed in 1925, and one season (1927–28) won 109 of 120 games. The team was ruled out of the circuit as "too strong" the following season. The Celtics gained a good deal of fame by making a number of tours that made their names bywords throughout the country.

The Celtics gained stature until they were playing over 150 games a season and winning 90 per cent of the time. They traveled a great deal and drew large crowds. At Cleveland in 1922 one of their games attracted 23,000 spectators. At first their home games were in New York's 71st Regiment Armory. Then they moved into the old Madison Square Garden and also appeared in the present Madison Square Garden until the team was disbanded in 1928.

The outstanding players on the Celtics included Joe Lapchick, Ernie Reich, Johnny Beckman, Pete Barry, Nat Holman, Chris Leonard, Dave Banks, George Haggerty, Dutch Dehnert, Elmer Ripley, Harry Brugge, Benny Borgman, "Stretch" Meehan, "Chief" Mueller and Jim Kane. Some became established college coaches after they retired from competition.

Holman, who gained recognition as one of the greats among the stars of that era, listed the following as among the best of the professionals:

Barney Sedran—Whirlwinds
Ed Wachter—Troy
Lou Wachter—Troy
Jack Inglis—Troy
Marty Friedman—Whirlwinds
Joe Brennan—Visitations
Joe Fogarty—Camden, N.J.
Blondy Hardman—Troy

The American League was a 9-city circuit when it was started in 1925. The professional season lasted six months and stars were paid $1,500 a month. Competition was suspended during the 1931–32 and 1932–33 seasons. It was resumed but the league never attained big-time prominence.

Professional basketball, on a large scale, did not take hold until well after World War II. The Basketball Association of America started league competition in 1946 and did not fare well at the beginning because it was competing with an older loop, the National Basketball League, which had been formed in 1937, for available playing talent.

In the summer of 1949 the two leagues merged and the way was cleared for the group, which operated under the name of the National Basketball Association, to concentrate on bringing the crowds into the arenas.

The first season found 17 cities in the circuit, which was divided into 3 divisions. The schedule called for more than 550 games.

There were too many weak teams in the loop and by the following season the league had been cut to 11 clubs in 2 divisions. Eight clubs functioned in 1957–58, by which time the league was operating on a sound basis.

Basketball was drawing so many sports fans that by 1970, the N.B.A. had accumulated 17 teams; 2 conferences, 4 divisions. The American Basketball Association came into existence during the 1967–68 season consisting of 11 teams, 2 divisions.

The A.B.A. brought back the 3-pt. field goal, taken from outside 25-ft. circle, from the old defunct A.B.L. hoping to add a new dimension to the game.

In 1972, Oscar Robertson became the second player in N.B.A. history to reach the 25,000-point mark; Wilt Chamberlain being the first player.

The Fabulous Harlem Globetrotters

(Courtesy of Wendell Smith, Sports Editor, *Pittsburgh Courier*, and a staff writer for the *Chicago Herald-American*.)

On a crisp January day in 1927, Abe Saperstein, a portly little man with big basketball ideas, took 5 players, a ramshackle flivver and a tattered road map and started one of the most amazing careers in the history of the sports world.

That was the unheralded and humble beginning of the Harlem Globetrotters. Since then they have grown to be one of the greatest sports aggregations.

They have toured millions of miles—from the barren wastes of Alaska to the tropical shores of·

Cuba; from Chicago and New York to such distant lands as Egypt, Japan, China, Hawaii, Spain, North Africa, England, France and Russia, as well as other more remote places.

Before the Globetrotters developed into an outstanding attraction and became international gypsies, they bounced around this country in jalopies that were as unique as their version of how basketball should be played.

In those early days they made annual visits to such out-of-the-way places as Roseberg, Ore.; Yakima, Wash., and Juneau, Alaska. No place was too small for this band of black cage magicians, no mode of transportation was too ancient. They have arrived at their destination via horse and wagon, dog sled and other comparatively crude means of transportation.

It has been a long, tedious journey along the road to basketball success for Saperstein and his spectacular, talented crew. All the highways from Bend, Ore., and Deer Lodge, Mont., to New York's famous Madison Square Garden and San Francisco's Cow Palace have not been smooth. At times their future was blurred by snow blizzards, driving rainstorms and even tornadoes.

But they always made it and now, by virtue of their perseverance and faith in the future, millions of people all over the world are flocking to see them perform. Now they travel by plane, train and boat. They put on their great show before capacity crowds in Chicago Stadium, Pasadena's spacious Rose Bowl, New York's Madison Square Garden, the Palais des Sports in Gay Paree, and other universally famous arenas. The name "Globetrotters" is, indeed, no misnomer.

Sensation attends them wherever they play. In 1952, for example, they shattered the all-time one-day American attendance mark for basketball when 35,548 fans saw them play the College All-Americans at Madison Square Garden in afternoon and night games. Then in 1953 they played before 36,256 fans in Memorial Coliseum, Los Angeles.

The Globetrotters played 176 games during their 1951–52 "regular" season. As soon as they had completed their United States schedule, they took off for Brazil, where they started the longest and greatest cage safari of all time.

They played in the following countries before returning to the United States: Brazil, Uruguay, Paraguay, Argentina, Chile, Peru, Ecuador, Colombia, Venezuela, England, France, Belgium, Holland, Germany, Switzerland, Spain, Portugal, North Africa, Italy, Greece, Turkey, Lebanon, Egypt, Thailand, Japan, China, Hawaii and the Philippines.

The reason the Globetrotters are such a magnetic attraction is probably because they refuse to take themselves seriously. They create the impression that they play the game with one purpose in mind—to entertain the fan. They combine basketball brilliance with a bagful of tricks and tomfoolery. One minute the fans are applauding them for their amazing shooting and whirlwind passing, the next for their side-splitting antics and superb ball handling.

A star of their hardwood extravaganza was Reece (Goose) Tatum, called "The Clown Prince of Basketball." He is a lanky, slow-motion type of player, whose extraordinary arms extend down to his knees. His arm span is 84 inches—widest and longest of any modern athlete. A native of Eldorado, Ark., he was 6 feet 3 inches tall, weighed 190 pounds and averaged 25 points per game. Tatum now had his own touring team, called the Harlem Magicians.

Another outstanding performer was Marques Haynes, a spectacular dribbler. Haynes hails from Sand Springs, Okla. He is a graduate of Langston University in Langston, Okla.

Other key men have included: Ermer Robinson, a one-hand push shot expert from San Diego, Calif.; Clarence Wilson, set-shot wizard who lives in Horse Cave, Ky., and came to the team from Tennessee State College in Nashville; Joshua Grider, also a Tennessee State alumnus and a native of Kansas City, Mo.; William (Rookie) Brown, the star of the movie "Harlem Globetrotters" and a native of Asbury Park, N.J.; and Sam Wheeler of St. Louis, Mo., who first attracted attention while playing for Philander Smith College in Little Rock, Ark. Walter Dukes, Seton Hall College All-American, and Wilt Chamberlain, the fabulous 7-footer who was two-time All-American at Kansas University.

Champions

AMATEUR

(Source: Official National Collegiate Athletic Association Basketball Guide. Reprinted with permission.)

National Collegiate

(Coaches in parentheses)

1939—Oregon (Howard Hobson)
1940—Indiana (Branch McCracken)
1941—Wisconsin (Harold Foster)
1942—Stanford (Everett Dean)
1943—Wyoming (Everett Shelton)
1944—Utah (Vadal Peterson)
1945—Oklahoma A. & M. (Henry Iba)
1946—Oklahoma A. & M. (Henry Iba)
1947—Holy Cross (Alvin Julian)
1948—Kentucky (Adolph Rupp)
1949—Kentucky (Adolph Rupp)
1950—City College of New York (Nat Holman)
1951—Kentucky (Adolph Rupp)
1952—Kansas (Forrest C. Allen)
1953—Indiana (Branch McCracken)
1954—LaSalle (Kenneth Loeffler)

1955—San Francisco (Phil Woolpert)
1956—San Francisco (Phil Woolpert)
1957—North Carolina (Frank J. McGuire)
1958—Kentucky (Adolph Rupp)
1959—California (Pete Newell)
1960—Ohio State (Fred R. Taylor)
1961-62—Cincinnati (Edward Jucker)
1963—Loyola (Ill.) George M. Ireland)
1964—UCLA (John R. Wooden)
1965—UCLA (John R. Wooden)
1966—Texas Western (Don Haskins)
1967—UCLA (John R. Wooden)
1968—UCLA (John R. Wooden)
1969—UCLA (John R. Wooden)
1970—UCLA (John R. Wooden)
1971—UCLA (John R. Wooden)
1972—UCLA (John R. Wooden)
1973—UCLA (John R. Wooden)

National Invitation
(At Madison Square Garden, New York.)

1938—Temple (Jim Usilton)
1939—Long Island University (Clair Bee)
1940—Colorado (Cox)
1941—Long Island University (Clair Bee)
1942—West Virginia (Raese)
1943—St. John's (Joe Lapchick)
1944—St. John's (Joe Lapchick)
1945—DePaul (Raymond Meyer)
1946—Kentucky (Adolph Rupp)
1947—Utah (Vadal Peterson)
1948—St. Louis (Edward Hickey)
1949—San Francisco (Peter Newell)
1950—City College of New York (Nat Holman)
1951—Brigham Young (Stanley Watts)
1952—La Salle (Kenneth Loeffler)
1953—Seton Hall (John Russell)
1954—Holy Cross (Lester Sheary)
1955—Duquesne (Donald Moore)
1956—Louisville (Bernard Hickman)
1957—Bradley (Chuck Orsborn)
1958—Xavier (James McCafferty)
1959—St. John's
1960—Bradley
1961—Providence
1962—Dayton
1963—Providence
1964—Bradley
1965—St. John's
1966—Brigham Young
1967—Southern Illinois
1968—Dayton
1969—Temple
1970—Marquette
1971—North Carolina
1972—Maryland
1973—Virginia Tech

National Assn. of Intercollegiate Athletics
(Formerly N.A.I.B.)

1938—Missouri State (Warrensburg)
1939—Southwestern (Kansas)

1940—Tarkio (Mo.)
1941—San Diego State
1942—Hamline
1943—Missouri State (Cape Girardeau)
1944—No competition
1945—Loyola (New Orleans)
1946—Southern Illinois
1947—Marshall
1948—Louisville
1949—Hamline
1950—Indiana State
1951—Hamline
1952-53—Missouri State (Springfield)
1954—St. Benedict's
1955—East Texas State
1956—McNeese State
1957-59—Tennessee A & I
1960—Lenoir Rhyne
1961—Grambling
1962—Prairie View A & M
1963—Pan American
1964—Rockhurst (Kansas City)
1965—Central State (Ohio)
1966—Oklahoma Baptist
1967—St. Benedict's College (Kansas)
1968—Central State (Ohio)
1969—Eastern New Mexico
1970-72—Kentucky State
1973—Guilford

NATIONAL COLLEGIATE—
  College Division

1957—Wheaton
1958—South Dakota
1959-60—Evansville
1961—Wittenberg
1962—Mt. St. Mary's
1963—South Dakota State
1964-65—Evansville
1966—Kentucky Wesleyan
1967—Winston-Salem State
1968-69—Kentucky Wesleyan
1970—Philadelphia Textile
1971—Evansville
1972—Roanoke
1973—Kentucky Wesleyan

Eastern League (Ivy)

Team

Year	W.	L.	Pct.
1902—Yale	5	3	.675
1903—Yale	7	3	.700
1904—Columbia	10	0	1.000
1905—Columbia	8	0	1.000
1906—Pennsylvania	9	1	.900
1907—Yale	9	1	.900
1908—Pennsylvania	8	0	1.000
1909—10—No competition			
1911—Columbia	7	1	.875
1912—Columbia	8	2	.800
1913—Cornell	7	1	.875

1914—Cornell—Columbia .	8	2	.800
1915—Yale	8	2	.800
1916—Pennsylvania*	9	2	.818
1917—Yale	9	1	.900
1918—Pennsylvania	9	1	.900
1919—No competition			
1920—Pennsylvania	10	0	1.000
1921—Pennsylvania	9	1	.900
1922—Princeton*	9	2	.818
1923—Yale	7	3	.700
1924—Cornell	8	2	.800
1925—Princeton	9	1	.900
1926—Columbia	9	1	.900
1927—Dartmouth*	8	3	.727
1928—Pennsylvania*	8	3	.727
1929—Pennsylvania	8	2	.800
1930—Columbia	9	1	.900
1931—Columbia	10	0	1.000
1932—Princeton*	9	2	.818
1933—Yale	8	2	.800
1934—Pennsylvania	10	2	.833
1935—Pennsylvania*	11	2	.846
1936—Columbia	12	0	1.000
1937—Pennsylvania	12	0	1.000
1938—Dartmouth	8	4	.667
1939—Dartmouth	10	2	.883
1940—Dartmouth	11	1	.917
1941—Dartmouth	10	2	.833
1942—Dartmouth*	11	2	.844
1943—Dartmouth	11	1	.917
1944—Dartmouth	8	0	1.000
1945—Pennsylvania	5	1	.833
1946—Dartmouth	7	1	.875
1947—Columbia	11	1	.917
1948—Columbia	11	1	.917
1949—Yale	9	3	.750
1950—Princeton	11	1	.917
1951—Columbia	12	0	1.000
1952—Princeton	10	2	.833
1953—Pennsylvania	10	2	.833
1954—Cornell*	12	3	.800
1955—Princeton*	11	4	.733
1956—Dartmouth	10	4	.714
1957—Yale	12	2	.857

1958-59—Dartmouth
1960-61—Princeton
1962—Columbia, Harvard (tie)
1963-65—Princeton
1966—Pennsylvania
1967—Princeton
1968—Columbia*
1969—Princeton
1970-72—Pennsylvania
*Won playoff.

Big Ten

Team

Year	W.	L.	Pct.
1906—Minnesota	7	1	.875
1907—Chi., Wis., Minn. ..	6	2	.750
1908—Chicago	8	1	.888
1909—Chicago	12	0	1.000
1910—Chicago	9	3	.750
1911—Purdue, Minn.	8	4	.667
1912—Wis., Purdue	12	0	1.000
1913—Wisconsin	12	0	1.000
1914—Wisconsin	12	0	1.000
1915—Illinois	12	0	1.000
1916—Wisconsin	11	0	1.000
1917—Illinois, Minnesota .	10	2	.833
1918—Wisconsin	9	3	.750
1919—Minnesota	10	2	.833
1920—Chicago	11	2	.846
1921—Mich., Wis., Purdue	8	4	.667
1922—Purdue	8	1	.888
1923—Iowa, Wisconsin ...	11	1	.917
1924—Wisc., Ill., Chicago .	8	4	.667
1925—Ohio State	11	1	.917
1926—Ind., Iowa, Mich. Pur.	8	4	.667
1927—Michigan	10	2	.833
1928—Indiana, Purdue ...	10	2	.833
1929—Michigan, Wisconsin	10	2	.833
1930—Purdue	10	0	1.000
1931—Northwestern	11	1	.917
1932—Purdue	11	1	.917
1933—Ohio St., Northw. .	10	2	.833
1934—Purdue	10	2	.833
1935—Ill., Wis., Purdue ..	9	3	.750
1936—Indiana, Purdue ...	11	1	.917
1937—Illinois, Minnesota .	10	2	.833
1938—Purdue	10	2	.833
1939—Ohio State	10	2	.833
1940—Purdue	10	2	.833
1941—Wisconsin	11	1	.017
1942—Illinois	13	2	.867
1943—Illinois	12	0	1.000
1944—Ohio State	10	2	.833
1945—Iowa	11	1	.917
1946—Ohio State	10	2	.833
1947—Wisconsin	9	3	.750
1948—Michigan	10	2	.833
1949—Illinois	10	2	.833
1950—Ohio State	11	1	.917
1951—Illinois	13	1	.929
1952—Illinois	12	2	.857
1953—Indiana	17	1	.944
1954—Indiana	12	2	.857
1955—Iowa	11	3	.786
1956—Iowa	13	1	.929
1957—Indiana, Michigan St.	10	4	.714
1958—Indiana	10	4	.714

1959—Michigan State
1960-62—Ohio State
1963—Illinois, Ohio State (tie)
1964—Michigan, Ohio State (tie)
1965-66—Michigan
1967—Indiana, Michigan State (tie)
1968—Ohio State*
1969—Purdue
1970—Iowa
1971—Ohio State
1972—Minnesota
1973—Indiana
*Won playoff.

Southeastern

Team

(Tournament determined champion through 1950, standings thereafter.)

Year and champion	Runner-up
1933—Kentucky	Mississippi State
1934—Alabama	Florida
1935—Louisiana State*	Kentucky
1936—Tennessee	Alabama
1937—Kentucky	Tennessee
1938—Georgia Tech	Mississippi
1939—Kentucky	Tennessee
1940—Kentucky	Georgia
1941—Tennessee	Kentucky
1942—Kentucky	Alabama
1943—Tennessee	Kentucky
1944—Kentucky	Tulane
1945—Kentucky	Tennessee
1946—Kentucky	Louisiana State
1947—Kentucky	Tulane
1948—Kentucky	Georgia Tech
1949—Kentucky	Tulane
1950—Kentucky	Tennessee
1951—Kentucky	
1952—Kentucky	
1953—L.S.U.	
1954—Kentucky	
1955—Kentucky	
1956—Alabama	
1957—Kentucky	
1958—Kentucky	
1959—Mississippi State	
1960—Auburn	
1961—Mississippi State	
1962—Mississippi State, Kentucky (tie)	
1963—Mississippi State	
1964—Kentucky	
1965—Vanderbilt	
1966—Kentucky	
1967—Tennessee	
1968-71—Kentucky	
1972—Kentucky, Tennessee (tie)	
1973—Kentucky	

*No tournament held. LSU claimed title on 12-0 record to Kentucky's 11-0.

Big Eight (formerly Big Seven)

Team

Year	W.	L.	Pct.
1929—Oklahoma	10	0	1.000
1930—Missouri	8	2	.800
1931—Kansas	7	3	.700
1932—Kansas	7	3	.700
1933—Kansas	8	2	.800
1934—Kansas	9	1	.900
1935—Iowa State	8	2	.800
1936—Kansas	10	0	1.000
1937—Kansas, Nebraska	8	2	.800
1938—Kansas	9	1	.900
1939—Missouri, Oklahoma	7	3	.700
1940—Kans., Okla., Mo.	8	2	.800
1941—Kansas, Iowa State	7	3	.700
1942—Kansas, Oklahoma	8	2	.800
1943—Kansas	10	0	1.000
1944—Iowa State, Oklahoma	9	1	.900
1945—Iowa State	8	2	.800
1946—Kansas	10	0	1.000
1947—Oklahoma	8	2	.800
1948—Kansas State	9	3	.750
1949—Oklahoma, Nebraska	9	3	.750
1950—Kans.,Nebr.,Kans. St.	8	4	.667
1951—Kansas State	11	1	.917
1952—Kansas	11	1	.917
1953—Kansas	10	2	.833
1954—Kansas, Colorado	10	2	.833
1955—Colorado	11	1	.917
1956—Kansas State	9	3	.750
1957—Kansas	11	1	.917
1958—Kansas State	10	2	.833
1959—Kansas State			
1960—Kansas State, Kansas (tie)			
1961—Kansas State			
1962—Colorado			
1963—Kansas State, Colorado (tie)			
1964—Kansas State			
1965—Oklahoma State			
1966-67—Kansas			
1968—Kansas State			
1969—Colorado			
1970—Kansas State			
1971—Kansas			
1972-73—Kansas State			

Missouri Valley

Team

Year	W.	L.	Pct.
1908—Kansas	7	2	.778
1909—Kansas	10	2	.833
1910—Kansas	13	1	.929
1911—Kansas	10	2	.833
1912—Kansas, Nebraska	10	2	.833
1913—Nebraska	10	5	.667
1914—Kansas	13	1	.929
1915—Kansas	13	1	.929
1916—Nebraska	8	0	1.000
1917—Kansas State	10	2	.833
1918—Missouri	15	1	.937
1919—Kansas State	10	0	1.000
1920—Missouri	17	1	.944
1921—Missouri	17	1	.944
1922—Missouri, Kansas	15	1	.937
1923—Kansas	16	0	1.000
1924—Kansas	15	1	.937
1925—Kansas	15	1	.937
1926—Kansas	16	2	.889
1927—Kansas	10	2	.833
1928—Oklahoma	18	0	1.000
1929—Washington	7	0	1.000
1930—Wash., Creighton	6	2	.750
1931—Creigh., Wash., Okla. A.&M.	5	3	.600
1932—Creighton	8	0	1.000

Year	W.	L.	Pct.
1933–Butler	9	1	.900
1934–Butler	9	1	.900
1935–Drake, Creighton	8	4	.667
1936–Drake, Okla. A.&M., Creighton	8	4	.667
1937–Oklahoma A.&M.	11	1	.917
1938–Oklahoma A.&M.	13	1	.929
1939–Okla. A.&M., Drake	11	3	.786
1940–Oklahoma A.&M.	12	0	1.000
1941–Creighton	9	3	.750
1942–Creigh.,Okla. A&M	9	1	.900
1943–Creighton	10	0	1.000
1944–Oklahoma A.&M.*	–	–	–
1945–Oklahoma A.&M.*	–	–	–
1946–Oklahoma A.&M.	12	0	1.000
1947–St. Louis	11	1	.917
1948–Oklahoma A.&M.	10	0	1.000
1949–Oklahoma A.&M.	9	1	.900
1950–Bradley	11	1	.917
1951–Oklahoma A.&M.	12	2	.857
1952–St. Louis	9	1	.900
1953–Oklahoma A.&M.	8	2	.800
1954–Oklahoma A.&M.	9	1	.900
1955–Tulsa, St. Louis	8	2	.800
1956–Houston	9	3	.750
1957–St. Louis	12	2	.857
1958–Cincinnati	13	1	.929
1959-61–Cincinnati			
1962–Cincinnati, Bradley (tie)			
1963–Cincinnati			
1964–Drake, Wichita State (tie)			
1965–Wichita State			
1966–Cincinnati			
1967-68–Louisville			
1969–Drake, Louisville (tie)			
1970–Drake			
1971–Drake, Louisville, St. Louis (tied)			
1972–Louisville			
1973–Memphis State			

*No Conference competition held, but Oklahoma A.&M. was voted title.

Southwest

Team Year	W.	L.	Pct.
1915–Texas	5	0	1.000
1916–Texas	6	0	1.000
1917–Texas	7	1	.875
1918–Rice	7	3	.700
1919–Texas	11	2	.846
1920–Texas A.&M.	16	0	1.000
1921–Texas A.&M.	10	2	.833
1922–Texas A.&M.	13	3	.812
1923–Texas A.&M.	15	3	.833
1924–Texas	20	0	1.000
1925–Oklahoma A.&M.	12	2	.857
1926–Arkansas	11	1	.917
1927–Arkansas	8	2	.800
1928–Arkansas	12	0	1.000
1929–Arkansas	11	1	.917
1930–Arkansas	10	2	.833
1931–Texas Christian	9	3	.750
1932–Baylor	10	2	.833
1933–Texas	11	1	.917
1934–Texas Christian	10	2	.833
1935–S.M.U., Rice, Ark.	9	3	.750
1936–Arkansas	11	1	.917
1937–Southern Methodist	10	2	.833
1938–Arkansas	11	1	.917
1939–Texas	10	2	.833
1940–Rice	10	2	.833
1941–Arkansas	12	0	1.000
1942–Rice, Arkansas	10	2	.833
1943–Texas, Rice	9	3	.750
1944–Arkansas, Rice	11	1	.917
1945–Rice	12	0	1.000
1946–Baylor	11	1	.917
1947–Texas	12	0	1.000
1948–Baylor	11	1	.917
1949–Rice, Baylor, Ark.	9	3	.750
1950–Arkansas, Baylor	8	4	.667
1951–Texas A.&M., Texas, T.C.U.	8	4	.667
1952–Texas Christian	11	1	.917
1953–Texas Christian	9	3	.750
1954–Rice, Texas	9	3	.750
1955–Southern Methodist	9	3	.750
1956–Southern Methodist	12	0	1.000
1957–Southern Methodist	11	1	.917
1958–Ark., So. Methodist	9	5	.643
1959–Texas Christian			
1960–Texas			
1961–Texas Tech			
1962–Texas Tech, Southern Methodist (tie)			
1963–Texas			
1964–Texas A & M			
1965–Southern Methodist, Texas (tie)			
1966-67–Southern Methodist			
1968–Texas Christian U.			
1969–Texas A & M			
1970–Rice			
1971–Texas Christian			
1972–Southern Methodist, Texas (tie)			

Pacific Coast (Pacific-8)

Team Year	W.	L.	Pct.
1916–California, Oreg. St.	5	3	.625
1917–Washington State	8	1	.889
1918–No competition			
1919–Oregon	10	4	.714
1920–Stanford	9	1	.900
1921–California, Stanford	8	3	.727
1922–Idaho	7	0	1.000
1923–Idaho	8	3	.727
1924–California	7	3	.700
1925–California	5	2	.734
1926–California	7	0	1.000
1927–California	7	0	1.000
1928–S. California	8	3	.727
1929–California	11	0	1.000

1930—So. California	9	3	.750
1931—Washington	16	3	.842
1932—California	11	3	.786
1933—Oregon State	14	5	.737
1934—Washington	16	3	.842
1935—So. California	13	2	.867
1936—Stanford	11	4	.733
1937—Stanford	12	2	.857
1938—Stanford	12	2	.857
1939—Oregon	16	2	.889
1940—So. California	12	2	.857
1941—Washington State	15	3	.833
1942—Stanford	13	2	.867
1943—Washington	14	4	.777
1944—California*	4	0	1.000
Washington*	15	1	.937
1945—Oregon*	13	6	.684
U.C.L.A.*	4	2	.667
1946—California	13	2	.867
1947—Oregon State	15	3	.833
1948—Washington	13	7	.650
1949—Oregon State	14	5	.737
1950—U.C.L.A.	12	2	.857
1951—Washington	13	5	.722
1952—U.C.L.A.	10	4	.714
1953—Washington	17	1	.944
1954—So. California	10	5	.667
1955—Oregon State	17	1	.944
1956—U.C.L.A.	16	0	1.000

1957-60—California
1961—Southern California
1962-65—U.C.L.A.
1966—Oregon State
1967-1973—U.C.L.A.
   *No inter-division playoff held, division winners named co-champions.

National A.A.U.

(Source: Amateur Athletic Union Official Basketball Guide.)

Men

1897—23d Street Y.M.C.A., New York
1898—No competition
1899—1900—Knickerbocker A.C., New York
1901—Ravenswood Y.M.C.A., Chicago
1902—03—No competition
1904—Buffalo (Germans) Y.M.C.A., Buffalo, N.Y.
1905—09—No competition
1910—Company F, Portage (Wis.) N.G.
1911—12—No competition
1913—14—Cornell (Armour Playground), Chicago
1915—Olympic Club, San Francisco
1916—University of Utah, Salt Lake City
1917—Illinois A.C., Chicago
1918—No competition
1919—Los Angeles A.C.
1920—New York University
1921—Kansas City A.C.
1922—Lowe and Campbell, Kansas City, Mo.
1923—Kansas City A.C.

1924—Butler University, Indianapolis
1925—Washburn College, Topeka, Kan.
1926—27—Hillyards, St. Joseph, Mo.
1928—29—Cook Paint Co., Kansas City, Mo.
1930—32—Henry Clothiers, Wichita, Kan.
1933—34—Diamond DX Oilers, Tulsa, Okla.
1935—Southern Kansas Stage Lines, Kansas City
1936—Globe Refiners, McPherson, Kan.
1937—Denver Safeways
1938—Healey Motors, Kansas City
1939—Denver Nuggets
1940—Phillips Oilers, Bartlesville, Okla.
1941—Twentieth Century-Fox, Hollywood, Calif.
1942—Denver American Legion
1943—48—Phillips Oilers
1949—Oakland (Calif.) Bittners
1950—Phillips Oilers
1951—Stewart Chevrolets, San Francisco
1952—53—Caterpillar Diesels, Peoria, Ill.
1954—Peoria Cats, Peoria, Ill.
1955—Phillips Oilers
1956—Buchan Bakers, Seattle, Wash.
1957—U.S. Air Force
1958—Peoria (Ill.) Cats
1959—Wichita Vickers
1960—Peoria (Ill.) Cats
1961—Cleveland Pipers
1962-63—Phillips 66ers
1964—Akron Goodyears
1965—Armed Forces All Stars
1966—Ford Mustangs
1967—Akron Goodyears
1968-72—Armed Forces All Stars

Women

1926—Pasadena (Calif.) A. and C.C.
1927—28—No competition
1929—Schepps Aces, Dallas, Tex.
1930—Sunoco Oilers, Dallas, Tex.
1931—Golden Cyclones, Dallas, Tex.
1932-33—Durant (Okla.) Cardinals
1934—36—Tulsa Business College
1937—Little Rock (Ark.) Flyers
1938—39—Galveston (Tex.) Anicos
1940—41—Lewis-Norwood Flyers, Little Rock, Ark.
1942—43—A.I.C., Davenport, Iowa
1944—45—Vultee Aircraft, Nashville, Tenn.
1946—Nashville (Tenn.) Goldblumes
1947—Atlanta (Ga.) Sports Arenas
1948-49—Nashville Goldblumes
1950—Nashville Business College
1951-53—Hanes Hosiery, Winston-Salem, N.C.
1954-57—Wayland Flying Queens, Plainview, Tex.
1958—Nashville Business College
1959—Wayland College
1960—Nashville Business College
1961—Wayland College
1962-69—Nashville Business College

1970-71—Hutcherson Flying Queens,
Plainview, Tex.
1972—J.F. Kennedy College, Nebraska

PROFESSIONAL

(Source: National Basketball Association.)

N.B.A. Championship Finals

1950—Minneapolis beat Syracuse, 4 games to 2
1951—Rochester beat New York, 4 games to 3
1952—Minneapolis beat New York, 4 games to 3
1953—Minneapolis beat New York, 4 games to 1
1954—Minneapolis beat Syracuse, 4 games to 3
1955—Syracuse beat Fort Wayne, 4 games to 3
1956—Philadelphia beat Fort Wayne, 4 games
    to 1
1957—Boston beat St. Louis, 4 games to 3
1958—St. Louis beat Boston, 4 games to 2
1959—Boston beat Minneapolis, 4 games to 0
1960—Boston beat St. Louis, 4 games to 3
1961—Boston beat St. Louis, 4 games to 1
1962—Boston beat Los Angeles, 4 games to 3
1963—Boston beat Los Angeles, 4 games to 2
1964—Boston beat San Francisco, 4 games to 1
1965—Boston beat Los Angeles, 4 games to 1
1966—Boston beat Los Angeles, 4 games to 3
1967—Philadelphia beat San Francisco, 4 games
    to 2
1968—Boston beat Los Angeles, 4 games to 2
1969—Boston beat Los Angeles, 4 games to 3
1970—New York beat Los Angeles, 4 games to 3
1971—Milwaukee beat Baltimore, 4 games to 0
1972—Los Angeles beat New York, 4 games to 1
1973—New York beat Los Angeles, 4 games to 3

N.B.A. All-Star Game

1951—East 111, West 94, at Boston
1952—East 108, West 91, at Boston
1953—West 79, East 75, at Fort Wayne
1954—East 98, West 93, at New York
1955—East 100, West 91, at New York
1956—West 108, East 94, at Rochester
1957—East 109, West 97, at Boston
1958—East 130, West 118, at St. Louis
1959—West 124, East 108, at Detroit
1960—East 125, West 115, at Philadelphia
1961—West 53, East 131, at Syracuse
1962—West 150, East 130, at St. Louis
1963—East 115, West 108, at Los Angeles
1964—East 111, West 107, at Boston
1965—East 124, West 123, at St. Louis
1966—East 137, West 94, at Cincinnati
1967—West 135, East 120, at San Francisco
1968—East 144, West 124, at New York
1969—East 123, West 112, at Baltimore
1970—East 142, West 135, at Philadelphia
1971—West 108, East 107, at San Diego
1972—West 112, East 110, at Los Angeles
1973—East 104, West 84, at Chicago

N.B.A. Individual Scoring Leaders

1949-50

	Games	Goals	Fouls	Pts.
George Mikan, Minneapolis	68	649	567	1,865
Alex Groza, Indianapolis	64	521	454	1,496
Frank Brian, Indianapolis	64	368	402	1,138
Max Zaslofsky, Chicago	68	397	321	1,115
Ed Macauley, St. Louis	67	351	379	1,081

1950-51

George Mikan, Minneapolis	68	678	576	1,932
Alex Groza, Indianapolis	66	492	445	1,429
Ed Macauley, Boston	68	459	466	1,384
Joe Fulks, Philadelphia	66	429	378	1,236
Frank Brian, Tri-Cities	68	363	418	1,114

1951-52

Paul Arizin, Philadelphia	66	548	578	1,674
George Mikan, Minneapolis	64	545	433	1,523
Bob Cousy, Boston	66	512	409	1,433
Ed Macauley, Boston	66	384	496	1,264
Bob Davies, Rochester	65	379	294	1,052

1952-53

Neil Johnston, Philadelphia	70	504	556	1,564
George Mikan, Minneapolis	70	500	442	1,442
Bob Cousy, Boston	71	464	479	1,407
Ed Macauley, Boston	69	451	500	1,402
Adolph Schayes, Syracuse	71	375	512	1,262

1953-54

Neil Johnston, Philadelphia	72	591	577	1,759
Bob Cousy, Boston	72	486	411	1,383
Ed Macauley, Boston	71	462	420	1,344
George Mikan, Minneapolis	72	441	424	1,306
Ray Felix, Baltimore	72	410	449	1,269

1954-55

Neil Johnston, Philadelphia	72	521	589	1,631
Paul Arizin, Philadelphia	72	529	454	1,512
Bob Cousy, Boston	71	522	460	1,504
Bob Pettit, Milwaukee	72	520	426	1,466
Frank Selvy, Milwaukee	71	452	444	1,348

1955-56

Bob Pettit, St. Louis	72	646	557	1,849
Paul Arizin, Philadelphia	72	617	507	1,741
Neil Johnston, Philadelphia	70	499	549	1,547
Clyde Lovelette, Minneapolis	71	594	338	1,526
Adolph Schayes, Syracuse	72	465	542	1,472

1956-57

Paul Arizin, Philadelphia	71	613	591	1,817
Bob Pettit, St. Louis	71	613	529	1,755
Adolph Schayes, Syracuse	72	496	625	1,617
Neil Johnston, Philadelphia	69	520	535	1,575
George Yardley, Ft. Wayne	72	522	503	1,547

1957-58

George Yardley, Detroit ..	72	673 655	2,001
Adolph Schayes, Syracuse	72	581 629	1,791
Bob Pettit, St. Louis	70	581 557	1,719
Clyde Lovellette, Cincinnati	71	679 301	1,659
Paul Arizin, Philadelphia .	68	483 440	1,406

1958-59

Bob Pettit, St. Louis	72	719 667	2,105
Jack Twyman, Cincinnati .	72	710 437	1,857
Paul Arizin, Philadelphia .	70	632 587	1,851
Elgin Baylor, Minneapolis .	70	605 532	1,742
Cliff Hagan, St. Louis	72	646 415	1,707

1959-60

Wilt Chamberlain, Philadelphia	72	1,065 577	2,707
Jack Twyman, Cincinnati .	75	870 598	2,388
Elgin Baylor, Minneapolis .	70	755 564	2,074
Bob Pettit, St. Louis	72	669 544	1,882
Cliff Hagan, St. Louis	75	719 421	1,859

1960-61

Wilt Chamberlain, Philadelphia	79	1,251 531	3,033
Elgin Baylor, Los Angeles .	73	931 676	2,538
Oscar Robertson, Cincinnati	71	756 653	2,165
Bob Pettit, St. Louis	76	769 582	2,120
Jack Twyman, Cincinnati .	79	796 405	1,997

1961-62

Wilt Chamberlain, Philadelphia	80	1,597 835	4,029
Walt Bellamy, Chicago ...	79	973 549	2,495
Oscar Robertson, Cincinnati	79	866 700	2,432
Bob Pettit, St. Louis	78	867 695	2,429
Jerry West, Los Angeles ..	75	799 712	2,310

1962-63

Wilt Chamberlain, Philadelphia	80	1,463 660	3,586
Elgin Baylor, Los Angeles	80	1,029 661	2,719
Oscar Robertson, Cincinnati	80	825 614	2,264
Bob Pettit, St. Louis	79	778 685	2,241
Walt Bellamy, Chicago ...	80	840 553	2,233

1963-64

Wilt Chamberlain, San Francisco	80	1,204 540	2,948
Oscar Robertson, Cincinnati	79	840 800	2,480
Bob Pettit, St. Louis	80	791 608	2,190
Walt Bellamy, Baltimore ..	80	811 537	2,159
Jerry West, Los Angeles ..	72	740 584	2,064

1964-65

Wilt Chamberlain, Philadelphia	80	1,063 408	2,534
Jerry West, Los Angeles ..	80	822 648	2,292
Oscar Robertson, Cincinnati	80	807 665	2,279
Sam Jones, Boston	80	821 428	2,070
Elgin Baylor, Los Angeles .	80	763 483	2,009

1965-66

	Games	Goals	Fouls	Pts.
Wilt Chamberlain, Philadelphia	79	1,078	501	2,649
Jerry West, Los Angeles ..	79	818	840	2,476
Oscar Robertson, Cincinnati	76	818	742	2,378
Rick Barry, San Francisco	80	818	569	2,059
Walt Bellamy, New York .	80	695	430	1,820

1966-67

Rick Barry, San Francisco	78	1,011	753	2,775
Oscar Robertson, Cincinnati	79	838	736	2,412
Wilt Chamberlain, Philadelphia	81	785	386	1,956
Jerry West, Los Angeles ..	66	645	602	1,892
Elgin Baylor, Los Angeles .	70	711	440	1,862

1967-68

Dave Bing, Detroit	79	835	472	2,142
Elgin Baylor, Los Angeles .	77	757	488	2,002
Wilt Chamberlain, Philadelphia	82	819	354	1,992
Earl Monroe, Baltimore ..	82	742	507	1,991
Hal Greer, Philadelphia ...	82	777	422	1,976

1968-69

Elvin Hayes, San Diego ...	82	930	467	2,327
Earl Monroe, Baltimore...	80	809	447	2,065
Bill Cunningham, Philadelphia	82	739	556	2,034
Bob Rule, Seattle	82	776	413	1,965
Oscar Robertson, Cincinnati	79	656	643	1,955

1969-70

Jerry West, Los Angeles ..	74	831	647	2,309
Lew Alcindor, Milwaukee .	82	938	485	2,361
Elvin Hayes, San Diego ...	82	914	428	2,256
Bill Cunningham, Philadelphia	81	802	510	2,114
Lou Hudson, Atlanta	80	830	371	2,031

1970-71

Lew Alcindor, Milwaukee .	82	1,063	470	2,596
John Havlicek, Boston ...	81	892	554	2,338
Elvin Hayes, San Diego ...	82	948	454	2,350
Dave Bing, Detroit	82	799	615	2,213
Lou Hudson, Atlanta	76	829	381	2,039

1971-72

Kareem Abdul-Jabbar (L. Alcindor), Milwaukee	81	1,159	504	2,822
Nate Archibald, Cincinnati	76	734	677	2,145
John Havlicek, Boston ...	82	897	458	2,252
Spencer Haywood, Seattle	73	717	480	1,914
Gail Goodrich, Los Angeles	82	826	475	2,127

1972-73

Nate Archibald, Kansas City-Omaha	80	1,028	663	2,719
Kareem Abdul-Jabbar, Milwaukee	76	982	328	2,292

Spencer Haywood, Seattle 77 889 473 2,251
Lou Hudson, Atlanta 75 816 397 2,029
Pete Maravich, Atlanta ... 79 789 485 2,063

A.B.A. Championship Finals

1968—Pittsburgh beat New Orleans, 4 games to 3
1969—Oakland beat Indiana, 4 games to 1
1970—Indiana beat Los Angeles, 4 games to 2
1971—Utah beat Kentucky, 4 games to 3
1972—Indiana beat New York, 4 games to 2
1973—Indiana beat Kentucky, 4 games to 3

A.B.A. All-Star Game

1968—East 126, West 120, at Indianapolis
1969—West 133, East 127, at Louisville, Ky.
1970—West 128, East 98, at Indianapolis
1971—East 126, West 122, at Greensboro, N.C.
1972—East 142, West 115, at Louisville, Ky.
1973—West 123, East 111, at Salt Lake City

N.B.A.-A.B.A. All-Star Game

1971—N.B.A. 125, A.B.A. 120
1972—N.B.A. 106, A.B.A. 104

A.B.A. Individual Scoring Leaders

1967-68

	Games	Goals*	Fouls	Pts.
Connie Hawkins, Pittsburgh	70	635	603	1,875
Doug Moe, New Orleans ..	78	665	551	1,884
Lavern Tart, Oakland-New Jersey	73	633	451	1,714
Darel Carrier, Kentucky ..	77	643	395	1,765
Larry Jones, Denver	76	602	530	1,742

1968-69

Rick Barry, Oakland	35	389	403	1,190
Connie Hawkins, Minnesota	47	493	425	1,420
Larry Jones, Denver	75	735	591	2,133
James Jones, New Orleans	77	763	521	2,050
Louie Dampier, Kentucky	78	514	308	1,933

1969-70

Spencer Haywood, Denver	84	986	547	2,519
Rick Barry, Washington ..	52	509	400	1,442
Bob Verga, Carolina	82	801	458	2,258
Don Freeman, Miami	79	761	626	2,163
Louie Dampier, Kentucky	82	545	447	2,125

1970-71

Dan Issel, Kentucky	83	938	604	2,480
Rick Barry, New York ...	59	613	451	1,734
John Brisker, Pittsburgh ..	79	809	430	2,315
Mack Calvin, Floridians ..	81	727	696	2,201
Charlie Scott, Virginia ...	84	886	456	2,276

1971-72

Charlie Scott, Virginia ...	73	956	525	2,524
Rick Barry, New York ...	80	829	641	2,518
Dan Issel, Kentucky	83	969	591	2,538
John Brisker, Pittsburgh ..	49	520	248	1,417
Ralph Simpson, Denver ..	84	917	457	2,300

1972-73

Julius Erving, Virginia ...	71	889	475	2,268
George McGinnis, Indiana	82	860	517	2,261
Dan Issel, Kentucky	84	899	485	2,292
Bill Cunningham, Carolina	84	757	472	2,028
Ralph Simpson, Denver ..	81	727	421	1,890

*Includes 3-point field goals.

Citizens Savings Athletic Foundation Selections

(Formerly Helms Athletic Foundation)

National Champions

	W.	L.
1901—Yale (No Coach)	10	4*
1902—Minnesota (Dr. L.J. Cooke)	11	0
1903—Yale (No Coach)	15	1
1904—Columbia (No Coach)	17	1*
1905—Columbia (No Coach)	19	1*
1906—Dartmouth (No Coach)	16	2
1907—Chicago (Joseph Raycroft)	20	2
1908—Chicago (Joseph Raycroft)	21	2
1909—Chicago (Joseph Raycroft)	12	0
1910—Columbia (Harry A. Fisher)	11	1*
1911—St. John's (Brooklyn) (C.B. Allen)	14	0
1912—Wisconsin (Walter Meanwell) ...	15	0
1913—U.S. Navy (Louis P. Wenzell) ...	9	0
1914—Wisconsin (Walter Meanwell) ...	15	0
1915—Illinois (Ralph R. Jones)	16	0
1916—Wisconsin (Walter Meanwell) ...	20	1
1917—Washington St. (J.F. Bohler)	25	1
1918—Syracuse (Edmund Dollard)	16	1
1919—Minnesota (Dr. L.J. Cooke)	13	0
1920—Pennsylvania (L.W. Jourdet)	22	1
1921—Pennsylvania (Edward McNichol)	21	2
1922—Kansas (Forrest C. Allen)	16	2
1923—Kansas (Forrest C. Allen)	17	1
1924—North Carolina (N.W. Shepard) ..	25	0
1925—Princeton (Albert Wittmer)	21	2
1926—Syracuse (Lewis Andreas)	19	1
1927—Notre Dame (George Keogan) ...	19	1
1928—Pittsburgh (H.C. Carlson)	21	0
1929—Montana State (S.R. Dyche)	35	2
1930—Pittsburgh (H.C. Carlson)	23	2
1931—Northwestern (Art Lonborg) ...	16	1
1932—Purdue (Ward Lambert)	17	1
1933—Kentucky (Adolph Rupp)	20	3
1934—Wyoming (Willard Witte)	26	3*
1935—New York U. (Howard Cann) ...	19	1
1936—Notre Dame (George Keogan) ...	22**	2
1937—Stanford (John Bunn)	25	2
1938—Temple (James Usilton)	23	2
1939—Long Island U. (Clair Bee)	24	0
1940—So. California (Justin Barry)	20	3
1941—Wisconsin (Harold Foster)	20	3
1942—Stanford (Everett Dean)	27	4
1943—Wyoming (Everett Shelton)	31	2

1944—Army (Edward Kelleher)	15	0
1945—Oklahoma A. & M. (Henry Iba)	27	4
1946—Oklahoma A. & M. (Henry Iba)	31	2
1947—Holy Cross (Alvin Julian)	27	3
1948—Kentucky (Adolph Rupp)	36	3
1949—Kentucky (Adolph Rupp)	32	2
1950—C.C.N.Y. (Nat Holman)	24	5
1951—Kentucky (Adolph Rupp)	32	2
1952—Kansas (Forrest C. Allen)	28	3
1953—Indiana (Branch McCracken)	23	3
1954—Kentucky (Adolph Rupp)	25	0
1955—San Francisco (Phil Woolpert)	28	1
1956—San Francisco (Phil Woolpert)	29	0
1957—No. Carolina (Frank J. McGuire)	32	0
1958—Kentucky (Adolph Rupp)	23	6
1959—California (Pete Newell)	25	4
1960—Ohio State (Fred Taylor)	25	3
1961—Cincinnati (Ed Jucker)	27	3
1962—Cincinnati (Ed Jucker)	29	2
1963—Loyola (Chicago) George Ireland)	29	2
1964—U.C.L.A. (John Wooden)	30	0
1965—U.C.L.A. (John Wooden)	28	2
1966—Texas Western (Don Haskins)	28	1
1967—U.C.L.A. (John Wooden)	30	0
1968—U.C.L.A. (John Wooden)	29	1
1969—U.C.L.A. (John Wooden)	29	1
1970—U.C.L.A. (John Wooden)	28	2
1971—U.C.L.A. (John Wooden)	29	1
1972—U.C.L.A. (John Wooden)	30	0
1973—U.C.L.A. (John Wooden)	30	0

*Undefeated in Collegiate Play
**One tie game played by Notre Dame

College Player-of-the-Year

1905—Chris Steinmetz, Wisconsin
1906—George Grebenstein, Dartmouth
1907—Gilmore Kinney, Yale
1908—Charles Keinath, Pennsylvania
1909—John Schommer, Chicago
1910—Harland "Pat" Page, Chicago
1911—Theodore Kiendl, Columbia
1912—Otto Stangel, Wisconsin
1913—Eddie Calder, St. Lawrence
1914—Gil Halstead, Cornell
1915—Ernest Houghton, Union
1916—George Levis, Wisconsin
1917—Ray Woods, Illinois
1918—William Chandler, Wisconsin
1919—Erling, Platou, Minnesota
1920—Howard Cann, New York University
1921—George Williams, Missouri
1922—Charles Carney, Illinois
1923—Paul Endacott, Kansas

1924—Charles Black, Kansas
1925—Earl Mueller, Colorado College
1926—John Cobb, North Carolina
1927—Victor Hanson, Syracuse
1928—Victor Holt, Oklahoma
1929—J.A. Thompson, Montana State
1930—Charles Hyatt, Pittsburgh
1931—Bart Carlton, Ada (Okla.) Teachers
1932—John Wooden, Purdue
1933—Forest Sale, Kentucky
1934—Wesley Bennett, Westminster
1935—Leroy Edwards, Kentucky
1936—John Moir, Notre Dame
1937—Angelo Luisetti, Stanford
1938—Angelo Luisetti, Stanford
1939—Chester Jaworski, Rhode Island State
1940—George Glamack, North Carolina
1941—George Glamack, North Carolina
1942—Stan Modzelewski, Rhode Island State
1943—George Senesky, St. Joseph's
1944—George Mikan, De Paul
1945—George Mikan, De Paul
1946—Robert Kurland, Oklahoma A. & M.
1947—Gerald Tucker, Oklahoma
1948—Ed Macauley, St. Louis
1949—Anthony Lavelli, Yale
1950—Paul Arizin, Villanova
1951—Richard Groat, Duke
1952—Clyde Lovellette, Kansas
1953—Robert Houbregs, Washington
1954—Tom Gola, La Salle
1955—Bill Russell, San Francisco
1956—Bill Russell, San Francisco
1957—Leonard Rosenbluth, North Carolina
1958—Elgin Baylor, Seattle
1959—Oscar Robertson, Cincinnati
1960—Oscar Robertson, Cincinnati
1961—Jerry Lucas, Ohio State
1962—Paul Hogue, Cincinnati
1963—Arthur Heyman, Duke
1964—Walter Hazzard, U.C.L.A.
1965—William Bradley, Princeton; Gail Goodrich, U.C.L.A.
1966—Cazzie Russell, Michigan
1967—Lew Alcindor, U.C.L.A.
1968—Lew Alcindor, U.C.L.A.
1969—Lew Alcindor, U.C.L.A.
1970—Pete Maravich, Louisiana St.; Sidney Wicks, U.C.L.A.
1971—Sidney Wicks, U.C.L.A.; Austin Carr, Notre Dame
1972—Bill Walton, U.C.L.A.
1973—Bill Walton, U.C.L.A.

All-Time All-American College Team

Forward	Victor Hanson	Syracuse	1925, 1926, 1927
Forward	John A. Thompson	Montana State	1927, 1928, 1929, 1930
Forward	Charles Hyatt	Pittsburgh	1928, 1929, 1930
Forward	Angelo Luisetti	Stanford	1936, 1937, 1938
Center	Jerry Lucas	Ohio State	1960, 1961, 1962
Center	George Mikan	De Paul	1943, 1944, 1945, 1946

Guard	Robert Kurland	Oklahoma A. & M.	1944, 1945, 1946
Guard	Edward McNichol	Pennsylvania	1915, 1916, 1917
Guard	Paul Endacott	Kansas	1921, 1922, 1923
Guard	John Wooden	Purdue	1930, 1931, 1932
Guard	Bill Russell	San Francisco	1954, 1955, 1956

All-American College Teams—Since 1920

1920

Forward—George Sweeney, Pennsylvania
Forward—Goege Gardner, Southwestern
Forward—Howard Cann, New York University
Forward—Forrest Di Bernardi, Westminster
Center—Charles Carney, Illinois
Center—George Williams, Missouri
Guard—Paul Hinkle, Chicago
Guard—Hubert Peck, Pennsylvania
Guard—Dan McNichol, Pennsylvania
Guard—Irving Cook, Washington University

1921

F—Arnold Oss, Minnesota
F—Forrest Di Bernardi, Westminster
F—Edward Durno, Oregon
F—R.D. Birkhoff, Chicago
C—George Williams, Missouri
C—Everett Dean, Indiana
G—Dan McNichol, Pennsylvania
G—Donald White, Purdue
G—Herbert Bunker, Missouri
G—Basil Hayden, Kentucky

1922

F—Charles Carney, Illinois
F—George Browning, Missouri
F—George Gardner, Southwestern
F—Ira McKee, Navy
C—William Grave, Pennsylvania
C—Marshall Hjelte, Oregon Aggies
G—Herbert Bunker, Missouri
G—Ray Miller, Purdue
G—Paul Endacott, Kansas
G—Arthur Loeb, Princeton

1923

F—Al Fox, Idaho
F—George Browning, Missouri
F—Ira McKee, Navy
F—James Lovely, Creighton
C—John Luther, Cornell
C—R.C. Carmichael, North Carolina
G—Arthur Loeb, Princeton
G—Paul Endacott, Kansas
G—Charles Black, Kansas
G—Herbert Bunker, Missouri

1924

F—John Cobb, North Carolina
F—R.C. Carmichael, North Carolina
F—Amory Gill, Oregon Aggies

F—James Lovely, Creighton
C—Tusten Ackerman, Kansas
C—Hugh Latham, Oregon
G—Harry Kipke, Michigan
G—Charles Black, Kansas
G—H.W. Middlesworth, Butler
G—Abb Curtis, Texas

1925

F—John Cobb, North Carolina
F—John Miner, Ohio State
F—Tusten Ackerman, Kansas
F—Victor Hanson, Syracuse
C—Gerald Spohn, Washburn
C—Earl Mueller, Colorado College
G—Burges Carey, Kentucky
G—Noble Kizer, Notre Dame
G—Carlos Steele, Oregon Aggies
G—Emanuel Goldblatt, Pennsylvania

1926

F—Victor Hanson, Syracuse
F—George Spradling, Purdue
F—John Cobb, North Carolina
F—Gale Gordon, Kansas
C—Albert Peterson, Kansas
C—Richard Doyle, Michigan
G—George Dixon, California
G—Carl Loeb, Princeton
G—Emanuel Goldblatt, Pennsylvania
G—Algot Westergren, Oregon

1927

F—Bennie Oosterbaan, Michigan
F—Victor Hanson, Syracuse
F—Ashworth Thompson, Montana State
F—Gerald Spohn, Washburn
C—John Nyikos, Notre Dame
C—Ross McBurney, Wichita
G—George Dixon, California
G—John Lorch, Columbia
G—Harry Wilson, Army
G—Syd Corenman, Creighton

1928

F—Bennie Oosterbaan, Michigan
F—Charles Hyatt, Pittsburgh
F—Ernest Simpson, Colorado College
F—Ashworth Thompson, Montana State
C—Victor Holt, Oklahoma
C—Charles Murphy, Purdue
G—Joseph Schaaf, Pennsylvania
G—Alfred James, Washington
G—Sykes Reed, Pittsburgh

G—Glen Rose, Arkansas

1929

F—Charles Hyatt, Pittsburgh
F—Ashworth Thompson, Montana State
F—Joseph Schaaf, Pennsylvania
F—Vern Corbin, California
C—Charles Murphy, Purdue
C—Frank Ward, Montana State
G—Carey Spicer, Kentucky
G—Eugene Lambert, Arkansas
G—Bruce Drake, Oklahoma
G—Harlow Rothert, Stanford

1930

F—Charles Hyatt, Pittsburgh
F—Branch McCracken, Indiana
F—Bart Carlton, Ada Teachers
F—Ashworth Thompson, Montana State
C—Charles Murphy, Purdue
C—Frank Ward, Montana State
G—John Wooden, Purdue
G—John Lehners, So. California
G—Paul McBrayer, Kentucky
G—Marshall Craig, Missouri

1931

F—Richard Linthicum, U.C.L.A.
F—Elwood Romney, Brigham Young
F—Carey Spicer, Kentucky
F—Bart Carlton, Ada Teachers
C—George Gregory, Columbia
C—Joseph Reiff, Northwestern
G—John Wooden, Purdue
G—Wesley Fesler, Ohio State
G—Ralph Cairney, Washington
G—Louis Berger, Maryland

1932

F—Elwood Romney, Brigham Young
F—Joseph Kintana, California
F—Ed Krause, Notre Dame
F—Les Witte, Wyoming
C—Forest Sale, Kentucky
C—Ad Dietzel, Texas Christian
G—John Wooden, Purdue
G—Dave Jones, Columbia
G—Louis Berger, Maryland
G—Allen Brachen, Providence

1933

F—Joseph Reiff, Northwestern
F—Jerome Nemer, So. California
F—Les Witte, Wyoming
F—Ken Fairman, Princeton
C—Forest Sale, Kentucky
C—Ed Lewis, Oregon State
G—Don Smith, Pittsburgh
G—Frank Baird, Butler
G—Elliott Loughlin, Navy
G—Ellis Johnson, Kentucky

1934

F—Robert Galer, Washington
F—Les Witte, Wyoming
F—John De Moisey, Kentucky
F—Harold Eifert, California
C—Wesley Bennett, Westminster
C—Lee Guttero, So. California
G—Wallace Myers, Texas Christian
G—Claire Cribbs, Pittsburgh
G—George Ireland, Notre Dame
G—Emmett Lowery, Purdue

1935

F—Wesley Bennett, Westminster
F—Al Bonniwell, Dartmouth
F—Jack Gray, Texas
F—Glen Roberts, Emory & Henry
C—Leroy Edwards, Kentucky
C—Lee Guttero, So. California
G—Claire Cribbs, Pittsburgh
G—William Nash, Columbia
G—George Ireland, Notre Dame
G—Omar Browning, Oklahoma

1936

F—Angelo Luisetti, Stanford
F—John Moir, Notre Dame
F—Robert Kessler, Purdue
F—Ike Poole, Arkansas
C—Paul Nowak, Notre Dame
C—Bill Kinner, Utah
G—William Nash, Columbia
G—Vernon Huffman, Indiana
G—Robert Egge, Washington
G—Norman Iler, Washington & Lee

1937

F—Angelo Luisetti, Stanford
F—Jewell Young, Purdue
F—John Moir, Notre Dame
F—John O'Brien, Columbia
C—Paul Nowak, Notre Dame
C—Bob Spessard, Washington & Lee
G—Fred Pralle, Kansas
G—Jules Bender, Long Island U.
G—Francis Murray, Pennsylvania
G—Merle Rousey, Oklahoma A. & M.

1938

F—Angelo Luisetti, Stanford
F—Jewell Young, Purdue
F—John Moir, Notre Dame
F—Bonnie Graham, Mississippi
C—Hubert Kirkpatrick, Baylor
C—Paul Nowak, Notre Dame
G—Fred Pralle, Kansas
G—John O'Brien, Columbia
G—Ignatius Volpi, Manhattan
G—Meyer Bloom, Temple

1939

F—Lauren Gale, Oregon
F—James Hull, Ohio State
F—Irving Torgoff, Long Island U.
F—Gus Broberg, Dartmouth
C—Chester Jaworski, Rhode Island State
C—Urgel Wintermute, Oregon
G—Jesse Renick, Oklahoma A. & M.
G—John Lobsinger, Missouri
G—Bobby Moers, Texas
G—Ernie Andres, Indiana

1940

F—Ralph Vaughn, So. California
F—Gus Broberg, Dartmouth
F—John Dick, Oregon
F—William Hapac, Illinois
C—George Glamack, North Carolina
C—Stanley Modzelewski, Rhode Island State
G—Jesse Renick, Oklahoma A. & M.
G—Bobby Moers, Texas
G—John Lobsinger, Missouri
G—Fred Beretta, Purdue

1941

F—Gus Broberg, Dartmouth
F—John Adams, Arkansas
F—Howard Engelman, Kansas
F—Gene Englund, Wisconsin
C—George Glamack, North Carolina
C—Stanley Modzelewski, Rhode Island State
G—Lee Huber, Kentucky
G—Milton Phelps, San Diego State
G—Walter O'Connor, Drake
G—Ray Sundquist, Washington State

1942

F—John Kotz, Wisconsin
F—Price Brookfield, West Texas State
F—James Pollard, Stanford
F—George Munroe, Dartmouth
C—Stanley Modzelewski, Rhode Island State
C—Bob Kinney, Rice
G—Scott Hamilton, West Virginia
G—Ray Evans, Kansas
G—Bud Millikan, Oklahoma A. & M.
G—Andrew Phillip, Illinois

1943

F—Robert G. Bishop, Washington State
F—Kenneth Sailors, Wyoming
F—George L. Senesky, St. Joseph's
F—Andy Phillip, Illinois
C—Gerald Tucker, Oklahoma
C—Bill Tom Closs, Rice
G—Raymond Evans, Kansas
G—William Morris, Washington
G—Robert Rensberger, Notre Dame
G—John Mahnken, Georgetown

1944

F—Dale Hall, U.S. Military Academy
F—Bob Dille, Valparaiso
F—Arnold Ferrin, Utah
F—Otto Graham, Northwestern & Colgate
C—Audley Brindley, Dartmouth
C—Robert Brannum, Kentucky
G—George Mikan, De Paul
G—Alva Paine, Oklahoma
G—Robert Kurland, Oklahoma A. & M.
G—Bill Henry, Rice

1945*

F—Bill Henry, Rice
F—Dale Hall, Army
F—Howie Schultz, Hamline
F—Max Morris, Northwestern
F—George Mikan, De Paul
F—Vince Hanson, Washington State
D—Robert Kurland, Oklahoma A. & M.
D—Adrian Back Jr., Navy
D—Walton Kirk Jr., Illinois
D—Herbert Wilkinson, Iowa

1946

F—Max Morris, Northwestern
F—Charles Black, Kansas
F—Leo Klier, Notre Dame
F—Tony Lavelli, Yale
F—Robert Kurland, Oklahoma A. & M.
F—George Mikan, De Paul
D—Sid Tanenbaum, New York U.
D—Jack Parkinson, Kentucky
D—Paul Huston, Ohio State
D—James Jordan, North Carolina

1947

F—Gerald Tucker, Oklahoma
F—John Hargis, Texas
F—George Kafton, Holy Cross
F—Ralph Hamilton, Indiana
F—Don Barksdale, U.C.L.A.
F—Ed Koffenberger, Duke
D—Sid Tanenbaum, New York U.
D—Arnold Ferrin, Utah
D—Ralph Beard, Kentucky
D—Leland Byrd, West Virginia

1948

F—Tony Lavelli, Yale
F—Murray Wier, Iowa
F—Richard Dickey, North Carolina State
F—Duane Klueh, Indiana State
C—Ed Macauley, St. Louis
C—Jack Nochols, Washington
D—Ralph Beard, Kentucky
D—Kevin O'Shea, Notre Dame
D—Arnold Ferrin, Utah
D—Andrew Wolfe, California

*Beginning in 1945 the Foundation selected players as forwards and defense men, making it possible for two centers to be chosen.

1949

F—Tony Lavelli, Yale
F—Ernest Vandeweghe, Colgate
F—Vince Boryla, Denver
F—Vern Gardner, Utah
C—Alex Groza, Kentucky
C—Ed Macauley, St. Louis
D—Ralph Beard, Kentucky
D—Robert Harris, Oklahoma A. & M.
D—William Erickson, Illinois
D—Slater Martin, Texas

1950

F—Robert Cousy, Holy Cross
F—Sam Ranzino, North Carolina State
F—William Sharman, So. California
F—Harold Haskins, Hamline
C—Paul Arizin, Villanova
C—Don Lofgran, San Francisco
D—Paul Unruh, Bradley
D—Richard Schnittker, Ohio State
D—Irwin Dambrot, C.C.N.Y.
D—John Pilch, Wyoming

1951

F—Richard Groat, Duke
F—Sam Ranzino, North Carolina State
F—William Mlkvy, Temple
F—Robert Zawoluk, St. John's
C—William Spivey, Kentucky
C—Clyde Lovellette, Kansas
D—Ernie Barrett, Kansas State
D—Gale McArthur, Oklahoma A. & M.
D—Melvin Hutchins, Brigham Young
D—Gene Melchiorre, Bradley

1952

F—Richard Groat, Duke
F—John O'Brien, Seattle
F—Cliff Hagan, Kentucky
F—Mark Workman, West Virginia
C—Charles Darling, Iowa
C—Clyde Lovellette, Kansas
D—Robert Zawoluk, St. John's
D—William Stauffer, Missouri
D—Rodney Fletcher, Illinois
D—Don Johnson, Oklahoma A. & M.

1953

F—Robert Houbregs, Washington
F—Robert Pettit, Louisiana State
F—John O'Brien, Seattle
F—Tom Gola, La Salle
C—Don Schlundt, Indiana
C—Walter Dukes, Seton Hall
D—Richard Knostman, Kansas State
D—Ernest Beck, Pennsylvania
D—B.H. Born, Kansas
D—Robert Mattick, Oklahoma A. & M.

1954

F—Cliff Hagan, Kentucky
F—Tom Gola, La Salle
F—Togo Palazzi, Holy Cross
F—Jesse Arnelle, Penn State
C—Robert Pettit, Louisiana State
C—Don Schlundt, Indiana
D—Robert Carney, Bradley
D—Richard Rosenthal, Notre Dame
D—Frank Selvy, Furman
D—Robert Mattick, Oklahoma A. & M.

1955

F—Tom Gola, La Salle
F—Dick Garmaker, Minnesota
F—Darrell Floyd, Furman
F—Edward Conlin, Fordham
C—Bill Russell, San Francisco
C—Don Schlundt, Indiana
D—Dick Hemric, Wake Forest
D—Richard Wilkinson, Virginia
D—Jack Stephens, Notre Dame
D—Richard Ricketts, Duquesne

1956

F—Bill Russell, San Francisco
F—Darrell Floyd, Furman
F—Robin Freeman, Ohio State
F—Thomas Heinsohn, Holy Cross
C—Charles Tyra, Louisville
C—Willie Naulls, U.C.L.A.
D—Leonard Rosenbluth, North Carolina
D—Harold Lear, Temple
D—Sihugo Green, Duquesne
D—Norman Stewart, Missouri

1957

F—Leonard Rosenbluth, North Carolina
F—Grady Wallace, South Carolina
F—Joseph Gibbon, Mississippi
F—Chet Forte, Columbia
C—Wilton Chamberlain, Kansas
C—Jim Krebs, Southern Methodist
D—Rod Hundley, West Virginia
D—Jim Ashmore, Mississippi State
D—Gary Thompson, Iowa State
D—Jack Quiggle, Michigan State

1958

F—Elgin Baylor, Seattle
F—Oscar Robertson, Cincinnati
F—Bob Boozer, Kansas State
F—Mike Farmer, San Francisco
C—Wilton Chamberlain, Kansas
C—Archie Dees, Indiana
G—Guy Rodgers, Temple
G—Dom Flora, Washington and Lee
G—Don Hennon, Pittsburgh

1959

F—Robert Boozer, Kansas State

F—John Cox, Kentucky
F—Oscar Robertson, Cincinnati
F—Jerry West, West Virginia
C—John Green, Michigan State
C—Bailey Howell, Mississippi State
G—Don Hennon, Pittsburgh
G—Louis Pucillo, North Carolina State
G—Alan Seiden, St. John's
G—Walter Torrence, U.C.L.A.

1960

F—Oscar Robertson, Cincinnati
F—Tom Sanders, New York Univ.
F—Jerry West, West Virginia
F—Tom Stith, St. Bonaventure
C—Darrall Imhoff, California
C—Jerry Lucas, Ohio State
G—Len Wilkens, Providence
G—James Darrow, Bowling Green
G—William Kennedy, Temple
G—Roger Kaiser, Georgia Tech.

1961

F—Tom Stith, St. Bonaventure
F—Bob Wiesenhahn, Cincinnati
F—John Rudometkin, So. California
F—Tony Jackson, St. John's
C—Jerry Lucas, Ohio State
C—Terry Dischinger, Purdue
G—Roger Kaiser, Georgia Tech
G—Chet Walker, Bradley
G—Larry Siegfried, Ohio State
G—Frank Burgess, Gonzaga

1962

F—Leonard Chappell, Wake Forest
F—John Foley, Holy Cross
F—John Havlicek, Ohio State
F—Arthur Heyman, Duke
C—Terry Dischinger, Purdue
C—Paul Hogue, Cincinnati
C—Jerry Lucas, Ohio State
C—Billy McGill, Utah
G—John Green, U.C.L.A.
G—Charles "Cotton" Nash, Kentucky
G—Rodney Thorn, West Virginia
G—Chester Walker, Bradley

1963

F—Art Heyman, Duke
F—Barry Kramer, New York Univ.
F—Ron Bonham, Cincinnati
F—Charles "Cotton" Nash, Kentucky
C—Nate Thurmond, Bowling Green
C—Paul Silas, Creighton
G—Rod Thorn, West Virginia
G—Jerry Harkness, Loyola (Ill.)
G—Eddie Miles, Seattle
G—Jim Rayl, Indiana

1964

F—Bill Bradley, Princeton
F—Charles "Cotton" Nash, Kentucky
F—Fred Hetzel, Davidson
F—Ron Bonham, Cincinnati
C—Walt Hazzard, U.C.L.A.
C—Dave Stallworth, Wichita
G—Gary Bradds, Ohio State
G—Jeff Mullins, Duke
G—Cazzie Russell, Michigan
G—Mel Counts, Oregon State

1965

F—Bill Bradley, Princeton
F—Rick Barry, Miami
F—Fred Hetzel, Davidson
F—Cazzie Russell, Michigan
C—Dave Stallworth, Wichita
C—Wayne Estes, Utah
G—Gail Goodrich, U.C.L.A.
G—Bill Cunningham, North Carolina
G—Dave Bing, Syracuse
G—John Austin, Boston College

1966

F—Dave Schellhase, Purdue
F—Dave Bing, Syracuse
F—Jack Marin, Duke
F—Dick Snyder, Davidson
C—Clyde Lee, Vanderbilt
C—Bob Verga, Duke
G—Cazzie Russell, Michigan
G—Jim Walker, Providence
G—Louis Dampier, Kentucky
G—Matt Guokas Jr., St. Joseph

1967

F—Clem Haskins, Western Kentucky
F—Westley Unseld, Louisville
F—Sonny Dove, St. John's
F—Elvin Hayes, Houston
C—Lew Alcindor, U.C.L.A.
C—Mel Daniels, New Mexico
G—Larry Miller, North Carolina
G—Bob Verga, Duke
G—Bob Lloyd, Rutgers
G—Jim Walker, Providence

1968

F—Elvin Hayes, Houston
F—Westley Unseld, Louisville
F—Lucius Allen, U.C.L.A.
F—Don May, Dayton
C—Lew Alcindor, U.C.L.A.
C—Bob Lanier, St. Bonaventure
G—Peter Maravich, Louisiana State U.
G—Larry Miller, N. Carolina
G—Calvin Murphy, Niagara
G—Jo Jo White, Kansas

1968-69
(NCAA Consensus)

C—Lew Alcindor, U.C.L.A.
F—Spencer Haywood, Detroit
G—Calvin Murphy, Niagara
G—Pete Maravich, L.S.U.
F—Rick Mount, Purdue
C—Dan Issel, Kentucky
F—Mike Maloy, Davidson
F—Bud Ogden, Santa Clara
G—Charlie Scott, North Carolina
G—Jo Jo White, Kansas

1969-70
(NCAA Consensus)

F—Rick Mount, Purdue
C—Bob Lanier, St. Bonaventure
G—Calvin Murphy, Niagara
G—Pete Maravich, L.S.U.
C—Dan Issel, Kentucky
G—Austin Carr, Notre Dame
G—Jimmy Collins, New Mexico State
G—John Roche, South Carolina
G—Charlie Scott, North Carolina
F—Sidney Wicks, U.C.L.A.

1970-71
(NCAA Consensus)

F—Howard Porter, Villanova
G—Austin Carr, Notre Dame
G—Johnny Neumann, Mississippi
F—Ken Durrett, La Salle
F—Sidney Wicks, U.C.L.A.
F—Curtis Rowe, U.C.L.A.
C—Jim Daniels, Western Kentucky
G—John Roche, South Carolina
G—Dean Meminger, Marquette
C—Artis Gilmore, Jacksonville

1971-72
(News Selections)

C—Bill Walton, U.C.L.A. (A.P., UPI)
G—Dwight Lamar, Southwestern Louisiana
    (AP, UPI)
G—Henry Bibby, U.C.L.A. (AP, UPI)
F—Ed Ratliff, Long Beach State (AP, UPI)
C—Jim Chones, Marquette (AP, UPI)
C—Tom Riker, South Carolina (AP, UPI)
G—Barry Parkhill, Virginia (AP, UPI)
F—Robert McAdoo, North Carolina (AP, UPI)
G—Allan Hornyak, Ohio State (AP, UPI)
G—Jim Price, Louisville (AP, UPI)
.F—Dwight Davis, Houston (AP)

1972-73
(AP News Selection)

G—Doug Collins, Illinois State
G—Dwight Lamar, Southwestern Louisiana
F—Ed Ratliff, Long Beach State
C—Bill Walton, U.C.L.A.

G—David Thompson, North Carolina State
C—Kermit Washington, American Univ.
F—Keith Wilkes, U.C.L.A.
G—Ernie DiGregorio, Providence
G—Kevin Joyce, South Carolina
C—Jim Brewer, Minnesota

Citizens Savings Basketball Hall of Fame (Helms Hall of Fame)

PLAYERS

Tusten Ackerman, Kansas
Lew Alcindor, U.C.L.A.
Elgin Baylor, Seattle
Wesley Bennett, Westminster, Pa.
Louis Berger, Maryland
Charles Black, Kansas
Robert Boozer, Kansas State
William Bradley, Princeton
Gus Broberg, Dartmouth
Arthur Browning, Missouri
Herbert Bunker, Missouri
Bart Carlton, Ada, Oklahoma Teachers
Richard Carmichael, North Carolina
Charley Carney, Illinois
Lewis Castle, Syracuse
Wilt Chamberlain, Kansas
William Chandler, Wisconsin
David Charters, Purdue
John Cobb, North Carolina
Robert Cousy, Holy Cross
Forrest De Bernardi, Westminster (Mo.)
Dave DeBusschere, Detroit
Terry Dischinger, Purdue
George Dixon, California
Walter Dukes, Seton Hall
Le Roy Edwards, Kentucky
Paul Endacott, Kansas
Wayne Estes, Utah State
Raymond Evans, Kansas
Arnold Ferrin, Utah
Harry Fisher, Columbia
Darrell Floyd, Furman
George Gardner, Southwestern, Kan.
George Glamack, North Carolina
Thomas Gola, La Salle
Emanuel Goldblatt, Pennsylvania
Gail Goodrich, U.C.L.A.
Richard Groat, Duke
Lee Guttero, S. California
Cyril Haas, Princeton
Cliff Hagan, Kentucky
Dale Hall, U.S. Army
Victor Hanson, Syracuse
Julian Hayward, Wesleyan
Walter Hazzard, U.C.L.A.
Dick Hemric, Wake Forest
Don Hennon, Pittsburgh
Bill Henry, Rice
Fred Hetzel, Davidson
Arthur Heyman, Duke
Paul Hinkle, Chicago

Ernest Houghton, Union
Marcus Hurley, Columbia
Charles Hyatt, Pittsburgh
Darrell Imhoff, California
George Ireland, Notre Dame
Charles Keinath, Pennsylvania
Theodore Kiendl, Pennsylvania
Gilmore Kinney, Yale
Edward Krause, Notre Dame
Robert Kurland, Oklahoma A. and M.
Anthony Lavelli, Yale
George Levis, Wisconsin
John Lobsiger, Missouri
Arthur Loeb, Princeton
Clyde Lovellette, Kansas
James Lovely, Creighton
Jerry Lucas, Ohio State
Angelo Luisetti, Stanford
Dan McNichol, Pennsylvania
Ed Macauley, St. Louis
Pete Maravich, Louisiana State
Robert Mattick, Oklahoma State
George Mikan, De Paul
Stanley (Stutz) Modzelewski, Rhode Island
Bobby Moers, Texas
John Moir, Notre Dame
Max Morris, Northwestern
Charles Murphy, Purdue
Charles "Cotton" Nash, Kentucky
William Nash, Columbia
Paul Nowak, Notre Dame
John O'Brien, Columbia
Arnold Oss, Minnesota
Harlan O. (Pat) Page, Chicago
Hubert Peck, Pennsylvania
Robert Pettit, Louisiana State
Andrew Phillip, Illinois
Fred Pralle, Kansas
Sam Ranzino, North Carolina State
Joseph Reiff, Northwestern
Jesse Renick, Oklahoma State
Richard Ricketts, Duquesne
Oscar Robertson, Cincinnati
Guy Rodgers, Temple
Elwood Romney, Brigham Young
Leonard Rosenbluth, North Carolina
Craig Ruby, Missouri
John Rudometkin, Co. Cal.
Bill Russell, San Francisco
Cazzie Russell, Michigan
John Ryan, Columbia
Forest Sale, Kentucky
Joseph Schaaf, Pennsylvania
Donald Schlundt, Indiana
John Schommer, Chicago
Alphonse Schumaker, Dayton
Carey Spicer, Kentucky
Gerald Spohn, Washburn
Chris Steinmetz, Wisconsin
George Sweeney, Pennsylvania
Helmer Swenholt, Wisconsin
Sid Tanenbaum, New York

John A. (Cat) Thompson, Montana State
Gerald Tucker, Oklahoma
Chester Walker, Bradley
Frank Ward, Montana State
Jerry West, West Virginia
Sidney Wicks, U.C.L.A.
George Williams, Missouri
Les Witte, Wyoming
John Wooden, Purdue
Ray Woods, Illinois
Jewell Young, Purdue
Robert Zawoluk, St. John's

PROFESSIONAL
All-Star Selections*

1947
(Basketball Association of America)

* From
*From N.B.A. Guide.

First Team

Joe Fulks, Philadelphia
Bob Feerick, Washington
Stan Miasek, Detroit
Bones McKinney, Washington
Max Zaslofsky, Chicago

Second Team

Ernie Calverley, Providence
Frank Baumholtz, Cleveland
John Logan, St. Louis
Chuck Halbert, Chicago
Fred Scolari, Washington

1948
(Basketball Association of America)

First Team

Joe Fulks, Philadelphia
Max Zaslofsky, Chicago
Ed Sadowski, Boston
Howie Dallmar, Philadelphia
Bob Feerick, Washington

Second Team

John Logan, St. Louis
Carl Braun, New York
Stan Miasek, Chicago
Fred Scolari, Washington
Buddy Jeanette, Baltimore

1949
(Basketball Association of America)

First Team

George Mikan, Minneapolis
Joe Fulks, Philadelphia
Bob Davies, Rochester
Max Zaslofsky, Chicago
Jim Pollard, Minneapolis

Second Team

Arnie Risen, Rochester
Bob Feerick, Washington
Bones McKinney, Washington
Ken Sailors, Providence
John Logan, St. Louis

1949

(National Basketball League)

First Team

Dick Mehen, Waterloo
Al Cervi, Syracuse
Don Otten, Tri-Cities
Frank Brian, Anderson
Gene Englund, Oshkosh

Second Team

Whitey Von Neida, Tri-Cities
Marko Todorovich, Sheboygan
Bill Closs, Anderson
Ward Gibson, Tri-Cities
Ralph Johnson, Anderson

1950

(National Basketball Association)

First Team

George Mikan, Minneapolis
Jim Pollard, Minneapolis
Alex Groza, Indianapolis
Bob Davies, Rochester
Max Zaslofsky, Chicago

Second Team

Frank Brian, Anderson
Fred Schaus, Fort Wayne
Adolph Schayes, Syracuse
Al Cervi, Syracuse
Ralph Beard, Indianapolis

1951

(National Basketball Association)

First Team

George Mikan, Minneapolis
Ed Macauley, Boston
Bob Davies, Rochester
Alex Groza, Indianapolis
Ralph Beard, Indianapolis

Second Team

Frank Brian, Tri-Cities
Vern Mikkelsen, Minneapolis
Adolph Schayes, Syracuse
Joe Fulks, Philadelphia
Dick McGuire, New York

1952

(National Basketball Association)

First Team

Paul Arizin, Philadelphia
Bob Cousy, Boston
George Mikan, Minneapolis
Ed Macauley, Boston
Bob Davies, Rochester
Adolph Schayes, Syracuse

Second Team

Vern Mikkelsen, Minneapolis
Jim Pollard, Minneapolis
Larry Foust, Fort Wayne
Bob Wanzer, Rochester
Andy Phillip, Philadelphia

1953

(National Basketball Association)

First Team

Bob Cousy, Boston
George Mikan, Minneapolis
Ed Macauley, Boston
Adolph Schayes, Syracuse
Neil Johnston, Philadelphia

Second Team

Vern Mikkelsen, Minneapolis
Bob Wanzer, Rochester
Bob Davies, Rochester
Andy Phillip, Fort Wayne
Bill Sharman, Boston

1954

(National Basketball Association)

First Team

Bob Cousy, Boston
Neil Johnston, Philadelphia
George Mikan, Minneapolis
Adolph Schayes, Syracuse
Harry Gallatin, New York

Second Team

Ed Macauley, Boston
Jim Pollard, Minneapolis
Carl Braun, New York
Bob Wanzer, Rochester
Paul Seymour, Syracuse

1955

(National Basketball Association)

First Team

Neil Johnston, Philadelphia
Bob Cousy, Boston
Adolph Schayes, Syracuse
Bob Pettit, Milwaukee
Larry Foust, Fort Wayne

Second Team

Vern Mikkelsen, Minneapolis

Harry Gallatin, New York
Paul Seymour, Syracuse
Slater Martin, Minneapolis
Bill Sharman, Boston

1956
(National Basketball Association)

First Team

Bob Pettit, St. Louis
Paul Arizin, Philadelphia
Neil Johnston, Philadelphia
Bob Cousy, Boston
Bill Sharman, Boston

Second Team

Adolph Schayes, Syracuse
Maurice Stokes, Rochester
Clyde Lovellette, Minneapolis
Slater Martin, Minneapolis
Jack George, Philadelphia

1957
(National Basketball Association)

First Team

Paul Arizin, Philadelphia
Adolph Schayes, Syracuse
Bob Pettit, St. Louis
Bob Cousy, Boston
Bill Sharman, Boston

Second Team

George Yardley, Fort Wayne
Maurice Stokes, Rochester
Neil Johnston, Philadelphia
Dick Garmaker, Minneapolis
Slater Martin, St. Louis

1958
(National Basketball Association)

First Team

Bob Cousy, Boston
Bill Sharman, Boston
Bob Pettit, St. Louis
George Yardley, Detroit
Adolph Schayes, Syracuse

Second Team

Bill Russell, Boston
Tom Gola, Philadelphia
Maurice Stokes, Cincinnati
Cliff Hagan, St. Louis
Slater Martin, St. Louis

1959
(National Basketball Association)

First Team

Bob Pettit, St. Louis

Elgin Baylor, Minneapolis
Bill Russell, Boston
Bob Cousy, Boston
Bill Sharman, Boston

Second Team

Cliff Hagan, St. Louis
Adolph Schayes, Syracuse
Paul Arizin, Philadelphia
Slater Martin, St. Louis
Richie Guerin, New York

1960
(National Basketball Association)

First Team

Bob Pettit, St. Louis
Elgin Baylor, Minneapolis
Wilt Chamberlain, Philadelphia
Bob Cousy, Boston
Oscar Robertson, Cincinnati

Second Team

Jack Twyman, Cincinnati
Adolph Schayes, Syracuse
Bill Russell, Boston
Richie Guerin, New York
Bill Sharman, Boston

1961
(National Basketball Association)

First Team

Elgin Baylor, Los Angeles
Bob Pettit, St. Louis
Wilt Chamberlain, Philadelphia
Bob Cousy, Boston
Oscar Robertson, Cincinnati

Second Team

Adolph Schayes, Syracuse
Tom Heinsohn, Boston
Bill Russell, Boston
Larry Costello, Syracuse
Gene Shue, Detroit

1962
(National Basketball Association)

First Team

Bob Pettit, St. Louis
Elgin Baylor, Los Angeles
Wilt Chamberlain, Philadelphia
Jerry West, Los Angeles
Oscar Robertson, Cincinnati

Second Team

Tom Heinsohn, Boston
Jack Twyman, Cincinnati
Bill Russell, Boston
Richie Guerin, New York
Bob Cousy, Boston

1963
(National Basketball Association)
First Team

Elgin Baylor, Los Angeles
Bob Pettit, St. Louis
Bill Russell, Boston
Oscar Robertson, Cincinnati
Jerry West, Los Angeles

Second Team

Tom Heinsohn, Boston
Bailey Howell, Detroit
Wilt Chamberlain, San Francisco
Bob Cousy, Boston
Hal Greet, Syracuse

1964
(National Basketball Association)
First Team

Oscar Robertson, Cincinnati
Elgin Baylor, Los Angeles
Jerry West, Los Angeles
Wilt Chamberlain, San Francisco
Bob Pettit, St. Louis

Second Team

Tom Heinsohn, Boston
Jerry Lucas, Cincinnati
Bill Russell, Boston
Hal Greer, Philadelphia
John Havlicek, Boston

1965
(National Basketball Association)
First Team

Elgin Baylor, Los Angeles
Jerry Lucas, Cincinnati
Bill Russell, Boston
Oscar Robertson, Cincinnati
Jerry West, Los Angeles

Second Team

Bob Pettit, St. Louis
Gus Johnson, Baltimore
Wilt Chamberlain, San Francisco-Philadelphia
Sam Jones, Boston
Hal Greer, Philadelphia

1966
(National Basketball Association)
First Team

Jerry Lucas, Cincinnati
Rick Barry, San Francisco
Wilt Chamberlain, Philadelphia
Oscar Robertson, Cincinnati
Jerry West, Los Angeles

Second Team

John Havlicek, Boston

Gus Johnson, Baltimore
Bill Russell, Boston
Sam Jones, Boston
Hal Greer, Philadelphia

1967
(National Basketball Association)
First Team

Rick Barry, San Francisco
Elgin Baylor, Los Angeles
Wilt Chamberlain, Philadelphia
Jerry West, Los Angeles
Oscar Robertson, Cincinnati

Second Team

Willis Reed, New York
Jerry Lucas, Cincinnati
Bill Russell, Boston
Sam Jones, Boston
Hal Greer, Philadelphia

1968
(National Basketball Association)
First Team

Oscar Robertson, Cincinnati
Dave Bing, Detroit
Wilt Chamberlain, Philadelphia
Jerry Lucas, Cincinnati
Elgin Baylor, Los Angeles

Second Team

Jerry West, Los Angeles
John Havlicek, Boston
Bill Russell, Boston
Willis Reed, New York
Hal Greer, Philadelphia

1969 N.B.A. All-Star Team
First Team

F—Bill Cunningham, Philadelphia
F—Elgin Baylor, Los Angeles
C—Wes Unseld, Baltimore
G—Oscar Robertson, Cincinnati
G—Earl Monroe, Baltimore

Second Team

F—John Havlicek, Boston
F—Dave DeBusschere, New York
C—Willis Reed, New York
G—Jerry West, Los Angeles
G—Hal Greer, Philadelphia

1970 N.B.A. All-Star Team
First Team

F—Bill Cunningham, Philadelphia
F—Connie Hawkins, Phoenix
C—Willis Reed, New York
G—Jerry West, Los Angeles
G—Walt Frazier, New York

Second Team

F—John Havlicek, Boston
F—Gus Johnson, Baltimore
C—Lou Alcindor, Milwaukee
G—Lou Hudson, Atlanta
G—Oscar Robertson, Cincinnati

1971 N.B.A. All-Star Team

First Team

F—Bill Cunningham, Philadelphia
F—John Havlicek, Boston
C—Lew Alcindor, Milwaukee
G—Jerry West, Los Angeles
G—Dave Bing, Detroit

Second Team

F—Gus Johnson, Baltimore
F—Bob Love, Chicago
C—Willis Reed, New York
G—Oscar Robertson, Milwaukee
G—Walt Frazier, New York

1972 N.B.A. All-Star Team

First Team

F—John Havlicek, Boston
F—Spencer Haywood, Seattle
C—Kareem Abdul-Jabbar, Milwaukee
G—Jerry West, Los Angeles
G—Walt Frazier, New York

Second Team

F—Bill Cunningham, Philadelphia
F—Bob Love, Chicago
C—Wilt Chamberlain, Los Angeles
G—Nate Archibald, Cincinnati
G—Archie Clark, Baltimore

1973 N.B.A. All-Star Team

First Team

F—Spencer Haywood, Seattle
F—Rick Barry, Golden State
C—Kareem Abdul-Jabbar, Milwaukee
G—Nate Archibald, Kansas City-Omaha
G—Jerry West, Los Angeles

Second Team

F—John Havlicek, Boston
F—Dave DeBusschere, New York
C—Dave Cowens, Boston
G—Walt Frazier, New York
G—Pete Maravich, Atlanta

Podoloff Cup Winners
(Most Valuable Player in N.B.A.)

1956—Bob Pettit, St. Louis
1957—Bob Cousy, Boston
1958—Bill Russell, Boston
1959—Bob Pettit, St. Louis
1960—Wilt Chamberlain, Philadelphia

1961-63—Bill Russell, Boston
1964—Oscar Robertson, Cincinnati
1965—Bill Russell, Boston
1966-68—Wilt Chamberlain, Philadelphia
1969—Wes Unseld, Baltimore
1970—Willis Reed, New York
1971—Lew Alcindor, Milwaukee
1972—Kareem Abdul-Jabbar (Alcindor), Milwaukee
1973—Dave Cowens, Boston

N.B.A. Rookie of the Year

1954—Don Meineke, Ft. Wayne
1955—Ray Felix, Baltimore
1956—Maurice Stokes, Rochester
1957—Tom Heinsohn, Boston
1958—Woody Sauldsberry, Philadelphia
1959—Elgin Baylor, Minneapolis
1960—Wilt Chamberlain, Philadelphia
1961—Oscar Robertson, Cincinnati
1962—Walt Bellamy, Chicago
1963—Terry Dischinger, Chicago
1964—Jerry Lucas, Cincinnati
1965—Willis Reed, New York
1966—Rick Barry, San Francisco
1967—Dave Bing, Detroit
1968—Earl Monroe, Baltimore
1969—Wes Unseld, Baltimore
1970—Lew Alcindor, Milwaukee
1971—Dave Cowens, Boston; Geoff Petrie, Portland (tie)
1972—Sidney Ricks, Portland
1973—Bob McAdoo, Buffalo

American Basketball Association
1968 A.B.A. All-Star Team

First Team

F—Connie Hawkins, Pittsburgh
F—Doug Moe, New Orleans
C—Mel Daniels, Minnesota
G—Larry Jones, Denver
G—Charlie Williams, Pittsburgh

Second Team

F—Roger Brown, Indiana
F—Cincy Powell, Dallas
C—John Beasley, Dallas
G—Larry Brown, New Orleans
G—Lou Dampier, Kentucky

1969 A.B.A. All-Star Team

First Team

F—Rick Berry, Washington
F—Cincy Powell, Dallas
C—Spencer Haywood, Denver
G—Larry Jones, Denver
G—Warren Armstrong, Washington

Second Team

F—Doug Moe, Carolina

F—Bob Netolicky, Indiana
C—Mel Daniels, Indiana
G—Louis Dampier, Kentucky
G—Don Freeman, Miami

1970 A.B.A. All-Star Team
First Team

F—Joe Caldwell, Carolina
F—John Brisker, Pittsburgh
C—Dan Issel, Kentucky
G—Mack Calvin, Florida
G—Charlie Scott, Virginia

Second Team

F—Roger Brown, Indiana
F—Bob Netolicky, Indiana
C—Zelmo Beaty, Utah
G—Glen Combs, Utah
G—Don Freeman, Utah & Texas

1971 A.B.A. All-Star Team
First Team

F—Rick Barry, New York
F—Roger Brown, Indiana
C—Mel Daniels, Indiana
G—Charlie Scott, Virginia
G—Mack Calvin, Florida

Second Team

F—John Brisker, Pittsburgh
F—Joe Caldwell, Carolina
C—Zelmo Beaty, Utah (tie)
C—Dan Issel, Kentucky (tie)
G—Larry Cannon, Denver
G—Don Freeman, Texas

1972 A.B.A. All-Star Team
First Team

F—Rick Barry, New York
F—Dan Issel, Kentucky
C—Artis Gilmore, Kentucky
G—Don Freeman, Dallas
G—Bill Melchionni, New York

Second Team

F—Willie Wise, Utah
F—Julius Erving, Virginia
C—Zelmo Beaty, Utah
G—Ralph Simpson, Denver
G—Charlie Scott, Virginia

1973 A.B.A. All-Star Team
First Team

F—Julius Erving, Virginia
F—Bill Cunningham, Carolina
C—Artis Gilmore, Kentucky
G—Mack Calvin, Carolina
G—George Thompson, Memphis

Second Team

F—Willie Wise, Utah

F—George McGinnis, Indiana
C—Mel Daniels, Indiana
G—Jimmy Jones, Utah
G—Ralph Simpson, Denver

A.B.A. Most Valuable Player

1968—Connie Hawkins, Pittsburgh
1969—Mel Daniels, Indiana
1970—Spencer Haywood, Denver
1971—Mel Daniels, Indiana
1972—Artis Gilmore, Kentucky
1973—Bill Cunningham, Carolina

A.B.A. Rookie of the Year

1968—Mel Daniels, Indiana
1969—Warren Armstrong, Oakland
1970—Spencer Haywood, Denver
1971—Dan Issel, Kentucky; Charlie
            Scott, Virginia (tie)
1972—Artis Gilmore, Kentucky
1973—Brian Taylor, New York

BASIC RULES

(From *Sports for Recreation,* edited by E.D.
Mitchell, A.S. Barnes and Company, New York.)

Basketball is a game usually played indoors by
2 teams of 5 players each—a center, 2 forwards
and 2 guards—in which a ball must be thrown
into elevated goals resembling baskets.

The playing area is a rectangular hardwood-
surface court with minimum dimensions of 74 by
42 feet and maximum dimensions of 94 by 50
feet. The side boundary lines are called sidelines,
with the end boundary lines known as end lines.
(There should be a minimum clearance space of 3
feet, preferably 10 feet, outside the court.) In
the center of the court is a circle with a radius of
2 feet surrounded by a restraining circle of 6-foot
radius. The court is divided into equal halves by a
line drawn through the center of the court
parallel to the end lines, equidistant between
them.

At each end of the court, midway between
the sidelines and 4 feet in front of the end line, is
a vertical surface known as a backboard. The
backboards may be rectangular or fan-shaped and
may be made of plate glass, steel or wood. The
rectangular boards are 48 inches vertically and 72
inches horizontally. The fan-shaped boards in
over-all dimensions measure 35 inches high and
54 inches wide, with a 29-inch radius. Attached
to the backboard at a point 10 feet above floor
level is a basket consisting of a 5/8-inch metal
ring 18 inches in diameter from which a white
cord net 15 to 18 inches in length is suspended.

At a distance of 15 feet in front of each backboard and parallel to the end lines is a free throw
line 12 feet long, the middle point of which is
the center of the free throw circle, which has a
6 foot radius, completing the free throw area,
outside of which all players but the thrower must
stand during a free throw circle. These 2 lines are

equidistant from the sidelines and 6 feet apart from each other.

A basketball is a round ball about 30 inches in circumference, with an airtight rubber case covered with brown leather. It weighs not less than 20 nor more than 22 ounces.

The object of the game is for a team to throw the ball through its basket from above and to keep the other team from securing possession of the ball and scoring. The game is started by a jump ball at the center circle. For a jump ball, both centers stand inside the center circle, an official tosses the ball into the air between them, and each attempts to tap the ball to a team-mate. (Jump balls also occur at other places on the floor when a held ball occurs, that is, when 2 opposing players have one or both hands securely on the ball.)

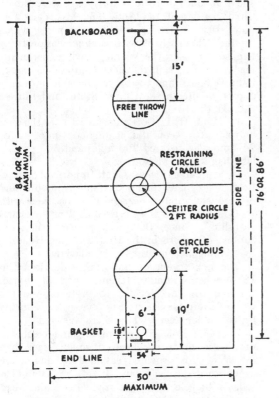

Basketball Court. (Taken from Sports for Recreation, edited by E. D. Mitchell, A. S. Barnes and Company, New York.)

In general, players may pass, throw, bat, roll or dribble (bounce) the ball, but may not run with it. They may not hold, push, charge, trip or impede the progress of an opponent by extending an arm, shoulder, hip, or knee. If they do so, they are charged with a personal foul and the offended player is permitted to throw 1 or more free throws, depending on the circumstances of the offense. For a free throw attempt, a player stands at the free throw line and is permitted an unobstructed opportunity to try to throw the ball through the basket. One point is awarded for each successful free throw, while a goal scored from the field counts 2 points. The team scored upon puts the ball in play by throwing it in from out of bounds behind the end line farthest from its own basket. A free throw also is permitted for a technical foul, which, in general, is an infraction of the rules that does not involve personal contact. In addition, there are certain restrictions in regard to handling the ball which are called violations and which award the ball out of bounds to the offended team.

College and adult games are customarily played in two 20-minute halves with a 15-minute intermission between the halves. High-school games are customarily played in four 8-minute quarters, with a 1-minute intermission between the first and second and the third and fourth quarters, and a 10-minute rest period between the halves. The team with the highest total of points at the end of the game is the winner. In case of a tie score, an overtime period of 3 to 5 minutes is played after a short intermission, as specified by the rules.

Professional rules vary only slightly from the amateur. The biggest difference is the 24-second rule in the professional game. It was designed to speed the game and thereby attract more fans. The rule requires that a team shoot within 24 seconds after acquiring possession of the ball. Another variation is that the professionals play 48 minutes—four 12-minute quarters.

In the women's game, 6 players usually make up one team and the court is divided into 2 zones. Lately, however, there has been a tendency toward 5-player teams in major competition. The players of each team are evenly split between the sections and are not permitted to leave them. Only the players in the attacking zone may try for a basket.

BICYCLE RACING

(Courtesy of Chester Nelsen, Sr., Records Chairman, Amateur Bicycle League of America, 4701 Natural Bridge, St. Louis, Mo., 63115)

Bicycle racing is a popular American and European sport. In the United States it is largely confined to enthusiastic amateurs, while abroad professional and amateur competitions flourish. In some areas of Eastern United States midget teams have been organized to interest youngsters

8 to 14 in the sport.

The idea of a self-propelled vehicle on wheels has intrigued mankind through many centuries, but it did not take definite form until 1690, when a two-wheeled contrivance made its appearance on the streets of Paris. The originator was M. de Sivrac, a Frenchman. The machine consisted of two wooden wheels, with upright posts on the sides of the wheels, such posts being joined together by a crossbar.

M. de Sivrac made one cardinal error, which condemned his device to oblivion. He forgot the need for pedals. Locomotion came about only when someone straddled the crossbar and then pushed the machine along by grounding the feet. The "rider" had to push the contraption along, instead of getting a ride. The invention quickly disappeared, and there were no further bicycle experiments of public knowledge until 1785, when another Frenchman, to fame unknown, launched a somewhat similar machine upon an abbreviated career.

The machine also had to be pushed. But the new inventor put the front wheel on a pivot, which permitted steering independently of the back wheel. The French of that era examined the creation, expressed doubt that a man ever could keep a two-wheeled machine in motion, in any fashion whatsoever and still maintain balance, and that "bike" also disappeared.

In 1789 a three-wheeled contrivance was created by two Frenchmen—Blanchard and Magurier. Comment concerning it appeared in the "Journal de Paris" on July 27, 1789. The newspaper, to distinguish the two different types, called the two-wheeler a "bicycle" and the three-wheeler a "tri-cycle." Cycle is a term used in astronomy and means circle; "bi" means two or twice and "tri" three, or thrice.

Dennis Johnson of England gained a patent on a three-wheeler in 1818. This also was propelled by shoving the feet along the ground. Johnson disposed of quite a few models but just when business was growing very brisk it was found that the pushing action caused varicose veins and the Johnson models promptly went out of favor.

In the same year—1818—Baron de Saverbrum of France produced a model which was the original of the later-day high-wheel bicycle. He made the front wheel much higher than the rear. He continued to increase the height of the front wheel and decrease the rear, until his final offering was a bike with a front wheel 64 inches tall and the rear only 12 inches high. It worked on the gear-rope principle, the rider pulling the rope. It wasn't popular because a man had to be an acrobat to keep it in motion. Too many riders were hurt in spills.

In 1821, Louis Gompertz of England perfected a different type gear rope, which, fundamentally, is the bicycle chain of today. And so, the great forward step was made. The next was in

1834, when Kirkpatrick McMillan, a blacksmith in Scotland, invented pedals with connecting rods. Later he constructed a tricycle, which had a gear shift, as well as pedals.

About 1865, Pierre Lallement, a Frenchman, brought forth a two-wheel bike, had it patented and took it to the United States in 1866. It was a "high-wheeler," made only of wood except for the tires, which were covered with iron. The Americans who tried to ride it in those days called it the "bone-shaker." Sales were few and Lallement soon was out of business.

However, by this time, the men with inventive minds conceded that the bicycle was something that belonged to a not very distant future. They concentrated on improving the bicycle to a point where it would be practical and, finally, indispensable. Hard rubber tires replaced the wooden and iron ones in 1868. Wire spokes were substituted for wood in 1869. The bike gained in popularity. A sewing machine company, which produced high wheels as a sideline, was profiting handsomely. As the years passed, experiments made with the high-wheeler provoked many improvements, and the bicycle became definitely a part of life in the United States and Europe through the 1880's.

In 1883, H. L. Cortis decided to set the first bicycle record—and did. Riding continuously for 24 hours, he covered 200 miles and 300 yards—less than 9 miles an hour.

In September, 1883, G. M. Hendrie of Springfield, Mass., later famous as an automobile and motorcycle builder, engaged in a road race with W. G. Rowe. It was advertised as "for the championship." Since that was perhaps the first contest of record in the United States, Hendrie, by winning, became the top-notch rider.

The next event of importance developed in 1884, when Thomas Stevens, using, of course, the high-wheeler, decided to "ride around the world." He returned after two years, announcing he had ridden "everywhere there was land."

In 1885, J. K. Starley of England created a bike with the front wheel not much larger than the rear. This provided easy riding, and made exceptional speed possible. It set the fashion for today's bicycle. Starley's original machines had hard rubber tires. In 1888, J. B. Dunlop, then a veterinary surgeon in Belfast, invented the pneumatic tires and the bicycle became tremendously popular thereafter. Through the 90's it furnished the chief outdoor diversion of Canadians, British and Americans.

The bicycle, equipped with the pneumatic tires, brought the sport of racing into increasing favor. There were road contests at different points, all over the United States. Since each race had a standard finish line, gentlemen with promotional instincts placed chairs at the finish lines and rented them. Later they erected small stands and sold seats. Still later, when customers demanded a prolonged view of races rather than just a sight of the finish, the promoters rented arenas, built saucer-like tracks, moved the sport indoors, and thus began the fabulous era of bike racing, the amateurs getting trophies, the pros taking cash and the promoters getting richer and richer.

The amateurs, however, rode indoors only in the winter. They preferred road racing to circling a saucer. The early-day amateur bike riders, training for some race, usually used the sidewalk, rather then the rutty roads. Such riders became known as "scorchers." When they ran down pedestrians, injuring many, killing some, town and city authorities passed laws, many still on the books, making it a crime for anyone to ride a bicycle on a sidewalk or along any pathway used by pedestrians.

The popularity of indoor professional sprints caused promoters to devise ways and means of separating the bike loving public from more of its cash. The result was the six-day race—a continuous performance—the first of which was the International, run in the old Madison Square Garden (New York) in 1891, the riders using the high-wheelers. From that year until 1899 the six-day race was a singles affair. Riders had to go it alone, pumping as long as they could, resting for a while, then resuming, for a grand total of 142 hours.

"Plugger Bill" Martin was the first winner, riding an old style bike to victory in 1891 and Charles Ashinger, also riding a high-wheeler, won in 1892.

In 1893, Albert Shock decided to experiment with the new style bike—the "safety"—such as is in vogue today. He won easily, and that was the end of the "bone-shaker" in bike racing annals, the "safety" coming into universal use.

The record under the one man plan—known as "go-as-you-please"—was 2,093.4 miles, made in 1898 by Charlie Miller, in Madison Square Garden. In that race the pace set by Miller practically wrecked the men who tried to follow him. Many of his rivals ended up in the hospital suffering exhaustion. This created condemnation of the sport. The promoters, sensing that something radical must be done to perpetuate six-day racing, introduced two-man teams the following year—1899—in New York.

The race was at 142 hours from 1899 to 1915, inclusive. In 1916 it was 143 hours and in 1917 was lengthened to 144 hours. Prior to 1920 there was only one annual race in New York. In 1920 it was decided to stage a contest in March and December, a custom which continued for many years.

From 1899 until 1916, when teams would finish with the same number of miles and laps, a man from each tied team would ride in a one-mile sprint. The team would be acclaimed winner whose representative won that sprint. In 1916

teams received points for winning various sprints during the week. If two or more teams completed the ride with exactly the same miles and laps, then the one having gained the highest number of sprint points became the winner. No ties resulted.

For many years six-day racing was confined to New York. Its popularity there influenced promoters in other cities to stage such races. They were successes, both in the United States and in Canada. These races followed each other so closely during the season that the circuit riders rarely had a week's rest at any time. But they did not complain. All this meant steady work for them.

In the heyday of the sport, riders with the biggest "crowd appeal" made from $10,000 to $15,000 a year. They worked on a flat guarantee from the promoter or a percentage of the receipts. The less spectacular cleared from $5,000 o $7,500, and shared with the stars in the distribution of prize money put up by spectators for winners of specified sprints.

Interest in the professional end of the sport in this country began to sag in the 1930's, and when the attendance at the six-day race in New York in 1939 took a sharp dip, the contests were abandoned in the present Madison Square Garden and were renewed there in the fall of 1961. However, grinds were held in various New York armories with moderate success.

On the amateur front, though, the popularity of bicycle racing continues at a high level, thanks to the efforts of the Amateur Bicycle League of America. The group, organized in 1920, is affiliated with the Union Cycliste Internationale, the world governing body of the sport, has an allied membership in the Amateur Athletic Union of the United States and is a charter member of the United States Olympic Committee. State or sectional championships are annually followed by contests for the United States title.

FAMOUS CYCLISTS

Walter Bardgett was considered the outstanding authority on bicycling racing in America until his death early in 1953. Bardgett raced all over the world from 1898 until about 1918 and was rated highly. Retiring from competition, Bardgett became editor of the *American Bicyclist,* the only regularly published cycling magazine in the country, and also reported the sport for various European publications. Bardgett, although asked repeatedly for his list of the top ten American cyclists, always named fifteen, it being his contention that he could not limit the list to ten. With the exception of Reggie Mc-Namara, Bardgett did not consider any rider after 1930 up to the caliber of those on his list because the professional sport has waned in this country ever since fire destroyed the New York Velodrome in 1929.

Bardgett's selections follow (the first three are named in order of preference; the others were rated of equal ability):

Frank L. Kramer, East Orange, N.J.; E. C. (Cannon) Bald, Buffalo, N.Y. (later of Pittsburgh); Iver Lawson, Salt Lake City, Utah; Tom Butler, Cambridge, Mass.; Tom Cooper, Detroit; Owen S. Kimble, Louisville, Ky.; Earl Kiser, Dayton, Ohio; Willie Fenn, Waterbury, Conn.; Floyd McFarland, San Jose, Calif.; Nat Butler, Cambridge, Mass.; Bobby Walthour Sr., Atlanta, Ga.; Major Taylor, Worcester, Mass.; Alfred Goullet, Newark, N.J.; Reggie McNamara, Newark, N.J.; Jackie Clarke, Newark, N.J.

TOUR OF FRANCE

The Tour of France is to bicycle racing what the World Series is to baseball. Interest in the sport in France each summer reaches its zenith and experts are numerous as the 100 or more riders wind their way through some 800 communities, pedal over mountain peaks from 4,000 to 7,000 feet in height and speed across the borders of Belgium, Spain, Switzerland and Italy. There are no controls, no customs, no formalities or other barriers in the way of the "Tour."

Cities and towns in France bid for the honor of having the grind of approximately 3,000 miles and usually 25 to 30 days (a day is called a "stage" and there is a winner for each stage) routed their way, so that the course is generally changed from year to year to fit in with the localities providing the best publicity and advertising facilities. A small army of trucks, vans, automobiles and motorcycles carries the equipment, supplies and the official party, which is made up of newspapermen, officials and trainers.

To win the Tour of France is considered cycling's highest honor—even higher than winning a world championship. Fausto Coppi, one of the great cyclists of all time, won the race twice in recent years, in 1949 and 1952. In his first triumph he covered 3,008 miles in 149 hours 40 minutes 49 seconds. In 1952 he was timed in 151 hours 57 minutes 20 seconds for about 3,000 miles.

Jacques Anquetil of France has won the coveted honor five times, in 1957, 1961, 1962, 1963, and 1964, while Eddy Merckx, of Belgium has won it the last four years.

Tour of France Winners*

1903—M. Garin, France
1904—H. Cornet, France
1905—L. Trousselier, France
1906—R. Pottier, France
1907—08—L. Petit-Breton, France
1909—F. Faber, Luxembourg
1910—O. Lapize, France

1911—G. Garrigou, France
1912—O. Defraye, Belgium
1913—14—P. Thys, Belgium
1915—18—No competition
1919—F. Lambot, Belgium
1920—P. Thys, Belgium
1921—L. Scieur, Belgium
1922—F. Lambot, Belgium
1923—H. Pelissier, France
1924—25—O. Bottechia, Italy
1926—L. Buysse, Belgium
1927—28—N. Franta', Luxembourg
1929—Dewaele, Belgium
1930—A. Leducq, France
1931—A. Magne, France
1932—A. Leducq, France
1933—G. Speicher, France
1934—A. Magne, France
1935—R. Maes, Belgium
1936—S. Maes, Belgium
1937—R. Lapebie, France
1938—Gino Bartali, Italy
1939—S. Maes, Belgium
1940—45—No competition
1946—*Jean Lazarides, France
1947—Jean Robic, France
1948—Gino Bartali, Italy
1949—Fausto Coppi, Italy
1950—Ferdinand Kubler, Switzerland
1951—Hugo Koblet, Switzerland
1952—Fausto Coppi, Italy
1953—Louison Bobet, France
1953—55—Louison Bobet, France
1956—Roger Walkowiak, France
1957—Jacques Anquetil, France
1958—Charley Gaul, Luxembourg
1959—Federico Bahamontes, Spain
1960—Gastone Nencini, Italy
1961—64—Jacques Anquetil, France
1965—Felice Gimondi, Italy
1966—Lucien Aimar, France
1967—Roger Pingeon, France
1968—Jan Janssen, Netherlands
1969—72—Eddy Merckx, Belgium
*Five-day race in 1946.

WORLD CHAMPIONS
Professional Motor-Paced (Track)

1895—James Michael, England
1896—A.A. Chase, England
1897—J.W. Stocks, England (walkover)
1898—R. Palmer, England
1899—H. Gibson, Canada
1900—C. Huret, France
1901—02—Thaddaus Robl, Germany
1903—Piet Dickentmann, Holland
1904—05—Robert Walthour, United States
1906—07—Louis Darragon, France
1908—F. Ryser, Switzerland
1909—11—Georges Parent, France
1912—George Wiley, United States

1913—Paul Guignard, France
1914—19—No competition
1920—Georges Seres, France
1921—Victor Linart, Belgium
1922—Leon Vanderstuyft, Belgium
1923—Paul Suter, Switzerland
1924—Victor Linart, Belgium
1925—Robert Grassin, France
1926—27—Victor Linart, Belgium
1928—Walter Sawall, Germany
1929—Georges Paillard, France
1930—Erich Moller, Germany
1931—Walter Sawall, Germany
1932—Georges Paillard, France
1933—Charles Lacquehay, France
1934—Erich Metze, Germany
1935—Charles Lacquehay, France
1936—A. Raynaud, France
1937—Walter Lohmann, Germany
1938—Erich Metze, Germany
1939—45—No competition
1946—Elio Frosio, Italy
1947—Raoul Lesueur, France
1948—Jean-Jacques Lamboley, France
1949—Elio Frosio, Italy
1950—Raoul Lesueur, France
1951—Jan Pronk, Holland
1952—Adolphe Verschueren, Belgium
1953—54—Adolphe Verschureren, Belgium
1955—Guillermo Timoner, Spain
1956—Graham French, Australia
1957—Paul De Paepe, Belgium
1958—Walter Bucher, Switzerland
1959—60—Guillermo Timoner, Spain
1961—Karl Marcell, West Germany
1962—Guillermo Timoner, Spain
1963—Leo Proost, Belgium
1964—65—Guillermo Timoner, Spain
1966—Romain DeLoof, Belgium
1967—68—Leo Proost, Belgium
1969—Jaap Oudkerk, Netherlands
1970—E. Rudolph, West Germany
1971—72—T. Verschueren, Belgium

Professional Sprint (Track)

1895—R.T.C. Protin, Belgium
1896—P. Bourrilon, France
1897—Willy Arend, Germany
1898—G.A. Banker, United States
1899—Major Taylor, United States
1900—Edm. Jacquelin, France
1901—03—Th. Ellegaard, Denmark
1904—Iver Lawson, United States
1905—Gabriel Poulain, France
1906—Th. Ellegaard, Denmark
1907—Emile Friol, France
1908—Th. Ellegaard, Denmark
1909—V. Dupre, France
1910—Emile Friol, France
1911—Th. Ellegaard, Denmark
1912—Frank L. Kramer, United States

1913—Walter Rutt, Germany
1914—19—No competition
1920—R. Spears, Australia
1921—24—Pete Moeskops, Holland
1925—E. Kauffman, Switzerland
1926—Pete Moeskops, Holland
1927—30—Lucien Michard, France
1931—W. Falck Hansen, Denmark
1932—37—Jos. Scherens, Belgium
1938—Arie Van Vliet, Holland
1939—45—No competition
1946—Jan Derksen, Holland
1947—Jos. Scherens, Belgium
1948—Arie Van Vliet, Holland
1949—51—Reg Harris, England
1952—Oskar Plattner, Switzerland
1953—Arie Van Vliet, Holland
1954—Reg Harris, Great Britain
1955—56—Antonio Maspes, Italy
1957—Jan Derksen, Holland
1958—Michel Rousseau, France
1959—62—Antonio Maspes, Italy
1963—Sante Gaiardoni, Italy
1964—Antonio Maspes, Italy
1965—Giuseppi Beghetto, Italy
1966—Giuseppi Beghetto, Italy
1967—Patrick Sercu, Belgium
1968—Giuseppe Beghetto, Italy
1969—Patrick Sercu, Belgium
1970—G. Johnson, Australia
1971—Leijin Loeveseijn, Netherlands
1972—R. van Lancker, Belgium

Professional Road

1927—Alfred Binda, Italy
1928—29—George Ronsse, Belgium
1930—Alfred Binda, Italy
1931—Learco Guerra, Italy
1932—Alfred Binda, Italy
1933—George Speicher, France
1934—Karel Kaers, Belgium
1935—Jean Aerts, Belgium
1936—Antonio Magne, France
1937—Elio Meulenberg, Belgium
1938—Marcel Kint, Belgium
1939—45—No competition
1946—Hans Knecht, Switzerland
1947—Theo. Middelkamp, Holland
1948—Alberic Schotte, Belgium
1949—Henri Van Steenbergen, Belgium
1950—Alberic Schotte, Belgium
1951—Ferdinand Kubler, Switzerland
1952—Heinz Mueller, Germany
1953—Fausto Coppi, Italy
1954—Louison Bobet, France
1955—Stan Ockers, Belgium
1956—57—Rik Van Steenbergen, Belgium
1958—Ercole Baldini, Italy
1959—Andre Darrigade, France
1960—61—Rik van Looy, Belgium
1962—Jean Stablenski, France

1963—Bennoni Beheyt, Belgium
1964—Jan Janssen, Holland
1965—Tommy Simpson, England
1966—Rudi Altig, West Germany
1967—Eddy Merckx, Belgium
1968—Vittorio Adorni, Italy
1969—Harm Ottenbros, Netherlands
1970—J.P. Monseré, Belgium
1971—Eddy Merckx, Belgium
1972—Marino Basso, Italy

Professional Pursuit

1946—Gerrit Peters, Holland
1947—Fausto Coppi, Italy
1948—Gerrit Schulte, Holland
1949—Fausto Coppi, Italy
1951—51—Antonio Bevilacqua, Italy
1952—53—Sid Patterson, Australia
1954—56—Guido Messina, Italy
1957—59—Roger Riviere, France
1960—61—Rudi Altig, West Germany
1962—Henk Nydam, Holland
1963—Leandro Faggin, Italy
1964—Ferdinand Bracke, Belgium
1965—66—Leandro Faggin, Italy
1967—Tijman Groen, Holland
1968—Hugh Porter, England
1969—Frederick Bracke, Belgium
1970—Hugh Porter, England
1971—Dirk Baert, Belgium
1972—Hugh Porter, England

Amateur Sprint (Track)

1893 (1 mile)—A. Zimmerman, United States
1893 (10 miles)—A. Zimmerman, United States
1894 (1 mile)—August Lehr, Germany
1894 (10 kilometers)—Jaap Eden, Holland
1895—Jaap Eden, Holland
1896—H. Reynolds, Ireland
1897—E. Schrader, Denmark
1898—Paul Albert, Germany
1899—T. Summersgill, England
1900—Didier-Nauts, Belgium
1901—E. Maitrot, France
1902—C. Piard, France
1903—A.L. Reed, England
1904—M. Hurley, United States
1905—J.S. Benyon, England
1906—F. Verri, Italy
1907—J. Devoissoux, France
1908—V.L. Johnson, England
1909—11—W.J. Bailey, England
1912—D. MacDougall, United States
1913—W.J. Bailey, England
1914—19—No competition
1920—M. Peeters, Holland
1921—M. Andersen, Denmark
1922—H.T. Johnson, England
1923—24—L. Michard, France
1925—Jaap Meyer, Holland
1926—A. Martinetti, Italy
1927—Mathias Engel, Germany

1928—W. Falck Hansen, Denmark
1929—A. Mazairac, Holland
1930—L. Gerardin, France
1931—Helge Harder, Denmark
1932—A. Richter, Germany
1933—Jac van Egmond, Holland
1934—Benedetto Pola, Italy
1935—Toni Merkens, Germany
1936—Arie Van Vliet, Holland
1937—38—J. Van De Wyver, Holland
1939—Jan Derksen, Holland
1940—45—No competition
1946—Oskar Plattner, Switzerland
1947—Reg Harris, England
1948—Mario Ghella, Italy
1949—Sid Patterson, Australia
1950—Maurice Verdeun, France
1951—52—Enzo Sacchi, Italy
1953—Marino Morettini, Italy
1954—Cyril Peacock, Great Britain
1955—Giuseppe Ogna, Italy
1956—57—Michel Rousseau, France
1958—59—Valentina Gasparelli, Italy
1960—Sante Gaiardoni, Italy
1961—62—Sergio Bianchetto, Italy
1963—Patrick Sercu, Belgium
1964—Pierre Trentin, France
1965—Omari Pkhakazde, Russia
1966—67—Daniel Morelan, France
1968—Luigi Beghetto, Italy
1969—71—Daniel Morelon, France

Amateur Motor-Paced

(Discontinued after 1914; road race substituted in 1921.)

1893—L.S. Meintjes, South Africa
1894—Wilhelm Henie, Norway
1895—M. Cordang, Holland
1896—F. Ponscarme, France
1897—E. Gould, England
1898—A.J. Cherry, England
1899—John A. Nelson, United States
1900—L. Bastien, France
1901—Sievers, Germany
1902—A. Gornemann, Germany
1903—A. Audemars, Switzerland
1904—05—Leon Meridith, England
1906—M. Bardonneau, France
1907—09—Leon Meridith, England
1910—H. Hens, Belgium
1911—Leon Meridith, England
1912—No competition
1913—Leon Meridith, England
1914—C. Blekemolen, Holland
1963—Romain DeLoof, Belgium
1964—Jaap Oudkerk, Holland
1965—Miguel Mas, Spain
1966—67—Piet De Witt, Holland
1968—Guiseppe Grassi, Italy
1969—Al Broom, Netherlands
1970—C. Stam, Netherlands
1971—Horst Gnas, West Germany

Amateur Road

1921—Gunnar Skold, Sweden
1922—D. Marsch, England
1923—L. Ferrario, Italy
1924—Andrew Leducq, France
1925—H. Hoevanaers, Belgium
1926—Octave Dayen, France
1927—Jean Aerts, Belgium
1928—Grandi, Italy
1929—P. Bertolassi, Italy
1930—G. Martano, Italy
1931—Henry Hansen, Denmark
1932—G. Martano, Italy
1933—Paul Egli, Switzerland
1934—Kees Pellenaars, Holland
1935—I. Mancini, Italy
1936—E. Buchwalder, Switzerland
1937—Adolfo Leoni, Italy
1938—Hans Knecht, Switzerland
1939—45—No competition
1946—Henri Aubry, France
1947—Alfio Ferrari, Italy
1948—Harry Snell, Sweden
1949—Henk J. Faanhof, Holland
1950—Jack Hoobin, Australia
1951—Gianni Ghidini, Italy
1952—Luciano Ciancola, Italy
1953—Riccardo Filippi, Italy
1954—Emile Van Cautier, Belgium
1955—Sante Ranucci, Italy
1956—Frans Mahn, Holland
1957—Louis Proost, Belgium
1958—59—Gustav Schur, East Germany
1960—Bernhard Eckstein, East Germany
1961—Jean Jourden, France
1962—Renaot Bongioni, Italy
1963—Flaviano Vicentini, Italy
1964—Eddy Merckx, Belgium
1965—Jacques Betheral, France
1966—Evert Dolman, Holland
1967—Graham Webb, Great Britain
1968—Vittorio Marcelli, Italy
1969—Leif Mortensen, Denmark
1970—Jorgen Schmidt, Denmark
1971—Regis Ovion, France

Amateur Pursuit

1946—Roger Rioland, France
1947—48—Guido Messina, Italy
1949—Knud E. Anderson, Denmark
1950—Sid Patterson, Australia
1951—Nino De Rossi, Italy
1952—Piet Van Heusden, Holland
1953—Gino Messina, Italy
1954—Leonardo Faggin, Italy
1955—Norman Sheil, England
1956—Ercole Baldini, Italy
1957—Carlo Simonigh, Italy
1958—Norman Sheil, Great Britain
1959—Rudi Altig, West Germany
1960—Marcel Delattre, France

1961—Hendrik Nydam, Holland
1962—Kay Jensen, Denmark
1963—Jean Walschaerts, Belgium
1964—66—Tijman Groen, Holland
1967—Gerrit Bongers, Holland
1968—Morgan Frey, Denmark
1969—70—Xavier Kurmann, Switzerland
1971—Martin Rodriguez, Colombia

UNITED STATES CHAMPIONS

Professional Motor-Paced (Track)

1900—01—Harry Elkes
1902—03—Robert Walthour Sr.
1904—Harry Caldwell
1905—08—H. McLean
1909—11—Elmer Collins
1912—13—George E. Wiley
1914—C. Carman
1915—George E. Wiley
1916—C. Carman
1917—18—George E. Wiley
1919—C. Carman
1920—25—George Chapman
1926—Victor Hopkins
1927—30—Franco Georgetti
1931—Charles Jaeger
1932—34—Alfred Letourneur
1935—Franco Giorgetti
1936—37—Gerard Debaets
1938—Tino Reboli
1939—Mike DeFilippo
1940—Gustav Kilian
1941—Mike DeFilippo
No further competition.

Professional Sprint (Track)

(Event discontinued after 1941)
1895—97—E.C. Bald
1898—Tom Butler
1899—Tom Cooper
1900—Major Taylor
1901—16—Frank L. Dramer
1917—Arthur Spencer
1918—Frank L. Kramer
1919—Ray Eaton
1920—Arthur Spencer
1921—Frank L. Kramer
1922—23—Willie Spencer
1924—Arthur Spencer
1925—Fred Spencer
1926—Willie Spencer
1927—Harris Horder
1928—29—Fred Spencer
1930—32—Cecil Walker
1933—George Dempsey
1934—36—Willie Honeman
1937—Mathias Engel
1938—Albert Sellinger
1939—George Shipman
1940—Mickey Francoise
1941—Tom Saetta

Amateur Sprint (Track)

1899—Frank L. Kramer
1900—Willie Fenn Sr.
1901—04—M.L. Hurley
1905—Matt Downey
1906—C. Sherwood
1907—W. Van den Dries
1908—Charley Stein
1909—Percy Lawrence
1910—11—Frank Blatz
1912—13—Donald McDougal
1914—Harry Kaiser
1915—Hans Ohrt
1916—17—John L. Staehle
1918—Gus Lang
1919—Charles Osterritter
1920—Fred Taylor
1921—Robert Walthour Jr.
1922—Willie Grimm
1923—Willie Fenn Jr.
1924—Paul Croley
1925—Charles Winter
1926—William Coles
1927—James Walthour Jr.
1928—Charles Ritter
1929—Sergio Matteini
1930—Dominick Tuccillo
1931—Arthur Rose
1932—Amos Hoffman
1933—Eddie Miller
1934—Robert Lipsett Jr.
1935—Albert Sellinger
1936—38—Mickey Francoise
1939—Howard Rupprecht
1940—Buster Logan
1941—Bob Stauffacher
1942—50—No competition
1951—Dave Rhoades
1952—Ronald Rhoades
1953—Richard Gatto (Mile)
1954—64—No competition
1965—Jack Simes
1966—Jack Disney
1967—Jack Simes
1968—Jack Disney
1969—Tim Mountford
1970—Skip Cutting
1971—72—Gary Campbell

Senior Pursuit

1965—Harry Cutting
1966—68—Dave Brink
1969-70—John Vande Velde
1971—72—Mike Neel

Senior 10-Mile (Track)

1965—William Kund
1966—Jim Rossi
1967—68—Steven Maaranen
1969—Jack Simes
1970—Bob Phillips

1971—Hans Nuerenberg
1972—Bob Phillips

Senior Amateur (Road)

1921—Arthur Nieminsky
1922—Carl Hambacher
1923—Charles Barclay
1924—Charles Winter
1925—26—Edward Merkner
1927—James Walthour Jr.
1928—R.J. Connor
1929—Sergio Matteini
1930—Robert Thomas
1931—34—No competition
1935—Cecil Hursey
1936—Jackie Simes
1937—Charles Bergna
1938—A. Jurca
1939—Martin Deras
1940—Furman Kugler
1941—Marvin Thomson
1942—44—No competition
1945—Ted Smith
1946—Don Hester
1947—48—Ted Smith
1949—Jimmy Lauf
1950—Robert Pfarr
1951—Gus Gatto
1952—Steve Hromjak
1953—Ronald Rhoades
1954—58—Jack Disney
1959—63—James Rossi
1964—Jackie Simes
1965—Michael Hiltner
1966—Bob Tetzlaff
1967—Bob Parsons
1968—John Howard
1969—Alan De Fever
1970—Mike Carnahan
1971—Steve Dayton
1972—John Howard

Junior Amateur (Road)

1922—Charles Smithson
1923—Samuel Dowell
1924—William Honeman
1925—Walter Bresnan
1926—Chester Atwood
1927—Ted Becker Jr.
1928—Bobby Thomas
1929—Tino Reboli
1930—George Thomas
1931—34—No competition
1935—36—David Martin
1937—Furman Jugler
1938—John Van Diest
1939—Frank Paul
1940—Harry Naismyth
1941—Andrew Bernardsky
1942—44—No competition
1945—Spencer Busch
1946—Don Sheldon

1947—Joe Cirone Jr.
1948—49—Donald Clausen
1950—Harry Backer
1951—Vaughan Angell
1952—John Chiselko
1953—Jack Hartman
1954—Bob Zumwalt Jr.
1955—Pat De Collibus
1956—Dave Staub
1957—Perry Metzler
1958—Jim Donovan
1959—Jackie Simes III
1960—Robert Fenn
1961—62—Alan Greco
1963—Jose Nin
1964—Tom McMilan
1965—Peter Senia
1966—Dave Johnson
1967—Jim Van Boven
1968—Tracy Wakefield
1969—Don Westell
1970—Henry Whitney
1971—Ralph Therrio
1972—Ted Waterbury

Women's Amateur Sprint

1966—Edith Johnson
1967—68—Nancy Burghart
1969—Audrey McElmury
1970—Jeanne Kloska
1971—Shiela Young
1972—Sue Novarra

Women's Amateur Pursuit

1966—Audrey McElmury
1967—68—Nancy Burghart
1969—70—Audrey McElmury
1971—Kathy Ecroth
1972—Clara Teyssier

Women's Amateur (Road)

1937—Doris Kopsky
1938—Dolores Amundsen
1939—Gladys R. Owens
1940—Mildred Jugler
1941—Jean Michels
1942—44—No competition
1945—46—Mildred M. Dietz
1947—50—Doris Travani
1951—Anna Piplak
1952—Jeanne Robinson
1953—54—Nancy Nieman
1955—Jeanne Robinson
1956—57—Nancy Nieman
1958—Maxine Conover
1959—Joanne Speckin
1960—61—Edith Johnson
1962—Nancy Burghart
1963—Edith Johnson
1964—65—Nancy Burghart
1966—Audrey McElmurray
1967—68—Nancy Burghart

1969—Donna Tobias
1970—Audrey McElmury
1971—Mary Jane Reoch
1972—Debby Bradley

New York Six-Day Winners

Year and Team		Miles
1899—Miller-Waller		2,733
1900—Elkes-MacFarland		2,628
1901—Walthour-MacEachern		2,555
1902—Leander-Krebs		2,477
1903—Walthour-Munroe		2,318
1904—Root-Dorion		2,386
1905—Root-Fogler		2,260
1906—Root-Fogler		2,292
1907—Rutt-Stol		2,312
1908—MacFarland-Moran		2,737
1909—Rutt-Clark		2,660
1910—Root-Moran		2,545
1911—Clark-Fogler		2,718
1912—Rutt-Fogler		2,661
1913—Goullet-Fogler		2,751
1914—Goullet-Grenda		2,759
1915—Grenda-Hill		2,700
1916—Dupuy-Egg		2,625
1917—Goullet-Magin		2,510
1918—McNamara-Magin		2,447
1919—Goullet-Madden		2,501
1920	(Mar.)—Goullet-Magin	2,447
	(Dec.)—Brocco-Coburn	2,289
1921	(Mar.)—Egg-Van Kempen	2,314
	(Dec.)—Brocco-Goullet	2,463
1922	(Mar.)—Grenda-McNamara	2,407
	(Dec.)—Goullet-Belloni	2,457
1923	(Mar.)—Goullet-Grenda	2,507
	(Dec.)—Kockler-Lawrence	2,519
1924	(Mar.)—Brocco-Buysse	2,454
	(Dec.)—Van Kempen-McNamara	2,368
1925	(Mar.)—Walthour-Spencer	2,397
	(Dec.)—Goosens-Debaets	2,394
1926	(Mar.)—McNamara-Giorgetti	2,109
	(Dec.)—McNamara-Linari	2,286
1927	(Mar.)—McNamara-Giorgetti	2,340
	(Dec.)—Spencer-Winter	2,522
1928	(Mar.)—Giorgetti-Debaets	2,162
	(Dec.)—Giorgetti-Spencer	2,290
1929	(Mar.)—Giorgetti-Debaets	2,135
	(Dec.)—Giorgetti-Debaets	2,270
1930	(Mar.)—Belloni-Debaets	2,330
	(Dec.)—Giorgetti-Broccardo	2,666
1931	(Mar.)—Letourneur-Guimbretiere	2,663
	(Dec.)—Letourneur-Guimbretiere	2,646
1932	(Mar.)—McNamara-Peden	2,602
	(Dec.)—Peden-Spencer	2,482
1933	(Mar.)—Letourneur-Debaets	2,500
	(Dec.)—Letourneur-Peden	2,487
1934	(Mar.)—Broccardo-Guimbretiere	2,472
	(Dec.)—Letourneur-Debaets	2,453
1935	(Mar.)—Letourneur-Giorgetti	2,359
	(Dec.)—Killian-Vopel	2,477
1936	(Mar.)—Killian-Vopel	2,572
	(Dec.)—Walthour-Crossley	2,499

1937	(Mar.)—Aerts-Debrucker	....	2,389
	(Dec.)—Killian-Vopel	....	2,435
1938	(Sep.)—Killian-Vopel	....	2,482
1939	(May)—Peden-Peden	....	2,388
	(Nov.)—Moretti-Yates	....	2,080
1940—47—No competition			
1948	(Mar.)—Giorgetti-DeBacco	.....	2,343
	(Oct.)—Bruneau-Saen	....	2,396
	(Nov.)—Giorgetti-Moretti	......	2,435
1949	(Mar.)—Diggelman-Koblet	......	2,384
	(Nov.)—Strom-Arnold	....	2,168

1950 (Mar.)—Rigoni-Terruzzi 2,081
1951—58—No competition
1959—Terruzzi—Faggin 1,218
1961—Plattner—von Buren 2,359

Event discontinued

Record—2,759 miles, Goullet-Grenda in 1914.

(For Olympic champions see section on Olympic games.)

UNITED STATES RECORDS

(Source: Chester Nelsen Sr., Records Chairman, Amateur Bicycle League of America)

Outdoor Banked Track—Unpaced Miles vs. Time

By — Ronald Skarin, Encino, California ....
... October 21, 1970

By — Wes Chowen, Encino, California ....
.. July 6, 1967

Miles	Time	Miles	Time
1	.2.13.6	13	.29.27.4
2	.4.27.9	14	.31.43.2
3	.6.42.1	15	.38.59.2
4	.8.55.5	20	.45.22.1
5	11.10.5	25	.56.48.3
6	13.24.3	30	1.08.24.2
7	15.39.7		
8	17.54.8		
9	20.11.1		
10	22.21.4		
11	24.43.6		
12	27.01.0		

Outdoor Banked Track—Distance Against Time

Miles	Time	Name and Place	Date
25 M 3975 Ft.	1 Hr.	Bob Best—San Francisco, California	June 12, 1960
47 M 5262 Ft.	2 Hr.	Bob Tetzlaff—Brown Deer, Wisconsin	October 4, 1960
64 M 5245 Ft.	3 Hr.	Paul Washak—Brown Deer, Wisconsin	August 15, 1960
84 M 2780 Ft.	4 Hr.	Paul Washak—Brown Deer, Wisconsin	August 15, 1960
103 M 4250 Ft.	5 Hr.	Paul Washak—Brown Deer, Wisconsin	August 15, 1960
122 M 5037 Ft.	6 Hr.	Paul Washak—Brown Deer, Wisconsin	August 15, 1960
141 M 3409 Ft.	7 Hr.	Paul Washak—Brown Deer, Wisconsin	August 15, 1960
159 M 3820 Ft.	8 Hr.	Paul Washak—Brown Deer, Wisconsin	August 15, 1960
178 M 682 Ft.	9 Hr.	Paul Washak—Brown Deer, Wisconsin	August 15, 1960
195 M 717 Ft.	10 Hr.	Paul Washak—Brown Deer, Wisconsin	August 15, 1960
212 M 717 Ft.	11 Hr.	Paul Washak—Brown Deer, Wisconsin	August 15, 1960
230 M 3645 Ft.	12 Hr.	Paul Washak—Brown Deer, Wisconsin	August 15, 1960

Outdoor Banked Track—Unpaced Competition

Miles	Time	Name and Place	Date
1000 Meters	1.09.7	Jackie Simes—Northbrook, Illinois	July 6, 1967
*1000 Meters	1.05.67	Olympic Games—Mexico City	1968
4000 Meters	5.05.4	John Vande Velde—Northbrook, Illinois	July 16, 1970
*4000 Meters	4.55.4	David Brink Olympics—Mexico City	1968
24 Mi., 1962 Ft.	1.0.00.0	Steve Pfeiffer—Chicago, Illinois	September 3, 1959

Outdoor Banked Track—Scratch Competition

Miles	Time	Name and Place	Date
½	59.9	Peter Senia, Jr.—Northbrook, Illinois	August 21, 1966
2	4.42.6	Chris Rose—Northbrook, Illinois	August 21, 1966
10	21.29	William Kund—Encino, California	August 1965

Road Competition—Scratch

Miles	Time	Name and Place	Date
¼	29.4	B.W. King, Atlantic City, New Jersey	September 16, 1922
1/3	38.6	Charles Winters—Chicago, Illinois	September 8, 1923
1	2.02	Henry Surman	August 8, 1908
1	2.02	R.L. Guthridge, Westfield, New Jersey	August 8, 1908
1	2.02	S.C. Haberle	August 8, 1908
2	4.43.2	Robert Parson—Milwaukee, Wisconsin	August 26, 1961
3	7.18.2	Don Sheldon—Columbus, Ohio	August 18, 1946
5	11.38	Vaughn Angell—Columbus, Ohio	August 5, 1951
15	34.14.6	Francois Mertens—Washington, D.C.	August 7, 1955
20	45.22	A.E. Wahl—Buffalo, New York	July 4, 1921
25	1.02.01.4	Rupert Walti—Belleville, New Jersey	May 8, 1955
30	1.10.48	Francois Mertens—Washington, D.C.	August 7, 1935
50	1.56.10.7	Jack Simes—Somerville, New Jersey	May 30, 1967
75	3.15.58	Eddie Doerr—St. Louis, Mo.	April 23, 1972
100	4.23.45	Donald Nelsen—St. Louis, Missouri	July 25, 1965
125	5.41.30	Bernard Dodd—Lake Merced, California	August 19, 1956
100 km	2.40.11	Arnold Uhrlass—Flemington, New Jersey	July 4, 1963
240.8	12.00.00	Ted Ernst—Pittsburgh, Pennsylvania	October 4, 1953

Road Competition—4 Man Team Unpaced

Distance	Time	Team and Place	Date
100 km	2.24.00.97	Wes Chowen, Bob Freund, Michael Hiltner, Bob Tetzlaff, Rome, Italy—Olympics	1960

Outdoor Banked Track—Pursuit Competition

Distance	Time	Team and Place	Date
4,000 Meters	4.39.3	4 Man Team: Skip Cutting, Steve Maaranen, John Van De Velde, Wayne Le Bombard, Encino, California	August 1968
*4,000 Meters	4.32.87	4 Man Team: Dave Chauner, Harry Cutting, Steve Maaranen, John Van De Valde, Olympic Games Mexico City	1968
4,000 Meters	5.10.1	2 Man Team: Hans Wolf, Arnold Uhrlass, Kissena Park, Flushing, New York City	September 1964

* High Altitude Record, Not Official

Outdoor Banked Track—Match Race Competition

Distance	Time	Name and Place	Date
Last 200 Meters	11.4	Jackie Simes—Copenhagen	June 5, 1962

Outdoor Banked Track—Unpaced Miles vs. Time—Women
By—Audrey McElmury, Encino, California ...... July 12, 1969

Miles	Time		
2	4.52.1	11	26.31.6
3	7.16.3	12	28.58.4
4	9.40.9	13	31.23.5
5	12.05.3	14	33.50.2
6	14.29.5	15	36.17
7	16.54.7	16	48.39.7
8	19.16.5	25	60.28.4
9	21.42.5	Distance for one hour:	
10	24.07.2	24 miles, 4098 feet, 9 inches	

Outdoor Banked Track—Women's Records

Distance	Time	Name and Place	Date
200 Meters, Flying Start	13.3	Edith Johnson—Northbrook, Illinois	August 1965
½ Mile	1.01.5	Edith Johnson—Brown Deer, Wisconsin	August 26, 1961
1 Mile	2.20.9	Nancy Burghart—St. Louis, Missouri	August 26, 1962
2 Mile	5.06	Elizabeth Burghart—St. Louis, Missouri	August 26, 1962
3,000 Meters	4.08.2	Audrey McElmury—Encino, California	July 7, 1968

Road Competition—Handicap

Miles	Time	Name and Place	Date
3	7.21	Jerome Steinert—Rye Beach, New York	September 12, 1909
5	12.28.4	J.B. Hawkins—Valley Stream, New York	November 8, 1908
10	23.08	Tom Bello—Floral Park, New York	September 12, 1909
13	30.56.6	Eugene Aickelin—Bronx, New York	May 20, 1923
15	34.52.8	Eugene Aickelin—Brooklyn, New York	June 24, 1923
20	49.55	Glenn A. Baxter—San Bernardino, California	May 12, 1917
25	57.15	Bernard Dodd—Oakland, California	October 14, 1956
50	1.58.05.6	Karl Napper—Commack, Long Island, N.Y.	May 7, 1961
60	2.17.38	William Yarwood—Camden to Atlantic Ct.	June 10, 1923
100	4.05.44	Francois Mertens—Wesbury, New York	June 8, 1952

Road Competition—Unpaced

Miles	Time	Name and Place	Date
1	2.08	Berthold Baker—Grant City, New Jersey	October 11, 1914
10	23.02.4	Mike Neel—Lake Merritt, Cal.	August 15, 1971
25	58.05	William Kund—Riverside, California	March 1965
60	2.35.09	John Sinibaldi—Paterson, New Jersey	June 9, 1935
90	4.23.58	Albert Marquart—Paterson, New Jersey	June 9, 1929
150	8.26.27	Joseph Kopsky—Floral Park, New York	May 5, 1912

Women's Road Records

25 Mile Scratch	1.04.44	Audrey McElmury—Riverside, California	April 1966
12 Hours Scratch, 217.4 Miles		Ruth Sibley—Pittsburgh, Pennsylvania	October 14, 1953

BILLIARDS

(Courtesy of Clement F. Trainer, The Union League of Philadelphia, 140 South Broad Street, Philadelphia, Pa., 19102, billiard historian and author of *History of the 18.2 Balk-Line Game of Billiards in the United States.*)

A textbook on the game of billiards, published at the turn of the century, touching on its historical aspects, quaintly observed, "Billiards was practically without a beginning. As with untold other excellences, so with that. Until merit is established, curiosity as to its origin rarely begins. When merit is acknowledged, it is too late to trace origin."

Little has been uncovered in the interim to alter that appraisal, but writers have continued to perpetuate those unsupported legends about which our anonymous author expressed such obvious misgivings. Chief of these would trace the beginnings of billiards to croquet or some similar outdoor game, brought indoors to escape the hazards of the weather, and date it from the fourteenth to the fifteenth century. Suffice it to say that the game today bears little resemblance to these tortured concepts, for, again drawing on our author, "whatever its old form, its new is essentially American," and this verdict, the irony of which could never have been foreseen, is as true today as when it was written.

Because today the various forms of the game on which this country placed its stamp are flourishing in Europe, Japan, and South America, while here it is but a shadow of its former self. Other than at the pocket game, professional competition, which furnished the inspiration for millions of less gifted players, is nonexistent; the great recreation rooms and academies, some of which housed a hundred or more tables, have all but disappeared, while private clubs, long the "high altars" of the game, have removed or greatly reduced their billiard facilities, and the game's devotees are but a ragged remnant of a once mighty army. A very modest renaissance, largely in the area of home tables, and virtually solely of the pocket variety, has occurred in the recent past, and it can only be hoped that a game that offers so much to its participants will one day, as has been the case with other sports, notably tennis, again take its rightful place in the sporting world.

As might be supposed, the game in this country derived from the English style, the size of the table being either six by twelve feet, or five and one half by eleven feet, with either four or six pockets. Four balls were used, consisting of a pure white "cue" ball for one player, a spotted white "cue" ball for his opponent, and two red "object" balls (the opponent's "cue" ball automatically became a third "object" ball for the striker). Points were scored by pocketing balls or by caroms, viz., causing the "cue" ball to strike two or three of the "object" balls. It was at this style of play that the first Tournament for the Championship of America was held in New York from June 1st to 9th, 1863, with Dudley Kavanaugh the winner in a field of eight players.

Prior to the construction of the pocketless table (the true billiard table), initial attempts at what was to become the basic billiard game were made by (1) reducing the number of balls to three, viz., two "cue" balls and one "object" ball, and (2) restricting the play simply to caroms—if in the process any one of the three balls was pocketed, no weight was given it, it was replaced at a designated spot, and the game proceeded.

Next evolved the two types of tables in use today—the true billiard table, sans pockets, with caroms as its sole objective, and a table employing six pockets, known as a "pool," or in later years, "pocket billiards," into which the direction of a designated ball was the sole object.

While the basic game of pool (pocket billiards) has remained virtually unchanged for three quarters of a century, the game of billiards passed through several phases. The pure carom game, played on a 5x10 table, with three balls, became the standard in the early 1870s, and the first Tournament for the Championship of the World at this style of play took place in New York from June 23rd to June 30th, 1973, ending in a tie among the first three of six contestants, with Albert Garnier emerging as the winner in the playoff.

However, the professionals of that era produced runs of such monotonous duration that increasingly restrictive measures were introduced to curtail them. The first device was the introduction of "balk" lines, lines drawn on the table restricting the areas in which caroms could be made. The first of such concepts took two forms, one consisting of four triangular spaces at each corner of the table, measuring fourteen by twenty eight inches (initially, a triangle measuring 5½ inches was explored), and the second a continuous line paralleling all four cushions, drawn six inches from the rail. Both of these types were described as the "Champion's Game," but were short lived. At the first style, in the New York tournament of November 11th to 24th, 1879, William Sexton and George F. Slosson tied for the lead in a field of eight, with Sexton winning the playoff. The second type received minimum acceptance, and both styles

passed from the competitive scene in 1885.

The other effort was the game of "cushion caroms," wherein a point was scored only if the "cue" ball struck at least one cushion prior to completing the carom. The first tournament at this style of play was held in New York from November 14th to 26th, 1881, and was won by Joseph Dion in a field of ten players. This version of the game enjoyed considerable popularity before it too passed from the scene.

The concept of balk-line as it ultimately developed appeared in the championship tournament held in Chicago from March 26th to April 6th, 1883, the lines then being drawn eight inches from and parallel with each rail, in the manner of the illustration at the end of this article, but without the small "anchor blocks," which did not appear until 1894. Jacob Schaefer, Sr. was the winner in a field of seven players.

By 1885, the lines were expanded to fourteen inches, and in a tournament held that year in New York from April 20th to 29th, George F. Slosson emerged the winner in a field of five. Later in the year the game received added impetus from a three-cornered tournament featuring the leading practitioners of the era— Slosson, Schaefer, and Vignaux. The original series ended in a tie, as did the first playoff, with Schaefer emerging the victor in the second.

In 1896 the full leap was made to eighteen inches, with a hybrid tournament combining 18.1 (a new concept—only one shot in "balk"), 18.2 (two shots in "balk"—the rules for this game, along with other major variations of the billiard game, are appended at the conclusion of this article), and cushion caroms, played in New York, Chicago and Boston. The first authentic tournament for the 18.1 championship of the world was played in New York from November 20th to December 4th, 1897, with George F. Slosson the winner in a field of five. This style of play, lacking the delicacy inherent in the 18.2 game, had a relatively short life, officially terminating in 1914, although abortive and controversial efforts were made to revive it in the mid twenties and thirties. Paris in 1903 was the site of the first tournament for the 18.2 Balk-Line Championship of the World, a game that has been described by one historian as "the highest standard by which the skill of the amateur and professional experts is measured," adding that it combined "all the beautiful and intricate features of the most fascinating of pastimes." It was the game that typified "billiards" to generations of Americans. This first tournament was won by the famed Frenchman Maurice Vignaux, whom America's own Willie Hoppe was to defeat three years later for the 18.1 crown at the age of eighteen. Following the Paris tournament, all of the remaining fourteen tournaments were played in the United States, the last being in Chicago in 1934, and players came here from France,

Belgium, Germany, and Japan to match their skills with the American players.

In 1937, as a last ditch effort to salvage the balk-line game, two final variations were introduced into this country. The first, known as 71.2, was a direct import from Europe, where it is still regularly played in the Pentathlon (71 refers to millimeters); the lines are so drawn as to eliminate any unrestricted area from the table, and result in six blocks. The second was an American variation of the preceding game, and was called 28.2, the 28, however, being in inches, to distinguish it from the first game. The distance of the lines from the rails was identical (28 inches equal 71 millimeters), but they were drawn so as to produce only four blocks, all restricted. Both games disappeared the following year with the demise of professional balk-line in this country.

The championship matches in the early part of the century were social affairs approximating the atmosphere of the opera, held in ballrooms of large hotels with spectators of both sexes attending in formal clothes. Four thousand people witnessed Hoppe's first match in this country upon his return from winning the 18.1 balk-line title abroad, and several years later he was to give a "command performance" at the White House.

A generation earlier George F. Slosson numbered among his pupils President Grant and King Edward VII of England, who once, as Prince of Wales, met Slosson in Liverpool with his private railroad car when he arrived with another pupil, the famed Adelina Patti. Other pupils included Mark Twain, Henry Ward Beecher, Robert G. Ingersoll, Charles A. Dana, and John McGraw. The game's "golden age" was in the twenties, when names like Hoppe, "young" Jake Schaefer, and Cochran were almost household words, to which the cognoscenti added those of Horemans of Belgium and Hagenlacher of Germany, each of these five men at one time holding the title of 18.2 balk-line champion of the world.

Willie Hoppe, of course, is the name best identified with the game by the American public, a fact that can readily be explained by the longevity of his reign: Hoppe won his first title in 1906 at the age of 18, although he had been in the public eye before that as the "boy wonder"; he won his last title in 1952, when he was approaching 65. No other American sports figure ever dominated his game to the extent that Hoppe did: it is an interesting commentary on the duration of his career that he competed against two generations of Schaefers, the famed "Wizard" whose final match was the successful defence of his 18.1 balk-line crown against Hoppe, and his illustrious son, "young Jake," the man who first interrupted Hoppe's long rule as champion at the 18.2 style of play. Despite Hoppe's long tenure, the younger Schaefer must,

in fact, be hailed as the finest balk-liner this country ever produced, raising the game to levels not seen before or since in America. One of his more spectacular performances, in championship competition, was to run the required 400 points "from the spot," his opponent never getting the opportunity to shoot.

With the public demand for a more challenging form of play, the three American balk-liners turned their attention in the mid-thirties to the three-cushion version of the game. While in no way disputing the statement of the previously quoted historian, the difficulty of the latter game can be readily grasped by the fact that whereas at that time an average of fifty points at each turn at the table was an acceptable measurement of professional skill at the balk-line style of play, an average of one at the three-cushion game occurs more in the breach than in the observance.

Previously, the role of three cushions had always been subordinated to that of balk-line; early in the century the *New York Times* had editorialized that the game "was not for spectators," because of the tendency of the earlier players to strive less to make a shot than to prevent their opponents from so doing, and as late as 1926 a Philadelphia paper referred to it as "a recently boomed style called three cushions. . . . Philadelphians know the game chiefly by hearsay." But the entrance of the three balk-liners advanced the game to front and center stage, and Hoppe, in particular, raised the game to new heights. In a tournament in 1940, he won all twenty of his games without a loss, fashioning a remarkable average of 1.16, meaning that he averaged one and one sixth point at this difficult game every time he shot. For the next twelve years, until his final triumph in 1952, Hoppe virtually dominated this style of play, but following his retirement there were a few sporadic competitive events, after which three cushions followed the fate of the balk-line game.

On the world scene, toward the end of the twenties, the three-cushion game received a new impetus, which in nowise has abated, from an unlikely source—the amateur player. The Union Mondiale de Billiard—the World Union of Billiards—is headquartered in Brussels, Belgium, and is the governing body of world amateur billiards. It has affiliates throughout Europe, Asia, South America, and, since 1966, the United States, where it is known as the Billiard Federation of the U.S.A. The latter is still a fledgling organization, its numerical membership grossly inferior to its European counterpart, as is, to a lesser degree, the skill of its players. While the world organization sponsors all of the major types of billiard games, emphasis is on the three-cushion game, in which it has conducted worldwide tournaments since 1928. In this period, during which the winning average has shown a steady increase, it has been won but once by an American, the beloved Edward L. Lee, of the New York Athletic Club, in 1936. Since 1963 through 1973 every tournament has been won by an extraordinary 36-year-old Belgian by the name of Raymond Ceulemans, whose lowest winning grand average during that time was 1.165 and his highest and most recent an incredible 1.479. Call it "improvement of the breed," but just as we have witnessed the breaking of the four-minute mile and the soaring of pole vaulters to unprecedented heights, so have the current players with the awesome statistics of their performances demonstrated their clear superiority over the greatest names in American billiard lore.

The best record for a 50-point championship tournament game in this country is 23 innings, achieved by three different players more than twenty years ago; with the speed up in the play, games now consist of 60 points, which Ceulemans has achieved in championship competition in 24 innings, for an amazing average of 2.50. . . . (an extraordinary performance by an American professional, Otto Reiselt, in 1926, however, should not go unnoticed; in "League" competition, which was the ultimate test in that day, he made 50 points in 16 innings, or an astronomic average of 3.125.) In the balk-line game, "young Jake" Schaefer's grand average of 57.14 against 5 competitors in the Chicago Tournament of 1925 marked the game's zenith in this country; in the European Pentathlon of 1972, which like its counterpart in the world of track features competition in several styles of play, the highest grand average at the balk-line style of play was 118.75, the second 109.09, the three following ranged from 81.24 to 69.13, while the two lowest averages were 57.03 and 34.56. In 1925, as noted above, Schaefer in one contest amassed the required 400 points in one inning, a feat never matched in the history of the game in this country; last year, in the aforementioned Pentathlon, two players accomplished it.

Thus far we have ignored the one phase of the game which, excepting its military bases overseas, America has never exported, pocket billiards. Oddly enough, it is this "poor relation" of the billiard family that has best survived, with activity and proficiency at the professional level at least comparable to the great names of its past like De Oro, Greenleaf, and Mosconi, and certainly with the largest residue of participants. It may tell something of the change in public tastes to recall Mosconi's statement that in the early thirties it was not uncommon for him to draw more spectators to one of his matches on Saturday evening in Chicago than the Bears football team did the following afternoon.

Whether this residue of interest, stimulated by the activity on the international scene, will become the nucleus for a revival of the game in this country remains very much on the knees of the gods.

CHAMPIONS AND RECORDS

The data that follows is drawn from games played in this country involving both native and foreign players, and contests in which Americans engaged outside the country. Under the then-prevailing circumstances, it is not unduly nationalistic to maintain that the champions listed and the records made during the respective periods covered were, in fact, "world" champions and "world" records, and were so recognized. Professionally, nothing has ever replaced on a worldwide scale the supervisory organization governing the several aspects of the game during the periods covered by this article, and today professional competition is almost as obsolete outside the United States as it is in this country. Reference has been made to the impressive amateur organization known as the Union Mondiale de Billard, but the names would not be recognized by a handful of Americans, and in the present state of the game in this country, the records, even if readily available, would be of little interest. At best, then, this article can be dismissed as a chronology of the game as it once existed under the American aegis, and a requiem for its passing.

At the outset, it should be noted, with no little regret, that the game has been poorly served by its would-be historians: a compilation of the demonstrable errors would contain sufficient material for a monograph that would fascinate a student of the game, and conceivably nauseate the casual reader. Secondly, the manner in which the game developed in this country was probably unique in the annals of sport. Almost from its inception it was under the sponsorship (domination?) of one or two equipment manufacturers, who subsequently merged, creating what was known with something less than affection among the players as "the billiard trust." With tactics that today would induce coronaries in the Department of Justice, they ruled the game with an iron hand: *they* donated the "championship emblem," and only contests played with *their* equipment were recognized as being for the "championship": Matches had to be "sanctioned"—Jake Schaefer, Jr. was compelled to retroactively renounce the 18.1 championship one year after the vanquished champion and the entire sporting world agreed he had won it; the title, it was declared, had been "vacated" by reason of inactivity, and a tournament would have to be held to determine the new champion. It never was, and it would be a brave historian who would presume to pontificate on 18.1 history subsequent to March 20, 1914. When Hoppe, the greatest gate attraction in the game's history, seriously entered three-cushion competition, he was barred from the following year's balk-line tournament—the game which he had previously dominated most of his life; from on high came the decree that he could not compete for both titles! The players occasionally rebelled, but since the leading performers were on the payroll of the manufacturer, they just as regularly returned, grumbling, to their appointed rounds. This situation to a degree is made to order for the historian, who up to a point can rationalize his version of history by adhering to the sequence of champions as revealed by the story of "sanctioned" matches; on the other hand, it conflicts with reality, and creates a credibility gap when, in the story of the 18.1 game, competition officially ceased in 1914, while contests billed in the press as being for the championship were held, and new records were being set, as late as 1938.

A minor problem in a list of champions, although one felt strongly by those involved, is simply one of mechanics, and part of the confusion in the records can be explained by the following factual illustration. Willie Hoppe was the undisputed champion at 18.2 balk-line in 1920, but lost his title to Jake Schaefer, Jr. in November of 1921, who, in turn, twice successfully defended it against challenges in 1922 before losing it to Hoppe in November of that year. Obviously, there are two ways of presenting these facts, viz.,

1920	Hoppe	Hoppe
1921	Hoppe	Schaefer
	Schaefer	
1922	Schaefer	Hoppe
	Hoppe.	

In the listings that follow, the shorter tabulation has been employed—in other words, it is implicit in the listings that the named champion for a given year was also champion for a *portion* of the following year until his successor emerged.

Another point that has provoked discussion arises from various circumstances, viz., war, depression, etc., during which there was no action at the championship level in a particular phase of the game. Thus, in the 18.2 balk-line field, Hoppe, correctly it is felt, is universally listed as champion from 1910 to 1920, despite the fact that between May, 1913 and October 1919, he did not engage in any "sanctioned" contests in defense of this title. Similarly, Schaefer is usually listed as the 18.2 titleholder from 1929 through 1933, despite the absence of championship competition from 1929 to 1934. In the boxing world, at least, custom seems to dictate that the champion is the champion until defeated, ousted by the sport's governing body, or retires.

A further question has been raised concerning championships acquired in tournaments and those won via the challenge route. In the game's heyday it was customary for the rules to provide that at least the two runners-up in a tournament

should have the right to challenge the winner for his title, thereby sustaining interest in the game between tournaments and affording residents of different sections of the country the opportunity of seeing the leading exponents of the game in competitive action as opposed to mere exhibitions. No distinction was ever made in the public's mind whether a man acquired his title in a tournament or via the challenge route, and the point seems without merit.

Finally, and more seriously, is the decision to list a man as a champion in those years when the competitive field was not as representative as might be desirable. Thus, in the three-cushion arena in 1938 the sole major tournament was in France, including, however, two leading American exponents, Cochran (the most recent champion) and Schaefer. It seemed not unfair to designate the winner of the tournament, Roger Conti, as champion for that year. Similarly, in 1939, the principal three-cushion event was a full season of "League" play, a lengthy round robin of competent professionals representing various cities throughout this country and Mexico, but excluding the "big three," Cochran, Hoppe, and Schaefer, who presumably felt that such a grind was beneath them, despite its status and their occasional participation in years past. Chamaco, the winner, has been designated as champion for that year. Conversely, although some records proclaim the existence of isolated three-cushion "champions" as far back as 1878, competition was not really formalized until the introduction of the Lambert Trophy in 1907, and the list begins with the winner of that event.

Concerning the pocket game, there has been a dilution of the authority of the game's "governing body" subsequent to 1957, and a proliferation of "championship" tournaments under varying auspices. The corresponding weakening of the validity of championship claims explains the termination of the titleholders at this particular date.

18.1 Balk-Line
Champions
1897—George F. Slosson
1898—Jacob (Jake) Schaefer, Sr.
    Frank C. Ives*
1901—02—Jacob (Jake) Schaefer, Sr.
1903—George B. Sutton (f)
1904—05—Maurice Vignaux
1906—William (Willie) F. Hoppe
1907—George B. Sutton (f)
    Jacob (Jake) Schaefer, Sr.
1908—George B. Sutton (f)
1909—George F. Slosson
    George B. Sutton
1910—11—William (Willie) F. Hoppe
1912—George B. Sutton
    Ora C. Morningstar
1913—14—William (Willie) F. Hoppe
*Voided on legal technicality   (f) Forfeit

Officially, the 18.1 game expired at this point, but in 1926 Jake Schaefer, Jr. successfully challenged Hoppe for his crown, and was hailed as champion by the press and sporting world. One year later Hoppe challenged Schaefer for the title, but at the last moment, under conflicting pressures from the omnipotent manufacturer and the promoter who arranged the match, Schaefer formally agreed to a nullification of the prior year's contest and renounced any claim to the title. To preclude a threatened lawsuit by the promoter, however, it was agreed that the match should proceed, billed as being not for the "world championship" but for "world supremacy"—a fascinating exercise in semantics. Schaefer again won.

18.1 Balk-Line (2)

In 1930, Hoppe, presumably proceeding on the theory that he had not actually lost his "world championship," accepted the challenge of Cochran for the "title." History repeated itself—the reigning powers refused to "sanction" the match, and again Hoppe lost. One year later he challenged Cochran, and this time won; in 1937 he successfully defended against the challenge of Schaefer. Thus far, at least, there was a plausible if somewhat bizarre logic to the sequence of claims, but in 1938 all logic appears to have gone out the window when in the last major match at this style of play Schaefer defeated Cochran in a contest that allegedly was for the 18.1 championship of the world.

Records

In the light of such a blurred background, it was thought appropriate to develop two sets of records, the first group covering the period through 1914 and the second derived from the subsequent controversial era. The "official" records, then, are as follows:

Type of Record	Holder	Pts.	Year
High run - game (500 points)	Frank Ives	140	1897
High run - match (1,000 points)	Willie Hoppe	110	1910
High avg. - game (500 points)	Frank Ives	31.25	1897
High grand avg. - match (1,000 points)	Willie Hoppe	22.22	1910
High grand avg. - tournament	Frank Ives	14.95	1897

In the period beginning in 1926, competition took the form solely of match play over more than one evening, in which style the performances for a single game are ignored and records recognized only for the match as a whole. In the six matches noted in the text, the highest run was 243 by Hoppe in 1931 in a match of 3,600 points, while the highest grand average of 34.61

was achieved by Schaefer in a match of similar duration in 1926; this latter statement ignores his grand average of 42.86 in the 1938 match with Cochran, which not only was abnormally brief (3 games of 200 points each), but also of doubtful legitimacy.

18.2 Balk-Line Champions

1903–05—Maurice Vignaux
1906—George F. Slosson
    George B. Sutton
1907—George B. Sutton
1908—William (Willie) F. Hoppe
1909—Ora C. Morningstar
    Calvin Demarest
1910—Harry P. Cline
    William (Willie) F. Hoppe
1911–20—William (Willie) F. Hoppe
1921—Jacob (Jake) Schaefer, Jr.
1922–24—William (Willie) F. Hoppe
1925—Jacob (Jake) Schaefer, Jr.
    Edouard J. Horemans
1926—Jacob (Jake) Schaefer, Jr.
    Eric Hagenlacher
1927—William (Willie) F. Hoppe
    Welker Cochran
    Jacob (Jake) Schaefer, Jr.
1928—Edouard J. Horemans
1929–33—Jacob (Jake) Schaefer, Jr.
1934—Welker Cochran

18.2 Balk-Line (2)

Type of Record	Holder	Pts.	Year
High run - game (400 points)	J. Schaefer, Jr.	400	1925
High run - game (500 points)	E.J. Horemans	244	1922
High run - match (1,500 points)	J. Schaefer, Jr.	432	1925
High avg. - game (400 points)	J. Schaefer, Jr.	400	1925
High avg. - game (500 points)	G.B. Sutton	100	1906
High grand avg. - match (1,500 pts.)	J. Schaefer, Jr.	93.75	1926
High grand avg. - tournament	J. Schaefer, Jr.	57.14	1925

Three Cushion Champions

1907—Harry P. Cline
1908—John W. Daly
    Thomas Hueston
    Alfredo De Oro
1909—Alfredo De Oro
1910—Fred Eames
    Thomas Hueston
    Alfredo De Oro
    John W. Daly

1911—Alfredo De Oro
1912—Joseph W. Carney
　　　John Horgan
1913—14—Alfredo De Oro
1915—George Moore
　　　William H. Huey
　　　Alfredo De Oro
1916—Charles Ellis
　　　Charles McCourt
　　　Hugh Heal
　　　George Moore
1917—Charles McCourt
　　　Robert L. Cannefax
　　　Alfredo De Oro
1918—Augie Kieckhefer
1919—Alfredo De Oro
　　　Robert L. Cannefax
1920—John (Johnny) Layton
1921—Augie Kieckhefer
　　　John (Johnny) Layton
1922—John (Johnny) Layton
1923—Tiff Denton
1924—25—Robert L. Cannefax
1926—Otto Reiselt
1927—Augie Kieckhefer
　　　Otto Reiselt
1928—30—John (Johnny) Layton
1931—Arthur Thurnblad
1932—Augie Kieckhefer
1933—Welker Cochran
1934—John (Johnny) Layton
1935—Welker Cochran
1936—William (Willie) F. Hoppe
　　　Welker Cochran
1937—Welker Cochran
1938—Roger Conti
1939—Joseph (Joe) Chamaco
1940—43—William (Willie) F. Hoppe
1944—46—Welker Cochran
1947—52—William (Willie) F. Hoppe
1953—Raymond (Ray) Kilgore
1954—Harold Worst

Records

Conventional tabulations of three cushion records frequently distinguish between performances in "league" games, "tournament" games, and "match" games. The distinction between the first two is subtle and rather narrow, similar to ignoring records set during the baseball season and recognizing only performances in the world series. In some years "league" games were the sole competition, in others they were followed at the conclusion of the season by tournaments that were confined to the players finishing in the top positions in the League. Obviously, the pressure to win a given game in a short tournament is greater than in a lengthy season, but the competition is no less real. The distinction as to match play is justified: matches involve from a few to a number of games, and are generally continuous, so that a player losing 50 to 40 in the first game

can be the leader at the end of the second game by reaching a cumulative total of 100 points before his opponent does. Thus, the opportunity for high runs are greater, viz., a man concluding one night's play with say a run of 8 resumes the following night with the balls in the exact position where he left them, and should he make 5 more points before missing, the performance goes into the record books as a run of 13. Conversely, higher averages are obviously easier to attain in the individual games in "league" or "tournament" play—a major run in a 50-point game influences the "average" much more than it would in the longer "match" contest. Accordingly, the following tabulation compresses a host of statistics into the five basic essentials:

Type of Record	Holder	Pts.	Year
High run - game (50 points)	Willie Hoppe	20	1928
High run - match (360 & 1,000 Points)	Willie Hoppe	15	1936-50
High avg. - game (50 points)	Otto Reiselt	3.13	1926
High grand avg. - match (1,400 points)	Willie Hoppe	1.18	1947
High grand avg. - tournament	Willie Hoppe	1.33	1950

Pocket Billiards Champions

1878—80—Cyrille Dion
　　　Samuel F. Knight
　　　Alonzo Morris
　　　Gottlieb Wahlstrom
　　　Samuel F. Knight
1881—Gottlieb Wahlstrom
1882—83—Albert Frey
1884—85—J.L. Malone
1886—Albert Frey
1887—J.L. Malone (f)
　　　Alfredo De Oro (f)
1888—Alfredo De Oro
　　　Albert Frey
　　　Frank Powers
1889—Albert Frey
　　　Alfredo De Oro
1890—Frank Powers
　　　H. Manning
1891—Frank Powers (f)
　　　Alfredo De Oro
1892—94—Alfredo De Oro
1895—William Clearwater
　　　Alfredo De Oro
1896—Frank Stewart (f)
1897—Grant Eby
　　　Jerome Keogh
1898—William Clearwater
　　　Jerome Keogh
1899—1900—Alfredo De Oro
1901—Frank Sherman
　　　Alfredo De Oro

1902—William Clearwater
    Grant Eby
1903—Grant Eby
1904—Alfredo De Oro
1905—Jerome Keogh (f)
    Alfredo De Oro
    Thomas Hueston (f)
1906—John Horgan
    Jerome Keogh (f)
    Thomas Hueston
1907—Thomas Hueston
1908—Frank Sherman
    Alfredo De Oro
    Thomas Hueston
1909—Charles Weston
    John Kling
    Thomas Hueston
1910—Jerome Keogh
    Alfredo De Oro
1911—Alfredo De Oro
1912—Edward Ralph
    Alfredo De Oro
1913—15—Benjamin (Bennie) Allen
1916—Emmet Blankenship
    John (Johnny) Layton
    Frank Taberski
1917—18—Frank Taberski
1919—24—Ralph Greenleaf
1925—Frank Taberski
1926—Ralph Greenleaf
1927—Erwin Rudolph
    Thomas Hueston
    Frank Taberski (f)
1928—Ralph Greenleaf
    Frank Taberski
1929—Ralph Greenleaf
1930—Erwin Rudolph
1931—32—Ralph Greenleaf
1933—Erwin Rudolph
1934—Andrew Ponzi
1935—36—James (Jimmy) Caras
1937—Ralph Greenleaf
1938—39—James (Jimmy) Caras
1940—Andrew Ponzi
1941—Willie Mosconi
    Erwin Rudolph
1942—Erwin Crane
    Willie Mosconi
1943—Andrew Ponzi
1944—45—Willie Mosconi
1946—Erwin Crane
1947—48—Willie Mosconi
1949—James (Jimmy) Caras
1950—54—Willie Mosconi
1955—Erwin Crane
    Willie Mosconi
1956—57—Willie Mosconi
(f) Forfeit

Records

Following the 1949 World Championship Tournament, the ruling body of the game, in a decision of doubtful wisdom, decreed that henceforth championship matches would be played on a table 4½' x 9', instead of the traditional and more demanding 5' x 10', and that the length of the games would be increased from 125 to 150 points. The records, accordingly, are tabulated for both sizes of equipment.

Type of Record	Holder	Pts.	Year
High run - game (125 pts.)	Andrew Ponzi	127*	1939
High avg. - game (125 pts.)	Willie Mosconi	125	1940
High run - game (150 pts,)	Willie Mosconi	150	1956
High avg. - game (150 pts.)	Willie Mosconi	150	1956
High run - match (5'x10')	Andrew Ponzi	153	1934
High run - match (4½'x9')	Irving Crane	160	1951

*A rare but not unheard of paradox, in which by reason of the maneuvering at the beginning of a game, a player before ever scoring will lose a point (in this instance two points) and then proceed to run out his string, resulting in a high run that exceeds the stipulated duration of the game.

BASIC RULES

(From *The Dictionary of Sports,* published by A.S. Barnes and Co., New York)

Billiards is a game played on a billiard table where an ivory or composition ball is stroked with a long slender stick (cue). The object is to stroke this ball (cue ball) so that it successively hits 2 other balls (object balls), thus scoring a carom or billiard which counts 1 point, the game being for a specified number of points. The player continues as long as he scores points, and then surrenders his turn or inning to his opponent. The chief American games commonly designated as "true" billiards are balking, straight rail, and 3-cushion carom, and all are played on a pocketless table. English billiards is played on a larger table with pockets, and points are scored both for caroms and pocketing the object balls. In the American game of pocket billiards, the sole objective is pocketing. In the United States all other varieties with pockets are usually called "pool." Thus "billiards," used alone, denotes "without pockets" in the United States, "with pockets" in England. The following is an alphabetical list of important varieties of billiards:

Balkline. A pocketless game in which lines (balklines) are drawn parallel to all cushions either 18" or 14" therefrom, 8 spaces (balks) thus being formed between the lines and the cushions (on the ninth space there are no restrictions in the center table). When the 2 object balls are within a given balk, the player may take 1 or 2 shots (depending on the specified game) before driving one of the object balls out of the balk—although it may return to the balk, permitting him an additional turn. Reason: to prevent an expert player from gathering the balls into a corner and making points indefinitely.

Besides these balks there are also 7" x 7" squares (anchors) where each balkline intersects a cushion, the balkline bisecting the anchor. There are thus 8 anchors, and the same rules apply as with the larger balks. Reason for anchors: an expert would otherwise nurse an object ball on each side of, but close to, a balkline and a cushion, and thus not be affected by the balk rule.

The balkline games are American, and there have been three main types, each with a numerical prefix. 18.2, the chief favorite of modern professionals, designates that the balklines are 18" from the cushions and that two shots may be made in balk or anchor. 14.2 is favored by amateurs, the balklines being 14" from the cushions, with the above 2-shot rule. 18.1, formerly played by professionals, but now rare, designates 18" balklines but that only one shot may be made in balk or anchor.

Cushion caroms. A game like straight rail billiards (listed hereunder) except that to score a point the cue ball must touch one or more cushions before completing the carom.

Fifteen-ball. A game like rotation (listed hereunder), except that the score is decided by the actual number of a pocketed ball. The numbers of the 15 balls (numbered 1—15) total 120; therefore the player who first scores 61 is the winner.

14.1 pocket billiards. A game played on a pocketed table with 15 colored object balls numbered 1—15. The game is started by setting them up in triangular shape at the far end of the table, and the object is to knock the object balls into pockets with the cue ball. On each shot the player must specify both the number of the object ball and the pocket aimed at, this being known as "calling the shot." When 14 have been pocketed they are again put in triangle formation with the apex vacant, and the game proceeds until the agreed-on number of points are scored.

Rotation. A game using the same table and balls as pocket billiards and similar except that a player must first pocket the No. 1 ball, then the No. 2, etc., in ascending order to No. 15. Additional balls pocketed on a given stroke count, provided the mandatory one is also pocketed. A game is won by the player who first pockets 8 balls.

Straight rail. A game played on a pocketless table, the objective being to score caroms. The cue ball need hit no cushions, and there are no balklines. Only 2 shots may be made in the crotch.

The crotch is a situation in which both object balls lie within a 4½" square at any corner. Only 3 caroms may be scored unless one or both balls are forced out of the crotch. Failing to do so on the third shot, the player loses his turn.

Three-cushion. A pocketless game in which the cue ball must touch a cushion or cushions 3 different times before the carom is completed. If the cue ball is in contact with a cushion at the start, this cushion does not count as one of the 3 even though the player strokes directly at it. Players lag for opening shot. Winner of lag has choice of cue balls. Once selection of cue balls has been made, the players must continue to use the same cue ball for the duration of the game.

All carom games are begun by lagging to determine rotation of play. If more than two players are involved, rotation of play may be determined by the players drawing lots.

When the game is played by two players or two sides (partners), each player or side has its own cue ball. When three or more players are involved, incoming player shoots still cue ball, unless, for example, one player is "standing" the other two. In this case, the player (a side) uses one cue ball, while the other two players (the other side) use the other cue ball.

To lag for break, two players select a cue ball, which is placed on the table within the head string. The red ball, meanwhile, has been spotted on the foot spot. The players, one lagging to the left of the red ball and the other to the right of the red ball, stroke the white balls to the foot cushion and return. The side rails may be touched by the ball in lagging, though it is not required. Player whose ball comes to rest nearest to the head rail wins the lag. The winner has the right to shoot the first shot or assign the break shot to his opponent.

Billiard Table and Equipment

A rectangular table with a slate surface covered with tight green felt is used for the game. In the United States "billiards," used by itself, denotes any of the varieties played without pockets, and therefore the table has none. In England pockets are used, and the American equivalent for such a table is "pocket billiard" or "pool" table. On all tables cushions of vulcanized rubber along the edges enable the ball to bounce therefrom.

Most tables have 3 small spots on which the balls are spotted at the start, and after they have been pocketed (in any pocket game) or knocked off the table. One spot is the exact center, the other 2 in line with it on the table's long axis, each being half way between the center spot and one of the end cushions.

The usual American table, with or without pockets, has a playing surface 10' x 5' and the height from the floor is about 2½'. The pocketed English table is about 12' x 6'. Pocket tables have 6 pockets—one in each corner, and one in each side cushion, half way between the end cushions, the pocket entrances about 5" wide. Some American pocket tables have detachable cushions which can close the pockets to permit playing of any of the pocketless games.

The standard length of cues is 57", but many great players used a shorter cue. Hoppe's cue was 54" long, the size used by Slosson, Schaefer Sr. and Ives. The weights vary from 15 ounces to 22. Hoppe's weighed 19½ ounces; Johnny Layton used one weighing 22 ounces, while the weight for Schaefer Sr. was only 18. Peterson used the

shortest of cues—53½"—but its weight was 21 ounces.

The average size tip for the cue is ½".

The ivory balls used in 3-cushion and balkline play are two sizes: 2 3/8 and 2 25/64" in diameter. The weight is 7½ ounces. The ivory ball used in pocket billiards is a trifle smaller. The object balls in pocket billiards are made of a composition material, are 2¼" in diameter and weigh a trifle less than 7 ounces.

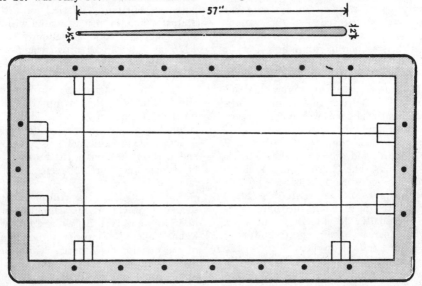

Billiard Table and Cue. This is the top of a balkline table. The balklines are either 14" or 18" from the cushions. The small squares (anchors) are 7" square. This type is illustrated because of the difficulty of textual explanation. For other types none of these lines would be drawn. In these there are three small spots, one in the exact center, the others near the head and foot, midway between the side cushions, so that the spots divide the table crosswise in four equal sections. If there are pockets, there are six—one in each corner and one in each of the side cushions, midway between the ends. (Taken from The Dictionary of Sports, *by Parke Cummings, A.S. Barnes and Company, New York.)*

BOBSLEDDING

The bobsled was developed from the sled of ancient times, which was merely a strip of animal skin stretched between smoothed strips of wood acting as runners. The first step in this evolution was the toboggan. It was conceived and developed about 1890 by a group of thrill-seeking American and English vacationers in Switzerland who were looking for something more daring than plodding through the Swiss Alps on snowshoes.

They laid out a course on the mountains around St. Moritz and were soon hurtling down the snow-clad slopes.

It soon was discovered that the toboggan was

too safe for this particular brand of daredevils, so they came up with the idea of mounting the toboggan on sled-like runners. This produced speeds far in excess of what the toboggan was capable of doing, but the light weight of the toboggan-sled, combined with the excessive speeds, caused the sled to lose its course and there were many serious accidents and some deaths.

The devotees of the toboggan, however, still were active and they formed an organization at St. Moritz called the Toboggan Club. New recruits for toboggan-sledding appeared in 1895 and they developed a much heavier sled than the original and added ballast to help keep it on the course. The new sleds were called "bob-sleds" and the group joined the Toboggan Club. The new group soon became dissatisfied with the safe and sane rules enforced by the Toboggan Club and withdrew to form its own organization under the name of "St. Moritz Bobsleigh Club" and mapped a course down the Swiss Alps called the Cresta Run.

The big sleighs in use at that time carried 5 passengers and the original racing rules stipulated that 2 passengers be women. In a short time stout men were substituted for the women because there were no females who cared to risk traveling over the treacherous run in bobsleds.

The first race on the Cresta Run was held as a feature of the first organized Bobsleigh Festival on Jan. 5, 1898. It was won by a crew that had G. St. Aubyn as the driver and Captain, Mrs. Shepley and Miss Davidson as women passengers, Major DeWinton the supercargo and H. N. P. Shaw the brake. Their time for the first of 2 heats was 3 minutes and the second heat took 2 minutes 54 seconds. The Cresta Run was much steeper than any courses built since, but, in comparison, present-day sleds travel equivalent-distance course in half the time.

Devotees gradually developed features on their sleds to increase their speed and as a consequence the Cresta Run proved to be too dangerous. An artificial run was built at St. Moritz in 1904 and was the first to be engineered for speed with comparative safety. Other winter sports centers soon followed and at the outbreak of World War II there were over 60 courses scattered along the mountainsides of Germany, Italy, Hungary, France, Austria, Switzerland, Czechoslovakia and other countries. Most of them were closed during the war years, but are now reopening.

Austria held the first national championships in 1908. Germany followed in 1910. In 1914 the first European title tests were run off. A hiatus in sports occurred during World War I, but the championships were resumed following the cessation of hostilities.

When the agitation for the inclusion of winter sports on the Olympic Games program was started, bobsleighing had so many supporters that the sport was included in the First Winter Games at Chamonix, France, in 1924. This was the first recognized international championship race and was won by a 4-man Swiss team driven by E. Scherrer.

In order for bobsleighing to be recognized in the Olympic picture, it was mandatory that an international governing body be formed to promulgate racing rules for the sport. In 1923 the Federation Internationale de Bobsleigh et Tobogganning was organized, with the bobsleigh clubs of the various countries the component parts of the group. This organization, abbreviated

to F.I.B.T., still governs the sport.

The first world championship under the F.I.B.T. was held in 1927 at St. Moritz. A 5-man English team driven by N. C. Martineau captured first place.

That year a group of Americans who had participated in the sport at St. Moritz petitioned the United States Olympic Committee for permission to represent this country in the Second Winter Olympics at St. Moritz in 1928. The request was granted and the group allied itself with the Amateur Athletic Union of the United States, which, in turn, affiliated with the F.I.B.T. The Americans took the Olympic competition in 1928 as Billy Fiske drove the 5-man crew to victory and a team piloted by J. Heaton finished second.

This success started a run of victories for the United States in the Olympic bobsled event. In the 1932 Games at Lake Placid, N.Y., the 2-man competition was added to the program and American teams finished 1, 2 in the 4-man event and first in the 2-man, the brother combination of Hubert and Curtis Stevens upsetting the pre-race predictions.

The United States continued its string of successes at Garmisch-Partenkirchen, Germany, in 1936 when Ivan Brown and Bob Washbond of Keene Valley, N.Y., took top 2-man honors.

The chain of American victories was not broken until 1952, when the best the United States could do was finish second in both events at Oslo, Norway.

When the Third Olympic Winter Games were awarded to Lake Placid, there was no engineered bobsled run on the American continent. However, ballyhoo based on the bobsled successes of the Americans in the 1928 Games bore fruit in a fund-raising campaign and Stanislaus Zentzytski, a well-known German engineer and run-builder, designed a course down the precipitous sides of Mount Van Hoevenberg, near Lake Placid. The mile-and-a-half run, which was built with New York State aid, is still the only bobrun in America. It is maintained by the New York State Conservation Department for racing and public riding.

In its original state the Mount Van Hoevenberg run had 26 major curves and has an average drop of 10 per cent, ranging from 8½ per cent to 15 per cent. Straightaways are 6½ feet wide, with the width on curves running from 10 to 22 feet. Some curves are 30 feet high, with nearly perpendicular walls. These walls are built of stone, while the straightaways are troughed with a back-fill of earth on each side. The run is iced with a mixture of snow and water which is plastered on with a trowel, templates being used as guides so that the curves will be built to engineered plans. After the run is iced, a coating of frosted snow is spread over it so that the runners on the sleds will bite in and maintain their course.

The upper half-mile of the original run was abandoned in 1938 for economy reasons. The resulting run is 5,013 feet long from starting line to finish. There is an intermediate starting point at the 2,323-foot mark and it is from this point that most novice and early winter senior races start.

The bobsleds themselves have been developed greatly since the first racing sleds. The initial step to gain speed was the placing of iron runners on the bottoms of the seld sides. These runners, used as late as the 1932 Olympics, were quarter-round strips of iron of unrestricted width, usually about three-quarters of an inch. Yankee ingenuity, however, quickly devised a plate runner inserted in wooden shoes, leaving about 2 inches of the plate exposed.

These plate runners were then ground down to ¼ to 3/8 of an inch and very nearly V'd on the bottom in order to reduce to a minimum the wearing surface on the ice and snow tracks. Different alloys of steel also were experimented with and the final formula was a fine grade of tool steel.

When the American sleds were equipped with these thin plate runners in the 1936 Olympic Games, the F.I.B.T. ruled against their use in all future races and also banned the V-type runner. While V-type plate runners had increased the speed of the sleds by about 12 seconds for the 1½-mile course, they also had a tendency to cut in on the run and damage the track. This was particularly true on the curves where big chunks would be gouged out of the ice covering. The F.B.I.T. stipulated that in the future no runner could be less than 8 millimeters wide for the 2-man sleds and 10 mm. for the 4-man. It also ruled that the bottoms of the runners must be true arcs of circles of the above-mentioned diameters.

The next development in the sled was the substitution of the steel plank for the wooden plank. This is the plank that connects the front and rear runners and on which the men sit. The steel plank was found to be much more flexible than the wooden type, allowing the sled to flex slightly when rounding curves, thus cutting down the friction between the runners and the ice. This important feature may be credited to the Linney brothers, Bill and Bob, of Lyon Mountain, N.Y., who ruled United States bobsledding circles in the late 1930's and 1940's.

To these mechanically-minded engineers also must go the credit for the next development in the sled. This was the installation of push-handles to insure a fast start. Previous to this innovation, in races with running starts, 2 of the 4-man crew sat on the sled while the other 2 pushed their backs and jumped on the sled after crossing the starting line. The handles are U-bars welded to the sides of the sled.

This flying start cuts seconds from the elapsed time of a race. When the Linneys sprang this feature on the racers during the 1939 season, every other sled became so equipped virtually overnight, but the jump the Linneys obtained by practice enabled them to out-distance the other teams.

The next innovation, the equipping of each runner of the sled with knee-action so that each runner acts independently of the others, is credited to Swiss manufacturers. This resulted in less loss of speed on curves because of the reduced friction of the runner. This feature first appeared in 1947 and all racing sleds were quickly equipped with the gadgets.

The final development of the racing sled into a mile-a-minute quarter-ton mogul of steel and aluminum is of recent vintage. This is the streamlining of the cowl of the sled. Although crude attempts had been made before the 1948 Olympic Games without marked success, repeated trials have succeeded in completely streamlining the sled and now all sleds have streamlined cowls.

Modern racing sleds are steered by either of 2 devices: by ropes attached to the front runners or with a wheel, as in an automobile. The rope steering is popular with European drivers, who claim that this type is more sensitive in detecting a skid and in bringing the sled out of a skid. American drivers use the wheel type exclusively, and this style is becoming popular in Europe.

The cost of a racing sled runs from approximately $600 for a machine-shop job, in which most of the work is by the prospective owner, to $1,250 for the best type factory-built European sled. Each sled should have at least 1 extra set of runners and some drivers carry several sets. These extra runners cost about $100 per set for the material and machine work.

Sled runners are built so they can be replaced in a matter of minutes if conditions require. Each driver has his own ideas as to the best length of runners and of the amount of roch they should have and where the most rock should be placed in the runner.

Even after the sled is built and ready for use there are always minor changes which the driver will want made, so that after every race the sled is taken from the run and tinkered with by the crew. They polish runners, change the position of the rock, etc.

This evolution of the present day racing sled has resulted in speeds as high as 89 miles per hour. When one realizes that the crew is sitting about 8 to 10 inches above the ground on a sled weighing over 500 pounds, travelling at close to 90 miles per hour, with the safety of the whole crew resting principally on the driver and, to a lesser extent, the brakeman, and where a single wrong move on the driver's part possibly can result in a serious accident, he sees why the sport of bobsledding has been called "The Champagne of Thrills."

The "bobsled" is so called because of the fact that in races the crew members other than the driver are called on to "bob" on straightaways to increase speed. This is a maneuver which with a well-trained crew can make a sled literally jump forward. The No. 2 and No. 3 men take orders from the brakeman, who calls for this move on long straightaways. These men, along with the brakeman, bend backward until almost lying supine and at the command "bob" jump forward into a sitting position, all acting in unison. At the brakeman's command they all bend backward again and repeat the maneuver. In a well-trained crew this can cut seconds from the elapsed time of a race. But the movements must be precise, with the whole crew acting in unison—otherwise the opposite effect is attained.

MOUNT VAN HOEVENBERG BOBRUN

The Mount Van Hoevenberg Bobrun, near Lake Placid, is maintained by the Conservation Department of the State of New York. It is usually open from the half-way mark for racing and public riding around the Christmas holidays. By mid-January the run is iced to the top and ready for use. The Conservation Department maintains sleds and furnished experienced drivers and brakemen for public riding. The sleds for this purpose are different from the racing sleds. They are not so swift and are safer. But a ride down the course is still quite an experience, combining the thrills of a roller coaster with those of being shot from a cannon.

Before experiencing these thrills, however, the prospective rider must sign a waiver and release, absolving the run management and the State from all claims of damages in case of accident. All racing crews also must sign this waiver, which also releases the club holding the race and all sports governing bodies from claims.

Spectators at racing events are kept informed of a sled's progress through a public address system. Before a sled starts the men in the booths give the all-clear signal, starting at the top. Such calls as "Clear at the top," "Clear at Shady," "Clear at Zig-Zag" are heard until all of the men in the booths have reported. The next call comes from the official starter at the top: "John Jones on the line—they're off."

As the sled races down the course the telephone men again go into action with something like this "Approaching Cliffside—riding high— they're through," Approaching Shady—got a skid—came out nicely—they're through," "Approaching finish—they're down."

Each booth man picks up as the sled approaches until the sled has crossed the finish line at the bottom. If there is a mishap, the person who sees it calls "86," which is the signal for "accident." An ambulance sled is rushed to the point of accident and a doctor and a nurse follow

in the auto ambulance to the nearest point on the access road to the scene of the mishap.

The race is held up until the track can be cleared. If the track has been damaged, red sawdust is used to mark the spot so that following drivers can steer clear of the site.

Loudspeakers are installed at various points on the run so that spectators, who can see only a single curve or straightaway may be kept informed of happenings throughout a race. In important contests the times are taken at intermediate points and announced. After the sled has crossed the finish line the computed time is given.

Crowds of 5,000 are frequent at the important races on the Mount Van Hoevenberg run. In Europe, where many of the courses are located near big population centers, gatherings of 20,000 and 25,000 are the rule.

Of the 60 or more bobsled runs in Europe at the outbreak of World War II, 21 of international specifications again were in operation in January, 1953. Their locations follow:

West Germany—Olympic bobrun at Garmisch-Partenkirchen, Hahnenklee-Bockswiese at Oberharz, Triberg at Schwarzwald in Neususbau, Winterberg at Sauerland in Neususbau.

East Germany—Oberhof, Schierke, Schreiberhau, Krummhubel, Friedrichsroda, Flinsberg, Schmiedeberg, Ilmenau.

France—Chamonix L'Alpe d'Huez.

Italy—Cortina d'Ampezzo.

Austria—Semmering, Igls.

Sweden—Solleftea.

Switzerland—St. Moritz, Engelberg.

TROPHIES

A trophy is awarded in each major event in the United States. The competition usually drawing the most entries is the National A.A.U. 4-man test, with the Billy Fiske Memorial Trophy the top prize. Fiske, a gallant and daring bobsledder, was only 17 years old when he drove a 5-man United States team to victory in the 1928 Olympic Winter Games at St. Moritz, Switzerland. He repeated the triumph 4 years later at Lake Placid, N.Y.

Fiske joined the Royal Air Force in England when World War II broke out in 1939. While returning from a mission he was wounded but landed his airplane. He died shortly after he was taken from the plane. Friends, headed by Alexis Thompson, a noted bobsledder, put up the trophy in his name in 1941. It is the most eagerly-sought award in bobsledding.

The Harold (Bubs) Monahan Trophy annually goes to the winners of the National A.A.U. 2-man championship. Monahan was a rising young bobsled pilot before he enlisted in the Royal Canadian Air Force in 1941. When the United States entered the conflict, Monahan transferred to the United States Air Force. He was on a mission over Italy when his plane was shot down over the Mediterranean and he was lost.

The Lowell Thomas International Trophies go to the victors in the 2- and 4-man North American championships. These cups were placed in competition in 1940 in the Lowell Thomas International Championships. Theyhave been awarded to the North American winners since 1947.

To the winners of the 2 competitions in the Adirondack Association A.A.U. title tests go the J. Hubert Stevens Memorial Trophies, donated in 1953 by Mrs. Stevens. J. Hubert Stevens, a member of a famous bobsledding family, won almost all the major titles, both 2- and 4-man, on the Mount Van Hoevenberg run and also won the 2-man Olympic title in 1932. He was captain of the United States Olympic team in 1936.

FAMOUS BOBSLEDDERS
Americans

Billy Fiske, Harold (Bubs) Monahan, J. Hubert Stevens, Curtis Stevens, F. Paul Stevens, Ray Stevens, Edward P. F. Eagan, Tippy Gray, Jay O'Brien, Bob an Bill Linney, Matthew Monahan Jr., Bucky Wells, Ivan E. Brown, Waightmann (Bud) Washbond, Francis Tyler, Alan M. Washbond, Stan Benham, Jack Heaton, Godfrey Dewey, Bill A'Amico, Jim Bickford, Marion Clark, Katharin Dewey, Donna Fox, Hunter Goodrich, Pat Martin, Lloyd Johnson, Arthur Tyler, Edward Seymour, John Helmer, Chuck Pandolph, Tuffield A. Latour, Paul Lamey, Robert Huscher.

Foreign

Felix Endrich, Reto Capadrutt and Fritz Feierabend of Switzerland; Anderl Ostler, Lorenz Nieberl, Werner Zahn, Franz Kemser and Hans Kilian of Germany; Freddie McAvoy and N. C. Martineau of England; Max Houben and Baron Lunden of Belgium; Count Rossi di Montelera and Lamberto Dalla Costa of Italy; Alex Papana of Rumania; Eugenio Monti and Sergio Sciorpaes, Italy.

CHAMPIONS AND RECORDS

World Championships

(Olympic winners recognized as world champions in Olympic years)

2-Man

Year	Heats	Time m. s.	Where held
1931—Hans Kilian—S. Huber, Germany	4	7:34.20	Oberhof, Germany
1932—J. Hubert Stevens—Curtis Stevens, United States	4	8:14.74	Lake Placid, N.Y.
1933—A. Papana—D. Hubert, Rumania	4	5:50.14	Schreiberhau, Germany
1934—A. Frim—V. Dimitriescu, Rumania	4	9:31.30	Engelberg, Switzerland
1935—Reto Capadrutt—E. Diener, Switzerland	2	3:31.72	Igls, Austria
1936—Ivan E. Brown—Alan M. Washbond, United States	4	5:29.29	Garmisch-Partenkirchen, Germany
1937—Fred McEvoy—B. H. Black, England	4	6:09.53	Cortina d'Ampezzo, Italy
1938—I. Fischer—R. Thielecke, Germany	4	5:34	St. Moritz, Switzerland
1939—Baron Lunden—J. Kuffer, Belgium	4	5:29.20	St. Moritz, Switzerland
1940—46—No competition			
1947—F. Feierabend—S. Waser, Switzerland	4	5:27.10	St. Moritz, Switzerland
1948—Felix Endrich—F. Waller, Switzerland	4	5:29.20	St. Moritz, Switzerland
1949—Felix Endrich—F. Waller, Switzerland	4	5:18.52	Lake Placid, N.Y.
1950—F. Feirabend—S. Waser, Switzerland	4	5:57.73	Cortina d'Ampezzo, Italy
1951—Anderl Ostler—Lorenz Nieberl, Germany	4	5:11.94	L'Alpe d'Huez, France
1952—Anderl Ostler—Lorenz Nieberl, Germany	4	5:25.54	Oslo, Norway
1953—Felix Endrich—Fritz Stockli, Switzerland	4	5:01.90	Garmisch-Partenkirchen, Germany
1954—Guglielmo Scheibmeier— Andre Zambelli, Italy	4	5:47.08	Cortina d'Ampezzo, Italy
1955—Fritz Feierabend— Harry Warbourton, Switzerland	4	5:33.28	St. Moritz, Switzerland
1956—Lamberto Dalla Costa—Giacoma Conti, Italy	4	5:30.14	Cortina d'Ampezzo, Italy
1957—Eugenio Monti— Renzo Alvera, Italy	4	5:17.94	St. Moritz, Switzerland
1958—Eugenio Monti— Renzo Alvera, Italy	4	5:05.78	Garmisch-Partenkirchen, Germany

1959—Eugenio Monti—
    Renzo Alvera, Italy 4   5:23.86   St. Moritz, Switzerland
1960—Eugenio Monti—Sergio Sciorpaes, Italy 4   —   Cortina, Italy
1961—Eugenio Monti—Sergio Sciorpaes, Italy 4   —   Lake Placid
1962—R. Ruatti—E. DeLorenzo, Italy 4   —   Garmisch, Germany
1963—E. Monti—S. Sciorpaes, Italy 4   4:27.04   Innsbruck, Austria
1964—A. Nash—R. Dixon, England 4   4:21.90   Innsbruck, Austria
1965—A. Nash—R. Dixon, England 4   5:11.30   St. Moritz, Switzerland
1966—E. Monti—S. Sciorpaes, Italy 4   5:07.52   Cortina d'Ampezzo, Italy
1967—E. Thaler—R. Durnthaler, Austria 2   1:55.43   Alpe D'Huez,France
1968—E. Monti—L. DePaolis, Italy 4   4:41.54   Grenoble, France
1969—N. DeZordo—A. Frassinelli, Italy 4   4:31.73   Lake Placid, U.S.
1970—H. Floth—J. Bader, W. Germany 4   5:05.39   St. Moritz, Switzerland
1971—M. Armano—G. Gaspari, Italy 2   2:22.80   Cervinia, Italy
1972—W. Zimmerer—P. Utzschneider, W. Germany . 4   4:57.07   Sapporo, Japan

4-Man

Year	Winner	Heats	Time m. s.	Where held
1924—Switzerland (E. Scherrer, A. Neveu, A. Schlaeppi, H. Schlaeppi)		4	5:45.54	Chamonix, France
1925-26—No competition				
1927 (5-man team)—England (N. C. Martineau, P. E. Diggle, N. A. Milles, P. Reid, E. R. Hall)		4	6:09.30	St. Moritz, Switzerland
1928 (5-man team)—United States (Billy Fiske, N. Taker, G. Mason, C. Gray, P. Parke)		2	3:20.50	St. Moritz, Switzerland
1929—No competition				
1930—Italy (F. Zanietta, G. Giasini, A. Dorini, G. Rossi)		4	11:29.95	Caux, Switzerland
1931—Germany (W. Zahn, R. Schmidt, Dr. F. Bock, E. Hinderfeld)		4	5:15.50	St. Moritz, Switzerland
1932—United States (Billy Fiske, Edward Eagan, C. Gray, Jay O'Brien)		4	7:53.68	Lake Placid, N.Y.
1933—No competition				
1934—Germany (Hans Kilian, F. Schwarz, H. Valta, S. Huber)		4	5:32.75	Garmisch-Partenkirchen, Germany
1935—Germany (Hans Kilian, A. Gruber, H. Valta, F. Schwarz)		4	5:33	St. Moritz, Switzerland
1936—Switzerland (P. Musy, A. Gartmann, C. Bouvier, J. Beerli)		4	5:19.85	Garmisch-Partenkirchen, Germany
1937—England (Fred McEvoy, D. S. Looker, C. P. Green, B. H. Black)		4	5:08.50	St. Moritz, Switzerland
1938—England (Fred McEvoy, D. S. Looker, C. P. Green, C. Mackintosch)		4	5:40.32	Garmisch-Partenkirchen, Germany
1939—Switzerland (F. Feirebend, H. Cattani, A. Hoerning, J. Beerli)		4	5:30.37	Cortina d'Ampezzo, Italy
1940-46—No competition				
1947—Switzerland (F. Feierabend, F. Waller, Felix Endrich, S. Wasser)		4	5:16.20	St. Moritz, Switzerland
1948—United States (Francis Tyler, Pat Martin, E. Rimkus, William D'Amico)		4	5:20.10	St. Moritz, Switzerland
1949—United States (Stan Benham, Pat Martin, William Casey, William D'Amico)		4	4:59.29	Lake Placid, N.Y.
1950—United States (Stan Benham, Pat Martin, James Atkinson, William D'Amico)		4	5:28.72	Cortina d'Ampezzo, Italy
1951—Germany (Anderl Ostler, Lorenz Nieberl, Xavier Leitl, M. Possinger)		2	2:24.98	L'Alpe d'Huez, France
1952—Germany (Anderl Ostler, Lorenz Nieberl, F. Kuhn, Franz Kemser)		4	5:07.84	Oslo, Norway
1953—United States (Lloyd Johnson, Pat Biesiadicki, Hubert Miller, Joseph Smith)		2	2:28.79	Garmisch-Partenkirchen, Germany

1954—Switzerland (Fritz Feierabend, Gottfried
    Diener, Harry Warbourton, Henrich
    Angst) 4   5:15.94 Corina d'Ampezzo, Italy
1955—Switzerland (Franz Kapus, Gottfried
    Diener, Robert Alt, Henrich Angst) 4   5:10.52 St. Moritz, Switzerland
1956—Switzerland (Franz Kapus, Gottfried Diener,
    Robert Alt, Henrich Angst) 4   5:10.44 Cortinz d'Ampezzo, Italy
1957—Switzerland (Hans Zoller, H. Theier,
    R. Kuderli, H. Lev) . . . .   5:11.45 St. Moritz, Switzerland
1958—Germany (Hans Roesch, Alfred Hammer,
    Walter Haller, Theo Bauer) 4   4:49.33 Garmisch-Partenkirchen, Germany
1959—United States (Art Tyler, Gary Sheffield,
    Parker Voorix, Tom Butler) 4   5:10.82 St. Moritz, Switzerland
1960—Italy—(Eugenio Monti, Rurio Nordi, Benito
    Regoni, Sergio Sciorpaes) 4   5:04.75 Cortina, Italy
1961—Italy (Eugenio Monti, Rurio Nordio, Benito
    Regioni, Sergio Sciorpaes) 2   2:18.40 Lake Placid, U.S.
1962—Germany (F. Schell, O. Goebl, J. Sterff,
    L. Siebert) 2   2:33.66 Garmisch, Germany
1963—Italy (S. Zardini, F. Della Torre,
    R. Mocellini, R. Bonagura) 4   4:19.34 Innsbruck, Austria
1964—Canada (V. Emery, P. Kirby
    D. Anakin, J. Emery) 4   4:14.46 Innsbruck, Austria
1965—Canada (V. Emery, M. Young,
    G. Presley, P. Kirby) 4   5:17.78 St. Moritz, Switzerland
1966-67—Canceled
1968—Italy (E. Monti, L. DePaolis, R. Zandonella,
    M. Armano) 2   2:17.39 Grenoble, France
1969—West Germany (W. Zimmerer, S. Geisreiter,
    W. Steinbauer, P. Utzschneider) 4   4:20.75 Lake Placid, U.S.
1970—Italy (N. DeZordo, R. Zandonella, M. Armano,
    L. DePaolis) 4   4:55.70 St. Moritz, Switzerland
1971—Switzerland (R. Stadler, M. Forster, K.
    Schaerer, P. Schaerer) 2   2:19.35 Cervinia, Italy
1972—Switzerland (J. Wicki, E. Hubacher, H.
    Leutenegger, W. Camichel) 4   4:43.07 Sapporo, Japan

North American Championships

At Mount Van Hoevenberg

2-Man

Asterisk indicates New Course.

Year	Heats	Course	Time m. s.
1931—J. Hubert Stevens—Arthur Adams, Lake Placid A.C.	4	1½ miles	8:52.80
1932—No competition			
1933—J. Hubert Stevens—Don Deloria, Adirondack B.C.	4	1½ miles	8:00.21
1934—Gilbert Colgate—Richard Lawrence, Sno Birds of Lake Placid Club .	4	1½ miles	7:57.31
1935—Ivan E. Brown—Alan M. Washbond, Keene Valley A.C.	4	1½ miles	8:05.20
1936—Matthew Monahan Jr.—Walter Morrison, Lake Placid	4	1½ miles	7:38.15
1937—No competition			
1938—Ivan E. Brown—Alan M. Washbond, Keene Valley A.C.	4	1 mile	4:53.60
1939—Ivan E. Brown—Alan M. Washbond, Keene Valley A.C.	4	1 mile	4:53.69
1940—Tuffield A. Latour—Paul Dupree, Saranac Lake Sports Assn.	4	1 mile	4:54.95
1941—Tuffield A. Latour—Paul Dupree, Saranac Lake B.C.	4	1 mile	4:56.57
1942—James Bickford—William D'Amico, Saranac Lake B.C.	4	1 mile	4:48.77
1943-45—No competition			
1946—Tuffield A. Latour—Richard Morse, Saranac Lake B.C.	4	1 mile	4:51.30
1947—Fred Fortune Jr.—Schuyler Carron, Lake Placid B.C.	4	1 mile	5:00.34
1948—Richard Surphlis—Henry Stearn, Saranac Lake B.C.	4	1 mile	5:27.83

	Heats	Course	Time m. s.
1949-50—No competition			
1951—Stan Benham—Patrick Martin, Sno Birds of Lake Placid Club	4	*1 mile	5:16.30
1952—Arthur Tyler—Edgar Seymour, Lake Placid B.C.	4	*1 mile	5:21.08
1953—Arthur Tyler—Edgar Seymour, Rochester B.C.	2	*1 mile	2:35.68
1954—Stan Benham—James Bickford, Sno Birds of Lake Placid Club	4	*1 mile	5:14.79
1955—No competition.			
1956—Stan Benham—Pat Martin, Sno Birds of Lake Placid Club	4	*1 mile	5:14.73
1957—John Helmer—Richard Cheverette, Lake Placid Sno Birds	4	*1 mile	5:00.61
1958—Tuffy Latour—Forest Morgan, Saranac Lake B. C.	4	*1 mile	5:00.91
1959—Fred Fortune—Jack Young, Lake Placid Sno Birds	4	*1 mile	4:58.33
1960—Eugenio Monti—Charles Pandalph (unattached)	4	1 mile	4:53.79
1961—No competition			
1962—Gary Sheffield—Gary Tennant, Lake Placid B.C.	4	---	5:12.90
1963—Eugenio Monti—Franco Gaspari, Italy	4	---	4:41.51
1964—Larry McKillip—Charles Hoffer, Saranac Lake B.C.	4	---	4:43.38
1965—William Thomas—John Mignacci, Hurricane B.C.	4	---	4:52.66
1966—Sergio Zardini—Peter Kirby, Canada	4	---	4:55.42
1967—Paul Lamey—Robert Lamey—Robert Huscher, U.S. Navy	4	---	4:50.19
1968—Charles McDonald—John Handley, Malone B.C.	4	1 mile	5:05.92
1969—Paul Lamey—Robert Huscher, U.S. Navy	4	1 mile	4:38.42
1970—Paul Lamey—Robert Huscher, U.S. Navy	4	1 mile	4:42.65
1971—Paul Lamey—Robert Huscher, U.S. Navy	4	1 mile	4:45.06

4-Man

Year Winner	Heats	Course	Time m. s.
1931—Saranac Lake Sports Assn. (Henry Homburger, Percy Bryant, Paul Stevens, Edmond Horton)	4	1½ miles	7:31.35
1932—Saranac Lake Sports Assn. (Henry Homburger, Percy Bryant, Paul Stevens, Edmond Horton)	2	1½ miles	3:48.34
1933—Adirondack B.C. (J. Hubert Stevens, John Shene, E. C. D. Cameron, Don Deloria)	4	1½ miles	7:12.51
1934—Sno Birds of Lake Placid Club (Raymond Stevens, Richard Lawrence, James Bickford, Crawford Merkle)	4	1½ miles	7:15.61
1935—Lake Placid A.C. (Curtis Stevens, Robert Martin, E. Hugh Varno, Crawford Merkle)	4	1½ miles	7:08.15
1936—Keene Valley A.C. (Aubrey Wells, Kurt Gelback, Melvin Luck, John Otis)	4	1½ miles	6:44.56
1937—No competition			
1938—Keene Valley A.C. (Aubrey Wells, Warren Martin, Hubert Nye, John Otis)	4	1 mile	4:24.90
1939—Lyon Mountain Miners (Robert J. Linney, Arthur Keysor, William Stacavitch, Angus Clain)	4	1 mile	4:40.85
1940—Republic Miners B.C. (William Linney, John Kerr, William Stacavitch, Angus Clain)	4	1 mile	4:28.14
1941—Republic Miners B.C. (William Linney, John Kerr, William Stacavitch, Angus Clain)	4	1 mile	4:27.71
1942—Saranac Lake B.C. (James Bickford, Lucien Miron, Richard Morse, Hugh Bickford)	4	1 mile	4:26.25
1943-45—No competition			
1946—Republic Miners B.C. (William Linney, William Stacavitch, Rufus Brickey, Thomas Hicks)	4	1 mile	4:24.30
1947—Ausable Forks American Legion B.S.C. (Joseph Meconi, Floyd Whisher, Harry Bombard, Franklyn Feattie)	2	1 mile	2:19.25
1948—Lake Placid B.C. (Stanley Benham, William Casey, James Atkinson, William Trombley)	4	1 mile	4:51.54
1949-50—No competition			
1951—Sno Birds of Lake Placid Club (Stanley Benham, Patrick Martin, James Atkinson, Howard Crossett)	4	*1 mile	4:51.90
1952—Saranac Lake B.C. (Robert Dupree, Ralph Hartman, Gerry Morgan, Robert Swain)	4	*1 mile	5:00.78

1953—Sno Birds of Lake Placid Club (Stanley Benham, Patrick
    Martin, James Atkinson, John Helmer)   2   *1 mile   2:26.29
1954-55—No competition.
1956—Sno Birds of Lake Placid Club (Stan Benham,
    Pat Martin, Chuck Pandolph, John Helmer   4   *1 mile   4:44.38
1957—Saranac Lake B.C. (Monroe Flagg, Neil Rogers,
    Walter Stahl, James Lamy)   4   *1 mile   4:46.61
1958—U.S. Air Force (Hill Moore, Ted Labernik,
    Robert Cloninger, Robert Dietz)   4   *1 mile   4:49.71
1959—Lake Placid Sno Birds (Stan Benham, Neil Rogers,
    Jim Lamy, Charles Pandolph)   4   *1 mile   4:44.48
1960—Eugenio Monti, Pat Neartin, Gary Sheffield, Charles
    Pandolph (unattached)   4   1 mile   4:38.66
1961—No competition
1962—Saranac Lake B.C. (Larry McKillip, Floyd Baumgartner,
    Neil Rogers, James Lamy)   4   ———   4:36.67
1963—Lake Placid B.C. (Bill Hickey, Bill Dundon,
    Reggie Benham, Charles Pandolph)   4   ———   4:32.78
1964—Italy (Sergio Zardini, Bill Baker,
    Paul Levesque, Charles Pandolph)   2   ———   2:18.48
1965—No competition
1966—Lake Placid B.C. (Joseph McKillip, James Strack,
    Robert Crowley, Michael Holbrock)   4   ———   4:42.86
1967—Lake Placid B.C. (Boris Said, David Dunn,
    Robert Crowley, Philip Duprey)   4   ———   4:33.14
1968—U.S. Air Force (Lester Fenner, Al Lowe,
    Allan Hachigian, John DeZalia)   4   1 mile   4:40.22
1969—No competition
1970—Lake Placid B.C. (Harry Peterson, Donald
    Fay, Ken Kesterman, Paul King)   4   1 mile   4:28.26
1971—U.S. Air Force (James Hickey, Larry Kilburn,
    James Bridges, Thomas Becker)   4   1 mile   4:30.73

National A.A.U. Championships

Senior 2-Man

Asterisk indicates New Course.

Year	Driver, brake and club	Heats	Course	Time m. s.
1931—J. Hubert Stevens—Arthur Adams, Lake Placid A.C.	4	1½ miles	8:52.80
1932—No competition			
1933—J. Hubert Stevens, Don Deloria, Adirondack B.C.	4	1½ miles	8:19.90
1934—Ivan E. Brown—Alan M. Washbond, Keene Valley A.C.	4	1½ miles	8:05.52
1935—J. Hubert Stevens—Paul Stevens, Adirondack B.C.	4	1½ miles	7:50.57
1936—Charles Storrin—Hubert Nye, Keene Valley A.C.	4	1½ miles	8:04.32
1937—No competition			
1938—Ivan E. Brown—Alan M. Washbond, Keene Valley A.C.	4	1 mile	4:52.63
1939—Ivan E. Brown—Alan M. Washbond, Keene Valley A.C.	4	1 mile	5:03.50
1940—Tuffield A. Latour—Paul Dupree, Saranac Lake Sports Assn	4	1 mile	5:04.31
1941—Tuffield A. Latour—Paul Dupree, Saranac Lake B.C.	4	1 mile	4:55.68
1942—Waightman (Bud) Washbond—Adrian Aubin, Lake Placid B.C.	4	1 mile	4:54.50
1943-45—No competition			
1946—Tuffield A. Latour—Richard Morse, Saranac Lake B.C.	4	1 mile	5:00.04
1947—Tuffield A. Latour—James Bickford, Saranac Lake B.C.	4	1 mile	5:14.59
1948—Richard Suphlis—Henry Stearn, Saranac Lake B.C.	4	1 mile	5:08.50
1949-50—No competition			
1951—Larry McKillip—Henry Stearn, Saranac Lake B.C.	4	*1 mile	5:36.78
1952—Arthur Tyler—Edgar Seymour, Lake Placid B.C.	4	*1 mile	5:21.08
1953—Arthur Tyler—Edgar Seymour, Rochester B.C.	4	*1 mile	5:19.30
1954—Stan Benham—James Bickford, Sno Birds of Lake Placid Club	4	*1 mile	5:11.61
1955—Waightman (Bud) Washbond—Pat Martin, Sno Birds of Lake Placid Club	4	*1 mile	5:04.16

	Heats	Course	Time m. s.
1956—Stan Benham—Pat Martin, Sno Birds of Lake Placid Club	4	*1 mile	5:03.86
1957—Stan Benham—Pat Martin, Sno Birds of Lake Placid Club	4	*1 mile	5:10.29
1958—No competition			
1959—T. Latour—F. Morgan, Saranac Lake B.C.	4	1 mile	5:10.55
1960—Eugenio Monti—Gary Sheffield (unattached)	4	1 mile	4:57.20
1961—William Dodge—Steven Phillips, Adirondack B.C.	4	1 mile	4:53.86
1962—Larry McKillip—James Lamy, Saranac Lake B.C.	4	1 mile	4:50.86
1963—Larry McKillip—James Lamy, Saranac Lake B.C.	4	———	4:47.75
1964—Larry McKillip—Charles Hoffer, Saranac Lake B.C.	4	———	4:46.43
1965—No competition			
1966—Howard Clifton—James Crall, Hurricane B.C.	4	———	4:57.82
1967—Gary Sheffield—Howard Silver, U.S. Air Force	4	———	4:44.99
1968—Gary Sheffield—Howard Silver, U.S. Air Force	4	1 mile	4:40.71
1969—Paul Lamey—Robert Huscher, U.S. Navy	4	1 mile	4:41.65
1970—Paul Lamey—Robert Huscher, U.S. Navy	4	1 mile	4:44.57
1971—Paul Lamey—Robert Huscher, U.S. Navy	4	1 mile	4:45.06

Senior 4—Man

(Driver named first; brake named last.)

Year Winner	Heats	Course	Time m. s.
1931—Saranac Lake Sports Assn. (Henry Homburger, Percy Bryant, Paul Stevens, Edmond Horton)	4	1½ miles	7:31.35
1932—Saranac Lake Sports Assn. (Henry Homburger, Percy Bryant, Paul Stevens, Edmond Horton)	2	1½ miles	3:48.34
1933—Lake Placid A.C. (Curtis Stevens, Charles Divine, Robert Martin, E. Hugh Varno)	4	1½ miles	7:15.50
1934—Lake Placid A.C. (Curtis Stevens, E. Hugh Varno, Robert Martin, Kenneth Wood)	4	1½ miles	7:29.42
1935—Lake Placid A.C. (Curtis Stevens, Robert Martin, E. Hugh Varno, Crawford Merkle)	4	1½ miles	7:03.40
1936—Keene Valley A. C. (Aubrey Wells, Kurt Gelback, Melvin Luck, John Otis)	4	1½ miles	7:02.37
1937—No competition			
1938—Keene Valley A.C. (Aubrey Wells, Warren Martin, Hubert Nye, John Otis)	4	1 mile	4:36.64
1939—Keene Valley A.C. (Aubrey Wells, Warren Martin, Hubert Nye, John Otis)	4	1 mile	4:46.41
1940—Sno Birds of Lake Placid Club (Katharin Dewey, Leo Martin, Pat Martin, Lawrence Straight)	4	1 mile	4:30.71
1941—Sno Birds of Lake Placed Club (Francis Tyler, E. Hugh Varno, Pat Martin, William D'Amico)	4	1 mile	4:37.58
1942—Saranac Lake B.C. (James Bickford, Richard Morse, Lucien Miron, Hugh Bickford)	4	1 mile	4:33.50
1943-45—No competition			
1946—Republic Miners B.C. (William Linney, William Stacavitch, Rufus Brickey, Thomas Hicks)	4	1 mile	4:25.96
1947—Saranac Lake B.C. (James Bickford, Patrick Buckley, Hugh Bickford, William Dupree)	4	1 mile	4:34.11
1948—Lake Placid B.C. (Stanley Benham, William Casey, James Atkinson, William Trombley)	4	1 mile	4:42.17
1949-50—No competition			
1951—Sno Birds of Lake Placid Club (Stanley Benham, Pat Martin, James Atkinson, Howard Crossett)	4	*1 mile	4:51.90
1952—Saranac Lake B.C. (Robert Dupree, Ralph Hartman, Gerry Morgan, Robert Swain)	4	*1 mile	5:00.78
1953—Sno Birds of Lake Placid Club (Stanley Benham, Pat Martin, James Atkinson, John Helmer)	4	*1 mile	4:53.40
1954—Sno Birds of Lake Placid Club (Stan Benham, Pat Martin, John B. Wells, John Helmer)	4	*1 mile	4:53.51
1955—Saranac Lake B.C. (Monroe Flagg, Lloyd Miller, James Lamy, Chuck Pandolph)	4	*1 mile	4:46.67

1956–Sno Birds of Lake Placid Club (Stan Benham,
Pat Martin, Chuck Pandolph, John Helmer) 4   *1 mile   4:47.95
1957–Sno Birds of Lake Placid Club (Stan Benham,
Pat Martin, Chuck Pandolph, John Helmer) 4   *1 mile   4:49.78
1958–Adirondack B.C. (Art Tyler, Doug Tyler, Parker Vooris, Tom Butler) 4   *1 mile   4:41.36
1959–Au Sable B.C. (B. Snow, R. Mousseau, C. Kemp, W. Dundon) 4   1 mile   4:52.28
1960–Saranac Lake B.C. (Joseph McKillip, Paul King,
Mike Peer, James Watson) 4   1 mile   4:46.69
1961–Saranac Lake B.C. (Larry McKillip, Mike Baumgartner,
Neil Rogers, James Lamy) 4   1 mile   4:42.08
1962–Saranac Lake B.C. (Larry McKillip, Floyd Baumgartner,
Neil Rogers, James Lamy) 4   1 mile   4:41.46
1963–Lake Placid B.C. (Bill Hickey, Bill Dundon,
Reggie Benham, Charles Pandolph) 4   ———   4:29.19
1964–U.S. Air Force (Lester Fenner, Dick Davies,
Dick Nichols, Eugene Dolan) 4   ———   4:41.17
1965–No competition
1966–Lake Placid B.C. (Joseph McKillip, James Strack,
Robery Crowley, Michael Holbrock) 4   ———   4:42.86
1967–Lake Placid B.C. (Bill Hickey, Robert Jessey,
Gary Martineau, Paul Savage) 4   ———   4:37.94
1968–U.S. Air Force (Lester Fenner, John DeZalia,
Al Lowe, Al Hatchigan) 4   1 mile   4:33.26
1969–Cleveland B.C. (Fred Fortune, Andy Kanaby,
Robert Goodspeed, James Lord) 2   1 mile   2:16.52
1970–U.S. Navy (Paul Lamey, Robert Huscher,
Errol Turner, William Caulson) 4   1 mile   4:33.99
1971–U.S. Air Force (James Hickey, Larry
Kilburn, James Bridges, Thomas Becker) 4   1 mile   4:30.73

BASIC RULES

Timing of a Race

Races are decided by the elapsed times of the different teams to negotiate the measured course. Only one sled is permitted on the course at a time. An electric clock in the timing room at the finish line is actuated by impulses from electric eyes at the start and finish. As the front of the sled crosses the starting line the "eye" at that point transmits its impulse to the clock, which starts recording on a tape, run by a printer connected to the clock, the elapsed seconds and minutes as the sled makes its run. As the front of the sled crosses the finish line, the electric eye at that point stops the clock and records on the tape the finish mark to the nearest second. The chief timer then measures this mark to the last recorded second and, by means of a Vernier scale, comes up with the elapsed time to the hundredth of a second. As races are often won by hundredths of a second, this measurement must be accurate. The writer acted as chief timer in the United States Olympic tryouts in 1935 when the 2 leading teams were exactly tied in elapsed time to the hundredth of a second at the end of 4 heats. The official time of each was 7 minutes 45.69 seconds for 4 mile-and-a-half heats. In such case the rules provide that the team with the fastest singled heat be declared the winner.

In addition to the electric timing, three stop watches time each heat of each sled and this time is recorded so that if by any mishap the electric timer ceases to function, the watch time may be used.

In championship races each sled makes 4 trips down the run and the combined time of the 4 heats constitutes the official time for the race. If weather conditions or other contingencies preclude the possibility of each team finishing 4 heats the race may be declared official after the second heat. Even if all sleds have finished 3 heats and possibly some of them have made their fourth run when the stoppage occurs the third and fourth heats are voided and the race reverts to the first 2 heats. This is because the early starters have an initial disadvantage through having to break in the track. This disadvantage is equalized in the later heats of a 2- or 4-heat race through the device of the order in which sleds start in a heat. However, a fair starting order cannot be worked out for a 3-heat race.

Specifications of Sleds, etc.

All sleds and crews entered in races must conform to certain restrictions promulgated in the rules of the F.I.B.T. The maximum weight of sleds must not exceed 507 lbs. for the 4-man sled or 363.6 lbs. for the 2-man. The length of the sled is restricted as is the width between runners, only one width being permitted. Minimum gauge of runners if prescribed. Only sleds constructed for the sitting position of crews are permitted. Crews may not lie prone on the sled. The latest rule change is a restriction of weights of crews.

On the 4-man bob the weight of the crew is limited to 880 pounds and on 2-man crews to 440. However, if the total weight of the crew falls short of these limits, ballast in the form of lead bars may be added to the sled to equalize the chances of a light crew against heavier opponents.

BOWLING

(Courtesy of Bruce Pluckhahn, American Bowling Congress, 5301 South 76 Street, Greendale, Wis., 53129, and Steve James, Editor of BOWLING Magazine.)

If there's anyone in the world of the 1970s who hasn't at least heard about bowling, he must live in a cave. And if you find a man who lives in a cave, he might just be tossing stones at sticks, or some such antics resembling the modern game of tenpins.

Bowling has become worldwide in scope and enjoyment, with international competition blossoming from the day-to-day activity performed by "Joe Bowlers" throughout the world who compete regularly in organized league play.

Organizations such as the American Bowling Congress, Women's International Bowling Congress, American Junior Bowling Congress, and the Federation Internationale des Quilleur have formulated rules to govern the sport. And the Bowling Proprietors Association of America, the Professional Bowlers Association, and the Professional Woman's Bowling Association have flourished and helped the game reach more people each year. The National Bowling Council, composed of the game's major integers, promotes bowling through a basic fundamental practice of united action from within.

Figures compiled by national pollsters reveal more than 40 million people bowl during a year. Of that, more than eight million (including members in Canada, Puerto Rico, Bermuda, Grand Bahamas, and foreign military installations) compete regularly in ABC, WIBC, and AJBC sanctioned competition.

Although the game now appeals to people of all walks of life, even though basic rule changes have not been altered, entering a bowling center today would give no clue to its origin.

Bowling has been traced to articles found in the tomb of an Egyptian child buried in 5200 B.C. The primitive implements included nine pieces of stone, to be set up as pins, at which the stone "ball" was rolled, the ball having first to roll through an archway made of three pieces of marble. Another ancient discovery was the Polynesian game of ula maika, also utilizing pins and balls of stone. The stones were to be rolled a distance of 60 feet, a distance which today still is one of the basic regulations of tenpins.

Another ancient form of bowls was played in the Italian Alps about 2,000 years ago. It involved the underhand tossing of stones at an object, differentiating it from the rolling of the stones, and is believed the origin of boccie, still a widely played game in Italy and among persons of Italian descent around the world. Basque quilles is another of the ancient European games, originating as an outdoor pastime using a wooden ball, probably made from tree roots, with a slot-like grip. The player held onto the ball as he swung it against the first of the three-foot-tall pins arranged in a large rectangular court. As that pin fell, hopefully to knock down its neighbor, the player rolled the ball toward the center of the court, trying to apply reverse spin that would send the ball ricocheting against several other pins. The pins were arranged in three rows of three each.

Bowling at pins probably originated in ancient Germany, not as a sport but as a religious ceremony. *Bowling,* written in the 19th century by William Pehle, secretary of the German Bowling Society and a member of the Berlin bowling club, revealed that as early as the third and fourth century, A.D., strange rites often would be held in the cloisters of churches. The parishioner would be told to place his ever-present *kegel*—the implement most Germans carried for sports and self protection—at one end of a runway resembling today's bowling lane. The kegel represented the *heide.* A stone was rolled at the heide, those successfully toppling it having cleansed themselves of sin. The practice was described in the chronicles of Paderborn, but evidently lasted less than two centuries.

The passage of time brought an increase in the size of the stone rolled at pins and eventually the ball came to be made of wood. In 1300, according to Pehle, some sections of Germany played a game with three pins; others used as many as 17. Martin Luther is credited with settling on the idea that nine was the ideal number of pins.

In his research, the German historian Pehle found numerous references to bowling, among them a game played at a great feast given the citizenry of Frankfurt in 1463.

The game spread into the lowland countries in

the 15th, 16th, and 17th centuries and also into Austria and Switzerland. The playing surface usually was wood. The roofing-over of the lanes, first done in London for lawn bowls around the year 1450, was the true beginning of modern bowling as an all-weather, around-the-clock game.

There is confusion about how and when bowling at pins came to the United States, arising from the interuse of the word *bowl* even though tenpins and lawn bowling have no physical resemblances. And why and when the 10th pin was added to the American game still is a mystery. It is believed tenpins was played in New York City in the 1820s. The earliest known reference to bowling at pins was made by Washington Irving in "Rip Van Winkle" (about 1818).

Regardless of how the game came into being, it became so popular by mid-19th century that indoor lanes were being built throughout Manhattan and the Bronx and on westward, in Syracuse, Buffalo, Cincinnati, Chicago, Milwaukee, and other cities with large German populations. Many were part of *turnvereins*—fraternal gymnastic societies—but they quickly spread to wide public usage. While gambling on the game became a problem in some areas, the lack of uniform playing rules and equipment specifications stifled the development as a whole. In 1875, delegates from nine bowling clubs in New York and Brooklyn met in Germania Hall in the Bowery and organized the National Bowling Association. This was the first attempt to bring order out of chaos and some of the legislation agreed on then still is in effect in modified form.

Still, disagreement raged between East and West, principally the alignment of New York state bowlers against everyone else to the West. On Sept. 9, 1895, the American Bowling Congress was organized in Beethoven Hall in New York City. The breach was healed, rules and equipment standards were developed—and adhered to—and the game as it finally was organized more than three-quarters of a century ago has remained basically unchanged. There have been numerous rules modifications, but no really significant alterations in equipment specifications other than those adopted to meet changes brought on by such technological advancements as automation and the invention of plastic, nylon, and other synthetics.

Once ABC came into the picture, bowling began its growth. Manufacturers discovered the field was lucrative enough to warrant their attention. Pins had been set mostly by hand, on pegs that popped out of the lane when the pinboy stepped on a treadle. Machines were designed to do this job. Only the best of top-grade maple was used in the pins. Balls had been made of lignum vitae, a tropical wood that was almost indestructible, except that it chipped and lost its shape. Suddenly all sorts of balls made of hard rubber,

still the basic ingredient, appeared. As many as 16 to 24 lanes were built into one building—pin palaces they were called—and nationally known players began to emerge. The game became a sport, even a livelihood, to many.

In 1901, ABC started its national tournament, attracting 41 five-man teams to a four-day gathering in Chicago. Other regional and national competition prospered as ABC involvement broadened. Promotion and publicity developed to the extent that in 1953, at its Golden Jubilee tournament (three years were lost because of World War II), the ABC tournament drew an entry of 8,180 teams or upwards of 41,000 individuals. Prize funds in the big event, which moves from city to city annually and for which lanes are specially installed for spans of nearly three months, have topped $700,000.

The ABC Masters tournament, held annually for the professionals and leading nonpros since 1951, is an added highlight of the three-month extravaganza. After a qualifying round, 64 players are pitted in head-to-head competition in a double elimination format. In 1971 at Detroit, professional Jim Godman rolled the first 300 game in final round action, which helped him move from the losers' bracket and deal Don Johnson two four-game losses.

The lifeblood of bowling is its league play. The highly organized, competitive league structure has made the trek to the lanes a way of life for millions, particularly during the fall and winter months. The trend toward higher handicaps, which in turn produce equalization to a greater extent between all teams in all leagues, and the popularity of the individual match-point system, which provides an extra dose of competition in addition to team play, has helped boost ABC membership over the four million mark. And WIBC, organized in 1916, has surpassed the three-million-member level. Together, the two organizations sponsor the American Junior Bowling Congress with its more than 700,000 boys and girls of college age and under.

League play in the three major membership organizations is sanctioned, meaning competition is conducted under rules laid down by the parent bodies, including the handling of prize funds by the adult leagues. About $150 million in league prize money, disbursed at season's end, is protected under ABC's automatic bonding program. WIBC has a similar program that protects upwards of $50 million in women's league funds. This carries over into tournament play, too, where the two groups sanction more than 15,000 tournaments annually. Prize funds, and their distribution, amounting to tens of millions of dollars, are protected against wrongful use and mishandling.

In October 1972, the organizations moved into a new combined national headquarters complex in the Milwaukee, Wisconsin, suburb of

Greendale. They maintain separate identity and operation but share expenses and work application wherever practical. Milwaukee has been ABC's home since 1907. WIBC had been headquartered in Columbus, Ohio, since 1927.

ABC's Hall of Fame, established in 1941, is the third oldest, preceded only by those of baseball (1936) and golf (1940). A vote is conducted each year and nearly 70 men have been enshrined, including several for meritorious service. The honorees are inducted in ceremonies on ABC tournament lanes. Bronze tablets are hung in the new National Bowling Hall of Fame and Museum in the headquarters complex in Milwaukee. The WIBC Hall of Fame, established in 1953 as "The Star of Yesteryear," also honors its women in the Milwaukee building.

WIBC has conducted an annual national championship for women since 1917, it too moving among the nation's large cities, but being held in commercial bowling centers. More than 48,000 women took part in the 1973 event in Las Vegas, Nevada, the 105-day duration and the entry of 9,644 five-player teams making it the largest tournament of its kind ever held. The previous high came in the 50th anniversary year, 1967, when 30,000 women took part in the annual tournament in Rochester, New York. WIBC also conducts a special event for the top women bowlers, the prestigious Queens tournament. It was begun in 1961, modeled after ABC's Masters tournament.

The largest individual tournament is the Petersen Classic, held for about seven months each year in Chicago, offering a first prize in excess of $35,000 and attracting more than 18,000 entrants, most of them men.

Steady growth boosted the bowling membership through its first 50 years, then the bowling "boom" began in the early 1950s with the approval by ABC of the first fully automated pinsetting machine. Pinboys had come into short supply during a wartime economy that continued into peacetime. The machines knew no physical limitations and actually made bowling a 24-hour recreation in some cities. Widespread air conditioning and architectural innovations lent their strong effects to the game, which also developed its total "family" aspects as more and more women took to the game and encouraged their children to do the same. Television was a great influence in popularizing the sport. National series were developed, "live" and "taped," that took bowling into people's living rooms and helped broaden the concept that bowling truly was a pursuit for everyone from "8 to 80."

There always have been competitors who stood above the rest, but never were they brought to the front more than in 1958 when the Professional Bowlers Association came on the scene. Whereas most of the game's stars had been semiprofessionals, maintaining regular employ-ment to supplement their earnings in league and tournament competition, the PBA quickly developed a "star" system and a tournament tour fashioned after that of professional golf. Helped by television, the PBA soon had its members playing for more than $1 million in yearly prize money. Don Carter, already a much-heralded performer, became "Mr. Bowling" in the late 1950s and was succeeded by Dick Weber in the '60s. Don Johnson appeared to be taking on the role in the early 70s. Their earnings and product endorsements put them into the $100,000-plus yearly income bracket and gave the game new stature.

The Bowling Proprietors Association of America, which recently moved its national headquarters to Dallas, Texas, from Chicago, has been a major influence on the structural level of the game since 1932. In addition to its trade association functions, BPAA conducted a number of tournaments for both men and women. Its most notable was the All-Star, a superb match game event that began as a Chicago Tribune promotion on Pearl Harbor day, Dec. 7, 1941, and continued under BPAA direction through May 1970. Then it was given over to the PBA, renamed the U.S. Open, and made a part of the PBA's regular winter tour.

As membership in the three groups—ABC, WIBC, and AJBC, plus the Youth Bowling Association of the BPAA—peaked at more than eight million, the leading manufacturers of equipment in the U.S. began to look elsewhere for markets. So did inventors in other countries who had been exposed to the phenomenal growth of the sport in the United States through their travels. Suddenly tenpins, the game that had crossed the Atlantic as a ninepin game years before, was on its way back to Europe. Foreseeing the development, some Britishers asked ABC to lend its aid in the formation of an association. The British Ten Pin Bowling Association came into being in 1961, its equipment specifications exactly those of the ABC, its rules only slightly modified. Australia followed suit and other countries hurried to restructure their regulations as tenpin centers were built in Paris, Antwerp, Berlin, and other cities. The British alone reached a playing membership of more than 40,000 in five years. Japan bowlers recently were swept up in the "boom" and centers went up—and up—with one Tokyo establishment boasting 504 lanes, by far the world's largest.

Informal international bowling competition had been held as early as 1892 when a team of Americans played in a bowling "festival" in Hamburg, Germany. After the turn of the century, teams from New York made several more trips to Germany. A group of Americans toured Sweden in 1923 and 1929, then hosted a number of European teams in matches held in New York in 1934. The first attempt to create a tenpin bowling organization on the Continent came in 1925. The group sponsored some scattered competition and in 1936 staged a series of bowling events concurrent with the summer Olympic Games in Berlin. More than 50 Americans made the trip, some today holding membership in the ABC Hall of Fame. It was the last international get-to-gether of any consequence until the Federation Internationale des Quilleurs came on the scene in 1951.

Seven European nations sent teams to the first World tournament of the FIQ in Helsinki, Finland, in 1954. Nine took part at Essen, Germany, in 1955, a dozen at Halsingbord, Sweden, in 1958 and 15 at Hamburg in 1960. The World meet moved to Mexico in 1963, when it was put on a four-year basis, and back to Malmo, Sweden, in 1967. Milwaukee, Wis., was host city for the 1971 event when 32 nations competed. The United States entered world competition in 1963 and has been a dominant factor ever since.

FIQ competition is held in zones—American, European, and Asian—at four-year intervals. FIQ headquarters are in Zurich, Switzerland. FIQ competition is held for nonprofessionals, and gold, silver, and bronze medals are awarded to the first three place finishers. The American style of alternating lanes after each frame is used, plus two European styles, one in which an entire game is bowled on one lane, the other in which half the game is bowled on one lane, the second half on the other.

Japan, a member of the Asiatic zone, boasts a general membership in excess of 70,000, while Canada has a tenpin population of almost 70,000. Some other leading areas and their bowling population include Sweden, 21,000; Australia, 24,000; Mexico, 11,000; Finland, 10,000; and Venezuela, 7,500.

There are no bowling centers in the United States that can match Japan's 504 lanes, but there are 39 establishments with 64 or more lanes. The largest is Willow Grove Park lanes in suburban Philadelphia with 116. The only other with more than 100 is Edison lanes in Edison, New Jersey, with 112. There are about 8,800 bowling centers in the U.S. having 139,000 lanes. Canada has 153 centers with 2,105 lanes. All told, ABC certifies more than 144,000 lanes annually in 9,350 establishments, figures that are down from early 1960 peaks of 11,476 establishments and 165,000 lanes. More than $30 million is spent on equipment annually.

Bowling is recreation to some; sport to others. Some form of the game probably is played by more peoples of the world than any other, with the possible exception of soccer football. The overall appeal is endless, which has been the main reason participation has increased so steadily over the years.

BIG PIN

FAMOUS BOWLERS
Men

A.B.C. Hall of Fame

Charter Members 1941
Joseph Bodis, Cleveland
Adolph Carlson, Chicago
Charley Daw, Milwaukee
John Koster, Nyack, N. Y.
Herbert Lange, Watertown, Wis.
Mort Lindsey, Stamford, Conn.
Hank Marino, Milwaukee
James Smith, Buffalo
Harry Steers, Chicago
Gilbert Zunker, Milwaukee

1951
Joseph Wilman, Chicago
1952
Ned Day, Milwaukee
1953
James Blouin, Chicago, Ill.
1954
Joseph Norris, Chicago
William Knox, Philadelphia
1955
James McMahon, Fair Lawn, N. J.

1957
Andy Varipapa, Hempstead, N. Y.
1958
Frank Benkovic, Milwaukee
1959
Walter Ward, Cleveland
George Young, Detroit
1960
Albert Brandt, Lockport, N. Y.
1961
William Sixty, Milwaukee
Phil Wolf, Chicago (Veterans committee selection)
1962
John Crimmins, Detroit
1963
E.D. Easter, Winston-Salem, N.C. (Veterans committee selection)
Basil Fazio, Detroit
Steve Nagy, Detroit
1964
Nelson Burton Sr., St. Louis

1965

Therman Gibson, Detroit

1966

Herbert (Buddy) Bomar, Chicago

1967

Fred Bujack, Sacramento, Calif.

Frank Kartheiser, Chicago
(Veterans committee selection)

Walter (Skang) Mercurio, Cleveland
(Veterans committee selection)

1968

William Bunetta, Fresno, Calif.

Louis Campi, Demont, N.J.

Alfred Faragalli, Wayne, N. J.

Russell Gersonde, Milwaukee

Edward Kawolics, Chicago

Joseph Kristof, Columbus, Ohio

Paul Krumske, Chicago

Charles O'Donnell, St. Louis

Conrad Schwoegler, Madison, Wis.

Louis Sielaff, Detroit

Tony Sparando, New York

Barney Spinella, Los Angeles

1969

Joe Joseph, Lansing, Mich.

John Martino, Syracuse, N. Y.
(Veterans committee selection)

1970

Donald Carter, Los Angeles

Richard Weber, St. Louis

1971

Edward Lubanski, Detroit

Otto Stein Jr., St. Louis
(Veterans committee selection)

Frank Thoma, Chicago
(Veterans committee selection)

1972

William Lillard, Houston, Texas

Martin Cassio, Rahway, N. J.
(Veterans committee selection)

1973

Raymond Bluth, St. Louis, Mo.

Edward Krems, Chicago, Ill.
(Veterans committee selection)

Meritorious Service Members
1963

*Peter Howley, Chicago

*Elmer H. Baumgarten, Milwaukee

Abraham L. Langtry, Milwaukee

Louis P. Petersen, Chicago

Jack Hagerty, Toledo

Charles O. Collier, Chicago

*—Originally elected to Hall of Fame;
moved to Meritorious section by Board action.

1966

Harold Allen, Detroit

1968

William Doehrman, Ft. Wayne, Ind.

Cornelius (Cone) Hermann, St. Louis

1969

R.F. Bensinger, Chicago

David A. Luby, Chicago

1970

Samuel Weinstein, Chicago

1971

Howard W. McCullough, Chicago

Sam Levine, Cleveland

1972

LeRoy Chase, Peoria, Ill.

Milton Raymer, Chicago, Ill.

1973

Walt Ditzen, Phoenix, Ariz.

Bowler-of-the-Year

(Selected by the Bowling Writers Association of America.)

1943—44—Ned Day

1945—Buddy Bomar

1946—Joseph Wilman

1947—Buddy Bomar

1948—Andy Varipapa

1949—Connie Schwoegler

1950—Junie McMahon

1951—Lee Jouglard

1952—Steve Nagy

1953—54—Don Carter

1955—Steve Nagy

1956—Bill Lillard

1957—58—Don Carter

1959—Ed Lubanski

1960—Don Carter

1961—Dick Weber

1962—Don Carter

1963—Dick Weber

1964—Billy Hardwick

1965—Dick Weber

1966—Wayne Zahn

1967—Dave Davis

1968—Jim Stefanich

1969—Billy Hardwick

1970—Nelson Burton, Jr.

1971—72—Don Johnson

All-American Teams

Bowling Magazine, the official publication of the American Bowling Congress began selecting All-American teams annually in 1956.

1956

Bill Lillard

Don Carter

Dick Hoover

Dick Weber

Steve Nagy

1957

Don Carter

Dick Hoover

Bill Lillard

Dick Weber

Lou Campi

1958
Don Carter
Tom Hennessey
Buzz Fazio
Ed Lubanski
Steve Nagy

1959
Ed Lubanski
Don Carter
Ray Bluth
Billy Welu
Tom Hennessey

1960
Don Carter
Billy Golembiewski
Ray Bluth
Dick Weber
Harry Smith

1961
Don Carter
Dick Weber
Ray Bluth
Billy Welu
Joe Joseph

1962
Don Carter
Dick Weber
Ray Bluth
Billy Golembiewski
Dick Hoover

1963
Don Carter
Dick Weber
Ray Bluth
Harry Smith
Billy Welu

1964
Billy Hardwick
Dick Weber
Billy Welu
Bob Strampe
Jim St. John

1965
Dick Weber
Billy Hardwick
Bob Strampe
Jim St. John
Bill Allen

1966
Dick Weber
Les Schissler
Bob Strampe
Nelson Burton Jr.

1967
Dave Davis
Les Schissler
Jim Stefanich
Dick Weber
Wayne Zahn

1968
Jim Stefanich
Dave Davis
Wayne Zahn
Bill Allen
Don Johnson

1969
Billy Hardwick
Dick Weber
Jim Godman
Dick Ritger
Don Johnson

1970
Nelson Burton, Jr.
Dave Soutar
Mike McGrath
Don Johnson
Dave Davis

1971
John Petraglia
Don Johnson
Dave Soutar
Mike Lemongello
Dick Weber

1972
Nelson Burton Jr.
Don Johnson
Earl Anthony
Barry Asher
Larry Laub

Bowler-of-the-Year (Women)

1948—49—Val Mikiel
1950—54—Marion Ladewig
1955—Sylvia Martin
1956—Anita Cantaline
1957—59—Marion Ladewig
1960—Sylvia Martin
1961—62—Shirley Garms
1963—Marion Ladewig
1964—LaVerne Carter
1965—Betty Kuczynski
1966—Joy Abel
1967—Mildred Martorella
1968—69—Dorothy Fothergill
1970—Mary Baker
1971—Paula Sperber

American Bowling Congress (Champions)

A.B.C. TOURNAMENTS
(Courtesy of Bruce Pluckhahn, American Bowling Congress.)

Champions

All-Events

	5-Man	2-Man	Ind.	Total
1901—Frank Brill	478	610	648	1,736
1902—John Koster	639	555	647	1,841
1903—Fred Strong	657	626	613	1,896

	5-Man	2-Man	Ind.	Total
1904—Martin Kern	536	621	647	1,804
1905—Jack G. Reilly	609	605	577	1,791
1906—J.T. Peacock	585	591	618	1,794
1907—H.C. Ellis	629	588	588	1,775
1908—Russell Crable	648	653	623	1,924
1909—James Blouin	656	578	651	1,885
1910—Thomas Haley	617	639	705	1,961
1911—Jimmy Smith	603	673	637	1,913
1912—Phil Sutton	571	644	628	1,843
1913—Ed Hermann	723	634	615	1,972
1914—William Miller	565	657	675	1,897
1915—Matty E. Faetz	646	624	606	1,876
1916—Frank Thoma	628	658	633	1,919
1917—H. Miller	693	649	603	1,945
1918—Harry Steers	569	715	675	1,959
1919—Mort Lindsey	664	579	690	1,933
1920—Jimmy Smith	575	700	640	1,915
1921—Abe Schiemann	658	687	564	1,909
1922—Barney Spinella	635	714	650	1,999
1923—William J. Knox	618	686	715	2,019
1924—A.F. Weber	683	638	654	1,975
1925—Clarence Long	708	624	645	1,977
1926—Harry Gerloski	655	656	670	1,981
1927—Barney Spinella	595	732	637	2,014
1928—Phil Wolf	657	650	630	1,937
1929—Otto Stein Jr.	637	691	646	1,974
1930—George Morrison	716	625	644	1,985
1931—Mike Mauser	639	687	640	1,966
1932—Hugh Stewart	672	616	692	1,980
1933—Gil Zunker	598	750	712	2,060
1934—Walt Reppenhagen	634	702	636	1,972
1935—Ora Mayer	648	692	682	2,022
1936—John Murphy	685	682	639	2,006
1937—Max Stein	658	707	705	2,070
1938—Donald Beatty	709	640	629	1,978
1939—Joseph Wilman	627	693	708	2,028
1940—Fred Fischer	688	667	646	2,001
1941—Harold Kelly	647	652	714	2,013
1942—Stanley Moskal	599	711	663	1,973
1943—45—No competition				
1946—Joseph Wilman	658	706	690	2,054
1947—Junie McMahon	576	649	740	1,965
1948—Ned Day	667	637	675	1,979
1949—John Small	552	722	667	1,941
1950—Frank Santore	662	611	708	1,981
1951—Tony Lindemann	656	663	686	2,005
1952—Steve Nagy	662	698	705	2,065
1953—Frank Santore	600	645	749	1,994
1954—Brad Lewis	636	698	651	1,985
1955—Fred Bujack	627	631	735	1,993
1956—Bill Lillard	683	674	661	2,018
1957—Jim Spalding	706	720	662	2,088
1958—Al Faragalli	641	719	683	2,043
1959—Ed Lubanski	700	652	764	2,116
1960—Vince Lucci	743	697	645	1,985
1961—Bob Brayman (Classic)	646	680	637	1,963
Luke Karan (Regular)	579	750	631	1,960
1962—Jack Winters (Classic)	679	792	676	2,147
Billy Young (Regular)	609	712	694	2,015
1963—Tom Hennessey (Classic)	615	651	732	1,998
Wilford (Bus) Oswalt (Regular)	682	677	696	2,055
1964—Billy Hardwick (Classic)	694	664	730	2,088
Les Zikes (Regular)	604	683	714	2,001
1965—Tom Hennessey (Classic)	577-611	668	693	2,549
Tom Hathaway (Regular)	589	694	639	1,922
1966—Les Schissler (Classic)	665	687	760	2,112
John Wilcox (Regular)	673	613	718	2,004
1967—Bob Strampe (Classic)	667	699	726	2,092
Gary Lewis (Regular)	620	719	671	2,010
1968—Jim Stefanich (Classic)	664	652	667	1,983
Vince Mazzanti (Regular)	732	600	639	1,971
1969—Larry Lichstein (Classic)	618	716	726	2,060
Eddie Jackson (Regular)	649	685	654	1,988
1970—Bob Strampe (Classic)	687	686	670	2,043
Mike Berlin (Regular)	688	647	669	2,004
1971—Gary Dickinson (Classic)	655	635	710	2,000
Al Cohn (Regular)	639	686	738	2,063
1972—Teata Semiz (Classic)	609	631	754	1,994
Mac Lowry (Regular)	691	669	666	2,026

Singles

1901—Frank Brill	648
1902—Fred Strong	649
1903—Dan A. Jones	683
1904—Martin Kern	647
1905—C.M. Anderson	651
1906—Frank Favour	669
1907—M.T. Levey*	624
R.T. Matek	624
1908—Archie Wengler	699
1909—Larry Sutton*	691
F. Bruggemann	691
1910—Thomas Haley	705
1911—James Blouin	681
1912—Larry Sutton	679
1913—F. Peterson	693
1914—William Miller	675
1915—Wallace H. Pierce	711

1916–Sam Schliman*	685	1969–Nelson Burton, Jr. (Classic)	732
B.Huesman	685	Greg Campbell (Regular)	751
E. Shaw	685	1970–Glenn Allison (Classic)	730
1917–Otto Kallusch	698	Jake Yoder (Regular)	744
1918–C.J. Styles	702	1971–Victor Iwlew (Classic)	750
1919–Harry Cavan	718	Al Cohn (Regular)	738
1920–Joe Shaw	713	1972–Teata Semiz (Classic)	754
1921–F. Smith	702	Bill Pointer (Regular)	739
1922–Walter Lundgren	729		
1923–Carl A. Baumgartner	724	**Doubles**	
1924–Harry E. Smyers	749	1901–J. Voorheis–C.K. Starr	1,203
1925–Al Green	706	1902–J. McLean–Harry Steers	1,237
1926–Ed Votel	731	1903–H. Collins–A. Selbach	1,227
1927–William Eggars	706	1904–H.H. Krause–C.H. Spies	1,184
1928–Henry Summers	705	1905–R. Rolfe–E. Stretch	1,213
1929–Adolph Unke	728	1906–J.N. Reed–E. Dresbach	1,247
1930–Larry Shotwell	774	1907–E.G. Richter–E. Bagley	1,164
1931–Walter Lachowski	712	1908–J. Chalmers–H. Kiene	1,254
1932–Otto Nitchke	731	1909–A. Schwoegler–T. Schwoegler	1,304
1933–Earl Hewitt	724	1910–A. Daiker–E. Wetterman	1,231
1934–Jerry Vidro	721	1911–L. Seiler–W. Hartley	1,246
1935–Don Brokaw	733	1912–N.P. Owen–P. Sutton	1,259
1936–Charles Warren	735	1913–P. Schultz–John Koster	1,291
1937–Eugene Gagliardi	749	1914–J. Negley–D. VanNess	1,245
1938–Knute Anderson	746	1915–H. Allen–R. Allen	1,297
1939–James Danek	730	1916–Frank Thoma–Hank Marino	1,279
1940–Ray Brown	742	1917–G. Satorius–W. Holzschuh	1,346
1941–Fred Ruff Jr.	745	1918–Harry Steers–Frank Thoma	1,335
1942–John Stanley	756	1919–O. Kallusch–E. Barnes	1,305
		1920–B. Spinella–C. Spinella	1,336
1943–45–No competition		1921–M. Erikson–E. Krems	1,301
1946–Leo Rollick	737	1922–O. Kallusch–A. Schiemann	1,314
1947–Junie McMahon	740	1923–Charles Daw–F. Wilson	1,358
1948–Lincoln Protich	721	1924–H. Thoma–C. Thoma	1,380
1949–Bernard Rusche	716	1925–E. Schupp–E. Karich	1,318
1950–Everett Leins	757	1926–C. Aston–P. Young*	1,355
1951–Lee Jouglard	775	F. Gardella–F. Tocco	1,355
1952–Al Sharkey	758	1927–M. Flick–Frank Snyder	1,317
1953–Frank Santore	749	1928–H. Will–J. Hradek	1,363
1954–Tony Sparando	723	1929–W. Klecz–P. Butler	1,353
1955–Eddie Gerzine	738	1930–J. Devine–Garry Heup	1,339
1956–George Wade	744	1931–E. Rafferty–C. Reilly	1,316
1957–Bob Allen	729	1932–Frank Benkovic–Charles Daw	1,358
1958–Ed Shay	733	1933–Gil Zunker–Frank Benkovic	1,415
1959–Ed Lubanski	764	1934–George Rudolph–John Ryan	1,321
1960–Paul Kulbaga	726	1935–Clyde Sumerix–Harry Souers	1,348
1961–Earl Johnson (Classic)	733	1936–Anthony Slanina–Mike Straka	1,347
Lyle Spooner (Regular)	726	1937–Virgil Gibbs–Nelson Burton	1,359
1962–Bob Poole (Classic)	759	1938–Don Johnson–Fonnie Snyder	1,337
Andy Renaldy (Regular)	720	1939–Philip Icuss–Murray Fowler	1,405
1963–Tom Hennessey (Classic)	732	1940–Herbert Freitag–Joe Sinke	1,346
Fred Delello (Regular)	744	1941–William Lee–Ray Farnes	1,346
1964–Billy Hardwick (Classic)	730	1942–Edward Nowicki–George Baier	1,377
Jim Stefanich (Regular)	726	1943–45–No competition	
1965–Bob Kennicutt (Classic)	697	1946–John Gworek–Henry Kmidowski	1,360
Ken Roeth (Regular)	700	1947–Edward Doerr Jr.–Len Springmeyer	1,356
1966–Les Schissler (Classic)	760	1948–James Towns–William Sweeney	1,361
Don Chapman (Regular)	761	1949–Donald Van Boxel–Gene Bernhardt	1,332
1967–Lou Mandragona (Classic)	736	1950–Willis Ebosh–Earl Linsz	1,325
Frank Perry (Regular)	723	1951–Bob Benson–Ed Marshall	1,334
1968–Dave Davis (Classic)	741	1952–John Klares–Steve Nagy	1,453
Wayne Kowalski (Regular)	738		

1953—Eddie Koepp—Joe Kissoff 1,339	1912—Brunswick All-Stars, New York . . 2,904
1954—Don McClaren—Billy Welu 1,335	1913—F. DeKnispels, New York 3,006
1955—George Pacropis—Harry Zoeller . . . 1,365	1914—New Haven, New Haven, Conn. . . 2,944
1956—Bill Lillard—Stan Gifford 1,331	1915—Barry-Kettlers, Chicago 2,907
1957—Ronnie Jones—Joe Meszaros 1,369	1916—Commodore Barrys, Chicago 2,905
1958—John Tucker—Jim Vienick 1,414	1917—Birk Bros., Chicago 3,061
1959—Barney Vehige—Gib Fischbach 1,372	1918—Aquila Cigars, St. Paul 3,022
1960—Andy Marzich—Dick Jensen 1,369	1919—Athearn Hotel, Oshkosh 2,992
1961—Don Ellis—Joe Kristof (Classic) . . . 1,331	1920—Brucks No. 1, Chicago 3,096
Joe Macaluso—Gene Herring	1921—Saunders, Toronto 2,066
(Regular) 1,342	1922—Lincoln Ins., Fort Wayne 2,998
1962—Glenn Allison—Dick Hoover (Classic) 1,431	1923—Nelson-Mitchells, Milwaukee . . . 3,139
John Gribin—Gary Madison (Regular) 1,376	1924—Herb's Indians, Cleveland 3,044
1963—Joe Joseph—Billy Golembiewski	1925—Weisser Bl. Rib., Buffalo 3,023
(Classic) 1,378	1926—Castany, Chicago 3,063
Wilford (Bus) Oswalt—Gerry	1927—Tea Shops, Milwaukee 3,199
Schmidt (Regular) 1,337	1928—Oh Henrys, Chicago 3,057
1964—Bob Strampe—Hal Jolley (Classic) 1,355	1929—Hub Recreation, Joliet, Ill. 3,063
Pat Russo—Tony Russo (Regular) 1,343	1930—D. Graff's & Sons, Kalamazoo . . . 3,100
1965—Larry Oakar—Bill Beach (Classic) . . 1,355	1931—S. & L. Motors, Chicago 3,013
Courtney (Buzz) Bosler—Dan Slak	1932—Jefferson Clothiers, Dayton 3,108
(Regular) 1,300	1933—Flaig's Opticians, Covington, Ky. . 3,021
1966—Jim Stefanich—Andy Rogoznica	1934—Stroh's Bohemian Beer, Detroit . . 3,089
(Classic) 1,361	1935—Wolfe Tire Serv., Niagara Falls, N.Y. 3,029
Tony Loiacano—Bob Kwiecien	1936—Falls City Hi-Bru, Indianapolis . . . 3,089
(Regular) 1,351	1937—Krakow Furniture, Detroit 3,118
1967—Norm Meyers—Harry Smith	1938—Birk Bros., Chicago 3,234
(Classic) 1,422	1939—Fife Electrics, Detroit 3,151
Mark Kuglitsch—Ron Wheeler	1940—Monarch Beer, Chicago 3,047
(Regular) 1,357	1941—Vogel Bros., Forest Park, Ill. 3,065
1968—Bill Tucker—Don Johnson (Classic) . 1,329	1942—Budweiser, Chicago 3,131
Richard Stark—Walt Roy	1943—45—No competition
(Regular) 1,325	1946—Llo-Dar Mar Bowl, Santa Monica,
1969—Don McCune—Jim Stefanich (Classic) 1,355	Calif. 3,023
Robert Maschmeyer—Charles Guedel	1947—Eddie & Earl Linsz, Cleveland . . . 3,032
(Regular) 1,379	1948—Washington Shirts, Chicago 3,007
1970—Dave Soutar—Nelson Burton, Jr.	1949—Jimmie Smith's, South Bend 3,027
(Classic) 1,431	1950—Pepsi-Cola, Detroit 2,952
Dick Selgo—Don Bredehoft	1951—O'Malley Oldsmobile, Chicago . . . 3,070
(Regular) 1,371	1952—E & B Beer, Detroit 3,115
1971—Barry Warshafsky—Bill Zuben	1953—Pfeiffer Beer, Detroit 3,181
(Classic) 1,357	1954—Tri Par Radio, Chicago 3,226
Tony Maresca—Bill Haley	1955—Pfeiffer Beer, Detroit 3,136
(Regular) 1,330	1956—Falstaff Beer, Chicago 3,092
1972—Barry Asher—Carmen Salvino 1,366	1957—Peter Hand Reserve Beer, Chicago 3,126
(Classic)	1958—Falstaff Beer, St. Louis, Mo. 3,210
Jerry Nutt—Bill Stanfield 1,350	1959—Pfeiffer Beers, Detroit 3,243
(Regular)	1960—A & A Asphalt, Detroit 3,096
*Won roll-off.	1961—Brentwood Bowl, San Francisco
	(Classic)* 5,983
Five-Man Team	Meyerland Builders, Houston
	(Regular) 3,134
1901—Standards, Chicago 2,720	1962—Carter Gloves, St. Louis (Classic)* 6,248
1902—Fidelia, New York 2,792	Strike N Spare Lanes, Chicago
1903—O'Leary's, Chicago 2,819	(Regular) 3,128
1904—Ansons, Chicago 2,737	1963—California Bombers, Los Angeles
1905—Guenther's No. 2, Chicago 2,795	(Classic)* 6,233
1906—Centurys, Chicago 2,794	Old Fitzgerald, Chicago (Regular) 3,180
1907—Furniture City, Grand Rapids . . . 2,775	1964—Falstaff Beer, St. Louis (Classic)* . 6.417
1908—Bonds, Columbus 2,927	300 Bowl, Pontiac, Mich. (Regular) 3,117
1909—Lipman's, Chicago 2,962	1965—Thelmal Lanes, Louisville, Ky.
1910—Cosmos, Chicago 2,880	(Classic)* 6,151
1911—Flenners, Chicago 2,924	

G. & C. McDermitt, Inc., East
McKeesport, Pa. (Regular) . . 3,074

1966—Ace Mitchell's Shur-Hooks, Akron
(Classic)* 6.536

Plaza Lanes, Saulte Ste. Marie,
Ontario, Canada (Regular) . . 3,066

1967—Balancer Glove, Fort Worth, Tex.
(Classic)* 6,298

Pinky's Bowl, Milwaukee, Wis.
(Regular) 3,327

1968—Bowl-Rite Supply, Joliet, Ill.
(Classic)* 6,285

Dave's Auto Supply, Philadelphia
(Regular) 3,084

1969—Dick Weber Wrist Masters, Santa Ana,
Calif. (Classic)* 6,413

PAC Advertising, Lansing, Mich.
(Regular) 3,165

1970—Merchant Enterprises, New York
(Classic) 3,154

Hamm's Beer, Minneapolis (Regular) 3,243

1971—Chester Iio Investments, Houston
(Classic) 3,081

Carter Tool & Die, Rochester, N.Y. 3,238

1972—Basch Advertising, New York (Classic)3,099

Hamm's Beer, Minneapolis (Regular) 3,101

*Classic Teams bowled six games.

All-Time Records

Team Totals
(Through 1972)

Ace Mitchell Shur-Hooks, Akron* (C) 1966 3,357
Pinky's Bowl, Milwaukee* 1967 3,327
Dick Weber Wrist Masters,
Santa Ana, Calif.* (C) 1969 3,281
Ebonite, Hopkinsville, Ky. (C) . . . 1970 3,253
The Five, Munster, Ind. (C) 1970 3,248
Hamm's Beer, Minneapolis* 1970 3,243
Pfeiffer Beer, Detroit* 1959 3,243
Fresno Bombers, Fresno, Calif. (C) 1962 3,241
Don Carter Gloves, St. Louis (C) . . 1967 3,240
Carter Tool & Die, Rochester, N.Y.* 1971 3,238
Balancer Gloves, Ft. Worth, Texas* (C)1967 3,235
Birk Brothers, Chicago* 1938 3,234
Bowl-Rite Bowling Supply,
Joliet, Ill.* (C) 1968 3,226
Tri-Par Radio, Chicago* 1954 3,226
Falstaff Beer, St. Louis (C) 1962 3,222
Falstaff Beer, St. Louis* 1958 3,210
Falstaff Beer, St. Louis* (C) 1964 3,210
Falstaff Beer, St. Louis* (C) 1964 3,207
Stroh's Beer, Detroit 1958 3,205
Falstaff Beer, San Antonio, Texas . 1958 3,205
Stroh's Beer, Detroit (C) 1963 3,204
Old Fitzgerald, Chicago 1959 3,202
Tea Shops, Milwaukee* 1927 3,199
Budweiser Beer, St. Louis 1958 3,198
Don Carter Bowling Gloves,
St. Louis* (C) 1962 3,196
Helin Tackle, Detroit (C) 1963 3,194

* Won championship (C) Classic Division

Team Games

Falstaff Beer, San Antonio, Texas   1958 1,226
Tea Shops, Milwaukee 1927 1,186
Columbia Tite-Line, San Antonio .   1968 1,183
Jones Dairy, Kingston, N.Y. 1962 1,177
Pfeiffer Beer, Detroit 1959 1,176
Calumet Syrup, Munster, Ind. 1971 1,173
Laurel Lanes, Warren, Ohio 1967 1,170
Birk Brothers, Chicago 1936 1,169
The Five, Munster, Ind. 1970 1,162
Fresno Bombers, Fresno, Calif. . . .   1962 1,162
Jalovec Dodge, Cleveland 1952 1,162
Heil Products, Milwaukee 1937 1,161
Hamm's Beer, Chicago 1960 1,152
Budweiser Beer, St. Louis 1959 1,149
Falstaff Beer, St. Louis 1964 1,149
Fresno Bombers, Fresno, Calif. . . .   1966 1,148
Lake Madison Resort, Sioux Falls, S.D.1962 1,147
Stroh's Beer, Detroit 1963 1,146
Hilliard Chevrolet, Kansas City, Mo. 1964 1,145
Waldorf Golden Bock, Cleveland . .   1937 1,142
Chester Iio Investments, Houston .   1971 1,138
Hamm's Beer, Chicago 1962 1,138
Leonard Sales, St. Louis 1959 1,138
Ace Mitchell Shur-Hooks, Akron, Ohio1966 1,138
The Five, Munster, Ind. 1970 1,136

Doubles Totals

John Klares—Steve Nagy* 1952 1,453
Glenn Allison—Dick Hoover* (C) .   1962 1,431
Dave Soutar—Nelson Burton Jr.* (C)   1970 1,431
Norm Meyers—Harry Smith* (C) . .   1967 1,422
Gil Zunker—Frank Benkovic* 1933 1,415
Jack Winters—John Till (C) 1962 1,414
Bill Tucker—Jim Vrenick* 1958 1,414
Murray Fowler—Phil Icuss* 1939 1,405
Dave Soutar—Bob Strampe (C) . . .   1967 1,395
Otto Jensen—Horace Fishbeck . . .   1939 1,394
Buzz Fazio—Tony Galati 1939 1,384
Clarence Thoma—Harry Thoma* . .   1924 1,380
Bob Maschmeyer—Charles Guedel*   1969 1,379
Billy Golembiewski—Joe Joseph* (C)   1963 1,378
George Baier—Ed Nowicki* 1942 1,377
John Gribin—Gary Madison* 1962 1,376
Eddie Jackson—Chuck Edmonson .   1969 1,373
Barney Vehige—Gib Fischbach* . .   1959 1,372
Dick Selgo—Don Bredehoft* 1970 1,371
Dale Seavoy—Tommy Tuttle (C) . .   1970 1,371
Andy Marzich—Dick Jensen* 1960 1,369
Bob Nickel—Joe Joseph 1958 1,369
Ron Jones—Joe Meszaros* 1957 1,369
Tony Malone—Ray Smith 1959 1,366
John Seebeck—Angelo Zanoni . . .   1942 1,365

* Won championship (C)—Classic Division

Doubles Games

John Gworek—Henry Kmidowski .   1946 544
Bob DeGraff—Marsh Robbins (C) .   1961 538
Dick Karas—Ed Kawolics 1958 531
Jerry Coplan—Gene Skelton 1962 528
Morris Kallay—Bud Stroster 1949 527

Norm Meyers–Harry Smith (C) ...	1967	527
Carmel Dragotta–Fred Pukall	1939	527
Charles Reinle–Rudy Riepel	1926	526
Jerry Dutler–Bill Schaufert (C) ...	1966	526
Clyde Hobbs–Joe Bolek	1958	525
William Mills–Paul Scribner	1925	525
Joe Dumesic–Carroll Davies	1946	524

(C)–Classic Division

Singles Totals

Lee Jouglard*	1951	775
Larry Shotwell*	1930	774
Ed Lubanski*	1959	764
Don Chapman	1966	761
Les Schissler (C)	1966	760
Fred Potter	1959	760
Bob Poole* (C)	1962	759
Al Sharkey*	1952	758
Everett Leins*	1950	757
John Stanley*	1942	756
Teata Semiz* (C)	1972	754
Greg Campbell*	1969	751
Vic Iwlew* (C)	1971	750
Frank Santore*	1953	749
Gene Gagliardi*	1937	749
Harry Smyers*	1924	749

*Won Championship (C)–Classic Division

All Events

Jack Winters* (C)	1962	2,147
Ed Lubanski*	1959	2,116
Les Schissler* (C)	1966	2,112
Bob Strampe* (C)	1967	2,092
Jim Spalding*	1957	2,088
Billy Hardwick* (C)	1964	2,088
Jim Stefanich (C)	1966	2,072
Max Stein*	1937	2,070
Steve Nagy*	1952	2,065
Al Cohn*	1971	2,063
Larry Lichstein* (C)	1969	2,060
Gil Zunker*	1933	2,060
Billy Hardwick (C)	1966	2,060

*Won Championship (C)–Classic Division

Three Games in Any Event

Jack Winters	(CD)	1962	792
Glenn Allison	(CD)	1962	780
Dick Ciprich	(CD)	1972	779
Lee Jouglard	(S)	1951	775
Larry Shotwell	(S)	1930	774
Allie Brandt	(D)	1933	771
Fred Weber	(T)	1934	768
William Volz	(D)	1924	768
Ray Farness	(D)	1941	767
Therm Gibson	(T)	1964	767
Ed Lubanski	(S)	1959	764
Don Chapman	(S)	1966	761
Fred Potter	(S)	1959	760
Les Schissler	(CS)	1966	760
Bob Poole	(CS)	1962	759

Consecutive 1,800 Series or Better

	Years	Starting Year	High	Low	Ave.
George Young, Detroit, Mich. ..	9	1950	1953	1814	207.86
Bob Strampe, Detroit, Mich. ..	8	1964	2753*	2415*	213.48
Joe Wilman, Chicago, Ill. ...	8	1939	2054	1801	210.17
Tommy Tuttle, King, N. C.	8	1964	2571*	2403*	209.25
Ed Kawolics, Chicago, Ill. ...	8	1937	1964	1827	207.84
Joe Bodis, Cleveland, Ohio	8	1925	1931	1801	205.90
Bill Beach, Sharon, Pa.. ...	7	1962	2675*	1810	209.48
Bud Horn, Jr., Los Angeles, Calif.	7	1966	2633*	1805	209.11
Joe Joseph, Detroit, Mich. ..	7	1962	2587*	2445*	208.87
Billy Golembiewski, Detroit, Mich. ..	7	1961	2601*	2419*	208.46
Junie McMahon, Chicago, Ill. ...	7	1942	1965	1803	207.42
Hal Kaminski, Milwaukee, Wis.	7	1966	1933	1804	206.67
Earl Anthony, Tacoma, Wash. .	7	1965	1977	1805	204.30
Jim Stefanich, Joliet, Ill.	6	1963	1974	2421*	211.97
Norm Meyers, St. Louis, Ill. ...	6	1962	2581*	2460*	210.44
Marvin Stoudt, Harrisburg, Pa. .	6	1966	1999	1805	208.54
Marty Cassio, Rahway, N. J. ..	6	1939	1943	1805	207.22
Dale Seavoy, Detroit, Mich. ..	6	1962	2577*	2443*	206.81
Don McClaren, St. Louis, Mo. ..	6	1949	1917	1810	206.75
Al Novak, Phila., Pa. , ...	6	1936	1912	1809	205.29
Lee Jouglard, Detroit, Mich. ..	6	1953	1878	1817	204.67
John Crimmins, Detroit, Mich. ..	6	1939	1863	1801	203.93

*Denotes 12 games due to Classic team format.

Consecutive 1,900 Series or Better

	Starting Year	All Events Totals				
Norm Meyers ..	1963	1,960	1,973	1,922	1,951	1,953
Don Carter	1951	1,909	1,932	1,920		
Steve Nagy	1951	1,976	2,065	1,928		
Therman Gibson	1953	1,935	1,901	1,911		
Dick Weber	1959	1,930	1,947	1,934		
Ed Lubanski ...	1969	1,922	1,959	1,902		

Two-Year Average Records
(Includes Two Best All-Events Scores in a Row)

	Starting Year	All Events Totals	Average
Steve Nagy, Cleveland, Ohio ..	1951	1976	2065–4041–224-9
Don McCune, Munster, Ind.	1969	2645	2038–4683–223
Bob Strampe, Detroit, Mich.....	1967	2753	1918–4671–222-9

Les Schissler,
Denver, Colo. .... 1966 2734 2581—5315—221-11
Dave Soutar,
Gilroy, Calif. .... 1969 2638 1990—4628—220-8
Gary Lewis,
Chicago, Ill. ..... 1967 2010 1946—3956—219-14
Joe Wilman,
Chicago, Ill. ..... 1942 1897 2054—3951—219-9

Jim Stefanich,
Joliet, Ill. 1964 1974 2421 2623 2504 2613—212-51
Billy Welu,
Houston 1955 1913 1922 1839 2029 1878—212-41
Bill Beach,
Sharon, Pa. 1963 1888 1810 2526 2675 1925—212-12
Ed Lubanski,
Detroit 1959 2116 1733 2494 2530 2571—211-50
Glenn Allison,
Los Angeles 1962 2680 1938 2600 2405 2662—211-47

Three-Year Average Records
(Includes Three Best All-Events Scores in a Row)

	Starting Year	All Events Totals		Average
Steve Nagy,				
Cleveland, Ohio ..	1951	1976 2065	1928—221-2	
Bob Strampe,				
Detroit, Mich.....	1966	2536 2752	1918—218-13	
Don McCune,				
Munster, Ind.	1968	2485 2645	2038—217-7	
Bill Beach,				
Sharon, Pa.......	1965	2526 2575	1925—215-31	
Dave Soutar,				
Gilroy, Calif.	1969	2638 1990	1838—215-16	
Therm Gibson,				
Detroit	1962	2589 2613	1898—215-5	
Bill Golembiewski,				
Detroit, Mich.....	1961	2493 2561	2601—215-2	
Jim Stefanich,				
Joliet, Ill.	1966	2623 2504	2613—215	
Les Schissler,				
Denver, Colo.	1966	2734 2581	2424—214-35	
Billy Welu,				
Houston	1956	1922 1839	2029—214-12	

Four-Year Average Records

	Starting Year	All Events Totals			Average
Bob Strampe,					
Detroit, Mich..	1967	2753 1918 2431	2043—217-14		
Dick Weber,					
St. Louis, Mo..	1957	1992 1838 1930	1947—214-3		
Billy Welu,					
St. Louis, Mo..	1955	1913 1922 1839	2029—213-35		
Steve Nagy,					
Cleveland, Ohio	1951	1976 2065 1928	1692—213-23		
Les Zikes,					
Chicago	1962	1906 1825 2001	1740—213-4		
Bill Beach,					
Sharon, Pa. ...	1965	2526 2675 1925	1821—213-1		
Billy Hardwick,					
Louisville, Ky.	1963	2502 2724 2267	2723—212-40		
Al Faragalli,					
Wayne, N.J. ..	1956	1904 1839 2043	1872—212-26		
Joe Wilman,					
Chicago, Ill. ..	1940	1878 1810 1897	2054—212-7		
Don McCune,					
Munster, Ind. .	1967	1739 2485 2645	2038—212-3		

Five-Year Average Records
(Includes Five Best All-Events Scores in a Row)

	Starting Year	All Events Totals				Average
Bob Strampe,						
Detroit, Mich.	1966	2536 2753 1918 2431	2043—216-17			
Joe Wilman,						
Chi., Ill.	1939	2028 1878 1810 1897	2054—214-17			
Dick Weber,						
St. Louis	1957	1992 1838 1930 1947	2544—213-27			
Dick Ritger,						
Hartford, Wis.	1966	2477 2612 2386 2512	1963—213-22			

Ten-Year Average Records
(Includes Ten Best All-Events Scores in a Row)

	Starting Year	All Events Totals		Average
Bob Strampe,		2544 2502 1721 2661 2415		
Detroit, Mich.	1961	2536 2753 1918 2431 2043-211-103		
Glenn Allison,		1863 2680 1938 2600 2405		
Los Angeles, Cal.	1961	2662 2459 2321 2491 2012-209-23		
Steve Nagy,		1976 2065 1928 1692 1786		
Cleveland-Det.-	1951	1847 1809 2033 1794 1812-208-22		
St. Louis				
Dick Weber,		1922 1838 1930 1947 2544		
St. Louis, Mo.	1957	1751 2417 2572 2341 2506-207-103		
Ed Lubanski,		2530 2571 2192 2415 2541		
Detroit, Mich.	1962	2385 2404 2515 1959 1902-207-23		
Joe Joseph,		2248 2564 2587 2445 2512		
Lansing, Mich.	1962	2481 2498 2380 1855 1842-207-22		
Billy Golembiewski,		1954 1816 1713 2493 2561		
Detroit, Mich.	1958	2601 2419 2478 2523 2436-207-17		
Junie McMahon,		1804 1980 1779 1803 1897		
Chicago, Ill.	1939	1965 1834 1863 1815 1891-207-1		
George Young,		1778 1818 1851 1953 1814		
Detroit, Mich.	1949	1819 1864 1859 1908 1951-206-75		
Joe Wilman,		2028 1878 1810 1897 2054		
Chicago, Ill.	1939	1830 1834 1801 1740 1737-206-69		
Norm Meyers		2319 2518 2581 2541 2460		
Los Angeles, Cal.	1961	2492 2560 2194 2519 1918-206-10		

Most Strikes In One Tournament

	Year	T	D	S	Total Strikes	Score
Jack Winters	1962	22	30	22	—74	2,147
Mac Lowry	1972	23	23	22	—68	2,026
Max Stein	1937	20	23	25	—68	2,070
Billy Knox	1923	19	24	24	—67	2,019
Al Cohn	1971	20	22	24	—66	2,063
Les Schissler	1966	19	21	26	—66	2,112
Gil Zunker	1923	15	26	23	—64	2,060
Fred Fischer	1940	22	21	20	—63	2,001
Joe Wilman	1946	19	23	21	—63	2,054
Jim Spalding ...	1957	21	24	18	—63	2,088
Jim Stefanich ...	1966	13	25	25	—63	2,072
John Wilcox	1966	23	16	25	—63	2,004
Tony Lindemann .	1951	20	20	22	—62	2,005
Ed Brosius	1951	18	22	22	—62	1,956
Lindy Faragalli ..	1958	21	21	20	—62	2,043
Steve Nagy	1951	22	19	20	—61	1,976
Ed Lubanski	1959	––	––		—61	2,116
Don Beatty	1938	23	21	17	—61	1,978
Fred Bujack	1953	19	23	19	—61	1,970
Ora Mayer	1935	20	21	19	—60	2,022
Joe Wilman	1939	14	22	24	—60	2,028
Steve Nagy	1952	16	22	21	—59	2,065

Fred Bujack	1955	15	19	25—59	1,993
John Murphy	1936	21	18	19—58	2,006
Therman Gibson	.1955	15	19	25—58	1,935

Most Strikes In One Event

	Event	Year	Total
Jack Winters	CD	1962	30
Glenn Allison	CD	1962	30
Larry Shotwell	S	1930	29
Don Chapman	S	1966	29
Teata Semiz	CS	1972	27
Ray Farness	D	1941	27
Don Whelan	CS	1963	27
Gil Zunker	D	1933	26
Junie McMahon	S	1947	26
Lee Jouglard	S	1951	26
Fred Olmsted	S	1958	26
Bill Pace	S	1959	26
Jack Reuther	S	1959	26
Luke Karan	D	1961	26
Al Koltz	D	1961	26
Dan Stachnik	T	1965	26
Les Schissler	CS	1966	26

Most Strikes In A Row

Billy Knox	Singles	1913	17
Les Schissler	(CT)	1967	17
Virgil Foster	Singles	1951	16

300 Games

William J. Knox	(S)	1913
Charles Reinlie	(D)	1926
Jack Karstens	(D)	1933
Carl Mensenberg	(S)	1935
Michael Blazek	(S)	1938
Wm. McGeorge	(S)	1939
George Pallage	(S)	1940
Michael Domenico	(D)	1940
Wm. Hoar	(D)	1941
Leo Rollick	(D)	1946
Vince Lucci	(D)	1951
Ray Mihm	(S)	1953
Tony Sparando	(S)	1954
Myron Ericksen	(S)	1955
Edward Shea	(S)	1958
Louis Facsko	(S)	1960
Robert DeGraff	(CD)	1961
Les Schissler	(CT)	1967
Lou Cioffi	(CS)	1967
John Caras	(S)	1968
Bill Tucker	(CD)	1968
Jake Yoder	(S)	1970
Eddy Patterson	(CS)	1971

299 Games

James Gilligan	(S)	1921
Frank Degen	(D)	1922
Joe Summermatter	(T)	1924
Frank B. Fabing	(D)	1929
Edward E. Judy	(S)	1929
Sidney Baker	(S)	1930

J.L. Winko	(D)	1932
Henry Fischer	(S)	1939
Lowell Jackson	(D)	1940
William Caskey	(T)	1941
Joe Heinreich	(S)	1942
William Brooks	(T)	1948
Samuel Dempsey	(S)	1948
Howard Rommel	(D)	1951
Dale Carter	(S)	1954
Stan Williams	(S)	1957
Dick Karas	(D)	1958
Tony Baldwin	(D)	1963
Willie Clark	(D)	1965
Charles Guedel	(D)	1969
Glenn (Pete) Lacell	(D)	1970
William Sawon	(D)	1970

Tournament Sites

	Teams
1901—Chicago	41
1902—Buffalo	61
1903—Indianapolis	78
1904—Cleveland	112
1905—Milwaukee	217
1906—Louisville	221
1907—St. Louis	244
1908—Cincinnati	361
1909—Pittsburgh	374
1910—Detroit	401
1911—St. Louis	415
1912—Chicago	596
1913—Toledo	502
1914—Buffalo	450
1915—Peoria	513
1916—Toledo	756
1917—Grand Rapids	714
1918—Cincinnati	654
1919—Toledo	796
1920—Peoria	900
1921—Buffalo	940
1922—Toledo	1,126
1923—Milwaukee	1,956
1924—Chicago	2,132
1925—Buffalo	2,200
1926—Toledo	1,876
1927—Peoria	1,452
1928—Kansas City	2,251
1929—Chicago	2,523
1930—Cleveland	2,443
1931—Buffalo	2,639
1932—Detroit	2,336
1933—Columbus	1,597
1934—Peoria	1,329
1935—Syracuse	2,837
1936—Indianapolis	2,853
1937—New York	4,017
1938—Chicago	4,957

1939—Cleveland	4,145
1940—Detroit	6,078
1941—St. Paul	5,797
1942—Columbus	5,742
1943—45—No competition	
1946—Buffalo	5,744
1947—Los Angeles	3,356
1948—Detroit	7,348
1949—Atlantic City	5,444
1950—Columbus	5,109
1951—St. Paul	5,195
1952—Milwaukee	7,735
1953—Chicago	8,180
1954—Seattle	3,178
1955—Fort Wayne	5,826
1956—Rochester, N.Y.	5,845
1957—Forth Worth	3,056
1958—Syracuse, N.Y.	5,434
1959—St. Louis	5,482
1960—Toledo	5,716
1961—Detroit	6,136
1962—Des Moines	5,234
1963—Buffalo, N.Y.	4,880
1964—Oakland, Calif.	3,742
1965—St. Paul, Minn.	5,412
1966—Rochester, N.Y.	5,163
1967—Miami Beach, Fla.	3,420
1968—Cincinnati, Ohio	5,897
1969—Madison, Wis.	6,238
1970—Knoxville, Tenn.	4,772
1971—Detroit, Mich.	6,193
1972—Long Beach, Calif.	4,732

OTHER A.B.C. Statistics

High Team Total—3,858, Budweisers, St. Louis, Mo., 1958.

High Team Game—1,342, Hook Grip Five, Lodi, N.J., 1950.

High Doubles Total—1,614, Billy Walden—Nelson Burton, Jr., 1970

High Doubles Game—587, Tom Dern—Ron Spohn, 1965

High Singles Total—886, Albert Brandt, 1939.

High All-Events (Total)—2,259, Frank Benkovic, 1932.

Most 300 Games—24, Elvin Mesqer; 17, George Billick.

Two 300 Scores—One Match

	Games				Total
March 5, 1924—					
Frank Carauna	300,	300,	247,	268	1,115*
Jan. 16, 1931—					
Jack Almer . . .	300,	227,	300		827
April 12, 1937—					
Charles Daw . .	300,	201,	300		801
Feb. 17, 1944—					
Hank Marino . .	300,	232,	300		832

			Games			Total
Feb. 24, 1960—						
Bill Flynn		234,	300,	300		834
Jan. 15, 1962—						
Ernest Babcock		238,	300,	300		838
May 11, 1965—						
Bob Briarton . .	234,	300,	205,	300		1,039
Jan. 4, 1968—						
Dick Stoeffler .		225,	300,	300		825
Sept. 9, 1969—						
Carl Phippin . .		300,	213,	300		813
May 12, 1970—						
Darylee Cox . .		243,	300,	300		843
Oct. 26, 1971—						
Herb Stechauner		300,	212,	300		812
April 21, 1972—						
Mike Durbin . .		248,	300,	300		848

*Four games to a league series prevalent in Buffalo then.

The A.B.C. recognized 16,970 scores of 300 from 1908 through July 31, 1972; 10,303 games of 299 and 6,778 games of 298, bowled on sanctioned lanes and in sanctioned competition.

A.B.C. Registered Team Members

Team totals given on five-year average basis 1900 to 1940; thereafter, totals are on annual basis.

1895—1896	60
1900—1901	200
1904—1905	631
1909—1910	1,400
1914—1915	2,100
1919—1920	5,100
1924—1925	12,000
1929—1930	43,000
1934—1935	41,000
1939—1940	132,000
1940—1941	163,000
1941—1942	190,000
1942—1943	150,000
1943—1944	151,000
1944—1945	172,000
1945—1946	184,000
1946—1947	251,000
1947—1948	286,000
1948—1949	311,000
1949—1950	322,000
1950—1951	325,147
1952—1953	356,713
1953—1954	375,377
1954—1955	395,905
1955—1956	438,424
1956—1957	489,321
1957—1958	591,933
1958—1959	714,395
1959—1960	872,605
1960—1961	1,040,592
1961—1962	1,155,586
1962—1963	1,240,634
1963—1964	1,267,518
1964—1965	1,263,678

1965–1966	1,248,427
1966–1967	1,217,436
1967–1968	1,203,479
1968–1969	1,165,284
1969–1970	1,169,341
1970–1971	1,184,768
1971–1972	1,223,557

National Match-Game Champions

In the early days of bowling, every section of the country had some kind of match-game champion. Frequently, in the more heavily populated bowling centers, several laid claim to the title.

More aptly, these "match-game" champions could have been described as "pet pair" title-holders. Usually they had a pair of favorite lanes on which few, if any, rivals could beat them.

One of the first bowlers to move from his home lanes and bowl against virtually anyone, anywhere, was the late Jimmy Smith, an ABC Bowling Hall of Fame member. In the period between 1915 and 1922, Smith generally was considered the unofficial match-game champion. Then in 1922 Louis P. Petersen of Chicago gathered the leading bowlers of the day for a match-game tournament. The winner was Jimmy Blouin of Blue Island, Ill., who defended his title successfully 5 times, then retired.

Frank Kartheiser of Chicago assumed Blouin's vacated title in 1926, lost it in 1927 to Charley Daw of Milwaukee. Adolph Carlson of Chicago unseated Daw in 1928, defeated Walter (Skang) Mercurio of Cleveland and then lost the title to Joe Scribner of Detroit in 1929. Joe Falcaro of Brooklyn wrested the title from Scribner in 1929, defended it successfully once, then fended off all challenges until 1933, when he forfeited the crown.

In 1933 the Bowling Proprietors Association of America took over the match-game championships, conducted an elimination tournament and crowned the winner, Joe Miller of Buffalo, the match-game champion when Falcaro forfeited his title. In the 1934-35 season, Otto Stein of St. Louis won the eliminations and defeated Miller. In the 1935-36 season, Hank Marino of Milwaukee won the eliminations, defeated Stein and held the title until he retired from match competition in 1938.

In 1938, Ned Day of Milwaukee won the eliminations, and defeated Lowell Jackson of St. Louis for the title. He defended his title twice and held it until 1942.

Meanwhile, the Chicago Tribune instituted the All-Star tournament on Dec. 7, 1941. John Crimmins of Detroit won the first event, but Day held the BPAA match-game title until he "gave" it to the All-Star in 1942.

All-Star/U.S. Open Champions (Men)

	Winning Average	*Petersen Point Margin
1941-42–J. Crimmins . . .	208-44	2.36
1942-43–C. Schwoegler .	217-33	35.47
1943–44–Ned Day	208-59	17.6
1944-45–Buddy Bomar . .	205-51	8.30
1945-46–Joe Wilman . . .	209-61	4.25
1946-47–Andy Varipapa .	213-34	6.12
1947-48–Andy Varipapa .	210-8	0.17
1948-49–C. Schwoegler .	213-49	5.04
1949-50–Junie McMahon	214-19	11.20
1950-51–Dick Hoover . .	210-14	1.22
1951-52–Junie McMahon	209-53	3.38
1952-53–Don Carter . . .	205-47	6.31
1953-54–Don Carter . . .	207-4	0.27
1954-55–Steve Nagy . . .	209-16	3.33
1955-56–Bill Lillard	207-32	0.08
1956-57–Don Carter . . .	209-48	3.03
1957-58–Don Carter . . .	213-56	2.44
1959–Billy Welu	210-8	1.22
1960–Harry Smith	212-31	4.21
1961–Bill Tucker	217-36	9.28
1962–Dick Weber	216-30	619-600†
1963–Dick Weber	220-37	642-591
1964–Bob Strampe	215-17	714-616
1965–Dick Weber	216-30	608-586
1966–Dick Weber	218-57	684-681
1967–Les Schissler	215-44	613-610
1968–Jim Stefanich	219-30	5-47
1969–Billy Hardwick . . .	225-35	8-0
1970–Bobby Cooper . . .	234-4	12-29
1971–Mike Lemongello .	215-30	194-186
1972–Don Johnson	215-14	233,224

† Starting 1962, new format.

*Petersen Point system–1 point for a game won and 1 for each 50 pins scored.

A.B.C. Masters Tournment

	Won	Lost	Ave.
1951–Lee Jouglard	6	1	201.29
1952–Willard Taylor	8	1	200.89
1953–Rudy Habetler	10	1	200.30
1954–Eugene Elkins	7	0	205.68
1955–Buzz Fazio	7	0	204.46
1956–Dick Hoover	7	1	209.28
1957–Dick Hoover	9	1	216.98
1958–Tom Hennessey	7	0	209.54
1959–Ray Bluth	7	0	214.93
1960–Bill Golembiewski . . .	7	0	206.46
1961–Don Carter	8	1	211.50
1962–Bill Golembiewski . . .	7	0	223.43
1963–Harry Smith	7	0	219.12
1964–Billy Welu	7	0	227.00
1965–Billy Welu	9	1	202.30
1966–Bob Strampe	7	0	219.29
1967–Lou Scalia	7	0	216.32
1968–Pete Tountas	9	1	220.38
1969–Jim Chestney	10	1	223.05
1970–Don Glover	9	1	215.25
1971–Jim Godman	9	1	229.20
1972–Bill Beach	8	1	220.75

All-Star/U.S. Open Leaders in Average

(Through 1972)	Yrs.	Games	Pins	Ave.
Nelson Burton, Jr., St. Louis	8	435	92,766	213.25
Billy Hardwick, Louisville	7	388	82,742	213.25
Dave Davis, Miami	10	543	114,872	211.55
Wayne Zahn, Tempe, Ariz.	8	466	98,432	211.22
Les Schissler, Denver, Colo.	7	448	94,365	210.63
Tommy Tuttle, King, N.C.	10	436	91,564	210.00
Bob Strampe, Detroit	7	420	88,132	209.83
Dick Weber, St. Louis	19	1,328	278,633	209.81
Bill Allen, Orlando, Fla.	6	399	83,712	209.80
Bill Johnson, New Orleans	8	353	73,678	208.71

All-Star/U.S. Open Tournament Champions
(Women)

SINGLES	Average	Petersen Points
1952-53—Marion Ladewig . .	204-11	154.39
1953-54—Marion Ladewig . .	197-0	148.29
1954-55—Sylvia Wene	193-4	142.30
1955-56—Anita Cantaline . .	190-10	144.40
1956-57—Marion Ladewig . .	197-12	150.16
1957-58—Merle Matthews . .	194-1	145.09
1959—Marion Ladewig	201-1	149.33
1960—Sylvia Wene	194-6	144.14
1961—Phyllis Notaro	196-19	144.13
1962—Shirley Garms	200-16	138.44
1963—Marion Ladewig		
1964—LaVerne Carter		
1965—Ann Slattery		
1966—Joy Abel		
1967—Gloria Bouvia		
1968-69—Dorothy Fothergill		
1970—Mary Baker		
1971—Paula Sperber		
1972—Lorrie Koch		

DOUBLES

1953-54—Marge Skelton—Pat Dryer
1954-55—Dorothy Aldred—Helen Shablis
1955-56—Elvira Toepfer—Anita Cantaline
1956-57—Tess Johns—Jean Schultz
1957-58—Mrs. Marion Ladewig—La Verne Carter
1959—Marion Ladewig—LaVerne Carter
1960—Venice Pelton—Stevie Balogh
1961—Nobu Asami—Helen Duval
1962—Joy Abel—Betty Kuczynski
1963—Elaine Hanzel—Bobbie Shaler
1964—Joy Abel—Betty Kuczynski
1965—Janet Harman—Donna Zimmerman
1966—Jessie Miller—Phyllis Notaro

(Event Discontinued)

Women's International Bowling Congress (Big Pin)

(Courtesy of A.W. (Augie) Karcher, Women's International Bowling Congress, 5301 South 76th Street, Greendale, Wis., 53129)

CHAMPIONS

All-Events	Score
1916-17—Mrs. A.J. Koester	1,423
1918—Mrs. Emma Jaeger	1,552
1919—Mrs. B. Husk	1,580
1920—Mrs. M. Leibrich	1,606
1921—Mrs. Emma Jaeger	1,557
1922—Mrs. R. Abraham	1,659
1923—Deane Fritz	1,582
1924—Mrs. Rose Steger	1,647
1925—Mrs. Grayce Garwood Hatch	1,703
1926—Mrs. E. Lackey	1,641
1927—Mrs. Grayce Garwood Hatch . . .	1,644
1928—Mrs. Emma Jaeger	1,713
1929—Mrs. Emma Jaeger	1,700
1930—Mrs. Selva Twyford	1,727
1931—Mrs. M. Schulte	1,742
1932—Marie Warmbier	1,807
1933—Mrs. Sally Twyford	1,765
1934—Mrs. Esther Ryan	1,763
1935—Marie Warmbier	1,911
1936—Ella Burmeister	1,683
1937—Mrs. Louise Stockdale	1,761
1938—Dot Burmeister Miller	1,843
1939—Ruth Troy	1,724
1940—Mrs. Tess Morris	1,777
1941—Mrs. Sally Twyford	1,799
1942—Nina Van Camp	1,888
1943—45—No competition	
1946—Catherine Fellmeth	1,835
1947—Marge Dardeen	1,826
1948—Virgie Hupfer	1,850
1949—Cecelia Winandy	1,840
1950—Marion Ladewig	1,796
1951—LaVerne Haverly Carter	1,788
1952—Virginia Turner	1,854
1953—Doris Knechtges	1,886

1954—Anne Johnson	1,880	1959—Mae Bolt	664
1955—Mrs. Marion Ladewig	1,890	1960—Marge McDaniels	649
1956—Doris Knechtges	1,867	1961—Elaine Newton	661
1957—Anita Cantaline	1,859	1962—Martha Hoffman	693
1958—Mae Ploegman Bolt	1,828	1963—Dot Wilkinson	653
1959—Pat McBride	1,927	1964—Jean Havlish	690
1960—Judy Roberts	1,836	1965—Doris Rudell	659
1961—Evelyn Teal	1,848	1966—Gloria Bouvia	675
1962—Flossie Argent	1,808	1967—Gloria Paeth	652
1963—Helen Shablis	1,849	1968—Norma Parks	691
1964—Jean Havlish	1,980	1969—Joan Bender	690
1965—Donna Zimmerman	1,833	1970—Dorothy Fothergill	695
1966—Kate Helbig	1,835	1971—Mary Scruggs	698
1967—Carol Miller	1,862	1972—D.D. Jacobson	737
1968—Janice Sue Reichley	1,889		
1969—Helen Duval	1,927		
1970—Dorothy Fothergill	1,984		
1971—Lorrie Koch	1,840		
1972—Mildred Martorella	1,877		

Doubles

	Score
1916-17—Mrs. Roy Acker—Mrs. Jack Reilly	1,011
1918—Mrs. Roy Acker—Mrs. Jack Reilly	1,012
1919—Mrs. Mae Butterworth—Mrs. Steib	1,042
1920—Mrs. E. Willig—Mrs. J. Walz	1,043
1921—Mrs. P. Ley—G. Legge	1,079
1922—Helen Sneider —Louise Sneider Stockdale	1,094
1923—Mrs. Zoe Quin—Mrs. A. Davis	1,038
1924—Mrs. G. Acker—Mrs. Grace Smith	1,124
1925—M. Baker—M. Elbert	1,119
1926—J. Laib—A. Higgins	1,086
1927—A. Burke—E. Kirg	1,100
1928—A. Weiler—E. Estes	1,155
1929—M. Smith—D. McQuade Miller	1,123
1930—F. Trettin—M. Warmbier	1,173
1931—Z. Baker—G. Pomeroy	1,145
1932—M. Frank—E. Kirg	1,218
1933—V. Peters—M. Kite	1,135
1934—F. Trettin—D. McQuade	1,190
1935—E. Haufler—Billy Simon	1,219
1936—Mrs. A. Lindemann—Mrs. L. Baldy	1,116
1937—Loranna Franke—Garnette Weber	1,230
1938—Florence Probert—Ethel Sablatnik	1,215
1939—Connie Powers—Betty Reus	1,130
1940—Tess Morris—Dot Burmeister Miller	1,181
1941—Jo Pittinger—Mary Jane Saracino	1,155
1942—Stella Hartrick—Clara Allen	1,204
1943—45—No competition	
1946—Virginia Facozio—Prudence Dusher	1,251
1947—Candace Miller—Emma Beard	1,245
1948—Margaret Franklin—Merle Mathews	1,188
1949—Estelle Svoboda—Ann Elyasevich	1,229
1950—Shirley Gantenbein—Flo Schick	1,216
1951—Sgt. Esther Cooke—Alma Denini	1,179
1952—Lorraine Quam—Martha Hoffman	1,206
1953—Doris Knechtges—Jane Grudzien	1,211
1954—Frances Stennett—Rose Gacioch	1,244
1955—Wyllis Ryskamp —Mrs. Marion Ladewig	1,264
1956—Betty Maw—Mary Quinn	1,242
1957—Nellie Vella—Jeannette Gryzlak	1,218
1958—Jean Schultz—Tess Johns	1,173
1959—Sylvia Wene Martin —Adele Isphording	1,263
1960—Jette Mooney—Freda Laiber	1,221

Singles

	Score
1916-17—Mrs. A.J. Koester	486
1918—Mrs. F. Steib	537
1919—Mrs. R. Littlefield	594
1920—Mrs. T. Humphreys	559
1921—Mrs. Emma Jaeger	579
1922—Mrs. Emma Jaeger	603
1923—Mrs. Emma Jaeger	594
1924—Alice Feeney	593
1925—Mrs. E. Reich	622
1926—Mrs. L. Weismann	579
1927—Mrs. F. Ehrhart	577
1928—Anita Rump	622
1929—Mrs. Agnes Higgins	637
1930—Anita Rump	613
1931—Mrs. Myrtle Schulte	650
1932—Audrey McVay	668
1933—Mrs. Sally Twyford	628
1934—Marie Clemensen	712
1935—Marie Warmbier	652
1936—Mrs. Ella Burmeister	612
1937—Mrs. Anna Gottine	647
1938—Mrs. Rose Warner	622
1939—Helen Hengstler	626
1940—Mrs. Sally Twyford	626
1941—Nancy Huff	662
1942—Tillie Taylor	659
1943—45—No competition	
1946—Val Mikiel	682
1947—Agnes Junker	650
1948—Shirlee Wernecke	696
1949—Mrs. Clara Mataya	658
1950—Cleo Stallkamp McGovern	669
1951—Ida Simpson	639
1952—Lorene Craig	672
1953—Marge Baginski	637
1954—Mrs. Helen Martin	668
1955—Nellie Vella	695
1956—Lucille Noe	708
1957—Eleanor Towles	664
1958—Ruth Hertel	622

1961–Georgienna Eakins–Betty Long .. 1,239
1962–Sandy Hooper–Jean Stevens 1,238
1963–Ann Heyman–Ruth Redfox 1,260
1964–Shirley Garms–Grace Werkmeister 1,248
1965–Betty Remmick–Mary Ann White 1,263
1966–Martha Morgan–Pat Spence 1,231
1967–Elaine Liburdi–Joan Oleske 1,252
1968–Pauline Stickler–Mary Lou Graham 1,250
1969–Gloria Bouvia–Judy Cook 1,315
1970–Gloria Bouvia–Judy Cook 1,256
1971–Dorothy Fothergill
    –Mildred Martorella 1,263
1972–Judy Roberts–Betty Remmick .. 1,247

Five-Woman Team   Score

1916-17–Progress, St. Louis 2,082
1918–Leffingwell, Chicago 2,479
1919–M. Butler, Toledo, Ohio 2,436
1920–Stein's Jr., St. Louis 2,454
1921–Grand B. and B. Co., Rockford, Ill. . 2,482
1922–Birk Cola Girls, Chicago 2,531
1923–Page Dairy, Toledo 2,348
1924–Albert Pick and Co., Chicago 2,477
1925–Estes Alibis, Chicago 2,518
1926–Taylor Trunks, Chicago 2,525
1927–Boyle Valves, Chicago 2,515
1928–Alberti Jewelers, Chicago 2,682
1929–Harveys Market Square Rec.,
    Kansas City, Mo. 2,538
1930–Finucane Ladies, Chicago 2,784
1931–Alberti Jewelers, Chicago 2,748
1932–Martin Breitt Realtors, St. Louis, Mo. 2,664
1933–Alberti Jewelers, Chicago 2,867
1934–Tommy Doll's Five, Cincinnati 2,616
1935–Alberti Jewelers, Chicago 2,765
1936–Easty Five, Cleveland 2,617
1937–Heil Uniform Heat, Milwaukee 2,685
1938–Heil Uniform Heat, Milwaukee 2,706
1939–Kornitz Pure Oil, Milwaukee 2,618
1940–Logan Square Buicks, Chicago 2,689
1941–Rovick Bowling Shoes, Chicago ... 2,661
1942–Logan Square Buicks, Boston 2,815
1943–45–No competition
1946–Silver Seal Soda, St. Louis 2,721
1947–Kornitz Pure Oil, Milwaukee 2,987
1948–Kathryn Creme Pact, Chicago 2,812
1949–Gears by Enterprise, Detroit 2,786
1950–Fanatorium Majors, Grand Rapids,
    Mich. 2,903
1951–Hickman Oldsmobile Whirlaway,
    Indianapolis 2,705
1952–Cole Furniture Five, Cleveland 2,854
1953–B. & B. Chevrolet, Detroit 2,931
1954–Marhoefer Weiners, Chicago 2,734
1955–Falstaff, Chicago 2,991
1956–Daniel Ryan, Chicago 2,880
1957–Colonial Broach Co., Detroit 2,881
1958–Allgauer Restaurant, Chicago 2,972
1959–Bill Snethkamp Chrysler 3,030
1960–Spare-Time Games 2,876
1961–Allgauer Restaurant 2,919
1962–Linbrook Bowl 3,061

1963–Linbrook Bowl, Anaheim, Calif. 2,841
1964–Allgauer's, Chicago 2,920
1965–Belmont Bowl Pro Shop, Chicago .. 2,929
1966–Gossard Girls, Chicago 2,755
1967–The Orphans, Los Angeles 2,970
1968–Hudepohl Beer, Cincinnati 2,923
1969–Fitzpatrick Chevrolet, Concord, Calif. 2,986
1970–Parker-Fothergill Pro Shop,
    Cranston, R.I. 3,034
1971–Koenig & Strey Real Estate,
    Wilmette, Ill. 2,891
1972–Angeltown Creations, Placentia, Calif. 2,838

QUEENS TOURNAMENT

1961–Janet Harman
1962–Dorothy Wilkinson
1963–Irene Monterosso
1964–D.D. Jacobson
1965–Betty Kuczynski
1966–Judy Lee
1967–Mildred Martorella
1968–Phyllis Massey
1969–Ann Feigel
1970–71–Mildred Martorella
1972–Dorothy Fothergill

TOURNAMENT SITES

	Teams
1916–17–St. Louis	8
1918–Cincinnati	32
1919–Toledo	40
1920–Chicago	84
1921–Cleveland	66
1922–Toledo	85
1923–St. Louis	106
1924–Indianapolis	126
1925–Cleveland	153
1926–Milwaukee	274
1927–Columbus	224
1928–Detroit	220
1929–Buffalo	307
1930–Louisville	354
1931–New York	242
1932–St. Louis	303
1933–Peoria	177
1934–Indianapolis	253
1935–Chicago	470
1936–Omaha	373
1937–Rochester	531
1938–Cincinnati	741
1939–Oklahoma City	548
1940–Syracuse	1,185
1941–Los Angeles	1,015
1942–Milwaukee	1,900
1943–45–No competition	
1946–Kansas City	1,543
1947–Grand Rapids	1,695
1948–Dallas	1,460
1949–Columbus	2,600
1950–St. Paul	2,208
1951–Seattle	1,714

1952—St. Louis	3,045
1953—Detroit	5,000
1954—Syracuse	4,538
1955—Omaha	2,684
1956—Miami	1,918
1957—Dayton	3,098
1958—San Francisco	2,587
1959—Buffalo	4,491
1960—Denver	3,060
1961—Fort Wayne	3,330
1962—Phoenix	2,642
1963—Memphis	3,358
1964—Minneapolis	5,071
1965—Portland	4,068
1966—New Orleans	4,083
1967—Rochester	6,094
1968—San Antonio	4,329
1969—San Diego	4,477
1970—Tulsa	4,894
1971—Atlanta	4,928
1972—Kansas City	5,898

TOP WORLD SCORES

Team
High 3 Games

	Season	Score
Freeway Washer & Stamping Co., Cleveland, Ohio	59-60	3,379
Strachota Milshore-Regent Lanes, Milwaukee, Wis.	67-68	3,273
Pitch's Lounge & Restaurant, Milwaukee, Wis.	70-71	3,248
Hickman Whirlaway, Indianapolis, Ind.	49-50	3,238
Shaw Lanes, Cleveland, Ohio	60-61	3,237
Jac-Ro Die & Engineering Corp., Detroit, Mich.	69-70	3,230
Schaefer Beer, Paramus, N.J.	67-68	3,215
Brodey's Lanes, Indianapolis, Ind. Ind.	56-57	3,211
Hudepohl Beer, Cincinnati, O.	64-65	3,205
Champion Auto Parts, San Francisco, Calif.	71-72	3,202

High 1 Game

	Season	Score
Pitch's Lounge & Restaurant, Milwaukee, Wis.	64-65	1,193
Freeway Washer & Stamping Co., Cleveland, Ohio	59-60	1,190
Freeway Washer & Stamping Co., Cleveland, Ohio	59-60	1,187
Triangle Lanes, Kansas City, Mo.	70-71	1,178
Sauter's Restaurant, Bergen County, N.J.	66-67	1,172
Shaw Lanes, Cleveland, Ohio	60-61	1,172
Strachota Milshore-Regent Lanes, Milwaukee, Wis.	67-68	1,168
Hickman Whirlaway, Indianapolis, Ind.	49-50	1,163
Jac-Ro Die & Engineering Corp., Detroit, Mich.	69-70	1,160
Elsie's Coffee Shop, Albany, Calif.	51-52	1,158

Individual
High 3 Games

	Season	Score
Beverly Ortner, Galva, Iowa	68-69	818
Ruby Chong, Oakland, Calif.	67-68	794
Janet Harman, Norwalk, Calif.	63-64	792
Mildred Martorella, Rochester, N.Y.	66-67	692
Anita Vollmer, Cincinnati, Ohio	66-67	791
Carol Beard, Torrance, Calif.	68-69	790
Angela Mica, St. Louis, Mo.	56-57	787
Hope Riccilli, La Habra, Calif.	67-68	781
Eleanor Timbrook, Concord, Calif.	69-70	781
Jean Stevens, Oklahoma City, Okla.	59-60	779

High League Average

	Season	Score
Mildred Martorella, Rochester, N.Y.	67-68	219
Mildred Martorella, Rochester, N.Y.	68-69	218
Mildred Martorella, Rochester, N.Y.	69-70	215
Maureen Harris, Madison, Wis.	70-71	212
Mildred Martorella, Rochester, N.Y.	66-67	212
Shirley Sjostrom, Bloomington, Minn.	69-70	211
Helen Duval, Berkeley, Calif.	70-71	210

WIBC Hall of Fame

Emma Jaeger, Toledo, Ohio, 1953
Grayce Hatch, Cleveland, Ohio, 1953
Goldie Greenwald, Cleveland, Ohio, 1953
Louise Stockdale, Buena Park, Calif., 1953
Marie Warmbier, Chicago, Ill., 1953
Dorothy Miller, Chicago, Ill., 1954
Philena Bohlen, Los Angeles, Calif., 1955
Floretta McCutcheon, Pasadena, Calif., 1956
Emily Chapman, Long Island, N.Y., 1957
Catherine Burling, Cincinnati, Ohio, 1958
Jo Mraz, Cleveland, Ohio, 1959
Violet Simon, San Antonio, Texas, 1960
Addie Ruschmeyer, White Plains, N.Y., 1961
Anita Rump, Fort Wayne, Ind., 1962
Esther Ryan, Milwaukee, Wis., 1963
Sally Twyford, Nashville, Ind., 1964
Myrtle Schulte, St. Louis, Mo., 1965
Deane Fritz, Toledo, Ohio, 1966
Madalene (Bee) Hochstadter, Chicago, Ill., 1967
Grace Smith, Albuquerque, N.M., 1968
Leona Robinson, Phoenix, Ariz., 1969
Catherine Fellmeth, Lake Geneva, Wis., 1970
Tess Small, Wisconsin Rapids, Wis., 1971
Stella Hartrick, Detroit, Mich., 1972

MERITORIOUS SERVICE

Jeannette Knepprath, Milwaukee, Wis., 1963
Nora Kay, Toledo, Ohio, 1964
Emma Phaler, Columbus, Ohio, 1965

Berdie Speck, St. Louis, Mo., 1966
Iolia Lasher, Albany, N.Y., 1967
Bertha McBride, St. Paul, Minn., 1968
Margaret Higley, San Jose, Calif., 1969
Ann Wood, Cincinnati, Ohio, 1970
Gertrude Rishing, Omaha, Neb., 1972

BASIC RULES BIG PIN BOWLING
Playing Rules and Equipment
Specifications for Tenpin Bowling

Tenpins is played on a lane made of maple and pine, or approved synthetic material, 62 feet, 10 3/8 inches long and 41½ inches wide, both with a ½-inch permitted tolerance. A depressed gutter running the length of each side of the lane can be up to 9 3/8 inches wide. The set of 10 pins are placed in a diamond shape with the point of the diamond in the center of the lane facing the bowler.

The bowler starts his walk toward the foul line on an approach that is a minimum of 15 feet in length. Most bowlers take either four or five steps, though more or less are acceptable. The ball is delivered onto the lane, slightly above the foul line, and the bowler's foot must stop short of the foul line or an electronic device will register a "foul," negating the delivery. It is 60 feet from the foul line to the center of the number one or headpin spot.

The lane must be free of depressions or grooves. One qualification for certification by the American Bowling Congress is that no portion of the lane may be more than 40/1000ths of an inch, about the thickness of a dime, from perfect levelness.

The human pinboy has virtually disappeared. Pins are set by automated equipment and there are automated scoring devices that record pinfall and maintain the scoresheet of two teams on a pair of lanes.

Most pins in use today have a plastic coating over a laminated maple core. They can weigh between 3 pounds, 2 ounces and 3 pounds, 10 ounces, the same range as for all-wood pins, of which almost none are used today because of the high cost and relative scarcity of high quality maple. Nonwood or synthetic pins have been approved for use in ABC/WIBC sanctioned competition and weigh between 3 pounds, 4 ounces and 3 pounds, 6 ounces. All pins are 15 inches in height and must meet rigid specifications for centers of balance, moisture content, design and measurements.

The bowling ball is made of a nonmetallic substance, usually hard rubber or plastic, with a circumference of 27 inches and not weighing more than 16 pounds. Most balls are drilled with a thumb and two finger holes but there are no limitations provided the ball is in balance on no less than six prescribed sides according to ABC specifications.

The object of the game is to knock down as many of the 10 pins as possible with the first delivery. The ultimate is a "strike"—toppling all the pins with the first roll—and 12 successive strikes constitute a 300 game, also called a perfect game.

The game consists of ten frames, with two deliveries per frame. If pins remain standing after the first ball, the object with the second delivery is to topple the remaining pins for a "spare." Failure to achieve this is a "miss" or "error," unless the first ball resulted in a "split"—two or more widely spaced pins (the headpin, or number one pin cannot be one of those still standing). Failure to convert the split with the second ball results in an "open" frame.

A strike is marked with an "x" and is worth ten points plus the count on the next two deliveries. Thus it is possible to score 30 points (pins) in one frame by rolling three consecutive strikes. If the first ball in the fourth frame knocks down nine pins, the score in the second frame becomes 59—the 30 pins in the first frame, ten each for the next two strikes, and the nine for the first ball in the fourth frame.

A spare counts 10 pins plus the count on the *first* ball in the next frame. Thus, if the first frame results in a spare and the first delivery in the second knocks down nine pins, the score in the first frame is 19. If the single pin is missed the score becomes 28. If the spare is made, the procedure from the first frame is continued.

National Duck Pin Bowling Congress

In the Spring of 1900, Wilbert Robinson and John J. McGraw, both baseball immortals and then co-owners of the Diamond Bowling Alleys, Baltimore, Md., introduced the game known as duck pins. Frank Van Sant, their alley manager, suggested a set of 10-pins be made over into little pins to conform with the 6-inch bowling ball which was used in the games of 5-back and cocked hat. John Ditmar, a Baltimore woodturner, produced the first set of "duck pins."

When Robinson and McGraw, whose hobby was shooting ducks, saw the little pins fly and scatter all over the place, they remarked that they looked like a flock of flying ducks. Bill Clarke, a sports writer on the *Baltimore Morning Sun*, in his story the following day, christened them duck pins, and the name stuck.

For the first 2 years the new duck pin was strictly a summer game, but in 1903 several regular leagues were organized. From then the game rapidly spread, first to Washington, D.C., and then up and down the Atlantic Seaboard until Sept. 8, 1927, when the National Duck Pin Bowling Congress was organized in order that a standardization of the "57 varieties" of rules might be attained, standards established for both the duck pins themselves and the alleys.

George Isemann of Washington was elected executive secretary and he directed the destinies of the game until his death in 1940. He was succeeded by Arville L. Ebersole, also of Washington, who has continued as executive secretary of the organization to the present.

From a modest first National tournament entry of 68 teams in Baltimore in 1928 the Congress has grown to a team entry of 1,444 teams in the 1967 tournament, more than 1,500 teams are anticipated in the 1973 tournament. Sanctioned league membership is 38,573 teams with 328,401 members, and the Congress is directed by an executive committee representing the states of Vermont, Massachusetts, Rhode Island, Connecticut, New Jersey, Pennsylvania, Ohio, Maryland, Virginia, West Virginia, North Carolina, South Carolina, Georgia and Florida and the District of Columbia and the Province of Quebec. It is estimated that more than 4,000,000 bowlers are active in the duck pin game.

The American Rubberband Duck Pin Bowling Congress, established in 1945, is an affiliate of the National Duck Pin Bowling Congress.

In bowling at hard pins, a bowler is permitted 3 balls. If he knocks over all with his first ball, it is a strike; if with 2, it is a spare. If with 3, he gets the total pins which have been knocked down.

A variation of duck pins is the rubberband game. The pins, which are encased in rubber, react differently from the hard pins when struck by the ball. In some states the bowler is permitted 2 balls, while in others he may toss 3.

Otherwise, the rules governing big pin bowling apply to both types of the duck pin game.

CHAMPIONS AND RECORDS

Hard pins unless otherwise specified.

(Courtesy of A.L. Ebersole, Executive Secretary, National Duckpin Bowling Congress, 711-14th Street, N.W., Washington, D.C., 20005)

National Tournament Champions

Men's All-Events	Score
1928—Howard Campbell	1,113
1929—Sam Benson	1,141
1930—Athol Millar	1,203
1931—Ray Barnes	1,179
1932—Charles Bauer	1,195
1933—Mike Bogino	1,279
1934—Joe Morelli	1,192
1935—John Waters	1,215
1936—William Dente	1,274
1937—William Tato	1,194
1938—W.S. McNew	1,226
1939—Nick Tronsky	1,240
1940—Nick Tronsky	1,283
1941—Nick Tronsky	1,198
1942—Jimmy Libertini	1,282
1943—45—No competition	
1946—Joe Radocy	1,250
1947—Frank Guethler	1,239
1948—Jack Kamerzel	1,231
1949—George Young	1,267
1950—Nova Hamilton	1,274
1951—Mike Litrenta	1,339
1952—Frank Hanley*	1,239
1953—Charles Kebart	1,306
1954—Frank D'Imperio	1,259
1955—Tom Fitzgerald	1,249
1956—August Recchia	1,200
1957—Pat Crescenzi	1,240
1958—Joseph Serapillia	1,227
1959—William Bursey	1,301
1960—James Chearno	1,292
1961—Fosco Fattorini	1,293
1962—James Jenkins	1,280
1963—Dave Volk	1,284
1964—James Wolfensberger	1,287
1965—Al Grandy	1,323
1966—William Glaeser	1,303
1967—Al Barnhart	1,335
1968—Lindsey Hammonds	1,334
1969—Sterling Fritz	1,333
1970—Paul Popowyck	1,319
1971—Don Meyd	1,336
1972—James Garton	1,292

*Won roll-off.

Men's Singles	Score
1928—Albert Fischer	403
1929—Howard Campbell*	430
Jack Whalen	430
1930—Jack Otto	432
1931—Jack Whalen	435
1932—William Arnold	428
1933—Howard Furlong	440
1934—Nick Tronsky	453
1935—John Bianchi	458
1936—Carl Frisk	445
1937—William E. Powell	439
1938—Astor Clarke*	448
Bob Liberto	448
1939—Nick Tronsky	447
1940—Eddie Johnson	482
1941—Julian Easterday	459
1942—Bill Krauss	456
1943—45—No competition	
1946—Charles Kebart	471
1947—Winny Guerke	445
1948—Mike Dziadik	466
1949—John Catino	480
1950—Hal Tucker	487
1951—Steve Witkowski*	457
Tom Stirling	457
1952—Frank Shanley	452
1953—Al Rush	457
1954—Vince Della	443
1955—Walter Surowiecki*	445

1956—Al Burrell	430	1967—J. Serapilia—R. Fratini	919
1957—Pat Crescenzi	444	1968—G. Haigh—R. Cleary	919
1958—Francis Toolin	456	1969—A. Grandy—J. Rosen	885
1959—Hilmar Spersschneider	473	1970—T. Zagryn—A. Petro	867
1960—Tony Della Rocco	485	1971—E. Brown—P. Sharpe	871
1961—Robert Goss	463	1972—C. Creamer—W.M. Jenkins	915
1962—Frank Chiodi	450	*Won roll-off.	
1963—Earl Hartman	464		
1964—Jesse Davis	465	**Men's Team**	Score
1965—Norwood Heselbach	486	1928—King Pins, Washington, D.C.	1,735
1966—Leon Stetson	458	1929—Recreation Centre, Baltimore, Md.	1,812
1967—Charles Guess	502	1930—Bethesda Bowling Alleys, Bethesda,	
1968—Andy Constantinople	489	Md.	1,805
1969—William Wall	485	1931—Sokol Rosebuds, Bridgeport, Conn.	1,762
1970—Travis Cook	473	1932—Silver Spring Bowling Alleys,	
1971—Joe Bitnwe	488	Silver Spring, Md.	1,819
1972—Wally Adams, Irvin		1933—Morgan Recreation, Hartford, Conn.	1,951
Wagner (tie)	468	1934—Connecticut Yankees, Stratford,	
*Won roll-off.		Conn.	1,943

		1935—Northeast Temple, Washington, D.C.	1,956
Men's Doubles	Score	1936—Blue Ribbons, Willimantic, Conn.	1,948
1928—Ray Von Dreele—F. Smith	779	1937—Borders Friction Stop, Springfield, Vt.	1,995
1929—Red Morgan—G. Friend	775	1938—Holland Five, Bridgeport, Conn.	1,968
1930—J. Mulroe—Paul Harrison	780	1939—Holland Five, Bridgeport, Conn.	1,933
1931—Eddie Espey—Paul Harrison	774	1940—Blue Ribbons, Willimantic, Conn.	2,057
1932—C. Bild—E. Blakeney	801	1941—Newfield Men, Bridgeport, Conn.	1,919
1933—Mike Bogino—Carl Frisk	821	1942—Savoia—Franklin, Baltimore, Md.	2,044
1934—Walter Megaw—J. Waters	789	1943—45—No competition	
1935—Charles Bauer—Wilmer Robey	831	1946—Casino Five, Meriden, Conn.	1,950
1936—A. Christopher—Andy Friar*	831	1947—Holland Five, Bridgeport, Conn.*	1,919
W. Williams—J. LaMastra	831	Bethesda Bowling Center, Wash-	
1937—Astor Clarke—Bill Krauss	809	ington, D.C.	1,919
1938—R. Haines—A. Felter	918	Ice Palace, Washington, D.C.	1,919
1939—Hal Tucker—T. Keene	828	1948—Davidson's Recreation, Baltimore,	
1940—T. Iannarone—G. Brown	843	Md.	1,978
1941—P. Motyl—Mike Dziadik	793	1949—Kingsway, Fairfield, Conn.	1,929
1942—Jimmy Libertini—R. Haines	884	1950—Valley Forge Beer, Washington, D.C.*	1,951
1943—45—No competition		Davidson's Spillway, Baltimore, Md.	1,951
1946—H. Roetzel—B. Powley	825	1951—Forest Park, Baltimore, Md.	2,034
1947—J. Radocy—A. Balducci	852	1952—Washington Club, Providence R.I.	1,933
1948—D. Cost—F. Micalizzi	808	1953—Broadway Candy & Tobacco Co.,	
1949—J. Aler—G. Young	891	Baltimore, Md.	2,031
1950—W. Stalcup—Cletus Pannell*	828	1954—Patterson, Baltimore, Md.	1,976
G. Hargett—H. Smith	828	1955—Guida's Dairy-Blue Ribbons, New	
1951—Nick Tronsky—Harry Peters	911	Britain, Conn.	1,988
1952—Mike Avon—Paul Jarman	929	1956—Arrow "77," Baltimore, Md.	1,900
1953—Carroll Hildebrand—Hal Tucker	841	1957—Langley Sport Center,	
1954—Dr. H. Carbaugh—C. Harshman	834	Washington, D.C.	1,894
1955—T. Fitzgerald—G. Vetos	861	1958—All-Stars, East Haven, Conn.	1,878
1956—A. Recchia—C. Becker	777	1959—Chevy Chase Chevrolt, Washington,	
1957—J. Mordarski—E. Wotton	836	D.C.	2,081
1958—R. DeMatteis—M. Carboni	854	1960—Pla-Mor Bowling Lanes, Arlington,	
1959—V. Marsch—F. Hugelmeyer	850	Va.	2,009
1960—A. Rush—D. Little*	874	1961—Airway Major, Warwick, R.I.	2,083
E. Wojonwski—D. Warfield	874	1962—W. Stalcup Furniture Co.,	
1961—W. Stalcup—P. Crescenzi	875	Washington, D.C.	1,933
1962—R. Rhue—O. Wynne	871	1963—Bregialio's Sausage, Stamford, Conn.	1,982
1963—B. Gochenour—L. Tommey	844	1964—Caithness Buick, Bethesda, Md.	2,044
1964—J. Wolfensberger—M. Alexander	882	1965—Bowl America, Baltimore, Md.	2,104
1965—F. Caruso—J. Ferrando	901	1966—Candee—Whitney, New Haven,	
1966—A. Onofrey—J. Mammone	854	Conn.	2,054

1967—La Perle's Memorials, Plainfield,
  Conn. 2,064
1968—Valley Oilers, Portland, Conn. 2,085
1969—Snelling & Snelling, Baltimore, Md. . 2,057
1970—Kahlua Hut, Washington, D.C. 2,054
1971—Auto Electric Service, Hagerstown,
  Md. 2,116
1972—Guida's Dairy, New Britain, Conn. . 2,070
*Won roll-off

Women's All-Events

	Score
1928—Irene Mischou	973
1929—Marjorie Smith*	975
Margaret Miltner	975
1930—Lorraine Gulli	1,051
1931—Pauline Ford	992
1932—Naomi Zimmerman	1,052
1933—Anne Griffin	1,081
1934—Lorraine Gulli	1,114
1935—Lorraine Gulli	1,065
1936—Lucille Young	1,169
1937—Ida Simmons	1,101
1938—Lorraine Gulli	1,130
1939—Ida Simmons	1,130
1940—Katherine Vick	1,161
1941—Drusilla Kellum	1,034
1942—Lucy Rose	1,126
1943—45—No competition	
1946—Lorraine Gulli*	1,087
Jean Hoyt	1,087
1947—Lorraine Gulli	1,117
1948—Lillian Young	1,184
1949—Maxine Allen	1,231
1950—Doris Leigh	1,121
1951—Betty Covelly	1,151
1952—Anne Wissman	1,186
1953—Gladys Broska	1,153
1954—Mary Kuebler	1,139
1955—Elizabeth Barger	1,152
1956—Betty Mooney	1,137
1957—Elizabeth Barger	1,198
1958—Lee Myers	1,126
1959—Frances Wilson	1,190
1960—Ethel Dize	1,259
1961—Jessie Falls	1,210
1962—Cecilia Rohlfing	1,215
1963—Laura Morgan	1,207
1964—Dorothy Czajka	1,205
1965—Betty Powers	1,190
1966—Elizabeth Barger	1,207
1967—Jean Stewart	1,260
1968—Mary Ann Mitchell	1,202
1969—Minerva Weisenborn	1,248
1970—Jean Harris	1,213
1971—Peggy Nichols	1,236
1972—Cathy Sanders	1,203
*Won roll-off.

Women's Singles

	Score
1928—Arline Roberge	372
1929—Margaret Miltner	374
1930—Margaret Holliday	350
1931—Lotta Janowitz	351
1932—Helen Clements	358
1933—Lois Clopton	397
1934—Florence La Barr	375
1935—Lorraine Gulli	423
1936—Lucille Young	418
1937—Ida Simmons*	416
1938—Mabelle Hering	375
1939—Mabelle Hering*	379
Ethel Brewer	379
1940—Ruth Hampel	413
1941—Carolyn McGinn	398
1942—Edna Hughes	428
1943—45—No competition	
1946—Kitty Sheuchik	405
1947—Flo Reynolds	410
1948—Betty Bainbridge	426
1949—Doris Leigh	418
1950—Estelle Warrington	399
1951—Lorraine Gulli	431
1952—Elizabeth Lowry	430
1953—Gladys Broska	425
1954—Elaine Perlin	399
1955—Edith Christensen	420
1956—Betty Mooney	391
1957—Margie Yeatts	428
1958—Mary Simmons	396
1959—Dorothy Cridlin*	432
Frances Wilson	432
1960—Inez Rhine	458
1961—Jessie Falls	458
1962—Alva Brown	434
1963—Donna Moissonnier	422
1964—Jean Morris	465
1965—Ruth King	428
1966—Cecilia Rohlfing	441
1967—Shirley McAneney	429
1968—Mary Ann Mitchell	447
1969—Gertha Wilson	438
1970—Lori LeBlanc, Patricia	
Price (tie)	431
1971—Sue Marchone	460
1972—Barbara Brown	451
*Won roll-off.

Women's Doubles

	Score
1928—B. Foote—Arline Roberge	625
1929—M. Whalen—Marjorie Smith	688
1930—M. Hassell—M. Degnan	662
1931—Margaret Miltner—Elsie Fischer	676
1932—E. McCurdy—Polly Dozier	694
1933—Margaret Holliday—Lotta Janowitz	747
1934—Evelyn Ream—Billie Butler	701
1935—Olivia Schmidt—Helen Randlett	764
1936—M. Stapleton—Ida Simmons	784
1937—Phyllis Wills—Dorothy Lawson	738
1938—O. Schmidt—Helen Randlett	737
1939—A. D'Lugo—C. Kirk	743
1940—E. Andrus—Katherine Vick	778
1941—H. Staron—N. Urdan	695
1942—M. MacDonnell—A. D'Lugo	772

1943–45–No competition		
1946–G. Bohn–L. Krahl	. . . .	711
1947–Ingomar Moen–Lorraine Gulli	. . . .	727
1948–M. Anderson–Ruth Zentz	. . . .	783
1949–R. Gould–Maxine Allen	. . . .	797
1950–E. Branch–B. Smith	. . . .	768
1951–A. Wissman–Naomi Wargo	. . . . . .	748
1952–Ruby Hovanic–R. Martinelli	. . . .	764
1953–Myrtle Liphard–Elizabeth Barger	. .	752
1954–L. Rakowski–J. Johnson	. . . .	787
1955–J. Dubiel–A. Plude	. . . .	766
1956–L. Farmer–H. Lawrence	. . . .	757
1957–R. Rainey–E. Kluttz	. . . .	760
1958–N. McNamara–A. Clark	. . . .	758
1959–R. Freeman–A. Atkinson	. . . .	774
1960–J. Robinson–E. Dize	. . . .	825
1961–N. Moissonier–D. Moissonnier	. . . .	837
1962–F. Perkins–B. Boyer	. . . .	793
1963–M. Fontana–M. Galloway	. . . .	787
1964–M. Wierdak–H. Sudol	. . . .	780
1965–P. Stroessner–B. Mooney	. . . .	813
1966–H. Pappas–G. Wilson	. . . .	811
1967–L. Morgan–J. Stewart	. . . .	803
1968–D. Shortt–J. Stewart	. . . .	780
1969–M. Mitchell–C. Dyak	. . . .	803
1970–M. Skidmore–M. Reed	. . . .	872
1971–B. Stewart–A. Roberts	. . . .	826
1972–T. Vaccaro–D. Czajka	. . . .	798

Women's Team

	Score
1928–Commercials, Washington, D.C. . . .	1,534
1929–King Pins, Washington, D.C.	1,572
1930–Recreation Girls, Baltimore, Md. . .	1,638
1931–John Blick Girls, Washington, D.C. .	1,533
1932–Burk & Co. Girls, Norfolk, Va.	1,630
1933–Recreation Girls, Baltimore, Md. . .	1,671
1934–Lucky Strike Girls, Washington, D.C.	1,762
1935–Tivoli Girls, Baltimore, Md.	1,606
1936–Lucky Strike Girls, Washington, D.C.	1,762
1937–Charlotte Bowling Center,	
Charlotte, N.C.	1,635
1938–WICC Yankee Network,	
Bridgeport, Conn.	1,729
1939–Diamond Cab, Baltimore, Md. . . .	1,688
1940–WICC Yankee Network, Bridgeport,	
Conn.	1,729
1941–Rendezvous Bowling Center,	
Washington, D.C.	1,651
1942–Eureka Md. Assurance,	
Baltimore, Md.	1,785
1943–45–No competition	
1946–All States Life Insurance Co.,	
Baltimore, Md.	1,755
1947–Dundalk Center, Baltimore, Md. . . .	1,740
1948–Frank's Restaurant, Hartford, Conn.	1,731
1949–Aristocrat Dairy-Recreation,	
Baltimore, Md.	1,759
1950–Frederick Generator-Franklin,	
Baltimore, Md.	1,802
1951–Sena's Recreation, Waterbury, Conn.	1,843
1952–Newfield Girls, Bridgeport, Conn. . .	1,727

1953–Frederick Generator-Franklin,	
Baltimore, Md.	1,749
1954–Hyattsville, Washington, D.C.	1,740
1955–Brunswick Red Crowns-Pimlico,	
Baltimore, Md.	1,800
1956–New Essex, Baltimore, Md.	1,737
1957–Brunswick Red Crowns,	
Baltimore, Md.	1,803
1958–Fulford's, Washington, D.C.	1,738
1959–Carousel-Eastway, Baltimore, Md. .	1,882
1960–Aristocrat Dairy, Baltimore, Md. . .	1,834
1961–Coppola Ford Girls, Bridgeport,	
Conn.	1,876
1962–Guilford Lanes, Baltimore, Md. . . .	1,826
1963–Pin Path, Baltimore, Md.	1,862
1964–Brunswick-Pikesville, Baltimore, Md.	1,834
1965–Crestlanes Five, Lynchburg, Va. . . .	1,840
1966–Phil-Mar Inn Major Girls,	
Baltimore, Md.	1,869
1967–Holiday Lanes, Manchester, Conn. .	1,911
1968–Johnnie's New & Used Cars, Baltimore,	
Md.	1,849
1969–Eudowood Gardens, Baltimore, Md.	1,871
1970–Johnnie's New & Used Cars,	
Baltimore, Md.	1,843
1971–Overlea Caterers, Baltimore, Md. . .	1,861
1972–Ports Sport Shop, Baltimore, Md. . .	1,902

Mixed Doubles

(Women named first.)

	Score
1931–Elsie Fischer–Paul Harrison	699
1932–Lorraine Gulli–F. Moore	714
1933–R. Quinn–Howard Furlong	772
1934–M. Jenson–Wallie Pipp	780
1935–E. Ellis–A. Clarke	735
1936–F. Maroney–F. O'Brien	768
1937–D. Dudley–B. Gauer	777
1938–M. Akers–W. Robey	762
1939–C. Kirk–H. Parsons	789
1940–Lucille Young–J. Talbert	806
1941–Ida Simmons–A. Liebler	802
1942–Caroline Hiser–P. Wolfe	771
1943–45–No competition	
1946–E. Kidd–C. Kidd	774
1947–Blanche Wooton–Billy Stalcup . . .	795
1948–H. Bourgery–T. Carpenter	793
1949–Audrey Atkinson–O. Ellis	791
1950–Elizabeth Barger–Bill Brozey	792
1951–Betty Covelly–H. Lanasa	807
1952–H. Ploss–Jack White	765
1953–Marion Hamilton–Larkin Weedon .	802
1954–F. Reynolds–H. Peters	794
1955–F. Kupec–G. Pelletier	792
1956–P. Heim–G. Young	809
1957–E. Cozza–J. Curran	804
1958–K. Foley–N. Chouniard	771
1959–A. Bafford–L. Kaye	810
1960–F. Hudson–J. Hudson	848
1961–G. Darchik–D. Riccio	831
1962–G. Darchik–D. Riccio	824

1963—P. Jones—F. Fattorini   842
1964—F. Dennis—M. Correnti   864
1965—B. Mooney—E. Hartman   830
1966—W. Guerrette—J. Ferrando   852
1967—S. Connor—W. Lookingland   884
1968—B. Conner—R. Tull   859
1969—F. Haas—D. Lopardo   867
1970—J. Stewart—A. Petro   876
1971—K. Vail—A. Hickox   843
1972—M. Orme—R. Marchone   830

Mixed Teams   Score

1961—Fairlanes Mixed, Charlotte, N.C. . . . 1,779
1962—O & R Mixed, Norfolk, Va. 1,701
1963—Vick's Electric Appliance,
            Rockville, Md. 1,818
1964—Chappel's American, Alexandria, Va. 1,819
1965—Buddy's Horseshoe Club,
            Richmond, Va. 1,894
1966—Chucking Five, Winchester, Va. . . . 1,834
1967—Regent Mixed, Richmond, Va. 1,878
1968—Mix Masters, Baltimore, Md. 1,842
1969—Scrubs, Hagerstown, Md. 1,912
1970—Pinlanders, Baltimore, Md. 1,899
1971—Dilling Heating Co., Kings
            Mountain, N.C. 1,936
1972—Swineford Florist, Richmond, Va. . . 1,946

World Records
(Through 1971-72 season.)

5-Man Team

                                                 Score
Single Game—Strike Masters,
            Baltimore, Md.   820
3-game-set—Holiday Lanes, Manchester,
            Conn.   2,271
5-game set—Bowlarama, Norfolk, Va. 3,403
10-game set—Park Circle Motor,
            Baltimore, Md.   6,460
15-game set—Popular Club Recreation,
            Baltimore, Md.   9,420
Consecutive victories—Koontz Dairy,
            Westminster, Md.   42
High Season Average—Suburban
            Trust, Hyattsville, Md. 663-106

4-Man Team

Single Game—Birschtein Studio,   Score
            Norfolk, Va.   655
3-game set—Wheelers Four,
            Norfolk, Va.   1,736

3-Man Team

Single game—Green Construction Co.,
            Walkersville, Md.   506
3-game set—Nastu Aces, Stratford,
            Conn.   1,339
4-game set—Executive Vending,
            Norfolk, Va.   1,729
5-game set—Carroll Hildebrand, Eli Pickus
            and Nova Hamilton, Baltimore, Md. 1,957

Men's Doubles
                                                 Score
Single Game—*Bob Cleary—Charles
            Earle   367
            *Frank Caruso—John Ferrando . .   367
3-game set—Ray Divver—Vincent Divver . .   959
4-game set—Roy DeVeau—Gerald Maloney   1,206
5-game set—Art Anderson—Bob Covel . . . 1,512
6-game set—Miles Phillips—Al
            Izzo, Jr.   1,661
7-game set—Steve Witkowski—
            Joe Genovesi   1,938
8-game set—Earl Campell-Lee Seim 2,128
9-game set—Nova Hamilton—
            Winny Guerke   2,431
10-game set—Maurice LaCroix—Joe
            Carey   2,779
14-game set—Richard Mattheisz—
            Ed Taylor   3,630
15-game-set—Leo Lacroix—Maurice
            Lacroix   4,021
16-game set—Earl Campbell—Lee Seim . . . 4,147
20-game set—Ben Kosky—Bill Dente 5,286
25-game-set—Art Anderson—Bob Covel . . 6,612
30-game-set—Art Anderson—Bob Covel . . 7,974
35-game-set—Art Anderson—Bob Covel . . 9,318
40-game-set—Art Anderson—Bob Covel . .10,682
45-game-set—Art Anderson—Bob Covel . .11,992
50-game-set—Art Anderson—Bob Covel . .13,228
55-game-set—Art Anderson—Bob Covel . .14,679
60-game-set—Art Anderson—Bob Covel . .16,004
65-game-set—Art Anderson—Bob Covel . .17,516
70-game-set—Art Anderson—Bob Covel . .18,958
75-game-set—Art Anderson—Bob Covel . .20,317
80-game-set—Art Anderson—Bob Covel . .21,666
85-game-set—Art Anderson—Bob Covel . .22,978
90-game-set—Art Anderson—Bob Covel . .24,354
95-game-set—Art Anderson—Bob Covel . .25,704
100-game-set—Art Anderson—Bob Covel . .26,899
Season High Average—Steve Foltz—
            Billy Moore 270-75
Season Average (2 bowlers per lane)—
            Ed Kovis—Harry Peters 264-28
*Tie.

Men's Individual
                                                 Score
Single game—Harry Suit   257
3-game-set—Robert Gallis   549
4-game-set—Don Norton   661
5-game-set—Frank Micalizzi   818
6-game-set—Abner Barnhart   986
7-game-set—Robert Fahrney 1,105
8-game-set—Adolph Petro 1,236
9-game-set—George Pelletier 1,382
10-game-set—Robert Covel 1,551
12-game-set—Abner Barnhart 1,868
15-game-set—Frank Micalizzi 2,250
16-game-set—James Wolfensberger 2,289
18-game-set—Arthur Anderson 2,671
20-game-set—LeRoy Christian 2,857
24-game-set—Henry Howard 3,467
25-game-set—LeRoy Christian 3,533

28-game-set—George Pelletier 3,932
30-game-set—LeRoy Christian 4,331
32-game-set—Henry Howard 4,541
35-game-set—Mike Bogino 4,764
40-game-set—Art Anderson 5,386
45-game-set—Art Anderson 6,044
50-game-set—Henry Howard 7,069
55-game-set—Art Anderson 7,481
60-game-set—Art Anderson 8,181
65-game-set—Art Anderson 8,942
70-game-set—Art Anderson 9,626
75-game-set—Art Anderson 10,301
80-game-set—Art Anderson 10,979
85-game-set—Art Anderson 11,640
90-game-set—Art Anderson 12,356
95-game-set—Art Anderson 13,058
100-game-set—Art Anderson 13,674
100-game-set (continuous bowling)—
    Gordon McIlwee 12,446
Season High Average—Joe
    Lombardo . . . . . : 142-48
Season Average (2 bowlers per lane)—
    James Wolfensberger 139-65

5-Woman Team	Score
Single game—Sea King Seafood, Baltimore, Md.	760
3-game-set—Hauswalk Bakery, Baltimore, Md.	708
5-game set—Pine Grove Dairy, Portsmouth, Va.	3,094
10-game set—Evening Star Champions, Washington, D.C.	5,438
Consecutive victories—Bookies, Richmond, Va.	37
Season High Average—Corona Auto Parts, Glastonbury, Conn.	603-11

3-Woman Team

	Score
Single game—Ladies Triple Team No. 1, Baltimore, Md.	450
3-game-set—O'Connor Vending, Richmond, Va.	1,221

4-Woman Team

	Score
Single game—Robertson Crabhouse No. 2, Washington, D.C.	615
3-game-set—Robertson Crabhouse No. 2, Washington, D.C.	1,704

Women's Doubles	Score
Single-game—Sue Brown—Virginia Siegel	348
3-game-set—Frances Kupec—Helen Sudol	887
4-game-set—Dorothy Clark—Jay Megaw	1,085
5-game set—Elizabeth Barger—Ethel Dize	1,298
6-game set—Carolyn Vallante— Muriel Tebbets	1,499
7-game set—Evelyn Traber— Martha Cleveland	1,694

8-game set—Thelma McDonough—
    Evelyn Brose 1,905
9-game set—Ida Simmons—Elizabeth Lieb . 2,139
10-game set—Elizabeth Barger—Ethel Dize 2,572
15-game set—Naomi Zimmerman—
    Ruth Zentz 3,397
20-game set—Dorothy O'Brien—
    Ida Simmons 4,500
Season average—Dorothy Bermani—
    Dorothy Czajka 252-68

Women's Individual	Score
Single game—Geraldine Gravino	253
3-game-set—Terry Vaccaro	511
4-game-set—Pauline Renahan	630
5-game-set—Mary Kuebler	767
6-game-set—Dorothy Hull	936
7-game-set—Gaye Winslow	1,029
8-game-set—Patricia Rinaldi	1,113
9-game-set—Jean Stewart	1,270
10-game-set—Mary Kuebler	1,420
12-game-set—Patricia Rinaldi	1,659
15-game-set—Jean Harris	2,057
16-game-set—Helen Sudol	2,139
18-game-set—Wilda Guerrette	2,385
20-game-set—Betty Stevens	2,794
24-game-set—Barbara Drinnon	2,920
25-game-set—Betty Stevens	3,459
30-game-set—Betty Stevens	4,087
35-game-set—Maxine Allen	4,525
40-game-set—Maxine Allen	5,124
45-game-set—Maxine Allen	5,779
50-game-set—Maxine Allen	6,433
55-game-set—Maxine Allen	6,953
60-game-set—Maxine Allen	7,622
65-game-set—Maxine Allen	8,244
70-game-set—Maxine Allen	8,906
75-game-set—Maxine Allen	9,537
Season average—Elizabeth Barger	135-79
Season average (2 bowlers per lane)— Cathy Dyak	131-65

Mixed Teams	Score
Single game—The Rollers, Washington, D.C.	841
3-game-set—Buddy's Horseshoe Club, Richmond, Va.	2,044
4-man single game—D.H. Stevens Co., Silver Spring, Md.	617
4-man 3-game-set—D.H. Stevens Co., Silver Spring, Md.	1,612

Mixed Doubles	Score
Single game—Maureen Gilberto— Howard Hampton	370
3-game-set—Pat Andreone—Bill Hughes . . .	933
4-game-set—Ethel Dize (498)—Dave Volk (660)	1,158
5-game-set—Elizabeth Barger (745)— Bill Brozey (699)	1,444

	Score
6-game-set—Virginia Siegel (800)—Ralph Gaddi (937)	1,737
7-game-set—Elizabeth Barger (997)—Bill Brozey (975)	1,972
8-game-set—Ethel Dize (1,000)—Dave Volk (1,201)	2,201
9-game-set—Doris Short (1,217)—Bill Barrett (1,286)	2,503
10-game-set—Elizabeth Barger (1,265)—Bill Brozey (1,471)	2,736
12-game-set—Ethel Dize—Dave Volk	3,249
15-game-set—Maxine Allen (1,933)—Dave Volk (2,045)	3,978
20-game set—Flo Reynolds (2,512)—Ray Anderson (2,613)	5,125
25-game-set—Maxine Allen (3,250)—Bradford Dunham (3,093)	6,343
30-game-set—Maxine Allen (3,898)—Dave Volk (3,970)	7,868
35-game-set—Maxine Allen (4,514)—Dave Volk (4,551)	9,065
40-game-set—Maxine Allen (5,110)—Dave Volk (5,215)	10,325
45-game set—Maxine Allen (5,771)—Dave Volk (5,886)	11,657
50-game-set—Maxine Allen (6,348)—Dave Volk (6,535)	12,883
55-game-set—Maxine Allen (6,953)—Dave Volk (7,245)	14,198
60-game set—Maxine Allen (7,622)—Dave Volk (7,876)	15,498
65-game-set—Maxine Allen (8,244)—Dave Volk (8,499)	16,743
70-game-set—Maxine Allen (8,906)—Dave Volk (9,176)	18,082
75-game-set—Maxine Allen (9,537)—Dave Volk (9,844)	19,381
Season Average (2 bowlers per lane)—Jean Harris—LeRoy Christian	267-71

World Rubberband Duck Pin Records

Men's Team

	Score
Single game—D. Carapellucci Co., Pittsburgh, Pa.	1,286
3-game-set—Speedy's Catering, Versailles, Pa.	3,449
Consecutive Victories—Times-News, Cumberland, Md.	46

Men's Doubles

	Score
Single game—Jim Vitale—Carl Trozzi and Bob Lowther—A.W. Alexander (tie)	498
3-game-set—Mickey Petrovic—William Pochek	1,284

4-game-set—Charles Negro—Lee Venanzi	1,561

Men's Individual

	Score
Single game—William Toprani, Monongahela, Pa.	345
3-game-set—Ray pirko	823
4-game-set—Robert Ihrig	946
5-game-set—Eli Freville	1,051
9-game-set—Billy Wallace	1,871
20-game-set—Eli Freville	3,872
32-game-set—Joseph Boxco	5,772

Women's Team

	Score
Single-game—Leon's Leonette, McKeesport, Pa.	1,002
3-game-set—Leon's Leonnette, McKeesport, Pa.	2,907
Consecutive victories-Louis Dodge, Pittsburgh, Pa.	40

Women's Doubles

	Score
Single game—Elaine Palm—Toni Hijek	461
3-game-set—Wilma Cancilla—Audrey Palm	1,147
4-game-set—Olga Suhoza—Peg Brown	1,384

Women's Individual

	Score
Single game—Several	300
3-game-set—Audrey Palm	688
4-game-set—Libby Nara	767
5-game-set—Gabrielle Jamieson	884
9-game-set—Martha Venturini	1,675

Mixed Team

	Score
(5 Bowlers)	
Single game—Dainty Apparel, Montreal	1,072
3-game-set—A. Sofio & Son, Montreal, Canada	2,819
(6 Bowlers)	
Single game—Twitter Open, Uniontown, Pa.	1,159
3-game-set—All Stars, McKeesport, Pa.	3,096

Mixed Doubles

	Score
Single game—Rose Mooney (241)—William Columbus (252)	493
3-game-set—Rose Mooney (664)—William Columbus (655)	1,319

BOXING

(Courtesy of Nat S. Fleischer's Ring Boxing Encyclopedia, 120 West 31st St., New York, N.Y., 10001)

To most people, boxing generally means fist fighting for a purse of money, i.e., prize fighting. But the sport has other facets. Colleges, schools, athletic clubs and other organizations conduct amateur bouts in which there is no prize money awarded to the contestants. Here the bouts are friendly ones of matching skills in the "Manly Art of Self Defense." Many youngsters start out in boxing for the physical benefits they derive from the exercises pursued in developing their skills. Some who develop great skill eventually turn professional and make boxing a career.

The origin of boxing is buried in antiquity. It has been found to have existed long before the Greeks and Romans indulged in and watched contests. Later it took a strong hold in England. It had a hard time establishing itself in this country. Not until about the turn of the century did it gain a measure of respect in the United States. Now, it is a prosperous activity, with bouts conducted in the largest arenas in the nation. Radio brought descriptions of fights to the home, and television has brought the fight itself into the home. A person now can see at least one or two main bouts weekly while sitting on his living room sofa. Having become a part of the regular television program, fights generally bring in higher fees from TV than from gate receipts.

Boxing is permitted in many states and territories by an enabling act, which specifically prohibits "prize fighting." But the amateurs and the professionals have been indulging in "prize fighting" for decades, and nobody in authority has done anything about it. All of it has been with the blessing of the boxing commissions.

Since Webster says that "a prize is something offered, or striven for in competition," it means that an amateur becomes a "prize fighter" any time he strives for a trophy, and all professionals who accept cash for their services also are "prize fighters." Therefore, there isn't, in the United States, any group of fighters that is not violating that part of the law which says that "prize fighting is barred."

What the legislators had in mind when drafting the law was to block bare-knuckle fighting under London Prize Ring Rules. The gentlemen, obviously, were under the impression that "prize fighting" and bare-knuckle warfare were one and the same, whereas anyone who accepts an award of any kind for participating in any type of fist fight becomes a "prize fighter," whether he uses gloves or bare fists.

In the old days of bare-knuckle bouts the folks who were fancy with their speeches referred to the bouts as "pugilistic contests." The less refined classified them as "prize fights,"

since the men fought for a purse put up by promoters or spectators, the money being split according to advance agreement—all to the winner, 90 per cent to the winner, 10 per cent to the loser, 80—20, 70—30 or 60—40.

In this modern age the spectators pay their money through the box office of a promoter, who acts as transmitting agent. He pays money, or awards a trophy, as the fighters agree upon in advance, retaining a share for his expenses, as was done in the bare-knuckle days. Thus, the principle of boxing awards of today hardly differs from that in the era of bare-knuckle duels.

The legislators determined to bar bare-knuckle battles, under London Prize Ring Rules, because they had the idea the bouts were brutal, while modern boxing was the "manly art of self-defense." The truth is that present-day fighting, with gloves encasing fists and with rounds of three minutes each, are more devastating than ever was known in bare-knuckle fighting.

In the old days if a fighter had to take more beating than he could absorb he merely slipped to the ground and that ended the round. His seconds hauled him to his corner and ministered to him, while he enjoyed 30 seconds of respite. If he still happened to be too woozy to stand up under a new onslaught, he needed only to totter to midring for the next round and fall down again, without being hit. That ended the round, and he was permitted another 30 seconds of rest.

A fighter could continue this procedure without having to suffer a blow for any period of time.

In the last of the bare-knuckle fights for the heavyweight title, between John L. Sullivan and Jake Kilrain in 1889, Kilrain was down almost as long as he was up, and he "coasted" many rounds without being struck a single punch by simply falling down, which ended the round, as specified in London Prize Ring Rules.

In boxing—"the refinement of pugilism"—a round must go three minutes. If a fighter is taking a terrific beating, he has a choice of continuing to take it or going down. If he goes down he must be up within 10 seconds, or be counted out as loser.

A few hundred ringmen have gone to their graves because of the beatings they had to take from gloved fists during the three minutes that make up a round of boxing today.

Thousands of boxers have been hauled to hospitals after their fights with gloves. Tens of thousands more have needed medical help.

Billy Papke, after mixing with Stanley Ketchel for the middleweight title during an exhibition of the "art of self defense," was so battered his sister did not recognize him and refused Papke entrance to his home. Jack Dempsey, using gloves, wrecked the face of Jess Willard in three rounds. Gene Tunney, with gloves, so hammered the face of Dempsey during their Philadelphia fight in 1926 that it was weeks before the former champion regained natural appearance.

In contrast, it is difficult for anyone to name a dozen, a half dozen, or even a few instances of death resulting from those "brutal" bare-knuckle contests under London Prize Ring Rules. Men took beatings, but never anything comparable with what others have taken in "boxing bouts," where gloves do little more than protect the fists of the striking fighter and where the rules require a man to withstand a blizzard of punches, lest he go down and be counted out.

John L. Sullivan was at his peak when the bare-knuckle days were about done and when Marquis of Queensberry Rules, which called for gloves and three-minute rounds, were becoming the vogue. It is not of record that Sullivan, with bare knuckles, ever seriously damaged foemen except the flabby, outmatched Kilrain, who was able to carry on for about 75 rounds, under a broiling sun. But when Sullivan put on gloves and proceeded into action against the "all comers" of his era and foes had to absorb three minutes of a Sullivan attack, John L. almost pulverized the vast bulk of them.

There are no records of a fighter who lost an eye during a battle under London Prize Ring Rules, which permitted gouging. But Harry Greb, Kid Norfolk and many others lost the sight of an eye by being gouged with a gloved thumb in one of those "art of self defense" performances, where gouging is barred.

It is the most grotesque chapter of many that have been written since the world was young and pugilism was new. For, when truth peeps out, it becomes apparent that while legislators ended bare-knuckle fighting and approved gloved warfare, they really were ruling out a reasonably safe and sane method of ring warfare, in which devastation was limited, and traded it for a "refined glove sport," which, in almost any given year, causes more deaths and more human wreckage than occurred during the whole history of bare-knuckle fighting.

In making modern rules, the legislators remembered only what they had read of bare-knuckle pugilism of ancient times and not the bare-knuckle sport that was bettered by regulations fathered by the immortal Jack Broughton and many others.

Pugilism, which gets its name from the Latin "pugil" is the description of "one who fights with his fists." It was assumed for a long time that the ancient Romans and Greeks were the first to feature such battles. But certain slabs and figurines found in a temple at Khafaje, near Bagdad in Mesopotamia, by Dr. E.A. Speiser and associates indicate that men fought with their fists and wrestled centuries before the Greeks and Romans. Dr. Speiser headed an exploration group, sent out more than 40 years ago and sponsored by the University of Pennsylvania and the American Schools of Oriental Research.

One stone slab showed two fighters squaring off. Another showed two wrestlers at grips, their hands touching each other's hips. The hands of the pugilists were well wrapped in leather, the earliest cestus. In the Roman language, "cestus" really meant belt, but was applied when leather was used to girdle anything, including the hands.

It was no great surprise to learn that men of centuries ago—no doubt the Sumerians—used wrestling and fistic tactics, since hands were weapons given to the earliest man. He used them to fight off savage beasts, and undoubtedly to conquer human enemies. In his less vengeful hours, man, striving for perfection in the use of hands in battle, no doubt practiced the fistic arts, and the specimens discovered by Dr. Speiser showed men at such performance.

There appears to have been a lapse in the pugilistic arts from the Mesopotamian era until about 1750 B.C., when the practice was revived in a minor way. In about 900 B.C., the most brutal features of pugilism were sponsored by Theseus, son of Aegeus, a Greek monarch, to provide battles that satisfied his craving for blood and death.

Theseus lived in an era when kings seized every muscular youth in the nation for service as a warrior. Those men were not, in the full sense, slaves. But they were subject at all times to the rule and the whim of the kings. Generally, they were used for war. When there was no war, they were permitted to remain in comparative idleness, but all the while it was demanded of them that they keep physically fit.

Since the Greeks were great believers in holidays and there was constant striving to put on thrilling programs, Theseus devised fist fighting according to rules that were certain to provoke high drama and tragedy. He requisitioned certain of his father's warriors (or gladiators), explained the rules for the method of sport that he had created and forced them into action.

The warriors, as required by the rules of Theseus, sat on flat stones facing each other, their noses almost touching. Their fists were encased in leather thongs. On signal, they started punching at each other. All battles were to a finish. It seems that only the death of the antagonist meant complete victory. Therefore, when one man had hammered the other into insensibility, he continued to punch until he had beaten him to death.

Some of the battles were too prolonged to be pleasing to Theseus. They delayed staging of other fights by fresh gladiators. Therefore, Theseus had the thongs studded with metal, which resulted in quicker finishes. As time went on, the thongs were fitted with something like metal spikes, some short, others long, and often the first few blows landed by a man crushed the face of his opponent, while the delivery of a dozen subsequent blows usually ended the battle—and the warrior.

Historians are inclined to grant the title of all-time champion to Theagenes, of Thasos, Greece, a man who could deliver blows with awesome power. After winning the championship by finishing off the champion who preceded him, Theagenes is credited with obliterating his next 1,425 opponents. He struck quickly; far more so than his rivals. He struck with shattering force. Therefore, since he usually got in the first punch and often injured the other fighter so horribly he could not retaliate, Theagenes went on and on, beating and killing a long succession of gladiators.

The Greeks were the first nation to exploit fist fighting. But when the Romans conquered Greece, they took a great fancy to the "sport." They developed their own fistic warriors, sent them against the best in Greece, and the Romans usually won. The Romans, in preparing their men to face the outstanding fighters in Greece, went to great extremes to provide their man with the most brutal kind of cestus and perhaps the barbarous fistic attachments that the Romans used explains why they were so successful against the Greeks.

When the Romans almost had obliterated the Grecian gladiators who were fistic performers, the Romans staged bouts among their countrymen. When so doing, they made some radical changes in the rules. They decided that legs had some value in such bouts, and required that the battling be from standing position. A limited space was marked off, into which the fighters might retreat in time of great danger. The Romans, to offset the "charity" in such an act toward the gladiators, made the cestus more and more pulverizing.

It is possible that the space allotted to the fighters in those years was circular, rather than squared, accounting for the word "ring," which is a fistic term that has been used to describe the squared off areas for fighters for centuries.

While pugilistic contests generally were reserved for certain holidays in ancient Rome and Greece, they also were part of the funeral ceremonies for some departed notables. It was the belief of the people that the spirit of the deceased lingered in the neighborhood of the mortal's existence. The aim was to arrange, as part of the burial service, something that would please the spirit. If the man in life had been interested in fistic duels, then such a performance was arranged to regale the spirit.

At the funeral of Hector, within the walls of Troy, Dares, then regarded as the most famous pugilist, roared challenges for a battle to death with anyone who had the courage to meet him.

None of the youths accepted. Dares voiced his contempt, whereupon Entellus, an old gladiator from Sicily who had been taught cestus warfare in earlier years by King Eryx, tossed his cestus, smeared with dried blood and brain fragments, into the ring—a gesture of acceptance.

Using all the cunning that he had gained through a long life as a cestus warrior, Entellus held off the rushing, dashing Dares, who, without inflicting great damage, wore himself out trying to kill Entellus. As Dares tired, the tide of battle turned, Entellus forged to the front and Dares cried out acknowledgment of defeat. The satisfied Entellus stopped punching, thus saving Dares' life. It was one of the few times in ancient pugilism when a beaten warrior was spared from death.

Homer, the blind poet, told of a pugilistic contest where the winner received as a prize a "jackass in good condition" and the loser a two-handled cup—for no known reason. Other immortal Greeks of the centuries before Christ left writings that dealt with pugilistic contests, and there have been found in Greece and Rome drawings showing that the pugilists wore leather ear guards—the only protection used in that era.

Winning gladiators in cestus duels always were greatly honored. They were the kings of athletes. Tributes were paid to them in long orations. Rich rewards were theirs. Caligula, eccentric Emperor of Rome and a great pugilistic enthusiast, imported gladiators from Campania and Africa. He matched them and rewarded each winner with a captive maiden as a prize.

Cestus warfare was popular through centuries in Greece and Rome, but finally a less sanguinary king, who saw no reason why the youthful stalwarts should be killed off every afternoon or evening to provide an extra thrill for the spectators, came to rule. He banned the cestus and told the warriors they would have to use bare fists—or quit battling altogether. Eventually, even the use of fists was barred, a Roman emperor, just before the dawn of the Christian Era claiming that fist fighting ruined, instead of helped, prospective warriors, and pugilism went into eclipse for many centuries.

With the exception of a single mention, and that mention has been referred to as "a preposterous instance," pugilism stayed in oblivion until something like 17 centuries later, when one meets up with it in England. There is nothing to equal the strange disappearance of pugilism over so prolonged a span of time, especially when one remembers pugilism was among man's earliest methods of battle.

One historian, and one alone, found a pugilistic revival between 30 B.C. and 1750 A.D. He claims to have discovered that a gentle priest, later canonized as St. Bernardine, caused his parishioners to substitute fist fights for knife duels in Siena, Italy, about 1201 A.D.

Siena was a town, like so many others, where tempers flared, honor was assailed and honor had to be avenged. This resulted in duels in which the vanquished and often the victor ended in their graves. It is recorded that the priest, aware that angered men would fight regardless, suggested the substitution of bare fists for lethal weapons. His parishioners harkened to his pleas.

The priest taught men and boys how to strike blows without breaking their hands. Most important, he demonstrated how arms could be used to block punches. His stress was upon defense, since he did not want anyone brutally damaged. His preachment was that each man was to "box up" the enemy attack—self defense—and thus began a boxing era that endured throughout the lifetime of the priest.

The priest, according to the historian, was wise enough to realize that men, even with "honor at stake," were not eager to invite death—for themselves. Paying heed to the pleas of the priest, the men of the congregation put away whatever were the weapons in use at the time and called on their fists alone. The priest became referee, ending all bouts when honor had been avenged and before one warrior had seriously injured the other.

With the death of the priest, fist fighting gradually ceased in Siena. All trace of it is lost in four more centuries. Then historians, in group formation, found that men in England settled grudges with their fists and that some men, superior to the rank and file, began to indulge in contests "for the fun of it," later for side bets or purses.

Thus, England is called the "Cradle of Pugilism."

There was a lot of fist fighting in England in the 17th Century, but it was chiefly in "rough-and-tumble" style. Men who engaged in encounters were privileged to wrestle, punch, or toss the other to the ground. The technique through those years called for throwing a man to the ground with such force as to bounce the energy from him. That usually continued for hours, and such bouts, because of their length, decreased in favor.

However, some men made it strictly a punching bout, as witness this item, which appeared in January, 1681, in the "London Protestant Mercury":

"Yesterday a match of boxing was performed before his Grace, the Duke of Albemarle, between his butler and his butcher. The latter won the prize, as he hath done many times before, being accounted, though but a little man, the best at that exercise in England."

The names of the fighters, the rules under which they fought and all important details are absent. But this is not surprising to those familiar with early history in England, especially as it concerned sports. The fight, or contest, was the thing. Who participated never was regarded as of much consequence—unless the individual was of royalty, nobility or the aristocracy. Even in more modern times, the English ignore names, or, if names are given, they lack identifying process. It is "Smith fought Brown," or "J. Smith fought R. Brown" and little more.

James Figg lives in history as one of England's great athletes and as the originator of bareknuckle fighting, largely because he departed from the custom of the times when involved in contests. Figg was an all-around athlete, a swordsman of ability and a fine wrestler, and was the pioneer in England to realize the value of a blow with fists. Figg, in battles with other men, never wasted time trying to wear them out with wrestling grips and crashing falls to the turf. He moved in as close as possible and when his rival made a grab for him Figg lashed out with his huge fists. Since the others did not try for defense, Figg's punches usually landed. He either knocked out the other man or rendered him helpless with a succession of blows.

Naturally, Figg became talked-about. Crowds turned out whenever he went into action. While all men were permitted to use their fists, Figg popularized punching and soon his quick dispatch of opponents won him great acclaim. His immediate attack with fists, without waiting until the rival was groggy from gouging, butting and falls, became known as "Figg's Fighting," which grew immensely in favor. Figg moved along to fame and to recognition as England's champion and later capitalized on it by becoming a teacher of the art of punching solidly to the jaw and body—mostly to the jaw.

Figg, born about 1696, when pugilism was gaining real momentum in England, began his career rather early and was winner of 15 successive fights going into 1719. He was acclaimed as England's best. He stood willing to fight anyone for a side bet, as was the custom of the times, but no one cared to risk money and give him battle. They figured to lose both. Figg was invincible, since he was as great at wrestling as anyone else and, additionally, knew the art of delivering punches with crushing force. Therefore, lacking opponents, Figg was forced into temporary retirement. However, his fame was such that there was created a demand for his services as a teacher and in 1719 he opened a place called "Figg's Academy for Boxing," where, for a fee, he taught the proper way to clench fists, how to punch expertly and indicated all the vulnerable spots of a foeman. The novices first were taught all the wrestling tricks and then were schooled in punching.

Figg later changed the name of his place to "Figg's Amphitheatre," which was located on Tottenham Court Road, London. His graduates opened "boxing schools" of their own and by 1728 and 1729 there were more than a dozen boxing academies in the metropolis of England.

Figg's role of teacher did not cause him to forget that he also was a "boxer." He fought whenever the chance offered. He met six foemen in 1720, one in 1721, several in 1723 and battled occasionally from then until 1730, when, undefeated and having reached the age of 34, he announced his retirement. He died of pneumonia in 1734.

Although boxing has been almost exclusively a masculine sport, it is a matter of record that in 1722, after Figg had popularized fist fighting in England, a pair of English women generated a great dislike for each other, with the result that in June, 1722, this advertisement appeared in a London paper:

"Challenge—I, Elizabeth Wilkinson, of Clerkenwell, having had some words with Hannah Hyfield, and requiring satisfaction, do invite her to meet me upon the stage and to box for three guineas ($15); each woman holding half a crown (a piece of money) in each hand, and the first woman that drops the money to lose the battle."

The fight never was put on. The women were willing—even wildly eager. They wanted to punch it out before a public audience. But the police advised the women that such an affair would violate decency as well as ethics, and they served notice that if the fight were attempted the women would be jailed. That cured both of the lust for battle in public.

Figg was the dominating authority on boxing while he lived. His basic rule was that the men must continue battling until there was a definite winner or loser. No rest periods were allowed. Figg's ideas prevailed until 1743, when Jack Broughton, a great fighter and student of the sport, created radical changes in answer to demands to "lessen the brutality of pugilism."

Broughton drew up a set of rules and introduced them at a bout on Aug. 10, 1743. Broughton was to act as referee that night and his original rules were intended only to govern that particular affair, as witness paragraph 3 below. In 1838 these rules were elaborated into the London Prize Ring Rules. The Broughton rules follow:

1. That a square of a yard be chalked in the middle of the stage; and every fresh set-to after a fall, or being parted from the rails, each second is to bring his man to the side of the square, and place him opposite to the other, and till they are fairly set to at the lines, it shall not be lawful for one to strike the other.

2. That, in order to prevent any disputes, the time a man lies after a fall, if the second does not bring his man to the side of the square within the space of half a minute, he shall be deemed a beaten man.

3. That in every main battle, no person whatever shall be upon the stage except the principals and their seconds; the same rule to be observed in by-battles, except that in the latter, Mr. Broughton is allowed to be upon the stage to keep decorum, and to assist gentlemen in getting to their places, provided always he does not interfere in the battle; and whoever pretends to infringe these rules to be turned immediately out of the house. Everybody is to quit the stage as soon as the champions are stripped, before set-to.

4. That no champion be deemed beaten unless he fails coming up to the line, in the limited time; or, that his own second declares him beaten. No second is to be allowed to ask his man's adversary any questions, or advise him to give out.

5. That in by-battles, the winning man to have two-thirds of the money given, shall be publicly divided upon the stage notwithstanding any private agreements to the contrary.

6. That to prevent disputes in every main battle, the principals shall, on the coming on the stage, choose from among the gentlemen present, two umpires, who shall absolutely decide all disputes that may arise about the battle; and if the two umpires cannot agree, the said umpires to choose a third, who is to determine it.

7. That no person is to hit his adversary when he is down, or seize him by the hair, the breeches, or any part below the waist; a man on his knees to be reckoned down.

The Broughton and London Prize Ring laws governed pugilism for many years until it was decided to elaborate on them and to clarify some points that did not seem clear. This led to the creation of the "Revised London Prize Ring Rules," which were the authority for bare-knuckle warfare from the middle of the 18th Century until the last bare-knuckle championship fight on July 8, 1889, between John L. Sullivan and Jake Kilrain.

Broughton is one of the few persons not of royalty who is buried in Westminster Abbey, London.

For about 100 years the London Prize Ring Rules were the only ones known to the sport. Then, because some tender-hearted persons decided that "pugilism is barbarous," the Marquis of Queensberry drafted his famous rules. The Marquis decided that gloves should succeed bare fists, but the idea wasn't original with him. An item in a Paris newspaper of Oct. 8, 1818, read:

"Yesterday at Aix-la-Chapelle (France) a great exhibition was made by English boxers. The two champions were built like Hercules and were naked to the waist. They entered the place with their hands guarded with huge padded gloves. After a severe contest, one of them, more adroit than his rival, struck him so violent a blow on the breast that he fell, and victory was thus decided."

Working along with Arthur Chambers, an English lightweight who later fought in the United States, the Marquis framed the rules that bear his name and first were presented in 1865. However, it was not until 1872, at a tournament in London, that the rules were followed in toto, all contestants wearing gloves and fighting three-minute rounds, with wrestling, throwing, gouging, etc., barred.

The men of 1872 fought for trophies—the first time anything like that had happened. Previously, all battles either were for financial prizes, side bets, or to settle grudges. Furthermore, the 1872 tournament classified the fighters, i.e., a lightweight was 140 pounds or less, a middleweight 158 or less, and all over 158 went into the heavy class. Prior to that time, fighters were not classified. The contests usually were limited to the big men—those from 160 pounds up. The smaller persons, as a rule, did not go in for battling except when there was a grudge and they were of comparable size.

Here are the Queensberry Rules:

Rule 1. To be a fair stand-up boxing match in a 24-foot ring, or as near that size as practicable.

Rule 2. No wrestling or hugging allowed.

Rule 3. The rounds to be of three minutes' duration, and one minute's time between rounds.

Rule 4. If either man fall through weakness or otherwise, he must get up unassisted, ten seconds to be allowed him to do so, the other man meanwhile to return to his corner, and when the fallen man is on his legs the round is to be resumed, and continued till the three minutes have expired. If one man fails to come to the scratch in the ten seconds allowed, it shall be in the power of the referee to give his award in favor of the other man.

Rule 5. A man hanging on the ropes in a helpless state, with his toes off the ground, shall be considered down.

Rule 6. No seconds or any other person to be allowed in the ring during the rounds.

Rule 7. Should the contest be stopped by any unavoidable interference, the referee to name the time and place as soon as possible for finishing the contest; so that the match must be won and lost, unless the backers of both men agree to draw the stakes.

Rule 8. The gloves to be fair-sized boxing gloves of the best quality and new.

Rule 9. Should a glove burst, or come off, it must be replaced to the referee's satisfaction.

Rule 10. A man on one knee is considered down, and if struck is entitled to the stakes.

Rule 11. No shoes or boots with springs allowed.

Rule 12. The contest in all other respects to be governed by revised rules of the London Prize Ring.

AMERICAN HISTORY

Pugilistic encounters were not favored in the early days of America. The few that had been staged before John L. Sullivan popularized the sport by using boxing gloves, were with bare fists under London Prize Ring Rules. Such a form of "sport" was barred and the police always were alert to make arrests whenever they heard of any bouts that were to be fought. As a consequence, such battles generally took place in isolated spots, before small crowds, and even the introduction of the Queensberry Rules, did not, for quite a few years, disturb American lethargy concerning fist fighting.

Jacob Hyer is recorded as America's first champion. All he did to gain title was beat a man in a grudge fight, in 1816, and claim he was champion. No one was interested enough to dispute him. There was a lapse of 24 years and then Jacob's son, Tom, having grown to powerful manhood, announced he was his father's successor as champion of the United States. By that time, there were reports drifting in from England about the activities of fighters there.

Tom Hyer fought a few times in 1840, once in 1841, beat Yankee Sullivan of the British Isles in 1849, and that was his last fight. He died in 1864.

During the 1850's and 1860's the United States was invaded by English pugilists who either fought among themselves or met some Americans who were long on brawn but short on skill. The battles drew small crowds.

Eventually, Paddy Ryan of the United States, who had about four fights in his lifetime, defeated Joe Goss, who held the English title, and that established Ryan as the world champion. Ryan met John L. Sullivan, was outclassed by a superior puncher, went down before an onslaught and that made Sullivan the champion of the universe, at bare-knuckle fighting under London Prize Ring Rules. It wasn't "a glorious victory" and Sullivan's title impressed no one. He was rated as just another of a succession of bruisers who gouged, butted, wrestled and punched without any science.

He realized that bare-knuckle warfare had no future; that it was condemned to eventual extinction. John L. was smart enough to see that if he continued merely as a bare-knuckle specialist, there was little profit in it for him—and Sullivan needed money, a lot of money. Since he had boxed with gloves frequently in Boston theatres, prior to defeating Ryan, he sensed the opportunity to demonstrate prowess with gloves in bouts under the Queensberry Rules, which police always tolerated.

Sullivan attempted a daring thing in 1882. He decided to go along with a theatrical troupe and try to feature the performances with exhibitions in the art of boxing by taking on sparring mates, with gloves, in three minutes of boxing, Queensberry Rules prevailing. Thus, the "nice people" of the country had their first chance to witness boxing bouts, which, in the past, barring a few places like Boston, never had been publicly presented.

As time went on, persons began to twit Sullivan. They said he showed up so well because he paid his partners to turn in an inferior performance. This angered Sullivan. He came out with a proposition that hit the jackpot and made his name famous throughout the land. It was the superlative gesture, and it immediately popularized boxing.

Sullivan offered $100 to any man, no matter how big or how heavy, that he could not knock out in four rounds. As the plan caught on and theatres all over America were jammed to see Sullivan against some "local pride," he increased the offer to the then fabulous sum of $500.

Yokels everywhere made the try for the prize. Youngsters decided they wanted to become invincible, "like Sullivan," and boxing schools grew rapidly through the 1880's. Meanwhile, as ringmen were developed in the United States, a horde of experienced fighters came here from Australia, and England sent some, too. The days of glory for the sport had dawned, and Sullivan continued to be the great, great missionary. His activity in the 1880's was concentrated chiefly in the theatres, on his "all-comers" excursions, but he did take on some noted fighters with gloves in actual battle and fought a 39-round bare-knuckle draw with Charlie Mitchell of England in Chantilly, France, March 10, 1888, for $2,500 a side, the bout ending because rain had made the ring a quagmire.

Sullivan made his last defense of his bare-knuckle championship against Kilrain in Richburg, Miss., July 8, 1889. He stopped Kilrain in the 75th round the latter being unable to "toe scratch" for the 76th. The time was 2 hours 16 minutes 23 seconds.

In September, 1892, Sullivan met James J. Corbett in New Orleans, with gloves and under Queensberry Rules. John L.'s bare-knuckle crown was not at stake. The fight, won by Corbett, was the first to determine the "heavyweight championship under Marquis of Queensberry Rules." Corbett knocked out Sullivan in the 21st and became the first heavyweight champion under Marquis of Queensberry Rules, requiring gloves and three-minute rounds.

Boxing was not legal in New Orleans at the time, but since bare fists were not used, the fight was tolerated. Boxing also was allowed in California, and other centers, where the contests involved only bare fists and London Prize Ring Rules. The first state to permit boxing was New York, which gave its legal blessing late in 1896, with Nevada close behind.

New York sanctioned fights as of November, 1896, at which time Nevada was busying itself with a law that made the Corbett-Robert Fitzsimmons fight legal for March 17, 1897. The Nevada law, so far as is known, never was repealed. But the New York attitude has been subjected to considerable legislative procedure.

The sport, so far as legislation was concerned, was in a rather bad way throughout the nation until New York adopted the Walker Law as of September, 1920.

The rules for boxing in New York, which became the Walker Law, were drafted, generally, by William A. Gavin of England, who arrived in the United States about 1919. His basic plan was a private club, patterned after the National Sporting Club in London, where boxing was to be staged only for members. Gavin sold stock in his International Sporting Club, which really represented memberships, the members including some of the most famous and wealthy Americans. He raised a fund of about $350,000, which was to be used to buy a site and erect a building.

However, late in 1919 while Gavin was making up his boxing rules he was informed that boxing, even in a private club, was barred by the law. He then took his ring rules to Albany, N.Y., where James J. Walker was Speaker of the Senate. Walker agreed to sponsor the bill, which called for legalization of boxing throughout the state. Gavin hired Tex Rickard to act as matchmaker for his club.

Frank Armstrong, a mining promoter, came to realize that the Walker Law would be adopted long before Gavin could complete his planned club and Armstrong gained a lease on Madison Square Garden. He influenced Rickard to resign his job with Gavin and to join him as co-promoter at Madison Square Garden. The Walker bill was passed in the middle of 1920 and Rickard proceeded with plans for his first Garden show on Sept. 1, 1920.

Meanwhile, Gavin's club was in the "dream" stage. Gavin declared he had spent "a great deal of money in Albany," and when pressed for building action, took a boat one midnight and sailed for home, and that was the end of the club and also the $350,000.

Rickard, therefore, had a monopoly on boxing, not only in New York but also elsewhere, almost entirely as a result of Gavin's work and the funds Gavin had spent. The sport, under the Gavin-ized rules, was a tremendous success from the start and Rickard made a fortune. When the lease on the old Garden was about to expire, Rickard formed the corporation that built the present Madison Square Garden, somewhat removed from the Madison Square section of New York City. It was opened Dec. 15, 1925.

The success of boxing in New York influenced men in other states to advocate its legalization, and the law makers quickly responded. Within a few years, the various state boxing commissions joined together under the standard of the National Boxing Association. But New York and a few other states remained aloof.

Boxing is conducted in all states according to the specific rules in those states, but members of the N.B.A. have acted in concert, as regards suspensions, recognition of champions, etc.—with New York continuing to go on its own. As a consequence there often have been two champions in the same division: the champion acclaimed by the N.B.A. and the other by New York. In most cases, the rival champions have met to determine the actual titleholder. In 1952, however, New York entered into an "elastic" agreement with the N.B.A.

The advent of television has become a great factor in the purse of a fighter. Championship fights frequently are televised on closed (theatre) or home circuits. In either case the TV fees are considerable. For non-title bouts the advertising sponsor pays a stated sum for the telecasting of a boxing program and the boxers on it receive stipulated shares.

HEAVYWEIGHT CHAMPIONS

From the time of Jim Figg's retirement in 1730 until Paddy Ryan established undisputed claim to the bare-knuckle heavyweight championship in 1880, there was almost ceaseless confusion as to who was king of the heavyweight division. Men won titles, discarded them and never tried a "comeback." Others retired, only to return, and matters were befuddled for almost 150 years. Out of the chaos of "who was champion, when and why," the following, perhaps, as an orderly array:

British Bare-Knuckle

1719—James Figg, first champion.

1730—Figg retired undefeated. Tom Pipes and Bill Gretting each acclaimed himself successor. Pipes won first fight, Gretting the second, Pipes the third.

1734—Jack Broughton knocked out both Pipes and Gretting and fought all comers for 16 years without defeat.

1750—Jack Slack knocked out Broughton in 14 minutes on April 11. Slack won by the use of a backhand punch, which broke Broughton's nose, injured both eyes and blinded him. The Duke of Cumberland, a great admirer, had bet $50,000 to $10,000 that Broughton would win, although Broughton was 46 at the time.

1754—First international fight July 29; Slack stopped Petit, giant Frenchman, 25 minutes.

1760—Billy Stevens (The Nailer) knocked out Slack and retired. Tom Faulkner, George Taylor and George Meggs claimed title.

1761—Faulkner beat Taylor and retired; Stevens came out of retirement. Meggs knocked out Stevens.

1762—George Millsom defeated Meggs twice.

1763—Tom Juchau knocked out Millsom.

1766—Bill Darts defeated Juchau.

1769—Tom Lyons beat Darts.

1770—Lyons retired and Peter Corcoran, 6-foot 7-inch Irish champion, claimed title; Darts disputed him.

1771—Corcoran stopped Darts with a single punch on May 18 (English Derby week) at Epsom. Captain J. O'Kelly, Corcoran's Irish backer and a wealthy horse owner, won about $175,000 in wagers. A story followed that Darts had "sold out" for $1,000. It never was proven. Apparently the fight was on the level for as time went on Corcoran demonstrated that he was the most paralyzing right-hand hitter of many generations. During his six years as champion he fought more than 20 men and stopped most of them with the first solid blow.

1776—Harry Sellers, 24-year-old giant primed by the English to whip Corcoran, succeeded in the effort, but only after suffering three successive one-punch knockdowns. The poorly trained Irishman rushed himself into weakness after that by chasing Sellers and, after 30 minutes of actual fighting, Corcoran's legs buckled under him, Sellers leaped to the attack and finished Corcoran.

1780—Duggan Fearns beat Sellers and retired.

1782—Jack Jarvis claimed title.

1783—Tom Jackling (real name Tom Johnson), a stevedore by occupation, then 33 years old, made his professional debut by knocking out Jarvis in 15 minutes; Jackling claimed title. Bill Warr, Steve Oliver and Croyden (The Drover) disputed him.

1795—Bill Hooper stopped Bill Woods.

1795—John Owens defeated Hooper but was ignored as champion because Daniel Mendoza, a Spanish Jew, had compiled a brilliant record and was rated then as the greatest fighter in the world. While all England was crying aloud for someone to "whip the foreigner" there came an answer from "Gentleman Jack" Jackson, college youth, intimate of royalty, pal of poets and aristocrats and one of the most loved men in England's history. Jackson had been a champion at college. In 1788 he met Bill A. Fewterell of Birmingham, a hoodlum and braggart, in a finish fight on June 9, in Smitham Bottom, Croyden, England; it was a bout that was forced on him because in a boyish way (he was 19 then) he had offered the idea that he could beat Fewterell. The Prince of Wales and hundreds from the nobility and aristocracy of England were at the ringside cheering Jackson, who knocked out the giant Fewterell in 1 hour and 47 minutes. On March 12, 1789, Jackson met George Ingleston, broke his leg in a fall after 20 minutes of fighting and retired until 1795, when the call came for someone to beat Mendoza.

1795—Jackson knocked out Mendoza in 4

rounds (11 minutes) on April 15 near Horn-church, Essex, England, Mendoza was a 4-to-1 favorite. Later in the year Jackson retired and opened a school for boxing, although he had been graduated in medicine. Lord Byron was one of his pupils and called him "The Emperor of Pugilism." For many years, by royal command, Jackson appeared in boxing exhibitions in the Palace, displaying his prowess before the Czar of Russia, King of Prussia and other visiting royalty.

1800—Jem Belcher, 18-year-old grandson of Jack Slack, an earlier champion, defeated Andrew Gamble and was recognized as title-holder. He defeated a dozen challengers—feared no man and dodged none—during his reign. In 1803 he lost an eye in an accident while playing racquets and retired.

1804—Henry Pearce (The Game Chicken) claimed title.

1805—Tom Cribb, aspirant for title, knocked out Bill Richmond in 1 hour and 30 minutes. Richmond was an American Negro and perhaps the first American to take up ring warfare as a profession.

1805—Sneering challenges from Pearce caused Belcher to come out of retirement and fight Pearce for a side bet of $2,500 each on Dec. 6 near Doncaster, England. Pearce centered his attack on Belcher's good eye, closed it, and the wholly blinded Belcher had to quit after 35 minutes.

While Pearce was champion, he visited a prison where languished John Gully, a butcher boy confined there because he could not pay his debts. Gully asked to spar with Pearce, who had been a boyhood friend in Bristol. Pearce agreed and Gully gave the champion a lathering. When this news reached Fletcher Reid, a gambler and an enemy of Pearce, he paid Gully's debts, arranged his release and had him trained for a fight with Pearce. They met Oct. 8, 1805, and Pearce stopped Gully.

1806—Pearce retired; Gully claimed title. Gully beat Bob Gregson of Lancashire, 35 rounds. Gully was not recognized as champion after the appearance of Cribb, a superior warrior, in 1807. However, Gully continued fighting until 1809. Then he took his savings and bought a tavern. He prospered and purchased race horses. Two of them won the classic English Derby. Others triumphed in rich stakes and added to his fortune. Gully became a member of Parliament. He died in 1863, leaving a $1,000,000 fortune.

1807—Tom Cribb claimed title, ignoring Gully, and challenged the one-eyed Belcher. They met for a $1,000 (each) side bet, April 8, in Moulsey Hurst, England. In the 18th round Belcher knocked Cribb senseless. Cribb was unconscious for over 60 seconds. Using a trick, the seconds of Cribb gained a two-minute rest for their man. Belcher broke his right hand in landing the punch. But one-eyed and one-handed he fought along until the 41st round before he was forced to quit.

1809—Cribb and Belcher battled again on Feb. 1, near Epsom Downs. Belcher, out of condition, was knocked out in 40 minutes. Before he could recover and leave the battlefield police arrived and arrested him. He served 28 days in jail. Coming out, he caught a cold. Tuberculosis developed. He died July 11, 1811, age 29.

1810—Cribb defeated Tom Molineaux, a Negro and the first American ever to fight for a world heavyweight title, on Dec. 10, 1810, at Copthall Common, in 40 rounds.

Molineaux, a slave in Virginia, whipped a Negro bully on a neighboring plantation and his delighted master gave Molineaux his freedom. Having heard about Richmond, he encouraged Tom to make a try in pugilism and furnished transportation to England. Molineaux whipped an "unknown" in Bristol, knocked out Tom Blake in 8 rounds and performed ditto against six other "unknowns." The men called themselves "unknowns" fearing they would lose "social prestige" if it were publicly known they had tangled with a Negro. Molineaux's total earnings for the eight fights was less that $350.

The success of Molineaux caused English sports to demand that Cribb "fight and whip the Yankee nigger." Cribb finally agreed and 20,000 persons gathered at the scene. Molineaux made a punching bag of Cribb for 30 rounds. Americans at the ringside then were offering 5 to 1 that the Negro would win. There were no takers. Cribb, not trained for so terrific a fight, seemed like a man without chance as the 30th ended.

With the opening of the 31st, Molineaux rushed Cribb and dropped him with a right-hand smash. Molineaux stumbled trying to get out of Cribb's way, lunged wildly to get his balance, lost it and pitched headlong into a ring post. The impact knocked him unconscious.

Both men were revived for the 32d and were shoved out on unsteady feet toward midring. They bumped, staggered and fell, ending the round. In the 33d, Cribb summoned a last ounce of energy, lifted his fist as they came out, and hit Molineaux in the face. The Negro went down and out. It was found he had fractured his skull in the collision with the post in the 31st round.

1811—Cribb again defeated Molineaux in a return match Sept. 28, at Wymondham, England, before a crowd of 40,000—the record up to that time. Cribb was in perfect fettle; Molineaux was but a shadow of his former self. Cribb led from start, broke Mokineaux's jaw in the 10th and finished the Negro in the 11th. Molineaux fought only a few times after that, earned trifling sums, drifted into oblivion in England and was found dead on Aug. 4, 1818, in an army barracks in Galway, Ireland.

1822—Cribb, having challenged "any fighter in the world" over a period of 11 years without getting an acceptance, retired at the age of 41.

1823—Tom Spring defeated Bill Neat and was grudgingly acknowledged champion, being called "the man whose punch cannot dent butter." He was sneered at for his lack of punching power. But Spring, a wizard with the left hand, took on the sluggers, beat their faces to a pulp and then flattened them. Eventually, England came to look upon this fast moving, wonderfully clever warrior with the flashing left jab as one of the marvels of all ring history. He was the pioneer of fistic science.

The first stands ever erected for a fight crowd were those erected for Spring's battle with Jack Langan, the Irish champion, on Jan. 7, 1824. The stands seated nearly 4,000 and were built in the outskirts of Worcester, safe from police interference. The builders guaranteed the fighters half the receipts if they would fight in front of the stand, which they did. The stand was packed—at 10 shillings ($2,50 then) per customer. An additional 22,000 standees viewed the fight.

Spring knocked out Langan in the 77th. His gross reward was $27,000. This was made up of Langan's side bet of $2,000, the $5,000 donation of the grandstand owners and "chip-ins" of $20,000 from the crowd, the fight being on the basis of winner-take-all.

1824—In a return match June 1, in Chichester, England, before a gathering of 30,000, Spring knocked out Langan in 76 rounds.

1825—Spring retired to become an innkeeper. He died in 1851. Tom Cannon and Jem Ward claimed title. Ward beat Cannon for a side bet of $2,500. Ward retired in 1831.

1833—James Burke, an English deaf mute, and Simon Byrne, the Irish titleholder, fought for the championship on May 30. Burke knocked out Byrne.

1835—Burke invaded the United States—the first English champion to visit America in quest of fights. He found the game almost nonexistent. He succeeded in getting Jim O'Rourke, a rough and tumble fighter, to meet him for a small side bet near New Orleans. The battle ended in 3 rounds—in a riot. Some months later Burke stopped Tom O'Connell, another bruiser, in 10 minutes of fighting near Harts Island, N.Y. Burke soon returned to England.

1839—Bendigo (real name William Thompson) became champion on Feb. 12 when he beat Burke in 10 rounds, near Appleby, England. Bendigo, 6 feet 2½ inches tall and weighing 210, was one of the most powerful men to hold title.

1840—Bendigo injured a knee in a fight with Ben Caunt, could not go on, and referee awarded bout to Caunt. Bendigo retired.

1845—Bendigo's knee regained strength, he challenged Caunt and knocked him out in 93 rounds, Sept. 9, near Stoney, Stratford, England.

1846—Bendigo again retired but in 1850 accepted the challenge of Tom Paddock and knocked him out in 49 rounds on June 5, 1850, near Mildenhall.

1851—Bendigo retired for third time. He had been arrested 28 times for violating the anti-fight law, had served 28 prison terms and had been lectured on the evils of sin each time while in jail. When he gave up pugilism, he became an evangelist.

1851—1855—No champion.

1856—Tom Sayers claimed title. He was generally recognized in 1859, after whipping Bob Brettle.

1860—John C. Heenan, an American, invaded England. In 1858, Heenan had fought John Morrissey for the American title and was beaten in eleven rounds, having broken his right hand in the first. Heenan challenged for a new match, but Morrissey retired. Heenan thereupon claimed the American title. No one disputed him. When he reached England he declared he was America's champion and wanted to fight Sayers for the world title. The men met April 17 in Barnboro near London. The fight ended in the 42d round (2 hours 20 minutes) when toughs broke into the ring.

In all the years since there has been argument as to who was ahead at the time. Americans at the ringside who had bet on Heenan maintained that Sayers was on the verge of a knockout and that the mob which halted the battle was made up of English who had wagered on Sayers.

1860—Sayers announced his retirement, never fought again and died in 1865.

1861—Jem Mace claimed title; so did Sam Hurst. Mace stopped Hurst in 8 rounds.

1862—Tom King challenged Mace and Mace beat him in 43 rounds in their first fight on Jan. 18, near Godstone, England. They met a second time in Medway, England, and King won the championship, whipping Mace in 21 rounds, Nov. 26. King received a belt emblematic of the English championship.

1863—Heenan, still in England, challenged King and they met Dec. 23 at Wadhurst, England, for the world championship and a reported side bet of $10,000. Heenan had King in such a desperate condition after the 18th round that King could not toe scratch with the call of "time." But the referee did not award to Heenan. King's seconds took all the time they needed to revive King while Heenan's handlers made futile demands for a decision for Heenan. When the fight was renewed the tide of battle quickly shifted, King administered a terrific beating to Heenan, and Heenan's seconds tossed in the towel in the 25th round.

1864—Mace repeatedly challenged King, who refused to meet him. King announced his retirement from the ring. Taking up rowing, he became one of England's greatest scullers. King's gambling operations on the English turf were extremely successful and when he died in 1888 he left over $300,000.

1865—After the death of Sayers in this year and when it became certain that King would fight no more, Mace put in a claim for the title which King had won from him, but Joe Goss disputed him.

1866—On May 24, Mace and Goss met in Farmingham, England. They sparred for nearly 20 minutes, neither striking a blow, shook hands and jumped out of the ring. Police were in the crowd and the men feared arrest if they actually started battle. On Aug. 6, they met again on the banks of the Thames River, outside of London. Mace won from Goss in 21 rounds and claimed the world title. He announced his willingness to meet all comers in England but none gave him a fight.

1868—Mace left for a tour of the United States.

American Bare-Knuckle

American heavyweight history did not begin with the arrival of Mace, but his presence eventually made possible the establishment of a world champion at bare-knuckle fighting. The history of pugilism in the United States follows:

1816—The first actual pugilistic encounter on American soil was in 1816 when Jacob Hyer defeated Tom Beasley; it was more a grudge fight than to determine any championship. However, when Hyer won, he stated that he could "lick everybody else in America." No one disputed him and Hyer jocosely declared that this made him champion. He never fought again.

1841—Tom Hyer, son of Jacob, claimed his father's laurels. He was 22, weight 205, was 6 feet 2½ inches tall. John McCluster disputed Hyer, and Tom beat McCluster with a few punches.

1849—Hyer met Yankee Sullivan, an experienced English battler who was here on an all-comers tour, and knocked out Sullivan in 16 rounds on Feb. 7, after which Hyer, failing to find anyone to give him action, retired.

1852—John C. Morrissey claimed the American championship, although his only qualification was the fact that he had beaten a few mining camp bruisers and had won on a foul from George Thompson, near Benicia, Calif., Aug. 31. Morrissey, born in Ireland in 1831, settled in New York with his folks when a youngster and went to California in the gold rush of '49.

1853—Morrissey defeated Yankee Sullivan, Oct. 12, in 37 rounds. Sullivan led for 36 rounds. During the 30-second rest period he lost his temper because of taunts from Morrissey's gang, which had gathered back of his corner. He jumped out of the ring and was busy beating up toughs when the referee called the men to "toe scratch." Sullivan either did not hear the call or paid no heed. He was busy swatting toughs. So

the referee, in keeping with the rules, gave the decision to Morrissey.

1858—Morrissey fought John C. Heenan in Long Point, Canada. Heenan, born in Troy, N.Y., went to California in his teens, and there gained the nickname of "Benicia Boy" because he lived in that town. Heenan broke his right hand in the first round of the fight with Morrissey, but carried on until the 11th, when he was forced to quit. Heenan challenged for a return match, but Morrissey refused and retired from the ring. Morrissey then went to Saratoga Springs, N.Y., entered politics, became a state senator and race track promoter. Morrissey died in 1878.

1859—Heenan claimed title and in 1860, unable to get action in the United States, sailed for England, fighting Tom Sayers in 1860 and Tom King in 1863.

1863—Owing to Heenan's continued absence from the United States, Joe Coburn and Mike McCoole became joint claimants for the American championship. Coburn knocked out McCoole in 63 rounds, May 5, Charleston, Md.

1865—Coburn announced retirement; McCoole claimed title.

1869—Tom Allen of England defeated Bill Davis in 43 rounds on Jan. 12, near St. Louis, and disputed McCoole's titular claims. Allen, who had settled in the United States, having whipped some Americans, claimed the American title. This was disputed by Mike McCoole. A fight was arranged to determine the "American Champion." McCoole and Allen met June 15 near St. Louis, McCoole winning on a questionable foul in nine rounds.

International Bare-Knuckle

1870—Mace, regarded as world champion by succession to King's vacated throne in England, stopped Allen, 10 rounds, May 10, near Kennersville, La.

1871—Mace and Coburn, who returned from retirement, fought twice without result. The first bout was halted by police. They met again near St. Louis, Nov. 30, fought 12 rounds, stopped punching without explanation, jumped out of the ring and the referee said "draw." Coburn again retired and never returned.

1873—Mace, 42 years old, retired. He devoted himself thereafter to teaching boxing in the United States and England and died in 1911 at the age of 80. McCoole and Allen, the ancient and rival claimants, fought again. They battled near St. Louis, Sept. 23, and Allen stopped McCoole in 7. McCoole retired. Allen called himself "World's Champion."

1876—Goss, rated next to Mace in England, arrived in the United States and challenged Allen. They went into action near Covington, Ky., Sept. 7. Goss was annihilating Allen, who took to fouling and was disqualified in the 27th. That victory made Goss the world champion under London Prize Ring Rules.

1880 (June 21)—Paddy Ryan, an American, knocked out Goss in the 87th round (1 hour 24 minutes) on May 30, near Colliers Station, W. Va., in a fight for the world championship. Date and time in dispute. Wheeling "Intelligencer," according to Boyd B. Stutler, Managing Editor, American Legion Magazine, fixed date as June 1 and time 1 hour 27 minutes. Ryan thus became the first American to hold the undisputed bareknuckle championship of the world. Ryan was born March 15, 1853, in Thurles, County Tipperary, Ireland; height, 5 feet 11 inches; weight in fighting prime, 200 pounds; career started 1880; ended 1886; won title in first recorded battle of his career. Men fought for side bet $1,000. Lost title in first defense on Feb. 7, 1882, being knocked out in 9 rounds by John L. Sullivan, Mississippi City, Miss., for a purse and side bet totaling $5,000. Summary of record: total fights, 4; won 1; lost 2; other stopped by police.

1882 (Feb. 7)—John L. Sullivan knocked out Ryan in 9 rounds in Mississippi City, Miss., and became the last of the bare-knuckle champions. The final bare-knuckle battle of Sullivan's career, and the last one of consequence on American soil, was held on July 8, 1889, in Richburg, Miss., when he stopped Jake Kilrain in 75 rounds. Sullivan never was defeated as a London Prize Ring champion and carried the title to his grave.

Sullivan was born in Boston, Oct. 15, 1858; died in Abington, Mass., Feb. 2, 1918. Height, 5 feet 10½ inches, weight in prime, 195. Started fighting 1878, last appearance 1896 in exhibition bout. May have engaged in private exhibitions later, but no official record. Statistical record: total matches, 37; won by knockout, 12; won decisions, 20; draws, 3; no decision, 1; knocked out once. Sullivan's last appearance with gloves was at a benefit with Tom Sharkey in 1896, although he engaged in a few impromptu matches later.

World-Queensberry Rules

It has been customary to say that the first battle for the heavyweight championship of the world under Marquis of Queensberry rules—with gloves and 3-minute rounds—was between James J. Corbett and John L. Sullivan, Sept. 7, 1892, in New Orleans. It also has been the custom to say that there was no Queensberry champion at the time and that this fight was to determine such titleholder; that Sullivan went into the ring regarded as the champion only because of the bare-knuckle crown he had won from Paddy Ryan in 1882.

However, in 1936 "Biddy" Bishop, veteran fight manager and promoter advised:

"Before me, as I write, is a printed program of a fight between Sullivan and Dominick F. Mc-

Caffery of Pittsburgh, in Chester Park, Cincinnati, Ohio, Aug. 29, 1885.

"It states specifically on the program that 'the fight will be under Marquis of Queensberry rules,' after which are printed the rules to govern the contest, which were:

" 'Six rounds to decide the Marquis of Queensberry glove contest for the championship of the world.'

"Billy Tait was the referee. Immediately after the sixth and final round ended, Tait jumped out of the ring, without announcing his decision. He went to Toledo, Ohio. Forty-eight hours after the fight ended, someone in Toledo reminded Billy that he had forgotten to make a decision. So Billy said: 'Sullivan won.'

"So," concluded Bishop, "that might make Sullivan the first Queensberry champion as well as the last of the bare-knuckle champions."

Corbett and Sullivan fought for a $25,000 purse and a $10,000 side bet at New Orleans, Sept. 7, 1892. Corbett, winner of almost every round, knocked out Sullivan in the 21st, and took the $35,000 and the title.

James J. Corbett—Born in San Francisco, Sept. 1, 1866. Height 6 feet 1 inch; weight in fighting prime, 187. Started fighting as amateur in neighborhood makeshift gymnasium in 1880. Became member Olympic A.C. in San Francisco in 1883 and won championship of club three months later, knocking out Dave Eisenman, who was club and also San Francisco champion. In 1885—86 Corbett left San Francisco for Salt Lake City, took name of Jim Dillon and fought two professionals, knocking out Frank Smith, 2 rounds, and boxing an 8-round draw with Donald McDonald. Went on exhibition tour with McDonald. Returned to San Francisco middle of 1886. Never fought as amateur thereafter. First actual fight with professional was in 1889 against Joe Choynski, boyhood rival who had turned pro. No purse or bets at stake in that fight; merely a grudge battle. Corbett knocked out Choynski and then decided to turn professional. Won title from John L. Sullivan on knockout, 21 rounds, New Orleans, La., Sept. 7, 1892; lost it to Bob Fitzsimmons, 14 rounds, Carson City, Nev., March 17, 1897; last fight with Jim Jeffries, Aug. 14, 1903, San Francisco, which he lost in 10 rounds, was for championship. Corbett died in New York in 1933.

Robert L. Fitzsimmons—Born Helsten, Cornwall, England, June 4, 1863; height, 6 feet; weight in prime, varied between 163 and 170. Fitz made first ring appearance as amateur in tournament in Timura, New Zealand, 1880, conducted by Jem Mace of England, former bareknuckle world champion. Fitz won championship, knocking out four men in one night. In 1881, stopped 5 men in one night, including Herbert Slade called "Great Maori." Afterward Fitz started fighting professionally, but was unable to get much action in New Zealand. From 1882 to 1888 he had 14 fights; won all of them by knockouts. Won Australian middleweight championship; lost it to Jim Hall, Feb. 10, 1890, after which he came to the United States. First fight in San Francisco, May 29, 1890, when he stopped Billy McCarthy in 9 rounds. Won world middleweight title from Jack Dempsey (The Nonpareil) in 1891 and won heavyweight crown on March 17, 1897, knocking out Corbett in 14 rounds. Never lost middleweight title, but lost heavyweight title in first defense, being stopped in 11 rounds by James J. Jeffries, June 9, 1899, Coney Island, N.Y. Last fight in 1914 when, after 35 years of ring warfare and at age 52, went six rounds, no decision, in Philadelphia with K.O. Sweeney. Died in Chicago in 1918.

James J. Jeffries—Born April 15, 1875, Carroll, Ohio; height, 6 feet 1½ inches, weight in fighting prime, between 215 and 220. Began fighting 1896, last fight 1910. Was sparring partner for Corbett in 1897. Won championship by knocking out Fitzsimmons, 11 rounds, Coney Island, N.Y., June 9, 1899. Actively defended title until 1903. After two years idleness, retired in 1905. Influenced to try "come-back" against Jack Johnson. Knocked out by Johnson, 15 rounds, Reno, Nevada, July 4, 1910, in last fight of career. Jeffries and Johnson fought for $101,000 purse on the basis of 60 per cent for winner, 40 for loser, Jeffries' end was $40,400. He also received $10,000 for training expenses and sold his picture rights for $66,666. His total, therefore, was $117,066. Tex Rickard and Jack Gleason of San Francisco promoted the match. Rickard was referee. Jeffries died in Burbank, Calif., on March 3, 1953.

Marvin Hart—Born Sept. 16, 1876, in Kentucky; height, 5 feet 11 inches; weight, 190. In 1905 promoter of Hark-Jack Root match, staged in Reno, announced winner should be acclaimed successor to Jeffries, and Jeffries refereed. Jeff always said he never had sanctioned "giving away" crown. Hart won by knocking out Root in 12 rounds but never made much ado about his "title." He lost it to Tommy Burns Feb. 23, 1906. Died at Fern Creek, Ky., Sept. 17, 1931.

Tommy Burns—Born Hanover, Canada, June 17, 1881; height, 5 feet 7 inches; weight in prime, 175. Started fighting, 1900. Last battle, 1920. On Feb. 23, 1906, Burns won a 20-round decision from Hart in San Francisco, claimed heavyweight title and proceeded to capitalize on it. In 1908 was matched with Jack Johnson for fight in Sydney, Australia, the purse being $30,000, a record sum at that time. Promoter was Hugh D. McIntosh. They met in the Sydney Stadium, Dec. 26, 1908, and Johnson whipped Burns so terrifically that police jumped in and stopped the fight in the 14th round. Stadium in which bout was held later became model for oval football stadiums in United States.

Jack Johnson—(Negro) Born March 31, 1878, Galveston, Tex.; height, 6 feet 1 inch; weight in prime, 205–220. Was battle royal fighter at 16, began professional career in 1899; fought last battle in 1927. Won technical championship by stopping Burns in 14 rounds, Sydney, Australia. Won actual title knocking out Jim Jeffries, Reno, July 4, 1910, in 15 rounds. He lost the title April 5, 1915, in Havana, Cuba, being knocked out by Jess Willard in 26 rounds.

Johnson won 60 per cent of the $101,000 purse ($60,600) for the Jeffries fight, received $10,000 for training expenses and sold his third of the pictures for $50,000 to net grand total $120,600.

Johnson was guaranteed $30,000 for Willard fight, which was last of any importance during his career; Johnson was killed in an automobile accident in 1946.

Jess Willard—Born Dec. 29, 1883, Pottawatomie County, Kansas; height, 6 feet 7 inches; weight, 235–265; started career 1911, last fight 1923. Won championship April 5, 1915, knocking out Jack Johnson, 26 rounds, in Havana. Lost to Jack Dempsey, July 4, 1919, when seconds tossed towel into ring after 3d round while Willard was sitting in his corner. Willard got nothing but training expenses for Johnson fight. In first defence, against Frank Moran in New York, 10 rounds, no decision. Newspaper unanimously gave popular decision to Willard. He was paid $47,500—the record for an indoor fight up to that time. Moran received $27,500. Willard received $100,000 guarantee for Dempsey fight; Dempsey $27,500. Willard announced retirement after the 1919 defeat but reappeared 1922. He was paid $25,000 for putting Floyd Johnson to sleep on the Milk Fund card, and about $125,000 for being whacked into a swoon by Luis Firpo. Willard again retired.

Jack Dempsey—Born June 24, 1895, Manassa, Colo.; real name William Harrison Dempsey; began fighting career around Utah and Colorado mining camps in 1912, weight then about 148; height, 6 feet 1½ inches; weight in heavyweight prime, 187–194. Won heavyweight title from Jess Willard, July 4, 1919, Toledo; knocked Willard down 7 times in first round, battered him in second and third; Willard's seconds tossed in towel before fourth round began; lost to Gene Tunney, Philadelphia, Sept. 23, 1926, on 10-round decision; announced retirement after second Tunney fight, Chicago, Sept. 22, 1927.

Dempsey started comeback tour Aug. 20, 1931. Ended Aug. 15, 1932. Met 175 opponents, taking on 2, 3 or 4 a night and knocked out over 100. When outpointed by Kingfish Levinsky in August, 1932, Dempsey fought a few more inconsequential bouts and then retired. He came back to action in 1940, scored three knockouts.

Gene Tunney (James Joseph Tunny)—Born New York, May 25, 1898; height, 6 feet 1 inch;

weight, 160 to 188; began career, 1917. Won American light-heavyweight title from Harry Greb. Won heavyweight championship from Jack Dempsey, Philadelphia, Sept. 23, 1926, on 10-round decision; gave Dempsey return match in 1927 in Chicago and retained crown by again winning 10-round decision; scored 12th round knockout over Tom Heeney, New Zealand July 26, 1928, and announced retirement August, 1928.

1928—After Tunney's retirement, New York State Athletic Commission ordered tournament to determine successor. Jack Sharkey and William L. (Young) Stribling became standouts. They met in Miami, Fla., Feb. 27, 1929, and Sharkey won a 10-round decision.

1929—Max Schmeling of Germany stopped Johnny Risko, 9 rounds, New York on Feb. 1, and on June 27 the German gained a 15-round decision over Paulino Uzcudun in New York.

1930 (June 12)—Max Schmeling met Sharkey in New York. Gate was $749,935 and attendance of 79,222, wound up in wild disorder, with Schmeling gaining decision because of a foul delivered in the 4th round, although the award was not made until after the bell had rung for the 5th round, which never was fought.

The punch landed after 2 minutes and 55 seconds of the 4th. Referee Jimmy Crowley and Charles Mathison, one of the judges, did not see the blow. Harold Barnes, other judge, declared he saw it and, upon his statement, Crowley disqualified Sharkey.

1930 (June 18)—New York Commission, by vote of 2 to 1 "elected" Schmeling heavyweight champion of the world. Members Farley and Phelan favored giving Schmeling the honor; Member Muldoon voted against it, taking attitude that Schmeling did not prove, by victory on a foul, that he was best of the heavyweights.

1931 (Jan. 7)—New York Commission dethroned Schmeling and suspended him in the Empire State when he refused to sign for a match with Jack Sharkey for June, 1931. Barred from New York, Schmeling met Stribling in Cleveland. Schmeling defeated Stribling on technical knockout in 15th round of scheduled 15-round battle, July 3, 1931. Referee George Blake stopped fight with 14 seconds to go. Stribling had been down once in 15th.

Attendance 37,396. Gross receipts, $349,415; net $265,345. Schmeling received $106,138.36 (40 per cent) Stribling $33,168.24 (12½ per cent). Blake received $2,500. Loss to promoters "around $50,000."

1932 (June 21)—Jack Sharkey defeated Schmeling, decision, 15 rounds New York. Bout drew gross $475,000, of which Schmeling received $182,750 and Sharkey $43,000.

1933 (June 28)—Primo Carnera won championship, Long Island City Bowl, knocking out Sharkey in 6th with right-hand uppercut. Paid

attendance 31,753, gross receipts $198,259.15 and net $163,772.80. Sharkey's share (42½ per cent) was $69,603.14 and Carnera's (10 per cent) $16,377.28. Milk Fund received $19,000 and Madison Square Garden's profit $40,000.

1934 (June 14)—Max Baer won title, defeating Primo Carnera on technical knockout 2 minutes and 16 seconds of 11th round when Referee Arthur Donovan stopped fight. Carnera knocked down 12 times in the 11 rounds. Gross attendance 56,000 with 52,268 paid. Gross receipts, $428,000, divided as follows: Federal tax, $42,800; State tax, $21,400; Baer's share, $40,927; Carnera's, $122,782; Jack Dempsey's (as co-promoter, having had Baer's contract), $24,556 ; Milk Fund, $36,380; Promotion expenses, $88,600; Madison Square Garden's profit, $50,555.

1935 (June 13)—James J. Braddock won title, defeating Baer on points, 15 rounds; Long Island Bowl. Attendance, 35,000; gross receipts, $205,366; net, $169,074; Baer's share, $88,805; Braddock, $31,244.

1937 (June 22)—Joe Louis (second Negro to hold world heavyweight title) knocked out James J. Braddock, 8th round, Chicago. Gross receipts $715,470. At the age of 23, Louis was the youngest to win the crown.

Louis was born May 13, 1914, in Lexington, Ala. He began his boxing career in Detroit and first gained attention by his performances in the Golden Gloves amateur tournaments. He turned professional in 1934, and from then until he came out of "retirement" in 1950 he suffered only one defeat—a 12-round knockout by Max Schmeling on June 19, 1936.

After winning the title from Braddock, Louis, 6 feet 1½ inches tall and at his best at about 200 pounds, made a record by successfully defending his crown twenty-five times before he "retired" on March 1, 1949. (For record, see table in this section of Louis' fights).

The heavyweight title was "frozen" during World War II, as Louis was with the armed forces. His first fight after being mustered out was with Billy Conn at Yankee Stadium on June 19, 1946, at which a record price of $100 was charged for a ringside seat. Louis knocked out Conn in the eighth round.

1949 (June 22)—Ezzard Charles, on the "retirement" of Louis, ascended to the championship by outpointing Jersey Joe Walcott in 15 rounds at Chicago. Charles then gained universal recognition as champion when Louis emerged from retirement to meet him. The pair fought at Yankee Stadium on Sept. 27, 1950, and Charles gained the decision in 15 rounds.

Before defeating Louis, Charles had defended his title claim successfully against Gus Lesnevich, Pat Valentino and Freddie Beshore. Following his conquest of Louis, Ezzard defeated Nick Barone, Lee Oma, Jersey Joe Walcott and Joey

Maxim.

1951 (July 18)—Jersey Joe Walcott knocked out Charles in 7 rounds in Pittsburgh to win the title. Walcott, whose correct name is Arnold Cream, was born on Jan. 31, 1914, and thus, at 37, became the oldest fighter in modern ring history to win the heavyweight title. Previously Fitzsimmons, who became champion at 35, held this distinction.

Walcott made one successful defense of the crown, outpointing Charles in Philadelphia on June 5, 1952. It was the fourth fight between them.

1952 (Sept. 23)—Rocky Marciano ended Walcott's reign by knocking out the New Jersey warrior in 13 rounds in Philadelphia. For Marciano the victory served as a climax to a career that embraced 43 winning professional fights. Most notable among his victims in his march to the title was Joe Louis, whom he knocked out in eight rounds at Madison Square Garden on Oct. 26, 1951. Marciano was born in Brockton, Mass., on Sept. 1, 1924. His correct name is Rocco Marchegiano.

An all-around athlete, Marciano once received a tryout as a catcher for the Chicago Cubs. During the war he served overseas with an amphibious unit.

1953 (May 15)—Marciano, in his first title defense, knocked out Walcott in 2:25 of the first round, at Chicago Stadium. Attendance (paid), 13,266; total attendance, 16,034; gross gate, $331,795; net gate, $253,462; television and radio, $300,000. Total net, $553,462; Marciano's share, $166,038; Walcott's share, $250,000.

Only five heavyweight title fights have ended quicker. The fastest was when Tommy Burns knocked out Jem Roche at Dublin, Ireland, March 17, 1908, in 1:28 of the first round.

1953 (Sept. 24)—Marciano knocked out Roland LaStarza in 1:31 of the 11th round at the Polo Grounds, New York. Attendance; 44,562; Receipts, $435,817.

1954 (June 17)—Marciano outpointed Ezzard Charles in 15 rounds at Yankee Stadium, New York. Attendance, 47,585; Receipts $543,092.

1954 (Sept. 17)—Marciano knocked out Charles in 2:36 of the eighth round at Yankee Stadium. Attendance, 34,330; Receipts, $352,654.

1955 (May 16)—Marciano knocked out Don Cockell of England in 0:59 of the ninth round at Kezar Stadium, San Francisco. Attendance, 15,235; Receipts, $196,720.

1955 (Sept. 21)—Marciano knocked out Archie Moore in 1:19 of the ninth round at Yankee Stadium. Attendance, 61,574; Receipts, $948,117.

1956 (April)—Marciano retired. He won all 49 of his professional bouts.

1956 (Nov. 30)—Floyd Patterson won the vacant world title by knocking out Archie Moore in 2:27 of the fifth round at Chicago Stadium. Attendance, 16,248; Receipts, $380,858.

1957 (July 29)—Patterson knocked out Tommy Jackson in 1:52 of the 10th round at Polo Grounds. Attendance, 17,443; Receipts, $156,936.

1957 (Aug. 22)—Patterson knocked out Pete Rademacher in 2:57 of the sixth round at Sicks' Stadium, Seattle, Wash. Attendance, 16,961; Receipts, $234,030. (Rademacher was the Olympic heavyweight champion and was making his first start as a professional fighter).

1958 (Aug. 18)—Patterson knocked out Roy Harris in the twelfth round at Los Angeles. Attendance, 21,680; Receipts, $234,183.

1959 (May 1)—Patterson knocked out Brian London of Blackpool, England, in 0:51 of the 11th round at Indianapolis (Ind.) Fair Grounds Coliseum. Attendance, 10,088; Receipts, $103,111.

1959 (June 26)—Ingemar Johansson of Goteborg, Sweden, knocked out Patterson in 2:03 of the 3rd round at Yankee Stadium, New York. Johansson became the first foreigner to hold the title since Primo Carnera in 1933. Attendance, 21,961.

1960 (June 20)—Patterson became the first man to regain the heavyweight title by knocking out Ingemar Johansson in 1:51 of the fifth round at the Polo Grounds, N.Y. Attendance, 31,892; Receipts, $824,891. Gate plus closed circuit TV—$2,468,278.

1961 (March 13)—Patterson knocked out Ingemar Johansson, 6 rounds, Miami Beach, Fla.

1961 (December 4)—Patterson knocked out Tom McNeeley, 4 rounds, Toronto, Canada.

1962 (September 25)—Charles "Sonny" Liston knocked out Floyd Patterson, 2:06 in the first round at Comiskey Park, Chicago to become the new heavyweight champion. Attendance, 17,000; Receipts, $4,000,000 (estimated).

1963 (July 22)—Liston knocked out Floyd Patterson in 2:10 of the first round at Las Vegas, Nevada.

1964 (February 25)—Cassius Clay (Muhammed Ali) won the title when Sonny Liston failed to answer the bell for the seventh round. Miami Beach, Florida.

1965 (May 25)—Cassius Clay (Muhammed Ali) knocked out Sonny Liston in Lewiston, Maine, in what was officially announced as a one minute knockout. Films showed that 1.42 had elapsed by the time the referee declared Liston out. The Timer declared he had clocked the knockout in one minute flat.

1965 (November 22)—Cassius Clay (Muhammed Ali) stopped Floyd Patterson in Las Vegas, Nevada, in 2.18 of the twelfth round. The referee halted the bout when Patterson, due to an injured back, plus the beating he had taken, was unable to defend himself.

1966 (March 29)—Cassius Clay (Muhammed

Ali) defended his title by defeating George
Chuvalo, Toronto, in Maple Leaf Gardens,
Toronto, Canada, by unanimous decision, 15
rounds.

1966 (May 21)—Cassius Clay (Muhammed
Ali) stopped Henry Cooper, London, in the Arsenal Stadium of London, England, in the sixth
round.

1966 (August 6)—Cassius Clay (Muhammed
Ali) knocked out Brian London in the Earl's
Court, London, England, in the third round.

1966 (September 10)—Cassius Clay (Muhammed Ali) knocked out Karl Mildenberger, Frankfurt, Germany, in 1.30 of the twelfth round.

1966 (November 14)—Cassius Clay (Muhammed Ali) stopped Cleveland Williams in the
Houston Astrodome, Houston, Texas, in 1.08 of
the third round.

1967 (February 6)—Cassius Clay (Muhammed
Ali) defended his title against Ernie Terrell at the
Houston Astrodome by a decision in 15 rounds.

1967 (March 22)—Cassius Clay (Muhammed
Ali) knocked out Zora Folley in the seventh
round at Madison Square Garden, N.Y.

The heavyweight title was vacated by the New
York State Athletic Commission and the World
Boxing Association when Cassius Clay (Muhammed Ali) was convicted of violating the United
States Selective Service laws by refusing to be
drafted.

1970 (February 16)—Joe Frazier stopped
Jimmy Ellis in five rounds to win the vacant title
at Madison Square Garden, N.Y. Frazier was
recognized as champion by New York Commission and held the title in five states while Ellis
was the World Boxing Association's champion via
elimination of an eight-man tournament.

1971 (March 8)—Joe Frazier defeated Cassius
Clay (Muhammed Ali) in 15 rounds at Madison
Square Garden in N.Y. Decision was unanimous,
with Frazier decking Clay in the 15th.

1972 (Jan. 15)—Joe Frazier stopped Terry
Daniels at 1:45 of the fourth round in New
Orleans.

1972 (May 26)—Joe Frazier retained his title
by defeating Ron Stander when Stander failed to
answer the bell for the fifth round in Omaha,
Neb.

LIGHT-HEAVYWEIGHT CHAMPIONS
(175 pounds)

Lou Houseman, a boxing promoter and newspaperman in Chicago, advanced the idea that
there were many pugilists who were too heavy
for the middleweight division, which then had a
158-pound limit, and too light to compete with
heavyweights. He advocated a light-heavyweight
class to bridge the gap, top weight to be 175
pounds. Houseman had reason to consider this
problem, for he managed Jack Root, who had
recently outgrown the middleweight division and
was to prove the outstanding contender for the

new championship.

1903 (April 22)—Jack Root outpointed Kid
McCoy in 10 rounds at Detroit to establish
strong claim to title.

1903 (July 4)—George Gardner knocked out
Jack Root, 12 rounds, Fort Erie, Ont., and was
awarded championship belt.

1903   Nov. 4)—Bob Fitzsimmons outpointed Gardner, 20-round decision. Fitzsimmons
weighed about 170 and Gardner about 165.

1905 (Dec. 20)—"Philadelphia" Jack O'Brien
knocked out Fitzsimmons, 13 rounds, San Francisco.

Tommy Burns, weighing inside the limit, gained a 20-round decision over O'Brien in Los
Angeles, May 8, 1907, but made no claim to the
championship.

Jack Dillon, in 1912 or 1913, having beaten
all the men from 160 pounds up to 175, claimed
the championship, but never attempted to capitalize on it.

1916 (Oct. 24)—Battling Levinsky outpointed
Jack Dillon, 12 rounds, Boston, Oct. 24, 1916,
whereupon Dan Morgan, the ballyhoo manager,
put new life into the division by loud cheering
over his "champion."

Levinsky lost in 1920 on a foul to Boy McCormick in Seattle, but McCormick never claimed title, went to his home in England and retired.

1920 (Oct. 12)—Georges Carpentier of France
knocked out Levinsky, 4 rounds, Jersey City,
N.J. Carpentier, having been titleholder of the
class in Europe, thus became the actual world
champion.

Gene Tunney outpointed Levinsky, 12
rounds, Jan. 23, 1922, gaining American championship. Harry Greb outpointed Tunney,
15 rounds, May 23, 1922. Tunney regained
American title by outpointing Greb, 15 rounds,
Feb. 23, 1923. Tunney relinquished claim to
American championship when he entered heavyweight ranks in 1925.

1922 (Sept. 24)—Battling Siki, a Senegalese
Negro, became champion by knocking out Carpentier, 6 rounds, Paris.

1923 (March 17)—Mike McTigue beat Siki, 20
rounds, Dublin, Ireland.

1925 (May 3)—Paul Berlenbach outpointed
McTigue, 15 rounds, New York.

1926 (July 26)—Jack Delaney won from
Berlenbach on points, 15 rounds, Brooklyn.
Delaney resigned title when he entered the
heavyweight class in 1927 and McTigue reclaimed the crown.

1927 (Oct. 7)—Tommy Loughran outpointed
McTigue, 15 rounds, New York.

Loughran resigned title in August, 1929, so
that he might enter heavyweight class. The New
York State Athletic Commission, in the autumn
of 1929, ordered a tournament to decide Loughran's successor. Jimmy Slattery of Buffalo outpointed Lou Scozza, 15 rounds, in the final in

Buffalo. Meanwhile, the National Boxing Association crowned Maxie Rosenbloom as king of the division, ignoring Slattery.

1930 (June 25)—Rosenbloom became undisputed light-heavyweight champion by outpointing Slattery, 15 rounds, Buffalo. He defeated Slattery in a return match in the summer of 1931. Soon afterward the N.B.A. vacated Rosenbloom's title, but he was still world champion in New York.

1934 (Nov. 16)—Bob Olin won from Rosenbloom, 15 rounds, New York.

1935 (Oct. 31)—John Henry Lewis (Negro) outpointed Olin, 15 rounds, St. Louis. In 1938, Lewis resigned as titleholder to campaign as a heavyweight.

1939—Melio Bettina and Tiger Jack Fox were the survivors of an elimination tournament to determine Lewis' successor.

1939 (Feb. 4)—Bettina knocked out Fox, 9 rounds, New York.

1939 (Sept. 25)—Billy Conn outpointed Bettina, 15 rounds, New York. In 1940, Conn resigned title to fight heavyweights.

1941 (Jan. 13)—Anton Christoforidis defeated Bettina, 15 rounds, Cleveland, and was recognized by N.B.A. as Conn's successor.

1941 (May 22)—Gus Lesnevich, New York's recognized champion, outpointed Christoforidis, 15 rounds, New York.

1941 (Aug. 26)—Lesnevich defeated Tami Mauriello, 15 rounds, New York, and became internationally recognized as champion. Title "frozen" during World War II, with Lesnevich in the service. He knocked out Freddie Mills in the 10th in London in 1946 and stopped Billy Fox in the same round in New York in 1947 in successful title defenses.

1948 (July 26)—Freddie Mills of England took the title from Lesnevich, 15 rounds, London.

1950 (Jan. 24)—Joey Maxim won the 175-pound championship by knocking out Mills in 10 rounds in London. Maxim's tenure as champion was distinguished mainly by his success in repulsing the bid for the title made by Ray Robinson, who at the time was the middleweight ruler. They fought at Yankee Stadium on June 25, 1952, at a thermometer reading of 104. Robinson, who was outweighed, 173 pounds to 157½, piled up a big lead in 13 rounds. The heat was too much for him, though, and he failed to come out for the 14th, in which round Maxim gained credit for a knockout victory.

1952 (Dec. 17)—Archie Moore became the light heavyweight champion of the world by outpointing Maxim in 15 rounds at St. Louis. Moore was born on Dec. 13,1916, making him the oldest titleholder in the history of the class.

1953 (June 24)—Moore outpointed Maxim in 15 rounds (split decision) at Ogden, Utah.

1954 (Jan. 27)—Moore outpointed Maxim in 15 rounds at Miami Stadium, Miami, Fla.

1954 (Aug. 11)—Moore knocked out Harold Johnson of Philadelphia in the 14th round at Madison Square Garden, New York.

1955 (June 22)—Moore knocked out Carl (Bobo) Olson os San Francisco in the third round at Polo Grounds, New York.

1956 (June 5)—Moore knocked our Yolande Pompey of Trinidad, B.W.I. in the 10th round at Harringay Arena, London.

1957 (Sept. 20)—Moore knocked out Tony Anthony of New York in the sixth round at the Olmpic Auditorium, Los Angeles.

1958 —Moore knocked out Yvon Durelle in the eleventh round at Montreal.

1959 (August 12)—Moore knocked out Durelle in 3 rounds at Montreal.

1961 (June 10)—Moore, stripped of his N.B.A. section of the title by official decree, retained the other part by decision over Giulio Rinaldi in 15 rounds at Madison Square Garden.

1961 (February 7)—Harold Johnson won the vacant N.B.A. crown by knocking out Jesse Bowdry in 9 at Miami Beach.

1961 (April 24)—Johnson held his part of the title by knocking out Von Clay in the second round at Philadelphia.

1961 (August 29)—Johnson won a 15-round decision over Eddie Cotton in a title bout.

1962 (May 12)—With Archie Moore no longer interested in this weight limit, Johnson won the complete title by outpointing Doug Jones in 15 rounds at Philadelphia.

1962 (June 23)—Johnson won a 15-round decision over Gustav Scholz at Berlin, Germany to keep title.

1963 (June1)—Willie Pastrano won the title by outpointing Harold Johnson over fifteen rounds at Las Vegas, Nevada.

1965 (March 30)—Jose Torres knocked out Willie Pastrano, New York City, in the ninth round to win the crown.

1966 (May 21)—Jose Torres defeated Wayne Thornton of Fresno, California, in Shea Stadium, Flushing, L.I., N.Y., unanimous decision, 15 rounds.

1966 (August 15)—Jose Torres defeated Eddie Cotton, Seattle, Wash., in the Convention Center of Las Vegas, unanimous decision.

1966 (December 16)—Jose Torres and Dick Tiger of Nigeria fought in Madison Square Garden, New York, in the title match. Tiger defeated Torres in a unanimous decision, 15 rounds.

1967 (May 16)—Dick Tiger successfully defended his title against Jose Torres by unanimous decision, Madison Square Garden, N.Y.

1967 (November 17)—Dick Tiger scored a knockout of Roger Rouse, in the 12th round, Las Vegas, Nevada.

1968 (May 24)—Bob Foster won the title from Dick Tiger by a knockout in 2.05 of the fourth round at Madison Square Garden.

MIDDLEWEIGHT CHAMPIONS
(158 until 1915; then 160 pounds)

Although the middleweight class was not recognized as a distinct division of pugilism until 1884, there were fights among men of that poundage prior to that time. The first was on April 13, 1867, when Tom Chandler defeated Dooney Harris in 33 rounds (bare knuckles) in San Francisco for a side bet of $5,000. Chandler claimed the "championship of my class." His weight was about 156 pounds. Chandler earlier had fought at weights ranging from 130 up.

In 1872, George Rooke challenged Chandler "at your class" but Chandler ignored it and Rooke claimed title. In 1874, Mike Donovan beat Rooke and, after defending title of a class that had no distinct part of pugilism until 1884, Donovan retired in 1882. It was two years later when George Fulljames termed it the "Middleweight Class" and challenged the world.

1884—Jack Dempsey, "The Nonpareil," accepted Fulljames' challenge. They fought in Toronto, Ont., Aug. 30, 1884, using heavy driving gloves instead of bare fists. Dempsey stopped Fulljames in the 22nd.

1889—George La Blanche knocked out Dempsey with the "pivot punch" but, owing to use of that blow, never was acknowledged as champion.

1891 (Jan. 14)—Bob Fitzsimmons stopped Dempsey, 13 rounds, New Orleans.

1894—Fitz made one successful defense of the middleweight crown, then became a heavyweight.

1897—Kid McCoy, "Philadelphia" Jack O'Brien, Tommy Ryan and others claimed the title. They never met at 158 pounds, which was the limit in early days, and there was no fully acknowledged champion until 1908. Although each claimant insisted he was champion, Ryan, who had graduated from the welters in 1897, as champion, was looked upon by many as having the best claim to the title.

1908—Stanley Ketchel claimed championship; so did Jack (Twin) Sullivan. Ketchel knocked out Sullivan, 20 rounds, San Francisco, Feb. 22.

1908 (Sept. 7)—Billy Papke knocked out Ketchel, 12 rounds, Los Angeles.

1908 (Nov. 26)—Ketchel knocked out Papke, 11 rounds, San Francisco.

1910—Ketchel was shot and killed in Conway Mo., by Walter Dipley, Oct. 15, and title became vacant.

1911—Papke claimed title as did Mike Gibbons and Eddie McGoorty.

1913—Frank Klaus won on foul, 15 rounds, in Paris, from Papke.

1913 (Dec. 23)—George Chip knocked out Klaus, 5 rounds, Pittsburgh.

1914 (April 7)—Al McCoy knocked out Chip, one round, Brooklyn.

1915—Weight limit for division set at 160 pounds.

1917 (Nov. 14)—Mike O'Dowd knocked out McCoy, 6 rounds, Brooklyn.

1920 (May 6)—Johnny Wilson outpointed O'Dowd, 12 rounds, New York, Decision created wild protest.

1921 (March 17)—Wilson outpointed O'Dowd, 15 rounds, New York, and became recognized as champion.

1923 (Aug. 31)—Harry Greb outpointed Wilson, 15 rounds, New York.

1926 (Aug. 19)—Tiger Flowers (first Negro to hold title) outpointed Greb, 15 rounds, New York.

1926 (Dec. 3)—Edward (Mickey) Walker defeated Flowers, 10 rounds, Chicago.

1931 (June 19)—Walker relinquished title, claiming it impossible to make weight. Fought Jack Sharkey one month later and his poundage was 169½.

The National Boxing Association and the New York State Athletic Commission each sponsored a tournament to determine Walker's successor. Gorilla Jones won the former, Ben Jeby the latter. Jones was disqualified in the 11th round of a bout with Marcel Thil in Paris, France, June 11, 1932, but Thil's inactivity caused N.B.A. to vacate title, Jeby gaining universal recognition.

1933 (Aug. 9)—Lou Brouillard knocked out Jeby 7, rounds, New York.

1933 (Oct. 30)—Vince Dundee outpointed Brouillard, 15 rounds, Boston.

1934 (Sept. 11)—Teddy Yarosz outpointed Dundee, 15 rounds, Pittsburgh.

1935 (Sept. 19)—Babe Risko outpointed Yarosz, 15 rounds, Pittsburgh, Yarosz on floor 3 times.

1936 (Feb. 19)—Freddy Steele outpointed Risko, 15 rounds, Seattle.

1937 (Sept. 23)—Fred Apostoli stopped Thil, who was recognized by some as champion because he had defeated Jones, on a foul, in the 11th round (June 11, 1932) while Jones was regarded as world champion.

1938 (Jan. 7)—In overweight match, in New York, with the title not at stake, Apostoli stopped Steele in the 9th, but, under conditions, could not claim title.

1938 (July 26)—Al Hostak knocked out Steele in 1st round, Seattle.

1938 (Nov. 1)—Solly Kreiger outpointed Hostak, 15 rounds, Seattle, gaining N. B. A. recognition as champion.

1939 (June 27)—Hostak knocked out Krieger in 4th, in Seattle.

1939 (Oct. 2)—Ceferino Garcia knocked out Apostoli in 7th, in New York. Recognized by New York as champion.

1940 (Jan. 29)—Tony Zale outpointed Hostak, 10 rounds, in Chicago, to become N.B.A.

champion.

1940 (May 24)—Ken Overlin outpointed Garcia, 15 rounds, New York, and Overlin was New York Commission's champion.

1941 (May 9)—Billy Soose outpointed Overlin, 15 rounds, New York.

1941 (Nov. 28)—Soose resigned as New York's middleweight champion.

1941 (Nov. 28)—Zale outpointed Georgie Abrams, three-time winner over Soose, and Zale became regarded by both factions as world champion.

Title "frozen" for duration of World War II since Zale was with the Armed Forces.

1946 (Sept. 27)—Zale, in first defense of title since 1941, knocked out Rocky Graziano in the 6th before 39,827, outdoors, New York. Gate $342,497.

1947 (July 16)—Graziano knocked out Zale, in the 6th, Chicago, before 18,947 who paid $422,918, the record gate for an indoor fight. Graziano, whose license had been suspended by New York Commission, was recognized as N.B.A. champion.

1948 (June 10)—Zale regained the championship by knocking out Graziano in 3 rounds in Newark, N.J.

1948 (Sept. 21)—Marcel Cerdan of Casablanca, French Morocco, stopped Zale in 12 rounds at Roosevelt Stadium in Jersey City, N.J.

1949 (June 16)—Jake La Motta of the Bronx became the champion by knocking out Cerdan in ten rounds in Detroit. La Motta had agreed to a return match with Cerdan, and the latter, flying to this country from his home to prepare for the match, was killed in a crash on the Azores on Oct. 27.

1951 (Feb. 14)—Ray Robinson, holder of the world welterweight championship, became a double titleholder by knocking out La Motta in 13 rounds in Chicago.

1951 (July 10)—Randy Turpin, Leamington, England, defeated Robinson by a decision in 15 rounds in London, to win the championship.

1951 (Sept. 12)—Robinson regained the championship by knocking out Turpin in 10 rounds at the Polo Grounds. It was a fine performance on Robinson's part, for he was only even on points with his opponent, but bleeding copiously from an eye cut, when he turned defeat into victory by overwhelming his foe, clubbing him so severely as to cause the referee to halt proceedings.

1952—On March 13, Robinson beat Carl (Bobo) Olson in a 15-round title defense in San Francisco. On April 16, Robinson knocked out Graziano in 3 rounds in a title fight in Chicago. On June 25, Robinson tried for Joey Maxim's light-heavyweight championship and was leading by a tremendous point-margin when he suffered heat prostration and failed to come up for the

14th round. Robinson weighed 157½ and Maxim 173.

On Dec. 18 Robinson announced his retirement from the ring to devote himself to a theatrical career. This decision terminated for a time the pugilistic activities of a boxer who had come to be regarded as one of the best athletes ever to participate in the sport. Engaging in more than 140 fights up to that point, Robinson was beaten only 3 times. Two setbacks he subsequently reversed. He was born in Detroit on May 3, 1920. His real name is Walker Smith. Sugar Ray later changed his mind about retirement and returned to ring action and made ring history by becoming a champion of the division five times.

1953 (June 9)—Randy Turpin of England outpointed Charles Humez of France in 15 rounds at London, to win the European title.

1953 (June 19)—Carl Olson outpointed Paddy Young of New York in 15 rounds at Madison Square Garden, New York, to win the American title.

1953 (Oct. 21)—Olson outpointed Turpin in 15 rounds at Madison Square Garden, to win the world title.

1954 (April 2)—Olson outpointed Kid Gavilan of Camaguey, Cuba, in 15 rounds at Chicago Stadium.

1954 (Aug. 20)—Olson outpointed Rocky Castellani of Cleveland, Ohio, in 15 rounds at the Cow Palace, San Francisco.

1954 (Dec. 15)—Olson knocked out Pierre Langlois of France in the 11th round at the Cow Palace, San Francisco.

1955 (Dec. 9)—Sugar Ray Robinson, coming out of retirement, knocked out Olson in the second round at the Chicago Stadium, to become three-time champion.

1956 (May 18)—Robinson knocked out Olson in the fourth round at Wrigley Field, Los Angeles.

1957 (Jan. 2)—Gene Fullmer of West Jordan, Utah, won the title by outpointing Robinson in 15 rounds at Madison Square Garden.

1957 (May 2)—Robinson gained the title for the fourth time by knocking out Fullmer in the 5th round at the Chicago Stadium.

1957 (Sept. 23)—Carmen Basilio of Chittenango, N.Y., won the title by outpointing (split decision) Robinson in 15 rounds at Yankee Stadium.

1958 (March 25)—Robinson won the title for the fifth time by outpointing (split decision) Basilio in 15 rounds at the Chicago Stadium. Robinson's feat of winning a division title five times is unparalleled in boxing history.

1959 (August 28)—After the N.B.A. vacated Robinson's title, Gene Fullmer met Carmen Basilio for the title. Fullmer knocked out Basilio in the 14th at San Francisco.

1960 (January 22)—Paul Pender won the "championship" in all but N.B.A. territory by a split decision over Ray Robinson in 15 rounds at Boston, Mass.

1961 (July 11)—Terry Downes knocked out Paul Pender in 9 at London and won that part of the title.

1962 (April 7)—Paul Pender won 15-round decision over Terry Downes at Boston, Mass., regaining title.

1962 (September 23)—Dick Tiger of Nigeria beat Gene Fullmer in 15 rounds at San Francisco, winning Fullmer's share of the title.

Tiger and Fullmer boxed a fifteen round draw in Las Vegas, Nevada, February 23, 1963. Then when a proposed match between Tiger and Pender fell through, Pender announced his retirement as champion on May 7, 1963. Tiger was then given universal recognition as world champion. He clinched his right to the crown when he stopped Fullmer in seven rounds at Ibadan, Nigeria, on August 10, 1963.

1963 (December 7)—Joey Giardello won the title by outpointing Dick Tiger at Atlantic City, N.J., in 15 rounds.

1965 (October 21)—Dick Tiger of Nigeria, regained the world title by gaining the unanimous decision over Joey Giardello in Madison Square Garden, at the end of 15 rounds.

1966 (April 25)—Emile Griffith, Weehawken, N.J., defeated Dick Tiger in Madison Square Garden, 15 rounds by a split decision.

1966 (July 13)—Emile Griffith defeated Joey Archer of New York, in Madison Square Garden, in 15 rounds by a split decision.

1967 (January 23)—Emile Griffith retained title with a unanimous decision over Joey Archer, in 15 rounds, at Madison Square Garden, N.Y.

1967 (April 17)—Nino Benvenuti dethroned Emile Griffith at Madison Square Garden by a 15 round decision.

1967 (Sept. 29)—Emile Griffith regained title from Nino Benvenuti, in 15 rounds, at Shea Stadium, N.Y.

1968 (March 4)—Nino Benvenuti regained the title by defeating Emile Griffith by unanimous decision.

1970 (November 7)—Carlos Monzon knocked out Nino Benvenuti in the 12th round to win the title at Rome, Italy.

WELTERWEIGHT CHAMPIONS

(145 and later 147 pounds)

In 1792, some small English fighters, calling themselves "Welters," a weight term used in English horse racing, started battling among themselves. The first of these champions was Paddington Tom Jones, weighing 145 pounds, who defeated all comers in 1792 and for several years later.

Class lapsed about 1795, was revived in 1815 and, from time to time for the next 60 or 70 years, the English welters fought each other but gained no real recognition, cared little who was "champion" and battled mainly for the side bets and the "hat passing" contributions of the spectators. However, the weight was always fixed at or under 145.

When fighting became fairly popular in the United States after the Civil War, some welters fought among themselves but without a championship until the late 1880's when Paddy Duffy, who had whipped all comers, announced that he was "verily the champion" with no one left to " fight" and went into retirement.

1892—"Mysterious" Billy Smith stopped Danny Needham, 14 rounds, San Francisco; claimed title.

1894—Tommy Ryan defeated Smith in 20 rounds, Minneapolis.

1897—Smith reclaimed the title when Ryan entered the middleweight ranks.

1900—Rube Ferns became champion when Smith fouled him in 21st round, Buffalo.

1900—Matty Matthews defeated Ferns, 15 rounds, Detroit.

1901—Ferns regained title when he knocked out Matthews, 10 rounds, Toronto.

1901—Joe Walcott (Negro) stopped Ferns, 5th round, Fort Erie, On., Dec. 18.

1904—Dixie Kid won on foul from Walcott, 20 rounds, San Francisco, but only a few experts recognized him as champion.

1904—Dixie Kid and Joe Walcott fought a 20-round draw, San Francisco.

1906—Honey Mellody won from Walcott, 15 rounds, Chelsea, Mass., and laid claim to the title.

1907—Mike (Twin) Sullivan defeated Mellody, 20 rounds, Los Angeles.

1910—Sullivan vacated title by becoming middleweight.

1910—Jimmy Clabby and Jimmy Gardner both claimed title, but Clabby was recognized when he gained the popular verdict over the Dixie Kid in a 10-round no-decision bout, New York.

1911—Clabby became a Middleweight and vacated title.

1911—Ray Bronson, Clarence (Kid) Ferns and many others claimed championship but they did not meet at division weights and title was really vacant until 1915.

1915 (Aug. 31)—Ted Lewis, British champion, defeated Jack Britton, outstanding United States welterweight, 12 rounds, in Boston, and claimed title, which was generally recognized. From then until 1919, Lewis and Britton fought over a dozen times, each winning and losing about the same number of times and alternating as champion.

1919 (March 17)—Jack Britton knocked out Lewis, 9 rounds, Canton, Ohio.

1922—Edward (Mickey) Walker won 15-round decision in New York from Britton.

1926 (May 20)—Pete Latzo won 10-round decision from Walker in Scranton, Pa.

1927 (June 3)—Joe Dundee won 15-round decision from Latzo, New York.

1929—Jackie Fields won on foul from Dundee, 2 rounds, in Detroit.

1930 (May 9)—Young Jack Thompson (Negro) outpointed Fields, 15 rounds, in Detroit, winning title.

1930 (Sept. 5)— Tommy Freeman won title at Cleveland by defeating Thompson, 15 rounds.

1931 (April 14)—Young Jack Thompson regained title in Cleveland by scoring technical knockout over Freeman, the latter being unable to answer bell for 12th round.

1931 (Oct. 23)—Lou Brouillard, Danielson, Conn., won title in Boston, outpointing Thompson, 15 rounds.

1932 (Jan. 28)—Fields outpointed Brouillard in Chicago, 10 rounds.

1933 (Feb. 22)—Young Corbett 3d outpointed Fields, San Francisco, 10 rounds.

1933 (June 5)—Jimmy McLarnin stopped Corbett, Los Angeles, 1 round.

1934 (May 28)—Barney Ross outpointed McLarnin, New York, 15 rounds.

1934 (Sept. 17)—McLarnin outpointed Ross, New York, 15 rounds.

1935 (May 28)—Ross defeated McLarnin, New York, 15 rounds.

1938 (May 31)—Henry Armstrong outpointed Ross, 15 rounds, New York.

1940 (Oct. 4)—Fritzie Zivic outpointed Armstrong, 15 rounds, New York.

1941 (July 29)—Freddie (Red) Cochrane outpointed Zivic, 15 rounds, Newark, N.J.

1942—Cochrane enlisted in United States Navy and title frozen for duration of World War II.

1946 (Feb. 1)—Marty Servo knocked out Cochrane in 4th, New York.

1946 (Aug.)—Servo refused a match with Ray Robinson, claiming nasal injury.

1946 (Sept. 3)—Because Servo did not agree to match with Robinson, New York Commission declared his title vacant. Servo then retired.

1946 (Dec. 20)—Robinson outpointed Tommy Bell, 15 rounds, New York, and gained recognition as champion.

1947 (June 4)—Robinson stopped Jimmy Doyle in 8 rounds for the title in Cleveland.

1947 (Dec. 19)—Robinson stopped Chuck Taylor in 6 rounds for the title in Detroit.

1948 (June 28)—Robinson outpointed Bernard Docusen for the title, 10 rounds, Chicago.

1949 (July 11)—Robinson outpointed Kid Gavilan for the title, 15 rounds, Philadelphia.

1950 (Aug. 9)—Robinson defeated Charlie Fusari for the title, 15 rounds, Jersey City.

1951—Robinson stopped Jake La Motta for the middleweight title in Chicago in 13 rounds on Feb. 14, and subsequently gave up the welterweight crown.

1951 (March 18)— Johnny Bratton won N.B.A. title by defeating Charlie Fusari, 15 rounds, Chicago.

1951 (May 18)—Kid Gavilan outpointed Bratton, 15 rounds, Chicago, and Billy Graham, 15 rounds, New York (Aug. 29), to pave the way for universal recognition.

1952 (Feb. 4)—Gavilan outpointed Bobby Dykes in 15 rounds at the Miami (Fla.) Stadium.

1952 (July 7)—Gavilan knocked out Gil Turner of Philadelphia in the 11th round at Municipal Stadium, Philadelphia.

1952 (Oct. 5)—Gavilan outpointed Billy Graham of New York in 15 rounds at the Gran Stadium, Havana, Cuba.

1953 (Feb. 11)—Gavilan knocked out Chuck Davey in the 10th round at the Chicago Stadium.

1953 (Sept. 18)—Gavilan outpointed Carmen Basilio of Chittenango, N.Y., in 15 rounds (split decision) at the War Memorial Auditorium, Syracuse, N.Y.

1953 (Nov. 13)—Gavilan outpointed Johnny Bratton of Chicago in 15 rounds at the Chicago Stadium.

1954 (Oct. 20)—Johnny Saxton of New York won the title by outpointing Gavilan in 15 rounds at Philadelphia.

1955 (April 1)—Tony DeMarco of Boston won the title by knocking out Johnny Saxton in the 14th round at the Garden, Boston.

1955 (June 10) Carmen Basilio won the title by knocking out DeMarco in the 12th round at the War Memorial Auditorium, Syracuse, N.Y.

1955 (Nov. 30)—Basilio retained the title by knocking out DeMarco in the 12th round at Boston.

1956 (March 14)—Johnny Saxton regained the title by outpointing Basilio in 15 rounds at the Chicago (Ill.) Stadium.

1956 (Sept. 12)—Basilio regained the title by knocking out Saxton in the ninth round at the War Memorial Auditorium, Syracuse, N. Y.

1957 (Feb. 22) —Basilio knocked out Saxton in the second round at the Arena, Cleveland. (After Basilio won the middleweight title from Robinson, Sept. 23, 1957, he vacated the 147-pound championship).

1958 (June 6)—Virgil Akins knocked out Vince Martinez in the fourth round at St. Louis, Mo., to win the crown vacated by Basilio.

1958 (Dec. 5)— Don Jordan outpointed Akins in 15 rounds at Los Angeles to gain the title.

1960 (May 27)—Benny "Kid" Paret won 15-round decision from Jordan, taking title at Las Vegas, Nevada.

1961 (April 1)—Emile Griffith knocked out Paret in 13th at Miami Beach, gaining title.

1961 (Sept. 30)—Paret regained title in decision over Griffith, 15 rounds at Madison

Square Garden.

1962 (March 4)–Griffith knocked out Paret in 12 rounds at Madison Square Garden to regain title. Paret died of injuries.

1962 (July 13)–Griffith retained title in decision over Ralph Dupas, 15 rounds at Las Vegas.

1962 (December 8)–Griffith retained title by knocking out Jorge Fernandez in nine rounds at Las Vegas.

1963 (March 21)–Luis Rodriquez won the title by outpointing Emile Griffith over 15 rounds at Los Angeles, Calif.

1963 (June 8)–Emile Griffith regained the title for the second time by outpointing Luis Rodriguez over 15 rounds in Madison Square Garden, New York, N.Y.

1964 (June 12)–Emile Griffith defeated Luis Rodriguez in Las Vegas, Nevada, in 15 rounds by a decision.

1965 (March 30)–Emile Griffith retained title by a decision over Jose Stable in 15 rounds, Madison Square Garden.

1965 (September 22)–Emile Griffith remained champion by defeating Brian Curvis in 15 rounds at Wembley Stadium of London, England.

1965 (December 10)–Emile Griffith decisioned Manuel Gonzales in Madison Square Garden in 15 rounds.

1966 (May 18)–Emile Griffith, by edict of the New York Commission, gave up his welterweight title after gaining the world middleweight championship. No champion is permitted by international rules, to hold two titles simultaneously.

1966 (November 28)–Curtis Cokes won the unanimous decision over Jean Josselin in the Dallas Municipal Auditorium in what was accepted as a bout to decide the successor to Griffith.

Cokes had gained the World Boxing Association title in an elimination by defeating Manuel Gonzalez of Texas and Luis Rodriguez of Miami. In the meantime, Josselin of France had defeated Brian Curvis of Wales for the European title.

1967 (May 19)–Curtis Cokes defended his title against F. Pavilla by a knockout in the 10th round, at Dallas, Texas.

1967 (October 2)–Curtis Cokes remained champion by defeating Charlie Snipes by a knockout in the 8th round, at Oakland, Calif.

1969 (April 17)–Jose Napoles of Mexico stopped Curtis Cokes in the 13th round to win the title at Los Angeles.

1970 (December 3)–Billy Backus dethroned Jose Napoles in the fourth round at Syracuse, N.Y.

1971 (June 4)–Jose Napoles regained the title in a rematch against Billy Backus at Syracuse in the eighth round.

LIGHTWEIGHT CHAMPIONS
(133 pounds–now 135)

This division in America was without real recognition until 1868, when Abe Hicken defeated Pete McGuire in Perrysville, Mo. They fought at 130 pounds and called themselves "lightweights." Hicken claimed title, no one disputed, and he eventually retired.

In 1872, Joe Collyer of England, on a visit to the United States, defeated Billy Edwards, of America and Arthur Chambers of England, who had helped the Marquis of Queensberry frame the Queensberry Rules. Collyer soon retired.

1879–Chambers fought John Clark in Chippewa Falls, Canada, March 27, with bare knuckles and for a belt to be emblematic of the championship. They agreed on 133 pounds ringside. Chambers won on a foul in 33 rounds and was regarded as world champion.

There was a lapse in title activity from then to 1884, inasmuch as Chambers had retired. In 1884, Jack (Nonpareil) Dempsey, then fighting around 130 to 135, was looked upon as champion but made no real claim to title.

Jack McAuliffe, who had won the amateur lightweight championship and turned professional in 1885, claimed title. Others disputed him. He fought and whipped them all through the next nine years and retired undefeated in 1893. McAuliffe's record embraced 10 fights won on knockouts, 32 won on decision and 9 draws.

1893–Kid Lavigne claimed title. His claim was generally recognized. After beating all Americans for three years, he took on Dick Burge, the English champion who came to the United States, and knocked him out in 17 rounds. That absolutely established the world title in American possession. Lavigne lost title on points, on July 3, 1899, in a 20-round battle with Frank Erne in Buffalo.

1901–Joe Gans knocked out Erne in the first round in Fort Erie, Canada, on May 12 (45 seconds). Erne previously had been knocked out in 3 rounds (in 1900) by Terry McGovern, who weighed only about 125, but it was a handicap match, the stipulation being Erne could not lose his title in that bout.

1908–Battling Nelson knocked out Gans, 17 rounds, San Francisco, July 4.

1910–Ad Wolgast won title from Nelson on Feb. 22 when referee stopped bout after the 40th round of a 45-round fight to save Nelson from further punishment. Fight was at Port Richmond, Calif.

1912–Willie Ritchie won on foul from Wolgast, 16 rounds, San Francisco, Nov. 28.

1914–Freddie Welsh outpointed Ritchie under British scoring rules in a 20-round fight, London, England.

1917–Benny Leonard technically knocked

out Welsh in 9 rounds on May 28, New York.

1924—Leonard retired undefeated.

1925—As outcome of elimination tournament through Winter and Spring 1924—1925, Jimmy Goodrich was acclaimed champion.

1925—Rocky Kansas defeated Goodrich on points, 15 rounds, Buffalo, Dec. 7.

1926—Sammy Mandell won title from Kansas, July 3, on points in 10-round fight in Chicago.

1930—Al Singer of New York knocked out Mandell in 1st round (1 minute 32 seconds), New York, July 17.

1930—Tony Canzoneri knocked out Singer in 1st round (1 minute 6 seconds), New York, Nov. 14.

1933—Barney Ross outpointed Canzoneri, 10 rounds, Chicago, June 23.

1935 (April 15)—Barney Ross relinquished title, being unable to make weight.

1935 (May 10)—Tony Canzoneri and Lou Ambers, joint claimants for Ross' crown, fought 15 rounds in New York. Canzoneri won decision and regained title.

1936 (Sept. 4)—Ambers outpointed Canzoneri, 15 rounds, New York.

1938 (Aug. 17)—Henry Armstrong outpointed Ambers, 15 rounds, New York.

1939 (Aug. 22)—Ambers regained title by outpointing Armstrong, 15 rounds, New York.

1940 (May 10)—Lew Jenkins knocked out Ambers, 3 rounds, in New York.

1941 (Dec. 19)—Sammy Angott defeated Jenkins, 15 rounds, in New York.

1942 (Nov. 13)—Angott announced resignation of title.

1942 (Dec.)—The New York Commission designated Beau Jack of Augusta, Ga., and Tippy Larkin of Garfield, N.J., as the topnotchers among the active lightweights and declared that the winner of a match between them would be acclaimed champion.

1942 (Dec. 18)—Beau Jack knocked out Tippy Larkin, 3 rounds, New York.

1943 (May 21)—Bob Montgomery outpointed Beau Jack, 15 rounds, New York.

1943 (Nov. 19)—Beau Jack outpointed Montgomery, 15 rounds, New York.

1943—The N.B.A. announced it would not recognize as champion anyone who did not defeat Angott, who then announced his return to the ring.

1943 (Oct. 27)—Angott outpointed Slugger White, 15 rounds, Los Angeles, and was reestablished as the N.B.A. champion.

1944 (March 3)—Montgomery outpointed Jack in New York and regained New York Commission's recognition as champion.

1944 (March 8)—Juan Zurita outpointed Angott, 15 rounds, Hollywood, Calif., and was acclaimed champion by N.B.A.

1945 (April 18)—Ike Williams of Trenton, N.J., knocked out Zurita, 2d round, Mexico City,

and became N.B.A. champion.

1946 (Sept. 4)—Williams knocked out Ronnie James, British Empire champion, 9 rounds, Cardiff, Wales.

1947 (August 4)—Ike Williams knocked out Montgomery, 6 rounds, Philadelphia, and gained clear claim to the title.

1951 (May 25)—Jimmy Carter of the Bronx knocked out Williams, 14 rounds, New York, to take the championship.

1952 (May 14)—Lauro Salas of Monterey, Mexico, outpointed Carter to gain title in 15 rounds at Los Angeles.

1952 (Oct. 15)—Carter recaptured title by outpointing Salas in 15 rounds in Chicago.

1953 (April 24)—Carter knocked out Tommy Collins of Boston in the fourth round at the Boston Garden.

1953 (June 12)—Carter knocked out George Araujo of Fox Point, R.I., in the 13th round at Madison Square Garden, New York.

1953 (Nov. 11)—Carter knocked out Armand Savoie of Montreal in the fifth round at the Forum, Montreal.

1954 (March 5)—Paddy DeMarco of Brooklyn won the title by outpointing Carter in 15 rounds at Madison Square Garden.

1954 (Nov. 17)—Carter regained the title by knocking out DeMarco in the 15th round at the Cow Palace, San Francisco.

1955 (June 29)—Wallace (Bud) Smith of Cincinnati won the title by outpointing Jimmy Carter in 15 rounds at the Garden, Boston.

1955 (Oct. 19)—Smith outpointed Carter in 15 rounds at Cincinnati.

1956 (Aug. 24)—Joe Brown of Baton Rouge, La., won the title by outpointing Smith in 15 rounds at Municipal Stadium, New Orleans, La.

1957 (Feb. 13)—Brown knocked out Smith in the 11th round at the Auditorium, Miami Beach, Fla.

1957 (June 19)—Brown knocked out Orlando Zulueta of Havana, Cuba, in the 15th round at the Coliseum, Denver, Colo.

1957 (Dec. 4)—Brown knocked out Joey Lopes of Sacramento, Calif., in the 11th round at the Chicago Stadium.

1958 (May 7)—Brown knocked out Ralph Dupas in the eighth round at Houston, Texas, to retain title.

1958 (July 23)—Brown outpointed Kenny Lane in 15 rounds at Houston.

1959 (Feb. 11)—Brown outpointed Johnny Busso in 15 rounds at Houston.

1959 (June 3)—Brown knocked out Paolo Rosi in 9 at Washington, D.C., to keep title.

1959 (December 2)—Brown knocked out Dave Charnley in 6 rounds at Houston, Texas, to keep title.

1960 (October 28)—Brown won 15 round decision over Cisco Andrade at Los Angeles to retain title.

1961 (April 15)—Brown beat Dave Charnley in 15 rounds at London, England and kept title.

1961 (October 28)—Brown outpointed Bert Somodio in 15 rounds at Quezon City, Philippines to keep title.

1962 (April 21)—Carlos Ortiz won the title by outpointing Joe Brown in 15 rounds at Las Vegas.

1962 (December 3)—Ortiz knocked out Teruo Kosaka in five rounds at Tokyo to keep title.

1965 (April 10)—Ismael Laguna won the title by gaining the majority decision over Carlos Ortiz in Panama City, Panama.

1965 (November 13)—Carlos Ortiz, New York, regained title by defeating Ismael Laguna, on points in 15 rounds at San Juan, Puerto Rico.

1966 (June 20)—Carlos Ortiz, New York, stopped Johnny Bizarro, of Erie, Pa., in the Civic Arena of Pittsburgh in 2.29 of the 12th round.

1966 (November 28)—Carlos Ortiz knocked out Flash Elorde in 2.01 of the 14th round in Madison Square Garden.

1967 (July 1)—Carlos Ortiz defeated Sugar Romos by a knockout in the 4th round at San Juan, Puerto Rico.

1967 (August 16)—Carlos Ortiz outpointed Ismael Laguna, in 15 rounds, at Shea Stadium, N.Y.

1968 (June 29)—Carlos Ortiz lost the title to Carlos (Teo) Cruz in a split decision at Santo Domingo.

1969 (Feb. 19)—Mando Ramos stopped Carlos (Teo) Cruz in the eleventh round at Los Angeles.

1970 (March 3)—Ismael Laguna regained the title by defeating Mando Ramos in nine rounds at Los Angeles.

1970 (Sept. 26)—Ken Buchanan of Scotland outpointed Ismael Laguna in 15 rounds held at San Juan, P.R.

1972 (June 26)—Roberto Duran kayoed Ken Buchanan in the 13th round to win the title at Madison Square Garden.

FEATHERWEIGHT CHAMPIONS
(118 and 122 pounds—now 126)

Ike Weir, called the "Belfast Spider," a Scotsman, was the first man actually rated as "champion of the featherweights." That was during the 1880's. He was challenged in 1887 by Harry Gilmore, an American, and declined. In 1889 Weir, visiting the United States, fought an 80-round draw with Frank Murphy of England near Kouts, Ind. Billy Murphy came here from New Zealand, defeated Weir in San Francisco on Jan. 13, 1890, and was universally regarded as world champion of the class.

1890—Murphy outgrew class and retired.

1890—George Dixon, American Negro, stopped Nunce Wallace of England, in London, 18 rounds, for side bet of $2,000 and championship. Between 1890 and 1899 Dixon was beaten several times but always declared he had not lost title, inasmuch as it was his idea the poundage should be 118, not 122, and that the opponents who had beaten him weighed over 118. Among those to whom he lost were Billy Plimmer (1893), Frank Erne (1896) and Solly Smith (1897). Plimmer weighed 121, Erne 122, and Smith 120.

1899—Terry McGovern knocked out Dixon, 8 rounds, New York, at 118 pounds, which Dixon had fixed as featherweight limit.

1901—Young Corbett knocked out McGovern, 2 rounds, at 126 pounds, in Hartford, Conn., but Corbett, who was growing bulkier daily, never made claim to title.

1904—With Corbett and McGovern both in lightweight class and poundage officially fixed at 122, Abe Attell claimed the title and so did "Brooklyn" Tommy Sullivan. Sullivan previously (early in 1904) had knocked out Young Corbett with both men fighting above division weight.

1904—Sullivan won from Attell, foul, 5 rounds, St. Louis, Oct. 13.

1908—Attell knocked out Sullivan, 4 rounds, San Francisco, April 30.

1912—Johnny Kilbane outpointed Attell, 20 rounds, San Francisco, Feb. 22.

1923—Eugene Criqui of France knocked out Kilbane, 6 rounds, New York, June 2.

1923—Johnny Dundee outpointed Criqui, 15 rounds, New York, July 26.

1925—Dundee outgrew division and retired from class.

1925–26—Louis (Kid) Kaplan was winner of elimination contest to determine Dundee's successor.

1927—Kaplan outgrew division and retired.

1927—Benny Bass and Red Chapman, ranking claimants, fought twice. Bass won first on foul in the 1st round in New York, Jan. 1. Bass outpointed Chapman 10 rounds, Philadelphia, Sept. 12, and was recognized as champion by N.B.A.

1928—Tony Canzoneri and Bass met in title match in New York, Feb. 10, and Canzoneri won 15-round decision.

1928—Andre Routis of France won title from Canzoneri, 15-round decision, New York, Sept. 28.

1929—Christopher (Battling) Battalino won title by outpointing Routis, 10 rounds, Hartford, Conn., Sept. 23.

1932—Battalino relinquished title in March, being unable to make divisional limit.

1932—Kid Chocolate stopped Lew Feldman, 12 rounds, New York, Oct. 13, for New York Commission tournament title. Tommy Paul outpointed Johnny Pena, 15 rounds, Detroit, May 26, for N.B.A. tournament title.

1933—Freddie Miller outpointed Paul, 10 rounds, Chicago, Jan. 13, for N.B.A. title.

1934—Chocolate relinquished title to compete

as lightweight, New York solons designating Baby Arizmendi-Mike Belloise winner as champion. Arizmendi outpointed Belloise, 15 rounds, New York, Aug. 30.

1936 (May 11)—Petey Sarron defeated Miller, 15 rounds, Washington, D.C.

1937 (Oct. 29)—Henry Armstrong knocked out Sarron, 6th round, New York.

1938—Armstrong resigned as champion, New York Commission then recognized Mike Belloise and Joey Archibald as outstanding.

1938 (Oct. 17)—Archibald outpointed Belloise, 15 rounds, New York.

1940 (May 20)—Harry Jeffra outpointed Archibald, 15 rounds, Baltimore.

1941 (May 12)—Archibald outpointed Jeffra, 15 rounds, Washington, D.C.

1941 (Sept. 11)—Chalky Wright knocked out Archibald, 11 rounds, Washington, D.C.

1942 (Nov. 20)—Willie Pep outpointed Wright, 15 rounds, New York.

Pep's title as champion in New York "frozen" while Pep was with the Armed Forces during World War II.

From 1942 through 1944 there were many claimants, foremost of whom were Sal Bartolo of Boston and Phil Terranova of New York. But when Pep came out of the Army he established his title securely by beating Bartolo and then defeating Chalky Wright once more. He also vanquished Terranova.

1948 (Oct. 29)—Sandy Saddler of Harlem took the title by knocking out Pep, 4 rounds, New York.

1949 (Feb. 11)—Pep regained the championship by outpointing Saddler, 15 rounds, New York.

1950 (Sept. 8)—Saddler again became champion by stopping Pep in 8 rounds at Yankee Stadium. The fight was one of the roughest in years; the rivals suffered suspension for disregarding rules .

1951—Saddler inducted into the Army.

1952—Attempts to produce an "interim" champion failed to impress the fans.

1953—None.

1954—None.

1955 (Feb. 25)—Sandy Saddler outpointed Teddy (Red Top) Davis in 15 rounds at Madison Square Garden, New York.

1956 (Jan. 18)—Sandy Saddler knocked out Gabriel (Flash) Elorde in the 13th round at the Cow Palace, San Francisco.

1957—Following an auto accident in which he was injured in 1956, Saddler retired and relinquished the title.

1957 (June 24)—After an elimination tournament, with Hogan (Kid) Bassey of Nigeria and Cherif Hamia of Algeria as the finalists, Bassey won the vacant championship by knocking out Hamia in the tenth round at Paris, in the Palais des Sports.

1958 (April 1)—Bassey retained his title by knocking out Ricardo Moreno in the third round at Los Angeles.

1959 (March 18)—Davey Moore knocked out Bassey in the 13th round at Los Angeles to win the title.

1960 (August 29)—Moore won 15 round decision over Kazuo Takayama at Tokyo to retain title.

1961 (April 8)—Moore knocked out Danny Valdez in one round at Los Angeles to keep title.

1961 (November 13)—Moore outpointed Kazuo Takayama in 15 rounds at Tokyo to retain title.

1962 (August 17)—Moore knocked out Olli Maeki in 2 rounds at Helsinki, Finland to keep title.

1963 (March 21)—Sugar Ramos won the title by stopping Davey Moore in the 11th round at Los Angeles, Calif.

1964 (September 26)—Vicente Saldivar won the title by stopping Sugar Ramos in the 12th round at Mexico City, Mexico.

1966 (February 12)—Vicente Saldivar, Mexico City, knocked out Floyd Robertson, Ghana, in 2.29 of the second round in Mexico City.

1966 (August 7)—Vicente Saldivar, Mexico City, defeated Mitsunori Seki, Japan, in Mexico City, in 15 rounds by a decision.

1967 (January 29)—Vicente Saldivar, Mexico City, knocked out Mitsunori Seki, Japan, in Mexico City, in the 7th round.

1967 (June 15)—Vicente Saldivar, Mexico City, defeated Howard Winstone, Wales, by a 15 round decision, at Cardiff, Wales.

1967 (October 14)—Vicente Saldivar, Mexico City, knocked out Howard Winstone, Wales, in the 12th round, at Mexico City. He then retired as featherweight champion.

1969 (Jan. 23)—Johnny Famechon defeated Jose Legra in a 15-round decision to win the vacant world title, held in London.

1970 (May 9)—Vicente Saldivar regained the title by defeating Johnny Famechon of Australia by a decision in 15 rounds. Famechon retired after his loss.

1970 (Dec. 11)—Kuniaki Shibata of Japan knocked out Vicente Saldivar in the 13th round. Bout held in Tijuana, Mexico.

1972 (May 19)—Clemente Sanchez of Mexico kayoed Kuniaki Shibata in the third round to win the title held at Tokyo.

1972 (Dec. 16)—Clemente Sanchez vacated his title. He no longer could make the weight. W.B.A. champion is Ernesto Marcel of Panama. W.B.C. awarded Spain's Jose Legra their crown. The ring's title remains vacant.

BANTAMWEIGHT CHAMPIONS
(105, 112 and 116—now 118)

In 1885, the smallest fighters were called "bantams"—or "little chickens." Of the group in

America—perhaps no more than 8 or 10 at most—Charlie Lynch was supposed to be best. He went to England in 1856 and was beaten in 95 rounds by Simon Finighty, the best English bantam. He met Finighty again in 1859, won in 43 rounds and claimed the world title. Lynch retired undefeated in 1861 and the division was inactive until 1887.

1887—Tom Kelly, weighing 105 pounds, claimed title.

1888—Kelly and George Dixon (Negro) fought 9-round draw.

1890—Dixon claimed championship with Kelly's retirement and was acclaimed as such.

1894—Dixon outgrew division and retired.

1894—Jimmy Barry fought Casper Leon, 112 pounds, Sept. 25, at Lamont, Ill., Barry knocking out Leon in 28 rounds.

1899—Barry retired undefeated and Terry McGovern claimed title. On Sept. 12, McGovern knocked out Pedlar Palmer of England, joint claimant, in 1 round, Tuckahoe, N.Y.

1900—McGovern retired.

1900—Harry Forbes claimed title. Forbes met all comers until 1903.

1903—Frankie Neil knocked out Forbes, 2 rounds, San Francisco, Aug. 13.

1904—Joe Bowker of England outpointed Neil, 20 rounds, London, Oct. 17.

1904—Bowker outgrew division and Digger Stanley claimed title, as did Jimmy Walsh of America. They met three times for the title. Stanley won the first, 15 rounds, decision, the second was a 15-round draw and Walsh won the vacant title on Oct. 20, 1905, by outpointing Stanley in 15 rounds in their third fight.

1907—Title vacated by both Walsh and Stanley.

1907—Johnny Coulon claimed title.

1910—Coulon defeated Jim Kendrick, British champion, 19 rounds, New Orleans. They fought for world championship at 116 pounds and that became recognized weight for division.

1914—Kid Williams knocked out Coulon, 3 rounds, Vernon, Calif., June 9.

1915—Williams lost on foul to Johnny Ertle, 5 rounds, St. Paul, Sept. 10, and Ertle claimed title. Owing to fact that there was much argument over whether punch was fair or foul about 50 per cent of the experts regarded Ertle as new champion and the other half insisted Williams was still champion.

1917—Pete Herman beat Williams in 20 rounds and because Ertle had not accomplished much since his foul victory over Williams, Herman was regarded as the real champion. Fight was in New Orleans, Jan. 9.

1920—Joe Lynch won title from Herman, 15 rounds, New York, Dec. 22.

1921—Herman regained championship, beating Lynch in a decision fight in Brooklyn, June 25.

1921—Johnny Buff defeated Herman, 15 rounds, New York, Sept. 23.

1922—Lynch knocked out Buff, 14 rounds, New York, July 10.

1924—Abe Goldstein outpointed Lynch, 15 rounds, New York, March 21.

1924—Eddie Martin outpointed Lynch, 15 rounds, New York, Dec. 19.

1925—Charles (Phil) Rosenberg outpointed Martin, 15 rounds, New York, March 20.

1927—Rosenberg, unable to make weight, forfeited title.

1927—28—Bud Taylor was recognized as bantam champion by the N.B.A. New York Commission had different ideas. It felt that title belonged to Kid Francis, Panama Al Brown (Negro) or to one of the others. Up to the end of 1931 there was no undisputed champion, but there were a half-dozen fighters claiming supremacy.

1931—Brown beat Eugene Huat of France, 15 rounds, Montreal, Quebec, Oct. 27, and strengthened title claim.

1932—Brown defeated Huat again, 10 rounds, Paris, June 18.

1934 (July)—N.B.A. declared title vacant through Brown's failure to defend. New York Commission followed N.B.A. The N.B.A. then inaugurated tournament. Bobby Leitham, Canadian champion, named outstanding contender. Sixto Escobar, Puerto Rican, knocked out Leitham, 7 rounds, Holyoke, Mass., repeated knockout in 5 rounds at Montreal to win Canadian title. N.B.A. then named Baby Casanova, Mexican, outstanding contender. Escobar stopped Casanova in 9 rounds in Montreal, receiving Seagram Belt, emblematic of Canadian championship, and recognition from the N.B.A. as the "defending champion."

1935 (Aug.)—Baltasar Sangchili outpointed Brown, 15 rounds, Spain, and won title in European opinion. The United States did not share in this belief and ignored Sangchili.

1935 (Aug. 26)—Lou Salica, rated as champion by New York Commission, defeated Escobar, 15 rounds, New York.

1935 (Nov. 15)—Escobar defeated Salica, 15 rounds, New York.

1937 (Sept. 23)—Harry Jeffra outpointed Escobar, 15 rounds, New York.

1938 (Feb. 20)—Escobar outpointed Jeffra, 15 rounds, in Puerto Rico.

1940—Escobar resigned title.

1941—George Pace regarded by N.B.A. as its champion; Lou Salica rated as champion by New York Commission.

1941 (Sept. 24)—Salica outpointed Pace, 10 rounds, New York.

1942 (Aug. 7)—Manuel Ortiz outpointed Salica, 12 rounds, Hollywood, Calif., and gained N.B.A. recognition as champion.

1947 (Jan. 7)—Harold Dade, Chicago Negro,

outpointed Ortiz, 15 rounds, San Francisco. It was Ortiz's 16th defense of title.

1947 (March 11)—Ortiz regained title, defeating Dade, 15 rounds, Los Angeles.

1950 (May 31)—Vic Toweel, Johannesburg, South Africa, became champion by defeating Ortiz, 15 rounds, Johannesburg.

1952 (Nov. 15)—Jimmy Carruthers of Paddington, New South Wales, Australia, took the title from Toweel by a 1-round knockout in Johannesburg.

1953 (March 21)—Jimmy Carruthers knocked out Vic Toweel in the 10th round at Johannesburg, South Africa.

1954 (May 2)—Jimmy Carruthers outpointed Chamrern Songkitrat of Thailand in 12 rounds at Bangkok, Thailand.

1954 (May 16)—Jimmy Carruthers retired as undefeated champion.

1954 (Sept. 19)—Robert Cohen of France won the title by outpointing Chamrern Songkitrat in 15 rounds at Bangkok.

1955 (March 9)—Raton Macias of Mexico knocked out Chamrern Songkitrat in the 11th round at San Francisco in a bout sanctioned by the National Boxing Association as for the world title. (It was not universally recognized, only in a few N.B.A. states).

1955 (Sept. 3)—Robert Cohen fought a 15-round draw with Willie Toweel to retain his championship at Johannesburg, South Africa.

1956 (June 29)—Mario D'Agata of Italy won the title by knocking out Robert Cohen in the sixth round at the Foro Italico Soccer Stadium, Rome.

1957 (April 1)—Alphonse Halimi of Algeria and France won the title by outpointing Mario D'Agata in 15 rounds at the Palais des Sports, Paris, France.

1957 (June 15)—Raton Macias of Mexico, the N.B.A. recognized champion, knocked out Dommy Ursua of the Philippines in the 11th round at the Cow Palace, San Francisco.

1957 (Nov. 6)—Alphonse Halimi won undisputed possession of the world championship by outpointing Raton Macias in 15 rounds at Wrigley Field, Los Angeles.

1958—There were no championship bouts in the bantamweight division.

1959 (July 8)—Joe Becerra knocked out Halimi in 3 rounds at Los Angeles to win title.

1960 (August 30)—Becerra knocked out in 8 rounds by Elroy Sanchez and retired. It was non-title bout.

1960 (October 15)—Alphonse Halimi won decision over Freddie Gilroy in London to gain European title.

1960 (November 18)—Eder Jofre knocked out Elroy Sanchez in 6 rounds at Los Angeles to get American title.

1961 (March 25)—Halimi refused to meet Jofre who then boxed Piero Rollo, Italian champion, knocked Rollo out in 10 rounds and gained recognition as world champion.

1962 (January 18)—Jofre stopped Johnny Caldwell of Ireland in 10 rounds at San Paulo, Brazil to keep title.

1962 (May 4)—Jofre knocked out Herman Marques in 10 rounds to keep title.

1962 (September 11)—Jofre knocked out Joe Medel of Mexico in 6 rounds, retaining title, now unbeaten in 45 bouts.

1965 (May 17)—Fighting Harada defeated Eder Jofre by a decision in 15 rounds in Tokyo, Japan, to win the bantam title.

1966 (June 1)—Fighting Harada, Japan, defeated Eder Jofre, Sao Paolo, Brazil, in Tokyo, 15 rounds, by a unanimous decision.

1967 (January 3)—Fighting Harada, Japan, defended his title in 15 rounds, against Jose Medel, by a decision, at Nagoya, Japan.

1967 (July 4)—Fighting Harada, Japan, outpointed B. Caraballo in 15 rounds, at Tokyo, Japan.

1968 (Feb. 26)—Lionel Rose of Australia beat Fighting Harada to win the world title by a unanimous decision in a bout held in Tokyo.

1969 (Aug. 22)—Ruben Olivares of Mexico kayoed Lionel Rose in the fifth round of a title match held in Los Angeles. Attendance—17,000.

1970 (Oct. 16)—Chu Chu Castillo, Mexico, stopped Ruben Olivares at 2:27 of the 14th round. On ring physician's advice. Bout held at Los Angeles.

1971 (April 2)—Ruben Olivares regained the title in a 15-round decision over Chu Chu Castillo at Los Angeles.

1972 (March 19)—Rafael Herrera stopped Ruben Olivares in 1:28 of the eighth round in bout held at Mexico City.

1972 (July 30)—Enrique Pinder won a 15-round decision over Mexico's Rafael Herrera. Bout held at Panama City.

FLYWEIGHT CHAMPIONS
(112 pounds)

This division was established in England early in 1910 and later the same year such a class was introduced in this country.

Young Zulu Kid, Frankie Mason and Johnny Rosner were the early claimants. Eventually the performances of Mason gained him ranking as American flyweight champion. Jimmy Wilde of England then was world champion, having knocked out Rosner in Liverpool, April 24, 1916.

1921—Johnny Buff won American title from Frankie Mason, 15 rounds, New Orleans, Feb. 11.

1922—Pancho Villa, a Filipino, knocked out Buff, 11 rounds, New York, Sept. 14.

1923—Frankie Genaro outpointed Villa, 15 rounds, New York, March 1.

In the spring of 1923, Wilde, the English champion, came to the United States and, although Genaro was American champion, Wilde elected to mix it with Villa.

1923—Villa knocked out Wilde in 7 rounds in New York on June 18 and became known as world champion.

1925—Villa died on July 14, San Francisco.

1925—Fidel La Barba outpointed Genaro, 10 rounds, and was recognized as world champion, San Francisco, Aug. 22.

1927—La Barba retired to enter college.

1927—29—No definite champion to succeed La Barba. For a while Corporal Izzy Schwartz was rated as titleholder by the New York Commission. This was because he beat Newsboy Brown on points, Dec. 16, 1927. But others defeated Schwartz and conditions in the division became scrambled. In an effort to determine actual champion, the commission directed that an elimination tournament be staged, which started in November, 1929.

1930—Midget Wolgast, Philadelphia, who with Black Bill, a Cuban, worked his way into the final, outpointed Black Bill in a 15-round bout in Madison Square Garden, New York, March 21, and was acknowledged champion by the New York Commission.

At the same time New Jersey elected Willie La Morte as champion and the N.B.A., representing nearly 30 states, settled upon Genaro. Wolgast was matched to meet Genaro in New York in May, 1930, but the bout was called off.

1930 (May 16)—Wolgast scored a technical knockout over La Morte in New York.

1930 (Aug. 6)—Genaro defeated La Morte, 10-round decision, New York.

1930 (Dec. 26)—Genaro and Wolgast fought 15-round draw.

1931 (Oct. 26)—Young Perez, French fighter from Tunis, knocked out Genaro in the 2d round, Paris.

1932—Perez recognized as flyweight champion in France, but England elected its own, Jackie Brown.

1933—N.B.A. recognized Brown as champion.

1934—New York Commission selected Midget Wolgast as champion. N.B.A. also recognized him.

1935—At end of year New York Commission rated Small Montana as its champion. The N.B.A. did not nominate anyone.

1935 (Sept. 8)—Benny Lynch knocked out Brown, 2d round, Manchester, England, and claimed world title.

1935 (Sept. 16)—Montana outpointed Wolgast, 10 rounds, Oakland, Calif., and claimed title.

1937 (Jan. 9)—Lynch outpointed Montana, 15 rounds, England, and became recognized world champion.

1938 (June 29)—Lynch resigned title.

1938 (Sept. 22)—Peter Kane, England, defeated Jackie Jurich, United States, 15 rounds, England, Jurich having claimed United States title while Kane was regarded as European champion.

1939 (Oct. 4)—Montana outpointed Jurich, 10 rounds, Hollywood, Calif.

1940—Because of World War II Kane was forced into retirement.

1942—Montana regarded as American champion.

1943—Jackie Paterson of Scotland rated as world champion in Nat Fleischer's "Ring Record Book."

1946 (July 10)—Paterson clinched claim to title, before 50,000 fans, Glasgow, Scotland, winning 15-round decision from Joe Curran, Liverpool, England.

1948 (March 23)—Rinty Monaghan gained title by stopping Paterson in Belfast, Monaghan's home town, in 7 rounds.

1950—Monaghan retired. On April 25, Terry Allen of Islington, England, gained the title through winning an elimination tournament bout against Honore Pratesi, 15 rounds, London.

1950 (Nov. 1)—Dado Marino of Honolulu beat Allen, 15 rounds, Honolulu.

1952 (May 19)—Yoshio Shirai, Tokyo, Japan, took the crown by beating Marino, 15 rounds, Tokyo.

1953 (May 18)—Yoshio Shirai of Japan outpointed Tanny Campo of The Philippines in 15 rounds at Tokyo, Japan.

1953 (Oct. 27)—Yoshio Shirai outpointed Terry Allen of England in 15 rounds at Tokyo, Japan.

1954 (May 23)—Yoshio Shirai outpointed Leo Espinosa of The Philippines in 15 rounds at Tokyo, Japan.

1954 (Nov. 26)—Pascual Perez of Argentina won the title by outpointing Yoshio Shirai in 15 rounds at Tokyo, Japan.

1955 (May 31)—Pascual Perez knocked out Yoshio Shirai in the fifth round at Tokyo, Japan.

1956 (Jan. 11)—Pascual Perez outpointed Leo Espinosa of The Philippines in 15 rounds at Luna Park, Buenos Aires, Argentina.

1956 (June 30)—Pascual Perez knocked out Oscar Suarez of Cuba in the 11th round at Montevideo, Uruguay.

1956 (Aug. 3)—Pascual Perez knocked out Ricardo Valdez of Argentina in the fifth round at Tandil, Argentina.

1957 (March 30)—Pascual Perez knocked out Dai Dower of Cardiff, Wales, in the first round at San Lorenzo de Almagra Soccer Stadium, Buenos Aires, Argentina.

1957 (Dec. 7)—Pascual Perez knocked out Young Martin of Spain in the third round at San Lorenzo de Almagra Soccer Stadium, Buenos Aires, Argentina. Perez also engaged in two other bouts, which were listed as non-title fights, but since the fighters weighed in under the class weight limit both times, the fights were automatically championship contests. On July 12 Perez outpointed Luis Angel Jiminez in 10 rounds at Buenos Aires. On Aug. 24 Perez knocked out Pablo Sosa in the third round at Tandil. Both bouts were scheduled 10-rounders.

1958 (April 19)—Perez retained the title by outpointing Ramon Arias in a 15-rounder at Caracas, Venezuela.

1958 (Dec. 15)—Perez gained a unanimous decision over Dommy Ursua in Manila.

1960 (April 16)—Pone Kingpetch won title in 15-round decision from Pascual Perez at Bangkok, Thailand.

1960 (September 22)—Kingpetch knocked out Perez in return bout in 8 rounds at Los Angeles, keeping title.

1961 (June 27)—Kingpetch won 15 round decision over Mitsunroi Seki at Tokyo to keep title.

1962 (May 30)—Kingpetch won 15 round decision over Kyo Noguchi at Tokyo to keep title.

1962 (October 10)—Masahiko Harada of Japan knocked out Pone Kingpetch in the eleventh round at Tokyo to win title.

1963 (January 12)—Pone Kingpetch became the first to regain the flyweight title when he decisioned Fighting Harada over 15 rounds at Bangkok, Thailand.

1963 (September 18)—Hiroyuki Ebihara won the title when he knocked out Pone Kingpetch in 2:07 of the first round at Tokyo, Japan.

1964 (January 23)—Pone Kingpetch regained the title when he decisioned Hiroyuki Ebihara over 15 rounds at Bangkok, Thailand.

1965 (April 23)—Salvatore Burruni won by a unanimous decision over Pone Kingpetch in a 15 round bout in Rome.

1966 (June 14)—Walter McGowan, Scotland, defeated Salvatore Burruni, Italy, in Tokyo in 15 rounds by a unanimous decision.

1966 (December 30)—Chartchai Choinoi of Thailand, in Bangkok, knockout defending champion Walter McGowan, Scotland, in the 9th round.

1967 (July 26)—Chartchai Choinoi, Thailand, defended his title against P. Keosuriya by a knockout in the 3d round, at Bangkok.

1967 (Sept. 19)—Chartchai Choinoi, Thailand, knocked out Walter McGowan, Scotland, in the

7th round, at London, England.

1969 (Feb. 23)—Efren Torres of Mexico stopped Chartchai Chionoi in the eighth round to win the world title. Bout held in Mexico City.

1970 (March 20)—Chartchai Chionoi regained his title by outpointing Efren Torres in a 15-round match held at Bangkok, Thailand.

1970 (Dec. 7)—Erbito Salvarria kayoed Chartchai Chionoi in the second round in a bout held at Bangkok.

FAMOUS FIGHTERS

(Nat Fleisher's all-time ranking of world boxers.)

HEAVYWEIGHTS—1, Jack Johnson; 2, James J. Jeffries; 3, Bob Fitzsimmons; 4 Jack Dempsey; 5, James J. Corbett; 6, Joe Louis; 7, Sam Langford; 8, Gene Tunney; 9, Max Schmeling; 10, Rocky Marciano.

LIGHT HEAVYWEIGHTS—1, Kid McCoy; 2, Philadelphia Jack O'Brien; 3, Jack Dillon; 4, Tommy Loughran; 5, Jack Root; 6, Battling Levinsky; 7, Georges Carpentier; 8, Tom Gibbons; 9, Jack Delaney; 10, Paul Berlenbach.

MIDDLEWEIGHTS—1, Stanley Ketchel; 2, Tommy Ryan; 3, Harry Greb 4, Mickey Walker; 5, Ray Robinson; 6, Frank Klaus; 7, Billy Papke; 8, Les Darcy; 9, Mike Gibbons; 10, Jeff Smith.

WELTERWEIGHTS—1, Joe Walcott; 2, Mysterious Billy Smith; 3, Jack Britton; 4, Ted Kid Lewis; 5, Dixie Kid; 6, Harry Lewis; 7, Willie Lewis; 8, Henry Armstrong; 9, Barney Ross; 10, Jimmy McLarnin.

LIGHTWEIGHTS—1, Joe Gans 2, Benny Leonard; 3, Owen Moran; 4, Freddy Welsh; 5, Battling Nelson; 6, George Kid Lavigne; 7, Tony Canzoneri; 8, Willie Ritchie; 9, Lew Tendler; 10, Ad Wolgast.

FEATHERWEIGHTS—1, Terry McGovern; 2, Jem Driscoll; 3, Abe Attell; 4, Willie Pep; 5, Johnny Dundee; 6, Young Grifo; 7, Johnny Kilbane; 8, Kid Chocolate; 9, George K.O. Chaney; 10, Louis Kid Kaplan.

BANTAMWEIGHTS—1, George Dixon; 2, Pete Herman, 3, Kid Williams; 4, Eder Jofre; 5, Joe Lynch; 6, Bud Taylor; 7, Johnny Coulon; 8, Frankie Burns; 9, Eddie Campi; 10, Panama Al Brown.

FLYWEIGHTS—1, Jimmy Wilde; 2, Pancho Villa; 3, Frankie Genaro; 4, Fidel La Barba; 5, Benny Lynch; 6, Elky Clark; 7, Johnny Buff; 8, Midget Wolgast; 9, Peter Kane; 10, Pascual Perez.

Records of World Champions
(Source: Nat Fleischer's Ring Record Book)

Following is a table breaking down the record of modern world champions, title claimants and American and junior champions:

	TB	KO	WD	WF	D	LD	LF	KO by	ND	NC
Aaron, Barney	6	0	4	0	1	1	0	0	0	0
Akins, Virgil	92	34	25	0	2	29	0	2	0	0

	TB	KO	WD	WF	D	LD	LF	KO by	ND	NC
Allen, Terry	76	18	42	2	1	10	0	3	0	0
Ambers, Lou	102	29	59	0	6	6	0	2	0	0
Angott, Sammy	125	22	72	0	8	22	0	1	0	0
Apostoli, Freddie	72	31	30	0	1	6	0	4	0	0
Archibald, Joey	106	28	32	0	5	32	1	8	0	0
Arizmendi, Baby	87	8	42	0	11	23	0	3	0	0
Armstrong, Henry	175	97	47	0	8	19	1	2	1	0
Attell, Abe	168	47	43	1	17	7	0	3	50	0
Attell, Monte	99	21	13	0	14	13	1	8	27	2
Backus, Billy	52	17	18	0	4	12	0	1	0	0
Baer, Buddy	54	43	5	0	0	4	1	1	0	0
Baer, Max	79	50	15	0	0	9	1	3	1	0
Baldwin, Caleb	15	0	13	0	1	1	0	0	0	0
Baldwin, Matty	188	22	50	5	50	24	1	1	35	0
Ballerino, Mike	96	8	32	0	14	19	0	5	13	0
Barry, Jimmy	70	39	20	0	9	0	0	0	0	2
Bartfield, Soldier	169	18	11	3	8	13	0	5	111	0
Bartolo, Sal	97	16	58	0	5	16	0	2	0	0
Basilio, Carmen	79	27	29	0	7	14	0	2	0	0
Bass, Benny	197	59	79	2	6	16	10	2	22	1
Bassey, Hogan	68	20	35	0	1	6	2	4	0	0
Battalino, Bat	88	24	34	0	3	24	1	1	0	1
Becerra, Joe	78	42	29	0	2	3	0	2	0	0
Belanger, Frenchie	62	13	24	0	7	15	1	2	0	0
Belloise, Mike	126	19	65	0	13	15	0	14	0	0
Benjamin, Joe	68	15	26	1	5	8	2	1	10	0
Benvenuti, Nino	90	35	42	5	1	4	0	3	0	0
Berg, Jackie Kid	197	59	89	14	9	18	0	8	0	0
Berlenbach, Paul	49	30	7	0	3	4	0	3	1	1
Bernstein, Jack	107	17	48	0	7	22	0	1	12	0
Bettina, Melio	99	36	46	0	3	10	0	3	1	0
Blackburn, Jack	103	22	15	1	12	1	0	2	50	0
Blitman, Harry	63	23	28	1	2	2	0	2	5	0
Bloom, Phil	175	15	27	1	11	18	1	3	99	0
Bogash, Lou	107	23	42	2	10	12	0	1	17	0
Bowen, Andy	26	7	11	0	6	0	0	1	1	0
Bowker, Joe	51	8	32	0	1	4	0	4	2	0
Braddock, Jim	85	26	25	0	3	20	0	2	7	2
Bratton, Johnny	86	32	27	0	3	21	0	3	0	0
Brennan, Bill	117	64	5	0	3	4	0	4	37	0
Britt, Jimmy	23	3	10	0	1	1	2	4	2	0
Britton, Jack	325	21	77	1	20	25	2	1	177	1
Broad, Kid	67	5	11	2	16	20	1	3	9	0
Brouillard, Lou	140	66	43	1	3	24	2	1	0	0
Brown, Jackie	129	36	58	3	7	17	4	4	0	0
Brown, Joe	160	48	56	0	12	2	1	9	0	2
Brown, Knockout	142	52	4	1	2	4	0	4	75	0
Brown, Newsboy	66	8	39	0	5	11	0	1	2	0
Brown, Panama Al	154	58	61	3	12	15	2	1	2	0
Buchanan, Ken	46	17	27	0	0	1	0	1	0	0
Buff, Johnny	94	13	15	0	4	9	0	7	45	1
Burns, Frankie	169	33	17	0	10	3	1	1	104	0
Burns, Tommy	60	36	10	0	8	4	0	1	1	0
Burrini, Salvatore	109	31	68	0	1	7	0	2	0	0
Caldwell, Johnny	28	13	12	0	0	1	0	2	0	0
Callahan, Mushy	60	18	25	0	4	10	0	2	1	0
Callura, Jackie	100	13	43	1	10	27	0	6	0	0
Campi, Eddie	102	19	45	0	8	5	0	2	22	1
Canzoneri, Tony	181	44	94	0	11	27	1	1	3	0
Carnera, Primo	99	66	18	2	0	5	1	6	0	1
Carney, Jem	10	0	7	0	2	0	1	0	0	0

	TB	KO	WD	WF	D	LD	LF	KO by	ND	NC
Carpentier, Georges	106	51	30	4	5	6	1	8	1	0
Carruthers, Jimmy	25	13	8	0	0	2	1	1	0	0
Carter, James	120	31	49	0	9	28	0	3	0	0
Carter, Kid	69	22	13	1	6	12	5	8	2	0
Castillo, Chucho	52	19	18	2	2	6	0	5	0	0
Cerdan, Marcel	113	66	43	0	0	1	2	1	0	0
Chambers, Arthur	14	9	1	1	2	0	0	1	0	0
Chandler, Tom	4	2	1	0	1	0	0	0	0	0
Chaney, Andy	133	17	51	1	11	13	0	4	36	0
Chaney, George KO	179	82	22	0	2	4	6	8	55	0
Charles, Ezzard	122	58	38	0	1	17	1	7	0	0
Chionoi, Chartchai	64	29	19	0	2	12	0	2	0	0
Chip, George	155	34	3	1	3	10	3	3	97	1
Chocolate, Kid	161	64	81	0	6	8	0	2	0	0
Choynski, Joe	77	25	22	3	6	4	0	0	6	1
Christoforidis, Anton	74	14	36	1	8	12	0	3	0	0
Clabby, Jimmy	155	40	37	2	20	16	1	4	34	1
Clark, Elky	44	20	9	0	4	10	0	1	0	0
Clay, Cassius (Muhammed Ali)	42	32	9	0	0	1	0	0	0	0
Cline, Jr. Patsy	100	16	5	1	1	0	1	4	71	1
Cochrane, Freddie	116	26	46	0	9	30	0	5	0	0
Coffey, Jim	62	34	1	0	1	0	0	4	22	0
Cohen, Robert	43	14	22	0	3	2	0	2	0	0
Cokes, Curtis	79	30	31	0	4	11	0	3	0	0
Collyer, Sam	15	0	9	0	1	4	0	1	0	0
Conley, Frankie	81	15	22	0	10	7	0	4	21	2
Conn, Billy	74	14	50	0	0	8	0	2	0	0
Corbett, James J.	33	9	11	0	6	1	1	3	2	0
Corbett, Young	104	34	19	0	12	6	0	8	25	0
Corbett III, Young	166	36	96	0	15	9	0	3	7	0
Coulon, Johnny	96	24	32	0	4	2	0	2	32	0
Cowler, Tom	73	37	7	1	1	3	2	2	10	0
Criqui, Eugene	115	40	54	0	8	11	0	12	0	0
Cross, Leach	154	25	16	2	2	5	1	4	99	0
Crouse, Buck	93	41	12	0	3	1	1	0	35	0
Cruz, Carlos Teo	57	13	29	0	2	10	1	2	0	0
Curtis, Dick	18	2	16	0	0	0	0	0	0	0
Dade, Harold	77	9	32	0	6	23	2	5	0	0
D'Agata, Mario	67	23	27	4	3	8	1	1	0	0
Darcy, Les	39	20	14	1	0	3	1	0	0	0
Delaney, Jack	86	42	27	1	3	7	0	3	2	1
Delmont, Al	157	38	55	1	35	11	0	0	17	0
DeMarco, Paddy	104	8	67	0	3	19	0	7	0	0
DeMarco, Tony	71	33	25	0	1	5	0	7	0	0
Dempsey, Jack	81	49	10	1	8	6	0	1	6	0
Dempsey, Nonpareil	68	8	40	0	8	1	0	2	4	0
Dillon, Jack	240	60	31	0	15	6	0	0	127	1
Dixie Kid	126	63	13	2	6	13	2	3	23	1
Dixon, George	150	30	47	1	37	21	1	4	9	0
Donovan, Mike	33	2	22	0	7	0	2	0	0	0
Downes, Terry	43	27	7	0	0	2	1	6	0	0
Downey, Bryan	118	18	19	0	14	8	1	0	57	1
Driscoll, Jim	71	27	25	1	6	0	1	1	10	0
Duffy, Paddy	36	14	9	1	11	0	0	1	0	0
Dundee, Joe	123	23	62	1	11	13	2	5	4	2
Dundee, Johnny	321	19	93	1	18	29	0	2	159	0
Dundee, Vince	150	27	85	0	13	18	0	1	5	1
Duran, Roberto	30	24	5	0	0	1	0	0	0	0
Ebihara, Hiroyuki	69	34	29	0	1	5	0	0	0	0
Elorde, Flash	80	23	39	0	2	24	0	2	0	0
Erne, Frank	40	10	11	1	12	2	0	4	0	0

	TB	KO	WD	WF	D	LD	LF	KO by	ND	NC
Ertle, Johnny	79	14	4	2	3	8	0	3	45	0
Escobar, Sixto	64	21	21	0	4	18	0	0	0	0
Famechon, Johnny	67	20	35	1	6	5	0	0	0	0
Farr, Tommy	104	23	48	0	11	18	1	3	0	0
Ferns, Jim	53	31	9	1	1	8	0	3	0	0
Fields, Jackie	84	28	41	1	2	8	0	1	2	1
Finnegan, Dick	68	16	36	0	2	8	0	1	5	0
Firpo, Luis	35	25	4	1	0	0	0	2	3	0
Fitzsimmons, Bob	41	23	5	0	1	0	1	6	5	0
Fitzsimmons, Young Bob	69	16	15	0	3	13	0	0	22	0
Fleming, Frankie	67	27	3	1	0	0	0	0	36	0
Flowers, Tiger	149	49	61	5	6	3	2	8	14	1
Flynn, Jim	113	39	12	3	15	7	1	15	21	0
Fogarty, Jack	20	8	11	0	0	0	0	1	0	0
Foley, Larry	22	16	1	0	4	0	0	0	1	0
Forbes, Clarence	79	19	24	1	20	9	1	5	0	0
Forbes, Harry	130	30	47	3	23	4	0	11	12	0
Foster, Bob	55	42	7	0	0	2	0	4	0	0
Fox, Tiger Jack	147	81	39	0	6	11	1	6	0	3
Frazier, Joe	29	25	4	0	0	0	0	0	0	0
Freeman, Tommy	185	69	75	0	17	13	0	3	8	0
Fullmer, Gene	64	24	31	0	3	4	0	2	0	0
Fulton, Fred	100	66	6	2	2	1	4	7	11	1
Galento, Tony	112	58	22	1	6	17	2	6	0	0
Gans, Joe	156	54	60	5	10	3	0	5	18	0
Garcia, Ceferino	116	57	24	0	9	20	1	5	0	0
Gardner, Billy	53	22	18	0	10	3	0	0	0	0
Gardner, George	65	19	20	2	10	5	1	5	2	1
Gavilan, Kid	143	27	79	0	6	30	0	0	0	1
Genaro, Frankie	129	19	59	5	9	16	2	4	15	0
Geoghegan, Owney	11	0	9	1	1	0	0	0	0	0
Giardello, Joey	133	32	68	0	7	21	0	4	1	0
Gibbons, Jack	41	14	22	0	1	4	0	0	0	0
Gibbons, Mike	127	38	23	1	4	3	0	0	58	0
Gibbons, Tom	106	47	10	0	1	2	1	1	43	1
Glover, Mike	92	18	13	1	2	4	0	0	53	0
Godfrey, George	26	8	3	0	9	0	2	4	0	0
Goldman, Charley	136	20	16	0	11	4	0	1	84	0
Goldstein, Abe	129	30	59	0	5	9	0	4	22	0
Goldstein, Ruby	55	34	16	0	0	0	0	5	0	0
Gomes, Harold	56	24	25	0	0	3	0	4	0	0
Goodrich, Jimmy	110	6	36	2	15	32	0	1	18	0
Graham, Bushy	127	37	63	1	6	11	1	2	6	0
Graves, Kid	157	35	24	3	28	3	1	1	62	0
Graziano, Rocky	83	52	14	1	6	7	0	3	0	0
Greb, Harry	290	46	64	1	3	5	0	2	168	1
Griffith, Emile	90	21	55	0	0	10	1	2	0	1
Griffo, Young	106	5	42	2	37	6	0	2	12	0
Grim, Joe	134	2	8	0	8	28	2	4	82	0
Halimi, Alphonse	50	21	19	1	1	5	0	3	0	0
Hamas, Steve	41	27	8	0	2	3	0	1	0	0
Harada, Masahiki	63	22	33	0	1	5	0	2	0	0
Harris, Harry	54	15	24	1	7	2	0	0	5	0
Hart, Marvin	48	20	4	5	4	3	0	4	8	0
Hawkins, Dal	54	16	17	1	8	3	1	7	1	0
Heeney, Tom	70	15	19	5	7	15	1	6	1	1
Herman, Pete	148	19	52	0	8	10	1	1	57	0
Hernandez, Carlos	71	39	17	0	4	6	0	5	0	0
Herrera, Aurelio	81	47	6	0	15	7	0	4	2	0
Herrera, Rafael	55	17	27	0	4	5	0	2	0	0
Hostak, Al	83	47	21	0	6	6	0	3	0	0

	TB	KO	WD	WF	D	LD	LF	KO by	ND	NC
Houck, Leo	212	21	137	0	11	8	1	0	34	0
Hudkins, Ace	76	18	31	1	5	10	2	1	7	1
Indrissano, Johnny	53	8	38	1	1	3	0	1	1	0
Jack, Beau	111	40	43	0	5	20	0	3	0	0
Jackson, Peter	38	12	16	1	3	1	0	2	1	2
Jackson, Willie	158	17	7	1	8	8	0	1	115	1
Jadick, Johnny	134	9	63	1	8	44	0	7	2	0
Jeannette, Joe	149	56	13	3	8	7	0	1	61	0
Jeby, Ben	73	22	32	0	4	12	0	2	0	1
Jeffra, Harry	120	27	66	0	7	17	0	2	0	1
Jeffries, Jim	23	16	4	0	2	0	0	1	0	0
Jenkins, Lew	109	47	19	0	5	26	0	12	0	0
Jofre, Eder	67	45	16	0	4	0	2	0	0	0
Johansson, Ingemar	28	17	8	1	0	0	0	2	0	0
Johnson, Harold	88	33	44	0	0	6	0	5	0	0
Johnson, Jack	113	44	30	4	14	1	1	5	14	0
Jones, Gorilla	141	53	44	0	13	21	2	0	5	3
Jordan, Don	75	17	33	0	1	20	0	3	1	0
Jurich, Jackie	82	8	53	0	7	7	0	7	0	0
Kane, Peter	95	51	33	1	2	3	0	4	0	1
Kansas, Rocky	165	32	32	0	7	8	2	3	81	0
Kaplan, Kid	131	17	84	0	10	9	1	3	7	0
Kelly, Hugo	76	17	18	0	24	7	0	4	6	0
Kelly, Spider	44	11	19	0	4	5	0	4	1	0
Kelly, Tommy	7	0	3	1	0	3	0	0	0	0
Ketchel, Stanley	61	46	3	0	4	2	0	2	4	0
Kilbane, Johnny	140	22	23	1	8	2	0	2	81	1
Kilrain, Jake	36	3	15	0	12	3	0	2	1	0
Kingpetcn, Pone	40	11	20	1	0	5	0	3	0	0
Klaus, Frank	89	25	20	4	2	2	0	2	34	0
Klick, Frankie	61	6	22	1	6	24	0	2	0	0
Klondike	7	1	0	0	2	1	0	2	1	0
Kramer, Danny	90	25	25	2	3	15	3	4	13	0
Krieger, Solly	111	53	27	0	7	21	0	3	0	0
LaBarba, Fidel	97	15	57	0	8	15	0	0	2	0
LaBlanche, George	62	16	12	0	6	11	2	14	1	1
Laguna, Ismael	74	36	28	0	1	9	0	0	0	0
LaMotta, Jake	106	30	53	0	4	15	0	4	0	0
Langford, Sam	247	98	37	1	31	19	0	4	58	2
Larkin, Tippy	151	57	79	0	1	3	0	10	0	1
Latzo, Pete	150	25	36	4	3	29	0	2	50	1
Lavigne, George	55	16	19	0	8	3	0	2	7	0
Ledoux, Charles	110	57	23	3	3	15	0	2	7	0
Lemos, Richie	77	26	25	0	3	20	3	0	0	0
Leon, Casper	99	29	33	1	22	8	2	3	1	0
Leonard, Benny	209	68	20	0	1	0	1	4	115	0
Lesnevich, Gus	76	21	36	0	5	9	0	5	0	0
Levinsky, Battling	272	25	40	1	13	13	2	4	174	0
Lewis, Harry	163	42	37	1	11	12	3	1	56	0
Lewis, John Henry	104	54	37	0	5	7	0	1	0	0
Lewis, Ted Kid	253	68	85	2	9	13	7	4	65	0
Lewis, Willie	155	57	24	0	14	7	0	9	44	0
Liston, Sonny	54	39	11	0	0	1	0	3	0	0
Loi, Duilio	125	25	89	1	7	3	0	0	0	0
Loughran, Tommy	172	18	77	1	8	21	0	2	45	0
Louis, Joe	71	54	13	1	0	1	0	2	0	0
Lynch, Benny	72	27	29	1	9	4	1	1	0	0
Lynch, Joe	134	29	13	0	15	13	0	0	64	0
McAuliffe, Jack	52	9	32	0	9	0	0	0	2	0
McCarthy, Cal	33	22	2	1	6	1	0	1	0	0
McCarty, Luther	25	16	0	0	0	0	0	1	8	0

	TB	KO	WD	WF	D	LD	LF	KO by	ND	NC
McCoy, Al	146	28	22	0	8	3	0	2	83	0
McCoy, Kid	105	35	45	1	9	2	0	4	9	0
McFarland, Packey	104	47	17	0	5	0	0	1	34	0
McGoorty, Eddie	128	41	24	0	10	7	2	6	38	0
McGovern, Hughey	33	4	11	1	3	0	0	0	14	0
McGovern, Terry	77	34	24	1	4	1	1	2	10	0
McGowan, Walter	40	14	18	0	1	3	0	4	0	0
McGraw, Phil	94	15	12	2	6	16	3	3	37	0
McLarnin, Jimmy	77	20	42	1	3	10	0	1	0	0
McPartland, Kid	94	23	40	0	13	8	3	3	4	0
McTigue, Mike	145	57	24	0	6	10	2	10	36	0
McVey, Sam	79	33	13	1	8	5	0	7	11	1
Macias, Raton	37	22	14	0	0	0	0	1	0	0
Maher, Peter	77	31	13	3	5	0	0	14	10	0
Malone, Jock	159	31	47	5	9	16	2	3	42	4
Maloney, Jim	66	24	24	2	1	4	3	7	1	0
Mandell, Sammy	168	28	53	1	8	11	1	5	60	1
Mandot, Joe	98	15	35	1	11	8	0	6	22	0
Mantell, Frank	101	23	14	1	18	13	1	5	25	1
Marciano, Rocky	49	43	6	0	0	0	0	0	0	0
Marino, Dado	74	21	35	1	3	11	0	3	0	0
Marino, Tony	40	7	19	0	2	10	0	2	0	0
Martin, Bob	101	87	0	0	1	5	1	2	5	0
Martin, Eddie	90	27	45	0	3	8	0	3	3	1
Mason, Frankie	212	45	19	0	11	4	0	5	127	1
Matthews, Matty	84	14	31	2	17	12	0	1	7	0
Maxim, Joey	115	21	61	0	4	27	1	1	0	0
Mellody, Honey	95	36	20	0	13	6	1	6	13	0
Miller, Freddie	237	43	156	2	5	23	2	1	4	1
Miller, Ray	111	31	43	1	4	23	2	0	7	0
Miller, Freddie	96	52	21	0	6	11	0	6	0	0
Miske, Billy	103	34	9	2	2	1	0	1	54	0
Mitchell, Charley	27	0	13	0	11	2	0	1	0	0
Mitchell, Pinky	79	9	2	1	4	7	1	4	50	1
Mitchell, Richie	79	10	3	0	2	2	0	6	54	2
Mitchell, Young	41	31	4	0	6	0	0	0	0	0
Moha, Bob	96	18	18	0	4	2	2	0	52	0
Monaghan, Rinty	51	19	22	1	1	6	1	1	0	0
Montana, Small	111	10	70	0	9	19	0	3	0	0
Montanez, Pedro	99	51	36	0	5	5	0	2	0	0
Montgomery, Bob	97	37	38	0	3	16	0	3	0	0
Montreal, Young	103	11	45	0	6	18	0	1	21	1
Monzon, Carlos	93	56	24	0	9	3	0	0	1	0
Moore, Archie	228	140	53	0	8	17	2	7	0	1
Moore, Davey	67	30	28	1	1	5	0	2	0	0
Moore, Mem. Pal	208	10	77	0	22	15	3	0	81	0
Moran, Chappie	9	1	5	0	0	2	0	1	0	0
Moran, Frank	60	24	8	2	2	6	0	5	13	0
Moran, Owen	106	25	37	0	6	10	5	2	21	0
Morgan, Tod	171	15	87	4	27	28	1	3	6	0
Morris, Carl	72	35	8	4	1	2	4	5	13	0
Murphy, Harlem Tommy	130	23	15	0	12	4	1	2	73	0
Murphy, Kid	70	24	14	0	16	4	1	3	14	0
Murphy, Torpedo Billy	90	17	32	0	14	15	0	9	1	2
Murphy, Harlem Tommy	131	23	15	0	13	4	1	2	73	0
Neil, Frankie	56	24	1	1	4	9	0	4	13	0
Nelson, Battling	132	38	20	1	19	15	2	2	35	0
Nichols, George	107	24	47	0	9	17	0	9	1	0
Nova, Lou	63	31	18	0	5	3	0	6	0	0
O'Brien, Phil. Jack	181	36	59	6	16	3	0	4	57	0
O'Dowd, Mike	115	35	16	1	3	7	0	1	52	0

	TB	KO	WD	WF	D	LD	LF	KO by	ND	NC
O'Gatty, Jimmy	47	22	5	0	1	7	0	4	7	1
O'Gatty, Packey	132	49	7	2	5	5	0	3	61	0
Olin, Bob	85	25	27	1	5	23	0	4	0	0
Olivares, Ruben	72	62	5	1	1	1	0	2	0	0
Olson, Bobo	109	42	49	0	2	9	0	7	0	0
Ortiz, Carlos	70	29	32	0	1	6	0	1	0	0
Ortiz, Manuel	122	45	47	0	3	26	0	1	0	0
Otto, Young	196	70	19	0	4	8	0	2	93	0
Overlin, Ken	147	23	103	0	7	12	0	1	0	1
Pace, George	42	15	18	0	2	5	0	1	1	0
Palmer, Pedlar	64	2	40	3	4	10	0	5	0	0
Palzer, Al	15	6	2	0	0	0	0	2	4	0
Papke, Billy	64	29	9	1	7	6	2	1	9	0
Paret, Bernardo	50	10	25	0	3	8	0	4	0	0
Pastrano, Willie	84	14	49	0	8	11	0	2	0	0
Paterson, Jackie	90	41	20	1	3	14	1	10	0	0
Patterson, Floyd	64	40	15	0	1	3	0	5	0	0
Paul, Tommy	113	28	48	2	9	20	3	2	1	0
Pelkey, Arthur	50	12	9	0	4	1	0	13	11	0
Pender, Paul	48	20	19	1	2	3	0	3	0	0
Pep, Willie	241	65	164	0	1	5	0	6	0	0
Perez, Pascual	91	56	27	0	1	4	0	3	0	0
Perez, Young	131	26	62	1	16	19	0	7	0	0
Perkins, Eddie	54	12	29	0	1	11	0	1	0	0
Petrolle, Billy	157	63	22	4	10	17	0	3	37	1
Pinder, Enrique	40	14	22	0	2	0	0	2	0	0
Pladner, Spider	122	34	61	1	10	11	2	3	0	0
Plimmer, Billy	38	8	17	0	5	4	0	1	3	0
Puryear, Earl	190	22	72	0	29	20	1	0	46	0
Ramos, Armundo	39	20	13	0	0	3	1	2	0	0
Ramos, Ultiminio	65	39	14	1	4	2	1	4	0	0
Reagan, Johnny	17	12	0	0	3	2	0	0	0	0
Reich, Al	29	15	0	0	1	2	0	6	5	0
Renault, Jack	86	32	25	1	1	14	2	2	7	2
Risko, Eddie	51	7	20	0	6	9	0	9	0	0
Risko, Johnny	128	21	44	0	5	34	7	2	15	0
Ritchie, Willie	71	8	27	1	4	8	0	1	22	0
Rivers, Joe	67	15	13	3	8	11	1	5	11	0
Robinson, Ray	202	109	66	0	6	8	0	1	1	1
Rodak, Leo	117	6	74	0	10	22	0	5	0	0
Rodel, Geo. Boer	42	11	7	3	2	0	1	7	11	0
Rodriguez, Luis	121	49	57	1	0	10	0	3	0	0
Rooke, George	7	1	1	0	1	1	1	2	0	0
Root, Jack	53	24	17	3	5	0	0	3	1	0
Rose, Lionel	47	11	29	0	0	4	0	3	0	0
Rosenberg, Charley	64	7	28	1	6	14	1	0	7	0
Rosenberg, Dave	57	9	30	0	4	6	3	0	5	0
Rosenbloom, Maxie	289	18	187	5	23	33	0	2	19	2
Rosner, Johnny	77	7	4	0	1	4	1	2	58	0
Ross, Barney	82	24	50	0	3	4	0	0	1	0
Routis, Andre	86	10	33	11	7	17	6	2	0	0
Ruhlin, Gus	42	16	10	0	2	3	0	3	8	0
Ryan, Tommy	109	48	37	1	9	1	1	1	11	0
Saddler, Sandy	162	103	41	0	2	14	1	1	0	0
Salas, Lauro	148	39	44	0	12	44	1	7	1	0
Saldivar, Vicente	38	25	10	1	0	0	1	1	0	0
Salica, Lou	90	13	49	0	11	16	0	1	0	0
Salvarria, Erbito	42	8	25	0	3	5	0	1	0	0
Sam, Young Dutch	11	0	11	0	0	0	0	0	0	0
Sanchez, Clemente	51	27	12	0	3	8	0	1	0	0
Sands, Dave	104	62	31	0	1	7	0	1	0	2

	TB	KO	WD	WF	D	LD	LF	KO by	ND	NC
Sangchilli, Baltazar	77	24	33	2	5	11	1	1	0	0
Sarron, Petey	103	18	56	1	8	15	3	1	1	0
Saxton, Johnny	66	21	33	1	2	4	0	5	0	0
Scalzo, Petey	111	46	43	0	6	12	0	3	1	0
Schaaf, Ernie	94	40	32	0	2	11	1	1	7	0
Schmeling, Max	71	39	14	3	5	5	0	5	0	0
Schwartz, Izzy	117	7	51	1	12	27	0	1	18	0
Scott, Phil	81	28	28	6	4	5	0	8	0	2
Seddons, George	6	5	0	0	1	0	0	0	0	0
Servo, Marty	56	15	34	0	2	2	0	2	1	0
Shade, Dave	149	10	83	0	12	15	1	1	26	1
Sharkey, Jack (H)	55	15	20	3	3	8	1	4	1	0
Sharkey, Jack (B)	168	4	8	2	15	15	0	0	115	0
Sharkey, Tom	54	37	1	2	5	3	1	2	3	0
Shaw, Battling	23	4	9	0	0	7	0	3	0	0
Shibata, Kuniaki	44	22	15	0	3	0	0	3	0	0
Shirai, Yoshio	42	15	20	0	1	4	0	2	0	0
Shugrue, Johnny	54	7	37	0	2	5	1	0	2	0
Shugrue, Young	88	16	5	0	1	5	0	0	61	0
Siki, Battling	74	29	25	0	1	10	1	1	6	1
Singer, Al	70	24	34	2	2	4	0	4	0	0
Slattery, Jimmy	128	45	62	2	1	9	0	5	2	2
Slavin, Frank	37	16	9	0	4	2	0	4	2	0
Smith, Gunboat	131	40	15	1	7	8	1	11	48	0
Smith, Jeff	178	46	51	2	3	8	1	1	65	1
Smith, Midget	78	5	28	1	4	19	0	0	21	0
Smith, Mys. Billy	82	13	15	2	28	4	10	4	6	0
Smith, Solly	45	6	13	1	17	3	2	1	2	0
Smith, Wallace	60	18	14	0	6	15	0	7	0	0
Soose, Billy	41	13	21	0	1	6	0	0	0	0
Stanley, Digger	66	10	36	0	6	10	1	1	2	0
Steele, Freddie	95	38	46	0	5	2	0	3	0	1
Stribling, Young	286	126	93	3	14	9	2	1	36	2
Suggs, Chick	168	37	72	2	10	31	4	4	8	0
Sullivan, Dave	59	10	16	2	16	8	3	2	2	0
Sullivan, J. Twin	138	20	32	1	41	10	2	6	26	0
Sullivan, John L.	75	16	15	0	3	0	0	1	40	0
Sullivan, M. Twin	69	18	17	0	14	3	0	4	13	0
Sullivan, Steve (Kid)	110	13	18	2	11	13	1	4	48	0
Taylor, Bud	159	35	34	1	6	16	3	4	60	0
Tendler, Lew	168	37	22	0	2	7	3	1	94	1
Terranova, Phil	99	29	38	0	11	18	0	3	0	0
Terris, Sid	107	12	70	3	4	7	1	4	6	0
Thil, Marcel	96	34	40	4	4	12	0	2	0	0
Thomas, Joe	50	17	7	0	3	5	0	6	12	0
Thompson, Johnny	139	47	34	3	20	18	5	1	11	0
Thompson, Yg. Jack	66	31	15	0	3	16	0	0	1	0
Tiger, Dick	81	26	35	0	3	16	0	1	0	0
Torres, Efren	58	31	17	0	1	6	0	3	0	0
Torres, Jose	45	29	12	0	1	2	0	1	0	0
Toweel Vic	32	14	13	1	1	1	0	2	0	0
Tunney, Gene	76	41	14	1	1	1	0	0	17	1
Turpin, Randy	75	45	17	4	1	3	0	5	0	0
Uzcudun, Paulino	70	31	18	1	3	14	2	1	0	0
Villa, Pancho	103	22	49	0	4	4	1	0	23	0
Walcott, Joe	150	34	45	2	30	17	3	4	15	0
Walcott, Jersey Joe	67	30	18	1	1	11	0	6	0	0
Walker, Mickey	148	58	35	0	4	11	2	5	32	1
Walsh, Jimmy	120	12	39	1	18	8	0	1	41	0
Ward, Georgie	113	26	15	1	1	14	1	3	51	1
Weinert, Charley	78	23	9	4	1	1	1	7	32	0

	TB	KO	WD	WF	D	LD	LF	KO by	ND	NC
Weir, Ike	41	12	17	0	8	2	0	1	1	0
Wells, Bomb. Billy	49	33	4	0	0	0	1	11	0	0
Wells, Matt	75	7	18	2	2	13	1	3	28	1
Welsh, Freddie	167	24	50	3	7	3	0	1	79	0
White, Charley	169	51	28	1	8	13	0	3	64	1
Wilde, Jimmy	140	77	48	1	2	1	0	3	8	0
Willard, Jess	36	20	4	0	1	3	1	2	5	0
Williams, Ike	153	60	64	0	5	18	0	6	0	0
Williams, Kid	204	48	53	6	7	8	6	3	73	0
Wills, Harry	102	45	17	0	2	1	3	4	27	3
Wilson, Jackie	120	17	55	2	5	33	1	5	1	1
Wilson, Johnny	122	43	20	1	2	17	2	2	34	1
Wolgast, Ad	135	38	21	1	14	6	4	2	49	0
Wolgast, Midget	147	11	85	0	15	29	0	6	1	0
Wright, Chalky	140	57	45	0	5	27	0	5	0	1
Yanger, Benny	84	25	25	1	20	5	0	5	3	0
Yarosz, Teddy	127	16	90	0	3	17	0	1	0	0
Zale, Tony	88	46	24	0	2	12	0	4	0	0
Zivic, Eddie	85	18	24	0	5	30	0	8	0	0
Zivic, Fritzie	230	80	74	1	10	61	0	4	0	0
Zivic, Jack	132	33	58	1	4	23	2	1	10	0
Zivic, Pete	151	46	61	0	10	16	1	5	12	0
Zulu Kid, Yg.	100	9	4	1	10	10	1	3	62	0
Zurita, Juan	85	22	50	0	1	9	0	3	0	0

LEGEND: TB—Total Bouts; KO—Knockouts Scored, WD—Decisions Won; WF—Fights Won on Fouls; D—Draws; LD—Decisions Lost; LF—Fights Lost on Fouls; KO By—Knocked Out by Opponent; ND—No Decision; NC—No Contest.

POLICE STOPPED: Bouts which were stopped by the police with no decision rendered were fought by the following fighters. (Two each) Nonpareil Jack Dempsey, Johnny Kilbane; (One each) Arthur Chambers, Joe Dundee, Joe Gans, George LeBlanche, Battling Nelson, Jack Root, Tommy Ryan and Kid Williams.

Nonpareil Jack Dempsey failed to stop opponents, per agreement, in four bouts. They are listed as "no decision" bouts.

Gene Tunney's totals do not include A.E.F. bouts.

Original Joe Walcott's totals do not include all-comers tour, 1893.

Marciano's Undefeated Record

Rocky Marciano had a unique record as a professional fighter. He engaged in 49 fights and won all, including 6 heavyweight title defenses, before retiring on April 27, 1956. Here is his record:

1947

March 17—Lee Epperson ....KO 3

1948

July 12—Harry Balzerian ....KO 1
July 19—John Edwards ....KO 1
Aug. 9—Bobby Quinn ....KO 3
Aug. 23—Eddie Ross ....KO 1
Aug. 30—Jimmy Weeks ....KO 1
Sept. 13—Jerry Jackson ....KO 1
Sept. 20—Bill Hardeman ....KO 1
Sept. 30—Gil Cardione ....KO 1
Oct. 4—Bob Jefferson ....KO 2
Nov. 29—Patrick Connolly ....KO 1
Dec. 14—Gilley Ferron ....KO 2

1949

March 31—Johnny Pretzie ....KO 5
March 28—Artie Donato ....KO 1
April 11—James Walls ....KO 3
May 2—Jimmy Evans ....KO 3
May 23—Don Mogard ....W 10
July 18—Harry Haft ....KO 3
Aug. 16—Pete Louthis ....KO 3
Sept. 26—Tommy DiGiorgio ....KO 4
Oct. 10—Ted Lowry ....W 10
Nov. 7—Joe Domonic ....KO 2
Dec. 2—Pat Richards ....KO 2
Dec. 19—Phil Muscato ....KO 5
Dec. 30—Carmine Vingo ....KO 6

1950

March 24—Roland LaStarza ....W 10
June 5—Eldridge Eatman ....KO 3
July 10—Gino Buonvino ....KO 10
Sept. 18—Johnny Shkor ....KO 6
Nov. 13—Ted Lowry ....W 10
Dec. 18—Bill Wilson ....KO 1

1951

Jan. 29—Keene Simmons .... KO 8
March 20—Harold Mitchell .... KO 2
March 26—Art Henri .... KO 9
April 30—Red Applegate .... W 10
July 12—Rex Layne .... KO 6
Aug. 27—Freddie Beshore .... KO 4
Oct. 26—Joe Louis .... KO 8

1952

Feb. 13—Lee Savold .... KO 6
April 21—Gino Buonvino .... KO 2
May 12—Bernie Reynolds .... KO 3
July 28—Harry Matthews .... KO 2
*Sept. 23—Jersey Joe Walcott .... KO 13

1953

May 15—Jersey Joe Walcott .... KO 1
Sept. 24—Roland LaStarza .... KO 11
*Won world heavyweight title.

1954

June 17—Ezzard Charles .... W 15
Sept. 17—Ezzard Charles .... KO 8

1955

May 16—Don Cockell .... KO 9
Sept. 21—Archie Moore .... KO 9

Professional Record of Joe Louis

1934

July 4—Jack Kracken, Chicago .... KO 1
July 11—Willie Davis, Chicago .... KO 3
July 29—Larry Udell, Chicago .... KO 2
Aug. 13—Jack Kranz, Chicago .... W 6
Aug. 27—Buck Everett, Chicago ...... KO 2
Sept. 11—Alex Borchuk, Detroit ...... KO 4
Sept. 25—Rudolph Wiater, Chicago .... W 10
Oct. 24—Art Sykes, Chicago .... KO 8
Oct. 30—Jack O'Dowd, Detroit .... KO 2
Nov. 14—Stanley Poreda, Chicago ..... KO 1
Nov. 30—Charley Massera, Chicago .... KO 3
Dec. 14—Lee Ramage, Chicago .... KO 8

1935

Jan. 4—Patsy Perroni, Detroit .... W 10
Jan. 11—Hans Birkie, Pittsburgh ...... KO 10
Feb. 21—Lee Ramage, Los Angeles .... KO 2
Mar. 8—Donald Barry, San Francisco .. KO 3
Mar. 28—Natie Brown, Detroit .... W 10
Apr. 13—Roy Lazer, Chicago .... KO 3
Apr. 24—Biff Benton, Dayton .... KO 2
Apr. 27—Roscoe Toles, Flint .... KO 6
May 3—Willie Davis, Peoria .... KO 2
May 5—Gene Stanton, Kalamazoo ..... KO 3
June 25—Primo Carnera,
    Yankee Stadium .... KO 6
Aug. 7—King Levinsky, Chicago ...... KO 1
Sept. 24—Max Baer, Yankee Stadium .. KO 4
Dec. 13—Paulino Uzcudum, Madison
    Square Garden .... KO 4

1936

Jan. 17—Charley Retzlaff, Chicago .... KO 1
June 19—Max Schmeling, Yankee
    Stadium .... KO by 12
Aug. 17—Jack Sharkey, Yankee Stadium KO 3
Sept. 22—Al Ettore, Philadelphia ..... KO 5
Oct. 9—Jorge Brescia, Madison Square
    Garden .... KO 3
Dec. 14—Eddie Simms, Cleveland ..... KO 1

1937

Jan. 11—Stanley Ketchel, Buffalo ..... KO 2
Jan. 27—Bob Pastor, Madison Square
    Garden .... W 10
Feb. 17—Natie Brown, Kansas City .... KO 4
June 22—James J. Braddock, Chicago .. KO 8
   (Won heavyweight championship of the world)
Aug. 30—Tommy Farr, Yankee Stadium W 15

1938

Feb. 23—Nathan Mann, Madison Square
    Garden .... KO 3
Apr. 1—Harry Thomas, Chicago .... KO 5
June 22-Max Schmeling, Yankee Stadium KO 1

                              KO 1

1939

Jan. 25—John Henry Lewis, Madison Sq.
    Garden .... KO 1
Apr. 17—Jack Roper, Los Angeles ... KO 1
June 28—Tony Galento, Yankee Stadium KO 4
Sept. 20—Bob Pastor, Detroit ...... KO 11

1940

Feb. 9—Arturo Godoy, Madison Square
    Garden .... W 15
Mar. 29—Johnny Paychek, Madison Square
    Garden .... KO 2
June 20—Arturo Godoy, Yankee Stadium KO 8
Dec. 16—Al McCoy, Boston .... KO 6

1941

Jan. 31—Red Burman, Madison Square
    Garden .... KO 5
Feb. 17—Gus Dorazio, Philadelphia .. KO 2
Mar. 21—Abe Simon, Detroit ...... KO 13
Apr. 8—Tony Musto, St. Louis ..... KO 9
May 23—Buddy Baer, Washington, D.C. W disq. 7
June 18—Billy Conn, Polo Grounds .. KO 13
Sept. 29—Lou Nova, Polo Grounds .. KO 6

1942

Jan. 9—Buddy Baer, Madison Square
    Garden .... KO 1
Mar. 27—Abe Simon, Madison Square
    Garden .... KO 6

1946

June 19—Billy Conn, Yankee Stadium KO 8
Sept. 18-Tami Mauriello, Yankee Stadium KO 1

1947

Dec. 5—Joe Walcott, Madison Square
Garden . . . .   W 15

1948

June 25—Joe Walcott, Yankee Stadium   KO 11

1950

Sept. 27—Ezzard Charles, Yankee Stadium L 15
(title bout)
Nov. 29—Cesar Brion, Chicago . . . . .   W 10

1951

Jan. 3—Freddie Beshore, Detroit . . . .   KO   4
Feb. 7—Omelio Agramonte, Miami, Fla.   W 10
Feb. 23—Andy Walker, San Francisco   KO 10
May 2—Omelio Agramonte, Detroit . .   W 10
June 15—Lee Savold, Madison Square
Garden . . . .   KO   6
Aug. 1—Cesar Brion, San Francisco . .   W 10
Aug. 15—Jimmy Bivins, Baltimore . . .   W 10
Oct. 26—Rocky Marciano, Madison Square
Garden . . . . KO by 8

Recapitulation—bouts, 71; knockouts, 54;
decisions, 13; knocked out by, 2; lost, 1.

Champion Earners

Three heavyweight champions earned over
$2,000,000 directly with their fists, and a fourth
—John L. Sullivan—grossed well beyond
$1,000,000, thanks to his prize ring fame.

The "Golden Trio" is made up of Joe Louis,
Jack Dempsey and Gene Tunney, in that order,
while Max Schmeling made the record for a
foreign fighter.

Joe Louis

Louis made his fortune the hard way, by
piling it up slowly through a long succession of
fights, whereas Dempsey gathered in over
$2,500,000 for six fights, and Tunney earned
over $1,700,000 in three ring appearances.

Louis, who turned professional in 1934 and
was paid $50 for his first contest, engaged in 12
contests and grossed a mere $4,757 that year.
For 14 fights in 1935, including meetings with
Primo Carnera, Max Baer and other "name"
fighters, he received $426,175.

Prior to joining the Armed Forces, the biggest
sum paid to Louis for any battle was $349,228,
for his second meeting with Max Schmeling in
1938. After the war, Louis hit the jackpot when
he knocked out Billy Conn, in 8 rounds, and was
paid $625,916. In his other excursion in 1946,
he received $103,611 for knocking out Tami
Mauriello in the first round. The earnings from
that bout put him in front of Dempsey who, up
to that time, was the champion purse winner in
fistic history.

It is interesting to note that when Louis failed
to regain the title in his "comeback" fight against
Ezzard Charles at the Yankee Stadium, New
York on Sept. 27, 1950, the attendance was only
13,561 and receipts $205,370, of which Louis
received $53,908.

Louis' ring earnings follow:

1934	$ 4,757
1935	426,175
1936	281,838
1937	253,262
1938	406,409
1939	301,995
1940	117,455
1941	471,892
1942	111,082
1943—45 (in service)	
1946 (2 fights)	729,527
1947 (1 fight)	75,968
1948 (1 fight)	252,522
1950 (2 fights)	63,908
1951 (8 fights)	302,869
Total	$3,799,659

Earnings from exhibition tours, radio and television commitments amounted to about
$500,000 from 1946 through 1952. Louis' com-
plete earnings estimated as $4,299,659.

Jack Dempsey

Jack Dempsey was a fighter for about 6 years
before winning the title from Jess Willard in
Toledo in 1919. But his earnings through those
years were relatively small and did not gross
more than $100,000.

In 9 fights from 1919 to 1927 he made
$2,712,079. After being beaten by Tunney a
second time, Dempsey retired, but later changed
his mind and made a "comeback" tour which
ended in Chicago, when he fared none too well
against Battling Levinsky. Dempsey appeared in
exhibitions up to 1940, or thereabouts.

However, Dempsey, unlike Louis and Tunney,
cashed in richly on his fistic popularity by picking up at least $3,000,000, in addition to his
actual fight earnings, by acting as referee at boxing and wrestling bouts or making public appearances of one kind or another—master of
ceremonies, etc.

Dempsey's earnings follow:

Prior to 1919	$100,000*
1919—Jess Willard	27,500
1920—Billy Miske	55,000
1920—Bill Brennan	100,000
1921—Georges Carpentier	300,000
1923—Tom Gibbons	265,000
1923—Luis Firpo	470,000
1926—Gene Tunney	718,868
1927—Jack Sharkey	350,711
1927—Gene Tunney	425,000

Comeback tour (1930–31) 250,000*

Total	$3,062,079
Earnings as referee, etc.	3,000,000
	$6,062,079

*Estimated.

Gene Tunney

Although Gene Tunney had more than 60 fights, before meeting Dempsey in 1926, his grand total of earnings was comparatively small. It perhaps was not more than $225,000. He never fought after winning from Tom Heeney in 1928.

Tunney's earnings:

Prior to 1926	$ 225,000
1926–Dempsey	200,000
1927–Dempsey	990,445
1928–Heeney	525,000
Total	$1,940,445

John L. Sullivan

John L. Sullivan earned $1,221,320 during his lifetime, but only a small part of it came through actual ring efforts. His biggest share for any fight was $14,000 when he took on Herbert Slade, in New York, 3 rounds, in 1883. His money prior to 1882, when he won the title by whipping Paddy Ryan, as listed in Nat Fleischer's "All-Time Ring Record Book" totalled $3,320 for six fights. Fleischer gives Sullivan's complete ring earnings with his fists as follows:

Prior to 1882	$ 3,320
1882–Paddy Ryan	5,000
1882–Jim Elliot	1,100
1882–Tug Wilson	12,000
1883–Charlie Mitchell	11,000
1883–Herbert Slade	14,000
1884–Dominick McCafferey	1,800
1884–John M. Lafflin	9,200
1884–Al Greenfield	6,800
1885–Al Greenfield	5,500
1885–Paddy Ryan	7,900
1885–Jack Burke	4,300
1885–Dominick McCafferey	8,500
1886–Frank Herald	2,300
1886–Paddy Ryan	6,500
1886–Duncan McDonald	2,800
1887–Patsy Cardiff	3,750
1888–Charlie Mitchell	4,000
1889–Jake Kilrain	10,500
1892–James J. Corbett	*
Total	$ 120,270
Theatrical tours and lecture tours .	1,101,050
	$1,221,320

*Fight was for $25,000 purse and side bets of $10,000 on winner-take-all basis. Sullivan lost.

Sullivan's tremendous popularity brought him big money when he went on his various tours, during some of which he took on all comers, offering $100, and later $500 to anyone he didn't knock out in four rounds; in others he was the star of some theatrical production, the best remembered being "Honest Hearts and Willing Hands," which was featured in 1891.

The first Sullivan tour in 1882–1883, with Billy Madden as manager, grossed $105,000. The richest was that of 1883–1884, when Sullivan earned $195,000. The other extremely successful tours, as shown in Fleischer's book, were 1886–1887, tour of England, $110,000; 1887, American tour, $62,000; 1890, tour, $27,000; 1891, Australian tour (August and September), $58,000; 1891, tour, "Honest Hearts and Willing Hands," $87,000; 1893–1894, tour, $45,500; 1895, tour, "East and West," $85,900; 1896, tour, $91,000; 1897, tour, $42,000; 1898, tour, $25,300.

From 1899 until 1916, Sullivan devoted the major portion of his time to vaudeville work and earned approximately $141,000. He died with very little of his vast earnings remaining.

Max Schmeling

Max Schmeling of Germany gathered in more American boxing dollars than any other foreigner, and only four Americans—Louis, Dempsey, Tunney and Sullivan—exceeded his total. Additionally, Schmeling made money through his fights in Europe, his exhibitions there and his showing of American-made films of his battles. He was the greatest harvester of all foreign fighters.

It is possible that Schmeling, who started on the road to fame by knocking out Johnny Risko, the "Rubber Man," in 1929, after being on the verge of a knockout defeat himself, picked up about $1,640,000 for his fights, including $160,000 in exhibitions, etc.

The two Jack Sharkey fights enriched him $356,750 ($182,750 and $174,000); the two Louis fights added close to $350,000. The Bill Stribling battle earned him $125,000; Mickey Walker, $54,000; Max Baer, $75,000; Paulino Uzcudun, $75,000, and so on. Nice pay for a man who, arriving in the United States in 1928, received $1,000 for his first fight and fought his last battle in an American ring against Louis in 1938.

Ring battles in the U.S. (1928 to 1939, inc.)	$1,100,000
Fight pictures (shown in Europe) .	80,000
Exhibition tours (U.S.)	160,000
Exhibitions and fights (in Europe) .	200,000
Earned after 1945	100,000
Total	$1,640,000

The Ring Magazine Merit Award

Since 1928, *The Ring* magazine has awarded a medal of gold and silver to "The Fighter of the Year," selected on the basis of his contribution to the skill and science to the sport, his sportsmanship and reputation. The selections:

1928—Gene Tunney
1929—Tommy Loughran
1930—Max Schmeling
1931—Tommy Loughran
1932—Jack Sharkey
1933—No award
1934—Barney Ross and Tony Canzoneri
1935—Barney Ross
1936—Joe Louis
1937—Henry Armstrong
1938—Joe Louis
1939—Joe Louis
1940—Billy Conn
1941—Joe Louis
1942—Ray Robinson
1943—Fred Apostoli
1944—Beau Jack
1945—Willie Pep
1946—Tony Zale
1947—Gus Lesnevich
1948—Ike Williams
1949—Ezzard Charles
1950—Ezzard Charles
1951—Ray Robinson
1952—Rocky Marciano
1953—Carl (Bobo) Olson
1954—Rocky Marciano
1955—Rocky Marciano
1956—Floyd Patterson
1957—Carmen Basilio
1958—Ingemar Johansson
1959—Ingemar Johansson
1960—Floyd Patterson
1961—Joe Brown
1962—Dick Tiger
1963—Cassius Clay
1964—Emile Griffith
1965—Dick Tiger
1966—No award
1967—Joe Frazier
1968—Nino Benvenuti
1969—Jose Napoles
1970—Joe Frazier
1971—Joe Frazier
1972—Cassius Clay (Muhammad Ali),
    Carlos Monzon (tie)

Boxing Hall of Fame

In 1954, *The Ring* instituted Boxing's Hall of Fame. The hall is located in *The Ring* Museum, Madison Square Garden, New York, N.Y. Annual selections are made in three groups—Pioneer, Old-Timers and Modern. The selections:

Pioneer

James Figg, Heavyweight
John Jackson, Heavyweight
Daniel Mendoza, Heavyweight
John Morrisey, Heavyweight
Tom Hyer, Heavyweight
Arthur Chambers, Lightweight
Jack McAuliffe, Lightweight
Tom Cribb, Heavyweight
Jem Mace, Heavyweight
John C. Heenan, Heavyweight
Jack Broughton, Heavyweight
Tom Sayers, Heavyweight
Young Griffo, Featherweight
John L. Sullivan, Heavyweight
Jack Dempsey, Middleweight
William Richmond, Heavyweight
William Thompson (Bendigo), Heavyweight
Peter Jackson, Heavyweight
Charley Mitchell, Heavyweight
Tom Molineaux, Heavyweight
John Gully, Heavyweight
Dan Donnelly, Heavyweight
Tom Spring, Heavyweight
Ned Price, Heavyweight
Jem Ward, Heavyweight
Sam Collyer, Lightweight
Jake Kilrain, Heavyweight
James (Deaf) Burke, Heavyweight
Barney Young Aaron, Lightweight
    and Welterweight
Jacob Hyer, Heavyweight
Joe Goss, Heavyweight
Professor Mike Donovan, Middleweight
Nobby Clark, Featherweight
Tom Chandler, Middleweight

Old-Timers

Stanley Ketchel, Middleweight
Jack Johnson, Heavyweight
James J. Jeffries, Heavyweight
Bob Fitzsimmons, Heavyweight
Joe Gans, Lightweight
James J. Corbett, Heavyweight
Terry McGovern, Featherweight
Abe Attell, Featherweight
Sam Langford, Middleweight
Joe Walcott, Welterweight
Jem Driscoll, Featherweight
George Dixon, Featherweight and Bantamweight
Les Darcy, Middleweight
Packy MacFarland, Lightweight
Kid McCoy, Welterweight
Battling Nelson, Lightweight
Mike Gibbons, Welterweight
Tommy Ryan, Middleweight
Ad Wolgast, Lightweight
Jimmy Wilde, Flyweight
Tom Sharkey, Heavyweight
Jack Dillon, Light Heavyweight
George Lavigne, Lightweight

Pete Herman, Bantamweight
Johnny Kilbane, Featherweight
Joe Choynski, Heavyweight
Freddie Welsh, Lightweight
Tommy Burns, Heavyweight
Pancho Villa, Flyweight
Jack Root, Light Heavyweight
Willie Ritchie, Lightweight
Tommy Gibbons, Light Heavyweight
Georges Carpentier, Light Heavyweight
Ted (Kid) Lewis, Welterweight
Johnny Coulon, Bantamweight
Owen Moran, Featherweight, England
Young Corbett II, Featherweight
Battling Levinsky, Light Heavyweight
Joe Jeannette, Heavyweight
Philadelphia Jack O'Brien, Light Heavyweight
Leo Houck, Middleweight
Jeff Smith, Middleweight
Kid Williams, Bantamweight
Harry Willis, Heavyweight
Tiger Flowers, Middleweight
Paul Berlenbach, Light Heavyweight
Billy Papke, Middleweight
Fidel Labarba, Featherweight

Modern

Jack Dempsey, Heavyweight
Joe Louis, Heavyweight
Henry Armstrong, Featherweight, Lightweight
   and Welterweight
Harry Greb, Middleweight
Gene Tunney, Heavyweight
Benny Leonard, Lightweight
Mickey Walker, Welterweight and Middleweight
Tony Canzoneri, Lightweight
Jimmy McLarnin, Welterweight
Barney Ross, Welterweight
Tommy Loughran, Light Heavyweight
Johnny Dundee, Featherweight
Tony Zale, Middleweight
Rocky Marciano, Heavyweight
Kid Chocolate, Featherweight
Jack Britton, Welterweight
Lew Tendler, Lightweight
Billy Petrolle, Lightweight
Marcel Cerdan, Middleweight
Willie Pep, Featherweight
Lou Ambers, Lightweight
James J. Braddock, Heavyweight
Billy Conn, Light Heavyweight
Kid Gavilan, Welterweight
Archie Moore, Light Heavyweight
Ray Robinson, Middleweight
Max Baer, Heavyweight
Jersey Joe Walcott, Heavyweight
Carmen Basilio, Middleweight and Welterweight
Max Schmeling, Heavyweight
Ezzard Charles, Heavyweight
Rocky Graziano, Middleweight
Sandy Saddler, Featherweight

Maxie Rosenbloom, Light Heavyweight
Beau Jack, Lightweight
Fritzi Zivic, Welterweight

Ring Names—Real Names

Lou Ambers—Louis D'Ambrosio
Sammy Angott—Samuel Engotti
Henry Armstrong—Henry Jackson
Hogan Kid Bassey—Okon Bassey Asuquo
Battling Battalino—Christopher Battalino
Joe Becerra—Jose Covarrubias
Bendigo—William Thompson
Jackie (Kid) Berg—Judah Bergman
Jack Bernstein—John Dodick
Joe Bowker—Tommy Mahon
Bill Brennan—William Brenner
Jack Britton—William Breslin
Knockout Brown—Valentine Braun
Johnny Buff—John Lesky
Tommy Burns—Noah Brusso
Mushy Callahan—Vincent Scheer
Chucho Castillo—Jesus Aguillera
Andy Chaney—Andrew Kwasnick
George Chip—George Chipulonis
Kid Chocolate—Eligio Sardinias
Bert Colima—Ephram Romero
Eddie Coulon—Edgar Francois
Young Corbett—William Rothwell
Young Corbett III—Ralph Giordano
Leach Cross—Louis Wallach
Jack Delaney—Ovila Chapdelaine
Tony DeMarco—Leonard Liotta
Jack Dempsey—William Harrison Dempsey
Jack (Nonpareil) Dempsey—John Kelly
Jack Dillon—Ernest Cutler Price
Dixie Kid—Aaron L. Brown
Carl Duane—Carl Yacconetti
Joe Dundee—Samuel Lazzaro
Johnny Dundee—Joseph Carrora
Vince Dundee—Vincent Lazzaro
Wildcat Ferns—Clarence McCubbins
Jackie Fields—Jacob Finkelstein
Tiger Flowers—Theo Flowers
"Fireman" Jim Flynn—Andrew Haymes
Joe Gans—Joseph Gaines
Kid Gavilan—Gerardo Gonzalez
Frankie Genaro—Frank Di Gennara
Joey Giardello—Carmine Tillelli
Jimmy Goodrich—James E. Moran
Bud Gorman—Earl Lovejay
Bushy Graham—Angelo Geraci
Rocky Graziano—Rocco Barbelo
Joe Grim—Saverio Giannone
Pete Herman—Peter Gulotta
Ben Hogan—Benediel Hagen
Beau Jack—Sidney Walker
Willie Jackson—Oscar Tobler
Ben Jeby—Morris Jebaltowski
Harry Jeffra—Ignazio Guiffi
Lew Jenkins—Verlin Jenks
Jack Johnson—John Arthur Johnson

Tom Johnson—Thomas Jackling
Gorilla Jones—William Jones
Rocky Kansas—Rocco Tozzo
Stanley Ketchel—Stanislaus Kiecal
George LaBlanche—George Blais
Benny Leonard—Benjamin Leiner
Battling Levinsky—Barney Lebrowitz
Ted (Kid) Lewis—Gershon Mendeloff
Joe Louis—Joseph Louis Barrow
Al McCoy—Albert Rudolph
Kid McCoy—Norman Selby
Eddie McGoorty—Edward Van Dusant
Sammy Mandell—Samuel Mandella
Rocky Marciano—Rocco Marchegiano
Cannonball Eddie Martin—Vittorio Martino
Joey Maxim—Joseph Berardinelli
Willie Meehan—Eugene Walcott
Young Mitchell—John Herget
Archie Moore—Archibald Wright
Rinty Monaghan—John Monaghan
Tod Morgan—Bert Pilkington
Torpedo Billy Murphy—Thomas W. Murphy
Battling Nelson—Oscar Nielson
"Philadelphia" Jack O'Brien—Joseph Hagen
Young Otto—Arthur Susskind
Willie Pep—William Papaleo
Urtiminio Sugar Ramos—Ultimo Zaqueira
Babe Risko—Henry Pylkowski
Willie Ritchie—Geary Steffen
Ray Robinson—Walker Smith
Jack Root—Janos Ruthaly
Charley Phil Rosenberg—Charles Green
Barney Ross—Barnet Rasofsky
Tommy Ryan—Joseph Youngs
Vicente Saldivar—Vincente Garcia
Baltazar Sangchilli—Baltasar Hevoas
Jack Sharkey—Joseph Paul Zukauskas
Battling Siki—Louis Phal
Frank Slavin—Sydney Cornstalk
Gunboat Smith—Edward Smyth
"Mysterious" Billy Smith—Amos Smith
Tom Spring—Thomas Winter
Kid Sullivan—Stephen Tricaro
Yankee Sullivan—James Ambrose
Joe Thomas—Joseph Daly
Young Jack Thompson—Cecil Lewis Thompson
Dick Tiger—Dick Ihetu
Gene Tunney—James Joseph Tunney
Pancho Villa—Francisco Guilledo
Jersey Joe Walcott—Arnold Raymond Cream
Freddie Welsh—Fred Hall Thomas
Charlie White—Charles Anchovitz
Kid Williams—John Gutenko
Johnny Wilson—John Panica
Midget Wolgast—Joseph Loscalzo
Chalky Wright—Albert Wright
Tony Zale—Anthony Zaleski

FAMOUS PROMOTERS

In the era before John L. Sullivan's reign as heavyweight champion, fight promoters were practically unknown. Pugilists or their backers put up side bets, winner take all, and it was a custom to pass the hat among the spectators, the funds so derived either going to the winner or being split 50-50, as the contestants may have decided.

The pioneer promoters, as we know fight promotion in the United States today, were a group identified with the Olympic Club, New Orleans, who put up $11,000 for a bout to be staged in its gymnasium on Jan. 14, 1891, between Bob Fitzsimmons and Jack (Nonpareil) Dempsey for the middleweight championship of the world. The California A.C. of San Francisco followed with a $10,000 purse for the James J. Corbett-Peter Jackson fight on May 21, 1901. The battle went 61 rounds before it was stopped by Referee Hiram Cook, who called it "no contest." Corbett declared he had received no part of the $10,000 and that Jackson told him, "I got only a few dollars."

The Olympic Club of New Orleans promoted the Fitzsimmons-Peter Maher bout on March 2, 1892, putting up $10,000, of which Fitz received $9,000 for stopping Maher in the 12th.

The same club then decided on a "championship carnival" for New Orleans during which three titles would be at stake. A total of $37,000 was put up, to be divided as follows: $20,000 for a heavyweight battle between Sullivan and Corbett; $10,000 for a lightweight championship bout between Jack McAuliffe and Billy Myers; $7,000 for a clash between George Dixon and Jack Skelly for the featherweight title.

The fights took place on Sept. 6, 7 and 8, 1892, and results were as follows:

Dixon stopped Skelly in 6 rounds.
Corbett knocked out Sullivan in the 21st.
McAuliffe defeated Myers in 15.

Promotions from then until the advent of James W. Coffroth of San Francisco generally were conducted by clubs or syndicates. But Coffroth went on his own and made some revolutionary changes.

Coffroth, in his 20's at the turn of the century and just graduated as a lawyer, visited New York, saw some ring battles there, and decided to promote in San Francisco. He staged some of the most important contests of the time, involving such men as Corbett, James J. Jeffries, Tom Sharkey, Fitzsimmons, Tommy Burns, Jack Johnson, Stanley Ketchel, George Gardner, "Philadelphia" Jack O'Brien, Jack (Twin) Sullivan, Billy Papke, Joe Walcott, Honey Mellody Mike (Twin) Sullivan, Joe Gans, Battling Nelson, Leach Cross, Dal Hawkins, Ad Wolgast, Abe Attell and many others.

Coffroth customarily paid the fighters 60 per cent and, on some occasions, 75 per cent of the gross receipts, which money they split either 60 per cent to the winner and 40 per cent to the loser, or 75—25, and, in a few instances, 90—10.

Coffroth promoted for about a dozen years, then abandoned boxing and promoted racing in Mexico and amassed a fortune. He died in 1943.

Tex Rickard was the next of the leading international promoters. He first came to notice when he offered $30,000 for a fight between Joe Gans and Battling Nelson in the mining town of Goldfield, Nev. His next major venture was in 1910 when he offered a $101,000 purse for the July 4 battle between Jim Jeffries and Jack Johnson, which was divided 60 per cent to the winner (Johnson) and 40 per cent to the loser. His next promotion of importance was in 1916 when he matched Jess Willard, heavyweight champion, against Frank Moran in Madison Square Garden, New York, with Willard guaranteed $100,000. In 1919 he guaranteed Willard $100,000 and Jack Dempsey $27,500 for their July 4 fight in Toledo.

In 1920, when boxing was legalized in New York, Rickard leased Madison Square Garden, gained control of boxing, and started the golden era of the sport. Unlike Coffroth, who dealt in percentages, Rickard took the gamble by guaranteeing certain sums to the fighters in important bouts. He gave Jack Dempsey $300,000 and Georges Carpentier $200,000 for their 1921 meeting in the bowl he built in Jersey City, N.J. The fight grossed $1,789,238, but Rickard's profit was small due to what he explained as "the political overhead."

He guaranteed Dempsey $450,000 and Tunney $200,000 for their first fight in Philadelphia, in 1926, giving Dempsey the option of taking 37½ per cent of the gate. The receipts were $1,895,733, and Dempsey's percentage share was $718,868.

For the 1927 fight in Chicago, Rickard agreed to give Tunney 37½ per cent of the gate, which reached $2,658,660. Tunney's share was $990,445, while Dempsey accepted a guarantee of $425,000.

Although Rickard suffered a few small losses in his many outdoor promotions, he generally was a big winner until he put on the Tunney-Tom Heeney championship contest June 6, 1928. He guaranteed Tunney $525,000, Heeney $100,000. The fight was not well patronized and Rickard admitted a loss of "around $200,000." That ended Rickard's guarantee policy, and fighters who fought thereafter under his other promotions worked on percentage. Rickard died in 1929.

The third great promoter was Hugh D. McIntosh of Australia, who died in Engalnd in 1941.

In 1908, Tommy Burns, who was a claimant of the world heavyweight title vacated by James J. Jeffries, arrived in Australia. Jack Johnson, the most persistent of Burns' challengers, had followed Burns to Europe, hoping to get a match, but Burns had sailed for the Antipodes.

About that time President Theodore Roosevelt had ordered the United States Navy, then on a good-will tour, to visit Australia. McIntosh felt that if he could arrange a bout between Johnson and Burns in Sydney, while the Navy was anchored there, he could draw a huge crowd of sailors. He offered Burns $20,000 to fight Johnson. Burns accepted. Johnson cabled acceptance of a smaller McIntosh offer and left for Australia, the fight being scheduled for Christmas Day, 1908. McIntosh designed and had built for the occasion a saucer-like stadium, which later became model for the American football bowls.

McIntosh refereed the fight, which was stopped by the police in the 14th because Burns was terribly beaten. McIntosh cleared over $50,000 on the fight, but explained:

"Australians supported it. I had counted on American sailors for a possible sell-out. Exactly two appeared in uniform. They started fighting and had to be evicted."

McIntosh had moving pictures made of that battle, showed them in Australia and New Zealand, took them to England, then toured the United States with them, and made about $200,000 of the films, which were novelties at the time.

Returning to Australia, McIntosh proceeded with many major promotions. He lured almost 100 noted American fighters to Sydney, including Billy Papke, Jimmy Clabby, Sam Langford, Sam McVey, Jim Barry, Porky Flynn, Eddie McGoorty, Billy Murray, K.O. Brown, Buck Crouse, Jeff Smith and George Chip. In later years, when he resumed promotion after a career in politics, as a newspaper publisher and as Australia's "theatrical czar," he imported William (Young) Stribling and other Americans who were starring in the early 1930's.

Mike Jacobs succeeded Rickard as the outstanding promoter and patterned his activities along the general percentage lines of Tex in the latter's later years.

Jacobs launched his promotional career on Jan. 24, 1934, with Barney Ross competing against Billy Petrolle. Later he ceased operating as an individual and headed the Twentieth Century Sporting Club. His first big outdoor show was in June, 1935, with Joe Louis opposing Primo Carnera. At that time Jacobs was in opposition to Madison Square Garden, headed by Jimmy Johnston. When Johnston resigned a year or two later, Jacobs took over the Madison Square Garden job. The gates drawn by the Jacobs shows exceeded by many millions of dollars the grand total achieved by other famous promoters in ring history.

Jacobs, who died Jan. 24, 1953, had promoted more than 500 fights before selling the Twentieth Century S.C. to James D. Norris of Chicago. Norris changed the name of the firm to the International Boxing Club and became the world's foremost promoter. Besides presenting fights in Madison Square Garden, Norris also ran shows in Detroit, Chicago, St. Louis and various other cities.

Among Norris' contemporary promoters are Jack Solomons of England and Jimmy Murray of San Francisco.

Other noted promoters were Dominick Tortorich and Marty Burke, New Orleans; Eddie Mack of Boston; Tom Andrews, promoter and manager; Floyd Fitzsimmons of Michigan; Jim Mullins, Chicago; Simon Flaherty, New York; "Uncle Tom" Carey of California; Mike Collins of Minneapolis; Ancil Hoffman, promoter and manager, and George Blake of California.

FAMOUS MANAGERS

Before John L. Sullivan became heavyweight champion in 1882, boxing managers were practically unknown. The fighters or their friends arranged all bout details. When Sullivan took to the stage, meeting all comers, offering $500 to any man he could not knock out within four rounds, Billy Madden, a sparring partner, took charge of the theatrical bookings and thus became the first of a long line of boxing managers.

In 1891, when James J. Corbett was seeking a match with Sullivan, he hired William A. Brady, then an obscure actor, to become his manager. Brady, who afterward managed James J. Jeffries, later became one of the leaders in the theatrical profession.

About the time Brady was handling Jeffries, another youngster became a pilot. His name was Sam Harris and his warrior was Terry McGovern. Harris later graduated into the theatrical business and achieved promotional fame there at least equal to Brady's. Charles H. (Parson) Davies was a well-known fight manager of about two generations ago; so were Willis Britt and Martin Julian, brother-in-law of Fitzsimmons, and Fitz's manager Sam Fitzpatrick also was well known.

Among the well-remembered boxing managers of the more modern years are:

Jack Kearns, who piloted Jack Dempsey to fame and fortune; Billy Gibson, who guided Gene Tunney and Benny Leonard to championships; Leo P. Flynn, who managed a stable of 25 to 50 fighters at one time; Joe Woodman and George Lawrence, who handled boxers for two generations; Charles Harvey, who specialized in importing European ringmen; Frank A. Churchill, who imported Filipinos; Francois Deschamps, who managed Georges Carpentier of France; Leon See, who discovered Primo Carnera; Harry Pollok, who managed Freddie Welsh and many other stars; Sammy Goldman, manager of several champions; George Engel, who brought Harry Greb from obscurity to greatness.

Also Tom O'Rourke, among the earliest of managers; Dan Morgan, who managed more than 500 fighters; Phil Glassman, developer of Lew Tendler; Paddy Mullins, manager of Harry Wills; Frank (Doc) Bagley, early manager of Tunney; Jimmy Bronson, who managed Bob Martin, heavyweight champion of the A.E.F. of 1918, and who discovered the Zivics; Scotty Montieth, handler of Johnny Dundee and a small army of others; William L. (Pa) Stribling of Georgia; Biddy Bishop, who was among the pioneers of his profession; Nat Lewis and Tom Walsh of Chicago, who managed Charlie White and hundreds of others; Dan Carroll, Johnny Buckley and Eddie Mack of Boston.

Others were James Dougherty, "Baron of Leiperville, Pa.," manager of George Godfrey; Eddie Kane and Eddie Long, who had a succession of stables in Chicago, which included Tom Gibbons, Sammy Mandell and Bud Taylor; also, Billy McCarney, Dan McKetrick, Tom McArdle, Frank Bachman, Joe Gould, Willie Gilzenberg, Lew Brix, Harry Lenny, all of New York; Tom Andrews, Milwaukee.

Also, Sam Pian and Art Winch of Chicago; Gig Rooney, Wad Wadhams, Ancil Hoffman, manager of Max and Buddy Baer, all of California; Charlie Rose, Lew Burston, Billy Duffy, Jack Bulger, Hymie Kaplan, Sol Gold, Frank Jacobs and Charlie Cook, all of New York, Lou Diamond of New Jersey and Tom McGinty and Jimmy Dunn of Brooklyn.

The list continues with Tom Jones, who managed Jess Willard into a championship; Jack Curley, partner of Jones, manager of wrestlers, as well as boxers, and a promoter of both sports; Mike Gibbons, who took to managing after his ring days were done; Gus Wilson, former trainer of Jack Dempsey; Chris Dundee of Pennsylvania; Eddie Mead, who handled many boxers, including Joe Lynch and Henry Armstrong; Jack Hurley, Jimmy DeForest, who trained Dempsey for his fight with Willard in 1919; Jim Mullin of Chicago; Joe Smith of Philadelphia, manager of Tommy Loughran and many more; Pop Foster, who made a fortune for Jimmy McLarnin by his shrewd matching of the Pacific Coast welterweight; Max Waxman, business manager for Jack Dempsey, and Tex Sullivan, New York.

Also, Joe Jacobs, who handled Max Schmeling during most of his fights in New York; Al Weill of New York, matchmaker and promoter, as well as manager; Clarence Gillespie of New York; Fred Digby, who specialized in handling boxers from the deep South; Jack Reddy; Tommy Simpson of California; Mike Collins of Minnesota; Gene Lutz, who trained Bill (Young) Stribling, Freddie Welsh and others; "John the Barber" Reisler, once manager of Jack Dempsey; Jimmy Kelly, Johnny Keyes and Phil Bernstein of New York.

And, of course, the picturesque, dynamic James J. Johnston of New York, who died in 1946. Johnston was a boxer in England in his youth. He came to New York and started managing fighters, most of them imported from England. In time, he was handling one of the largest stables in this country. In an effort to develop a great heavyweight, Johnston once invited all ambitious big men to New York to appear in a heavyweight tournament. About 100 arrived. They were matched up, and, when it was all over, Johnston, who weighed about 140, wanted to bet he could whip any of the giants— and found no takers.

Johnston promoted on his own. Later he became matchmaker for Madison Square Garden. When Mike Jacobs, with Joe Louis as his fistic "ace," began to promote in opposition to the Garden in 1935, a war was on between Johnston and Jacobs. When Louis rose to the heights, with Jacobs holding a promotional contract with him, and the Garden was without contracts with high-class fighters, Johnston left the Garden promotional job, Jacobs took over, and Johnston then organized his own fight club, calling it the "30th Century Sporting Club" because Jacobs had called his the "20th Century Sporting Club." Lacking contracts with the talented fighters, Johnston soon ceased to operate as a promoter and resumed managing and, with his usual showmanship, gained titular matches for mediocre fighters and made fortunes for all of them.

FAMOUS REFEREES

George Siler was perhaps the most famous of all the referees. He started officiating in the bare-knuckle days when fights were for side bets and the admirers of each warrior backed their choices heavily. When the decision went against their man, the losers usually were wrathy, put much of the blame for defeat on the referee, and the ring arbiters of those years led a zestful and interesting life.

Siler, who refereed for about three decades, was the hero of many hair-breadth escapes, with his bravery and resourcefulness carrying him out of the zone of physical danger.

Siler refereed in thousands of bouts and, in his heyday, always was the first choice of fighters going into battle with the title at stake. Those men respected Siler, not merely for his splendid ring judgment, but also because of his rugged honesty.

Prof. John Duffy was another old-timer who was a favorite among the boxers. He refereed the Sullivan-Corbett fight in New Orleans in 1892 and many of the later-day battles in which Bob Fitzsimmons figured. John Fitzpatrick of New Orleans was the referee for the last of the bare-knuckle heavyweight bouts—the one between John L. Sullivan and Jake Kilrain in 1889.

Al Smith of New York, Captain Bill Daley of Boston, Colonel Alexander Brewster, Billy Mahoney, Billy Tate, Wyatt Earp, who usually went into the ring with a gun in his holster;

Hiram Cook and Bob Lynd were famous in their time.

Eddie Graney of San Francisco came along a little later and was the headliner for a decade. He refereed practically all the bouts promoted by James W. Coffroth and at least 30 of them involved some sort of championship.

Sports writers have gained their share of fame as referees: Jack Sheehan of Boston, Ed Smith, Chicago; Bat Masterson, New York; Otto Floto, Denver, Colo.; E.W. Dickerson, Grand Rapids, Mich.; Fred Digby, New Orleans; Joseph Murphy, St. Louis; Tom Andrews, Milwaukee; George Barton, Minneapolis; Ed W. Cochrane, Kansas City and Chicago—those and scores of others.

Jack Welch was a fine referee. Willard Bean of Salt Lake City, Harry Stout of Milwaukee, "Honest" John Kelly and George Blake of Los Angeles also were excellent officials.

Many ringmen, sometimes during their active careers but usually after retirement, have taken to refereeing: Corbett, Fitzsimmons, Jeffries, Tom Sharkey, Jack McAuliffe, and, in a later day, Jess Willard, Gunboat Smith, Benny Leonard, Bill Stribling, Jack Dempsey, Gene Tunney, with Dempsey reaping a small fortune for his work as referee.

Jimmy Bronson, once of Joplin, Mo., later of New York, promoter, manager and referee, officiated in about 3,000 bouts that were staged among the soldiers in Europe in the 1917–1918 war. These, added to the others, amateur and professional, in which he figured through more than 30 years, may give him the distinction of rendering more ring decisions than any other referee, living or dead.

Arthur Donovan, Harry Kessler and Ruby Goldstein, a former fighter, are the best known of modern-day referees. Since ring rules were changed over 25 years ago, ending the single official system and providing two judges, as well as the referee, the importance of the latter has become minimized. Whereas in other days the referee was the absolute judge from whose opinion there was no appeal, he now is one voice in a chorus of three, and can be outvoted by the judges.

Edward J. Neil Trophy

(Awarded each year by New York Boxing Writers' Association.)

1938—Jack Dempsey
1939—Billy Conn
1940—Henry Armstrong
1941—Joe Louis
1942—Sgt. Barney Ross
1943—U.S. boxers in service
1944—Lt. Comdr. Benny Leonard, U.S.M.S.
1945—James J. Walker
1946—Tony Zale
1947—Gus Lesnevich

1948—Ike Williams
1949—Ezzard Charles
1950—Ray Robinson
1951—Joe Walcott
1952—Rocky Marciano
1953—Kid Gavilan
1954—Carl Olson
1955—Carmen Basilio
1956—Floyd Patterson
1957—Carmen Basilio
1958—Archie Moore
1959—Ingemar Johansson
1960—Floyd Patterson
1961—Gene Fullmer
1962—Dick Tiger
1963—Emile Griffith
1964—Willie Pastrano
1965—Cassius Clay (Muhammed Ali)
1966—Dick Tiger
1967—Carlos Ortiz
1968—Bob Foster
1969—Joe Frazier
1970—Ken Buchanan
1971-72—Joe Frazier

James J. Walker Memorial Award

(Awarded annually by New York Boxing Writers' Association for meritorious service.)

1940—James J. Walker
1941—Gene Tunney
1942—No award
1943—Nat Fleischer
1944—John J. Phelan
1945—James J. Johnston
1946—Mike Jacobs
1947—James A. Farley
1948—Dan Morgan
1949—Abe J. Greene
1950—Wilbur Wood
1951—Edward P.F. Eagan
1952—George A. Barton
1953—Dr. Vincent A. Nardiello
1954—James J. Braddock
1955—Harry Mendel
1956—Frank Graham
1957—Jack Dempsey
1958—Sam Taub
1959—Marv Jenson
1960—Ned Brown
1961—Dr. Alexander Schiff
1962—Dr. Mal Stevens
1963—Harry Markson
1964—Mickey Walker
1965—Jack Cuddy
1966—Nat Fleischer
1967—Joe Louis
1968—John Condon
1969—Murray Goodman
1970—Don Dunphy
1971—Teddy Brenner

LONGEST AND SHORTEST FIGHTS

Longest Bare-Knuckle Fights

James Kelly and Jack Smith (6 hours 15 minutes) , near Melbourne, Australia, Oct. 19, 1856.

Mike Madden and Bill Hays, 185 rounds (6 hours 3 minutes), at Edenbridge, England, July 17, 1849.

Madden and Jack Grant, 140 rounds (5 hours 45 minutes), Woking, England, Dec. 12, 1848.

Con Orem, blacksmith, and Hugh O'Neil, miner, fought 175 rounds (about 5 hours 30 minutes), Virginia City, Mont., for "lightweight championship" and $100 side bet. Referee called it a draw, after stopping fight, which for time and rounds is American record for bare knuckles.

J. Fitzpatrick and James O'Neil, Berwick, Me., Dec. 4, 1860 (4 hours 20 minutes).

(Note: In bare-knuckle fighting, the number of rounds was never consequential. The time length of the fight was the important thing because, under London Prize Ring Rules, a round ended when a man fell or was knocked or thrown to the ground. Some rounds lasted many minutes, others only a second or two.)

Longest Fights with Gloves

(Each round the regulation 3-minute round of today)

110 rounds (7 hours 19 minutes)—Andy Bowen vs. Jack Burke, April 6, 1893, New Orleans. Referee called it "no contest" when fighters refused to continue.

100 rounds (6 hours 39 minutes)—Danny Needham vs. Patsy Kerrigan, Feb. 27, 1890, San Francisco. Draw.

77 rounds (5 hours 8 minutes)—Harry Sharpe knocked out Frank Crosby, Feb. 2, 1892, Nameoki, Ill. (Longest fight under Marquis of Queensberry Rules to end in a knockout.)

76 rounds (5 hours 3 minutes 45 seconds)—W. Sheriff (The Prussian) and J. Welch, April 20, 1884, Philadelphia. Draw.

Shortest Fights with Gloves

The record appears to be a 10-second kayo in the first round on April 3, 1936, between Al Carr and Lew Massey at New Haven, Ct. Although it was listed as 10 seconds, the bout was stopped in 7 seconds as Massey rested on the canvas.

Al Couture knocked out Ralph Walton in 10½ seconds, at Lewiston, Me., Sept. 23, 1946.

RINGDOM'S FAMOUS POEM

The first Jack Dempsey, known as "The Nonpareil," whose name was Kelly, was born in Ireland. He arrived in New York as a boy and eventually went to work as a cooper. He attended a boxing show in 1883—he then was 21—and when one of the headliners failed to appear, Kelly volunteered as substitute and gave his name as Jack Dempsey.

He won that fight, indulged in others, was victorious, quit the cooperage trade and embarked upon a ring career. Campaigning from 1883 to 1888 and weighing no more than 150 pounds at most, he never was defeated, although he battled more than 60 men, taking on all sizes from welters to heavies. On Aug. 27, 1889, he met George La Blanche in San Francisco. In the 22d round, La Blanche pivoted completely around, with his right arm stuck out straight like a stick, and it struck Dempsey with the impact of a whirling crowbar and dropped him for the count.

That was the first time the pivot punch was used—and the last. It has been perpetually barred.

Dempsey never recovered from that defeat. In his next fight Feb. 18, 1890—he won from Australian Billy McCarthy, but he lacked the dash and the spirit of the other years. On Jan. 14, 1891, Bob Fitzsimmons stopped him in 13 rounds in New Orleans and won Dempsey's middleweight title. Jack outpointed Mike Keough in 4 rounds in 1893, drew with McCarthy in 20 in 1894 and lost the last battle of his career to Tommy Ryan at Coney Island, N.Y., 3 rounds, Jan. 18, 1895.

Dempsey took sick a short time later. On June 8, 1895, he made his final public appearance at a benefit given for him in New York. Hoping to regain his shattered health, he left for the West a short while later, but died in Portland, Ore., Nov. 1, 1895.

M.J. McMahon of Portland, who had been Dempsey's attorney, was so touched by the neglect of Dempsey at his death by presumed friends and hurrahing admirers of other years, that he wrote the now world-famous poem. He had 1,000 copies made and distributed them among Dempsey's friends. Being modest, he did not sign his name.

The poem first was printed anonymously in the *Portland Oregonian* on Dec. 10, 1899, and eventually was reprinted around the world. Dempsey's friends, who had forgotten him so soon after his death in 1895, came rallying with funds to erect a tombstone and on this is now inscribed the poem which follows:

The Nonpareil's Grave

(1)

Far out in the wilds of Oregon,
  On a lonely mountain side,
Where Columbia's mighty waters,
  Roll down to the ocean side;
Where the giant fir and cedar
  Are imaged in the wave,
O'ergrown with firs and lichens,
  I found Jack Dempsey's grave.

(2)

I found no marble monolith,
  No broken shaft, or stone,
Recording sixty victories,
  This vanquished victor won;
No rose, no shamrock could I find,
  No mortal here to tell
Where sleeps in this forsaken spot
  Immortal Nonpareil.

(3)

A winding wooden canyon road
  That mortals seldom tread,
Leads up this lonely mountain,
  To the desert of the dead.
And the Western sun was sinking
  In Pacific's golden wave
And those solemn pines kept watching,
  Over poor Jack Dempsey's grave.

(4)

Forgotten by ten thousand throats,
  That thundered his acclaim,
Forgotten by his friends and foes,
  Who cheered his very name.
Oblivion wraps his faded form,
  But ages hence shall save
The memory of that Irish lad
  That fills poor Dempsey's grave.

(5)

Oh, Fame, why sleeps thy favored son
  In wilds, in woods, in weeds,
And shall he ever thus sleep on,
  Interred his valiant deeds.
'Tis strange New York should thus forget
  Its "bravest of the brave"
And in the fields of Oregon,
  Unmarked, leave Dempsey's grave.

AMATEUR BOXING

The sport of amateur boxing has thrived through more than four decades as a result of the activities of the member associations of the Amateur Athletic Union. Many youngsters who gained national amateur championships later became famous as professionals.

The A.A.U., through its many affiliated organizations, has encouraged amateur boxing, with the bouts limited to three rounds and with officials under strict instructions to halt proceedings before any outclassed youngster is hurt. It is humane boxing at its best—definitely a sport, not a license for a superior man to annihilate the inferior. The A.A.U. encourages boxing under its rules for all classes and this results annually in thousands of contests around the land.

Through a series of eliminations the A.A.U. weeds out the mediocre, so that when the finals for the National championships are fought, the competing youngsters are superbly conditioned for as many bouts as they may be asked to wage. The winners, as a consequence, emerge from a starting group that may number thousands.

The A.A.U. originally put on championships in the 105, 108, 125, 145, 158 and 168-pound classes, then changed the weight limits to 112, 118, 126, 135, 147, 160, 175 and heavyweight in the more modern era. To conform with international rules, the A.A.U. added two classes and shifted the weights in some of the other divisions, starting in 1952. The set-up now calls for the following classes: 112, 119, 125, 132, 139, 147, 156, 165, 178 and heavyweight. In 1968 a new class was added, the light flyweight division, 106 pound limit.

Boxing has been popular in colleges for many years, and contests, like the A.A.U. matchings, are so arranged that no one is badly hurt in any struggle to gain fame. The collegians have their own eliminations which determine their champions but, very often, a collegian finds his way into the A.A.U. eliminations.

United States Amateur Champions

(Source: Official Amateur Athletic Union Boxing Guide)

Light Flyweight
(Limit 106 pounds)

1968—Harland Marbley
1969—Dennis Mince
1970—Elijah Cooper
1971—Gary Griffin
1972—Davey Armstrong

Flyweight Class
(Limit 105 pounds, 1888–1912; 108 pounds, 1913–1921; 112 pounds starting in 1922)

1888—D. O'Brien
1889 (March)—M. Rice
1889 (Dec.)—D. O'Brien
1890—T. Murphy
1891—J.D. Millen
1892—No competition
1893—G. Ross
1894—J. Madden
1895—J. Salmon
1896—J. Mylan
1897—G.W. Owens
1898—No competition
1899—David Watson
1900—W. Cullen
1901—J. Brown
1902—W. Schumaker
1903—R. McKinley
1904—J. O'Brien
1905—Fred Stingel
1906—James Carroll
1907—J.J. O'Brien
1908—Angus McDougal

1909—Arthur Sousa
1910—James Rothwell
1911—John Fallon
1912—James Lynch
1913—Barney Snyder
1914—J. Downs
1915—Howard Root
1916—Thomas Darcy
1917—Thomas Fall
1918—Joe Wiles
1919—D. Kamins
1920—A.J. DeVito
1921—John Hamm
1922—T.P. McManus
1923—Al Bender
1924—Fidel La Barba
1925—Alfred Rollinson
1926—Lawrence Lyons
1927—Harry Liebenson
1928—Hyman Miller
1929—James Kerr
1930—George Ostrow
1931—Babe Triscaro
1932—Louis Salica
1933—Tony Valore
1934—Thomas Barry
1935—John Marcelline
1936—Jackie Wilson
1937—William Speary
1938—Robert Carroll
1939—Jose Mercado
1940—Johnny Manalo
1941—Lawrence Torpy
1942—LeRoy Jackson
1943—Anthony Peppi
1944—Cecil Schoonmaker
1945—Keith Hamilton
1946—David Buna
1947—Robert Holiday
1948—Frank Sodano
1949—John Ortega
1950—Sherman Nelson
1951—William Peacock
1952—Billy Hill
1953—Robert Singleton
1954—Charles Branch
1955—Heji Shimabukuro
1956—57—Albert Pell
1958—Ray Perez
1959—Gil Yanez
1960—Wayman Gray
1961—Peter Gonzales
1962—George Colon
1963—Lucas Matseke
1964—Melvin Miller
1965—Sam Goss
1966—Nickey Pirola
1967—Rolland (Boom Boom) Miller
1968—Kenny Bazer
1969—Caleo Long
1970—Eduardo Santiago
1971—72—Bobby Lee Hunter

Bantamweight Class

(Limit 115 pounds, 1888–1921; 118 pounds, 1922–1951; 119 pounds starting in 1952.)

1888–W.H. Rocap
1889 (April)–W.H. Rocap
1889 (Dec.)–W. Kenny
1890–B. Weldon
1891–G.F. Connolly
1892–No competition
1893–M.J. Hallihan
1894–R. McVeigh
1895–E. Horen
1896–J.J. Gross
1897–Charles Fahey
1898–No competition
1899–William Wildner
1900–H. Murphy
1901–George Young
1902–F. Fieg
1903–Thomas Stone
1904–Jerry Casey
1905–Sam Moss
1906–Harry Baker
1907–Henry Meyers
1908–M.J. Carroll
1909–Joe Gorman
1910–John Gallant
1911–13–Thomas Reagan
1914–S. Phillips
1915–Tony Vatlin
1916–Ben Valgar
1917–J. Tomasulo
1919–Ashton Donze
1920–J. Hutchinson
1921–George Daly
1922–Sidney Terris
1923–Harry Marcus
1924–Jack Tripoli
1925–August Gotto
1926–Joe Katish
1927–Thomas Paul
1928–John Daley
1929–Albion Holden
1930–Abie Miller
1931–Joseph Ferrante
1932–Jimmy Martin
1933–Angelo Tardugno
1934–Armond Sicilia
1935–Troy Bellini
1936–William Joyce
1937–Morris Parker
1938–39–William Speary
1940–Angel Ambrosano
1941–Raymond Brown
1942–Bernard Docussen
1943–Earl O'Neil
1944–Nick Saunders
1945–Amos Aitson
1946–Tsaneshi Naruo
1947–Gorky Gonzales
1948–Bill Morgan
1949–James Mitchell

1950–Mickey Mars
1951–Ernest DeJesus
1952–David Moore
1953–Thomas Nethercott
1954–Billy Ramos
1955–John Cereghin
1956–Don Whaley
1957–Hemon Marguez
1958–Charles Branch
1959–Fred Griffin
1960–Oscar German
1961–John Howard
1962–Victor Melendez
1963–Gerry Lott
1964–Art Jones
1965–George Colon
1966–Jose Marquez
1967–Earl Large
1968–Sam Goss
1969–Terry Pullen
1970–Robert Mullins
1971–Richardo Carreras
1972–John David

Featherweight Class

(Limit 125 pounds, 1889–1921; 126 pounds, 1922–1951; 125 pounds again starting in 1952.)

1889 (April)–J. Brown
1889 (Dec.)–J. Gorman
1890–J. Schneering
1891–W.H. Horton
1892–No competition
1893–W.H. Horton
1894–C. Miner
1895–L. Campbell
1896–No competition
1897–Joseph McCann
1898–No competition
1899–John Burns
1900–01–J. Scholes
1902–Joe McCann
1903–Ambrose J. McGarry
1904–T.F. Fitzpatrick
1905–Willie Cornell
1906–W.J. Leonard
1907–T.J. Fitzpatrick
1908–E.J. Walsh
1909–T.J. Fitzpatrick
1910–Frank Smith
1911–Frank Hufnagle
1912–John Cooper
1913–Walter Hitchen
1914–V. Pokorni
1915–Arthur Strawhacker
1916–William Morris
1917–Earl Baird
1918–James Fruzetti
1919–William P. Corbett
1920–S. Seeman
1921–Dan Gartin
1922–George Fifield
1923–Terry Park

1924—Joe Salas
1925—Ray Alfano
1926—Patsy Rufalo
1927—Christopher Battalino
1928—Harry Devine
1929—Martin Zuniga
1930—Ray Meyers
1931—Anthony Sarpati
1932—Richard Carter
1933—Louis Barisano
1934—Edwin Waling
1935—Al Netlow
1936—Joseph Church
1937—Edgar Waling
1938—39—William Eddy
1940—Frank Robinson
1941—Francis Leonard
1942—James Marlo
1943—Jackie Floyd
1944—Major Jones
1945—Virgil Franklin
1946—Leo Kelly
1947—Wallace Smith
1948—Teddy Fittipaldo
1949—Benny Apostadiro
1950—Sammy Rodgers
1951—Len Walters
1952—Mac Martinez
1953—Robert Tenquer
1954—Stan Fitzgerald
1955—Joe Charles
1956—Harry Smith
1957—Rubin Pizarro
1958—John (Patrick) Britt
1959—Roy Houpe
1960—George Foster
1961—Ralph Ungricht
1962—Steven Freeman
1963—Victor Baerga
1964—Charles Brown
1965—Lawrence Hines
1966—Robert Lozada
1967—Roy DeFilippis
1968—George McGarvey
1969—Joe Bennett
1970—Ray Lunny
1971—Ricky Boudreaux
1972—Herman Artis

Lightweight Class
(Limit 135 pounds, 1888—1951; 132 pounds starting in 1952.)
1888—T. Thompson
1889 (April)—E.F. Walker
1889 (Dec.)—W.F. McGarry
1890—J. Rice
1891—O.H. Ziegler
1892—No competition
1893—H.M. Leeds
1894—C.J. Gehring
1895—J. Quinn
1896—James Pyne

1897—Ed Dix
1898—No competition
1899—G. Jensen
1900—J. Hopkins
1901—J.F. Mumford
1902—John Dillon
1903—John Leavy
1904—Goliath Jones
1905—Ambrose J. McGarry
1906—Lew Powell
1907—Joseph Doyle
1908—J. Denning
1909—William Shevlin
1910—William Volk
1911—James Jarvis
1912—Al Wambsgans
1913—M.J. Crowley
1914—D. Stosh
1915—M.J. Crowley
1916—17—Thomas Murphy
1918—Thomas O'Malley
1919—Frank B. Cassidy
1920—Thomas Murphy
1921—Ben Ponteau
1922—Joe Ryan
1923—John T. McManus
1924—Fred Boylstein
1925—Jim McGonigan
1926—Thomas Lown
1927—Francis Burke
1928—29—Steve Halaiko
1930—Alex Santora
1931—Al Gomez
1932—Nat Bor
1933—Frank Eagan
1934—Norbet Meehan
1935—William Beauhold
1936—Thomas Pallatin
1937—Joseph Kelly
1938—Richard Ford
1939—George Toy
1940—Paul Matsumoto
1941—Tommy Moyer
1942—Robert McQuillan
1943—Charles Hunter
1944—Joey D'Amato
1945—Jetson Arnold
1946—Joseph Discopeli
1947—48—Johnny Gonsalves
1949—Charles Adkins
1950—George Justice
1951—James Hackney
1952—John Barnes
1953—Frank Smith
1954—Garnet Hart
1955—Jack Puscas
1956—Bill Cherry
1957—Gene Grisham
1958—Adam Ellison
1959—Quincy Daniels
1960—Brian O'Shea
1961—Woodie Marcus

1962—George Foster
1963—Manuel Rameriz
1964—Ronnie Harris
1965—Herb Dolloson
1966—68—Ronnie Harris
1969—Juan Ruis
1970—James Parks
1971—James Busceme
1972—Norman Goins

Light-Welterweight Class
(Limit 139 pounds.)

1952—Isaac Vaughn
1953—Juan Alvarez
1954—Robert Shell
1955—Robert Cofer
1956—Tommy Thomas
1957—58—Vincent Shomo
1959—Brian O'Shea
1960—Vincent Shomo
1961—Brian O'Shea
1962—Jackie Range
1963—Harold Finley
1964—Freddie Ward
1965—Ray Garay
1966—67—James Wallington
1968—Joe Louis Valdez
1969—Rudy Bolos
1970—Quiencelan Daniel
1971—Ray Seales
1972—Carlos Palomino

Welterweight Class
(Limit 145 pounds, 1897–1921; 147 pounds since 1922.)

1897—98—A. McIntosh
1899—Percy McIntyre
1900—01—J.J. Dukelow
1902—Charles McCann
1903—John Leavy
1904—C.T. Mitchell
1905—H.L. McKinnon
1906—William McDonald
1907—W.J. Kirkland
1908—William Rolfe
1909—M.J. McNamara
1910—Hillard Lang
1911—John Fisher
1912—13—Charles Askins
1914—M. Woldman
1915—August Ratner
1916—Eugene Brosseau
1917—Daniel O'Connor
1918—James Sullivan
1919—Dave Rosenberg
1920—J. Schroendorf
1921—Charles Jennkissen
1922—Harry D. Simons
1923—John Rini
1924—Al Mello
1925—Bernard Barde

1926—Edward Tiernan
1927—28—Tommy Lown
1929—Leslie Baker
1930—Charles Kelly
1931—32—Edward Flynn
1933—William Celebron
1934—Danny Farrar
1935—Jimmy Clark
1936—Leo Sweeney
1937—Johnny Marquez
1938—James O'Malley
1939—Cozy Storace
1940—Henry Brimm
1941—Dave Andrews
1942—Willard Buckless
1943—Charles Cooper
1944—Joe Gannon
1945—Abe Lee
1946—Robert Takeshita
1947—Jackie Keough
1948—Eugene Linscott
1949—Maurice Harper
1950—Gil Turner
1951—Rudolph Gwinn
1952—Andy Anderson
1953—Fred Terry
1954—Joseph Bethea
1955—Walter Sabbath
1956—Jackson Brown
1957—Don Hullinger
1958—Grey Gauvin
1959—Vernon Vincent
1960—61—Phil Baldwin
1962—Wade Smith
1963—Wade Smith
1964—Jessie Valdez
1965—Hodgeman Lewis
1966—Roland Pryor
1967—Kim Booker
1968—Mike Colbert
1969—70—Armando Muniz
1971—Sammy Maul
1972—Freddie Washington

Light-Middleweight Class
(Limit 156 pounds)

1952—Ernest Anthony
1953—William Collins
1954—John Houston
1955—56—Frank Davis
1957—Dennis Moyer
1958—Williams Pickett
1959—60—Wilbert McClure
1961—Bobby Pasquale
1962—Roy McMillan
1963—John Howard
1964—Toby Gibson
1965—Conrad Williams
1966—John Howard
1967—Arthur Davis
1968—William Beeler
1969—Larry Carlisle

1970—Jesse Valdez
1971—Billy Daniels
1972—Henry Johnson

Middleweight Class
(Limit 160 pounds through 1951; 165 pounds starting in 1952.)

1888—P. Cahill
1889 (April)—P. Cahill
1889 (Dec.)—W.H. Stuckey
1890—P. Cahill
1891—W.H. Stuckey
1892—No competition
1893—A. Black
1894—O. Harney
1895—M. Lewis
1896—George Schwegler
1897—A. McIntosh
1898—No competition
1899—A. McIntosh
1900—04—W. Rodenbach
1905—Charles Mayer
1906—Henry Fincke
1907—W. McKinnon
1908—Henry Hall
1909—Dan Sullivan
1910—William Beckman
1911—Napoleon Boutelier
1912—Arthur Sheridan
1913—14—William Barrett
1915—16—Adolph Kaufman
1917—Eugene Brosseau
1918—Martin Burke
1919—21 Sam Lagonia
1922—William Antrobus
1923—Homer Robertson
1924—Ben Funk
1925—Clayton Frye
1926—Arthur Flynn
1927—Joseph Hanlon
1928—Harry H. Henderson
1929—Ray Lopez
1930—Ring Larsen
1931—Frank Fullam
1932—Fred Caserio
1933—Tom Chester
1934—Fred Apostoli
1935—David Clark
1936—Jimmy Clark
1937—Ted Cerwin
1938—Bradley Lewis
1939—Ezzard Charles
1940—Joey Maxim
1941—James Mulligan
1942—43—Samson Powell
1944—Frank Sweeney
1945—Allen Faulkner
1946—Harold Anspach
1947—Nick Ranieri
1948—Raymond Bryan
1949—Albert Raymond

1950—Wes Echols
1951—Thomas Nelson
1952—Floyd Patterson
1953—Bryant Thompson
1954—Donald McCray
1955—56—Paul Wright
1957—Alex Ford
1958—Jose Torres
1959—Jimmy McQueen
1960—61—Leotis Martin
1962—Richard Gosha
1963—Robert Williams
1964—Will Cross
1965—George Cooper
1966—Martin Berzewdki
1967—Leonard Hutchins
1968—Alfred Jones
1969—Larry Ward
1970—John Mangum
1971—Joey Hadley
1972—Michael Colbert

Light-Heavyweight Class
(Limit 168 pounds in 1906; 175 pounds, 1913—1951—1966; 178 pounds starting in 1952.)

1906—Tad Riordan
1907—12—No competition
1913—Joe Brown
1914—W. Hanna
1915—Edward C. Carr
1916—Patrick McCarthy
1917—Ted Jamieson
1918—John McMinimen
1919—Al Roche
1920—J. Burke
1921—Mangu Larsen
1922—Charles McKenna
1923—Harry Fay
1924—Tom Kirby
1925—26—Henry Lamar
1927—George Hoffman
1928—Leon Lucas
1929—Martin Levandowski
1930—Frank Tucker
1931—Antone Poloni
1932—Homer Brandis
1933—Max Marek
1934—Joe Louis
1935—Joseph Bauer
1936—John Lasinski
1937—Tim Hill
1938—William Muldune
1939—James Reeves
1940—Victor Hutton
1941—Shelton Bell
1942—43—Robert Foxworth
1944—Ray Standifer
1945—Richard Nutt
1946—Robert Foxworth
1947—48—Grant Butcher

1949—Delopez Oliver
1950—Eldridge Thompson
1951—John Boutilier
1952—Eldridge Thompson
1953—Frank Perry
1954—Warren Lister
1955—56—John Horne
1957—Lindy Lindimoser
1958—Sylvester Banks
1959—60—Cassius Clay
1961—Bob Christopherson
1962—William Joiner
1963—Fred Lewis
1964—Bob Christopherson
1965—No competition
1966—67—John Griffin
1968—Leonard Hutchins
1969—Dave Matthews
1970—Nathaniel Jackson
1971—Marvin Johnson
1972—Hernando Molyneaux

Heavyweight Class
(Over 175 pounds, 1890—1951; over 178 pounds
starting in 1952.)

1890—N.F. Doherty
1891—A. Isaaca
1892—No competition
1893—D.A. Whilhere
1894—J. Kennedy
1895—W.D. Osgood
1896—Geo. Schwegler and J.G. Eberle (draw)
1897—D. Herty
1898—No competition
1899—1900—J.B. Knipe
1901—William Rodenbach
1902—03—Emery Payne
1904—W. Rodenbach
1905—Emery Payne
1906—W. Schulken
1907—Emery Payne
1908—Thomas Kennedy
1909—Phillip Schlossberg
1910—W.W. Barbour
1911—John Serino
1912—John Silverio
1913—A.J. Reich
1914—P.L. Kelly
1915—A. Sheridan
1916—Carlo Armstrong
1917—John Gaddi
1918—Martin Burke
1919—Edward Eagan
1920—K. Wicks
1921—Gordon Munce
1922—John Wilman
1923—Thomas Kirby
1924—E.G. Greathouse
1925—Joe Woods
1926—Armand Emanuel
1927—Milo Mallory
1928—George Hoffman

1929—Ralph Ficucello
1930—31—Jack Pallat
1932—Fred Feary
1933—Izzy Richeter
1934—Stanley Evens
1935—Louis Nova
1936—Willard Dean
1937—James Robinson
1938—Daniel Merritt
1939—Tony Novak
1940—Wallace Cross
1941—Ragan Kinney
1942—Paul Komar
1943—Walter Moore
1944—Richard Vaughn
1945—46—Charles Lester
1947—Willie Clemmons
1948—Coley Wallace
1949—Rex Layne
1950—51—Norval Lee
1952—Jack Scheberies
1953—Pete Rademacher
1954—Reuben Vargas
1955—George Moore
1956—Jim McCarter
1957—Lee Williams
1958—59—James Blythe
1960—Harold Espey
1961—Rudy Davis
1962—Wyce Westbrook
1963—Vic Brown
1964—Buster Mathis
1965—Boone Kirkman
1966—James Howard
1967—Forest Ward
1968—George Foreman
1969—Ernie Shaver
1970—Ronnie Lyle
1971—Duane Bobick
1972—Nick Wells

Golden Gloves

The Golden Gloves was originated and sponsored in 1927 by *The New York Daily News*. Limited at first to amateur boxers in the metropolitan district, it spread to Chicago the following year and has since grown to be national and international in scope.

For purposes of competition, the nation is divided into two Golden Gloves areas, East and West. In each area local tournaments are conducted. Following these, Eastern championships are held annually in New York and Western championships in Chicago. The grand climax comes when the Eastern champions meet the Western champions in the annual Intercity Golden Gloves matches.

W.R. Fritzinger, promotion manager of The News and president of The News Welfare Association, Inc., which sponsors the Golden Gloves, spoke for amateur boxing as a whole when he said:

"The voluntary entrance of a boy into an amateur boxing tournament stamps him as a brave man.

"Each knows that it is the severest test a man can have in sport. Maybe he will be thumped into oblivion in his first bout, but his heart was right or he wouldn't have entered. He knows that every time he pokes his head through the ropes he has to face an adversary whose one purpose is to knock him out.

"Golden Gloves champions have been found in strange places. Boys who went into it as a lark, or on a dare, or doubting themselves, suddenly have found themselves under the spotlight's glare before 20,000 spectators fighting for the championship. It happens as quickly as that. Boys who were novices in January have come into the March finals with skill and confidence. The huge throng will peg two or three of the contestants, possibly more, as outstanding professional prospects and they probably will be right.

"But we never have been interested in conducting Golden Gloves as an incubator for professional boxing. Our objective is to give these boys a chance to express themselves, to share the spotlight for a moment, to build their bodies and, above all, their characters.

"The magnitude of the Golden Gloves activities is shown by the fact that the 16 Chicago representatives in the intercity tournament often are survivors of an army of more than 15,000 competitors, while New York's 16 champions were developed in bouts involving even more original starters."

In addition to its service as a youth development activity, the Golden Gloves also serves as an ever growing source of funds for worthy charitable organizations. The net proceeds of Golden Gloves tournaments everywhere are contributed to such organizations and, over a period of years, contributions by The News Welfare Association in New York City alone have totaled over $650,000.

The vast majority of boys who compete in the Golden Gloves do not turn to professional boxing as a career. Many of those who do, however, go on to the heights of boxing fame. In 1945 seven of the eight world professional champions were graduates of the Golden Gloves.

Among the outstanding fighters of recent years who got their start in the Golden Gloves have been Ray Robinson, Jimmy Carter, and Gus Lesnevich, all of New York City, and such others as Joe Louis, Ezzard Charles, Joey Maxim, Rocky Marciano, Melio Bettina , Tony Zale, Barney Ross, Sal Bartolo, Lou Salica, Petey Scalzo, Harold Dade, each of whom has held a world championship.

All Golden Gloves competition is sanctioned by the Amateur Athletic Union and is conducted according to the rules of that organization.

Though the National A.A.U. now conducts its championships at eleven weight divisions, the Golden Gloves has nine standard weights, 106, 112, 118, 126, 135, 147, 160, 175 pound and heavyweight. Sub-novice bouts in each of the weight classes are also conducted. There are no draws in amateur boxing and a decision must be rendered by the officials, either two judges and a referee, or three judges.

Arch Ward, late sports editor of *The Chicago Tribune,* launched the Golden Gloves idea on an international basis by arranging All-American and All-European title bouts. They continued until 1940, when World War II forced their cancellation. International activity was resumed in the post-war years.

National Collegiate Champions

Competition held only in the years indicated.

Individual

112 Pounds

1932—Pete D'Allesandro, Temple
1948—Ernie Charboneau, Michigan State
1952—Ray Kuboyama, Hawaii
1956—Dean Plemmons, Wisconsin
1957—Edwardo Labastida, California Polytech
1958—T.C. Chung, San Jose State
1959—Heiji Shimabukura, College of Idaho

(No national championships held since 1959)

115 Pounds

1936—Mickey Brutto, West Virginia
1937—Roy Petragallo, Washington State
1938—David Bernstein, Catholic University

118 Pounds

1932—David A. Stoop, Penn State

119 Pounds

1948—S. Gremban, Wisconsin
1952—Frank Echevarria, Idaho
1953—Vic Kobe, Idaho State
1954—Gary Garber, Maryland
1955—Bobby McCullom, Idaho State
1956—Choken Maekawa, Michigan State
1957—Dave Abeyta, Idaho State
1958—Robert Tafoya, San Jose State
1959—Ron Nichols, San Jose State
1960—Ron Nichols, San Jose State

120 Pounds

1938—Sewele Whitney, Loyola (New Orleans)
1940—41—Ted Kara, Idaho
1942—Donald Harper, Southwestern
Louisiana Institute
1943—Bill Zurakowski, Michigan State

125 Pounds

1936—Robert Fadner, Wisconsin
1937—Carl Eckstrum, North Dakota

1938—Benny Alperstein, Maryland
1947—Gerald AuClair, Syracuse
1949—Wilbert Moss, Louisiana State
1950—Mac Martinez, San Jose State
1951—52—Neil Ofsthun, Minnesota
1953—Mike Guerrero, San Jose State
1954—55—Seiji Naya, Hawaii
1956—Bobby Soileau, Louisiana State
1957—Cyril Okamota, Idaho State
1958—Dave Abeyta, Idaho State
1959—Bobby Cornwall, Washington State
1960—Dave Nelson, San Jose State

126 Pounds

1932—Albert Wertheimer, Syracuse

127 Pounds

1939—Ted Kara, Idaho
1940—Sewele Whitney, Loyola (New Orleans)
1941—Frank Kara, Idaho
1942—Dick Miyagawa, San Jose State
1943—Charles Davey, Michigan State
1948—Douglas Ellwood, Louisiana State

130 Pounds

1947—Glenn Hawthorne, Penn State
1949—50—Ted Thrash, Louisiana State
1951—Jack Melson, Washington State

132 Pounds

1952—Archie Slaten, Miami (Florida)
1953—Paddy Garver   Idaho State
1954—55—Vince Palumbo, Maryland
1956—58—Richard Rall, Washington State
1959—Nick Akana, San Jose State
1960—Brown McGhee, Wisconsin

135 Pounds

1932—Robert Goldstein, Virginia
1936—Frank Goodman, Penn State
1937—Ben Alperstein, Maryland
1938—Julian Benoit, Idaho
1939—Gene Rankin, Wisconsin
1940—John Joca, Florida
1941—42—Gene Rankin, Wisconsin
1943—Davie Knight, Washington State
1947—Charles Davey, Michigan State
1949—Leonard Walker, Idaho
1950—51—Everett Conley, Washington State

136 Pounds

1948—Charles Davey, Michigan State

139 Pounds

1952—Chuck Adkins, San Jose State
1953—Calvin Clary, Louisiana State
1954—55—John Granger, Syracuse
1956—Dick Bartman, Wisconsin
1957—Ronald Rall, Idaho State
1958—Melvin Stroud, San Jose State
1959—Joe Bliss, Nevada
1960—Steve Kubas, San Jose State

145 Pounds

1936—Danny Farrar, Duke
1937—Rolly Shumway, Idaho
1938—Maynard Harlow, Virginia
1939—Omar Crocker, Wisconsin
1940—Snyder Parham, Louisiana State
1941—Elton Tobiasson, California Aggies
1942—Warren Jollymore, Wisconsin
1943—Cliff Lutz, Wisconsin
1947—Cliff Lutz, Wisconsin
1949—Charles Davey, Michigan State
1950—Leonard Walker, Idaho
1951—Gerald Black, Michigan State

147 Pounds

1948—D. Dickinson, Wisconsin
1952—Bob Morgan, Wisconsin
1953—Pat Sreenan, Wisconsin
1954—55—Herb Odom, Michigan State
1956—Gilliam McLane, Louisiana State
1957—Bill Haynes, Idaho State
1958—Walt Shephardson, Idaho State
1959—Buddy Rausch, Idaho State
1960—Mills Lane, Nevada

148 Pounds

1932—James Lewis, Penn State

155 Pounds

1936—Ord Fink, Syracuse
1937—Ed McKinnon, Washington State
1938—Steve Wilkerson, Mississippi
1939—40—Woodrow Swancutt, Wisconsin
1941—Rodney Belaire, Louisiana State
1942—Cliff Lutz, Wisconsin
1943—Don Miller, Wisconsin
1947—Herbert Carlson, Idaho
1949—Wayne Fontes, San Jose State
1950—Eli Thomas, Gonzaga
1951—Dick Murphy, Wisconsin

156 Pounds

1952—53—Ellsworth Webb, Idaho State
1954—Bob Meath, Wisconsin
1955—Anthony DiBiase, Virginia
1956—Vince Ferguson, Wisconsin
1957—Jim Flood, Sacramento State
1958—Jess Klinnenberg, Washington State
1959—Terry Smith, Sacramento State
1960—Jerry Turner, Wisconsin

160 Pounds

1932—Dennis Flynn, Loyola (New Orleans)
1948—Herbert Carlson, Idaho

165 Pounds

1936—Ray Jefferis, Syracuse
1937—Ray Matulewicz, Duke
1938—Sam Littlepage, West Virginia
1939—Fred Stant, Catholic University
1940—41—Laune Erickson, Idaho
1942—Kenneth Rathbun, Virginia

1943—Myron Miller, Wisconsin
1947—John Ledenski, Wisconsin
1949—Colin Connell, Minnesota
1950—Herb Carlson, Idaho
1951—Eli Thomas, Gonzaga
1952—Gordon Gladson, Washington State
1953—Tom Hickey, Michigan State
1954—Gordon Gladson, Washington State
1955—Max Voshall, San Jose State
1956—57—Roger Rouse, Idaho State
1958—Jim Flood, Sacramento State
1959—Charley Mohr, Wisconsin
1960—Stuart Bartell, San Jose State

175 Pounds

1932—Theofiel Wageman, New Hampshire
1936—Ray Matulewicz, Duke
1937—38—Louis Schmidt, Virginia
1939—Truman Torgerson, Wisconsin
1940—John Webster, Idaho
1941—Paul Scally, Penn State
1942—43—George Makris, Wisconsin
1947—Laune Erickson, Idaho
1949—Carl Bernardo, Miami (Fla.)
1950—Carl Maxey, Gonzaga
1951—Charles Spieser, Michigan State

176 Pounds

1948—Calvin Vernon, Wisconsin

178 Pounds

1952—Charles Spieser, Michigan State
1953—Ray Zale, Wisconsin
1954—Adam Kois, Penn State
1955—Gordon Gladson, Washington State
1956—Orville Pitts, Wisconsin
1957—Dale Leathem, Idaho State
1958—59—John Horne, Michigan State
1960—John Horne, Michigan State

Heavyweight

1932—Doyless Hill, Tulane
1936—Tom Pontecarvo, Western Maryland
1937—Harry Mullins, Mississippi State
1938—Ashby Dickerson, West Virginia
1939—Rene Trochesset, Louisiana State
1940—Nick Lee, Wisconsin
1941—Louis Campbell, Southwestern Louisiana Institute
1942—Salvatore Mirabito, Syracuse
1943—Verdayne John, Wisconsin
1947—Arthur Saey, Miami
1948—Vito Parisi, Wisconsin
1949—Marty Crandell, Syracuse
1950—Charles M. Drazenovich, Penn State
1951—52—Robert Ranck, Wisconsin
1953—Art Statum, North Carolina A.&T.
1954—Mike McMurtry, Idaho State
1955—Crowe Peele, Louisiana State
1956—Truman Sturdevant, Wisconsin
1957—Hal Espy, Idaho State
1958—Archie Milton, San Jose State

1959—Hal Espy, Idaho State
1960—Archie Milton, San Jose State

Team

1932—Penn State
1933—35—No competition
1936—Syracuse
1937—Washington State
1938—Catholic U., Virginia, West Virginia (tie)
1939—Wisconsin
1940—41—Idaho
1942—43—Wisconsin
1944—46—No competition
1947—48—Wisconsin
1949—Louisiana State
1950—Idaho, Gonzaga (tie)
1951—Michigan State
1952—Wisconsin
1953—Idaho State
1954—Wisconsin
1955—Michigan State
1956—Wisconsin
1957—Idaho State
1958—60—San Jose State

BASIC RULES*

Boxing is a contest of attacking and defending. Each contest is a bout—a set number of rounds—the length varying with the rules in effect. The purpose of the sport is to outbox or outclass the opponent, leading to his defeat by a knockout, a technical knockout, or a decision.

Boxing takes place in a square area, called a ring, not less than 18 nor more than 20 feet square. It is surrounded by three 1-inch ropes with cloth wrappings. For an elevated ring, a 2-inch padding extends at least 6 inches on the platform or "apron" beyond the roped area. If the ring is on floor level, an additional 2-inch pad extends 3 feet beyond the ropes.

The boxer uses a padded glove, or a mitt, consisting of a thumb and a main part—for the protection of the opponent as well as the fist of the boxer. Amateur Athletic Union rules specify 8-ounce gloves for divisions up to the 147-pound (welterweight) class; 10-ounce for classes heavier than that. Intercollegiate rules specify a 12-ounce minimum. Interscholastic rules recommend 10-ounce gloves up to and including the featherweight class and 12 ounces in all other classes. In professional fights in the United States, 8-ounce gloves are used generally, except in championship matches, in which 6-ounce gloves are the rule.

In amateur boxing a bout usually consists of three 2-minute rounds; in professional circles a round is three minutes long and the contests vary from 4 rounds to 15, with 6, 8 and 10-round bouts common. Fifteen rounds is the usual distance for a professional championship bout.

Each contestant may have the assistance of two seconds. The seconds are not permitted to

*Taken from Sports for Recreation, by E.D. Mitchell, A.S. Barnes & Co., New York.

speak, signal, or coach the contestants during the round. They must remain seated, entering the ring only between rounds and at the termination of the contest.

There are certain regulations concerning the conduct of the contestants and the types of blows that they may employ. The major infractions in boxing include hitting below the belt; holding an opponent with one hand and hitting with the other while doing so; hitting an opponent who is down or who is getting up after being floored; pushing or butting, with head or shoulder, or using the knee, and delivering a clubbing blow at the back of the neck (rabbit punch).

Professional boxing in America generally has a "no foul rule." It decrees that no bout may be awarded to a boxer who is hit a low blow (below the belt) because the wearing of a foul-proof cup is mandatory in most states. However, the offending boxer usually loses the round. If the fouling is repeated and deliberate, after warnings, disqualification, suspension and a fine may result.

Amateur intercollegiate rules specify disqualification for a deliberate low blow. If it is unintentional the fouled boxer has 3 minutes in which to recover. If he cannot do so in that time, the bout is terminated and decided on the points recorded up to that time.

It should be noted that the "no foul rule" applies only to the low blow.

A contestant is considered down (floored) under the following conditions:

1. When any part of his body other than his feet is on the floor.

2. When he is hanging helplessly over the ropes.

3. When he is outside or between the ropes.

4. When he is rising after being knocked down.

In professional boxing, when a contestant is down his opponent must retire to a neutral corner and remain there until the fallen boxer regains his feet. In intercollegiate competition, when a contestant is down his opponent must retire to a far corner and shall not resume boxing until ordered to do so by the referee.

In professional boxing, when a contestant goes down the referee takes up the count from the knockdown timekeeper, an official who uses a stopwatch to count the down (knockdown) time the instant the boxer goes down. The watch is started when the down occurs. If the referee consumes, for instance, 3 seconds in seeing that a boxer goes to a neutral corner, the knockdown timekeeper indicates this by turning the count over to him at 4. It is a knockout when a contestant is down 10 seconds or when the referee declares a technical knockout.

A "technical knockout," according to Parke Cummings' "The Dictionary of Sports,"† is "a knockout declared by the referee when he decides that a boxer cannot continue, regardless of whether or not the boxer has been counted out. It is also a technical knockout when, for any reason, a boxer fails to continue a bout at the beginning of a new round. In intercollegiate and interscholastic boxing, however, this technical knockout provision does not apply to a disabling cut in a dual meet. If this occurs in the first round the bout is declared a draw. If in the second or third round, the decision goes to the boxer who is ahead on points at the time."

†A.S. Barnes and Co. New York.

CANOEING

(Courtesy of William A. Smoke, National Paddling Committee, E. Riverside Drive, R.T. 1, Box 83, Buchanan, Mich., 49107)

A means of transportation in years long gone by, the canoe today to a great extent has lost its utilitarian function and is used largely as an instrument of recreation and racing, though it still on occasion is highly useful in such matters as exploration. The canoe in its various forms has been used for transportation from unrecorded times in many lands. The more primitive the region, the greater the need for a simple canoe. It played an enormous role in the settlement of North America. In the pioneer days, the settlers pushed westward in the red man's birch bark canoe over waterways, which literally served as highways.

In modern times the canoe has been devel-

oped into a medium for competitive sport and for recreation. It remains the craft in which much undeveloped land still is cruised for the sake of sport and in a spirit of exploration.

W. Van B. Claussen of Washington, D.C., formerly of New York, an outstanding authority on the subject, has written the following:

"Where and when the canoe 'evolved' is neither recorded in history, nor has any savant deduced the fact with any degree of certainty.

"Dugout canoes, crude in form and workmanship but nevertheless actual manmade artifacts, have been ascribed upon good evidence to the Stone Age. How many centuries earlier occurred the popularly conceived transition from a crude floating log, to two logs lashed together for greater stability, to a raft of logs for added carrying capacity, to a hollowed log—or dugout—for greater speed, yet satisfactory capacity, is anybody's guess.

"The interesting point is that so many truly primitive forms still persist in everyday use, in spite of the fact that the peoples using them are well acquainted with more modern and efficient craft, encountered in their ordinary pursuit of commerce. The principal factor in this persistence of earlier types is, of course, the greater ease with which these can be constructed of locally available materials, and with the use of simpler tools; and that, in spite of apparent crudeness, the designs of such craft usually are well suited to the local conditions.

"While the origin of the canoe may be shrouded in mystery and speculation, certain it is that the use of this type craft for sporting and recreational purposes among civilized peoples can definitely be ascribed to a British barrister, John Macgregor, as a result of his development of the Bob Roy type canoe in 1865, and the books he wrote of his subsequent cruising throughout Europe, Scandinavia and the Holy Land.

"Macgregor popularized canoeing as a sport. July 26th of this same year, 1865, saw the founding of the Royal Canoe Club at a meeting called by Macgregor at the Star and Garter Inn near London. Through the consequent activity, additional types of canoes were developed until by 1868 the 300 or more at the main clubhouse and at its branches on the Humber, the Mersey and at Oxford fell into general classifications as 'racers,' 'light boats' and 'Rob Roys'—each serving both as a paddling and as a sailing craft.

"About this same time, history has it that France adopted canoeing as a sport. It must have been in a desultory manner, however, since, prior to 1938, Frenchmen did not appear often in international competition; there have been but two well known French canoe clubs. Their devotees of the sport have handed down no heritage of canoeing literature.

"It was in 1871 that a group of enthusiasts, led by William L. Alden and M. Roosevelt Schuyler, organized the New York Canoe Club, at what is now St. George, Staten Island, N.Y. This start quickly led to the formation of other clubs. Some of these early clubs that are still in existence are: New York Canoe Club; Buffalo Canoe Club, N.Y.; Knickerbocker Canoe Club, Edgewater, N.J.; and Red Dragon Canoe Club, Philadelphia, Pa.

"Many small groups of ardent canoeists affiliated themselves with existing local rowing clubs and cruised and raced under the boat clubs' burgee.

"On Aug. 3, 1880, a group of 25 prominent canoeists met at Crosbyside Park, Lake George, N.Y., and organized the American Canoe Assoc-

iation, electing Alden, commodore of the N.Y.C.C. as the first commodore of the association, and Nathaniel H. Bishop, famous for his 1874 cruise from Quebec to the Gulf of Mexico in the paper canoe Maria Theresa as the first secretary-treasurer.

"Other names among the founders, famous in canoeing history, were Arthur Brentano, Nicholas Longworth, Adolph Lowenthal, Dr. A.C. Neide, J.H. Rushton, and William P. Stephens.

"Shortly after the founding of the A.C.A., there came into being the Canadian Canoe Association to coordinate the activities of the Canadian clubs and to facilitate the holding of competition both in paddling and sailing with the A.C.A., whose summer headquarters then centered around Grindstone Island, one of the Thousand Islands of the St. Lawrence River. Subsequently, the A.C.A. acquired from the Canadian government title to 'Sugar Island,' between Gananoque, Canada, and Clayton, N.Y., as official camp and regatta site.

"Similarly, the British Canoe Association was founded to administer the national and international interests of the various British clubs. However, probably because of the individualistic spirit of the British canoeists, the B.C.A. never seemed to attain an atmosphere of permanency, and through the years it has undergone various metamorphoses, emerging once as a section of the Camping Clubs of Great Britain and more recently as the British Canoe Union.

"Within a few years of its founding, the infant American Canoe Association began to acquire an impressive collection of elaborate trophies presented for permanent competition in various types of races in paddling, or in sailing, canoes, according to the personal interest of the donor and his desire to promote the development of a particular class. Some 18 or 20 of these trophies of the 1880's are still in competition and bear the names of many famous American and Canadian winners."

Claussen was one of those instrumental in bringing world organization into canoeing. In the early 1920's he began correspondence with foreign clubs that ultimately resulted in the formation of a world canoeing federation under the name of International Representation for the Canoeing Sport (I.R.K.).

Dr. Max Eckert of the Deutscher Kano Verband (D.K.V.) was elected president of the first Congress. Through the I.R.K., the 19 member nations applied for and received recognition for canoeing as an Olympic sport. It was not until the Olympics in Berlin in 1936 that canoe races were conducted as official events. However, before the I.R.K. was formed, a crew from the Washington (D.C.) Canoe Club made up of Harry Knight, Hank Larkin and Charles (Bud) Havens participated in a demonstration in the

VIIIth Olympiad in Paris in 1924 on the Seine. Three other nations were entered.

There were 19 nations in the Berlin Olympics for 9 events at 1,000 and 10,000 meters. A third place by Ernest Riedel of the Pendleton C.C. of Yonkers, N.Y., in the 10,000-meter K-1 race was the best United States performance.

The old I.R.K. was reorganized between the 1936 Games and the resumption of Olympic competition after the war. The new world organization was the International Canoe Federation (I.C.F.), with J. Asschier of the Swedish Kayak Association as president. There were 17 nations in the federation.

The canoeing events in the first post-war Olympics were on London's Thames. There were 8 events at 1,000 and 10,000 meters for men, 1 at 500 meters for women. For the United States, Stephen Lysak and Stephen Macknowski of the Yonkers (N.Y.) C.C. took first in the 10,000-meter C-2 event and second in the 1,000-meter C-2. Frank Havens of the Washington C.C. was second in the 10,000-meter C-1 event.

For the 1952 Olympics at Helsinki, Finland, 20 nations were entered for the same program as 4 years previously. Havens was first in the 10,000-meter C-1 race, breaking the world record by 3 minutes.

The American Canoe Association (ACA) is the organization sanctioned by the International Olympic Committee to pick Olympic teams for the Olympic games which are held every four years. Within the ACA falls an activities committee called the National Paddling Committee (NPC) which is responsible for all aspects of flatwater Olympic canoe and kayak racing. Among some of its functions, the NPC governs the rules and regulations of the sport, conducts the National and North American Championships each year, and sponsors a scholastic and collegiate racing program. This competition has brought about a change in American Canoe Association racing and equipment. Only 2 types of fine cedar V-bottom racing canoes were used here previously. One was a 16-footer with a 30-inch beam, used for one man and tandem competition and known as a "peanut." The other was a 20-foot craft with 30-inch beam for 4-man use, known as a "club four."

For the 1948 Games, a number of I.C.F. single-seater and 2-seater racing kayaks were imported for use in the senior double-blade events at Olympic metric distances. The single-seat kayak (K-1) is 17 feet long with a 20-inch beam. The K-2 measures approximately 21 feet with a 21½-inch beam. For senior single-blade events, the old "peanut" was supplanted by the I.C.F. racing canoe of 17 feet by 29½ inches for either 1-man or tandem crews (C-1 and C-2).

The most recent development is an effort to introduce in this country the 4-man I.C.F. racing kayak (K-4). It measures about 36 feet by 23½ inches.

In 1964 for the first time ever, the American girls won medals in the women's singles and doubles.

One of the old trophies still in competition is the International Challenge Cup. It was put up in 1885 by the New York Canoe Club as a perpetual challenge sailing prize. Through the years, though not annually, it has been contested for keenly in decked sailing canoes with sliding seats by American, Canadian and British clubs.

OUTSTANDING CANOEISTS

No other canoeist has dominated the national championships over a long period the way Ernest Riedel of the Pendleton Canoe Club in Yonkers, N.Y., did in his specialty, the 1-man double blade competition. Riedel gained his first title in 1930 and his last in 1948, registering 11 victories during that time. He did even better in the international races between the United States and Canada by winning the 1-man double blade Championship Trophy at a mile in successive years from 1923 to 1935 and following this with triumphs in 1938, 1940, 1941, 1946 and 1947.

Riedel also represented the United States in the 1936 Olympic Games at Berlin, Germany, and his best was a third in the 10,000-meter 1-man kayak event. He was picked to represent the United States in 1940 and 1944, but the war prevented the staging of the Games. He also competed in the 1948 Olympics.

Another who rates with the greats in the sport is Harry (Pop) Knight of the Washington Canoe Club, the only man ever to be on the winning side in 4 national title events in a year, a feat he performed twice. In 1932 he captured the 1-man single blade and shared the championships in tandem single blade, 4-man single blade and 4-man double blade competitions. Four years later he gained top laurels in the tandem single blade, 4-man single blade, tandem double blade and 4-man double blade events.

Other United States senior titles gained by Knight were the tandem single blade and tandem double blade in 1931; 4-man single, 4-man double and tandem double in 1933; 4-man single, tandem double and 4-man double in 1934 and tandem single in 1935.

Frank Havens of the Washington Canoe Club currently is one of the world's outstanding single blade men. He won the United States championship in 1950, 1951, 1952, 1954, 1956 and 1957 and capped his victories here by capturing the 10,000 meter race at the 1952 Olympic Games in the world record time of 57 minutes, 41 seconds. The next day he finished second in the 1,000-meter single blade test, 1.1 seconds behind the victor.

Stephen Lysak of the Yonkers (N.Y.) Canoe Club won his first national championship in the

1-man single blade event in 1936 and has been on a number of tandem and 4-man single blade championship crews. In 1948 he and his tandem partner, Stephen Macknowski, won the 10,000-meter single blade race at the London Olympics and placed second in the 1,000 meters. They also took the 1948 national title. Lysak built the canoe he used in the Olympic Games.

Frank Krick and John Haas of Philadelphia were one of the best tandem single blade combinations this country ever produced. They won national titles in 1946, 1947, 1949, 1954 and 1956 and finished fifth in the 10,000 meters in the 1952 Olympics, when Krick was 43 years old and Haas was 41.

Krick has been picked twice before to represent the United States in the Olympic Games, but had to pass up both opportunities. In 1936 he was paired with Stanley Cimokowski, whose citizenship papers did not arrive in time for the team to accept the berth. In 1940 the war prevented the pair from competing. This tandem won the United States single blade championship in 1938, 1939 and 1940.

William Gaehler of the Pendleton C.C. was an outstanding team man and partner. He paired with Al Gottlieb, W. Lofgren, W. Collis and Riedel to win national double blade titles in 1935, 1937, 1938, 1940 and 1941. He also was a member of the national 4-man double blade teams in 1930, 1931, 1935 and 1937 and was named to the Olympic teams in 1936 and 1940.

Andy Weigand won the single blade National championship four times (1965, 1967, 1970, 1971), teamed with Dennis Van Valkenburgh, Andy Toro, and Roland Muhlen to win the 2-man single-blade race in 1965, 1969, 1971–72. He also won the 2-man kayak in 1969 with Jerry Welborn his teammate plus being a crewman the 1972 national 4-man single blade champions.

Another Weigand who has winning ways is Pete. Winner of the 1-man kayak in 1969 and 1972, he teamed up with John Glair to win the 2-man kayak nationals in 1965–66, teamed with John Van Dyke to win in 1967 and again in 1972 with Bob Hoag as his teammate. The 4-man single blade winner in 1972 had Pete Weigand as a crewman while the 4-man kayak saw him winning with teammates in 1965–66 and again in 1972.

WINNERS OF MAJOR EVENTS

International Challenge Cup

1886—C. Bowyer Vaus, New York C.C.
1887—No competition
1888—Reginald S. Blake, New York C.C.
1889—No competition
1890—H. Lansing Quich, New York C.C.
1891—T.E.H. Barrington, New York C.C.
1892—T.S. Oxholm, New York C.C.

1893—94—No competition
1895—Paul Butler, New York C.C.
1896—1912—No competition
1913—14—Leo Friede, New York C.C.
1915—32—No competition
1933—Uffa Fox and Roger DeQuincey,
           Royal C.C., Great Britain
1934—35—No competition
1936—Roger DeQuincey, Royal C.C.,
           Great Britain
1937—47—No competition
1948—R. St. John, Royall C.C., Great Britain
1949—51—No competition
1953—54—No competition
1952—Louis Whitman, New York C.C.
1955—United States (Adolph Morse, Louis Whitman, Frank Jordaens, Joe Farrugia) defeated British team, 33¼ to 26.
(No further competition.)

U.S. Paddling Champions

One-Man Single Blade

1930—William Gaehler
1931—Charles Robinson
1932—Harry Knight
1933—Howard LaBrant
1934—35—Eric Rodman
1936—Stephen Lysak
1937—Leo Hickey
1938—Ernest Riedel
1939—Howard Woodward
1940—Theodore Blackman
1941—Joe Ryan
1942—45—No competition
1946—Andrew Kulakowich
1947—William Havens Jr.
1948—Andrew Macknowski
1949—Andrew Kulakowich
1950—52—Frank Havens
1953—George Byers
1954—Frank Havens
1955—George Byers
1956—57—Frank Havens
1958—Paul Donohue
1959—60—Steven Hernek
1961—Frank Havens
1962—R. van de Muelebroecke
1963—William Gates
1964—Dennie Van Valkenburgh
1965—Andy Weigand
1966—Jim O'Rourke
1967—Andy Weigand
1968—William Gates
1969—Andy Toro
1970—71—Andy Weigand
1972—Roland Muhlen

Two-Man Single Blade

1930—W. Gaehler—C. Robinson
1931—H. Knight—K. Knight
1932—H. Knight—E. Rodman

1933—E. Volante—T. Blackman
1934—J. Zaboy—A. Kropoff
1935—H. Knight—E. Rodman
1936—H. Knight—R. Ackad
1937—A. Springel—K. Nelson
1938—40—S. Cimokowski—F. Krick
1941—Joe Ryan—L. Kruppa
1942—45—No competition
1946—47—F. Krick—J. Haas
1948—S. Lysak—S. Macknowski
1949—F. Krick—J. Haas
1950—F. Boutilier—D. Bingham
1951—53—George Byers—Daniel Bingham
1954—Frank Krick—John Haas
1955—John Pagkos—John Haas
1956—Frank Krick—John Haas
1957—Richard Moran—Arnold Demus
1959—F. Krick—Kastner
1960—61—W. Hasse—R. van de Muelebroecke
1962—F. Havens—C. Lundmark
1963—64—James O'Rourke—Joseph Dronzek
1965—Andy Weigand—Dennis Van Valkenburgh
1966—Robert Fletcher—Dennis Murphy
1967—68—Michael Ansley—Stephen Ansley
1969—Andy Weigand—Andy Toro
1970—Andy Toro—Dick Soules
1971—Andy Weigand—Andy Toro
1972—Andy Weigand—Roland Muhlen

One-Man Kayak

1930—32—Ernest Riedel
1933—Gerald Mosher
1934—Adam Balko
1935—Ernest Riedel
1936—Harold Bruns
1937—38—Ernest Riedel
1939—William Havens Jr.
1940—41—Ernest Riedel
1942—45—No competition
1946—48—Ernest Riedel
1949—Andrew Kulakowich
1950—Michael Budrock
1951—John J. Anderson
1952—Richard Moran
1953—Michael Budrock
1954—Bob Dermond
1955—John Pagkos
1956—Raymond Clark
1957—Dave Merwin
1958—Ken Wilson
1959—Joseph Redela
1960—Paul Beecham
1961—Donald Dodge
1962—Charles Lundmark
1963—Bill Jewell
1964—Tony Ralphs
1965—John Van Dyke
1966—John Glair
1967—John Van Dyke
1968—John Pickett
1969—Peter Weigand

1970—Harry Krawczyk
1971—Tony Ralphs
1972—Peter Weigand

Two-Man Kayak

1930—C. Robinson—E. Riedel
1931—H. Knight—Rothrock
1932—C. Wilkie—J. Haas
1933—34—H. Knight—E. Rodman
1935—G. Gaehler—A. Gottlieb
1936—H. Knight—J. Long
1937—W. Gaehler—W. Lofgren
1938—W. Gaehler—E. Riedel
1939—E. Trilling—W. Havens Jr.
1940—W. Gaehler—W. Collis
1941—W. Gaehler—E. Riedel
1942—45—No competition
1946—47—A. Springel—E. Riedel
1948—A. Springel—F. Oldal
1949—A. Kulakowich—S. Lysak
1950—51—P. Bochnewich—J. Anderson
1952—53—Thomas Horton—John Eiseman
1954—Art Potter—John VanDyke
1955—John Pagkos—Russell Dermond
1956—Raymond Clark—Wally Haase and John
            Pagkos—Russell Dermond (tie)
1957—Ken Wilson—Robert O'Brien
1958—Russell Dermond—Greg Anderson
1959—Nick Tottossy—Joseph Redela
1960—Kenneth Wilson—John Wolters
1961—Russell Dermond—Michael Pagkos
1962—William Kelly—Neil O'Keefe
1963—64—Bill Jewell—Gert Grigoleit
1965—Pete Weigand—John Glair
1966—Pete Weigand—John Glair
1967—John Van Dyke—Pete Weigand
1968—Bill Bragg—Robert Haris
1969—Andy Weigand—Jerry Welborn
1970—Harry Krawczyk—Gene Krawczyk
1971—Tony Ralphs—Bill Leach
1972—Pete Weigand—Bob Hoag

Four-Man Single Blade

1930—31— Pendleton C.C., Yonkers, N.Y. (W.
            Gaehler, E. Dreher, E. Riedel, C. Rob-
            inson)
1932—Washington C.C. (H. Knight, E. Fore, H.
            Vollmer, E. Rodman)
1933—34— Washington C.C. (H. Knight, R.
            Ackad, H. Vollmer, E. Rodman)
1935—Pendleton C.C. (W. Gaehler, E. Dreher, L.
            Kruppa, E. Riedel)
1936—Washington C.C. (H. Knight, R. Ackad, W.
            Long, E. Trilling)
1937—Pendleton C.C. (E. Riedel, A. Gottlieb, W.
            Lofgren, W. Yeager)
1938—Cacawa C.C., Philadelphia (S. Cimokow-
            ski, F. Krick, J. Holland, J. Haas)
1939—Yonkers C.C. (A. Kulakowich, M. Kula-
            kowich, J. Lysak, S. Lysak)
1940—Yonkers C.C. (M. Kulakowich, C.

Schefler, J. Paretti, J. Alkonis)

1941—Yonkers C.C. (S. Macknowski, J. Daniels, R. Dunford, S. Lysak)

1942—45— No competition

1946—Yonkers C.C. (S. Macknowski, S. Lysak, M. Kulakowich, J. Paretti)

1947—Washington C.C. (W. Rhodes, W. Havens Jr., E. Trilling, F. Havens)

1948—Yonkers C.C. (A. Macknowski, S. Macknowski, S. Lysak, R. Dunford)

1949—Yonkers C.C. (S. Lysak, R. Dunford, J. Papot, K. Twitchell)

1950—Samoset C.C., West Roxbury, Mass. (B. Boutillier, D. Bingham, G. Byers, R. Mozer)

1951—Quinneboquin C.C., West Roxbury, Mass. (P. Doherty, R. Spillane, P. Donahue, R. Moran)

1952—Samoset C.C. (P. Donohue, D. Bingham, G. Byers, R. Moran)

1953—Samoset C.C. (Arnold Demis, William Anderson, Daniel Bingham, George Byers)

1954—Philadelphia C.C. (J. Haas, H. Rotzell, R. Harrington, F. Krick)

1955—Philadelphia C.C. (H. Rotzell, R. Harrington, J. Barnitz, F. Krick)

1956—Philadelphia C.C. (F. Krick, J. Haas, H. Rotzell, J. Barnitz)

1957—Yonkers C.C. (S. Messur, A. Springel, A. Geraty, D. Kelley)

1958—Potomac B.C. (W. Haase, Parker, Love, van de Muelebroecke)

1959—Yonkers C.C. (Bubrock, Manley, Bouchnevich, Messur)

1960—Potomac B.C. (W. Haase, W. Schuette, R. Caviola, R. van de Muelebroecke)

1961—Washington C.C. (L. Stitzenberger, A. Weigand, D. Van Valkenbergh, T. Palmby)

1962—Washington C.C. (F. Havens, A. Weigand, D. Van Valkenbergh, J. Beerbower)

1963—64—Potomac B.C. (R. Cavaiola, W. Smith, W. Haase, R. Van de Meulebroecke)

1965—Yonkers Canoe Club (Anderson, Parretti, J. Dronzek, J. O'Rourke)

1966—Columbia C.C. (D. Murphy, R. Fletcher, Gardner, Robinson)

1967—Washington C.C. (M. Ansley, S. Ansley, R. Jobber, A. Weigand)

1968—Washington C.C. (M. Ansley, S. Ansley, R. Jobber, Herneck)

1969—Unattached (W. Wilkins, P. Runnels, M. Guenther, R. Muhlen)

1970—Inwood N.Y. (R. Effinger, E. Rumayor, J. McCarthy, J. Maginness)

1971—Washington C.C. (B. Merritt, Smith, M. Ware, T. Scribner)

1972—Rusty Pelican O.A. (A. Weigand, R. Muhlen P. Weigand, D. Landenwitch)

Four-Man Kayak

1930—31—Pendleton C.C., Yonkers, N.Y. (E. Riedel, W. Gaehler, E. Freher, C. Robinson)

1932—Washington C.C. (S. Cimokowski, F. Krick, J. Haas, C. Wilkie)

1933—Washington C.C. (S. Cimokowski, F. Krick, J. Holland, J. Haas)

1934—Washington C.C. (H. Bruns, W. Bruns, E. Balko, W. Gaehler)

1935—Pendleton C.C. (E. Volante, T. Blackman, W. Hasenfus, J. Hasenfus)

1936—Washington C.C. (S. Lysak, H. Bruns, J. Lysak, E. Balko)

1937—Pendleton C.C. (W. Gaehler, E. Riedel, A. Gottlieb, W. Lofgren)

1938—Yonkers C.C. (H. Bruns, S. Schefler, J. Lysak, S. Lysak)

1939—Washington C.C. (E. Trilling, W. Havens Jr., H. Knight, K. Romjue)

1940—Yonkers C.C. (H. Bruns, S. Lysak, A. Russak, M. Kulakowich)

1941—Pendleton C.C. (E. Riedel, Joe Ryan, W. Gaehler, A. Springel)

1942—45—No competition

1946—Washington C.C. (W. Rhodes, H. Havens Jr., E. Trilling, H. Vollmer)

1947—Pendleton C.C. (A. Springel, B. Folks, E. Riedel, W. Lavach)

1948—Pendleton C.C. (A. Springel, E. Riedel, F. Oldal, John Ryan)

1949—Pendleton C.C. (A. Springel, E. Riedel, F. Oldal, W. Lavach)

1950—51—Yonkers C.C. (M. Budrock, J. Anderson, P. Bochnewich, R. Dunford)

1952—Potomac B.C., Washington (T. Horton, W. Schuette, J. Eiseman Jr., T. Kimball)

1953—Potomac B.C. (Paul Beachum, Thomas Jones, Andy Potter, William Haase)

1954—Yonkers C.C. (T. Budrock, J. Pagkos, H. Weidner, M. Budrock)

1955—Yonkers C.C. (J. Pagkos, A. Geraty, G. Barker, J. Anderson)

1956—Potomac B.C. (R. Clark, P. Yaeger, T. Jones, W. Haase)

1957—Potomac B.C. (K. Clark, W. Haase, W. Schuette, T. Horton)

1958—Yonkers C.C. (G. Anderson, R. Dermond, E. Budrock, S. Messur)

1959—Inwood C.C. (Wilson, Wolters, O'Brian, Feicht)

1960—Turkeyfoot K.C. (D. Merwin, A. Stuckey, J. Jerome, J. Klippert)

1961—Niles C.C. (D. Dodge, G. Grigolett, J. Huber, B. Albert)

1962—Inwood C.C. (B. Kelly, N. O'Keefe, T. Healy, E. Feicht)

1963—Inwood C.C. (W. Kelley, T. Healy, K. Wilson, N. O'Keefe)

1964—California K.C. (T. Ralphs, B. Jewell, W. Richards, G. Grigoleit)
1965—66—Potomac B.C. (J. Van Dyke, J. Redela, J. Glair, P. Weigand)
1967—Washington C.C. (J. Brosius, W. Schuette, Armstrong, C. Lundmark)
1968—New York A.C. (E. Heincke, A. Libertini, J. Beczak, N. O'Keefe)
1969—New York A.C. (E. Heincke, F. Albert, A. Libertini, J. Beczak)
1970—Sebago C.C. (H. Krawczyk, G. Krawczyk, E. Walsh, J. Greifenberger)
1971—Washington C.C. (A. Whitney, J. Brosius, S. Dragon, J. Goodrow)
1972—Rusty Pelican O.A. (P. Weigand, J. Van Cleave, B. Hoag, B. Leach)

Canoe Tilt

1959—Frank Havens—William Havens
1960—62—Frank Havens—Charles Lundmark
1963—Adolph Springel—Ernest Riedel
1964—72—No competition

LADIES

Single Kayak

1959—Mary Ann Duchai
1960—61—Glorianne Perrier
1962—Francine Fox
1963—Glorianne Perrier
1964—Marcia Jones
1965—Marcia Smoke and Sperry Jones (tie)
1966—72—Marcia Smoke

Double Kayak

1959—60—Mary Ann Duchai—Diane Jerome
1961—Glorianne Perrier—Nell Fisher
1962—Marcia Jones—Eileen Murphy
1963—64—Glorianne Perrier—Francine Fox
1965—Francine Fox—Glorianne Perrier
1966—1970—Marcia Smoke—Sperry Rademaker
1971—Marcia Smoke—Kathy Mosolino
1972—Marcia Smoke—Sperry Rademaker

4-Woman Kayak

1962—Niles K.C. (No names)
1963—Niles K.C. (M. Jones, Murphy, S. Jones, Rupp)
1964—Potomac B.C. (E. Murphy, D. Smith N. major, S. Gantz)
1965—Washington C.C. (F. Fox, G. Perrier, D. Smith, Farley)
1966—67—Michigan P.C. (M. Smoke, S. Rademaker, C. Corson, P. Petraites)
1968—Orlando C.C. (M. Smoke, S. Rademaker, C. Corson, P. Petraites)
1969—Washington C.C. (B. Scribner, J. Gray, C. Haermann, B. Merritt)
1970—Niles K.C. (M. Smoke, S. Rademaker, D. Jenkins, D. Darnall)
1971—Niles K.C. (M. Smoke, M. Flood, D. Jenkins, K. Mosolino)
1972—Niles K.C. (M. Smoke, M. Flood, L. Flood, S. Rademaker)

Team Point Winners

1930—31—Pendleton C.C.
1932—33—Washington C.C.
1934—Yonkers C.C.
1935—36—Washington C.C.
1937—40—Yonkers C.C.
1941—Inwood C.C.
1942—45—No competition
1946—Yonkers C.C.
1947—Pendleton C.C.
1948—Yonkers C.C.
1949—Pendleton C.C.
1950—51—Yonkers C.C.
1952—Samoset C.C.
1953—54—Potomac B.C.
1955—58—Yonkers C.C.
1959—62—Washington C.C.
1963—Niles C.C.
1964—California K.C.
1965—Washington C.C.
1966—Potomac B.C.
1967—Washington C.C.
(Discontinued)

CHECKERS

Nearly everyone knows how to play checkers. A favorite gift to children is a checker set, and it takes little time for a child to catch on to the game. However, though this leads to the impression that it is not a profound activity, the impression is incorrect. To become a master at the game requires the ability to think seriously and an analytical mind.

In the Middle Ages, checkers was deprecated as "chess for ladies," and this estimate persists in the name of the game in many modern languages—French, jeu des dames; German, damen-spiel; Italian, giuoco della dama, etc. The English name "draughts" is probably a reference to the pieces. The American name, checkers, refers to the use of a checkered board.

As with chess, the origin of checkers has been traced to remotest antiquity on evidence that proves nothing but that some board game was then played, advises Geoffrey Mott-Smith, an authority on games. Boards and pieces found in the tombs of the Pharaohs have been ascribed by various writers to chess, checkers, pachisi, mill, etc., and might with equal persuasion be cited to show an ancient origin for Camelot, a proprietary game launched about 25 years ago.

The fact appears to be that many of these board games developed from a primitive game, and that this ancestor also has survived almost unchanged as modern pachisi (parcheesi). Historians place the earliest clear evidence of chess in the 7th Century A. D. the first unmistakable account of checkers is in a Spanish book of 1547 A.D., by Antonio Torquemada. From this book we can conjecture that the game was played some centuries earlier.

The first serious attempt to analyze the strategy of checkers was made by a French mathematician, Pierre Mallet, in a book published in 1668. In 1800, the publication by Joshua Sturges of his *Guide to the Game of Draughts* launched an unparalleled period of activity by British players and theorists, who discovered and formulated all the basic principles of play.

Other leading writers on checkers were William Payne (1756), J. Drummond (1838) and Andrew Anderson (1844). Also James Lees, Joseph Gould, H.D. Lyman, R.E. Bowen, F.W. Drinkwater, Franke Dunne, Dr. T.J. Brown, J.D. Janvier and F. Tescheleit. Among important contributors to the problem collections of Lyman and Gould were Fred Allen, David Gourlay, W. Leggett, J. Robertson, J. Smith and G. Whitney.

Contemporary writers include Newell W. Banks, Willie Ryan, Tom Wiswell, Ben Boland, Millard Hopper, E.A. Smith, Leonard Hall, Ken Grover and Art Reisman.

Their books are read and studied by thousands all over the world. One of the latest volumes in the field is *Championship Chess and Checkers,** by Larry Evans and Wiswell. Nearly 1,000 books have been published on checkers in the last 200 years or more.

Today the game is well organized and Wiswell, Walter Hellman, Marion Tinsley, Banks and other masters are constantly on tour or writing books on this old and fascinating hobby.

In the United States the governing body is the American Checker Federation. It conducts a biennial tournament to determine the national champion, as well as numerous sectional and local events.

The chief international events in checkers have been team matches between countries. The first such event was between England and Scotland in 1884. The Scots won. In 1905, England sent a team to the United States and the British triumphed. In 1927 an American team beat the British by 96—20.

Continuing analysis has brought "go-as-you-please" checkers near to exhaustion. That is, if given free choice of opening, a modern expert can surely draw a game—he need risk losing only if he tries to win. With infallible play on both

*A.S. Barnes and Company, N.Y.

sides the game is undoubtedly a draw. In the middle of the last century, the percentage of drawn games in tournament play rose to inordinate heights. Andrew Anderson, the first modern world champion, and James Wyllie, in a championship match, played the same drawn game 54 times, neither player caring to risk loss by departing from "the book."

Walter Hellman won the world title in 1948 by defeating Asa Long, who had held the title for 15 years. The score was two games to one, with 37 ties, one which lasted eight hours. Since then Hellman has held the title for all but four of the last 25 years.

Modern tournament play therefore uses a plan to force contestants to be prepared for all possible openings, not merely the most favorable. In the "2-move restriction" plan, the 47 playable combinations of a Black first move and a White answer are written on cards and to begin a match between 2 players a card is drawn at random. Each contestant must take the Black and White sides of the prescribed opening in 2 separate games. National championships use a 3-move restriction, with 142 openings.

The rules of checkers are not the same throughout the world. In fact, the small divergences in the rules, making enormous differences in strategy, have created several distinct variants. In Spanish draughts, a king may move any distance along an open diagonal, like a bishop in chess. In Italian draughts, a single man may not capture a king . Polish draughts (so-called because advocated in a book written in ·1736 by a Pole residing in Paris) uses a 10-inch x 10-inch board with 20 pieces on each side. The British-American variant is believed to have sprung from Spanish draughts in the 16th Century.

Freestyle Checkers, also known as Spanish Checkers, was won by Enrique "King Chico" Freeman in the First World Freestyle Championship in 1964 by defeating Mexico's Eligio Rodriquez in a 24-game series. He has held the title since then.

FAMOUS PLAYERS

The best-known of the old-time players include Andrew Anderson of Scotland, first of the modern champions; James Wyllie, Anderson's successor as universal titleholder; Robert D. Yates, James Ferrie, Richard Jordan, Robert Martins, W.R. Barker, J.A. Kear, R.D. Petterson and William Strickland. Other notables in the game were Charles F. Barker, J.P. Reed, J. Lear, C. Hefter, C.H. Freeman, Willie Gardner, A.J. Heffner, P. Thirkell, A.E. Greenwood, R. Stewart, Richard Jordan and Alfred Jordan.

The modern list includes Newell W. Banks, Asa A. Long, Edwin F. Hunt, Tom Wiswell, Millard Hopper, Walter Hellman, Marion Tinsley, Basil Case, J. Marshall, J.T. Bradford, Alex Cameron, Charles Jolly, Harold Freyer, Harry

Lieberman, Chris Nelson, Derek Oldbury, Fraser, and Elbert Lowder.

A.S. Wheeler of the Ontario Checker Association listed the following as among Canada's greatest players: William Fleming, champion from 1867 to 1890; E.R. Jacques, Ed Kelly, Angus Crawford, J. Brown, W. Dodds, A. Fulton, L. Flannagan, E. Slavin, E.V. Thompson, E. Martin, N. Stephen and W.R. Fraser.

CHESS

Chess is considered a game of the intellectuals. It demands a keen and alert mind and concentration of the highest order, and it is a serious game, perhaps the most serious played by man. It is played throughout the civilized world. However, it has perhaps fewer followers than any other sport, even though the game has been played for centuries.

Chess dates back to antiquity. How far back is not absolutely known. In 1938, Dr. A.E. Speiser, heading a group of scientists in an exploration sponsored by the University of Pennsylvania and the American School of Oriental Research, excavated pieces of terra cotta believed to have been used as chess "men" in Mesopotamia 6,000 years ago.

The discovery was made on the fourteenth level of the site of ancient Tepe Gawra in Northern Iraq, which belongs, according to some scientists, to the El Obeid period, which existed 5,500 to 6,000 years ago. Some authorities on chess raise a question about the terra cotta pieces being chessmen, since no board of any kind was found with them. But the scientists answer that with the statement that years earlier there was uncovered a circular board belonging to the Byzantine Era, which might have been a chess board, thus, tracing back chess 50 or more centuries.

The exact origin of the game always has been shrouded in the mists, with confusion created by so many different nations claiming the honor for inventing this complicated universal game.

The Greeks, Romans, Babylonians, Arabs, Hindus, Castilians, Irish, Mesopotamians, Welsh, Hebrews, Chinese, Scythians and Araucanians all have been credited with founding chess. Some historians claim that King Solomon thought up the mental pastime; others give the honor to Japeth, to Shem, to Xerxes, the philosopher, while many insisted—until a short time ago—that chess was invented by the Chinese Mandarin, Han Sing, during the reign of Kao Tsu, otherwise Pin Lang, then a king, and later Emperor of China (174 B.C.).

It was declared that Han Sing, commanding an army invading the Shen Si country and seeking some way to keep his soldiers entertained while idle in winter quarters, devised chess, calling it Choke-Choo-Hong-Ki, meaning "science of wars." Thus, it was not only a game, but a method of schooling troops. To support this contention, those who had espoused the cause of Han Sing, pointed out that chess moves were akin to those made in the military strategy.

However, Han Sing was effaced as a possible originator of chess in 1930 by the discovery of a crude chess board, chess men and markers in the tomb of King Tut-Ankh-Amen of Egypt, who died more than 1,200 years before the birth of the Chinese Mandarin. That gave temporary honors to Tut and his Egyptians, but the Speiser findings place their laurels in jeopardy.

Chess now is almost the universal name of the game. But it has had many others through its long existence. The Hindus called it "Chaturanga"; the ancient Persians named it "Shatranj." The Romans referred to it as "Ludus Latrun Culorum" and the Chinese name for it was "Chong Ki." In early Ireland it was "Fifth Cheall," the Welsh named it "Tawlbwrdd." In Italy it was "Sacci Alla Rabiosa," while the Spaniards called it "Axedrez de La Drama." The old English name was "Check." The French called it "Echecs," and there is some dispute as to whether "chess" was derived from the English or the French.

The first writings on the game now known as chess were in 1200 A.D. (some fix the date as 1300 A.D.) by Jacobus de Cessolis, a Dominican Friar of Italy. He called his treatise "Liber De Moribus Hominum et Officiis Nobilium Super Ludo Scacorum." This later was translated into French by Jehan De Vignay, and in 1474 William Caxton, an Englishman, translated De Vignay's work into English.

Caxton's translation was not published until 1479. It was printed that year in Cologne (Germany) and appeared under the title of *The Game and Playe of Chesse*. There was such a demand for the book that late in 1479 Caxton decided upon a second printing. His intent was to have the work done in Cologne, but there was a print shop in London—just organized—which assured Caxton it could duplicate the printing of Cologne in metal type. Caxton gave that shop the order, and it is believed that the book was the first ever printed from metal type in England.

Caxton's treatise standardized play for a while but his basic rules did not endure. The Italians soon deviated from Caxton's regulations. In the 16th Century, Spain and other countries adopted the rules of Italy. So did England—eventually. This resulted in international play, with the greatest players being Italians and Spaniards.

Perhaps more books have been written on chess than deal with any other game that has been played. The hobby of many wealthy chess enthusiasts throughout the world has been the accumulation of volumes dealing with chess. The result has been several vast libraries devoted entirely to the game.

Ruy Lopez of Spain was the first player to gain recognition as a great master of the method of blindfold play. His system was copied by other Spaniards in the period from 1550 to about 1570. Meanwhile, Italy was developing some wizards and soon made championship claims.

The first tournament of consequence was in 1562 A.D., when two famous Italian players, Paolo Boi and Giovanni Leonardo da Cutri, went to Spain, met Santa Maria, Lopez, Busnardo and Ciron, a brilliant quartet—and defeated them all.

Giacchino Greco of Italy was ranked as the greatest chess player in the 17th Century and François André Danican, famous French musical composer, known as "Philidor" in chess circles, was the champion of the 18th Century. He defeated the best in his own country, the champions of Spain, the finest players in England and then, while in London in 1744, when he was only 21 years of age, met Philip Stamma, a marvelous Syrian, and, in a match of 10 games, won 8 and lost 1, the other being a draw.

Philidor long was credited with being the first man ever to play—and to win—at chess while blindfolded. He imposed that handicap upon himself so that in games with other players the competition might be more equal. But Philidor, who died in 1795, was not the creator of blindfold chess. Lopez had played it 2 centuries earlier. Nor was Lopez the originator. The Arabs and Persians, as early as the 11th Century, had blindfolded themselves in matches with inferior players, so as to minimize their advantage in skill.

Stamma rallied from defeat by Philidor to become not only a master, but also to be acclaimed the pioneer in modern chess technique. He was a native of Aleppo, Syria, and was an interpreter of Oriental languages for the King of England stationed in London. Near the middle of the 18th Century, he published a book in which he outlined 100 artificial end positions, and this, with his later notations, increased interest in the game because it put the greater stress upon strategy.

Chess dates its great advance in popularity from the era of Stamma, whose feats determined others to try to eclipse him, or, at least, equal him.

Another Frenchman—Louis de la Bourdonnais—succeeded Philidor as a champion of France. He won the international title by defeating Alexander Macdonnell, the greatest in England, in a series of matches. After de la Bourdonnais, who died in 1840, had passed his peak,

Alexandre Deschapelles (1780—1847) became recognized as the champion.

In 1843, Pierre de Saint-Amant, a pupil of de la Bourdonnais, and Howard Staunton of London were matched in Paris "for the international championship." Staunton won. He scored later victories over some remarkable players from other parts of Europe and became the promoter of the first real international chess tournament. He staged it in connection with the World's Exhibition in London in 1851, which year marked the beginning of a new era in the sport.

The championship was won by Prof. Adolph Anderssen of Germany, but Staunton continued to acclaim himself "European Champion." He proceeded to issue challenges as European champion and in 1858, Paul Morphy (1837—1884) of New Orleans, one of the greatest chess masters of all ages, accepted and sailed to Europe to test Staunton's skill.

Morphy had won the American championship in 1857, in the first United States tournament, held in New York. In one match, Louis Paulsen devoted 14 hours 28 minutes to thinking before making one move. Morphy defeated him, anyway.

Morphy never gained the opportunity to meet Staunton. The "European Champion," upon Morphy's arrival, told him he would meet him "at some later date." Morphy toured Europe while awaiting Staunton's action. Morphy defeated Anderssen, the conqueror of Staunton, and a score of others of international fame. He won so easily that the matches bore no resemblance to contests. Europe joined America in declaring Morphy champion of the world, whereupon enthusiasts of both continents demanded that Staunton meet Morphy or retire. Staunton replied by announcing his retirement in 1858. He never played in a tournament again. He died in 1874.

Morphy returned to the United States in 1859. His health broke in 1860. He retired from play and died in 1884.

Upon Morphy's resignation as champion, Professor Anderssen reclaimed the title. He was disputed by Wilhelm Steinitz. They met in 1866, Steinitz winning. Steinitz, an Austrian, became a resident of the United States in 1883. He retained the title until 1894, when he was conquered by Dr. Emanuel Lasker of Berlin. Lasker was champion from 1894 until 1921, when he was defeated by Jose R. Capablanca of Havana, Cuba. The latter reigned until 1927, when he was dethroned by Dr. Alexander A. Alekhine of Paris. In 1935, Alekhine was defeated by Dr. Max Euwe of Holland. On Dec. 7, 1937, Dr. Alekhine regained the crown by defeating Euwe at The Hague.

International chess play ended with the outbreak of war in Europe, although in Russia, in 1940, a tournament called "International" was put on and resulted in a tie between Igor Bondarevsky of Rostov and Andreas Lilienthal of Budapest. In 1942, there was staged in Munich, Germany, the "European Championship Tournament." This was won by Goosta Stoltz of Sweden; Dr. Alekhine tied for second with Erik Lunden of Sweden. The other contestants were from Germany and Denmark.

Geoffrey Mott-Smith of New York, a leading authority, advises on the following post-war developments in the game:

"The first international team match to be conducted by radio was between the United States and the U.S.S.R., Sept. 1–4, 1945. The American team consisted of Arnold S. Denker, Samuel Reshevsky, Reuben Fine, Israel Horowitz, Isaac Kashdan, Herman Steiner, Albert Pinkus, H. Seidman, Abraham Kupchik and Anthony Santasiere. The Russians were Mikhail Botvinnik, Vassily Smyslov, I. Boleslavsky, Salo Flohr, A. Kotov, Bondarevsky, Lilienthal, V. Ragozin, N. Makogonov and David Bronstein.

"Each man played two games with his opposite number on the other team. The Russian team won by 15½ to 4½. The sensation of the event was the defeat of Reshevsky and Fine, considered America's strongest players, by the official No. 2 and No. 3 players of Russia. U.S.S.R. has an elaborate system of national ranking based on achievement; it involves less personal judgment than does the United States tennis ranking. The United States has no system of national ranking in chess.

"In September, 1946, a new era of international team matches was inaugurated when an American team traveled to Russia to play a face-to-face match. Again ten Americans faced ten Russians, each pair of same number playing two games. The American team was Reshevsky, Fine, Denker, Horowitz, Kashdan, Steiner, Pinkus, A. Kevitz, A.W. Dake and O. Ulvestad. The Russian team was made up of Botvinnik, P. Keres, Smyslov, Boleslavsky, Kotov, Flohr, Ragozin, Bondarevsky, Lilienthal and Bronstein.

"The Russians won by 12½ to 7½. Again the remarkable feature was the superiority of the Russian team at the top. The first three American players earned only 1 point altogether, out of a possible 6.

" The first of the major international tournaments since the end of the war was held at Groningen, Holland, in 1946. Botvinnik was the winner, with 14½ games won, 4½ lost. Second honors went to Dr. Euwe, 14–5, and third to Smyslov. Denker made the best American showing, with a 9½–9½ record.

"Botvinnik was crowned world champion by winning a round-robin tournament in 1948, the other participants being Smyslov, Keres, Reshevsky and Euwe. Fine of the United States was invited but did not attend. These players were selected by world opinion as the logical contenders.

"The difficulty of arranging a match between Botvinnik and any challenger outside the Soviet orbit has led to the recognition of an unofficial 'Western championship,' which was won in 1952 by Reshevsky in a match against Miguel Najdorf of Argentina."

In 1957 Vassily Smyslov of Russia dethroned Botvinnik in a challenge match for the world title. Smyslov did not hold the title long. Early in 1958 he played a match against Botvinnik in Moscow, and the latter won to become the world ruler again.

Bobby Fischer defeated former world champion Tigran Petrosian of the U.S.S.R. on Oct. 26, 1971 and won the right to play the current world champion, Boris Spassky. Fischer became the first American to reach the final step in the elimination series. On Sept. 1, 1972, the 29-year old Fischer defeated Spassky in the 21st game of a 24-game series, winning $156,000 of a $250,000 purse. It was the first time in 25 years that the title had passed out of Russian hands.

WORLD CHAMPIONS

Mr. Mott-Smith declared in an article for the Encyclopaedia Britannica:

"The strongest players of their time, and therefore regarded by later generations as 'World Champions' were:

1747–1795–Francois Philidor, France
1815–1820–Alexandre Deschapelles, France
1820–1840–Louis de la Bourdonnais, France
1843–1851–Howard Staunton, England
1851–1858–Adolph Anderssen, Germany
1858–1859–Paul Morphy, United States
1862–1866–Adolph Anderssen

"In 1866 Anderssen was defeated in a match by Wilhelm Steinitz of Austria, who then laid claim to the title of 'World Champion.' Rightly, for he was undoubtedly the strongest player of his day. Steinitz successfully defended his title in formal matches against Blackburne, Zukertort, Tchigorin (twice) and Gunsberg. His unparalleled reign of 28 years was brought to a close in 1894, when he was defeated by a young German player, Dr. Emanuel Lasker.

"The 'official' world champions, since the title was first used, have been as follows:

1866–1894–Wilhelm Steinitz, Vienna
1894–1921–Dr. Emanuel Lasker, Berlin
1921–1927–Jose R. Capablanca, Havana
1927–1935–Dr. Alexander A. Alekhine, Paris
1935–1937–Dr. Max Euwe, Holland
1937–1946–Dr. Alekhine*
1948–1956–Mikhail Botvinnik, Russia
1957–Vassily Smyslov, Russia
1958–59–Mikhail Botvinnik, Russia
1960–Mikhail Tal, Russia

1961–62–Mikhail Botvinnik, Russia
1963–68–Tigran Petrosian, Russia
1969–71–Boris Spassky, Russia
1972–Bobby Fisher, United States
*Dr. Alekhine died in 1946 and the title was left vacant.

Other Famous International Players

Specialists in blindfold play have been Joseph H. Blackburne (England), Reti, Alekhine, and (contemporary) George Koltanowski (U.S.)

The only women ever to achieve the status of an international master was Mrs. Vera Menchik Stevenson, a Russian who married an English engineer. She was killed in the bombing of London in World War II. Russia has produced another woman champion in Nona Gaprindashvili, who has won the Women's World Championship since 1969.

Contemporary United States players include: Frank Reshevsky, Fine, Larry Evans, Denker, Kashdan, Edward Lasker, Horowitz, Dake, Kevitz, Herbert Seidman, Arthur Bisguier, William Lombardy, and Bobby Fischer, Benko, Robert and Donald Byrne. Active in chess journalism: Irving Chernev, Byrne and George Koltanowski.

Other famous names: Frank Marshall, Dr. Ossip S. Bernstein, Julius Breyer, Edgar Colle, R. Charousek, R. Duras, E. Eliskases, K. Gilg, E. Gruenfeld, Carlos Guimard, Paul Johner, Hans Kmoch, Boris Kostich, Lilienthal, Georg Marco, Jacques Mieses, Mario Monticelli, K. Opocensky, V. Pirc, Svetozar Gligoric, H. Pilnik, Arturito Pomar, V. Ragosin, A. Rabinovich, S. Rosselli, Fritz Saemisch, Rudolf Spielmann, Gideon Stahlberg, G. Stolz, Mir Sultan Khan, Rudolf Teichmann, Carlos Torre, Dr. S. Trifunovic, Dr. Milan Vidmar, Simon Winawer, Bent Larsen, Boris Spassky, Vassily Smyslov and Paul Keres.

UNITED STATES CHAMPIONS

Prior to 1936, the United States championship was decided by a match between the recognized champion and a challenger.

The first American champion was Morphy. His successor was George H. Mackenzie of New York, who held the title from 1871 to 1887. From then until 1894, Max Judd of St. Louis and Simon Lipschultz reigned. Jackson W. Showalter of Georgetown, Ky., was the next champion, in 1894. The same year Albert B. Hodges of Staten Island, N.Y., captured the laurels only to relinquish them to Showalter before the year was out. The Kentuckian ruled until 1897, when Harry Nelson Pillsbury of Boston took over and held the title until he died in 1906. Showalter returned to the No. 1 position and held it until displaced in 1909.

"Frank Marshall, one of the greatest chess masters of all time," relates Mott-Smith, "gained the crown in 1909 and continued as champion through 1935.

"Samuel Reshevsky of New York won the 1936 title in tournament play, repeating in 1938, 1940 and in 1942, the contest being biennial. Reshevsky did not compete in 1944 and Arnold S. Denker of New York won. Reshevsky was back in 1946 and regained the championship, winning 16 of 18 games. The title went to Herman Steiner of Los Angeles in 1948 and Larry Evans of New York won it in 1951, the event not being held for three years.

"Evans held the title through 1953. In 1954 Arthur B. Bisguier began a 4-year reign. Bisguier was succeeded by a rising 15-year-old star, Bobby Fischer. The Brooklyn (N.Y.) high school lad gained additional honors in Europe and appears destined for big things in international competition. Larry Evans regained the title in 1968 only to lose to Sam Reshevsky in 1969. Bobby Fischer again took the title in 1971 and 1972 besides winning the World Championship in 1972, the first American to gain that distinction.

"Mrs. Mary Bain, Mrs. Gisela K. Gresser and N. May Karff have had a monopoly on the women's championship for the last fifteen years or so."

United States Men's Champions

1852-62–Paul Morphy
1871-1887–George H. Mackenzie
1887-92–Max Judd
1892-94–Simon Lipshultz
1894–Jackson W. Showalter
1897-1906–Harry Nelson Pillsbury
1906-09–Jackson W. Showalter
1909-36–Frank J. Marshall
1936-44–Samuel Reshevsky
1944-46–Arnold S. Denker
1948–Herman Steiner
1951-53–Larry Evans
1954-57–Arthur B. Bisguier
1958-61–Robert Fischer
1962–Larry Evans
1963-67–Robert Fischer
1968–Larry Evans
1969–70–Samuel Reshevsky
1971-72–Bobby Fischer

COLLEGIATE CONFERENCES

NATIONAL COLLEGIATE ATHLETIC ASSOCIATION

The National Collegiate Athletic Association, with a membership of more than 765 colleges, universities, athletic conferences affiliated associations and associate institutions, is a national organization with legislative and educational functions, devoted to the promotion of uniform and high standards of intercollegiate athletic administration and competition, based on a premise that undergraduate athletics is an integral part of the educational function.

History

As a result of the alarming number of football injuries, Chancellor MacCracken of New York University called a conference of colleges on Dec. 9, 1905, to determine whether the game of football should be abolished or reformed. Thirteen Eastern institutions attended the meeting, at which it was decided to institute certain reforms. A second conference was called Dec. 28, 1905, with the representatives of 62 institutions in attendance. A football rules committee of seven was appointed and an amalgamation with the former American Football Rules Committee was accomplished to form a single rules committee.

At the same conference, preliminary plans were made for a national body to assist in the formulation of sound requirements for intercollegiate athletics, particularly football, and the name of Intercollegiate Athletic Association of the United States was suggested. This body was conceived as an educational organization, with neither legislative nor executive functions. At a meeting on March 31, 1906, a constitution and by-laws were adopted. The first annual convention of the Intercollegiate Athletic Association was held at the Murray Hill Hotel in New York on Dec. 29, 1906. At the fifth annual convention, Dec. 29, 1910, the name of the organization was changed to the National Collegiate Athletic Association.

Functions

Historically, the National Collegiate Athletic Association was conceived as an educational organization, except in the writing of playing rules for the various intercollegiate sports and in its conduct of national collegiate meets and tournaments.

The educational or advisory functions of the association were pursued by the statements of policy contained in its constitution and in the discussions at its annual meetings.

The first constitution contained a set of eligibility rules suggested as minimum requirements where local conditions permitted but not conditions of membership. These rules provided that competition should be limited to those taking full-time work at the institution, limited competition to four years, required a year of residence before eligibility for transferring students and established a penalty of one year's ineligibility for football players failing to continue in class attendance for two-thirds of the year in which they played. These rules were coupled with other provisions to govern practices with regard to recruiting and subsidizing.

The constitution was re-written in 1939 to include explicit "Standards for the Conduct of Intercollegiate Athletics," adherence to which was to be a condition of membership with a constitutional provision for the expulsion of nonconforming members.

World War II prevented further pursuit of that policy, which was endorsed by formal ratification of the new constitution in 1941. In 1946 there occurred new efforts to tighten the qualifications for membership as a means for standardizing intercollegiate athletic practices and at its annual meeting in January, 1948, the association approved a set of fundamental principles for the conduct of intercollegiate athletics to which members were required to subscribe.

At the 1951 convention, certain sections of the constitution were deleted, relating to the award of financial aid to athletes, and it was voted to revamp the enforcement machinery. At the following convention, the accredited delegates again adopted additional requirements for sound athletic administration and created a membership committee as its enforcement arm.

At its 47th annual convention in 1953, the association vested in its Council, a 17-man policy-directing agency, the power to discipline members who failed to observe the rules and regulations of the association. The convention took a historic step by providing the council with the authority to direct members to refrain from competition with member institutions which fail to observe the association's requirements.

Since that time a number of member institutions have been penalized for rules infractions.

The N.C.A.A. is the rules-making body for intercollegiate sports. These rules are made by committees of the association appointed at the annual convention. The rules committees draft the codes for college football, soccer, boxing, track and field, lacrosse, swimming, wrestling, ice hockey, skiing, fencing, gymnastics, and jointly with other organizations which follow the rules, for basketball. The high schools have representation on the track and field, swimming and wrestling rules committees and in a semi-official manner for football.

An important function of the association is the promotion of intercollegiate athletic competition in all sports, and that is a further function of the rules committees. One device employed in that direction is the publication, along with playing rules, of guide books for the various sports which include records, seasonal results, schedules, playing statistics and technical and general information on the game.

Further, the association conducts national collegiate championship meets or tournaments in the following sports: cross-country, golf, tennis, basketball, baseball, boxing, gymnastics, wrestling, ice hockey, swimming, fencing and track and field.

The elected officers of the N.C.A.A. consist of a president, secretary-treasurer and vice presidents in each of the eight N.C.A.A. districts. The officers with the vice presidents and seven members-at-large comprise the council, which acts as a guiding, advisory and policy group. An executive committee of nine administers the business of the association between annual meetings. The N.C.A.A. employs an executive director and maintains executive offices at Kansas City, Mo., as well as a service branch in New York City.

The N.C.A.A. also holds membership in the United States Olympic Association, with representation among its elected officers, its executive committee and on committees for nine of the Olympic sports which are conducted as a part of the intercollegiate athletic program. Collegiate officers of the Olympic Association are Asa S. Bushnell of the Eastern College Athletic Conference, secretary, and Wilson, who is vice president. As a part of its Olympic responsibilities the N.C.A.A. has undertaken a campaign to finance the participation of the college and ex-college athletes in the Olympic Games.

After the 1972 Olympic Games, the N.C.A.A. withdrew from the U.S. Olympic Committee stressing the need for reorganization. It had withdrawn once before, in 1926, in an effort to gain parity with the Amateur Athletic Union on Games Committees.

A new proposal to reconstruct the N.C.A.A. is being considered when members meet this August in a special convention. The formulated proposal basically is: three divisions in all sports. Division I would be made up of large institutions, Division II would be small state institutions, and Division III would be small liberal arts colleges.

The proposal would allow each school to select its division, except football. The Football Statistics and Classification Committee has determined 121 universities will be in Division I competition. A full program in eight of the 17 recognized sports would be required with a major program in at least two sports for Division I institutes. Division II schools would be required to have four sports programs, one in each of the three seasons.

The number of scholarships would be limited under the new financial aid proposals. One other proposal to be approved is the admission of women to the sports programs. The N.C.A.A. Council recommended throwing open tournament and meet competition in any of the 17 recognized sports to both men and women.

Purposes

To uphold the principle of institutional control of, and responsibility for, all collegiate sports in conformity with the constitution and by-laws of the association.

To stimulate and improve intramural and intercollegiate sports.

To encourage the adoption by its constituent members of strict eligibility rules to comply with satisfactory standards of scholarship, amateur standing, and good sportsmanship.

To formulate, copyright and publish rules of play for the government of collegiate sports.

To preserve collegiate athletic records.

To supervise the conduct of regional and national collegiate athletic contests under the auspices of this association and establish rules of eligibility therefor.

To cooperate with other amateur athletic organizations in the promotion and conduct of national and international athletic contests.

To study any phases of competitive athletics and establish standards therefor, to the end that colleges and universities of the United States may maintain their athletic activities on a high plane.

To legislate through by-laws or resolution of a convention upon any subjects of general concern to the members in the administration of intercollegiate athletics.

Services

(a) Publishes "Official Guides" in nine sports. They include the official playing rules, college schedules, informative articles on the construction of playing fields and the conduct of meets and tournaments and a year-end review in each sport, including the results of the season's play and other pertinent information.

(b) Provides a large film library, covering play in national meets and tournaments, for use without charge by member institutions.

(c) Conducts national meets and tournaments in 12 sports and enforces eligibility rules for this competition, including the one-year residence rule, one-year transfer rule and other basic eligibility requirements.

(d) Finances a service branch known as the National Collegiate Athletic Bureau, which collects, compiles and distributes the official statistics of college football, basketball and track; publishes and distributes the Official N.C.A.A. Rules Books and Guides, which contain the results, future schedules, records and other valuable information; and, generally, performs other functions commonly associated with a publishing and record-keeping agency.

(e) Provides financial and other assistance to various groups interested in the promotion and encouragement of intercollegiate and intramural athletics; actively assists the various national coaches associations in projects which provide better teaching, better competition and sounder administration.

(f) Participates in the United States Olympic movement, aiding in fund raising and providing coaches and athletes for American teams.

(g) Serves as the over-all, national administrative and legislative body for universities and colleges of the United States on matters of intercollegiate athletics.

Among the direct advantages to be enjoyed by a member institution are:

1. An active member is entitled to vote on all issues before the association.

2. It may be represented by as many as three accredited delegates and an unlimited number of visiting delegates at the annual convention.

3. Its athletes and teams are eligible for meets and tournaments of the association.

4. Its representatives are eligible for all elective offices and committee assignments.

5. Its schedules and playing records for each intercollegiate sport are carried in full in the official guides of the association for the particular sport involved.

6. Its athletic director automatically receives a complimentary copy of each guide and rule book published by the association.

7. An active member is automatically included in the national statistical service for football, basketball and track.

8. An active member is entitled to use the various 16 mm. films of N.C.A.A. championship events, without charge other than payment of postage.

9. An active member is eligible to participate in the N.C.A.A. Intercollegiate Athletic Group Insurance Program, which provides catastrophe medical coverage for athletes engaged in practice, play or transport.

10. Its president, faculty representative and athletic director automatically receive all literature of the association, including the results of studies and surveys undertaken by the association.

11. In effect, the association is the universities and colleges of the nation speaking of and acting on athletic matters at the national level. As a result, the N.C.A.A. serves as a vehicle for its members with resultant direct and indirect benefits. For example:

Legislation is enacted to deal with athletic problems when they spread across regional lines and members concur that national action is needed.

Studies are conducted as a means to developing solutions to athletic problems, such as the recent surveys on television, post-season events, length and time of play and practice seasons, etc.

The association, through its officers and various committees, serves as a counseling agency in the field of college athletic administration.

Membership

The association's membership is composed of 765 total members, including 664 colleges and universities; 44 active allied conferences; 30 associate institutions and 27 affiliated organizations.

Publications

(a) Guides

Official N.C.A.A. Football Guide
Official N.C.A.A. Basketball Guide
Official N.C.A.A. Swimming Guide
Official N.C.A.A. Track and Field Guide
Official N.C.A.A. Soccer Guide
Official N.C.A.A. Lacrosse Guide
Official N.C.A.A. Boxing Guide
Official N.C.A.A. Ice Hockey Guide
Official N.C.A.A. Wrestling Guide

(b) Record Books

Official Collegiate Football Record Book
Official Collegiate Basketball Record Book
(Abridged newsstand editions of the guides, minus certain sections including the rules)

(c) Rule Books

Official N.C.A.A. Football Rules Book
Official N.C.A.A. Basketball Rules Book
(These publications contain the rules of the sport only)

(d) Official Basketball Score Book, including the official scoring rules.

(e) The N.C.A.A. Yearbook, which contains the annual year-end reports of the district vice presidents and tournaments and rules committees, the list of officers and committees, the proceedings of the annual convention and the financial reports of the association.

(f) Special periodicals from time to time.

(For N.C.A.A. champions, see individual sports.)

EASTERN COLLEGE ATHLETIC CONFERENCE

The Eastern College Athletic Conference, with a membership of 213 colleges, first came into being on Jan. 1, 1938, as the Central Office for Eastern Intercollegiate Athletics. Where there are now 19 organizations in cooperative affiliation with the E.C.A.C., there were only 14 such groups at the beginning. Formerly a federation of these intercollegiate associations and leagues, the E.C.A.C. was transformed in 1947 into an organization of colleges.

The E.C.A.C. territory embraces 11 New England and Middle Atlantic states and the District of Columbia, and the member institutions include large and small colleges and universities, private, state and municipal institutions.

The E.C.A.C. differs from the majority of the other major college conferences throughout the country because it is not a playing conference, in which every team within the group meets all or most of the others in the various sports. However, the majority of the conference members enter into intercollegiate competition with one another either through dual games and contests, or in the championships and tournaments of the several leagues and associations.

The Conference has exacting rules of eligibility affecting competition by its members. These rules include rigid provisions regarding amateurism, scholastic standing, college residence, student transfers, years of participation, and non-collegiate competition during and outside of the regular college term. The principles and policies for the conduct of intercollegiate athletics embodied in the E.C.A.C. code entail definite limitations on financial aid to athletes, and they bar the recruiting and subsidization of players.

The E.C.A.C.'s various rules, regulations, principles and policies are framed and enacted by the membership; they are interpreted by the Conference's committees on eligibility and on principles and policies; they are applied individually by the member institutions.

Backbone of rules enforcement in the Conference is this procedure: "The president of each member institution shall file annually with the Commissioner of the Conference a 'declaration of principles', confirming that member institution's continuing support of and adherence to the Constitution, principles and policies, rules of eligibility, and resolutions of the Conference."

Essential and significant features of the E.C.A.C. rules include the following:

(1) Varsity competition for freshmen is permitted only at the smaller member colleges granted special waivers on enrollment. (Enrollments of 750 or less male undergraduates.)

(2) The customary rules apply for period of competition; an athlete who is not eligible for varsity participation as a freshman may have only three years of such activity, and this competition must be concluded within five years of the date of his entrance into college.

(3) Transfer students must be in residence at a member college for a full calendar year before they can gain athletic eligibility.

(4) Non-collegiate competition is allowed only with the specific approval of a student's own athletic director or the director's official representative; most outside competition is barred in basketball.

(5) Recruiting cannot entail special inducements.

(6) There may be no discrimination for or against an athlete in entrance qualifications, in academic pursuits, or in other collegiate procedures.

(7) Where financial aid is granted, need or high scholarship or both must be definitely established; such aid may be awarded only by the regular agency of the college constituted for this purpose.

(8) Athletes may compete *against* professionals but not on teams *with* them.

(9) Mere signing of a professional contract brings immediate and permanent loss of eligibility.

All Eastern College Athletic Conference member colleges are accredited by the regional accrediting agencies having direct jurisdiction over the areas in which the institutions are located. These are the Middle States Association of Colleges and the New England Association of Colleges. Lack of such accreditation prevents election to membership for an applicant college.

The E.C.A.C. is an allied member of the National Collegiate Athletic Association, and 103 of its members hold individual membership in the N.C.A.A. and are active in the affairs of that organization. The E.C.A.C's Commissioner and Assistant Commissioner are both members of the National Association of Collegiate Commissioners, and through this latter body keep in close touch with the activities of the 10 other major sport conferences throughout the United States.

The E.C.A.C. supervises annual tournaments and championship competitions either on a Conference basis or for the affiliated organizations in baseball, rowing, track, basketball, swimming, ice hockey, gymnastics, fencing, lightweight football, golf, tennis and wrestling. Outstanding events include the E.C.A.C., Holiday Basketball Festival; the I.C.A.A.A.A. indoor, outdoor and cross country championships; the Intercollegiate Rowing Association's Regatta at Syracuse; the Eastern Association of Rowing Colleges Sprint Regatta; the Intercollegiate Fencing Association team and individual championships; the Eastern Intercollegiate Wrestling Association's Tourney; and the Heptagonal Games Association's indoor and outdoor meets.

Game officials for most Conference members are supervised and appointed by the Commissioner and the E.C.A.C. staff in football, basketball, baseball, gymnastics, soccer, track, fencing, wrestling, and hockey.

Early in December of each year the E.C.A.C. conducts a two-day schedule-making convention at which the athletic directors arrange thousands of sports events in short order and with a minimum of complication.

Organizations Affiliated with E.C.A.C.

Collegiate Basketball Officials Bureau
Eastern Association of Rowing Colleges
Eastern College Hockey Association
Eastern Intercollegiate Baseball League
Eastern Intercollegiate Basketball
    Association
Eastern Intercollegiate Football Association

Eastern Intercollegiate 150-Lb. Football League
Eastern Intercollegiate Golf Association
Eastern Intercollegiate Gymnastic League
Eastern Intercollegiate Golf Association
Eastern Intercollegiate Gymnastic League
Eastern Soccer Officials Bureau
Eastern Intercollegiate Swimming League
Eastern Intercollegiate Tennis Association
Eastern Intercollegiate Wrestling Association
Heptagonal Games Association (Track and Field)
Intercollegiate Association of Amateur Athletes of America (Track and Field)
Intercollegiate Fencing Association
Intercollegiate Rowing Association
Metropolitan Intercollegiate Track and Field Association
Middle Atlantic Collegiate Track and Field Association

WESTERN (BIG TEN) CONFERENCE

The Intercollegiate Conference of Faculty Representatives grew out of a meeting of the presidents of seven universities of the Middle West. This meeting, called by President Smart of Purdue University, was held in Chicago on Jan. 11, 1895, for the purpose of considering the regulation and control of intercollegiate athletics. At that meeting rules covering certain phases of intercollegiate athletics were formulated, and an organization for regulation and control of athletic activities, consisting of appointed faculty representatives, one from each institution, was set up.

The faculty representatives held their first meeting on Feb. 8, 1896. The minutes of that gathering refer to the "Intercollegiate Conference of Faculty Representatives." It is from that reference that the organization commonly known as the "Western Conference," "Big Ten," or "Intercollegiate Conference" derives its official title used herein. The conference, thus, is an association, the primary purpose of which is to insure faculty control and the regulation of intercollegiate athletics as institutional activities, and harmonious intercollegiate relationships among member institutions.

At the time of its organization, the conference was composed of seven members, as follows: University of Chicago, University of Illinois, University of Michigan, University of Minnesota, Northwestern University, Purdue University and University of Wisconsin.

On Dec. 1, 1899, Indiana University and the State University of Iowa were admitted to membership. Ohio State University was admitted on April 6, 1912. The University of Michigan, which withdrew from the conference on Jan. 14, 1908, was, on June 9, 1917, invited to return, and resumed membership on Nov. 20, 1917. The University of Chicago withdrew from the conference as of June 30, 1946. Michigan State

College was admitted to membership on May 20, 1949.

A significant advance in the regulation of intercollegiate athletics was inaugurated by two special conferences, which, at the call of President Angell of the University of Michigan, met in Chicago on Jan. 19–20 and March 9, 1906. As a result of these conferences, the faculty representatives on March 10, 1906, officially adopted the following regulations:

1. Eligible players must have met all entrance requirements, completed a full year's work and one year of residence.

2. Graduate students not eligible, and the competition of an individual student limited to three years.

3. No freshman intercollegiate competition allowed.

4. No training tables or training quarters permitted.

5. A drastic reduction in football schedules (five games).

6. Coaches to be appointed only by university bodies, in regular ways, and at moderate salaries.

Up to 1912 there was no restriction upon the member institutions as to their representatives; the requirement was simply that they be members of the faculty. Two institutions in that year were represented by men who were devoting their full time to the work in physical education and athletics. At the conference meeting on April 6, 1912, a recommendation from the conference presidents was presented, proposing that the conference consist of two representatives from each institution, "one of whom at least should not be connected with the department of physical training."

This proposal was defeated by a vote of 6 to 2. By a similar vote, however, it was provided that "the faculty representative of each university in the conference must be a person who receives no pay for any services connected with athletics or the department of physical culture."

At a special meeting on Sept. 26, 1918, the conference suspended "its activities as a controlling body," at the same time tendering to the War Department "its services in carrying on athletic activities, both intermural and intercollegiate, in and among its members." It declared its former authority in effect again on Dec. 7, 1918.

Another significant development in the control and management of intercollegiate athletic affairs in the conference is found in the growth of responsibility of the athletic directors. By 1922 the administration of intercollegiate athletic activities in the member institutions had become largely vested in athletic directors—men of professional rank devoting their full time to the task. By that time it had become customary for these officers of the member institutions to hold regular meetings, usually at the same time and place as the sessions of the faculty representatives. These meetings gave opportunity for better schedule-making and for the drawing up of "agreements" governing the conduct of athletics.

A further significant step was taken in 1922 in the creation of the office of commissioner of athletics, the incumbent of which was not only "to study athletic problems of the various Western Conference universities and assist in enforcing the eligibility rules which govern Big Ten athletics," but also to conduct "an educational campaign looking toward the development of better sportsmanship, belief in the amateur law and understanding of the values of competitive athletics."

In July of that year Maj. John L. Griffith was appointed to the office and served continuously until his death on Dec. 7, 1944. Since that date Kenneth L. Wilson, formerly director of athletics at Northwestern University, has served as commissioner.

Even this brief historical sketch of the conference's development should record the organization of the graduate directors, an alumni body organized in 1901 for the purpose of conducting a conference track meet. Through the long early periods when the majority of the conference schools had no directors of athletics, this alumni committee rendered valuable service by supplementing most effectively the work of the faculty representatives. Not only the track and field championships, but also other championships, as they naturally developed in tennis, swimming, cross-country, etc., were efficiently handled by this graduate directors' group.

The graduate directors' group retired from active service on Jan. 14, 1926. At that time, the active duties in administration were taken over by the directors of athletics of the conference universities.

SOUTHERN CONFERENCE

The Southern Conference was organized in 1921 for the purpose of promoting and conducting intercollegiate athletics as a wholesome activity for college students and establishing uniform eligibility regulations.

Since its organization, the conference has had as its basic eligibility regulations, a strict transfer rule, an academic requirement of 24 semester or 36 quarter hours for varsity participation and a freshman rule, except during war years.

Originally, the conference was composed of the following institutions: University of Maryland, University of Virginia, Virginia Military Institute, Washington and Lee University, Virginia Polytechnic Institute, University of North Carolina, North Carolina State College, University of South Carolina, Clemson College, University of Tennessee,

Vanderbilt University, University of the South, University of Kentucky, University of Georgia, Georgia Institute of Technology, University of Mississippi, Mississippi State College, University of Louisiana, Tulane University, University of Alabama, Alabama Polytechnic Institute, and the University of Florida. Duke University joined the conference in 1927.

In 1932 the institutions from the states of Kentucky, Tennessee, Florida, Georgia, Alabama, Louisiana and Mississippi withdrew from the Southern Conference and formed the Southeastern Conference. The University of Maryland, University of Virginia, Virginia Military Institute, Washington and Lee University, Virginia Polytechnic Institute, University of North Carolina, Duke University, North Carolina State College, University of South Carolina and Clemson College continued as the Southern Conference. Since 1932, Furman University, The Citadel, Wake Forest College, Davidson College, The College of William and Mary, University of Richmond, George Washington University and the University of West Virginia have joined the conference. In 1937 the University of Virginia withdrew from the conference.

The office of commissioner was established Jan. 1, 1951. The position is held by Wallace Wade, a former noted football coach. The conference is controlled and operated by full-time faculty representatives, appointed by the president of each member institution. The officers of the conference are a president, vice president and secretary-treasurer, and the three compose the executive committee, which conducts the affairs of the conference between meetings.

At the spring meeting of the conference in May, 1953, seven members, Clemson, Duke, Maryland, North Carolina, North Carolina State, South Carolina and Wake Forest, withdrew to form a new "smaller, compact" group. The secessionists called their organization the Atlantic Coast Conference.

ATLANTIC COAST CONFERENCE

In 1953, seven members withdrew from the Southern Conference because of its unwieldiness and formed the Atlantic Coast Conference. The University of Virginia also became a member of the new group.

SOUTHEASTERN CONFERENCE

In the early 1920's the original Southern Conference was formed with the membership list comprising in most part the larger schools then in the Southern Intercollegiate Athletic Association. The new organization was called the Southern Intercollegiate Conference at the time it was formed at Atlanta, Ga., at a meeting held Feb. 25–26, 1921. On Dec. 7, 1923, after all of the present members of the Southeastern Conference had joined the parent organization, the name was changed to the Southern Conference.

Vanderbilt had come into the group on Dec. 8, 1922, and the University of the South of Sewanee, Tenn., joined one year later to bring the roster of membership to 23.

In 1932 it became apparent that the Southern Conference was too large and unwieldly for good competition. A division along geographical lines was agreed on by representatives and the Southeastern Conference was formed.

The new group consisted of 13 colleges in Georgia, Florida, Kentucky, Tennessee, Alabama, Mississippi and Louisiana. With the exception of the University of the South, which dropped out in 1940, the original members still belong to the circuit. They are the University of Kentucky, University of Tennessee, Vanderbilt University, Georgia Institute of Technology, University of Georgia, University of Florida, University of Mississippi, Mississippi State College, University of Alabama, Tulane University, Louisiana State University and Alabama Polytechnic Institute (Auburn).

In recent years the group set up a central bureau and chose Bernie Moore, a former football coach, as commissioner. The organization has its headquarters in the Redmont Hotel, Birmingham, Ala.

SOUTHWEST ATHLETIC CONFERENCE

On May 6, 1914, representatives of eight Southwestern educational institutions met in Dallas, Tex., at the Oriental Hotel for the purpose of considering the formation of a Southwest Intercollegiate Athletic Conference. The following institutions were presented: Baylor University, University of Oklahoma, Southwestern University, Oklahoma A. and M. College of Texas, Louisiana State University, University of Arkansas, and the University of Texas. On Dec. 8, 1914, representatives of the following institutions accepted the provisions of the conference and became charter members of the Southwest Intercollegiate Athletic Conference: A. and M. College of Texas, Baylor University, Oklahoma A. and M. College, the Rice Institute, Southwestern University, University of Arkansas, University of Oklahoma, and the University of Texas. The first officers of the organization were: president, W.T. Mather, University of Texas; vice president, John Corbett, Oklahoma A. and M. College; secretary-treasurer, P.H. Arbuckle, Rice Institute.

In 1916, the word "Intercollegiate" was dropped from the chartered name of the organization, and "Southwest At letic Conference" became the official name. In the same year, Southwestern University withdrew from the conference and, in 1918, Southern Methodist University was admitted. Phillips University was admitted in 1919, but dropped out in 1921. The University of Oklahoma withdrew from membership in 1920. Texas Christian University was elected to membership in 1922 and Oklahoma A. and M. withdrew in May, 1925. Texas Tech recently was admitted to membership.

Champions were declared for the year 1915 in football, basketball, track, and baseball. The conference recognized other sports and sponsored championship competition in them as follows: tennis, 1916; cross-country, 1920; golf, 1925; swimming, 1930; fencing, 1938.

The work of the faculty representatives, while not as well known to the public as that of the coaches and athletic directors, has been important in the development of the conference. The foresight and diligence of such men as W.T. Mather, the University of Texas; A.C. Love, Texas A. and M.; Henry Trantham, Baylor University; W.H. Watkins, the Rice Institute, and J.C. Futrall, University of Arkansas, made possible the formation and early development of the conference.

The fine leadership and long service of such men as Ike Ashburn, Charles E. Friley, E.J. Kyle, T.D. Brooks, C.W. Crawford and D.W. Williams of Texas A. and M.; B.N. Wilson, J.S. Waterman and Robert A. Leflar of the University of Arkansas; J.T. McCants of Rice; J.S. McIntosh of Southern Methodist University; E.W. McDiarmid and Gayle Scott of Texas Christian University; D.A. Penick, W.E. Metzenthin, J.C. Dolley and Byron E. Short of the University of Texas; James W. St. Clair, executive secretary of the conference from 1938 to 1945; James H. Stewart, executive secretary from 1945 to 1950; Howard O. Grubbs, executive secretary since 1950, and members of the present conference faculty committee have been responsible for the high standards and perfection of structure of the now constituted Southwest Athletic Conference.

MISSOURI VALLEY CONFERENCE

Midwestern athletic history was made at the old Midland Hotel in Kansas City, Mo., on Jan. 12, 1907, when eight faculty members representing five universities met in the first preliminary gathering to form the Missouri Valley Conference.

Prof. Clark W. Hetherington probably could be called "Father of the Missouri Valley Conference," for it was at his suggestion that the first meeting was held. Professor Hetherington and Dr. W.J. Monilaw represented the University of Missouri; Mark Catlin, the University of Iowa; Captain Workizer, the University of Nebraska; Prof. C.M. Woodward, Washington University, while the University of Kansas sent three delegates—Dr. James Naismith, inventor of basketball, and Prof. A.T. Walker and W.C. Lansdon.

Five schools formally organized the conference at a second Kansas City meeting Feb. 16, 1907. Washington University and the state universities of Missouri, Iowa, Nebraska and Kansas formed the group.

The first Missouri Valley athletic championship to be decided was in football in 1907 when Iowa and Nebraska tied for top honors with a victory apiece. The first track meet was held in May, 1908, at Kansas City. The Missouri Valley Basketball League was formed Nov. 10, 1908, with Washington, Missouri and Kansas constituting a Southern Division and Nebraska, Iowa State and Drake making up the Northern Division. A championship play-off series between Northern and Southern winners was arranged.

The conference was increased to seven on March 15, 1908, at Kansas City, when Drake University and Iowa State College were voted in. This line-up prevailed until May 26, 1911, when Iowa withdrew to join the Western Conference. In 1912, Kansas State took Iowa's place, being admitted Dec. 26.

There have been few dull moments in the Valley ever since. Grinnell was admitted Dec. 13, 1918. Nebraska was suspended from the conference during 1919 and 1920. The University of Oklahoma was admitted Dec. 5, 1919, and Oklahoma A. and M. College Dec. 6, 1924, when the conference was expanded to ten members.

In 1928, Missouri, Iowa State, Oklahoma, Kansas and Kansas State withdrew to form a separate conference.

Creighton was admitted and took part in the 1928 football campaign. Butler, admitted in 1932, withdrew in 1934, the same year Tulsa and Washburn College were admitted. St. Louis University was admitted Jan. 16, 1937, increasing the number of schools to eight.

After World War II, Washington University, Washburn College and Creighton withdrew. Bradley University and the University of Detroit entered for the 1949 football campaign and the University of Houston was admitted June 19, 1950, in time to be included on the 1950–51 basketball schedule.

Since then the membership has fluctuated rather frequently. For example, Bradley and Drake withdrew and then re-entered. More than 20 schools have held membership at one time or another.

PACIFIC COAST INTERCOLLEGIATE ATHLETIC CONFERENCE

The Pacific Coast Intercollegiate Athletic Conference was founded on Dec. 2, 1915, at the Oregon Hotel, Portland, Ore., by representatives of the University of California, University of Oregon, Oregon State College and the University of Washington. The three latter schools, then members of the Northwest Conference, and California, which at that time had just resumed competition in American football after a 10-year period of playing rugby, joined together to form the conference in order to broaden the scope of their athletic competition.

One year later at Seattle, Wash., Stanford University and Washington State College applied for membership and were accepted. The entry of the United States into the war a few months later brought a temporary cessation of regular intercollegiate competition among the varsity teams of the member schools. In 1919 competition was resumed on an even larger scale than before the war.

The University of Idaho and the University of Southern California were admitted in 1922. The following year, because of the great distances between the California and northwest members of the conference, Northern and Southern Divisions were formed for competition in all sports except football, which remained on a conference-wide basis. The membership further was enlarged with the addition of Montana State University in 1924 and U.C.L.A. in 1927.

In 1940 the office of commissioner was established and Edwin N. Atherton was appointed to that position. Victor O. Schmidt succeeded Atherton on the latter's death in 1944. The commissioner's responsibilities include the enforcement and interpretation of the conference athletic code, and conducting of conference business between the semi-annual meetings of the conference representatives and the appointment of football and basketball officials for conference games.

World War II curtailed athletic competition in 1943, although the majority of the member schools did not entirely drop intercollegiate athletics. By 1946 the conference was back in normal competition with its ten member schools participating in approximately 1,500 athletic contests per year.

Montana State resigned from the conference, effective Aug. 12, 1950, to join the Mountain States Conference.

In 1958 dissatisfaction over penalties inflicted on several members for alleged code violations led to the decision of these schools to announce their intention to withdraw from the conference in 1959 and 1960. This appears to have spelled the doom of the conference. Schmidt resigned as commissioner.

Later, Washington, California, U.C.L.A. and Southern California announced the formation of the Athletic Association of Western Universities to succeed the dying Pacific Coast Conference.

OTHER CONFERENCES

(Source: *The Blue Book of College Athletics,* published by the Rohrich Corporation, 1940 East 6th St., Cleveland, Ohio, 44114).

ARKANSAS INTERCOLLEGIATE CONFER-
ENCE (AIC)—Arkansas A&M, Arkansas AM&N,
Arkansas College, Arkansas Tech, College of the
Ozarks, Harding College, Hendrix College, Hen-
derson State, Southern State, Ouachita, State
College of Arkansas.

ATLANTIC COAST CONFERENCE (ACC)—
Clemson, Duke, North Carolina State, U. of
Maryland, U. of North Carolina at Chapel Hill,
Wake Forest, Virginia.

ATLANTIC INTERCOLLEGIATE ATHLETIC
ASSOCIATION—St. Mary's, Dalhousie, Acadie,
St. Francis Xavier, New Brunswick, Mount Alli-
son, U. of de Moncton, St. Thomas, Prince
Edward Island, Memorial Univ. of Newfound-
land.

BIG EIGHT—Iowa State, Kansas State, Colorado,
Kansas, Missouri, Nebraska, Oklahoma, Oklahoma State.

BIG SKY ATHLETIC CONFERENCE (BSAC)—
Boise State, Gonzaga, Idaho State, Idaho, Mon-
tana State, Montana, Northern Arizona, Weber
State.

BIG STATE ATHLETIC CONFERENCE
(BSAC)—East Texas Baptist, Huston-Tillotson,
St. Edward's, St. Mary's, Southwestern, Texas
Lutheran, Texas Wesleyan.

BIG TEN (INTERCOLLEGIATE CONFER-
ENCE OF FACULTY REPRESENTA-
TIVES)—Illinois, Indiana, Iowa, Michigan State,
Michigan, Minnesota, Northwestern, Ohio State,
Purdue, Wisconsin.

CALIFORNIA COLLEGIATE ATHLETIC
ASSOCIATION (CCAA)—California State at Ful-
lerton, California Polytechnic-San Luis Obispo,
California Polytechnic-Pomona, California-River-
side, San Fernando Valley State, California
State-Northridge, California State-Bakersfield.

CAROLINAS INTERCOLLEGIATE A.C.—
Athletic Christian, Catawba, Elon, Guilford, High
Point, Lenoir Rhyne, Mars Hill, Newberry, Pfeif-
fer, Presbyterian.

CENTRAL ATLANTIC COLLEGE CONFER-
ENCE (CACC)—Bloomfield, Dowling, Kings,
Marist, Nyack, Southampton.

CENTRAL COLLEGIATE CONFERENCE
(CCC)—Bowling Green State, Central Michigan,
DePaul, Drake, Eastern Michigan, Indiana State,
Indiana, Kansas, Kent State, Kentucky State,
Loyola (Chicago), Marquette, Michigan State,
Northern Illinois, Notre Dame, South Illinois,
Toledo, U.S. Air Force Academy, Wayne State,

Western Illinois, Western Michigan.

CENTRAL INTERCOLLEGIATE A.A.—Eliza-
beth City State, Fayetteville State, Hampton
Institute, Johnson C. Smith, Livingstone, The
Norfolk State, St. Augustine's, St. Paul's, Shaw,
Virginia State, Virginia Union, Winston-Salem
Teachers.

COLLEGE ATHLETIC CONF.—Centre College,
Southwestern at Memphis, Univ. of the South,
Washington and Lee, Washington.

COLLEGE CONFERENCE OF ILLINOIS AND
WISCONSIN (CCIW)—Augustana, Carroll, Car-
thage, Elmhurst, Illinois Wesleyan, Millikin,
North Central, North Park, Wheaton.

COLONIAL INTERCOLLEGIATE SOCCER
CONF.—Barrington, Eastern Nazarene, Gordon,
Massachusetts Maritime Academy, Nasson, New
England, St. Francis, Southeastern Massa-
chusetts.

DELAWARE VALLEY CONFERENCE
(DVC)—Eastern, Lincoln U., Philadelphia College
of Bible, Philadelphia College of Pharmacy &
Science, Rutgers Col. of South Jersey, Salisbury
State.

DIXIE INTERCOLLEGIATE ATHLETIC CON-
FERENCE (DIAC)—Christopher Newport Col-
lege, Greensboro, Lynchburg, Methodist College,
North Carolina Wesleyan, St. Andrews, U. of
North Carolina at Greensboro, Virginia Wesleyan.

EASTERN ASSN. OF ROWING COLLEGES—
Boston University, Brown, Columbia, Cornell,
Dartmouth, Harvard, M.I.T., Navy, Northeastern,
Pennsylvania, Princeton, Rutgers, Syracuse, Wis-
consin, Yale.

EASTERN COLLEGE ATHLETIC CONFER-
ENCE (ECAC)—213 colleges.

EASTERN COLLEGE BASKETBALL ASSOC.—
180 colleges.

EASTERN COLLEGE HOCKEY ASSOCIATION
(ECHA)—Army, Babson, Boston College, Boston
State, Boston U., Bowdoin, Brown, Clarkson,
Colby, Colgate, Connecticut, Cornell, Dart-
mouth, Harvard, MIT, Massachusetts, Merrimack,
Middlebury, New Hampshire, Northeastern,
Norwich, Pennsylvania, Princeton, Providence,
RPI, St. Lawrence, Vermont, Yale.

EASTERN INTERCOLLEGIATE ATHLETIC
ASSOCIATION—Amherst, Assumption, Bates,
Boston State, Bowdoin, Brandeis, Central Con-
necticut State, Coast Guard, Colby, Middlebury,
MIT, Providence, Southern Connecticut State,

Springfield College, Trinity, Tufts, Wesleyan, Williams, Worchester Polytechnic.

EASTERN COLLEGIATE JUDO ASSOCIATION (ECJA)—Boston, Columbia, U. of Connecticut, Cornell, Florida State, Georgetown, Housatonic Community College, Howard, Juniata, Lehigh, Maritime, Maryland, Massachusetts, Newark College of Engineering, Newark State College, Northeastern, Old Dominion, Puerto Rico College of Agriculture, Catholic U. of Puerto Rico, Puerto Rico College of Cayey, Interamerican U. of Puerto Rico, Puerto Rico, Pratt Institute, Princeton, Rensselaer Polytechnic Institute, St. John's, Slippery Rock State College, South Florida, Stony Brook, Tallahassee Community College, Temple, Towson State, U.S. Military Academy, Virginia Military Institute, William Paterson College of N.J., Yale.

EASTERN COLLEGE SOCCER ASSOCIATION (ECSA)—45 colleges.

EASTERN FOOTBALL CONFERENCE (EFC)—Central Connecticut State, Bridgeport, Glassboro State (N.J.), Montclair State (N.J.), Southern Connecticut State.

EASTERN INTERCOLLEGIATE BASEBALL LEAGUE—Army, Brown, Columbia, Cornell, Dartmouth, Harvard, Navy, Pennsylvania, Princeton, Yale.

EASTERN INTERCOLLEGIATE FOOTBALL ASSOCIATION (EIFA)—Adelphi, Albright, Alfred, Amherst, Army, Bates, Boston College, Boston University, Bowdoin, Bridgeport, Brown, Bucknell, Buffalo, Colby, Colgate, Columbia, Connecticut, Cornell, Cortland, Dartmouth, Delaware, Gettysburg, Hamilton, Harvard, Hobart, Hofstra, Holy Cross, Ithaca, Lafayette, Lehigh, Maine, Massachusetts, Merchant Marine Academy, Montclair, Muhlenberg, Navy, New Hampshire, Pennsylvania, Penn State, Pittsburgh, C.W. Post, Princeton, Rhode Island, R.P.I., University of Rochester, Rutgers, St. Lawrence, Southern Connecticut, Syracuse, Temple, Upsala, Vermont, Villanova, Wagner, West Virginia, Yale.

EASTERN INTERCOLLEGIATE GOLF ASSN.—Army, Brown, Colgate, Columbia, Cornell, Dartmouth, Georgetown, Harvard, Holy Cross, Navy, Pennsylvania, Penn State, Pittsburgh, Princeton, Syracuse, Yale.

EASTERN INTERCOLLEGIATE GYMNASTIC LEAGUE—Army, Massachusetts, Navy, Penn State, Pittsburgh, Springfield, Syracuse, Temple.

EASTERN INTERCOLLEGIATE LIGHTWEIGHT FOOTBALL LEAGUE—Army, Columbia, Cornell, Navy, Pennsylvania, Princeton, Rutgers.

EASTERN INTERCOLLEGIATE SWIMMING LEAGUE—Army, Cornell, Dartmouth, Harvard, Navy, Pennsylvania, Princeton, Yale.

EASTERN INTERCOLLEGIATE TENNIS ASSN.—Army, Brown, Columbia, Cornell, Dartmouth, Harvard, Navy, Pennsylvania, Princeton, Yale.

EASTERN INTERCOLLEGIATE WRESTLING ASSN.—Army, Colgate, Columbia, Cornell, F. and M., Harvard, Lehigh, Navy, Pennsylvania, Penn State, Pittsburgh, Princeton, Rutgers, Syracuse, Temple, Yale.

EVERGREEN INTERCOLLEGIATE ATHLETIC—Central Washington, Eastern Washington, Puget Sound, Western Washington, Whitworth.

FAR WESTERN INTERCOLLEGIATE ATHLETIC—California State College (Hayward), University of California at Davis, Chico State, Humboldt State, Sacramento State College, San Francisco State, Sonoma State.

FRONTIER CONFERENCE—Carroll, Eastern Montana, Montana Tech, Northern Montana, Rocky Mountain, Western Montana.

GATEWAY INTERCOLLEGIATE ATHLETIC CONFERENCE (GIAC)—Dominican, Lakeland, Milton, Northland, Northwestern (Wisc.)

GEORGIA INTERCOLLEGIATE ATHLETIC—Berry, LaGrange, Piedmont, Shorter, West Georgia, Valdosta, Georgia Southwestern.

GOLDEN STATE ATHLETIC—California Baptist, Life College, L.A. Baptist College, Pacific Christian College.

GREAT PLAINS ATHLETIC CONFERENCE (GPAC)—Fort Hays Kansas State College, Kansas State College of Pittsburg, Kansas State Teachers (Emporia), Southern Colorado State College, Nebraska (Omaha), Northern Colorado, Washburn.

GREATER BOSTON COLLEGE ATHLETIC CONFERENCE—Boston College, Boston, Brandeis, Harvard, MIT, Northeastern, Tufts.

GULF STATE CONFERENCE (GSC)—Louisiana Tech, McNeese State, Northeast Louisiana, Nicholls State, Northwestern Louisiana, Southeastern Louisiana, Southwestern Louisiana.

HEART OF AMERICA CONFERENCE (HAC)—Baker, Central Methodist College, College of Emporia, Graceland, William Jewell, Missouri Valley, Ottawa, Tarkio.

HEPTAGONAL GAMES ASSN.–Army, Brown, Columbia, Cornell, Dartmouth, Harvard, Navy, Pennsylvania, Princeton, Yale.

HOOSIER-BUCKEYE COLLEGIATE CONFERENCE– (BCC)–Anderson, Bluffton, Defiance, Earlham, Findlay, Hanover, Manchester, Taylor, Wilmington.

ILLINOIS-INDIANA COLLEGIATE SOCCER CONFERENCE–DePauw, Earlham, Lake Forest, MacMurray, Principia, Wabash, Wheaton.

INDIANA COLLEGIATE CONFERENCE (ICC)–Butler, DePauw, Evansville, St. Joseph's, Valparaiso, Indiana Central, Wabash.

INDIANA INTERCOLLEGIATE ATHLETIC–Anderson, Ball State Teachers, Bethel, Butler, Concordia, DePauw, Earlham, Evansville, Fort Wayne Bible, Franklin, Goshen, Grace, Hanover, Huntington, Manchester, Marian, Indiana Central, Indiana State Teachers, Indiana State (Evansville), Indiana Tech, Indiana, Notre Dame, Northwood Institute, Oakland City, Purdue, Rose Polytechnic, St. Benedict, St. Francis, St. Joseph, Taylor, Tri-State, Valparaiso, Vincennes, Wabash.

INTERCOLLEGIATE ASSOCIATION OF AMATEUR ATHLETES OF AMERICA(ICAAAA)–86 colleges.

INTERCOLLEGIATE BOXING ASSN. OF AMERICA–Catholic University, Maryland, Penn State, Syracuse, Army, Virginia, Western Maryland.

INTERCOLLEGIATE FENCING ASSOCIATION (IFA)–Army, C.C.N.Y., Columbia, Cornell, Harvard, M.I.T., Navy, N.Y.U., Pennsylvania, Penn State, Princeton, Rutgers, Yale.

INTERCOLLEGIATE ROWING ASSN.–Columbia, Cornell, Navy, Pennsylvania, Syracuse.

INTERCOLLEGIATE SOCCER FOOTBALL ASSOCIATION OF AMERICA (ISFAA)–100 colleges.

INTERNATIONAL COLLEGIATE HOCKEY ASSOCIATION (ICHA)–Lake Superior, Bemidji State, Wisconsin State Univ. Superior, Lake Hoad.

IOWA INTERCOLLEGIATE ATHLETIC–Buena Vista, Central, Dubuque, Luther, Simpson, Upper Iowa, Wartburg, William Penn.

IVY LEAGUE–Brown, Columbia, Cornell, Dartmouth, Harvard, Pennsylvania, Princeton, Yale.

JAMES A. NAISMITH INTERCOLLEGIATE BASKETBALL–St. Francis, Nasson, Bryant, Barrington, Babson Institute, Gordon.

KANSAS COLLEGE ATHLETIC–McPherson, Kansas Wesleyan, Bethany, College of Emporia, Bethel, Friends University, Sterling, St. Mary of the Plains, Southwestern, Tabor.

KENTUCKY INTERCOLLEGIATE ATHLETIC–Berea, Campbellsville, Cumberland, Union, Pikeville.

KNICKERBOCKER BASEBALL CONFERENCE–Adelphi, Brooklyn, Hunter, Kings Port, Lehman, New York Tech, Pace, Pratt, Queens, Stony Brook.

KNICKERBOCKER BASKETBALL CONFERENCE–Brooklyn, Brooklyn Polytechnic Institute, Lehman, Queens, Pace, Pratt, Yeshiva, Stony Brook, King's Point.

LITTLE THREE–Williams College, Amherst College, Wesleyan U.

LONE STAR CONFERENCE OF TEXAS–Abilene Christian, Angelo State, East Texas State, Howard Payne, Sam Houston State, Southwest Texas State, Stephen F. Austin, Sul Ross State, Tarleton State, Texas College of Arts and Industries.

MAINE INTERCOLLEGIATE A.A.–Bates, Bowdoin, Colby, Maine.

MARITIME INTERCOLLEGIATE ATHLETIC–Acadia, Dalhousie, King's, Mount Allison, St. Francis Xavier, St. Mary's, St. Thomas, U. of New Brunswick, Memorial, Prince Edward Island.

MASON-DIXON INTERCOLLEGIATE–Bridgewater, Catholic University, Gallaudet, Hampden-Sydney, Johns Hopkins, Loyola, Mount St. Mary's, Randolph Macon, Roanoke, Baltimore, Washington, Western Maryland, Shepherd College, Towson State.

METROPOLITAN COLLEGIATE BASEBALL–CCNY, Fairleigh Dickinson, C.W. Post, Iona, LIU, Manhattan, St. Francis, (NY), Seton Hall, Wagner.

METROPOLITAN COLLEGIATE SWIMMING CONFERENCE–Adelphi, Columbia, St. John's, St. Francis, Brooklyn, Hunter, H.H. Lehman, CCNY, Monmouth, Manhattan, Brooklyn Poly., Queens, LIU, Seton Hall, U.S. Merchant Marine Academy, N.Y.S. Merchant Marine Academy.

METROPOLITAN INTERCOLLEGIATE BASKETBALL ASSN.—Fordham, Manhattan, N.Y.U., St. John's, Wagner.

METROPOLITAN INTERCOLLEGIATE SOCCER—Adelphi, Baruch, Brooklyn, CCNY, Fairleigh-Dickinson, Hunter, Lehman, LIU, Manhattan, Merchant Marine, Montclair State, N.Y. Tech., C.W. Post, Pratt, Queens, St. Francis (N.Y.), Seton Hall, Stony Brook.

METROPOLITAN INTERCOLLEGIATE TRACK AND FIELD ASSN.—Adelphi, CCNY, Columbia, Fairleigh-Dickinson, Fordham, Iona, Manhattan, NYU, C.W. Post, Rutgers, St. John's, Seton Hall.

MICHIGAN COLLEGIATE—Detroit College, Lake Superior State, Michigan Lutheran, Northwood Institute.

MICHIGAN INTERCOLLEGIATE A.A.—Adrian, Alma, Calvin, Hope, Kalamazoo, Olivet, Albion.

MID-AMERICAN CONFERENCE—Bowling Green State, Central Michigan, Eastern Michigan, Kent State, Miami, Ohio U., Toledo, Western Michigan.

MID-CENTRAL—Concordia, Grace, Huntington, Indiana Institute of Tech., St. Francis, Tri-State.

MIDDLE ATLANTIC STATES COLLEGIATE ATHLETIC CONFERENCE—Albright, American, Bucknell, Delaware Valley, Delaware, Dickinson, Drexel Institute of Tech., Drew, Elizabethtown, F. and M., Gettysburg, Haverford, Hofstra, Johns Hopkins, Juniata, Lafayette, La Salle, Lebanon Valley, Lehigh, Lycoming, Moravian, Muhlenberg, P.M.C., St. Joseph's, Stevens Tech, Susquehanna, Swarthmore, Temple, Scranton, Ursinus, Wagner, Washington, West Chester Teachers, Western Maryland, Wilkes, Philadelphia Col. of Textiles & Science, Rider, Upsala.

MID-EASTERN ATHLETIC CONFERENCE—Delaware State, Howard, Morgan State N.C.A.&T. State U., North Carolina Central, South Carolina State, U. of Maryland-E.S.

MIDDLE EASTERN COLLEGE ATHLETIC—Iona, King's, LeMoyne, St. Francis, Siena, Scranton.

MID-OHIO—Bluffton, Cedarville, Defiance, Findlay, Malone, Wilmington.

MIDWEST COLLEGIATE ATHLETIC—Beloit, Carleton, Coe, Cornell, Grinnell, Knox, Lawrence, Monmouth, Ripon, St. Olaf.

MIDWEST INTERCOLLEGIATE VOLLEYBALL—Ball State, Calvin, Earlham, George Williams, Indiana Institute of Tech., Indiana, Michigan State, Ohio State, Toledo, U. of Illinois (Chicago), Purdue.

MIDWESTERN COLLEGIATE SOCCER CONFERENCE—Calvin, Hope, Wheaton, Lake Forest, MacMurray, Walbash, Earlham.

MINNESOTA INTERCOLLEGIATE ATHLETIC—Augsburg, Concordia, Gustavus Adolphus, Hamline, Macalester, St. John's, St. Mary's of Minnesota (Duluth Branch).

MISSOURI INTERCOLLEGIATE ATHLETIC—Central Missouri State, Lincoln, Northeast Missouri State Teachers, Northwest Missouri State, Southeast Missouri State, Southwest Missouri State, Missouri (at Rolla).

MISSOURI VALLEY CONFERENCE (MVC)—Bradley, Drake, Louisville, Memphis State, New Mexico State, North Texas State, Tulsa, St. Louis, West Texas State, Wichita State.

MOUNTAIN INTERCOLLEGIATE WRESTLING—Colorado Mines, Western State, Adams State, Colorado State University, Air Force Academy, Denver, Utah State, Weber State, Idaho State, Montana State, Montana, Northern Arizona, Northern Colorado.

NATIONAL ASSOCIATION OF INTERCOLLEGIATE ATHLETICS—is an association of some 560 colleges and universities of the U.S.A. and Canada.

NATIONAL COLLEGIATE ATHLETIC ASSOC. (NCAA)—765 total; including 664 colleges and universities; as active members, 44 allied conferences, 30 associate institutions and 27 affiliated organizations.

NATIONAL COLLEGIATE JUDO ASSOCIATION (NCJA)—150 colleges and universities, judo clubs and/or teams.

NATIONAL INTERCOLLEGIATE SQUASH RACQUETS ASSOC.—Adelphi, Amherst, Air Force, Army, Bowdoin, Cornell, Dartmouth, Hamilton, Harvard, Hobart, Fordham, Franklin & Marshall, MIT, Navy, Pennsylvania, Princeton, Queens (Ontario), Trinity, Wesleyan, Washington & Lee, Western Ontario, Williams, Yale, York (Ontario).

NEW ENGLAND COLLEGE ATHLETIC CONFERENCE—Assumption, American International, Amherst, Babson Institute, Bates, Boston College, Boston University, Bowdoin, Brandeis, Bridgeport, Brown, Clark, Colby, Connecticut,

Dartmouth, Hartford, Harvard, Holy Cross, Lowell Tech, Maine, M.I.T., Massachusetts, Merrimack, Springfield, St. Anselm's, St. Michael's, Suffolk, Trinity, Tufts, U.S. Coast Guard Academy, Vermont, Wesleyan, Williams, Worcester Polytech, Yale, Bridgewater State, Central Connecticut State, Middlebury College, Nasson College, New Hampshire, Northeastern, Norwich, Providence College, Southern Connecticut State, Stonehill, Bentley, Boston State, Bryant, Castleton State, Eastern Connecticut State, New Haven, Nichols State, Plymouth State, Quinnipac of Rhode Island, Sacred Heart, Salem State, U. of Maine (Portland-Gorham), Westfield State, Windham, Worcester State.

NEW ENGLAND INTERCOLLEGIATE AMATEUR ATHLETIC ASSN.–Amherst, Bates, Boston College, Boston University, Bowdoin, Brandeis, Brown, Colby, Connecticut, Holy Cross, Massachusetts, M.I.T., Maine, New Hampshire, Northeastern, Norwich, Providence, Rhode Island, Springfield, Trinity, Tufts, Vermont, U.S. Coast Guard Academy, Wesleyan, Williams, Worcester Polytech, Central Connecticut State College, Hartford, Southern Connecticut, Assumption, Bentley, Boston State, Dartmouth, Merrimack, St. Anselm's.

NEW ENGLAND INTERCOLLEGIATE FOOTBALL ASSOCIATION–Bridgewater State, Central Connecticut State, Coast Guard Academy, Maine Maritime Academy, Middlebury, Nichols, Northeastern, Norwich, Springfield, Trinity, Tufts, Wesleyan, Williams, Worcester Polytechnical Institute, Assumption, Curry, Fairfield, Hartford, Western Connecticut State, Providence, St. Michael's, Stonehill, Western N.E. State, New Haven, Norwalk Community College.

NEW ENGLAND INTERCOLLEGIATE LACROSSE LEAGUE–Amherst, Bowdoin, Brandeis, Brown, Dartmouth, Harvard, Holy Cross, Massachusetts, M.I.T., Middlebury, New Hampshire, Nichols, Trinity, Tufts, Wesleyan, Williams, W.P.I., Yale.

NEW ENGLAND STATE COLLEGE ATHLETIC CONFERENCE–Westfield State, Boston State, North Adams State, Worcester State, Lowell State, Fitchburg State, Salem State, Bridgewater State, Eastern Connecticut State, Gorham State, Farmington State, Plymouth State, Keene State, Rhode Island College, Johnson State, Castleton State, Lyndon State.

NEW JERSEY STATE COLLEGE–Glassboro State, Jersey City State, Montclair State, Newark State, Paterson State, Trenton State.

NEW YORK STATE COLLEGIATE TRACK AND FIELD–Alfred, Brockport State, Buffalo,

Buffalo State, Cortland State, Hamilton College, Harpur, Hartwick, Ithaca, LeMoyne, Oswego State, Plattsburgh State, Rensselaer Tech., Roberts Wesleyan, Rochester, Union.

NORTH CENTRAL INTERCOLLEGIATE ATHLETIC–North Dakota State, North Dakota, South Dakota State, South Dakota, Morningside, Augustana, Mankato State, Northern Iowa.

NORTH DAKOTA COLLEGE ATHLETIC–Dickinson State Teachers, Jamestown College, Mayville State Teachers Minot State Teachers, Valley City State Teachers, Wahpeton State School of Science.

NORTHEAST COLLEGE CONFERENCE–Thomas, Unity, U. of Maine (Framington), Husson, Maine Maritime Academy, U. of Maine (Machais), Ricker, U. of Maine (Presque Isle), U. of Maine (Fort Kent), New Brunswick.

NORTH-EAST COLLEGIATE BASKETBALL LEAGUE–Bridgeport, Central Connecticut, Merrimack, Sacred Heart, St. Anselm's, Southern Connecticut, Stonehill.

NORTHERN ILLINOIS INTERCOLLEGIATE CONFERENCE–Aurora, Judson, Rockford, Trinity, Concordia, Illinois Benedictine.

NORTHERN INTERCOLLEGIATE–Bemidji State, Mankato State, Moorhead State, St. Cloud State, Winona State, U. of Minnesota (Morris), Southwest Minnesota State.

OHIO ATHLETIC–Capital, Dension, Heidelberg, Marietta, Mount Union, Muskingum, Oberlin, Ohio Wesleyan, Otterbein, Wittenberg, Wooster, Baldwin Wallace, Hiram, Kenyon.

OHIO VALLEY–Eastern Kentucky State, Middle Tennessee State, Morehead State, Murray State, Tennessee Polytechnic, Western Kentucky, East Tennessee State, Austin Peay State.

OKLAHOMA COLLEGIATE ATHLETIC–Central State, East Central State, Northeastern State, Northwestern State, Oklahoma Baptist, Phillips, Southeastern State, Panhandle State, Cameron State, Langston U., Southwestern State.

PACIFIC COAST ATHLETIC ASSOCIATION (PCAA)–California State (Long Beach), California State (Los Angeles), Fresno State, San Diego State, San Jose State, U. of California (Santa Barbara), U. of the Pacific.

PACIFIC-8 CONFERENCE–U. of California (Berkeley), Oregon, Oregon State, U. of Southern California, Stanford, UCLA, Washington, Washington State.

PACIFIC NORTHWEST CONFERENCE—College of Idaho, Lewis & Clark, Linfield, Pacific Lutheran, Whitman, Willamette, Whitworth.

PACIFIC NORTHWEST INTERCOLLEGIATE A.C.—College of Idaho, Lewis & Clark, Linfield, Pacific, Pacific Lutheran, Whitman, Willamette.

PENNSYLVANIA STATE TEACHERS—State Teachers Colleges at Bloomsburg, California, Cheyney, Clarion, East Stroudsburg, Edinboro, Indiana, Kutztown, Lock Haven, Mansfield, Millersville, Shippensburg, Slippery Rock, West Chester.

PENN-OHIO SWIMMING & DIVING ASSN.—Youngstown, Slippery Rock State College, Carnegie Institute of Tech., Cleveland State U., Lock Haven State College, Grove City College, Westminster College, Indiana State, Ashland College.

PRAIRIE COLLEGE—Blackburn, Greenville, Illinois College, Iowa Wesleyan, Eureka College, Olivet Nazarene College.

PRESIDENTS' ATHLETIC—Case Institute of Technology, John Carroll, Western Reserve, Thiel, Washington and Jefferson, Allegheny, Bethany.

ROCKY MOUNTAIN ATHLETIC—Adams State College, Southern Utah College, Colorado School of Mines, Fort Lewis College, Regis College, Westminster College (Salt Lake), Western New Mexico, Western State College (Colorado).

ROCKY MOUNTAIN INTERCOLLEGIATE SOCCER LEAGUE—Colorado College, Colorado School of Mines, Colorado State, Regis College, Colorado, Denver, Wyoming, U.S. Air Force Academy, Colorado Alpine, Rockmont, Metro State, Baptist Bible.

SOUTHERN CONFERENCE (SC)—The Citadel, Davidson, East Carolina, Furman, Richmond, VMI, William and Mary, Appalachin State.

SOUTHERN INTERCOLLEGIATE ATHLETIC—Alabama State College, Alabama A&M College, Albany, State, Benedict College, Bethune-Cookman College, Clark College, Fisk, Florida A&M, Fort Valley State College, Knoxville College, Lane College, Morehouse College, Morris Brown College, Tuskegee Institute, Miles College, Savannah State College.

SOUTHERN STATES CONFERENCE (SSC)—Athens College, Columbus College, Huntingdon, Spring Hill, St. Bernard, Montevallo, William Carey College.

SOUTHERN NEW ENGLAND—State College of Bridgewater; Southeastern Massachusetts, Quinnipiac, Nichols, Bryant.

SOUTHLAND—Abilene Christian College, Arkansas State College, Lamar, Louisiana Tech, McNeese State, Southwestern Louisiana, U. of Texas at Arlington.

SEABOARD ATHLETIC CONFERENCE (SAC)—Barrington, Eastern Nazarene, Gordon, The King's College.

SOUTH DAKOTA INTERCOLLEGIATE CONFERENCE (SDIC)—Black Hills State, Dakota State, Dakota Wesleyan, Huron, Northern State, South Dakota School of Mines and Technology, U. of South Dakota at Springfield.

SOUTH EASTERN CONFERENCE (SEC)—Alabama, Auburn, Florida, Georgia, Kentucky, Louisiana State, Mississippi, Mississippi State, Tennessee, Vanderbilt.

SOUTHERN CALIFORNIA INTERCOLLEGIATE ATHLETIC CONFERENCE (SCIAC)—California Institute of Technology, Claremont-Harvey Mudd College, Occidental, Pomona, U. of Redlands, Whittier, LaVerne.

SOUTHWEST ATHLETIC CONFERENCE (SAC)—Arkansas, Baylor, Rice, Southern Methodist, Texas, Texas A&M, Texas Christian, Texas Tech, Houston.

STATE UNIVERSITIES OF NEW YORK ATHLETIC—State University of New York Colleges of Education at Brockport, Buffalo, Cortland, Fredonia, Geneseo, New Paltz, Oneonta, Oswego, Plattsburgh, Potsdam.

TENNESSEE INTERCOLLEGIATE ATHLETIC—Chattanooga, East Tennessee State, Memphis State, Maryville, Southwestern, University of the South, Middle Tennessee State, David Lipscomb, Union, Tennessee Polytechnic, Austin Peay State, Belmont, Bethel, Carson-Newman, Lambuth, Milligan, Bryant, Christian Brothers, Fisk, Knoxville, Lemoyne, Peabody, Tennessee A&I, Tennessee Wesleyan, Tennessee, Trevecca Nazarene, U. of Tennessee at Martin, Vanderbilt.

TRI-STATE COLLEGE CONFERENCE—Bethel, Concordia, Northwestern, Sioux Falls, Yankton, Westmar.

TRI-STATE INTERCOLLEGIATE BOWLING—North Dakota, North Dakota State, North Dakota State School of Science, Northern State College, U. of Minnesota (Morris), Wisconsin State U. (River Falls), Wisconsin State U. (LaCrosse), St. Olaf College, Mankato State College.

UNITED STATES INTERCOLLEGIATE LA-
CROSSE ASSN—Membership containing 88 colleges and universities.

UPPER NEW YORK STATE SWIMMING ASSN.
—Buffalo, Buffalo State, Niagara, Brockport
State, St. Bonaventure, Rochester, Oneonta
State, Oswego State, Colgate, Syracuse, Union
College, Rensselaer Polytech., Plattsburgh State.

VOLUNTEER STATE ATHLETIC—Bethel,
David Lipscomb, Lincoln Memorial, Union, Milligan, Belmont, Tennessee (Martin Branch), Carson-Newman, King, Tennessee Wesleyan, Tus-
culum, Christian Brothers College, Union,
Lemoyne-Owen.

WEST COAST ATHLETIC—Loyola University
(Los Angeles), Pepperdine College, St. Mary's
College (Calif.), San Francisco, Santa Clara,
Seattle, U. of Nevada at Reno, U. of Nevada at
Las Vegas.

WEST VIRGINIA INTERCOLLEGIATE ATH-
LETIC—Alderson-Broaddus, Beckley, Bluefield
State, Concord, Davis & Elkins, Fairmont, Glen-
ville, Morris Harvey, Salem, Sheppard State, West

Virginia Tech, West Virginia Wesleyan, West
Liberty State, Wheeling, West Virginia State.

WESTERN ATHLETIC—Arizona State, Brigham
Young, Colorado State, Arizona, New Mexico,
Texas at El Paso, Utah, Wyoming.

WESTERN COLLEGIATE HOCKEY ASSN.—
Colorado College, Denver, Michigan College of
Mining & Technology, Michigan State, Michigan,
U. of Minnesota (Duluth), U. of Minnesota
(Minneapolis), Notre Dame, North Dakota,
Wisconsin.

WESTERN NEW YORK INTERCOLLEGIATE
BASEBALL—Buffalo State Teachers College,
Buffalo, Canisius, Niagara, St. Bonaventure.

WISCONSIN STATE UNIVERSITY—State Colleges at Eau Claire, LaCrosse, Oshkosh, Platte-
ville, River Falls, Stevens Point, Stout, Superior,
Whitewater.

YANKEE CONFERENCE—Boston, Connecticut,
College of Holy Cross, Maine, Massachusetts,
New Hampshire, Rhode Island, Vermont.

CRICKET

Cricket is played on a comparatively small
scale in the United States, but it is a leading
British sport. Britons view the sport in the same
manner that Americans take to baseball. The
game, which is played at a much slower tempo
than baseball, spread from the British Isles to
most of British possessions and commonwealths.
It commands large amounts of newspaper space,
particularly during the playing of Test matches
and The Ashes, the world series of cricket.
However, though these events generate great
interest, there is no unseemly celebration of
victory. Unlike American baseball fans, Britons
don't push, shove or shout, and the police are
not needed to keep them off the playing area.
The seeking of autographs is frowned upon.
Nevertheless, in the case of big matches, work
stops while the Britons watch their television sets
or listen to radio accounts of the play.

Cricket in England, Australia, New Zealand,
South Africa, the West Indies and, to a degree,
Canada, is a sport for the masses as well as the
classes. Records are kept as scrupulously as are
those in baseball and football in the United
States, and some of the finest sports literature
has been written about the game. One London
collector has 3,852 different books and
pamphlets on the game. In the United States,

K.A. Auty, M.B.E., of Chicago, Ill., is reputed to
have the largest library of cricket books and
"cricketana" in this hemisphere.

While all logical evidence points to the English
as inventors of the game, some historians think
that the name cricket is derived from croquet, a
game that was popular in France before the
beginning of cricket. They believe that the
French might have devised a crude form of
cricket as an offshoot of croquet and that the
English borrowed the idea and perfected it into
modern cricket.

Historians point out that there is a French
word "crequet," pronounced "krick kay" and
that this is evidence that France created the game
and named it. However, cricket was unknown in
France through the years when it was gaining
great favor in England around the 12th or 13th
Century. Further, the word "croquet" did not
make its appearance in the French language until
1478, when, obviously, it was used to describe a
sport that existed in England.

English historians, while insisting that cricket
originated and developed in England, do not
know the approximate date when it first was
played, where it was played, or how it gained its
name. One authority thought that it came from
"crice" (or cryce), which was a word in old

English meaning "staff" (or stick). This appears to be far fetched because staff is used to describe a marker used in lawn bowls. R. Cotgraves' "Dictionarie of the French and English Tongues" of 1611 translates the French word "crosse" as follows: "A cricket, staffe, or crooked staffe, where-with bois (boys) play at cricket."

The man who compiled that dictionary knew that cricket was played in England in 1611—and sooner—but sheds no light on whether it also was played in France. He merely states that "crosse in French means a cricket stick.

The origin of cricket, which once seemed destined to become the national game of the United States, is still in dispute. According to Strutt, and authority, cricket was a development of "club ball," but details as to "club ball" are not available.

A drawing in the Kings Library in London, dated 1344, establishes cricket as a well organized and commanding sport at that time. Historians are inclined to agree that the game began in either the 12th or 13th Century. The drawing shows a cricket bowler with a batter facing him. The batter has his bat upside down, resting on the ground, as if in a waiting position.

Edward IV decided that play at "Hands In and Hands Out," apparently the name of the game in 1477, interfered with compulsory practice at archery. He forbade its continuance and fixed a fine and two years imprisonment for players and a fine and three years in jail for anyone who permitted the game to be played on his property. The ban endured for generations. Later rulers became tolerant toward cricket and play eventually was resumed openly, without incurring royal penalty.

What is believed to be the oldest book containing the earliest reference to the playing of cricket is in the possession of the Guildford Corporation of Surrey, England.

It is the record of the Quarter Sessions. In it are minutes for an inquiry held in the year 1597-98 concerning the wrongful enclosure of a piece of land.

John Derrick, Gentleman, "one of the queene's majesties coroners of the county of Surrey" gave evidence that "when he was a scholler in the free school of Guildeford he and several of his fellows did run and play there at crickett and other plaies."

The progress of the game was not rapid, nor without opposition. In 1620, Oliver Cromwell was denounced because he had participated in the "disreputable game of cricket," and the town of Maidstone was classified as "profane" because some youths played the game on Sundays.

Cricket, under attack in England for many years, won a great victory in 1748, when it was ruled as a legal sport by the Court of the Kings Bench, the decision being on a request from cricket enthusiasts. The court decided: "It

(cricket) is a very manly game, not bad in itself, but only bad in the ill use made of it by wagering more than 10 pounds on it, wagering being bad, and against the law."

In earliest cricket play, there were no wickets. The players cut two circular holes in the turf. A batsman was put out by the ball being thrown into the hole before the bat was grounded into the "crease," which was a line 48 inches in front of the hole. A type of wicket was invented about 1700.

The first recorded match was played between Kent and Surrey in 1728 and there was a game of some importance in Gloucestershire in 1729.

In 1744, there was a revision of the rules that had governed earlier competition, the London Cricket Club sponsoring the changes. In 1777, three stumps were introduced. The measurements were 22 x 6 inches, increased to 24 x 7 in 1788, to 26 x 7 in 1816 and to 27 x 8 in 1817, with two bails (cross pieces) added. The dimensions now, after experiments of 8 inches minimum and 28 inches maximum and ratified in 1947, are 9 inches x 27 inches. The bails, 4 3/8 inches in length, must not project more than half an inch above the top of the stumps. The weight of the cricket ball, fixed at about 5½ to 5¾ ounces in 1774, never has been changed. The width of the bat at its widest part, fixed at 4¼ inches in 1774, remains unchanged. The length must not be more than 38 inches.

Modern cricket stems from the historical meeting of the Marylebone Cricket Club at London in 1788, at which time all previous rules were revised and the basis of the game definitely established. The M.C.C was first known as the Artillery Ground Club; the name was changed to the White Conduit Cricket Club in 1780 and to its present name—Marylebone Cricket Club—in 1787. Since that date, the club has become, in many ways, the Supreme Court of cricket throughout the British Isles, Australia, New Zealand, South Africa, India and the West Indies.

In the late 1960s, the M.C.C. introduced one-day games on Sundays to attract the dwindling crowds. It also revised an old rule allowing stars from overseas to play for English county teams without qualifying by two years' residency.

The most famous term in cricket is "The Ashes," an outgrowth of the Test Match between England and Australia in England in 1882, some years after the first meeting between the countries.

In August of that year, playing at the Kennington Oval, Australia scored 63 in its first innings and England countered with 101. The Australians were all out for 122 in the second innings, and when England went to bat the second time needing only 85 runs for victory, it seemed that the hosts would emerge triumphant. But the English failed against the brilliant bowling of Frederick R. Spofforth and scored only 77 runs, giving Australia the victory by a 7-run margin.

The following day an epitaph, with a black-edged border, appeared in The Sporting Times of London. It read:

"In Affectionate Remembrance of English Cricket Which Died at the Oval on 29th of August, 1882. Deeply lamented by a large circle of sorrowing friends and acquaintances. R.I.P. N.B. The body will be cremated, and the ashes taken to Australia."

The next year when Hon. Ivo Bligh, later Lord Darnley, took an English team to Australia he was asked to "bring back the ashes." When the team reached Melbourne, a group of women solemnly presented to Bligh an earthenware urn 5 inches high, which was filled with ashes and bore the inscription:

"When Ivo goes back with the urn, the urn,
Studds, Steel, Read and Tylecote, return,
    return,
The welkin will ring loud,
The great crowd will feel proud,
Seeing Barlow and Bates with the urn, the
    urn,
And the rest coming home with the urn."

The urn and the ashes remained in the possession of Lord Darnley until his death. They were formally presented to the Marylebone Cricket Club in the summer of 1928 and continue to stand in the "long room" among other historic treasures of cricket.

The highlights relative to cricket as a game in England and the Dominions, revealed by H. Archie Richardson's research are:

1707—Cricket recognized as being among recreations for people of England.

1728—In first county match, Kent played Sussex, for a side bet.

1744—Cricket laws appeared, sponsored by London Cricket Club, perhaps a revision of earlier code.

1748—Cricket legally ruled as an honorable sport in England.

1772—Hampshire played Kent, near Canterbury, before what then was record crowd—20,000.

1775—Three stumps, 22 x 6 inches, used for first time; pitch was 22 yards in length.

1806—First Gentlemen's versus Players (professionals) game.

1820—William C. Ward, Marylebone C.C., scored 278 runs against Norfolk, a record.

1827—First Oxford-Cambridge match.

1846—Scoreboard used for first time—at Lord's Cricket Grounds.

1853—Cane-handled bats, invented by Nixon, put into use for first time.

1866—Practice nets introduced at Lord's Grounds.

1873—County championship play started in England.

1876-77—First Test Match played between Australia and England in Australia.

1880—England-Australia Test Matches played for first time in England.

1885—Five Test Matches played for first time.

1895—Albert C. MacLaren made 424 runs in England—then a record.

1898—Board of Control instituted.

1913—Covering ends of wickets permitted.

1915—William G. Grace, greatest of English players died. Career covered 1864–1908 period. Scored 54,896 runs, captured 2,876 wickets.

1927—Victoria (Australia) scored 1,107 runs, record for one team.

1930—Donald G. Bradman, Australia, established world record, 452 runs, not out.

1938—England, in Test Matches, established record, 903 for 7 wickets, Leonard Hutton scoring 364 runs for Test Match record.

1939—Bradman tied Charles B. Fry's record for 6 centuries, 6 consecutive innings.

1945—Walter R. Hammond, England, established world record with two centuries for 7th time.

1953—John B. (Jack) Hobbs, England, first professional cricket player to be knighted.

1958—Surrey won English county championship for record seventh successive time; Garfield Sobers, a West Indian player, scored 365 not out to set world record for Test Match. Sobers passed the record in about 3 hours less time than the 13 hours 20 minutes it took Hutton to set the previous record. Hanif Mohammad of Pakistan set the record for the longest innings when he scored 337 in 16 hours 13 minutes.

Australia won the "Ashes" in 1958 under the captaincy of Richie Benaud and continued to dominate until England retook the urn in the 1970s.

Cricket in the United States

Cricket was well known in the eastern part of what is now the United States as early as 1747. It was brought here by the early British settlers. Many of the earliest baseball players in the United States previously were cricketers. Harry Wright, organizer and manager of the first professional baseball club—the Cincinnati Red Stockings—had been a professional cricketer. The pioneer terms used in baseball were those used in cricket. Even the first uniforms worn by the American ball players were almost exact copies of those used by Englishmen in cricket play. And the same applied to the wearing apparel of the early American lawn tennis players.

From the 1840's to the 1860's cricket seemed certain to be adopted by Americans with the same enthusiasm shown in England. But the game lapsed in favor of the faster and more immediately-concluded game that became American baseball. Only in a few sections of the United States, notably in New York, Pennsylvania, Illinois and California, are organized competitions staged annually on a scale comparable to that of former years.

H. Archie Richardson gathered the following data regarding the sport in America:

1751—First newspaper report of a match in America, New York's team defeating London, 166 to 130.

1809—Cricket played in Boston.

1832—Philadelphia Union Cricket Club formed.

1843—Cricket team organized at University of Pennsylvania.

1844—James Turner, Philadelphia Unions, scored 120 runs, first time the "century" was bettered in North America.

1849—Chicago team played Milwaukee.

1859—George Parr of England organized a team, paying each player $450 and expenses. Team toured principal cities in the eastern part of United States. Match at Hoboken drew 24,000 patrons.

1860—Cricket team organized at University of Michigan.

1872—English team, headed by William G. Grace, toured United States.

1896—Philadelphia scored America's greatest victory, defeating Australian stars, 282 to 222.

1897—Philadelphia team toured England.

1906—J. Barton King of Philadelphia established American record, 344 runs.

1907—University of Pennsylvania team toured British Isles.

1908—William H. Saven of Princeton, N.J., first American to play for "Gentlemen of England."

1912—Patrick Higgins of Los Angeles made American record with 7 "centuries" during season.

1955—Dennis Silk, born in California on Oct. 10, 1931, was elected captain of Cambridge University.

1958—Pakistani team toured United States, playing at New York, Philadelphia and Washington, D.C.

In 1973, the U.S. Cricket Assoc. was asked to participate in the ninth Maccabiah Games held at Ganei Tikvah, Israel. Searching for a team for the "Jewish Olympics" was not an easy task with only 150 cricket clubs in the U.S., and perhaps 2,500 members, 20 of which are Jews.

Cradle of Cricket in the United States
(Courtesy of Hermann Helms.)

The remarkable Newhall family of Philadelphia, which at one time could muster a full cricket eleven among the male members of three generations, was chiefly responsible for the development of the game in that city and raising it, nationally and internationally, to a high level. No other city has attained similar distinction. It was mainly due to the Newhalls' efforts, supported by the social circles in which they moved, that the great country clubs, like the Germantown and Merion Cricket Clubs, were organized, and focused upon the Quaker City the attention of the British cricketing world. These two influential clubs continue to exist, retaining the original names but, sad to relate, golf and tennis have moved in, crowding cricket out.

Those clubs, with the Belmont, Young America and Philadelphia Cricket Clubs cooperating, made it possible for American players to contend on even terms with English, Canadian and Australian opponents. Naturally, this condition led to visits by foreign teams on tour and to trips abroad—to Canada and England—by groups composed for the most part of native American players.

One of these journeys took the Philadelphians to Halifax, Nova Scotia, to play all-Halifax and the British Garrison stationed there at the time. Such was the warm hospitality of their "Bluenose" hosts that a trophy, reminiscent of the occasion, was carried back to the City of Brotherly Love. Later, this trophy was utilized when the "Halifax Cup" competition was organized. Presently, we hear of Philadelphia teams fairly bearding the lion in his den, invading England and meeting county clubs on even terms and with honor.

With the advent of World War I, a complete change slowly but surely enveloped this brightest era for cricket on this side of the Atlantic. Old reliables came to the end of their careers and there were none to take their places. The grip on popular favor gradually lessened until now the interest still maintained is but a shadow of former enthusiasm.

The story has been vividly recalled and authentically recorded by Dr. John A Lester, captain of two of the touring American elevens, in "A Century of Philadelphia Cricket," published in 1951 by the University of Pennsylvania Press. Great names like J. Barton King, kingpin of them all; George S. Patterson, Arthur M. Wood, F. Hermann Bohlen, Percy H. Clark, W. P. O'Neill, J. Henry Scattergood, William R. Wister, H. McGiverin, George W. Pepper, the Scott brothers and "four Newhalls" are given full credit for their accomplishments. This volume is dedicated to the memory of the Newhalls, "who established cricket in Philadelphia."

In 1899, Prince K. S. Ranjitsinhji made a memorable visit to the United States, bringing with him such famous amateurs as A. C. MacLaren, A. E. Stoddard, G. I. Jessop, B. J. T. Bosanquet and S. M. J. Woods. The Indian Prince, one of the great batsmen of all time, introduced an unorthodox but effective style of batting. His fearlessness, in the face of all manner of bowling, was equaled only by the later Don Bradman.

New York City and Environs

Cricket flourished in New York City and environs during the 1890's and the early decades of the 20th Century, and was nurtured by many clubs under the direction of the Metropolitan District Cricket League, New York Cricket Association and the New York and New Jersey Cricket Association. It was an attractive scene that was presented on the Parade Grounds back of Prospect Park in Brooklyn, where, on Saturday afternoons and holidays, half a dozen clubs, including Brooklyn, Kings County, Manhattan and Bedford, pitched their tents throughout the length and center of the field, with baseball nines skirting the fences on both sides.

Livingston, Staten Island, was and still is a stronghold of the game. Walker Park, now administered by the City of New York, was named in memory of the son of R. St. George Walker, then president of the Staten Island Cricket and Tennis Club, who died in combat during World War I. It was the scene of many international matches. The Brooklyn, Staten Island and Paterson clubs were still carrying on, 50 years later, and together with two in Philadelphia—General Electric and Fairmount—constitute the New York and Metropolitan Cricket Association.

Heroic figures on the cricket creases of early days were M. R. Cobb, F. F. Kelly, F. J. Prendergast, Harry Coyne, J. L. Poole, Alfred Tyrrell, A. S. Durrant, Archie Brown, R. G. Ormsby, E. G. Hull, L. C. K. Wood, C. A. Dewhurst, John Brebner and J. L. Poyer. It was Brown, of Brooklyn, who, in two "not out" innings against Lord Hawke's team at Livingston, scored 95 runs off the fast bowling of S. M. J. Woods of Somerset.

Organized with the help of tennis players back in 1873, the Staten Island club is the oldest of all the cricket clubs within the metropolitan area of New York City. Always it could present elevens of Championship caliber, and the trophies captured over the years are many.

Among the organizers of the original Metropolitan District Cricket League, of which the Rev. W.S. Rainsford was the first president, were C. A. McCully, Jerome Flannery, Harry Manley, Joseph G. Davis, W. J. Wood, James D. Boyd, John Howard Lacey and Clifford G. Turner.

Julian L. Poyer, who in the annals of the Brooklyn Cricket Club is credited with 26 centuries for his team, of which he was captain from 1905 to 1907, was born in Trinidad during 1882 and acquired skill and experience in first class and cup matches among Caribbean cricketers. He joined Brooklyn in 1902 and served also as vice president. He was president for seven years until 1949. During his long career here it was rare when he did not stand at the top of the batting averages in his club or when playing in matches for league or association championships.

Another executive of ability and long service was the secretary of the Brooklyn Cricket Club, Vincent H. Cockeram, also born in 1882, in London. He joined the club in 1912 and was secretary for 28 years consecutively. He was vice president once, treasurer eight times and in 1953 was honored with the presidency.

Aside from the honorary positions held by R. St. George Walker in the Staten Island Cricket Club, the secretarial tenure of John Brebner for 20 years is noteworthy.

UNITED STATES FACTS AND FIGURES

J. Barton King of the Belmont Club, Philadelphia, is ranked as the greatest all-around cricketer produced in the United States. In first-class matches he scored 2,673 runs. His highest score was a record 344 runs. He captured 529 wickets at an average cost of 12.48 runs per wicket. He was the only American to capture more than 100 wickets during a tour of England in 1908, taking 115 at an average of 10.48 runs per wicket. He captured more than 2,000 wickets in all his matches. King is credited with giving his greatest batting performance against Surrey in England in 1903, when he had 133 not out, and 98 run out.

Julian L. Poyer of the Brooklyn Cricket Club is rated as the best modern batsman. He won the New York and Metropolitan Cricket Association batting championship 19 times and New York—New Jersey C.A. honors 4 times. His aggregate for championship matches was 9,716 runs in 270 innings; 71 times not out; scored 20 centuries. His highest single score was 124 not out. He had an average of 48.77 runs per innings.

Patrick J. Higgins of the Los Angeles Cricket Club set a United States record for most centuries in one season when he made 7 in 1912. His scores by innings: 159, 100, 100, 121, 182, 110, 240 not out. Grand total—1,012 runs.

Highest Partnership—340 runs, William Robertson (206 not out) and A. G. Sheath (118 not out), San Francisco Bohemians, 1894.

Largest Team Score—689 runs, G. S. Patterson's team against A. M. Woods' team, Philadelphia, Aug. 21-22, 1894.

Greatest Victory by an American Team in United States—Philadelphia defeated Australia by an innings and 60 runs. Scores: Australia, 121 and 101 runs; Philadelphia, 282 runs.

FAMOUS PLAYERS
(Compiled by H. Archie Richardson.)

Australian

Sir Donald Bradman of Australia, modern cricket's most prolific run-scorer, was born in 1908. His first-class career extended from 1927 through 1949. He made 118 runs in his debut in first-class cricket. His record follows:

Scored 300 or more runs in an innings 6 times.

Scored 200 or more runs in an innings 37 times.

Scored 117 centuries in first-class cricket (record for Australian).

Scored 118 runs in first appearance in first-class cricket in 1927.

Scored 100 or more runs 6 successive innings (1938–39 season), equaling record made by Charles B. Fry of England in 1901.

Most centuries (by Australian in England) – 13, in 1938.

Most centuries in Australian season–8, during 1937–38.

Twice scored 1,000 runs in England before the end of May (no Englishman did this more than once).

Highest aggregate in Australia–1,690 (1928–29).

Scored more than 1,000 runs in a season 16 times.

Only Australian to score 2,000 or more runs during each of four tours of England.

Record number of centuries in Test Matches– 29 (19 against England, 4 against Indian, 4 against South Africa, 2 against West Indies).

Scored most double centuries in Australia vs. England Test Matches–8.

Highest aggregate in one series of Test Matches –974 runs, in England in 1930.

Shares world second-wicket record (with William H. Ponsford)–451 runs against England in 1934.

Shares world fifth-wicket record (with Sydney G. Barnes)–405 runs against England at Sydney, Australia, during 1946-47 season.

Highest Individual Scores

Runs	For	Against	At	Season
*452	New S. Wales	Queensland	Sydney	1920-30
369	S. Australia	Tasmania	Adelaide	1935-36
357	S. Australia	Victoria	Melbourne	1935-36
*340	New S. Wales	Victoria	Sydney	1928-29
334	Australia	England	Leeds	1930
304	Australia	England	Leeds	1934

*Not out.

Frederick R. Spofforth, Australia's greatest bowler. Among many sensational performances captured 764 wickets in 1878 and 763 in 1880.

Montague A. Noble. Has best all-around record for Test Matches. He scored 1,905 runs and captured 115 wickets in 38 matches. Also

among best captains.

Victor Trumper, an outstanding batsman. Scored 2,263 runs in Test Matches.

Charles G. Macartney. Holds high scoring record for single innings by Australian in England with 345 runs.

Hughie Trumble. Captured most wickets in Test Matches–141.

Clement Hill. Scored 2,660 runs in Test Matches.

Sydney Gregory. Scored 2,193 runs in Test Matches.

Warwick W. Armstrong scored 2,172 runs in Test Matches.

English

William G. Grace. Born 1848. Played 44 seasons of first-class cricket (1865–1908). Scored 54,896 runs, captured 2,876 wickets, made 126 centuries.

John B. Hobbs. Played from 1903 through 1935. Holds world aggregate record for first-class cricket with 61,237 runs; second in Test Match aggregate with 3,636 runs, scored 12 centuries in Test Matches; leads in centuries in first-class matches with 197.

Walter R. Hammond. Holds record for Test Matches in Australia, with 905 runs. Aggregate for career (1920–1947– 50,486 runs. Made 78 catches in 1928 and 10 in one match the same year.

E. (Patsy) Hendren. Scored 57,610 runs in 32 seasons; made 718 catches.

Wilfred R. Rhodes (1898–1930). Scored 39,797 runs, captured 4,188 wickets; made 1,708 runs and captured 109 wickets in Test Matches.

Herbert Sutcliffe (1919–1945). Scored 50,135 runs, 149 centuries, and with Percy Holmes holds world record for first-wicket partnership with 555 runs.

BASIC RULES

A team is made up of 11 players, consisting of a bowler (pitcher), point, cover point, mid off, mid on, short slip, third man, square leg, deep mid off, deep mid on, wicket keeper (catcher).

There are, however, 21 different positions on the field and are taken up at the discretion of the captain, who places an attacking or defensive field according to the state of the game and the condition of the wicket.

A regulation or championship match (or game) consists of two complete innings, with all players on both sides having one turn at bat in each innings. A player remains at bat until he is put out. Some great batsmen can score 100 or more runs in one turn at bat and a match may last as long as six days.

In most major games play starts at 11:30 A.M. or noon and ends about 6 or 6:30 P.M., depending upon agreement between the captains.

There are no foul balls in cricket. The batsman can hit the ball to the front of him, draw it to either side or pull it in back of him.

Substitutions are not permitted, except when a player is injured.

The ball used is 5½ to 5¾ ounces in weight and a fraction smaller in size than a baseball, but with a thicker, harder leather cover.

The cane-handled bat is shaped much like a baseball bat, but the batting half of it is flat. It is shaped like a paddle and must not be more than 4½ inches wide, 38 inches in length.

No baseball park in the United States is large enough to serve as a cricket field. The minimum cricket grounds should be at least 450 x 500 feet, and one about 525 x 550 is preferable so that the maximum distance may be gained on hard drives.

Two wickets are used. They are made up of three stumps, 28 inches high, and so spaced that the width of the wicket is 9 inches. On top of the wickets are placed little strips of wood, called bails, 4 3/8 inches in length.

The wickets are 22 yards (66 feet) apart, the bowler's position being at one wicket, the batsman's at the other, as compared with 60 feet 6 inches between the batsman and the pitcher in baseball.

The game requires two umpires—one at each wicket.

The first turn at bat is decided by the flip of a coin.

When the defending team takes the field the offensive team puts one man at each wicket and these men constitute a batting team. The bowler can make as long a run as he wishes before delivering the ball, but he must make delivery before crossing the "crease"—a white line—which is 66 feet from the batsman's wicket. The bowler is not permitted to bend his arm in delivery.

The object of the bowler is to try to bowl (pitch with straight arm) out of the reach of the bat and knock down the bail, in which case the batsman is out. The batsman, of course, is the defender of the wicket, and his other purpose is to hit the ball as far as he can and score runs.

A famous term in bowling is the "hat trick." This is credited to a bowler who knocks over, or captures, by means of catches, three or more wickets with successive deliveries. In an earlier day, a hat was presented to all such bowlers.

One of the confusing features of cricket from the viewpoint of the American, who is chiefly familiar with baseball, is that two bowlers operate in each game. When the starting bowler has delivered six "fair balls" from his end, the umpire calls "over." A man at the other wicket, designated by the captain, then becomes the bowler, bowling to the batter at the opposite wicket, while the starting bowler takes the place of his "assistant" in field play. In view of the fact that the change in the bowling direction exactly reverses the frontal attack of the batsman, the fielders change position to conform.

After the second bowler has pitched 6 "fair balls," the team again changes position, the first bowler resumes bowling, and they so alternate until the game's end, unless a change in bowlers is necessary. In such cases, a new bowler is chosen by the captain, from the men already in action on the field.

When the batsman hits the ball, he runs for the other wicket, while his batting partner runs for the one just vacated by the batsman. If they both reach the wicket in safety, that counts one run for the batter. If it is an extra long hit, they keep on running, and a run is scored every time the batsman reaches the opposite wicket. The batsman who happens to be at the wicket opposite the bowler, becomes the batsman when

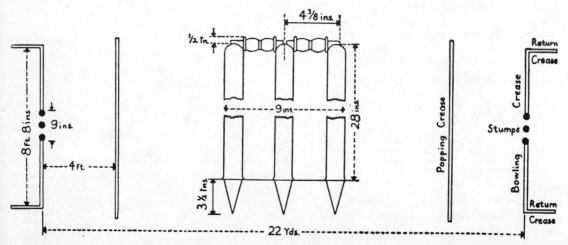

Cricket Field. The detailed drawings are of the stumps which appear at the ends of the field. (Taken from "The Laws of Cricket," published by Educational Production Ltd., London.)

the running has ceased.

When a batsman is put out, the man next on the batting order goes to the wicket and this continues until all eleven men have had a turn at bat. Then the opposing team goes to bat.

The partner of the last man "out," of course, had no one to remain with him at bat, and, thus, in scoring this man is marked as "not out."

The batsman can be put out in various ways. He can be bowled out by the bowler hitting his wicket; he can be put out if any opposing player catches his hit on the fly; if he hits (breaks) the wicket with his bat while hitting at the ball; a fielder, with the ball, can "run him out" by hitting a wicket with the ball, while the batsman is out of crease (safety zone); the wicket keeper can stump him by hitting the wicket or bails with the ball when the batsman is out of the crease, and a bowler can dismiss the batsman lbw (leg before wicket) on an appeal to the umpire directly behind the flight of the ball and if the umpire considers the ball would have hit the wicket had it not been obstructed by any part of the batman's person except his hand.

Retiring a player is equivalent to "taking a wicket."

CURLING

Winter may be a time of hibernation, athletically speaking, for many persons, but there are many who prefer to continue to be engaged in some sort of athletic endeavor during the period when the nights are long and the days short. From this group no doubt came the creators of the sport of Curling.

Just who originated curling, where and when is not known. This is a game played on ice, and thus a product of the cold countries. But which cold country is a matter for debate that has continued through the centuries the sport has endured.

Scotland claims credit for its creation. So does Flanders. But there is no evidence that anything similar to curling existed in any part of the Netherlands before Scotland had elevated curling to the status of a major sport. So the honor appears to belong to Scotland.

A pond drained near Dunblane about 75 years ago revealed a curling stone on which was carved "1551." It had two handles attached. This is evidence that the game was established in Scotland four centuries ago, which pre-dates some claims by the Netherlands advocates.

It has been customary to refer to curling as "the game of lawn bowls played on ice." The Scots become indignant and insist that curling is a radically different and wholly original game. Facts do not bear them out.

Lawn bowling existed in Scotland for centuries before curling. It was Scotland's national outdoor summer game. Then came curling, somewhere between 1520 and 1550. Then and ever since, the principle of play has been very much like lawn bowling.

In Curling, players push a huge stone along the ice toward a "tee" (a fixed object), the game getting its name from the right or left spin given a played stone which causes it to proceed in an arc to the right or left. This change in direction of a played stone is known as the "curl" of a stone. In lawn bowling, the players cast a biased ball at a jack, the big trick being to get a twist into it whenever sending the ball at its object. Though their game is on ice, curlers do not use skates.

In ancient times the stones usually were irregular, square-edged affairs, and even wood blocks were used. The rounded stones made their appearance in 1800 and since then have come into universal use. Canadians substituted iron for stone years ago, when there was no limit as to weight. The irons then ranged from 45 to 115 pounds. Since stones have been standardized as to size, Canadians ceased using iron and resumed using stone, all of which comes from Scotland.

A good lawn bowler soon becomes a good curler—and vice versa. In fact, most lawn bowlers who live in northern climes go in for curling during the winter, and the curlers in the winter are on the bowling greens in the summer.

More than 400 songs have been written and dedicated to curling, and it frequently has been praised in pulpits as "a splendid sport for man to indulge in."

The oldest curling club in existence is the Dudingston Curling Society, organized in Edinburgh, Jan. 17, 1795. This group played according to its own rules until 1834 when the "Amateur Curling Club of Scotland" was formed. The new organization decided that there should be a standardization of the rules and went into convention with the Dudingston and other outstanding clubs of that period. Curling as a regulated sport dates from that time, but the "Amateur Curling Club" ceased to function as a separate unit after Nov. 15, 1838, and was merged into the Grand Caledonian Curling Club, which became the ruling body for the sport throughout the world.

In 1842, Queen Victoria of England visited Scotland and attended a curling contest. Immediately after the departure of the Queen, who praised the game, the name of the club was changed to "Royal Caledonian Curling Club," by which it since has been known.

At the time of its founding, the Caledonian had a pioneer membership of 28 clubs. This had increased to 500 in 1880, to 700 in 1900, and its roll now contains the names of more than 1,000 clubs.

The sport was introduced in Canada about 1807 and the United States about 1820. It is believed that the New York Caledonian Curling Club is the oldest continuous curling club in the U.S. with records dating back to 1855 and is the only remaining charter member club of the Grand National, organized June 26, 1867. For the first 70 years it made infinitely more progress in this country than in Canada. The original United States club was the "Orchard Lakes" of Pontiac, Mich., and the members influenced the creation of many other organizations along the Canadian border. With Canada apathetic toward curling, Scotland challenged the United States in the winter of 1902-03, and this resulted in the first international match.

The great American curlers then were concentrated in the Utica, Schenectady and Saranac, N.Y., area. But the St. Andrew's Golf Club, north of Yonkers, had many Scots as members who were fine curlers. They organized a team in 1903, or 1904, at the joint suggestion of members Peter Fletcher and Nicholas Murray Butler, later president of Columbia University. St. Andrew's put together a fine squad that was conspicuous for many years in the sport.

While players in New York State kept the winter game alive in the East, it spread in popularity to states around the Great Lakes and on the Canadian border, where there was a reasonable assurance of ice for steady play. Wisconsin became an important curling state and developed many outstanding rinks.

In 1938 a team of 50, representing the Royal Caledonian Curling Club of Scotland, toured Canada and the United States. They were excellent players and sportsmen and demonstrated the fine art of the draw game as compared with the running game, which is becoming more popular on this side of the ocean.

In 1950 a Canadian team visited Scotland and in 1952 a team from the United States also visited Scotland at the invitation of the Royal Club. Both tours were highly successful.

The Royal Caledonian Curling Club is known as the "Mother Club" and has affiliated clubs in Canada, the United States, New Zealand and Sweden. In Canada the Dominion Curling Association is the over-all club, although many member clubs of the D.C.A. have direct affiliation with the "Mother Club."

There are three major organizations in the United States, the Grand National Curling Club of America, the Mid-West Curling Association and the United States Women's Curlers Association, the latter now having a membership of over 4680 players.

About the turn of the century Canada supplanted the United States as the stronghold of curling on the North American continent. There are so many teams—both men's and women's—in the various provinces that many insist it is Canada's national winter game, numerically, at least. There are about 1,581 clubs in the Dominion.

While curling generally is regarded as "an old man's game," it has gained many youngsters as devotees, both here and in Canada. There are teams of youngsters, the middle-aged and the elderly; teams for men, teams for women, and an occasional mixed team. In some districts, curling challenges ice hockey for popularity among the youth proving, as so many have contended, that it is "the ageless game."

Once curling makes its impress upon a novice, it never ceases its pressure. "Once a curler, always a curler," is the saying. Youngsters continue to play into old age; oldsters play until no energy is left for participation. The zest of contest is one thing; the social side of the game is something else—and a big lure. It's always "hail fellows, well met" when curlers go into action, and a "nip" while the wintry breezes blow. The warmth the "nip" produces and the gay comradeship in the game makes it beloved by devotees.

FAMOUS CURLERS, TEAMS, TROPHIES

Famous curling clubs in the United States include the Utica (N.Y.) C.C., which began winning championships in 1882 and hasn't stopped. In virtually all competitions for American trophies—the Mitchell Gold Medal, the W. Fred Allen Memorial, the Paterson Memorial Medal and the Gordon Champion Rink Medal, to mention some—the Uticas have been consistent winners and the full number of their victories is a chapter unto itself.

The Thistle C.C. is another which achieved fame, medals and cups. The Yonkers C.C. of the olden days always had talented players. The Saranac Lake C.C. is richly endowed with trophies won by its members through the years. The old Van Courtlandt C.C. of New York City and the St. Andrew's Golf Club of Mount Hope, N.Y., have had teams of top caliber.

Other well-known American clubs of the past and present are Pines C.C., St. Paul C.C., Mohawk Golf Club, New York Caledonian C.C., founded in 1855; Ardsley (N.Y.) C.C., Schenectady (N.Y.) C.C., The Country Club, Brookline, Mass.; Milwaukee C.C., Granite C.C. of Detroit, Jersey City C.C., Terrace City C.C., Nashua (N.H.) C.C., Portage City C.C. and Cambria C.C.

Most treasured Canadian prize is the Macdonald's Brier Tankard, emblematic of the

Dominion championship. This competition annually brings together the outstanding rinks from each of the eleven provinces in Canada. To reach this select circle, each province holds open competitions and follows with round-robin play-offs for district winners.

Recognized as the world's largest tournament, year in and year out, is the Manitoba Bonspiel, held at Winnipeg.

Another big Canadian event is the annual Quebec International Bonspiel, with the Lieutenant-Governor's Trophy a chief award.

Great Canadian teams of the past and present include Hamilton Thistles, Torontos, Toronto Granities, Galt C.C., Lindsay C.C., Orillas, Owen Sound C.C., Collingwoods, Toronto Queen City C.C., Toronto Lakeviews, Toronto High Parks, Royal Montreals, Montreal Thistles, Caledonias, Heather, St. Lawrence. Winnipeg Granites, Winnipeg Thistles, Strathconas of Winnipeg and the Thistle C.C. and Carleton C.C. of New Brunswick.

Among the champion women's teams of Dominion prominence have been The Toronto Queen City C.C., Torontos, Toronto Granites, regarded as the greatest of all; Thornhill C.C., the Orillas, Strathconas of Winnipeg, Granites of Winnipeg and the Dauphins of Manitoba.

The Gordon International Medal Matches have been bringing Canadian and American teams together in competition since 1884. The matches are between clubs representing the Canadian Branch of the Royal Caledonian Curling Club and the Grand National Curling Club of America. From 16 to 20 clubs usually represent a side. In recent years the results have been about even. The Thistles, Heathers and Caledonias have the best club record among the Canadians, while the Utica C.C. has been the most successful American entry.

From 1959 through 1967, the Scotch Cup, sponsored by the Scotch Whisky Association, was an "unofficial" world championship, involving (initially) Canada and Scotland. In 1961, the U.S. entered the competition with Sweden joining in 1962, Norway and Switzerland in 1964, France in 1966, and Germany in 1967. Air Canada took over the sponsorship in 1968, renaming the trophy, Silver Broom. Two new nations have been added for the 1973 world championship, Denmark and Italy.

CANADIAN CHAMPIONS

(Courtesy of Joseph E. Milano, Grand National Curling Club of America.)

Teams and skips in parentheses

1927—Nova Scotia (Halifax C.C., Murray Mac-Neill)
1928—Manitoba (Strathcona C.C., Winnipeg, Gordon Hudson)
1929—Manitoba (Strathcona C.C., Gordon Hudson)
1930—Manitoba (Granite C.C., Winnipeg, Howard Wood)
1931—Manitoba (Strathcona C.C., Robert J. Gourley)
1932—Manitoba (Granite C.C., James Congalton)
1933—Alberta (Royal C.C., Edminton, C.R. Manahan)
1934—Manitoba (Strathcona C.C., Leo Johnson)
1935—Ontario (Thistle C.C., Hamilton, Gordon Campbell)
1936—Manitoba (Strathcona C.C., J.K. Watson)
1937—Alberta (Royal C.C., Edminton, C.R. Manahan)
1938—Manitoba (Glenboro C.C., Albert Gowanlock)
1939—Ontario (Granite C.C., Kitchener, Bert C. Hall)
1940—Manitoba (Granite C.C., Howard Wood)
1941—Alberta (Calgary C.C., T.F.H. Palmer)
1942—Manitoba (Strathcona C.C., J.K. Watson)
1943-45—No competition
1946—Alberta (Sedgewick C.C., W. Rose)
1947—Manitoba (Deer Lodge C.C., Winnipeg, J. Welsh)
1948—British Columbia (Trail C.C., T. D'Amour)
1949—Manitoba (Strathcona C.C., J.K. Watson)
1950—Northern Ontario (Kirkland Lake C.C., T. Ramsay)
1951—Nova Scotia (Glooscap C.C., Kentville, H.D. Oyler)
1952—Manitoba (Fort Rouge C.C., Winnipeg, William Walsh)
1953—Manitoba (Dauphin, Albert Gowanlock)
1954—Alberta (Edmonton Granites, Matt Baldwin)
1955—Saskatchewan (Avonlea, Garnet Campbell)
1956—Manitoba (Fort Rouge C.C., Winnipeg, William Walsh)
1957-58—Alberta (Edmonton C.C., Matt Baldwin)
1959-60—Regina (E.M. Richardson)
1961—Edmonton (H.J. Gervais)
1962—Regina (E.M. Richardson)
1963—Saskatchewan (E. Richardson)
1964—British Columbia (L. Dagg)
1965—Manitoba (T. Braunstein)
1966—Alberta (R. Northcott)
1967—Ontario (A Phillips)
1968-69—Calgary, Alberta (R. Northcott)
1970-71—Manitoba (D. Duguid)
1972—Edmonton (O. Meleschuk)
1973—Regina (H. Mazinke)

U.S. NATIONAL

(Marshall Field Trophy)

Skips in parentheses

1957—Minnesota (H. Lauber)
1958—Michigan (C.D. Fisk)
1959—Minnesota (F. Kleffman)
1960—No. Dakota (O. Gilleshammer)
1961—Washington (Dr. F. Crealock)
1962—Minnesota (F. Kleffman)
1963—Michigan (M. Slyziuk)

1964—Minnesota (F.H. Magie Jr.)
1965—Wisconsin (R. Somerville)
1966—No. Dakota (Dr. J.B. Zbacnik)
1967—Washington (B. Roberts)
1968-69—Wisconsin (R. Somerville)
1970—North Dakota (A. Tallackson)
1971—North Dakota (D. Dalziel)
1972—North Dakota (R. LaBonte)

GORDON INTERNATIONAL MEDAL RECORD

Trophy donated by Robert Gordon of New York for competition between rinks in the Canadian Branch of the Royal Caledonian Curling Club and the Grand National Curling Club of America.

1884—United States 36, Canada 28, at Montreal.
1885-87—No competition
1888—Canada 68, United States 28, at Montreal.
1889—Canada 62, United States 27, at Montreal.
1890—Canada 43, United States 31, at Albany, N.Y.
1891—Canada 55, United States 43, at Montreal.
1892-93—No competition
1894—United States 44, Canada 24, at Albany, N.Y.
1895—Canada 40, United States 24, at Montreal.
1896—Canada 43, United States 26, at Albany, N.Y.
1897-98—No competition
1899—Canada 58, United States 33, at Montreal.
1900—United States 46, Canada 22, at Utica.
1901—Canada 53, United States 19, at Montreal.
1902—No competition
1903—Canada 44, United States 25, at Utica, N.Y.
1904—United States 39, Canada 34, at Montreal.
1905—Canada 34, United States 32, at Utica, N.Y.
1906—Canada 35, United States 33, at Montreal.
1907—Canada 38, United States 31, at Utica, N.Y.
1908—Canada 49, United States 28, at Montreal.
1909—United States 59, Canada 45, at Utica, N.Y.
1910—Canada 147, United States 77, at Montreal.
1911—United States 149, Canada 137, at Boston.
1912—Canada 161, United States 136, at Montreal.
1913—Canada 176, United States 137, at Boston.
1914—Canada 418, United States 280, at Montreal.
1915—United States 183, Canada 148, at Utica, N.Y.
1916-18—No competition
1919—Canada 353, United States 226, at Montreal.
1920—Canada 189, United States 187, at Utica, N.Y.
1921—Canada 403, United States 227, at Montreal.
1922—United States 219, Canada 204, at Utica, N.Y.
1923—Canada 424, United States 297, at Montreal.
1924—United States 180, Canada 173, at Utica, N.Y.
1925—Canada 382, United States 214, at Montreal.
1926—Canada 287, United States 251, at Utica, N.Y.
1927—Canada 453, United States 335, at Montreal.
1928—United States 278, Canada 254, at Utica, N.Y.
1929—Canada 403, United States 373, at Montreal.
1930—Canada 271, United States 205, at Utica, N.Y.

1931—Canada 304, United States 278, at Montreal.
1932—Canada 232, United States 208, at Saranac Lake, N.Y.
1933—Canada 252, United States 164, at Montreal.
1934—Canada 194, United States 135, at Brookline, Mass.
1935—United States 185, Canada 179, at Montreal.
1936—United States 228, Canada 118, at Utica, N.Y.
1937—Canada 211, United States 176, at Montreal.
1938—United States 227, Canada 145, at Montreal.
1939—United States 238, Canada 164, at Utica, N.Y.
1940—Canada 215, United States 177, at Montreal.
1941—Canada 272, United States 205, at Montreal.
1942—United States 360, Canada 359, at Montreal.
1943—Canada 389, United States 320, at Montreal.
1944—Canada 348, United States 326, at Montreal.
1945—No competition
1946—United States 408, Canada 273, at Utica, N.Y.
1947—Canada 382, United States 304, at Montreal.
1948—United States 166, Canada 141, at Brookline, Mass.
1949—Canada 342, United States 312, at Montreal.
1950—United States 332, Canada 299, at Utica, N.Y.
1951—Canada 413, United States 366, at Montreal.
1952—United States 287, Canada 264, at Schenectady, N.Y.
1953—Canada 269, United States 165, at Montreal.
1954—United States 472, Canada 436, at Brookline Mass.
1955—Canada 603, United States 373, at Montreal.
1956—United States 384, Canada 344, at Utica, N.Y.
1957—Canada 516, United States 379, at Montreal.
1958—United States 340, Canada 319, at Schenectady, N.Y.
1959—Canada 519, United States 336, at Montreal
1960—Canada 448, United States 395, at Boston
1961—Canada 492, United States 344, at Montreal
1962—United States 392, Canada 387, at Utica
1963—Canada 321, United States 311, at Montreal
1964—United States 458, Canada 422, at Albany
1965—Canada 525, United States 413, at Montreal
1966—United States 444, Canada 356, at Boston
1967—Canada 504, United States 367, at Montreal
1968—Canada 417, United States 333, at Ardsley-on-Hudson, N.Y.
1969—United States 367, Canada 362, at Montreal
1970—Canada 476, United States 376, Schenectady, N.Y.
1971—Canada 387, United States 318, at Montreal
1972—Canada 338, United States 325, at Winchester, Mass.
1973—Canada 28, United States 14*, at Montreal
*Scoring changed from total stones to games won.

Recapitulation (Through 1973)

Canada 52
United States 26

AIR CANADA SILVER BROOM
(Courtesy of Douglas D. Maxwell, Executive Director, World Curling Championship)
Skips in Parentheses
1959-60—Canada (Ernie Richardson)
1961—Canada (Hec Gervais)
1962-63—Canada (Ernie Richardson)
1964—Canada (Lyall Dagg)
1965—United States (Bud Somerville)
1966—Canada (Ron Northcott)
1967—Scotland (Chuck Hay)
1968-69—Canada (Ron Northcott)
1970-71—Canada (Don Duguid)
1972—Canada (Orest Meleschuk)
1973—Sweden (Kjell Oscarius)

WOMEN

The United States Women's Curling Association originated in 1947, with a nucleus of five clubs. In February, 1949, the first Women's Bonspiel was sponsored by the USWCA in Wauwatosa, Wis. By 1973, the USWCA had a 76-member organization with over 4,680 members, covering 17 states.

U.S. Women's Champions
(Courtesy of Mrs. M.J. Schulenburg, President, United States Women's Curling Association)
Skips in parenthesis
1949—Winnipeg, Manitoba (Mrs. Doris Fraser)
1950—Indian Hill Squaws (Mrs. Herbert Kochs)
1951—Wauwatosa Granites (Mrs. Roy Hansen)
1952—Toronto Granites (Mrs. Robert Amell)
1953-55—Wauwatosa Granites (Mrs. Erwin Nell)
1956—Chicago Heathers (Mrs. Ernest Wentcher)
1957—Chicago Heathers (Mrs. Frank Pollen)
1959—Skokie Thistles (Mrs. Donald Jones)
1961—The Country Club (Mrs. C. Campbell Patterson)
1962—Wauwatosa Granites (Mrs. Steuart Tray)
1963—Westchester Wicks (Mrs. George Marsh)
1964—Skokie Thistles (Mrs. John G. Butler)
1965—Indian Hill Squaws (Mrs. John Bulger)
1966—St. Paul Bonnie Spielers (Mrs. Ronald Taylor)
1967—Utica Glengarries (Mrs. Stanley Storms)
1968—St. Paul Bonnie Spielers (Mrs. Jerome Schwab)
1969—Pardee Pipers (Mrs. Alfred Miller)
1970—Duluth Women's Curling Club (Mrs. Charles Evingson)
1971—North Shore Lassies (Mrs. Alfred Krumholz, Jr.)
1972—Wilmette Wil-Wicks (Mrs. Gerry Duguio)

BASIC RULES OF CURLING

The stones used now are standardized at 38 pounds, 36 inches in circumference and 4½ inches in height (maximum measurements). If a stone is broken during a game, no substitution is permitted. The player continues with the largest fragment.

Curling is played on ice, usually in an indoor rink. Each team is made up of 4 men. The "tee" lines are 38 yards apart; the total length of the rink is 42 yards. At each end is a "hack," or foothold, imbedded in the ice from which each player delivers his stones. Each player curls two stones alternately with his opponent.

B.J. Paulson, "skip" of the Wauwatosa Curling Club of Wisconsin, describing the technique of play, wrote:

"The curling stone is dished on both top and bottom. One side is sharp, for 'keen ice,' the other side is smooth for 'slow ice.' A hole is broached through the center of the rock, with a square counter-sink at either end to receive the square head of a bolt, which passes through the stone and is screwed into a goose-neck handle. The stone is delivered by means of this handle.

"Bolt and handle can be removed and replaced quickly when it becomes necessary to 'turn' the stone, depending upon ice conditions.

"The player swings the stone back, clear of the ice much in the same manner as one who is delivering a Bowling ball and skims the surface of ice with a smooth follow-through. At the instant he releases the stone, the player gives the handle either an in-turn or an out-turn, which is accomplished by a twist of the wrist that gives the stone a one-quarter turn and imparts to it the 'curling' action, which is nothing more nor less than a long curve. The amount of force put into the 'shot' depends upon the condition of the ice and the orders of the 'skip.'

"Each team comprises the lead man, who is usually the novice; the No. 2 man, who plays second; the No. 3 man, next to the 'skip' in proficiency, and the 'skip,' or captain.

"The 'skip' always figures out the plays and designates with his broom on the ice where he wants the stone laid which is being played by his team member. He then calls for either an 'in-turn' or an 'out-turn,' a 'running shot,' a 'guard,' etc., holds his broom on the ice, the position of his broom designating the mark at which the player shoots. The 'skip' also calls for whatever 'weight' he thinks the play requires—that is, the amount of force to put into the stone as it is delivered, in order to stop at the point where the 'skip' wants it laid.

"The broom has a two-fold purpose. In addition to being a pointer, in the skip's hands, it is used by supporting players to sweep frost or moisture from in front of the moving stone, permitting it to carry farther.

"After all 16 stones have been played, that 'end' is completed and the score for that 'end' is counted. The scoring side receives 1 point for each stone inside the 'House' that is not canceled by reason of an opponent's stone lying closer to the center, the 'House' being the designation given to the 'target,' embracing the entire area inside the outer ring. If a stone is lying on the outside of the outer ring, with the edge of the stone barely overhanging the ring, this stone is called a 'hanger' and counts the same value as any stone inside of the 'House,' provided it is not canceled by an opponent's stone. Sometimes a long 'hanger' is the only count in cases where vicious 'dog eat dog' play has been carried on (or exceptionally poor playing), with each side 'cleaning house.' That is, taking out opponent's stones with 'running shots.'

"The customary game consists of ten or twelve 'ends,' although fourteen or more 'ends' are frequently played. In case of a tie score, an extra 'end' is played to determine the winner.

"The ice is kept scrupulously clean and should be as level as a billiard table, free from humps, bulges and cracks. Before a game is started, the players light their pipes, get out their brooms and wide-blade steel scraper, scrape down the ice to remove all inequalities, then sweep off every particle of 'scrapings,' and then 'pebble' the ice. This last is a very important operation and con-

sists of spraying warm water on the ice, accomplished by means of a special sprinkler with a straight handle at the bottom of it. The 'pebbler,' accompanied by a player carrying a bucket of warm water, walks backward down the rink, and swings the water-filled sprinkler over his head in a wide, rhythmic arc to throw the water uniformly across the ice, from side to side. Usually the sprinkler has to be filled half a dozen times in pebbling the length of the rink.

"At temperatures of around 20° or 25° above zero, the 'pebble' will 'set' within five or ten minutes and the ice is then ready for play. The 'pebble' is accurately descriptive, as the drops of hot water, sprinkled on the ice, raise tiny 'ice knobs' on which the stones ride. Without this 'pebble,' it would be impossible to control the stones. The 'pebble' helps to impart the necessary 'curl' to the stones as they slide over the ice, so a 'good pebble' is an essential part of the game."

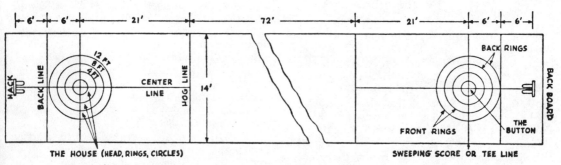

Curling Rink. (Taken from "Sports for Recreation," edited by E. D. Mitchell, A. S. Barnes and Company, New York.)

DOG RACING

GREYHOUND (DOG) RACING

(Courtesy of Walter J. Buchele, Author of **Greyhound Racing Guide**, P.O. Box 885, Keokuk, Iowa)

The sport of GREYHOUND (DOG) RACING today was derived from the ancient sport of coursing. Coursing in itself means the pursuit of running game with dogs that follow by sight instead of by scent. Such dogs, having exceptional speed, were used in the pursuit of wild game as far back as 5000 B.C. Of these, the greyhound has proven best suited to Dog Racing as it has developed as today's sport.

Early racing of greyhounds was also known as coursing and today some of this terminology is used in naming races at a track, such as Flagler Course," "Southland Course," etc.

Greyhound activities can be traced back for centuries through prose, poetry and art. The general appearance of the greyhound and its speed have been consistent characteristics for thousands of years. From drawing and inscriptions found in ancient tombs in Egypt it has been determined that the greyhound was owned and used for the pleasure of the nobility of the era. It is said in some circles that Cleopatra was the "First Lady" of the greyhound.

Apparently the migration of the greyhound occurred in the Middle ages as history places them in Rome and then in the British Isles. One could probably attribute the fact that greyhound racing is known as "The Sport of Queens" to its English ancestry.

The first coursing organization was the "Swaffham Club" started in Norfolk, England in 1776 by Lord Orford. A code of laws for coursing was written by Thomas Mowbray, the Duke of Norfolk under the reign of Queen Elizabeth. Coursing increased in popularity and by 1836 the "Waterloo Cup" was established and it became the most widely attended coursing event in the world. With the increased interest in greyhounds, the formation of coursing clubs grew in England and Ireland.

Interest had spread to the United States, or what there was of it at the time, and in 1896 the National Coursing Association was formed. Strangely enough, coursing in this country appeared in the West and Mid-West, not on the East Coast as one might think. The greyhounds were used with antelope instead of rabbits in the first described coursing events. Coursing with the hare or rabbits came into its own in Nebraska and South Dakota where rabbits were plentiful. Public sentiment against killing of rabbits in coursing events brought about the use of the mechanical rabbit or lure. The first attempts to use a mechanical lure were made in England in 1876 and in this country in 1907.

Coursing, using live rabbits, is still in effect today in certain areas and as specific events. The greatest advance however has occurred in greyhound racing with the use of the mechanical rabbit or lure. Increased growth and expansion have occurred since the early 1930s with the legalization of paramutuel betting in various states.

With the formation of the American Greyhound Track Operators Association (AGTOA) in 1960 and their continued efforts to maintain the highest standards in racing and to protect the public interests, the sport should continue to grow.

Greyhound Racing is one of the most fascinating sports today and the way to enjoy it the most is to learn as much as possible about it. Were the Greyhounds to run in fenced lanes it would be far less difficult to predict the outcome. It is the free-running of greyhounds with accompanying incidents, accidents and casualties that adds the gamble to the outcome.

Greyhound Racing Programs are a combination Program and Racing Form Sheet. Each race is set up to give complete entry information and with it is usually included the record of the last six races in which each greyhound has raced (past performances).

The Past Performance lines as printed in the Program are the RACING FORM of the sport of Greyhound Racing. To find the real nature and enjoyment of the sport one has only to learn the complete makeup and meaning of all aspects of the Past Performance Charts. By their evaluation, as regards the eight greyhounds in a race, one can determine reasonably well the possibilities of the race. This learning process can *not* be accomplished in a short space of time. To learn, one must have an interest in the sport, and learning will produce enjoyment and results.

Each greyhound has a Past Performance record and as printed in a Program it consists of its six recent races. This covers a period of one month's racing, more or less, under normal racing frequency at a track. The period of time depends on the number of greyhounds in the grade as this has a measure of control on the frequency of racing. The six races do give a resume of the racing form of each greyhound for the past month and help in evaluating its present capabilities. Complete information on each greyhound's past performance can be obtained by back-checking through a PROGRAM LIBRARY. This allows a fan to get information on downgraded greyhounds that is not available in one program.

The occasional fan will, of necessity, have to depend on the past performance record as printed in the program. Once understood it will furnish a big percentage of the necessary information for successful betting and enjoyment of the sport. For the occasional fan the use of known handicappers' selections should not be overlooked.

Greyhounds must be registered with the National Coursing Association (NCA) in order to compete on AGTOA and other approved tracks.

"Breedings must be reported to the Keeper of the Stud Book within ten days from date of breeding, and the litter must be registered and tattooed within sixty days from the date of whelping."

"All litters of puppies shall be registered and tattooed within sixty days from date of their birth, the color, the markings and distinguishing features and tattoo numbers of each puppy shall be shown by bertillon as prescribed by the Association, with the number of the litter in the left ear and with the numbers designating the month, and year that they were whelped, and with the letter identifying the individual in the right ear."

All racing greyhound Owners must have an Owner's License.

A greyhound can be owned by one person or have a number of persons under a shared ownership. When a greyhound has multiple Owners, the names of all Owners must be known and listed for that greyhound.

All greyhounds owned by an individual or a Kennel are covered by that individual's or kennel's Owner's License.

An operating Licensed Kennel contracts with a track to furnish a specified number of greyhounds to race for the duration of a meeting, usually 25 to 30 in number. During the meeting, should any greyhound become injured, disabled, drop out or be ruled out by the judges, the kennel must furnish a replacement.

Kennels are allowed to replace greyhounds that are doing poorly. Such greyhounds are of little or no value to either the owner or the track. The track is interested in having the best races possible with capable greyhounds. A greyhound that is not earning is of no value to the kennel.

The age at which a greyhound can begin its racing career is governed by this regulation in Florida: "No greyhound under the age of twelve months can run in an official race other than races fashioned for greyhounds of the same age." Other states operate under the rules of the state; check the state of your interest.

Actually most greyhounds start their careers in racing from sixteen months to two years of age. The day the greyhound is whelped (born) starts its age.

The length of time a greyhound races is dependent on its capability. Present standards and practice finds most greyhounds withdrawn from racing by the time they reach six years of age. Winning capability and its earnings must be the governing factors in keeping a greyhound in competition. Racing is the business of a kennel or owner and they do not keep nonpaying greyhounds on the racing circuit.

Greyhounds that race after reaching six years of age are few and far between, they are the exception and worthy of note when found.

In order to get the most enjoyment from greyhound racing one must understand the GRADING system used. Greyhounds can be classified as Self-grading, in other words, each greyhound determines its Grade by its wins and losses in racing.

"From Rule 305 B - 1.13 (1) Before the opening of a racing meet, the Racing Secretary, after sufficiently schooling all greyhounds and considering their past performances, shall classify and assign them to their proper grade."

Even at the beginning of a meeting the performance of each greyhound in its schooling races largely determines its grade. For example: At its last track a greyhound had achieved Grade A and was in that grade at the finish of the meeting. Its schooling races at the new track showed by performance that the greyhound was in line with Grade B so the Racing Secretary classified it in Grade B. Now the greyhound will, by its own performance, either remain in Grade B or advance to Grade A by winning first place in a scheduled race.

For the entire meeting at this track each greyhound then becomes its own classifier, moving up-grade or down-grade, depending on its own wins and losses.

Greyhound Tracks are located in various countries of the world including the following: United States, Mexico, England, Ireland, Spain, France, Italy, and Indochina, just to name a few. All countries do not operate under the same regulations. Greyhound races are made up having seven, eight, and nine greyhounds as the number in each race, and this too depends on the country involved.

The United States tracks use eight greyhounds per race. Presently, i.e., 1973, there are nine states in the United States that have legalized greyhound racing. These have a total of thirty-eight greyhound tracks with two more new ones under construction. A number of other states are in various stages of progress in the process of legalization of greyhound racing.

Greyhound races are scheduled by licensed tracks through the State Racing Commission of the state in which the track is located. The length of time each track operates, called a meeting, can range from a few programs to 120 or more days. Programs are scheduled as matinees (afternoons) and night programs. Matinees are usually made up of eleven races and start at 1:00 or 1:30 P.M. Night programs are greater in number and are usually made up of twelve races and start at 7:45 or 8:00 P.M.

BETTING

Many of the people attending Greyhound Racing are those that can be classified as vacation fans. This is particularly true at southern tracks that are in operation during the winter months as in Florida and Arizona. Such fans may not follow greyhound racing closely but are interested in racing as entertainment during their vacation. These fans can enjoy the excitement of greyhound races even though their knowledge of the sport may be limited.

Betting is a part of the sport and inexperienced fans should not play the greyhounds blindly. Competent help in handicapping is available to all fans and it is advisable to follow the selections of a known handicapper. It is well to check handicapper's selections after each race to see which one Lady Luck is riding with that night. Regardless of how much any one person may know about handicaping the greyhounds it is an accepted fact in all betting that Lady Luck can be and is involved in the outcome in one way or another. If not, the percentage of correct selections would figure to be the same for each handicapper every night, and it is not the same.

Many persons that attend the races regularly use a known handicapper's selections. The handicappers as listed are well versed in the sport and are employed to give a selection service to be used by the racing fan. This can be considered a reasonable thing to do because the handicappers are operating in their vocation the same as any experienced person in a trade or profession.

Many fans use the track or newspaper HANDICAPPERS' selections in making their bets when attending the races. Handicappers are employed by the track and by local newspapers in the track area; their selections for the greyhound races are printed for use by racing fans as a matter of information.

Such handicappers are very well acquainted with the sport and are well versed as to which factors best determine a greyhound's possibility of winning a race or being in the money. Even with their know-how it is well to point out that they do not always agree; there is still the element of personal opinion that comes into play. Also, there are times when the handicapper's selections miss entirely. When this occurs do not discount the handicapper's ability to make selections.

In this connection two points should be emphasized:

1. Always remember that greyhounds are free running and the starts, bumps, spills, and turns have a lot to do with the race; that first turn usually takes the heaviest toll.
2. As greyhounds are free running and self-grading, any greyhound in a race is a possible winner.

In the program the track handicapper's selections are printed at the bottom of the sheet for each race. Each selection gives the number of the greyhound picked for first, second, and third places in the race. At some tracks four places are picked. The most used names for track handicappers are CHARTMAN, RAILBIRD, and TRACKMAN. Combining the selection of two or more handicappers is listed as CONSENSUS, which implies the best selection by taking all handicappers' picks into consideration.

Example	1st	2nd	3rd
Railbird	1	4	8
Trackman	7	4	8
Chartman	4	1	6

Of these three the Consensus would be . . . .

Consensus	4	1	7

Statistics sometimes are available on handicappers' selections as shown by the following table printed in the Flagler Track program of Dec. 20, 1967.

HANDICAPPERS' SCOREBOARD
(Through 1,214 races)

Selector	Winners	Quinielas	Total
Concensus	336	331	667
Chartman	333	309	642
Dillon, Miami News . . .	319	309	628
Railbird	322	302	624
Elliot, Miami Herald . .	318	297	615
Trackman	298	305	603

In checking this statistical table and using the Consensus figures:

On Winners	336 payoffs in 1214 races —approximately 25%
On Quinielas	331 payoffs in 1214 races —approximately 25%

To use or not to use handicapper's selections is entirely at the option of the fan and the decision is that of the fan.

Under the pari-mutuel system of betting the public does not bet against the track but rather the track acts as the agent and clearing house for the bets. The state law authorizes a definite percentage for the track operation and a tax for the state; this total percentage amounts to 15 to 20 percent, check state law; the balance of the amount bet is returned to the public.

Ticket issuing machines at most race tracks are by the American Totalisator Company. As the tickets are sold the transactions are automatically registered and the amount and number of tickets sold on each greyhound feeds into an electronic odds-computer. The odds are computed and posted on the Oddsboard automatically at regular intervals. The payoff prices are computed by calculators, audited by state officials, and then posted as official.

The ticket issuing machines are automatically locked when the post bell rings, *no purchase* can be made after the bell sounds.

Greyhound racing tracks are usually sized at one-fourth of a mile and are oval in shape. Difference in distance from the front track to the back track is normally the reason for the difference between tracks of the length of the stretch. All tracks do not use the same diameter circle for the ends of the oval. Another marked variation is the width of the running lane which is from 17 to 30 feet; a 22-foot width is the one most used.

The track layout above is a graphic illustration of greyhound racing tracks in general. The quarter mile oval track works best for the length races generally used which are 5/16 mile, 3/8 mile and 7/16 mile or slight variations from these lengths.

Starting boxes can be placed permanently, as illustrated, for the different distances and using one finish line. Races as follows:

For 5/16 mile race—

Starting box to finish line is 1/16 mile plus one round of 1/4 mile equals the 5/16 mile race.

For 3/8 mile race—

Starting box to finish line is 1/8 mile plus one round of 1/4 mile equals the 3/8 mile race.

For 7/16 mile race—

Starting box to finish line is 3/16 mile plus one round of 1/4 mile equals the 7/16 mile race.

In every race the greyhounds go past the finish line in the first part of the race and then make one complete quarter mile run back to the finish line. The exception to this would be a 3/16 mile race which would start from the 7/16 starting box and come around the track to the finish line.

The majority of the tracks use an inside lure, that is, the mechanical rabbit travels the oval of the infield of the track.

The lure starts and stops at the place marked "R" on the track layout above. It is electrically operated and can move at variable speeds. As it is mounted on a wheeled carriage and runs on a track, it is not silent. The greyhounds can hear the approach of the lure as it travels toward the starting box which they occupy. They are ready for the chase when the doors of the starting box open.

The announcer at the track usually has a pet name for the lure such as "Here comes the Bunny" or "Speedy" and one that is used is "Squeaky."

The two points marked "C-1" and "C-2" on the track illustration are the locations of the curtains that are drawn across the track, confining the greyhounds at the end of the race. Curtain C-1 is drawn across first. It is just ahead of where the lure stops behind a screen. The greyhounds come to this curtain and are stopped; when all are past curtain C-2, it is drawn, confining the greyhounds in the area of the track. Handlers then retrieve the greyhounds and take them back to the lockout kennels.

Sooner or later tracks will eliminate use of confining curtains.

TRACK LAYOUT
SCHEMATIC
CHECK TRACK ATTENDED FOR LOCAL DIFFERING CONDITIONS

3/8 MILE
1980 FEET
START

7/16 MILE 2310 FEET
START

3/8 OFF CALL
STRETCH CALL
FOR 5/16 & 3/8

5/16-1/8 MILE CALL
3/8-1/4 MILE CALL

USUAL TRACK IS 1/4 MILE 1320 FEET
NOT TO SCALE

R   C-1

5/16 OFF CALL

FINISH

START

C-2

5/16 MILE 1650 FEET   FINISH

**Greyhound races are run in a
counter-clockwise direction**

DOG SHOWS

Yards and yards of prize ribbons and great numbers of silver trophies are presented annually to winners at dog shows. There also can be financial rewards. With the tremendous rise in interest, the showing of dogs has developed an economic aspect to go along with its sporting features. The exhibitors of pedigreed show dogs engage in spirited, sometimes fierce, competition in pursuit of the blue ribbon.

Originally, that is to say back in the 1870's, sport was the raison d'être of the dog show. An exhibition gave the owner an opportunity to display his pet, and if the animal won gave him a keen sense of pride. The competition was a lot of fun. Everyone had a good time at the show and exhibited sportsmanship as well as dogs. With the

passage of time, however, the attitude of some exhibitors changed vastly.

Show dogs are of two different groups. Some really are house pets in what might be called the "off season" and are entered in important competitions during the show season. Others are trouped around the country, from one show to another, and rarely have a chance to lead the life of a house pet.

Some owners make a business of displaying and breeding their dogs; others, taking pride in their pets and, feeling they are of championship or near championship caliber, enter them in near-by shows. Some dogs are placed in the charge of professional handlers when emerging from puppyhood and become troupers; others are handled only by their owners, who show them when they please.

The dog whose career is to be displayed at shows leads a different life from the ordinary pet, especially if he is a winner of prizes and ranks high among the best of his breed. He may have a potential value from $1,000 to $20,000 through winnings or breeding. He is treated like royalty. He is carefully guarded. Compared to the liberties accorded the ordinary dog, the show-trouper has very few. But the routine is not difficult for him, since usually he knows no other.

Dogs as large as the enormous Kodiak bears roamed this earth during the Paleocene Period, millions of years ago, according to historians. Skeletons of more than 60 distinct species have been taken from the Crazy Mountain region in Montana and 14 of these were positively identified by Dr. Gaylord Simpson of the American Museum of Natural History.

These ancient animals were termed "bear dogs" by Dr. Simpson, and their official name is Arctocyoidae. They had awesome teeth, powerful bones, but small brain cavities.

In later periods, dogs decreased in size until today none of the wild dogs weighs as much, or is as large, as the giants of the domesticated group, which includes the St. Bernard, Great Dane, Newfoundland and the huge Mastiff of Tibet. The bulkiest of these does not scale better than 200 pounds, while the smallest of the toy breeds weighs about one pound.

Domesticated dogs are descended from the wild dog, naturally mated with wolves, jackals and coyotes, after which these offspring were scientifically bred to produce the many varieties of today. The American Kennel Club, governing organization in the United States, recognizes 118 distinct breeds of dogs, all belonging to one or another of the six major classifications: Sporting, Hound, Working, Terrier, Toy and Non-Sporting.

The number of possible standard breeds is unlimited, depending only upon the success of experiments by breeders to establish a new type. Whenever there is any cross-breeding, the first result is a litter of "mongrels." But if this cross-breeding results in a distinct new species, with blooded ancestry on both sides, and if the breeder applies for recognition of this dog as a standard breed, the governing organization may grant it, provided the dog continues to breed true to his type.

An instance:

Fifty years ago the Sealyham dog did not exist officially. Yet in 1924, in 1927 and later this type was selected the best of all the breeds shown at Westminster Kennel Club show in New York, the blue-ribbon event of American dogdom. This dog resulted from the pique of a retired British Army officer over nuisance done to the river bank of his estate in Wales.

When Captain John Edwardes retired from the King's service, he settled down in his home at Haverfordwest in Pembrokeshire, Wales. He discovered that badgers and otters were over-running the banks of his property fronting on the Sealy River. He could not find a dog with legs short enough to crawl into the otter holes and still retain enough speed and durability to run with hounds, and thus be of value in various kinds of hunts.

Captain Edwardes then proceeded to breed a species.

He is believed to have used various breeds, including the Dandie Dinmont, the West Highland White, the Bull Terrier and the Pembroke Welsh Corgi.

The result was the dog of his desire, which he named the Sealyham—after the river.

He registered the dog for breeding purposes and the usual investigation was made. The dog was found to be a distinct species and registration was accepted. However, in keeping with A.K.C. rules, no new breed is accepted until it breeds true to its kind over several generations.

Many of today's breeds were unknown 100 or 150 years ago. They were developed by the process used by Captain Edwardes. Other breeds have come down through the centuries, unchanged in size, without any cross-breeding, and argument long has existed as to which of such species is the oldest.

The "Complete Dog Book," issued by the American Kennel Club and dealing with the origin of about 112 breeds, does not settle the dispute. Rather, the contributed articles merely tend to complicate the situation.

The Saluki Club of America had this to say:

"The Saluki, the Royal Dog of Egypt, is perhaps the oldest known breed of domesticated dog, a distinct breed and type as long ago as 329 B.C., when Alexander the Great invaded India. The Saluki is claimed to be as old as the earliest known civilization, the claim being made that the hounds shown on the earliest carvings look more like the Saluki than any breed (a greyhound body, with feathered ears, tail and legs).

"Exactly the same hound appears on the Egyptian tombs, 2100 B.C., and more recent excavations of the still older Sumerian Empire, estimated at 7000–6000 B.C., have produced carvings of striking resemblance to the Saluki.

"Whenever one sees the word 'dog' in the Bible, it means Saluki."

Concerning the Afghan, an article without authorship line, states:

"It was near Jebel Musa, or the Mountains of Moses, between the Gulf of Suez and the Gulf of Akaba, that the breed now known as the Afghan hound first became a recognizable type of dog. This spot, long held sacred by the Jews and Christians alike—where Moses delivered the Ten Commandments, was a part of Ancient Egypt at the time when the Afghan's existence was first mentioned on papyrus.

"The document that thus forms the cornerstone of the history of the Afghan hound has been attributed to the period 4000–3000 B.C., and it mentions a dog so many times there can be little doubt.

"According to Major H. Blackstone, an English authority who made the translation, the dog is referred to as Cynocephalus, which may be literally translated as baboon or freely translated as monkey-faced hound. The illustrations of the dogs found on the tombs of the time offer convincing proof that even the Afghan hound's head was suggestive of a baboon."

Discussing the Greyhound, which has a body like the Saluki, but does not have the Saluki's feathered ears, tail or legs, another unidentified author says:

"The first knowledge of the Greyhound comes in the Tomb of Amten, in the valley of the Nile, regarded by Egyptologists as belonging to the Fourth Dynasty, which in modern chronology would be between 4000 and 3000 B.C. The carvings of this tomb show dogs of unmistakable Greyhound type in the separate scenes. The dogs have ring tails.

"While the old Egyptian scenes establish the Greyhound as a recognizable type at a very early date, the first complete description of this breed was written by Ovid, who lived from 63 B.C. to 17 A.D. Reading this, one can have little doubt that the dog of ancient times is the same as the dog of today."

The Norwegian Elkhound Association contributed this to the volume:

"In Vista Cave at Jaeren, in Western Norway, a Norwegian Elkhound's skeleton was uncovered among the stone implements in a stratum dating back to 5000–4000 B.C."

The Mastiff Club of America stated:

"The term 'Mastiff' describes a group of dogs rather than a single breed. It is supposed to have originated in Asia. Cassel finds drawings on Egyptian monuments of typical mastiffs dating back to 3000 B.C. Carser describes the Old English mastiff in his account of the invasion of Britain in 55 B.C. They fought beside their masters against the Romans."

Some historians declare that Mastiffs before the Christian Era weighed between 250 and 300 pounds, and the Assyrian kings on fete days sent the most powerful into pits to fight lions.

The "Complete Dog Book," in another unsigned article, which dealt with the Chow Chow, stated:

"There was discovered, not so very long ago, a bas-relief, dating back to the Han Dynasty, about 150 B.C. That definitely places the Chow as a hunting dog in that period. While this establishes the breed as more than 2,000 years old, it is

believed by many authorities that the Chow goes back much further."

An article dealing with the Italian Greyhound said:

"There is strong evidence that the Italian Greyhound was an effete favorite in the ancient days of Pompeii."

Jack Baird of Hartford, Conn., an international authority on dogs and their breeding, points out that articles in the "Complete Dog Book," are by experts on certain breeds and that the A.K.C. does not offer such articles as its own conclusions. Baird states that all breeds of today trace back through one cross or another to such basic species as the Afghan, Saluki, Greyhound and Tibetan Mastiff, and perhaps one or two more.

In feudal times in England the Saluki was so highly regarded that none but royalty and nobility was permitted to own one, and to kill such a dog was a crime punishable by death.

The Saluki, like the Greyhound, is almost devoid of a sense of smell and hunts entirely by sound and sight. They are rated as the fastest dogs that run, but for sustained speed the all-time champion is the Fox Hound. Many such hounds have been timed running a mile in a trifle more than 2 minutes, and the astonishing thing is that they can maintain for hours a rate of speed that is impossible by other swift dogs.

The bloodhound, a breed developed by William the Conqueror, has the keenest sense of smell of any dog on earth. He originally was called "the blooded hound," meaning that his breeding was the purest possible. But this became distorted, and so the most mournful looking, most inoffensive of all dogs owns the most savage-sounding name.

The Irish Wolfhound is the tallest of all dog breeds, the male measuring from 31 to 34 inches and weighing about 120 pounds on the average, while the female averages 28 inches and 90 pounds.

In the 1870's a great deal of friendly dispute about the sleekness of their dogs caused many breeders in the United States to group together to promote the first dog show in the United States. That was in Gilmore's Gardens, New York, and the show lasted three days—May 8–9–10, 1877. It was so genuinely enjoyed and so successful that it was determined to have an annual show thereafter. The Westminster Kennel Club, sponsor of the exhibition, has conducted such shows ever since.

The earliest Westminster shows—1877, 1878, 1879 —were at Gilmore's Gardens. The 1882 to 1890 shows, inclusive, were in the American Institute Building, New York. Those of 1912, 1913 and 1914 were in Grand Central Palace. Madison Square Garden has been the site since that time.

There were 1,177 dogs in the pioneer show of

1877—but only 15 or 20 breeds.

The record entry was in 1937, when 3,146 dogs were judged and that, perhaps, will be the New York perpetual record, because it was ruled, some years ago, that the entry list must be limited to 2,500 although the restriction has been made flexible, and the list has gone somewhat higher.

The record for entries in any American show—indoor or outdoor—was established with 4,456 for the 1939 Morris and Essex. Since it was revived following World War II the event was limited to a number of invited breeds. The record for entries by one owner was set at Morris and Essex in 1936 when Dr. A. P. Munn of Long Branch, N.J., arrived with four vans containing 101 dogs.

The world's largest dog show is Crufts in London with 8,397 entries in 1970.

All dogs, to be eligible for the different classes at the accepted shows, must be registered and the pedigree of a dog becomes authentic only when traceable through the A.K.C. records.

Each breed is judged by an authority on that breed. The rules of judging and of awarding points differ with each breed. What may be a point-winning feature with one breed is ignored in another.

For instance, in judging a Siberian Husky, only six factors are involved, as follows:

	Pts.
General Appearance and Conduct	20
Head and Ears	20
Body and Shoulders	20
Legs and Feet	15
Coat	15
Tail	10
Perfect score would be	100

In comparison, this is how points are determined in judging Scottish Terriers:

	Pts.
Skull	5
Muzzle	5
Eyes	5
Ears	10
Neck	5
Chest	5
Body	15
Legs and Feet	10
Tail	2½

Coat	15
Size	10
Color	2½
General Appearance	10
	100

The Mastiff and the Newfoundland must be judged on 12 different points, the Borzoi (Russian Wolfhound) on 11 and the Irish Wolfhound on 15—head, ears, eyes, teeth, neck, shoulders, chest, etc.

Dogs are judged in their breed classes first. Then they are judged on a group basis, i.e., Sporting, Hound, Working, Terrier, Toy and Non-Sporting. From the group winners the judge selects the best in show.

In theory, the dog named as best in the show is the one scoring closest to the perfection of the breed standard.

In 1948 the Westminster Kennel Club made it a real championship show by requiring that all entries, except puppies, must have won a blue ribbon in a regular A.K.C. show.

The success and the popularity of the earliest dog shows in New York influenced breeders in other communities to originate exhibitions of their own.

Most picturesque of all shows, and the most famous of those that took place outdoors, was the Morris and Essex Kennel Club exhibit at Madison, N.J., on the border of Morris and Essex Counties. The show was originated in 1920 as an indoor display, but Mrs. M. Hartley Dodge, niece of the late John D. Rockefeller, decided in 1927 that indoor shows made for conditions too cramped for the dogs and the spectators. So she held it outdoors that year and thereafter until 1958 when it was discontinued.

The Morris and Essex is staged on what was a polo field on the Dodge estate, known as Giralda Farms. To provide shelter from torrid sunshine or rain, tents are set up. These have increased until now more canvas is raised than is used by the biggest circus.

The show is a one-day affair, starting at 10 A.M. and ending in the early evening. There is one judge for each breed. Attendance has ranged from 500 to 40,000. Money goes out in prizes for winning owners, or for silver cups and ribbons.

WESTMINSTER KENNEL CLUB

Year	Best in Show	Breed	Owner
1907—Ch. Warren Remedy		Fox Terrier (smooth)	Winthrop Rutherfurd
1908—Ch. Warren Remedy		Fox Terrier (smooth)	Winthrop Rutherfurd
1909—Ch. Warren Remedy		Fox Terrier (smooth)	Winthrop Rutherfurd
1910—Ch. Sabine Rarebit		Fox Terrier (smooth)	Sabine Kennels
1911—Ch. Tickle Em Jock		Scottish Terrier	A. Albright, Jr.
1912—Ch. Kenmore Sorceress		Airedale Terrier	William P. Wolcott
1913—Ch. Strathway Prince Albert		Bulldog	Alex H. Stewart
1914—Ch. Brentwood Hero		Old English Sheepdog	Mrs. Tyler Morse

Year	Dog	Breed	Owner
1915—Ch. Matford Vic	Old English Sheepdog	George W. Quintard
1916—Ch. Matford Vic	Old English Sheepdog	George W. Quintard
1917—Ch. Conejo Wycollar Boy	Fox Terrier (wire)	Mrs. Roy A. Rainey
1918—Ch. Haymarket Faultless	Bull Terrier	R.H. Elliot
1919—Ch. Briergate Bright Beauty	Airedale Terrier	G.L.L. Davis
1920—Ch. Comejo Wycollar Boy	Fox Terrier (wire)	Mrs. Roy A. Rainey
1921—Ch. Midkiff Seductive	Cocker Spaniel	William T. Payne
1922—Ch. Boxwood Barkentine	Airedale Terrier	Frederic C. Hood
1923—No best in show award		
1924—Ch. Barberryhill Bootlegger	Sealyham Terrier	Bayard Warren
1925—Ch. Governor Moscow	Pointer	Robert F. Maloney
1926—Ch. Signal Circuit	Fox Terrier (wire)	Halleston Kennels
1927—Ch. Pinegrade Perfection	Sealyham Terrier	Frederic C. Brown
1928—Ch. Talavera Margaret	Fox Terrier (wire)	R.M. Lewis
1929—Land Loyalty of Bellhaven	Collie	Mrs. Florence B. Ilch
1930—Ch. Pendley Calling of Blarney	Fox Terrier (wire)	John G. Bates
1931—Ch. Pendley Calling of Blarney	Fox Terrier (wire)	John G. Bates
1932—Ch. Nancolleth Markable	Pointer	Giralda Farms
1933—Ch. Warland Protector of Shelterock	Airedale Terrier	S.M. Stewart
1934—Ch. Flornell Spicy Bit of Halleston	Fox Terrier (wire)	Halleston Kennels
1935—Ch. Nunsoe Duc de la Terrace of Blakeen	Poodle (standard)	Blakeen Kennels
1936—Ch. St. Margaret Magnificent of Clairedale	Sealyham Terrier	Clairedale Kennels
1937—Ch. Flornell Spicy Piece of Halleston	Fox Terrier (wire)	Halleston Kennels
1938—Daro of Maridor	English Setter	Maridor Kennels
1939—Ferry v. Rauhfelsen of Giralda	Doberman Pinscher	Giralda Farms
1940—Ch. My Own Brucie	Cocker Spaniel	H.E. Mellenthin
1941—Ch. My Own Brucie	Cocker Spaniel	H.E. Mellenthin
1942—Ch. Wolvey Pattern Edgerstoune	West Highland (white) Terrier	Mrs. John G. Winant
1943—Ch. Pitter Patter of Piperscroft	Miniature Poodle	Mrs. P.H.B. Frelinghuysen
1944—Ch. Flornell Rare-Bit of Twin Ponds	Welsh Terrier	Mrs. Edward P. Alker
1945—Shieling's Signature	Scottish Terrier	Mr. and Mrs. T.H. Snethen
1946—Ch. Hetherington Model Rhythm	Fox Terrier (wire)	Mr. and Mrs. T.H. Carruthers, 3d
1947—Ch. Warlord of Mazelaine	Boxer	Mr. and Mrs. R.C. Kettles Jr.
1948—Ch. Rock Ridge Night Rocket	Bedlington Terrier	Mr. and Mrs. W.A. Rockefeller
1949—Ch. Mazelaine's Zazarac Brandy	Boxer	Mr. and Mrs. John P. Wagner
1950—Ch. Walsing Winning Trick of Edgerstoune	Scottish Terrier	Mrs. John G. Winant
1951—Ch. Bang Away of Sirrah Crest	Boxer	Dr. and Mrs. R.C. Harris
1952—Ch. Rancho Dobe's Storm	Doberman Pinscher	Mr. and Mrs. Len Carey
1953—Ch. Rancho Dobe's Storm	Doberman Pinscher	Mr. and Mrs. Len Carey
1954—Ch. Carmor's Rise and Shine	Cocker Spaniel	Mrs. Carl E. Morgan
1955—Ch. Kippax Fearnought	Bulldog	Dr. John A. Saylor
1956—Ch. Wilber White Swan	Toy Poodle	Bertha Smith
1957—Ch. Shirkhan of Grandeur	Afghan	Dorothy Chenade and Sunny Shay
1958—Ch. Puttencove Promise	Standard Poodle	Mr. and Mrs. George K. Putnam
1959—Ch. Fontclair Festoon	Miniature Poodle	Dunwalke Kennels
1960—Ch. Chick T'Sun of Caversham	Pekingese	Mr. & Mrs. C.C. Venable
1961—Ch. Cappoquin Little Sister	Toy Poodle	F. Micelson
1962—Ch. Elfinbrook Simon	West Highland (white) terrier	Wishing Well Kennel
1963—Ch. Wakefield's Black Knight	English Springer Spaniel	Mrs. W.J.S. Borie
1964—Ch. Courtenay Fleetfoot of Pennyworth	Whippet	Pennyworth Kennels
1965—Ch. Carmichaels Fanfare	Scottish Terrier	Mr. and Mrs. Charles C. Stalter

1966—Ch. Zeloy Mooremaides Magic .. Wire Fox Terrier .... Mrs. Marion G. Bunker
1967—Ch. Bardene Bingo .... Scottish Terrier ..... E.H. Stuart
1968—Ch. Stingray of Derryabah ..... Lakeland Terrier .... Mr. & Mrs. James A. Farrell, Jr.
1969—Ch. Glamoor Good News ...... Skye Terrier .... Walter & Mrs. Adele F. Goodman
1970—Ch. Arriba's Prima Donna ...... Boxer .... Dr. & Mrs. P.J. Pagano and
                                                            Dr. Theodore S. Fickles
1971—Ch. Chinoe's Adamant James ... English Springer
                                     Spaniel .... Dr. Milton Prickett
1972—Ch. Chinoe's Adamant James ... English Springer
                                     Spaniel .... Dr. Milton Prickett

Westminster Winners by Breeds

Fox Terrier (Wire)	10	Poodle (Standard)	2
Airedale Terrier	4	Poodle (Toy)	2
Fox Terrier (Smooth)	4	Bedlington Terrier	1
Cocker Spaniel	4	Bull Terrier	1
Boxer	4	Collie	1
Doberman Pinscher	3	English Setter	1
Old English Sheepdog	3	Welsh Terrier	1
Scottish Terrier	5	West Highland (white) terrier	2
Sealyham Terrier	3	Afghan Hound	1
Pointer	2	Pekingese	1
Bulldog	2	English Springer Spaniel	3
Poodle (Miniature)	2	Whippet	1
Lakeland Terrier	1	Skye Terrier	1

Westminster Entries—1877-1972

Year Dogs	Year Dogs	Year Dogs	Year Dogs	Year Dogs	Year Dogs
1877—1,177	1893—1,319	1909—1,936	1925—2,078	1941—2,548	1957—2,594
1878—1,002	1894—1,344	1910—1,963	1926—2,261	1942—2,388	1958—2,569
1879— 953	1895—1,406	1911—2,070	1927—2,133	1943—2,351	1959—2,544
1880—1,115	1896—1,409	1912—1,929	1928—2,410	1944—2,510	1960—2,547
1881—1,113	1897—1,438	1913—1,893	1929—2,412	1945—2,653	1961—2,548
1882—1,259	1898—1,330	1914—1,921	1930—2,673	1946—2,597	1962—2,566
1883— 970	1899—1,530	1915—1,711	1931—2,516	1947—2,589	1963—2,633
1884—1,100	1900—1,516	1916—1,704	1932—2,350	1948—2,540	1964—2,607
1885— 950	1901—1,549	1917—1,886	1933—2,240	1949—2,559	1965—2,648
1886—1,026	1902—1,678	1918—1,644	1934—2,462	1950—2,532	1966—2,603
1887— 976	1903—1,650	1919—1,560	1935—2,837	1951—2,522	1967—2,961
1888—1,178	1904—1,709	1920—1,624	1936—2,920	1952—2,451	1968—2,580
1889—1,436	1905—1,752	1921—1,754	1937—3,146	1953—2,561	1969—2,530
1890—1,372	1906—1,956	1922—1,796	1938—3,093	1954—2,572	1970—2,611
1891—1,375	1907—1,999	1923—1,827	1939—3,069	1955—2,537	1971—3,031
1892—1,163	1908—2,000	1924—1,782	1940—2,738	1956—2,560	1972—3,093

MORRIS AND ESSEX KENNEL CLUB

1927—Ch. Higgins' Red Pat .... Irish Setter .... William W. Higgins
1928—Ch. Delf Discriminate of Pinegrade ... Sealyham Terrier ...... Pinegrade Kennels
1929—Ch. Little Emir .... Pomeranian .... Mrs. V. Matta
1930—Ch. Weltona Frizzette of Wildoaks .... Fox Terrier (wire) ..... Mr. and Mrs. R.C. Bondy
1931—Ch. Fionne v Loheland of Walnut
        Hall .... Great Dane .... Harkness Edwards
1932—Ch. Lone Eagle of Earlsmoor .... Fox Terrier (wire) ..... Dr. and Mrs. S. Milbank
1933—Eppingeville of Blarney .... Fox Terrier (wire) ..... John G. Bates
1934—Ch. Gunside Babs of Hollybourne .... Sealyham Terrier ...... S.L. Froelich
1935—Ch. Milson O'Boy .... Irish Setter .... Mrs. Cheever Porter
1936—Ch. Mr. Reynal's Monarch .... Harrier .... Armory L. Haskell
1937—Ch. Sturdy Max .... English Setter .... Maridor Kennels

1938—Ch. Ideal Weather	Old English Sheepdog . .	Leonard Collins
1939—Ch. My Own Brucie	Cocker Spaniel	H.E. Mellenthin
1940—Ch. Blakeen Jung Frau	Poodle (standard)	Blakeen Kennels
1941—Ch. Nornay Saddler	Fox Terrier (smooth) . . .	Wissaboo Kennels
1942—45—No shows		
1946—Ch. Benbow's Beau	Cocker Spaniel	Robert A. Gusman
1947—Ch. Rock Ridge Night Rocket	Bedlington Terrier	Mr. and Mrs. W.A. Rockefeller
1948—Ch. Rock Ridge Night Rocket	Bedlington Terrier	Mr. and Mrs. W.A. Rockefeller
1949—Ch. Walsing Winning Trick of Edgerstoune	Scottish Terrier	Mrs. John G. Winant
1950—Ch. Tyronne Farm Clancy	Irish Setter	Jack Spear
1951—Ch. Rock Falls Colonel	English Setter	William T. Holt
1952—Ch. Wyretex Wyns Traveller of Trucote	Fox Terrier (wire)	Mrs. Leonard Smit
1953—Ch. Toplight Template of Twin Ponds	Welsh Terrier	Mrs. Edward P. Alker
1954—No competition		
1955—Ch. Baroque of Quality Hill	Boxer	Mr. and Mrs. John P. Wagner
1956—Ch. Roadcoach Roadster	Dalmatian	Mrs. Sydney K. Allman Jr.
1957—Ch. Fircot L'Ballerine of Maryland . . .	Miniature Poodle	Seafren Kennels
1958—No further competition.		

LIST OF DOG BREEDS

(Recognized by the American Kennel Club in 1972)

There are four requirements for acceptance: the dogs must breed true to type; the dogs of breed must exist in this country in considerable numbers; they must be spread around the country widely in the hands of many owners, and not be localized in the hands of a few, and present practice requires the organization of a breed club that is fairly representative of the owners. The last previous acceptance was that of the Akita and the Bichon Frise in 1971.

Affenpinschers
Afghan Hounds
Airedale Terriers
Akitas
Alaskan Malamutes
Australian Terrier
Basenjis
Basset Hounds
Beagles
Bedlington Terriers
Belgian Malinois
Belgian Sheepdog
Belgian Tervuren
Bernese Mountain Dogs
Bichon Frise
Bloodhounds
Border Terriers
Borzois
Boston Terriers
Bouviers des Flandres
Boxers
Briards
Bulldogs
Bullmastiff
Bull Terriers

Cairn Terriers
Chihuahuas
Chow Chows
Collies
Coonhounds (Black and Tan)
Dachshunds
Dalmatians
Dandie Dinmont Terriers
Deerhounds (Scottish)
Doberman Pinschers
English Toy Spaniels
Foxhounds (American)
Foxhounds (English)
Fox Terriers
French Bulldogs
German Shepherd Dogs
German Wire-haired Pointers
Giant Schnauzers
Great Danes
Great Pyrenees
Greyhounds
Griffons (Brussels)
Griffons (Wire-haired Pointing)
Harriers
Irish Terriers
Italian Greyhounds
Japanese Spaniels
Keeshonden
Kerry Blue Terriers
Komondorok
Kuvaszok
Lakeland Terriers
Lhasa Apsos
Maltese
Manchester Terriers
Mastiffs
Newfoundlands
Norwegian Elkhounds
Norwich Terriers

Old English Sheepdogs
Otter Hounds
Papillons
Pekingese
Pinschers (Miniature)
Pointers
Pointers (German Shorthaired)
Pomeranians
Poodles
Pugs
Pulik
Retrievers (Chesapeake Bay)
Retrievers (Curly-coated)
Retrievers (Flat-coated)
Retrievers (Golden)
Retrievers (Labrador)
Rhodesian Ridgebacks
Rottweilers
St. Bernards
Salukis
Samoyeds
Schipperkes
Schnauzers (Standard)
Schnauzers (Miniature)
Scottish Terriers
Sealyham Terriers
Setters (English)

Setters (Gordon)
Setters (Irish)
Shetland Sheepdogs
Shih Tzu
Siberian Huskies
Silky Terriers
Skye Terriers
Spaniels (American Water)
Spaniels (Brittany)
Spaniels (Clumber)
Spaniels (Cocker)
Spaniels (English Cocker)
Spaniels (English Springer)
Spaniels (Field)
Spaniels (Irish Water)
Spaniels (Sussex)
Spaniels (Welsh Springer)
Staffordshire Terriers
Vizslas
Weimaraners
Welsh Corgis (Cardigan)
Welsh Corgis (Pembroke)
Welsh Terriers
West Highland White Terriers
Whippets
Wolfhounds (Irish)
Yorkshire Terriers

FENCING

(Courtesy of Amateur Fencers League of America, 249 Eton Place, Westfield, N.J., 07090)

Fencing began as a form of combat. Over the centuries it became outmoded as a means of warfare and it gradually evolved into dueling. Today it is a sport of skill, alertness and fast footwork. It has developed into a popular sport, particularly in colleges.

Fencing, which is the art of armed personal offense and defense, originated as a form of deadly combat long before the Christian Era and continued as such for 2,000—perhaps more—years. Probably the oldest known sword is the short sword with its blade of bronze, found in the tomb of Saragon the first King of Ur. This would date the pioneer fencing weapon at 5,000 or more years, according to historians.

The most treasured blade in the world is the Divine Sword of Japan. It is over 2,000 years old and is called the Rusanagino Tsurugi. It was brandished by Prince Yamato Takeruno Mikoto, and legend has it that he used it first to cut down blazing grass which surrounded him and then whirled it with victorious result at his enemies in Eastern Japan. When the sword was moved on Nov. 1, 1935, to a new building in the Atusta Shrine at Nagoya, the occasion called for a national holiday in Japan and a ceremony in which over 500,000 took part. Thus one of the largest crowds in history assembled to pay homage to a fencing device of only legendary value.

From the time of Saragon of ancient Ur until the 12th or 13th Centuries A.D., the sword was not in general use for the reason that the blade was of bronze, which could not hold a sharp edge. Although sword combats —spears were used in earlier days—were common long before Christ, duels as the accepted means of settling disputes did not come into vogue until centuries afterward and it was this custom that gave fencing a tremendous impetus.

The early duels were to the death. Since no gentleman could afford to refuse a challenge for fear of social ostracism, all men gave much of their time and energy to learning the art of swordsmanship. Even today, when fencing is usually practiced only for sport's sake, there are instances of dueling to settle disputes. In most modern duels, however, the rules end the contest when one man has drawn the other's blood. Furthermore, modern fencers the world over frown on this vestige of the past and it is seldom indeed that a principal in the modern duel is an active participant in the sport.

Several countries lay claim to the origin of fencing as a sport, and each has a convincing basis for its claim. During the 14th Century the Germans decided that dueling could be a form of sport as well as a fight to the death. They pioneered duels with blunted sword points, and an official determined who was superior after a fixed length of time. A manuscript dated 1410 A.D. describes fencing as a sport in Germany, leading to the conclusion that it may have been established 50 or 60 years earlier, or near the middle of the 14th Century. The Marxbruder (Fencing) Guild of Lowenberg existed in 1383.

These data relative to fencing in Germany in the 14th Century weaken Italy's claim to creation of the sport because there was no fencing in Italy until the 15th Century. However, the sword used in the early years in Germany was a heavy, clumsy weapon, 32 to 36 inches in length, without a hand guard. The use of such a weapon set early German fencing apart from modern fencing, which is more directly traceable to Spain, Italy and France. The inventor of the hand guard, which he called pas d'ane, was Gonzalvo de Cordova, a Spanish army captain who died in 1515 and whose sword is in the Madrid Museum.

A singular fact concerning the growth in popularity of fencing is that it gained its greatest momentum after gunpowder had ended the bow and arrow as major weapons in warfare. The aristocracy of Europe clambered out of its suits of armor as soon as bullets started to pierce the metal that had once protected them. These men earlier had called on the sword only to attack. Not needing protection, they had not learned defensive tactics and so had to appeal to the commoners to teach them the strategy of defense with the sword.

Schools for teaching fencing sprang up all over Europe, with the upper classes in the roll of students. Many of the teachers previously had earned a livelihood by putting on sword exhibitions with carnivals that toured the countryside. There was, for a time, opposition to fencing schools and it is noted that around the 15th Century in England, one Roger, who described himself as a "master," was indicted on the charge of "keeping a fencing school for divers men, and enticing sons of respectable persons to waste time and spend the property of their parents in bad practices."

Achille Marozzo of Italy perhaps was the first to write a booklet on fencing (1536), and what probably was the first treatise of its kind in English is Silver's "Brief Introductions on My Paradoxes of Defense" (1599). Roy S. Tinney, an American who began fencing in 1898 and devoted many years to teaching the sport as a hobby, declared:

"The use of the sword for defense as well as offense was first evolved and presented to the world by Camillo Agrippa of Milan, living in Rome. He was not a fencing master. He was a gentleman and engineer and a great mathematician. He worked in collaboration with Michael Angelo, who drew the illustrations for Agrippa's book 'A Treatise on the Science of Arms,' published in Rome in 1553.

"Fencing is an art and an education, a sport with a lure peculiarly its own. Backed by centuries of tradition, idealized in prose and poetry, skill in swordsmanship is universally admired. Fencers exemplify a quality so few possess—poise.

Silhouettes of the Targets

A. Target: foil
B. Target: épée
C. Target: sabre

"Fencing has been and always will be enjoyed by a highly intelligent minority; those possessing the moral courage, the self-discipline, the quiet determination required to become proficient in a sport that calls for the highly perfected technique of the golfer, the explosive energy of the sprinter and the split-second decisions demanded of the boxer and the tennis player.

"It demands greater powers of analysis than any other sport."

Along in 1570, Henri Saint-Didier of France gave names to the major movements in fencing (disengage, coupe, double, redoublement and priz-de-fer) and most of them endure to this day as the international language for the sport. Prior to this time it was customary for the different nations to use their own languages.

The first radical departure from the various swords of early years was introduced about 1680 by Count Koenigsmarken of Poland. The upper half of his blade was very wide, but just below the middle it tapered severely. Further, his blade was triangular and hollowed on all three sides. The French, referring to his type of sword, for some unknown reason called it "Colichemarder" so that today that sword of revolutionary design is still known as the Colichemarder. The epee and saber of modern use are improvements in some fashion of the basic Koenigsmarken idea.

The swords and skills of swordsmen were often called into action in the United States, as well as in Europe, to wage duels. There was fencing in the United States—and much fatal dueling—in Revolutionary War days and for some generations thereafter, but duels to "avenge honor" ceased after the Civil War and fencing became the exclusive property of sportsmen.

The modern sport is subject to a few conventional rules, but otherwise differs little in fundamental technique from its more martial counterpart. Prior to the 18th Century the movements had to be formalized and restricted because of danger to face and eyes. With the introduction of the wire-mesh mask, however, the game became more flexible and the tendency was toward lighter and more flexible weapons. The result is that today's contests place a premium on speed and coordination and give little if any advantage to sheer strength.

Prior to 1891 the sport of fencing in the United States was under the general supervision of the Amateur Athletic Union. In that year the active fencers established an autonomous organization and, under the leadership of Dr. Graeme M. Hammond, the Amateur Fencers League of America became, and still is, the governing body in this country.

The AFLA had 57 active divisions in the United States in 1972 with headquarters in New Jersey. It was affiliated with the AAU, the U.S. Olympic Association, and the Federation Internationale d'Escrime, the international governing body for fencing. The development of the Amateur Fencers League of America, subsequent to the administration of Dr. Hammond, has been in the capable hands of Col. Henry Breckinridge, F. Barnard O'Connor, Leon M. Schoonmaker, Harold Van Buskirk, Dr. John R. Huffman, Dernell Every, Miguel A. de Capriles, Jose R. de Capriles, Donald S. Thompson, Dr. Paul Makler, Norman Lewis, Alan M. Ruben, and Stephen B. Sobel. Membership in the AFLA is open to all persons interested in the sport of fencing. The official magazine is *American Fencing*. In 1972, it was estimated that there were 400,000 fencers in the United States.

FAMOUS SWORDSMEN

Men

One of the greatest swordsmen of an early era was Chevalier de Saint Georges, a half-breed from Guadalupe. Another was Italy's fabulous Di Grassi. Chevalier de'Eon de Beaumont (1728—1810), peerless in his time, moved from France to England and there founded the family that has been illustrious in the fencing history of England.

The two greatest swordsmen of modern times are Nedo Nadi and Aldo Nadi of Italy. Aldo Nadi, began to fence when he was 4 years old and won his first championship at the age of 12.

Other great professional champions and masters have been: Louis Merignac, Kirchoffer, Louis Rondelle, Raoul Clery and Emile Gouspy of France; A.J. Corbesier, George Heintz and Clovis Deladrier of Belgium; Eugene Pini, Guiseppe (Beppo) Nadi, A. Greco and Italo Santelli of Italy; George Santelli of Hungary; Aurelio Garcia Campo and Julio Martinez Castello of Spain, and B. Bertrand, Leon Bertrand and Edgar Seligman of England. The professional today is almost exclusively a teacher of fencing—a fencing master or "maitre d'armes."

The list of great international amateur fencers includes Lucien Gaudin, E. Gravelotte, P. Cattiau, Georges Buchard, Roger Ducret and Christian d'Oriola of France; Paul Anspach of Belgium; G. Gaudini, O. Puliti, A. Montano, Gustavo Marzi and Eduardo Mangiarotti of Italy; E. Fuchs, A. Gombos, G. Piller, E. Kabos, Aladar Gerevich, Rudolf Karpati and G. Kovacs of Hungary; Lord Derborough, Charles de Beaumont and Emrys Lloyd of England; R. L. Heide of Norway; A. E. W. de Jong of Holland; Ramon Fonst of Cuba, and George C. Calnan and Joseph L. Levis of the United States.

The outstanding American champions include W. Scott O'Connor, Dr. B. F. O'Connor, R. O. Haubold, Charles G. Bothner, G. Kavanaugh, A. V. Z. Post, Dr. Graeme M. Hammond, Charles T. Tatham, A. G. Anderson, A. E. Sauer, George H. Breed, Sherman Hall, Dr. F. W. Allen, C. R. McPherson, William H. Russell, Leo G. Nunes, George C. Calnan, Nickolas Muray, Miguel A. de Capriles, Dr. John R. Huffman, Hugh V. Alessandroni, Dr. Norman C. Armitage, Gustave M. Heiss, Dernell Every, Thomas J. Sands, Warren A. Dow, Jose R. de Capriles, Dean Cetrulo, Dr. Tibor Nyilas, Norman Lewis, Silvio Giolito, Dr. Daniel Bukantz and Albert Axelrod.

In almost every case, the great champions reach their peak between the ages of 28 and 35 and the average competitive life of a fencer covers a span of over 25 years.

Women

The title of greatest woman fencer of all time probably belongs to Ilona Elek of Hungary. Miss Elek was the Olympic champion in 1936 and 1948 and world champion in 1934, 1935 and 1951. Other outstanding international fencers include Helene Mayer of Germany, Elen Preis of Austria, Irene Camber of Italy and Karen Lachmann of Denmark. Three American women performed with distinction in Olympic competition: Mrs. Maria Cerra Tishman, Mrs. Janice York Romary and Mrs. Maxine Mitchell.

In the early days of women's fencing in the United States Adeline Gehrig, sister of baseball's immortal Lou, was the outstanding national champion. Another star of that period was Mrs. C.H. Voorhees. In later years the outstanding champions were Mrs. Florence Schoonmaker, Marion Lloyd, Dorothy Locke, Mrs. Helena M. Dow, Miss York and Mrs. Mitchell.

Miss Mayer came to live in the United States in 1933 and won the National championship eight times between 1934 and 1946.

The foil is the only weapon used by women.

Champions

WORLD
Men's Foil
*1896—E. Gravelotte, France
*1900—E. Coste, France
*1904—A.V.Z. Post, Cuba
*1906—Dillon-Cavanagh, France
*1912—Nedo Nadi, Italy
*1920—Nedo Nadi
*1924—Roger Ducret, France
 1926—G. Chiavacci, Italy
 1927—O. Puliti, Italy
*1928—Lucien Gaudin, France
 1929—O. Puliti
 1930—Giulio Gaudini, Italy
 1931—R. Lemoine, France
*1932—Gustavo Marzi, Italy
 1933—G. Guaragna, Italy
 1934—Giulio Gaudini
*1936—Giulio Gaudini
 1937—Gustavo Marzi
 1938—G. Guaragna
 1947—Christian d'Oriola, France
*1948—Jean Buhan, France
 1949—Christian d'Oriola
 1950—Renzo Nostini, Italy
 1951—Manlio di Rosa, Italy
*1952—54—Christian d'Oriola
 1955—Gyuricza, Hungary
*1956—Christian d'Oriola
 1957—Mihaly Fulop, Hungary
 1958—Gian Carlo Bergamini, Italy
 1959—Allan Jay, Great Britain
 1960—Victor Jdanovich, U.S.S.R.
 1961—Richard Parulski, Poland
 1962—Gherman Sveshnikov, U.S.S.R.

 1963—Jean-Claude Magnan, France
*1964—Egon Franke, Poland
 1965—Jean-Claude Magnan, France
 1966—German Svechnikov, U.S.S.R.
 1967—Viktor Poutiatin, U.S.S.R.
*1968—Ion Drimba, Rumania
 1969—70—Fredrich Wessel, West Germany
 1971—Vasily Stankovich, U.S.S.R.
*1972—Witold Woyda, Poland

Men's Epee
*1896—E. Gravelotte
*1900—Ramon Fonst, Cuba
*1904—Ramon Fonst
 1906—Comte de la Falaise, France
*1908—G. Alibert, France
*1912—Paul Anspach, Belgium
*1920—A. Massard, France
 1921—Lucien Gaudin, France
 1922—R. Herde, Norway
 1923—W. Brower, Holland
*1924—C. Delporte, Belgium
 1926—G.C. Tainturier, France
 1927—Georges Buchard, France
*1928—Lucien Gaudin
 1929—30—P. Cattiau, France
 1931—Georges Buchard
*1932—G. Cornaggia-Medici, Italy
 1933—Georges Buchard
 1934—P. Dunay, Hungary
 1935—H. Drakenberg, Sweden
*1936—Franco Riccardi, Italy
 1937—B. Schmetz, France
 1938—M. Pecheux, France
 1947—G. Artigas, France

*1948—Luigi Cantone, Italy
1949—D. Mangiarotti, Italy
1950—Mogens Luchow, Denmark
1951—*52—Eduardo Mangiarotti, Italy
1953—Josef Sacovics, Hungary
1954—Eduardo Mangiarotti
1955—Anglesio, Italy
*1956—Carlo Pavesti, Italy
1957—Armand Movyal, France
1958—H. William Hoskyns, England
1959—Gerard Lafranc, France
1960—Giuseppe Delfino, Italy
1961—Jacque Guittet, France
1962—Istevan Kausz, Hungary
1963—Roland Losert, Austria
*1964—Grigory Kriss, U.S.S.R.
1965—Zoltan Nemere, Hungary
1966—Aleksis Nikantchikov, U.S.S.R.
1967—Aleksis Nikantchikov, U.S.S.R.
*1968—Gyozo Kulcsar, Hungary
1969—Bogdan Andrzejewski, Poland
1970—Alexi Nikanchikov, U.S.S.R.
1971—Grigor Kriss, U.S.S.R.
*1972—Tibor Fenyvesi, Hungary

Men's Saber
*1896—G. Georgiadis, Greece
*1900—Comte de la Falaise, France
*1904—M. de Diaz, Cuba
1906—G. Georgiadis
*1908—E. Fuchs, Hungary
*1912—E. Fuchs
*1920—Nedo Nadi, Italy
1922—23—A.E.W. De Jong, Holland
*1924—Alexandre Posta, Hungary
1925—J. Garay, Hungary
1926—27—A. Gombos, Hungary
*1928—E. Terztyansky, Hungary
1929—J. Glycais, Hungary
1930—31—George Piller, Hungary
*1932—George Piller
1933—34—Endre Kabos, Hungary
1935—Aladar Gerevich, Hungary
*1936—Endre Kabos
1937—G. Kovacs, Hungary
1938—A. Montano, Italy
1947—A. Montano
*1948—Aladar Gerevich
1949—G. Dare, Italy
1950—Jean Levavasseur, France
1951—Aladar Gerevich
*1952—G. Kovacs
1953—Paul Kovacs, Hungary
1954—Rudolf Karpati, Hungary
1955—Aladar Gerevich
*1956—Rudolf Karpati
1957—Jerzy Pawlowski, Poland
1958—Yakov Rylski, Russia
1959—60—Rudolf Karpati, Hungary
1961—Iakov Rylskii, U.S.S.R.
1962—Zoltan Horvath, Hungary
1963—Yakov Rylski, U.S.S.R.

*1964—Tibor Pezsa, Hungary
1965—66—Jerzy Pawlowski, Poland
1967—Mark Rakita, U.S.S.R.
*1968—Jerzy Pawlowski, Poland
1969—Victor Sidiak, U.S.S.R.
1970—Tibor Pezsa, Hungary
1971—Michele Maffei, Italy
*1972—Victor Sidiak, U.S.S.R.

*Champion determined at Olympic Games. Prior to 1934, when the world title was first recognized officially, the European champion was considered the world titleholder. Competition held only in years designated.

Men's Team Foil
*1904—Cuba
*1920—Italy
*1924—France
*1928—Italy
*1932—France
*1936—Italy
*1948—France
*1952—53—France
1954—*56—Italy
1957—Hungary
1958—France
1959—66—U.S.S.R.
1967—Rumania
*1968—France
1969—70—U.S.S.R.
1971—France
*1972—Poland

Men's Team Epee
*1906—Germany
*1908—France
*1912—Belgium
*1920—Italy
*1924—France
*1928—Italy
*1932—France
*1936—Italy
*1948—France
*1952—*56—Italy
1957-58—Italy
1959—Hungary
1960—Italy
1961—U.S.S.R.
1962—France
1963—Poland
*1964—Hungary
1965—66—France
1967—U.S.S.R.
*1968—Hungary
1969—U.S.S.R.
1970—72—Hungary

Men's Team Saber
*1904—Cuba
*1906—Germany
*1908—Hungary
*1912—Hungary
1920—Italy

*1924—Italy
*1928—Hungary
*1932—Hungary
*1936—Hungary
*1948—Hungary
*1952-*56—Hungary
1957—58—Hungary
1959—Poland
1960—Hungary
1961—63—Poland
*1964—65—U.S.S.R.
1966—Hungary
1967—71—U.S.S.R.
*1972—Italy

Women's Foil
*1924—Mrs. E.O. Ossier, Denmark
*1928—29—Helene Mayer, Germany
1930—J. Adams, Belgium
1931—Helene Mayer
*1932—Elen Preis, Austria
1933—G. Neligan, Great Britain
1934—35—Ilona Elek, Hungary
*1936—Ilona Elek
1937—Helene Mayer
1938—M. Sediva, Czechoslovakia
1939—46—No competition
1947—Elen Preis
*1948—Ilona Elek
1949—Elen Preis
1950—Renée Garillhe, France, and Elen Preis
　　　　(tie)
1951—Ilona Elek
*1952—Irene Camber, Italy
1953—Irene Camber, Italy
1954—Karen Lachmann, Denmark
1955—Domolki, Hungary
*1956—Gillian Sheen, Great Britain
1957—Alexandra Zabelina, Russia
1958—Valentina Kisseleva, Russia
1959—Efimova, U.S.S.R.
1960—61—Heide Schmid, Germany
1962—Olga Szabo, Rumania
1963—*64—Ildiko Ujlak-Rejto Hungary
1965—Galina Gorokhova, U.S.S.R.
1966—Tatyana Samusenko, U.S.S.R.
1967—Alexandra Zabelina, U.S.S.R.
*1968—69—Elana Novikova Belova, U.S.S.R.
1970—Galina Gorokova, U.S.S.R.
1971—Marie Chantal Demaille, France
*1972—Antonella Ragno, Italy

Woman's Foil Team
1932—Denmark
1933—35—Hungary
1936—Germany
1937—Hungary
1947—48—Denmark
1950—51—France
1952—55—Hungary
1956—U.S.S.R.
1957—Italy
1958—U.S.S.R.

1959—Hungary
*1960—61—U.S.S.R.
1962—*64—Hungary
1965—66—U.S.S.R.
1967—Hungary
*1968—U.S.S.R.
1969—Rumania
1970—*72—U.S.S.R.
　　*Olympic Championships in this event were begun only in 1960. Prior to that there were only World Team Championships in Olympic years.

UNITED STATES
Men's Foil
1892—W. Scott O'Connor
1893—William T. Heintz
1894—Charles G. Bothner
1895—A.V.Z. Post
1896—G. Kavanaugh
1897—Charles G. Bothner
1898—No competition
1899—G. Kavanaugh
1900—F. Townsend
1901—Charles T. Tatham
1902—J.P. Parker
1903—F. Townsend
1904—05—Charles G. Bothner
1906—S.D. Breckinridge
1907—C. Waldbott
1908—W.L. Bowman
1909—O.A. Dickinson
1910—G.K. Bainbridge
1911—George H. Breed
1912—Sherman Hall
1913—P.J. Meylan
1914—S.D. Breckinridge
1915—O.A. Dickinson
1916—A.E. Sauer
1917—Sherman Hall
1918—No competition
1919—20—Sherman Hall
1921—F.W. Honeycutt
1922—H.M. Raynor
1923—R. Peroy
1924—Leo G. Nunes
1925—28—George C. Calnan
1929—Joseph L. Levis
1930—31—George C. Calnan
1932—33—Joseph L. Levis
1934—Hugh V. Alessandroni
1935—Joseph L. Levis
1936—Hugh Alessandroni
1937—Joseph L. Levis
1938—Dernell Every
1939—Norman Lewis
1940—Dernell Every
1941—Dean Cetrulo
1942—43—Warren A. Dow
1944—A. Snyder
1945—Dernell Every
1946—Jose R. de Capriles
1947—Dean Cetrulo
1948—Nathaniel Lubell

1949—Daniel Bukantz
1950—51—Silvio Giolito
1952—53—Daniel Bukantz
1954—Joseph L. Levis
1955—Albert Axelrod
1956—Sewall Shurtz
1957—Daniel Bukantz
1958—Albert Axelrod
1959—Joseph Paletta
1960—Albert Axelrod
1961—Lawrence Anastasi
1962—63—Edwin Richards
1964—Herbert Cohen
1965—Robert Russell
1966—Max Geuter (Germany)
1967—68—Heizaburo Okawa (Japan)
1969—Carl Borack
1970—Albert Axelrod
1971—Uriah Jones
1972—Joseph Freeman

Men's Epee
1892—F. Barnard O'Connor
1893—Graeme M. Hammond
1894—R.O. Haubold
1895—Charles G. Bothner
1896—A.V.Z. Post
1897—Charles G. Bothner
1898—No competition
1899—M. Diaz
1900—W.D. Lyon
1901—03—Charles T. Tatham
1904—Charles G. Bothner
1905—W. Scott O'Connor
1906—W. Grebe
1907—W.D. Lyon
1908—Paul Benzenberg
1909—10—A. de la Poer
1911—George H. Breed
1912—A.V.Z. Post
1913—A.E. Sauer
1914—F.W. Allen
1915—J.A. MacLaughlin
1916—William H. Russell
1917—Leo G. Nunes
1918—No competition
1919—William H. Russell
1920—R.W. Dutcher
1921—C.R. McPherson
1922—Leo G. Nunes
1923—George C. Calnan
1924—Leo G. Nunes
1925—William H. Russell
1926—Leo G. Nunes
1927—Harold Van Buskirk
1928—Leo G. Nunes
1929—F.S. Righeimer
1930—M. Pasche
1931—Miguel A. de Capriles
1932—Leo G. Nunes
1933—34—Gustave M. Heiss
1935—Thomas J. Sands

1936—Gustave M. Heiss
1937—Thomas J. Sands
1938—Jose R. de Capriles
1939—L. Tingley
1940—F. Seibert
1941—Gustave M. Heiss
1942—Henrique Santos
1943—R. Driscoll
1944—Miguel A. de Capriles
1945—Max Gilman
1946—A. Wolff
1947—James Strauch
1948—50—Norman Lewis
1951—Jose R. de Capriles
1952—Abelardo Menendez
1953—Donald Thompson
1954—Sewall Shurtz
1955—56—Abram Cohen
1957—58—Richard Berry
1959—Henry Kolowrat
1960—David Micahnik
1961—Lt. Robert Beck
1962—Gilbert Eisner
1963—Lawrence Anastasi
1964—Paul Pesthy
1965—Joseph Elliott
1966—68—Paul Pesthy
1969—Stephen Netburn
1970—Joseph Elliott
1971—72—James Melcher

Men's Saber
1892—R.O. Haubold
1893—94—Graeme M. Hammond
1895—97—Charles G. Bothner
1898—No competition
1899—G. Kavanaugh
1900—J.L. Ervin
1901—03—A.V.Z. Post
1904—A.G. Anderson
1905—K.B. Johnson
1906—07—A.G. Anderson
1908—G.W. Postgate
1909—A.E. Sauer
1910—J.T. Shaw
1911—A.G. Anderson
1912—C.A. Bill
1913—A.G. Anderson
1914—W. Von Blejenburgh
1915—16—Sherman Hall
1917—Arthur S. Lyon
1918—No competition
1919—Arthur S. Lyon
1920—Sherman Hall
1921—C.R. McPherson
1922—Leo G. Nunes
1923—L.M. Schoonmaker
1924—J.E. Gignoux
1925—Joseph Vince
1926—Leo G. Nunes
1927—28—Nickolas Muray
1929—Leo G. Nunes

1930—Norman C. Armitage
1931—33—John R. Huffman
1934—36—Norman C. Armitage
1937—38—John R. Huffman
1939—43—Norman C. Armitage
1944—Tibor Nyilas
1945—Norman C. Armitage
1946—Tibor Nyilas
1947—James Flynn
1948—Dean Cetrulo
1949—Umberto Martino
1950—53—Tibor Nyilas
1954—George Worth
1955—Richard Dyer
1956—Tibor Nyilas
1957—58—Daniel Magay
1959—Tomas Orley
1960—Eugene Hamori
1961—Daniel Magay
1962—Michael Dasaro
1963—Eugene Hamori
1964—Attila Keresztes
1965—Alex Orban
1966—67—Al Morales
1968—Anthony J. Keane
1969—72—Alex Orban

Men's Three-Weapon
(Competition discontinued after 1950)
1907—G. Reimherr
1908—09—W.L. Bowman
1910—V.P. Curti
1911—J.T. Shaw
1912—Sherman Hall
1913—L.A. MacLaughlin
1914—W. Von Blejenburgh
1915—Sherman Hall
1916—No record
1917—S. Pitt
1918—No competition
1919—20—Sherman Hall
1921—22—Leo G. Nunes
1923—R. Peroy
1924—J.W. Dimond
1925—J.E. Gignoux
1926—Leo G. Nunes
1927—George C. Calnan
1928—Leo G. Nunes
1929—Joseph L. Levis
1930—Leo G. Nunes
1931—32—John R. Huffman
1933—34—Miguel A. de Capriles
1935—38—John R. Huffman
1939—Jose R. de Capriles
1940—John R. Huffman
1941—42—Miguel A. de Capriles
1943—46—No competition
1947—Miguel A. de Capriles
1948—50—Tibor Nyilas

Men's Team Foil
1906—Boston A.C. (W.L. Bowman, F.W. Allen, S. Cabot)

1907—New York A.C. (A.G. Anderson, V.P. Curti, W.D. Lyon)
1908—09—New York A.C. (G.K. Bainbridge, W.L. Bowman, V.P. Curti)
1910—11—New York A.C. (W.L. Bowman, V.P. Curti, J.E. Gignoux)
1912—Fencers Club (G.H. Breed, S. Hall, A.V.Z. Post)
1913—New York A.C. (P.W. Allison, J.E. Gignoux, J.A. MacLaughlin)
1914—15—Washington F.C. (H. Breckinridge, S.D. Breckinridge, J.A. MacLaughlin)
1916—New York A.C. (No Data)
1917—New York A.C. (P.W. Allison, S. Hall, L.G. Nunes)
1918—No competition
1919—New York A.C. (S. Hall, B.F. O'Connor, S. Pitt)
1920—New York A.C. (S. Hall, L.G. Nunes, S. Pitt)
1921—Washington F.C. (H. Breckinridge, F.W. Honeycutt, H. Rayner)
1922—Fencers Club (H. Breckinridge, A.S. Lyon, P. Meylan)
1923—Fencers Club (G.H. Breed, H. Breckinridge, R. Peroy)
1924—Fencers Club (G.H. Breed, H. Breckinridge, A.P. Walker Jr.)
1925—Fencers Club (G.C. Calnan, R. Peroy, A.P. Walker Jr.)
1926—Fencers Club (H. Breckinridge, G.C. Calnan, R. Peroy)
1927—New York A.C. (J. Aabye, J.C. Falkenberg, L.G. Nunes)
1928—Fencers Club (G.C. Calnan, D. Every, J.L. Levis)
1929—Fencers Club (D. Every, J.L. Levis, S. Robbins)
1930—Boston A.C. (E.H. Lane, E.L. Lane, J. Levis)
1931—32—Fencers Club (H.V. Alessandroni, G.C. Calnan, D. Every)
1933—Fencers Club (H.V. Alessandroni, W.J. Block, D. Every)
1934—Fencers Club (H.V. Alessandroni, W.J. Block, J.L. Levis)
1935—Fencers Club (H.V. Alessandroni, N. Muray, W.T. Pecora 2d)
1936—Fencers Club (H.V. Alessandroni, I.B. Cantor, N. Muray)
1937—University F.C. (J.R. de Capriles, M.A. de Capriles, W.A. Dow)
1938—Salle Santelli (J.R. de Capriles, M.A. de Capriles, W.A. Dow)
1939—Salle Santelli (J.R. de Capriles, M.A. de Capriles, W.A. Dow, N. Lewis)
1940—Salle Santelli (A. Axelrod, J.R. de Capriles, D. Cetrulo)
1941—42—New York A.C. (W.A. Dow, D. Every, S. Giolito, J.R. Huffman)
1943—46—No competition

1947–New York A.C. (W.A. Dow, D. Every, S. Giolito, R. Ozol)

1948–New York A.C. (W.A. Dow, D. Every, W. Goldsmith)

1949–50–Fencers Club (D. Bukantz, N. Lubell, A. Prokop, C. Steinhardt)

1951–Fencers Club (D. Bukantz, L. Kellerman, N. Lubell, E. Vebell)

1952–Salle Santelli (A. Axelrod, A. Kwartler, L. Turk)

1953–Fencers Club (D. Bukantz, C. Ettinger, N. Lubell, J. Strauch)

1954–Salle Santelli (A. Axelrod, R. Goldstein, A. Kwartler, N. Lewis)

1955–Fencers Club (D. Bukantz, J.R. de Capriles, H. Goldsmith, N. Lubell)

1956–Fencers Club (D. Bukantz, N. Lubell, A. Prokop, A. Seeman)

1957–Fencers Club (D. Bukantz, H. Goldsmith, N. Lubell, A. Seeman)

1958–Fencers Club (D. Bukantz, H. Goldsmith, C. Steinhardt, A. Seeman)

1959–New York Univ. (Dasaro, Davis, Glazer)

1960–New York A.C. (Giolito, Haaf, Keane)

1961–New York A.C. (Giolito, Mooney, Richards, Spinella)

1962–Fencers Club (Axelrod, Bukantz, Goldsmith, Seemen)

1963–Fencers Club (Axlerod, Cohen, Glazer, Goldsmith)

1964–Salle Santelli (Gaylor, Jones, Kwartler, Russell)

1965–New York F.C. (Axelrod, Checkes, Grafton, Margolis)

1966–New York F.C. (Axelrod, Cohen, Grafton)

1967–Los Angeles F.A. (Okawa, Berger, Elliott, Shimizu)

1968–Salle Santelli (Russell, Jones, Kamhi, Lang)

1969–Salle Csiszar (Campbell, M. Davis, Anastasi, Morgan)

1970–Salle Santelli (Russell, Schmatolla, Lang)

1971–New York A.C. (Walter Krause, J. Kestler, A. Davis, Mannino)

1972–Salle Santelli (Jones, Kamhi, Schmatolla, Russell)

Men's Team Epee

1906–New York A.C. (C.G. Bothner, G.M. Hammond, S. McCullough)

1907–New York A.C. (C.G. Bothner, V.P. Curti, W.D. Lyon)

1908–Fencers Club (G.H. Breed, W.S. O'Connor, C.T. Tatham)

1909–N.Y. Turn Verein (J. Allaire, P. Benzenberg, G. Reimerr)

1910–11–New York A.C. (W.L. Bowman, V.P. Curti, J.E. Gignoux)

1912–Fencers Club (G.H. Breed, P.J. Meylan, A. de la Poer)

1913–Boston A.A. (F.W. Allen, O.D. MacLaughlin, F. Schenck)

1914–New York A.C. (W. Von Blejenburgh, W.D. Bowman, J.E. Gignoux)

1915–Washington F.C. (C.L. Boune, S.D. Breckinridge, J.A. MacLaughlin)

1916–New York A.C. (W.L. Bowman, V.P. Curti, L.G. Nunes)

1917–West Point Officers Club (G. Halsington, W.H. Wilbur, W.H. Young)

1918–No competition

1919–New York A.C. (V.P. Curti, W.L. Gottshall, S. Pitt)

1920–Boston A.A. (E.R. Gay, W.H. Russell, E. Wallen)

1921–Washington F.C. (H. Breckinridge, F.W. Honeycutt, H. Rayner)

1922–Fencers Club (G.H. Breed, P.J. Meylan, A.S. Lyon)

1923–Washington Square F.C. (N. Muray, D. Waldhaus, C.V. Webb)

1924–Yale University (H.J. Boulton, H.H. Brown, E.P. Mengel)

1925–Fencers Club (G.C. Calnan, W.H. Russell, A.P. Walker Jr.)

1926–Fencers Club (H. Breckinridge, G.C. Calnan, A.P. Walker Jr.)

1927–Boston A.A. (E.H. Lane, F.L. Lane, C.C. Shears)

1928–Fencers Club (G.C. Calnan, R.C. Elwell, A.P. Walker Jr.)

1929–Washington Square F.C. (F.M. Bianco, K. Inukai, P. Mijer)

1930–University F.C. (M.A. de Capriles, M. Kapner, E.H. Sorenson)

1931–University F.C. (J.R. de Capriles, M.A. de Capriles, M. Kapner)

1932–Fencers Club (G.C. Calnan, G.M. Heiss, T. Jaeckel)

1933–Fencers Club (G.M. Heiss, T. Jaeckel, M. Pasche)

1934–36–Fencers Club (G.M. Heiss, T. Jaeckel, T. Sands)

1937–Fencers Club (W. Cornett, R. Driscoll, A. Skrobisch)

1938–New York A.C. (J.V. Grombach, L.G. Nunes, F.R. Weber)

1939–Fencers Club (N.C. Armitage, G.M. Heiss, T. Jaeckel)

1940–Salle Santelli (J.R. de Capriles, M.A. de Capriles, N. Lewis)

1941–Fencers Club (R. Driscoll, G.M. Heiss, T. Jaeckel, A. Skrobisch)

1942–New York A.C. (N. Muray, L.G. Nunes, H. Santos)

1943–46–No competition

1947–Salle Santelli (J.R. de Capriles, R. Goldstein, N. Lewis)

1948–Salle Santelli (J.R. de Capriles, R. Goldstein, N. Lewis, M. Metzger)

1949–Salle Santelli (J.R. de Capriles, M. Metzger, P. Mijer, P. Moss)

1950–Salle Santelli (R. Goldstein, M. Metzger, N. Lewis)

1951—Fencers Club (J.R. de Capriles, A. Skrobisch, J. Strauch, E. Vebell)
1952—Northern Ohio, Cleveland (W. Durrett, H. Fried, S. Thompson, W. Henry)
1953—Salle Santelli (P. Moss, R. Goldstein, N. Lewis, L. Turk)
1954—Fencers Club (J.R. de Capriles, A. Skrobisch, J. Strauch, E. Vebell)
1955—Salle Santelli (R. Goldstein, W. Henry, P. Mijer, P. Moss)
1956—Salle Csiszar (R. Dyer, P. Makler, A. Ruben)
1957—Michigan (R. Berry, B. Calkins, R. Martinez, R. Pinchuk)
1958—Michigan (R. Berry, G. Calkins, R. Martinez, G. Pinter)
1959—Pentathlon (A. Anastasi, P. Pesthy, R. Stoll)
1960—U.S. Navy (J. Margolis, J. Paletta, R. Wommack)
1961—N.Y.A.C. (M. Alexander, R. King, J. Powell, R. Spinella)
1962—N.Y.A.C. (P. Pesthy, J. Powell, R. Spinella)
1963—U.S. Modern Pentathlon (Moore, Morales, Stoll)
1964—New York A.C. (Pesthy, Powell, Richards)
1965—Salle Csiszar (Balla, Byer, Hamori, Micahnik)
1966—Salle Csiszar (Anastasi, Kolowrat, Micahnik)
1967—Salle Csiszar (Kolowrat, Micahnik, Netburn)
1968—Salle Csiszar (Anastasi, Netburn, Micahnik, Miller)
1969—Salle Mori (Scott, Elliott, Christie)
1970–72—New York A.C. (Masin, Pesthy, Netburn)

Men's Team Saber
1910—New York A.C. (A.G. Anderson, C.A. Bill, F.J. Byrne)
1911—New York A.C. (A.G. Anderson, C.A. Bill, V.P. Curti)
1912–13—New York A.C. (A.G. Anderson, C.A. Bill, F.J. Byrne)
1914—Fencers Club (A.S. Lyon, S. Pitt, J.T. Shaw)
1915—New York A.C. (A.G. Anderson, V.P. Curti, S. Hall)
1916—Fencers Club (No Data)
1917—New York A.C. (S. Hall, L.G. Nunes, S. Pitt)
1918–19—No competition
1920—Philadelphia F.C. (J.G. Bartol, A.R. Clapp, J.B. Parker)
1921—New York A.C. (S. Hall, C.R. McPherson, L.G. Nunes)
1922—New York A.C. (J.G. Bartol, C.R. McPherson, L.G. Nunes)

1923—New York A.C. (E.S. Acel, J.E. Gignoux, L.H. Weld)
1924—Fencers Club (R. Peroy, L.M. Schoonmaker, H. Van Buskirk)
1925—Fencers Club (P. Calle, G.C. Calnan, R. Peroy)
1926—New York A.C. (J.E. Gignoux, L.G. Nunes, J. Vince)
1927—New York A.C. (E.S. Acel, L.G. Nunes, J. Vince)
1928—New York A.C. (J.E. Gignoux, N. Muray, L.G. Nunes)
1929—New York A.C. (E.S. Acel, J.R. Huffman, N. Muray)
1930—New York A.C. (E.S. Acel, B. de Nagy, L.G. Nunes)
1931—New York A.C. (J.R. Huffman, B. de Nagy, L.G. Nunes)
1932—New York A.C. (J.R. Huffman, N. Muray, L.G. Nunes)
1933—New York A.C. (E.S. Acel, J.R. Huffman, B. de Nagy)
1934—Fencers Club (N.C. Armitage, A. Muray, N. Muray)
1935—Salle d'Armes Vince (P.W. Bruder, J.A. Cerra, S.T. Stewart Jr.)
1936—New York A.C. (E.S. Acel, J.R. Huffman, B. de Nagy)
1937—New York A.C. (E.S. Acel, J.R. Huffman, S.T. Stewart Jr.)
1938—New York A.C. (J.R. Huffman, R. Marson, S.T. Stewart Jr.)
1939—New York A.C. (E.S. Acel, J.R. Huffman, R. Marson)
1940—New York A.C. (E.S. Acel, J.R. Huffman, R. Marson, N. Muray)
1941—Salle Santelli (M.A. de Capriles, D. Cetrulo, T. Nyilos, G.V. Worth)
1942—New York A.C. (J.R. Huffman, R. Marson, R. Muray)
1943–46—No competition
1947—Salle Santelli (M.A. de Capriles, D. Cetrulo, T. Nyilas, G.V. Worth)
1948—Salle Santelli (D. Cetrulo, J. Gorlin, T. Nyilas, G.V. Worth)
1949—Salle Santelli (J. Gorlin, A. Kwartler, T. Nyilas, G.V. Worth)
1950—New York A.C. (J.H. Flynn, R. Marson, N. Muray, S.T. Stewart Jr.)
1951—New York A.C. (J.H. Flynn, R. Marson, N. Muray)
1952—Salle Santelli (T. Nyilas, A. Kwartler, A. Treves, S. Gorlin)
1953—Salle Santelli (T. Nyilas, G. Worth, A. Kwartler, S. Gorlin)
1954—Salle Santelli (S. Gorlin, A. Kwartler, T. Nyilas, G. Worth)
1955—Salle Santelli (S. Gorlin, T. Nyilas, A. Treves, G. Worth)
1956—Salle Santelli (R. Blum, S. Gorlin, T. Nyilas, A. Treves)

1957–San Francisco (G. Domolky, D. Magay, T. Orley)

1958–Salle Santelli (G. Worth, A. Kwartler, C. Pellaghy, R. Blum)

1959–Salle Santelli (R. Blum, A. Kwartler, C. Pallaghy, G. Worth)

1960–Pannonia A.C. (J. Baker, G. Biagini, A. Orban, T. Orley)

1961–Pannonia A.C. (J. Baker, G. Biagini, D. Magay, A. Orban)

1962–N.Y.A.C. (A. Keresztes, T. Nyllas, T. Orley, L. Pongo)

1963–New York A.C. (Kerszles, Pariser, Pongo, Richards)

1964–Salle Csiszar (Balla, Hamori, Krajcir, Makler)

1965–New York A.C. (Garbatini, Morales, Orban, Pongo)

1966–New York A.C. (Dasaro, Morales, Orban, Keane)

1967–New York A.C. (Dasaro, Keane, Morales, Orban)

1968–New York A.C. (Keane, Orban, Morales, Gall)

1969–New York A.C. (Gall, Morales, Keane, Orban)

1970–New York A.C. (Gall, Pongo, Morales, Keane)

1971–Salle Csiszar (Balla, Battle, Makler, Mayer)

1972–New York A.C. (Orban, Keane, Gall, Morales)

Men's Team Three-weapon

1906–New York A.C. (S. McCullough, G.M. Hammond K.B. Johnson)

1907–New York A.C. (G.K. Bainbridge, W.D. Lyon, A.G. Anderson)

1908–New York A.C. (V.P. Curti, W.D. Lyon, A.G. Anderson)

1909–Fencers Club (G.H. Breed, A. de la Poer, A.V.Z. Post)

1910–Fencers Club (G.H. Breed, E. Adams, A.V.Z. Post)

1911–12–Fencers Club (G.H. Breed, A. de la Poer, A.V.Z. Post)

1913–New York A.C. (P.W. Allison, J.A. MacLaughlin, A.G. Anderson)

1914–New York A.C. (P.W. Allison, J.A. MacLaughlin, W. Von Blejenburgh)

1915–New York A.C. (P.W. Allison, V.P. Curti, A. Hall)

1916–Fencers Club (P.J. Meylan, G.H. Breed, A.S. Lyon)

1917–New York A.C. (P.W. Allison, L.G. Nunes, S. Pitt)

1918–19–No competition

1920–New York A.C. (S. Hall, L.G. Nunes, S. Pitt)

1921–Fencers Club (G.H. Breed, W. Twyeffort, L.M. Schoonmaker)

1922–New York A.C. (J. Aabye, L.G. Nunes, C.R. McPherson)

1923–Washington Square F.C. (C.V. Webb, P. Mijer, N. Muray)

1924–Fencers Club (R. Peroy, G.H. Breed, L.M. Schoonmaker)

1925–Fencers Club (R. Peroy, G.C. Calnan, P. Calle)

1926–Fencers Club (G.C. Calnan, C. Bardiani, H. Van Buskirk)

1927–New York A.C. (J. Aabye, L.G. Nunes, J. Vince)

1928–Fencers Club (G.C. Calnan, A.P. Walker, Jr., H. Van Buskirk)

1929–Fencers Club (J.L. Levis, C. Lamar, N.C. Armitage)

1930–New York A.C. (L.G. Nunes, J.V. Grombach, N. Muray)

1931–Salle d'Armes Vince (G. Cetrulo, J. Barmack, P.W. Bruder)

1932–Fencers Club (H.V. Alessandroni, T. Jaeckel, N.C. Armitage)

1933–Fencers Club (G.C. Calnan, T. Jaeckel, N.C. Armitage)

1934–New York A.C. (D. Every, L.G. Nunes, J.R. Huffman)

1935–Fencers Club (H.V. Alessandroni, T. Jaeckel, N.C. Armitage)

1936–37–Salle Santelli (W.A. Dow, J.R. de Capriles, M.A. de Capriles)

1938–New York A.C. (D. Every, N. Muray, J.R. Huffman)

1939–Salle Santelli (W.A. Dow, J.R. de Capriles, M.A. de Capriles, P. Lubart)

1940–New York A.C. (W.A. Dow, L.G. Nunes, J.R. Huffman)

1941–Salle Santelli (J.R. de Capriles, P. Mijer, T. Nyilas)

1942–New York A.C. (D. Every, H. Santos, J.R. Huffman)

1943 to 1946–No competition

1947–48–Salle Santelli (D. Cetrulo, J.R. de Capriles, T. Nyilas)

1949–Salle Santelli (A. Axelrod, J.R. de Capriles, G.V. Worth)

1950–Salle Santelli (A. Axelrod, N. Lewis, G.V. Worth)

1951–New York A.C. (D. Every, H. Santos, J.H. Flynn)

1952–Salle Santelli (A. Axelrod, R. Goldstein, G.V. Worth)

1953–Salle Santelli (A. Kwartler, R. Goldstein, G. Worth)

1954–Salle Santelli (A. Axelrod, R. Goldstein, N. Lewis, G. Worth)

1955–Fencers Club (D. Bukantz, H. Goldsmith, A. Skrobisch, A. Cohen)

1956–U.S. Air Force (R. Goldman, H. Kolowrat, T. Carhart)

1957–Michigan (B. Krieger, R. Berry, W. Goering)

1958—New England (A. Axelrod, R. Pew, W. Andre, E. Richards)

1959—Fencers Club (Seeman, Cohen, Farber, Kolowraf)

1960—N.Y.A.C. (Keane, Spinella, Pallaghy)

1961—Salle Csiszar (Davis, Micahnik, Anastasi, Hamori)

1962—Fencers Club (Mayer, Axelrod, Adams)

1963—U.S. Modern Pentathlon (Dasaro, Stoll, Morales)

1964—New York A.C. (Richards, Pesthy, Keresztes)

Event Discontinued

Women's Foil

1912—A. Baylis
1913—Mrs. W.H. Dewar
1914—M. Stimson
1915—Jessie Pyle
1916—Mrs. C.H. Voorhees
1917—Florence Walton
1918—19—No competition
1920—23—Adeline Gehrig
1924—Mrs. C.H. Hopper
1925—26—Mrs. Florence Schoonmaker
1927—S. Stern
1928—Marion Lloyd
1929—Mrs. Florence Schoonmaker
1930—Mrs. Harold Van Buskirk
1931—Marion Lloyd
1932—33—Dorothy Locke
1934—35—Helene Mayer
1936—Mrs. Joanne de Tuscan
1937—39—Helene Mayer
1940—Helena Mroczkowska
1941—42—Helene Mayer
1943—Helena Mroczkowska
1944—Madaline Dalton
1945—Maria Cerra
1946—Helene Mayer
1947—48—Mrs. Helena Mroczkowska Dow
1949—Polly Craus
1950—51—Janice-Lee York
1952—Mrs. Maxine Mitchell
1953—Paula Sweeney
1954—55—Mrs. Maxine Mitchell
1956—57—Mrs. Janice Lee Romary
1958—Mrs. Maxine Mitchell
1959—Pilar Roldan
1960—61—Janice Lee Romary
1962—Yoshie Takeucji
1963—Harriet King
1964—66—Janice Romary
1967—Harriet King
1968—Janice Romary
1969—Ruth White
1970—71—Harriet King
1972—Ruth White

Women's Foil Team

1956—So. Cal. (M. Mitchell, J. Romary)
1957—So. Cal. (I. Hoblit, M. Mitchell, J. Romary)

1958—Salle Lucia (A. Genton, H. King, C. Kwartler, P. Schwabe)

1959—Los Angeles A.C. (J. Despars, M. Mitchell, F. Talleg)

1960—Salle Lucia (A. Genton, H. King, P. Schwabe)

1961—Salle Santelli (A. Drungis, S. Pierce, B. Santelli, J. Romary)

1962—So. Cal. (M. Ichiyasu, B. Linkmeyer, M. Mitchell, J. Romary)

1963—Fencers Club (Brill, Dalton, Dardia, Sokol)

1964—Pannonia A.C. (Angell, Holloway, King, Lucero)

1965—Salle Santelli

1966—Pannonia A.C. (Angell, Magay, King)

1967—Salle Vince (Rose, Saurer, Romary)

1968—Salle Santelli (O'Connor, Reid, Pierce)

1969—Salle Santelli (O'Connor, Reid, O'Donnell)

1970—New York F.C. (White, Adamovich, Genton)

1971—West End F.C. (Brown, Mitchell, Burton)

1972—Salle Santelli (O'Connor, O'Donnell, Reid, Chesney)

National Collegiate

(Courtesy of Jeffrey Tishman, Amateur Fencers League of America)

Team Three-weapon

1941—Northwestern
1942—Ohio State
1943—46—No competition
1947—New York University
1948—City College of New York
1949—Army, Rutgers (tie)
1950—Navy
1951—52—Columbia
1953—Pennsylvania
1954—Columbia, N.Y.U., tie
1955—Columbia
1956—Illinois
1957—New York University
1958—Illinois
1959—Navy
1960—61—New York University
1962—Navy
1963—Columbia
1964—Princeton
1965—Columbia
1966—67—New York University
1968—Columbia
1969—Pennsylvania
1970—New York University
1971—Columbia, N.Y.U. (tie)
1972—Univ. of Detroit

Foil

1941—Edward McNamara, Northwestern
1942—Byron Krieger, Wayne
1943—46—No competition

1947—Abraham Balk, New York University
1948—Albert Axelrod, City College of New York
1949—Ralph Tedeschi, Rutgers
1950—51—Robert Nielsen, Columbia
1952—Harold Goldsmith, City College of
    New York
1953—Edward Nober, Brooklyn College
1954—Robert Goldman, Pennsylvania
1955—Herman Velasco, Illinois
1956—Ralph DeMarco, Columbia
1957—58—Bruce Davis, Wayne
1959—Joe Paletta, Navy
1960—Eugene Glazer, New York University
1961—62—Herbert Cohen, New York University
1963—Jay Lustig, Columbia
1964—Bill Hicks, Princeton
1965—Joe Nalven, Columbia
1966—Al Davis, New York University
1967—Mike Gaylor, New York University
1968—Gerard Esponda, San Francisco State
1969—Anthony Kestler, Columbia
1970—Walter Krause, New York University
1971—72—Tyrone Simmons, Univ. of Detroit

Epee

1941—G.H. Boland, Illinois
1942—Dan Burtt, Ohio State
1943—46—No competition
1947—Abraham Balk, New York University
1948—William Bryan, Navy
1949—Richard Bowman, Army
1950—Thomas Stuart, Navy
1951—Daniel Chafetz, Columbia
1952—James Wallner, New York University
1953—Jack Tori, Pennsylvania
1954—Henry Kolowrat, Princeton
1955—Donald Tadrawski, Notre Dame
1956—Kinmont Hoitsma, Princeton
1957—James Margolis, Columbia
1958—59—Roland Wommack, Navy
1960—Gilbert Eisner, New York University
1961—Jerry Halpren, New York University
1962—Thane Hawlins, Navy
1963—Lawrence Crum, Navy
1964—65—Paul Pesthy, Rutgers
1966—Bernhardt Herman, Iowa
1967—George Masin, New York University
1968—Don Sieja, Cornell
1969—James Wetzler, Pennsylvania
1970—John Nadas, Case Western Reserve Univ.
1971—George Szunyogh, New York University
1972—Ernesto Fernandez, Pennsylvania

Saber

1941—William Meyer, Dartmouth
1942—Andre Deladrier, St. John's
1943—46—No competition
1947—Oscar Parsons, Temple
1948—50—Alex Treves, Rutgers
1951—Chamberless Johnston, Princeton
1952—53—Robert Parmacek, Pennsylvania
1954—Steve Sobel, Columbia
1955—Barry Pariser, Columbia

1956—Gerald Kaufman, Columbia
1957—Bernie Balaban, New York University
1958—Art Schankin, Illinois
1959—Al Morales, Navy
1960—Mike Dasaro, New York University
1961—Israel Colon, New York University
1962—Barton Nisonson, Columbia
1963—Bela Szentivanyi, Wayne
1964—Craig Bell, Illinois
1965—Howard Goodman, New York University
1966—Paul Apostol, New York University
1967—68—Todd Makler, Pennsylvania
1969—Norman Braslow, Pennsylvania
1970—72—Bruce Soriano, Columbia

Intercollegiate Fencing Association

Team Three-Weapon

1923—Army
1924—Navy
1925—Navy, Yale (tie)
1926—Yale
1927—Army
1928—29—Yale
1930—Army, Yale (tie)
1931—Army
1932—Yale
1933—New York University
1934—Columbia
1935—38—New York University
1939—Navy
1940—42—New York University
1943—Navy
1944—47—No competition
1948—C.C.N.Y.
1949—50—New York University
1951—Columbia
1952—New York University
1953—Navy
1954—Columbia
1955—Cornell
1956—57—Navy
1958—Columbia
1959—61—New York University
1962—N.Y.U., Columbia (tie)
1963—Columbia
1964—Navy
1965—Columbia
1966—New York University
1967—Pennsylvania
1968—New York University
1969—Princeton
1970—71—New York University
1972—Columbia

BASIC RULES

In all types of fencing bouts the object is to touch the opponent with the weapon and at the same time prevent him from scoring a touch. The bouts are conducted on a rubber or cork-linoleum strip 6 feet wide and approximately 50 feet long. All the fencing must take place within the limits of this area and penalties are imposed upon the fencer who crosses the boundaries. The bouts are ruled by a jury, of which one man is the director and the other two or four are judges. The director is in charge of the bout and stands about 10 feet away from the strip at an equal distance from the contestants. The judges are assigned to watch the fencers and advise the director when they see a touch scored. The director awards the touches, applies the rules and controls the play by the commands of "On Guard," "Fence" and "Halt."

Three types of weapons are used: foil, epee and saber. While the basic principles are similar, there are structural differences and varying conventions of play which should be noted.

The Foil

The foil is the direct descendant of the short dress sword. It has a flexible rectangular blade with a blunt point and a bell guard 4.7 inches in diameter. Its maximum over-all weight is about 17 ounces and its over-all length a little over 43 inches.

The foil is a conventional weapon. The rules provide that touches, to be valid, must be made with the point on a target, which includes the trunk of the body from the top of the collar to the groin lines in the front and to a horizontal line across the tops of the hip bones on the back. For women, the target is the same.

Touches scored on the head, arms or legs are called "foul," but carry no penalty other than halting the bout and nullifying any subsequent touches until the play is ordered to resume by the director. The contestant scoring 5 valid touches (4 in women's bouts) is declared the winner.

Major competitions use electrical apparatus for judging touches.

Generally speaking, the contestant who is attacked must defend himself (parry) before assuming the offensive (riposte). The attacker is said to have the "right of way." A successful parry gains for the defendant the "right of way." Where both fencers are hit simultaneously, the touch is awarded to the one who has the "right of way."

The Epee

The epee is a modern counterpart of the dueling sword. The blade is triangular and rigid and has several small sharp prongs at the tip so as to catch on the opponent's uniform. The guard is large (5.4 inches in diameter), the over-all weight is 27 ounces. It is the same length as the foil.

In this weapon, a hit may be scored on any part of the body and there are no conventions of "right of way." Whoever hits first is awarded the touch and if both men hit simultaneously a "double touch" is scored and each contestant is credited with a touch. If, as a result of a double touch, the score becomes 5-5, the bout is continued until one fencer scores a winning touch. If

time should expire, however, and the score is tied at any score, both men lose (except in collegiate and scholastic fencing, where the bout is continued until a decisive result is reached). Otherwise the first fencer to score five touches is the winner.

A special feature of the epee and foil is the electrical judging apparatus. A small spring at the tip of the weapon is depressed when a touch is scored and an electrical contact is made which registers on a central control box and indicates which fencer has scored. The contact shuts off a relay so that any touch scored subsequently by the other contestant will not register. Where both contestants hit within a fixed fraction of a second, a double touch is recorded by the machine.

The Saber

The saber is approximately the same weight and length as the foil. It has a flexible triangular blade with cutting edges along the entire front and one-third of the back edge. Its guard is large (5.5 inches in diameter) and curved so that one section is attached to the pommel at the back of the weapon.

Modern saber fencing is nearest to the technique of the old rapier. Both the point and the cutting edges of the blade are used to score touches. Valid touches must land on the body at any point above the waist, including the arms and the head. Touches on the legs are "foul" and have the same effect as in foil. The contestant scoring five valid touches first is declared the winner.

The saber is perhaps the most spectacular of the three weapons because the movements are wider and easier to follow. Touches can often be heard, as well as seen, and the drama is heightened by the clash of steel. As in foil, the conventions of "right of way" are applied to touches which land more or less simultaneously.

EQUIPMENT

The personal equipment of a fencer includes the following:

A uniform made of strong material which will cover the neck, trunk, arms and legs of the body. The cost of a uniform runs from $32.00 up, but any heavy white duck trousers will suffice, and a jacket may be purchased for $14.00.

A wire mesh mask is another necessity and costs about $10.00.

A padded glove (for the weapon hand only) is available for $5.00.

Weapons are not expensive. A nonelectric foil costs $7.00, a nonelectric epee about $9.00 and a sabre about $10.00. An electric foil sells for about $18.00 and an electric epee for about a dollar less. Replacement blades for all weapons are available beginning at $4.00.

(For Olympic champions see section on Olympic Games.)

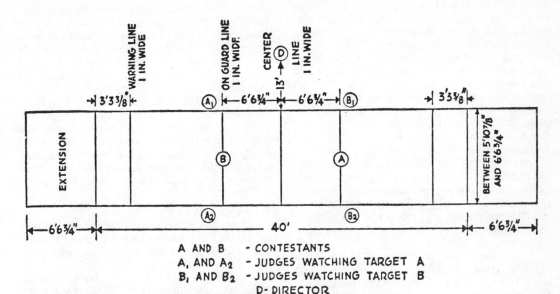

A AND B   - CONTESTANTS
A, AND A₂ - JUDGES WATCHING TARGET A
B, AND B₂ - JUDGES WATCHING TARGET B
D- DIRECTOR

The Fencing Strip. (Taken from "Sports for Recreation," edited by E. D. Mitchell, A. S. Barnes and Company, New York.)

FIELD HOCKEY—MEN

Believed to be the oldest stick-and-ball game, field hockey is played in many parts of the world. It has not as yet caught on to any great extent in this country. The game is supposed to have originated in Persia about 2000 B.C. and it was played in various parts of Europe during the Middle Ages. In England it was forbidden, along with certain other sports, because it interfered with practice in archery, the basis of national defense.

The modern game was developed in England around the middle of the last century and it has spread to many countries. It has been played in the Olympic Games since 1908, but by men only.

The game had been played in a desultory sort of way at various points in the United States prior to 1926. However, in that year a group in New York City and Westchester County, headed by Henry K. Greer of Rye, N.Y., took up the game and attempted to arrange regular matches between men's teams. They were introduced to hockey by Miss Louise Roberts, an English coach at Rosemary Hall School for girls at Greenwich, Conn., who later became Mrs. Greer.

On Oct. 28, 1928, at the Germantown Cricket Club in Philadelphia what is believed to be the first organized match between American men's teams took place, the participants being Westchester Field Hockey Club of Rye and German-

town Cricket Club. Westchester was the victor, 2–1. Since then there has been regular competition and there now are regularly organized teams in Westchester County, New York City, Philadelphia, Baltimore and Washington. There also were six teams in and about Los Angeles before World War II but these have not been reorganized. The game is played on a less organized basis by other groups in various parts of the country.

In view of the fact that field hockey was to be played in the Olympic Games of 1932, the United States Olympic Committee asked the American group to organize themselves for Olympic competition. Accordingly, in 1930 the Field Hockey Association of America was formed to control the men's sport and this association became affiliated with the American Olympic Association and with the Federation Internationale de Hockey.

The United States has been represented by men's field hockey teams in the Olympic Games of 1932, 1936 and 1948. The caliber of the American Olympic teams has improved greatly since 1932. The Olympic teams of 1936 and 1940 gave good accounts of themselves. In actual place scoring they were not successful, but their standard of competition was high. In 1936 they lost to the great world champion team of India, 7–0, which is considered an excellent performance. India defeated Germany in the final, 8—1. In a practice match in 1948, the English team managed to defeat the Americans, 1—0, on a penalty goal.

The game has been making strides in the Rye, N.Y., and Greenwich, Conn., areas in recent years and tournament cup competition has developed. Teams also have gone on tours.

Field hockey is one of the few truly amateur games, there being no professional field hockey. The international governing bodies are the International Hockey Board, comprised of England, Scotland, Ireland and Wales, and the Federation Internationale de Hockey, which has approximately 30 countries in its membership, including the United States. Starting with the holding of the Olympic Games in London a liaison between these bodies was worked out and they promulgated the same rules.

Today the leading countries in this sport are India, England, the Netherlands, Germany and Pakistan. Along with cricket, field hockey has the distinction of being the national game of India. India has dominated every Olympic competition. The sports writers covering the Games of 1932 at Los Angeles voted the performance of the Indian team the outstanding exhibition of skill in any sport.

The Indian type of play features short, controlled passes as opposed to the European type, in which the tendency is to hit the ball about the field more. Furthermore, the players in India and Pakistan use sticks with a short toe. By using these sticks and employing a left-handed grip well behind the stick they are able to reverse the stick without changing the grip and thus attain remarkable ball control. The conventional long-toed stick will strike the ground and fail to contact the ball properly if it is reversed in this manner. European players are gradually adopting the short-toed stick.

The United States always has attempted to follow the Indian type of play as closely as possible, although using some of the European technique. This type of play is easily adopted by men familiar with such passing games as basketball, lacrosse and ice hockey. American men take to the game readily once they play it, but it has spread very slowly. This is partly because of the difficulty in obtaining proper publicity, the general impression in the United States being that it is a woman's game.

The reason it has not spread more rapidly from the geographical standpoint is that it is necessary that certain rules, which might seem somewhat technical, be thoroughly understood and that the game be umpired properly. The umpiring is difficult as a good deal of judgment is called for as to whether or not to call fouls.

To avoid confusion and the development of conflicting variations of the game it has been thought best to make haste slowly and to expand

from well-informed centers. This lesson has been learned from the experience of certain European countries. Schools and colleges have not so far had room on their busy athletic programs for this new sport and programs of the hockey clubs were greatly reduced temporarily during World War II.

Field hockey is an ideal team sport to be played even after school and college days. Although very vigorous, it is not conducive to injury and many men play well into their 40's. It is interesting to note that the Mount Washington Club of Baltimore, Md., perennial National champion in lacrosse, has adopted field hockey as its fall sport.

FAMOUS PLAYERS

Famous international players include Shoveler of England, Haag and Weiss of Germany, van den Berg and Esser of the Netherlands and Dhyan Chand and Pinninger of India.

Some of the best American players have been Mike O'Brien and Kurt Orban of Westchester, Horace Disston of Philadelphia and Bill Stude of Baltimore. Frank Leslie-Jones of Rye, N.Y., one of the originators of the modern British-Indian style of play, coached the American Olympic teams of 1932 and 1936. Henry K. Greer coached the 1948 team.

BASIC RULES

Field hockey is played on a field 100 yards long and 60 yards wide. The goals are 7 feet high and 12 feet wide.

The ball originally was a cricket ball (similar to a baseball) but plastic balls now are also approved. It weighs 5½ to 5¾ ounces and it is 8 13/16 to 9¼ inches in circumference. The average stick is 36 to 38 inches long and weighs 18 to 22 ounces. To prevent stinging the handle is laminated and is attached to the solid head by glue and binding. The striking surface is flat on the left side only and only the flat surface may be used.

There are 11 players on a team, 5 forwards, 3 halfbacks, 2 fullbacks and a goalkeeper. A goal, which counts 1 point, may be scored only from within a semi-circle (striking circle) described 16 yards from the goal. Two halves of 35 minutes each are played and in international competition no substitutions are allowed, even for injury. Time out is permitted only in case of injury.

In general strategy field hockey is similar to soccer football. However, one big difference is that no obstruction is allowed—that is, it is forbidden to place one's body between the opponent and the ball. The reason for this rule and for the one-sided stick rule is that the sticks are relatively heavy and are used for hard striking. Consequently, if it were permitted to defend the ball with the body the game would become quite dangerous. The goalkeeper wears heavy pads and is the only one allowed to kick the ball or stop it with the foot. All players, however, may stop the ball with the hand.

The game is started and re-started after each goal by a bully in the center of the field. A bully occurs when two players stand at opposite sides of the ball and tap the ground and each other's sticks alternately three times before putting the ball in play. If the ball is hit over the goal line by the attackers without a goal being scored the game is re-started by a bully on the nearer 25-yard line. If the ball is hit over the goal line accidentally by the defense a corner is taken, the defenders all being behind the goal line and the attackers being outside the striking circle until the ball is hit in from the corner of the field by one of the attackers.

If the defenders hit the ball over the goal line intentionally or commit a foul within the circle, a penalty corner is taken, the only difference being that the attacker hits the ball out from a point on the goal line 10 yards from either goal-post. In the case of other fouls a free hit is awarded the team opposed to the offender on the spot where the infraction occurred. When the ball goes over the side line it is rolled in by hand by a player of the team opposed to the player who last touched it.

An important point is that the umpire refrains from enforcing a penalty where he believes that to enforce it would give an advantage to the offending team. There is one umpire for each half of the field.

The offside rule is similar to that in soccer except that three opponents are required to place a player on-side if he is ahead of the ball and in the attacking half of the field. In most respects the rules are the same as those used by the women but the play is different due to the superior strength of wrist, speed and aggressiveness of men.

The playing surface is usually grass covered, but in India most of the grounds are of hard dirt. In England and most of continental Europe the game is played through the fall, winter and spring, but in the United States weather conditions permit play only in the fall and spring.

(For Olympic champions see section on Olympic Games.)

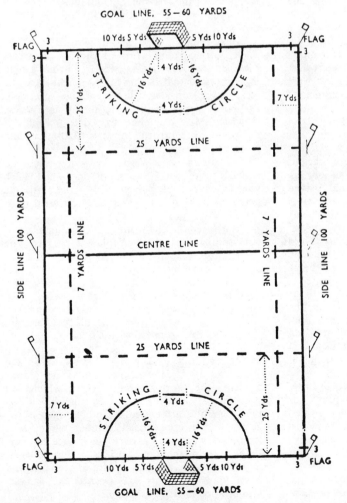

Field Hockey Playing Area.

(Taken from "Rules of the Game of Hockey," issued under the authority of the International Hockey Board.

FIELD HOCKEY—WOMEN

(Courtesy Betty Shellenberger, U.S. Field Hockey Association, Inc.,
107 School House Lane, Philadelphia, Pa. 19144)

Women's Field Hockey is one of the sports for which we are indebted to England. It was brought here at the turn of the century when women were beginning to discard high-buttoned shoes, felt hats and tight corsets, and they took up the game eagerly.

The ancient game is almost the exclusive property of women and girls in colleges and schools, or the fashionable feminine set along the Atlantic Seaboard.

When the athletes, tiring of running, wrestling and jumping contests, sought other forms of diversion in the old days, they either rolled pebbles at a fixed object or tried their hand at hitting pebbles for distance with tree branches.

The pebble-rolling idea was the forerunner of such modern sports as lawn bowling, curling, etc., and the batting idea has been carried through the ages to become the great-granddaddy of all the games now played with a ball and stick, such as baseball, cricket, golf, lacrosse and others.

The principle of field hockey was well known to ancient nations. The Greeks of about 2,500 years ago played a game similar to it. One meets up with it some centuries later in France, where it bore the name "hoquet." The English were fascinated by it and took it to their homeland under the name of "hokay," the French pronunciation. The English spelled it "hockey," later giving it pronunciation in keeping with its English spelling.

It wasn't called field hockey in the precarious generations when it was in favor, and out, in England. It was discarded, revived and played under haphazard rules. "Hockey" was the name it went under and not until the advent and development of ice hockey was the ancient sport classified as "field hockey" in order to avoid confusion with the newer game.

Field hockey made some strides after being put to new rules at a meeting in London in 1875, but not enough to satisfy the groups with its interest at heart. In fact, not until the Wimbledon Hockey Club, founded in 1883, tightened some laws, discarded others and replaced them with new regulations that speeded play and made the contests more exciting, did the game develop and expand in Europe.

Until 1887 field hockey was the exclusive property of men, being regarded as too rough for women. In that year, however, the women played the game, adopted it and proceeded to popularize it throughout the world. The men's game in England, France, India and other foreign countries still continues in high favor, however.

Field hockey was played occasionally in the United States in the 1880's and 1890's, but there is little of record concerning it. How often it was indulged in by men, if at all, is not established. The game's first definite mention in this country came when a group of women from England formed the Livingston Hockey Association at Staten Island, N.Y. The experiment was not prolonged and after a few brief seasons the organization ceased to exist.

In late August of 1901 the foundation of field hockey in this country was laid at a session of the Harvard Summer School when Constance M.K. Applebee of the British College of Physical Education, here to study anthropometry (measurement of the human body), demonstrated the game on the small concrete courtyard outside the Harvard gymnasium.

The demonstration came about after an afterclass discussion of the relative merits of British and American women athletes among Miss Applebee, Harriet I. Ballintine, another member of the class; Dr. Dudley Sargent, the instructor, and Dr. Tait MacKenzie, a visiting professor.

According to Lora Segall, writing in "The Eagle," official publication of the United States Field Hockey Association, Miss Ballintine "laughingly attested that if both Miss Applebee and she were to be considered representative specimens the point would have to terminate in a draw. However, Miss Applebee refused to accept this decision. She turned to Miss Ballintine and pleasantly asserted:

" 'The contest, if we must view it as such, has actually not been quite a fair one. An English woman cannot be judged athletically until she performs in field hockey. It is the national sport for our women.'

"Surprised at the confused countenances of her companions, Miss Applebee pursued the subject further and discovered that no one had any knowledge of the sport of which she spoke.

" 'Why, then I must show you!' she stated."

Miss Applebee put on the demonstration game the next day, with a collection of ice hockey sticks, shinny sticks and an indoor baseball. Chalk was used to mark off the field.

Miss Ballintine, director of physical education at Vassar College, saw the possibilities in the game and asked Miss Applebee to teach Vassar students the sport. With 24 sticks, which had been left at Spalding's after an Englishman had unsuccessfully attempted to interest men in the game, and a cricket ball painted white, Miss Applebee went to Vassar to introduce hockey. Later she taught the sport at other colleges, including Wellesley, Smith, Mount Holyoke and Bryn Mawr and in 1922 opened her famous Mount Pocono Hockey Camp.

Although the game gained in popularity and clubs were organized in the Philadelphia area, it was not until 1920 that an American team went to England. Partly from that impetus and the increasing interest developed in the colleges, a group of enthusiastic and far-sighted women gathered to form the United States Field Hockey Association.

An organization meeting was held on Jan. 21, 1922, with Miss Applebee presiding. Mrs. Edward B. Krumbhaar of Philadelphia was elected the first president and served until 1925, followed by Cynthia M. Wesson, 1925–27 and 1938–41; Anne B. Townsend, 1927–32; Gertrude Hooper, 1932–38; Suzanne R. Cross, 1945–47; Ethel T. Kloberg, 1947–49, Anne Lee Delano, 1949–53, and Dr. Nancy Sawin, 1954–1959; Ethlyn A. Davis, 1960–63; Grace Robertson, 1964-1971. Mrs. Phyllis S. Weikart has served as president since 1972.

Interest in the sport in the United States has increased through the years. In 1922 there were 4 local associations with a combined membership of 24 active clubs and 65 allied members; in 1972 there were 53 local associations with a membership of more than 336 active clubs and about 1,000 schools and colleges. It is estimated that there are more than 65,000 players in this country. The sport, ideal for women and girls eager for team play where speed, accuracy of action and endurance are factors, now extends from coast to coast. Air travel now enables the teams from the Pacific Coast to participate regularly in the national tournaments.

The U.S.F.H.A. is divided into 9 sections with local associations assigned to each section. Each local association must have at least 3 active clubs. Players in these clubs must be at least 16 years of age and the majority of the players are those who are out of school or college and who play for sheer enjoyment. The hockey association is a truly amateur group whose players pay all expenses whether in this country or abroad.

Over a week-end in November, each section holds a tournament among its local associations and at the end names its first and reserve teams, individuals being chosen from the various competing teams by a selection committee. The National tournament, at which these sectional teams play, is held during Thanksgiving week-end, with a local association as hostess, thus taking the best hockey to all areas. Except during the war years from 1942 to 1945, this tournament has been held annually other than in 1936 when the U.S.F.H.A. was hostess for the conference of the International Federation of Women's Hockey Associations.

There is no championship award but over the years the Philadelphia Association has proved the strongest. From the players on the sectional teams, a Selection Committee chooses All-United States and Reserve teams.

In 1922 and 1923 the All-England Women's Hockey Association sent 8 coaches to this country. In 1925, 1954, and 1969, the Irish Ladies Hockey Union sent over a squad; English players were here in 1928, 1947, 1961, and 1971. The Scottish W.H.A. had teams here in 1931 and 1951. The Welsh W.H.A. toured in 1957. The year 1965 saw the visit of a combined team of players from Great Britain and Ireland. In 1966, the Jamaica W.H.A. sent a squad and in 1967, the Australian and New Zealand teams played a number of games here on their way home from the 1967 I.F.W.H.A. Conference. Teams from the Guyana W.H.A. and the women's section of the Royal Netherlands Hockey Association toured in 1968. Australia and Scotland will again be sending touring teams in 1973.

The U.S.F.H.A. has progressed immeasurably and the standard of play improved by our teams visiting other countries. Teams were sent to England in 1924, to the International Conference in Denmark in 1933, followed by a tour of the continent and the British Isles; to Australia in 1938, to British Guiana in 1939, to England, Scotland and the Netherlands in 1948 and to the International Conference in South Africa in 1950. In 1956, a United States team toured Australia and New Zealand and did very very well, winning 19 matches and losing 6. However, American teams did not fare well on English tours in 1953 and 1955, but in 1962 tied England 3-3 in the feature match of the year before 55,000 at Wembley Stadium, London.

The U.S.F.H.A. has continued to take an active part in the international phases both here and abroad. In 1953, a U.S.F.H.A. team participated in the fifth triennial conference of the International Federation of Women's Hockey Associations at Folkestone, England, and then toured the British Isles. To celebrate the diamond jubilee of the All England Women's Hockey Association, a U.S.F.H.A. team played England in the first international match under floodlights at the Arsenal Stadium, London, in October, 1955. In 1956, the sixth I.F.W.H.A. conference was held in Sydney, Australia and following the conference, the U.S.F.H.A. team toured Queensland, Australia, New Zealand, and played one match in Fiji. A visit to South Africa was made in 1958, and in 1959 a representative group was scheduled to attend the I.F.W.H.A. conference in Amsterdam, the Netherlands, and tour continental Europe.

In 1963, the U.S.F.H.A. was hostess to the eighth conference of the I.F.W.H.A. and entertained delegates and players from 22 countries. Then 14 teams toured to various sections of the United States. In 1965 and 1972, a U.S. team played in Jamaica and the 1967 team toured in Germany before participating with 18 other teams in the ninth conference of the I.F.W.H.A. in Cologne, Germany. Continuing a policy of trying to provide more international play, U.S.F.H.A. Touring Teams were sent to Guyana in 1969 and Zambia in 1970; the U.S.F.H.A. team which attended the 10th Conference of the I.F.W.H.A. in Auckland, New Zealand in 1971 also played in Sri Lanka (Ceylon), Australia, Malaysia, Hong Kong, and Japan during this tour. In 1973 U.S.F.H.A. teams will play in Argentina and in the 75th Anniversary celebration tournament of the Royal Netherlands Hockey Association with 7 other countries. This team will also tour in England. The 11th Conference of the I.F.W.H.A. will be held in Edinburgh, Scotland in 1975 while Canada will hostess the event in 1979.

In addition to the foreign tours, the U.S.F.H.A. has sent teams to remote areas or to help groups in need of coaching, starting as early as 1926 to Ohio and Indiana, 1930 to California, Oregon and Washington, 1936 to the South, and in 1940 to the West and South.

Very shortly after the organization of the U.S.F.H.A. it was recognized that a large part of the development of the sport was dependent upon officials and in 1924 both the Umpiring and Rules Committee were formed. With the establishment of the Women's International Hockey Rules Board in 1967, their "Code of Rules" is the one now played by all member countries of the I.F.W.H.A. These rules are published in connection with the Division of Girls and Women's Sports of the American Association of Health, Physical Education and Recreation.

The Umpiring Committee, in the belief that good umpiring promotes good playing, provides for the rating of umpires to raise the standard of play and furnishes clubs and schools with lists of rated umpires in addition to providing other services. There are now more than 900 rated umpires. To those who have shown outstanding ability and service, the parent body gives a U.S.F.H.A. Honorary Umpire award which parallels the highest rank for players. The recipients of this award are: Marjorie Auster, Anne Lee Delano, Mrs. Emily J. Magoon, Caryl Newhof, Jane Shurmer, Dr. Nancy Sawin, Mrs. Elinor Taylor, Mrs. Helen Allen, Mrs. Marion Mulford, Betty Richey, Mary Bottaro, Mrs. Claire Harden, Blanche Brogden, Mrs. Helen Carty, Evelyn Fine, Evelyn Haldeman, Ruth Stevenson, Dorothy Sullivan, Mrs. Marion Earl, Margaret Jesseph, Mrs. Beatrice Thomas.

The U.S.F.H.A. confers honorary membership on those who have contributed meritorious service toward the objectives of the organization. The honorary members include Mrs. Edward Krumbhaar, Helen Ferguson, Constance M.K. Applebee, Cynthia Wesson, Anne Townsend,

Gertrude Hooper, Anne Toomey, May Fogg, Helen Bina, Barbara Stregeigh, Anne Lee Delano, Dorothy Franklin, Frances Pierce, Mrs. Elizabeth Burger Jackson, Anna Espenschade, Alfreda Mosscrop, Marion Pettit, Bessie Rudd, Betty Richey, Harriet Walton, Marjorie Strang, Mrs. Joyce Cran Barry, Ethlyn A. Davis, Frances Homer, Harriet Rogers, Betty Shellenberger, Mrs. Frances S. Blomfield, Sophie Dickson, Ethel Kloberg, Dr. Nancy Sawin, Elizabeth Cooper, Grace Robertson, Bess Taylor, Caroline Haussermann and Elizabeth Williams.

The officers of the U.S.F.H.A. serve for a term of 2 years without restriction on re-election. In 1949 the office of executive secretary was created to provide a permanent position for the ever-increasing activities. In carrying out its objective "to spread, further and advance the best interests of field hockey for women and girls in the United States," the association offers many services, such as "The Eagle," a magazine published four times during the playing season; an equipment chairman to locate and distribute used equipment to groups otherwise unable to play; current information on new equipment and its availability; an extension committee, offering coaches or demonstration games; an insurance chairman, publicity and promotion, services to colleges and technical service which prepares and distributes motion picture films and film loops, bulletin board material and booklets.

The International Federation of Women's Hockey Associations, of which the U.S.F.H.A. is a charter member, was organized in 1927 with a membership of 8 countries for the purpose of furthering the best interests of the game among women of all nations, to promote friendly intercourse among players and to work for uniformity of rules. The first Triennial Conference was held in Geneva in 1930, the next in Copenhagen in 1933, with teams from Denmark, Great Britain, Germany, the Netherlands and America attending. At that time, Mrs. Krumbhaar and Miss Townsend, both of the United States, were elected president and secretary, respectively.

In 1936 the conference was held in Philadelphia, with the foreign teams touring the country before or after the tournament. The 1939 conference, which was to have been held in England, had to be canceled and it was not until 1950 that world conditions permitted the next conference, held in South Africa. All who have a part in these international games feel justifiable pride in the organization and its accomplishments. The membership in the Federation now totals 35 countries.

Although in the United States one finds the gatherings limited to enthusiasts (or close relatives of the players), a tremendous achievement in the women's phase of the game took place in London, on March 3, 1951, when the international match between England and Ireland was staged before a record crowd of more than 30,000 at Wembley Stadium. It had been a bold venture to hold a game in such surroundings, but that success was topped in 1952 when 45,000 saw England defeat Scotland, 9–2.

"Women's Hockey Field," the magazine edited by Marjorie Pollard, for many years one of England's outstanding forwards, stated:

"Wembley was achieved without the glamour and clamour of cup, trophies, points or pools. It was done without any assistance whatsoever from the majority of the national newspapers. It was done because of the solidarity and loyalty among hockey players. Those are roundly reassuring qualities and it was good to see them demonstrated on such an occasion. They give heart, increase courage, and supply determination to go forward still further."

Women's sports, too, go a long way in establishing international friendship and good will, and hockey players the world around have shown remarkably convincing ability to initiate and carry out large-scale programs.

OUTSTANDING PLAYERS

Anne B. Townsend, who played at forward, center halfback and left fullback, is considered the greatest American field hockey player. She was the All-American captain—meaning, in fact, the ranking player, from 1923 through 1936, except in 1933. Frances Elliott, a goalkeeper, was named captain in 1933 and again in 1947.

Miss Townsend, Miss Elliott, Barbara Strebeigh, and Alice Putnam Willetts (left halfbacks), Vonnie Gros (right fullback), Betty Richey, Betty Shellenberger and Mrs. Mary Ann Harris (forwards) were on either the United States or Reserve team for 10 or more consecutive years. Patricia Kenworthy Nuckols (center halfback), Anne McConaghie Volp (left inner) and Dr. Nancy Sawin each have been named many times since 1940, although no national teams were selected from 1942 through 1945. Others who have been honored with numerous selections are Adele Boyd (left fullback), Phyllis Stadler (center forward), and Betty Miller (right wing) 8 times; Mrs. Ruth Heller Aucott (center halfback); Kitty McLean, Angela Geraci Poisson, and Mrs. Bonnie Heuer (right halfbacks) 7 times; Alison Hersey (left wing) and Gertrude Dunn (forward and halfback) and Joan Moser (center forward) 6 times.

Left Wing—Betty Richey, Marjorie Harrowell, Betty Cadbury, Alison Hersey.

Left Inners—Anne McConaghie Volp, Elenore Pepper, May Howe, Virginia Vanderbeck, Mrs. Mary Ann Harris.

Centers—Betty Shellenberger, Kitty Weiner DuBois, Hilda Anderson, Phyllis Stadler, Joan Moser.

Right Inners—Barbara Newhall Newlin, Barbara Strohbar Clement, Betty White, Catherine Kendig Clegg, Joan Edenborn, Gertrude Dunn.

Right Wings—Anne Parry Tillman, Suzanne R. Cross, Helen Howe, Rosemary Deniken, Betty Miller.

Left Halfbacks—Alice Putnam, Barbara Strebeigh, Jean Chapin Dolat, Margot Cunningham.

Center Halfbacks—Patricia Kenworthy Nuckols, Betty Taussig, Jean Graham, Priscilla Bartol, Helen Libby, Mrs. Ruth Heller Aucott.

Right Halfbacks—Kitty McLean, Harriet Walton, Dorothy Moffett, Anne Pugh, Angela Geraci, Bonnie Heuer.

Left Fullbacks—Anne Page, Jane Adair Cameron-Smith, Anne Lee Delano, Adele Boyd.

Right Fullbacks—Anne B. Townsend, Selina Silleck, Helena Wheeler, Frances Pierce, Geraldine Thaete Shipley, Dr. Nancy Sawin, Vonnie Gros.

Goalkeepers—Frances Elliott, Elizabeth Burger, Barbara Crowe, Marie Kerstetter, Mrs. Patricia Zelley, Patricia Zimmerman, Trudy Kesting.

Note: No United States teams named 1942 through 1945; also 1936, when the 1935 team participated in the International Conference.

ALL-UNITED STATES TEAMS

1924
First Team
Left Wing—Mary Tyler
Left Inner—Margaret Wiener
Center—Louise Fessenden
Right Inner—Susan Goodman
Right Wing—Mary Adams
Left Half—Jean Ware
Center Half—Anne Townsend (Capt.)
Right Half—Kitty McLean
Left Back—Virginia Carpenter
Right Back—Hildegarde Jacob
Goal—Helen Ferguson and Mrs. V. Baker

1925
First Team
LW—Mrs. Donald Wilbur
LI—Elizabeth Waidner
C—Margaret Wiener
RI—Susan Goodman
RW—Martha Brewer
LH—Mrs. W.W. Brown
CH—Anne Townsend (Capt.)
RH—Kitty McLean
LB—Hildegarde Jacob
RB—Alice Jones
G—Helen Ferguson

1926
First Team
LW—Mary Adams

LI—Anne Townsend (Capt.)
C—Carol Rice
RI—Betty Cadbury
RW—Martha Brewer
LH—Anne Page
CH—Kitty McLean
RH—Priscilla Bartol
LB—Hildegarde Jacob
RB—Agnes Bergen
G—Mrs. Lewis Taylor

1927
First Team
LW—Mrs. Donald Wilbur
LI—Anne Townsend (Capt.)
C—Carol Rice
RI—Betty Cadbury
RW—Janet Seeley
LH—Peggy Waidner
CH—Kitty McLean
RH—Peggy Ferguson
LB—Kathryn Snyder
RB—Mildred Buchanan
G—Helen Ferguson

1928
First Team
LW—Claribel Smith
LI—Agnes Rogers
C—Louise Lynah
RI—Betty Cadbury
RW—Peggy Waidner
LH—Barbara Strebeigh
CH—Anne Townsend (Capt.)
RH—Kitty McLean
LB—Anne Page
RB—Agnes Bergen
G—Frances Elliott

1929
First Team
LW—Claribel Smith
LI—Agnes Rogers
C—Helen Davenport
RI—Betty Cadbury
RW—Suzanne Cross
LH—Barbara Strebeigh
CH—Anne Townsend (Capt.)
RH—Kitty McLean
LB—Priscilla Bartol
RB—Anne Pugh
G—Hannah Praxl

1930
First Team
LW—Betty Cadbury
LI—Janet Kendig
C—Katherine Wiener
RI—Mary Apollinio
RW—Suzanne Cross
LH—Barbara Strebeigh
CH—Anne Townsend (Capt.)

RH—Kitty McLean
LB—Anne Page
RB—Anne Pugh
G—Leeta McWilliams

1931
First Team
LW—Betty Cadbury
LI—Betty Richey
C—Katherine Wiener
RI—Mary Apollinio
RW—Suzanne Cross
LH—Barbara Strebeigh
CH—Anne Townsend (Capt.)
RH—Priscilla Bartol
LB—Barbara Black
RB—Geraldine Thaete
G—Frances Elliott

1932
First Team
LW—Betty Cadbury
LI—Virginia Vanderbeck
C—Katherine Wiener
RI—Virginia Bourquardez
RW—Suzanne Cross
LH—Barbara Strebeigh
CH—Anne Townsend (Capt.)
RH—Anne Pugh
LB—Barbara Black
RB—Geraldine Thaete
G—Frances Elliott

1933
First Team
LW—Agnes Rodgers
LI—Virginia Vanderbeck
C—Adele Loysen
RI—Elizabeth Richey
RW—Emma Disston
LH—Betty Taussig
CH—Anne Townsend
RH—Anne Pugh
LB—Lucille Burnham
RB—Geraldine Thaete
G—Frances Elliott (Capt.)

1934
First Team
LW—Marjorie Harrowell
LI—May Howe
C—Katherine Wiener
RI—Virginia Bourquardez
RW—Helen Howe
LH—Barbara Strebeigh
CH—Anne Townsend (Capt.)
RH—Anne Pugh
LB—Anne Page
RB—Frances Pierce
G—Barbara Crowe

1935
First Team
LW–Elizabeth Toulmin
LI–May Howe
C–Anne Townsend (Capt.)
RI–Catherine Kendig
RW–Helen Howe
LH–Helena Wheeler
CH–Betty Taussig
RH–Helen Libby
LB–Barbara Black
RB–Geraldine Thaete Shipley
G–Barbara Crowe

1936 Squad
Elizabeth Toulmin
May Howe
Anne Townsend (Capt.)
Catherine Kendig
Helen Howe
Helena Wheeler
Betty Taussig
Helen Libby
Barbara Black
Geraldine Thaete Shipley
Barbara Crowe
Frances Elliott
Frances Pierce
Barbara Strebeigh
Anne Pugh
Betty Richey
Virginia Bourquardez
Suzanne Cross
Katherine Wiener

1937
A Squad
Anne Delano
Frances Elliott
Betty Richey
Anne Townsend

B Squad
Jane Adair
Barbara Crowe
Marion Edwards
Marion Fuller
Louise Gray
Marjorie Harrowell
Virginia Meryweather
Anne Parry
Frances Pierce
Gretchen Schuyler
Selina Silleck
Harriet Walton
Eliza Lawson Washburn
Evelyn Weinicke

1938
First Team
LW–Marjorie Harrowell
LI–Betty Richey
C–Virginia Meryweather
RI–Catherine Kendig Clegg
RW–Anne Parry
LH–Barbara Strebeigh
CH–Betty Taussig
RH–Margaret Meyer
LB–Anne Page
RB–Anne Townsend (Capt.)
G–Frances Elliott

1939
First Team
LW–Winifred Wolff
LI–Barbara Strobhar
C–Betty Shellenberger
RI–Lucy Jane Hedberg
RW–Marjorie Harrowell
LH–Barbara Strebeigh
CH–Betty Taussig
RH–Louise Orr
LB–Christine Hamilton
RB–Frances Pierce
G–Helen Park

1940
First Team
LW–Margaret Cornwell
LI–Anne McConaghie
C–Betty Shellenberger
RI–Barbara Strobhar
RW–Anne Parry
LH–Barbara Strebeigh
CH–Betty Taussig Flersham
RH–Louise Orr
LB–Patricia Kenworthy
RB–Helen Tomlinson
G–Helen Park

1941
First Team
LW–Margaret Cornwell
LI–Anne McConaghie
C–Betty Shellenberger
RI–Barbara Strobhar
RW–Betty Richey
LH–Jane Adair Cameron-Smith
CH–Patricia Kenworthy
RH–Dorothy Sullivan
LB–Frances Pierce
RB–Helen Tomlinson
G–Frances Elliott

1942–45–No Selections
1946
First Team
LW–Betty Richey
LI–Anne McConaghie Volp
C–Betty Shellenberger
RI–Barbara Newhall Newlin
RW–Betty White
LH–Alice Putnam

CH—Patricia Kenworthy (Capt.)
RH—Dorothy Moffett
LB—Anne Delano
RB—Selina Silleck
G—Alice Willey

1947
First Team

LW—Elenore Pepper
LI—Marion E. Dougherty
C—Betty Shellenberger
RI—Barbara Strobhar Clement
RW—Barbara Newhall Newlin
LH—Alice Putnam
CH—Patricia Kenworthy
RH—Harriet Walton
LB—Anne Delano
RB—Anne Townsend (Capt.)
G—Frances Elliott

1948
First Team

LW—Betty Shellenberger
LI—Anne McConaghie Volp
C—Hilda Anderson
RI—Anna J. Westervelt
RW—Betty White
LH—Alice Putnam
CH—Jean Graham
RH—Mary Louise Roberts
LB—Nancy Sawin
RB—Patricia Kenworthy Nuckols
G—Elizabeth Burger (Capt.)

1949
First Team

LW—Betty Shellenberger
LI—Anne McConaghie Volp
C—Hilda Anderson
RI—Beth Ralph
RW—Elenore Pepper
LH—Alice Putnam
CH—Dorothy Moffett
RH—Jean Chapin Dolat
LB—Anne Delano
RB—Elyse DuBois
G—Elizabeth Burger (Capt.)

1950
First Team

LW—Elenore Pepper
LI—Anne McConaghie Volp
C—Hilda Anderson
RI—Betty Shellenberger
RW—Betty Richey
LH—Alice Putnam
CH—Patricia Kenworthy Nuckols
RH—Jean Graham
LB—Anne Delano (Capt.)
RB—Nancy Sawin
G—Elizabeth Burger

1951
First Team

LW—Betty Shellenberger (Co-Capt.)

LI—Anne McConaghie Volp (Co-Capt.)
C—Betty White
RI—Barbara Newhall Newlin
RW—Patricia Damminger
LH—Alice Putnam
CH—Jean Graham
RH—Patricia Kenworthy Nuckols
LB—Dorothy Moffett
RB—Nancy Sawin
G—Marie Kerstetter

1952
First Team

LW—Betty Shellenberger
LI—Anne McConaghie Volp (Co-Capt.)
C—Elenore Pepper Merkh
RI—Betty White (Co-Capt.)
RW—Marie Bird
LH—Alice Putnam Willetts
CH—Patricia Kenworthy Nuckols
RH—Bertha Nolan
LB—Dorothy Moffett
RB—Nancy Sawin
G—Elizabeth Burger

1953
First Team

LW—Marie Oliver
LI—Anne Volp
CF—Marlene Lochner
RI—Betty Shellenberger
RW—Jean Siterlet
LH—Alice Willets
CH—Patricia Nuckols
RH—Anne LeDuc
LB—Mary Fetter
RB—Nancy Sawin
G—Beatrice Thomas

1954
First Team

LW—Joan Schenerlein
LI—Anne Volp
CF—Elenore Pepper
RI—Joan Edenborn
RW—Betty Shellenberger
LH—Alice P. Willetts
CH—Patricia K. Nuckols
RH—Blanche Prendergast
LB—Nancy Sawin
RB—Mary Fetter
G—Elizabeth Burger

1955
First Team

LW—Betty Shellenberger
LI—Anne Volp
CF—Beth Ralph
RI—Joan Edenborn
RW—Rosemary Deniken
LH—Alice Willetts
CH—Ruth Heller
RH—Angela Geraci
LB—Helen Gibson

RB—Mary Fetter
G—Jenepher Price

1956
First Team

LW—Kate Barrett
LI—Anne Volp
CF—Norma Simmons
RI—Rosemary Deniken
RW—Joan Edenborn
LH—Margot Cunningham
CH—Nancy Sawin
RH—Angela Geraci
LB—Elizabeth Williams
RB—Joan Paul
G—Jenepher Shillingford

1957
First Team

LW—Kate Barrett
LI—Anne Volp
CF—Helen Callas
RI—Joan Edenborn
RW—Rosemary Deniken
LH—Jean Dolat
CH—Ruth Aucott
RH—Angela Geraci
LB—Betty Richey
RB—Carol Haussermann
G—Pat Zimmerman

1958
First Team

LW—Betty Shellenberger
LI—Eleanor Keady
CF—Phyllis Stadler
RI—Rosemary Blankley
RW—Lee Chadbourne
LH—Margot Cunningham
CH—Ruth Aucott
RH—Angela Geraci
LB—Betty Richey
RB—Vonnie Gros
G—Pat Zimmerman

1959
First Team

LW—Alison Hersey
LI—Mary Ann Leight
CF—Phyllis Stadler
RI—Rosemary D. Blankley
RW—Lee Chadbourne
LH—Margot Cunningham
CH—Gertrude Dunn
RH—Angela Geraci
LB—Adele Boyd
RB—Vonnie Gros
G—Patricia Zimmerman

1960
First Team

LW—Betty Shellenberger
LI—Mary Ann Leight
CF—Phyllis Stadler

RI—Gertrude Dunn
RW—Joan Edenborn
LH—Margot Cunningham
CH—Ruth Aucott
RH—Angela Geraci
LB—Adele Boyd
RB—Vonnie Gros
G—Patricia Zelley

1961
First Team

LW—Alison Hersey
LI—Mary Ann Leight
CF—Phyllis Stadler
RI—Gertrude Dunn
RW—Joan Edenborn
LH—Margot Cunningham
CH—Barbara Longstreth
RH—Angela Geraci
LB—Adele Boyd
RB—Vonnie Gros
G—Patricia Zelley

1962
First Team

LW—Alison Hersey
LI—Mary Ann Leight
CF—Phyllis Stadler
RI—Gertrude Dunn
RW—Betty Miller
LH—Ruth Aucott
CH—Barbara Longstreth
RH—Lynne Crosley
LB—Adele Boyd
RB—Vonnie Gros
G—Patricia Zelley

1963
First Team

LW—Phyllis Stadler
LI—Mary Ann Leight
CF—Elenore Pepper
RI—Joan Edenborn
RW—Betty Miller
LH—Margery Orris
CH—Gertrude Dunn
RH—Lynne Reichert
LH—Adele Boyd
RF—Vonnie Gros
G—Patricia Zimmerman

1964
First Team

LW—Lois Dawson
LI—Mary Ann Harris
CF—Phyllis Stadler
RI—Gertrude Dunn
RW—Betty Miller
LH—Margery Orris
CH—Ruth Aucott
RH—Lynne Reichert
LF—Adele Boyd
RF—Vonnie Gros
G—Patricia Zimmerman

1965
First Team
LW—Alison Hersey
LI—Mary Ann Harris
CF—Phyllis Stadler
RI—Sue Day
RW—Sally Wilkins
LH—Margery Orris
CH—Faye Bardman
RH—Marilyn O'Neill
LF—Adele Boyd
RF—Vonnie Gros
G—Trudy Kesting

1966
First Team
LW—Alison Hersey
LI—Mary Ann Harris
CF—Joan Moser
RI—Sue Day
RW—Betty Miller
LH—Judy Smiley
CH—Faye Bardman
RH—Bonnie Smith
LF—Adele Boyd
RF—Vonnie Gros
G—Patricia Zelley

1967
First Team
LW—Alison Hersey
LI—Mary Ann Harris
CF—Barbara Leighton
RI—Sally Wilkins
RW—Betty Miller
LH—Ruth Aucott
CH—Faye Bardman
RH—Bonnie Smith
LF—Sue Honeysett
RF—Vonnie Gros
G—Patricia Zelley

1968
First Team
LW—Dale Philippi
LI—Mary Ann Harris
CF—Joan Moser
RI—Joy Chamberlain
RW—Betty Miller
LH—Val Miller
CH—Beverly Miller
RH—Bonnie Smith
LB—Marcia Miglio
RB—Vonnie Gros
G—Trudy Kesting

1969
First Team
LW—Dale Philippi
LI—Mary Ann Harris
CF—Joan Moser
RI—Robin Cash
RW—Betty Miller
LH—Val Miller

CH—Judy Smiley
RH—Bonnie S. Heuer
LB—Sune Honeysett
RB—Vonnie Gros
G—Trudy Kesting

1970
First Team
LW—Sherrill Vaughan
LI—Mary Ann Harris
CF—Joan Moser
RI—Robin Cash
RW—Betty Miller
LH—Sandy Wood
CH—Sue Honeysett
RH—Bonnie S. Heuer
LB—Marcia M. Johnson
RB—Vonnie Gros
G—Trudy Kesting

1971
First Team
LW—Sherrill Vaughan
LI—Mary Ann Harris
CF—Robin Cash
RI—Joan Moser
RW—Shelby Pontz
LH—Val Miller
CH—Judy Smiley
RH—Bonnie S. Heuer
LB—Diane Wright
RB—Holly Alden
G—Trudy Kesting

1972
First Team
LW—Sherrill Vaughan
LI—Mary Ann Harris
CF—Joan Moser
RI—Robin Cash
RW—Dee Dustin
LH—Pam Hixon
CH—Val Miller
RH—Bonnie S. Heuer
LB—Mrs. Marcia M. Johnson
RB—Diane Wright
G—Gwen Wentz

BASIC RULES

The game is played on a field 90 to 100 yards in length, 50 to 60 yards in width. A smaller field is used for junior play.

A goal counts 1 point and is scored when the ball passes wholly over the goal line between the goalposts. To score a goal the ball must be touched by an attacker's stick within the striking circle.

The striking circle is a white line 4 yards long, parallel to, and 16 yards from, the goal line. This line is continued to meet the goal line by two quarter circles, each with a goalpost as center. The goalposts are placed in the center of each goal line and consist of two perpendicular posts, 4 yards apart, joined together by a horizontal crossbar 7 feet from the ground. The two posts and the cross-bar should be 2 inches wide and not more than 3 inches deep.

Nets should be firmly fixed to the posts and crossbar and to the ground behind the goals so that there is no gap for the ball to pass through.

Two center forwards start a game by alternately touching their opponent's stick and then the ground three times, after which each is free to play the ball, which is stationary. This is known as a "bully." A bully is also used to start the game after a point is scored. When the ball goes out of bounds over the end line, it is put into play by a free hit taken by one of the defending team 16 yards from the goal line exactly opposite the spot where it crossed the end line. No player is allowed to stand within 5 yards of the two players participating in the bully.

When the ball goes out of bounds along the side-lines, it is rolled in by a player of the opposing team to that of the player who last touched the ball before it passed over the sideline. The ball must be rolled in, not bounced, and must touch the ground within 1 yard of the point where it crossed the line.

The ball has a white leather cover and weighs not less than 5½ nor more than 5¾ ounces; its circumference is not less than 8¾ and not more than 9¼ inches. The stick has a flat face only on its left side. Left-handed sticks are barred. Sticks of 18 to 20 ounces have been found to be sufficiently heavy. Some are manufactured in this country, but better sticks are still imported from England. The goalkeepers are protected by wide pads and heavy cleated shoes, with such reinforcements as individuals find necessary. Many players wear shin guards and cleated sneakers are a great help on grass. Shoes with metal cleats or spikes are not permitted.

Playing time of a game is a maximum of two 35-minute halves; a minimum of two 15-minute halves. There is no overtime play if a game is tied. A team is made up of 11 players, 5 forwards, 3 halfbacks, 2 fullbacks and a goalkeeper, but this formation is not compulsory.

The usual uniform is a short kilt with a colored blouse and knee socks, although American rules specify that each team shall have a costume of distinguishing color.

Two umpires officiate, dividing the field and not changing ends. If necessary, there may also be timekeepers and scorekeepers.

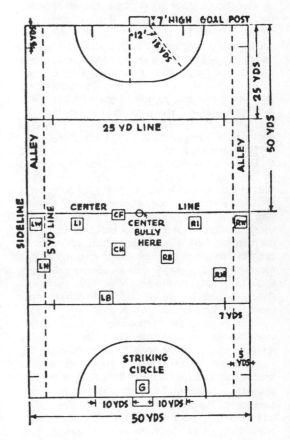

Field for Women's Field Hockey, showing starting positions of players. (Taken from "Sports for Recreation," edited by E. D. Mitchell, A. S. Barnes and Company, New York.)

FIELD TRIALS

(Courtesy William F. Brown, *"American Field"* Magazine,
222 West Adams Street, Chicago, Ill. 60606)

The intelligence and ability of the sporting dog are vividly displayed in field trials, a rapidly growing recreational activity in America. The dogs compete formally under natural and artificial hunting rules, and thousands of sportsmen get a real thrill from engaging their dogs in this activity.

In the early days of using specialized hunting breeds, the contests were more or less impromptu, advises William F. Brown, Editor, "American

Field" Magazine, Chicago, and author of "Field Trials."* Breeders and owners and trainers, proud of the prowess of their dogs, engaged in friendly arguments as to who had the better hunting dogs, the better-trained performers. The upshot of such amiable discussions was a challenge for a hunt under the judgment of an experienced sportsman, who would serve as an impartial official and set out

*A. S. Barnes & Co., New York.

similar tests for the dogs and render a decision as to which was the better. With the passage of time and as more people became involved in such events, the contests took on an aspect of formality and not only were the tests standardized, but rules also promulgated that governed the running of what became known as "Field Trials."

The sport cannot boast of a background in antiquity. The first public trial of which there is a complete record was held at Cannock Chase, a beautiful country estate, near Stafford, England, on May 1, 1866, when a group of keen sportsmen met for the purpose of trying their Pointers and Setters in actual competition in order to ascertain their real qualities as compared one with the other. A tentative affair had been held at Southill the year before, but the event at Stafford is regarded as the true beginning of the sport in Great Britain.

The inaugural public trial in America took place on Oct. 8, 1874, near Memphis, Tenn., sponsored by the Tennessee State Sportsmen's Association. This initial "Grand Field Trial" for the best Setter or Pointer attracted nine starters of local reputation, but brought out far greater interest and enthusiasm among owners and breeders than had been anticipated. The judging at this first American field trial was on the basis of so many points for each piece of good work, with the following scale of points governing: Nose, 30; pace and style, 20; breaking, 20; pointing style and staunchness 15; backing 10; roading, 5.

Subsequently the method of judging underwent various developments. The point system was replaced by the "heat system," wherein each dog was in direct competition with its bracemate and a winner was declared for every heat, with respective winners rebraced until a final result was achieved. In vogue at the present time is the so called "spotting system." This means "spotting" out the best dogs in the stake—for one dog is in competition against all the others; his performance is weighed against that of not only his immediate bracemate, but also of all the other dogs who compete in the particular stake. Field trials may be divided into several classifications:

(1) Pointing Dog Trials, for Pointers, English Setters, Irish Setters, Gordon Setters, Brittany Spaniels, German Shorthaired Pointers, Wire-Haired Pointing Griffons, Drahthaars, Weimaraners and Vizslas, to name the breeds that point their game.

(2) Beagle Trials, with 13-inch and 15-inch classes, and competition on rabbits.

(3) Spaniel Trials, for the accepted Spaniel breeds, chiefly for English Springer Spaniels and Cocker Spaniels. The dog is required to hunt the ground within ordinary shooting range, find game and upon flushing, stop immediately, assume a sitting position, exhibit steadiness to wing and shot, then retrieve on command. Pheasants and ducks are ordinarily used in licensed trials; pigeons in sanctioned meets. Land work receives the greater emphasis, although water tests are provided.

(4) Retriever Trials, for the recognized Retriever breeds, notably Labradors, Goldens, Chesapeake Bays, Irish Water Spaniels, Curly-Coated and Flat-Coated Retrievers. The function of the Retriever is to mark the fall of game, on order go briskly to the fall, recover the game and return rapidly to deliver right up to hand. Upland game birds and waterfowl are provided; land and water tests are given.

(5) Hound Trials, of different kinds for the various hound breeds. Fox hound meets have been esteemed over a goodly term of years; Coon hound trials have gained in popularity, and there are contests for Bassets.

Although there are the five general classifications enumerated, the average gunner is likely to think of a field trial in terms of bird dogs because the competitions for Pointers and Setters antedated all other forms of hunting dog competitions and continue the most popular. It was not until nearly a third of a century after American Pointer and Setter trials became a matter of public record in 1874 that Beagle trials began. In this country, Spaniel trials made their debut about 1924 and Retriever trials later.

All of the recognized Pointing dog trials are under the auspices of the American Field and the Amateur Field Trial Clubs of America. Individual clubs, as well as the parent breed organizations, promote field trial competitions. There are nearly 850 recognized bird dog trials held annually. These meets embrace over 2,700 individual stakes and approximately 40,000 purebred Pointing dogs compete in these events.

The leading stakes include the American Field Futurities on quail and pheasant, the National championship at Grand Junction, Tenn., a blue-ribbon event that was established in 1896; the National Free-for-All Quail championship, Continental Quail championship, the Prairie Chicken championships, National Pheasant championship, Grand National Grouse championship and the National Amateur championships.

The major Pointing dog trials are over contiguous courses, run on quail, pheasant, prairie chicken, ruffed grouse, woodcock, chukars and Hungarian partridge. One-course field trials also are popular in the excess of 300 individual sportsmen's clubs that sponsor recognized Pointing dog trials.

Beagle trials also are numerous and the clubs operate under the supervision of the Federation of Beagle Clubs. For Spaniel trials, the parent organizations are the English Springer Spaniel Club of America and the American Spaniel Club. The National Retriever Club functions for the recognized Retriever trials. For the Spaniels, a National Springer championship has been staged since 1947. A National Cocker championship was run for the first time in December, 1953. A National Retriever championship has been run since the early 1940's.

The object of field trials is the promotion and development of the high-class hunting dog. The aim is to provide competition of the highest kind among pure bred dogs of the classifications defined, to stimulate enthusiasm among owners and to act as a practical guide for breeders by setting a high standard of performance, thus bringing to the fore dogs that as progenitors will improve the breed. The American Field and the Field Dog Stud Book, an authentic all-breed registry, maintain comprehensive records of recognized field trials so that fanciers may obtain reliable information as to a dog's winning record and the victories gained by his progeny.

Field trials spread the gospel of game conservation and educate the hunter to a fuller appreciation of the work of his dogs. The sport is a mighty influence in the important work of protection and propagation to assure perpetuation of America's game life.

Field trials are professional and amateur; various stakes distribute cash prizes or trophy awards. Succinctly, an amateur is defined as one who does not receive any remuneration whatsoever for training or handling a dog other than his own. There are different age classifications, but it may be best to include here "Minimum Requirements for Field Trials for All Pointing Breeds," as adopted by the Amateur Field Trial Clubs of America, the American Field Publishing Company of Chicago, Ill., and the Field Dog Stud Book.

Wins will not be recognized and recorded unless the trial and/or each stake in which such win is made conforms to the following conditions:

1. The name of the club, place and date of the trial, and the secretary's name and address must be announced in an issue of the American Field bearing a publication date at least seven (7) days before the trials are to be run, and entry blanks, with complete description of each stake, be available to owners and handlers at least six (6) days before the date of the drawing.

2. Recognized stakes are:

Puppy Stakes—from Jan. 1 to June 30 in each year for dogs whelped on or after Jan. 1 of the year preceding. From July 1 to Dec. 31 in each year for dogs whelped on or after June 1 of the year preceding.

Derby Stakes—from July 1 to Dec. 31 in each year for dogs whelped on or after Jan. 1 of the year preceding, and from Jan. 1 to June 30 in each year for dogs whelped on or after Jan. 1 of two years preceding.

All-Age Stakes—For dogs of any age.

An "Open" stake is one in which there are no limitations with respect to either dogs or handlers. An "Amateur" stake is one in which all handlers are amateurs as defined by the By-Laws of the Amateur Field Trial Clubs of America.

Winners in Members' and Shooting Dog All-Age Stakes will be recorded but winners of Children, Ladies, Brace, and other stakes not conforming to the foregoing definitions will not be recognized.

Championship Winners' Stakes and Futurities—Wins will be recorded only in such amateur events of this character as are recognized by the Amateur Field Trial Clubs of America, and in such Open events as are recognized by the American Field Publishing Company and the Field Dog Stud Book.

3. The minimum length of heats for all stakes other than Puppy Stakes shall be thirty (30) minutes on the basis of the time that an average brace takes to negotiate the course. In the case of one-course trials, no more than eight (8) minutes of the thirty (30) shall be spent in the birdfield. Minimum length of heats for Puppy Stakes shall be fifteen (15) minutes.

4. A stake must be drawn no later than the night before the day the stake is advertised to be run.

5. Dogs shall not be substituted after the draw.

6. Braces shall be run, and handled, as drawn, unless given prior consent of the judges, which consent must not be given for the purpose of accommodating owners, handlers, or dogs that are not available when reached in the regular order of the draw. In the case of withdrawals, the bracemates of such withdrawn dogs may be run together at the discretion of the judges. Bitches which come in season, braced with a male, are scratched.

7. No entry shall be accepted after a stake is drawn.

8. No more than one brace of dogs shall be run on a course or any part of a course at the same time, irrespective of whether the dogs are in the same stake or in different stakes.

9. Stakes shall be run only on recognized game birds whose flight shall not be impaired by caging, hobbling, wing clipping, brailing, or in any other manner.

10. Bitches in season shall not be permitted to run in one-course trials. In multiple course trials, they may start only if, in the opinion of the judges, it can be accomplished under conditions which will insure absolute fairness to other entries.

Wins will not be recorded, or if recorded, will be cancelled if made at a trial or in a stake not conforming to the above requirements.

It is recommended that courses contain sufficient bird cover and suitable objectives to induce intelligent searching by the dogs. Birdfields, if used, should be of adequate size to permit a dog to hunt without excessive hacking and with cover sufficient to hold birds. A variety of cover and objectives is desirable. Five (5) acres is suggested as a minimum area for a birdfield.

CHAMPIONS

National Bird Dog   *No champion in 1897, 1938, 1944, 1965.*

Year	Name	Breed & Sex	Sire	Dam	Owner	Handler
1896	Count Gladstone IV	Setter dog	Count Noble	Ruby's Girl	Avent and Hitchcock	J.M. Avent
1898	Tony's Gale	Setter dog	Antonio	Nellie G	Eldred Kennels	D.E. Rose
1899	Joe Cumming	Setter dog	Antonio	Picciola	W.W. Titus	W.W. Titus
1900	Lady's Count Gladstone	Setter dog	Count Gladstone IV	Dan's Lady	G.G. Williamson	D.E. Rose
1901	Sioux	Setter bitch	Count Gladstone IV	Hester Prynne	Avent and Duryea	J.M. Avent
1902	Sioux	Setter bitch	Count Gladstone IV	Hester Prynne	Avent and Duryea	J.M. Avent
1903	Geneva	Setter bitch	Tony Boy	Lena Belle	Pierre Lorillard	Charles Tucker
1904	Mohawk II	Setter dog	Tony Boy	Countess Meteor	Avent and Duryea	J.M. Avent
1905	Alambagh	Setter dog	Dash Antonio	Eldred Lark	Hobart Ames	C.E. Buckle
1906	Pioneer	Setter dog	Count Whitestone	Bonnie Doone	G.N. Clemson	E. Shelley
1907	Prince Whitestone	Setter dog	Count Whitestone	Queen Lilia	T.T. Pace	T.T. Pace
1908	Count Whitestone II	Setter dog	Count Whitestone	Mecca's Lady	Dr. H.B. McMaster	E.D. Garr
1909	Manitoba Rap	Pointer dog	Ripple	Lady Cyrano Rush	Thomas Johnson	C.H. Babcock
1910	Monora	Setter bitch	Mohawk II	Tankas	J.M. Avent	J.M. Avent
1911	Eugene M	Setter dog	Rosco Gladstone	Irene Cooper	Frank Reily	W.H. Elliott
1912	Commissioner	Setter dog	Count Whitestone	Flossie May Fly	W.R. Craig	J.M. Avent
1913	Phillipides	Setter dog	Prince Rodney	Mary Tudor	Fred S. Hall	J.A. Gude
1914	Comanche Frank	Pointer dog	Fishel's Frank	Lady Johns	U.R. Fishel	J.M. Avent
1915	La Besita	Setter bitch	Fishel's Frank	El Beso	F.M. Stephenson	W.H. Beazell
1916	John Proctor	Pointer dog	John Proctor	Miss Mariutch	A.L. Curtis	C.H. Babcock
1917	Mary Montrose	Pointer bitch	Comanche Frank	Lorna Doone	William Ziegler Jr.	R.K. Armstrong
1918	Joe Muncie	Setter dog	Jack Muncie	Miss Mathews	Benjamin Weil	J.M. Avent
1919	Mary Montrose	Pointer bitch	Comanche Frank	Lorna Doone	William Ziegler Jr.	H.A. Tomlinson
1920	Mary Montrose	Pointer bitch	Comanche Frank	Lorna Doone	William Ziegler Jr.	H.A. Tomlinson
1921	Ferris' Jake	Pointer dog	John Proctor	Lady Ferris	C.F. Griffith	Mack Pritchette
1922	Becky Broom Hill	Pointer bitch	Broom Hill Dan	Nell's Queen Cott	L.L. Haggin	Chesley Harris
1923	Becky Broom Hill	Pointer bitch	Broom Hill Dan	Nell's Queen Cott	L.L. Haggin	Chesley Harris
1924	Doughboy	Pointer dog	Nicholas Spettel	Kelona Lady	E.J. Rowe	J.W. Martin
1925	Becky Broom Hill	Pointer bitch	Broom Hill Dan	Nell's Queen Cott	L.L. Haggin	Chesley Harris
1926	Feagin's Mohawk Pal	Setter dog	Molemon	Mary Jepp	E.M. Tutwiler	Forrest Dean
1927	McTyre	Pointer dog	Milligan's Dan	McPherson's Choice	Jacob France	Chesley Harris
1928	Feagin's Mohawk Pal	Setter dog	Molemon	Mary Jepp	E.M. Tutwiler Jr.	Forrest Dean
1929	Mary Blue	Pointer bitch	James Ben Hur	Lee's Grace	W.C. Teagle	Chesley Harris
1930	Feagin's Mohawk Pal	Setter dog	Molemon	Mary Jepp	E.M. Tutwiler Jr.	Forrest Dean
1931	Mary Blue	Pointer bitch	James Ben Hur	Lee's Grace	W.C. Teagle	Chesley Harris
1932	Susquehanna Tom	Pointer dog	Highland Boy	Rap's Joy	Lebanon Kennels	Jake Bishop
1933	Rapid Transit	Pointer dog	The Hottentot	Milligan's Jane	A.G.C. Sage	Clyde Morton
1934	Norias Annie	Pointer bitch	John Willing Jr.	Ben Hur's Countess	W.C. Teagle	C.H. Harris
1935	Homewood Flirtatious	Pointer bitch	Seaview Rex	Wilder's Orange Lady	Homewood Kennels	F.E. Bevan
1936	Sulu	Pointer bitch	The Hottentot	Lue's Sue	A.G.C. Sage	Clyde Morton
1937	Air Pilot's Sam	Pointer dog	Air Pilot	Nancy F	Ed Farrior	Ed Farrior
1939	Sport's Peerless Pride	Setter dog	Sport's Peerless	Gore's Blue Bonnie	L.M. Bobbitt	W.D. English
1940	Lester's Enjoy's Wahoo	Pointer dog	Enjoy	Lester's Mary Lou	Dr. B.S. Lester	John S. Gates
1941	Ariel	Pointer dog	Air Pilot's Sam	Lullaby	A.G.C. Sage	Clyde Morton
1942	Luminary	Pointer dog	Doctor Blue Willing	Lullaby	A.G.C. Sage	Clyde Morton
1943	Ariel	Pointer dog	Air Pilot's Sam	Lullaby	A.G.C. Sage	Clyde Morton
1945	Ariel	Pointer dog	Air Pilot's Sam	Lullaby	A.G.C. Sage	Clyde Morton
1946	Mississippi Zev	Setter dog	Peerless Eugene M	Red Flapper	Dr. W.R. Trapp	J.E. Bufkin

Year	Name	Breed & Sex	Sire	Dam	Owner	Handler
1947	Saturn	Pointer dog	Luminary	Hostess	A.G.C. Sage	Clyde Morton
1948	Peter Rinski	Pointer dog	Tennessee Dare Devil	Lady Willing Lady	R.R. Waugh	Ray Smith
1949	Sierra Joan	Pointer bitch	Air Pilot Sammy	Titan's Girl	H.E. McGonigal	Howard Kirk
1950	Shore's Brownie Doone	Pointer dog	Claussen's Ran. Doone	Devotion's Kate	G.M. Livingston	G.A. Evans Jr.
1951	Paladin	Pointer dog	Ariel	Titan's Girl	A.G.C. Sage	Clyde Morton
1952	Shore's Brownie Doone	Pointer dog	Ariel	Titan's Girl	Estate of A.G.C. Sage	Clyde Morton
1953	Shore's Brownie Doone	Pointer dog	Claussen's Ranger Doone	Devotion's Kate	Mrs. G.M. Livingston	George A. Evans
1954	Warhoop Jake	Pointer dog	Lester's Enjoy's Wahoo	Spunky Willing Diane	Dr. H.E. Longsdorf	Ed Mack Farrior
1955	Lone Survivor	Pointer dog	Luminary	Titanette	Dr. S.R. Calame	Leon Covington
1956	Palamonium	Pointer dog	Paladin	Pandemonium's Dianah	Jimmy Hinton	Clyde Morton
1957	Wayriel Allegheny Sport	Pointer dog	Wayriel Jack	Allegheny Shendon Brownie	R.W. Riggins and Dr. J.A. Bays	Herman Smith
1958	The Arkansas Ranger	Pointer dog	Running Wrangler	Ranger Bows	M.F. Mitchell	Jack Harper
1959	Palamonium	Pointer dog	Paladin	Pandemonium's Dianah	Jimmy Hinton	Clyde Morton
1960	Home Again Mike	Pointer dog	The Haberdasher	Ariel's Spunky Fireball	W.C. Jones	Paul Walker
1961	Spacemaster	Pointer dog	Fast Delivery	Knolwood Selene	Ralph Daniel	Paul Walker
1962	Home Again Hattie	Pointer bitch	Home Again Mike	Hattie of Arkansas	W.E. Johnson	Jack Harper
1963	Stormy Tempest	Pointer dog	Stormy Mike	Anytime	Dr. W.G. Arney and S.W. Hart	Gene Lunsford
1964	War Storm	Pointer dog	Warhoop Jake	Satilla Little Jane	B. McCall	John S. Gates
1966	Safari	Pointer bitch	Mercer Miller	Mercer Mill Judy	S.H. Vredenburgh	John Rex Gates
1967	Satilla Virginia Lady	Pointer bitch	Satilla Midnight Sun	Lady Bess	Dr. F.M. Phillippi	Dr. F.M. Phillippi
1968	Riggins White Knight	Pointer dog	Major Lexington Boy	Stanley's Candy	Dr. Nicholas E. Palumbo	D. Hoyle Eaton
1969	Red Water Rex	Pointer dog	Tiny Wahoo	Sea Island Gale	E.B. Alexander & W.T. Pruitt	D. Hoyle Eaton
1970	Johnny Crockett	Setter dog	Wonsover's Crockett Jed	Patterson's Flying Lady	H.P. Sheely	W.C. Kirk
1971	Wrapup	Pointer bitch	Riggins White Knight	Bar Lane Dot	Jimmy Hinton & Jack T. Payne	Billy Morton
1972	The Texas Squire	Pointer dog	Flush's Country Squire	Flush's Royal Sally	Edwin Brown	John Rex Gates

NATIONAL AMATEUR QUAIL

Year	Name	Breed & Sex	Sire	Dam	Owner	Handler
1918	Fairy Beau	Setter Dog	Beau Danstone	Fairy Legend	H.D. Kirkover	H.D. Kirkover
1919	Phil's Speed Ben	Setter Dog	Phil S	S's Nellie Rodfield	W.H. Smathers	W.H. Smathers
1921	Riley Frush	Setter Dog	Paliacho	Louise Danstone II	Dr. P.K. Phillips	Dr. P.K. Phillips
1922	Eugene M's Jim	Setter Dog	Eugene M	Lulu S	Dr. O.D. Stickney	Dr. O.D. Stickney
1923	Maid's Eugene	Setter Dog	Eugene M	Lamberton's Maid	C.L. Carter	J.H. Jenkins
1925	Seaview Rex	Pointer Dog	Tarheel John	Greycourt	Dr. O.D. Stickney	R.W. Norman
1927	Dan Woolton's Dauntless	Pointer Dog	Cole's Dan Woolton	Iuka Bess	John Dunn	John Dunn
1928	Junedale Allie	Pointer Bitch	Great Island Devil	Ruth Virginia Proctor	Dr. F.H. Lahey	Dr. F.H. Lahey
1930	Bill's Bob	Pointer Bitch	Buente's Jack Proctor	Concho Black Beauty	Cecil S. Proctor	Cecil S. Proctor
1931	Belle the Devil	Pointer Bitch	Great Island Devil	Ridgefield Queen	Ray. Hoagland	Ray. Hoagland
1932	Bill's Bob	Pointer Bitch	Buente's Jack Proctor	Concho Black Beauty	Cecil S. Proctor	Cecil S. Proctor
1933	Comanche Quelle	Pointer Bitch	Muscogee Frank	Jean Milady	Dr. C.E. Wagg	Dr. C.E. Wagg
1934	Shanghai Express	Pointer Dog	Richardson's Policeman	Touchstone Retrieving Roxy	Dr. F.H. Lahey	Dr. F.H. Lahey
1935	Black Hawk Kid	Setter Dog	Hawk's Ben	Clitemnestra K	Carl E. Duffield	Carl E. Duffield
1936	Chimes Mississippi Jack	Pointer Dog	Chimes Tenn. Fred	Comanche Gypsy Broomhill	B.C. Goss	B.C. Goss
1937	Sport's Peerless Pride	Setter Dog	Sport's Peerless	Gore's Blue Bonnie	L.M. Bobbitt	L.M. Bobbitt
1938	Nepken Carolina Jake	Pointer Dog	Nepken Carolina Bill	Gaines Old Gold	Dr. W.F. Vail	Dr. W.F. Vail
1939	Lady Norias	Pointer Bitch	Norias Little Man	Winamac Pritchette	A.D. Noe Jr.	A.D. Noe Jr.
1940	Javelin	Pointer Dog	Doctor Blue Willing	Belinda Dainty	W.W. Vandeveer	W.W. Vandeveer
1941	Spunky Creek Coin	Pointer Dog	Village Boy	Spunky Creek Amazon	Ernest J. Shaffer	Ernest J. Shaffer
1942	Bobbitt's Peerless Pride	Setter Dog	Sport's Peerless Pride	Equipoise	L.M. Bobbitt	L.M. Bobbitt
1943	Our Congersman	Pointer Dog	Congersman	Nola	Fred H. Clarkson	Fred H. Clarkson

Year	Name	Breed & Sex	Sire	Dam	Owner	Handler
1944	Lebanon Tim	Pointer Dog	Scalper	Sam's Topsy	Lebanon Kennels	Harold Watson
1945	Dr. Sam's Titania	Pointer Bitch	Air Pilot Sammy	Titan's Girl	Dr. S.O. Black	Dr. S.O. Black
1946	Mississippi Zev	Setter Dog	Peerless Eugene M	Red Flapper	Dr. W.R. Trapp	Dr. W.R. Trapp
1947	Satilla Sam	Pointer Dog	Pilot Sam's Seaview	Spunky Creek Jill	Lester Varn	Lester Varn
1948	Briscoe's Carolina Doughgirl	Pointer Bitch	Baconrind's Doughboy Rap	Sam's Sooner Sue	Powel Briscoe	Powel Briscoe
1949	Briscoe's Carolina Doughgirl	Pointer Bitch	Baconrind's Doughboy Rap	Sam's Sooner Sue	Powel Briscoe	Powel Briscoe
1950	Commander's Frank	Setter dog	Flight Commander	Clematis	Carl E. Duffield	Carl E. Duffield
1951	Chasseur	Pointer dog	Ariel	Lebanon Joy	Lebanon Kennels	E.H. Vare
1952	Commander's Hightone Beau	Setter dog	Flight Commander	Clematis	C.E. Duffield and Mrs. Archie Taylor	C.E. Duffield
1953	Commander's Hightone Beau	Setter dog	Flight Commander	Clematis	C.E. Duffield and Mrs. Archie Taylor	C.E. Duffield
1954	McCallum's Perfection	Pointer bitch	Wayriel	Ariel's Spunky Ria	Richard S. Seward	Robert H. Larson
1955	Paladin's Jubilee	Pointer bitch	Paladin	Pandemonium's Dianah	C.A. Hinton Jr.	C.A. Hinton Jr.
1956	Home Again Mike	Pointer dog	The Haberdasher	Ariel's Spunky Fireball	W.C. Jones	W.C. Jones
1957	Home Again Mike	Pointer dog	The Haberdasher	Ariel's Spunky Fireball	W.C. Jones	W.C. Jones
1958	Gunsmoke	Pointer dog	Satilla Sam	Luminary's Kate	Herbert N. Holmes Jr.	Herbert N. Holmes Jr.
1959	Northwester	Pointer dog	Home Again Mike	Whispering Winds	Guy H. Lewis Jr.	Guy. H. Lewis Jr.
1960	Seairup	Pointer dog	Titanup	Sierra June	Dr. G.E. Oehler	Dr. G.E. Oehler
1961	Pineland Johnny	Pointer dog	Satilla Wahoo Pete	Pineland Alice	M.C. Fleming	M.C. Fleming
1962	Mack's Chief Warhoop	Pointer dog	Warhoop Jake	Satilla Luminary Ruth	Berol and Franks	Martin Best Jr.
1963	Kilsyth Sparky	Pointer dog	Q's Delivery Doone	Resthaven Doone Gal	Mrs. G.M. Livingston	Bill Allen
1964	Vendetta	Pointer dog	Cronus	Constant	Harold S. Sharp	Herbert R. Ingram
1965	Primos Rowdy	Pointer dog	Holly Lyn Joe	Sutherland's Belle	Frank Stout	Frank Stout
1966	La Strega	Pointer dog	Rambling Rebel Jackson	Rambling Rebel Lady	Lloyd Reeves	Joe W. Bales
1967	Haberdasher's Southerner	Pointer dog	The Haberdasher	Huntland Paladin's Limoge	Dr. W.R. McCall	Dr. W.R. McCall
1968	Rinski Little Sam	Pointer dog	Wayriel Allegheny Dan	Rinski Flying Girl	J.R. McClain	J.R. McClain
1969	A Rambling Rebel	Pointer dog	Rambling Rebel Dan	Homerun Bess	W.S. Richardson	C.R. Scarborough
1970	Gunsmoke's Admiration	Pointer bitch	Gunsmoke	Colonial Rose M	H.N. Holmes	H.N. Holmes
1971	Haberdasher's Royal Ace	Pointer dog	Paladin's Royal Heir	Mike's Madonna	Dr. W.H. McCall	Dr. W.H. McCall
1972	Hill's Stylish Sam	Pointer dog	Paladin's Kentucky Joe	Dick's Palamonium Babe	Pete Frierson & Mrs. G. Frierson Salter	Pete Frierson

NATIONAL FREE-FOR-ALL

Year	Name	Breed & Sex	Sire	Dam	Owner	Handler
1916	John Proctor	Pointer dog	Fishel's Frank	Miss Mariutch	A.L. Curtis	C.H. Babcock
1917	De Soto Frank	Pointer dog	Fishel's Frank	Alford's John's Fancy	A.G.C. Sage	J.L. Halloway
1918	Candy Kid	Setter dog	Vallejo	Bond's Gypsy	C.E. Duffield	Chesley H. Harris
1919	Jay R's Boy	Setter dog	Jay R. Whitestone	Trixie Danstone	Dr. T.H. Clark	Edw. Farrior
1920	Jay R's Boy	Setter dog	Jay R. Whitestone	Trixie Danstone	Dr. T.H. Clark	Edw. Farrior
1921	Shore's Ben	Setter dog	Ben's Sport	Mollie Cummings	Dr. A.F. Stone	John W. Martin
1922	Becky Broom Hill	Pointer bitch	Broom Hill Dan	Nell's Queen Cott	L.L. Haggin	Chesley H. Harris
1923	Muscle Shoals' Jake	Pointer dog	Ferris' Jake	Harris' Lady Pauper	James C. Foster Jr.	Edw. Farrior
1924	Muscle Shoals' Jake	Pointer dog	Ferris' Jake	Harris' Lady Pauper	James C. Foster Jr.	Mack Pritchette
1925	McTyre	Pointer dog	Milligan's Dan	McPherson's Choice	Jacob France	Chesley H. Harris
1926	Manrico	Pointer dog	Ferris' Jake	Griffith's Deenoya	C.E. Griffith	Pete Dixon
1927	McTyre	Pointer dog	Milligan's Dan	McPherson's Choice	Jacob France	Chesley H. Harris
1928	Ireland's Greymist	Pointer bitch	Griffith's Jack	Burger's Johanna	H. Glenn Ireland	Mack Pritchette
1929	Superlette	Pointer bitch	James Ben Hur	Doughboy's Kelona Lady	A.G.C. Sage	Clyde Morton
1930	Mary Blue	Pointer bitch	Milligan's Dan	Lee's Grace	W.C. Teagle	Chesley H. Harris
1931	Superlette	Pointer bitch	Milligan's Dan	Doughboy's Kelona Lady	A.G.C. Sage	Clyde Morton
1932	Superlette	Pointer bitch	Milligan's Dan	Doughboy's Kelona Lady	A.G.C. Sage	Clyde Morton
1933	Norias Roy	Pointer dog	News Boy	Norias Lady	W.C. Teagle	Prather Robinson

Year	Name	Breed and Sex	Sire	Dam	Owner	Handler
1934	Spunky Creek Joann	Pointer bitch	Muscle Shoals' Jake	Ireland's Greymist	Mrs. Nina Billingslea	Mack Pritchette
1935	Shanghai Express	Pointer dog	Richardson's Policeman	Touchstone Retrieving Roxy	G.M. Livingston	Henry Gilchrist
1936	Air Pilot's Sam	Pointer dog	Air Pilot	Nancy F	L.D. Johnson	Ed. Mack Farrior
1937	Timbuctoo	Pointer dog	The Hottentot	Lue's Sue	A.G.C. Sage	Ed. Mack Farrior
1938	Norias Aeroflow	Pointer bitch	Norias Jeff	Norias Kate	W.C. Teagle	Chesley H. Harris
1939	Air Pilot's Sam	Pointer dog	Air Pilot	Nancy F	L.D. Johnson	Edw. Farrior
1940	Rockabye Baby	Pointer bitch	Joe Willing	Lullaby	A.G.C. Sage	Clyde Morton
1941	The Texas Ranger	Pointer dog	Rex's Tarheel Jack	Miss Nellie Knolwood	D.B. McDaniel	Jack P. Harper
1942	Luminary	Pointer dog	Doctor Blue Willing	Lullaby	A.G.C. Sage	Clyde Morton
1943	The Texas Ranger	Pointer dog	Rex's Tarheel Jack	Miss Nellie Knolwood	D.B. McDaniel	Jack P. Harper
1944	Ariel	Pointer dog	Air Pilot's Sam	Lullaby	A.G.C. Sage	Clyde Morton
1945	Ariel	Pointer dog	Air Pilot's Sam	Lullaby	A.G.C. Sage	Clyde Morton
1946	Saturn	Pointer dog	Luminary	Hostess	A.G.C. Sage	Clyde Morton
1947	Texan Boy	Pointer dog	The Texas Ranger	Nola II	D.B. McDaniel	Jack P. Harper
1948	Pandemonium	Pointer dog	Homerun Harrigan	Flying Girl	A.G.C. Sage	F.W. Frazier
1949	Pandemonium	Pointer dog	Homerun Harrigan	Flying Girl	A.G.C. Sage	F.W. Frazier
1950	Fast Delivery	Pointer dog	Delivery Boy	Ends Up	A.B. Bobbitt	Paul Walker
1951	Warhoop Jake	Pointer dog	Lester's Enjoy's Wahoo	Spunky Willing Diane	Dr. H.E. Longsdorf	Ed. Mack Farrior
1952	Warhoop Jake	Pointer dog	Lester's Enjoy's Wahoo	Spunky Willing Diane	Dr. H.E. Longsdorf	Ed. Mack Farrior
1953	Hall's Stonecroft Babe	Pointer bitch	Tyson	Gold Flame	Mrs. A.A. Hall	Howard Kirk
1954	Lone Survivor	Pointer dog	Luminary	Titanette	Dr. E.R. Calame	Leon Covington
1955	Palamonium	Pointer dog	Paladin	Pandemonium's Dianah	James Hinton	Clyde Morton
1956	Volcano	Pointer dog	Tyson	Ranger's Ariel Girl	Marc F. Mitchell	Jack Harper
1957	Medallion	Pointer dog	Satilla Wahoo Pete	Sheila's Dot	S.H. Vredenburgh	John S. Gates
1958	Medallion	Pointer dog	Satilla Wahoo Pete	Sheila's Dot	S.H. Vredenburgh	John S. Gates
1959	Storm Trooper	Pointer dog	Stormy Mike	Bettie Shanks	B. McCall	John S. Gates
1960	Home Again Hattie	Pointer bitch	Home Again Mike	Hattie of Arkansas	V.E. Johnson	Jack Harper
1961	Farmer's Secret Weapon	Pointer dog	Secret Weapon Boy	Farmer's Lady Tyson	Peter Lusardi	P.A. Brousseau
1962	Stormy Tempest	Pointer dog	Stormy Mike	Anytime	Dr. W.G. Arney & S.W. Hart	Gene M. Lunsford
1963	Canon	Pointer dog	Tradition	Storm's Judy	Jimmie Hinton	Jimmie Hinton
1964	War Storm	Pointer dog	Warhoop Jake	Satilla Little Jane	B. McCall	John S. Gates
1965	Paladin's Royal	Pointer dog	Paladin's Royal Heir	Mike's Madonna	Rogers H. Hays	John Rex Gates
1966	Jorwick's Dixiecrat	Pointer dog	Storm's Romance	Neill Bickerstaff's Marry	G.G. Jordan	Winfred Campbell
1967	Riggins White Knight	Pointer dog	Major Lexington Boy	Stanley's Candy	R.W. Riggins	Dexter Hoyle Eaton
1968	Air Control	Pointer dog	Airflight	Sara Lee	W.W. Till	David Grubb
1969	Oklahoma Flush	Pointer dog	Paladin's Royal Flush	Baconrind's Sandy	R.M. Kyes	John Rex Gates
1970	Wrapup	Pointer bitch	Riggins White Knight	Bar Lane Dot	Jimmy Hinton & J.T. Payne	Billy Morton
1971	Wrapup	Pointer bitch	Riggins White Knight	Bar Lane Dot	Jimmy Hinton & J.T. Payne	Billy Morton
1972	Ormond Smart Alec	Pointer dog	Morris Warhoop Doc	Ranger's Atakapa Lady	Mr. & Mrs. F.J. Matthew III	D. Hoyle Eaton

NATIONAL DERBY

Year	Name	Breed and Sex	Sire	Dam	Owner	Handler
1920	The Ace	Pointer dog	Big Six	Gray's Lady Queen	A.G.C. Sage	J.L. Holloway
1921	Stylish Wasp	Pointer bitch	Stylish Palmetto	Peggie Montrose	Miss Marion du Pont	R.K. Armstrong
1922	Duquesne Nell	Pointer bitch	Mount Riga Rap	Patsey Jane Proctor	J.H. Elder	Ed. Farrior
1923	Kohinoor	Pointer dog	Blue Diamond's Frank	Miss Fearless Diamond	A.G.C. Sage	J.L. Holloway
1924	Inquisitive Lady	Setter bitch	Braeburnie's Heir	Piava	C.W. Campbell	Ed. Farrior
1925	Belle the Devil	Pointer bitch	Great Island Devil	Ridgefield Queen	Joseph Crane Jr.	Joseph Crane Jr.
1926	Jess Reynolds Diamond	Pointer bitch	Highland Boy	Floretta Hawk	M.S. Hughes	Ed. Farrior
1927	The Laird	Pointer dog	Highland Boy	Deuce of Spades	A.G.C. Sage	J.L. Holloway
1928	Mingo	Pointer bitch	Muscle Shoals' Jake	Zipporah	Mrs. F.R. Billingslea	Mack Pritchette

Year	Name	Breed & Sex	Sire	Dam	Owner	Handler
1929	Air Pilot	Pointer dog	Muscle Shoals' Jake	Ferris Blanche Cash	H.D. Whitaker	Ed. Farrior
1930	Susquehanna Tom	Pointer dog	Highland Boy	Rap's Joy	Lebanon Kennels	Jake Bishop
1931	Trego	Pointer dog	Mack Pritchette	Rag Speedy's Bonita	G.R. Feltman	John Campbell
1932	Gangster	Pointer dog	John Willing Jr.	Myers Ruth	Miss Emmy Haggin	Prather Robinson
1933	Sun Beau	Pointer dog	Cushbawn Billy	Becky Jake	W.C. McIntosh	Mack Pritchette
1934	Norias Esso	Pointer dog	Norias Roy	Myers Ruth	W.C. Teagle	Prather Robinson
1935	Alabama Scrambles	Pointer dog	Kremlin	Myers Ruth	Jacob France	C.H. Harris
1936	Norias Aeroflow	Pointer bitch	Norias Jeff	Norias Kate	W.C. Teagle	Prather Robinson
1937	Lester's Lonnie Munger	Pointer dog	Glenn's Greymist Jake	Lester's Silver Moon	Dr. B.S. Lester	J.S. Gates
1938	Rockabye Baby	Pointer bitch	Joe Willing	Lullaby	A.G.C. Sage	Clyde Morton
1939	Nightcap	Pointer dog	Hot Toddy	Pittsview Girl	A.G.C. Sage	Clyde Morton
1940	Surracho	Pointer dog	Aborigine	Hostess	W.F. Miller	Ed Mack Farrior
1941	Contact	Pointer dog	Propeller	Belvedere	Lebanon Kennels	Mack McGrady
1942	Astra	Pointer bitch	Luminary	Tarantella	A.G.C. Sage	Clyde Morton
1943	Kilsyth Belle B	Pointer bitch	Allegheny Sam	Aborigine's Seaview Girl	G.M. Livingston	George Crangle
1944	Bonsoir	Pointer dog	Nightcap	Rockabye Baby	A.G.C. Sage	Clyde Morton
1945	Oration	Pointer dog	Homerun Harrigan	Flying Girl	A.G.C. Sage	Clyde Morton
1946	Wayside Butch	Pointer dog	Wayside Herzogg	Susie Crow	E.H. Anderson	C.H. Lonon
1947	Stargazer	Pointer dog	Saturn	Lullaby Lady	A.G.C. Sage	Clyde Morton
1948	Westerner	Pointer dog	Ariel	Miss McMeda	A.G.C. Sage	Clyde Morton
1949	Warhoop Jake	Pointer dog	Lester's Enjoy's Wahoo	Spunky Willing Diane	H.R. Ingram	Ed Mack Farrior
1950	Shady Lady O	Pointer bitch	Ariel's Mondino Pete	Lawless Becky	I.C. Ownbey	Gladden Miller
1951	Ariel Hobo's Becky	Pointer bitch	Ariel Hobo Joe	Airacobra's Little Joe	William Welch	John H. Parker
1952	Wistful	Pointer bitch	Paladin	Lullaby Breeze	Fred W. Shappert	F.W. Frazier
1953	Palamonium	Pointer dog	Paladin	Pandemonium's Dianah	James Hinton	Clyde Morton
1954	Storm Trooper	Pointer dog	Stormy Mike	Bettie Shanks	George Suttle	Edward Farrior
1955	Turnto	Setter dog	Commander's Hightone Beau	Sport's Jill	G.R. Feltman	Ray Smith
1956	Jeff of Arkansas	Pointer dog	Running W Wrangler	Ranger Bows	G.B. Oliver	Jack Harper
1957	The Arkansas Ranger	Pointer dog	Running W Wrangler	Ranger Bows	Mrs. G.B. Oliver	Jack Harper
1958	Honest Injun	Pointer bitch	Ginza	Miss Melee	Len C. Enos	Robert Lee
1959	Safari	Pointer bitch	Mercer Killer	Mercer Mill Judy	S.H. Vredenburgh	John S. Gates
1960	Tradition	Pointer bitch	Overbrook's Explorer	Net's Judy	Jimmie Hinton	Clyde Morton
1961	Riggins White Knight	Pointer dog	Major Lexington Boy	Stanley's Candy	R.W. Riggins	Hoyle Eaton
1962	Canon	Pointer dog	Tradition	Storm's Judy	Jimmie Hinton	Clyde Morton
1963	Dixie Deb	Pointer bitch	Briarsfield Ace	Warhoop Sister	J.D. Morrow & Adolph Troppendahl	Marshall Loftin
1964	Royal Heir	Pointer dog	Paladin's Royal Heir	Sea Island Anna	J.D. Spears	John S. Gates
1965	Air Control	Pointer dog	Airflight	Sara Lee	W.W. Till	David Grubb
1966	Autumn's Memories	Pointer bitch	Paladin's Royal Flush	Hedgeliner	Roger H. Hays	Fred Arant
1967	Flush's Country Squire	Pointer dog	Paladin's Royal Flush	Streamliner	J.B. Braswell Jr.	John Rex Gates
1968	Boom Town	Pointer dog	Red Water Rex	Jeff's Lady	D.W. Bonaguidi	D. Hoyle Eaton
1969	Royal Gusto	Pointer dog	Paladin's Royal Flush	Bittersweet	Quail Capital Kennels	John Rex Gates
1970	Rebel Knight	Pointer dog	Riggins White Knight	Pasadena Lady	R.R. Brown Jr.	D. Hoyle Eaton
1971	Orion Flush	Pointer dog	Sandstorm Jake	Ripley Creek Ranee	Dr. Olin Thompson	John Rex Gates
1972	Hardy's Scarlet Georgia	Pointer bitch	Spacerider	Scarlet Rebel K	C.L. Hardy Jr.	Ted Gardner

ALL-AMERICA CLUB'S OPEN CHICKEN

Year	Name	Breed & Sex	Sire	Dam	Owner	Handler
1912	Comanche Frank	Pointer dog	Fishel's Frank	Lady Johns	U.R. Fishel	J.M. Avent
1913	John Proctor	Pointer dog	Fishel's Frank	Miss Mariutch	A.L. Curtis	C.H. Babcock
1914	Babblebrook Joe	Setter dog	Mohawk II	Early Dawn	Louis McGrew	E.D. Garr

Year	Winner	Breed	Sire	Dam	Owner	Handler
1915	John Proctor	Pointer dog	Fishel's Frank	Miss Mariutch	A.L. Curtis	C.H. Babcock
1916	Candy Kid	Setter dog	Vallejo	Bond's Gypsy	C.E. Duffield	C.H. Harris
1917	Candy Kid	Setter dog	Vallejo	Bond's Gypsy	C.E. Duffield	C.H. Harris
1918	Candy Kid	Setter dog	Vallejo	Bond's Gypsy	C.E. Duffield	George Payton
1919	Mary Montrose	Pointer bitch	Comanche Frank	Lorna Doone	William Ziegler Jr.	H.A. Tomlinson
1920	Jersey Jo-Jo	Setter dog	Tim Wise	Duchess S	Frank Reily	Joseph Crane
1921	Comanche Zig Field	Pointer dog	Comanche Frank	Topsy Girl	C.E. Griffith	C.H. Harris
1922	Doughboy	Pointer dog	Nicholas Spettel	Kelona Lady	E.J. Rowe	J.W. Martin
1923	Doughboy	Pointer dog	Nicholas Spettel	Kelona Lady	E.J. Rowe	J.W. Martin
1924	Inquisitive Lady	Setter bitch	Braeburnie's Heir	Piava	C.W. Campbell	Ed. Farrior
1925	McTyre	Pointer dog	Milligan's Dan	McPherson's Choice	Jacob France	C.H. Harris
1926	Highland Boy	Pointer dog	Ferris' Manitoba Rap	Rags' Dell	E.R. Coleman	Jake Bishop
1927	Sobig	Pointer dog	Omar	Rubaiyat's Adair	Weil and Ray	J.M. Avent
1928	Miss Mayfair	Pointer bitch	Winston	Wheeler's Jackinette	F.S. Groves	John Campbell
1929	Mary Blue	Pointer bitch	James Ben Hur	Lee's Grace	W.C. Teagle	Chesley H. Harris
1930	Mad Anthony	Pointer dog	Orrwod's Beautiful Jake	Queen of Arnaud	C.H. Reynolds	Frank Cummins
1931	Schoolfield	Pointer dog	Tip of Joyeuse	Appalachian Mary	Ambrose Gaines	Luther Smith
1932	Algonquin	Pointer dog	Highland Boy	Rap's Joy	Lebanon Kennels	Jake Bishop
1933	Norias Roy	Pointer dog	News Boy	Norias Lady	W.C. Teagle	Prather Robinson
1934	Air Pilot's Sam	Pointer dog	Air Pilot	Nancy F	L.D. Johnson	Edward Farrior
1935	Doctor Blue Willing	Pointer dog	Doctor Norman	Miss Willing	L.D. Johnson	Edward Farrior
1936	Chimes Mississippi Jack	Pointer dog	Chimes Tennessee Fred	Comanche Gypsy Broomhill	B.C. Goss	George Payton
1937	Propeller	Pointer dog	Tweed	Creole Sue	Lebanon Kennels	Mack McGrady
1938	Little Eva	Pointer bitch	Pearl River Dan	Robin's Fleetest	W.J. McGee	Ed. Mack Farrior
1939	Norias Aeroflow	Pointer bitch	Norias Jeff	Norias Kate	W.C. Teagle	C.H. Harris
1940	War Admiral	Pointer dog	Doctor Blue Willing	Seaview Rex's Dixie	Dr. T.G. Jones	E.E. Downs
1941	Young's Billie	Pointer dog	Jim Peters	Frost's White Boots	H.J. Yoakum	V.E. Humphreys
1942	Titan	Pointer dog	Spunky Creek Boy	Spunky Creek Joann	George Mallers	W.D. English
1943	Way Yonder	Pointer dog	Spunky Creek Boy	Mary B Willing	Dr. H.E. Longsdorf	W.D. English
1944	Lebanon Tim	Pointer dog	Scalper	Sam's Topsy	Lebanon Kennels	W.D. English
1945	Lebanon Tim	Pointer dog	Scalper	Sam's Topsy	Lebanon Kennels	W.D. English
1946	Medic	Pointer dog	Medico	Mackay Point Sis	Dr. A.S. Bumgardner	Howard Kirk
1947	Sierra Joan	Pointer bitch	Air Pilot Sammy	Titan's Girl	H.E. McGonigal	Lee Worstell
1948	Bomberette	Pointer bitch	Air Pilot Sammy	Titan's Girl	J.T. Payne	Howard Kirk
1949	Sierra Joan	Pointer bitch	Air Pilot Sammy	Titan's Girl	H.E. McGonigal	Leon Covington
1950	Marvelous Jack	Pointer dog	Marvelous	Smith's Peggy Jane	C.L. Little	Ed. Mack Farrior
1951	Warhoop Jake	Pointer dog	Lester's Enjoy's Wahoo	Spunky Willing Diane	Dr. H.E. Longsdorf	Ed Farrior
1953	Excello	Pointer dog	Fast Delivery	Pernal	Dr. H.E. Longsdorf	John S. Gates
1955	Stanton's Victory	Pointer bitch	Stanton	Juneaire	C.F. Mueller	E.A. Weddle
1956	Brownaire Tommy	Pointer dog	Shore's Brownie Doone	Aviette	F.S. Oosterhoudt	Ed Mack Farrior
1957	Tyrolean	Pointer dog	Tyson	Surracho's Spunky Girl	C.C. Jones	John S. Gates
1958	Le Baron	Pointer dog	Satilla Wahoo Pete	Sheila's Dot	O.D. Carlton	John S. Gates
1959	Medallion II	Pointer dog	Medallion	Stanton's June	Dr. W.B. Griffin	Leon Covington
1960	Notus	Pointer dog	Westerner	Forshalee Titaness	B.M. Hogan	John S. Gates
1961	Safari	Pointer bitch	Mercer Miller	Mercer Mill Judy	S.H. Vredenburgh	
1962	Cancelled	—	—	—	—	—
1963	John Oliver	Pointer dog	Jeff of Arkansas	Ranger's Texas Sally	John Dale Jr.	Jack Harper
1964	Maxim	Pointer dog	Nightcap's Ranger Tyson	Palamonium's Jill	S.H. Vredenburgh	John S. Gates
1965	Bellemeade Ranger	Pointer dog	The Arkansas Ranger	Katherine of Claylick	Dr. Vernon Hutton, Jr.	John Rex Gates
1966	Safari	Pointer bitch	Mercer Miller	Mercer Mill Judy	S.H. Vredenburgh	John Rex Gates
1967	Precise	Pointer dog	Paladin's Royal Heir	The Prodigy	R.M. Kyes	John Rex Gates

Year	Name	Breed & Sex	Sire	Dam	Owner	Handler
1968	The Hurricane	Pointer dog	Tiny Wahoo	Stanley's Candy	John Dale Jr.	John Rex Gates
1969	Flush's Country Squire	Pointer dog	Paladin's Royal Flush	Streamliner	J.B. Braswell	John Rex Gates
1970	No trial held					
1971	Oklahoma Flush	Pointer dog	Paladin's Royal Flush	Baconrind's Sandy	S.H. Vredenburg	John Rex Gates
1972	Miller's Miss Knight	Pointer bitch	Riggins White Knight	Delivery Bertha Mae	R.H. Hays	Faye Throneberry

NEW ENGLAND BIRD DOG

Sponsored by the Association of New England Field Trial Clubs

Year	Name	Breed & Sex	Sire	Dam	Owner	Handler
1930	Miss Magpie of Ware	Pointer bitch	Master Robert	Dot of Stagmount	A.B. Field	L.B. Chapman
1933	Ghoststone's Sue Riley	Setter bitch	Ghoststone	Yendor's Sue Riley	T.P. Whittemore	H.G. Silver
1934	Granite State Mischief	Setter bitch	Racketeer	Granite State Special	W.H. Shaw	H.G. Silver
1935	Village Gangster	Pointer dog	Village Boy	Mad Anthony's Babe	C.W. Stevens	Michael Seminatore
1936	Lady B Gay	Setter bitch	Florendale Lou's Beau	Miss Gay Girl	Dr. L.J. Hyde	Dr. L.J. Hyde
1937	Garrison Hill Frank	Pointer dog	Oronoke Pilot	Garrison Hill Mary	L.H. Newkirk, Jr.	W.M. Colby
1938	Chief Inspector	Setter dog	Pepper Martin	Florenbeau Lou	Michael Seminatore	Michael Seminatore
1940	Chicora Delight	Setter bitch	Chicora Citation	Lassie Porter	W. Lee White	Michael Seminatore
1941	Granite State Highboy	Pointer dog	Lexington Jake	Country Lass	C.H. Fraser	W.M. Colby
1942	Chicora Delight	Setter bitch	Chicora Citation	Lassie Porter	W. Lee White	Michael Seminatore
1943	Granite State Hipower	Pointer dog	Lexington Jake	Country Lass	E.F. Clark	W.M. Colby
1945	Sam L's Fiora	Setter bitch	Gym	Vogan's Onachye	Sam Light	Larry Tuttle
1946	Sam L's Skyscraper	Setter dog	Sam L's Skyrocket	Ralph's Peerless Starlight	Sam Light	Larry Tuttle
1948	Merrylee Patsy	Pointer bitch	Bet's Country Boy	Granite State Merrylee	Burt Terrell	Mike Seminatore
1949	Contender's Spunky Delight	Pointer bitch	Joe Contender	Spunky Creek Ella	Henry Berol	Mike Seminatore
1950	Contender's Spunky Delight	Pointer bitch	Joe Contender	Spunky Creek Ella	Henry Berol	Mike Seminatore
1951	Sam L's Skyhigh	Setter dog	Equity	Skyrocket's Starpoise	Sam Light	Larry Tuttle
1952	Sam L's Hadaway	Setter dog	Sam L's Skyhigh	Fiora Sky	Sam Light	Rich Tuttle
1953	Masterman's Countess	Setter bitch	Chief Masterman	Color Bearer	W. Lee White	Mike Seminatore
1954	Surracho's Texas Boy	Pointer dog	The Texas Traveler	Surracho's Spunky Girl	Henry Berol	Mike Seminatore
1955	Granite Valley Bid	Pointer bitch	Joe Contender	Pilgrim Maid	R. McAllister III	F.E. Harwarth
1956	Tancanhoosen Hunter	Pointer dog	Tancanhoosen Brook	Tick Thomee	L.F. Bissell	Carl Beattie
1958	Title withheld					
1959-60	Dona's Sammy	Setter dog	Tulagi Chief	Beau Essig's Donna	Florence E. Harwarth	Walter Robertshaw
1961	Hickory Pride	Setter dog	Invader	Trigger Girl	W. Lee White	Mike Seminatore
1962	General Rodfield Inspector	Setter dog	Masterman Rodfield	Chief's Lady Ginger	S.S. Johnston	Michael Seminatore
1963	*Collinswood Ripper	Setter dog	Hightone's Rip	Retinsue	F.A. DeBlase	Wink Griffin
1964	*Hickory's Delight	Setter bitch	Hickory Pride	Leading Lady	Dr. J.R. Seminatore	Mike Seminatore
1965	*Piscataqua Samson	Pointer dog	Piscataqua Sam	Polkadot Peg	Roland Prairie	Thelmar Page
1966	Berk Boy	Pointer dog	Berkshire Joe	Berkshire Spunky Girl	F.J. Wills, Jr.	Oddone Piazza
1967	Pride's Delight	Setter bitch	Hickory Pride	Evening Delight	C.P. Fogg	E.L. Frisella
1968	Jungle Doctor	Pointer dog	Music Maker	Willing Sue	A.J. Valeri	A.J. Valeri
1969	Strawberry Fly	Setter bitch	Elhew Jungle	Potato Patch Sue	Dr. A.H. Nitchman	Dr. A.H. Nitchman
1970	Chief's Justice	Setter dog	Commander's Jet Stream	Hickory's Delight	Michael Seminatore	Michael Seminatore
1971	Manunka Chunk Smokey	Setter dog	Grouse Ridge Smokey	Wonsover Donna Belle	H.A. & Margaret Searles	Bill Conlin

* —Placed First—Title Withheld.

DOMINION CLUB'S CHICKEN

Year	Name	Breed & Sex	Sire	Dam	Owner	Handler
1936	Air Pilot's Sam	Pointer dog	Air Pilot	Nancy F	L.D. Johnson	Ed Farrior

Year	Name	Breed & Sex	Sire	Dam	Owner	Handler
1937	Navasota Shoals Jake	Pointer dog	More Muscle Jake	Navasota Fenno	W.V. Bowles	Clyde Anderson
1938	Propeller	Pointer dog	Tweed	Creole Sue	Lebanon Kennels	Mack McGrady
1939	Peerless Par	Setter dog	Sport's Peerless	Paliacho's Polly III	R.E. Rooke	G.A. Story
1940	Farmwood Traveler	Pointer dog	Congersman	Farmwood Macaroni	U.M. Fleischmann	Sam Yount
1941	Mercer Mill Jake	Pointer dog	Mississippi Broomhill Jake	Fae's Village Anne	B.C. Goss	J.S. Gates
1942	Tarheelia's Lucky Strike	Pointer dog	Lexington Jake	Tarheelia's Best Bet	G.M. Livingston	George Crangle
1943	Ariel	Pointer dog	Air Pilot's Sam	Lullaby	A.G.C. Sage	Clyde Morton
1944	Homerun Dixie Mike	Pointer dog	Homerun Dixie Dan	Carolina's Betty Prickett	E.L. Hart	Lou Palmer
1945	Arrowsmith	Pointer dog	Lester's Enjoy's Wahoo	Manley's Joyeuse Ann	Dr. G.E. Fisher	John Gates
1946	Saturn	Pointer dog	Luminary	Hostess	A.G.C. Sage	Clyde Morton
1947	Bomber Commander's John	Pointer dog	Bomber Commander	Ichauway's Peggy	George Sears	John Gates
1948	Wayside Butch	Pointer dog	Wayside Herzogg	Susie Crow	E.H. Anderson	C.H. Lonon
1949	Doctor Robin	Pointer dog	Spot Robbin	Almon's Lady Shoals	Grant Sturman	T.M. Lunsford
1950	Agrippa	Pointer dog	Lester's Enjoy's Wahoo	Tip's Village Girl	F.T. Holliday	John Gates
1951	Greenwood Bill	Pointer dog	Dawn's Village Bill	Greenwood Gale	H.M. Beattie	John Gates
1952	Satilla Wahoo Pete	Pointer dog	Satilla Sam	Fisher's Wahoo Mary	J. E. McClanahan and Joseph Sanford	John Gates
1953	Title withheld					
1954	Satilla Wahoo Pete	Pointer dog	Satilla Sam	Fisher's Wahoo Mary	H.E. Eyster	John Gates
1955	Crawford's Junior's Lady	Pointer bitch	Oboy Jake Jr.	Lummie	Bruce Harris	E.A. Weddle
1956	Susan Peters	Pointer bitch	Satilla Wahoo Pete	Sheila's Dot	H.E. Weil	John Gates
1957	Riggins Spunky Pete	Pointer dog	Ranger's Spunky Pete	Riggins Lady Saturn	R.W. Riggins	Herman Smith
1958	Dick's Derby Day	Pointer dog	Fast Delivery	Riggins Lady Saturn	W.A. Ambrose	Herman Smith
1959	Susan Peters	Pointer bitch	Satilla Wahoo Pete	Sheila's Dot	H.E. Weil	John Gates
1960	Susan Peters	Pointer bitch	Satilla Wahoo Pete	Sheila's Dot	H.E. Weil	John Gates
1961	Gunsmoke's Jewel	Pointer bitch	Gunsmoke	Santee Susan	Dr. T.J. Lattimore	P.A. Brousseau
1962	Polaris Pete	Pointer dog	John B. Lane	Whispering Breeze	Dr. H.H. Vaughan	John S. Gates
1963	War Storm	Pointer dog	Warhoop Jake	Satilla Little Jane	B. McCall	John S. Gates
1964	Technique	Pointer dog	Dandy Town	Golden Smoke	J.D. Spears	John S. Gates
1965	Highway Man	Pointer dog	Llano Man	Wayriel's Saturn Lady	George Georghegan	W.F. Rayl
1966	Social Climber	Pointer dog	Gunsmoke	Trenchant Barb	H.E. Weil	John Rex Gates
1967	Safari	Pointer bitch	Mercer Miller	Mercer Miller Judy	S.H. Vredenburgh	John Rex Gates
1968	Flaming Star	Setter dog	Turnto's Hightone Pete	Miss Boo's Loch	Mrs. G.G. Jordan	Herman Smith
1969	Hill's Stylish Sam	Pointer dog	Paladin's Kentucky Joe	Dick's Palamonium Babe	Quail Capital Kennels	John Rex Gates
1970	Texas Allegheny Pete	Pointer dog	Texas Allegheny Sport	Home Again Lou	Blue Morrow	John Rex Gates
1971	Saladin	Pointer dog	Riggins White Knight	Rex's Rexannie	Dr. D.E. Hawthorne	Harve Butler

AMERICAN FIELD PHEASANT DOG FUTURITY

Year	Name	Breed & Sex	Sire	Dam	Owner	Handler
1934	1st—Farmwood Macaroni	Pointer bitch	Yankee Doodle Jack	Farmwood Lou	U.M. Fleischmann	Sam Yount
	2d—Farmwood Yankee	Pointer dog	Yankee Doodle Jack	Farmwood Lou	U.M. Fleischmann	Sam Yount
	3d—Bill's Faith	Pointer bitch	Nepken Carolina Bill	Sunoco Girl	J.F. Carlisle	G.M. Crangle
1935	1st—Tip's Topsy's Top	Pointer dog	Village Boy	Tip's Topsy	J.F. Carlisle	G.M. Crangle
	2d—Allegheny Schoolgirl	Pointer bitch	Schoolfield	Rosedale Mite	R.H. Clemmer	R.H. Clemmer
	3d—Farmwood Thunder	Pointer dog	The Coming Storm	Farmwood Flit	U.M. Fleischmann	Sam Yount
1936	1st—Lawless Boy	Pointer dog	Village Boy	Lawless Lady	J.E. Cain Jr.	W.D. English
	2d—Spunky Creek Coin	Pointer dog	Village Boy	Spunky Creek Amazon	Mrs. N. Billingslea	Mack Pritchette
	3d—Jack's Bill	Pointer dog	Rosedale Jack	Camden Peggy	Mrs. E.H. Ellis	James Crangle
1937	1st—Village Red Light	Pointer dog	Village Boy	Tarheelia Win	L.H. Newkirk Jr.	A.C. Biggi
	2d—Shore's Doctor Doone	Pointer dog	Shore's Jack Doone	Wild Bill's Lue	F.C. Ash	Earl Crangle
	3d—Shore's Wild Lady	Pointer bitch	Shore's Jack Doone	Shore's Lemon Lady	Dr. T.W. Shore	Sam Yount

Year	Placement and Dog	Breed/Sex	Sire	Dam	Owner	Handler
1938	1st—Gaiety Gaines	Pointer bitch	Rex's Tarheel Jack	Highland Bimpkins Girl	C.F. Gaines	Earl Crangle
	2d—Farmwood Mischief	Pointer bitch	Farmwood Yankee	Shore's Pearl Doone	U.M. Fleischmann	Sam O. Yount
	3d—Miss Pilot Doone	Pointer bitch	Air Pilot	Shore's Mary Doone	Dr. F.O. Foard	Marvin Yount
1939	1st—Yankee Doodle Supreme	Pointer dog	Yankee Doodle Jack	Village Boy's Betty	A.D. Noe Jr.	W.D. English
	2d—Farmwood Fleece	Pointer bitch	Farmwood Yankee	Radio Beam	U.M. Fleischmann	Sam O. Yount
	3d—Pathfinder Highland Rex	Pointer dog	Rex's Tarheel Jack	Highland Bimpkins Girl	F.C. Ash	G.M. Crangle
1940	1st—Allegheny Sam	Pointer dog	Air Pilot's Sam	Grover's Tippy Joy	Dr. L.O. Crumpler	W.D. English
	2d—Tarheel's Sassy Jane	Pointer bitch	Rex's Tarheel Jack	Highland Bimpkins Girl	S.G. Bayly	Marvin Yount
	3d—Kushla Creek Babe	Pointer dog	Spunky Creek Boy	Kushla Dixie	C.D. Garrison	E.M. Farrior
1941	1st—Lenape E Z-Stride	Pointer dog	Bill's Stylish Tom	Skip's Spunky Girl	F.D. Foster	F.E. Bevan
	2d—Peerless Pride's Pal	Setter dog	Bobbitt's Peerless Pride	Peerless Stylish Lady	L.M. Bobbitt	L.M. Bobbitt
	3d—Homerun Dixie Mike	Pointer dog	Homerun Dixie Dan	Carolina's Betty Prickett	Miss C.L. Phelps	C.L. Prickett
1942	1st—Farmwood Falcon	Pointer dog	Farmwood Yankee	Radio Beam	U.M. Fleischmann	S.O. Yount
	2d—Atlas	Pointer dog	Air Pilot's Sam	Seaview's Polkadot	Euclid Claussen	F.E. Bevan
	3d—Pilot Sam's Seaview	Pointer dog	Air Pilot's Sam	Seaview's Polkadot	C.F. Taylor	G.M. Crangle
1943	1st—Farmwood Florida	Pointer bitch	Farmwood Yankee	Farmwood Blondy	U.M. Fleischmann	S.O. Yount
	2d—Palmer's Linda	Pointer dog	Dr. Sam's Charlie	Doctor Sam's Princess	S.W. Palmer	S.W. Palmer
	3d—Market Wise	Pointer dog	Rex's Tarheel Jack	Knolwood Lady	T.H. Mofield	W.D. English
1944	1st—Allitas Shoals Jackie	Pointer dog	Bobbitt's Stylish Jake	Knolwood Lady	Mrs. Lester Varn	G.M. Crangle
	2d—Sixty H	Pointer bitch	Missouri Pete	Waskada Dream	W.F. Oliver	W.D. English
	3d—Ichaloy	Pointer dog	Spunky Creek Boy	Ichaby Fanny	H.W. Helwig	W.L. Cosner
1945	1st—Home Again Harrigan	Pointer dog	Homerun Harrigan	Dr. Sam's Bobbie	Jack Reider	F.E. Bevan
	2d—Tip Top Bob	Pointer dog	Pilot Sam's Seaview	Crumpler's Carolina Nell	E.J. Laney	Herman Smith
	3d—Satilla Sam	Pointer dog	Hirshfield's Pegasus	Spunky Creek Jill	Lester Varn	Earl Crangle
1946	1st—Hirshfield's Pegasus II	Pointer dog	Hirshfield's Pegasus	Hirshfield's Spunky Village	Dr. A.C. Hirschfield	G.M. Crangle
	2d—Hootn Tootn Newton	Pointer dog	Claussen's Green Light	Homewood China Doll	Euclid Claussen	F.E. Bevan
	3d—Island Park Schooner	Pointer dog	Island Park Boy	Air Pilot's Dixie	Dr. H.D. Chamberlain	O.S. Redman
1947	1st—Snaparoon	Pointer dog	Ariel Ace	Jake's Rose	Robert Tuttle	W.L. Cosner
	2d—Siwanoy	Pointer dog	Baconrind's Doughboy Rap	Sam's Sooner Sue	A.L. Gamber	A.L. Gamber
	3d—Ariel's Radar	Pointer dog	Ariel Ace	Jake's Rose	Rufe Watson	G.M. Crangle
1948	1st—Kilsyth Jack Citation	Pointer dog	Shore's Brownie Doone	Norias Algiers	G.M. Livingston	G.A. Evans
	2d—Carousel	Pointer dog	Air Way	Forty Four	W.F. Barden	Ed Farrior
	3d—Tyrone	Pointer dog	Tyson	Gold Flame	E.A. Ruff	Howard Kirk
1949	1st—Fast Special Delivery	Pointer dog	Fast Delivery	Delivery Boy's Girl	W.C. Jones	Herman Smith
	2d—Ichaloy Goldenrod	Pointer dog	Ichaloy	Jake's Village Dot	C.G. Holt	W.L. Cosner
	3d—Fast Air Delivery	Pointer dog	Fast Delivery	Delivery Boy's Girl	A.B. Bobbitt	Paul Walker
1950	1st—Kilsyth Dixie Sam	Pointer dog	Kilsyth Delivery Doc	Ends Up	G.M. Livingston	G.A. Evans Jr.
	2d—Mr. Tyson	Pointer dog	Tyson	Ranger's Amanda Willing	C.A. Rugg	Pete Smith
	3d—Hayrack	Pointer dog	Louisiana Hayride	Spunky Boy's Cookie	Dr. R.H. Lillie	Lee Hoffman
1951	1st—Rumson Farm Hayride	Pointer dog	Louisiana Hayride	Nightcap's Aurora	Raymond Hoagland	Earl C. Crangle
	2d—Hayride	Pointer dog	Shore's Brownie Doone	Nightcap's Aurora	Dr. H.E. Longsdorf	Earl C. Crangle
	3d—Hayride	Pointer dog	Fast Delivery	Kilsyth Delivery Dot	Mrs. G.M. Livingston	George A. Evans
1952	1st—Newman's Delivery Dan	Pointer dog	Shore's Brownie Doone	Frank's Delivery Frankie	E.J. Newman	Fred Arant Jr.
	2d—Kilsyth Dixie Ace	Pointer dog	Tyson	Aviette	Geraldine Livingston	George A. Evans
	3d—Spunky Tyson's Mike	Pointer dog	The Haberdasher	Spunky Creek Pilot	Millar Buchanan	W.L. Cosner
1953	1st—Builder	Pointer dog	Ranger's Spunky Pete	Bonsoir's Lady Jill	Dr. H.E. Longsdorf	Paul Walker
	2d—Spunky Pete's Honey	Pointer dog	Shore's Brownie Doone	Ranger's Spunky Mary	Dr. W.H. Wallingford	Herman Smith
	3d—Kilsyth Florida Rebel	Pointer bitch	Shore's Brownie Doone	Kilsyth Delivery Dot	Mrs. G.M. Livingston	George A. Evans
1954	1st—Kilsyth White Chief	Pointer dog	Fast Delivery	Kilsyth Honey	Mrs. G.M. Livingston	Paul Walker
	2d—Fast Delivery Belle	Pointer bitch	Spunky Tyson's Mike	Nightcap Girl	Murtis Lee Carver	W.L. Cosner
	3d—Natty Netty	Pointer dog	Paladin	Village's Lady Pilot	A.J. Schorr	John Thompson
1955	1st—Tool Steel Man	Pointer dog	Tyson	Sierra Doone	Mrs. Betty Hoover	Pete Smith
	2d—Hodge's Tyson	Pointer dog	Tyson	Yon Dot	H.D. Hodge and B.W. Calvin	

Year	Placement	Breed/Sex	Sire	Dam	Owner	Handler
	3d—Slugger's Patti	Setter bitch	Louisville Slugger	Astral	Alton B. King	J.O. Dunn
1956	1st—Northwester	Pointer dog	Home Again Mike	Whispering Winds	Guy H. Lewis Jr.	Paul Walker
	2d—Tick's Lexington Jake	Pointer dog	Elhew Marksman	Hunt's Lexington Judy	Edward Emerson Jr.	Edw. Emerson Jr.
	3d—Carsilio	Pointer dog	Rumson Farm Haymaker	Dotty Pegasus	Harry Hanley	Earl C. Crangle
1957	1st—Rambling Rebel Dan	Pointer dog	Newman's Delivery Dan	Alicia's Image	J.M. Culp	Fred Arant
	2d—Sirtoga Stormy Mack	Pointer dog	Sirtoga	Stormy Kate	C.I. Dover	Paul Walker
	3d—Tancanhoosen Stony Crag	Pointer dog	Satilla Wahoo Pete	Greenwood Anna	L.F. Bissell	W.R. Conlin
1958	1st—Resthaven Spunky Bill	Pointer dog	Tarengo Spunky Boy	Aric's Spunky Fireball	Harold A. Crane	Fred Arant Jr.
	2d—Vaga	Pointer dog	The Haberdasher	Rumson Farm Attraction	C.H. Edwards	Paul Walker
	3d—Tag Me	Pointer dog	Medallion	Winsome Dinah	Mrs. Philip Donehoo	Earl C. Crangle
1959	1st—Elhew Zeus	Pointer dog	Elhew Marksman	Santee Susan	Robert G. Wehle	Robert G. Wehle
	2d—Gunsmoke's Jewel	Pointer bitch	Gunsmoke	Accolade's Empress	Dr. T.J. Lattimore	P.A. Brousseau
	3d—Bloody Mary	Pointer bitch	Luminary's Agrippa Ben	Satilla Mary	W.S. Gabhart Jr.	Paul Walker
1960	1st—Satilride	Pointer dog	Rumson Farm Hayride	Miskristie	H.H. Townshend	Earl Crangle
	2d—Knightime Fred	Pointer dog	Q's Delivery Doone	Delivery's Little Kate	Dr. E.G. Knight	Fred Arant Jr.
	3d—Teller	Pointer bitch	Cassell's Mr. Ike	Homerun Best	O.E. Massey	P.A. Brousseau
1961	1st—Homerun Johnny	Pointer dog	Rambling Rebel Dan	Sandy Milos	Claudia Lee Phelps	Fred Arant Jr.
	2d—Airflight	Pointer dog	Airway Traveler	Elhew Empress	H.S. Harrington	Bob Cline
	3d—Elhew Muldoon	Pointer dog	Elhew Zeus	Elhew Dior	Robert G. Wehle	Paul Walker
1962	2d—Tagson	Pointer dog	Elhew Sharpshooter	Step Easy	R.G. Wehle	R.G. Wehle
	3d—Mike's Home Again	Pointer dog	Tag Me	Rico Paladin's Belles	Mrs. D.S. McClain	Earl C. Crangle
1963	1st—Blue Coast	Pointer dog	Mike's Delivery	Thorne	W.P. Snow	Fred Arant Jr.
	2d—Susie Mac	Pointer bitch	Rambling Rebel Dan	Belle Doone	A.R. Smith	Pete Smith
	3d—Carolina Magnolia	Pointer bitch	Rambling Rebel Dan	Country Nan	W.B. McCullough, Jr.	Fred Arant
1964	1st—Mingo	Pointer bitch	Rambling Rebel Dan	Homerun Sis	Martin C. Best and Leslie R. Tichenor	Fred Arant
	2d—Cross Over	Pointer dog	Homerun Robert	Annie's Graceful Girl	Leslie R. Tichenor and Martin C. Best	Fred Arant
	3d—Comstock	Pointer dog	Marquis Ghost	LaGrange City Girl	J.B. Bell and M.C. Best	Fred Arant
1965	1st—Resthaven Bill Again	Pointer bitch	Resthaven Spunky Bill	Crossup	Dr. F.S. McKnight	Lee Hoffman
	2d—Rambling Fastback	Pointer dog	Rambling Ramrod	Rambling Belle	H.A. Crane	Fred Arant
	3d—Coho	Pointer dog	Latham's White King	John Oliver's Susie	C.R. Scarborough	Fred E. Bevan
1966	1st—Roz's Image	Pointer dog	Rambling Rebel Dan	Homerun Rozette	R.H. Morrison	Fred Arant Jr.
	2d—Amberjack	Pointer bitch	Warhoop's Dapper Dick	Tani's Speedy	S.R. Cline	Bob Lamb
	3d—Homerun Jim	Pointer dog	Homerun Johnny	Homerun Sis	E. John Asfeld	George W. Hodge
1967	1st—Storm Glider's Jess	Pointer dog	Mr. Glider	Jennie Gal	W.H. Wimmer	Fred Arant
	2d—Knight's Country Dude	Pointer dog	Riggins White Knight	Bar Lane Dot	Bill Coates	Phil Brousseau
	3d—Towery's Rambling Pat	Pointer bitch	Snowhill Rambling Bob	Bar Lane Sue	Clem R. Vaught	Fred Arant
1968	1st—Toronado's Star	Setter bitch	Toronado	Sparkling Flame	Don Towery	Fred Arant Jr.
	2d—Spiritmaster	Pointer dog	La Strega	Hootenanny	E.A. DiMonte	George J. Bevan
	3d—Flying Heels Bob	Pointer dog	La Strega	Gwynedd Cathy	T.C. Manous	George J. Bevan
1969	1st—Double Rebel	Pointer dog	A Rambling Rebel	Hollybourne Cricket	Lloyd Reeves	Fred Arant Jr.
	2d—Flush's Image	Pointer dog	Paladin's Royal Flush	Drug's Jane Delivery	C.R. Scarborough	Orin Brown
	3d—Double Rebel Dan	Pointer dog	A Rambling Rebel	Hollybourne Cricket	Roger Kyes	Fred Arant Jr.
1970	1st—Mister Dave	Pointer dog	Medallion Quail Finder	Tiny Wahoo's Louisa	W.S. Richardson	David Grubb
	2d—Conversation	Pointer bitch	Guy's Joe	Sabre Dance	E.C. Juntti	David Grubb
	3d—Gwynedd's Joy	Pointer dog	Spiritmaster	Gwynedd Cathy	R.H. Clark	George J. Bevan
1971	1st—Fast Astro Boy	Pointer dog	Fast Drug Delivery	Spunky's Space Nell	W.T. Holmes	David Grubb
	2d—Yankee Sentry	Pointer dog	Sentry	Radiant	Bernard Girard	Bill Conlin
	3d—Shalimar	Pointer dog	Sentry	Buie's Kate	William S. Cioffi	David Grubb
					W.T. Jowett	

AMERICAN FIELD QUAIL FUTURITY WINNERS

Year	Name	Breed & Sex	Sire	Dam	Owner	Handler
1944	1st—Oration	Pointer dog	Homerun Harrigan	Flying Girl	A.G.C. Sage	Clyde Morton
	2nd—Night Hawk	Pointer dog	Nightcap	Pilot's Blue Willing	A.G.C. Sage	Clyde Morton
	3rd—Rex Village Frank	Pointer dog	Rex Village Boy	Blue Willing Countess	J.L. Martin	E.B. Epperson
	4th—Torchbearer	Setter dog	Little Smoky	Peerless Tar Girl	D.B. McDaniel	Jack Harper
1945	1st—Bolero	Pointer dog	Nightcap	Tarantella	A.G.C. Sage	Clyde Morton
	2nd—Miss Nappie	Pointer bitch	Charlobart	Blue Willing Countess	Dr. M.W. Rigsbee	E.A. Weddle
	3rd—Big One	Pointer dog	Accolade	Titania	J.C. Ward	Ed Farrior
	4th—Luminary's Doctor Blue	Pointer dog	Luminary	Newman's Lady	B.G. Guinn	E.B. Epperson
1946	1st—Pandemonium	Pointer dog	Homerun Harrigan	Flying Girl	A.G.C. Sage	Clyde Morton
	2nd—Fain's Fleetfoot	Pointer dog	Suavity	Little June	Lamar Fain	Leon Covington
	3rd—Dr. Sam's Spartan	Pointer dog	Sam's Uptown Jack	Carolina Air Dot	Dr. S.O. Black	F.E. Bevan
	4th—Drug Topic	Pointer dog	Spot Robbin	Almon's Lady Shoals	Otis Brown	G.M. Lunsford
1947	1st—Tennessee Zev	Setter dog	Mississippi Zev	Mohawk's Peerless Kate	W.L. Nichol	J. Earl Bufkin
	2nd—Westerner	Pointer dog	Ariel	Miss McMeda	A.G.C. Sage	Clyde Morton
	3rd—Ariel's Louisiana Lou	Pointer bitch	Ariel	Saturna	E.B. Smith	B.F. Epperson
	4th—Penafore Rahn	Pointer dog	Air Pilot Sammy	Titan's Susanna	G.R. Feltman	Ray Smith
1948	1st—Kilsyth Forshalee Rocky	Pointer dog	Darby's Tip	Forshalee Kay's Kate	Mrs. G.M. Livingston	G.A. Evans
	2nd—Jhok	Pointer dog	Tyson	Gold Flame	M.F. Mitchell	Howard Kirk
	3rd—Ariel Hobo Joe	Pointer dog	Ariel	Miss Dress Parade	William Welch	John H. Parker
	4th—Desperado	Pointer dog	Bonsoir	Spunky's Spunkylette	T.H. Mofield	T.M. Lunsford
1949	1st—Fast Air Delivery	Pointer dog	Fast Delivery	Delivery Boy's Girl	A.B. Bobbitt	Paul Walker
	2nd—Mobile's King Fish	Pointer dog	Warlock	Lullaby Willing Girl	G.L. Donoghue	C.W. House
	3rd—Cross Spring	Pointer dog	Field Judge	Bettie Shanks	George Suttle	Ed Mack Farrior
	4th—Bart	Pointer bitch	Charlobart	Ware's Maryland Marge	A.R. Dahl	John Thompson
1950	1st—Satilla Wahoo Pete	Pointer dog	Satilla Sam	Fisher's Wahoo Mary	Leonard Waldron	J.S. Gates
	2nd—Ariel Hobo's Becky	Pointer bitch	Ariel Hobo Joe	Airacobra's Little Joe	William Welch	John Parker
	3rd—Beelertown Lady	Pointer bitch	Sammy's Air Pilot	The Lancaster Gal	Dr. R.B. Baird Jr.	W.C. Lawson
	4th—Merry Apple Jack	Pointer bitch	Faraway	Lady Mac McCord	G.W. Crews	G.A. Evans
1951	1st—Kilsyth Dynamite Goodloe	Pointer dog	Shore's Brownie Doone	Kilsyth Delivery Dot	Mrs. G.M. Livingston	Earl Crangle
	2nd—Rumson Farm Hayride	Pointer dog	Louisiana Hayride	Nightcap's Aurora	Raymond Hoagland	F.W. Frazier
	3rd—Tyrolean	Pointer dog	Tyson	Surracho's Spunky Girl	R.W. Norman	J.S. Gates
	4th—Top Cadet	Pointer dog	Fast Delivery	Spunky's Spunkylette	H.E. Weil	John H. Gardner
1952	1st—Crafty	Pointer dog	Knockdown	Weiser's Winnie	John H. Gardner	John S. Gates
	2nd—Mercer Millrace	Pointer dog	Greenwood Bill	Sheila's Dot	B.C. Goss	Ray Smith
	3rd—Equity's Tennessee Lady	Setter bitch	Tennessee Zev	Miss Dixie Henson	R.K. Dinning	Lee Worstell
	4th—Paho	Pointer bitch	Drug News	Wahoo's Aviatrix	Bruce Lewis	Frank Dimke
1953	1st—Storm Trooper	Pointer dog	Stormy Mike	Bettie Shanks	B. McCall	Paul Walker
	2nd—Builder	Pointer dog	The Haberdasher	Bonsoir's Lady Jill	Dr. H.E. Longsdorf	George A. Evans
	3rd—Kilsyth Georgia Rebel	Pointer dog	Shore's Brownie Doone	Kilsyth Delivery Dot	Mrs. G.M. Livingston	John S. Gates
	4th—Greenwood's Ghost	Pointer dog	Greenwood Bill	Luminist	H.M. Beattie	Paul Walker
1954	1st—Fast Delivery Belle	Pointer bitch	Fast Delivery	Nightcap Girl	Miss Murtis L. Carver	Herman Smith
	2nd—The Tuxedo Queen	Pointer bitch	Satilla Wahoo Pete	Luminary's Jane	F.M. Cassell	Frank Dimke
	3rd—Stormy Voyage	Pointer bitch	Stormy Mike	Tip's Jane	B. McCall	John Gardner
	4th—Homestake	Pointer bitch	Knockdown	Wings Away	W.A. Howell	Ed Farrior
1955	1st—John Storm	Pointer dog	Stormy Mike	Dandy Bow	B. McCall	Jack Harper
	2nd—Knockout	Pointer dog	Knockdown	Guion's Penny	William Cox	E.B. Epperson
	3rd—Hattie of Arkansas	Pointer bitch	Running W Wrangler	Ranger Bows	Mrs. G.B. Oliver	Herman Smith
	4th—Riggins Spunky Pete	Pointer dog	Ranger's Spunky Pete	Riggins Lady Saturn	Friel M. Cassell	Ed Farrior
1956	1st—Warhoop Storm	Pointer dog	Warhoop Jake	Storm's Kate	B. McCall	Ed Farrior
	2nd—Le Baron	Pointer dog	Satilla Wahoo Pete	Sheila's Dot	S.H. Vredenburgh	E.M. Farrior

Year	Place & Name	Breed	Sire	Dam	Owner	Handler
1957	3rd–Chuckaluck	Setter dog	Sam L's Skyhigh	Taylor's Peerless Lou	C.H. Kinnard	Bill Taylor
	4th–Drug Queen	Pointer bitch	Greenwood Bill	Pete's Wahoo Bell	W.L. Lane and C.D. Duke Jr.	E.M. Farrior
	No Champion					
1958	1st–Medallion II	Pointer dog	Medallion	Stanton's June	Dr. W.B. Griffin	John S. Gates
	2nd–The Prodigy	Pointer bitch	Fast Delivery	Paladin's Swan	A.B. Bobbitt	Paul Walker
	3rd–Maelstrom	Pointer dog	Sarasota	Peter's Stormy Girl	Edwin Brown	John S. Gates
	4th–Hollier's Hayride	Pointer dog	Fred Hayride	Dot Spunky Creek	J.O. Carter	W.L. Cosner
1959	1st–Gunsmoke's Jewel	Pointer bitch	Gunsmoke	Santee Susan	Dr. T.J. Lattimore	John S. Gates
	2nd–Dixie Springtime	Pointer bitch	Medallion	Sugarplum	M.W. Ramage Jr.	John S. Gates
	3rd–Lucy's Lad	Pointer dog	Sarasota	Pete's Wahoo Bell	H.E. Weil	John S. Gates
	4th–Bouncing Babe	Pointer bitch	Porter's	Princess Pat	E.T. Thatcher	Ray Smith
1960	1st–Riggins White Knight	Pointer dog	Major Lexington Boy	Stanley's Candy	R.W. Riggins	D. Hoyle Eaton
	2nd–Ranger Satilla Dot	Pointer bitch	The Arkansas Ranger	Satilla's Omega Dot	Dr. H.R. Foreman	Ray Smith
	3rd–Wayriel Ben	Pointer dog	Wayriel Allegheny Sport	Tyran	George M. Davis	Roy D. Jones
	4th–Misty Morn	Pointer bitch	Tyfame's Kentucky Rufus	Delight	J.H. Hurdle	J. Nathan Cottrell Jr.
1961	1st–Gunsmoke's Yon Way	Pointer dog	Gunsmoke Titanup's	Windy Way	J.D. Bayer	Howard Kirk
	2nd Berol's Wrangler Sum	Pointer dog	Tiny Wahoo	Wrangler's Village Linda	Berol Kennels	Bob Lee
	3rd–Satilla Midnight Imp	Pointer bitch	Satilla Midnight Sun	Lady's Bess	Dr. Frank M. Phillipi	Don Dixon
	4th–Little Dandy	English setter dog	The Arkansas Fury	Security May	G.L. Morris Jr.	Ray Smith
1962	1st–War Exterminator	Pointer dog	War Storm	Sugarplum	Chester C. Coon	John S. Gates
	2nd–Jemador	Pointer dog	Holly Lyn Joe	Fantasy Pat	County Animal Hospital	John H. Gardner
	3rd–Look On	Pointer dog	Forward Look	Survivor's Wahoo Lou	Mrs. R.K. Archbell	Ray Smith
	4th–Dark Secret	Pointer dog	Wayriel Allegheny Sport	Ranger's Spunky Belle	Joe W. Bales	George Bevan
1963	1st–Fast Jake	Pointer dog	Fast Drug Delivery	Renfro Delivery Girl	A.B. Bobbitt	Paul Walker
	2nd–Broomhill	Pointer dog	Hedgerow	Mercer Miller	Dr. H.H. Vaughan	John Rex Gates
	3rd–Gwynedd Bill	Pointer dog	Haberdasher's Stormy Hayride	Stormy Tyke	W.T. Holmes	George Bevan
	4th–Rambling Nellie	Pointer bitch	Rambling Rebel Dan	Doug's Pepper	C.R. Scarborough	Fred Arant
1964	1st–Doctor's Stormy Mack	Pointer dog	Storm's Romance	Lynes Fast Judy	Dr. D.E. Hawthorne	E.B. Epperson
	2nd–Timberline Becky	Pointer bitch	Paladin's Royal Heir	Sugarplum	Bunny Lynes	M.G. Lynes
	3rd–Sugarshack	Pointer bitch	War Storm	Medallion's Kitty	Tom Peacock	Bob Lamb
	4th–Our Nominee	Pointer dog	Riggins White Knight	Deep Run Dot	Ray N. Barto	Dexter Hoyle Eaton
1965	1st–Stuart's Rambling Rebel	Pointer dog	Rambling Rebel Dan	Bar Lane Dot	Guy H. Lewis	Fred Arant
	2nd–Knight's Automation	Pointer bitch	Riggins White Knight	Hedgeline	R.W. Riggins	Dexter Hoyle Eaton
	3rd–Royal Flush's Hotshot	Pointer dog	Paladin's Royal Flush	Karen's Dapple Sue	R.H. Hays	John Rex Gates
	4th–Crewman	Pointer dog	David of Arkansas	Homerun Sis	W.H. Jarrett	G.W. Rodgers
1966	1st–Homerun Jim	Pointer dog	Homerun Johnny	Renfro Delivery Lady	W.H. Wimmer	Fred Arant, Jr.
	2nd–Drug's Joe Delivery	Pointer dog	Fast Drug Delivery	Jacqueline	A.B. Bobbitt	Paul Walker
	3rd–Warhoop Dapper Jack	Pointer dog	Warhoop's Dapper Dick	Berol's Seariup Girl	O.N. Bennett	Herman Smith
	4th–Berol's Muffin Man	Pointer dog	Vandetta	Baconrind's Sandy	Henry Berol	Bob Herrington
1967	1st–Oklahoma Flush	Pointer dog	Paladin's Royal Flush	Renfro Delivery Lady	Dr. I.J. Hammond	John Rex Gates
	2nd–Bud's Dan	Pointer dog	Fast Drug Delivery	Ranger's Wayriel Sue	W.W. Williamson Jr.	George J. Bevan
	3rd–Flop's Man	Pointer dog	Palamonium's Big Parade	Baconrind's Sandy	L.H. Morrison Jr.	John Gardner
	4th–Paladin's Royal Gold	Pointer bitch	Paladin's Royal Flush		K.L. Keesee	John Rex Gates
1968	1st–Jorwick's Papa J	Pointer dog	Jorwick's Dixiecrat	Jorwick's Delilah	G.G. Jordan	Collier Smith
	2nd–Spiritmaster	Pointer dog	La Strega	Hootenanny	T.C. Manous	G.J. Bevan
	3rd–Doctor's Stormy Rex	Pointer dog	Doctor's Stormy Mack	Moneymaker	Dr. F.D. Coffield	E.B. Epperson
	4th–Beth's White Knight	Pointer dog	Riggins White Knight	Misty Morn	H.T. Ingram	Collier Smith
1969	1st–Homerun Buddy	Pointer dog	Homerun Johnny	Homerun Sis's Dot	Claudia L. Phelps	Fred Arant, Jr.
	2nd–Doctor I J	Pointer dog	Riggins White Knight	Survivor's Ranger Katie	Dr. I.J. Hammond	D.H. Eaton
	3rd–Miller's Miss Star	Setter bitch	Flaming Star	Miller's Miss Coon	Anthony Imbesi	Collier Smith
	4th–Flush's Image	Pointer dog	Paladin's Royal Flush	Drug's Jane Delivery	R.M. Kyes	Bud Brown

Year	Placement	Breed	Sire	Dam	Owner	Breeder
1970	1st—Hiway	Pointer dog	Gunset	Silencer	D.C. Sharp	Ernest Allen
	2nd—Red Water Tex	Pointer dog	Red Water Rex	Arkansas Texas Sally	S.E. Austin	Faye Throneberry
	3rd—Endeavor	Pointer bitch	The Matador	Frostoria	David H. Myers	Bud Daugherty
	4th—Orion Flush	Pointer dog	Sandstorm Jake	Ripley Creek Ranee	Dr. O.D. Thompson	John Rex Gates
1971	1st—Haberdasher's Heir	Pointer dog	Melody Heir	Stormy Becky	Dr. W.H. McCall	John Rex Gates
	2nd—Cardinal	Pointer bitch	Red Water Rex	Arkansas Flashie Flush	W.H. Jarrett	Roy D. Jines
	3rd—Red Water Dawn	Pointer dog	Red Water Rex	Sudan Smokey Dawn	Ray & Charlotte Lenz	John Gardner
	4th—Fast Astro Boy		Fast Drug Delivery	Spunky's Space Nell	Bernard Girard	David Grubb

FOOTBALL

Football, first played in the United States in 1869, has become the nation's No. 1 autumn sport. Hundreds of colleges and thousands of high schools play each Saturday. The National Football League, had grown to 14 member clubs in the early 1960s, played a schedule of 14 season games following a pre-season list of five contests each. It was divided into two conferences and the winners of these groups met for the championship, usually on the first Sunday after Christmas. These championships were carried on coast-to-coast television and had an audience estimated near 50 million.

Millions more watch college and professional games on television each week.

For the fourth time since the birth of the N.F.L., another league, this time the American Football League, was attempting to challenge the parent league. Previous leagues had been the American Football League of 1926, built around Harold "Red" Grange; the American League of 1936-37; the All America Football Conference of 1946-49.

Professional football was blessed with an endless supply of able players produced by the colleges at no expense to the professional teams. In return, the N.F.L. had always stuck to a policy of refraining from luring football players away from school until each player's class had graduated. This maintained a friendly relationship not enjoyed by professional baseball which had made a habit of breaking up the education of many young baseball players.

Players range from the 270-pound tackles in the professional league to the undersized 7-year-olds using a home-made football on the sandlots. Professional salaries range as high as $100,000 a year, with the average in the neighborhood of $20,000.

Football, as we know it today, is a far cry from its parent game, soccer, which originated in England about the 11th Century. Where football may have been played earlier, if at all, is left to the guesswork of historians.

One of that group reached the conviction that the ancient Greeks played football under the name of harpastum. That's about as much as the guess embraces. Nothing is said as to the rules or form of play. The game is supposed to have originated in Sparta, have been adopted by the Romans and banned by a ruler of Rome about the dawn of the Christian Era.

Since the Greeks, and then the Greeks and the Romans, indulged in Olympic Games for many centuries, in which they featured the sports known to those times, it is rather strange that football—if it existed—never found its way to any Olympic program. Nor was it ever mentioned as a means of contest between the rival nations at any time. Beyond one nonchalant mention by a historian, it has no place in history.

It has been declared by the historian who "discovered" football in long-ago Greece that, after acceptance of the sport by the Romans, it was ruled out by Augustus Caesar, first emperor of Rome (63 B.C.—14 A.D.), as being too "gentle" a game to fit soldiers for war. Nowhere is such an edict officially credited to Augustus. It does not seem to be written anywhere in ancient history that warriors were trained for battle by indulgence in sport games. That's a modern procedure.

Therefore, the game credited to the Greeks, lacking anything more than passing mention by one historian, might have been a game of fancy—not fact.

The second mention given to football as an "ancient game" is by Dr. E. Norman Gardiner, in his volume "Athletics of the Ancient World," published by the Oxford University Press in England, in which he quotes the following from papers written, perhaps in the late 19th Century, by Prof. H.A. Giles:

"An old Chinese writer, speaking of the town of Lin-tzu, says there were none among its inhabitants who did not perform with pipes, or some string instrument, fight cocks, race dogs, or play football."

Since "football" comes from the English of "futeballe," the Chinese, if they ever did play football, had another word for it. What that word was escaped Professor Giles. The professor quoted the writings of a Chinese poet, in which the poet referred to the game as "football." Whether he actually called it "football," or by some Chinese name, which the professor translated into "football," is not clear.

It was stated by Professor Giles that the ball used was round, made of 8 pointed strips of leather, filled with hair, and that footballs, filled with air, were introduced in 500 A.D.

The findings of Professor Giles must be astonishing to other historians. First of all, he credits natives of exactly one town in ancient China indulging in the game. China, neither ancient nor modern, ever gave much of its time to games that were combative. The Chinese, even in these days, while indulging in a few competitive games, generally skip the combative. It is, seemingly, an inherited dislike, come down through the centuries. Yet Professor Giles had Chinese indulging in football at a time when no other nation was devoting itself to the game, if one excludes the fanciful play credited to Greece.

What makes the Giles "discovery" most remarkable is that he learned about something that was going on in China through at least 8 centuries (300 B.C. to 500 A.D.), which has escaped the thousand and one men who devoted themselves to search into the past history of China. Giles, and Giles alone, found football in China. Can Giles be right—and all the others wrong?

The professor does not say why football disappeared from China without a trace—and lacked a trace, during those 800 years, that eluded all other searchers. There is nothing in Chinese art, literature or anything else come down from ancient centuries as proof that the Chinese ever played at football, which is a game of no interest to the modern Chinese.

Authentic history has it that some few years after the Danes vacated England, which they had occupied from about 1016 to 1042, workmen, excavating an old battlefield, uncovered a skull that undeniably was that of a Dane. These men, like all English, still smouldering with memories of Danish imperialism, kicked at the skull to show their feelings. Then all the others took to kicking the skull back and forth, and work actually was neglected while the boot was being applied to the defunct Dane's head.

Boys, seeing this, sensed a new form of diversion. They dug around and also found a skull. Some boys were barefoot; others wore shoes none too stout. The concussion caused by kicking voided their anticipated pleasure, but they retained the idea, and shortly thereafter one of the boys appeared with an inflated cow bladder and, thus, the basic principle of football was born.

Football, beginning between 1050 and 1075, found quick favor among the English. Perhaps that was because the natives came to regard each inflated bladder as the skull of a hated Dane, and they could kick it savagely without the aftermath of bruised toes.

Entering the 12th Century, football, without any basic rules, became something with mob-scene embroidery. Players of adjacent towns would meet at some midway spot. The bladder would be thrown down, as a signal for action, and then, with scores, and sometimes hundreds of players on each side, action would get under way. Apparently the rules provided that the team was winner which kicked the ball into the middle of the rival town. Play was accompanied by lusty yelling, and it is written that when victorious players came charging into small towns, kicking the football through the main streets, the non-combatant villagers became terrified. Shop keepers closed their stores and shoppers remained indoors until the tumult and shouting had died.

The authorities were asked to halt this random, roving game with its extra high jinks, lest the hoydenish fellows knock down small buildings, as well as fleeing pedestrians. The disciples of this game of "kicking the Dane's head" were commanded to confine their activity to a vacant area, or abandon the sport entirely.

That marked the beginning of standardization of the game. A field was marked off with boundaries somewhat similar to those governing soccer today. A point was scored whenever the ball was kicked over the goal line of the other team. The rules did not fix the number of players, but it was stipulated that "both sides must have an approximately equal number of players," and that meant anywhere from 19 to 50 on a side, depending upon how many craved action.

Until then the game had no definite name. It was called "kicking the Dane's head," "kicking the bladder" and similar descriptions. But in the 12th Century, it officially became "futballe" and soon its popularity exceeded that of many sports of early England. In fact, so many English indulged in "futballe," to the exclusion of all else during leisure hours, that King Henry II (1154—1189) became alarmed because his subjects were neglecting the compulsory practice of archery. He ordered "futballe" performers to "cease playe" and accomplished his purpose when he threatened imprisonment, not only for the performers, but also for the owners of land whereon the barred game was played.

So effective was King Henry's order that at the time of his death in 1189 football was little more than a fragrant memory. The ban was continued by succeeding rulers for more than 400 years, but because of the tolerance of certain monarchs, the game was played occasionally and, thus, the principles of the sport passed from one generation to another.

Early in the 16th Century some Irishmen in Dublin, ignoring the rule in England concerning football, created what is known today as Gaelic football. This emboldened the English to resume play at "futballe," but it was done furtively for many decades, until the ascent to the English throne in 1603 of James I of the House of Stuart.

By that time, firearms had succeeded archery as a superior means of attack in warfare. There was no further need for the subjects to sharpen up on bow and arrow practice. When an appeal was made to James to revoke the law of Henry and permit "futballe playe," James not only lifted the bars, which had been down for more than 4 centuries, but also gave the game his blessing. He said that he regarded football as a clean, honorable and manly pastime; one that tended to develop character, as well as the physical self, and that he sincerely hoped that England would resume football play with enthusiasm.

England did just that—and more. Football teams came into existence everywhere. Cities, towns and villages became famous—or otherwise—depending upon the prowess of their football teams. There was no national governing association, but play was reasonably standardized and where there was conflict in rules when different town teams faced each other, this was bridged by mutual agreement between the captains.

Football, from its start in England in the 11th Century until the middle of the 19th Century, was strictly a kicking game, first merely across a goal line. In the later years of revival, goal posts and cross bars came into existence. Picking up and running with the ball was barred and never happened until the year 1823 with the appearance of William Ellis of Rugby College. (See rugby chapter for details.)

Originally, football was the term used to describe a game by which a ball was propelled by the foot alone. The game created, unconsciously, by Ellis, became known as rugby, to distinguish it from the original sport. When rugby became increasingly popular in England, the advocates of the original game met and ruled to adhere strictly to kicking. In time, such game became known as "soccer." (See soccer chapter for details.)

While the English were enjoying football in the Middle Ages, the Irish, deciding they would like such a form of sport but regarding the English game as a bit too tame, devised their own style of play, which now is known as Gaelic football. It probably is the roughest football

game. (See Gaelic football chapter for details.) Early in the 19th Century, the third method of playing football was brought about by Ellis, as mentioned above.

The next football style came about when American collegians blended soccer with rugby and added some methods of play that made it a game apart from all others.

The Canadians play at soccer and rugby, but created a game of their own that departs from both soccer and rugby and is called Canadian football. The Australians also originated a distinct method.

In recent years another manner of football play was introduced in the United States, designed for youngsters. It calls for teams of 6 players, instead of the usual 11, and operates under rules that are intended to prevent mass plays.

So, the off-shoots of the original game, which started in England more than 900 years ago, are:

American Football (College and Professional)
6-man Football
Australian Rules Football
Canadian Football
Gaelic Football
Rugby
Soccer

American College Football

American football exists today because of McGill University of Montreal, Canada, and the courtesy of Harvard, the host team at 2 football games in Cambridge, Mass., May 14 and 15, 1874.

At Harvard in the spring of 1871, a group of students got together and started to play, with the permission of President Elliot, what was called the "Boston Game." It was different from the informal, unorganized kicking game that had been banned by the faculty in the 1860's in that the ball—round, inflated and made of rubber—could be picked up at any time and the holder could run with it if pursued.

It also was different from the game that Princeton and Rutgers played in the first intercollegiate football game at New Brunswick, N.J., Nov. 6, 1869. That game was played under a modification of the London Football Association rules, with 25 men to a side, and was the game of soccer, in which no running with the ball is permitted and the ball may be advanced only by the foot, head or shoulder. Columbia, which joined Princeton and Rutgers in a series of games in 1870, and Yale, which was to enter the intercollegiate lists in 1872 in a game with Columbia, also played association football or soccer, with variations.

When, in the fall of 1873, Yale invited Harvard, Princeton, Columbia and Rutgers to a

convention at the Fifth Avenue Hotel in New York to draft a code of rules and organize the Intercollegiate Football Association, Harvard declined to attend. It refused because of the belief that the "Boston Game" was irreconcilable with the game the other 4 were playing.

It has been said that Harvard's decision was the most momentous in the history of football in the United States—that if it had accepted the invitation and gone along with Yale, Princeton, Columbia and Rutgers in the adoption of the code they drafted in New York, the American game would never have evolved and soccer would have been established as the intercollegiate sport.

The rules drafted at the Fifth Avenue Hotel on Oct. 19, 1873, were based on the "association" style of game. They were patterned upon those adopted by the Princeton Foot Ball Association on its organization Oct. 15, 1871, and the Yale Football Association, formed Oct. 31, 1872.

Harvard, which organized its own Foot Ball Club Dec. 3, 1872, for games between classes, had to look elsewhere than to Yale, Princeton, Columbia and Rutgers for intercollegiate competition because of rules differences. So it welcomed a proposal that came from McGill University for a series of games. Two games were played in the spring of 1874 at Cambridge and a third at Montreal in the fall. It was agreed that the first of the 2 at Cambridge should be played under Harvard's rules and the second under McGill's rules, which were the rules of the English game of rugby.

So, on May 15, 1874, the game of rugby was introduced to the United States at Cambridge. This was an historic date in American football. Following upon Harvard's refusal to attend the 1873 convention that adopted a soccer code, the game with McGill set the stage for the evolution of football as played in the United States—a game distinctly American and not British.

The Harvard rules for the "Boston Game" permitted a player to pick up the ball at any time and also to run with it if pursued, as has been noted above. But, as William R. Tyler of the class of 1874 wrote in the "Harvard Advocate": "There were many points of difference from the rugby game. It (Harvard's game) was eminently a kicking, as distinguished from a running and tackling, game. The rules ... existed only in tradition. We went to work to learn the rugby game, but I should question if there were 3 men in college who had ever seen the egg-shaped ball. ... A dropkick was an unknown and almost incredible feat, and the intricacies of 'off side,' 'free kick,' 'put out' and such commonplaces of the game seemed inextricable mysteries to novices like us."

The first game at Cambridge, played under Harvard rules, resulted in victory for the home team, 3 goals to 0. The second, under rugby rules, ended in a scoreless tie. It was agreed to play 15 men on a side, but 4 members of the McGill team were unable to make the trip at the last minute and there were only 11 to a side.

The results were unimportant. The significant thing was that Harvard liked the rugby game so much that it adopted the rugby rules. Yale and Princeton in turn followed Harvard's action. So the battle was won that was to decide the pattern of a new game—a game stemming from rugby but gradually, step by step, departing from rugby in the evolution reflecting American inventive genius and characteristics.

As enthusiasm for the new rugby game grew at Harvard there awakened a desire to play Yale. On Oct. 16, 1875, representatives of the 2 colleges met at Springfield, Mass., and agreed upon the "Concessionary Rules." Under these the first game in what was to become and remain for many years the classic of the gridiron was played on Nov. 13, 1875. The game was largely rugby, with Harvard agreeing to certain changes of a soccer nature and Yale conceding to play 15 men on a side instead of the 11 it advocated. Yale had fielded elevens since it met a visiting English team from Eton in the first international football match played in this country in 1873, winning by 2 goals to 1. The game marked the first time 11 men had played on a side.

Harvard defeated Yale, 4 goals to 0, and Yale,

won over to the rugby game, adopted it in 1876. In their meeting that year Harvard agreed to Yale's request for 11-man teams but finally the number was changed to 10. This time the Elis won, 1 goal to 0.

Two Princetonians were observers at the first Harvard-Yale game and became sold on rugby. With much effort they persuaded their college to switch to this game and Princeton adopted it in early November, 1876. More than that, it sent invitations to Yale, Harvard, Rutgers and Columbia, inviting them to join Princeton in a convention at Springfield. There, at Massasoit House, on Nov. 23, 1876, the code of the Rugby Union was adopted with some changes and a new Intercollegiate Football Association was formed.

So the die was cast for rugby rather than soccer, and shortly the evolution from rugby into the American game was to get under way. It started in 1880 with the appearance of the quarterback and the substitution of scrimmage for the English scrum, the reduction of the players from 15 to 11 to a side and the naming of the team positions. Then came the establishment of downs and the origin of the use of signals in 1882. These were the forerunners of the far-reaching changes and innovations having to do with blocking, tackling, forward passing, shifts and formations that were to bring forth a game of such speed, skill and clever strategic maneuvers as to establish football as by far the king of intercollegiate sports throughout the land and bring millions of spectators into the stadiums annually.

It is not definitely established when football under soccer rules was imported into the United States. A form of association football, with ill-defined rules and no set number of players, was among the pastimes of townspeople and schoolboys in the Eastern United States until colonial days. Herbert Manchester, in his book, "Four Centuries of Sport in America," disclosed that some species of football was played at both Harvard and Yale as far back as the 1820's, but it was more a means to "haze" freshmen than regulation play. It appears that the newcomers at each school were forced into what might be called a football game by the sophomores. The "freshies" were supposed to kick the ball. The sophs made a habit of missing their kicks at the ball and kicked the newcomers instead. The agitated "freshies" soon were kicking back, and this brought about a lot of "class-day" injuries.

The authorities at both schools took cognizance of this and in the 1830's forbade such "games." Football then lapsed, so far as the records are concerned, until after the Civil War, and in 1869 Princeton and Rutgers met in the first intercollegiate game at New Brunswick, N.J., as mentioned previously.

But it was, meanwhile, known as a sport and was played in the United States between the

1830's and 1869. Henry Chadwick, called the "Father of American Baseball," wrote a booklet in 1866 for the "Dime Library," published by Beadle and Co. of New York, in which he outlined rules for play at football, as well as cricket. Chadwick touched not only on soccer, but also on rugby; but no heed was paid to rugby by the colleges, the soccer game being preferred.

A woodcut is in existence showing the First Maryland Regiment playing a game, undoubtedly soccer, at Camp Johnson in Winchester, Va., in 1861, with almost the entire regiment participating. The field was full of players. There are no details as to the kind of game, rules, or the outcome. This cut alone is proof that the game did exist, in some fashion, prior to the Princeton-Rutgers saga that was written in 1869.

Rutgers defeated Princeton, 6 to 4, in that first collegiate game, at soccer rules, Nov. 6, 1869—Rutgers' last victory over the Tigers until 1938. Princeton was unwilling to take the Nov. 6 result as a criterion of football worth between the colleges and challenged for a return match, Nov. 13, 1869, which Rutgers accepted.

Princeton won the return match, 8-0.

Princeton went into the second game, making full use of a blood-chilling cry that was a result of the Civil War. It was a rebel yell, which the Confederates had called upon when going into battle with the Union Army. The Princetons figured it might frighten the Rutgers athletes, if properly vocalized, at psychological moments, and perhaps it did. Anyway, when a play was about to get into motion, or had gone into motion, Princeton called on its yell, which had been classified as a "Scarer," and emerged as victor by the score of 8 to 0.

Princeton, it appears, had used the yell in the first game, but without much luck. It interfered with their play, since it required a lot of breath, which the game also demanded. The wily Princetons schooled some of their fellow students in the rebel call before the second game began, and when the players ran out of wind, the few students from Princeton, who were on the sidelines, let loose.

This yelling was the beginning of the custom of cheering at football games, urging on one's team, and resulted, in time, in the fancy yells of today, plus the singing of songs intended to arouse the favored team to greater effort.

One of the quaint facts regarding the first Princeton-Rutgers game, in which William S. Gummere captained Princeton and William Leggett captained Rutgers, is that Judge Irving Hall Lane of Flemington, N.J., the last survivor of that 1869 game, sat in for the Princeton-Rutgers duel on Nov. 5, 1938, when Rutgers, after a lapse of 69 years, again defeated Princeton, 20–18. Judge Lane, then 87, died a few days later, but had lived long enough to see Rutgers conquer Princeton for the first time

since his own student days.

When the details of the first 2 Princeton-Rutgers games were wafted around, undergraduates along the Atlantic Seaboard became intrigued. Columbia put together a team in 1870 and played both Princeton and Rutgers that year—at soccer. There were no games in 1871. Yale organized in 1872 and scheduled 1 game, defeating Columbia, 3 goals to 0—at soccer.

Cornell organized for informal campus games early in 1873 and one of its students, corresponding with a friend at the University of Michigan, learned that Michigan had some footballers. This resulted in an exchange of challenges and agreement upon a game to be played on neutral ground—Cleveland—30 men to a side. Naturally, the students had to get permission to absent themselves from studies. When President White of Cornell had perused the request, he made the rather classic decision:

"I will not permit 30 men to travel 400 miles merely to agitate a bag of wind."

As stated, Princeton, Rutgers, Columbia and Yale held the first football meeting late in 1873, Harvard abstaining and playing its first intercollegiate game in 1874 with McGill. Stevens entered the lists in 1873, Tufts in 1874, City College of New York and Wesleyan in 1875, Pennsylvania in 1876 and Trinity College of Hartford in 1877. In 1878 Michigan appeared in the Middle West.

The new American Intercollegiate Football Association of 1876, with a pioneer membership of 5 colleges—Princeton, Rutgers, Columbia, Harvard and Yale—decided that autumn perhaps was better than the spring for such a rugged game as football, and the schedule was made for games in the fall of 1876. In addition, the members wrote out the first set of rules to govern the then-hybrid game and universal play that year deviated for the first time from the soccer of earlier seasons.

As time went on, the rules makers continually tinkered with the laws and, eventually, the game ceased to be a blend of soccer and rugby and became very definitely a distinct game, hardly related to the fundamental play of either soccer or rugby.

An accurate and amusing description of the evolution of football was given by the late John W. Heisman, a player of a long gone era, later a coach for 36 years and after that an athletic director until his death in 1936. Heisman wrote:

"I played football first in 1886 on a high school team in Western Pennsylvania. I was at Brown University in '87 and '88, and '89, '90 and '91 I played at Penn.

"The length of the field between goal lines in the old days was 110 yards, not 100, as at present. That made longer runs possible. There were no 5-yard stripe lines running across the field. There were no linesmen, and no line sticks. The referee kept track of distance by just dropping a handkerchief where he guessed the ball was last put into play. The players of both sides would slyly try to move that handkerchief, while some team-mate engaged the referee in a discussion of the rules. So we varied action by kicking a handkerchief, as well as a football.

"We had gotten down to 11 men on a team even so long ago as that, but, as a rule, teams carried only 4 substitutes, even while on a trip, and trips sometimes meant playing two or three games on successive days, so as to be sure to take in enough money at the gate to defray the expenses of the trip.

"The time of the playing halves of a game in those days was 45 minutes, not 30 minutes, 'as now. Furthermore, the game was not divided into quarters as now, so there is today a rest period we never had in the old days. Players of my time had to be real iron men, because we played 2 games each week—Wednesdays and Saturdays.

"Once a game started, a player could not leave unless he actually was hurt, or, at least, pleaded injury. Accordingly, whenever the captain wanted to put a fresh player into action he whispered, 'Get your arm hurt, or something.' In one game my captain whispered to me: 'Get your neck broke, Heisman.'

"We wore jerseys and shorts of great variety. We had no helmets or pads of any kind; in fact, one who wore home-made pads was regarded as a sissy. Hair was the only head protection we knew, and in preparation for football we would let it grow from the first of June.

"Many college men of that day, especially divinity and medical students, permitted their beards to grow. Often they were referred to as 'Gorillas.' The divinity students couldn't answer back—I mean, in the right way.

"We didn't have many sweaters in those days, but we all wore snug fitting canvas jackets over our jerseys. You see, the tackling in that day wasn't clean-cut, and around the legs, as it is today. All too often it was wild, haphazard clutching with the hands, and when runners wore loose garments they were often stopped by a defensive player grabbing a handful of loose clothing. Some players wore pants, or jackets, of black horsehair. When you made a fumbling grab, you lost your fingernails.

"In those pioneer years, arguments followed most every decision the referee made. The whole team took part, so that half the time the officials scarcely knew who was captain. More than that, every player was privileged to argue as much as he pleased with any and every player of the opposition. The player who was a good linguist always was a priceless asset.

"We practiced every afternoon as players do now, but as we had no forward pass in the game

then, we put in large chunks of time on sprinting and getting down field under punts. As a result of this I have no hesitation in saying our punting of those bygone years was decidedly better than what we witness today.

"Falling on the ball also was deemed a very important essential of a player's education. We had little concentrated work on practical tackling, or instruction in its technique. That was something we were supposed to figure out for ourselves, as it was much the same when it came to interference. But with or without special instruction, we were past masters at tackling around the neck. There was a rule against it but that rule was, I am sure, broken oftener than any other in the book.

"Line charging? Very little scientific thought had been put on that department of play before the dawn of the present century. Nearly all linesmen, as a rule, lined up squarely against those who played the same positions on the opposing team. They didn't crouch or squat or play low. They mostly stood bolt upright and fought it out with each other hammer and tongs, tooth and nail, fist and feet. Fact is, you didn't stand much chance of making the line those days unless you were a good wrestler and fair boxer.

"Certain ingenious plays featured early-day sport that were quite as startling and unique as is the forward pass of today. First was the flying wedge, invented in 1892 and brought out by Harvard. The play was promptly copied by almost every team in the country.

"Today we start the game with a kick-off, but in those days it was a fake kick, the center merely touching the ball to his toe and then tossing it back to a team-mate who ran with it while the rest of the team gave him what interference it could.

"In the flying wedge, however, 9 of the players of the team withdrew about 20 yards from mid-field and at a signal these 9, in two lanes, started simultaneously and at full speed, converging on a point indicated by the ball. By the time they arrived at the ball, they had worked up a stupendous mass momentum, and the interference they gave for the runner was something wonderful to behold, and terrible to stop.

"In 1894 Coach Woodruff, at Penn, drafted the principle of the flying wedge for his famous flying interference, which could be put into operation by the team that had the ball in every scrimmage down. This consisted in starting the tackle and end ahead of the snapping of the ball. They swung back together, between their line and the backfield, and then kept on to reinforce the work of their companion tackle and end, on the other side of the ball. Just before they hit the defensive line the ball went into play, and the results were again almost as disastrous to the defense as was the flying wedge. These 2 plays were quite as spectacular and thrilling as any that the modern game has produced. So unstoppable were they, however, that the Rules Committee was forced to legislate them out of existence within a few years in order to preserve the proper balance between offense and defense.

"One of the greatest drawbacks of the game 50 years ago was the fact that there was no neutral zone between the two scrimmage lines. There was only an imaginary scrimmage line drawn through the center of the ball. Naturally the rush line players of both teams were constantly striving to crowd this imaginary hair line, in order to get the jump on their opponents.

This led to endless wrangling between teams and officials as to how many players were a hair's breadth over this hair line on each down. This resulted in so much charging and counter-charging, pushing and wrestling, that it often took the quarterback a full minute to get the ball in play.

"Bert Walters, a former captain of Harvard, introduced in 1903 the idea of the present neutral zone—a great improvement.

"In the old days, players of one side were permitted to grab hold of their runners anywhere they could and pull, push or yank him along in any direction that would make the ball advance. Sometimes 2 enemy tacklers would be clinging to the runner's legs, and trying to hold him back, while several team-mates of the runner had hold of his arms, head, hair, or wherever they could attach themselves, and were pulling him in the other direction. I still wonder how some of the ball carriers escaped dismemberment.

"Some backs had leather straps, like valise handles, sewed or riveted on the shoulders of their jackets and on the hips of their trousers, so as to offer good handholds for their team-mates.

"Wouldn't it make your eyes pop out if you were attending a football game today and saw the defensive ends going out 30 or 40 feet from their adjacent tackle? Well, that's where defensive ends played in those days. Why? Because a defensive end was not asked, or expected, to do anything much beyond keeping the opposing runner from getting around his end. So they tried to take good care that it shouldn't happen, by playing so close to the boundary that the runner had to go out of bounds to pass them.

"We were allowed only 3 downs in those days, but were required to gain only 5 yards on those 3 tries.

"Whenever the ball went out of bounds it was not brought in 10 paces and put in play on that spot, as is the case nowadays. Instead, both rush lines faced each other at right angles to the boundary line. The man who had recovered the ball out of bounds brought it to the spot where it went out, and threw it out into the field of play with both sides scrambling to recover it."

Football of the 1880's and going into the 1890's put the stress on brawn. Since Yale and Harvard were important in football, the big youths of the nation, ready for a college career, usually chose those institutions, since it meant a chance to become a member of the champion squad. Those who passed up Yale and Harvard usually showed up at Princeton, Pennsylvania or Columbia, and such institutions became the abiding places of giants in an era when gigantic players meant possible football crowns.

In 1905, Penn was matched to meet Swarthmore, whose team was built around Bob Maxwell, a 250-pound lineman of high speed and great strength. Penn knew that victory over Swarthmore would be insured only if Maxwell were put out of commission early. So the word was out, "Get Maxwell," and the Penn players made a valiant effort, with 11 men concentrating on reducing Maxwell to wreckage at the earliest possible time. They took "dead aim" at the Swarthmore giant and submitted him to a merciless battering.

Maxwell stuck it out, but when he tottered off the field his face was a bloody wreck. Some photographer snapped him, and the photo of the mangled Maxwell, appearing in a newspaper, caught the attention of the then President Theodore Roosevelt. It so angered him that he issued an ultimatum that if rough play in football were not immediately ruled out, he would abolish it by executive edict.

The Rules Committee of Football, meeting in the winter of 1905—06 and determined to save the game, legalized the forward pass, even as it forbade some of the more dangerous scrimmages. The forward pass became legal with the start of the 1906 season and the game was somewhat revolutionized.

However, Columbia, one of the foremost among the football pioneers, abandoned the game as did many colleges along the Pacific Coast, where rugby was substituted in some instances, soccer in others. Although permitted to forward pass by the new regulations, the colleges along the Atlantic Seaboard rarely called the play into action. One of the first major colleges to use a forward pass was Yale, in 1906. Failing in all other offensive attempts against Harvard, it tried a forward pass. The play succeeded and Yale won, 6 to 0.

A Notre Dame team of pipsqueak size made the forward pass what it is today, after major colleges had slighted it as a possible weapon for something like 7 years.

Army had a gap in its 1913 schedule and was looking around for some "soft touch" to tune up its players for later contests against rugged foes. The Army schedule-maker heard about little-known Notre Dame and offered $1,000 to Notre Dame if it would care to meet Army. The little Western institution accepted, although $1,000 was just about enough to send 15 of its players from Indiana to West Point, N.Y.

Gus Dorais, quarterback, and Knute Rockne, an end for Notre Dame, worked at the Cedar Point (Ohio) vacation resort in the summer of 1913. Knowing the Army game was ahead and nursing a slim hope for victory, Dorais and Rockne practiced the forward pass on the beach of Lake Erie in their leisure hours. Dorais perfected himself as a pitcher and Rockne as a catcher. They had the trick down to a fine science when they returned to school in the autumn.

However, prior to the Army game, it was decided to school someone else in catching passes, since it was figured that if Rockne were the only receiver, he quickly would be smothered. Therefore, Pliska, a back, was tutored privately, and in due time Notre Dame moved on to West Point and took the field against the Army giants.

Dorais proceeded to put the forward pass into operation. His pitches baffled the Army men. Army players stood around helplessly for a while, then, with Dorais ready for a new offensive play, swirled around Rockne, who had been highly successful in ripping off tremendous yardage on aerials. Thereupon, Dorais passed to Pliska and continued to alternate his pitches, to the bewilderment of Army.

Notre Dame defeated Army, 35 to 13, and "made" the forward pass as an attacking weapon. Those young gentlemen also "made" Notre Dame as a football institution, and the rise of the college from football obscurity to greatness dates from that spectacular debut along the banks of the Hudson River.

The unexpected result of the Army-Notre Dame game did more to popularize football with the masses than any that had ever been played. It gave courage to the smaller colleges, whose squads were made up chiefly of light men. It demonstrated that a light team, using the pass, could fight on even terms with the bulky squads devoted to line play or hurricanic charges around the flanks. It ended the day when brawn was the determining factor in football conflict.

Pittsburgh, like Notre Dame, was virtually unknown in football until it specialized in the forward pass. It later hired the renowned Glenn (Pop) Warner as coach, and in 1916 Pittsburgh's team had such fine success that it gained rating as the national champion. Other small colleges —Washington and Jefferson, Centre (of Kentucky), etc.—depending upon a passing attack, leaped quickly into the rays of the national spotlight, and the era when "might is right" in American football passed into history.

The first college to number its football players was Washington and Jefferson in 1908. The idea was picked up from the practice of numbering track athletes. For some reason, Washington and Jefferson abandoned the system shortly there-

after and players were not numbered again until 1913, when Amos Alonzo Stagg made the experiment at University of Chicago. Prior to then, colleges generally took the attitude that the players were recognizable without numbers to the students and the graduates, and it didn't matter whether the other patrons at games knew who they were. The confusion in the minds of the spectators, who could not identify competing players, was augmented on rainy days when the players became so smeared with mud that even the rival uniforms lost distinguishing colors.

Since there were no loudspeakers and megaphones were not used and since few colleges used a scoreboard in any part of the grounds, spectators often left games not knowing who had made the scores and, on some occasions, not sure who had won the game. One reporter of the era became muddled during a closing play of a rather important game (Army–Navy) and flashed a game-winning touchdown for the wrong team. Repeatedly, backfield men who, long before, had retired to the benches, were credited with making touchdowns, or field goals, that were the work of their substitutes. Explanations of who made tackles during important plays rarely was attempted by writers, because few knew, as a certainty, who was in action.

The Chicago Daily News of Nov. 24, 1913, commenting on the numbering of Chicago players, stated:

"Numbering football players, the plan tried by Coach Stagg of the University of Chicago, proved a great success in its try-out in the Wisconsin game Saturday at Marshall Field. The Maroon players bore big white numbers on their backs and it was easy for spectators to distinguish which man took the ball on each occasion. Spectators were more than pleased with the manner in which the plan worked out."

Despite the action at Chicago and Pittsburgh, which delighted the patrons, the idea of numbering players was rejected for quite a few years by major colleges and did not become a general practice until the early 1920's.

Football moved along in popularity, gradually, until the first World War. Play during the progress of the conflict was abbreviated. At the war's conclusion, football became a prime favorite and the enormous crowds that turned out for stellar contests soon piled up sufficient treasury reserves to enable many colleges to build huge stadiums, which cost from $500,000 into the millions. But the sustained interest in the sport, even though seat prices were doubled and tripled in some instances, made it possible for colleges to pay all indebtedness, and to have enough surplus annually to support many other forms of sport in colleges which sports, because of small attendance, could not pay their own way.

The Yale Bowl, opened in 1914, was the most

magnificent structure of its kind in the world at the time. Many other stadiums were built after Yale had led the way, but not many have been of the true bowl shape, such as the plant at New Haven. Many have been on the horseshoe pattern. Some schools, in areas where big league baseball parks operate, decided against the expense of erecting their own stadiums and rent the baseball fields for important contests.

World War II affected football attendance considerably, as a result of transportation restrictions, but with the fighting ended before the 1945 football season began, the crowds returned in greater force than ever before. The 1949 attendance shattered all records at the autumnal sport, which in the long-ago generally attracted fewer than a corporal's guard of students, even though admission was free.

Shortly after the post-war boom in the sport, a new problem—television—arose. Since the development of video on a national basis, the authorities, notably the powerful National Collegiate Athletic Association, have imposed certain restrictions, such as permitting only one game to be televised nationally each Saturday during the regular season.

Although the majority claim that the televising of a big game is hurting the attendance at other games, a strong minority have made their presence felt. No satisfactory solution has come out of the controversy, which may go on for years. With or without television, large crowds generally have turned out to watch winning teams, a fact of life common to most team sports.

CHRONOLOGICAL HISTORY OF COLLEGE FOOTBALL

1869—Princeton and Rutgers pioneered intercollegiate football at New Brunswick, N.J., playing games on successive Saturdays—Nov. 6 and Nov. 13. Rutgers won the first, 6 to 4 and Princeton took the second, 8 to 0, both games under soccer rules.

1870—Columbia organized and played both Rutgers and Princeton—soccer rules.

1872—Yale created a football team and played one game, beating Columbia, 3 to 0—soccer rules.

1873—Late in year, Princeton, Rutgers, Columbia and Yale met and drafted a code, with soccer rules prevailing. Harvard declined to join.

1874 (May 14)—Harvard defeated McGill under "Boston Game" rules, 3 goals to 0, at Cambridge, Mass.

1874 (May 15)—Harvard played McGill University at rugby, introduced by McGill. The game ended in a 0—0 tie.

1875—Yale and Harvard met for the first time, and predominating "Concessionary Rules" were rugby, as advocated by Harvard. Harvard won, 4 goals to 0.

1876—American Intercollegiate Football Association created at Springfield, Mass., membership being Princeton, Rutgers, Columbia, Harvard and Yale. Yale claimed first championship, defeating Harvard, Columbia and Princeton, with E.V. Baker as Yale captain. Rules governing game were those of Rugby Union with changes. A goal was made equal to 4 touchdowns.

1877—15 players constituted a team, arranged as follows: 9 men on rush line, 1 quarterback, 2 halfbacks, 1 three-quarter back and 2 fullbacks. Length of game 90 minutes.

1878—It was decided that players were to discard tights and wear canvas pants and jackets.

1880—Number of players on a side reduced from 15 to 11 and names of the positions originated. Rugby "scrum" abandoned in favor of a crude scrimmage line, out of which has developed the modern scrimmage line. Position of the quarterback in the scrimmage created, placing him to receive snapback of the ball. He is forbidden to carry the ball. Playing field standardized at 110 x 53 yards, replacing original 140 x 70 yards.

1881—In case of a tie, 2 additional periods of 15 minutes each were ordered to be played.

1882—Introduction of the rule on "downs" and "yards" to gain, as follows: "If, on 3 consecutive downs, a team has not advanced ball 5 yards, or lost 10 yards, it must give up ball to other side at the spot where the final down is made." Signals originated this year. In beginning they consisted of sentences, later of letters beginning sentence. They became numbers in 1885. Teams standardized as follows: 7 forwards, 1 quarterback, 2 halfbacks, 1 fullback. Four touchdowns were given precedence over goal from the field; 2 safeties were made equal to touchdown.

1883—Reorganization of officials provided for 2 judges, 1 to be selected by each team, and 1 impartial referee, the latter's decree to be final.

1883—Numerical scoring introduced with these values: safeties, 1 point; touchdowns, 2 points; goal from touchdown, 4 points; goal from field, 5 points. Referee ordered to take out time for all unnecessary delays. Numerical scoring amended at end of 1884 season to make touchdown 4 points; safety, 2 points; goal after touchdown, 2 points. Origin of interference, then called "guarding."

1885—Harvard faculty prohibited football for the season.

1887—Pennsylvania and Rutgers met in an indoor football game, Madison Square Garden, New York, the first contest under such conditions.

1888—Rule prohibited blocking with extended arms; tackling extended to point below waist but not below knees.

1889—Walter Camp made first All-America selections.

1890—Yale team appeared wearing extra-long hair—first time this had been featured.

1894—Withdrawal of Harvard and Pennsylvania from association wrecked organization and football was without governing body. University Athletic Club of New York invited Harvard, Pennsylvania, Princeton and Yale to form a rules committee, which was done. It made elaborate revision of code. It was decided that officials should consist of an umpire, referee and linesman; length of game reduced from 90 minutes to 70 minutes, divided into 2 halves; no player should lay hands upon an opponent unless the opponent had ball, and that no play should be allowed in which more than 3 men started before ball was in play.

1895—American Intercollegiate Football Association disbanded.

1897—Point scoring changed to following: touchdown, 5 points; goal after touchdown, 1; field goal, 5, safety, 2.

1902—Teams required to change goals following a touchdown or goal from the field.

1904—Value of field goal reduced to 4 points.

1905—1906—Football sank to its lowest depths, owing to great number of deaths and crippling injuries resulting from mass plays where brute strength and great weight were the determining factors. Many college presidents either banned football or threatened to do so unless something was done immediately. Parents of many football players forbade them to play. President Theodore Roosevelt said game must be made safer. With the fate of the game hanging in the balance, football leaders met in the winter of 1905—06, ruled out practically all mass formations, prohibited hurdling, permitted the forward pass and other "safety" rules.

1906—Forward pass introduced. Officials to consist of referee, 2 umpires and linesman. Length of game reduced to 60 minutes, divided into 2 halves of 30 minutes each. Distance to gain on downs increased to 10 yards. First forward pass reported thrown by Wesleyan against Yale, with Moore passing and Van Tassel receiving. Yale overwhelmed Wesleyan despite it. In the same season, Yale is reported to have completed a pass against Harvard for a touchdown, Yale winning the game, 6 to 0, the pass constituting the only score.

1907—Office of field judge was created; one of the 2 umpires was eliminated.

1908—Washington and Jefferson occasionally numbered its players, a college innovation that was not continued as a regular thing at W. & J.

1909—Value of field goal reduced to 3 points—the rule today.

1910—Player withdrawn from game for any reason was permitted to return to play in subsequent period. Game divided into quarters of 15 minutes each, instead of old rule of 30-minute halves. Time out between first and second, and

third and fourth quarters fixed at 1 minute, with 30 minutes out for rest between halves.

1912—Teams allowed 4 downs to advance ball 10 yards instead of 3. Dimensions of field reduced to 100 yards with extra space of 10 yards behind each goal, the latter being zone in which forward pass might be legally caught by the offensive side. Kick-off, formerly delivered from middle of field, changed to the 40-yard line. Kick-off following a touchback removed from the 25-yard line to the 20-yard line. Value of touchdown increased from 5 to 6 points.

1913—Chicago players numbered in game against Wisconsin.

1915—Numbering of players started at University of Pittsburgh.

1917—Substitutes prohibited from talking with members of team upon the field until after completion of their first play.

1922—Ball put in scrimmage on 5-yard line for try for extra point. Previously try for extra point was made from where scorer crossed goal line.

1924—Kick-off made from middle of field. Players required to come to full stop on shift plays.

1925—Victor of toss given choice of receiving kick-off or kicking-off to opponent; 40-yard line again restored as line of the kick-off. Clipping forbidden. Walter Camp died.

1926—Penalty of down and loss of 5 yards imposed for incompleted forward passes after first one in same series of downs.

1927—Goal posts set 10 yards back of goal line. Time limit of 30 seconds placed on putting ball in play after it was ready for play. Limit of 15 seconds placed on "huddle." Pause of 1 second imposed on shift. Fumbled punt declared a dead ball.

1929—Run with fumble recovered by opposition prohibited. Try for point after touchdown made from scrimmage at 2-yard line.

1930—Backward passes and fumbles going out of bounds between goal lines awarded to team last touching ball.

1932—Ball became dead the instant any portion of the carrier, excepting hands and feet, touched the ground. Edward K. Hall, editor of the Football Guide, died.

1933—Side zone of 10 yards created. This applied when ball became dead; play was resumed 10 yards in from boundary. Clipping definition was made to include running into the back of a player not carrying ball.

1937—No second kick-off allowed if ball was kicked out of bounds between goal lines. Ball went into play on receiving team's 20-yard line. Rule required players to wear numerals on front as well as back.

1938—Side zone increased to 15 yards.

1939—Penalty for pass hitting ineligible player fixed at loss of down, plus 15-yard penalty.

1940—Time for putting ball into play, including huddle, fixed at 25 seconds, instead of 30. Penalty later fixed at 5 yards.

1941—Free substitutions permitted, except during last 2 minutes of first half.

1942—5-yard penalty for illegal delay of game.

1943—1944—No changes during war. During this period, about 350 colleges abandoned football for duration.

1945—Team making second consecutive kick-off out of bounds was penalized by opposition getting ball on its 40-yard line.

1946—Number of "times out" allowed each team increased from 3 to 4. Size of numerals worn by players ordered increased.

1947—Running shift eliminated.

1948—Use of tee for all place kicks legalized. Specify scrimmage at receiving team's restraining line after second out-of-bounds kick-off.

1949—New definition of clipping to protect the player below the waist only on blocks thrown from behind. Blockers required to keep fists against chest. Linemen on offense not to pass neutral zone on a forward pass until the pass was touched.

1950—The fair catch abolished. The use of elbows in offensive and defensive blocking curbed. The prohibition of flying blocks and tackles deleted.

1951—The fair catch restored—Player to signal intention by raising one hand clearly above head and waving it from side to side. The penalty for an illegal shift reduced to 5 yards.

1953—The free substitution rule dating from 1941 killed, ending the use of the "two-platoon" system that caused so much controversy following its introduction and the use of separate offensive and defensive elevens.

1953—Jim Thorpe, who in 1950 was voted the greatest football player in the half-century poll of The Associated Press, died.

1955—Substitution rule liberalized to permit a player who participated in the first down of a period then was withdrawn from the game to return once during that period. The four-minute segments at the end of each half were eliminated. Waving of hand no longer required in signal for fair catch.

1958—In the first change in scoring values since 1912, a team scoring a touchdown received the option of trying for a 1 or 2-point conversion. A successful place-kick or drop-kick on the conversion attempt was worth 1 point; a successful run or pass 2 points. The conversion attempt, formerly from the 2-yard line, was moved back to the 3. Substitution rule again liberalized to allow a player to enter the game twice each quarter. Offensive blockers restricted to use of "only one arm and that hand" while contacting opponent.

1959—At its January convention, the Rules Committee adopted the proposal to widen the goal posts by 4 feet 10 inches to 24 feet. The posts had been 19 feet 2 inches wide.

FOOTBALL WRITERS ASSOCIATION OF AMERICA

Press associations and newspapers have assigned writers to report football conflicts for almost fifty years. Although more writers and more radio and television sportscasters have been engaged during the last twenty years in reporting football than any other major sport, it was not until 1941 that the writers organized into an association, following in some degree the pattern set by the baseball writers, the boxing writers and the turf writers.

Bert McGrane of the Des Moines (Iowa) "Register," who is secretary of the organization, advised:

"The Football Writers Association of America was conceived Aug. 28, 1941. The foundation of the association was laid at that time, the complete structure introduced as a working organization Dec. 5, 1941.

"From a nucleus of 8 founders, the Football Writers Association of America numbered about 500 members at the close of the 1952 season. The phenomenal growth of the organization was accomplished in spite of the fact that the United States was at war within 2 days after the formal launching of the association.

"No major football game on the college front escapes the eyes of members of the association. Through most of the states, even in Honolulu, from the congested population centers through the more sparsely settled strongholds of football, the association is represented.

"Its purposes:

"1. To promote the best interests of football.

"2. To encourage and recognize outstanding achievements in sportsmanship, in play, coaching, sports writing, or in other fields contributing to the advancement of the game, by awarding trophies or citations for exceptional performance.

"3. To standardize the forms and methods in the compilation of football statistics.

"4. To secure better facilities and better regulation of working conditions in the football stadia pressboxes.

"5. To bring closer friendship among the writers of football throughout the United States.

"6. To promote, through the mutual exchange of opinions and viewpoints and otherwise, better understanding and harmony between the football writers as a group and those with whom they work, the coaches, players, athletic directors, publicity directors, faculty representatives, conference commissioners and others.

"Football's Man of the Year was the first award of the Football Writers Association of

America. Inaugurated in 1942, it goes annually to the person adjudged by the Football Writers Association members to have made, through his character, leadership, initiative or ability, the greatest contribution to the game."

The Grantland Rice Award, made annually after the bowl games, is the F.W.A.A.'s national title choice. The Award was initiated after the 1954 season.

Players

ALL-AMERICA SELECTIONS

A special N.C.A.A. Committee formed in 1954 proved, after exhaustive research, that credit for the selection of the first All-America football team in 1889 should go to Caspar Whitney, a leading sports authority in New York City in the early 1890's, instead of the former Yale star, Walter Camp, as popularly believed. Camp himself gives sole credit to Whitney for the selections from 1889 through 1896 even though the listings were under Camp's name in "Harper's Weekly." However, Camp skillfully promoted All-America teams, chose them himself beginning in 1897, and his selections appeared in "Collier's Weekly," a national magazine, until his death on March 14, 1925. Grantland Rice succeeded Camp as the selector for the magazine through 1947.

Rice combined with the Football Writers Association of America in 1948 to make selections for "Look" Magazine until his death in 1954.

Walter Camp's Selections—1889—1924

1889

End—Arthur Cumnock, Harvard
Tackle—Hector W. Cowan, Princeton
Guard—John Cranston, Harvard
Center—William J. George, Princeton
Guard—William W. Heffelfinger, Yale
Tackle—Charles O. Gill, Yale
End—Amos Alonzo Stagg, Yale
Quarterback—Edgar Allen Poe, Princeton
Halfback—James T. Lee, Harvard
Halfback—Roscoe H. Channing Jr., Princeton
Fullback—Knowlton Ames, Princeton

1890

E—Frank W. Hallowell, Harvard
T—Marshall Newell, Harvard
G—Jesse B. Riggs, Princeton
C—John Cranston, Harvard
G—William W. Heffelfinger, Yale
T—William C. Rhodes, Yale
E—Ralph H. Warren, Princeton
Q—Dudley Dean, Harvard
H—John Corbett, Harvard
H—Lee McClung, Yale
F—Sheppard Homans Jr., Princeton

1891

E—Frank A. Hinkey, Yale
T—Wallace C. Winter, Yale
G—William W. Heffelfinger, Yale
C—John W. Adams, Pennsylvania
G—Jesse B. Riggs, Princeton
T—Marshall Newell, Harvard
E—John A. Hartwell, Yale
Q—Phillip King, Princeton
H—Everett J. Lake, Harvard
H—Lee McClung, Yale
F—Sheppard Homans Jr., Princeton

1892

E—Frank A. Hinkey, Yale
T—A. Hamilton Wallis, Harvard
G—Bert Waters, Harvard
C—William H. Lewis, Harvard
G—Arthur L. Wheeler, Princeton
T—Marshall Newell, Harvard
E—Frank W. Hallowell, Harvard
Q—Vance McCormick, Yale
H—Charles Brewer, Harvard
H—Phillip King, Princeton
F—Harry C. Thayer, Pennsylvania

1893

E—Frank A. Hinkey, Yale
T—Langdon Lea, Princeton
G—Arthur L. Wheeler, Princeton
C—William H. Lewis, Harvard
G—William O. Hickok, Yale
T—Marshall Newell, Harvard
E—Thomas S. Trenchard, Princeton
Q—Phillip King, Princeton
H—Charles Brewer, Harvard
H—Franklin B. Morse, Princeton
F—Frank S. Butterworth, Yale

1894

E—Frank A. Hinkey, Yale
T—Bert Waters, Harvard
G—Arthur L. Wheeler, Princeton
C—Phillip T. Stillman, Yale
G—William O. Hickok, Yale
T—Langdon Lea, Princeton
E—Charles Gelbert, Pennsylvania
Q—George T. Adee, Yale
H—Arthur Knipe, Pennsylvania
H—George H. Brooke, Pennsylvania
F—Frank S. Butterworth, Yale

1895

E—Norman Cabot, Harvard
T—Langdon Lea, Princeton
G—Charles M. Wharton, Pennsylvania
C—Al Bull, Pennsylvania
G—Dudley Riggs, Princeton
T—Fred T. Murphy, Yale
E—Charles Gelbert, Pennsylvania
Q—Clinton R. Wyckoff, Cornell
H—S. Brinckerhoff Thorne, Yale
H—Charles Brewer, Harvard
F—George H. Brooke, Pennsylvania

1896

E—Norman Cabot, Harvard
T—William W. Church, Princeton
G—Charles M. Wharton, Pennsylvania
C—Robert R. Gailey, Princeton
G—Wiley Woodruff, Pennsylvania
T—Fred T. Murphy, Yale
E—Charles Gelbert, Pennsylvania
Q—William M. Fincke, Yale
H—Edgar N. Wrightington, Harvard
H—Addison W. Kelly, Princeton
F—John Baird, Princeton

1897

FIRST TEAM

E—Garrett Cochran, Princeton
T—Burr C. Chamberlain, Yale
G—T. Truxton Hare, Yale
C—Alan E. Doucette, Harvard
G—Gordon Brown, Yale
T—John Outland, Pennsylvania
E—John A. Hall, Yale
Q—Charles A.H. DeSaulles, Yale
H—Benjamin H. Dibblee, Harvard
H—Addison W. Kelly, Princeton
F—John Minds, Pennsylvania

SECOND TEAM

E—Boyle, Pennsylvania
T—Rodgers, Yale
G—Chadwick, Yale
C—Cadwalader, Yale
G—Rinehart, Lafayette
T—Scales, Army
E—McKeever, Cornell
Q—Young, Cornell
H—Nesbitt, Army
H—Fultz, Brown
F—McBride, Yale

THIRD TEAM

E—Moulton, Harvard
T—Hillebrand, Princeton
G—Bouve, Harvard
C—Overfield, Pennsylvania
G—McCracken, Pennsylvania
T—Donald, Harvard
E—Tracy, Cornell
Q—Baird, Princeton
H—Bannard, Princeton
H—Walbridge, Lafayette
F—Wheeler, Princeton

1898

FIRST TEAM

E—Lew R. Palmer, Princeton
T—A.R.T. Hillebrand, Princeton
G—T. Truxton Hare, Pennsylvania
C—Peter Overfield, Pennsylvania
G—Gordon Brown, Yale
T—Burr C. Chamberlain, Yale
E—John W. Hallowell, Harvard
Q—Charles D. Daly, Harvard

H—John Outland, Pennsylvania
H—Benjamin H. Dibblee, Harvard
F—Clarence B. Herschberger, Chicago

SECOND TEAM

E—Poe, Princeton
T—Steckle, Michigan
G—McCracken, Pennsylvania
C—Cunningham, Michigan
G—Boal, Harvard
T—Haughton, Harvard
E—Cochrane, Harvard
Q—Kennedy, Chicago
H—Richardson, Brown
H—Warren, Harvard
F—O'Dea, Wisconsin

THIRD TEAM

E—Folwell, Pennsylvania
T—Sweetland, Cornell
G—Randolph, Penn State
C—Jaffray, Harvard
G—Reed, Cornell
T—Foy, Army
E—Smith, Army
Q—Kromer, Army
H—Raymond, Wesleyan
H—Benedict, Nebraska
F—Romeyn, Army

1899

FIRST TEAM

E—David C. Campbell, Harvard
T—A.R.T. Hillebrand, Princeton
G—T. Truxton Hare, Pennsylvania
C—Peter Overfield, Pennsylvania
G—Gordon Brown, Yale
T—George S. Stillman, Yale
E—Arthur Poe, Princeton
Q—Charles D. Daly, Harvard
H—Isaac Seneca, Carlisle
H—Josiah H. McCracken, Pennsylvania
F—Malcolm L. McBride, Yale

SECOND TEAM

E—Hallowell, Harvard
T—Wheelock, Carlisle
G—Edwards, Princeton
C—Cunningham, Michigan
G—Wright, Columbia
T—Wallace, Pennsylvania
E—Coombs, Pennsylvania
Q—Kennedy, Chicago
H—Richardson, Brown
H—Slaker, Chicago
F—Wheeler, Princeton

THIRD TEAM

E—Snow, Michigan
T—Alexander, Cornell
G—Trout, Lafayette
C—Burnett, Harvard
G—Burden, Harvard
T—Pell, Princeton

E—Hamill, Chicago
Q—Hudson, Carlisle
H—McLean, Michigan
H—Weekes, Columbia
F—O'Dea, Wisconsin

1900

FIRST TEAM

E—David C. Campbell, Harvard
T—James R. Bloomer, Yale
G—Gordon Brown, Yale
C—Herman P. Olcott, Yale
G—T. Truxton Hare, Pennsylvania
T—George S. Stillman, Yale
E—John W. Hallowell, Harvard
Q—William M. Fincke, Yale
H—George B. Chadwick, Yale
H—William Morley, Columbia
F—Perry T.W. Hale, Yale

SECOND TEAM

E—Gould, Yale
T—Wallace, Pennsylvania
G—Wright, Columbia
C—Sargent, Harvard
G—Sheldon, Yale
T—Lawrence, Harvard
E—Coy, Yale
Q—Daly, Harvard
H—Weekes, Columbia
H—Sawin, Harvard
F—Cure, Lafayette

THIRD TEAM

E—Smith, Army
T—Alexander, Cornell
G—Teas, Pennsylvania
C—Page, Minnesota
G—Belknap, Navy
T—Farnsworth, Army
E—Van Hoevenberg, Columbia
Q—Williams, Iowa
H—Reiter, Princeton
H—Sharpe, Yale
F—McCracken, Pennsylvania

1901

FIRST TEAM

E—David C. Campbell, Harvard
T—Oliver F. Cutts, Harvard
G—William J. Warner, Cornell
C—Henry C. Holt, Yale
G—William G. Lee, Harvard
T—Paul B. Bunker, Army
E—Ralph T. Davis, Princeton
Q—Charles D. Daly, Army
H—Robert P. Kernan, Harvard
H—Harold Weekes, Columbia
F—Thomas H. Graydon, Harvard

SECOND TEAM

E—Bowditch, Harvard
T—Blagden, Harvard
G—Barnard, Harvard

C—Rachman, Lafayette
G—Hunt, Cornell
T—Wheelock, Carlisle
E—Swan, Yale
Q—De Saulles, Yale
H—Purcell, Cornell
H—Ristine, Harvard
F—Cure, Lafayette

THIRD TEAM

E—Henry, Princeton
T—Pell, Princeton
G—Olcott, Yale
C—Fisher, Princeton
G—Teas, Pennsylvania
T—Goss, Yale
E—Gould, Yale
Q—Johnson, Carlisle
H—Heston, Michigan
H—Morley, Columbia
F—Schoelkopf, Cornell

1902

FIRST TEAM

E—Thomas L. Shevlin, Yale
T—James J. Hogan, Yale
G—John R. DeWitt, Princeton
C—Henry C. Holt, Yale
G—Edgar T. Glass, Yale
T—Gilbert Kinney, Yale
E—Edward Bowditch, Harvard
Q—Foster Rockwell, Yale
H—George B. Chadwick, Yale
H—Paul B. Bunker, Army
F—Thomas H. Graydon, Harvard

SECOND TEAM

E—Sweeley, Michigan
T—Pierce, Amherst
G—Warner, Cornell
C—Boyers, Army
G—Goss, Yale
T—Knowlton, Harvard
E—Davis, Princeton
Q—Weeks, Michigan
H—Barry, Brown
H—Metcalf, Yale
F—Bowman, Yale

THIRD TEAM

E—Metzger, Pennsylvania
T—Farr, Chicago
G—Lerum, Wisconsin
C—McCabe, Pennsylvania
G—Marshall, Harvard
T—Schacht, Minnesota
E—Farmer, Dartmouth
Q—Daly, Army
H—Foulke, Princeton
H—Heston, Michigan
F—Torney, West Point

1903

FIRST TEAM

E—Howard H. Henry, Princeton
T—James J. Hogan, Yale
G—John R. DeWitt, Princeton
C—H.J. Hooper, Dartmouth
G—Andrew Marshall, Harvard
T—Daniel W. Knowlton, Harvard
E—Charles D. Rafferty, Yale
Q—James E. Johnson, Carlisle
H—William Heston, Michigan
H—J. Dana Kafer, Princeton
F—Richard Smith, Columbia

SECOND TEAM

E—Davis, Princeton
T—Thorp, Columbia
G—Riley, Army
C—Strathern, Minnesota
G—Gilman, Dartmouth
T—Schacht, Minnesota
E—Shevlin, Yale
Q—Whitam, Dartmouth
H—Nichols, Harvard
H—Mitchell, Yale
F—R. Miller, Princeton

THIRD TEAM

E—Redden, Michigan
T—Turner, Dartmouth
G—Bezdec, Wisconsin
C—Bruce, Columbia
G—Piekarski, Pennsylvania
T—Maddock, Michigan
E—Rogers, Minnesota
Q—Harris, Minnesota
H—Gravar, Michigan
H—Stankard, Holy Cross
F—Salmon, Notre Dame

1904

FIRST TEAM

E—Thomas L. Shevlin, Yale
T—James L. Cooney, Princeton
G—Frank Piekarski, Pennsylvania
C—Arthur C. Tipton, Army
G—Gilbert Kinney, Yale
T—James J. Hogan, Yale
E—Walter H. Eckersall, Chicago
Q—Vincent Stevenson, Pennsylvania
H—Daniel J. Hurley, Harvard
H—William Heston, Michigan
F—Andrew L. Smith, Pennsylvania

SECOND TEAM

E—Weede, Pennsylvania
T—Thorp, Columbia
G—Gilman, Dartmouth
C—Roraback, Yale
G—Tripp, Yale
T—Curtiss, Michigan
E—Gillespie, Army

Q—Rockwell, Yale
H—Reynolds, Pennsylvania
H—Hubbard, Amherst
F—Mills, Harvard

THIRD TEAM

E—Glaze, Dartmouth
T—Butkiewicz, Pennsylvania
G—Short, Princeton
C—Torrey, Pennsylvania
G—Thorpe, Minnesota
T—Doe, Army
E—Rothgeb, Illinois
Q—Harris, Minnesota
H—Hoyt, Yale
H—Vaughan, Dartmouth
F—Bender, Nebraska

1905

FIRST TEAM

E—Thomas L. Shevlin, Yale
T—Otis Lamson, Pennsylvania
G—Roswell C. Tripp, Yale
C—Robert Torrey, Pennsylvania
G—Francis H. Burr, Harvard
T—Beaton H. Squires, Harvard
E—Ralph Glaze, Dartmouth
Q—Walter H. Eckersall, Chicago
H—Howard Roome, Yale
H—John H. Hubbard, Amherst
F—James McCormick, Princeton

SECOND TEAM

E—Catlin, Chicago
T—Forbes, Yale
G—Thompson, Cornell
C—Flanders, Yale
G—Schulte, Michigan
T—Curtiss, Michigan
E—Marshall, Minnesota
Q—Hutchinson, Yale
H—Morse, Yale
H—Sheble, Pennsylvania
F—Von Saltza, Columbia

THIRD TEAM

E—Levene, Pennsylvania
T—Berthke, Wisconsin
G—Fletcher, Brown
C—Gale, Chicago
G—Maxwell, Swarthmore
T—Biglow, Yale
E—Tooker, Princeton
Q—Crowell, Swarthmore
H—Hammond, Michigan
H—Findlay, Wisconsin
F—Bezdek, Chicago

1906

FIRST TEAM

E—Robert W. Forbes, Yale
T—Horatio Biglow, Yale

G—Francis H. Burr, Harvard
C—W.T. Dunn, Penn State
G—Elmer Ives Thompson, Cornell
T—James L. Cooney, Princeton
E—L. Carpar Wister, Princeton
Q—Walter H. Eckersall, Chicago
H—John W. Hayhew, Brown
H—William F. Knox, Yale
F—Paul L. Veeder, Yale

SECOND TEAM

E—Dague, Navy
T—Draper, Pennsylvania
G—Ziegler, Pennsylvania
C—Hockenberger, Yale
G—Dillon, Princeton
T—Osborn, Harvard
E—Marshall, Minnesota
Q—Jones, Yale
H—Hollenback, Pennsylvania
H—Wendell, Harvard
F—McCormick, Princeton

THIRD TEAM

E—Levene, Pennsylvania
T—Weeks, Army
G—Kersberg, Harvard
C—Hunt, Carlisle
G—Christy, Army
T—Northcroft, Navy
E—Exendine, Carlisle
Q—E. Dillon, Princeton
H—Morse, Yale
H—Manier, Vanderbilt
F—Garrels, Michigan

1907

FIRST TEAM

E—W.H. Dague Jr., Navy
T—Dexter Draper, Pennsylvania
G—Gus Ziegler, Pennsylvania
C—Adolph Schulz, Michigan
G—William W. Erwin, Army
T—Horatio Biglow, Yale
E—Clarence F. Alcott, Yale
Q—T.A. Dwight Jones, Yale
H—John W. Wendell, Harvard
H—Edwin H.W. Harlan, Princeton
F—James McCormick, Princeton

SECOND TEAM

E—Exendine, Carlisle
T—Horr, Syracuse
G—Rich, Dartmouth
C—Grant, Harvard
G—Thompson, Cornell
T—O'Rourke, Cornell
E—Scarlett, Pennsylvania
Q—Dillon, Princeton
H—Marks, Dartmouth
H—Hollenback, Pennsylvania
F—Coy, Yale

THIRD TEAM

E—Wister, Princeton
T—Lang, Dartmouth
G—Goebel, Yale
C—Phillips, Princeton
G—Krider, Swarthmore
T—Weeks, Army
E—McDonald, Harvard
Q—Steffen, Chicago
H—Capron, Minnesota
H—Hauser, Carlisle
F—Douglas, Annapolis

1908

FIRST TEAM

E—Hunter Scarlett, Pennsylvania
T—Hamilton Fish, Harvard
G—William A. Goebel, Yale
C—Charles J. Nourse, Harvard
G—Clarke W. Tobin, Dartmouth
T—Mark E. Horr, Syracuse
E—George H. Schildmiller, Dartmouth
Q—Walter P. Steffen, Chicago
H—Frederick M. Tibbott, Princeton
H—William A. Hollenback, Pennsylvania
F—Edwin H. Coy, Yale

SECOND TEAM

E—Dennie, Brown
T—Siegling, Princeton
G—Andrus, Yale
C—Philoon, Army
G—Messmer, Wisconsin
T—O'Rourke, Cornell
E—Reifsnider, Navy
Q—Cutler, Harvard
H—Ver Wiebe, Harvard
H—Mayhew, Brown
F—Walder, Cornell

THIRD TEAM

E—Page, Chicago
T—Draper, Pennsylvania
G—Van Hook, Illinois
C—Brusse, Dartmouth
G—Hoar, Harvard
T—Northcroft, Navy
E—Johnson, Army
Q—Miller, Pennsylvania
H—Thorpe, Carlisle
H—Gray, Amherst
F—McCaa, Lafayette

1909

FIRST TEAM

E—Adrien E. Regnier, Brown
T—Hamilton Fish, Harvard
G—Albert Benbrook, Michigan
C—Carroll T. Cooney, Yale
G—Hamlin F. Andrus, Yale
T—Henry H. Hobbs, Yale
E—John R. Kilpatrick, Yale

Q—John McGovern, Minnesota
H—Stephen H. Philben, Yale
H—W.M. Minot, Harvard
F—Edward H. Coy, Yale

SECOND TEAM

E—Bankhart, Dartmouth
T—Lilley, Yale
G—Goebel, Yale
C—P. Withington, Harvard
G—Tobin, Dartmouth
T—McKay, Harvard
E—Braddock, Pennsylvania
Q—Howe, Yale
H—Allerdice, Michigan
H—Magidsohn, Michigan
F—Marks, Dartmouth

THIRD TEAM

E—Page, Chicago
T—Siegling, Princeton
G—L. Withington, Harvard
C—Farnum, Minnesota
G—Fisher, Harvard
T—Casey, Michigan
E—McCaffrey, Fordham
Q—Sprackling, Brown
H—Corbett, Harvard
H—Miller, Notre Dame
F—McCaa, Lafayette

1910

FIRST TEAM

E—John R. Kilpatrick, Yale
T—Robert G. McKay, Harvard
G—Albert Benbrook, Michigan
C—Ernest B. Cozens, Pennsylvania
G—Robert T. Fisher, Harvard
T—James Walker, Minnesota
E—Stanfield Wells, Michigan
Q—W. Earl Sprackling, Brown
H—Percy Wendell, Harvard
H—Talbot T. Pendleton, Princeton
F—E. LeRoy Mercer, Pennsylvania

SECOND TEAM

E—L. Smith, Harvard
T—Scully, Yale
G—Weir, Army
C—Morris, Yale
G—Brown, Navy
T—Smith, Brown
E—Daley, Dartmouth
Q—Howe, Yale
H—Dalton, Navy
H—Field, Yale
F—McKay, Brown

THIRD TEAM

E—Eyrich, Cornell
T—Grimm, Washington
G—Metzger, Vanderbilt
C—Sisson, Brown

G—Butzer, Illinois
T—Shonka, Nebraska
E—Dean, Wisconsin
Q—McGovern, Minnesota
H—Taylor, Oregon
H—Ramsdell, Pennsylvania
F—H. Corbett, Harvard

1911

FIRST TEAM

E—Sanford B. White, Princeton
T—Edward J. Hart, Princeton
G—Robert T. Fisher, Harvard
C—Henry H. Ketcham, Yale
G—Joseph M. Duff Jr., Princeton
T—Leland S. Devore, Army
E—Douglass M. Bomeisler, Yale
Q—Arthur Howe, Yale
H—Percy Wendell, Harvard
H—Jim Thorpe, Carlisle
F—J.P. Dalton, Navy

SECOND TEAM

E—Smith, Harvard
T—Munk, Cornell
G—Scruby, Chicago
C—Bluthenthal, Princeton
G—McDevitt, Yale
T—Scully, Yale
E—Very, Penn State
Q—Sprackling, Brown
H—Morey, Dartmouth
H—Camp, Yale
F—Rosenwald, Minnesota

THIRD TEAM

E—Ashbaugh, Brown
T—Buser, Wisconsin
G—Francis, Yale
C—Weems, Navy
G—Arnold, Army
T—Brown, Navy
E—Kallett, Syracuse
Q—Capron, Minnesota
H—Mercer, Pennsylvania
H—Wells, Michigan
F—Hudson, Trinity

1912

FIRST TEAM

E—Samuel M. Felton, Harvard
T—Wesley T. Englehorn, Dartmouth
G—Stanley B. Pennock, Harvard
C—Henry H. Ketcham, Yale
G—W. John Logan, Princeton
T—Robert P. Butler, Wisconsin
E—Douglass M. Bomeisler, Yale
Q—George M. Crowther, Brown
H—Charles E. Brickley, Harvard
H—Jim Thorpe, Carlisle
F—E. LeRoy Mercer, Pennsylvania

SECOND TEAM

E—Very, Penn State
T—Probst, Syracuse
G—Cooney, Yale
C—Parmenter, Harvard
G—Kulp, Brown
T—Trickey, Iowa
E—Hoeffel, Wisconsin
Q—Pazzetti, Lehigh
H—Morey, Dartmouth
H—Norgren, Chicago
F—Wendell, Harvard

THIRD TEAM

E—Ashbaugh, Brown
T—Shaughnessy, Minnesota
G—Bennett, Dartmouth
C—Bluthenthal, Princeton
G—Brown, Navy
T—Devore, Army
E—Jordan, Bucknell
Q—Bacon, Wesleyan
H—Hardage, Vanderbilt
H—Baker, Princeton
F—Pumpelly, Yale

1913

FIRST TEAM

E—Robert H. Hogsett, Dartmouth
T—Harold R. Ballin, Princeton
G—Stanley B. Pennock, Harvard
C—Paul R. Des Jardien, Chicago
G—J.H. Brown Jr., Navy
T—Nelson S. Talbot, Yale
E—Louis A. Merillat, Army
Q—Ellery C. Huntington Jr., Colgate
H—James Craig, Michigan
H—Charles E. Brickley, Harvard
F—Edward W. Mahan, Harvard

SECOND TEAM

E—Fritz, Cornell
T—Butler, Wisconsin
G—Busch, Carlisle
C—Marting, Yale
G—Ketcham, Yale
T—Weyand, Army
E—Hardwick, Harvard
Q—Wilson, Yale
H—Spiegel, Washington and Jefferson
H—Guyon, Carlisle
F—Eichenlaub, Notre Dame

THIRD TEAM

E—Solon, Minnesota
T—Halligan, Nebraska
G—Munns, Cornell
C—Paterson, Michigan
G—Talman, Rutgers
T—Storer, Harvard
E—Rockne, Notre Dame
Q—Miller, Penn State

H—Baker, Princeton
H—Nergren, Chicago
F—Whitney, Dartmouth

1914

FIRST TEAM

E—Huntington Hardwick, Harvard
T—Harold R. Ballin, Princeton
G—Stanley B. Pennock, Harvard
C—John J. McEwan, Army
G—Ralph D. Chapman, Illinois
T—Walter H. Trumbull, Harvard
E—John E. O'Hearn, Cornell
Q—Milton P. Ghee, Dartmouth
H—John Moulbetsch, Michigan
H—Frederick J. Bradlee, Harvard
F—Edward W. Mahan, Harvard

SECOND TEAM

E—Merillat, Army
T—Nash, Rutgers
G—Jordan, Texas
C—Des Jardien, Chicago
G—Shenk, Princeton
T—Patterson, Washington and Jefferson
E—Brann, Yale
Q—Barrett, Cornell
H—Spiegel, Washington and Jefferson
H—Cahall, Lehigh
F—LeGore, Yale

THIRD TEAM

E—Solem, Minnesota
T—Halligan, Nebraska
G—Spears, Dartmouth
C—Cruikshank, Washington and Jefferson
G—Meacham, Army
T—Weyand, Army
E—Overesch, Navy
Q—Wilson, Yale
H—Pogue, Illinois
H—Talman, Rutgers
F—Whitney, Dartmouth

1915

FIRST TEAM

E—Bert Baston, Minnesota
T—Joseph A. Gilman, Harvard
G—C.W. Spears, Dartmouth
C—Robert Peck, Pittsburgh
G—Christopher Schlachter, Syracuse
T—Earl C. Abell, Colgate
E—Murray N. Shelton, Cornell
Q—Charles Barrett, Cornell
H—Richard S.C. King, Harvard
H—Bart Macomber, Illinois
F—Edward W. Mahan, Harvard

SECOND TEAM

E—Herron, Pittsburgh
T—Buck, Wisconsin
G—Hogg, Princeton

C—Cool, Cornell
G—Black, Yale
T—Van der Graaf, Alabama
E—Higgins, Penn State
Q—Watson, Harvard
H—Tibbott, Princeton
H—Oliphant, Army
F—Talman, Rutgers

THIRD TEAM

E—Heyman, Washington and Jefferson
T—Cody, Vanderbilt
G—Dadmun, Harvard
C—McEwan, Army
G—Taylor, Auburn
T—Halligan, Nebraska
E—Squier, Illinois
Q—Russell, Chicago
H—Abraham, Oregon Aggies
H—Mayer, Virginia
F—Berryman, Penn State

1916

FIRST TEAM

E—Bert Baston, Minnesota
T—D. Belford West, Colgate
G—Clinton R. Black Jr., Yale
C—Robert Peck, Pittsburgh
G—Harrie D. Dadmun, Harvard
T—C.E. Horning, Colgate
E—George C. Moseley, Yale
Q—O.C. Anderson, Colgate
H—Elmer G. Oliphant, Army
H—Frederick D. Pollard, Brown
F—Charles W. Harley, Ohio State

SECOND TEAM

E—Herron, Pittsburgh
T—Ward, Navy
G—Hogg, Princeton
C—McEwan, Army
G—Backman, Notre Dame
T—Gates, Yale
E—Miller, Pennsylvania
Q—Purdy, Brown
H—LeGore, Yale
H—Casey, Harvard
F—Berry, Pennsylvania

THIRD TEAM

E—Coolidge, Harvard
T—Beckett, Oregon
G—Garrett, Rutgers
C—Phillips, Georgia Tech
G—Seagraves, Washington
T—Ignico, Washington and Jefferson
E—Vowell, Tennessee
Q—Curry, Vanderbilt
H—Gilroy, Georgetown
H—Driscoll, Northwestern
F—McCreight, Washington and Jefferson

1917 Service Teams

(Usual selections omitted because of war conditions.)

FIRST TEAM

E—Rasmussen, Nebraska (Grant)
T—Beckett, Oregon (Mare Island)
G—Black, Yale (Newport Reserve)
C—Callahan, Yale (Newport Reserve)
G—Allemdinger, Michigan (Fort Sheridan)
T—West, Colgate (Dix)
E—Gardiner, Carlisle (Custer)
Q—Watkins, Colgate (Mineola)
H—Casey, Harvard (Boston Navy Yard)
H—Minot, Harvard (Devens)
F—Smith, Michigan (Great Lakes)

SECOND TEAM

E—Ellenberger, Cornell (Dix)
T—Moriarty (Coast Naval Reserve)
G—Thurman, Virginia (Jackson)
C—Hommand, Kansas (Funston)
G—Withington, Harvard (Funston)
T—Blacklock, Michigan A. and M. (Great Lakes)
E—Mitchell (Mare Island Marines)
Q—Anderson, Colgate (Dix)
H—Shiverick, Cornell (Grant)
H—Barrett, Cornell (Newport Reserves)
F—Maxfield, Lafayette (Fort Slocum)

THIRD TEAM

E—Dennit, Brown (Funston)
T—Robertson, Dartmouth (Dodge)
G—Snyder (91st Division, Lewis)
C—White, Yale (Jackson)
G—Holder (91st Division, Lewis)
T—Lathrop, Notre Dame (Grant)
E—Hunt (Coast Naval Reserve)
Q—Costello, Georgetown (Custer)
H—O'Boyle, Georgetown (Pelham)
H—Blaire, Maryland (Upton)
F—Thayer, Pennsylvania (Meade)

Army and Navy players are not included, nor are there any from the southern camps, since these had not completed their schedules in time for selection.

1918

FIRST TEAM

E—Paul Robeson, Rutgers
T—Leonard Hilty, Pittsburgh
G—L.A. Alexander, Syracuse
C—Ashel Day, Georgia Tech
G—L.S. Perry, Navy
T—Louis C. Usher, Syracuse
E—Robert Hopper, Pennsylvania
Q—Frank L. Murray, Princeton
H—Thomas Davies, Pittsburgh
H—Wolcott Roberts, Navy
F—Frank Steketee, Michigan

SECOND TEAM

E—Weeks, Brown
T—Henry, Washington and Jefferson
G—Stahl, Pittsburgh
C—Depler, Illinois
G—Scaffe, Navy
T—Ripple, North Carolina State
E—Fincher, Georgia Tech
Q—Robb, Columbia
H—Frisch, Fordham
H—McLaren, Pittsburgh
F—Flowers, Georgia Tech

THIRD TEAM

E—Schwarzer, Syracuse
T—Goetz, Michigan
G—Huggins, Brown
C—Callahan, Princeton
G—Gordon, California
T—Neylon, Pennsylvania
E—Tressel, Washington and Jefferson
Q—Ackley, Syracuse
H—Eckberg, Minnesota
H—Kelley, Rutgers
F—Butler, Navy

1919

FIRST TEAM

E—Robert Higgins, Penn State
T—D. Belford, West, Colgate
G—L.A. Alexander, Syracuse
C—James R. Weaver, Centre
G—A.F. Youngstrom, Dartmouth

T—Wilbur F. Henry, Washington and Jefferson
E—Henry Miller, Pennsylvania
Q—Alvin T. McMillin, Centre
H—Edward Casey, Harvard
H—Charles W. Harley, Ohio State
F—Ira E. Rodgers, West Virginia

SECOND TEAM

E—Weston, Wisconsin
T—Ingwersen, Illinois
G—Denfield, Navy
C—Bailey, West Virginia
G—Depler, Illinois
T—Grimm, Washington
E—Dumoe, Lafayette
Q—Strubing, Princeton
H—Trimble, Princeton
H—Oss, Minnesota
F—Braden, Yale

THIRD TEAM

E—Blaik, Army
T—Slater, Iowa
G—Clark, Harvard
C—Callahan, Yale
G—Pixley, Ohio State
T—Cody, Vanderbilt
E—Roberts, Centre

Q—Boynton, Williams
H—Steers, Oregon
H—Gillo, Colgate
F—Robertson, Dartmouth

1920

FIRST TEAM

E—Charles R. Carney, Illinois
T—J. Stanton Keck, Princeton
G—J. Timothy Callahan, Yale
C—Herbert Stein, Pittsburgh
G—Thomas S. Woods, Harvard
T—Ralph Scott, Wisconsin
E—W.E. Fincher, Georgia Tech
Q—Donald B. Lourie, Princeton
H—Gaylord R. Stinchcomb, Ohio State
H—Charles Way, Penn State
F—George Gipp, Notre Dame

SECOND TEAM

E—Urban, Boston College
T—Goetz, Michigan
G—Wilkie, Navy
C—Cunningham, Dartmouth
G—Alexander, Syracuse
T—McMillan, California
E—LeGendre, Princeton
Q—McMillin, Centre
H—Garrity, Princeton
H—Davies, Pittsburgh
F—French, Army

THIRD TEAM

E—Ewen, Navy
T—Voss, Detroit
G—Breidster, Army
C—Havemeyer, Harvard
G—Trott, Ohio State
T—Dickens, Yale
E—Muller, California
Q—Boynton, Williams
H—Haines, Penn State
H—Leech, Virginia Military Institute
F—Horween, Harvard

1921

FIRST TEAM

E—Harold P. Muller, California
T—Russell F. Stein, Washington and Jefferson
G—Frank J. Schwab, Lafayette
C—Henry Vick, Michigan
G—John F. Brown, Harvard
T—Charles E. McGuire, Chicago
E—James B. Roberts, Centre
Q—Aubrey Devine, Iowa
H—Glenn Killinger, Penn State
H—Malcolm P. Aldrich, Yale
F—Edgar L. Kaw, Cornell

SECOND TEAM

E—Swanson, Nebraska
T—Slater, Iowa

G—Trott, Ohio State
C—Larsen, Navy
G—Bedenk, Penn State
T—Keck, Princeton
E—Kiley, Notre Dame
Q—McMillin, Centre
H—Owen, Harvard
H—Davies, Pittsburgh
F—Mohardt, Notre Dame

THIRD TEAM

E—Crisler, Chicago
T—Into, Yale
G—Pucelik, Nebraska
C—Stein, Pittsburgh
G—Whelchel, Georgia
T—McMillan, California
E—Stephens, California
Q—Lourie, Princeton
H—French, Army
H—Barchet, Navy
F—Barron, Georgia Tech

1922

FIRST TEAM

E—W.H. Taylor, Navy
T—C. Herbert Treat, Princeton
G—Frank J. Schwab, Lafayette
C—Edgar W. Garbisch, Army
G—Charles J. Hubbard, Harvard
T—John Thurman, Pennsylvania
E—Harold P. Muller, California
Q—Gordon C. Locke, Iowa
H—Edgar L. Kaw, Cornell
H—Harry G. Kipke, Michigan
F—John W. Thomas, Chicago

SECOND TEAM

E—Kirk, Michigan
T—Waldorf, Syracuse
G—Cross, Yale
C—Bowser, Pittsburgh
G—Setron, West Virginia
T—Neidlinger, Dartmouth
E—Bomar, Vanderbilt
Q—Smythe, Army
H—Morrison, California
H—Owen, Harvard
F—Barron, Georgia Tech

THIRD TEAM

E—Kopf, Washington and Jefferson
T—Below, Wisconsin
G—McMillen, Illinois
C—Peterson, Nebraska
G—Dickinson, Princeton
T—Gulian, Brown
E—Kadesky, Iowa
Q—Uteritz, Michigan
H—Jordan, Yale
H—Barchet, Navy
F—Castner, Notre Dame

1923

FIRST TEAM

E—Lynn Bomar, Vanderbilt
T—Century A. Milstead, Yale
G—Charles J. Hubbard, Harvard
C—Jack Blott, Michigan
G—Joseph Bedenk, Penn State
T—Frank L. Sundstrom, Cornell
E—Homer Hazel, Rutgers
Q—George R. Pfann, Cornell
H—Harold E. Grange, Illinois
H—Earl Martineau, Minnesota
F—William N. Mallory, Yale

SECOND TEAM

E—MacRae, Syracuse
T—Wiederquist, Washington and Jefferson
G—Brown, Notre Dame
C—Lovejoy, Yale
G—Aschenbach, Dartmouth
T—Deibel, Lafayette
E—Tallman, West Virginia
Q—Richeson, Yale
H—Wilson, Penn State
H—Tryon, Colgate
F—Stevens, Yale

THIRD TEAM

E—Stout, Princeton
T—Beam, California
G—Carney, Annapolis
C—Garbisch, Army
G—Johnson, Texas A. and M.
T—Bassett, Nebraska
E—Luman, Yale
Q—Dunn, Marquette
H—Koppisch, Columbia
H—Bohren, Pittsburgh
F—Nevers, Stanford

1924

FIRST TEAM

E—H.B. Bjorkman, Dartmouth
T—Edward F. McGinley, Pennsylvania
G—Edliff Slaughter, Michigan
C—Edgar Garbisch, Army
G—E.C. Horrell, California
T—Ed Weir, Nebraska
E—Charles Berry, Lafayette
Q—Harry Stuhldreher, Notre Dame
H—Harold E. Grange, Illinois
H—Walter Koppisch, Columbia
F—Homer Hazel, Rutgers

SECOND TEAM

E—Wakefield, Vanderbilt
T—Beattie, Princeton
G—Abramson, Minnesota
C—Lovejoy, Yale
G—Pondelik, Chicago
T—Waldorf, Syracuse
E—Lawson, Stanford

Q—Slagle, Princeton
H—Pond, Yale
H—Wilson, Washington
F—Crowley, Notre Dame

THIRD TEAM

E—Mahaney, Holy Cross
T—Wissinger, Pittsburgh
G—Fleckenstein, Iowa
C—Walsh, Notre Dame
G—Mahan, West Virginia
T—Growdy, Chicago
E—Fraser, Army
Q—Stivers, Idaho
H—Imlay, California
H—Keefer, Brown
F—Strader, St. Mary's

Grantland Rice's Selections—1925-53

(In Collier's 1925 through 1947; in Look, with
cooperation of The Football Writers Association
of America (from 1948 through 1953).

1925

E—Oosterbaan, Michigan
T—Weir, Nebraska
G—Diehl, Dartmouth
C—McMillan, Princeton
G—Hess, Ohio State
T—Chase, Pittsburgh
E—Thayer, Pennsylvania
Q—Grange, Illinois
H—Oberlander, Dartmouth
H—Wilson, Washington
F—Nevers, Stanford

1926

E—Winslett, Alabama
T—Sprague, Army
G—Shively, Illinois
C—Boeringer, Notre Dame
G—Connaughton, Georgetown
T—Wickhorst, Navy
E—Hanson, Syracuse
Q—Friedman, Michigan
H—Kaer, Southern California
H—Baker, Northwestern
F—Joesting, Minnesota

1927

E—Oosterbaan, Michigan
T—Raskowski, Ohio State
G—Smith, Notre Dame
C—Charlesworth, Yale
G—Crane, Illinois
T—Smith, Pennsylvania
E—Nash, Georgia
Q—Drury, Southern California
H—Cagle, Army
H—Welch, Pittsburgh
F—Joesting, Minnesota

1928

E—Fesler, Ohio State
T—Getto, Pittsburgh
G—Post, Stanford
C—Pund, Georgia Tech
G—Burke, Navy
T—Pommerening, Michigan
E—Haycraft, Minnesota
Q—Harpster, Carnegie Tech
H—Cagle, Army
H—Scull, Pennsylvania
F—Strong, New York University

1929

E—Donchess, Pittsburgh
T—Nagurski, Minnesota
G—Gannon, Notre Dame
C—Ticknor, Harvard
G—Montgomery, Pittsburgh
T—Sleight, Purdue
E—Schoonover, Arkansas
Q—Carideo, Notre Dame
H—Cagle, Army
H—Glasgow, Iowa
F—Welch, Purdue

1930

E—Fesler, Ohio State
T—Sington, Alabama
G—Koch, Baylor
C—Ticknor, Harvard
G—Beckett, California
T—Rhea, Nebraska
E—Dalrymple, Tulane
Q—Carideo, Notre Dame
H—Dodd, Tennessee
H—Pinckert, Southern California
F—Macaluso, Colgate

1931

E—Smith, Georgia
T—Quatse, Pittsburgh
G—Munn, Minnesota
C—Morrison, Michigan
G—Hickman, Tennessee
T—Schwegler, Washington
E—Dalrymple, Tulane
Q—Wood, Harvard
H—Schwartz, Notre Dame
H—Rentner, Northwestern
F—Shaver, Southern California

1932

E—Moss, Purdue
T—Smith, Southern California
G—Summerfelt, Army
C—Ely, Nebraska
G—Corbus, Stanford
T—Kurth, Notre Dame
E—Nisbett, Washington
Q—Newman, Michigan
H—Zimmerman, Tulane

H—Hitchcock, Auburn
F—Heller, Pittsburgh

1933

E—Skladany, Pittsburgh
T—F. Wistert, Michigan
G—Corbus, Stanford
C—Bernard, Michigan
G—Rosenberg, Southern California
T—Crawford, Duke
E—Larson, Minnesota
Q—Warburton, Southern California
H—Purvis, Purdue
H—Feathers, Tennessee
F—Sauer, Nebraska

1934

E—Don Hutson, Alabama
T—Bill Lee, Alabama
G—George Barclay, North Carolina
C—George Shotwell, Pittsburgh
G—Bill Bevan, Minnesota
T—Bob Reynolds, Stanford
E—Frank Larson, Minnesota
Q—Bobby Grayson, Stanford
H—Bill Wallace, Rice
H—Fred Borries, Navy
F—Pug Lund, Minnesota

1935

E—Gaynell Tinsley, Louisiana State
T—Dick Smith, Minnesota
G—John Weller, Princeton
C—Darrell Lester, Texas Christian
G—Inwood Smith, Ohio State
T—Truman Spain, Southern Methodist
E—Jim Moscrip, Stanford
Q—Riley Smith, Alabama
H—Jay Berwanger, Chicago
H—Bobby Wilson, Southern Methodist
F—Bobby Grayson, Stanford

1936

E—Gaynell Tinsley, Louisiana State
T—Ed Widseth, Minnesota
G—Max Starcevich, Washington
C—Alex Wojciechowicz, Fordham
G—Steve Reid, Northwestern
T—Averill Daniell, Pittsburgh
E—Larry Kelley, Yale
Q—Sammy Baugh, Texas Christian
H—Clint Frank, Yale
H—Ray Buivid, Marquette
F—Sam Francis, Nebraska

1937

E—Andy Bershak, North Carolina
T—Ed Franco, Fordham
G—Leroy Monsky, Alabama
C—Clark Hinkle, Vanderbilt
G—Joe Routt, Texas A. and M.
T—Vic Markov, Washington

E—Jerome Holland, Cornell
Q—Clint Frank, Yale
H—Marshall Goldberg, Pittsburgh
H—Byron White, Colorado
F—Sam Chapman, California

1938

E—Bowden Wyatt, Tennessee
T—Ed Beinor, Notre Dame
G—Ralph Heikkinen, Michigan
C—Ki Aldrich, Texas Christian
G—Sid Roth, Cornell
T—Ed McKeever, Cornell
E—Waddy Young, Oklahoma
Q—Davey O'Brien, Texas Christian
H—Bob MacLeod, Dartmouth
H—Vic Bottari, California
F—Marshall Goldberg, Pittsburgh

1939

E—Frank Ivy, Oklahoma
T—Nick Drahos, Cornell
G—Harry Smith, Southern California
C—John Schiechl, Santa Clara
G—Ed Molinski, Tennessee
T—Joe Boyd, Texas A. and M.
E—Esco Sarkkinen, Ohio State
Q—Paul Christman, Missouri
H—Nile Kinnick, Iowa
H—Tom Harmon, Michigan
F—Banks McFadden, Clemson

1940

E—Dave Rankin, Purdue
G—Bob Reinhard, California
T—Bob Suffridge, Tennessee
C—Rudy Mucha, Washington
G—Augie Lio, Georgetown
T—Alf Bauman, Northwestern
E—Gene Goodreault, Boston College
Q—Frankie Albert, Stanford
H—Tom Harmon, Michigan
H—George Franck, Minnesota
F—John Kimbrough, Texas A. and M.

1941

E—John Rokisky, Duquesne
T—Ernie Blandin, Tulane
G—Endicott Peabody, Harvard
C—Vic Banonis, Detroit
G—Bernie Crimmins, Notre Dame
T—Bob Reinhard, California
E—Mal Kutner, Texas
Q—Frankie Albert, Stanford
H—Bruce Smith, Minnesota
H—Bill Dudley, Virginia
F—Bob Westfall, Michigan

1942

E—Dave Schreiner, Wisconsin
T—Robin Olds, Army
G—Julius Franks, Michigan
C—Joe Domnanovieh, Alabama

G—Lynn Houston, Ohio State
T—Dick Wildung, Minnesota
E—Don Currivan, Boston College
Q—Paul Governali, Columbia
H—Billy Hillenbrand, Indiana
H—Frank Sinkwich, Georgia
F—Mike Holovak, Boston College

1943

E—Herb Hein, Northwestern
T—Jim White, Notre Dame
G—Merv Pregulman, Michigan
C—Casimir Myslinski, Army
G—Pat Filley, Notre Dame
T—Art McCaffrey, College of Pacific
E—Pete Pihos, Indiana
Q—Angelo Bertelli, Notre Dame
H—Creighton Miller, Notre Dame
H—Bob Odell, Pennsylvania
F—Bill Daley, Michigan

1944

E—Paul Walker, Yale
T—John Ferraro, Southern California
G—John Green, Army
C—Caleb Dan Warrington, Auburn
G—Bill Hackett, Ohio State
T—Don Whitmire, Navy
E—Pete Tinsley, Georgia Tech
Q—Doug Kenna, Army
H—Bob Jenkins, Navy
H—Les Horvath, Ohio State
F—Bob Fenimore, Oklahoma A. and M.

1945

E—Dick Duden, Navy
T—George Savitsky, Pennsylvania
G—Warren Amling, Ohio State
C—Vaughn Mancha, Alabama
G—John Green, Army
T—DeWitt Coulter, Army
E—Hubert Bechtol, Texas
Q—Herman Wedemeyer, St. Mary's
H—Glenn Davis, Army
H—Harry Gilmer, Alabama
F—Felix Blanchard, Army

1946

E—Henry Foldberg, Army
T—Dick Huffman, Tennessee
G—Weldon Humble, Rice
C—Paul Duke, Georgia Tech
G—Johnny Mastrangelo, Notre Dame
T—George Connor, Notre Dame
E—Burr Baldwin, U.C.L.A.
Q—Johnny Lujack, Notre Dame
H—Glenn Davis, Army
H—Charlie Trippi, Georgia
F—Felix Blanchard, Army
Utility back—Arnold Tucker, Army

1947

E—Bill Swiacki, Columbia

T—George Connor, Notre Dame
G—Joe Steffy, Army
C—Dick Scott, Navy
G—Steve Suhey, Penn State
T—Bob Davis, Georgia Tech
E—Paul Cleary, Southern California
Q—Johnny Lujack, Notre Dame
H—Ray Evans, Kansas
H—Tony Minisi, Pennsylvania
F—Bob Chappuis, Michigan

1948

E—Dick Rifenburg, Michigan
T—Leo Nomellini, Minnesota
G—Bill Healy, Georgia Tech
C—Chuck Bednarik, Pennsylvania
G—Joe Henry, Army
T—Leon Hart, Notre Dame
E—Art Weiner, North Carolina
B—Johnny Rauch, Georgia
B—Doak Walker, Southern Methodist
B—Emil Sitko, Notre Dame
B—Jackie Jensen, California

1949

E—Leon Hart, Notre Dame
T—Wade Walker, Oklahoma
G—Ed Bagdon, Michigan State
C—Clayton Tonnemaker, Minnesota
G—Rod Franz, California
T—Al Wahl, Michigan
E—Jim Williams, Rice
B—Arnold Galiffa, Army
B—Doak Walker, Southern Methodist
B—Charlie Justice, North Carolina
B—Emil Sitko, Notre Dame

1950

OFFENSIVE TEAM

E—Ernest Curtis, Vanderbilt
T—James Weatherall, Oklahoma
G—Robert Ward, Maryland
C—Redmond Finney, Princeton
G—Lewis McFadin, Texas
T—Robert Gain, Kentucky
E—Dan Foldberg, Army
B—Bob Reynolds, Nebraska
B—Victor Janowicz, Ohio State
B—Kyle Rote, Southern Methodist
B—Bob Williams, Notre Dame

DEFENSIVE TEAM

E—Bill McColl, Stanford
T—Holland Donan, Princeton
G—Ted Daffer, Tennessee
G—Robert Momsen, Ohio State
T—Albert Tate, Illinois
E—Dorne Dibble, Michigan State
Linebacker—Elmer Stout, Army
Linebacker—Les Richter, California
B—Edward Withers, Wisconsin
B—Richard Sprague, Washington

Safety—Buddy Jones, Oklahoma

1951

OFFENSIVE TEAM

E—Stan Williams, Baylor
T—Don Coleman, Michigan State
G—Nick Liotta, Villanova
C—Doug Moseley, Kentucky
G—Ray Beck, Georgia Tech
T—Jack Little, Texas A. and M.
E—Bill McColl, Stanford
B—Larry Isbell, Baylor
B—Hank Lauricella, Tennessee
B—John Karras, Illinois
B—Dick Kazmaier, Princeton

DEFENSIVE TEAM

E—Frank McPhee, Princeton
E—Pat O'Donahue, Wisconsin
T—Bill Pearman, Tennessee
T—Jim Weatherall, Oklahoma
G—Chet Millett, Holy Cross
G—Bob Ward, Maryland
L—Pat Cannamela, Southern California
L—Les Richter, California
H—Ollie Matson, San Francisco
H—Bobby Dillon, Texas
Safety—Al Brosky, Illinois

1952

OFFENSIVE TEAM

E—Bernie Flowers, Purdue
T—Hal Miller, Georgia Tech
G—Elmer Willhoite, Southern California
C—Tom Catlin, Oklahoma
G—John Michels, Tennessee
T—Kline Gilbert, Mississippi
E—Tom Stolhandske, Texas
B—Jack Scarbath, Maryland
B—Billy Vessels, Oklahoma
B—Gene Filipski, Villanova
B—Paul Giel, Minnesota

DEFENSIVE TEAM

E—Frank McPhee, Princeton
E—Don Voss, Wisconsin
T—Dick Modzelewski, Maryland
T—Eldred Kraemer, Pittsburgh
G—Frank Kush, Michigan State
G—Harley Sewell, Texas
L—Donn Moomaw, U.C.L.A.
L—George Morris, Georgia Tech
B—Gil Reich, Kansas
B—John Lattner, Notre Dame
Safety—Jim Sears, Southern California

1953 (22-man team)

E—Ken Buck, College of Pacific
E—John Carson, Georgia
E—Don Dohoney, Michigan State
E—Carlton Massey, Texas
T—Art Hunter, Notre Dame

T—Stan Jones, Maryland
T—Ed Meadows, Duke
T—Jack Shanafelt, Pennsylvania
G—Milt Bohart, Washington
G—Ray Correll, Kentucky
G—Crawford Mims, Mississippi
G—J.D. Roberts, Oklahoma
C—Matt Hazeltine, California
C—Jerry Hilgenberg, Iowa
Q—Bob Garrett, Stanford
Q—Jackie Parker, Mississippi State
B—Alan Ameche, Wisconsin
B—Paul Cameron, U.C.L.A.
B—J.C. Caroline, Illinois
B—Paul Giel, Minnesota
B—Kosse Johnson, Rice
B—John Lattner, Notre Dame

Associated Press Selections

1925

E—Oosterbaan, Michigan
T—Weir, Nebraska
G—Diehl, Dartmouth
C—McMillan, Princeton
G—Sturhahn, Yale
T—Chase, Pittsburgh
E—Tully, Dartmouth
Q—Grange, Illinois
H—Wilson, Washington
H—Oberlander, Dartmouth
F—Nevers, Stanford

1926

E—Hanson, Syracuse
T—Wickhorst, Navy
G—Connaughton, Georgetown
C—Boeringer, Notre Dame
G—Shively, Illinois
T—Sprague, Army
E—Winslett, Alabama
Q—Friedman, Michigan
H—Baker, Northwestern
H—Kaer, Southern California
F—Joesting, Minnesota

1927

E—Oosterbaan, Michigan
T—Hake, Pennsylvania
G—Webster, Yale
C—Bettencourt, St. Mary's
G—Smith, Notre Dame
T—Sprague, Army
E—Shiver, Georgia
Q—Spears, Vanderbilt
H—Welch, Pittsburgh
H—Drury, Southern California
F—Joesting, Minnesota

1928

E—Franklin, St. Mary's
T—Pommerening, Michigan
G—Burke, Navy

C—Howe, Princeton
G—Post, Stanford
T—Speer, Georgia Tech
E—Van Sickle, Florida
Q—Clark, Colorado College
H—Cagle, Army
H—Carroll, Washington
F—Strong, New York University

1929

E—Fesler, Ohio State
T—Sleight, Purdue
G—Cannon, Notre Dame
C—Ticknor, Harvard
G—Schwartz, California
T—Nagurski, Minnesota
E—Donchess, Pittsburgh
Q—Carideo, Notre Dame
H—Cagle, Army
H—Uansa, Pittsburgh
F—Holm, Alabama

1930

E—Fesler, Ohio State
T—Sington, Alabama
G—Metzger, Notre Dame
C—Ticknor, Harvard
G—Woodworth, Northwestern
T—Edwards, Washington State
E—Baker, Northwestern
Q—Carideo, Notre Dame
H—Schwartz, Notre Dame
H—Pinckert, Southern California
F—Macaluso, Colgate

1931

E—Dalrymple, Tulane
T—Marvil, Northwestern
G—Munn, Minnesota
C—Yarr, Notre Dame
G—Hoffman, Notre Dame
T—Schwegler, Washington
E—Smith, Georgia
Q—Wood, Harvard
H—Schwartz, Notre Dame
H—Pinckert, Southern California
F—Rentner, Northwestern

1932

E—Moss, Purdue
T—Kurth, Notre Dame
G—Summerfelt, Army
C—Ely, Nebraska
G—Vaught, Texas Christian
T—Smith, Southern California
E—Martinez-Zorilla, Cornell
Q—Heller, Pittsburgh
H—Newman, Michigan
H—Hitchcock, Auburn
F—Zimmerman, Tulane

1933

E—Geisler, Centenary

T—Crawford, Duke
G—Schammel, Iowa
C—Bernard, Michigan
G—Corbus, Stanford
T—Schwammel, Oregon State
E—Skladany, Pittsburgh
Q—Warburton, Southern California
H—Lund, Minnesota
H—Buckler, Army
F—Sauer, Nebraska

1934

E—Frank Larson, Minnesota
T—Bill Lee, Alabama
G—Les Hartwig, Pittsburgh
C—Darrell Lester, Texas Christian
G—George Barclay, North Carolina
T—Bob Reynolds, Stanford
E—Don Hutson, Alabama
Q—Bobby Grayson, Stanford
H—Fred Borries, Navy
H—Bill Wallace, Rice
F—Pug Lund, Minnesota

1935

E—Gaynell Tinsley, Louisiana State
T—Larry Lutz, California
G—John Weller, Princeton
C—Darrell Lester, Texas Christian
G—Paul Tangora, Northwestern
T—Dick Smith, Minnesota
E—Bill Shuler, Army
Q—Riley Smith, Alabama
H—Jay Berwanger, Chicago
H—Bobby Wilson, Southern Methodist
F—Bobby Grayson, Stanford

1936

E—Gaynell Tinsley, Louisiana State
T—Ed Widseth, Minnesota
G—Max Starcevich, Washington
C—Mike Basrak, Duquesne
G—Joe Routt, Texas A. and M.
T—Averill Daniell, Pittsburgh
E—Larry Kelley, Yale
Q—Clint Frank, Yale
H—Ray Buivid, Marquette
H—Ace Parker, Duke
F—Sam Francis, Nebraska

1937

E—Chuck Sweeney, Notre Dame
T—Ed Franco, Fordham
G—Joe Routt, Texas A. and M.
C—Clark Hinkle, Vanderbilt
G—Leroy Monsky, Alabama
T—Tony Matisi, Pittsburgh
E—Jerome Holland, Cornell
Q—Clint Frank, Yale
H—Byron White, Colorado
H—Marshall Goldberg, Pittsburgh
F—Sam Chapman, California

1938

E—Jerome Holland, Cornell
T—Ed Beinor, Notre Dame
G—Ralph Heikkinen, Michigan
C—Ki Aldrich, Texas Christian
G—Ed Bock, Iowa State
T—Al Wolff, Santa Clara
E—Waddy Young, Oklahoma
Q—Davey O'Brien, Texas Christian
H—Parker Hall, Mississippi
H—John Pingel, Michigan
F—Marshall Goldberg, Pittsburgh

1939

E—Paul Severin, North Carolina
T—Harley McCollum, Tulane
G—Harry Smith, Southern California
C—John Schiechl, Santa Clara
G—Ed Molinski, Tennessee
T—Nick Drahos, Cornell
E—Buddy Kerr, Notre Dame
Q—Nile Kinnick, Iowa
H—Tom Harmon, Michigan
H—Banks McFadden, Clemson
F—John Kimbrough, Texas A. and M.

1940

E—Paul Severin, North Carolina
T—Nick Drahos, Cornell
G—Bob Suffridge, Tennessee
C—Chet Gladchuck, Boston College
G—Warren Alfson, Nebraska
T—Bob Reinhard, California
E—Buddy Elrod, Mississippi State
Q—Frankie Albert, Stanford
H—Tom Harmon, Michigan
H—George Franck, Minnesota
F—John Kimbrough, Texas A. and M.

1941

E—Dave Schreiner, Wisconsin
T—Dick Wildung, Minnesota
G—Endicott Peabody, Harvard
C—Darrell Jenkins, Missouri
G—Ralph Fife, Pittsburgh
T—Bob Reinhard, California
E—Mal Kutner, Texas
Q—Frankie Albert, Stanford
H—Bill Dudley, Virginia
H—Frank Sinkwich, Georgia
F—Bruce Smith, Minnesota

1942

E—Dave Schreiner, Wisconsin
T—Dick Wildung, Minnesota
G—Garrard Ramsey, William and Mary
C—Joe Domnanovich, Alabama
G—Chuck Taylor, Stanford
T—Clyde Johnson, Kentucky
E—Bob Shaw, Ohio State
Q—Glenn Dobbs, Tulsa
H—Paul Governali, Columbia
H—Frank Sinkwich, Georgia
F—Mike Holovak, Boston College

1943

E—Joe Parker, Texas
T—Jim White, Notre Dame
G—John Steber, Georgia Tech
C—Casimir Myslinski, Army
G—George Brown, Navy
T—Pat Preston, Duke
E—Ralph Heywood, Southern California
Q—Bob Odell, Pennsylvania
H—Creighton Miller, Notre Dame
H—Otto Graham, Northwestern
F—Bill Daley, Michigan

1944

E—Pete Tinsley, Georgia Tech
T—Don Whitmire, Navy
G—Bill Hackett, Ohio State
C—Calebdan Warrington, Auburn
G—Hamilton Nichols, Rice
T—John Ferraro, Southern California
E—Hub Bechtol, Texas
Q—Les Horvath, Ohio State
H—Glenn Davis, Army
H—Bob Fenimore, Oklahoma, A. and M.
F—Felix Blanchard, Army

1945

E—Hubert Bechtol, Texas
T—DeWitt Coulter, Army
G—John Green, Army
C—Vaughn Mancha, Alabama
G—Warren Amling, Ohio State
T—Albert Nemetz, Army
E—Richard Duden, Navy
Q—Herman Wedemeyer, St. Mary's
H—Robert Fenimore, Oklahoma A. and M.
H—Glenn Davis, Army
F—Felix Blanchard, Army

1946

E—Burr Baldwin, U.C.L.A.
T—George Connor, Notre Dame
G—Weldon Humble, Rice
C—Paul Duke, Georgia Tech
G—Alex Agase, Illinois
T—Richard Huffman, Tennessee
E—Elmer Madar, Michigan
Q—John Lujack, Notre Dame
H—Charles Trippi, Georgia
H—Glenn Davis, Army
F—Felix Blanchard, Army

1947

E—Paul Cleary, Southern California
T—Bob Davis, Georgia Tech
G—Steve Suhey, Penn State
C—Charles Bednarik, Pennsylvania
G—William Fischer, Notre Dame
T—Richard Harris, Texas

E—William Swiacki, Columbia
B—John Lujack, Notre Dame
B—Robert Chappuis, Michigan
B—Ray Evans, Kansas
B—Doak Walker, Southern Methodist

1948

E—Dick Rifenburg, Michigan
T—Leo Nomellini, Minnesota
G—Paul Burris, Oklahoma
C—Charles Bednarik, Pennsylvania
G—Rod Franz, California
T—William Fischer, Notre Dame
E—Barney Poole, Mississippi
B—Bobby Jack Stuart, Army
B—Doak Walker, Southern Methodist
B—Charlie Justice, North Carolina
B—Art Murakowski, Northwestern

1949

E—Leon Hart, Notre Dame
T—James Martin, Notre Dame
G—Rod Franz, California
C—Clayton Tonnemaker, Minnesota
G—John Schweder, Pennsylvania
T—Wade Walker, Oklahoma
E—James Williams, Rice
B—Arnold Galiffa, Army
B—Doak Walker, Southern Methodist
B—Charlie Justice, North Carolina
B—Emil Sitko, Notre Dame

1950

OFFENSIVE TEAM

E—Dan Foldberg, Army
T—Jim Weatherall, Oklahoma
G—Lewis McFadin, Texas
C—Bill Vohaska, Illinois
G—Bob Ward, Maryland
T—Bob Gain, Kentucky
E—Don Stonesifer, Northwestern
B—Don Heinrich, Washington
B—Bob Reynolds, Nebraska
B—Everett Grandelius, Michigan State
B—Dick Kazmaier, Princeton

DEFENSIVE TEAM

E—Frank Anderson, Oklahoma
T—Al Carapella, Miami
G—Les Richter, California
G—Ted Daffer, Tennessee
T—Al Wahl, Michigan
E—Don Menasco, Texas
Linebacker—Elmer Stout, Army
Linebacker—Irvin Holdash, North Carolina
B—Bob Williams, Notre Dame
B—Vic Janowicz, Ohio State
B—Eddie Salem, Alabama

1951

OFFENSIVE TEAM

E—Bill McColl, Stanford

T—Bob Toneff, Notre Dame
G—Bob Ward, Maryland
C—Doug Moseley, Kentucky
G—Marvin Matuszak, Tulsa
T—Don Coleman, Michigan State
E—Bob Carey, Michigan State
B—Dick Kazmaier, Princeton
B—Hank Lauricella, Tennessee
B—Hugh McElhenny, Washington
B—Larry Isbell, Baylor

DEFENSIVE TEAM

E—Pat O'Donahue, Wisconsin
T—Jim Weatherall, Oklahoma
G—Ray Beck, Georgia Tech
G—Joe Palumbo, Virginia
T—Bill Pearman, Tennessee
E—Dewey McConnell, Wyoming
L—Keith Flowers, Texas Christian
L—Les Richter, California
B—Bobby Dillon, Texas
B—Al Brosky, Illinois
B—Ollie Matson, San Francisco

1952

OFFENSIVE TEAM

E—Tom Stolhandske, Texas
E—Frank McPhee, Princeton
T—Kline Gilbert, Mississippi
T—Dave Suminski, Wisconsin
G—John Michels, Tennessee
G—Marvin Matuszak, Tulsa
C—Pete Brown, Georgia Tech
B—Billy Vessels, Oklahoma
B—Paul Giel, Minnesota
B—Don Heinrich, Washington
B—Jack Scarbath, Maryland

DEFENSIVE TEAM

E—Don Branby, Colorado
E—Tom Scott, Virginia
T—J.D. Kimmel, Houston
T—Charlie Lapradd, Florida
G—Frank Kush, Michigan State
G—Steve Eisenhauer, Navy
L—Richard Tamburo, Michigan State
L—Donn Moomaw, U.C.L.A.
B—Jim Sears, Southern California
B—Johnny Lattner, Notre Dame
B—Bobby Moorhead, Georgia Tech

1953

E—Don Dohoney, Michigan State
E—Sam Morley, Stanford
T—Stan Jones, Maryland
T—Jack Shanafelt, Pennsylvania
G—J.D. Roberts, Oklahoma
G—Crawford Mims, Mississippi
C—Larry Morris, Georgia Tech
B—Paul Giel, Minnesota
B—Johnny Lattner, Notre Dame
B—Paul Cameron, U.C.L.A.

B—Kosse Johnson, Rice

1954

E—Ron Beagle, Navy
E—Frank McDonald, Miami (Fla.)
T—Jack Ellena, U.C.L.A.
T—Rex Boggan, Mississippi
G—Bud Brooks, Arkansas
G—Ralph Chesnauskas, Army
C—Kurt Burris, Oklahoma
B—Ralph Guglielmi, Notre Dame
B—Howard Cassady, Ohio State
B—Dicky Moegle, Rice
B—Alan Ameche, Wisconsin

1955

E—Ron Beagle, Navy
E—Howard Schnellenberger, Kentucky
T—Paul Wiggin, Stanford
T—Frank D'Agostino, Auburn
G—Jim Brown, U.C.L.A.
G—Pat Bisceglia, Notre Dame
C—Bob Pellegrini, Maryland
B—Earl Morrall, Michigan State
B—Howard Cassady, Ohio State
B—Tommy McDonald, Oklahoma
B—Jim Swink, Texas Christian

1956

E—Joe Walton, Pittsburgh
E—Ron Kramer, Michigan
T—Alex Karras, Iowa
T—John Witte, Oregon State
G—Bill Glass, Baylor
G—Jim Parker, Ohio State
C—Jerry Tubbs, Oklahoma
B—Tommy McDonald, Oklahoma
B—Johnny Majors, Tennessee
B—Jim Brown, Syracuse
B—Don Bosseler, Miami (Fla.)

1957

E—Jim Phillips, Auburn
E—Dick Wallen, U.C.L.A.
T—Alex Karras, Iowa
T—Lou Michaels, Kentucky
G—Aurelius Thomas, Ohio State
G—Bill Krisher, Oklahoma
C—Dan Currie, Michigan State
B—King Hill, Rice
B—Dick Christy, North Carolina State
B—Jim Pace, Michigan
B—John Crow, Texas A. and M.

1958

E—Jim Houston, Ohio State
E—Buddy Dial, Rice
T—Ted Bates, Oregon State
T—Brock Strom, Air Force Academy
G—Zeke Smith, Auburn
G—George Deiderich, Vanderbilt
C—Bob Harrison, Oklahoma
B—Randy Duncan, Iowa

B—Billy Cannon, Louisiana State
B—Bill Austin, Rutgers
B—Pete Dawkins, Army

1959

E—Marlin McKeever, Southern California
E—Fred Mautino, Syracuse
T—Dan Lanphear, Wisconsin
T—Don Floyd, Texas Christian
G—Roger Davis, Syracuse
G—Bill Burrell, Illinois
C—Maxie Baughan, Georgia Tech
B—Bob Schloredt, Washington
B—Jim Mooty, Arkansas
B—Billy Cannon, Louisiana State
B—Charley Flowers, Mississippi

1960

E—Dan LaRose, Missouri
E—Mike Ditka, Pittsburgh
T—Ken Rice, Auburn
T—Bob Lilly, Texas Christian
G—Tom Brown, Minnesota
G—Ben Balme, Yale
C—Roy McKasson, Washington
B—Jake Gibbs, Mississippi
B—Joe Bellino, Navy
B—Pervis Atkins, New Mexico State
B—Bob Ferguson, Ohio State

1961

E—Jerry Hillebrand, Colorado
E—Bill Miller, Miami
T—Merlin Olsen, Utah State
T—Billy Neighbors, Alabama
G—Dave Behrman, Michigan State
G—Roy Winston, Louisiana State
C—Alex Kroll, Rutgers
B—Sandy Stephens, Minnesota
B—Ernie Davis, Syracuse
B—Jim Saxton, Texas
B—Bob Ferguson, Ohio State

1962

E—Pat Richter, Wisconsin
E—Dave Robinson, Penn State
T—Bobby Bell, Minnesota
T—Don Brumm, Purdue
G—John Treadwell, Texas
G—Damon Bame, Southern California
C—Lee Roy Jordan, Alabama
B—Terry Baker, Oregon State
B—Jerry Stovall, Louisiana State
B—George Mira, Miami (Florida)
B—George Saimes, Michigan State

1963

E—Bob Lacey, North Carolina
E—Dave Parks, Texas Tech
T—Scott Appleton, Texas
T—Carl Eller, Minnesota
G—Bob Brown, Nebraska
G—Damon Bame, Southern California

C—Richard Butkus, Illinois
Q—Roger Staubach, Army
B—Jim Sidle, Auburn
B—Sherman Lewis, Michigan State
B—Billy Lothridge, Georgia

1964

OFFENSIVE TEAM

E—Fred Biletnikoff, Florida State
E—Larry Elkins, Baylor
T—Jim Wilson, Georgia
T—Larry Kramer, Nebraska
G—Tommy Nobis, Texas
G—Bill Fisk, Southern California
C—Pat Killorin, Syracuse
B—John Huarte, Notre Dame
B—Bob Timberlake, Michigan
B—Gale Sayers, Kansas
B—Donnie Anderson, Texas Tech

DEFENSIVE TEAM

E—Harold Wells, Purdue
E—Allen Brown, Mississippi
T—Dan Kearley, Alabama
T—John Van Sicklen, Iowa State
L—Dick Butkus, Illinois
L—Steve DeLong, Tennessee
L—Ron Caveness, Arkansas
B—Tucker Frederickson, Auburn
B—Clarence Williams, Washington State
B—Arnie Chonko, Ohio State
B—Cosmo Iacavazzi, Princeton

1965

OFFENSIVE TEAM

E—Howard Twilley, Tulsa
E—Charles Casey, Florida
T—Karl Singer, Purdue
T—Glen Ray Hines, Arkansas
G—Dick Arrington, Notre Dame
G—Tom Nobis, Texas
C—Paul Crane, Alabama
Q—Steve Juday, Michigan State
B—Don Anderson, Texas Tech
B—Mike Garrett, Southern California
B—Jim Grabowski, Illinois
K—Charley Gogolak, Princeton

DEFENSIVE TEAM

E—Aaron Brown, Minnesota
E—Ed Weisacosky, Miami (Fla.)
T—Walt Barnes, Nebraska
T—Loyd Phillips, Arkansas
MG—George Patton, Georgia
LB—Dwight Kelley, Ohio State
LB—Frank Emanuel, Tennessee
LB—Carl McAdams, Oklahoma
B—Nick Rassas, Notre Dame
B—John Roland, Missouri
B—George Webster, Michigan State

1966

OFFENSIVE TEAM

E—Jack Clancy, Michigan
E—Ray Perkins, Alabama
T—Cecil Dowdy, Alabama
T—Gary Bugenhagen, Syracuse
G—Tom Regner, Notre Dame
G—LaVerne Allers, Nebraska
C—Jim Breland, Georgia Tech
Q—Steve Spurrier, Florida
B—Mel Farr, U.C.L.A.
B—Nick Eddy, Notre Dame
B—Clint Jones, Michigan State

DEFENSIVE TEAM

E—Bubba Smith, Michigan State
E—Tom Greenlee, Washington
T—Loyd Phillips, Arkansas
T—George Patton, Georgia
MG—Wayne Meylan, Nebraska
LB—Paul Naumoff, Tennessee
LB—Jim Lynch, Notre Dame
LB—Bob Matheson, Duke
DB—George Webster, Michigan State
DB—Frank Loria, Virginia Tech

1967

OFFENSIVE TEAM

E—Denis Homan, Alabama
E—Ron Sellers, Florida State
T—Ron Yary, Southern California
T—Edgar Chandler, Georgia
G—Gary Cassells, Indiana
G—Rich Stotter, Houston
C—Bob Johnson, Tennessee
Q—Gary Beban, U.C.L.A.
H—O.J. Simpson, Southern California
H—Leroy Keyes, Purdue
F—Larry Csonka, Syracuse
K—Jerry DePoyster, Wyoming

DEFENSIVE TEAM

E—Ted Hendricks, Miami (Fla.)
E—Kevin Hardy, Notre Dame
T—Dennis Byrd, North Carolina State
T—Greg Pipes, Baylor
MG—Wayne Meylan, Nebraska
LB—Adrian Young, Southern California
LB—Granville Liggins, Oklahoma
LB—Bill Hobbs, Texas A & M
DB—Tom Schoen, Notre Dame
DB—Frank Loria, Virginia Tech
DB—Dick Anderson, Colorado

1968

OFFENSIVE TEAM

E—Ted Kwalick, Penn State
E—Ron Sellers, Florida State
T—Mike Montler, Colorado
T—Dave Foley, Ohio State
G—Charles Rosenfelder, Tennessee
G—Jim Barnes, Arkansas
C—John Didion, Oregon State

Q—Terry Hanratty, Notre Dame
B—O.J. Simpson, So. California
B—Leroy Keyes, Purdue
B—Chris Gilbert, Texas

DEFENSIVE TEAM

E—Ted Hendricks, Miami (Fla.)
E—John Zook, Kansas
T—Bill Stanfill, Georgia
T—Joe Greene, No. Texas State
MG—Ed White, California
LB—Steve Kiner, Tennessee
LB—Dennis Onkotz, Penn State
LB—Mike Widger, Virginia Tech
DB—Jake Scott, Georgia
DB—Roger Wehrli, Missouri
DB—Al Worley, Washington

1969

OFFENSIVE TEAM

E—Carlos Alvarez, Florida
E—Walker Gillette, Richmond
T—Bob McKay, Texas
T—Sid Smith, Southern California
G—Chip Kell, Tennessee
G—Bridges, Houston
C—Rodney Brand, Arkansas
Q—Mike Phipps, Purdue
B—Jim Otis, Ohio State
B—Steve Owens, Oklahoma
B—Bob Anderson, Colorado

DEFENSIVE TEAM

E—Jim Gunn, Southern California
E—Phil Olsen, Utah State
T—Mike Reid, Penn State
T—Mike McCoy, Notre Dame
MG—Jim Stillwagon, Ohio State
LB—Don Parish, Stanford
LB—Steve Kiner, Tennessee
LB—Dennis Onkotz, Penn State
DB—Buddy McClinton, Auburn
DB—Steve Curtis, Michigan
DB—Jack Tatum, Ohio State

1970

OFFENSIVE TEAM

E—Jim Braxton, West Virginia
WR—Elmo Wright, Houston
WR—Ernie Jennings, Air Force
T—Dan Dierdorf, Michigan
T—Bob Newton, Nebraska
G—Chip Kell, Tennessee
G—Larry DiNardo, Notre Dame
C—Don Popplewell, Colorado
Q—Joe Theismann, Notre Dame
B—Steve Worster, Texas
B—Don McCauley, North Carolina

DEFENSIVE TEAM

E—Bill Atessis, Texas
E—Charlie Weaver, USC

T—Rock Perdoni, Georgia Tech
T—Dick Bumpas, Arkansas
MG—Jim Stillwagon, Ohio State
LB—Jack Ham, Penn State
LB—Mike Anderson, Louisiana State
LB—Jerry Murtaugh, Nebraska
DB—Jack Tatum, Ohio State
DB—Tom Casanova, Louisiana State
DB—Dave Elmendorf, Texas A & M

1971

OFFENSIVE TEAM

E—Doug Kingsriter, Minnesota
E—Terry Beasley, Auburn
T—Jerry Sisemore, Texas
T—John Vella, Southern California
G—Reggie McKenzie, Michigan
G—Royce Smith, Georgia
C—Tom Brahaney, Oklahoma
Q—Pat Sullivan, Auburn
B—Greg Pruitt, Oklahoma
B—Ed Marinaro, Cornell
B—Lydell Mitchell, Penn State

DEFENSIVE TEAM

E—Smylie Gebhart, Georgia Tech
E—Walt Patulski, Notre Dame
T—Larry Jacobson, Nebraska
T—Mel Long, Toledo
MG—Rich Glover, Nebraska
LB—Dave Chaney, San Jose State
LB—Jeff Siemon, Stanford
LB—Mike Taylor, Michigan
DB—Clarence Ellis, Notre Dame
DB—Bobby Majors, Tennessee
DB—Tom Myers, Syracuse

1972

OFFENSIVE TEAM

E—Johnny Rodgers, Nebraska
E—Charles Young, Southern California
T—Jerry Sisemore, Texas
T—John Hicks, Ohio State
G—Ron Rusnak, North Carolina
G—John Hannah, Alabama
C—Tom Brahaney, Oklahoma
Q—John Hufnagel, Penn State
B—Otis Armstrong, Purdue
B—Greg Pruitt, Oklahoma
B—Woodrow Green, Arizona State

DEFENSIVE TEAM

E—Willie Harper, Nebraska
E—Roger Goree, Baylor
T—Derland Moore, Oklahoma
T—Greg Marx, Notre Dame
LB—Richard Wood, Southern California
LB—John Skorupan, Penn State
LB—Randy Gradishar, Ohio State
MG—Rich Glover, Nebraska
DB—Calvin Jones, Washington
DB—Robert Popelka, Southern Methodist
DB—Brad Van Pelt, Michigan State

United Press International Selections—
(Selections from 1926-1957, U.P., from 1958 on,
U.P.I.)

1926

E—Broda, Brown
T—Wickhorst, Navy
G—Hess, Ohio State
C—Butler, Pennsylvania
G—Connaught, Georgetown
T—Lassman, New York U.
E—Hanson, Syracuse
Q—Friedman, Michigan
H—Hamilton, Navy
H—Rogers, Pennsylvania
F—Karow, Ohio State

1927

E—Oosterbaan, Michigan
T—Hibbs, Southern California
G—Smith, Notre Dame
C—Charlesworth, Yale
G—Hansen, Minnesota
T—Hake, Pennsylvania
E—Shiver, Georgia
Q—Drury, Southern California
H—Flannagan, Notre Dame
H—Welch, Pittsburgh
F—Joesting, Minnesota

1928

E—Phillips, California
T—Pommerening, Michigan
G—Robesky, Stanford
C—Pund, Georgia Tech
G—Gibson, Minnesota
T—Douds, Washington and Jefferson
E—Fesler, Ohio State
Q—Harpster, Carnegie Tech
H—Strong, New York U.
H—Cagle, Army
F—Carroll, Washington

1929

E—Donchess, Pittsburgh
T—Hammon, Southern Methodist
G—Cannon, Notre Dame
C—Ticknor, Harvard
G—Montgomery, Pittsburgh
T—Nagurski, Minnesota
E—Tappaan, Southern California
Q—Carideo, Notre Dame
H—McEver, Tennessee
H—Hufford, Washington
F—Welch, Purdue

1930

E—Fesler, Ohio State
T—Sington, Alabama
G—Metzger, Notre Dame
C—Ticknor, Harvard
G—Wisniewski, Fordham

T—Lubratovich, Wisconsin
E—Baker, Northwestern
Q—Carideo, Notre Dame
H—Schwartz, Notre Dame
H—Moffett, Stanford
F—Macaluso, Colgate

1931

E—Dalrymple, Tulane
T—Kurth, Notre Dame
G—Munn, Minnesota
C—Miller, Purdue
G—Baker, Southern California
T—Quatse, Pittsburgh
E—Cronkite, Kansas State
Q—Shaver, Southern California
H—Schwartz, Notre Dame
H—Rentner, Northwestern
F—Cain, Alabama

1932

E—Skladany, Pittsburgh
T—Smith, Southern California
G—Summerfelt, Army
C—Gracey, Vanderbilt
G—Corbus, Stanford
T—Kurth, Notre Dame
E—Moss, Purdue
Q—Newman, Michigan
H—Zimmerman, Tulane
H—Heller, Pittsburgh
F—Christensen, Utah

1933

E—Manske, Northwestern
T—Crawford, Duke
G—Rosenberg, Southern California
C—Bernard, Michigan
G—Schwammel, Iowa
T—F. Wistert, Michigan
E—Geisler, Centenary
Q—Warburton, Southern California
H—Franklin, Oregon State
H—Buckler, Army
F—Purvis, Purdue

1934

E—Don Hutson, Alabama
T—Dick Steen, Syracuse
G—Bill Bevan, Minnesota
C—George Shotwell, Pittsburgh
G—Regis Monahan, Ohio State
T—Clyde Carter, Southern Methodist
E—Jim Moscrip, Stanford
Q—Bobby Grayson, Stanford
H—Millard (Dixie) Howell, Alabama
H—Fred Borries, Navy
F—Francis (Pug) Lund, Minnesota

1935

E—Gaynell Tinsley, Louisiana State
T—Ed Widseth, Minnesota

G—Inwood Smith, Ohio State
C—Gomer Jones, Ohio State
G—Sidney Wagner, Michigan State
T—Dick Smith, Minnesota
E—Wayne Millner, Notre Dame
Q—Sammy Baugh, Texas Christian
H—Bobby Wilson, Southern Methodist
H—Jay Berwanger, Chicago
F—Bobby Grayson, Stanford

1936

E—Gaynell Tinsley, Louisiana State
T—Ed Widseth, Minnesota
G—Max Starcevich, Washington
C—Bob Herwig, California
G—John Lautar, Notre Dame
T—Averill Daniell, Pittsburgh
E—Larry Kelley, Yale
Q—Sammy Baugh, Texas Christian
H—Clarence (Ace) Parker, Duke
H—Ed Goddard, Washington State
F—Sam Francis, Nebraska

1937

E—Chuck Sweeney, Notre Dame
T—Ed Franco, Fordham
G—Joe Routt, Texas A. and M.
C—Alex Wojciechowicz, Fordham
G—Vard Stockton, California
T—Frank Kinard, Mississippi
E—John Wysocki, Villanova
Q—Byron (Whizzer) White, Colorado
H—Sam Chapman, California
H—Clint Frank, Yale
F—Marshall Goldberg, Pittsburgh

1938

E—Bill Daddio, Pittsburgh
T—Al Wolff, Santa Clara
G—Bob Suffridge, Tennessee
C—Ki Aldrich, Texas Christian
G—Ralph Heikkinen, Michigan
T—Ed Beinor, Notre Dame
E—John Wysocki, Villanova
Q—Davey O'Brien, Texas Christian
H—Eric Tipton, Duke
H—Parker Hall, Mississippi
F—Marshall Goldberg, Pittsburgh

1939

E—Ken Kavanaugh, Louisiana State
T—Harry Stella, Army
G—Harry Smith, Southern California
C—John Haman, Northwestern
G—Bob Suffridge, Tennessee
T—Nick Drahos, Cornell
E—Esco Sarkkinen, Ohio State
Q—John Kimbrough, Texas A. and M.
H—Nile Kinnick, Iowa
H—Tom Harmon, Michigan
F—George Cafego, Tennessee

1940

E—Dave Rankin, Purdue
T—Nick Drahos, Cornell
G—Marshall Robnett, Texas A. and M.
C—Rudy Mucha, Washington
G—Bob Suffridge, Tennessee
T—Alf Bauman, Northwestern
E—Gene Goodreault, Boston College
Q—Frankie Albert, Stanford
H—George Franck, Minnesota
H—Tom Harmon, Michigan
F—John Kimbrough, Texas A. and M.

1941

E—Bob Dove, Notre Dame
T—Dick Wilding, Minnesota
G—Endicott Peabody, Harvard
C—Darrell Jenkins, Missouri
G—Ray Frankowski, Washington
T—Ernie Blandin, Tulane
E—John Rokiskey, Duquesne
Q—Bruce Smith, Minnesota
H—Frank Sinkwich, Georgia
H—Bill Dudley, Virginia
F—Bob Westfall, Michigan

1942

E—Bob Dove, Notre Dame
T—Dick Wilding, Minnesota
G—Alex Agase, Illinois
C—Spencer Moseley, Yale
G—Harvey Hardy, Georgia Tech
T—Albert Wistert, Michigan
E—Dave Schreiner, Wisconsin
Q—Paul Governali, Columbia
H—Billy Hillenbrand, Indiana
H—Frank Sinkwich, Georgia
F—Mike Holovak, Boston College

1943

E—John Yonakor, Notre Dame
T—Jim White, Notre Dame
G—Pat Filley, Notre Dame
C—Casimir Myslinski, Army
G—Alex Agase, Purdue
T—Don Whitmire, Navy
E—Ralph Heywood, Southern California
Q—Angelo Bertelli, Notre Dame
H—Creighton Miller, Notre Dame
H—Tony Butkovich, Purdue
F—Bill Daley, Michigan

1944

E—Jack Dugger, Ohio State
T—Bill Willis, Ohio State
G—Ben Chase, Navy
C—Jack Tavener, Indiana
G—Joe Stanowicz, Army
T—Don Whitmire, Navy
E—Barney Poole, Army
Q—Les Horvath, Ohio State
H—Bob Jenkins, Navy

H—Glenn Davis, Army
F—Felix Blanchard, Army

1945

E—Hank Foldberg, Army
T—DeWitt Coulter, Army
G—John Green, Army
C—Vaughn Mancha, Alabama
G—Warren Amling, Ohio State
T—George Savitsky, Pennsylvania
E—Dick Duden, Navy
Q—Bob Fenimore, Oklahoma A. and M.
H—Glenn Davis, Army
H—Herman Wedemeyer, St. Mary's (Calif.)
F—Felix Blanchard, Army

1946

E—Hank Foldberg, Army
T—George Connor, Notre Dame
G—Waldron Humble, Rice
C—Paul Duke, Georgia Tech
G—Alex Agase, Illinois
T—Warren Amling, Ohio State
E—Burr Baldwin, U.C.L.A.
Q—Johnny Lujack, Notre Dame
H—Glenn Davis, Army
H—Charlie Trippi, Georgia
F—Felix Blanchard, Army

1947

E—Bill Swiacki, Columbia
T—George Connor, Notre Dame
G—Joe Steffy, Army
C—Chuck Bednarik, Pennsylvania
G—Bill Fischer, Notre Dame
T—John Ferraro, Southern California
E—Barney Poole, Mississippi
B—Bob Chappuis, Michigan
B—Doak Walker, Southern Methodist
B—Bobby Layne, Texas
B—Johnny Lujack, Notre Dame

1948

E—Leon Hart, Notre Dame
T—Leo Nomellini, Minnesota
G—Bill Fischer, Notre Dame
C—Chuck Bednarik, Pennsylvania
G—Paul Burris, Oklahoma
T—Alvin Wistert, Michigan
E—Dick Rifenberg, Michigan
B—Doak Walker, Southern Methodist
B—Charlie Justice, North Carolina
B—Jackie Jensen, California
B—Stan Heath, Nevada

1949

E—Leon Hart, Notre Dame
T—Leo Nomellini, Minnesota
G—Rod Franz, California
C—Clayton Tonnemaker, Minnesota
G—Ed Bagdon, Michigan State
T—Alvin Wistert, Michigan
E—Art Weiner, North Carolina

B—Emil Sitko, Notre Dame
B—Doak Walker, Southern Methodist
B—Bob Williams, Notre Dame
B—Arnold Galiffa, Army

1950

E—Dan Foldberg, Army
T—Bob Gain, Kentucky
G—Les Richter, California
C—Jerry Groom, Notre Dame
G—Lewis (Bud) McFadin, Texas
T—Jim Weatherall, Oklahoma
E—Bill McColl, Stanford
B—Vic Janowicz, Ohio State
B—Kyle Rote, Southern Methodist
B—Leon Heath, Oklahoma
B—Bob Williams, Notre Dame

1951

E—Bill McColl, Stanford
T—Don Coleman, Michigan State
G—Les Richter, California
C—Dick Hightower, Southern Methodist
G—Bob Ward, Maryland
T—Jim Weatherall, Oklahoma
E—Bob Carey, Michigan State
B—Dick Kazmaier, Princeton
B—Johnny Karras, Illinois
B—Vito (Babe) Parilli, Kentucky
B—Hank Lauricella, Tennessee

1952

E—Bernie Flowers, Purdue
T—Dick Modzelewski, Maryland
G—Elmer Willhoite, Southern California
C—Donn Moomaw, U.C.L.A.
G—John Michels, Tennessee
T—Hal Miller, Georgia Tech
E—Frank McPhee, Princeton
B—Billy Vessels, Oklahoma
B—Jack Scarbath, Maryland
B—Johnny Lattner, Notre Dame
B—Don McAuliffe, Michigan State

1953

E—Carlton Massey, Texas
T—Art Hunter, Notre Dame
G—J.D. Roberts, Oklahoma
C—Larry Morris, Georgia Tech
G—Crawford Mims, Mississippi
T—Stan Jones, Maryland
E—Don Dohoney, Michigan State
B—Johnny Lattner, Notre Dame
B—Paul Cameron, U.C.L.A.
B—Paul Giel, Minnesota
B—J.C. Caroline, Illinois

1954

E—Max Boydston, Oklahoma
T—Jack Ellena, U.C.L.A.
G—Calvin Jones, Iowa
C—Kurt Burris, Oklahoma
G—Bud Brooks, Arkansas

T—Sid Fournet, Louisiana State
E—Don Holleder, Army
B—Ralph Guglielmi, Notre Dame
B—Howard Cassady, Ohio State
B—Dicky Moegle, Rice
B—Alan Ameche, Wisconsin

1955

E—Ron Kramer, Michigan
T—Bruce Bosley, West Virginia
G—Virgil (Bo) Bolinger, Oklahoma
C—Bob Pellegrini, Maryland
G—Calvin Jones, Iowa
T—Norm Masters, Michigan State
E—Ron Beagle, Navy
B—Howard Cassady, Ohio State
B—Jim Swink, Texas Christian
B—Paul Hornung, Notre Dame
B—Jon Arnett, Southern California

1956

E—Ron Kramer, Michigan
T—John Witte, Oregon State
G—Jim Parker, Ohio State
C—Jerry Tubbs, Oklahoma
G—Bill Glass, Baylor
T—Lou Michaels, Kentucky
E—Joe Walton, Pittsburgh
B—Tommy McDonald, Oklahoma
B—Johnny Majors, Tennessee
B—Paul Hornung, Notre Dame
B—Jim Brown, Syracuse

1957

E—Jim Phillips, Auburn
T—Alex Karras, Iowa
G—Bill Krisher, Oklahoma
C—Don Stephenson, Georgia Tech
G—Al Ecuyer, Notre Dame
T—Lou Michaels, Kentucky
E—Jim Gibbons, Iowa
B—John Crow, Texas A. and M.
B—Walt Kowalczyk, Michigan State
B—Clendon Thomas, Oklahoma
B—Bob Anderson, Army

1958

E—Buddy Dial, Rice
T—Ted Bates, Oregon State
G—Al Ecuyer, Notre Dame
C—Bob Harrison, Oklahoma
G—John Guzik, Pittsburgh
T—Brock Strom, Air Force Academy
E—Sammy Williams, Michigan State
B—Billy Cannon, Louisiana State
B—Pete Dawkins, Army
B—Randy Duncan, Iowa
B—Bob White, Ohio State

1959

E—Monty Stickles, Notre Dame
E—Bill Carpenter, Army
T—Dan Lanphear, Wisconsin
T—Don Floyd, Texas Christian
G—Roger Davis, Syracuse
G—Bill Burrell, Illinois
C—Maxie Baughan, Georgia Tech
B—Richie Lucas, Penn State
B—Billy Cannon, Louisiana State
B—Ron Burton, Northwestern
B—Charley Flowers, Mississippi

1960

E—Mike Ditka, Pittsburgh
E—Dan LaRose, Missouri
T—Bob Lilly, Texas Christian
T—Ken Rice, Auburn
G—Tom Brown, Minnesota
G—Joe Romig, Colorado
C—E.J. Holub, Texas Tech
B—Jake Gibbs, Mississippi
B—Joe Bellino, Navy
B—Ernie Davis, Syracuse
B—Bob Ferguson, Ohio State

1961

E—Gary Collins, Maryland
E—Pat Richter, Wisconsin
T—Merlin Olsen, Utah State
T—Billy Neighbors, Alabama
G—Joe Romig, Colorado
G—Roy Winston, Louisiana State
C—Alex Kroll, Rutgers
B—Sandy Stephens, Minnesota
B—Ernie Davis, Syracuse
B—Jim Saxton, Texas
B—Bob Ferguson, Ohio State

1962

E—Pat Richter, Wisconsin
E—Hal Bedsole, Southern California
T—Bobby Bell, Minnesota
T—Jim Dunaway, Mississippi
G—John Treadwell, Texas
G—Jack Cvercko, Northwestern
C—Lee Roy Jordan, Alabama
B—Terry Baker, Oregon State
B—Jerry Stovall, Louisiana State
B—Mel Renfro, Oregon
B—George Saimes, Michigan State

1963

E—Vern Burke, Oregon State
E—James Kelley, Notre Dame
T—Scott Appleton, Texas
T—Carl Eller, Minnesota
G—Bob Brown, Nebraska
G—Richard Redmans, Washington
C—Richard Butkus, Illinois
Q—Roger Staubach, Army
B—Gale Sayers, Kansas
B—Sherman Lewis, Michigan State
B—Jay Wekinson, Duke

1964

E—Jack Snow, Notre Dame
E—Larry Elkins, Baylor
T—Larry Kramer, Nebraska
T—Ralph Neely, Oklahoma
G—Rich Redman, Washington
G—Tommy Nobis, Texas
C—Dick Butkus, Illinois
B—John Huarte, Notre Dame
B—Gale Sayers, Kansas
B—Jerry Rhome, Tulsa
B—Jim Grabowski, Illinois

1965

OFFENSIVE TEAM

E—Howard Twilley, Tulsa
E—Freeman, White, Nebraska
T—Glen Ray Hines, Arkansas
T—Sam Ball, Kentucky
G—Dick Arrington, Notre Dame
G—Doug Van Horn, Ohio
C—Paul Crane, Alabama
Q—Bob Griese, Purdue
B—Mike Garrett, Southern California
B—Donny Anderson, Texas Tech
B—Jim Grabowski, Illinois

DEFENSIVE TEAM

E—Aaron Brown, Minnesota
E—Charles Smith, Michigan State
T—Loyd Phillips, Arkansas
T—Bill Yearby, Michigan
LB—Tom Nobis, Texas
LB—Carl McAdams, Oklahoma
LB—Dwight Kelly, Ohio State
B—Nick Rassas, Notre Dame
B—George Webster, Michigan State
B—John Roland, Missouri
B—Bruce Bennett, Florida

1966

OFFENSIVE TEAM

E—Gene Washington, Michigan State
E—Jack Clancy, Michigan
T—Cecil Dowdy, Alabama
T—Ron Yary, Southern California
G—Tom Regner, Notre Dame
G—LaVerne Allers, Nebraska
C—Jim Breland, Georgia Tech
Q—Steve Spurrier, Florida
B—Nick Eddy, Notre Dame
B—Mel Farr, U.C.L.A.
B—Floyd Little, Syracuse

DEFENSIVE TEAM

E—Bubba Smith, Michigan State
E—Tom Greenlee, Washington
T—Loyd Phillips, Arkansas
T—Pete Duranko, Notre Dame
MG—Wayne Meylan, Nebraska
LB—Jim Lynch, Notre Dame
LB—Paul Naumoff, Tennessee

DB—George Webster, Michigan State
DB—Nate Shaw, Southern California
DB—Tom Beier, Miami (Fla.)
DB—Martine Bercher, Arkansas

1967

OFFENSIVE TEAM

E—Jim Seymour, Notre Dame
E—Dennis Homan, Alabama
T—Ron Yary, Southern California
T—Edgar Chandler, Georgia
G—Rich Stotter, Houston
G—Harry Olszewski, Clemson
C—Bob Johnson, Tennessee
Q—Gary Beban, U.C.L.A.
H—O.J. Simpson, Southern California
H—Leroy Keyes, Purdue
F—Larry Csonka, Syracuse

DEFENSIVE TEAM

E—Ted Hendricks, Miami (Fla.)
E—Tim Rossovich, Southern California
T—Kevin Hardy, Notre Dame
T—Dennis Byrd, North Carolina State
MG—Granville Liggins, Oklahoma
LB—Adrian Young, Southern California
LB—Don Manning, U.C.L.A.
DB—Tom Schoen, Notre Dame
DB—Bobby Johns, Alabama
DB—Frank Loria, Virginia Tech
DB—Al Dorsey, Tennessee

1968

OFFENSIVE TEAM

E—Jim Seymour, Notre Dame
E—Ted Kwalick, Penn State
T—Dave Foley, Ohio State
T—George Kunz, Notre Dame
G—Charles Rosenfelder, Tennessee
G—Guy Dennis, Florida
C—John Didion, Oregon State
Q—Terry Hanratty, Notre Dame
H—O.J. Simpson, So. California
H—Leroy Keyes, Purdue
F—Bill Enyart, Oregon State

DEFENSIVE TEAM

E—Ted Hendricks, Miami (Fla.)
E—John Zook, Kansas
T—Bill Stanfill, Georgia
T—Joe Greene, No. Texas State
MG—Chuck Kyle, Purdue
LB—Dennis Onkotz, Penn State
LB—Bill Hobbs, Texas A&M
DB—Roger Wehrli, Missouri
DB—Mike Battle, So. California
DB—Jake Scott, Georgia
DB—Al Worley, Washington

1969

OFFENSIVE TEAM

E—Carlos Alvarez, Florida

E—Jim Mandich, Michigan
T—Sid Smith, Southern California
T—Bob McKay, Texas
G—Chip Kell, Tennessee
G—Larry DiNardo, Notre Dame
C—Rodney Brand, Arkansas
Q—Mike Phipps, Purdue
B—Steve Owens, Oklahoma
B—Jim Otis, Ohio State
B—Bob Anderson, Colorado

DEFENSIVE TEAM

E—Jim Gunn, Southern California
E—Phil Olsen, Utah State
T—Mike McCoy, Notre Dame
T—Mike Reid, Penn State
MG—Jim Stillwagon, Ohio State
LB—Steve Kiner, Tennessee
LB—Dennis Onkotz, Penn State
DB—Glenn Cannon, Mississippi
DB—Steve Curtis, Michigan
DB—Neal Smith, Penn State
DB—Buddy McClinton, Auburn

1970

OFFENSIVE TEAM

E—Tom Gatewood, Notre Dame
E—Ernie Jennings, Air Force
T—Dan Dierdorf, Michigan
T—Bob Wuensch, Texas
G—Chip Kell, Tennessee
G—Larry DiNardo, Notre Dame
C—Don Popplewell, Colorado
Q—Jim Plunkett, Stanford
B—Steve Worster, Texas
B—John Brockington, Ohio State
B—Ed Marinaro, Cornell

DEFENSIVE TEAM

E—Bill Atessis, Texas
E—Charlie Weaver, Southern California
T—Rock Perdoni, Georgia Tech
T—Joe Ehrmann, Syracuse
MG—Jim Stillwagon, Ohio State
LB—Jack Ham, Penn State
LB—Mike Anderson, Louisiana State
LB—Jack Tatum, Ohio State
DB—Larry Willingham, Auburn
DB—Clarence Ellis, Notre Dame
DB—Mike Sensibaugh, Ohio State
DB—Bill McClard, Arkansas

1971

OFFENSIVE TEAM

E—Johnny Rodgers, Nebraska
E—Terry Beasley, Auburn
T—Jerry Sisemore, Texas
T—Dave Jayner, Penn State
G—Royce Smith, Georgia
G—Reggie McKenzie, Michigan
C—Tom DeLeone, Ohio State
Q—Pat Sullivan, Auburn

B—Ed Marinaro, Cornell
B—Greg Pruitt, Oklahoma
B—Johnny Musso, Alabama

DEFENSIVE TEAM

E—Walt Patulski, Notre Dame
E—Willie Harper, Nebraska
T—Larry Jacobson, Nebraska
T—Mel Long, Toledo
LB—Mike Taylor, Michigan
LB—Jackie Walker, Tennessee
LB—Jeff Siemon, Stanford
DB—Tommy Casanova, Louisiana State
DB—Clarence Ellis, Notre Dame
DB—Brad Van Pelt, Michigan State
DB—Bobby Majors, Tennessee

1972

OFFENSIVE TEAM

E—Johnny Rodgers, Nebraska
E—Charles Young, Southern California
T—Jerry Sisemore, Texas
T—Pete Adams, Southern California
G—Ron Rusnak, North Carolina
G—John Hannah, Alabama
C—Tom Brahaney, Oklahoma
Q—Bert Jones, Louisiana State
B—Otis Armstrong, Purdue
B—Greg Pruitt, Oklahoma
B—Woodrow Green, Arizona State

DEFENSIVE TEAM

E—Bruce Bannon, Penn State
E—Willie Harper, Nebraska
T—Dave Butz, Purdue
T—Greg Marx, Notre Dame
MG—Rich Glover, Nebraska
LB—Randy Gradishar, Ohio State
LB—Jamie Rotella, Tennessee
DB—Cullen Bryant, Colorado
DB—Randy Logan, Michigan
DB—Conrad Graham, Tennessee
DB—Brad Van Pelt, Michigan State

MAJOR-COLLEGE CHAMPIONS

Pass Receiving

1937—Jim Benton, Arkansas
1938—Sam Boyd, Baylor
1939—Ken Kavanaugh, Louisiana State
1940—Eddie Bryant, Virginia
1941—Henry Stanton, Arizona
1942—Cullen Rogers, Texas A. and M.
1943—Neil Armstrong, Oklahoma A. and M.
1944-45—Reid Moseley, Georgia
1946—Neil Armstrong, Oklahoma A. and M.
1947—Barney Poole, Mississippi
1948—John O'Quinn, Wake Forest
1949—Art Weiner, North Carolina
1950—Gordon Cooper, Denver
1951—Dewey McConnell, Wyoming
1952—Ed Brown, Fordham

1953—John Carson, Georgia
1954—Jim Hanifan, California
1955—Hal Burnine, Missouri
1956—Art Powell, San Jose State
1957—Stuart Vaughn, Utah
1958—Dave Hibbert, Arizona
1959—Chris Burford, Stanford
1960—Hugh Campbell, Washington State
1961—Hugh Campbell, Washington State
1962—Vern Burke, Oregon State
1963—Lawrence Elkins, Baylor
1964—Howard Twilley, Tulsa
1965—Howard Twilley, Tulsa
1966—Glenn Meltzer, Wichita State
1967—Bob Goodridge, Vanderbilt
1968—Ron Sellers, Florida State
1969—Jerry Hendren, Idaho
1970—Mike Mikolayunas, Davidson
1971—Tom Reynolds, San Diego State
1972—Tom Forzani, Utah State

Punting
1937—John Pingel, Michigan State
1938—Jerry Dowd, St. Mary's
1939—Harry Dunkle, North Carolina
1940-41—Owen Price, Texas Mines
1942—Bob Cifers, Tennessee
1943—Harold Cox, Arkansas
1944—Bob Waterfield, U.C.L.A.
1945—Howard Maley, Southern Methodist
1946—John Galvin, Purdue
1947—Leslie Palmer, North Carolina State
1948—Charlie Justice, North Carolina
1949—Paul Stombaugh, Furman
1950—Zack Jordan, Colorado
1951—Chuck Spaulding, Wyoming
1952—Desmond Koch, Southern California
1953—Zeke Bratkowski, Georgia
1954—A.L. Terpening, New Mexico
1955—Don Chandler, Florida
1956—Kirk Wilson, U.C.L.A.
1957—Dave Sherer, Southern Methodist
1958—Bobby Walden, Georgia
1959—John Hadl, Kansas
1960—Dick Fitzsimmons, Denver
1961—Joe Zugar, Arizona State (Tempe)
1962—Joe Don Looney, Oklahoma
1963—Danny Thomas, S.M.U.
1964—R. Lambert, Mississippi
1965—Dave Lewis, Stanford
1966—Ron Widby, Tennessee
1967—Zenon Andrusyshyn, UCLA
1968—Danny Pitcock, Wichita
1969—Ed Marsh, Baylor
1970—Marv Bateman, Utah
1971—Marv Bateman, Utah
1972—Ray Guy, Southern Mississippi

Scoring
1937—Byron White, Colorado
1938—Parker Hall, Mississippi
1939—John Polanski, Wake Forest
1940—Tom Harmon, Michigan

1941—Bill Dudley, Virginia
1942—Bob Steuber, Missouri
1943—Steve Van Buren, Louisiana State
1944—Glenn Davis, Army
1945—Felix Blanchard, Army
1946—Gene Roberts, Chattanooga
1947—Lu Gambino, Maryland
1948—Fred Wendt, Texas Mines
1949—George Thomas, Oklahoma
1950—Bobby Reynolds, Nebraska
1951—Ollie Matson, San Francisco
1952—Jackie Parker, Mississippi State
1953—Earl Lindley, Utah State
1954—Art Luppino, Arizona
1955—Jim Swink, Texas Christian
1956—Clendon Thomas, Oklahoma
1957—Leon Burton, Tempe State
1958—Dick Bass, College of Pacific
1959—Pervis Atkins, New Mexico State
1960—Bob Gaiters, New Mexico State
1961—James Pilot, New Mexico State
1962—Jerry Logan, West Texas State
1963—Dave Casinelli, Memphis State;
          Cosmo Iacavazzi, Princeton (tie)
1964—Brian Piccolo, Wake Forest
1965—Howard Twilley, Tulsa
1966—Ken Hebert, Houston
1967—Leroy Keyes, Purdue
1968—Jim O'Brien, Cincinnati
1969—Steve Owens, Oklahoma
1970—Brian Bream, Air Force
1971—Ed Marinaro, Cornell
1972—Harold Henson, Ohio State

Rushing
1937—Byron White, Colorado
1938—Len Eshmont, Fordham
1939—John Polanski, Wake Forest
1940—Al Ghesquire, Detroit
1941—Frank Sinkwich, Georgia
1942—Rudy Mobley, Hardin-Simmons
1943—Creighton Miller, Notre Dame
1944—Wayne Williams, Minnesota
1945—Bob Fenimore, Oklahoma A. and M.
1946—Rudy Mobley, Hardin-Simmons
1947—Wilton Davis, Hardin-Simmons
1948—Fred Wendt, Texas Mines
1949—Johnny Dottley, Mississippi
1950—Wilford White, Tempe State
1951—Ollie Matson, San Francisco
1952—Howard Waugh, Tulsa
1953—J.C. Caroline, Illinois
1954-55—Art Luppino, Arizona
1956—Jim Crawford, Wyoming
1957—Leon Burton, Tempe State
1958—Dick Bass, College of Pacific
1959—Pervis Atkins, New Mexico State
1960—Bob Gaiters, New Mexico State
1961—James Pilot, New Mexico State
1962—James Pilot, New Mexico State
1963—Dave Casinelli, Memphis State
1964—Brian Piccolo, Wake Forest

1965–Mike Garrett, Southern California
1966–Ray McDonald, Idaho
1967–O.J. Simpson, Southern California
1968–O.J. Simpson, Southern California
1969–Steve Owens, Oklahoma
1970–Ed Marinaro, Cornell
1971–Ed Marinaro, Cornell
1972–Pete Van Valkenburg, Brigham Young

Passing
1937-38–Davey O'Brien, Texas Christian
1939–Kay Eakin, Arkansas
1940–Billy Sewell, Washington State
1941–Bud Schwenk, Washington (Mo.)
1942–Ray Evans, Kansas
1943–Johnny Cook, Georgia
1944–Paul Rickards, Pittsburgh
1945–Al Dekdebrun, Cornell
1946–Travis Tidwell, Auburn
1947–Chuck Conerly, Mississippi
1948–Stan Heath, Nevada
1949–Adrian Burk, Baylor
1950–Don Heinrich, Washington
1951–Don Klosterman, Loyola (Calif.)
1952–Don Heinrich, Washington
1953–Bob Garrett, Stanford
1954–Paul Larson, California
1955–George Welsh, Navy
1956–John Brodie, Stanford
1957–Ken Ford, Hardin-Simmons
1958–Buddy Humphrey, Baylor
1959–Dick Norman, Stanford
1960–Harold Stephens, Hardin Simmons
1961–Chon Gallegos, San Jose State
1962–Don Trull, Baylor
1963–Don Trull, Baylor
1964–Jerry Rhome, Tulsa
1965–Bill Anderson, Tulsa
1966–John Eckman, Wichita State
1967–Terry Stone, New Mexico
1968–Chuck Hixson, S.M.U.
1969–John Reaves, Florida
1970–Sonny Sixkiller, Washington
1971–Brian Sipe, San Diego State
1972–Dave Strock, Virginia Tech

Total Offense
1937–Byron White, Colorado
1938–Davey O'Brien, Texas Christian
1939–Ken Washington, U.C.L.A.
1940–Johnny Knolla, Creighton
1941–Bud Schwenk, Washington (Mo.)
1942–Frank Sinkwich, Georgia
1943–Bob Hoernschemeyer, Indiana
1944-45–Bob Fenimore, Oklahoma A. and M.
1946–Travis Tidwell, Auburn
1947–Fred Enke Jr., Arizona
1948–Stan Heath, Nevada
1949-50–Johnny Bright, Drake
1951–Dick Kazmaier, Princeton
1952–Ted Marchibroda, Detroit
1953–Paul Larson, California

1954–George Shaw, Oregon
1955–George Welsh, Navy
1956–John Brodie, Stanford
1957–Bobby Newman, Washington State
1958–Dick Bass, College of Pacific
1959–Dick Norman, Stanford
1960–Bill Kilmer, UCLA
1961–Dave Hoppman, Iowa State
1962–Terry Baker, Oregon State
1963–George Mira, Miami (Fla.)
1964–Jerry Rhome, Tulsa
1965–Bill Anderson, Tulsa
1966–Virgil Carter, Brigham Young
1967–Sal Olivas, New Mexico State
1968–Greg Cook, Cincinnati
1969–Dennis Shaw, San Diego State
1970–Pat Sullivan, Auburn
1971--Gary Huff, Florida State
1972–Dave Strock, Virginia Tech

SCORING LEADERS

Points	Total
1912–James Thorpe, Carlisle	198
1913–J. (Al) Spiegel, W. and J.	127
1914–John Imlay, Missouri Mines	180
1915–J.N. DePrato, Michigan State	188
1916–Ivan H. Grove, Henry-Kendall	196
1917–William A. Ingram, Navy	162
1918–No record	
1919–Ira Rodgers, West Virginia	147
1920–James Leech, V.M.I.	210
1921–A.C. Bowser, Bucknell	91
1922–B. Kingsley, Franklin Marshall	120
1923–John Levi, Haskell	149
1924–John Levi, Haskell	112
1925–Charles Flournoy, Tulane	128
1926–Mayes McClain, Haskell	253
1927–Myles Lane, Dartmouth	125
1928–Kenneth Strong, N.Y.U.	153
1929–Eugene McEver, Tennessee	130
1930–Leonard Macaluso, Colgate	145
1931–Robert Campiglio, West Liberty T	145
1932–Louis Bush, Mass. State	114
1933–Peter Young, Bluefield Institute	108
1934–Bill Shepherd, Western Maryland	133
1935–Ray Zeh, Western Reserve	112
1936–Charles Thomas, Delta (Ala.) T.	119
1937–Douglas Locke, St. Mary's (Tex.)	160
1938–Edward Smith, Rust (Miss.)	122
1939–Lloyd Madden, Colorado Mines	141
1940–John Hunt, Marshall (W. Va.)	162
1941–Bill Dudley, Virginia	134
1942–Ed McGovern, Rose Poly (Ind.)	165
1943–Robert Steuber, DePauw	129
1944–Glenn Davis, Army	120
1945–Walt Trojanowski, Connecticut	132
1946–Joe Carter, Florida A. & I.	152
1947–Darwin Horn, Pepperdine	115
Chuck Schoenherr, Wheaton	115
1948–Ted Scown, Sul Ross State	168
1949–Sylvester Polk, Maryland State	129
1950–Bobby Reynolds, Nebraska	157

1951—Paul Yackey, Heidelberg	132	1944—Glenn Davis, Army	20
1952—Al Conway, William Jewell	133	1945—Walt Trojanowski, Connecticut	22
1953—Leo Lewis, Lincoln (Mo.)	132	1946—Gene Roberts, Chattanooga	18
1954—Art Luppino, Arizona	166	1947—Darwin Horn, Pepperdine	19
1955—Nate Clark, Hillsdale	144	Chuck Schoenherr, Wheaton	19
1956—Larry Houdek, Kansas Wesleyan	114	1948—Ted Scown, Sul Ross State	28
1957—Len Lyles, Louisville	132	1949—Sylvester Polk, Maryland State	19
1958—Carl Herakovich, Rose Poly	168	George Thomas, Oklahoma	19
1959—Garney Henley, Huron	141	1950—Carl Taseff, John Carroll	23
1960—Bill Cooper, Muskingum	152	1951—Paul Yackey, Heidelberg	22
1961—James Pilot, New Mexico State	138	1952—Al Conway, William Jewell	22
1962—Mike Goings, Bluffton (Ohio)	132	1953—Leo Lewis, Lincoln (Mo.)	22
1963—Dave Casinelli, Memphis State;		1954—Art Luppino, Arizona	24
Cosmo Iacavazzi, Princeton (tie)	84	1955—Nate Clark, Hillsdale	24
1964—Brian Piccolo, Wake Forest	111	1956—Larry Houdek, Kansas Wesleyan	19
1965—Howard Twilley, Tulsa	127	1957—Len Lyles, Louisville	21
1966—Ken Hebert, Houston	113	1958—Carl Herakovich, Rose Poly	25
1967—Leroy Keyes, Purdue	114	1959—Garney Henley, Huron	22
1968—Jim O'Brien, Cincinnati	142	1960—Bob Gaiters, New Mexico State	23
1969—Steve Owens, Oklahoma	138	Bill Cooper, Muskingum	23
1970—Don McCauley, North Carolina	126	1961—Pete Pedro, West Texas State	22
1971—Ed Marinaro, Cornell	148	1962—Mike Goings, Bluffton (Ohio)	22
1972—Harold Henson, Ohio State	120	1963—Dave Casinelli, Memphis State	14

Touchdowns

1912—James Thorpe, Carlisle	25	Cosmo Iacavazzi, Princeton (tie)	14
1913—J. (Al) Spiegel, W. and J.	21	1964—Brian Piccolo, Wake Forest	17
1914—John Imlay, Missouri Mines	30	1965—Floyd Little, Syracuse	19
1915—J.M. DePrato, Michigan State	24	1966—Lee Jones, Buffalo	16
1916—John J. Gilroy, Georgetown	22	1967—Leroy Keyes, Purdue	19
1917—William A. Ingram, Navy	19	1968—O.J. Simpson, Southern California	22
R. Cornog, Swarthmore	19	1969—Steve Owens, Oklahoma	23
1918—No record		1970—Don McCauley, North Carolina	21
1919—Ira Rodgers, West Virginia	19	1971—Lydell Mitchell, Penn. State	29
1920—James Leech, V.M.I.	26	1972—Harold Henson, Ohio State	20
1921—Eddie Kaw, Cornell	15		
1922—B. Kingsley, Franklin & Marshall	20		
1923—John Levi, Haskell	24	**TROPHY WINNERS**	
1924—John Levi, Haskell	18		
1925—Charles Flournoy, Tulane	19	**John W. Heisman Memorial**	

1926—George Wilson, Lafayette 20

(Originated by the Downtown Athletic Club of New York and awarded to the country's outstanding player as voted by sports writers.)

1927—John Janoski, Duke	19		
1928—Kenneth Strong, N.Y.U.	21		
1929—Eugene McEver, Tennessee	21	1935—Jay Berwanger (back), Chicago	
Clark Hinkle, Bucknell	21	1936—Larry Kelley (end), Yale	
1930—Leonard Macaluso, Colgate	19	1937—Clint Frank (quarterback), Yale	
Albert Greeves, Mt. Morris	19	1938—Davey O'Brien (quarterback), Texas Christian	
1931—Robert Campiglio, West Liberty State	22	1939—Nile Kinnick (back), Iowa	
1932—Louis Bush, Mass. State	19	1940—Tom Harmon (back), Michigan	
1933—Peter Young, Bluefield Institute	18	1941—Bruce Smith (back), Minnesota	
1934—John Oravec, Williamette	20	1942—Frank Sinkwich (back), Georgia	
1935—Kenneth Noble, Baldwin-Wallace	16	1943—Angelo Bertelli (quarterback), Notre Dame	
R. Nori, DeKalb (Ill.) Teachers	16	1944—Leslie Horvath (quarterback), Ohio State	
Edward Stanley, Williams	16	1945—Felix Blanchard (back), Army	
1936—Charles Thomas, Delta (Ala.) T.	19	1946—Glenn Davis (back), Army	
Norman Schoen, Baldwin-Wallace	19	1947—Johnny Lujack (quarterback), Notre Dame	
1937—Doug Locke, St. Mary's (Tex.)	26	1948—Doak Walker (back), Southern Methodist	
1938—Edward Smith, Rust (Miss.)	20	1949—Leon Hart (end), Notre Dame	
1939—Lloyd Madden, Colorado Mines	23	1950—Vic Janowicz (back), Ohio State	
1940—John Hunt, Marshall (W.Va.)	27	1951—Dick Kazmaier (back), Princeton	
1941—Bill Dudley, Virginia	18	1952—Billy Vessels (back), Oklahoma	
1942—Ed McGovern, Rose Poly (Ind.)	23	1953—Johnny Lattner (back), Notre Dame	
1943—Robert Steuber, DePauw	19	1954—Alan Ameche, (back), Wisconsin	
		1955—Howard Cassady (back), Ohio State	

1956—Paul Hornung (quarterback), Notre Dame
1957—John Crow (back), Texas A. & M.
1958—Pete Dawkins (back), Army
1959—Billy Cannon (back), Louisiana State
1960—Joe Bellino (back), Navy
1961—Ernie Davis (back), Syracuse
1962—Terry Baker (back), Oregon State
1963—Roger Staubach (quarterback), Navy
1964—John Huarte (quarterback), Notre Dame
1965—Mike Garrett (back), Southern California
1966—Steve Spurrier (quarterback), Florida
1967—Gary Beban (quarterback), UCLA
1968—O.J. Simpson (back), Southern California
1969—Steve Owens (back), Oklahoma
1970—Jim Plunkett (quarterback), Stanford
1971—Pat Sullivan (quarterback), Auburn
1972—Johnny Rodgers (end), Nebraska

Teams

NATIONAL CHAMPIONS

(Courtesy of William M. Peterez, Ph. D., Archivist, Univ. of Southern California)

The Helms Athletic Foundation began selecting the number one team starting in 1889 until 1923.

From 1924 through 1940, the Dickenson system of grading was used to rank the teams for national championship trophies. The Jack F. Rissman Trophy was in competition from 1924 until it was retired by Notre Dame in 1930. The Knute Rockne Trophy, first offered in 1931, was retired by Michigan in 1940.

The Associated Press poll of sports writers, which was originated in 1936, and the United Press International ratings of 35 leading coaches, started in 1950, annually determine the ranking of the nation's college football teams.

Since 1941, the final writers poll of each season, conducted by The Associated Press, has been used toward determining permanent possession of the Dr. Henry L. Williams Trophy (1941-47, retired by Notre Dame), the Rev. J. Hugh O'Donnell Trophy (1948-56, retired by Oklahoma) and the AP Trophy (for which competition started in 1957).

United Press superseded by merger of U.P. and INS. in 1958 after making selections from 1950 to 1957, annually awards the United Press International Trophy to the selected by its rating board of coaches.

The Football Writers Association of America, through its Selection Committee, began to choose a national champion in 1954. The F.W.A.A. champion, who receives the Grantland Rice Award, is selected following the bowl games.

In 1959, the National Football Foundation & Hall of Fame awarded the General Douglas MacArthur Trophy for their selection.

Year	Team	W.	L.	T.
1889	Princeton	10	0	0
1890	Harvard	11	0	0
1891	Yale	13	0	0
1892	Yale	13	0	0
1893	Princeton	11	0	0
1894	Yale	16	0	0
1895	Pennsylvania	14	0	0
1896	Princeton	10	0	1
1897	Pennsylvania	15	0	0
1898	Harvard	11	0	0
1899	Harvard	10	0	1
1900	Yale	12	0	0
1901	Michigan	11	0	0
1902	Michigan	11	0	0
1903	Princeton	11	0	0
1904	Pennsylvania	12	0	0
1905	Chicago	11	0	0
1906	Princeton	9	0	1
1907	Yale	9	0	1
1908	Pennsylvania	11	0	1
1909	Yale	10	0	0
1910	Harvard	8	0	1
1911	Princeton	8	0	2
1912	Harvard	9	0	0
1913	Harvard	9	0	0
1914	Army	9	0	0
1915	Cornell	9	0	0
1916	Pittsburgh	8	0	0
1917	Georgia Tech	9	0	0
1918	Pittsburgh	4	1	0
1919	Harvard	9	0	1
1920	California	9	0	0
1921	Cornell	8	0	0
1922	Cornell	8	0	0
1923	Illinois	8	0	0
1924	Notre Dame	10	0	0
1925	Dartmouth	8	0	0
1926	Stanford	10	0	1
1927	Illinois	7	0	1
1928	Southern California	9	0	1
1929	Notre Dame	9	0	0
1930	Notre Dame	10	0	0
1931	Southern California	10	1	0
1932	Michigan	8	0	0
1933	Michigan	7	0	1
1934	Minnesota	8	0	0
1935	Southern Methodist	12	1	0
1936	Minnesota	7	1	0
1937	Pittsburgh	9	0	1
1938	Texas Christian	11	0	0
1939	Texas A. and M.	11	0	0
1940	Minnesota	8	0	0
1941	Minnesota	8	0	0
1942	Ohio State	9	1	0
1943	Notre Dame	9	1	0
1944	Army	9	0	0
1945	Army	9	0	0
1946	Notre Dame	8	0	1
1947	Notre Dame	9	0	0
1948	Michigan	9	0	0
1949	Notre Dame	10	0	0

Year	Team	W	L	T
1950 .. Oklahoma (AP, UP)		10	1	0
1951 .. Tennessee (AP, UP)		10	1	0
1952 .. Michigan State (AP, UP)		9	0	0
1953 .. Maryland (AP, UP)		10	1	0
1954 .. Ohio State (AP)		10	0	0
U.C.L.A. (UP)		9	0	0
1955 .. Oklahoma (AP, UP)		11	0	0
1956 .. Oklahoma (AP, UP)		10	0	0
1957 .. Auburn (AP)		10	0	0
1957 .. Ohio State (UP)		9	1	0
1958 .. Louisiana State (AP,UPI)		11	0	0
1959 .. Syracuse (AP, UPI)		11	0	0
1960 .. Minnesota (AP, UPI)		8	2	0
1961 .. Alabama (AP, UPI)		11	0	0
1962 .. Southern California (AP, UPI)		9	0	0
1963 .. Texas (AP, UPI)		10	0	0
1964 .. Alabama (AP, UPI)		10	0	0
1965 .. Michigan State (UPI)		10	0	0
Alabama (AP)		8	1	1
1966 .. Notre Dame (AP, UPI)		9	0	1
1967 .. Southern California(AP, UPI)		9	1	0
1968 .. Ohio State (AP, UPI)		9	0	0
1969 .. Texas (AP, UPI)		10	0	0
1970 .. Nebraska (AP)		10	0	1
Texas (UPI)		10	0	0
1971 .. Nebraska (AP, UPI)		12	0	0
1972 .. Southern California (AP, UPI)		11	0	0

NATIONAL ASSOCIATION OF INTERCOLLEGIATE ATHLETICS (N.A.I.A.)

Champions (Small Colleges)

1957—Pittsburg (Kansas) State
1958—NE Oklahoma (Tahlequah) State
1959—Texas A-I
1960—Lenoir Rhyne
1961—Pittsburg (Kansas) State
1962—Central Oklahoma (Edmund) State
1963—St. John's University (Collegeville)
1964—Concordia (Minn.) College and Sam Houston State
1965—St. John's University (Collegeville)
1966—Waynesburg (Pa.) College
1967—Fairmont (W. Virginia)
1968—Troy State (Ala.)
1969—Texas A & I
1970—Texas A & I
1971—Livingston (Ala.)
1972—East Texas State

ASSOCIATED PRESS YEARLY RANKINGS

1936

1. Minnesota
2. Louisiana State
3. Pittsburgh
4. Alabama
5. Washington
6. Santa Clara
7. Northwestern
8. Notre Dame
9. Nebraska
10. Pennsylvania

1937

1. Pittsburgh
2. California
3. Fordham
4. Alabama
5. Minnesota
6. Villanova
7. Dartmouth
8. Louisiana State
9. Notre Dame
10. Santa Clara

1938

1. Texas Christian
2. Tennessee
3. Duke
4. Oklahoma
5. Notre Dame
6. Carnegie Tech
7. Southern California
8. Pittsburgh
9. Holy Cross
10. Minnesota

1939

1. Texas A. and M.
2. Tennessee
3. Southern California
4. Cornell
5. Tulane
6. Missouri
7. U.C.L.A.
8. Duke
9. Iowa
10. Duquesne

1940

1. Minnesota
2. Stanford
3. Michigan
4. Tennessee
5. Boston College
6. Texas A. and M.
7. Nebraska
8. Northwestern
9. Mississippi State
10. Washington

1941

1. Minnesota
2. Duke
3. Notre Dame
4. Texas
5. Michigan

6. Fordham
7. Missouri
8. Duquesne
9. Texas A. and M.
10. Navy

1942

1. Ohio State
2. Georgia
3. Wisconsin
4. Tulsa
5. Georgia Tech
6. Notre Dame
7. Tennessee
8. Boston College
9. Michigan
10. Alabama

1943

1. Notre Dame
2. Iowa Pre-Flight
3. Michigan
4. Navy
5. Purdue
6. Great Lakes
7. Duke
8. Del Monte Pre-Flight
9. Northwestern
10. March Field

1944

1. Army
2. Ohio State
3. Randolph Field
4. Navy
5. Bainbridge
6. Iowa Pre-Flight
7. Southern California
8. Michigan
9. Notre Dame
10. Fourth Air Force

1945

1. Army
2. Alabama
3. Navy
4. Indiana
5. Oklahoma A. and M.
6. Michigan
7. St. Mary's
8. Pennsylvania
9. Notre Dame
10. Texas

1946

1. Notre Dame
2. Army
3. Georgia
4. U.C.L.A.
5. Illinois
6. Michigan
7. Tennessee
8. Louisiana State

9. North Carolina
10. Rice

1947

1. Notre Dame
2. Michigan
3. Southern Methodist
4. Penn State
5. Texas
6. Alabama
7. Pennsylvania
8. Southern California
9. North Carolina
10. Georgia Tech

1948

1. Michigan
2. Notre Dame
3. North Carolina
4. California
5. Oklahoma
6. Army
7. Northwestern
8. Georgia
9. Oregon
10. Southern Methodist

1949

1. Notre Dame
2. Oklahoma
3. California
4. Army
5. Rice
6. Ohio State
7. Michigan
8. Minnesota
9. Louisiana State
10. College of Pacific

1950

1. Oklahoma
2. Army
3. Texas
4. Tennessee
5. California
6. Princeton
7. Kentucky
8. Michigan State
9. Michigan
10. Clemson

1951

1. Tennessee
2. Michigan State
3. Maryland
4. Illinois
5. Georgia Tech
6. Princeton
7. Stanford
8. Wisconsin
9. Baylor
10. Oklahoma

1952

1. Michigan State
2. Georgia Tech
3. Notre Dame
4. Oklahoma
5. Southern California
6. U.C.L.A.
7. Mississippi
8. Tennessee
9. Alabama
10. Texas

1953

1. Maryland
2. Notre Dame
3. Michigan State
4. Oklahoma
5. U.C.L.A.
6. Rice
7. Illinois
8. Georgia Tech
9. Iowa
10. Virginia

1954

1. Ohio State
2. U.C.L.A.
3. Oklahoma
4. Notre Dame
5. Navy
6. Mississippi
7. Army
8. Maryland
9. Wisconsin
10. Arkansas

1955

1. Oklahoma
2. Michigan State
3. Maryland
4. U.C.L.A.
5. Ohio State
6. Texas Christian
7. Georgia Tech
8. Auburn
9. Notre Dame
10. Mississippi

1956

1. Oklahoma
2. Tennessee
3. Iowa
4. Georgia Tech
5. Texas A. and M.
6. Miami (Fla.)
7. Michigan
8. Syracuse
9. Michigan State
10. Oregon State

1957

1. Auburn
2. Ohio State
3. Michigan State
4. Oklahoma
5. Navy
6. Iowa
7. Mississippi
8. Rice
9. Texas A. and M.
10. Notre Dame

1958

1. Louisiana State
2. Iowa
3. Army
4. Auburn
5. Oklahoma
6. Air Force Academy
7. Wisconsin
8. Ohio State
9. Syracuse
10. Texas Christian

1959

1. Syracuse
2. Mississippi
3. Louisiana State
4. Texas
5. Georgia
6. Wisconsin
7. Texas Christian
8. Washington
9. Arkansas
10. Alabama

1960

1. Minnesota
2. Mississippi
3. Iowa
4. Navy
5. Missouri
6. Washington
7. Arkansas
8. Ohio State
9. Alabama
10. Duke

1961

1. Alabama
2. Ohio State
3. Texas
4. Louisiana State
5. Mississippi
6. Minnesota
7. Colorado
8. Michigan State
9. Arkansas
10. Utah State

1962

1. Southern California
2. Wisconsin
3. Mississippi
4. Texas
5. Alabama
6. Arkansas
7. Louisiana State

8. Oklahoma
9. Penn State
10. Minnesota

1963

1. Texas
2. Navy
3. Pittsburgh
4. Illinois
5. Nebraska
6. Auburn
7. Mississippi
8. Oklahoma
9. Alabama
10. Michigan State

1964

1. Alabama
2. Arkansas
3. Notre Dame
4. Michigan
5. Texas
6. Nebraska
7. Louisana State
8. Oregon State
9. Ohio State
10. Southern California

1965

1. Alabama
2. Michigan State
3. Arkansas
4. Nebraska
5. U.C.L.A.
6. Missouri
7. Tennessee
8. Southern California
9. Notre Dame
10. Texas Tech

1966

1. Notre Dame
2. Michigan State
3. Alabama
4. Georgia
5. U.C.L.A.
6. Nebraska
7. Purdue
8. Georgia Tech
9. Miami (Fla.)
10. Southern Methodist

1967

1. Southern California
2. Tennessee
3. Oklahoma
4. Indiana
5. Notre Dame
6. Wyoming
7. Oregon State
8. Alabama
9. Purdue
10. Penn State

1968

1. Ohio State
2. Penn State
3. Texas
4. So. California
5. Notre Dame
6. Arkansas
7. Kansas
8. Georgia
9. Missouri
10. Purdue

1969

1. Texas
2. Ohio State
3. Nebraska
4. Tennessee
5. Louisiana State
6. Notre Dame
7. Michigan
8. Arizona State
9. Arkansas
10. Auburn

1970

1. Nebraska
2. Notre Dame
3. Texas
4. Tennessee
5. Ohio State
6. Arizona State
7. Louisiana State
8. Stanford
9. Michigan
10. Auburn

1971

1. Nebraska
2. Oklahoma
3. Colorado
4. Alabama
5. Penn State
6. Michigan
7. Georgia
8. Arizona State
9. Tennessee
10. Stanford

1972

1. So. California
2. Oklahoma
3. Ohio State
4. Alabama
5. Penn State
6. Auburn
7. Texas
8. Michigan
9. Nebraska
10. Louisiana State

UNITED PRESS INTERNATIONAL YEARLY RATINGS

1950

1. Oklahoma
2. Texas

3. Tennessee
4. California
5. Army
6. Michigan
7. Kentucky
8. Princeton
9. Michigan State
10. Ohio State

1951

1. Tennessee
2. Michigan State
3. Illinois
4. Maryland
5. Georgia Tech
6. Princeton
7. Stanford
8. Wisconsin
9. Baylor
10. Texas Christian

1952

1. Michigan State
2. Georgia Tech
3. Notre Dame
4. (Tie). Oklahoma
4. (Tie). Southern California
6. U.C.L.A.
7. Mississippi
8. Tennessee
9. Alabama
10. Wisconsin

1953

1. Maryland
2. Notre Dame
3. Michigan State
4. U.C.L.A.
5. Oklahoma
6. Rice
7. Illinois
8. Texas
9. Georgia Tech
10. Iowa

1954

1. U.C.L.A.
2. Ohio State
3. Oklahoma
4. Notre Dame
5. Navy
6. Mississippi
7. Army
8. Arkansas
9. Miami (Fla.)
10. Wisconsin

1955

1. Oklahoma
2. Michigan State
3. Maryland
4. U.C.L.A.
5. Texas Christian
6. Ohio State
7. Georgia Tech

8. Notre Dame
9. Mississippi
10. Auburn

1956

1. Oklahoma
2. Tennessee
3. Iowa
4. Georgia Tech
5. Texas A. and M.
6. Miami (Fla.)
7. Michigan
8. Syracuse
9. Minnesota
10. Michigan State

1957

1. Ohio State
2. Auburn
3. Michigan State
4. Oklahoma
5. Iowa
6. Navy
7. Rice
8. Mississippi
9. Notre Dame
10. Texas A. and M.

1958

1. Louisiana State
2. Iowa
3. Army
4. Auburn
5. Oklahoma
6. Wisconsin
7. Ohio State
8. Air Force Academy
9. Texas Christian
10. Syracuse

1959

1. Syracuse
2. Mississippi
3. Louisiana State
4. Texas
5. Georgia
6. Wisconsin
7. Washington
8. Texas Christian
9. Arkansas
10. Penn State

1960

1. Minnesota
2. Iowa
3. Mississippi
4. Missouri
5. Washington
6. Navy
7. Arkansas
8. Ohio State
9. Kansas
10. Alabama

1961

1. Alabama
2. Ohio State
3. Louisiana State
4. Texas
5. Mississippi
6. Minnesota
7. Colorado
8. Arkansas
9. Michigan State
10. Utah State

1962

1. Southern California
2. Wisconsin
3. Mississippi
4. Texas
5. Alabama
6. Arkansas
7. Oklahoma
8. Louisiana State
9. Penn State
10. Minnesota

1963

1. Texas
2. Navy
3. Pittsburgh
4. Illinois
5. Nebraska
6. Auburn
7. Mississippi
8. Oklahoma
9. Alabama
10. Michigan State

1964

1. Alabama
2. Arkansas
3. Notre Dame
4. Michigan
5. Texas
6. Nebraska
7. Louisiana State
8. Oregon State
9. Ohio State
10. Southern California

1965

1. Michigan State
2. Arkansas
3. Nebraska
4. Alabama
5. U.C.L.A.
6. Missouri
7. Tennessee
8. Notre Dame
9. Southern California
10. Texas Tech

1966

1. Notre Dame
2. Michigan State
3. Alabama

4. Georgia
5. U.C.L.A.
6. Purdue
7. Nebraska
8. Georgia Tech
9. Southern Methodist
10. Miami (Fla.)

1967

1. Southern California
2. Tennessee
3. Oklahoma
4. Notre Dame
5. Wyoming
6. Indiana
7. Alabama
8. Oregon State
9. Purdue
10. U.C.L.A.

1968

1. Ohio State
2. So. California
3. Penn State
4. Georgia
5. Texas
6. Kansas
7. Tennessee
8. Notre Dame
9. Arkansas
10. Oklahoma

1969

1. Texas
2. Penn State
3. Arkansas
4. Southern California
5. Ohio State
6. Missouri
7. Louisiana State
8. Michigan
9. Notre Dame
10. U.C.L.A.

1970

1. Texas
2. Ohio State
3. Nebraska
4. Tennessee
5. Notre Dame
6. Arizona State
7. Louisiana State
8. Stanford
9. Michigan
10. Auburn

1971

1. Nebraska
2. Alabama
3. Oklahoma
4. Michigan
5. Penn State
6. Auburn
7. Colorado

8. Georgia
9. Arizona State
10. Louisiana State

1972

1. So. California
2. Oklahoma
3. Ohio State
4. Alabama
5. Texas
6. Michigan
7. Auburn
8. Penn State
9. Nebraska
10. Louisiana State

CONFERENCE CHAMPIONS

Ivy League

The Ivy League was an informal group of Eastern Colleges from the turn of the century until 1956, when it organized formally for football competition. Army and Navy dropped out of the informal league several years before the start of formal circuit competition and are not members now.

1900—Yale (won 5, lost 0)
1901—Harvard (6–0)
1902—Yale (3–0–1)
1903—Princeton (4–0)
1904—Pennsylvania (4–0)
1905—Yale (5–0); Penn (4–0)
1906—Princeton (4–0–1)
1907—Penn (3–0); Dartmouth (1–0)
1908—Harvard (3–0)
1909—Yale (4–0); Penn (2–0)
1910—Pennsylvania (2–0)
1911—Princeton (3–0–1)
1912—Harvard (4–0)
1913—Harvard (5–0); Dartmouth (2–0)
1914—Cornell (2–0)
1915—Cornell (2–0)
1916—Brown (2–0)
1917—Pennsylvania (2–0)
1918—Pennsylvania (1–0)
1919—Navy (1–0)
1920—Dartmouth (3–0)
1921—Cornell (3–0); Navy (2–0)
1922—Cornell (3–0); Princeton (2–0)
1923—Yale (4–0); Cornell (3–0)
1924—Pennsylvania (2–0)
1925—Dartmouth (3–0); Penn (3–0)
1926—Brown (3–0)
1927—Yale (5–0)
1928—Army (2–0); Navy (2–0)
1929—Dartmouth (4–2)
1930—Army (2–1)
1931—Cornell (3–1)
1932—Army (3–0); Brown (3–0)
1933—Princeton (5–0)
1934—Navy (3–0)
1935—Princeton (6–0)
1936—Dartmouth (5–0–1)

1937—Dartmouth (4–0–2)
1938—Cornell (3–0–1)
1939—Cornell (4–0)
1940—Pennsylvania (5–0–1)
1941—Pennsylvania (6–1–0)
1942—Navy (4–1)
1943—Navy (4–0)
1944—Army (3–0)
1945—Army (2–0)
1946—Yale (4–1–1); Harvard (3–1–0); Penn (3–1–0)
1947—Pennsylvania (4–0)
1948—Cornell (4–0)
1949—Cornell (5–1)
1950—Princeton (5–0)
1951—Princeton (6–0)
1952—Pennsylvania (4–0)
1953—Cornell (3–0–2)
1954—Yale (4–2); Cornell (4–2)
1955—Princeton (6–1)
1956—Yale (7–0)
1957—Princeton (6–1)
1958—Dartmouth (6–1)
1959—Pennsylvania (6–1)
1960—Yale (7–0)
1961—Columbia (6–1); Harvard (6–1)
1962—Dartmouth (7–0)
1963—Dartmouth (6–1); Princeton (6–1)
1964—Princeton (7–0)
1965—Dartmouth (7–0)
1966—Harvard (6–1); Dartmouth (6–1)
1967—Yale (7–0)
1968—Yale (6–0–1), Harvard (6–0–1)
1969—Princeton (6–1), Dartmouth (6–1), Yale (6–1)
1970—Dartmouth (9–0)
1971—Dartmouth (8–1), Cornell (8–1)
1972—Dartmouth (5–1–1)

Western (Big Ten)

1896–97—Wisconsin
1898—Michigan
1899—Chicago
1900—Minnesota, Iowa
1901—Michigan, Wisconsin
1902—Michigan
1903—Michigan, Minnesota
1904—Michigan, Minnesota
1905—Chicago
1906—Minnesota, Wisconsin
1907–08—Chicago
1909—Minnesota
1910—Illinois, Minnesota
1911—Minnesota
1912—Wisconsin
1913—Chicago
1914—Illinois
1915—Illinois, Minnesota
1916–17—Ohio State
1918–19—Illinois
1920—Ohio State
1921—Iowa

1922—Iowa, Michigan, Chicago
1923—Illinois, Michigan
1924—Chicago
1925—Michigan
1926—Michigan, Northwestern
1927—28—Illinois
1929—Purdue
1930—Michigan, Northwestern
1931—Michigan, Northwestern, Purdue
1932—33—Michigan
1934—Minnesota
1935—Minnesota, Ohio State
1936—Northwestern
1937—38—Minnesota
1939—Ohio State
1940—41—Minnesota
1942—Ohio State
1943—Michigan, Purdue
1944—Ohio State
1945—Indiana
1946—Illinois
1947—48—Michigan
1949—Ohio State, Michigan
1950—Michigan
1951—Illinois
1952—Wisconsin, Purdue
1953—Michigan State, Illinois
1954—55—Ohio State
1956—Iowa
1957—Ohio State
1958—Iowa
1959—Wisconsin
1960—Minnesota, Iowa
1961—Ohio State
1962—Wisconsin
1963—Illinois
1964—Michigan
1965—66—Michigan State
1967—Indiana, Purdue, Minn.
1968—Ohio State
1969—Michigan, Ohio State
1970—Ohio State
1971—Michigan
1972—Ohio State

Big Eight

1928—29—Nebraska
1930—Kansas
1931—33—Nebraska
1934—Kansas State
1935—37—Nebraska
1938—Oklahoma
1939—Missouri
1940—Nebraska
1941—42—Missouri
1943—44—Oklahoma
1945—Missouri
1946—47—Oklahoma, Kansas
1948—59—Oklahoma
1960—Missouri
1961—Colorado
1962—Oklahoma

1963—66—Nebraska
1967—Oklahoma
1968—Kansas, Oklahoma
1969—Missouri, Nebraska
1970—71—Nebraska
1972—Oklahoma

Southeastern

1933—Alabama
1934—Tulane, Alabama
1935—36—Louisiana State
1937—Alabama
1938—Tennessee
1939—Tennessee, Georgia Tech, Tulane
1940—Tennessee
1941—Mississippi State
1942—Georgia
1943—44—Georgia Tech
1945—Alabama
1946—Georgia, Tennessee
1947—Mississippi
1948—Georgia
1949—Tulane
1950—Kentucky
1951—Georgia Tech, Tennessee
1952—Georgia Tech
1953—Alabama
1954—55—Mississippi
1956—Tennessee
1957—Auburn
1958—Louisiana State
1959—Georgia
1960—Mississippi
1961—Alabama, Louisiana State
1962—63—Mississippi
1964—65—Alabama
1966—Alabama, Georgia
1967—Tennessee
1968—Georgia
1969—Tennessee
1970—Louisiana State
1971—72—Alabama

Southern

1922—Georgia Tech
1923—Vanderbilt
1924—26—Alabama
1927—28—Georgia Tech
1929—Tulane
1930—Alabama, Tulane
1931—Tulane
1932—Tennessee, Auburn
1933—Duke
1934—Washington and Lee
1935—36—Duke
1937—North Carolina
1938—39—Duke
1940—Clemson
1941—Duke
1942—William and Mary
1943—45—Duke

1946—North Carolina
1947—William and Mary
1948—Clemson
1949—North Carolina
1950—Washington and Lee
1951—Maryland, V.M.I.
1952—Duke
1953—56—West Virginia
1957—V.M.I.
1958—West Virginia
1959—V.M.I.
1960—V.M.I.
1961—Citadel
1962—V.M.I.
1963—Virginia Tech
1964—65—West Virginia
1966—East Carolina, William & Mary
1967—West Virginia
1968—Richmond
1969—Richmond, Davidson
1970—William & Mary
1971—Richmond
1972—East Carolina

Atlantic Coast

1953—54—Duke
1955—Maryland, Duke
1956—Clemson
1957—North Carolina State
1958—Clemson
1959—Clemson
1960—Duke
1961—Duke
1962—Duke
1963—North Carolina State, North Carolina
1964—North Carolina State
1965—Duke, South Carolina
1966—67—Clemson
1968—North Carolina St.
1969—South Carolina
1970—Wake Forest
1971—72—North Carolina

Missouri Valley

1907—Nebraska
1908—Kansas
1909—Missouri
1910—12—Nebraska
1913—Missouri
1914—15—Nebraska
1916—Nebraska, Missouri
1917—Kansas
1918—No award
1919—Missouri
1920—Oklahoma
1921—22—Nebraska
1923—Kansas
1924—25—Missouri
1926—Nebraska
1927—Missouri
1928—29—Drake

1930—Drake, Oklahoma A. & M.
1931—Drake
1932—Oklahoma A. & M.
1933—Drake, Oklahoma A. & M.
1934—Washington
1935—Washington, Tulsa
1936—Tulsa, Creighton
1937—38—Tulsa
1939—Washington
1940—43—Tulsa
1944—45—Oklahoma A. & M.
1946—47—Tulsa
1948—Oklahoma A. & M.
1949—Detroit
1950—51—Tulsa
1952—Houston
1953—Oklahoma A. & M., Detroit
1954—Wichita
1955—Wichita, Detroit
1956—57—Houston
1958—North Texas State
1959—North Texas State, Houston
1960—Wichita
1961—Wichita
1962—Tulsa
1963—Cincinnati, Wichita State
1964—Cincinnati.
1965—Tulsa
1966—North Texas State, Tulsa
1967—North Texas State
1968—69—Memphis State
1970—Louisville
1971—Memphis State
1972—Louisville, West Texas, Drake

Southwest

1915—Baylor
1916—No award
1917—Texas A.& M.
1918—No award
1919—Texas A. & M.
1920—Texas
1921—Texas A. & M.
1922—Baylor
1923—Southern Methodist
1924—Baylor
1925—Texas A. & M.
1926—Southern Methodist
1927—Texas A. & M.
1928—Texas
1929—Texas Christian
1930—Texas
1931—Southern Methodist
1932—Texas Christian
1933—No award
1934—Rice
1935—Southern Methodist
1936—Arkansas
1937—Rice
1938—Texas Christian
1939—Texas A. & M.
1940—Texas A. & M., S.M.U.

1941–Texas A. & M.
1942–43–Texas
1944–Texas Christian
1945–Texas
1946–Arkansas, Rice
1947–48–Southern Methodist
1949–Rice
1950–Texas
1951–Texas Christian
1952–Texas
1953–Rice, Texas
1954–Arkansas
1955–Texas Christian
1956–Texas A. & M.
1957–Rice
1958–Texas Christian
1959–Arkansas, Texas, Texas Christian
1960–Arkansas
1961–Arkansas, Texas
1962–63–Texas
1964–65–Arkansas
1966–Southern Methodist
1967–Texas A & M
1968–Texas, Arkansas
1969–72–Texas

Rocky Mountain (Skyline)

1938–Utah
1939–Colorado
1940–41–Utah
1942–Colorado, Utah
1943–44–Colorado
1945–Denver
1946–Utah State, Denver
1947–48–Utah
1949–50–Wyoming
1951–53–Utah
1954–Denver
1955–Colorado A. & M.
1956–Wyoming
1957–Utah
1958–Wyoming
1959–Wyoming
1960–Wyoming, Utah State
1961–Wyoming, Utah State
   (Conference dissolved, effective in 1962)

Western Athletic Conference

1962–63–New Mexico
1964–Utah, New Mexico, Arizona
1965–Brigham Young
1966–68–Wyoming
1969–72–Arizona State

Pacific Coast

1916–Washington
1917–Washington State
1918–No competition
1919–Oregon, Washington
1920–23–California
1924–Stanford
1925–Washington

1926–Stanford
1927–Southern California, Stanford
1928–29–Southern California
1930–Washington State
1931–32–Southern California
1933–Oregon, Stanford
1934–Stanford
1935–California, U.C.L.A., Stanford
1936–Washington, Southern California
1937–38–California
1939–Southern California
1940–Stanford
1941–Oregon State
1942–U.C.L.A.
1943–45–Southern California
1946–U.C.L.A.
1947–Southern California
1948–California, Oregon
1949–50–California
1951–Stanford
1952–Southern California
1953–55–U.C.L.A.
1956–Oregon State
1957–Oregon State, Oregon
1958–California
   (Conference dissolved, effective in 1959.)

PACIFIC EIGHT

1959–Southern California, UCLA, Washington
1960–Washington
1961–UCLA
1962–Southern California
1963–Washington
1964–Oregon State, Southern California
1965–U.C.L.A.
1966–69–Southern California
1970–71–Stanford
1972–Southern California

EASTERN CHAMPIONS
   (August V. Lambert Memorial Trophy.)

1936–Pittsburgh
1937–Pittsburgh
1938–Carnegie Tech
1939–Cornell
1940–Boston College
1941–Fordham
1942–Boston College
1943–Navy
1944–Army
1945–Army
1946–Army
1947–Pennsylvania
1948–Army
1949–Army
1950–Princeton
1951–Princeton
1952–Syracuse
1953–Army
1954–Navy
1955–Pittsburgh

1956—Syracuse
1957—Navy
1958—Army
1959—Syracuse
1960—Navy, Yale
1961—Penn State
1962—Penn State
1963—Navy
1964—Penn State
1965—Dartmouth
1966—Syracuse
1967—69—Penn State
1970—Dartmouth
1971—72—Penn State

BOWL GAMES

In 1915 the city of Pasadena, Calif., decided to stage a football game as part of its Rose Festival on Jan. 1, 1916. Washington State was the outstanding Pacific Coast Conference team in 1915 and was given the privilege of inviting an Eastern team to meet it in the Pasadena Bowl. Washington State defeated Brown, 14 to 0, and that was the beginning of the bowl games of post-season football, although in 1902 there had been a bowl game—Michigan vs. Stanford, which Michigan won, 49 to 0.

In 1917, Oregon State played Pennsylvania in the Pasadena Rose Bowl. The 1918 and 1919 bowl games were between service elevens. In 1920, Harvard defeated Oregon, 7 to 6, and there was a game at Pasadena every New Year from then until Jan. 1, 1942, when war conditions caused transfer of the contest to the Duke Stadium in Durham, N.C. Play was resumed in the Rose Bowl in 1943.

In 1946 it was decreed that the Rose Bowl games, for a 5-year period beginning in 1947, were to be between the winner of the Pacific Coast Conference title and the Western Conference champion. The pact has been renewed several times.

The success of the early Rose Bowl games brought about the origination of other post-season contests, usually played Jan. 1 of the year directly following the end of the football season. Among the earliest of such games was the East-West series, which started in San Francisco in 1925. Stars from Eastern college teams meet those of the West, with the net proceeds going to the Charity Committee of the Masonic Shrine.

Rose Bowl

The Rose Bowl contest at Pasadena, Calif., was first known as the "Tournament of Roses Association Game." The name was changed to "Rose Bowl Game" in 1923, the year in which the present stadium was dedicated. Harlan W. Hall of Pasadena is credited with naming the stadium the "Rose Bowl."

1902—Michigan 49, Stanford 0
1916—Washington State 14, Brown 0
1917—Oregon 14, Pennsylvania 0
1918—Mare Island Marines 19, Camp Lewis Army 7
1919—Great Lakes Navy 17, Mare Island Marines 0
1920—Harvard 7, Oregon 6
1921—California 28, Ohio State 0
1922—Wash. & Jeff. 0, California 0
1923—So. California 14, Penn State 3
1924—Navy 14, Washington 14
1925—Notre Dame 27, Stanford 10
1926—Alabama 20, Washington 19
1927—Alabama 7, Stanford 7
1928—Stanford 7, Pittsburgh 6
1929—Georgia Tech 8, California 7
1930—So. California 47, Pittsburgh 14
1931—Alabama 24, Wash. State 0
1932—So. California 21, Tulane 12
1933—So. California 35, Pittsburgh 0
1934—Columbia 7, Stanford 0
1935—Alabama 29, Stanford 13
1936—Stanford 7, So. Methodist 0
1937—Pittsburgh 21, Washington 0
1938—California 13, Alabama 0
1939—So. California 7, Duke 3
1940—So. California 14, Tennessee 0
1941—Stanford 21, Nebraska 13
1942—Oregon St. 20, Duke 16 (at Durham)
1943—Georgia 9, UCLA 0
1944—So. California 29, Washington 0
1945—So. California 25, Tennessee 0
1946—Alabama 34, So. California 14
1947—Illinois 45, UCLA 14
1948—Michigan 49, So. California 0
1949—Northwestern 20, California 14
1950—Ohio State 17, California 14
1951—Michigan 14, California 6
1952—Illinois 40, Stanford 7
1953—So. California 7, Wisconsin 0
1954—Mich. State 28, UCLA 20
1955—Ohio State 20, So. California 7
1956—Mich. State 17, UCLA 14
1957—Iowa 35, Oregon St. 19
1958—Ohio State 10, Oregon 7
1959—Iowa 38, California 12
1960—Washington 44, Wisconsin 8
1961—Washington 17, Minnesota 7
1962—Minnesota 21, UCLA 3
1963—So. California 42, Wisconsin 37
1964—Illinois 17, Washington 7
1965—Michigan 34, Oregon St. 7
1966—UCLA 14, Mich. State 12
1967—Purdue 14, So. California 13
1968—So. California 14, Indiana 3
1969—Ohio State 27, So. California 16
1970—So. California 10, Michigan 3
1971—Stanford 27, Ohio State 17
1972—Stanford 13, Michigan 12
1973—So. California 42, Ohio State 17

Orange Bowl (Miami)

1933—Miami (Fla.) 7, Manhattan 0
1934—Duquesne 33, Miami (Fla.) 7
1935—Bucknell 26, Miami (Fla.) 0
1936—Catholic U. 20, Mississippi 19
1937—Duquesne 13, Miss. State 12
1938—Auburn 6, Mich. State 0
1939—Tennessee 17, Oklahoma 0
1940—Georgia Tech 21, Missouri 7
1941—Miss. State 14, Georgetown 7
1942—Georgia 40, TCU 26
1943—Alabama 37, Boston Col. 21
1944—LSU 19, Texas A&M 14
1945—Tulsa 26, Georgia Tech 12
1946—Miami (Fla.) 13, Holy Cross 6
1947—Rice 8, Tennessee 0
1948—Georgia Tech 20, Kansas 14
1949—Texas 41, Georgia 28
1950—Santa Clara 21, Kentucky 13
1951—Clemson 15, Miami (Fla.) 14
1952—Georgia Tech 17, Baylor 14
1953—Alabama 61, Syracuse 6
1954—Oklahoma 7, Maryland 0
1955—Duke 34, Nebraska 7
1956—Oklahoma 20, Maryland 6
1957—Colorado 27, Clemson 21
1958—Oklahoma 48, Duke 21
1959—Oklahoma 21, Syracuse 6
1960—Georgia 14, Missouri 0
1961—Missouri 21, Navy 14
1962—LSU 25, Colorado 7
1963—Alabama 17, Oklahoma 0
1964—Nebraska 13, Auburn 7
1965—Texas 21, Alabama 17
1966—Alabama 39, Nebraska 28
1967—Florida 27, Georgia Tech 12
1968—Oklahoma 26, Tennessee 24
1969—Penn State 15, Kansas 14
1970—Penn State 10, Missouri 3
1971—Nebraska 17, Louisiana St. 12
1972—Nebraska 38, Alabama 6
1973—Nebraska 40, Notre Dame 6

Sugar Bowl (New Orleans)

1935—Tulane 20, Temple 14
1936—TCU 3, LSU 2
1937—Santa Clara 21, LSU 14
1938—Santa Clara 6, LSU 0
1939—TCU 15, Carnegie Tech 7
1940—Texas A&M 14, Tulane 13
1941—Boston Col. 19, Tennessee 13
1942—Fordham 2, Missouri 0
1943—Tennessee 14, Tulsa 7
1944—Georgia Tech 20, Tulsa 18
1945—Duke 29, Alabama 26
1946—Oklahoma A&M 33, St. Mary's 13
1947—Georgia 20, No. Carolina 10
1948—Texas 27, Alabama 7
1949—Oklahoma 14, No. Carolina 6
1950—Oklahoma 35, LSU 0
1951—Kentucky 13, Oklahoma 7

1952—Maryland 28, Tennessee 13
1953—Georgia Tech 24, Mississippi 7
1954—Georgia Tech 42, West Virginia 19
1955—Navy 21, Mississippi 0
1956—Georgia Tech 7, Pittsburgh 0
1957—Baylor 13, Tennessee 7
1958—Mississippi 39, Texas 7
1959—LSU 7, Clemson 0
1960—Mississippi 21, LSU 0
1961—Mississippi 14, Rice 6
1962—Alabama 10, Arkansas 3
1963—Mississippi 17, Arkansas 13
1964—Alabama 12, Mississippi 7
1965—LSU 13, Syracuse 10
1966—Missouri 20, Florida 18
1967—Alabama 34, Nebraska 7
1968—LSU 20, Wyoming 13
1969—Arkansas 16, Georgia 2
1970—Mississippi 27, Arkansas 22
1971—Tennessee 34, Air Force 13
1972—Oklahoma 40, Auburn 22
1973—Oklahoma 14, Penn State 0

Cotton Bowl (Dallas)

1937—TCU 16, Marquette 6
1938—Rice 28, Colorado 14
1939—St. Mary's 20, Texas Tech 13
1940—Clemson 6, Boston Col. 3
1941—Texas A&M 13, Fordham 12
1942—Alabama 29, Texas A&M 21
1943—Texas 14, Georgia Tech 7
1944—Randolph Field 7, Texas 7
1945—Oklahoma A&M 34, TCU 0
1946—Texas 40, Missouri 27
1947—Arkansas 0, LSU 0
1948—So. Methodist 13, Penn State 13
1949—So. Methodist 21, Oregon 13
1950—Rice 27, No. Carolina 13
1951—Tennessee 20, Texas 14
1952—Kentucky 20, TCU 7
1953—Texas 16, Tennessee 0
1954—Rice 28, Alabama 6
1955—Georgia Tech 14, Arkansas 6
1956—Mississippi 14, TCU 13
1957—TCU 28, Syracuse 27
1958—Navy 20, Rice 7
1959—TCU 0, Air Force 0
1960—Syracuse 23, Texas 14
1961—Duke 7, Arkansas 6
1962—Texas 12, Mississippi 7
1963—LSU 13, Texas 0
1964—Texas 28, Navy 6
1965—Arkansas 10, Nebraska 7
1966—LSU 14, Arkansas 7
1967—Georgia 24, So. Methodist 9
1968—Texas A&M 20, Alabama 16
1969—Texas 36, Tennessee 13
1970—Texas 21, Notre Dame 17
1971—Notre Dame 24, Texas 11
1972—Penn State 30, Texas 6
1973—Texas 17, Alabama 13

Sun Bowl

(At El Paso, Tex.)
1936—Hardin-Simmons 14, New Mexico State 14
1937—Hardin-Simmons 34, Texas Mines 6
1938—West Virginia 7, Texas Tech 6
1939—Utah 26, New Mexico 0
1940—Catholic U. 0, Arizona State (Tempe) 0
1941—Western Reserve 26, Ariz. State (Tempe) 13
1942—Tulsa 6, Texas Tech 0
1943—2d Air Force 13, Hardin-Simmons 7
1944—Southwestern 7, New Mexico 0
1945—Southwestern 35, U. of Mexico 0
1946—New Mexico 34, Denver 24
1947—Cincinnati 18, Virginia Tech 6
1948—Miami (Ohio) 13, Texas Tech 12
1949—West Virginia 21, Texas Mines 12
1950—Texas Western 33, Georgetown 20
1951—West Texas State 14, Cincinnati 13
1952—Texas Tech 25, College of Pacific 14
1953—College of Pacific 26, Miss. Southern 7
1954—Texas Western 37, Mississippi Southern 14
1955—Texas Western 47, Florida State 20
1956—Wyoming 21, Texas Tech 14
1957—George Washington 13, Texas Western 0
1958—Louisville 34, Drake 20
1959—Wyoming 14, Hardin Simmons 6
1960—New Mexico State 28, North Texas State 8
1961—New Mexico State 20, Utah State 13
1962—Villanova 17, Wichita 9
1963—West Texas State 15, Ohio University 14
1964—Oregon 21, Southern Methodist 14
1965—Georgia 7, Texas Tech 0
1966—Texas Western 13, Texas Christian 12
1967—Wyoming 28, Florida State 20
1968—Texas (El Paso) 14, Mississippi 7
1969—Auburn 34, Arizona 10
1969—(Dec.) Nebraska 45, Georgia 6
1970—(Dec.) Georgia Tech 17, Texas Tech 9
1971—(Dec.) LSU 33, Iowa State 15
1972—(Dec.) North Carolina 32, Texas Tech 28

Gator Bowl

(At Jacksonville, Fla.)
1946—Wake Forest 26, South Carolina 14
1947—Oklahoma 34, North Carolina State 13
1948—Maryland 20, Georgia 20
1949—Clemson 24, Missouri 23
1950—Maryland 20, Missouri 7
1951—Wyoming 20, Washington and Lee 7
1952—Miami (Fla.) 14, Clemson 0
1953—Florida 14, Tulsa 13
1954—Texas Tech 35, Auburn 13
1955—Auburn 33, Baylor 13
1956—Vanderbilt 25, Auburn 13
1957—Georgia Tech 21, Pittsburgh 14
1958—Tennessee 3, Texas A.&M. 0
1958—(Dec. 27)—Mississippi 7, Florida 3
1959—Mississippi 7, Florida 3
1960—Arkansas 14, Georgia Tech 7
1961—Florida 13, Baylor 12
1962—Penn State 30, Georgia Tech 15

1963—Florida 17, Penn State 7
1964—North Carolina 35, Air Force 0
1965—Florida State 36, Oklahoma 19
1966—Georgia Tech 31, Texas Tech 21
1967—Tennessee 18, Syracuse 12
1968—Florida State 17, Penn State 17
1969—Missouri 35, Alabama 10
1969—(Dec.) Florida 14, Tennessee 13
1971—Auburn 35, Mississippi 28
1972—Georgia 7, North Carolina 3
1973—Auburn 24, Colorado 3

Astro-Blue Bonnet Bowl (Houston)

1959—Clemson 23, TCU 7
1960—Texas 3, Alabama 3
1961—Kansas 33, Rice 7
1962—Missouri 14, Georgia Tech 10
1963—Baylor 14, LSU 7
1964—Tulsa 14, Mississippi 7
1965—Tennessee 27, Tulsa 6
1966—Texas 19, Mississippi 0
1967—Colorado 31, Miami (Fla.) 21
1968—SMU 28, Oklahoma 27
1969—Houston 36, Auburn 7
1970—Oklahoma 24, Alabama 24
1971—Colorado 29, Houston 17
1972—Tennessee 24, LSU 17

East-West (Shrine Classic)

(At San Francisco)
1925—(Dec. 26)—West 6, East 0
1927—West 7, East 3
1927—(Dec. 26)—West 16, East 6
1928—(Dec. 29)—East 20, West 0
1930—East 19, West 7
1930—(Dec. 27)—West 3, East 0
1932—East 6, West 0
1933—West 21, East 13
1934—West 12, East 0
1935—West 19, East 13
1936—East 19, West 3
1937—East 3, West 0
1938—East 0, West 0
1939—West 14, East 0
1940—West 28, East 11
1941—West 20, East 14
1942—West 6, East 6 (at New Orleans)
1943—East 13, West 12
1944—East 13, West 13
1945—West 13, East 0
1946—West 7, East 7
1947—West 13, East 9
1948—East 40, West 9
1949—East 14, West 12
1950—East 28, West 6
1951—West 16, East 7
1952—East 15, West 14
1953—East 21, West 20
1954—West 31, East 7
1955—East 13, West 12
1956—East 29, West 6

1957—West 7, East 6
1958—West 27, East 13
1959—East 26, West 14
1960—West 21, East 14
1961—East 7, West 0
1962—West 21, East 8
1963—East 25, West 19
1964—East 6, West 6
1965—West 11, East 7
1966—West 22, East 7
1967—East 45, West 22
1968—East 16, West 14
1968—(Dec.)—West 18, East 7
1969—(Dec.)—West 15, East 0
1971—(Jan.)—West 17, East 13
1971—(Dec.)—West 17, East 13
1972—(Dec.)—East 9, West 3

North-South (Shrine All-Stars)

Formerly at Baltimore, Md.; Knoxville, Tenn., and Birmingham, Ala.; now at Miami. Game usually played in December.)

1932—South 7, North 6
1933—No game
1934—North 7, South 0
1935—38—No games
1939—(Jan. 2)—North 7, South 0
1939—(Dec. 30)—South 33, North 20
1940—North 14, South 12
1941—South 16, North 0
1942—South 24, North 0
1943—No game
1944—South 24, North 7
1945—North 26, South 0
1946—South 20, North 13
1947—South 33, North 6
1948—North 19, South 13
1949—South 27, North 13
1950—North 20, South 14
1951—South 14, North 9
1952—South 35, North 7
1953—South 21, North 21
1954—South 20, North 0
1955—South 20, North 17
1956—South 20, North 7
1957—North 17, South 7
1958—North 23, South 20
1959—South 49, North 20
1960—North 27, South 17
1961—North 41, South 14
1962—North 35, South 16
1963—South 15, North 14
1964—North 37, South 30
1965—South 16, North 14
1966—North 27, South 26
1967—North 27, South 14
1968—North 24, South 0
1968—(Dec.)—North 3, South 0
1969—(Dec.)—North 31, South 10
1970—(Dec.)—North 28, South 7

1971—(Dec.)—South 7, North 6
1972—(Dec.)—North 17, South 10

Blue-Gray

(At Montgomery, Ala. Game usually played in December.)

1938—Blue 7, Gray 0
1939—Gray 33, Blue 20
1940—Blue 14, Gray 12
1941—Gray 16, Blue 0
1942—Gray 24, Blue 0
1943—No college game
1944—Gray 24, Blue 7
1945—Blue 26, Gray 0
1946—Gray 20, Blue 13
1947—Gray 33, Blue 6
1948—Blue 19, Gray 13
1949—Gray 27, Blue 13
1950—Gray 31, Blue 6
1951—Gray 20, Blue 14
1952—Gray 28, Blue 7
1953—Gray 40, Blue 20
1954—Blue 14, Gray 7
1955—Gray 20, Blue 19
1956—Blue 14, Gray 0
1957—Gray 21, Blue 20
1958—Blue 16, Gray 0
1959—Blue 20, Gray 8
1960—Blue 35, Gray 7
1961—Gray 9, Blue 7
1962—Blue 10, Gray 6
1963—Gray 21, Blue 14
1964—Blue 10, Gray 6
1965—Gray 23, Blue 19
1966—Blue 14, Gray 9
1967—Blue 22, Gray 16
1968—Gray 28, Blue 7
1969—Blue 6, Gray 6
1970—Gray 38, Blue 7
1971—Gray 9, Blue 0
1972—Gray 27, Blue 15

RECORDS OF FAMOUS SERIES
Army-Navy

Date	Site
Nov. 29, 1890	
Navy 24, Army 0	West Point, N.Y.
Nov. 28, 1891	
Army 32, Navy 16	Annapolis, Md.
Nov. 26, 1892	
Navy 12, Army 4	West Point, N.Y.
Dec. 2, 1893	
Navy 6, Army 4	Annapolis, Md.
1894-98—No games	
Dec. 2, 1899	
Army 17, Navy 5	Franklin Field, Philadelphia
Dec. 1, 1900	
Navy 11, Army 7	Franklin Field, Philadelphia
Nov. 30, 1901	
Army 11, Navy 5	Franklin Field, Philadelphia
Nov. 29, 1902	
Army 22, Navy 8	Franklin Field, Philadelphia
Nov. 28, 1903	
Army 40, Navy 5	Franklin Field, Philadelphia

Nov. 26, 1904
Army 11, Navy 0 . . . . Franklin Field, Philadelphia
Dec. 2, 1905
Army 6, Navy 6 . . . . Princeton, N.J.
Dec. 1, 1906
Navy 10, Army 0 . . . . Franklin Field, Philadelphia
Nov. 30, 1907
Navy 6, Army 0 . . . . Franklin Field, Philadelphia
Nov. 28, 1908
Army 6, Navy 4 . . . . Franklin Field, Philadelphia
1909—No game
Nov. 26, 1910
Navy 3, Army 0 . . . . Franklin Field, Philadelphia
Nov. 25, 1911
Navy 3, Army 0 . . . . Franklin Field, Philadelphia
Nov. 30, 1912
Navy 6, Army 0 . . . . Franklin Field, Philadelphia
Nov. 29, 1913
Army 22, Navy 9 . . . . Polo Grounds, New York
Nov. 28, 1914
Army 20, Navy 0 . . . . Franklin Field, Philadelphia
Nov. 27, 1915
Army 14, Navy 0 . . . . Polo Grounds, New York
Nov. 25, 1916
Army 15, Navy 7 . . . . Polo Grounds, New York
1917-18—No games
Nov. 29, 1919
Navy 6, Army 0 . . . . Polo Grounds, New York
Nov. 20, 1920
Navy 7, Army 0 . . . . Polo Grounds, New York
Nov. 26, 1921
Navy 7, Army 0 . . . . Polo Grounds, New York
Nov. 25, 1922
Army 17, Navy 14 . . . . Philadelphia
Nov. 24, 1923
Army 0, Navy 0 . . . . Polo Grounds, New York
Nov. 29, 1924
Army 12, Navy 0 . . . . Baltimore Stadium
Nov. 28, 1925
Army 10, Navy 3 . . . . Polo Grounds, New York
Nov. 27, 1926
Army 21, Navy 21 . . . . Soldiers Field, Chicago
Nov. 26, 1927
Army 14, Navy 9 . . . . Polo Grounds, New York
1928-29—No games
Dec. 13, 1930
Army 6, Navy 0 . . . . Yankee Stadium, New York
Dec. 12, 1931
Army 17, Navy 7 . . . . Yankee Stadium, New York
Dec. 3, 1932
Army 20, Navy 0 . . . . Franklin Field, Philadelphia
Nov. 25, 1933
Army 12, Navy 7 . . . . Franklin Field, Philadelphia
Dec. 1, 1934
Navy 3, Army 0 . . . . Franklin Field, Philadelphia
Nov. 30, 1935
Army 28, Navy 6 . . . . Franklin Field, Philadelphia
Nov. 28, 1936
Navy 7, Army 0 . . . . Municipal Stadium, Philadelphia
Nov. 27, 1937
Army 6, Navy 0 . . . . Municipal Stadium, Philadelphia
Nov. 26, 1938
Army 14, Navy 7 . . . Municipal Stadium, Philadelphia
Dec. 2, 1939
Navy 10, Army 0 . . . Municipal Stadium, Philadelphia
Nov. 30, 1940
Navy 14, Army 0 . . . Municipal Stadium, Philadelphia
Nov. 29, 1941
Navy 14, Army 6 . . . Municipal Stadium, Philadelphia
Nov. 28, 1942
Navy 14, Army 0 Thompson Stadium, Annapolis, Md.
Nov. 27, 1943
Navy 13, Army 0 . . Michie Stadium, West Point, N.Y.
Dec. 2, 1944
Army 23, Navy 7 . . . . Baltimore Stadium
Dec. 2, 1945
Army 32, Navy 13 . . Municipal Stadium, Philadelphia

Nov. 30, 1946
Army 21, Navy 18 . . Municipal Stadium, Philadelphia
Nov. 29, 1947
Army 21, Navy 0 . . . Municipal Stadium, Philadelphia
Nov. 27, 1948
Army 21, Navy 21 . . Municipal Stadium, Philadelphia
Nov. 26, 1949
Army 38, Navy 0 . . . Municipal Stadium, Philadelphia
Dec. 2, 1950
Navy 14, Army 2 . . . Municipal Stadium, Philadelphia
Dec. 1, 1951
Navy 42, Army 7 . . . Municipal Stadium, Philadelphia
Nov. 29, 1952
Navy 7, Army 0 . . . . Municipal Stadium, Philadelphia
Nov. 28, 1953
Army 20, Navy 7 . . . Municipal Stadium, Philadelphia
Nov. 28, 1954
Navy 27, Army 20 . . Municipal Stadium, Philadelphia
Nov. 26, 1955
Army 14, Navy 6 . . . Municipal Stadium, Philadelphia
Dec. 1, 1956
Army 7, Navy 7 . . . . Municipal Stadium, Philadelphia
Nov. 30, 1957
Navy 14, Army 0 . . . Municipal Stadium, Philadelphia
Nov. 29, 1958
Army 22, Navy 6 . . . Municipal Stadium, Philadelphia
Nov. 28, 1959
Navy 43, Army 12 . . Municipal Stadium, Philadelphia
Nov. 26, 1960
Navy 17, Army 12 . . Municipal Stadium, Philadelphia
Dec. 2, 1961
Navy 13, Army 7 . . . Municipal Stadium, Philadelphia
Dec. 1, 1962
Navy 34, Army 14 . . Municipal Stadium, Philadelphia
1963—Navy 21, Army 15 . . . . Municipal Stadium, Phil.
1964—Army 11, Navy 8 . . . . . Municipal Stadium, Phil.
1965—Army 7, Navy 7 . . . . . . Municipal Stadium, Phil.
1966—Army 20, Navy 7 . . . . . Municipal Stadium, Phil.
1967—Navy 19, Army 14 . . . . Municipal Stadium, Phil.
1968—Army 21, Navy 14
1969—Army 27, Navy 0
1970—Navy 11, Army 7
1971—Army 24, Navy 23 . . J.F. Kennedy Stadium, Phil.
1972—Army 23, Navy 15 . . J.F. Kennedy Stadium, Phil.

Games won—Army 36, Navy 31, Tied—6.

Yale-Harvard

g—goal; t—touchdown; s—safety.   Site

1875—Harvard 4g 2t, Yale 0g 0t . . . . . New Haven
1876—Yale 1g 0t, Harvard 0g 2t . . . . . New Haven
1877—No game
1878—Yale 1g 0t 2s, Harvard 0g 0t 13s Boston
1879—Yale 0g 0t 2s, Harvard 0g 0t 4s New Haven
1880—Yale 1g 1t 2s, Harvard 0g 0t 9s Boston
1881—Yale 0g 0t 0s, Harvard 0g 0t 4s New Haven
1882—Yale 1g 3t 0s, Harvard 0g 0t 2s Cambridge
1883—Yale 23, Harvard 2 . . . . New York
1884—*Yale 52, Harvard 0 . . . . New Haven
1885—No game
1886—Yale 29, Harvard 4 . . . . Cambridge
1887—Yale 17, Harvard 8 . . . . New York
1888—No game
1889—Yale 6, Harvard 0 . . . . Springfield
1890—Harvard 12, Yale 6 . . . . Springfield
1891—Yale 10, Harvard 0 . . . . Springfield
1892—Yale 6, Harvard 0 . . . . Springfield
1893—Yale 6, Harvard 0 . . . . Springfield
1894—Yale 12, Harvard 4 . . . . Springfield
1895—96—No games

1897—Yale 0, Harvard 0 . . . . Cambridge
1898—Harvard 17, Yale 0 . . . . New Haven
1899—Yale 0, Harvard 0 . . . . Cambridge
1900—Yale 28, Harvard 0 . . . . New Haven
1901—Harvard 22, Yale 0 . . . . Cambridge
1902—Yale 23, Harvard 0 . . . . New Haven
1903—Yale 16, Harvard 0 . . . . Cambridge
1904—Yale 12, Harvard 0 . . . . New Haven
1905—Yale 6, Harvard 0 . . . . Cambridge
1906—Yale 6, Harvard 0 . . . . New Haven
1907—Yale 12, Harvard 0 . . . . Cambridge
1908—Harvard 4, Yale 0 . . . . New Haven
1909—Yale 8, Harvard 0 . . . . Cambridge
1910—Yale, 0, Harvard 0 . . . . New Haven
1911—Yale 0, Harvard 0 . . . . Cambridge
1912—Harvard 20, Yale 0 . . . . New Haven
1913—Harvard 15, Yale 5 . . . . Cambridge
1914—Harvard 36, Yale 0 . . . . New Haven
1915—Harvard 41, Yale 0 . . . . Cambridge
1916—Yale 6, Harvard 3 . . . . New Haven
1917—18—No games
1919—Harvard 10, Yale 3 . . . . Cambridge
1920—Harvard 9, Yale 0 . . . . New Haven
1921—Harvard 10, Yale 3 . . . . Cambridge
1922—Harvard 10, Yale 3 . . . . New Haven
1923—Yale 13, Harvard 0 . . . . Cambridge
1924—Yale 19, Harvard 6 . . . . New Haven
1925—Yale 0, Harvard 0 . . . . Cambridge
1926—Yale 12, Harvard 7 . . . . New Haven
1927—Yale 14, Harvard 0 . . . . Cambridge
1928—Harvard 17, Yale 0 . . . . New Haven
1929—Harvard 10, Yale 6 . . . . Cambridge
1930—Harvard 13, Yale 0 . . . . New Haven
1931—Yale 3, Harvard 0 . . . . Cambridge
1932—Yale 19, Harvard 0 . . . . New Haven
1933—Harvard 19, Yale 6 . . . . Cambridge
1934—Yale 14, Harvard 0 . . . . New Haven
1935—Yale 14, Harvard 7 . . . . Cambridge
1936—Yale 14, Harvard 13 . . . . New Haven
1937—Harvard 13, Yale 6 . . . . Cambridge
1938—Harvard 7, Yale 0 . . . . New Haven
1939—Yale 20, Harvard 7 . . . . Cambridge
1940—Harvard 28, Yale 0 . . . . New Haven
1941—Harvard 14, Yale 0 . . . . Cambridge
1942—Yale 7, Harvard 3 . . . . New Haven
1943—44—No games
1945—Yale 28, Harvard 0 . . . . New Haven
1946—Yale 27, Harvard 14 . . . . New Haven
1947—Yale 31, Harvard 21 . . . . New Haven
1948—Harvard 20, Yale 7 . . . . Cambridge
1949—Yale 29, Harvard 6 . . . . New Haven
1950—Yale 14, Harvard 6 . . . . Cambridge
1951—Yale 21, Harvard 21 . . . . New Haven
1952—Yale 41, Harvard 14 . . . . Cambridge
1953—Harvard 13, Yale 0 . . . . New Haven
1954—Yale 13, Harvard 9 . . . . Cambridge
1955—Yale 21, Harvard 7 . . . . New Haven
1956—Yale 42, Harvard 14 . . . . Cambridge
1957—Yale 54, Harvard 0 . . . . New Haven
1958—Harvard 28, Yale 0 . . . . Cambridge
1959—Harvard 35, Yale 6 . . . . New Haven
* Harvard lists 1884 score as 48—0.

1960—Yale 39, Harvard 6 . . . . Cambridge
1961—Harvard 27, Yale 0 . . . . New Haven
1962—Harvard 14, Yale 6 . . . . Cambridge
1963—Yale 20, Harvard 6 . . . . New Haven
1964—Harvard 18, Yale 14 . . . . Cambridge
1965—Harvard 13, Yale 0 . . . . New Haven
1966—Harvard 17, Yale 0 . . . . Cambridge
1967—Yale 24, Harvard 20 . . . . New Haven
1968—Harvard 29, Yale 29 . . . . Cambridge
1969—Yale 7, Harvard 0 . . . . New Haven
1970—Harvard 14, Yale 12 . . . . Cambridge
1971—Harvard 35, Yale 16 . . . . New Haven
1972—Yale 28, Harvard 17 . . . . Cambridge
Games won—Yale 49, Harvard 32, Tied 8.

Yale-Princeton

Site

1873—Princeton 3g, Yale 0g . . . . New Haven
1874—75—No games
1876—Yale 2g, 1t, Princeton 0g, 0t . . Hoboken
1877—*Yale 0g, 2t, Princeton 0g, 0t . Hoboken
1878—Princeton 1g, Yale 0g . . . . Hoboken
1879—Yale 0g, 0t, Princeton 0g, 0t . . Hoboken
1880—Yale 0g, 0t, Princeton 0g 0t . . . New York
1881—Yale 0g, 0t, Princeton 0g 0t . . . New York
1882—Yale 2g, Princeton 1g . . . . New York
1883—Yale 6, Princeton 0 . . . . New York
1884—†Yale 6, Princeton 4 . . . . New York
1885—Princeton 6, Yale 5 . . . . New Haven
1886—†Yale 4, Princeton 0 . . . . Princeton
1887—Yale 12, Princeton 0 . . . . New York
1888—Yale 10, Princeton 0 . . . . New York
1889—Princeton 10, Yale 0 . . . . New York
1890—Yale 32, Princeton 0 . . . . Brooklyn
1891—Yale 19, Princeton 0 . . . . New York
1892—Yale 12, Princeton 0 . . . . New York
1893—Princeton 6, Yale 0 . . . . New York
1894—Yale 24, Princeton 0 . . . . New York
1895—Yale 20, Princeton 10 . . . . New York
1896—Princeton 24, Yale 6 . . . . New York
1897—Yale 6, Princeton 0 . . . . New Haven
1898—Princeton 6, Yale 0 . . . . Princeton
1899—Princeton 11, Yale 10 . . . . New Haven
1900—Yale 29, Princeton 5 . . . . Princeton
1901—Yale 12, Princeton 0 . . . . New Haven
1902—Yale 12, Princeton 5 . . . . Princeton
1903—Princeton 11, Yale 6 . . . . New Haven
1904—Yale 12, Princeton 0 . . . . Princeton
1905—Yale 23, Princeton 4 . . . . New Haven
1906—Yale 0, Princeton 0 . . . . Princeton
1907—Yale 12, Princeton 10 . . . . New Haven
1908—Yale 11, Princeton 6 . . . . Princeton
1909—Yale 17, Princeton 0 . . . . New Haven
1910—Yale 5, Princeton 3 . . . . Princeton
1911—Princeton 6, Yale 3 . . . . New Haven
1912—Yale 6, Princeton 6 . . . . Princeton

*Since only goals counted toward winning a game, this was called a tie game by the referee.

†Games in 1884 and 1886 were stopped by referee because of darkness and were recorded as ties. Yale was leading in both games when play ended. Under the Association rules of the 1880's, two full halves had to be played in order to make a game official.

1913—Yale 3, Princeton 3 ....New Haven
1914—Yale 19, Princeton 14 ....Princeton
1915—Yale 13, Princeton 7 ....New Haven
1916—Yale 10, Princeton 0 ....Princeton

1917—18—No games

1919—Princeton 13, Yale 6 ....New Haven
1920—Princeton 20, Yale 0 ....Princeton
1921—Yale 13, Princeton 7 ....New Haven
1922—Princeton 3, Yale 0 ....Princeton
1923—Yale 27, Princeton 0 ....New Haven
1924—Yale 10, Princeton 0 ....Princeton
1925—Princeton 25, Yale 12 ......New Haven
1926—Princeton 10, Yale 7 ....Princeton
1927—Yale 14, Princeton 6 ....New Haven
1928—Princeton 12, Yale 2 ....Princeton
1929—Yale 13, Princeton 0 ....New Haven
1930—Yale 10, Princeton 7 ....Princeton
1931—Yale 51, Princeton 14 ......New Haven
1932—Yale 7, Princeton 7 ....Princeton
1933—Princeton 27, Yale 2 ....New Haven
1934—Yale 7, Princeton 0 ....Princeton
1935—Princeton 38, Yale 7 ....New Haven
1936—Yale 26, Princeton 23 ......Princeton
1937—Yale 26, Princeton 0 ....New Haven
1938—Princeton 20, Yale 7 ....Princeton
1939—Princeton 13, Yale 7 ....New Haven
1940—Princeton 10, Yale 7 ....Princeton
1941—Princeton 20, Yale 6 ....New Haven
1942—Yale 13, Princeton 6 ....Princeton
1943—Yale 27, Princeton 6 ....New Haven

1944—No game

1945—Yale 20, Princeton 14 ......Princeton
1946—Yale 30, Princeton 2 ....New Haven
1947—Princeton 17, Yale 0 ....Princeton
1948—Princeton 20, Yale 14 ......New Haven
1949—Princeton 21, Yale 13 ......Princeton
1950—Princeton 47, Yale 12 ......New Haven
1951—Princeton 27, Yale 0 ....Princeton
1952—Princeton 27, Yale 21 ......New Haven
1953—Yale 26, Princeton 24 ......Princeton
1954—Princeton 21, Yale 14 ......New Haven
1955—Princeton 13, Yale 0 ....Princeton
1956—Yale 42, Princeton 20 ......New Haven
1957—Yale 20, Princeton 13 ......Princeton
1958—Princeton 50, Yale 14 ......New Haven
1959—Yale 38, Princeton 20 ......Princeton
1960—Yale 43, Princeton 22 ......New Haven
1961—Princeton 26, Yale 16 ......Princeton
1962—Princeton 14, Yale 10 ......New Haven
1963—Princeton 27, Yale 7 ....Princeton
1964—Princeton 35, Yale 14 ......New Haven
1965—Princeton 31, Yale 6 ....Princeton
1966—Princeton 13, Yale 7 ....New Haven
1967—Yale 29, Princeton 7 ....Princeton
1968—Yale 42, Princeton 17 ......New Haven
1969—Yale 17, Princeton 14 ......Princeton
1970—Yale 27, Princeton 22 ......New Haven
1971—Yale 10, Princeton 6 ....Princeton
1972—Yale 31, Princeton 7 ....New Haven

Games won—Yale 48, Princeton 37, Tied 8.

Princeton-Harvard

Site

1877 (spring)—Harvard 1g, 2t,
   Princeton 1t ....Cambridge
1877 (fall)—Princeton 1g, 1t, Harvard 1t Hoboken
1878—Princeton 1t, Harvard 0 ....Boston
1879—Princeton 1g, Harvard 0 ......Hoboken
1880—Princeton 2g, 2t, Harvard 1g, 1t New York
1881—Princeton 0, Harvard 0 ....New York
1882—Harvard 1g, 1t, Princeton 1g ....Cambridge
1883—Princeton 26, Harvard 7 ......Princeton
1884—Princeton 36, Harvard 6 ......Cambridge
1885—No game
1886—Princeton 12, Harvard 0 ......Princeton
1887—Harvard 12, Princeton 0 ......Cambridge
1888—Princeton 18, Harvard 6 ......Princeton
1889—Princeton 41, Harvard 15 .....Cambridge
1890—94—No games
1895—Princeton 12, Harvard 4 ......Princeton
1896—Princeton 12, Harvard 0 ......Cambridge
1897—1910—No games
1911—Princeton 8, Harvard 6 ....Princeton
1912—Harvard 16, Princeton 6 ......Cambridge
1913—Harvard 3, Princeton 0 ....Princeton
1914—Harvard 20, Princeton 0 ......Cambridge
1915—Harvard 10, Princeton 6 ......Princeton
1916—Harvard 3, Princeton 0 ....Cambridge
1917—18—No games
1919—Princeton 10, Harvard 10 .....Princeton
1920—Princeton 14, Harvard 14 .....Cambridge
1921—Princeton 10, Harvard 3 ......Princeton
1922—Princeton 10, Harvard 3 ......Cambridge
1923—Harvard 5, Princeton 0 ....Princeton
1924—Princeton 34, Harvard 0 ......Cambridge
1925—Princeton 36, Harvard 0 ......Princeton
1926—Princeton 12, Harvard 0 ......Cambridge
1927—33—No games
1934—Princeton 19, Harvard 0 ......Cambridge
1935—Princeton 35, Harvard 0 ......Princeton
1936—Princeton 14, Harvard 14 .....Cambridge
1937—Harvard 34, Princeton 6 ......Princeton
1938—Harvard 26, Princeton 7 ......Cambridge
1939—Princeton 9, Harvard 6 ....Princeton
1940—Princeton 0, Harvard 0 ....Cambridge
1941—Harvard 6, Princeton 4 ....Princeton
1942—Harvard 19, Princeton 14 .....Cambridge
1943—45—No games
1946—Harvard 13, Princeton 12 .....Princeton
1947—Princeton 33, Harvard 7 ......Cambridge
1948—Princeton 47, Harvard 7 ......Princeton
1949—Princeton 33, Harvard 13 .....Cambridge
1950—Princeton 63, Harvard 26 .....Princeton
1951—Princeton 54, Harvard 13 .....Cambridge
1952—Princeton 41, Harvard 21 .....Princeton
1953—Princeton 6, Harvard 0 ....Cambridge
1954—Harvard 14, Princeton 9 ......Princeton
1955—Harvard 7, Princeton 6 ....Cambridge
1956—Princeton 35, Harvard 20 .....Princeton
1957—Princeton 28, Harvard 20 .....Cambridge
1958—Princeton 16, Harvard 14 .....Princeton
1959—Harvard 14, Princeton 0 ......Cambridge

1960—Princeton 14, Harvard 12 . . . . . Princeton
1961—Harvard 9, Princeton 7 . . . . Cambridge
1962—Harvard 20, Princeton 0 . . . . . . Princeton
1963—Harvard 21, Princeton 7 . . . . . . Cambridge
1964—Princeton 16, Harvard 0 . . . . . Princeton
1965—Princeton 14, Harvard 6 . . . . . Cambridge
1966—Princeton 18, Harvard 14 . . . . Princeton
1967—Princeton 45, Harvard 6 . . . . . . Cambridge
1968—Harvard 9, Princeton 7 . . . . Princeton
1969—Princeton 51, Harvard 20 . . . . Cambridge
1970—Harvard 29, Princeton 7 . . . . . Princeton
1971—Princeton 21, Harvard 10 . . . . . Cambridge
1972—Princeton 10, Harvard 7 . . . . . Princeton
 Games won—Princeton 38, Harvard 22, Tied 5

Notre Dame-Army

1913—Notre Dame 35, Army 7
1914—Army 20, Notre Dame 7
1915—Notre Dame 7, Army 0
1916—Army 30, Notre Dame 10
1917—Notre Dame 7, Army 2
1918—No game
1919—Notre Dame 12, Army 9
1920—Notre Dame 27, Army 17
1921—Notre Dame 28, Army 0
1922—Army 0, Notre Dame 0
1923—Notre Dame 13, Army 0
1924—Notre Dame 13, Army 7
1925—Army 27, Notre Dame 0
1926—Notre Dame 7, Army 0
1927—Army 18, Notre Dame 0
1928—Notre Dame 12, Army 6
1929—Notre Dame 7, Army 0
1930—Notre Dame 7, Army 6
1931—Army 12, Notre Dame 0
1932—Notre Dame 21, Army 0
1933—Notre Dame 13, Army 12
1934—Notre Dame 12, Army 6
1935—Army 6, Notre Dame 6
1936—Notre Dame 20, Army 6
1937—Notre Dame 7, Army 0
1938—Notre Dame 19, Army 7
1939—Notre Dame 14, Army 0
1940—Notre Dame 7, Army 0
1941—Army 0, Notre Dame 0
1942—Notre Dame 13, Army 0
1943—Notre Dame 26, Army 0
1944—Army 59, Notre Dame 0
1945—Army 48, Notre Dame 0
1946—Army 0, Notre Dame 0
1947—Notre Dame 27, Army 7
1948—56—No games.
1957—Notre Dame 23, Army 21
1958—Army 14, Notre Dame 2
1959—64—No games
1965—Notre Dame 17, Army 0
1966—Notre Dame 35, Army 0
1967-68—No game
1969—Notre Dame 45, Army 0
1970—Notre Dame 51, Army 10
1971-72—No Game
 Games won—Notre Dame 28, Army 8, Tied 4.

HIGH SCORES

Single Games

1900—Dickinson 227, Haverford Gr. School 0
1916—**Georgia Tech 222, Cumberland (Tenn.) 0
1922—King (Tenn) 206, Lenoir-Rhyne 0
1916—*St. Viator (Ind.) 205, Lane College
  Chicago 0
1922—Roanoke (Va.) 187, Randolph-Macon
  Academy 0
1916—Edmond Teachers (Okla.) 183, Oklahoma
  Methodist 0
1917—Oklahoma 179, Kingfisher 0
1918—Albion (Mich.) 178, Detroit Navy Camp 0
1920—Arizona 167, Camp H. J. Jones 0

 * Leo Schlick made 12 touchdowns and kicked 28 of
29 extra points for a game-scoring record of 100 points.
 **Game reduced to 45 minutes.

Season

Year	College	W	L	T	For	Agst.
1886 ..	Harvard	12	2	0	765	41
1888 ..	Yale	13	0	0	694	0
1886 ..	Yale (a)	9	0	1	687	4
1889 ..	Yale	15	1	0	661	31
1887 ..	Harvard	10	1	0	660	23
1902 ..	Michigan	11	0	0	644	12
1887 ..	Princeton	9	0	0	637	25
1888 ..	Harvard	12	1	0	635	32
1920 ..	Henry-Kendall (b) .	10	1	1	622	21
1904 ..	Minnesota	12	0	0	618	12
1888 ..	Princeton	11	1	0	609	16
1919 ..	Henry-Kendall	8	0	1	592	27
1891 ..	Harvard	13	1	0	588	26
1949 ..	College of the Pacific	11	0	0	575	66
1904 ..	Michigan	10	0	0	567	22
1916 ..	Henry-Kendal	10	0	0	566	33
1903 ..	Michigan	11	0	1	565	6
1914 ..	Missouri Mines	8	0	0	560	0
1926 ..	Haskell	12	0	1	558	63
1890 ..	Harvard	11	0	0	555	12
1901 ..	Michigan	11	0	0	550	0
1887 ..	Yale	9	0	0	515	12
1960 ..	Florida A-M	9	1	0	515	73
1915 ..	Vanderbilt	9	1	0	514	38
1944 ..	Second Air Force (Colo.)	10	4	1	513	76
1972 ..	Arizona State	9	2	0	513	261
1920 ..	California	9	0	0	510	14
1944 ..	Randolph Field (Texas)	12	0	0	508	19
1971 ..	Nebraska	13	0	0	507	104
1922 ..	Phillips (Oklahoma)	7	0	0	506	74
1961 ..	Florida A-M	10	0	0	506	39
1912 ..	Carlisle Indian School	12	1	1	505	NA
1944 ..	Army	9	0	0	504	35

(a) Princeton game called because of darkness
(b) Now Tulsa University.

All-Time Scoring Record
Harvard (1886)

82—Tufts	0
46—Tufts	0
28—Pennsylvania	0
54—M.I.T.	0
59—M.I.T.	0
62—M.I.T.	0
70—Dartmouth	0
34—Wesleyan	0
44—Stevens	0
86—Andover	0
158—Exeter	0
38—Grads	0
0—Princeton	12
4—Yale	29
765	41

HARVARD'S RECORD—1886—1891

Year	W	L	Points For	Agst.
1886	12	2	765	41
1887	10	1	660	23
1888	12	1	635	32
1889	9	2	419	53
1890	11	0	555	12
1891	13	1	588	26
Total	67	7	3,622	187

Harvard averaged 603 2/3 points per season.

UNDEFEATED, UNTIED, UNSCORED-ON TEAMS

(Playing at least 6 games)

Year	College	Won	Points
1888	Yale	13	694
1891	Yale	13	488
1892	Yale	13	435
1898	Kentucky	7	181
1901	Michigan	11	550
1902	Nebraska	11	185
1902	South Dakota	9	216
1906	Washington State	6	44
1907	Oregon State	6	137
1909	Yale	10	209
1910	Illionis	7	89
1910	Pittsburgh	9	282
1914	Missouri Mines	8	560
1917	Texas A-M	8	270
1919	Texas A-M	10	275
1925	Danville (Ind.) Teachers	6	203
1926	Trinity (Iowa)	6	182
1928	College of Emporia	7	175
1931	Mount St. Charles (Montana)	6	192
1932	Colgate	9	264
1933	DePauw	7	136
1933	California Poly (San Luis Obispo)	7	78
1934	*Murray (Okla.) Aggies	9	196
1938	**Duke	9	114
1939	**Tennessee	10	212

* Lost one game 7-0, later forfeited to Murray.
** Defeated in Rose Bowl Game.

MICHIGAN'S POINT-A-MINUTE TEAMS

Year	Games	W	L	T	Points For	Agst.
1901	11	11	0	0	550	0
1902	11	11	0	0	644	12
1903	12	11	0	1	565	6
1904	10	10	0	0	567	22
1905	13	12	1	0	495	2
Totals	57	55	1	1	2,821	42

Michigan, which averaged 564 1/5 points per season, lost to Chicago, 2-0, in the last game in 1905.

KNUTE ROCKNE'S COACHING RECORD AT NOTRE DAME

Year	W	L	T	Points For	Agst.
1918	3	1	2	133	39
1919	9	0	0	229	47
1920	9	0	0	251	44
1921	10	1	0	375	41
1922	8	1	1	222	27
1923	9	1	1	275	37
1924	10	0	0	285	54
1925	7	2	1	200	64
1926	9	1	0	210	38
1927	7	1	1	158	57
1928	5	4	0	99	107
1929	9	0	0	145	38
1930	10	0	0	265	74
Total	105	12	5	2,847	667

Average points per game: N.D. 23, opponents 5. Consecutive victory record, 20 (won 9 straight in 1919; 9 in 1920; and beat Kalamazoo and De Pauw in first 2 games in 1921, then lost to Iowa, 10 to 7).

Defeats were: 1918, Michigan State, 7—13; 1921, Iowa, 7—10; 1922, Nebraska, 6—14; 1923, Nebraska, 7—14; 1925 (2), Army, 0—27, and Nebraska, 0—17; 1926, Carnegie Tech., 0—19; 1927, Army, 0—18; 1928 (4), Wisconsin, 6—22; Georgia Tech., 0—13; Carnegie Tech., 7—27; Southern California, 14—27.

Ties were: 1918, Great Lakes, 7—7; Nebraska, 0—0; 1922, Army, 0—0; 1925, Penn State, 0—0; 1927, Minnesota, 7—7.

Miscellany

ANNUAL COLLEGE FOOTBALL ATTENDANCE

The Service Bureau of the National Collegiate Athletic Association compiles annual attendance records for all four-year colleges, including non-members of the N.C.A.A.

The attendance, excluding post-season games:

1947	15,248,000	(estimated paid)
1948	15,248,000	(estimated paid)
1949	15,675,000	(estimated paid)
1950	15,172,000	(estimated paid)
1951	14,272,000	(estimated paid)
1952	14,196,000	(estimated paid)
1953	13,754,000	(estimated paid)
1954	14,091,000	(estimated paid)
1955	14,211,000	(estimated paid)
1956	14,866,000	(estimated paid)
1957	18,290,724	(total)
1958	19,280,709	(total)
1959	19,615,344	(total)
1960	20,403,409	(total)
1961	20,677,604	(total)
1962	21,227,162	(total)
1963	22,237,094	(total)
1964	23,354,477	(total)
1965	24,682,572	(total)
1966	25,275,899	(total)
1967	26,430,639	(total)
1968	27,025,846	(total)
1969	27,626,160	(total)
1970	29,465,604	(total)
1971	30,455,442	(total)
1972	30,828,802	(total)

BASIC RULES

American football is played on a field 100 yards in length and 53-1/3 yards wide. The goalposts in the college game are placed centrally 10 yards back of each goal line to prevent possible injury to players through collision with the uprights; in the professional game the posts are exactly on the lines on the ends of the playing field.

Goalposts must not exceed 20 feet in height. They are 24 feet apart, with a horizontal crossbar 10 feet from the ground.

The ball is prolate spheroid in shape, with a circumference not less than 28 inches and no more than 28½ inches; the short axis shall measure no less than 21¼ and no more than 21½ inches; the length of the long axis shall measure not less than 11 inches nor more than 11¼. The weight of the ball shall be between 14 and 15 ounces and when inflated for play shall have a pressure of not less than 12½ pounds, nor more than 13½ pounds.

Play is divided into four periods of 15 minutes each; one minute rest is permitted between the first and second periods and between the third and fourth, with a 15-minute intermission between halves. The professionals take a 20-minute intermission.

The college game is supervised by five officials—referee, umpire, field judge, linesman and electric-clock operator. The professionals use a back judge instead of an electric-clock operator.

Eleven players constitute a team: a center, two guards, two tackles, two ends, a quarterback, two halfbacks and a fullback. Substitutions may be made at any time, but in the college game, a player may enter the game only twice each quarter.

Play is started with a kick-off of the ball into enemy territory. Determination as to which team shall kick off or receive is made by the toss of a coin. The team receiving must gain 10 yards in four downs (plays) immediately following the run-back play or forfeit possession of the ball to the opposing team at the point of failure. It may give up possession of the ball at any time by kicking to its opponent.

The ball may be advanced (1) by running or plunging and (2) by forward or lateral passing.

The ball may not be advanced by kicking without forfeiture to the other team. However, a score may be made by successful placement or drop kicking.

Points are scored as follows:

6 points for a touchdown, which means when a ball is carried, or successfully passed and caught, beyond the enemy goal line.

1 or 2 points for a conversion. After a touchdown, the scoring side can run or pass the ball for 2 points or kick for 1 point, in any event with the play starting on the 3-yard line (in college games). In professional football, conversion attempts are made from the 2-yard line and are worth 1 point. In the event the ball is passed, or carried, over the line, it may be carried across anywhere within the playing boundaries. If kicked, it must go between the goalposts and over the crossbar.

3 points for a goal from the field. This is accomplished by a drop kick, meaning the ball is dropped to the ground and kicked on the rebound, or a placement kick, meaning the ball is passed to one player who holds it on the ground in position for a team-mate to kick it. Drop and placement kicks are successful only if ball clears crossbar between uprights of goalposts.

2 points for a safety. Where a man in possession of the ball is downed back of his goal line, it counts 2 points for the other side provided the impetus that put the ball back of the goal line came from the side defending that goal. Otherwise it is a touchdown and no points are given.

The other form of kicking is called punting. The ball is dropped toward the instep and kicked by the instep toward enemy territory. The punt play is made when it is deemed wiser to surrender the ball than to retain possession.

Under college rules, in the event a game is forfeited the official score shall be 1 to 0. It is interesting to note, however, that in the professional National Football League only the commissioner has the right to forfeit a game. Whereas the colleges abolished the free sub-

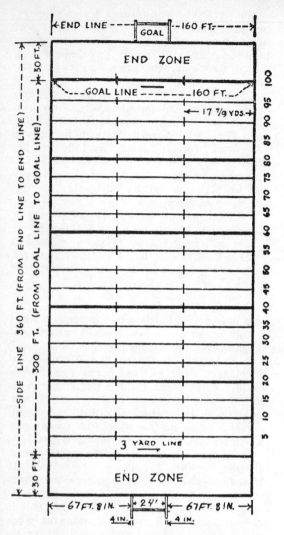

Football Field. This is a field for amateur rules. In the professional game the goal posts are on the goal line instead of the end line. (Taken from "The Dictionary of Sports," by Parke Cummings, A. S. Barnes and Company, New York.)

stitution rule in 1953 because of limited manpower and increased costs, the professionals still maintain the provision and a player may enter and leave a contest at any time.

Another difference is the rule on when a player is downed. In the collegiate phase, a play stops when any portion of the ball carrier's body, except the hands and feet, touches the ground. The professional may get up and continue until the referee blows his whistle signifying that the runner has been downed.

American football is a game freighted with many rules and about 60 penalties for roughness, clipping, punching, tripping and other unsportsmanlike conduct, for unnecessarily delaying the game, for offside, etc.

Professional Football

Professional football in America hurdled some stupendous barriers and became a popular sport.

It was a fight almost all the way—a fight that brought discouragement as new obstacles were hoisted in front of the sponsors. But professional football, assailed so vigorously by college coaches and alumni, survived by some miracle and basks now in the glorious light of a victory well won.

Dr. Harry A. March stated in his book "Pro Football" that the town of Latrobe, Pa., near Pittsburgh, was the stage for the first professional football match, Aug. 31, 1895—Latrobe versus Jeanette, Pa.

The Latrobe team, related Dr. March, originally was managed and sponsored by the Y.M.C.A. and all games were played on Saturday. As the time neared for the game with Jeanette, the Latrobe regulars, who seemed to be in on a profit-sharing basis, found themselves minus an experienced quarterback. Having heard about John Brallier (later a dentist in Latrobe), who had starred for Indiana Normal, they offered him $10 and expenses. Brallier accepted and became football's first professional.

Pittsburgh was the first large city to have an all-professional team. Among the earliest "pro" clubs were the Duquesnes of Pittsburgh, the Olympics of McKeesport, Pa., and the Orange A.C. of Newark, N.J., organized in 1896 or 1897.

In 1902 and 1903 teams were organized in Canton and Massillon, Ohio, each being backed by wealthy men. The line-ups sparkled with college graduates. Willie Heston, Michigan's immortal back, was a member of the Canton squad. He received $600 and expenses for one game—the only time he ever played as a professional. He broke a leg on the first play.

As early as 1914 the college coaches battled vigorously against the professional sport. It was intimated that collegians, turned pro, could not maintain honor or honesty in their new surroundings. Much was said, and plenty was quoted, that college football and professionalism never would mix in post-graduate days.

But certain collegians loved to play the game. Since they had played it "for free" through many years, the idea of having a few more whirls with the pigskin and getting real cash for such performance was a lure they could not resist. Therefore, despite orations of the college coaches, graduated football stars in increasing number joined the professional ranks.

Nevertheless, it was a discouraging fight for the pros. They had the players to guarantee highclass contests. But college coaches and "old grads" raised so loud a cry against the professional sport that for many seasons they just didn't have the crowds. The foes of pro football had, for a while, succeeded in blackening the sport to such extent that fans generally stayed away from the professional games.

The American Professional Football Association was founded in June, 1920. Few people attended the games. At the season's end it folded, and the college coaches joined in loud boasts of "I told you so."

But Joseph F. Carr of Columbus, Ohio, thought the idea had merit. He rallied the somewhat demoralized professional forces in 1921 and organized what is the National Football League of today. Few cared to take a chance with the new league, despite Carr's high optimism. Franchise costs were fixed at bargain rates, some selling for as low as $50. In 1962 they were worth $10,000,000 and upward.

The league went into action in 1921 but for many years it was a struggle. Carr was fortunate in surrounding himself with magnates who were willing to gamble on a distant future. Just how bleak things were through the early years is shown by the fact that a game between the New York Giants and Chicago Bears attracted 80 customers, only a trifle more than the number of players on the premises.

But that was the low point. Interest in the sport perked thereafter. The league continued to have trouble for a while in getting collegians of All-America variety, since such men demanded far more than the club owners could pay. They met that situation by hiring players of less fame, who were willing to play largely for "the fun of it," plus a little cash each week.

The crowds, impressed by the earnestness of the athletes, if not by their names, patronized pro football in increasing numbers. Soon the clubs were breaking even. As time went on, they hired famous players at terms such men demanded and still showed profits. Red ink was discarded and the financial numerals were in the black.

Magnates, who had been constant losers, became big winners. The National League and all its playing units continued to show mounting profits. The crowds increased and the New York Giants, Chicago Bears and other clubs profited handsomely.

Among the interesting incidents in the career of the National Football League, as prepared by George Strickler, are the following:

1920—The American Professional Football Association was organized, with Jim Thorpe, formerly of Carlisle, as president. Franchises cost $100. The venture was not a financial success, and when the season concluded, the organization was in a bad way.

1921—A new group took over the A.P.F.L., with Joseph F. Carr as president. Franchises were doled out at $50 each. During the season, the league was in difficulty on many occasions,

certain teams disbanded and new ones were prevailed upon to take the field. During the season there were 23 different teams represented in the league. The Staley A.C. of Decatur, Ill., known as the "Chicago Bears" because they played their games in Chicago, won the championship.

1922—Name of organization changed to National Football League. Staley A.C. franchise transferred to Chicago. In first player deal the Chicago Bears paid $100 to Rock Island for Ed Healey, former Dartmouth tackle. The earliest sale of a professional player was concluded in 1920, during the first year of the A.P.F.L., when Akron sold Bob Nash to Columbus for $300.

1925—Tim Mara, with Billy Gibson, then managing Boxer Gene Tunney, as some sort of a partner, bought New York Giants franchise for $2,500. Chicago Bears signed Harold (Red) Grange.

1925—Revolutionary change for betterment of professional football came about when Grange, greatest halfback of the era, quit the University of Illinois and went on a football tour, sponsored by Charles C. (Cash and Carry) Pyle. Grange, heading one team, played against all-star squads in different cities and attracted huge crowds for that era. The tour directed attention to professional football more than had been accomplished before, and the presence of Grange did much to benefit the sport. Grange toured the following season, too, and his profits from both years were estimated at $80,000 to $100,000.

1926—Milwaukee fined $500 for playing four high school boys in league game. League ruled no collegians eligible for play until complete college career was concluded. This was brought about because Grange had quit Illinois after end of football season to become pro, not waiting to complete school course. Result was criticism of league for "kidnaping tactics." Teams limited to minimum of 15, maximum of 18 players.

1929—Chicago Cardinals became first pro team to go to training camp, choosing Coldwater, Mich.

1930—Player limit fixed at 20 maximum, 16 minimum.

1931—Chicago Bears, Green Bay Packers and Portsmouth (Ohio) teams fined $1,000 each for using players whose classes had not been graduated from college.

1933—Goal posts returned to goal line. Forward passes legal from any spot back of scrimmage. League divided and sectional play-offs were started.

1934—In first pro vs. college All-Stars game, Chicago Bears and collegians played scoreless tie in Chicago.

1936—Player limit maximum increased to 25.

1936—First collegian gained by draft, adopted in 1935, was Jay Berwanger of the University of

Chicago. He was awarded to Philadelphia. Rules gave weaker clubs first chance at drafting eligible college players.

1937—Boston franchise transferred and team became Washington "Redskins."

1938—Beginning of professional All-Star game (later called Pro Bowl games).

1940—Detroit club fined $5,000 for "tampering" with Clyde (Bulldog) Turner who, under the draft rules, belonged to the Chicago Bears. Player limit increased to 33 maximum, 22 minimum.

1941—Elmer F. Layden, formerly of Notre Dame, became "High Commissioner" of National League. Later Layden was elected for a 5-year term.

1943—Player limit reduced to 28 for one year. Reaffirmed in 1944.

1945—League roster showed that 638 players had been with Armed Forces. Player limit restored to 33 maximum.

1946—League limited to 10 teams. Layden resigned as commissioner. Bert Bell of Philadelphia succeeded him. Cleveland team transferred to Los Angeles. All-America Conference, a rival league, founded. Cleveland Browns won Western Division title and New York Yankees won Eastern title. Cleveland triumphed in play-off, 14-9

1947—In January, Charles Trippi, a star halfback from the University of Georgia, received many bids to play both professional baseball and football. He accepted the offer of Charles W. Bidwill, owner of the Chicago Cardinals, which was reported to be $100,000 for 4 years. This made Trippi the highest salaried pro player in the history of the game. All-time attendance record for professional football established when 2,448,848 spectators saw the 60 N.F.L. regular-season games plus the exhibition and world championship contests. Average attendance at regular-season games was 30,624.

1948—Player limit increased to 35.

1949—On Dec. 9, Bell and J. Arthur Friedlund, who represented the All-America Conference, announced a merger of the two leagues. The combination ended a costly war in which each league tried to outbid the other for college stars and efforts were made to lure players from one league to the other. The All-America Conference, formed in 1946, lasted four seasons. Baltimore, Cleveland and San Francisco of the A.A.C. joined the 10 teams of the N.F.L.

1950—Player limit set at 32 maximum, 25 minimum. N.F.L. divided into American and National conferences. Cleveland was put in the former Eastern Division, which was re-named the American Conference. Baltimore and San Francisco landed in the former Western Division, re-named the National Conference. Cleveland, which won every league championship in the 4-year existence of the A.A.C., won the N.F.L. championship by defeating Los Angeles, 30 to 28.

1951—Withdrawal of Baltimore left N.F.L. a 12-team circuit. Player limit set at 33 maximum, 25 minimum. Pro bowl game established at Los Angeles (Jan. 14) bringing together the stars of each division. Browns' domination of pro football ended by Los Angeles in title play-off, 24-17.

1953—Baltimore granted a franchise. Designation of American and National conferences abandoned in favor of Eastern and Western conferences. The set-up: Eastern Conference—Chicago Cardinals, Cleveland Browns, New York Giants, Philadelphia Eagles, Pittsburgh Steelers, Washington Redskins. Western Conference — Baltimore Colts, Chicago Bears, Detroit Lions, Green Bay Packers, Los Angeles Rams, San Francisco 49ers.

1954—Bert Bell received a new 12-year contract as league president and commissioner.

1957—Player limit increased to 35. League season attendance record broken for the sixth successive year. The 72 regular-season games drew 2,836,318 paying spectators, an average of 39,388 per game. A record crowd of 102,368 watched the Los Angeles Rams beat the San Francisco Forty-niners, 37-24, at the Los Angeles Coliseum on Nov. 10.

1958—Bonus pick eliminated. League attendance increased 5.98 per cent to 3,006,124, an average of 41,752 per game and a record for the seventh straight year.

1959—No rule changes. On August 14th, first organizational meeting for American Football League under leadership of Lamar Hunt. Six teams represented — New York, Dallas, Los Angeles, Minneapolis, Denver, Houston, with Buffalo and Boston admitted in October. Bert Bell, commissioner of the N.F.L. since 1946, died of a heart attack on October 11th. Austin H. Gunsel named president of the office of the commissioner until annual N.F.L. meeting in January 1960. Joe Foss named A.F.L. commissioner for 3-year term.

1960—Pete Rozelle named N.F.L. commissioner. Lamar Hunt named first A.F.L president for 1-year term. A.F.L. adopted 14-game home-and-home schedule and approved withdrawal of Minneapolis due to stadium problems. Two-point option on points-after-touchdown adopted by A.F.L. Oakland completed team lineup for A.F.L.'s first season divided into Eastern Division (Boston, Buffalo, Houston, New York) and Western Division (Dallas, Denver, Los Angeles, Oakland). Lettering of players' names on backs of jerseys adopted by A.F.L. The N.F.L. awarded Dallas a 1960 franchise and Minnesota a 1961 franchise to a 14-team expansion. Both leagues agreed on a "No Tampering" verbal pact relative to players' contracts. N.F.L. Chicago Cardinals transferred to St. Louis.

1961—Los Angeles Chargers' franchise transferred to San Diego. K.S. (Bud) Adams elected A.F.L. president for 1961. Canton, Ohio, was chosen as site of Professional Football Hall of Fame.

1962—The first NFL rule change in four years made it illegal to grab face mask of any player. AFL voted to make scoreboard clock official timing device. Pete Rozelle reelected as NFL Commissioner for new five-year term. AFL Commissioner Joe Foss given new five-year contract. The AFL filed anti-trust suit against NFL, charging monopoly and conspiracy in player signings, television, and expansion. AFL lost suit.

1963—AFL founder, Lamar Hunt, moved the Dallas Texans to Kansas City. The New York Titans (AFL) franchise bought by sydicate, headed by D. (Sonny) Werblin, changed name to Jets. Commissioner Pete Rozelle suspended Paul Hornung, Green Bay halfback, and Detroit tackle Alex Karras for betting on their own teams and other NFL games. Five other Detroit players fined.

1964—NFL Commissioner Rozelle reinstated Paul Hornung and Alex Karras after reviewing their cases. AFL Commissioner Joe Foss given three-year contract commencing in 1965.

1965—The NFL pledged not to sign a contract or any document with college players until after their season, including Bowl games, was completed. A sixth official, the line judge, was added for each NFL game. His duties: timekeeping and checking action at the line of scrimmage. The color of NFL officials' penalty flags changed from white to bright gold. Atlanta awarded NFL franchise. The AFL voted to expand by two teams for the 1966 season, with Miami gaining the 9th franchise.

1966—Joe Foss resigned after six years as AFL Commissioner. Al Davis, General Manager and Coach of Oakland Raiders, named new commissioner but terminated his term after three months. Milt Woodard took over the presidential duties. The NFL goal posts standardized (off-set from goal line; colored bright gold; uprights extend 20 feet above crossbar and will not be less than 3 nor 4 inches in diameter). The NFL and AFL entered into an agreement to form combined league of 24 teams, expanding to 26 by 1968. Pete Rozelle named as Commissioner. Leagues to play separate schedules until 1970, but will meet, starting in 1967, in a championship game, and will play each other in preseason. Congress passed special legislation between NFL and AFL to exempt them from Anti-trust action. New Orleans became 16th franchise for NFL.

1967—NFL realigned into 4 four-team divisions for the 1967-68-69 seasons with the Coastal (Atlanta, Baltimore, Los Angeles and San Francisco) and Central (Chicago, Detroit, Green Bay and Minnesota) Divisions making up the Western Conference. The Eastern Conference had the Capitol Division (Dallas, New Orleans, Philadelphia, Washington) and the Century Division (Cleveland, New York, Pittsburgh, St. Louis) for the 1967 season. Divisional champions would play off for the conference title and the right to meet in the championship game. New York and New Orleans switch divisions in 1968 but return to 1967 alignment in 1969. Owners voted by resolution for single standard goal post and to line the playing field with a six-foot wide white restraining strip. Cincinnati became AFL's 10th franchise. Arthur Modell elected president of NFL until 1968.

1968—AFL and NFL owners voted to require by 1970 all member teams to play in a stadium with a 50,000-seat capacity.

1969—AFL interdivision playoffs, with winner in one division playing runner-up in other, voted new postseason format in 1969 only. Monday night games televised in 1970-71-72. Commissioner Pete Rozelle announced that the Baltimore Colts, Cleveland Browns, and Pittsburgh Steelers had agreed to join the present 10 AFL teams to form new 13-team American Conference in the National Football League in 1970. The remaining 13 teams in the NFL would form the National Conference. Each would realign into three divisions, the conference champions meeting each year in the Super Bowl. The 13 American Conference teams are in the following 3 divisions: Central—Cincinnati, Cleveland, Houston, Pittsburgh; Eastern—Baltimore, Boston, Buffalo, Miami, New York Jets; Western—Denver, Kansas City, Oakland, San Diego. AFL and NFL owners voted to conduct open inter-conference trading between the present 26 teams from Jan. 19 to Mar. 1, 1970.

1970—The 13-team National Football Conference was realigned into three divisions: Eastern—Dallas, New York Giants, Philadelphia, St. Louis, Washington; Central—Chicago, Detroit, Green Bay, Minnesota; Western—Atlanta, Los Angeles, New Orleans, San Francisco. Art Modell resigned as president of NFL and Milt Woodard resigned as AFL president. Lamar Hunt elected AFC president and George Halas, Chicago Bears owner, elected NFC president for 2-year terms. NFL owners adopted the following rule changes: 1. names of players on backs of jerseys, directly above number; 2. ball to be Wilson brand with signature of commissioner of league; 3. point after touchdown worth one point; 4. official time of game to be scoreboard time unless there is no clock or it is faulty. Line judge would then be official timer. Vince Lombardi, executive vice president and coach of The Washington Redskins and former general manager-coach of the Green Bay Packers, died on Sept. 3.

1971—NFL owners approved a change in the playing rules making it a "judgment call" for determining intentional grounding of a pass to prevent loss of yardage. The Boston Patriots name changed to New England Patriots. Dan Reeves, president and general manager of the Los Angeles Rams, died on April 15th.

1972—In-bound markers for NFL playing field changed leaving 18 feet, 6 inches (the width of a goal post crossbar) in the middle.

PROFESSIONAL STATISTICS

(Courtesy Suzanne Treat, editor *The Encyclopedia of Football*, A.S. Barnes & Co.)

PRO FOOTBALL HALL OF FAME
(Canton, Ohio)

Player	Year Elected
Cliff Battles	1968
Samuel Baugh	1963
Charles Bednarik	1967
Jim Brown	1971
Guy Chamberlin	1965
Jack Christiansen	1970
Earl Clark	1963
James Conzelman	1964
Arthur Donovan	1968
John Driscoll	1965
William Dudley	1966
Albert Edwards	1969
Tom Fears	1970
Daniel Fortmann	1965
Otto Graham	1965
Harold Grange	1963
Joseph Guyon	1966
George Halas	1963
Edward Healey	1964
Melvin Hein	1963
Wilbur Henry	1963
Arnold Herber	1966
Bill Hewitt	1971
Clarke Hinkle	1964
Elroy Hirsch	1968
Robert Hubbard	1963
Donald Hutson	1963
Walter Kiesling	1966
Frank Kinard	1971
Earl Lambeau	1963
Robert Layne	1967
Sidney Luckman	1965
William Lyman	1964
Gino Marchetti	1972
Ollie Matson	1972
George McAfee	1966
Hugh McElhenny	1970
John McNally	1963
August Michalski	1964
Wayne Millner	1968

Marion Motley	1968
Bronko Nagurski	1963
Ernest Nevers	1963
Leo Nomellini	1969
Steven Owen	1966
Ace Parker	1972
Joe Perry	1969
Pete Pihos	1970
Andy Robustelli	1971
Ernie Stautner	1969
Kenneth Strong	1967
Joseph Stydahar	1967
James Thorpe	1963
Y.A. Tittle	1971
George Trafton	1964
Charles Trippi	1968
Emlen Tunnell	1967
Clyde Turner	1966
Norm Van Brocklin	1971
Steven Van Buren	1965
Robert Waterfield	1965
Alex Wojciechowicz	1968

Non-players	Year Elected
Bert Bell	1963
Charles Bidwill	1967
Paul Brown	1967
Joseph Carr	1963
Lamar Hunt	1972
Vince Lombardi	1971
Tim Mara	1963
George Marshall	1963
Earle Neale	1969
Hugh Ray	1966
Daniel Reeves	1967
Arthur Rooney	1964

United Savings Helms Hall of Fame
(For professional football)

AGAJANIAN, Benjamin—Kicker, Pittsburgh, Philadelphia, New York, Los Angeles, Green Bay (N.F.L.); Los Angeles, Green Bay (N.F.L.); Los Angeles (A.A.F.C.); Los Angeles, Dallas (A.F.L.) 1945—1961.

ALBERT, Frank— Back, San Francisco, 1946—52.

ARNETT, Jon— Back, Los Angeles and Chicago Bears, 1957—66.

BANDUCCI, Bruno— Guard, Philadelphia, San Francisco (A.A.F.C.), San Francisco, 1944—54.

BATTLES, Clifford— Back, Boston and Washington, 1932—37.

BAUGH, Samuel— Back, Washington, 1937—52.

BEDNARIK, Charles— Center, Philadelphia, 1949—62.

BELL, DeBenneville "Bert", owner Philadelphia Eagles, 1933—45; Commissioner National Football League, 1946—59.

BENTON, James— End, Cleveland Rams, Chicago Bears, Los Angeles, 1938—47.

BIDWELL, Charles— owner Chicago Cardinals, 1933—47.

BLOOD, John (McNally)—Back, Milwaukee, Duluth, Pottsville, Green Bay and Pittsburgh, 1925—39.

BRAY, Raymond— Guard, Chicago Bears, Green Bay, 1939—52.

BRITO, Eugene— End, Washington, Los Angeles, 1951—60.

BROWN, James— Back, Cleveland Browns, 1957—65.

BROWN, Paul— Coach, Cleveland Browns (A.A.F.C.), 1946—49; Cleveland Browns, 1950—62; Cincinnati Bengals (AFL-AFC) 1968—72.

CANADEO, Anthony— Back, Green Bay, 1941—52.

CARR, Joseph F.— First president of the National Football League, 1921—39.

CLARK, Earl (Dutch)—Back, Portsmouth and Detroit, 1931—38.

CONERLY, Charles— Quarterback, New York, 1948—61.

CONZELMAN, James— Qback, Decatur, Rock Island, Milwaukee, Detroit Panthers, Providence, 1920—29.

DONOVAN, Arthur— Tackle, Baltimore, New York Yanks, Dallas Texans, 1950—61.

DRISCOLL, John (Paddy)—Back, Chicago Cardinals and Bears, 1921—29.

DUDLEY, William— Back, Pittsburgh, Detroit, Washington, 1942—53.

EDWARDS, Albert (Turk)—Tackle, Boston and Washington, 1932—40.

FEARS, Tom— End, Los Angeles, 1948—56.

FLAHERTY, Ray— End, New York Giants and Yankees, 1927—35.

FORTMANN, Daniel— Guard, Chicago Bears, 1936—42.

GIFFORD, Frank— Back, New York Giants, 1952—64.

GRAHAM, Otto— Back, Cleveland, 1946—55.

GRANGE, Harold (Red)—Back, Chicago Bears and New York Yankees, 1925—34.

GROZA, Lou— Tackle, Cleveland, 1946—59.

HALAS, George— End, coach, Chicago Bears, 1921—59.

HEIN, Melvin— Center, New York Giants, 1931—45.

HENRY, Wilbur— Tackle, Canton, New York Giants, Akron, Stapletons and Pottsville, 1920—28.

HERBER, Arnold— Back, Green Bay and New York Giants, 1930—45.

HEWITT, William— End, Chicago Bears and Philadelphia, 1932—39, 1943.

HINKLE, Clark— Back, Green Bay, 1932—41.

HIRSCH, Elroy— End, Chicago Rockets and Los Angeles, 1946—57.

HUBBARD, Robert (Cal)—Tackle, Green Bay Pittsburgh and New York Giants, 1927—36.

HUNTER, Arthur— Center, Green Bay, Cleveland, Los Angeles Rams, Pittsburgh, 1954—65.

HUTSON, Donald— End, Green Bay, 1935—45.

KIESLING, Walter— Guard, Duluth, Pottsville, Boston, Chicago Cardinals, Chicago Bears, Green Bay, Pittsburgh, 1926—38; coach Pittsburgh, 1954—56.

KILROY, Frank— Guard, Philadelphia, 1943—56.

LAMBEAU, Earl— Back, coach, Green Bay, Chicago Cardinals, Washington, 1921—54.

LAYNE, Robert— Qback, Chicago Bears, New York Bulldogs, Detroit, Pittsburgh, 1948—62.

LeBARON, Edward— Qback, Washington, Dallas Cowboys, 1952—63.

LEEMANS Alphonse (Tuffy)—Back, New York Giants, 1936—43.

LOMBARDI, Vincent— Coach, Green Bay, 1959—67; Washington, 1969—70; General Manager, Green Bay, 1968.

LUCKMAN, Sidney— Back, Chicago Bears, 1939—50.

LYMAN, Roy— Tackle, Canton, Cleveland, Chicago Bears, 1922—34.

McAFEE, George— Back, Chicago Bears, 1940—50.

McELHENNY, Hugh— Back, San Francisco, Minnesota, New York Giants, Detroit, 1952—64.

MANDERS, John— Back, Chicago Bears, 1933—40.

MARA, Timothy J.— owner New York Giants, 1925—58.

MARCHETTI, Gino— End, Dallas Texans, Baltimore, 1952—66.

MARSHALL, George Preston—owner Boston and Washington Redskins, 1932—62.

MARTIN, James— Linebacker, Kicker, Cleveland, Detroit, Baltimore, Washington, 1950—64.

MATSON, Ollie— Back, Chicago Cardinals, Los Angeles, Detroit, Philadelphia, 1952—66.

MEADOR, Edward— Back, Los Angeles (NFL-NFC), 1959—70.

MOTLEY, Marion— Back, Cleveland Browns (A.A.F.C.), Cleveland, Pittsburgh, 1946—55.

MUSSO, George— Guard, Chicago Bears, 1933—44.

NAGURSKI, Bronko— Back, Chicago Bears, 1930—37, 1943.

NEALE, Earle— Coach, Philadelphia, 1941—50.

NESSER, Al— End, Akron, Columbus, New York Giants, 1920—28; Cleveland Indians, 1931.

NEVERS, Ernest— Back, Duluth and Chicago Cardinals, 1926—31.

NOMELLINI, Leo— Tackle, San Francisco, 1950—63.

OWEN, Stephen— Tackle, coach, New York Giants, 1926—53.

PARKER, Raymond— Back, Detroit, Chicago Cardinals, 1935—43; Co-coached, Chicago Cardinals, 1949; Coached, Detroit, 1951—56, Pittsburgh 1957—64.

PAUL, Don— Linebacker, Los Angeles, 1948—55.

PERRY, Fletcher Joe—Back, San Francisco, 1948—49 A.A.F.C. and 1950—61 N.F.L.

PIHOS, Peter– End, Philadelphia, 1947–55.

REEVES, Daniel– Owner, Cleveland-Los Angeles Rams, 1941–71.

RENFRO, Ray– Back, Cleveland, 1952–63.

RICHTER, Les– Linebacker, Los Angeles, 1954–62.

ROBUSTELLI, Andy– End, Los Angeles, New York Giants, 1951–64.

ROTE, Kyle– End, New York Giants, 1951–61.

ROTE, Tobin– Qback, Green Bay, Detroit, San Diego (AFL), Denver (AFL), 1950–66.

ST. CLAIR, Robert– Tackle, San Francisco, 1953–63.

SEARS, Vistor– Tackle, Philadelphia, 1941–51.

SHAW, Lawrence– coach, San Francisco, 1950–54; Philadelphia, 1958–60.

SPRINKLE, Ed– End and Guard, Chicago Bears, 1944–55.

STAUTNER, Ernest– Tackle, Pittsburgh, 1950–63.

STORCK, Carl L. Sec-Treas. N.F.L., 1921–39, President 1939–40.

STRONG, Kenneth– Back, Stapletons and New York Giants, 1929–47.

STYDAHAR, Joseph– Tackle, coach, Chicago Bears and Los Angeles Rams, Chicago Cardinals, 1936–54.

THORPE, James– Back, Canton, Cleveland, Oorang, Rock Island and New York Giants, 1920–26.

TITTLE, Yelverton– Quarterback, San Francisco, New York, Baltimore, 1950–62 N.F.L.; Baltimore 1948–49 A.A.F.C.

TRAFTON, George– Center, Chicago Bears, 1920–32.

TRIPPI, Charles– Back, Chicago Cardinals, 1947–55.

TUNNELL, Emlen– Back, New York, Green Bay, 1948–61.

TURNER, Clyde– Center, Chicago Bears, 1940–51.

VAN BROCKLIN, Norman–Quarterback, Los Angeles, Philadelphia, 1949–60.

VAN BUREN, Steve–Back, Philadelphia Eagles, 1944–51.

WALKER, Doak– Back, Detroit, 1950–55.

WATERFIELD, Robert– Back, Cleveland Rams and Los Angeles, 1946–52.

WEBSTER, Alex– Back, New York Giants, 1955–64; coach, New York Giants, 1969–72.

WILLIAMS, Fred– Tackle, Chicago Bears, Washington, 1952–65.

WOJCIECHOWICZ, Alexander– Center, Detroit and Philadelphia, 1938–50.

YOUNGER, Paul– Back, Los Angeles, Pittsburgh, 1949–58.

All-League Selections
National Football League/Conference
(Colleges in parentheses.)
1931
END–LaVern Dilweg, Green Bay (Marquette)

END–Morris (Red) Badgro, New York (Southern California)

TACKLE–Robert (Cal) Hubbard, Green Bay (Geneva)

TACKLE–George Christensen, Portsmouth (Oregon)

GUARD–August Michalske, Green Bay (Penn State)

GUARD–Denver Gibson, New York (Grove City)

CENTER–Frank McNally, Chicago Cards (St. Mary's)

QUARTERBACK– Earl (Dutch) Clark, Portsmouth (Colorado)

HALFBACK–Harold (Red) Grange (Illinois)

HALFBACK–Johnny Blood (McNally), Green Bay (St. John, Minn.)

FULLBACK–Ernie Nevers, Chicago Cards (Stanford)

1932
E–Ray Flaherty, New York (Gonzaga)
E–Luke Johnsos, Chicago Bears (Northwestern)
T–Robert (Cal) Hubbard, Green Bay
T–Albert (Turk) Edwards, Boston (Washington State)
G–Jules Carlson, Chicago Bears (Oregon State)
G–Walter Kiesling, Chicago Cards (St. Thomas)
C–Nathan Barrager, Green Bay (Southern California)
QB–Earl (Dutch) Clark, Portsmouth
HB–Arnie Herber, Green Bay (Regis)
HB–Roy (Father) Lumpkin, Portsmouth (Georgia Tech)
FB–Bronko Nagurski, Chicago Bears (Minnesota)

1933
E–Bill Hewitt, Chicago Bears (Michigan)
E–Morris (Red) Badgro, New York
T–Robert (Cal) Hubbard, Green Bay
T–Albert (Turk) Edwards, Boston
G–Herman Hickman, Brooklyn (Tennessee)
G–Joe Kopcha, Chicago Bears (Chattanooga)
C–Melvin Hein, New York (Washington State)
QB–Harry Newman, New York (Michigan)
HB–Glenn Presnell, Portsmouth (Nebraska)
HB–Cliff Battles, Boston (West Virginia Wesleyan)
FB–Bronko Nagurski, Chicago Bears

1934
E–Bill Hewitt, Chicago Bears (Michigan)
E–Morris (Red) Badgro, New York
T–George Christensen, Detroit
G–Denver Gibson, New York
G–Joe Kopcha, Chicago Bears
C–Melvin Hein, New York
QB–Earl (Dutch) Clark, Detroit
HB–Beattie Feathers, Chicago Bears (Tennessee)
HB–Ken Strong, New York (New York University)
FB–Bronko Nagurski, Chicago Bears

1935
E–Bill Smith, Chicago Cards (Washington)

E—Bill Karr, Chicago Bears (West Virginia)
T—Bill Morgan, New York
T—George Musso, Chicago Bears (Milligan)
G—Joe Kopcha, Chicago Bears
G—August Michalske, Green Bay
C—Melvin Hein, New York
QB—Earl (Dutch) Clark, Detroit
HB—Ed Danowski, New York (Fordham)
HB—Ernie Caddel, Detroit (Stanford)
FB—Mike Mikulak, Chicago Cards (Oregon)

1936

E—Bill Hewitt, Philadelphia
E—Don Hutson, Green Bay (Alabama)
T—Albert (Turk) Edwards, Boston
T—Ernie Smith, Green Bay (Southern California)
G—Lon Evans, Green Bay (Texas Christian)
G—Grover Emerson, Detroit (Texas)
C—Melvin Hein, New York (Washington State)
QB—Earl (Dutch) Clark, Detroit
HB—Cliff Battles, Washington
HB—Alphonse (Tuffy) Leemans, New York (George Washington)
FB—Clark Hinkle, Green Bay (Bucknell)

1937

E—Bill Hewitt, Philadelphia
E—Gaynell Tinsley, Chicago Cards (Louisiana State)
T—Joe Stydahar, Chicago Bears (West Virginia)
T—Albert (Turk) Edwards, Washington (Washington State)
G—Lon Evans, Green Bay
G—George Musso, Chicago Bears
C—Melvin Hein, New York
QB—Earl (Dutch) Clark, Detroit
HB—Cliff Battles, Washington
HB—Sammy Baugh, Washington (Texas Christian)
FB—Clark Hinkle, Green Bay

1938

E—Don Hutson, Green Bay
E—Gaynell Tinsley, Chicago Cards
T—Ed Widseth, New York (Minnesota)
T—Joe Stydahar, Chicago Bears
G—Daniel Fortmann, Chicago Bears (Colgate)
G—Russ Letlow, Green Bay (San Francisco)
C—Melvin Hein, New York
QB—Clarence (Ace) Parker, Brooklyn (Duke)
HB—Ed Danowski, New York (Fordham)
HB—Lloyd Cardwell, Detroit (Nebraska)
FB—Clark Hinkle, Green Bay

1939

E—Don Hutson, Green Bay
E—Jim Poole, New York (Mississippi)
T—Joe Stydahar, Chicago Bears
T—Jim Barber, Washington (San Francisco)
G—Daniel Fortmann, Chicago Bears
G—Johnny Del Isola, New York (Fordham)
C—Melvin Hein, New York
QB—Davey O'Brien, Philadelphia (Texas Christian)
HB—Alphonse (Tuffy) Leemans, New York

HB—Andy Farkas, Washington (Detroit)
FB—Bill Osmanski, Chicago Bears (Holy Cross)

1940

E—Don Hutson, Green Bay
E—Perry Schwartz, Brooklyn (California)
T—Joe Stydahar, Chicago Bears
T—Frank Kinard, Brooklyn (Mississippi)
G—Daniel Fortmann, Chicago Bears
G—John Wiethe, Detroit (Xavier, Cincinnati)
C—Melvin Hein, New York
QB—Clarence (Ace) Parker, Brooklyn
HB—Sammy Baugh, Washington
HB—Byron (Whizzer) White, Detroit (Colorado)
FB—John Drake, Cleveland (Purdue)

1941

E—Don Hutson, Green Bay
E—Perry Schwartz, Brooklyn
T—Frank Kinard, Brooklyn
T—Wilbur Wilkin, Washington (St. Mary's)
G—Daniel Fortmann, Chicago Bears
G—Joe Kuharich, Chicago Cards (Notre Dame)
C—Clyde (Bulldog) Turner, Chicago Bears (Hardin-Simmons)
QB—Sid Luckman, Chicago Bears (Columbia)
HB—Cecil Isbell, Green Bay (Purdue)
HB—George McAfee, Chicago Bears (Duke)
FB—Clark Hinkle, Green Bay

1942

E—Don Hutson, Green Bay
E—Bob Masterson, Washington (Miami)
T—Wilbur Wilkin, Washington
T—Lee Artoe, Chicago Bears (Santa Clara)
G—Daniel Fortmann, Chicago Bears
G—Bill Edwards, New York (Baylor)
C—Clyde (Bulldog) Turner, Chicago Bears
QB—Sid Luckman, Chicago Bears
HB—Cecil Isbell, Green Bay
HB—Bill Dudley, Pittsburgh (Virginia)
FB—Gary Famiglietti, Chicago Bears (Boston University)

(Official selections discontinued after 1942.)

1943
(Associated Press)

E—Don Hutson, Green Bay
E—Ed Rucinski, Chicago Cards (Indiana)
T—Frank Kinard, Brooklyn
T—Al Blozis, New York (Georgetown)
G—Dick Farman, Washington (Washington State)
G—Daniel Fortmann, Chicago Bears
C—Clyde (Bulldog) Turner, Chicago Bears
QB—Sid Luckman, Chicago Bears
HB—Sammy Baugh, Washington
HB—Harry Clark, Chicago Bears (West Virginia)
FB—Tony Canadeo, Green Bay (Gonzaga)

(United Press)

E—Don Hutson
E—Ed Rucinski
T—Vic Sears, Philadelphia-Pittsburgh (Oregon State)

T—Al Blozis
G—Dick Farman
G—Daniel Fortmann
C—Clyde (Bulldog) Turner
QB—Sid Luckman
HB—Sammy Baugh
HB—Harry Clark
FB—Ward Cuff, New York (Marquette)

1944
(Associated Press)
E—Don Hutson, Green Bay
E—Joe Aguirre, Washington (St. Mary's)
T—Albert Wistert, Philadelphia (Michigan)
T—Frank Kinard, Brooklyn
G—Len Younce, New York (Oregon State)
G—Riley Matheson, Cleveland (Texas Mines)
C—Clyde (Bulldog) Turner, Chicago Bears
QB—Sid Luckman, Chicago Bears
HB—Frank Sinkwich, Detroit (Georgia)
HB—Steve Van Buren, Philadelphia (Louisiana State)
FB—Bill Paschal, New York (Georgia Tech)

1945
(Associated Press)

E—Don Hutson, Green Bay
E—Jim Benton, Cleveland (Arkansas)
T—Albert Wistert, Philadelphia
T—Frank Cope, New York
G—Riley Matheson, Cleveland
G—Bill Radovich, Detroit (Southern California)
C—Charlie Brock, Green Bay (Nebraska)
QB—Bob Waterfield, Cleveland (U.C.L.A.)
HB—Steve Van Buren, Philadelphia
HB—Steve Bagarus, Washington (Notre Dame)
FB—Bob Westfall, Detroit (Michigan)

(United Press)

E—Don Hutson
E—Steve Pritko, Cleveland (Villanova)
T—Albert Wistert
T—Emil Uremovich, Detroit (Indiana)
G—Riley Matheson
G—Bill Radovich
C—Charlie Brock
QB—Sammy Baugh, Washington
HB—Bob Waterfield
HB—Steve Van Buren
FB—Ted Fritsch, Green Bay (Stevens Point Teachers)

1946
(Associated Press)

E—Jim Benton, Los Angeles Rams
E—Jim Poole, New York Giants (Mississippi)
T—Frank Kinard, New York Yankees
T—Albert Wistert, Philadelphia
G—Riley Matheson, Los Angeles Rams
G—Bill Radovich, Los Angeles Dons
C—Clyde (Bulldog) Turner, Chicago Bears
B—Bob Waterfield, Los Angeles Rams
B—Glenn Dobbs, Brooklyn (Tulsa)

B—Orban (Spec) Sanders, New York Yankees (Texas)
B—Ted Fritsch, Green Bay

(United Press)

E—Jim Benton
E—Ken Kavanaugh, Chicago Bears (Louisiana State)
T—Albert Wistert
T—Jim White, New York (Notre Dame)
G—Ausgustino (Gus) Lio, Philadelphia (Georgetown)
G—Riley Matheson
C—Clyde (Bulldog) Turner
QB—Bob Waterfield
HB—Bill Dudley, Pittsburgh (Virginia)
HB—Frank Filchock, New York (Indiana)
FB—Ted Fritsch

1947
(Associated Press)
E—Mac Speedie, Cleveland (Utah)
E—Bruce Alford, New York Yankees (Texas Christian)
T—Albert Wistert, Philadelphia
T—Dick Huffman, Los Angeles Rams (Tennessee)
G—Riley Matheson, Los Angeles Rams
G—Bruno Banducci, San Francisco (Stanford)
C—Clyde (Bulldog) Turner, Chicago Bears
B—Sid Luckman, Chicago Bears (Columbia)
B—Otto Graham, Cleveland (Northwestern)
B—Steve Van Buren, Philadelphia
B—Orban (Spec) Sanders, New York Yankees

(United Press)

E—Ken Kavanaugh, Chicago Bears
E—Mal Kutner, Chicago Cards (Texas)
T—Albert Wistert
T—Fred Davis, Chicago Bears (Alabama)
G—Len Younce, New York
G—William Moore, Pittsburgh (Loyola, New Orleans)
C—Vince Banonis, Chicago Cards (Detroit)
QB—Sid Luckman
HB—Steve Van Buren
HB—Sammy Baugh, Washington
FB—Marlin (Pat) Harder, Chicago Cards (Wisconsin)

1948
(Associated Press)
E—Mal Kutner, Chicago Cardinals
E—Mac Speedie, Cleveland
T—Dick Huffman, Los Angeles Rams
T—Bob Reinhard, Los Angeles Dons (California)
G—Garrard Ramsey, Chicago Cards (William and Mary)
G—Dick Barwegan, Baltimore (Purdue)
C—Clyde (Bulldog) Turner, Chicago Bears
B—Otto Graham, Cleveland
B—Charlie Trippi, Chicago Cards (Georgia)
B—Steve Van Buren, Philadelphia
B—Marion Motley, Cleveland (Nevada)

(United Press)

E—Pete Pihos, Philadelphia (Indiana)
E—Mal Kutner
T—Albert Wistert, Philadelphia
T—Dick Huffman
G—Ray Bray, Chicago Bears (Western Michigan)
G—Garrard Ramsey
C—Clyde (Bulldog) Turner
QB—Sammy Baugh, Washington
HB—Steve Van Buren
H—Charlie Trippi
FB—Marlin (Pat) Harder, Chicago Cards

1949

(Associated Press)

E—Mac Speedie, Cleveland
E—Pete Pihos, Philadelphia
T—Arnold Weinmeister, New York Yankees (Washington)
T—Dick Huffman, Los Angeles Rams
G—Dick Barwegan, Baltimore
G—Garrard Ramsey, Chicago Cards
C—Fred Naumetz, Los Angeles Rams (Boston College)
B—Otto Graham, Cleveland
B—Steve Van Buren, Philadelphia
B—Bob Waterfield, Los Angeles Rams
B—Chet Mutryn, Buffalo (Xavier of Ohio)

(United Press)

E—Pete Pihos
E—Tom Fears, Los Angeles (U.C.L.A.)
T—Vic Sears, Philadelphia (Oregon State)
T—Dick Huffman
G—Ray Bray, Chicago Bears
G—Garrard Ramsey
C—Fred Naumetz
QB—Bob Waterfield
HB—Steve Van Buren
HB—Tony Canadeo, Green Bay (Gonzaga)
FB—Marlin (Pat) Harder, Chicago Cards

1950

(Associated Press)

E—Tom Fears, Los Angeles
E—Dan Edwards, New York Yanks (Georgia)
T—George Connor, Chicago Bears (Notre Dame)
T—Arnie Weinmeister, New York Giants
G—Dick Barwegan, Chicago Bears (Purdue)
G—Joe Signaigo, New York Yanks (Notre Dame)
C—Charles (Chuck) Bednarik, Philadelphia (Pennsylvania)
QB—Johnny Lujack, Chicago Bears (Notre Dame)
HB—Doak Walker, Detroit (Southern Methodist)
HB—Joe Geri, Pittsburgh (Georgia)
FB—Marion Motley, Cleveland

(United Press)

E—Tom Fears
E—Mac Speedie, Cleveland
T—George Connor
T—Arnie Weinmeister
G—Dick Barwegan
G—Bill Willis, Cleveland (Ohio State)

C—Clayton Tonnemaker, Green Bay (Minnesota)
QB—Johnny Lujack
HB—Doak Walker
HB—Joe Geri
FB—Marion Motley

1951

(Associated Press—Offensive Team)

E—Elroy Hirsch, Los Angeles (Wisconsin)
E—Leon Hart, Detroit (Notre Dame)
T—George Connor, Chicago Bears
T—Leo Nomellini, San Francisco (Minnesota)
G—Lou Creekmur, Detroit (William and Mary)
G—Dick Barwegan, Chicago Bears
C—Victor Lindskog, Philadelphia (Stanford)
QB—Otto Graham, Cleveland (Northwestern)
HB—Doak Walker, Detroit
HB—Dub Jones, Cleveland (Tulane and Louisiana State)
FB—Ed Price, New York Giants (Tulane)

(Associated Press—Defensive Team)

E—Larry Brink, Los Angeles (Northern Illinois)
E—Len Ford, Cleveland (Michigan)
T—Arnie Weinmeister, New York Giants
T—Al DeRogatis, New York Giants (Duke)
G—Bill Willis, Cleveland
G—Lester Bingaman, Detroit (Illinois)
*LB—Charles (Chuck) Bednarik, Philadelphia (Pennsylvania)
*LB—Paul Younger, Los Angeles (Grambling)
HB—Jerry Shipkey, Pittsburgh (U.C.L.A.)
HB—Otto Schnellbacher, New York Giants (Kansas)
Safety—Emlen Tunnell, New York Giants (Iowa)
* Linebacker.

(United Press—Offensive Team)

E—Elroy Hirsch
E—Dante Lavelli, Cleveland (Ohio State)
T—Lou Groza, Cleveland (Ohio State)
T—DeWitt (Tex) Coulter, New York Giants Army)
G—Louis Creekmur
G—Dick Barwegan
C—Frank Gatski, Cleveland (Marshall)
B—Otto Graham
B—Doak Walker
B—Bill Jones
B—Dan Towler, Los Angeles (Washington and Jefferson)

(United Press—Defensive Team)

E—Len Ford
E—Leon Hart
T—Arnie Weinmeister
T—George Connor, Chicago Bears
G—Bill Willis
G—Jon Baker, New York Giants (California)
LB—Tony Adamle, Cleveland (Ohio State)
LB—Charles (Chuck) Bednarik
HB—Otto Schnellbacher
HB—Warren Lahr, Cleveland (Western Reserve)
Safety—Emlen Tunnell

1952

(Associated Press—Offensive Team)

E—Cloyce Box, Detroit (West Texas State)
E—Gordon Soltau, San Francisco (Minnesota)
T—George Connor, Chicago Bears
T—Leo Nomellini, San Francisco
G—Lou Creekmur, Detroit
G—Lou Groza, Cleveland
C—Frank Gatski, Cleveland
B—Bobby Layne, Detroit (Texas)
B—Hugh McElhenny, San Francisco (Washington)
B—Ed Price, New York Giants
B—Dan Towler, Los Angeles

(Associated Press—Defensive Team)

E—Len Ford, Cleveland
E—Pete Pihos, Philadelphia
T—Arnold Weinmeister, New York
T—Thurman McGraw, Detroit (Colorado A. and M.)
G—Stan West, Los Angeles (Oklahoma)
G—Bill Willis, Cleveland
LB—Charles (Chuck) Bednarik, Philadelphia
LB—Jerry Shipkey, Pittsburgh
HB—Jack Christiansen, Detroit (Colorado A. & M.)
HB—Ollie Matson, Chicago Cards (San Francisco)
Safety—Emlen Tunnell, New York

(United Press—Offensive Team)

E—Mac Speedie, Cleveland
E—Gordon Soltau
T—Lou Groza, Cleveland
T—Leo Nomellini
G—Lou Creekmur
G—Bill Fischer, Chicago Cards (Notre Dame)
C—William Walsh, Pittsburgh (Notre Dame)
QB—Otto Graham, Cleveland
HB—Hugh McElhenny
HB—Dan Towler
FB—Ed Price

(United Press—Defensive Team)

E—Len Ford
E—Larry Brink, Los Angeles
T—Arnie Weinmeister
T—Thurman McGraw
G—Stan West
G—Lester Bingaman, Detroit
LB—Charles (Chuck) Bednarik
LB—George Connor
HB—Jim Smith, Detroit (Iowa)
HB—Herb Rich, Los Angeles (Vanderbilt)
Safety—Emlen Tunnell

1953

(Associated Press—Offensive Team)

E—Pete Pihos, Philadelphia
E—Elroy Hirsch, Los Angeles
T—George Connor, Chicago Bears
T—Lou Groza, Cleveland
G—Lou Creekmur, Detroit
G—Dick Stanfel, Detroit

C—Frank Gatski, Cleveland
B—Otto Graham, Cleveland
B—Hugh McElhenny, San Francisco
B—Doak Walker, Detroit
B—Joe Perry, San Francisco (Compton Junior College)

(Associated Press—Defensive Team)

E—Len Ford, Cleveland
E—Andy Robustelli, Los Angeles (Arnold)
T—Arnold Weinmeister, New York
T—Leo Nomellini, San Francisco
G—Les Bingaman, Detroit
G—Bill Willis, Cleveland
LB—Chuck Bednarik, Philadelphia
LB—Don Paul, Los Angeles (Washington State)
HB—Tommy Thompson, Cleveland (William and Mary)
HB—Tom Keane, Baltimore (West Virginia)
Safety—Jack Christiansen, Detroit

(United Press—Offensive Team)

E—Pete Pihos
E—Dante Lavelli, Cleveland
T—Lou Groza
T—Lou Creekmur
G—Dick Stanfel
C—Bruno Banducci, San Francisco
C—Frank Gatski
QB—Otto Graham
HB—Hugh McElhenny
HB—Dan Towler, Los Angeles
FB—Joe Perry

(United Press—Defensive Team)

E—Len Ford
E—Norm Willey, Philadelphia (Marshall)
T—Arnold Weinmeister
T—Leo Nomellini
C—Les Bingaman
G—Dale Dodrill, Pittsburgh (Colorado A. and M.)
LB—George Connor
LB—Tommy Thompson
HB—Jack Christiansen
HB—Tom Keane
Safety—Ken Gorgal, Cleveland (Purdue)

1954

(Associated Press—Offensive Team)

E—Pete Pihos, Philadelphia
E—Bob Boyd, Los Angeles (Loyola of Los Angeles)
T—Lou Creekmur, Detroit
T—Lou Groza, Cleveland
G—Dick Stanfel, Detroit
G—Bruno Banducci, San Francisco
C—Bill Walsh, Pittsburgh
QB—Otto Graham, Cleveland
HB—Doak Walker, Detroit
HB—Ollie Matson, Chicago Cards
FB—Joe Perry, San Francisco

(Associated Press—Defensive Team)

E—Len Ford, Cleveland
E—Norm Willey, Philadelphia
T—Leo Nomellini, San Francisco
T—Art Donovan, Baltimore (Boston College)
G—Les Bingaman, Detroit
G—Dale Dodrill, Pittsburgh
LB—Chuck Bednarik, Philadelphia
LB—Joe Schmidt, Detroit (Pittsburgh)
HB—Tom Landry, New York (Texas)
HB—Bobby Dillon, Green Bay (Texas)
Safety—Jack Christiansen, Detroit

(United Press—Offensive Team)

E—Pete Pihos
E—Harlon Hill, Chicago Bears (Florence Teachers)
T—Lou Groza
T—Lou Creekmur
G—Bruno Banducci
G—Dick Stanfel
C—Bill Walsh
QB—Otto Graham
HB—Doak Walker
HB—Ollie Matson
FB—Joe Perry

(United Press—Defensive Team)

E—Len Ford
E—Norm Willey
T—Leo Nomellini
T—Art Donovan
G—Les Bingaman
G—Frank Kilroy, Philadelphia (Temple)
LB—Chuck Bednarik
LB—Roger Zatkoff, Green Bay (Michigan)
HB—Jim David, Detroit (Colorado A. and M.)
HB—Tom Landry
Safety—Jack Christiansen

1955
(Associated Press—Offensive Team)

E—Harlon Hill, Chicago Bears
E—Pete Pihos, Philadelphia
T—Lou Groza, Cleveland
T—Bill Wightkin, Chicago Bears (Notre Dame)
G—Stan Jones, Chicago Bears (Maryland)
G—Duane Putnam, Los Angeles (College of Pacific)
C—Frank Gatski, Cleveland
QB—Otto Graham, Cleveland
HB—Ollie Matson, Chicago Cards
HB—Frank Gifford, New York (Southern California)
FB—Alan Ameche, Baltimore (Wisconsin)

(Associated Press—Defensive Team)

E—Gene Brito, Washington (Loyola of Los Angeles
E—Andy Robustelli, Los Angeles
T—Art Donovan, Baltimore
T—Bob Toneff, San Francisco (Notre Dame)

G—Bill George, Chicago Bears
LB—Roger Zatkoff, Green Bay
LB—Joe Schmidt, Detroit
HB—Will Sherman, Los Angeles (St. Mary's)
HB—Bobby Dillon, Green Bay
Safety—Jack Christiansen, Detroit
Safety—Emlen Tunnell, New York

(United Press—Offensive Team)

E—Harlon Hill
E—Billy Wilson, San Francisco (San Jose State)
T—Lou Groza
T—Bob St. Clair, San Francisco (Tulsa and University of San Francisco)
G—Abe Gibron, Cleveland (Purdue)
G—Bill Austin, New York (Oregon State)
C—Frank Gatski
QB—Otto Graham
HB—Ollie Matson
HB—Ron Waller, Los Angeles (Maryland)
FB—Alan Ameche

(United Press—Defensive Team)

E—Gene Brito
E—Len Ford, Cleveland
T—Art Donovan
T—Don Colo, Cleveland (Brown)
G—Dale Dodrill, Pittsburgh
LB—Chuck Bednarik, Philadelphia
LB—George Connor, Chicago Bears
HB—Don Paul, Cleveland
HB—Will Sherman
Safety—Jack Christiansen
Safety—Bobby Dillon

1956
(Associated Press—Offensive Team)

E—Harlon Hill, Chicago Bears
E—Bill Howton, Green Bay (Rice)
T—Lou Creekmur, Detroit
T—Roosevelt Brown, New York (Morgan State)
G—Stan Jones, Chicago Bears
G—Dick Stanfel, Washington
C—Larry Strickland, Chicago Bears (North Texas State)
QB—Bobby Layne, Detroit
HB—Frank Gifford, New York
HB—Ollie Matson, Chicago Cards
FB—Rick Casares, Chicago Bears (Florida)

(Associated Press—Defensive Team)

E—Andy Robustelli, New York
E—Gene Brito, Washington
T—Rossevelt Grier, New York (Penn State)
T—Art Donovan, Baltimore
G—Bill George, Chicago Bears (Wake Forest)
LB—Joe Schmidt, Detroit
LB—Les Richter, Los Angeles (California)
HB—Dick Lane, Chicago Cards (Scottsbluff Junior College)
HB—Jack Christiansen, Detroit

Safety—Emlen Tunnell, New York
Safety—Yale Lary, Detroit (Texas A.&M.)

(United Press—Offensive Team)

E—Harlon Hill
E—Bill Howton
T—Lou Creekmur
T—Roosevelt Brown
G—Stan Jones
G—Dick Stanfel
C—Charlie Ane, Detroit (Southern California)
QB—Bobby Layne
HB—Frank Gifford
HB—Ollie Matson
FB—Rick Casares

(United Press—Defensive Team)

E—Andy Robustelli
E—Gene Brito
T—Roosevelt Grier
T—Ernie Stautner, Pittsburgh (Boston College)
G—Bill George
LB—Joe Schmidt
LB—Chuck Bednarik, Philadelphia
HB—Emlen Tunnell
HB—Dick Lane
Safety—Jack Christiansen
Safety—Bobby Dillon, Green Bay

1957
(Associated Press—Offensive Team)

E—Billy Wilson, San Francisco
E—Bill Howton, Green Bay
T—Lou Creekmur, Detroit
T—Roosevelt Brown, New York
G—Duane Putnam, Los Angeles
G—Dick Stanfel, Washington
C—Jim Ringo, Green Bay (Syracuse)
QB—Y.A. Tittle, San Francisco (Louisiana State)
HB—Frank Gifford, New York
HB—Ollie Matson, Chicago Cards
FB—Jimmy Brown, Cleveland (Syracuse)

(Associated Press—Defensive Team)

E—Gino Marchetti, Baltimore
   (University of San Francisco)
E—Gene Brito, Washington
T—Leo Nomellini, San Francisco
T—Art Donovan, Baltimore
G—Bill George, Chicago Bears
LB—Joe Schmidt, Detroit
LB—Marv Matuszak, San Francisco (Tulsa)
HB—Jack Christiansen, Detroit
HB—Bobby Dillon, Green Bay
Safety—Jack Butler, Pittsburgh (St. Bonaventure)
Safety—Milt Davis, Baltimore (U.C.L.A.)

(United Press—Offensive Team)

E—Billy Wilson
E—Bill Howton
T—Roosevelt Brown
T—Lou Groza, Cleveland

G—Dick Stanfel
G—Duane Putnam
C—Bill Strickland, Chicago Bears
QB—Y.A. Tittle
HB—Frank Gifford
HB—Ollie Matson
FB—Jimmy Brown

(United Press—Defensive Team)

E—Gino Marchetti
E—Andy Robustelli, New York
T—Art Donovan
T—Leo Nomellini
LB—Joe Schmidt
LB—Bill George
LB—Marv Matuszak
HB—Jack Butler
HB—Yale Lary, Detroit
Safety—Bobby Dillon
Safety—Jack Christiansen

1958
(Associated Press—Offensive Team)

E—Ray Berry, Baltimore (Southern Methodist)
E—Del Shofner, Los Angeles (Baylor)
T—Roosevelt Brown, New York
T—Jim Parker, Baltimore (Ohio State)
G—Dick Stanfel, Washington
G—Duane Putnam, Los Angeles
C—Ray Wietecha, New York (Northwestern)
QB—Johnny Unitas, Baltimore (Louisville)
HB—Lenny Moore, Baltimore (Penn State)
HB—Jon Arnett, Los Angeles
   (Southern California)
FB—Jimmy Brown, Cleveland

(Associated Press—Defensive Team)

E—Gino Marchetti, Baltimore
E—Andy Robustelli, New York
T—Gene Lipscomb, Baltimore
   (Miller High School, Detroit)
T—Ernie Stautner, Pittsburgh
LB—Sam Huff, New York (West Virginia)
LB—Joe Schmidt, Detroit
LB—Bill George, Chicago Bears
HB—Jack Butler, Pittsburgh
HB—Yale Lary, Detroit
Safety—Jim Patton, New York (Mississippi)
Safety—Bobby Dillon, Green Bay

(United Press International—Offensive Team)

E—Ray Berry
E—Del Shofner
T—Roosevelt Brown
T—Jim Parker
G—Dick Stanfel
G—Duane Putnam
C—Ray Wietecha
QB—Johnny Unitas
HB—Lenny Moore
HB—Jon Arnett
FB—Jimmy Brown

(United Press International—Defensive Team)

E—Gino Marchetti
E—Gene Brito, Washington
T—Gene Lipscomb
T—Ernie Stautner
LB—Joe Schmidt
LB—Sam Huff
LB—Bill George
HB—Jack Butler
HB—Yale Lary
Safety—Jim Patton
Safety—Bobby Dillon

1959
Offensive Team

E—Berry, Baltimore (A.P., U.P.I.)
E—Shofner, Los Angeles (A.P., U.P.I.)
T—Brown, New York (A.P., U.P.I.)
T—Parker, Baltimore (A.P., U.P.I.)
G—Smith, Cleveland (A.P., U.P.I.)
G—Jones, Chicago (A.P.)
G—Spinney, Baltimore (U.P.I.)
C—Ringo, Green Bay (A.P., U.P.I.)
QB—Unitas, Baltimore (A.P., U.P.I.)
HB—Gifford, New York (A.P., U.P.I.)
HB—Moore, Baltimore (A.P.)
HB—Smith, San Francisco (U.P.I.)
FB—Brown, Cleveland (A.P., U.P.I.)

Defensive Team

E—Marchetti, Baltimore (A.P., U.P.I.)
E—Robustelli, New York (A.P., U.P.I.)
T—Lipscomb, Baltimore (A.P., U.P.I.)
T—Nomellini, San Francisco (A.P., U.P.I.)
LB—Huff, New York (A.P., U.P.I.)
LB—George, Chicago (A.P., U.P.I.)
LB—Schmidt, Detroit (A.P., U.P.I.)
HB—Woodson, San Francisco (A.P., U.P.I.)
HB—Butler, Pittsburgh (A.P., U.P.I.)
S—Derby, Pittsburgh (U.P.I.)
S—Patton, New York (A.P., U.P.I.)
S—Nelson, Baltimore (A.P.)

1960
Offensive Team

E—Berry, Baltimore (A.P., U.P.I.)
E—Randle, St. Louis (A.P., U.P.I.)
T—Parker, Baltimore (A.P., U.P.I.)
T—Gregg, Green Bay (A.P.)
T—Brown, New York (U.P.I.)
G—Smith, Cleveland (A.P., U.P.I.)
G—Kramer, Green Bay (A.P.)
G—Jones, Chicago (U.P.I.)
C—Ringo (A.P., U.P.I.)
QB—Van Brocklin, Philadelphia (A.P., U.P.I.)
HB—Hornung, Green Bay (A.P., U.P.I.)
HB—Moore, Baltimore (A.P., U.P.I.)
FB—Brown, Cleveland (A.P., U.P.I.)

Defensive Team

E—Marchetti, Baltimore (A.P., U.P.I.)
E—Robustelli, New York (A.P., U.P.I.)

E—Atkins, Chicago (U.P.I.)
T—Jordan, Green Bay (A.P., U.P.I.)
T—Karras, Detroit (A.P., U.P.I.)
LB—Bednarik, Philadelphia (A.P., U.P.I.)
LB—George, Chicago (A.P., U.P.I.)
LB—Forester, Green Bay (A.P., U.P.I.)
HB—Brookshier, Philadelphia (A.P., U.P.I.)
HB—Lane, Detroit (U.P.I.)
HB—Woodson, San Francisco (A.P.)
S—Norton, St. Louis (A.P., U.P.I.)
S—Patton, New York (A.P., U.P.I.)

1961
Offensive Team

E—Shofner, New York (A.P., U.P.I.)
E—Phillips, Los Angeles (A.P., U.P.I.)
T—Brown, New York (A.P., U.P.I.)
T—Gregg, Green Bay (U.P.I.)
T—Parker, Baltimore (A.P.)
G—Thurston, Green Bay (A.P., U.P.I.)
G—Smith, Cleveland (A.P., U.P.I.)
C—Ringo, Green Bay (A.P., U.P.I.)
QB—Jurgenson, Philadelphia (A.P., U.P.I.)
HB—Hornung, Green Bay (A.P., U.P.I.)
HB—Moore, Baltimore (A.P., U.P.I.)
FB—Brown, Cleveland (A.P., U.P.I.)

Defensive Team

E—Marchetti, Baltimore (A.P., U.P.I.)
E—Katcavage, New York (A.P., U.P.I.)
T—Jordan, Green Bay (A.P., U.P.I.)
T—Karras, Detroit (A.P., U.P.I.)
LB—Schmidt, Detroit (A.P., U.P.I.)
LB—Forester, Green Bay (A.P., U.P.I.)
LB—George, Chicago (A.P.)
LB—Currie, Green Bay (U.P.I.)
HB—Barnes, New York (A.P., U.P.I.)
HB—Whittenton, Green Bay (A.P., U.P.I.)
S—Patton, New York (A.P., U.P.I.)
S—Lane, Detroit (A.P.)
S—Sample, Pittsburgh (U.P.I.)

1962
Offensive Team

E—Shofner, New York (A.P., U.P.I.)
E—R. Kramer, Green Bay (A.P.)
E—Ditka, Chicago (U.P.I.)
T—R. Brown, New York (A.P., U.P.I.)
T—Gregg, Green Bay (A.P., U.P.I.)
G—J. Kramer, Green Bay (A.P., U.P.I.)
G—Parker, Baltimore (A.P.)
G—Thurston, Green Bay (U.P.I.)
C—Ringo (A.P., U.P.I.)
QB—Tittle, New York (A.P., U.P.I.)
HB—Mitchell, Washington (A.P., U.P.I.)
HB—Perkins, Dallas (A.P.)
HB—Bass, Los Angeles (U.P.I.)
FB—Taylor, Green Bay (A.P., U.P.I.)

Defensive Team

E—Marchetti, Baltimore (A.P., U.P.I.)
E—W. Davis, Green Bay (A.P.)
E—Katcavage, New York (U.P.I.)

T—R. Brown, Detroit (A.P., U.P.I.)
T—Jordan, Green Bay (A.P.)
T—A. Karras, Detroit (U.P.I.)
LB—Schmidt, Detroit (A.P., U.P.I.)
LB—Currie, Green Bay (A.P., U.P.I.)
LB—Forester, Green Bay (A.P., U.P.I.)
HB—Adderly, Green Bay (A.P., U.P.I.)
HB—Lane, Detroit (A.P., U.P.I.)
S—Patton, New York (A.P., U.P.I.)
S—Lary, Detroit (A.P., U.P.I.)

1963
Offensive Team

E—Shofner, New York (A.P., U.P.I.)
E—Ditka, Chicago (A.P., U.P.I.)
T—Brown, Roosevelt, New York (U.P.I.)
T—Gregg, Green Bay (A.P., U.P.I.)
T—Schafrath, Cleveland (A.P.)
G—Kramer, J., Green Bay (A.P., U.P.I.)
G—Parker, Baltimore (A.P.)
G—Gray, St. Louis (U.P.I.)
C—Ringo, Green Bay (A.P., U.P.I.)
Q—Tittle, New York (A.P., U.P.I.)
B—Mason, Minnesota (A.P., U.P.I.)
B—Conrad, St. Louis (A.P., U.P.I.)
B—Brown, James, Cleveland (A.P., U.P.I.)

Defensive Team

E—Atkins, Chicago (A.P., U.P.I.)
E—Katcavage, New York (A.P., U.P.I.)
T—Jordan, Green Bay (A.P., U.P.I.)
T—Brown, Roger, Detroit (A.P., U.P.I.)
LB—George, Chicago (A.P., U.P.I.)
LB—Fortunato, Chicago (A.P., U.P.I.)
LB—Forester, Green Bay (A.P.)
LB—Pardee, Los Angeles (U.P.I.)
HB—Lynch, New York (A.P., U.P.I.)
HB—Lane, Detroit (U.P.I.)
HB—Adderley, Green Bay (A.P.)
S—Petitbon, Chicago (A.P., U.P.I.)
S—Wilson, St. Louis (U.P.I.)
S—Taylor, Chicago (A.P.)

1964
Offensive Team

E—Clark, Dallas (A.P.)
E—Ditka, Chicago (A.P., U.P.I.)
E—Mitchell, Washington (U.P.I.)
T—Gregg, Green Bay (A.P., U.P.I.)
T—Schafrath, Cleveland (A.P., U.P.I.)
G—Parker, Baltimore, (A.P., U.P.I.)
G—Gray, St. Louis (A.P., U.P.I.)
C—Tinglehoff, Minnesota (A.P., U.P.I.)
Q—Unitas, Baltimore (A.P., U.P.I.)
B—Moore, Baltimore (A.P., U.P.I.)
B—Morris, Chicago (A.P., U.P.I.)
B—Brown, Cleveland (A.P., U.P.I.)

Defensive Team

E—Marchetti, Baltimore (A.P., U.P.I.)
E—Davis, Green Bay (A.P., U.P.I.)
T—Jordan, Green Bay (A.P., U.P.I.)

T—Lilly, Dallas (A.P., U.P.I.)
LB—Nitschke, Green Bay (A.P., U.P.I.)
LB—Fortunato, Chicago (A.P., U.P.I.)
LB—Baughan, Philadelphia (A.P.)
LB—Walker, Detroit (U.P.I.)
B—Fischer, St. Louis (A.P., U.P.I.)
B—Boyd, Baltimore (A.P., U.P.I.)
S—Krause, Washington (A.P., U.P.I.)
S—Wood, Green Bay (A.P., U.P.I.)

1965
Offensive Team

E—Parks, San Francisco (A.P., U.P.I.)
E—Retzlaff, Philadelphia (A.P., U.P.I.)
T—Schafrath, Cleveland (A.P., U.P.I.)
T—Brown, Philadelphia (A.P.)
T—Gregg, Green Bay (U.P.I.)
G—Parker, Baltimore (A.P., U.P.I.)
G—Gregg, Green Bay (A.P.)
G—Gray, St. Louis (U.P.I.)
C—Tingelhoff, Minnesota (A.P., U.P.I.)
Q—Unitas, Baltimore (A.P., U.P.I.)
B—Sayers, Chicago (A.P., U.P.I.)
B—Orr, Baltimore (A.P.)
B—Collins, Cleveland (U.P.I.)
B—Brown, Cleveland (A.P., U.P.I.)

Defensive Team

E—Davis, Green Bay (A.P., U.P.I.)
E—Jones, Los Angeles (A.P., U.P.I.)
T—Lilly, Dallas (A.P., U.P.I.)
T—Karras, Detroit (A.P., U.P.I.)
LB—Walker, Detroit (A.P., U.P.I.)
LB—Butkus, Chicago (A.P.)
LB—Fortunato, Chicago (A.P.)
LB—Nitschke, Green Bay (U.P.I.)
LB—Houston, Cleveland (U.P.I.)
B—Adderley, Green Bay (A.P., U.P.I.)
B—Boyd, Baltimore (A.P., U.P.I.)
S—Wood, Green Bay (A.P., U.P.I.)
S—Krause, Washington (A.P., U.P.I.)

1966
Offensive Team

E—Hayes, Dallas (A.P., U.P.I.)
E—Mackey, Baltimore (A.P., U.P.I.)
T—Brown, R., Philadelphia (A.P., U.P.I.)
T—Gregg, Green Bay (A.P., U.P.I.)
T—Kramer, Green Bay (A.P., U.P.I.)
G—Thomas, San Francisco (A.P.)
G—Gordy, Detroit (U.P.I.)
C—Tingelhoff, Minnesota (A.P., U.P.I.)
Q—Starr, Green Bay (A.P., U.P.I.)
B—Sayers, Chicago (A.P., U.P.I.)
B—Studstill, Detroit (A.P., U.P.I.)
B—Kelly, Cleveland (A.P., U.P.I.)

Defensive Team

E—Davis, Green Bay (A.P., U.P.I.)
E—Jones, Los Angeles (A.P., U.P.I.)
T—Lilly, Dallas (A.P., U.P.I.)
T—Olson, Los Angeles (A.P., U.P.I.)
LB-Howley, Dallas (A.P., U.P.I.)

LB—Nitschke, Green Bay (A.P., U.P.I.)
LB—Caffey, Green Bay (A.P., U.P.I.)
B—Adderly, Green Bay (A.P., U.P.I.)
B—Boyd, Baltimore (U.P.I.)
B—Green, Dallas (A.P.)
S—Wood, Green Bay (A.P., U.P.I.)
S—Wilson, St. Louis (A.P., U.P.I.)

1967
Offensive Team

E—Taylor, Washington (A.P., U.P.I.)
E—Smith, St. Louis (U.P.I.)
E—Mackey, Baltimore (A.P.)
T—Neely, Dallas (A.P., U.P.I.)
T—Gregg, Green Bay (A.P., U.P.I.)
G—Kramer, Green Bay (A.P., U.P.I.)
G—Hickerson, Cleveland (A.P., U.P.I.)
C—Tingelhoff, Minnesota (U.P.I.)
C—DeMarco, St. Louis (A.P.)
Q—Unitas, Baltimore (A.P., U.P.I.)
B—Kelly, Cleveland (A.P., U.P.I.)
B—Sayers, Chicago (A.P., U.P.I.)
B—Jones, New York (U.P.I.)
B—Richardson, Baltimore (A.P.)

Defensive Team

E—Jones, Los Angeles (A.P., U.P.I.)
E—Davis, Green Bay (A.P., U.P.I.)
T—Olsen, Los Angeles (A.P., U.P.I.)
T—Lilly, Dallas (A.P., U.P.I.)
LB—Robinson, Green Bay (A.P., U.P.I.)
LB—Butkus, Chicago (U.P.I.)
LB—Baughan, Los Angeles (U.P.I.)
LB—Nobis, Atlanta (A.P.)
LB—Howley, Dallas (A.P.)
B—Jeter, Green Bay (A.P., U.P.I.)
B—Green, Dallas (A.P., U.P.I.)
S—Wood, Green Bay (A.P., U.P.I.)
S—Meador, Los Angeles (U.P.I.)
S—Wilson, St. Louis (A.P.)

1968
Offensive Team
E—Hayes, Dallas (A.P.)
E—Warfield, Cleveland (U.P.I.)
E—Mackey, Baltimore (A.P., U.P.I.)
T—Neely, Dallas (A.P., U.P.I.)
T—Brown, Philadelphia (A.P.)
T—Vogel, Baltimore (U.P.I.)
G—Hickerson, Cleveland (A.P., U.P.I.)
G—Mudd, San Francisco (A.P., U.P.I.)
C—Tingelhoff, Minnesota (A.P., U.P.I.)
Q—Morrall, Baltimore (A.P., U.P.I.)
B—Kelly, Cleveland (A.P., U.P.I.)
B—Sayers, Chicago (A.P., U.P.I.)
B—McNeil, San Francisco (A.P., U.P.I.)

Defensive Team

E—Jones, Los Angeles (A.P., U.P.I.)
E—Eller, Minnesota (A.P., U.P.I.)
T—Olsen, Los Angeles (A.P., U.P.I.)
T—Lilly, Dallas (A.P., U.P.I.)

ML—Butkus, Chicago (A.P., U.P.I.)
LB—Howley, Dallas (A.P.)
LB—Curtis, Baltimore (A.P., U.P.I.)
LB—Robinson, Green Bay (U.P.I.)
CB—Boyd, Baltimore (A.P., U.P.I.)
CB—Barney, Detroit (A.P., U.P.I.)
S—Wilson, St. Louis (A.P., U.P.I.)
S—Meador, Los Angeles (A.P.)
S—Wood, Green Bay (U.P.I.)

1969
Offensive Team

E—Jefferson, Pittsburgh (A.P., U.P.I.)
E—Collins, Cleveland (A.P., U.P.I.)
E—Abramowicz, New Orleans (A.P.)
E—Smith, Washington (A.P., U.P.I.)
T—Brown, Los Angeles (A.P., U.P.I.)
T—Neely, Dallas (A.P., U.P.I.)
G—Hickerson, Cleveland (A.P., U.P.I.)
G—Mack, Los Angeles (U.P.I.)
G—Niland, Dallas (A.P.)
C—Tingelhoff, Minnesota (A.P., U.P.I.)
Q—Gabriel, Los Angeles (A.P., U.P.I.)
B—Sayers, Chicago (A.P., U.P.I.)
B—Hill, Dallas (A.P., U.P.I.)

Defensive Team

E—Jones, Los Angeles (A.P., U.P.I.)
E—Eller, Minnesota (A.P., U.P.I.)
T—Olsen, Los Angeles (A.P., U.P.I.)
T—Lilly, Dallas (A.P.)
T—Page, Minnesota (U.P.I.)
LB—Butkus, Chicago (A.P., U.P.I.)
LB—Howley, Dallas (A.P., U.P.I.)
LB—Robinson, Green Bay (A.P., U.P.I.)
CB—Barney, Detroit (A.P., U.P.I.)
CB—Adderley, Green Bay (A.P.)
CB—Green, Dallas (U.P.I.)
S—Wilson, St. Louis (A.P., U.P.I.)
S—Meador, Los Angeles (A.P., U.P.I.)

1970
Offensive Team

E—Washington, San Francisco (A.P., U.P.I.)
E—Gordon, Chicago (A.P., U.P.I.)
E—Sanders, Detroit (A.P., U.P.I.)
T—Brown, Los Angeles (A.P., U.P.I.)
T—Banaszek, San Francisco (A.P.)
T—McMillan, St. Louis (U.P.I.)
G—Gillingham, Green Bay (A.P., U.P.I.)
G—Mack, Los Angeles (A.P.)
G—Niland, Dallas (U.P.I.)
C—Tingelhoff, Minnesota (A.P.)
C—Flanagan, Detroit (U.P.I.)
Q—Brodie, San Francisco (A.P., U.P.I.)
B—Brown, Washington (A.P., U.P.I.)
B—Johnson, New York Giants (A.P.)
B—Lane, St. Louis (U.P.I.)

Defensive Team

E—Eller, Minnesota (A.P., U.P.I.)
E—Humphrey, Atlanta (A.P.)

E—Jones, Los Angeles (U.P.I.)
T—Page, Minnesota (A.P., U.P.I.)
T—Olsen, Los Angeles (A.P., U.P.I.)
MLB—Butkus, Chicago (A.P., U.P.I.)
LB—Howley, Dallas (A.P., U.P.I.)
LB—Naumoff, Detroit (A.P.)
LB—Stallings, St. Louis (U.P.I.)
CB—Johnson, San Francisco (A.P., U.P.I.)
CB—Renfro, Dallas (A.P.)
CB—Wehrli, St. Louis (U.P.I.)
S—Wilson, St. Louis (A.P., U.P.I.)
S—Lockhart, New York Giants (A.P.)
S—Krause, Minnesota (U.P.I.)

1971
Offensive Team

E—Washington, San Francisco (A.P., U.P.I.)
E—Grim, Minnesota (U.P.I.)
E—Jefferson, Washington (A.P.)
E—Sanders, Detroit (A.P., U.P.I.)
T—Yary, Minnesota (A.P., U.P.I.)
T—McMillan, St. Louis (U.P.I.)
T—Wright, Dallas (A.P.)
G—Mack, Los Angeles (A.P., U.P.I.)
G—Niland, Dallas (A.P.)
G—Gillingham, Green Bay (U.P.I.)
C—Blue, San Francisco (A.P., U.P.I.)
Q—Staubach, Dallas (A.P.)
Q—Landry, Detroit (U.P.I.)
B—Brockington, Green Bay (A.P., U.P.I.)
B—Owens, Detroit (A.P.)
B—Brown, Washington (U.P.I.)

Defensive Team

E—Eller, Minnesota (A.P., U.P.I.)
E—Humphrey, Atlanta (A.P., U.P.I.)
T—Page, Minnesota (A.P., U.P.I.)
T—Lilly, Dallas (A.P., U.P.I.)
MLB—Butkus, Chicago (A.P., U.P.I.)
LB—Pardee, Washington (A.P., U.P.I.)
LB—Wilcox, San Francisco (A.P., U.P.I.)
CB—Johnson, San Francisco (A.P., U.P.I.)
CB—Renfro, Dallas (A.P.)
CB—Wehrli, St. Louis (U.P.I.)
S—Bradley, Philadelphia (A.P., U.P.I.)
S—Green, Dallas (A.P.)
S—Krause, Minnesota (U.P.I.)

1972*
Offensive Team

E—Washington, San Francisco
E—Jackson, Philadelphia
E—Tucker, New York Giants
T—Wright, Dallas
T—Yary, Minnesota
G—Niland, Dallas
G—Mack, Los Angeles
C—Blue, San Francisco
Q—Tarkenton, Minnesota
B—Brown, Washington
B—Brockington, Green Bay
K—Marcol, Green Bay

Defensive Team

E—Humphrey, Atlanta
E—Eller, Minnesota
T—Lilly, Dallas
T—Page, Minnesota
MLB—Butkus, Chicago
LB—Wilcox, San Francisco
LB—Hanburger, Washington
CB—Johnson, San Francisco
CB—Barney, Detroit
S—Bradley, Philadelphia
S—Krause, Minnesota
P—Chapple, Los Angeles

* Sporting News Selections

ALL-LEAGUE SELECTIONS
(American Football League/Conference)

From 1960 to 1967, the all-league teams were
selected by either the players or coaches. The
newspaper selections since 1967 are listed below.

1967
Offensive Team

E—Sauer, New York Jets (A.P., U.P.I.)
E—Cannon, Oakland (A.P., U.P.I.)
T—Mix, San Diego (A.P., U.P.I.)
T—Tyrer, Kansas City (A.P.)
T—Schuh, Oakland (U.P.I.)
G—Talamini, Houston (A.P., U.P.I.)
G—Sweeney, San Diego (A.P., U.P.I.)
C—Otto, Oakland (A.P., U.P.I.)
Q—Lamonica, Oakland (A.P., U.P.I.)
B—Garrett, Kansas City (A.P., U.P.I.)
B—Nance, Boston (A.P., U.P.I.)
FL—Alworth, San Diego (A.P., U.P.I.)

Defensive Team

E—Davidson, Oakland (A.P., U.P.I.)
E—Holmes, Houston (A.P., U.P.I.)
T—Buchanan, Kansas City (A.P., U.P.I.)
T—Keating, Oakland (A.P., U.P.I.)
MLB—Buoniconti, Boston (A.P., U.P.I.)
LB—Webster, Houston (A.P., U.P.I.)
LB—Bell, Kansas City (A.P., U.P.I.)
CB—Farr, Houston (A.P., U.P.I.)
CB—McCloughan, Oakland (A.P., U.P.I.)
S—Saimes, Buffalo (A.P., U.P.I.)
S—Robinson, Kansas City (A.P., U.P.I.)

1968
Offensive Team

E—Alworth, San Diego (A.P., U.P.I.)
E—Sauer, New York Jets (A.P., U.P.I.)
E—Whalen, Boston (A.P., U.P.I.)
T—Mix, San Diego (A.P., U.P.I.)
T—Tyrer, Kansas City (A.P., U.P.I.)
G—Sweeney, San Diego (A.P., U.P.I.)
G—Upshaw, Oakland (A.P., U.P.I.)
C—Otto, Oakland (A.P., U.P.I.)
Q—Namath, New York Jets (A.P., U.P.I.)

B—Robinson, Cincinnati (A.P., U.P.I.)
B—Dixon, Oakland (A.P., U.P.I.)

Defensive Team

E—Philbin, New York Jets (A.P., U.P.I.)
E—Jackson, Denver (A.P., U.P.I.)
T—Buchanan, Kansas City (A.P., U.P.I.)
T—Birdwell, Oakland (A.P., U.P.I.)
MLB—Lanier, Kansas City (A.P.)
MLB—Connors, Oakland (U.P.I.)
LB—Webster, Houston (A.P., U.P.I.)
LB—Bell, Kansas City (A.P., U.P.I.)
CB—Farr, Houston (A.P., U.P.I.)
CB—Brown, Oakland (A.P., U.P.I.)
S—Grayson, Oakland (A.P., U.P.I.)
S—Robinson, Kansas City (A.P., U.P.I.)

1969
Offensive Team

E—Biletnikoff, Oakland (A.P.)
E—Alworth, San Diego (U.P.I.)
E—Maynard, New York Jets (A.P.)
E—Wells, Oakland (U.P.I.)
E—Trumpy, Cincinnati (A.P., U.P.I.)
T—Tyrer, Kansas City (A.P., U.P.I.)
T—Schuh, Oakland (A.P., U.P.I.)
G—Budde, Kansas City (A.P.)
G—Upshaw, Oakland (A.P., U.P.I.)
G—Sweeney, San Diego (U.P.I.)
C—Otto, Oakland (A.P., U.P.I.)
Q—Lamonica, Oakland (A.P., U.P.I.)
B—Little, Denver (A.P., U.P.I.)
B—Snell, New York Jets (A.P., U.P.I.)

Defensive Team

E—Jackson, Denver (A.P., U.P.I.)
E—Philbin, New York Jets (A.P., U.P.I.)
T—Elliott, New York Jets (A.P., U.P.I.)
T—Buchanan, Kansas City (A.P., U.P.I.)
MLB—Buoniconti, Miami (A.P., U.P.I.)
LB—Webster, Houston (A.P., U.P.I.)
LB—Bell, Kansas City (A.P., U.P.I.)
CB—Brown, Oakland (A.P., U.P.I.)
CB—Byrd, Buffalo (A.P., U.P.I.)
S—Grayson, Oakland (A.P., U.P.I.)
S—Robinson, Kansas City (A.P., U.P.I.)

1970
Offensive Team

E—Briscoe, Buffalo (A.P., U.P.I.)
E—Biletnikoff, Oakland (A.P.)
E—Wells, Oakland (U.P.I.)
E—Trumpy, Cincinnati (A.P.)
E—Reed, Houston (U.P.I.)
T—Tyrer, Kansas City (A.P., U.P.I.)
T—Hill, New York Jets (A.P., U.P.I.)
G—Upshaw, Oakland (A.P.)
G—Sweeney, San Diego (A.P.)
G—Budde, Kansas City (U.P.I.)
G—Hickerson, Cleveland (U.P.I.)
C—Otto, Oakland (A.P., U.P.I.)

Q—Lamonica, Oakland (A.P., U.P.I.)
B—Little, Denver (A.P., U.P.I.)
B—Dixon, Oakland (A.P., U.P.I.)

Defensive Team

E—Jackson, Denver (A.P., U.P.I.)
E—Brown, Kansas City (A.P.)
E—Smith, Baltimore (U.P.I.)
T—Elliott, New York Jets (A.P., U.P.I.)
T—Buchanan, Kansas City (A.P.)
T—Greene, Pittsburgh (U.P.I.)
MLB—Lanier, Kansas City (A.P., U.P.I.)
LB—Bell, Kansas City (A.P., U.P.I.)
LB—Russell, Pittsburgh (A.P., U.P.I.)
CB—Marsalis, Kansas City (A.P., U.P.I.)
CB—Brown, Oakland (A.P., U.P.I.)
S—Robinson, Kansas City (A.P., U.P.I.)
S—Logan, Baltimore (A.P., U.P.I.)

1971
Offensive Team

E—Taylor, Kansas City (A.P., U.P.I.)
E—Warfield, Miami (A.P., U.P.I.)
E—Morin, Cleveland (A.P., U.P.I.)
T—Tyrer, Kansas City (A.P., U.P.I.)
T—Hill, New York Jets (U.P.I.)
T—Brown, Oakland (A.P.)
G—Little, Miami (A.P., U.P.I.)
G—Sweeney, San Diego (A.P., U.P.I.)
C—Curry, Baltimore (A.P., U.P.I.)
Q—Griese, Miami (A.P., U.P.I.)
B—Csonka, Miami (A.P., U.P.I.)
B—Little, Denver (A.P., U.P.I.)

Defensive Team

E—Smith, Baltimore (A.P., U.P.I.)
E—Stanfill, Miami (U.P.I.)
E—Brown, Kansas City (A.P.)
T—Greene, Pittsburgh (A.P., U.P.I.)
T—Reid, Cincinnati (A.P., U.P.I.)
MLB—Lanier, Kansas City (A.P., U.P.I.)
LB—Hendricks, Baltimore (A.P., U.P.I.)
LB—Bell, Kansas City (A.P., U.P.I.)
CB—Brown, Oakland (A.P., U.P.I.)
CB—Marsalis, Kansas City (U.P.I.)
CB—Thomas, Kansas City (A.P.)
S—Houston, Houston (U.P.I.)
S—Scott, Miami (A.P., U.P.I.)
S—Volk, Baltimore (A.P.)

1972*
Offensive Team

E—Biletnikoff, Oakland
E—Warfield, Miami
E—Chester, Oakland
T—Brown, Oakland
T—Hill, New York Jets
G—Little, Miami
G—Van Dyke, Pittsburgh
C—Otto, Oakland
Q—Namath, New York Jets
B—Harris, Pittsburgh

B—Simpson, Buffalo
B—Csonka, Miami
K—Gerela, Pittsburgh

Defensive Team

E—Stanfill, Miami
E—Bethea, Houston
T—Greene, Pittsburgh
T—Reid, Cincinnati
LB—Lanier, Kansas City
LB—Russell, Pittsburgh
LB—Bell, Kansas City
CB—Brown, Oakland
CB—Parrish, Cincinnati
S—Anderson, Miami
S—Scott, Miami
P—Wilson, Kansas City
*Sporting News Selections

N.F.L. Most Valuable Player

(Winners of Joe F. Carr Trophy)

1938—Mel Hein (center), New York
1939—Parker Hall (halfback), Cleveland
1940—Ace Parker (halfback), Brooklyn
1941—Don Hutson (end), Green Bay
1942—Don Hutson (end), Green Bay
1943—Sid Luckman (quarterback), Chicago Bears
1944—Frank Sinkwich (quarterback), Detroit
1945—Bob Waterfield (quarterback), Cleveland
1946—Bill Dudley (halfback), Pittsburgh
(Award discontinued after 1946)

CHAMPIONSHIP PLAY-OFFS

1933—Chicago Bears 23, New York Giants 21 (at Chicago, Dec. 17)
1934—New York Giants 30, Chicago Bears 13 (at New York, Dec. 9)
1935—Detroit Lions 26, New York Giants 7 (at Detroit, Dec. 15)
1936—Green Bay Packers 21, Boston Redskins 6 (at New York, Dec. 13)
1937—Washington Redskins 28, Chicago Bears 21 (at Chicago, Dec. 12)
1938—New York Giants 23, Green Bay Packers 17 (at New York, Dec. 11)
1939—Green Bay Packers 27, New York Giants 0 (at Milwaukee, Dec. 10)
1940—Chicago Bears 73, Washington Redskins 0 (at Washington, Dec. 8)
1941—Chicago Bears 37, New York Giants 9 (at Chicago, Dec. 21)
1942—Washington Redskins 14, Chicago Bears 6 (at Washington, Dec. 13)
1943—Chicago Bears 41, Washington Redskins 21 (at Chicago, Dec. 26)
1944—Green Bay Packers 14, New York Giants 7 (at New York, Dec. 17)
1945—Cleveland Rams 15, Washington Redskins 14 (at Cleveland, Dec. 16)
1946—Chicago Bears 24, New York Giants 14 (at New York, Dec. 15)

1947—Chicago Cardinals 28, Philadelphia Eagles 21 (at Chicago, Dec. 28)
1948—Philadelphia Eagles 7, Chicago Cardinals 0 (at Philadelphia, Dec. 19)
1949—Philadelphia Eagles 14, Los Angeles Rams 0 (at Los Angeles, Dec. 18)
1950—Cleveland Browns 30, Los Angeles Rams 28 (at Cleveland, Dec. 24)
1951—Los Angeles Rams 24, Cleveland Browns 17 (at Los Angeles, Dec. 23)
1952—Detroit Lions 17, Cleveland Browns 7 (at Cleveland, Dec. 28)
1953—Detroit Lions 17, Cleveland Browns 16 (at Detroit, Dec. 27)
1954—Cleveland Browns 56, Detroit Lions 10 (at Cleveland, Dec. 26)
1955—Cleveland Browns 38, Los Angeles Rams 14 (at Los Angeles, Dec. 26)
1956—New York Giants 47, Chicago Bears 7 (at New York, Dec. 30)
1957—Detroit Lions 59, Cleveland Browns 14 (at Detroit, Dec. 29)
1958—*Baltimore Colts 23, New York Giants 17 (at New York, Dec. 28)
1959—Baltimore 31, New York 16 (at Baltimore, Dec. 27, 1959)
1960—Philadelphia 17, Green Bay 13 (at Philadelphia, Dec. 26, 1960)
1961—Green Bay 37, New York 0 (at Green Bay, Dec. 31, 1961)
1962—Green Bay 16, New York 7 (at New York Dec. 30, 1962)
1963—Chicago 14, New York 10 (at Chicago, Dec. 29, 1963)
1964—Cleveland 27, Baltimore 0 (at Cleveland, Dec. 27, 1964)
1965—Green Bay 23, Cleveland 12 (at Green Bay, Jan. 2, 1966)
1966—Green Bay 34, Dallas 27 (at Dallas, Jan. 1, 1967)
1967—Green Bay 21, Dallas 17 (at Green Bay, Dec. 31, 1967)
1968—Baltimore 34, Cleveland 0, (at Cleveland, Dec. 29, 1968)
1969—Minnesota 27, Cleveland 7, (at Minnesota, Jan. 4, 1970)
1970—Dallas 17, San Francisco 10, (at San Francisco, Jan. 3, 1971)
1971—Dallas 14, San Francisco 3, (at Dallas, Jan. 2, 1972)
1972—Washington 26, Dallas 3 (at Washington, Dec. 31, 1972)
*Sudden-death overtime.

American Football League—
Conference Championship Playoffs

1960—Houston 24, San Diego 16, (at Houston, Jan. 1, 1970)
1961—Houston 10, San Diego 3, (at San Diego, Dec. 24, 1961)

1962—*Kansas City 20, Houston 17, (at Houston, Dec. 23, 1962)

1963—San Diego 51, Boston 10, (at San Diego, Jan. 5, 1964)

1964—Buffalo 20, San Diego 7, (at Buffalo, Dec. 26, 1964)

1965—Buffalo 23, San Diego 0, (at San Diego, Dec. 26, 1965)

1966—Kansas City 31, Buffalo 7, (at Buffalo, Jan. 1, 1967)

1967—Oakland 40, Houston 7, (at Oakland, Dec. 31, 1967)

1968—New York Jets 27, Oakland 23, (at New York, Dec. 29, 1968)

1969—Kansas City 17, Oakland 7, (at Oakland, Jan. 4, 1970)

1970—Baltimore 27, Oakland 17, (at Baltimore, Jan. 3, 1971)

1971—Miami 21, Baltimore 0, (at Miami, Jan. 2, 1972)

1972—Miami 21, Pittsburgh 17, (at Pittsburgh, Dec. 31, 1972)

*Sudden-death overtime

Interleague Playoff—Super Bowl

1966—Green Bay (NFL) 35, Kansas City (AFL) 10, (at Los Angeles, Jan. 15, 1967)

1967—Green Bay (NFL) 33, Oakland (AFL) 14, (at Miami, Jan. 14, 1968)

1968—New York Jets (AFL) 16, Baltimore (NFL) 7, (at Miami, Jan. 12, 1969)

1969—Kansas City (AFL) 23, Minnesota (NFL) 7, (at New Orleans, Jan. 11, 1970)

1970—Baltimore (AFC) 16, Dallas (NFC) 13, (at Miami, Jan. 17, 1971)

1971—Dallas (NFC) 24, Miami (AFC) 3, (at New Orleans, Jan 16, 1972)

1972—Miami (AFC) 14, Washington (NFC) 7, (at Los Angeles, Jan. 14, 1973)

Champions and Divisional Winners

The National Football League was divided into two divisions in 1933, with the Eastern (E) winner meeting the Western (W) in the championship play-off. League split into American (A) and National (N) conferences in 1950. Early in 1953 the names of the divisions were changed to Eastern and Western conferences. In 1970, the National Football Conference was divided into three divisions: Eastern (E), Western (W), and Central (C). The winner of each division, plus a fourth qualifier, competed in playoff games to determine conference champion.

Year Team	W	L	T	Pct.
1921—Chicago Bears (Staley's)	10	1	1	909
1922—Canton Bulldogs	10	0	2	1.000
1923—Canton Bulldogs	11	0	1	1.000
1924—Cleveland Bulldogs	7	1	1	.875
1925—Chicago Cardinals	11	2	1	.846
1926—Frankford Yellow Jackets	14	1	1	.933
1927—New York Giants	11	1	1	.917
1928—Providence Steamrollers	8	1	2	.888
1929—Green Bay Packers	12	0	1	1.000
1930—Green Bay Packers	11	3	1	.786
1931—Green Bay Packers	12	2	0	.857
1932—Chicago Bears	7	1	6	.875
1933—Chicago Bears (W)	10	2	1	.833
1933—New York Giants (E)	11	3	0	.786
1934—New York Giants (E)	8	5	0	.615
1934—Chicago Bears (W)	13	0	0	1.000
1935—Detroit Lions (W)	7	3	2	.700
1935—New York Giants (E)	9	3	0	.750
1936—Green Bay Packers (W)	10	1	1	.909
1936—Boston Redskins (E)	7	5	0	.587
1937—Washington Redskins (E)	8	3	0	.727
1937—Chicago Bears (W)	9	1	1	.900
1938—New York Giants (E)	8	2	1	.800
1938—Green Bay Packers (W)	8	3	0	.727
1939—Green Bay Packers (W)	9	2	0	.818
1939—New York Giants (E)	9	1	1	.900
1940—Chicago Bears (W)	8	3	0	.727
1940—Washington Redskins (E)	9	2	0	.818
1941—Chicago Bears (W)	10	1	0	.909
1941—New York Giants (E)	8	3	0	.727
1942—Washington Redskins (E)	10	1	0	.909
1942—Chicago Bears (W)	11	0	0	1.000
1943—Chicago Bears (W)	8	1	1	.889
1943—Washington Redskins (E)	6	3	1	.667
1944—Green Bay Packers (W)	8	2	0	.800
1944—New York Giants (E)	8	1	1	.889
1945—Cleveland Rams (W)	9	1	0	.900
1945—Washington Redskins (E)	8	2	0	.800
1946—Chicago Bears (W)	8	2	1	.800
1946—New York Giants (E)	7	3	1	.700
1947—Chicago Cardinals (W)	9	3	0	.750
1947—Philadelphia Eagles (E)	9	4	0	.692
1948—Philadelphia Eagles (E)	9	2	1	.818
1948—Chicago Cardinals (W)	11	1	0	.917
1949—Philadelphia Eagles (E)	11	1	0	.917
1949—Los Angeles Rams (W)	8	2	2	.800
1950—Cleveland Browns (A)	11	2	0	.846
1950—Los Angeles Rams (N)	10	3	0	.769
1951—Los Angeles Rams (N)	8	4	0	.667
1951—Cleveland Browns (A)	11	1	0	.917
1952—Detroit Lions (N)	9	3	0	.750
1952—Cleveland Browns (A)	8	4	0	.667
1953—Detroit Lions (W)	10	2	0	.833
1953—Cleveland Browns (E)	11	1	0	.917
1954—Detroit Lions (W)	9	2	1	.818
1954—Cleveland Browns (E)	9	3	0	.750
1955—Los Angeles Rams (W)	8	3	1	.727
1955—Cleveland Browns (E)	9	2	1	.818
1956—Chicago Bears (W)	9	2	1	.818
1956—New York Giants (E)	8	3	1	.727
1957—Detroit Lions (W)	8	4	0	.667
1957—Cleveland Browns (E)	9	2	1	.818
1958—Baltimore Colts (W)	9	3	0	.750
1958—New York Giants (E)	9	3	0	.750
1959—Baltimore (W)	9	3	0	.750
1959—New York (E)	10	2	0	.833
1960—Green Bay (W)	8	4	0	.666
1960—Philadelphia (E)	10	2	0	.833

1961—Green Bay (W)	11	3	0	.786	1964—Buffalo (E)	12	2	0	.857
1961—New York (E)	10	3	1	.769	1964—San Diego (W)	8	5	1	.615
1962—Green Bay (W)	13	1	0	.929	1965—Buffalo (E)	10	3	1	.769
1962—New York (E)	12	2	0	.857	1965—San Diego (W)	9	2	3	.818
1963—Chicago (W)	11	1	2	.917	1966—Kansas City (W)	11	2	1	.846
1963—New York (E)	11	3	0	.786	1966—Buffalo (E)	9	4	1	.692
1964—Baltimore (W)	12	2	0	.857	1967—Oakland (W)	13	1	0	.929
1964—Cleveland (E)	10	3	1	.769	1967—Houston (E)	9	4	1	.692
1965—Green Bay (W)	10	3	1	.769	1968—New York (E)	11	3	0	.786
1965—Cleveland (E)	11	3	0	.786	1968—*Oakland (W)	12	2	0	.857
1966—Green Bay (W)	12	2	0	.857	1969—Kansas City (W)	11	3	0	.786
1966—Dallas (E)	10	3	1	.769	1969—Oakland (W)	12	1	1	.923
1967—Green Bay (W)	9	4	1	.692	1969—New York (E)	10	4	0	.714
1967—Dallas—(E)	9	5	0	.643	1969—Houston (E)	6	6	2	.500
1968—Baltimore (W)	13	1	0	.929	1970—Baltimore (E)	11	2	1	.846
1968—Cleveland (E)	10	4	0	.714	1970—Oakland (W)	8	4	2	.667
1969—Minnesota (W)	12	2	0	.857	1970—**Miami (E)	10	4	0	.714
1969—Cleveland (E)	10	3	1	.769	1970—Cincinnati (C)	8	6	0	.571
1970—Dallas (E)	10	4	0	.714	1971—Miami (E)	10	3	1	.769
1970—San Francisco (W)	10	3	1	.769	1971—**Baltimore (E)	10	4	0	.714
1970—Minnesota (C)	12	2	0	.857	1971—Cleveland (C)	9	5	0	.643
1970—*Detroit (C)	10	4	0	.714	1971—Kansas City (W)	10	3	1	.769
1971—Dallas (E)	11	3	0	.786	1972—Miami (E)	14	0	0	1.000
1971—San Francisco (W)	9	5	0	.643	1972—Pittsburgh (C)	11	3	0	.786
1971—Minnesota (C)	11	3	0	.786	1972—Oakland (W)	10	3	1	.750
1971—*Washington (E)	9	4	1	.692	1972—**Cleveland (C)	10	4	0	.714
1972—Washington (E)	11	3	0	.786					
1972—*Dallas (E)	10	4	0	.714					
1972—Green Bay (C)	10	4	0	.714					
1972—San Francisco (W)	8	5	1	.607					

*Divisional Playoff
**Fourth Qualifier for Playoffs

*Fourth Qualifier for Playoffs

NFC Divisional Playoffs

Three divisions: Eastern (E), Central (C), and Western (W). *Fourth qualifier for playoffs.

1970—Dallas (E) 5, *Detroit (C) 0
1970—San Francisco (W) 17, Minnesota (C) 14
1971—Dallas (E) 20, Minnesota (C) 12
1971—San Francisco (W) 24, *Washington (E) 20
1972—*Dallas (E) 30, San Francisco (W) 28
1972—Washington (E) 16, Green Bay (C) 3

American Football League— Conference Divisional Winners

The league was formed with two divisions in 1960: Eastern (E) and Western (W). In 1970, the merger of AFL and NFL into the National Football League with two conferences, AFC and NFC; each with three divisions—Eastern (E), Western (W), and Central (C) and a fourth qualifier determined the champion after interconference playoffs.

Year Team	W	L	T	Pct.
1960—Houston (E)	10	4	0	.714
1960—Los Angeles (W)	10	4	0	.714
1961—Houston (E)	10	3	1	.769
1961—San Diego (W)	12	2	0	.857
1962—Dallas (W)	11	3	0	.786
1962—Houston (E)	11	3	0	.786
1963—San Diego (W)	11	3	0	.786
1963—*Boston (E)	7	6	1	.538

AFC Divisional Playoffs

In 1969, the AFL competed in interdivisional playoffs—the first- and second-placed team of each division in playoffs for championship. In 1970, the three division leaders plus a fourth qualifier competed in playoffs to determine conference champion and the right to play in the Super Bowl. The three divisions: Eastern (E), Central (C), and Western (W).

1969—Kansas City (W) 13, New York (E) 6
1969—Oakland (W) 56, Houston (E) 7
1970—Baltimore (E) 17, Cincinnati (C) 0
1970—Oakland (W) 21, *Miami (E) 14
1971—**Miami (E) 27, Kansas City (W) 24
1971—*Baltimore (E) 20, Cleveland (C) 3
1972—Miami (E) 20, *Cleveland (C) 14
1972—Pittsburgh (C) 13, Oakland (W) 7

* Fourth Qualifier for Playoffs
** Sudden-Death Overtime

Team Departmental Champions

Total Yards Gained

1932—Chicago Bears	2,755
1933—New York Giants	2,970
1934—Chicago Bears	3,750
1935—Chicago Bears	3,454
1936—Detroit	3,703
1937—Green Bay	3,201
1938—Green Bay	3,037
1939—Chicago Bears	3,988
1940—Green Bay	3,400

1941—Chicago Bears 4,265	1946—Green Bay 1,765
1942—Chicago Bears 3,900	1947—Los Angeles 2,171
1943—Chicago Bears 4,045	1948—Chicago Cards 2,560
1944—Chicago Bears 3,239	1949—Philadelphia 2,607
1945—Washington 3,549	1950—New York Giants 2,336
1946—Los Angeles 3,763	1951—Chicago Bears 2,408
1947—Chicago Bears 5,053	1952—San Francisco 1,905
1948—Chicago Cards 4,694	1953—San Francisco 2,230
1949—Chicago Bears 4,873	1954—San Francisco 2,498
1950—Los Angeles 5,420	1955—Chicago Bears 2,388
1951—Los Angeles 5,506	1956—Chicago Bears 2,468
1952—Cleveland Browns 4,352	1957—Los Angeles 2,142
1953—Philadelphia 4,811	1958—Cleveland 2,526
1954—Los Angeles 5,187	1959—Cleveland 2,149
1955—Chicago Bears 4,316	1960—St. Louis (NFL) 2,356
1956—Chicago Bears 4,537	Oakland (AFL) 2,056
1957—Los Angeles 4,143	1961—Green Bay (NFL) 2,350
1958—Baltimore 4,539	Dallas (AFL) 2,189
1959—Baltimore 4,458	1962—Buffalo (AFL) 2,480
1960—Houston (AFL) 4,936	Green Bay (NFL) 2,460
—Baltimore (NFL) 4,245	1963—Cleveland (NFL) 2,639
1961—Houston (AFL) 6,288	San Diego (AFL) 2,203
—Philadelphia (NFL) 5,112	1964—Green Bay (NFL) 2,276
1962—New York (NFL) 5,005	Buffalo (AFL) 2,040
—Houston (AFL) 4,971	1965—Cleveland (NFL) 2,331
1963—San Diego (AFL) 5,153	San Diego (AFL) 2,085
—New York (NFL) 5,024	1966—Kansas City (AFL) 2,274
1964—Buffalo (AFL) 5,206	Cleveland (NFL) 2,166
—Baltimore (NFL) 4,779	1967—Cleveland (NFL) 2,139
1965—San Francisco (NFL) 5,270	Houston (AFL) 2,356
—San Diego (AFL) 5,188	1968—Chicago (NFL) 2,377
1966—Dallas (NFL) 5,145	Kansas City (AFL) 2,227
—Kansas City (AFL) 5,114	1969—Dallas (NFL) 2,276
1967—New York (AFL) 5,152	Kansas City (AFL) 2,220
—Baltimore (NFL) 5,008	1970—Dallas (NFC) 2,300
1968—Oakland (AFL) 5,696	Miami (AFC) 2,082
—Dallas (NFL) 5,117	1971—Miami (AFC) 2,429
1969—Dallas (NFL) 5,122	Detroit (NFC) 2,376
—Oakland (AFL) 5,036	1972—Miami (AFC) 2,960
1970—Oakland (AFC) 4,829	Chicago (NFC) 2,360
—San Francisco (NFC) 4,503	
1971—Dallas (NFC) 5,035	
—San Diego (AFC) 4,738	**Yards Passing**
1972—Miami (AFC) 5,036	
—New York (NFC) 4,483	In 1972, the system for rating passing was changed. Teams rated in four categories: percentage of completions, average yards gained per

Yards Rushing

pass attempt, percentage of interceptions, and percentage of touchdown passes per attempt.

1932—Chicago Bears 1,770	1932—Chicago Bears 1,013
1933—Boston Redskins 2,367	1933—New York Giants 1,335
1934—Detroit 2,763	1934—Green Bay 1,165
1935—Chicago Bears 2,096	1935—Green Bay 1,416
1936—Detroit 2,885	1936—Green Bay 1,629
1937—Detroit 2,074	1937—Green Bay 1,398
1938—Detroit 1,893	1938—Washington 1,536
1939—Chicago Bears 2,043	1939—Chicago Bears 1,965
1940—Chicago Bears 1,818	1940—Washington 1,887
1941—Chicago Bears 2,156	1941—Chicago Bears 2,002
1942—Chicago Bears 1,881	1942—Green Bay 2,407
1943—Phila.—Pitts 1,730	1943—Chicago Bears 2,310
1944—Philadelphia 1,663	1944—Washington 2,021
1945—Cleveland Rams 1,714	

1945–Cleveland Rams	1,857
1946–Los Angeles	2,080
1947–Washington	3,336
1948–Washington	2,861
1949–Chicago Bears	3,055
1950–Los Angeles	3,709
1951–Los Angeles	3,296
1952–Cleveland Browns	2,566
1953–Philadelphia	3,089
1954–Chicago Bears	3,104
1955–Philadelphia	2,472
1956–Los Angeles	2,419
1957–Baltimore	2,388
1958–Pittsburgh	2,752
1959–Baltimore	2,753
1960–Houston (AFL)	3,203
Baltimore (NFL)	2,956
1961–Houston (AFL)	4,392
Philadelphia (NFL)	3,605
1962–Denver (AFL)	3,404
Philadelphia (NFL)	3,385
1963–Baltimore (NFL)	3,296
Houston (AFL)	3,222
1964–Houston (AFL)	3,527
Chicago (NFL)	2,841
1965–San Francisco (NFL)	3,487
San Diego (AFL)	3,103
1966–New York (AFL)	3,464
Dallas (NFL)	3,023
1967–New York (AFL)	3,845
Washington (NFL)	3,730
1968–San Diego (AFL)	3,623
Dallas (NFL)	3,026
1969–Oakland (AFL)	3,271
San Francisco (NFL)	3,158
1970–San Francisco (NFC)	2,923
Oakland (AFC)	2,865
1971–San Diego (AFC)	3,134
Dallas (NFC)	2,786
1972–Miami (AFC)	2,076
New York (NFC)	2,461

Points Scored

1932–Green Bay (14 games)	.152
1933–New York Giants (14)	.244
1934–Chicago Bears (13)	.286
1935–Chicago Bears (12)	.192
1936–Green Bay (12)	.248
1937–Green Bay (11)	.220
1938–Green Bay (11)	.223
1939–Chicago Bears (11)	.298
1940–Washington (11)	.245
1941–Chicago Bears (11)	.396
1942–Chicago Bears (11)	.376
1943–Chicago Bears (10)	.303
1944–Philadelphia (10)	.267
1945–Philadelphia (10)	.272
1946–Chicago Bears (11)	.289
1947–Chicago Bears (12)	.363
1948–Chicago Cards (12)	.395
1949–Philadelphia (12)	.364

1950–Los Angeles (12)	.466
1951–Los Angeles (12)	.392
1952–Los Angeles (12)	.349
1953–San Francisco (12)	.372
1954–Detroit (12)	.337
1955–Cleveland (12)	.349
1956–Chicago Bears (12)	.363
1957–Los Angeles (12)	.307
1958–Baltimore (12)	.381
1959–Baltimore (12)	.374
1960–New York (AFL) (14)	.382
Cleveland (NFL) (12)	.362
1961–Houston (AFL) (14)	.513
Green Bay (NFL) (14)	.391
1962–Green Bay (NFL) (14)	.415
Dallas (AFL) (14)	.389
1963–New York (NFL) (14)	.448
San Diego (AFL) (14)	.399
1964–Baltimore (NFL) (14)	.428
Buffalo (AFL) (14)	.400
1965–San Francisco (NFL) (14)	.421
San Diego (AFL) (14)	.340
1966–Kansas City (AFL) (14)	.448
Dallas (NFL) (14)	.445
1967–Oakland (AFL) (14)	.468
Los Angeles (NFL) (14)	.398
1968–Oakland (AFL) (14)	.453
Dallas (NFL) (14)	.431
1969–Minnesota (NFL) (14)	.379
Oakland (AFL) (14)	.377
1970–San Francisco (NFC) (14)	.352
Baltimore (AFC) (14)	.321
1971–Dallas (NFC) (14)	.406
Oakland (AFC) (14)	.344
1972–Miami (AFC) (14)	.385
San Francisco (NFC) (14)	.353

Individual Champions
Scoring (NFL–NFC)

	Touch-downs	Extra points	Field goals	Total points
1932–Earl (Dutch) Clark, Portsmouth	4	6	3	39
1933–Ken Strong, New York Giants	6	13	5	64
Glenn Presnell, Portsmouth	6	10	6	64
1934–Jack Manders, Chicago Bears	3	31	10	79
1935–Earl (Dutch) Clark, Detroit	6	16	1	55
1936–Earl (Dutch) Clark, Detroit	7	19	4	73
1937–Jack Manders, Chicago Bears	5	15	8	69
1938–Clark Hinkle, Green Bay	7	7	3	58
1939–Andy Farkas, Washington	11	2	0	68
1940–Don Hutson, Green Bay	7	15	0	57

1941—Don Hutson, Green
Bay 12 20 0 92
1942—Don Hutson, Green
Bay 17 33 1 138
1943—Don Hutson, Green
Bay 12 36 3 117
1944—Don Hutson, Green
Bay 9 31 0 85
1945—Steve Van Buren,
Philadelphia 18 2 0 110
1946—Ted Fritsch, Green
Bay 10 13 9 100
1947—Pat Harder, Chi-
cago Cards 7 39 7 102
1948—Pat Harder, Chi-
cago Cards 6 53 7 110
1949—Pat Harder, Chi-
cago Cards 8 45 3 102
Gene Roberts, New
York Giants 17 0 0 102
1950—Doak Walker, De-
troit 11 38 8 128
1951—Elroy Hirsch, Los
Angeles 17 0 0 102
1952—Gordon Soltau, San
Francisco 7 34 6 94
1953—Gordon Soltau, San
Francisco 6 48 10 114
1954—Bobby Walston,
Philadelphia 11 36 4 114
1955—Doak Walker, De-
troit 7 27 9 96
1956—Bobby Layne,
Detroit 5 33 12 99
1957—Sam Baker,
Washington 1 29 14 77
Lou Groza, Cleve-
land 0 32 15 77
1958—Jim Brown,
Cleveland 18 0 0 108
1959—Paul Hornung,
Green Bay 7 31 7 94
1960—Paul Hornung,
Green Bay 15 41 15 176
1961—Paul Hornung,
Green Bay 10 41 15 146
1962—James Taylor,
Green Bay 19 0 0 114
1963—Don Chandler,
New York 0 52 18 106
1964—Leonard Moore,
Baltimore 20 0 0 120
1965—Gale Sayers,
Chicago 22 0 0 132
1966—Bruce Gossett,
Los Angeles 0 29 28 113
1967—James Bakken,
St. Louis 0 36 27 117
1968—Leroy Kelly,
Cleveland 20 0 0 120
1969—Fred Cox,
Minnesota 0 43 26 121

1970—Fred Cox,
Minnesota (NFC) 0 35 30 125
1971—Curt Knight,
Washington (NFC) 0 27 29 114
1972—Chester Marcol,
Green Bay (NFC) 0 29 33 128

Scoring (AFL—AFC)

	Touch-downs	Extra points	Field goals	Total points
1960—Gene Mingo, Denver (AFL)	6	33	18	123
1961—Gino Cappelletti, Boston (AFL)	8	48	17	147
1962—Gene Mingo, Denver (AFL)	4	32	27	137
1963—Gino Cappelletti, Boston (AFL)	2	35	22	113
1964—Gino Cappelletti, Boston (AFL)	7	36	25	155
1965—Gino Cappelletti, Boston (AFL)	9	27	17	132
1966—Gino Cappelletti, Boston (AFL)	6	35	16	119
1967—George Blanda, Oakland (AFL)	0	56	20	116
1968—Jim Turner, New York (AFL) . .	0	43	34	145
1969—Jim Turner, New York (AFL) . .	0	33	32	129
1970—Jan Stenerud, Kansas City (AFC) .	0	26	30	116
1971—Garo Yepremian, Miami (AFC)	0	33	28	117
1972—Bobby Howfield, New York Jets (AFC)	0	40	27	121

Ball Carrying

	Yards gained	Attempts
1932—Bob Campiglio, Stapleton (N.Y.)	504	104
1933—Cliff Battles, Boston	737	146
1934—Beattie Feathers, Chicago Bears	1,004	101
1935—Doug Russell, Chicago Cards	499	140
1936—Tuffy Leemans, New York Giants	830	206
1937—Cliff Battles, Washington .	874	216
1938—Byron White, Pittsburgh . .	567	152
1939—Bill Osmanski, Chicago Bears	699	121
1940—Byron White, Detroit	514	146
1941—Clarence Manders, Brooklyn	486	111
1942—Bill Dudley, Pittsburgh . . .	696	162
1943—Bill Paschal, New York Giants	572	147
1944—Bill Paschal, New York Giants	737	196

1945—Steve Van Buren,
    Philadelphia 832 143
1946—Bill Dudley, Pittsburgh 604 146
1947—Steve Van Buren,
    Philadelphia 1,008 217
1948—Steve Van Buren,
    Philadelphia 945 201
1949—Steve Van Buren,
    Philadelphia 1,146 263
1950—Mario Motley, Cleveland
    Browns 810 140
1951—Eddie Price, New York
    Giants 971 271
1952—Dan Towler, Los Angeles .. 894 156
1953—Joe Perry, San Francisco ... 1,018 192
1954—Joe Perry, San Francisco ... 1,049 173
1955—Alan Ameche, Baltimore ... 961 213
1956—Rick Casares, Chicago
    Bears 1,126 234
1957—Jim Brown, Cleveland 942 202
1958—Jim Brown, Cleveland 1,527 257
1959—Jim Brown, Cleveland 1,329 290
1960—Jim Brown, Cleveland (NFL) 1,257 215
    Abner Haynes, Dallas (AFL) 875 156
1961—Jim Brown, Cleveland (NFL) 1,408 305
    Billy Cannon, Houston (AFL) 948 200
1962—Jim Taylor, Green Bay (NFL) 1,474 272

Cookie Gilchrist, Buffalo
    (AFL) 1,096 214
1963—Jim Brown, Cleveland (NFL) 1,863 291
    Clem Daniels, Oakland (AFL) 1,099 215
1964—Jim Brown, Cleveland (NFL) 1,446 280
    Cookie Gilchrist, Buffalo
    (AFL) 981 230
1965—Jim Brown, Cleveland (NFL) 1,544 289
    Paul Lowe, San Diego (AFL) 1,121 222
1966—Jim Nance, Boston (AFL) .. 1,458 299
    Gale Sayers, Chicago (NFL) . 1,231 229
1967—Jim Nance, Boston (AFL) .. 1,216 269
    Leroy Kelly, Cleveland (NFL) 1,205 235
1968—Leroy Kelly, Cleveland (NFL) 1,239 248
    Paul Robinson, Cincinnati
    (AFL) 1,023 238
1969—Gale Sayers, Chicago (NFL) . 1,032 236
    Dick Post, San Diego (AFL) . 873 182
1970—Larry Brown, Washington
    (NFC) 1,125 237
    Floyd Little, Denver (AFC) . 901 209
1971—Floyd Little, Denver (AFC) . 1,133 284
    John Brockington, Green
    Bay (NFC) 1,105 216
1972—O.J. Simpson, Buffalo (AFC) 1,251 292
    Larry Brown, Washington
    (NFC) 1,216 285

Pass Receiving

	Caught	Yards	Touchdowns
1932—Luke Johnsos, Chicago Bears	24	321	2
1933—John Kelley, Brooklyn	21	219	3
1934—Joe Carter, Philadelphia	16	237	3
1935—Tod Goodwin, New York Giants	26	432	4
1936—Don Hutson, Green Bay	34	526	9
1937—Don Hutson, Green Bay	41	552	7
1938—Gaynell Tinsley, Chicago Cards	41	516	1
1939—Don Hutson, Green Bay	34	846	6
1940—Don Looney, Philadelphia	58	707	4
1941—Don Hutson, Green Bay	58	738	10
1942—Don Hutson, Green Bay	74	1,211	17
1943—Don Hutson, Green Bay	47	776	11
1944—Don Hutson, Green Bay	58	866	9
1945—Don Hutson, Green Bay	47	834	9
1946—Jim Benton, Los Angeles	63	981	6
1947—Jim Keane, Chicago Bears	64	910	10
1948—Tom Fears, Los Angeles	51	698	4
1949—Tom Fears, Los Angeles	77	1,013	9
1950—Tom Fears, Los Angeles	84	1,116	7
1951—Elroy Hirsch, Los Angeles	66	1,495	17
1952—Mac Speedie, Cleveland	62	911	5
1953—Pete Pihos, Philadelphia	63	1,049	10
1954— Pete Pihos, Philadelphia	60	872	10
Billy Wilson, San Francisco	60	830	5
1955—Pete Pihos, Philadelphia	62	864	7
1956—Billy Wilson, San Francisco	60	889	5
1957—Billy Wilson, San Francisco	52	757	6
1958— Ray Berry, Baltimore	56	794	9
Pete Retzlaff, Philadelphia	56	766	2
1959—Raymond Berry, Baltimore	66	959	14

1960—Lionel Taylor, Denver (AFL)	92	1,235	12
Raymond Berry, Baltimore (NFL)	74	1,298	10
1961—Lionel Taylor, Denver (AFL)	100	1,176	4
Jim Phillips, Los Angeles (NFL)...............	78	1,092	5
1962—Lionel Taylor, Denver (AFL)	77	908	4
Bobby Mitchell, Washington (NFL)	72	1,384	11
1963—Lionel Taylor, Denver (AFL)	78	1,101	10
Bobby Joe Conrad, St. Louis (NFL)	73	967	10
1964—Charley Hennigan, Houston (AFL)	101	1,546	8
Johnny Morris, Chicago (NFL)...............	93	1,200	10
1965—Lionel Taylor, Denver (AFL)	85	1,131	6
Dave Parks, San Francisco (NFL)	80	1,344	12
1966—Lance Alworth, San Diego (AFL)	73	1,383	13
Charley Taylor, Washington (NFL)...........	72	1,119	12
1967—George Sauer, New York (AFL)	75	1,189	6
Charley Taylor, Washington (NFL)...........	70	990	9
1968—Clifton McNeil, San Francisco (NFL)	71	994	7
Lance Alworth, San Diego (AFL)	68	1,312	10
1969—Dan Abramowicz, New Orleans (NFL)	73	1,015	7
Lance Alworth, San Diego (AFL)	64	1,003	4
1970—Dick Gordon, Chicago (NFC)	71	1,026	13
Marlin Briscoe, Buffalo (AFC)	57	1,036	8
1971—Fred Biletnikoff, Oakland (AFC)	61	929	9
Bob Tucker, New York (NFC)	59	791	4
1972—Harold Jackson, Philadelphia (NFC)	62	1,048	4
Fred Biletnikoff, Oakland (AFC)...............	58	802	7

Forward Passing

In 1972, the system for rating passers was changed. Qualifiers rated in four categories: percentage of completions, average yards gained per pass attempt, percentage of interceptions, and percentage of touchdown passes per attempt, rather than total touchdown passes as in the past.

	Passes	Com-pleted	Yards	Touch-downs	Intercepted
1932—Arnie Herber, Green Bay	101	37	639	9	9
1933—Harry Newman, New York Giants	132	53	963	8	17
1934—Arnie Herber, Green Bay	115	42	799	8	12
1935—Ed Danowski, New York Giants	113	57	795	9	9
1936—Arnie Herber, Green Bay	173	77	1,239	9	13
1937—Sammy Baugh, Washington.............	171	81	1,127	7	14
1938—Ed Danowski, New York Giants	129	70	848	8	8
1939—Parker Hall, Cleveland Rams...........	208	106	1,227	9	13
1940—Sammy Baugh, Washington.............	177	111	1,367	12	10
1941—Cecil Isbell, Green Bay	206	117	1,479	15	11
1942—Cecil Isbell, Green Bay	268	146	2,021	24	14
1943—Sammy Baugh, Washington.............	239	133	1,754	23	19
1944—Frank Filchock, Washington...........	147	84	1,139	13	9
1945—Sammy Baugh, Washington.............	182	128	1,669	11	4
1946—Bob Waterfield, Los Angeles...........	251	127	1,747	18	17
1947—Sammy Baugh, Washington.............	354	210	2,938	25	15
1948—Tommy Thompson, Philadelphia	246	141	1,965	25	11
1949—Sammy Baugh, Washington.............	255	145	1,903	18	14
1950—Norm Van Brocklin, Los Angeles	233	127	2,061	18	14
1951—Bob Waterfield, Los Angeles...........	176	88	1,566	13	10
1952—Norm Van Brocklin, Los Angeles	205	113	1,736	14	17
1953—Otto Graham, Cleveland Browns........	258	167	2,722	11	9
1954—Norm Van Brocklin, Los Angeles	260	139	2,637	13	21
1955—Otto Graham, Cleveland	185	98	1,721	15	8
1956—Ed Brown, Chicago Bears	168	96	1,667	11	12
1957—Tom O'Connell, Cleveland	110	63	1,229	9	8
1958—Eddie LeBaron, Washington	145	79	1,365	11	10
1959—Charles Conerly, New York	194	113	1,706	14	4

1960—Milt Plum, Cleveland (NFL)	250	151	2,297	21	5
Jack Kemp, Los Angeles (AFL)	406	211	3,018	20	25
1961—George Blanda, Houston (AFL)	362	187	3,330	36	22
Milt Plum, Cleveland (NFL)	302	177	2,416	18	10
1962—Len Dawson, Dallas (AFL)	310	189	2,759	29	17
Bart Starr, Green Bay (NFL)	285	178	2,438	12	9
1963—Y.A. Tittle, New York (NFL)	367	221	3,145	36	14
Tobin Rote, San Diego (AFL)	286	170	2,510	20	17
1964—Len Dawson, Kansas City (AFL).......	354	199	2,879	30	18
Bart Starr, Green Bay (NFL)	272	163	2,144	15	4
1965—Rudy Bukich, Chicago (NFL)	312	176	2,641	20	9
John Hadl, San Diego (AFL)	348	174	2,798	20	21
1966—Bart Starr, Green Bay (NFL)	251	156	2,257	14	3
Len Dawson, Kansas City (AFL)	284	159	2,527	26	10
1967—C.A. Jurgensen, Washington (NFL)	508	288	3,747	31	16
Daryl Lamonica, Oakland (AFL)	425	220	3,228	30	20
1968—Len Dawson, Kansas City (AFL)........	224	131	2,109	17	9
Earl Morrall, Baltimore (NFL)...........	317	182	2,909	26	17
1969—C.A. Jurgensen, Washington (NFL)	442	274	3,102	22	15
Greg Cook, Cincinnati (AFL)	197	106	1,854	15	11
1970—John Brodie, San Francisco (NFC)	378	223	2,941	24	10
Daryl Lamonica, Oakland (AFC)	356	179	2,516	22	15
1971—Roger Staubach, Dallas (NFC)	211	126	1,882	15	4
Bob Griese, Miami (AFC)	263	145	2,089	19	9
1972—Norm Snead, New York (NFC)	325	196	2,307	17	12
Earl Morrall, Miami (AFC)	150	83	1,360	11	7

All-Star Game

The All-Star game, originated by the late Arch Ward, sports editor of The Chicago Tribune, is an annual classic held at Soldier Field, Chicago, in which the best of the college senior players of the preceding season and the champion team of the National Football League meet for the benefit of charitable institutions of all denominations. A trophy is presented to the outstanding college player, as determined by the judges as the most valuable to his team in the game.

1934—Chicago Bears 0, All-Stars 0
1935—Chicago Bears 5, All-Stars 0
1936—Detroit Lions 7, All-Stars 7
1937—All-Stars 6, Green Bay Packers 0
1938—All-Stars 28, Washington Redskins 16
1939—New York Giants 9, All-Stars 0
1940—Green Bay Packers 45, All-Stars 28
1941—Chicago Bears 37, All-Stars 13
1942—Chicago Bears 21, All-Stars 0
1943—All-Stars 27, Washington Redskins 7
1944—Chicago Bears 24, All-Stars 21
1945—Green Bay Packers 19, All-Stars 7
1946—All-Stars 16, Los Angeles Rams 0
1947—All-Stars 16, Chicago Bears 0
1948—Chicago Cardinals 28, All-Stars 0
1949—Philadelphia Eagles 38, All-Stars 0
1950—All-Stars 17, Philadelphia Eagles 7
1951—Cleveland Browns 33, All-Stars 0
1952—Los Angeles Rams 10, All-Stars 7
1953—Detroit Lions 24, All-Stars 10
1954—Detroit Lions 31, All-Stars 6
1955—All-Stars 30, Cleveland Browns 27
1956—Cleveland Browns 26, All-Stars 0

1957—New York Giants 22, All-Stars 12
1958—All-Stars 35, Detroit Lions 19
1959—Baltimore Colts 29, All-Stars 0
1960—Baltimore Colts 32, All-Stars 7
1961—Philadelphia Eagles 28, All-Stars 14
1962—Green Bay Packers 42, All-Stars 20
1963—All-Stars 20, Green Bay 17
1964—Chicago 28, All-Stars 17
1965—Cleveland 24, All-Stars 16
1966—Green Bay 38, All-Stars 0
1967—Green Bay 27, All-Stars 0
1968—Green Bay 34, All-Stars 17
1969—New York Jets (AFL) 26, All-Stars 24
1970—Kansas City (AFC) 24, All-Stars 3
1971—Baltimore (AFC) 24, All-Stars 17
1972—Dallas (NFC) 20, All-Stars 7

Pro Bowl

1938—New York Giants 13, All-Stars 10 (at Los Angeles)
1939—Green Bay Packers 16, All-Stars 7 (at Los Angeles)
1940—Chicago Bears 28, All-Stars 14 (at Los Angeles)
1941—Chicago Bears 35, All-Stars 24 (at New York)
1942—All-Stars 17, Washington Redskins 14 (at Philadelphia)
1943—50— No games
1951—American Conference 28, National Conference 27 (at Los Angeles)
1952—National Conference 30, American Conference 13 (at Los Angeles)

1953–National Conference 27, American Conference 7 (at Los Angeles)

1954–Eastern Conference 20, Western Conference 9 (at Los Angeles)

1955–Western Conference 26, Eastern Conference 19 (at Los Angeles)

1956–Eastern Conference 31, Western Conference 30 (at Los Angeles)

1957–Western Conference 19, Eastern Conference 10 (at Los Angeles)

1958–Western Conference 26, Eastern Conference 7 (at Los Angeles)

1959–Eastern Conference 28, Western Conference 21 (at Los Angeles)

1960–Western Conference 38, Eastern Conference 21

1961–Western Conference 34, Eastern Conference 31

1962–Western Conference 31, Eastern Conference 30

1963–East Conference 30, Western Conference 20

1964–Western Conference 31, Eastern Conference 17

1965–Western Conference 34, Eastern Conference 14

1966–Eastern Conference 36, Western Conference 7

1967–Eastern Conference 20, Western Conference 10

1968–Western Conference 38, Eastern Conference 20

1969–Western Conference 10, Eastern Conference 7

1970–Western Conference 16, Eastern Conference 13

1971–National Conference 27, American Conference 6

1972–American Conference 26, National Conference 13

1973–American Conference 33, National Conference 28

Rules

For rules of professional football see Basic Rules section under American College Football.

Six-Man Football

The comparatively new American game of football with a team of 6 players to a side has made remarkable progress since its beginning in 1934.

It was devised as a sport for youth who loved to play for the fun of it and to reduce the possibility of injury to a minimum. The game provides excitement and action and has made such rapid strides that today at least 30,000 teams play it, enjoy it and are wholly unconcerned as to whether 1,000 or 10 persons see them in action.

The story of 6-man football is that of a man, a former football player, who recognized the danger in the American game of football for immature, undeveloped youngsters and the need of a game suited to the small schools, and proceeded to devise a contest in which play provided the maximum of action and the minimum of injury risk.

Stephen E. Epler, who played end for Cotner College (Lincoln, Neb., 1932) originated the 6-man football game in 1934 while coaching at Chester (Neb.) High School. His brain child was designed for junior colleges, high schools, grammar schools and boys' clubs.

Epler proceeded to develop the game after

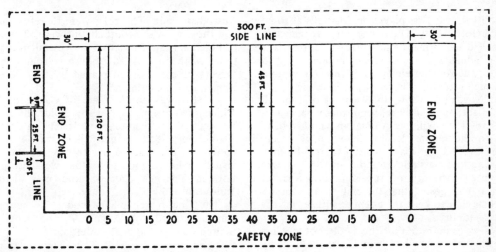

Six-Man Football Field. (Taken from "Sports for Recreation," edited by E. D. Mitchell, A. S. Barnes and Company, New York.)

Dean Mommey, superintendent of the Chester schools, had pointed out that although small boys liked to play football, the regular 11-man team game was impractical for them and fraught with considerable danger because of their immaturity.

During late spring and the summer of 1934, Epler worked on the new game. He decided that a 6-man team meant the field would be rather free for a passing and running attack. To avoid the danger that is present in regulation 11-man football scrimmages, he ruled that a man receiving the ball behind the line of scrimmage could not carry it beyond. Thus, a player was required to kick or pass, and, to encourage kicking, 4 points were awarded for a field goal.

A team consists of a center, 2 ends, a quarterback, a halfback and a fullback—3 men on the line, 3 back of it. The normal field is 240 x 120 feet, as compared with 300 x 160 in 11-man football. The basic rules of the 11-man game apply to the 6-man sport, and the equipment is about the same. The official 6-man football rules first were issued in 1938. The National 6-Man Committee, with Epler as chairman, is part of the National Federation of State High School Athletic Associations.

When Epler outlined his new game in August, 1934, several schools showed interest, but none cared to risk the money for equipment. In this emergency, the late W.H. Roselius, then coach at Hebron College, agreed to lend the needed things, and a game was arranged between a combination chosen from the high schools in Chester and Hardy, and another recruited from the Alex-andria and Belvidere high schools, all in Nebraska.

This pioneer contest was staged under the floodlights of the Hebron College field on Sept. 26, 1934, was well attended and, fittingly, ended in a 19-19 tie. In 1948, Chester High School first staged the Epler Bowl Game as an annual 6-man classic.

"The geographic expansion of the game since then has been very rapid," reports Epler. "It spread to 9 states in 1935, to 17 in 1936, to 45 by 1941. As early as 1938 Canadian and Hawaiian teams were playing it."

In 1953 there were more than 30,000 teams in the United States alone, compared with the 100 or fewer of 1934. With the thousands of intramural 6-man teams, many of which use the pass and touch variety, the number of participants in 6-man football may exceed that of the 11-man game.

The game was not created with the audience-appeal idea. "It was to be just clean and safe fun for youngsters. Spectators were not important," stated Epler. "It merely was necessary for the boys to arrive at the playing field and go into action, and usually they arrived.

"Therefore, 6-man football not merely survived, but went on to increasing popularity. This is so because boys like to kick a ball, they like to throw it and the game gives them generous chances. They have done much with the sport, in advancing it into national popularity."

Since 1947 the game has had its own magazine, "The Six-Man Football Magazine," edited by C. J. O'Connor of Baltimore, listing national, individual and team records for 6-man football.

Australian Football

(Courtesy of Don. V. Selth, Canberra, Australia)

Football was first played in Australia at some time before 1850. There were no recognizable rules, and according to one historian football was "only indulged in at festivals or holidays, just to interest the rougher elements of the colony, and with such prizes as a barrel of porter or ale."

In November 1850, three games of football took place, apparently with no rules whatsoever. In 1856, T. W. Wills, an Australian who had been sent to the famous Rugby School in Warwickshire, England, for his education returned home. He was a first-class cricketer and, in 1857, he was appointed secretary of the Melbourne Cricket Club and suggested that the club should form a football club to keep the cricketers fit during the winter months.

Wills was definite that the method of tackling opposing players, which was common in rugby and which resembles the tackle of American football, should not be permitted in the Australian code. The rules were therefore basically those of rugby football, but were adapted to make them appropriate for Australian conditions, with further adaption to include some aspects of the football played by the "rougher elements of the colony."

In this way some traces of Gaelic football, which had been played by goldminers who immigrated to Australia from Ireland in the Gold Rushes of 1851, found their way into the Australian code, and a few features of the game that later became soccer football were also incorporated. The new code was known as Victorian Rules football.

The first match played under the new rules was advertised for August 7, 1858, between Scotch College and the Melbourne Church of England grammar school. There were forty players on each side and the first team to kick two goals was to be declared the winner. However, with eighty men in the game and the goal posts nearly half a mile apart, scoring was very difficult. After three hours Scotch College kicked a goal, but no further score resulted before nightfall. Two weeks later the game was resumed, but neither school scored a goal on that day. A week later the two teams again resumed the match but again neither side scored and the game was officially declared to be a draw.

There are four uprights at each end, without crossbars. The two inner ones are about 20 feet high and are called goal posts. If the ball is kicked between the two goal posts, with any kind of kick and at any height, a goal is scored. If it is touched by an opponent or kicked between a goal post and one of the outer posts one point is scored. In 1899, the size of teams was reduced from twenty to eighteen players and it has remained at this number ever since.

Matches are played in the winter with each season consisting of twenty games. At the end of these twenty games the four leading teams play semi-final and final matches to decide the premiership winner. In Melbourne, a city of 2.3 million people, it is not uncommon for 200,000 to watch the six V.F.L. matches that are played every Saturday afternoon. In addition, there are many other minor leagues in the city, suburbs, and country areas.

The two outstanding features of the game are the long kick, usually by drop-kicks but occasionally by punts, and the overhead catching known in Australian Rules as high marking. The longest drop-kick in competition is 83 yards.

There is no specified size of a playing field. All fields are oval in shape, usually about 180 yards in length and about 160 yards in width. The ball is similar in shape to the grid iron and rugby footballs, but not quite so tapered at each end.

Playing time consists of four quarters of twenty-five minutes. There are no time-out periods and the play is therefore continuous. A player is allowed to run with the ball provided he bounces it on the ground every ten yards. But the ball can be kicked five or six times as quickly as it can be carried and therefore running with the ball is uncommon.

The medal winners awarded each year to the outstanding players in the three major football states have been:

VICTORIA
(Brownlow Medal)

1924—E. Greeves
1925—C. Watson
1926—I. Warne-Smith
1927—S. Coventry
1928—I. Warne-Smith
1929—A. Collier
1930—S. Judkins
1931-32—H. Bunton

1933—W. Smallhorn
1934—R. Reynolds
1935—H. Bunton
1936—D. J. Ryan
1937-38—R. Reynolds
1939—M. Whelan
1940—D. Fothergill, H. Matthews (tie)
1941—N. Ware
1942-45—Suspended during war.
1946—Dr. Don Cordner
1947—B. Deacon
1948—W. Morris
1949—R. Clegg
1950—A. Ruthven
1951—B. Smith
1952—R. Wright
1953—W. Hutchison
1954—R. Wright
1955—F. Goldsmith
1956—P. Box
1957—B. Gleeson
1958—N. Roberts
1959—R. Skilton
1960—J. Schultz
1961—J. James
1962—A. Lord
1963—R. Skilton
1964—G. Collis
1965-66—I. Stewart
1967—R. Smith
1968—R. Skilton
1969—K. Murray
1970—P. Bedford
1971—I. Stewart
1972—L. Thompson

WESTERN AUSTRALIA
(Sandover Medal)

1921—T. Outridge
1922—H. Boyd
1923—W. Thomas
1924—J. Gosnell
1925—G. Owens
1926—J. Leonard
1927—J. Craig
1928—J. Rocchi
1929—W. Thomas
1930—E. J. Flemming
1931—L. G. Richards
1932—K. Hough
1933-34—S. C. Clarke
1935—L. Daly, G. Krepp (tie)
1936—G. Maloney
1937—F. Jenkins
1938-39—H. W. Bunton
1940—E. O'Keefe
1941—H. W. Bunton
1942—L. Bowen
1943—T. Moriarty
1944—J. D. Davis
1945—G. Bailey
1946—Loughbridge

1947—C. Lewington	1930—W. Scott
1948—M. McIntosh	1931—J. Sexton
1949—G. Maffina	1932—S. M. Pontifex
1950—J. D. Conway	1933—W. K. Dunn
1951—F. Buttsworth	1934—G. B. Johnston
1952—S. Marth	1935—J. Cockburn
1953-54—M. McIntosh	1936—W. B. McCallum
1955—J. Todd	1937—J. H. Hawke
1956—G. Farmer	1938—R. B. Quinn
1957—J. Clarke	1939—J. Pash
1958—E. Kilmu Ray	1940—M. Brock
1959—B. Foley	1941—M. Boyall
1960—G. Farmer	1942-44—Suspended during war.
1961—N. Beard	1945—R. B. Quinn
1962—H. Bunton, Jr.	1946-47—R. Hank
1963—R. Sorell	1948-49—Ron Phillips
1964—B. Cable	1950—Ian McKay
1965-66—W. Walker	1951—John Marriott
1967—W. Walker, J. Parkinson (tie)	1952—L. Fitzgerald
1968—B. Cable	1953—J. Deane
1969—M. Brown	1954—L. Fitzgerald
1970—P. Dalton	1955—L. Head
1971—D. Hollins	1956—D. Boyd

SOUTH AUSTRALIA
(Magarey Medal)

	1957—R. Benton
	1958—L. Head
	1959—L. Fitzgerald
1898—A. Green	1960—B. Barbary
1899—S. Malin	1961—J. Halbert
1900—Not known	1962—K. Eustice
1901—P. Sandland	1963—L. Head
1902—T. McKenzie	1964—G. Motley
1903—S. Wave	1965—G. Window
1904—Not known	1966—R. Kneebone
1905-6—T. McKenzie	1967—T. Obst
1907—J. Mack	1968—B. Robran
1908—J. Terney	1969—D. Phillis
1909—H. R. Head	1970—B. Robran
1910—S. Hoskin	1971—R. Ebert
1911—H. V. Cumberland	
1912—D. Lowe	
1913—T. Leahy	
1914—J. Ashley	
1915—F. F. Barry	
1919-21—D. Moriarty	
1922—R. Barnes	
1923—H. Riley	
1924—W. Scott	
1925—A. G. Lill	
1926-27—B. McGregor	
1928—J. Handby	
1929—R. Snell	

Among other champions, past and present, are Dick Lee, Gordon Coventry, Bruce McGregor (Father of Ken), Jack Dyer, "Cazzer" Cazaly, Dave McNamara (holder of several distance kicking records), Ivo Warne-Smith, Laurie Nash, Norm Smith, Jack Mueller, Ron Barassi, Darrel Baldock, Den Farmer, Ron Todd, Bob Quinn, Bob Hank, Dick Reynolds (who played 320 senior games before his retirement), Jack Sheedy (337 games), Bob Skilton, Merve McIntosh, Lou Richards, Graham Farmer (who holds the Australian record of 356 games), Ted Whitten (321 games), and Ian Stewart.

Canadian (Rugby) Football

(Courtesy of J. G. Gaudaur, Commissioner, Canadian Football League, 11 King St., West; Suite 908, Toronto 1, Ontario)

Although a game similar to English rugger had been played in Canada since the middle of the 19th century, Canadian football was first organized with the establishment of the Canadian Rugby Union in 1891, and was composed of teams from Eastern Canada including the colleges. The game stems from English rugger which had 15 men on a side and as late as 1920 there were 14 men on a team. Two of them were called "side-scrimmagers," one on each side of the "center-scrimmager" who "heeled" the ball out to put it in play.

The side-scrims were dropped in 1921 and the center then began to put the ball in play with a direct pass as in American football. However there were and still are 12 men on a team, the twelfth man usually being called a flanker back on offense and a defensive halfback or line backer on defense.

Although the game has been played as an organized sport since 1891 it wasn't until 1909 that the game attracted any national significance. That year, Earl Grey who was the Governor General of Canada, donated a trophy known as the Grey Cup, which was to be emblematic of the Amateur Rugby Championship of Canada. This trophy was first competed for in 1909 by two Toronto teams, the University of Toronto and the Parkdale Club. At this first Grey Cup game there were approximately 3800 people in attendance and the gross revenue from all sources was $2,616.00.

In 1921 a League which had been operating in Western Canada joined the Canadian Rugby Union and competed that year, for the first time, in the National Championship Grey Cup game with Edmonton losing to Toronto by the score of 23-0. The attendance at the game was 9,558 and the gross revenue from all sources was a record $9,991.00.

Frank (Shag) Shaughnessy, ex-president of the International Baseball League, who played with and captained Notre Dame just after the turn of the century, became the first professional football coach in Canada with McGill University in Montreal, in 1912.

He immediately introduced American tactics to the game, such as the secondary defense, two-man blocking on opening holes in the line, etc. It was Shag who persuaded the rules makers to drop the two side-scrims in 1921 and to adopt the direct pass from center. Shag campaigned for the forward pass for many years, but it didn't become part of the Canadian game until 1931.

After 1935 the Canadian Colleges dropped out of contention and by 1938 there were only three leagues competing within the framework of the Canadian Rugby Union for the now much coveted Grey Cup. In the East there were two leagues, The Inter-Provincial Rugby Football Union which was more or less semi-pro in that some players were paid and the Ontario Rugby Football Union which was strictly amateur. In the West the league was called the Western Inter-Provincial Rugby Union. That year (1938) the Grey Cup game was played in Toronto between the Toronto Argonauts of the Inter-Provincial Football Union and the Winnipeg Blue Bombers of the Western League. The attendance at this game was 18,778 and the gross revenue from all sources had now increased to $17,545.00.

In 1950 the modern era of Canadian Professional Football began. The year previous, the all-America Conference Professional League in the U.S. ceased operations and many of the top pro stars from that league flooded into Canada. In that year the two pro leagues, the Inter-Provincial Rugby Football Union in the East and the Western Inter-Provincial Rugby Football Union in the west imported, not only the highly skilled American pros and college rookies, but American coaches as well. The game was now out and out pro with all players getting paid. The increased standard of play on the field was immediately reflected at the gate. That year the Toronto Argonauts once again played the Winnipeg Blue Bombers for the Grey Cup game in Toronto. A sellout crowd of 27,101 attended the game and the gross revenue from all sources had grown to a new record of $65,622.00. By the mid 1950s the football terminology which was a hold over from the early rugger days, had completely disappeared and had become identical to that used in the United States. Also by that time television had entered the picture and by 1955 the Grey Cup game, which that year was played in the West for the first time at Vancouver, attracted a sellout crowd of 39,491 and the gross revenue had jumped to a new record $198,360.00.

The next two years were to see the Inter-Provincial Rugby Union and the Western Inter-Provincial Rugby Union revise and modernize their constitutions to become organizations known as the Eastern Football Conference and the Western Football Conference respectively. The member clubs of the Eastern Conference were the Montreal Alouette Football Club Inc., the Ottawa Football Club Limited, the Argonaut Football Club Limited and the Hamilton Tiger-Cat Football Club Limited.

The member clubs of the Western Football Conference were B. C. Lions Football Club, Stampeder Football Club Limited, Edmonton Eskimo Football Club, The Saskatchewan Roughrider Football Club and the Winnipeg Football Club.

In 1959 the Canadian Football League was formed with the Eastern Football Conference and the Western Football Conference, forming the Eastern and Western divisions of the Canadian Football League respectively with G. Sydney Halter named the Commissioner of the League.

In 1961 approximately 2,000,000 admissions were purchased to watch Canadian Pro Football and the gross revenue to all clubs from all sources was approximately $8,000,000. The Grey Cup Game gross revenue that year exploded to an amazing new record of $499,500.00 for the one game. A survey revealed that approximately 9,000,000 people attended the game, listened to it on radio, or watched it on T.V.

In 1971, the revenue for the Grey Cup game

had increased to a gross figure of $766,945.00.

Many top ranking U.S. College football players, on graduation, decide to play their Pro football in Canada, many of them living there the year around and continuing to live there after their football days are over.

The number of college players has increased to such a measure that 70% of the C.F.L.'s teams are made up of U.S. players, including many All-Americans.

The Canadian Rugby Union continued to exist, but as the body that governs minor football in Canada. Each year the Canadian Football League donates $55,000.00 to this League to assist Minor Football.

Expansion of U.S. football teams into Canada was rejected by C.F.L. owners in 1971. New York was hopeful of a franchise after wide interest of TV viewers was expressed when 108 stations broadcasted C.F.L. games.

Difference between Canadian and American Football Rules—

There are three main fundamental differences. First, in the Canadian game there are 12 men on a team instead of 11, with the extra man playing offensively as a flanker with the defensive man playing the position of a defensive halfback. Secondly, there are only three downs to make the 10 yards instead of four. Thirdly, there is no fair catch in Canadian football when receiving a kick. The punt receivers have no alternative but to catch the ball and attempt to advance it and are required to do this with no blockers. The players covering the punt, however, are required to be no closer than five yards to the punt receiver when he catches the ball. Further, a single point can be scored by punting the ball over the goal line if the punt receivers are unable to run it out of the end zone which is 25 yards in depth. Further, if the punt receivers do receive a punt in the end zone and run it out say to the one yard line, they will be required to scrimmage from there.

The field size in Canada is 110 yards by 65 yards instead 100 x 50 and this of course places a greater emphasis on quarterback maneuverability and outside running speed. Also, the linemen instead of being lined up nose to nose so to speak, must be a yard apart. This of course gives the offense a great advantage and combined with the fact that all backs may be in motion in the Canadian game, offsets the fact that there are three downs instead of four.

The game is played in four quarters of 15 minutes each with a halftime intermission of 20 minutes. There are *no* time outs.

Penalties are marked off for 5, 10, 15, or 25 yards, according to the infraction. Rough play (piling on, clipping, slugging) will cost you 25. There is no yardage difference between offensive and defensive penalties.

CANADIAN FOOTBALL CHAMPIONS
1892—Osgoode Hall (Ontario)
1893—Queen's (Intercollegiate)
1894—Ottawa University (Quebec Union)
1895—University of Toronto
1896-97—Ottawa University (Quebec Union)
1898—Ottawa (Ontario Union)
1899—No competition
1900—Ottawa (Ontario Union)
1901—Ottawa University (Quebec Union)
1902—Ottawa (Ontario Union)

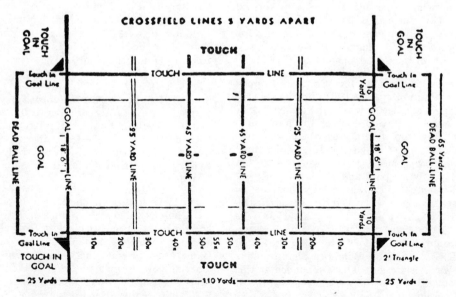

Canadian Football Field.
(Taken from the "Official Rules of the Canadian Rugby Union.")

1903-04—No competition
1905—University of Toronto (Ontario Union)
1906—Hamilton (Ontario)
1907—Montreal (Interprovincial)
1908—Hamilton (Interprovincial)
1909-11—University of Toronto (Intercollegiate)
1912—Hamilton Alerts (Ontario)
1913—Hamilton (Interprovincial)
1914—Toronto Argonauts (Interprovincial)
1915—Hamilton (Interprovincial)
1916-19—No competition
1920-21—Toronto Argonauts (Interprovincial)
1922-25—Queen's University (Intercollegiate)
1926—Ottawa (Interprovincial)
1927—Toronto Balmy Beach (Ontario)
1928-29—Hamilton Tigers (Interprovincial)
1930—Toronto Balmy Beach (Ontario)
1931—Montreal A.A.A. (Interprovincial)
1932—Hamilton Tigers (Interprovincial)
1933—Toronto Argonauts (Interprovincial)
1934—Sarnia Imperials (Ontario)
1935—Winnipeg (Western)
1936—Sarnia Imperials (Ontario)
1937-38—Toronto Argonauts (Interprovincial)
1939—Winnipeg (Western)
1940—Ottawa (Interprovincial)

1941—Winnipeg (Western)
1942—Toronto R.C.A.F. Hurricanes (Ontario)
1943—Hamilton Wildcats (Ontario)
1944—St. Hyacinthe (Quebec Union)
1945-47—Toronto Argonauts (Interprovincial)
1948—Calgary (Western)
1949—Montreal (Interprovincial)
1950—Toronto Argonauts (Interprovincial)
1951—Ottawa (Interprovincial)
1952—Toronto Argonauts (Interprovincial)
1953—Hamilton (Big Four)
1954-56—Edmonton (W.I.F.U.)
1957—Hamilton (Big Four)
1958—Winnipeg (W.I.F.U.)
1959—Winnepeg
1960—Ottawa
1961-62—Winnipeg
1963—Hamilton Tiger-Cats
1964—Vancouver Lions
1965—Hamilton Tiger-Cats
1966—Saskatchewan Rough Riders
1967—Hamilton Tiger-Cats
1968-69—Ottawa Rough Riders
1970—Montreal Alouettes
1971—Calgary Stampeders
1972—Hamilton Tiger-Cats

GAELIC FOOTBALL

Which sport is the roughest? That question brings many answers. One sport that ranks high in the vote-getting is Gaelic Football, sometimes referred to as unmitigated mayhem. Like the Indian game of baggataway in Canada, Gaelic football at first was played with enormous numbers of men on each side; there were few, if any, rules and the playing field stretched many square miles and a game, which could be called more properly a near-riot, sometimes lasted all day.

The average Irishman is of the opinion that Gaelic football has been played in the homeland for a thousand years or more.

"How else," he will demand, "would it have been possible for the Irish to have developed so many men of fabulous courage, strength and such great physical skill through so many centuries?"

However, the Gaelic game is an off-shoot of football as it was originated, about 800 or 900 years ago in England, with the Irish mixing the kicking game with a few distinct ideas of their own as to what should go on during football conflict. The result is a game that tests the strength of the brawniest of men, puts acid to the thing called courage and makes the Gaelic form of play unique.

Ireland isn't the only place where Gaelic football is played, but the Irish seem to be the only ones who play it twice, or more.

Sports enthusiasts who have seen all forms of football and judged impartially declare that Gaelic football is the game of games if you are seeking swift-changing panoramas, brilliant speed, reckless daring, wild courage and sustained action.

The origin of Gaelic football as a separate game, as well as the date, is in dispute, but it is known to have been very popular in Dublin in 1527. The old game was different from that of today. The size of the team was not limited. All the able-bodied in one town played against those of another, or parish played against parish. The size of the teams scaled between 25 and 100. An effort was made to keep them numerically even, but this rarely happened, and frequently one team had from 5 to 30 more players than its rival.

In some of the earlier centuries the rules provided that a game start at a point in dead center between two rival parishes. That might have been two miles, or ten miles, from either parish line. The team that advanced the ball across the boundary line of the rival parish won.

Games in the far-flung years were very ceremonial. There was a dancing contest among the colleens as a preliminary. After that the master of ceremonies went to midfield and addressed the crowd. The players wore caps, from which fluttered ribbons of distinguishing color.

A master of ceremonies in a game between Lusk and Swords in 1721 treated the spectators to something unique when he canted this poem, one of Ireland's classics so far as athletics are concerned:

"Ye champions of fair Lusks and ye of Swords,
"View well this ball, the present of your lords,
"To outward view, three folds of bullock's hide,

"With leather thongs bound fast on every side,
"A mass of finest hay concealed from sight,
"Conspire at once to make it firm and light."

In those days there was no rest period, teams playing until one or another scored a goal, which ended the contest.

At the turn of the 18th century the game was popular throughout Ireland, and the reading of a poem or song before the battle began was still in vogue. But after the game was under way, there was no singing and nothing poetic, especially in the Nanny, Meath and Boyne River districts, where teams from opposite sides of the streams played each other according to their own particular rules, none of them chummy.

Because punching at the ball was permitted, many eyes were blackened, noses broken and mouths cut by players who seemingly aimed their punches at the ball but actually drove them into enemy faces. The real strategy of the game, as explained by an Irish player, was to mess up the other man's face as soon as possible, because a man with two swollen eyes couldn't follow the ball so well as one with clear vision. Players often started the season by getting a pair of black eyes, and they remained discolored until the season was over.

About a hundred years ago Gaelic football had no official name, and the innocent bystanders classified it as a free-for-all fight. The whole idea was to get the ball beyond the other team's goal line, and never mind what means were necessary to accomplish the purpose. The game was called "Rough and Tumble" in one part of Ireland prior to 1884. In another, it was "Corner to Corner." West Kerry called it "Cad" because the ball was a leather-covered cow's bladder. The refined persons referred to the ball as a "liathroid coise."

In 1884 the men of Tipperary met Waterford—34 to a side—near Carrick-on-Suir. It was like a world war—without mechanical weapons. The fierce struggle ended in a scoreless tie when one of the contestants kicked the ball out of the neighborhood. After the players had calmed down, they decided that the game might be better if there were some standard rules.

Dan and Maurice Davin of Carrick, spectators at the combat and important citizens in the community, agreed that something ought to be done to save the Irish lads for posterity. So, with Michael Cusack of Clare and some of the players, the Davins drew a set of rules that softened the game slightly. They formed the Gaelic Athletic Association at a big meeting in Hayes Hotel in Thurles, Ireland, on Nov. 1, 1884. Since then it has been the ruling body for the sport.

There are 15 men to a side in Gaelic football. The performers are not permitted to throw, but can dribble, as in basketball, kick along the ground, punt or punch the ball. Inasmuch as each side is eager to advance toward the rival goal line, there is bristling action during every minute, split into two halves of 30 minutes each.

One point is scored for kicking or punching the ball over the crossbar and 3 are tallied if the ball is punched or kicked into the net. When a team is close to the enemy goal posts, the action becomes furious with the advancing side using every trick to score and the defenders calling upon all they have to roll back the assault, gain possession of the ball and start an advance of their own.

Beginning in 1931 and until England went to war, the winners of the All-Ireland championship visited the United States and played the crack teams in this country which, as a rule, are made up of "graduates" of the Irish game. Most American teams are centered around New York City.

Gaelic football players in Ireland are not paid. If they go on tours, they are paid a sum of money by the club equivalent to what they would have earned at their trade or profession.

The fact that the men accept fees for playing while away from home does not put them into the professional class, according to Irish standards, and they remain amateurs.

Missionaries of the game have tried to popularize it throughout Europe and in other places, without success. Folks gaze in awe at what happens during an exhibition of this sport, and since most of them are interested in living a few years longer, they refuse to become players, but they never fail to go into raptures over the wild action and the terrific body collisions, which they witness as spectators and which the Irish players classify as "a bit of fun."

The game in Ireland is organized on a county basis. Usually all 32 counties, including the four in Northern Ireland, have teams from senior classification down the parish districts. The teams play all summer and from the senior teams each county selects an all-star team to represent it in the National Cup competition. The all-Ireland championship matches the county selected teams in an elimination tournament, with one defeat bringing elimination. The two surviving teams play for the championship, a one-game affair that draws as many as 90,000 spectators.

The G.A.A. is so dedicated to the fostering and preservation of the Irish games that it bars

Gaelic football players from watching or engaging in "foreign" games, such as soccer, rugby or cricket. The penalty is suspension from Gaelic games for one year. Continued activity can lead to a lifetime suspension.

In recent years, the all-Ireland Gaelic football and hurling champions have resumed their annual visits to this country to play against selected teams from New York. One of the biggest upsets of these engagements occurred at the Polo Grounds in 1958, when the New York teams won both the football and hurling contests.

Many of the players on the selected teams were born in Ireland and learned the games there before migrating to this country. At times the United States has been permitted by the ruling body, the Gaelic Athletic Association of Ireland, to compete in the National League finals.

The ruling body in this country is the Gaelic Athletic Association, located in New York City. It is affiliated with the G.A.A. of Ireland.

While most of the activity is centered in the New York area, teams also have been formed in Boston, Chicago, San Francisco, Los Angeles, Detroit, Syracuse and Rochester, Philadelphia, Newark, Bridgeport, Hartford, Springfield, Mass., Boston and Holyoke, as well as in England and Canada.

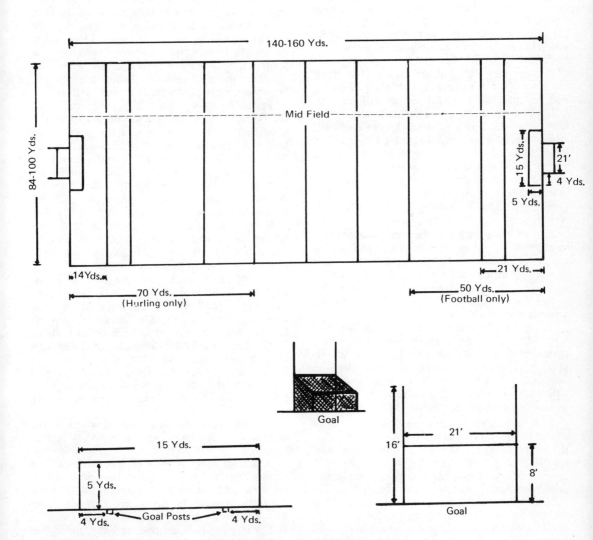

Gaelic Football and Hurling Field

GOLF

One of the most rapidly growing sports, particularly in the United States, is golf. The game of hitting a ball into a cup is largely a participant sport, though many tournaments draw large numbers of spectators. It is a game of discipline, hope and despair. It also is an ideal form of nonstrenuous exercise. With the rise in the number of devotees has come an advancement in the clubs and balls. The tools of today's golfer are a far cry from the equipment used in the early days of the sport, which is generally accepted to have been invented in Scotland in comparatively modern times. However, some historians claim it was originated before the Christian Era, thereby confusing the game's history.

Historians belonging to the strange clan that always has opposed crediting the moderns or comparative moderns with originating anything hazard the guess that shepherds, in a time long before the Christian Era, may have indulged in the game of golf. They point to the curved sticks and intimate that the sheep tenders could have used them to hit pebbles.

Perhaps they did. But any driving that took place was just for distance and not in keeping with the rules laid down for the game of golf.

Long after it had become definitely established that the Scots invented the game of golf, as it is played now, the usual thing happened. A historian disputed what was evident. He observed a drawing of a Hollander leaning against a slim stick with a knob at the end and immediately offered the conclusion that the Dutch had pioneered the game, insisting the stick was a golf club, called the driver in later years.

Beyond the drawing, there never was anything to support the claim that the Dutch had played golf before the Scots. In fact, neither the Dutch of later centuries nor those of today have shown interest in the game, whereas golf has played a conspicuous role in the history of Scotland for many centuries.

The story of the game in earliest time is rather peculiar, since it deals much more with edicts against play than it does with progress or development. Through a great many generations in Scotland golf gets mention on history's pages only through some rule prohibiting it, as issued by one or another of the monarchs.

Golf is known to have enjoyed some vogue about 1440. It became much too popular with the public to please James II, ruler in the land of the heather in 1457, and that year he prevailed upon Parliament to enact a rule, during the month of March, making it unlawful for anyone to play at "golfe" because indulgence used up the leisure of the people, who could put it to better advantage by the practice of archery.

In that era, the bow and arrow were the chief weapons of warfare, and throughout the British Isles there was constant fear of invasion by enemies. Male citizens were required, by regal demand, to devote a portion of each day to perfecting markmanship. Whenever a citizen of England or Scotland, although having complied with the law, began indulging in sport of some kind, the king regarded it as a waste of time, lengthened the archery practice hours and prohibited the sport, or ruled against it in some fashion, to force the people to better themselves with bows and arrows.

James IV of Scotland (1488-1513) developed into a fair sort of golfer and continued to play the game because it fascinated him.

Mary, the granddaughter of James IV and daughter of James V, learned golf in early girlhood and was sent later to France to be educated. Just what term was used to explain the golf ball chaser, prior to that era, is not known. But when Mary was in France, she referred to the youths as "cadets," meaning pupils. The pronunciation, in France, was "cad-day," and later, in Scotland, and then in England, the term was adopted, the pronunciation being as in France, but it was spelled both "caddy" and "caddie."

James V followed his golf-playing father onto the throne of Scotland. He was not an enthusiast about golf, but did not oppose the game. When Mary, the first woman golfer, became Queen of Scots in 1542 she played golf openly, gave it her blessing, and the sport advanced thereafter. During her reign, there was founded the most famous of golf courses—St. Andrews of Scotland—which came into existence about 1552.

Some years after Mary's death in 1587, certain elements made a new effort to blot out golf. The best they could do was to have a law written prohibiting play on Sundays.

Chiefly, golf was a game for club members. The Royal Blackheath Club may have been founded in 1608 so that a place could be provided for play at golf. The Edinburgh Burgess Golfing Society may have been created about 1735, the Honorable Company of Edinburgh Golfers came into existence in 1744 and the Royal and Ancient Golf Club was operating in 1754. The latter club sponsored a tournament of some sort, in the same year, but the details are lacking.

The St. Andrews old course, now one of the outstanding in the world, is 6,883 yards in length.

Although there is little of record concerning golf in Scotland from 1800 to the end of 1859, the first tournament took place in 1860 at the Prestwick course in Scotland. This, in time, became known as the famous British Open. A belt was put up as a prize, and the conditions were that it was to become the personal property of the man winning thrice.

In that era the topnotch golfers were Willie Park Sr. and Tom Morris Sr. More or less, they dominated what little competition went on. Park won the title in 1860, becoming the first recognized champion. Morris won in 1861 and 1862 and Park won in 1863, to make it 2-all. When the veterans met again in 1864, Morris was the winner. In 1865 another tournament was arranged and competition was "open to anyone," which is how the event came to be known as the "Open Championship." At the time, there was no real distinction between amateurs and professionals. The "Open" meant that play, which previously had been limited to Scotland and which seemed to include, chiefly, the players at Prestwick, could be indulged in by any one who cared to enter competition.

A. L. Srath won the title in 1865.

Tom Morris Jr., as good as his father, perhaps better, retired by winning a belt in 1868, 1869 and 1870. There was no championship in 1871. The lapse must have saddened the enthusiasts of the time, since they met, late in 1871, decided upon resumption of the tournament in 1872 and resolved that play, instead of being always at Prestwick, be shifted around to the different courses in Scotland.

By that time, golf enthusiasm had been stirred in England, which, previously, had been rather apathetic toward the game. English players felt they had a chance against the stars of Scotland and some moved into action in the revived championship of 1872. But Tom Morris Jr., the finest player of his time, won his fourth straight victory in 1872.

In the earliest days of golf, the ball was made of feathers. These were stuffed as tightly as possible into a small bag of very thin leather. When the packing was completed, the opening was sewed. The liveliness of the ball depended upon how well it had been stuffed. But no matter how packed, it was not a ball that enabled drivers to get great distances.

A ball, with a leather cover and stuffed with feathers, came into the possession of George C. Paris of New Britain, Conn., some years ago. Its age was guessed at more than a century. Several tests were made to determine its possible maximum distance. The ball was driven up to 175 yards. The later gutta percha was a superior ball, so far as driving range was concerned, but 200 to 225 yards were rated as "remarkable" for a drive.

In 1848, after many experiments, the gutta percha ball was adopted. It was possible to drive it farther and putt it in truer fashion than the feather ball. It continued to be the only type of golf ball until 1899 when the rubber ball, invented in the United States, was introduced.

Throughout his career, Tom Morris Jr. employed the "gutty" ball. Yet in 36 holes of play at Prestwick in 1870, he used only 149 strokes, a record that was never effaced while play was at 36 holes and the gutta percha ball was in use. Since that would be 298 for 72 holes, with a ball that limited the distance, the performance of Morris, stands out as truly brilliant.

The beginnings of golf in North America are not clearly recorded. There were organizations that functioned as "golf clubs" and mention was made of "golf greens" back in the 18th Century in both South Carolina and Georgia, but there is nowhere any record of play at the game of golf.

There are some guesses that the game, then in swaddling clothes as a public game even in Scotland, was brought to what now is the United States by Scottish regiments and played occasionally during the Revolutionary War. The only supporting evidence is that a decade or so after the war there were "golf clubs" in the United States.

But their chief function seemed to be to serve as places for folks to get together to dine or dance. There is nothing in the paid advertisements used by those organizations to indicate that a game of golf ever was played.

In 1906, the father of Charles (Chick) Evans, the great links star of a later day, made a search through papers printed in the latter part of the 18th Century and into the 19th for material for his American bibliography. The senior Evans found quite a few notices in the form of paid advertisements inserted by officials of "golf clubs," but nothing that dealt with a contest at golf.

The Charleston (S.C.) "City Gazette." of Oct. 13, 1795, carried this advertisement:

"Notice—The anniversary of the Golf Club will be held on Saturday next, at the Club House, Harleston's Green, where members are requested to attend at one o'clock."

The "ad" was signed by William Milligan, as secretary, and the officers were James Gairdner (or Gardiner), president; William Blacklock, vice president, with Milligan as both secretary and treasurer.

A somewhat similar "ad" appeared in October, 1796, and another on Oct. 12, 1797. The latter referred to the organization as the "South Carolina Golf Club."

In 1798, James Johnston Jr. succeeded Milligan as secretary and was issuing notices. On Sept. 29, 1798, Johnston had this notice printed:

"At an anniversary meeting of the Golf Club, on the 8th instant, it was resolved that every member who does not, on or before the 16th instant, signify his intention to the secretary of continuing in the club, will be considered as having his seat vacated."

There is framed in the Savannah (Ga.) Golf Club the following invitation:

"The honor of Miss Eliza Johnson's presence is requested to a ball to be given by the members of the Golf Club in this city, (Savannah, Ga.) at the Exchange, on Tuesday evening, the 13th inst, at 7 o'clock."

The invitation is dated at Savannah, December, 1811, and signed by George Hogarth, as treasurer, and George Woodruff, Robert Mackay, John Craig and James Dickson as "managers."

According to a succession of "ads" in the Savannah "Daily Republican," the Savannah Golf Club had meetings from then to Jan. 7, 1820, after which affairs of the club ceased to be a matter for advertising and its further activities are not a part of the records. But in 1818 and 1819, according to the "Republican," the meetings chiefly were at the home of Mrs. Gribbins, "who kept a boarding house on the bay."

In all the advertising, covering a period of about 15 years, none mentioned play at golf by any members of either the Charleston or Savannah Golf Clubs.

Ships' officers, either from Scotland or England, probably Scotland, sailing into Canada and having shore leisure, introduced golf to Canada. The exact year is not known. It may have been in the late 1850's or early 1860's. A 3-hole course was built in Montreal and a similar one in Quebec. As early as 1873, the Canadians had become sufficiently interested in the new sport to determine it should have a governing body to lay down the rules.

The result was the creation on the North American continent of the first club organized for play at golf. The meeting, which launched the game on its official career, was in the office of John S. Sidney of Montreal on Nov. 4, 1873, and the original club soon was renamed the Royal Montreal Golf Club, now the most powerful in the Dominion.

The Canadian Amateur championship tournament was staged for the first time in 1895, the Open in 1904 and the Canadian Professional title first was competed for in 1912. But in the years before Canada believed that title play was necessary, golf was a great favorite among Canadian clubmen. Each important match was ceremonial, the players being required to wear red coats and white flannel trousers, while the captain had to don white gloves when making the opening drive.

The story of golf—the actual game—in the United States, begins in the 1880's.

Joseph Mickle Fox, a Philadelphian, learned about golf on a trip to Scotland in 1884 and introduced the game at his summer home in Foxburg, Pa., in 1885. This led to the founding of the Foxburg Golf Club in 1887, and the club, still in existence, is probably the oldest one in the United States.

John G. Reid, a Scotsman living in the Yonkers (N.Y.) area, introduced the game to his friends in Yonkers on Feb. 22, 1888, and this introduction had a more telling effect on the development of the game here.

Months earlier, Robert Lockhart, a friend of Reid's, had gone to Scotland and Reid asked him to bring back some balls and clubs. Almost as soon as they were put into Reid's hands, he invited friends to watch him in an exhibition, and to join him in play. The inclement weather did not halt Reid's experiment, nor keep his comrades from joining him in a cow pasture in Yonkers. John B. Upham, who also was versed in golf, joined the group, which included, in addition to Reid, and Upham, Henry O. Talmadge, Harry Holbrook, Kingman Putnam and Alexander P. W. Kinnan. Reid and Upham demonstrated the technique to their friends.

However, before elaborate play could start, the famous blizzard struck the New York area, in March, 1888, and for weeks, the ground either was blanketed with snow or too soft to be playable.

When the sextet again proceeded with play, taking turns in using the limited supply of clubs and being careful not to lose the treasured balls, it was found the small course was not adequate. This led to the taking over of a 30-acre piece of land at North Broadway and Shonnard Place, owned by John C. Shotts, a German butcher. The golfers never bothered to pay Shotts lease or rental money. They just laid out a 6-hole course, played when they chose and ignored Shotts, who, it seemed, made no objection.

When summer came, so did new equipment— from Scotland. By that time, the group's members had become addicts. The men played on Sundays, as well as weekdays, and were the subjects of sermons by various preachers. Passersby watched the action occasionally and classified as "ridiculous folly" the practice of hitting a ball and then tracking it down, merely to hit it again.

On Nov. 14, 1888, Reid gave a dinner party, attended by Upham, Holbrook, Talmadge and Putnam. The gentlemen decided they should band into a golf organization and at a meeting decided to call themselves the "St. Andrew's Golf Club of Yonkers," honoring the famous St. Andrews Club in Scotland. Lockhart and Gilbert Turner were elected to membership. On March 22, 1889, when the club met again, J. C. Ten Eyck became a member, as did S. H. Fitch, Kinnan, Colonel Heermance and E. I. Loiselle.

On March 30, 1889, the first mixed foursome went into action. Upham was teamed with Mrs. Reid, while Reid's partner was Carrie Low. Mrs. Reid and Upham won by 1½ holes, the rule then giving each pair half a point when a hole was halved.

In the spring of 1892 the club, having a membership of 13 active players, had to move from the old course. A new 6-holer was constructed on Palisade Avenue. There was an apple tree near the first tee. On warm days, players took off their outer clothing, hung it on the tree, and this led to their being called the "Apple Tree Gang." By then folks across the Hudson River who had seen the "Apple Tree Gang" at play built their own courses.

Another old course is the Middlesboro Club in Middlesborough, Ky. Howard J. Douglas, secretary-treasurer of the Middlesborough Chamber of Commerce, advised, in February, 1947:

"Our Middlesboro course of 9 holes was completed in 1889. It was built by English people, who had come here to open this section, our town being laid out as an industrial iron center, in 1890.

"The Middlesboro Club has been in continuous use since its opening in 1889 and not many changes have been made, beyond adding some new territory."

Going into 1894 there were crude links at Paterson, Lakewood, New Brunswick, Montclair, and elsewhere in New Jersey, with other organizations playing at golf in New York State. Tuxedo and Newburgh had courses; the Ardsley and Knollwood Clubs were constructed at White Plains. Later, Rye, N.Y., built its famous Apawamis course and Greenwich, Conn., added a links to its Fairfield Club grounds. Additionally, there were Shinnecock and Meadow Brook on Long Island and Richmond on Staten Island—all this within six or seven years after Reid and Lockhart had put on their exhibition.

All clubs except St. Andrew's had 9-hole courses. St. Andrew's, with its 6-holer, was referred to as a "cow pasture course." The members resented that, took over the General Jacob Odell farm on the Saw Mill River Parkway in Westchester County, N.Y., gave a farewell party at the "Apple Tree Gang" quarters and went into new quarters on Dec. 29, 1893.

In 1894 a group of golfers, most of them centered in the East, decided to have a tournament to determine a champion. It was announced it would be "open to the world," and, thus, it became known as the "United States Open." So far as can be established, anyone could compete.

The first Open was at St. Andrew's in the summer of 1894 and was at match play. Willie Dunn defeated Willie Campbell, 2 up, to win the title. Two "Amateur championships" were held that same year, at Newport, R.I., and at the St. Andrew's course and were won by W. G. Lawrence and L. B. Stoddard, respectively.

Late in 1894 clubmen who were leaders in the sport determined to organize in order to conduct recognized championships, to adopt rules of play and to regulate the question of amateur status. It was felt that there should be a national body to standardize the sport and to act as a court of appeals.

The call was for a "general meeting of golf clubs" on Dec. 22, 1894, but only five responded with delegates. They were St. Andrew's (Mount Hope, N.Y.), The Country Club (Brookline, Mass.), Newport (R.I.) Golf Club and Shinnecock Hills, Southampton, Long Island representing the East, and this Chicago Golf Club, the sole representative from the West. The organization that was created became known as the United States Golf Association, which then and since, has been the controlling body for the sport in this country.

The enormous growth of the association from its modest beginning of five clubs is shown by the fact that 4,000 clubs and courses are now affiliated with it.

The pioneers of the U.S.G.A. conducted their first amateur championship in 1895 at Newport, with 32 competitors. It found C. B. Macdonald the winner over C. E. Sands by the comfortable margin of 12 holes up and 11 to play. Horace Rawlins won their first Open championship on the same course the next day with a 36-hole score of 173.

Women had taken an interest in the new game almost from its beginning in Yonkers, and when a tournament was planned to determine the men's amateur champion in 1895, they decided to have a tourney of their own. This resulted in the first U.S.G.A. Women's Amateur championship in 1895. There were thirteen contestants and play was at the new Meadow Brook Club course on Long Island. It was at medal play and Mrs. C. S. Brown was the winner with 132 strokes for 18 holes. The following year the event was changed to match play and has so continued.

During the larger part of the first two decades of its existence as a championship-play game in the United States, golf had very little public appeal. The amateur players were, for the main part, members of clubs which had their own courses. The professionals were few in number and were made up mainly of the teaching group. They entered the Open, to an increasing extent, but golf continued to be a game folks read about only at tournament time.

In 1913, Harry Vardon and Ted Ray, English stars, came over for the Open, which was played at Brookline, Mass. Since they were such superlative golfers, it was conceded that the title would go to one or the other. The match exploded into headlines when a 20-year-old American youth, Francis Ouimet of Boston, who in earlier years had been a caddy, tied both Vardon and Ray at 304.

The next sensation came in the play-off. The amazing Ouimet, unknown up to that time, won the championship, turning in a sizzling 72 for 18 holes, while the mighty Vardon's best was 77 and Ray floundered in with 78.

The increase in public interest in the game dated from then. The exploit of Ouimet was told and retold. People who knew about the game only vaguely suddenly had a desire to play. Some joined clubs. In some cities, public courses were laid out. More and more were added to the number as time went on and golf leaped into remarkable popularity, with millions of players in the United States and over 5,700 courses before the outbreak of World War II.

Ouimet's feat not only gave impetus to the game itself, but brought many teachers from abroad to take jobs with the new clubs, while some men, who had been amateurs, turned professional and increased that group to such an extent that it was felt, late in 1915, the clan should have an organization and a tournament of its own.

Rodman Wanamaker, a multi-millionaire merchant who was keen about golf and interested in the welfare of the professionals, invited a group to luncheon at the Taplow Club, New York, Jan. 17, 1916. At the meeting, the Professional Golfers' Association of America was launched. It arranged for its first tournament at a meeting on April 10, when the name of the organization definitely was decided upon and new rules were drafted.

The first tournament was in 1916, directed by George Frothingham, first president of the unit. James M. Barnes was the pioneer winner, defeating Jock Hutchison, 1 up, at the Siwanoy (Bronxville, N.Y.) course. World War I stopped play in 1917 and 1918, but Barnes was the winner again in 1919. Hutchison took the honors in 1920 and the following year saw the surge of Walter Hagen.

The professionals, of course, were dominant in their own field, but when it came to Open championship play they had certain spotlight difficulties after Robert T. Jones Jr., of Georgia reached his prime. He continued to blight the pathways of his golfing rivals until he retired after the 1930 season.

Jones had a habit of getting into Open play-offs starting in 1923, and thereafter the pros had to beat the great amateur to gain any distinction. It was not always an easy task. Jones finished second in the Open of 1922; won the Open in 1923, was second in 1924, lost the play-off to Willie MacFarlane in 1925, won again in 1926, tied with Johnny Farrell in 1928 only to be beaten in the play-off, won the play-off in 1929 and won in 1930.

About a score of years ago, there were so few open and professional tournaments that the champion money winner was able, with a lot of luck, to pick up only a pittance, compared with the sums that are possible today. In 1934, Paul Runyan was the headliner as regards money won for an entire season of play, and his total for that year was $6,767. Since Runyan, like all other professionals, had to pay his traveling expenses, caddy fees, etc., it meant that at the end of the season he had paid out about $6,765 for the chance to earn $6,767, meaning his net income

for being the champion tournament player was $2. Others less successful than Runyan finished the year with deficits.

In 1935 there were 34 tournaments open to professional competition. The gross value was $135,000. The big money winner was Johnny Revolta, with $9,543. The balance of the prize money was divided among 226 other contestants.

Since then, largely through the influence of Fred Corcoran, a promoter, the amount of money put up as prizes was tremendously increased. The vast difference wrought by the efforts of Corcoran is shown by the fact that in 1945, the No. 1 earner, Byron Nelson, earned a total of $52,511. Other golfers, even those who finished far down the list, won more than their operating expenses.

In 1952, Julius Boros, who won the United States Open championship and also a $25,000 purse, the largest posted up to that time, at the Tam O'Shanter Country Club, near Chicago, was the leading money-winner with $37,032.97. Fourteen others won at least $10,000. In 1956, Ted Kroll was high with $72,835. With the increase of tournaments and prize money, by 1963 Arnold Palmer was leading money-winner with $128,230. In 1972 Jack Nicklaus won $280,482.

Women professionals became numerous enough to organize after World War II, and under the guidance of Hope Seignious of Greensboro, N.C., they formed the Women's Professional Golfers' Association. Patty Berg was the first president.

This organization conducted Open championships in 1946, 1947 and 1948. In 1949 there was a reorganization which resulted in the formation Ladies' Professional Golfers' Association, with Miss Berg as president and Corcoran as tournament director. This group continued the Open championships through 1952.

In 1953 the United States Golf Association assumed responsibility for the women's Open championship at the request of the L.P.G.A. At the same time Mrs. Mildred Didrikson Zaharias succeeded Miss Berg as president.

Today there are some 3 million female golfers in the country, with the number of lady pros increasing every year, the average age being between 25 and 30 and about 90 percent of them single. Two of the richest female golfers are Hall of Famer Mickey Wright, who has won almost $350,000, and the all-time money-winner at $500,000, Kathy Whitworth.

The game of golf gained its first national headquarters in January, 1951, when the U.S.G.A. opened "Golf House" at 40 East Thirty-eighth Street, New York, N.Y. "Golf House" serves not only as the U.S.G.A. headquarters, but also as a museum and library in which are preserved records of the game from its beginnings, old and modern clubs and balls, old and modern books and magazines and record books, clubs of champion players, photographs of U.S.G.A. champions and teams and a variety of other exhibits.

"Golf House" was purchased through the contributions of golfers and golf clubs and associations and is open for inspection every weekday.

During 1951 the U.S.G.A. and the Royal and Ancient Golf Club of St. Andrews, Scotland, engaged in negotiations abroad leading to the adoption of a uniform code of rules, which became effective generally throughout the world in 1952. Through the first half of the 20th Century the two bodies had made several revisions in their separate codes so that they had been getting further and further apart in details. The only difference now between the two codes is in the size of the ball. A slightly smaller ball is used in Great Britain because of the different conditions of wind and terrain prevailing there.

The weight and diameter of the golf ball have been subjected to many changes, all designed to create a ball with a maximum carry. The present official ball in the United States weighs 1.62 ounces and is 1.68 inches in diameter.

Bogey was the first term used in golf to indicate a score an ordinary golfer should make and generally was known as "Colonel Bogey." It came into use in the early days of the game abroad.

As accuracy increased and the players scored much better, the term bogey passed out of use. The skill of a player, thereafter, came to be measured by how close he could come to par. Par is fixed by a yardage scale and came into existence in the United States in the early years of the 20th Century to provide a basis for handicapping. Though technically incorrect, bogey is frequently used today to indicate a one-over-par score for a hole.

FAMOUS PLAYERS

Men

Allan Robertson, St. Andrews, Scotland, professional, undefeated, died in 1858; Tom Morris Jr., St. Andrews, won 4 British Opens (1868, 1869, 1870, 1872), died at the age of 24; Harry Vardon, England, won 6 British Opens (1896, 1898, 1899, 1903, 1911, 1914) and the United States Open (1900); John Ball, Hoylake, England, won 8 British Amateurs (1888, 1890, 1892, 1894, 1899, 1907, 1910, 1912) and was the first amateur to win the British Open (1890); Harold Hilton, Hoylake, won 4 British Amateurs (1900, 1901, 1911, 1913), the United States Amateur (1911) and 2 British Opens (1892, 1897).

Also, Francis Ouimet, Boston, first amateur to win the United States Open (1913) and a double winner of the United States Amateur (1914, 1931); Walter Hagen, Rochester, N.Y., won 2 United States Opens (1914, 1919), broke the British dominance in the British Open by win-

ning 4 times (1922, 1924, 1928, 1929) and won 5 United States P.G.A. championships (1921, 1924, 1925, 1926, 1927); Gene Sarazen, New York, won 2 United States Opens (1922, 1932), the British Open (1932) and 3 United States P.G.A. titles (1922, 1923, 1933) the 1935 Masters, the 1954 P.G.A. Seniors; Robert T. Jones Jr., Atlanta, Ga., amateur, won 13 major championships (between 1923 and 1930) and made his "Grand Slam" by winning the British Amateur, British Open, United States Open and United States Amateur (1930); Ben Hogan, Fort Worth, Tex., won the United States Open in 1948, suffered serious injuries in an automobile accident in 1949 and then won it again in 1950, 1951, and 1953; won 2 P.G.A. crowns (1946, 1948); Arnold Palmer won the British Open (1961, 1962) and U.S. Open (1960); Lee Trevino won 2 U.S. Opens (1968, 1971), the British Open (1971, 1972), and Canadian Open (1971); Jack Nicklaus won the Augusta Masters in 1972, the P.G.A. (1963, 1971), the U.S. Open 3 times (1962, 1967, 1972), and the British Open (1966, 1970).

Women

Beatrix Hoyt, New York, won 3 United States championships (1896, 1897, 1898); Mrs. Dorothy Campbell Hurd, North Berwick, Scotland, and Philadelphia, won 2 British (1909, 1911), 3 United States (1909, 1910, 1924) and 3 Canadian (1910, 1911, 1912); Gladys Ravenscroft, England, won the British (1912) and the United States (1912); Alexa Stirling, Atlanta, won 3 United States (1916, 1919, 1920) and 2 Canadian (1920, 1934); Joyce Wethered, England, won 4 British (1922, 1924, 1925, 1929). Also, Mrs. Glenna Collett Vare, Philadelphia, won 6 United States (1922, 1925, 1928, 1929, 1930, 1935), 2 Canadian (1923, 1924) and was twice runner-up in the British (1929, 1930); Pam Barton, England, won both the British and United States (1936); Patty Berg, Minneapolis, won the United States Women's Amateur (1938) and the first Women's Open (1946); Mrs. Mildred Didrikson Zaharias, Tampa, Fla., won the United States Amateur (1946), was the first American to win the British Amateur (1947) and also won 3 United States Women's Opens (1948, 1950, 1954); Louise Suggs, Atlanta, won the United States Amateur (1947), the British Amateur (1948) and 2 United States Women's Opens (1949, 1952); Jo Anne Gunderson Carner won the U.S. Amateur 4 times (1957, 1960, 1966, 1968), and the U.S. Open in 1971; Mary Mills won the L.P.G.A. in 1964, 1973, and the Women's U.S. Open in 1963; Kathy Whitworth won the L.P.G.A. in 1967, 1971.

BOBBY JONES–RECORDS AND "GRAND SLAM"

Little debate will be provoked if Robert T.

Jones Jr. of Atlanta, Ga., is nominated as the greatest amateur golfer of all time.

He won his first title in 1911—the junior championship of Atlanta—when he was 9. He won three invitation tournaments in Atlanta in 1915. He won four championships in 1916—when he was 14—including the Georgia State title. And in the same year he made his first appearance in the United States Amateur.

In 1930, as a climax to his career, Jones made the "Grand Slam" in golf. He won the British Amateur and the British Open, returned here and won the U.S.G.A. Open and then the U.S.G.A. Amateur. The feat, never accomplished before, or since, follows:

British Amateur—May, at St. Andrews, Scotland. Drew bye in the first round; defeated Sidney Roper, 3 and 2; defeated Cowan Shankland, 5 and 3; defeated Cyril J.H. Tolley, defending champion, 1 up (19 holes); defeated G. O. Watt, 4 and 2; defeated H. R. Johnson, 1929 U.S. amateur champion, 1 up; defeated Eric W. Fiddian, 4 and 3; defeated George Voigt in semi-finals, 1 up; defeated Roger H. Wethered in final, 7 and 6.

British Open—June, at Hoylake. Qualified with 150. Then shot 70, 72, 74, 75—291 in field of 400.

U.S.G.A. Open—July, at Interlachen, Minneapolis—Shot 71, 73, 68, 75—287.

U.S.G.A. Amateur—September, at Merion Cricket Club—Sept. 22, shot 69 to lead first-round qualifiers; Sept. 23, shot 73 to make his total 142, winning medal; Sept. 24, defeated C. Ross Somerville, 5 and 4, and defeated J. G. Hoblitzel, 5 and 4 (both at 18 holes); Sept. 25, defeated Fay Coleman, 6 and 5 (36 holes); Sept. 26, defeated Jess Sweetser, 9 and 8 (36 holes); Sept. 27, defeated Eugene Homans, 8 and 7, in final.

Highlights of Jones' Career

1911 (Age 9)—Won junior championship cup of Atlanta Athletic Club.

1912 (Age 10)—Lost in semi-final round of junior champhionship at Atlanta Athletic Club.

1913 (Age 11)—Played his first 80-stroke round at East Lake Course.

1915 (Age 13)—Qualified in Southern Amateur, but lost in second round.

1916 (Age 14)—Won Georgia State Amateur championship. Jones, playing in his first National Amateur championship, beat E. M. Byers and F. W. Dyer, then lost to Bob Gardner, 4 and 3, in third round at Merion. Bob qualified with a 74 for the first round and an 89 on the second.

1917 (Age 15)—Won Southern Amateur championship.

1919 (Age 17)—Lost to S. Davidson Herron, 5 and 4, in final of National Amateur championship. Finished in tie for second in Canadian Open.

1920 (Age 18)—Won Southern Amateur. Tied for medal with F. J. Wright Jr., with 154 in National Amateur, but was beaten in semi-final round by Frances Ouimet, 6 and 5. Jones playing in his first National Open, tied for eighth place with 299, four strokes behind the winner, Ted Ray.

1921 (Age 19)—Jones qualified with 151 in the National Amateur, then beat Clarence Wolff, 12 and 11, and Dr. O. F. Willing, 9 and 8, but lost to Willie Hunter, 2 and 1, in the third round. Tied for fifth in National Open with 303, fourteen strokes behind the winner, Jim Barnes. Withdrew from British Open after scoring 78 and 74 because he was dissatisfied with his playing. Lost to Allen Graham in fourth round of British Amateur.

1922 (Age 20)—Tied for second in National Open with 289, one stroke behind the winner, Gene Sarazen. Lost to Jess Sweetser, 8 and 7, in semi-final round of National Amateur. Won Southern Amateur. Won both matches in Walker Cup competition.

1923 (Age 21)—Won National Open for first time, beating Bobby Cruickshank in play-off, 76 to 78. Jones had regular rounds of 71, 73, 76, 76—296 and Cruickshank 73, 72, 78, 73. Qualified for National Amateur with 149, tying for the medal with Chick Evans. Lost to Max Marston, 2 and 1, in second round.

1924 (Age 22)—Won National Amateur for first time, beating George Von Elm, 9 and 8, in final. Finished second in National Open with 300, three strokes behind the winner, Cyril Walker. Won singles, lost foursome match in Walker Cup play.

1925 (Age 23)—Won National Amateur, defeating Watts Gunn, 8 and 7, in final. Lost to Willie Macfarlane in National Open playoff, 72 to 73, after each had finished regulation play with 291's.

1926 (Age 24)—Qualifying with scores of 66, 68 at Sunningdale, Bobby went on to St. Anne's and became the first American amateur to win the British Open title, with a 72-hole aggregate of 291. Won National Open with 293. Won National Amateur medal with 143, but lost to George Von Elm, 2 and 1, in final. Lost to Andrew Jamieson, 4 and 3, in British Amateur quarter-finals. Won both Walker Cup matches.

1927 (Age 25)—Finished in quadruple tie for eleventh in National Amateur. Won National Amateur, beating Chick Evans,

8 and 7, in final. Won British Open with record score of 285.

1928 (Age 26)—Won National Amateur, defeating T. Philip Perkins, 10 and 9, in final. Lost to Johnny Farrell in National Open playoff, 143-144, after both finished regular play with 294's. Won both Walker Cup matches.

1929 (Age 27)—Tied with Eugene V. Homans for National Amateur medal with 149, but lost to Johnny Goodman, 1 up, in first round. Tied Al Espinosa for first in National Open and then won 36-hole play off, 141 to 164.

1930 (Age 28)—Won British Open for third time with score of 291. Won British Amateur first time. Won National Open fourth time. Won National Amateur fifth time. Won both Walker Cup matches.

Golf Champions and Statistics

UNITED STATES U.S.G.A. Open

Year and champion	1st	2d	3d	4th	Tot.	Site
		Rounds				
1894 (match play)—Willie Dunn (a)						St. Andrew's
1895—Horace Rawlins	45	46	41	41	173	Newport
1896—James Foulis	78	74	—	—	152	Shinnecock Hills
1897—Joe Lloyd	83	79	—	—	162	Chicago
1898—Fred Herd	84	85	75	84	328	Myopia Hunt Club
1899—Willie Smith	77	82	79	77	315	Baltimore
1900—Harry Vardon (England)	79	78	76	80	313	Chicago
1901—Willie Anderson (b)	84	83	83	81	331	Myopia Hunt Club
1902—Lawrence Auchterlonie	78	78	74	77	307	Garden City G.C.
1903—Willie Anderson (c)	73	76	76	82	307	Baltusrol
1904—Willie Anderson	75	78	78	72	303	Glen View
1905—Willie Anderson	81	80	76	77	314	Myopia Hunt Club
1906—Alex Smith	73	74	73	75	295	Onwentsia
1907—Alex Ross	76	74	76	76	302	Philadelphia
1908—Fred McLoed (d)	82	82	81	77	322	Myopia Hunt Club
1909—George Sargent	75	72	72	71	290	Englewood
1910—Alex Smith (e)	73	73	79	73	298	Philadelphia
1911—John J. McDermott (f)	81	72	75	79	307	Chicago
1912—John J. McDermott	74	75	74	71	294	Buffalo
1913—Francis Ouimet (g)	77	74	74	79	304	Brookline
1914—Walter Hagen	68	74	75	73	290	Midlothian
1915—Jerome D. Travers	76	72	73	76	297	Baltusrol
1916—Charles Evans Jr.	70	69	74	73	286	Minikahda
1917-18—No competition						
1919—Walter Hagen (h)	78	73	75	75	301	Brae Burn
1920—Edward (Ted) Ray (England)	74	73	73	75	295	Inverness
1921—James M. Barnes	69	75	73	72	289	Columbia
1922—Gene Sarazen	72	73	75	68	288	Skokie
1923—Robert T. Jones Jr. (i)	71	73	76	76	296	Inwood
1924—Cyril Walker	74	74	74	75	297	Oakland Hills
1925—Willie Macfarlane (j)	74	67	72	78	291	Worcester
1926—Robert T. Jones Jr.	70	79	71	73	293	Scioto
1927—Tommy Armour (k)	78	71	76	76	301	Oakmont
1928—Johnny Farrell (l)	77	74	71	72	294	Olympia Fields
1929—Robert T. Jones Jr. (m)	69	75	71	79	294	Winged Foot
1930—Robert T. Jones Jr.	71	73	68	75	287	Interlachen
1931—Billy Burke (n)	73	72	74	73	292	Inverness
1932—Gene Sarazen	74	76	70	66	286	Fresh Meadow
1933—Johnny Goodman	75	66	70	76	287	North Shore
1934—Olin Dutra	76	74	71	72	293	Merion
1935—Sam Parks Jr.	77	73	73	76	299	Oakmont
1936—Tony Manero	73	69	73	67	282	Baltusrol
1937—Ralph Guldahl	71	69	72	69	281	Oakland Hills
1938—Ralph Guldahl	74	70	71	69	284	Cherry Hills

1939—Byron Nelson (o)	72	73	71	68	284	Philadelphia
1940—W. Lawson Little Jr. (p)	72	69	73	73	287	Canterbury
1941—Craig Wood	73	71	70	70	284	Colonial
1942—No championship (q)						
1943-45—No competition						
1946—Lloyd Mangrum (r)	74	70	68	72	284	Canterbury
1947—Lew Worsham (s)	70	70	71	71	282	St. Louis
1948—Ben Hogan	67	72	68	69	276	Riviera
1949—Cary Middlecoff	75	67	69	75	286	Medinah
1950—Ben Hogan (t)	72	69	72	74	287	Merion
1951—Ben Hogan	76	73	71	67	287	Oakland Hills
1952—Julius Boros	71	71	68	71	281	Northwood
1953—Ben Hogan	67	72	73	71	283	Oakmont
1954—Ed Furgol	71	70	71	72	284	Baltusrol
1955—Jack Fleck (u)	76	69	75	67	287	Olympic
1956—Cary Middlecoff	71	70	70	70	281	Oak Hill
1957—Dick Mayer (v)	70	68	74	70	282	Inverness
1958—Tommy Bolt	71	71	69	72	283	Southern Hills
1959—Bill Casper Jr.	71	68	69	74	282	Winged Foot
1960—Arnold Palmer	72	71	72	65	280	Cherry Hills
1961—Gene Littler	73	68	72	68	281	Oakland Hills
1962—Jack Nicklaus	72	70	72	69	283	Oakmont
1963—Julius Boros	71	74	76	72	293	Brookline
1964—Ken Venturi	72	70	66	70	278	Congressional
1965—Gary Player	70	70	71	71	282	Bellerive
1966—Billy Casper	69	68	73	68	278	Olympic
1967—Jack Nicklaus	71	67	72	65	275	Baltusrol
1968—Lee Trevino	69	68	69	69	275	Oak Hill
1969—Orville Moody	71	70	68	72	281	Champions
1970—Tony Jacklin	71	70	70	70	281	Hazeltine
1971—Lee Trevino (w)	70	72	69	69	280	Merion
1972—Jack Nicklaus	71	73	72	74	290	Pebble Beach
1973—Johnny Miller	71	69	76	63	279	Oakmont

(a) Dunn beat Willie Campbell, 2 up.

(b) Anderson beat Alex Smith in play-off, 85-86.

(c) Anderson beat David Brown in play-off, 82-84.

(d) McLeod beat Willie Smith in play-off, 77-83.

(e) Smith beat John J. McDermott and Mac-Donald Smith in play-off, 71 to McDermott's 75 and Smith's 77.

(f) McDermott beat M. J. Brady and G. O. Simpson in play-off, 80 to Brady's 82 and Simpson's 85.

(g) Ouimet beat Harry Vardon and Edward (Ted) Ray in play-off, 72 to Vardon's 77 and Ray's 78.

(h) Hagen beat M. J. Brady in play-off, 77-78.

(i) Jones beat Bobby Cruickshank in play-off, 76-78.

(j) Macfarlane beat Robert T. Jones Jr. in 36-hole play-off, 147-148.

(k) Armour beat Harry Cooper in play-off, 76-79.

(l) Farrell beat Robert T. Jones Jr. in 36-hole play-off, 143-144.

(m) Jones beat Al Espinosa in 36-hole play-off, 141-164.

(n) Burke beat George Von Elm in second 36-hole play-off, 148-149, after each scored 149 in first play-off.

(o) Nelson beat Denny Shute in first play-off, 68-78, but was tied by Craig Wood. Nelson beat Wood, 70-73, in second play-off.

(p) Little beat Gene Sarazen, 70-73, in play-off.

(q) In 1917, Jock Hutchison, with a 292, won an Open Patriotic Tournament for the benefit of the American Red Cross at the White-marsh Valley Country Club. In 1942, Ben Hogan, with a 271, won a Hale America National Open Tournament for the benefit of the Navy Relief Society and United Service Organizations at the Ridgemoor Country Club.

(r) Mangrum beat Victor Ghezzi and Byron Nelson in second play-off, 72 to Ghezzi's and Nelson's 73. Each shot a 72 on first play-off.

(s) Worsham beat Sam Snead in play-off, 69-70.

(t) Hogan beat Lloyd Mangrum and George Fazio in play-off, 69 to Mangrum's 73 and Fazio's 75.

(u) Fleck beat Ben Hogan in play-off, 69-72.

(v) Mayer beat Cary Middlecoff in play-off, 72-79.

(w) Trevino defeated Jack Nicklaus, 68-71, in 18-hole play-off.

Two tournaments were held prior to 1895, both in 1894. One was a medal play competition at the Newport Golf Club which W. G. Lawrence won with a score of 188 for 36 holes; the other was a match play competition at the St. Andrew's Golf Club won by L. B. Stoddard, who beat Charles B. Macdonald, 1 up.

U.S.G.A. Amateur

1895—Charles B. Macdonald beat C. E. Sands, 12 and 11, at Newport (R.I.) G.C.

1896—H. G. Whigham beat J. G. Thorp, 8 and 7, at Shinnecock Hills (N.Y.) G.C.

1897—H. G. Whigham beat W. R. Betts, 8 and 6, at Chicago G.C., Wheaton, Ill.

1898—Findlay S. Douglas beat W. B. Smith, 5 and 3, at Morris County G.C., Morristown, N.J.

1899—H. M. Harriman beat Findlay S. Douglas, 3 and 2, at Onwentsia Club, Lake Forest, Ill.

1900—Walter J. Travis beat Findlay S. Douglas, 2 up, at Garden City (N.Y.) G.C.

1901—Walter J. Travis beat W. E. Egan, 5 and 4, at C.C. of Atlantic City, Atlantic City, N.J.

1902—L. N. James beat E. M. Byers, 4 and 2, at Glen View G.C., Golf, Ill.

1903—Walter J. Travis beat E. M. Byers, 5 and 4, at Nassau C.C., Glen Cove, N.Y.

1904—H. Chandler Egan beat Fred Herreshoff, 8 and 6, at Baltusrol G.C., Short Hills, N.J.

1905—H. Chandler Egan beat D. E. Sawyer, 6 and 5, at Chicago G.C., Wheaton, Ill.

1906—E. M. Byers beat G. S. Lyon, 2 up, at Englewood (N.J.) G.C.

1907—Jerome D. Travers beat Archibald Graham, 6 and 5, at Euclid Club, Cleveland.

1908—Jerome D. Travers beat Max Behr, 8 and 7, at Garden City G.C.

1909—R. A. Gardner beat H. Chandler Egan, 4 and 3, at Chicago G.C.

1910—W. C. Fownes Jr. beat W. K. Wood, 4 and 3, at The Country Club, Brookline, Mass.

1911—Harold H. Hilton beat Fred Herreshoff, 1 up (37 holes), at Apawamis Club, Rye, N.Y.

1912—Jerome D. Travers beat Charles Evans Jr., 7 and 6, at Chicago G.C.

1913—Jerome D. Travers beat J. G. Anderson, 5 and 4, at Garden City G.C.

1914—Francis Ouimet beat Jerome D. Travers, 6 and 5, at Ekwanok C.C., Manchester, Vt.

1915—Robert A. Gardner beat J. G. Anderson, 5 and 4, at C.C. of Detroit, Grosse Point Farms, Mich.

1916—Charles Evans Jr. beat Robert A. Gardner, 4 and 3, at Merion Cricket Club, Haverford, Pa.

1917-18—No competition

1919—S. D. Herron beat Robert T. Jones Jr., 5 and 4, at Oakmont (Pa.) C.C.

1920—Charles Evans Jr. beat Francis Ouimet, 7 and 6, at Engineers C.C., Roslyn, N.Y.

1921—Jesse P. Guilford beat Robert A. Gardner, 7 and 6, at St. Louis C.C.

1922—Jess W. Sweetser beat Charles Evans Jr., 3 and 2, at The Country Club, Brookline.

1923—Max R. Marston beat Jess W. Sweetser, 1 up (38 holes), at Flossmoor (Ill.) C.C.

1924—Robert T. Jones Jr. beat George Von Elm, 9 and 6, at Merion Cricket Club.

1925—Robert T. Jones Jr. beat Watts Gunn, 8 and 7, at Oakmont C.C.

1926—George Von Elm beat Robert T. Jones Jr., 2 and 1, at Baltusrol G.C.

1927—Robert T. Jones Jr. beat Charles Evans Jr., 8 and 7, at Minikahda Club, Minneapolis.

1928—Robert T. Jones Jr. beat T. Philip Perkins, 10 and 9, at Brae Burn C.C., West Newton, Mass.

1929—Harrison R. Johnston beat Dr. O. F. Willing, 4 and 3, at Pebble Beach Course, Del Monte, Calif.

1930—Robert T. Jones Jr., beat Eugene Homans, 8 and 7, at Merion C.C.

1931—Francis Ouimet beat Jack Westland, 6 and 5, at Beverly C.C., Chicago.

1932—C. Ross Somerville beat Johnny Goodman, 2 and 1, at Baltimore C.C.

1933—George T. Dunlap Jr. beat Max R. Marston, 6 and 5, at Kenwood C.C., Cincinnati.

1934—W. Lawson Little Jr. beat David Goldman, 8 and 7, at The Country Club, Brookline.

1935—W. Lawson Little Jr. beat Walter Emery, 4 and 2, at C.C. of Cleveland.

1936—John W. Fischer beat Jack McLean, 1 up (37 holes), at Garden City G.C.

1937—Johnny Goodman beat Ray Billows, 2 up, at Alderwood G.C., Portland, Ore.

1938—Willie Turnesa beat B. Patrick Abbott, 8 and 7, at Oakmont C.C.

1939—Marvin Ward beat Ray Billows, 7 and 5, at North Shore C.C., Glen View, Ill.

1940—Richard D. Chapman beat W. B. McCullough, 11 and 9, at Winged Foot G.C., Mamaroneck, N.Y.

1941—Marvin Ward beat B. Patrick Abbott, 4 and 3, at Omaha (Neb.) F.C.

1942-45—No competition

1946—Ted Bishop beat Smiley Quick, 1 up (37 holes), at Baltusrol G.C.

1947—Robert H. Riegel beat Johnny Dawson, 2 and 1, at Pebble Beach Course.

1948—Willie Turnesa beat Ray Billows, 2 and 1, at Memphis (Tenn.) C.C.

1949—Charles R. Coe beat Rufus King, 11 and 10, at Oak Hill C.C., Rochester, N.Y.

1950—Sam Urzetta beat Frank R. Stranahan, 1 up (39 holes), at Minneapolis G.C.

1951—Billy Maxwell beat Joseph F. Gagliardi, 4 and 3, at Saucon Valley C.C., Bethlehem, Pa.

1952—Jack Westland beat Al Mengert, 3 and 2, at Seattle (Wash.) G.C.

1953—Gene Littler beat Dale Morey, 1 up, at Oklahoma City (Okla.) G. C.

1954—Arnold Palmer beat Robert Sweeny, 1 up, at C.C. of Detroit, Mich.

1955—Harvie Ward beat William Hyndman 2d, 9 and 8, at C.C. of Virginia, Richmond, Va.

1956—Harvie Ward beat Chuck Kocsis, 5 and 4, at Knollwood C.C., Lake Forest, Ill.

1957—Hillman Robbins beat Frank (Bud) Taylor, 5 and 4, at The Country Club, Brookline, Mass.

1958—Charles Coe beat Tommy Aaron, 5 and 4, at Olympia C.C., San Fransisco, Calif.

1959—Jack Nicklaus beat Charles R. Coe, 1 up, at Broadmoor C.C. Colorado Springs, Colo.

1960—Deane Beman beat Robert W. Gardner, 6 and 4, at St. Louis C.C., Clayton, Mo.

1961—Jack Nicklaus beat H. Dudley Wysong, 8 and 6, at Pebble Beach C.C., Del Monte, Calif.

1962—Labron Harris Jr. beat Downing Gray, 1 up, at Pinehurst C.C., North Carolina.

1963—Deane Beman beat R. H. Sikes, 2 and 1, at Wakonda C.C., Des Moines, Ia.

1964—Bill Campbell defeated Ed Tutwiler, 1 up, at Canterbury G.C., Cleveland, Ohio.

1965—Bob Murphy beat Bob Dickson, 291 to 292, at Southern Hills C.C., Tulsa, Okla.

1966—Gary Cowan beat Deane Beman, 285-75 to 285-76, at Merion G.C., Ardmore, Penn.

1967—Bob Dickson defeated Vinnie Giles, 285 to 286, at Colorado Springs, Colorado.

1968—Bruce Fleisher defeated Vinnie Giles, 284 to 285, at Columbus, Ohio.

1969—Steve Melnyk defeated Vinnie Giles, 286 to 291, at Oakmont (Pa.) C.C.

1970—Lanny Wadkins beat Tom Kite, Jr., 279 to 280, at Waverly C.C., Portland, Ore.

1971—Gary Cowan defeated Eddie Pearce, 280 to 283, at Wilmington (Del) C.C.

1972—Vinnie Giles 3rd defeated Ben Crenshaw and Mark Hayes, 285 to 288, at Charlotte, N.C.

Professional Golfers Association

1916—James M. Barnes beat Jock Hutchison, 1 up, at Siwanoy C.C., Bronxville, N.Y.

1917-18—No competition

1919—James M. Barnes beat Fred McLeod, 5 and 4, at Engineers C.C., Roslyn, N.Y.

1920—Jock Hutchison beat J. Douglas Edgar, 1 up, at Flossmoor (Ill.) C.C.

1921—Walter Hagen beat James M. Barnes, 3 and 2, at Inwood (N.Y.) C.C.

1922—Gene Sarazen beat Emmet French, 4 and 3, at Oakmont (Pa.) C.C.

1923—Gene Sarazen beat Walter Hagen, 1 up (38 holes), at Pelham (N.Y.) C.C.

1924—Walter Hagen beat James M. Barnes, 2 up at French Lick Springs (Ind.) G.C.

1925—Walter Hagen beat William Mehlhorn, 6 and 5, at Olympia Fields (Ill.) C.C.

1926—Walter Hagen beat Leo Diegel, 5 and 3, at Salisbury Links, Salisbury Plains, N.Y.

1927—Walter Hagen beat Joe Turnesa, 1 up, at Cedar Crest C.C., Dallas.

1928—Leo Diegel beat Al Espinosa, 6 and 5, at Five Farms Course, Baltimore, C.C.

1929—Leo Diegel beat Johnny Farrell, 6 and 4, at Hillcrest C.C., Los Angeles.

1930—Tommy Armour beat Gene Sarazen, 1 up, at Fresh Meadow C.C., Flushing, N.Y.

1931—Tom Creavy beat Denny Shute, 2 and 1, at Wannamoisett C.C., Rumford, R.I.

1932—Olin Dutra beat Frank Walsh, 4 and 3, at Keller Links, St. Paul.

1933—Gene Sarazen beat Willie Goggin, 5 and 4, at Blue Mound C.C., Wauwatosa, Wis.

1934—Paul Runyan beat Craig Wood, 1 up (38 holes), at Park Club, Buffalo, N.Y.

1935—Johnny Revolta beat Tommy Armour, 5 and 4, at Twin Hills C.C., Oklahoma City, Okla.

1936—Denny Shute beat Jimmy Thomson, 3 and 2, at Pinehurst (N.C.) C.C.

1937—Denny Shute beat Harold McSpaden, 1 up (37 holes), at Pittsburgh F.C., Aspinwall, Pa.

1938—Paul Runyan beat Sam Snead, 8 and 7, at Shawnee, C.C., Shawnee-on-Delaware, Pa.

1939—Henry Picard beat Byron Nelson, 1 up (37 holes), at Pomonok C.C., Flushing, N.Y.

1940—Byron Nelson beat Sam Snead, 1 up, at Hershey (Pa.) C.C.

1941—Vic Ghezzi beat Byron Nelson, 1 up (38 holes), at Cherry Hills, C.C. Denver.

1942—Sam Snead beat Cpl. Jimmy Turnesa, 2 and 1, at Seaview C.C., Absecon, N.J.

1943—No competition

1944—Bob Hamilton beat Byron Nelson, 1 up, at Manito G. and C.C., Spokane, Wash.

1945—Byron Nelson beat Sam Byrd, 4 and 3, at Moraine C.C., Dayton, Ohio.

1946–Ben Hogan beat Ed Oliver, 6 and 4, at Portland (Ore.) C.C.

1947–Jim Ferrier beat Chick Harbert, 2 and 1, at Plum Hollow G.C., Detroit.

1948–Ben Hogan beat Mike Turnesa, 7 and 6, at Norwood Hills C.C., St. Louis.

1949–Sam Snead beat Johnny Palmer, 3 and 2, at Hermitage C.C., Richmond, Va.

1950–Chandler Harper beat Henry Williams Jr., 4 and 3, Scioto C.C., Columbus, Ohio.

1951–Sam Snead beat Walter Burkemo, 7 and 6, at Oakmont C.C.

1952–Jim Turnesa beat Chick Harbert, 1 up, at Big Spring G.C., Louisville.

1953–Walter Burkemo beat Felice Torza, 2 and 1, at Birmingham (Mich.) C.C.

1954–Chick Harbert beat Walter Burkemo, 4 and 3, at Keller Links, St. Paul, Minn.

1955–Doug Ford beat Cary Middlecoff, 4 and 3, at Meadow Brook C.C., Northville, Mich.

1956–Jack Burke beat Ted Kroll, 3 and 2, at Blue Hill C.C., Canton, Mass.

1957–Lionel Hebert beat Dow Finsterwald, 2 and 1, at Miami Valley Club, Dayton, Ohio.

1958–Dow Finsterwald, 276, Havertown, Pa.

(Note: In 1958, the tournament was changed to 72-hole medal play.)

1959–Bob Rosburg, 277, Minneapolis C.C.

1960–Jay Herbert, 281, Firestone, C.C.

1961–Jerry Barber, 277, beat Don January in playoff, 67 to 68, Dunedin, Fla.

1962–Gary Player, 278, Aromink C.C., Newton Square, Pa.

1963–Jack Nicklaus, 279, Dallas (Texas) A.C. C.C.

1964–Bobby Nichols, 271, Columbus C.C.

1965–Dave Marr, 280, Laurel Valley G.C., Ligonier, Penn.

1966–Al Geiberger, 280, Firestone C.C., Akron, Ohio.

1967–Don January won playoff, 69 to 71, over Don Massengale, at Columbine Country Club, Littleton, Colorado.

1968–Julius Boros, 281, at Pecan Valley C.C., San Antonio, Tex.

1969–Ray Floyd, 276, at National Cash Register C.C., Dayton, Ohio.

1970–Dave Stockton, 279, at Southern Hills C.C., Tulsa, Okla.

1971–Jack Nicklaus, 281, at Palm Beach (Fla.) Gardens.

1972–Gary Player, 281, at Birmingham, Mich.

Augusta Masters

Year and winner	Score
1934–Horton Smith	284
1935–Gene Sarazen*	282
1936–Horton Smith	285
1937–Byron Nelson	283
1938–Henry Picard	285
1939–Ralph Guldahl	279
1940–Jimmy Demaret	280
1941–Craig Wood	280
1942–Byron Nelson	280
1943-45–No competition	
1946–Herman Keiser	282
1947–Jimmy Demaret	281
1948–Claude Harmon	279
1949–Sam Snead	282
1950–Jimmy Demaret	283
1951–Ben Hogan	280
1952–Sam Snead	286
1953–Ben Hogan	274
1954–Sam Snead*	289
1955–Cary Middlecoff	279
1956–Jack Burke	289
1957–Doug Ford	283
1958–Arnold Palmer	284
1959–Art Wall Jr.	284
1960–Arnold Palmer	282
1961–Gary Player	280
1962–Arnold Palmer*	280
1963–Jack Nicklaus	286
1964–Arnold Palmer	276
1965–Jack Nicklaus	271
1966–Jack Nicklaus*	288
1967–Gay Brewer	280
1968–Bob Goalby	277
1969–George Archer	281
1970–Billy Casper*	279
1971–Charles Coody	279
1972–Jack Nicklaus	286

* Won play-off.

National Intercollegiate Individual

(Conducted by the Intercollegiate Golf Association of America from 1897 through 1938; by the National Collegiate Athletic Association since 1939.)

1897–Louis P. Bayard Jr., Princeton

1898 (spring)–John Reid Jr., Yale

1898 (fall)–James F. Curtis, Harvard

1899–Percy Pyne 2d, Princeton

1900–No competition

1901–H. Lindsley, Harvard

1902 (spring)–Charles Hitchcock Jr., Yale

1902 (fall)–H. Chandler Egan, Harvard

1903–F. O. Reinhart, Princeton

1904–A. L. White, Harvard

1905–Robert Abbott, Yale

1906–W. E. Clow Jr., Yale

1907–Ellis Knowles, Yale

1908–H. H. Wilder, Harvard

1909–Albert Seckel, Princeton

1910–Robert E. Hunter, Yale

1911–George C. Stanley, Yale

1912–F. C. Davison, Harvard

1913–Nathaniel Wheeler, Yale

1914–Edward P. Allis 3d, Harvard

1915–Francis R. Blossom, Yale

1916–J. W. Hubbell, Harvard
1917-18–No competition
1919–A. L. Walker Jr., Columbia
1920–Jess W. Sweetser, Yale
1921–J. Simpson Dean, Princeton
1922–Pollock Boyd, Dartmouth
1923-24–Dexter Cummings, Yale
1925-26–G. Fred Lamprecht, Tulane
1927–Watts Gunn, Georgia Tech
1928–M. J. McCarthy Jr., Georgetown
1929–Tom Aycock, Yale
1930-31–George T. Dunlap Jr., Princeton
1932–John W. Fischer Jr., Michigan
1933–Walter Emery, Oklahoma
1934–Charles R. Yates, Georgia Tech
1935–Ed White, Texas
1936–Charles Kocsis, Michigan
1937–Fred Haas Jr., Louisiana State
1938–John P. Burke, Georgetown
1939–Vincent D'Antoni, Tulane
1940–F. Dixon Brooke, Virginia
1941–Earl Stewart, Louisiana State
1942–Frank Tatum Jr., Stanford
1943–Wallace Ulrich, Carleton
1944–Louis Lick, Minnesota
1945–John Lorms, Ohio State
1946–George Hamer, Georgia
1947–Dave Barclay, Michigan
1948–Bobby Harris, San Jose State
1949–Harvie Ward, North Carolina
1950–Fred Wampler, Purdue
1951–Tom Nieporte, Ohio State
1952–Jim Vickers, Oklahoma
1953–Earl Moeller, Oklahoma A. and M.
1954–Hillman Robbins, Memphis State
1955–Joe Campbell, Purdue
1956–Rick Jones, Ohio State
1957–Rex Baxter, Houston
1958–Phil Rodgers, Houston
1959–Dick Crawford, Houston
1960–Dick Crawford, Houston
1961–Jack Nicklaus, Ohio
1962–Kermit Zarley, Houston
1963–R. H. Sikes, Arkansas
1964–Jerry Potter, Miami (Fla.)
1965–Marty Fleckman, Houston
1966–Bob Murphy, Florida
1967–Hale Irwin, Colorado
1968–Grier Jones, Oklahoma State
1969–Bob Clark, Calif. State (L.A.)
1970–John Mahaffey, Houston
1971–Ben Crenshaw, Texas
1972–Ben Crenshaw, Texas, and
       Tom Kite, Texas (tie)

National Intercollegiate Team

1897–Yale
1898 (spring)–Harvard
1898(fall)–Yale
1899–Harvard
1900–No competition
1901–Harvard

1902 (spring)–Yale
1902 (fall)–Harvard
1903-04–Harvard
1905-13–Yale
1914–Princeton
1915–Yale
1916–Princeton
1917-18–No competition
1919-20–Princeton
1921–Dartmouth
1922-23–Princeton
1924-26–Yale
1927-30–Princeton
1931-33–Yale
1934-35–Michigan
1936–Yale
1937–Princeton
1938-39–Stanford
1940–Princeton, Louisiana State (tie)
1941–Stanford
1942–Stanford, Louisiana State (tie)
1943–Yale
1944–Notre Dame
1945–Ohio State
1946–Stanford
1947–Louisiana State
1948–San Jose State
1949-52–North Texas State
1953–Stanford
1954–Southern Methodist
1955–Louisiana State
1956-60–Houston
1961–Purdue
1962–Houston
1963–Oklahoma State
1964-67–Houston
1968–Florida
1969-70–Houston
1971-72–Texas

Public Links

The United States Golf Association began its Amateur Public Links Championship in 1922. The Standish Cup was put up for winners of the men's individual title and the Harding Cup was awarded to the winners of the team competition. Starting in 1923, the teams first represented cities and later qualifying sections.

The inaugural tournament drew 140 entries for individual play and was won by Edmund R. Held of St. Louis. Currently the entries run into the thousands.

1922–Edmund R. Held
1923–Richard J. Walsh
1924–Joseph Coble
1925–R. J. McAuliffe
1926–Lester Bolstad
1927-29–C. F. Kaufmann
1930–Robert E. Wingate
1931–Charles Ferrera
1932–R.L. Miller
1933–Charles Ferrera

1934—David A. Mitchell
1935—Frank Strafaci
1936—B. Patrick Abbott
1937—Bruce N. McCormick
1938—Al Leach
1939—Andrew Szwedko
1940—Robert C. Clark
1941—William M. Welch
1946—Smiley Quick
1947—Wilfred Crossley
1948—Michael R. Ferentz
1949—Ken Towns
1950—Stan Bielat
1951—Dave Stanley
1952—Omer L. Bogan
1953—Ted Richards
1954—Gene Andrews
1955—Sam Kocsis
1956—Junie Buxbaum
1957—Don Essig
1958—Dan Sikes
1959—Bill Wright
1960—Verne Callison
1961—Dick Sikes
1962—Dick Sikes
1963—Bobby Lunn
1964—Bill McDonald
1965—Arne Dokka
1966—Monty Kaser
1967—Vern Callison
1968—Gene Towry
1969—John Jackson, Jr.
1970—Bob Risch
1971—Fred Haney
1972—Bob Allard*
* Won Playoff.

Ladies Professional Golf Association

1955—Beverly Hanson beat Louise Suggs, 4 and 3, at Orchard Ridge C.C., Ft. Wayne, Ind.
1956—Marlene Hagge won sudden-death playoff over Patty Berg after 291 tie, at Forest Lake C.C., Detroit, Mich.
1957—Louise Suggs beat Wiffi Smith, 285 to 288, at Churchill Valley C.C., Pittsburgh, Penn.
1958—Mickey Wright beat Fay Crocker, 288 to 294, at Churchill Valley C.C., Pittsburgh, Penn.
1959—Betsy Rawls beat Patty Berg, 288 to 289, at Sheraton Hotel C.C., French Lick, Ind.
1960—Mickey Wright beat Louise Suggs, 292 to 295, at Sheraton Hotel C.C., French Lick, Ind.
1961—Mickey Wright beat Louise Suggs, 287 to 296, at Stardust C.C., Las Vegas, Nev.
1962—Judy Kimball beat Shirley Spork, 282 to 286, at Stardust C.C., Las Vegas, Nev.

1963—Mickey Wright beat Mary Mills, Mary Faulk, Louise Suggs, 294 to 296, at Stardust C.C., Las Vegas, Nev.
1964—Mary Mills beat Mickey Wright, 278 to 280, at Stardust C.C., Las Vegas, Nev.
1965—Sandra Haynie beat Clifford A. Creed, 279 to 280, at Stardust C.C., Las Vegas, Nev.
1966—Gloria Ehret beat Mickey Wright, 282 to 285, at Stardust C.C., Las Vegas, Nev.
1967—Kathy Whitworth beat Shirley Englehorn, 284 to 285, at Pleasant Valley C.C., Sutton, Mass.
1968—Sandra Post beat Kathy Whitworth, 294-68 to 294-75, in playoff at Pleasant Valley C.C., Sutton, Mass.
1969—Betsy Rawls beat Carol Mann, 293 to 297, at Concord G.A., Kiamesha Lake, N.Y.
1970—Shirley Englehorn beat Kathy Whitworth, 285-74 to 285-78, in playoff at Pleasant Valley C.C., Sutton, Mass.
1971—Kathy Whitworth beat Kathy Ahern, 288 to 292, at Pleasant Valley C.C., Sutton, Mass.
1972—Kathy Ahern beat Janie Blalock, 293 to 299, at Pleasant Valley C.C., Sutton, Mass.
1973—Mary Mills beat Betty Burfeindt, 288 to 289, at Pleasant Valley C.C., Sutton, Mass.

U.S.G.A. Women's Amateur

1895 (medal play)— Mrs. C.S. Brown, 132, at Meadow Brook G.C., Westbury, N.Y.
1896—Beatrix Hoyt beat Mrs. A. Turnure, 2 and 1, at Morris County G.C., Convent, N.J.
1897—Beatrix Hoyt beat Miss N.C. Sargent, 5 and 4, at Essex County Club, Manchester, Mass.
1898—Beatrix Hoyt beat Maude K. Wetmore, 5 and 3, at Ardsley Club, Ardsley-on-Hudson, N.Y.
1899—Ruth Underhill beat Mrs. Caleb F. Fox, 2 and 1, at Philadelphia C.C., Bala, Pa.
1900—Frances C. Griscom beat Margaret Curtis, 6 and 5, at Shinnecock Hills (N.Y.) G.C.
1901—Genevieve Hecker beat Lucy Herron, 5 and 3, at Baltusrol G.C., Short Hills, N.J.
1902—Genevieve Hecker beat Miss L.A. Wells, 4 and 3, at The Country Club, Brookline, Mass.
1903—Bessie Anthony beat Miss J.A. Carpenter, 7 and 6, at Chicago G.C., Wheaton, Ill.
1904—Georgiana Bishop beat Mrs. E.F. Sanford, 5 and 3, at Merion Cricket Club, Haverford, Pa.

1905—Pauline Mackay beat Margaret Curtis, 1 up, at Morris County G.C.
1906—Harriot S. Curtis beat Miss M.B. Adams, 2 and 1, at Brae Burn C.C., West Newton, Mass.
1907—Margaret Curtis beat Harriot S. Curtis, 7 and 6, at Midlothian C.C., Blue Island, Ill.
1908—Kate C. Harley beat Mrs. T.H. Polhemus, 6 and 5, at Chevy Chase (Md.) Club.
1909—Dorothy Campbell beat Mrs. Ronald H. Barlow, 3 and 2, at Merion Cricket Club.
1910—Dorothy Campbell beat Mrs. G.M. Martin, 2 and 1, at Homewood C.C., Flossmoor, Ill.
1911—Margaret Curtis beat Lillian Hyde, 5 and 3, at Baltusrol G.C.
1912—Margaret Curtis beat Mrs. Ronald H. Barlow, 3 and 2, at Essex County Club.
1913—Gladys Ravenscroft beat Marion Hollins, 2 up, at Wilmington (Del.) C.C.
1914—Mrs. H. Arnold Jackson (Kate Harley) beat Elaine V. Rosenthal, 1 up, at Nassau C.C., Glen Cove, N.Y.
1915—Mrs. C.H. Vanderbeck beat Mrs. William A. Gavin, 3 and 2, at Onwentsia Club, Lake Forest, Ill.
1916—Alexa Stirling beat Mildred Caverly, 2 and 1, at Belmont Springs C.C., Waverly, Mass.
1917—18—No competition
1919—Alexa Stirling beat Mrs. William A. Gavin, 6 and 5, at Shawnee C.C., Shawnee-on-Delaware, Pa.
1920—Alexa Stirling beat Mrs. Dorothy Campbell Hurd, 5 and 4, at Mayfield C.C., Cleveland.
1921—Marion Hollins beat Alexa Stirling, 5 and 4, at Hollywood G.C., Deal, N.J.
1922—Glenna Collett beat Mrs. William A. Gavin, 5 and 4, at Greenbrier G.C., White Sulphur Springs, W.Va.
1923—Edith Cummings beat Alexa Stirling, 3 and 2, at Westchester-Biltmore C.C., Rye, N.Y.
1924—Mrs. Dorothy Campbell Hurd beat Mary K. Browne, 7 and 6, at Rhode Island C.C., Nyatt, R.I.
1925—Glenna Collett beat Mrs. Alexa Stirling Fraser, 9 and 8, at St. Louis C.C.
1926—Mrs. Helen B. Stetson beat Mrs. Wright D. Goss, 3 and 1, at Merion Cricket Club.
1927—Mrs. Miriam Burns Horn beat Maureen Orcutt, 5 and 4, at Cherry Valley Club, Garden City, N.Y.
1928—Glenna Collett beat Virginia Van Wie, 13 and 12, at Virginia Hot Springs G. and T.C., Hot Springs, Va.
1929—Glenna Collett beat Mrs. Leona Pressler, 4 and 3, at Oakland Hills C.C., Birmingham, Mich.

1930—Glenna Collett beat Virginia Van Wie, 6 and 5, at Los Angeles C.C.
1931—Helen Hicks beat Mrs. Glenna Collett Vare, 2 and 1, at C.C. of Buffalo, Buffalo, N.Y.
1932—Virginia Van Wie beat Mrs. Glenna Collett Vare, 10 and 8, at Salem C.C., Peabody, Mass.
1933—Virginia Van Wie beat Helen Hicks, 4 and 3, at Exmoor C.C., Highland Park, Ill.
1934—Virginia Van Wie beat Dorothy Traung, 2 and 1, at Whitemarsh C.C., Chestnut Hill, Pa.
1935—Mrs. Glenna Collett Vare beat Patty Berg, 3 and 2, at Interlachen C.C., Minneapolis.
1936—Pamela Barton (England) beat Mrs. Maureen Orcutt Crews, 4 and 3, at Canoe Brook C.C., Summit, N.J.
1937—Mrs. Estelle Lawson Page beat Patty Berg, 7 and 6, at Memphis (Tenn.) C.C.
1938—Patty Berg beat Mrs. Estelle Lawson Page, 6 and 5, at Westmoreland C.C., Wilmette, Ill.
1939—Betty Jameson beat Dorothy Kirby, 3 and 2, at Wee Burn Club, Noroton, Conn.
1940—Betty Jameson beat Jane Cothran, 2 and 1, at Del Monte (Calif.) G. and C.C.
1941—Mrs. Betty Hicks Newell beat Helen Sigel, 5 and 3, at The Country Club, Brookline, Mass.
1942—45—No competition
1946—Mrs. Mildred Didrikson Zaharias beat Mrs. Clara Callender Sherman, 10 and 9, at Sunset Hills C.C., Tulsa, Okla.
1947—Louise Suggs beat Dorothy Kirby, 2 up, at Franklin Hills C.C., Franklin, Mich.
1948—Grace Lenczyk beat Helen Sigel, 4 and 3, at Pebble Beach Course, Del Monte, Calif.
1949—Mrs. Mark A. Porter beat Dorothy Kielty, 3 and 2, at Merion G.C., Ardmore, Pa.
1950—Beverly Hanson beat Mae Murray, 6 and 4, at Atlanta (Ga.) Athletic Club.
1951—Dorothy Kirby beat Claire Doran, 2 and 1, at Town and C.C., St. Paul.
1952—Mrs. Jacqueline Pung beat Shirley McFedters, 2 and 1, at Waverley C.C., Portland, Ore.
1953—Mary Lena Faulk beat Polly Riley, 3 and 2, at Rhode Island C.C., Providence R.I.
1954—Barbara Romack beat Mickey Wright, 4 and 2, at Allegheny C.C., Sewickley, Pa.
1955—Pat Lesser beat Jane Nelson, 7 and 6, at Myers Park, C.C., Charlotte, N.C.
1956—Marlene Stewart beat JoAnne Gunderson, 2 and 1, at Meridians Hills, C.C., Indianapolis, Ind.
1957—JoAnne Gunderson beat Mrs. Anne Casey Johnstone, 8 and 6, Sacramento, Calif.

1958—Anne Quast beat Barbara Romack, 3 and 2, Danbury, Conn.

1959—Barbara McIntire beat Joanne Goodwin, 4 and 3, at Congressional C.C., Washington D.C.

1960—JoAnne Gunderson beat Jean Ashley, 6 and 5, at Tulsa (Okla.) C.C.

1961—Anne Quast Decker defeated Phyllis Preuss, 14 and 13, at Tacoma (Wash.) C.&G.C.

1962—JoAnne Gunderson beat Ann Baker, 9 and 8, at Rochester (N.Y.) C.C.

1963—Anne Quast Welts beat Peggy Conley, 2 and 1, at Taconic G.C., Williamstown, Mass.

1964—Barbara McIntire defeated JoAnne Gunderson, 3 and 2, at Prairie Dunes C.C., Hutchinson, Kan.

1965—Jean Ashley beat Anne Quast Welts, 5 and 4, at Lakewood C.C., Denver, Colo.

1966—JoAnne Gunderson Carner beat Marlene Stewart Streit, by 41 holes, at Sewickley Heights G.C., Sewickley, Pa.

1967—Lou Dill beat Jean Ashley, 5 and 4, at Annandale G.C., Pasadena, Calif.

1968—JoAnne Gunderson Carner beat Anne Quast Welts, 5 and 4, at Birmingham (Mich.) C.C.

1969—Catherine Lacoste defeated Shelley Hamlin, 3 and 2, at Las Colinas C.C., Irving, Tex.

1970—Martha Wilkinson beat Cynthia Hill, 3 and 2, at Wee Burn C.C., Darien, Conn.

1971—Laura Baugh defeated Beth Barry, 1 up, 36 holes, at Atlanta (Ga) C.C.

1972—Mary Anne Budke beat Cynthia Hill, 5 and 4, at St. Louis (Mo.) C.C.

U.S. Women's Open

1946 (match play)—Betty Berg beat Betty Jameson, 5 and 4, at Spokane (Wash.) C.C.

1947—Betty Jameson, 295, Starmouth Forest C.C., Greensboro, N.C.

1948—Mrs. Mildred Didrikson Zaharias, 300, Atlantic City C.C., Northfield, N.J.

1949—Louise Suggs, 291, Prince Georges G. and C.C., Landover, Md.

1950—Mrs. Mildred Didrikson Zaharias, 291, Rolling Hills, C.C., Wichita, Kan.

1951—Betsy Rawls, 293, Druid Hills G.C., Atlanta, Ga.

1952—Louise Suggs, 284, Bala G.C., Philadelphia.

1953—Betsy Rawls, 302, C.C. of Rochester, N.Y.

1954—Mrs. Mildred Didrikson Zaharias, 291, Salem C.C., Peabody, Mass.

1955—Fay Crocker, 299, Wichita (Kan.) C.C.

1956—Mrs. Kathy Cornelius,* 302, Northland Hills C.C., Duluth, Minn.

1957—Betsy Rawls, 299, Winged Foot G.C., Mamaroneck, N.Y.

1958—Mickey Wright, 290, Forest Lake C.C., Pontiac, Mich.

1959—Mickey Wright, 287, at Churchill Valley C.C., Pittsburgh, Pa.

1960—Betsy Rawls, 292, at Worcester (Mass.) C.C.

1961—Mickey Wright, 293, at Baltusrol G.C., Springfield, N.J.

1962—Murle Lindstrom, 301, at Dunes G.C., Myrtle Beach, S.C.

1963—Mary Mills, 289, at Kenwood C.C., Cincinnati, Ohio.

1964—Mickey Wright,* 290, San Diego C.C., Chula Vista, Calif.

1965—Carol Mann, 290, Atlantic City C.C., Northfield, N.J.

1966—Sandra Spuzich, 297, at Hazeltine National G.C., Chaska, Minn.

1967—Catherine Lacoste ‡, 294, at Hot Springs (Va.) G.&T.C.

1968—Sue Maxwell Berning, 289, at Moselem Springs G.C., Reading, Pa.

1969—Donna Caponi, 294, at Scenic Hills C.C., Pensacola, Fla.

1970—Donna Caponi, 287, at Muskogee (Okla.) C.C.

1971—JoAnne Gunderson Carner, 288, at Erie, Pa.

1972—Sue Maxwell Berning, 299, at Winged Foot, Mamaroneck, N.Y.

* Won Play-off.

‡ Amateur

Women's Eastern Amateur

1906—Fanny C. Osgood 178
1907—Mary B. Adams 189
1908—Fanny C. Osgood 171
1909—Mary B. Adams 185
1910—Fanny C. Osgood 357
1911—Mrs. Ronald H. Barlow 272
1912—Mrs. Ronald H. Barlow 261
1913—Mrs. Ronald H. Barlow 296
1914—Mrs. H. Arnold Jackson 172
1915—Mrs. C. H. Vanderbeck 186
1916—Mrs. William A. Gavin 260
1917-18—No competition
1919—Mrs. Ronald H. Barlow 177
1920—Mrs. Ronald H. Barlow 170
1921—Mrs. C. H. Vanderbeck 178
1922—Glenna Collett 246
1923—Glenna Collett 248
1924—Glenna Collett 163
1925—Maureen Orcutt 166
1926—Mrs. G. Henry Stetson 253
1927—Glenna Collett 250
1928—Maureen Orcutt 253
1929—Maureen Orcutt 241
1930—Frances Williams 254

1931—Helen Hicks 263
1932—Mrs. Glenna Collett Vare 232
1933—Charlotte Glutting 160
1934—Maureen Orcutt 244
1935—Mrs. Glenna Collett Vare 237
1936—Edith Quier 243
1937—Charlotte Glutting 240
1938—Maureen Orcutt 223
1939—Mrs. H. Warren Beard 241
1940—Grace Amory 236
1941—Mrs. Marion Turpie McNaughton ... 244
1942-45—No competition
1946—Laddie Irwin 234
1947—Maureen Orcutt 234
1948—Pat O'Sullivan 229
1949—Maureen Orcutt 240
1950—Peggy Kirk 232
1951—Patricia O'Sullivan 235
1952—Helen Sigel 230
1953—Mary Ann Downey
1954—Mrs. Mae Murray Jones
1955—Mary Ann Downey
1956—Mrs. Norman Woolworth
1957—Joanne Goodwin
1958—Mary Patton Janssen
1959—Mrs. E. J. McAuliffe
1960—Mrs. Philip J. Cudone
1961—Marge Burns
1962—Helen Sigel Wilson
1963—Phyllis Preuss
1964—Nancy Roth
1965—Nancy Roth
1966—Nancy Roth Syms
1967—Phyllis Preuss
1968—JoAnne Gunderson Carner
1969—Mrs. Mark Porter
1970-71—Lancy Smith
1972—Alice Dye
1973—Lancy Smith
Play-offs in 1931, 1937.

1927—Glenna Collett
1928—Mrs. Opal S. Hill
1929-30—Glenna Collett
1931-33—Maureen Orcutt
1934—Charlotte Glutting
1935—Estelle Lawson
1936—Deborah Verry
1937—Mrs. Estelle Lawson Page
1938—Jane Cothran
1939-41—Mrs. Estelle Lawson Page
1942—Louise Suggs
1943—Dorothy Kirby
1944-45—Mrs. Estelle Lawson Page
1946—Louise Suggs
1947—Mrs. Mildred Didrikson Zaharias
1948—Louise Suggs
1949—Peggy Kirk
1950-51—Patricia O'Sullivan
1952—Barbara Romack
1953—Patricia O'Sullivan
1954—Joyce Ziske
1955—Wiffi Smith
1956—Marlene Stewart
1957—Barbara McIntire
1958—Mrs. Philip Cudone
1959—Ann Casey Johnstone
1960—Barbara McIntire
1961—Barbara McIntire
1962—Clifford Ann Creed
1963—Nancy Roth
1964—Phyllis Preuss
1965—Barbara McIntire
1966—Nancy Roth Syms
1967—Phyllis Preuss
1968—Mrs. Alice Dye
1969—Phyllis Preuss
1970—Hollis Stacy
1971—Barbara McIntire
1972—Jane Bastanchury Booth
1973—Beth Barry

Women's North and South Amateur

1903-04—Mrs. Myra D. Paterson
1905—M. H. Dutton
1906—Mrs. Myra D. Paterson
1907—M. B. Adams
1908—Julia Mix
1909—Mary Fownes
1910—Mrs. C. H. Vanderbeck
1911—Louise Elkins
1912—Mrs. J. R. Price
1913—Lillian Hyde
1914—F. Harvey
1915-16—Mrs. Ronald H. Barlow
1917—Elaine V. Rosenthal
1918—Mrs. Dorothy Campbell Hurd
1919—Mrs. Ronald H. Barlow
1920-21—Mrs. Dorothy Campbell Hurd
1922-24—Glenna Collett
1925—Mrs. Melvin Jones
1926—Louise Fordyce

Women's Southern Amateur

1911—Mrs. Roger Smith
1912—Mrs. F. G. Jones
1913—Mrs. F. W. Daley
1914—Mrs. F. G. Jones
1915-16—Alexa Stirling
1917—Mrs. K. G. Duffield
1918—No competition
1919—Alexa Stirling
1920-21—Mrs. David C. Gaut
1922—Mrs. Dozier Lowndes
1923—Mrs. David C. Gaut
1924—Mrs. Dozier Lowndes
1925—Mrs. John Armstrong
1926—Marion Turpie
1927—Mrs. Dalton Raymond
1928—Marion Turpie
1929—Margaret Maddox
1930—Mrs. David C. Gaut
1931—Mrs. Marion Turpie Lake

1932—Mrs. Ben Fitzhugh
1933—Aniela Gorczyca
1934—Betty Jameson
1935—Mary Rogers
1936—Mrs. Mark McGarry
1937—Dorothy Kirby
1938-39—Marion Miley
1940—Mrs. Frank Goldthwaite
1941—Louise Suggs
1942-45—No competition
1946—Mrs. Estelle Lawson Page
1947—Louise Suggs
1948—Polly Riley
1949—Margaret Gunther
1950-51—Polly Riley
1952—Kathy McKinnon
1953-54—Polly Riley
1955—Mrs. Scott Probasco
1956—Mary Ann Downey
1957—Clifford Ann Creed
1958—Mrs. Mary Ann Reynolds
1959—Judy Eller
1960—Judy Eller
1961—Polly Riley
1962—Clifford Anne Creed
1963—Mrs. Paul Hendrix
1964—Nancy Roth
1965—Phyllis Preuss
1966—Nancy Roth Syms
1967—Mrs. Teddy Boddie
1968—Phyllis Preuss
1969—Mrs. John Rathmell
1970—Kathy Hite
1971-72—Beth Barry

1933—Lucille Robinson
1934—Mrs. Leona Cheney
1935—Marion Miley
1936—Dorothy Traung
1937—Marion Miley
1938—Patty Berg
1939—Edith Estabrooks
1940—Betty Jameson
1941—Mrs. Russell Mann
1942—Betty Jameson
1943-44—Dorothy Germain
1945—Phyllis Otto
1946-47—Louise Suggs
1948—Dorothy Kielty
1949—Helen Sigel
1950—Polly Riley
1951—Marjorie Lindsay
1952—Polly Riley
1953-54—Claire Doran
1955—Pat Lesser
1956—Anne Quast
1957—Meriam Bailey
1958—Barbara McIntire
1959—JoAnne Gunderson
1960—Ann Casey Johnstone
1961—Anne Quast Decker
1962—Carol Sorenson
1963—Barbara McIntire
1964-65—Barbara Fay White
1966—Peggy Conley
1967—Dorothy Germain Porter
1968—Catherine Lacoste, France
1969-70—Jane Bastanchury
1971—Beth Barry
1972—Debbie Massey

Women's Western Amateur

1901-03—Bessie Anthony
1904—Frances Everett
1905-06—Mrs. C. L. Dering
1907—Lillian French
1908—Mrs. W. France Anderson
1909—Vida Llewellyn
1910—Mrs. Thurston Harris
1911-12—Caroline Painter
1913—Myra Helmer
1914—Mrs. H. D. Hammond
1915—Elaine V. Rosenthal
1916-17—Mrs. F. C. Letts Jr.
1918—Elaine V. Rosenthal
1919—Mrs. Perry W. Fiske
1920—Mrs. F. C. Letts Jr.
1921—Mrs. Melvin Jones
1922—Mrs. David C. Gaut
1923—Miriam Burns
1924—Edith Cummings
1925—Mrs. S. L. Reinhardt
1926—Dorothy Page
1927-28—Mrs. Leona Pressler
1929—Mrs. Opal S. Hill
1930—Mrs. Miriam Burns Tyson
1931-32—Mrs. Opal S. Hill

Women's Trans-Mississippi Amateur

1927—Mrs. Miriam Burns Horn
1928-29—Mrs. Opal S. Hill
1930—Mrs. H. S. Clarke
1931—Mrs. Opal S. Hill
1932—Mrs. Walter Beyer
1933—Phyllis Buchanan
1934—Mrs. Opal S. Hill
1935-36—Marion Miley
1937—Betty Jameson
1938-39—Patty Berg
1940—Betty Jameson
1941—Mrs. Russell Mann
1942-45—No competition
1946—Mrs. Mildred Didrikson Zaharias
1947-48—Polly Riley
1949—Betsy Rawls
1950—Marjorie Lindsay
1951—Mary Ann Downey
1952—Mrs. Lyle Bowman
1953—Edean Anderson
1954—Vonnie Colby
1955—Polly Riley
1956—Wiffie Smith
1957—Mrs. James Ferrie

1958—Marjorie Lindsay
1959—Ann Casey Johnstone
1960—Sandra Haynie
1961—JoAnne Gunderson
1962—Jean Thompson
1963—Judy Bell
1964—Carol Sorenson
1965—Sharon Miller
1966—Roberta Albers
1967—Jane Bastanchury
1968—Mrs. Michael Skala
1969—Jane Bastanchury
1970—Martha Wilkinson
1971—Jane Bastanchury
1972—Michelle Walker, England

Women's National Intercollegiate

1941—Eleanor Dudley, Alabama
1942-45—No competition
1946—Phyllis Otto, Northwestern
1947—Shirley Spork, Michigan State Normal
1948—Grace Lenczyk, Stetson
1949—Marilynn Smith, Kansas
1950—Betty Rowland, Rollins
1951—Barbara Bruning, Wellesley
1952—Mary Ann Villegas, St. Mary's Dominican
1953—Pat Lesser, Seattle
1954—Nancy Reed, George Peabody
1955—Jackie Yates, Redlands
1956—Marlene Stewart, Rollins
1957—Meriam Bailey, Northwestern
1958—Carol Ann Pushing, Carleton
1959—Judy Eller
1960—JoAnne Gunderson
1961—Carol Sorenson
1962—Claudia Lindor
1963—Patti Shook
1964—Roberta Albers
1965—Judy Hoetmer
1966—Joyce Kazmierski
1967—Martha Wilkinson
1968—Gail Sykes, Odessa (Tex.) College
1969—Jane Bastanchury, Arizona State
1970—Cathy Gaughan, Arizona State
1971—Shelley Hamlin,
1972—Ann Laughlin, Miami (Fla.)

GREAT BRITAIN
British Open

1860—Willie Park Sr., 174, Prestwick
1861—Tom Morris Sr., 163, Prestwick
1862—Tom Morris Sr., 163, Prestwick
1863—Willie Park Sr., 168, Prestwick
1864—Tom Morris Sr., 167, Prestwick
1865—A. L. Strath, 162, Prestwick
1866—Willie Park Sr., 169, Prestwick
1867—Tom Morris Sr., 170, Prestwick
1868—Tom Morris Jr., 170, Prestwick
1869—Tom Morris Jr. 154, Prestwick
1870—Tom Morris Jr., 149, Prestwick

1871—No competition
1872—Tom Morris Jr., 166, Prestwick
1873—Tom Kidd, 179, St. Andrews
1874—Mungo Park, 159, Musselburgh
1875—Willie Park Sr., 166, Prestwick
1875—Bob Martin, 176, St. Andrews
1876—Jamie Anderson, 160, Musselburgh
1877—No competition
1878—Jamie Anderson, 157, Prestwick
1879—Jamie Anderson, 170, St. Andrews
1880—Bob Ferguson, 162, Musselburgh
1881—Bob Ferguson, 170, Prestwick
1882—Bob Ferguson, 171, St. Andrews
1883—W. L. Fernie (a), 159, Musselburgh
1884—Jack Simpson, 160, Prestwick
1885—Bob Martin, 171, St. Andrews
1886—D. L. Brown, 157, Musselburgh
1887—Willie Park Jr., 161, Prestwick
1888—Jack Burns, 171, St. Andrews
1889—Willie Park Jr. (a), 155, Musselburgh
1890—John Ball, 164, Prestwick
1891—Hugh Kirkaldy, 166, St. Andrews
1892—H. H. Hilton, 305, Muirfield
1893—W. Auchterlonie, 322, Prestwick
1894—J. H. Taylor, 326, Sandwich
1895—J. H. Taylor, 322, St. Andrews
1896—Harry Vardon (a), 316, Muirfield
1897—H. H. Hilton, 314, Hoylake
1898—Harry Vardon, 307, Prestwick
1899—Harry Vardon, 310, Sandwich
1900—J. H. Taylor, 309, St. Andrews
1901—James Braid, 309, Muirfield
1902—Alex Herd, 307, Hoylake
1903—Harry Vardon, 300, Prestwick
1904—Jack White, 296, Sandwich
1905—James Braid, 318, St. Andrews
1906—James Braid, 300, Muirfield
1907—Arnaud Massy, 312, Hoylake
1908—James Braid, 291, Prestwick
1909—J. H. Taylor, 295, Deal
1910—James Braid, 299, St. Andrews
1911—Harry Vardon (a), 303, Sandwich
1912—Ted Ray, 295, Muirfield
1913—J. H. Taylor, 304, Hoylake
1914—Harry Vardon, 306, Prestwick
1915-19—No competition
1920—George Duncan, 303, Deal
1921—Jock Hutchison (a), 296, St. Andrews
1922—Walter Hagen, 300, Sandwich
1923—A. G. Havers, 295, Troon
1924—Walter Hagen 301, Hoylake
1925—Jim Barnes, 300, Prestwick
1926—Robert T. Jones Jr., 291, Royal Lytham, St. Anne's
1927—Robert T. Jones Jr., 285, St. Andrews
1928—Walter Hagen, 292, Sandwich
1929—Walter Hagen, 292, Muirfield
1930—Robert T. Jones Jr., 291, Hoylake
1931—Tommy Armour, 296, Carnoustie
1932—Gene Sarazen, 283, Princes, Sandwich
1933—Densmore Shute (a), 292, St. Andrews
1934—Henry Cotton, 283, Sandwich

1935—Alfred Perry, 283, Muirfield
1936—A. H. Padgham, 287, Royal Liverpool
1937—Henry Cotton, 290, Carnoustie
1938—R. A. Whitcombe, 295, Sandwich
1939—Richard Burton, 290, St. Andrews
1940-45—No competition
1946—Sam Snead, 290, St. Andrews
1947—Fred Daly, 293, Hoylake
1948—Henry Cotton, 284, Gullane, Muirfield
1949—Bobby Locke (a), 283, Sandwich, Deal
1950—Bobby Locke, 279, Troon, Lochgreen
1951—Max Faulkner, 285, Portrush
1952—Bobby Locke, 287, Royal Lytham, St. Anne's
1953—Ben Hogan, 282, Carnoustie
1954—Peter Thomson, 283, Royal Birkdale
1955—Peter Thomson, 281, St. Andrews
1956—Peter Thomson, 286, Royal Liverpool
1957—Bobby Locke, 279, St. Andrews
1958—Peter Thomson (a), 278, St. Anne's
1959—Gary Player, 284, Muirfield
1960—Kel Nagle, 278, Inverness
1961—Arnold Palmer, 284, Birkdale
1962—Arnold Palmer, 276, Troon
1963—Bob Charles, 277, St. Anne's
1964—Tony Lema, 279, St. Andrews
1965—Peter Thomson, 285, Royal Birkdale
1966—Jack Nicklaus, 282, Muirfield C., Scotland
1967—Roberto De Vicenzo, 278, Hoylake
1968—Gary Player, 289, Carnoustie, Scotland.
1969—Tony Jacklin, 280, St. Anne's, England
1970—Jack Nicklaus (a), 283, St. Andrews, Scotland
1971—Lee Trevino, 278, at Birkindale, Southport, Eng.
1972—Lee Trevino, 278, at Muirfield, Scotland
1973—Tom Weiskoph, 276, at Troon, Scotland

(a)Won play-off. In 1892 competition was extended to 72 holes.

American winners—Hutchison (1921), Hagen (1922, 1924,1928, 1929), Barnes (1925), Jones (1926, 1927, 1930), Armour (1931), Sarazen (1932), Shute (1933), Snead (1946), Hogan (1953), Palmer (1961, 1962), Lema (1964), Nicklaus (1966, 1970), Trevino (1971, 1972), Tom Weiskoph (1973). Amateur winners—Ball, Hilton, Jones.

British Amateur

1885—A. F. MacFie beat Horace G. Hutchinson, 7 and 6, Hoylake.
1886— Horace G. Hutchinson beat Henry Lamb, 7 and 6, St. Andrews.
1887—Horace G. Hutchinson beat John Ball, 1 up, Hoylake.
1888—John Ball beat J. E. Laidlay, 5 and 4, Prestwick.
1889—J. E. Laidlay beat John Ball, 2 and 1, St. Andrews.
1890—John Ball beat J. E. Laidlay, 4 and 3, Hoylake.

1891—J. E. Laidlay beat Harold H. Hilton, 1 up (20 holes), St. Andrews.
1892—John Ball beat Harold H. Hilton, 3 and 1, Sandwich.
1893—Peter Anderson beat J. E. Laidlay, 1 up, Prestwick.
1894—John Ball beat S. M. Ferguson, 1 up, Hoylake.
1895—L. M. B. Melville beat John Ball, 1 up (19 holes), St. Andrews.
1896—F. G. Tait beat Harold H. Hilton, 8 and 7, Sandwich.
1897—A. J. T. Allan beat James Robb, 4 and 2, Muirfield.
1898—F. G. Tait beat S. M. Ferguson, 7 and 5, Hoylake.
1899—John Ball beat F. G. Tait, 1 up (37 holes), Prestwick.
1900—Harold H. Hilton beat James Robb, 8 and 7, Sandwich.
1901—Harold H. Hilton beat J. L. Low, 1 up, St. Andrews.
1902—C. Hutchings beat S. H. Fry, 1 up, Hoylake.
1903—R. Maxwell beat H. G. Hutchinson, 7 and 5, Muirfield.
1904—Walter J. Travis (U.S.) beat Edward Blackwell, 4 and 3, Sandwich.
1905—A. G. Barry beat Hon. O. Scott, 3 and 2, Prestwick.
1906—James Robb beat C. C. Lingen, 4 and 3, Hoylake.
1907—John Ball beat C. A. Palmer, 6 and 4, St. Andrews.
1908—E. A. Lassen beat H. E. Taylor, 7 and 6, Sandwich.
1909—R. Maxwell beat Capt. C. K. Hutchinson, 1 (37 holes), Muirfield.
1910—John Ball beat C. Aylimer, 10 and 9, Hoylake.
1911—Harold H. Hilton beat E. A. Lassen, 4 and 3, Prestwick.
1912—John Ball beat Abe Mitchell, 1 up (38 holes), Westward Ho!
1913—Harold H. Hilton beat Robert Harris, 6 and 5, St. Andrews.
1914—J. L. Jenkins beat C. O. Hezlet, 3 and 2, St. Andrews.
1915-19—No competition
1920—Cyril Tolley beat Robert A Gardner, 1 up (37 holes), Muirfield.
1921—Willie Hunter beat A. J. Graham, 12 and 11, Hoylake.
1922—E. W. E. Holderness beat John Caven, 1 up, Prestwick.
1923—Roger H. Wethered beat Robert Harris, 7 and 6, Deal.
1924—E. W. E. Holderness beat E. F. Storey, 3 and 2 St. Andrews.
1925—Robert Harris beat K. F. Fradgley, 13, and 12, Westward Ho!

1926—Jess W. Sweetser (U.S.) beat A. F. Simpson, 6 and 5, Muirfield.

1927—Dr. William Tweddell beat D. E. Landale, 7 and 6, Hoylake.

1928—T. Philip Perkins beat Roger H. Wethered, 6 and 4, Prestwick.

1929—Cyril J. H. Tolley beat John N. Smith, 4 and 3, Sandwich.

1930—Robert T. Jones Jr. (U.S.) beat Roger H. Wethered, 7 and 6, St. Andrews.

1931—Eric Martin-Smith beat John DeForest, 1 up, Westward Ho!

1932—John DeForest beat Eric Fiddian, 3 and 1, Muirfield.

1933—Hon. Michael Scott beat T. A. Bourn, 4 and 3, Hoylake.

1934—W. Lawson Little Jr. (U.S.) beat James Wallace, 14 and 13, Prestwick.

1935—W. Lawson Little Jr. (U.S.) beat Dr. William Tweddell, 1 up, Royal Lytham, St. Anne's.

1936—Hector Thomson beat Jim Ferrier, 2 up, St. Andrews.

1937—Robert Sweeny (U.S.) beat Lionel Munn, 3 and 2 Sandwich.

1938—Charles Yates (U.S.) beat Cecil Ewing, 3 and 2, Troon.

1939—Alex Kyle beat Andrew Duncan, 2 and 1, Hoylake.

1940-45—No competition

1946—James Bruen beat Robert Sweeny (U.S.), 4 and 3, Birkdale.

1947—Willie Turnesa (U.S.) beat Dick Chapman (U.S.), 3 and 2, Carnoustie.

1948—Frank R. Stranahan (U.S.) beat Charles Stowe, 5 and 4, Sandwich.

1949—S. Max McCready beat Willie Turnesa (U.S.), 2 and 1, Portmarnock.

1950—Frank R. Stranahan (U.S.) beat Dick Chapman (U.S.), 8 and 6, St. Andrews.

1951—Dick Chapman (U.S.) beat Charles R. Coe (U.S.), 5 and 4, Porthcawl.

1952—Harvie Ward (U.S.) beat Frank R. Stranahan (U.S.), 6 and 5, Prestwick.

1953—Joe Carr (Ireland) beat Harvie Ward (U.S.), 2 up, Hoylake.

1954—Doug Bachli beat William C. Campbell (U.S.), 2 and 1, Muirfield.

1955—Joe Conrad (U.S.) beat Alan Slater, 3 and 2, St. Anne's.

1956—John Beharrel beat Leslie Taylor, 5 and 4, Troon.

1957—Reid Jack (Scotland), beat Harold Ridgley (U.S.), 2 and 1, Formby.

1958—Joe Carr (Ireland) beat Alan Thirwell (England), 3 and 2.

1959—Deane Beman (U.S.)

1960—Joe Carr

1961—Michael Bonallack

1962—Richard Davies (U.S.)

1963—Michael Lunt

1964—Gordon Clarke

1965—Mike Bonnallack

1966—Bobby Cole

1967—Bob Dickson (U.S.)

1968-70—Mike Bonallack

1971—Steve Melnyk (U.S.)

1972—Trevor Homer

The Hon. Michael Scott won in 1933 at the age of 55 and is the oldest player to win a major national championship. Walter J. Travis was Australian-born, but represented the United States when he won in 1904.

Women's British Amateur

1893-95—Lady Margaret Scott

1896—A. B. Pascoe

1897—E. C. Orr

1898—L. Thomson

1899—M. Hezlet

1900—R. K. Adair

1901—M. A. Graham

1902—M. Hezlet

1903—R. K. Adair

1904—Lottie Dod

1905—B. Thompson

1906—Mrs. Kennion

1907—M. Hezlet

1908—M. Titterton

1909—Dorothy Campbell

1910—Grant Suttie

1911—Dorothy Campbell

1912—Gladys Ravenscroft

1913—Muriel Dodd

1914—Cecil Leitch

1915-19—No competition

1920-21—Cecil Leitch

1922—Joyce Wethered

1923—Doris Chambers

1924-25—Joyce Wethered

1926—Cecil Leitch

1927—Thion de la Chaume

1928—Nanette LeBlan

1929—Joyce Wethered

1930—Diana Fishwick

1931-33—Enid Wilson

1934—Mrs. Andrew Holm

1935—Wanda Morgan

1936—Pamela Barton

1937—Jessie Anderson

1938—Mrs. Andrew Holm

1939—Pamela Barton

1940-45—No competition

1946—Mrs. Jean Hetherington

1947—Mrs. Mildred Didrikson Zaharias (U.S.)

1948—Louise Suggs (U.S.)

1949—Frances Stephens

1950—Vicomtesse de Saint Sauveur

1951—Mrs. P. G. McCann

1952—Moira Paterson

1953—Marlene Stewart

1954—Frances Stephens

1955—Jessie Valentine
1956—Wiffi Smith (U.S.)
1957—Philomena Garvey
1958—Mrs. George Valentine
1959—Elizabeth Price
1960—Barbara McIntire
1961—Mrs. A. D. Spearman
1962—Mrs. Marley Spearman
1963—Mlle. B. Varangot
1964—Carol Sorenson
1965—Mlle. B. Varangot
1966-67—Elizabeth Chadwick
1968—Brigette Varangot
1969—Catharine Lacoste
1970—Dinah Oxley
1971-72—Michelle Walker

CANADA

Canadian Open

1904—J. H. Oke	156
1905—George Cumming	148
1906—Charles Murray	170
1907—Percy Barrett	306
1908—Albert Murray	300
1909—Karl Keffer	309
1910—Daniel Kenny	303
1911—Charles Murray	314
1912—George Sargent	299
1913—Albert Murray	314
1914—Karl Keffer	300
1915-18—No competition	
1919—J. Douglas Edgar	278
1920—J. Douglas Edgar	298
1921—W. H. Trovinger	293
1922—Al Watrous	303
1923—Clarence W. Hackney	295
1924—Leo Diegel	285
1925—Leo Diegel	295
1926—Macdonald Smith	283
1927—Tommy Armour	288
1928—Leo Diegel	282
1929—Leo Diegel	274
1930—Tommy Armour	277
1931—Walter Hagen	282
1932—Harry Cooper	290
1933—Joe Kirkwood	282
1934—Tommy Armour	287
1935—Gene Kunes	288
1936—W. Lawson Little Jr.	271
1937—Harry Cooper	285
1938—Sam Snead	277
1939—Harold McSpaden	292
1940—Sam Snead	281
1941—Sam Snead	274
1942—Craig Wood	275
1943-44—No competition	
1945—Byron Nelson	268
1946—George Fazio	278
1947—Bobby Locke	268
1948—Charles Congdon	280

1949—E. J. Harrison	271
1950—Jim Ferrier	271
1951—Jim Ferrier	273
1952—Johnny Palmer	263
1953—Dave Douglas	273
1954—Pat Fletcher	280
1955—Arnold Palmer	265
1956—Doug Sanders*	273
1957—George Bayer	271
1958—Wes Ellis	267
1959—Doug Ford	
1960—Art Wall Jr.	
1961—Jackey Cupit	
1962—Ted Kroll	
1963—Doug Ford	
1964—Kel Nagle	
1965—Gene Littler	
1966—Don Massengale	
1967—Art Wall, Jr.	
1968—Bob Charles	
1969—Tommy Aaron	
1970—Kermit Zarley	
1971—Lee Trevino	
1972—Gay Brewer	

Play-offs in 1920, 1930, 1931, 1938, 1940, 1946, 1967, 1969, 1971.

*Amateur

Canadian Amateur

1895—T. H. Harley
1896—Stewart Gillespie
1897—W. A. H. Kerr
1898—George S. Lyon
1899—Vere C. Brown
1900—George S. Lyon
1901—W. A. H. Kerr
1902—F. R. Martin
1903—George S. Lyon
1904—Percy Taylor
1905-07—George S. Lyon
1908—Alex Wilson Jr.
1909—E. Legge
1910—Fritz Martin
1911—G. H. Hutton
1912—George S. Lyon
1913—G. H. Turpin
1914—George S. Lyon
1915-18—No competition
1919—William McLuckie
1920—C. B. Grier
1921—Frank Thompson
1922—C. C. Fraser
1923—W. J. Thompson
1924—Frank Thompson
1925—Donald D. Carrick
1926—C. Ross Somerville
1927—Donald D. Carrick
1928—C. Ross Somerville
1929—Eddie Held
1930-31—C. Ross Somerville
1932—Gordon Taylor

1933-34—Albert W. Campbell
1935—C. Ross Somerville
1936—Fred Haas Jr.
1937—C. Ross Somerville
1938—Ted Adams
1939—Kenneth Black
1940-45—No competition
1946—Henry Martell
1947-48—Frank R. Stranahan
1949—Dick Chapman
1950—Bill Mawhinney
1951—Walter McElroy
1952—Larry Bouchey
1953—Don Cherry
1954—Harvie Ward
1955-56—Moe Norman
1957—Nick Weslock
1958—Bruce Castator
1959—Johnny Johnston
1960—Keith Alexander
1961—Gary Cowan
1962—Reginald Taylor
1963—Nick Weslock
1964—Nick Weslock
1965—George Henry
1966—Nick Weslock
1967—Stuart Jones
1968—Jim Doyle
1969—Wayne McDonald
1970—Allen Miller
1971—Dick Siderowf*
1972—Doug Roxburgh
*Won Playoff

P.G.A. Money-Winning Champions

Year	Player	Total
1941—Ben Hogan		$18,358.00
1942—Ben Hogan		13,143.00
1943—No records kept.		
1944—Byron Nelson		37,967.69
1945—Byron Nelson		63,335.66
1946—Ben Hogan		42,556.36
1947—Jimmy Demaret		27,936.83
1948—Ben Hogan		36,812.00
1949—Sam Snead		31,593.83
1950—Sam Snead		35,758.83
1951—Lloyd Mangrum		26,088.83
1952—Julius Boros		37,032.97
1953—Lew Worsham		34,002.00
1954—Bob Toski		65,891.24
1955—Julius Boros		63,121.55
1956—Ted Kroll		72,835.83
1957—Dick Mayer		65,835.00
1958—Arnold Palmer		42,607.50
1959—Art Wall Jr.		53,167.60
1960—Arnold Palmer		75,262.85
1961—Gary Player		64,540.45
1962—Arnold Palmer		81,448.83
1963—Arnold Palmer		128,230.00
1964—Jack Nicklaus		113,284.00
1965—Jack Nicklaus		140,752.00
1966—Billy Casper		121,944.00
1967—Jack Nicklaus		188,998.08
1968—Billy Casper		205,168.00
1969—Frank Beard		175,223.00
1970—Lee Trevino		157,037.00
1971—Jack Nicklaus		244,490.00
1972—Jack Nicklaus		280,482.00

Women's P.G.A. Money-Winning Champions

Year	Player	Total
1948—Babe Zaharias		$3,400
1949—Babe Zaharias		4,650
1950—Babe Zaharias		14,800
1951—Babe Zaharias		15,087
1952—Betsy Rawls		14,503
1953—Louise Suggs		19,816
1954—Patty Berg		16,011
1955—Patty Berg		16,497
1956—Marlene Bauer Hagge		20,235
1957—Patty Berg		16,272
1958—Beverly Hanson		12,639
1959—Betsy Rawls		26,774
1960—Louise Suggs		16,892
1961—Mickey Wright		22,236
1962—Mickey Wright		21,641
1963—Mickey Wright		31,269
1964—Mickey Wright		29,800
1965—Kathy Whitworth		28,658
1966—Kathy Whitworth		33,517
1967—Kathy Whitworth		44,004
1968—Kathy Whitworth		59,097
1969—Carol Mann		49,447
1970—Kathy Whitworth		31,544
1971—Kathy Whitworth		43,534
1972—Kathy Whitworth		57,919

INTERNATIONAL TEAM MATCHES

American golf has developed five international team matches.

The oldest is that between amateur teams representing the United States and Great Britain for the Walker Cup. It was originated in 1922 and is held every other year, the site alternating between the countries. The cup was given by G. Herbert Walker, who was president of the United States Golf Association in 1920. The United States team is selected by the U.S.G.A. and the British team by the Royal and Ancient Golf Club of St. Andrews, Scotland. Each team consists of eight players and usually two alternates.

The next oldest is that between professional teams representing the United States and Great Britain for the Ryder Cup. This series was inaugurated in 1926 and also is held every other year, the site alternating between the countries. The cup was presented by Samuel Ryder of England, a patron of professional golf in Great Britain. The United States team is selected by the Professional Golfers Association of America and the British team by the Professional Golfers

Association of Great Britain. Each team consists of eight players and usually two alternates.

The only women's match is between amateur teams representing the United States and the British Isles for the Curtis Cup. The series started in 1930 and also is held every other year, the site alternating. The United States team is selected by the U.S.G.A. and the British team by the Ladies' Golf Union. The cup was donated by the Misses Harriot and Margaret Curtis, who between them won four U.S.G.A. Women's Amateur championships between 1906 and 1912. Each team consists of six players and usually two alternates.

The match for the Americas Cup among amateur teams representing the United States, Canada and Mexico was originated in 1952 and is held every other year, the site rotating among the three countries. The teams consist of six players and one alternate, and each team plays the other two teams simultaneously. The cup was donated by Jerome P. Bowes Jr., the president of the Western Golf Association in 1950-51. The teams are selected by the U.S.G.A., the Royal Canadian Golf Association and the Asociacion Mexicana de Golf.

The series for the Hopkins Cup also began in 1952 and is played annually between professional teams representing the United States and Canada. The teams are selected by the P.G.A.'s of the respective countries. There are six players and an alternate on each team. The cup was donated by John Jay Hopkins.

Walker Cup (Biennial)
(Competition between United States and British amateurs.)

1922—U.S. 8, G.B. 4, at National Golf Links of America, Southampton, N.Y.
1923—U.S. 6, G.B. 5 (1 match halved), at St. Andrews, Scotland.
1924—U.S. 9, G.B. 3, at Garden City (N.Y.) C.C.
1926—U.S. 6, G.B. 5 (1 match halved), at St. Andrews.
1928—U.S. 11, G.B. 1, at Chicago G.C., Wheaton, Ill.
1930—U.S. 10, G.B. 2, at Royal St. George's G.C., Sandwich, England.
1932—U.S. 8, G.B. 1 (3 matches halved), at The Country Club, Brookline, Mass.
1934—U.S. 9, G.B. 2 (1 match halved), at St. Andrew's, Scotland.
1936—U.S. 9, G.B. 0 (3 matches halved), at Pine Valley G.C., Clementon, N.J.
1938—G.B. 7, U.S. 4 (1 match halved), at St. Andrews.
1947—U.S. 8, G.B. 4, at St. Andrews.
1949—U.S. 10, G.B. 2, at Winged Foot G.C., Mamaroneck, N.Y.
1951—U.S. 6, G.B. 3, at Birkdale G.C., Southport, England.
1953—U.S. 9, G.B. 3, at Kittansett C., Marion, Mass.

1955—U.S. 10, G.B. 2, at St. Andrews, Scotland.
1957—U.S. 8, G.B. 3, at Minneapolis, Minn.
1959—U.S. 9, G.B. 3, at Muirfield, Scotland.
1961—U.S. 11, G.B. 1, at Seattle C.C.
1963—U.S. 12, G.B. 8, at Turnberry G.C., Alisa, Scotland.
1965—U.S. 11, G.B. 11, at Baltimore Maryland
1967—U.S. 13, G.B. 7, at Sandwich, England.
1969—U.S. 10, G.B. 8, at Milwaukee, Wis.
1971—G.B. 13, U.S. 11, at St. Andrews, Scotland.
Informal match in 1921 at Hoylake, England, was won by U.S., 9 to 3.

Ryder Cup (Biennial)
(United States vs. British professionals)
1927—U.S. 9½, G.B. 2½, at Worcester, Mass.
1929—G.B. 7, U.S. 5, at Moortown, England.
1931—U.S. 9, G.B. 3, at Columbus, Ohio.
1933—G.B. 6½, U.S. 5½, at Southport, England.
1935—U.S. 9, G.B. 3, at Ridgewood (N.J.) C.C.
1937—U.S. 8, G.B. 4, at Southport
1947—U.S. 11, G.B. 1, at Portland, Ore.
1949—U.S. 7, G.B. 5, at Ganton, England.
1951—U.S. 9½, G.B. 2½, at Pinehurst, N.C.
1953—U.S. 6½, G.B. 5½, at Wentworth, England.
1955—U.S. 8, G.B. 4, at Palm Springs, Calif.
1957—G.B. 7, U.S. 4, at Lindrick, England.
1959—U.S. 8½, G.B. 3½, at Palm Desert, Calif.
1961—U.S. 14½, G.B. 9½, at St. Anne's, England.
1963—U.S. 23, G.B. 9, at East Lake C.C., Atlanta, Ga.
1965—U.S. 19½, G.B. 12½, at Southport, England.
1967—U.S. 23½, G.B. 8½, at Houston, Texas
1969—U.S. 16, G.B. 16, at Southport, England.
1971—U.S. 18½, G.B. 13½, at St. Louis, Mo.
Informal match in 1926 at Wentworth, England, was won by Great Britain, 13½ to 1½.

Curtis Cup (Biennial)
(United States vs. British Isles—women amateurs)
1932—U.S. 5½, B.I. 3½, at Wentworth, England.
1934—U.S. 6½, B.I. 2½, at Chevy Chase, Md.
1936—U.S. 4½, B.I. 4½, at Gleneagles, Scotland.
1938—U.S. 5½, B.I. 3½, at Manchester, Mass.
1948—U.S. 6½, B.I. 2½, at Southport, England.
1950—U.S. 7½, B.I. 1½, at Buffalo, N.Y.
1952—B.I. 5, U.S. 4, at Muirfield, Scotland.
1954—U.S. 6, B.I. 3, at Ardmore, Pa.
1956—B.I. 5, U.S. 4, at Sandwich, England.
1958—B.I. 4½, U.S. 4½, at West Newton, Mass.
   (As defenders, British Isles retained cup.)
1960—U.S. 6½, B.I. 2½, at Lindrick, Nottinghamshire, England.
1962—U.S. 8, B.I. 1, at Broadmoor C.C., Colorado Springs, Colo.
1964—U.S. 10½, B.I. 7½, at Wales, Great Britain.
1966—U.S. 13, B.I. 5, at Hot Springs, Va.
1968—U.S. 10½, G.B. 7½, at Royal County Down, Newcastle, Northern Ireland.

1970—U.S. 11½, G.B. 6½, at Brae Burn C.C., West Newton, Mass.

1972—U.S. 10, G.B. 8, at Western Gailes, Scotland.

Informal match in 1930 at Sunningdale, England, was won by the British Isles, 8 to 6.

RECORDS U.S. LOW SCORES

Lowest 72-Hole Score—257 (60, 68, 64, 65), by Mike Souchak, Feb. 17-20, 1955, Brackenridge Park, San Antonio, Tex.

Lowest 54-Hole Score—189, Chandler Harper, Brackenridge Park, San Antonio, Tex., (last 3 rounds).

Lowest 36-Hole Score—122, Sam Snead, Greenbrier Open, May 16-17, 1959.

Lowest 18-Hole Score—59, Sam Snead, White Sulphur Springs, W. Va., May 16, 1959.

Lowest 9-Hole Score—25, A.J. "Bill" Burke, St. Louis, Mo., May 20, 1970.

BASIC RULES

A round of golf is 18 holes. The holes may be of any length, usually from 100 to 600 yards. Matches may be at 18, 36, 54 or 72 holes, as the pre-contest rules may determine.

There are two methods of competition: match play and stroke (medal) play. Match play is usually 18 or 36 holes when championships are involved. Stroke play usually is 72 holes.

In match play the result is determined by who wins the most holes. The one taking the fewest number of strokes to put the ball into cup is winner of that particular hole; if the players take an equal number, the hole is halved and neither scores.

In stroke play the winning of individual holes is ignored. The contest is won by the player requiring the fewest strokes to negotiate the number of holes specified.

Fourteen clubs are permitted to be used in a round of golf. In an earlier era they had names. Now each is numbered, except the putter. Wooden clubs, with their numbers and the names they once bore are:

No. 1 Driver	No. 3 Spoon
No. 2 Brassie	No. 4 Cleek

The wood used for the club heads is persimmon or is laminated. Iron-headed clubs are:

No. 1 Driving Iron	No. 6 Spade Mashie
No. 2 Midiron	No. 7 Mashie Niblick
No. 3 Mid Mashie	No. 8 Lofter
No. 4 Mashie Iron	No. 9 Niblick
No. 5. Mashie	No. 10 Wedge

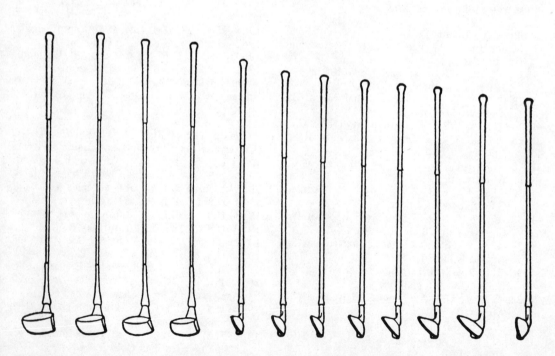

Golf Clubs. From left to right are the driver (No. 1 wood); brassie (No. 2 wood); spoon (No. 3 wood); spoon (No. 4 wood); No. 2 iron, No. 3 iron (long irons); No. 4 iron, No. 5 iron, No. 6 iron (medium irons); No. 7 iron, No. 8 iron (short irons); putter. (Taken from "The Dictionary of Sports," by Parke Cummings, A.S. Barnes and Company, New York.)

GYMNASTICS

Gymnastics consists of a wide range of exercises that build various muscles of the body, such as wrist, back, arm, etc. The exercises include tumbling, vaulting, climbing and balancing. Detail of execution is a major part of the scoring. To reach the top the gymnast must undergo rigid training and strict disciplining of mind and body. He also must try to develop new and difficult routines. But despite his achievements, the gymnast seldom receives public acclaim. He is among the world's least publicized athletes. Gymnasts execute, in a single evening, acts of greater daring and perform more valiantly more muscular feats than some baseball and football players are called upon to do in an entire season. But their activities lack the so-called "mob appeal," and all the gymnasts in America do not attract in an entire year as many spectators as are lured to a baseball park for a big game.

Therefore, gymnasts rarely make even the minor headlines and the remarkable heroics performed by so many are, at best, condensed into a grudgingly-given paragraph in a few newspapers.

Gymnastics is a word from ancient Greek. It means athletic, or disciplinary, exercises. Gymnasium also is Greek and describes the ground, or place, for gymnastic performance. Calisthenics, while linked with gymnastics, are a lighter form of exercise.

Paul W. Krempel of Los Angeles, one of the great gymnasts of about three decades ago, quoted the word gymnasium as meaning "a place where exercises are practiced; to train naked, or lightly clad." He stated that in Grecian antiquity a gymnasium was an institution common to the town, which, at first, was simply an open place for exercises, but to which were added baths, porticos, chambers, often adorned with works of art and forming a place for lectures and schools of philosophers.

Greek rulers of by-gone times decreed that the males must strive for physical perfection, which led to the creation of outdoor gymnasiums. The original indoor places in many instances were vast hypaethral buildings, with a colonnade around the four interior sides. These structures had to be large enough to contain a running track, a field for the weight, discus and javelin throwers, bathrooms with hot and cold water, rubbing rooms where the athletes were anointed with oil and an adequate supply of dressing rooms. In a way, the gymnastics of ancient times were the track and field sports of today, with some variations.

Although in modern times weight lifting is a sport separate from gymnastics, the Greeks coupled the routine of both sports for their young men. The students were required to run, jump, throw weights, discus and javelin; they lifted weights and wrestled. When the time neared for an Olympiad, each gymnasium had its tryouts for youngsters, and each one was urged to compete in all the events on the program. The ones scoring the highest number of points were chosen to represent that particular gymnasium at the Olympiad.

Inasmuch as the Greek boys in their late teens or early 20's spent the major part of each day at the gymnasiums, taking only an occasional hour for recess, it was ruled that all gymnasiums must include adequate grounds, with many shade trees, to provide a restful spot for the students. This resulted in the construction of promenades, refreshment booths, benches, etc., some covered, others uncovered.

In a short while, the fair maidens of Greece began to drop into the gardens and wait for the boy friends to come out and visit between classes. Soon the oldsters of the cities began to appear in the gardens outside the gymnasiums, and, with the flight of time, gymnasium grounds became popular day-time meeting places and, in a way, pioneered the picnic grounds of much later centuries.

There were three gymnasiums in Athens—the Lyceum, the Academia and the Cynosarges—and there were scores of others scattered throughout the nation. Excavations have disclosed some huge gymnasiums in Alexandria, Olympia, Pergamon, Hierapolis, Aphrodisias, Delos, Asos and Troas. Every city of consequence in ancient Greece had a gymnasium of some sort, just as every village in the United States has some school or general place for meetings.

The gymnasium idea was adopted by the Romans after they had conquered Greece, but when the Olympiads were abolished in 392 A.D. by the Roman Emperor Theodosius and physical training no longer was compulsory, gymnasiums were closed as training places. However, the learned men of the Empire decided that they should not be wholly abandoned. They reopened the gymnasiums and taught the arts and sciences within the walls, and that really was the start of the school house of today.

In the earliest years of gymnastics in the United States, the sport was indulged in chiefly by immigrants from Europe, where such exercises were extremely popular. The sons of these people, too, went in for gymnastics in the clubs organized by their fathers and grandfathers, and for a long while the sport was dominated by foreign groups.

After the Amateur Athletic Union assumed national control in 1897, other clubs, where gymnastics had been unknown before, developed their own stars. Year after year the monopoly which the foreign born, or first generation

Americans, had on the titles, became weaker, as fourth, fifth and sixth-generation Americans took to the sport. But at no time has the so-called American been able to roll back the foreign-born to a secondary role for any prolonged period.

Quite a few years ago, the colleges began to tutor gymnastics, and in 1940 the first college team in the history of the sport—the University of Illinois—captured the national championship and tied for it in 1941. Since then the high schools and junior high schools have been featuring gymnastics and are developing performers who compare with the greatest foreigners.

Roy E. Moore, then chairman of the National A.A.U. Gymnastics Committee, commenting on the 1952 Olympic Games in the "Gymnastics Yearbook," reported that a record number of twenty-three nations sent teams to Helsinki, Finland. In addition, several countries were represented by individuals, giving the men a total of 183 competitors.

Moore said that the facilities provided by the Finnish gymnastic body were the best ever for the Games and pointed out that the United States, in finishing in the upper third bracket, or eighth place, had made a very creditable showing.

The Russians, entering the competition for the first time, won the team title and had the individual all-around winner in Tchoukarine. Edward Scrobe and Bob Stout made the best showing for the Americans and Moore, in an article in the "Amateur Athlete," stated that this duo would have made any of the teams that took part in the Olympics. Moore's findings were based on complete summaries of every event.

Russian athletes excelled again in the 1956 Olympics. Russia continued to dominate the Olympics through the 1972 games in the women's division but Japan cornered the gold medals in the men's.

In 1969, the A.A.U. and N.C.A.A. separated gymnastics from trampoline, tumbling, and rebound tumbling competition.

FAMOUS GYMNASTS AND TEAMS
Men

Of all the gymnasts in this country, Alfred Jochim undoubtedly was the greatest and of all the clubs featuring the sport the Swiss Turn Verein of Hudson County, N.J., of which Jochim was a member, was the most amazing.

Jochim flashed into fame by winning the A.A.U. all-around title in 1925, repeated in 1926, 1927, 1928, 1929 and 1930 and came back in 1933 to gain his seventh crown. George Wheeler, of the First U.P. Community House, Pittsburgh, is the runner-up with five championships—1937, 1938, 1939, 1940 and 1941.

The Swiss Turn Verein won its first team championship in 1926, lost in 1927, regained the title in 1928 and was unbeaten until 1940, when Illinois stopped its phenomenal streak. The Swiss lost again in 1941, climbed back to the throne in 1942, but surrendered to Penn State College's great team in 1943. At all times it has been very powerful, and it has been a case of "beat the Swiss and win the title."

The first all-around champion was Earl Linderman of Camden, N.J., in 1897. Others include O. Steffen, New York, 3 times a title winner; John F. Bissinger, New York, twice; E. C. Brendlin, Camden, N.J.; Anton Heida, Philadelphia; Fred Steffens, Brooklyn, twice; Frank Jirasek, Cedar Rapids, Iowa, twice; Paul Krimmel, New York, twice; Franz Kanis, Newark, N.J., three times a champion; Peter Hol, New York, twice; Joseph Oszy, New York, twice; Curtis Rottman, New York, twice; Frank Kriz, New York, twice; Jochim; Frank Haubold, New Jersey, twice; Frank Cumiskey, New Jersey, five times; Fred H. Meyer, New York; Wheeler, five times; Arthur E. Pitt, Union Hill, N.J. three times; William Roetzheim, a collegian, three times; Robert Stout, Philadelphia, twice.

Among the famous teams, in addition to the Swiss Turn Verein, have been Newark T.V., Norwegian T.V. and A.C., Los Angeles School of P.E., New York A.C., West Side Y.M.C.A., New York; Bohemian Gym Assn., New York; New York T.V., Los Angeles A.C., National Turners, Newark, N.J.; University of Illinois, Philadelphia Turngemeinde and Florida State.

Edward A. Hennig of Cleveland won his first A.A.U. Indian club swinging title in 1904, tied in 1911 and won in 1933, 1936, 1937, 1939, 1940, 1942, 1945, 1946, 1947, 1950 and 1951, which is quite a record for sustained athletic excellence. He also won the club swinging at the 1904 Olympic Games.

Women

The first A.A.U. championships for women, staged in 1931, found Roberta C. Ranck of Philadelphia as the all-around titleholder. Her specialties were the side horse and parallel bars. The next all around champion was Consetta Caruccio of Baltimore, who won in 1933 and repeated in 1934. Then, in succession, came Thera Steppich of Long Island, Jennie Caputo, Newark, N.J., Pearl Perkins and Helm McKee of Philadelphia, Margaret Weissmann of New York.

Miss Perkins (later Mrs. Nightingale) won two other championships and Miss McKee repeated in 1944. Clara M. Schroth of Philadelphia won successive titles in 1945 and 1946, then won four straight from 1949 to 1952, the latter year as Mrs. Lomady. Helen Schifano of Elizabeth, N.J., took the crown in 1947 and 1948.

The Philadelphia Turngemeinde, the National Turners of Newark, N.J., Germania T.V. of Baltimore, the New York T.V. and the Swiss Lincoln

T.V. of Chicago have developed some of the best women's teams.

NATIONAL A.A.U. CHAMPIONS

Men
All-Around

1897—Earl Linderman
1898-1900—O. Steffen
1901—John F. Bissinger
1902—E. C. Brendlin
1903—John F. Bissinger
1904—Anton Heida
1905-06—No competition
1907-08—Fred Steffens
1909-10—Frank Jirasek
1911-12—Paul Krimmel
1913-15—Franz Kanis
1916—Peter Hol
1917—B. Jorgensen
1918—Joseph Oszy
1919—Peter Hol
1920—Joseph Oszy
1921—Curtis Rottman
1922—Frank Kriz
1923—Curtis Rottman
1924—Frank Kriz
1925-30—Alfred Jochim
1931-32—Frank Haubold
1933—Alfred Jochim
1934—Frank Cumiskey
1935—Frederick H. Meyer
1936—Frank Cumiskey
1937-41—George Wheeler
1942-44—Arthur E. Pitt
1945-47—Frank Cumiskey
1948—Edward Scrobe
1949-51—William Roetzheim
1952-53—Robert Stout
1954—Charles Simms
1955—Karl Schwenzfeier and John Miles (tie)
1956-59—John Beckner
1960—Fred Orlofsky
1961—Nobuyuki Aihara
1962—Donald Tonry
1963-66—Makoto Sakamoto
1967—Yoshi Hayasaki
1968—Makoto Sakamoto
1969—Mauno Nissinen
1970-71—Yoshi Takei
1972—Makoto Sakamoto

Flying Rings

1885-94—Robert Stoll
1895-96—No competition
1897-1900—C. Berndt
1901—P. M. Kempf
1902—E. F. Kunath
1903—Paul M. Kemp
1904—Herman T. Glass
1905-06—No competition
1907—E. F. Kunath

1908-15—J. D. Gleason
1916-18—Otto A. Poll
1919-20—J .D. Gleason
1921—John Kristufek
1922—J. D. Gleason
1923—A. Pfeiffer
1924—E. Kremla
1925-27—Paul W. Krempel
1928—George J. Gulack
1929—Alfred Jochim
1930—Paul W. Krempel
1931—Arthur Gilmore
1932—W. Denton
1933-34—Arthur Gilmore
1935—George J. Gulack
1936—Joseph Goldenburg
1937—Arthur Gilmore
1938—Arthur E. Pitt
1939-41—Joseph Goldenburg
1942—Louis R. Fina
1943—J. William Buffa
1944—Frank Cumiskey
1945—Waldemir Baskovich
1946—William Bonsall
1947—Waldemir Baskovich
1948—J. William Buffa
1949—Waldemir Baskovich
1950—George Wickler, Marcus Gilden (tie)
1951—John Miles
1952—George Wickler
1953—George Wickler (Still Rings)
1954—Leonard Harris (Still Rings)
1955— John Miles (Still Rings)
Samuel Bailie (Flying Rings)
1956— Richard Beckner (Still Rings)
Fred Hoerner (Flying Rings)
1957— Attila Takach, Armando Vega (Tie, Still Rings)
Tom Darling (Flying Rings)
1958—Ken Cheney
1959-61—Thomas Darling
1962—Charles Denney
(No Further Competition)

Free Calisthenics

1921—Curtis Rottman
1922—B. Jorgensen
1923—Alfred Jochim
1924—Frank Kriz
1925—E. Preiss
1926-27—Paul Krempel
1928-34—Alfred Jochim
1935—Frank Cumiskey
1936—Fred H. Meyer
1937-41—George Wheeler
1942-45—Arthur E. Pitt
1946—Paul E. Fina
1947—Ray Sorensen
1948-49—Robert Stout
1950-51—Ara Hairabedian
1952—Jean Cronstedt

1953—Robert Stout
1954—Don Faber
1955—John Beckner
1956—Chick Cicio
1957-58—Attila Takach
1959—Jamile Ashmore
1960—Armando Vega
1961—Nobuyuki Aihara
1962—Donald Tonry
1963—Armando Vega
1964—Rich Pascale
1965—Makoto Sakamoto
1966—Toby Towson
1967—Makoto Sakamoto
1968-70—Toby Towson
1971-72—Yoshi Takei

Horizontal Bar

1885—R. Molineux
1886-87—F. J. Hosp
1888-89—R. Molineux
1890—G. Ahl
1891-92—C. Bayer
1893—H. Zettler
1894—C. Bayer
1895-96—No competition
1897-1900—C. Berndt
1901—John F. Bissinger
1902—E. C. Brendlin
1903—Anton Jahoda
1904—Anton Heida, Edward A. Hennig (tie)
1905-06—No competition
1907—A. Schnall
1908—Fred Steffens
1909—No competition
1910—Paul Krimmel
1911—Edward A. Hennig
1912—Paul Krimmel
1913-15—Franz Kanis
1916—B. Jorgensen
1917—F. Hell
1918—Curtis Rottman
1919—Peter Hol
1920-23—Curtis Rottman
1924—Frank Kriz
1925—Curtis Rottman
1926—Alfred Jochim
1927—Harold G. Newhart
1928-30—Alfred Jochim
1931—Gustav Schmelcher
1932—Michael Schuler
1933—Jack Holst
1934-36—Frank Cumiskey
1937—Chester Phillips
1938—George Wheeler
1939—C. M. Phillips
1940—Arthur E. Pitt
1941—George Wheeler
1942-43—Arthur E. Pitt
1944-46—Frank Cumiskey
1947—Edward Scrobe
1948—Frank Cumiskey

1949—Edward Scrobe
1950—William Roetzheim
1951—Harold S. Lewis, William Roetzheim (tie)
1952—Robert Stout
1953—Charles Simms
1954—Jean Cronstedt
1955-57—Abie Grossfeld
1958—John Beckner
1959—Arthur Sherlock
1960—John Beckner
1961—Takashi Mitsukuri
1962—Robert Lynn
1963—Makoto Sakamoto
1964—Ron Barak
1965-68—Makoto Sakamoto
1969—John Ellas
1970-71—Yoshi Takei
1972—Makoto Sakamoto

Still Rings

1959—Jamile Ashmore
1960—Fred Orlofsky
1961—Nobuyuki Aihara
1962—Carl Wolf
1963-64—Armando Vega
1965-66—Makoto Sakamoto
1967—Sei Ito
1968—Steve Cohen
1969—Robert Emery
1970-72—Yoshi Takei

Indian Clubs

1885-87—Joseph D. Harris
1888—F. Schroeder
1889-90—No competition
1891—C. E. Smith
1892—J. H. Dougherty
1893-94—Joseph D. Harris
1895—T. Mert
1896-97—No competition
1898—Joseph D. Harris
1899-1903—F. Metz Jr.
1904—Edward A. Hennig
1905-06—No competition
1907—R. C. Wilson
1908—George A. Lynn
1909-10—Joseph D. Harris
1911—Edward A. Hennig, Joseph Savage (tie)
1912-14—Ray W. Dutcher
1915-16—J. L. McCloud
1917-18—Ray W. Dutcher
1919—J. L. McCloud
1920—Ray W. Dutcher
1921—J. L. McCloud
1922-28—Ray W. Dutcher
1929-30—Robert Job
1931—James Nicoll
1932—Phil Ehrenberg
1933—Edward A. Hennig
1934—James Nicoll
1935—Moses J. Firestone
1936-37—Edward A. Hennig

1938–Victor Krygowski
1939-40–Edward A. Hennig
1941–Vernon S. Gilmore
1942–Edward A. Hennig
1943–Vernon S. Gilmore
1944–William Wintersteen
1945-47–Edward A. Hennig
1948-49–George Hearn
1950-51–Edward A. Hennig
1952–No competition
1953–Don Holder
(No further competition)

Long Horse

1897–Earl Linderman
1898–John F. Bissinger
1899–O. Steffen
1900-01–John F. Bissinger
1902–Anton Jahoda
1903–John F. Bissinger
1904–Anton Heida, George Eyser (tie)
1905-06–No competition
1907–L. Spann
1908–Joseph Gregor
1909-10–William Heisler
1911–Joseph Gregor
1912-13–Paul Krimmel
1914–Franz Kanis
1915-16–Peter Hol
1917–V. Winsjansen
1918–Frank Kriz
1919–Paul Krempel
1920–V. Winsjansen
1921–Curtis Rottman
1922–Frank Kriz
1923–Curtis Rottman
1924–Max Wandrer
1925–Fred Berg
1926–Adolph Zink
1927–Fred Berg
1928–Rudolf Hradecky
1929–Adolph Zink
1930-34–Alfred Jochim
1935–Frederick H. Meyer
1936–Rudolf Hradecky
1937-41–George Wheeler
1942–Arthur E. Pitt
1943–Lt. Newton Loken, U.S.N.
1944–Rudolf Hradecky
1945–Frank Cumiskey
1946–Rudolf Hradecky
1947–Lt. Col. Robert C. Sears, Rudolf
        Hradecky (tie)
1948–Joseph Kotys
1949–William Tom
1950–Jack Barnes
1951–Edward Scrobe
1952–Archie Durham
1953–Robert Stout
1954–Charles Simms
1955–John Miles
1956–Charles Simms

1957–Armando Vega
1958-59–Donald Tonry
1960–Larry Banner
1961–Takashi Mitsukuri
1962–Wilhelm Weiler
1963-64–Armando Vega
1965–Makoto Sakamoto
1966–Fred Roethlisberger
1967–Sei Ito
1968–Makoto Sakamoto
1969–Paul Tickenoff
1970–John Crosby
1971–Barry Slotten
1972–Melvin Hill

Parallel Bars

1885–A. H. Beck
1886–H. S. Pettit
1887–O. Fuchs
1888–B. Klein
1889-90–G. Ahl
1891–B. Klein
1892–C. Bayer
1893–G. Ahl
1894–E. Buehler
1895-96–No competition
1897-1900–O. Steffen
1901–E. C. Brendlin
1902–Joseph Buner
1903–E. C. Brendlin
1904–George Eyster
1905-06–No competition
1907–A. Schnall
1908–George Ketcham
1909-10–Frank Jirasek
1911-12–W. Dittman
1913–Paul Krimmel
1914-15–Franz Kanis
1916–Peter Hol
1917-18–B. Jorgensen
1919–Peter Hol
1920–Joseph Oszy
1921–Curtis Rottman
1922–Frank Kriz
1923-25–Walter Meyer
1926–Alfred Jochim
1927–Michael Schuler
1928-29–Alfred Jochim
1930–Paul W. Krempel, Herman Witzig (tie)
1931–Alfred Jochim
1932–Frank Haubold
1933-34–Alfred Jochim
1935–Frederick H. Meyer
1936–Arthur E. Pitt
1937-41–George Wheeler
1942–Arthur E. Pitt, Harold Zimmerman (tie)
1943–Solomon P. Small
1944-45–Frank Cumiskey
1946–Edward Scrobe
1947–Lt. Col. Robert C. Sears
1948-49–Joseph Kotys

1950—Edward Scrobe
1951—Joseph Kotys
1952—Edward Scrobe
1953—John Beckner
1954—Jean Cronstedt
1955—Edward Scrobe
1956—John Beckner
1957—Armando Vega
1958—John Beckner
1959—John Beckner, Edward Scrobe (tie)
1960—Armando Vega, Fred Orlofsky (tie)
1961—Nobuyuki Aihara
1962—Donald Tonry
1963-64—Armando Vega
1965—Makoto Sakamoto
1966—Makoto Sakamoto, Greg Weiss (tie)
1967—Yoshi Hayasaki
1968—Makoto Sakamoto
1969—Yoshi Hoyasaki
1970—Yoshi Takei
1971—Brent Simmons
1972—Yoshi Takei

Side Horse

1897—T. Hartel
1898—O. Steffen
1899-1901—John F. Bissinger
1902—Joseph Buner
1903—John F. Bissinger
1904—Anton Heida
1905-06—No competition
1907-09—Roy E. Moore
1910—A. Klar
1911—T. Simmons
1912-13—Roy E. Moore
1914-15—Franz Kanis
1916—Joseph Oszy
1917—I. C. Zenker
1918—Joseph Oszy
1919—Paul W. Krempel
1920—Charles M. Cremer
1921—Curtis Rottman
1922—Joseph B. Richter
1923—Charles M. Cremer
1924—Joseph B. Richter
1925—Charles M. Cremer
1926-28—Alfred Jochim
1929-31—Frank Haubold
1932—Frank Cumiskey
1933—Alfred Jochim
1934-35—William L. Taylor
1936-37—Frank Cumiskey
1938-40—George Wheeler
1941—William L. Taylor
1942—Frank Cumiskey
1943—Arthur E. Pitt
1944—Alex Julian
1945-47—Frank Cumiskey
1948—Stephen Greene
1949-50—Eugene Rabbitt
1951—William Roetzheim, Eugene Rabbitt (tie)

1952—Eugene Rabbitt
1953—William Roetzheim
1954—Robert Diamond
1955—James Brown
1956—Joseph Kotys
1957-58—Arthur Shurlock
1959—John Beckner
1960—Garland O'Quinn
1961—Shuji Tsurumi
1962—William Buck
1963—Greg Weiss
1964—Russ Mills
1965—Makoto Sakamoto
1966—Makoto Sakamoto, Steve Cohen (tie)
1967—Arne Lascari
1968—John Russo
1969—Dave Thor
1970—Charlie Morse
1971—Ken Liehr
1972—Theodore Marcy

Tumbling

1885—No competition
1886—W. Haas
1887-92—No competition
1893—P. Steier
1894—W. Haas
1895-96—No competition
1897-98—W. Haas
1899-1900—George Steier
1901—Frank Hamilton
1902-03—Paul E. Steier
1904-06—No competition
1907-08—A. Schnall
1909-10—Henry Jacknal
1911-14—M. J. Bedford
1915—Joseph F. Dunn
1916-21—Arthur W. Nugent
1922-24—Joseph F. Dunn
1925-26—David H. Sharpe
1927—E.V. Klinker
1928-29—William J. Hermann
1930—Leo Vandendaele
1931—William J. Hermann
1932—Rowland Wolfe
1933—Edwin Gross
1934—Kenneth Carter
1935—Charles J. Keeney
1936-37—Frank Wells
1938-39—Joe Giallombardo
1940-43—George Szypula
1944—Harold Frey
1945—Irvin E. Bedard
1946—Andrew Pasinski
1947—Charles W. Thomson
1948-50—Irvin E. Bedard
1951-54—Richard Browning
1955-56—James Sebbo
1957—Jeff Austin
1958—L. Nocera
1959—62—Harold Holmes
1963—Phil Voaz

1964–Rusty Mitchell
1965–Kean Day
1966–Phil Voaz
1967–Tom Proulx
1968–Doug Boger
(Discontinued)

Rope Climb

(20 feet–hands alone)

1888–Robert Stoll
1889–F.A. Lang
1890–J. Hoffman
1891-94–B. Sanford
1895-96–No competition
1897-98–B. Sanford
1899-1903–Edward Kunath
1904–George Eyser
1905-06–No competition
1907–Edward Kunath
1908–Joseph T. Smith
1909–Edward Kunath
1910–T. Anastas
1911–G.F. Septhon
1912–T. Anastas
1913-14–E. Lindenbaum
1915–R. Illig
1916-17–F. Siebert
1918–L. Weissman
1919–K. Fintzelberg
1920–L. Weissman
1921–George Taylor
1922-23–L. Weissman
1924–J.T. Andreasen
1925-27–Manfred Kraemer
1928–John R. Waterman
1929–Manfred Kraemer
1930–Leonard Stern
1931–Gustav Baack
1932-33–Randall Bryden
1934–Herman Dock
1935–Roman N. Pieo
1936–Harrison Houston
1937–Roman N. Pieo
1938-39–Stanley Ellison
1940-41–Roman N. Pieo
1942–Charles Senft
1943–Charles Lebow
1944-46–Stephen Greene
1947–Garvin E. Smith
1948-50–Don Perry
1951–Richard Browning
1952-54–Don Perry
1955–Robert Hammond
1956-58–Robert Manning
1959–Garvin Smith
1960–N.D. Hulme
1961–Robert Winter
1962–Steven Leidner
(Discontinued)

Rebound Tumbling

1959–Ronald Munn

1960–Larry Snyder
1961–Thomas Osterland
1962–Frank Schmitz
1963-66–Wayne Miller
1967-68–David Jacobs
(Discontinued)

Trampoline

1962–Frank Schmitz
1963–Wayne Miller
1964–Wayne Miller
1965–Jim Yongue
1966–Wayne Miller
1967-68–David Jacobs
(Discontinued)

Team

1914-15–Newark (N.J.) Turn Verein
1916-17–Norwegian Turn and Athletic Club
1918–National Turners, Newark, N.J.
1919–Los Angeles School of Physical Training
1920–New York Athletic Club
1921–New York Turn Verein
1922–New York Athletic Club
1923-24–New York Turn Verein
1925–Los Angeles A.C.
1926–Swiss Turn Verein of Hudson County, N.J.
1927–New York Turn Verein
1928-39–Swiss Turn Verein of Hudson County,
        N.J.
1940–University of Illinois
1941–University of Illinois, Bohemian Gymnastic
        Association Sokol, New York (tie)
1942–Swiss Gymnastic Society, Union City, N.J.
1943–Pennsylvania State College
1944–Swiss Gymnastic Society, Union City, N.J.
1945–Pennsylvania State College
1946-47–Swiss Gymnastic Society, Union City,
        N.J.
1948–Pennsylvania State College
1949–University of Illinois Navy Pier
1950–Los Angeles Athletic Club
1951–Florida State University
1952–Philadelphia Turners
1953–Florida State Gymkana
1954–Los Angeles Turners
1955–Florida State Gymkana
1956–No competition
1957-59–Los Angeles Turners
1960–Penn State
1961–Southern Illinois
1962-64–Los Angeles Turners
1965-66–Southern Connecticut Gym Club
1967–Northwestern Louisiana State
1968–No competition
1969–Husky Gym Club, Seattle
1970-72–New York A.C.

Women
All-Around

1931–Roberta C. Ranck
1932–No competition

1933–34–Consetta Caruccio
1935–Thera Steppich
1936–Jennie Caputo
1937–Pearl Perkins
1938–Helm McKee
1939–Margaret Weissmann
1940–No competition
1941–Mrs. Pearl Perkins Nightingale
1942–No competition
1943–Mrs. Pearl Perkins Nightingale
1944–Helm McKee
1945–46–Clara M. Schroth
1947–48–Helen Schifano
1949–51–Clara M. Schroth
1952–Mrs. Clara Schroth Lomady
1953–54–Ruth Grulkowski
1955–Ernestine Russell
1956–Sandra Ruddick
1957–Muriel Davis
1958–59–Ernestine Russell
1960–Gail Sontgerath
1961–Kazuki Kadowaki
1962–Dale McClements
1963–Muriel Grossfeld
1964–Marie Walther
1965–Doris Fuchs Brause
1966–Linda Metheny
1967–Carolyn Hacker
1968–Linda Metheny
1969–Joyce Tanac
1970–72–Linda Metheny

Flying Rings

1933–35–Thera Steppich
1936–Consetta Caruccio
1937–Mary Conlin
1938–Margaret Weissmann
1939–Andrea J. Barbustiak
1940–No competition
1941–Margaret Weissmann
1942–No competition
1943–Pearl Perkins
1944–45–Helm McKee
1946–Clara M. Schroth
1947–Helen Schifano
1948–51–Clara M. Schroth
1952–No competition
1953–Clara Urban
1954–No competition
1955–Doris Fuchs
1956–No competition
1957–Louise Wright
(No further competition)

Calisthenics

1931–Dorothy M. Rossenbach
1932–No competition
1933–Consetta Caruccio
1934–Thera Steppich
1935–Consetta Caruccio, Adelaide Meyer (tie)
1936–Jennie Caputo
1937–Consetta Caruccio

1938–Margaret Weissmann
1939–Andrea J. Barbustiak
1940–43–No competition
1944–46–Clara M. Schroth
1947–Helen Schifano
1948–Clara M. Schroth
1949–Mrs. Meta Elste
1950–51–Clara M. Schroth
1952–Mrs. Clara Schroth Lomady
1953–Ruth Grulkowski
1954–55–Ernestine Russell
1956–58–Muriel Davis
1959–Betty Maycock
1960–64–Muriel Grossfeld
1965–Dale McClements
1966–68–Linda Metheny
1969–Joyce Tanac
1970–72–Linda Metheny

Indian Clubs

1941–Mrs. Roberta Ranck Bonniwell
1942–No competition
1943–44–Elsie Carlile
1945–49–Margaret Dutcher
1950–51–Mrs. Roberta Ranck Bonniwell
(No further competition)

Parallel Bars

1931–Roberta C. Ranck
1932–No competition
1933–Thera Steppich
1934–Consetta Caruccio
1935–Thera Steppich
1936–Jennie Caputo
1937–Pearl Perkins
1938–Andrea J. Barbustiak
1939–Helen Schifano
1940–No competition
1941–Pearl Perkins
1942–No competition
1943–Pearl Perkins
1944–Helm McKee
1945–Marian Twining
1946–Clara M. Schroth
1947–Meta Neumann
1948–Helen Schifano
1949–50–Clara M. Schroth
1951–Mrs. Marian Twining Barone
1952–Mrs. Clara Schroth Lomady
1953–Barbara Cortilet
1954–Louise Wright
1955–Ernestine Russell
1956–57–Sandra Ruddick
1958–Myra Perkins
1959–Marta Nagy
1960–Muriel Grossfeld
1961–Doris Fuchs
1962–Gail Sontgerath
1963–Muriel Grossfeld
1964–Doris Fuchs
1965–Linda Metheny
1966–Doris Fuchs Brause

1967–Linda Metheny
1968–Doris Fuchs Brause
1969–Joyce Tanac
1970–Linda Metheny
1971–72–Roxanne Pierce

Side Horse
1931–Roberta C. Ranck
1932–No competition
1933–Roberta C. Ranck
1934–36–Mary Conlin
1937–Jennie Caputo
1938–Consetta Caruccio
1939–Andrea J. Barbustiak
1940–No competition
1941–Pearl Perkins
1942–No competition
1943–Pearl Perkins
1944–Clara M. Schroth
1945–Clara M. Schroth, Marian Twining (tie)
1946–47–Helen Schifano
1948–49–Clara M. Schroth
1950–Mrs. Marian Twining Barone
1951–Clara M. Schroth
1952–Mrs. Clara Schroth Lomady
1953–Ruth Grulkowski
1954–Louise Wright
1955–Ernestine Russell
1956–57–Sandra Ruddick
1958–59–Ernestine Russell
1960–Betty Maycock
1961–Kazuki Kadowaki
1962–Dale McClements
1963–Avis Tieber, Beverly Averyt (tie)
1964–Avis Tieber
1965–Doris Fuchs Brause
1966–Vera Govaerts
1967–Carolyn Hacker
1968–69–Joyce Tanac
1970–Adele Gleaves
1971–Roxanne Pierce
1972–Nancy Theis

Tumbling
1938–Helen Matkowsky
1939–42–Vera Tipowitz
1943–44–Bernice Nebelong
1945–46–Leonora Owens
1947–48–Jo Ann Matthews
1949–Marie Armstrong
1950–51–Joanne Slocum
1952–57–Barbara Galleher
1958–59–Teresa Montefusco
1960–Avis Tieber
1961–62–Barbara Galleher
1963–64–Judy Wills
1965–Barbara Gallagher
1966–68–Judy Wills
(Discontinued)

Balance Beam
1941–51–Clara M. Schroth
1952–Mrs. Meta Elste
1953–54–Ruth Grulkowski
1955–Ernestine Russell
1956–Sandra Ruddick
1957–Muriel Davis
1958–Ernestine Russell
1959–Muriel Davis
1960–Gail Sontgerath
1961–Kazuki Kadowaki
1962–64–Muriel Grossfeld
1965–Marie Walther
1966–Linda Metheny
1967–Carolyn Hacker
1968–Linda Metheny
1969–Joyce Tanac
1970–Linda Metheny
1971–Linda Metheny; Theresa
      Fileccia (tie)
1972–Linda Metheny

Rebound Tumbling
1961–Barbara Galleher
1962–Beverly Avery
1963–64–Judy Wills
1965–No competition
1966–68–Judy Wills
(Discontinued)

Trampoline
1962–Beverly Averyt
1963–64–Judy Wills
1965–Beverly Averyt
1966–68–Judy Wills
(Discontinued)

Team Drill
1941–Panzer College
1942–No competition
1943–(Brooklyn (N.Y.) Central Y.M.C.A.
1944–Panzer College
1945–Elizabeth (N.J.) Y.W.H.A.
1946–Panzer College
1947–Elizabeth Y.M. and Y.W.H.A.
1948–Philadelphia Turners
1949–Lincoln Turners, Chicago
1950–Swiss Turn Verein, Paterson, N.J.
1951–Lincoln Turners, Chicago
1952–No competition
1953–Florida State Gymkana
1954–American Sokol, Eastern District (N.J.)
(No further competition.)

NATIONAL COLLEGIATE CHAMPIONS
All-Around
1938–39–Joe Giallombardo, Illinois
1940–Joe Giallombardo and Lou Fina, Illinois
      (tie)
1941–Courtney Shanken, Chicago

1942—Newt Loken, Minnesota
1948—Ray Sorenson, Penn State
1949-50—Joe Kotys, Kent State
1951—William Roetzheim, Florida State
1952—Jack Beckner; Southern California
1953-54—Jean Cronstedt, Penn State
1955—Karl Schwenfeier, Penn State
1956—Don Tonry, Illinois
1957—Armando Vega, Penn State
1958—Abie Grossfeld, Illinois
1959—Armando Vega, Penn State
1960—Jay Werner, Penn State
1961—Gregor Weiss, Penn State
1962—Robert Lynn, Southern California
1963—Gil Larose, Michigan
1964—Ron Barak, Southern California
1965—Mike Jacobson, Penn State
1966-67—Steve Cohen, Penn State
1968—Makoto Sakamoto, Southern California
1969—Mauno Nissinen, Washington
1970-71—Yoshi Hayasaki, Washington
1972—Steve Hug, Stanford

Flying Rings

1938—Joe Giallombardo, Illinois
1939—Ron Hall, Southern California
1940—Bill Butler, Navy
1941—Del Daly, Minnesota
1942—Jim Parker, Navy
1948—George Hayes, Temple
1949—Jerry Todd, Southern California
1950—Bob Schneider, Navy
1951—Mel Stout, Michigan State
1952—Jack Sharp, Florida State
1953—Ken Bartlett, Minnesota
1954—Manuel Procopio, Penn State
1955—George Wikler, Southern California
1956—Fred Hoerner, Navy
1957-58—Tom Darling, Pittsburgh
1959-60—Jay Werner, Penn State
1961—Frank Snay, Navy
(Discontinued)

Still Rings

1959—Armando Vega, Penn State
1960—Sam Garcia, Southern California
1961—Fred Orlofsky
1962-63—Dale Cooper, Michigan State
1964—Chris Evans, Arizona State
1965—Glenn Gailis, Iowa
1966—Ed Gunny, Michigan State
1967—Josh Robison, California
1968—Pat Arnold, Arizona
1969—Paul Vexler, Penn State, Ward Maythaler,
     Iowa, (tie)
1970—Dave Seal, Indiana State
1971—Charles Ropiequet, Southern Illinois
1972—Dave Seal, Indiana State

Free Exercise

1941—Lou Fina, Illinois

1953—Bob Sullivan, Illinois
1954—Jean Cronstedt, Penn State
1955—Don Faber, U.C.L.A.
1956—Jamile Ashmore, Florida State
1957—Norman Marks, Los Angeles State
1958—Abie Grossfeld, Illinois
1959—Don Tonry, Illinois
1960—Ray Hadley, Illinois
1961-62—Robert Lynn, Southern California
1963—Tom Seward, Penn State, and Mike
     Henderson, Michigan (tie)
1964—Rusty Mitchell, Southern Illinois
1965-66—Frank Schmitz, Southern Illinois
1967—Dave Jacobs, Michigan
1968-69—Toby Towson, Michigan State
1970—Tom Prouix, Colorado State
1971—Stormy Eaton, New Mexico
1972—Odess Lovin, Oklahoma

Horizontal Bar

1938—Bob Sears, Army
1939—Adam Walters, Temple
1940—Norm Boardman, Temple
1941—Newt Loken, Minnesota
1942—Norm Boardman, Temple
1948—Joe Calvetti, Illinois
1949—Bob Stout, Temple
1950—Joe Kotys, Kent State
1951—William Roetzheim, Florida State
1952—Charles Simms, Southern California
1953—Hal Lewis, Navy
1954—Jean Cronstedt, Penn State
1955—Carlton Rintz, Michigan State
1956—Ronnie Amster, Florida State
1957-58—Abie Grossfeld, Illinois
1959-60—Stanley Tarshis, Michigan State
1961—Bruno Klaus, Southern Illinois
1962—Robert Lynn, Southern California
1963—Gil LaRose, Michigan
1964—Ron Barak, Southern California
1965—Jim Curzi, Michigan State, and Mike
     Jacobson, Penn State (tie)
1966—Rusty Rock, San Fernando Valley State
1967—Rich Grigsby, San Fernando Valley State
1968—Makoto Sakamoto, Southern California
1969—Bob Manna, New Mexico
1970—Yoshi Hayasaki, Washington
1971—Brent Simmons, Iowa State
1972—Tom Linder, Southern Illinois

Long Horse

1938—Erwin Beyer, Chicago
1939—Marv Forman, Illinois
1940-42—Earl Shanken, Chicago
1948—Jim Peterson, Minnesota
1962—Bruno Klaus, Southern Illinois
1963—Gil LaRose, Michigan
1964—Sid Oglesby, Syracuse
1965—Dan Millman, California
1966—Frank Schmitz, Southern Illinois

1967—Paul Mayer, Southern Illinois
1968—Bruce Colter, Los Angeles State
1969—Dan Bowles, California; Jack McCarthy,
Illinois (tie)
1970—Doug Boger, Arizona
1971—Pat Mahoney, San Fernando Valley
1972—Gary Morava, Southern Illinois

Parallel Bars

1938—Erwin Beyer, Chicago
1939—Bob Sears, Army
1940—Bob Hanning, Minnesota
1941—Caton Cobb, Illinois
1942—Hal Zimmerman, Penn State
1948—Ray Sorenson, Penn State
1949—Joe Kotys, Kent State, and Mel Stout,
Michigan State (tie)
1950—Joe Kotys, Kent State
1951-52—Jack Beckner, Southern California
1953-54—Jean Cronstedt, Penn State
1955—Carlton Rintz, Michigan State
1956-57—Armando Vega, Penn State
1958—Ted Muzyczko, Michigan State
1959—Armando Vega, Penn State
1960—Robert Lynn, Southern California
1961—Fred Tijerina, Southern Illinois
Jeff Cardinalli, Springfield
1962—Robert Lynn, Southern California
1963—Arno Lascari, Michigan
1964—Ron Barak, Southern California
1965-66—Jim Curzi, Michigan State
1967-68—Makoto Sakamoto, Southern California
1969-70—Ron Rapper, Michigan
1971—Brent Simmons, Iowa State; Tom Dunn,
Penn State (tie)
1972—Dennis Mazur, Iowa State

Side Horse

1938-39—Erwin Beyer, Chicago
1940—Harry Koehnemann, Illinois
1941-42—Caton Cobb, Illinois
1948—Steve Greene, Penn State
1949—Joe Berenato, Temple
1950—Eugene Rabbitt, Syracuse
1951—Joe Kotys, Kent State
1952—Frank Bare, Illinois
1953—Carlton Rintz, Michigan State
1954—Robert Lawrence, Penn State
1955—Carlton Rintz Michigan State
1956—James Brown, Los Angeles State
1957—John Davis, Illinois
1958—Bill Buck, Iowa
1959—Art Shurlock, California
1960-61—James Fairchild, Southern California
1962—Mike Aufrecht, Illinois
1963-64—Russ Mills, Yale
1965—Bob Elsinger, Springfield
1966—Gary Hoskins, Los Angeles State
1967—Keith McCanless, Iowa
1968—Jack Ryan, Colorado
1969—Keith McCanless, Iowa

1970—John Russo, Wisconsin; Russ Hoffman,
Iowa State (tie)
1971-72—Russ Hoffman, Iowa State

Trampoline

1948—Gay Hughes, Illinois
1949-51—Edsel Buchanan, Michigan
1952—Dick Gutting, Florida State
1953—Bob Hazlett, Iowa
1954—James Norman, Iowa
1955—Richard Albershardt, Indiana
1956—Don Harper, Florida State
1957—Glenn Wilson, Western Illinois
1958—Don Harper, Ohio State
1959—Ed Cole, Michigan
1960—Larry Snyder, Illinois
1961—Tom Gompf, Michigan
1962—Steven Johnson, Michigan State
1963—Gary Erwin, Michigan
1964—Gary Erwin, Michigan
1965—Frank Schmitz, Southern Illinois
1966—Wayne Miller, Michigan
1967—Dave Jacobs, Michigan
1968—George Huntzicker, Michigan
(Discontinued)

Tumbling

1938-40—Joe Giallombardo, Illinois
1941—John Adkins, Illinois
1942—George Szypula, Temple
1948-49—Charlie Thompson, California
1950—Irving Bedard, Illinois
1951-52—Bob Sullivan, Illinois
1953—James Sebbo, Syracuse
1954—Richard Browning, Illinois
1955—Lloyd Cochran, Southern California
1956—Dan Lirot, Illinois
1957-58—Frank Hailand, Illinois
1959—Dave Dulaney, Penn State
1960—Alvin Barasch, Illinois
1961—Jack Ryder, Florida State
1962—Rusty Mitchell, Southern Illinois
1963—Hal Holmes, Illinois
1964—Rusty Mitchell, Southern Illinois
(Discontinued)

Rope Climb

1938—Bob Sears, Army
1939—Ray Belardi, Army
1940—Stan Ellison, Navy
1941—Courtney Shanken, Chicago
1942—Dale Cox, Navy
1948-49—Ken Foreman, Southern California
1950-51—Leo Minotti, Syracuse
1952—John Claybrook, Army
1953-54—Don Perry, U.C.L.A.
1955—Robert Hammond, U.C.L.A.
1956—Philip Mullen, Penn State
1957-58—Garvin Smith, Los Angeles
1959—Don Littlewood, Penn State

1960—Nelson Hulme, Navy
1961-62—Paul Davis, California
(Discontinued)

Rebound Tumbling

1964—Gary Erwin, Michigan
1965—No competition
1966—Wayne Miller, Michigan
1967—Dave Jacobs, Michigan
1968—George Huntzicker, Michigan
(Discontinued)

Team

1938—Chicago
1939-42—Illinois
1943-47—No competition
1948—Penn State
1949—Temple
1950—Illinois
1951-52—Florida State
1953-54—Penn State
1955-56—Illinois
1957—Penn State
1958—Illinois, Michigan State (tie)
1959-61—Penn State
1962—Southern California
1963—Michigan
1964—Southern Illinois
1965—Penn State
1966-67—Southern Illinois
1968—California
1969—Iowa
1970—Michigan
1971—Iowa State
1972—Southern Illinois

GYMNASTIC EVENTS AND RULES

The gymnastic events in international championships are:

Free Calisthenics
Long Horse
Side Horse
Horizontal Bar
Parallel Bars
Still Rings
All-Around

Other than international events may include the following:

Tumbling
Rope Climbing
Flying (Swinging) Rings
Trampoline

The all-around competition includes all the six international events, with the grand total performance to be the determining factor.

One compulsory and one optional exercise is required for the horizontal bar, free calisthenics, long horse, side horse, parallel bars and still rings. All contestants must execute the compulsory exercise. The optional is an exercise of the contestants' choosing in which they feel they will appear at their best. The judges, usually 5 in number, score the contestants on both exercises, taking into account the degree of difficulty in performing the exercise, execution of the movement and the form displayed.

Tumbling is limited to 4 routines of not over 2 minutes duration on either 1 mat or several secured together. If any competitor touches the floor on either side of the mat while performing a straight mat routine, it is considered poor form and points are deducted accordingly.

On the flying rings, the combination must be performed with the rings in motion, maintaining an angle of at least 40 degrees. In rope climbing, each contestant gets 2 chances, with the fastest time deciding the winner. The rope is 1½ inches and the climb 20 feet. The athlete starts from a sitting position on the floor, both legs fully extended.

Trampoline competition consists of 3 sequences, with the first and second followed by 10-second rest stops. Each sequence must consist of a reasonable number of preparatory bounces, then the performer is allowed a maximum of 8 contacts with the trampoline bed. Club swinging, which was discontinued in 1954, requires 1 trial of 4 minutes. Each club must weigh 1 pound, and the dropping of a club ends the exercise.

Free calisthenics includes rhythmic movements combined with balance, strength and tumbling routines. The optional exercise must last not more than 2 minutes nor less than 1½ and must be performed without hand apparatus.

(For Olympic champions see section on Olympic Games.)

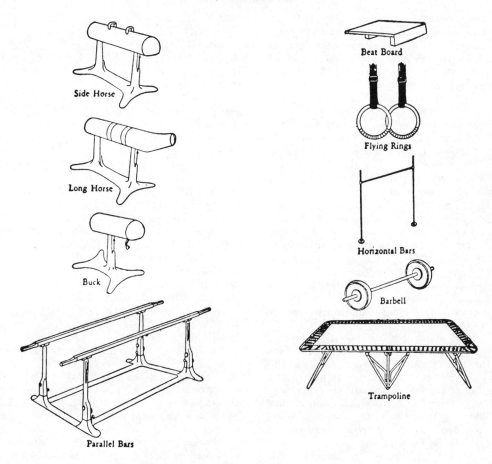

Gymnastics Apparatus. (Taken from "The Dictionary of Sports," by Parke Cummings, A. S. Barnes and Company, New York.)

HANDBALL

With the great emphasis placed on physical fitness in the United States today, Handball is growing in popularity as a conditioning sport. Competitors frequently lose several pounds in a strenuous match. Sedentary persons often keep in trim by playing handball. Courts are most frequently found in Y.M.C.A.'s, athletic clubs and college gymnasiums.

The Irish originated handball in the 10th Century, and this game undoubtedly was the parent of tennis.

The early name of the game in Ireland and England was "Fives"—five fingers to the hand.

Handball was a favorite sport in Ireland for centuries, but it made little progress until about 100 years ago, when one Meham Baggs, a Tipperary enthusiast, developed into a wizard by reason of the fact that he could control his shots in such a way as to make the ball spin, curve and do tricks on the rebound—to the utter bewilder-

ment of his rivals, who quickly learned all about "screw tosses" and the other tricks of the mighty Baggs, and then proceeded to give him real competition.

English schools adopted Handball many years ago. The game has enjoyed continued vogue, especially at Eton, where a fine player is a person of distinction.

One of the famous players of the 18th and 19th Centuries was John Cavanagh of St. Giles. Upon his death in 1819, a great tribute was paid to him in the newspaper, "Examiner," which included the following:

"Cavanagh is dead, and has not left his peer behind him. When he touched the ball, there was end to the chase. His eye was certain, his hand fatal, his presence of mind complete. He could do what he pleased, and he always knew exactly what to do. There was not only nobody equal, but nobody second to him."

Among the stars in Ireland in the 1870's was Phil Casey, who migrated to Brooklyn about 1882 and was amazed to learn that there were no handball courts in the United States and no players, except the idle ones, who, like himself, had come from British shores.

Casey quickly struck up an acquaintanceship with several of them, produced some of the balls he had brought from Ireland, and they proceeded with their game, batting the ball against convenient brick walls. But this was not satisfactory because the rough surfaces of the walls made it impossible to get the required spin, and so the technique of the game suffered.

By this time, people in the neighborhood, watching Casey and his companions, became interested and expressed a desire to play. Casey invited them and then sensed the opportunity to go commercial—to his own financial advantage. Getting the required capital, Casey built a handball court. It was 65 feet long, 25 feet wide, had a front wall 30 feet high and side walls of 25. His place was well patronized, and Casey used his profits to build other courts.

The "graduates" of the Casey school spread the gospel of handball and soon the game was played in almost every important center in this country. In places where there was not enough population to support an official court, the game was played against walls of wood or brick, and there wasn't a fireman in the land who didn't devote some of his leisure to playing handball against the side of the firehouse.

In 1887 or 1888, Bernard McQuade, a native of Ireland, then in New York, announced that he was a better man than Casey, and if Casey didn't think so he would meet Casey to determine the American championship. Casey quickly answered by defeating McQuade, and then decided to become world champion by the simple process of playing—and defeating—John Lawlor, then champion of Ireland.

The match was arranged for a $1,000 side bet, the first 10 games to be played in Cork, Ireland, the next 11 in the United States; the man taking the first 11 games to be acknowledged as world champion. Lawlor won 6 and Casey 4 in Ireland. In the United States, Casey took 7 straight.

Casey met all comers from then until 1900, when he ran out of opponents and announced his retirement. Soon afterward, the game, as a professional sport, withered and might have slipped into obscurity if it had not been for the Amateur Athletic Union. This organization saw the merits of handball, planned for its future, and, in 1897, conducted its first tournament, which returned Michael Eagan of Jersey City, by way of Galway, Ireland, as the first champion.

About 25 years ago Robert W. Kendler of Chicago put on a virtual one-man drive to increase interest in the sport, which is under the jurisdiction of the A.A.U. He was instrumental in the founding of the United States Handball Association.

The U.S.H.A. was organized in 1951, according to Mort Leve, as a "Players' Fraternity" to promote further the game and improve existing tournament conditions.

A title tournament was held in 1951 in competition with the A.A.U. The 1952 championships were conducted jointly and in December of that year, at the annual A.A.U. convention, a five-year pact was signed by the groups, with both pledged to "encourage greater participation in the sport of amateur handball." Agreement also was reached on recognition of A.A.U. traveling permits and amateur codes.

Leve adds that the U.S.H.A. since its founding has made much progress, with record entries in national events. Exhibition tours sponsored by the U.S.H.A. have "spread the gospel" and a monthly magazine devoted exclusively to handball is published. The magazine is Ace, 505 North Michigan Avenue, Chicago 11, Ill.

Among the successful U.S.H.A. innovations are the national intercollegiate, junior and masters tournaments.

Until 1900, the handball courts had 4 walls, each 22 feet high, with a playing surface of 46 x 22 feet. Only the hard handball was used. But activities on bathing beaches created the idea for a 1-wall court and brought the soft handball into use. Now the hard handball game is virtually extinct.

The bathers, seeking diversion while relaxing after a swim, played handball with a tennis ball, batting it against any near-by wall. Many enthusiasts, who had wanted to own and operate a court and who found the cost of a regulation 4-wall court too high, saw in the 1-wall court the realization of their ambitions.

One-wall courts first made their appearance on the bathing beaches in the Greater New York district, in 1913 and 1914. Soon they mushroomed elsewhere—on other beaches, in public halls, gymnasiums, etc. The popularity of this new type of handball spread to all parts of the country and handball was back again in high favor. Today there are more than 8,000 courts in the U.S. alone, with the main popularity centered in large metropolitan areas such as New York, Chicago, and Los Angeles.

The first National A.A.U. senior four-wall championship was staged in Los Angeles in 1919, and William Ranft of Los Angeles was the winner. The first National A.A.U. one-wall championship was held in New York in 1924 and was won by Jack Byrnes of New York.

One-wall handball, originating in Brooklyn, still is very popular there. Numerous 1-wall courts are in operation in the public parks of Greater New York.

Women rarely play the 4-wall game, but hundreds of thousands indulge in the 1-wall game, especially during the summer, either on the beaches or in one of the civic playgrounds, which teem with handball courts.

FAMOUS PLAYERS
Four-Wall Softball

William F. Ranft, J. Lacey, George Retzer, Max Gold, G. Klawiter, R. Retzer, Maynard Laswell, Joe Gordon, and Andy Berry, all of Los Angeles; Dr. Carl Haedge, St. Paul; Art Shinners, Milwaukee; Joe Murray and John J. Condon, San Francisco; R. Serrenberg and J. Bathey, Detroit; A. W. Paynter, Alfred Banuet, L. McMillan, J. Donovan, all of San Francisco; H. Dworman, Joe Griffin, John Bell, W. Kamman, and A. Schaufelberger, all of Detroit; Sam Atcheson, Memphis; Joe Platak, Chicago, ranked by many as the champion of champions; George Nelson, Baltimore, and Victor Hershkowitz of Brooklyn, a sensation in recent years.

Also, Angelo Trulio, Edward Hahn, Daniel Shea, Arthur Lennon, Frank Coyle, Edward Linz, Pat McDonough and John J. Dunwoody, all of New York; Leo Manka and Henry F. Herz Jr., of Brooklyn; Walter Plekan, Buffalo, and Gus Lewis and Charles Ruggles, Hollywood Calif.; Jack Clements, San Francisco, and Jack Emas, Philadelphia.

One-Wall Softball

Jack Byrnes, Harry Mearns, Simon LaFarge, Fred Schmidt, Morton Alexander, A. Aiello, John Seamon, William Sackman, Sam Buxbaum, Murray Vernon, Sol Goldman, Mike Schmookler, Seymour Alexander, Irving Jacobs, Harry Goldstein, Dan Levinson, Dave Margolis, Joseph Garber, Hershkowitz, Jack Londin, William Lauro, Irving Newman, George Gluckler, Harry Michitsch and the Obert brothers, Rubrecht, Oscar and Carl.

Present era of great players: Jim Jacobs, Johnny Sloan, Dave Graybill, Paul Haber, Marty Decatur, three Obert brothers, Oscar, Carl and Rubrecht (Ruby) . . . Phill Collins, Stuffy Singer, Bob Bourbeau . . . Canadian and former Ireland champion, Joey Maher . . . Ken Scheneider, Bus Lewis, Bob Lindsay, Pete Tyson, Dr. Stan London, Jack McDonald, Phil Elbert.

A.A.U. CHAMPIONS
Four-Wall Softball Singles

1919—William Ranft
1920—Max Gold
1921—Dr. Carl Haedge
1922—Art Shinners
1923—Joe Murray
1924-26—Maynard Laswell
1927—George Nelson
1928—Joe Griffin
1929-31—Alfred Banuet
1932—Angelo Trulio
1933—34—Sam Atcheson
1935—41—Joe Platak
1942—Jack Clements
1943—Joe Platak
1944—Frank Coyle
1945—Joe Platak
1946—Angelo Trulio
1947—48—Gus Lewis
1949—Victor Hershkowitz
1950—Ken Schneider
1951—Joseph Brady
1952—Victor Hershkowitz
1953—Thomas Ginty
1954—William Lauro
1955—Sam Costa
1956—Jimmy Jacobs
1957—Bob Brady
*1958—John Sloan
†1959—John Sloan
1960—James Jacobs
1961—Oscar Obert
1962—Carl Obert
1963—64—Oscar Obert
1965—Pat Kirby
1966—67—No competition
1968—Bill Yambrick
1969—Pat Kirby
1970—Dr. Steve August
1971—Pat Kirby
1972—Lou Russo

*Combined A.A.U.–U.S.H.A.–Y.M.C.A. "World Series"
†Combined A.A.U.–Y.M.C.A. tournament.

Four-Wall Softball Doubles

1919—Ranft—Lacey
1920—Klawiter—Retzer
1921—Spiegel—Asselin
1922—Laswell—Gold
1923—Bathey—Serrenberg
1924—McMillan—Donovan
1925—Kamman—Dworman
1926—McMillan—Donovan
1927—Kamman—Dworman
1928—Kamman—Schaufelberger
1929—Banuet—McMillan
1930—Banuet—Paynter
1931—Bathe—Dworman
1932—Trulio—Laswell
1933—Goudreau—Endzvick
1934—Hertz—Manka
1935—36—Berry—Gordon
1937—Platak—Weiller
1938—39—Coyle—Linz
1940—Gordon—Goldsmith
1941—Coyle—Linz
1942—Gordon—Goldsmith
1943—Gordon—Smith
1944—Platak—Quinn
1945—Atcheson—Dettwiller
1946—Coyle—Linz
1947—Haber—Samson
1948—Gluckler—Pahl

1949—Lewis—Haber
1950—Coyle—Baier
1951—Brady—Keays
1952—Coyle—Baier
1953—55—Abate—Ingrassia
1956—57—Sloan—Collins
*1958—Sloan—Collins
†1959—Sloan—Collins
1960—Sloan—Collins
1961—O. Obert—R. Obert
1962—O. Obert—R. Obert
1963—64—Oscar and Ruby Obert
1965—Ruby and Carl Obert
1966—67—No competition
1968—Ruby and Oscar Obert
1969—Ray Neveau—Simie Fein
1970—Terry Muck—Bill Yambrick
1971—72—Simie Fein—Ray Neveau

*Combined   A.A.U.—U.S.H.A.—Y.M.C.A.   "World
Series"
†Combined A.A.U.—Y.M.C.A. tournament.

Junior Four-Wall Softball Singles

1920—No competition
1921—P.J. McDonagh
1922—Maynard Laswell
1923—A.C. Hobelman
1924—J. Rodgers Flannery
1925—J.R.T. Hedeman
1926—J. Schaumer
1927—Tom Bolan
1928—Pat Young
1929—F. Olney
1930—Ed Hahn
1931—Angelo Trulio
1932—John Endzevick
1933—Charles Mentz
1934—K.E. Walter
1935—H. Herz
1936—J. Goudreau
1937—Jack Clements
1938—Walter Plekan
1939—Joe Gordon
1940—George Brotemarkle
1941—Ken Schneider
1942—Gus Lewis
1943—Bill Baier
1944—Joe Kulwicki
1945—Jack Srenco
1946—J. Emas
1947—Joseph Brady
1948—H. Schrutt
1949—Mal Dorfman
1950—Solly Newman
1951—Alvis Grant
1952—Edward Wilson
1953—Jimmy Jacobs
1954—No competition
1955—Sam Costa
1956—Harry Hyde
1957—Dick Langdon
1958—Oscar Obert

1959—No competition
1960—Marty Decatur
1961—F. Coyle
1962—C. Benham
1963—72—No competition

Junior Four-Wall Softball Doubles

1920—Henry—Smith
1921—Butler—Groden
1922—Micus—Byrne
1923—Straub—Flannery
1924—Schildecker—Sward
1925—Bolan—Owen
1926—Spalty—Hunt
1927—Hill—Hern
1928—Endzevick—Johnson
1929—Powers—Goube
1930—Hahn—Dunwoody
1931—Barry—Trulio
1932—Goudreau—Brown
1933—Ruddy—Coyle
1934—Manka—Herz
1935—Bruck—Knopp
1936—Berko—Bauer
1937—Goldsmith—McGinnis
1938—Schwartz—Pearlman
1939—Badham—Warren
1940—Phelan—Miller
1941—Schneider—Silver
1942—Dressler—Lappen
1943—Kendler—Baier
1944—Ehrlers—Corwin
1945—Klayman—Berg
1946—Abate—Gaughran
1947—Badham—Weisman
1948—Brennan—H. Schrutt
1949—Lehman—Meyer
1950—Gordon—DiRe
1951—Daum—McKay
1952—DiOrio—Serzen
1953—Decker—Rose
1954—No competition
1955—Emas—Dorfman
1956—Beattie—Hyde
1957—Langdon—Appenzeller
1958—Obert—Pushkal
1959—No competition
1960—C. Obert—R. Obert
1961—Boissiree—Aguila
1962—Laskow—Kramberg
1963—72—No competition

One-Wall Softball Singles

1924—Jack Byrnes
1925—26—No competition
1927—28—Murray Vernon
1929—Mike Schmookler
1930—Fred Schmidt
1931—Seymour Alexander
1932—No competition
1933—Irving Jacobs
1934—Harry Goldstein

1935—Jack Londin
1936—Dave Margolis
1937—Harry Goldstein
1938—Joseph Garber
1939—Harry Michitsch
1940—Morton Alexander
1941—Arthur Wolfe
1942—Joseph Garber
1943—46—No competition
1947—48—Victor Hershkowitz
1949—Murray Orenstein
1950—Victor Hershkowitz
1951—Arthur Locker
1952—53—Victor Hershkowitz
1954—Rubrecht Obert
1955—56—Harold Hanft
1957—Victor Hershkowitz
1958—59—Oscar Obert
1960—Carl Obert
1961—Steve Sandler
1962—Carl Obert
1963—Ken Davidoff
1964—Oscar Obert
1965—Ken Davidoff
1966—67—Steve Sandler
1968—Marty Decatur
1969—Steve Sandler
1970—Mark Levine
1971—72—Steve Sandler

One-Wall Softball Doubles

1924—Sackman—Buxbaum
1925—No competition
1926—Schwartz—Seaman
1927—28—Goldman—Seaman
1929—Galowin—Alexander
1930—Goldman—Alexander
1931—Aiello—Seaman
1932—No competition
1933—Alexander—Londin
1934—35—Levinson—Margolis
1936—C. Alexander—M. Alexander
1937—39—Goldstein—Baskin
1940—41—Alexander—Hecht
1942—Hershkowitz—Orenstein
1943—46—No competition
1947—Geller—Gluckler
1948—Hershkowitz—Wolfe
1949—Orenstein—Baskin
1950—Schwartz—Blank
1951—Alexander—Elmaleh
1952—Kirzner—Andrews
1953—Kravitz—Kirzner
1954—Russel—Lightsy
1955—R. Obert—O. Obert
1956—Hershkowitz—Locker
1957—61—Obert—Obert
1962—Davidoff—Eisenberg
1963—64—Oscar and Ruby Obert
1965—H. Eisenberg—Dave Norvid
1966—Ken Holmes—Wally Ulbrich
1967—Carl and Ruby Obert

1968—69—Marty Decatur—Steve Sandler
1970—Marty Decatur—Artie Reyer
1971—Kenny Davidoff—Howie Eisenberg
1972—Marty Decatur—Marty Katzen

One-Wall Masters Doubles

1963—Vic Hershkowitz—Phil Silverstein
1964—No competition
1965—No competition
1966—Mal Cohen—Lou Wigden
1967—Ray Gershen—Julie Stack
1968—Bob Brady—Bob McGuire
1969—Al Goldstein—Nat Schifter
1970—Sal Chiovari—Jules Stack
1971—Lou Caputo—Bill Taub

Four-Wall Masters Singles

1970—Ray Elliott
1971—72—Tom Schoendorf

Four-Wall Masters Doubles

1963—Jack Weitz—William Gluck
1964—No competition
1965—Vic Hershkowitz—Sam Costa
1966—67—No competition
1968—69—Bob Brady—Bob McGuire
1970—Mike Lalaeff—Tony Klimek
1971—72—Cecil Lloyd—Alvis Grant

U.S.H.A. NATIONAL CHAMPIONS

Four-Wall Singles

1951—Walter Plekan
1952—Vic Hershkowitz
1953—Bob Brady
1954—Vic Hershkowitz
1955—57—Jimmy Jacobs
1958—59—John Sloan
1960—Jimmy Jacobs
1961—John Sloan
1962—63—Oscar Obert
1964—65—Jim Jacobs
1966—67—Paul Haber
1968—Simon (Stuffy) Singer
1969—71—Paul Haber
1972—Fred Lewis

Four-Wall Doubles

1951—52—Frank Coyle—Bill Baier
1953—Sam Haber—Harry Dreyfus
1954—56—Sam Haber—Ken Schneider
1957—Phil Collins—John Sloan
1958—59—Phil Collins—John Sloan
1960—Jimmy Jacobs—Dick Weisman
1961—John Sloan—Vic Hershkowitz
1962—63—Jimmy Jacobs—Marty Decatur
1964—John Sloan—Phil Elbert
1965—Jimmy Jacobs—Marty Decatur
1966—Pete Tyson—Bob Lindsay
1967—68—Jim Jacobs—Marty Decatur
1969—Lou Kramberg—Lou Russo

1970—Carl and Ruby Obert
1971—Ray Neveau—Simie Fein
1972—Kent Fusselman—Al Drews

Four-Wall Masters Singles

1969—John Scopis
1970—Tom Ciasulli
1971—72—Rudy Stradburger

Four-Wall Masters

(One partner age 40 or over; the other 45 or over)
1952—53—Ray Laser—Bob Kendler
1954—George Brotemarkle—Bart Hackney
1955-56—Joe Shane—Alex Boisseree
1957-60—George Brotemarkle—Bill Feivou
1961—Gus Louis—Frank Coyle
1962—Gus Louis—Bob Kendler
1963—Bob Brady—Bill Keays
1964-67—Ken Schneider—Gus Lewis
1968—Bob Brady—Bob McGuire
1969—Ken Schneider—Gus Lewis
1970—Bob Brady—Bill Keays
1971—Arnold Aguilar—Irv Simon
1972—Ken Schneider—Paul Elbert

BASIC RULES

The standard four-wall court is 40 feet long, 20 feet high, 20 feet wide, with back wall height of minimum of 12 feet. Halfway between the front and backwalls a line is drawn across the court (short line). Lines should be 1½ inches wide. Five feet in front of the center line and parallel with it is another line (service line.) The space between these lines is known as the service zone. The service box, in which the partner of the server stands while the service is being made, is an area in the service zone 18 inches from and parallel to the sidewall. A service box is drawn on each side of the court.

The standard 1-wall court is 34 x 20 feet with a wall that is 16 feet high. The side lines should extend 3 feet past the backline. Sixteen feet back from the wall, a line is drawn across the court (short line). Nine feet back of this line, on each side of the court, there is a small line extending inward from the sideline 4 inches. This designates the serving area.

The hollow-centered pressurized ball is of black rubber about 1 7/8 inches in diameter and weighing about 2.3 ounces. Players wear soft gloves usually for the protection of their hands.

Play is started by a service which consists of dropping the ball to the floor and on the rebound striking the ball with one hand so that it hits the frontwall first and then rebounds beyond the short line to the floor before hitting the ceiling (contrary to all other major wall games, the ball may be hit into the ceiling), backwall or sidewalls. The receiver has the option of returning "shorts" on the first service. A short is an other-wise legal serve that fails to carry over the short line or that hits the ceiling, backwall or sidewalls before striking the floor back of the short line. A player who serves a second consecutive short loses the serve. A legal return is made by hitting the ball either on the volley (playing the ball before it strikes the floor) or on the first bounce so that it strikes the frontwall before falling on the floor, and may strike any of the walls or the ceiling on its way to the frontwall. If successfully returned, the ball is kept in play until one of the players fails to make a return. If missed by the receiver, a point is awarded to the server, while a miss on the part of the server takes him out of the serving. Twenty-one points constitute a game.

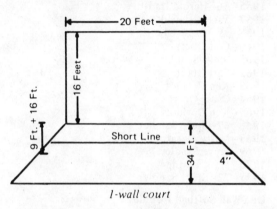

1-wall court

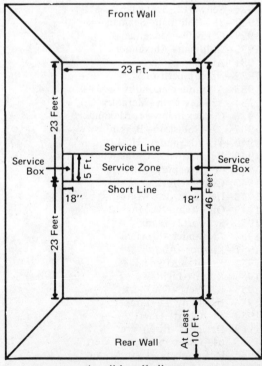

4-wall handball court

(Courtesy of Larry Evans, Publicity Director, The U.S. Trotting Assoc., 750 Michigan Ave., Columbus, Ohio, 43215)

THE HARNESS HORSE

Often considered a "Johnny-Come-Lately" sport, harness racing actually goes back to the dawn of recorded history and horses racing while drawing two-wheeled carts long preceded horse racing with a rider perched in a saddle.

John Hervey, the eminent horse historian, has pointed out that the horse originated as a small dwarf-like animal and only gradually evolved to its present size, partly through environment and partly through efforts of long-ago fanciers of the breed.

Baked clay tablets unearthed in Asia Minor about 40 years ago carry a comprehensive treatise on horse training dictated by one Kik-kulis, head trainer or master of the horse for King Suppliuliumas of Mitanni, a country later known as Cappadocia and for many ages part of the Assyro-Babylonian empire. Almost 900 lines of script have been found covering preparation of the horse for training, his diet, grooming and preparations for training him for speed at the trot. At the end of 144 days, he was ready either for the race course, the hunting field or the battle-field. They didn't have the alternative of the dog food can or the glue pot since all this was written in 1350 B.C. or more than 3,000 years ago.

Horse racing at the ancient Grecian Olympics began about 1000 B.C. and it wasn't until some 200 years later that horseback races were inaugurated at the Olympics. Considering that Olympic participants of that day were kings, princes and persons of great wealth who scoured the ancient world for good horses, it is reasonable to assume that horse evolution and breeding had not produced an animal large enough to be ridden until about 800 B.C., while it is evident that they had been driven in harness for many hundreds of years prior to that date.

Many reasons have been advanced for the disappearance of the trotter from history for a period of more than 2,000 years until he once more appeared in modern history. Warfare and its needs plus the painstaking care necessary to train a trotter undoubtedly played a part. However, 200 years ago the so-called Norfolk Trotter appeared and was bred as a road-horse—not as a race horse, although human nature undoubtedly provided the "hot-rodder" of the 18th century with the opportunity to compete with his neighbor along the country roads.

Trotting in this country was given a great impetus with the importation in 1788 of Messenger, a grey thoroughbred stallion who had distinguished himself on the race tracks of England. He continued as a successful sire of runners in this country but it became apparent as

time elapsed that he had founded here a separate and distinct breed of trotters which far surpassed all others in speed and quality. When his sons and daughters were put to breeding, their progeny became widely known as superior performers.

What is a trotter? What is a pacer? What distinguishes the harness horse from a runner?

Both trotting and pacing are acquired, not natural, gaits. When trotting, the left front leg and right rear leg go forward together, then the right front and left rear. When pacing, the left front and left rear move forward simultaneously, then the right front and right rear giving a sort of rolling motion to the gait, and often described as piston-like or sidewheeling.

At speed, the natural gait of a horse is the gallop and when urged a horse will run (or gallop) by nature. Just as in a human runner, speed is attained by training and the Kentucky Derby, Preakness and Belmont stakes winners of thoroughbred racing attained fame by running—and fast!

A trotter is trained to stay on the trot and to trot fast. If he breaks gait, goes offstride and into a gallop, he must be pulled up and back into the trotting stride—not disqualifying him but usually costing any hope of winning. The same rules apply to the pacer. He must pace.

The first recorded mile in less than three minutes while trotting was registered in 1806 by a gelding named Yankee. Nothing is known of the breeding of Yankee but the mark was made at Harlem, N.Y., where a well-known trotting track flourished for many years.

By 1839, this had been reduced to 2:32 when Dutchman trotted under the guidance of be-whiskered Hiram Woodruff, the dean of the early 19th century reinsmen, and six years later the grey mare, Lady Suffolk, became the first 2:30 trotter in harness with a 2:29½ effort at Hoboken, N.J.

This record still was standing when William Rysdyck's Hambletonian was foaled at Chester, N.Y. This bay colt was destined to become the "Great Father" of the modern standardbred horse, the latter a name to distinguish the harness horse from the thoroughbred and came from the breeding aim to develop a horse who could trot or pace in standard time—now 2:20 or faster.

Hambletonian's prowess as a sire was fantastic and his stud fee soon soared to the then unheard of fee of $500, and business was brisk. Hambletonian never raced but 99% of the harness horses racing today can trace back in breeding lines to Hambletonian, and the greatest of modern trotting classics is aptly named in honor of this stallion.

Most trotting races of the early 19th century were on horseback and Currier & Ives prints graphically depict many of the great contests of the day with all horses in perfect trotting stride and the erect riders allowing their mustaches to flow in the breeze as they head toward the finish line and the stands packed with spectators.

The Hall of Fame of the Trotter at Goshen, N.Y., a small city which a hundred years ago was the main seat of harness racing and breeding in the nation, features many of these colorful displays in its exhibit rooms.

The high-wheeled sulky was the racing conveyance from the decade prior to the Civil War and these high wheelers careened around the tracks until 1892 when the bicycle-wheel sulky was invented.

In the 50 years from Lady Suffolk's time until the '90's, the trotting record gradually had been cut from 2:29½ to 2:08¼ but the new type sulky resulted in more than a four-second drop the next season, and the first mile trotted in two minutes came in 1903 when Lou Dillon was timed in that figure at Readville, Mass.

The pacers, meanwhile had reached two minutes in 1897 when Star Poiter was clocked in 1:59¼. Then came Dan Patch, often called the greatest harness horse of all time.

On the early 20th-century tracks, with equipment considered crude by modern standards, Dan Patch climaxed his brilliant career by pacing a mile in an official 1:55¼. This mark stood until 1938 when Billy Direct lowered the pacing standard to 1:55, and Greyhound reached 1:55¼ on the trot, records which were set only a day apart at Lexington, Ky.

The 1:55 barrier stood 22 years before Adios Butler paced in 1:54 3/5 on Lexington's mile track and came back a year later to pace a stunning 1:55 3/5 over the Delaware, O., half-mile track to cut more than two seconds from the small-track mark. Albatross equalled this half-mile track record in 1972.

Bret Hanover, a three-time Harness Horse of the Year, lowered the pacing record to 1:53 3/5 in 1966 and Steady Star unleashed a stunning 1:52 in 1971 at Lexington for the current mark. Nevele Pride, ended a 31-year reign for Greyhound in 1969 when he trotted in 1:54 4/5 at Indianapolis.

The Standardbred trotter and pacer of today, through a long period of selective breeding, have become greatly refined in type as compared with their ancestors of the foundation period. In many ways they almost approach the Thoroughbred in form, finish and elegance, while the better specimens are among the world's finest road horses in the horse show world. As a rule a height of from 15½ to 16 hands prevails. It was formerly the idea that, in order to allow free play of the limbs, the harness horse should have unusual bodily length, sometimes showing as much as a hand (4 inches) greater in that measurement than in his height. But that type of conformation has been superseded and the champion Greyhound, for example, is taller than he is long. He is also much taller than the average trotter, being almost 16½ hands high. On the other hand, the pacing champion, Billy Direct, was a small horse, being over a hand lower than Greyhound.

Through the formative period, long-distance racing of the most severe description prevailed. Gradually there evolved from this the system of best three heats in five (or more if necessary) which was universal until after the turn of the century, when owing to the marked increase in speed, movement toward a shortening of distances was ushered in. Today, at the current night meetings, where pari-mutuel wagering is a part of the program, the field of horses goes one dash of from six furlongs to two miles in distance. Though there is some of this "odd-distance" racing, even at night meetings the route usually is a straight mile dash.

On the Grand Circuit and fair circuits, two-heat races, best two in three, with three heats very often the limit, usually rules. On pari-mutuel tracks which also belong to the Grand Circuit, dash racing is the usual fare. Most tracks still are regulation mile or one-half mile in circumference, but three-quarters and five-eighths sizes also are approved and gaining popularity.

Saddle and wagon racing have been discontinued, the former many decades ago. In the beginning colt racing was unknown, for harness horses were then necessarily mature and well-seasoned animals. But with the upbuilding and specialization of the Standard breed, extreme speed, long tediously produced by intensive training, has become an innate characteristic, born with the foal.

The extraordinary degree to which this prevails today is demonstrated by the blazing times posted by two-year-olds of both gaits since 1944 when Titan Hanover, a trotter, sped to the first 2:00 mile by a two-year-old. It took nine more years before a two-year-old pacer reached 2:00, a 1:58 3/5 performance by Adios Boy. But the two-year-old trotting mark now stands at 1:58 2/5, set by Nevele Pride in 1967, and Ricci Reenie Time paced in 1:56 1/5 in 1972.

One of the strong points of the Standard breed is the fact that champions can be and have been bred in all parts of the United States, as well as in Canada. Of the five successive world champions since the trotting record was placed below 2:00, the first, Lou Dillion, 1:58½, was bred in California; the second, Uhlan, 1:58, in Massachusetts; the third, Peter Manning, 1:56¾, in Illinois; the fourth, Greyhound, 1:55¼, in Kentucky; and the fifth, Nevele Pride, 1:54 3/5, in Pennsylvania.

From Dan Patch, bred in Indiana, the pacing kings have been Billy Direct, 1:55, bred by a Massachusetts owner; Adios Harry, 1:55, in Delaware; Adios Butler, 1:54 3/5, in New York; Bret Hanover, 1:53 3/5, in Pennsylvania; and Steady Star, 1:52, in Tennessee.

Some horses perform creditably at both gaits. The World's Champion double-gaited horse is Steamin' Demon who paced in 1:58 4/5 and trotted in 1:59 1/5. Fastest double-gaited mare was Calumet Evelyn who paced in 1:59¼ and trotted in 1:59½.

However, some families now predominate in pacers with most of the colts going to this gait naturally. Among these are the families of The Abbe, Abbedale, Grattan, and Billy Direct. Many colts from other families are first tried as trotters. If they show no trotting aptitude, or are more inclined to pace, they are put to pacing. Much of the change is accomplished by shoeing and the use of hopples to keep on the pacing gait.

Adios is the greatest stallion of any breed. Although he died in 1965, the lifetime earnings of his get had soared to $19,563,190 through 1972.

A powerful influence in the evolution of the trotter and the steady reduction of the speed limit, aside from the great work of the breeders, has been that of the trainers and drivers, many of whom also have been breeders as well. The immense improvement in their methods and skill, as compared with those of the formative period, has contributed greatly to progress, the betterment of gain, and manners most particularly.

THE UNITED STATES TROTTING ASSOCIATION

All harness racing today in the United States and Maritime Provinces of Canada is conducted under the guidance of the United States Trotting Association.

This Association was organized in 1938 and 1939 by a group of representative horsemen from all sections of the country who previously held membership in one of the three sponsoring or governing bodies. This move welded all Standardbred racing interests under one roof, for the first time in the history of the sport as we know it today, for it centralized authority and made possible an administrative procedure far more efficient and effective than ever before realized.

Before this time various sections of the country managed their version of the sport much as they pleased. Three outstanding groups preceded the organization which we have now: the United States Trotting Association, American Trotting Association and the National Trotting Association. Until they were combined, trainers and owners often never knew, for sure, just which organization they were racing under and therefore were always in doubt as to what racing rules were to be followed, for each had its own dictums.

All harness racing functions were soon after joined into one main location at Hartford, Conn. but centralized in Columbus, Ohio in 1948.

For full representation and to alleviate any unequal distribution of power, the country was divided into ten districts with an eleventh formed in the Maritime Provinces of Canada. Each district has at least three directors, with more heavily member-populated districts entitled to additional directors with a maximum of five. These men are elected by members of the Association in each district who are, in all cases, drivers, owners, breeders, track operators and officials. There is no doubt under this system that everyone concerned definitely is given a voice in conducting the sport.

Once each year a national meeting of all district directors is held, forming a caucus of the whole, at which time all problems confronting the sports are discussed and rules passed to regulate the following year's activities. Each district also holds annual meetings of all members at which time directors are elected and recommendations forwarded to the National Board of Directors.

The U.S.T.A. has adopted the policy of electing a president to run its affairs. He serves as head executive officer carrying out the wishes of the entire board. This position is comparable now to other well known commissioner posts in the world of sports except that the president is elected for a four-year term.

It is the primary duty of the U.S.T.A. to maintain a central record system and clearing house for the sport of harness racing on a nation-wide scale. Through its registration department all horses of the Standard breed are listed and their blood lines and ownership recorded, leading to improvement of the breed.

Officials such as judges and starters are licensed, as are drivers. This assures the best and most capable personnel to handle race meetings.

Each district board serves as a hearing panel of penalized cases for all infractions committed in its territory. Any driver, owner, groom, or operator, if penalized by track stewards (judges), has the right to appeal his case to the annual meeting of this board for further hearing or ask for special hearing which is provided for under the by-laws of the association. Decisions on the part of this district board of review may be further appealed to the national appeals board in its annual sessions.

The president has the right to issue or refuse membership to any track for a meeting if, in his opinion, the meeting "would be to the detriment of the sport." He also can refuse membership to any driver or owner for the same reason.

A force of field representatives under the direction of the association's Executive Vice

President is at the constant call of tracks for aid of any nature and these representatives are continually on the "go" during the racing season.

Programs from tracks are sent to the U.S.T.A. program department and a close check is made on all of them. When it becomes apparent that the program department of a specific track is falling below the superior standards which are required, a U.S.T.A. representative visits the track and reviews the situation. Through this means, the national programming standard is maintained at a high level.

The U.S.T.A. also maintains both publicity relations departments, providing information, public research, and photographic services to all tracks, and promoting the sport through the nation's newspapers, magazines and airwaves.

GRAND CIRCUIT

Like every other sport, harness racing has its "big league." In this case it is the Grand Circuit. Organized back in 1873 with four member tracks "mainly for the purpose of setting up a definite itinerary for horse owners" it has grown to include not only the cream of the sulky world in racing competition but has developed into a gigantic circuit for America's top trotters and pacers.

In the world of professional sport the Ragin' Grand, as it is sometimes termed, stands as an unique organization. In a nation which has made sports big business the Circuit wholesomely supervises the operation of a multi-million dollar sports industry on a mutual trust, almost avocational basis.

Starting with four member tracks in its original charter it has progressed through the years up until the present time to a point where there have been over 50 tracks holding membership at one time or another.

Growth can well be measured by total purses now dispensed across the Circuit's entourage. In the first year of existence prize money amounted to $170,000. Of late years drivers have competed for purses amounting to over $7,000,000 annually.

Each track sponsoring a Grand Circuit meeting is considered a member and has representation on the Board of Stewards. It is this Board which formulates its policies, awards dates, elects officers and conducts general affairs of the organization. To prove further that it is a non-profit organization each track conducting a meeting pays weekly dues which are used to finance the entire undertaking.

Primarily an organization for colt racing, The Grand Circuit starts its season in the South in March but doesn't get into gear in the North until 2 months later when the two- and three-year-olds are first reaching competitive level. Then comes a series of twenty or more weekly sessions at tracks stretching across the country with an itinerary of 20,000 miles and presenting many of the major colt stakes.

PARI-MUTUEL TRACKS

Harness racing on the modern pari-mutuel basis was first staged at Roosevelt Raceway, located at Westbury, Long Island, near New York City, in 1940, and has mushroomed in the space of a little over 30 years into one of the nation's top spectator sports.

With night raceways, modern presentations, and the introduction of the starting gate, the sport changed rapidly from America's smaller towns and an essentially rural atmosphere to an outstanding attraction for the metropolitan sports fans.

Major raceways now are located in or near such cities as New York, Chicago, Los Angeles, Philadelphia, Washington, Baltimore, San Francisco, Buffalo, Rochester, Syracuse, Albany, Detroit, Cleveland, Columbus, Boston, Cincinnati, Dayton, Wilmington, Louisville, St. Louis, Portland, Me., Pittsburgh, Wilkes-Barre, and many others. A total of 86 pari-mutuel meetings, of more than two weeks duration, were scheduled for 1973.

Attendance at pari-mutuel plants skyrocketed to more than 27 million in 1971 and almost as high in 1972. Millions more watched the sport at fairs where attendance figures are often undetermined, but the spectator total is among the top five sports.

From only a few thousand dollars in 1940, the wagering total had soared to $2,080,819,478 in 1972.

The states which legalize pari-mutuels at harness races profited handsomely with $162,329,393 going into state treasuries in 1972.

The rise in harness racing at the raceways is reflected in purses paid to horsemen and the consequent boom in the breeding industry. Purses reached $105,595,669 in 1972 as compared to the $1,857,591 paid in 1940, while 39,013 trotters and pacers saw action.

The rise of wagering meetings has made harness racing a year-around sport with racing in California and Florida during the winter months as well as in New York, Michigan, Illinois, Delaware, Massachusetts, New Hampshire, and Vermont. Most northern tracks, however, don't get underway until at least a hint of spring is in the air.

FAIR CIRCUITS

Before the advent of pari-mutuel harness tracks in the United States, by far the major portion of Standard bred news came out of the hundreds of fair meetings scattered here, there, and everywhere, at the nation's crossroads. The smaller fair circuits, made up of anywhere from four to twenty tracks, still make up the lion's share of meetings conducted in the sport.

The sport of harness racing is a popular rural attraction and has its roots in the rural areas. Whereas there are approximately 100 large pari-mutuel meetings and Grand Circuit stops each season, staging the highly publicized races, there are more than 300 small fair meetings sponsored by county fair boards in practically every state in the Union.

Fair Circuits are a boon to the small stable owner or the individual who perhaps owns his horse and who finds untold pleasure in driving his trotter or pacer himself. They are many times organized on a well formulated plan giving the participants a planned itinerary to follow during the summer months.

Feature races are planned and maintained as yearly attractions at individual meetings.

Many horsemen have had fears in the past few years that perhaps the life of the small fair did not hold much promise, due to the problems of present day. However, those who govern the sport and the horsemen themselves will never permit the "fair meetings" to vanish. It is the life blood of harness racing.

TROTTING'S TRIPLE CROWN

Harness racing's counterpart to the famed Kentucky Derby remains the Hambletonian, sponsored by the Hambletonian Society and first raced in 1926 at Syracuse, N. Y., but the nation's three-year-old trotters now have three lucrative targets each year.

The Hambletonian had a purse over the $144,590 mark in 1960. This race, held at Du Quoin, Ill., beginning in 1957, has gained more distinction and publicity than any other event the harness world ever has known. Conducted on the 2-in-3 heat plan, the Hambletonian is the goal of all trainers and owners—if you win it, you're on top!

The Hambletonian has been raced at Syracuse, Lexington, Ky., Yonkers, N. Y., and at Goshen, N. Y., where it was a fixture for many years before being moved to Du Quoin, Ill., after the 1956 renewal. A lavish show-case has been provided for the traditional classic at this Southern Illinois track in the heart of the farm belt, but metropolitan fans by the thousands make the annual trek to Du Quoin for the trotting spectacle.

Oldest of the "Triple Crown" features is the Kentucky Futurity, a feature of the Lexington Trots meeting at Lexington, Ky., each autumn, and the grand finale for strictly three-year-old trotting competition. The Futurity steadily has been increased in value until now it ranks well above the $60,000 mark.

The Yonkers Futurity on the half-mile Yonkers Raceway oval in Yonkers, N. Y., rounds out the "Triple Crown" events and is a one-dash affair. Also in the $100,000 purse category, as is the Yonkers Futurity, are the Dexter at Roosevelt Raceway and the Colonial at Liberty Bell Park in Philadelphia.

PACING'S TRIPLE CROWN

The hitherto "forgotten" three-year-old pacers were given their first major purse when the Little Brown Jug classic was inaugurated in 1946 at Delaware, O., and held there annually since that date.

Now the "Jug" has companion attractions in the William H. Cane Futurity at Yonkers Raceway and the Messenger Stake at Roosevelt Raceway, both metropolitan New York tracks.

All of the "Triple Crown" pacing events are contested over half-mile tracks with the heat plan in effect for the Little Brown Jug and single dashes deciding the Cane and the Messenger. All have purses in the $100,000 plus category along with two newcomers in this age and gait class—the Adios at The Meadows track near Washington, Pa., and the L. K. Shapiro stake at Hollywood Park near Los Angeles.

In 1944 a nationwide contest was conducted by the group planning the race at Delaware, O., and the name selected was Little Brown Jug in honor of the famous world champion pacer of the 19th centrtury.

THE RACE

A change in the system of racing has taken place in the past few years to enable the sport to keep up with modern trends and furnish better entertainment for the race-going public.

Previously, horses were raced on the three-heat plan, which gradually gave way to the two-in-three system. In races of this type, the same field of horses was brought out three and four times during an afternoon—to fans it was like going to a moving picture show and seeing the same picture again and again. Also, the former way of starting was crude and tedious, for at times it took a half-hour or more before the word "Go" was given by the starter.

Today, the sport is changing fast to "dash" racing, in which a field goes to the post once during a program and then makes way for new fields. In stake racing and at rural fair meetings, the change has been slower, and although the oldtime "scoring system" of starting has almost completely vanished from the scene, heat racing still persists.

One of the outstanding factors in the upsurge of interest in harness racing, which has increased its popularity ten fold in the past ten years, is the mobile starting gate. This mechanical barrier was introduced at Roosevelt Raceway on Long Island in 1946. It was designed by Steve Phillips who got his idea from watching a moving picture crew photograph horses from the rear end of a car in 1937.

All meetings, with few exceptions, now use the starting gate. Even the smaller fairs have adopted its use.

The initial gate has prospered and has served as the general pattern of all gates now used. It is constructed by using the lever system of arms extending from an especially constructed body of a high powered car. When in motion and getting a field of horses "away" the arms are extended, affording positions for eight horses in back of it across the track. At the word "go" the starter by virtue of a compressed air system causes the arms to be brought back on each side of the car giving the horses a clear field.

This mechanical means of starting a field of harness horses has practically abolished the old scoring system.

Every driver carries a stop-watch, during the course of a race, and separately times the horse he is driving, attempting at all times to save his mount as much as possible until the final brush through the home stretch to the wire.

The choice position is the "Pole," or next to the inside rail. This horse gets a slight head start but often the horse drawing the pole position is not fast enough to hold it, and an opponent takes it away from him.

Most top drivers prefer to get the pole position and then "cover up" their mounts by letting one or two horses pass them going to the front as windbreakers. Then, if the breaks are with him he will pull out during the final quarter mile often winning or at least putting up a capable drive.

In harness racing, drivers are required to keep their horses on gait but a "break" does not mean a disqualification unless the driver fails to pull the horse to its proper gait.

FAMOUS HORSES
Adios

The bidding was tense at the Lexington, Ky., harness horse auction in 1948 when the stallion Adios was being sold. Delvin Miller of Meadowlands, Pa., finally bought him with a bid of $21,000—and there were many who thought the already-famous trainer had made a misguided purchase. Yet, only seven years later, Miller sold Adios to a syndicate composed of Hanover Shoe Farm of Hanover, Pa., Max C. Hempt of Mechanicsburg, Pa., and himself for $500,000 and kept the stallion at his Meadowlands Farm.

The sale price in 1955 was four times higher than any Standardbred horse had brought before but none of the owners ever regretted their purchase.

Adios quickly established himself as the greatest pacing sire of all time and the earnings of his offspring now have vaulted him into the No. 1

position as the top stallion of any breed in history. Although he died in 1965, the lifetime earnings of his progeny had soared to $19,563,190 through 1972.

Sons such as Bullet Hanover, Adios Harry, Adios Butler, Adios Boy, Bret Hanover, and daughters Countess Adios and Dottie's Pick rewrote the sport's record books for a decade or more.

Adios was a champion pacer in his own right with a mark of 1:57½. He was foaled at Two Gaits Farm in Indianapolis, where he was sired by Hal Dale out of Adioo Volo. At two, he won the Fox Stake and Geers Stake, and at three, he won the Geers and Matron Stakes. Rupert Parker was his trainer-driver during his colt campaigns, while Frank Ervin drove him in later seasons.

Adios Butler

Fastest harness horse of all time on both mile and half-mile tracks! That was the amazing record owned by Adios Butler when he was retired from racing at the close of the 1961 season.

On October 4, 1960, he streaked around the "Old Red Mile" track at Lexington, Ky., in 1:54 3/5 to erase the 1:55 record set 22 years before by Billy Direct. Even more outstanding, in the opinion of many, was his 1:55 3/5 mile on the half-mile track at Delaware, O., on Sept. 21, 1961. At Delaware, he cut more than two full seconds from the 1:57 4/5 record he previously had shared with Bye Bye Byrd. Tracks one-half mile in circumference, where the horse must cope with sharper turns and go around twice, usually are considered about three seconds "slower" than mile ovals.

Sired by the great Adios, Adios Butler cost trainer Paige West only $6,000 as a yearling with George Phalen as co-owner. Angelo Pellillo purchased Phalen's half-interest before Adios Butler's three-year-old season for $17,500, and West and Pellillo shared Adios Butler's $150,255 earnings in 1959. In that year, Adios Butler won the "Triple Crown" of pacing—the Messenger Stakes, the Cane Pace and the Little Brown Jug.

West and Pelilla syndicated their star for $600,000 in 1960, retaining a half-interest themselves. Adios Butler won $173,114 that season and wound up with his world championship record. As a five-year-old in 1961, he lost only once in 14 races and boosted his lifetime earnings to $509,844.

Billy Direct

Billy Direct, the fastest harness horse the world had ever known, like Greyhound, was "born 20 years too soon." Were he racing today Billy Direct, a pacer, would have vast earnings instead of the paltry $12,040 that is credited to him. Billy Direct was foaled in Tennessee in 1934. He was bred by H. H. Ridge of Haverhill,

Mass., and was a son of Napoleon Direct-Gay Forbes. That mating had earlier produced Forbes Direct, a 2:00 pacer.

Billy Direct showed promise sufficiently early in his 2-year-old form to bring a $2,000 offer from Nathan Smith, Lowell, Mass., which was accepted. Billy made his first start July 7, 1936. He won 7 of 9 starts and early in 1937 was sold to P. J. Downey of Worcester, Mass., and Dan McConville of Ogdensburg, N. Y., and went into the hands of the great Canadian trainer, Vic Fleming.

Late in his 3-year-old form, Billy Direct paced a mile in a race in 1:58, a mark which stood for pacers of any age until 1951, when Good Time lowered it.

A year later, on Sept. 28, 1938, Billy Direct was slated to start in a free-for-all pace at Lexington, Ky. There was a faulty start and Billy Direct and one other horse pulled up, thinking that the recall bell had been sounded. It had not and Billy Direct was declared distanced. Fleming, knowing his horse to be razor sharp, requested to be permitted to go in a time trial and Billy Direct responded with a mile in 1:55.

Later he was retired to stud and at Hanover Shoe Farms turned out some of the greatest horses of all time, including Tar Heel (sold at 3 for $125,000), Ensign Hanover and Dudley Hanover, both Little Brown Jug winners, and Direct Rhythm, whose mile in 1:56 1/5 in 1952 was the fastest since Billy's own.

Billy Direct died in 1947. His record:

Years	Age	Sts.	1st.	2nd.	3rd.	4th.	Unpl.
1936	2	9	7	0	2	0	0
1937	3	20	19	0	0	1	0
1938	4	20	15	1	2	0	2
1939	5	6	6	0	0	0	0
		55	47	1	4	1	2

Dan Patch

Perhaps no other horse in the history of harness racing is as well-known as Dan Patch. Performing just after the turn of the century, Dan Patch was a horse so far ahead of his time that even today, when two-minute miles are more common, only two have bettered his series of 30 within that magic figure. Dan never lost a race, and of 56 heats he lost but two. In both instances, he came back to win easily the second heat and the decision.

Dan Patch was foaled in 1896 out of the mare Zelica, property of Dan Messner, Jr., of Oxford, Ind. Messner had taken his mare, a $255 bargain purchase, to Chebanse, Ill., to be bred to the famed stallion Joe Patchen.

Under the easy handling of John Wattles, his 73-year-old trainer, Dan was worked lightly as a colt, beginning his training at three and entering a race for the first time when he was four. He won that race at Boswell, Ind., turning in a best heat of 2:22¼. By 1902 Dan Patch had cut his record to 2:03¾ and had run out of competition.

During the previous winter Dan was purchased by M.E. Sturgis of Buffalo for $20,000 and in December of 1902 the New Yorker sold the already-famed pacer to M.W. Savage of Minneapolis for $60,000. Savage displayed true affection for his great horse and once refused an offer of $180,000 for him.

In 1903 Dan Patch lowered the world's record to 1:56¼ and in 1904 to 1:56. The following year, pacing behind a thoroughbred runner whose sulky bore a wind and dust shield on the back, he cut the record to 1:55¼. In 1906, Dan was clocked in 1:55 before 90,000 spectators at the Minnesota State Fair, but by now the runner in front bearing windshield had been ruled illegal and this 1:55 never was officially recognized and Dan remains credited with 1:55¼.

The bay retired undefeated with nine world records after 1909 exhibition and was returned to Savage, Minn. There the final chapter of Dan Patch and his devoted owner was written. Both horse and man were stricken with heart ailments in July, 1916. On July 11, Dan Patch died. Savage died the following day.

Goldsmith Maid

The most amazing trotting horse that ever lived was Goldsmith Maid. A farm animal until 6, she was raced only once until she was 8, then she fractured a vast succession of records, made her fastest time at 19 and was still a champion at 20.

Over her grave in Fashion Stud Farm, Trenton, N. J., is a monument bearing this inscription:

"Here lies Goldsmith Maid, Queen of Trotters for seven years. Born in Sussex County, 1857, died here September 23, 1885. Best record 2:14, made at Boston in 1874. Earned $364,200, the world's record. Driven by Budd Doble. Owned by Henry N. Smith."

The sire of Goldsmith Maid was Alexander's Abdallah. The dam was hauling a cart for J. Vermerule, a hat peddler, when John B. Decker of Deckerstown, N.J., saw her. He took a fancy to the mare, purchased her for a trifling sum, and bred her to Alexander's Abdallah. The first foal was Goldsmith Maid, originally named The Maid.

Decker tried to make a harness horse of The Maid, but failed. This horse, which became the gentlest of creatures in her later years, was unruly in her youth. Decker made various attempts to drive her. She either tore the harness to shreds or kicked the buggy apart.

A short time later Decker sold the mare to his nephew, John H. Decker, for $350. He tried to train her, failed and sold her to "Jersey Bill" Thompson, who finally broke her to harness after many weary months and got her to a race. She won it but the date, place and other details are unknown.

Later, "Jersey Bill" and his partner, Billy Bodine, went to Washingtonville, N.Y., near Newburgh, and put on a 3-hour demonstration of her speed for Alden Goldsmith, who was in the market for a fast trotter. Goldsmith bought The Maid and an old buggy, for $1,000, rechristened her "Goldsmith Maid" and turned her over to Bodine for training.

Goldsmith Maid was 8 when Goldsmith entered her in a race at Goshen, N.Y., for a $100 purse. She won both heats—2:36 and 2:37.

Goldsmith sold her in 1869—she was 12—to Budd Doble and Barney Jackman for $15,000, and Goldsmith thought he had negotiated a keen deal. Doble and Jackman made over $100,000 with her. They sold her to Harry N. Smith of Trenton for $32,000. She was 14 then. Smith had intended to retire her to the stud, but she still seemed to have speed. So he campaigned her and Goldsmith Maid, racing for Smith until she was 20, earned over $100,000. However, she was generally so superior to her competition that much of the money was gained in exhibition races—trotting alone in an effort to beat her own time.

Goldsmith Maid was undefeated through 1871, 1872, 1873 and 1874. In 1875, although beaten once in a 4-heat race by Lula in Rochester, N.Y., on Aug. 14, she was the undisputed champion at the year's end.

Altogether, Goldsmith Maid trotted in 426 heats and won more than 350. She earned $364,200 and appeared in her last race at the age of 20. She died at 28 of pneumonia.

Greyhound

Greatest trotter in the history of harness racing. That appraisal of Greyhound would draw little dissension from horsemen and fans alike for the gray gelding was truly a super horse.

From his three-year-old season in 1935 through 1940, his last season of competition, Greyhound won 59 of 64 heats and lost only one race. His greatest day came on Sept. 29, 1938 when in the gathering dusk at Lexington, Ky., he was timed in 1:55¼, a record at that time. A year earlier, when he was five, Greyhound had first equalled the 1:56¾ world record of Peter Manning, set in 1922, then had established a new standard of 1:56. These memorable trials also were at Lexington.

The tall, gangling Greyhound was a depression era foal, arriving in 1932 as the product of Guy Abbey and Elizabeth. Henry H. Knight of Nicholasville, Ky., owner of Elizabeth, gelded Greyhound as a yearling and sent him to a fall sale at Indianapolis. There the future trotting champion was purchased for $900 by E. J. Baker of St. Charles, Ill., who placed him in the hands of his

trainer-driver Sep Palin. Baker's horses for many years had been under the supervision of Palin, who, early in Greyhound's two-year-old season, predicted a bright career for this promising gray.

Greyhound improved rapidly, closing out his first year of competition with six straight victories. Then, as a three-year-old in 1935, Greyhound began his complete domination of his gait. He was an easy winner of the Hambletonian and finished the season undefeated. At four he lost on the half-mile track at Goshen, N. Y., but it was the last time Greyhound was to know defeat.

Greyhound's record:

Year	Age	Sts.	1st.	2nd.	3rd.	4th.	Unpl.
1934	2	18	12	2	1	2	1
1935	3	20	18	0	1	1	0
1936	4	17	15	2	0	0	0
1937	5	2	2	0	0	0	0
1938	6	10	10	0	0	0	0
1939	7	0	0	0	0	0	0
1940	8	15	14	1	0	0	0
		82	71	5	2	3	1

Hambletonian

On May 5, 1849, a crippled mare foaled a colt under a clump of oak trees on the farm of Jonas Seeley in Orange County, N. Y.

This colt was destined to be called the "Father of the Breed," and 99% of harness horses racing today trace back in pedigree to this colt who was to be officially called Hambletonian 10, but usually just plain Hambletonian.

Seeley's hired man, William Rysdyk, used all his resources to buy the colt (with the mare thrown into the deal) for $125, and later made a fortune when Hambletonian proved to be a stallion without equal.

Hambletonian rarely appeared in harness and the fastest time ever announced for him for a mile test was 2:48½, very good for a 3-year-old in this mid-19th century but slow by modern standards. Yet, almost every champion today traces directly back to this colt foaled by a 17-year-old mare known only as the Bellfounder mare—called because of her sire, Bellfounder. Abdallah was Hambletonian's sire.

In a period from 1851 through 1875, 24 seasons, Hambletonian sired 1,331 foals—unprecedented in all harness horse history. His stud fee started at $25 and rose to $500, an unheard of sum in those days, and Rysdyk became a wealthy man.

The most famous trotting race in the world, The Hambletonian Classic for three-year-olds, honors the name of this peerless stallion.

Rosalind

Rosalind, a contemporary of the great Greyhound, established the fastest trotting mile by a mare in harness history, a 1:56¾ performance in

October, 1938, at Lexington, Ky.

Foaled in 1933, Rosalind was bred by Ben F. White who presented the filly to his son, Gibson. The elder White had driven Scotland, sire of Rosalind, to his record of 1:59¼ and had both bred and driven her dam, Alma Lee. White's connection with Rosalind's family stretched back 30 years and Rosalind was a rewarding climax to that association.

After a brilliant season at two, Rosalind won seven of eight races in 1936 including the historic Hambletonian. In 1938 when she was five, Rosalind trotted 1:57¼ at Syracuse, N. Y., to lower Nedda's 16-year-old mark by a full second. Later in that same season Rosalind reduced her time to 1:57 at Lexington, Ky., and four days later, on Oct. 4, was clocked at Lexington in the record 1:56¾.

In 1939, her last racing season, Rosalind started only three times but two of the starts were for record-breaking miles hitched to pole with Greyhound. The first came at Syracuse in 1:59 and the second at Indianapolis in 1:58¼, both well under the previous team mark of 2:03¼. She then retired with a record of 24 wins, seven seconds and one third.

Rosalind and her owner, Gibson White, are central subjects of one of the finest children's stories ever written—*Born to Trot* by Marguerite Henry.

Bret Hanover

Whatever records for pacers existed before the mid-1960's were smashed by the remarkable Bret Hanover, named "Harness Horse of the Year" in each of his three racing seasons, 1964, 1965 and 1966. In his relatively brief career, before being retired to stud duty, the son of Adios-Brenna Hanover finished in the money in all of his 68 starts. His 62 victories, five seconds, and a third earned $922,616, an all-time record at the end of 1966.

He broke two minutes 31 times, beating Dan Patch's total of 30 two-minute miles. His 1:53 3/5 in a time trial at Lexington, Ky., was the fastest mile ever recorded by a harness horse. Against competition, as a three year old, Bret Hanover paced a 1:55 mile over the Indianapolis, Indiana mile track and a 1:57 on the Delaware, Ohio, half-mile, both world records.

Bret was purchased by Richard Downing of Shaker Heights, Ohio for $50,000 at a 1963 yearling auction. He was then turned over to Frank Ervin for training. In his first racing season he went unbeaten in 24 starts. His stake victories included the Fox, L. B. Sheppard, Roosevelt Futurity, and McMahon Memorial with earnings of $173,298, a record for his age. These achievements gained his first "Harness Horse of the Year" award, the first two year old to be so honored.

When Bret Hanover lost to Adios Vic in mid-1965, it ended a 35 race winning streak. He lost twice more to Vic but won 21 other races. Winning the pacers' Triple Crown of the Little Brown Jug, Messenger, and Cane Futurity, along with the Commodore and Matron Stakes and $341,784 again brought top honors at year-end.

In his last racing season, Bret earned $407,534 by winning 17 of 20 starts including wins in the American-National Maturity, the H.T.A., the Empire, and the Realization. His record time trial at Lexington and third consecutive "Harness Horse of the Year" honors closed out his racing career.

Nevele Pride

Notional, irritable, and downright ornery at times, Nevele Pride also was the fastest trotter in history when he retired from the track in 1969. He earned $873,238 while winning 57 times in 67 starts over three seasons and set world records as a two-year-old, three-year-old, and four-year-old.

He snapped tips from grooms' fingers, nipped unwary shoulders and kicked at dignitaries in winner's circles across the nation—but when he laid his ears back and pounded down the homestretch to another record, crowds roared approval of the horse who simply overpowered his opponents.

Bred by Mr. and Mrs. E. C. Quin in Pennsylvania and purchased at private sale by Nevele Acres of Ellenville, N. Y. who later sold a half-ownership to Louis Resnick, a neighbor, Nevele Pride was trained throughout his career by Stanley Dancer.

Sired by Star's Pride, top sire of trotters in the 1960s, Nevele Pride won 26 of 29 starts as a 2-year-old including a 1:58 2/5 world record at Lexington, Ky., in 1967. The following year, he swept the Hambletonian and the other major three-year-old trotting classics and posted a 1:56 3/5 mile at Indianapolis, a world record for that age.

As a four-year-old, he took Greyhound's 31-year-old world record off the books with a 1:54 4/5 mile before a horde of hysterical Hoosiers at Indianapolis. But at least as important was the world record he set at Saratoga Springs, N. Y., when he trotted a mile on that half-mile sized track in 1:56 4/5—almost two full seconds under the former 1:58 3/5 mark.

Now a stallion at Stoner Creek Stud in Kentucky, his progeny made their debut on the tracks as two-year-olds in 1973.

Albatross

Owner Bert James thought Albatross should bring $7,000 at the Harrisburg, Pa., yearling sale in the fall of 1969, and when bidding halted at $6,800 James bought the colt back. Later that day he agreed to sell Albatross for $6,500 but the buyer failed to show up at the appointed time, and James reluctantly took the colt back to Washington, Pa., and turned him over to Harry Harvey to train.

The rest is a story Hollywood would reject as too improbable for belief.

By Meadow Skipper out of Voodoo Hanover, Albatross won 14 of 17 starts in 1970 and earned $183,540 and a mile record of 1:57 4/5, capped by his selection as Two-Year-Old Pacer of the Year in the U. S. Trotting Association poll of harness writers at year end.

Syndicated by James in January, 1971, for $1,250,000 Albatross began his 3-year-old campaign under the tutelage of Stanley Dancer. He won 25 of 28 starts and $558,009 with a record 1:54 4/5 in a race at Lexington, a feat he performed twice the same day. The major event he lost was the Little Brown Jug when he was edged by Nansemond. Voting for Harness Horse of the Year was almost a formality.

It was little more than that in 1972 after Albatross had won 20 of 26 starts and lowered the world race record to 1:54 3/5 on the 5/8 mile track at Chicago's Sportsman's Park.

But early in the 1972 season, the outlook was not good as Albatross lost his first three starts and his syndicate owners disagreed on policy. The result was that Albatross was resyndicated, this time for $2,500,000, and trainer Dancer was retained in the sulky for a year which brought $414,921 in purses and a lifetime $1,201,470 in earnings for the horse nobody wanted as a yearling.

At the end of 1972, he had earned more than any pacer in the world and was headed for a stallion career at Hanover Shoe Farms in Pennsylvania.

Harness Horse of the Year
(U.S.T.A. poll of harness writers)

1947—Victory Song (trotter)
1948—Rodney (trotter)
1949—Good Time (pacer)
1950—Proximity (trotter)
1951—Pronto Don (trotter)
1952—Good Time (pacer)
1953—Hi-Lo's Forbes (pacer)
1954—Stenographer (trotter)
1955-56—Scott Frost (trotter)
1957—Torpid (pacer)
1958—Emily's Pride (trotter)
1959—Bye Bye Byrd (pacer)
1960-61—Adios Butler (pacer)
1962—Su Mac Lad (trotter)
1963—Speedy Scot (trotter)
1964-66—Bert Hanover (pacer)
1967-69—Nevele Pride (trotter)
1970—Fresh Yankee (trotter)
1971-72—Albatross (pacer)

Leading Sires of Two-Minute Horses
(Through 1972)

(Only the initial 2:00 record of a performer is credited)

Sire	Trotters	Pacers	Total
Adios, p, TT1:57 1/2m	1	78	79
Tar Heel, p, TT1:57m	0	67	67
Good Time, p, 1:57 4/5m	0	62	62
Bye Bye Byrd, p, 1:56 1/5m	0	33	33
Volomite, 3, 2:03 1/4m	11	22	33
Greentree Adios, p,2,2:00 4/5m	0	24	24
Star's Pride, 1:57 1/5m	20	4	24
Scotland, TT1:59 1/4m	12	11	23
Hoot Mon, 3, 2:00m	11	10	21
Dancer Hanover, p, TT1:56 4/5m	0	20	20
Gene Abbe, p, TT2:00 3/5m	0	20	20
Thorpe Hanover, p, 1:58 2/5m	0	20	20
Bret Hanover, p, TT1:53:3/5m	0	19	19
Bullet Hanover, p, 3,TT1:55 3/5m	0	17	17
Poplar Byrd, p, 1:59 3/5m	0	17	17
Rodney, TT1:57 2/5m	14	3	17

Leading Drivers of Two-Minute Horses
(Through 1972)

DRIVER	Trotters	Pacers	Total
Joe O'Brien	13	56	69
Delvin Miller	9	45	54
John Simpson, Sr.	11	29	40
William Haughton	7	32	39
Frank Ervin	10	26	36
Stanley Dancer	7	28	35
Wayne Smart	6	22	28
Del Cameron	2	21	23
George Sholty	2	20	22
Jack Bailey	1	21	22
Robert Williams	2	20	22
Gene Riegle	1	19	20

Total Two-Minute Drives
(Through 1972)

DRIVER	Trotters	Pacers	Total
Joe O'Brien	39	140	179
Stanley Dancer	49	115	164
Frank Ervin	19	89	108
William Haughton	12	87	99
Delvin Miller	14	80	94
John Simpson, Sr.	19	71	90
S. F. Palin	31	33	66
George Sholty	4	54	58
James Dennis	1	56	57
Robert Williams	7	47	54
Gene Riegle	1	51	52
Ralph Baldwin	23	23	46
Wayne Smart	5	40	45
Del Cameron	3	41	44
Howard Beissinger	14	26	40

PREPARING THE HORSE FOR A RACE*

Harness horses, whether they are performing at a night pari-mutuel track or at an afternoon county fair meeting, are warmed up thoroughly before they are raced. Most of them have at least six warm-up miles under their belts before they parade to the post.

Individual warming-up patterns vary according to conditioning beliefs of trainers and the known habits of their horses. Sluggish horses, for instance, may need additional miles to get them tuned to racing pitch. Frail horses, on the other hand, may be warmed up fewer miles in order to conserve their strength. But in general, with variations allowed for trainers and horses, a trotter or pacer is prepared for his racing engagement in the following manner:

Even though prior notice may have been served through controlled feeding (big eaters may be deprived of their hay rations on race day) earlier in the day, actual preparation for the race begins about 2 hours before post time.

The horse is led from his stall at that hour and hitched to a jog cart. He wears nothing but the harness. The boots, poles, shadow rolls, hobbles etc. that he will require when he races, are not in place.

Usually the groom does the driving on this first warm-up trip, which consists of the horse being jogged the wrong way (clockwise) of the track for 2½-3 miles and then being turned and going the right way a leisurely mile that is usually timed at about 2:45.

The horse is then taken back to his stall—by this time he is usually being warmed up out of the paddock—sponged down and covered with a blanket that is called a cooler.

After a 20-30 minute wait, the horse is hitched to the jog cart again and is ready for what is known as his second warm-up mile. This time he is wearing most of his racing gear and usually the trainer, or his assistant, is in the cart. After 2 scores, the horse trots or paces his mile in about 2:30 and is returned to his paddock stall. Once more he is sponged down and allowed to blow out. This time, because he has gone a faster warm-up mile, he is allowed 30-40 minutes before post time.

For the final warm-up mile the horse is hitched to a sulky, the actual racing vehicle, for the first time. The regular driver is at the reins. The speed of this final mile depends on the caliber of the horse and how fast his race is expected to go. If the race is expected to go in about 2:10—and we are considering here races on half-mile tracks—the horse probably will be warmed up in 2:18. If the race is for horses that can go at 2:05, the mile will probably be around 2:12.

*From the Trotting and Pacing Guide, compiled and edited by Larry Evans and Walter Adamkosky and published by the United States Trotting Association.

And if the race is for the fastest of the trotting and pacing horses, the final mile will vary between 2:08 and 2:12, with a very fast half or quarter tacked on the end of the mile.

The same sponging and blowing out procedure is repeated after this warm-up trip and the horse is ready to race.

HARNESS RACING GLOSSARY*

Horses

FREE-LEGGED PACER—A pacer that races without hopples, the leg harness that guides the horse's stride.

MAIDEN—Horse, mare or gelding that has never won a heat or race at the gait being raced.

FREE-FOR-ALL—Horses (or races for such horses) that have won considerable money and must race in fast classes. Means "free for all" to enter and open to all horses, regardless of earnings.

STANDARDBRED—Pure bred trotting or pacing horses. Non-Standard horse is a cross-bred horse or one that can't be traced in breeding far enough to qualify for Standard registration.

GREEN HORSE—One that has never trotted or paced in a public race or against time.

Equipment

BRACE BANDAGES—Resilient bandages on the legs of horses worn in some cases in an effort to support lame legs, worn in other cases to protect a horse from cutting and skinning his legs while racing.

CHECK REIN—Line running from the bit to the top of the horse's head, then to the saddle hook to keep a horse's head up. Trotters and pacers commonly race with heads high to maintain a balanced, reaching stride.

CRAB BIT—Bit with prongs extending at the horse's nose. Purpose is to tip the horse's head up and help prevent him from ducking his head, bowing his neck and pulling hard on the rein.

JOG CART—A cart longer and heavier than a racing sulky, used in warm-up miles because it's more comfortable for the driver than a sulky.

OPEN BRIDLE—Bridle without blinds or blinkers covering the eyes. Some bridles are rigged with blinds that shut off vision to the rear and side and a few horses are raced with goggles or "peekaboo" blinds.

STANDING HALTER—Similar to martingale, it is a strap that runs from the girth to a tight halter on the horse's head. It helps keep him from throwing his head up and going into a break.

SULKY OR BIKE—Light racing rig with bicycle type wheels used in harness races. The sulkies

*From the Trotting and Pacing Guide

weigh from 29 to 37 pounds, usually have hardwood shafts and cost about $400. Aluminum and steel sulkies have been introduced recently.

Racing and Training

BLOWOUT—A workout prior to the race, usually the day before.

BREAKING—When a horse leaves his gait and "breaks" into a gallop. A trotter or pacer must remain on that gait in a race. If he makes a break, the driver must immediately pull him back to his gait.

DASH—Races decided in a single trial.

HEAT—One trip in a race that will be decided by winning 2 or more trials.

JOGGING—A slow warm-up or exercise of several miles with the horse going the wrong way of the track.

LUGGING AND PULLING—Some horses pull on the reins, "lug" on one rein, or bear out or in with the driver, making it hard to drive them and rate the mile at an even clip.

ON THE LIMB—Lapped on horses at the pole or rail so that there's no chance to get in. A horse out "on the limb" has farther to go and usually tires and falls back, unless he is far superior to other horses in the race.

RATING—Maintaining an even rate of speed and timing finishing rush. Harness horses are rated to a fraction of a second in miles. Unlike running horses, which run the first quarter fastest and slow up in each succeeding quarter, the trotters and pacers usually negotiate the finishing quarter fastest.

SCORING—Preliminary warming-up of horses before the start. The horses are turned near the starting point and hustled away as they will in the race.

Statistics

(Courtesy of The United States Trotting Association, Columbus, O.)

WORLD CHAMPIONSHIP RECORDS

This compilation recognizes as Champions those horses that have made the fastest time at their gait, age, sex either against time or in a race at one mile. This is the distance upon which the sport of light harness racing has been built and established.

Trotting on Mile Track

All Age

Nevele Pride, b h 4, by Star's Pride-Thankful (1969: Stanley Dancer) Indianapolis, Ind . . TT1:54 4/5
Rosalind, b m 5, by Scotland-Alma Lee (1938: Ben F. White) Lexington, Ky. TT1:56 3/4
Greyhound, g g 6, by Guy Abbey-Elizabeth (1938: S.F.Palin) Lexington, Ky. TT1:55 1/4

Two-Year-Olds

Nevele Pride, b c, by Star's Pride-Thankful (1967: Stanley Dancer) Lexington, Ky. 1:58 2/5
Impish, b f, by The Intruder-Ilo Hanover (1961: Frank Ervin) Lexington, Ky. 1:58 3/5
Argo Kid, b g, by Speedster-Lady's One (1963: Wilbur Long) Lexington, Ky. and
   Old Glory, b g, by Star's Pride-Briana Hanover (1969: Glen Garnsey) Lexington, Ky. . 2:02 3/5
   and Record Mat, br g by Diplomat Hanover-Record Express (1967: F. Ervin)
   Lexington, Ky. TT2:02 3/5

Three-Year-Olds

Super Bowl, b c, by Star's Pride-Pillow Talk (1972: Stanley Dancer) Du Quoin, Ill. 1:56 2/5
Emily's Pride, b f by Star's Pride-Emily Scott (1958: Flave Nipe) Lexington, Ky. and
   Yankee Lass, b f by Florican-Yankee Maid (1958: Frank Ervin) Lexington, Ky. and
   Expresson, br f by Diplomat Hanover-Record Express (1959: F. Ervin, Lexington, Ky. and
   Worth Seeing, br f by Worthy Boy-Jon Hanover (1962: Stanley Dancer) Lexington, Ky. TT1:58
Savoir, br g by Star's Pride-Spicy Song (1971: James Arthur) Lexington, Ky. 1:58 1/5

Four-Year-Olds

Nevele Pride, b h by Star's Pride-Thankful (1969: Stanley Dancer) Indianapolis, Ind . . . TT1:54 4/5
Fresh Yankee, b m by Hickory Pride-Pert Yankee (1967: Sanders Russell) Lexington, Ky. TT1:57 1/5
Greyhound, g g by Guy Abbey-Elizabeth (1936: S. F. Palin) Springfield, Ill. 1:57 1/4

Trotting On Five-Eighths Mile Track

All Age

Nevele Pride, b h by Star's Pride-Thankful (1969: Stanley Dancer Laurel, Md. and
   Speedy Crown, b h 4 by Speedy Scot-Missile Toe (1972: H. Beissinger) Columbus, O. . 1:58
Fresh Yankee, b m by Hickory Pride-Pert Yankee (1970: Joe O'Brien) Philadelphia, Pa. . 1:58 4/5
Savoir, br g 3 by Star's Pride-Spicy Song (1971: James Arthur)Philadelphia, Pa. 1:58 4/5

Two-Year-Olds

Super Bowl, b c by Star's Pride-Pillow Talk (1971: Vernon Dancer) Philadelphia, Pa. 2:01 4/5
Sparkling Molly, b f by Star's Pride-Sparkling Rhythm (1968: John Chapman) Phila. Pa. . 2:03
Wire to Wire, b g by Egyptian Candor-Hailstorm (1969: Del Cameron) Atlantic City, N.J. 2:06 4/5

Three-Year-Olds

Nevele Pride, b c by Star's Pride-Thankful (1968: Stanley Dancer) Philadelphia, Pa. 1:59
Delmonica Hanover, b f by Speedy Count-Delicious (1972: Benoit Cote) Montreal, Que. . 2:00 1/5
Savoir, br g by Star's Pride-Spicy Song (1971: James Arthur) Philadelphia, Pa. 1:58 4/5

Four-Year-Olds

Nevele Pride, b h by Star's Pride-Thankful (1969: Stanley Dancer) Laurel, Md. and
    Speedy Crown, b h by Speedy Scot-Missile Toe (1972: Howard Beissinger) Columbus, O. 1:58
Worth Seeing, br m by Worthy Boy-Jen Hanover (1963: Stanley Dancer) Philadelphia, Pa. and
    Jes R. Hoot, br m by Hoot Mon-Jessie Colby (1966: James Michaels) Laurel, Md. . . . 1:59 4/5
Savoir, br g by Star's Pride-Spicy Song (1972: James Arthur) Cicero, Ill. 1:59

Trotting on Half-Mile Track

All Age

Nevele Pride, b h 4 by Star's Pride-Thankful (1969: Stanley Dancer) Saratoga Springs, N.Y. 1:56 4/5
Armbro Flight, br f 3 by Star's Pride-Helicopter (1965: Joe O'Brien) Delaware, O. 1:59 1/5
Greyhound, g g 5 by Guy Abbey-Elizabeth (1937: S. F. Palin) Historic Track, Goshen, N.Y. TT1:59 3/4

Two-Year-Olds

Ayres, b c by Star's Pride-Arpege (1963: John F. Simpson) Delaware, Ohio 2:00 1/5
Impish, b f by The Intruder-Ilo Hanover (1961: Frank Ervin, Delaware, Ohio 2:03 3/5
Mustard Seed, b g by Midland Hanover-Jessie King (1965: Harold Dancer, Sr.) Saratoga
    Springs, N. Y. 2:05 3/5

Three-Year-Olds

Songcan, b c by Florican-Ami Song (1972: George Sholty) Delaware, Ohio 1:58 3/5
Armbro Flight, br f by Star's Pride-Helicopter (1965: Joe O'Brien) Delaware, O. 1:59 1/5
Savoir, br g by Star's Pride-Spicy Song (1971: James Arthur) Delaware, Ohio 1:59 4/5

Four-Year-Olds

Nevele Pride, b h by Star's Pride-Thankful (1969: Stanley Dancer) Saratoga Springs, N.Y. 1:56 4/5
Flamboyant, br m by Florican-Megs Melody (1968: John Chapman) Yonkers, N.Y. 2:00 2/5
Speedy Play, b g by Speedster-Gentle Play (1966: Warren Cameron) Wilmington, Del. . . . 2:01 2/5

Pacing on Mile Track

All Age

Steady Star, b h 4 by Steady Beau-Avaway (1971: Joe O'Brien) Lexington, Ky. TT1:52
Tarport Lib, b f 3 by Thorpe Hanover-Adios Betty (1966: H. Beissinger) Lexington, Ky. . 1:56 2/5
Cardigan Bay, b g 8 by Hal Tryax-Colwyn Bay (1965: Stanley Dancer) Inglewood, Calif. and
    Easy Prom b g 5 by Easy Adios-Promway (1967: Robt. Farrington) Inglewood, Calif. . 1:57 2/5

Two-Year-Olds

Ricci Reenie Time, b c by Race Time-Ricci Reenie (1972: Harold Dancer Jr.) Lexington, Ky.1:56 1/5
Decorum, b f by Meadow Skipper-Good Taste (1971: Stanley Dancer) Lexington, Ky. 1:57 1/5
Timely Beauty, b f by Good Time-Lorraine (1962: Frank Ervin) Lexington, Ky. TT1:57 1/5
Corsican, br g by Lusty Song-Napoleon's Mite (1957: Harry Dailey) Lexington, Ky. 1:59 4/5

Three-Year-Olds

Steady Star, b c by Steady Beau-Avaway (1970: Joe O'Brien) Lexington, Ky. TT1:54
Tarport Lib, b f by Thorpe Hanover-Adios Betty (1966: Howard Beissinger) Lexington, Ky. 1:56 2/5
Big Kahuna, b g by Quick Pick-Debbie Jeno (1971: Jack Williams, Jr.) Inglewood, Calif. . 1:58 2/5

Four-Year-Olds

Steady Star, b h 4 by Steady Beau-Avaway (1971: Joe O'Brien) Lexington, Ky. TT1:52
Dottie's Pick, b m by Adios-Pick Up (1956: Delvin Miller) Inglewood, Calif. TT1:56 4/5
Ace Of Spades, blk g by Jerry The First-Lady Attorney (1961: Paige West) Inglewood, Calif. 1:57 4/5

Pacing On Five-Eighths Mile Track

All Age

Albatross, b h 4 by Meadow Skipper-Voodoo Hanover (1972: Stanley Dancer) Cicero, Ill. 1:54 3/5
Miss Conna Adios, b m 6 by Adios Senator-Americonna Direct (1969: Tom Lewis)

Wilmington, Del. and Romalie Hanover, b f 3 by Dancer Hanover-Romola Hanover
(1972:Roland Beaulieu) Montreal, Que.. 1:57 3/5
Dancing David, b g 7 by Famed Abbey-Watchim's Princess (1967: Robt. Farrington)
Cicero, Ill.. 1:58

Two-Year-Olds

Truluck, b c by Torpid-Monel (1969: George Sholty) Philadelphia, Pa............... 1:58 2/5
Romalie Hanover, b f by Dancer Hanover-Romola Hanover (1971: Arthur Hult) Phila. Pa. and
Pammy Lobell, b f by Airliner-Prelude Lobell (1971: Bernard Webster) Philadelphia, Pa. 2:00 1/5
To Ri Boy, b g by Adios Harry-Chuckel (1972: Thomas Lewis) Columbus, O. 1:59 2/5

Three-Year-Olds

Romeo Hanover, ch c by Dancer Hanover-Romola Hanover (1966: Geo. Sholty) Cicero, Ill. 1:56 1/5
Romalie Hanover, b f by Dancer Hanover-Romola Hanover (1972: Roland Beaulieu)
Montreal Que... 1:57 3/5
Frosty Clay, b g by Ellroy Clay-Fay Frost (1970: Gene Riegle) Columbus, Ohio 1:58 4/5

Four-Year-Olds

Albatross, b h by Meadow Skipper-Voodoo Hanover (1972: Stanley Dancer) Cicero, Ill. . 1:54 3/5
Miss Conna Adios, b m by Adios Senator-Americonna Direct (1969: Tom Lewis) Phila. Pa. 1:57 4/5
Mark Dean, b g by Noble Dean-Jo's Adios (1972: William Herman) Wilmington, Del. 1:58 4/5

Pacing On Half-Mile Track

All Age

Albatross, b h 4 by Meadow Skipper-Voodoo Hanover (1972: Stanley Dancer)
Delaware, Ohio.. 1:55 3/5
Adios Butler, b h 5 by Adios-Debby Hanover (1961: Eddie Cobb) Delaware, Ohio TT1:55 3/5
Bret's Pet, b f 3 by Bret Hanover-War Sand (1972:William Roseboom) Delaware, Ohio ... 1:57 4/5
Cardigan Bay, b g 8 by Hal Tryax-Colwyn Bay (1964: Vernon Dancer) Yonkers, N. Y. ... 1:58 1/5

Two-Year-Olds

Columbia Hanover, br c by Good Time-Mitzi Eden (1969: Roland Beaulieu) Yonkers, N. Y. and
J. R. Skipper, b c by Meadow Skipper-Good Dena (1972: Greg Wright) Delaware, Ohio 1:58 4/5
Real Hilarious, b f by Shadow Wave-Seascape (1972: Lew Williams) Northfield, Ohio 2:00 2/5
Corsican, br g by Lusty Song-Napoleon's Mite (1957: Harry Dailey) Saratoga Springs, N. Y. 2:02 3/5

Three-Year-Olds

Strike Out, ch c by Bret Hanover-Golden Miss (1972: Keith Waples) Delaware, Ohio 1:56 3/5
Bret's Pet, b f by Bret Hanover-War Sand (1972: William Roseboom) Delaware, Ohio 1:57 4/5
Skipper Gene, ch g by Gene Abbe-Karen O (1965: Fred Cheney) Maywood, Ill. and
Clever Napoleon, b g by Napoleon Hanover-Goldie Chico (1971: Terry Holton)
Delaware, O. 2:00 3/5

Four-Year-Olds

Albatross, b h by Meadow Skipper-Voodoo Hanover (1972: Stanley Dancer) Delaware, Ohio 1:55 3/5
Meadow Elva, br m by Thorpe Hanover-Julia Frost (1968: Delmer Insko) Yonkers, N. Y.. 1:59 2/5
W. W. Smith, b g by Thorpe Hanover-Beatrice Adios (1968:Howard Parker) Saratoga
Springs, N. Y. 1:58 4/5

MILE RECORDS BY THE WORLD CHAMPION TROTTERS

Nevele Pride, bh, 4, by Star's Pride; Indianapolis, Ind., 1969 (S. Dancer) 1:54 4/5
Greyhound, g g, 6, by Guy Abbey; Lexington, Ky., 1938 (S. F. Palin) 1:55 1/4
Greyhound, g g, 5, by Guy Abbey; Lexington, Ky., 1937 (S. F. Palin) 1:56
Greyhound, g g, 5, by Guy Abbey; Lexington, Ky., 1937 (S. F. Palin) 1:56 3/4
Peter Manning, b g, 6, by Azoff; Lexington, Ky., 1922 (T. W. Murphy) 1:56 3/4
Peter Manning, b g, 6, by Azoff; Columbus, Ohio, 1922 (T. W. Murphy) 1:57
Peter Manning, b g, 5 by Azoff; Lexington, Ky., 1921 (T. W. Murphy) 1:57 3/4
Peter Manning, b g, 5, by Azoff; Syracuse, N.Y., 1921 (T. W. Murphy) 1:58
Uhlan, b g, 8, by Bingen; Lexington, Ky., 1912 (Charles Tanner) 1:58
Lou Dillon, ch m, 5, by Sidney Dillon; Memphis, Tenn., 1903 (Millard Sanders) 1:581/2
Lou Dillon, ch m, 5, by Sidney Dillon; Readville, Mass., 1903 (Millard Sanders) 2:00
Cresceus, ch h, 7, by Robert McGregor; Columbus, Ohio, 1901 (G. H. Ketcham) 2:02 1/4
Cresceus, ch h, 7, by Robert McGregor; Cleveland, Ohio, 1901 (G. H. Ketcham) 2:02 3/4
The Abbot, b g, 7, by Chimes; Terre Haute, Ind., 1900 (E. F. Geers) 2:03 1/4
Alix, b m, 6, by Patronage; Galesburg, Ill., 1894 (Andres McDowell) 2:03 3/4

Nancy Hanks, b m, 6, by Happy Medium; Terre Haute, Ind., 1892 (Budd Doble) 2:04
Nancy Hanks, b m, 6, by Happy Medium; Independence, Iowa, 1892 (Budd Doble) 2:05 1/4
Nancy Hanks, b m, 6, by Happy Medium; Chicago, Ill., 1892 (Budd Doble) 2:07 1/4
Sunol, b m, 5, by Electioneer; Stockton, Calif., 1891 (Charles Marvin) 2:08 1/4
Maud S., ch m, 11, by Harold; Cleveland, Ohio, 1885 (W. W. Bair) 2:08 3/4
Maud S., ch m, 10, by Harold; Lexington, Ky., 1884 (W. W. Bair) 2:09 1/4
Maud S., ch m, 10, by Harold; Cleveland, Ohio, 1884 (W. W. Bair) 2:09 3/4
Jay-Eye-See, bl g, 6, by Dictator; Providence, R. I., 1884 (E. D. Bither) 2:10
Maud S., ch m, 7, by Harold; Rochester, N.Y., 1881 (W. W. Bair) 2:10 1/4
Maud S., ch m, 7, by Harold; Pittsburgh, Pa., 1881 (W. W. Bair) 2:10 1/2
Maud S., ch m, 6, by Harold; Chicago, Ill., 1880 (W. W. Bair) 2:10 3/4
St. Julien, b g, 11, by Volunteer; Hartford, Conn., 1880 (Orrin Hickok) 2:11 1/4
St. Julien, b g, 11, by Volunteer; Rochester, N.Y., 1880 (Orrin Hickok) 2:11 3/4
Maud S., ch m, 6, by Harold; Rochester, N.Y., 1880 (W. W. Bair) 2:11 3/4
St. Julien, b g, 10, Volunteer; Oakland, Calif., 1879 (Orrin Hickok) 2:12 3/4
Rarus, b g, 11, by Conklin's Abdallah; Cleveland, Ohio, 1878 (John Splan) 2:13 1/4
Rarus, b g, 11, by Conklin's Abdallah; Cleveland, Ohio, 1878 (John Splan) 2:14
Goldsmith Maid, b m, 17, by Abdallah; Boston, Mass., 1874 (Budd Doble) 2:14
Goldsmith Maid, b m, 17, by Abdallah; Rochester, N.Y., 1874 (Budd Doble) 2:14 3/4
Goldsmith Maid, b m, 17, by Abdallah; Buffalo, N.Y., 1874 (Budd Doble) 2:15 1/2
Goldsmith Maid, b m, 17, by Abdallah; East Saginaw, Mich., 1874 (Budd Doble) 2:16
Goldsmith Maid, b m, 17, by Abdallah; East Saginaw, Mich., 1874 (Budd Doble) 2:16 1/2
Occident, br g, 10, by Doc; Sacramento, Calif., 1873 (George Tennant) 2:16 3/4
Goldsmith Maid, b m, 15, by Abdallah; Boston, Mass., 1872 (Budd Doble) 2:16 3/4
Goldsmith Maid, b m, 14, by Abdallah; Milwaukee, Wis., 1871 (Budd Doble) 2:17

MILE RECORDS BY THE WORLD CHAMPION PACERS

Steady Star, b h, 4, by Steady Beau; Lexington, Ky., 1971 (Joe O'Brien) 1:52
Bret Hanover, b h, 4, by Adios; Lexington, Ky., 1966 (Frank Ervin) 1:53 3/5
Bret Hanover, b h, 4, by Adios; Vernon, N.Y., 1966 (Frank Ervin) 1:54
Adios Butler, b h, 4, by Adios; Lexington, Ky., 1960 (Paige West) 1:54 3/5
Adios Harry, br h, 4, by Adios; Vernon, N.Y., 1955 (Luther Lyons) 1:55
Billy Direct, b h, 4, by Napoleon Direct; Lexington, Ky., 1938 (Vic Fleming) 1:55
Dan Patch, br h, 9, by Joe Patchen; Lexington, Ky., 1905 (H. C. Hersey) 1:55 1/4*
Dan Patch, br h, 8, by Joe Patchen; Memphis, Tenn., 1904 (H. C. Hersey) 1:56
Dan Patch, br h, 7, by Joe Patchen; Memphis, Tenn., 1903 (M. E. McHenry) 1:56 1/4
Dan Patch, br h, 7, by Joe Patchen; Brighton Beach, N.Y., 1903 (M. E. McHenry) 1:59
Star Pointer b h, 8, by Brown Hal; Readville, Mass., 1897 (D. McClary) 1:59 1/4
John R. Gentry, b h, 7, by Ashland Wilkes; Glen Falls, N.Y., 1896 (W. J. Andrews) 2:00 1/2
John R. Gentry, b h, 7, by Ashland Wilkes; Glen Falls, N.Y., 1896 (W. J. Andrews) 2:01 1/2
Robert J., b g, 6, by Hartford; Terre Haute, Ind., 1894 (E. F. Geers) 2:01 1/2
Robert J., b g, 6, by Hartford; Indianapolis, Ind., 1894 (E. F. Geers) 2:02 1/2
Robert J., b g, 6, by Hartford; Fort Wayne, Ind., 1894 (E. F. Geers) 2:03 3/4
Flying Jib, b g, 8, by Algona; Chicago, Ill., 1893 (John Kelly) 2:04
Mascot, b g, 7, by Deceive; Terre Haute, Ind., 1892 (W. J. Andrews) 2:04
Hal Pointer, b g, 8, by Tom Hal; Chicago, Ill., 1892 (E. F. Geers) 2:05 1/4
Direct, b h, 6, by Director; Independence, Iowa, 1891 (George Starr) 2:06
Johnston, b g, 7, by Joe Bassett; Chicago, Ill., 1884 (John Splan) 2:06 1/4
Johnston, b g, 6, by Joe Bassett; Chicago, Ill., 1883 (Peter V. Johnston) 2:10
Johnston, b g, 6, by Joe Bassett; Chicago, Ill., 1883 (Peter V. Johnston) 2:11 3/4
Little Brown Jug, br g, 6, by Tom Hal; Hartford, Conn., 1881 (W. H. McCarthy) 2:11 3/4
Sleepy Tom, ch g, 11, by Tom Rolfe; Chicago, Ill. 1879 (S. C. Phillips) 2:12 1/4
Sleepy Tom, ch g, 11, by Tom Rolfe; Columbus, Ohio, 1879 (S. C. Phillips) 2:14 1/2
Rowdy Boy, bl g, 10, by Bull Pup; East Saginaw, Mich., 1879 (C. W. Forth) 2:15
Sweetzer, g g, 10, by Tom Crowder; Oakland, Calif., 1878 (A. M. Wilson) 2:15
*With Windshield.

GROWTH OF HARNESS RACING

Year	Horses Starting	Purses	USTA Members	Tracks	Horses Registere
1972	39,013	$105,595,669.00	36,518	409	11,842
1971	37,617	97,593,634.00	34,622	417	11,654

1970 .... 35,465	89,280,537.00	32,725	429	11,981
1969 .... 33,188	80,683,497.00	31,561	434	11,851
1968 .... 30,919	71,004,560.00	29,466	440	10,232
1967 .... 28,789	61,851,457.00	26,774	432	11,803
1966 .... 26,756	58,679,557.00	24,846	436	9,128
1965 .... 25,359	53,123,148.00	23,617	446	8,386
1964 .... 23,525	47,130,980.00	22,203	446	8,212
1963 .... 21,664	41,069,036.93	20,918	442	7,822
1962 .... 19,563	35,375,000.00	19,251	441	7,392
1961 .... 18,694	32,635,694.33	17,272	431	7,353
1960 .... 17,702	31,581,922.54	15,593	454	6,794
1959 .... 16,666	29,748,582.31	15,122	462	5,517
1958 .... 15,906	27,572,830.48	13,481	454	5,485
1957 .... 15,212	24,249,842.69	12,680	467	4,700
1956 .... 14,622	21,862,611.30	12,267	482	4,660
1955 .... 14,548	20,626,774.10	11,754	489	4,512
1954 .... 13,997	18,961,265.17	11,352	497	4,496
1953 .... 13,194	18,832,740.79	10,669	503	4,885
1952 .... 11,927	16,052,772.91	9,776	501	3,871
1951 .... 11,187	13,119,753.57	8,731	518	4,879
1950 .... 10,281	11,522,684.44	8,411	546	4,386
1949 .... 9,798	11,362,785.09	7,821	593	4,140
1948 .... 9,323	9,805,079.05	7,353	612	3,460
1947 .... 8,563	7,528,870.98	7,352	625	3,247
1946 .... 7,757	6,290,600.00	5,918	598	2,418
1945 .... 5,679	3,445,906.13	5,531	485	2,117
1944 .... 5,029	2,634,977.58	3,871	437	1,948

LEADING MONEY-WINNING TROTTERS, ALL TIME

(Listed here are the leading money-winning trotters as far back as winnings were reported. The figures are based on race winnings and do not include the totals from exhibitions and races against time. Horses are credited only with net winnings during the years when winnings were calculated on a net basis.)

Horse	Record	Sex	Sire	Year Raced	Money Won
Une de Mai	2:00 1/5	b m	Kerjacques	1967-72	$1,619,463*
Fresh Yankee	TT1:57 1/5	b m	Hickory Pride	1965-72	1,294,252*
Roquepine	(No U.S.)	br m	Atus II	1963-69	956,161*
Su Mac Lad	1:58 4/5	b g	Potomac Lad	1956-65	885,095
Nevele Pride	TT1:54 4/5	b h	Star's Pride	1967-69	873,238
Tidalium Pelo	(No U.S.)	bl h	Jidalium	1966-72	758,603*
Dayan	TT1:55 4/5	b h	Hickory Smoke	1968-72	668,974
Speedy Scot	3,1:56 4/5	b h	Speedster	1962-65	650,909
Duke Rodney	3,1:59	br h	Rodney	1960-66	639,408
Elaine Rodney	3,1:58 3/5	br m	Rodney	1959-68	610,685*
Super Bowl	3,1:56 2/5	b h	Star's Pride	1971-72	601,006
Tornese	(No. U.S.)	ch h	Tabac Blond	1955-61	546,404*
Speedy Crown	3,1:57 1/5	b h	Speedy Scot	1970-72	545,495
Carlisle	TT1:57	br h	Hickory Pride	1965-69	544,136
Noble Victory	1:55 3/5	br h	Victory Song	1964-66	522,391
Grandpa Jim	1:58 4/5	br h	Newport Star	1966-71	501,051
Armbro Flight	3,1:59	br m	Star's Pride	1964-66	493,602
Fine Shot	3,2:02 3/5	br h	Sharpshooter	1967-72	490,774
Agaunar	2:02 1/5h	ch m	Oriole	1965-72	486,457*
Earl Laird	1:59 4/5	bl g	Jean Laird	1962-71	477,034
Darn Safe	1:59	br g	Darnley	1953-63	475,738
Eileen Eden	3,2:01 1/5	ch m	Spectator	1965-71	475,000*
Flamboyant	2:00 2/5h	br m	Florican	1966-68	449,665
Quick Pride	3,1:58 1/5	br h	Hickory Pride	1970-72	440,233
Dartmouth	2:00 1/5h	bl h	Victory Song	1963-65	429,397
Savoir	3,1:58 1/5	br g	Star's Pride	1970-72	428,677
Lindy's Pride	3,1:57 3/5	b h	Star's Pride	1968-70	396,209

* Included estimated foreign earnings.

LEADING MONEY WINNING PACERS, ALL TIME

(Listed here are the leading money winning pacers as far back as winnings were reported. The figures are based on race winnings and do not include totals from exhibitions and races against time. Dan Patch engaged in many remunerative exhibitions, but did not accumulate large earnings. Horses are credited only with net winnings during the years when winnings were recorded on the net basis.)

Horse	Record	Sex	Sire	Year Raced	Money Won
Albatross	1:54 3/5f	b h	Meadow Skipper	1970-72	$1,201,470
Rum Customer	3,1:56	b h	Poplar Byrd	1967-71	1,001,548
Cardigan Bay	1:57 2/5	b h	Hal Tryax	1959-68	1,000,837*
Bret Hanover	TT1:53 3/5	b h	Adios	1964-66	922,616
Laverne Hanover	3,1:56 3/5f	br h	Tar Heel	1968-71	868,557
Overcall	1:57 1/5f	b h	Capetown	1965-69	783,948
Henry T. Adios	1:57 4/5	b h	Adios	1960-64	706,698
Romeo Hanover	3,1:56 1/5f	ch h	Dancer Hanover	1965-67	658,505
Fulla Napoleon	3,1:57 1/5	b h	Dale Frost	1967-70	582,279
Song Cycle	1:58	br h	Walter McKlyo	1965-72	559,255
Bye Bye Byrd	TT1:56 1/5	b h	Poplar Byrd	1957-61	554,257
Best Of All	1:56 2/5	b h	Good Time	1966-68	548,899
Irvin Paul	1:58 3/5f	b g	Gene Abbe	1959-67	548,518
Adios Butler	TT1:54 3/5	b h	Adios	1958-61	509,844
Nardin's Byrd	3,1:59h	b h	Bye Bye Byrd	1966-69	507,341
Race Time	3,1:57	b h	Good Time	1963-65	486,955
Romulus Hanover	3,1:57 1/5f	ch h	Dancer Hanover	1966-68	483,750
Super Wave	1:57f	b h	Shadow Wave	1968-71	481,370
Horton Hanover	1:58f	br h	Star's Pride	1967-72	473,122
Adios Vic	3,1:56 3/5	b h	Adios	1964-68	455,841
Strike Out	3,1:56 3/5h	ch h	Bret Hanover	1971-72	454,063
Nansemond	4,1:56 1/5f	b h	Tar Heel	1970-72	448,436
Timely Knight	1:58 1/5f	b h	Good Time	1965-72	448,669
Meadow Skipper	3,1:55 1/5	br h	Dale Frost	1962-65	428,057
Kentucky	3,1:57	br h	Tar Heel	1969-72	421,395
Most Happy Fella	3,TT1:55	b h	Meadow Skipper	1969-70	419,033
Mr. Budlong	1:58 1/5	br g	Bud Mite	1958-69	416,208

*Included estimated foreign earnings.

Leading Money-Winners by Years—
Trotters

Year	Horse	Won		Year	Horse	Won
1890	McDoel	$ 9,800		1913	Etawah	24,498
1891	Little Albert	11,575		1914	Peter Volo	33,572
1892	Nightingale	16,550		1915	Peter Scott	50,535
1893	Oro Wilkes	13,425		1916	Mabel Trask	33,720
1894	Beuzetta	23,880		1917	Early Dreams	23,745
1895	Oakland Baron	11,475		1918	Nella Dillon	15,689
1896	Rose Croix	11,000		1919	McGregor the Great	24,947
1897	Rilma	14,406		1920	Peter Manning	26,550
1898	John Nolan	16,500		1921	Jeannette Rankin	28,220
1899	Idolita	18,000		1922	Czar Worthy	22,800
1900	Cresceus	13,250		1923	Favonian	21,145
1901	Cresceus	22,874		1924	Mr. McElwyn	24,875
1902	Lord Derby	57,625		1925	Trumpet	29,275
1903	Billy Burke	33,300		1926	Guy McKinney	68,742
1904	Sweet Marie	23,825		1927	Iosola's Worthy	56,638
1905	Angiola	12,929		1928	Spencer	55,036
1906	Nut Boy	19,430		1929	Walter Dear	57,509
1907	Sonoma Girl	28,950		1930	Hanover's Bertha	59,877
1908	Allen Winter	38,600		1931	Calumet Butler	38,115
1909	Margin	27,000		1932	The Marchioness	52,327
1910	Dudie Archdale	29,234		1933	Mary Reynolds	20,826
1911	R.T.C.	31,900		1934	Lord Jim	13,138
1912	Baden	35,700		1935	Greyhound	26,712

1936	Rosalind	37,834
1937	Shirley Hanover	20,023
1938	McLinn Hanover	31,201
1939	Peter Astra	45,242
1940	Spencer Scott	40,981
1941	Bill Gallon	29,118
1942	The Ambassador	20,559
1943	Volo Song	29,966
1944	Yankee Maid	30,865
1945	Titan Hanover	35,273
1946	Victory Song	43,608
1947	Hoot Mon	56,810
1948	Egan Hanover	67,567
1949	Bangaway	74,438
1950	Proximity	87,175
1951	Pronto Don	80,850
1952	Sharp Note	101,625
1953	Newport Dream	94,933
1954	Katie Key	69,637
1955	Scott Frost	186,101
1956	Scott Frost	85,851
1957	Hoot Song	114,877
1958	Emily's Pride	118,830
1959	Diller Hanover	149,897
1960	SuMac Lad	159,662
1961	SuMac Lad	245,750
1962	Duke Rodney	206,113
1963	Speedy Scot	244,403
1964	Speedy Scot	235,710
1965	Dartmouth	252,348
1966	Noble Victory	210,696
1967	Carlisle	232,243
1968	Nevele Pride	427,440
1969	Lindy's Pride	323,997
1970	Fresh Yankee	359,002
1971	Fresh Yankee	293,950
1972	Super Bowl	436,258

Pacers

1890	Cricket	$ 7,100
1891	Hal Pointer	11,375
1892	Flying Jib	13,700
1893	May Marshall	9,200
1894	Robert J.	29,875
1895	Joe Patchen	15,600
1896	Planet	8,150
1897	Star Pointer	22,875
1898	Lady of the Manor	11,450
1899	Hal B.	13,862
1900	Connor	9,875
1901	Audubon Boy	19,650
1902	Direct Hal	25,550
1903	Star Hal	11,150
1904	Morning Star	15,900
1905	Bolivar	10,220
1906	Ardelie	10,977
1907	Leland Onward	8,820
1908	The Eel	16,300
1909	George Gano	18,600

1910	The Abbe	17,650
1911	Branham Baughman	14,630
1912	Joe Patchen	27,100
1913-14	No record	
1915	Hal Boy	35,066
1916	Ben Ear	12,515
1917	Ben Ali	10,310
1918	Directum J.	13,217
1919	Grace Direct	16,980
1920	Hal Mahone	11,562
1921	Jimmy McKerron	14,385
1922	Margaret Dillon	12,337
1923	Anna Bradford's Girl	13,444
1924	Baron Worthy	20,095
1925	Ribbon Cane	27,320
1926	Jean Grattan	24,285
1927	Bert Abbe	29,812
1928	Grattan Bars	41,475
1929	Labrador	22,190
1930	May E. Grattan	32,317
1931	Toll Gate	12,029
1932	Zombro Hanover	13,767
1933	Laurel Hanover	4,927
1934	Calumet Evelyn	9,358
1935	Calumet Evelyn	6,543
1936	Dusty Hanover	9,321
1937	Chief Consul	11,154
1938	Blackstone	14,724
1939	William Cash	5,951
1940	Blackhawk	11,073
1941	Court Jester	20,700
1942	Adios	16,188
1943	Attorney	13,308
1944	True Chief	24,768
1945	Ensign Hanover	31,327
1946	Ensign Hanover	34,368
1947	April Star	51,570
1948	Dr. Stanton	48,820
1949	Good Time	58,766
1950	Scottish Pence	73,387
1951	Tar Heel	66,629
1952	Good Time	110,299
1953	Keystoner	59,131
1954	Red Sails	66,615
1955	Adios Harry	98,900
1956	Adios Harry	129,912
1957	Torpid	113,982
1958	Belle Acton	167,887
1959	Bye Bye Byrd	212,433
1960	Bye Bye Byrd	187,612
1961	Adios Butler	180,250
1962	Henry T. Adios	220,302
1963	Overtrick	208,833
1964	Race Time	199,292
1965	Bret Hanover	341,784
1966	Bret Hanover	407,534
1967	Romulus Hanover	277,636
1968	Rum Customer	355,618
1969	Overcall	373,150
1970	Most Happy Fella	387,239
1971	Albatross	558,009
1972	Albatross	459,921

LEADING-MONEY WINNING DRIVERS

1972	Herve Filion	$2,473,265
1971	Herve Filion	1,915,945
1970	Herve Filion	1,647,837
1969	Delmer Insko	1,635,463
1968	William R. Haughton	1,654,172
1967	William R. Haughton	1,305,773
1966	Stanley F. Dancer	1,218,403
1965	William R. Haughton	889,943
1964	Stanley F. Dancer	1,051,538
1963	William R. Haughton	790,086
1962	Stanley F. Dancer	760,343
1961	Stanley F. Dancer	674,723
1960	Delvin G. Miller	567,282
1959	William R. Haughton	711,435
1958	William R. Haughton	816,659
1957	William R. Haughton	586,950
1956	William R. Houghton	572,945
1955	William R. Haughton	599,445
1954	William R. Haughton	415,577
1953	William R. Haughton	374,527
1952	William R. Haughton	311,728
1951	John F. Simpson	333,136
1950	Delvin Miller	306,814
1949	Clinton Hodgins	184,109
1948	Ralph N. Baldwin	153,223

LEADING DASH-WINNING DRIVERS

1972	Herve Filion	605
1971	Herve Filion	543
1970	Herve Filion	486
1969	Herve Filion	394
1968	Herve Filion	407
1967	Robert G. Farrington	277
1966	Robert G. Farrington	283
1965	Robert G. Farrington	310
1964	Robert G. Farrington	312
1963	Donald Busse	201
1962	Robert Farrington	203
1961	Robert G. Farrington	210
1960	Delmer M. Insko	156
1959	William D. Gilmour	165
1958	William R. Haughton	176
1957	William R. Haughton	156
1956	William R. Haughton	167
1955	William R. Haughton	168
1954	William R. Haughton	153
1953	William R. Haughton	116
1952	Levi Harner	129
1951	John R. Simpson	118
1950	John F. Simpson	111
1949	Clinto Hodgins	128
1948	Harry Burright	129

High Priced Horses Sold at Auction

Price	Horse & Age When Sold	Purchaser & Year of Purchase
*$210,000	Good Humor Man, b c 1	Vernon Gochneaur, Aurora, Ohio (1971)
130,000	Painter, b h 8	Two Gaits Farm, Castleton Farm & Marson Farm, Indianapolis, Ind. (1962)
125,000	Tar Heel, bl c 3	Hanover Shoe Farms, Hanover, Pa. (1951)
125,000	Dexter Hanover, b c 1	Thomas A. & Mildred Dexter, Pearl River, N.Y.; Arthur W. Dexter, Jr. & Alice Schmidt, Nanuet, N.Y.; Apache Stable, Orlando, Fla.
117,000	Miracle Tip, b c 1	Messenger Stable, Chicago, Ill. & Cliff Baker Ranches, Los Angeles, Calif. (1970)
115,000	Nevele Bigshot, b c 1	Nevele Acres, Ellenville, N.Y. (1968)
113,000	Speedy Streak, b c 1	Gainseway Farm, Lexington, Ky. (1965)
110,000	Speedy Flight, br c 1	Messenger Stable, Chicago, Ill. (1969)
110,000	Romette Hanover, b f 1	L-Bar Farms, Goshen, N.Y. & Capital Hill Farms, Montreal, Que. & J. Elgin Armstrong, Brampton, Ont. (1972)
107,000	Buttonwood Pride, br c 1	Herbert Zimmerman, New York, N.Y. (1972)
106,000	Menges Hanover, b c 1	Side Wheeler Stable, New Egypt, N.J. (1968)
105,000	Dancer Hanover, b c 1	Stanley Dancer syndicate, New Egypt, N.J. (1958)
105,000	Bart Hanover, b c 1	Rose Hild Breeding Farm, New Hope, Pa. & Egyptian Acre Stable, New Egypt, N.J. (1967)
101,000	Romalie Hanover, b f 1	Dr. & Mrs. George Smith, Jr.; George A. Smith III & Barbara Johnson, Byram, Conn.
100,000	Brad Hanover, ch c 1	Lehigh Stables, New Egypt, N.J. (1966)
100,000	Nevele Major, br c 1	Nevele Acres, Ellenville, N.Y. (1967)
100,000	Solicitor, b c 3	Hanover Shoe Farms, Hanover, Pa. (1951)

*Record for yearling.

TYPES OF RACES TO BE OFFERED

(U. S. Trotting Assn. Rule 9, Sect. 13 for 1973)

In presenting a program of racing, the racing secretary shall use exclusively the following types of races:

1. Stakes and Futurities
2. Early Closing and Late Closing Events.
3. Conditioned Races.
4. Claiming Races
5. Preferred races limited to the fastest horses at the meeting. These may be Free-For-All

Races, JFA, or Invitationals. Horses to be used in such races shall be posted in the Race Secretary's office and listed with the Presiding Judge. Horses so listed shall not be eligible for conditioned overnight races unless the conditions specifically include horses on the preferred list. Twelve such races may be conducted during a 6-day period of racing at tracks distributing more than $100,000 in overnight purses during such period and not more than 10 such races shall be conducted at other tracks during a 6-day period of racing, provided that at least two of these races are for three-year-olds, four-year-olds, or combined three and four-year-olds. At tracks which race less than 5 days per week, not more than ten such races may be conducted during a 6-day period. Purses offered for such races shall be at least 15% higher than the highest purse offered for a conditioned race programmed the same racing week.

No 2-year-old or 3-year-old will be eligible to be placed on the preferred or invitational list to race against older horses until it has won 7 races unless requested by the owner or authorized agent. The owner or authorized agent may withdraw such request at his discretion.

Where a meeting is in progress in December and continues in January of the subsequent year, races and earnings won at that meeting may be computed in determining whether a horse may be placed on the preferred list.

6. Classified races are permitted when authorized by the State Racing Commission.

Classification Terms

CLASSIFIED RACE—Race arranged by a handicapper regardless of the money winning eligibility of the horses.

CONDITIONED RACE—With specific conditions such as non-winners at the meeting, non-winners of a certain amount of money in the past year, etc.

CLAIMING RACE—A race in which every horse starting therein may be claimed (purchased for the advertised amount) in conformity with the rules.

EARLY CLOSING PURSE—Race for a definite amount fixed in the published conditions and to which entries closed at least six weeks preceding the race.

FUTURITY—A futurity is an event in which the competing animal was nominated before being foaled (mares are nominated while carrying colts). Prominent harness futurities include the Kentucky Futurity, Horseman Futurity, Reading Futurity, Review Futurity, and several sponsored by state organizations.

OVERNIGHT EVENT—Race for which entries closed not more than three days (omitting Sundays) or less before the race.

STAKE—Race which will be contested in a year

subsequent to its closing and in which all nominating and starting fees are added to the purse.

CHRONICLES OF HISTORIC AND RICH EVENTS

The Acorn
Two-Year-Old Filly Trot
Historic Track, Goshen, N.Y.

Yr	Purse	Winning Horse & Driver	Fastest Heat
45	$ 4,854.	Deanna (Gibson White)	R2.04
46	5,475.	Nymph Hanover (Thomas Berry)	2.12¼h
47	6,426.	Song Girl (John Caton)	2.12.1h
48	9,539.	Martha Doyle (Frank Ervin)	2.10 h
49	8,854.	Honor Bright (Henry Myott)	a2.11.2h
50	9,582.	Royal Blood (Paul Vineyard)	2.14.2h
51	11,530.	Vesta's Worthy (Franklin Safford)	2.09.4h
52	11,777.	Lively Lady (Delvin Miller)	2.09.2h
53	13,929.	Stenographer (Delvin Miller)	2.11.3h
54	11,875.	Wilda Hanover (Frank Ervin)	b2.11 h
55	12,143.	Blythe Hanover (Frank Ervin)	c2.09.4h
56	13,181.	Charming Barbara (Wm. Haughton)	2.07 h
57	13,904.	Yankee Lass (Frank Ervin)	2.09 h
58	14,031.	Pompon (Harry Pownall, Sr.)	d2.11 h
59	14,147.	Farr's Pride (Harry Pownall, Sr.)	e2.09.3h
60	17,592.	Gay Fabrina (Howard B. Camden)	f2.08.1h
61	14,788.	Sprite Rodney (Frank Ervin)	g2.08.3h
62	18,003.	Delicious (Delvin Miller)	h2.06.4h
63	18,382.	A.C.'s Jennie (Sanders Russell)	2.09 h
64	17,830.	Frosty Song (Ralph Baldwin)	2.09.4h
65	18,193.	Coalition (Frank Ervin)	2.07 h
66	13,265.	Kimberly Dutchess (Ralph Baldwin)	2.06.3h
67	14,645.	Viv Hanover (Stanley Dancer)	2.07.1h
68	15,213.	Dillers Fleur (Malcom Weaver)	i2.07.4h
69	9,870.	Dancing Flower (Chris Boring)	2.08.4h
70	12,202.	Keystone Selene (Delvin Miller)	2.06 h
71	10,000.	Franella Hanover (George Sholty)	2.07.2h
72	13,398.	Colonial Charm (Glen Garnsey)	2.07.3h

a By Honor Bright and Mysteria.
b By Arvilla Hanover.
c By Nora Frost.
d By Matora Hanover.
e By Elaine Rodney.
f By Meadow Farr.
g By Sprite Rodney and Tercel.
h By Buff Hanover.
i By Quintina Hanover.

The Adios
†Three-Year-Old Colt Pace
The Meadows, Meadow Lands, Pa.

Yr	Purse	Winning Horse & Driver	Fastest Heat
67	$85,510.	Romulus Hanover (Wm. Haughton)	R1.57.3f
68	93,320.	Bye and Large (George Sholty)	2.00.1f
69	88,970.	Laverne Hanover (Wm. Haughton)	2.01 f
70	86,740.	Most Happy Fella (Stanley Dancer)	a1.59.2f
71	88,800.	Albatross (Stanley Dancer)	1.58.3f
72	92,110.	*	b1.58.1f

* Strike Out (Keith Waples) finished x-2-dh1 Jay Time (Gene Riegle) finished x-3-dh1.
a By Columbia George.   b By Lynden Bye Bye.
† Three-Year-Old Open Pace before 1972.

The American Classics
*Invitational Trot
Hollywood Park, Inglewood, Calif.

Yr	Purse	Winning Horse & Driver	Fastest Heat
55	$75,000.	Scott Frost (Joe O'Brien)	a 1.59.3
56	75,000.	Scott Frost (Joe O'Brien)	1.58.3
57	75,000.	Galophone (W.R. Walker)	2.00.2
58	75,000.	Charming Barbara (Wm. Haughton)	2.00.1
59	85,000.	Senator Frost (Richard Buxton)	1.57.3
60	85,000.	Silver Song (Howard Camden)	1.59.1
61	80,000.	Air Record (George Sholty)	1.58.2
62	50,000.	Duke Rodney (Wm. Haughton)	2.16.1
63	50,000.	Porterhouse (Earle Avery)	2.15
64	50,000.	Marco Hanover (Richard Buxton)	2.14
65	50,000.	Armbro Flight (Joe O'Brien)	2.15.3
66	50,000.	Earl Laird (R.J. Williams)	R2.13.2

67	60,000.	Grandpa Jim (Robert Farrington)	2.13.4
68	75,000.	Lady B. Fast (Wm. Popfinger)	2.15.2
69	100,000.	Fresh Yankee (Glen Garnsey)	2.15
70	100,000.	Dayan (Wm. Myer)	R2.13.2
71	100,000.	Fresh Yankee (Joe O'Brien)	2.20.4
72	100,000.	Dayan (Wm. Myer)	2.19.4

a By Gayleway.   *1 1/8-miles dash since 1962.

The American Classics
†Invitational Pace
Hollywood Park, Inglewood, Calif.

Yr	Purse	Winning Horse & Driver	Fastest Heat
55	$75,000. *		a1.57.2
56	75,000.	Dottie's Pick (Delvin Miller)	1.57.4
57	75,000.	Widower Creed (Jim Wingfield)	1.58.3
58	75,000.	Gold Worthy (Wayne Smart)	b1.56.3
59	75,000.	Sunbelle (Joe O'Brien)	1.57.2
60	75,000.	Adios Butler (Edward Cobb)	1.55.3
61	80,000.	Adios Butler (Paige West)	1.57.3
62	50,000.	Irvin Paul (Charles L. King)	2.11.1
63	50,000.	Gamecock (Joe O'Brien)	2.13.3
64	50,000.	Meadow Skipper (Earle Avery)	2.11.3
65	50,000.	Cardigan Bay (Stanley Dancer)	2.12.3
66	50,000.	True Duane (Chris Boring)	R2.09.1
67	60,000.	Easy Prom (Robert Farrington)	2.13.3
68	75,000.	Overcall (Delmer Insko)	2.15.3
69	100,000.	Overcall (Delmer Insko)	2.11.1
70	100,000.	Laverne Hanover (George Sholty)	2.14.4
71	100,000.	Albatross (Stanley Dancer)	2.13.4
72	100,000.	Albatross (Stanley Dancer)	2.11.3

* Time's Square (McKinley Kirk) finished 4-3-1;
Hillsota Earle Avery) finished 1-4-3.
a By Diamond Hal.
† 1 1/8-miles dash since 1962.

The American-National Maturity
Four-Year-Old Trot
Sportsman's Park, Cicero, Ill.

Yr	Purse	Winning Horse & Driver	Fastest Heat
59	$68,032.	Senator Frost (Richard Buxton)	2.01.3f
60	61,196.	Tie Silk (Philippe Dussault)	2.02.2f
61	70,848.	Merrie Duke (John Patterson, Sr.)	2.06 f
62	59,944.	Duke Rodney (Wm. Haughton)	2.00.1f
63	63,639.	Tercel (Harry Pownall, Sr.)	2.03 f
64	66,201.	Speedy Scot (Ralph Baldwin)	2.00.3f
65	59,478.	Dartmouth (Ralph Baldwin)	2.02.4f
66	83,462.	Noble Victory (Stanley Dancer)	R1.59.2f
67	89,580.	Carlisle (Wm. Haughton)	1.59.3f
68	69,728.	Proven Freight (James Dennis)	2.02 f
69	70,396.	Snow Speed (Ralph Baldwin)	R1.59.2f
70	67,324.	Armbro Jet (Joe O'Brien)	2.03.1f
71	65,694.	Keystone Brian (Edward Dunnigan)	*
72	66,645.	Savoir (James Arthur)	1.59 f

* Time disallowed due to disqualification of Timothy T.

The American-National Maturity
Four-Year-Old Pace
Sportsman's Park, Cicero, Ill.

Yr	Purse	Winning Horse & Driver	Fastest Heat
59	$54,879.	Bye Bye Byrd (Clint Hodgins)	1.58.2f
60	61,196.	Adios Butler (Edward Cobb)	2.01.1f
61	61,222.	Merrie Gesture (Edward Kelly)	2.00 f
62	72,425.	Henry T. Adios (Stanley Dancer)	1.59.2f
63	86,030.	Coffee Break (George Sholty)	2.00 f
64	83,278.	Delightful Time (George Sholty)	2.00.3f
65	80,731.	Race Time (Ralph Baldwin)	1.59.1f
66	71,418.	Bret Hanover (Frank Ervin)	1.58.2f
67	80,719.	Song Cycle (Wm. Shuter)	1.59.2f
68	83,612.	Best of All (R.J. Williams)	R1.57.1f
69*	49,533.	Careless Time (Joe Marsh, Jr.)	2.01.1f
	49,533.	Rum Customer (Wm. Haughton)	2.00.1f
70	92,350.	Lightning Wave (Wm. Shuter)	2.04.1f
71	104,000.	Kentucky (Bruce Nickells)	1.59.3f
72	80,425.	Albatross (Stanley Dancer)	2.00 f

* Raced in two divisions.

American Trotting Championship
*Invitational Trot
Roosevelt Raceway, Westbury, N.Y.

Yr	Purse	Winning Horse & Driver	Fastest Heat
46	$25,000.	Doctor Spencer (H.C. Fitzpatrick)	2.03 h

47	25,000.	Proximity (Clint Hodgins)	2.02.2h
48	25,000.	Sidney Hanover (Franklin Safford)	2.03.2h
49	25,000.	Chris Spencer (Harry Whitney)	2.04.1h
50	25,000.	Proximity (Clint Hodgins)	2.03.2h
51	25,000.	Demon Hanover (Harrison Hoyt)	2.03.1h
52	25,000.	Silver Riddle (Clint Hodgins)	2.37.2h
53	25,000.	Florican (Harold Miller)	2.33 h
54	25,000.	Royal Pastime (C.J. Champion)	2.36.3h
55	25,000.	Jamie (Robert Parkinson)	2.33.3h
56	25,000.	Galophone (W.R. Walker)	2.33.1h
57	25,000.	Trader Horn (Wm. Haughton)	2.36 h
58	25,000.	Demon Rum (C.J. Champion)	2.36.1h
59	50,000.	Jamin (Jean Riaud)	2.34.1h
60	50,000.	Silver Song (Howard Camden)	2.33.2h
61	50,000.	Merrie Duke (John Patterson, Sr.)	2.33.3h
62	50,000.	Porterhouse (Earle Avery)	2.32.3h
63	50,000.	Su Mac Lad (Stanley Dancer)	2.33.1h
64	50,000.	Speedy Scot (Ralph Baldwin)	R2.31.2h
65	50,000.	Speedy Scot (Ralph Baldwin)	2.34 h
66	50,000.	Noble Victory (Stanley Dancer)	R2.31.2h
67	50,000.	Perfect Freight (James Dennis)	2.33 h
68	50,000.	Carlisle (Wm. Haughton)	2.34.2h
69	50,000.	Nevele Pride (Stanley Dancer)	2.33 h
70	50,000.	Dayan (Wm. Myer)	2.32.1h
71	50,000.	Dart Hanover (Herve Filion)	2.34 h
72	50,000.	Speedy Crown (Howard Beissinger)	2.34 h

* 1¼-miles dash since 1952.

Atlantic Seaboard Circuit Pace
Non-Winners of $35,000 in 1971, Conditioned
Laurel, Md., Aug. 3

Yr	Purse	Winning Horse & Driver	Fastest Heat
64	$40,250.	Camden Adios (Wm. Savage)	2.04.3h
65	40,750.	Truant Hanover (Fred Parks)	2.04.1h
66	60,000.	Smokeover N. (Wm. Haughton)	R2.01.2h
67	47,500.	Niagara Byrd (Clint Galbraith)	2.02.4h
68	44,750.	Jerry Gauman (Herve Filion)	2.02 h
69	40,000.	Pine Hill Time (Richard Welch)	2.04.1h
70	25,000.	Lord Roger (Robert Stiles, Jr.)	2.04 h
71*	25,000.	Sundancer D. (Harold J. Dancer)	2.02.4h
71†	25,000.	Majestic Jerry (Henri Filion)	2.03 h
72	50,000.	Tarport Skipper (John Chapman)	2.00 f

* Summer Final division.
† Fall Final division.

Battle of the Brandywine
Three-Year-Old Pace
Brandywine Rcy., Wilmington, Del.

Yr	Purse	Winning Horse & Driver	Fastest Heat
60*	$29,800.	Knight Time (James Boring)	2.01.4h
	29,800.	Betting Time (Clint Hodgins)	2.02.2h
61*	28,000.	Adios Don (Howard Camper)	2.00.2h
	28,000.	Al Sam (Earl Beede)	2.02.1h
62	32,000.	Adora's Dream (Jack Williams, Jr.)	2.00.1h
63	29,700.	Country Don (Marcel Dostie)	2.02.2h
64	30,900.	Vicar Hanover (Wm. Haughton)	2.01 h
65	33,800.	Rivaltime (George Sholty)	2.01.3h
66*	24,300.	Money Wise (Wm. Riddick)	2.04 h
	24,300.	Overcall (John Patterson, Sr.)	2.03.1h
67	34,500.	Romulus Hanover (Wm. Haughton)	2.00 h
68	33,100.	Fulla Napoleon (Richard Thomas)	2.00.1h
69	33,900.	Super Wave (Jack Kopas)	1.59.4h
70	35,900.	Columbia George (Roland Beaulieu)	1.58.4f
71	50,000.	Albatross (Stanley Dancer)	R1.57.1f
72*	37,500.	Shadow Star (Jack Kopas)	1.59.2f
	37,500.	Silent Majority (Vernon Dancer)	1.57.2f

* Raced in two divisions.

The Belle Acton
Two-Year-Old Filly Pace
Roosevelt Raceway, Westbury, N.Y.

Yr	Purse	Winning Horse & Driver	Fastest Heat
60	$22,764.	Sweet Miriam (Frank Darish)	2.06.1h
61	25,442.	Ritzy Hanover (Howard Camper)	2.05.2h
62	24,583.	Timely Beauty (Frank Ervin)	2.05.1h
63	24,524.	Sand Tart (Delvin Miller)	2.03.1h
64	26,979.	Beloved Hanover (Stanley Dancer)	2.03.2h
65	26,821.	Bonjour Hanover (Stanley Dancer)	2.06.3h
66	29,074.	Sunrise Hanover (C.J. Champion)	2.07 h
67	29,922.	Timely Drummond (Keith Waples)	2.06.3h
68	28,088.	Scotch Jewel (Ralph Baldwin)	R2.02.4h

Yr	Purse	Winning Horse & Driver	Fastest Heat
69	27,928.	Sprinkle (John W. Smith, Sr.)	2.05.2h
70	29,222.	Keystone Memento (Stanley Dancer)	2.04.3h
71	28,905.	Hope Diamond (Wm. Popfinger)	2.04 h
72	32,627.	Skippers Dream (John Chapman)	2.04.3h

The Bronx
*Three-Year-Old Filly Pace
Yonkers, N.Y., May 18

Yr	Purse	Winning Horse & Driver	Fastest Heat
57	$22,947.	Newport Judy (Adelbert Cameron)	2.13 h
58	25,163.	Kwik (C.J. Fitzpatrick, Jr.)	2.10.4h
59	23,352.	Honick Rainbow (Stanley Dancer)	2.11.1h
60	25,765.	Rapid Transit (Hugh Bell)	2.12.4h
61	45,470.	Sweet Miriam (Frank Darish)	2.11 h
62	44,402.	Stand By (Wm. Haughton)	2.10.4h
63	54,702.	Harry's Laura (Clint Hodgins)	2.02.4h
64	39,791.	Bit O'Sugar (Wm. Haughton)	2.05.1h
65	39,933.	Balenzano (George Phalen)	2.03.4h
66	35,407.	Bonjour Hanover (Stanley Dancer)	2.02.1h
67	25,000.	Meadow Elva (John Chapman)	2.01.3h
68	35,000.	Quickie Hanover (Clint Hodgins)	2.03.3h
69	35,000.	Scotch Jewel (Glen Garnsey)	2.07.1h
70	26,660.	Timely News (Wm. Gilmour)	2.03.1h
71	27,247.	Overdrawn (Warren Cameron)	2.02.3h
72	27,700.	Pammy Lobell (Wm. Haughton)	R2.01.1h

* 1 1/16-miles dash before 1963.

The Buckeye State
Two-Year-Old Pace
Ohio State Fair, Columbus, Ohio

Yr	Purse	Winning Horse & Driver	Fastest Heat
58	$23,850.	Butch Harmony (Clyde Snook)	2.05.3h
59	26,100.	Major Goose (Richard Buxton)	a2.05 h
60	28,000.	Good Counselor (David McClain)	b2.06.2h
61	29,600.	Coffee Break (George Sholty)	2.03 h
62	27,850.	Victoria Lind (Wayne Smart)	2.05 h
63	26,450.	Jug Time (Wayne Smart)	2.03 h
64	29,250.	Tuxedo Hanover (Wayne Smart)	2.03.3h
65	26,800.	True Duane (Chris Boring)	2.10 h
66	31,000.	What A Flash (Clarence Newhart)	2.04 h
67	30,500.	Nob Hill (Wm. Haughton)	2.02.4h
68	30,650.	Turn Right (James Eades)	c2.05.3h
69	31,300.	Double Ohio (Jack Morgan)	2.04 h
70	32,650.	Frisky Hill (Herbert Miller)	2.04.1h
71	36,650.	Jay Time (Gene Riegle)	R2.00.2h
72	32,159.	Sunrise Time (Michael Zeller)	2.01.4h

a By Major Goose and Edgewood Royal.
b By Chance Pick.
c By Expresso Digaren.

The William H. Cane Futurity
*Three-Year-Old Pace
Yonkers, N.Y.

Yr	Purse	Winning Horse & Driver	Fastest Heat
55	$71,040.	Quick Chief (Wm. Haughton)	2.11.1h
56	71,570.	Noble Adios (John Simpson, Sr.)	2.09.2h
57	66,952.	Torpid (John Simpson, Sr.)	2.09.1h
58	60,457.	Raider Frost (Hugh Bell)	2.08.1h
59	64,457.	Adios Butler (Clint Hodgins)	2.09 h
60	65,245.	Countess Adios (Delvin Miller)	2.08 h
61	110,950.	Cold Front (Clint Hodgins)	2.08.3h
62	117,542.	Ranger Knight (Clint Hodgins)	2.13.1h
63	163,187.	Meadow Skipper (Earle Avery)	1.58.4h
64	123,191.	Race Time (George Sholty)	2.01.4h
65	125,236.	Bret Hanover (Frank Ervin)	2.01 h
66	126,915.	Romeo Hanover (Wm. Myer)	1.59.4h
67	150,000.	Meadow Paige (Wm. Haughton)	2.03 h
68	150,000.	Rum Customer (Wm. Haughton)	1.59.4h
69	100,000.	Kat Byrd (Eldon Harner)	2.02.2h
70	102,770.	Most Happy Fella (Stanley Dancer)	R1.58.3h
71	106,795.	Albatross (Stanley Dancer)	2.00 h
72	107,097.	Hilarious Way (John Simpson, Jr.)	2.02.2h

* 1 1/16-miles dash before 1963.

Castleton Farm Stake
Two-Year-Old Trot
Du Quoin, Ill., Aug. 30

Yr	Purse	Winning Horse & Driver	Fastest Heat
46	$12,042.	Way Yonder (Thomas Berry)	2.05¼

Yr	Purse	Winning Horse & Driver	Fastest Heat
47	19,773.	Adeline Hanover (Gibson White)	2.05.3
48	25,446.	Miss Tilly (Fred Egan)	2.05
49	23,540.	Florican (Harry Pownall, Sr.)	a2.04
50	32,398.	Scotch Rhythm (Ralph Baldwin)	2.06
51	32,119.	Duke of Lullwater (John Simpson, Sr.)	2.04.2
52	26,070.	Elby Hanover (Hugh Bell)	2.03.2
53	26,186.	Newport Dream (Adelbert Cameron)	2.01.3
54	23,589.	Butch Hanover (Joe O'Brien)	b2.03.4
55	22,356.	Saboteur (Wayne Smart)	2.03.3
56	22,703.	Major Newport (Adelbert Cameron)	c2.04.1
57	24,366.	Mix Hanover (Frank Ervin)	2.04.1
58	27,455.	Diller Hanover (John Chapman)	2.04.1
59	27,398.	Blaze Hanover (Joe O'Brien)	2.03.2
60	23,945.	Matastar (Harry Pownall, Sr.)	d2.02.1
61	25,715.	Gallant Hanover (Lou Huber, Jr.)	2.01.3
62	23,314.	Florlis (Harry Pownall, Sr.)	e2.01.1
63	22,282.	Big John (Eddie Wheeler)	f2.02.3
64	25,289.	Noble Victory (Stanley Dancer)	2.00.2
65	28,011.	*	g2.08
66	22,186.	**	h2.03.4
67	23,599.	Nevele Pride (Stanley Dancer)	R1.58.4
68	29,858.	Nardins Gayblade (Wm. Haughton)	i2.04.4
69	30,365.	Victory Star (Vernon Dancer)	2.02.1
70	28,377.	Hoot Speed (Glen Garnsey)	j1.59.1
71	25,604.	Songcan (Gilles Lachance)	2.00
72	28,961.	South Bend (Howard Beissinger)	k2.01

* Kerry Way (Frank Ervin) finished 2-1; Amastar (Gordon Larlee) finished 1-2.
** Cardinal Jamie (George Sholty) finished 1-3; Kimberly Dutchess (Ralph Baldwin) finished 3-1.
a By Lusty Song.
b By Scott Frost.
c By Bond Hanover.
d By Peter Frost.
e By Speedy Scot.
f By Dartmouth.
g By Kerry Way.
h By Cardinal Jamie.
i By Nevele Major and Lindys Pride.
j By Noble Gesture.
k By Blitzen.

Coaching Club Trotting Oaks
Three-Year-Old Fillies
Historic Track, Goshen, N.Y.

Yr	Purse	Winning Horse & Driver	Fastest Heat
41	$ 5,845.	Florimel (Harry Pownall, Sr.)	2.10¾h
42	4,061.	Follow Me (Eddie Havens)	2.11¾h
43	7,657.	Barbara Babcock (Ben White)	2.04¾
44	7,791.	Emily Scott (Fred Egan)	2.06¼
45	10,007.	Beatrice Hanover (Harry Pownall, Sr.)	2.04¾
46	11,443.	Onolee Hanover (Franklin Safford)	2.08¼h
47	10,034.	Nymph Hanover (Thomas Berry)	2.09.1h
48	14,011.	Adeline Hanover (Gibson White)	a2.08.1h
49	15,299.	Martha Doyle (Frank Ervin)	2.05 h
50	14,935.	Honor Bright (John Simpson, Sr.)	2.08.1h
51	17,911.	Betsy Volo (Delvin Miller)	2.06.3h
52	18,485.	Crystal Hanover (Henry Myott)	2.07.1h
53	15,284.	Bewitch (Henry Myott)	2.05 h
54	18,299.	Stenographer (Delvin Miller)	2.06 h
55	15,819.	Arvilla Hanover (Wm. Haughton)	2.07 h
56	14,404.	Egyptian Princess (Earle Avery)	2.04 h
57	17,018.	Charming Barbara (Wm. Haughton)	2.06.1h
58	19,019.	Anna Dares (John Simpson, Sr.)	2.05 h
59	18,028.	Matora Hanover (John Simpson, Sr.)	b2.05.2h
60	17,746.	Elaine Rodney (Clint Hodgins)	2.03.4h
61	22,212.	Meadow Farr (Delvin Miller)	2.04 h
62	15,921.	Impish (Frank Ervin)	2.02.4h
63	14,208.	Kentucky Belle (Ralph Baldwin)	2.04.3h
64	14,760.	A.C.'s Jennie (Sanders Russell)	c2.06.3h
65	16,278.	Armbro Flight (Joe O'Brien)	2.03.2h
66	14,053.	Mary Donner (Frank Ervin)	2.03.1h
67	12,978.	Flamboyant (Wm. Haughton)	2.04 h
68	11,942.	Daring Speed (Clint Hodgins)	2.05.4h
69	14,981.	Flowing Speed (John Chapman)	2.03.4h
70	10,736.	Vanaro (Wm. Popfinger)	R2.02.1h
71	10,000.	My Own Star (Ralph Baldwin)	2.05.3h
72	10,000.	Franella Hanover (George Sholty)	2.06 h

a By Mighty Sister.   c By Speedy Victory.
b By Lady Belvedere.

The Colonial
Three-Year-Old Trot
Liberty Bell Park, Philadelphia, Pa.

Yr	Purse	Winning Horse & Driver	Fastest Heat
68	$100,000.	Nevele Pride (Stanley Dancer)	R1.59 f
69	100,000.	Lindys Pride (Howard Beissinger)	2.00.1f
70	102,275.	Timothy T. (John Simpson, Jr.)	2.03.1f
71	103,120.	Savoir (James Arthur)	1.59.1f
72	100,000.	Super Bowl (Stanley Dancer)	2.02 f

The Commodore
Three-Year-Old Pace
Roosevelt Raceway, Westbury, N.Y.

Yr	Purse	Winning Horse & Driver	Fastest Heat
63	$35,237.	Meadow Skipper (Delvin Miller)	2.01.4h
64	37,150.	Iron Rail (Stanley Dancer)	2.02.3h
65	35,800.	Bret Hanover (Frank Ervin)	1.59.2h
66	25,000.	Romeo Hanover (Wm. Myer)	2.03 h
67	34,425.	Romulus Hanover (Wm. Haughton)	2.01.1h
68	33,106.	Fulla Napoleon (Richard Thomas)	2.01.3h
69	25,000.	Steady Brave (Loring Norton)	2.05 h
70	30,850.	Columbia George (Roland Beaulieu)	R1.58.2h
71	32,200.	Albatross (Stanley Dancer)	1.59.4h
72*	22,625.	Hilarious Way (John Simpson, Jr.)	2.02.4h
	23,625.	Silent Majority (Stanley Dancer)	2.00 h

* Raced in two divisions.

The Debutante Stake
Two-Year-Old Filly Pace
Historic Track, Goshen, N.Y.

Yr	Purse	Winning Horse & Driver	Fastest Heat
47	$ 2,546.	Marion Direct (Paul Vineyard)	2.13.2h
48	5,074.	Television (C.P. Chappell)	2.11.1h
49	4,989.	Our Time (Frank Ervin)	2.09.4h
50	7,933.	Gay Sadie (Franklin Safford)	2.09.2h
51	8,736.	Galleta (Delvin Miller)	2.08.1h
52	11,394.	Precious Hal (Ralph Baldwin)	a2.07.4h
53	10,225.	Phantom Lady (Frank Ervin)	2.08 h
54	10,291.	Poplar Juliann (Delvin Miller)	b2.07.2h
55	10,449.	Elizabeth D. (Wayne Smart)	2.06 h
56	9,663.	Adios Fancy (Franklin Safford)	c2.06.2h
57	9,505.	Traffic Lady (John Simpson, Sr.)	2.08 h
58	10,565.	Wonderful Time (Frank Ervin)	2.06 h
59	11,262.	Jan Hanover (Wm. Haughton)	2.04.1h
60	12,110.	Vivian's Adios (Delvin Miller)	2.05.1h
61	13,231.	Ritzy Hanover (Howard Camper)	2.06 h
62	12,517.	Timely Beauty (Frank Ervin)	2.04.2h
63	15,053.	Poplar Wick (Delmer Insko)	d2.07.2h
64	19,015.	Beloved Hanover (Stanley Dancer)	2.03.4h
65	14,800.	Bonjour Hanover (Stanley Dancer)	2.03.4h
66	15,542.	Ember Hanover (Richard Thomas)	R2.02.3h
67	15,617.	Mildred Pierce (Earle Avery)	e2.05.2h
68	18,576.	Scotch Jewel (Ralph Baldwin)	2.04.2h
69	18,497.	Betty Hanover (Stanley Dancer)	2.03.1h
70	16,170.	Keystone Memento (Stanley Dancer)	2.03 h
71	12,422.	Saucy Wave (Harry Harvey)	2.04.4h
72	14,898.	All Alert (Glen Garnsey)	f2.04.3h

a By Adios Ann.
b By Big Bertha and Bunny Chief.
c By Maxine's Dream.
d By Timely Choice.
e By Scuse Me.
f By Real Hilarious.

The Dexter Cup
†Three-Year-Old Trot
Roosevelt Raceway, Westbury, N.Y.

Yr	Purse	Winning Horse & Driver	Fastest Heat
60	$73,129.	Quick Song (Ralph Baldwin)	2.10.4h
61	83,175.	Matastar (Harry Pownall, Sr.)	2.10.1h
62	89,721.	Lord Gordon (John Patterson, Sr.)	2.11 h
63	80,376.	Speedy Scot (Ralph Baldwin)	2.11.2h
64	78,222.	Dartmouth (Stanley Dancer)	2.08.4h
65	79,886.	Armbro Flight (Joe O'Brien)	2.03.3h
66	87,180.	Carlisle (Wm. Haughton)	2.07.2h
67	183,463.	Flamboyant (Wm. Haughton)	2.04.3h
68	166,746.	Nevele Pride (Stanley Dancer)	2.02.2h
69	173,455.	Lindys Pride (Howard Beissinger)	2.03.3h
70	111,514.	Marlu Pride (Herve Filion)	R2.01.2h
71	107,686.	Quick Pride (Stanley Dancer)	2.03 h

| 72 | 100,000. | Songcan (George Sholty) | 2.02.4h |

† 1 1/16-miles dash before 1965.

The Founders Gold Cup
Three-Year-Old Trot
Vernon, N.Y.

Yr	Purse	Winning Horse & Driver	Fastest Heat
67	$25,000.	Keystone Pride (Wm. Haughton)	2.02
68	25,000.	Nevele Pride (Stanley Dancer)	R1.58.4
69	30,000.	Dayan (Fred Bradbury)	2.03.1
70	30,000.	Timothy T. (John Simpson, Jr.)	1.58.4
71	57,530.	Keystone Hilliard (Vernon Dancer)	a1.59.3
72	46,015.	Super Bowl (Stanley Dancer)	R1.58.3

a By Speedy Crown.

The Fox Stake
Two-Year-Old Pace
Indiana State Fair, Indianapolis, Ind.

Yr	Purse	Winning Horse & Driver	Fastest Heat
27	$14,887.	Red Pluto (S.F. Palin)	2.06
28	11,841.	Baron Hall (John Case)	2.09½
29	11,996.	Capital Stock (W.J. Hodson)	2.06½
30	8,568.	Corporal Lee (Lyman Brusie)	2.06½
31	8,352.	Calumet Cheater (Thomas Berry)	2.02½
32	6,447.	Logan Scott (W.T. Britenfield)	a2.02
33	3,325.	Laurel Hanover (Thomas Berry)	2.08
34	4,303.	The Auctioneer (S.F. Palin)	2.12½
35	7,076.	Worthy Grattan (Warren Dennis)	2.04½
36	9,051.	Dusty Hanover (Henry Thomas)	2.04
37	9,450.	The Widower (Vic Fleming)	2.05½
38	10,495.	Blackstone (H.M. Parshall)	2.04
39	11,980.	William Cash (W.T. Britenfield)	2.05
40	14,920.	Blackhawk (Delvin Miller)	b2.03¼
41	16,965.	Court Jester (Rupert Parker)	2.04¼
42	16,240.	Adios (Rupert Parker)	2.05¾h
43	12,703.	Attorney (Earnest Smith)	2.06¼h
44	15,690.	True Chief (Thomas Berry)	2.06½h
45	19,651.	Ensign Hanover (S.F. Palin)	2.09½h
46	20,585.	Poplar Byrd (Thomas Berry)	c2.02
47	29,019.	Knight Dream (Franklin Safford)	2.01.2
48	32,159.	Good Time (Frank Ervin)	2.03.2
49	29,358.	Our Time (Frank Ervin)	2.03.2
50	33,477.	Solicitor (Delvin Miller)	d2.03.1
51	33,680.	Thunderclap (Edgar Leonard)	e2.04.4
52	32,942.	Iosola's Ensign (Wayne Smart)	2.03
53	41,137.	Meadow Pace (Joe O'Brien)	f2.01.2
54	29,444.	Captain Adios (Delvin Miller)	g2.02
55	26,578.	Bachelor Hanover (Wm. Haughton)	h2.00.4
56	34,815.	Torpid (John Simpson, Sr.)	1.59.4
57	42,131.	Thorpe Hanover (Delvin Miller)	i2.00.2
58	46,436.	Meadow Al (Joe O'Brien)	2.00.3
59	50,469.	Bullet Hanover (John Simpson, Sr.)	R1.57
60	42,193.	Adios Cleo (John Simpson, Sr.)	1.59.2
61	55,635.	Coffee Break (George Sholty)	1.58.1
62		–Rain--	
63	57,351.	Race Time (Ralph Baldwin)	1.58
64	54,308.	Bret Hanover (Frank Ervin)	1.58
65	58,559.	Romeo Hanover (Wm. Myer)	1.59
66	61,718.	Best of All (James Hackett)	1.59.2
67	67,037.	Golden Money Maker (Harold J. Dancer)	1.58.4
68	67,341.	Laverne Hanover (Wm. Haughton)	j1.59.4
69	71,327.	Truluck (George Sholty)	1.57.4
70	71,030.	Albatross (Harry Harvey)	1.58.3
71	68,112.	Strike Out (John Hayes)	1.58
72	76,492.	*	k1.57.2

* Ricci Reenie Time (Harold J. Dancer) finished 2-1; Faraway Bay (Richard Buxton) finished 1-2.

a By His Majesty.
b By Victorious Hal.
c By Goose Bay.
d By Tar Heel.
e By Thunderclap and Silent Waters.
f By Excellent Chief.
g By American Way.
h By Greentree Adios.
i By Raider Frost.
j By Santas Fury.
k By Ricci Reenie Time.

The Goshen Cup
Two-Year-Old Pace
Historic Track, Goshen, N.Y.

Yr	Purse	Winning Horse & Driver	Fastest Heat
49	$10,000.	Irish Hal (H.C. Fitzpatrick)	2.08.3h

50	10,000.	Tar Heel (Wm. Haughton)	2.07.2h
51	10,000.	Gander (Hugh Bell)	a2.06.4h
52	12,850.	Knight Star (Franklin Safford)	b2.07.1h
53	16,450.	Parker Byrd (Frank Ervin)	2.05 h
54	10,000.	Adios Evret (Robert Myer)	2.04.3h
55	11,950.	Queen's Knight (Franklin Safford)	2.04.4h
56	13,950.	Airliner (Ned Bower)	2.07.3h
57	13,350.	Pat Rainbow (Clint Hodgins)	2.07 h
58	13,800.	Adios Day (Ned Bower)	c2.04.4h
59	16,350.	Muncy Hanover (Earle Avery)	2.04.1h
60	15,450.	Henry T. Adios (Stanley Dancer)	d2.05.1h
61	13,350.	Play Bill (Frank Ervin)	2.04.3h
62	15,300.	Majestic Hanover (Stanley Dancer)	2.04.1h
63	17,400.	Vicar Hanover (Wm. Haughton)	2.04.1h
64	17,700.	Bret Hanover (Don C. Miller)	2.03 h
65	21,300.	Overcall (*John Patterson, Jr.)	2.01.4h
66	14,323.	Romulus Hanover (Wm. Haughton)	R2.01.2h
67	13,090.	Fulla Napoleon (Richard Thomas)	2.02 h
68	18,559.	Laverne Hanover (Wm. Haughton)	2.02.4h
69	20,357.	Sir Carlton (Leroy Copeland)	e2.03.3h
70	17,481.	Count Bret (Herve Filion)	2.03.4h
71	11,922.	Cory (George Sholty)	2.03.2h
72	16,212.	Valiant Bret (John Wilcutts)	2.03.1h

* John Patterson, Sr., drove first elimination heat.
a By David Caudle.   d By Adios Don.
b By Iosola's Ensign.   e By Ideal Donut.
c By Adios Chief.

The Governor's Cup
Three-Year-Old Trot
Ohio State Fair, Columbus, Ohio

Yr	Purse	Winning Horse & Driver	Fastest Heat
58	$18,025.	La Belle (Richard Buxton)	2.04.4h
59	21,175.	Leading Song (Virgil Butt)	a2.05.4h
60	22,950.	Ava Song (Edwin Boyer)	2.05.1h
61	23,950.	Air Medal (Wayne Smart)	2.03.4h
62	24,000.	Talent Scout (Howard Beissinger)	Rb 2.03.1h
63	21,200.	Van's First (Edwin Boyer)	2.06.3h
64	21,600.	Silver Ghost (Bruce Nickells)	c 2.04.4h
65	23,600.	Spud Coaltown (Bruce Nickells)	2.05 h
66	23,300.	Gay Sam (Joseph Lighthill)	2.04.1h
67	21,800.	High N Away (Gene Riegle)	2.05.4h
68	24,650.	Doralee (Wayne Smart)	d2.04.2h
69	22,250.	Game Pride (Wayne Smart)	e2.05.4h
70	23,850.	Tammie Hill (Edward Dunnigan)	f2.04.1h
71	25,500.	Another Love (Gene Riegle)	2.04 h
72	23,150.	Killbuck Mary (Richard Buxton)	R2.01.4h

a By Pioneer.   d By Doralee and Johnny U.
b By Top Pro.   e By Abe.
c By Silver Ghost and   f By Witch of Endor.
     Argo Kid.

The Greyhound
*Two-Year-Old Trot—Review Futurity
Illinois State Fair, Springfield, Ill.

Yr	Purse	Winning Horse & Driver	Fastest Heat
42	$ 5,018.	Volo Song (Ben White)	2.08¾ h
43	4,825.	Enac (Rupert Parker)	2.12¾ h
44	9,823.	Algiers (H. C. Fitzpatrick)	2.07
45	12,546.	Bombs Away (S.F. Palin)	2.05½
46	14,234.	Way Yonder (Thomas Berry)	2.06
47	14,368.	Rollo (Adelbert Cameron)	a2.06.2
48	20,650.	Miss Tilly (Fred Egan)	2.05.3
49	16,809.	Florican (Harry Pownall, Sr.)	b2.06.2
50	23,162.	Mighty Fine (Delvin Miller)	2.04.4
51	21,840.	Duke of Lullwater (John Simpson, Sr.)	c2.04.3
52	16,664.	Elby Hanover (Hugh Bell)	2.05.3
53	22,628.	Newport Dream (Adelbert Cameron)	2.02.3
54	18,358.	Childs Hanover (Frank Ervin)	2.04.1
55	16,250.	Saboteur (Wayne Smart)	2.03.1
56	17,114.	Double Scotch (Eugene Mattucci)	d2.03.4
57	20,030.	Way Cloud (W.R. Walker)	2.03.4
58	23,288.	Diller Hanover (John Chapman)	2.06
59	23,719.	Blaze Hanover (Joe O'Brien)	2.03
60	18,311.	Matastar (Harry Pownall, Sr.)	2.02.3
61	22,307.	Gallant Hanover (Lou Huber, Jr.)	2.03.1
62	19,483.	Speedy Scot (Ralph Baldwin)	2.01.4
63	17,842.	Dartmouth (Lawrence Garton)	2.03.3
64	20,300.	Marengo Hanover (John Simpson, Sr.)	2.03.3
65	26,127.	Amastar (Gordon Larlee)	e2.02.3

66	23,230.	Speedy Streak (Frank Ervin)	2.04.3
67	26,244.	Nevele Pride (Stanley Dancer)	R2.00.1
68	32,480.	Lindys Pride (Howard Beissinger)	2.01.1
69	37,150.	Timothy T. (John Simpson, Sr.)	2.02.1
70	33,050.	Hoot Speed (Glen Garnsey)	2.01.2
71	28,070.	Super Bowl (Vernon Dancer)	2.04.3
72	35,440.	Volstar Hanover (Joe O'Brien)	2.01

a By Adeline Hanover   d By Double Scotch and
b By Lusty Song.   Hoot Song.
c By Hardy Hanover.   e By Governor Armbro.
* Stake prior to 1967.

The Hambletonian
Three-Year-Old Trot
Du Quoin, Ill.

Yr	Purse	Winning Horse & Driver	Fastest Heat
26	$ 73,451.	Guy McKinney (Nat Ray)	2.04¾
27	54,694.	Iosola's Worthy (Marvin Childs)	2.03¾
28	66,226.	Spencer (W.H. Lessee)	2.02½
29	60,309.	Walter Dear (Walter Cox)	2.02¾
30	56,859.	Hanover's Bertha (Thomas Berry)	2.03
31	50,921.	Calumet Butler (R.D. McMahon)	2.03¼
32	49,489.	The Marchioness (Wm. Caton)	a2.01¼
33	40,459.	Mary Reynolds (Ben White)	2.03¾
34	25,845.	Lord Jim (H.M. Parshall)	2.02¾
35	33,321.	Greyhound (S.F. Palin)	2.02¼
36	35,643.	Rosalind (Ben White)	2.01¾
37	37,912.	Shirley Hanover (Henry Thomas)	2.01½
38	37,962.	McLin Hanover (Henry Thomas)	2.02¼
39	40,502.	Peter Astra (H.M. Parshall)	2.04¼
40	43,658.	Spencer Scott (Fred Egan)	2.02
41	38,729.	Bill Gallon (Lee Smith)	2.05
42	38,954.	The Ambassador (Ben White)	2.04
43	42,298.	Volo Song (Ben White)	2.02½
44	33,577.	Yankee Maid (Henry Thomas)	2.04
45	50,196.	Titan Hanover (Harry Pownall, Sr.)	2.04
46	50,995.	Chestertown (Thomas Berry)	2.02½
47	46,267.	Hoot Mon (S.F. Palin)	2.00
48	59,941.	Demon Hanover (Harrison Hoyt)	2.02
49	69,791.	Miss Tilly (Fred Egan)	2.01.2
50	75,209.	Lusty Song (Delvin Miller)	2.02
51	95,263.	Mainliner (Guy Crippen)	2.02.3
52	87,637.	Sharp Note (Bion Shively)	2.02.3
53	117,117.	Helicopter (Harry Harvey)	b2.01.3
54	106,830.	Newport Dream (Adelbert Cameron)	2.02.4
55	86,863.	Scott Frost (Joe O'Brien)	2.00.3
56	100,603.	The Intruder (Ned Bower)	2.01.2
57	111,126.	Hickory Smoke (John Simpson, Sr.)	2.00.1
58	106,719.	Emily's Pride (Flave Nipe)	1.59.4
59	125,283.	Diller Hanover (Frank Ervin)	2.01.1
60	147,481.	Blaze Hanover (Joe O'Brien)	c1.59.3
61	131,573.	Harlan Dean (James Arthur)	1.58.2
62	116,612.	A.C.'s Viking (Sanders Russell)	1.59.3
63	115,549.	Speedy Scot (Ralph Baldwin)	d1.57.3
64	115,281.	Ayres (John Simpson, Sr.)	1.56.4
65	122,245.	Egyptian Candor (Adelbert Cameron)	e2.03.4
66	122,540.	Kerry Way (Frank Ervin)	1.58.4
67	122,650.	Speedy Streak (Adelbert Cameron)	2.00
68	116,190.	Nevele Pride (Stanley Dancer)	1.59.2
69	124,910.	Lindys Pride (Howard Beissinger)	1.57.3
70	143,630.	Timothy T. (John Simpson, Jr.)	f1.58.2
71	129,770.	Speedy Crown (Howard Beissinger)	1.57.2
72	119,090.	Super Bowl (Stanley Dancer)	R1.56.2

a By Hollyrood Dennis.   d By Florlis.
b By Morse Hanover.   e By Armbro Flight.
c By Quick Song and   f By Formal Notice.
     Hoot Frost.

The Hambletonian Filly Stake
Three-Year-Old Trot
Du Quoin, Ill.

Yr	Purse	Winning Horse & Driver	Fastest Heat
71	$31,500.	Gay Blossom (Glen Garnsey)	R2.00
72	32,480.	Sara Lane Hanover (Joe O'Brien)	2.00.1

Hanover Colt Stake
Two-Year-Old Trot
Liberty Bell Park, Philadelphia, Pa.

Yr	Purse	Winning Horse & Driver	Fastest Heat
65*	$16,277.	Governor Armbro (Joe O'Brien)	2.07.1f
	16,477.	Proud Vic (Marcel Dostie)	2.05.4f

66	28,228.	Keystone Pride (Wm. Haughton)	2.05.2f
67	26,277.	Nevele Pride (Stanley Dancer)	2.03.3f
68*	17,011.	Dayan (John Wilcutts)	2.03.4f
	17,011.	Gun Runner (Earle Avery)	2.03.1f
69	29,828.	Victory Star (Vernon Dancer)	2.03.4f
70	26,202.	Quick Pride (Delvin Miller)	2.04.3f
71	27,391.	Super Bowl (Vernon Dancer)	R2.01.4f
72	26,482.	Arnie Almahurst (Gene Riegle)	2.05 f

* Raced in two divisions.

Hanover Colt Stake
Two-Year-Old Pace
Liberty Bell Park, Philadelphia, Pa.

Yr	Purse	Winning Horse & Driver	Fastest Heat
65*	$16,785.	Overcall (John Patterson)	2.01.4f
	16,785.	Effrat Hanover (Joe O'Brien)	2.02.2f
	16,785.	Tarport Paul (Delvin Miller)	2.03.1f
66†	22,314.	Romulus Hanover (Wm. Haughton)	2.02 f
	22,314.	Nardins Byrd (Wm. Haughton)	2.01.1f
67	40,027.	Batman (Adelbert Cameron)	2.06 f
68†	23,826.	Hammerin Hank (George Sholty)	2.02 f
	23,826.	Laverne Hanover (Wm. Haughton)	2.00.1f
69†	23,782.	Columbia George (Roland Beaulieu)	1.59.3f
	23,982.	Truluck (George Sholty)	R1.59 f
70†	21,593.	Nansemond (Herve Filion)	2.00.1f
	21,593.	Veri Special (Herve Filion)	1.59.2f
71†	22,190.	Strike Out (Wm. Gilmour)	1.59.1f
	22,190.	Berry Hanover (Vernon Dancer.)	2.01 f
72	40,222.	Valiant Bret (Harry Tudor)	2.10.3f

* Raced in three divisions. † Raced in two divisions.

Hanover Colt Stake
Three-Year-Old Trot
Liberty Bell Park, Philadelphia, Pa.

Yr	Purse	Winning Horse & Driver	Fastest Heat
66	$24,605.	Carlisle (Wm. Haughton)	2.02.2f
67	27,378.	Keystone Pride (Wm. Haughton)	2.02.1f
68	24,371.	Snow Speed (Ralph Baldwin)	R1.59.3f
69	25,981.	Dayan (Fred Bradbury)	2.02.2f
70	25,876.	Timothy T. (John Simpson, Jr.)	2.03.4f
71	22,102.	Speedy Crown (Howard Beissinger)	1.59.4f
72	19,741.	Super Bowl (Stanley Dancer)	2.01.3f

Hanover Colt Stake
Three-Year-Old Pace
Liberty Bell Park, Philadelphia, Pa.

Yr	Purse	Winning Horse & Driver	Fastest Heat
66	$29,705.	Romeo Hanover (George Sholty)	2.01.2f
67	31,878.	Meadow Paige (Herve Filion)	1.59.1f
68	35,839.	Fulla Napoleon (Richard Thomas)	2.01.2f
69	36,036.	Laverne Hanover (Wm. Haughton)	2.00 f
70	33,521.	Truluck (John Wilcutts)	R1.57.3f
71	27,252.	Nansemond (Herve Filion)	1.58.1f
72	26,166.	Strike Out (John Hayes, Sr.)	2.01.3f

The Hanover Filly Stake
Two-Year-Old Trot
Liberty Bell Park, Philadelphia, Pa.

Yr	Purse	Winning Horse & Driver	Fastest Heat
47	$10,079.	Tilly Trott (S.F. Palin)	2.08.2
48	11,826.	Martha Doyle (Frank Ervin)	2.12
49	11,166.	Mysteria (Delvin Miller)	2.13.3
50	13,324.	Betsy Volo (Delvin Miller)	2.03.3
51	16,041.	Kimberly Mine (John Simpson, Sr.)	2.04.3
52	15,164.	*	a2.03.1
53	19,159.	Stenographer (Delvin Miller)	2.03.1
54	16,167.	Columbia Hanover (John Simpson, Sr.)	b2.03
55	16,953.	Egyptian Princess (Earle Avery)	2.02
56	16,452.	Cassin Hanover (Fred Egan)	2.02.3
57	18,628.	Yankee Lass (Frank Ervin)	2.02.4
58	17,096.	Merrie Annabelle (John Patterson, Sr.)	2.00
59	17,625.	Carlene Hanover (Ralph Baldwin)	2.02
60	20,053.	Florikash (Wayne Smart)	2.01.4
61	18,155.	Impish (Frank Ervin)	R1.58.3
62	20,321.	Star Act (Joe O'Brien)	2.01.3
63	20,685.	A.C.'s Jennie (Sanders Russell)	2.03
64	23,013.	Armbro Flight (Joe O'Brien)	2.06.4

65†	16,860.	Mary Donner (Frank Ervin)	2.06.4f
	16,860.	Kerry Way (Frank Ervin)	2.07.1f
66	26,337.	Flamboyant (Wm. Haughton)	2.04.4f
67	27,412.	Ole Hanover (James Hackett)	2.09.1f
68	26,229.	Sparkling Molly (John Chapman)	2.03 f
69†	16,478.	Lovester (Chas. Clark, Jr.)	2.05 f
	16,278.	Misty Ayres (Jerry Graham)	2.06 f
70	25,250.	Keystone Selene (Delvin Miller)	2.04 f
71	25,901.	Killbuck Mary (Richard Buxton)	2.03.3f
72	26,143.	Colonial Charm (Glen Garnsey)	2.04.2f

* Earl's Song (Wayne Smart) finished 2-1; Fiesta Hanover (John Simpson, Sr.) finished 1-2.
a By Earl's Song.   b By Sweet Talk.
† Raced in two divisions.

The Hanover Filly Stake
Two-Year-Old Pace
Liberty Bell Park, Philadelphia, Pa.

Yr	Purse	Winning Horse & Driver	Fastest Heat
47	$ 8,527.	Marion Direct (Paul Vineyard)	2.08
48	10,273.	Miss Morris Chief (Joe O'Brien)	a2.07.1
49	12,316.	Beryl Hanover (Gibson White)	2.11.1h
50	12,576.	Floating Dream (McKinley Kirk)	2.00.4
51	15,178.	Silent Waters (John Simpson, Sr.)	2.03
52	15,049.	Pleasant Surprise (McKinley Kirk)	2.02
53	19,389.	Adios Betty (Delvin Miller)	2.01.3
54	18,295.	Step Lively (Joe O'Brien)	2.02.2
55	18,678.	Flaming Arrow (Edward Cobb)	b2.02
56	18,102.	Good Counsel (Frank Ervin)	2.02
57	18,578.	Traffic Lady (John Simpson, Sr.)	2.02
58	18,596.	Great Pleasure (Robert Altizer)	2.01.4
59	18,175.	Countess Adios (Delvin Miller)	R1.59.2
60	16,853.	Way Wave (Ralph Baldwin)	2.01
61	19,455.	Stancy Hanover (Wayne Smart)	c2.00
62	17,971.	Timely Beauty (Frank Ervin)	2.02
63	20,185.	Poplar Wick (Delbert Insko)	1.59.3
64	27,713.	Bewitch Hanover (John Simpson, Sr.)	2.02.3
65†	18,910.	Tarport Lib (Delvin Miller)	2.02.3
	18,910.	Bonjour Hanover (Stanley Dancer)	2.02 f
66	33,237.	Meadow Elva (Wm. Haughton)	2.03.2f
67†	19,406.	Armbro Indigo (Joe O'Brien)	2.03.2
	19,606.	Keystone Widow (Wm. Riddick)	2.04 f
68†	21,295.	Adiola Hanover (Howard Beissinger)	2.02 f
	21,295.	Shadow Mir (Herve Filion)	2.01.2f
69†	20,654.	Fanny Hail (Edward Dunnigan)	2.03.2f
	20,454.	Bardot Hanover (Keith Waples)	2.05.2f
70‡	16,093.	Jo Hanover (C.J. Fitzpatrick)	2.02.2f
	16,093.	Good Bret (Harold J. Dancer)	2.03 f
	16,093.	Truthful Waverly (Herve Filion)	2.02.2f
71†	20,825.	Myrtle Direct (Herman Graham, Jr.)	2.02.1f
	20,825.	Romalie Hanover (Arthur Hult)	2.00.1f
72	33,643.	Shifting Scene (Chas. Clark,Jr.)	2.01.4f

a By Dotty Direct.   c By Ritzy Hanover.
b By Princess Adios.
† Raced in two divisions.   ‡ Raced in three divisions

The Hanover Filly Stake
Three-Year-Old Trot
Liberty Bell Park, Philadelphia, Pa.

Yr	Purse	Winning Horse & Driver	Fastest Heat
48	$10,884.	Voluptuous (Thomas Berry)	2.05
49	12,688.	Lady Jeritza (Adelbert Cameron)	a2.03.3
50	11,051.	Honor Bright (John Simpson, Sr.)	2.04.1
51	14,186.	Neola Hanover (Wilbur Ehlen)	2.12.4
52	16,374.	Lu Peck (H.C. Fitzpatrick)	2.02.1
53	15,451.	Earl's Song (Wayne Smart)	2.00.2
54	18,986.	Stenographer (Delvin Miller)	2.00.4
55	14,960.	Sweet Talk (Wayne Smart)	2.02
56	14,078.	Nimble Colby (Ralph Baldwin)	2.00.2
57	14,652.	Charming Barbara (Wm. Haughton)	2.00.3
58	16,028.	Emily's Pride (Flave Nipe)	b2.00.1
59	16,946.	Sara Black (W.R.Walker)	2.00
60	13,925.	Carlene Hanover (Ralph Baldwin)	c2.01
61	16,353.	Meadow Farr (Joe O'Brien)	Rd1.59.4
62	14,205.	Worth Seein (Ralph Baldwin)	2.01.1
63	15,271.	Elma (John Simpson, Sr.)	2.01.1
64	17,653.	Golden Make It (Joe O'Brien)	e2.01.1
65	22,113.	Armbro Flight (Joe O'Brien)	2.02.1f
66	21,620.	Fresh Yankee (Sanders Russell)	2.04 f
67	24,037.	Lana Hanover (Vernon Dancer)	2.05.4f
68†	19,445.	Arbida Hanover (John Simpson, Sr.)	2.04.1f
	19,445.	Daring Speed (Clint Hodgins)	2.04 f

69†	17,509.	Extra Bonus (Clifford Boyd)	2.04.1f
	17,709.	Tarport Farr (Wm. Gilmour)	2.05.2f
70	24,492.	Vanaro (Wm. Popfinger)	2.02.3f
71	20,020.	Noble Gal (Herman Graham, Jr.)	2.02.2f
72	20,326.	Delmonica Hanover (Jn. Simpson, Jr.)	2.04.4f

a By Rosamond. d By Air Medal.
b By Sandalwood. e By Speedy Victory.
c By Elaine Rodney.
† Raced in two divisions.

The Hanover Filly Stake
Three-Year-Old Pace
Liberty Bell Park, Philadelphia, Pa.

Yr	Purse	Winning Horse & Driver	Fastest Heat
48	$ 9,619.	Marion Direct (Paul Vineyard)	2.11.1
49	12,688.	Romola Hal (Adelbert Cameron)	2.02.3
50	11,396.	Direct Gal (John Caton)	2.01.3
51	12,634.	Meda Volo (Delvin Miller)	2.00.3
52	15,512.	Silent Waters (Delvin Miller)	2.03
53	12,404.	Pleasant Surprise (McKinley Kirk)	2.01
54	13,236.	Phantom Lady (Frank Ervin)	1.59.4
55	15,305.	Dottie's Pick (Delvin Miller)	a2.00.4
56	15,228.	Flaming Arrow (Edward Cobb)	R1.58.2
57	14,652.	Quick Pick Up (John Simpson, Sr.)	1.59.3
58	16,228.	Sunbelle (Joe O'Brien)	1.59.4
59	17,546.	Quick Lady (Olin Davis)	1.58.4
60	15,225.	Countess Adios (Delvin Miller	1.59.4
61	15,453.	Way Wave (Ralph Baldwin)	1.58.3
62	15,605.	Stand By (Wm. Haughton)	2.00.3
63	14,471.	Timely Beauty (Frank Ervin)	b1.59.3
64	16,535.	Adiolia (George Sholty)	2.03.1
65†	14,506.	Rescued (James Arthur)	2.02 f
	14,506.	Colleen Napoleon (Richard Thomas)	2.03 f
66	23,720.	Bonjour Hanover (Stanley Dancer)	2.02 f
67	27,237.	Meadow Elva (Wm. Haughton)	2.01.1f
68†	20,568.	Sunnie Tar (Joe O'Brien)	1.59.2f
	20,568.	Trotwood Tootie (Delvin Miller)	2.01.3f
69	29,649.	Nevele Dream (John Simpson Jr.)	2.00.4f
70	30,872.	Bardot Hanover (Herve Filion)	2.01 f
71	24,525.	Keystone Memento (Ronald Dancer)	2.01 f
72	24,155.	Romalie Hanover (Roland Beaulieu)	1.59.2f

a By Amber Rodney. b By Glad Rags.
† Raced in two divisions.

The E. Roland Harriman
Two-Year-Old Trot
Yonkers, N. Y.

Yr	Purse	Winning Horse & Driver	Fastest Heat
64	$ 57,622.	Noble Victory (Stanley Dancer)	2.05.2h
65*	75,000.	Governor Armbro (Joe O'Brien)	2.07.2h
	75,000.	Bonus Boy (Adelbert Cameron)	2.06.4h
66	100,000.	Flamboyant (Wm. Haughton)	2.09.2h
67	100,000.	Nevele Pride (Stanley Dancer)	2.05.2h
68*	37,500.	Gun Runner (Earle Avery)	2.06.2h
	37,500.	Adam Eden (Wm. Myer)	2.08 h
69	50,320.	Victory Star (Vernon Dancer)	2.07.2h
70	49,495.	Quick Pride (Delvin Miller)	2.04 h
71	45,948.	Super Bowl (Vernon Dancer)	R2.02.3h
72	41,971.	Colonial Charm (Glen Garnsey)	2.06 h

* Raced in two divisions.

The Horseman Stake
Two-Year-Old Trot
Indiana State Fair, Indianapolis, Ind.

Yr	Purse	Winning Horse & Driver	Fastest Heat
38	$ 8,335.	Peter Astra (H.M. Parshall)	2.05¼
39	9,375.	Kuno (Harry Whitney)	a2.05
40	15,495.	Bill Gallon (Lee Smith)	2.04
41	14,875.	Colby Hanover (Fred Egan)	2.05½
42	13,335.	Volo Song (Ben White)	2.06¼h
43	13,120.	Eva's Boy (Wayne Smart)	2.09¼h
44	17,480.	Titan Hanover (Harry Pownall, Sr.)	2.05¾h
45	18,311.	Deanna (Ben White)	2.07 h
46	17,536.	Hoot Mon (Fred Egan)	2.04¼
47	26,405.	Rollo (Adelbert Cameron)	2.06.2
48	33,846.	Miss Tilly (Fred Egan)	2.06
49	32,992.	Florican (Harry Pownall, Sr.)	b2.02.1
50	40,748.	Mighty Fine (Delvin Miller)	2.04.2
51	34,716.	Duke of Lullwater (John Simpson, Sr.)	2.03.4
52	30,695.	Newport Star (Adelbert Cameron)	2.06.1
53	32,484.	Newport Dream (Adelbert Cameron)	2.03.4
54	28,041.	Galophone (Houston Stone)	c2.04.3
55	26,276.	Saboteur (Harry Pownall, Sr.)	2.05.2
56	23,770.	Bond Hanover (Joe O'Brien)	d2.04
57	37,112.	Sharpshooter (Harry Pownall, Sr.)	e2.05.1
58	41,598.	Diller Hanover (John Chapman)	2.03.1
59	43,701.	Blaze Hanover (Joe O'Brien)	f2.01.2
60	42,469.	Harlan Dean (Delvin Miller)	2.01.2
61	51,927.	Safe Mission (Joe O'Brien)	g2.03.3
62		--Rain--	
63	47,173.	Smart Rodney (Wm. Haughton)	2.03.3
64	51,643.	Noble Victory (Stanley Dancer)	R2.00.1
65	47,291.	Kerry Way (Frank Ervin)	2.02.4
66	41,308.	Kimberly Dutchess (Ralph Baldwin)	h2.04.3
67	36,858.	Nevele Pride (Stanley Dancer)	2.02.1
68	47,435.	Nevele Major (Stanley Dancer)	i2.02.2
69	44,589.	Nevele Rascal (Stanley Dancer)	2.03.1
70	44,262.	Noble Gesture (Herman Graham, Jr.)	2.01.1
71	34,084.	*	j2.03
72	46,320.	Blitzen (Herman Graham, Jr.)	2.02.1

* Star's Chip (Stanley Dancer) finished 2-1; Super Bowl (Vernon Dancer) finished 1-2.

a By Spencer Scott. g By Gallant Hanover and Safe Mission.
b By Lusty Song.
c By Butch Hanover. h By Halifax Hanover.
d By Major Newport. i By The Prophet.
e By Gang Awa. j By Star's Chip.
f By Uncle Sam.

The Horseman Futurity
Three-Year-Old Trot
Indiana State Fair, Indianapolis, Ind.

Yr	Purse	Winning Horse & Driver	Fastest Heat
07	$ 4,000.	Kentucky Todd (Harry Stinson)	2.09
09	4,000.	Baroness Virginia (Samuel Fleming)	2.13¼
11	6,500.	Mainleaf (Richard Curtis)	2.09¼
13	6,277.	Etawah (Edward Geers)	2.01¾
14	6,625.	Ortolan Axworthy (Alonzo McDonald)	2.08¼
15	6,552.	Native Spirit (Bert Shank)	2.08¼
16	4,900.	Bingen Silk (J.B. Chandler)	2.07¼
17	3,598.	Harvest Gale (Walter Cox)	2.08¾
18	4,188.	Peter June (Edward Geers)	2.05½
19	4,839.	Periscope (John Dodge)	2.06¼
20	6,406.	Arion Guy (Harry Stokes)	2.05¼
21	5,500.	Nelson Dillon (Joseph Serrill)	2.05½
22	5,242.	Peter Earl (Nat Ray)	2.05¼
23	4,902.	The Senator (Alonzo McDonald)	2.07½
24	4,379.	Mr. McElwyn (Ben White)	2.03¾
25	4,394.	Sam Williams (Walter Cox)	2.06¼
26	5,933.	Charm (Ben White)	2.08¼
27	7,665.	Iosola's Worthy (Thomas Berry)	2.05¾
28	7,712.	Etta Volo (W.K. Dickerson)	2.04½
29	8,468.	Volomite (Walter Cox)	2.04½
30	7,454.	Legality (H.M. Parshall)	2.06½
31	6,428.	Protector (Wm. Caton)	2.02¼
32	6,105.	The Marchioness (Wm. Caton)	2.02
33	6,805.	Brown Berry (Fred Egan)	2.03¼
34	4,293.	Vitamine (Wm. Caton)	2.01¾
35	3,088.	Greyhound (S.F. Palin)	2.05
36	3,235.	Bill Strang (W.K. Dickerson)	2.02¾
37	3,141.	Southland (Fred Egan)	2.03½
38	5,155.	McLin (Henry Thomas)	2.01¾
39	3,160.	Lyrmite (Thomas Berry)	2.07
40	4,480.	Spencer Scott (Fred Egan)	2.01¼
41	4,792.	Bill Gallon (Lee Smith)	2.01
42	5,979.	Pay Up (Lee Smith)	2.07¼ h
43	7,084.	Darnley (Harry Whitney)	2.04¾ h
44	4,290.	Yankee Maid (Henry Thomas)	2.05¼ h
45	3,755.	Voltite (S.F. Palin)	2.05¼ h
46	5,475.	Victory Maid (S.F. Palin)	2.01¾
47	6,465.	Way Yonder (Adelbert Cameron)	2.03.2
48	12,130.	Egan Hanover (Ralph Baldwin)	2.02.3
49	15,493.	Bangaway (Ralph Baldwin)	2.05
50	12,803.	Lusty Song (Delvin Miller)	2.02
51	23,685.	Scotch Rhythm (Ralph Baldwin)	2.04.4
52	24,707.	Sharp Note (Bion Shively)	2.01
53	24,456.	Kimberly Kid (Thomas Berry)	2.01.3
54	22,502.	Darn Safe (B.J. Schue)	2.00.3

			Fastest Heat
55	20,741.	Galophone (Wm. Haughton)	2.01
56	20,656.	Nimble Colby (Ralph Baldwin)	2.03.3
57	20,489.	Hoot Song (Ralph Baldwin)	2.01.4
58	22,708.	Sandalwood (Ralph Baldwin)	2.01.2
59	26,251.	Expresson (Frank Ervin)	2.01.4
60	32,265.	Quick Song (Ralph Baldwin)	2.00.3
61	36,895.	Spectator (Ralph Baldwin)	1.59.4
62	37,517.	Safe Mission (Joe O'Brien)	a2.03
63	39,549.	Speedy Scot (Ralph Baldwin)	1.59.1
64	36,843.	Dartmouth (Ralph Baldwin)	2.00.2
65	38,496.	Armbro Flight (Joe O'Brien)	b1.57.2
66	36,879.	Carlisle (Wm. Haughton)	c2.00.2
67	35,303.	Dazzling Speed (Stanley Dancer)	d2.00.2
68	34,737.	Nevele Pride (Stanley Dancer)	R1.56.3
69	41,563.	Nevele Major (Stanley Dancer)	2.02.4
70	38,565.	Formal Notice (James Arthur)	2.00.4
71	35,737.	Hoot Speed (Glen Garnsey)	1.59.3
72	32,080.	Super Bowl (Stanley Dancer)	1.59.3

a By Lord Gordon.   c By Polaris
b By Noble Victory. d By Speed Model.

The Horseman Futurity
Three-Year-Old Pace
Indiana State Fair, Indianapolis, Ind.

Yr	Purse	Winning Horse & Driver	Fastest Heat
07	$ 2,100.	Betty Brent (Vance Nuckols)	2.12½
09	2,000.	Maggie Winder (Henry Jones)	2.06½
11	3,366.	Miss De Forest (Alonzo McDonald)	2.07¾
13	3,381.	Homer Baughman (Crit Davis)	2.12¼
14	3,567.	Bud Elliott (Frank Jones)	2.14¼
15	3,528.	General Todd (Guy Rea)	2.04¼
16	2,670.	Alice Jolla (C.A. Valentine)	2.17¼
17	1,983.	Rex De Forest (Walter Cox)	2.11½
18	2,370.	Liberty Mac (Wm. Hasch)	2.09¼
19	2,598.	Goldie King (T.W. Murphy)	2.10¾
20	2,362.	Tramp Safe (Harry Stokes)	2.04½
21	2,000.	Peter Henley (T.W. Murphy)	2.08¼
22	2,056.	Peter Etawah (T.W. Murphy)	2.06¾
23	1,859.	Anna Bradford's Girl (Ben White)	2.05¾
24	1,791.	Marion C. (W.T. Candler)	2.11½
25	1,876.	Hollywood Abigail (J.L. Dodge)	2.12½
26	2,358.	Highland Scott (T.W. Murphy)	2.06½
27	4,127.	Hollyrood Jacquelyne (Harry Stokes)	2.03¾
28	3,448.	Trampunion (Marvin Childs)	2.07¼
29	3,719.	Petroguy (S.F. Palin)	2.06¾
30	3,606.	Calumet Adam (R.D. McMahon)	2.07½
31	3,134.	Calumet Brownie (Fred Egan)	2.02
32	3,338.	Raider (Fred Egan)	2.03
33	2,449.	Daniel Hanover (Thomas Berry)	2.03
34	1,875.	Calumet Evelyn (Victor Fleming)	2.07¾
35	1,749.	Calumet Fingo (Ray Nohlechek)	a2.09½
36	1,469.	Jack Orr (W.K. Dickerson)	2.02
37	1,689.	Frisco Dale (Homer Walton)	2.04¾
38	1,839.	Chief Counsel (H.M. Parshall)	2.01¾
39	1,327.	Alban (Harry Whitney)	2.07¼
40	2,385.	William Cash (W.T. Britenfield)	2.01¼
41	2,151.	Wilmington (H.C. Fitzpatrick)	2.04¼
42	2,591.	Margamite (John Simpson, Sr.)	2.08 h
43	3,043.	King's Counsel (H.M. Parshall)	2.09½ h
44	2,350.	Filly Direct (Wayne Smart)	2.08¾ h
45	1,829.	Jimmy Creed (Claude Wright)	2.09½ h
46	4,025.	Honest Truth (McKinley Kirk)	2.05¾
47	5,265.	Norris Hanover (Henry Myott)	2.02.4
48	9,730.	Knight Dream (Franklin Safford)	2.01.3
49	11,593.	Stormyway (Ralph Baldwin)	2.02.4
50	14,604.	Quilla Hanover (John Simpson, Sr.)	2.00.4
51	15,385.	Floating Dream (McKinley Kirk)	2.01
52	17,103.	Thunderclap (Hugh Bell)	2.01.3
53	19,356.	Keystoner (Frank Ervin)	2.00
54	19,922.	Diamond Hal (Joe O'Brien)	b2.00.3
55	19,741.	Meadow Ace (Adelbert Cameron)	1.59
56	14,898.	Adioscot (James Arthur)	c2.00.3
57	21,187.	Torpid (John Simpson, Sr.)	1.59.3
58	18,332.	Bye Bye Byrd (Donald Taylor)	1.59.3
59	26,558.	Newport Admiral (Adelbert Cameron)	1.59.1
60	24,394.	Bullet Hanover (John Simpson, Sr.)	1.59.2
61	32,402.	Tarport Jimmy (James Arthur)	d2.00.3
62		--Rain--	
63	28,991.	Sly Yankee (Stanley Dancer)	e1.58.3
64	29,869.	McMoe (James Hackett)	f2.00.3
65	34,838.	Adios Vic (James Dennis)	Rg1.55
66	30,329.	Romeo Hanover (George Sholty)	1.58.4
67	32,053.	Best of All (James Hackett)	1.57.2

68	40,437.	Rum Customer (Wm. Haughton)	1.56.3
69	37,913.	Laverne Hanover (Wm. Haughton)	1.59
70	38,515.	Columbia George (Roland Beaulieu)	1.56.4
71	40,507.	Gamely (George Sholty)	1.56.4
72	37,030.	Hilarious Way (John Simpson, Jr.)	1.56.4

a By Kent Bumpas.   e By Meadow Russ.
b By Queen's Adios.   f By Torpedo.
c By Noble Adios.   g By Bret Hanover.
d By Adios Cleo.

The Hudson
*Three-Year-Old Filly Trot
Yonkers, N.Y.

Yr	Purse	Winning Horse & Driver	Fastest Heat
57	$21,117.	Taffy Hanover (S.L. Caton)	2.16.4h
58	24,762.	Lumber Along (Philip Corley)	2.17.2h
59	23,122.	Thalia Hanover (John Simpson, Sr.)	2.15.3h
60	26,405.	Darcie Hanover (Levi Harner)	2.15.2h
61	44,780.	Speedy Princess (Earle Avery)	2.13 h
62	45,882.	Worth Seein (Stanley Dancer)	2.19 h
63	47,372.	Cheer Honey (Don C. Miller)	2.04.2h
64	35,131.	Golden Make It (George Sholty)	R2.04.1h
65	35,783.	Armbro Flight (Joe O'Brien)	2.06.4h
66	32,947.	Coalition (Olof Widell)	2.06.4h
67	25,000.	Flamboyant (Wm. Haughton)	2.08.1h
68†	17,500.	Partys Over (Richard Thomas)	2.05.2h
	17,500.	Daring Speed (Clint Hodgins)	2.04.2h
69	35,000.	Charmette Hanover (John Patterson,Sr.)	2.04.3h
70	25,160.	Sweet Freight (George Sholty)	2.05.4h
71	25,747.	Waverly Hostess (Herve Filion)	2.06.3h
72	24,200.	Speedy Carlene (Stanley Dancer)	2.05 h

† Raced in two divisions.
* 1 1/16-miles dash before 1963.

Illinois State Fair Colt Stake
Two-Year-Old Trot
Illinois State Fair, Springfield, Ill.

Yr	Purse	Winning Horse & Driver	Fastest Heat
52	$40,537.	Steve Tell (Dale Ainsworth)	2.14.1h
53	56,075.	Bagdad (Dale Ainsworth)	a2.11.2
54	58,025.	Gracie Colleen (Thomas Wilburn)	2.07.2
55	53,637.	Peggy Key (Olen Humphres)	2.08.2
56	57,787.	Su Mac Lad (John Peat)	2.09.2
57	44,450.	Miss Scotbed (Thomas Graham)	2.07.2
58	43,350.	Duchess Ronald (Thomas Graham)	2.09.1
59	44,725.	Prince Jamie (Fred Spencer)	2.07.4
60	45,300.	Volarie (Howard Camper)	2.07.3
61	43,975.	Paul's Best (B.J. Schue)	2.06
62	44,700.	Windy Skeeter (Roland Michaud)	2.07.4
63	43,400.	Private Bud (Donald Busse)	b2.08.4
64	43,050.	Joe Brooke (Leslie Redshaw)	R2.05.2
65	43,425.	Dangerous Storm (Joe O'Brien)	2.07.2
66	42,725.	Rock Springs Jane (Joe O'Brien)	2.08.3
67	49,600.	Moon Baby (Ralph Baldwin)	c2.07.4
68	49,775.	Frosty Rader (Ardie Speed)	d2.07.3
69	50,375.	Skippio (Bruce Nickells)	e2.05.2
70	49,600.	Col W. (*Thomas Graham)	2.03.3
71†	24,812.	Lincoln's Apache (Jack Leonard)	2.09.1
	24,812.	Charm Date (Harry Burright)	2.08
72	48,650.	Soxy Byrd (K.M. Rutherford)	2.06

* Joe O'Brien drove 3rd and 4th elimination heats.
a By Aggie O.   † Raced in two divisions.
b By Lucinda's Key. d By Gallant Trip.
c By Lead Off Man.   e By Rader Guy.

Illinois State Fair Colt Stake
Two-Year-Old Pace
Illinois State Fair, Springfield, Ill.

Yr	Purse	Winning Horse & Driver	Fastest Heat
52	$40,537.	Gene Jester (Jack Williams)	2.07.4
53	56,075.	John Sitzmann (Russell Britenfield)	a2.07.1
54	58,225.	Eclipse Queen (Barney Thomason)	2.07.3
55	55,437.	Double Mc (John Ackerman)	2.05.2
56	60,387.	Sunny Byrd (J. Edgar Leonard)	2.04.2
57	48,000.	Bye Bye Byrd (Donald Taylor)	b2.04
58	52,950.	Roxburgh Leonard (Glen Kidwell)	c2.04
59	52,050.	Hark Win (John Cisna)	2.04
60	50,775.	Nibble Byrd (Gene Riegle)	2.03.3
61	46,600.	Crystal Byrd (Glen Kidwell)	2.01.4
62	48,675.	Fly Fly Byrd (Joe O'Brien)	2.03.3

63	47,775.	Don Parker (Gene Riegle)	2.06.2
64	47,950.	Lan Dow (Joe O'Brien)	d2.03.2
65	49,725.	Jimmy's Pilot (Delbert Insko)	2.01.4
66	47,600.	King Noble (Joe O'Brien)	2.02
67	55,275.	John L. Purdue (Howard Beissinger)	2.03.1
68	58,800.	Active Don (Glen Kidwell)	R2.00
69	59,375.	Monas Byrd (Delmer Insko)	e2.01.3
70	57,900.	Arcadia Jake (Norman Thompson)	f2.01.3
71†	20,233.	Cash Top (Daryl Busse)	2.04.3
	20,233.	*	g2.03.4
	20,233.	Perfect Weapon (Ray Gillilan)	2.03.1
72	62,300.	Stormy Filter (Jerry Graham)	h2.04

* Hardy Vonian (Gene Riegle) finished 1-2; Go Brave (Joe O'Brien) finished 2-1.

a By Atomic Rocket. f By Nite Brook.
b By Fleet Bird. g By Hardy Vonian.
c By Billy. h By Stormy Filter and
d By Rail Chief. Slippin By.
e By Janitor Jim.
† Raced in three divisions.

Illinois State Fair Colt Stake
Three-Year-Old Trot
Illinois State Fair, Springfield, Ill.

Yr	Purse	Winning Horse & Driver	Fastest Heat
53	$56,075.	Still Better (Glenn Hawkins)	2.08
54	55,500.	Bishop's First (Russell Rose)	2.09.4
55	52,912.	Marathon Hanover (Houston Stone)	2.03.2
56	52,862.	An Ka Da (J. Edgar Leonard)	a2.05.3
57	42,224.	Cindy Gal (Wm. Carney)	b2.04.3
58	44,325.	Lady Ann Reed (Stanley Dancer)	c2.02.4
59	42,650.	Greve (J. Edgar Leonard)	2.04.4
60	43,550.	*	d2.02.3
61	42,900.	Volarie (Howard Camper)	2.04.1
62	43,625.	Rona Farcry (J.W. Smith)	2.04.3
63	43,175.	Windy Skeeter (Roland Michaud)	e2.05.3
64	41,400.	Eyre Royal (Thomas Graham)	2.04
65	42,600.	Royal Escort (Jack Hankins)	2.06.3
66	41,925.	Princess Randolph (Donald Busse)	f2.05.2
67	48,825.	Dandy Date (Harry Braden)	g2.03.4
68	48,125.	Empire Squire (Forest Price)	2.03.4
69	49,400.	Nancys Darnley (Stanley Dancer)	h2.04.4
70	49,250.	Ballards Red Coat (Homer Ballard)	2.04
71†	24,237.	Clyde Oaks (Wm. Shuter)	2.03.4
	24,237.	**	Ri2.02.1
72	49,100.	Dangerous Russ (Wm. Carney)	2.04.2

* Petunia's Filly (Del Cronk) finished 2-1-dh1; Volation's Key (Herman Graham, Jr.) finished 2-1-dh1.
** Eddy Oakley (Daryl Busse) finished 1-2; Jays Gal (Clayton Mangus) finished 2-1.

a By Scotch Treat. g By Dangerous Luck.
b By Ronald's Carol. h By Breezy Hill.
c By Hardy Junior and i By Eddy Oakley.
Louie Yates. † Raced in two divisions.
d By Petunia's Filly.
e By Windy Skeeter and Royal Que.
f By Melody Dynamite.

Illinois State Fair Colt Stake
Three-Year-Old Pace
Illinois State Fair, Springfield, Ill.

Yr	Purse	Winning Horse & Driver	Fastest Heat
53	$56,075.	B'Haven (Emanuel Worsham)	2.03.3
54	57,500.	Peter Van Gundy (Mel Harmening)	2.06.4
55	53,712.	Frisco Flyer (John Simpson, Sr.)	2.02.3
56	55,462.	Coburn Frost (Wayne Smart)	2.04
57	43,600.	Sunny Byrd (Wm. Rouse)	2.01
58	44,750.	Bye Bye Byrd (Donald Taylor)	1.59.4
59	48,575.	Royal Ronald (Thomas Graham)	a2.02.4
60	46,600.	Fiddler's Green (Thomas Graham)	b2.00.3
61	47,000.	H.D. Counsel (Dwayne Pletcher)	c2.00.4
62	42,725.	Thomas Purdue (Joe O'Brien)	2.00.2
63	44,100.	Fly Fly Byrd (Joe O'Brien)	d2.03.3
64	43,900.	Bob Yates (A. George Shaw)	e1.59.4
65	45,100.	Chicago King (Lucien Fontaine)	2.05.3
66	45,575.	Jimmys Pilot (Delbert Insko)	f2.00
67	51,700.	Shore Will (George Sholty)	g2.00.1
68	53,350.	Shoestring (Marshall Schue)	1.59.3
69	54,200.	Active Don (Glen Kidwell)	R1.58.4
70	66,625.	Janitor Jim (Ray Wagner)	h1.59.2
71†	19,066.	*	i2.01.2
	19,066.	**	j2.01

	19,066.	Arcadia Jake (John Ackerman)	1.59.1
72	60,674.	Chaw (Dwayne Pletcher)	1.59.4

* Guy Daniel (Harry Burright) finished 1-2; Parker Royal (Glen Kidwell) finished 2-1.
** Poco Pilot (Jack Hankins) finished 1-2; Skipper Time (John Ackerman) finished 2-1.

a By Bert Yates. f By Blaze Byrd.
b By Gunmor. g By Shore Will and
c By Daddio. King Noble.
d By Fly Fly Byrd and h By Poplar Mark.
Byrd Yates. i By Guy Daniel.
e By Bosco Rosco. j By Poco Pilot.
†Raced in three divisions.

International Stallion Stake
Two-Year-Old Trot
Lexington, Ky.

Yr	Purse	Winning Horse & Driver	Fastest Heat
71	$33,403.	*	Ra1.59.4
72	36,190.	**	b2.01.2

* Super Bowl (Vernon Dancer) finished 2-1; Flush (George Sholty) finished 1-2.
** Arnie Almahurst (Gene Riegle) finished 2-1; South Bend (Michael Zeller) finished 1-2.
a By Super Bowl. b By Arnie Almahurst.

International Stallion Stake
Two-Year-Old Pace
Lexington, Ky.

Yr	Purse	Winning Horse & Driver	Fastest Heat
71	$43,963.	Kit Hanover (Joe O'Brien)	Ra1.57.2
72	52,470.	Ricci Reenie Time (Harold Dancer, Jr.)	b2.01.1

a By Entrepreneur. b By Valiant Bret.

International Stallion Stake
Two-Year-Old Filly Trot
Lexington, Ky.

Yr	Purse	Winning Horse & Driver	Fastest Heat
71	$16,481.	Delmonica Hanover (John Simpson, Sr.)	R2.00.3
72	18,810.	Amalulu (Herman Graham, Jr.)	a2.01.4

a By Ah So.

International Stallion Stake
Two-Year-Old Filly Pace
Lexington, Ky.

Yr	Purse	Winning Horse & Driver	Fastest Heat
71	$19,341.	Romalie Hanover (Arthur Hult)	2.06.4
72	26,180.	Skippers Dream (Gene Riegle)	R1.59.2

The Jugette
Three-Year-Old Filly Pace
Delaware, Ohio

Yr	Purse	Winning Horse & Driver	Fastest Heat
71	$30,414.	Jefferson Time (Bernard Webster)	2.00.1h
72	35,460.	Romalie Hanover (Roland Beaulieu)	Ra1.57.4h

a By Brets Pet.

Kentucky Futurity
Three-Year-Old Trot
Lexington, Ky.

Yr	Purse	Winning Horse & Driver	Fastest Heat
93	$11,850.	Oro Wilkes (J.A. Goldsmith)	2.14½
94	26,430.	Beuzetta (Guss Macey)	2.14½
95	20,000.	Oakland Baron (W.W. Milam)	2.16¼
96	16,250.	Rose Croix (M.E. McHenry)	2.14
97	10,000.	Thorn (O.A. Hickok)	2.13¼
98	10,000.	Peter the Great (P.V. Johnson)	2.12½
99	10,000.	Boralma (Guss Macey)	2.11½
00	10,000.	Fereno (Ed Benyon)	2.10¾
01	10,000.	Peter Sterling (J.B. Chandler)	2.11½
02	14,000.	Nella Jay (F.D. McKey)	2.14¼
03	14,000.	Sadie Mac (A.McDonald)	2.12¾
04	16,000.	Grace Bond (W.J. Andrews)	2.09¼
05	16,000.	Miss Adbell (A. McDonald)	2.09¾
06	17,000.	Siliko (M. McHenry & W. McCarthy)	2.11¼

Yr	Purse	Winning Horse & Driver	Fastest Heat
07	17,000.	General Watts (M. Bowerman)	2.11
08	16,000.	The Harvester (E.F. Geers)	2.08¾
09	16,000.	Baroness Virginia (T.W. Murphy)	2.07¼
10	16,000.	Grace (Mc McDevitt)	2.08
11	16,000.	Peter Thompson (J.L. Serrill)	2.07½
12	16,000.	Manrico B. (W.G. Durfee)	2.07¼
13	16,000.	Etawah (E.F. Geers)	2.05¾
14	16,000.	Peter Volo (T.W. Murphy)	2.03½
15	16,000.	Mary Putney (R.D. McMahon)	2.05½
16	16,000.	Volga (Ben White)	2.04½
17	16,000.	The Real Lady (T.W. Murphy)	2.03¾
18	16,000.	Nella Dillon (J.L. Serrill)	2.05¼
19	14,000.	Periscope (J.L. Dodge)	2.04½
20	14,000.	Arion Guy (Harry Stokes)	2.04¾
21	14,000.	Rose Scott (T.W. Murphy)	2.03½
22	14,000.	Lee Worthy (Ben White)	2.03¾
23	14,000.	Ethelinda (Walter Cox)	2.03½
24	14,000.	Mr. McElwyn (Ben White)	2.02
25	14,000.	Aileen Guy (Ben White)	2.03¾
26	14,000.	Guy McKinney (Nat Ray)	2.06¾
27	14,000.	Iosola's Worthy (Marvin Childs)	2.05¼
28	14,000.	Spencer (W.H. Leese)	2.05
29	14,000.	Walter Dear (Walter Cox)	2.02¾
30	14,000.	Hanover's Bertha (Thomas Berry)	2.00
31	14,000.	Protector (Wm. Caton)	1.59¼
32	14,000.	The Marchioness (Wm. Caton)	2.02
33	14,000.	Meda (Ben White)	2.03¼
34	14,000.	Princess Peg (S.F. Palin)	2.00¾
35	12,000.	Lawrence Hanover (Henry Thomas)	2.00¾
36	10,000.	Rosalind (Ben White)	2.03
37	9,295.	Twilight Song (Ben White)	2.01¼
38	9,570.	McLin Hanover (Henry Thomas)	2.00¾
39	9,000.	Peter Astra (H.M. Parshall)	2.02½
40	9,075.	Spencer Scott (Fred Egan)	2.02
41	8,330.	Bill Gallon (Lee Smith)	2.02¼
42 to 45 inclusive -- Not Raced --			
46	25,781.	Victory Song (S.F. Palin)	2.00½
47	36,905.	Hoot Mon (S.F. Palin)	2.04 1/5
48	50,071.	Egan Hanover (Ralph Baldwin)	2.03.2
49	57,154.	Bangaway (Ralph Baldwin)	2.05.2
50	54,665.	Star's Pride (Harry Pownall, Sr.)	2.02
51	66,659.	Ford Hanover (John Simpson, Sr.)	2.01.2
52	66,231.	Sharp Note (Bion Shively)	2.00
53	67,485.	Kimberly Kid (Thomas Berry)	2.00.3
54	63,121.	Harlan (Delvin Miller)	2.01
55	62,702.	Scott Frost (Joe O'Brien)	2.00.3
56	53,731.	Nimble Colby (Ralph Baldwin)	2.02
57	50,460.	Cassin Hanover (Fred Egan)	2.02.1
58	53,330.	Emily's Pride (Flave Nipe)	a1.59.1
59	53,810.	Diller Hanover (Ralph Baldwin)	2.01.1
60	64,040.	Elaine Rodney (Clint Hodgins)	1.58.3
61	59,330.	Duke Rodney (Eddie Wheeler)	b1.58.1
62	55,230.	Safe Mission (Joe O'Brien)	1.59.1
63	61,128.	Speedy Scot (Ralph Baldwin)	1.57.1
64	57,096.	Ayres (John Simpson, Sr.)	1.58.1
65	65,133.	Armbro Flight (Joe O'Brien)	1.59.3
66	61,602.	Governor Armbro (Joe O'Brien)	2.00.2
67	58,642.	Speed Model (Arthur Hult)	c1.59.3
68	57,398.	Nevele Pride (Stanley Dancer)	R1.57
69	64,757.	Lindys Pride (Howard Beissinger)	1.59
70	76,351.	Timothy T. (John Simpson, Jr.)	1.59.4
71	63,415.	Savoir (James Arthur)	1.58.1
72	56,210.	Super Bowl (Stanley Dancer)	1.59

a By Senator Frost.   c By Rocket Speed.
b By Caleb.

The Lady Maud
Three-Year-Old Filly Pace
Roosevelt Raceway, Westbury, N.Y.

Yr	Purse	Winning Horse & Driver	Fastest Heat
60	$26,972.	Hodge Podge (Alfred Thomas)	2.03.1h
61	28,776.	Truly Rainbow (Walter Welch)	2.07.1h
62	38,810.	Cathy J. Hanover (Stanley Dancer)	2.02.2h
63	33,831.	Harry's Laura (Clint Hodgins)	2.05.3h
64	39,315.	Bit O'Sugar (Wm. Haughton)	2.03.4h
65	50,639.	Woodlawn Drummond (Keith Waples)	2.04.2h
66	37,321.	Bonjour Hanover (Stanley Dancer)	2.01.3h
67	38,716.	Poplar Evalynda (George Sholty)	2.03.2h
68	40,254.	Thorpe Marge (Wm. Haughton)	2.03.3h
69	44,344.	Supple Yankee (Stanley Dancer)	2.03.3h
70	44,083.	Betty Hanover (Harold J. Dancer)	R2.01.2h
71	44,992.	Jefferson Time (Bernard Webster)	2.05 h
72	46,177.	Romalie Hanover (Roland Beaulieu)	2.01.4h

The Lady Suffolk
*Three-Year-Old Filly Trot
Roosevelt Raceway, Westbury, N.Y.

Yr	Purse	Winning Horse & Driver	Fastest Heat
60	$20,176.	Elaine Rodney (Clint Hodgins)	2.13.2
61	26,325.	Speedy Princess (Earle Avery)	2.12.2h
62	27,723.	Impish (Frank Ervin)	2.12.1h
63	25,461.	Campus Queen (Ralph Baldwin)	2.14.1h
64	28,574.	Speedy Victory (W.R. Walker)	2.12.4h
65	27,062.	Arabesque (Delmer Insko)	2.07 h
66	30,060.	Starlight Way (George Sholty)	2.05.1h
67	36,053.	Lana Hanover (Vernon Dancer)	2.07.3h
68	33,890.	Jostle (John Simpson, Sr.)	2.06.2h
69	44,988.	Flowing Speed (John Chapman)	2.04.2h
70	38,571.	Tammie Hill (George Sholty)	2.03.3h
71	39,962.	Egyptian Jody (Stanley Dancer)	2.04.4h
72	35,000.	Delmonica Hanover (John Chapman)	R2.02.4h

*1 1/16-miles dash before 1965.

La Paloma Pace
Two-Year-Old Fillies
Yonkers, N.Y.

Yr	Purse	Winning Horse & Driver	Fastest Heat
64	$21,207.	Balenzano (Delmer Insko)	2.05.3h
65	25,000.	Bonjour Hanover (Stanley Dancer)	2.11.2h
66	25,000.	Meadow Elva (Stanley Dancer)	2.03.3h
67	25,000.	Berinda Hanover (John Simpson, Jr.)	2.07 h
68*	12,500.	Evalina Lobell (Wm. Myer)	2.07.2h
	12,500.	Fiesta Lobell (Stanley Dancer)	2.06.2h
69	25,660.	Revolve (Delmer Insko)	2.05.3h
70	25,247.	Evelyn Hanover (Delmer Insko)	2.04.3h
71	28,448.	Romalie Hanover (Arthur Hult)	R2.02.3h
72	29,971.	Jambo Belle (Merritt Dokey)	2.03.2h

* Raced in two divisions.

The Little Brown Jug
Three-Year-Old Pace
Delaware, Ohio

Yr	Purse	Winning Horse & Driver	Fastest Heat
46	$35,358.	Ensign Hanover (Wayne Smart)	a2.02¾h
47	38,200.	Forbes Chief (Adelbert Cameron)	2.05 h
48	47,528.	Knight Dream (Franklin Safford)	2.07.1h
49	58,281.	Good Time (Frank Ervin)	2.03.2h
50	56,525.	Dudley Hanover (Delvin Miller)	2.02.3h
51	66,280.	Tar Heel (Adelbert Cameron)	2.00 h
52	60,463.	Meadow Rice (Wayne Smart)	2.01.3h
53	54,972.	Keystoner (Frank Ervin)	b2.02.3h
54	69,332.	Adios Harry (Morris MacDonald)	c2.02.2h
55	66,608.	Quick Chief (Wm. Haughton)	d2.00 h
56	52,666.	Noble Adios (John Simpson, Sr.)	2.00.4h
57	73,528.	Torpid (John Simpson, Sr.)	2.00.4h
58	65,252.	Shadow Wave (Joe O'Brien)	2.01 h
59	76,582.	Adios Butler (Clint Hodgins)	1.59.2h
60	66,510.	Bullet Hanover (John Simpson, Sr.)	e1.58.3h
61	70,069.	Henry T. Adios (Stanley Dancer)	1.58.4h
62	75,038.	Lehigh Hanover (Stanley Dancer)	1.58.4h
63	68,294.	Overtrick (John Patterson, Sr.)	1.57.1h
64	66,590.	Vicar Hanover (Wm. Haughton)	f2.00.4h
65	71,447.	Bret Hanover (Frank Ervin)	1.57 h
66	74,616.	Romeo Hanover (George Sholty)	1.59.3h
67	84,778.	Best of All (James Hackett)	g1.59 h
68	104,226.	Rum Customer (Wm. Haughton)	1.59.3
69	109,731.	Laverne Hanover (Wm. Haughton)	2.00.2h
70	100,110.	Most Happy Fella (Stanley Dancer)	1.57.1h
71	102,994.	Nansemond (Herve Filion)	1.57.2
72	104,916.	Strike Out (Keith Waples)	R1.56.3h

a By Royal Chief.   e By Bullet Hanover and
b By Newport Chief.   Muncy Hanover.
c By Phantom Lady.   f By Combat Time.
d By Dottie's Pick.   g By Nardins Byrd.

The Little Brown Jug Trial
Three-Year-Old Pace
Hazel Park, Mich.

Yr	Purse	Winning Horse & Driver	Fastest Heat
56	$20,100.	Bachelor Hanover (Wm. Haughton)	2.02
57	18,400.	Adios Express (Joe O'Brien)	2.14.2
58	20,650.	O.F. Brady (Wayne Smart)	2.02.4h
59	22,050.	Vicki's Jet (Wm. Rouse)	a2.03.3h
60	21,850.	Dancer Hanover (Delvin Miller)	b2.01 h

61	21,150.	Henry T. Adios (Stanley Dancer)	2.03.3h
62	19,400.	Adora's Dream (Jack Williams, Jr.)	2.04.1h
63	19,500.	Country Don (Marcel Dostie)	2.03.1h
64	21,000.	Bengazi Hanover (George Sholty)	R1.57.3f
65	19,500.	Bret Hanover (Frank Ervin)	R1.57.3f
66	21,050.	True Duane (Chris Boring)	1.58.3f
67	25,350.	Romulus Hanover (Wm. Haughton)	1.58.2f
68	27,000.	Bye and Large (George Sholty)	2.00 f
69	30,000.	Laverne Hanover (Wm. Haughton)	1.59.2f
70	17,000.	Columbia George (Roland Beaulieu)	1.58 f
71	23,000.	Albatross (Stanley Dancer)	2.03.3f
72	29,700.	Silent Majority (Wm. Haughton)	2.02 f

a By Meadow Al. b By Muncy Hanover.

The Little Pat
†Two-Year-Old Pace--Review Futurity
Illinois State Fair, Springfield, Ill.

Yr	Purse	Winning Horse & Driver	Fastest Heat
42	$ 5,378.	King's Counsel (H.M. Parshall)	2.07 h
43	3,389.	Attorney (Art Blackwell)	2.10 h
44	7,973.	True Chief (Thomas S. Berry)	2.05
45	8,936.	Ensign Hanover (S.F. Palin)	2.04¼
46	12,851.	Poplar Byrd (Thomas Berry)	2.04¾
47	14,374.	Friscoway (H.C. Fitzpatrick)	2.02.4
48	15,727.	Good Time (K.R. Cartnal)	2.04
49	16,923.	Our Time (Frank Ervin)	2.06.4
50	18,737.	Tar Heel (Adelbert Cameron)	2.03.2
51	19,515.	Thunderclap (Hugh Bell)	a2.02.1
52	17,402.	Iosola's Ensign (Wayne Smart)	2.03.4
53	21,883.	Queen's Adios (Wayne Smart)	b2.01
54	17,022.	Captain Adios (Delvin Miller)	c2.04.1
55	15,301.	Buckeye (James Fitzpatrick)	d2.01.1
56	20,020.	Adios Express (Joe O'Brien)	e2.02.1
57	16,130.	Thorpe Hanover (Delvin Miller)	2.00.3
58	21,213.	Adios Day (Delvin Miller)	f2.01.2
59	17,473.	Bullet Hanover (John Simpson, Sr.)	1.59.1
60	16,264.	Lang Hanover (James Hackett)	g2.01.4
61	15,171.	Coffee Break (George Sholty)	2.00.2
62	15,505.	Overtrick (John Patterson, Sr.)	2.01.1
63	16,362.	Ripping Good (Frank Ervin)	h2.02.1
64	19,570.	Bret Hanover (Frank Ervin)	R1.58.2
65	20,388.	Overcall (John Patterson, Sr.)	2.01.4
66	21,822.	Armbro Hurricane (James Dennis)	2.00
67	28,869.	Rum Customer (Wm. Haughton)	i1.58.4
68	30,880.	Laverne Hanover (Wm. Haughton)	1.59.2
69	42,350.	Ideal Donut (Joe O'Brien)	j1.58.4
70	33,650.	*	k1.59.1
71	34,670.	Hilarious Way (John Simpson, Jr.)	1.59.1
72	37,040.	Ricci Reenie Time (Harold J. Dancer)	R1.58.2

* Winning Worthy (Herman Graham, Jr.) finished 5-1; Race Byrd (Glen Garnsey) finished 1-5.

a By Meadow Rice. g By High Test.
b By Parker Byrd. h By Lancelot Hanover.
c By Libby's Boy. i By Meadow Brick.
d By Adioscot. j By Race Time Boy.
e By Devastator. k By Winning Worthy.
f By Adios Chief.
† Stake prior to 1967.

Lou Dillon Trot
Two-Year-Old Fillies
Yonkers, N.Y.

Yr	Purse	Winning Horse & Driver	Fastest Heat
64	$19,707.	Armbro Flight (Joe O'Brien)	2.07.3h
65*	18,750.	Justly Scottish (Donald Niccum)	2.07.3h
	18,750.	Little Miss Mitzie (Wm. Haughton)	2.08.2h
66	25,000.	Flamboyant (John Chapman)	2.07.1h
67	25,000.	Ole Hanover (James Hackett)	2.09.4h
68	25,000.	Jounce (John Chapman)	2.08.4h
69	25,660.	Little Victory (Ted Dennis)	2.09.1h
70	26,747.	Sonata Hill (Edward Dunnigan)	2.05.3h
71	27,448.	Delmonica Hanover (John Chapman)	R2.04.2h
72	26,971.	Honeysuckle Rose (Harold McKinley)	2.12 h

* Raced in two divisions.

Matron Stake
Three-Year-Old Trot
Wolverine Raceway, Livonia, Mich.

Yr	Purse	Winning Horse & Driver	Fastest Heat
10	$ 6,274.	Colorado E. (Guss Macey)	2.07¼
11	6,166.	Peter Thompson (Joseph Serrill)	2.08¼
12	5,491.	Baldy McGregor (W.J. Andrews)	2.08
13	6,835.	Dillon Axworthy (Joseph Serrill)	2.10¼
14	5,252.	Peter Volo (T.W. Murphy)	2.13¾
15	7,443.	Rusticoat (W.J. Andrews)	2.08¼
16	5,888.	Expressive Lou (T.W. Murphy)	2.11
17	5,851.	Miss Bertha Dillon (Joseph Serrill)	2.03¼
18	5,977.	David Guy (T.W. Murphy)	2.05¼
19	6,925.	Periscope (John Dodge)	2.04½
20	6,700.	Sister Bertha (Joseph Serrill)	2.06¾
21	9,000.	Guardian Trust (R.D. McMahon)	2.06¼
22	7,350.	Lee Worthy (Ben White)	2.05½
23	7,380.	Hollyrood Leonard (Norman Tallman)	2.05¼
24	6,080.	Mr. McElwyn (Ben White)	2.03½
25	7,265.	Sam Williams (Walter Cox)	2.05¾
26	8,505.	Guy McKinney (Nat Ray)	2.04½
27	8,700.	Kashmir (Ben White)	2.05¼
28	8,230.	Nelly Signal (Nat Ray)	2.04½
29	7,970.	Volomite (Walter Cox)	2.05
30	6,720.	Hanover's Bertha (Thomas Berry)	2.05½
31	6,165.	Protector (Will Caton)	2.03¾
32	6,370.	Brevere (Ben White)	2.04¼
33	5,300.	Spencer McElwyn (Marvin Childs)	a2.04¼
34	2,880.	Emily Stokes (Fred Egan)	b2.03¼
35	4,105.	Greyhound (S.F. Palin)	2.03¼
36	4,060.	Rosalind (Ben White)	2.04¼
37	3,300.	Schnapps (Will Caton)	2.04½
38	4,085.	Professor (George Bennett)	2.02¾
39	5,150.	Peter Astra (H.M. Parshall)	2.05
40	4,427.	Spencer Scott (Fred Egan)	2.03
41	5,638.	Perpetual (H.M. Parshall)	2.04¼
42	6,506.	Pay Up (Lee Smith)	2.08½
43	5,430.	Volo Song (Ben White)	2.05½
44	3,856.	Yankee Maid (Henry Thomas)	2.05
45	3,376.	Tompkins Hanover (A.S. Rodney)	2.08¾
46	4,349.	Chestertown (Thomas Berry)	2.04½
47	7,771.	Nymph Hanover (Thomas Berry)	2.09 h
48	9,749.	Demon Hanover (Harrison Hoyt)	2.10.4h
49	8,229.	Guy Ambassador (H.C. Fitzpatrick)	c2.04.3
50	6,629.	Star's Pride (Harry Pownall, Sr.)	2.11.4
51	10,777.	Scotch Rhythm (Ralph Baldwin)	2.04.4
52	12,248.	Scotch Victor (Joe O'Brien)	2.06.3
53	17,856.	Kimberly Kid (Thomas Berry)	2.01.3
54	19,542.	Prince Victor (Harry Pownall, Sr.)	d2.00.3
55	18,079.	Childs Hanover (Frank Ervin)	2.03.2
56	19,049.	Nimble Colby (Ralph Baldwin)	2.03.1
57	20,523.	Hoot Song (Ralph Baldwin)	2.01.3
58	20,477.	Sandalwood (Ralph Baldwin)	2.02
59	19,344.	Diller Hanover (Frank Ervin)	e2.00.2
60	21,441.	Uncle Sam (Lou Huber, Jr.)	R1.59.3
61	17,262.	Caleb (John Simpson, Sr.)	2.05 h
62	26,525.	Sprite Rodney (Frank Ervin)	2.07.3h
63	20,825.	Speedy Scot (Ralph Baldwin)	2.02.2h
64	20,829.	Dartmouth (Ralph Baldwin)	2.07 h
65	24,998.	Egyptian Candor (Stanley Dancer)	2.06.3h
66	24,680.	Bonus Boy (Adelbert Cameron)	2.07 h
67	22,137.	Halifax Hanover (Joe O'Brien)	2.09.3h
68	17,278.	Master Yankee (James Larente)	2.10.3h
69	25,000.	Wealthy (Stanley Dancer)	2.09.1h
70	25,000.	Gallant Prince (Stanley Dancer)	2.06.2
71	25,000.	Noble Gesture (Herman Graham, Jr.)	2.00.3
72	25,000.	Mr. Colwell (Chas. Norris, Jr.)	2.02.3

a By King Ben. d By Darn Safe.
b By Reynolda. e By Tie Silk.
c By Guy Ambassador and Atomic Maid.

Matron Stake
Three-Year-Old Pace
Wolverine Raceway, Livonia, Mich.

Yr	Purse	Winning Horse & Driver	Fastest Heat
10	$ 2,166.	Leftwich (James Healey)	2.12
11	2,043.	Miss DeForest (Alonzo McDonald)	2.10
12	1,938.	Herman Wenger (T.W. Murphy)	2.13¼
13	2,155.	Tillie Tipton (T.W. Murphy)	2.13½
14	1,050.	Anna Bradford (T.W. Murphy)	2.12
15	1,269.	General Todd (Guy Rea)	2.06
16	1,046.	Rose Magee (T.W. Murphy)	2.22
17	898.	Donna Lola (Robert Wright)	2.10¼
18	793.	Direct the Work (J.O. McAllister)	2.06½
19 to 30 inclusive – Not Raced –			
31	1,405.	Calumet Brownie	2.04
32	1,080.	Raider (Fred Egan)	2.04
33	925.	Calumet Dubuque (Harry Stokes)	2.03½
34	556.	Laurel Hanover	
35	870.	George Washington (Will Caton)	2.06

36	1,350.	Erla (Victor Fleming)	2.04
37	1,295.	Fred Hamer (Harry McKay)	2.05
38	1,460.	Chief Counsel (H.M. Parshall)	2.03½
39	1,760.	Blackstone (H.M. Parshall)	2.03¾
40	1,815.	Fearless Peter (H.M. Parshall)	2.04¼
41	1,406.	Bell Boy (Victor Fleming)	2.04
42	1,965.	Supreme Hal (Franklin Safford)	2.07 h
43	1,879.	Adios (Rupert Parker)	2.06¼
44	2,484.	Attorney (Art Blackwell)	2.04½
45	1,561.	True Chief (Thomas Berry)	2.03½
46	1,854.	Ensign Hanover (S.F. Palin)	2.03¼
47	5,179.	Goose Bay (J.D. Mahoney)	a2.04.3h
48	5,429.	E.J. Hal (Neal Houslet)	2.07.4
49	6,903.	Good Time (Frank Ervin)	2.01.3
50	6,870.	Dudley Hanover (Harry Pownall, Sr.)	2.09
51	6,920.	Tar Heel (Delvin Miller)	2.02.2h
52	7,875.	Meadow Rice (Delvin Miller)	2.03 h
53	16,731.	Keystoner (Frank Ervin)	2.00.3
54	14,248.	Meadow Pace (Joe O'Brien)	1.59.4
55	13,526.	Sea Eagle (H.C. Fitzpatrick)	2.01.2
56	14,534.	Adioway (Joe O'Brien)	b2.01
57	17,806.	Meadow Rhythm (B.J. Schue)	c2.03
58	10,379.	Bye Bye Byrd (Donald Taylor)	2.00
59	16,005.	Newport Admiral (Adelbert Cameron)	2.02.1
60	8,796.	Bullet Hanover (John Simpson, Sr.)	1.59
61	9,608.	High Test (Frank Ervin)	2.03 h
62	18,894.	Coffee Break (George Sholty)	2.01.4h
63	20,575.	*	2.02.2h
64	20,755.	Race Time (Ralph Baldwin)	2.04.4h
65	21,434.	Bret Hanover (Frank Ervin)	2.02.4h
66	23,211.	Carry Man (Philip Corley)	2.03.1h
67	29,302.	Nevele Dancer (Stanley Dancer)	2.04.1h
68	23,858.	Batman (Bruce Nickells)	2.04 h
69	25,000.	Laverne Hanover (Wm. Haughton)	2.02.1h
70	25,000.	Most Happy Fella (Stanley Dancer)	1.59
71	25,000.	Albatross (Stanley Dancer)	R1.58.2
72	25,000.	Breadwinner (Adelbert Cameron)	1.59.2

* Delightful Time (George Sholty) and James B. Hanover (Delbert Insko) finished in a dead heat for first.

a By Shamrock Joe.   c By Cheyenne Goose.
b By Steamin' Demon.

McMahon Memorial
Two-Year-Old Pace
Du Quoin, Ill.

Yr	Purse	Winning Horse & Driver	Fastest Heat
46	$11,825.	Poplar Byrd (Thomas Berry)	2.03¼
47	16,104.	Friscoway (H.C. Fitzpatrick)	2.04
48	19,871.	Good Time (Frank Ervin)	2.03.2
49	25,035.	Beryl Hanover (Gibson White)	2.04.4
50		--Rain--	
51	30,969.	Gander (Hugh Bell)	2.03
52	26,645.	Iosola's Ensign (Wayne Smart)	a2.02.2
53	28,831.	Meadow Pace (Joe O'Brien)	2.01
54	24,279.	Meadow Leo (B.J. Schue)	b2.01.4
55	21,206.	Buckeye (James Fitzpatrick)	2.01.2
56	26,843.	Adios Express (Joe O'Brien)	c2.04
57	25,976.	Painter (John Simpson, Sr.)	d2.00.3
58	28,720.	Adios Day (Delvin Miller)	2.00.3
59	24,638.	Bullet Hanover (John Simpson, Sr.)	2.01.4
60	23,945.	Adios Cleo (John Simpson, Sr.)	2.00.1
61	23,530.	Raceaway (Joe O'Brien)	2.00.2
62	22,279.	Overtrick (John Patterson, Sr.)	1.59.4
63	24,352.	Race Time (Ralph Baldwin)	2.03.2
64	24,944.	Bret Hanover (Frank Ervin)	2.00
65	26,631.	Overcall (John Patterson, Sr.)	e2.07.4
66	24,371.	Best of All (James Hackett)	1.58.1
67	26,704.	Rum Customer (Wm. Haughton)	2.00.2
68	28,248.	Laverne Hanover (Wm. Haughton)	1.59.4
69	32,176.	Truluck (George Sholty)	1.57.2
70	28,377.	High Ideal (George Sholty)	2.01.3
71		--Rain--	
72	34,880.	Ricci Reenie Time (Harold J. Dancer)	R1.57

a By Gosling.   d By Thorpe Hanover.
b By American Way.   e By Meadow Lenco.
c By Newport Duke.

The Messenger Stake
Three-Year-Old Pace
Roosevelt Raceway, Westbury, N.Y.

Yr	Purse	Winning Horse & Driver	Fastest Heat
56	$ 71,500.	Belle Acton (Wm. Haughton)	2.01.2h

57	100,084.	Meadow Lands (Delvin Miller)	a2.04.4
58	108,565.	O'Brien Hanover (James Jordan)	2.01.4h
59	110,994.	Adios Butler (Clint Hodgins)	2.00.1h
60	142,786.	Countess Adios (Delvin Miller)	2.02.1h
61	145,377.	Adios Don (Howard Camper)	2.02.4h
62	169,430.	Thor Hanover (John Simpson, Sr.)	2.01.1h
63	146,324.	Overtrick (John Patterson, Sr.)	2.00.4
64	150,960.	Race Time (Ralph Baldwin)	2.01.2h
65	151,252.	Bret Hanover (Frank Ervin)	2.02 h
66	169,885.	Romeo Hanover (George Sholty)	2.01 h
67	178,064.	Romulus Hanover (Wm. Haughton)	R1.59.1h
68	189,018.	Rum Customer (Wm. Haughton)	2.01.4h
69	182,976.	Bye Bye Sam (Stanley Dancer)	2.02.3h
70	123,450.	Most Happy Fella (Stanley Dancer)	2.02.3h
71	114,977.	Albatross (Stanley Dancer)	2.00.2h
72	154,733.	Silent Majority (Wm. Haughton)	2.01.4h

a By Adios Express.

The Midwest Derby
Three-, Four- and Five-Year-Old Pace
Sportsman's Park, Cicero, Ill.

Yr	Purse	Winning Horse & Driver	Fastest Heat
65	$50,000.	Adios Marches (Wm. Shuter)	1.59.3f
66	50,000.	Transient (Dwayne Pletcher)	2.00.3f
67	50,000.	Star Carrier (Richard Farrington)	2.00.4f
68	50,000.	Careless Time (Joe Marsh, Jr.)	2.02.1f
69	50,000.	Tanner (Alvin Stanke)	R1.59.2f
70	50,000.	Teffe (Dwayne Pletcher)	2.03.2f
71	50,000.	Michigan Mack (Ralph Mapes)	2.04.3f
72	50,000.	Game Guy (Daryl Busse)	2.02.4f

National Pacing Derby
*Invitational
Roosevelt Raceway, Westbury, N.Y.

Yr	Purse	Winning Horse & Driver	Fastest Heat
46	$25,000.	April Star (Wm. Fleming)	2.03¾h
47	25,000.	Direct Express (Paul Vineyard)	2.02.2h
48	25,000.	Goose Bay (Ralph Baldwin)	2.03 h
49	25,000.	Jimmy Creed (Jimmie Cruise)	2.02 h
50	25,000.	Good Time (Frank Ervin)	2.02.1h
51	25,000.	Prince Jay (Wilbur Beattie)	2.04.1h
52	25,000.	Good Time (Frank Ervin)	2.31.3h
53	25,000.	Direct Rhythm (Delvin Miller)	2.33.4h
54	25,000.	Prince Adios (Clint Hodgins)	2.31.4h
55	25,000.	Adios Boy (Howard Camden)	2.32.2h
56	25,000.	Diamond Hal (Joe O'Brien)	2.33.4h
57	25,000.	Diamond Hal (Joe O'Brien)	2.31.4h
58	25,000.	Duane Hanover (Wm. Haughton)	2.33.4h
59	50,000.	Bye Bye Byrd (Clint Hodgins)	**
60	50,000.	Bye Bye Byrd (Clint Hodgins)	2.31.3h
61	50,000.	Adios Butler (Edward Cobb)	2.31.3h
62	50,000.	Irvin Paul (Charles King)	R2.29.3h
63	50,000.	Irvin Paul (Charles King)	2.34.2h
64	50,000.	Tarquinius (George Sholty)	2.31 h
65	50,000.	Cardigan Bay (Stanley Dancer)	2.34.4h
66	50,000.	Cardigan Bay (Stanley Dancer)	2.34.2h
67	50,000.	True Duane (Chris Boring)	2.32.4h
68	50,000.	Best of All (Robert Williams)	2.32.2h
69	50,000.	Overcall (Delmer Insko)	2.33 h
70	50,000.	Horton Hanover (Joe O'Brien)	2.30.1h
71	50,000.	Super Wave (Jack Kopas)	2.32.3h
72	50,000.	Albatross (Stanley Dancer)	2.33.3h

*1¼-miles dash since 1952.
**Time disallowed due to disqualification of Speedy Pick.

The Ohio State
Two-Year-Old Trot
Ohio State Fair, Columbus, Ohio

Yr	Purse	Winning Horse & Driver	Fastest Heat
58	$20,750.	Royal Flash (Claude Wright)	2.11.4h
59	23,400.	Merrie Duke (John Patterson, Sr.)	2.05.3h
60	26,100.	Miss Demon Song (David McClain)	2.08.3h
61	26,500.	Lord Valentine (George Sholty)	2.09.3h
62	29,000.	Fred Walker (George Sholty)	R2.04.3h
63	22,800.	Speedy Count (Wm. Haughton)	2.05 h
64	25,600.	Spud Coaltown (Bruce Nickells)	2.09 h
65	25,800.	Frosty Tip (Bert Amos, Sr.)	2.09 h
66	25,400.	High N Away (Gene Riegle)	2.10.3h
67	27,500.	Fashion Hill (Adelbert Cameron)	2.05.2h
68	24,900.	Hiland Hill (Richard Hackett)	2.08.4h
69	26,400.	Art Hill (John Edmunds)	2.07.1h

70	27,200.	Sonata Hill (Wm. Haughton)	2.06 h
71	27,400.	Killbuck Mary (Richard Buxton)	2.05.2h
72	27,100.	Travelogue (Terry Holton)	2.05 h

The Proximity
Two-Year-Old Filly Trot
Roosevelt Raceway, Westbury, N.Y.

Yr	Purse	Winning Horse & Driver	Fastest Heat
60	$23,064.	Meadow Farr (James Jordan)	2.05.3h
61	25,745.	Worth Seein (Stanley Dancer)	R2.04.4h
62	23,083.	Cheer Honey (Frank Ervin)	2.06.4h
63	29,524.	Golden Make It (George Sholty)	2.06.4h
64	28,179.	Armbro Flight (Joe O'Brien)	2.06.2h
65	28,321.	Kerry Way (Stanley Dancer)	2.07.3h
66	27,074.	Flamboyant (Wm. Haughton)	2.09.1h
67	29,422.	Pompanette (Earle Avery)	2.11 h
68	29,288.	Sparkling Molly (John Chapman)	2.07 h
69	30,328.	Dancing Flower (Chris Boring)	2.09 h
70	31,122.	Keystone Selene (Delvin Miller)	2.07.3h
71	27,905.	Franella Hanover (George Sholty)	2.07.1h
72	30,627.	Colonial Charm (Glen Garnsey)	2.05.3h

The Realization
*Four-Year-Old Trot
Roosevelt Raceway, Westbury, N.Y.

Yr	Purse	Winning Horse & Driver	Fastest Heat
62	$67,105.	Duke Rodney (Wm. Haughton)	2.08.4h
63	85,663.	Sprite Rodney (Frank Ervin)	2.12.3h
64	91,381.	Speedy Scot (Ralph Baldwin)	2.09.3h
65	100,195.	Dartmouth (Ralph Baldwin)	2.09.1h
66	89,111.	Perfect Freight (Delmer Insko)	2.08.3h
67	88,664.	Carlisle (Wm. Haughton)	2.14 h
68	99,561.	Flamboyant (Wm. Haughton)	2.12 h
69	88,670.	Nevele Pride (Stanley Dancer)	R2.07.2h
70	94,335.	Pridewood (Wm. Haughton)	2.12.3h
71	101,469.	Timothy T. (John Simpson, Jr.)	2.11 h
72	92,505.	Speedy Crown (Howard Beissinger)	2.09.4h

* 1 1/16-miles dash.

The Realization
*Four-Year-Old Pace
Roosevelt Raceway, Westbury, N.Y.

Yr	Purse	Winning Horse & Driver	Fastest Heat
62	$74,805.	Henry T. Adios (Stanley Dancer)	2.08.1h
63	93,163.	Lehigh Hanover (Stanley Dancer)	2.09 h
64	104,381.	Overtrick (John Patterson, Sr.)	2.06.4h
65	87,695.	Race Time (Ralph Baldwin)	2.08.2h
66	86,111.	Bret Hanover (Frank Ervin)	2.12.2h
67	91,664.	Romeo Hanover (George Sholty)	2.08 h
68	98,132.	Best of All (Robert Williams)	2.08.2h
69	93,123.	Adios Waverly (Herve Filion)	2.07.3h
70	98,835.	Bye Bye Sam (Stanley Dancer)	2.07.4h
71	102,969.	Windy Way (Robert J. Williams)	2.08.2h
72	91,000.	Albatross (Stanley Dancer)	R2.06 h

* 1 1/16-miles dash.

Review Futurity
Three-Year-Old Trot
Illinois State Fair, Springfield, Ill.

Yr	Purse	Winning Horse & Driver	Fastest Heat
94	$21,575.	B.B.P. (Frank Loomis)	2.13¾
95 to 98 inclusive -- Not Raced --			
99	20,000.	Idolita (Thomas Marsh)	2.12½
00	5,000.	Mobel (Edward Benyon)	2.16¾
01	5,000.	The Rowellen (James Golden)	2.16¼
02	5,000.	The Rajah (Charles Lyons)	2.14¾
03	5,000.	Ethel's Pride (Scott Hudson)	2.15
04	7,000.	Alta Axworthy (A.L. Thomas)	2.10½
05	7,000.	Susie N. (T.W. Murphy)	2.11
06	7,000.	Governor Francis (W.O. Foote)	2.11½
07	7,000.	General Watts (M. Bowerman)	2.09½
08	7,000.	The Harvester (E.F. Geers)	2.10½
09	7,000.	Czarevna (Thomas Nolan)	2.09½
10	6,500.	Native Belle (T.W. Murphy)	2.07¾
11	6,500.	Atlantic Express (John Dickerson)	2.08¼
12	6,500.	Adlon (John Dickerson)	2.08¼
13	9,000.	Don Chenault (H.C. Stinson)	2.06¼
14	8,500.	Peter Volo (T.W. Murphy)	2.07¼
15	8,500.	Mary Putney (R.D. McMahon)	2.08¼
16	8,500.	Volga (Ben White)	2.07¼
17	6,500.	The Real Lady (T.W. Murphy)	2.04¼
18	6,000.	David Guy (T.W. Murphy)	2.05¾
19	6,000.	Periscope (John Dodge)	2.07¼
20	6,000.	Sister Bertha (Joseph Serrill)	2.05¼
21	6,000.	Rose Scott (T.W. Murphy)	2.04¼
22	6,000.	Peter Earl (Nat Ray)	2.04¼
23	6,000.	The Senator (Alonzo McDonald)	2.04¼
24	6,235.	Mr. McElwyn (Ben White)	2.05¼
25	6,235.	Aileen Guy (Ben White)	2.04¾
26	6,235.	Guy McKinney (Nat Ray)	2.05½
27	6,235.	Iosola's Worthy (Marvin Childs)	2.04¾
28	6,235.	Guy Abbey (Victor Fleming)	2.04¾
29	6,235.	Walter Dear (Walter Cox)	2.05½
30	8,500.	Hanover's Bertha (Thomas Berry)	2.01¼
31	8,500.	Protector (Will Caton)	2.03¾
32	3,525.	The Marchioness (Will Caton)	2.02
33	1,160.	Calumet Delco (H.M. Parshall)	2.05¾
34	1,560.	Lord Jim (H.M. Parshall)	2.04½
35	1,610.	Greyhound (S.F. Palin)	2.00
36	1,700.	Ruth M. Mac (Thomas Berry)	2.04¼
37	1,475.	Delphia Hanover (Henry Thomas)	2.05¼
38	1,740.	Earl's Mr. Will (Thomas Berry)	2.03¾
39	1,815.	Peter Astra (H.M. Parshall)	2.05
40	1,825.	Earl's Moody Guy (Thomas Berry)	2.02¼
41	2,210.	Bill Gallon (Lee Smith)	2.04¾
42	3,882.	Cannon Ball (Harry Whitney)	2.05½h
43	4,013.	Volo Song (Ben White)	2.08¼h
44	5,726.	Pearl Harbor (Omer Amundsen)	2.05 h
45	5,573.	Doctor Spencer (Henry Thomas)	2.00½
46		--Rain--	
47	7,274.	Way Yonder (Houston Stone)	2.04.1
48	11,039.	Egan Hanover (Ralph Baldwin)	2.02.4
49	15,128.	Bangaway (Ralph Baldwin)	2.03
50	14,135.	Lusty Song (Delvin Miller)	2.03.2
51	17,138.	Spennib (Fay Fitzpatrick)	a2.02.3
52	15,679.	Hit Song (Harry Pownall, Sr.)	2.01.2
53	17,190.	Kimberly Kid (Thomas Berry)	2.01
54	18,277.	Prince Victor (James Hackett)	2.01.2
55	17,600.	Scott Frost (Joe O'Brien)	2.01.3
56	15,889.	Bold Rodney (Robert Parkinson)	2.01
57	19,174.	Double Scotch (Joe O'Brien)	2.01.2
58	17,518.	Mc Colby (Dana Cameron)	b2.01.2
59	18,742.	Diller Hanover (Ralph Baldwin)	2.01
60	22,794.	Uncle Sam (Lou Huber, Jr.)	2.00.1
61	18,533.	Caleb (John Simpson, Sr.)	1.58.3
62	21,528.	*	c2.01.1
63	24,125.	**	d1.59.4
64	20,660.	Ayres (John Simpson, Sr.)	1.59
65	21,512.	Noble Victory (Stanley Dancer)	1.59.3
66	18,171.	Kerry Way (Frank Ervin)	2.00.1
67	20,931.	Dazzling Speed (Stanley Dancer)	e1.59.4
68	16,730.	Snow Speed (Ralph Baldwin)	f1.58.3
69	22,000.	Lindys Pride (Howard Beissinger)	2.00.3
70	26,900.	Timothy T. (John Simpson, Jr.)	2.01.1
71	29,250.	Hoot Speed (Glen Garnsey)	Rg1.58.1
72	21,970.	Super Bowl (Stanley Dancer)	1.59.3

* Nathaniel (Harry Pownall, Sr.) finished 1-2; Safe Mission (Joe O'Brien) finished 2-1.
** Glidden Hanover (Eddie Wheeler) finished 2-1; Cheer Honey (Frank Ervin) finished 1-2.

a By Scotch Rhythm.
b By Great Lullwater.
c By Nathaniel.
d By Glidden Hanover.
e By Speedy Streak.
f By Nevele Pride.
g By Quick Pride.

Review Futurity
Three-Year-Old Pace
Illinois State Fair, Springfield, Ill.

Yr	Purse	Winning Horse & Driver	Fastest Heat
29	$ 1,500.	Axworthy Pride (Frank Cares)	a2.07
30	2,000.	Calumet Adam (R.D. McMahon)	2.01¼
31	2,150.	Lady Vonian (H.M. Parshall)	2.03½
32	1,175.	Raider (Fred Egan)	2.02½
33	1,030.	Gene Volo (H.C. Fitzpatrick)	2.06¼
34	800.	Highland Millie (Ben White)	2.07¾
35	1,420.	Wedgemere Volo (H.M. Parshall)	2.03¼
36	1,550.	Little Pat (Charles Lacey)	2.01
37	1,545.	Hal Cochato (S.F. Palin)	2.00½
38	1,330.	Chief Counsel (H.M. Parshall)	1.58¼
39	1,385.	Blackstone (H.M. Parshall)	2.00
40	1,525.	Fearless Peter (H.M. Parshall)	2.01¼
41	1,525.	Bell Boy (H.M. Parshall)	2.04¼
42	3,632.	Voloway (Henry Thomas)	b2.05 h

43	2,463. Purdue Hal (S.F. Palin)	2.02¼h
44	4,127. Attorney (Art Blackwell)	2.05½h
45	3,872. True Chief (Thomas Berry)	2.01¼
46	--Rain--	
47	7,327. Forbes Chief (Adelbert Cameron)	2.01.3
48	9,335. Atomic Bomb (Delvin Miller)	c2.01.4
49	12,903. Good Time (Frank Ervin)	2.01.2
50	12,502. Quilla Hanover (John Simpson, Sr.)	2.01.4
51	11,509. Tar Heel (Delvin Miller)	1.59.4
52	10,745. Voting Trust (B.J. Schue)	2.01
53	12,254. Dutch Dandy (Wayne Smart)	d1.59.1
54	15,241. *	e1.59.1
55	15,202. Sea Eagle (H.C. Fitzpatrick)	2.00.3
56	13,411. Adioscot (Delvin Miller)	2.00.2
57	14,864. Torpid (John Simpson, Sr.)	1.59.4
58	14,638. Thorpe Hanover (Delvin Miller)	1.59.2
59	19,470. Bristol Hanover (Delvin Miller)	1.59
60	12,286. Dancer Hanover (Delvin Miller)	2.00
61	15,720. Adios Don (Howard Camper)	f1.57.4
62	16,765. Coffee Break (George Sholty)	1.57
63	14,486. James B. Hanover (Delbert Insko)	2.00.1
64	17,810. Race Time (Ralph Baldwin)	2.00.2
65	15,562. **	g1.59.2
66	12,821. Fashion Tip (James Dennis)	1.58.2
67	13,681. Best of All (James Hackett)	R1.57
68	16,150. ***	h1.58.4
69	16,280. Bye Bye Sam (Stanley Dancer)	2.03
70	22,650. Race Time Boy (Wm. Haughton)	i1.59
71	25,350. Winning Worthy (Herman Graham, Jr.)	1.57.2
72	17,170. Hilarious Way (John Simpson, Jr.)	R1.55.2

* Diamond Hal (Joe O'Brien) finished 2-1; Meadow
   Gold (James Arthur) finished 1-2.
** Bret Hanover (Frank Ervin) finished 2-1; Adios
   Vic (James Dennis) finished 1-2.
*** Ozzie Hanover (Gene Riegle) finished 2-1;
    Nevele Romeo (Stanley Dancer) finished 1-2.

a By Lee Strathmore and	e By Diamond Hal.
Axloretta (four-heat race).	f By Lang Hanover.
b By Lilydale.	g By Bret Hanover.
c By E.J. Hal.	h By Ozzie Hanover.
d By Marvel Way.	i By Toliver Hanover.

W.N. Reynolds Memorial
Two-Year-Old Trot
Buffalo Raceway, Hamburg, N.Y.

Yr	Purse	Winning Horse & Driver	Fastest Heat
51	$11,092.	Theme Song (B.J. Schue)	2.12.4h
52	13,920.	Singing Sword (Delvin Miller)	a2.14 h
53	12,505.	Brevity Hanover (Delvin Miller)	2.10 h
54	12,597.	Colbymite (Ralph Baldwin)	2.09.4h
55	12,269.	Valiant Rodney (Dana Cameron)	2.07.3h
56	17,067.	Demon Rum (C.J. Champion)	2.12.4h
57	10,007.	Sharpshooter (Harry Pownall, Sr.)	2.10 h
58	12,075.	Larue Hanover (S.L. Caton)	2.12.3h
59	14,986.	Blaze Hanover (Joe O'Brien)	2.08.4h
60	13,633.	Mr. Pride (Wm. Haughton)	2.08.2h
61	17,043.	Hickory Hill (Wm. Haughton)	2.08.1h
62*	8,989.	B.F. Coaltown (Harry Short)	2.08 h
	8,989.	Incorporator (Wm. Haughton)	2.13.4h
63*	8,831.	Late Frost (Delvin Miller)	2.10 h
	8,831.	Space Freight (John Simpson, Jr.)	2.11.4h
64*	9,415.	Ben Hur (Don C. Miller)	2.11.3h
	9,415.	Egyptian Candor (Stanley Dancer)	2.09.3h
65	18,493.	Ideal Rodney (Wm. Haughton)	2.09 h
66	19,429.	Drummond R.C. (Keith Waples)	2.09.1h
67	18,360.	Nevele Pride (Stanley Dancer)	2.07.4h
68	19,729.	Nevele Major (Stanley Dancer)	R2.06.4h
69	20,385.	Victory Star (Vernon Dancer)	R2.06.4h
70*	12,108.	A.C.'s Orion (Wm. Haughton)	2.13 h
	12,008.	Thai (Joe O'Brien)	2.15 h
71*	12,475.	Songcan (Gilles Lachance)	2.14.3h
	12,475.	Hambo Hope (John Schroeder)	2.14 h
72	25,050.	Walter Be Good (Bernard Webster)	2.07.3h

a By Lee Gallon.
* Raced in two divisions.

The Roosevelt Futurity
Two-Year-Old Pace
Roosevelt Raceway, Westbury

Yr	Purse	Winning Horse & Driver	Fastest Heat
60	$71,881.	Adios Cleo (John Simpson, Sr.)	2.04.2h
61	86,533.	Meadow Grayson (James Arthur)	2.02.4h
62	79,249.	Steady Beau (Delmer Insko)	2.02.1h

63	49,062. Bengazi Hanover (Robert Frame)	2.02.4h
64	52,427. Bret Hanover (Frank Ervin)	2.02.3h
65	51,643. Romeo Hanover (Wm. Myer)	2.03 h
66	52,149. Romulus Hanover (Wm. Haughton)	2.04 h
67	49,345. Fulla Napoleon (Richard Thomas)	2.05 h
68	83,365. Laverne Hanover (Wm. Haughton)	2.02.2h
69	93,986. Truluck (George Sholty)	2.03.3h
70	92,360. Albatross (Harry Harvey)	R2.00.4h
71	81,216. Strike Out (Wm. Gilmour)	2.01.4h
72	79,881. Otaro Hanover (Herve Filion)	2.03 h

Roosevelt International Trot
*Invitational
Roosevelt Raceway, Westbury, N.Y.

Yr	Purse	Winning Horse & Driver	Fastest Heat
59	$50,000.	Jamin (France) (Jean Riaud)	3.08.3h
60	50,000.	Hairos II (Holland) (Willem Geersen)	2.34 h
61	50,000.	Su Mac Lad (U.S.) (Stanley Dancer)	2.34.2h
62	50,000.	Tie Silk (Canada) (Keith Waples)	2.34.1h
63	50,000.	Su Mac Lad (U.S.) (Stanley Dancer)	2.32.3h
64	50,000.	Speedy Scot (U.S.) (Ralph Baldwin)	2.32.3h
65	100,000.	Pluvier III (Sweden) (Gunnar Nordin)	2.36.2h
66	100,000.	Armbro Flight (Canada) (Joe O'Brien)	R2.31.3h
67	100,000.	Roquepine (France) (Henri Levesque)	2.43.4h
68	100,000.	Roquepine (France) (J-R Gougeon)	2.38.3h
69	100,000.	Une de Mai (France) (J-R Gougeon)	2.33.2h
70	125,000.	Fresh Yankee (Canada) (Joe O'Brien)	2.35.1h
71	125,000.	Une de Mai (France) (J-R Gougeon)	2.34.4h
72	125,000.	Speedy Crown (U.S.) (H. Beissinger)	2.35.1h

* 1½-miles dash in 1959; a ¼-miles dash since 1960.

The L.K. Shapiro Stake
Three-Year-Old Pace
Hollywood Park, Inglewood, Calif.

Yr	Purse	Winning Horse & Driver	Fastest Heat
71	$100,000.	Albatross (Stanley Dancer)	R1.58.2
72	106,550.	Silent Majority (Wm. Haughton)	1.59

The Lawrence B. Sheppard
Two-Year-Old Pace
Yonkers, N.Y.

Yr	Purse	Winning Horse & Driver	Fastest Heat
64	$57,622.	Bret Hanover (Frank Ervin)	2.02.1h
65	100,000.	Romeo Hanover (Wm. Myer)	2.01 h
66	100,000.	Nardins Byrd (Delmer Insko)	2.03.2h
67	100,000.	Fulla Napoleon (Richard Thomas)	2.01.2h
68	50,000.	Hammerin Hank (George Sholty)	2.03 h
69	49,320.	Columbia George (George Sholty)	R1.58.4h
70	53,495.	Albatross (Harry Harvey)	2.02 h
71	44,948.	Shadow Star (Jack Kopas)	2.02 h
72*	25,985.	Valiant Bret (John Chapman)	2.02 h
	24,985.	Armbro Nesbit (Duncan MacDonald)	1.59.4h

* Raced in two divisions.

The Su Mac Lad
Three-Year-Old Colt & Gelding Trot
Yonkers, N.Y.

Yr	Purse	Winning Horse & Driver	Fastest Heat
67	$25,000.	Halifax Hanover (Joe O'Brien)	2.04.1h
68	25,000.	Nevele Pride (Stanley Dancer)	2.04 h
69	25,000.	Gun Runner (Earle Avery)	2.04.1h
70	24,660.	Gil Hanover (Wm. Haughton)	2.02.4h
71	24,247.	A.C.'s Orion (Wm. Haughton)	2.06.2h
72	50,000.	Dayan (Wm. Myer)	R2.01.4h

The Tattersalls Pace
Three-Year-Olds
Lexington, Ky.

Yr	Purse	Winning Horse & Driver	Fastest Heat
71	$52,866.	Albatross (Stanley Dancer)	R1.54.4
72	46,141.	Strike Out (Keith Waples)	1.58.2

Arthur S. Tompkins Memorial
Two-Year-Old Trot
Hazel Park, Mich.

Yr	Purse	Winning Horse & Driver	Fastest Heat
27	$14,700.	Spencer (Alonzo McDonald)	2.07¾
28		--Rain--	
29	8,950.	Main McElwyn (Ben White)	2.07¾
30	5,000.	Chestnut Burr (W.T. Britenfield)	2.08¼
31	4,000.	Hollyrood Robin (Fred Egan)	2.06¼
32	4,000.	Hollyrood Portia (Wm. Crozier)	a2.07¼
33	2,000.	Sturdy (Harry Brusie)	2.04¾
34	1,800.	Greyhound (S.F. Palin)	2.06¾
35	1,800.	Rosalind (Ben White)	2.04¾
36	2,500.	Schnapps (Ben White)	2.07½
37	2,500.	Blair (Vic Fleming)	2.05½
38	3,000.	Nibble Hanover (Harry Whitney)	b2.05½
39	4,000.	Earl's Moody Guy (Thomas Berry)	2.09¾
40	4,000.	Bill Gallon (Lee Smith)	2.07
41	4,000.	Cannon Ball (Harry Whitney)	2.07
42	4,000.	Volo Song (Ben White)	2.07¼
43	4,000.	Yankee Maid (Henry Thomas)	2.09½
44	5,000.	Titan Hanover (Harry Pownall, Sr.)	2.07
45	5,000.	Bombs Away (S.F. Palin)	2.07¼
46	5,000.	Rodney (Bion Shively)	2.07½
47	5,000.	Judge Moore (Eugene Pownall)	c2.05.3
48	5,000.	Miss Tilly (Fred Egan)	2.07.4
49	5,000.	Lusty Song (H.M. Parshall)	2.03.2
50	10,000.	Scotch Rhythm (Ralph Baldwin)	2.06.1
51	10,000.	Hit Song (Harry Pownall, Sr.)	2.06
52	19,400.	Singing Sword (†Harry Harvey)	d2.08.2
53	22,200.	Newport Dream (Adelbert Cameron)	2.03
54	11,800.	Galophone (Wm. Haughton)	2.03.4
55	21,200.	Charlotte Frost (Thomas Berry)	2.04.3
56	15,600.	Bond Hanover (Joe O'Brien)	e2.06.3
57	16,039.	Mix Hanover (Frank Ervin)	f2.06.3
58	14,119.	Diller Hanover (Ralph Baldwin)	2.06
59	14,076.	Uncle Sam (Lou Huber, Jr.)	2.04
60	9,742.	Caleb (John Simpson, Sr.)	g2.04.1
61	10,543.	Gallant Hanover (Lou Huber, Jr.)	2.08
62	17,175.	Speedy Scot (Ralph Baldwin)	2.05.3h
63	13,275.	Dartmouth (Ralph Baldwin)	2.06.3h
64	13,150.	Florican Flash (Gene Riegle)	2.13.2h
65	13,150.	Carlisle (Wm. Haughton)	2.10.2h
66	12,150.	Floral Hanover (Delvin Miller)	2.10.4h
67	11,475.	Mata Gay (Carl E. Quinn)	2.13 h
68	13,150.	Tarport Devlin (Delvin Miller)	2.05.1f
69	23,980.	Keystone Brian (Wm. Haughton)	2.06.1f
70	16,592.	A.C.'s Orion (Wm. Haughton)	2.09.2f
71	15,622.	Star's Chip (Stanley Dancer)	2.08.1f
72	25,072.	Super Bowl (Stanley Dancer)	R2.02.4f

† Delvin Miller drove second elimination heat.
a By Sir Raleigh.
b By Peter Astra.
c By Madison Hanover.
d By Singing Sword and Kimberly Kid.
e By Hoot Song.
f By Gang Awa.
g By Spectator.

Westbury Futurity
Two-Year-Old Trot
Roosevelt Raceway, Westbury, N.Y.

Yr	Purse	Winning Horse & Driver	Fastest Heat
60	$71,881.	Duke Rodney (Eddie Wheeler)	2.05.3h
61	85,135.	Sprite Rodney (Frank Ervin)	R2.04.3h
62	77,349.	Speedy Scot (Ralph Baldwin)	R2.04.3h
63	49,062.	Dartmouth (Ralph Baldwin)	2.05.4h
64	50,427.	Noble Victory (Wm. Haughton)	2.05.1h
65	56,643.	Kerry Way (Frank Ervin)	2.06.3h
66	54,149.	Pay Dirt (Earle Avery)	2.07.4h
67	51,845.	Nevele Pride (Stanley Dancer)	2.05 h
68	96,865.	Dayan (John Wilcutts)	2.06 h
69	90,986.	Gunner (Malcom Weaver)	2.06.4h
70	74,360.	Quick Pride (Delvin Miller)	2.06 h
71	71,716.	Super Bowl (Vernon Dancer)	2.06.1h
72	77,881.	Burning Speed (Glen Garnsey)	2.06.2h

The Westchester
Three-Year-Old Colt & Gelding Pace
Yonkers, N.Y.

Yr	Purse	Winning Horse & Driver	Fastest Heat
67	$25,000.	Romulus Hanover (Wm. Haughton)	2.01.1h
68	25,000.	Rum Customer (Wm. Haughton)	2.00.3h
69	25,000.	Kat Byrd (Eldon Harner)	2.02.4h
70	26,160.	Most Happy Fella (Stanley Dancer)	R1.59 h
71	25,247.	Albatross (Stanley Dancer)	1.59.3h
72	54,500.	Keystone Pat (Ronald Waples)	2.01 h

The Yonkers Futurity
*Three-Year-Old Trot
Yonkers, N.Y.

Yr	Purse	Winning Horse & Driver	Fastest Heat
55	$73,840.	Scott Frost (Joe O'Brien)	2.12 h
56	77,170.	Add Hanover (John Simpson, Sr.)	2.12.4h
57	57,812.	Hoot Song (Ralph Baldwin)	2.16.1h
58	56,157.	Spunky Hanover (Howard Camper)	2.13.3h
59	56,397.	John A. Hanover (Stanley Dancer)	2.11 h
60	74,265.	Duke of Decatur (Delvin Miller)	2.13.3h
61	100,330.	Duke Rodney (Eddie Wheeler)	2.10.3h
62	105,422.	A.C.'s Viking (Sanders Russell)	2.10.4h
63	135,127.	Speedy Scot (Ralph Baldwin)	2.03.3h
64	116,691.	Ayres (John Simpson, Sr.)	R2.01.3h
65	122,236.	Noble Victory (Stanley Dancer)	2.02 h
66	123,375.	Polaris (George Sholty)	2.06 h
67	150,000.	Pomp (Harry Pownall, Sr.)	2.04.4h
68	150,000.	Nevele Pride (Stanley Dancer)	2.03.3h
69	100,000.	Lindys Pride (Howard Beissinger)	2.03 h
70	106,770.	Victory Star (Vernon Dancer)	2.03.4h
71	110,795.	Quick Pride (Stanley Dancer)	2.02.4h
72	93,097.	Super Bowl (Stanley Dancer)	2.02 h

* 1 1/16-miles dash before 1963.

IMPORTANT RULES

Uniform rules and regulations for light harness racing are enacted and enforced by The United States Trotting Association. All the rules are important but some have special significance. In the hope that fans may gain a better working knowledge of the rules, some of the more important ones follow:

Rule 16.—STARTING.

Section 1. With Starting Gate.—

(a) **Starter's Control.**—The Starter shall have control of the horses from the formation of the parade until he gives the word "go."

(b) **Scoring.**—After one or two preliminary warming up scores, the Starter shall notify the drivers to fasten their helmet chin straps and come to the starting gate. During or before the parade the drivers must be informed as to the number of scores permitted.

(c) The horses shall be brought to the starting gate as near one-quarter of a mile before the start as the track will permit.

(d) **Speed of Gate.**—Allowing sufficient time so that the speed of the gate can be increased gradually, the following minimum speeds will be maintained:

(1) For the first 1/8 mile, not less than 11 miles per hour.
(2) For the next 1/16 of a mile not less than 18 miles per hour.
(3) From that point to the starting point, the speed will be gradually increased to maximum speed.

(e) On mile tracks horses will be brought to the starting gate at the head of the stretch and the relative speeds mentioned in sub-section (d) above will be maintained.

(f) **Starting Point.**—The starting point will be a point marked on the inside rail a distance of not less than 200 feet from the first turn. The Starter shall give the word "go" at the starting point.

(g) WHEN A SPEED HAS BEEN REACHED IN THE COURSE OF A START THERE SHALL BE NO DECREASE EXCEPT IN THE CASE OF A RECALL.

(h) **Recall Notice.**—In case of a recall, a light plainly visible to the driver shall be flashed and a recall sounded, but the starting gate shall proceed out of the path of the horses. **At extended pari-mutuel tracks in the case of a recall, wherever possible, the starter shall leave the wings of the gate extended and gradually slow the speed of the gate to assist in stopping the field of horses. In an emergency, however, the starter shall use his discretion to close the wings of the gate.**

(i) There shall be no recall after the word "go" has been given and any horse, regardless of his position or an accident, shall be deemed a starter from the time he entered into the Starter's control unless dismissed by the Starter.

(j) **Breaking Horse.**—The Starter shall endeavor to get all horses away in position and on gait but no recall shall be had for a breaking horse except as provided in (k) (5).

(k) **Recall—Reasons For.**—The Starter may sound a recall only for the following reasons:

(1) A horse scores ahead of the gate.

(2) There is interference.

(3) A horse has broken equipment.

(4) A horse falls before the word "go" is given.

(5) Where a horse refuses to come to the gate before the gate reaches the pole 1/8 of a mile before the start, the field may be turned.

(l) **Penalties.**—A fine not to exceed $100, or suspension from driving not to exceed 15 days, or both, may be applied to any driver, by the Starter for:

(1) Delaying the start.

(2) Failure to obey the Starter's instructions.

(3) Rushing ahead of the inside or outside wing of the gate.

(4) Coming to the starting gate out of position.

(5) Crossing over before reaching the starting point.

(6) Interference with another driver during the start.

(7) Failure to come up into position.

A hearing must be granted before any penalty is imposed.

Rule 18.—Driving Rule

Section 1. Although a leading horse is entitled to any part of the track except after selecting his position in the home stretch, neither the driver of the first horse or any other driver in the race shall do any of the following things, which shall be considered violation of driving rules:

(a) Change either to the right or left during any part of the race when another horse is so near him that in altering his position he compels the horse behind him to shorten his stride, or causes the driver of such other horse to pull him out of his stride.

(b) Jostle, strike, hook wheels, or interfere with another horse or driver.

(c) Cross sharply in front of a horse or cross over in front of a field of horses in a reckless manner, endangering other drivers.

(d) Swerve in and out or pull up quickly.

(e) Crowd a horse or driver by "putting a wheel under him."

(f) "Carry a horse out" or "sit down in front of him," take up abruptly in front of other horses so as to cause confusion or interference among the trailing horses, or do any other act which constitutes what is popularly known as helping.

(g) Let a horse pass inside needlessly.

(h) Laying off a normal pace and leaving a hole when it is well within the horse's capacity to keep the hole closed.

(i) Commit any act which shall impede the progress of another horse or cause him to "break."

(j) Change course after selecting a position in the home stretch and swerve in or out, or bear in or out, in such manner as to interfere with another horse or cause him to change course or take back.

(k) To drive in a careless or reckless manner.

(l) Whipping under the arch of the sulky, the penalty for which shall be no less than 10 days suspension.

Breaking Rule

(a) When any horse or horses break from their gait in trotting or pacing, their drivers shall at once, where clearance exists, take such horse to the outside and pull it to its gait.

(b) The following shall be considered violations of Section 12 (a):

(1) Failure to properly attempt to pull the horse to its gait.

(2) Failure to take to the outside where clearance exists.

(3) Failure to lose ground by the break.

(c) If there has been no failure on the part of the driver in complying with 12 (b), (1), (2), and (3), the horse shall not be set back unless a contending horse on his gait is lapped on the hind quarter of the breaking horse at the finish.

(d) The Judges may set any horse back one or more places if in their judgment any of the above violations have been committed.

14. If in the opinion of the Judges, a driver

allows his horse to break for the purpose of fraudulently losing a heat, he shall be liable to the penalties elsewhere provided for fraud and fouls.

TROTTER

Diagonally gaited horse. Moves with a high-stepping, straight ahead gait with left front and right hind legs moving forward in unison. The trotter usually wears a heavier shoe than a pacer (average: 8 oz.); the length of his front toe is usually longer (3¾"−3 7/8"); and his angle (that formed by the front of the foot and the sole of the foot) is usually a little more acute (46-48 degrees). The trotter is generally shod "flat" in front, that is, he usually wears level shoes, and usually wears a swedge shoe (a creased shoe which provides traction when the horse's hind foot hits the ground) behind.

Equipment Worn By Trotters

ELBOW BOOTS− Sheepskin lined pads worn high on front legs to protect elbows (points at rear and bottom of shoulders) from the front feet as they are folded back in top stride. Needed on high gaited trotters.

HIND SHIN BOOTS−Leather protecting guards on the lower hind legs. Prevent cuts and bruises from the front shoes which graze the hind legs of some trotters.

TOE WEIGHTS− Brass or lead weights weighing from two to four ounces. They are clipped to the edge of the front hoofs to extend a horse's stride.

QUARTER BOOTS− Close fitting boots on the front heel to protect the tender quarter (heel of the foot) from being cut by the hind shoes.

MARTINGALE− A strap, running from the girth between the horse's front legs, to the reins which are threaded through the rings at the end of the martingale. Helps prevent horse from tossing and raising head.

PACER

Laterally gaited horse. Moves with a swaying motion swinging the right front and right hind legs forward at the same time. The pacer usually wears a lighter shoe than the trotter (average: 5 oz.); the length of his front toe is usually shorter (3½"−3 5/8") and his angle (that formed by the front of the foot and the sole of the foot) is usually less acute (48-50 degrees). The pacer generally wears a flat or half round shoe in front and a combination shoe, half round inside− swedge outside, behind. The swedge part increases traction thus widening the horse's gait and lessening possibility of the hind foot hitting a front leg. The half round portion presents a rounded edge and lessens the danger of serious injury in the event such "crossfiring" does occur.

Equipment Worn By Pacers

HOBBLES−Leather straps encircling the front and hind legs of a pacer on the same side to keep those legs moving in unison and to help the horse maintain its gait. The straps running over the horse's back and to the haunches are known as hobble hangers.

SHADOW ROLL− A large sheepskin-type roll worn just above a horse's nose and just below his eyes. It cuts off the horse's view of the track so that he won't shy at shadows, pieces of paper or other objects.

KNEE BOOTS−Boots fitted around the knees and held up by suspenders (usually white) over the horse's withers. They protect the knees from blows from the opposite foot, especially on turns where a horse is more likely to break stride if he "brushes his knees."

HEAD POLE−A cue (usually a billiard cue with a hole bored in the handle to accommodate a leather thong) fastened alongside horse's head and neck to keep his head straight.

GAITING STRAP−Strap strung inside shafts of sulky to keep the horse from swinging the rear end to the right and left and traveling sideways on his gait.

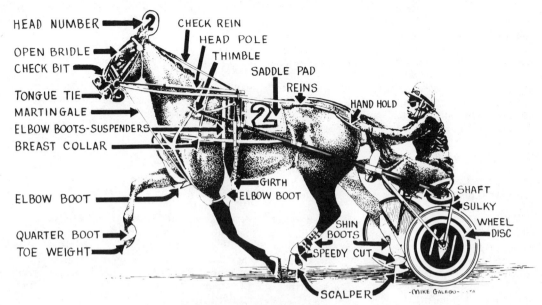

HEAD NUMBER
OPEN BRIDLE
CHECK BIT
TONGUE TIE
MARTINGALE
ELBOW BOOTS-SUSPENDERS
BREAST COLLAR
ELBOW BOOT
QUARTER BOOT
TOE WEIGHT

CHECK REIN
HEAD POLE
THIMBLE
SADDLE PAD
REINS
HAND HOLD

GIRTH
ELBOW BOOT

SHIN BOOTS
SPEEDY CUT

SHAFT
SULKY
WHEEL
DISC

SCALPER

-MIKE GALEGO-

EQUIPMENT COMMONLY WORN BY
THE TROTTER

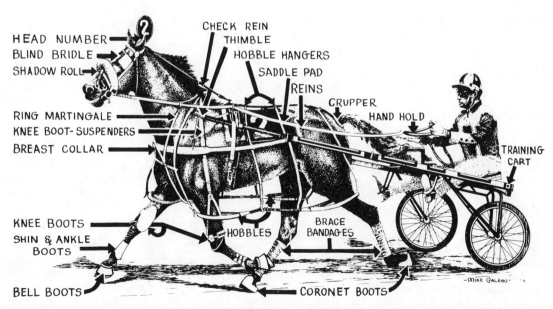

HEAD NUMBER
BLIND BRIDLE
SHADOW ROLL
RING MARTINGALE
KNEE BOOT-SUSPENDERS
BREAST COLLAR
KNEE BOOTS
SHIN & ANKLE BOOTS
BELL BOOTS

CHECK REIN
THIMBLE
HOBBLE HANGERS
SADDLE PAD
REINS
CRUPPER
HAND HOLD

TRAINING CART

HOBBLES
BRACE BANDAGES

CORONET BOOTS

-MIKE GALEGO-

EQUIPMENT COMMONLY WORN BY
THE PACER

HORSE RACING

Frequently called the Sport of Kings, horse racing in recent decades has zoomed in popularity. The thoroughbred sport has been showing annual increases in attendance, wagering, revenue to states and purses. The success of racing has brought about enormous modernization of tracks and parks. No longer are the horse parks shabby establishments catering only to the wealthy who are interested in the improvement of the breed and unsavory characters looking for an easy dollar. The plants now are bright and shiny and some are the last word in comfort and beauty. A cross section of America can usually be found in attendance. Some parks even cater to family groups, though minors are not allowed to bet.

The history of the horse has intrigued man since he first became aware of the animal's existence.

The horse may have been, in almost dwarfish size, the first of the world's animals. Certainly his existence is traced back farther than others by scientists.

Beyond the dog, the horse has been more intimately identified with man than any other animal because he has been a beast of burden and a means of sport. His beginning, progress and development, therefore, have been subjected to unceasing study.

No animal that ever inhabited this earth has made so many appearances, disappearances and reappearances as the horse in his parade of 45,000,000 years, during which he has grown from a height of less than 1 foot to the gigantic Percheron of this day, 16.1 to 16.3 hands. (A hand is 4 inches.)

The age of the horse is, or course, a guess by scientists or historians. It may be 45,000,000 years, 4,500,000 years, 450,000 or a mere 4,500 years. No one ever has furnished absolute evidence.

The origin of the horse has been puzzling because the horse, the ass and the zebra belong to the same family. There has been uncertainty whether a certain skeleton was that of a horse, or of his relatives, the ass and the zebra. Each has a single hoof, meaning that it is solid and without toes, making this species distinct from all other animals.

The history of the horse on the North American continent is typical of that of the horse throughout the world, so far as his eccentric existence is concerned.

The horse inhabited what is now America 45,000,000 years ago and then disappeared, without a trace, for 25,000,000 years. He reappeared, larger than before, remained a while—and again he was gone. He returned about 1,000,000 years ago, grown still larger, only to fade again. There is no further fossilized record of him until about 25,000 years ago. After which he once more vanished, to remain unknown on the North American continent until the 16th Century when Hernando Cortez, the invader, brought horses from Spain to Mexico. Some of those stayed, to become founders of the family of wild horses in North America.

The skeleton of the oldest horse known to science is on display in the museum of Amherst (Mass.) College. Its age is estimated at 45,000,000 years. Horses may have existed before then, but there are no fossils to prove it. The skeleton was resurrected in June, 1903, from the "Bad Lands" of Wyoming, near Grey Gull River, by Professor Frederic Brewster and a group of his students. Professor Brewster, who died in Alaska in 1937, called the skeleton "Eohippus Borealis," meaning the "Dawn Horse." Eohippus Borealis is 11 inches (not feet) in height and is established definitely as a horse because of bone formations, single hoof and other structure that classifies him.

The prehistoric horse long since has disappeared from life and remains only in fossil form. The oldest known breed of horse of continuous existence is the "Przewalski Wild Horse," an inhabitant of the Gobi desert region for at least 6,000 years. The next oldest breed still existing is the horse of Northern Africa, founder of the thoroughbred family of today.

Until 1881 it was assumed that the horse of Arabia was the oldest. But in that year, Colonel N. W. Przewalski, while exploring in Gobi, picked up some skin and bones, studied them, was mystified, and had them shipped to Russia. The colonel's first conclusion, reached while in the desert, was that the skin and bones were those of horses, yet the horse, up to then, never had been seen in those parts.

Put to test, the remains were identified by Russian scientists as being those of a complete horse, and the age of the skeleton was fixed as "at least 6,000 years." The excited Przewalski immediately returned to Gobi to hunt for live horses, knowing that if he found them, he would be the possessor of perhaps the oldest specimen of horse of continuous breeding. The quest was successful. The colonel captured more than a score of wild horses, which since have borne his name. He shipped them to Russia. Comparison of them was made with the skeletons. They were identical—and thus the proof that the 6,000-year-old fossil was that of the

Przewalski wild horse of today. This wild horse is about 53 inches high, with huge bones, and an enormous head, with legs much shorter but far stronger than any other breed.

Other explorations revealed an animal called the "Steppe Horse" inhabiting the high places of Mongolia. He never has been found outside the cold, mountainous regions, and although he differs somewhat in conformation from the wild horse of the Gobi desert, it is believed that he is a member of that family.

Historians declare that the first domesticated horse made its appearance in Egypt about 1500 B.C., some saying it came out of Libya, others holding to the Manetho theory that it was brought into Egypt by wandering tribes, never identified as to race, and known only as Hyksos, which means "direction whence they came."

The generally accepted version relative to the known origin of the domesticated horse, from which the thoroughbred springs, is this:

The shepherd kings of Egypt, a peaceful group, were succeeded by the ruthless Thebans, who conquered many nations and added them to the empire that was Egypt.

About 1500 B.C., the Theban pharaohs attacked Libya, a land of seafaring people who at one time occupied almost the entire northern coast of Africa, with the exception of the Delta of the Nile. Libya had surrendered territory gradually until 1500 B.C., when the Thebans drove down upon them and they were holding only a small portion of the land that once had been theirs. They had become an isolated people.

The Egyptians, seeking booty to take back to their king, noticed an animal unlike any they ever had seen before. It was the horse—diminutive as compared with the horse of today—yet the exact species from which the modern race horse has been developed.

Many horses were seized and taken to Egypt by the victorious army. Their average height was 42 inches. They were presented to the king, and it was explained to him the Libyans hitched these animals to a vehicle and used them for hauling. The king, quickly recognizing the usefulness of the horse in military campaigns, sent couriers to Libya with the message that instead of exacting the usual tribute of gold, jewels and precious stones, he would take horses.

The Libyan horse was far different in conformation from any of the wild horses. It had a much smaller head, frailer bones and longer, thinner legs. Obviously, it could not have been an offspring of wild horses. It was different from the zebra, and just as different from the ass. Historians cannot vision the horse of Libya as the outcome of chance mating of the zebra, or the ass, with the wild

horse. So there is—and ever will be—doubt as to the exact beginning of this distinct breed of horse that came out of Libya into Egypt about 1500 B.C. and was ancestor of the "hot blooded horse," or thoroughbred of today.

The Egyptians practically stripped the Libyans of their horses and proceeded with elaborate breeding plans. They used the horses to haul carts or freight light supplies of war. Other nations sought to buy horses, but not until she had an over-supply, would Egypt sell. The price was exorbitant. Further, the Egyptians would not sell mares, nor any non-castrated horses before turning them over to the purchasing nation. They, thus, originated the practice of gelding the horse.

Perhaps the outstanding breeder of all time was Darius (521-485 B.C.), who, while reigning in Persia, had more than 50,000 brood mares. Darius was the first to concentrate on breeding larger and stronger horses in the hope they could carry soldiers on their backs. In the time of Darius, the horse was 13 to 13½ hands (52 to 56 inches) in height and weighed between 500 and 600 pounds. The thoroughbred today measures 62 to 65 inches, and the average well proportioned horse will weigh about 1,050 pounds in racing prime. The horse of Darius was much too small and frail for horsebacking use.

The ambition of Darius never was realized, but those who followed him carried on the experiment. Inch by inch, a taller horse—and a heavier, stronger horse—was developed. Just who was first to ride a horse is not known. The saddle is mentioned as existing in crude form somewhat prior to 350 A.D. Quite likely, men rode bareback generations before then, and probably the first horseback riding was in the 3d Century.

On the other hand, the ancient saddle may have been for the ass, which was strong enough for saddle riding before the Christian Era.

But it remained for Mohammed (570-632 A.D.) to popularize horseback riding. Having founded a new religion, he was eager that his disciples carry the fundamentals of it to far places in the fastest possible time. Therefore he mounted them on horses. The sight of the riders astride the horses created astonishment. The combination was held in awe and superstitious reverence, and the missionaries were given most eager audience, thus aiding the ambitions of Mohammed for converts.

The thoroughbred did not appear in any number in Europe until the 8th Century, when the Arabs drove the Goths out of Spain and took control. They brought with them bands of Arabian horses, using them both for hauling and under saddle. Breeding farms were created in Spain and within 100 years the thoroughbred was well established. But those horses, like the pure Arabians of today, although far stronger than the original horses from Libya, were no more than 14 hands to 14½ hands (56 to 58 inches) tall.

The Arabian horses of the 9th, 10th and 11th centuries, incapable of carrying a man far, could travel at high speed over a short distance. This interested King Henry I (1100-1135 A.D.) of England so much that he ordered the purchase of an Arabian stallion in Spain in 1110 A.D. and bred it with the slow but powerful mares that belonged to the ancient species of England, dating back centuries in the matter of continuous existence.

The result was a horse that had strength, speed and was of definite value in warfare. Henry promptly ordered some Arabian mares and started extensive breeding. When the Arabs were driven out of Spain in 1121 A.D., taking with them the best of the horses that had not been killed in battle, Henry made future purchases from Morocco.

For many generations, the breeding of Arabian and Moroccan horses in England was confined to royalty, and the foals of pure Arabian or Morocco blood became known as "Royal Horses." Eventually, wealthy aristocrats, wishing fast horses of their own, imported Arabians and Moroccans, and the result was that England soon had both a new breed of horses as the result of cross-mating and increasing numbers of pure Arabians, or Moroccans.

Owners of purebreds finally became involved in friendly arguments as to which horse was faster and which owner was the better rider. That marked the beginning of horse racing in England. There were no race courses. Men just plotted out 4 miles and that was the racing strip. The 4-mile route was the regulation racing distance because that had been the standard for chariot races of the Olympiads of more than 15 centuries earlier and custom maintained 4 miles as the perfect route for equine contests.

The first public race course was the Smithfield Track in London, built about 1174 A.D. The date of its opening generally is regarded as the birthday of organized racing under saddle. Horsemen, not content to race only when Smithfield conducted an abbreviated meeting, scheduled contests in their neighborhoods. The popularity of these caused proprietors of fairs to arrange a race as a special feature of each program, and soon no fair throughout England was regarded as complete without at least one horse race.

Until 1512, men raced merely for the "glory of it," but in that year the promoters of the fair in Chester, England, which was a well established racing center, gave a wooden ball, festooned with flowers, as a prize to the winner—the first racing trophy. In 1540, a silver ball was substituted. Its value was 4 shillings ($1). In 1607 some towns became very extravagant and awarded golf balls—or, rather, gold shells—worth about $10.

The blundering of a silversmith in 1609 brought about the custom of three prizes for a race. The contest of that year was to be held at Chester, and Robert Ambrye, its sheriff, was to put up the prize. He ordered a silver ball but rejected it as being of "inferior workmanship." The silversmith made another try—and once again Ambrye was not content. But the third ball suited him. On race day, Ambrye found himself possessed of 3 silver balls. What to do? He pondered—and created an idea. The best ball would go to the winner, next best for second place and the other to the rider of the horse finishing third.

The widowed Queen Anne of England (1702-1714) originated the sweepstakes idea—racing for a cash award. While her husband (King Charles) was alive, she had a small string of racers, but took little active part in the sport which, by that time, had taken a firm hold upon the English. However, ascending the throne in 1702, she quickly gave royal approval to horse racing, encouraged it and ran her horses in the important contests.

In 1703, Queen Anne put up a silver plate, worth about $20, for the big race at Doncaster. Each year until 1710 her offering was the same. In 1710 she donated a gold cup (worth $300) and fixed the rules for competition, limiting races to 6 horses, each to carry 168 pounds, best 2-heats-in-3, each heat to be of 4 miles. This race was greeted with so much praise that Queen Anne gave a $500 gold cup to the winner of the 1711, 1712, and 1713 races. She ran her horse Pepper in the 1712 contest and Mustard in 1713—without success.

Queen Anne changed the rules in 1714. As usual, she donated a $500 cup, but insisted that owners of all starters put up 10 guineas ($50), winner to take all. Thus cash prizes originated. Star, the Queen's horse, won the first actual money-race in history.

To Anne also belongs much of the credit for standardizing the breeding of horses. Until her time, the breeding had been haphazard. She ruled that a certain number of stallions and brood mares be selected as founders of a family of "thoroughbred horses," meaning horses whose blood lines could be traced back directly to Arabia. But her plan was not carried out for several decades.

After the middle of the 18th Century, racing in England had become so popular and interest in the outcome of the contests so great that a publication—the "English Racing Calendar"—was originated for the purpose of printing results. The "Calendar" was alone in the turf field until 1791, when the "English Stud-Book" was created. The "Calendar" in its beginning was not very particular about its listings. It was only necessary for a horse to have "performed creditably" on the turf to gain recognition. The "Stud—Book" also accepted horses that had raced well, upon the assumption that none but a well-bred horse could race well.

Eventually, when the number of horses became greater and there was much cross-breeding, the "Stud-Book" changed its attitude. It determined that horses to be eligible for listing must be descended from certain thoroughbred, or "blooded," royalty, which had been Anne's idea. But which was royalty? It was determined, finally, that the founding sires should be those from which had descended Matchem, Herod (or King Herod) and Eclipse, which trio had been considered great during their careers. Further, it was decided that when the tap root of those horses was established, such horses and all their descendants should be known as "thoroughbreds," a distinct type, the word meaning that the horse had been thoroughly, or scientifically, bred, in keeping with the highest English standards.

Matchem, foaled in 1748, was found to have descended from Godolphin's Arabian stallion. Herod, foaled in 1758, traced to Byerly's (or Byerley's) Turkish stallion. Eclipse, so named because he was foaled in 1764, the year of a total eclipse, traced to Darley's Arabian. Thus, automatically, all horses which descended from the 3 founding stallions—Godolphin's, Byerly's and Darley's—were ranked as thoroughbreds. The same designation was applied to all horses that had descended from the later-day Matchem, Herod and Eclipse.

Byerly's Turk was so called because he was owned by a man named Byerly, and was supposed to be of Barb, or Turkish, origin. But it never was definitely established where the horse had been foaled or what was his exact breeding. All that is known is that he was taken to Ireland about 1689, put into stud and by the turn of the 18th Century was producing horses with fine speed.

Darley's Arabian was so named because he was owned by a man named Darley, who had purchased him at Aleppo, a town in Syria, about 1704 and had shipped him to his brother in York, England. The offspring of this Arabian were beautifully formed, had splendid endurance and were very fast. The greatness of Eclipse made the Darley line famous.

The third of the founding trio was Godolphin's Arabian, although some insist that he was a Barb, meaning he was bred in Barbary, which was the habitat of the Moors. This sire, destined to become one of the most remarkable in all the world, had an amazing career.

Originally, he was sent as a gift by the Emperor of Morocco to King Louis XIV of France. The Emperor regarded him as the finest horse in his country. He hoped that Louis would ride him and then retire him for breeding, but for some unknown reason, Louis not only did not ride him and did not breed him, but gave him away or sold him. There is a lapse of several years in history of this horse, and then he reappeared in 1724 on the streets of Paris, hauling a cart.

An Englishman named Coke took notice of this cart horse as the driver pulled him to a stop. A keen judge of horseflesh, Coke recognized regal lines and struck up a bargain with the owner. Coke purchased the horse for $15 and shipped him to a Mr. Williams, who owned the James Coffee House in London and who was a breeder on a small scale. Williams didn't think much of the gift. He spoke about the horse to a patron—Lord Godolphin. His Lordship examined the horse and, like Coke, recognized him as a pure Arabian. Godolphin offered to buy him from Williams, and Williams responded by giving the horse to Godolphin as an outright gift.

Godolphin sent the stallion to his breeding farms and then forgot him until an emergency arose. He had intended breeding his mare, Rexanna, to his best stallion, but that stallion had taken sick. Rather than lose the opportunity to breed Rexanna, he mated her with the gift horse. The result was a foal that was named Lath. It became a sensational performer. Immediately Godolphin started to hunt for the ancestry of his gift stallion. He went to Williams, who communicated with Coke, who located the man who had sold the horse. Coke, using the information supplied, ran down all clues and finally learned that this was the stallion that an Emporer had given to a King. Since Godolphin's Arabian had sired other splendid horses, as had his sons, and grandsons, he was selected to complete the trio.

Thus these 3 became the founding stallions of the 3 lines of English thoroughbreds, which endure to this day.

Racing gained greatly in popularity in England all through the 18th Century, but it had one great drawback as the breeding became intensified. Contests were at 4 miles and most races were on the heat system—best 2-of-3. This meant that a horse had to run 8 miles, and possibly 12, under saddle in a single afternoon—too grueling a task for any but those that had reached 5, 6 or 7 years of age.

Breeders of race horses, thus, were placed in a position of supporting a horse for many years before it had a chance to earn its oats and hay money. But a change was wrought in 1776 by Colonel St. Leger, a breeder who lived near Doncaster, England. He decided that 3-year-olds were strong enough to run at least 2 miles in an afternoon, and arranged a race "for 3-year-old colts at 2 miles, 1 heat to decide." It attracted 6 entries and the event was won by St. Leger's own horse, Sampson. The race had no name, but with its second running in 1777, became known as "St. Leger's Race," and since then has been officially called the St. Leger, oldest stakes race in the world.

In 1779 the 12th Earl of Derby felt something should be done to provide action for 3-year-old fillies which were not eligible for the St. Leger. He thereupon carded a race at the Epsom course for "3-year-old fillies," the distance to be a mile and a half, "*one heat to decide.*" That race, too, had no name, but quickly came to be called the "Epsom Oaks" in honor of his Lordship's estate at Epsom —which is its name today. The Earl's horse, Bridget, was winner of the first Oaks.

In 1780, while continuing the Oaks as a race exclusively for fillies, the Earl established another. It was to be at a mile and a half for "3-year-old horses," meaning it was open to both sexes. He didn't name that one, either, but the public started to call it "Derby's race at Epsom." This was changed to "Epsom's Derby," and it still is so called in England, although around the world it is known as the "English Derby."

Although the distance of the St. Leger was fixed at 2 miles, and the Oaks and Derby at 1½ miles, they never have been run at those routes. Because of a measuring error the first St. Leger was over a course of 1 mile 6 furlongs and 132 yards. Another, and later, blunder made the Epsom distance 1 mile, 881 yards, instead of 1 mile 880 yards. The same course was used when the Epsom (English) Derby was originated. The routes never have been changed; the Derby continues at a mile and a half, plus an extra yard; the St. Leger at a mile, 6 furlongs, 132 yards.

While the era between 1700 and 1750 was of importance in the advancement of racing in England, that between 1751 and 1799 was even more epoch-making. It saw the launching of the "Racing Calendar" and of the famous "Stud-Book." It brought about the establishment of the founding stallions for thoroughbred purposes and standardized the breeding of horses. In addition, the Jockey Club was founded in the latter part of the 18th Century. It drafted racing laws and arranged for rules of conduct, which endure unto this day. It took over control of the "Stud Book," which registered all breeding of thoroughbreds, and fashioned many regulations, relative to the mating of horses, as well as to the racing of them.

The Jockey Club, an informal group of horse owners at the outset, rose to ranking as the most powerful organization in the history of the sport. While its decrees, even today, are supposed to be imposed only upon racing in England, the mandates generally are accepted by all turf organizations in the world.

The Jockey Club was organized informally at the Thatcher House on St. James Street, London, in 1751. The small group of horsemen met again in 1752 to discuss the future of horse racing and decided to call itself the Jockey Club. It was without an official name up to then. The assembled gentlemen arranged some sketchy rules to govern the sport, contributed money toward the purchase of land and laid out plans for the building of a small house, which was to be known as "the clubhouse," at which all the members would meet.

Until about 1758, the Jockey Club did not take itself very seriously. Its interest chiefly was in races in which members intended to run horses, or in tracks where they proposed to campaign. The gentlemen soon became aware that certain abuses had come into the sport. Since no other group was interested in the development of clean racing, the Jockey Club took on the task and eventually became the Supreme Court in all disputes.

In 1762 the members decided that the colors of each should be registered with the club, and the first list included 18 names. The club made a few more rules changes. In 1780 it sanctioned a race among 2-year-olds. In 1786 the Prince of Wales was included as a member and from then on the Jockey Club became the recognized leader in turf affairs in England, and its regulations became the pattern for racing throughout the world.

It was ruled about 1790 that the membership of the Jockey Club be limited to 50, but that there could be additional members in honorary roles. There has not been any change since then.

The Jockey Club controls the "Stud-Book." In all instances of dispute, it rules what horses shall be or shall not be registered. A horse to be eligible must trace in direct line to one or another of the founding stallions, or he does not get his name into the "Stud-Book." There are no exceptions.

The fundamental rules for horse racing, as outlined 150 to 175 years ago by the pioneers of the Jockey Club in England, still govern the sport. There have been certain changes or additions to conform with the modernization of the sport, but breeders, owners, trainers, jockeys and racing officials still hew to the line that was drawn by the gentlemen who met long ago in the little coffeehouse in London.

RACING IN AMERICA

Horses were non-existent on the modern North American continent until the arrival of Cortez in 1519. He brought with him horses from Spain, most of them Arabians or Barbs. A number escaped while Cortez was sweeping westward through Mexico and by natural breeding they increased, starting the wild horse family in Mexico and Latin America.

The horse family in what now is the United States was founded by the animals brought here about 1540 by Francisco Vasquez Coronado, who rode northward from Mexico, crossing the Rio Grande, to explore a region that now is Kansas. He took 260 horses along on that journey and practically all escaped. These bred and multiplied. They roamed north into Canada, south into Mexico, and some of the Mexican horses came into the United States, while some French Normans, a huge type taken into Canada by the French settlers, escaped and joined the horses in what became the United States. This brought about the development of the wild horse of all sizes and shapes on the North American continent.

The history of horse racing in this country begins in New York State, and not in Virginia, as was popularly supposed. The first known turf race in Virginia was on April 10, 1674, which was 9 years after New York had put on a race, of which there is detailed record.

Col. Richard Nicolls, who arrived in 1664 as the first English Governor of New York, succeeding the Dutch governor, determined to start horse racing as one of his first acts. In February, 1665, after various conferences with his staff, he called a public meeting at what now is Hempstead, Long Island. He declared that he had decided upon a series of horse races, and added:

"These races shall not be so much for the divertisement of youth as for encouraging the bettering of the breed of horses which, through neglect, has been impaired."

Nicolls recognized the need for a better breed of horses than existed in the Colonies. Those horses, for the most part, were of a Dutch strain, having been imported by the Hollanders when they ruled the New York area. Such animals were heavy, slow and awkward. They were suitable for rough farm work, but lacked speed for horsebacking. Nicolls sought horses that had speed and, thus, encouraged racing, feeling that a succession of contests might develop swiftness in the animals.

As a result of the conclave, a race course was mapped out near Hempstead. It was called the "Newmarket Course," honoring a place in England. It is assumed there was a race at Hempstead in 1665, another in 1666 and another in 1667. But that is supposition. There is no documentary or other evidence. However, it is absolutely established that there was a race in March, 1668, because there now is among the Yale University collection of old silver, a porringer given to the winner of the 1668 contest. That piece of silver is regarded as the oldest of American manufacture.

On it is inscribed:

"1668, wunn att. hanstead planes."

The initials of the maker are P. V. B., which might have meant Peter Van Brough, famous Albany silversmith of that era.

Nothing on the dish establishes the identity of the winner, but a scroll, plus circumstances uncovered by a long investigation, would indicate that the victorious horse owner of 1668 was Captain Sylvester Salisbury, an English Army officer who was a conspicuous figure in those days.

Colonel Nicolls returned to England late in 1668. Governor Frank Lovelace, his successor, announced in 1669 that there would be a race at "Newmarket Course" for 2 silver cups, and that the subscription "is 1 crown each, or its equivalent in goode wheate,"—the first sweepstakes race in this country. Lovelace thus carried on the experiment started by Nicolls.

Final proof that New York, and not Virginia, was the cradle of horse racing in what now is the United States is found in the writings of Daniel Denton. He was a delegate to a religious assembly in New York in 1665. His father was the first minister of the historic Presbyterian Church, established in Hempstead in 1664. Denton, returning to England in 1670, wrote of Long Island:

"Toward the middle of the island lyeth a plain sixteen miles long and four broad, where you will find neither stick nor stone to hinder the horses' heels, or endanger them in their races, and once a year the best horses in the land are brought hither to try their swiftness. The swiftest are rewarded with a silver cup."

There is argument among historians as to which was the first pure thoroughbred brought to the colony from England. One faction states:

"Bully Rock was the first blooded English

racing stallion shipped to this country, and 1730 is the approximate year. Bully Rock was bred to (Dutch) American mares for several seasons. In 1738, or 1739, there was shipped to this country an English race mare, named Bay Bolton. She was bred to Bully Rock in 1740, and the foal was the first thoroughbred born on American soil."

Another group ignores the existence of both Bully Rock and Bay Bolton and declares:

"Sometime prior to 1750, Governor Ogle, of Maryland, owned a horse named Spark, which had been presented to him by Lord Baltimore, who also had imported Queen Mab, by Musgroves, a gray Arab mare, from England. Colonel Tasker, at about that time, imported Selima, a daughter of Godolphin's Arabian, and Colonel Colville imported a mare which he named Miss Colville, but which was registered in the English stud book as Wilkes Old Hautboy.

"Colonel Taylor imported Jenny Cameron, a mare, and it is further known that there was imported, about 1747, the stallion Monkey, by Lonsdale, a bay Arab, which was about 22 years old when brought here. A famous stallion—Jolly Roger—came here in about 1762, and he was followed in 1764 by Fearnaught, son of Regulus-Silvertail, and represented the best blood in England. Morton's Traveller was imported in 1768."

Although New York pioneered horse racing in the United States, Virginia gave it the greatest impetus through the 17th and into the 18th centuries. Some of the races were just for the "fun of it," others were for trophies put up by some community that wished to feature an equine duel, but most of them were for side bets with only 2 horses competing.

There were at least 5 race tracks in Virginia in the 1680's and in the Virginia State Library at Richmond is a notice concerning a horse race that was run in Henrico County in October, 1678.

The following facts concerning early racing on this continent are reprinted from "Annals of American Sport," Vol. XV, "The Pageant of America," (c) Yale University Press:

"As early as 1750 the New York Postboy (a newspaper) reported that 'upward of seventy chairs and chaises' and many more horses were carried across the Brooklyn ferry the day before the opening race at Newmarket (on Salisbury Plain, Long Island).

"For less formal race meetings especially those which settled disputes between the Morrisses and the De Lanceys, there were courses in Manhattan (New York City). A beautiful one lay in the region of the Lispenard meadows in Greenwich Village ... The De Lanceys maintained a private track fronting on the Bowery."

The Revolutionary War sent racing into eclipse for a while, but almost immediately afterward, there was a rapid recovery. Quite a few thoroughbred stallions, and some thoroughbred mares, were imported and put to stud services along the Atlantic Seaboard, while in Kentucky, the early settlers in the Lexington district not only concentrated on breeding horses, which they had brought from Virginia, but also went in for racing on a rather grand scale for that particular era.

The Kentuckians didn't wait for race tracks to settle their arguments as to which man had the better horse, or which was the superior rider. They put up their bets and rode a designated distance along the travelled byways of Lexington. Those races became of such frequent occurrence that the townsfolk who were not participating made a series of complaints.

In 1793 the town trustees of Lexington, Ky., ruled horsemen off the main street—now South Broadway—because the charging horses frightened the citizens. In 1797 there was erected outside of Lexington the first race track in Kentucky, known as "Williams Race Track." When this became too small and outmoded, a new one was built and opened in 1828. It continued to operate until 1935—a span of 107 years.

Mambrina, a thoroughbred filly, sired in England, by Mambrino, who also was sire of Messenger, famous in harness horse lore, appeared in the United States in 1787. She was then about 2 years old. In 1788, Messenger reached the United States by way of Philadelphia. Both Mambrina and Messenger were assigned to stud duty. In 1798, Diomed, winner of the first Epsom (English) Derby, reached here, being imported for breeding purposes by a Colonel Hoomes, perhaps of Virginia. Diomed cost Hoomes about $250.

Baronet, another thoroughbred, arrived soon afterward, and the flow of both thoroughbred stallions and mares to the United States increased through succeeding years.

Diomed lived to be about 30, and was a great success as a stallion. He sired, among others, Peacemaker, who raced a 2-mile heat, in 1803, under 168 pounds, in 3 minutes and 54 seconds. It remained as a record for almost 3 decades. Many other of Diomed's get, most of them produced through mating with mediocre mares, became noted for their high speed under saddle.

Duroc, bred to Miller's Damsel, a daughter of Messenger, produced American Eclipse, one of the most famous horses ever raced in the United States. He stepped along a 1-mile, 2-mile and 3-mile heats and outran everything sent against him. While he was being hailed by Northerners as the fastest horse in America, an audacious challenge came from the Southland.

Col. William R. Johnson of Peterburg, Va., heading a syndicate of "Southern gentlemen," asked whether the owner cared to race American Eclipse against the "champion of the South" for a side bet of $10,000, which was important money in that era. The colonel stated that the "champion of the South" had not been determined by the "Southern gentlemen," but that if the proposition were accepted, there would be elimination races, after which the "Southern gentlemen" would designate which horse was to race against American Eclipse.

The challenge was accepted, and the race was scheduled for the summer of 1823 at the Union Course on Long Island. When folks in New York and near-by places were told that a big delegation of Southern racing enthusiasts would accompany the "Southern champion" and would be prepared to wager heavily on him, the Northerners were in high glee. They figured that American Eclipse was the superior of every horse in the United States.

The colonel and a delegation from the Southland moved northward in the spring of 1823, taking along several horses. After various workouts, it was announced that John Richards was the one chosen to race against American Eclipse. But John Richards went lame, almost on the eve of the race, and the doughty colonel said that Henry, sometimes called Sir Henry, would be the substitute.

Reports have it that thousands of Southerners moved northward for the race and almost all visitors were rich with funds, to be bet on the Southern horse. The Northerners thought American Eclipse so superior to any horse in the world that they offered odds and took all bets, as specified by the canny gentlemen from the South. John C. Stevens, who later became part owner of the yacht "America," which won the international race with England in 1851, was among the 60,000 reported present at the Union Course, and Stevens, a heavy gambler, bet a fortune on American Eclipse to win.

The race was at 4-mile heats, best 2 of 3, and American Eclipse, by taking the second and third heats, won the race. This created an impression that the Northerners had profited handsomely on the race, but the truth is they had been outslicked by the wily Southerners, and actually were big losers.

In races, under the heat system, there is betting on each individual heat, and also on the race outcome. The folks from Dixieland avoided betting on the race itself. They wagered heavily on the result of the first heat. The Northerners, thinking American Eclipse was invincible, regardless of conditions, backed American Eclipse very handsomely for the first heat.

The result was a financial jolt for the citizens who had backed American Eclipse.

The folks from the South were well aware that American Eclipse, in a 3-heat race, could beat John Richards, Henry or any other horse. So they avoided betting on the outcome of the race itself. The big money went on Henry to beat American Eclipse in the first heat—that is, the Southern money went that way. The Northerners did not, at the time, realize they were being tricked.

The people from the New York region assumed that the "Southern gentlemen" would be shooting for the $10,000 purse, which is what the "slickers" from the South had hoped. The Northerners did not know the Johnson crowd was willing to lose the $10,000, for the chance to make a coup on the first heat.

Practically the entire bulk of the money brought up from the South was bet that Henry would win the first heat. The Northern crowd covered it, not knowing that the strategy of the Southerners called for Henry to win the first heat, even if it broke him down for the rest of the race.

The jockey on Henry called on his horse for utmost speed at "go" for the first heat and rode him at a dizzy rate for the entire 4 miles. The rider on American Eclipse, of course, refused to keep step with the flying Henry, since he wanted to conserve the energy of his horse for the succeeding heats, so as to win the $10,000.

Henry won the first heat, just as the clever Southern syndicate had figured, in 7:37½, which ranks as superlative speed for a 4-mile trip even to this day. The gentlemen from the South collected their winnings on the heat and generally ignored the offers of wagers on the second heat. They knew Henry had nothing left. Therefore, the boys in the North had little chance to win back any of their losses on the second and third heats, which were taken by American Eclipse in 7:49 and 8:42. Henry being beaten almost half a mile in the final heat.

After a lapse of 13 years, the same Colonel Johnson sauntered back into the picture with the suggestion for another North-South contest. The colonel said he had been hearing a lot about Post Boy, champion of the North, but he was sure his friend, Col. John Crowell of Alabama had a much faster horse in John Bascombe. Another race was arranged:

another bet of $10,000 per side was made; Union Race Course once more was chosen as the site and conditions were the same—best 2-of-3, each heat to be 4 miles. Another enormous crowd attended.

This time the Northerners determined not to be outsmarted by the gentlemen from the South. They stipulated that the wager on the outcome of the race itself must be equal to that on the first heat. The smiling Southerners agreed, and the result made the Southern crowd rich in funds once again.

On that occasion, the gentlemen from the South, knowing all about Post Boy's top speed and his durability and also knowing that John Bascombe was a truly great horse, figured they were operating with an ace in the hole. They bet the Northerners that John Bascombe would take the first heat, also the second heat, and that he would win in straight heats. They took $2 against their $1 that the Southern horse would win two heats in a row.

John Bascombe did not let them down. He won the first heat in 7:49, and the Southerners tossed their profits, and their original stake, betting he also would win the second. In horse terms, they played something of a parlay. John Bascombe won the second heat—and thus the race—in 7:57½, and Post Boy never was close.

Johnson and his jubilant troupe of "Southern gentlemen" then retired to the home acres, wealthier by far than they ever had been before. Estimates have been made fixing $1,000,000 as the sum the group won when Henry took that first heat, and another $1,000,000 when John Bascombe won both heats and the race.

Two other North-South contests featured racing in the 19th Century. The first was for the usual side bet of $10,000 involving Fashion, owned by William Gibbons of New Jersey, and Boston, owned by Nathaniel Reeves of Virginia. It was best 2-of-3 heats of 4 miles each, with the Union Race Course as the scene. The race was on May 20, 1842, and Fashion, one of the really great American Racers of the last century, won in straight heats, taking the first in 7:32, which was a world record, and the second in 7:45.

In 1845 there was another intersectional race, with Fashion again representing the North and Peytona, owned by Thomas Kirham of Alabama, solidly supported by the South. Fashion had grown old and the years had dulled his speed, but the Northerners thought that Fashion still was able to defeat any horse in the world. They wagered accordingly and rued the act. Peytona won in straight heats, 7:39¼ and 7:45¼. That just about ended the North-South racing, the Northerners being

"broke," and the Southerners needing no more cash.

The Civil War, which created such great demands for horses for cavalry purposes, made America aware of its need for the fastest type of horses. This focused attention upon horses of the thoroughbred species. A great number of American horses were cross breeds. Not many could be traced back directly to the 3 founding sires in England. Therefore, as soon as it was possible, wholesale importation of pure thoroughbreds, whose strain was not diluted with other blood, was started.

The present day American tribe of Fair Play horses traces back to Matchem, by way of the sire West Australian. The Herod blood flows in the veins of all the descendants of Lexington, perhaps the grandest of American stallions, and also is present in the Royal Minstrel group. Eclipse, through his son, the oddly named Pot-8-OS, comes down through the Ben Brush and Domino family in the United States.

Racing was given real impetus during the Civil War by John Morrissey, who launched the pioneer meeting at Saratoga Springs, N.Y., in 1864. Morrissey had been a bare-knuckle prize fighter in the days of his youth. Later he went into politics, and became wealthy. He settled in Saratoga and because he liked horse racing launched a meeting in that city where notables gathered.

Morrissey liked money and saw a chance to gain a lot of it with a race meeting at Saratoga during the month of August. The place then was a noted health resort, and folks had much idle time, especially in the afternoon. Morrissey built a race course, influenced horsemen to ship to Saratoga for a meeting, arranged stakes races and was liberal about purse money for the cheaper grade of horses.

The aristocratic Travers family of New York was identified with racing in the big city and so Morrissey, catering to the classes, named his first stakes race the "Travers." It still is being run and is the oldest contest of its kind in the United States.

The result of organized racing under Morrissey's control at Saratoga convinced men elsewhere that racing could be launched successfully in major fashion. Previously, the meetings had been of 1 or 2 days each. Marylanders constructed the Pimlico track for 1870 operations in Baltimore, and a group in New Orleans built the Fair Grounds course, the idea being to have reasonably prolonged meetings, as Morrissey had done at Saratoga. It was opened in 1873.

There had been racing of a sort in different parts of New York State, Virginia, Kentucky and elsewhere. There had been tracks of no great consequence both in Lexington and Louisville, Ky. But the sport took on "big time" status, in Kentucky with the opening of Churchill Downs in 1875. Tracks began to mushroom in or near the larger cities in all parts of the United States through the late 1870's and into the 1880's, during which time the importation of thoroughbreds from England greatly increased. Meanwhile, owners of horses established their own farms, and this brought about the breeding of the American thoroughbred, tracing down from the founding sires in England.

The earliest wagering in this country was just between owners or spectators, who had different ideas as to the outcome of the contests. Later, auction pools were introduced. Bookmakers made their first appearance on the new tracks about 1873. They were from England. The pioneer perhaps was James Kelly, who took pre-race bets about 1871, but did not operate at the tracks. After the English bookmakers had showed the way, Americans became bookmakers and supplanted them late in the 1870's.

Pari-mutuel wagering, which originated in 1865 in France, was tried in New York in the middle 1870's. It was not popular and soon was discarded. The machines were introduced at Churchill Downs in 1878, but were dropped in 1889. The bookmakers, who had to pay a rental to do business, complained that the machines, operated by the track, which deducted 5% of the money handled for its share, were interfering with the bookmakers' business.

Bookmaking, which was devised in England in the early part or middle of the 19th Century, was the only form of wagering on the New York tracks from the 1870's until 1940, when it was legislated out and pari-mutuels succeeded it. Bookmaking also was the only form of wagering in Kentucky from 1889 to 1908, when civic authorities in Louisville ruled against it and Col. Matt J. Winn resurrected the old pari-mutuel machines that had been used both in Kentucky and New York and used them, and also revived auction pool wagering "until the storm blows over" in Louisville.

The ban on bookmaking never was lifted in Louisville. Colonel Winn continued the mutuels and finally discarded the auction pools. The success of mutuels in Louisville influenced Pimlico and other tracks, harassed by authorities waging war on bookmakers, to use the machine form of wagering.

The "reform wave," which started to roll about 1906 and continued for quite a few years, ended major racing everywhere except in Kentucky and Maryland going into 1912. Track operators in both those states used pari-mutuel machines, and, thus, escaped condemnation. The success of the mutuels in Maryland and Kentucky caused legislatures, one by one, to legalize pari-mutuel wagering, even as they obliterated bookmaking, and, beginning in 1940, bookmaking was gone from all the states and machine wagering was legal in more than 20 states, with the blessings of the legislatures and the governors.

Racing from the time of Morrissey in the 1860's until into the 1890's moved along in the United States without much governing control. The stewards for each track made the rules. The racing people generally observed them. In any big crisis, an appeal for guidance was sent to the Jockey Club in London. The track operators, usually, worked on a "gentleman's agreement" basis, and there was little conflict in the schedules for race meetings.

Some small sectional groups took over supervision, in a minor way, of the affairs of racing in their own territories, but these hardly were of consequence. In time, abuses crept into the sport, and, as a result, a number of men, identified with racing in New York state, which was the axis of the sport in the United States, decided to create a jockey club that would control affairs.

The resultant Jockey Club of New York proceeded to control the sport.

The oldest turf organization of continuous existence in America is the Maryland Jockey Club, created in 1743 to supervise racing activities at the track then operated at Annapolis. The club never tried to expand its power beyond the borders of Maryland, but it continued to be the sole governing force in the state until creation of the State Racing Commission.

Racing in New York*

It was some 300-odd years ago that New York became incorporated as a city. It was about 12 years later that New Yorkers first had a formally laid-out race course to patronize and quite a few years later—April of 1903—when Jamaica opened its doors and provided the reason for 1953's Golden Jubilee, which was climaxed at this course by the $100,000 Wood Memorial.

Racing came to the district, as it came to every other part of the world, when the first pair of owners decided to prove who had the faster horse. But it was not until the English took Nieuw Amsterdam from the Dutch and re-christened it New York in honor of the Duke of York, that any formal racing took place. That was in 1665, a year that, incidentally, saw the city's first mayor, Tom Willett from Plymouth who had been appointed to serve in this capacity.

*From New York Racing Associations Service Bureau's Press information Booklet.

It wasn't the first mayor, however, but the first colonial governor, Richard Nicolls, who inaugurated a meeting on the flatlands of Long Island known as the Hempstead Plain, not far from the site of present-day Belmont Park. This was the first known race track in America and the museum at Yale University owns the first known trophy, a silver porringer discovered about 60 years ago in a New York shop and bearing the inscription: "1668. wunn att. hanstead planes."

Jamaica started in 1902 when a wooded section of sparsely populated country was cleared and work started on a race course. Jimmy Holmes, now working with Bert Morgan in track photography but from his boyhood a follower of racing, has recalled these days in an article published by The Blood-Horse.

"There were two ways of reaching it," he writes, "by the Long Island Railroad, or by a dinky trolley-car line which left from old Washington (now 160th Street) and Jamaica Avenue. It opened on April 27th, 1903. The first officials were William H. Reynolds, president; Philip J. Dwyer, manager; George F. Dobson, secretary, and Walter E. Edwards, racing secretary. Edward Maher was track superintendent and Chris J. FitzGerald the starter.

"Jamaica presented a far different appearance than it does today. There was a huge wooden grandstand with betting shed and field stand alongside. A five-furlong chute, which may have been used once but never thereafter, extended from the upper turn. A highly ornamental club house, a saddling shed (the only building now left) and a jockey house completed the appointments. Stables were in the corner adjacent to Baisley Boulevard.

"The opening, which followed the spring meeting at Aqueduct, greeted such belles and beaux as Lillian Russell, glamor girl of her time, and 'Diamond Jim' Brady. Such bigtime gamblers as 'Bet-a-million' Gates, John A. Drake, Davy Johnson, W. E. D. Stokes, Louis V. Bell and Alex Shields were giving much business to 65 bookmakers in the 'big ring,' including such as Morty Lynch, 'Humming Bird' Tyler, Johnny Walters and Eddie Burke.

"Owners' names appearing in the program included William C. Whitney, August Belmont, Sydney Paget, James R. Keene, Davy Johnson, and Richard T. Wilson. Nationally known jockeys of the period were George Odom, Johnny Bullman, Willie Shaw, Grover Cleveland Fuller, Tommy Burns and Frank O'Neill.

"Feature of the opening day and one of the early spring classics of the time was the Excelsior Handicap, a jaunt of 1-1/16 miles for a purse of $10,000. The winner was

Blackstock, a four-year old bay colt by Hanover—Mannie Himyar, by Himyar, bred and owned by the Hon. William C. Whitney, trained by John W. Rogers and ridden by Fuller."

From that beginning, Jamaica has continued to play a major part in the sport in New York, and in the nation. It was at this plant on Memorial Day of 1945 that the biggest crowd in the history of New York racing—and one of the four or five biggest race crowds of America—came to watch the day's sport, 64,670 by a turnstile count.

Always very popular with the average race follower in New York, Jamaica played a prominent role in racing's war effort during World War II when it was used frequently for the combined meetings of the New York Racing Associations when they raised millions for the war effort.

Jamaica, of course, is not the oldest in New York. Here in the Metropolitan area, Aqueduct owns that distinction, having been opened for its inaugural meet on Sept. 27, 1894. And upstate at Saratoga Springs, where racing's national museum is maintained, there is the oldest active race course in America, the Historic Union Avenue course of the Saratoga Association to which the leading horses and racing figures repair each season during the month of August. The guns of Gettysburg had not been long silent when the first meeting was held at Saratoga on the morning of Aug. 2, 1864.

Though Governor Nicolls' course on the Hempstead Plains was the first carefully laid out one in New York—as well as the country—there were others that continued to mushroom in or right outside the city, only to be overgrown by the rapidly expanding metropolis. This continued up to the first days of this century, when Brooklyn had something like 3 half-milers, and from 1880 to 1910 Brooklyn and Long Island (of which Brooklyn is a part) had at times as many as 6 major tracks in operation.

Some historians claim a crowd of 75,000 for a North-South match race held during the 1850's at the old Union Avenue Course, which was at about the juncture of Rockaway Boulevard and Atlantic Avenue. It was probably a smaller crowd, but these events drew tremendous interest and extras were published by the papers of the day.

Sheepshead Bay, Gravesend and Brighton Beach were 3 sites where racing's tradition in New York had its foundation. Nowadays there is little "Winter Book" activity. Back then, winter books were very active on the Brooklyn Handicap at Gravesend and the Suburban at Sheepshead Bay.

But much, much earlier than these events,

there was the first stakes ever run in New York, over a course—exact location lost in time—somewhere on Manhattan Island. It was called the New York Subscription Plate, first run in 1725. In the Metropolitan Museum of Art there is a silver bowl on which is inscribed "This Plate won by a Horse cal'd Old Tenor Belonging to Lewis Morris, Jun'r, Octb're ye 11, 1751."

According to the carefully prepared "Thoroughbred Racing and Breeding," put out by the Thoroughbred Racing Associations of the United States, "It was at the course on Church Farm, so called because it was one of the holdings of Trinity Church, that the first known business venture in race track management was made. Management of the Church Farm in 1736 was in the hands of one Francis Child, who also happened to be the innkeeper in the vicinity. Child advertised in the New York Gazette that: 'All persons coming into the field, the subscribers and winning horses only excepted, are to pay six pense each to the owner of the grounds.'"

Some of the richest tradition of racing in New York—which saw the foundation of a great many of the stakes now carried on at Belmont Park—was born in the tracks to the north of the city, or in its northern boroughs, during the closing days of the past century and the opening ones of this.

These were Jerome Park, located in the Fordham district, and Morris Park, about 2 miles to the East. Jerome Park was brought into being and took its name from Leonard W. Jerome the maternal grandfather of Winston Churchill. He purchased land from the Bathgate estate in 1865 and Jerome Park was opened in 1866. For a good many years it flourished as a center for polo, coaching parties and various forms of horse sport as well as racing.

In 1887 it became apparent the city was about to take over Jerome Park and John A. Morris, grandfather of the present president of Jamaica, who, with his father Francis Morris—whose filly, Ruthless, had won the first running of the Belmont Stakes—had been in racing for a good many years, was asked to find a new site. He first favored Van Cortlandt Park, but soon learned the city had other plans for this site also and finally settled on a spot about 2 miles East of Jerome Park.

Racing opened at Morris Park in August, 1889, and it continued through 1904. The Westchester Racing Association had organized and leased Morris Park in 1895 and it carred over to Belmont in 1905 many of the traditional races. It was, for instance, at Jerome Park that the Belmont Stakes was run for the first time, and it continued through the racing at Morris, shifting to Belmont with

the opening there.

So racing started its second half-century at Jamaica with 1953 and approaches its fourth century in the country, carrying with it a tradition handed down from the men and women who carved a country out of the wilderness they found here in the new world.

In 1955, a nonprofit organization, eventually called the New York Racing Association, bought the four tracks in New York State and embarked on a program of improvement. The group, composed of leading men in horse racing, worked out a plan designed to make the sport more attractive. Renovation costing millions was made at Belmont and Saratoga and construction of a new track and plant at Aqueduct was started. Jamaica was scheduled to be abandoned when the new Aqueduct track was ready to open in 1959.

The Jockey Club*

Racing today is spread throughout the United States; it takes place during all four seasons of the year and millions of persons attend. It is not any exaggeration to say the pattern for all of this was laid by The Jockey Club. Wherever racing is held in the country, the basic principles under which it is conducted were laid down by The Jockey Club.

There has, of course, been horse racing in this country since colonial time, but it is only during the past 50 years or so, dating to the closing years of the past century, that the sport has had uniformity of rules and administration. These grew out of the desire of the horsemen themselves, the men racing, who were anxious to have a recognizable pattern of racing wherever they might go.

Prior to 1891 each racing association operated under rules of its own making. At that time a board of control was established in New York, with its members including racing associations as well as owners, but the divergent interests of the group prevented the uniformity that was sought. So in 1893 a meeting of owners and trainers was held and the following resolutions adopted:

"It is proposed at the instance of and at the request of a large number of the owners and breeders in the United States that a Jockey Club be formed with a roll of, say, fifty.

"Its purpose to be, not only to encourage the development of the Thoroughbred horse, but to establish racing on such a footing that it may command the interest as well as the confidence and favorable opinion of the public.

"That this Club shall be formed with a

*From New York Racing Associations Service Bureau's Press Information Booklet.

membership as above stated, which is to include the present members of the Board of Control, or such of them as may be in accord with the purposes and objects which they proposed new organization is intended to accomplish, viz.:

"First: To establish a firm authority over all racing upon all the Associations' courses which may come under its control.

"Second: To punish offenders against accepted racing laws.

"Third: To protect the interests of the public and thereby insure its confidence and support.

"Fourth: To maintain and disperse exact justice in respect to all questions pertaining to racing, or the interests of racing, which may affect the welfare of the associations which may race under the rules of this proposed organization and which are incident to the ownership of properties."

The Jockey Club was incorporated in February, 1894, and since then its aims and purposes have been as expressed in the resolution calling for the formation. Soon after its inception, it adopted Rules of Racing, based on those that the English Jockey Club had in force after 140 years of experience. These rules, with amendments and modernizations, are the rules under which races are held in the United States.

As racing, under the impetus of pari-mutuel popularity, spread throughout the country, various states enacted racing laws and set up commissions to supervise the sport. In New York the State Racing Commission came into being at about the same time as The Jockey Club and together they have conducted the sport in the state.

The Jockey Club continued to offer advice and aid wherever it could in setting up racing and, on the occasion of the club's 50th anniversary in 1944, the National Association of State Racing Commissioners adopted a resolution of appreciation for presentation to The Jockey Club that praised "its constant diligence and supervision (which) has brought the sport to a peak of high efficiency in supervision (and) wishes it continued success in its endeavors to improve the sport."

Today probably the biggest part of The Jockey Club's work is in the registration bureau at its offices at 250 Park Avenue, New York City. Here the name, breeding and pertinent facts about every thoroughbred horse racing in the country are filed and cross-indexed.

This, or course, is part of the task of maintaining the American Stud Book. The first attempt to maintain a record of American racing was made in 1829 with the

publication of the "American Turf Register and Sport Magazine." In 1868, Col. Saunders D. Bruce began the publication of "The American Stud Book" to record the pedigree of the American thoroughbred. The Jockey Club took over the custody of the American Stud Book in 1896 and its careful guardianship assures the purity of breed and protection to breeders and the race-going public.

There is one room at The Jockey Club that is not like an office. This is the library and the board room. Here, in locked bookcases which line the walls, are old publications priceless in their historical value and the walls are hung with some of the finest racing paintings in the world. In this room are held the meetings of officers and stewards (directors), who have set so much of the style of racing through the years.

In another part of the offices, elaborate color files are maintained where a new owner can learn immediately whether the colors he wants already are in use and where owners can register this identification for life if they desire.

Among other things done by The Jockey Club is the maintenance of its breeding bureau at Avon, N.Y., where stallions and, quite frequently, mares donated by members are made available to farmers and breeders at minimum cost. For years, for instance, William Woodward's Triple Crown winner, Omaha, stood at a stud fee of $15.

The Jockey Club established, contributes to and, through its stewards, operates The Jockey Club Foundation for the benefit of deserving and impoverished persons, such as trainers and jockeys, who formerly participated in racing and The Jockey Club chairman administers a $250,000 charitable trust set up in 1932 by the late John G. Cavanagh for the purpose.

The club maintains during the racing season a regular training program for officials, designed to produce men capable of handling the specialized work of conducting a race meeting. This course had been opened to all members of the Thoroughbred Racing Associations of the United States by The Jockey Club without charge and there have been men taking the course from many states and from Canada and Cuba.

The club maintains a record of all leases of horses between owners, partnership agreements and the assumed names under which horses are raced, establishing a record of persons interested directly or indirectly in a particular horse.

There are 3 officers of the club—chairman, vice chairman and secretary-treasurer—and 9 stewards, whose duties are those of directors and whose terms of office are divided so that they will not expire simultaneously. None of the officers or stewards receives any recompense.

Thoroughbred Racing Associations of the United States, Inc.

(Courtesy of John I. Day Jr., T.R.A.)

While each race track is an integral part of the racing industry as a whole, each was, until the early 1940's, an independent operation. In the decade preceding Pearl Harbor, racing had been undergoing a noticeable expansion as more and more state governments recognized it as a source of revenue and enacted sponsoring legislation.

When suddenly the country found itself at war, the need for unified action by thoroughbred racing became all the more apparent. In March of 1942 representatives of all phases of thoroughbred racing met in Chicago to plan the coordination of the sport's adjustment to war conditions.

Out of that meeting came the formation of the Thoroughbred Racing Associations of the United States, Inc., nationally known today as the T.R.A. Twenty-two race tracks were represented in the organization of T.R.A. and by December of 1942, when the body held its first annual meeting, it had a membership of 32 tracks. In 1962 there were 46, and by 1973, there were 53 tracks listed.

The following tracks are members of TRA:

Popular Name	Corporate Name	Location
Ak-Sar-Ben	Knights of Ak-Sar-Ben	Omaha, Neb.
Aqueduct	New York Racing Association, Inc.	Ozone Park, N.Y.
Arizona Downs	Arizona Downs, Inc.	Phoenix, Arizona
Assiniboia Downs	Assiniboia Enterprises Ltd.	Winnipeg, Canada
Atlantic City	Atlantic City Racing Association, Inc.	McKee City, N.J.
Belmont Park	New York Racing Association Inc.	Elmont, New York
Blue Bonnets	Blue Bonnets Raceway, Inc.	Montreal Canada
Bowie	Southern Maryland Agricultural Association	Bowie, Maryland
Calder	Calder Race Course, Inc.	Miami, Florida
Centennial	Centennial Turf Club, Inc.	Littleton, Colo.
Churchill Downs	Churchill Downs, Inc.	Louisville, Ky.
Continental	Continental Thoroughbred Racing Assoc.	Philadelphia, Pa.
Cranwood	Cranwood Racing Club, Inc.	North Randall, Ohio
Delaware Park	Delaware Racing Association	Stanton, Delaware
Detroit	Detroit Racing Association, Inc.	Livonia, Michigan
Eagle Downs	Eagle Downs Racing Association	Philadelphia, Pa.
Exhibition Park	British Columbia Jockey Club	Vancouver, B.C.
Finger Lakes	Finger Lakes Racing Association, Inc.	Farmington, N.Y.
Florida Downs	Florida Downs & Turf Club	Oldsmar, Fla.
Fort Erie	The Ontario Jockey Club	Fort Erie, Canada
Great Barrington	Barrington Fair Association	Great Barrington, Mass.
Green Mountain	Green Mountain Racing Corp.	Pownal, Vermont
Greenwood	The Ontario Jockey Club	Toronto, Canada
Hialeah	Hialeah Park, Inc.	Hialeah, Florida
Hollywood Park	Hollywood Turf Club	Inglewood, Calif.
Keeneland	Keeneland Association, Inc.	Lexington, Ky.
La Mesa Park	Northeastern New Mexico Fair Association	Raton, N.M.
Latonia	Kentucky Jockey Club	Florence, Kentucky
Laurel	Laurel Race Course, Inc.	Laurel, Maryland
Lincoln Downs	Burrillville Racing Association	Lincoln, R.I.
Longacres	Washington Jockey Club	Renton, Wash.
Marlboro	Southern Maryland Agricultural Fair Association	Upper Marlboro, Md.
Miles Park	Louisville Racing Corporation	Louisville, Ky.
Monmouth Park	Monmouth Park Jockey Club	Oceanport, N.J.
Narragansett Park	Narragansett Racing Association	Pawtucket, R.I.
Northampton	Hampshire, Franklin & Hampden Agricultural Soc.	Northampton, Mass.
Oaklawn Park	Oaklawn Jockey Club	Hot Springs, Ark.
Oak Tree	Oak Tree Racing Association	Arcadia, Calif.
Penn National	Pennsylvania National Turf, Inc.	Grantville, Pa.
Pimlico	The Maryland Jockey Club	Baltimore, Md.
Playfair	Inland Empire Racing Association, Inc.	Spokane, Wash.
Randall	Randall Racing Club, Inc.	Cleveland, Ohio
Rockingham Park	The New Hampshire Jockey Club, Inc.	Salem Depot, N.H.

Santa Anita	Los Angeles Turf Club, Inc.	Arcadia, Calif.
Santa Fe Downs	Santa Fe Downs, Inc.	Santa Fe, New Mexico
Saratoga	New York Racing Association, Inc.	Saratoga Springs, N.Y.
Shamrock	Shamrock Association, Inc.	Wilkes-Barre, Pa.
Summit	Summit Racing Club, Inc.	North Randall, Ohio
Thistledown	Thistledown Racing Club, Inc.	Warrensville, Ohio
Timonium	Maryland State Fair & Agricultural Society of Baltimore County	Timonium, Md.
Tropical Park	Tropical Park, Inc.	Miami, Florida
Turf Paradise	Turf Paradise, Inc.	Phoenix, Arizona
Woodbine	The Ontario Jockey Club	Ontario, Canada

The immediate activities of T.R.A. were obvious. Besides meeting with such Washington agencies as the ODT, OPA and WMC, the T.R.A. facilitated the setting up of relief programs at race tracks that met with the approval of the Bureau of Internal Revenue and that, under the auspices of the Turf Committee of America, netted over $25,000,000 for various war agencies and charities.

Meanwhile, the T.R.A. also served as a coordinating factor in the relationship between the race tracks and other groups in racing such as The Jockey Club, the National Association of State Racing Commissioners, the American Trainers' Association, the Jockeys' Guild and the Horsemen's Benevolent and Protective Association.

The long-range objectives of the group were stated in the certificate of incorporation as follows:

"To promote and coordinate the patriotic and charitable activities of the thoroughbred racing associations of the United States; to maintain and promote public interest in thoroughbred racing; to improve the operations affecting thoroughbred racing; to prepare and distribute information of all kinds which may be useful in developing and improving the business of the thoroughbred racing associations of the United States."

It is obvious that the organizers of the T.R.A. were thinking beyond the duration of the war and recognized the need for organization and co-operative thought which had been felt for some years.

Plans which had been formulated prior to the war's end were put in effect a few months after the conflict terminated with the setting up of a national organization of an investigative nature known as the Thoroughbred Racing Protective Bureau, under the direction of Spencer J. Drayton, executive secretary. Drayton assembled a staff of investigators for the most part made up of men with previous experience in the Federal Bureau of Investigation. The new organization started functioning on Jan. 15, 1946.

By the middle of 1946, the T.R.P.B. was in full operation, with headquarters in New York City—field offices in Baltimore, Chicago and Los Angeles and seasonal offices in Boston, Miami and New Orleans. The T.R.P.B. is wholly finanaced by the member tracks of the T.R.A. at an average annual cost of about $450,000. Member tracks, in all, spend over $3,000,000 each year to insure that the public is furnished an honest, clean racing spectacle, as well as to protect their patrons from undesirables.

Nor was racing content to rest once the Thoroughbred Racing Protective Bureau was organized and functioning. In 1947 the T.R.A. adopted a code of standards which was, in effect, a forthright statement of policy for thoroughbred racing.

The code constituted one of the most stringent regulatory measures ever voluntarily adopted by any sport or industry and it has met with the full approval of other groups in the sport, such as The Jockey Club, American Trainers' Association, the National Association of State Racing Commissioners and other horsemen's and breeders' organizations.

T.R.A. Code of Standards

SECTION I

Racing—Racing must be honest and highly competitive, and, as a spectacle, must be vitally interesting and entertaining. There are fundamentally two groups to be served, the spectators and the contestants.

All member tracks of the association must be certain that these fundamental principles are fully maintained. Any failure will merit and receive prompt punitive action.

SECTION II

Reporting of Corrupt Practices or Violations of the Rules of Racing—Each member track of the association shall institute and require observance of the following rule: Any official or employee of a member track of the association, or any person engaged in racing during the meeting, or his employees, or any badge holder, who (1) is approached in any manner by any person attempting to bribe or to fix or otherwise influence the result of any racing contest; (2) or who shall come into possession of knowledge concerning any violation of the Rules of Racing or any violation of law in connection with the running of a race, shall immediately report the information to the stewards of the race course for complete investigation by the Thoroughbred Racing Protective Bureau, and for such other action on the part of the stewards as the case may warrant or as may be required by the rules of the State Racing Commission.

SECTION III

"Come-back" Money—No member track of the association shall provide or permit to be provided any convenience or facilities for the use of bookmakers, betting commissioners, their agents, or their employees. No facilities will be provided or permitted for the handling of "come-back" money at the track. The maintenance of credit accounts, the payment of commissions in any form, the providing of telephone or other communication services and any other form of aid to bookmakers, betting commissioners, their agents, or their employees will be prohibited.

SECTION IV

Wire Services—Member tracks of the association may grant wire service privilege and any other form of communication service privileges only to legitimate and approved news outlets which do not directly or indirectly service bookmakers, betting commissioners or their agents or employees.

SECTION V

Touting and Tip Sheets—It is desirable to protect the public while in attendance at race tracks from the activities of individuals engaged in touting. The hawking of touting propositions or tip sheets on the property of race tracks is a highly undesirable practice and lowers the status of racing and shall be prohibited.

This does not preclude the sale of newspapers, racing publications and approved selectors sheets at designated places.

SECTION VI

Fingerprinting—In order to protect the public and to prevent undesirable individuals from engaging in horse racing, each member track of the association shall require that all of its officers, officials and employees, and concessionnaires and their employees be fingerprinted. Further, it shall be required that all those actively participating in racing horses at a member track be fingerprinted.

SECTION VII

Jockey Club Registration Certificates—Each member track of the association shall require that The Jockey Club Registration Certificate of each horse brought to the track be delivered on arrival to a designated official of the track, to be retained by such official until the departure of the horse.

A receipt for the certificate shall be given to the owner and the member track shall assume responsibility for the certificate until its return to the proper owner.

Commencing with foals of 1950, each member track shall require that all transfers of title be properly recorded in the space provided on the reverse side of The Jockey Club Registration Certificate. Any transfers not so recorded will not be recognized and the Thoroughbred will be ineligible to start—except that the Stewards of the meeting may excuse any horse from this requirement for cause, permitting it to start and providing an opportunity for the owner to meet this requirement.

SECTION VIII

Delegation of Responsibility of Management—No member track of the association shall permit encroachment by any individual group, committee, or organization upon the functions of management.

(a) The allotment of stall space for any race meeting shall be considered the sole and exclusive function of the member track of the association. In performing this responsibility, no member track shall delegate or share this responsibility with any individual, committee, group or organization. Each member track of the association, in alloting stall space, shall be guided by the primary consideration of securing the best available competition and maintaining the highest standards of racing.

(b) The appointment of stewards and other racing officials shall be the sole and exclusive responsibility of the racing association. This responsibility shall not be delegated to or shared by any individual, committee, group or organization except in those cases where such delegation or sharing of responsibilities is required by law.

SECTION IX

Awards and Bonuses to Non-employees—No member track of the association shall pay awards or bonuses to anyone other than the owners, breeders or nominators of the horses in any contest. This regulation does not apply to payments to employees of the racing association.

SECTION X

Solicitation of Competition—No member track of the association shall solicit competition for races by offering to, or paying, owners, trainers, or jockeys, monetary inducements in any form, including expenses other than the advertised purses or trophies. A member track, however, may defray the expenses of competitors coming from or returning to places outside the continental limits of the United States. Proper vanning expenses may be paid by a track from stables in immediate vicinity.

No member track shall attempt to procure entries by assigning unfair weights and/or by divulging handicap weights before the scheduled time of their publication.

SECTION XI

Solicitation of Wagering—The solicitation of wagering by track management through the use of public address or other similar means shall be prohibited.

This provision does not preclude the periodic announcement concerning post time and the daily double.

SECTION XII

Night Racing—There shall be no racing between sunset and sunrise.

SECTION XIII

Safety and Security—As a responsibility to the public, it is incumbent upon member tracks of the association at all times to provide facilities that afford safety and security.

Member tracks of the association shall make every effort to eliminate any condition which constitutes a possible hazard in this respect.

Each member track of the association shall take steps to install protective facilities in the stable areas and paddocks in order to prevent tampering with horses or the soliciting of personnel in these areas to engage in illegal activities.

Member tracks of the association will give earnest consideration to all recommendations submitted by the Thoroughbred Racing Protective Bureau pertaining to matters of safety and security.

SECTION XIV

Cooperation with Officials of the Thoroughbred Racing Associations and the Thoroughbred Racing Protective Bureau—Each member track of the Thoroughbred Racing Associations shall cooperate in furnishing to the officials of the Thoroughbred Racing Associations such information as the officials, acting in their official capacity, may request and which may be of benefit to the Thoroughbred Racing Associations as a whole. The member tracks of the association, when information comes to their attention regarding individuals, conditions, or practices detrimental to racing, shall transmit such information to the Thoroughbred Racing Protective Bureau for consideration, correlation and appropriate action.

SECTION XV

Penalties for Non-compliance with Code—In the event a member track of the association violates any provision of this code the directors of the Thoroughbred Racing Associations may—after informing the association member a hearing thereon—suspend or expel that member from the Thoroughbred Racing Associations, providing, however, a vote of a majority of the entire membership of the board of directors shall be required for such suspension or expulsion.

SECTION XVI

Conflicts with State and Local Laws—In the event that any provisions of this code are in conflict with any state statutes, local ordinances, or rules of state racing commissions, such provisions are to be considered modified to conform with such statutes or ordinances.

SECTION XVII

Tattoo Branding for Identification—No thoroughbred shall be permitted to start at a member track unless The Jockey Club Registration Certificate number has been officially tattooed by the T.R.P.B. beneath the upper lip of the horse for identification purposes—except that the stewards of the meeting may excuse any horse from this requirement for cause, permitting it to start and providing an opportunity for the owner to meet the tattoo requirement.

SECTION XVIII

No member track at any time shall knowingly permit or knowingly tolerate betting with bookmakers, betting commissioners, their agents or employees either on the track or by telephone or by other communication to or from the track.

SECTION XIX

Any activity, conduct or association on the part of officers or directors of a member track that brings justifiable public criticism against the member track, the Association or Thoroughbred racing constitutes grounds for suspension or expulsion.

National Museum of Racing
Saratoga Springs, N.Y.

A number of outstanding figures in the horse racing world organized the National Museum of Racing, Inc. A charter was granted by the New York State Board of Regents in October, 1950, Mrs. Elaine E. Mann, executive secretary of the Museum reports.

The purpose of the organization was to establish a museum for the collection, preservation and exhibition of books, documents, statuary, paintings, films, memorials and any and all kinds of articles associated with the history and development of horse racing and the breeding of thoroughbred horses.

The displays were housed in Canfield's Casino 1951 to 1954. The cornerstone for the present building, which is situated directly across from Saratoga Racetrack, the oldest operating track in the United States, was laid in April, 1955, and the formal opening, attended by Gov. W. Averell Harriman of New York, was held in August, 1955. In 1957 a wing was added to house paintings of distinguished persons dedicated to racing.

In the Museum's collection are more than 100 portraits of great American horses, including Man o' War, Exterminator, Fair Play, Equipoise and Nashua. In addition there are gold and silver trophies, racing plates, bronze statuettes, 160 sets of famous racing silks and portraits of jockeys.

A notable part of the Museum is the Hall of Fame in which tribute is paid to outstanding horses, jockeys and trainers.

Following are those enshrined in the Hall of Fame:

Hall of Fame

HORSES (Year of Birth)

Armed (1941)	Dr. Fager (1964)	Jolly Roger (1922)	Regret (1912)
Artiful (1902)	Eclipse (1888)	Kingston (1884)	Roseben (1909)
Beldame (1901)	Elkridge (1938)	Lexington (1850)	Salvator (1886)
Ben Brush (1893)	Equipoise (1928)	Longfellow (1867)	Sarazen (1921)
Blue Larkspur (1926)	Exterminator (1915)	Luke Blackburn	Seabiscuit (1933)
Boston (1833)	Fair Play (1905)	(1877)	Sir Archy (1805)
Broomstick (1901)	Gallant Fox (1927)	Man o' War (1917)	Sir Barton (1916)
Buckpasser (1963)	Gallorette (1942)	Miss Woodford	Swaps (1952)
Bushranger (1930)	Good and Plenty	(1880)	Sysonby (1902)
Cicada (1959)	(1900)	Nashua (1952)	Tom Fool (1949)
Citation (1945)	Grey Lag (1918)	Native Dancer (1950)	Top Flight (1929)
Colin (1905)	Hanover (1884)	Neji (1950)	Twenty Grand (1928)
Commando (1898)	Hindoo (1878)	Old Rosebud (1911)	Twilight Tear (1941)
Count Fleet (1940)	Imp (1894)	Omaha (1932)	War Admiral (1934)
Discovery (1931)	Jay Trump (1957)	Peter Pan (1904)	Whirlaway (1938)
Domino (1891)	Kelso (1957)		

TRAINERS

Guy Bedwell	John M. Gaver	H.A. Jones	James Rowe, Sr.
P.M. Burch	T.J. Healey	A.J. Joyner	D.M. Smithwick
W.P. Burch	Sam Hildreth	Henry McDaniel	H.J. Thompson
J. Dallett Byers	Max Hirsch	William Molter	M.H. VanBerg
William Duke	John Hyland	W.F. Mulholland	Robert W. Walden
Frank E. Childs	Hirsch Jacobs	John Rogers	William Winfrey
James E. Fitzsimmons	B.A. Jones		

JOCKEYS

Frank D. Adams (s)	Henry Griffin	Isaac Murphy	Earl Sande
John H. Adams	William Hartack	Ralph Neves	Carroll Schilling
Edward Arcaro	Charles Kurtsinger	Joseph Notter	Bill Shoemaker
Ted Atkinson	William Knapp	Winnie O'Connor	James Stout
Steve Brooks	John Loftus	George Odom	Todhunter Sloan
Frank Coltiletti	John Longden	Frank O'Neill	Fred Taral
Buddy Ensor	Danny Maher	Gil Patrick	Nash Turner
Laverne Fator	Linus McAtee	Sam Purdy	George Woolf
Mack Garner	James McLaughlin	John Reiff	Raymond Workman
Edward Garrison	Walter Miller	Alfred Robertson	

(s) Steeplechase rider.

New York Racing Association

In 1955, a new idea in the operation of horse racing tracks was germinated and now appears to be bearing fruit. The new idea was that of nonprofit operation of New York State's tracks. Because the corporations running the state's track found their shares of mutuel take inadequate and for other reasons, the physical facilities were allowed to fall into disrepair. The deterioration was going on while attendance at racing meets was increasing rapidly. It became apparent to prominent persons in the field that something had to be done if New York racing was to be kept on a first-class plane.

A number of these prominent persons who were interested in thoroughbred horse racing studied the situation and came up with the idea of a nonprofit organization to conduct racing in the state. At first the group was called the Greater New York Association. The name later was changed to the New York Racing Association. The group succeeded in getting favorable legislation of Albany, the state capital. A 25-year franchise was granted and the state made concessions in the matter of take. This enabled the association to obtain loans from banks for the purpose of purchasing the four state tracks, Belmont, Aqueduct, Jamaica and Saratoga, and for plant improvements. It was decided to improve the Belmont and Saratoga tracks, build a completely new track and plant at Aqueduct and eventually abandon Jamaica. The total cost was estimated at about $60,000,000.

Horseman's Benevolent and
Protective Association

Probably the largest racing organization is the Horsemen's Benevolent and Protective Association, consisting of about 17,000 owners, breeders and trainers of thoroughbred horses. Comprising 15 geographical divisions in this country and Canada, which is subdivided into three regions, the H.B.P.A., as the horsemen call their group, was founded in 1940 and was the outgrowth of a horsemen's organization started that year at Rockingham Park, Salem, N.H., by Philip Bieber, a young horse owner and trainer from New York. Bieber was the first president of his brain child, then known as the "Horse Retirement Fund." The organization was originally designed to eliminate bad racing stock by paying their owners to retire them, but the group abandoned the idea and later included a charitable and benevolent program. It was incorporated under the name of the Horsemen's Benevolent and Protective Association.

Sunny Jim Fitzsimmons, famous as the developer of Gallant Fox, Omaha, Johnstown and many other great horses, was the first national president, and Judge Joseph A. Murphy, a racing official, the first national adviser.

During the years the organization has dispensed about $1,500,000 for doctors' bills and charity among racing people. During the course of racing disasters, such as the "Swamp Fever" epidemic of 1948 and various race track fires it has raised another $100,000 to help racing people.

In addition, it has carried on a persistent campaign resulting in the increase by millions of dollars of purse distribution by the race tracks, sometimes with the members refusing to race their horses when the tracks failed to provide what the organization has felt were equitable purses. The H.B.P.A. also has campaigned for improved living conditions on the backstretch for the men who care for the horses and must live with them to properly attend to their duties.

Members are quick to point out that the H.B.P.A. is not a trade union, that its members perform no services for hire, but that the organization is what its name implies, a benevolent and protective group safeguarding the interests of those who have capital invested in thoroughbred

breeding and racing stock. The only dues paid are a 1 per cent (maximum $25) deduction of each purse that the owner's or trainer's horses win.

National headquarters are at Suite 1038, Pennsylvania Bldg., 425 13th St., N.W., Washington, D.C. 20004.

Steeplechase Racing

The first jumping race in the United States was a hurdle contest in 1834, at the Washington (D.C.) Jockey Club Park "for gentlemen (amateur) riders."

Jumping courses were built in many of the tracks of other days, but many were abandoned, and jumping races have been continued only at these major tracks: Belmont, Aqueduct and Saratoga, in New York; Delaware Park, near Wilmington; Pimlico, Laurel, and Agua Caliente, Mex.

However, a great many hunt clubs are banded in the National Steeplechase and Hunt Association and feature steeplechasing and hurdling.

BETTING
Bookmaking

In the early period of horse racing in England it was customary, when friend raced friend, for each to make a side bet, the pay-off to be made when the race was run. As the sport expanded and strangers raced strangers, with each eager to make a side bet, but neither trusting the other, the money was posted with a reputable citizen, who became known as the "stakes holder."

As more and more races were added, increasing the number of wagers, the stakeholders protested against continuance of their pay-less jobs. They pointed out it took too much of their time. The horsemen influenced them to continue holding stakes on the promise that 5 per cent of the total stake could be deducted before the pay-off as remuneration.

As the years went on and the public wanted to wager, too, the task became too complicated for the stakeholders. Thus the bookmaking idea was born.

The old-time stakeholders became the bookmakers. They arranged odds against each horse in the race, based on their ideas of its chance for victory. The odds were so arranged that, theoretically, the bookmakers would have a profit of 5 per cent on each race. Later-day bookmakers increased their percentage to 8, 10 or 12, according to their desires.

In calculating bookmaking percentages, top and bottom figures of the quotation are totalled, the gross divided into 100 and the result multiplied by the bottom figure. If there is a 4-horse race, and the bookmaker calculated to have about a 5 per cent book, his odds would be about like this:

Horse A ...... 6 to 5 .... 45.45%
Horse B ...... 2 to 1 .... 33.33%
Horse C ...... 5 to 1 .... 16.66%
Horse D ...... 9 to 1 .... 10.00%

Total 105.44%

The bookmaker would be, theoretically, taking in $105.44, paying back $100, and thus profiting 5 per cent or $5.44.

If he wanted to make 10 per cent, he could reduce the odds on Horse A to even money. That would make the percentage on that horse 50 and increase the grand total to $110, of which the bookmaker would keep $10, or approximately 10 per cent.

A "Dutch book" is one where the bookmaker offers such odds that if he gets a balanced book he must be a loser. A "Dutch book," in the instance stated earlier, would result if the bookmaker had odds like this:

Horse A ...... 9 to 5 .... 35.71%
Horse B ...... 2 to 1 .... 33.33%
Horse C ...... 7 to 1 .... 12.50%
Horse D ...... 10 to 1 .... 9.09%

Total 90.63%

Such a book theoretically would produce only $90.63 and the bookmaker, having to pay out $100, would lose, $9.37 on each $100.

The term "round book" is used to describe one wherein the odds would be such that the bookmaker would take in $100, and, having to pay out $100, would come out even, and his book would be a "rounder."

Table for Figuring Bookmaker's Percentage

1 to 5	83.33	4 to 1	20.00
2 to 5	71.42	4½ to 1	18.19
3 to 5	62.50	5 to 1	16.66
4 to 5	55.55	6 to 1	14.29
1 to 1	50.00	7 to 1	12.50
6 to 5	45.45	8 to 1	11.11
7 to 5	41.67	9 to 1	10.00
8 to 5	38.46	10 to 1	9.09
9 to 5	35.71	11 to 1	8.33
2 to 1	33.33	12 to 1	7.69
11 to 5	31.25	13 to 1	7.14
12 to 5	29.41	14 to 1	6.66
2½ to 1	28.57	15 to 1	6.25
13 to 5	27.78	20 to 1	4.76
14 to 5	26.31	25 to 1	3.85
3 to 1	25.00	30 to 1	3.23
16 to 5	23.81	40 to 1	2.44
17 to 5	22.72	50 to 1	1.96
3½ to 1	22.23	60 to 1	1.64
18 to 5	21.73	75 to 1	1.32
19 to 5	20.83	100 to 1	.99

Pari-Mutuel Betting

Pari-mutuel betting was introduced about 90 years ago by a Parisian businessman, Pierre Oller, and, as the name implies, is based on the idea of "betting among ourselves." Oller, it seems, liked to bet on horse races, but disliked taking the arbitrary odds posted by bookmakers and so set about introducing a system whereby bets were pooled and the odds on the winning horse determined by the amount in the pool in relation to the number of winning tickets to be redeemed. This is still the principle of pari-mutuel betting, but the further development of the totalizator has improved it insofar as the player is concerned.

Pari-mutuel betting today is more or less taken for granted by racing people, but many non-racegoers know nothing about it.

Before a race, the first set of approximate odds flashed on the totalizator board in the infield is called a "morning line." These are purely speculative odds, calculated by a man employed for that purpose and serving as a guide to the trend the betting might take. After the actual betting has been in progress for several minutes, the "morning line" is taken down and approximate odds, calculated according to the actual amount bet on each horse in relation to the total amount in the pool, are flashed on the board. These odds continue to reflect the changes in the betting.

It makes no difference to the race track whether the favorite wins (an event sometimes disastrous to an individual bookmaker), or a long shot wins. In either event, the state and the track get their legally prescribed amounts from the commission and tax deducted from the pool.

The totalizator, through which the wagers are made, is one of the most important items of mechanical equipment ever adopted by racing; it has, in effect, done for pari-mutuel betting what the linotype machine did for printing. What was once a series of manual and mental manipulations is now done by pressing a button.

The ticket-vending machine prints and issues the betting tickets at the rate of 50 per minute. An adaptation of the dial telephone system sorts, adds and transmits totals to the indicator boards in the calculating room which show, at all times, how much is bet on each horse in each pool. This information is flashed on the public indicator board every 90 seconds.

The first completely electrical totalizator was conceived and built in the United States in 1927 and 1928 and taken to England in 1929. There it was adopted by the English Race Course Betting Board and put into general use throughout Britain.

It was not until 1933 that the first of these totalizators was adopted by an American track— Arlington Park, Chicago, Ill. Today, it is in general use at all of the major tracks.

The totalizator also eliminated the possibility of error or dishonest handling of tickets, each being accounted for by mechanical and electrical impulses that register each transaction immediately until the locking of all vending machines concludes the betting.

Operation of the enormous adding machine that is the totalizator requires a highly specialized and well organized staff. Depending upon the size of the track and the day of operation, the mutuel staff ranges from 400 to 900 men who operate 100 to 350 vending machines. Recording, checking and rechecking of the betting transactions involve the use of more than 150 different and vari-colored printed forms.

The main part of the mutuel crew is made up of ticket sellers and cashiers. Meanwhile, crews in the money room are sorting and counting and furnishing the cashiers with needed denominations of currency; calculators are flashing approximate odds about 15 times for each race; ticket checkers are accounting for cashed tickets, and sheet writers are auditing the whole operation. Machine supervisors change the code die for each race, set the meters back to zero and see that the ticket-vending machine is supplied with ticket paper.

Thus, the modern totalizator absolutely assures honesty of the entire betting operation, and guarantees that each bettor will, after the deduction of the authorized commission and tax, obtain the exact proportion and share of the total amount bet to which he is entitled.

The "daily double" was introduced for pari-mutuel wagering by Leo Dandurand at Connaught Park (Ottawa) in 1930. It was an original idea. The quinella was borrowed from Rio de Janeiro in 1931, with Dandurand and James Munroe as joint sponsors. It was first tried at King's Park in Montreal.

Pari-mutuel wagering in the United States is legal in the following 26 states:

Arizona, Arkansas, California, Colorado, Delaware, Florida, Idaho, Illinois, Kentucky, Louisiana, Maine, Maryland, Massachusetts, Michigan, Montana, Nebraska, Nevada, New Hampshire, New Jersey, New Mexico, New York, Ohio, Oregon, Pennsylvania, Rhode Island, South Dakota, Vermont, Washington, West Virginia, and Wyoming.

Not all these states have pari-mutuel devices or conduct racing.

State legislatures determine how great a percentage of money in the betting pools at race tracks is to be deducted for transfer to state treasuries. In addition, states usually take odd cents, called "breakage," since pay-offs are not made in pennies. The breakage system was introduced to this country with the coming of the pari-mutuel machines in the 1870's.

The state percentages:

20%—Montana, Wyoming
19%—Maine
18%—Arizona, New Mexico, Vermont
17%—Florida, New Jersey, New York, Ohio, Pennsylvania, Rhode Island
16½%—Nevada
16%—Arkansas, Colorado, Delaware, Illinois, Louisiana, Massachusetts, New Hampshire, Washington, West Virginia
15¾%—California
15%—Idaho, Kentucky, Maryland, Michigan, Oregon, South Dakota
14%—Nebraska

Highest Pay-offs to Players—U. S.*

In the early days of pari-mutuel wagering in the United States, the minimum ticket on a horse was $5. In 1889, at Churchill Downs, Louisville, Ky., the minimum was reduced to $2 when sales lagged, but show tickets were not sold. In 1908 the $5 minimum was re-established. In 1911 the minimum again was reduced to $2, at Latonia, Ky., and included place and show tickets as well. That system is still the standard.

The top pay-offs that follow deal with tickets sold on the $2 basis:

Year	Horse	Track	Odds
†1912—Wishing Ring	Latonia, Ky	$941.75 to 1
1933—Augeas	Tijuana, Mex.	419.00 to 1
1910—Muzzeta W.	Lexington, Ky.	414.35 to 1
1933—King Jack	Tijuana, Mex.	409.00 to 1
1934—Trycook	Hagerstown, Md.	404.00 to 1
1968—Waverly Steps	Woodbine	387.10 to 1
1923—Fincastle	Havana, Cuba	350.30 to 1
1923—Lt. W.J. Murray	Havana, Cuba	347.00 to 1
1930—Miss Fountain	Havana, Cuba	341.80 to 1
1938—Playmay	Santa Anita, Calif.	335.70 to 1
1968—Fleetglow	Green Mountain	329.40 to 1
1941—Meadow Money	Lincoln Fields, Ill.	325.20 to 1
1932—Nanamay	Tanforan, Calif.	301.10 to 1
1933—Zombro	Charles Town, W.Va.	295.00 to 1
1913—Cadeau	Pimlico, Md.	287.55 to 1
1937—Escohigh	Tropical Park, Fla.	284.50 to 1
1949—Luxuriant	Narragansett Park, R.I.	282.00 to 1

†Wishing Ring's place price was $321.30 to 1.

Record Bookmaking Pay-off—500 to 1, on Petonia, Washington Park, 1894, and Bright Skies, Oakland, 1909.

Record Mutuels Pay-off on Place—$484.55 to 1, on Baal, Hialeah Park, 1932.

Record Mutuels Pay-off on Show—$87.40 to 1, on Carbine's Goldy, Alamo Downs, Texas, 1936.

*The above, and most of the other statistics in the horse racing section, compiled by John I. Day, Jr., Thoroughbred Racing Associations of the United States; Robert F. Kelley and Pat O'Brien, New York Racing Associations Service Bureau, and Sid Feder.

Most of the statistics are reproduced from the American Racing Manual by special permission of the copyright owners, Triangle Publications, Inc.

Other Record Pay-Offs

World's Longshot Record—3,400 to 1, November, 1929. Mrs. Answorth, wife of a Liverpool (England) physician, picked Coole in hurdle race at Haydack Park, England, and bet 2 shillings ($.50). Coole won and Mrs. Answorth received $1,705. The previous record was 3,037 to 1 on Robledo at Shanghai, China, earlier in 1929.

Largest Pay-offs on $5 Win Tickets—

Pay-off	Horse	Track	Date
$1,178.00	Nickajack	Jerome Park, N.Y.	Oct. 12, 1872
1,078.20	Wapakoneta	Saratoga, N.Y.	July 17, 1882
956.30	Camel	Louisville, Ky.	Oct. 5, 1909
760.00	Col. Sprague	Washington Park, Ill.	May 18, 1882
760.00	Harvard	Brighton Beach, N.Y.	Aug. 19, 1887

Record $2 Daily Double Pay-offs in North America—

Pay-off	Horses	Year	Track
$15,005.00	Pawn-Selected Set	1972	Lincoln Downs, R.I.
12,724.80	Rocklite-Slick Trick	1954	Tijuana, Mexico
10,772.00	Joy Bet-Merry Caroline	1939	Washington Park, Ill.
9,826.80	Miss Warcreus-Johnny Green	1964	Caliente Race Track, Mexico
8,711.40	Oriolo-Covinan	1960	Golden Gate, Calif.
8,614.40	Mighty Tough-Detach	1945	Rockingham Park, N.H.
8,505.80	Pilot Me-Shadydale Impact	1968	Pompano Park, Fla.
7,725.60	Goldwater-Blueonia	1956	Tijuana, Mexico
7,711.20	Hollybon-Last Waltz	1947	Dade Park, Ky.
7,205.40	Wannoah-Arakay	1935	Tropical Park, Fla.

European record—$11,650 for a 60-cent wager (18,892 to 1), Oct. 30, 1935, on England's "Autumn Double" when Near Relation won Cesarewitch Handicap and Commander III won the Cambridgeshire.

Canadian record—$8,498.35 for $5 ticket, (odds of $1,698.97 to $1), at Thorncliffe Park, Toronto, Sept. 17, 1932.

Quinella record (means picking horses to finish 1, 2 in a race)—$3,100.75 for $2 ticket. Entrap and Grand Duchess, 7th race, Sept. 12, 1932, Thorncliffe (Toronto); $3,000.50 for $2, Visa and Jack D'Or, July 26, 1934, King's Park (Montreal).

Shortest Price on Winners—1 to 100—on Man o' War 3 times in 1920. Lowest possible price in pari-mutuel system, by law, is 1 to 20 in states where breakage is to the nickel and 1 to 10 where breakage is to the dime.

Freakish Pay-offs—Sweep Vestal won the first race at Charles Town, W.Va., on Dec. 17, 1934, but no win ticket had been sold on her. In keeping with the rules of pari-mutuel wagering, Sweep Vestal was ignored as winner in pay-offs, and those who bet on second horse—Tiny Miss—to win were paid off. Sweep Vestal's pay-off for place was $105.80 for $2 and for show $7.80. Those who bet Tiny Miss to win received $6.80 for each $2 ticket.

On March 24, 1930, St. John's Park, near Jacksonville, Fla., Miss Scotia would have paid $121.60 for a $2 win ticket. She ran second. The mutuel pay-off on place was $3 for a $2 ticket, odds of 1 to 2. The race was won by Wagtail, 1-to-2 favorite. Wagtail paid $2.70 for place.

Perhaps racing's most remarkable long-shot day was on Tuesday, Sept. 20, 1949. Here are some of the pay-offs:

At Narragansett Park, R.I.—Luxuriant returned $566.80, $125.60 and $52.40 on $2 tickets across the board, a New England record. At Belmont Park, N.Y.—Bert's Reward won at $127.10, $21.50 and $9. At Atlantic City, N.J.—Gro-Up came home at $45.60, $16.20 and $9.60. At Marlboro, Md.—Playblix paid $123.20, $28 and $7.20.

Tropical Park in Coral Gables, Fla., had quite a "long-shot day" on Dec. 29, 1937. Earl Porter won the first race at $97.30 for $2. In the 2d race Texas Tommy was the winner at $77.80. The daily double paid $873.40 for $2. Geologist finished first at $55.60 in the 3d race. Escohigh won the 6th race and returned $571 for $2.

On successive days, April 22 and 23, 1941, the daily double at Bay Meadows, Calif., paid $3,610 and $3,935.20 for $2.

Only one ticket was sold on the $10,772.40-to-$2 American record daily double at Washington Park in 1939. Claude E. Elkins, 40-year-old bowling alley keeper of Anna, Ill., owned it, and he was not even at the track to cash the ticket. He wired the selections and the money. Joy Bet paid $131.40 for $2 and Merry Caroline $20 for $2.

Eight horses, a record, figured in a pay-off at the Fair Grounds in New Orleans in 1938. The winner was Catomar, at $12.40, $3.60 and $2.20 across the board. He was grouped in the mutuel "field" with 3 other horses. Carvola, an entry with White Cockade, finished 2d, making a total of 6. Gato, who took 3d, was an entry with Shining Heels, bringing the number to 8.

On Nov. 16, 1938, Mrs. R. E. Dwyer and Helen O'Brien of Washington, D.C., went into partnership on a daily double ticket on Charles F. and James Boy at Bowie, Md. Charles F. won and paid $19.10; James Boy won and paid $80.60. The women had the only ticket sold on that combination and collected $6,754.

Harry Topsy of Jersey City, N.J., at Tropical Park on March 18, 1935, played a daily double that consisted of Wannoah and Arakay. It clicked and Topsy collected the entire pool of $7,205.40.

On Feb. 1, 1934, at the Fair Grounds in New Orleans, Sister Zoe's odds were 1 to 10 to win, and Sallie Bourland's odds were $413.80 to $1 win. They both finished in the money and paid $2.20—1 to 10—to show—the absolute minimum.

On St. Patrick's Day, 1938, Charles McNutt, deputy sheriff of Pulaski County, Ark., coupled Peggy Torch and Miss Firefly. The combination won and McNutt collected the entire pool—$6,002.80.

On Sept. 8, 1949, eight straight favorites swept the card at Del Mar track in California, an unusual occurrence in racing. Top price of the day was $8.60 for $2. An 8-horse parlay would have returned $10,483.77 for $2.

Perhaps the record "error" of all time occurred at Hialeah Park in Florida on Feb. 2, 1939, when John R. Brain, a mutuel clerk, was asked for a $10 ticket on Horse No. 8 in the seventh race and he punched out a ticket on No. 7 by mistake. The customer refused it, so Brain gave him a ticket on No. 8. Since no other player came along to buy the ticket on No. 7, Brain had to put $10 of his own into the pool and take the ticket himself. The No. 7 horse, Fleet Step, won the race, paying $196.60 for $2.

When the American horse, Battleship, won the English Grand National at 40 to 1 in 1948, and Barbadeche took the Bickerstaffe Plate at 55 to 1, it was discovered only one 10-shilling ($2.50) ticket had been sold on this double combination. The net pool was $25,310. An unidentified man presented the single ticket and collected at odds of better than 10,000 for 1.

Calculating a Parlay

For lightning calculations of parlay pay-offs:

Multiply pay-offs on the 2 successful horses, then divide by 4, after which multiply by the number of dollars bet.

For example: One horse paid $4.60; the other $10, in a 2-horse parlay. Multiply $4.60 by $10: $46. Dividing by 4 gives $11.50—a profit of $10.50. Then multiply by the number of dollars played.

On a 3-horse parlay, multiply the 3 winning tickets and divide by 8, which will give the money due for a $1 bet (including the original $1). For instance: The horses paid $4, $6 and $20. Four times 6 is $24, and 20 times that is $480. Dividing by 8 gives $60, which is due for each $1 bet (the $1, of course, being included in the $60).

On a 4-horse parlay, multiply the pay-offs and then divide by 16. For a 5-horse parlay, divide by 64.

U.S. ATTENDANCE, WAGERING AND REVENUE TO STATES FROM TAXES

Year	Attendance	Mutuel Handle
1950	22,525,567	1,394,185,004
1951	23,807,892	1,591,038,310
1952	26,434,903	1,915,220,517
1953	27,969,331	2,064,572,984
1954	27,425,637	2,017,825,498
1955	27,773,999	2,060,000,801
1956	29,032,932	2,179,777,236
1957	30,617,824	2,236,101,618
1958	30,862,247	2,241,289,105
1959	32,204,142	2,466,996,600
1960	32,935,583	2,524,996,670
1961	34,934,571	2,608,070,937
1962	36,654,290	2,642,596,023
1963	38,091,417	2,855,600,544
1964	39,186,519	3,057,898,763
1965	38,957,281	3,113,348,035
1966	47,020,456	3,076,247,370
1967	40,308,763	3,322,826,349
1968	29,329,199	2,541,031,674*
1969	29,139,005	2,634,125,187*
1970	30,353,202	2,787,492,810*
1971	31,820,851	2,956,804,686*
1972	30,805,461	2,959,614,159*

*TRA Tracks only.

U.S. TOTAL RACING DAYS AND RACES

(If only one track operates on a certain day, that indicates one day of racing; if 2, 5 or 10 operate it means 2, 5 or 10 racing days.)

Year	Days	Races
1920	1,022	6,897
1921	1,074	7,250
1922	1,182	8,045
1923	1,319	8,991
1924	1,456	10,007
1925	1,656	11,579
1926	1,713	12,065
1927	1,680	11,832
1928	1,613	11,465
1929	1,599	11,133
1930	1,653	11,477
1931	1,660	11,690
1932	1,518	10,835
1933	1,746	12,680
1934	1,959	14,261
1935	2,133	15,830
1936	2,033	15,344
1937	2,140	16,250
1938	2,140	16,243
1939	2,199	16,967
1940	2,096	16,041
1941	2,162	16,912
1942	2,228	17,593
1943	2,052	16,094
1944	2,396	19,228
1945	2,480	19,587
1946	3,020	23,940
1947	3,134	24,884
1948	3,183	25,388
1949	3,309	26,832
1950	3,290	26,932
1951	3,394	27,856

Year	Days	Races
1952	3,515	29,051
1953	3,635	30,069
1954	3,685	30,467
1955	3,827	31,757
1956	3,979	33,445
1957	4,120	34,982
1958	3,910	33,325
1959	4,218	36,579
1960	4,304	37,661
1961	4,641	40,744
1962	4,772	41,766
1963	5,203	45,449
1964	5,326	46,922
1965	5,283	47,335
1966	5,254	46,814
1967	5,344	47,811
1968	5,553	49,777
1969	5,825	52,315
1970	6,242	56,676
1971	6,394	57,467
1972	6,624	59,410

MONEY DISTRIBUTION AT U.S. RACE TRACKS

(Purses and stakes.)

Year	Amount
1908	$4,351,691
1909	3,146,695
1910	2,942,333
1911	2,337,957
1912	2,391,625
1913	2,929,963
1914	2,994,525
1915	2,853,037
1916	3,842,471
1917	4,066,258
1918	3,425,347
1919	4,642,865
1920	7,773,407
1921	8,435,083
1922	9,096,215
1923	9,675,811
1924	10,825,446
1925	12,577,270
1926	13,884,820
1927	13,935,619
1928	13,332,361
1929	13,417,827
1930	13,674,160
1931	13,084,154
1932	10,082,757
1933	8,516,325
1934	10,443,495
1935	12,794,418
1936	12,994,605
1937	14,363,562
1938	14,946,609
1939	15,312,839
1940	15,911,167
1941	17,987,225
1942	18,138,118
1943	18,555,680
1944	29,159,099
1945	32,300,060
1946	49,291,024
1947	53,932,141
1948	54,436,063
1949	52,317,078
1950	50,102,099
1951	55,551,124
1952	63,950,236
1953	72,870,819
1954	74,225,611
1955	76,643,696
1956	81,311,581
1957	85,300,966
1958	85,467,082
1959	92,848,541
1960	93,741,552
1961	98,846,843
1962	103,525,712
1963	113,122,209
1964	121,777,847
1965	126,463,984
1966	130,653,813
1967	139,170,738
1968	150,644,478
1969	168,713,911
1970	185,625,110
1971	201,435,894
1972	210,607,722

FAMOUS TRAINERS

Ben A. Jones and his son Horace Allyn (Jimmy) Jones have made Calumet Farm the power in the stakes-horsefield in the past decade or so and the Joneses have saddled a record number of 8 Kentucky Derby winners, starting with Lawrin in 1938.

The leader in the selling-plater field is Hirsch Jacobs, who has trained more than 22,000 winners since 1926. Jacobs handled Stymie, whom he purchased for $1,500 from the King Ranch and then developed into a money-winning champion with earnings of more than $900,000.

Others outstanding in the field include "Sunny Jim" Fitzsimmons, who has saddled more than 200 stakes winners in more than a half-century; Max Hirsch; James Rowe Sr. and Jr.; Andrew J. Joyner; H. Guy Bedwell; Samuel C. Hildreth; Henry McDaniel; J. D. Mikel; George Alexandra; Dave Womeldorff; Stanley Lipiec; Willie Molter; R. H. McDaniel, and J. W. Healy.

Also, August (Sarge) Swenke; George M. Odom; Roscoe Goose; Andy Schuttinger; Lou Schaefer; the Christmas brothers of Maryland—Ed, Frank and Yancey; Preston Burch; W. T. (Fatty) Andersen; Clyde Van Dusen; C. E. (Boots) Durnell; Pete Coyne; Ed Corrigan; John Morris; H. J. (Derby Dick) Thompson, who trained 4 Kentucky Derby winners; "Whistling Bob" Smith, and "Silent Tom" Smith.

Others include Mose Shapoff; Frank J. Kearns; Earl Sande; John M. Gaver; R. O. Higdon; Frank Catrone; Clarence Buxton; R. A. Coward; T. J. Healey; Steve Judge; A. G. Tarn; Phil Bieber; Eugene Jacobs; Ed Haughton; T. H. Heard Jr.; Tom McCreery; W. F. Mulholland; A. A. Baroni; Freddie Hopkins; J. H. (Bud) Stotler; John B. Partridge; Roy Waldron; H. L. Fontaine; Mose Goldblatt; W. C. (Bill) Winfrey; Duval A. Headley, J. P. (Sammy) Smith, V. R. Wright, and Charles Whittingham.

Max Hirsch, the veteran conditioner who trained Bold Venture and Assault, had at least one day of notable disappointment. On Nov. 8, 1938, Hirsch started a 5-horse entry in a race at Pimlico, which, naturally, was made favorite. Fast Flight, one of the 5, finished first. But he was disqualified—and under the rules of racing the numbers of all others in the entry also were taken down, including Just Once, who had finished third.

The oldest active turfman is believed to have been Tom Cheek, who died a few years ago. He trained his stable until his death at the age of 104.

Leaders In Winners Saddled

Year	Trainer	Winners
1907	James Rowe	70
1908	Andrew J. Joyner	71
1909	H. Guy Bedwell	122
1910	F. Ernest	105
1911	W. B. Carson	72
1912	H. Guy Bedwell	84
1913	H. Guy Bedwell	87
1914	H. Guy Bedwell	84
1915	H. Guy Bedwell	97
1916	H. Guy Bedwell	123
1917	H. Guy Bedwell	66
1918	K. Spence	58
1919	K. Spence	96
1920	K. Spence	74
	S. A. Clopton	74
1921	Samuel C. Hildreth	85
1922	Henry McDaniel	78
	J. A. Parsons	78
1923	C. B. Irwin	147
1924	J. A. Parsons	93
1925	J. J. Duggan	70
1926	W. Perkins	82
1927	Samuel C. Hildreth	72
1928	J. F. Schorr	65
	J. Reed	65
1929	L. Gentry	74
1930	C. B. Irwin	92
1931	J. D. Mikel	72
1932	G. Alexandra	76
1933	Hirsch Jacobs	116
1934	Hirsch Jacobs	127
1935	Hirsch Jacobs	114
1936	Hirsch Jacobs	177
1937	Hirsch Jacobs	134
1938	Hirsch Jacobs	109
1939	Hirsch Jacobs	106
1940	D. Womeldorff	108
1941	Hirsch Jacobs	123
1942	Hirsch Jacobs	133
1943	Hirsch Jacobs	128
1944	Hirsch Jacobs	117
1945	Stanley Lipiec	127
1946	Willie Molter	122
1947	Willie Molter	155
1948	Willie Molter	184
1949	Willie Molter	129
	W. H. Bishop	129
1950	R. H. McDaniel	156
1951	R. H. McDaniel	164
1952	R. H. McDaniel	168
1953	R.H. McDaniel	211
1954	R. H. McDaniel	206
1955	F. H. Merrill, Jr.	154
1956	V. R. Wright	177
1957	V. R. Wright	192
1958	F. H. Merrill, Jr.	171
1959	V. R. Wright	172
1960	F. H. Merrill Jr.	143
1961	V. R. Wright	178
1962	W. H. Bishop	162
1963	H. Jacobson	140
1964	H. Jacobson	169
1965	H. Jacobson	200
1966	L. Cavalaris Jr.	175
1967	Everett Hammond	200
1968	Jack Van Berg	256
1969	Jack Van Berg	239
1970	Jack Van Berg	282
1971	Dale Baird	245
1972	Jack Van Berg	286

Leaders in Money Won

Year	Trainer	Winners	Horses Winnings
1935—J. H. Stotler		87	$303,005
1936—James Fitzsimmons		42	193,415
1937—R. McGarvey		46	209,925
1938—Earl Sande		15	226,495
1939—James Fitzsimmons		45	266,205
1940—Tom Smith		14	269,200
1941—Ben A. Jones		70	475,316
1942—John Gaver		48	406,547
1943—Ben A. Jones		73	267,915
1944—Ben A. Jones		60	601,660
1945—Tom Smith		52	510,655
1946—Hirsch Jacobs		99	560,077
1947—H. A. (Jimmy) Jones		85	1,334,805
1948—H. A. (Jimmy) Jones		81	1,118,670
1949—H. A. (Jimmy) Jones		76	948,583
1950—Preston M. Burch		96	637,754
1951—John Gaver		45	637,242
1952—Ben A. Jones		29	662,137
1953—H. Trotsek		54	1,028,873
1954—W. Molter		136	1,107,860
1955—J. Fitzsimmons		66	1,270,055
1956—W. Molter		142	1,227,402
1957—H. A. Jones		70	1,150,910
1958—W. Molter		69	1,116,544
1959—W. Molter		71	847,290
1960—H. Jacobs		97	748,349
1961—H. A. Jones		62	759,856
1962—M. A. Tenney		58	1,099,474
1963—M. A. Tenney		40	860,703
1964—W. C. Winfrey		61	1,350,534
1965—H. Jacobs		91	1,331,628
1966—E. A. Neloy		93	2,456,250
1967—E. A. Neloy		72	1,776,089
1968—E. A. Neloy			1,233,101
1969—Elliott Burch			1,067,936
1970—C. Whittingham			1,302,354
1971—C. Whittingham			1,737,115
1972—C. Whittingham			1,734,020

JOCKEYS

Famous Jockeys

Perhaps the most publicized of all jockeys was Tod Sloan, who started his career in the United States and completed it in England. Sloan, with abnormally short legs, popularized the short stirrups. He leaned well over the neck of his horse and this position became known as the "monkey crouch" in England. At first, Sloan was scoffed at for using the position, but the style was adopted by the English riders when Sloan proved a consistent winner.

Sloan was rated a great judge of pace. He was a strategist on a horse and was daring to an extreme. He had a great pair of hands and used them to control the wildest horses; he was a crack billiards player and a near-champion with a rifle. The short stirrup that Sloan made famous was devised by Charles Verplank.

Many veterans regard Isaac Murphy, a Negro jockey, as the greatest. Murphy was at his best between 1884 and about 1890, and had, perhaps, the highest winning average of all. Almost all his riding was in the South and Middle West until the late 1880's. Then he shifted his operations to New York and was sensational there. He added to his fame by his excellent handling of Salvator and Freeland, two of the top horses of the era.

Ed (Snapper) Garrison is another immortal. He had a habit of holding back with his horse until the stretch run. He always came on like a whirlwind as he flashed past the stands. His finishes were so spectacular and so often repeated that it has been customary since his time to refer to a tight race climax as a "Garrison finish."

Some are inclined to brush aside claims for Sloan, Murphy and Garrison and insist that Jimmy McLaughlin was the greatest jockey. He was keen, resourceful, an excellent judge of pace and a rider who knew no fear.

Earl Sande, Eddie Arcaro, Johnny Longden, Ted Atkinson, Willie Shoemaker and Bill Hartack are generally regarded as the best jockeys developed in the last 3 or 4 decades. Sande, who preceded the others by a number of years, first gained acclaim while riding for Commander J. K. L. Ross of Canada. He shifted to Harry Sinclair's Rancocas Stable and completed his major career in the famous colors of William Woodward's Belair Stud.

Willie Shoemaker tops all jockeys in the money-winning department. Up to the 1972 season, Shoemaker's mounts had won $46,731,086. He had 6,267 winners.

Johnny Longden, who retired in 1966 after 40 years of racing, had 6,026 winners and won $24,665,800. Eddie Arcaro, racing for 31 years, retired in 1961 with 4,779 first place winners. He won $30,039,543.

Atkinson has won the acclaim of turf followers by his excellent handling of mounts. He captured the riding championship in 1944 and 1946.

Other outstanding jockeys:

Walter Miller, who brought home 388 winners in 1906; Eugene Hildebrand; Winnie O'Connor; Jimmy Winkfield; Fred Taral; Willie Shaw; Dick Clawson; Danny Maher; Sam Doggett; Jack Martin; Eddie Martin; John and Jimmie Lamley; Arthur Redbern; Andy Hamilton; Willie and Eddie Dugan; Otto Wonderly; Herman Radtke; J. (Soup) Perkins; G. Covington; Tommy Burns; Dave Nicol; George M. Odom; Willie (Daredevil) Fitzpatrick; "Monk" Overton; Alonzo Clayton; Johnny, Lester and Charlie Reiff; Isaac Lewis; H. (Iceman) Spencer, and Roscoe Troxler.

Also, Roscoe Goose; Frankie Robinson; Johnny Maiben; Carol Shilling; Jimmy Butwell; Andy Schuttinger; Mack Garner; Willie Knapp; Mark Fator; Laverne Fator; Buddy Ensor; Johnny Loftus; Linus (Pony) McAtee; Raymond (Sonny) Workman; Eddie Ambrose; "Chick" Lang; Ivan Parke; Ted Rice; Albert Johnson; Willie Crump; Johnny McTaggart; Eddie Taplin; Tommy McTaggart; Joe Notter; Clarence Kummer; Clarence Turner; R. Lyne; George Ellis; Jake Heupel; Frankie Keough, and L. Lyke.

The list continues with Alfred Robertson; J. C. (Red) Pollard; Georgie Woolf; Eddie Pool; Don Meade; Carroll Bierman; Johnny Adams; Basil James; Johnny Gilbert; Conn McCreary; Eric Guerin; Lou Schaefer; Jackie Westrope; Sammy Renick; Bobby Permane; Wayne Wright; Job D. Jessop; Doug Dodson; Arnold Kirkland; Jimmy Stout; Steve Brooks; Nick Wall; Ferril Zufelt, Dave Gorman; Hedley Woodhouse; Anthony DeSpirito, Joe Culmone; Willie Shoemaker; Bill Hartack; Ralph Neves; Sam Boulmetis; Bob Ussery, Bill Boland; Walter Blum; Avelino Gomez; Braulio Baeza, and Ismael Valenzuela.

Famous Steeplechase Jockeys

Conspicuous among the professional steeplechase jockeys of the past and present:

Nat Ray; F. Williams; W. Allen; V. Powers; R. H. Crawford; Dolly Byers; C. Mergler; C. Smoot; M. Hunt; W. G. Collins; F. Slate; F. Bellhouse; E. Kennedy; E. Roberts; W. Owen; D. Marzani; F. D. Adams; H. Harris; J. Magee; G. Walker; J. Penrod; A. P. Smithwick, and Tommy Walsh and Joe Aitcheson, Jr. Tom Roby was a star when a serious injury ended his riding career.

George H. (Pete) Bostwick is rated as the best gentleman (amateur) jockey of all time, with Rigan McKinney and Foxhall Keene high on the list.

All-Time U.S. Leaders

When Johnny Longden won with Fleet Diver at Hollywood Park in Inglewood, Calif., on May 15, 1952, he became the first American jockey to ride 4,000 winners. Only the English jockey, Gordon Richards, has ridden more winners than

Longden. The 49-year-old Richards, who was made a knight by Queen Elizabeth in 1953, celebrated by winning England's Epsom Derby for the first time in 28 attempts. He gained his 4,670th victory with Sir Victor Sassoon's Pinza. The queen's colt, Aureole, finished second. Longden subsequently surpassed Richards, who retired to become a trainer.

United States Champions
   (Winners ridden.)

Year	Jockey	Mts.	1st	2d	3d
1900.	C. Mitchell	854	195	140	139
1901.	W. O'Connor	1,047	253	221	192
1902.	J. Ranch	1,069	276	205	181
1903.	G. C. Fuller	918	229	152	122
1904.	E. Hildebrand	1,169	297	230	171
1905.	D. Nicol	861	221	143	136
1906.	Walter Miller	1,384	388	300	199
1907.	Walter Miller	1,194	334	226	170
1908.	V. Powers	1,260	324	264	185
1909.	V. Powers	704	173	121	114
1910.	G. Garner	947	200	188	153
1911.	T. Koerner	813	162	133	112
1912.	P. Hill	967	168	141	129
1913.	M. Buxton	887	146	131	136
1914.	John McTaggart	787	157	132	106
1915.	Mack Garner	775	151	118	90
1916.	Frank Robinson	791	178	131	124
1917.	Willie Crump	803	151	140	101
1918.	Frank Robinson	864	185	140	108
1919.	C. Robinson	896	190	145	126
1920.	James Butwell	721	152	129	139
1921.	Chick Lang	696	135	110	105
1922.	Mark Fator	859	188	153	116
1923.	Ivan Parke	718	173	105	95
1924.	Ivan Parke	844	205	175	121
1925.	A. Mortensen	987	187	145	138
1926.	R. Jones	1,172	190	163	152
1927.	L. Hardy	1,130	207	192	151
1928.	J. Inzelone	979	150	141	124
1929.	M. Knight	863	149	132	133
1930.	H. R. Riley	861	177	145	123
1931.	H. Roble	1,174	173	173	155
1932.	John Gilbert	1,050	212	144	160
1933.	Jackie Westrope	1,224	301	235	235
1934.	Maurice Peters	1,045	227	179	147
1935.	C. Stevenson	1,099	206	169	146
1936.	Basil James	1,106	245	195	161
1937.	John Adams	1,265	260	186	177
1938.	John Longden	1,150	236	168	171
1939.	Donald Meade	1,284	255	221	180
1940.	Earl Dew	1,377	287	201	180
1941.	Donald Meade	1,164	210	185	158
1942.	John Adams	1,120	245	185	150
1943.	John Adams	1,069	228	159	171
1944.	Theodore Atkinson	1,539	287	231	213
1945.	Job D. Jessop	1,085	290	182	168
1946.	Theodore Atkinson	1,377	233	213	173
1947.	John Longden	1,327	316	250	195
1948.	John Longden	1,197	319	223	161
1949.	Gordon Glisson	1,347	270	217	181
1950.	Joe Culmone	1,676	388	283	218
	Willie Shoemaker	1,640	388	266	230
1951.	Charles Burr	1,319	310	232	192
1952.	Anthony DeSpirito	1,482	390	247	212
1953.	W. Shoemaker	1,683	485	302	210
1954.	W. Shoemaker	1,251	380	221	142
1955.	W. Hartack	1,702	417	298	215
1956.	W. Hartack	1,387	347	252	184
1957.	W. Hartack	1,283	341	208	178
1958.	W. Shoemaker	1,133	300	185	137
1959.	W. Shoemaker	1,285	347	230	159
1960.	W. Hartack	1,402	307	247	190
1961.	J. Sellers	1,394	328	212	227
1962.	R. Ferraro	1,755	352	252	226
1963.	W. Blum	1,704	360	286	215
1964.	W. Blum	1,577	324	274	170
1965.	J. Davidson	1,582	319	228	190
1966.	A. Gomez	996	318	173	142
1967.	J. Velasquez	1,939	438	315	270
1968.	A. Cordero, Jr.	1,662	345	278	219
1969.	L. Snyder	1,645	352	290	243
1970.	S. Hawley	1,908	452	313	265
1971.	L. Pincay, Jr.	1,627	380	288	214
1972.	S. Hawley		367		

The 30 per cent win average compiled by Shoemaker in 1954 is the highest by any jockey. The runner-up average of 29 was set in 1953, also by Shoemaker.

Leading Money-Winning Jockeys, Annually

Until 1946, no jockey ever rode the winners of $1,000,000 in one year. Since then the achievement has become fairly common. In 1957, eight riders surpassed the million mark, with Bill Hartack hitting $3,060,501.

Following are the yearly money-winning riders since 1946:

Year	Rider	Winnings
1946	Ted Atkinson (233)	$1,036,825
1947	Doug Dodson (141)	1,429,949
1948	Eddie Arcaro (188)	1,686,230
1949	Steve Brooks (209)	1,316,817
1950	Eddie Arcaro (195)	1,410,160
1951	Willie Shoemaker (257)	1,329,890
1952	Eddie Arcaro (188)	1,859,591
1953	Willie Shoemaker (485)	1,784,187
1954	Willie Shoemaker (380)	1,876,760
1955	Eddie Arcaro (158)	1,864,796
1956	Bill Hartack (347)	2,343,955
1957	Bill Hartack (341)	3,060,501
1958	Willie Shoemaker (300)	2,961,693
1959	Willie Shoemaker (347)	2,843,133
1960	Willie Shoemaker (274)	2,123,961
1961	Willie Shoemaker (304)	2,690,819
1962	Willie Shoemaker (311)	2,916,844
1963	Willie Shoemaker (271)	2,526,925
1964	Willie Shoemaker (246)	2,649,553
1965	Braulio Baeza (270)	2,582,702
1966	Braulio Baeza (298)	2,951,022
1967	Braulio Baeza (256)	3,088,888

1968—Braulio Baeza (201) 2,835,108
1969—Jorge Velasquez (258) 2,542,315
1970—Laffit Pincay, Jr. (269) 2,626,526
1971—Laffit Pincay, Jr. (380) 3,784,377
1972—Laffit Pincay, Jr. (—) 3,225,827

Leading Steeplechase Jockeys in U.S.

Year	Jockey	Mts.	Winners
1905	N. Ray	51	19
1906	N. Ray	53	18
1907	H. Boyle	43	15
1908	McKinley	78	27
1909	Donohue	27	13
1910	J. Lynch	37	16
1911	F. Williams	67	25
1912	W. Allen	61	27
1913	W. Allen	74	21
	J. Kermath	74	21
1914	W. Allen	55	15
1915	F. Williams	77	28
1916	F. Williams	52	20
1917	V. Powers	39	15
1918	D. Byers	49	16
1919	R. H. Crawford	53	21
1920	R. H. Crawford	43	18
1921	D. Byers	48	15
1922	R. H. Crawford	53	22
1923	C. Mergler	55	14
1924	L. Cheyne	55	13
1925	R. Haynes	34	13
1926	R. H. Crawford	48	15
1927	L. Cheyne	45	10
	C. Smoot	53	10
1928	D. Byers	31	15
1929	H. Jeffcott	38	9
1930	W. Hunt	23	10
1931	F. Bellhouse	37	13
1932	W. Collins	57	10
1933	W. Collins	58	16
1934	F. Slate	37	12
1935	F. Bellhouse	59	17
1936	P. McGinnis	28	9
1937	A. Bauman	35	13
1938	E. Kennedy	44	17
1939	J. Penrod	66	15
1940	J. McCulloch	45	14
1941	T. Roby	55	13
1942	E. Roberts	58	15
	G. Walker	78	15
1943	W. Owne	112	22
1944	W. Owen	118	24
1945	W. Owen	104	22
1946	J. Magee	80	28
	F. D. Adams	106	28
1947	T. Field	68	25
1948	D. Marzani	99	24
1949	F. D. Adams	114	23
1950	F. D. Adams	82	21
1951	F. D. Adams	100	35
1952	F. D. Adams	84	23
1953	F. D. Adams	93	22

1954	F. D. Adams	103	38
1955	F. D. Adams	127	31
1956	A. P. Smithwick	99	21
1957	A. P. Smithwick	112	29
1958	A. P. Smithwick	138	39
1959	J. Murphy	87	20
1960	T. Walsh	121	29
1961	J. Aitcheson Jr.	141	36
1962	A. P. Smithwick	147	29
1963	J. Aitcheson Jr.	160	38
1964	J. Aitcheson Jr.	141	40
1965	D. Small Jr.	143	27
1966	T. Walsh	157	37
1967	J. Aitcheson Jr.	149	36
1968	J. Aitcheson Jr.	148	33
1969	J. Aitcheson Jr.	145	32
1970	J. Aitcheson Jr.	112	25
1971	J. Fishback	95	26

LEADING MONEY-WINNING OWNERS
(Since 1940)

1940—Charls S. Howard ....$ 334,120
1941—Calumet Farm 475,091
1942—Greentree Stable 414,432
1943—Calumet Farm 267,915
1944—Calumet Farm 601,660
1945—Maine Chance Farm 589,170
1946—Calumet Farm 564,095
1947—Calumet Farm 1,402,436
1948—Calumet Farm 1,269,710
1949—Calumet Farm 1,128,942
1950—Brookmeade Stable 651,399
1951—Greentree Stable 637,242
1952—Calumet Farm 1,283,197
1953—A. G. Vanderbilt 987,306
1954—King Ranch 837,615
1955—Hasty House Farm 832,879
1956—Calumet Farm 1,057,383
1957—Calumet Farm 1,150,910
1958—Calumet Farm 946,262
1959—Cain Hoy Stable 742,081
1960—C. C. Whitney 1,039,091
1961—Calumet Farm 759,856
1962—R. C. Ellsworth 1,154,454
1963—Ellsworth Stable 1,096,863
1964—Wheatley Stable 1,073,572
1965—Marion H. Van Berg 895,246
1966—Wheatley Stable 1,225,861
1967—Hobeau Farm 1,120,143
1968—Marion H. Van Berg 1,105,388
1969—Marion H. Van Berg 1,453,679
1970—Marion H. Van Berg 1,347,289
1971—S. Sommer 1,523,508
1972—S. Sommer 1,605,896

LEADING BREEDERS

Latest figures indicate there are about 1,645 farms in the United States where breeding thoroughbreds is a business.

Following are the most successful breeders annually, in point of races won and money earned by products they bred:

LEADING BREEDERS
(Since 1940)

Year	Leader (races won)	Races won	Leader (money)	Horses' earnings
1940	Arthur B. Hancock	302	Joseph E. Widener	$ 317,961
1941	Willis S. Kilmer	256	Calumet Farm	528,211
1942	Arthur B. Hancock	333	Greetree Stable	536,173
1943	Arthur B. Hancock	346	Arthur B. Hancock	619,049
1944	Arthur B. Hancock	322	Calumet Farm	990,612
1945	Mereworth Stud	307	Coldstream Stud	791,477
1946	Arthur B. Hancock	350	Mereworth Stud	962,677
1947	Mereworth Stud	358	Calumet Farm	1,807,432
1948	Mereworth Stud	330	Calumet Farm	1,559,850
1949	Mereworth Stud	347	Calumet Farm	1,515,181
1950	Mereworth Stud	313	Calumet Farm	1,090,286
1951	Mereworth Stud	299	Calumet Farm	1,198,107
1952	Mereworth Stud	270	Calumet Farm	2,060,590
1953	Mereworth Farm	246	Calumet Farm	1,573,803
1954	Calumet Farm	201	Calumet Farm	1,139,609
1955	Henry H. Knight	223	Calumet Farm	999,737
1956	Henry H. Knight	293	Calumet Farm	1,528,727
1957	Henry H. Knight	284	Calumet Farm	1,469,473
1958	Henry H. Knight	260	Claiborne Farm	1,414,355
1959	King Ranch	227	Claiborne Farm	1,322,595
1960	E. P. Taylor	267	C. V. Whitney	1,193,181
1961	E. P. Taylor	265	Calumet Farm	1,078,894
1962	Edward P. Taylor	263	Rex C. Ellsworth	1,678,769
1963	Edward P. Taylor	300	Rex C. Ellisworth	1,465,069
1964	Edward P. Taylor	305	Bieber-Jacobs Stable	1,301,677
1965	Edward P. Taylor	290	Bieber-Jacobs Stable	1,994,649
1966	Edward P. Taylor	162	Bieber-Jacobs Stable	1,575,027
1967	Edward P. Taylor	288	Bieber-Jacobs Stable	1,575,414
1968	Edward P. Taylor	280	Clairborne Farm	1,493,189
1969	Edward P. Taylor	302	Claiborne Farm	1,331,485
1970	Harbor View Farm	366	Harbor View Farm	1,515,861
1971	Harbor View Farm	394	Harbor View Farm	1,739,214
1972	Harbor View Farm	326	Leslie Combs 2nd	1,578,851

Horses

SPEED

Speed determines class among race horses. The faster the horse, the higher the class credited to him.

There are classy sprinters and classy routers (distance racers). The super-horse, of course, is one that can beat both the sprinter and distance runners. Man o' War was a super-horse. He stepped out in front with the call of "go," headed sprinters over the short route and was in front of distance horses at the end. On the other hand, through 1934 and 1935, King Saxon was peerless as a sprinter. He could carry his terrific speed up to a mile and sixteenth, but usually, after that, he had nothing left.

Cavalcade, the sensation of 1934, was strictly a router. Up to a mile, he never was conspicuous in a race. Ordinary sprinters beat him at 6 or 7 furlongs, but after the mile mark he gained speed and came on with a terrific burst.

A horse is regarded in his running prime at 3 and 4 years. Beyond that age, the normal class horse begins to lose his swiftness. He no longer can match bursts with the younger horses and, therefore, loses ranking. The slower he gets, the more precipitate is his descent and he continues to be dropped in class until the owner finds a class wherein he is still fast enough to win.

A race horse will step between 50 and 60 feet per second. On hard, fast courses, like Arlington, Belmont, Saratoga or Golden Gate Fields, which were built for speed, a great horse can run a mile in 1:35 or better, whereas at ordinary tracks the same animal would do well to beat 1:40.

Inasmuch as the average horse is over 8 feet in length with neck stretched out, if he is travelling at the rate of 54 feet per second he negotiates what is equivalent to nearly 7 times his own length in 1 second.

Man o' War, one of the mightiest striding horses of all time, is credited with average leaps of 27 feet, meaning he made two jumps per second, even in comparatively slow time.

An ordinary horse in the selling plater division (a non-stakes horse), running on a fair sort of track, will do a mile in 1 minute, 40 seconds, a total 100 seconds—a speed average 52.8 feet per second.

A horse, racing only 2 furlongs, can "turn on the heat" all the way. Bob Wade ran 2 furlongs at Butte, Mont., in 21¼ seconds in 1890. He averaged within a fraction of 60 feet per second.

In contrast, Market Wise, stepping 2 miles in 3:20 4/5 in 1941, averaged 52.5, while Sotemia, holder of the 4-mile mark of 7:10 4/5, made in 1912 at Churchill Downs, averaged 49 feet.

HANDICAPPING AND SCALE OF WEIGHTS

Even without the obstacles encountered en route, it is probable that racing would never have grown to the point it has were it not for the handicapping system. When several horses race against one another and one is obviously the fastest, there is not much point in racing those same horses again until, in some way, the fast animal can be so handicapped that there is some possibility of his being beaten by the others.

The present system of handicapping is the result of an immense amount of study and observation. It took many years of watching horses perform under different burdens before a set scale could be established that would be fair to all those who came into its scope. A definite grade was established in England by Honorable John Henry Rous, and it worked so well that it was brought to America without any major changes and is now as old as American racing. The scale itself assigns a specified amount of weight to be carried by all age groups during each month of the year. This scale holds true only when horses of two different ages are competing against each other, and since all horses share a common birthdate, January 1st, the discrepancies are nil.

While the scale of weights is used to its greatest advantage when a horse is competing against an older, or younger, adversary, it also has great use as a base weight for the track handicappers to go on. If three-year-olds are running in a race that is exclusively for their age group, the track handicapper will usually take the one he thinks best of the group and assign him scale weight. That is to say, the weight that he would carry against an older horse at that time of year. Then the handicapper will assign lesser weights to the rest of the field in the order of his estimation of their merit, giving all the fairest chance to win the race and thus provide competition, the essence of racing.

If the top weight in the above example wins that race, he will pick up additional weight in his next start and so on until either he has proved that he can concede twenty pounds to his opposition and thus assure himself a niche in turf history, or a lesser weight will win and the top-weighted horse will then not have to carry such a burden in his next start.

But all races are not handicaps. There are multitudes of races for the younger age groups with rich purses that allow a horse to amass a fortune in winnings without ever having to concede a pound of weight to his adversary. These races are called "sweepstakes" or stakes races. They require that all horses carry the same weight and that the owners enter a nomination fee for their horses more than 72 hours before the race is run. America's Triple Crown—The Kentucky Derby, the Preakness and The Belmont Stakes—are good examples of this type of race. Another type of race for the younger horses that does not fall into the handicap category is the produce event. In a race like this, the horse is nominated with a fee before he is born and then additional payments along the line furnish the winner with a huge purse. The Belmont Futurity annually nets its winner more than $80,000 from all its nominating fees.

If a horse is not good enough to run in the rich events when he is young he then moves down the scale to the allowance division. In this grade, horses compete with certain allowances made for amount of money earned and number of races run, in an effort to even the race. Should the horse still not be able to compete in this class he is dropped to the claiming races where he is entered to be claimed for a certain fee each time he competes. In a race like this the owner can only enter a horse for the amount he thinks he is worth since another owner can put up the claiming price and take the horse by dropping a check in the claim box before the race.

There are many other types of races with conditions set to attract the most horses and provide the most interesting race. The conditions for the different types of races reach extremes also. A few years back, one track had a race for which gray horses only were eligible. Needless to say, the publicity value of such an event exceeded the actual purse, but it did provide interest. Some tracks have races open only to horses foaled in the state where the track is located while other states have demanded, and received, allowances for horses having been foaled within their boundaries.

As many types of races as there are, they are all styled with the same purpose in mind, namely to provide the most thrilling sport for the customers. Any manner in which that aim is achieved is considered good handicapping.

FAMOUS THOROUGHBREDS

Opinions differ as to the greatest American-foaled thoroughbred. Man o' War, who won 20 of 21 races in 1919-1920, was voted the No. 1 horse in the half-century poll of The Associated

Press in 1950, but that was before Citation became the first horse in history to pass the $1,000,000 mark in earnings.

Man o' War was campaigned only as a 2- and 3-year-old. He established 5 American track records. Except, perhaps, in his memorable race with John P. Grier at Aqueduct in 1920, Man o' War never really was pressed in competition. His only defeat came when he was virtually left at the post.

Exterminator's career was different. He raced from the time he was 2 until he was 9—and always was a stakes competitor. He won 50 of 100 official starts, was second 17 times and third on 17 other occasions. He had a number of trainers; he found all sizes and types of jockeys on his back, all with different temperaments and riding methods. He won in all types of going and at distances ranging from 5½ furlongs to 2¼ miles, under huge weight packages.

Some, the old-timers rate Sysonby as the fastest of all horses and the greatest, too. They point out that he won 14 of his 15 starts before his career was abruptly ended, and that he earned $184,438, a trememdous amount in his generation.

Other famous American horses:

Whirlaway, one-time money-winning king; Count Fleet, 3-year-old sensation in 1943; Equipoise, a former holder of the mile record; Roamer, "mile king" of another era; Colin, unbeaten in his 2 racing years; Hindoo, the "wonder horse" through 1880, 1881, 1882; Domino, who held the money-winning crown for a quarter of a century, and Sarazen, one of the fastest horses of any generation.

Also, Citation; Commando; Ben Halladay; The Parader; Lamplighter; Twenty Grand; Sir Barton, first winner of the Triple Crown (Kentucky Derby, Preakness and Belmont Stakes); Gallant Fox; Omaha; Alsab, who was purchased for $700 and developed into a champion; Sun Beau, who held the money-winning title for a number of years; Zev; Salvator; Tenny; Henry of Navarre; Whiskbroom II; Blue Larkspur; Discovery, a great

weight-carrier; War Admiral; Crusader; Roseben; Mate; Challedon; Johnstown; Whichone; Display; Victorian; Morvich, and Reigh Count, sire of Count Fleet and a standout performer in the United States and England.

The list continues with Osmand; Market Wise; Kingston; Grey Lag; Calvacade; Jack High; Omar Khayyam; Peter Pan; Hanover; Hourless; Iron Mask; Billy Kelly; Africander; Fair Play; Dark Secret; Borrow; Hermis; The Porter; Sir Martin; Banquet; Tea Tray; Imp; Ladkin; Plaudit; Parole; Ten Broeck; American Flag; Proctor Knott; Spokane; Audacious; Old Rosebud; Tippety Witchett; Mad Hatter; Sun Briar; Balko; Cudgel; Ben Ali; Jamestown; Ben Brush, and the modern Stymie; Assault; First Fiddle; Armed; Eight Thirty; Devil Diver; One Count; Tom Fool; Native Dancer, Nashua; Round Table; Gallant Man, and Bold Ruler. Included in this list are: Sword Dancer, Gun Bow, Northern Dancer, Tom Rolfe, Roman Brother, Kelso, Damascus, Buckpasser, Arts and Letters, Dr. Fager, Fort Marcy, and Secretariat.

Included among the great fillies and race mares were:

Top Flight; Regret, only filly to win the Kentucky Derby; Mollie McCarthy; Miss Woodford; Blue Girl; Eugenia Burch; Beldame; Colonial Girl; Hamburg Belle; Lady Amelia; Maskette; Artful; Firenze; Fairy Star; Pan Zareta; The Butterflies; Startle; Careful; Flamma; Viva America; Glade; Princess Doreen; Black Maria; Mata Hari, and Bateau.

Also, Nellie Flag; Cleopatra; Anita Peabody; Nellie Morse; Prudery; Handy Mandy; Alcibiades; Easter Stockings; Rose of Sharon; Suntica; Paradisical; Flying Lil; Nimba; Jacola; Edith Cavell; Snowflake; Black Helen; Petrify; Level Best; Miss Dogwood; Vagrancy; Mar-Kell; Miss Keeneland; Twilight Tear; Beaugay; Busher; Honeymoon; First Flight; Bridal Flower; Busanda; Lithe; But Why Not; Bed o' Roses; Bewitch; Next Move; Doubledogdare, and Idun. Including, Quill, Tosmah, Bowl of Flowers, Cicada, Moccasin, Gallant Bloom, Shuvee.

Man o' War's Record

(Bred by August Belmont. Owned by Glen Riddle Farm.)

1919

Date	Track	Race	Dist.	Wt.	Fin.	Time	Odds	Earnings
June 6	Belmont Park	Purse	5/8 st	115	1	:59	3-5	$ 500
June 9	Belmont Park	Keene Memorial Stakes	5 1/2f st	115	1	1:05 3/5	7-10	4,200
June 21	Jamaica	Youthful Stakes	5 1/2f	120	1	1:06 3/5	1-2	3,850
June 23	Aqueduct	Hudson Stakes	5/8	130	1	1:01 3/5	1-10	2,825
July 5	Aqueduct	Tremont Stakes	3/4	130	1	1:13	1-10	4,800
Aug. 2	Saratoga	United States Hotel Stakes	3/4	130	1	1:12 2/5	9-10	7,600
Aug. 13	Saratoga	Sanford Memorial Stakes	3/4	130	2	1:11 1/5	11-20	700
Aug. 23	Saratoga	Grand Union Hotel Stakes	3/4	130	1	1:12	11-20	7,600
Aug. 30	Saratoga	Hopeful Stakes	3/4	130	1	1:13	9-20	24,600
Sept. 13	Belmont Park	Belmont Futurity	3/4 st	127	1	1:11 3/5	1-2	26,650

st—Straightaway.

Total $83,325

1920

Date	Track	Event	Dist.	Wt.		Time		Earnings
May 18	Pimlico	Preakness Stakes	1 1/8	126	2	1:51 3/5	4-5	$23,000
May 29	Belmont Park	Withers Stakes	1	118	1	1:35 4/5	1-7	4,825
June 12	Belmont Park	Belmont Stakes	1 3/8	126	1	2:14 1/5	1-25	7,950
June 22	Jamaica	Stuyvesant Handicap	1	135	1	1:41 3/5	1-100	3,850
July 10	Aqueduct	Dwyer Stakes	1 1/8	126	1	1:49 1/5	1-5	4,850
Aug. 7	Saratoga	Miller Stakes	1 3/16	131	1	1:56 3/5	1-30	4,700
Aug. 21	Saratoga	Travers Stakes	1 1/4	129	1	2:01 4/5	2-9	9,275
Sept. 4	Belmont Park	Lawrence Realization Stakes	1 5/8	126	2	2:40 4/5	1-100	15,040
Sept. 11	Belmont Park	Jockey Club Stakes	1 1/2	118	1	2:28 4/5	1-100	5,850
Sept. 18	Havre de Grace	Potomac Handicap	1 1/16	138	1	1:44 4/5	15-100	6,800
Oct. 12	Kenilworth Park	Kenilworth Park Gold Cup	1 1/4	120	1	2:03	1-20	80,000

Total $166,140

RECAPITULATION

	Age	Starts	1st	2d	3d	Unp.	Earnings
1919	2	10	9	1	0	0	$ 83,325
1920	3	11	11	0	0	0	166,140
Totals		21	20	1	0	0	$249,465

(Man o' War died on Nov. 1, 1947.)

Citation's Record
Stakes Victories

1947

Date	Event	Dist.	Wt.	Time	Earnings
July 30	Elementary Stakes	3/4	122	1:10 3/5	$17,300
Oct. 4	Belmont Futurity	6 1/2	122	1:15 4/5	78,430
Nov. 8	Pimlico Futurity	1 1/16	119	1:48 4/5	36,675

1948

Date	Event	Dist.	Wt.	Time	Earnings
Feb. 11	Seminole Handicap	7/8	112	1:23	8,525
Feb. 18	Everglades Handicap	1 1/8	126	1:49	7,200
Feb. 28	Flamingo Stakes	1 1/8	126	1:48 4/5	43,500
Apr. 17	Chesapeake Stakes	1 1/16	122	1:45 4/5	19,750
May 1	Kentucky Derby	1 1/4	126	2:05 2/5	83,400
May 15	Preakness Stakes	1 3/16	126	2:02 2/5	91,870
May 29	Jersey Stakes	1 1/4	126	2:03	43,300
June 12	Belmont Stakes	1 1/2	126	2:28 1/5	77,700
July 5	Stars and Stripes	1 1/8	119	1:49 1/5	38,000
Aug. 28	American Derby	1 1/4	126	2:01 3/5	66,450
Oct. 2	Jockey Club Gold Cup	2	117	3:21 3/5	72,700
Oct. 16	Empire City Gold Cup	1 5/8	119	2:42 4/5	75,600
Oct. 29	*Pimlico Special	1 3/16	120	1:59 4/5	10,000
Dec. 11	Tanforan Handicap	1 1/4	123	2:02 4/5	31,800

1950

Date	Event	Dist.	Wt.	Time	Earnings
June 3	Golden Gate Mile	1	128	1:33 3/5	14,550

1951

Date	Event	Dist.	Wt.	Time	Earnings
July 4	American Handicap	1 1/8	123	1:48 2/5	33,000
July 14	Hollywood Gold Cup	1 1/4	120	2:01	100,000

*Walkover.

Record by Years

	Age	Starts	1st	2d	3d	Unp.	Earnings
1947	2	9	8	1	0	0	$155,680
1948	3	20	19	1	0	0	709,470
1949	4	0	0	0	0	0	— —
1950	5	9	2	7	0	0	73,480
1951	6	7	3	1	2	1	147,130
Total		45	32	10	2	1	$1,085,760

Nashua's Record
Stake Victories

1954

Date	Event	Dist.	Wt.	Time	Earnings
May 12	Belmont Juvenile	5/8	117	0:58	$ 12,150
Aug. 28	Hopeful	6½	122	1:17 4/5	57,050
Oct. 9	Belmont Futurity	6 1/2	122	1:15 3/5	88,015

1955

Date	Event	Dist.	Wt.	Time	Earnings
Feb. 26	Flamingo Stakes	1 1/8	122	1:49 3/5	104,600
Mar. 26	Florida Derby	1 1/8	122	1:53 1/5	100,000
Apr. 23	Wood Memorial	1 1/8	126	1:50 3/5	75,100
May 28	Preakness Stakes	1 3/16	126	1:54 3/5	67,550
June 11	Belmont Stakes	1 1/2	126	2:29	83,700
July 2	Dwyer Stakes	1 1/4	126	2:03 4/5	37,200
July 16	Arlington Classic	1	126	1:35 1/5	91,675
Aug. 31	Washington Park match race	1 1/4	126	2:04 1/5	100,000
Oct. 15	Jockey Club Gold Cup	2	119	3:24 4/5	52,850

1956

Date	Event	Dist.	Wt.	Time	Earnings
Feb. 18	Widener Handicap	1 1/4	127	2:02	92,600
May 5	Grey Lag Handicap	1 1/8	128	1:50 3/5	37,100
May 19	Camden Handicap	1 1/8	129	1:49 1/5	22,750
July 4	Suburban Handicap	1 1/4	128	2:00 4/5	55,900
July 14	Monmouth Handicap	1 1/4	129	2:02 4/5	78,200
Oct. 13	Jockey Club Gold Cup	2	124	3:20 2/5	36,600

Record by Years

	Age	Starts	1st	2nd	3rd	Unp.	Earnings
1954	2	8	6	2	0	0	$192,865
1955	3	12	10	1	1	0	752,550
1956	4	10	6	1	0	3	343,150
Total		30	22	4	1	3	$1,288,565

FAMOUS STEEPLECHASERS

Good and Plenty; Alfar; Grandpa; Hibler; Duke of Duluth; Cherry Malotte; Skibbereen; Jolly Roger; Fairmont; Duettiste; Earlocker; Shannon River; Bushranger; Erne II; Lorenzo; Billy Barton; Battleship; Ossabaw; Ruller; Green Cheese; Arc Light; Tourist II; Expectation; Bagatelle; The Brook; Amagansett; Roiter; Elkridge; Cottesmore; Chenango; National Anthem; Lion Heart; Iron Shot; Annibal; The Welkin; John M. P.; Brother Jones; Oedipus; Rouge Dragon; Trough Hill; Niji; Shipboard; King Commander and The Mast. Also included are Amber Driver, Bon Nouvel, Mako, L'Escargot, Top Bid, and Shadow Brook.

CHAMPIONS
Triangle Publications Poll

(Selections by staffs of Daily Racing Form and Morning Telegraph.) Starting in 1971, the annual champions were determined in a combined poll of the staff members of Daily Racing Form and The Morning Telegraph, plus The Board of Selection of the T.R.A. and members of the National Turf Writers Association.

Horse of the Year

1936—Granville	1961—Kelso
1937—War Admiral	1962—Kelso
1938—Seabiscuit	1963—Kelso
1939—Challedon	1964—Kelso
1940—Challedon	1965—Roman Brother
1941—Whirlaway	1966—Buckpasser
1942—Whirlaway	1967—Damascus
1943—Count Fleet	1968—Dr. Fager
1944—Twilight Tear	1969—Arts and Letters
1945—Busher	1970—Fort Marcy
1946—Assault	1971—Ack Ack
1947—Armed	1972—Secretariat
1948—Citation	
1949—Capot	
1950—Hill Prince	
1951—Counterpoint	
1952—One Count	
1953—Tom Fool	
1954—Native Dancer	
1955—Nashua	
1956—Swaps	
1957—Bold Ruler	
1958—Round Table	
1959—Sword Dancer	
1960—Kelso	

Handicap Division

Horse	Filly
1936—Discovery	————
1937—Seabiscuit	————
1938—Seabiscuit	Marica
1939—Kayak II	Lady Maryland
1940—Challedon	War Plumage
1941—Mioland	Fairy Chant
1942—Whirlaway	Vagrancy
1943—Market Wise	Mar-Kell
Devil Diver	
1944—Devil Diver	Twilight Tear
1945—Stymie	Busher
1946—Armed	Gallorette
1947—Armed	But Why Not
1948—Citation	Conniver
1949—Coaltown	Bewitch
1950—Noor	Two Lea
1951—Hill Prince	Bed o' Roses
1952—Crafty Admiral	Real Delight
1953—Tom Fool	Sickle's Image
1954—Native Dancer	Parlo
1955—High Gun	Misty Morn
1956—Swaps	Blue Sparkler
1957—Dedicate	Pucker Up
1958—Round Table	Bornastar
1959—Sword Dancer	Tempted
1960—Bald Eagle	Royal Native
1961—Kelso	Airman's Guide
1962—Kelso	Primonetta
1963—Kelso	Cicada
1964—Kelso	Tosmah
1965—Roman Brother	Old Hat
1966—Buckpasser	Open Fire
1967—Damascus	Straight Deal
1968—Dr. Fager	Gamely
1969—Arts and Letters	Gallant Bloom
1970—Fort Marcy	Shuvee
1971—Ack Ack	Shuvee
1972—Autobiography	Typecast

3-Year-Olds

Colt	Filly
1936—Granville	————
1937—War Admiral	————
1938—Stagehand	————
1939—Challedon	Unerring
1940—Bimelech	————
1941—Whirlaway	Painted Veil
1942—Alsab	Vagrancy
1943—Count Fleet	Stefanita
1944—By Jimminy	Twilight Tear
1945—Fighting Step	Busher
1946—Assault	Bridal Flower
1947—Phalanx	But Why Not
1948—Citation	Miss Request
1949—Capot	Two Lea, Wistful (tie)
1950—Hill Prince	Next Move
1951—Counterpoint	Kiss Me Kate
1952—One Count	Real Delight
1953—Native Dancer	Grecian Queen
1954—High Gun	Parlo

1955—Nashua	Misty Morn
1956—Needles	Doubledogdare
1957—Bold Ruler	Bayou
1958—Tim Tam	Idun
1959—Sword Dancer	Royal Native
1960—Kelso	Berlo
1961—Carry Back	Bowl of Flowers
1962—Jaipur	Cicada
1963—Chateaugay	Lamb Chops
1964—Northern Dancer	Tosmah
1965—Tom Rolfe	What a Treat
1966—Buckpasser	Lady Pitt
1967—Damascus	Furl Sail
1968—Stage Door Johnny	Dark Mirage
1969—Arts and Letters	Gallant Bloom
1970—Personality	Office Queen
1971—Canonero II	Turkish Trousers
1972—Key to The Mint	Susan's Girl

2-Year-Olds

Colt	Filly
1936—Pompoon	————
1937—Menow	————
1938—El Chico	Inscoelda
1939—Bimelech	Now What
1940—Our Boots	Level Best
1941—Alsab	Petrify
1942—Count Fleet	Askmenow
1943—Platter	Durazna
1944—Pavot	Busher
1945—Star Pilot	Beaugay
1946—Double Jay	First Flight
1947—Citation	Bewitch
1948—Blue Peter	Myrtle Charm
1949—Hill Prince	Bed o' Roses
1950—Battlefield	Aunt Jinny
1951—Tom Fool	Rose Jet
1952—Native Dancer	Sweet Patootie
1953—Porterhouse	Evening Out
1954—Nashua	High Voltage
1955—Needles	Doubledogdare
1956—Barbizon	Leallah
1957—Nadir	Idun
1958—First Landing	Quill
1959—Warfare	My Dear Girl
1960—Hail to Reason	Bowl of Flowers
1961—Crimson Satan	Cicada
1962—Never Bend	Smart Deb
1963—Hurry to Market	Castle Forbes
1964—Bold Lad	Queen Empress
1965—Buckpasser	Moccasin
1966—Successor	Regal Gleam
1967—Vitriolic	Queen of the Stage
1968—Top Knight	Gallant Bloom
1969—Silent Screen	Fast Attack
1970—Hoist the Flag	Forward Gal
1971—Riva Ridge	Numbered Account
1972—Secretariat	La Prevoyante

Sprinter

1947—Polynesian	1949—Delegate
1948—Coaltown	1950—Sheilas Reward

1951—Sheilas Reward
1952—Tea-Maker
1953—Tom Fool
1954—White Skies
1955—Berseem
1956—Decathlon
1957—Decathlon
1958—Bold Ruler
1959—Intentionally

1960—64—No selection
1965—Affectionately
1966—Impressive
1967—Dr. Fager
1968—Dr. Fager
1969—Ta Wee
1970—Ta Wee
1971—Ack Ack
1972—Chou Croute

Steeplechaser

1942—Elkridge
1943—Brother Jones
1944—Rouge Dragon
1945—Mercator
1946—Elkridge
1947—War Battle
1948—American Way
1949—Trough Hill
1950—Oedipus
1951—Oedipus
1952—Jam
1953—The Mast
1954—King Commander
1955—Neji
1956—Shipboard

1957—58—Neji
1959—Ancestor
1960—Benguala
1961—Peal
1962—Barnabys Bluff
1963—Amber Diver
1964—65—Bon Nouvel
1966—Mako
1967—Quick Pitch
1968—Bon Nouvel
1969—L'Escargot
1970—Top Bid
1971—Shadow Brook
1972—Soothsayer

Grass Horse

1953—Iceberg II
1954—Stan
1955—St. Vincent
1956—Career Boy
1957—58—Round Table
1959—Round Table
1960—No selection
1961—T.V. Lark
1962—No selection
1963—Mongo

1964—No selection
1965—Parka
1966—Assagai
1967—Fort Marcy
1968—Dr. Fager
1969—Hawaii
1970—Fort Marcy
1971—Run the Gantlet
1972—Cougar II

Thoroughbred Racing Association Poll

(Selections based on poll of handicappers at
T.R.A. tracks.) Starting in 1971, the annual
champions were determined in a combined poll
of staff members of *Daily Racing Form* and the
Morning Telegram, the T.R.A. and the National
Turf Writers Association.

American Champion

1950—Hill Prince
1951—Counterpoint
1952—Native Dancer
1953—Tom Fool
1954—Native Dancer
1955—Nashua
1956—Swaps
1957—Dedicate
1958—Round Table
1959—Sword Dancer
1960—Kelso

1961—Kelso
1962—Kelso
1963—Kelso
1964—Kelso
1965—Roman Brother
1966—Buckpasser
1967—Damascus
1968—Dr. Fager
1969—Arts and Letters
1970—Personality

Handicap Division

Horse	Filly or Mare
1950—Noor	Two Lea
1951—Hill Prince	Bed o' Roses
1952—Crafty Admiral	Next Move
1953—Tom Fool	Sickle's Image
1954—Native Dancer	Lavender Hill
1955—High Gun	Parlo
1956—Swaps	Blue Sparkler
1957—Dedicate	Pucker Up
1958—Round Table	Bornastar
1959—Round Table	Tempted
1960—Bald Eagle	Royal Native
1961—Kelso	Airman's Guide
1962—Kelso	Primonetta
1963—Kelso	Cicada
1964—Kelso	Old Hat
1965—Roman Brother	Old Hat
1966—Bold Bidder	Summer Scandal
1967—Buckpasser	Straight Deal
1968—Dr. Fager	Gamely
1969—Nodouble	Gamely
1970—Nodouble	Shuvee

3-Year-Olds

Colt	Filly
1950—Hill Prince	Next Move
1951—Counterpoint	Kiss Me Kate
1952—One Count	Real Delight
1953—Native Dancer	Grecian Queen
1954—High Gun	Parlo
1955—Nashua	Misty Morn
1956—Needles	Doubledogdare
1957—Bold Ruler	Bayou
1958—Tim Tam	Idun
1959—Sword Dancer	Silver Spoon
1960—Kelso	Berlo
1961—Carry Back	Bowl of Flowers
1962—Jaipur	Cicada
1963—Chateaugay	Lamb Chops
1964—Northern Dancer	Tosmah
1965—Tom Rolfe	What a Treat
1966—Buckpasser	Lady Pitt
1967—Damascus	Gamely
1968—Stage Door Johnny	Dark Image
1969—Arts & Letters	Gallant Bloom
1970—Personality	Fanfreluche

2-Year-Olds

Colt	Filly
1950—Battlefield	Aunt Jinny
1951—Tom Fool	Rose Jet
1952—Native Dancer	Sweet Patootie
1953—Porterhouse	Evening Out
1954—Nashua	High Voltage
1955—Nail	Nasrina
1956—Barbizon	Romanita
1957—Jewel's Reward	Idun
1958—First Landing	Quill
1959—Warfare	My Dear Girl
1960—Hail to Reason	Bowl of Flowers

1961—Crimson Satan	Cicada
1962—Never Bend	Smart Deb
1963—Hurry to Market	Castle Forbes
1964—Bold Lad	Queen Empress
1965—Buckpasser	Moccasin
1966—Successor	Regal Gleam
1967—Vitriolic	Queen of the Stage
1968—Top Knight	Process Shot
1969—Silent Screen	Tudor Screen
1970—Hoist the Flag	Forward Gal

Steeplechaser

1950—Oedipus	1961—Peal
1951—Oedipus	1962—Barnaby's Bluff
1952—Oedipus	1963—Amber Diver
1953—The Mast	1964—Bon Nouvel
1954—King Commander	1965—Bon Nouvel
1955—Neji	1966—Tuscalee
1956—Shipboard	1967—Quick Pitch
1957-58—Neji	1968—Bon Nouvel
1959—Ancestor	1969—L'Escargot
1960—Benguala	1970—Top Bid

Money-Winning Leaders

In the early days of horse racing the value of an animal generally was measured by his earnings. The values of stakes were so standardized that what a horse won in a season, or a lifetime, was something of a gauge by which he could be judged.

In the 1890's, when Domino earned $170,790 (in 1893, as a 2-year-old), it had great meaning. He had won more than any 2-year-old of his time. He was greatness personified. The standard continued for better than 25 years. The value of a 2-year-old was compared against the grand earning performance of Domino. But as time went on conditions changed. Money added to stakes was increased fabulously. A modern horse could win, as a result of stakes appreciation, double or triple what was possible for Hindoo and other old-timers.

Races that were worth $10,000 or $15,000 in the heyday of Man o' War, Exterminator, etc., have skyrocketed. Both great horses are far down on the money list—Exterminator with $252,996 for 8 racing years, and Man o' War with $249,465 for two years of sensational exploits, during which he won 20 to 21 starts. By comparison with horses of a later day, both Exterminator and Man o' War are "dubs" as earners.

Therefore, the earnings of horses of the old days, insignificant with those of the moderns, are no criterion. They lived—those old idols—in an era of "small change."

Both Exterminator and Man o' War, in action these past few years, would have, by winning equivalent stakes, pushed their incomes close to the $1,000,000 mark, but they are close only to the quarter-million. Therefore, the modern horse, picking up $500,000, or thereabouts, is not to be considered their superior because of the numerals. He is to be regarded merely as fortunate, since he was foaled at a time when even obscure races net moderns more in an afternoon than was possible for Colin, Discovery, Domino, Hindoo, Exterminator, Equipoise, Man o' War, Salvator, Sarazen and Sysonby to earn in an entire season.

Therefore, no horse of class is to be judged by the money he has won.

All-Time
(Through 1972)

	Sts.	1st	2d	3d	Amount
Kelso	63	39	12	2	$1,977,896
Round Table	66	43	8	5	1,749,869
Buckpasser	31	25	4	1	1,462,014
Nashua	30	22	4	1	1,288,565
Carry Back	61	21	11	11	1,241,165
Damacus	32	21	7	3	1,176,781
Fort Marcy	75	21	18	14	1,109,791
Citation	45	32	10	2	1,085,760
Native Diver	81	37	7	12	1,026,500
Dr. Fager	22	18	2	1	1,002,642
Swoon's Son	51	30	10	3	970,605
Roman Brother	42	16	10	5	943,473
Stymie	131	35	33	28	918,485
T. V. Lark	72	19	13	6	902,194
Shuvee	44	16	10	6	890,445
Swaps	25	19	2	2	848,900
Nodouble	42	13	11	5	846,749
Sword Dancer	39	15	7	4	829,610
Candy Spots	22	12	5	1	824,718
Mongo	46	22	10	4	820,766
Armed	81	41	20	10	817,475
Find	110	22	27	27	803,615
Gun Bow	42	17	8	4	798,722
Grimson Satan	58	18	9	9	796,007
In Reality	27	14	9	2	795,824
Native Dancer	22	21	1	0	785,240
Cicada	42	23	8	6	783,674
First Landing	37	19	9	2	779,577
Bold Ruler	33	23	4	2	764,204
Bally Ache	31	16	9	4	758,522
Straight Deal	99	21	21	9	733,020
Quicken Tree	74	15	9	13	718,303

Unbeaten 2-Year-Old Champions

Year	Horse	Races Won
1873	Rutherford	1
1879	Sensation	8
1886	Tremont	13
1889	El Rio Rey	9
1893	Domino	9
1894	The Butterflies	3
1907	Colin	12
1914	Regret	3
1920	Tryster	6
1921	Morvich	11
1930	Vanderpool*	11
1931	Top Flight	7
1938	El Chico	7
1939	Bimelech	6
1944	Pavot	8
1952	Native Dancer	9
1957	Idun (filly)	8
1965	Moccasin (filly)	8

*Vanderpool finished second to Equipoise, beaten 3 lengths, but Equipoise was disqualified.

Leading United States Sires
(Since 1940)

Year and Sire	Races Won	Money
1940—Sir Gallahad III (f) .	102	$ 305,610
1941—Blenheim II (e)	64	378,981
1942—Equipoise	82	437,141
1943—Bull Dog (f)	172	372,706
1944—Chance Play	150	431,100
1945—War Admiral	59	591,352
1946—Mahmoud (f)	101	683,025
1947—Bull Lea	126	1,259,718
1948—Bull Lea	147	1,334,027
1949—Bull Lea	165	992,002
1950—Heliopolis	167	852,292
1951—Count Fleet	124	1,160,847
1952—Bull Lea	136	1,630,655
1953—Bull Lea	107	1,155,846
1954—Heliopolis (e).....	148	1,406,638
1955—Nasrullah (i)	69	1,433,660
1956—Nasrullah (i)	106	1,462,413
1957—Princequillo	147	1,698,427
1958—Princequillo	110	1,394,540
1959—Nasrullah	141	1,434,543
1960—Nasrullah	122	1,419,683
1961—Ambiorix	148	936,976
1962—Nasrullah	107	1,474,831
1963—Bold Ruler	56	917,531
1964—Bold Ruler	88	1,457,156
1965—Bold Ruler	90	1,091,924
1966—Bold Ruler	107	2,306,523
1967—Bold Ruler	135	2,249,272
1968—Bold Ruler	99	1,988,427
1969—Bold Ruler	90	1,357,144
1970—Hail to Reason	82	1,400,839
1971—Northern Dancer ..	93	1,288,580
1972—Round Table	——	1,199,933

Note: Of above stallion champions, all bred in United States except: (e) England, (f) France, (i) Ireland.

RECORDS
World

Distance	Horse, age, weight, track and location	Date	Time
1/4	Big Racket, 4, 111, Hipodromo de las Americas, Mexico City, Mexico	Feb. 5, 1945	0:20 4/5
2 1/2 f. ...	Tie Score, 5, 115, Hipodromo de las Americas, Mexico City, Mexico	Feb. 5, 1946	0:26 4/5
3/8	Atoka, 6, 105, Butte, Mont.	Sept. 7, 1906	0:33 1/2
3 1/2 f. ...	Joe Blair, 5, 115, Juarez, Mexico	Feb. 5, 1916	0:39
3 1/2	Deep Sun 7, 120, Shenandoah Downs, Charles Town, W. Va.	July 11, 1959	0:39
Y2	Tamran's Jet, 2, 118, Sunland Park, Sunland, N.M.	Mar. 22, 1968	0:44 4/5
	Crimson Saint, 2, 119, Oakland Park, Hot Springs, Ark.	Apr. 1, 1971	0:44 4/5
	Mighty Mr. A., 3, 116, Sportsman's Park, Cicero, Ill.	Nov. 1, 1971	0:44 4/5
	Thief of Bagdad, 5, 114, Sportsman's Park, Cicero, Ill.	Nov. 5, 1971	0:44 4/5
4 1/2	Kathryn's Doll, 2, 111, Turf Paradise, Phoenix, Ariz.	Apr. 9, 1967	0:50 2/5
	Dear Ethel, 2, 114, Miles Park, Louisville, Ky.	July 4, 1967	0:50 4/5
5/8	Zip Pocket, 3, 122, Turf Paradise, Phoenix, Ariz.....................	Apr. 22, 1967	0:55 2/5
5 1/2 f. ...	Zip Pocket, 3, 129, Turf Paradise, Phoenix, Ariz.	Nov. 19, 1967	1:01 3/5
5 3/4 f. ...	Fighting Fox, 4, 126, Empire City, Yonkers, N.Y.	July 8, 1939,	1:07 2/5
	Doublrab, 4, 130, Empire City, Yonkers, N.Y.	July 18, 1942	1:07 2/5
3/4	*Gelding by Blink-Broken Tendril, 3, 123, Brighton, England	Aug. 6, 1929	1:06 1/5
3/4	Vale of Tears, 6, 120, Ak-Sar-Ben, Omaha, Neb.	June 7, 1969	1:07 2/5
6 1/2 f. ...	Turbulator, 4, 115, Longacres, Seattle, Wash.	Aug. 16, 1970	1:14
7/8	El Drag, 4, 115, Hollywood Park, Inglewood, Calif.	May 21, 1955	1:20
7/8	Native Diver, 6, 126, Hollywood Park, Inglewood, Calif.	May 22, 1965	1:20
1 mi.	Dr. Fager, 4, 134, Arlington Park, Arlington, Ill.	Aug. 24, 1968	1:32 1/5
1 mi. 70 yd.	Drill Site, 5, 115, Garden State Park, Cherry Hill, N.J.	Oct. 12, 1964	1:38 4/5
1 mi. 70 yd.	Pass the Brandy, 7, 114, Arlington Park, Arlington, Ill.	July 25, 1970	1:38 4/5
1 1/16	Swaps, 4, 130, Hollywood Park, Inglewood, Calif.	June 23, 1956	1:39
1 1/8	Pink Pigeon, 4, 116, Santa Anita, Arcadia, Calif.	Mar. 27, 1969	1:45 4/5
1 3/16	Fleet Bird, 4, 123, Golden Gate Fields, Albany, Calif.	Oct. 24, 1953	1:52 3/5
1 1/4	Quilche, 6, 115, Santa Anita, Arcadia, Calif.	Feb. 23, 1970	1:58
1 3/8	Quilche, 6, 115, Hollywood Park, Inglewood, Calif.	Apr. 25, 1970	2:11 3/5
1 1/2	Fiddle Isle, 5, 124, Santa Anita, Arcadia, Calif.	Mar. 31, 1970	2:23
1 9/16	Lone Wolf, 5, 115, Keeneland, Lexington, Ky.	Oct. 31, 1961	2:37 3/5
1 5/8	Swaps, 4, 130, Hollywood Park, Inglewood, Calif.	July 25, 1956	2:38 1/5
1 mi. 5 1/2 f.	Distribute, 9, 109, River Downs, Cincinnati, Ohio	Sept. 7, 1940	2:51 3/5
1 3/4	Swartz Pete, 6, Alexandra Park, Auckland, New Zealand	Jan. 1, 1966	2:50 4/5
1 7/8	El Moro, 8, 116, Delaware Park, Wilmington, Del	July 22, 1963	3:11 4/5
2	Polazel, 3, 142, Salisbury, England	July 8, 1924	3:15
2 mi. 40 yd.	Winning Mark, 4, 107, Thistle Down Park, Cleveland, Ohio	July 20, 1940	3:29 2/5
2 mi. 70 yd.	Iberis, 4, 122, Hawthorne, Cicero, Ill.	Oct. 15, 1969	3:30 3/5
2 1/16	Midafternoon, 4, 126, Jamaica, Jamaica, N.Y........................	Nov. 15, 1956	3:29 3/5
2 1/8	Centurion, 5, 119, Newbury, England	Sept. 29, 1923	3:35
2 3/16	Santiago, 5, 112, Narragansett Park, Pawtuckey, R.I.	Sept. 27, 1941	3:51 1/5
2 1/4	Dakota, 4, 116, Longfield, England	May 27, 1927	3:37 3/5
2 3/8	Wiki Jack, 4, 97, Tijuana, Mexico	Feb. 8, 1925	4:15
2 1/2	Miss Grillo, 6, 118, Pimlico, Baltimore, Md.	Nov. 12, 1948	4:14 3/5
2 5/8	†Worthman, 5, 101, Tijuana, Mexico	Feb. 22, 1925	4:51 2/5
2 3/4	Shot Put, 4, 126, Washington Park, Homewood, Ill.	Aug. 14, 1940	4:48 4/5
2 7/8	‡Bosh, 5, 100, Tijuana, Mexico	Mar. 8, 1925	5:23
3	Farragut, 4, 113, Agua Caliente, Mexico	Mar. 9, 1941	5:15
3 3/8	Winning Mark, 4, 104, Washington Park, Homewood, Ill.	Aug. 21, 1940	6:13
4	Sotemia, 5, 119, Churchill Downs, Louisville, Ky.	Oct. 7, 1912	7:10 4/5

† Track heavy.   ‡ Track sloppy.

3/4 mile course at Brighton is started from a hill and is down grade to within one-third of a mile of the finish.

Straight Course

Distance	Horse, age, weight, track and location	Date	Time
1/4	Red Jones, 7, 126, Cranwood Race Course, Warrensville Heights, Ohio	Oct. 21, 1958	0:21 1/5
1/4	Bekky's Star, 2, 115, Sunland Park, Sunland, N.M.	Feb. 12, 1968	0:21 1/5
	Wandering Boy, 6, 118, Turf Paradise, Phoenix, Ariz.	Dec. 5, 1965	0:21 1/5
2 1/2f....	Meditacao, 2, 113, Hipodrome de las Americas, Mexico City, Mex	Apr. 2, 1970	0:26 2/5
3/8	King Rhymer, 2, 118, Santa Anita Park, Arcadia, Calif.	Feb. 27, 1947	0:32
1/2	Sonido, 2, 111, Hipodromo La Rinconada, Caracas, Ven.	June 28, 1970	0:44 2/5
4 1/2 f. ...	The Pimpernel, 2, 118, Belmont Park, Elmont, N.Y.	May 17, 1951	0:49 4/5
	Reneged, 2, 118, Belmont Park, Elmont, N.Y.	June 7, 1955	0:49 4/5
5/8	Indigenous, 4, 131, Epsom Downs, Epsom, Eng.	June 2, 1960	0:53 3/5
5 1/2 f. ..	Delegate, 7, 113, Belmont Park, Elmont, N.Y.	Oct. 10, 1951	1:01 3/5
3/4	Vestment, 2, 115, Belmont Park, Elmont, N.Y.	Oct. 15, 1954	1:07 4/5
6 1/2 f. ...	Porter's Mite, 2, 119, Belmont Park, Elmont, N.Y.	Sept. 17, 1938	1:14 2/5
	Native Dancer, 2, 122, Belmont Park, Elmont, N.Y.	Sept. 27, 1952	1:14 2/5
*Abt. 7/8 .	High Strung, 2, 122, Belmont Park, Elmont, N.Y.	Sept. 15, 1928	1:19
7/8	First Edition, 4, 126, Hurst Park, Hampton Court, England	May 25, 1926	1:20
1	Alizarene, 4, 120, Chepstow, Eng.	June 28, 1947	1:32 3/5
1 1/4	Banquet, 3, 108, Monmouth Park, New Jersey	July 17, 1890	2:03 3/4

* 165 feet short of 7/8 mile.

Record Prices for Sires

The record price for a horse occurred in 1970 for $5,440,000. Nijinsky II, the first English Triple Crown winner in 35 years, was bought by a syndicate of 32 shares, $170,000 each.

Today there are now 46 stallions syndicated for $1 million or more.

Horse	Year	Price
Nijinsky	1970	....$5,444,000
Vaguely Noble	1968	5,000,000
Buckpasser	1967	4,800,000
Dr. Fager	1968	3,200,000

Bold Reason	1971	3,200,000
Arts and Letters* ...	1970	3,000,000
Raise a Native	1967	2,625,000
Damascus	1968	2,560,000
Graustark	1966	2,400,000
Northern Dancer	1970	2,400,000
Kauai King	1966	2,160,000
Sir Ivor	1970	2,080,000
Le Fabuleux	1971	2,080,000
Swaps	1957	2,000,000
Dancer's Image	1968	2,000,000
*Estimated		

Record Prices for Yearlings

Year	Name	Pedigree	Buyer	Price
1970 .	Crowned Prince (c) ..	Raise a Native-Gay Hostess ...	Frank McMahon	$510,000
1968 .	Reine Enchanteur (f)	Sea-Bird-Libra	W.P. Rosso	405,000
1968 .	Exemplary (c)	Fleet Nasrullah-Sequence	Ada L. Martin Stable	280,000
1970 .	Our Beloved (f)	Hail to Reason-Affectionately .	John W. Jacobs (Agent) ..	256,000
1967 .	Majestic Prince (c) ..	Raise a Native-Gay Hostess ...	Frank McMahon	250,000
1971 .	(Unnamed) (c)	Buckpasser-Casaque Grise	Mrs. Marion du Pont Scott	235,000
1968 .	Love of Learning (f) .	Hail to Reason-Cosmah	J.E. Burch (Agent)	225,000
1971 .	Mr. Prospector (c) ...	Raise a Native-Gold Digger ...	A.I. Savin	220,000
1968 .	Burd Alane (c)	Sea-Bird-Sofarsogood	Watermill Farm	210,000
1969 .	Knight's Honor (c) ..	Round Table-Vestment	Bert W. Martin	210,000
1969 .	Shalimar Gardens (f) .	Raise a Native-Sailor Princess .	Happy Valley Farm	205,000

(c) Colt; (f) Filly

U.S. FOAL REGISTRATIONS

(Since 1940)

Year	Foals		
1940	6,559	1956	9,791
1941	6,784	1957	10,076
1942	6,352	1958	11,159
1943	5,839	1959	11,935
1944	5,400	1960	12,550
1945	5,600	1961	13,461
1946	6,478	1962	14,161
1947	7,600	1963	15,911
1948	8,200	1964	17,347
1949	8,481	1965	18,768
1950	9,036	1966	20,131
1951	8,581	1967	21,754
1952	8,413	1968	22,977
1953	9,062	1969	24,033
1954	9,031	1970	24,954
1955	9,195	1971	25,000

WINNERS OF STAKES RACES

Racing's "Triple Crown"

The best-known horse races in this country are three events for 3-year-olds—the Kentucky Derby at Churchill Downs, the Preakness Stakes at Pimlico and the Belmont Stakes at Belmont Park. These races combined are known as the "Triple Crown" of the American turf. The Derby now is at a mile and a quarter, the Preakness at a mile and three-sixteenths and the Belmont at a mile and a half.

Only nine horses, starting with Sir Barton in 1919, have won all three classics. The others were Gallant Fox (1930), Omaha (1935), War Admiral (1937), Whirlaway (1941), Count Fleet (1943), Assault (1946), Citation (1948), and Secretariat (1973).

The tabulations on these three races were compiled and copyrighted by Triangle Publications, Inc. (Daily Racing Form and Morning Telegraph) and are reprinted by special permission.

Kentucky Derby

Churchill Downs; 3-year olds; 1-¼ miles

Year	Winner	Jockey	Wt.	Net val.
1875	Aristides	Lewis	100	$2,850
1876	Vagrant	Swim	97	2,950
1877	Baden Baden	Walker	100	3,300
1878	Day Star	Carter	100	4,050
1879	Lord Murphy	Schauer	100	3,550
1880	Fonso	G Lewis	105	3,800
1881	Hindoo	J. McLaughlin	105	4,410
1882	Apollo	Hurd	102	4,560
1883	Leonatus	W. Donohue	105	3,750
1884	Buchanan	I. Murphy	110	3,990
1885	Joe Cotton	Henderson	110	4,630
1886	Ben Ali	P. Duffy	118	4,890
1887	Montrose	I. Lewis	118	4,200
1888	Macbeth II	Covington	115	4,740
1889	Spokane	Kiley	118	4,970
1890	Riley	I. Murphy	118	5,460
1891	Kingman	I. Murphy	122	4,680
1892	Azra	A. Clayton	122	4,230
1893	Lookout	Kunze	122	4,090
1894	Chant	Goodale	122	4,020
1895	Halma	Perkins	122	2,970
1896	Ben Brush	Simms	117	4,850
1897	Typhoon II	F. Garner	117	4,850
1898	Plaudit	Simms	117	4,850
1899	Manuel	Taral	117	4,850
1900	Lieutenant Gibson	Boland	117	4,850
1901	His Eminence	Winkfield	117	4,850
1902	Alan-a-Dale	Winkfield	117	4,850
1903	Judge Himes	H. Booker	117	4,850
1904	Elwood	Prior	117	4,850
1905	Agile	J. Martin	122	4,850
1906	Sir Huon	R. Troxler	117	4,850
1907	Pink Star	Minder	117	4,850
1908	Stone Street	A. Pickens	117	4,850
1909	Wintergreen	V. Powers	117	4,850
1910	Donau	Herbert	117	4,850
1911	Meridian	G. Archibald	117	4,850
1912	Worth	C.H. Shilling	117	4,850
1913	Donerail	R. Goose	117	5,475
1914	Old Rosebud	J. McCabe	114	9,125
1915	Regret	J. Nutter	112	11,450
1916	George Smith	J. Loftus	117	9,750
1917	Omar Khayyam	C. Borel	117	16,600
1918	Exterminator	W. Knapp	114	14,700
1919	Sir Barton	J. Loftus	112½	28,825
1920	Paul Jones	T. Rice	126	30,375
1921	Behave Youself	C. Thompson	126	38,450
1922	Morvich	A. Johnson	126	53,775
1923	Zev	E. Sande	126	53,600
1924	Black Gold	J.D. Mahoney	126	52,775
1925	Flying Ebony	E. Sande	126	52,950
1926	Bubbling Over	A. Johnson	126	50,075
1927	Whiskery	L. McAtee	126	51,000
1928	Reigh Count	C. Lang	126	55,375
1929	Clyde Van Dusen	L. McAtee	126	53,950
1930	Gallant Fox	E. Sande	126	50,725
1931	Twenty Grand	C. Kurtsinger	126	48,725
1932	Burgoo King	E. James	126	52,350
1933	Brokers Tip	D. Meade	126	48,925
1934	Cavalcade	M. Garner	126	28,175
1935	Omaha	W. Saunders	126	39,525
1936	Bold Venture	I. Hanford	126	37,725
1937	War Admiral	C. Kurtsinger	126	52,050
1938	Lawrin	E. Arcaro	126	47,050
1939	Johnstown	J. Stout	126	46,350
1940	Gallahadion	C. Bierman	126	60,150
1941	Whirlaway	E. Arcaro	126	61,275
1942	Shut Out	W.D. Wright	126	64,225
1943	Count Fleet	J. Longden	126	60,725
1944	Pensive	C. McCreary	126	64,675
1945	Hoop, Jr.	E. Arcaro	126	64,850
1946	Assault	W. Mehrtens	126	96,400
1947	Jet Pilot	E. Guerin	126	92,160
1948	Citation	E. Arcaro	126	83,400
1949	Ponder	S. Brooks	126	91,600
1950	Middleground	W. Boland	126	92,650
1951	Count Turf	C. McCreary	126	98,050
1952	Hill Gail	E. Arcaro	126	96,300
1953	Dark Star	H. Moreno	126	90,050
1954	Determine	R. York	126	102,050
1955	Swaps	W. Shoemaker	126	108,400
1956	Needles	D. Erb	126	123,450
1957	Iron Liege	W. Hartack	126	107,950
1958	Tim Tam	I. Valenzuela	126	116,400
1959	Tomy Lee	W. Shoemaker	126	119,650
1960	Venetian Way	W. Hartack	126	114,850
1961	Carry Back	J. Sellers	126	120,500
1962	Decidedly	W. Hartack	126	119,650
1963	Chateaugay	B. Baeza	126	108,900
1964	Northern Dancer	W. Hartack	126	114,300
1965	Lucky Debonair	W. Shoemaker	126	112,000
1966	Kauai King	D. Brumfield	126	120,500
1967	Proud Clarion	R. Ussery	126	119,700
1968	Dancer's Image*	R. Ussery	126	122,600
1969	Majestic Prince	W. Hartack	126	113,200
1970	Dust Commander	M. Manganello	126	127,800
1971	Canonero II	G. Avila	126	145,500
1972	Riva Ridge	R. Turcotte	126	140,300
1973	Secretariat	R. Turcotte	126	155,050

* Purse taken away from Dancer's Image and awarded to Forward Pass.

Preakness Stakes

Pimlico Race Course; 3-year-olds; 1-3/16 miles.

Year	Winner	Jockey	Wt.	Net val.
1873	Survivor	G. Barbee	110	$ 1,800
1874	Culpepper	M. Donohue	110	1,900
1875	Tom Ochiltree	L. Hughes	110	1,900
1876	Shirley	G. Barbee	110	1,950
1877	Cloverbrook	C. Holloway	110	1,600
1878	Duke of Magenta	C. Holloway	110	2,100
1879	Harold	L. Hughes	110	2,550
1880	Grenada	L. Hughes	110	2,000

1881 Saunterer ......W. Costello	110	1,950
1882 Vanguard .....W. Costello	110	1,250
1883 Jacobus........G. Barbee	110	1,635
1884 Knight of Ellerslie		
S.H. Fisher	110	1,905
1885 Tecumseh ...J. McLaughlin	118	2,160
1886 The Bard .....S.H. Fisher	118	2,050
1887 Dunbine ....W. Donoghue	118	1,675
1888 Refund .....F. Littlefield	118	1,185
1889 Buddhist .....H. Anderson	118	1,130
1894 Assignee ....F. Taral	122	1,830
1895 Belmar ....F. Taral	115	1,350
1896 Margrave ....H. Griffin	115	1,350
1897 Paul Karvar ....Thorpe	108	1,420
1898 Sly Fox ....W. Simms	120	1,500
1899 Half Time .....R. Clawson	102	1,580
1900 Hindus ....H. Spencer	110	1,900
1901 The Parader ......Landry	118	1,605
1902 Old England ....L. Jackson	118	2,240
1903 Flocarline ....W. Gannon	113	1,875
1904 Bryn Mawr .E. Hilderbrand	108	2,355
1905 Cairngorm ....W. Davis	114	2,200
1906 Whimsical .....W. Miller	108	2,355
1907 Don Enrique ..G. Mountain	107	2,260
1908 Royal Tourist ...E. Dugan	112	2,455
1909 Effendi ....W. Doyle	116	3,225
1910 Layminster ......R. Estep	84	3,300
1911 Watervale ......E. Dugan	112	2,700
1912 Colonel Halloway, C. Turner	107	1,450
1913 Buskin........J. Butwell	117	1,670
1914 Holiday ....A. Schuttinger	108	1,355
1915 Rhine Maiden .D. Hoffman	104	1,275
1916 Damrosch .....L. McAfee	115	1,380
1917 Kalitan ....E. Haynes	116	4,800
1918 War Cloud ......J. Loftus	117	12,250
1918 Jack Hare Jr.......C. Peak	115	11,250
1919 Sir Barton ......J. Loftus	126	24,500
1920 Man o' War ...C. Kummer	126	23,000
1921 Broomspun ...F. Coltiletti	114	43,000
1922 Pillory ....L. Morris	114	51,000
1923 Vigil ....B. Marinelli	114	52,000
1924 Nellie Morse ...J. Merimee	121	54,000
1925 Coventry ......C. Kummer	126	52,700
1926 Display ....J. Maiben	126	53,625
1927 Bostonian ....A. Abel	126	53,100
1928 Victorian .....R. Workman	126	60,000
1929 Dr. Freeland ...L. Schaefer	126	52,325
1930 Gallant Fox ......E. Sande	126	51,925
1931 Mate ....G. Ellis	126	48,225
1932 Burgoo King .....E. James	126	50,375
1933 Head Play ...C. Kurtsinger	126	26,850
1934 High Quest ......R. Jones	126	25,175
1935 Omaha ......W. Saunders	126	25,325
1936 Bold Venture ....G. Woolf	126	27,325
1937 War Admiral .C. Kurtsinger	126	45,600
1938 Dauber ....M. Peters	126	51,875
1939 Challedon ....G. Seabo	126	53,710
1940 Bimelech ......F.A. Smith	126	53,230
1941 Whirlaway ......E. Arcaro	126	49,365
1942 Alsab..........B. James	126	58,175
1943 Count Fleet ....J. Longden	126	43,190
1944 Pensive ......C. McCreary	126	60,075

1945 Polynesian ....W.D. Wright	126	66,170
1946 Assault ......W. Mehrtens	126	96,620
1947 Faultless ......D. Dodson	126	98,005
1948 Citation ....E. Arcaro	126	91,870
1949 Capot ....T. Atkinson	126	79,985
1950 Hill Prince ......E. Arcaro	126	56,115
1951 Bold ....E. Arcaro	126	83,110
1952 Blue Man .....C. McCreary	126	86,135
1953 Native Dancer ...E. Guerin	126	65,200
1954 Hasty Road .....E. Arcaro	126	91,000
1955 Nashua ......W. Hartack	126	76,550
1956 Fabius ....E. Arcaro	126	84,250
1957 Bold Ruler ..I. Valenzuela	126	65,250
1958 Tim Tam ....J. Adams	126	97,900
1959 Royal Orbit ...W. Harmatz	126	136,200
1960 Bally Ache .....R. Ussery	126	121,000
1961 Carry Back ......J. Sellers	126	126,200
1962 Greek Money ....J. Rotz	126	135,800
1963 Candy Spots, W. Shoemaker	126	127,500
1964 Northern Dancer,W. Hartack	126	124,200
1965 Tom Rolfe ...R. Turcotte	126	128,100
1966 Kauai King ..D. Brumfield	126	129,000
1967 Damascus ..W. Shoemaker	126	141,500
1968 Forward Pass .I. Valenzuela	126	142,700
1969 Majestic Prince .W. Hartack	126	129,500
1970 Personality ...E. Belmonte	126	151,300
1971 Canonero II ......G. Avila	126	137,400
1972 Bee Bee Bee ....E. Nelson	126	135,300

Belmont Stakes
Belmont Park; 3-year-olds; 1-½ miles.

Year Winner	Jockey	Wt.	Net val.
1867 Ruthless .....J. Gilpatrick	107	$1,850
1868 General Duke ....R. Swim	110	2,800
1869 Fenian..........C. Miller	110	3,350
1870 Kingfisher ......W. Dick	110	3,750
1871 Harry Bassett ....W. Miller	110	5,450
1872 Joe Daniels ......J. Rowe	110	4,500
1873 Springbok ....J. Rowe	110	5,200
1874 Saxon ....G. Barbee	110	4,200
1875 Calvin ....R. Swim	110	4,450
1876 Algerine .....W. Donohue	110	3,700
1877 Cloverbrook ..C. Holloway	110	5,200
1878 Duke of Magenta .L. Hughes	118	3,850
1879 Spendthrift ....Evans	118	4,250
1880 Grenada ....L. Hughes	118	2,800
1881 Saunterer .....T. Costello	118	3,000
1882 Forester ....J. McLaughlin	118	2,600
1883 Geo. Kinney..J. McLaughlin	118	3,070
1884 Panique .....J. McLaughlin	118	3,150
1885 Tyrant ....P. Duffy	118	2,710
1886 Inspector B .J. McLaughlin	118	2,720
1887 Hanover ....J. McLaughlin	118	2,900
1888 Six Dixon ...J. McLaughlin	118	3,440
1889 Eric ....W. Hayward	118	4,960
1890 Burlington ......S. Barnes	125	8,560
1891 Foxford ......E. Garrison	118½	5,070
1892 Patron ....W. Hayward	122	6,610
1893 Comanche .....W. Simms	117	5,310
1894 Henry of Navarre, W. Simms	117	6,680
1895 Belmar ....F. Taral	119	2,700
1896 Hastings ....H. Griffin	122	3,025

1897 Scottish Chieftain			
	J. Scherrer	115	3,550
1898 Bowling Brook	F. Littlefield	122	7,810
1899 Jean Bereaud . . .	R. Clawson	122	9,445
1900 Ildrim	N. Turner	126	14,790
1901 Commando	H. Spencer	126	11,595
1902 Masterman	J. Bullman	126	13,220
1903 Africander	J. Bullman	126	12,285
1904 Delhi	G. Odom	126	11,575
1905 Tanya	E. Hilderbrand	121	17,240
1906 Burgomaster	L. Lyne	126	22,700
1907 Peter Pan	G. Mountain	126	22,765
1908 Colin	J. Notter	126	22,765
1909 Joe Madden	E. Dugan	126	24,550
1910 Sweep	J. Butwell	126	9,700
1913 Prince Eugene . .	R. Troxler	109	2,825
1914 Luke McLuke . .	M. Buxton	126	3,025
1915 The Finn	G. Byrne	126	1,825
1916 Friar Rock	E. Haynes	126	4,100
1917 Hourless	J. Butwell	126	5,800
1918 Johren	F. Robinson	126	8,950
1919 Sir Barton	J. Loftus	126	11,950
1920 Man o' War . . .	C. Kummer	126	7,950
1921 Grey Lag	E. Sande	126	8,650
1922 Pillory	C.H. Miller	126	39,200
1923 Zev	E. Sande	126	38,000
1924 Mad Play	E. Sande	126	42,880
1925 American Flag . .	A. Johnson	126	38,500
1926 Crusader	A. Johnson	126	48,550
1927 Chance Shot	E. Sande	126	60,910
1928 Vito	C. Kummer	126	63,430
1929 Blue Larkspur . . .	M. Garner	126	59,650
1930 Gallant Fox	E. Sande	126	66,040
1931 Twenty Grand,	C. Kurtsinger	126	58,770
1932 Faireno	T. Malley	126	55,120
1933 Hurryoff	M. Garner	126	49,490
1934 Peace Chance .	W.D. Wright	126	43,410
1935 Omaha	W. Saunders	126	35,480
1936 Granville	J. Stout	126	29,800
1937 War Admiral .	C. Kurtsinger	126	38,020
1938 Pasteurized	J. Stout	126	34,530
1939 Johnstown	J. Stout	126	37,020
1940 Bimelech	F.A. Smith	126	35,030
1941 Whirlaway	E. Arcaro	126	39,770
1942 Shut Out	E. Arcaro	126	44,520
1943 Count Fleet	J. Longden	126	45,340
1944 Bounding Home,	G.L. Smith	126	55,000
1945 Pavot	E. Arcaro	126	52,675
1946 Assault	W. Mehrtens	126	75,400
1947 Phalanx	R. Donoso	126	78,900
1948 Citation	E. Arcaro	126	77,700
1949 Capot	T. Atkinson	126	60,900
1950 Middleground . . .	W. Boland	126	61,350
1951 Counterpoint . .	D. Gorman	126	82,000
1952 One Count	E. Arcaro	126	82,400
1953 Native Dancer . . .	E. Guerin	126	82,500
1954 High Gun	E. Guerin	126	89,000
1955 Nashua	E. Arcaro	126	83,700
1956 Needles	D. Erb	126	83,600
1957 Gallant Man .	W. Shoemaker	126	77,300
1958 Cavan	P. Anderson	126	73,440
1959 Sword Dancer,	W. Shoemaker	126	93,535

1960 Celtic Ash	W. Hartack	126	96,785
1961 Sherluck	B. Baeza	126	104,900
1962 Jaipur	W. Shoemaker	126	109,550
1963 Chateaugay	B. Baeza	126	101,700
1964 Quadrangle	M. Ycaza	126	110,850
1965 Hail to All	J. Sellers	126	104,150
1966 Amberoid	W. Boland	126	117,700
1967 Damascus . .	W. Shoemaker	126	104,950
1968 Stage Door Johnny			
	H. Gustines	126	117,700
1969 Arts and Letters . .	B. Baeza	126	104,050
1970 High Echelon . . .	J.L. Rotz	126	115,000
1971 Pass Catcher	W. Blum	126	97,710
1972 Riva Ridge . . .	R. Turcotte	126	93,540
1973 Secretariat	R. Turcotte	126	90,120

Other Major Stakes in U.S.

(From The American Racing Manual)

Alabama Stakes

Saratoga; 3-year-old fillies; 1¼ miles.

Year	Jockey	Wt.	Win. val.
1872 Woodbine	Gradwell	107	$ 2,650
1873 Minnie W.	Ponton	107	3,050
1874 Regardless	Sparling	107	3,100
1875 Olitipa	Evans	107	2,800
1876 Merciless	Sparling	107	2,850
1877 Susquehanna	Hayward	107	3,450
1878 Belle	Hayward	113	2,800
1879 Ferida	Hughes	113	3,300
1880 Glidelia	W. Donohue	113	2,600
1881 Thora	W. Donohue	113	1,450
1882 Belle of Runnymede .	Stoval	113	3,250
1883 Miss Woodford			
	J. McLaughlin	113	3,050
1884 Tolu	Blaylock	113	3,500
1885 Ida Hope	I. Murphy	113	3,225
1886 Millie	J. McLaughlin	113	3,550
1887 Grisette	West	108	3,000
1888 Bella B.	J. McLaughlin	115	3,675
1889 Princess Bowling .	I. Murphy	114½	2,650
1890 Sinaloa II	Barnes	113	3,750
1891 Sallie McClelland .	Anderson	112	2,075
1892 Ignite	Clayton	112	2,475
1897 Poetess	C. Thorpe	114	1,425
1901 Morningside	N. Turner	116	1,900
1902 Par Excellence	Redfern	116	3,850
1903 Stamping Ground . . .	Fuller	116	4,625
1904 Beldame	O'Neill	124	3,850
1905 Tradition	W. Davis	124	4,850
1906 Running Water . . .	W. Miller	116	3,850
1907 Kennyetto	Notter	116	3,850
1908 Mayfield	C.H. Shilling	106	3,850
1909 Maskette	Scoville	124	3,850
1910 Ocean Bound .	C.H. Shilling	124	3,850
1913 Flying Fairy	T. Davies	113	1,455
1914 Addie M.	C. Burlingame	113	1,740
1915 Waterblossom . . .	E. Martin	126	1,160
1916 Malachite	L. Lyke	109	1,720
1917 Sunbonnet	J. Loftus	124	3,850
1918 Eyelid	L. Ensor	117	6,575
1919 Vexatious	E. Ambrose	114	7,265

1920 Cleopatra	L. McAtee	126	7,275
1921 Prudery	L. Fator	124	7,275
1922 Nedna	F. Keogh	114	8,050
1923 Untidy	E. Sande	124	8,950
1924 Priscilla Ruley	J. Maiben	117	9,925
1925 Maid at Arms	A. Johnson	124	10,625
1926 Rapture	L. McAtee	124	9,275
1927 Nimba	H. Thurber	124	12,925
1928 Nixie	D. McAuliffe	121	11,550
1929 Aquastella	P. Walls	121	11,775
1930 Escutcheon	L. McAtee	117	13,875
1931 Risque	E. Steffen	121	14,200
1932 Top Flight	R. Workman	126	12,225
1933 Barn Swallow	D. Meade	124	11,525
1934 Hindu Queen	L. Humphries	111	11,050
1935 Alberta	S. Coucci	111	7,350
1936 Floradora	D. Brammer	111	7,525
1937 Regal Lily	H. Richards	123	7,475
1938 Handcuff	J. Westrope	125	8,275
1939 War Plumage	M. Peters	124	10,100
1940 Salaminia	D. Meade	111	9,450
1941 War Hazard	C. McCreary	114	8,975
1942 Vagrancy	J. Stout	114	8,950
1943 Stefanita	C. McCreary	117	11,425
1944 Vienna	J. Stout	114	18,170
1945 Sicily	T. Atkinson	110	21,015
1946 Hypnotic	E. Guerin	124	18,250
1947 But Why Not	E. Guerin	126	17,975
1948 Compliance	T. Atkinson	112	16,900
1949 Adile	E. Arcaro	112	17,000
1950 Busanda	R. Permane	108	15,850
1951 Kiss Me Kate	E. Arcaro	126	15,250
1952 Lily White	T. Atkinson	109	17,000
1953 Sabette	J. Higley	114	18,800
1954 Parlo	E. Arcaro	121	20,550
1955 Rico Reto	W. Boland	113	20,750
1956 Tournure	E. Guerin	115	18,600
1957 Here and There	E. Nelson	113	20,450
1958 Tempted	R. Ussery	113	18,712
1959 High Bid	H. Morena	113	37,230
1960 Make Sail	M. Ycaza	118	38,205
1961 Primonetta	W. Shoemaker	121	35,555
1962 Firm Policy	J. Sellers	121	37,050
1963 Tona	M. Sorrentino	114	37,310
1964 Miss Cavandish	H. Grant	124	36,530
1965 What A Treat	J.L. Rotz	118	41,080
1966 Natashka	W. Shoemaker	121	36,790
1967 Gamely	W. Shoemaker	118	39,130
1968 Gay Matelda	J.L. Rotz	118	36,920
1969 Shuvee	J. Davidson	124	35,360
1970 Fanfreluche	R. Turcotte	118	38,415
1971 Lauries Dancer	S. Hawley	118	35,280
1972 Summer Guest	R. Turcotte	121	32,640
1973 Desert Vixen	J. Velasquez	119	34,620

Not run from 1893 to 1896, from 1898 to 1900, inclusive, nor in 1911 or 1912. Distance 1 1/8 miles prior to 1901, in 1904 and from 1906 to 1916, inclusive; 1 1/16 miles in 1901, 1902, and on the turf in 1903; 1 5/16 miles in 1905. Stamina finished first in 1908, but was disqualified. Bonnet Ann finished first in 1942, but was disqualified. Run at Belmont Park in 1943, 1944 and 1945. Lady Pitt finished first in 1966, but was disqualified and placed second. Heartland finished first in 1968 but was disqualified and placed second.

American Derby

Arlington Park; 3-year-olds; 1-1/8 miles.

Year	Jockey	Wt.	Win. val.
1884 Modesty	I. Murphy	117	$10,700
1885 Volante	I. Murphy	123	9,570
1886 Silver Cloud	I. Murphy	121	8,160
1887 C.H. Todd	Hamilton	118	13,690
1888 Emperor of Norfolk	I. Murphy	123	14,340
1889 Spokane	T. Kiley	121	15,400
1890 Uncle Bob	T. Kiley	115½	15,260
1891 Strathmeath	Covington	112	18,610
1892 Carlsbad	R. Williams	122	16,930
1893 Boundless	E. Garrison	122	49,500
1894 Rey el St'a A'ta	E. Van Kuren	122	19,750
1898 Pink Coat	W. Martin	127	9,225
1900 Sidney Lucas	J. Bullman	122	9,425
1901 Robert Waddell	J. Bullman	119	19,275
1902 Wyeth	L. Lyne	122	19,875
1903 The Picket	Helgesen	115	27,025
1904 Highball	G.C. Fuller	122	26,325
1916 Dodge	F. Murphy	126	6,850
1926 Boot to Boot	A. Johnson	121	89,000
1927 Hydromel	L. McDermott	116	22,750
1928 Toro	E. Ambrose	126	21,925
1929 Windy City	L. McDermott	118	47,550
1930 Reveille Boy	W. Fronk	118	51,300
1931 Mate	G. Ellis	126	48,675
1932 Gusto	S. Coucci	118	48,200
1933 Mr. Khayyam	P. Walls	121	23,410
1934 Cavalcade	M. Garner	126	23,310
1935 Black Helen	D. Meade	118	25,025
1937 Dawn Play	L. Balaski	116	25,400
1940 Mioland	J. Adams	123	44,900
1941 Whirlaway	A. Robertson	126	44,975
1942 Alsab	G. Woolf	126	60,850
1943 Askmenow	G. Woolf	115	56,150
1944 By Jimminy	G. Woolf	122	61,650
1945 Fighting Step	G. South	118	68,950
1946 Eternal Reward	R. Campbell	118	83,450
1947 Fervent	D. Dodson	118	70,950
1948 Citation	E. Arcaro	126	66,450
1949 Ponder	S. Brooks	126	66,150
1950 Hill Prince	E. Arcaro	126	60,050
1951 Hall of Fame	T. Atkinson	122	61,200
1952 Mark-Ye-Well	E. Arcaro	120	103,325
1953 Native Dancer	E. Arcaro	128	66,500
1954 Errard King	S. Boulmetis	124	68,900
1955 Swaps	W. Shoemaker	126	89,600
1956 Swoon's Son	E. Arcaro	122	102,600
1957 Round Table,	W. Shoemaker	126	100,350
1958 Nadir	M. Ycaza	120	144,600
1959 Dunce	L.C. Cook	126	93,700
1960 T.V. Lark	J. Sellers	123	70,500

1961 Beau Prince	S. Brooks	112	71,400
1962 Black Sheep	J. Longden	117	71,250
1963 Candy Spots,	W. Shoemaker	126	65,833
1964 Roman Brother	F. Alvarez	122	89,300
1965 Tom Rolfe	W. Shoemaker	126	83,100
1966 Buckpasser	B. Baeza	128	84,100
1967 Damascus	W. Shoemaker	126	75,000
1968 Forward Pass	I. Valenzuela	123	70,600
1969 Fast Hilarious,	L. Pincay, Jr.	114	55,000
1970 The Pruner	B. Baeza	117	65,300
1971 Bold Reason	L. Pincay, Jr.	124	81,950
1972 Dubassoff	J. Vasquez	117	72,800
1973 Bemo	W. Passmore	117	69,400

No racing in Chicago in 1895, 1896, 1897, 1899, 1905 and 1906. Not run from 1905 to 1915, inclusive, nor from 1917 to 1925, inclusive. Run at old Washington Park, Chicago, Ill., up to and including 1904. Run at Hawthorne in 1916. Not run in 1936, 1938 nor 1939. Distance 1½ miles from 1884 to 1915, inclusive, and in 1926 and 1927; 1¼ miles in 1916 and from 1928 to 1951, inclusive, and from 1962 to 1965 inclusive; 1 3/16 miles from 1955 to 1957, inclusive.

Arlington Classic

Arlington Park; 3-year olds; 1 mile

Year Winner	Jockey	Wt.	Win. val.
1929 Blue Larkspur	M. Garner	126	$59,900
1930 Gallant Fox	E. Sande	126	64,750
1931 Mate	A. Robertson	126	73,650
1932 Gusto	S. Coucci	126	76,600
1933 Inlander	R. Jones	118	32,755
1934 Cavalcade	M. Garner	126	30,325
1935 Omaha	W.D. Wright	126	28,975
1936 Granville	J. Stout	126	28,400
1937 Flying Scot	J. Gilbert	123	27,375
1938 Nedayr	W.D. Wright	121	27,500
1939 Challedon	H. Richards	126	35,600
1940 Sirocco	G. Woolf	121	37,935
1941 Attention	C. Bierman	121	42,450
1942 Shut Out	E. Arcaro	126	69,700
1943 Slide Rule	F. Zufelt	120	53,450
1944 Twilight Tear	L. Haas	114	62,050
1945 Pot o' Luck	D. Dodson	119	67,150
1946 The Dude	M. Duhon	119	76,850
1947 But Why Not	W. Mehrtens	117	71,500
1948 Papa Redbird	R.L. Baird	122	66,600
1949 Ponder	S. Brooks	126	65,450
1950 Greek Song	O. Scurlock	120	58,950
1951 Hall of Fame	T. Atkinson	120	62,975
1952 Mark-Ye-Well	E. Arcaro	112	105,375
1953 Native Dancer	E. Guerin	126	97,725
1954 Errard King	S. Boulmetis	120	104,475
1955 Nashua	E. Arcaro	126	91,675
1956 Swoon's Son	D. Erb	120	102,000
1957 Clem	C. McCreary	117	105,950
1958 A Dragon Killer	J. Combest	117	101,100
1959 Dunce	L.C. Cook	117	78,700
1960 T.V. Lark	J. Sellers	120	85,500
1961 Globemaster	J. Rotz	119	72,900

1962 Ridan	A. Gomez	123	64,750
1963 Candy Spots,	W. Shoemaker	126	86,833
1964 Tosmah	S. Boulmetis	115	69,000
1965 Tom Rolfe	W. Shoemaker	124	62,500
1966 Buckpasser	B. Baeza	125	63,000
1967 Dr. Fager	B. Baeza	120	61,000
1968 Exclusive Native			
	I. Valenzuela	113	63,000
1969 Ack Ack	B. Baeza	120	66,800
1970 Corn off the Cob			
	E. Belmonte	117	64,500

Run at Washington Park in 1943, 1944 and 1945. Distance 1-¼ miles prior to 1952. Renamed Grand Prix Stakes in 1971.

Arlington-Washington Futurity

Arlington Park; 2-year-olds; 6 Furlongs

Year Winner	Jockey	Wt.	Win. val.
1962 Candy Spots,	W. Shoemaker	122	$142,250
1963 Golden Ruler	H. Hinojosa	122	112,500
1964 Sadair	W. Shoemaker	122	134,925
1965 Buckpasser	B. Baeza	122	190,475
1966 Diplomat Way,	W. Shoemaker	122	195,200
1967 T.V. Commercial			
	P. Anderson	122	105,895
1967 Vitriolic	W. Shoemaker	122	105,895
1968 Strong Strong	D. Gargan	122	212,850
1969 Silent Screen	J.L. Rotz	122	206,075
1971 Hold Your Peace			
	C. Marquez	122	45,000
1971 Governor Max	C. Perret	122	45,000
1972 Shecky Greene	C. Marquez	122	103,020
1973 Lover John	R. Ussery	122	97,470

Distance 7/8 mile prior to 1971. Run in two divisions in 1967 and 1971. Court Recess finished third in the 1967 second division, but was disqualified. Not run in 1970.

Arlington-Washington Lassie Stakes

Arlington Park; 2-year-old Fillies; 6½ Furlongs

Year Winner	Jockey	Wt.	Win. val.
1929 Capture	E. Shropshire	117	9,175
1930 Risque	E. Steffen	117	6,650
1931 Top Flight	A. Robertson	120	19,125
1932 Hilena	R. Workman	119	17,900
1933 Mata Hari	R. Jones	117	21,670
1934 Motto	R. Workman	119	22,510
1935 Forever Yours	D. Meade	117	25,790
1936 Apogee	E. Steffen	122	21,020
1937 Theen	I. Anderson	117	15,630
1938 Inscoelda	C. Rollins	117	17,540
1939 Now What	R. Workman	122	18,820
1940 Blue Delight	A. Snyder	119	17,250
1941 Petrify	R. Donoso	117	17,200
1942 Fad	A. Craig	117	25,980
1943 Twilight Tear	N. Jemas	113	26,460
1944 Expression	F. Zufelt	119	28,900
1945 Beau Gay	J. Adams	119	35,900
1946 Four Winds	I. Anderson	119	51,000
1947 Bewitch	D. Dodson	119	47,150
1948 Pail of Water	W. Mehrtens	119	40,350

1949 Dutchess Peg . . . . S. Brooks	119	45,125
1950 Shawnee Squaw . A. Rivera	119	43,865
1951 Princess Lygia . . .K. Church	119	45,580
1952 Fulvous . . . . S. Brooks	119	53,275
1953 Queen Hopeful . . J. Adams	119	66,565
1954 Delta . . . . S. Brooks	119	62,750
1955 Judy Rullah . . . . . . D. Erb	119	57,335
1956 Leallah . . . . . . .W. Hartack	119	56,010
1957 Poly Hi . . . . E. Guerin	119	65,025
1958 Dark Vintage . J. Heckmann	119	63,850
1959 Monarchy . . . . . . S. Brooks	119	61,950
1960 Colfax Maid . . . . S. Brooks	119	59,350
1961 Rudoma . . . . . . W. Hartack	116	38,500
1962 Smart Deb . . . . . . M. Ycaza	119	44,900
1963 Sari's Song . W. Shoemaker	119	61,505
1964 Admiring . . . . . .W. Hartack	119	77,815
1965 Silver Bright . . . .J. Nichols	119	111,265
1966 Mira Femme . I. Valenzuela	119	96,525
1967 Shenow . . . . . L. Pincay, Jr.	119	92,500
1968 Process Shot . . . C. Baltazar	119	80,000
1969 Clover Lane . W. Shoemaker	119	80,000

Distance 5½ furlongs prior to 1932; ¾ mile from 1932 to 1961, inclusive. Run at Washington Park in 1943, 1944, and 1945. Run as Arlington Lassie Stakes prior to 1963. Not run in 1970, 1971, or 1972.

Beldame Handicap
Belmont Park; 3-year-olds and over; fillies and mares; 1 1/8 miles.

Year Winner Age	Jockey	Wt.	Win. val.
1905 Flip Flap . . . . Shaw	116	$ 1,570
1906 Veil . . . . Shaw	120	1,380
1907 Berry Maid . . . . . . .Sumter	119	1,565
1909 Imprudent . . . . . . E. Dugan	108	1,050
1917 Enfilade . . . . .J. Loftus	126	1,450
1918 Pen Rose . . . A. Schuttinger	117	1,825
1919 Thelma K. . . . . .C. Kummer	116	2,350
1920 Crocus . . . . .L. Ensor	118	3,725
1921 My Reverie . . . . . C. Turner	120	3,825
1922 Miss Star . . . . E. Taplin	107	4,150
1923 Tree Top . . . . . F. Coltiletti	115	4,525
1924 Superlette . . . . L. Fator	118	3,725
1925 Patricia J. . . . . L. Fator	112	3,875
1926 Frilette . . . . J. Maiben	114	4,125
1927 One Hour . . . . . . .G. Fields	118	3,850
1928 Triskette . . . . . . .W. Kelsay	112	3,925
1929 The Beasel . . . . . .W. Kelsay	119	4,300
1930 Blind Lane . . . . . . .P. Walls	118	4,525
1931 Stagecraft . . . . . .M. Garner	123	2,655
1932 Tickory Tock . . . . .P. Walls	110	1,425
1939 Nellie Bly (3) . . . J. Renick	102	10,100
1940 Fairy Chant (3), I. Anderson	119	14,050
1941 Fairy Chant (4), I. Anderson	123	14,450
1942 Barrancosa (7) . . . E. Arcaro	116	
Vagrancy (3) . . . J. Stout	119	7,800
1943 Mar-Kell (4) . B. Thompson	126	20,050
1944 Donitas First (3)T. Atkinson	112	18,530
1945 War Date (3) . . A. Kirkland	119	24,100
1946 Gallorette (4) . . . .J. Jessop	126	39,300
1946 Bridal Flower (3), A. DeLara	114	39,300

1947 Snow Goose (3),T. Atkinson	106	41,500
1947 But Why Not (3) . E. Arcaro	120	42,250
1948 Conniver (4) . . . D. Dodson	121	49,700
1949 Miss Request (4) . E. Arcaro	113	53,600
1950 Next Move (3) . N. Combest	116	47,400
1951 Thelma Berger (4)		
W. Shoemaker	110	49,300
1952 Next Move (5) . . . E. Guerin	125	43,400
1952 Real Delight (3) . E. Arcaro	126	42,400
1953 Atalanta (5) . .H.B. Wilson	121	47,600
1954 Parlo (3) . . . . . . .H. Guerin	116	45,500
1955 Lalum (3) . . . . . H. Moreno	116	50,800
1956 Levee (3) . . . . .R. Broussard	115	48,100
1957 Pucker Up (4),W. Shoemaker	125	51,200
1958 Outer Space (4) W. Harmatz	117	44,595
1959 Tempted (4) . . . . E. Nelson	125	42,905
1960 Berlo (3) . . . . E. Guerin	119	57,615
1961 Airman's Guide (4),H. Grant	123	62,400
1962 Cicada (3) . . W. Shoemaker	118	87,750
1963 Oil Royalty (5) . . M. Ycaza	123	56,972
1964 Tosmah (3) . . .S. Boulmetis	118	52,552
1965 What A Treat (3) . J.L. Rotz	118	53,430
1966 Summer Scandal (4)W. Blum	123	55,380
1967 Mac's Sparkler (5)W. Boland	123	53,235
1968 Gamely (4) . . L. Pincay, Jr.	123	53,202
1969 Gamely (5). . . L. Pincay, Jr.	123	52,877
1970 Shuvee (4) . . . . R. Turcotte	123	54,437
1971 Double Delta (5) . K. Knapp	123	49,710
1972 Susan's Girl (3)L. Pincay, Jr.	118	67,680

Distance 5 furlongs and for 2-year-old fillies in 1905, 1906, 1907, 1909, and from 1917 to 1932, inclusive. Not run in 1908, nor from 1910 to 1916, inclusive, nor from 1933 to 1938, inclusive. Distance 1 1/16 miles in 1939. Barrancosa and Vagrancy dead-heated for first place in 1942. Run in 2 divisions in 1946, 1947 and 1952. Run at Aqueduct from 1939 to 1956, inclusive; in 1959 and from 1962 to 1968, inclusive.

Benjamin F. Lindheimer Handicap
Arlington Park; 3-year-olds and over; 1 3/16 miles (Turf Course)

Year Age	Jockey	Wt.	Win. val.
1962 Prove It (5) . . . . H. Moreno	130	$31,900
1963 The Axe II (5) . . . J.L. Rotz	127	66,450
1964 Master Dennis (4)		
D. Brumfield	116	68,750
1965 Brambles (5). . . . K. Knapp	115	33,700
1966 Toulore (4) . . . . B. Moreira	116	34,400
1967 Fusilier Boy (4) . H. Moreno	114	73,100
1968 War Censor (5) . . . .E. Fires	116	68,850
1969 Tampa Trouble (4) .E. Fires	112	68,100
1970 Te Vega (5) . . . . C. Baltazar	114	40,500
1970 Kerry's Time (4)		
J.R. Anderson	112	40,500
1971 Princess Pout (5), J. Cruguet	117	71,400

Distance 1¼ miles (main course) in 1962; 1½ miles in 1963, 1964 and 1966. Fast Hilarious finished first in the 1970 first division but was disqualified and placed third. Run in two divisions in 1970. Not run in 1972.

Brooklyn Handicap
Aqueduct; 3-year-olds and over; 1¼ miles.

Year	Age Jockey	Wt.	Win. val.
1887 Dry Monopole (4)			
	A. McCarthy	106	$5,850
1888 The Bard (5) . . W. Hayward	125		6,925
1889 Exile (7) . . . . . A. Hamilton	116		6,900
1890 Castaway II (4) . . . W. Bunn	128		6,900
1891 Tenny (5) . . . . Barnes	128		14,800
1892 Judge Morrow (5)			
	A. Covington	116	17,750
1893 Diablo (7) . . . . . . F. Taral	112		17,750
1894 Dr. Rice (4) . . . . . F. Taral	112		17,750
1895 Hornpipe (4) . . A. Hamilton	105		7,750
1896 Sir Walter (6) . . . . F. Taral	113		7,750
1897 Howard Mann (4) H. Martin	106		7,750
1898 Ornament (4) . . . . T. Sloan	127		7,800
1899 Banastar (4) . . . . D. Maher	110		7,800
1900 Kinley Mack (4) . P. McCue	122		7,800
1901 Conroy (3) W. O'Connor	102½		7,800
1902 Reina (4) . . . . W. O'Connor	104		7,800
1903 Irish Lad (3) . . . . F. O'Neill	103		14,950
1904 The Picket (4) . . E. Helgesen	119		15,800
1905 Delhi (4) . . . . T. Burns	124		15,800
1906 Tokalon (5) . . . . . W. Bedell	108		15,800
1907 Superman (3) . . . W. Miller	99		15,800
1908 Celt (3) . . . . J. Notter	106		19,750
1909 King James (4) . . E. Dugan	126		3,850
1910 Fitz Herbert (4) . E. Dugan	130		4,800
1913 Whisk Broom II (6)J. Notter	130		3,125
1914 Buckhorn (5) . . J. McCahey	113		3,350
1915 Tartar (5) . . . . J. McTaggart	103		3,850
1916 Friar Rock (3) . . . E. Haynes	108		3,850
1917 Borrow (9) . . . . . W. Knapp	117		4,850
1918 Cudgel (4) . . . . L. Lyke	129		4,850
1919 Eternal (3) . A. Schuttinger	105		4,850
1920 Cirrus (4) . . . . L. Ensor	108		5,850
1921 Grey Lag (3) . . . . . L. Fator	112		7,600
1922 Exterminator (7)A. Johnson	135		7,600
1923 Little Chief (4) . . . E. Sande	114		7,600
1924 Hephaistos (5) . . . J. Maiben	106		7,600
1925 Mad Play (4) . . . . . L. Fator	123		7,600
1926 Single Foot (4) . . C. Turner	110		11,950
1927 Peanuts (5) . . . . H. Thurber	112		13,150
1928 Black Panther (4) J. Maiben	105		13,750
1929 Light Carbine (6) . G. Rose	97		14,300
1930 Sortie (5) . . . . P. Walls	111		10,800
1931 Questionnaire (4)			
	R. Workman	127	13,900
1932 Blenheim (4) . . . . . H. Mills	109		9,800
1933 Dark Secret (4) . . . H. Mills	115		3,380
1934 Discovery (3) . . J. Bejshak	113		2,925
1935 Discovery (4) . . J. Bejshak	123		10,200
1936 Discovery (5) . . . L. Fallon	136		10,575
1937 Seabiscuit (4) . . . J. Pollard	122		18,025
1938 The Chief (3) . . J. Longden	105		18,450
1939 Cravat (4) . . . . B. James	126		18,250
1940 Isolated (7) . . . . . . J. Stout	119		16,900

Year	Jockey	Wt.	Win. val.
1941 Fenelon (4) . . . . . . J. Stout	119		19,250
1942 Whirlaway (4) . . . . G. Woolf	128		23,650
1943 Devil Diver (4) . . S. Brooks	123		23,200
1944 Four Freedoms (4)E. Arcaro	116		39,720
1945 Stymie (4) . . . . . R. Permane	116		39,120
1946 Gallorette (4) . . . . J. Jessop	118		41,100
1947 Assault (4) . . . . . E. Arcaro	133		38,100
1948 Conniver (4) . . T. Atkinson	114		39,300
1949 Assault (6) . . . . D. Gorman	122		40,600
1950 My Request (5) T. Atkinson	119		41,000
1951 Palestinian (5) .S. Boulmetis	121		39,000
1952 Crafty Admiral (4)E. Guerin	116		41,700
1953 Tom Fool (4) . T. Atkinson	136		37,900
1954 Invigorator (4) . . E. Arcaro	114		40,500
1955 High Gun (4) . . . . E. Arcaro	132		37,900
1956 Dedicate (4) . . . . E. Arcaro	114		37,600
1957 Portersville (5) . . E. Nelson	116		37,700
1958 Cohoes (4) . . . . . . J. Ruane	110		36,450
1959 Babu (5) . . . . . . C. McCreay	112		72,545
1960 On-and-On (4) I. Valenzuela	118		70,010
1961 Kelso (4) . . . . E. Arcaro	136		73,320
1962 Beau Purple (5) . .W. Boland	116		71,240
1963 Cyrano (4) . . . . . R. Ussery	113		72,800
1964 Gun Bow (4) . . . . . W. Blum	122		71,500
1965 Pia Star (4) . . . . . . J. Sellers	121		69,680
1966 Buckpasser (3) . . . B. Baeza	120		69,615
1967 Handsome Boy (4)			
	E. Belmonte	116	69,355
1968 Damascus (4) . . . M. Ycaza	130		71,110
1969 Nodouble (4) . E. Belmonte	127		70,850
1970 Dewan (5) . . . L. Pincay, Jr.	118		69,810
1971 Never Bow (5) . . . R. Ussery	126		69,060
1972 Key to the Mint (3) B. Baeza	112		70,860

Not run in 1911 and 1912. Run at Belmont Park in 1913, and at Gravesend prior to 1911; at Jamaica Race Course from 1956 to 1959, inclusive. Distance 1 1/8 miles from 1915 to 1939, inclusive; 1 3/16 miles 1956 to 1959, inclusive.

Californian Stakes
Hollywood Park; 3-year-olds and over; 1 1/6 mi.

Year	Jockey	Wt.	Win. val.
1954 Imbros . . . . J. Longden	118		$75,300
1955 Swaps . . . . D. Erb	115		63,700
1956 Porterhouse . . I. Valenzuela	118		63,700
1957 Social ClimberW. Shoemaker	119		70,700
1958 Seaneen . . . . J. Longden	109		62,200
1959 Hillsdale . . . . T. Barrow	123		66,800
1960 Fleet Nasrullah . J. Longden	119		65,200
1961 First Balcony . . . . E. Burns	115		67,700
1962 Cadiz . . . . W. Harmatz	111		71,200
1963 Winonly . . . . . . J. Leonard	115		77,300
1964 Mustard Plaster . J. Leonard	111		70,500
1965 Viking Spirit . . . . K. Church	115		67,900
1966 Travel Orb . . . . W. Harmatz	112		75,100
1967 Biggs . . . . W. Harmatz	112		74,200
1968 Dr. Fager . . . . B. Baeza	130		74,600
1969 Nodouble . . . E. Belmonte	127		70,400
1970 Baffle . . . . J. Lambert	113		62,800
1971 Cougar II . . . W. Shoemaker	124		81,100
1972 Cougar II . . . W. Shoemaker	127		76,400

Carter Handicap

Belmont Park: 3-year-olds and over; 7/8 mile.

Year	Age	Jockey	Wt.	Win val.
1895* Charade (6)		Doggett	100	$ 600
1896† Deerslayer (4)		Doggett	110	675
1897‡ Premier (4)		Coylie	114	540
1898‡ The Manxman (4)		Lewis	114	1,350
1899 D. of Middleburg (3)		Sullivan	106	1,470
1900 Box (6)		Maher	125	1,560
1901 Motley (4)		Shaw	110	1,570
1902 Ethics (4)		H. Cochran	106	1,645
1903 Ahumada (3)		J. Martin	101	2,735
1904 Beldame (3)		F. O'Neill	103	7,710
1905 Ormonde's Right (4)		W. Davis	110	7,140
1906 Roseben (5)		Lyne	129	7,850
1907 Glorifier (5)		Mountain	119	7,850
1908 Jack Atkin (4)		Musgrave	122	6,850
1910 Gretna Green (6)		G. Burns	105	1,925
1914 Roamer (3)		M. Buxton	109	1,925
1915 Phosphor (3)		J. Loftus	116	1,925
1916 Trial by Jury (4)		E. Campbell	121	1,925
1917 Old Rosebud (6)		A. Schuttinger	130	2,825
1918 Old Koenig (5)		G. Byrne	122	2,825
1919 Naturalist (5)		C. Fairbrother	132	2,825
1920 Audacious (4)		F. Keogh	117	3,850
1921 Audacious (5)		C. Kummer	126	7,300
1922 Knobbie (4)		L. Fator	120	7,600
1923 Little Celt (3)		C. Turner	116	7,400
1924 Sarazen (3)		E. Sande	118	6,900
1925 Silver Fox (3)		L. Fator	114	8,150
1926 Macaw (3)		L. McAtee	123	
Nedana (4)		L. Fator	119	4,750
1927 Happy Argo (4)		F. Weiner	119	9,250
1928 Osmand (4)		E. Sande	122	9,250
1929 Osmand (5)		W. Garner	132	8,900
1930 Flying Heels (3)		W. Kelsay	118	7,650
1931 Flying Heels (4)		C. Kurtsinger	125	7,400
1932 Happy Scot (4)		A. Robertson	117	6,100
1933 Caterwaul (3)		R. Workman	114	600
1934 Open Range (3)		E. Litz'berger	95	895
1935 King Saxon (4)		C. Rainey	127	6,850
1936 Clang (4)		E. Litzenberger	110	7,200
1937 Aneroid (4)		C. Rosengarten	123	8,875
1938 Airflame (4)		R. Workman	119	7,400
1939 Fighting Fox (4)		J. Stout	119	7,600
1940 He Did (7)		G. Woolf	124	8,400
1941 Parasang (4)		B. James	114	6,375
1942 Doublrab (4)		B. Thompson	120	7,250
1943 Devil Diver (4)		G. Woolf	126	7,150
1944 Brownie (5)		E. Guerin	115	
Bossuet (4)		J. Stout	127	
Wait A Bit (5)		G.L. Smith	118	3,623
1945 Apache (6)		J. Stout	130	7,945
1946 Flood Town (4)		W. Mehrtens	113	8,125
1947 Rippey (4)		O. Scurlock	112	19,750
1948 Gallorette (6)		J. Jessop	122	20,550
1949 Better Self (4)		D. Gorman	126	20,350
1950 Guillotine (3)		T. Atkinson	109	16,950
1951 Arise (5)		E. Guerin	122	16,000
1952 Northern Star (4)		T. Atkinson	115	20,250
1953 Tom Fool (4)		T. Atkinson	135	41,700
1954 White Skies (5)		J. Stout	133	44,200
1955 Bobby Brocato (4)		R. Broussard	116	43,000
1956 Red Hannigan (5)		P. J. Bailey	114	40,400
1957 Portersville (5)		T. Atkinson	111	40,800
1958 Bold Ruler (4)		E. Arcaro	135	37,620
1959 Jimmer (4)		J. Ruane	108	37,490
1960 Yes You Will (4)		L. Adams	122	38,205
1961 Chief of Chiefs (4)		J. Leonard	116	38,805
1962 Merry Ruler (4)		J. Sellers	119	38,545
1963 Admiral's Voyage (4)		R. Broussard	126	37,830
1964 Ahoy (4)		H. Grant	133	37,505
1965 Viking Spirit (5)		K. Church	123	35,620
1966 Davis II (6)		C. Stone	116	37,440
1967 Tumiga (3)		B. Feliciano	113	36,790
1968 In Reality (4)		J. Velasquez	124	36,270
1969 Promise (4)		R. Ussery	124	37,440
1970 Tyrant (4)		R. Ussery	117	36,010
1971 Native Royalty (4)		J.L. Rotz	112	35,280
1972 Leematt (4)		M. Venezia	116	34,200

*Distance 1¼ miles. †1 1/8 miles ‡1 1/16 miles. ‡About 7/8 mile (150 feet short). 6½ furlongs from 1899 to 1902, inclusive, and in 1933 and 1934. Not run in 1909, 1911, 1912 and 1913. Run as purse race in 1933 and 1934. Macaw and Nedana dead-heated for first in 1926. In 1944 Brownie, Bossuet and Wait A Bit dead-heated for first. Run at old Aqueduct from 1895 to 1945, inclusive, and from 1947 to 1955, inclusive; at new Aqueduct from 1960 to 1967, inclusive.

Century Handicap

Hollywood Park; 3-year-olds and up; 1 3/8 miles (Turf Course)

Year	Jockey	Wt.	Win val.
1968 Model Fool (5)	M. Ycaza	115	$49,750
1969 Pinjara (4)	W. Shoemaker	118	45,650
1970 Quilche (6)	J. Lambert	115	46,750
1971 Big Shot II (6)	R. Rosales	111	58,100
1972 Cougar II (6)	W. Shoemaker	121	56,000

Distance 1 1/8 miles in 1968.

Champagne Stakes

Belmont Park; 2-year-olds; 1 mile.

Year	Jockey	Wt.	Win val.
1867 Sarah B.	Washington	97	$ 1,250
1868 Cottrill	C. Miller	100	850
1869 Finesse	C. Miller	97	1,200
1870 Madam Dudley	W. Miller	97	1,350
1871*Grey Planet	Donohue	100	1,500
1872 Minnie W.	Sparling	97	1,050
1873 Grinstead	Feakes	100	1,750
1874 Hyder Ali	Donohue	100	1,850
1875 Virginius	W. Clarke	100	2,100
1876 Bombast	Barrett	110	1,950
1877 Albert	Barbee	110	1,900

1878	Belinda	Sparling	107	1,275	1941	Alsab	C. Bierman	122	9,500

1878 Belinda .... Sparling 107   1,275
1879 Carita .... Evans 107   2,050
1880 Lady Rosebery ....
　　　　　　J. McLaughlin 107   1,175
1881 Macduff .... Fisher 110   1,150
1882 Breeze .... Shauer 108   1,325
1883 Leo .... Shauer 110   1,350
1884 Eachus ... J. McLaughlin 115   1,225
1885 Dew Drop .... Olney 122   1,775
1886 Connemarra ....
　　　　　　A. McCarthy, Jr. 112   2,100
1887 Cascade .... Church 102   1,875
1888 Radiant ...... W. Donohue 115   2,650
1889 June Day .... Barnes 118   1,975
1890†Hoodlum ...... Covington 106   2,500
1891 Azra .... Clayton 108   3,470
1892 Ramapo .... Doggett 111   3,780
1893 Sir Excess .... Taral 123   6,320
1894 Salvation .... Taral 113   4,880
1895 Ben Brush .... Simms 120   2,350
1896 The Friar ...... Littlefield 118   3,050
1897 Plaudit ..... R. Williams 125   2,250
1898 Lothario .... Maher 107   3,250
1899 Kilmarnock .... Odom 112   3,585
1900 Garry Herrmann .. Bullman 117   2,765
1901 Endurance by Right ....
　　　　　　O'Connor 119   4,375
1902 Meltonian .... Redfern 107   5,435
1903 Stalwart .... W. Hicks 112   6,135
1904 Oiseau .... Odom 122   6,600
1905 Perverse .... Shaw 119   6,255
1906 Kentucky Beau ... W. Miller 119   5,910
1907 Colin .... W. Miller 122   5,700
1908 Helmet .... Notter 122   5,625
1909 Fauntleroy ..... McCahey 122   1,060
1914 Paris .... M. Buxton 110   1,205
1915 Chicle ...... T. McTaggart 112   1,065
1916 Vivid ...... A. Schuttinger 105   1,455
1917 Lanius ...... F. Robinson 110   1,650
1918 War Pennant .... E. Taplin 106½   2,525
1919 Cleopatra ..... L. McAtee 107   3,575
1920 Grey Lag .... L. Ensor 111½   4,150
1921 Surf Rider .... L. Fator 107   4,400
1922 Nassau ..... C. Fairbrother 112   4,650
1923 Sarazen .... E. Sande 112   5,225
1924 Beatrice .... G. Fields 109   6,275
1925 Bubbling Over .. A. Johnson 122   4,550
1926 Valorous ...... L. McAtee 112   5,750
1927 Oh Say .... F. Fields 114   6,025
1928 Healy .... W. Kelsay 115   5,825
1929 Whichone ..... L. McAtee 127   5,825
1930 Mate .... L. Fator 119   6,050
1931 Sweeping Light F. Coltiletti 116   5,525
1932 Dynastic .... C. Kurtsinger 119   4,025
1933 Hadagal ..... L. Humphries 116   2,170
1934 Balladier ..... W.D. Wright 124   3,520
1935 Brevity ...... W.D. Wright 113   4,875
1936 Privileged ...... E. Arcaro 122   4,200
1937 Menow ..... C. Kurtsinger 113   4,225
1938 Porter's Mite .... B. James 119   4,650
1939 Andy K. ...... J. Longden 124   5,875
1940 Monday Lunch .. E. Arcaro 110   9,675

1941 Alsab .... C. Bierman 122   9,500
1942 Count Fleet .... J. Longden 116   9,375
1943 Pukka Gin .... T. Atkinson 113   10,125
1944 Pot o' Luck .... R. Permane 106   15,950
1945 Marine Victory . D. Padgett 116   15,665
1946 Donor .... J. Jessop 116   20,550
1947 Vulcan's Forge . A. Kirkland 110   22,650
1948 Capot .... T. Atkinson 110   24,300
1949 Theory .... S. Brooks 113   23,150
1950 Uncle Miltie . H. Woodhouse 122   24,050
1951 Armageddon. W. Shoemaker 122   24,050
1952 Laffango .... N. Shuk 122   25,600
1953 Fisherman .. H. Woodhouse 122   25,700
1954 Flying Fury .... H. Moreno 122   24,700
1955 Beau Fond ..... E. Arcaro 122   22,700
1956 Not Run
1957 Jewel's Reward ....
　　　　　　W. Shoemaker 122   84,225
1958 First Landing .. E. Arcaro 122   96,870
1959 Warfare ..... I. Valenzuela 122   138,195
1960 Roving Minstrel . H. Moreno 122   108,035
1961 Donut King ..... M. Ycaza 122   146,800
1962 Never Bend ..... M. Ycaza 122   129,675
1963 Roman Brother .. J.L. Rotz 122   152,150
1964 Bold Lad .... B. Baeza 122   116,825
1965 Buckpasser ...... B. Baeza 122   163,875
1966 Successor .... B. Baeza 122   148,325
1967 Vitriolic .... B. Baeza 122   119,500
1968 Top Knight ..... M. Ycaza 122   110,450
1969 Silent Screen .... J.L. Rotz 122   128,150
1970 Limit to Reason ...
　　　　　　J. Velasquez 122   145,025
1971 Riva Ridge .... R. Turcotte 122   117,090
1972 Stop the Music .. J.L. Rotz 122   87,900

Run at Morris Park prior to 1905. *Distance reduced to ¾ mile from 1 mile. Run at Jerome Park previous to 1890. †Distance increased from ¾ mile to 1 mile. Distance 7/8 mile from 1891 to 1904, inclusive; Widener Course (165 feet less than 7/8 mile) from 1905 to 1932, inclusive. Not run from 1910 to 1913, inclusive, not in 1956. 6½ furlongs (Widener Course) from 1933 to 1939, inclusive. Run at Aqueduct in 1959 and from 1963 to 1967, inclusive. Hoist The Flag finished first in 1970 but was disqualified. Secretariat finished first in 1972 but was disqualified and placed second.

Charles H. Strub Stakes
Santa Anita Park; 4-year-olds; 1¼ miles.

Year		Jockey	Wt.	Win. val.
1963 Crimson Satan .	H. Hinojosa	118	$92,400
1964 Gun Bow ...	W. Shoemaker	117	87,000
1965 Duel	M. Ycaza	112	79,600
1966 Bold Bidder .	W. Shoemaker	119	89,500
1967 Drin	L. Pincay Jr.	117	84,800
1968 Most Host	W. Harmatz	114	73,700
1969 Dignitas........	F. Alvarez	115	81,300
1970 Snow Sporting,	L. Pincay, Jr.	114	84,500
1971 War Helm	J. Sellers	115	87,100
1972 Unconscious,	W. Shoemaker	114	85,300

Distance 1 1/8 miles in 1970. Nodouble finished first in 1969 but was disqualified and placed second.

Coaching Club American Oaks
Belmont Park; 3-year-old fillies; 1½ miles.

Year	Jockey	Wt.	Win. val.
1917 Wistful	W.J. O'Brien	124	$ 2,300
1918 Rose d'Or	L. Ensor	111	5,050
1919 Polka Dot	L. Ensor	111	7,790
1920 Cleopatra	L. McAtee	117	4,075
1921 Flambette	E. Sande	112½	4,850
1922 Prudish	L. Morris	111	11,700
1923 How Fair	A. Johnson	112½	11,775
1924 Princess Doreen	H. Stutts	121	12,875
1925 Fl. Nightingale			
	L. McDermott	111	13,400
1926 Edith Cavell	F. Coltiletti	117	12,100
1927 Nimba	H. Thurber	111	15,775
1928 Bateau	E. Sande	121	14,825
1929 Sweet Verbena	J. Maiben	114	16,625
1930 Snowflake	L. Schaefer	121	19,600
1931 Tambour	F. Coltiletti	121	15,000
1932 Top Flight	R. Workman	121	15,075
1933 Edelweiss	J. Gilbert	114	12,550
1934 Lady Reigh	D. Meade	111	9,575
1935 Black Helen	D. Meade	121	7,750
1936 High Fleet	J. Gilbert	111	10,575
1937 Dawn Play	L. Balaski	121	10,575
1938 Creole Maid	H. Richards	121	10,425
1939 War Plumage	N. Wall	116	11,500
1940 Damaged Goods	J. Gilbert	121	12,550
1941 Level Best	A. Robertson	121	10,275
1942 Vagrancy	T. Malley	121	15,425
1943 Too Timely	G. Woolf	121	13,250
1944 Twilight Tear	C. McCreary	121	12,495
1945 Elpis	J. Adams	121	15,215
1946 Hypnotic	P. Miller	121	21,180
1947 Harmonica	J. Adams	121	48,200
1948 Scattered	W. Mehrtens	121	43,700
1949 Wistful	S. Brooks	121	48,700
1950 Next Move	E. Guerin	121	44,500
1951 How	E. Arcaro	121	46,800
1952 Real Delight	E. Arcaro	121	45,100
1953 Grecian Queen	E. Guerin	121	45,500
1954 Cherokee Rose	H. Moreno	121	43,900
1955 High Voltage	T. Atkinson	121	45,800
1956 Levee	H. Woodhouse	121	41,100
1957 Willamette	J. Choquette	121	48,800
1958 A Glitter	A. Valenzuela	121	45,792
1959 Resaca	M. Ycaza	121	58,512
1960 Berlo	E. Guerin	121	55,262
1961 Bowl of Flowers	E. Arcaro	121	75,806
1962 Bramalea	R. Ussery	121	78,081
1963 Lamb Chop	H. Gustines	121	78,244
1964 Miss Cavandish	H. Grant	121	79,544
1965 Marshua	R. Broussard	121	84,175
1966 Lady Pitt	W. Blum	121	77,919
1967 Quillo Queen	E. Cardone	121	85,637
1968 Dark Mirage	M. Ycaza	121	75,562
1969 Shuvee	J. Davidson	121	77,756
1970 Missile Belle	P. Anderson	121	87,019

1971 Our Cheri Amour	J. Kurtz	121	78,975
1972 Summer Guest	R. Turcotte	121	66,360
1973 Magazine	A. Cordero	121	70,200

Distance 1 1/8 miles in 1917; 1¼ miles in 1918 and from 1959 to 1970, inclusive; 1 3/8 miles from 1919 to 1941, inclusive, and from 1944 to 1958, inclusive. Run as a handicap prior to 1928. Run at Aqueduct from 1963 to 1967, inclusive.

Colonial Cup International Steeplechase
Springdale Course; 4-year-olds and up; 2 mi and 6½ furlongs

Year	Age	Jockey	Wt.	Win. val.
1970 Top Bid (6)		J. Aitcheson	160	$63,000
1971 Inkslinger (4)		T. Carberry	149	63,000
1972 Soothsayer (5)		J. Aitcheson	151	60,000

Delaware Handicap
Delaware Park; 3-year-old and up; 1¼ miles

Year First	Age	Jockey	Wt.	Win. val.
1937 Rosenna (3)		M. Peters	108	$ 8,125
1938 Marica (5)		R. Dotter	125	8,300
1939 Shangay Lily (7)		R. Donoso	113	9,175
1940 Tedbriar (3)		J. Lynch	108½	9,625
1941 Dotted Swiss (4)		M. Peters	114	9,550
1942 Monida (5)		A. DeLara	112	8,850
1944 Everget (3)		A. Kirkland	113	8,975
1945 Plucky Maud (4)		R. Permane	115	12,450
1946 Bridal Flower (3)		A. DeLara	111	20,200
1947 Elpis (5)		L. Hansman	108	22,200
1948 Miss Grillo (6)		I. Hanford	119	20,850
1949 Allie's Pal (4)		R.J. Martin	114	19,950
1950 Adile (4)		J. Gilbert	119	21,650
1951 Busanda (4)		E. Guerin	126	42,600
1952 Kiss Me Kate (4)		R. Nash	126	43,250
1953 Grecian Queen (3)		T. Atkinson	114	84,600
1954 Gainsboro Girl (4)		A. Catalano	113	101,800
1955 Parlo (4)		E. Guerin	128	99,900
1956 Flower Bowl (4)		L. Batcheller	112	104,875
1957 Princess Turia (4)		W. Hartack	119	110,875
1958 Endine (4)		E. Nelson	111	106,875
1959 Endine (5)		P.J. Bailey	117	98,312
1960 Quill (4)		R. Ussery	125	94,750
1961 Airmans Guide (4)		H. Grant	121	104,687
1962 Seven Thirty (4)		L. Adams	120	92,375
1963 Waltz Song (5)		S. Mellon	116	112,062
1964 Old Hat (5)		B. Thornburg	113	79,254
1965 Steeple Jill (4)		J. Ruane	123	80,122
1966 Open Fire (5)		F. Lovato	110	79,930
1967 Straight Deal (5)		R. Ussery	125	76,879
1968 Politely (5)		A. Cordero, Jr.	126	76,476
1969 Obeah (4)		J.L. Rotz	113	74,168
1970 Obeah (5)		L. Moyers	114	85,215
1971 Blessing Angelica (3)		J. Vasquez	111	80,860

1972 Blessing Angelica (4) . . . .

E. Belmonte 114 74,000

Run as New Castle Handicap prior to 1955. Not run in 1943. Distance 1 1/16 miles prior to 1951.

Derby Trial
Churchill Downs; 3-year-olds; 1 mile.

Year	Jockey	Wt.	Win. val.
1938 The Chief . . . . . .G. Woolf	117	$ 2,145
1939 Viscounty . . . . .C. Bierman	110	2,150
1940 Bimelech . . . . . .F.A. Smith	118	2,170
1941 Blue Pair . . . . . .J. Richard	115	2,045
1942 Valdina Orphan .C. Bierman	111	2,305
1943 Ocean Wave . . . . . . W. Eads	112	2,290
1944 Broadcloth . . . . . .F. Zufelt	110	4,400
1945 Burning Dream . D. Dodson	111	4,570
1946 Rippey . . . . .F. Zufelt	110	9,775
1947 Faultless . . . . . D. Dodson	118	9,075
1948 Citation . . . . E. Arcaro	118	8,525
1949 Olympia . . . . . . E. Arcaro	118	9,000
1950 Black George . . . . E. Nelson	112	9,850
1951 Fanfare . . . . D. Dodson	112	10,250
1952 Hill Gail . . . . E. Arcaro	118	9,775
1953 Dark Star . . . . . H. Moreno	115	11,650
1954 Hasty Road . . . . . J. Adams	118	11,700
1955 Flying Fury . . .C. McCreary	118	11,200
1956 Fabius . . . . .W. Hartack	112	13,050
1957 Federal Hill . . . .W. Carstens	122	10,500
1958 Tim Tam . . . . I. Valenzuela	122	10,380
1959 Open View . . . . . .K. Korte	116	10,385
1960 Beau Purple . . . . . E. Guerin	116	10,770
1961 Crozier . . . . B. Baeza	122	10,627
1962 Roman Line . . . . J. Cobest	122	10,432
1963 Bonjour . . . . W. Shoemaker	122	10,530
1964 Hill Rise . . . W. Shoemaker	122	10,432
1965 Bold Lad . . . . . .W. Hartack	122	10,237
1966 Exhibitionist . . E. Belmonte	122	10,237
1967 Barbs Delight . .W. Hartack	116	10,627
1968 Proper Proof . . . . .J. Sellers	122	10,627
1969 Ack Ack . . . . M. Ycaza	122	10,432
1970 Admiral's Shield . J. Nichols	119	10,725
1971 Vegas Vic . . . . . . .H. Grant	119	13,910
1972 Key To The Mint . B. Baeza	122	14,560

Dixie Handicap
Pimlico; 3-year-olds and over; 1½ miles.

Year	Jockey	Wt.	Win val.
1870 Preakness . . . . . . .Hayward	110	$ 6,400
1871 Harry Bassett . . . . . .Rowe	110	6,500
1872 Hubbard . . . . McCabe	110	13,200
1873 Tom Bowling . . . . . . Swim	110	4,000
1874 Vandalite . . . . .Houston	107	13,200
1875 Tom Ochiltree . . . . . . Evans	110	4,350
1876 Vigil . . . . .Spillman	110	4,300
1877 King Faro . . . . . . Walker	110	4,450
1878 Duke of Magenta . . . Hughes	110	4,200
1879 Monitor . . . . .Hughes	107	4,850
1880 Grenada . . . . Hughes	110	4,200
1881 Crickmore . . . . .Hughes	107	3,550
1882 Monarch . . . . Schauer	110	3,500

1883 George Kinney			
	J. McLaughlin	110	3,600
1884 Loftin . . . . .Stoval	112½	3,595
1885 East Lynne . . .W. Donohue	115	3,595
1886 The Bard . . . . . W. Hayward	118	3,290
1887 Hanover . . . .J. McLaughlin	123	4,560
1888 Taragon . . . . . . W. Hayward	123	4,040
1902 Adelaide Prince W.L. Powers	113	1,530
1903 Colonsay . . . . . . .W.C. Daly	114	1,750
1904 The Southerner . M. Corbett	116	3,310
1924 Chacolet (6) . . . .M. Garner	116	24,840
1925 Sarazen (4) . . . . .E. Sande	130	25,950
1926 Sarazen (5) . . . . . F. Weiner	128	24,550
1927 Mars (4) . . . . . F. Coltiletti	124	26,375
1928 Mike Hall (4) . . H. Richards	110	24,975
1929 Diavolo (4) . . . . .J. Maiben	112	27,600
1930 Sandy Ford (4) . F. Catrone	106	26,025
1931 Paul Bunyan (5)			
	E. Gianelloni	110	15,425
1932 Gallant Knight (5)H. Schutte	121	14,550
1933 Stepenfetchit (4) .E. Steffen	112	5,100
1934 Equipoise (6) .R. Workman	130	4,190
1935 Only One (4) . . . .R. Merritt	108	4,520
1936 Dark Hope (7) . . . .R. Jones	113	9,500
1937 Calumet Dick (5) J. Wagner	108	9,450
1938 Pompoon (4) . . . . .G. Woolf	118	20,950
1939 Sir Damion (5) . . D. Meade	113	22,025
1940 Honey Cloud (6) . . H. Mora	115	18,250
1941 Haltal (4) . . . .C. McCreary	110	19,850
1942 Whirlaway (4) . . . E. Arcaro	128	19,275
1943 Riverland (5) . . . . S. Brooks	123	17,775
1944 Sun Again (5) . .F.A. Smith	120	25,700
1945 Rounders (6)F. Remerscheid	118	25,400
1946 Armed (5) . . . . . D. Dodson	130	25,700
1947 Assault (4) . . . . .E. Arcaro	129	24,700
1948 Fervent (4) . . . .N.L. Pierson	121	21,950
1949 Chains (4) . . . . .J.D. Jessop	109	21,150
1950 Loser Weeper (5)N. Combest	108	18,450
1951 County Delight (4)J. Nichols	114	18,650
1952 Alerted (4) . . . . . . R. Sisto	112	20,400
1953 Royal Vale (5) .J. Westrope	120	18,800
1954 Straight Face (4) . .B. Green	115	19,500
1955 St. Vincent (4) . . .B. James	126	20,250
1956 Chevation (5) . . . C. Rogers	117	21,000
1957 Akbar Khan (5) . . E. Nelson	113	19,675
1958 Pop Corn (4) . . . . .J. Ruane	110	19,650
1959 One-Eyed King (5) M. Ycaza	120	18,712
1960 Shield Bearer (5) . . N. Shuk	114	19,070
1961 Hunter's Rock (3) F. Lovato	111	19,857
1962 Wise Ship (5) . . .H. Gustines	123	41,437
1963 Cedar Key (3) . . . . . .T. Lee	110	40,885
1964 Will I Rule (4) . R. Turcotte	118	40,852
1965 Or et Argent (4) . .W. Blum	116	22,847
1965 Flag (5) . . . . .T. Lee	114	22,945
1966 Knightly Manners (5) T. Lee	112	37,830
1967 War Censor (4) . . . .E. Fires	125	38,740
1968 High Hat (4) . .R. Broussard	116	36,270
1969 Czar Alexander (4)			
	W. Hartack	122	37,895
1970 Fort Marcy (6) J. Velasquez	124	37,375
1971 Chompion (6) . . . . M. Hole	119	36,920
1972 Onandaga (6) . . . . J. Kurtz	118	38,350

Run as Dinner Party Stakes in 1870; as Reunion Stakes from 1872 to 1888, inclusive. Run at Benning, Washington, D.C., at 1¾ miles, for three-year-olds, in 1902, 1903 and 1904. Distance 2 miles, for three-year-olds, from 1870 to 1888, inclusive. 1 3/16 miles from 1924 to 1952, inclusive. Not run from 1889 to 1901, inclusive, nor from 1905 to 1923, inclusive. Run at 1 1/8 miles in 1953 and 1954; 1 3/8 miles from 1955 to 1959, inclusive. Run in two divisions in 1965. Fort Marcy finished first in 1971 but was disqualified and placed fourth.

Dwyer Handicap
Aqueduct; 3-year-olds; 1¼ miles.

Year	Jockey	Wt.	Win. val.
1887 Hanover	J. McLaughlin	118	$2,675
1888 Emperor of Norfolk	I. Murphy	118	3,740
1889 Cynosure	Fitzpatrick	118	4,790
1890 Burlington	Barnes	118	6,960
1891 Russell	Taylor	122	5,270
1892 Patron	Hayward	122	5,240
1893 Rainbow	Littlefield	122	4,350
1894 Dobbins	Simms	122	5,340
1895 Keenan	Griffin	122	4,640
1896 Handspring	Doggett	122	7,800
1897 Octagon	Simms	122	7,960
1898 The Huguenot	Spencer	122	7,750
1899 Ahom	H. Martin	119	7,750
1900 Petruchio	Spencer	108	8,475
1901 Bonnibert	Spencer	112	7,750
1902 Major Daingerfield	Odom	118	7,750
1903 Whorler	F. O'Neill	118	7,750
1904 Bryn Mawr	Lyne	118	10,000
1905 Cairngorm	W. Davis	118	5,390
1906 Belmere	F. O'Neill	118	9,475
1907 Peter Pan	W. Miller	126	10,475
1908 Fair Play	E. Dugan	114	13,350
1909 Joe Madden	E. Dugan	126	9,225
1910 Dalmatian	C.H. Shilling	122	2,300
1913 Rock View	T. McTaggart	123	2,150
1914 Roamer	J. Butwell	117	2,300
1915 Norse King	J. Butwell	111	2,275
1916 Chicle	T. McTaggart	116	2,950
1917 Omar Khayyam	A. Collins	125	3,850
1918 War Cloud	M. Buxton	124	4,850
1919 Purchase	W. Knapp	118	4,850
1920 Man o' War	C. Kummer	126	4,850
1921 Grey Lag	E. Sande	123	7,100
1922 Ray Jay	C. Ponce	117	7,150
1923 Dunlin	C. Lang	123	7,150
1924 Ladkin	J. Maiben	123	7,750
1925 American Flag	A. Johnson	126	8,900
1926 Crusader	E. Sande	123	15,000
1927 Kentucky II	J. Maiben	108	18,500
1928 Genie	W. Kelsay	110	19,600
1929 Grey Coat	S. O'Donnell	117	19,450
1930 Gallant Fox	E. Sande	126	11,500
1931 Twenty Grand	C. Kurtsinger	126	11,500
1932 Faireno	T. Malley	124	12,200
1933 War Glory	J. Gilbert	118	4,250
1934 Rose Cross	S. Coucci	116	4,090
1935 Omaha	W.D. Wright	126	9,200
1936 Mr. Bones	J. Gilbert	119	8,500
1937 Strabo	S. Renick	116	10,750
1938 The Chief	G. Woolf	119	8,900
1939 Johnstown	J. Stout	126	9,250
1940 Your Chance	W.D. Wright	116	9,650
1941 Whirlaway	E. Arcaro	126	8,075
1942 Valdina Orphan	C. Bierman	116	21,150
1943 Vincentive	J. Gilbert	111	19,600
1944 By Jimminy	T. Atkinson	114	39,170
1945 Wildlife	T. Atkinson	116	38,835
1946 Assault	W. Mehrtens	126	40,700
1947 Phalanx	R. Donoso	126	40,800
1948 My Request	T. Atkinson	121	39,200
1949 Shackleton	R. Bernhardt	111	38,000
1950 Greek Song	O. Scurlock	116	27,400
1951 Battlefield	E. Arcaro	121	39,800
1952 Blue Man	C. McCreary	126	39,300
1953 Native Dancer	E. Guerin	126	38,100
1954 High Gun	E. Guerin	126	39,300
1955 Nashua	E. Arcaro	126	37,200
1956 Riley	T. Atkinson	112	30,400
1957 Bureaucracy	W. Boland	114	30,500
1958 Victory Morn	E. Guerin	115	29,270
1959 Waltz	S. Boulmetis	121	52,515
1960 Francis S.	P.J. Bailey	119	34,565
1961 Hitting Away	H. Woodhouse	119	54,340
1962 Cyane	E. Nelson	116	54,957
1963 Outing Class	R. Ussery	122	55,250
1964 Quadrangle	M. Ycaza	126	53,170
1965 Staunchness	R. Ussery	114	53,397
1966 Mr. Right	E. Cardone	110	53,527
1967 Damascus	W. Shoemaker	128	54,177
1968 Stage Door Johnny	H. Gustines	129	53,235
1969 Gleaming Light	L. Adams	112	52,747
1970 Judgable	R. Woodhouse	108	54,892
1971 Jim French	A. Cordero, Jr.	125	49,020
1972 Cloudy Dawn	W. Hartack	118	51,525

Distance 1½ miles in 1887, from 1898 to 1909, inclusive, and from 1926 to 1934, inclusive; 1 5/16 miles in 1925; 1 1/8 miles from 1915 to 1924, inclusive, and from 1935 to 1939, inclusive. Not run in 1911 and 1912. Run at Gravesend from 1887 to 1910, inclusive, and at Belmont Park in 1913. Run as Brooklyn Derby prior to 1918. Snow Ridge finished first in 1940 but was disqualified. Distance 1 3/16 miles 1956 to 1959, inclusive. Run at Belmont Park in 1957 and 1958; Jamaica Race Course in 1956 and 1959. Run as Dwyer Stakes prior to 1956.

Flamingo Stakes
Hialeah Park; 3-year-olds; 1 1/8 miles.

Year	Jockey	Wt.	Win. val.
1926 Torcher	S. Griffin	117	$4,450
1929 Upset Lad	J.H. Burke	118	8,600
1930 Titus	A. Robertson	118	9,900
1931 Lightning Bolt	C. Kurtsinger	118	10,800
1932 Evening	R. Leischman	113	9,725

1933 Charley O. . . . . . . J. Gilbert 118 10,475
1934 Time Clock . . . . .M. Garner 114 10,075
1935 Black Helen . . . . . D. Meade 113 15,600
1936 Brevity . . . . . .W.D. Wright 120 20,050
1937 Court Scandal . . .E. Steffen 120 20,900
1938 Lawrin . . . . . .W.D. Wright 120 20,100
1939 Technician . . . . I. Hanford 118 20,000
1940 Woof Woof . . . I. Anderson 118 22,450
1941 Dispose . . . . . A. Robertson 120 20,200
1942 Requested . . . . . . E. Arcaro 122 28,150
1944 Stir Up . . . . E. Arcaro 118 14,825
1946 Round View, L. Hildebrandt 118 29,600
1947 Faultless . . . . A. Snider 118 49,500
1948 Citation . . . . A. Snider 126 43,500
1949 Olympia . . . . . T. Atkinson 126 48,500
1950 Oil Capitol . . . .K. Church 126 44,800
1951 Yildiz . . . . . . .W. Mehrtens 117 50,000
1952 Blue Man . . . . .C. McCreary 117 47,450
1952 Charlie McAdam . . . .
               S. Boulmetis 117 47,450
1953 Straight Face. . T. Atkinson 122 116,400
1954 Turn-to . . . . H. Moreno 122 96,400
1955 Nashua . . . . E. Arcaro 122 104,600
1956 Needles . . . . D. Erb 117 111,600
1957 Bold Ruler . . . . E. Arcaro 122 94,200
1958 Tim Tam . . . . .W. Hartack 122 97,800
1959 Troilus . . . . .C. Rogers 122 86,070
1960 Bally Ache . . . . . R. Ussery 122 90,880
1961 Carry Back . . . . . .J. Sellers 122 84,370
1962 Prego . . . . L. Adams 122 88,530
1963 Never Bend . . . . . M. Ycaza 122 88,140
1964 Northern Dancer . . . .
               W. Shoemaker 122 89,830
1965 Native Charger . . J.L. Rotz 122 93,340
1966 Buckpasser . W. Shoemaker 122 88,660
1967 Reflected Glory . . . .
               J. Velasquez 122 93,990
1968 Wise Exchange E. Belmonte 122 89,050
1969 Top Knight . . . . . M. Ycaza 122 95,160
1970 My Dad George . . . .
               R. Broussard 122 104,910
1971 Executioner . . . J. Vasquez 122 100,750
1972 Hold Your Peace,C. Marquez 122 86,190
1973 Our Native . . . . J. Vasquez 122 91,520

Not run in 1927, 1928, 1943 nor 1945. Run at Tampa in 1926. Run as Florida Derby prior to 1937; run in 2 divisions in 1952. Jewel's Reward finished first in 1958 but was disqualified and placed second. Sunrise County finished first in 1962 but was disqualified and placed third. Iron Ruler finished first in 1968 but was disqualified and placed second.

Florida Derby
Gulfstream Park; 3-year-olds; 1 1/8 miles.

Year	Jockey	Wt.	Win val.
1952 Sky Ship . . . . R. Nash		114	$17,550
1953 Money Broker . . .A. Popara		117	88,000
1954 Correlation . W. Shoemaker		119	100,000
1955 Nashua . . . . E. Arcaro		122	100,000
1956 Needles . . . . D. Erb		117	95,200

1957 Gen. Duke . . . . .W. Hartack 122 73,400
1958 Tim Tam . . . . . .W. Hartack 122 77,900
1959 Easy Spur . . . . .W. Hartack 122 75,300
1960 Bally Ache . . . . . . R. Ussery 122 79,500
1961 Carry Back . . . . . .J. Sellers 122 75,100
1962 Ridan . . . . M. Ycaza 122 85,800
1963 Candy Spots, W. Shoemaker 122 74,700
1964 Northern Dancer . . . .
               W. Shoemaker 122 76,500
1965 Native Charger . . J.L. Rotz 122 79,800
1966 Williamston Kid . . . .
               R. L. Stevenson 122 83,400
1967 In Reality . . . . .E. Fires 122 99,400
1968 Forward Pass . D. Brumfield 122 94,000
1969 Top Knight . . . . . M. Ycaza 122 81,800
1970 My Dad George,R. Broussard 122 103,600
1971 Eastern Fleet . . . . .E. Maple 118 82,680
1972 Upper Case . . R. Turcotte 118 107,760
1973 Royal and Regal . . W. Blum 122 78,120

Abe's First finished first in 1966 but was disqualified and placed fourth.

Futurity Stakes
Belmont Park; 2-year-olds; 6½ furlongs

Year	Jockey	Wt.	Win val.
1888 Proctor Knott . . . S. Barnes		112	$40,900
1889 Chaos . . . . G. Day		109	54,500
1890 Potomac . . . . .A. Hamilton		115	67,675
1891 His Highness .J. McLaughlin		130	61,675
1892 Morello . . . . . . W. Hayward		118	40,450
1893 Domino . . . . F. Taral		130	48,855
1894 The Butterflies . .H. Griffin		112	48,710
1895 Requital . . . . . . .H. Griffin		115	53,190
1896 Ogden . . . . . . .F. Turbiville		115	43,790
1897 L'Alouette . . . .R. Clawson		115	34,290
1898 Martimas . . . . .H. Lewis		118	36,610
1899 Chacornac . . . . . H Spencer		114	30,630
1900 Ballyhoo Bey . . . .T. Sloan		112	33,580
1901 Yankee . . . . . W. O'Connor		119	36,850
1902 Savable . . . . L. Lyne		119	44,500
1903 Hamburg Belle . . .G. Fuller		114	36,600
1904 Artful . . . . . .E. Hildebrand		114	40,830
1905 Ormondale . . . .A. Redfern		117	32,960
1906 Electioneer . . . . . .W. Shaw		117	36,880
1907 Colin . . . . .W. Miller		125	26,640
1908 Maskette . . . . . . .J . Notter		118	26,110
1909 Sweep . . . . .J. Butwell		126	24,100
1910 Novelty . . . . . .C.H. Shilling		127	25,360
1913 Pennant . . . . C Borel		119	15,060
1914 Trojan . . . . . .C. Burlingame		117	16,010
1915 Thunderer . . . . . .J. Notter		122	16,590
1916 Campfire . . . . .J. McTaggart		125	17,340
1917 Papp . . . . L. Allen		127	15,600
1918 Dunboyne . . A. Schuttinger		127	23,360
1919 Man o' War . . . . . .J. Loftus		127	26,650
1920 Step Lightly . . . . F. Keogh		116	35,870
1921 Bunting . . . . . . F. Coltiletti		117	39,700
1922 Sally's Alley . . .A. Johnson		116	47,550
1923 St. James . . . . T. McTaggart		130	64,810
1924 Mother Goose . . L. McAtee		114	65,730
1925 Pompey . . . . .L. Fator		127	58,480

1926 Scapa Flow	L. Fator	122	65,980
1927 Anita Peabody	C. Lang	124	91,790
1928 High Strung	L. McAtee	122	97,990
1929 Whichone	R. Workman	125	105,730
1930 Jamestown	L. McAtee	130	99,600
1931 Top Flight	R. Workman	127	94,780
1932 Kerry Patch	P. Walls	122	88,690
1933 Singing Wood	R. Jones	122	81,700
1934 Chance Sun	W.D. Wright	122	77,510
1935 Tintagel	S. Coucci	122	66,450
1936 Pompoon	H. Richards	127	55,630
1937 Menow	C. Kurtsinger	119	56,800
1938 Porter's Mite	B. James	119	57,045
1939 Bimelech	F.A. Smith	126	57,710
1940 Our Boots	E. Arcaro	119	65,800
1941 Some Chance	W. Eads	122	57,900
1942 Occupation	G. Woolf	126	57,890
1943 Occupy	G. Woolf	126	55,635
1944 Pavot	G. Woolf	126	53,890
1945 Star Pilot	A. Kirkland	126	52,940
1946 First Flight	E. Arcaro	123	73,350
1947 Citation	A. Snider	122	78,430
1948 Blue Peter	E. Guerin	126	88,510
1949 Guillotine	T. Atkinson	122	87,585
1950 Battlefield	E. Arcaro	122	81,715
1951 Tom Fool	T. Atkinson	122	86,710
1952 Native Dancer	E. Guerin	122	82,845
1953 Porterhouse	W. Boland	122	92,875
1954 Nashua	E. Arcaro	122	88,015
1955 Nail	H. Woodhouse	122	100,425
1956 Bold Ruler	E. Arcaro	122	91,145
1957 Jester	P.J. Bailey	122	81,005
1958 Intentionally,	W. Shoemaker	122	80,690
1959 Weatherwise	E. Arcaro	122	88,470
1960 Little Tumbler,	R. Broussard	119	85,191
1961 Cyane	M. Ycaza	122	85,650
1962 Never Bend	W. Shoemaker	122	94,347
1963 Bupers	A. Gomez	122	90,974
1964 Bold Lad	B. Baeza	122	85,566
1965 Priceless Gem	W. Blum	119	93,827
1966 Bold Hour	J.L. Rotz	122	91,084
1967 Captain's Gig,	W. Shoemaker	122	90,493
1968 Top Knight	M. Ycaza	122	88,283
1969 High Echelon	J.L. Rotz	122	92,807
1970 Salem	J.L. Rotz	122	99,333
1971 Riva Ridge	R. Turcotte	122	87,636
1972 Secretariat	R. Turcotte	122	83,320

Distance 1,263 yards 1 foot from 1892 to 1901, inclusive; ¾ mile prior to 1892 and from 1902 to 1924, inclusive; about 7/8 mile from 1925 to 1933, inclusive. Run at Sheepshead Bay until 1910. Run at Saratoga in 1910, 1913 and 1914; at Aqueduct in 1959, 1960 and from 1962 to 1967, inclusive. Not run in 1911 and 1912. Run over old straight course prior to 1926. Over Widener Straight Course, 1926 to 1958, inclusive.

Garden State Stakes
Garden State Park; 2-year-olds; 1 1/16 miles.

Year Winner	Jockey	Wt.	Net. val.
1953 Turn-to	H. Moreno	122	$151,282

1954 Summer Tan	E. Guerin	122	151,096
1955 Prince John	A. Valenzuela	122	157,918
1956 Barbizon	W. Hartack	122	168,430
1957 Nadir	W. Hartack	122	155,047
1958 First Landing	E. Arcaro	122	175,965
1959 Warfare	I. Valenzuela	122	157,485
1960 Carry Back	J. Sellers	122	160,782
1961 Crimson Satan			
	W. Shoemaker	122	180,819
1962 Crewman	W. Shoemaker	122	164,118
1963 Hurry to Market	W.M. Cook	122	190,374
1964 Sadair	M. Ycaza	122	181,020
1965 Prince Saim	J. Culmone	122	187,167
1966 Successor	B. Baeza	122	188,475
1967 Bugged	E. Belmonte	122	188,721
1968 Beau Brummel	B. Baeza	122	187,596
1969 Forum	W. Blum	122	198,375
1970 Run the Gantlet	J.L. Rotz	122	211,392
1971 Riva Ridge	R. Turcotte	122	176,334
1972 Secretariat	R. Turcotte	122	179,199

Grand National Steeplechase
Belmont Park; 4-year-olds and over; 2½ miles

Year	Age	Jockey	Wt.	Win val.
1899 Trillion (8)	Mr. W.C. Hayes	163	$ 6,150
1900 Philae (5)	Donahue	153	6,525
1901 Sacket (6)	Carson	137	6,100
1902 Geo. W. Jenkins (4).	Ray	133	5,525
1903 Plohn (6)	Ray	141	6,050
1904 St. Jude (4)	Ray	142	5,450
1905 Mackey Dwyer (5)	Holman	149	5,210
1906 Good and Plenty (6)	Ray	170	5,675
1907 Alfar (5)	Owens	143	5,500
1908 Kara (5)	McAfee	138	4,775
1909 Sir Wooster (5)	Davidson	155	740
1910 Rossfenton (4)	W. Allen	138	1,275
1913 Penobscot (4)	Wolke	140	1,845
1914 Relluf (7)	T. Tuckey	157	1,650
1915 Mission (6)	B. Haynes	148	1,785
1916 Hibler (7)	T. Parrette	140	1,860
1917 Expectation (6)	B. Haynes	144	1,895
1918 St. Charlcote (6)	C. Smoot	158	1,755
1919 Stonewood (7)	V. Powers	148	2,150
1920 Square Dealer (6)	V. Powers	154	2,075
1921 Earlocker (5)	W. Mahoney	142	3,675
1922 Lytle (8)	R.H. Crawford	136	3,575
1923 Sea Tale (7)	J. Pierce	158	3,675
1924 Dan IV. (6)	N. Kennedy	158	4,100
1925 Moseley (5)	C. Smoot	138	6,350
1926 Erne II. (5)	R.H. Crawford	149	6,550
1927 Jolly Roger (5)			
	R.H. Crawford	165	34,750
1928 Jolly Roger (6)			
	R.H. Crawford	167	35,850
1929 Arc Light (5)	A. Bauman	151	34,450
1930 Tourist II. (5)	W. Hunt	148	28,350
1931 Green Cheese (4)			
	Mr. R. McK'y	140	28,250
1932 Tourist II. (7)	G. Cooper	158	8,200
1933 Best Play (4)	A. Bauman	132	4,850
1934 Battleship (7)			
	Mr. C.K. Bassett	147	5,900

1935 Snap Back (6) ... W.N. Ball	137	6,050
1936 Bushranger (6) ...H. Little	172	5,750
1937 Sailor Beware (5) .H. Little	153	9,200
1938 Annibal (5)Mr. R. McKinney	156	8,100
1939 Whaddon Chase (4)J. Penrod	146	9,300
1940 Cottesmore (5) ....F. Slate	160	14,850
1941 Speculate (5) ..... T. Roby	142	14,350
1942 Cottesmore (7) ....F. Slate	155	13,950
1943 Brother Jones (7) G. Walker	150	14,500
1944 Burma Road (5) ..J. Magee	136	13,385
1945 Mercator (6) .....W. Owen	142	15,005
1946 Elkridge (8) .... E. Roberts	151	21,425
1947 Adaptable (6) ....J. Rich	147	20,700
1948 American Way (6)D. Marzani	144	22,350
1949 His Boots (4)... D. Marzani	141	15,550
1950 Trough Hill (8) ...H. Harris	150	16,450
1951 Oedipus (5) ...... A. Foot	140	16,750
1952 Sea Legs (6) .. F.D. Adams	136	19,550
1953 His Boots (8).....E. Carter	141	20,350
1954 Shipboard (4) .... A. Foot	152	19,000
1955 Neji (5) ...... F.D. Adams	163	19,200
1956 Shipboard (6) ... A. Foot	164	19,500
1957 Neji (7) ... A.P. Smithwick	168	21,450
1958 Neji (8) ... A.P. Smithwick	173	17,932
1959 Sun Dog (5) .....T. Walsh	137	18,030
1960 Sun Dog (5)..... T. Walsh	145	17,640
1961 Independence (9) .T. Walsh	138	18,232
1962 Barnabys Bluff (4) T. Walsh	153	28,100
1963 Tuscarora (7) ....T. Walsh	160	18,135
1964 Bon Nouvel (4)....		
A.P. Smithwick	156	18,297
1965 Mako (5) ....T. Walsh	142	17,842
1966 Bampton Castle (9)....		
J. Aitcheson	141	17,907
1967 Golpista (9)... D. Small Jr.	146	25,691
1968 Bampton Castle (11)....		
J. Aitcheson	160	25,057
1969 High Patches (5)D. Small, Jr.	144	25,659
1970 Lake Delaware (7)		
D. Small Jr.	154	25,366
1971 ShadowBrook (7) L. O'Brien	155	24,240

Run at Morris Park prior to 1905; at Aqueduct in 1959, 1961, and from 1963 to 1967, inclusive. Distance about 2½ miles prior to 1916; about 3 miles from 1916 to 1956, inclusive, and in 1959, 1961, and 1963; about 3 1/8 miles in 1957, 1958, 1960, and 1962; 3 1/8 miles in 1968; 3 miles in 1964, through 1967, 1969, and 1970. In 1930 Arc Light finished first but was disqualified.

Grand Prix
Arlington Park; 3-year-olds; 1 mile

Year	Jockey	Wt.	Win val.
1971 Son Ange .....C. Baltazar	114	$68,400

Arlington Classic prior to 1971. Not run in 1972.

Grey Lag Handicap
Aqueduct; 3-year-olds and over; 1 1/8 miles.

Year	Age	Jockey	Wt.	Win val.
1941 Dit (4).....A. Robertson	112	$ 8,075
1942 Marriage (6) ..J. Longden	109	13,600

1943 Boysy (7) ...... J. Cavens	114	14,150
1944 First Fiddle (5) .J. Longden	119	12,325
1945 Stymie (4) .....R. Permane	121	10,640
1946 Stymie (5).. H. Woodhouse	127	24,750
1947 Assault (4) ...W. Mehrtens	128	32,325
1949 Royal Governor (5)....		
O. Scurlock	114	20,600
1950 Lotowhite (3) ... K. Stuart	103	20,350
1951 Cochise (5) ... O. Scurlock	122	18,700
1952 Tom Fool (3) . T. Atkinson	119	42,200
1953 Find (3)........ E. Guerin	115	44,700
1956 Nashua (4) ... T. Atkinson	128	37,100
1957 Kingmaker (4)... R. Ussery	116	38,800
1958 Oh Johnny (5).. W. Boland	119	37,750
1959 Vertex (5) ....S. Boulmetis	130	54,887
1960 Sword Dancer (4) . E. Arcaro	126	44,800
1961 Mail Order (5) ... L. Adams	123	56,420
1962 Ambiopoise (4) .. R. Ussery	115	55,770
1963 Sunrise County (4)J.L. Rotz	118	55,152
1964 Saidam (5) ..... M. Ycaza	114	53,527
1965 Quita Dude (5) I. Valenzuela	115	55,282
1966 Selari (4) ....J. Sellers	113	54,697
1967 Moontrip (6) ...A. Cordero	112	54,405
1968 Bold Hour (4) ... J.L. Rotz	113	55,250
1969 Bushido (3) ..... L. Adams	113	37,960
1970 Arts and Letters (4)B. Baeza	128	55,022
1971 Judgable (4) .. R. Turcotte	112	51,420
1972 Droll Role (4) ....E. Maple	109	50,085
1973 Summer Guest (3)		
J. Vasquez	116	86,850

Distance 1-1/16 miles in 1949 and 1950; 7/8 mile in 1969. Not run in 1948, 1954 and 1955. Run at Jamaica Race Course prior to 1960. In 1967, Advocator finished first but was disqualified.

Gulfstream Park Handicap
Gulfstream Park; 3-year-olds and over; 1¼ miles.

Year	Age	Jockey	Wt.	Win val.
1946 Do-Reigh-Mi (5) .B. Strange	112	$11,000
1947 Armed (6) ..... D. Dodson	129	23,000
1948 Rampart (6) .....M. Basile	108	20,050
1949 Coaltown (4).. O. Scurlock	128	13,000
1950 Chicle II. (5) H. Woodhouse	125	9,750
1951 Ennobled (5) ..... J. Stout	113	9,500
1952 Crafty Admiral (4) C. Errico	114	19,850
1953 Crafty Admiral (5)K. Church	128	37,400
1954 Wise Margin (4) .. K. Stuart	106	43,500
1955 Mister Black (6) . J. Adams	113	42,100
1956 Sailor (4) ......W. Hartack	119	83,300
1957 Bardstown (5) ..W. Hartack	130	76,400
1958 Round Table (4)		
W. Shoemaker	130	69,800
1959 Vertex (5) ....S. Boulmetis	125	80,700
1960 Bald Eagle (5) ... M. Ycaza	126	71,400
1961 Tudor Way (5) .W. Hartack	124	74,000
1962 Jay Fox (4) .... L. Gilligan	112	72,800
1963 Kelso (6) .... I. Valenzuela	130	70,500
1964 Gun Bow (4) W. Shoemaker	125	76,600
1965 Ampose (4) .....K. Knapp	112	71,900
1966 First Family (4) ...E. Fires	112	74,200
1967 Pretense (4) ......J. Sellers	126	97,600

1968 Gentleman James (4) . . . .

R. Grubb	110	86,000

1969 Court Recess (4) . M. Miceli 108 86,400
1970 Snow Sporting (4) A. Pineda 118 83,600
1971 Fast Hilarious (5) . C. Perret 116 77,040
1972 Executioner (4) . . C. Barrera 114 80,880
1973 West Coast Scout (5) . . . .

L. Adams	116	80,880

Run as Gulfstream Handicap and for 4-year-olds and over in 1946. Run as a purse race from 1949 to 1951, inclusive. Yorky finished first in 1962 but was disqualified and placed second.

Hawthorne Gold Cup Handicap

Hawthorne; 3-year-olds and over; 1¼ miles.

Year	Horse	Jockey	Wt.	Win val.
1928	Display (5)	J. Maiben	126	$20,200
1929	Sun Beau (4)	F. Coltiletti	126	21,900
1930	Sun Beau (5)	F. Coltiletti	126	23,800
1931	Sun Beau (6)	J. Maiben	126	20,700
1932	Plucky Play (5)	G. Woolf	126	21,450
1933	Equipoise (5)	R. Workman	126	17,250
1935	Discovery (4)	J. Bejshak	126	11,125
1937	Sahri II. (6)	F.A. Smith	110	11,125
1938	Esposa (6)	N. Wall	120	10,825
1939	Challedon (3)	H. Richards	120	10,900
1946	Jack's Jill (4)	J. Higley	111	19,450
1947	Be Faithful (5)	W. Garner	116	38,500
1948	Billings (3)	M. Peterson	122	39,700
1949	Volcanic (4)	A.D. Rivera	125	38,100
1950	Dr. Ole Nelson (4)	G. Porch	110	19,750
1951	Seaward (6)	A. Gomez	113	27,250
1952	To Market (4)	W. Boland	123	39,800
1953	Sub Fleet (4)	S. Brooks	115	67,350
1954	Rejected (4)	E. Guerin	123	61,550
1955	Hasseyampa (4)	B. Fisk	111	55,200
1956	Dedicate (4)	W. Boland	120	80,750
1957	Round Table (3)	W. Harmatz	121	75,950
1958	Round Table (4)			
		W. Shoemaker	126	73,250
1959	Day Court (4)	H. Moreno	113	71,300
1960	Kelso (3)	E. Arcaro	117	88,900
1961	T.V. Lark (4)	J. Longden	113	78,250
1962	Beau Purple (5)	W. Boland	123	82,250
1963	Admiral Vic (3)	M. Solomone	122	78,500
1964	Going Abroad (4)			
		R. Broussard	120	77,100
1965	Moss Vale (4)	R. Baldwin	116	79,600
1966	Bold Bidder (4)	P. Anderson	121	75,200
1967	Dr. Fager (3)	B. Baeza	123	72,360
1968	Nodouble (3)	M. Heath	117	83,680
1969	Nodouble (4)	E. Belmonte	125	74,280
1970	Gladwin (4)	R. Turcotte	115	81,320
1971	Twice Worthy (4)			
		L. Pincay, Jr.	119	73,880
1972	Droll Role (4)	E. Maple	111	69,780

Not run in 1934, 1936 nor from 1940 to 1945, inclusive. Weight-for-age prior to 1937.

Hollywood Gold Cup
Invitational Handicap

Hollywood Park; 3-year-olds and over; 1¼ miles.

Year	Horse	Age	Jockey	Wt.	Win val.
1938	Seabiscuit (5)		G. Woolf	133	$37,150
1939	Kayak, II. (4)		G. Woolf	125	35,075
1940	Challedon (4)		G. Woolf	133	36,200
1941	Big Pebble (5)		J. Westrope	119	62,475
1944	Happy Issue (4)				
			H. Woodhouse	119	60,600
1945	Challenge Me (4)				
			A. Skoronski	108	48,230
1946	Triplicate (5)		B. James	113	79,900
1947	Cover Up (4)		R. Permane	117	73,500
1948	Shannon II. (7)		J. Adams	116	67,600
1949	Solidarity (4)		R. Neves	115	100,000
1950	Noor (5)		J. Longden	130	100,000
1951	Citation (6)		S. Brooks	120	100,000
1952	Two Lea (6)		H. Moreno	113	100,000
1953	Royal Serenade (5)				
			J. Longden	113	100,000
1954	Correspondent		J. Longden	110	100,000
1955	Rejected (5)		G. Glisson	118	100,000
1956	Swaps (4)		W. Shoemaker	130	100,000
1957	Round Table (3)				
			W. Shoemaker	109	100,000
1958	Gallant Man (4)				
			W. Shoemaker	130	100,000
1959	Hillsdale (4)		T. Barrow	124	100,000
1960	Dotted Swiss (4)		E. Burns	107	100,000
1961	Prince Blessed (4)				
			J. Longden	114	102,100
1962	Prove It (5)		H. Moreno	125	102,100
1963	Cadiz (7)		E. Burns	111	102,100
1964	Colorado King (5)		R. York	118	102,100
1965	Native Diver (6)		J. Lambert	124	102,100
1966	Native Diver (7)		J. Lambert	126	102,100
1967	Native Diver (8)		J. Lambert	123	102,100
1968	Princessnesian (4)		D. Pierce	117	102,100
1969	Figonero (4)		A. Pineda	115	102,100
1970	Pleasure Seeker (4)				
			L. Pincay, Jr.	114	102,100
1971	Ack Ack (5)		W. Shoemaker	134	100,000
1972	Quack (4)		D. Pierce	115	100,000

Not run in 1942 and 1943. Run at Santa Anita Park in 1949. Run under regular nomination procedure prior to 1971.

Hollywood Juvenile Championship

Hollywood Park; 2-year-olds, ¾ mile.

Year	Horse	Jockey	Wt.	Win. val.
1938	Unerring	J. Adams	119	$ 2,015
1939	Polymelior	R. Neves	118	8,320
1940	Flying Choice	J. Longden	115	7,600
1941	Phar Rong	G. Woolf	122	
	Madie Greenock	P. Martinez	119	6,200
1944	Realization	R. Neves	115	17,750
1944	Post Graduate	H.Woodhouse	115	15,650
1945	Favorito	J. Craigmyle	114	21,540
1946	U Time	L. Balaski	114	21,900
1947	Zenoda	R. Neves	111	16,800
1948	Star Fiddle	H. Trent	118	21,050
1949	Thanks Again	F. Chojnacki	116	31,100
1950	Gold Capitol	R. Neves	113	28,600
1951	Prudy's Boy	G. Lasswell	114	24,900

1952 Little Request	J. Longden	122	20,350	
1953 Arrogate	E. LeBlanc	116	44,500	
1954 Blue Ruler	S. Brooks	113	45,700	
1955 Bold Bazooka	R. York	116	47,200	
1956 Lucky Mel	J. Longden	122	61,450	
1957 Old Pueblo	E. Arcaro	116	49,000	
1958 Tomy Lee	W. Shoemaker	122	51,600	
1959 Noble Noor	D. Pierce	113	117,700	
1960 Pappa's All	G. Taniguchi	122	97,050	
1961 Rattle Dancer	R. Yanez	116	102,800	
1962 Y Flash	R. Campas	116	69,100	
1962 Noti	E. Burns	116	69,100	
1963 Malicious	I. Valenzuela	119	65,150	
1963 Nevada Bin	R. York	116	66,150	
1964 Charger's Kin	P. Moreno	122	86,075	
1964 Neke	L. Gilligan	116	86,075	
1965 Port Wine	W. Shoemaker	122	111,500	
1966 Forgotten Dreams	A. Maese	122	101,300	
1967 Jim White	W. Hartack	122	120,050	
1968 Fleet Kirsch	A. Pineda	122	125,850	
1969 Insubordination	L. Pincay, Jr.	122	101,850	
1970 Fast Fellow	D. Tierney	122	106,400	
1971 Royal Owl	W. Shoemaker	122	101,000	
1972 Bold Liz	J. Tejeira	122	83,000	
1973 Century's Envoy	J. Lambert	122	78,500	

Run as Starlet Sweepstakes prior to 1940; as Starlet Stakes from 1940 to 1958, inclusive. Phar Rong and Madie Greenock dead-heated for first place in 1941. Not run in 1942 and 1943. Run at Santa Anita in 1949. Distance 5½ furlongs in 1938; 7/8 mile in 1944 and 1945; 1 1/16 miles in 1950. In 1957, Strong Ruler finished first but was disqualified and placed third. Run in two divisions in 1944, 1962, 1963 and 1964.

Hopeful Stakes
Saratoga; 2-year-olds; 6½ furlongs.

Year	Jockey	Wt.	Win val.
1903 Delhi	C. Gannon	112	$22,275
1904 Tanya	E. Hildebrand	127	29,790
1905 Mohawk II.	A. Redfern	130	16,490
1906 Peter Pan	W. Knapp	130	17,640
1907 Jim Gaffney	D. Nicol	115	17,500
1908 Helmet	J. Notter	115	10,990
1909 Rocky O'Brien	V. Powers	122	17,160
1910 Novelty	A. Thomas	130	19,140
1913 Bringhurst	Loftus	113	4,100
1914 Regret	J. Notter	127	9,590
1915 Dominant	J. Notter	130	9,150
1916 Campfire	J. McTaggart	130	18,850
1917 Sun Briar	W. Knapp	130	30,600
1918 Eternal	A. Schuttinger	115	30,150
1919 Man o' War	J. Loftus	130	24,600
1920 Leonardo II	A. Schuttinger	115	33,850
1921 Morvich	A. Johnson	130	34,900
1922 Dunlin	C. Kummer	115	38,950
1923 Diogenes	C. Ponce	115	46,800
1924 Master Charlie	G. Babin	130	48,700
1925 Pompey	L. Fator	127	42,850
1926 Lord Chaucer	F. Coltiletti	115	48,850
1927 Brooms	J. Maiben	115	55,750
1928 Jack High	G. Ellis	127	54,100

1929 Boojum	R. Workman	117	54,750
1930 Epithet	W. Kelsay	117	55,000
1931 Tick On	P. Walls	117	45,950
1932 Ladysman	R. Jones	130	41,400
1933 Bazaar	D. Meade	119	35,550
1934 Psychic Bid	M. Garner	122	24,250
1935 Red Rain	R. Workman	124	38,400
1936 Maedic	E. Litzenberger	122	32,600
1937 Sky Larking	A. Robertson	119	31,450
1938 El Chico	N. Wall	126	42,550
1939 Bimelech	F.A. Smith	122	33,750
1940 Whirlaway	J. Longden	122	37,850
1941 Devil Diver	J. Skelly	119	35,950
1942 Devil's Thumb	C. McCreary	122	31,750
1943 Bee Mac	S. Young	119	33,300
1944 Pavot	G. Woolf	126	51,775
1945 Star Pilot	A. Kirkland	112	55,195
1946 Blue Border	A. DeLara	122	46,450
1947 Relic	J. Adams	114	48,200
1948 Blue Peter	E. Guerin	126	47,750
1949 Middleground	D. Gorman	114	44,050
1950 Battlefield	E. Guerin	122	47,550
1951 Cousin	E. Guerin	122	51,700
1952 Native Dancer	E. Guerin	122	51,450
1953 Artismo	D. Gorman	122	58,900
1954 Nashua	E. Arcaro	122	57,050
1955 Needles	J. Choquette	122	50,000
1956 King Hairan	E. Arcaro	122	48,400
1957 Rose Trellis	F. Lovato	122	40,075
1958 First Landing	E. Arcaro	122	36,700
5959 Tompion	W. Shoemaker	122	73,434
1960 Hail to Reason	R. Ussery	122	76,602
1961 Jaipur	E. Arcaro	122	76,229
1962 Outing Class	D. Pierce	122	76,407
1963 Traffic	M. Ycaza	122	72,394
1964 Bold Lad	B. Baeza	122	72,231
1965 Buckpasser	B. Baeza	122	71,614
1966 Bold Hour	J.L. Rotz	122	70,005
1967 What a Pleasure	B. Baeza	122	74,083
1968 Top Knight	M. Ycaza	122	80,145
1969 Irish Castle	B. Baeza	122	73,044
1970 Proudest Roman	J.L. Rotz	122	85,117
1971 Rest Your Case	J. Vasquez	122	77,355
1972 Secretariat	R. Turcotte	121	51,930

Not run in 1911 and 1912. Distance ¾ mile prior to 1925. Run over Widener Course at Belmont Park in 1943, 1944 and 1945.

Invitational Turf Handicap
Hollywood Park; 3-year-olds and over; 1½ miles (turf course).

Year	Age	Jockey	Wt.	Win. val.
1969 Fort Marcy (5)		M. Ycaza	124	$55,000
1970 Fiddle Isle (5)		W. Shoemaker	128	55,000
1971 Cougar II (5)		W. Shoemaker	127	68,750

Run as Hollywood Invitational Turf Handicap prior to 1971 and Ford Pinto Invitational Turf Handicap in 1971.

Jersey Derby
Garden State Park; 3-year olds; 1 1/8 miles.

Year	Jockey	Wt.	Win. val.
1960 Bally Ache	R. Ussery	126	$77,995

1961 Ambiopoise . . . . . R. Ussery	126	80,600
1962 Jaipur . . . . L. Adams	126	84,955
1963 Candy Spots W. Shoemaker	126	78,715
1964 Roman Brother . . F. Alvarez	126	81,445
1965 Hail to All . . . . . . J. Sellers	126	86,905
1966 Creme dela Creme		
D. Brumfield	126	89,635
1967 In Reality . . . . E. Fires	126	77,480
1968 Out of the Way .E. Belmont	126	87,555
1969 Al Hattab . . . . M. Hole	126	89,115
1970 Personality . . . E. Belmonte	126	83,460
1971 Bold Reasoning . J. Vasquez	126	87,360
1972 Smiling Jack . . . . F. Iannelli	126	89,180

Crimson Satan finished first in 1962 but was disqualified and placed third. In 1967, Dr. Fager finished first but was disqualified to fourth.

Jockey Club Gold Cup
Aqueduct; 3-year-olds and over; 2 miles.

Year Age Jockey	Wt.	Win. val.
1919 Purchase . . . . . . C. Kummer	118	$ 5,350
1920 Man o' War (3) .C. Kummer	118	5,850
1921 Mad Hatter (5) . . . E. Sande	125	12,100
1922 Mad Hatter (6) . . . E. Sande	125	12,700
1923 Homestretch (3) . . . C. Lang	114	11,300
1924 My Play (5) . A. Schuttinger	125	14,150
1925 Altawood (4) . . . . . E. Sande	120	13,050
1926 Crusader (3) . . . . J. Maiben	114	13,300
1927 Chance Play (4) . . . E. Sande	125	12,000
1928 Reigh Count (3) . . . C. Lang	114	10,850
1929 Diavolo (4) . . . . . J. Maiben	125	10,900
1930 Gallant Fox (3) . . . E. Sande	118½	10,300
1931 Twenty Grand (3)		
C. Kurtsinger	114	10,400
1932 Gusto (3) . . . . . B. Hanford	114	9,950
1933 Dark Secret (4) . . . .H. Mills	125	6,400
1934 Dark Secret (5)		
C. Kurtsinger	125	6,200
1935 Firethorn (3) . . . . E. Arcaro	117	6,550
1936 Count Arthur (4) . J. Stout	124	6,750
1937 Firethorn (5) . . H. Richards	124	6,050
1938 War Admiral (4)		
W.D. Wright	124	5,500
1939 Cravat (4) . . . . . . B. James	124	5,550
1940 Fenelon (3) . . . . . . J. Stout	114	6,700
1941 Market Wise (3) . . . B. James	114	7,325
1942 Whirlaway (4) . . . G. Woolf	124	18,350
1943 Princequillo (3) C. McCreary	117	18,500
1944 Bolingbroke (7) .R. Permane	125	17,645
1945 Pot o' Luck (3) . D. Dodson	114	18,335
1946 Pavot (4) . . . . E. Arcaro	124	18,250
1947 Phalanx (3) . . . . R. Donoso	117	17,850
1948 Citation (3) . . . . . E. Arcaro	117	72,700
1949 Ponder (3) . . . . . . S. Brooks	117	36,300
1950 Hill Prince (3) . . . E. Arcaro	117	36,000
1951 Counterpoint (3)D. Gorman	117	35,600
1952 One Count (3) . . D. Gorman	117	52,100
1953 Level Lea (3) . . . .W. Boland	117	55,100
1954 High Gun (3) . . . . E. Arcaro	119	55,150
1955 Nashua (3) . . . . . E. Arcaro	119	52,850
1956 Nashua (4) . . . . . E. Arcaro	124	36,600

1957 Gallant Man (3)		
W. Shoemaker	119	53,850
1958 Inside Tract (4) C. McCreary	124	·52,417
1959 Sword Dancer (3) E. Arcaro	119	70,790
1960 Kelso (3) . . . . E. Arcaro	119	70,205
1961 Kelso (4) . . . . E. Arcaro	124	68,770
1962 Kelso (5) . . . . I. Valenzuela	124	70,785
1963 Kelso (6) . . . . I. Valenzuela	124	70,785
1964 Kelso (7) . . . . I. Valenzuela	124	70,590
1965 Roman Brother (4) B. Baeza	124	71,500
1966 Buckpasser (3) . . .B. Baeza	119	71,825
1967 Damascus (3) W. Shoemaker	119	69,290
1968 Quicken Tree (5) W. Hartack	124	71,370
1969 Arts and Letters (3)		
B. Baeza	119	69,030
1970 Shuvee (4) . . . . R. Turcotte	121	70,785
1971 Shuvee (5) . . . .J. Velasquez	121	66,900
1972 Autobiography (4)		
A. Cordero, Jr.	124	68,220

Run as Jockey Club Stakes in 1919 and 1920. Run at 1½ miles in 1919 and 1920. In 1927 Brown Bud finished first but was disqualified. Run at Belmont Park from 1919 to 1959, inclusive; in 1962 to 1968.

John B. Campbell Handicap
Bowie Race Course; 3-year-olds and over; 1 1/16 miles.

Year Jockey	Wt.	Win. val.
1954 Joe Jones (4) . . C. McCreary	116	$20,050
1955 Social Outcast (4) E. Guerin	125	55,600
1956 Sailor (4) . . . . . . W. Hartack	122	74,750
1957 Dedicate (5) . . . .W. Boland	124	75,150
1958 Promised Land (4)		
I. Valenzuela	121	73,645
1959 Vertex (5) . . . . S. Boulmetis	124	74,595
1960 Yes You Will (4) . L. Adams	115	74,010
1961 Conestoga (4) . R.L. Gilbert	111	76,992
1962 Yorktown (5) . . . J. Nickols	116	75,335
1963 Kelso (6) . . . . I. Valenzuela	131	71,337
1964 Mongo (5) . . . . . . J.L. Rotz	126	71,110
1965 Lt. Stevens (4) . . T. Barrow	117	74,750
1966 Tosmah (5) . . .S. Boulmetis	118	74,490
1967 Quinta (4) . . . . . . S. Brooks	113	72,800
1968 In Reality (4) . . C. Baltazar	122	72,215
1969 Juvenile John (4)		
J. Giovanni	113	74,815
1970 Best Turn (4) . . C. Baltazar	114	39,910
1970 Mitey Prince (5) . . P. Kallai	112	39,910
1971 Bushido (5) . . . . . E. Nelson	114	75,140
1972 Favorecidian (5)W. Passmore	117	54,762
1972 Boone the Great (4)		
T. Agnello	112	56,062
1973 Vertee (4) . . . . . . J. Ruane	116	58,695
1973 Delay (5) . . . . J. Canessa	113	58,695

Distance 1 1/8 miles in 1954. Run as John B. Campbell Memorial Handicap prior to 1959. Run in two divisions in 1970, 1972, and 1973.

Lawrence Realization Stakes
Belmont Park; 3-year-olds; 1½ miles (turf course)

Year Jockey	Wt.	Win. val.
1889 Salvator . . . . .J. McLaughlin	122	$34,100

1890 Tournament .. W. Hayward	112½	25,300
1891 Potomac ..... A. Hamilton	119	30,850
1892 Tammany .....E. Garrison	119	28,470
1893 Daily America ...W. Simms	107	24,150
1894 Dobbins ....W. Simms	122	33,400
1895 Bright Phoebus ...L. Reiff	115	29,700
1896 Requital ......A. Clayton	119	17,365
1897 The Friar .....F. Littlefield	115	18,125
1898 Hamburg ....T. Sloan	122	13,875
1899 Ethelbert ......H. Spencer	118	12,890
1900 Prince of Melbourne		
H. Spencer	126	14,325
1901 The Parader ..... P. McCue	126	13,555
1902 Major Daingerfield G. Odom	123	12,875
1903 Africander .....J. Bullman	126	18,635
1904 Ort Wells ....F. O'Neill	126	20,945
1905 Sysonby ....D. Nicol	126	17,935
1906 Accountant .....J. Martin	126	16,260
1907 Dinna Ken ....G. Mountain	123	16,880
1908 Fair Play ....E. Dugan	126	17,685
1909 Fitz Herbert ....V. Powers	122	14,900
1910 Sweep ....J. Notter	126	9,755
1913 Rock View .. T. McTaggart	127	2,475
1916 Star Hawk ....H.H. Phillips	117	2,775
1917 Omar Khayyam . M. Buxton	126	5,950
1918 Johren ......F. Robinson	126	10,725
1919 Vexatious ......W. Knapp	123	20,540
1920 Man o' War ....C. Kummer	126	15,040
1921 Touch Me Not . F. Coltiletti	126	17,850
1922 Kai-Sang ....E. Sande	126	21,400
1923 Zev ....E. Sande	126	24,410
1924 Aga Khan ......J. Maiben	116	25,120
1925 Marconi ....K. Noe	116	26,500
1926 Espino ....L. Fator	126	26,100
1927 Nimba ....H. Thurber	123	29,470
1928 Reigh Count .....C. Lang	126	28,430
1929 The Nut ......M. Garner	119	31,760
1930 Gallant Fox ......E. Sande	126	29,610
1931 Twenty Grand C. Kurtsinger	126	29,700
1932 Faireno ....T. Malley	126	24,985
1933 War Glory ......J. Gilbert	123	21,400
1934 Carry Over .....T. Malley	116	18,110
1935 Firethorn ......E. Arcaro	119	16,780
1936 Granville ....J. Stout	126	19,550
1937 Unfailing ....F. Kopel	112	19,590
1938 Magic Hour ....J. Longden	112	16,800
1939 Hash ....E. Arcaro	119	18,750
1940 Fenelon ....J. Stout	123	18,070
1941 Whirlaway ...A. Robertson	126	23,050
1942 Alsab ....G. Woolf	126	7,900
1943 Fairy Manhurst .J. Longden	109	7,475
1944 By Jimminy .....G. Woolf	126	13,805
1945 Pot o' Luck .. D. Dodson	126	20,060
1946 School Tie .... T. Atkinson	110	18,300
1947 Cosmic Bomb . O. Scurlock	114	19,050
1948 Ace Admiral .. T. Atkinson	114	20,400
1949 Ponder ....S. Brooks	126	15,500
1950 Bed o' Roses .. N. Combest	107	15,600
1951 Counterpoint ..D. Gorman	126	15,700
1952 Mark-Ye-Well ... E. Arcaro	118	20,000
1953 Platan ....C. McCreary	110	20,150
1954 Fisherman .. H. Woodhouse	122	18,900

1955 Thinking Cap .. P.J. Bailey	114	18,250
1956 Riley ....T. Atkinson	120	18,450
1957 Promised Land		
H. Woodhouse	114	19,800
1958 Martins Rullah		
W. Shoemaker	117	17,900
1959 Middle Brother .. E. Arcaro	120	18,225
1960 Kelso ....E. Arcaro	120	35,800
1961 Sherluck ....B. Baeza	123	35,490
1962 Battle Joined .... M. Ycaza	116	37,245
1963 Dean Carl ......R. Ussery	120	36,530
1964 Quadrangle ..... M. Ycaza	126	35,165
1965 Munden Point .S. Boulmetis	116	35,880
1966 Buckpasser ......B. Baeza	126	35,490
1967 Successor ....B. Baeza	116	35,620
1968 Funny Fellow ....B. Baeza	116	36,595
1969 Oil Power .....J. Cruguet	116	34,970
1970 Kling Kling .....J. Cruguet	114	37,310
1971 Specious ....E. Maple	111	34,740
1972 Halo ....B. Baeza	114	35,280

Run as Realization prior to 1899. Run at Sheepshead Bay prior to 1913; at Aqueduct in 1959, 1961, and from 1963 to 1967, inclusive. Not run in 1911, 1912, 1914, and 1915. Distance 1 5/8 miles from 1889 to 1913, inclusive, and from 1918 to 1969, inclusive. Run on main course prior to 1970. In 1919 Over There finished first but was disqualified.

Louisiana Derby

Fair Grounds, New Orleans; 3-year-olds; 1 1/8 miles.

Year	Jockey	Wt.	Win. val.
1920 Damask ......E. Ambrose	118	$ 4,975
1923 Amole ......J.D. Mooney	118	9,180
1924 Black Gold ..J.D. Mooney	126	14,750
1925 Quatrain ....H. Stutts	126	17,350
1926 Bagenbaggage .... E. Blind	116	9,800
1927 Boo ....G. Johnson	114	14,250
1928 Jack Higgins ....C.E. Allen	118	15,450
1929 Calf Roper ... F. Coltiletti	117	15,825
1930 Michigan Boy ...J. Shelton	117	9,225
1931 Spanish Play ... C. Landolt	120	7,475
1932 Lucky Tom ....A. Pascuma	120	9,375
1933 Col. Hatfield .....C. Meyer	116	4,750
1934 Hickory Lad ...J. Westrope	113	2,870
1935 McCarthy ......P. Keester	117	2,150
1936 Rushway ......J. Longden	116	3,900
1937 Grey Count .... C. Corbett	116	7,730
1938 Wise Fox ......J. Longden	114	9,510
1939 Day Off ....E. Arcaro	114	9,510
1943 Amber Light . J. Longden	120	10,750
1944 Olympic Zenith ...N. Jemas	117	11,525
1946 Pellicle ...... A. LoTurco	117	11,675
1947 Carolyn A. ...... R. Nash	118	15,700
1948 Bovard ...... W. Saunders	111	11,500
1949 Rookwood J. Delahoussaye	111	11,600
1950 Greek Ship ......C. Errico	123	12,900
1951 Whirling Bat .. P. Anderson	111	15,900
1952 Gushing Oil .....A. Popara	111	16,400
1953 Matagorda ..... P.J. Bailey	111	31,875
1954 Gigantic ...R. McLaughlin	111	36,325

1955 Roman Patrol .. D. Dodson	123	34,175
1956 Reaping Right .. R.L. Baird	111	35,525
1957 Federal Hill ....W. Carstens	123	33,275
1958 Royal Union . J. Heckmann	114	34,850
1959 Master Palynch		
R. Broussard	115	35,600
1960 Tony Graff .. W. Chambers	111	35,975
1961 Bass Clef ......R. Baldwin	111	37,700
1962 Admiral's Voyage		
R. Broussard	121	38,150
1963 City Line ...... R.L. Baird	119	31,750
1964 Grecian Princess		
K. Broussard	116	33,300
1965 Dapper Delegate		
J. Heckmann	121	33,900
1966 Blue Skyer ...R. Broussard	116	36,000
1967 Ask the Fare ... D. Holmes	115	36,550
1968 Kentucky Sherry J. Combest	118	37,500
1969 King of the Castle		
C.H. Marquez	115	35,700
1970 Jim's Alibhi .... R. Baldwin	115	38,850
1971 Northfields ......W. Blum	118	38,550
1972 No Le Hace ... P. Rubbicco	118	50,000
1973 Leo's Pisces ......B. Breen	115	50,000

Run at Jefferson Park prior to 1932. Not run in 1921, 1922, 1940, 1941, 1942 nor 1945.

Man o' War Stakes

Belmont Park; 3-year-olds and over; 1½ miles (turf course).

Year	Jockey	Wt.	Win. val.
1959 Dotted Line (6).. W. Boland	111	$71,732
1959 Tudor Era (6) .. W. Hartack	124	72,382
1960 Harmonizing (6) ..J. Ruane	126	70,530
1961 Wise Ship (4) ...H. Gustines	108	65,000
1962 Beau Purple (5) ..W. Boland	126	74,620
1963 The Axe II (5) ... J.L. Rotz	126	73,905
1964 Turbo Jet II (4) ...H. Grant	126	72,670
1965 Hill Rise (4) .... M. Ycaza	126	73,255
1966 Assagai (3) ..... L. Adams	121	72,865
1967 Ruffled Feathers (3)		
D. Hidalgo	121	75,465
1968 Czar Alexander (3)		
J. Velasquez	121	75,530
1969 Hawaii (5) ....J. Velasquez	126	73,645
1970 Fort Marcy (6) J. Velasquez	126	75,465
1971 Run the Gantlet (3)		
R. Woodhouse	121	67,200
1972 Typecast (6) A. Cordero, Jr.	123	70,380

Run in two divisions in 1959. Run as Man o' War Handicap in 1959 and 1961. Distance 1 5/8 miles in 1961 and from 1963 to 1967, inclusive. Run at Aqueduct in 1959, 1961, and from 1963 to 1967, inclusive.

Massachusetts Handicap

Suffolk Downs; 3-year-olds and over; Abt. 1½ miles (turf course).

Year	Age	Jockey	Wt.	Win. val.
1935 Top Row (4) .....G. Woolf	116	$18,750
1936 Time Supply (5)R. Workman	121	23,500
1937 Seabiscuit (4) ... J. Pollard	130	51,780
1938 Menow (3) ....N. Wall	107	40,550

1939 Fighting Fox (4) .. J. Stout	113	49,250
1940 Eight Thirty (4) H. Richards	126	46,550
1941 War Relic (3).. T. Atkinson	102	48,350
1942 Whirlaway (4) ....G. Woolf	130	43,850
1943 Market Wise (5) .V. Nodarse	126	39,650
1944 First Fiddle (5) .J. Longden	124	41,850
1945 First Fiddle (6) .J. Longden	121	42,750
1946 Pavot (4) ..... A. Kirkland	120	47,750
1947 Stymie (6) ....C. McCreary	128	41,150
1948 Beauchef (5) ... R. Donoso	115	47,250
1949 First Nighter (4) . J. Renick	104	39,200
1950 Cochise (4) .....E. Arcaro	120	21,400
1951 One Hitter (5) . T. Atkinson	113	22,000
1952 To Market (4) ...W. Boland	110	32,600
1953 Royal Vale (5) .J. Westrope	125	43,300
1954 Wise Margin (4) .. K. Stuart	111	43,100
1955 Helioscope (4) .S. Boulmetis	126	36,000
1956 Midafternoon (4) W. Boland	110	38,200
1957 Greek Spy (4) ....E. Guerin	118	39,100
1958 Promised Land (4)		
P. Anderson	119	36,255
1959 Air Pilot (5) ... J. Leonard	116	53,880
1960 Talent Show (5)....		
R. Broussard	117	35,865
1961 Polylad (5) .....E. Arcaro	112	37,505
1962 Air Pilot (8) ....L. Moyers	105	37,115
1963 Crimson Satan (4)		
H. Hinojosa	124	38,545
1964 Smart (5) ......E. Nelson	115	35,880
1965 Smart (6) ......E. Nelson	117	36,205
1966 Fast Count (3) .M. Venezia	108	53,430
1967 Good Knight (5) ..K. Karte	113	40,153
1968 Out of the Way (3)J.L. Rotz	112	39,682
1969 Beau Marker (4) .L. Moyers	109	36,741
1970 Semillant (5) ....J. Cruguet	113	54,730
1971 Chompion (6) .J. Velasquez	116	54,421

Distance 1 1/8 miles prior to 1948. 1¼ miles from 1948 to 1969, inclusive. Run on main course prior to 1970. Day Court finished first in 1959 but was disqualified and placed second.

Matron Stakes

Belmont Park; 2-year-old fillies; ¾ mile.

Year	Jockey	Wt.	Win. val.
1892 Sir Francis ....Garrison	118	$36,770
1893 Domino ....Taral	128	24,560
1894 Agitator ....Taral	111	31,310
1899 Indian Fairy .....J. Slack	111	16,697
1900 Beau Gallant ..... Bullman	125	16,297
1901 Heno ....Odom	122	17,593
1902†Grey Friar .....N. Turner	124	12,180
1902 Eugenia Burch ......Odom	122	6,790
1903†The Minute Man . F. O'Neill	117	8,035
1903 Armenia ....W. Hicks	112	5,525
1904†Bedouin .... Shaw	114	12,725
1904 Sandria ....Hildebrand	104	13,345
1905†Burgomaster ....Lyne	124	10,405
1905 Perverse ....Lyne	109	10,485
1906†Ballot ....Radtke	122	10,250
1906 Adoration ......W. Miller	116	9,030
1907†Colin ....W. Miller	129	9,340
1907 Stamina ....W. Knapp	119	8,940

1908†Helmet	Notter	124	9,625
1908 Maskette	Notter	124	5,895
1909†Radium Star	Creevy	114	8,995
1909 Greenvale	Gilbert	111	8,535
1910†Naushon	J. Glass	125	9,485
1910 Bashti	C.H. Shilling	117	8,655
1914†Pebbles	J. Butwell	130	1,130
1914 Charter Maid	J. McTaggart	110	1,045
1923 Tree Top	F. Coltiletti	109	4,150
1924 Blue Warbler	D. Hurn	127	10,625
1924 Taps	A. Johnson	119	15,075
1926 Pantella	L. McAtee	124	18,275
1927 Glade	G. Ellis	114	21,025
1928 Dreadnaught	S. O'Donnell	115½	21,725
1929 Dustemall	L. McAtee	115	25,250
1930 Baba Kenny	J. Smith	115	24,650
1931 Top Flight	R. Workman	127	23,750
1932 Barn Swallow	E. James	115	20,575
1933 High Glee	J. Gilbert	115	18,800
1934 Nellie Flag	E. Arcaro	115	20,550
1935 Beanie M.	D. Meade	119	11,900
1936 Wand	H. Richards	115	12,075
1937 Merry Lassie	J. Longden	123	10,900
1938 Dinner Date	A. Robertson	119	16,700
1939 Miss Ferdinand	J. Westrope	115	14,825
1940 Misty Isle	W.D. Wright	119	15,710
1941 Petrify	R. Donoso	119	17,710
1942 Good Morning	H. Lindberg	109	9,525
1943 Boojiana	T. Atkinson	119	7,900
1944 Busher	E. Arcaro	119	22,530
1945 Beaugay	A. Kirkland	123	23,500
1946 First Flight	E. Arcaro	123	35,535
1947 Inheritance	D. Dodson	123	35,060
1948 Myrtle Charm	T. Atkinson	119	37,805
1949 Bed o' Roses	E. Guerin	119	40,210
1950 Atalanta	H. Woodhouse	119	38,690
1951 Rose Jet	H. Woodhouse	119	44,830
1952 Is Proud	C. McCreary	119	40,960
1953 Evening Out	O. Scurlock	119	41,345
1954 High Voltage	E. Arcaro	119	49,330
1955 Doubledogdare	E. Arcaro	119	48,620
1956 Romanita	E. Guerin	119	43,020
1957 Idun	W. Hartack	119	42,900
1958 Quill	P.J. Bailey	119	42,610
1959 Heavenly Body	M. Ycaza	119	58,224
1960 Rose Bower	J. Rotz	119	58,635
1961 Cicada	W. Shoemaker	119	61,028
1962 Smart Deb	R. Ussery	119	63,869
1963 Hasty Matelda	J. Combest	119	63,596
1964 Candalita	R. Ussery	119	63,680
1965 Moccasin	L. Adams	119	67,717
1966 Swiss Cheese	J.L. Rotz	119	68,659
1967 Queen of the Stage	B. Baeza	119	64,733
1968 Gallant Bloom	E. Belmonte	119	62,634
1969 Cold Comfort	J. Velasquez	119	68,484
1970 Bonnie and Gay R. Woodhouse		119	68,009
1971 Numbered Account	B. Baeza	119	60,309
1972 La Prevoyante	J. Le Blanc	119	59,874

Run at Morris Park prior to 1905. For colts and fillies prior to 1902. †For colts (run in two divisions—one for colts and one for fillies—from 1902 to 1914, inclusive). Run at Pimlico by special arrangement in 1910. Not run in 1895, 1896, 1897, 1898, 1911, 1912, 1913, nor from 1915 to 1922, inclusive. Run over the old straight course prior to 1926; run over main course in 1941; Widener Course from 1926 to 1940, inclusive, and from 1942 to 1958, inclusive. In 1947 Bewitch finished first but was disqualified. Run at Aqueduct in 1960 and from 1962 to 1968, inclusive.

Metropolitan Handicap

Belmont Park; 3-year-olds and over; 1 mile.

Year	Age	Jockey	Wt.	Win. val.
1891 Tristan (6)		Taylor	114	$ 7,300
1892 Pessara (4)		Taral	117	12,200
1893 Charade (4)		Doggett	107½	13,740
1894 Ramapo (4)		Taral	117	6,145
1896 Counter Tenor (4)		Hamilton	115	3,850
1897 Voter (3)		Lamley	99	3,850
1898 Bowling Brook (3)		P. Clay	102	4,280
1899 Filigrane (3)		Clawson	102	6,750
1900 Ethelbert (4)		Maher	126	6,250
1901 Banastar (6)		Odom	123	6,810
1902 Arsenal (3)		J. Daly	90	8,920
1903 Gunfire (4)		T. Burns	109	11,080
1904 Irish Lad (4)		Shaw	123	10,880
1905 Sysonby (3)		Shaw	107	
Race King (4)		L. Smith	97	5,655
1906 Grapple (4)		Garner	97	10,850
1907 Glorifier (5)		Garner	119	10,650
1908 Jack Atkin (4)		C.H. Shilling	128	9,620
1909 King James (4)		G. Burns	125	3,785
1910 Fashion Plate (4)		M. McGee	105	3,800
1913 Whisk Broom II (6)		Notter	126	3,500
1914 Buskin (4)		C. Fairbrother	114	4,200
1915 Stromboli (4)		C. Turner	118	2,325
1916 The Finn (4)		A. Schuttinger	120	3,350
1917 Ormesdale (4)		J. McTaggart	111	3,850
1918 Trompe La Mort (3) L. McAtee			102	3,865
1919 Lanius (4)		J. Loftus	115½	3,865
1920 Wildair (3)		E. Ambrose	107	3,865
1921 Mad Hatter (5)		E. Sande	127	8,150
1922 Mad Hatter (6)		E. Sande	129	8,550
1923 Grey Lag (5)		E. Sande	133	7,600
1924 Laurano (3)		H. Thurber	101	9,150
1925 Sting (4)		B. Breuning	114	8,625
1926 Sarazen (5)		F. Weiner	129	9,125
1927 Black Maria (4)		F. Coltiletti	116	8,225
1928 Nimba (4)		H. Thurber	114	8,575
1929 Petee-Wrack (4)		S. O'Donnell	120	8,600
1930 Jack High (4)		L. McAtee	110	8,275
1931 Questionnaire (4) R. Workman			122	7,575
1932 Equipoise (4)		R. Workman	127	7,425
1933 Equipoise (5)		R. Workman	128	4,725
1934 Mr. Khayyam (4)		R. Jones	119	3,480
1935 King Saxon (4)		C. Rainey	118	7,225
1936 Good Harvest (4)		S. Renick	107	6,650
1937 Snark (4)		J. Longden	112	6,675

1938 Danger Point (4) . E. Arcaro	112	8,450
1939 Knickerbocker (3) F.A. Smith	100	7,500
1940 Third Degree (4) . E. Arcaro	123	10,400
1941 Eight Thirty (5) H. Richards	132	10,250
1942 Attention (4) . . . D. Meade	124	11,300
1943 Devil Diver (4) . . .G. Woolf	117	10,900
1944 Devil Diver (5) T. Atkinson	134	10,080
1945 Devil Diver (6) T. Atkinson	129	18,280
1946 Gallorette (4) . .J.D. Jessop	110	22,050
1947 Stymie (6) . . . . . . .B. James	124	21,650
1948 Stymie (7) . . . .C. McCreary	126	21,200
1949 Loser Weeper (4)		
H. Woodhouse	105	21,400
1950 Greek Ship (3) H. Woodhouse	106	22,450
1951 Casemate (4) . . . D. Gorman	115	26,000
1952 Mameluke (4) . . . .G. Porch	112	25,200
1953 Tom Fool (4) . T. Atkinson	130	25,800
1954 Native Dancer (4) E. Guerin	130	28,300
1955 High Gun (4) . .A. DeSpirito	130	25,500
1956 Midafternoon (4) W. Boland	111	37,700
1957 Traffic Judge (5) . E. Arcaro	118	44,600
1958 Gallant Man (4)		
W. Shoemaker	130	37,620
1959 Sword Dancer (3)		
W. Shoemaker	114	74,235
1960 Bald Eagle (5) . . . M. Ycaza	128	73,130
1961 Kelso (4) . . . . E. Arcaro	130	74,100
1962 Carry Back (4) . . . .J. Rotz	123	72,735
1963 Cyrano (4) . . . . . R. Ussery	113	74,815
1964 Olden Times (6) H. Moreno	119	75,010
1965 Gun Bow (5) . . . . .W. Blum	130	72,540
1966 Bold Lad (4) . . . . .B. Baeza	132	75,140
1967 Buckpasser (4) . . . B. Baeza	130	70,980
1968 In Reality (4) . . . J.L. Rotz	124	70,135
1969 Arts and Letters (3)		
J. Cruguet	111	75,725
1970 Nodouble (5) . . . J. Tejeira	126	74,490
1971 Tunex (5) . . . . . . .J. Ruane	113	72,960
1972 Executioner (4) E. Belmonte	119	70,920

Run at Morris Park prior to 1905. Distance 1 1/8 miles prior to 1897. Sysonby and Race King dead-heated for first place in 1905. Not run in 1895, 1911 nor 1912. In 1934 Equipoise finished first but was disqualified. Run at Aqueduct from 1960 to 1967, inclusive, and in 1969.

Michigan Mile and One-Eighth Handicap
Detroit Park; 3-year-olds and over; 1 1/8 miles.

Year	Jockey	Wt.	Win. val.
1949 Sir Sprite (8) . . . . . .H. Hart	120	$ 5,805
1950 Fancy Flyer (5)		
M.N. Gonzalez	115	6,175
1951 Kings Hope (3) . .L.C. Cook	102	1,950
1952 Bully Boy (5) S. Armstrong	114	6,500
1953 Second Avenue (6)		
C. Bierman	114	39,750
1954 Spur On (6) . . . . P.J. Bailey	114	42,925
1955 Greatest (5) . . . . .T. Barrow	114	40,525
1956 Nonnie Jo (5) . . .L.C. Cook	111	38,900
1957 My Night Out (4)E.J. Knapp	111	38,320
1958 Nearctic (4) . . . B. Sorensen	114	40,009

1959 Total Traffic (5)		
H. Hinojosa	110	40,350
1960 Little Fritz (5) .W.A. Peake	116	42,600
1961 American Comet (5)		
E.J. Knapp	114	39,780
1962 Beau Prince (4) . . S. Brooks	115	39,000
1963 Crimson Satan (4)		
H. Hinojosa	128	38,285
1964 Going Abroad (4)		
R. Broussard	120	30,727
Tibaldo (4) . . . . .D. Gargan	112	30,727
1965 Old Hat (6) . . .R. Gallimore	115	59,410
1966 Stanislas (4) . . . .D. Gargan	109	74,425
1967 Estreno II (6) . .H. Marquez	112	81,770
1968 Nodouble (3) . . . M. Heath	111	80,145
1969 Calandrito (4) C.H. Marquez	115	65,000
1970 Fast Hilarious (4)		
C. Marquez	116	81,900
1971 Native Royalty (4)		
R.J. Campbell	116	85,930

Run on turf in 1949 at Detroit Fair Grounds. Run as a purse race in 1951 and 1952. Run as Michigan Mile from 1949 to 1956, inclusive, and in 1958; as Michigan Mile and One-Sixteenth in 1957, and from 1959 to 1964, inclusive. Going Abroad and Tibaldo dead-heated for first place in 1964.

Pimlico-Laurel Futurity
Laurel Race Course; 2-year-olds; 1 1/16 miles.

Year	Jockey	Wt.	Win. val.
1921 Morvich . . . . . . .A. Johnson	122	$42,750
1922 Blossom Time . .A. Johnson	119	41,015
1922 Sally's Alley . . .A. Johnson	116	41,015
1923 Beau Butler . . .G.W. Carroll	122	54,030
1924 Stimulus . . . . . .H. Thurber	122	49,220
1925 Canter . . . . C. Turner	117	53,350
1926 Fair Star . . . . . O. Bourassa	119	59,660
1927 Glade . . . . L. Morris	114	53,310
1928 High Strung . . . . L. McAtee	122	50,750
1929 Flying Heels . . . .W. Kelsay	117	55,810
1930 Equipoise . . . .R. Workman	119	50,360
1931 Top Flight . . . .R. Workman	119	56,170
1932 Swivel . . . . J. Gilbert	116	62,430
1935 Hollyrood . . . . . S. Coucci	122	45,850
1936 Matey . . . . H. Richards	119	25,300
1937 Nedayr . . . . . .W.D. Wright	122	28,140
1938 Challedon . . . . . . .G. Seabo	119	28,770
1939 Bimelech . . . . . .F.A. Smith	122	33,230
1940 Bold Irishman . . . J. Gilbert	122	33,830
1941 Contradiction .K. McCombs	122	33,910
1942 Count Fleet . . . .J. Longden	119	30,820
1943 Platter . . . . .C. McCreary	119	33,440
1944 Pot o' Luck . . . . D. Dodson	122	35,130
1945 Star Pilot . . . . . A. Kirkland	122	36,365
1946 Jet Pilot . . . . J. Gilbert	122	37,615
1947 Citation . . . . D. Dodson	119	36,675
1948 Capot . . . . T. Atkinson	119	47,325
1949 Oil Capitol . . .E.J. Knapp	122	48,755
1950 Big Stretch . . . T. Atkinson	122	45,090
1951 Cajun . . . . N. Shuk	122	46,450

1952 Isasmoothie . . . . B. Mitchell	119	59,410
1953 Errard King . . . S. Boulmetis	122	61,450
1954 Thinking Cap . . D. Dodson	122	53,870
1955 Nail . . . . H. Woodhouse	122	67,980
1956 Missile . . . . . . P. Anderson	122	71,235
1957 Jewel's Reward		
W. Shoemaker	122	115,347
1958 Intentionally W. Shoemaker	122	168,020
1959 Progressing . H. Woodhouse	122	71,635
1960 Garwol . . . . . I. Valenzuela	122	67,046
1961 Crimson Satan W. Shoemaker	122	72,585
1962 Right Proud . . . L. Leonard	122	72,637
1963 Quadrangle . . . . W. Hartack	122	110,012
1964 Sadair . . . . M. Ycaza	122	110,913
1965 Spring Double . H. Hinojosa	122	134,543
1966 In Reality . . . . . . J.L. Rotz	122	121,667
1967 Vitriolic . . . . B. Baeza	122	113,015
1968 King Emperor . E. Belmonte	122	114,380
1969 High Echelon . . . M. Ycaza	122	114,803
1970 Limit to Reason .J. Cruguet	122	123,526
1971 Riva Ridge . . . R. Turcotte	122	90,733
1972 Secretariat . . . . R. Turcotte	122	83,395

Run in two divisions in 1922. Distance 1 mile prior to 1929. Not run in 1933 nor 1934. In 1936 Privileged finished first but was disqualified. Fathers Image finished first in 1965 but was disqualified and placed second. Run as Pimlico Futurity in 1966 and at Pimlico Race Course prior to 1966. Run as Laurel Futurity in 1972.

San Juan Capistrano Handicap

Santa Anita Park; 4-year-olds and over (by invitation); about 1¾ miles; (turf course).

Year Age Jockey	Wt.	Win. val.
1935 Head Play (5) . C. Kurtsinger	115	$ 9,100
1936 Whopper (4) . . W. Saunders	112	10,950
1937 Seabiscuit (4) . . . J. Pollard	120	9,200
1938 Indian Broom (5)		
H. Richards	110	8,700
1939 Cravat (4) . . . . . J. Westrope	118	25,200
1940 Mioland . . . . J. Adams	117	10,250
1941 Mioland (4) . . . . L. Haas	130	44,310
1945 Bric a Bac (4) . C. McCreary	122	36,840
1946 Triplicate (5) . . . . . J. Jessop	111	40,030
1949 Miss Grillo (7) . . . J. Adams	117	38,100
1950 Noor (5) . . . . . . J. Longden	117	40,400
1951 Be Fleet (4) . . . . J. Longden	114	37,800
1952 Intent (4) . . . . . . E. Guerin	122	33,200
1953 Intent (5) . . . . . . E. Arcaro	126	65,100
1954 By Zeus (4) . . . . . . R. York	110	73,100
1955 St. Vincent (4) .J. Longden	123	69,800
1956 Bobby Brocato (5)		
G. Taniguchi	124	68,900
1957 Corn Husker (4) . E. Arcaro	116	69,400
1958 Promised Land (4)		
I. Valenzuela	121	70,000
1959 Royal Living (4) . R. Neves	117	70,700
1960 Amerigo (5) . . . W. Hartack	122	73,800
1961 Don't Alibi (5)		
W. Shoemaker	118	68,100

1962 Olden Times (4)		
W. Shoemaker	119	73,000
1963 Pardao (5) . . . I. Valenzuela	119	70,600
1964 Cedar Key (4) . . . M. Ycaza	115	53,100
1964 Mr. Consistency (6)		
K. Church	125	54,100
1965 George Royal (4)J. Longden	116	75,000
1966 George Royal (5)J. Longden	118	75,000
1967 Niarkos (7) . . . . . A. Pineda	120	75,000
1968 Niarkos (8) . . . . . A. Pineda	121	75,000
1969 Petrone (5) . . . . . .J. Sellers	122	75,000
1970 Fiddle Isle (5)		
W. Shoemaker	125	50,000
1970 Quicken Tree (7) .F. Alvarez	124	50,000
1971 Cougar II (5) W. Shoemaker	126	75,000
1972 Practicante (6) L. Pincay, Jr.	118	75,000

Distance 1 1/8 miles prior to 1939; 1 1/16 miles in 1940, 1½ miles in 1939, 1941, and from 1945 to 1949, inclusive; 1¾ miles from 1950 to 1953, inclusive; 1½ miles in 1954. For 3-year-olds in 1940; for 3-year-olds and over in all other years prior to 1968. Not run from 1942 to 1944, inclusive; nor in 1947 and 1948. Run in two divisions in 1964. Fiddle Isle and Quicken Tree dead-heated for first place in 1970.

Santa Anita Derby

Santa Anita Park; 3-year-olds; 1 1/8 miles.

Year Jockey	Wt.	Win. val.
1935 Gillie . . . . S. Coucci	126	$19,650
1936 He Did . . . . . . W.D. Wright	126	26,000
1937 Fairy Hill . . . . . . M. Peters	121	45,425
1938 Stagehand . . . .J. Westrope	118	42,350
1939 Ciencia . . . . . . .C. Bierman	115	41,850
1940 Sweepida . . . . .R. Neves	120	43,850
1941 Porter's Cap . . . . . .L. Haas	120	44,975
1945 Bymeabond . . . . . .G. Woolf	119	37,250
1946 Knockdown . . .R. Permane	122	74,680
1947 On Trust . . . . . .J. Longden	118	81,750
1948 Salmagundi . . . .J. Longden	118	79,850
1949 Old Rockport . . .G. Glisson	118	94,700
1950 Your Host . . . .J. Longden	118	89,800
1951 Rough 'n Tumble E. Arcaro	118	81,500
1952 Hill Gail . . . . . T. Atkinson	118	92,900
1953 Chanlea . . . . E. Arcaro	118	84,500
1954 Determine . . . . . . R. York	118	84,800
1955 Swaps . . . . .J. Longden	118	90,400
1956 Terrang . . . . W. Shoemaker	118	111,700
1957 Sir William . . . . H. Moreno	118	95,900
1958 Silky Sullivan W. Shoemaker	118	83,400
1959 Silver Spoon . . . . . R. York	113	95,300
1960 Tompion . . . W. Shoemaker	118	83,300
1961 Four-and-TwentyJ. Longden	118	100,100
1962 Royal Attack . . . .E. Burns	118	107,100
1963 Candy Spots W. Shoemaker	118	98,300
1964 Hill Rise . . . . .D. Pierce	118	87,400
1965 Lucky Debonair		
W. Shoemaker	118	89,300
1966 Boldnesian . . . . . . .W. Blum	118	96,900
1967 Ruken . . . . .F. Alvarez	118	94,900
1968 Alley Fighter . L. Pincay, Jr.	120	102,100
1969 Majestic Prince .W. Hartack	120	87,200

1970 Terlago	.... W. Shoemaker	120	96,400
1971 Jim French	.A. Cordero, Jr.	120	88,400
1972 Solar Salute	.. L. Pincay, Jr.	120	88,000
1973 Sham	.... L. Pincay, Jr.	120	79,400

Distance 1 1/16 miles prior to 1938; 1¼ miles in 1947. Not run from 1942 to 1944, inclusive.

Santa Anita Handicap

Santa Anita Park; 4-year-olds and over; 1¼ miles

Year Age	Jockey	Wt.	Win. val.
1935 Azucar (7)	...... G. Woolf	117	$108,400
1936 Top Row (5)	.. W.D. Wright	116	104,600
1937 Rosemont (5)	. H. Richards	124	90,700
1938 Stagehand (3)	.....N. Wall	100	91,450
1939 Kayak II. (4)	.... J. Adams	110	91,100
1940 Seabiscuit (7)	... J. Pollard	130	86,650
1941 Bay View (4)	......N. Wall	108	89,360
1945 Thumbs Up (6)	.J. Longden	130	82,925
1946 War Knight (6)	.. J. Adams	115	101,220
1947 Olhaverry (8)	. M. Peterson	116	98,900
1948 Talon (6)	.... E. Arcaro	122	102,500
1949 Vulcan's Forge (4)	....		
	D. Gorman	119	102,000
1950 Noor (5)	......J. Longden	110	97,900
1951 Moonrush (5)	..J. Longden	114	97,900
1952 Miche (7)	...... J. Covalli	115	104,100
1953 Mark-Ye-Well (4)	. E. Arcaro	130	97,900
1954 Rejected (4)	W. Shoemaker	118	105,900
1955 Poona II (4)	W. Shoemaker	117	103,200
1956 Bobby Brocato (5)	....		
	J. Longden	118	97,900
1957 Corn Husker (4)	..R. Neves	105	103,600
1958 Round Table (4)	....		
	W. Shoemaker	130	97,900
1959 Terrang (6)	.....W. Boland	116	97,900
1960 Linmold (4)	.....D. Pierce	110	97,900
1961 Prove It (4)	. W. Shoemaker	115	100,000
1962 Physician (5)	.....D. Pierce	114	100,000
1963 Crozier (5)	......B. Baeza	122	100,000
1964 Mr. Consistency (6)	....		
	K. Church	120	102,100
1965 Hill Rise (4)	.....D. Pierce	120	100,000
1966 Lucky Debonair (4)	....		
	W. Shoemaker	124	100,000
1967 Pretense (4)	. W. Shoemaker	118	100,000
1968 Mr. Right (5)	.... M. Yanez	115	100,000
1969 Nodouble (4)	.E. Belmonte	122	100,000
1970 Quicken Tree (7)	.F. Alvarez	118	100,000
1971 Ack Ack (5)	W. Shoemaker	130	100,000
1972 Triple Bend (4)	.. D. Pierce	129	105,000

Not run in 1942, 1943 nor 1944. In 1952 Intent finished first but was disqualified and placed second. For 3-year-olds and over prior to 1969.

Selima Stakes

Laurel Park; 2-year-old fillies; 1 1/16 miles.

Year	Jockey	Wt.	Win. val.
1926 Fair Star	..... O. Bourassa	114	$23,370
1927 Bateau	.... E. Ambrose	115	23,985
1928 Current	.........E. Pool	111	22,370

1929 Khara	.........L. Fator	109	24,730
1930 Tambour	......L. Schaefer	112	26,070
1931 Laughing Queen	.J. Bejshak	114	23,370
1932 Notebook	........H. Mills	114	23,790
1933 Jabot	........R. Workman	113	22,175
1934 Nellie Flag	...... E. Arcaro	122	22,420
1935 Split Second	.... E. Arcaro	111	20,580
1936 Talma Dee	. . . A. Robertson	111	22,480
1937 Jacola	....W.D. Wright	114	24,430
1938 Big Hurry	.....F.A. Smith	114	25,890
1939 War Beauty	.. A. Robertson	114	26,560
1940 Valdina Myth	. H. Richards	119	23,580
1941 Ficklebush	...K. McCombs	107	24,600
1942 Askmenow	....C. Bierman	111	21,900
1943 Miss Keeneland	.F.A. Smith	111	20,750
1944 Busher	.........E. Arcaro	117	25,780
1945 Athene	......W. Mehrtens	111	33,790
1946 Bee Ann Mac	....A. DeLara	114	41,840
1947 Whirl Some	.... D. Dodson	116	40,340
1948 Gaffery	..........C. Kirk	114	39,220
1949 Bed o' Roses	.... E. Guerin	116	40,010
1950 Aunt Jinny	........N. Wall	122	37,170
1951 Rose Jet	...... E. Guerin	115	38,380
1952 Tritium	..........R. Nash	114	42,330
1953 Small Favor	.... P. McLean	116	44,910
1954 High Voltage	.... E. Arcaro	119	50,810
1955 Levee	......R. Broussard	119	49,930
1956 Lebkuchen	....J. Longden	119	47,000
1957 Guide Line	.....W. Boland	114	46,280
1958 Rich Tradition	..W. Boland	119	37,646
1959 La Fuerza	....S. Boulmetis	114	38,497
1960 Good Move	..... E. Guerin	119	37,080
1961 Tamarona	........J. Sellers	119	35,743
1962 Fool's Play	......J. Sellers	119	34,053
1963 My Card	... B. Thornburg	119	55,360
1964 Marshua	... W. Chambers	119	59,208
1965 Moccasin	.......L. Adams	119	57,603
1966 Regal Gleam	.... M. Ycaza	122	78,107
1967 Syrian Sea	....E. Belmonte	119	67,814
1968 Shuvee	...... R. Turcotte	122	67,080
1969 Predictable	..... R. Ussery	119	76,362
1970 Patelin	...... L. Pincay, Jr.	119	73,502
1971 Numbered Account	B. Baeza	122	77,720
1972 La Prevoyante	..J. Le Blanc	122	76,043

Distance 1 mile prior to 1941. Run at Pimlico in 1943.

Suburban Handicap

Aqueduct; 3-year-olds and over; 1¼ miles.

Year Age	Jockey	Wt.	Win. val.
1884 Gen. Munroe (6)	W. Donohue	124	$ 4,945
1885 Pontiac (4)	.....H. Olney	102	5,855
1886 Troubadour (4)	....		
	W. Fitzpatrick	115	5,697
1887 Eurus (4)	........G. Davis	102	6,065
1888 Elkwood (5)	....W. Martin	119	6,812
1889 Raceland (4)	...E. Garrison	120	6,900
1890 Salvator (4)	.....I. Murphy	127	6,900
1891 Loantaka (5)	....M. Bergen	110	9,900
1892 Montana (4)	...E. Garrison	115	17,750
1893 Lowlander (5)	P. McDermott	105	17,750

1894 Ramapo (4) ...... F. Taral	120	12,070	
1895 Lazzarone (4) . A. Hamilton	115	4,730	
1896 Henry of Navarre (5)			
H. Griffin	129	5,850	
1897 Ben Brush (4) ... W. Simms	123	5,850	
1898 Tillo (4) ...... A. Clayton	119	6,800	
1899 Imp (5) .... N. Turner	114	6,800	
1900 Kinley Mack (4) . P. McCue	125	6,800	
1901 Alcedo (4) ..... H. Spencer	112	7,800	
1902 Gold Heels (4) .O. Wonderly	124	7,800	
1903 Africander (3) ... .G. Fuller	110	16,490	
1904 Hermis (5) ..... A. Redfern	127	16,800	
1905 Beldame (4) ... .F. O'Neill	123	16,800	
1906 Go Between (5) ... W. Shaw	116	16,800	
1907 Nealon (4) ...... W. Dugan	113	16,800	
1908 Ballot (4) ...... .J. Notter	127	19,750	
1909 Fitz Herbert (3) . E. Dugan	105	3,850	
1910 Olambala (4) . .G. Archibald	115	4,800	
1913 Whisk Broom II. (6)			
J. Notter	139	3,000	
1915 Stromboli (4) ... C. Turner	122	3,925	
1916 Friar Rock (3) ... M. Garner	101	3,450	
1917 Boots (6) .... J. Loftus	122	4,900	
1918 Johren (3) .... F. Robinson	110	5,850	
1919 Corn Tassel (5) ... L. Ensor	108	5,200	
1920 Paul Jones (3)			
A. Schuttinger	106	6,350	
1921 Audacious (5) . .C. Kummer	120	8,100	
1922 Captain Alcock (5) C. Ponce	108	8,200	
1923 Grey Lag (5) ..... E. Sande	135	7,800	
1924 Mad Hatter (8) ... E. Sande	125	9,150	
1925 Sting (4) ..... B. Breuning	122	11,300	
1926 Crusader (3) ... J. Callahan	104	13,150	
1927 Crusader (4) ...C. Kummer	127	11,875	
1928 Dolan (4) ..... J. Callahan	105	13,675	
1929 Bateau (4) .... E. Ambrose	112	14,100	
1930 Petee-Wrack (5) ...E. Sande	122	11,850	
1931 Mokatam (4) . A. Robertson	123	11,200	
1932 White Clover II. (6)			
R. Workman	115	11,100	
1933 Equipoise (5) .R. Workman	132	7,250	
1934 Ladysman (4) ... S. Coucci	114	5,750	
1935 Head Play (5) C. Kurtsinger	114	12,175	
1936 Firethorn (4) .. H. Richards	116	12,125	
1937 Aneroid (4) .C. Rosengarten	110	10,950	
1938 Snark (5) ...... J. Longden	120	17,050	
1939 Cravat (4) ..... J. Westrope	121	17,750	
1940 Eight Thirty (4) H. Richards	127	19,850	
1941 Your Chance (4) . D. Meade	114	25,200	
1942 Market Wise (4) ...B. James	124	27,800	
1943 Don Bingo (4) ... J. Renick	104	27,600	
1944 Aletern (5) ... H. Lindberg	108	39,210	
1945 Devil Diver (6) .. E. Arcaro	132	34,995	
1946 Armed (5) ..... D. Dodson	130	43,000	
1947 Assault (4) ..... E. Arcaro	130	40,100	
1948 Harmonica (4) . W. Mehrtens	109	39,700	
1949 Vulcan's Forge (4) E. Arcaro	124	43,200	
1950 Loser Weeper (5)N. Combest	115	41,400	
1951 Busanda (4) ..... K. Stuart	102	42,100	
1952 One Hitter (6) . T. Atkinson	112	41,900	
1953 Tom Fool (4) . T. Atkinson	128	40,400	
1954 Straight Face (4)T. Atkinson	118	44,400	

1955 Helioscope (4) .E. Boulmetis	128	61,150	
1956 Nashua (4) ..... E. Arcaro	128	55,900	
1957 Traffic Judge (5) . E. Arcaro	124	58,450	
1958 Bold Ruler (4) ... E. Arcaro	134	53,360	
1959 Bald Eagle (4) ... M. Ycaza	119	71,635	
1960 Sword Dancer (4) E. Arcaro	125	69,165	
1961 Kelso (4) .... E. Arcaro	123	72,735	
1962 Beau Purple (5) . .W. Boland	115	68,380	
1963 Kelso (6) .... I. Valenzuela	133	70,525	
1964 Iron Peg (4) ..... M. Ycaza	116	71,500	
1965 Pia Star (4) ...... J. Sellers	117	70,720	
1966 Buffle (3) .... R. Turcotte	110	72,085	
1967 Buckpasser (4) ... B. Baeza	133	71,370	
1968 Dr. Fager (4) ..... B. Baeza	132	69,615	
1969 Mr. Right (6) A. Cordero, Jr.	117	69,550	
1970 Barometer (5)			
A. Cordero, Jr.	111	71,565	
1971 Twice Worthy (4). .J. Ruane	116	69,240	
1972 Hitchcock (6) ..C. Marquez	112	67,980	
1973 Key To The Mint (4)			
B. Baeza	126	65,700	

Run at Sheepshead Bay prior to 1913, at Belmont Park from 1913 to 1960, inclusive. Not run in 1911, 1912 nor 1914.

Sunset Handicap

Hollywood Park; 3-year-olds and over; 2 miles (turf course).

Year	Jockey	Wt.	Win. val.
1938 Ligaroti (6) . N. Richardson		122	$ 4,200
1939 Sorteado (4) ..... R. Neves		109	9,500
1940 Kayak II. (5) .... J. Adams		131	13,750
1941 King Torch (4) . .J. Deering		105	18,950
1946 Historian (5) .. O. Scurlock		121	37,150
1947 Cover Up (4) ...R. Permane		122	32,000
1948 Drumbeat (3) ..T. Williams		100	33,100
1949 Ace Admiral (4) J. Longden		122	34,650
1950 Hill Prince (3) ... E. Arcaro		128	35,300
1951 Alderman (4) ..J. Westrope		112	34,400
1952 Great Circle (5) . R. Heather		112	31,700
1953 Lights Up (6) ..J. Westrope		114	60,400
1954 Fleet Bird (5) ....R. Neves		115	63,200
1955 Social Outcast (5) E. Guerin		121	64,400
1956 Swaps (4) .. W. Shoemaker		130	64,400
1957 Find (7) ....R. Neves		119	66,000
1958 Gallant Man (4)			
W. Shoemaker		132	61,500
1959 Whodunit (4) .... R. York		110	63,700
1960 Dotted Swiss (4) ..E. Burns		120	63,100
1961 Whodunit (6) ... M. Ycaza		117	52,800
1962 Prove It (5) . W. Shoemaker		129	55,000
1963 Arbitrage (5) ..... P. Moreno		110	50,350
1964 Colorado King (5)			
W. Shoemaker		124	50,650
1965 Terry's Secret (3) .A. Maese		116	48,000
1966 O'Hara (4) .... .D. Pierce		113	52,650
1967 Hill Clown (4)W. Shoemaker		109	63,500
1968 Fort Marcy (4) L. Pincay, Jr.		122	73,500
1969 Petrone (5) ......J. Sellers		124	61,450
1970 One For All (4)L. Pincay, Jr.		114	75,350

1971 Over The Counter (7) . . . .
J. Lambert 114 80,650
1972 Typecast (6) . . . . . J. Sellers 121 78,350

Run as Aloha Handicap in 1938 and 1939. Distance 1 1/8 miles in 1938 and 1950; 1½ miles in 1939, 1940, 1967, and 1968; 1 5/8 miles from 1941 to 1949, inclusive, and from 1951 to 1966, inclusive. Run on main course prior to 1967. Not run from 1942 to 1945, inclusive. Run at Santa Anita Park in 1949.

Travers Stakes
Saratoga; 3-year-olds; 1¼ miles.

Year	Jockey	Wt.	Win. val.
1864 Kentucky	Gilpatrick	100	$ 2,950
1865 Maiden	Sewell	97	3,400
1866 Merrill	Abe	100	3,500
1867 Ruthless	Gilpatrick	103	2,850
1868 The Banshee	Smith	97	3,150
1869 Glenelg	C. Miller	110	3,000
1870 Kingfisher	C. Miller	110	4,950
1871 Harry Bassett	W. Miller	110	5,600
1872 Joe Daniels	J. Rowe	110	5,500
1873 Tom Bowling	R. Swim	110	5,400
1874 Attila	Barbee	110	5,050
1875 D'Artagnan	Barbee	110	4,850
1876 Sultana	Hayward	107	3,700
1877 Baden Baden	Sayers	110	4,550
1878 Duke of Magenta	Hughes	118	4,250
1879 Falsetto	I. Murphy	118	4,950
1880 Grenada	Hughes	118	3,750
1881 Hindo	J. McLaughlin	118	2,950
1882 Carley B.	Quantrell	115	3,450
1883 Barnes	J. McLaughlin	118	3,400
1884 Rataplan	Fitzpatrick	118	4,150
1885 Bersan	Spellman	118	4,025
1886 Inspector B.	J. McLaughlin	118	3,825
1887 Carey	Blaylock	118	3,825
1888 Sir Dixon	J. McLaughlin	118	4,625
1889 Long Dance	Barnes	118	3,700
1890 Sir John	Bergen	118	4,925
1891 Vallera	R. Williams	122	2,900
1892 Azra	Clayton	122	2,750
1893 Stowaway	McDermott	107	2,450
1894 Henry of Navarre	Taral	125	2,350
1895 Liza	Griffin	104	1,125
1897 Rensselaer	Taral	126	1,425
1901 Blues	Shaw	126	6,750
1902 Hermis	Rice	111	6,750
1903 Ada Nay	F. O'Neill	106	8,150
1904 Broomstick	T. Burns	129	5,850
1905 Dandelion	Shaw	111	8,350
1906 Gallavant	W. Miller	111	5,800
1907 Frank Gill	Notter	129	5,800
1908 Dorante	J. Lee	116	5,800
1909 Hilarious	Scoville	129	5,800
1910 Dalmatian	C.H. Shilling	129	4,825
1913 Rock View	T. McTaggart	129	2,725
1914 Roamer	J. Butwell	123	3,000
1915 Lady Rotha	M. Garner	106	2,150
1916 Spur	J. Loftus	129	3,125
1917 Omar Khayyam	J. Butwell	129	5,350
1918 Sun Briar	W. Knapp	120	7,700
1919 Hannibal	L. Ensor	120	9,835
1920 Man o' War	A. Schuttinger	129	9,275
1921 Sporting Blood	L. Lyke	116	10,275
1922 Little Chief	L. Fator	123	11,325
1923 Wilderness	B. Marinelli	120	13,550
1924 Sun Flag	F. Keogh	115	14,675
1925 Dangerous	C. Kummer	115	13,425
1926 Mars	F. Coltiletti	123	15,050
1927 Brown Bud	L. Fator	120	29,925
1928 Petee-Wrack	S. O'Donnell	117	30,550
1929 Beacon Hill	A. Robertson	117	21,825
1930 Jim Dandy	F.J. Baker	120	27,050
1931 Twenty Grand	L. McAtee	126	33,000
1932 War Hero	J. Gilbert	115	23,150
1933 Inlander	R. Jones	126	21,050
1934 Observant	L. Humphries	112	14,650
1935 Gold Foam	S. Coucci	112	14,675
1936 Granville	J. Stout	127	14,700
1937 Burning Star	W.D. Wright	117	14,550
1938 Thanksgiving	E. Arcaro	117	14,400
1939 Eight Thirty	H. Richards	117	16,575
1940 Fenelon	J. Stout	122	17,425
1941 Whirlaway	A. Robertson	130	16,900
1942 Shut Out	E. Arcaro	130	17,825
1943 Eurasian	S. Brooks	112	19,850
1944 By Jimminy	E. Arcaro	126	25,015
1945 Adonis	C. McCreary	110	28,680
1946 Natchez	T. Atkinson	124	24,750
1947 Young Peter	T. May	124	19,375
1948 Ace Admiral	T. Atkinson	108	19,650
1949 Arise	C. Errico	108	16,600
1950 Lights Up	G. Hettinger	110	16,350
1951 Battlefield	E. Arcaro	123	15,000
1952 One Count	E. Guerin	126	16,450
1953 Native Dancer	E. Guerin	126	18,850
1954 Fisherman	H. Woodhouse	120	19,500
1955 Thinking Cap	P.J. Bailey	120	19,150
1956 Oh Johnny	H. Woodhouse	116	33,200
1957 Gallant Man	W. Shoemaker	126	29,500
1958 Piano Jim	R. Ussery	112	29,920
1959 Sword Dancer	M. Ycaza	126	51,962
1960 Tompion	W. Hartack	126	53,165
1961 Beau Prince	S. Brooks	126	54,210
1962 Jaipur	W. Shoemaker	126	53,722
1963 Crewman	E. Guerin	120	52,910
1964 Quadrangle	M. Ycaza	126	52,032
1965 Hail to All	J. Sellers	123	56,777
1966 Buckpasser	B. Baeza	126	53,690
1967 Damascus	W. Shoemaker	126	52,065
1968 Chompion	J. Cruguet	114	55,802
1969 Arts and Letters	B. Baeza	126	69,290
1970 Loud	J. Vasquez	114	73,385
1971 Bold Reason	L. Pincay, Jr.	120	66,420
1972 Key to the Mint	B. Baeza	117	66,600
1973 Annihilate 'Em	R. Turcotte	120	68,280

In 1874 race resulted in a dead-heat, Attila winning the run-off in 3:08¾. Distance 1¾ miles prior to 1890; 1½ miles in 1890, 1891 and 1892; 1¼ miles in 1893, 1894 and 1897; 1 1/8 miles in 1895, 1901, 1902 and 1903. Not run in 1896, 1898, 1899, 1900, 1911 nor 1912. In 1915 Trial by Jury finished first but was disqualified. Run as Travers Midsummer Derby from 1927 to 1932, inclusive. Run at Belmont Park in 1943, 1944 and 1945.

United Nations Handicap (Turf Course)

Atlantic City; By invitation only; 3-year-olds and over; 1 3/16 miles.

Year	Jockey	Wt.	Win. val.
1953 Iceberg II (5) . . J. Contreras		120	$43,050
1954 Closed Door (5) W. Hartack		117	50,000
1955 Blue Choir (4) . . W. Hartack		126	73,600
1956 Career Boy (3) S. Boulmetis		116	65,000
1957 Round Table (3)			
	W. Shoemaker	118	65,000
1958 Clem (4) . . . W. Shoemaker		113	65,000
1959 Round Table (5)			
	W. Shoemaker	136	65,000
1960 T.V. Lark (3) . . . .J. Sellers		120	65,000
1961 Oink (4) . . . . . . L. Gilligan		119	65,000
1962 Mongo (3) . . . . .C. Burr		117	65,000
1963 Mongo (4) . . . W. Chambers		124	75,000
1964 Western Warrior (5)			
	H. Gustines	114	75,000
1965 Parka (7) . . . . .W. Blum		119	75,000
1966 Assagai (3) . . . . . L. Adams		118	65,000
1967 Flit-To (4) . . H. Woodhouse		110	65,000
1968 Dr. Fager (4) . . . . . B. Baeza		134	65,000
1969 Hawaii (5) . . . .J. Velasquez		124	75,000
1970 Fort Marcy (6) J. Velasquez		125	75,000
1971 Run the Gantlet (3)			
	R. Woodhouse	117	65,000
1972 Acclimatization (4)			
	C. Barrera	113	65,000

Washington Park Handicap

Arlington Park; 3-year-olds and over; 1 mile.

Year	Age	Jockey	Wt.	Win. val.
1926 Smiling Gus (3) .L. Edwards			97	$10,710
1927 Girl Scout (5) . . .S. Cooper			104	6,490
1929 Misstep (4) . . C. McCrossen			124	5,510
1930 Misstep (5) . . E. Shropshire			126	6,410
1931 Tannery (4) . . . . . R. Heigle			112	6,210
1932 Gold Step (5) . . H. Schutte			107	5,290
1933 No More (5) . . . . E. Arcaro			109	2,295
1934 Isaiah (4) . . . . .J. Kacala			110	2,240
1935 Late Date (6) A. Robertson			111	4,220
1936 Where Away (4) C. Corbett			115	8,080
1938 Dora May (5) .K. McCombs			108	1,650
1939 Star Boarder (3) .A. Bodiou			105	4,350
1940 War Plumage (4) . . .N. Wall			110	24,800
1941 Big Pebble (5) . .J. Westrope			120	25,500
1942 Marriage (6) . . . C. Corbett			114	25,200
1943 Thumbs Up (4) . . .O. Grohs			120	
Royal Nap (3) .W. Mehrtens			107	25,950
1944 Equifox (7) . . . . .A. Bodiou			113	40,700
1945 Busher (3) . . . . .J. Longden			115	40,200
1946 Armed (5) . . . . . D. Dodson			130	39,300
1947 Armed (6) . . . . . D. Dodson			130	37,500
1948 Fervent (4) . . .N.L. Pierson			120	36,000
1949 Coaltown (4) . . . . S. Brooks			130	34,800

1950 Inseparable (5) . .K. Church		110	33,000
1951 Curandero (5) . . .A. Gomez		115	113,950
1952 Crafty Admiral (4)E. Guerin		128	119,900
1953 Sickle's Image (5)W.M. Cook		106	108,500
1954 Pet Bully (6) . . . W. Hartack		119	110,900
1955 Jet Action (4)W. Shoemaker		120	96,000
1956 Swaps (4) . . W. Shoemaker		130	85,750
1957 Pucker Up (4)W. Shoemaker		111	80,800
1958 Clem (4) . . . . .J. Sellers		110	94,175
1959 Round Table (5)			
W. Shoemaker		132	72,650
1960 T.V. Lark (3) . . . .J. Sellers		116	68,600
1961 Chiefs of Chiefs (4)			
C. Meaux		112	72,900
1962 Prove It (5) . W. Shoemaker		131	68,450
1963 Crimson Satan (4)			
H. Hinojosa		126	68,150
1964 Gun Bow (4) . . . . .W. Blum		132	69,750
1965 Take Over (4) . L. Kunitake		110	68,600
1966 Bold Bidder (4) P. Anderson		120	64,200
1967 Handsome Boy (4)			
E. Belmonte		122	58,000
1968 Dr. Fager (4) . . . . . B. Baeza		134	67,700
1969 Night Invader (3)			
D.E. Whited		112	68,050
1970 Doc's T.V. (4) . D.E. Whited		114	33,900
1971 Well Mannered (4)			
M. Solomone		120	33,500
1972 Staunch Avenger (4)			
D. Whited		114	34,000
1973 Burning On (5) . D. Richard		114	32,800

Not run in 1928 nor 1937. Distance ¾ mile from 1927 to 1934, inclusive, and in 1938; 1¼ miles in 1926, 1935, and 1936, and from 1940 to 1950, inclusive; 1 1/8 miles in 1959, 1963, and 1964.

Washington D.C. International

Laurel Race Course; 3-year-olds and over; By invitation only; 1½ miles (turf course).

Year	Age	Jockey	Wt.	Win. val.
1952 Wilwyn (4) . . . . . E. Mercer			126´	$32,500
1953 Worden II (4) . . .C. Smirke			126	50,000
1954 Fisherman (3) . . . E. Arcaro			122	50,000
1955 El Chama (4) R. Bustamante			126	50,000
1956 Master Boing (3)				
		G. Chancelier	122	70,000
1957 Mahan (6) . . . .S. Boulmetis			126	70,000
1958 Sailor's Guide (6) .H. Grant			126	70,000
1959 Bald Eagle (4) . . . M. Ycaza			126	70,000
1960 Bald Eagle (5) . . . M. Ycaza			126	70,000
1961 T.V. Lark (4) . .J. Longden			126	70,000
1962 Match II (4)				
		Y. Saint-Martin	128	70,000
1963 Mongo (4) . . . W. Chambers			126	90,000
1964 Kelso (7) . . . . I. Valenzuela			126	90,000
1965 Diatome (3) . . .J. DeForge			120	90,000
1966 Behistoun (3) . . J. DeForge			120	90,000
1967 Fort Marcy (3) . . M. Ycaza			120	90,000
1968 Sir Ivor (3) . . . . . L. Piggott			120	100,000
1969 Karabas (4) . . . . .L. Piggott			127	100,000

1970 Fort Marcy (6) ....
                J. Velasquez 127 100,000
1971 Run the Gantlet (3) ....
                R. Woodhouse 120 100,000
1972 Droll Role (4) ....B. Baeza 127 100,000
Tudor Era finished first in 1958 but was disqualified.

Distance about 1½ miles from 1952 to 1958, inclusive.

Widener Handicap
Hialeah Park; 3-year-olds and over; 1¼ miles.

Year Age	Jockey	Wt.	Win. val.
1936 Mantagna (4)	E. Litzenberger	109	$10,150
1937 Columbiana (4)	H. Le Blanc	109	52,000
1938 War Admiral (4)	C. Kurtsinger	130	49,550
1939 Bull Lea (4) ...	I. Anderson	119	46,450
1940 Many Stings (5)	R. Donoso	109	52,000
1941 Big Pebble (5)	G. Seabo	109	51,800
1942 The Rhymer (4)	E. Arcaro	111	53,950
1944 Four Freedoms (4)	E. Arcaro	109½	29,350
1946 Armed (5)	D. Dodson	128	45,700
1947 Armed (6)	D. Dodson	129	43,900
1948 El Mono (4)	P. Roberts	112	43,800
1949 Coaltown (4)	T. Atkinson	123	42,300
1950 Royal Governor (6)	C. Rogers	118	43,000
1951 Sunglow (4)	D. Dodson	116	54,100
1952 Spartan Valor (4)	J. Stout	119	51,300
1953 Oil Capitol (6)	C. McCreary	114	93,200
1954 Landlocked (4)	J. Heckmann	116	102,200
1955 Hasty Road (4)	J. Adams	122	95,400
1956 Nashua (4)	E. Arcaro	127	92,600
1957 Bardstown (5)	W. Hartack	126	82,200
1958 Oligarchy (4)	S. Boulmetis	108	92,800
1959 Bardstown (7)	S. Brooks	124	87,240
1960 Bald Eagle (5)	M. Ycaza	123	89,700
1961 Yorky (4)	J. Sellers	116	81,770
1962 Yorky (5)	S. Brooks	120	87,620
1963 Beau Purple (6)	W. Boland	125	83,460
1964 Mongo (5)	W. Chambers	125	85,020
1965 Primordial II (8)	S. Hernandez	118	88,140
1966 Pia Star (5)	J. Sellers	117	87,620
1967 Ring Twice (4)	W. Boland	111	81,640
1968 Sette Bello (6)	E. Fires	110	92,950
1969 Yumbel (8)	F. Toro	112	89,180
1970 Never Bow (4)	E. Belmonte	112	86,970
1971 True North (5)	R. Woodhouse	114	96,850
1972 Good Counsel (4)	A. Cordero, Jr.	111	93,990

Run as Widener Challenge Cup Handicap prior to 1938. Not run in 1943 nor 1945.

Withers Stakes
Aqueduct; 3-year-olds; 1 mile.

Year	Jockey	Wt.	Win. val.
1874 Dublin	Ponton	110	$3,200
1875 Aristides	Swim	110	4,150
1876 Fiddlesticks	Feakes	110	3,500
1877 Bombast	Barrett	110	4,200
1878 Duke of Magenta	Hughes	118	3,500
1879 Dan Sparling	Kelly	118	5,305
1880 Ferncliffe	Barrett	118	3,800
1881 Crickmore	Hughes	115	4,275
1882 Forester	J. McLaughlin	118	4,600
1883 Geo. Kinney	J. McLaughlin	118	2,990
1884 Panique	Fitzpatrick	118	3,240
1885 Tyrant	P. Duffy	118	3,070
1886 Biggonet	Maynard	113	3,260
1887 Hanover	J. McLaughlin	118	3,490
1888 Sir Dixon	Fitzpatrick	118	3,620
1899 Diablo	Godfrey	121	5,380
1890 King Eric	Garrison	110	8,140
1891 Picknicker	F. Littlefield	117	4,190
1892 Tammany	Garrison	122	7,460
1893 Dr. Rice	Taral	122	9,470
1894 Domino	Taral	122	7,100
1895 Lucania	Reiff	109	2,700
1896 Handspring	Simms	122	2,550
1897 Octagon	Simms	119	2,550
1898 The Huguenot	Spencer	122	3,815
1899 Jean Bereaud	Clawson	122	4,450
1900 Kilmarnock	N. Turner	126	5,470
1901 The Parader	Landry	126	5,020
1902 Compute	Shaw	126	4,815
1903 Shorthose	Haack	126	6,395
1904 Delhi	Odom	126	5,750
1905 Blandy	W. Davis	126	6,220
1906 Accountant	J. Martin	126	6,850
1907 Frank Gill	Notter	126	7,775
1908 Colin	Notter	126	12,090
1909 Hilarious	Butwell	126	11,070
1910 The Turk	M. McGee	126	3,000
1913 Rock View	Buttwell	118	2,325
1914 Charlestonian	C. Burlingame	115	2,900
1915 The Finn	G. Byrne	118	1,425
1916 Spur	J. Loftus	118	2,900
1917 Hourless	J. Butwell	118	5,475
1918 Motor Cop	E. Taplin	118	7,100
1919 Sir Barton	J. Loftus	118	8,075
1920 Man o' War	C. Kummer	118	4,825
1921 Leonardo II	A. Schuttinger	118	5,475
1922 Snob II	C. Kummer	118	17,050
1923 Zev	E. Sande	118	18,300
1924 Bracadale	E. Sande	118	19,000
1925 American Flag	A. Johnson	118	19,600
1926 Haste	E. Sande	118	22,800
1927 Chance Shot	E. Sande	118	23,250
1928 Victorian	R. Workman	118	22,300
1929 Blue Larkspur	M. Garner	118	28,250
1930 Whichone	R. Workman	118	26,150
1931 Jamestown	L. McAtee	118	27,300
1932 Boatswain	A. Robertson	118	21,600
1933 The Darb	A. Robertson	118	20,550
1934 Singing Wood	R. Jones	118	16,000
1935 Rosemont	W.D. Wright	118	11,250
1936 White Cockade	E. Litzenberger	118	18,200
1937 Flying Scot	J. Gilbert	118	15,050
1938 Menow	C. Kurtsinger	118	15,000
1939 Johnstown	J. Stout	118	15,750

1940 Corydon .... E. Arcaro	118	16,650
1941 King Cole ...... J. Gilbert	118	20,300
1942 Alsab .... B. James	126	15,500
1943 Count Fleet .... J. Longden	126	12,700
1944 Who Goes There J. Longden	126	16,150
1945 Polynesian .... W.D. Wright	126	19,125
1946 Hampden ...... E. Arcaro	126	20,320
1947 Faultless ...... D. Dodson	126	20,950
1948 Vulcan's Forge . D. Dodson	126	20,100
1949 Olympia ...... E. Arcaro	126	21,150
1950 Hill Prince ..... E. Arcaro	126	20,700
1951 Battlefield ...... E. Arcaro	126	20,600
1952 Armageddon ..... R. York	126	22,000
1953 Native Dancer ... E. Guerin	126	23,050
1954 Jet Action .... J. Contreras	126	26,250
1955 Traffic Judge .... E. Arcaro	126	21,850
1956 Oh Johnny . H. Woodhouse	126	20,100
1957 Clem .... C. McCreary	126	19,100
1958 Sir Robby ...... E. Guerin	126	19,362
1959 Intentionally .... M. Ycaza	126	58,072
1960 John William H. Woodhouse	126	74,950
1961 Hitting Away H. Woodhouse	126	38,935
1962 Jaipur ..... W. Shoemaker	126	38,090
1963 Get Around ..... B. Baeza	126	39,650
1964 Mr. Brick .... R. Ussery	126	40,105
1965 Flag Raiser ..... R. Ussery	126	39,000
1966 Indulto .... J.L. Rotz	126	38,935
1967 Dr. Fager .... B. Baeza	126	37,895
1968 Call Me Prince ...W. Boland	126	38,220
1969 Ack Ack .... M. Ycaza	126	37,765
1970 Hagley .... R. Turcotte	126	38,805
1971 Bold Reasoning . J. Vasquez	126	35,100
1972 Key to the Mint ..B. Baeza	126	35,400

Run at Jerome Park prior to 1890; at Morris Park from 1891 to 1904, inclusive. Not run in 1911 nor 1912. Run at Jamaica Race Course at 1 1/16 miles in 1956. At Belmont Park from 1905 to 1955, inclusive, and from 1957 to 1959, inclusive. Gleaming Light finished first in 1969 but was disqualified and placed fifth.

Wood Memorial

Aqueduct; 3-year-olds; 1 1/8 miles.

Year	Jockey	Wt.	Win. val.
1925 Backbone .... I. Parke	110	$ 7,600
1926 Pompey ...... B. Breuning	120	8,700
1927 Saxon .... G. Ellis	117	9,050
1928 Distraction .. D. McAuliffe	120	11,300
1929 Essare .... M. Garner	110	11,000
1930 Gallant Fox ...... E. Sande	120	10,150
1931 Twenty Grand C. Kurtsinger	120	10,200
1932 Universe ...... L. McAtee	120	10,400
1933 Mr. Khayyam ..... P. Walls	122	3,760
1934 High Quest ..... D. Bellizzi	120	3,990
1935 Today .... R. Workman	112	11,350
1936 Teufel ..... E. Litzenberger	112	10,775
1937 Melodist ...... J. Longden	120	19,150
1938 Fighting Fox ..... J. Stout	120	17,450
1939 Johnstown .... J. Stout	120	17,675
1940 Dit .... L. Haas	120	19,225
1941 Market Wise .... D. Meade	120	16,650
1942 Requested .... W.D. Wright	120	22,900

1943 Count Fleet .... J. Longden	126	20,150
1944 Stir Up .... E. Arcaro	126	19,625
1944 Lucky Draw ... J. Longden	126	20,115
1945 Jeep .... A. Kirkland	126	18,945
1945 Hoop Jr. .... E. Arcaro	126	18,945
1946 Assault ...... W. Mehrtens	126	22,600
1947 Phalanx .... E. Arcaro	126	31,325
1947 I Will .... E. Arcaro	126	31,625
1948 My Request .... D. Dodson	126	34,600
1949 Olympia .... E. Arcaro	126	31,850
1950 Hill Prince ..... E. Arcaro	126	34,500
1951 Repetoire ..... P. McLean	126	35,250
1952 Master Fiddle .. D. Gorman	126	45,200
1953 Native Dancer ... E. Guerin	126	87,000
1954 Correlation . W. Shoemaker	126	86,000
1955 Nashua ...... T. Atkinson	126	75,100
1956 Head Man ...... E. Arcaro	126	42,400
1957 Bold Ruler ..... E. Arcaro	126	40,800
1958 Jewel's Reward .. E. Arcaro	126	37,575
1959 Manassa Mauler R. Broussard	126	55,915
1960 Francis S. .. W. Shoemaker	126	60,465
1961 Globemaster ...... J. Rotz	126	56,062
1962 Admiral's Voyage		
W. Shoemaker	126	59,702
1963 No Robbery .... J.L. Rotz	126	59,020
1964 Quadrangle .... W. Hartack	126	58,012
1965 Flag Raiser ..... R. Ussery	126	60,222
1966 Amberoid ...... W. Boland	126	74,425
1967 Damascus .. W. Shoemaker	126	73,060
1968 Dancer's Image .. R. Ussery	126	73,775
1969 Dike .... J. Velasquez	126	72,085
1970 Personality.... E. Belmonte	126	76,570
1971 Good Behaving . C. Baltazar	126	67,320
1972 Upper Case ... R. Turcotte	126	71,040

Run as Wood Stakes prior to 1927. Distance 1 mile and 70 yards from 1925 to 1939, inclusive; 1 1/16 miles from 1940 to 1951, inclusive. Run in two divisions in 1944, 1945 and 1947. In 1956 Golf Ace finished first but was disqualified and placed second. Run at Jamaica Race Course prior to 1960. Sunrise County and Admiral's Voyage dead-heated for first place in 1962; Sunrise County was disqualified and placed second.

Woodward Stakes

Belmont Park; 3-year-olds and over; 1¼ miles.

Year	Jockey	Wt.	Win. val.
1954 Pet Bully (6) ... W. Hartack	126	$43,700
1955 Traffic Judge (3) . E. Arcaro	118	40,000
1956 Mister Gus (5) I. Valenzuela	126	52,950
1957 Dedicate (5) ... W. Hartack	126	70,500
1958 Clem (4) ... W. Shoemaker	126	71,080
1959 Sword Dancer (3) E. Arcaro	120	70,170
1960 Sword Dancer (4) E. Arcaro	126	71,730
1961 Kelso (4) .... E. Arcaro	126	71,240
1962 Kelso (5) .... I. Valenzuela	126	74,880
1963 Kelso (6) .... I. Valenzuela	126	70,720
1964 Gun Bow (4) ..... W. Blum	126	70,330
1965 Roman Brother (4) B. Baeza	126	71,240
1966 Buckpasser (3) ... B. Baeza	121	73,190
1967 Damascus (3) W. Shoemaker	120	70,070

1968 Mr. Right (5)...H. Gustines 126 69,420
1969 Arts and Letters (3)B. Baeza 120 68,900
1970 Personality (3) E. Belmonte 121 71,435
1971 West Coast Scout (3)....

J.L. Rotz 121 67,860
1972 Key to the Mint (3) B. Baeza 119 69,300
Distance 1 mile in 1954, 1 1/8 miles in 1955.
Run at Aqueduct in 1959, 1960, and from 1962
to 1967, inclusive. Cougar II finished first in
1971 but was disqualified and placed third.

Foreign Stakes Winners
(From American Racing Manual)
Epsom Derby
Epsom Downs, England; 3-year-olds; 1½ miles.

Distance one mile prior to 1784. Distance 1½
miles since 1939. Run at Newmarket from 1915
to 1918, inclusive and from 1940 to 1945,
inclusive, and called the New Derby Stakes.

Year	Winner	Owner	Win. val.
1780	Diomed	Sir C. Bunbury	$ 5,620
1781	Y. Eclipse	Mr. O'Kelly	6,255
1782	Assassin	Lord Egremont	5,500
1783	Saltram	Mr. Parker	5,000
1784	Sergeant	Mr. O'Kelly	5,125
1785	Aimwell	Lord Clermont	4,375
1786	Noble	Mr. Panton	5,000
1787	Sir P. Teazle	Lord Derby	4,500
1788	Sir Thomas	Prince of Wales	4,625
1789	Skyscraper	Duke of Bedford	4,652
1790	Rhadamanthus	Lord Grosvenor	4,750
1791	Eager	Duke of Bedford	4,625
1792	John Bull	Lord Grosvenor	4,875
1793	Waxy	Sir F. Poole	6,500
1794	Daedalus	Lord Grosvenor	6,125
1795	Spread Eagle	Sir F. Standish	6,500
1796	Didelot	Sir F. Standish	6,500
1797	Colt by Fidget	Duke of Bedford	5,000
1798	Sir Harry	Mr. Cookson	5,375
1799	Archduke	Sir F. Standish	5,000
1800	Champion	Mr. Wilson	5,250
1801	Eleanor	Sir C. Bunbury	4,375
1802	Tyrant	Duke of Grafton	4,750
1803	Ditto	Sir H. Williamson	4,625
1804	Hannibal	Lord Egremont	4,625
1805	Card. Beaufort	Lord Egremont	6,250
1806	Paris	Lord Foley	5,875
1807	Election	Lord Egremont	5,875
1808	Pan	Sir H. Williamson	5,500
1809	Pope	Duke of Grafton	6,375
1810	Whalebone	Duke of Grafton	6,500
1811	Phantom	Sir J. Shelley	7,500
1812	Octavius	Mr. Ladbrook	7,125
1813	Smolensko	Sir C. Bunbury	7,375
1814	Blucher	Lord Stawell	7,125
1815	Whisker	Duke of Grafton	7,500
1816	Prince Leopold	Duke of York	7,250
1817	Azor	Mr. Payne	8,625
1818	Sam	Mr. Thornhill	8,500
1819	Tiresias	Duke of Portland	8,250
1820	Sailor	Mr. Thornhill	7,875
1821	Gustavus	Mr. Hunter	7,875
1822	Moses	Duke of York	7,625
1823	Emilius	Mr. Udny	8,375
1824	Cedric	Sir J. Shelley	8,875
1825	Middleton	Lord Jersey	9,000
1826	Lap Dog	Lord Egremont	9,000
1827	Mameluke	Lord Jersey	13,500
1828	Cadland	Duke of Rutland	13,000
1829	Frederick	Mr. Gratwicke	12,750
1830	Priam	Mr. Chifney	13,500
1831	Spaniel	Lord Lowther	15,500
1832	St. Giles	Mr. Ridsdale	14,375
1833	Dangerous	Mr. Saddler	17,625
1834	Plenipotentiary	Mr. Batson	17,125
1835	Mundig	Mr. Bowes	16,750
1836	Bay Middleton	Lord Jersey	18,125
1837	Phosphorus	Lord Berner	14,000
1838	Amato	Sir G. Heatcote	18,265
1839	Bloomsbury	Mr. W. Ridsdale	19,500
1840	Little Wonder	Mr. Robertson	19,125
1841	Coronation	Mr. Rawlinson	21,875
1842	Attila	Colonel Anson	24,500
1843	Cotherstone	Mr. Bowes	21,250
184-	Orlando	Colonel Peel	21,750
1845	Merry Monarch	Mr. Gratwick	20,000
1846	Pyrrhus the First	Mr. Gully	26,500
1847	Cossack	Mr. Pedley	26,500
1848	Surplice	Lord Clifton	28,000
1849	T. Flying Dutchman	Lord Eglinton	31,875
1850	Voltigeur	Lord Zetland	29,375
1851	Teddington	Sir J. Hawley	26,875
1852	Dan. O'Rourke	Mr. Bowes	24,350
1853	W. Australian	Mr. Bowes	26,500
1854	Andover	Mr. Gully	29,250
1855	Wild Dayrell	F. Popham	24,125
1856	Ellinton	Admiral Harcourt	28,125
1857	Blink Bonny	W. L'Anson	27,750
1858	Beadsman	Sir J. Hawley	26,615
1859	Musjid	Sir J. Hawley	33,250
1860	Thormanby	Mr. Merry	30,500
1861	Kettledrum	Colonel Towneley	30,500
1862	Caractacus	Mr. Snewing	32,125
1863	Macaroni	R.C. Naylor	34,500
1864	Blair Athol	W. L'Anson	32,500
1865	Gladiateur	C'nt F. deLagrange	34,375
1866	Lord Lyon	R. Sutton	37,750
1867	Hermit	Mr. Chaplin	35,000
1868	Blue Gown	Sir J. Hawley	34,000
1869	Pretender	J. Johnstone	31,125
1870	Kingcraft	Lord Falmouth	38,875
1871	Favonius	B. Rothschild	25,625
1872	Cremorne	H. Savile	24,250
1873	Doncaster	Mr. Merry	24,125
1874	Geo. Frederick	W.S. Cartwright	26,750
1875	Calopin	Prince Batthany	24,750
1876	Kisber	A. Baltazzi	27,875
1877	Silbio	Lord Falmouth	30,250
1878	Sefton	W.S. Crawfurd	29,125
1879	Sir Bevvs	Mr. Acton	35,125
1880	Bend Or	D. of Westminster	31,875
1881	Iroquois†	P. Lorillard	29,625
1882	Shotover	D. of Westminster	23,875
1883	St. Blaise	Sir F. Johnstone	25,750
1884	*St. Gatien	J. Hammond	
	Harvester	Sir J. Willoughby	24,500
1885	Melton	Lord Hastings	22,625
1886	Ormonde	D. of Westminster	23,500
1887	Mer. Hampton	Mr. Abington	22,625
1888	Ayrshire	Duke of Portland	18,375
1889	Donovan	Duke of Portland	20,250
1890	Sanfoin	Sir J. Miller	29,700
1891	Common	Sir F. Johnstone	27,550
1892	Sir Hugo	Lord Bradford	34,900
1893	Isinglass	Mr. McCalmont	27,575
1894	Ladas	Lord Rosebery	27,250
1895	Sir Visto	Lord Rosebery	27,250
1896	Persimmon	Prince of Wales	27,250
1897	Galtee More	Mr. Gubbins	27,250
1898	Jeddah	J. Larnach	27,250
1899	Flying Fox	D. of Westminster	27,250
1900	Diamond Jubilee	Prince of Wales	27,250
1901	Volodyovski†	W.C. Whitney	28,350
1902	Ard Patrick	J. Gubbins	27,250
1903	Rock Sand	Sir J. Miller	32,500
1904	St. Amant	L. de Rothschild	32,250
1905	Cicero	Lord Rosebery	32,250
1906	Spearmint	Maj. E. Loder	32,250
1907	Orby†	R. Croker	32,250

Year	Winner	Owner	Value
1908	Signorinetta	Chev. Ginistrelli	32,250
1909	Minoru	King Edward	32,250
1910	Lemberg	Mr. Fairie	32,250
1911	Sunstar	J.B. Joel	32,250
1912	Tagalie	W. Raphael	32,250
1913	Aboyeur	A.P. Cunliffe	32,250
1914	Durbar II†	H.B. Duryea	32,250
1915	Pommern	S. Joel	12,000
1916	Fifinella	E. Hulton	14,500
1917	Gay Crusader	Mr. Fairie	10,250
1918	Gainsborough	Lady Jas. Douglas	20,000
1919	Grand Parade	Lord Glanely	32,250
1920	Spion Kop	Maj. G. Loder	32,250
1921	Humorist	J.B. Joel	32,250
1922	Captain Cuttle	Lord Woolavington	51,250
1923	Papyrus	Ben Irish	56,800
1924	Sansovino	Lord Derby	59,025
1925	Manna	H.E. Morris	55,475
1926	Coronach	Lord Woolavington	51,750
1927	Call Boy	Frank Curzon	63,075
1928	Felstead	Sir H. C'liffe-Owen	58,025
1929	Trigo	W. Barnett	59,825
1930	Blenheim	H.H. Aga Khan	50,180
1931	Cameronian	J.A. Dewar	48,640
1932	April the Fifth	T. Walls	34,056
1933	Hyperion	Lord Derby	49,182
1934	Windsor Lad	H.H.M. of Raj'pla	46,760
1935	Bahram	H.H. Aga Khan	46,080
1936	Mahmoud	H.H. Aga Khan	49,670
1937	Mid-Day Sun	Mrs. G.B. Miller	47,205
1938	Bois Roussel	P. Beatty	43,644
1939	Blue Peter	Lord Rosebery	42,680
1940	Pont l'Eveque	F. Darling	23,803
1941	Owen Tudor	Mrs. M'D'ald-Buc'n	18,003
1942	Watling Street	Lord Derby	15,530
1943	Straight Lead	Miss Dorothy Paget	17,552
1944	Ocean Swell	Lord Rosebery	23,604
1945	Dante	Sir Eric Ohlson	33,356
1946	Airborne	J.E. Ferguson	38,662
1947	Pearl Diver	B.G. de Waldner	38,788
		H.H. Aga Khan	49,936
1948	My Love		
		Leon Volterra	
1949	Nimbus	Mrs. M. Glenister	56,980
1950	Galcador	Marcel Boussac	51,030
1951	Arctic Prince	Joseph McGrath	54,264
1952	Tulyar	H.H. Aga Khan	57,353
1953	Pinza	Sir Victor Sassoon	53,530
1954	Never Say Die†	R. Sterling Clark	47,485
1955	Phil Drake	Mme. Suzy Volterra	52,365
1956	Lavadin	Pierre Wortheimer	58,389
1957	Crepello	Sir Victor Sassoon	52,245
1958	Hard Ridden	Sir Victor Sassoon	56,196
1959	Parthia		101,018
1960	St. Paddy		92,546
1961	Psidium		96,734
1962	Larkspur		113,568
1963	Relko		98,948
1964	Santa Claus		201,787
1965	Sea-Bird		182,843
1966	Charlottown		208,600
1967	Royal Palace		173,370
1968	†Sir Ivor		140,460
1969	Blakeney		151,460
1970	†Nijinsky II		149,546
1971	†Mill Reef	Paul Mellon	117,900
1972	†Roberto	John Galbreath	164,931

† American bred or owned.

* Dead Heat.

Grand National Steeplechase

Liverpool, England; 6-year-olds and over; 4 miles 856 yards (Aintree Course)

Year	Winner	Owner	Value
1839	Lottery	J. Elmore	——
1840	Jerry	Mr. Villebois	——
1841	Charity	Lord Craven	——
1842	Gaylad	J. Elmore	——
1843	Vanguard	Lord Chesterfield	——
1844	Pioneer	Mr. Quartermaine	——
1845	Cure All	W.S. Crawfurd	——
1846	Pioneer	Mr. Adams	——
1847	Matthew	Mr. Courtenay	——
1848	Chandler	Capt. Little	——
1849	Peter Simple	Mr. S. Mason Jr.	$4,025
1850	Abd el Kader	Mr. Osborne	——
1851	Abd el Kader	Mr. Osborne	——
1852	Miss Mowbray	T.F. Mason	3,400
1853	Peter Simple	Capt. Little	——
1854	Bourton	Mr. Moseley	——
1855	Wanderer	Mr. Dennis	——
1856	Freetrader	W. Barnet	——
1857	Emigrant	G. Hodgman	5,575
1858	Little Charley	C. Capel	——
1859	Half Caste	Mr. Willoughby	4,200
1860	Anatis	C. Capel	——
1861	Jealousy	J. Bennett	4,925
1862	Huntsman	Visc't de Namur	——
1863	Emblem	Lord Coventry	4,275
1864	Emblematic	Lord Coventry	——
1865	Alcibiade	B.J. Angell	5,175
1866	Salamander	Mr. Studd	——
1867	Cortolvin	Duke of Hamilton	8,300
1868	The Lamb	Lord Poulett	7,850
1869	The Colonel	Mr. Weyman	8,800
1870	The Colonel	M. Evans	7,325
1871	The Lamb	Lord Poulett	8,325
1872	Casse Tete	E. Brayley	7,275
1873	Disturbance	Capt. Machell	9,800
1874	Reugny	Capt. Machell	9,450
1875	Pathfinder	H. Bird	9,700
1876	Regal	Capt. Machell	7,550
1877	Austerlitz	F.G. Hobson	6,450
1878	Shifnal	J. Nightingall	8,450
1879	The Liberator	G. Moore	9,500
1880	Empress	P. Ducrot	6,250
1881	Woodbrook	Capt. Kirkwood	4,900
1882	Seaman	Lord Manners	6,675
1883	Zoedone	Prince C. Kinsky	4,625
1884	Voluptuary	H.F. Boyd	5,175
1885	Roquefort	A. Cooper	5,175
1886	Old Joe	Mr. Douglas	6,805
1887	Gamecock	E. Jay	6,080
1888	Playfair	Col. E.W. Baird	5,905
1889	Frigate	M.A. Maher	6,170
1890	Ilex	G. Masterman	8,325
1891	Come Away	W.G. Jameson	8,400
1892	Father O'Flynn	C.G. Wilson	8,400
1893	Cloister	C.G. Duff	9,825
1894	Why Not	Capt. C.H. Fenwick	9,875
1895	W.M.F. Borneo	J. Widger	9,875
1896	The Soarer	Lord Wavertree	9,875
1897	Manifesto	H.M. Dyas	9,875
1898	Drogheda	C.G. Adams	9,875
1899	Manifesto	J.G. Bulteel	9,875
1900	Ambush II	Prince of Wales	9,875
1901	Grudon	B. Bletsoe	9,875
1902	Shannon Lass	A. Gorham	10,000
1903	Drumcree	J.S. Morrison	10,000
1904	Moifaa	G.Ḣ. Gollan	10,000
1905	Kirkland	F. Bibby	10,125
1906	Ascetic's Silver	Prince Hatzfeldt	10,875
1907	Eremon	S. Howard	12,000
1908	Rubio†	Maj. F. Douglas-Pennant	12,000
1909	Lutteur III	J. Hennessy	12,000
1910	Jenkinstown	S. Howard	12,000
1911	Glenside	F. Bibby	12,500
1912	Jerry M	Mr. C.G. Assheton-Smith	16,000
1913	Covertcoat	Sir C.G. Assheton-Smith	15,850
1914	Sunloch	T. Tyler	17,575

Year	Horse	Owner	Value
1915	Ally Sloper	Lady Nelson	17,575
1916	*Bermouth	P.F. Heybourn	5,750
1917	*Ballymacad	Sir G. Bullough	6,025
1918	*Poethlyn	Mrs. H. Peel	4,925
1919	*Poethlyn	Mrs. H. Peel	17,950
1920	Troytown	Major Gerrard	21,800
1921	Shaun Spadah	T. McAlpine	39,925
1922	Music Hall	Hugh Kershaw	35,000
1923	Sgt. Murphy†	Stephen Sanford	36,100
1924	Master Rob't	Lord Airlie	40,825
1925	Double Chance	Major D. Goold	40,600
1926	Jack Horner	C. Schwartz	31,550
1927	Sprig	Mrs. M. Partridge	41,075
1928	Tipperary Tim	H.S. Kenyon	55,900
1929	Gregalach	Mrs. M.A. G'm'll	64,625
1930	Shaun Goilin	W. Midwood	48,650
1931	Grakle	C.R. Taylor	37,240
1932	Forbra	W. Parsonage	28,577
1933	Kellsboro Jack†	Mrs. F.A. Clark	36,725
1934	Golden Miller	Miss D. Paget	36,325
1935	Reynoldstown	Maj. Noel F'rlong	32,725
1936	Reynoldstown	Maj. Noel F'rlong	35,100
1937	Royal Mail	H. Lloyd Thomas	33,225
1938	Battleship†	Mrs. M. Scott	37,545
1939	Workman	Sir A. Maguire	31,966
1940	Bogskar	Lord Stalbridge	16,887
1946	Lovely Cottage	Jock Morant	35,300
1947	Caughoo	J.J. McDowell	39,728
1948	Sheila's Cottage	John Proctor	36,428
1949	Russian Hero	W.F. Williamson	37,868
1950	Freebooter	Mrs. L. Brotherton	27,942
1951	Nickel Coin	Jeffrey Royle	24,766
1952	Teal	Harry Lane	25,110
1953	Early Mist	J.H. Griffin	26,407
1954	Royal Tan	J.H. Griffin	24,288
1955	Quare Times	Mrs. C. Welman	25,085
1956	E.S.B.	Mrs. L. Carver	24,416
1957	Sundew	Mr. & Mrs. Geoffrey Kohn	24,831
1958	Mr. What†	David Jones Coughlan	38,414
1959	Oxo		38,200
1960	Merryman		36,775
1961	Nicolaus Silver		51,156
1962	Kilmore		69,985
1963	Ayala		59,682
1964	Team Spirit		56,784
1965†	Jay Trump		61,715
1966	Anglo		62,334
1967	Foinavon		74,597
1968	Red Alligator		42,835
1969	Highland Wedding		42,138
1970	Gay Trip		35,530
1971	Specify		37,200
1972	Well To Do		66,990
1973	Red Rum.		63,175

*Substitute race. †American bred or owned. Not run from 1941 through 1945, inclusive.

Melbourne Cup

Melbourne, Australia; 3-year-olds and over; 3,200 meters

Year	Age	Jockey	Wt.	Win. val.
1861 Archer	(5)	J. Cutts	133	$ --
1862 Archer	(6)	J. Cutts	142	--
1863 Banker	(3)	H. Chifney	74	--
1864 Lantern	(3)	S. Davis	87	--
1865 Toryboy	(7)	E. Kavanagh	98	--
1866 The Bard	(3)	W. Davis	85	--
1867 Tim Whiffler	(5)	I. Driscoll	123	--
1868 Glencoe	(4)	C. Stanley	127	--
1869 Warrior	(6)	S. Morrison	122	--
1870 Nimblefoot	(7)	J. Day	92	--
1871 The Pearl	(5)	J.T. Kavanagh	101	--
1872 The Quack	(6)	W. Enderson	108	--
1873 Don Juan	(4)	W. Wilson	96	--
1874 Haricot	(4)	P. Pigott	91	--
1875 Wollomai	(6)	R. Batty	106	--
1876 Briseis	(3)	P. St. Albans	88	--
1877 Chester	(3)	P. Pigott	96	--
1878 Calamia	(5)	T. Brown	114	--
1879 Darriwell	(5)	S. Cracknell	102	--
1880 Grand Fleneur	(3)	T. Hales	98	--
1881 Zulu	(4)	J. Gough	80	--
1882 The Assyrian	(5)	C. Hutchins	111	--
1883 M'rtini Henri	(3)	J. Williamson	103	--
1884 Malua	(5)	A. Robertson	135	--
1885 Sheet Anchor	(7)	M. O'Brien	109	--
1886 Arsenal	(4)	W. English	103	--
1887 Dunlop	(5)	T. Sanders	115	--
1888 Mentor	(4)	M. O'Brien	115	--
1889 Bravo	(6)	J. Anwin	119	--
1890 Carbine	(5)	R. Ramage	145	51,150
1891 Malvolio	(4)	G. Redfern	116	50,620
1892 Glenloth	(5)	G. Robson	111	49,835
1893 Tarcoola	(8)	H. Cripps	116	35,750
1894 Patron	(4)	H. Dawes	129	--
1895 Auraria	(5)	J. Stevenson	102	--
1896 Newhaven	(3)	H. Gardiner	111	20,740
1897 Gaulus	(4)	S. Callinan	106	20,840
1898 The Grafter	(5)	J. Gough	128	21,460
1899 Merriwee	(3)	V. Turner	104	21,965
1900 Clean Sweep	(3)	A. Richardson	98	21,985
1901 Revenue	(5)	F. Dunn	108	30,585
1902 The Victory	(4)	R. Lewis	124	23,420
1903 Lord Cardigan	(3)	N. Godby	92	31,620
1904 Acrasia	(7)	T. Clayton	104	33,160
1905 Blue Spec	(6)	F. Bullock	112	31,870
1906 Poseidon	(3)	T. Clayton	104	31,630
1907 Apologue	(5)	W. Evans	107	24,545
1908 Lord Nolan	(3)	J.R. Flynn	94	25,635
1909 Prince Foote	(3)	W.H. McL'n	106	27,185
1910 Comedy King	(4)	W.H. McL'lan	109	30,890
1911 The Parisian	(6)	R. Cameron	121	33,210
1912 Piastre	(4)	A. Shanahan	107	32,880
1913 Posinatus	(5)	A. Shanahan	98	36,345
1914 Kingsburgh	(4)	G. Meddick	96	38,200
1915 Patrobas	(3)	R. Lewis	104	38,700
1916 Sasanof	(3)	F. Foley	95	34,775
1917 West Court	(5)	W.H. McL'lan	117	29,895
1918 Night Watch	(5)	W. Duncan	93	30,680
1919 Artilleryman	(3)	R. Lewis	104	36,450
1920 Poitrel	(6)	K. Bracken	140	36,550
1921 Sister Olive	(3)	E. O'Sullivan	93	40,860
1922 King Ingoda	(4)	A. Wilson	99	52,740
1923 Bitalli	(4)	A. Wilson	98	52,440
1924 Backwood	(6)	P. Brown	114	50,995
1925 Windbag	(4)	J. Munro	130	52,450
1926 Spearfelt	(5)	H. Cairns	129	49,560
1927 Trivalve	(4)	R. Lewis	104	49,990
1928 Statesman	(4)	J. Munro	112	46,845
1929 Nightmarch	(4)	R. Reed	128	47,110
1930 Phar Lap	(4)	J. Pike	138	46,145
1931 White Nose	(5)	N. Percival	98	35,000
1932 Peter Pan	(3)	W. Duncan	104	24,500
1933 Hall Mark	(3)	J. O'Sullivan	106	26,009
1934 Peter Pan	(5)	D. Munro	136	41,000
1935 Marabou	(4)	K. Voitre	109	40,000
1936 Wotan	(4)	O. Phillips	110	36,000
1937 The Trump	(5)	A. Reed	117	36,000
1938 Catalogue	(8)	F. Shean	116	28,000
1939 Rivette	(6)	E. Preston	97	39,540
1940 Old Rowley	(7)	A. Knox	110	22,309
1941 Skipton	(3)	W. Cook	104	17,967
1942 Colonus	(4)	H. McCloud	100	16,957
1943 Dark Felt	(6)	V. Hartney	116	24,871
1944 Sirius	(4)	D. Munro	117	17,853
1945 Rainbird	(4)	W. Cook	105	40,000
1946 Russia	(6)	D. Munro	126	35,000
1947 Hiraji	(4)	J. Purtell	109	30,269
1948 Rimfire	(6)	R. Neville	100	50,000

1949 Foxzami (4)	W. Fellows	120	12,500
1950 Comic Court (5)	P. Glennon	131	38,400
1951 Delta (5)	N. Sellwood	131	31,360
1952 Dalray (4)	W. Williamson	132	31,500
1953 Wodalla (4)	R.J. Purtell	116	22,050
1954 Rising Fast (5)	J. Purtell	131	43,400
1955 Toparoa (7)	N. Sellwood	106	23,625
1956 Evening Peal (4)	G. Podmore	112	33,600
1957 Straight Draw (5)	N. McGrowdie	117	49,550
1958 Baystone (6)	M. Schumaker	121	30,000
1959 MacDougal (6)	P. Glennon	123	33,600
1960 Hi Jinx (5)	W. Smith	108	56,000
1961 Lord Fury (4)	R. Selkrig	105	46,480
1962 Even Stevens (5)	L. Coles	117	31,500
1963 Gatum Gatum (5)	J. Johnson	110	43,120
1964 Polo Prince (6)	R. Taylor	115	43,023
1965 Light Fingers (4)	R. Higgins	116	46,462
1966 Galilee (4)	J. Miller	125	41,300
1967 Red Handed (7)	R. Higgins	121	46,251
1968 Rain Lover (4)	J. Johnson	114	41,300
1969 Rain Lover (5)	J. Johnson	133	51,100
1970 Baghdad Note (5)	E. Didham	119	51,100
1971 Silver Knight (4)	R. Marsh	121	69,900

Distance 2 miles prior to 1972.

Prix de l'Arc de Triomphe

Longchamp, Paris, France; 3-year-olds and over; weight for age; 1½ miles.

Year	Age	Jockey	Wt.	Win. val.
1920 Comrade (3)	F. Bullock	121	$14,369
1921 Ksar (3)	G. Stern	121	24,691
1922 Ksar (4)	F. Bullock	133	28,615
1923 Parth (3)	O'Neill	121	20,197
1924 Massine (4)	Sharpe	133	16,800
1925 Priori (3)	M. Allemand	121	22,370
1926 Biribi (3)	D. Torterolo	121	13,748
1927 Mon Talisman (3)	C.H. S'blat	121	21,778
1928 Kantar (3)	A. Esling	122	22,054
1929 Ortello (3)	P. Caprioli	121	26,278
1930 Motrico (4)	M. Fruhinsholtz	133	25,958
1931 Pearl Cap (3)	C.H. Semblat	119	24,000
1932 Motrico (6)	C.H. Semblat	133	20,028

1933 Crapom (4)	P. Caprioli	122	21,229
1934 Brantome (3)	C. Bouillon	122	26,717
1935 Samos (3)	W. Sibbritt	119	26,800
1936 Corrida (4)	C. Elliott	129	25,000
1937 Corrida (4)	C. Elliott	129	34,000
1938 Eclair au Chocolat (3)	C. B'illon	122	27,131
1941 Le Pacha (3)	P. Francolon	119	600,000f
1942 Djebel (5)	J. Doyasbere	133	1,000,000f
1943 Verso II. (3)	G. Duforez	119	1,000,000f
1944 Ardan (3)	J. Doyasbere	119	1,200,000f
1945 Nikellora (3)	W. Johnstone	116	1,200,000f
1946 Caracalla (4)	C. Elliott	133	16,666
1947 Le Paillon (5)	F. Rochetti	133	41,666
1948 Migoli (4)	C. Smirke	132	52,095
1949 Coronation (3)	R. Poincelet	119	105,603
1950 Tantieme (3)	J. Doyasbere	122	79,457
1951 Tantieme (4)	J. Doyasbere	133	71,250
1952 Nuccio (4)	R. Poincelet	132	84,999
1953 La Sorellina (3)	M. Larraun	119	91,801
1954 Sica Boy (3)	R. Johnston	122	92,640
1955 Ribot (3)	E. Camici	122	86,450
1956 Ribot (4)	E. Camici	132	88,000
1957 Oroso (4)	S. Boullenger	132	112,000
1958 Ballymoss (4)	A. Breasley	132	106,198
1959 Saint Crespin III (3)	G. Moore	122	98,298
1960 Puissant Chef (3)	M. Garcia	122	128,385
1961 Molvedo (3)	E. Camici	122	120,000
1962 Soltikoff (3)	M. Depalmas	122	227,000
1963 Exbury (4)	J. DeForge	133	196,933
1964 Prince Royal II (3)	R. Poincelet	122	216,000
1965 Sea-Bird (3)	T.P. Glennon	122	240,035
1966 Bon Mot (3)	F. Head	122	219,172
1967 Topyo (3)	W. Pyers	122	224,000
1968 Vaguely Noble (3)	W. Williamson	122	235,946
1969 Levmoss (3)	W. Williamson	132	213,188
1970 Sassafras (3)	Y. St. Martin	122	248,364
1971†Mill Reef (3)	G. Lewis	122	251,847
1972 San San (4)	F. Head	122	283,000

Not run in 1939 and 1940. Run at Le Tremblay in 1944. Value of franc not established from 1941 to 1945, inclusive. Value shown is estimated gross. In 1959 Saint Crespian III and Midnight Sun deadheated for first; following objection Saint Crespin III was placed first and Midnight Sun second. † American-bred and/or owned.

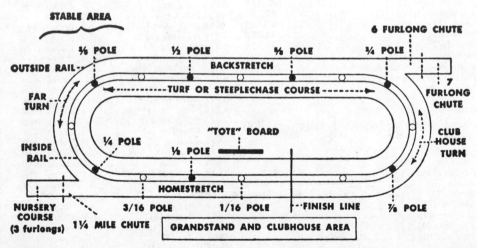

Layout of Mile Track for Horse Racing. (Taken from "The Dell 1953 Racing Almanac," by John I. Day Jr. and Rowland Barber. Reprinted by permission of Western Printing and Lithographing Company, New York.)

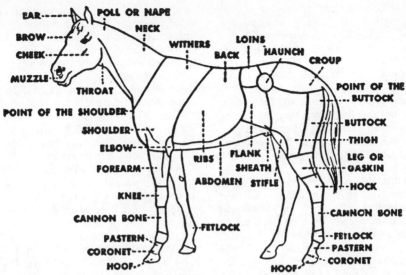

Conformation of Horse. (Taken from "The Dell 1953 Racing Almanac," by John I. Day Jr. and Rowland Barber. Reprinted by permission of Western Printing and Lithographing Company, New York.)

HORSESHOE PITCHING

THE HISTORY OF HORSESHOE PITCHING

The game of horseshoe pitching originated in the army camps of the Roman empire around 150 A.D., shortly after the Romans began protecting the feet of their horses with iron footwear, a trick they had learned from their Asiatic rivals, the Parthians.

The old Greek pastime of throwing the discus had become quoit throwing and was quite popular among the officers and the nobility. The common soldiers and camp followers, lacking the expensive equipment for quoits, or the discus, substituted the iron footwear of their horses and evolved an accuracy type game by tossing them at a target, usually a stake.

Roman legions spread the game to England where the twin games of quoits and horseshoe pitching developed together, civilians preferring quoits while the military was partial to horseshoes. English settlers and soldiers brought the two games to America and quoits was quite popular on the Atlantic seaboard. Gradually, quoits declined in popularity and almost disappeared as a game, being supplanted by horseshoe pitching which spread westward with our pioneers. Horseshoe stakes could be found alongside almost every blacksmith shop in the early days of our country.

The game continued popular in rural America as the country developed and horseshoe pitching contests became the order of the day at family reunions, holiday celebrations and County Fairs. This led to the formation of local and neighborhood horseshoe pitching clubs. The first such club of record was at Meadville, Pa. in 1892 and about the same time in East Liverpool, O. A club with 600 members was formed in Long Beach, Calif. in 1900, the first on the Pacific coast.

By the turn of the century, play in organized clubs and formal contests was most prevalent in Kansas and Missouri. There are records of team tournaments held in Convention Hall in Kansas City, Mo. in 1900 and at Independence, Mo. in 1902. Detailed accounts of a team match between Ottawa, Kan. and Kansas City, Kan. for a side bet of $100 still exist in the files of the National Horseshoe Pitchers' Association.

A big tournament was staged in 1905 at Kansas State College in Manhatten, Kan., the doubles championship being won by Robert Pierce and A. B. Argenbright of Kansas City while the individual title was won by Frank Jackson of Kellerton, Ia., who later won the World title many times and became the legendary figure of the game.

Finally, in 1909, at Bronson, Kan. a promoter staged a tourney "open to anyone in the world" and posted a large sum of money and a belt symbolic of the World Championship as prizes. This affair attracted a great many players from all over the midwest and was won by Frank

Jackson of Kellerton, Ia., who was undoubtedly the best horseshoe pitcher of his day. The National Association has since recognized this tournament as the first World Tournament.

During these early years of organized horseshoe pitching the rules were a hodge-podge of conflicting provisions, different scoring values and unregulated equipment. This choatic condition threatened the existence of the game. Each section of the country, even adjoining neighborhoods, used stakes of different heights set a distances ranging from 36 to 50 feet apart. The shoes had no definite dimensions or weight and scoring values varied greatly.

To correct this situation a meeting was held in 1914. Representatives of local clubs from all over the midwest attended. After studying the various rules in use, a unified code of rules and playing procedures was drawn up and approved. Arrangements were made to hold an official World Tournament the following year, and an organization known as the Grand League of American Horseshoe Pitchers was formed. This was the beginning of the present National Horseshoe Pitchers' Association of America.

The World Tournament was held as scheduled in 1915 at Heathwood Park in Kansas City, Kan., and was won by the famous Frank Jackson of Iowa, who defended his title successfully against all comers for the next three years. The original rules called for stakes eight inches high placed 38½ feet apart. Shoes weighed between two pounds and two pounds three ounces. Ringers counted five points, leaners three and shoes within six inches of the stake one point. The provision for "cancellation" scoring, whereby two shoes of a like value thrown by opposing players in the same frame cancel each other was also written into the rules. An official game consisted of 21 points.

Frank Jackson dominated the game so completely that no official World Tournaments were held during the next three years, but in 1919 the Sunshine Pleasure Club in St. Petersburg, Fla. staged a World Tournament which was won by Fred Brust of Columbus, O., and the players formed a group known as the National League of Horseshoe and Quoit Players.

This group improved the rules and staged both winter and summer World Tournaments in 1920, and in 1921 under the guidance of Ben Leighton held a World Tournament at St. Paul, Minn. in co-operation with the Grand League of American Horseshoe Players. The two groups combined to form the present National Horseshoe Pitchers' Association of America, commonly known as the N.H.P.A., which was incorporated as a non-profit group that year and has functioned ever since as the official governing body of the game.

During the ensuing years, the N.H.P.A. has promoted the game on both the recreational and competitive levels, improved the playing rules,

equipment and procedures, and sponsored and sanctioned championship tournaments on local, state, regional and national levels. Without the influence and efforts of the N.H.P.A. the game of horseshoe pitching would probably have withered away and died many years ago.

Fred Brust of Columbus, O., winner of the 1919 World Title, was the first to manufacture horseshoes specifically for the game. Dave Cottrell of New York and Ben Leighton of Minnesota, both early N.H.P.A. officials, were the first to design scoresheets for the orderly and accurate compiling of tournament results. Ray Howard of Ohio published The Horseshoe World from 1920 to 1943 and did much to promote and further the game and the N.H.P.A.

Other N.H.P.A. officials to whom horseshoe pitchers owe a debt of gratitude are Leland Mortenson of Iowa, Jack Claves of Missouri and "Pop" Woodfield of Washington, D.C.

The restrictions of World War II almost ended the game, but the efforts of Harvey Clear of California and Arch Stokes of Utah kept the N.H.P.A. and the game alive and provided a firm basis for postwar development.

In more recent years the monthly magazine published by Byron Jaskulek of New York City and the administration of the N.H.P.A. by Arch Gregson and Elmer Beller, both of California, has carried on the work of their predecessor. The association publishes a monthly magazine, The Horseshoe Pitchers' News Digest, which is edited by Ellis Cob of Illinois.

The game of horseshoes has moved from the farms and backyards and picnic groves into our municipal parks where more than 90 percent of the game is played today on regulation clay courts equipped with concrete pitching platforms and usually with floodlights for night play.

The game has experienced considerable growth in the past decade during which time under the direction of its executive secretary Robert Pence the National Horseshoe Pitchers' Association has increased it membership more than fourfold. The organization now has official state chapters in 49 states and seven provinces of Canada, each with numerous local club affiliates. The number of championship tournaments and organized local leagues has kept pace with this growth.

The 1972 World and National Tournament at Greenville, Ohio attracted a record number of more than 500 entrants from 41 states and three provinces of Canada. Also for the first time players from overseas took part with several entrants from South Africa. This is an eleven-day event with morning, afternoon, and night sessions played on a battery of 18 or more floodlighted courts with an many as 5,000 spectators.

The 1973 tournament will be held indoors for the first time with the Redwood Empire Horseshoe Club of Eureka, Calif. the host. Normally an outdoor game, there has been a big increase in the number of indoor horseshoe facilities in the past five years.

The caliber of play and competition has also improved tremendously. National champions of grandfather's day would have a tough time to even win an average city or county tournament against the players of today.

There has been a steady influx of outstanding young players. Dan Kuchcinski of Erie, Pa. had three World titles to his credit in the Men's division at the age of 21. Other ranking contend-ers still in their early twenties or less include Ross Stevenson of Canada, Paul Day and Mark Seibold of Indiana and Donnie and Gary Roberts of Ohio.

Walter Ray Williams of Eureka, Calif. won the World Junior title at the age of 12 in 1972 with a ringer average of 89.2 percent. He is only one of a number of outstanding Juniors under the age of 17.

Presently the National Horseshoe Pitchers' Association is headed by Ralph Dykes of Lombard, Ill., President, and Robert Pence of Gary, Ind., Secretary.

WORLD HORSESHOE PITCHING CHAMPIONS
(Courtesy of The National Horseshoe Pitchers' Association of America)

No competition in years not listed.

Men

Year	Winner
1909	Frank Jackson
1915	Frank Jackson
1919	Fred M. Brust
1920	George May
1920	Frank Jackson
1921	Charles Bobbitt (winter)
1921	Frank Jackson (summer)
1922	Frank Lundin
1923	Harold Falor (15 yrs. old)
1923	George May
1924	C. C. Davis (winter)
1924-25	Putt Mossman
1926	Frank Jackson (winter)
1927	C. C. Davis (winter)
1927	C. C. Davis (summer)
1928	C. C. Davis
1929	Blair Nunnmaker
1933	Ted Allen (World's Fair)
1934-36	Ted Allen
1937	Fernando Isais
1938-40	Ted Allen
1941	Fernando Isais
1946	Ted Allen
1947-52	Fernando Isais
1953	Ted Allen
1954	Guy Zimmerman
1955-57	Ted Allen
1958	Fernando Isais
1959	Ted Allen
1960	Don Titcomb
1961	Harold Reno
1962	Paul Focht
1963	John Monasmith
1964	Harold Reno
1965	Elmer Hohl (Canada)
1966	Curt Day
1967	Dan Kuchcinski
1968	Elmer Hohl (Canada)
1969-70	Dan Kuchcinski
1971	Curt Day
1972	Elmer Hohl (Canada)

Women

Year	Winner
1920	Marjorie Voohries
1921	Mrs. J. R. Mathews
1922	Mrs. Mayme Francisco (winter)
1922	Mrs. C. A. Lanham (summer)
1923	Mrs. Mayme Francisco (winter)
1923	Mrs. Mayme Francisco (summer)
1924	Mrs. C. A. Lanham (winter)
1924	Mrs. C. A. Lanham (summer)
1925	Mrs. C. A. Lanham (winter)
1926	Mrs. George Brouillette (winter)
1927	Mrs. George Brouillette (winter)
1927	Mrs. C. A. Lanham (summer)
1928	Mrs. Mayme Francisco (winter)
1928	Mrs. C. A. Lanham (summer)
1929	Mrs. Mayme Francisco (winter)
1933	Caroline Schultz (summer)
1934	Caroline Schultz
1935	Mrs. Esther James (summer)
1948-49	Mrs. Anna Lindquist
1950	Mrs. Pat DeLeary
1951-52	Mrs. Sarah Byers
1953	Pat DeLeary
1954	*Katie Gregson
1955	Hazel Harris
1956	Vicki Chapelle
1957	Gertsie Lou Selby
1958	Vicki Chapelle
1959	Vicki Chapelle
1960	Esta McKee
1961	Vicki Chapelle
1962	Sue Gillespie
1963	Vicki Chapelle Winston
1964-65	Sue Gillespie
1966-67	Vicki Chapelle Winston
1968	Lorraine Thomas
1969	Vicki Chapelle Winston
1970-72	Ruth Hangen

*Won in three-way play-off.

SENIORS (Over 60 years)

Year	Winner
1960	W. O. Maxwell
1961-62	Joseph Wilkinson

1963	. . . . . .	Ralph Navarro
1964-65	. . . .	Harold Tuttle
1966-70	. . . .	John Paxton
1971	. . . . . .	Stan Manker
1972	. . . . . .	Ray Miller

INTERMEDIATES (Between 60 and 65 Years)

1967	. . . . . .	Wayne Winston
1968-69	. . . .	Francis Winetrout
1970-71	. . . .	Art Holter
1972	. . . . . .	Abe Austin

JUNIORS (Under 17 years)

1951-53	. . . .	David Loucks
1954-55	. . . .	Byron Bowman
1956	. . . . . .	Robert Madsen
1957	. . . . . .	Rodney Hilton
1958	. . . . . .	William Backer
1959	. . . . . .	Donald Roberts
1960	. . . . . .	Harold Brown
1961-64	. . . .	Gary Roberts
1965	. . . . . .	Ross Stevenson (Canada)
1966	. . . . . .	Mark Seibold
1967-68	. . . .	Farron Eisemann
1969	. . . . . .	Mark Seibold
1970	. . . . . .	Bill Holland
1971-72	. . . .	Walter Ray Williams

Junior Girls (under 17 years)

1967	. . . . . .	Bonita Seibold
1968	. . . . . .	Carolan Truman
1969	. . . . . .	Mary Lee
1970	. . . . . .	Peggy Smith
1971-72	. . . .	Jennifer Reno

WORLD HORSESHOE PITCHING RECORDS

Tournament

Ringer Percentage (31 games) — 87.5 — Casey Jones — 1948.

Ringer Percentage (35 games) — 88.5 — Elmer Hohl — 1968.

Total Ringers (35 games) — 2,903 — Ralph Maddox — 1964.

Double Ringers (35 games) — 1,173 — Ralph Maddox — 1964.

Most Shoes Pitched (35 games) — 3,586 — John Rademacher — 1968.

Single Game

Ringer Percentage — 100 — Guy Zimmerman — 1948; Elmer Hohl — 1968.

Total Ringers — 175 — Glen Henton — 1965.

Double Ringers — 80 — Glen Henton — 1965.

Consecutive Ringers — 72 — Ted Allen — 1951.

HORSESHOE PITCHING HALL OF FAME

Established in 1965 by the National Horseshoe Pitchers' Assoc., honoring famous individuals in the game dating back to 1909. One to three members may be elected annually.

Ted Allen	David Cottrell
Elmer Beller	C. C. Davis
Ellis Cobb	Curt Day
Archie Gregson	Blair Nunamaker
Elmer Hohl	Bob Pence
Raymond Howard	Jimmy Risk
Fernando Isais	Arch Stokes
Frank Jackson	Vicki Winston
Casey Jones	Harry Woodfield
Putt Mossman	Guy Zimmerman

ARCH STOKES MEMORIAL AWARD

Awarded annually by the National Association to the individual who contributed the most to the game of horseshoe pitching during the year.

1958 .	Elmer Beller	1966 .	Reinhard Backer
1959 .	Archie Gregson	1967 .	Will Gullickson
1960 .	Harold Craig	1968 .	Ralph Dykes
1961 .	Robert Pence	1969 .	Leo McGrath
1962 .	Ellis Cobb	1970 .	Wally Shipley
1963 .	Ted Allen	1971 .	Hal Hanania
1964 .	Ottie Reno	1972 .	Rollin Futrell
1965 .	Irwin Carlberg		

BASIC RULES AND REQUIREMENTS

The game of horseshoes is essentially an accuracy-type game in which the players toss objects in the form of horseshoes at a target in the form of an iron stake.

The required equipment for a game is two stakes fastened securely in the ground 40 feet apart and two horseshoes for each player. The stakes should be of iron or soft steel one inch in diameter protruding 14 inches above the ground and leaning two or three inches toward each other.

The game was originally played with real horseshoes, but now shoes manufactured specifically for the game are used. These simulate a real horseshoe and cannot exceed two and one-half pounds in weight. The tips which form the open end have rolled down edges called heel calks and the closed end has a toe calk. These calks cannot extend more than ¾ of an inch from the blade of the shoe. The opening between the heel calks cannot exceed more than three and one-half inches and the overall length of the shoe cannot exceed seven and one-half inches.

Each stake is placed in the center of an area six feet square called the pitcher's box. Players toss their shoes from within the confines of this box. In casual or picnic games the boundaries of this box are imaginary and the stakes are simply driven into the ground 40 feet apart.

Permanent facilities such as backyard courts, municipal park and playground courts, and those used by organized clubs have the stakes anchored in concrete or wooden blocks to hold them firmly in place. Generally these courts have two hard surface pitching platforms 18 inches wide and six feet long at each stake from which the players toss their shoes. These platforms are constructed inside the confines of the pitcher's box on opposite sides leaving an area six feet long by three wide in the middle. This is the target area with the stake in the middle and the better courts have his area filled with potter's or blue clay to a depth of six to eight inches. This clay is kept in a moist or puttylike condition so the shoes will not bounce or roll. Some courts use loam or sand as a substitute for the clay.

The object of the game is to pitch the horseshoe so that it comes to rest encircling the stake, or failing in that comes to rest as close to the stake as possible. Games may be singles (the "walking" game with two players as opponents) or doubles (the "partners" game with four players).

The players toss a coin to determine who starts the game by pitching first. Each player pitches two successive shoes at the opposite stake; then they travel to the opposite stake, tally the score, and pitch back to the other stake.

The doubles game has two opponents at one stake and their partners at the other stake. One pair of partners compete as a unit against the other set of partners, thus no walking between stakes is necessary. Otherwise the game is played the same as the singles or "walking" game. The points scored by one player and his partner at the opposite stake are added together as the game progresses against the total accumulated by the other pair of partners.

Basic rules to be observed are as follows:

1. A player must pitch each shoe from inside the outer edges (foul lines) of the pitcher's box and at least 18 inches from the stake. If any portion of a player's foot extends over the foul line before he releases the shoe that particular pitch is a foul and does not count in the scoring.

2. A player must stand at the rear of the pitcher's box while his opponent is delivering his shoes and must not talk or make any distracting noises or movements. A player violating this rule loses the value of both shoes pitched in that particular frame.

3. A player cannot walk to the opposite end until both players have pitched their shoes in a frame.

4. A shoe that strikes the ground outside the pitcher's box or on the hard surface of the pitching platforms and then bounces into scoring distance does not count in the scoring.

5. A shoe that breaks when pitched does not count and another shoe must be pitched in its place.

6. Shoes must not be moved until the score of that frame is tallied and should not be touched except in the process of measuring to determine the score. Players violating this rule lose the value of the shoes they pitched in that frame.

Scoring rules:

A frame consists of each player pitching two shoes at the opposite stake.

A "ringer" is a shoe that encircles the stake in such a manner that a straightedge can be laid across the open end of the shoe touching both prongs without touching the stake.

A shoe leaning against the stake has the same value as one touching the stake but lying on the ground.

When each player throws a "ringer" or when each player throws two "ringers" in a frame the "ringers" cancel each other.

Shoes of opposing players that are equal distance from the stake in the same frame are regarded as ties and cancel each other, the next closest shoe scoring one point providing it is within six inches of the stake.

Shoes must be within six inches of the stake to count in the scoring. This distance may be increased for novices and beginners.

The player who scores in a frame pitches first in the next frame. If no points are scored in a frame the player who pitched last in that frame pitches first in the next frame.

Scoring values:

A game consists of enough frames for one player to accumulate 50 points. Local rules may lower this official game figure. Years ago an official game consisted of 21 points and this total is still used in many picnic and casual type games.

A player scores one (1) point in a frame when one of his shoes is closer to the stake than either of his opponent's shoes providing it is within six inches of the stake.

A player scores one (1) point in a frame when he and his opponent each have a "ringer" and his remaining shoe is closer to the stake than his opponent's remaining shoe, providing it is within six inches of the stake.

A player scores two (2) points in a frame when both of his shoes are within six inches of the stake and closer than either of his opponent's shoes.

A player scores three (3) points in a frame when one of his shoes is a "ringer" providing his opponent does not have a "ringer" in that frame.

A player scores three (3) points in a frame when both of his shoes are "ringers" and one of his opponent's shoes is a "ringer."

A player scores four (4) points in a frame when one of his shoes is a "ringer" and his remaining shoe is within at least six inches of the stake and closer than either of his opponent's shoes.

A player scores six (6) points in a frame when both of his shoes are "ringers" and neither of his opponent's shoes are "ringers".

Three-handed games between three players, commonly called "cut-throat games," are played under the same rules except that a player who does not have a "ringer" in a frame is out of contention in that frame and the points are determined between the two remaining players on the same basis as in a two-handed game.

Women and juniors pitch a distance of 30 feet. This distance may be reduced for extremely young players. Otherwise the rules are the same. The age for junior players is generally set at below 17 years.

HORSE-SHOE COURT LAYOUT

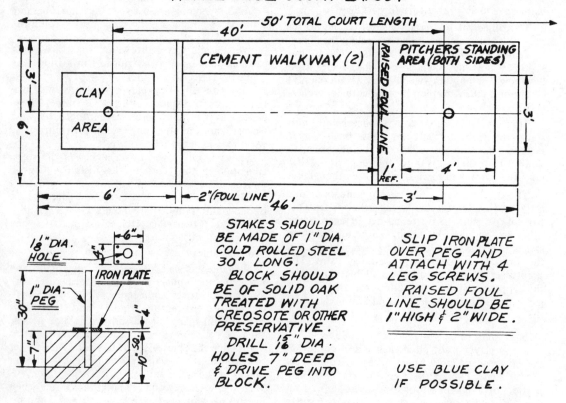

STAKES SHOULD BE MADE OF 1" DIA. COLD ROLLED STEEL 30" LONG.

BLOCK SHOULD BE OF SOLID OAK TREATED WITH CREOSOTE OR OTHER PRESERVATIVE.

DRILL 1⅝" DIA. HOLES 7" DEEP & DRIVE PEG INTO BLOCK.

SLIP IRON PLATE OVER PEG AND ATTACH WITH 4 LEG SCREWS.

RAISED FOUL LINE SHOULD BE 1"HIGH & 2"WIDE.

USE BLUE CLAY IF POSSIBLE.

HORSE SHOWS

Before the development and widespread distribution of the automobile, the horse played a vital role in man's work and play. Naturally, owners of horses became fond and proud of them and were eager to match them against the animals of others.

One phase of this competition evolved into the horse show, and in the beginning contests involved equine-minded persons of all social classes. The first horse show was held in 1883. In the 1890's the horse show became a great annual social event for the "aristrocracy" in the New York area. The biggest shows on this continent are held yearly in New York, Harrisburg, Pa.; Toronto, Ont., and Kansas City, Mo.

The first show was democratic, as to the horses on display and the customers who wan-

dered around Gilmore's Gardens, an exhibition place in New York, which predated the Old Madison Square Garden.

But for no reason ever fully explained, society seized upon the Horse Show as a place to display its precious jewels and gaudy finery. The custom continues, and the opening of the National Horse Show vies with the annual opening at the Metropolitan Opera House for splendor.

The pioneer event in Gilmore's Gardens by the newly organized National Horse Show Association of America—Oct. 22 to 26, 1883—was "open to all comers," and almost all possible comers in the way of equine species were on the premises.

There were 165 exhibitors and 299 competing horses. Prancing thoroughbreds, high stepping trotters—these were housed under the same roof as fire-engine horses, buggy-horses, street-car horses, delivery-wagon horses, Shetland ponies, policemen's mounts, mighty draught horses, average farm horses and even a few donkeys—were among the entries to give the final touch to the occasion.

High drama was added to the first show by the appearance for a jog around the track of Goldsmith Maid, the most beloved trotting horse of her time. This magnificent speed marvel, then 26, acted like a modest prima donna while on parade, and the chronicles of the times stated that "Goldsmith Maid was greeted by wildest enthusiasm."

The success of that first show, enjoyed by exhibitors and audience alike, decided the promoters to make it an annual event and there has been a horse show in New York every year since, except in 1889, when Gilmore's Gardens was torn down, and some of the war years—1914, 1943, 1944, 1945. The show was moved to the old Madison Square Garden in 1890 and was staged there until the building was demolished. Then it was moved to the new Garden.

The second show—that of 1884—with its collection of ponies that were worth about $25 each and its full-sized horses of mediocre breeding, was featured by the entrance of a team of roadsters owned by J. B. Houston of New York and valued at $20,000. They won the championship of the show and a cup valued at $300. Immediately the wealthy owners of other superb horses began reaching for entry blanks, and the Horse Show soon became the place where horsemen had a chance to display their equine stars.

Within a decade, the Horse Show went very social. The display of animals became secondary to the display of gowns and cloaks. It was an annual gathering place of beauty, aristrocracy and wealth. A word picture was sketched in The New York Times some years ago by Charles Smith, then one of the few persons still alive who had seen the first Horse Show and all succeeding ones.

"In the 90's," Smith pointed out, "New York society took over the Horse Show for its very own. Society women spent huge sums for clothes and for gems with intent to display them for the first time at the Horse Show and bedazzle all beholders.

"The average spectators crowded the promenades and viewed society as it sat enthroned in boxes of old Madison Square Garden, which was new then, and a magnificent edifice for the times.

"In 1896 a newspaper made a cost estimate of $13,000, for morning, afternoon and evening gowns, and wraps, properly to outfit a society woman for the show.

"One woman of note in the 90's left her box in the early days of the show to avoid the stares of the promenaders. She couldn't endure the ordeal. This woman was the famous beauty and actress, Lily Langtry.

"The greatest crowd of earlier days was at the show in 1895 when the Duke of Malborough and his bride of a day, the former Miss Consuelo Vanderbilt, were among the spectators. Gowns and corsage bouquets were crushed and men's immaculate shirt fronts disarranged as the crowd milled in front of the box of W. K. Vanderbilt, father of the bride, eager to see the new Duchess and her husband. But the newlyweds, both plainly dressed, sat in ordinary seats just behind the box and were unnoticed.

"I still can see E. Barry Wall, the Beau Brummel of New York, with his high pointed collar, driving his tandem cart in the ring, and the late August Belmont, judging classes, 50 years ago.

"Recollection is still fresh of the visit of the Prince of Wales, later Edward VIII, who abdicated the throne, at a matinee performance in 1919. He was a very personable, democratic young man, who held his bowler hat in one hand, and fumbled with his tie with the other, while receiving a tremendous ovation.

"One of the amusing things of an earlier era was the search for a horse that had been entered but couldn't be located. It was at the height of the hunt that a serious fellow, studying the entry blank, came to conclude—and rightly so—that the entry had been made by a wag. The name of the horse given was 'Street Car, by Rapid Transit, out of Electric.' "

During the period from 1883 to 1913, the National Horse Show officials awarded 10,000 prizes to 7,398 exhibitors who had made 38,000 entries in the 3,317 different events. After 1913 came a radical change. There was a general weeding out of events that had been exclusively for work horses of one type or another, simply because these almost had ceased to exist, because of the motorizing of street cars, fire engines and various other conveyances.

Substituting for the original events were new ones especially framed for the new breed of show horses. In the years since, the trend has been more and more in that direction until today, almost the only horse that has a chance to win is one bred especially for such a task, or a thoroughbred or a standard-bred trained thoroughly.

The success of the early New York shows led to the staging of similar, but much less elaborate, events elsewhere in the United States. As these increased in number, there was formed the American Horse Shows Association, with headquarters in New York, which became the supervising body.

In the years since horse shows became established entertainment features there have been bred special species of horse—the hackney and saddle horse—for horse show purpose. Great stress has been put on different gaits at which horses can travel, the three-gaited and especially the five-gaited horse being greatly in favor. Quite a few types of horses are bred only for show purposes and during the peak of their careers are shipped around the nation to compete for rich prizes.

The horse show now is a year-round sport—indoors in the winter, outdoors in the warm months.

Some of the smaller shows award only ribbons and cups. The others, additionally, offer cash.

Owning show horses is strictly a rich man's sport because the prizes that can be won, even by the champions, hardly equal the maintenance cost. Some years ago there was much comment because a show horse won $2,780, which was something of a record. The money won still left the owner about $700 to $1,200 short of enough to pay for the animal's upkeep.

Of course, if an owner develops a great stallion or mare, this animal will recompense him somewhat with stud fees or by sale to a breeder. The gifted five-gaited Gold Digger sold for $10,000 and this more than repaid for his original cost and maintenance.

Perhaps the greatest show horse of all time was Sweetheart-on-Parade—an aptly-named mare. She won the Grand National championship for five-gaited horses twice—1931 and 1932—in an apparent climax of a brilliant career. She then was retired by her owner, Mrs. H. P. Roth.

During the next three years there was considerable praise for newer champions and comparisons were made of them with Sweetheart-on-Parade. While there was much hurrahing over the younger mares that had been gaining glory with Sweetheart in retirement, Mrs. Roth created a surprise by bringing her back and entering her in the mares' division of the Board of Governors Stake in Kansas City, Oct. 24, 1935.

Sweetheart-on-Parade, then a bit old, still had enough class to conquer all opposition and she was adjudged the champion and winner of the $500 prize, a tremendously popular triumph.

The program for the show in New York, which usually runs along for eight days, includes 115 to 125 different events. They bring sectional champions of the season into competition with each other, as well as against former national champions.

The New York program is so arranged as to give competitive opportunity to practically all types of show horses. There are contests for the three-gaited horses (walk, trot and canter), the five-gaited horses (walk, trot, canter, step and pace, known as slow gait, and the rack, a very fast gait), many events for saddle horses; there are contests for jumping horses and for horses trained for the hunts.

There are driving contests—singles, teams and tandems—for experienced harness horses and also novices, for experienced and novice drivers, for women as well as men. But the popular event is the competition for the military, in which the greatest horsemen from all parts of the world meet the best American riders in a series of daredevil jumping contests.

While the hackneys, the new type saddle horse, the harness horses, the thoroughbred jumpers, the inter-bred hunters and other types usually compete in their own classes, there are many competitions open to any horse its owner might care to enter. The decisions are made by men who are authorities on the capabilities conformation or championship requirements of the breed they are judging.

The hackney and the modern hunter horse, especially the former, are developments of an intense desire on the part of the British to get distinct types of show horses. The hackney was produced by breeding an Arabian sire to a Norfolk trotting mare. The direct result was a colt named Shales, differing radically from both parents in conformation, and, when used as a stallion, was immediately capable of reproducing his own distinctive kind.

In producing the distinct breed called the "saddle horse," the horsemen first mated a thoroughbred stallion with a trotting mare. Then they bred another thoroughbred stallion to the crossbred mare which resulted from the first mating. This procedure was continued until they had a horse of their desire, who was named "Gaines Denmark 61," shortened to "Denmark"; and he was established as the founder of the species.

The New York group discontinued its shows when World War II produced transportation difficulties for men and animals. Many smaller shows also were suspended. The New York show was resumed in 1946, with all the social fanfare and grandeur of the last fifty or fifty-five years, which have made this exhibition unique, and, in a way, the most extraordinary of its kind in the world.

In 1972 a total of 17,500 horse shows were held, 4,500 of them in the U.S. and Canada. The American Horse Shows Association sponsored 90 shows in the U.S. and Canada with $2 million in prizes being offered. The association is concerned with promoting the interests of the sport, making and enforcing uniform rules, licensing judges, settling disputes, maintaining permanent records and disseminating information.

Each year it keeps records of what amount to national championship standings in the many horse show divisions. The championships are determined on a point basis for several shows and the silver trophies distributed to winners at the annual winter meeting are eagerly sought.

HURLING

(Courtesy of Thomas C. Curran, Secretary, New York Gaelic Athletic Association)

Hurling is as traditionally Irish as the shamrock, and as ancient as the Round Towers of the Emerald Isle. History records that the game was played in Ireland centuries before the coming of St. Patrick. Lovers of the sport read with pride of the great hurling feats and other athletic achievements of Cuchulain, a Munster Prince who while journeying to the great Annual Athletic Hostings at Tara, seat of the High Kings of Ireland in County Meath, amused himself by striking a hurling ball into the air many yards ahead and repeating this feat as he ran without allowing the ball to touch the ground. In this manner he arrived on the plains of Tara, to the consternation of the other athletes assembled there, and was cordially received by the beautiful Queen Maeve.

"Hurling," advised Wedger Meagher, Sports Editor of the "Irish Echo" of New York, "is a game that looks dangerous to the uninitiated, and spectators seeing it for the first time wonder why there are not many serious injuries. Rarely do players get badly hurt and while minor cuts and bruises may be frequent, serious accidents are comparatively few.

"Hurling is a scientific game, and in order to attain proficiency in the art the game must be taken up at an early age for it requires years of intensive practice to attain the efficiency necessary for big-time competition. Like all other games, hurling has become modernized. A century ago in Ireland it was parish against parish with teams of unlimited numbers. The game was usually started on the boundary between the parishes, and the team that succeeded in taking the ball a certain distance into its own territory was declared victorious.

"When the Gaelic Athletic Association was founded in Ireland in 1884 rules governing Hurling and Gaelic Football were made; goal and point posts were introduced, and a team was made up of twenty-one players. Some years later the number of players on a team was reduced to seventeen and still later to the present number of fifteen.

"The Gaelic Athletic Association controls hurling throughout the thirty-two countries of Ireland and does not recognize the much disputed British Border, which cuts off the six counties of Ulster.

"It is interesting to note that the competition for the All-Ireland championship has been held annually since 1887 without interruption except in 1888 when the teams toured the United States.

"Emigrant Irish hurlers continued to play the game in the land of their adoption, with the result that long before the Gaelic Athletic Association was formed in New York in 1914, hurling and Gaelic football were played in the principal cities along the Eastern seaboard, in Chicago and San Francisco.

"Celtic Park, in Queens, Long Island, headquarters of the famous Irish-American A.C., which produced many Olympic track and field champions, was for years the venue for hurling and Gaelic football in New York. But in recent years Croke Park, 240th Street and Broadway, has become the 'Home of the Gaels'.

ALL-IRELAND CHAMPIONS

1887—Tipperary	1909—Kilkenny	1931—Cork	1953—Cork
1888—No competition	1910—Wexford	1932—Kilkenny	1954—Cork
1889—Dublin	1911—Kilkenny	1933—Kilkenny	1955—Wexford
1890—Cork	1912—Kilkenny	1934—Limerick	1956—Wexford
1891—Kerry	1913—Kilkenny	1935—Kilkenny	1957—Kilkenny
1892—Cork	1914—Clare	1936—Limerick	1958—Tipperary
1893—Cork	1915—Leix	1937—Tipperary	1959—Waterford
1894—Cork	1916—Tipperary	1938—Dublin	1960—Wexford
1895—Tipperary	1917—Dublin	1939—Kilkenny	1961-62—Tipperary
1896—Tipperary	1918—Limerick	1940—Limerick	1963—Kilkenny
1897—Limerick	1919—Cork	1941—Cork	1964-65—Tipperary
1898—Tipperary	1920—Dublin	1942—Cork	1966-67—Kilkenny
1899—Tipperary	1921—Limerick	1943—Cork	1968—Wexford
1900—Tipperary	1922—Kilkenny	1944—Cork	1969—Tipperary
1901—London-Irish	1923—Galway	1945—Tipperary	1970—Cork
1902—Cork	1924—Dublin	1946—Cork	1971—Tipperary
1903—Cork	1925—Tipperary	1947—Kilkenny	1972—Kilkenny
1904—Kilkenny	1926—Cork	1948—Waterford	
1905—Kilkenny	1927—Dublin	1949—Tipperary	
1906—Tipperary	1928—Cork	1950—Tipperary	
1907—Kilkenny	1929—Cork	1951—Tipperary	
1908—Tipperary	1930—Tipperary	1952—Cork	

BASIC RULES OF HURLING

The game is played on a field 140 yards long and 80 yards wide. A team consists of 15 players. The ball used is 9 to 10 inches in circumference, and in weight it ranges between 3¼ and 4 ounces. Generally, it has a cork center, with a cover of horsehide. The stick (hurley) is something like a field hockey stick—curved, with a rather broad blade. There is no standard as to the weight. The stick is 4 inches at its widest part, tapering off toward each end, and is 3 feet long.

Scoring can be accomplished in two ways: if the ball, hurled by the stick, lands in the net strung between the goal posts, it counts 3 points; if over the crossbar between the goal posts, 1 point. The goal posts are 16 feet high, 21 feet apart, with a crossbar 8 feet above the ground.

The trick of the game is for the player to catch the ball on the stick, run with it, if he can, and then hurl it. The player is not permitted to pick the ball off the ground with his hand; he must do so with his stick. The player may pick the ball off his stick; but he cannot run with it, or throw it with his hand.

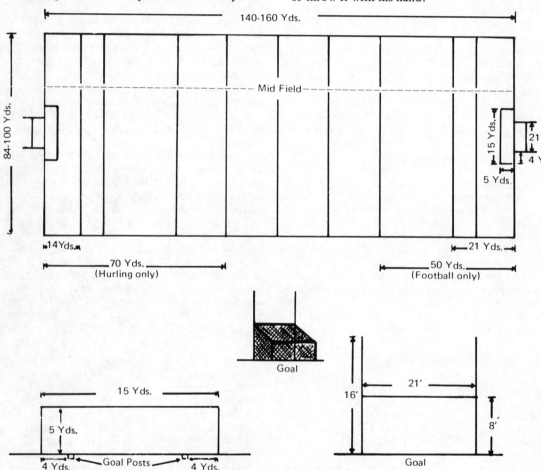

Gaelic Football and Hurling Field

ICE BOATING

Two things are necessary for ice boating—ice and courage. Unfortunately for devotees of the sport the former is frequently missing, particularly in the East. Sometimes the hardy ice boat sailors have to wait years and years for a good go at their sport. But they don't mind it. Even though there are years when they can get in only a couple of days of sailing over frozen water, these hardy outdoorsmen are ready for a spin at every opportunity.

Ice boating, like water boating, has undergone a great change in the past 25 years. Formerly a rich man's sport, with boats costing several thousands of dollars and professional skippers and crews the order of the day whenever an important trophy was at stake, the sport today is confined almost entirely to small, light, but extremely fast boats, often built by their owners.

These are so easily carried on top of a car that fans no longer wait for ice on their home waters, but travel far afield to regattas, taking advantage of modern highways and cars to widen their area of active sailing. By traveling in this way, it is possible for the iceboater to sail from early December until late March in a normally cold winter. Even in recent years with record-breaking mildness of weather, the mountain lakes of Northwestern New Jersey have furnished fine iceboating.

In a severe winter, when these lakes are snowed under, there will be ice on the waters of the Hudson, Navesink and Shrewsbury rivers, as well as the Great South Bay along Long Island's outer beach. Similar variations of conditions are possible in the Mid-Western iceboating region, comprising roughly the states of Wisconsin, Michigan, Northern Ohio and Northern Illinois, as well as the province of Ontario, immediately adjacent to these states.

Between these two areas, stretching roughly from Buffalo to Newburgh, N.Y., there is a wide belt that suffers severely from snow, and does not get sufficient rainy or warm weather to cut the snow down. As a result, throughout this region, the sport never has prospered, though a few boats will be found on almost every sizable lake.

The Dutch seem to have been the first iceboaters, although the Finns and Lapps and others living around the Baltic Sea no doubt contrived some sort of "sailing sleigh," as the Austrians call it, at a very early date. We have an actual drawing of a Dutch iceboat dating from 1790 and a photo taken in 1937 showing identical boats taking passengers for rides in the Netherlands. These Dutch craft were really boats, since they were simply the regular summer sailing craft, with a strong cross plank under the hull near the bow, having a runner at each end, and a sharp iron shoe on the bottom of the boat's regular rudder, at the stern. Any iceboater can see at a glance that although these cannot be fast, because of their baggy sails and generally inefficient rig, they are no doubt very rugged, able to carry a dozen or more people, and need inspire no fear of thin ice.

Similar boats no doubt appeared along the banks of the Dutch-settled Hudson River at an early date. We do know that in 1790 one Oliver Booth sailed an iceboat on the frozen river at Poughkeepsie, N.Y. Within a few years similar craft were sailing the frozen waters around Red Bank and Long Branch, N.J.

Immediately after the Civil War, interest in sports gained rapidly, and iceboating was no exception. The Poughkeepsie Ice Yacht Club was formed in 1869, followed within a few years by the New Hamburgh and Hudson River Ice Yacht Clubs. The latter organization, located at Hyde Park, N.Y., flourished under the patronage of a large group of millionaire sportsmen, including Archibald Rogers and John E. Roosevelt, an uncle of President Franklin Delano Roosevelt, who was himself an officer of the club at one time.

The club fleet in 1900 mustered over 50 yachts, including 6 giants of the First Class, with over 600 square feet of sail. The 2 most famous yachts of this club were Rogers' Jack Frost, probably the best designed, built and equipped ice yacht of her day, and John Roosevelt's Icicle, of almost identical design. Jack Frost, a five-time winner of the Ice Yacht Challenge Pennant of America, had the advantage of a meticulously built backbone, or keel, contributed by no less a master than Nat Herreshoff of Bristol, R.I., and all her fittings and rigging were the finest that could be had.

Icicle also won this prize banner 4 times. She is being carefully preserved on the Roosevelt estate and may be seen on exhibition, along with a smaller boat owned by Franklin D. Roosevelt, in the Roosevelt Memorial Library at Hyde Park. As an interesting sidelight on the grand manner in which these Hudson River families lived, Icicle was almost entirely constructed of choice butternut timbers grown right on the Roosevelt estate. Her builder was Jacob Buckhout of Poughkeepsie, who, with his son George, was far and away the country's foremost iceboat designer and builder until 1930—that is, during the era of the big boat, the wealthy owner and the professional skipper. Smaller boats were built and sailed more often than the big ones, but never won major trophies.

The development of the sport at Long Branch and Red Bank followed a similar pattern and the boats were similar to those of the Hudson. From 1883 to 1902 the North Shrewsbury Ice Boat and Yacht Club of Red Bank sent its best boats to the Hudson to challenge for the Ice Yacht Challenge Pennant of America on 7 occasions. To the credit of Icicle and Jack Frost, the record shows they never lost a race, and the Pennant never left the Hudson. It reposes in the Roosevelt Memorial Library, alongside the Icicle, while a replica has been returned to competition under the sponsorship of the Eastern Ice Yachting Association and is currently held by the Pewaukee Ice Yacht Club of Wisconsin.

Iceboating on the Hudson died after 1902, and the centers of activity shifted to the Jersey rivers mentioned above, as well as to the Mid-West where the sport became active and flourishing in Kalamazoo, Mich., and Madison and Oshkosh, Wis. The boats in use were still almost all of the basic Hudson River pattern, consisting of a single fore-and-aft stick or spar, called "backbone" or "keelson," mounted just ahead of its midpoint on a broad, flexible wooden plank called the "runner plank," which had a runner mounted at each of its extremities. The third running blade was pivoted through the after end of the backbone and controlled by a tiller. The helmsman and crew man (only 2 men sailed these huge boats as a rule) clung precariously to a shallow, elliptical tray just ahead of the steering runner.

The mast was stepped on the backbone, several feet ahead of the runner plank. The rig, almost without exception, was jib-and-mainsail.

From 1879, when H. Relyea built the Robert Scott on the Hudson, until 1947, when Carl Bernard and Frank Tetzlaff constructed the Mary B. at Madison, the only changes made in design of this stern-steering type of yacht were refinements of materials and rigging.

To the credit of the older boats go the speed records, too. In 1885, Commodore James Weaver sailed the Scud at 107 miles an hour on the Navesink River at Red Bank; in 1907 Commodore Elisha Price sailed the Clarel at 144 miles an hour on the Shrewsbury River at Long Branch; in 1908 the Wolverine of Kalamazoo, Mich., sailed the fastest 20 miles to windward and return recorded to 1953, covering the course from a standing start in 39 minutes 4 seconds. There is a record of 4 yachts sailing together down the Hudson from Poughkeepsie to New Hamburgh (9 miles) at an average of 84 miles an hour! Clearly, in those days, the iceboat was the fastest vehicle man had yet produced, and when considered in the light of the fact that it has no engine of any kind, its performances still seem phenomenal.

Speeds of these magnitudes are not commonplace in iceboating, but they have been repeatedly accomplished by well-rigged and well-sailed boats when conditions were favorable—plenty of room, clear, hard ice and a strong wind. To the uninitiated, sailing faster than the wind is hard to believe, yet it is by just this means that such speeds are made. As far as experiments show, about the best the iceboat can accomplish is approximately 4 times the speed of the wind that is blowing at the time. This speed is not a simple phenomenon to explain, but if it is borne in mind that (1) the boat is sailing *across* the wind and is not being pushed along by it and (2) by her very motion the boat creates an increase in the velocity of the wind she sails with, it may become more understandable. The truth of the matter is that the boat *never* sails faster than the wind that is driving her.

On a day with a gentle breeze of 8 to 10 miles strength, a well-handled iceboat can sail 35 to 40 miles an hour and her occupants will feel a regular gale in their faces as she does it. The limit to this process is set by the fact that the faster the boat moves, the more the wind tends to strike her from straight ahead. The boat whose sail can

develop driving power at the smallest wind angle off dead ahead is the boat that will develop the greatest speed.

These principles were only vaguely known in the early days, and the traditional jib-and-mainsail rig with rudder at the stern was so firmly entrenched that experiments with other types of rig and hull design were few and far between and usually unsuccessful.

The fact that the terrific forward thrust sometimes lifted the steering runner from the ice, sending the whole boat into a mad spin, was accepted as one of the facts of iceboating, annoying but incurable. Perfect tuning of the boat and perfect handling by the sailor could minimize but never could eliminate this built-in tendency to become unmanageable in strong winds.

About 1931, Starke Meyer of Milwaukee, Wis., began experimenting with models of iceboats and became convinced that a boat with steering runner at the bow and runner-plank aft, like a tricycle, would not spin. He reasoned that the downward and forward thrust of the mast, now located between steering runner and runner-plank, could serve only to increase rudder traction, rather than the opposite. There was no doubt of the correctness of his reasoning when his first bow-steerer easily ran away from all competition in her first season on the ice.

But other revelations were yet to come. Following the well-established belief that a winning boat had to be a big boat, Meyer's early bow-steerers were relatively large craft, carrying 250 square feet of sail—Class B of the Northwestern Ice Yachting Association. Like all experimenters, Meyer learned the hard way that to be safe, a bow-steering iceboat must be long enough and wide enough to carry her sail in a strong wind without excessive "hiking"—rearing up on 2 runners.

Sailing one windy day, his boat hiked high and fast, and capsized. Her mast shattered and the hull fell on him. After weeks in the hospital, he recovered, but the story of his accident nearly stopped development of the bow-steerer before it had really started.

The idea then appeared in a new form—a bow-steering boat again, but this time with a sail of only 75 square feet. To the amazement of all, this little marvel could sail safely and fast long after bigger boats had been forced to quit by the gale. For it was now clear that the bow-steerer would not spin—that she was inherently correctly balanced and directionally stable. It remained only for experiment to determine the best proportions of length to width to size and height of sail plan to minimize the capsizing hazard and produce a real racer.

Within a decade the job was done. By 1940 wild experiments were the exception rather than the rule they had been only 3 years previously. The design had crystallized by reason of a great resurgence of interest in the sport, prompted by the low cost, ease of construction and amazing performance of these small bow-steerers. The 75-square-foot sail area class enjoyed a rapid growth and by 1950 was winning not only its own class races, but also open and free-for-all events of all sorts. The days of the big boat, the wealthy owner and the professional skipper are gone and probably will never return. They were picturesque and grand, but the little modern boats have broadened the appeal of the sport tremendously.

Other classes still exist, but very few boats are built in them, and it is safe to predict that as the older large boats are discarded, they will not be replaced. As final evidence of what has happened, in March 1953, the Pewaukee Ice Yacht Club won the Ice Yacht Challenge Pennant of America from the Fox Lake Ice Yacht Club of Chicago at Lake Geneva, Wis. Three races were sailed, each of 20 miles, half to windward and half to leeward. All 3 races broke the old record of Wolverine referred to above, and the time for the final heat, 29 minutes 4 seconds, probably will stand for some time. All boats sailing were 75-square foot "Skeeters," as they are called. Wolverine carried 650 square feet of canvas. All 4 boats traveled to the race site on top of ordinary automobiles. When Wolverine left her home port, a special freight car was required. These Skeeters weigh about 300 pounds, Wolverine nearly a ton.

Iceboats since the earliest times have been classified for racing purposes by measuring their sail area. This relatively simple system served to encourage experiments with both hull and rig, since no penalty was incurred by building an unconventional boat, and the matter of seaworthiness, responsible for many of the limitations placed on sailboat designers, was obviously not a factor.

Reflecting the progress of the sport, the classes set up by the Hudson River Ice Yacht Club, and followed at Long Branch and Red Bank also, before 1900 were as follows:

First Class—Over 600 square feet
Second Class—450 to 600 square feet
Third Class—300 to 450 square feet
Fourth Class—225 to 300 square feet
Fifth Class—Under 225 square feet

By 1923, although the Hudson River was no longer an active center, the classes recognized by the Northwestern Ice Yachting Association were the following:

Class A—250 to 350 square feet
Class B—175 to 250 square feet
Class C—Up to 175 square feet

The few remaining boats of over 350-square-foot sail area were raced for various challenge cups and trophies, but were already so scarce that they did not warrant recognition as a class. Classification in the East followed suit and in 1923 both Red Bank and Long Branch recognized Class A as 200—350 square feet and Class B at "under 200 square feet."

By 1935 the Northwestern Association recognized the growth of smaller-sized boats and added Class D, 75 to 125 square feet, and Class E, up to 75 square feet.

In 1937 seven active Eastern clubs formed the Eastern Ice Yachting Association, patterned after the 25-year-old Northwestern Association and recognizing the same classes, with a minor difference: the 250-foot class is known as Class X, so as to allow the 200-foot class to retain its identity and connection with several pre-association trophies. Membership in both these associations varies as their various member clubs prosper, but in general the Eastern Association includes a group of clubs in the New York—New Jersey—Connecticut area.

The growth of the smallest recognized class—E, at 75 square feet—was so rapid that by 1939 there was a need for a single-class organization devoted to this class alone, after the example of the International Star Class and other similar "1-design" classes in water yachting.

Accordingly, the International Skeeter Association was founded, with headquarters in Chicago, since the greatest activity and development in this class were taking place in the Northern Illinois Southern Wisconsin area. The term "Skeeter," at first loosely applied to any bow-steering iceboat, was limited to the 75-square-foot class once this association was formed.

Activity was also brisk around Detroit, where Lake St. Clair offers a wide expanse of sailable ice, and although Detroit remains one of the last strongholds of the really big boats, it likewise rapidly became the center of experimentation and development in Class E, with the emphasis on high, narrow sails, as contrasted with the lower, more squatty sail plans developed on the Western side of Lake Michigan.

Toronto and Hamilton, Ont., came to life also, and the bow springboard, a short, springy plank extending forward of the regular bow and carrying the steering runner, was developed by Gordon Reid of Toronto.

Many names are connected with this recent and very active development period, but outstanding are those of Ted Mead, Chicago, who turned a toy into a racing yacht; Harry Nye, Chicago, who finally discovered how to cut a sail for an iceboat (because of the high air-speed over an iceboat's sail, it must be shaped differently, be made of more rugged material, and even mounted on the spars in a different way from typical sailboat practice); Howard Boston, Detroit, who discovered how to cut an iceboat sail of nylon; Gordon Reid, inventor of the bow springboard, and Elmer Millenbach of Detroit, probably the finest and most consistent skipper, as well as one of the topflight designers and builders of modern small racers. Millenbach's Renegade, though smaller than the typical Skeeter and carrying only 68 square feet of sail, has established such an outstanding record of victories, not only in the Skeeter (75-square-foot) Class, but also unlimited free-for-all competition against everything, that she was made the prototype of a real One-Design Class, with identical construction, dimensions, materials and weights required of all members.

Most of these racing Skeeters are single-seaters, precluding the possibility of carrying a passenger for pleasure sailing, or for instruction in handling an iceboat. The need for a 2-seater boat was felt both in the East and the West and crystallized in the founding in 1948 of a second 1-design class, this time in the East, appropriately called the "Yankee," with an orthodox 2-seater as the accepted design. Although relatively slow at first, Yankees now are competing on even terms with single-seater racers.

Both the Northwestern and the Eastern associations try to conduct annual championship regattas, to which members clubs may send their best boats in all recognized classes. In 1953 the Northwestern Association voted to admit the few remaining boats of over 350 square feet to Class A so that any iceboat in the Mid-West is eligible to take part.

The International Skeeter Association held its 1953 championship regatta on Lake Geneva, Wis. Fifty boats appeared at the starting line for the 5-race series. The winner, with 3 firsts, a second and a third, was Frank Trost's unnamed yacht No. V–80. In second place, with 1 first, 2 seconds, a third and a fourth, was Renegade III, and third, scoring 9–3–4–3–1, was Thunderjet, owned by William Perrigo of Milwaukee.

In 1951, the New Hamburgh Ice Yacht Club, inactive for 25 years since the Hudson River failed to provide safe ice, turned over custody and stewardship of the famous Ice Yacht Challenge Pennant of America, first put up by them in 1881, to the Eastern Ice Yachting Association. When an examination disclosed that the original silk streamer, some 30 feet in length, was too weak to stand handling, it was decided to place it in the Roosevelt Memorial Library at Hyde Park, under glass.

A replica was made of nylon and placed in competition at any open invitation regatta at Greenwood Lake, N.J., Feb. 18, 1951. All known clubs in the world were invited to compete. Most distant challengers were Ed Rollberg, representing the Fox Lake (Ill.) Ice Yacht Club and Millenbach. Rollberg won a close series from Millenbach, both easily defeating 15 Eastern clubs.

Weather prevented racing for the Pennant in 1952, but on March 1, 1953, Fox Lake defended the trophy against a challenge from the Pewaukee Ice Yacht Club, Pewaukee, Wis., at Lake Geneva. Bill Perrigo, sailing Thunderjet, and Frank Trost, at the helm of Tuscarora, captured the Pennant for Pewaukee. Trost, in Tuscarora, and Chuck Kotovic, sailing Snow Goose, successfully defended in 1954. Kotovic and Perrigo retained the honors for Pewaukee in 1955. In 1956, Kotovic and Tom Norris, at the helm of Seabiscuit III, defended successfully, as did Trost, with Perrigo again, and Kotovic, with Snow Goose, in 1957. Poor ice conditions prevented competition for the Pennant in 1958.

Since this trophy is open to any size boat and to any club in the world, it is the top award in the sport.

In the Mid-West, interest in the larger boats is kept alive by competition for 2 fine cups, both by tradition open only to the boats of Class A and larger, though there seems to be nothing in the actual wording of their Deeds of Gift to prevent challenge by smaller yachts. Older, and for the larger class (originally over 600 square feet) is the Stuart Cup, put up in 1903, and in recent years held alternately by Madison, Oshkosh and Detroit.

The second large-boat trophy is the Hearst Cup, put up in 1904 by William Randolph Hearst for competition in the 450-foot class, since then opened to Class A at 350.

Before World War II, European iceboating was very active and well organized, under the Europaeischen Ice Yachting Union. Member nations included Sweden. Latvia, Esthonia, Germany, Austria. Competition was held annually in several classes, and 1 One-Design class of about the same size as our Class C. No bow-steering boats were used and rigs were almost universally single-sail, or "cat"; the backbone was a hull, or fuselage, with pilot and passenger sitting upright, and steering done by a wheel. All these elements are characteristic of the American bow-steerer, which has been proven over and over again to be much faster. Although contact never was formally established across the Atlantic, correspondence and comparisons of ideas went on with the result that Americans, borrowing freely the efficient cat rig, fuselage backbone and safe, comfortable pilot's position, developed the modern terrifically fast racer when they made it into a bow-steering design.

On the other hand, Europeans refused to use the bow-steerer, no doubt because of some ill-fated poorly-designed first attempt. Since the war some iceboating is again carried on in Germany, and Sweden has continued on right through the years. It is hoped that international, and possibly Olympic, iceboating may soon become a reality.

ICE HOCKEY

Among the most action-packed sports is Ice Hockey. A swift moving game, Ice Hockey provides rough body contact and demands skillful skating and expert stickhandling. A well-organized passing attack is a treat to behold. Most professional players are Canadians, who start developing their skills at any early age. With the recent increase in artificial ice rinks, especially at colleges and preparatory schools, the caliber of play by United States athletes has improved.

Although the origin of ice hockey, it is agreed by competent authorities, can be placed in Eastern Canada in the second half of the 19th Century, the birthplace and date of the sport long have been the subjects of debate.

The debates might have made pleasant off-season or "hot stove league" discussions for generations and generations of devotees had not a movement begun some years ago to establish a Hockey Hall of Fame.

The governing officials of hockey decided upon the plan of awarding the site of the Hall of Fame to the community that could best produce evidence that it was the game's birthplace. The strongest bids were made by Montreal, Kingston and Halifax.

To the satisfaction of the accredited committee appointed by the Canadian Amateur Hockey Association, Kingston offered the best claims and thus to that Ontario city was awarded the Hall of Fame.

With such designation, of course, went official hockey's blessings to that community as the birthplace of the ice sport. Bitter repercussions resulted. The once pleasant debate had become very much of a sore point with, for example, some Montreal inhabitants. The subject now had become a cause of rapidly rising blood pressure in some people.

The findings of the three-man investigating committee—its members were William A. Hewitt, George Slater and Capt. James T. Sutherland—traced the game in Kingston back to 1855. The first players were members of Her Majesty's Royal Canadian Rifles, an Imperial Army unit, and the scene of their activity was the harbor to the rear of Tête du Pont barracks. Indeed, there even was a suggestion that as early as the 1830's hockey (or shinny, one of several sports from which ice hockey is said to have been derived) was played in the Kingston area.

On the subject of derivation, incidentally, there is vagueness, too. Some experts have traced the game to field hockey, others to shinny, or hurley, and still others to the European game of bandy. The word "hockey" is said to be an Anglicization of "hoquet," the French term for a shepherd's stick, which resembles the stick with which hockey is played.

Counterclaims from Montreal concerning the birth of hockey insisted that whatever game was played elsewhere, the first game of true ice hockey was played in Montreal by teams of McGill University students in 1875. Complicating this contention, however, was research which indicated that the McGill student responsible for introducing the sport to his college—his name was J. G. A. Creighton—had brought it to the campus from his home town of Halifax!

However, in time many became convinced that the Kingston Hall of Fame would not be realized. Consequently, National Hockey League officials approached leaders of the Canadian National Exhibition in Toronto, where Canada's Sports Hall of Fame had been established, with the idea of a Hockey Hall of Fame. Agreement was reached and the opening of the official International Hockey Hall of Fame took place on August 26, 1961.

Despite difficulty in establishing the precise birthplace of modern ice hockey in Canada, there is firm and definite record of the growth of ice hockey since the 1880's. Leagues and associations were established in Ontario cities, and in Montreal and other Quebec cities. A few years later there was activity in the prairie provinces and on Canada's West coast.

The first league was a four-team organization in Kingston, established in 1885. Its members were the Royal Military College, Queen's University (the first champions), Kingston Athletics and the Kingston Hockey Club.

The Stanley Cup was first presented to the team winning the championship of Canada in 1893. Today its possession represents world supremacy in the professional realm.

Lord Kilcoursie, aide to Lord Stanley of Preston, then Governor General of the Dominion, had become an enthusiast of hockey and prevailed upon Lord Stanley to donate the prize. The original silverware cost 10 pounds ($48.66). The first winner was the Montreal A.A.A.

Professional hockey teams made their appearance in the early 1900's and in a short time the regulations concerning possession of the Stanley Cup were altered to provide that "This trophy is to be presented to the team winning the professional hockey championship of the world."

From 1912 through 1925 the champions of the Pacific Coast League (embracing teams from Canada and the United States) met the Eastern titleholders for the Stanley Cup. When big league hockey was disbanded in the West, partially because of the progress made by the National Hockey League in the United States, the cup in 1926 became identified solely with the N.H.L. and each year since the latter league's teams compete in post-season play-offs for its possession.

The predecessor of the N.H.L. was the National Hockey Association, disbanded in 1917 due to internal squabbling. From 1926 to the present the N.H.L. has functioned as hockey's only major league. From 1942 to 1967 the league was composed of six teams—Boston Bruins, Chicago Black Hawks, Detroit Red Wings, Montreal Canadiens, New York Rangers, and Toronto Maple Leafs.

Beginning with the 1967-68 season the N.H.L. embarked on a major expansion. Six teams became league members and formed a new West Division. The teams, were: Oakland Seals, Los Angeles Kings, Minnesota North Stars, Philadelphia Flyers, Pittsburgh Penguins, and the St. Louis Blues. The six older franchises are grouped in the East Division.

Hockey's expansion has not been limited to Canada and the United States. Amateur teams operate throughout the world under the control of the Ligue Internationale de Hockey sur Glace (International Ice Hockey Federation). Hockey has been on the Winter Olympic program since 1920.

ICE HOCKEY IN THE UNITED STATES

There is some question about the site where ice hockey was introduced in the United States. The first appearance of the sport can be traced to 1893 and to 2 specific places—Yale University, New Haven, Conn., and Johns Hopkins University, Baltimore, Md.

Two Yale tennis stars, Malcolm G. Chace and Arthur E. Foote, who had visited Canada for tournaments, became enthusiastic about hockey while there and brought the game back to their campus.

There also is recorded a report of a Montreal visitor, C. Shearer, who, while studying at Johns Hopkins University, formed a team of students and induced a Quebec team to visit Baltimore to engage the collegians in a contest.

It is conceivable, too, these events took place simultaneously. The influence of Chace and Foote is suggested in connection with the first hockey league formed in the United States.

It was the Amateur Hockey League, organized in New York in November, 1896, with 4 teams. The first league game ever held in this country brought together the St. Nicholas and the Brooklyn Skating Clubs, one month after the Amateur Hockey League was founded.

In the St. Nicholas line-up were 3 ranking American tennis players. They were H. W. Slocum, R. D. Wrenn and W. A. Larned, and among them they won the United States singles championship 14 times. Chace, a 3-time intercollegiate title winner, teamed with Wrenn in 1895 to win the United States doubles championship. It is conceivable that the Yale collegians prompted other tennis players to try ice hockey as an off-season pursuit.

There is evidence of others besides Shearer promoting hockey in Baltimore. Another Canadian, S. Alf Mitchell, along with a Baltimorean named W. A. Bisnaw, is credited with stimulating hockey activity in the period between 1893 and 1895.

Incidentally, a league was formed in Baltimore only 2 months after the Amateur Hockey League was established in New York. It was identified as the Baltimore Hockey League.

The sport spread rapidly in the United States. By the winters of 1895—96 and 1896—97, teams were playing throughout New England, in Philadelphia, Pittsburgh, Chicago and Washington, D.C.

The first professional team in the United States was a fabulous array known as Portage Lakers, from the small Michigan mining town of Houghton. The Lakers won 24 of 26 games their first year, 1903.

The Pacific Coast League of Canada admitted a member from the United States, Portland, Ore., in 1914, and a year later Seattle, Wash., also entered the circuit. In 1917 the Seattle Metropolitans won the league championship and went on to acquire the Stanley Cup, the first United States team to achieve the feat.

Boston became the first United States member of the National Hockey League in 1924.

Amateur hockey has enjoyed steadily increasing popularity in this country since its establishment more than 70 years ago. The original Amateur Hockey League in New York changed its name to the American Amateur Hockey League in later years as it expanded to take in teams from other cities. It encountered trouble at the time of World War I, supervision of the sport skipping from one body to another, but since the formation of the Amateur Hockey Association of the United States in 1937 its progress has been excellent.

CHRONOLOGICAL HISTORY OF HOCKEY

1855—First recorded ice hockey activity in Kingston, Ont., was played by the Royal Canadian Rifles, an Imperial Army unit.

1875—Formal rules created by students at McGill University, Montreal.

1885—First hockey league organized in Kingston, Ont.

1893—Stanley Cup placed in competition. Hockey introduced to the United States at Yale University in New Haven, Conn., and at Johns Hopkins University, Baltimore, Md.

1896—First United States Hockey league organized in New York City.

1909—The National Hockey Association, forerunner of the present National Hockey League, was established.

1917—The National Hockey Association was disbanded and on Nov. 22 the National Hockey League was organized in Montreal. The Montreal

Canadiens, Montreal Wanderers, Ottawa, Quebec and the Toronto Arenas were admitted to the league. Quebec held a franchise, but decided not to operate that season. Frank Calder was elected president and secretary-treasurer. The first league games were played Dec. 19, 1917. Toronto was the only city that had artificial ice.

1918—When the Westmount Arena, home of the Wanderers, burned, the team dropped out of the league. The 3 playing zones, and forward passing in center area came into existence. The tabulation of assists began.

1919—Quebec Bulldogs operated their franchise in the N.H.L. The Toronto Arenas changed their name to Toronto St. Pats.

1920—Hamilton Tigers replaced Quebec. Goalkeepers were allowed to pass the puck forward in the defensive areas. Ice hockey was included at the Olympic Games for the first time.

1924—Boston Bruins became first United States team to join the National League. The Montreal Maroons also entered the circuit, giving Montreal 2 teams.

1925—Hamilton Tigers' franchise was sold to New York Americans for $75,000. The third United States club, the Pittsburgh Pirates, also entered the league.

1926—Biggest single year in history of N.H.L. Three United States teams, New York Rangers, Chicago Black Hawks and Detroit Cougars, were admitted to the league. It was now a 10-team circuit and was divided into 2 sections: the Canadian Division had Toronto Maple Leafs (changed name from St. Pats), Ottawa Senators, Montreal Canadiens, Montreal Maroons and New York Americans; the American Division consisted of Boston Bruins, New York Rangers, Chicago Black Hawks, Detroit Cougars and Pittsburgh Pirates. The Stanley Cup came into the exclusive possession of the league. The season schedule of 44 games for each team was inaugurated.

1927—Forward passes were allowed in all attacking zones.

1928—Legislation removed all restrictions from forward passes in all zones.

1930—Pittsburgh franchise was transferred to Philadelphia, where a team known as the Quakers operated for one season. Detroit changed name from Cougars to Falcons.

1931—Philadelphia dropped out of league. Ottawa retired for a year. N.H.L. schedule increased to 48 games for each club.

1932—Ottawa resumed play for 2 seasons.

1933—Detroit changed nickname from Falcons to Red Wings.

1934—Ottawa franchise transferred to St. Louis. The team was called St. Louis Eagles and consisted of most of the Ottawa players. The penalty shot made its appearance.

1935—St. Louis dropped out of the league, leaving the membership at 8 teams.

1937—The Amateur Hockey Association of the United States was organized.

1938—The Montreal Maroons withdrew from the N.H.L.

1941—New York Americans changed name to Brooklyn Americans.

1942—Brooklyn Americans withdrew from league. This left the present 6 teams—Montreal Canadiens, Toronto Maple Leafs, Boston Bruins, New York Rangers, Detroit Red Wings and Chicago Black Hawks. Schedule increased to 50 games for each team.

1943—Frank Calder, president of the National League since its inception, died in Montreal in February. Mervyn (Red) Dutton, former manager of the New York Americans, succeeded him.

1946—Dutton retired as president prior to opening of 1946—47 season and was succeeded by Clarence S. Campbell. The schedule increased to 60 games for each team.

1949—Schedule increased to 70 games each.

1953—Acceptance of James Norris Memorial Trophy.

1954—Interleague draft modified to insure availability of players.

1956—Saturday afternoon games played and televised.

1959—The waiver price in the N.H.L was increased from $15,000 to $20,000, the first change in price in 6 years. Under the league system, each club makes up a protected list of 20 players. Any other player on its roster or anywhere in its farm system may then be drafted by other clubs.

1960—N.H.L. Clubs allowed to dress 16 players exclusive of goalkeepers for a game.

1961—Hockey Hall of Fame at the C.N.E., Toronto, officially opened on August 26 by Prime Minister John G. Diefenbaker and U.S. Ambassador Livingston T. Merchant.

1961—Gordie Howe, Detroit Red Wings, becomes first individual to play in 1,000 N.H.L. games.

1962—N.H.L. teams agree on unrestricted draft of players 17 years or younger.

1964—Conn Smythe Trophy presented to N.H.

1966—Lester Patrick Trophy presented to N.H.

1967—Six U.S. teams join the N.H.L. making it a 12-team, two division circuit. The new franchises are: Los Angeles Kings, Oakland Seals, Minnesota North Stars, Philadelphia Flyers, Pittsburgh Penguins, St. Louis Blues.

—Schedule increased to 74 games.

1968—Prince of Wales Trophy presented to Eastern Division winner, Campbell Bowl presented to Western Division. An award for perserverance, sportsmanship, and dedication to hockey was created to commemorate Bill Masterton, a center for the Minnesota North Stars, who died while playing a game in January 1968.

1970—Expansion of National League from 12 to 14 teams, with the Vancouver Canucks and Buffalo Sabres admitted, brought realignment of teams—Chicago shifting to Western Division and the two new teams going into the Eastern Division for 1970—71 season.

1972—Newly formed World Hockey Association, a 12-member pro circuit, would compete against the N.H.L. in the 1972—73 season. The W.H.A. teams were split into two divisions: East-ern and Western. The Quebec Nordiques, New England Whalers, New York Raiders, Ottawa Nationals, Cleveland Crusaders, and Philadelphia Blazers made up the Eastern Division. The Western consisted of Los Angeles Sharks, Alberta Oilers, Houston Aeros, Minnesota Fighting Saints, Chicago Cougars, and Winnipeg Jets. The N.H.L. expanded their teams to 16 with the addition of the New York Islanders in the East and the Atlanta Flames in the West.

Professional Hockey

Honored Players
International Hockey Hall of Fame

Headquarters of the Hall of Fame is located in the Hockey Hall of Fame Building at the Canadian National Exhibition in Toronto. Elections are made periodically by the Hockey Hall of Fame Committee after nomination by the Hall of Fame Selection Committee, made up of 11 experts. Entry is possible in three classifications—players, builders of the sport, and referees. At the end of 1971 there were a total of 180 honored members, comprising 131 players, 42 builders, and 7 referees.

National Hockey Hall of Fame

America's first shrine to hockey is currently under construction with opening ceremonies due June 21, 1973. The first group of enshrinees is expected to number 15 with annual additions to be between 3 and 5 members. The U.S. Hockey Hall of Fame is located in Eveleth, Minnesota, 55734, honoring American players, coaches, referees, and administrators who have made significant contributions to the game.

National League All-Star Teams

The N.H.L. has given official recognition to All-Star first and second teams beginning with the 1930-31 season. Since 1946-47, the league has rewarded every player picked to the All-Star teams with a bonus. Currently, the teams are selected by a panel of hockey writers and broadcasters from each league city.

1930—1931

First Team	Position	Second Team
Gardiner Chicago	Goal	Thompson, T., Boston
Shore, Boston	Defense	Mantha, Mont. Canadiens
Clancy, Toronto	Defense	Johnson, N.Y. Rangers
Morenz, Mont. Canadiens	Center	Boucher, N.Y. Rangers
Cook, W., N.Y. Rangers	Right Wing	Clapper, Boston
Joliat, Mont. Canadiens	Left Wing	Cook, B., N.Y. Rangers

1931—1932

First Team	Position	Second Team
Gardiner, Chicago	Goal	Worters, N.Y. Americans
Shore, Boston	Defense	Mantha, Mont. Canadiens
Johnson, N.Y. Rangers	Defense	Clancy, Toronto
Morenz, Mont. Canadiens	Center	Smith, H., Montreal Maroons
Cook, W., N.Y. Rangers	Right Wing	Conacher, C., Toronto
Jackson, Toronto	Left Wing	Joliat, Mont. Canadiens

1932—1933

First Team	Position	Second Team
Roach, Detroit	Goal	Gardiner, Chicago
Shore, Boston	Defense	Clancy, Toronto
Johnson, N.Y. Rangers	Defense	Conacher, L., Mont. Maroons
Boucher, F., N.Y. Rangers	Center	Morenz, Mont. Canadiens
Cook, W., N.Y. Rangers	Right Wing	Conacher, C., Toronto
Northcott, Mont. Maroons	Left Wing	Jackson, Toronto

1933—1934

First Team	Position	Second Team
Gardiner, Chicago	Goal	Worters, N.Y. Americans
Clancy, Toronto	Defense	Shore, Boston
Conacher, L., Chicago	Defense	Johnson, N.Y. Rangers
Boucher, F., N.Y. Rangers	Center	Primeau, Toronto

Conacher, C., Toronto	Right Wing	Cook, W., N.Y. Rangers
Jackson, Toronto	Left Wing	Joliat, Mont. Canadiens

1934–1935

Chabot, Chicago	Goal	Thompson, T., Boston
Shore, Boston	Defense	Wentworth, Mont. Maroons
Seibert, N.Y. Rangers	Defense	Coulter, Chicago
Boucher, F., N.Y. Rangers	Center	Weiland, Detroit
Conacher, C., Toronto	Right Wing	Clapper, Boston
Jackson, Toronto	Left Wing	Joliat, Mont. Canadiens

1935–1936

Thompson, Boston	Goals	Cude, Mont. Canadiens
Shore, Boston	Defense	Seibert, Chicago
Siebert, Boston	Defense	Goodfellow, Detroit
Smith, H., Mont. Maroons	Center	Thomas, Toronto
Conacher, C., Toronto	Right Wing	Dillon, N.Y. Rangers
Schriner, N.Y. Americans	Left Wing	Thompson, P., Chicago

1936–1937

Smith, N., Detroit	Goal	Cude, Mont. Canadiens
Siebert, Mont. Canadiens	Defense	Seibert, Chicago
Goodfellow, Detroit	Defense	Conacher, L., Mont. Maroons
Barry, Detroit	Center	Chapman, N.Y. Americans
Aurie, Detroit	Right Wing	Dillon, N.Y. Rangers
Jackson, Toronto	Left Wing	Schriner, N.Y. Americans

1937–1938

Thompson, T., Boston	Goal	Kerr, N.Y. Rangers
Shore, Boston	Defense	Coulter, N.Y. Rangers
Siebert, Mont. Canadiens	Defense	Seibert, Chicago
Cowley, Boston	Center	Apps, Toronto
Dillon, N.Y. Rangers Drillon, Toronto	Right Wing	—————— ——————
Thompson, P., Chicago	Left Wing	Blake, Mont. Canadiens

1938–1939

Brimsek, Boston	Goal	Robertson, N.Y. Americans
Shore, Boston	Defense	Seibert, Chicago
Clapper, Boston	Defense	Coulter, N.Y. Rangers
Apps, Toronto	Center	Colville, N., N.Y. Rangers
Drillon, Toronto	Right Wing	Bauer, Boston
Blake, Mont. Canadiens	Left Wing	Gottselig, Chicago

1939–1940

Kerr, N.Y. Rangers	Goal	Brimsek, Boston
Clapper, Boston	Defense	Coulter, N.Y. Rangers
Goodfellow, Detroit	Defense	Seibert, Chicago
Schmidt, Boston	Center	Colville, N.Y. Rangers
Hextall, N.Y. Rangers	Right Wing	Bauer, Boston
Blake, Mont. Canadiens	Left Wing	Dumart, Boston

1940–1941

Broda, Toronto	Goal	Brimsek, Boston
Clapper, Boston	Defense	Seibert, Chicago
Stanowski, Toronto	Defense	Heller, N.Y. Rangers
Cowley, Boston	Center	Apps, Toronto
Hextall, N.Y. Rangers	Right Wing	Bauer, Boston
Schriner, Toronto	Left Wing	Dumart, Boston

1941–1942

Brimsek, Boston	Goal	Broda, Toronto
Seibert, Chicago	Defense	Egan, N.Y. Americans
Anderson, T., N.Y. Americans	Defense	McDonald, W., Toronto
Apps, Toronto	Center	Watson, N.Y. Rangers
Hextall, N.Y. Rangers	Right Wing	Drillon, Toronto
Patrick, Lynn, N.Y. Rangers	Left Wing	Abel, Detroit

1942–1943

Mowers, Detroit	*Goal*	Brimsek, Boston
Seibert, Chicago	*Defense*	Crawford, Boston
Stewart, J., Detroit	*Defense*	Hollett, Boston
Cowley, Boston	*Center*	Apps, Toronto
Carr, L., Toronto	*Right Wing*	Hextall, N.Y. Rangers
Bentley, D., Chicago	*Left Wing*	Patrick, Lynn, N.Y. Rangers

1943–1944

Durnan, Mont. Canadiens	*Goal*	Bibeault, Toronto
Seibert, Chicago	*Defense*	Bouchard, Mont. Canadiens
Pratt, Toronto	*Defense*	Clapper, Boston
Cowley, Boston	*Center*	Lach, Mont. Canadiens
Carr, L., Toronto	*Right Wing*	Richard, Mont. Canadiens
Bentley, D., Chicago	*Left Wing*	Cain, Boston

1944–1945

Durnan, Mont. Canadiens	*Goal*	Karakas, Chicago
Bouchard, Mont. Canadiens	*Defense*	Harmon, Mont. Canadiens
Hollet, Detroit	*Defense*	Pratt, Toronto
Lach, Mont. Canadiens	*Center*	Cowley, Boston
Richard, Mont. Canadiens	*Right Wing*	Mosienko, Chicago
Blake, Mont. Canadiens	*Left Wing*	Howe, S., Detroit

1945–1946

Durnan, Mont. Canadiens	*Goal*	Brimsek, Boston
Crawford, Boston	*Defense*	Reardon, Mont. Canadiens
Bouchard, Mont. Canadiens	*Defense*	Stewart, J., Detroit
Bentley, M., Chicago	*Center*	Lach, Mont. Canadiens
Richard, Mont. Canadiens	*Right Wing*	Mosienko, Chicago
Stewart, G., Toronto	*Left Wing*	Blake, Mont. Canadiens

1946–1947

Durnan, Mont. Canadiens	*Goal*	Brimsek, Boston
Reardon, Mont. Canadiens	*Defense*	Stewart, Detroit
Bouchard, Mont. Canadiens	*Defense*	Quackenbush, Detroit
Schmidt, Boston	*Center*	Bentley, Chicago
Richard, Mont. Canadiens	*Right Wing*	Bauer, Boston
Bentley, D., Chicago	*Left Wing*	Dumart, Boston

1947–1948

Broda, Toronto	*Goal*	Brimsek, Boston
Quackenbush, Detroit	*Defense*	Reardon, Mont. Canadiens
Stewart, J., Detroit	*Defense*	Colville, N., N.Y. Rangers
Lach, Mont. Canadiens	*Center*	O'Connor, N.Y. Rangers
Richard, Mont. Canadiens	*Right Wing*	Poile, Chicago
Lindsay, Detroit	*Left Wing*	Stewart, G., Chicago

1948–1949

Durnan, Mont. Canadiens	*Goal*	Rayner, N.Y. Rangers
Quackenbush, Detroit	*Defense*	Harmon, Mont. Canadiens
Stewart, J., Detroit	*Defense*	Reardon, Mont. Canadiens
Abel, Detroit	*Center*	Bentley, D., Chicago
Richard, Mont. Canadiens	*Right Wing*	Howe, G., Detroit
Conacher, R., Chicago	*Left Wing*	Lindsay, Detroit

1949–1950

Durnan, Mont. Canadiens	*Goal*	Rayner, N.Y. Rangers
Mortson, Toronto	*Defense*	Reise, Detroit
Reardon, Mont. Canadiens	*Defense*	Kelly, Detroit
Abel, Detroit	*Center*	Kennedy, Toronto
Richard, Mont. Canadiens	*Right Wing*	Howe, G., Detroit
Lindsay, Detroit	*Left Wing*	Leswick, N.Y. Rangers

1950–1951

| Sawchuk, Detroit | *Goal* | Rayner, N.Y. Rangers |

Kelly, Detroit	*Defense*	Thomson, Toronto
Quackenbush, Boston	*Defense*	Reise, Detroit
		Abel, Detroit
Schmidt, Boston	*Center*	Kennedy, Toronto
Howe, G., Detroit	*Right Wing*	Richard, Mont. Canadiens
Lindsay, Detroit	*Left Wing*	Smith, S., Toronto

1951–1952

Sawchuk, Detroit	*Goal*	Henry, Boston
Kelly, Detroit	*Defense*	Buller, N.Y. Rangers
Harvey, Mont. Canadiens	*Defense*	Thomson, Toronto
Lach, Mont. Canadiens	*Center*	Schmidt, Boston
Howe, G., Detroit	*Right Wing*	Richard, Mont. Canadiens
Lindsay, Detroit	*Left Wing*	Smith, S., Toronto

1952–1953

Sawchuk, Detroit	*Goal*	McNeil, Mont. Canadiens
Kelly, Detroit	*Defense*	Quackenbush, Boston
Harvey, Mont. Canadiens	*Defense*	Gadsby, Chicago
Mackell, Boston	*Center*	Delvecchio, Detroit
Howe, G., Detroit	*Right Wing*	Richard, Mont. Canadiens
Lindsay, Detroit	*Left Wing*	Olmstead, Mont. Canadiens

1953–1954

Lumley, Toronto	*Goal*	Sawchuck, Detroit
Kelly, Detroit	*Defense*	Gadsby, Chicago
Harvey, Mont. Canadiens	*Defense*	Horton, Toronto
Mosdell, Mont. Canadiens	*Center*	Kennedy, Toronto
Howe, G., Detroit	*Wing*	Richard, M., Mont. Canadiens
Lindsay, Detroit	*Wing*	Sandford, Boston

1954–1955

Lumley, Toronto	*Goal*	Sawchuck, Detroit
Harvey, Mont. Canadiens	*Defense*	Goldham, Detroit
Kelly, Detroit	*Defense*	Flaman, Boston
Beliveau, Mont. Canadiens	*Center*	Mosdell, Mont. Canadiens
Richard, M., Mont. Canadiens	*Wing*	Geoffrion, Mont. Canadiens
S. Smith, Toronto	*Wing*	Lewicki, N.Y. Rangers

1955–1956

Plante, Mont. Canadiens	*Goal*	Hall, Detroit
Harvey, Mont. Canadiens	*Defense*	Kelly, Detroit
Gadsby, N.Y. Rangers	*Defense*	Johnson, T., Mont. Canadiens
Beliveau, Mont. Canadiens	*Center*	Sloan, Toronto
Richard, M., Mont. Canadiens	*Wing*	Howe, G., Detroit
Lindsay, Detroit	*Wing*	Olmstead, Mont. Canadiens

1956–1957

Hall, Detroit	*Goal*	Plante, Mont. Canadiens
Harvey, Mont. Canadiens	*Defense*	Flaman, Boston
Kelly, Detroit	*Defense*	Gadsby, N.Y. Rangers
Beliveau, Mont. Canadiens	*Center*	Litzenberger, Chicago
Howe, G., Detroit	*Wing*	Richard, M., Mont. Canadiens
Lindsay, Detroit	*Wing*	Chevrefils, Boston

1957–1958

Hall, Chicago	*Goal*	Plante, Mont. Canadiens
Harvey, Mont. Canadiens	*Defense*	Flaman, Boston
Gadsby, N.Y. Rangers	*Defense*	Pronovost, Detroit
Richard, H., Mont. Canadiens	*Center*	Beliveau, Mont. Canadiens
Howe, G., Detroit	*Right Wing*	Bathgate, N.Y. Rangers
Moore, Mont. Canadiens	*Left Wing*	Henry, N.Y. Rangers

1958–1959

Plante, Mont. Canadiens	*Goal*	Sawchuck, Detroit
Johnson, Mont. Canadiens	*Defense*	Pronovost, Detroit
Gadsby, N.Y. Rangers	*Defense*	Harvey, Mont. Canadiens

Beliveau, Mont. Canadiens	*Center*	Richard, H., Mont. Canadiens
Bathgate, N.Y. Rangers	*Wing*	Howe, Detroit
Moore, Mont. Canadiens	*Wing*	Delvecchio, Detroit

1959–1960

Hall, Chicago	*Goal*	Plante, Mont. Canadiens
Harvey, Mont. Canadiens	*Defense*	Stanley, Toronto
Pronovost, Detroit	*Defense*	Pilote, Chicago
Beliveau, Mont. Canadiens	*Center*	Horvath, Boston
Howe, Detroit	*Wing*	Geoffrion, Mont. Canadiens
Hull, Chicago	*Wing*	Prentice, N.Y. Rangers

1960–1961

Bower, Toronto	*Goal*	Hall, Chicago
Harvey, Mont. Canadiens	*Defense*	Stanley, Toronto
Pronovost, Detroit	*Defense*	Pilote, Chicago
Beliveau, Mont. Canadiens	*Center*	Richard, H., Mont. Canadiens
Geoffrion, Mont. Canadiens	*Wing*	Howe, Detroit
Mahovlich, Toronto	*Wing*	Moore, Mont. Canadiens

1961–1962

Plante, Montreal Canadiens	*Goal*	Hall, Chicago
Harvey, New York Rangers	*Defense*	Brewer, Toronto
Talbot, Montreal Canadiens	*Defense*	Pilote, Chicago
Mikita, Chicago	*Center*	Keon, Toronto
Bathgate, New York Rangers	*Wing*	Howe, Detroit
Hull, Chicago	*Wing*	Mahovlich, Toronto

1962–1963

Hall, Chicago	*Goal*	Sawchuck, Detroit
Pilote, Chicago	*Defense*	Horton, Toronto
Brewer, Toronto	*Defense*	Vasko, Chicago
Mikita, Chicago	*Center*	Richard, H. Mont. Canadiens
Howe, Detroit	*Wing*	Bathgate, N.Y. Rangers
Mahovlich, Toronto	*Wing*	Hull, Chicago

1963–1964

Hall, Chicago	*Goal*	Hodge, Mont. Canadiens
Pilote, Chicago	*Defense*	Vasko, Chicago
Horton, Toronto	*Defense*	Laperriere, Mont. Canadiens
Mikita, Chicago	*Center*	Beliveau, Mont. Canadiens
Wharram, Chicago	*Wing*	Howe, Detroit
Hull, Chicago	*Wing*	Mahovlich, Toronto

1964–1965

Crozier, Detroit	*Goal*	Hodge, Mont. Canadiens
Pilote, Chicago	*Defense*	Gadsby, Detroit
Laperriere, Mont. Canadiens	*Defense*	Brewer, Toronto
Ullman, Detroit	*Center*	Mikita, Chicago
Provost, Mont. Canadiens	*Wing*	Howe, Detroit
Hull, Chicago	*Wing*	Mahovlich, Toronto

1965–1966

Hall, Chicago	*Goal*	Worsley, Mont. Canadiens
Pilote, Chicago	*Defense*	Stapleton, Chicago
Laperriere, Mont. Canadiens	*Defense*	Stanley, Toronto
Mikita, Chicago	*Center*	Beliveau, Mont. Canadiens
Howe, Detroit	*Wing*	Rousseau, Mont. Canadiens
Hull, Chicago	*Wing*	Mahovlich, Toronto

1966–1967

Giacomin, N.Y. Rangers	*Goal*	Hall, Chicago
Pilote, Chicago	*Defense*	Horton, Toronto
Howell, N.Y. Rangers	*Defense*	Orr, Boston
Mikita, Chicago	*Center*	Ullman, Detroit
Wharram, Chicago	*Wing*	Howe, Detroit
Hull, Chicago	*Wing*	Marshall, N.Y. Rangers

1967–1968

Worsley, Mont. Canadiens	*Goal*	Giacomin, N.Y. Rangers
Orr, Boston	*Defense*	Neilson, N.Y. Rangers
Horton, Toronto	*Defense*	Tremblay, J.C., Mont. Canadiens
Mikita, Chicago	*Center*	Esposito, Boston
Howe, Detroit	*Wing*	Gilbert, N.Y. Rangers
Hull, Chicago	*Wing*	Bucyk, Boston

1968–1969

Hall, St. Louis	*Goal*	Giacomin, N.Y. Rangers
Orr, Boston	*Defense*	Green, Boston
Horton, Toronto	*Defense*	Harris, Mont. Canadiens
Esposito, Boston	*Center*	Beliveau, Mont. Canadiens
Howe, Detroit	*Wing*	Cournoyer, Mont. Canadiens
Hull, Chicago	*Wing*	Mahovlich Detroit

1969–1970

T. Esposito, Chicago	*Goal*	Giacomin, N.Y. Rangers
Orr, Boston	*Defense*	Brewer, Detroit
Park, N.Y. Rangers	*Defense*	Laperriere, Mont. Canadiens
P. Esposito, Boston	*Center*	Mikita, Chicago
Howe, Detroit	*Wing*	McKenzie, Boston
Hull, Chicago	*Wing*	Mahovlich, Detroit

1970–1971

Giacomin, N.Y. Rangers	*Goal*	Plante, Toronto
Orr, Boston	*Defense*	Park, N.Y. Rangers
Tremblay, Mont. Canadiens	*Defense*	Stapleton, Chicago
P. Esposito, Boston	*Center*	Keon, Toronto
Hodge, Boston	*Wing*	Cournoyer, Mont. Canadiens
Bucyk, Boston	*Wing*	Hull, Chicago

1971–1972

T. Esposito, Chicago	*Goal*	Dryden, Mont. Canadiens
Orr, Boston	*Defense*	White, Chicago
Park, N.Y. Rangers	*Defense*	Stapleton, Chicago
P. Esposito, Boston	*Center*	Ratelle, N. Y. Rangers
Gilbert, N.Y. Rangers	*Wing*	Cournoyer, Mont. Canadiens
Hull, Chicago	*Wing*	Hadfield, N.Y. Rangers

1972–1973

Dryden, Mont. Canadiens	*Goal*	T. Esposito, Chicago
Orr, Boston	*Defense*	White, Chicago
LaPointe, Mont. Canadiens	*Defense*	Gibbs, Minnesota
P. Esposito, Boston	*Center*	Mikita, Chicago
Cournoyer, Mont. Canadiens	*Wing*	Pappin, Chicago
Martin, Buffalo	*Wing*	Hull, Chicago

AWARD WINNERS

Trophies are presented each season for individual excellence. Two—the Vezina and the Ross—are given automatically on statistical results. The others are determined by vote, hockey writers, radio broadcasters and telecasters from each league city participating in the poll. A seventh trophy, the Conn Smythe Trophy, is awarded for outstanding performance in the Stanley Cup playoffs. League governors select the winner. Still another award, the Lester Patrick Trophy, given annually to an individual for outstanding service to hockey in the United States, was first presented in 1967.

Hart Trophy
(Most valuable player.)

1923–24—Frank Nighbor, Ottawa
1924–25—Billy Burch, Hamilton
1925–26—Nels Stewart, Montreal Maroons
1926–27—Herb Gardiner, Montreal Canadiens
1927–28—Howie Morenz, Montreal Canadiens
1928–29—Roy Worters, N.Y. Americans
1929–30—Nels Stewart, Montreal Maroons
1930–32—Howie Morenz, Montreal Canadiens
1932–33—Eddie Shore, Boston
1933–34—Aurel Joliat, Montreal Canadiens
1934–36—Eddie Shore, Boston
1936–37—Babe Siebert, Montreal Canadiens

1937—38—Eddie Shore, Boston
1938—39—Toe Blake, Montreal Canadiens
1939—40—Ebbie Goodfellow, Detroit
1940—41—Bill Cowley, Boston
1941—42—Tommy Anderson, N.Y. Americans
1942—43—Bill Cowley, Boston
1943—44—Babe Pratt, Toronto
1944—45—Elmer Lach, Montreal Canadiens
1945—46—Max Bentley, Chicago
1946—47—Maurice Richard, Montreal Canadiens
1947—48—Buddy O'Connor, N.Y. Rangers
1948—49—Sid Abel, Detroit
1949—50—Chuck Rayner, N.Y. Rangers
1950—51—Milt Schmidt, Boston
1951—53—Gordon Howe, Detroit
1953—54—Al Rollins, Chicago
1954—55—Ted Kennedy, Toronto
1955—56—Jean Beliveau, Montreal Canadiens
1956—57—Gordon Howe, Detroit
1957—58—Gordon Howe, Detroit
1958—59—Andy Bathgate, N.Y. Rangers
1959—60—Gordon Howe, Detroit
1960—61—Bernie Geoffrion, Montreal Canadiens
1961—62—Jacques Plante, Montreal Canadiens
1962—63—Gordon Howe, Detroit
1963—64—Jean Beliveau, Montreal Canadiens
1964—65—Bobby Hull, Chicago
1965—66—Bobby Hull, Chicago
1966—67—Stan Mikita, Chicago
1967—68—Stan Mikita, Chicago
1968—69—Phil Esposito, Boston
1969—70—Bobby Orr, Boston
1970—71—Bobby Orr, Boston
1971—72—Bobby Orr, Boston
1972—73—Bobby Clarke, Philadelphia

Ross Trophy

(Individual scoring champion.)

The trophy first was placed in competition in 1947—48 to give additional designation and honor to the league's point-scoring leader. Previous scoring champions are also listed.

	Goals	A'ts	Pts.
1917—18—Joe Malone, Mont. Canadiens	44	..	44
1918—19—Newsy Lalonde, Mont. Canadiens	23	9	32
1919—20—Joe Malone, Quebec	39	6	45
1920—21—Newsy Lalonde, Mont. Canadiens	33	8	41
1921—22—Punch Broadbent, Ottawa	32	14	46
1922—23—Babe Dye, Toronto	26	11	37
1923—24—Cy Denneny, Ottawa	22	1	23
1924—25—Babe Dye, Toronto	38	6	44
1925—26—Nels Stewart, Mont. Maroons	34	8	42
1926—27—Bill Cook, N.Y. Rangers	33	4	37
1927—28—Howie Morenz, Mont. Canadiens	33	18	51
1928—29—Ace Bailey, Toronto	22	10	32
1929—30—Cooney Weiland, Boston	43	30	73
1930—31—Howie Morenz, Mont. Canadiens	28	23	51
1931—32—Harvey Jackson, Toronto	28	25	53
1932—33—Bill Cook, N.Y. Rangers	28	22	50
1933—34—Charlie Conacher, Toronto	32	20	52
1934—35—Charlie Conacher, Toronto	36	21	57
1935—36—Dave Schriner, N.Y. Americans	19	26	45
1936—37—Dave Schriner, N.Y. Americans	21	25	46
1937—38—Gordon Drillon, Toronto	26	26	52
1938—39—Toe Blake, Mont. Canadiens	24	23	47
1939—40—Milt Schmidt, Boston	22	30	52

	Goals	A'ts	Pts.
1940—41—Bill Cowley, Boston	17	45	62
1941—42—Bryan Hextall, N.Y. Rangers	24	32	56
1942—43—Doug Bentley, Chicago	33	40	73
1943—44—Herb Cain, Boston	36	46	82
1944—45—Elmer Lach, Mont. Canadiens	26	54	80
1945—46—Max Bentley, Chicago	31	30	61
1946—47—Max Bentley, Chicago	29	43	72
1947—48—Elmer Lach, Mont. Canadiens	30	31	61
1948—49—Roy Conacher, Chicago	26	42	68
1949—50—Ted Lindsay, Detroit	23	55	78
1950—51—Gordon Howe, Detroit	43	43	86
1951—52—Gordon Howe, Detroit	47	39	86
1952—53—Gordon Howe, Detroit	49	46	95
1953—54—Gordon Howe, Detroit	33	48	81
1954—55—Bernie Geoffrion, Mont. Canadiens	38	37	75
1955—56—Jean Beliveau, Mont. Canadiens	47	41	88
1956—57—Gordon Howe, Detroit	44	45	89
1957—58—Dickie Moore, Mont. Canadiens	36	48	84
1958—59—Dickie Moore, Mont. Canadiens	41	55	96
1959—60—Bobby Hull, Chicago	39	42	81
1960—61—Bernie Geoffrion, Mont. Canadiens	50	45	95
*1961—62—Bobby Hull, Chicago	50	34	84
1962—63—Gordon Howe, Detroit	38	48	86
1963—64—Stan Mikita, Chicago	39	50	89
1964—65—Stan Mikita, Chicago	28	59	87
1965—66—Bobby Hull, Chicago	54	43	97
1966—67—Stan Mikita, Chicago	35	62	97
1967—68—Stan Mikita, Chicago	40	47	87
1968—69—Phil Esposito, Boston	49	77	126
1969—70—Bobby Orr, Boston	33	87	120
1970—71—Phil Esposito, Boston	76	76	152
1971—72—Phil Esposito, Boston	66	67	133
1972—73—Phil Esposito, Boston	55	75	130

*Andy Bathgate of the N.Y. Rangers also scored 84 points, but Hull was awarded the Ross Trophy on the basis of more goals scored, 50-28.

Calder Memorial Trophy

(Rookie of the Year.)

For 4 seasons, the league's leading rookie was selected, although no trophy existed symbolic of this honor. In 1936-37, Frank Calder, N.H.L. president, placed in competition a trophy bearing his name. Following his death, the league in 1942-43 continued this award as the Calder Memorial Trophy.

1932—33—Carl Voss, Detroit
1933—34—Russ Blinco, Mont. Maroons
1934—35—Dave Schriner, N.Y. Americans
1935—36—Mike Karakas, Chicago
1936—37—Syl Apps, Toronto
1937—38—Cully Dahlstrom, Chicago
1938—39—Frank Brimsek, Boston
1939—40—Kilby Macdonald, N.Y. Rangers
1940—41—Johnny Quilty, Mont. Canadiens
1941—42—Grant Warwick, N.Y. Rangers
1942—43—Gaye Stewart, Toronto
1943—44—Gus Bodnar, Toronto
1944—45—Frank McCool, Toronto
1945—46—Edgar Laprade, N.Y. Rangers
1946—47—Howie Meeker, Toronto
1947—48—Jim McFadden, Detroit
1948—49—Pentti Lund, N.Y. Rangers
1949—50—Jack Gelineau, Boston
1950—51—Terry Sawchuk, Detroit
1951—52—Bernie Geoffrion, Mont. Canadiens
1952—53—Lorne Worsley, N.Y. Rangers
1953—54—Camille Henry, N.Y. Rangers

1954—55—Eddie Litzenberger, Chicago
1955—56—Glenn Hall, Detroit
1956—57—Larry Regan, Boston
1957—58—Frank Mahovlich, Toronto
1958—59—Ralph Backstrom, Mont. Canadiens
1959—60—Bill Hay, Chicago
1960—61—Dave Keon, Toronto
1961—62—Bob Rousseau, Mont. Canadiens
1962—63—Kent Douglas, Toronto
1963—64—Jacques Laperriere, Mont. Canadiens
1964—65—Roger Crozier, Detroit
1965—66—Brit Selby, Toronto
1966—67—Bobby Orr, Boston
1967—68—Derek Sanderson, Boston
1968—69—Danny Grant, Minnesota
1969—70—Tony Esposito, Chicago
1970—71—Gil Perreault, Buffalo
1971—72—Ken Dryden, Mont. Canadiens
1972—73—Steve Vickers, New York Rangers

Lady Byng Memorial Trophy
(Sportsmanship and gentlemanly conduct.)

The Lady Byng Trophy was placed in competition in the 1924—25 season. Following the death in 1949 of Lady Byng, whose husband had been Canada's Governor General at the time she presented the original trophy, the league perpetuated the award in her memory.

1924—26—Frank Nighbor, Ottawa
1926—27—Billy Burch, N.Y. Americans
1927—31—Frank Boucher, N.Y. Rangers
1931—32—Joe Primeau, Toronto
1932—35—Frank Boucher, N.Y. Rangers
1935—36—Doc Romnes, Chicago
1936—37—Marty Barry, Detroit
1937—38—Gordon Drillon, Toronto
1938—39—Clint Smith, N.Y. Rangers
1939—41—Bobby Bauer, Boston
1941—42—Syl Apps, Toronto
1942—43—Max Bentley, Chicago
1943—44—Clint Smith, N.Y. Rangers
1944—45—Bill Mosienko, Chicago
1945—46—Toe Blake, Mont. Canadiens
1946—47—Bobby Bauer, Boston
1947—48—Buddy O'Connor, N.Y. Rangers
1948—49—Bill Quackenbush, Detroit
1949—50—Edgar Laprade, N.Y. Rangers
1950—51—Red Kelly, Detroit
1951—52—Sid Smith, Toronto
1952—54—Red Kelly, Detroit
1954—55—Sid Smith, Toronto
1955—56—Earl Reibel, Detroit
1956—57—Andy Hebenton, N.Y. Rangers
1957—58—Camille Henry, N.Y. Rangers
1958—59—Alex Delvecchio, Detroit
1959—60—Don McKenney, Boston
1960—61—Red Kelly, Toronto
1961—62—Dave Keon, Toronto
1962—63—Dave Keon, Toronto
1963—64—Ken Wharram, Chicago
1964—65—Bobby Hull, Chicago
1965—66—Alex Delvecchio, Detroit

1966—67—Stan Mikita, Chicago
1967—68—Stan Mikita, Chicago
1968—69—Alex Delvecchio, Detroit
1969—70—Phil Goyette, St. Louis
1970—71—John Bucyk, Boston
1971—72—Jean Ratelle, New York Rangers
1972—73—Gil Perreault, Buffalo

Vezina Trophy
(Best goalkeeper record.)

The trophy was presented by Leo Dandurand, Louis Letourneau and Joe Cattarinich, former owners of the Montreal Canadiens, in memory of Georges Vezina, the Canadiens' outstanding goaltender who collapsed during a game in 1925 and died a few months later.

1926—29—George Hainsworth, Mont. Canadiens
1929—30—Tiny Thompson, Boston
1930—31—Roy Worters, N.Y. Americans
1931—32—Charlie Gardiner, Chicago
1932—33—Tiny Thompson, Boston
1933—34—Charlie Gardiner, Chicago
1934—35—Lorne Chabot, Chicago
1935—36—Tiny Thompson, Boston
1936—37—Norman Smith, Detroit
1937—38—Tiny Thompson, Boston
1938—39—Frank Brimsek, Boston
1939—40—Dave Kerr, N.Y. Rangers
1940—41—Turk Broda, Toronto
1941—42—Frank Brimsek, Boston
1942—43—Johnny Mowers, Detroit
1943—47—Bill Durnan, Mont. Canadiens
1947—48—Turk Broda, Toronto
1948—50—Bill Durnan, Mont. Canadiens
1950—51—Al Rollins, Toronto
1951—53—Terry Sawchuk, Detroit
1953—54—Harry Lumley, Toronto
1954—55—Terry Sawchuk, Detroit
1955—60—Jacques Plante, Mont. Canadiens
1960—61—Johnny Bower, Toronto
1961—62—Jacques Plante, Mont. Canadiens
1962—63—Glenn Hall, Chicago
1963—64—Charlie Hodge, Mont. Canadiens
1964—65—Terry Sawchuk and Johnny Bower, Toronto
1965—66—Lorne Worsley and Charlie Hodge, Mont. Canadiens
1966—67—Denis DeJordy and Glenn Hall, Chic.
1967—68—Lorne Worsley and Rogatien Vachon, Mont. Canadiens
1968—69—Glenn Hall and Jacques Plante, St. Louis
1969—70—Tony Esposito, Chicago
1970—71—Ed Giacomin and Gilles Villemure, N.Y. Rangers
1971—72—Tony Esposito and Gary Smith, Chic.
1972—73—Ken Dryden, Mont. Canadiens

James Norris Memorial Trophy
(Best defenseman)

This award was presented by the four children

of the late James Norris in memory of their father, former owner-president of the Detroit Red Wings. Since the 1953-54 season it has been presented annually to the "regular defense player who demonstrates throughout the season the greatest all-around ability in that position."

1953−54−Red Kelly, Detroit
1954−58−Doug Harvey, Mont. Canadiens
1958−59−Tom Johnson, Mont. Canadiens
1959−61−Doug Harvey, Mont. Canadiens
1961−62−Doug Harvey, New York Rangers
1962−63−Pierre Pilote, Chicago
1963−64−Pierre Pilote, Chicago
1964−65−Pierre Pilote, Chicago
1965−66−Jacques Laperriere, Mont. Canadiens
1966−67−Harry Howell, N.Y. Rangers
1967−68−Bobby Orr, Boston
1968−69−Bobby Orr, Boston
1969−70−Bobby Orr, Boston
1970−71−Bobby Orr, Boston
1971−72−Bobby Orr, Boston
1972−73−Bobby Orr, Boston

Conn Smythe Trophy
(Most valuable player in Stanley Cup playoffs)

1964−65−Jean Beliveau, Mont. Canadiens
1965−66−Roger Crozier, Detroit
1966−67−Dave Keon, Toronto
1967−68−Glenn Hall, St. Louis Blues
1968−69−Serge Sevard, Mont. Canadiens
1969−70−Bobby Orr, Boston
1970−71−Ken Dryden, Mont. Canadiens
1971−72−Bobby Orr, Boston
1972−73−Yvan Cournoyer, Mont. Canadiens

OTHER STATISTICS
Stanley Cup Winners

The Stanley Cup, emblematic of the world professional championship, came into the possession of the N.H.L. in 1917.

1893−Montreal A.A.A.
1894−Montreal A.A.A.
1895−Montreal Victorias
1896−Winnipeg Victorias
1897−98−Montreal Victorias
1899−(February)−Montreal Victorias
1899−(March)−Montreal Shamrocks
1900−Montreal Shamrocks
1901−Winnipeg Victorias
1902−Montreal A.A.A.
1903−05−Ottawa Silver Seven
1906−Montreal Wanderers
1907−(January)−Kenora Thistles
1907−(March)−Montreal Wanderers
1908−Montreal Wanderers
1909−Ottawa Senators
1910−Montreal Wanderers
1911−Ottawa Senators
1912−13−Quebec Bulldogs
1914−Toronto Ontarios
1915−Vancouver Millionaires
1916−Montreal Canadiens
1917−Seattle Metropolitans
1918−Toronto Arenas
1919−Series unfinished*
1920−21−Ottawa Senators
1922−Toronto St. Pats
1923−Ottawa Senators
1924−Montreal Canadiens
1925−Victoria Cougars
1926−Montreal Maroons
1927−Ottawa Senators
1928−New York Rangers
1929−Boston Bruins
1930−31−Montreal Canadiens
1932−Toronto Maple Leafs
1933−New York Rangers
1934−Chicago Black Hawks
1935−Montreal Maroons
1936−37−Detroit Red Wings
1938−Chicago Black Hawks
1939−Boston Bruins
1940−New York Rangers
1941−Boston Bruins
1942−Toronto Maple Leafs
1943−Detroit Red Wings
1944−Montreal Canadiens
1945−Toronto Maple Leafs
1946−Montreal Canadiens
1947−49−Toronto Maple Leafs
1950−Detroit Red Wings
1951−Toronto Maple Leafs
1952−Detroit Red Wings
1953−Montreal Canadiens
1954−55−Detroit Red Wings
1956−60−Montreal Canadiens
1961−Chicago Black Hawks
1962−64−Toronto Maple Leafs
1964−66−Montreal Canadiens
1966−67−Toronto Maple Leafs
1967−68−Montreal Canadiens
1968−69−Montreal Canadiens
1969−70−Boston Bruins
1970−71−Montreal Canadiens
1971−72−Boston Bruins
1972−73−Montreal Canadiens

*Five games had been played in the final series between the Montreal Canadiens and Seattle, champion of the Pacific Coast League, when the competition was ended because of an influenza epidemic.

Stanley Cup Playoff Series

With the league divided into two divisions, the first and third, and second and fourth place clubs in each division met in a 4-out-of-7-game series. The winners then met in a 4-out-of-7-game series to decide the division winner. The winners of this series met in a 4-out-of-7-game series for the Stanley Cup.

1967−68
Preliminary Series
East Division
Mont. Canadiens beat Boston, 4 games to 0.
Chicago beat N.Y. Rangers, 4 games to 2.

West Division
St. Louis beat Philadelphia, 4 games to 3.
Minnesota beat Los Angeles, 4 games to 3.
Semi-Final Round
Mont. Canadiens beat Chicago, 4 games to 1.
St. Louis beat Minnesota, 4 games to 3.

1968–69
Preliminary Series
East Division
Mont. Canadiens beat N.Y. Rangers, 4 games to 0.
Boston beat Toronto, 4 games to 0.
West Division
St. Louis beat Philadelphia, 4 games to 0.
Los Angeles beat Oakland, 4 games to 3.
Semi-Final Round
Mont. Canadiens beat Boston, 4 games to 2.
St. Louis beat Los Angeles, 4 games to 0.

1969–70
Preliminary Series
East Division
Chicago beat Detroit, 4 games to 0.
Boston beat N.Y. Rangers, 4 games to 2.
West Division
St. Louis beat Minnesota, 4 games to 2
Pittsburgh beat Oakland, 4 games to 0
Semi-Final Round
Boston beat Chicago, 4 games to 0.
St. Louis beat Pittsburgh, 4 games to 2.

1970–71
Preliminary Series
East Division
Mont. Canadiens beat Boston, 4 games to 3.
N.Y. Rangers beat Toronto, 4 games to 2.
West Division
Chicago beat Philadelphia, 4 games to 0.
Minnesota beat St. Louis, 4 games to 2.
Semi-Final Rounds
Mont. Canadiens beat Minnesota, 4 games to 2.
Chicago beat N.Y. Rangers, 4 games to 3.

1971–72
Preliminary Series
East Division
Boston beat Toronto, 4 games to 1.
N.Y. Rangers beat Mont. Canadiens, 4 games to 2.
West Division
Chicago beat Pittsburgh, 4 games to 0.
St. Louis beat Minnesota, 4 games to 3.
Semi-Final Round
Boston beat St. Louis, 4 games to 0.
N.Y. Rangers beat Chicago, 4 games to 0.

1972–73
Preliminary Series
East Division
Mont. Canadiens beat Buffalo, 4 games to 2.
N.Y. Rangers beat Boston, 4 games to 1.
West Division
Philadelphia beat Minnesota, 4 games to 2.
Chicago beat St. Louis, 4 games to 1.

Semi-Final Round
Mont. Canadiens beat Philadelphia, 4 games to 1.
Chicago beat N.Y. Rangers, 4 games to 1.

National Hockey League Champions
(Regular season.)

1917–18—Toronto Arenas
1918–19—Montreal Canadiens
1919–21—Ottawa Senators
1921–22—Toronto St. Pats
1922–23—Ottawa Senators
1923–25—Montreal Canadiens
1925–26—Montreal Maroons
*1926–27—Ottawa Senators
*1927–28—New York Rangers
1928–30—Boston Bruins
1930–31—Montreal Canadiens
1931–32—New York Rangers
1932–33—Toronto Maple Leafs
1933–34—Detroit Red Wings
1934–35—Toronto Maple Leafs
1935–37—Detroit Red Wings
1937–38—Toronto Maple Leafs
1938–41—Boston Bruins
1941–42—New York Rangers
1942–43—Detroit Red Wings
1943–47—Montreal Canadiens
1947–48—Toronto Maple Leafs
1948–55—Detroit Red Wings
1955–56—Montreal Canadiens
1956–57—Detroit Red Wings
1957–62—Montreal Canadiens
1962–63—Toronto Maple Leafs
1963–64—Montreal Canadiens
1964–65—Detroit Red Wings
1965–66—Montreal Canadiens
1966–67—Chicago Black Hawks
1967–68—Montreal Canadiens (East Division)
      Philadelphia Flyers (West Division)
1968–69—Montreal Canadiens (Eastern)
      St. Louis Blues (Western)
1969–70—Chicago Black Hawks (Eastern)
      St. Louis Blues (Western)
1970–71—Boston Bruins (Eastern)
      Chicago Black Hawks (Western)
1971–72—Boston Bruins (Eastern)
      Chicago Black Hawks (Western)
1972–73—Montreal Canadiens (Eastern)
      Chicago Black Hawks (Western)

*No intersectional playoffs took place during these years as the top three teams in each division played off to determine a divisional champion.

The National Hockey League history dates to the year 1909, when what had been the Eastern Canada Hockey Association and the Federal League combined to form the National Hockey Association. Champions of the predecessor leagues are listed below.

National Hockey Association
1909–10—Montreal Wanderers
1910–11—Ottawa Senators

1911–13–Quebec Bulldogs
1913–14–Toronto Ontarios
1914–15–Ottawa Senators
1915–17–Montreal Canadiens

Eastern Canada Hockey Association
1905–08–Montreal Wanderers
1908–09–Ottawa

Federal League
1903–04–Montreal Wanderers
1904–05–Ottawa Silver Seven
1905–06–Smith's Falls
1906–07–Ottawa Vic's

International Hockey League Champions
(First professional hockey league)

1903–04–Portage Lakes of Houghton, Michigan
1904–05–Calumet, Michigan
1905–06–Portage Lakes of Houghton, Michigan
1906–07–Portage Lakes of Houghton, Michigan

Stanley Cup Play-off Records
Team

Longest game–Detroit Red Wings 1, Montreal Maroons 0, March 24–25, 1936, at Montreal; winning goal (by Mud Bruneteau) scored at 16:30 of 6th overtime period (at 2:25 A.M.) . . . . .176m. 30s.

Shortest overtime game–Detroit Red Wings 2, New York Americans 1, March 19, 1940, winning goal (by Syd Howe) scored at 25 seconds of 1st overtime period . . . . .60m. 25s.

Most goals, one game–Montreal Canadiens, March 30, 1944, against Toronto, score 11–0. 11

Most goals, both teams, one game–Montreal Canadiens 8, Chicago 7, May 8, 1973 15

Individual

Most goals–Maurice Richard, Montreal Canadiens, 15 play-offs. 82

Most assists–Gordon Howe, Detroit, 18 play-offs 91

Most points–Gordon Howe, Detroit, 65 goals, 91 assists, 18 play-offs 156

Most goals, one season's playoffs–Yvan Cournoyer, Montreal Canadiens, 1973 15

Most assists, one season's play-offs–Stan Mikita, Chicago Black Hawks, 1962 15

Most points, one season's play-offs–Stan Mikita, Chicago, 6 goals, 15 assists, 1962 21

Most goals, one game–Maurice Richard, Montreal Canadiens, March 23, 1944, against Toronto 5

Most assists, one game–Toe Blake, Montreal Canadiens, March 23, 1944, against Toronto; Maurice Richard, Montreal Canadiens, March 27, 1956, against New York Rangers; Bert Olmstead, Montreal Canadiens, March 30, 1957, against New York Rangers; Don McKenney, Boston Bruins, April 5, 1958, against New York Rangers. 5

Most points, one game–Dickie Moore, Mon-

treal Canadiens, 2 goals, 4 assists, March 25, 1954, against Boston 6

Quickest goal–Gordon Howe, Detroit, April 1, 1954, against Toronto . . . . 9 secs.

Most shutouts by goalie–Turk Broda, Toronto, 13 play-offs 13

Most shutoffs by goalie, one season's play-offs–Clint Benedict, Montreal Maroons, 1928, against Ottawa, Montreal Canadiens, New York Rangers; Dave Kerr, New York Rangers, 1937, against Montreal Maroons and Detroit; Frank McCool, Toronto, 1945, against Montreal Canadiens and Detroit; Terry Sawchuk, Detroit, 1952, against Toronto and Montreal Canadiens 4

Stanley Cup Scoring Leaders
(Since 1927.)

	Games	G'ls	As'ts	Pts.
1927–Harry Oliver, Boston	8	4	2	6
Perk Galbraith, Boston	8	3	3	6
Frank Frederickson, Boston	8	2	4	6
1928–Frank Boucher, N.Y. Rangers	9	7	1	8
1929–Butch Keeling, N.Y. Rangers	6	3	0	3
Andy Blair, Toronto	4	3	0	3
Ace Bailey, Toronto	4	1	2	3
1930–Dit Clapper, Boston	6	4	2	6
1931–Cooney Weiland, Boston	5	6	3	9
1932–Frank Boucher, N.Y. Rangers	7	3	6	9
1933–Cecil Dillon, N.Y. Rangers	8	8	2	10
1934–Larry Aurie, Detroit	9	3	7	10
1935–Baldy Northcott, Mont. Maroons	7	4	1	5
Harvey Jackson, Toronto	7	3	2	5
Marvin Wentworth, Mont. Maroons	7	3	2	5
1936–Buzz Boll, Toronto	9	7	3	10
1937–Marty Barry, Detroit	10	4	7	11
1938–Johnny Gottselig, Chicago	10	5	4	9
1939–Bill Cowley, Boston	12	3	11	14
1940–Phil Watson, N.Y. Rangers	12	3	6	9
Neil Colville, N.Y. Rangers	12	2	7	9
1941–Milt Schmidt, Boston	11	5	6	11
1942–Don Grosso, Detroit	12	8	6	14
1943–Carl Liscombe, Detroit	10	6	8	14
1944–Toe Blake, Mont. Canadiens	9	7	11	18
1945–Joe Carveth, Detroit	14	5	6	11
1946–Elmer Lach, Mont. Canadiens	9	5	12	17
1947–Maurice Richard, Mont. Canadiens	10	6	5	11
1948–Ted Kennedy, Toronto	9	8	6	14
1949–Gordon Howe, Detroit	11	8	3	11
1950–Pentti Lund, N.Y. Rangers	12	6	5	11
1951–Maurice Richard, Mont. Canadiens	11	9	4	13
Max Bentley, Toronto	11	2	11	13
1952–Ted Lindsay, Detroit	8	5	2	7
Floyd Curry, Mont. Canadiens	11	4	3	7
Metro Prystai, Detroit	8	2	5	7
Gordon Howe, Detroit	8	2	5	7
1953–Ed Sandford, Boston	11	8	3	11
1954–Dickie Moore, Mont. Canadiens	11	5	8	13
1955–Gordon Howe, Detroit	11	9	11	20
1956–Jean Beliveau, Mont. Canadiens	10	12	7	19
1957–Bernie Geoffrion, Mont. Canadiens	10	11	7	18
1958–Fleming Mackell, Boston	12	5	14	19
1959–Dickie Moore, Mont. Canadiens	11	5	12	17
1960–Henri Richard, Mont. Canadiens	8	3	9	12
Bernie Geoffrion, Mont. Canadiens	8	2	10	12
1961–Gordon Howe, Detroit	11	4	11	15
Pierre Pilote, Chicago	12	3	12	15
1962–Stan Mikita, Chicago	12	6	15	21
1963–Gordon Howe, Detroit	11	7	9	16
Norm Ullman, Detroit	11	4	12	16
1964–Gordon Howe, Detroit	14	9	10	19
1965–Bobby Hull, Chicago	14	10	7	17
1966–Norm Ullman, Detroit	12	6	9	15
1967–Jim Pappin, Toronto	12	7	8	15
1968–Bill Goldsworthy, Minnesota	14	8	7	15
1969–Phil Esposito, Boston	10	8	10	18
1970–Phil Esposito, Boston	14	13	14	27
1971–Frank Mahovlich, Montreal	20	14	13	27
1972–Phil Esposito, Boston	15	9	15	24
1973–Yvan Cournoyer, Montreal	17	15	10	25

Regular-Season Records
Team

Most points, one season (2 points for a victory, 1 for a tie)—Detroit Red Wings, 1950-51 101

Fewest points, one season—Philadelphia Quakers, 1930-31 12

Longest unbeaten streak—Boston, 15 victories, 8 ties, 1940-41 . . . . 23 games

Longest unbeaten streak at home—Montreal Canadiens, 24 victories, 4 ties, 1943-44 and 1944-45 . . . . 28 games

Longest unbeaten streak on road—Boston, 9 victories, 6 ties, 1940-41; Detroit, 10 victories 5 ties, 1951-52 . . . . 15 games

Longest non-winning streak—New York Rangers, 21 losses, 4 ties, 1943-44 and 1944-45 . . . . 25 games

Longest losing streak—Philadelphia Quakers, 1930-31 . . . . 15 games

Longest non-shutout record—New York Rangers, Nov. 1940, to Dec. 31, 1942 . . . 117 games

Most tie games, one season—Montreal Canadiens, 1962-63 23

Fewest tie games, one season—Boston, 1929-30 1

Most goals, one season—Boston, 1970-71 399

Fewest goals, one season—Philadelphia Quakers, 1930-31 76

Most goals, one game—Montreal Canadiens, March 3, 1920, against Quebec Bulldogs, score 16-3 16

Most consecutive goals, one game—Detroit, Jan. 23, 1944, against New York Rangers, score 15-0 15

Most goals, one period—Detroit, in third period, against New York Rangers, Jan. 23, 1944 (final score: 15-0) 8

Most goals, both teams, one game—Montreal Canadiens 14, Toronto 7, Jan. 10, 1920 21

Most goals against, one season—New York Rangers, 1943-44 .310

Fewest goals against, one season—Ottawa Senators, 1925-26 42

Most goals against, one game—New York Rangers, Jan. 23, 1944, lost to Detroit, 15-0 .15

Most penalty minutes, one season—Detroit Red Wings, 1964-65 1,121

Individual

Most goals, one season—Phil Esposito, Boston, 1970-71 76

Most assists, one season—Bobby Orr, Boston, 1970-71 102

Most points, one season—Phil Esposito, Boston, 1970-71, 76 goals, 76 assists 152

Most goals, one game—Joe Malone, Quebec Bulldogs, Jan. 31, 1920, against Toronto St. Pats 7

Most assists, one game—Billy Taylor, Detroit, March 16, 1947, against Chicago 7

Most points, one game—Maurice Richard, Montreal Canadiens, Dec. 28, 1944, 5 goals, 3 assists, against Detroit; Bert Olmstead, Montreal Canadiens, Jan. 9, 1954, 4 goals, 4 assists against Chicago 8

Longest goal-scoring streak—Punch Broadbent, 16 games Ottawa Senators, 1921-22

Quickest goal—Ron Martin, New York Americans, Dec. 4, 1932, against Montreal Canadiens; Ted Kennedy, Toronto, Oct. 24, 1953 against Boston . . . . 8 secs.

Fastest 2 goals—Nels Stewart, Montreal Maroons, Jan. 3, 1931, in second period, against Boston . . . . 4 secs.

Fastest 3 goals—Bill Mosienko, Chicago, March 23, 1952, in third period, against New York Rangers . . . . .21 secs.

Most penalty minutes, one season—Keith Magnuson, Chicago Black Hawks, 1970-71 . .291

Most consecutive games played—Andy Hebenton, 1955-56 through 1963-64, while playing for New York and Boston . . . . .630 (plus 22 play-off games)

Fewest goals allowed by goalie, one season—Alex Connell, Ottawa Senators, 1925-26 42

Most shutouts for goalie, one season—George Hainsworth, Montreal Canadiens, 1928-29 . . .22

Most consecutive shutouts for goalie—Alex Connell, Ottawa Senators, 1927-28 6

Individual Penalty Leaders

Year	Player and team	Minutes
1917–18—	No record	
1918–19—	Joe Hall, Mont. Canadiens	85
1919–20—	Cully Wilson, Toronto	79
1920–21—	Bert Corbeau, Mont. Canadiens	86
1921–22—	Sprague Cleghorn, Mont. Canadiens	63
1922–23—	Billy Boucher, Mont. Canadiens	52
1923–24—	Bert Corbeau, Toronto	55
1924–25—	Billy Boucher, Mont. Canadiens	92
1925–26—	Bert Corbeau, Toronto	121
1926–27—	Nels Stewart, Mont. Maroons	133
1927–28—	Eddie Shore, Boston	166
1928–29—	Red Dutton, Mont. Maroons	139
1929–30—	Joe Lamb, Ottawa	119
1930–31—	Harvey Rockburn, Detroit	118
1931–32—	Red Dutton, N.Y. Americans	107
1932–33—	Red Horner, Toronto	144
1933–34—	Red Horner, Toronto	126
1934–35—	Red Horner, Toronto	125
1935–36—	Red Horner, Toronto	167
1936–37—	Red Horner, Toronto	124
1937–38—	Red Horner, Toronto	82
1938–39—	Red Horner, Toronto	85
1939–40—	Red Horner, Toronto	87
1940–41—	Jimmy Orlando, Detroit	99
1941–42—	Jimmy Orlando, Detroit	81
1942–43—	Jimmy Orlando, Detroit	89
1943–44—	Mike McMahon, Mont. Canadiens	98
1944–45—	Pat Egan, Boston	86
1945–46—	Jack Stewart, Detroit	73
1946–47—	Gus Mortson, Toronto	133

1947–48–Bill Barilko, Toronto 147
1948–49–Bill Ezinicki, Toronto 145
1949–50–Bill Ezinicki, Toronto 144
1950–51–Gus Mortson, Toronto 142
1951–52–Gus Kyle, Boston 127
1952–53–Maurice Richard, Mont. Canadiens 112
1953–54–Gus Mortson, Chicago 132
1954–55–Fern Flaman, Boston 150
1955–56–Lou Fontinato, N.Y. Rangers . . . 202
1957–58–Lou Fontinato, N.Y. Rangers . . . 152
1958–59–Ted Lindsay, Chicago 184
1959–60–Carl Brewer, Toronto 150
1960–61–Pierre Pilote, Chicago 165
1961–62–Lou Fontinato, Mont. Canadiens . 167
1962–63–Howie Young, Detroit 273
1963–64–Vic Hadfield, N.Y. Rangers 151
1964–65–Carl Brewer, Toronto 177
1965–66–Reg Fleming, Boston-N.Y. Rangers 166
1966–67–John Ferguson, Mont. Canadiens . 177
1967–68–Barclay Plager, St. Louis 153
1968–69–Forbes Kennedy, Toronto 219
1969–70–Keith Magnuson, Chicago 213
1970–71–Keith Magnuson, Chicago 291
1971–72–Bryan Watson, Pittsburgh 210
1972–73–Steve Durbano, St. Louis 229

ALL-STAR GAME

1947–All-Stars 4, Toronto 3.
1948–All Stars 3, Toronto 1.
1949–All-Stars 3, Toronto 1.
1950–Detroit 7, All-Stars 1.
1951–First Team 2, Second Team 2, at Toronto.
1952–First Team 1, Second Team 1, at Detroit.
1953–All-Stars 3, Montreal Canadiens 1.
1954–All-Stars 2, Detroit 2.
1955–Detroit 3, All-Stars 1.
1956–All-Stars 1, Montreal Canadiens 1.
1957–All-Stars 5, Montreal Canadiens 3.
1958–Montreal Canadiens 6, All-Stars 3.
1959–Montreal Canadiens 6, All-Stars 1.
1960–All-Stars 2, Montreal Canadiens 1.
1961–All-Stars 3, Chicago 1.
1962–Toronto 4, All-Stars 1.
1963–Toronto 3, All-Stars 3.
1964–All-Stars 3, Toronto 2.
1965–All-Stars 5, Montreal Canadiens 2.
1966–Montreal Canadiens 3, All-Stars 0.
1967–Toronto 4, All-Stars 3.
1968–East All-Stars 3, West All-Stars 3
1969–East All-Stars 2, West All-Stars 1.
1970–West All-Stars 2, East All-Stars 1.
1971–East All-Stars 3, West All-Stars 2.
1972–East All-Stars 5, West All-Stars 4

WORLD HOCKEY ASSOCIATION

League formed in 1972-73 season consisting of six teams in two divisions, east (E) and west (W). Quarterfinal playoffs are between first place winners and fourth-place team, and the second- and third-placed team in a best-of-seven series. The winners of this series then meet in a best-of-seven semi-final series for division champion. The finals are a best-of-seven series for the AVCO World Trophy.

World Hockey Association Standings

1972-73	Won	Lost	Tied	Pts.	Goals For	Goals Agnst.
New England Whalers (E)	46	30	2	94	318	263
Winnipeg Jets (W)	43	31	4	90	285	249

Quarterfinal Series

1972–73

East

New England Whalers beat Ottawa Nationals, 4 games to 1
Cleveland Crusaders beat Philadelphia Blazers, 4 games to 0

West

Winnipeg Jets beat Minnesota Fighting Saints, 4 games to 1
Houston Aeros beat Los Angeles Sharks, 4 games to 2

Semi-Final Series

1972–73

New England beat Cleveland, 4 games to 1
Winnipeg beat Houston, 4 games to 0

AVCO World Trophy

(Trophy salutes AVCO Financial Services, prime sponsors and benefactors of WHA)

1972–73

New England beat Winnipeg, 4 games to 0

Scoring Leaders

1972–73	Goals	Assists	Points
Andre Lacroix, Philadelphia	50	74	124

Most Valuable Player

(Selected by sports writers and broadcasters in WHA cities)

1972–73–Bobby Hull, Winnipeg Jets

All-Star Teams

East	1972–73		West
Cheevers, Cleveland . .	Goal	. . .	Wakely, Winnipeg
Tremblay, Quebec . . .	Defense		Hornung, Winnipeg
Shmyr, Cleveland . . .	Defense		Crashley, Los Angeles
Ward, New York	Center	.	Bordeleau, Winnipeg
Jarrett Cleveland	Wing	. .	Hull, Winnipeg
Webster, New England	Wing	. .	Connelly, Minnesota

All-Star Game

1972–73–East 6, West 2

AMERICAN LEAGUE

Champions

The American League, top-ranking minor professional league, is an outgrowth of 2 leagues— the International and the Canadian-American. In 1936, the latter leagues were merged and became the International-American League. In 1940, the name was shortened to its present title.

Canadian-American League

1927–28–Springfield
1929–Boston
1930–Springfield
1931–Springfield
1932–Providence
1933–Boston
1934–Providence
1935–Boston
1936–Philadelphia

International League

1930–Cleveland
1931–Windsor
1932–33–Buffalo
1934–London
1935–36–Detroit

International-American League

1937–Syracuse Stars
1938–Providence Reds
1939–Cleveland Barons
1940–Providence Reds

American League

1941–Cleveland Barons
1942–Indianapolis Capitols
1943–44–Buffalo Bisons
1945–Cleveland Barons
1946–Buffalo Bisons
1947–Hershey Bears
1948–Cleveland Barons
1949–Providence Reds
1950–Indianapolis Capitols
1951–Cleveland Barons
1952–Pittsburgh Hornets
1953–54–Cleveland Barons
1955–Pittsburgh Hornets
1956–Providence Reds
1957–Cleveland Barons
1958–59–Hershey Bears
1960–62–Springfield Indians
1963–Buffalo Bisons
1964–Cleveland Barons
1965–66–Rochester Americans
1967–Pittsburgh Hornets
1968–Rochester Americans
1969–Hershey Bears
1970–Buffalo Bisons
1971–Springfield
1972–Nova Scotia

WESTERN LEAGUE

Champions

Organized under the name of Pacific Coast League in 1944 as an amateur circuit. Became a professional league for the 1948-49 season. Changed name to present title in 1952.

Pacific Coast League (amateur)

1944–45–Seattle Iron Men
1946–Vancouver Canucks
1947–Los Angeles Monarchs
1948–Vancouver Canucks

Pacific Coast League (professional)

1949–San Diego Skyhawks
1950–New Westminster Royals
1951–Victoria Cougars
1952–Saskatoon Quakers

Western League

1953–Edmonton Flyers
1954–Calgary Stampeders
1955–Edmonton Flyers
1956–Winnipeg Warriors
1957–Brandon Regals
1958–Vancouver Canucks
1961–Portland Buckaroos
1962–Edmonton Flyers
1963–San Francisco Seals
1964–San Francisco Seals
1965–Portland Buckaroos
1966–Victoria Maple Leafs
1967–Seattle Totems
1968–Seattle Totems
1969–Vancouver Canucks
1970–Vancouver Canucks
1971–Portland Buckaroos
1972–Denver Spurs

Amateur Hockey

WORLD CHAMPIONS

Ligue Internationale de Hockey sur Glace
(International Ice Hockey Federation)

*1920–Canada	(Winnipeg Falcons)
*1924–Canada	(Toronto Granites)
*1928–Canada	(Toronto Varsity Grads)
1930–Canada	(Toronto Canadas)
1931–Canada	(Manitoba Grads)
*1932–Canada	(Winnipeg Winnipegs)
1933–United States	(Boston Olympics)
1934–Canada	(Saskatoon Quakers)
1935–Canada	(Winnipeg Monarchs)
*1936–Great Britain	(National Team)
1937–Canada	(Kimberley Dynamiters)
1938–Canada	(Sudbury Wolves)
1939–Canada	(Trail Smoke Eaters)
1940–46–No competition	
1947–Czechoslovakia	(National Team)
*1948–Canada	(Ottawa RCAF Flyers)
1949–Czechoslovakia	(National Team)
1950–Canada	(Edmonton Mercurys)
1951–Canada	(Lethbridge Maple Leafs)
*1952–Canada	(Edmonton Mercurys)
1953–Sweden	(Three Crowns)
1954–Russia	(Moscow)
1955–Canada	Penticton V's
1956–Russia	(Moscow)
1957–Sweden	(Three Crowns)
1958–Canada	(Whitby Dunlops)
1959–Canada	(Belleville McFarlands)
*1960–United States	(AHAUS Team)
1961–Canada	(Trail Smoke Eaters)

1962—Sweden   (Three Crowns)
1963—Russia
*1964—Russia
1965—Russia
1966—Russia
1967—Russia
*1968—Russia
1969—Russia
1970—Russia
1971—Russia
1972—Czechoslovakia

  * Also Olympic Champions. During Olympic years the L.I.H.G. conducts the championship as part of the Olympic Games.

  Note—Canada won a world championship competition held in 1911 in Switzerland. However, this was not an L.I.H.G. sponsored event.

EUROPEAN CHAMPIONS

1910—Great Britain
1911—Bohemia
1912—Results scratched by L.I.H.G.
1913—Belgium
1914—Bohemia
1915—19—No competition
*1920—Czechoslovakia
1921—Sweden
1922—Czechoslovakia
1923—Sweden
1924—France
1925—Czechoslovakia
1926—Switzerland
1927—Austria
*1928—Sweden
1929—Czechoslovakia
1930—Germany
1931—Austria
1932—Sweden
1933—Czechoslovakia
1934—Germany
1935—Switzerland
*1936—Great Britain
1937—Great Britain
1938—Great Britain
1939—Switzerland
1940—46—No competition
1947—Czechoslovakia
*1948—Czechoslovakia
1949—Czechoslovakia
1950—Switzerland
1951—Sweden
*1952—Sweden
1953—Sweden
1954—Russia
1955—Russia
*1956—Russia
1957—Sweden
1958—Russia
1959—Russia
*1960—Russia
1961—Czechoslovakia
1962—Sweden
1963—Russia

*1964—Russia
1965—Russia
1966—Russia
1967—Russia
*1968—Russia
1969—Russia
1970—Russia
1971—Czechoslovakia
1972—Czechoslovakia
*Olympic competition.

  After the first few years of organized league play U.S. national amateur hockey championship claims were equally valid from winners of either of the two most powerful, if widely separated, leagues. The American Amateur Hockey League (A.A.H.L.)—first league organized in the U.S.—operated in the New York City vicinity beginning in 1896. The American Amateur Hockey Association (A.A.H.A.), founded in 1913, was composed largely of teams from the Minnesota and Michigan mining areas.

  The International Skating Union made the first attempt to govern ice hockey in the U.S. on a national basis, including the determination of a national champion; its supervision began in 1917. However, the champions of the American Amateur Hockey Association retained a valid claim on the national championship, partly because of the loosely organized operations of the International Skating Union, and partly because of the high caliber of A.A.H.A. hockey. The A.A.H.L. had ceased operations after the 1916-17 season.

  In October, 1920, the United States Amateur Hockey Association (U.S.A.H.A.) was formed. The A.A.H.A. affiliated with the new organization. Shortly before, by virtue of an agreement with the International Skating Union and the Amateur Athletic Union (A.A.U.), the U.S.A.H.A. was recognized as the sole governing body for amateur hockey in the U.S. During the next several years the U.S.A.H.A. champion was recognized as the national champion.

  However, the U.S.A.H.A. declined in the late 1920's and the A.A.U. voted to assume control of the sport preceding the 1930-31 season. Until the conclusion of the 1936-37 season, the A.A.U. annual tournament provided the U.S. national champion.

  With the establishment of the Amateur Hockey Association of the U.S. (A.H.A.U.S.) in 1937 another short period of dual national champions was inaugurated, lasting through 1948. Ironically, neither organization has been able to conduct a national senior open championship in recent years although the A.H.A.U.S., which dominates amateur hockey, conducts national championships in eight lower classifications.

  A listing of all national champions through the years, and their trophy awards, follows.

American Amateur Hockey League

1896–97–New York Athletic Club
1897–98–New York Athletic Club
1898–99–Brooklyn Skating Club
1899–1900–Crescent Athletic Club, New York
1900–01–Crescent Athletic Club
1901–02–Crescent Athletic Club
1902–03–Crescent Athletic Club
1903–04–Wanderers Hockey Club, New York
1904–05–Crescent Athletic Club
1905–06–Crescent Athletic Club
1906–07–St. Nicholas Skating Club, New York
1907–08–Crescent Athletic Club
1908–09–New York Athletic Club
1909–10–New York Athletic Club
1910–11–Crescent Athletic Club
1911–12–Crescent Athletic Club
*1912–13–Hockey Club of New York
1913–14–St. Nicholas Hockey Club, New York
1914–15–St. Nicholas Hockey Club
1915–16–Boston Athletic Association, Boston, Mass.
1916–17–Boston Athletic Association
*Beginning this season the champion received the A.A.H.L. Championship Trophy.

American Amateur Hockey Association
(MacNaughton Cup)

1913–14–Cleveland Athletic Club, Cleveland, Ohio
1914–15–American Soo, Sault Ste. Marie, Michigan
1915–16–St. Paul Athletic Club, St. Paul, Minn.
1916–17–St. Paul Athletic Club, St. Paul, Minn.
1917–19–No competition
1919–20–Canadian Soo, Sault Ste. Marie, Ontario, Canada

International Skating Union
(Fellowes Cup)

1917–18–Pittsburgh Athletic Association
1918–19–No competition
1919–20–Pittsburgh Athletic Association

United States Amateur Hockey Association
(Fellowes Cup)

1920–21–Cleveland Hockey Club, Cleveland, Ohio
1921–22–Westminster Hockey Club, Boston, Mass.
1922–23–Boston Athletic Association, Boston, Mass.
1923–24–Pittsburgh Yellow Jackets, Pittsburgh, Penn.
1924–25–Pittsburgh Yellow Jackets, Pittsburgh, Penn.
1925–26–Minneapolis Rockets, Minneapolis, Minn.

Amateur Athletic Union of the U.S.

1930–31–Crescent Athletic Club, New York

1931–32–Atlantic City Sea Gulls
1932–33–Atlantic City Sea Gulls
1933–34–White Star Athletic Club, Detroit
1934–35–Baby Ruth Hockey Club, Chicago
1935–36–No competition
1936–37–Boston Olympics
1937–38–Boston Olympics
1938–39–Cleveland American Legion
1939–40–University of Minnesota
1940–41–St. Nicholas Hockey Club, New York
1941–42–Boston College
1943–46–No competition
1946–47–Hanover (New Hampshire) Indians
1947–48–Colgate University
1949–72–No competition

Amateur Hockey Association of the U.S.
(National Senior Open Trophy–formerly the A.A.H.L. Championship Trophy, 1913-17)

1937–38–Hershey Bears
1938–39–New York Rovers
1939–40–Detroit Holzbaugh Fords
1940–41–Atlantic City Sea Gulls
1941–42–New York Rovers
1942–43–U.S. Coast Guard Cutters, Baltimore
1943–44–U.S. Coast Guard Cutters, Baltimore
1944–45–Seattle Ironmen
1945–46–Vancouver Canucks, British Columbia, Canada
1946–47–Boston Olympics
1947–48–Toledo Mercurys
1948–49–Spokane Flyers
1949–50–Chatham Maroons, Ontario, Canada (Eastern U.S.)
Spokane Flyers (Western U.S.)
1950–51–Toledo Mercurys
1951–52–Johnstown Jets
1952–53–Cincinnati Mohawks
1953–54–Great Falls (Montana) Americans
1954–72–No competition

Eastern Hockey League
Regular Season Champions
(Mayor Walker Trophy)

1933–34–Atlantic City Sea Gulls
1934–35–Crescent Athletic Club, New York
1935–36–Hershey Bears
1936–37–Atlantic City Sea Gulls (First Half)
  *Hershey Bears (Second Half)
1937–38–Hershey Bears
1938–39–New York Rovers
1939–40–Baltimore Orioles
1940–41–Washington (D.C.) Eagles
1941–42–New York Rovers
1942–43–U.S. Coast Guard Cutters, Baltimore
1943–44–Boston Olympics
1944–45–Boston Olympics
1945–46–Boston Olympics
1946–47–New York Rovers
1947–48–Baltimore Clippers
1948–49–League did not operate
1949–50–Toledo Buckeyes

1950—51—Johnstown Jets
1951—52—Johnstown Jets
1952—53—Springfield (Mass.) Indians
1953—54—League did not operate
1954—55—Clinton Comets
1955—56—New Haven Blades
1956—57—Charlotte Clippers
1957—58—Charlotte Clippers
1958—59—Clinton Comets
1959—60—Johnstown Jets
1960—61—Greensboro Generals
1961—62—Clinton Comets
1962—63—Greensboro Generals
1963—64—Johnstown Jets
1964—65—Nashville Dixie Flyers
1965—66—Long Island Ducks
1966—67—Nashville Dixie Flyers
1967—70—Clinton Comets
1971—72—Charlotte Checkers
*Won play-off

International Hockey League

(Championship determined by play-offs; winner awarded Joseph Turner Memorial Trophy)

1945—46—Detroit Auto Club
1946—47—Windsor Spitfires
1947—48—Toledo Mercurys
1948—49—Windsor Spitfires
1949—50—Chatham (Ontario) Maroons
1950—51—Toledo Mercurys
1951—52—Toledo Mercurys
1952—57—Cincinnati Mohawks
1957—58—Indianapolis Chiefs
1958—59—Louisville Rebels
1959—60—St. Paul Saints
1960—61—St. Paul Saints
1961—62—Muskegon (Mich.) Zephyrs
1962—63—Fort Wayne Komets
1963—64—Toledo Blades
1964—65—Fort Wayne Komets
1965—66—Port Huron (Mich.) Flags
1966—67—Toledo Blades
1968—Muskegon Mohawks
1969—70—Dayton Gems
1971—Port Huron Flags
1972—Port Huron Wings

National Collegiate A.A.

1948—Michigan
1949—Boston College
1950—Colorado College
1951—53—Michigan
1954—Rensselaer Polytechnic Institute
1955—56—Michigan
1957—Colorado College
1958—Denver
1959—North Dakota
1960—61—Denver
1962—Michigan Tech
1963—North Dakota
1964—Michigan
1965—Michigan Tech

1966—Michigan State
1967—Cornell
1968—69—Denver
1970—Cornell
1971—72—Boston
1973—Wisconsin

Pentagonal (Ivy) Hockey League

1934—Dartmouth
1935—Yale
1936—37—Harvard
1938—39—Dartmouth
1940—Yale
1941—Princeton
1942—43—Dartmouth
1944—46—No competition
1947—49—Dartmouth
1950—51—Brown
1952—Yale
1953—Princeton
1954—58—Harvard
1959—60—Dartmouth
1961—63—Harvard
1964—Dartmouth
1965—Brown
1966—73—Cornell

Western Collegiate Hockey Association

1952—Colorado College
1953—54—Minnesota
*1955—Colorado College
1956—Michigan
1957—Colorado College
1958—North Dakota
1959—League inactive
1960—61—Denver
1962—Michigan Tech
1963—64—Denver
1965—66—Michigan Tech
1966—67—North Dakota
1968—69—Denver
1970—Minnesota
1971—Michigan Tech.
1972—Denver

*Since 1955 W.C.H.A. champions awarded the Mac-Naughton Cup, formerly national championship trophy of the American Amateur Hockey Association, 1913-20, and championship trophy of successor leagues through 1950.

Effective with the 1965-66 season the MacNaughton Cup was awarded to the WCHA team finishing first during the regular season; in prior seasons the cup and championship went to the play-off winner.

CANADIAN CHAMPIONS
Allan Cup Winners

Emblematic of the Canadian senior amateur championship.)

1908—Ottawa Cliffsides
1909—Queen's University
1910—St. Michael's College
1911—12—Winnipeg Victorias
1913—Winnipeg Hockey Club
1914—Regina Victorias

1915—Winnipeg Monarchs
1916—Winnipeg 61st Battalion
1917—Toronto Dentals
1918—Kitchener
1919—Hamilton Tigers
1920—Winnipeg Falcons
1921—University of Toronto
1922–23—Toronto Granites
1924—Sault Ste. Marie Soo Greyhounds
1925–26—Port Arthur Bearcats
1927—University of Toronto Grads
1928—University of Manitoba
1929—Port Arthur Bearcats
1930—Montreal A.A.A.
1931—Winnipegs
1932—Toronto Nationals
1933–34—Moncton Hawks
1935—Halifax Wolverines
1936—Kimberly Dynamiters
1937—Sudbury Tigers
1938—Trail Smoke Eaters
1939—Port Arthur Bearcats
1940—Kirkland Lake Blue Devils
1941—Regina Rangers
1942—Ottawa R.C.A.F. Flyers
1943—Ottawa Commandos
1944—Quebec Aces
1945—No competition
1946—Calgary Stampeders
1947—Montreal Royals
1948—Edmonton Flyers
1949—Ottawa Senators
1950—Toronto Marlboros
1951—Owen Sound Mercurys
1952—Fort Frances Canadians
1953—Kitchener-Waterloo Dutchmen
1954—Penticton (B.C.) V's
1955—Kitchener-Waterloo Dutchmen
1956—Vernon (B.C.) Canadians
1957—Whitby Dunlops
1958—Belleville McFarlands
1959—Whitby Dunlops
1960—Chatham Maroons
1961—Galt Terriers
1962—Trail Smoke Eaters
1963—Windsor Bulldogs
1964—Winnipeg Maroons
1965—Sherbrooke Beavers
1966—Drumheller Miners
1967—Drummondville (Que.) Eagles
1968—Victoriaville (Que.) Tigers
1969—Galt Hornets
1970—Spokane Jets
1971—Galt Hornets
1972—Spokane Jets

Memorial Cup Winners

(Emblematic of the Canadian junior amateur championship.)

1919—University of Toronto Schools
1920—Toronto Canoe Club

1921—Winnipeg Falcons
1922—Fort William G.W.V.A.
1923—University of Manitoba
1924—Owen Sound Greys
1925—Regina Pats
1926—Calgary Canadiens
1927—Owen Sound Greys
1928—Regina Monarchs
1929—Toronto Marlboros
1930—Regina Pats
1931—Winnipeg Elmwood Millionaires
1932—Sudbury Wolves
1933—Newmarket Redmen
1934—St. Michael's, Toronto
1935—Winnipeg Monarchs
1936—West Toronto Nationals
1937—Winnipeg Monarchs
1938—St. Boniface Seals
1939–40—Oshawa Generals
1941—Winnipeg Rangers
1942—Portage La Prairie Terriers
1943—Winnipeg Rangers
1944—Oshawa Generals
1945—St. Michael's, Toronto
1946—Winnipeg Monarchs
1947—St. Michael's, Toronto
1948—Port Arthur Bruins
1949—Montreal Royals
1950—Montreal Canadiens
1951—Barrie Flyers
1952—Guelph Biltmores
1953—Barrie Flyers
1954—St. Catherines Teepees
1955–56—Toronto Marlboros
1957—Flin Flon Bombers
1958—Ottawa-Hull Canadiens
1959—Winnipeg Braves
1960—St. Catherine Tee Pees
1961—St. Michael's, Toronto
1962—Hamilton Red Wings
1963—Edmonton Oil Kings
1964—Toronto Marlboros
1965—Niagara Falls Flyers
1966—Edmonton Oil Kings
1967—Toronto Marlboros
1968—Niagara Falls Flyers
1969–70—Montreal Canadiens
1971—Quebec Remparts
1972—Cornwall (Que.) Royals

(For Olympic champions see section on Olympic Games.)

BASIC RULES

(From E.D. Mitchell's "Sports for Recreation," A.S. Barnes and Company, New York.)

Ice hockey, a goal game, is played on an ice surface (rink) by a team of 6 players. The objective is to propel the puck (disk) along the ice and shoot it into the opponent's goal. Each score (goal) counts 1 point.

The rink is a rectangular field of ice which

need not be of any specified size as long as it is at least 60 by 160 feet. The usual rink is 185 to 200 feet long and 85 feet wide. At either end of the rink is a goal cage placed at least 10 feet out from the end of the backboards. This cage consists of a net which encloses the sides and back and which is supported by two upright posts 4 feet high and 6 feet apart. The net extends back at least 17 inches from the top and extends down to the ice. A goal line painted red connects the bases of the posts. The distance between the goals is not specified. Around the border of the ice is a wooden wall (sideboard) 4 feet high and painted white. Two blue lines drawn crosswise divide the rink into 3 equal playing areas or zones: offensive, center, and defensive zone. The professional National Hockey League rink has a red line dividing the playing area into two equal parts.

An amateur rink has 5 face-off spots; the professional rink, 13. The amateur spots are red, 12 inches in diameter. In the amateur rink, 2 are in each end zone, each 15 feet out from the goal line and midway between the sideboards and nearest cage (goal) post. One is in the exact center of the rink. All are surrounded with face-off circles. These are 2-inch-wide blue circles of 10-foot radius which surround the red face-off spots and center spot. In the amateur rink there is a penalty-shot restraining line 25 feet in front of each goal.

The puck is a disk of vulcanized rubber 3 inches in diameter and 1 inch thick, black in color and about 5½ to 6 ounces in weight.

A wooden stick, consisting of a long handle with a blade on the end, is used to propel the puck. The length, top of handle to heel, may not exceed 53 inches; the blade length may not exceed 14¾ inches. The height of the blade may not exceed 3 inches except for the goalkeeper's (3½ inches). Most stick blades have a slight bevel in one or the other direction and are accordingly "right-handed" or "left-handed" to accommodate players who shoot right or left-handed. Neutral sticks are not beveled. Angles formed with the blade and the handle vary; the degree of this angle is known as the lie. The stick of the defense man should be as long as possible and as heavy as the player can comfortably handle.

The skate is of tubular aliminum with a steel blade, which is narrow and somewhat curved. The radius (curve) is such that neither speed (sharp radius on the figure skate cuts speed) nor turning ability (no radius on the long flat racing skate makes turning difficult) is unduly sacrificed. Most hockey players have the blades of their skates "rockered" so that only a few inches are flat on the ice. This greatly aids maneuverability. Goalkeepers, of course, use a flat edge. The skate is permanently attached to a heel-less shoe which is sometimes equipped with a hard box toe for protection.

To protect the body, a light shoulder pad and hip pad are used. The goalkeeper is subjected to more hard shots than any other player and, consequently, wears body protectors, large goal pads and padded gauntlets. The other players want as much freedom as possible and so use only light, padded hockey gloves, shin guards and knee guards.

The team consists of a goalkeeper, right defense, left defense, center, right wing and left wing. Whenever the puck is faced at the center of the rink, the goalkeeper stands directly in front of his goal net at the end of the rink. A few yards in front of him are the right and left defense. The center, the hub around whom the attack revolves at the start of each play, faces off at center. Out to each side of the rink are the respective wings, right and left.

At the start of the game, the puck is put in play in the center ice spot by a face-off. The referee drops the puck on the ice between the sticks of the rival centers, at the same time giving the signal to play. The centers try to get possession of the puck and send it out to the wings. The face-off occurs when the game begins, at the beginning of each period, after a goal is scored, after the puck goes out of bounds, after a foul is committed, and after an off-side whistle has blown.

One great advantage of the game is the lack of complicated rules. The rules involve varying periods of suspension for rough play, and every effort is made to check unnecessary roughness by this means.

Penalties are classified according to the severity of the offense into minor, major, misconduct and disqualification, and the offending player must remain in a penalty box for a stated number of minutes, or, in some cases, leave the game. The penalty box, usually on the side of the rink opposite the players' bench, accommodates 8 persons, including the game timekeeper, penalty timekeeper and scorers. Minor penalties include technical violations, such as holding the puck with the hands or gloves or substituting too soon; also personal infractions, such as holding an opponent. The penalty is 2 minutes' suspension from the game. Major penalties include serious infractions, such as tripping or holding to prevent a score, charging from behind, dangerous cross-checking and the like; and the penalty is 5 minutes' suspension. Misconduct penalties are awarded in case of foul or abusive language, and the penalty is 10 minutes' suspension with, however, a substitute allowed after 2 minutes of play. Disqualification penalties are for deliberate attempts to injure an opponent and call for suspension for the balance of the game. The player who is disqualified is not allowed in the penalty box. His substitute must enter the penalty box and serve the penalty time before entering the game.

The attack is led by the center and 2 wings, who try to advance the puck into the opponents' goal by a succession of passes and shots. Body-checking or blocking with the hip or shoulder is permissible if done from the front or side, but not from the back. Blocking is accomplished by getting in front of the opponent so that he has to go around. The puck may also be blocked with the body, stick or hand, provided it is not carried forward. Hitting or lifting an opponent's stick with one's own is permitted. However, if undue force is used, this is classed as slashing and is penalized.

Stick checking is of 3 types: poke check, hook check and sweep check. In the poke check the defensive man pokes the blade of his stick at the puck in an attempt to knock it away from the attacker's possession. In the hook check he lays his stick flat on the ice and as the attacker goes past him he tries to hook the puck away from the attacker. In the sweep check the defen-sive man sweeps his stick along the ice at the puck attempting to knock it away from the puck carrier's possession.

The defense is generally led by the 2 defense men, who are responsible for protecting the area from the defensive blue line to their own goal. Not infrequently one of these men is able to take the offensive and skate toward the opposing goal with the puck. Generally, if one of the defense does take the puck down the ice, one of the wings interchanges with him and takes care of his territory until he returns. A defense man must be able to skate and handle a puck as well as a forward.

The game consists of three 20-minute periods, with an intermission of 10 minutes between periods. An important rule of the game requires that the man with puck precede his mates across the blue line on the attacking team's side of the rink.

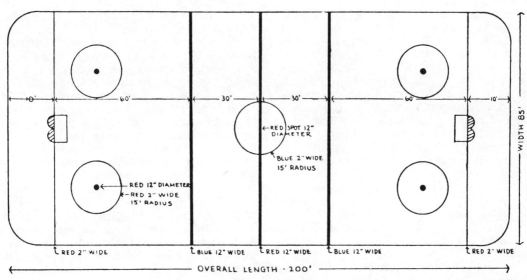

Professional Ice Hockey Rink.

ICE SKATING—FIGURE

Form and grace are the keynotes of figure skating. In contrast to the speed skater, who bends his body forward, the figure skater stands upright, expending less effort and achieving a smoother stroke. The skates have curved blades, enabling the skater to make sharp turns and spins. The invention of the steel blade gave impetus to the sport of skating, but figure skating grew at a slow pace until Sonja Henie appeared on the scene.

The beguiling lady from Norway made several million dollars through her gracefulness and amazing skill on ice skates. She pioneered the route that others have taken to fame and fortune.

The skate, the ski and the snowshoe have a common value: they enable humans to travel on snow and ice. But which was first—the skate, ski or snowshoe—is a matter that long has been debated.

In the northern countries of Europe the winters always bring much snow and ice. And long ago man, finding it necessary to travel despite the hardships, devised a winter means of locomotion. But whether he first called on small bones, which served him as skates; large bones, which were ski runners, or first devised the earliest of snowshoes is not known, nor will it ever be established.

So far as the skate is concerned, the first "blades" were made of the small bones of animals, perhaps with the joints hacked off, or at least ground down in some fashion, to make the runner as smooth as possible. They were succeeded centuries later by wooden-bladed skates. Whether wood was first used for skis or for skates we still do not know.

Certain drawings from the Middle Ages show the ancient gods of the Northland, who were supposed to have existed a few thousand years earlier, wearing huge skates, or skis, with turned-up toes. This indicates that the artists took considerable license with the legendary figures of the misty ages of equipping them with turned-up wooden runners, which were unknown until long after the gods had been discarded.

The word skate quite likely is derived from the Dutch "schaats," but it is not certain whether the Dutch, Finns, Swedes or Norwegians first used skates. Nor is it established which was foremost in the development of skis, skates and snowshoes. But it is definitely known that Scotland is the place where skating became a sport and where, as a sport, it gained early impetus and acquired a momentum that sent it whirling to the cold countries of the world.

So early as 1642 A.D., the Scots organized the Skating Club of Edinburgh. Just exactly what form of skating was called upon by the Scots of that era to provide them with entertainment is not known. As time went on, more skating clubs came into existence in Scotland, which, in addition to being the home of the skating sport, is the land where the game of curling on ice was devised.

The club in Edinburgh followed soon after the creation of the iron skate, which supplanted the wooden blade. The first iron skates were fashioned in 1572, and although progress on them was sluggish in comparison with that on the modern steel-bladed skates, they must have been a great improvement over the skates of heavily waxed wooden runners.

Skating made considerable progress as a sport after the middle of the 17th Century, and history notes that an American artist, Benjamin West, who spent a great deal of time in Europe, was the first to win a skating championship. The time is fixed as in the 1770's, but the place and other details are not matters of accurate record.

The Scots, who moved to Canada in early times along with other settlers from Europe, took their iron skates with them, and Canada had a skating carnival before the turn of the 19th Century. The Canadian weather was such that

skates, skis and snowshoes were of great need, and the new Canadians, by way of Scotland, England and France, found enjoyment in skating matches in their leisure hours.

There was, at the same time, skating in the northern parts of New England, but there is not much evidence concerning the use of skates for sport's sake. In fact, the skating sport made little more than spasmodic progress until 1850, when E. W. Bushnell of Philadelphia revolutionized affairs with a pair of skates with steel blades, which he sold for $30, a large amount of money at that time.

Bushnell was swamped with orders, since the steel skate was the perfect answer to the demand of centuries. He filled as many as he could. Other men started to make steel skates and as increased production lowered the price the skates were sold in all parts of the world where there was ice.

Bushnell's skates gave the devotees of the sport a fine chance to indulge in twists and turns on ice and on blades that did not have to be sharpened with every few dozen strokes. And it was an American, Jackson Haines, who revolutionized the art of skating.

Haines was a ballet master. After the outbreak of the Civil War in the United States, business fell away sharply. Haines knew that Vienna liked dancing, especially the waltz and late in 1863 he shifted his base of operations to Austria.

While in Vienna in 1864, Haines noticed that the people liked to skate, but they moved around in what seemed to be aimless fashion. Haines offered the idea that skating should be to music, that the waltz could be transferred to ice, as could other dance movements.

Haines then became a ballet teacher of ice skaters. He devised the movements, and his pupils followed him. He glided, waltzed, twisted and spiraled, as ballet dancers do. Thus, he originated a new form of skating that was copied throughout Europe and later was adopted in Canada and the United States.

The transplanted American also performed many novelty acts on ice, including the difficult feat of skating on stilts. His fame spread the width of Europe. He became known as the "American Ice Master," and when he died in Finland in 1875 a monument was erected to his memory. On his tombstone he was hailed as the "American Skating King."

Haines, who had established schools in Austria and many other countries, was succeeded by many of his pupils. They spread the doctrine of Haines to all nations where skating was a sport. The graduates of Haines improvised, to a certain extent, but the major movements in figure skating today—called "fancy skating" in an earlier generation—stem from those outlined by the master.

Louis Rubinstein, a Canadian, was the first famous figure skater on the North American continent. He visited Europe during the early 1870's and became a pupil of Haines. Returning to Canada, he schooled many of his friends and the result was the formation on Nov. 30, 1878, of the Amateur Skating Association of Canada, the first group of its kind in North America.

Americans became interested in the figures on ice made by Rubinstein and his club members and, in 1887, there was created in Philadelphia the Skating Club of the United States, which was the pioneer group in this country to take up skating after the Haines pattern.

Rubinstein was the Canadian champion from 1878 until 1889. He won the American title in open competition in 1888 and 1889. He climaxed his career in 1890 by going to St. Petersburg (now Leningrad), Russia, where he defeated the greatest European skaters to become world champion.

Beyond the Philadelphia area, where interest in figure skating was concentrated among 20 to 30 persons, there was little concern about such skating in the United States until 1908, when Irving Brokaw of New York went to Europe, studied skating there, returned to the United States and lectured on the fine qualities of figure skating.

Through Brokaw's efforts, the first national fancy (or figure) skating tournament for "the United States championship, with competition open to the world," was put on in New Haven, Conn., in 1914. Theresa Weld of Massachusetts won the women's singles. Norman N. Scott of Montreal won the men's singles, while the pairs championship went to Scott and Jeanne Chevalier, also of Canada.

A year later the new sport went into eclipse and remained so until 1918 because of the war. Mrs. R. S. Beresford of England won the women's title in 1918 and Nathaniel W. Niles of the United States became the men's champion. The tournament lapsed in 1919 and was resumed in 1920. Miss Weld returned to the throne and Sherwin C. Badger won the men's competition, while Miss Weld and Niles captured the pairs crown.

For the next few years the women's division was highlighted by Miss Weld, who had become Mrs. Blanchard, Beatrix Loughran of Boston and Maribel Y. Vinson of Boston and New York. Niles, Badger, Roger Turner of Philadelphia and Robin E. Lee, was originally from Minnesota but competed for a New York club, dominated the men's section. Figure skating was known chiefly as a sport that interested few persons, who skated for titles in the presence of "crowds" that embraced little more than friends and relatives of the contestants.

Meanwhile, Sonja Henie was making little nicks in the Hall of Fame of skatedom in Europe. She took up figure skating when she was about 7 and was so clumsy her older brother recom-

mended to the parents that the skates be taken from her lest she break her neck.

At 10 she won the figure skating championship of Norway—her first title—in 1924. The complete amateur record of the "Girl in White," a title conferred upon Miss Henie because she always wore a white costume in competition, follows:

World (10)—1927, 1928, 1929, 1930, 1931, 1932, 1933, 1934, 1935, 1936.

Olympic (3)—1928, 1932, 1936.

Norwegian (6)—1924, 1925, 1926, 1927, 1928, 1929.

European (8)—1929, 1930, 1931, 1932, 1933, 1934, 1935, 1936.

Prior to Miss Henie's appearance in the 1936 Olympic competition at Garmisch Partenkirchen, Germany, she received a proposition from Jeff Dixon, an Amercian promoter operating in Paris. He told her if she won he would star her in a skating act in Paris. But she had to win. Otherwise, it was no deal.

In the 1936 Olympics, Miss Henie, who previously in Olympic contests had won with considerable ease because of her fine execution of the compulsory figures, as well as those of her own devising, met the greatest opposition of her amateur career. Exactly what did happen in Germany before Miss Henie was declared winner by a margin as wide as a shaved pencil point remained a subject of controversy for many years.

Her stoutest competition came from Cecelia Cooledge of England and Vur-Anne Hulton of Sweden. Reports which seeped from Germany after Miss Henie had been declared the champion were garbled. One had it that the judges had decided upon Miss Cooledge as the winner, but when a protest was made by Miss Henie, they ordered a skate-off, which was won by Miss Henie. Another stated there was an exact tie and that Miss Henie won in the skate-off. Anyway, the final score was Miss Henie, 424.5 points; Miss Cooledge, 418.1; Miss Hulton, 394.7.

Regardless, Miss Henie emerged the winner, to the discomfiture of the English, who had been certain Miss Colledge was the most graceful and marvelous woman skater in the world—in 1936. Miss Henie at once abandoned the amateur ranks, sought out Dixon and went through with her contract with him.

Then she journeyed to the United States and plans were made to feature the 5-foot, 110-pound star from Norway in a skating act, beginning with the 1936-37 season.

The tour of 1936-37, which had been tagged before it started "a calamity show," was a sensational success. This was followed by a tour a year later. The moving picture people in Hollywood wanted her to star in an ice show. She starred in one, then another. Her tours enriched her beyond her own dreams. Within a short time, she ceased to play under the auspices of someone else and arranged to produce her own shows, familiar as the "Hollywood Ice Review."

After she had set the pattern for ice carnivals, others followed. Oscar Johnson and Eddie Shipstad of Minnesota, who had been making a little money here and there clowning on ice, assembled their carnival. After a struggle, it succeeded.

There was Miss Henie's "Hollywood Ice Revue" on tour; there were the Shipstad and Johnson shows. Others came into existence. The "Ice Cycles." the "Ice Capades." the "Ice Follies," part of the Shipstad and Johnson chain or belonging to others. The ice carnivals, unknown in the United States before Miss Henie's time, became gigantic spectacles, which drew crowded houses throughout the land.

Miss Henie played to between 15,000,000 and 20,000,000 customers in her first 15 years as a trouper. Those appearances grossed $25,000,000 to $30,000,000. The other shows, becoming of much more importance and magnitude gradually, have lured millions through the turnstiles since 1940, and all those who followed the trail blazed by the little Norwegian girl have profited. She died in 1969.

The financial success of Miss Henie influenced Miss Vinson, the American champion, and many foreign women stars to turn professional. They vied with each other in the effort to put on more and more elaborate routines and to perform more and more difficult feats, and many created some sensational acts.

Many of the men skaters also turned "pro," but none ever gained the individual popularity accorded the women. The men usually served in supporting roles, on a salary basis, or received a percentage—a small one—of the tour profits.

In recent years America has produced a figure skater who ranks with the all-time greats in the sport. He is Richard T. Button of Englewood, N.J., who in 1952 turned professional by signing a contract for $150,000 to make limited appearances in an ice show.

Button, before leaving the amateur ranks, proved over and over again that he was outstanding in the men's international and national competition. He started on the road to fame by winning the United States championship in 1946 at the age of 16, the youngest ever to hold the title. When he closed the book on his simon-pure career he was credited with 5 straight world championships, 7 consecutive United States titles (to equal Roger Turner's mark) and 2 Olympic titles in the post-World War II renewals of the Games. He also won 3 successive North American crowns.

In 1949, Button, while a student at Harvard University, was in possession of the 5 major titles—Olympic, world, North American, European and United States—an unprecedented feat. That year Button also was the victor in the voting for Sullivan Trophy, the Amateur Athletic

Union's outstanding award.

That the United States still had accomplished figure skaters despite the removal of Button from the picture was demonstrated in the 1953 world championships when the two major crowns went to Americans. Hayes Alan Jenkins of Colorado Springs, Colo., picked up where Button left off in the men's singles and Tenley Albright of Newton Center, Mass., gave the United States its first women's universal titleholder. Miss Albright completed an unprecedented "triple" in 1953 by also winning the North American and United States championships.

Miss Albright, who retired from competition shortly after the 1956 Olympics in order to pursue medical studies, in turn was succeeded by the talented Carol Heiss of New York City.

In recent years two female skaters have achieved worldwide acclaim: Peggy Fleming, World Champion from 1966 to 1968, U. S. winner from 1964 to 1968 and North American Champion in 1967; and Janet Lynn, the 20-year-old who won 5 National Championships and an Olympic bronze medal. Both have turned pro.

FAMOUS FIGURE SKATERS
Men

The great American figure skaters of the past and present include Richard T. Button, Sherwin C. Badger, Roger Turner, Robin E. Lee, Eugene Turner, Robert Specht, Arthur R. Vaughan Jr., Hayes Allan Jenkins, Nathaniel W. Niles and Norman Scott. Roger Turner is tied with Button as the holder of most national titles. Badger took the United States championships for 5 straight years, starting in 1920. Lee also won 5 titles in successive years. Jenkins followed Button as world, North American and United States champion, and was succeeded by his brother, David, who has been world and United States champion since 1957.

D. McI. Hodgson, Melville Rogers, 5 times a titleholder, and Montgomery Wilson, a 9-time champion, were among Canada's top performers.

Europe has produced a number of outstanding figure skaters, including Karl Schafer of Austria, who was world champion from 1930 through 1936. Willi Boeckl, another Austrian, was the universal titleholder from 1925 through 1928. Ulrich Salchow of Sweden won 10 world crowns, 5 in a row from 1901 to 1905, missing in 1906, then starting another succession of 5 in 1907.

In 1972 the Russian skaters, Aleksei Ulanov and Irina Rodnina, were the sixth couple to win the World Pairs Championship for the fourth time.

Women

Sonja Henie, on her record, rates as the greatest of women figure skaters. Prior to her time, Mrs. Otto von Szabo Plank of Austria, Lily Kronberger of Hungary and Meray Horvath of Hungary were great among the great. Megan Taylor of England was the successor to the laurels carried by Cecelia Cooledge and after her came Jeannette Altwegg to be England's greatest. Madge Syers was the English champion shortly after the turn of the century.

One of the best was the beautiful Canadian blonde, Barbara Ann Scott of Ottawa, who won the 1947 European championship in competition against a star-studded field. Miss Scott followed that by winning the world championship in 1947 and the world and Olympic titles in 1948. Later she became the featured performer in professional ice shows.

Mrs. Theresa Weld Blanchard of Brookline, Mass., was the first women's champion in this country. The veterans still acclaim her as America's best. She captured the inaugural competition in 1914. Miss Weld returned as queen again in 1920 and repeated in 1921, 1922, 1923, and 1924. She won the pairs title with Niles in 1918 and in 1920, 1921, 1922, 1923, 1924, 1925, 1926 and 1927.

Beatrix Loughran won the singles in 1925, 1926, and 1927 and the pairs with Badger in 1930, 1931 and 1932. Maribel Y. Vinson monopolized the throne in the late 1920's and in the Thirties reigning in 1928, 1929, 1930, 1931, 1932, 1933 1935, 1936 and 1937. Suzanne Davis of Philadelphia broke Miss Vinson's chain of victories in 1934. Another to run up a long string of triumphs in the title competition was Gretchen Merrill, who ruled from 1943 through 1948.

Other champions were Joan Tozzer, Jane Vaughn (Mrs. Sullivan) and Yvonne Sherman, who captured successive titles in 1949 and 1950. Sonya Klopfer was the 1951 queen and Tenley Albright the victor from 1952 through 1956. Miss Albright also captured 2 world titles and the 1956 Olympic laurels.

Miss Albright reigned supreme through the 1956 Olympic Games. In the world championships that year, she was succeeded by a new American star, Carol Heiss, who had been a close second to Miss Albright in the Olympics. Miss Albright then retired from competition in order to pursue medical studies and Miss Heiss has dominated the women's singles since.

In the 1960's and early 1970's Peggy Fleming and Janet Lynn of the U.S., Karen Magnussen of Canada, and Beatrix Schuba of Austria were champions either in World or National championships for single performers. In pairs competition in the U.S., Cynthia and Ronald Kauffman captured the title 3 years running, while Judy Schwomeyer and James Sladky won the dance competition from 1968 through 1972.

CHAMPIONS
World
Men
1890—Louis Rubenstein, Canada

1896—Gilbert Fuchs, Germany
1897—Gustav Hugel, Austria
1898—H. Grenander, Sweden
1899-1900—Gustav Hugel, Austria
1901-05—Ulrich Salchow, Sweden
1906—Gilbert Fuchs, Germany
1907-11—Ulrich Salchow, Sweden
1912-13—Firtz Kachler, Austria
1914—Gosta Sandahl, Sweden
1915-21—No competition
1922—Gillis Grafstrom, Sweden
1923—Fritz Kachler, Austria
1924—Gillis Grafstrom, Sweden
1925-28—Willi Boeckl, Austria
1929—Gillis Grafstrom, Sweden
1930-36—Karl Schafer, Austria
1937-38—Felix Kaspar, Austria
1939—Graham Sharp, England
1940-46—No competition
1947—Hans Gerschweiler, Switzerland
1948-52—Richard T. Button, United States
1953-56—Hayes Alan Jenkins, United States
1957-59—David Jenkins, United States
1960—Alain Giletti, France
1961—No competition
1962—Donald Jackson, Canada
1963—Donald McPherson, Canada
1964—Manfred Schnellodorfer, West Germany
1965—Alain Calmat, France
1966-68—Emmerich Danzer, Austria
1969-70—Tim Wood, United States
1971-72—Ondrej Nepela, Czechoslovakia

Women
1906-07—Madge Syers, England
1908-11—Lily Kronberger, Hungary
1912-14—Meray Horvath, Hungary
1915-21—No competition
1922-26—Mrs. Otto von Szabo Plank, Austria
1927-36—Sonja Henie, Norway
1937—Cecelia Cooledge, England
1938-39—Megan Taylor, England
1940-46—No competition
1947-48—Barbara Ann Scott, Canada
1949-50—Aja Vrzanova, Czechoslovakia
1951—Jeannette Altwegg, England
1952—Jacqueline du Bief, France
1953—Tenley Albright, United States
1954—Gundi Busch, Germany
1955—Tenley Albright, United States
1956-60—Carol Heiss, United States
1961—No competition.
1962-64—Sjoukje Dijkstra, Netherlands
1965—Petra Burka, Canada
1966-68—Peggy Fleming, United States
1969-70—Gabriele Seyfert, East Germany
1971-72—Beatrix Schuba, Austria

Pairs
1908—A. Hubler—H. Burker, Germany
1909—Mr. and Mrs. Johnson, England

1910—A. Hubler—H. Burger, Germany
1911—L. Eilers—W. Jakobsson, Finland
1912—Mr. and Mrs. Johnson, England
1913—Helene Engelmann—K. Meijstrick,
  Austria
1914—Mr. and Mrs. W. Jakobsson, Finland
1915-21—No competition
1922—Helene Engelmann—
  Alfred Berger, Austria
1923—Mr. and Mrs. W. Jakobsson, Finland
1924—Helene Engelmann—
  Alfred Berger, Austria
1925—Mrs. Otto von Szabo Plank—
  Ludwig Wrede, Austria
1926—Andree Joly—Pierre Brunet, France
1927—Mrs. Otto von Szabo Plank—
  Ludwig Wrede, Austria
1928—Andree Joly—Pierre Brunet, France
1929—Lilli Scholz—Otto Kaiser, Austria
1930—Mr. and Mrs. Pierre Brunet, France
1931—Emelia Rotter—Laszlo Szollas, Hungary
1932—Mr. and Mrs. Pierre Brunet, France
1933-35—Emelia Rotter—
  Laszlo Szollas, Hungary
1936-39—Maxi Herber—Ernst Baier, Germany
1940-46—No competition
1947-48—Micheline Lannoy—
  Pierre Baugniet, Belgium
1949—Andrea Kekessy—Ede Kiraly, Hungary
1950—Karol and Peter Kennedy,
  United States
1951—Ria Baran—Paul Falk, Western Germany
1952—Mrs. Ria Baran Falk—
  Paul Falk, Western Germany
1953—John and Jennifer Nicks, England
1954-55—Frances Dafoe—Norris Bowden, Canada
1956—Elizabeth Schwarz—Kurt Oppelt, Austria
1957-60—Barbara Wagner—Robert Paul, Canada
1961—No competition
1962—Maria and Otto Jelinek, Canada
1963-64—Marika Kilius—Hans-Jurgen—
  Baulmer, West Germany
1965—68—Ljudmila Belousova—Oleg
  Protopopov, Russia
1969—72—Irina Rodnina—Aleksei
  Ulanov, Russia

Dance

1950—Lois Waring—Michael McGean (United
  States)
1951—55—Jean Westwood—Lawrence Demmy
  (Great Britain)
1956—Pamela Weight—Paul Thomas (Great
  Britain)
1957—58— June Markham—Courtney Jones
  (Great Britain)
1959—60—Doreen Denny—Courtney Jones(Great
  Britain)
1961—Cancelled
1962—Eva Romanove— Pavel Roman (Czechoslavakia)
1962—65—Eva Romanove—Pavel Roman (Czech-

oslavakia)
1966—69—Diane Towler—Bernard Ford (Great
  Britain)
1970—72— Ljudmila Pakhomova—Aleksandr
  Gorshkov (Russia)

United States
Men

1914—Norman N. Scott
1915—17—No competition
1918—Nathaniel W. Niles
1919—No competition
1920—24—Sherwin C. Badger
1925—Nathaniel W. Niles
1926—C.I. Christenson
1927—Nathaniel W. Niles
1928—34—Roger Turner
1935—39—Robin E. Lee
1940—41—Eugene Turner
1942—Robert Specht
1943—Arthur R. Vaughan Jr.
1944—45—No competition
1946—52—Richard T. Button
1953—56—Hayes Alan Jenkins
1957—60—David Jenkins
1961—Bradley Lord
1962—Monty Hoyt
1963—Thomas Litz
1964—Scott Allen
1965—Gary Visconti
1966—Scott Allen
1967—Gary Visconti
1968—70—Tim Wood
1971—John Misha Petkevich
1972—Ken Shelley

Women

1914—Theresa Weld
1915—17—No competition
1918—Mrs. R.S. Beresford
1919—No competition
1920—Theresa Weld
1921—24—Mrs. Theresa Weld Blanchard
1925—27—Beatrix Loughran
1928—33—Maribel Y. Vinson
1934—Suzanne Davis
1935—37—Maribel Y. Vinson
1938—40—Joan Tozzer
1941—Jane Vaughn
1942—Mrs. Jane Vaughn Sullivan
1943—48—Gretchen Merrill
1949—50—Yvonne Sherman
1951—Sonya Klopfer
1952—56—Tenley Albright
1957—60—Carol Heiss
1961—Laurence R. Owen
1962—Barbara Pursley
1963—Lorraine Hanlon
1964—68—Peggy Fleming
1969—72—Janet Lynn

Pairs

1914—Jeanne Chevalier—Norman N. Scott

1915–17–No competition
1918–Theresa Weld–Nathaniel W. Niles
1919–No competition
1920–Theresa Weld–Nathaniel W. Niles
1921–27–Mrs. Theresa Weld Blanchard–
        Nathaniel W. Niles
1928–29–Maribel Y. Vinson–Thornton Coolidge
1930–32–Beatrix Loughran–Sherwin C. Badger
1933–Maribel Y. Vinson–George E.B. Hill
1934–Grace E. Madden–James L. Madden
1935–37–Maribel Y. Vinson–George E.B. Hill
1938–40–Joan Tozzer–M. Bernard Fox
1941–Donna Atwood–Eugene Turner
1942–44–Doris Schubach–Walter Noffke
1945–46–Donna Jeanne Pospisil–Jean
        Pierre Brunet
1947–Yvonne Sherman–Robert Swenning
1948–52–Karol and Peter Kennedy
1953–56–Carole Ann Ormaca–Robin Greiner
1957–Nancy Rouillard–Ronald Ludington
1958–60–Nancy and Ronald Ludington
1961–Maribel Y. Owen–Dudley Richards
1962–Dorothyann Nelson–Pieter Kollen
1963–64–Judianne and Jerry Fotheringill
1965–Vivian and Ronald Joseph
1966–69–Cynthia and Ronald Kauffman
1970–72–Jo Jo Starbuck–Ken Shelley

Dance (Gold)

1960–Margie Ackles–Charles W. Phillips, Jr.
1961–Diane Sherbloom–Larry Pierce
1962–Yvonne Littlefield–Peter F. Betts
1963–Sally Schantz–Stanley Urban
1964–Darlene Streich–Charles Fetter, Jr.
1965–66–Kristin Fortune–Dennis Sveum
1967–Lorna Dyer–John Carrell
1968–72–Judy Schwomeyer–James Sladky

Canadian
Men

1920–Norman N. Scott
1921–22–D. McI. Hodgson
1923–Melville Rogers
1924–John Z. Machado
1925–28–Melville Rogers
1929–35–Montgomery Wilson
1936–37–Osborn Colson
1938–39–Montgomery Wilson
1940–41–Ralph McCreath
1942–Michael Kirby
1943–44–No competition
1945–Nigel Stephens
1946–Ralph McCreath
1947–Norris Bowden
1948–Wallace Diestelmeyer
1949–50–Roger Wickson
1951–53–Peter Firstbrook
1954–58–Charles Snelling
1959–62–Donald Jackson
1963–Donald McPherson
1964–Charles Snelling
1965–67–Donald Knight

1968–69–Jay Humphry
1970–David McGillivray
1971–72–Toller Cranston

Women

1920–21–Jeanne Chevalier
1922–23–D. Jenkins
1924–Constance Wilson
1925–26–Cecil Smith
1927–Constance Wilson
1928–M. Barclay
1929–30–Constance Wilson
1931–35–Mrs. Constance Wilson Samuel
1936–Eleanor O'Meara
1937–Dorothy Caley
1938–Eleanor O'Meara
1939–Mary Rose Thacker
1940–Nora McCarthy
1941–Mary Rose Thacker
1942–Mrs. Mary Rose Baer
1943–No competition
1944–48–Barbara Ann Scott
1949–51–Suzanne Morrow
1952–Marlene E. Smith
1953–54–Barbara Gratton
1955–57–Carol Jane Pachl
1958–59–Margaret Crosland
1960–63–Wendy Griner
1964–66–Petra Burka
1967–Valerie Jones
1968–Karen Magnussen
1969–Linda Carbonetto
1970–72–Karen Magnussen

North American
(Biennial Competition)
Men

1923–Sherwin C. Badger, United States
1925–27–Melville Rogers, Canada
1929–31–33–35–37–39–Montgomery Wilson,
        Canada
1941–Ralph McCreath, Canada
1943–45–No competition
1947–49–51–Richard T. Button, United States
1953–55–Hayes Alan Jenkins, United States
1957–David Jenkins, United States
1959–61–Donald Jackson, Canada
1963–Donald McPherson, Canada
1965–Gary Visconti, United States
1967–Donald Knight, Canada
1969–Tim Wood, United States
1971–John Misha Petkevich, United States

Women

1923–Mrs. Theresa Weld Blanchard,
        United States
1925–27–Beatrix Loughran, United States
1929–Constance Wilson, Canada
1931–33–35–Mrs. Constance Wilson Samuel,
        Canada
1937–Maribel Y. Vinson, United States
1939–41–Mary Rose Thacker, Canada

1943—No competition
1945—47—Barbara Ann Scott, Canada
1949—Yvonne Sherman, United States
1951—Sonya Klopfer, United States
1953—55—Tenley Albright, United States
1957—59—Carol Heiss, United States
1961—Laurence R. Owen, United States
1963—Wendy Griner, Canada
1965—Petra Burke, Canada
1967—Peggy Fleming, United States
1969—Janet Lynn, United States
1971—Karen Magnussen, Canada

Pairs

1923—Dorothy Jenkins—A.G. McLennan, Canada
1925—Mrs. Theresa Weld Blanchard—Nathaniel W. Niles, United States
1927—Marion McDougall—Chauncey Bangs, Canada
1929—Constance and Montgomery Wilson, Canada
1931—33—Mrs. Constance Wilson Samuel—Montgomery Wilson, Canada
1935—Maribel Y. Vinson—George E.B. Hill, United States
1937—Veronica Clarke— Ralph McCreath, Canada
1939—Joan Tozzer— Ralph McCreath, Canada
1941—Eleanor O'Meara—Ralph McCreath, Canada
1943—45— No competition
1947—Suzanne Morrow— Wallace Diestelmeyer, Canada
1949—51—Karol and Peter Kennedy, United States
1953—55—Frances Dafoe—Norris Bowden, Canada
1957—59—Barbara Wagner—Robert Paul, Canada
1961—Maria and Otto Jelinek, Canada

1963—Debbi Wilkes— Guy Revell, Canada
1965—Vivian and Ronald Joseph, United States
1967-69—Cynthia and Ronald Kauffman, United States
1971—Jo Jo Starbuck—Ken Shelley, United States

Dance

1947—49—Lois Waring—Walter Bainbridge
1951—Carmel and Edward Bodel
1953—Carol Peters—Daniel Ryan
1955—Carmel and Edward Bodel
1957—59—Geraldine Fenton—William McLachlan
1961—Virginia Thompson—William McLachlan
1963—Paulette Doan—Kenneth Ormsby
1965—67—Lorna Dyer—John Carrell
1969—Donna Taylor—Bruce Lennie
1971—Judy Schwomeyer—Jim Sladky

(For Olympic champions see section on Olympic Games.)

BASIC RULES

Skaters striving for figure championships, either singles or pairs, go through routines far different from those in ice carnivals. In the latter, they strive for the novel, the dramatic and the picturesque. But the title seekers must perform routines, the execution of which generally is monotonous to the beholders, accounting for the lack of popularity of such contests.

Determination of the champion is on the point system, the contestants indulging in both school figures and free style. Under new figure skating rules, compulsory figures were reduced from six to three, counting 40%; a new short program of compulsory moves which prescribed free-skating elements was adopted (20%); and free-skating was awarded the remaining 40%.

ICE SKATING—SPEED

Once skates were invented, it was inevitable that skaters would engage in tests of speed. As skates improved so did the clockings. The development of the long, narrow metal blade enabled the racer to increase his speed vastly.

There have been Canadian speed skating championships for men since 1887, and in the United States speed championships for more than 60 years. The tournaments to determine the North American championships among the men began in 1891. In 1921 there was originated both the United States and the North American races for women, while Canada had its first contest for women much earlier.

Winter sports events became part of the Olympic Games program for the first time in

1924 at Chamonix, France.

Some of the speed skaters in this country and Canada also participate in barrel-jumping contests.

MEN'S WORLD CHAMPIONS

(Source: James L. Hawkins, U.S. International Skating Assoc., 10 S. Broadway, Suite 1800, St. Louis, Mo., 63102.

The winner of three of the four races automatically becomes the all-around champion. If no skater wins three of the four events, the competitor completing all the races and attaining the lowest total of points is champion. The number of seconds taken for the 500-meter race counts as the number of points for that event;

for 1,500 meters one-third of the number of seconds; for 5,000 meters one-tenth and for 10,000 meters one-twentieth.

All-Around

1893—Jaap Eden, Holland
1894—Kein Sieger (point leader, but not champion)
1895-96—Jaap Eden
1897—I.K. McCullock, Canada
1898—99—Peder Ostlund, Norway
1900—Edvard Engelsaas, Norway
1901—Franz Wathen, Finland
1902—03—Kein Sieger (point leader, but not champion)
1904—Sigurd Mathisen, Norway
1905—C.C.J. de Koning, Holland
1906—07—Kein Sieger (point leader, but not champion)
1908—09—Oscar Mathisen
1910—11—Nicolai Strunnikoff, Russia
1912—14—Oscar Mathisen
1915—21—No competition
1922—Harald Strom, Norway
1923—Clas Thunberg, Finland
1924—Roald Larsen, Norway
1925—Clas Thunberg, Finland
1926—Ivar Ballangrud, Norway
1927—Bernt Evensen, Norway
1928—29—Clas Thunberg
1930—Michael Staksrud, Norway
1931—Clas Thunberg
1932—Ivar Ballangrud
1933—Hans Engnestangen, Norway
1934—Bernt Evensen, Norway
1935—Michael Staksrud
1936—Ivar Ballangrud
1937—Michael Staksrud
1938—Ivar Ballangrud
1939—Birger Wasenius, Finland
1940—46—No competition
1947—Lasse Parkkinnen, Finland
1948—Odd Lundberg, Norway
1949—Kornel Pajor, Hungary
1950—Hjalmar Andersen, Norway
1951—Hjalmar Andersen
1952—Hjalmar Andersen
1953—Oleg Goncharenko, Russia
1954—Boris Shilkov, Russia
1955—Sigge Ericsson, Sweden
1956—Oleg Goncharenko
1957—Knut Johannesen, Norway
1958—Oleg Goncharenko, Russia
1959—Juhani Jaevinen, Finland
1960—Boris Stenin, U.S.S.R.
1961—Henk van der Grift, Netherlands
1962—Viktor Kosischin, U.S.S.R.
1963—John Nilsson, Sweden
1964—Knut Johannesen, Norway
1965—Per Ivar Moe, Norway
1966—67—Kees Verkerk, Netherlands

1968—Fred Anton Maier, Norway
1969—Dag Fornaess, Norway
1970—72—Ard Schenk, Netherlands

Sprint

1972—Leo Linkovesi, Finland

500 Meters

1893—Jaap Eden, Holland (0:51.8)
1894—Oscar Fredriksen, Norway, and Jaap Eden, Holland (0:50.4)
1895—Oscar Fredriksen (0:48.2)
1896—Jaap Eden (0:50.2)
1897—Alfred Naess, Norway (0:46.8)
1898—Julius Seyler, Germany (0:47.2)
1899—Peder Ostlund, Norway (0:50.5)
1900—Peder Ostlund (0:46.2)
1901—Franz Wathen, Finland (0:54)
1902—Rudolf Gundersen, Norway (0:47)
1903—Franz Wathen (0:49.4)
1904—Rudolf Gundersen (0:46.6)
1905—Martinus Lordahl, Norway (0:49.8)
1906—John Wikander, Finland (0:50.8)
1907—Oluf Steen, Norway (0:47.4)
1908—John Wikander (0:44.8)
1909—Oscar Mathisen, Norway (0:45.6)
1910—Oscar Mathisen (0:46.3)
1911—Nicolai Strunnikoff, Russia (0:46.4)
1912—Oscar Mathisen (0:44.2)
1913—Oscar Mathisen (0:46)
1914—Oscar Mathisen (0:45.3)
1915—21—No competition
1922—Roald Larsen, Norway (0:43.6)
1923—Clas Thunberg, Finland (0:45.2)
1924—Clas Thunberg (0:45)
1925—Clas Thunberg (0:44.7)
1926—Roald Larsen (0:44.7)
1927—Roald Larsen; Clas Thunberg and I. Korpela, Finland (0:46.3)
1928—Roald Larsen (0:43.1)
1929—Clas Thunberg (0:43.1)
1930—Haakon Pedersen, Norway (0:43.8)
1931—Clas Thunberg (0:44.1)
1932—Bernt Evensen, Norway (0:44.5)
1933—Hans Engnestangen, Norway (0:43.5)
1934—Haakon Pedersen (0:49.9)
1935—Harry Haraldsen, Norway (0:43.6)
1936—Delbert Lamb, United States (0:42.6)
1937—Georg Krog, Norway (0:42.9)
1938—Hans Engnestangen (0:41.8)
1939—Hans Engnestangen (0:44.8)
1940—46—No competition
1947—Sverre Farstad, Norway (0:44.3)
1948—Konstantin Kudrjavtsev, Russia (0:43.9)
1949—Kenneth Henry, United States (0:46.3)
1950—John Werket, United States (0:47.3)
1951—Susumu Naito, Japan (0:43)
1952—Kenneth Henry (0:43.4)
1953—Toivo Salonen, Finland (0:43.1)
1954—Evgeni Grishin, Russia (0:44.1)
1955—Toivo Salonen (0:42.6)
1956—Juri Mikhailov, Russia (0:41.9)

1957—Yevgeni Grishin, Russia (0:42.3)
1958—Robert Merkulov, Russia (0:44.2)
1959—Gennady Voronin, Russia (0:42.4)
1960—Evgenii Grishin, U.S.S.R. (0:40.5)
1961—Evgenii Grishin, U.S.S.R. (0:41.7)
1962—Evgenii Grishin, U.S.S.R. (0.41.7)
1963—Eugeni Grishin, Russia (0:39.8)
1964—Keiichi Suzuki, Japan (0:41.1)
1965—Keiichi Suzuki, Japan (0:40.7)
1966—Tom Gray, United States (0:40.9)
1967—Keiichi Suzuki, Japan (0:40.9)
1968—Keiichi Suzuki, Japan (0:40.3)
1969—Keiichi Suzuki, Japan (0:40.1)
1970—Magne Thomassen, Norway (0:40.15)
1971—Dag Fornaess, Norway (0:41.33)
1972—Ard Schenk, Netherlands and Roar
        Gronvold, Norway (tie) (0:40.14)

1,500 Meters

1893—Jaap Eden, Holland (2:48.2)
1894—Einar Halvorsen, Norway (2:35.6)
1895—Jaap Eden (2:25.4)
1896—Jaap Eden (2:36.2)
1897—I.K. McCullock, Canada (2:40.8)
1898—Peder Ostlund, Norway (2:23.6)
1899—Peder Ostlund (2:45)
1900—Edvard Engelsaas, Norway (2:38.4)
1901—Franz Wathen, Finland (2:43.4)
1902—Rudolf Gundersen, Norway (2:34.4)
1903—Johan Schwartz, Norway (2:59)
1904—Sigurd Mathisen, Norway (2:35.8)
1905—C.C.J. de Koning, Holland (2:41)
1906—Rudolf Gundersen (2:41.6)
1907—Anti Wiklund, Finland (2:33)
1908—Oscar Mathisen, Norway (2:20.8)
1909—Oscar Mathisen (2:27.4)
1910—Oscar Mathisen (2:32.6)
1911—Nicolai Strunnikoff, Russia (2:26)
1912—Oscar Mathisen (2:20.8)
1913—Oscar Mathisen (2:24.4)
1914—Oscar Mathisen (2:26.1)
1915—21—No competition
1922—Clas Thunberg, Finland (2:22.8)
1923—Roald Larsen, Norway (2:24.9)
1924—Roald Larsen (2:27.8)
1925—Clas Thunberg (2:23)
1926—Ivar Ballangrud, Norway (2:25.4)
1927—Clas Thunberg (2:24.1)
1928—Clas Thunberg (2:18.8)
1929—Clas Thunberg (2:21.9)
1930—Michael Staksrud, Norway (2:23.4)
1931—Clas Thunberg (2:24.4)
1932—Ivar Ballangrud (2:24.8)
1933—Clas Thunberg (2:22.8)
1934—Bernt Evensen, Norway (2:30.1)
1935—Ivar Ballangrud (2:23.4)
1936—Ivar Ballangrud (2:17.4)
1937—Hans Engnestangen, Norway (2:19.5)
1938—Hans Engnestangen (2:15.9)
1939—Birger Wasenius, Finland (2:30.7)
1940—46—No competition
1947—Sverre Farstad, Norway (2:21)

1948—John Werket, United States (2:22.3)
1949—John Werket (2:30.8)
1950—John Werket (2.32.1)
1951—Wim van der Voort, Holland (2:17.7)
1952—Wim van der Voort (2:21.3)
1953—Boris Shilkov, Russia (2:18.1)
1954—Boris Shilkov (2:22.3)
1955—Oleg Goncharenko, Russia (2:20.6)
1956—Boris Shilkov (2:11.6)
1957—Boris Shilkov (2:13.9)
1958—Oleg Goncharenko (2:17.7)
1959—Toivo Salonen, Finland (2:15.8)
1960—Boris Stenin, U.S.S.R. (2:10.7)
1961—Henk van der Grift, Netherlands (2:16.8)
1962—Boris Stenin, U.S.S.R. (2:13.5)
1963—Lo Chin-huan, China (2:09.2)
1964—Nils Aaness, Norway (2:12.0)
1965—Per Ivar Moe, Norway (2:08.0)
1966—Kees Verkerk, Netherlands (2:12.9)
1967—Ard Schenk, Netherlands (2:09.1)
1968—Magne Thomassen, Norway (2:07.1)
1969—Kees Verkerk, Netherlands (2:08.7)
1970—Ard Schenk, Netherlands (2:04.4)
1971—Ard Schenk, Netherlands (2:04.8)
1972—Ard Schenk, Netherlands (2:03.06)

5,000 Meters

1893—Jaap Eden, Holland (9:59)
1894—Einar Halvorsen, Norway (9:32)
1895—Jaap Eden (8:41)
1896—Jaap Eden (9:03.2)
1897—I.K. McCullock, Canada (9:25.4)
1898—Peder Ostlund, Norway (8:52.2)
1899—Peder Ostlund (9:54.6)
1900—Edvard Engelsaas, Norway (9:34.2)
1901—Rudolf Gundersen, Norway (9:56.8)
1902—J. Wiinikainen, Finland (9:20.6)
1903—G. Kiseleff, Russia (10:08)
1904—Sigurd Mathisen, Norway (9:28.2)
1905—C.C.J. de Koning, Holland (9:17.6)
1906—N. Sedoff, Russia (9:45.2)
1907—Gunnar Stromsten, Finland (9:27.6)
1908—Oscar Mathisen, Norway (8:55.4)
1909—Evgeni Burnoff, Russia (8:45)
1910—Magnus Johansen, Norway (9:27.9)
1911—Nicolai Strunnikoff, Russia (9:10.2)
1912—Oscar Mathisen (8:45.2)
1913—W. Ippolitoff, Russia (8:43.4)
1914—Oscar Mathisen (9:20.6)
1915—21—No competition
1922—Harald Strom, Norway (8:26.5)
1923—Jakob Melnikoff, Russia (9:06.2)
1924—Roald Larsen, Norway (8:54.5)
1925—Clas Thunberg, Finland (8:43.3)
1926—Ivar Ballangrud, Norway (8:42.7)
1927—Bernt Evensen, Norway (8:53.5)
1928—Ivar Ballangrud (8:28.8)
1929—Ivar Ballangrud (9:03.2)
1930—Michael Staksrud, Norway (8:28.7)
1931—Ossi Blomqvist, Finland (8:58.6)
1932—Ivar Ballangrud (8:37.6)

1933—Ivar Ballangrud (8:42.5)
1934—Birger Wasenius, Finland (10:03)
1935—Michael Staksrud (8:30)
1936—Ivar Ballangrud (8:32.5)
1937—Max Stiepl, Austria (8:28.6)
1938—Ivar Ballangrud (8:20.2)
1939—Charles Mathisen (9:31)
1940—46—No competition
1947—Lasse Parkkinnen, Finland (8:33.7)
1948—Kees Broekman, Holland (8:37.5)
1949—Kornel Pajor, Hungary (9:09.4)
1950—Hjalmar Andersen, Norway (9:15.4)
1951—Hjalmar Andersen (8:27.9)
1952—Hjalmar Andersen (8:16.8)
1953—Oleg Goncharenko, Russia (8:26)
1954—Oleg Goncharenko (8:21.9)
1955—Knut Johannesen, Norway (8:33)
1956—Oleg Goncharenko (8:07.7)
1957—Knut Johannesen (8:08.9)
1958—Vladimir Shilikovski, Russia (8:31.5)
1959—Jan Pesman, Holland (8:12.1)
1960—Valerii Kotov, U.S.S.R. (8:06.1)
1961—Ivar Nilsson, Sweden (7:58.0)
1962—Ivar Nilsson, Sweden (8:03.2)
1963—John Nilsson, Sweden (7:34.3)
1964—Knut Johannesen, Norway (7:41.3)
1965—John Nilsson, Sweden (7:33.3)
1966—Kees Verkerk, Netherlands (7:42.8)
1967—Kees Verkerk, Netherlands (7:30.4)
1968—Fred Anton Maier, Norway (7:25.0)
1969—Kees Verkerk, Netherlands (7:24.1)
1970—Jan Bols, Netherlands (7:28.6)
1971—Ard Schenk, Netherlands (7:18.8)
1972—Ard Schenk, Netherlands (7:22.84)

10,000 Meters

1893—Oscar Fredriksen, Norway (20:21.4)
1894—Jaap Eden, Holland (19:12.4)
1895—Jaap Eden (17:56)
1896—Jaap Eden (18:52.4)
1897—I.K. McCullock, Canada (20:02.4)
1898—Peder Ostlund, Norway (18:40)
1899—Jan Greve, Holland (20:36.8)
1900—Edvard Engelsaas, Norway (20:09.4)
1901—Franz Wathen, Finland (20:13.2)
1902—J. Wiinikainen, Finland (19:09.6)
1903—Th. Bonsnaes, Norway (22:15)
1904—Sigurd Mathisen, Norway (19:31)
1905—C.C.J. de Koning, Holland (19:16)
1906—N. Sedoff, Russia (19:03.6)
1907—Gunnar Stromsten, Finland (19:09.6)
1908—Oscar Mathisen, Norway (18:01.8)
1909—Evgeni Burnoff, Russia (18:17.4)
1910—Nicolai Strunnikoff, Russia (18:34)
1911—Nicolai Strunnikoff (18:13)
1912—Oscar Mathisen (17:46.3)
1913—W. Ippolitoff, Russia (17:37.8)
1914—W. Ippolitoff (18:47.6)
1915—21—No competition
1922—Harald Strom, Norway (17:37.5)
1923—Harald Strom (17:58.4)
1924—Uno Pietila, Finland (18:05.9)

1925—Uno Pietila (18:01.5)
1926—Ivar Ballangrud, Norway (18:09.1)
1927—Bernt Evensen, Norway (18:05.8)
1928—Armand Carlsen, Norway (17:17.4)
1929—Michael Staksrud, Norway (17:57)
1930—Ivar Ballangrud (17:53.7)
1931—Ossi Blomqvist, Finland (18:22.2)
1932—Ivar Ballangrud (17:58)
1933—Eddie Schroeder, United States (17:43.6)
1934—Armand Carlsen, Norway (19:03.5)
1935—Michael Staksrud (17:48.5)
1936—Birger Wasenius, Finland (17:51.4)
1937—Max Stiepl, Austria (17:25.3)
1938—Ivar Ballangrud and Charles Mathisen,
    both Norway (17:14.4)
1939—Alfons Berzins, Latvia (19:19.5)
1940—46—No competition
1947—Reidar Liaklev, Norway (17:37)
1948—Kees Broekman, Holland (17:48.8)
1949—Kornel Pajor, Hungary (18:42)
1950—Hjalmar Andersen, Norway (17:40.8)
1951—Hjalmar Andersen (19:31.8)
1952—Hjalmar Andersen (17:03.5)
1953—Oleg Goncharenko, Russia (17:22.2)
1954—Oleg Goncharenko (17:38.7)
1955—Sigge Ericsson, Sweden (17:09.8)
1956—Torstein Seiersten, Norway (16:43.3)
1957—Knut Johannesen, Norway (16:33.9)
1958—Knut Johannesen (17:08.3)
1959—Knut Johannesen (17:00.8)
1960—Jan Pesman, Netherlands (16:53.7)
1961—Viktor Kosichkin, U.S.S.R. (16:35.9)
1962—John Nilsson, Sweden (16:29.4)
1963—John Nilsson, Sweden (15:53.0)
1964—Knut Johannesen, Norway (16:06.9)
1965—John Nilsson, Sweden (15:47.7)
1966—Kees Verkerk, Netherlands (16:21.6)
1967—Kees Verkerk, Netherlands (15:51.7)
1968—Fred Anton Maier, Norway (15:26.8)
1969—Jan Bols, Netherlands (16:02.9)
1970—Jan Bols, Netherlands (15:22.6)
1971—Ard Schenk, Netherlands (15:01.6)
1972—Ard Schenk, Netherlands (15:22.09)

WOMEN'S WORLD CHAMPIONS
All-Around

1947—Verne Lesche, Finland
1948—50—Maria Isakova, Russia
1951—John Huttunen, Finland
1952—Lidia Selikhova, Russia
1953—Khalida Schegoleeva, Russia
1954—Lidia Selikhova, Russia
1955—Rimma Zhukova, Russia
1956—Zofia Kondakova, Russia
1957—58—Inga Voronina, Russia
1959—Tamara Rylova, Russia
1960—61—Valentina Stenina, Russia
1962—Inga Voronina, Russia
1963—64—Lidia Skoblikova, Russia
1965—Inga Voronina, Russia
1966—Valentina Stenina, Russia
1967—68—Stien Kaiser, Netherlands

1969–Lasma Kauniste, Russia
1970–Atje Keulen-Deelstra, Netherlands
1971–Nina Statkevich, Russia
1972–Atje Keulen-Deelstra, Netherlands

Women's Sprint
1972–Monika Pflug, West Germany

NATIONAL, INTERNATIONAL, NORTH AMERICAN CHAMPIONS

| * | International | N | National |
| NA | North American | US | U. S. Open |

Men's Outdoor
1891–92–Joseph Donoghue
1893–95–John S. Johnson
1896–97–John Nilsson
1898–99–No competition
1900–Leroy See
1901–07–Morris Wood
1908–10–Edmund Lamy
1911–14–Robert McLean
1915–Russell Wheeler*
1916–Harry Cody
1917–Arthur Staff
1918–19–No competition
1920–Everett McGowan,* Roy McWhirter
1921–Charles Jewtraw, Joseph Moore*
1922–Roy McWhirter, William Steinmetz*
1923–Harry Kashkey (N), Charles Jewtraw*
1924–Charles I. Gorman*
1925–Francis A. Allen
1926–O'Neill Farrell*
1927–No competition
1928–Lloyd Guenther
1929–Allen Potts (N), Jack Shea (NA)
1930–Jack Shea (N), Ross Robinson (NA)
1931–Frank Stack (NA)
1932–James Webster
1933–Melvin Johnston
1934–James Webster (N), Edward Schroeder (NA)
1935–37–Marvin Swanson (N)
1938–Vic Ronchetti (N, NA)
1939–Charles Leighton (NA), Ken Batholomew (N)
1940–Leo Freisinger (NA, N)
1941–42–Ken Bartholomew (NA, N)
1943–46–No competition
1947–Ken Bartholomew (N), Mario Trafeli (NA)
1948–George Fisher (NA, N)
1949–Ray Blum (N)
1950–Ken Bartholomew (N), Ray Blum (NA)
1951–Ken Bartholomew (N)
1952–Ken Bartholomew (N); Terry Browne, Art Longsjo and Ray Blum tied for NA
1953–Ken Bartholomew (N)
1954–Ken Bartholomew (N), Art Longsjo (NA)
1955–Ken Bartholomew (N), Jay Hasbrouck (NA)
1956–Ken Bartholomew (N, NA)
1957–Ken Bartholomew, Bobby Snyder (N, tie) Jim Campbell (NA)
1958–Gene Sandvig (N), Andy Korenak (NA)

1959–Ken Bartholomew (N); Keith Meyer and Gene Sandvig (NA tie)
1960–Ken Bartholomew (N), Tom Augustitis (NA)
1961–Edward Rudolph (N), Arnold Uhrlass (NA)
1962–Floyd Bedbury (N), Kick Hunt (NA)
1963–Tom Gray (N); Edward Rudolph and Bud Campbell (NA tie)
1964–N. Blatchford (N)
1965–Richie Wurster (N), Bob Fenn (US)
1966–Richie Wurster (N), Bill Lanigan (US)
1967–Mike Passarella (N), John Wurster (US)
1968–Pete Cefalu (N)
1969–Pete Cefalu (N), Richard Wurster (US)
1970–Pete Cefalu (N), Richard Wurster (NA)
1971–Jack Walters (N), Richard Wurster (NA)
1972–Barth Levy (N, NA)

Women's Outdoor
1921–23–Gladys Robinson*
1924–25–Rose Johnson*
1926–Leila B. Potter,* Lois Littlejohn (N)
1927–No competition
1928–Elsie Muller
1929–Loretta Neitzel
1930–Leila B. Potter*
1931–No competition
1932–Helen Bina
1933–Kit Klein
1934–Dorothy Franey (N), Kit Klein (NA)
1935–Kit Klein (N)
1936–Dorothy Franey (N)
1937–Maddy Horn (N)
1938–Janet Milne (NA), Mary Dolan (N)
1939–40–Maddy Horn (N, NA)
1941–46–No competition
1947–Betty Mitchell (NA), Geraldine Scott (N)
1948–Betty Mitchell (NA), Lorraine Sabbe (N)
1949–Lorraine Sabbe (N)
1950–Betty Mitchell (NA), Janice Christopher-son (N)
1951–Tie between Barbara Marchetti and Gwen-dolyn DuBois (N)
1952–Barbara Marchetti (N); Miss Marchetti, Doreen McLeod tied for NA
1953–Pat Gibson (N)
1954–Mrs. Barbara M. DeSchepper (NA), Pat Gibson (N)
1955–Pat Gibson (NA, N)
1956–Pat Gibson (NA, N)
1957–Mary Maland (N), Jeanne Robinson (NA)
1958–Mrs. Jeanne Robinson Omelenchuk (N, NA)
1959–Mrs. Jeanne Robinson Omelenchuk (N)
1960–Mary Novak
1961–Jean Ashworth
1962–Mrs. Jeanne Robinson Omelenchuk (N, NA)
1963–Jean Ashworth (N), Jean Omelenchuk (NA)
1964–Diane White (N)
1965–Jean Omelenchuk (N, US)
1966–Diane White (N), Jean Ashworth (US)
1967–Jean Ashworth (N, US)

1968—Helen Lutsch (N)
1969—Sally Blatchford (N), Sue Bradle (US)
1970—Sheila Young (N, NA)
1971—Sheila Young (N), Ruth Moore (NA)
1972—Ruth Moore and Nancy Thorne (N tie),
      Judy Spraggs (NA)

Men's Indoor

1906—07—Morris Wood
1908—10—Edmund Lamy
1911—14—Robert McLean
1915—Russell Wheeler*
1916—Anton O'Sickey
1917—Arthur Staff
1918—20—No competition
1921—24—Joe Moore*
1925—Edward Meyers
1926—27—No competition
1928—Allen Potts (N)
1929—Percy Johnson (NA)
1930—No competition
1931—32—Frank Stack (NA)
1933—Alex Hurd (NA)
1934—35—No competition
1936—Alex Hurd (NA)
1937—Marvin Swanson (NA), Leo Freisinger (N)
1938—Frank Stack (NA), Leo Freisinger (N)
1939—41—No competition
1942—H. Van Putten (NA)
1943—47—No competition
1948—Al Broadhurst (NA)
1949—50—Edgar Dame Jr. (NA)
1950—Emanuel Babayan (N)
1951—No competition
1952—Ray Blum (NA)
1953—Jim Campbell (N), Edgar Dame (NA)
1954—Art Longsjo (NA), Bob Olson (N)
1955—Bill Disney (NA), Bill Disney and Jay
      Hasbrouck (tied for N)
1956—Kenneth LeBel (NA, N)
1957—Steve Stenson (N), Jack Disney (NA)
1958—Jack Disney (N), Jim Campbell (NA)
1959—Steve Stenson, Dick Hunt (N), Donal Beam
      (NA)
1960—Terry McDermott (N), Steve Stenson (NA)
1961—Keith Meyer and Bob McCarthy (N tie),
      Terry McDermott (NA)
1962—Charles Aedo (N), Ken LeBel (NA)
1963—Bud Campbell (N), Robert McCarthy (NA)
1964—John Keith (N), Bob Fenn (US)
1965—Bud Campbell (N), Bob Fenn (US)

1966—Bill Lanigan (N), John Keith (US)
1967—Bill Lanigan (N), Bud Campbell (US)
1968—John Keith (N), Bill Lanigan (US)
1969—Bill Lanigan (N, US)
1970—Barth Levy (N), Bill Noyes (NA)
1971—Pete Cefalu and Jack Walters (N tie),
      Pat Maxwell (NA)
1972—Barth Levy (N), Bill Noyes (NA)

Women's Indoor

1921—22—Gladys Robinson*
1923—27—No competition
1928—Elsie Muller (N)
1929—Faith Schoen (NA)
1930—31—Loretta Neitzel (N)
1932—Kit Klein (NA)
1933—Maddy Horn (NA)
1934—35—No competition
1936—Dorothy Franey (NA)
1937—Dorothy Franey (NA), Maddy Horn (N)
1938—Eleanor T. Dyer (NA), Maddy Horn (N)
1939—41—No competition
1942—Elaine Gordon (NA)
1943—47—No competition
1948—49—Lorraine Sabbe (NA)
1950—Barbara Marchetti (N, NA)
1951—No competition
1952—Janet Bachman (NA)
1953—Barbara Marchetti (N)
1954—Mrs. Barbara Marchetti DeSchepper
      (N, NA)
1955—Mrs. Barbara M. DeSchepper (N, NA)
1956—Pat Underhill (NA), Marion Finch (N)
1957—Jean Ashworth (N, NA)
1958—Mary Novak (N), Jean Ashworth (NA)
1959—Jean Ashworth
1960—61—Mary Novak
1962—Dian White, Karen Kaper (NA)
1963—Jean Ashworth (N), Darlene Sechanic
      (NA)
1964—Edith Johnson (N, US)
1965—Diane White (N, US)
1966—Diane White (N), Jean Ashworth (US)
1967—Sally Blatchford (N, US)
1968—Mary Blair (N), Sally Blatchford and
      Cathy Crowe (US tie)
1969—Mary Blair (N), Cathy Crowe (US)
1970—Cathy Crowe (N), Sue Bradle (NA)
1971—Cathy Crowe (N), Carole Moore (NA)
1972—Michele Conroy (N, NA)

WORLD OUTDOOR RECORDS
Men

Distance (meters)	Time	Name and Country	Site	Date
500	0:38.0	Leo Linkovesi, Finland	Davos, Switzerland	Jan. 2, 1972
		Erhard Keller, W. Germany	Inzell, W. Germany	Mar. 4, 1972
		Hasse Borjes, Sweden	Inzell, W. Germany	Mar. 4, 1972
1,000	1:18.5	Erhard Keller, W. Germany	Inzell, W. Germany	Mar. 4, 1972
1,500	1:58.7	Ard Schenk, Netherlands	Davos, Switzerland	Jan. 16, 1971

Distance (meters)	Time	Name and Country	Site	Date
3,000	2:28.5	Ard Schenk, Netherlands	Inzell, W. Germany	Mar. 2, 1972
5,000	7:09.8	Ard Schenk, Netherlands	Inzell, W. Germany	Mar. 4, 1972
Sprint	155,800 Pts.	Erhard Keller, W. Germany	Inzell, W. Germany	Mar. 4-5, 1972
All-around	167,420 Pts.	Ard Schenk, Netherlands	Inzell, W. Germany	Mar. 4-5, 1972

Women

500	0:42.5	Anne Henning, United States	Davos, Switzerland	Jan. 7, 1972
1,000	1:27.3	Anne Henning, United States	Davos, Switzerland	Jan. 8, 1972
1,500	2:15.8	Stien Kaiser, Netherlands	Davos, Switzerland	Jan. 15, 1972
3,000	4:46.5	Stien Kaiser, Netherlands	Davos, Switzerland	Jan. 16, 1972
5,000	9:01.6	Rimma Zhukova, Russia	Alma Ata, Russia	Jan. 24, 1953
Sprint	175.730 Pts.	Ruth Schleiermacher, E. Germany	Inzell, W. Germany	Feb. 1971
All-around	182,805 Pts.	Atje Keulen-Deelstra, Netherlands	Inzell, W. Germany	Jan. 15-16, 1972

U.S. AMATEUR OUTDOOR RECORDS

Senior Men

Distance	Time	Name and Country	Site	Date
220 yards	0:17.8	Richard McDermott	St. Paul	Jan. 29, 1961
440 yards	0:34.3	Pete Cefalu	St. Paul	Jan. 31, 1970
880 yards	1:12.5	Dan Carrol	St. Paul	Feb. 1, 1969
¾ mile	1:55.8	Clas Thunberg	Saranac Lake, N.Y.	Feb. 15, 1926
1 mile	2:35.3	Bobby Fenn	St. Paul	Feb. 1, 1969
2 miles	5:24.6	Richard Wurster	St. Paul	Jan. 31, 1970
3 miles	8:19.6	Ross Robinson	Lake Placid, N.Y.	Feb. 14, 1930
5 miles	14:05.6	Mike Woods	St. Paul	Jan. 29, 1972

(400-meter track)

1 mile	2:29.7	Del Lamb	Oslo, Norway	Feb. 19, 1948

Senior Women

220 yards	0:20.2	Maddy Horn	Saranac Lake, N.Y.	Feb. 11, 1939
	0:20.2	Pat Gibson	St. Paul, Minn.	Jan. 30, 1955
440 yards	0:38.1	Leah Poulos	St. Paul	Jan. 31, 1970
880 yards	1:22.1	Nancy Thorne	St. Paul	Jan. 30, 1972
¾ mile	2:12.4	Jean Omelenchuk	St. Paul	Jan. 23, 1965
1 mile	2:53.3	Jean Ashworth	St. Paul	Jan. 27, 1963

U.S. AMATEUR INDOOR RECORDS
(Track 12 Laps or Under)

Senior Men

Distance	Time	Name	Place	Date
220 yards	0:18.0	Fred Robson	Boston	Jan. 13, 1911
1/6 mile	0:23.8	Charles Gorman	St. John, N.B.	Mar. 1, 1927
440 yards	0:36.8	Charles Gorman	St. John, N.B.	Feb. 27, 1925
880 yards	1:15.6	Ben O'Sickey	Pittsburgh	Mar. 1, 1916
¾ mile	2:00.4	Percy Johnson	Cleveland	Mar. 2, 1928
1 mile	2:41.2	Morris Wood	Pittsburgh	Feb. 13, 1904
		Fred Robson	Pittsburgh	Feb. 13, 1904
1½ mile	4:25.0	Edmund Lamy	Cleveland	Jan. 27, 1910
2 miles	5:54.8	Robert Hackenbach	St. Paul	Jan. 30, 1937
3 miles	8:58.8	Percy Johnson	Pittsburgh	Feb. 19, 1927
4 miles	13:41.8	Joe Moore	Brooklyn	Feb. 7, 1927
5 miles	15:42.2	Frank Stack	Chicago	Feb. 8, 1930

Senior Women

220 yards	0:21.6	Dorothy Franey	St. Paul	Feb. 15, 1936
1/6 mile	0:31.0	Dorothy Franey	St. Louis	Feb. 25, 1933
440 yards	0:41.0	Jean Ashworth	Champaign	Mar. 9, 1963
880 yards	1:23.3	Jean Ashworth	Champaign	Mar. 10, 1963
¾ mile	2:15.8	Sally Blatchford	Champaign	Mar. 12, 1967
1 mile	3:04.3	Jean Ashworth	Champaign	Mar. 9, 1963

(Track 13 laps or over)

Senior Men

440 yds.	0:37.6	Greg Moklen	Los Angeles	Mar. 18, 1972
880 yds.	1:16.0	Pete Cefalo	Los Angeles	Mar. 18, 1972
¾ mile	2:00.5	Bill Lanigan	Flushing	Mar. 9, 1968
1 mile	2:42.1	Bill Noyes	St. Louis	1969
2 miles	5:45.5	Bill Noyes	Madison	Mar. 8, 1970

Senior Women

440 yds.	0:42.0	Barbara De Schepper	Edmonton	Apr. 23-25, 1953
880 yds.	1:25.7	Michele Conroy	Los Angeles	Mar. 18, 1972
¾ mile	2:10.2	Susan Bradle	Madison	Mar. 7, 1970
1 mile	2:58.9	Susan Bradle	Madison	Mar. 8, 1970

JAI-ALAI

A distinct Latin flavor pervades the sport of jai-alai. Though it has been tried in Chicago and New York, Miami, Fla., is the only United States city presenting the sport. Among the reasons cited for its failure to prosper elsewhere are the difficulty of obtaining major league players and laws restricting betting.

Jai-alai, pronounced "hi-li," means "merry festival" in the Basque language. This name was adopted by the Cubans when the game was imported to their shores in 1900. Jai-alai is known by the name of "pelota" (ball) in Spain.

Dispute exists as to where the game originated. One faction states that Hernando Cortez (1485–1547) learned that early Aztecs had played it long before he invaded Mexico in 1519 and that he carried the idea back to Andalusia. Other historians say jai-alai is just a game of handball, with variations supplied by the Basques. They started with the bare hand, then progressed to a flat bat, a short basket and finally the long curved wicker basket or "cesta." The methods of play are similar to those of handball on a large scale.

The ball in jai-alai is harder and heavier than a golf ball and has been clocked at better than 150 miles per hour. This makes movement of the jai-alai ball the fastest in any sport. It is constructed of virgin de-para rubber from Brazil. The ball is hand wound by a process taking many hours. A layer of linen thread is added and then two coats of goat skin. Each ball costs $25 and when the outer goat skin is scratched, it must be replaced. The ball is approximately three-quarters the size of a regulation baseball.

The cesta has a glove at the top. Each player has his preference as to the size of the basket. It has a chestnut frame and ribs and the reeds used to weave it into a permanent, durable shape are grown atop the mountains of Northern Spain. These reeds are very light but extremely strong. Each player has his favorite "cestero" or basket-maker and these technicians are highly skilled in their trade.

Jai-alai was introduced into the United States during the World's Fair at St. Louis in 1904. Later it was played in Chicago and was successful until the law permitting gambling on the sport was revised. Jai-alai was then taken to New Orleans and was successful until the betting law was changed. In 1924 the game was inaugurated as a tourist attraction in Miami, Fla. The Biscayne Jai-Alai Fronton,* now called Miami Jai-Alai, was completed in 1926. The first fronton was destroyed by a hurricane in the same year. In 1933 the State of Florida legalized pari-mutuel wagering for horses, dogs and jai-alai. The game in Miami has been a constant and growing success. The Miami seasons runs 100 nights from mid-December to mid-April. The popularity of the sport has been growing steadily (in 1959, games were televised into the New York area from Tijuana, Mexico), and, consequently, there has been an increase in the amount of money wagered. The attendance averages more than 3,500 per night.

Jai-alai also is played in Italy, Spain, Southern France, Cuba, Mexico and the Philippines. The game has been played in Egypt, Belgium and China.

At present, the big league of modern jai-alai is Miami, Mexico City and Havana, Cuba. The management of these frontons are supporting three schools in the Basque country of Spain. They admit boys from the ages of 8 to 13 for instruction. When the lads improve enough to play professionally, they are put under contract by the Spanish impresarios and play in Spain. After a year of professional competition, the best are selected for Western Hemisphere competition.

Wagering on jai-alai follows the same pattern as that employed at horse tracks. A program normally features ten separate games, each game being comparable to a horse race in that pay-offs provide for win, place and show. The players or teams are designated by post positions.

*A fronton is a court or building used for jai-alai.

Games are divided into singles and doubles. In singles, each player is a betting unit, while in doubles matches each team of two players comprises a betting unit. The quiniela bet originated with jai-alai. Two post positions are selected in quiniela wagering and to win they must finish first and second, or second and first. The pay-offs for a $2 ticket often run over $100.

Recently a new type of wagering, called "quiniela exacta" was introduced. It is like the quiniela, except that the bettor must pick the exact order, i.e., first and second. This new form has paid more than $700 for a $2 ticket.

The stars of jai-lai make up to $3,500 per month and can play the year round. Travel expenses and medical care are provided by the management of the fronton.

BASIC RULES

Jai-alai is the simplest of ball games and requires in its basic form only a man, a ball and a wall. The man must throw the ball against the wall, causing the ball to land within certain specified limitations and then return the ball to the wall before it bounces twice, advises L. Stanley Berenson of the Miami Jai-Alai. In the American version of jai-alai, the wall is the "frontis," the granite main wall of the jai-alai fronton, where the game is played. And, rather than simply being thrown against the wall, the pelota is hurled at incredible speed by the cesta, which is strapped to the player's wrist so snugly it becomes a powerful extension of the arm.

The singles game, played between two men, follows these lines: The server must bounce the ball once on the floor at the service line. Then he scoops up the ball as it bounces and throws it to the front wall. The ball must return from the wall and land in "fair" territory. Then the opponent must in one motion catch and return the ball to the wall in the wall's "fair" portion. In turn, his return must remain within the boundary of the court.

Points are scored when a player fails to return a service, either by missing the ball entirely or by throwing it too low or too high on the front wall; by throwing it into the wire screens overhead and on one side of the court, or by throwing it to the front wall in such a manner that it does not land in the fair zone after hitting the wall. The player losing the point must retire from the court, and the player winning the point continues to play until he has in turn been "set down," or scores the required number of points to win the game. If the game point is to 7, then there will be 8 players in the game—always 1 player more than the game point.

There is an added touch to jai-alai that demands not one wall, but three, a front, side, and backwall. The American jai-alai fronton is 176 feet long, and when a player throws the pelota to the frontwall, it often bounces off the sidewall, to the players' left as they face the frontwall, serving to keep the ball in the court and to form a base for the two "playing walls"—the front and backwalls. There is no fourth wall on a jai-alai court. Instead there is a wire screen to allow the spectators to watch the game without being struck by the ball.

The player or team (jai-alai often is played with two players to a team, "doubles," as in tennis) reaching game point first is the automatic winner. The player or team having the second highest number of points is the runner-up and so on. Players tied when another player reaches game point finish out the scoring by means of round-robin play-offs.

Recently a new system of scoring, called the American Qualifying and Finals Elimination

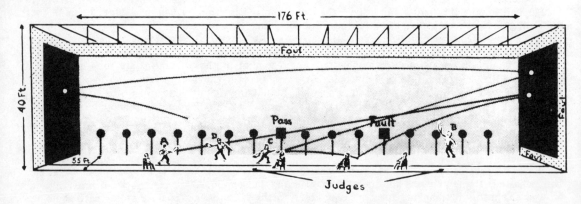

Jai-Alai. Server (A) throws to front wall. Opponent (B) misses the ball, but his teammate (C) takes it on the bounce, returns it to the front wall, causing player (D) to get ready for a rebote shot. Ball's speed is 150 miles per hour.

System, was devised for use at the Miami fronton.

Under the new system there are 8 post positions, playing to 5 points in the following manner: The game starts with the usual elimination system, but when a post position makes 3 points he has qualified and doesn't have to play again until 2 other posts have qualified by also making 3 points each against the balance of the field. The 3 finalists play off as follows: To win the game a post must either (1) defeat the other 2 posts in 2 straight points, arriving at the designated 5 points, or (2) defeat 1 post and lose to the other, in which case, 2 posts will be tied at 4 points each and these 2 posts will then play 1 point. At the conclusion of that point, 1 post will have 5 points, the loser of that point will still have 4 points for place and the post that was put down his first time up will be awarded show position. If condition (1) exists, the 2 posts who have not scored will play 1 point to establish place and show position. Naturally, the first post to qualify will serve to the second post in the finals and the winner of that point will serve the third qualifier.

LACROSSE—MEN

(Courtesy of Craig E. Taylor, Executive Secretary,
Lacrosse Hall of Fame, Homewood, Baltimore, Md., 21218)

Lacrosse is one of the few games that can be considered to be stirctly North American in origin. It is one of the fastest games, requiring skill, speed and endurance. It is a great favorite in American colleges, and since it is played in the spring it lures many collegiate football players, who find it an exciting way to keep in trim.

Lacrosse is a development of the Canadian Indian game of baggataway, perhaps played by the aborigines for centuries before adoption and standardization by the white settlers of Canada.

Lacrosse is played indoors as well as outdoors, but the indoor play, experimented with on various occasions, never has been in much favor. The greater appeal is made by the outdoor sport.

The Indians played baggataway under rules somewhat different from those that govern lacrosse today. But they had the original idea, and the Canadians merely made some improvements.

When the pioneer French Canadians first saw the Indians at play, they were impressed by the peculiar formation of the head of the stick used in the game. They didn't know what name the Indians had for their sport, but when describing it to fellow French Canadians they talked about "lacrosse"—the stick—which reminded them of a bishop's crozier.

And so, even before they adopted the game, the invaders of Canada had named it.

The early Indians used a different strategy for baggataway from the whites of this period. Their technique called for crippling as many of the opposing players as possible by "accidental" smashes with the stick. When the opposing teams had been whittled down, those left played the game as it should be played, and made an effort to gain victory by scoring.

The stellar baggataway games among the Indians always called for considerable ceremony. Some were preceded by a big pow-wow, a feast and wild dancing; others involved only religious ceremonies before the game, with the feast and the dancing afterward. The women, who were the rooters, ran up and down the sidelines beating men of their tribes with stout switches to urge them on to more furious and inspired action.

Baggataway did not limit the size of the team nor of the field. As many could play as had the desire. But the rival chieftains always were careful that the aggregations were comparatively even as to numbers. Teams ranged from 75 to 200 men on a side. Sometimes as many as a thousand participated.

Medicine men were the referees and, generally, the goal lines. In the beginning, the spots where the rival medicine men stood served as the goal lines. If either chose to wander or became absentminded and went for a long hike, the line moved right along with him. Often the line shifted from 5 to 10 miles in the course of play.

A game of baggataway was used as the medium to perpetrate the worst massacre in Canadian history on June 4, 1763. Stories differ as to who inspired it. One authority states that Pontiac, the famous Ottawa chief who was friendly with the French and hated the English, who then controlled Canada, was the evil genius, and that the game was between the visiting Ojibway and Sac Indians.

J. B. Patterson, in "Black Hawk's Biography" (Black Hawk was the outstanding Sac Indian in all history) has a somewhat different version—and perhaps the correct one. Patterson states that the Chippewas then were the inhabitants in the district where the fort—Michillimackinac (now Mackinac)—was located, and that the Sacs had sent a large delegation to visit with the Chippewas, the arrival being just before the birthday of King George III of England (June 4), a date that always was marked by celebrations among the English.

Word was sent by the Chippewas to Captain Etherington, in charge of the fort, that a baggataway game in honor of the King's birthday would be played between the Chippewas and the Sacs. The soldiers and transients who were staying at the fort were invited to attend but Etherington, suspicious, replied that his men would not leave the fort.

The Indians then stated that the game would be staged near the fort, so that the dwellers need not leave it to witness the contest. Play started in the vicinity of the fort and roved up and down for perhaps an hour. Many of the soldiers, trappers and traders who were in the fort finally walked outside and stood up or sat on the ground and watched the progress of the contest, leaving the gate to the fort wide open.

Squaws were seated on the sidelines. All were heavily blanketed, although the day was extremely warm. No significance was attached to this by the soldiers, it being regarded merely as a peculiarity of the Indian women. Suddenly, as the play was within a short distance of the fort, a signal was called by one of the chiefs. The Indians dropped their sticks, rushed to the squaws who passed them tomahawks from under their blankets, and dashed toward the fort.

Patterson's story has it that only three whites survived. Captain Etherington and Lieutenant Leslie were seized and carried away, but released a short time later. Alexander Henry escaped and, while in New York in 1824, turned author and told the story of the massacre in his "Travels and Adventures in Canada and the Indian Territories."

It is not clearly established when the baggataway game of the Indians was so altered that the new style of play became lacrosse.

F. M. Van Wagner of McGill University, Montreal, who has made a hobby of tracing the development of sports in Canada, found the following in an old program of 1894, sponsored by the Canadian Wheelman's Association:

"The early records of the 'national game' have yet to be traced. As far as can be ascertained, the first recorded match was played between teams of Iroquois and Algonquin Indians in September, 1834, at the Pierre race course (Montreal)."

That contest was in an enclosure. Since baggataway was a roving game some rules changes had to be made to conform with the limited space. Further, the Indians, playing before a white gathering, needed some understandable rules for the enclosed play. This, then, might have been the beginning of lacrosse as a definite game.

The Van Wagner findings further disclosed:

"An old Montreal resident (in 1894) claims to have played a game much like lacrosse in 1839, near what now is Richmond Square on St. Antoine Street, but there is little evidence that white men handled the 'crease' until 1842.

"The Olympic Club, which was organized in 1842, held yearly athletic meetings, and to highlight the program a game of lacrosse was played either between Indian teams or a white team against Indians. When whites played Indians, the whites usually had 7 men against 5 Indians. At the meeting on Aug. 28 and 29, 1844, a match of lacrosse was played between 12 Indians the first day and on the second day the whites played against the Indians, the aborigines winning."

Van Wagner's search revealed that lacrosse games were played at the Olympic sports meeting of 1848 and 1851, and in the latter year white men beat the Indians for the first time. The Olympic Club disbanded in the 1850's, but many members joined in forming the Montreal Lacrosse Club in 1856—the first organization to be devoted to the game that had been hewed out of ancient baggataway.

With the creation of that club, the rules were changed so as to fit the ideas of the white men and, at the annual sports meeting in September, 1857, two rival club teams played a game.

In 1858 the second club for lacrosse play—the Hochelaga—came into existence. The Beaver Club was formed in 1859 and in 1860 the "Montreal Lacrosse Club" changed its name to the "Lacrosse Club of Montreal" and absorbed the Hochelagas. In 1861 it re-adopted the name of the Montreal Lacrosse Club.

Dr. George W. Beers, a Montreal dentist, became the "father of lacrosse" in the middle 1860's by framing a set of rules with the assistance of Montreal Club members and instituting other changes. The old Indian ball of hair stuffed in deerskin was discarded for a ball of hard rubber. The stick was enlarged and improved, the number of players standardized at 12 to a side with positions definitely established. The positions were goal, point, cover point, three defense, center, three attack, outside home and inside home.

These changes occurred in 1867, with the formation of the National Lacrosse Association and the introduction of lacrosse to Great Britain and France through a tour of W. B. Johnson of Montreal with eighteen Caughnawage Indians. An association similar to Canada's subsequently was formed in England.

There was no change in the number of players until 1933, when teams were reduced to 10, the size that prevails today.

Hal Walker, a sports writer for the Toronto Globe and Mail, advised:

"Lacrosse was exclusively an amateur game in Canada until after the turn of the 20th Century. Then some cities, desiring the publicity that would accrue from representation by a crack lacrosse team, began to ship pay envelopes secretly to some state players. In time, this was done rather openly. This game went into eclipse with the First World War, but had a healthy revival along in 1919. By 1920 this had produced in Ontario the best-balanced teams Canada ever had.

"This pro game—maybe it should be called gratuity game—called for 12-man teams. Toronto had some fine combinations, known as the Maitlands, St. Simons, Young Torontos and Riversides. The cities of Orangeville, Weston, Brampton, Mimico, St. Catharines and Niagara Falls were very well represented. In Toronto, crowds of 5,000 to 8,000 turned out for the Saturday afternoon games.

"But, through lack of proper guidance, the professional game went into decay and lacrosse has been an amateur outdoor game since about 1932.

"In the 1930's, they devised an indoor lacrosse game called 'box lacrosse.' The players in Toronto and Montreal were ill-fitted for this venture. Some were veterans beyond their peak; others were green youngsters. The games were in enclosed places, in the summer, and the people refused to sit in the sweltering arenas and watch lopsided games. The league died early and nobody—except the ill-advised promoters—was saddened."

Charles W. Rowan, secretary-treasurer of the Ontario Lacrosse Association, advised that the entire "Canadian lacrosse picture is that of Box-la, a 6-man style, with a 16-player maximum per team in each game." The positions are: goalkeeper, right defense, left defense, center, right home and left home. Each team is permitted 9 substitute players and 1 substitute goalkeeper. "Lacrosse is a wonderful game and is the most historical of our North American team sports," Rowan added.

Lacrosse in the United States

Once the game had been established firmly in Canada, it was not long in crossing the border to the United States. Clubs were organized in New York City, Elmira, N.Y., and Bradford, Pa. They included the New York University Club and the Park Lacrosse Club of Brooklyn, formed in 1877. Others begun at that time were the Ravenswood Club, composed largely of New York City residents from Canada, and the New York Lacrosse Club, made up of New York Athletic Club members.

There was a tournament at Gilmore's Gardens in New York in 1877, another the following year. Included in the latter tournament were teams of Iroquois and Onondaga Indians. The United States Amateur Lacrosse Association was formed in 1879.

College lacrosse, which flourishes today under the banner of the United States Intercollegiate Lacrosse Association, got its start with the organization of the N.Y.U. team. Harvard was the second college with a team. The Crimson's was formed in 1881. Princeton started the following year.

The intercollegiate association was formed in 1882 with Harvard, Princeton and Columbia as the members. Yale and N.Y.U. were admitted the following year. In 1884 a number of players from various colleges and clubs had one of the most successful European tours ever enjoyed by United States athletes.

At a dinner in the 1920's the intercollegiate association began the annual practice of naming an All-American team and a secondary team. Since there are too many teams playing nowadays for all teams to play one another, a committee studies all the records and establishes a champion. The team thus established receives the Wilson Wingate Trophy.

The committee also picks the outstanding defensive player of the year. He gets the William Schmeisser Memorial Trophy. Other prizes, some of them sectional, are the Lou Umstead Trophy for the best player in the state of Pennsylvania, the Maryland Lacrosse Association's Men's Trophy for the best player in Maryland, the Jack Turnbull Trophy for the best "attack" player, the C. Markland Kelly Trophy for the best goalie and the Ohio Lacrosse Trophy, donated by A. C. McCormick of Akron.

In 1930, when a combined Oxford-Cambridge squad visited the United States, J. D. Flannery put up a trophy for a game between the Englishmen and Syracuse, the best American college team of that year. The Oxford-Cambridge team won. There has been no play for the trophy since.

Lacrosse is played all over the country, enjoying its greatest popularity in and near Baltimore. Crowds of 10,000 are attracted when top-flight teams meet. During the 1932 Olympic Games at Los Angeles, over 150,000 turned out to watch three contests.

The game is popular in secondary schools, as well as at colleges and clubs. In the five years before World War II and in the years since, the sport has made more progress in player and spectator appeal than at any other time.

Lacrosse Overseas

Lacrosse gained footholds in England and Australia at about the same time—1877 in Great Britain, 1874 Down Under. An association was formed in the south of England in 1882 and Canada's rules were adopted.

Australia had 163 teams and 2,614 players before World War II. About 2,000 players volunteered for war service. With the end of hostilities, the game began an upward trend.

ALL-AMERICAN SELECTIONS

1927

Goal	Gazee, Navy
Point	Gamache, Harvard
Cover Point	Biddison, Johns Hopkins
First Defense	Trapnell, Hobart
Second Defense	McFarland, Colgate
Third Defense	Clark, Syracuse (Capt.)
Center	Land, Johns Hopkins
Third Attack	Crosswaite, Maryland
Second Attack	Roberts, Rutgers
First Attack	Painter, Syracuse
Out Home	Thulin, Princeton
In Home	Hull, Navy

1928

G—Street, Maryland
P—Harrington, Syracuse
CP—Mallonee, Johns Hopkins
FD—Spring, Navy
SD—Born, Army
TD—Alton, Rutgers
C—Lang, Johns Hopkins (Capt.)
TA—Larrison, Colgate
SA—Roberts, Rutgers
FA—Painter, Syracuse
OH—Biddison, Johns Hopkins
IH—Linkous, Maryland

1929

G—Richardson, Colgate
P—Boucher, St. John's
CP—Brophy, Syracuse
FD—Schoales, Cornell
SD—Loan, Maryland
TD—Spring, Navy
C—Fenn, Steven Tech
TA—Scarlet, Princeton
SA—Potter, Union
FA—Parrish, Navy
OH—Huggins, Yale
IH—Evans, Maryland

1930

G—Kelly, Maryland, and Evanson, Rutgers
P—Kearney, Rutgers, and E. Lotz, St. John's
CP—Utz, Pennsylvania, and Hall, Johns Hopkins
FD—Jenifer, Princeton, and Heagy, Maryland
SD—Brophy, Syracuse, and Galbraith, Hobart
TD—Spring, Navy, and Cornbrooks, St. John's
C—Page, Colgate, and Smith, Yale
TA—Gould, Dartmouth, and Rosen, N.Y.U.
SA—Finegan, Union, and Allen, Navy
FA—Stevens, Yale, and Turnbull, Johns Hopkins
H—Evans, Maryland, and Champion, Cornell
H—Latimer, Rutgers, and Pool, St. John's

1931

G—Rinehart, Springfield, and Armacost, St. John's

P—P. Lotz, St. John's, and Knauss, Rutgers
P—Deekman, Maryland, and E. Lotz, St. John's
FD—Zimmerman, Army, and James, Navy
SD—Galbraith, Hobart, and Hagar, Union
TD—Fisher, Union, and Brinkley, Harvard
C—Pugh, Maryland, and Smith, Yale
TA—Ziegler, St. John's, and Pottenger, Army
SA—Guild, Johns Hopkins, and Beggs, Yale
FA—Stevens, Yale, and Pike, Swarthmore
H—Latimer, Rutgers, and Turnbull, Johns Hopkins
H—Pool (Capt.), St. John's, and Ronkin, Maryland

1932

G—Porter, Navy, and Brooks, Princeton
P—Summerfelt, Army, and Nicholson, Maryland
P—Lotz, St. John's, and Obersheiner, Hobart
FD—Tuller, Cornell, and Cronin, Rutgers
SD—Kranz, Dartmouth, and Morris, St. John's
TD—Lang, Johns Hopkins, and Norris, Maryland
C—Pugh, Maryland, and Packard, Johns Hopkins
TA—Pottenger, Army, and Wyatt, Union
SA—Guild, Johns Hopkins, and Beggs, Yale
FA—Turnbull (Capt.), Johns Hopkins, and Julian, Rutgers
H—Latimer, Rutgers, and Welch, Syracuse
H—Ronkin, Maryland, and Kelly, Johns Hopkins

1933

(Beginning of 10-man teams.)

G—Shea, Dartmouth, and Brooks, Princeton
P—Ward, Rutgers, and Train, Yale
CP—Summerfelt, Army, and Lamont, St. John's
FD—Yearley, Johns Hopkins, and Krans, Dartmouth
SD—Sothoron, Maryland, and Wands, Pennsylvania
C—Pugh, Maryland, and Tibbets, Army
SA—Finnegan, Union, and Lang, Johns Hopkins
FA—Ives, Johns Hopkins, and Pike, Swarthmore
OH—Kelly, Johns Hopkins, and Winslow, Cornell
IH—Schwab, Princeton, and Ferguson, Navy

1934

G—Johnson, Hobart, and Reinhold, Washington
P—Lamond, St. John's, and Opdyke, Rutgers
CP—Siber, Maryland, and Train, Yale
FD—Yearley, Johns Hopkins, and Stillman, Army
SD—Ceppi, Princeton, and Sothoron, Maryland
C—Beeler, Johns Hopkins, and Tibbets, Army
SA—Humphreys, Rutgers, and Foote, Union
FA—Kelly, Johns Hopkins, and Delaney, Syracuse
OH—Robbins, Syracuse, and Lang, Johns Hopkins
IH—Wardell, Princeton, and Smith, St. John's

1935

G—Johnson, Hobart, and Ruhling, Johns Hopkins
P—Lamond, St. John's, and Nye, Pennsylvania
CP—Silbert, Maryland, and Swindell, Johns Hopkins
FD—VanMeter, Rutgers, and True, Army
SD—Donahue, St. John's, and Rombro, Maryland

C—Jensen, Syracuse, and Truxton, Army
SA—Ward, Navy, and Thomas, Maryland
FA—Wardell, Princeton, and Koth, Penn State
OH—Robbins, Syracuse, and Smith, St. John's
IH—Ellinger, Maryland, and England, Harvard

1936

G—Kelly, Maryland, and Britten, Princeton
P—Ennis, Maryland, and Witherspoon, Harvard
CP—Naylor, Johns Hopkins, and Jontos, Syracuse
FD—True, Army, and Swindell, Johns Hopkins
SD—Hammann, St. John's, and Rabbit, Maryland
C—Truxton, Army, and Smith, Navy
SA—Palcanis, Rutgers, and Brill, Maryland
FA—Ferris, Hobart, and Smith, Union
OH—Ellinger, Maryland, and Christhilf, Maryland
IH—Smith, St. John's, and Warner, Yale

1937

G—Kelly, Maryland, and Hallock, Rutgers
P—Robinson, Princeton, and Naylor, Johns
    Hopkins
CP—Witherspoon, Harvard, and Soucek, Navy
FD—Swindell, Johns Hopkins, and Melig, Navy
SD—Kelley, Navy, and McLean, Princeton
C—Truxton, Army, and Morison, Syracuse
SA—Dering, Princeton, and Hammann, St. John's
FA—Ferris, Hobart, and Smith, Union
OH—Ellinger, Maryland, and Scott, Army
IH—Smith, St. John's, and Neilson, Maryland

1938

G—James, Navy
P—Bradley, Army
CP—Foedisch, Princeton
FD—Player, Navy
SD—Rowe, St. Johns
C—Perry, Rutgers
SA—Lindsay, Maryland
FA—Sherburne, Army
OH—Miller, Navy
IH—Neilson, Maryland

1939

G—James, Navy
P—Mulitz, Maryland
CP—Wilson, Army
FD—Tolson, Hopkins
SD—Meade, Maryland
C—Stephens, Pennsylvania
SA—Henry, Yale
FA—Ferris, Hobart
OH—Hendrix, Navy
IH—Buck, St. John's

1940

G—Turner, Princeton
P—Frontezak, Army
CP—Mulitz, Maryland
FD—Tolsen, Hopkins
SD—Ritter, Penn State
C—Donnelly, Swarthmore
SA—Evans, Rutgers
FA—Ferris, Hobart
OH—Nevares, Maryland

IH—King, Princeton

1941

G—Campbell, Princeton
P—Tolson, Johns Hopkins
CP—Shawn, Johns Hopkins
FD—Brady, Navy
SD—Mueller, Maryland
C—Donnelly, Swarthmore
SA—Thigpen, Army
FA—Thomas, Johns Hopkins
OH—Wilder, Dartmouth
IH—Fitch, Hobart

1942

G—Campbell, Princeton
P—Kaestner, Johns Hopkins
CP—Gehman, Princeton
FD—Smith, Army
SD—Brady, Navy
C—Schmidt, Rutgers
SA—Dell, Yale
FA—Thomas, Johns Hopkins
OH—Weisheit, Princeton
IH—Fitch, Hobart

1943

G—Courtney, Loyola
P—Tiedeberg, Stevens Tech
CP—Ditmar, Maryland
FD—Riepe, Johns Hopkins
SD—Ochenrider, Navy
C—Green, Drexel
SA—Guild, Johns Hopkins
FA—Hoyert, Maryland
OH—Booze, Navy
IH—Palmer, Princeton

1944

G—L. B. Broughton, Army
P—J. W. Donaldson, Army
CP—Fred Alner, Cornell
FD—Vince T. Anania, Navy
SD—Jack Heldberg, Stevens Tech
C—H. D. Hume, Navy
SA—John Mott, Stevens Tech
FA—Brooks Tunstall, Cornell
OH—R. Merriam, Dartmouth
IH—R. H. Groves, Army

1945

G—John J. Albright, Navy
P—Norman Mallory, Army
CP—Charles Merdinger, R.P.I.
FD—Charles Guy, Navy
SD—John G. Hedberg, Stevens Tech
C—William Devens, Army
SA—Herbert Stiles, Navy
FA—Harry McCloskey, Swarthmore
OH—William Stites, Army
IH—Richard Groves, Army

1946

G—Jerry Courtney, Johns Hopkins
P—Robert Fetters, Maryland

CP—Clarence Hewitt, Johns Hopkins
FD—James Carrington, Navy
SD—Edward Hanson, Navy
C—William Devens, Army
SA—Ernest L. Ransome, Princeton
FA—Lee Chambers, Navy
OH—Leonard Gaines, Princeton
IH—A. Hausman, Army

1947

G—Geroge Baron, C.C.N.Y.
P—Frederick Allner, Princeton
CP—Lloyd Bunting, Johns Hopkins
FD—John McEnery, Army
SD—Wilson Fewster, Johns Hopkins
C—James Hartinger, Army
SA—Henry Fish, Princeton
FA—Brooke Tunstall, Johns Hopkins
OH—Daymon Jordan, R.P.I.
IH—Leonard Gaines, Princeton

1948

Goal . . . . John Rust, Army
Defense . . . . .Charles Gilfallen, Duke
Defense . . . . Frederick Allner, Princeton
Defense . . . . .John McEnery, Army
Midfield . . . . .James Hartinger, Army
Midfield . . . . Henry Fish, Princeton
Midfield . . . . Ray Greene, Johns Hopkins
Attack . . . . . . .Brooke Tunstall, Johns Hopkins
Attack . . . . .Lee Chambers, Navy
Attack . . . . .Daymon Jordan, R.P.I.

1949

G—Richard Seth, Navy
D—Phillip Ryan, Navy
D—Robert Proutt, Virginia
D—Lloyd Bunting, Johns Hopkins
M—James Adams, Johns Hopkins
M—James Hartinger, Army
M—William Fuller, Syracuse
A—Lee Chambers, Navy
A—William Powell, R.P.I.
A—Oliver Shepard, Johns Hopkins

1950

G—William Clements, Washington and Lee
D—Phil Ryan, Navy
D—Lloyd Bunting, Johns Hopkins
D—Kinloch Yellott, Yale
M—Robert Sandell, Johns Hopkins
M—William Fuller, Syracuse
M—Richard Coons, R.P.I.
A—William Hooper, Virginia
A—Richard Powell, R.P.I.
A—Don Hahn, Princeton

1951

G—Joseph Sollers Jr., Johns Hopkins
D—William Hubbell, Maryland
D—Bruno Giordano, Army
D—Charles Golfillan, Duke
M—Redmond Finney, Princeton
M—Edward Meyer, Army

M—Lester Eustace, R.P.I.
A—Donald Hahn, Princeton
A—William Hooper Jr., Virgina
A—Ray Wood, Washington College

1952

G—William Larash, Maryland
D—William Hubbell, Maryland
D—Robert Bickel, Duke
D—Wallace Beneville, Rutgers
M—Avery Blake Jr., Swarthmore
M—Kenneth Miller, Princeton
M—Albert Lorenzen, Army
A—Gordon Jones, Virginia
A—Lester Eustace, R.P.I.
A—Emil Budnitz, Johns Hopkins

1953

G—John Johnson, Army
D—William Shoop, R.P.I.
D—David Tait, Princeton
D—H. Edwin Semler, Johns Hopkins
M—Donovan Kniss, Navy
M—Richard Young, Drexel
M—Thomas Compton, Virginia
A—Ralph Willis, Princeton
A—Emil Budnitz, Johns Hopkins
A—Avery Blake Jr., Swarthmore

1954

G—John Jones, Navy
D—Stanley Swanson, Navy
D—Furlong Baldwin, Princeton
D—Edward Anderson, Duke
M—James Grieves, Virginia
M—Bruce Yancey, Syracuse
M—Oliver Combs, Army
A—Peter Leone, Army
A—George Corrigan, Maryland
A—William Hunter, Navy

1955

G—Clement Malin, Dartmouth
D—John Raster, Navy
D—John Simmons, Maryland
D—Carl Orent, Hofstra
M—Si Ulcickas, Navy
M—Robert Kelley, Rutgers
M—James Keating, Maryland
A—Charles Wicker, Maryland
A—Percy Williams, Navy
A—John Griffis, R.P.I.

1956

G—James Kappler, Maryland
D—John Simmons, Maryland
D—John Pendergast, Yale
D—Peter Wagner, R.P.I.
M—James Keating, Maryland
M—Robert Kelley, Rutgers
M—Arlyn Marshall, Johns Hopkins
A—Charles Wicker, Maryland
A—Stuart Lindsay, Syracuse
A—John Howard, Washington College

1957

G—Jim Kappler, Maryland
D—Ben Glyphis, Army
D—Doug Levick, Princeton
D—Walt Mitchell, Johns Hopkins
M—Joe Seivold, Washington College
M—Ernie Betz, Maryland
M—James Brown, Syracuse
A—Billy Morrill, Johns Hopkins
A—Mickey Webster, Johns Hopkins
A—Jack Daut, Rutgers

1958

G—James Lewis, Washington and Lee
D—Douglas G. Levick, Princeton
D—Walter B. Mitchell, Johns Hopkins
D—Donald Tillar, Army
M—Ernest J. Betz, Maryland
M—Paul Loewer, Baltimore
M—Joseph Seivold, Washington
A—William K. Morrill Jr., Johns Hopkins
A—Richard Corrigan, Maryland
A—James Webster Jr., Johns Hopkins

1959

G—Randall Mail, Dartmouth
D—William Morton, Dartmouth
D—Robert Schwartzberg, Maryland
D—Donald Tillar, Army
M—John Heyd, Princeton
M—Agostino DiMaggio, Washington
M—Charles Getz, Army
A—John Howland, Rutgers
A—James Webster, Johns Hopkins
A—William Morrill Jr., Johns Hopkins

1960

G—Edward Nippard, Baltimore
D—Jack O. Horton, Princeton
D—John P. MacNealey, Johns Hopkins
D—William S. Carpenter, Army
M—David L. Dresser, Cornell
M—Herman T. Eubanks, Army
M—Richard R. Pariseau, Navy
A—Howard Albrecht, Baltimore
A—Karl Rippelmeyer, Navy
A—Robert S. Miser, Army

1961

G—Howard Kringard, Princeton
D—Neal Reich, Navy
D—Mike Byrne, Johns Hopkins
D—Richard Bruckner, Army
M—Clayton Beardmore, Maryland
M—Sam Wilder, Army
M—Junior Kelz, Baltimore
A—Jerry Schmidt, Johns Hopkins
A—Thomas W. Mitchell, Navy
A—Henry Peterson, Virginia

1962

G—Deeley Nice, Virginia
D—Timothy Callard, Princeton
D—Fred Lewis, Navy

D—Robert Fuellhart, Army
M—Richard Finley, Syracuse
M—Al Biddison, Army
M—James Levasseur, Virginia
M—Roger Kisiel, Navy
M—Clayton Beardmore, Maryland
M—Henry Ciccarone, Johns Hopkins
A—George Tracy, Navy
A—Grady H. Watts, Harvard
A—Jerry Shmidt, Johns Hopkins

1963

G—A. Norm Webb, Jr., Army
D—Anthony (Mac) Caputo, Virginia
D—Michael D. Coughlin, Navy
D—Jan Berzins, Johns Hopkins
M—Robert Grose, Yale
M—Homer Schwartz, Johns Hopkins
M—Bill King, Dartmouth
M—Gray (Tuck) Henry, Princeton
M—Snowden Hoff, Virginia
M—Donald C. MacLaughlin, Navy
A—John Valestra, Rutgers
A—George P. Tracy, Navy
A—Ray Altman, Maryland

1964

G—Norm Webb, Army
D—Mike Buckley, Army
D—Jim Campbell, Navy
D—Mike Coughlin, Navy
M—Fred Betz, Maryland
M—Roy Buckner, Army
M—Snowden Hoff, Virginia
M—Mike Herriott, Dartmouth
M—Homer Schwartz, Johns Hopkins
M—John Taylor, Navy
A—Tom Sheckells, Army
A—Jim Lewis, Navy
A—John Valestra, Rutgers

1965

G—John Schofield, Maryland
D—Bob Radcliffe, Army
D—Charles Benoit, Yale
D—Pat Donnelly, Navy
M—Tim Vogel, Army
M—Dick Peterson, Virginia
M—Stephen Mallonee, Johns Hopkins
M—John Kenworthy, Maryland
M—Neil Henderson, Navy
M—Brian Lantier, Navy
A—Gerald Pfeiffer, Johns Hopkins
A—Tom Sheckells, Army
A—Jim Lewis, Navy

1966

G—Richard Alter, Brown
D—John Baker, Princeton
D—Al Pastrana, Maryland
D—Ben Kaestner, Johns Hopkins
M—John McKissock, Dartmouth
M—Frank Kobes, Army
M—George Armiger, Brown

M—Jerry Schnydman, Johns Hopkins
M—Richard Salmon, Navy
M—Howard Crisp, Navy
A—Bruce Cohen, Cornell
A—John Heim, Maryland
A—Jim Lewis, Navy

1967

G—Milton Hilliard, Cornell
D—Benjamin Kaestner, John Hopkins
D—Carl Tamulevich, Navy
D—John Baker, Princeton
M—John McIntosh, Navy
M—Alan Davey, Navy
M—James Chalfant, Washington College
M—Jerome Schnydman, Johns Hopkins
M—Bruce Hinkle, Maryland
M—Glynn Hale, Army
A—Joseph Cowan, Johns Hopkins
A—John Heim, Maryland
A—Christopher Pettit, Army

1968

G—Milton Hilliard, Cornell
G—Malcolm Ogilvie, Navy
D—Carl Tamulevich, Navy
D—Michael Clark, Johns Hopkins
D—Peter Coy, Virginia
M—John McIntosh, Navy
M—Steve Pfeiffer, Maryland
M—Charles Goodell, Johns Hopkins
A—Joe Cowan, Johns Hopkins
A—H. D. McCarty, Johns Hopkins
A—Peter Cramblot, Army

1969

G—James Eustace, Virginia
D—Mike Clark, Johns Hopkins
D—Dick Luecke, Army
D—John Padgett, Navy
M—Charles Coker, Johns Hopkins
M—Harry MacLaughlin, Navy
M—Charles Goodell, Johns Hopkins
A—Joseph Cowan, Johns Hopkins
A—Peter Cramblet, Army
A—Mark Webster, Cornell

1970

G—Leonard Supko, Navy
D—Gregory Murphy, Navy
D—Robert MacCool, Johns Hopkins
D—G. Douglas Hilbert, Virginia
M—Charles Coker, Johns Hopkins
M—James Potter Jr., Virginia
M—Harry MacLaughlin, Navy
A—Peter Cramblett, Army
A—Thomas Cafaro, Army
A—Mark Webster, Cornell

1971

G—Robert Rule, Cornell
D—John Burnap, Cornell
D—John Overs, Hofstra
D—Tom Schildwachter, Virginia
M—Ronn Liss, Army

M—Robert Shaw, Cornell
M—Pete Eldridge, Virginia
A—Tom Cafaro, Army
A—Al Rimmer, Cornell
A—Jay Connor, Virginia

1972

G—Les Matthews, Johns Hopkins
D—Ed Haugevik, Rutgers
D—Larry Story, Yale
D—Tom O'Leary, Army
M—Pete Eldredge, Virginia
M—Rick Kowalchuk, Johns Hopkins
M—Doug Schreiber, Maryland
A—John Kaestner, Maryland
A—Jack Thomas, Johns Hopkins
A—Jay Connor, Virginia

HALL OF FAME

Dr. Roland Abercrombie, Johns Hopkins (1958)
Fred C. Alexander, Harvard (1963)
Gordon Armstrong, Johns Hopkins (1969)
Gaylord (Peck) Auer, No college (1968)
Henry F. Baker, Swarthmore (1964)
Norris Barnard, Swarthmore (1959)
Thomas N. Biddison, Sr., Johns Hopkins (1963)
Fred Billings, Navy (1962)
Avery F. Blake, Swarthmore, Pennsylvania
    (1961)
John W. Boucher, St. John's (1967)
Frank Breyer, Johns Hopkins (1964)
Albert A. Brisotti, New York Univ. (1958)
C. Brower, Hobart (1959)
Carlton P. Collins, Cornell (1958)
Walter T. Collins, Yale (1964)
Laurie D. Cox, Harvard (1957)
William A. Davis, (1959)
Joseph H. Deckman, Maryland (1965)
Charles Ellinger, Maryland (1969)
Milton Erlanger, Johns Hopkins (1966)
William (Moon) Evans, Maryland (1966)
John E. Faber, Maryland (1963)
Carlton J. Ferris, Hobart (1971)
Fred Fitch, Syracuse (1961)
Royce Flippin, Navy (1966)
Henry Ford, Swarthmore (1962)
Henry S. Frank, Johns Hopkins (1965)
Waldemar H. Fries, Cornell (1959)
Morris Gilmore, Navy (1968)
Avery (Red) Gould, Dartmouth (1966)
Lorne R. Guild, Johns Hopkins (1967)
William J. Harkness, Union (1961)
Carl Hartdegen, Lehigh (1963)
Russell S. Hawkins, Sr., Brown (1967)
Albert B. Heagy, Maryland (1965)
Frederic (Rip) Hewitt, Maryland (1971)
William Hudgins, Johns Hopkins (1959)
James D. Iglehart, St. John's (1968)
Victor F. Jenkins, Syracuse (1967)
Joseph J. Julien, Rutgers (1965)
Caleb Kelly, Johns Hopkins (1969)
Donaldson Kelly, Johns Hopkins (1966)

John F. Kelly, Maryland (1969)
J. Sarasfield Kennedy, Crescent A.C. (1960)
Andrew Kirkpatrick, St. John's (1958)
John Knipp, Johns Hopkins (1959)
Francis L. Kraus, Hobart (1964)
Philip E. Lamb, Swarthmore (1965)
Gibbs La Motte, Mt. Washington Club (1969)
Fred C. Linkous, Maryland (1967)
William Logan, Johns Hopkins (1969)
Edwin L. Lotz, St. John's (1966)
Philip L. Lotz, St. John's (1968)
Irving Lydecker, Syracuse (1960)
Malcolm MacIntyre, Yale (1966)
William Madden, Johns Hopkins (1961)
C. Gardner Mallonee, Johns Hopkins (1960)
Charles E. Marsters, Harvard (1957)
Ivan M. Marty, Maryland (1970)
Harland Meistrell, Princeton (1962)
Cyrus C. Miller, New York Univ. (1957)
Leon Miller, City College of N.Y. (1960)
Miller Moore, Pennsylvania (1964)
William H. Moore, III, Johns Hopkins (1961)
W. Kelso Morrill, Johns Hopkins (1961)
Howard Myers, Jr., Virginia (1971)
W. Oster Norris, St. John's (1962)
Claxton J. O'Connor, St. John's (1964)
John G. Paige, Colgate (1960)
Sifford Pearre, Johns Hopkins (1967)
Robert Poole, St. John's (1963)
Edwin Powell, Maryland (1964)
Gordon Pugh, Maryland (1968)
Victor Ross, Syracuse (1962)
William C. Schmeisser, Johns Hopkins (1957)
Herbert Scott, Crescent A.C. (1960)
Roy Simmons, Syracuse (1964)
Winthrop A. Smith, Yale (1968)
Arthur Finn Spring, Navy (1971)
Victor Starzenski, Stevens Tech (1959)
Jason Stranahan, Union (1963)
Thomas Strobhar, Johns Hopkins (1959)
Edward M. Stuart, Johns Hopkins (1960)
Fritz R. Stude, Johns Hopkins (1970)
Conrad J. Sutherland, Princeton (1961)
Roy Taylor, Cornell (1957)
Glenn N. Thiel, Syracuse (1965)
Ferris Thomsen, Swarthmore & St. John's (1963)
F. Morris Touchstone, Army (1960)
Thomas Truxton, Army (1970)
Douglas Turnbull, Johns Hopkins (1962)
John I. Turnbull, Johns Hopkins (1966)
Albert W. Twitchell, Rutgers (1967)
Reginald Van Truitt, Maryland (1959)
Harry E. Wilson, Army (1963)
Fred Wyatt, Union (1969)
W. Caspari Wylie, Maryland (1959)
Church Yearley, Johns Hopkins

UNITED STATES CHAMPIONS
Intercollegiate

The Wingate Trophy, emplematic of the championship of the United States Intercol-legiate Lacrosse Association, was first awarded in 1936.

1881-82—Harvard
1833—Yale
1884-85—Princeton
1886-1901—Records not available
1902—Johns Hopkins
1903-04—Records not available
1905—Columbia, Cornell, Harvard, Swarthmore (tie)
1906—Cornell, Johns Hopkins (tie)
1907—Cornell, Johns Hopkins (tie)
1908—Harvard, Johns Hopkins (tie)
1909—Harvard, Columbia, Johns Hopkins (tie)
1910—Harvard, Swarthmore (tie)
1911—Harvard, Johns Hopkins (tie)
1912—Harvard
1913—Harvard, Johns Hopkins (tie)
1914—Cornell, Lehigh (tie)
1915—Harvard, Johns Hopkins (tie)
1916—Cornell, Lehigh (tie)
1917—Stevens Tech, Lehigh (tie)
1918—No champion
1919—Stevens Tech, Johns Hopkins (tie)
1920—Syracuse, Lehigh (tie)
1921—Lehigh
1922—Syracuse
1923—Johns Hopkins
1924-25—Syracuse
1926-27—Johns Hopkins
1928—Johns Hopkins, Maryland, Navy, Rutgers (tie)
1929—*Navy, Union
1930-31—St. John's (Baltimore)
1932-35—No champions
1936—Maryland
1937—Maryland, Princeton (tie)
1938—Navy
1939-40—Maryland
1941—Johns Hopkins
1942—Princeton
1943—Navy
1944—Army
1945—Army, Navy (tie)
1946—Navy
1947-48—Johns Hopkins
1949—Johns Hopkins, Navy (tie)
1950—Johns Hopkins
1951—Army, Princeton (tie)
1952—Virginia, Rensselaer Polytech (tie)
1953—Princeton
1954—Navy
1955-56—Maryland
1957—Johns Hopkins
1958—Army
1959—Army, Maryland, Johns Hopkins (3-way tie)
1960—Navy
1961—Army, Navy (tie)
1962—Navy
1963-66—Navy
1967—Johns Hopkins, Navy, Maryland (3-way tie)

1968—Johns Hopkins
1969—Johns Hopkins, Army (tie)
1970—Johns Hopkins, Navy (tie)
1971—Cornell
1972—Virginia

*St. John's of Baltimore was generally regarded as the national champion, but was ineligible for official recognition because the school was not then a member of the U.S.I.L.A.

North-South Game

The annual highlight of the intercollegiate lacrosse season is the North-South game, which brings together the best players from each section.

1940—North 6, South 5
1941—South 7, North 6
1942—North 6, South 3
1943—South 9, North 5
1944-45—No games
1946—North 14, South 14
1947—North 15, South 3
1948—North 11, South 6
1949—South 11, North 6
1950—North 12, South 8
1951—North 12, South 11
1952—South 15, North 7
1953—South 12, North 9
1954—North 13, South 11
1955—South 12, North 11
1956—South 20, North 10
1957—North 14, South 10
1958—South 26, North 6
1959—South 10, North 9
1960—South 13, North 12
1961—South 13, North 9
1962—South 14, North 4
1963—South 14, North 11
1964—*American 12, National 10
1965—North 15, South 10
1966—South 13, North 5
1967—North 7, South 5
1968—North 9, South 8
1969—South 12, North 11
1970—South 11, North 10
1971—North 9, South 6
1972—South 18, North 14

*Called the All-American Classic

United States Open

1934-36—Mount Washington L.C.
1937—Baltimore A.C.
1938-40—Mount Washington L.C.
1941—Johns Hopkins
1942—Mount Washington L.C.
1943-45—No competition
1946-50—Mount Washington L.C.
1951—Baltimore L.C.
1952-53—Mount Washington L.C.
1954—Mount Washington L.C., Navy (tie)
1955—Mount Washington L.C., Maryland (tie)
1956—Maryland

1957—Johns Hopkins, Mount Washington L.C. (tie)
1958—Army
1959-60—Mt. Washington (Baltimore)
1961—Baltimore Lacrosse Club
1962—Mt. Washington (Baltimore)
1963—Baltimore University Club
1964—Mt. Washington L.C.
1965—Baltimore University Club
1966-67—Mt. Washington L.C.
1968-71—Long Island L.C.
1972—Carling's L.C.

BASIC RULES

(From "Lacrosse," by W. Kelso Morrill, published by A. S. Barnes and Company, New York.)

Lacrosse is played on a field 110 yards long by not less than 60 yards, not more than 70 yards wide. The goals are 80 yards apart, with 15 yards of playing territory behind each goal.

Each goal consists of two poles 6 feet apart, extending 6 feet above the ground and joined by a rigid top cross-bar. The poles (about 2 inches in diameter) are fitted with a pyramid-shaped cord netting of not more than 1½ inches mesh. Although the 2-inch pipe is the best, many teams use 1-inch pipe and some use wooden posts. The netting is fastened to a stake in the ground at a point 7 feet in back of the center of the goal. The netting must be fastened close to the ground to prevent the ball from passing through it.

A circle around the goal is known as the goal crease. This circle has a radius of 9 feet and should be clearly marked by a white line. The center of the circle is midway between the goal posts.

The boundary lines are composed of two side lines and two end lines. These are marked in white, as is a center line, drawn across the middle of the field perpendicular to the side lines. The field must have a white line 10 yards in length, parallel to the center line, 20 yards directly in front of each goal. The territory extending from these lines to the end lines is called the goal area. Also there must be a white line 20 yards long on each side of the field and parallel to the side lines. These lines extend 10 yards on either side of the center line. The territory between these lines and the side lines is called the wing area. The wing area is designated by lines on each side of the field 20 yards long and 20 yards away from the center of the field, parallel with the sidelines and extending 10 yards on each side of the center line.

Ten players compose a team. Although the original names of the players are retained for historic reasons, it has been found less confusing to call the three players who play closest to their own goal, the defense men; the players who play both attack and defense, the midfield players, one of whom is the center; and the three men who play closest to their opponent's goal, the attack players. The tenth man is, of course, the goal keeper. Sometimes the words "close defense" or "close attack" are used to distinguish these men from the midfielders. The point, cover point, and first defense are the defense men; the second defense, center, and second attack are the midfielders; and the first attack, out home, and in home are the attack men.

Before each game the players of the opposing teams line up at the center of the field facing each other with their left sides toward the goal they are defending. Originally, the reason for this line-up was to enable the officials to inspect the players' equipment, since in the early days there was considerable use of illegal sticks and illegal shoes. Now, the purpose is to allow the players to meet their opponents. This method of lining up for each contest is unique to lacrosse and extremely colorful.

Before play starts at the center of the field, the players are confined to the following positions on the field: the center at the center of the field; one midfielder in one wing area and the remaining midfielder in the other; the attack in the attack goal area; and the goalie and defense in the defense goal area. So long as the proper number of players is in the assigned area, it does not matter which position any one man plays throughout the game. For example, at the face-off, a close-attack man could face the ball and the center play in the attack goal area. In case a penalty has deprived a team of one or more players, that team is exempt from confining its players to the wing and attack goal areas to the extent of the number of players in the penalty box. It also has a right to choose in which area it shall exercise its exemption.

As soon as the game starts, all players are released from their assigned positions and are allowed the freedom of the field within its boundaries, with one exception: three attack men and four defense men must always remain on their respective sides of the center line.

Besides a marked field to play on and a pair of goals, it is necessary to have a ball, and each player must have a stick, helmet, gloves and uniform. It is illegal for any player to participate in any of the play without a stick in his hand.

The ball is of India rubber sponge, not less than 7¾ inches, not more than 5 to 5¼ ounces in weight. When dropped from a height of 72 inches upon a hardwood floor, it should have a bounce of not less than 45 inches and not more than 49 inches.

The stick is known as a crosse, from which the game derives its name. Sticks are either right- or left-handed, although today almost everyone plays with a right-handed stick.

The stick is made up of the handle and the head (net or face) joined together at the throat. The net is bound on either side by a wall. Both walls may be made of wood or plastic, or one of wood or plastic and the other of cat-gut. For a right-handed stick, the right wall is always wooden or plastic; for a left-handed stick, the left wall is always wooden or plastic. The net may be made of leather, clock-cord or cat-gut. The guard is a mat of leather or rawhide that prevents the ball from being held fast in the narrow part of the net. There must be no peculiar fastening to the net that might make it difficult for the ball to be dislodged by an opponent.

The pocket is that portion of the net that holds the ball. The pocket is adjustable. Each player should develop or "break in" the pocket of his own stick. To keep the wall straight and stiff, the strings forming the pocket and the wall should be loosened after each practice or game and then tightened before the next one begins. In wet weather, the player should oil the net strings slightly, to keep them from becoming taut and lifeless, but never the wall.

The width of the stick may not be more than 12 nor less than 7 inches, and the length may not be more than 6 nor less than 3 feet. The length of the stick varies with the individual player's ability to handle it efficiently. Four face sizes are commonly used: a small face for the close attack (7 to 8 inches), a medium-size face for the midfield players (8 inches), a larger face for the close-defense (10 inches) and a still larger face for the goalie (12 inches).

The attacking player uses a stick with a small face to enable him to make short, snappy passes, to allow him to shoot quickly from any position and to permit him to dodge without losing the ball. The close-defense player prefers a stick with a large net and a long handle to enable him to intercept passes, block shots and prevent dodging. The midfield players are both attack and defense players, and hence their sticks must be medium in both the size of the net and the length of the handle. The goalkeeper uses a stick with the largest face of all in order to help him stop the ball from going into the goal.

The object of each side is to put the ball into the goal of the opponent and to prevent it from going into their own goal, and all the running, dodging, passing and checking tend to that end. A goal counts 1 point.

The ball may not be touched by the hands except by the goalkeeper when attempting to prevent the scoring of a goal. The ball is kept in play by being carried, thrown or batted with the stick, or kicked in any direction within the confines of the playing field.

A game is 60 minutes in length, divided into 4 quarters of 15 minutes each. There is a 1-minute interval between the first and second quarters and between the third and fourth quarters. Between the second and third quarters is an intermission of 10 minutes during which interval the teams may leave the field. If at the end of the regular playing time the score is tied, play is resumed after an intermission of 5 minutes for two 5-minute periods. Whichever team scores the greatest number of goals in the two overtime periods is declared the winner. If the score is still tied at the end of these periods, the game is declared a tie.

At the beginning of each quarter and after each goal is scored, play is started in the center of the field by a draw or face-off between the two center players. The two centers put the backs of the nets of their sticks together at the center of the field so that the plane of the stick is perpendicular to the playing field and parallel to the center line. The centers allow their sticks to rest upon the ground and crouch facing the goals they are attacking. The referee places the ball between and touching the two nets and starts play by blowing a whistle. At the whistle, each center attempts to have his team get possession of the ball, either by controlling it himself or by passing it to a teammate.

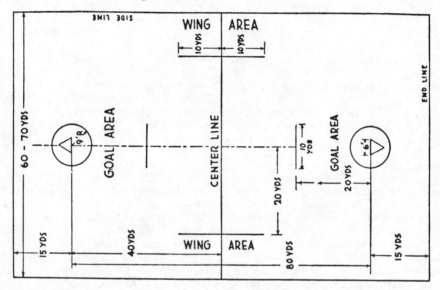

Men's Lacrosse Field. (Taken from "Sports for Recreation," edited by E. D. Mitchell, A. S. Barnes and Company, New York.)

LACROSSE—WOMEN

Though lacrosse is indigenous to the North American continent, the women's game largely owes its rise to England. It is quite different from the men's game, requiring no brawn and no body contact. It is a game of speed and skill, and the only similarity to the men's game is in the name and general shape of the stick or "crosse." Since there is no body contact, such equipment as helmets, padding and heavy gloves is not required. The rules and manner of playing are different from the men's game.

The dissimilarity in the men's and women's games follows the difference in their histories. The men's game stems more directly from the original American Indian "tribal warfare" version; whereas, the game played by the women was modified greatly as it made its way to England. In the 1860's a visiting team from Canada played before Queen Victoria—and with their traditional feeling for sport, the English saw in lacrosse the possibilities of a game of high skill; whereupon they modified the game and formed suitable rules.

It was first played by women in the English private schools in the early 1900's. English women's sports instructors "introduced" the game here while teaching in American schools and colleges. About 1912 Sargent College in Boston and Sweet Briar College in Virginia were playing the game. In the early 1920's there is record of Bryn Mawr College and Rosemary Hall School in Greenwich, Conn., practicing stick-work. By 1926, Baltimore schools had started playing and, in the latter part of the 1920's, Joyce Cran started a program at Wellesley College. At this time there were also "club" matches in Baltimore.

The start of the United States Association followed shortly after at Constance M. K. Applebee's "Hockey Camp" in Mount Pocono, Pa. Miss Applebee had introduced field hockey to American women in 1901 and had remained on through the years to assist in the development of the game. Her camp was attended by many of the hockey players who wanted to get into condition for the autumn contests. A very large impetus to the start of lacrosse came through the efforts of Joyce Reilly, one of the English coaches who urged those attending camp to try lacrosse, American and English physical education instructors who wished to further the game of lacrosse also were active in American hockey playing, and during an annual visit to the Pocono camp, in 1931, the United States Women's Lacrosse Association was launched, with Mrs. Joyce Cran Barry as the first president.

The members went back to the areas where they taught, to interest others in the game and form groups known as "local associations"—the first ones being organized in Boston, New York, Philadelphia and Baltimore.

In 1933 the first National tournament was held at Greenwich, Conn. In 1934 a team of English players visited America under the leadership of Kathleen Lockley who, with the newly established U.S.W.L.A., spread interest and knowledge of the sport. A return invitation was extended to our American association and in 1935 a group of 16 went to England to play with the English clubs. On their return to America the players were able to pass on what they had learned. The English paid a return visit in 1936 and several stayed on to act as coaches.

In the intervening years, the game grew steadily in the United States, in numbers and in quality. In 1949 the U.S.W.L.A. extended an invitation to another English team to visit this country. This visit was returned in 1951, when a United States team made a tour of the British Isles. It was not until this latter tour that America was able to compete on an international level. The Americans lost by 12—3 to the All-England team and 8—6 to Wales, but succeeded in defeating Scotland, 6—3, and Ireland, 10—5.

In 1969, Australia invited two teams, one from England and the other from the U.S., to coach and play in exhibition games. The tour became worldwide and included games in New Zealand, Hong Kong, Tokyo, and the Netherlands.

The game has spread to parts of the South, to the Midwest and to the West Coast. There are approximately 100 colleges and schools offering lacrosse to women and, as many of the institutions taking up lacrosse have, in later years, been physical education training schools, the game is experiencing a rapid spread.

In the inter-association play, Philadelphia always has fielded strong teams. The outstanding individual player in women's lacrosse—placing on the honorary All-American team for 21 of the 25 years the National tournament has been held—is Betty Richey of the Physical Education Department at Vassar College. This may well be a world record for women in amateur sports.

The specifications on equipment and rules* of the game have been set by the United States Women's Lacrosse Association. Schools and colleges offering lacrosse affiliate with the U.S.W.L.A., which is the official body governing American women's lacrosse activities and represents the United States women in international activities. The U.S.W.L.A. offers assistance in starting lacrosse programs, keeps an eye on standards of equipment and maintains a service on films and written material for instructional purposes.

OUTSTANDING PLAYERS

In addition to Betty Richey, the list of leading United States players includes: Elizabeth Toulmin, Suzanne Cross, Anne Delano, Eugenia Slaymaker, Betty White, Betty Shellenberger, Gretchen Schuyler, Jane Vache, Helena Wheeler, Jane Adair Smith, Dorothy Benson, Patricia Kenworthy Nuckols, Alice Putnam Willetts, Virginia Allen, Lucille Burnham, Betsy Crothers, Evelyn DuPont Donaldson, Susan Lamb, Jane Brown Peck, Anne Pugh LeBoutillier, Anne Townsend, Clorinda Saragosa, Gloria Heath, Gayle Meacham, Roberta Brennan, Judy Devlin, Mary Fetter and Lee Chadbourne,

Honorary memberships in the United States Women's Lacrosse Association were conferred for outstanding contributions upon 10 persons in the first 20 years of the group's existence. The list includes: Mrs. Joyce Cran Barry, Martha Butler Klug, Anne Pugh LeBoutillier, Betty Richey, Gretchen Schuyler and Helena Wheeler of the United States and M. O. Newbold, Kathleen Lockley, Marjorie Lockley Buxton and Anne Dudley Smith of England. Also included are: Suzanne Cross, Gertrude Hooper, Margaret Boyd, Gloria Heath, Rosabelle Sinclair, Anne Lee Delano, Jane Vaché, Betty Shellenberger, Ann Coakley, Jane Oswald, and Mary Fetter Semanik.

*The official rules appear in the National Section's Women's Athletics Field Hockey-Lacrosse Guide, published by the American Association for Health, Physical Education and Recreation, 1201 Sixteenth St., N. W., Washington, D.C. 20036.

UNITED STATES SELECTIONS

(Courtesy of United States Women's Lacrosse Association.)

1933

All-American

Goal	Natalie Sullivan
Point	Anne Townsend
Cover Point	Bettie Freeman
Third Man	Lucille Burnham

Left Defense Wing . . . . Elizabeth Toulmin
Right Defense Wing . . . . Suzanne Cross
Center . . . . Anne Pugh
Left Attack Wing . . . . .Elizabeth Glidden
Right Attack Wing . . . . Betty Richey
Third Home . . . . Jane Adair
Second Home . . . . Constance Morton
First Home . . . . Elizabeth Bonthron

1934

All-American

G—Natalie Sullivan
P—Lillian Scott
CP—Lucille Burnham
3d M—Anne Townsend
LDW—Dorothy Benson
RDW—Suzanne Cross
C—Elizabeth Toulmin
LAW—Anne Pugh
RAW—Anne Paxson
3d H—Jane Adair
2d H—Betty Richey
1st H—Elizabeth Bonthron

1935

All-American

G—Barbara Crowe
P—Lillian Scott
CP—Bettie Freeman
3d M—Lucille Burnham
LDW—Suzanne Cross
RDW—Florence Hoff
C—Elizabeth Toulmin
LAW—Gretchen Schuyler
RAW—Betty Richey
3d H—Anne Pugh
2d H—Elizabeth Bonthron
1st H—Virginia Allen

1936

All-American

G—Barbara Crowe
P—Lillian Scott
CP—Bettie Freeman
3d M—Anne Townsend
LDW—Lucille Burnham
RDW—Florence Hoff
C—Elizabeth Toulmin
LAW—Jane Adair
RAW—Anne Pugh
3d H—Betty Richey
2d H—Virginia Allen
1st H—Gretchen Schuyler

1937

All-American

G—Barbara Crowe
P—Dorothy Benson
CP—Beth Wilbur
3d M—Natalie Park
LDW—Virginia Bourguardez
RDW—Suzanne Cross
C—Elizabeth Toulmin

LAW—Jane Adair
RAW—Betty Richey
3d H—Virginia Allen
2d H—Gretchen Schuyler
1st H—Helen Lilly

1938

All-American

G—Gretchen Schuyler
P—Doris Armstrong
CP—Dorothy Sullivan
3d M—Anne Townsend
LDW—Grace Willett
RDW—Dorothy Benson
C—Elizabeth Toulmin
LAW—Dorothy Tashjian
RAW—Jane Adair
3d H—Betty Richey
2d H—Virginia Allen
1st H—Ethel Myers

1939

All-American

G—Betty Riegel
P—Bunnie Struthers
CP—Beth Wilbur
3d M—Natalie Park
LDW—Suzanne Cross
RDW—Grace Willett
C—Elizabeth Toulmin
LAW—Evelyn Horn
RAW—Anne Delano
3d H—Betty Richey
2d H—Gretchen Schuyler
1st H—Ethel Myers

1940

All-American

G—Betty Riegel
P—Helena Wheeler
CP—Pat Kenworthy
3d M—Natalie Park
LDW—Dorothy Benson
RDW—Suzanne Cross
C—Elizabeth Toulmin
LAW—Jessie Disston
RAW—Ruth Stevenson
3d H—Betty Richey
2d H—Betty Shellenberger
1st H—Ethel Myers

1941

All-American

G—Gloria Heath
P—Helena Wheeler
CP—Pat Kenworthy
3d M—Beth Wilbur
LDW—Suzanne Cross
RDW—Dorothy Benson
G—Elizabeth Toulmin
LAW—Harriet Wickham
RAW—Mary Conklin
3d H—Betty Richey

2d H—Betty Shellenberger
1st H—Naomi Wright

1942

All-American

G—Ruth Thalheimer
P—Pat Kenworthy
CP—Helena Wheeler
3d M—Anna Kohout
LDW—Suzanne Cross
RDW—Leslie Wead
C—Jessie Disston
LAW—Naomi Wright
RAW—Mary Conklin
3d H—Betty Richey
2d H—Betty White
1st H—Betty Shellenberger

1943

All-American

G—Margaret Sheahan
P—Leslie Wead
CP—Pat Kenworthy
3d M—Ruth Servais
LDW—Eugenia Slaymaker
RDW—Agnetta Powell
C—Naomi Wright
LAW—Betty White
RAW—Anne Delano
3d H—Betty Richey
2d H—Betty Shellenberger
1st H—Jacqueline Fehling

1944

All-American

G—Catherine Christie
P—Molly Boileau
CP—Eugenia Slaymaker
3d M—Betsy Crothers
LDW—Ruth Servais
RDW—Agneta Powell
C—Phyllis Levine
LAW—Anne Delano
RAW—Betty Richey
3d H—Betty Shellenberger
2d H—Alice Putnam
1st H—Barbara Nason

1945

All-American

G—Margaret Sheahan
P—Molly Boileau
CP—Eugenia Slaymaker
3d M—Betsy Crothers
LDW—Agneta Powell
RDW—Leslie Wead
C—Anne Delano
LAW—Katherine Downing
RAW—Betty White
3d H—Betty Richey
2d H—Alice Putnam
1st H—Barbara Nason

1946

All-American

G—Jane Brown
P—Helena Wheeler
CP—Eugenia Slaymaker
3d M—Betsy Crothers
LDW—Evelyn Donaldson
RDW—Harriet Hebden
C—Alvera Bolland
LAW—Jane Vache
RAW—Betty White
3d H—Betty Richey
2d H—Betty Shellenberger
1st H—Gretchen Schuyler

1947

All-American

G—Jane Brown
P—Helena Wheeler
CP—Pat Kenworthy
3d M—Betsy Crothers
LDW—Eugenia Slaymaker
RDW—Alice Roberts
C—Alvera Bolland
LAW—Jane Vache
RAW—Betty White
3d H—Betty Richey
2d H—Betty Shellenberger
1st H—Alice Putnam

1948

All-American

G—Gretchen Schuyler
P—Susan Lamb
CP—Nora Burton Licata
3d M—Phoebe Lukens
LDW—Evelyn Donaldson
RDW—Alice Roberts
C—Elizabeth Toulmin
LAW—Jane Vache
RAW—Alice Putnam
3d H—Deborah Morris
2d H—Betty Richey
1st H—Betty Cooke

1949

All-American

G—Jane Brown
P—Ruth Stevenson
CP—Susan Lamb
3d M—Ellen Ward
LDW—Eugenia Slaymaker
RDW—Alice Roberts
C—Helen Dixon
LAW—Jane Vache
RAW—Betty White
3d H—Anne Delano
2d H—Betty Richey
1st H—Margaret Malcolm

1950

All-American

G—Jane Brown

P—Gayle Meacham
CP—Susan Lamb
3d M—Evelyn Donaldson
LDW—Eugenia Slaymaker
RDW—Clorinda Lauretano
C—Anne Wilkinson
LAW—Jane Vache
RAW—Betty White
3d H—Anne Delano
2d H—Betty Richey
1st H—Lois Linton

1951

All-American

G—Gloria Heath
P—Helena Wheeler
CP—Susan Lamb
3d M—Evelyn Donaldson
LDW—Marion Phillips
RDW—Patricia Told
C—Ann Coakley
LAW—Jane Vache
RAW—Anne Delano
3d H—Betty Richey
2d H—Alice Putnam
1st H—Lois Linton

1952

All-American

G—Gloria Heath
P—Gayle Meacham
CP—Mary Fetter
3d M—Dorothy Moffett
LDW—Eugenia Slaymaker
RDW—Cynthia McKelvey
C—Anne Loveman
LAW—Nancy Vadner
RAW—Anne Delano
3d H—Betty Richey
2d H—Margot Cunningham
1st H—Lois Linton

1953

All-American

G—Roberta Brennan
P—Gayle Meacham
CP—Mary Fetter
3d M—Dorothy Moffett
LDW—June Biedler
RDW—Clorinda Saragosa
C—Betty Nawrath
LAW—Nancy Vadner
RAW—Betty White
3d H—Mildred Barnes
2d H—Betty Shellenberger
1st H—Betty Richey

1954

All-American

G—Roberta Brennan and Gloria Heath
P—Gayle Meacham
CP—Mary Fetter
3d M—Dorothy Moffett

LDW—Eugenia Slaymaker
RDW—Clorinda Saragosa
C—Lee Chadbourne
LAW—Betty Richey
RAW—Betty Shellenberger
3d H—Judy Devlin
2d H—Mrs. Alice Willetts
1st H—Margot Cunningham

1955

All-American

G—Roberta Brennan
P—Gayle Meacham
CP—Mary Fetter
3d M—Jane Oswald
LDW—Eugenia Slaymaker
RDW—Anne Capolino
C—Lee Chadbourne
LAW—Elizabeth Swett
RAW—Betty King
3d H—Judy Devlin
2d H—Alice Willetts
1st H—Margot Cunningham

1956

All-American

G—Roberta Brennan
P—Gayle Meacham
CP—Mary Fetter
3d M—Barbara J. Hall
LDW—Christine Fazzi
RDW—Clorinda Saragosa
C—Lee Chadbourne
LAW—Kate Barrett
RAW—Eleanor Keady
3d H—Mildred Barnes
2d H—Helen Allen
1st H—Barbara Heylmun

1957

All-American

G—Gloria Heath
P—Gayle Meacham
CP—Mary Fetter
3d M—Barbara Hall
LDW—Clorinda Saragosa
RDW—Gertrude Dunn
C—Jane Oswald
LAW—Ellie Keady
RAW—Sue Gordy
3d H—Betty Shellenberger
2d H—Judy Devlin
1st H—Barbara Heylmun

1958

All-American

G—Bobbie Brennan
P—Gayle Meacham
CP—Mary Fetter
3d M—Jane Oswald
LDW—Lee Chadbourne
RDW—Gertrude Dunn
C—Judy Devlin

LAW—Sue Gordy
RAW—Eleanor Keady
3d H—Mildred Barnes
2d H—Betty Shellenberger
1st H—Barbara Heylmun

1959

All-American

1st H—Barbara Heylmun
2d H—Betty Manuel
3d H—Judy Devlin
LAW—Sue Gordy
RAW—Kate Barrett
C—Mildred Barnes
LDW—Jean Dolat
RDW—Lee Chadbourne
3d M—Jane Oswald
CP—Mary Fetter
P—Gayle Meacham
G—Roberta Brennan

1960

All-American

1st H—Mildred Barnes
2d H—Barbara Heylmun
3d H—Margot Cunningham
LAW—Lyn Crosley
RAW—Eleanor Keady
C—Lee Chadbourne
LDW—Vonnie Gros
RDW—Gertrude Dunn
3d M—Anne Newell
CP—Mary Fetter
P—Gayle Meacham
G—Roberta Brennan

1961

All-American

1st H—Barbara Longstreth
2d H—Margot Cunningham
3d H—Mildren Barner
RAW—Eleanor Keady
LAW—Lyn Crosley
C—Ann Wieland
RDW—Gertrude Dunn
LDW—Vonnie Gros
3d M—Anne Newell
CP—Mary Fetter
P—Gayle Meacham
G—Roberta Brennan

1962

All-American

1st H—Barbara Longstreth
2d H—Margot Cunningham
3d H—Kate Barrett
RAW—Lyn Crosley
LAW—Enid Clinchard
C—Alison Hersey
RDW—Margaret McNally
LDW—Gertrude Dunn
3d M—Anne Newell
CP—Vonnie Gros

P—Natalie Smith
G—Pat Zelly

1963

All-American

1st H—Barbara Longstreth
2d H—Kate Barrett
3d H—Margot Cunningham
LAW—Enid Russell
RAW—Agnes Bixler
C—Alison Hersey
LDW—Gertrude Dunn
RDW—Margaret McNally
3d M—Anne Robertson
CP—Vonnie Gros
P—Natalie Smith
G—Roberta Brennan

1964

All-American

1st H—Jackie Pitts
2d H—Barbara Longstreth
3d H—Sue Day
LAW—Enid Russell
RAW—June Belli
C—Alison Hersey
LDW—Judy Smiley
RDW—Margaret McNally
3d M—Ann Robertson
CP—Vonnie Gros
P—Nathalie Smith
G—Roberta Brennan

1965

All-American

1st H—Jackie Pitts
2d H—Enid Russell
3d H—Sue Day
LAW—Lee Bush
RAW—Kate Barrett
C—Alison Hersey
LDW—Sandy Boehringer
RDW—Judy Smiley
3d M—Sue Honeysett
CP—Vonnie Gros
P—Nathalie Smith
G—Karen Burke

1966

All-American

1st H—Jackie Pitts
2d H—Enid Russell
3d H—Sue Day
LAW—Alison Hersey
RAW—Judy Hedges
C—Ann Sage
LDW—Judy Smiley
RDW—Nathalie Smith
3d M—Mary Rue
CP—Sue Honeysett
P—Sandra Lawson
G—Karen Burke

1967

All-American

1st H—Barbara Longstreth
2d H—Enid Russell
3d H—Mickey Waldman
LAW—Alison Hersey
RAW—Priscilla Taylor
C—Judy Hedges
LDW—Judy Smiley
RDW—Vonnie Gros
3d M—Sue Honeysett
CP—Nathalie Smith
P—Sandra Lawson
G—Karen Burke

1968

All-American

1st H—Alison Hersey
2d H—Enid Russell
3d H—Mickey Waldman
LAW—Priscilla Taylor
RAW—Tina Sloan
C—Judy Hedges
LDW—Judy Smiley
RDW—Vonnie Gros
3d M—Sue Honeysett
CP—Nathalie Smith
P—Sandy Boehringer
G—Linda Swarts

1969

All-American

1st H—Jacquelin Pitts
2d H—Alison Hersey
3d H—Mickey Waldman
LAW—Janet Lippincott
RAW—Tina Sloan
C—Judy Hedges
LDW—Judy Smiley
RDW—Vonnie Gros
3d M—Ann Sage
CP—Sue Honeysett
P—Nathalie Smith
G—Linda Swarts

1970

All-American

1st H—Jacquelin Pitts
2d H—Alison Hershel
3d H—Agnes Bixler
RAW—Tina Sloan
LAW—Beth Anders
C—Judy Hedges
RDW—Janet Smith
LDW—Judy Smiley
3d M—Nathalie Smith
CP—Sue Honeysett
P—Gail Allebach
G—Linda Swarts

1971

All-American

1st H—Jacquelin Pitts

2d H—Sharon Weld
3d H—Agnes Bixler
RAW—Tina Sloan
LAW—Janet Lippincott
C—Judy Hedges
LDW—Judy Smiley
RDW—Janet Smith
3d M—Diane Wright
CP—Sue Honeysett
P—Gail Allebach
G—Linda Swarts

EQUIPMENT

The equipment requirements are moderate—a lacrosse "package" consists of 24 crosses, 2 dozen balls and goal nets. Leg pads such as those used by field hockey goalies serve well for the lacrosse goalkeeper, and the only additional equipment needed is the chest protector.

The regulation baseball chest protector serves satisfactorily. Those designed especially for lacrosse have an extension covering the thigh.

It has been a precaution for schools to require their goalkeepers to wear a face mask. All players wear rubber "sneakers" with rubber cleats.

The crosse shall not exceed four feet in length or nine inches in its widest part. The weight of the crosse should not be more than 20 ounces. The ball shall be of rubber sponge, not less than 7¾ nor more than 8 inches in circumference. It shall weigh not less than 4½ nor more than 5¼ ounces.

The goal is framed by 2 square posts 6 feet apart and 6 feet high joined by a rigid top cross bar. The netting of 1½ inch mesh or smaller is attached from the goal posts to a point on the ground 6 feet behind the center of the goal line.

BASIC RULES

The game of lacrosse for women is played on a field 90 to 110 yards in length. There are no boundaries other than natural ones and the play progresses from a center "draw" through aerial passes, the object being to place the ball in the opponent's "goal." There are 12 players on a team stretched from end to end the length of the field, each player closely marked by her opponent. To hamper an opponent's movement toward goal, positioning of defense players on the field is utilized, forcing the attack to change pace or to pass, giving the defense an opportunity to gain control of the ball by an interception or when possible by a light tap on the opponent's crosse to dislodge the ball.

The movements of "cradling" to keep the ball in the crosse, catching and overarm passing follow the natural rhythmic movement of the body—the upright position is excellent for carriage of the body and lacrosse rates high from a physical education standpoint, as well as being excellent "sport."

A circle (goal crease) having a radius of 8½

feet measured from the center of the goal mouth limits the advance of the attack. For a goal (1 point) to count, neither the stick nor feet of any

Center Circle
10 yard radius

Right Defense
Wing

Right Attack
Wing

Goalkeeper

Point

Coverpoint

Thirdman

Center

Left Defense
Wing

Third Home

Left Attack
Wing

Second Home

First Home

Goal-6 ft. wide & high
Goal Crease-8½ ft. radius
Distance between Goals
90 to 110 yards

Lacrosse Field and Positions. (United States Women's Lacrosse Association.) In this diagram, which is not drawn to scale, just the 12 positions on one team are shown. The team is attacking the goal at the bottom.

attack player may cross over the crease either during or after a shot. Nor may the goalkeeper be "checked" while she is within the bounds of the crease. A player may, however, run through the crease to field a wide ball, but no player may run across the crease while in possession of the ball. The goalkeeper may not utilize the immunity of the crease by pulling the ball back into the crease unless both her feet remain inside the bounds of the crease.

The only fouls are rough checking, impeding a player's progress by reaching across her shoulder when tackling from behind, holding down an opponent's crosse, guarding the crosse with raised elbow or hand, touching the ball with the hands (only the goalkeeper may "put away" a ball with her hands, but she may not catch it in her hands), intentionally kicking the ball.

The penalty for a foul is a "free position." When the whistle is blown, all players "stand" where they are (except the goalkeeper, who may resume her place) and the umpire indicates where the player taking the free position is to stand. No player may be nearer than 5 yards to this player. When the whistle is blown by the umpire, the play proceeds. The player with the ball may shoot, pass or run.

As the rules are few, an umpire in lacrosse is called upon to exercise discretion in preventing roughness—and she may call a player for any action she considers dangerous. She also exercises discretion in calling the ball "out of bounds" when it is sent quite far afield, into grandstands, hedges, obstructions, etc.—such "natural boundaries" usually being agreed upon with the two captains before the game. In addition to the field umpire, it is common practice to have one goal umpire at each end to watch particularly for crease infringements. An alternate method is to use two field umpires with the field divided diagonally so that each is able to cover one goal.

A game consists of 25-minute halves, with a 10-minute intermission. If the contest is tied, there is no overtime play.

LAWN BOWLS

(Courtesy of Harold L. Esch, American Lawn Bowls Association,
P.O. Box 6141-C, Orlando, Fla., 32803)

The game of lawn bowling is enjoying a renascence in this country. Popular years ago, the sport declined for a period and then interest began to grow. In the last two decades or so it has made rapid advances. Young and old are taking it up and the game has spread to all sections of the nation.

Some historians are of the belief that the most primitive game, after running, jumping, throwing

and wrestling, is lawn bowling, generally called "bowls" in most British countries. Others pass the credit to what now is field hockey. The actual result may be a tie.

In lawn bowling, the principle of the game, in very earliest times, was to roll a round pebble at an object; the field hockey idea called for using a stick and hitting the pebble, either at some other object or just for distance. Neither game called for equipment that nature did not provide.

Historians are agreed that the origin of lawn bowls is shrouded in mystery. They conclude it was a game of antiquity, becoming a game of consequence in early Egypt and later in Greece and Rome. There exist sculptured vases, plaques, etc., to indicate that lawn bowls was played at least 3,500 or 4,000 years ago and that it found some favor among royalty and the aristocracy of the times, but was indulged in mainly by the older rulers.

It is not established by what name lawn bowling—bowls or bowles—was known in the mist shrouded ages. But when the Caesars ruled Rome the game was played there as "boccie," by which the sport still is known to Italians. Boccie appears to be an improvement of the ancient game, whereas lawn bowling, which originated in England and Scotland, and where it gained its name of bowls, originally spelled "bowles," is a variation of "boccie."

The Romans carried the "boccie" idea with them into Northern Europe, and indications are that the sport was indulged in there as early as the 10th Century. There is conclusive proof, furnished by writings, that the English were playing it in the 12th Century, under the name of "bowles." The career of the sport from then on is easy to trace because "bowls" or "bowles," later called "bowling" and finally "lawn bowling," to distinguish it from the game where balls are cast at wooden pins, was a very controversial subject in early England.

Bowls was so well established in England in 1299 that a group of players formed the Southampton Town Bowling Club that year. This pioneer club still is in existence and matches are regularly played on the original green, laid out over 600 years ago.

Bowls, as a sport in England, has been praised more and condemned more than perhaps any game ever played—praised by those who were fascinated by it; condemned by those who regarded it as a "vicious form of gambling." Things came to such a pass in the 16th Century that King Henry VIII issued an edict in 1511 in which he declared that "the game of bowles is an evil because the alleys are operated in conjunction with saloons, or dissolute places, and bowling has ceased to be a sport, and rather a form of vicious gambling."

Henry's ban against bowling was continued by succeeding rulers, and actually was not lifted until 1845. However, none of Henry's successors made a serious effort to crush bowling, the chief reason being that almost every English monarch was a bowler—royal estates were equipped with greens. The word "green" designated the plot of ground allotted for the game, this area being divided into as many bowling "alleys" as the owner could provide, each "alley" being 20 feet wide and 120 feet long.

In 1579, Stephen Gosson, in his "School of Abuse," launched a bitter tirade against bowls, declaring that "common bowling alleys are but moths that eat up the credit of many idle citizens." He drew a ghastly word picture of the suffering, poverty and starvation that had come to wives and children of those who bowled on the common alleys and lost in their gambling.

However, not all persons felt toward bowls as did Gosson, In "The Book of Sports" (1618), King James I recommended the game to his son. King Charles I was a good bowler and always eager to bet on himself. He often visited Richard Shute, a merchant whose bowling green on Barking Hill was one of the finest in England, and upon one occasion Charles is reported to have lost 1,000 pounds to Shute.

The Scots, who adopted the game in the 16th Century, took to it with so much enthusiasm that it was for a long time the national sport. To the Scots belongs the credit for improving on many of the rules and standardizing play. This was done gradually through nearly 3 centuries, and in 1848—49 the Scots, headed by W. W. Mitchell (1803—1884), one of the greatest bowls authorities that ever lived, framed the laws which, almost in toto, govern today.

There has been certain confusion as to when the game of lawn bowls was introduced to America. This is because in earlier eras both lawn bowls and the game of bowling at pins were called "bowling" in the United States. However, it would seem that lawn bowls was introduced about 1690, whereas the pin game arrived no sooner than 1800, and gets its first real mention in Washington Irving's story, "Rip Van Winkle."

Lawn bowling and bowling at pins are not related games.

Boston and New York were the earliest strongholds of lawn bowls. As early as 1714 the "Boston News Letter" carried an advertisement which was reprinted in Herbert Manchester's book "Four Centuries of Sport in America." The "ad" read:

"The Bowling Green, formerly belonging to Mr. James Ivers, Cambridge Street, now belongs to Mr. Daniel Stevens, of the British Coffee House, where all gentlemen, merchants, and others, having a mind to recreate themselves, shall be accommodated."

Manchester also found that in 1732 the city authorities in New York had leased to John Chambers, Peter Bayard and Peter Jay "a piece of land at the lower end of Broadway fronting the fort, for the purpose of a bowling green." This became the famous "Bowling Green" district of the metropolis, and although the bowlers long since have disappeared and the greens have become a part of Battery Park, the name "Bowling Green" remains as descriptive of that part of downtown New York.

Lawn bowling spread from New York and

Boston to many other cities along the Atlantic Seaboard and was the game of games until the Revolutionary War. Then play abruptly ceased. However, after the end of the conflict, the "craze" for bowling no longer existed. The sport was practically non-existent for 100 years, only to be reintroduced and lifted back to popularity by Christian Schepflin of Dunellen, N.J.

Schepflin had gone to England and then to Scotland and became a bowling enthusiast. Returning to New Jersey, he laid out a bowling green, explained the game to his friends and neighbors, and the revival was under way. Soon there were clubs throughout New Jersey, in New York, Philadelphia and adjacent points, with the trend then westward and to the south.

There were so many bowlers and so many clubs up to 1915, without any governing body, that it was decided to create one that would standardize rules, arrange tournaments and regulate play. This brought about formation of the American Lawn Bowling Association at Buffalo, N.Y., in that year.

In the last thirty-five years, lawn bowling again has gained high favor. The sport, once the exclusive property of elderly people, was adopted with enthusiasm by the youngsters. Just how well youth fared in its adventure in this sport is shown by the fact that the National championship in 1934 was won by 16-year-old Fred Chaplin Jr. of Brooklyn.

There are now nearly 200 lawn bowling clubs in the United States, including many public greens. In the 1930's the Works Project Administration (WPA), taking cognizance of the enthusiasm over lawn bowling, installed greens in important parks in cities throughout the nation. There also are many bowling greens in municipal playgrounds and there are more than 10,000 players scattered over the land.

Lawn bowling has world-wide scope among the English-speaking people and recent statistics show that many people have taken up the sport in the various countries in recent years. Perhaps the greatest growth has been in Australia. That country listed 8,352 members in 1911. By 1953 it boasted 91,343 members while today they have 250,000 men and some over 100,000 women.

Similar figures exist in other countries. South Africa has 40,000 members; New Zealand 45,000; England 225,000; Scotland 60,000; Wales 15,000 and so on.

The indoor game has taken on such great popularity throughout the British Isles that new halls and clubhouses are being built to house the sport on carpet—good play in all weather.

Canada has some 10,000 bowlers from Nova Scotia to British Columbia. Montreal hosted a six-country round robin championship in connection with the "Expo '67" with the USA, England, Scotland, Ireland, and Wales joining Canada

for this event.

Sixteen countries competed in the First World Lawn Bowls Championships in Sydney, Australia, in October of 1966. Participants included, besides Australia, were New Zealand, Papua-New Guinea, Fiji, South Africa, Rhodesia, Malawi, Kenya, Hong Kong, England, Ireland, Scotland, Wales, Canada, USA and Island of Jersey. The second World Bowls Championships were played in Worthing, England in June 1972, and in addition to the countries that participated in the first championship, Israel and the Island of Guernsey were added.

Other countries active in lawn bowls includes Brazil, Argentina, Egypt, Zambia, Japan and Swaziland.

Divisions have been organized in the American Lawn Bowling Association. Data supplied by Harold L. Esch of Orlando, Fla., one of America's outstanding authorities on the game, shows that those divisions fan out from the Atlantic to the Pacific, from the Canadian Border to the Gulf of Mexico, with California and Florida the great winter tournament centers.

"The Archie G. Bennett Trophy," points out Esch, "was the prize for the winner in the East-West Division play. Among the great teams that have competed for this treasure are those which represented Brooklyn, Buffalo, Chicago, Orlando, Fla., Beverly Hills, Calif., and Pasadena, Calif.

"There are regional associations, as well as divisions, connected with the national body. There also are state leagues."

FAMOUS TROPHIES

Championship play in the United States has had its share of tournament trophies. In many cases trophies have been donated in the names of famous players. Among these are the Charles S. Rettie Memorial Trophy, in competition for the first event in the National tournament in memory of Mr. Rettie, who for many years was the secretary-treasurer of the American Lawn Bowling Association.

Among the most coveted trophies are those presented by Spalding Inn, Whitefield, New Hampshire and The Inn, Buck Hill Falls, Pa. The Spalding Inn trophy goes to the top singles player in the country. The Buck Hill Falls award is presented annually to the best doubles players.

Other National tournament awards are the Chicago Cup, Wisconsin Trophy, California Trophy, Lakeside (Chicago) Trophy, Western New York Trophy, National Open Singles Trophy and the Metropolitan (New York) Trophy.

The Charles J. Fox International Lawn Bowls Cup, for competition between Great Britain and the United States along the lines of the Davis Cup matches in tennis, is another important award.

American Lawn Bowls Association

Singles

1928—David White
1929—William Kidd
1930—Dr. J.A. Sherwood
1931—Cancelled—Rain
1932—S.A. Tulloch
1933—James McArthur
1934—Fred Chaplin Jr.
1935—Robert Pollock
1936—E.J. Leinert
1937—William Milmine
1938—Nate Waddington
1939—George Davidson
1940—41—Arthur H. Hartley
1942—43—No competition
1944—Richard Auld
1945—No competition
1946—Arthur H. Hartley
1947—Floyd Taylor
1948—Richard Auld
1949—John Proctor
1950—Richard Folkins
1951—George Robbins
1952—Hugh Folkins
1953—John Stevenson
1954—Richard Folkins
1955—Harry P. Hope
1956—Pete Campbell
1957—Richard Folkins
1958—Harold L. Esch
1959—Thomas Stirrat
1960—Arthur H. Hartley
1961—R.L. "Lundy" Fullerton
1962—63—John Henderson
1964—Ezra Wyeth
1965—Arthur H. Hartley
1966—Robert Roulston
1967—Alexander "Bob" Veitch
1968—James Grainger
1969—Bert Littler
1970—Barrie McFadden
1971—Ezra Wyeth
1972—Douglas MacArthur

Doubles

1920—Thomas Grieve—Thomas Turnbull
1921—No record
1922—Don Calderwood—R. Dott
1923—James Kershaw—Thomas Turnbull
1924—Randall—Donaldson
1925—Orkney—Stuart
1926—Dr. W.H. Johnson—Dr. C.C. Cott
1927—John Green—Sim Robertson
1928—Harry Wright—Tom Williams
1929—S. Maxwell—James Watson
1930—Duncan Smith—William Milmine
1931—Dr. J.A. Sherwood—Dr. C.C. Cott
1932—Duncan Gillies—Paul Neilson
1933—Albert Dehner—Hap Dehner
1934—S.A. Tulloch—R.A. Dunlop
1935—Robert Savage—J. Freeburn

1936—J. Shailor—S. Craig
1937—L.D. McArthur—L.M. McArthur
1938—Dr. R.W. Sendker—Earl Meek
1939—Richard Auld—Frank Whistler
1940—John McEwen—Dr. S.A. MacKenzie
1941—Richard Auld—A.G. Merrin
1942—43—No competition
1944—James Johnstone—J.S. Gardner
1945—No competition
1946—Robert Savage—V. Byrne
1947—J.G. Calderwood—A.L. Graham
1948—John Proctor—William Smith
1949—David Campbell—Malcolm Carlson
1950—Richard Folkins—Hugh Folkins
1951—Richard Auld—Tom Stirrat
1952—Richard Folkins—Hugh Folkins
1953—A.A. Gilchrist Sr.—A.A. Gilchrist Jr.
1954—Hugh Folkins—Richard Folkins
1955—Jeff Smith—Frank C. Wilson
1956—John Milne—John McArthur
1957—Richard Folkins—Frank D. Murray
1958—G. Clyde—A. Armstrong
1959—L. Graham—David Cameron
1960—61—J.H. Davis—Dr. C.H. Brereton
1962—H.T. Morgan—Eugene Tincher
1963—Harold Esch—John Henderson
1964—Harry Whitescarver—William Lloyd
1965—John Clark—Howard Wilson
1966—William Ducklow—Howard Wilson
1967—C.I. Dickinson—C.E. Dickinson
1968—Dave Stephen—J.C. Sneddon
1969—Al Hughes—Harold Esch
1970—Dave Dakers—Jim Candelet
1971—Ezra Wyeth—Neil McInnes
1972—John Patterson—Louis Hebert

Rinks

The following awards have been presented in this competition: M.F. Robertson Trophy (1918—27); second M.F. Robertson Trophy (1928—37); McGuire-Lockie Memorial Trophy (1938—44); Charles S. Rettie Memorial Trophy (1946 to date).

(Skips in parentheses.)

1918—Roselawn L.B.C., Pawtucket, R.I. (Thomas Hampson)
1919—20—Fall River (Mass.) L.B.C. (James Violet)
1921—Buffalo (N.Y.) L.B.C. (Dr. F.W. McGuire)
1922—23—St. Andrews Club, Buffalo, N.Y. (William MacPhail)
1924—25—Buffalo B.G.C. (Alexander Simpson)
1926—Buffalo L.B.C. (W. Stan Hayes)
1927—Buffalo L.B.C. (Dr. W.H. Johnson)
1928—Thistle L.B.C., Hartford, Conn. (C.S. Rettie)
1929—Boston B.G.C. (H. Edwards)
1930—Buffalo L.B.C. (E.J. Leinert)
1931—Boston B.G.C. (Robert Russell)
1932—Buffalo L.B.C. (W. Stan Hayes)
1933—Pasadena (Calif.) L.B.C. (Albert Dehner)
1934—Boston B.G.C. (David Dakers)

1935—New York City L.B.C. (George Reid)
1936—Pasadena L.B.C. (Albert Dehner)
1937—Chicago L.B.C. (L.M. McArthur)
1938—Fernleigh L.B.C., Hartford, Conn. (W.A. Ebbets)
1939—Essex County L.B.C., Bloomfield, N.J. (Edward Peill)
1940—Buffalo L.B.C. (E.J. Leinert)
1941—Detroit L.B.C. (J.S. Weir)
1942—43— No competition
1944—Boston B.G.C. (David Dakers)
1945—No competition
1946—Washington Park L.B.C., Chicago (Robert Savage)
1947—Vancouver (B.C.) L.B.C. (A. Ciro)
1948—Chicago L.B.C. (John Proctor)
1949—Chicago L.B.C. (L.D. McArthur)
1950—Arroyo Seco L.B.C., Los Angeles (Richard Folkins)
1951—Fernleigh L.B.C. (Dr. C. Deming)
1952—Vancouver South L.B.C. (Wally Kenmuir)
1953—Chicago L.B.C. (Robert Savage)
1954—Arroyo Seco L.B.C. (Richard Folkins)
1955—New York L.B.C. (Alexander L. Ripley)
1956—Thistle L.B.C., Hartford, Conn. (Robert Dickson)
1957—Arroyo Seco L.B.C. (Richard Folkins)
1958—Chicago L.B.C. (Robert Savage)
1959—San Francisco L.B.C. (Clive Forrester)
1960—St. Petersburg L.B.C. (Dr. C.H. Brereton)
1961—Galt, Ontario (J.S. Muir)
1962—Arroyo Seco L.B.C. (Richard Folkins)
1963—Detroit (J. Colin Sneddon)
1964—Pawtucket, R.I. (James Candelet)
1965—Streetsville, Ontario (Harvey Andrew)
1966—Niagara Falls, N.Y. (John Anderson)
1967—Pomona, Calif. (L. Clark)
1968—Milwaukee (Otto Gerhardt)
1969—Oakland, Calif. (Rob Quillen)
1970—London, Ontario (Ken McIntyre)
1971—Pawtucket, R.I. (Jim Candelet)
1972—Toronto, Ontario (Albert Templeman)

DIVISIONAL CHAMPIONS
Eastern
Singles
(Robert D. Kay Trophy)

1947—Ray Northam
1948—George Thayer
1949—John McPoland
1950—Richard Auld
1951—No competition
1952—Alex. Thompson
1953—Thomas Stirrat
1954—Gordon Calton
1955—Harry Edwards
1956—No competition
1957—John Chisholm
1958—Russell Williams
1959—David Dakers
1960—James Graham
1961—No competition

1962—Thomas Howitt
1963—Joseph Brisco
1964—65—James Graham
1966—No competition
1967—Joseph Stevenson
1968—Robert Russell
1969—Robert Roulston
1970—Robert Wallbank
1971—Al Cline
1972—No competition

Doubles
(Brunswick Trophy)

1947—Robert Russell—John Anderson
1948—David Cameron—Thomas Atkins
1949—N. Gallogly—Frank Hamilton
1950—George Hope—Frank Hamilton
1951—No competition
1952—Jack Beacom—Ken Crozier
1953—John Milne—John McArthur
1954—Pete Campbell—Andrew Latta
1955—Thomas Hope—George Hope
1956—No competition
1957—Andrew Logan—Ziggie Kochan
1958—James Smart—William Gilbert
1959—Irvine Clifford—William Smith
1960—George Hopkins—Albert Warham
1961—No competition
1962—David Dakers—Thomas Howitt
1963—James Graham—Hugh Gallagher
1964—John McArthur—John Milne
1965—Harry Engstrom—William Scheer
1966—No competition
1967—Daniel Tomchik—Edwin Roach
1968—Jim Candelet—Joe Briscoe
1969—Jim Law—Bill Deacon
1970—W. Tewksbury—Bill Kaestle
1971—Jim Candelet—Bob Brandon
1972—No competition

Rinks
(McGuire-Lockie Trophy)

1947—Thistle L.B.C., Hartford (George Davidson)
1948—Hyde Park L.B.C., Niagara Falls, N.Y. (Richard Auld)
1949—Essex County L.B.C., Bloomfield, N.J. (A. Buchanan)
1950—Bridgeport (Conn.) L.B.C. (Simpson Crowe)
1951—No competition
1952—Boston L.B.C. (David Dakers)
1953—54—Smithfield Avenue L.B.C., Pawtucket, R.I. (James Candelet)
1955—New York City L.B.C. (John McPoland)
1956—No competition
1957—Cunningham B.G.C., Milton, Mass. (J. Earl Tays)
1958—Providence (R.I.) B.G.C. (Ray Sayer)
1959—Springfield, Mass. (Albert Ward)
1960—Essex County L.B.C., Bloomfield, N.J. (Archie Buchanan)
1961—No competition

1962—Essex County L.B.C., Bloomfield, N.J. (Jack Forbes)
1963—Hyde Park L.B.C., Niagara Falls, N.Y. (John Anderson)
1964—Smithfield Avenue L.B.C., Pawtucket, R.I. (James Candelet)
1965—Essex County L.B.C., Bloomfield, N.J. (Robert Lindsay)
1966—No competition
1967—Essex County L.B.C., Bloomfield, N.J. (Joseph Stevenson)
1968—Pawtucket, R.I., (Jim Candelet)
1969—Merriton, Ontario (Tom Park)
1970—Trenton, N.J., (Tom Currie)
1971—Pawtucket, R.I., (Jim Candelet)
1972—No competition

Central

Singles
(Robert Whitehead Trophy)

1947—L.L. McClow
1948—L.D. McArthur
1949—No competition
1950—David Campbell
1951—David Hunter
1952—A.A. Gilchrist Sr.
1953—No competition
1954—H. Breckenridge
1955—Willis J. Tewksbury
1956—57—Daniel Gillan
1958—No competition
1959—Charles Casey
1960—Lachlan McArthur
1961—Robert Savage
1962—Walter Sneddon
1963—No competition
1964—James Johnstone
1965—Howard McGaffney
1966—John Murdoch
1967—Dr. Thomas Davis
1968—No competition
1969—Dr. Thomas Davis
1970—Ross Brown
1971—George Madden
1972—Ben True

Doubles
(Reed Memorial Trophy)

1947—A. Stewart—William Crerar
1948—W. Bolderson—George Snedden
1949—No competition
1950—Hugh Crerar—William Crerar
1951—David Hunter—D. Murray
1952—John Cordes—Dan Penny
1953—No competition
1954—John McGregor—David Stephen
1955—George Fyfe—John Proctor
1956—Dr. John Huston—Neil McCairns
1957—Daniel Penny—Jack Young
1958—No competition
1959—Charles Casey—Joseph Ibe
1960—Robert Savage—Peter Purden
1961—Dr. John Huston—Neil McCairns

1962—W.J. Tewksbury—Leonard Snyder
1963—No competition
1964—Percy Stevenson—J. Miller
1965—John Deist—Charles Low
1966—Joe Ferguson—J. Guthrie
1967—Herbert Jeske—Howard Walker
1968—No competition
1969—William Miller—Ross Brown
1970—Bert MacWilliams—Al Shilito
1971—Bert MacWilliams—J. Stewart
1972—Lachlan MacArthur—Ken Martin

Rinks
(Budd Trophy)

1947—Chicago L.B.C. (S. Hainey, skip)
1948—Chicago L.B.C. (Robert Savage)
1949—No competition
1950—Columbus Park L.B.C., Chicago (David Greenough)
1951—Detroit East L.B.C., Detroit (James Cosgrove)
1952—Columbus Park L.B.C. (George Fyfe)
1953—No competition
1954—Detroit L.B.C. (John Brown)
1955—Columbus Park L.B.C. (Hugh Crerar)
1956—Columbus Park L.B.C. (David Campbell)
1957—Sherman Park L.B.C., Milwaukee (Howard Walker)
1958—No competition
1959—Racine, Wis., L.B.C. (Edward Nelson)
1960—61—Sherman Park L.B.C., Milwaukee (Howard Walker)
1962—Clearwater, Fla. L.B.C. (W.J. Tewksbury)
1963—No competition
1964—Columbus Park L.B.C., Oak Park, Ill. (Read Rogers)
1965—Buffalo, N.Y. (C. Parr)
1966—Columbus Park L.B.C., Oak Park, Ill. (John Murdoch)
1967—Lakeside, Chicago, Ill. (Roger McArthur)
1968—No competition
1969—Columbus Park L.B.C., Oak Park, Ill. (John Murdoch)
1970—Milwaukee— Lake Park (Neil McCairns)
1971—Lakeside, Chicago, Ill. (Doug MacArthur)
1972—Milwaukee— Lake Park (Ed Erdtmann)

Northwest

Singles
(Robert Pratt Trophy)

1934—August Frank
1936—36—Robert M. Mark
1937—Ernest Griffiths
1938—William Clarke
1939—August Frank
1940—Henry Roeder
1941—James Murdock
1942—William Clarke
1943—William Davy
1944—45—Floyd Garlick
1946—James Christie
1947—Robert Coulter
1948—Hugh Taylor

1949—Floyd Garlick
1950—Scott Keenlyside
1951—A.J. Underhill
1952—No competition
1953—Ernest F. Myers
1954—Alex. Houston
1955—R.A. Bindley
1956—Alex Houston
1957—No competition
1958—Roy Sparrow
1959—Peter Solberg
1960—61—Thomas Owens
1962—No competition
1963—Peter Solberg
1964—Bruce Matheson
1965—Andrew Rae
1966—Alex Johnston
1967—No competition
1968—Doug Coyle
1969—Arley Hudson
1970—Tom Dixon
1971—Joe Patelli
1972—Al Fultz

Doubles
(William Clarke Memorial Trophy since 1945)
1934—Vern Warren—William Clarke
1935—L.M. Wilkinson—Ivan Dickinson
1936—Henry Roeder—Art Miller
1937—Charles Middleton—Frank Holert
1938—J. Corbitt—Ivan Dickinson
1939—William Seeber—J. McCallum
1940—Ivan Dickinson—Art Miller
1941—J. Darbyshire—Cameron LeRoy
1942—Rain prevented completion of play
1943—August Frank—Henry Roeder
1944—Ivan Dickinson—Art Miller
1945—Del Sparrow—Roy Sparrow
1946—47—A. Quartermaine—Scott Keenlyside
1948—R. MacKenzie—A.B. Findlay
1949—H.L. Dawes—F.A. Dawes
1950—C.E. Dinkinson—J. MacCallum
1951—A. Hunter—Wally Kenmuir
1952—No competition
1953—Charles Middleton—Ernest Griffiths
1954—Lew Thomas—Ernest F. Myers
1955—A. Morrison—Sherman Siddons
1956—A. Morrison—Sherman Siddons
1957—No competition
1958—Sherman Siddons—A. Morrison
1959—Harry Rees—J. Morrison
1960—J.O. Jones—Edward Collins
1961—Sherman Siddons—Arthur Morrison
1962—No competition
1963—Andrew Rae—David Lyons
1964—James Langlow—David Cameron
1965—Ernest Myers—Harry Butler
1966—William Veale—Murdo McRae
1967—No competition
1968—Bert Littler—Lou Sousae
1969—C. Dickinson—C. Dickinson, Jr.
1970—Ed Willgress—Lewis Storm

1971—Bob Boehm—Arley Hudson
1972—M.M. Morrison—Alvin Olson

Rinks
(For Edwin James Trophy since 1945)
1934—Vancouver, B.C. (Bell)
1935—Tacoma, Wash. (E. McNeil)
1936—Bellingham, Wash. (Art Miller)
1937—Tacoma (H. Kinney)
1938—Vancouver (D. MacKenzie)
1939—Bellingham (Henry Roeder)
1940—Seattle (Charles Middleton)
1941—Seattle (Ernest Griffiths)
1942—Seattle (J. Anderson)
1943—Bellingham (Henry Roeder)
1944—Renton, Wash. (R. Pratt)
1945—Bellingham (J. McCallum)
1946—Victoria, B.C. (G. Marconini)
1947—New Westminister B.C., Vancouver (Roy Sparrow)
1948—Vancouver (H. Taylor)
1949—Vancouver (Wally Kenmuir)
1950—Arroyo Seco L.B.C., Los Angeles, Calif. (Len Hughes)
1951—Vancouver (Alex Houston)
1952—No competition
1953—New Westminister B.C. (Les Register)
1954—Vancouver (Alex Houston)
1955—Tacoma (Ernest F. Myers)
1956—Stanley Park L.B.C., Vancouver B.C. (R.C. Elliott)
1957—No competition
1958—Queen City L.B.C., Seattle, Wash. (Gordon Martin)
1959—Queen City L.B.C. (James Sheriff)
1960—Vancouver (A. Morrison)
1961—New Westminister L.B.C. (Roy Sparrow)
1962—No competition
1963—Jefferson Park L.B.C., Seattle (Jack Davidson)
1964—Dunbar L.B.C., Vancouver, B.C. (J. Leitch)
1965—66—Queen City L.B.C., Seattle (Ernest Myers)
1967—No competition
1968—Vancouver B.C. (Charles Burns)
1969—Portland, Oregon (Si Berry)
1970—Queen City, Seattle (Clarence Dickinson)
1971—Portland, Oregon (Jack McDougal)
1972—Queen City, Seattle (W. Mattocks)

Southeast
Singles
(St. Petersburg Trophy)
1952—Arthur H. Hartley
1953—Willis J. Tewksbury
1954—Arthur H. Hartley
1955—No competition
1956—Arthur H. Hartley
1957—Willis J. Tewksbury
1958—Arthur H. Hartley
1959—Willis J. Tewksbury
1960—No competition
1961—62—Arthur H. Hartley

1963—Cancelled—Rain
1964—Maurice Merriken
1965—No competition
1966—Arthur H. Hartley
1967—Clovis C. Lutz
1968—Cancelled
1969—Willis J. Tewksbury
1970—No competition
1971—Ken McIntyre
1972—Lee Grimshaw

Doubles
(Clearwater Trophy)
1952—Harry R. Hall—Neil Felker
1953—Arthur H. Hartley—W.G. (Bill) Hay
1954—Major C.L. Marsh—Lou L. Heaton
1955—No competition
1956—Willis J. Tewksbury—Frank H. Greening
1957—Frank C. Wilson—Jeff Smith
1958—William H. Young—George T. Langton
1959—Harry P. Hope—J.E. Smith
1960—No competition
1961—Arthur H. Hartley—D. Gordon MacKenzie
1962—J.H. Davis—C.H. Brereton
1963—Harry Hope—Jeff Smith
1964—Howard Wilson—George Meyer
1965—No competition
1966—Arthur H. Hartley—Edward J. Hayden
1967—Chester Pegg—Frank Osborne
1968—Willis Tewksbury—Walter Roy
1969—Howard Wilson—John Clark
1970—No competition
1971—Willis Tewksbury—Ray Grove, Jr.
1972—Harry Hope—Jeff Smith

Trebles
(J. Lester Esch Memorial Trophy)
1952—St. Petersburg (Fla.) L.B.C. (Harry R. Hall)
1953—St. Petersburg (Fla.) L.B.C. (D.R. Swisher)
1954—St. Petersburg L.B.C. (Willis J. Tewksbury)
1955—No competition
1956—St. Petersburg L.B.C. (Frank C. Wilson)
1957—Orlando L.B.C. (Harold L. Esch)
1958—St. Petersburg L.B.C. (Stewart A. Tulloch)
1959—Harry P. Hope—J.E. Smith—J.H. Davis
1960—No competition
1961—Clearwater, Fla. (W.J. Tewksbury)
1962—Streetsville, Ontario (Frank Pedgeon)
1963—Clearwater, Fla. (Clovis C. Lutz)
1964—St. Petersburg, Fla. (William Greaves)
1965—No competition
1966—Pawtucket, R.I. (James F. Candelet)
1967—Orlando, Fla. (Harold L. Esch)
1968—69—St. Petersburg, Fla. (Howard Wilson)
1970—No competition
1971—St. Petersburg, Fla. (Harry Hope)
1972—Bradenton, Fla. (Dave Strain)

Southwest

Singles
(Andrew C. Getty Trophy)
1951—J. Cobb

1952—Ray Veitch
1953—Percy Georgeson
1954—Richard W. Folkins
1955—T. Moorcroft
1956—Andy Lockhart
1957—Arnold Lees
1958—Peter Smith
1959—No competition
1960—Richard W. Folkins
1961—Cleve Forrester
1962—Carroll F. Chase
1963—Dan Howarth
1964—No competition
1965—Alf Andersen
1966—N. McInnes
1967—Harry Soderstrom
1968—Donald Buckley
1969—No competition
1970—Thomas Stirrat
1971—No competition
1972—William Mumma

Doubles
(North Division Trophy)
1951—Ken G. Landgraf—J. Armstrong
1952—Richard W. Folkins—Hugh Folkins
1953—Percy Georgeson—L. Graham
1954—Richard W. Folkins—Hugh Folkins
1955—Carroll F. Chase—Frank D. Murray
1956—Arnold Lees—W. Moore
1957—David Cameron—R. Russell
1958—R.W. Folkins—Frank Murray
1959—No competition
1960—Carl C. Waterbury—Roy Carver
1961—Robert Gordon—Arnold Lees
1962—Robert Gordon—Arnold Lees
1963—A. Benno—A. Richardson
1964—No competition
1965—Richard Folkins—Frank Murray
1966—Alex Veitch—Ezra Wyeth
1967—Roy Carver—Ash Ashley
1968—Neil McInnes—Ezra Wyeth
1969—No competition
1970—Robert Russell—Dan Howarth
1971—No competition
1972—Doug Coyle—Harry Soderstrom

Triples
(Irving C. Lewis Trophy)
1951—Oakland, Calif. (Ray Veitch)
1952—Exposition Park, Los Angeles (A. Buchan)
1953—San Francisco, Calif. (A. Lockhart)
1954—Arroyo Seco L.B.C., Los Angeles (Richard W. Folkins)
1955—Pasadena, Calif. (Carroll F. Chase)
1956—Beverly Hills, Calif. (L. Biggs)
1957—Oakland, Calif. (A. Veitch, Jr.)
1958—Arroyo Seco L.B.C., Los Angeles (R.W. Folkins)
1959—No competition
1960—Arroyo Seco L.B.C. (Richard W. Folkins)
1961—Beverly Hills L.B.C. (C.C. Waterbury)
1962—Santa Barbara L.B.C. (J. Coleman)

1963–Oakland, Calif. (Ralph Gordon)
1964–No competition
1965–Oakland, Calif. (Robert Quillen)
1966–Pasadena, Calif. (Carroll Chase)
1967–San Francisco, Calif. (John DaLuz)
1968–Arroyo Seco L.B.C., Los Angeles (Neil McInnes)
1969–No competition
1970–San Francisco L.B.C. (Clive Forrester)
1971–No competition
1972–MacKenzie Park L.B.C., Santa Barbara (G. Cormack)

Pacific Inter-Mountain Division

Singles
1971–Richard Folkins
1972–Joe DeLuz

Doubles
1971–Rob Quillen–Jeff Weatherly
1972–Rob Quillen–Harry Soderstrom

Triples
1971–Graham Jarvis, Tom Duncalf, Tom Owens
1972–Doug Coyle, Frank Souza, Alex. Lockhart

Open National Marl
(At St. Petersburg, Fla.)
Singles
(R. Stewart Brown Trophy presented 1934-1962; Dr. Weston Krupp Trophy from 1963 to date.)
1926–Dr. C. H. Burritt
1927–Charles G. Blake
1928–Andrew Laing
1929–Charles D. Gordon
1930–Alex M. Crawford
1931–F. W. Goodliffle
1932–Harry Salisbury
1933–George Reid
1934-35–Alex M. Crawford
1936–Neil C. Felker
1937–Alex M. Crawford
1938–Dr. Weston Krupp
1939–Neil C. Felker
1940–Dr. Weston Krupp
1941–Robert C. Whitehead
1942–Dr. Weston Krupp
1943–Alex M. Crawford
1944–George Reid
1945–John McKirdie
1946–Neil C. Felker
1947–Arthur H. Hartley
1948–Louis J. Siller
1949–David M. Fockler
1950–Frank C. Wilson
1951–Arthur H. Hartley
1952–Fred J. Harrington
1953–Thomas Lawson
1954–Stewart A. Tulloch
1955–Arthur H. Hartley
1956–Stewart A. Tulloch
1957-58–Arthur H. Hartley
1959–David Dunkerley

1960–Fred Harrington
1961–D. E. Anderson
1962–Arthur H. Hartley
1963–Alex L. Ripley
1964–Donald Belford
1965–Howard B. Wilson
1966-67–Alex L. Ripley
1968–Art Brown
1969–John Clark
1970–Arthur H. Hartley
1971–Willis Tewksbury
1972–Noel Farr
(Trophy retired in 1962 and presented to Mr. Hartley.)

Scotch Doubles
(George Smith Trophy presented from 1938-62; Steward A. Tulloch Trophy from 1963 to date.)
1926–O. A. Feine–J. W. Tesky
1927–H. H. Davison–John Rennie
1928–Dr. C. A. Gilchrist–Thomas Holmes
1929–Jacob Taylor–Harry McGibbon
1930–Fred Wilkinson–Vondye J. Hesse
1931–Walter Dundas–J. E. Trelford
1932–T. C. Reed –J. Lester Esch
1933–H. H. Davison–Ross Ormerod
1934–A. M. McGill–Henry Moffat
1935–Jacob Taylor–Frank Whitehall
1936–37–Alex M. Crawford–Dr. Weston Krupp
1938–J. T. Conley–Joseph Rankine
1939–Dr. J. B. Jupp–William H. Miles
1940–Roy B. Osgood–Arthur Howard
1941–Arthur H. Hartley–Frank R. Callahan
1942–W. Stan Hayes–Frank Greening
1943–Alex M. Crawford–Arthur Howard
1944–Claude Lapsley–Morris Jay
1945–Dr. J. B. Jupp–Frank Greening
1946–C. C. McDonald–R. J. Alexander
1947–Arthur H. Hartley–Sam W. Little
1948–A. A. Gilchrist Sr.–John P. Heighton
1949–Dr. J. B. Jupp–Fred J. Harrington
1950–Frank C. Wilson–C. Lorne Reburn
1951–John Young–J. A. Matheson
1952–D. R. Swisher–Col. E. R. Holmes
1953–Neil Felker–L. J. Siller
1954–Frank C. Wilson–Jeff Smith
1955–Dr. R. W. Sendker–Willis J. Tewksbury
1956–A. G. Cascadden–Dr. C. E. Knister
1957–Arthur H. Hartley–D. Gordon MacKenzie
1958–Norman H. Richardson–Raymond Jantzen
1959–Arthur H. Hartley–Fred J. Harrington
1960–C. Lorne Reburn–Robert R. Ramsey
1961-62–Howard Wilson–Fred Harrington
1963–Alex L. Ripley–Hugh McLaren
1964–David E. Anderson–Duncan Gillies
1965–William Crerar–Roy T. Marr
1966–67–Alex L. Ripley–Walter Smith
1968–Willis J. Tewksbury–William Smith
1969–Peter Purden–Tom Rodgers
1970–71–Willis Tewksbury–Ray Grove, Jr.
1972–Harry Hope–Jeff Smith

Rinks

ST. PETERSBURG TIMES TROPHY (donated by the newspapers of St. Petersburg, Fla.)

(Skips named first.)

1927—Harry H. Davison, A.D. Perry, G.C. Mc-Eldowney, John Rennie

1928—J.F. Wooster, Charles A. Godman. G.E. McLachlan, A. Provan

1929—Jacob Taylor, Peter M. Lytle, Harry Mc-Gibbon, Robert E. Marshall

1930—Alex M. Crawford, J.E. Trelford, A. Provan, E.C. McDonald

1931—George Smith, A.S. Young, Charles L. McNaughton, A.D. Perry

1932—T.C. Reed, Jacob Taylor, William J. Pickard, J. Lester Esch

1933—Ira F. Myers, George Smith, W. Miller Scott, A.S. Young

1934—C. Lorne Reburn, W. Miller Scott, Charles L. McNaughton, Fred W. Silvester

1935—C. Lorne Reburn, W. Miller Scott, Fred W. Silvester, A.D. Perry

1936—Alex M. Crawford, Dr. Weston Krupp, Charles D. Gordon, G.L. Allen

1937—T.C. Reed, J.W. Shelley, W. Miller Scott, A.M. Allen

1938—Roy B. Osgood, J.A. Sheppard, Jacob Taylor, R.W. Coward

1939—Neil Felker, William H. Miles, Dr. J.B. Jupp, C.M. Keith

1940—Edward J. Leinert, W. Stan Hayes, Walter W. Dundas, C.W. Lines

1941—*David Rees, John McKirdie, H.A. Burdick

1942—Alex M. Crawford, A.A. Little, Arthur Howard

1943—David Deans, David Rees, A.A. Gilchrist Sr.

1944—Alexander Smart, John Beattie, John Riley

1945—George Reid, John Young, Charles Schrenker

1946—D.C. Nale, W.M. Bristol, J. Harry Cunningham

1947—Dr. J.B. Jupp, Harry L. Sanborn, Louis J. Siller

1948—Norman H. Richardson, C. Lorne Reburn, Charles Schrenker

1949—Dr. C.H. Brereton, A.G. Cascadden, Fred J. Harrington

1950—Neil Filker, Fred J. Harrington, Louis J. Siller

1951—Dr. Weston Krupp, Jeffrey E. Smith, Sam W. Little

1952—Dr. Weston Krupp, Jeffrey E. Smith, J.A. Matheson

1953—Hugh Burgess, J.C. Clark, David Porter

1954—Arthur H. Hartley, Olaf Kling, H.S. (Tiny) Buck

1955—Ross Flintoff, W. Merlin Letcher, Joseph C. Ward

1956—D.E. Anderson, Dr. R.W. Sendker, Willis J. Tewksbury

1957—J.H. Smith, Jack Stewart, George Webster

1958—Fred J. Harrington, C. Lorne Reburn, Jeff Smith

1959—Alex Barbour, Raymond Jantzen, George Webster

1960—Dr. Weston Krupp, William Young, J.H. Davis

1961—D.E. Anderson, R.P. Bolling, Ray Jantzen

1962—Martin Dow, Frank C. Wilson, David Porter

1963—Donald Belford, Tom Flemming, George Webster

1964—Donald Belford, George Webster, John Clark

1965—Darrell Swisher, Smith Graham, George Meyer

1966—Harry Thatcher, James Wilson, Daniel McGregor

1967—Alex L. Ripley, Walter Smith, Dr. C.H. Brereton

1968—Jack Dodds, William Kurtz, George Green

1969—W.J. Tewksbury, Walter Roy, Chas. Buckingham

1970—Harry Hope, George Meyer, Jeff Smith

1971—George Marr, A. Gepp, F. Ingram

1972—W.J. Tewksbury, Ray Grove Jr., Peter Milroy

*Beginning in 1941 play was changed from rinks to trebles.

UNITED STATES CHAMPIONSHIPS

Closed competition limited to citizens of the United States and representing each of the five geographical divisions of the A.L.B.A.

Singles

(Spalding Inn, Whitefield, New Hampshire Trophy)

1957—Leonard Schofield

1958—59—Willis Tewksbury

1960—Arnold Lees

1961—James Candelet

1962—Howard S. Walker

1963—64—Willis Tewksbury

1965—Ezra Wyeth

1966—James Candelet

1967—Willis J. Tewksbury

1968—George E. Dunn

1969—Willis J. Tewksbury

1970—Clive Forrester

1971—James F. Candelet

1972—Neil McInnes

Doubles

(Buck Hill Falls, Pa., Trophy)

1958—Robert Savage—Peter Purden

1959—James Candelet—Robert Smart

1960—Thomas Stirrat—Fred Howarth

1961—Albert Presutti—George Dunn

1962—Harold L. Esch—Claude K. Swafford

1963—Robert Russell—Dan Howarth

1964—Robert Russell—Donald Buckley
1965—Arthur Hartley—Edward Hayden
1966—William Kaestle—Stephen Horwath
1967—Harold L. Esch—Alfred G. Hughes
1968—James F. Candelet—Robert Smart
1969—Alex S. Lockhart—Clive Forrester
1970—F. Ray Grove, Jr.—Willis J. Tewksbury
1971—Robert McGaffney—William Miller
1972—Neil McInnes—Ezra Wyeth

International Match

Between teams representing the United States and the Province of Ontario, Canada.

1941—Canada 121, United States 119
1942—Canada 137, United States 109
1943—Canada 150, United States 109
1944—45—No competition
1946—Canada 130, United States 94
1947—United States 121, Canada 111
1948—Canada 98, United States 90
1949—Canada 141, United States 88

1950—United States 127, Canada 117
1951—Canada 114, United States 108
1952—United States 145, Canada 109
1953—United States 115, Canada 109
1954—United States 166, Canada 87
1955—Canada 129, United States 124
1956—United States 150, Canada 91
1957—United States 95, Canada 92
1958—United States 135, Canada 105
1959—Canada 108, United States 87
1960—No competition
1961—Canada 101, United States 90
1962—65—No competition
1966—Canada 121, United States 106
(Discontinued)

WORLD LAWN BOWLS CHAMPIONSHIP

Singles

1966—David Bryant, England
1972—Mal Evans, Wales

DISTANCE TO JACK VARIES FROM 85 TO 100 FEET

WHITE JACK IS SMALLER THAN PLAYERS' BOWLS.
• INDICATES WHITE JACK
● INDICATES PLAYERS' BOWLS

GREEN IS SURROUNDED BY DITCH INTO WHICH BOWLS FALL IF ROLLED TOO STRONGLY.

44 YDS

19' TO 21' RINK

RUBBER MAT 44 YDS CANVAS

Lawn Bowls. (Taken from Sport for the Fun of It, by John R. Tunis, A. S. Barnes and Company New York.)

Doubles

1966—Geoff Kelley—Bert Palm, Australia

1972—Cecekio Delgado—Eric Liddell, Hong Kong

Triples

1966—John Dobbie, Athol Johnson, Don Collins, Australia

1972—Richard Folkins, Clive Forrester, William Miller, United States

Fours

1966—W. O'Neill, G. Jolly, R. Buchan, N. Lash, New Zealand

1972—N. King, C. Stroud, T. Hayward, P. Line, England

Women

Singles

1969—Gladys Doyle, Papua-New Guinea

Doubles

1969—Elsie McDonald, May Cridlan, South Africa

Triples

1969—Sarah Sundelowitz, Yetta Emanuel, Cathy Bidwell, South Africa

Fours

1969—S. Sundelowitz, Y. Emanuel, M. Cridland, C. Bidwell, South Africa

BASIC RULES

Bowling on the green is a combination of ten pins and horseshoes. It also bears a resemblance to curling. It may be played in singles, doubles, trebles or 4-man.

In the 4-man game, the players are designated as follows: "lead" or first player, second player, third player and skip (captain). These players are frequently called a rink of players. The two skips decide who shall roll first by a toss. The winner has his choice. Thereafter, the winner of each previous head (end) plays first. A head terminates when all bowlers on both sides have bowled their balls toward one end. The player shooting first rolls the jack ball and then his own two bowls alternately with the lead player of the opponents. The second players follow and roll their two bowls alternately, next the third players, and finally the skips. The player must have a foot on the mat when rolling his bowl.

The jack is a small white ball weighing 10 ounces and is 2½ inches in diameter. Any time a bowler knocks the jack outside the rink boundary, or less than 25 yards from the bowling mat, the opposing side then can cast the jack anew, but shall not play first. The mat is 14 by 24 inches.

The object of the game is to get the bowl as close as possible to the jack ball. It is permissible to knock opponents' bowls away from the jack. For each bowl closer to the jack than any bowls of the opponents, 1 point is scored. (This is similar to scoring in horseshoes.) Twenty-one ends usually constitute a game, although it may be any stipulated number of shots, heads, or length or time agreed upon by the players prior to the start of the game. In singles play, the game is 21 points.

Expert bowlers are adept at curving the bowl, using both a forehand curve and a backhand curve. The forehand breaks to the left while the backhand goes off to the right.*

The average "bowling green" is about 120 feet square, and is divided into rinks. Each rink is 20 feet wide and 120 feet long, official measurement. The greens are carpet-like grass surfaces similar to the finest golf putting greens and are maintained with the utmost care. In some instances, where grass is difficult to maintain the year around, a sand-surfaced court, sometimes called "marl," is constructed. This is a combination of clay and sand molded together to give a hard yet smooth and even playing surface.

A bank 2 feet high and a ditch 18 inches deep surround the green. The bowls range in size from 4 13/16 to 5 1/8 inches in diameter and vary in weight from 3 pounds 2 ounces to 3 pounds 8 ounces. They are biased—meaning unbalanced. Because of this, they can be made to curve as much as 4 feet in a 100-foot roll. An expert can put a spin on his bowl so that when it collides with an opponent's it stays almost at the point of impact instead of following through.

The 4-man team is the true game. Of this, the "skip" is the commander. He directs play, telling his men where to aim the bowl and his word is law. The doubles game often is referred to as "Scotch Doubles" because of the fact that this particular type of playing has gained such great favor in Scotland.

*The above from "Sports for Recreation," edited by E.D. Mitchell, A.S. Barnes and Company, New York.

MISCELLANEOUS
Aerial Tennis

The origin of Aerial Tennis can be traced back to the Chinese sport called Battledore and Shuttlecocks. The original bats, or paddles, were made entirely of wood but, later, the best paddles were made by stretching parchment, or cat gut, over a wooden head. With the idea of a gut racket the people of India conceived the game of Poona, which the Duke of Beaufort, an Englishman, later played and called Badminton in honor of his ancestral home, the Badminton house.

The first birdies were sometimes made of rubber but, most often, they were made of cork, filled with lead, and crowned with feathers which gave the birdies the appearance of a battling game cock. Logically, the birdie was later termed "shuttlecock".

The game of Aerial Tennis as we know it, in 1968, was revived by a Mr. Hudson of Cincinnati, Ohio, who went back to the original idea of using a wooden paddle. Mr. Hudson encountered a problem in making the birdies. He made them out of sea-gull feathers and because it is illegal to kill sea-gulls in the United States he had to obtain the feathers from Canada—a costly and involved process.

A few years later, Kenneth Sells, of Kansas City, discovered that birdies could be produced more economically by using white turkey feathers. In Kansas City the court size was changed. It was changed from thirty feet by fifty feet, to twenty-six feet by fifty feet. The game Aerial Tennis began to spread slowly throughout the United States and increased in popularity when used by the Armed Services for training and recreation during World War II. The growth of Aerial Tennis has become so rapid that it will be only a matter of time before this once exclusive game gains the esteem it deserves.

The game is played by batting a feather birdie, twice the size and weight of a Badminton birdie, over a seven foot net, with a wooden paddle that measures seventeen and one-half inches in length. The objective is to place the birdie in such a manner that it is impossible for an opponent to return it.

Associated Press Mid-Century Poll

(Courtesy of The Associated Press.)

In 1950, the AP asked sports experts in the United States to select the greatest athletes and outstanding events in various fields during the first half of the 20th Century. The leaders in the balloting follow:

GREATEST MALE ATHLETE

1. Jim Thorpe
2. Babe Ruth
3. Jack Dempsey
4. Ty Cobb
5. Bob Jones
6. Joe Louis
7. Red Grange
8. Jesse Owens
9. Lou Gehrig
10. Bronko Nagurski
11. Jackie Robinson
12. Bob Mathias
13. Walter Johnson
14. Glenn Davis
15. Bill Tilden
16. Glenn Cunningham
17. Glenn Morris
18. Cornelius Warmerdam

GREATEST BASEBALL PLAYER

	Votes
1. Babe Ruth	253
2. Ty Cobb	116
3. Lou Gehrig	8
4. Walter Johnson	7
5. Joe DiMaggio	5
6. Hans Wagner	2
7. Christy Mathewson	2

GREATEST FIGHTER

	Votes
1. Jack Dempsey (heavyweight)	251
2. Joe Louis (heavyweight)	104
3. Henry Armstrong (126–147 lbs.)	16
4. Gene Tunney (heavyweight)	6
5. Benny Leonard (lightweight)	5
6. Jack Johnson (heavyweight)	4
7. Jim Jeffries (heavyweight)	2

One vote each—Bob Fitzsimmons (heavyweight); Sam Langford (heavyweight); Mickey Walker (middleweight); Ray Robinson (welterweight); Joe Gans (lightweight).

GREATEST FOOTBALL PLAYER

	Votes
1. James Thorpe, Carlisle	170
2. Harold (Red) Grange, Illinois	138
3. Bronko Nagurski, Minnesota	38
4. Ernie Nevers, Stanford	7
5. Sammy Baugh, Texas Christian	7
6. Don Hutson, Alabama	6
7. George Gipp, Notre Dame	4
8. Charles Trippi, Georgia	3

Two votes each—Sid Luckman, Columbia, Steve Van Buren, Louisiana State; Willie Heston, Michigan; Chick Harley, Ohio State.

One vote each—Wilbur Henry, Washington and Jefferson; Bennie Oosterbaan, Michigan; Nile Kinnick, Iowa; Glenn Dobbs, Tulsa; Glenn Davis, Army; Clyde Turner, Hardin-Simmons; Doak Walker, Southern Methodist; Frank Albert, Stanford; Felix (Doc) Blanchard, Army; Charley Brickley, Harvard.

GREATEST GOLFER

	Votes
1. Bob Jones	293
2. Ben Hogan	40
3. Walter Hagen	29
4. Byron Nelson	17
5. Sam Snead	6
6. Gene Sarazen	4
7. Joyce Wethered	2
8. Harry Vardon	1

GREATEST TENNIS PLAYER

	Votes
1. Bill Tilden	310
2. Jack Kramer	32
3. Donald Budge	31
4. Mrs. Helen Wills Moody	12
5. Suzanne Lenglen	2

One vote each—Bill Johnston, Fred Perry, Ellsworth Vines, Mrs. Molla Bjurstedt Mallory.

GREATEST BASKETBALL PLAYER

1. George Mikan
2. Hank Luisetti
3. Nat Holman
4. Charley (Chuck) Hyatt
5. Alex Groza

GREATEST SWIMMER

	Votes
1. Johnny Weissmuller	132
2. Hironoshin Furuhashi	20
3. Adolph Kiefer	11
4. Duke Kahanamoku	10
5. Gertrude Ederle	8
6. Bill Smith	7
7. Ann Curtis	7
8. Alan Ford	6
9. Helene Madison	6
10. Esther Williams	5
11. Eleanor Holm	5

GREATEST TRACK AND FIELD PERFORMER

	Votes
1. Jesse Owens	201
2. Jim Thorpe	74
3. Paavo Nurmi	31
4. Glenn Cunningham	30
5. Cornelius Warmerdam	12
6. Mildred Didrikson Zaharias	9
7. Charley Paddock	8
8. Gunder Hagg	5
9. Bob Mathias	5
10. Mrs. Fanny Blankers-Koen	3

GREATEST THOROUGHBRED

1. Man o' War
2. Citation
3. Whirlaway
4. Seabiscuit
5. Exterminator

GREATEST FEMALE ATHLETE

1. Mildred Didrikson Zaharias (golf, track)
2. Helen Wills Moody (tennis)
3. Stella Walsh (track and field)
4. Fanny Blankers-Koen (track)
5. Gertrude Ederle (swimming)
6. Suzanne Lenglen (tennis)
7. Alice Marble (tennis)
8. Ann Curtis (swimming)
9. Sonja Henie (figure skating)
10. Helen Stephens (track and field)
11. Eleanor Holm (swimming)
12. Patty Berg (golf)
13. Helene Madison (swimming)
14. Glenna Collett Vare (golf)
15. Mary K. Browne (golf, tennis)
16. Eleonora Sears (hiking, tennis, squash racquets)
17. Helen Jacobs (tennis)
18. Louise Suggs (golf)
19. Joyce Wethered (golf)
20. Zoe Ann Olsen (swimming)
21. Barbara Ann Scott (figure skating)
22. Mildred Burke (wrestling)

GREATEST UPSET

	Votes
1. Boston Braves' four-straight World Series victory over Philadelphia Athletics in 1914	128
2. Gene Tunney's victory over Jack Dempsey in their first heavyweight title fight in 1926	53
3. Centre College's 6—0 football victory over Harvard in 1921	40
4. Jim Braddock's victory over Max Baer for world heavyweight title in 1935	24
5. Upset's victory over Man o' War in 1919	21
6. Max Schmeling's knockout of Louis in 1936	12
7. Notre Dame's 35—13 football victory over Army in 1913	10
8. Dempsey's knockout of Jess Willard in 1919	7
9. Holy Cross' 55—12 football victory over Boston College in 1942	7
10. Navy's 21—21 football tie with Army in 1948	7
11. New York Yankees' World Series victory over Brooklyn in 1949	4
12. Cincinnati's World Series victory over Chicago White Sox in 1919	4
13. Columbia's 7—0 Rose Bowl football victory over Stanford in 1934	3
14. Auburn's 14—13 football victory over Alabama in 1949	3
15. Chicago Bears' 73—0 football victory over Washington in 1940	3
16. Carnegie Tech's 27—7 football victory over Notre Dame in 1926	3

MOST DRAMATIC EVENT

	Votes
1. Dempsey-Firpo fight in 1923	70
2. Babe Ruth "calling" World Series homer in 1932	66
3. Dempsey-Tunney "long count" fight in 1927	43
4. Lou Gehrig's farewell appearance in 1939	23
5. Grover Alexander's strikeout of Tony Lazzeri in 1926 World Series	21
6. Notre Dame's 18—13 football victory over Ohio State in 1935	17
7. Red Grange's feats (he scored 5 touchdowns) against Michigan in 1924	13
8. Babe Ruth's farewell in 1948	13
9. Floyd Bevens' near no-hitter in 1947 World Series	12
10. Joe Louis' first-round knockout of Max Schmeling in 1938	12

Association of Sports Museums and Halls of Fame

The thought for the development of an Association of Sports Museums and Halls of Fame was conceived in 1971 by Buck Dawson, Director of the International Swimming Hall of Fame, Fort Lauderdale, Flordia.

The purpose of the Association is that of co-ordinating the activities of the various sports museums and halls of fame in North America, and striving to be helpful to all.

The founding president was Buck Dawson. At convention meeting at the Naismith Memorial Basketball Hall of Fame, Springfield, W.R. Bill Schroeder was elected President-Secretary-Treasurer of the Association for 1972-73.

Lee Williams and Bruce Pluckhahn were elected Vice-Presidents, as Buck Dawson, Philip Pines, Bruce Pluckhahn, W.R. Bill Schroeder, Don Sarno and Lee Williams were designated members of the Board of Directors for 1972-73.

The 1973 convention meeting of the Association will be held, possibly in October, in Los Angeles, as Citizens Savings Hall (new name) will coordinate.

Sports Museums and Halls of Fame

Aquatic Hall of Fame and Museum of Canada, 436 Main Street, Winnipeg, Manatoba R3B 1B2, Canada, Vaughan L. Baird, Chairman

Canada Sports Hall of Fame, Canadian National Exhibition, Toronto 2B, Ontario, Canada, M.H. "Lefty" Reid, Curator

Canadian Football Hall of Fame, City Hall Plaza, Hamilton, Ontario, Canada, Larry Smith, Director

Citizens Savings Hall (new name, April 1, 1973), 9800 South Sepulveda Boulevard, Los Angeles, California 90045, W.R. Bill Schroeder, Managing Director

Hall of Fame of the Trotter, 240 Main Street, Goshen, New York, Philip A. Pines, Director

Hockey Hall of Fame, Exhibition Park, Toronto, Ontario, Canada, M.H. "Lefty" Reid, Curator and Secretary

International Softball Congress Hall of Fame (Long Beach, California), 9800 South Sepulveda Boulevard, Los Angeles, California 90045, Donald Sarno, Director

International Softball Congress Hall of Fame (Long Beach, California), 9800 South Sepulveda Boulevard, Los Angeles, California 90045, Donald Sarno, Director

International Swimming Hall of Fame, 1 Hall of Fame Drive, Fort Lauderdale, Florida 33316, Buck Dawson, Director

National Bowling Hall of Fame and Museum (Milwaukee), 5301 South 76th Street, Greendale, Wisconsin 53129, Bruce Pluckhahn, Director

National Cowboy Hall of Fame and Western Heritage Center, 1700 N.E. 63rd Street, Oklahoma City, Oklahoma 73111, Dean Krakel, Managing Director

Naismith Memorial Basketball Hall of Fame, Box 175, Springfield, Massachusetts 01109, Lee Williams, Director

San Diego Hall of Champions (Associate Member), Balboa Park, San Diego, California 92101, Captain Arthur T. Emerson, Jr., USN (Ret.), Director

The National Football Foundation and Hall of Fame, 17 East 80th Street, New York City, New York 10021, James L. McDowell, Executive Director

The National Ski Hall of Fame, Ishpeming, Michigan 49849, Ray Leverton, Curator

United States Figure Skating Association Museum (USFSA), 1240 Soldiers Field Road, Boston, Massachusetts, Benjamin T. Wright, Chairman (65 Foster Road, Belmont, Massachusetts 02178)

United States Hockey Hall of Fame, Box 657 Eveleth, Minnesota, Roger Godin, Director

Ball Games

A combination of circumstances during the last 2 generations has brought about the creation and development of a large number of ball games, many unknown to the public that does not visit the playgrounds.

The Playground Association of America, now the National Recreation Association, was formed in 1906 by a group of public-spirited citizens who felt that, since cities had become congested and there was a dearth of playing fields, something should be done to provide playgrounds for youngsters.

After the playgrounds had been established, the association devised sports to fit the limited areas. The programs for play included a variety of games which called for a ball and stick.

The success of this enterprise influenced school boards to encourage games in schoolyards, so that the muscular effort would build strength and health. Thus, the children could have games before school and during recess, and resume play at the recreation centers after school hours.

The playground movement received great impetus from the Federal Government, which set aside huge sums of money to construct and equip playgrounds in every city and hamlet where there was a need for organized play.

Some areas were large; others were small. In fact, most of them were so small that when fitted out with archery ranges, horseshoe courts, lawn bowling greens, shuffleboard courts, tennis courts, etc., there wasn't much room left for baseball and softball diamonds and so on.

More youngsters wanted to play baseball or softball than the diamonds could accommodate. Girls wanted to have a "go" at some game where a ball was the principal part of the equipment. Some did play basketball and volleyball, but the basketball and volleyball courts, too, were limited in number. And so the playground supervisors imported games from elsewhere, and invented their own.

Tether ball was imported from England, where it was a great favorite. A pole is planted with its top 10 feet from the ground. A piece of string is tacked to the top of the pole and on the other end of the string is a tennis ball, which, when at rest, is 2 feet 6 inches from the ground.

The rival players use the ordinary tennis racquet. The idea is to hit the ball toward the opponent so that it swings on its string and winds around the pole. If it winds down to a black line 6 feet from the ground you are the winner. Meanwhile, your opponent is trying to wind the ball on your side.

A variation of baseball that has taken hold in and around St. Louis, Mo., is corkball. The game, which was devised by habitués of a combination boarding house-saloon, originally was played with a broomstick and a bung from a beer barrel. The bat now is 38 inches long and not more than an inch and a half at its widest part. The ball is round and made of cork wound with string and has a horsehide cover. Generally there are 5 players on a side and a game lasts 5 innings. The positions are designated as catcher, pitcher, left fielder, center fielder and right fielder.

Basket goal is an offshoot of basketball and is little more than goal shooting practice. Giant volleyball was developed from volleyball. Among the other games are:

Captain's ball, end ball, newcomb ball, drive ball, toss ball, punch ball, bee ball, tom ball, speed ball, fist ball, long ball, bounce ball, pin ball, score ball, bottle ball, curtain ball, cabinet ball, recreation ball, playground ball, lee ball, beat ball, line ball, one o' gang, corner ball, post ball, bounce hand baseball, triangle ball, hit ball, sprint ball, stick ball and others.

Boccie

(From E.D. Mitchell's "Sports for Recreation," A.S. Barnes and Company, New York.)

Boccie (pronounced "bott-chee") is an Italian bowling game little known in the United States except in communities with a high percentage of European population. Yet the game has every factor to assure acceptance and permanency in a recreation program. Facilities and equipment are easily and inexpensively acquired and maintenance cost is slight; playing rules are simple and quickly understood; physical requirements are low enough to attract men, women and children; games go quickly and no 2 are exactly alike, thus sustaining interest; games may be played indoors or outdoors.

There is no regulation court for boccie, but 60 by 10 feet seems to be an average installation. This space is enclosed by 10- or 12-inch wooden sides and somewhat higher wooden ends to serve as backstops. Many installations have shallow troughs about 3 inches deep at either end of the court to keep balls bowled too hard from returning to the playing field.

The playing surface is level and when of hard dirt, a mixture of clay and sand is preferable.

The equipment consists of 8 balls having a diameter of 4½ inches, plus a smaller "jack" ball 2¾ inches in diameter. Four large balls are marked by engraved bands or by color to distinguish them from the other 4. The best balls are made of *lignum vitae*, said to be the heaviest wood in the world; however, less expensive composition balls, similar to bowling balls, are obtainable. Some difficulty may be experienced in purchasing regulation 4½-inch boccie balls, in which case 5-inch duckpin balls are a possible substitute.

Two, 4 or 8 players are split into 2 teams. When 8 compete, 2 players from each side are stationed at opposite ends of the court and play alternate frames or innings.

Sides match to determine which uses the plain balls and which the marked balls, and which has the honor of starting. A player from the winning side begins the game by tossing the jack ball from one end of the court any distance he pleases toward the other end. The same player then tries to roll or toss one of his large balls as close to the jack ball as possible. His side then steps back and does not bowl again until the opponents have succeeded in getting one of their balls closest to the jack. This procedure continues until one side has used all its balls, whereupon the other side is entitled to bowl its remaining balls. The partners play alternately.

Balls must be delivered underhand; they may

be thrown through the air or bowled, as the player chooses. A player must deliver the ball before overstepping a line indicated by marks placed on the side walls 4 feet down the court from the back edge of the playing area, but not counting the trough. It is permissible to change the location of the jack ball by hitting it and to knock away an opponent's ball. A ball thrown or hit out of the court is out of play. If the jack is hit out of court, it is returned to a spot in the middle of the far edge of the playing surface. The side that wins a point, or points, in each frame, begins play in the next frame; play is in the opposite direction down court from the previous frame. Shots banked from the wooden sides are permitted.

One point is awarded for every ball of a side closer to the jack ball than the closest ball of the opponents. The game is 12 points, except when the opposing side has 11 points; when this occurs, play is continued until one side has a clear advantage of 2 points. A match is the best 2 of 3 games.

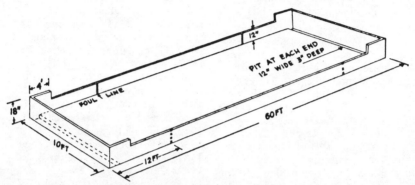

Boccie Court. (Taken from "Sports for Recreation," edited by E.D. Mitchell, A.S. Barnes and Company, New York.)

Citizens Savings Athletic Foundation

(Formerly Helms Athletic Foundation)

The Citizens Savings Athletic Foundation has a most interesting history, which dates back to the year 1936.

Helms Athletic Foundation was instituted and funded by Paul H. Helms, and developed by Managing Director W.R. Bill Schroeder on October 15, 1936, at Los Angeles, California.

Under the banner of Helms, the Athletic Foundation enjoyed 34 eventful years of operation in the interest of wholesome sports.

After headquartering in downtown Los Angeles for twelve years, the Athletic Foundation moved into impressive Helms Hall, sports shrine, which was dedicated on October 17, 1948. Paul H. Helms and the Helms family provided the funds for the erection of the sports shrine.

In July of 1970, the Helms family found it impossible to continue to sponsor the Athletic Foundation and sports shrine. For two months, both were without sponsorship. However, operation was continued.

In the meantime, there were numerous offers by organizations, in various sections of the country, to serve as continuing sponsors. However, Managing Director Schroeder elected to join forces with United States and Loan Association of California.

On October 6, 1970, United Savings Helms Athletic Foundation and United Savings Helms Hall became realities, as quarters for both were moved from Venice Boulevard in West Los Angeles, to 9800 South Sepulveda Boulevard, Los Angeles, in the International Airport area.

In March of 1973, United Savings and Citizens Savings & Loan Association completed a merger, providing for an expansion of operations for both. It was then that the Athletic Foundation was designated Citizens Savings Athletic Foundation, and the sports shrine was named Citizens Savings Hall.

Originally, in 1936, the Athletic Foundation fashioned an extensive awards program, reaching all levels—junior, high school, amateur, college, and professional. Making use of the Bill Schroeder sports library as the source, the Athletic Foundation delved deeply into sports research.

Subsequently, the Athletic Foundation developed awards programs for Athlete of the Month, Athlete of the Year, and Halls of Fame for many sports and categories. The most significant awards which were developed, in 1949, were those for the World Trophy.

The World Trophy, serving to recognize the foremost amateur athlete of each of the six areas of the world—Africa, Asia, Australia, Europe, and North and South America—annually. Selections date back to the year 1896, that in which the first of the Modern Olympic Games was held.

World Trophy silver plaque awards are granted each year. The permanent trophy, standing more than 6 feet in height, is made of gold, silver, and bronze, resting upon a marble base. It is lodged in Citizens Savings Hall.

Citizens Savings Halls of Fame include those for Athletic Trainers, Automobile Racing, Badminton, Baseball, Basketball, Boxing, Fencing, Football, Golf, Gymnastics, Handball, Rowing, Soaring, Swimming and Diving, Synchronized Swimming, Tennis, Track and Field, Volleyball, Weightlifting, Winter Sports, and Wrestling.

The Athletic Foundation also conducts Halls of Fame programs for College Athletic Directors, College Sports Information Directors, and the National Association of Intercollegiate Athletics.

Since its inception in 1936, the Athletic Foundation has been involved in countless numbers of civic activities, of sports kind.

The current Board which acts upon Citizens Savings Athletic Foundation awards selections is composed of Jim Cour, Bud Furillo, Fred Hessler, Tom Kelly, Bill Shirley, Allin Slate, Jack Stevenson, Gil Stratton, W.R. Bill Schroeder, and Elwood A. Teague, chairman.

NORTH AMERICA WORLD TROPHY SELECTIONS

1896—Robert Garrett (track and field)
1897—Robert D. Wrenn (Tennis)
1898—Juliette P. Atkinson (tennis)
1899—T. Truxton Hare (football)
1900—Alvin C. Kraenzlein (track and field)
1901—Charles Daly (football)
1902—William A. Larned (tennis)
1903—Walter J. Travis (golf)
1904—James D. Lightbody (track and field)
1905—May Sutton (tennis)
1906—Walter Eckersall (football, baseball, track and field)
1907—Martin J. Sheridan (track and field)
1908—Melvin Sheppard (track and field)
1909—Charles M. Daniels (swimming)
1910—Fred C. Thomson (all-round)
1911—Hazel Hotchkiss (tennis)
1912—James Thorpe (track, all-round)
1913—Maurice E. McLoughlin (tennis)
1914—Francis Ouimet (golf)
1915—Jerome D. Travers (golf)
1916—J.E. (Ted) Meredith (track and field)
1917—Molla Bjurstedt (tennis)
1918—Avery Brundage (track and field)

1919—William Johnston (tennis)
1920—Charles W. Paddock (track and field)
1921—William T. Tilden 2d (tennis)
1922—Thomas Hitchcock Jr. (polo)
1923—John Weissmuller (swimming)
1924—Harold Grange (football)
1925—Ernest Nevers (football, baseball, basketball)
1926—Robert T. Jones Jr. (golf)
1927—Benjamin Oosterbaan (football, baseball, basketball)
1928—Percy Williams (track and field)
1929—Helen Wills (tennis)
1930—Glenna Collett (golf)
1931—Helene Madison (swimming)
1932—H. Ellsworth Vines (tennis)
1933—Glenn Cunningham (track and field)
1934—W. Lawson Little (golf)
1935—Jesse Owens (track and field)
1936—Glenn Morris (track and field, all-round)
1937—J. Donald Budge (tennis)
1938—Angelo Luisetti (basketball)
1939—Alice Marble (tennis)
1940—J. Gregory Rice (track and field)
1941—Robert L. Riggs (tennis)
1942—Cornelius Warmerdam (track and field)
1943—Gilbert Dodds (track and field)
1944—Ann Curtis (swimming)
1945—Glenn Davis (football, all-round)
1946—Pauline Betz (tennis)
1947—John A. Kramer (tennis)
1948—Robert Mathias (track and field, all-round)
1949—Melvin Patton (track and field)
1950—Richard H. Attlesey (track and field)
1951—Robert E. Richards (track and field)
1952—Horace Ashenfelter (track and field)
1953—Malvin Whitfield (track and field)
1954—Wes Santee (track and field)
1955—Patricia McCormick (diving)
1956—Parry O'Brien (track and field)
1957—Robert Gutowski (track and field)
1958—Rafer Johnson (track and field, all-round)
1959—Ray Norton (track and field)
1960—Wilma Rudolph (track and field)
1961—Ralph Boston (track and field)
1962—Terry Baker (football, basketball)
1963—Brian Sternberg (track and field)
1964—Alfred Oerter (track and field)
1965—Michael Garrett (football, baseball)
1966—James Ryun (track and field)
1967—Randy Matson (track and field)
1968—Robert Beamon (track and field)
1969—Bill Toomey (track and field)
1970—Gary Hall (swimming)
1971—Pat Matzdorf (track and field)
1972—Mark Spitz (swimming)

Codeball

Dr. William E. Code of Chicago invented the little known sport of Codeball in the late 1920's. During World War II it was one of the games recommended in the Armed Forces Sports Program.

As with most physicians, Dr. Code was called

upon for many years to recommend some form of exercise, not too vigorous, which might tone muscles and, at the same time, better the condition of the patient. Dr. Code responded with a game that bears his name and is of two distinct kinds: one outdoors, the other indoors. The game was first introduced at the Lake Shore Athletic Club, Chicago.

The only similarity between the indoor and outdoor versions is that the same ball is used, the ball being 6 inches in diameter and weighing 12 ounces.

The indoor game is "codeball-in-the-court," the outdoor is "codeball-on-the-green." The indoor game is something like handball, except that the feet, and not the hands, are used. The outdoor game follows, generally, the rules of golf, but the ball is propelled by the feet alone.

The indoor game requires that the ball be kicked on the fly or on the first bounce off the court walls. The hands aren't permitted to touch the ball except when the player is getting ready to serve. The kicking process is recommended for developing balance and skill. More or less, handball rules and scoring govern codeball-in-the-court.

The outdoor game provides for teeing off, as in golf, with the ball being kicked off the tee. All progress must be by kicking. Upon reaching the green the player, to hole out, must kick the ball into an inverted cone-shaped bowl with a top opening 18 inches wide. The cone is 7½ inches deep and has a base 41 inches in diameter. The player negotiating the "bowl" in the least number of kicks wins the hole in match play, the one completing the course, which is 14 holes—or bowls—in the least number of kicks is the winner in medal competition.

There is no standard distance for codeball-on-the-green, just as there is none in golf. The course is laid out according to the terrain. The distance between bowls varies, as it does in golf. There are short holes and long holes.

The original game was codeball-in-the-court. But the older folks decided it was a bit too strenuous. So it was bequeathed to youth, and the newer game of codeball-on-the-green was originated for the oldsters who, along with younger people, find it fun without being exacting.

The *Amateur Athlete,* the official organ of the Amateur Athletic Union, discussing codeball, said:

"Since its introduction, codeball has made rapid strides. The indoor version was given impetus by numerous athletic clubs, colleges, and Y.M.C.A.'s, where handball courts were available. One of the first cities to lay out a public course for 'codeball-on-the-green' was Miami, Fla. The school children there took to the game in great numbers, and then the tourists discovered it and liked it.

"By the end of 1932 'codeball-in-the-court' was firmly established as a playground recreation, installations having been made in many public parks for outdoor play against walls in Kokomo, Rock Island, Fort Wayne, Louisville, Toledo, Dayton, Chicago and other cities. By then, too, the game of codeball-on-the-green had been established as an adjunct to many private and public golf courses and in summer camps.

"The game has been introduced in hospitals as a recreation for patients and convalescents. The United States War Veterans' Hospital at North Chicago, Elgin State Hospital for mental cases in Elgin and Hines Memorial Hospital in Chicago were among the first to recognize the therapeutic values of codeball and made the game available to patients."

Codeball in both forms gained a great number of converts during the war and its popularity since then has been on the increase. Dr. Code declared:

"Codeball-on-the-green is a nice, easy game. It can be played leisurely. But codeball-in-the-court is radically different. It calls for almost the ultimate in speed, an alert eye, a high order of kicking skill and plenty of stamina. It's a rugged sort of sport, even though there is no body contact, and the average football player, taking up the court game, usually suffers early embarrassment over his misses in kicks at the fast moving ball."

A special demonstration of codeball-on-the-green was staged at the Olympic Village, Helsinki, Finland, prior to the 1952 Olympic Games. Much interest was exhibited and information was sought by groups from Egypt, India, Mexico, Australia, Germany, Brazil, Venezuela, Denmark, England, France, Japan and other countries.

Fieldball

(Originally known as Field Handball)

The Germans originated the game and named it field handball. It was so described on the Berlin Olympic Games program of 1936.

Some years prior to 1936, Americans adopted the game, under its original name—field handball. After World War II broke out in Europe, resentment against the Germans was such that the name of the game, so far as the Americans were

concerned, was changed and Americans call it fieldball.

Fieldball is played with a ball about the size of a soccer football, but the rules prohibit all players, except the goalkeeper, from kicking it. It is a throwing, passing and punching game. The players may catch the ball or they may strike it with their fists. If they catch it, they are permitted to throw for the goal or pass to a teammate. They may not run with it.

The game bears no relation to handball. The Germans gave it that name simply because the hands are involved. Fieldball is likened by some to soccer, while others refer to it as a form of outdoor basketball, except that goal posts are used.

A team is made up of 11 players, and the game is played on a field either 100 yards long and 60 yards wide or 110 x 70. There are goals at each end of the playing field.

Play begins in the center of the field. The object is to throw the ball or bat it with the fist between the goal posts of the opposing team. If successful, 1 point is scored. Whenever a team has scored, play is resumed in midfield. A player on the team that has been scored against makes the first throw, which usually is a pass to a teammate.

A referee and 4 linesmen supervise the game. The referee calls violations and metes out free and penalty throws, as may be required.

Fieldball is very fast, with sustained action, and has grown greatly in favor in the United States, especially in the playgrounds that are of sufficient size to provide a regulation field.

Metric Equivalents

All English-speaking countries used yards, feet and inches in determining distance in athletic contests until the end of 1931. Meanwhile, other nations used the metric system, which operates on the decimal basis.

Since all Olympic distances and time are on the metric system, the Amateur Athletic Union of the United States decided late in 1931 to use the metric plan for outdoor meets, but keep yardage for indoor contests. The Intercollegiate A.A.A.A. immediately followed and, since 1932, the metric distances and time have been used for A.A.U. and I.C.A.A.A.A. contests.

The National Collegiate A.A. continues to use yards, feet and inches, and also the old method of timing after experimenting with metric measurements for its outdoor meets from 1933 to 1936, inclusive.

STANDARD MEASUREMENTS

A meter is 39.37 inches.

100 meters equals 109 yards 1 foot 1 inch.

110 meters equals 120 yards 10 7/10 inches.

600 meters equals 656 yards 6 inches.

800 meters equals 874 yards 2 feet 8 inches.

1,500 meters equals 1,640 yards 1 foot 3 inches.

3,000 meters equals 1 mile 1,520 yards 2 feet 6 inches.

5,000 meters equals 3 miles 188 yards 2 inches.

10,000 meters equals 6 miles 376 yards 4 inches.

.0016 equals 1/16 inch.

.0031 equals 1/8 inch.

.0063 equals 1/4 inch.

.0127 equals 1/2 inch.

A kilometer equals 1,000 meters (0.621370 mile).

METERS TRANSLATED TO FEET AND INCHES

Meters		Meters	
1	... 3 ft. 3.37 in.	3	... 9 ft. 10.11 in.
2	... 6 ft. 6.74 in.	4	...13 ft. 1.48 in.
5	...16 ft. 4.85 in.	30	...98 ft. 5.10 in.
6	...19 ft. 8.22 in.	35	...114 ft. 9.95 in.
7	...22 ft. 11.59 in.	40	...131 ft. 2.80 in.
8	...26 ft. 2.96 in.	45	...147 ft. 7.65 in.
9	...29 ft. 6.33 in.	50	...164 ft. .50 in.
10	...32 ft. 9.70 in.	60	...196 ft. 10.20 in.
15	...49 ft. 2.55 in.	70	...229 ft. 7.90 in.
20	...65 ft. 7.40 in.	75	...246 ft. .75 in.
25	...82 ft. .25 in.	80	...262 ft. 5.60 in.

The A.A.U., in its "Official Track and Field Handbook," Rule 19, dealing with records, states:

"For measuring, or checking, courses, where no metric tape is available, the following table will be acceptable:

50 meters	164.04 ft.
60 meters	196.86 ft.
100 meters	328.1 ft.
200 meters	656.2 ft.
300 meters	984.3 ft.
400 meters	1,312.4 ft.
500 meters	1,640.5 ft.
600 meters	1,968.6 ft.
800 meters	2,624.7 ft.
1,000 meters	3,280.9 ft.
1,500 meters	4,921.3 ft.
2,000 meters	6,561.7 ft.
3,000 meters	9,842.6 ft.
4,000 meters	13,123.4 ft.
5,000 meters	16,404.3 ft.
6,000 meters	19,685.1 ft.
7,000 meters	22,966.0 ft.
8,000 meters	26,246.8 ft.
9,000 meters	29,527.0 ft.
10,000 meters	32,808.5 ft."

RELATION OF METERS TO YARDS

Meters	Miles	Yards	Feet	In.
1	0	1	0	3.37
2	0	2	0	10.11
4	0	4	1	1.48
5	0	5	1	4.85
10	0	10	2	9.70
20	0	21	2	7.40

30	0	32	2	5.10	800	0	874	2	8.00
40	0	43	2	2.80	1,000	0	1,093	1	10.00
50	0	54	2	.50	1,500	0	1,640	1	3.00
60	0	65	1	10.20	1,600	0	1,749	2	4.00
70	0	76	1	7.90	2,000	1	427	0	8.00
80	0	87	1	5.60	3,000	1	1,520	2	6.00
90	0	98	1	3.30	5,000	3	188	0	2.00
100	0	109	1	1.00	10,000	6	376	0	4.00
110	0	120	0	10.70	20,000	12	752	0	8.00
200	0	218	2	2.00	25,000	15	940	0	10.00
300	0	328	0	3.00	30,000	18	1,128	1	0.00
400	0	437	1	4.00					
500	0	546	2	5.00					

26 miles 385 yards equals 42,195.1 meters.

Paddle Tennis

(And Platform Paddle Tennis)

Paddle tennis was invented after World War I by Frank P. Beal, secretary of the Community Council of New York, to provide children with a game that would enable them to learn the rudiments of lawn tennis. He conducted the first tournament at Washington Square Park in New York City in 1924.

Platform paddle tennis, a later creation, was originated by Fessenden S. Blanchard and James K. Cogswell of Scarsdale, N.Y., and calls for the use of a covered platform on which the game can be played, thus making it a year-round pastime.

Beal, a tennis enthusiast who felt that a child was too small to learn the game of tennis with his limited strength and his lack of durability, which tennis requires, constructed a court half the size of one used for lawn tennis. He substituted light paddles for the heavier racquets, and the youngsters, on their 39 x 18-foot double court, get a lot of fun and exercise.

The net is 30 inches high, and it is possible that the idea for the game came from the tennis played on a court of limited size and with a low net, on the decks of ocean liners (deck tennis).

The ball is of sponge rubber and the paddle is of laminated wood, so light that a child can swing it easily.

The game became a great favorite among youngsters. Play teaches them the technique of lawn tennis and when they outgrow paddle tennis they usually show immediate progress at the other sport. The game spread beyond the public playground areas and courts were built on the beaches in the Greater New York area.

Since Beal launched the game, it has extended in popularity to all parts of the United States, and many thousands of courts have been made available for play.

Older persons watched the children for a while, then gave the game a try and became converts. The result is that a large army of adults now indulges in paddle tennis. Among the grown-ups who were first to test out paddle tennis were Cogswell and Blanchard. They became so enthusiastic about it that they devised the platform idea, so that play could be indulged in during all seasons and under all weather conditions.

The platform is roofed over. At first, the topping was canvas. This was discarded for solid material. The platform is portable. Furthermore, it is so arranged that lights can be attached to the ceilings for play under the floodlights.

The court devised by Blanchard, since play was for oldsters rather than youngsters, measures 44 x 20 feet. The ball also is of sponge rubber, but the paddles are heavier and somewhat bigger, to suit the older and stronger players.

Blanchard became such a paddle tennis devotee that he did not stop with pioneering the platform idea for the game. He wrote a book, "Paddle Tennis," published by A.S. Barnes and Company, which deals with the history of the sport, and the technique of play. This book has done much to influence adults to take up the sport.

As early as 1938, there were so many paddle tennis players that it was felt a national organization was needed to supervise the sport. This resulted in the formation of the United States Paddle Tennis Association, which is the governing body of a game played in practically every state in the Union and in the outlying territories.

Paddle tennis rules vary somewhat from those of lawn tennis, though the fundamentals of play are identical. In adult competition only one serve is allowed in paddle tennis and if it is a fault the server loses the point. The entire court is in bounds in singles following service. Youngsters, however, are permitted 2 serves and all play is confined to the singles court.

Playing the ball off the backstops and sidewalls is permitted in platform paddle tennis.

Skate Sailing

(Courtesy of Basil Kamener, Sec., Skate-Sailing Association of America,
4 Manor Rd., Livingston, N. J., 07039

Skate sailing, as a sport, is practiced in the United States within a narrow zone of the country below the "snow belt" of New England, and above the more temperate areas, where lakes and rivers don't freeze to a safe thickness for sailing. This zone includes lakes in New Jersey, New York, Connecticut, and Pennsylvania in the eastern part of the country, Ohio in the middle of the country, and Wisconsin in the mid-west. Sailing is also practiced on lakes and rivers in Canada and the Scandinavian countries. These areas are conducive to skate sailing because winter snows are generally light, and with occasional thaws and refreezing, the surfaces are restored to make sailing possible. A slight snowfall, covering cracks and ice fishing holes, can make sailing hazardous.

In order to sail, one only needs a pair of skates, a sail, strong legs, ice, and wind. The most popular sail in use today is called "the Hopatcong Racing Sail." It is named after a lake in New Jersey where sailing is very popular. Its design was conceived in 1917 by W. Van B. Claussen, and has undergone very little change since that time. Newer modern materials have been substituted for the original cotton sailcloth and spruce spars, but the dimensions have not varied. Wind tunnel tests have proven the geometry to be correct in placing the center of pressure of the sail on the shoulder of the sailor, where it belongs. Varying the dimensions tends to cause twisting and unbalancing of the sailor. A properly constructed sail is effortless to hold and easy to control.

The Hopatcong sail is constructed of a nylon or dacron sailcloth, sewn with the outside edges parallel to the warp or selvage of the material. Depending on the number of square feet desired, the sail is from 8 to 10 feet high in the front and tapers to 4 to 5 feet at the rear. Both the front and rear edges of the sail have pockets sewn in them the width of the sail to receive jib and tail bows of a flexible material such as rattan or fiberglass to assist in stretching the material taut. Stretching is accomplished by attaching a boom to the center of the jib bow and, with a lashing cord of dacron, nylon, or cotton, pulling the tail bow toward the opposite end of the boom. The boom is about one foot longer than the sail. A mast serves to stretch the sail in the vertical direction and provide a means of holding the sail. Spars are usually made in sections and joined with ferrules to provide ease in portability.

When in use, the boom of the sail rests on the shoulder, and the sailor grasps the mast with one or both hands below the boom. The sailor tacks across the wind just as a boat would, but on ice, speeds of 40 to 50 miles an hour can easily be attained. In order to change direction, the sailor grasps the mast with one hand on each side of the boom, and holding the sail horizontally overhead, glides into the wind in a smooth curve. As he comes about, the sailor lightly drops the sail on the opposite shoulder and continues sailing in the opposite direction, with the sail between his body and the wind. Jibing, or turning downwind can be done, but if the sailor is not moving fast enough, the sail tends to be blown over his head. Sailing on a downwind tack, speeds 2 and ½ times the wind velocity are attainable. Sailing directly downwind, speeds less than the wind speed are attained due to frictional losses.

Most skate sailors own several sails of different sizes so that the appropriate sail can be chosen for the wind conditions of the day. On a gusty day with 30-mile-an-hour winds, a 25-square-foot sail might be more than enough to handle, but on a mild day, 65 square feet might be easily handled.

Skates used for sailing are similar to racing skates but a little longer. The blades are from 18 to 21 inches long with a slight "rock" or curve at the rear to enable one to lean back slightly to raise the tips when rough ice is encountered. Figure and hockey skates are generally unsatisfactory due to their short length and resulting instability in the direction of travel. The long blade of the sailing skate glides over small cracks and smooths out the bumps on the ice.

Clothing worn for sailing is similar to that which a skier or snowmobiler wears. Some sailors wear floatable jackets and protective head gear. Most of them carry ice awls and lengths of light cord or rope to assist themselves and others in case anyone goes through thin ice, or accidentally sails into open water. Skate sailers follow safety procedures similar to other sports—never sail alone is a cardinal rule.

The Skate Sailing Association of America, organized in 1922, to promote skate sailing, holds races whenever weather conditions permit. In the past two years (1971, 1972) unsuccessful attempts have been made to hold a National meet in Sandusky, Ohio between eastern, mid-western, and the Ohio sailors, racing on Sandusky Bay. The weather has been most uncooperative, but attempts will continue to hold this meet in future years. Races are held on a triangular course with each leg approximately half a mile long. A handicap system is established to give the heavier and slower sailors a chance to win. Sails used in competition are limited in size to one square foot of sail area to each 2 and ½ pounds of the sailor's weight.

Timing and Photo-Finishes

Electrical timing of sports events has progressed slowly for 2 main reasons—the possibility of failure and high cost. As an example, anything—from a dog to a piece of paper or a sea gull—can break a beam of light and stop a timing machine. This is but one of hundreds of booby traps that lie in wait for those who would develop an electrical timing system for sports events. Therefore, there are few places, other than for the timing of automobile and airplane short speed records, where electrical timing is employed without hand timing as a standby. And in practically all sports it is the hand timing that is "official."

There are 2 "electrical" systems employed in international sports championships—mechanical watches operated by electrical control and an electrically-driven clock actuated electrically. There are various systems now being used in one sport or another. The start is recorded by the breaking of a thread, by the tripping of a timing gate, by the breaking of a beam of light, by contact of the firing pin of a starting pistol, or acoustically, by the report of the firing pistol. All are designed to start the watches, whether electrical or mechanical. The finish is recorded usually by the breaking of a beam of light. With mechanical watches, this stops them; with electric systems, the clock usually is not stopped, but photographed. With mechanical watches, the limit of timing is to a tenth of a second. With electrical clocks, the limit is approximately ½ of 1/100th of a second.

The idea of photographing the finish of a race and, at the same time recording the elapsed time, was fathered by Gustavus T. Kirby, president emeritus of the United States Olympic Committee. He sparked the idea about 1926 when he was chairman of the Advisory Committee of the Intercollegiate Association of Amateur Athletes of America. A similar idea occurred to C. H. Fetter, then an electronic engineer of Western Electric, a subsidiary of American Telephone and Telegraph Co. Joining forces in 1931, they perfected what was known as the Kirby Two-Eyed Camera.

The basic instrument was a standard 16-millimeter motion picture camera operated at 128 frames per second and with a double lens so arranged that a portion of film of each frame could photograph a disk clock which registered time to 1/100th of a second. This camera was official for judging for the 1932 Olympics at Los Angeles and was official for timing the decathlon.

The clock of the Kirby camera was essentially a Veeder counter driven by a specially constructed 200-cycle, standard frequency generator controlled by a tuning fork. Ordinary house current is, of course, accurate only to within a few seconds at best and is, therefore, impractical for driving a sports timing watch where accuracy to a few thousandths of a second is essential.

The creation of the Kirby system was a major development. The cost was about $50,000. This factor, plus other technical details, precluded the use of the Kirby outfit at any but the most important meets. Similar considerations have limited the use of electrical timing.

The Kirby camera antedated the "photo-finish camera" of horse racing by a few years. Horse race cameras employ a strip of film which is moved past a slit at approximately the speed of the horse. The principle is old and slit cameras were first made in France by Debrie in 1929 for the non-sporting use of photographing the numbers on passing freight cars for the purpose of identification. The application of time to the slit camera in the United States started in 1938, when the first patent application was filed by Harry Bellock.

The basic idea of replacing hand timers with electrical gadgets goes back at least to 1905 and in the Longines collection of sports pictures is one taken about that period showing a short indoor track with a start and stop registered by broken threads.

Electrical timing in tenths of seconds is not necessarily more accurate than hand timing. Years of field experience have shown that with precisely synchronized watches, 3 out of 4 and often 4 out 4 expert timers will agree to the precise tenth of a second. There is nothing inherent in an all-electrical system that guarantees accuracy.

The present international rules in virtually all sports specify 4 hand timers, 1 of which is an alternate. If 3 watches register the same time, that is official. If 2 of 3 register the same time, that is official. If the 3 watches register different times, the middle time is official. If one varies from the others by more than 3/10ths of a second, the fourth, or alternate, watch thereupon becomes official and is counted with the other 2.

The photo-electric eye mentioned at the beginning must be developed so that it will respond not to a momentary image, such as an arm or ski pole, but only to the passage of something substantial like an entire human body. The problems of terrain complicate the use of photo-electric eyes.

Snow produces reflections and salt such as is found on the automobile speed runs at Bonneville, Utah, is even worse. In this salt bed area, the operation of any electrical equipment is difficult. Communication between start and stop is variously arranged, usually with copper wire of low resistance. When the wire is laid in snow, it requires special arctic insulation. It must be elevated above salt.

A great deal of work has been done with shortwave radio to tie start and finish together. The pitfalls are many. Freezing of batteries is a serious hazard in skiing. Longines has had long experience with this problem and was the first to receive a transmitting license for sports timing in the United States and in Canada, as well as in Switzerland and Norway.

After many years of work, Longines developed what seems to be the perfected apparatus. It is a 15-watt frequency modulation (FM) unit that provides for transmission of both voice and signal. It has a range of 50 miles under good conditions, and of at least 5 miles in highly industrialized areas or over ore-laden rocks in high mountain terrain. Large investments in research in electrical sports timing equipment are currently being made by Longines and Omega, another watch company.

Developments of both of these companies were tested in the 1952 Olympics, where the Longines equipment was used for the winter events and the Omega in the Summer Games. In their photofinish timing camera, Omega has followed the slit principle. Longines continued with the basic Kirby idea, but added three-dimensional effect.

Pictures taken at 65 frames per second are stereoscopic. The Longines camera can be used for judging or can pick up and photograph on the same film a special electrical clock which is accurate to 1/100,000th of a second. It records time to a 100th of a second or rough fraction and can automatically time the arrival of contestants separated by as little as 1/10th of a second. The automatic developing device, essential to all of such photographic equipment, produces a picture in 4 seconds.

The Longines electric timer is dual; if one unit breaks down, the other automatically takes over. The timer is portable with self-contained battery supply and quartz crystal frequency generator.

It is not surprising that international athletic organizations have been loathe to recognize electrical equipment "officially." The Kirby camera received the blessing of the Amateur Athletic Union of the United States for official timing, but not that of the Olympic Committee. It was approved by the International Federation of Aviation for timing aviation records. However, the Kirby system has not been used for many years. The Longines electrical timing equipment has been approved for official record making by the International Association of Recognized Automobile Clubs.

Electrically actuated mechanical watches are mandatory in international ski championships conducted under the auspices of the Federation Internationale de Ski (F.I.S.). Automobile speed trials, such as mile runs under the sanction of the American Automobile Association, on the salt beds of Utah, are timed electrically by apparatus developed under the supervision of the A.A.A. Longines electrically actuated equipment, both for close circuit races and mile trials, with both shortwave radio and wire connections have been approved by the American Power Boat Association.

International track rules make hand timing with 4 watches, as described above, mandatory, but local bodies may approve electrical timing.

After the introduciton of the Photochart camera at the Del Mar track in California in 1937, there was the inevitable development of a combination camera and timing device that would record the order of finishes and time the races as well.

The first such combination—as developed by engineers of the Bulova Watch Company, Photochart Corporation, and Beckman and Whitley, California engineers, was the Bulova Phototimer. It was introduced for use in track and field during the 1948 indoor season.

From that introduction the Phototimer developed into an adjunct to the judging and timing of officials. The Amateur Athletic Union of the United States, the National Collegiate Athletic Association and other bodies adopted regulations requiring the study of pictures whenever the races are so close that the officials cannot agree on the outcome.

The Bulova Phototimer became an official instrument for use in aiding the judges and timers at the United States Olympic trials, the annual indoor and outdoor championships, I.C.A.A.A.A. and virtually every other major American meet, including those held at Madison Square Garden in New York.

After the development of the Bulova Phototimer there emerged a similar device in Europe by the Omega Watch Company. The Omega Electric Eye camera determined that Lindy Remigino of the United States team was the 100-meter winner over Herb McKenley after an exceedingly close finish in the 1952 Olympic Games at Helsinki, Finland.

There is another device in use in horse and trotting races. It is called the Teletimer, an electronic device that times the races but does not photograph the finishes.

Since the introduction of the Photochart camera, which photographs finishes, what used to be a rarity in horse racing, the dead heat, has become quite commonplace. The same development has occurred in track and field. The most important dead heat photographed was in the United States Olympic trials at Los Angeles in June, 1952, when Jim Gathers of the Army Air Force and Dean Smith of the University of Texas were declared tied for third place in the 100-meter dash. This was the first official dead heat called in track and as a result both went to Helsinki.

Another historic decision caused by the Bulova Phototimer was in the first reversal of an announced result of a major race, the Baxter Mile finish of the 1952 New York Athletic Club Games at Madison Square Garden. This race could have been called a dead heat. At first, Don Gehrmann was declared the winner over Fred Wilt, but 40 minutes later the decision was reversed after a study of the photograph and Wilt was declared the winner.

As a result of this race the A.A.U. adopted the following rule: "Where an approved photographic device is properly used at the finish of a race, the chief judge, if he believes it may be of aid to the judges, may withhold announcement of the order of finish until after examination of the photograph."

The Photochart and Phototimer cameras operate on the "slit" principle. There is no shutter operating in the cameras, which "see" the finish line through a narrow vertical slit, which is always open. The 35 mm. film moves past the slit at the same proportionate speed as the horses or runners. The objects are photographed continuously as they reach and pass the finish line on which the camera is trained.

Each horse or runner is photographed as he hits the finish line. Under normal conditions, the picture will separate noses of horses to less than 1/32d of an inch. The entire finish is recorded on 4 or 5 inches of film and can be developed in less than 2 minutes. Positive prints, 8 x 10 inches, have been ready for the judges within 70 seconds after the finish of a race.

This method of photography has become standard all over the world. The original Photochart camera has been placed in the Museum of Racing at Saratoga Springs, N.Y. The Photochart Company, directly and indirectly, operates at practically every American track, flat and harness, and at most dog tracks. Its equipment is used throughout South America—Argentina, Brazil, Peru, Chile, Venezuela, etc.— and there are other companies operating similar cameras in England, India, Australia, South Africa and other parts of the world.

The Bulova Phototimer was a succeeding development to the Photochart. The idea was conceived by Arde Bulova, the company's chairman of the board, while watching the Photochart operate at the race track. Engineers developed the electric timing device. The electronic timer imprints time, in hundredths of a second, along the margin of the film so that the picture reveals the order of finish, the name and date of the event and the time of each contestant.

Time-study tests proved that the electric time averages 4-8 100ths of a second slower than expert timing with fine hand watches. The Bulova timer is put into operation at the sound of the starter's gun by a radio pick-up and stops and times the runners photographically at the finish line. Human timers are a fraction slower reacting to the starting gun and stopping their watches.

According to E. C. Bredin in his book, "Running and Training," the electrical timer first was used in England in the 1890's. Bredin observed that whenever the electric device was called into operation, it showed men speeding faster than was shown by the watches held by the hand timers.

The old electric timer was operated by current that passed along a line attached to the trigger of the starter's pistol, with the other end attached to the tape at the finish line. The breaking of the tape stopped the timing.

The American Teletimer Corporation, the operator of the Teletimer, was organized in New York State in 1938, and the first installation was made at the Pimlico race track in the fall of that year.

The Teletimer depends upon photo-electric cells and narrow beams of light that are directed against these cells for the starting and stopping of the timing registers. The operation follows:

A light projector is installed at every 16th pole along the outside rail of the racing strip. The light or beam is directed into the photo-electric cell with its amplifying equipment at the corresponding pole along the inside rail of the racing strip. The beam projectors and photo-electric cell equipments are connected by means of cables to a console in the booth that usually forms one end of the totalizator board. The face of the booth is made up of electric light indicators upon which the time appears as the race progresses.

After the horses leave the starting gate, the leading horse breaks the beam across the track at the official starting pole and the impulse resulting instantaneously sets the timing registers into operation. The timing registers are complicated switching devices similar to those in use at telephone exchanges, and count and add time in fifths of seconds.

When the leading horse breaks the beam at the poles a quarter of a mile from the starting position, the resulting electrical impulse stops the timing register for that distance and the time of the ¼-mile automatically appears on the face of the booth. Similar means record the time for the ½-mile, ¾-mile, mile and finish.

The system employs the "magic brain," which prevents any electrical impulses caused by breaking of beams from operating the timing registers before the horses reach the required position, thus preventing the wrong time from appearing on the board.

The Teletimer is in use at many major race tracks in this country and is being used at some of the major trotting tracks as well.

Trophies

Baseball, America's "national game," which has been in the forefront for nearly 100 years, seems to be the only sport in the United States that gained major ranking without the award of an important trophy for individual or team achievement.

Trophies in sports that predate baseball have been an accepted gesture for almost a century; trophies for sports, presumably inconsequential compared with baseball since the 1870's, have become famous. The word "trophy," derived from the Greek, means a monument to victory on battlefields.

Each Grecian military triumph of ancient times was commemorated by placing a slab on a tree nearest to the spot that marked the successful turning point of battle. The Greeks first used a wooden slab, but soon abandoned it for more durable ones because of the rules and ethics of the times. One of the rules was that no slab ever could be repaired or replaced, the idea being that if this were done it would reopen old wounds when warfare of the past should be only a memory.

However, the Greeks, ethics or no ethics, were determined that there should be a lasting memento. Noticing that wooden slabs quickly perished under the whiplash of the wind and the onrush of years, they used armor plate. This was serviceable, but had a tendency to rust and to blend into the color of the tree bark.

After experimentation, the Greeks hit upon silver as the proper metal for a trophy. This was very white and shiny and glittered in the sunlight—until weather tarnished it. After that proud Greeks would slip up in the night with some metal polish, shine the silver and have it glittering again so that all might read and know from the inscription that this marked the spot where the Greeks had proved their greatness as warriors.

When Greece staged its first major Olympic Games in 776 B.C., it determined to award a trophy—the symbol of victory—to all winners. But the trophy wasn't metal. It was a wreath made of the olive leaves from the trees on the sacred Mount Olympus. Soon the rulers heard laments; the leaves quickly perished and there was nothing the champion could display as proof of his prize-winning prowess.

Then was originated the custom of permitting each champion to return to his home city and build a monument or erect a trophy to the memory of his valiant deed. In most instances the champions contented themselves with a plaque tacked to a tree in a conspicuous place, but many rich athletes, or those with wealthy admirers, built statues to themselves in the public places of their cities or towns.

The Romans, after conquering Greece, not only continued the practice of awarding olive leaves to winners and allowing them to erect monuments, but after the dawn of the Christian Era awarded bits of silver to the winners, which the champions could show at any time, as proof of their status in athletic realms.

The Olympics were banned in 392 A.D. by Emperor Theodosius because the Greeks and the Romans mingled in too many side-issue brawls, and the awarding of trophies to Olympic athletes came to an end.

There is no further mention of bestowal of trophies until 1512 A.D. when it is discovered that the town of Chester, England, cradle of horse racing, awarded a wooden ball festooned with flowers to the winner of the annual 4-mile horse race at the fair. In 1540 it was decided to substitute a silver shell, in the shape of a ball, in place of the wooden ball. This shell had an intrinsic value of about $1. Silver continued to be the only trophy metal until 1607 when in England an elaborate gold ball was substituted. It was hollow and worth about $10.

The awarding of silver balls continued in England until 1703, when Queen Anne put up a silver plate worth $20 to go to the winner of a horse race. Each year from 1703 to 1709 she awarded silver plate of increasing worth. In 1710 she donated a gold plate with a value of $300 and in 1714, the last year of her life, she thought up the cup idea, so that toasts might be sipped from a trophy, and awarded a $500 gold cup— the first ever presented. Incidentally, the queen's horse—Star—won the race and the trophy.

The first silver trophy donated in what later became the United States but which then was a British colony was for a horse race run on "Hansted Plaines" (Hempstead, Long Island), March 25, 1668. The award was put up by Col. Richard Nicolls, the first British Governor of New York, who was eager to encourage the sport, believing this would bring about intensive breeding in a land where horses were few and "scrubby" in size.

The race—and the trophy—was won by Capt. Sylvester Salisbury, a British army officer. It was in the shape of a porringer and had on it the initials "P. V. B." believed to be those of Peter Van Brugh, a well-known silversmith of the time who lived in Albany, N.Y. The porringer, of solid silver, was regarded as the oldest piece of silver created within the United States and is now a part of the Mabel Brady Gawan Collection at Yale University.

The oldest continuous trophy is that given to the winning crew of novice oarsmen for a race of about 4½ miles on the River Thames (England), between London Bridge and Chelsea. It was established in 1715 in the will of Thomas Doggett, an English actor, who provided that the race should be run "every year, on the same day, forever." The race is known as Doggett's Coat and Badge, since the trophy is an orange-colored livery (coat) and a badge, representing Liberty.

Perhaps the next oldest trophy is the cup that was awarded to the winner of the first Grand Challenge (rowing race) of the British Henley, which originated in 1839 and has been awarded since then.

Next perhaps was the cup for a yacht race in 1851 as part of the London Exposition ceremonies of that year. The cup, costing about $500, was donated by the Royal Yacht Club of England. It was won by the United States schooner, America, but not much consideration was given to the conquest at the time. English sailors, filled with pride of accomplishment, felt they would regain the cup "in due time." But more than $75,000,000 has been spent in the effort—and the America's Cup still remains in the United States.

Going into the latter part of the 19th Century it became a custom, when a fistic title was at stake, for the "sports" of the day to "chip in" enough money to buy a belt as a trophy for the winner. It was a continuation of an infrequent practice in bare-knuckle ring days in England in the 18th Century.

In the 1860's, when the first golf tournament was arranged in Scotland, a belt was put up to become the permanent property of the man first to win three successive annual championships. Tom Morris Jr. retired the belt by winning the British Open in 1868, 1869, and 1870.

Other sports then were progressing toward organization and tournaments. But a switch was made from belts to medals for individuals because few men wore belts in those years and the medal became the thing to give, although in later years, when promoters wished to become elaborate with their gifts, they awarded plates, cups, etc., some of silver, others of gold.

One of the unwritten rules of the time was that if there was only one prize, it was to be of silver; if 2, then the first was gold, the second silver; if 3, the third was of bronze—a method of award that has come down to the present.

The rules regarding trophies differ, according to the wishes of the donor. When the award merely is a medal, the recipient usually gets permanent possession. If it is a cup or a piece of plate, it may become the permanent possession of the winner, or it may be a temporary possession, to be turned over to the man or team that subsequently defeats the holder. In such cases, the holder or holders of the trophy receive a small reproduction for permanent possession.

Within the last generation, new trophies of national or international importance have been donated. But the years have added to the tradition and glory associated with many trophies, which so often have been in the limelight, and so gallantly fought for and defended.

Trophies are awarded to champions, championship teams, or crews, in many other branches of sports. Some are sponsored by individuals, some by the governing organizations, others by writer groups, some by newspapers, some by the Citizens Savings Athletic Foundation. Each trophy carries its own conditions.

In some instances the winner gets the trophy outright; in others, the winner receives a small copy of the major trophy. In still others, the event must be won twice or three times before permanent possession is gained.

The donor of a trophy always is permitted to stipulate the conditions concerning the award and, of course, all contestants abide by them.

A trophy, incidentally, regardless of its intrinsic value, does not taint the amateur accepting it. If an amateur takes as much as $1 in cash as a prize offering, it tends to professionalize him, but he may accept a trophy of any value without violating his amateur status.

(For additional information on trophies see individual sections.)

MOTORBOATING

One of the fastest growing sports since World War II has been motorboating. With the trend toward suburban living has come the realization of the advantages of motorboating. Millions have become boat-minded and have found that they can enjoy the sport at modest cost. Further, it is a sport and recreation that can be enjoyed by all members of the family.

A boat can be the central point of a week-end holiday or a summer vacation. With the aid of a trailer, boats can be transported from one waterway to another, from one lake to another and from one river to another. Thus Northerners have become acquainted with Southern rivers, lakes, etc., and vice versa. Westerners visit Eastern and Southern waters and their waters are "discovered" by boatmen from other sections of the country.

Boating has associated sports, also, such as water skiing, skin diving and fishing.

The original gasoline-driven boat putt-putted a few yards on the River Seine in Paris, then quit. That was 1887, after Gottlieb Daimler, having discovered internal combustion, sought some vehicle that might quiver into action when fitted with his motor. He experimented successfully with the bicycle to make the first motorcycle and two years later he hitched a similar device to the rear of a rowboat and that was the pioneer outboard motorboat.

There is a lapse between Daimler's trial of 1887 until 1896, when a successful motorboat made its appearance in United States water. It was called a "naphtha launch." There are no details except that it was an ordinary rowboat to which a crude naphtha-driven engine was attached, and was probably used by a lobster fisherman. Although the motorboat is a development of the late 19th Century, there is little information on its career until 1900.

Immediately after the start of the 20th Century the value of the naphtha-driven engine was realized. English engineers began to develop engines with a powerful drive. The American builders joined with them and impetus was given when Sir Alfred Harmsworth, later Lord Northcliffe, made motorboating a sporting event and donated a racing trophy in 1903.

The winner of the first Harmsworth race was a boat named "Napier," of English registry. Its speed was 18 nautical miles an hour. In comparison, Gar Wood, on Sept. 20, 1932, drove "Miss America X" at the rate of 124.86 land miles an hour on the St. Clair River near Algonac, Mich. The present world record for an unlimited hydroplane is held by Roy Duby, driver of "Miss U. S. 1," which traveled at the rate of 200.419 miles per hour at Guntersville, Ala., on April 17, 1962, on a mile straightaway course.

John Cobb went faster on Sept. 29, 1952, when his jet-propelled "Crusader" was clocked at 206.8 miles per hour on Loch Ness, Scotland, but before the Englishman could complete the number of runs necessary to make his record official, the boat disintegrated and Cobb was killed. In 1954, on Lake Mead, Nevada, Donald Campbell of England broke the so-called water barrier that is supposed to exist around the 200 m.p.h. mark. On Nov. 16, he made an official record of 216.2 m.p.h. and 193 on the second. On Sept. 19, 1956, he raised the record to 225.36 on Lake Coniston, England. He followed this with a new record of 239.07 on Lake Coniston on Nov. 7, 1957. Then on Nov. 10, 1958, he increased it to 248.62. In each instance he used one of his jet-propelled "Bluebirds." In June 1967, Lee Taylor drove his jet-propelled "Hustler" 285.213 miles per hour at Guntersville, Ala.

The fastest performance by any motorboat through 1910 was the 33.6 m.p.h. turned in by F. K. Burnham's "Dixie III" in winning the Gold Cup competition that year. After that time, however, speed was accelerated by the adoption of the George F. Crouch principle in boat building. He designed the first V-shaped, concave bottom while constructing a boat called the "Pan IV."

When Sir Malcolm Campbell made 141.75 m.p.h. in the British-built unlimited hydroplane

"Bluebird" in 1939, many authorities on boat building said that this was the maximum speed at which a craft could travel. Two reasons were given. One was that it seemed impossible to construct a higher-powered engine and the second was that no hull could be built to withstand greater water pressure.

However, new applications of metal, plywood and plastics have developed stronger construction and now it is believed that the ultimate speed of boats will be determined by the physical limits of the drivers.

At the present time there are more than 5,000 owners and drivers campaigning race boats in the United States under the red and blue burgee of the American Power Boat Association. Fully 2,000 others participate as official designers, engine experts, hull builders and fuel blenders.

Major race meets in the United States are under the auspices of the A.P.B.A., and speeds made in these events are eligible for consideration as world records by the Union of International Motor Boating, which has its headquarters in Europe.

That motorboating is on the rise in the United States is shown by the fact that in 1952 the A.P.B.A. sanctioned 223 inboard, outboard and stock outboard regattas in the 15 regions covering the country. It was the first time since the organization was founded in 1903 that it had approved more than 200 competitive events, an increase of about 16 per cent over the previous year. Today over 600 regattas are sanctioned annually in the United States and Canada.

Pointing up the interest in boating is the annual National Motor Boat Show staged every January in New York under the auspices of the National Association of Engine and Boat Manufactureres. Thousands are attracted daily during the run of the exposition, which has on display every conceivable type of craft and accessory of interest to the recreational devotee.

GOLD CUP AND HARMSWORTH TROPHY

The most historic international race is that for the Harmsworth Trophy, originated in 1903, while the outstanding competition on a national scale has been for the Gold Cup, first held on the Hudson River in 1904. Both races are for unlimited hydroplanes.

The chronology of the Harmsworth competition shows 9 straight victories for Gar Wood's various "Miss Americas" in as many tests staged between 1920 and 1933. Since that time the race has been held infrequently. Stanley Dollar was the winner with "Skip-A-Long" in 1949, Stanley S. Sayres took the trophy as a result of the victory by "Slo-Mo-Shun IV" in 1950 and William Waggoner's Shanty I, driven by Lieut. Col. Richard Schlieg, won in 1956.

Speeds in the Gold Cup race range from 23.6 m.p.h. for the best heat in 1904 to 109.28 m.p.h. in 1957.

AMERICAN POWER BOAT ASSOCIATION

The American Power Boat Association, the supervisory body for motorboat racing in the United States, celebrated its Golden Jubilee in November, 1953. It was founded in 1903 when the necessity arose for the establishment of a governing body to create and enforce the rules of power boat racing in this country.

The earliest motorboat racing on record was in the Hudson River and in Alexandria Bay, Thousand Islands, both in New York State, just after the turn of the century. A year after the founding of the A.P.B.A., the first Gold Cup race was held at the Columbia Yacht Club on the Hudson River. It was won by a 59-foot displacement "runabout," Standard, owned by C. C. Riotte, averaging 23.6 m.p.h. over a 32-mile course. Not until 16 years later did a motorboat in competition surpass the mile-a-minute mark when Wood turned the trick in his original Miss America.

In the early 1920's inboard runabout and hydroplane regattas were annual fixtures in many cities of the United States. The sport of cruiser racing on a handicap basis was popular, particularly for such long distance events as the New York-Block Island race of the New York Athletic Club. It was in this era that outboard motorboats entered the racing scene, and a place was made for them in the A.P.B.A.'s over-all picture. This brought into boat racing many youngsters and persons with small incomes who could not afford the larger, more expensive inboards.

The history of the A.P.B.A. is not only a history of motorboat racing in the United States, but also a history of the modernization of all recreational motor-driven craft, pioneered on ther race courses and then incorporated into the designs of family pleasure boats by the country's builders. The racing programs of the A.P.B.A. have developed an awareness of boating as a recreation for sportsmen in all income brackets and in turn have stimulated increased participation in competitive events. Modern regatta programs offer a wide variety of racing classes to spectators and participants in the sport.

UNITED STATES POWER SQUADRONS

After a rapid and truly impressive growth, especially since World War II, the largest yachting and pleasure boating body in the country is now by a wide margin the energetic United States Power Squadrons, with more than 18,400 members in 141 unit squadrons. It operates in inland as well as coastal states and in some of the territories and possessions.

This is a non-commercial body of skippers and navigators which has as its primary object teaching men and women how to handle and navigate yachts safely and to study the science of boat operating. From its earliest days, it has had as exofficio members on its national governing body a number of admirals and other high-ranking officers of the United States Navy, Coast Guard, Coast and Geodetic Survey, Merchant Marine, Naval Observatory and other government agencies.

Without exception, unit squadrons hold free instruction courses of study, customarily 10 to 12 weeks long. Some of the branch squadrons conduct as many as 5 of these free instruction programs of study in a year. They are open to men and women and upper teen-agers. After learning the rudiments of small-boat handling, rules of the road, the compass, charts, aids to navigation, yacht etiquette, etc., many take a final examination and apply for formal admission into a squadron. There is no compulsion to join and some do not.

Although women are not eligible for membership, they are welcomed in the instruction courses and may receive a special certificate on passing the final examination. Subsequent programs of study cover 4 or sometimes 5 years and permit members to pass through the grades of advanced pilot, junior navigator and finally to the exalted rating of navigator which involves celestial studies in higher mathematics. Special instruction programs have been evolved by some of the squadrons in seamanship, sailing and such special areas as motor mechanics and meteorology or weather prediction.

Although a small headquarters staff is maintained, the U.S.P.S. members serve unselfishly and without recompense as instructors and test markers because of what has become a deep and genuine interest in teaching and spreading the gospel of safe boat handling. Members customarily wear unique insignia on their uniforms, including tridents, merit marks, etc.

The United States Power Squadrons trace their origin to 1912 in the Boston Yacht Club where motor-driven boats were just coming into favor and where Vice Commodore Roger Upton was placed in special charge of the motorboat division of the club fleet.

By early 1914 two other similar units had been organized, one at Portland, Me., and one along the Hudson River in New York City. The United States Power Squadrons were formally organized on Feb. 2, 1914, at a meeting of representatives of a number of yacht clubs held at the New York Y.C. Commodore Upton was elected the first chief commander and it is noteworthy that Charles F. Chapman of New York, to whom was given the coveted No. 1 certificate, became the first treasurer.

Early requirements to have squadron drills and maneuvers modeled along the operation of a naval fleet later were discontinued, although many who served in the Navy and Army, including the amphibious forces during World Wars I and II, received some of their pre-service training in Power Squadron instruction courses.

Motorboating Statistics

(Courtesy of the American Power Boat Association,
22811 Greater Mack St., Clair Shores, Mich., 48080)

HARMSWORTH TROPHY WINNERS

(Competition only in years indicated.)

Year	Winner	Boat	Owner	Course	Speed
1903	England	Napier I	S.F. Edge	Queenstown, Ireland	19.53
1904	France	Trefle-A-Quatre	E. B. Thurbon	Dolent, England	26.63
1905	England	Napier II	S. F. Edge	Arachon, France	26.03
1906	England	Yarrow-Napier	Lord Montague and L. de Rothschild	Solent, England	15.48
1907	United States	Dixie I	E. J. Schroeder	Solent, England	31.78
1908	United States	Dixie II	E. J. Schroeder	Huntington Bay, N.Y.	31.35
1910	United States	Dixie III	F. K. Burnham	Huntington Bay, N.Y.	36.04
1911	United States	Dixie IV	F. K. Burnham	Huntington Bay, N.Y.	40.28
1912	England	Maple Leaf IV	E. Mackay-Edgar	Huntington Bay, N.Y.	43.18
1913	England	Maple Leaf IV	E. Mackay-Edgar	Osborne Bay, England	57.45
1920	United States	Miss America I	Garfield A. Wood	Osborne Bay, England	61.51
1921	United States	Miss America II	Garfield A. Wood	Detroit River	59.75
1926	United States	Miss America V	Garfield A. Wood	Detroit River	61.118
1928	United States	Miss America VII	Garfield A. Wood	Detroit River	59.325
1929	United States	Miss America VII	Garfield A. Wood	Detroit River	75.287
1930	United States	Miss America IX	Garfield A. Wood	Detroit River	77.233
1931	United States	Miss America VIII	George Wood	Detroit River	85.861
1932	United States	Miss America X	Garfield A. Wood	Lake St. Clair	78.489
1933	United States	Miss America X	Garfield A. Wood	St. Clair River	86.939
1949	United States	Skip-A-Long	Stanley Dollar	Detroit River	94.285
1950	United States	Slo-Mo-Shun IV	Stanley S. Sayres	Detroit River	100.680
1956	United States	Shanty I	William Waggoner Jr.	Detroit River	89.750
1959	Canada	Miss Supertest III	J. G. Thompson	Detroit River	99.789
1960	Canada	Miss Supertest III	J. G. Thompson	Lake Ontario	115.483
1961	Canada	Miss Supertest III	J. G. Thompson	Lake Ontario	98.218

Speed is in statute miles per hour. The Maple Leaf IV was the first hydroplane to win, all predecessors having been displacement craft.

GOLD CUP WINNERS

Year	Winner and owner	Winner's Best Heat speed m.p.h.
1904	Standard, C.C. Riotte	23.6
1904	Vingt-Et-Un II, W. Sharpe Kilmer	25.3
1905	Chip, J. Wainwright	15.9
1906	Chip II, J. Wainwright	20.6
1907	Chip II, J. Wainwright	20.8
1908	Dixie II, E.J. Schroeder	30.9
1909	Dixie II, E.J. Schroeder	32.9
1910	Dixie III, F.K. Burnham	33.6
1911	Mit II, J.H. Hayden	36.1
1912	P.D.Q. II, Alfred G. Miles	44.5
1913	Ankle Deep, C.S. Mankowski	50.49
1914	Baby Speed Demon II, Paula Blackton	48.5
1915	Miss Detroit, Miss Detroit P.B.A.	49.7
1916	Miss Minneapolis, Miss Minneapolis B.A.	36.8
1917	Miss Detroit II, Garfield A. Wood	56.5
1918	Miss Detroit III, Detroit Yachtsmen	52.1
1919	Miss Detroit III, Garfield A. Wood	56.3
1920	Miss America, Garfield A. Wood	70.0
1921	Miss America, Garfield A. Wood	56.5
1922	Packard-Chris-Craft, J.G. Vincent	40.6
1923	Packard-Chris-Craft, J.G. Vincent	44.4
1924	Baby Bootlegger, Caleb Bragg	46.4
1925	Baby Bootlegger, Caleb Bragg	48.4
1926	Greenwich Folly, G.H. Townsend	49.22
1927	Greenwich Folly, G.H. Townsend	50.99
1928	No competition	
1929	Imp, R.F. Hoyt	50.489
1930	Hotsy Totsy, V. Kliesrath	56.05
1931	Hotsy Totsy, V. Kliesrath-R. Hoyt	54.92
1932	Delphine IV, Horace E. Dodge	59.21
1933	El Lagarto, George Reis	60.866
1934	El Lagarto, George Reis	58.06
1935	El Lagarto, George Reis	57.582
1936	Impshi, Horace E. Dodge	47.12
1937	Notre Dame, Herbert Mendelsohn	68.645
1938	Alagi, Theo Rossi	66.08
1939	My Sin, Z.G. Simmons Jr.	67.05
1940	Hotsy Totsy III, Sidney Allen	51.316
1941	My Sin, Z.G. Simmons Jr.*	52.509
1942–45	No competition	
1946	Tempo VI, Guy Lombardo	70.878
1947	Miss Peps V, Walter, Roy and Russell Dossin	57.02
1948	Miss Great Lakes, Albin Fallon	52.89
1949	My Sweetie, Horace E. Dodge	78.645
1950	Slo-Mo-Shun IV, Stanley S. Sayres	80.892
1951	Slo-Mo-Shun V, Stanley S. Sayres	91.766
1952	Slo-Mo-Shun IV, Stanley S. Sayres	84.355

1953—*Slo-Mo-Shun IV*, Stanley S. Sayres 95.268	1964—*Miss Bardahl*, Ole Bardahl 108.104
1954—*Slo-Mo-Shun V*, Stanley S. Sayres 99.784	1965—*Miss Bardahl*, Ole Bardahl 110.655
1955—*Gale V*, Joseph Schoenith 100.954	1966—*Tahoe Miss*, Harrah's 97.861
1956—*Miss Thriftway*, G.E. Rhodes 100.906	1967—*Miss Bardahl*, Ole Bardahl 104.691
1957—*Miss Thriftway*, Willard Rhodes 109.828	1968—*Miss Bardahl*, Ole Bardahl ....
1958—*Hawaii Kai III*, L.N. Welsch 108.734	1969—*Miss Budweiser*, B. Little
1959—*Maverick*, W.T. Waggoner 104.033	T. Friedkin 103.587
1960—No competition	1970—*Miss Budweiser*, Hydros, Inc. 101.848
1961—*Miss Century 21*, Willard Rhodes 99.676	1971—*Miss Madison*, Miss Madison, Inc. 101.522
1962—*Miss Century 21*, Willard Rhodes 100.102	1972—*Atlas Van Lines*, Atlas Van Lines 103.547
1963—*Miss Bardahl*, Ole Bardahl 114.650	* Only contestant.

PRESIDENT'S CUP WINNERS

(At Washington, D.C.)

Course—3 heats of 15 statute miles each.

Year	Boat	Owner	m.p.h.				
1926—*Cigarette*	L.G. Hamersley	55.20	1953—*Slo-Mo-Shun V* ...	Stanley Sayres	91.070
1927 *Miss Syndicate* ...	Horace E. Dodge ...	51.62	1954—*Gale IV*	Joseph Schoenith .	91.378
1928—No competition			1955 *Miss U.S.*	George Simon	100.148
1929—*Imp*	Richard F. Hoyt ...	47.131	1956 *Hawaii Kai III* ...	Edgar Kaiser	100.009
1930 *Hotsy-Totsy*	R. Hoyt-V. Kliesrath	54.93	1957 *Hawaii Kai III* ...	L.N. Welsch	93.317
1931—*El Lagarto*	George Reis	51.148	1958 *Miss U.S. I* ...	George Simon	97.280
1932—*Delphine IV*	Mrs. R.T. Baker	57.162	1959 *Wahoo*	William Boeing Jr. .	107.119
1933—*El Lagarto*	George Reis	55.555	1960 *Miss Detroit* ...	Charles Thompson ..	100.878
1934—*El Lagarto*	George Reis	57.216	1961 *Miss Century 21* .	Willard Rhodes ..	103.523
1935—*Notre Dame*	Herbert Mendelsohn	52.80	1962—*Miss Century 21* .	Willard Rhodes	109.157
1936 *Ma-Ja*	Jack Rutherford ...	57.252	1963—*Miss Exide*	Hydros, Inc. ....
1937 *Notre Dame* ...	Herbert Mendelsohn	64.516	1964 *Miss Smirnoff* ...	Gale Enterprises ...
1938—*Alagi*	Theo Rossi	62.285	1965 No competition
1939 *Miss Canada III* ..	E.A. Wilson	51.83	1966 *Notre Dame* ...	Fraser McDonald ...
1940 *Notre Dame*	Herbert Mendelsohn	65.790	1967 No competition
1941-45—No competition			1968 *Miss Eagle Electric*, Warner Gardner ....
1946—*Miss Great Lakes* .	Albin Fallon	69.632	1969 No competition
1947 *Miss Peps V*	Dossin Bros.	64.114	1970 *Myr Sheet Metal*, .	Bill Muncey ....
1948 *Such Crust*	Jack Schafer	73.409	1971 *Atlas Van Lines*, .	Bill Muncey ....
1949—No race*			1972 *Pride of Pay 'n Pak*, Bill Sterett, Jr. 109.090
1950 *Miss Pepsi*	Dossin Bros.	83.450	
1951 *Miss Pepsi*	Dossin Bros.	78.611	*My Sweetie, piloted by Bill Cantrell, won the first
1952 *Miss Pepsi*	Dossin Bros.	84.472	heat in 11 minutes 27-4/10 seconds. The water too rough for the second and third heats.

MOTOR BOAT RECORDS

Five Miles Competition (1-2/3 Mile Course)

Class Inboard	m.p.h. Speed	Date	Where Made	Boat Name	Driver
7 Litre (Div. 1) ..101.580	. 10/4/69	Issaquah, Wash.	*Record 7*	George Babcock
7 Litre (Div. II) ...93.071	10/31/71	Havasu Landing, Calif. ...	*Sagres II*	Antonio Rodrigues
280 Hydro 86.331	. 10/1/72	Issaquah, Wash.	*Buccaneer*	John Leach
5 Litre 93.946	. 2/8/70	St. Petersburg, Fla.....	*Miss Washington D.C.*	Charles Dunn, Jr.
225 Hydro 91.001	. 2/6/72	St. Petersburg, Fla.	*Country Boy*	Joe Siracusa
150 Hydro 83.333	. 6/14/70	Harrison Hot Springs, B.C.	*La Cucaracha*	Glenn Brewer
145 Hydro......74.938	. 2/14/71	St. Petersburg, Fla.	*Lil 'Lectron*	Willard Wilson
98 Hydro 78.261	. 2/6/71	St. Petersburg, Fla.	*First Mortgage*	Richard L. Cooper
850 Hydro 74.938	12/30/62	San Diego, Calif.	*Piranha*	Mickey Remund
44 Hydro 54.695	. 7/26/69	Red Bank, N.J.	*Jinx*	James Campbell
Cracker Box 77.653	. 7/30/72	Seattle, Wash.	*Cracker Jack*	Carl Thornhill
44 Run 50.448	. 2/8/58	St. Petersburg, Fla.	*My Sin*	Bob Mutschler
Jersey Speed Skiff 61.898	.. 6/6/71	Washington, D.C.	*Flying Karpet*	Herbert Moore
Ski Rac. Run 90.543	. 8/20/72	Red Bank, N.J.....	*Yankee Stealer*	Mario Squillace
Super Stock 89.910	. 5/30/71	Seattle, Wash.	*Krazy Kanaka*	Don Due
B Rac. Run 68.886	. 7/24/66	Merced, Calif.	*Lil 'Bee*	Ernie Rose
E Rac. Run 83.682	. 5/24/70	San Diego, Calif.	*Go For Broke*	Bud Murphy
K Rac. Run......98.630	. 7/30/72	Seattle, Wash.	*Liberty*	Gordon Jennings
E Ser. Run 69.471	. 2/7/70	St. Petersburg, Fla.	*Second Mortgage* ...	Ted Neuweiler, Jr.
F Ser. Run 77.787	.. 2/7/70	St. Petersburg, Fla.	*Dancing Bear*	R. Curtis Brayer

Class Outboard	m.p.h. Speed	Date	Where	Boat	Driver
M Hydro	47.269	9/16/72	Yelm, Wash.	Frantic I	Mike Carson
A Hydro	72.464	9/16/72	Yelm, Wash.	W-82	Ron Anderson
B Hydro	75.345	3/2/69	Lakeland, Fla.	W-3	Bob Hering
C Hydro	82.418	3/2/69	Lakeland, Fla.	J-2	John Schubert
D Hydro	84.906	3/2/69	Lakeland, Fla.	J-2	John Schubert
F Hydro	83.256	3/5/67	Lakeland, Fla.	Spooker XXII	Jerry Waldman
C Ser. Hydro (Sect. 1)	56.074	2/10/63	St. Petersburg, Fla.	Y-64	Homer Kincaid
A Rac. Run	65.526	9/18/65	Yelm, Wash.	84-R	Lee Sutter
B Rac. Run	67.039	9/18/66	Yelm, Wash.	Tite-Rope	Kay Harrison
C Rac. Run	70.838	9/17/72	Yelm, Wash.	Lil' Fox	Richard Fuchslin
D Rac. Run	73.559	9/14/68	Yelm, Wash.	Lil' Fox	Richard Fuchslin
F Rac. Run	70.505	9/14/68	Yelm, Wash.	Lil' Fox	Richard Fuchslin
C Ser. Run (Sect. 1)	51.814	2/9/64	St. Petersburg, Fla.	CE-11	Ronald Messenger

Modified Outboard

A Mod. Hydro	51.993	9/4/72	Dayton, Ohio	6-H	John Wearly
B Mod. Hydro	56.926	9/4/72	Dayton, Ohio	6-H	John Wearly
C Mod. Hydro	57.878	9/4/72	Dayton, Ohio	96-H	Donald Dennis
D Mod. Hydro	66.667	9/4/72	Dayton, Ohio	Bad News	Mike Doran
E Mod. Hydro	69.284	9/4/72	Dayton, Ohio	Bad News	Mike Doran
A Mod. Run	49.234	9/4/72	Dayton, Ohio	Mike	Mike O'Brien
B Mod. Run	53.381	9/4/72	Dayton, Ohio	Mike	Mike O'Brien
C Mod. Run	54.315	9/4/72	Dayton, Ohio	Banana	Harry Brinkman
D Mod. Run	59.840	9/4/72	Dayton, Ohio	Green Hornet	James Miner
E Mod. Run	57.766	9/4/72	Dayton, Ohio	17-V	Burt Hoefs

Stock Outboard

J Stock Run	30.790	9/18/71	Yelm, Wash.	Brad's Dumbo	Brad Shuman
A Stock Run	48.780	9/20/70	Yelm, Wash.	Tuna	Craig Selvidge
B Stock Run	57.016	9/18/71	Yelm, Wash.	Mr. Active	Earl Garrison
C Stock Run	55.901	9/17/67	Yelm, Wash.	Joker	Thomas Scheidt
D Stock Run	59.980	9/16/72	Yelm, Wash.	74-H	Richard Lovelace
36 Stock Run	49.478	6/11/72	Dayton, Ohio	Then Came the Bear	Bernie Schaller
J Stock Hydro	32.503	9/14/69	Yelm, Wash.	Janny's J	Janis Lee
A Stock Hydro	52.632	9/19/71	Yelm, Wash.	Mini Brute II	Roy Miner
B Stock Hydro	63.604	9/19/71	Yelm, Wash.	The Willy Bandersnatch	Bob Wartinger
C Stock Hydro	61.834	9/19/65	Yelm, Wash.	Costamesado	Ralph Thede
D Stock Hydro	68.285	9/18/65	Yelm, Wash.	177-R	Tom O'Neill

GOLD CUP HISTORIC PERFORMANCES

Figures in parentheses indicate miles — 2½ mile course — *3 mile course

Event-Distance	Speed m.p.h.	Date	Where	Boat Name	Driver	Owner
Gold Cup Lap (2½)	111.663	9/28/69	San Diego, Calif.	Myr's Special	Dean Chenowith	Gale Enterprises, Inc.
Gold Cup Lap (3)	120.356	8/4/65	Seattle, Wash.	Miss Exide	Bill Brow	Milo Stoen
Gold Cup Heat (15)	103.906	9/28/69	San Diego, Calif.	Myr's Special	Dean Chenowith	Gale Enterprises, Inc.
Gold Cup Heat (15)*	112.172	8/8/65	Seattle, Wash.	Miss Exide	Bill Brow	Milo Stoen
Gold Cup Heat (30)*	109.823	8/11/57	Seattle, Wash.	Hawaii Kai III	Jack Regas	Henry J. Kaiser
Gold Cup Race (60)*	105.119	7/7/63	Detroit, Mich.	Miss Bardahl	Ronald Musson	Ole Bardahl
Gold Cup Qualifying (1 Lap)	116.883	9/27/69	San Diego, Calif.	Notre Dame	Leif Borgerson	U-7, Inc.
Gold Cup Qualifying (1 Lap)*	120.300	1958	Seattle, Wash.	Maverick	Bill Stead	W.T. Waggoner, Jr.
Gold Cup Qualifying (2 Laps)	113.066	9/24/69	San Diego, Calif.	Miss U.S.	Bill Muncey	U.S. Equipment Co.
Gold Cup Qualifying (3 Laps)*	119.998	1958	Seattle, Wash.	Maverick	Bill Stead	W.T. Waggoner, Jr.

MOTORCYCLING

The motorcycle is a versatile vehicle. It can be used for a variety of purposes—business, military, recreation and sport. It is a particular favorite of adventurous youngsters. It also was the first vehicle driven by a motor. Naturally, racing competition began soon after the development of the motorcycle.

When Gottlieb Daimler of Germany perfected

internal combustion in 1885 by using gasoline, he built an engine and, not having a carriage to use for experimental purposes, attached it to the front of his bicycle. The result was not a grand success, but Daimler did prove that the engine could propel a bicycle.

The engineers of that early day concentrated on a machine that could convey several persons, and, therefore, the development of the motorcycle was delayed until the automobile had been well advanced in construction. Thus, the motorcycle did not gain concentrated attention until after the dawn of the 20th Century.

A Belgian put together the first actual motorcycle early in 1900. This creation was followed within a few months by the building of a somewhat similar device in the United States.

George Hendee of Springfield, Mass., was the first American to build a definite motorcycle. Hendee started work on his machine in 1901 and had it ready for 1902, calling it "The Indian Motorcycle." A short time later the Davidson brothers of Milwaukee, Wis., who had been tinkering with the motorcycle principles in 1901, introduced the first Harley-Davidson model.

The earliest machines were equipped with a crude belt drive, and the pioneer builders had their little joke about it, saying that "it takes 4 hours' effort to keep it running 2 minutes." However, in the years since then motorcycles have been developed to a point where they not only serve as racing, sport and transportation vehicles but are in great commercial use. They have been tremendously valuable in warfare.

The first known record for an endurance run was made by Hendee on July 4, 1902, from New York to Boston. The second was from New York to Waltham, Mass., 250 miles, in 16 hours 30 minutes. The first hill climb was at Boston on May 30, 1904. The event was won by Charles Gustafson, and created considerable comment because a "gas buggy" was able to climb a steep hill. The first race of importance was won by George Holden in Brooklyn in 1903 in the "wonderful time" of 14 minutes 57 1/5 seconds for 10 miles.

The equipment improved and machines became faster. In 1912, Lee Humiston rode an Excelsior motorcycle at the rate of 100 miles per hour. The speed was regarded as amazing.

In 1934, E. Henne of Germany was credited with an average of 152.86 m.p.h., which then stood as the world record for motorcycles. He bettered his record in 1937 by going 174 m.p.h. over a measured mile. Both records were established on BMW motorcycles. The latter mark withstood challenges until April 12, 1950, when Wilhelm Herz turned in a world mark for 2-wheelers by doing a measured mile at 180 miles per hour. It was established with a streamlined, supercharged 500 cc. NSU machine on the Munich-Ingolstadt autobahn in Germany.

Since even the narrowest roads are suitable for motorcycles, they were first used for transcontinental runs in the United States. They could travel through spots that were inaccessible to automobiles. This is still the case. Motorcycle clubs throughout the United States are taking an active part in civil defense. They serve as emergency communications couriers, auxiliary police and in many other capacities where traversing difficult terrain quickly is of prime importance.

The earliest transcontinental rider, and the most famous, was "Cannonball" Baker. He hung up the pioneer Los Angeles-to-New York mark of 8 days 21 hours 16 minutes. Thereafter Baker virtually became a commuter between the coasts and repeatedly smashed his records.

In Baker's heyday, he held most of the endurance and many of the speed records. Since his time engines of mightier power have been built, providing infinitely greater speed. Although all of Baker's great performances have been surpassed, he remains, in motorcycle memory, as perhaps the greatest all-round rider of all time.

Motorcycle racing in this country is held under the auspices of the American Motorcycle Association, with headquarters at Westerville, Ohio. Prior to World War II, which forced the cancellation of all motorcycle racing, the association sanctioned between 900 and 1,000 race meets each year. For the 1972 season, the A.M.A. sanctioned upwards of 5,000 events.

The great racing centers were on the hard sands of Daytona Beach, Fla., and the speedways at Langhorne, Pa., and Springfield, Ill. However, many records were made at Syracuse, N.Y.; Altoona, Pa.; Oakland, Calif.; Salem, N.H.; Beverly Hills, Calif.; Bakersfield, Calif.; Fresno, Calif.; Milwaukee, Wis.; Toledo, Ohio; San Luis Obispo, Calif., and on the salt surface course at Bonneville, Utah.

The outstanding contest is the 200-mile National championship event held annually at Daytona Beach. This race draws contestants from all parts of the United States and Canada and attracts crowds of more than 20,000. It has become known as the "Indianapolis of Motorcycle Racing."

FAMOUS RIDERS

Joining Baker in the top circle are many remarkable riders, with Ralph Hepburn and Johnny Seymour among the outstanding. None ever was more of a daredevil than Hepburn, who was at his peak in 1920-22, and later became an automobile racer. Hepburn, driving a 61" motorcycle, made mile, 5-mile, 10-mile, 25-mile, 200-mile and 300-mile marks on dirt tracks more than 45 years ago, when travel on such tracks always was fraught with danger.

Hepburn turned the mile on dirt in 39 3/5 seconds, which has been bettered only once, by

Jim Davis, whose performance was on the faster, safer speedway. Hepburn's greatest feat, perhaps, was on July 4, 1921, at Dodge City, Kan., where he negotiated 300 miles on dirt in 3 hours 30 minutes 3 seconds, an average of about 90 miles an hour—one of the most amazing of all feats for durability at high speed.

Seymour was Hepburn's great rival and, like Hepburn, he was a man of remarkable skill and had a scorn for danger. He drove every cycle to the maximum speed.

Other great riders include: Curley Fredericks, Bill Minnick, Davis, Joe Petrali, who was outstanding for a decade; Otto Walker, Sam Riddle, F.T. Scott, Otho Wilson, Miny Waln, Fred Ludlow, Floyd Dreyer, Tuffy Jacobs, Lester Foote, S.M.B. McKinney, Arthur Pechar, Paul Anderson, Bill Huber, who was at his best when the war ended the sport; Mel Rhoades, Frenchy Castonguay, Arther Hafer, Lester Hillbish, Woodsie Castonguay, Ed Kretz, Louis Guanella, Fred Ham, William Mathews, Blackie Bullock, Joe Leonard, Everett Brashear, Bobby Hill, Howard Mitzel and Brad Andres. Included are: Mert Lawwill, Fred Nix, Bart Markel, Gene Romero, Calvin Rayborn, Dick Mann, Gary Nixon, Mark Brelsford.

Many motorcycle stars started out racing bicycles. And some motorcycle champions became pilots of speedway automobiles. Other riders, who were outstanding in other fields, after quitting the motordromes, and the roadways of the nation, included:

Gen. Simon Buckner, United States Army, who became head of Alaska Command; Sir Malcolm Campbell, auto racer; Clark Gable, movies and aviation gunner; Charles Lindbergh, aviator; Tyrone Power, movies; Clarence Chamberlain, aviator; Douglas Corrigan, aviator; Bill Cummings, auto racer; Mauri Rose, auto racer; Bob Young, movies; Bob Montgomery, movies; Chet Lauck (Lum), radio; Norris Goff (Abner), radio; Daniel Frohman, theater; Zeppo Marx, movies; Jon Hall, movies; Wallace Beery, movies; Andy Devine, movies; Dennis Morgan, movies; Edgar Bergen, radio and movies; Van Johnson, movies; John Payne, movies; Roy Rogers, movies; Dick Powell, movies; Allan Jones, movies; Preston Foster, movies; Francis Burnham, mortorboat driver.

A.M.A. Champions and Records

NATIONAL CHAMPIONS

1936

Dirt Track Race, Class A—Joe Petrali
Speedway—Lester Billbish
Night Speedway—Benny Kaufman
Endurance Run—Oscar Lenz
Road Race—Ed Kretz
Tourist Trophy—H. Marshall
Miniature Tourist Trophy (45 cu. in.)—Curtis Duty
Miniature Tourist Trophy (80 cu. in.)—Hap Jones

HILL CLIMBING

45 Cubic Inch, Class A—Joe Petrali
45 Cubic Inch, Expert—Howard Mitzel
45 Cubic Inch, Class B—Harold Seamans
80 Cubic Inch, Class B—Harold Seamans

1937

Dirt Track—Robert Beatty
Speedway—Ed Kretz
Night Speedway—Benny Kaufman
Endurance—Junior Muehlenbeck
Road—Ed Kretz
Tourist Trophy (100 miles)—Al Aunapu
Miniature Tourist Trophy (45 cu. in.)—Tommy Hayes
Miniature Tourist Trophy (80 cu. in.)—Tommy Hayes.

HILL CLIMBING

45-Cubic Inch, Class A—Joe Petrali
45-Cubic Inch, Expert—Joe Petrali
45-Cubic Inch, Class B—Harold Seamans
80-Cubic Inch, Class B—Harold Seamans

1938

Dirt Track, Class A—Fred Toscani
Dirt Track, Class C—Woodsie Castonguay
Speedway—Ed Kretz
Road—Ben Campanale
Endurance—Ted Konecny
Tourist Trophy (50 miles)—Milt Iverson
Tourist Trophy (100 miles)—Milt Iverson
Tourist Trophy (200 miles)—Ed Kretz
Miniature Tourist Trophy Racing (45 cu. in.)—J.B. Jones
Miniature Tourist Trophy Racing (80 cu. in.)—Tommy Hayes

HILL CLIMBING

Class A—Joe Petrali
Expert—Willard Bryan
Class B—Pat Ronco
Class C—John Powers

1939

Dirt Track (25 miles)—Stan Witinski
Dirt Track (50 miles)—Lester Hillbish
Speedway (100 miles)—Robert Sparks
Speedway (200 miles)—Jack Cottrell
Road—Ben Campanale
Endurance—Junior Muehlenbeck
Tourist Trophy (50 miles)—Ernie Holbrook
Tourist Trophy (100 miles)—Charles Daniels
Tourist Trophy (200 miles)—Bob Hallowell
Miniature Tourist Trophy (45 cu. in.)—J.B. Jones
Miniature Tourist Trophy (80 cu. in.)—Tommy Hayes

HILL CLIMBING
45-Cubic Inch, Class A—Willard Bryan
45-Cubic Inch, Expert—Howard Mitzel
45-Cubic Inch, Class B—A.W. French
74-Cubic Inch, Class B—Harold Seamans

1940

Dirt Track—Mel Rhoades
Speedway (100 miles)—Ed Kretz
Speedway (200 miles)—Louis Guanella
Road (100 miles)—Babe Tancrede
Road (200 miles)—Babe Tancrede
Endurance—Earl Robinson
Tourist Trophy (50 miles)—Ted Edwards
Tourist Trophy (100 miles)—Ted Edwards
Miniature Tourist Trophy (45 cu. in.)—J.B. Jones
Miniature Tourist Trophy (80 cu. in.)—Tommy
  Hayes

HILL CLIMBING—CLASS A
45-Cubic Inch, Class A—Willard Bryan
45-Cubic Inch, Expert—Willard Bryan
45-Cubic Inch, Class B—Harold Seamans and Darrel Bryan (tie)
74-Cubic Inch, Class B—Harold Seamans

1941

Dirt Track—Frenchy Castonguay
Speedway (100 miles)—Tommy Hayes
Speedway (200 miles)—Ernie Holbrook
Road (100 miles)—June McCall
Road (200 miles)—Billy Mathews
Tourist Trophy (45 cu. in.)—J.B. Jones
Tourist Trophy (80 cu. in.)—Tommy Hayes
Tourist Trophy (50 miles)—Tommy Hayes
Endurance—No competition

HILL CLIMBING—CLASS A
45-Cubic Inch, Class B—Darrel Bryan
74—Cubic Inch, Class A—Tom Paradise
74-Cubic Inch, Expert—Willard Bryan

1942—45—No competition

1946

Dirt Track—Chet Dykgraaf
Speedway (100 miles)—John Speigelhoff
Road (100 miles)—Ed Kretz
Endurance—Claude Goulding
Miniature Tourist Trophy (45 cu. in.)—Herman
  Dahlke
Miniature Tourist Trophy (80 cu. in.)—Ray Tur-
  sky

HILL CLIMBING—CLASS A
45-Cubic Inch, Class B—Tan Hemmis
45-Cubic Inch, Qualifying—Tan Hemmis
74-Cubic Inch, Class A—Clem Murdaugh
74-Cubic Inch, Expert—Clem Murdaugh

1947

Speedway (100 miles)—Ed Guill
Night Speedway—Cordy Milne
Endurance—Julius Kroeger

DIRT TRACK
5 Miles (½-mile track)—Leo Anthony

10 Miles (½-mile track)—Leo Anthony
10 Miles (mile track)—Floyd Emde
25 Miles (mile track)—Jimmy Chann

ROAD
100 Miles—Alli Quattrocchi
200 Miles—John Spiegelhoff

TOURIST TROPHY
45-Cubic Inch—Lowell Rettinger
80-Cubic Inch—Herman Dahlke
50 Miles—Ed Rush
100 Miles—Ray Tanner

HILL CLIMBING—CLASS A
45-Cubic Inch, Class B—Herb Fletcher
45-Cubic Inch, Qualifying—Herb Fletcher
74-Cubic Inch, Class A—Roy Burke
74—Cubic Inch, Expert—Clem Murdaugh

1948

Speedway (100 miles)—Ed Kretz
Endurance—Earl Flanders

DIRT TRACK
3 Miles (½-mile track)—Leo Anthony
5 Miles (½-mile track)—Paul Albrecht
8 Miles (½-mile track)—Buck Brigance
10 Miles (mile track)—Billy Huber and Bobby
  Hill (dead heat)
15 Miles (mile track)—Jimmy Chann
25 Miles (mile track)—Jimmy Chann

ROAD
100 Miles—Joe Weatherly
200—Miles—Floyd Emde

TOURIST TROPHY
45-Cubic Inch—Bill Miller
80-Cubic Inch—Billy Douglas
50 Miles—Bill Magurany
100 Miles—Ed Kretz

HILL CLIMBING—CLASS A
45-Cubic Inch, Class B—Joe Hemmis
45-Cubic Inch, Class B Qualifying—T. Hemmis
74-Cubic Inch, Class A—Sam Kakabar
74-Cubic Inch, Expert—Al Skrelunas

1949

Speedway (100 miles)—Jimmy Chann
Endurance Run—Bert Cummings
Cross-Country Run—Aub LeBard

DIRT TRACK
5 Miles—Paul Albrecht
7 Miles (½-mile track)—Claud Dawson
8 Miles (½-mile track)—Paul Albrecht
10 Miles (½-mile track)—Bobby Hill
10 Miles (mile track)—Paul Albrecht
15 Miles (mile track)—Jimmy Chann
20 Miles (mile track)—Horace Travis
25 Miles (mile track)—Jimmy Chann

ROAD
100 Miles—Joe Weatherly
200 Miles—Dick Klamfoth

TOURIST TROPHY

45-Cubic Inch—Bill Miller
80-Cubic Inch—Roger Soderstrom

HILL CLIMBING—CLASS A

45-Cubic Inch, Class B—Buddy Cosgrove
45-Cubic Inch, Class B Qualifying—Buddy Cosgrove
74-Cubic Inch, Class A—Earl Buck
74-Cubic Inch, Expert—Howard Mitzel

1950

Speedway (100 miles)—Billy Huber
Endurance Run (600 miles)—Del Kuhn

DIRT TRACK

5 Miles (½-mile track)—Bill Tuman
7 Miles (½-mile track)—Paul Albrecht
8 Miles (½-mile track)—Bill Tuman
10 Miles (½-mile track)—Joe Weatherly
15 Miles (mile track)—Larry Headrick
20 Miles (mile track)—Larry Headrick
25 Miles (mile track)—Larry Headrick

ROAD

100 Miles—Bill Miller
200 Miles—Billy Mathews

TOURIST TROPHY

45-Cubic Inch—Roger Soderstrom
80-Cubic Inch—Roger Soderstrom

HILL CLIMBING—CLASS A

45-Cubic Inch, Class B—Don Farrow
45-Cubic Inch, Class B Qualifying—Paul Allen
74-Cubic Inch, Class A—Willard Bryan
74-Cubic Inch, Expert—Willard Bryan

1951

Speedway (100 miles)—Billy Huber
Endurance Run (500 miles)—Joe Gee
Cross-Country (150 miles)—Aub LeBard

DIRT TRACK

5 Miles (½-mile track)—Lowell Rettinger
7 Miles (½-mile track)—Dick Klamfoth
8 Miles (½-mile track)—Ernie Beckman
10 Miles (½-mile track)—Dick Klamfoth
15 Miles (mile track)—Bobby Hill
20 Miles (mile track)—Kenny Eggers
25 Miles (mile track)—Bobby Hill

ROAD

100 Miles—Dick Klamfoth
200 Miles—Dick Klamfoth

TOURIST TROPHY

45-Cubic Inch—Jimmy Phillips
80-Cubic Inch—Jimmy Phillips

HILL CLIMBING—CLASS A

45-Cubic Inch, Class B—Larry Sutter
45-Cubic Inch, Class B Final—Louis Corriere
74-Cubic Inch, Class A—Willard Bryan
74-Cubic Inch, Expert Final—Pete Eubelacker

1952

Speedway (100 miles)—Richard Fisher
Speedway (200 miles)—Bobby Hill

Endurance Run (500 miles)—Frank Piasecki
Cross-Country—John McLaughlin
Catalina Grand National—Nick Nicholson

DIRT TRACK

5 Miles (½-mile track)—Everett Brashear
7 Miles (½-mile track)—Albert Gunter
8 Miles (½-mile track)—Ernie Beckman
10 Miles (½-mile track)—Bobby Hill
5 Miles (mile track)—Bobby Hill
10 Miles (mile track)—Bobby Hill
15 Miles (mile track)—Paul Goldsmith
20 Miles (mile track)—Bill Tuman
25 Miles (mile track)—Bobby Hill

ROAD

100 Miles—Dick Klamfoth
200 Miles—Dick Klamfoth

TOURIST TROPHY

45-Cubic Inch—Bill Miller
80-Cubic Inch—Roger Soderstrom

HILL CLIMBING—CLASS A

45-Cubic Inch, Class B—Larry Franz
45-Cubic Inch, Class B Final—Larry Franz
74-Cubic Inch, Class A—Earl Buck
74-Cubic Inch, Expert Final—Howard Mitzel

1953

Speedway (100 miles)—Paul Goldsmith
Speedway (200 miles)—Bill Tuman
Endurance Run (500 miles)—Don Pink
24-Hour Run (650 miles)—Don Pink

DIRT TRACK

5 Miles (½-mile track)—Joe Leonard
10 Miles (½-mile track)—Everett Brashear
5 Miles (mile track)—Everett Brashear
10 Miles (mile track)—Bobby Hill
15 Miles (mile track)—Bobby Hill
20 Miles (mile track)—Joe Leonard
25 Miles (mile track)—Bill Tuman

ROAD

50 Miles—Joe Leonard
100 Miles—E. Fisher
200 Miles—Paul Goldsmith

TOURIST TROPHY

45-Cubic Inch—Joe Leonard
80-Cubic Inch—Roger Soderstrom

HILL CLIMBING—CLASS A

45-Cubic Inch Amateur—Philip Rockwell
45-Cubic Inch Amateur Final—Duane Nealen
74-Cubic Inch Professional—R.J. Nealen
74-Cubic Inch Professional Final—Howard Mitzel

1954

Speedway (100 miles)—Everett Brashear
Endurance Run—B. Penton
Cross-Country—R. Burke
Class C Grand National—Joe Leonard

DIRT TRACK

5 Miles (½-mile track)—Al Gunter
5 Miles (1-mile track)—Eugene Thiessen

6 Miles (½-mile track)—Dick Klamfoth
7 Miles (½-mile track)—Charles Carey
8 Miles (½-mile track)—Charles Carey
8 Miles (1-mile track)—Joe Leonard
9 Miles (½-mile track)—Joe Leonard
10 Miles (½-mile track)—Paul Goldsmith
20 Miles (1-mile track)—Joe Leonard
25 Miles (1-mile track)—Joe Leonard

ROAD

50 Miles—H. Fearey
75 Miles—Joe Leonard
100 Miles—Joe Leonard
125 Miles—K. Eggers
200 Miles—Bobby Hill

TOURIST TROPHY

45-Cubic Inch—Joe Leonard
80-Cubic Inch—Joe Leonard

HILL CLIMBING—CLASS A

45-Cubic Inch Amateur—W. Lyle
45-Cubic Inch Amateur Final—Duane Nealen
74-Cubic Inch Professional—R.J. Nealen
74-Cubic Inch Professional Final—R.J. Nealen

1955

Speedway (100 miles)—Brad Andres
Endurance Run—Sal Scirpo
Cross-Country—Bill Postel
Class C Grand National—Brad Andres

DIRT TRACK

5 Miles (½-mile track)—Everett Brashear
6 Miles (½-mile track)—Don Tindall
7 Miles (½-mile track)—Al Gunter
8 Miles (½-mile track)—Paul Goldsmith
9 Miles (½-mile track)—Joe Leonard
10 Miles (½-mile track)—Everett Brashear
15 Miles (1-mile track)—Everett Brashear
20 Miles (1-mile track)—Everett Brashear
25 Miles (1-mile track)—Everett Brashear

ROAD

50 Miles—Joe Leonard
75 Miles—Brad Andres
100 Miles—Brad Andres
125 Miles—Brad Andres
200 Miles—Brad Andres

TOURIST TROPHY

45-Cubic Inch—Joe Leonard
80-Cubic Inch—E. Kretz Jr.

HILL CLIMBING—CLASS A

45-Cubic Inch Amateur—W. Lyle
45-Cubic Inch Amateur Final—L. Corriere
74-Cubic Inch Professional—Howard Mitzel
74-Cubic Inch Professional Final—R.J. Nealen

1956

Speedway (100 miles)—Everett Brashear
20 Miles (mile track)—Joe Leonard

DIRT TRACK

10 Miles (½-mile track)—Everett Brashear
20 Miles (mile track)—Joe Leonard

ROAD

100 Miles—Brad Andres

TOURIST TROPHY

45-Cubic Inch—Brad Andres
80-Cubic Inch—Joe Leonard

HILL CLIMBING—CLASS A

45-Cubic Inch, Amateur—Philip Rockwell
74-Cubic Inch, Professional—Howard Mitzel

1957

Endurance Run (500 miles)—Eddie Day
Cross-Country—Buck Smith
Class A Scrambles—Bud Ekins
Class C Grand National—Joe Leonard

DIRT TRACK

5 Miles (½-mile track)—Carroll Resweber
10 Miles (½-mile track)—Carroll Resweber
25 Miles (mile track)—Joe Leonard
50 Miles (mile track)—Joe Leonard

ROAD

100 Miles—Joe Leonard
200 Miles—Joe Leonard

TOURIST TROPHY

45-Cubic Inch—Al Gunter
80-Cubic Inch—George Everett

HILL CLIMBING—CLASS A

45-Cubic Inch, Amateur—Charles Jacob
74-Cubic Inch, Professional—Duane Nealen

1958

Cross-Country—Buck Smith
Endurance Run (250 miles)—John Penton
Endurance Run (500 miles)—John Penton
Class C Grand National—Carroll Resweber

DIRT TRACK

5 Miles (½-mile track)—Carroll Resweber
10 Miles (½-mile track)—Dick Klamfoth
15 Miles (½-mile track)—Dick Klamfoth
20 Miles (mile track)—Carroll Resweber
25 Miles (mile track)—Everett Brashear
50 Miles (mile track)—Joe Leonard

ROAD

100 Miles—Brad Andres
200 Miles—Joe Leonard

TOURIST TROPHY

45-Cubic Inch—George Everett
80-Cubic Inch—Dick Dorresteyn

HILL CLIMBING—CLASS A

45-Cubic Inch, Amateur—Gordon Mitzel
74-Cubic Inch, Professional—Earl Buck

1959

Cross Country—Bud Ekins
Endurance Run (250 miles)—John Penton
Endurance Run (500 miles)—Sal Scirpo
Class C Grand National—Carroll Resweber

DIRT TRACK

5 Mile (½-mile track)—Carrol Resweber
8 Mile (½-mile track)—Sammy Tanner

10 Mile (½-mile track)—Dick Klamfoth
15 Mile (½-mile track)—Dick Klamfoth
25 Mile (1-mile track)—Carroll Resweber
50 Mile (1-mile track)—Carroll Resweber

ROAD

100 Miles—Brad Andres
200 Miles—Brad Andres

TOURIST TROPHY

45-Cubic Inch—Dick Mann
80-Cubic Inch—Duane Buchanan

HILL CLIMBING—CLASS A

45-Cubic Inch—Harold Werner
80-Cubic Inch—Joe Hemmis

1960

ENDURANCE RUNS

100 Miles—Fred Barber
150 Miles—John Quick
200 Miles—John Penton
250 Miles—John Toth
500 Miles—John Penton
Class C Grand National—Carroll Resweber

DIRT TRACK

5 Mile (½-mile track—Carroll Resweber
8 Mile (½-mile track)—Al Gunter
10 Mile (½-mile track)—Carroll Resweber
15 Mile (½-mile track)—Carroll Resweber
20 Mile (1-mile track)—Carroll Resweber
25 Mile (1-mile track)—Everett Brashear
50 Mile (1-mile track)—Troy Lee

ROAD

100 Miles—Dick Mann
150 Miles—Brad Andres
200 Miles—Brad Andres

TOURIST TROPHY

45-Cubic Inch—Joe Leonard
80-Cubic Inch—Bart Markel

HILL CLIMBING—CLASS A

45-Cubic Inch, Amateur—Vic Salvadore
74-Cubic Inch, Professional—Charles Jacobs

1961

Formula A Short Track—Carroll Resweber

ENDURANCE RUNS

125 Mile—Jack Wright
150 Mile—John Penton
175 Mile—William Baird
200 Mile—Schyler Ball
250 Mile—John Penton
500 Mile—Lewis Atkinson
Class C Grand National—Carroll Resweber

DIRT TRACK

5 Mile (½-mile track)—Carroll Resweber
8 Mile (½-mile track)—Neil Keen
10 Mile (½-mile track)—Carroll Resweber
15 Mile (½-mile track)—Dick Mann
25 Mile (1-mile track)—Joe Leonard
50 Mile (1-mile track)—Carroll Resweber

ROAD

100 Miles—Joe Leonard
150 Miles—Carroll Resweber
200 Miles—Roger Reiman

TOURIST TROPHY

45-Cubic Inch—Bart Markel
80-Cubic Inch—Joe Leonard

1962

Cross Country—Eddie Mulder
Class A Short Track—Carroll Resweber
TT Scrambles, Heavyweight—Leroy Guthrie
TT Scrambles, Lightweight—Richard Gariepy

ENDURANCE RUNS

125 Miles—John Penton
150 Miles—Bill Baird
250 Miles—John Penton
400 Miles—Max Bubeck
500 Miles—John Wright

Class C Grand National—Bart Markel

ROAD

100 Miles—Dick Mann
120 Miles—Tony Murguia
130 Miles—Carroll Resweber
150 Miles—Carroll Resweber
200 Miles—Don Burnett

TOURIST TROPHY

45-Cubic Inch—Bart Markel
80-Cubic Inch—Dick Hammer
Combined—Dick Dorresteyn

HILL CLIMBING—CLASS A

45-Cubic Inch, Amateur—Phillip Petrick
80-Cubic Inch, Professional—Joe Hemmis

1963

Cross Country—Ed Mulder
Class A Short Track—Gary Nixon
Scrambles Open Class—Clark White
Scrambles 500 cc Class—Don Spargur
Scrambles 250cc Class—Bill Holcomb

ENDURANCE RUNS

100 Mile—Bill Baird
125 Mile—Bill Baird
150 Mile—Sal Scirpo
200 Mile—Al Rogers
250 Mile—Sox Brookhart
500 Mile—Bert Wieland

Endurance Grand National—Bill Baird

Formula C Grand National—Dick Mann

DIRT TRACK

5 Mile (½-mile track)—George Roeder
8 Mile (½-mile track)—Al Gunter
10 Mile (½-mile track)—Ronnie Rall
15 Mile (½-mile track)—Ronnie Rall
20 Mile (1-mile track)—George Roeder
50 Mile (1-mile track)—George Roeder

ROAD

50 Mile—Gary Nixon
100 Mile—Jody Nicholas

150 Mile—Jody Nicholas
200 Mile—Ralph White

TOURIST TROPHY

Lightweight—Bark Markel
Heavyweight—Sid Payne
50 Lap—Dick Mann

HILL CLIMBING—FORMULA A

45-Cubic Inch Amateur—Glen Kyle
74-Cubic Inch Professional—Phil Petrick

1964

Cross-Country—Mike Patrick
Class C Short Track—Roger Reiman
Scrambles, Heavyweight—Charles Vincent
Scrambles, Lightweight—Bill Holcomb
24-Hour Marathon—David Mungenast

ENDURANCE RUNS

100 Miles—David Barnes
125 Miles—John Penton
150 Miles—Bill Baird
175 Miles—Bill Baird
200 Miles—Joe Kremer
250 Miles—Sox Brookhart
500 Miles—Buck Smith

Endurance Grand National—Bill Baird
Formula C Grand National—Roger Reiman

DIRT TRACK

5 Mile (½-mile track)—Bart Markel
7 Mile (½-mile track)—George Roeder
8 Mile (½-mile track)—Sam Tanner
10 Mile (½-mile track)—Bart Markel
12 Mile (½-mile track)—Bart Markel
15 Mile (½-mile track)—George Roeder
20 Mile (1-mile track)—Gary Nixon
50 Mile (1-mile track)—Sam Tanner

ROAD

50 Miles—Dick Mann
100 Miles—Larry Schafer
150 Miles—Dick Mann
175 Miles—Dick Mann
200 Miles—Roger Reiman

TOURIST TROPHY

Lightweight—Ronnie Rall
Heavyweight—Dick Mann
50 Lap—Dave Palmer

HILL CLIMBING—FORMULA A

45-Cubic Inch Amateur—Tom Reiser
74-Cubic Inch Professional—Joe Hemmis

HILL CLIMBING—FORMULA C

80-Cubic Inch Expert—Richard Clay
45-Cubic Inch Expert—Lydian Ascenzi
80-Cubic Inch Novice—Gene Walker
45-Cubic Inch Novice—Gene Walker

1965

Cross Country—Ron Nelson
Class C Short Track—Gary Nixon
Scrambles Open Class—Dallas Baker
Scrambles 500cc Class—Dan Kelly
Scrambles 250cc Class—Steven Scott

Hare Scrambles—Gary Conrad
24-Hour Marathon—Jim White

ENDURANCE RUNS

100 Mile—Robert Fusan
125 Mile—Eugene Esposito
150 Mile—Bill Baird
175 Mile—Bill Baird
200 Mile—Malcolm Smith
250 Mile—Robert Fusan
500 Mile—Bill Decker

Endurance Grand National—Bill Baird
Formula C Grand National—Bart Markel

DIRT TRACK

8 Mile (½-mile track)—Sam Tanner
10 Mile (½-mile track)—George Roeder
12 Mile (½-mile track)—Bart Markel
15 Mile (½-mile track)—Bart Markel
20 Mile (1-mile track)—Mert Lawwill
50 Mile (1-mile track)—Ralph White

ROAD

75 Mile—Gary Nixon
80 Mile 250cc—Dick Mann
100 Mile—Ralph White
110 Mile—Ralph White
120 Mile—Ralph White
150 Mile—Dick Mann
200 Mile—Roger Reiman

TOURIST TROPHY

Lightweight—Bart Markel
Heavyweight—Ed Mulder
30 Lap—Dave Palmer
50 Lap—Sid Payne

HILL CLIMBING—FORMULA A

45-Cubic Inch Amateur—Beese Wendt
74-Cubic Inch Professional—Glen Kyle

1966

Cross Country—Gary Conrad
Class C Short Track—Bart Markel
Hare Scrambles—Dick Vick
24-Hour Marathon—David Mungenast

ENDURANCE RUNS

125 Mile—Eugene Esposito
150 Mile—John Young
175 Mile—Bill Baird
200 Mile—Bob Steffen
250 Mile—John Young
400 Mile—Robert Chase
500 Mile—John Penton

Endurance Grand National—Bill Baird
Formula C Grand National—Bart Markel

DIRT TRACK

5 Mile (½-mile track)—Sam Tanner
7 Mile (½-mile track)—Babe DeMay
8 Mile (½-mile track)—Sam Tanner
10 Mile (½-mile track)—Bart Markel
15 Mile (½-mile track)—Sam Tanner
20 Mile (1-mile track)—Fred Nix
50 Mile (1-mile track)—Gary Nixon

ROAD

75 Mile—Cal Rayborn
110 Mile—Gary Nixon
200 Mile—Buddy Elmore

TOURIST TROPHY

20 Lap—Ed Mulder
30 Lap—Ed Mulder
50 Lap—Ed Mulder

HILL CLIMBING—FORMULA A

45-Cubic Inch Amateur—Beese Wendt
74-Cubic Inch Professional—Glen Kyle

1967

Class C Short Track—Gary Nixon
Hare and Hound—Russell Coppage
Hare Scrambles—Steve Hurd
24-Hour Marathon—William Brandom

ENDURANCE RUNS

75 Mile—John Young
100 Mile—Robert Fusan
125 Mile—George Newsom
135 Mile—Jack McLane, Jr.
150 Mile—Bill Baird
175 Mile—Bill Baird
200 Mile—Jack McLane, Jr.
250 Mile—John Penton
500 Mile—Dave Ekins

Grand National—Gary Nixon
Grand National Endurance—Bill Baird

DIRT TRACK

5 Mile (½-mile track)—Bart Markel
7 Mile (½-mile track)—George Roeder
8 Mile (½-mile track)—Dan Haaby
9 Mile (½-mile track)—Fred Nix
10 Mile (½-mile track)—Fred Nix
12 Mile (½-mile track)—Dick Mann
15 Mile (½-mile track)—Bart Markel
20 Mile (1-mile track)—Gary Roeder

ROAD RACE

75 Miles—Gary Nixon
100 Miles—Gary Nixon
110 Miles—Cal Rayborn
200 Miles—Gary Nixon

TOURIST TROPHY

20 Lap—Dick Mann
30 Lap—Mert Lawwill
50 Lap—Gordon Van Leeuwen

HILL CLIMBING—FORMULA A

45-Cubic Inch, Amateur—Jack Taylor
74—Cubic Inch, Professional—Joe Hemmis

1968

Grand National Gary Nixon

DIRT TRACK   Where Made

5 Mile (½-mile track) Ronnie Rall ..... Livonia, Mich.
8 Mile (½-mile track) Mert Lawwill .... Gardena, Calif.
9 Mile (½-mile track) Fred Nix   ..Oklahoma City, Okla.
10 Mile (½-mile track) Gary Nixon ...Columbus, Ohio
11 Mile (½-mile track) Mert Lawwill .... Salinas, Calif.
12 Mile (½-mile track) Bart Markel ...... Reading, Pa.

13 Mile (½-mile track)—Bart Markel ....Richmond, Va.
14 Mile (½-mile track)—Bart Markel ....San Jose, Calif.
15 Mile (½-mile track)—Bart Markel ....Louisville, Ky.
10 Mile (1-mile track)—Fred Nix ..... Santa Rosa, Calif.
15 Mile (1-mile track)—Fred Nix .... Sedalia, Mo.
20 Mile (1-mile track)—Fred Nix .... Portland, Ore.
25 Mile (1-mile track) Fred Nix .... Sacramento, Calif.

TOURIST TROPHY

20 Lap Bart Markel .... Peoria, Ill.
25 Lap—Gene Romero .... Lincoln, Neb.
30 Lap—Gordon Van Leeuwen ....Castle Rock, Wash.
50 Lap Gordon Van Leeuwen .... Gardena, Calif.

ROAD RACES

Miniature— Walter Fulton, 3rd .... Heidelberg, Pa.
100-Mile Calvin Rayborn .... Indianapolis, Ind.
110-Mile Calvin Rayborn .... Indianapolis, Ind.
200-Mile Calvin Rayborn .... Daytona Beach, Fla.

SHORT TRACK

Indoor—Gary Nixon .... Houston, Tex.
Outdoor Fred Nix .... Hinsdale, Ill.

HILL CLIMB

45-Cubic Inch Professional B Jack Taylor
74-Cubic Inch Professional A Earl Bowly

1969

Grand National Mert Lawwill

DIRT TRACK   Where Made

10 Mile Bart Markel .... Terre Haute, Ind.
20 Mile Larry Palmgren .... Santa Rosa, Calif.
30 Mile Larry Palmgren .... Indianapolis, Ind.
56 ½ Mile Fred Nix .... Nazareth, Pa.

TOURIST TROPHY

20 Lap Gordon Van Leeuwen .... Houston, Tex.
25 Lap Ed Wirth .... Hinsdale, Ill.
30 Lap Mert Lawwill .... Castle Rock, Wash.
50 Lap Mark Brelsford .... Gardena, Calif.

ROAD RACES

30 Lap Miniature Calvin Rayborn ..... Heidleberg, Pa.
100 Mile Fred Nix .... Loudon, N.H.
110-Mile Calvin Rayborn .... Indianapolis, Ind.
125 Mile Art Baumann .... Sears Point, Calif.
200 Mile Calvin Rayborn .... Daytona Beach, Fla.

SHORT TRACK

Indoor 25 Lap Ronnie Ball .... Houston, Tex.
Outdoor 25 Lap Dick Mann .... Hinsdale, Ill.

1970

Grand National—Gene Romero

DIRT TRACK   Where Made

20 Lap Mile—Gene Romero .... Sedalia, Mo.
50 Lap—Chuck Palmgren .... Nazareth, Pa.
50 Mile—Gene Romero .... Sacramento, Calif.

TOURIST TROPHY

20 Lap Indoor—Jim Rice .... Houston, Tex.
25 Lap—Eddie Mulder .... Hinsdale, Ill.
50 Lap—Mert Lawwill .... Gardena, Calif.

ROAD RACES

100 Mile—Gary Nixon .... Loudon, N.H.
125 Mile—Ron Grant .... Kent, Wash.
200 Mile—Dave Aldana .... Talladega, Ala.
200 Mile—Dick Mann .... Daytona Beach, Fla.

SHORT TRACK

Indoor—25 Lap—Mert Lawwill .... Houston, Tex.

1971

Grand National Dick Mann

DIRT TRACK	Where Made	DIRT TRACK	Where Made
10 Miles—Dave Sehl	Louisville, Ky.	25 Mile—Jim Rice	Colorado Springs, Colo.

TOURIST TROPHY

20 Lap Indoor—Dick Mann	Houston, Tex.	20 Lap Indoor—John Hateley	Houston, Tex.
30 Lap Outdoor—Lewis Burres	Castle Rock, Wash.	25 Lap Outdoor—Dick Mann	Peoria, Ill.
50 Lap Outdoor—Mark Brelsford	Gardena, Calif.		

ROAD RACES

100 Miles—Dick Mann	Mt. Pocono, Pa.	100 Mile—Gary Fisher	Loudon, N.H.
125 Miles—Kel Carruthers	Atlanta, Ga.	125 Mile—Cal Rayborn	Monterey, Calif.
200 Miles—Yvon Duhamel	Talledega, Ala.	200 Mile—Yvon Duhamel	Talladega, Ala.
200 Miles—Dick Mann	Daytona Beach, Fla.	200 Mile—Don Emde	Daytona Beach, Fla.
		250 Mile—Paul Smart	Ontario, Calif.

SHORT TRACK

25 Lap Indoor—Jim Odom	Houston, Tex.	25 Lap Outdoor—Mark Brelsford	Gardena, Calif.

HILL CLIMB

Professional A—Glen Kyle

Inter-AMA 250 c.c. moto-cross—Gary Jones

1972

Grand National—Mark Brelsford

OLYMPIC GAMES

Without question the Olympic Games stand as the oldest and most truly international of all sports competitions. Born in antiquity, banned and then revived, the Games are now held every four years. The majority of the countries of the world send their outstanding athletes in various sports to these contests. The athletes live and fraternize in an Olympic village at the site of the Games, which are designed to promote good will among the nations. The competition draws visitors from all over the world. Various cities bid for the Summer and Winter Games.

The Games have a rich and historic background. They were originated by the Greeks long before the Christian Era and held regularly until 392 A.D. They were banned in that year by a Roman emperor, after having been in existence 11 centuries. In 1896, after a lapse of 1,500 years, the Games were revived, appropriately enough, in Athens, Greece, and have been staged since, except for interruptions caused by World Wars I and II.

Few happenings of antiquity have been subjected to so much research or dealt with in more detail by historians than the Olympic Games. These Games highlighted much of the history of ancient Greece and of Rome when it was the most powerful empire in the world. There is some confusion as to how the Games originated, but the story of the Games dating from 776 B.C. has been rather well preserved.

In Greek, the word "Olympiad" concerns a measure of time and means a period embracing four years. The "Olympic Games" took place at the end of every "Olympiad," or, in reverse explanation, they marked the beginning of a new "Olympiad." So much is established fact. But historians never have been sure of the origin and purpose of the "Olympic Games."

Many are of the belief that the earliest ceremonies started about 1453 B.C. and were not meant as athletic carnivals but were really memorial services. It is thought that, originally, the ceremonies were a civic or tribal custom to honor those who had died within an Olympiad, since Greeks did not measure time year by year as is the present custom, but by a period of four years.

It might have been a day, or a period of days, for mourning, much like the American Memorial Day.

The ancient Greeks held the belief that when a person died the spirit remained in the neighborhood where the person had lived. They thought that such spirits were watching over the scenes that had been known in life. Since that was the belief and since the surviving relatives and friends were eager to please, records of the favorite activities of a person were kept for guidance after death.

Therefore, when the passing of an Olympiad or the dawn of a new one was to be marked, a program was arranged at which things that had interested the departed in life would be displayed before the watching spirits. This could account for the great variety of the ancient programs, which included oratory, art of various kinds, music, recitals of poetry, as well as athletic contests.

In 1453 B.C. and for centuries later, Greece was known as Hellas. It was not a united country. Unrelated tribes warred with one another. There were many cities independent of each other—and jealous. There was no king of Hellas, as a nation. The ruler of each city was king only of that city. But through many centuries, politicians, philosophers and the wise men of the land tried earnestly to forge a united nation of those tribes, cities, towns and villages.

Legend has it that the idea for the Olympics originated with the Idaean Heracles, a crafty diplomat. But regardless of its source, the suggestion was favorably received. Chieftains agreed to send their best athletes, orators, musicians, etc., into events at Mount Olympus, but refused to abandon their individual ceremonies which had been tribal custom for over 600 years.

The leaders in the movement for a united Greece readily agreed. The tribes, therefore, continued to have their usual ceremonies and they became tryout places for all those who aspired to participate in what came to be the national contests.

It is not of undisputed record what was the exact term used to describe the most ancient of those affairs, but it is known that the expression "Olympic Games" was put into use in 776 B.C., when it became the custom to celebrate an Olympiad at the sacred mountain in Greece. By that time the ceremonies, no matter what their character in earlier times, took on something of a carnival air, although retaining certain religious principles.

Cleosthenes, King of Pisa; Lycurgus, King of Sparta, and Iphitus, King of Elis, are supposed to have promoted the first Olympic games in 776 B.C. On a discus, uncovered centuries later, was inscribed the laws that were to govern the Games and under them appeared the names of Lycurgus and Iphitus. The discus was a symbol of mighty muscles in that era. The man who could throw the discus farthest was ranked as the greatest athlete in the land.

Those who argued that the establishment of national peace and understanding might be accomplished through the "get-together" principle of the Games were correct. The warring tribes and the quarreling cities forgot their bitterness, almost with the first Olympic Games and Greece soon became a united nation.

Mount Olympus, on the Greek-Macedonian border and somewhat removed from the center of Greek culture, was chosen as the site for the Games for certain reasons. Foremost, it was supposed to be the abiding place of the gods, and it was felt they would bless the ceremonies. Secondly, the remoteness of the spot prevented the rise of jealousy among the rulers that might have occurred had any particular city been chosen. In addition, the base of Mount Olympus was such that an enormous crowd could be accommodated.

One of the strictest rules of the Olympic Games barred women, not merely as participants but also as spectators. Some women, overcome by curiosity, became "knot-hole" peepers or tree climbers. Those who were caught usually were put to death because the Games still were regarded as religious ceremonies and the law of the ancient Greeks prohibited women at such functions.

The women eventually retaliated with Games of their own. These took place every four years, but did not happen in the same year as the Olym-

pics. They were called Heraea and were founded by Hippodameia as a celebration of her marriage to Pelops.

There does not seem to be any authentic record as to when women finally were permitted to witness the Olympic Games, but it is presumed that this courtesy was extended not many generations after the Pherenice incident, one of the dramatic moments in ancient Olympiad history.

Pherenice was the mother of Peisidorous, a pugilist. She was so anxious to second her son in a fight that she slipped into the Stadium in male garb. When Peisidorous won, the mother's elation was such that she forgot her caution, took him in her arms and caressed him. An investigation followed. Pherenice's identity was disclosed. She was put on trial. She pleaded about love and motherhood. The judges ordered her freed, after long deliberation, but ruled that in the future all trainers would have to appear naked at the Games.

Some Olympiads later, with the advent of new rules with more tolerance toward women, the ban against them as spectators was lifted, but they never were allowed to compete.

In the earliest of the ancient Games, contestants wore loin cloths, but in 720 B.C. these were abandoned—after an accident. Orsippus of Megara, who wasn't considered as having a chance in a foot race, lost his loin cloth during the running and, "unimpeded," gained victory by a wide margin. The athletes in the remaining contests of that Olympiad discarded their cloths, and from then on, through a period of many years, the men competed only in nature's garb.

The Olympic Games, until Rome conquered Greece, were limited to free-born Greeks with unblemished reputation. None that ever had violated the most insignificant rule of the nation—or of manhood—could compete. The highest honor that Greece could bestow was to permit a man to participate in the Olympic Games.

There are no data as to what events beyond foot racing made up the first Olympus programs. But as time went on and the famous gymnasiums of Greece devised new athletic diversions, there were additions to the program, each being more elaborate than the preceding. Foot racing and discus throwing were the earliest favorites, and later came wrestling, jumping and pugilism.

Beginning with the 14th Olympiad, a double race was run. The earlier race had been once around the Stadium. The new event consisted of running from one end of the Stadium to the other and back again. Later a distance race—12 times around the Stadium was introduced. The pentathlon was added in the 18th Olympiad.

In 652 B.C., for the 25th Olympiad, there was added the Pancratium, which was a combination of wrestling and pugilism and featured the cestus as a weapon for attack.

Chariot races, dealt with so stirringly in the

novel "Ben Hur," also were introduced in the 25th Olympiad. The horses, small and not very strong, hauled vehicles called chariots, which were very light and generally two-wheeled.

For several centuries the Olympic Games were limited to adults. But eventually boys were admitted into sprinting, jumping and similar contests, where there was no great drain on stamina.

It is noted that almost all events added to succeeding programs were on the athletic side. There was no new stress on arts and sciences. However, one of the additions, which certainly was not athletic, was for "honorable political activity." The award to the champion of this group was the highest. Usually it was a wreath of gold leaves.

The Games reached their zenith in Greece in 464 B.C. By that time Greece was a united nation and the greatest ambition of every community was to have an Olympic champion.

The young men, hopeful of appearing in the Games, went into strenuous training a year in advance. This was done at the call of the king's heralds, who went to all the principal cities and towns of the land. A month before the Games, in which Greeks alone were permitted to participate up to that time, there was a preliminary test for all entrants. Those who did not meet a certain standard of athletic ability, or who were found guilty of a crime or sacrilege, regardless of physical skill, were eliminated.

Prior to the Games, at the height of their glory, all contestants and officials made a pilgrimage to the statue of the god Zeus. There the athletes took an oath to abide by the judges' rulings and make no protest under any circumstances. The judges swore they would be fair. This was followed by a prayer by each competitor for victory, with the qualification of "only if I am best."

Then came the procession to the scene of the Games and as the parade moved through the streets the players were implored by their neighbors and kinfolk to gain victory. Entering the Stadium, the various squads were exhorted by the most famous orators from their cities to give their best, to be fair and clean and to win for the home city.

A trumpet was sounded to signal each event. As soon as the sounding ceased, heralds hurried through the Stadium and, pointing out to the crowd each competing athlete, announced the youth's name, home city, athletic records and other pertinent data.

When the contest was over, the trumpet again was blown—this time for silence. The judges announced the winner, a branch from a palm tree was placed in his hand and a wreath, made of the leaves of the wild olive trees that grew in the sacred altis, was put on his head.

At the conclusion of the five-day festival, the winners were escorted to the statue of Zeus, where they gave prayers of thanks. Then there were impressive closing ceremonies followed by a formal banquet, where orators, poets, musicians and other notables praised the triumphant warriors.

Returning to his home, preceded by a procession, each victor was showered with more honors. He entered the city through a hole in the city's wall made especially for such entry. The idea of ripping a hole in the wall was to point out that a city, possessed of an athlete of such prowess, need have no further fear of harm from enemies and an unbroken wall was an unnecessary protection.

The winner then was wined and dined lavishly—at public expense. Gifts were forced upon him. He was exempted from taxation. All a city could do to show its delight over housing so illustrious a human as an Olympic winner was done. As a climax, he was permitted to build a monument to himself in any part of the city he chose. If he lacked funds, the wealthy townsmen subscribed the necessary money.

The Olympic Games continued to be exclusively the property of the Greeks until after 456 B.C., in which year Greece was conquered by the Romans. Greece lost its separate identity, becoming a province of the Roman Empire. For several Olympiads, the Greeks were the sole participants, the Games being under supervision of the Romans.

The Romans, as spectators, took a great interest in the Games and encouraged their youth to strive for perfection in the sports played by the Greeks. Then the youngsters of Rome entered the contests and competed with the Greeks.

The Games, conducted amicably for many generations, eventually encountered discord and then scandal. The Greeks charged that the Roman champions had capitalized on their newly-gained fame by going on tours and accepting cash, or some material equivalent, for making public appearances. The Romans denied the accusation and continued to participate in Olympic Games, despite protests from the Greeks over the amateur status of some of their entries. This led to increasing bitterness between them.

During one of the subsequent Olympiads, the Romans, angered by the Greek charges of professionalism, went on a rampage. They set fire to buildings used to house athletes and wrecked about everything that was wreckable in and around the Stadium. When the dust had settled and the fury had ebbed, Emperor Theodosius of Rome decided that the Olympic Games had become a public nuisance and issued an order abolishing them, after the Olympiad of 392 A.D.

That ended the Olympic Games after an uninterrupted span of over 1,100 years.

When Rome, including its province of Greece, was conquered by barbarians in 476 A.D., one of the first seizures was of the sacred statue of Zeus on Olympus. This was 60 feet tall, made of ivory and studded with gold bars. The barbarians took the statue as a trophy. Many years later it was destroyed in a fire.

An earthquake in the 6th Century wrecked the Stadium at Olympus and later a landslide buried the ruins under the dirt and stones to a depth of nearly 20 feet. In the 1870's German archaeologists began to remove the soil overlying the site of the ancient Games, and the task was completed in 1881.

A young French baron, Pierre de Coubertin of Paris, was responsible for the rebirth of the Olympic Games after a lapse of 15 centuries.

Motivated by a conviction that a better understanding among men of all nations would be a result of a revival of the Games on a world basis, de Coubertin, after several years of preliminary study and discussion, made his first formal Olympic Games proposal at a meeting of the Athletic Sports Union in Paris in 1892.

The baron's proposal did not gain an enthusiastic response. In fact, a less determined individual might have been discouraged sufficiently to discard his "dream."

However, at an athletic congress in 1894, to which came representatives of many countries, de Coubertin enlisted support for his program. Before the congress had disbanded, his dream became reality. The assembled delegates voted to celebrate the first modern Olympic Games in 1896 and chose, as a fitting site, the City of Athens, the capital of Greece.

Even at this point, de Coubertin had imposing obstacles to surmount. The financial burdens were huge and the citizens of Greece were without means to proceed with preparations for the Games. This problem was overcome when George Averoff, a merchant of Alexandria, Egypt, posted 1,000,000 drachmas to the credit of the Olympic Committee. Construction of a stadium on the outskirts of Athens followed and the stage was set for the Games in April, 1896.

The First U.S. Team

Not much publicity was given to the 1896 revival of the Olympics in the United States, the project being regarded as European. But the idea captivated a small group of American athletes, who decided to participate. Since there was no American Olympic Committee, there was no money for the trip.

However, Robert Garrett, a Princeton student, influenced three college mates to go along with him on the trip, Garrett supplying the money for expenses. The Princeton group was made up of Garrett, who had done some shot-putting and had performed in the jumps; Francis A. Lane, a sprinter; Herbert B. Jamison, a middle-distance man, and Albert C. Tyler, a pole vaulter.

James B. Connolly, a Harvard freshman, having heard of the plans, asked permission to go

along and paid his expenses. Meanwhile, Boston Athletic Association officials, learning that others wanted to compete, raised a fund to defray their expenses, and that is how Thomas Curtis, Thomas E. Burke, Ellery H. Clark, William W. Hoyt and Arthur Blake joined the American team, which set off for Europe and encountered a succession of difficulties before it arrived at Athens.

Clark, in later years, wrote a book, "Reminiscences of an Athlete," in which he detailed the excursion of the Americans. He explained that Blake, who was eager to get into the Games, had talked to Arthur Burnham, an influential member of the Boston A.A., and that Burnham had been instrumental in raising the money to send the Boston A.A. combination along with the Princeton group and Connolly. John B. Graham, coach at the club, was named to accompany the squad, acting as coach and manager.

The team sailed from New York on March 20, 1896, on a small tramp steamer, which did not usually carry passengers and whose only passengers on the journey were the American youngsters, who were unable to exercise in the cramped space. The ship arrived at Naples, Italy, about April 1, and then, and only then, did the young Americans come to realize that the Games were to start April 6, not the 18th, as they had supposed.

The date had been given out officially according to a Greek calendar, which differed from the American. The squad had fewer than five days to get from Naples into action at Athens, and the only way open was to take a miserable little boat, which was ready to sail from Naples to Patras, Greece. The athletes engaged passage and made Patras late at night on April 5. They had exactly 10 hours to get from there to Athens, and arrived just in time for the call of athletes for the first events, the trial heats of the 100-meter race.

The first final of a 12-event program was the hop, step and jump. All the entrants moved to the starting spot, and Connolly tagged along. He was asked who he was and he answered:

"Connolly of the United States."

Connolly went into competition with Europe's best and leaped 45 feet. It was better than anybody else could do and Connolly became the first Olympic Games champion to be crowned in 15 centuries.

The Americans, to the last man, were not in condition. The travel to Naples had cramped their muscles; the trip to Patras had given them no chance to unkink them. The all-night train ride to Athens had made things worse. But they put a man in 10 of the events and won 9 championships.

After Connolly's victory Garrett won the shotput and followed with a triumph in the discus throw. Hoyt, tall and slim, entered the pole vault. He outleaped everybody else, to give the United States its fourth straight championship. Clark won both the high jump and the broad jump. Burke was an easy winner in the 100 meters and the 400, while Curtis outsped his rivals in the 110-meter hurdles.

Blake made a try for the 800-meter title. He was off to a fine lead and held it until 100 meters from the finish. Then lack of training through the previous 17 days exacted its toll, Blake had to slow his pace and E.H. Black of England went on to victory. Blake ran in the marathon but collapsed after 15 miles.

The Americans passed up the 1,500 meters but with 9 victories in 10 tries piled up the most remarkable record in the entire history of track and field in the modern Olympic Games.

For the purpose of comparison here are the winning times—or distances—for the 12 track and field events which made up the 1896 Olympics, and the marks for the same events in the 1972 Games at Munich, Germany:

	1896	1972
100-meter dash .	12 seconds	10.1 seconds
400-meter run .	54.2 seconds	44.7 seconds
800-meter run .	2 min. 11 sec.	1 min. 45.9 sec.
1,500-meter run	4 min. 33.2 sec.	3 min. 36.3 sec.
Marathon	2 hr. 55 min. 20 sec.	2 hr. 12 min. 19.7 sec.
High Jump	5 ft. 11¼ in	7 ft. 3¾ in.
Pole Vault	10 ft. 9¾ in.	18 ft. ½ in.
Broad Jump . . .	20 ft. 9 ¾ in.	27 ft. ½ in.
Hop, Step, and Jump . . .	45 ft.	56 ft. 11 in.
Shot-Put	36 ft. 2 in.	69 ft. 6 in.
Discus	95 ft. 7½ in.	211 ft. 3½ in.

Recent History

The First World War prevented the holding of the Olympic Games in 1916. They were resumed in 1920, with Antwerp, Belgium, the locale. Paris followed as host in 1924 and Amsterdam, the Netherlands, entertained the athletes in 1928.

In 1932 nearly 2,500 athletes, representing more than 40 nations, competed in the Summer Games at Los Angeles and the Winter Games at Lake Placid, N.Y., as the United States conducted the program for the first time since 1904.

Four years later the Games shifted to Germany, where considerable energy was expended in making them the most fabulous in modern history. No expense was spared, no effort was too great to create for Germany the honor of having arranged the most stupendous of sport carnivals. The winter events were at Garmisch-Partenkirchen in the Bavarian Alps in February, 1936, and were highly successful. The summer contests were staged in Berlin. The Games were held in the Reich Sports Grounds, specially built for the occasion on a 325-acre plot. The stands had seating arrangements for 100,000.

Almost 4,000 athletes from 43 nations competed at Berlin after the torch to light the Olympic Flame in the arena was carried from Olympia, Greece, to Germany by a relay of more than 3,000 bearers. The Germans won the unofficial team title, but it remained for an American Negro, Jesse Owens, to put on one of the greatest individual performances ever recorded at the Games. Owens won three championships (100 and 200-meter dashes and broad jump) and gained a fourth gold medal as a member of America's winning 400-meter relay team.

The International Olympic Committee voted to hold the 1940 Winter Games at Garmisch-Partenkirchen, which would have given the German resort the honor of being the first to stage the contests twice, and the Summer Games were awarded to Tokyo, but World War II canceled the plans and prevented the 1944 Games.

The Games were resumed in 1948, with the summer program taking place in London, England, and the winter contests at St. Moritz, Switzerland. Little Finland performed a magnificent feat in taking care of the wants of nearly 6,000 athletes at Helsinki in 1952. Oslo, Norway, was the site of the winter competition.

In 1956, the Summer Games were held in the Southern Hemisphere for the first time, at Melbourne, Australia. With crowds of about 100,000 daily they were one of the most successful programs held. Warfare in Egypt and an uprising in Hungary reduced the field from a record 75 nations to 67. The equestrian competition was held in Stockholm, Sweden, and drew athletes from 69 countries. The Winter Games were held at Cortina d'Ampezzo, Italy.

The 1960 games were held at Rome, Italy, following the Winter Games at Squaw Valley, Calif.

Mexico City was the 1968 site with 114 nations competing.

Tragedy overshadowed the 1972 Games held at Munich, West Germany. Arab terrorists assassinated 11 members of the Israeli team. Despite widespread demands the Games be discontinued, Israel agreed with Olympic officials to resume competition the next day.

Although a limited ice skating program had been included in the Olympics of 1908 and 1920, the French Olympic Organizing Committee staged the first Winter Olympic Games at Chamonix in 1924, the year the Games proper were awarded to Paris. The Winter Games have been held regularly since.

The revived Olympic Games of 1896 were moderately successful, but not spectacular. Comparatively few nations sent contestants, because the idea was new and not altogether attractive in view of the fact that public-spirited citizens, chiefly, had to furnish the expense money for the athletes. Furthermore, with the exception of the United States and Great Britain, few countries had athletes sufficiently skilled in track and field events to hope for any degree of success.

However, as the idea was carried on, many European nations previously without representation in the Olympic Games, began to develop their young men in the technique of track and field competition. Gradually more nations took part, and the Finns, unknown in the 1896 Olympic Games, gained victories in various events so early as 1912.

As time went on, the Olympic program was greatly expanded from the 12-event program of 1896. Track and field events for the men reached close to 40 for the 1936 Olympiad, and, additionally, there were contests in rowing, swimming, boxing, fencing, cycling, wrestling, water polo, equestrian, gymnastics, hockey, soccer, pistol, revolver and rifle shooting, trapshooting, weight lifting, as well as contests or exhibitions, in art, literature, etc.

When winter sports were put on the program for the first time in 1924, the competition included speed and figure skating, skiing, hockey and bobsledding.

Women made their first appearance in the modern Olympics in 1912, confining themselves to diving and swimming. In 1928 they were privileged to compete among themselves in a special series of track and field events.

FAMOUS PERFORMERS
Men

The individual voted by American sports writers and broadcasters in an Associated Press poll as the outstanding United States athlete of the first half of the 20th Century did not fail to include Olympic triumphs among his many accomplishments. Nowhere in the Olympic records, however, are his deeds recorded.

He was Jim Thorpe, the Indian from Carlisle school, who won the decathlon and the pentathlon at the 1912 Games in Stockholm. Charges that Thorpe had violated his amateurism by playing semi-professional baseball prior to the Games were made later—and Thorpe was compelled to return his medals.

Before his death on March 28, 1953, several efforts were made to effect the return of Thorpe's medals to him but none of the movements took hold.

These were Thorpe's accomplishments at Stockholm in the pentathlon:

200-Meter Dash—First, 22.9 seconds.
1,500-Meter Run—First, 4 min. 44.8 sec.
Broad Jump—First, 23 ft. 2¼ in.
Discus—First, 116 ft. 8¼ in.
Javelin—Third, 153 ft. 2¾ in. Hugo Wieslander, Sweden, was first with 162 ft. 1 in.

Following is Thorpe's Olympic decathlon record:

100-Meter Dash—Two-way tie for third, 11.2 sec. Scott Jacobsson, Sweden, and Eugene Mercer, United States, tied for first with 11 sec.

400-Meter Run—Fourth, 52.2 sec. Eugene Mercer, United States, was first with 49.9 sec.
1,500-Meter Run—First, 4 min. 40.1 sec.
110-Meter Hurdles—First, 15.6 sec.
High Jump—First, 6 ft. 1½ in.
Shot Put—First, 42 ft. 3¼ in.
Discus—Third, 121 ft. 3¾ in. G.W. Philbroke, United States, was first with 136 ft. 4.2 in.
Pole Vault—Four-way tie for third, 10 ft. 7¾ in. Mercer was first with 11 ft. 9.7 in.
Broad Jump—Third, 22 ft. 3¼ in. C. Lomberg, Sweden, was first with 22 ft. 6.6 in.
Javelin—Fourth, 149 ft. 11 in. Wieslander first with 176 ft. 4.2 in.
Point scores—Thorpe 8,413, Wieslander 7,724, Holmer 7,348, Donahue 7,083.

Ray C. Ewry, a New Yorker, won more Olympic gold medals than any other competitor. In 1900 and 1904, he was the victor in the standing broad jump, the standing high jump and the standing hop, step and jump. In 1906 and 1908, he won the standing broad jump and the standing high jump for a total of 10 gold medals. Ewry's specialties no longer are a part of the Olympic program. Paavo Nurmi has the next best record. The Peerless Finn won seven track championships.

Swimmer Mark Spitz of California achieved seven gold medals in the 1972 games, more than any individual athlete in one session, setting 4 world records in the process.

Other outstanding United States track and field performers were Alvin C. Kraenzlein, Archie Hahn, Jim Lightbody, Harry Hillman, Paul Pilgrim, Martin Sheridan, Mel Sheppard, Pat McDonald, Matt McGrath, Ralph Craig, Charley Paddock, Ray Barbuti, Eddie Tolan, Jesse Owens, Harrison Dillard, Mal Whitfield, Mel Patton, Charles Moore Jr., Horace Ashenfelter, Jim Bausch, Bob Mathias, Bill Carr, John Woodruff, Johnny Hayes, Forrest Towns, Charles Bacon, F. Morgan Taylor, Glenn Hardin, Roy Cochran, Sabin Carr, Bob Richards, Earle Meadows, Leo Sexton, Ralph Rose, Ken Carpenter, Glenn Morris, Ted Meredith, Harold Osborn, Bobby Morrow and Parry O'Brien.

Finnish greats also included Hannes Kolehmainen, Willie Ritola, Lauri Lehtinen, A.O. Stenroos, Rolmari Iso-Hollo and Lasse Viren.

England had Harold Abrahams, Eric Liddell, Douglas Lowe, Tom Hampson and Lord David Burghley.

Stars from other countries were Emil Zatopek of Czechoslovakia, Arthur Wint and George Rhoden of Jamaica, W.J. Sherring, Bobby Kerr and Percy Williams of Canada, Luigi Beccali and Adolfo Consolini of Italy, Jack Lovelock of New Zealand, Gaston Reiff of Belgium, Juan Zabala and Delfo Cabrera of Argentina, Robert Tisdall, Patrick O'Callaghan and Ron Delany of Ireland, Joseph Barthel of Luxemburg, John Winter of Australia, E. Lemming and Arne Ahman of Sweden, Vladimir Kuts of Russia and Adhemar da Silva of Brazil, Kipchose Keino of Kenya and John Akii-Bua, Uganda.

Women

Mrs. Fanny Blankers-Koen of the Netherlands; Mildred Didrikson (Mrs. Zaharias), Helen Stephens, Elizabeth Robinson, Jean Shiley, Lillian Copeland, Alice Coachman and Mildred McDaniel of the United States; Micheline Ostermeyer of France; Marjorie Jackson, Mrs. Shirley Strickland de la Hunty and Betty Cethbert of Australia; Ethel Catherwood of Canada; Gisela Mauermayer of Germany and Yvette Williams of New Zealand.

Team Scoring

Although the Olympic fathers do not recognize point scoring by nations, heavy emphasis has been placed on this aspect of the Games by newspaper correspondents from all over the world who report the progress of the competition to their homelands.

De Coubertin, in establishing the modern Olympics, made it clear that his intent was to crown individuals, not nations.

Yet every four years much of the dramatic impact of the competition stems from the battle for unofficial team points. This point contest perhaps reached its heights at Helsinki in 1952 when Communist Russia participated for the first time. The team fight between the Soviet and the United States, leading exponents of opposing political philosophies, frequently stole newspaper headlines from the feats of individuals.

Generally accepted in the United States is a scoring system allotting 10 points to the winner of an event, 5 to the second-place contestant, 4 for third and 3, 2, 1 for fourth, fifth, and sixth.

Not until the next-to-last day of the 1952 Olympics did the United States clinch the "championship." The Games ended with the Americans scoring 614 points to Russia's 553½.

One valid criticism of this point-scoring system is that it gives equal weight to all events. The winner of an obscure event earns as many points for his country as does the 100-meter dash victor in track. Yet track and field is regarded as the principal reason for the Olympics. Without this sport on the program, it is unlikely the Olympics would continue to attract world-wide attention. Indeed, many authorities believe the Games would cease to exist without footracing.

The Olympic Oath

"We swear that we will take part in the Olympic Games in loyal competition, respecting the regulations which govern them and desirous of participating in them in the true spirit of sportsmanship for the honor of our country and for the glory of sport."

Sites of the Games

Year Summer	Winter
1896—Athens, Greece	
1900—Paris, France	
1904—St. Louis, Missouri	
1906—Athens, Greece	
1908—London, England	
1912—Stockholm, Sweden	
1916—Not held	
1920—Antwerp, Belgium	
1924—Paris, France	Chamonix, France
1928—Amsterdam, Holland	St. Moritz, Switzerland
1932—Los Angeles, California	Lake Placid, New York
1936—Berlin, Germany	Gamisch-Partenkirchen, Germany
1940—Not held	Not held
1944—Not held	Not held
1948—London, England	St. Moritz, Switzerland
1952—Helsinki, Finland	Oslo, Norway
1956—*Melbourne, Australia	Cortina d'Ampezzo, Italy
1960—Rome	Squaw Valley, Calif.
1964—Tokyo, Japan	Innsbruck, Austria
1968—Mexico City, Mexico	Grenoble, France
1972—Munich, Germany	Sapporo, Japan

*Because of Australia's quarantine on horses, the equestrian competition was held at Stockholm, Sweden.

Summer Games Competitors

Year and site	Entries
1896—Athens	484
1900—Paris	427
1904—St. Louis	595
1906—Athens	901
1908—London	2,082
1912—Stockholm	3,282
1920—Antwerp	2,741
1924—Paris	3,385
1928—Amsterdam	3,905
1932—Los Angeles	1,700
1936—Berlin	3,959
1948—London	6,000
1952—Helsinki	5,781
1956—Melbourne	*4,000
1964—Tokyo	*6,000
1968—Mexico City	*7,500
1972—Munich	*8,000

*Approximate.

Records and Champions

RECORDS
Track and Field—Men

Event	Record	Holder and country	Year	Where Made
100 meters	9.9s	Jim Hines, U.S.	1968	Mexico City
200 meters	19.8s	Tommie Smith, U.S.	1968	Mexico City
400 meters	43.8s	Lee Evans, U.S.	1968	Mexico City
800 meters	1m. 44.3s	Ralph Doubell, Australia	1968	Mexico City
1,500 meters	3m. 34.9s	Kipchoge Keino, Kenya	1968	Mexico City
5,000 meters	13m. 26.4s	Lasse Viren, Finland	1972	Munich
10,000 meters	27m. 38.4s	Lasse Viren, Finland	1972	Munich
Marathon	2h. 12m. 11.2s	Abebe Bikila, Ethiopia	1964	Tokyo
20,000-meter walk	1 hr. 26m. 42.45	Peter Frenkel, E. Germany	1972	Munich
50,000-meter walk	3 hr. 56m. 11.6s	Bernd Kannenberg, W. Germany	1972	Munich
110-meter hurdles	13.2s	Rod Milburn, U.S.	1972	Munich
400-meter hurdles	47.8s	John Akii–Bua, Uganda	1972	Munich
3,000-meter steeple chase	8m. 23.6s	Kipchoge Keino, Kenya	1972	Munich
400-meter relay	38.2s	United States (C. Green, M. Pender, R. Smith, J. Hines)	1968	Mexico City
	38.2s	United States (L. Black, R. Freeman, L. James, L. Evans)	1972	Munich
1,600-meter relay	2m. 56.1s	United States (V. Matthews, R. Freeman, L. James, L. Evans)	1968	Mexico City
High jump	7 ft. 4¼ in.	Dick Fosbury, U.S.	1968	Mexico City
Broad jump	29 ft. 2½ in.	Bob Beamon, U.S.	1968	Mexico City
Triple jump	57 ft. ¾ in.	Victor Saneyev, Russia	1968	Mexico City
Pole vault	18 ft. ½ in.	Wolfgang Nordwig, E. Germany	1972	Munich
Discus	212 ft. 6½ in.	Al Oerter, U.S.	1968	Mexico City
Javelin	296 ft. 10 in.	Klaus Wolferman, W. Germany	1972	Munich
16 lb. Shot-put	69 ft. 6 in.	Wladyslaw Komar, Poland	1972	Munich
16 lb. Hammer	247 ft. 8½ in.	Anatoli Bondarchuk, Russia	1972	Munich
Decathlon	8,454 pts.	Nikolai Avilov, Russia	1972	Munich

Track and Field—Women

Event	Record	Holder and country	Year	Where Made
100 meters	11.0s	Wilma Rudolph, U.S.	1960	Rome
		Wyomia Tyus, U.S.	1968	Mexico City
200 meters	22.4s	Renate Stecher, E. Germany	1972	Munich
400 meters	51.0s	Monika Zehrt, E. Germany	1972	Munich
800 meters	1m. 58.6s	Hildegard Falck, W. Germany	1972	Munich
80-meter hurdles	10.3s	Maureen Caird, Australia	1968	Mexico City
100-meter hurdles	12.6s	Annelie Ehrhardt, E. Germany	1972	Munich
400-meter relay	42.8s	United States (B. Ferrell, M. Bailes, M. Netter, W. Tyus)	1968	Mexico City
	42.8s	West Germany (C. Krause, I. Mickler, A. Richter, H. Rosendahl)	1972	Munich
High jump	6 ft. 2¾ in.	Iolanda Balas, Rumania	1964	Tokyo
Discus	218 ft. 7 in.	Faina Melnik, Russia	1972	Munich
Javelin	209 ft. 7 in.	Ruth Fuchs, E. Germany	1972	Munich
Broad jump	.22 ft. 4½ in.	V. Viscopoleanu, Romania	1968	Mexico City
Shot-Put	69 ft.	Nadezhda Chizhova, Russia	1972	Munich
Pentathlon	4,801 pts.	Mary Peters, Great Britain	1972	Munich

Swimming—Men

Event	Record	Holder and country	Year	Where Made
100-meter freestyle	51.2s	Mark Spitz, U.S.	1972	Munich
200-meter freestyle	1m. 52.8s	Mark Spitz, U.S.	1972	Munich
400-meter freestyle	4m. 00.3s*	Brad Cooper, Australia	1972	Munich

* (By disqualification of Rick DeMont, U.S.)

| 1,500-meter freestyle | 15m. 52.6s | Mike Burton, U.S. | 1972 | Munich |
| 100-meter backstroke | 56.6s | Roland Matthes, E. Germany | 1972 | Munich |

200-meter backstroke	2m. 02.8s	Roland Matthes, E. Germany	1972	Munich
100-meter breaststroke	1m. 04.9s	Nobutaka Taguchi, Japan	1972	Munich
200-meter breaststroke	2m. 21.5s	John Hencken,U.S.	1972	Munich
100-meter butterfly	54.3s	Mark Spitz, U.S.	1972	Munich
200-meter butterfly	2m. 00.7s	Mark Spitz, U.S.	1972	Munich
200-meter individual medley	2m. 07.2s	Gunnar Larsson, Sweden	1972	Munich
400-meter individual medley	4m. 32s	Gunnar Larsson, Sweden	1972	Munich
400-meter medley relay	3m. 48.2s	United States (M. Stamm, T. Bruce, M. Spitz, J. Heidenreich)	1972	Munich
400-meter freestyle relay	3m. 26.4s	United States (D. Edgar, J. Murphy J. Heidenreich, M. Spitz)	1972	Munich
800-meter freestyle relay	7m. 38.8s	United States (J. Kinsella, F. Tyler, S. Genter, M. Spitz)	1972	Munich

Swimming—Women

100-meter freestyle	58.6s	Sandra Neilson, U.S.	1972	Munich
200-meter freestyle	2m. 03.6s	Shane Gould, Australia	1972	Munich
400-meter freestyle	4m. 19.0s	Shane Gould, Australia	1972	Munich
800-meter freestyle	8m. 53.7s	Keena Rothhammer, U.S.	1972	Munich
100-meter backstroke	1m. 05.8s	Melissa Belote, U.S.	1972	Munich
200-meter backstroke	2m. 19.2s	Melissa Belote, U.S.	1972	Munich
100-meter breaststroke	1m. 13.6s	Cathy Carr, U.S.	1972	Munich
200-meter breaststroke	2m. 41.7s	Beverly Whitfield, Australia	1972	Munich
100-meter butterfly	1m. 03.3s	Mayumi Aoki, Japan	1972	Munich
200-meter butterfly	2m. 15.6s	Karen Moe, U.S.	1972	Munich
200-meter individual medley	2m. 23.1s	Shane Gould, Australia	1972	Munich
400-meter individual medley	5m. 03.0s	Gail Neall, Australia	1972	Munich
400-meter medley relay	4m. 20.7s	United States (M. Belote, C. Carr, D. Deardurff, S. Neilson)	1972	Munich
400-meter freestyle relay	3m. 55.2s	United States (S. Neilson, J. Kemp, J. Barkman, S. Babashoff)	1972	Munich

SUMMER GAMES CHAMPIONS, 1896–1972

Track and Field—Men
(Events on current Olympic program)

100-Meter Dash

1896—Thomas E. Burke, United States ... 12 s.
1900—F.W. Jarvis, United States .... 10.8s.
1904—Archie Hahn, United States .... 11 s.
1906—Archie Hahn, United States .... 11.2s.
1908—Reggie Walker, South Africa ...... 10.8s.
1912—Ralph C. Craig, United States ..... 10.8s.
1920—Charles W. Paddock, United States . 10.8s.
1924—Harold Abrahams, Great Britain ... 10.6s.
1928—Percy Williams, Canada .... 10.8s.
1932—Eddie Tolan, United States .... 10.3s.
1936—Jesse Owens, United States .... 10.3s.
1948—Harrison Dillard, United States .... 10.3s.
1952—Lindy Remigino, United States .... 10.4s.
1956—Bobby Morrow, United States ..... 10.5s.
1960—Armin Hary, Germany .... 10.2s.
1964—Robert Hayes, United States ...... 10.0s.
1968—Jim Hines, United States 9.9s
1972—Valeri Borzov, Russia .... 10.1s.

200-Meter Dash

1900—J.W.B. Tewksbury, United States .. 22.2s.
1904—Archie Hahn, United States .... 21.6s.
1908—Bobby Kerr, Canada .... 22.4s.
1912—Ralph C. Craig, United States ..... 21.7s.
1920—Allan Woodring, United States .... 22 s.
1924—Jackson V. Scholz, United States .. 21.6s.

1928—Percy Williams, Canada .... 21.8s.
1932—Eddie Tolan, United States .... 21.1s.
1936—Jesse Owens, United States .... 20.7s.
1948—Melvin E. Patton, United States .... 21.1s.
1952—Andy Stanfield, United States ..... 20.7s.
1956—Bobby Morrow, United States ..... 20.6s.
1960—Livio Berruti, Italy .... 20.5s.
1964—Henry Carr, United States .... 20.3s.
1968—Tommie Smith, United States 19.8s
1972—Valeri Borzov, Russia 20.0s

400-Meter Run

1896—Thomas E. Burke, United States ... 54.2s.
1900—Maxey Long, United States .... 49.4s.
1904—Harry Hillman, United States ...... 49.2s.
1906—Paul Pilgrim, United States .... 53.2s.
1908—Wyndham Halswelle, Great Britain (walkover) .... 50 s.
1912—Charles Reidpath, United States ... 48.2s.
1920—Bevil Rudd, South Africa .... 49.6s.
1924—Eric Liddell, Great Britain .... 47.6s.
1928—Ray Barbuti, United States .... 47.8s.
1932—William A. Carr, United States ..... 46.2s.
1936—Archie Williams, United States .... 46.5s.
1948—Arthur Wint, Jamaica .... 46.2s.
1952—George Rhoden, Jamaica .... 45.9s.
1956—Charley Jenkins, United States .... 46.7s.
1960—Otis Davis, United States .... 44.9s.
1964—Michael Larrabee, United States ... 45.1s.
1968—Lee Evans, United States .... 43.8s.
1972—Vincent Matthews, United States .. 44.7s.

800-Meter Run

1896—E.H. Flack, Great Britain 2:11
1900—A.E. Tysoe, Great Britain 2:01.4
1904—Jim D. Lightbody, United States . 1:56
1906—Paul Pilgrim, United States 2:01.2
1908—Mel Sheppard, United States 1:52.8
1912—Ted Meredith, United States 1:51.9
1920—A.G. Hill, Great Britain 1:53.4
1924—Douglas Lowe, Great Britain 1:52.4
1928—Douglas Lowe, Great Britain 1:51.8
1932—Tom Hampson, Great Britain . . . 1:49.8
1936—John Woodruff, United States . . . 1:52.9
1948—Mal Whitfield, United States 1:49.2
1952—Mal Whitfield, United States 1:49.2
1956—Tom Courtney, United States . . . 1:47.7
1960—Peter Snell, New Zealand 1:46.3
1964—Peter Snell, New Zealand 1:45.1
1968—Ralph Doubell, Australia 1:44.3
1972—Dave Wottle, United States 1:45.9

1,500-Meter Run

1896—E.H. Flack, Great Britain 4:33.2
1900—C. Bennett, Great Britain 4:06
1904—Jim D. Lightbody, United States . 4:05.4
1906—Jim D. Lightbody, United States . 4:12
1908—Mel Sheppard, United States 4:03.4
1912—Arnold Jackson, Great Britain . . . 3:56.8
1920—A.G. Hill, Great Britain 4:01.8
1924—Paavo Nurmi, Finland 3:53.6
1928—Harry Larva, Finland 3:53.2
1932—Luigi Beccali, Italy 3:51.1
1936—Jack Lovelock, New Zealand 3:47.8
1948—Henri Eriksson, Sweden 3:49.8
1952—Joseph Barthel, Luxemburg 3:45.2
1956—Ron Delany, Ireland 3:41.2
1960—Herbert Elliott, Australia 3:35.6
1964—Peter Snell, New Zealand 3:38.1
1968—Kipchoge Keino, Kenya 3:34.9
1972—Pekka Vasala, Finland 3:36.3

5,000-Meter Run

1912—Hannes Kolehmainen, Finland . . . 14:36.6
1920—Joseph Guillemot, France 14:55.6
1924—Paavo Nurmi, Finland 14:31.2
1928—Willie Ritola, Finland 14:38
1932—Lauri Lehtinen, Finland 14:30
1936—Gunnar Hoeckert, Finland 14:22.2
1948—Gaston Reiff, Belgium 14:17.6
1952—Emil Zatopek, Czechoslovakia . . . 14:06.6
1956—Vladimir Kuts, Russia 13:39.6
1960—Murray Halberg, New Zealand . . . 13:43.4
1964—Robert Schul, United States 13:48.8
1968—Mohamed Gammoudi, Tunisia . . . 14:05.0
1972—Lasse Viren, Finland 13:26.4

10,000-Meter Run

1912—Hannes Kolehmainen, Finland . . . 31:20.8
1920—Paavo Nurmi, Finland 31:45.8
1924—Willie Ritola, Finland 30:23.2
1928—Paavo Nurmi, Finland 30:18.8
1932—Janusz Kusocinski, Poland 30:11.4
1936—Ilmari Salminen, Finland 30:15.4
1948—Emil Zatopek, Czechoslovakia . . . 29:59.6
1952—Emil Zatopek, Czechoslovakia . . . 29:17
1956—Vladimir Kuts, Russia 28:45.6
1960—Petr Bolotnikov, Russia 28:32.2
1964—William Mills, United States 28:24.4
1968—Naftali Temu, Kenya 29:27.4
1972—Lasse Viren, Finland 27:38.4

Marathon

1896—Spiridon Loues, Greece 2:55:20
1900—Michel Teato, France 2:59
1904—T.J. Hicks, United States 3:28:53
1906—W.J. Sherring, Canada 2:51:23.6
1908—John J. Hayes, United States . . . 2:55:18
1912—K.K. McArthur, South Africa . . 2:36:54.8
1920—Hannes Kolehmainen, Finland . . 2:32:35.8
1924—A.O. Stenroos, Finland 2:41:22.6
1928—El Ouafi, France 2:32:57
1932—Juan Zabala, Argentina 2:31:36
1936—Kitei Son, Japan 2:29:19.2
1948—Delfo Cabrera, Argentina 2:34:51.6
1952—Emil Zatopek, Czechoslovakia . . 2:23:03.2
1956—Alain Mimoun, France 2:25
1960—Bekele Abebe, Ethiopia 2:15:16.2
1964—Bekele Abebe, Ethiopia 2:12:11.2
1968—Mamo Wolde, Ethiopia 2:20:26.4
1972—Frank Shorter, United States . . . 2:12:19.7

110-Meter Hurdles

1896—Tom Curtis, United States . . . . 17.6s.
1900—Alvin Kraenzlein, United States . . . . 15.4s.
1904—F.W. Schule, United States . . . . 16 s.
1906—R.G. Leavitt, United States . . . . 16.2s.
1908—Forrest Smithson, United States . . . 15.0s.
1912—F.W. Kelly, United States . . . . 15.1s.
1920—Earl Thomson, Canada . . . . 14.8s.
1924—D.C. Kinsey, United States . . . . 15.0s.
1928—Sam Atkinson, South Africa . . . . . . 14.8s.
1932—George Saling, United States . . . . . 14.6s.
1936—Forrest Towns, United States . . . . . 14.2s.
1948—William Porter, United States . . . . . 13.9s.
1952—Harrison Dillard, United States . . . . 13.7s.
1956—Lee Calhoun, United States . . . . . . 13.5s.
1960—Lee Calhoun, United States . . . . . . 13.8s.
1964—Hayes Jones, United States . . . . . . 13.6s.
1968—Willie Davenport, United States . . . 13.3s.
1972—Rod Milburn, United States . . . . . . 13.2s.

400-Meter Hurdles

1900—J.W.B. Tewksbury, United States . . 57.6s.
1904—Harry Hillman, United States . . . . . 53.0s.
1908—Charles Bacon, United States . . . . . 55.0s.
1920—Frank Loomis, United States . . . . . 54.0s.
1924—F. Morgan Taylor, United States . . 52.6s.
1928—Lord David Burghley, Great Britain . 53.4s.
1932—Robert Tisdall, Ireland . . . . 51.8s.
1936—Glenn Hardin, United States . . . . . 52.4s.
1948—Roy Cochran, United States . . . . . 51.1s.
1952—Charles Moore Jr., United States . . 50.8s.
1956—Glenn Davis, United States . . . . . . 50.1s.
1960—Glenn Davis, United States . . . . . . 49.3s.
1964—Warren Jay Cowley, United States . 49.6s.
1968—Dave Hemery, Great Britain . . . . . 48.1s.
1972—John Akii-Bua, Uganda . . . . 47.8s.

3,000-Meter Steeplechase

1920—P. Hodge, Great Britain 10:02.4
1924—Willie Ritola, Finland 9:33.6
1928—Toivo Loukola, Finland 9:33.6
1932—Volmari Iso-Hollo, Finland *10:33.4
1936—Volmari Iso-Hollo, Finland 9:03.8
1948—Thure Sjoistrand, Sweden 9:04.6
1952—Horace Ashenfelter, United States 8:45.4
1956—Chris Brasher, Great Britain 8:41.2
1964—Gaston Roelants, Belgium 8:30.8
1968—Amos Biwott, Kenya 8:51.0
1972—Kipchoge Keino, Kenya 8:23.6
*Ran extra lap by mistake

20,000-Meter Walk

1956—Leonid Spirine, Russia 1:31:27.4
1960—Vladimir Golubnichiy, Russia . . . 1:34:07.2
1964—Kenneth Mathews, Great Britain . 1:29:34.0
1968—Vladimir Golubnichiy, Russia . . . 1:35:58.4
1972—Peter Frenkel, E. Germany 1:26:42.4

50,000-Meter Walk

1932—T.W. Green, Great Britain 4:50:10
1936—Harold Whitlock, Great Britain . . 4:30:41.4
1948—John Ljunggren, Sweden 4:41:52
1952—Guiseppe Bordoni, Italy 4:28:07.8
1956—Norman Read, New Zealand 4:30:42.8
1960—Donald Thompson, Great Britain 4:25:30.0
1964—Abdon Pamich, Italy 4:11:12.4
1968—Christoph Hohne, E. Germany . . 4:20:13.6
1972—Bernd Kannenberg, W. Germany . 3:56:11.6

400-Meter Relay

1912—Great Britain . . . . 42.4s.
1920—United States . . . . 42.2s.
1924—United States . . . . 41.0s.
1928—United States . . . . 41.0s.
1932—United States . . . . 40.0s.
1936—United States . . . . 39.8s.
1948—United States . . . . 40.6s.
1952—United States . . . . 40.1s.
1956—United States . . . . 39.5s.
1960—Germany 39.5*
1964—United States . . . . 39.0s.
1968—United States . . . . 38.2s.
1972—United States . . . . 38.2s.
(* U.S. team finished first in 39.4 but was disqualified for passing baton outside legal zone.)

1,600-Meter Relay

1908—United States 3:27.2
1912—United States 3:16.6
1920—Great Britain 3:22.2
1924—United States 3:16
1928—United States 3:14.2
1932—United States 3:08.2
1936—Great Britain 3:09
1948—United States 3:10.4
1952—Jamaica, B.W.I. 3:03.2
1956—United States 3:04.8
1960—United States 3:02.2
1964—United States 3:00.7
1968—United States 2:56.1
1972—Kenya 2:59.8

Running High Jump

1896—Ellery Clark, United States .5 ft. 11 1/4 in.
1900—I. K. Baxter, United States . . .6 ft. 2 4/5 in.
1904—Sam Jones, United States . . . . . .5 ft. 11 in.
1906—Con Leahy, Ireland . . . . .5 ft. 9 7/8 in.
1908—H. F. Porter, United States . . . . . .6 ft. 3 in.
1912—Alma Richards, United States . . .6 ft. 3 in.
1920—Dick Landon, United States . .6 ft. 4 1/4 in.
1924—Harold Osborn,
    United States . . . . .6 ft. 5 15/16 in.
1928—Robert W. King,
    United States . . . . .6 ft. 4 3/8 in.
1932—D. McNaughton, Canada . . . .6 ft. 5 5/8 in.
1936—Cornelius Johnson, United
    States . . . . .6 ft. 7 15/16 in.
1948—John Winter, Australia . . . . .6 ft. 6 in.
1952—Walter Davis, United States . . 6 ft. 8.32 in.
1956—Charley Dumas,
    United States . . . . .6 ft. 11 1/4 in.
1960—Robert Shavlakadze, Russia . . . . .7 ft. 1 in.
1964—Valer Brumel, Russia . . . . . .7 ft. 1 3/4 in.
1968—Dick Fosbury, United States .7 ft. 4 1/4 in.
1972—Yuri Tarmak, Russia . . . . . . .7 ft. 3 3/4 in.

Running Broad Jump

1896—Ellery Clark, United States .20 ft. 9 3/4 in.
1900—Alvin Kraenzlein, United
    States . . . . .23 ft. 6 7/8 in.
1904—Myer Prinstein, United States . .24 ft. 1 in.
1906—Myer Prinstein, United
    States . . . . .23 ft. 7 1/2 in.
1908—Frank Irons, United States . .24 ft. 6 1/2 in.
1912—A. L. Gutterson, United
    States . . . . .24 ft. 11 1/4 in.
1920—William Petterssen, Sweden .23 ft. 5 1/2 in.
1924—DeHart Hubbard, United
    States . . . . .24 ft. 5 1/8 in.
1928—Edward B. Hamm, United
    States . . . . .25 ft. 4 3/4 in.
1932—Edward Gordon,
    United States . . . . 25 ft. 3/4 in.
1936—Jesse Owens,
    United States . . . . .26 ft. 5 21/64 in.
1948—Willie Steele,
    United States . . . . .25 ft. 8 in.
1952—Jerome Biffle,
    United States . . . . 24 ft. 10.03 in.
1956—Gregory Bell,
    United States . . . . .20 ft. 8 1/4 in.
1960—Ralph Boston,
    United States . . . . .26 ft. 7 3/4 in.
1964—Lynn Davies,
    Great Britain . . . . .26 ft. 5 3/4 in.
1968—Bob Beamon,
    United States . . . . .29 ft. 2 1/2 in.
1972—Randy Williams,
    United States . . . . 27 ft. 1/2 in.

Pole Vault

1896—William W. Hoyt,
    United States . . . . .10 ft. 9 3/4 in.
1900—I. K. Baxter,
    United States . . . . .10 ft. 9 9/10 in.

1904—C.E. Dvorak, United States .... 11 ft. 6 in.
1906—Gouder, France .... 11 ft. 6 in.
1908—A.C. Gilbert, United States .... 12 ft. 2 in.
　　　E.T. Cook Jr., United States ... 12 ft. 2 in.
1912—H. J. Babcock,
　　　United States .... 12 ft. 11 1/2 in.
1920—Frank Foss, United States ..... 13 ft. 5 in.
1924—Lee Barnes,
　　　United States .... 12 ft. 11 1/2 in.
　　　Glenn Graham,
　　　United States .... 12 ft. 11 1/2 in.
1928—Sabin W. Carr,
　　　United States .... 13 ft. 9 3/8 in.
1932—William Miller,
　　　United States .... 14 ft. 1 7/8 in.
1936—Earle Meadows,
　　　United States .... 14 ft. 3 1/4 in.
1948—Guinn Smith,
　　　United States .... 14 ft. 1 1/4 in.
1952—Robert Richards,
　　　United States .... 14 ft. 11.14 in.
1956—Robert Richards,
　　　United States .... 14 ft. 11 1/2 in.
1960—Donald Bragg,
　　　United States .... 15 ft. 5 1/8 in.
1964—Fred M. Hansen,
　　　United States .... 16 ft. 8 3/4 in.
1968—Bob Seagren,
　　　United States .... 17 ft. 8 1/2 in.
1972—Wolfgang Nordwig,
　　　E. Germany .... 18 ft. 1/2 in.

16-Lb. Shot-Put

1896—Robert Garrett, United States .. 36 ft. 2 in.
1900—Richard Sheldon,
　　　United States .... 46 ft. 3 1/8 in.
1904—Ralph Rose, United States ..... 48 ft. 7 in.
1906—Martin Sheridan,
　　　United States .... 40 ft. 4 4/5 in.
1908—Ralph Rose,
　　　United States .... 46 ft. 7 1/2 in.
1912—Pat McDonald, United States ... 50 ft. 4 in.
1920—Willie Porhola, Finland .... 48 ft. 7 1/8 in.
1924—Clarence Houser,
　　　United States .... 49 ft. 2 1/2 in.
1928—John Kuck,
　　　United States .... 52 ft. 11/16 in.
1932—Leo Sexton,
　　　United States .... 52 ft. 6 3/16 in.
1936—Hans Woellke,
　　　Germany .... 53 ft. 1 13/16 in.
1948—Wilbur Thompson,
　　　United States .... 56 ft. 2 in.
1952—Parry O'Brien,
　　　United States .... 57 ft. 1.43 in.
1956—Parry O'Brien, United States .. 60 ft. 11 in.
1960—William Nieder,
　　　United States .... 64 ft. 6 3/4 in.
1964—Dallas C. Long,
　　　United States .... 66 ft. 8 1/4 in.
1968—Randy Matson,
　　　United States .... 67 ft. 4 3/4 in.

1972—Wladyslaw Komar,
　　　Poland .... 69 ft. 6 in.

Discus Throw

1896—Robert Garrett,
　　　United States .... 95 ft. 7 1/2 in.
1900—Rudolph Bauer,
　　　Hungary .... 118 ft. 2 9/10 in.
1904—Martin Sheridan,
　　　United States .... 128 ft. 10 1/2 in.
1906—Martin Sheridan,
　　　United States .... 136 ft. 2/3 in.
1908—Martin Sheridan,
　　　United States .... 134 ft. 2 in.
1912—A. R. Taipale, Finland ..... 148 ft. 3.9 in.
1920—E. Niklander, Finland .... 146 ft. 7 in.
1924—Clarence Houser,
　　　United States .... 151 ft. 5 1/4 in.
1928—Clarence Houser,
　　　United States .... 155 ft. 2 4/5 in.
1932—John Anderson,
　　　United States .... 162 ft. 4 7/8 in.
1936—Kenneth Carpenter,
　　　United States .... 165 ft. 7 29/64 in.
1948—Adolfo Consolini, Italy ...... 173 ft. 2 in.
1952—Simeon Iness,
　　　United States .... 180 ft. 6.85 in.
1956—Al Oerter, United States .... 184 ft. 11 in.
1960—Al Oerter, United States .... 194 ft. 2 in.
1964—Al Oerter, United States .. 200 ft. 1 1/2 in.
1968—Al Oerter, United States .. 212 ft. 6 1/2 in.
1972—Ludvik Danek,
　　　Czechoslovakia .... 211 ft. 3 1/2 in.

Javelin Throw

1906—E. Lemming, Sweden .... 175 ft. 6 in.
1908—E. Lemming, Sweden .... 179 ft. 10 1/2 in.
1912—E. Lemming, Sweden .... 198 ft. 11 1/4 in.
1920—Jonni Myyra, Finland .... 215 ft. 9 3/4 in.
1924—Jonni Myyra, Finland .... 205 ft. 6 3/4 in.
1928—E. H. Lundquist,
　　　Sweden .... 218 ft. 6 1/8 in.
1932—Matti Jarvinen, Finland ... 238 ft. 6 1/8 in.
1936—Gerhard Stoeck,
　　　Germany .... 235 ft. 8 13/32 in.
1948—Kaj. Rautavaara,
　　　Finland .... 228 ft. 10 1/2 in.
1952—Cy Young, United States .. 242 ft. 0.78 in.
1956—Egil Danielsen, Norway ... 281 ft. 2 1/4 in.
1960—Viktor Cybulenko,
　　　Russia .... 277 ft. 8 3/8 in.
1964—Pauli Nevala, Finland ..... 271 ft. 2 1/4 in.
1968—Yanis Lusis, Russia ...... 295 ft. 7 1/4 in.
1972—Klaus Wolferman,
　　　W. Germany .... 296 ft. 10 in.

16-Lb. Hammer Throw

1900—John Flanagan,
　　　United States .... 167 ft. 4 in.
1904—John Flanagan,
　　　United States .... 170 ft. 4 1/4 in.
1908—John Flanagan,
　　　United States .... 170 ft. 4 1/4 in.

1912—Matt McGrath,
United States ....177 ft. 7 in.
1920—Pat Ryan, United States ...173 ft. 5 5/8 in.
1924—Fred Tootell,
United States ....174 ft. 10 1/4 in.
1928—Patrick O'Callaghan,
Ireland ....168 ft. 7 1/2 in.
1932—Patrick O'Callaghan,
Ireland ....176 ft. 11 1/8 in.
1936—Karl Hein, Germany ....185 ft. 4 1/16 in.
1948—Imre Nemeth, Hungary ..183 ft. 11 1/2 in.
1952—Josef Csarmak, Hungary . 197 ft. 11.67 in.
1956—Harold Connolly,
United States ....207 ft. 3 1/2 in.
1956—Harold Connolly,
United States ....207 ft. 3 1/2 in.
1960—Vasiliy Rudenkov,
Russia ....220 ft. 1 5/8 in.
1964—Romuald Klim, Russia ....228 ft. 9 1/2 in.
1968—Gyula Zsivotsky, Hungary ....240 ft. 8 in.
1972—Anatoli Bondarchuk,
Russia ....247 ft. 8 1/2 in.

Triple Jump

1896—James B. Connolly, United States .. 45 ft.
1900—Myer Prinstein,
United States ....47 ft. 4 1/4 in.
1904—Myer Prinstein,
United States .... 47 ft.
1906—P. O'Connor, Ireland ....46 ft. 2 in.
1908—T. J. Ahearne,
Great Britain ....48 ft. 11 1/4 in.
1912—G. Lindblom, Sweden .....48 ft. 5 1/8 in.
1920—V. Tuulos, Finland ....47 ft. 6 7/8 in.
1924—A. W. Winter, Australia ...50 ft. 11 1/8 in.
1928—Mikio Oda, Japan .....49 ft. 10 13/16 in.
1932—Chuhei Nambu, Japan ....51 ft. 7 in.
1936—Naoto Tajima, Japan .....52 ft. 5 5/16 in.
1948—Arne Ahman, Sweden ....50 ft. 6 1/4 in.
1952—Adhemar da Silva, Brazil ... 53 ft. 2.59 in.
1956—Adhemar da Silva, Brazil ...53 ft. 7 1/2 in.
1960—Jozef Schmidt, Poland ....55 ft. 1 3/4 in.
1964—Jozef Schmidt, Poland .....55 ft. 3 1/2 in.
1968—Victor Saneyev, Russia ..... 57 ft. 3/4 in.
1972—Victor Saneyev, Russia ......56 ft. 11 in.

Decathlon

1912—Hugo Wieslander, Sweden ... 7,724.495
1920—H. Loveland, Norway 6,804.35
1924—Harold Osborn, United States 7,710.775
1928—Paavo Yrjola, Finland 8,053.29
1932—James Bausch, United States . 8,462.235
1936—Glenn Morris, United States ..*7,900
1948—Bob Mathias, United States ..*7,139
1952—Bob Mathias, United States ..†7,887
1956—Milton Campbell, United
States 7,937
1960—Rafer Johnson, United States . 8,392
1964—Willi Holdorf, Germany 7,887
1968—Bill Toomey, United States .. 8,193
1972—Nikolai Avilor, Russia 8,454

*Scoring system revised. †Scoring System Revised
again.

Modern Pentathlon

1952—Lars Hall, Sweden 32
1956—Lars Hall, Sweden 4,833
1960—Ferenc Nemeth, Hungary 5,024
1964—Ferenc Nemeth, Hungary 5,116
1968—Bjoern Ferm, Sweden 4,964
1972—Andras Balczo, Hungary 5,412

Track and Field—Men
(Discontinued events)

60-Meter Run

1900—Alvin Kraenzlein, United States.... 7s
1904—Archie Hahn, United States .... 7s.

5-Mile Run

1906—H. Hawtrey, Great Britain 26:11.8
1908—E.R. Voight, Great Britain 25:11.2

200-Meter Hurdles

1900—Alvin Kraenzlein, United States . 25.4s.
1904—Harry Hillman, United States ... 24.6s.

2,500-Meter Steeplechase

1900—George Orton, United States.... 7:34
1904—Jim D. Lightbody, United States 7:36.9

3,200-Meter Steeplechase

1908—A. Russell, Great Britain 10:47.8

4,000-Meter Steeplechase

1900—C. Rimmer, Great Britain 12:58.4

3,000-Meter Team Race

1912—United States .... 9 pts.
1920—United States .... 10 pts.
1924—Finland .... 8 pts.

3-Mile Team Race

1908—Great Britain .... 6 pts.

5,000-Meter Team Race

1900—Great Britain .... 26 pts.

8,000-Meter Cross-Country

1912—Hannes Kolehmainen, Finland .. 45:11.6

8,000-Meter Cross-Country, Team

1912—Sweden .... 10 pts.

10,000-Meter Cross-Country

1920—Paavo Nurmi, Finland *27:15
1924—Paavo Nurmi, Finland 32.54.8
*Error in distance.

10,000-Meter Cross-Country, Team

1920—Finland .... 10 pts.
1924—Finland .... 11 pts.

1,500-Meter Walk

1906—George V. Bonhag, United States 7:12.6

3,000-Meter Walk

1920—Ugo Frigerio, Italy 13:14.2

3,500-Meter Walk

1908—G.E. Larner, Great Britain 14:55

10,000-Meter Walk

1912—George Goulding, Canada 46:28.4
1920—Ugo Frigerio, Italy 48:06.2
1924—Ugo Frigerio, Italy 47:49.0

1948—John Mikaelsson, Sweden 45:13.2
1952—John Mikaelsson, Sweden 45:02.8

10-Mile Walk

1908—G.E. Larner, Great Britain 1:15:57.4

Standing High Jump

1900—Ray C. Ewry, United States .....5 ft. 5 in.
1904—Ray C. Ewry, United States ...4 ft. 11 in.
1906—Ray C. Ewry, United States ..5 ft. 1 5/8 in.
1908—Ray C. Ewry, United States .....5 ft. 2 in.
1912—Platt Adams, United States ..5 ft. 4 1/8 in.

Standing Broad Jump

1900—Ray C. Ewry, United States .10 ft. 6 2/5 in.
1904—Ray C. Ewry, United States .11 ft. 4 7/8 in.
1906—Ray C. Ewry, United States ...10 ft. 10 in.
1908—Ray C. Ewry, United States 10 ft. 11 1/4 in.
1912—C. Tsicilitiras, Greece .... 11 ft. 1/4 in.

Standing Hop, Step and Jump

1900—Ray C. Ewry, United States .34 ft. 8 1/2 in.
1904—Ray C. Ewry, United States .34 ft. 7 1/4 in.

16-lb. Shot Put—Both Hands

1912—Ralph Rose, United States 90 ft. 10 9/16 in.

Discus Throw—Both Hands

1912—A. R. Taipale, Finland ....271 ft. 1 1/8 in.

Discus Throw—Greek Style

1906—W. Jaervinen, Finland ....115 ft. 4 in.
1908—Martin Sheridan, United States 124 ft. 8 in.

Javelin Throw—Free Style

1908—E. Lemming, Sweden .....178 ft. 7 1/2 in.

Javelin Throw—Both Hands

1912—J. J. Saaristo, Finland ...358 ft. 11 1/2 in.

56-Lb. Weight Throw

1904—E. Desmarteau, Canada ....34 ft. 4 in.
1920—Pat McDonald,
    United States ....36 ft. 11 5/8 in.

All-Around Championship

1904—T.P. Kiely, Great Britain ..... 6,036 pts.

Pentathlon

1906—H. Mellander, Sweden .... 24 pts.
1912—F.R. Bie, Norway .... 16 pts.
1920—E.R. Lehtonen, Finland .... 18 pts.
1924—E.R. Lehtonen, Finland .... 14 pts.

Track and Field—Women

100-Meter Dash

1928—Elizabeth Robinson, United
    States .... 12.2s.
1932—Stella Walsh, Poland .... 11.9s.
1936—Helen Stephens, United States .. 11.5s.
1948—Fanny Blankers-Koen,
    Netherlands .... 11.9s.
1952—Marjorie Jackson, Australia ..... 11.5s.
1956—Betty Cuthbert, Australia .... 11.5s.
1960—Wilma Rudolph, United States .. 11.0s.
1964—Wyomia Tyus, United States .... 11.4s.
1968—Wyomia Tyus, United States .... 11.0s.
1972—Renate Stecher, E. Germany .... 11.1s.

200-Meter Dash

1948—Fanny Blankers-Koen,
    Netherlands .... 24.4s.
1952—Marjorie Jackson, Australia ..... 23.7s.
1956—Betty Cuthbert, Australia ...... 23.4s.
1960—Wilma Rudolph, United States .. 24.0s.
1964—Edith McGuire, United States ... 23.0s.
1968—Irene Szewinska, Poland .... 22.5s.
1972—Renate Stecher, E. Germany .... 22.4s.

400-Meter Dash

1964—Betty Cuthbert, Australia ...... 52.0s.
1968—Colette Besson, France .... 52.0s.
1972—Monika Zehrt, E. Germany ..... 51.0s.

800-Meter Run

1928—Linda Radke, Germany 2:16.8
1960—Ljudmila Shevcova, Russia 2:04.3
1964—Ann Packer, Great Britain 2:01.1
1968—Madeline Manning, United States 2:00.9
1972—Hildegard Falck, W. Germany ... 1:58.6

1,500-Meter Run

1972—Ludmila Bragina, Russia 4:01.4

80-Meter Hurdles

1932—Mildred Didrikson, United States 11.7s.
1936—Trebisonda Villa, Italy .... 11.7s.
1948—Fanny Blankers-Koen,
    Netherlands .... 11.2s.
1952—Shirley Strickland de la Hunty,
    Australia .... 10.9s.
1956—Shirley Strickland, Australia .... 10.7s.
1960—Irina Press, Russia .... 10.8s.
1964—Karin Balzer, Germany .... 10.5s.
1968—Maureen Caird, Australia ...... 10.3s.

100-Meter Hurdles

1972—Annelle Ehrhardt, E. Germany .. 12.6s.

400-Meter Relay

1928—Canada .... 48.4s.
1932—United States .... 47 s.
1936—United States .... 46.9s.
1948—Netherlands .... 47.5s.
1952—United States .... 45.9s.
1956—Australia .... 44.5s.
1960—United States .... 44.5s.
1964—Poland .... 43.6s.
1968—United States .... 42.8s.
1972—West Germany .... 42.8s.

1,600-Meter Relay

1972—East Germany 3:23.0

Running High Jump

1928—Ethel Catherwood, Canada .....5 ft. 3 in.
1932—Jean Shiley, United States ...5 ft. 5 1/4 in.
1936—Ibolya Csak, Hungary ....5 ft. 3 in.
1948—Alice Coachman,
    United States ....5 ft. 6 1/8 in.
1952—Esther Brand, South Africa .. 5ft. 5 3/4 in.
1956—Mildred McDaniel,
    United States ....5 ft. 9 1/4 in.

1960—Iolanda Balas, Russia . . . . 6 ft. 3/4 in.
1963—Iolanda Balas, Rumania . . . . .6 ft. 2 3/4 in.
1968—Miloslava Reskova,
Czechoslovakia . . . . .5 ft. 11 3/4 in.
1972—Uirke Meyfarth,
W. Germany . . . . .6 ft. 2 3/4 in.

Running Broad Jump

1948—Olga Gyarmati, Hungary . . .18 ft. 8 1/4 in.
1952—Yvette Williams,
New Zealand . . . . 20 ft. 5.66 in.
1956—Elzbieta Krzesinska,
Poland . . . . .20 ft. 9 3/4 in.
1960—Vyera Krepkina, Russia . . .20 ft. 10 3/4 in.
1964—Mary Rand, Great Britain . . . . .22 ft. 2 in.
1968—V. Viscopoleanu,
Rumania . . . . .22 ft. 4 1/2 in.
1972—Heidemarie Rosendahl,
W. Germany . . . . .22 ft. 3 in.

Shot Put

1948—Micheline Ostermeyer,
France . . . . .45 ft. 1 1/2 in.
1952—Galina Zybina, Russia . . . . . 50 ft. 2.58 in.
1958—Tamara Tychkevitch, Russia . . .54 ft. 5 in.
1960—Tamara Press, Russia . . . . . .56 ft. 9 7/8 in.
1964—Tamara Press, Russia . . . . .59 ft. 6 in.
1968—Margitta Gummel, E. Germany .64 ft. 4 in.
1972—Nadezhda Chizhova, Russia . . .69 ft. 0 in.

Discus Throw

1928—H. Konopacka, Poland . . .129 ft. 11 7/8 in.
1932—Lillian Copeland,
United States . . . . .133 ft. 2 in.
1936—Gisela Mauermayer,
Germany . . . . .156 ft. 3 3/36 in.
1948—Micheline Ostermeyer,
France . . . . .137 ft. 6 1/2 in.
1952—Nina Romaschkova,
Russia . . . . .168 ft. 8 1/2 in.
1956—Olga Fikotova,
Czechoslovakia . . . . .176 ft. 1 1/2 in.
1960—Nina Ponomareva, Russia .180 ft. 8 1/4 in.
1964—Tamara Press, Russia . . . .187 ft. 10 3/4 in.
1968—Lia Manolin, Rumania . . . .191 ft. 2 1/2 in.
1972—Faina Melnik, Russia . . . . .218 ft. 7 in.

Javelin Throw

1932—Mildred Didrikson,
United States . . . . .143 ft. 4 in.
1936—Tilly Fleischer, Germany . .148 ft. 2 3/4 in.
1948—H. Baume, Austria . . . . .149 ft. 6 in.
1952—Dana Zatopekova,
Czechoslovakia . . . . 165 ft. 7.05 in.
1956—Inessa Iaounzem, Russia . . . . .176 ft. 8 in.
1960—Elvira Ozolina, Russia . . . . . . .183 ft. 8 in.
1964—Mihaela Penes, Rumania . .198 ft. 7 1/2 in.
1968—Angela Nemeth, Hungary . . 198 ft. 1/2 in.
1972—Ruth Fuchs, E. Germany . . . . .209 ft. 7 in.

Pentathlon
Points
1964—Irina Press, Russia 5,246
1968—Ingred Becker, W. Germany 5,098
1972—*Mary Peters, Great Britain 4,801
*Point system changed.

Swimming—Men

50 Yards

1904—Zoltan de Holomay, Hungary . . 28s.

100 Meters

1896—Alfred Hajos, Hungary 1:22.2
1900—Jarvis, Great Britain 1:16.4
1904—Z. de Holomay, Hungary *1:02.8
1906—Charles Daniels, United States . 1:13
1908—Charles Daniels, United States . 1:05.8
1912—Duke P. Kahanamoku, U.S. . 1:03.4
1920—Duke P. Kahanamoku, U.S. . 1:01.4
1924—John Weissmuller, United States 59 s.
1928—John Weissmuller, United States 58.6s.
1932—Y. Miyazaki, Japan . . . . 58.2s.
1936—Ferenc Czik, Hungary . . . . 57.6s.
1948—Walter Ris, United States . . . . . 57.3s.
1952—Clarke Scholes, United States . . 57.4s.
1956—Jon Henricks, Australia . . . . . . 55.4s.
1960—John Devitt, Australia . . . . 55.2s.
1964—Donald A. Schollander, U.S. . . 53.4s.
1968—Mike Wenden, Australia . . . . . . 52.2s.
1972—Mark Spitz, United States . . . . . 51.2s.
* 100 yards.

200 Meters

1900—F.C. Lane, Australia 2:25.2
1904—Charles Daniels, United States . *2:44.2
1968—Mike Wenden, Australia 1:55.2
1972—Mark Spitz, United States 1:52.8
*220 yards.

400 Meters

1900—Jarvis, Great Britain . . . . ——
1904—Charles Daniels, United States . 6:16.2
1906—Otto Sheff, Austria *6:23.8
1908—H. Taylor, Great Britain 5:36.8
1912—G.R. Hodgson, Canada 5:24.4
1920—Norman Ross, United States . . . 5:26.8
1924—John Weissmuller, United States 5:04.2
1928—Albert Zorilla, Argentina 5:01.6
1932—Clarence Crabbe, United States 4:48.4
1936—Jack Medica, United States 4:44.5
1948—Bill Smith, United States 4:41
1952—Jean Boiteux, France 4:30.7
1956—Murray Rose, Australia 4:27.3
1960—Murray Rose, Australia 4:18.3
1964—Donald A. Schollander, U.S. . . . 4:12.2
1968—Mike Burton, United States . . . 4:09.0
1972—†Brad Cooper, Australia 4:00.3
* 440 yards.
†(Rick DeMont, U.S., won event in 4:00.3 but was
disqualified for using unauthorized medication)

500 Meters

1896—Paul Neumann, Austria 8:12.6

880 Yards

1904—Emil Rausch, Germany 13:11.4

1,200 Meters

1896—Gutmann, Hungary 18:22.2

1,500 Meters

1908—H. Taylor, Great Britain 22:48.4

1912—G.R. Hodgson, Canada	22:00
1920—Norman Ross, United States ...	22:23.2
1924—A.M. Charlton, Australia	20:06.6
1928—Arne Borg, Sweden	19:51.8
1932—K. Kitamura, Japan	19:51.6
1936—Norboru Terada, Japan	19:13.2
1948—Jimmy McLane, United States .	19:18.5
1952—Ford Konno, United States ...	18:30
1956—Murray Rose, Australia	17:58.9
1960—John Konrads, Australia	17:19.6
1964—Robert Windle, Australia	17:07.1
1968—Mike Burton, United States ...	16:38.9
1972—Mike Burton, United States ...	15:52.6

1,600 Meters

1906—H. Taylor, Great Britain	28:28

1 Mile

1904—Emil Rausch, Germany	27:18.2

100-Meter Backstroke

1904—Walter Brock, Germany	*1:16.8
1908—A. Bieberstein, Germany	1:24.6
1912—Harry Hebner, United States ..	1:21.2
1920—Warren Kealoha, United States .	1:15.2
1924—Warren Kealoha, United States .	1:13.2
1928—George Kojac, United States ...	1:08.2
1932—M. Kiyokawa, Japan	1:08.6
1936—Adolph Kiefer, United States ..	1:05.9
1948—Allen Stack, United States	1:06.4
1952—Yoshinobu Oyakawa, U.S.	1:05.4
1956—David Thiele, Australia	1:02.2
1960—David Thiele, Australia	1:01.9
1968—Roland Matthes, E. Germany ..	58.7
1972—Roland Matthes, E. Germany ..	56.6
* 100 yards.	

200-Meter Backstroke

1964—Jed R. Graef, United States ...	2:10.3
1968—Roland Matthes, E. Germany ..	2:09.6
1972—Roland Matthes, E. Germany ..	2:02.8

100-Meter Breaststroke

1968—Don McKenzie, United States ...	1:07.7
1972—Nobutaka Taguchi, Japan	1:04.9

200-Meter Breaststroke

1908—F. Holman, Great Britain	3:09.2
1912—Walter Bathe, Germany	3:01.8
1920—H. Malmroth, Sweden	3:04.4
1924—R.D. Skelton, United States	2:56.6
1928—Y. Tsuruta, Japan	2:48.8
1932—Y. Tsuruta, Japan	2:45.4
1936—Detsuo Hamuro, Japan	2:42.5
1948—Joe Verdeur, United States	2:39.3
1952—John Davies, Australia	2:34.4
1956—Masura Furukawa, Japan	2:34.7
1960—William Mulliken, United States .	2:37.4
1964—Ian O'Brien, Australia	2:27.8
1968—Felipe Munoz, Mexico	2:28.7
1972—John Hencken, United States ...	2:21.5

100-Meter Butterfly

1968—Doug Russell, United States	55.9s.
1972—Mark Spitz, United States	54.3s.

200-Meter Butterfly

1956—William Yorzyk, United States ..	2:19.3
1960—Michael Troy, United States	2:12.8
1964—Kevin Barry, Australia	2:06.6
1968—Carl Robie, United States	2:08.7
1972—Mark Spitz, United States	2:00.7

400-Meter Breaststroke

1904—George Zahanus, Germany	*7:23.6
1912—Walter Bathe, Germany	6:29.6
1920—H. Malmroth, Sweden	6:31.8
* 440 yards.	

200-Meter Individual Medley

1968—Charles Hickcox, United States ..	2:12.0
1972—Gunnar Larsson, Sweden	2:07.2

400-Meter Individual Medley

1964—Richard W. Roth, United States .	4:45.4
1968—Charles Hickcox, United States ..	4:48.4
1972—Gunnar Larsson, Sweden	4:32.0

400-Meter Free Style Relay

1964—United States	3:33.2
1968—United States	3:31.7
1972—United States	3:26.4

400-Meter Medley Relay

1960—United States	4:05.4
1964—United States	3:58.4
1968—United States	3:54.9
1972—United States	3:48.2

800-Meter Freestyle Relay

1908—Great Britain	10:55.6
1912—Australia	10:11.6
1920—United States	10:04.4
1924—United States	9:59.4
1928—United States	9:36.2
1932—Japan	8:58.4
1936—Japan	8:51.5
1948—United States	8:46
1952—United States	8:31.1
1956—Australia	8:23.6
1960—United States	8:10.2
1964—United States	7:52.1
1968—United States	7:52.3
1972—United States	7:38.8

1,000-Meter Team Race

1906—Hungary	17:16.2

Plunge for Distance

1904—W.E. Dickey, Unites States ...	62 ft. 6 in.

Underwater

1900—Devendeville, France	60 meters

Springboard Dive

1904—Dr. G.E. Sheldon, United States .	12 2/3
1906—Gottlob Walz, Germany	——
1908—A. Zurner, Germany	85 1/2
1912—Paul Gunther, Germany	6
1920—L.E. Kuehn, United States	6
1924—A.C. White, United States	7
1928—Pete Desjardins, United States ..	185.04
1932—Michael Galitzen, United States .	161.38
1936—Dick Degener, United States	163.57

1948—Bruce Harlan, United States 163.64
1952—David Browning, United States .. 205.29
1956—Bob Clotworthy, United States.. 159.56
1960—Gary Tobian, United States 170.00
1964—Kenneth R. Sitzberger,
      United States 159.90
1968—Bernie Wrightson, United States . 170.15
1972—Vladimir Vasin, Russia 594.09
*Point system changed.

Fancy High Dive

1912—Erik Adlerz, Sweden 7
1920—Clarence E. Pinkston, U.S. 7
1924—A.C. White, United States 9

Plain High Dive

1908—H. Johanssen, Sweden 83.70
1912—Erik Adlerz, Sweden 7
1920—Arvid Wallman, Sweden 7
1924—Richard Eve, Australia 13½

Platform Dive

1928—Pete Desjardins, United States .. 98.74
1932—Harold Smith, United States 124.80
1936—Marshall Wayne, United States .. 113.58
1948—Dr. Sammy Lee, United States .. 130.05
1952—Dr. Sammy Lee, United States .. 156.28
1956—Juan Capilla, Mexico 152.44
1960—Robert Webster, United States .. 165.56
1964—Robert Webster, United States .. 148.58
1968—Klaus Dibiasi, Italy 164.18
1972—Klaus Dibiasi, Italy *504.12
*Point system changed.

Water Polo

1904—United States
1908—Great Britain
1912—Great Britain
1920—Great Britain
1924—France
1928—Germany
1932—Hungary
1936—Hungary
1948—Italy
1952—Hungary
1956—Hungary
1960—Italy
1964—Hungary
1968—Yugoslavia
1972—Russia

Swimming—Women
100 Meters

1912—Fanny Durack, Australia 1:22.2
1920—Ethelda Bleibtrey, United States. 1:13.6
1924—Ethel Lackie, United States 1:12.4
1928—Albina Osipowich, United States 1:11
1932—Helene Madison, United States .. 1:06.8
1936—Rita Mastenbroek, Netherlands.. 1:05.9
1948—Greta Andersen, Denmark 1:06.3
1952—Katalin Szoke, Hungary 1:08.8
1956—Dawn Frazer, Australia 1:02
1960—Dawn Fraser, Australia 1:01.2
1964—Dawn Fraser, Australia 59.5

1968—Jan Henne, United States 1:00.0
1972—Sandra Neilson, United States   58.6

200-Meter Freestyle

1968—Debbie Meyer, United States ... 2:10.5
1972—Shane Gould, Australia 2:03.6

300 Meters

1920—Ethelda Bleibtrey, United States. 4:34

400 Meters

1924—Martha Norelius, United States .. 5:45.4
1928—Martha Norelius, United States .. 5:42.8
1932—Helene Madison, United States .. 5:28.5
1936—Rita Mastenbroek, Netherlands.. 5:26.4
1948—Ann Curtis, United States 5:17.8
1952—Valerie Gyenge, Hungary 5:12.1
1956—Lorraine Crapp, Australia 4:56.6
1960—Christine von Salta, United States 4:50.6
1964—Virginia Duenkel, United States . 4:43.3
1968—Debbie Meyer, United States ... 4:31.8
1972—Shane Gould, Australia 4:19.0

800-Meter Freestyle

1968—Debbie Meyer, United States ... 9:24.0
1972—Keena Rothhammer, U.S. 8:53.7

100-Meter Backstroke

1924—Sybil Bauer, United States 1:23.2
1928—Marie Braun, Holland 1:22
1932—Eleanor Holm, United States ... 1:19.4
1936—Dina Senff, Netherlands 1:18.9
1948—Karen Harup, Denmark 1:14.4
1952—Joan Harrison, South Africa 1:14.3
1956—Judy Grinham, Great Britain ... 1:12.9
1960—Lynn Burke, United States 1:09.3
1964—Cathy Ferguson, United States .. 1:07.7
1968—Kaye Hall, United States 1:06.2
1972—Melissa Belote, United States ... 1:05.8

200-Meter Backstroke

1968—Pokey Watson, United States ... 2:24.8
1972—Melissa Belote, United States ... 2:19.2

100-Meter Breaststroke

1968—Djurdjica Bjedov, Yugoslavia ... 1:15.8
1972—Cathy Carr, United States 1:13.6

200-Meter Breaststroke

1924—Lucy Morton, Great Britain 3:33.2
1928—Hilde Schrader, Germany 3:12.6
1932—Clare Dennis, Australia 3:11.7
1936—Hideko Maehata, Japan 3:03.6
1948—Nel van Vliet, Netherlands 2:57.2
1952—Eva Szekely, Hungary 2:51.7
1956—Ursula Happe, Germany 2:53.1
1960—Anita Lonsbrough, Great Britain 2:49.5
1964—Galina Prozumenschikova, Russia 2:46.4
1968—Sharon Wichman, United States . 2:44.4
1972—Beverly Whitfield, Australia 2:41.7

100-Meter Butterfly

1956—Shelley Mann, United States 1:11
1960—Carolyn Schuler, United States .. 1:09.5
1964—Sharon Stouder, United States .. 1:04.7
1968—Lynn McClements, Australia 1:05.5

1972—Mayumi Aoki, Japan 1:03.3

200-Meter Butterfly

1968—Ada Kok, Netherlands 2:24.7
1972—Karen Moe, United States 2:15.6

400-Meter Freestyle Relay

1912—Great Britain 5:52.8
1920—United States 5:11.6
1924—United States 4:58.8
1928—United States 4:47.6
1932—United States 4:38
1936—Netherlands 4:36
1948—United States 4:29.2
1952—Hungary 4:24.4
1956—Australia 4:17.1
1960—United States 4:08.9
1964—United States 4:03.8
1968—United States 4:02.5
1972—United States 3:55.2

200-Meter Individual Medley

1968—Claudia Kolb, United States 2:24.7
1972—Shane Gould, Australia 2:23.1

400-Meter Individual Medley

1964—Donna DeVarona, United States . 5:18.7
1968—Claudia Kolb, United States 5:08.5
1972—Gail Neall, Australia 5:03.0

400-Meter Medley Relay

1960—United States 4:41.1
1964—United States 4:33.9
1968—United States 4:28.3
1972—United States 4:20.7

Plain High Dive   Points

1912—Greta Johansson, Sweden 39.9
1920—Miss Fryland, Denmark 6
1924—Caroline Smith, United States . . . 9

Springboard Dive   Points

1920—Aileen Riggin, United States 9
1924—Elizabeth Becker, United States . 8
1928—Helen Meany, United States 78.62
1932—Georgia Coleman, United States . 87.52
1936—Marjorie Gestring, United States . 89.28
1948—Vickie Draves, United States 108.74
1952—Patricia K. McCormick,
       United States 147.30
1956—Patricia K. McCormick,
       United States 142.36
1960—Ingrid Kramer, Germany 155.81
1964—Ingrid Engle-Dramer, Germany . . 145.00
1968—Sue Gossick, United States 150.77
1972—Micki King, United States . . . . . . * 450.03
*Point system changed.

Platform Dive

1928—Elizabeth B. Pinkston, U.S. 31.60
1932—Dorothy Poynton, United States 40.26
1936—Dorothy Poynton Hill, U.S. 33.93
1948—Vickie Draves, United States 67.87
1952—Patricia K. McCormick, U.S. 79.37
1956—Patricia K. McCormick, U.S. 84.85
1960—Ingrid Kramer, Germany 91.28
1964—Lesley Bush, United States 99.80

1968—Milena Duchkova,
       Czechoslovakia 109.59
1972—Ulrika Knape, Sweden *390.00
*Point system changed

Archery

Men, Individual

1972—John Williams, United States

Women, Individual

1972—Doreen Wilber, United States

Double York Round

1904—Phil Bryant, United States
1908—W. Dodd, Great Britain

Double American Round

1904—Phil Bryant, United States

Team Round

1904—United States

Continental Round

1908—M. Grisot, France

Bird Shooting—Standing Target

1920—Van Meer, Belgium
1920—Belgium (team)

Bird Shooting—Moving Target

1920—Van Innis, Belgium
1920—Belgium (team)

National Round—Women

1908—Miss Q. Newell, Great Britain

Double National Round—Women

1904—Mrs. M.C. Howell, United States

Double Columbia Round—Women

1904—Mrs. M.C. Howell, United States

Team Championship—Women

1904—United States

Baseball

1912—United States (demonstration)
1936—United States (demonstration)

Basketball

1904—United States (demonstration)
1936—United States
1948—United States
1952—United States
1956—United States
1960—United States
1964—United States
1968—United States
1972—Russia

Boxing

Light Flyweight

1968—Francisco Rodriguez, Venezuela
1972—Gyoergy Gedo, Hungary

Flyweight

1904—George V. Finnegan, United States (105 lb.)
1920—Frank Genaro, United States
1924—Fidel La Barba, United States
1928—Anton Kocsis, Hungary
1932—Stephen Enekes, Hungary

1936—Willi Kaiser, Germany
1948—Pascuel Perez, Argentina
1952—Nate Brooks, United States
1956—Terence Spinks, Great Britain
1960—Gyula Torok, Hungary
1964—Fernando Atzori, Italy
1968—Ricardo Delgado, Mexico
1972—Gherghi Kostadinov, Bulgaria

Bantamweight

1904—O.L. Kirk, United States (115 lb.)
1920—Walker, South Africa
1924—W.H. Smith, South Africa
1928—Vittorio Tamagnini, Italy
1932—Horace Gwynne, Canada
1936—Ulderico Sergo, Italy
1948—Tibor Csik, Hungary
1952—Pentti Hamalainen, Finland
1956—Wolfgang Behrendt, Germany
1960—Oleg Grigoryev, Russia
1964—Takao Sakurai, Japan
1968—Valery Sokolov, Russia
1972—Orlando Martinez, Cuba

Featherweight

1904—O.L. Kirk, United States
1920—Fritsch, France
1924—John Fields, United States
1928—L. Van Klaveren, Holland
1932—Carmelo A. Robledo, Argentina
1936—Oscar Casanova, Argentina
1948—Ernesto Formenti, Italy
1952—Jan Zachara, Czechoslovakia
1956—Vladimir Safronov, Russia
1960—Francesco Musso, Italy
1964—Stanislav Stepashkin, Russia
1968—Antonio Roldan, Mexico
1972—Boris Kousnetsov, Russia

Lightweight

1904—H.J. Spanger, United States
1920—Samuel Mosberg, United States
1924—Harold Nielsen, Denmark
1928—Carlo Orlandi, Italy
1932—Lawrence Stevens, South Africa
1936—Imre Harangi, Hungary
1948—Gerry Dreyer, South Africa
1952—Aureliano Bolognesi, Italy
1956—Richard McTaggart, Great Britain
1960—Kaximierz Pazdzior, Poland
1964—Jozef Grudzien, Poland
1968—Ronnie Harris, United States
1972—Jan Szcepanski, Poland

Light Welterweight

1952—Charles Adkins, United States
1956—Vladimir Enguibarian, Russia
1960—Bohumil Nemecek, Czechoslavakia
1964—Jerzy Kulej, Poland
1968—Jerzy Kulej, Poland
1972—Ray Seales, United States

Welterweight

1904—Al Young, United States
1920—Schneider, Canada

1924—J.S. Delarge, Belgium
1928—Edward Morgan, New Zealand
1932—Edward Flynn, United States
1936—Sten Suvio, Finland
1948—Julius Torma, Czechoslovakia
1952—Zygmunt Chychla, Poland
1956—Necolae Linca, Rumania
1960—Giovanni Benvenuti, Italy
1964—Marian Kasprzyk, Poland
1968—Manfred Wolke, East Germany
1972—Emilio Correa, Cuba

Light Middleweight

1952—Laszlo Papp, Hungary
1956—Laszlo Papp, Hungary
1960—Wilbert McClure, United States
1964—Boris Lagutin, Russia
1968—Boris Lagutin, Russia
1972—Dieter Kottysch, West Germany

Middleweight

1904—Charles Mayer, United States
1920—H.W. Mallin, Great Britain
1924—H.W. Mallin, Great Britain
1928—Piero Toscani, Italy
1932—Carmen Barth, United States
1936—Jean Despeaux, France
1948—Laszlo Papp, Hungary
1952—Floyd Patterson, United States
1956—Gennady Chatkov, Russia
1960—Edward Crook, United States
1964—Valery Popenchenko, Russia
1968—Christopher Finnegan, Great Britain
1972—Viatcheslav Lemechev, Russia

Light Heavyweight

1920—Edward Eagan, United States
1924—H.J. Mitchell, Great Britain
1928—Victoria Avendano, Argentina
1932—David E. Carstens, South Africa
1936—Roger Michelot, France
1948—George Hunter, South Africa
1952—Norvel Lee, United States
1956—James Boyd, United States
1960—Cassius Clay, United States
1964—Cosimo Pinto, Italy
1968—Dan Pozdniak, Russia
1972—Mate Pavlov, Yugoslavia

Heavyweight

1904—Sam Berger, United States
1920—Rawson, Great Britain
1924—Otto Von Porat, Norway
1928—Jurido Rodriguez, Argentina
1932—Santiago A. Lovell, Argentina
1936—Herbert Runge, Germany
1948—Rafael Iglesias, Argentina
1952—Edward Sanders, United States
1956—Pete Rademacher, United States
1960—Francesco De Piccoli, Italy
1964—Joseph Frazier, United States
1968—George Foreman, United States
1972—Teofilo Stevenson, Cuba

Canoeing

Kayak Singles—1,000 Meters

1936—Gregor Hradetzky, Austria
1948—Gert Fredriksson, Sweden
1952—Gert Fredriksson, Sweden
1956—Gert Fredriksson, Sweden
1960—Erik Hansen, Denmark
1964—Rolf Peterson, Sweden
1968—Mihaly Hesz, Hungary
1972—Aleksandr Shaparenko, Russia

Kayak Singles Slalom

1972—Siegbert Horn, East Germany

Kayak Singles—10,000 Meters

1936—Ernst Krebs, Germany
1948—Gert Fredriksson, Sweden
1952—Thorvald Stromberg, Finland
1956—Gert Fredriksson, Sweden

Canadian Singles—1,000 Meters

1936—Francis Amyot, Canada
1948—Josef Holecek, Czechoslovakia
1952—Josef Holecek, Czechoslovakia
1956—Leon Rottman, Rumania
1960—Janos Parti, Hungary
1964—Jurgen Eschert, Germany
1968—Tibor Tatai, Hungary
1972—Ivan Patzaichin, Rumania

Canadian Singles Slalom

1972—Reinhard Eiben, East Germany

Canadian Singles—10,000 Meters

1948—F. Capek, Czechoslovakia
1952—Frank Havens, United States
1956—Leon Rottman, Rumania

Kayak Pairs—1,000 Meters

1936—Austria (Adolf Kainz, Alfons Dorfner)
1948—Sweden (H. Berglund, L. Klingstroem)
1952—Finland (K. Wires, Y. Hietanen)
1956—Germany (M. Scheuer, M. Miltenberger)
1960—Sweden (Gert Fredriksson, Sven Sjodelius)
1964—Sweden (Sven Sjodelius, Gunnar Utterberg)
1968—Russia (Aleksandr Shaparenko, Vladimir Morozov)
1972—Russia (Nicolai Gorbachev, Viktor Kratassyuk)

Kayak Pairs—10,000 Meters

1936—Germany (Paul Wevers, Ludwig Lamden)
1948—Sweden (G. Akerlund, H. Wetterstroem)
1952—Finland (K. Wires, Y. Hietanen)
1956—Hungary (J. Uranyi, L. Fabian)

Folding Kayak Singles—10,000 Meters

1936—Gregor Hradetzky, Austria

Folding Kayak Pairs—10,000 Meters

1936—Sweden (Sven Johansson, Eric Bladstroem)

Kayak Fours—1,000 Meters

1964—Russia (Nikolay Chuzhikov, Anatoly Grishin, Viacheslav Ionov, Vladimir Morozov)
1968—Norway (Steiner Amudsen, Egil Soby, Tore Berger, Jan Johansen)
1972—Russia (Filatov, Morozov, Stezenko, Didenko)

Canadian Pairs—1,000 Meters

1936—Czechoslovakia (Vladimir Syrovatka, F. Jan Brzak)
1948—Czechoslovakia (J. Brzak, B. Kudrna)
1952—Denmark (B. Rasch, F. Haunstoft)
1956—Rumania (A. Dumitru, S. Ismailciuc)
1960—Russia (Leonid Geyshter, Sergey Makarenko)
1968—Rumania (Ivan Patzaichan, Serghei Covaliov)
1972—Russia (Vladas Chessyunas, Yuri Lobanov)

Canadian Pairs Slalom

1972—East Germany (Walter Hofman, Rolf-Dieter Amend)

Canadian Pairs—10,000 Meters

1936—Czechoslovakia (Vaclav Mottle, Zdenek Skrdlant)
1948—United States (S. Lysak, S. Macknowski)
1952—France (G. Turlier, J. Laudet)
1956—Russia (P. Kharine, G. Botev)

Kayak Singles Relay—2,000 Meters

1960—Germany (Dieter Krause, Gunther Perleberg, Paul Lange, Friedhelm Wentzke)

Kayak Singles (Women)—500 Meters

1948—K. Hoff, Denmark
1952—Sylvia Saimo, Finland
1956—Elisavota Dementieva, Russia
1960—Antonina Seredina, Russia
1964—Ludmila Khvedosiuk, Russia
1968—Ludmila Pinaeva, Russia
1972—Yulia Ryabchinskaya, Russia

Kayak Singles Slalom—Women

1972—Angelika Bahmann, East Germany

Kayak Pairs (Women)—500 Meters

1960—Russia (Maria Shubina, Antonina Seredina)
1964—Germany (Roswitha Esser, Annemarie Zimmerman)
1968—West Germany (Annemarie Zimmermann, Roswitha Esser)
1972—Russia (Ludmila Pinaeva, Ekaterina Kuryshko)

Cycling

Road Race—Individual

1896—Konstantinidis, Greece
1906—Vast, Bardonneau, France (tie)
1912—R. Lewis, South Africa
1920—H. Stenquist, Sweden
1924—A. Blanchonnet, France
1928—H. Hansen, Denmark
1932—Attilio Pavesi, Italy
1936—R. Charpentier, France
1948—J. Bayaert, France
1952—Andrae Noyelle, Belgium
1956—Ercole Baldini, Italy

1960—Viktor Kapitonov, Russia
1964—Mario Zanin, Italy
1968—Pierfranco Vianelli, Italy
1972—Hennie Kuiper, Netherlands

Road Race—Team

1912—Sweden
1920—France
1924—France
1928—Denmark
1932—Italy
1936—France
1948—Belgium
1952—Belgium
1956—France
1960—Italy
1964—Holland
1968—Netherlands
1972—Russia

1,000-Meter Scratch

1896—Emile Masson, France (2,000 meters)
1900—Taillendier, France
1906—Francesco Verri, Italy
1908—Void, time limit exceeded
1920—Maurice Peeters, Holland
1924—Lucien Michard, France
1928—R. Beaufrand, France
1932—Jacobus van Edmond, Holland
1936—Toni Merkens, Germany
1948—Mario Ghella, Italy (920 meters)
1952—Enzo Sacchi, Italy
1956—Michel Rousseau, France
1960—Sante Gaiardoni, Italy
1964—Giovanni Pettenella, Italy
1968—Daniel Morelon, France
1972—Daniel Morelon, France

2,000-Meter Tandem

1906—Great Britain (Matthews, Rushen)
1908—France (Schilles, Auffray)
1920—Great Britain (Ryan, Lance)
1924—France (Choury, Cugnot)
1928—Holland (Leene, van Dijk)
1932—France (Perrin, Chaillot)
1936—Germany (Ihbe, Lorenz)
1948—Italy (Teruzzi, Perona)
1952—Australia (Cox, Mockridge)
1956—Australia (Browne, Marchanti)
1960—Italy (Sergio Bianchetto, Giuseppe Beghetto)
1964—Italy (A. Damiano, S. Bianchetto)
1968—France (D. Morelon, P. Trentin)
1972—Russia (V. Semenets, I. Tselovalnikov)

4,000-Meter Team Pursuit

1908—Great Britain
1920—Italy
1924—Italy
1928—Italy
1932—Italy
1936—France
1948—France
1952—Italy
1956—Italy

1960—Italy
1964—Germany
1968—Denmark
1972—West Germany

4,000 Meter Individual Pursuit

1964—Jiri Daller, Czechoslovakia
1968—Daniel Rebillard, France
1972—Knut Knudsen, Norway

1,000-Meter Time Trial

1928—W. Falck-Hansen, Denmark
1932—E.L. Gray, Australia
1936—Arie Gerrit van Vliet, Holland
1948—J. Dupont, France
1952—Russell Mockridge, Australia
1956—Leondro Faggin, Italy
1960—Sante Gaiardoni, Italy
1964—Patrick Sercu, Belgium
1968—Pierre Trentin, France
1972—Neils Fredborg, Denmark

333.3-Meter Time Trial

1896—Emile Masson, France
1906—Francesco Verri, Italy

660-Yard Sprint

1896—Emile Masson, France
1906—V.L. Johnson, Great Britain

5 Kilometers

1906—Francesco Verri, Italy
1908—Ben Jones, Great Britain

10 Kilometers

1906—P. Mason, France

20 Kilometers

1906—W.J. Pett, Great Britain
1908—C. Kingsbury, Great Britain

50 Kilometers

1920—H. George, Belgium
1924—J. Willems, Holland

100 Kilometers

1896—C. Flameng, France
1908—C. Bartlett, Great Britain

12-Hour Race

1896—A. Schmall, Austria

Equestrian Events

3-Day Event (Individual)

1912—Lt. A. Nordlander, Sweden
1920—Lt. De Moerner, Sweden
1924—A.D.C. Van Der Voort Van Zijp, Holland
1928—Lt. C.F. Pahud de Mortanges, Holland
1932—Lt. C.F. Pahud de Mortanges, Holland
1936—Ludwig Stubbendorf, Germany
1948—Capt. B. Chevallier, France
1952—Hans von Blixen-Finecke, Sweden
1956—Lt. Petrus Kastenman, Sweden
1960—Lawrence Morgan, Australia
1964—Mauro Checcoli, Italy
1968—Jean-Jacques Guyon, France
1972—Richard Meade, Great Britain

3-Day Event (Team)

1912—Sweden (Nordlander, Aldercreutz, Casparsson)
1920—Sweden (H. Morner, Lundstrom, von Braun)
1924—Holland (van Zijp, de Mortanges, G. de Kruiff Sr.)
1928—Holland (C.F. Pahud de Mortanges, G.P. De Kruyff, A.D.C. Van Der Voort Van Zijp)
1932—United States (Earl F. Thomson, Edwin Y. Argo, Harry D. Chamberlin)
1936—Germany (Ludwig Stubbendorf, Rudolf Lippert, Konrad Freiherr von Wangenheim)
1948—United States (F.S. Henry, C.H. Anderson, Earl F. Thomson)
1952—Sweden (von Blixen-Finecke, Stahre, Frolen)
1956—Great Britain (Frank Weldon, Bertie Hill, Laurence Rook)
1960—Australia (William Roycroft, Neale Lavis, Lawrence Morgan)
1964—Italy (M. Checcoli, P. Angioni, G. Ravano)
1968—Great Britain (Allhusen, Meade, Jones)
1972—Great Britain (Gordon-Watson, Parker, Meade, Phillips)

Dressage (Individual)

1912—Capt. C. Bonde, Sweden
1920—Capt. Lundblad, Sweden
1924—E.V. Linder, Sweden
1928—C.F. von Langen, Germany
1932—F. Lesage, France
1936—H. Pollay, Germany
1948—Capt. H. Moser, Switzerland
1952—Henri St. Cyr, Sweden
1956—Maj. Henri St. Cyr, Sweden
1960—Sergey Filatov, Russia
1964—Henri Chammartin, Switzerland
1968—Ivan Kizimov, Russia
1972—Lisejott Linsenhoff, W. Germany

Dressage (Team)

1928—Germany (Von Langen, Linkenbach, Von Litzbeck)
1932—France (Lesage, Marion, Jousseaume)
1936—Germany (Pollay, Gerhard, Von Oppeln-Bronikowski)
1948—Sweden (Boltenstern St. Cyr, Persson)
1952—Sweden (St. Cyr, Stahre, Frolen)
1956—Sweden (St. Cyr, Persson, Boltenstern)
1964—Germany (H. Boldt, R. Klimke, J. Neckermann)
1968—West Germany (J. Neckermann, R. Klimke, L. Linsenhoff)
1972—Russia (Petushkova, Kizimov, Kalita)

Prix de Nations (Individual Jumping)

1912—Capt. J. Cariou, France . . . . 186 pts.
1920—Lt. Lequio, Italy 2   faults
1924—Lt. Gemuseus, Switzerland 6   faults
1928—F. Ventura, Czechoslovakia . . . . no faults
1932—Takeichi Nishi, Japan 8   faults

1936—Kurt Hasse, Germany 4   faults
1948—H. Cortes, Mexico . . . . .6¼ faults
1952—Pierre d'Oriola, France 8   faults
1956—Hans Gunther Winkler, Germany 4   faults
1960—Raimondo D'inzeo, Italy . . . . . .12 faults
1964—P. Jonquieres d'Oriola, France . .9   faults
1968—William Steinkraus, United States 4   faults
1972—Graziano Mancinelli, Italy 8   faults

Prix de Nations (Team)

1912—Sweden (Lewenhaupt, Kilman, von Rosen) . . . . 545 pts.
1920—Sweden (von Rosen, Loenig, Norling) .14 faults
1924—Sweden (Thelning, Stahle, Lundstrom) . . . . 42.25 faults
1928—Spain de los Truxillos, Morenes, Fernandez) . . . . .4 faults
1932—All teams participating disqualified.
1936—Germany (v. Barnekow, Hasse, Brandt) .44 faults
1948—Mexico (Cortes, Uriza, Valdes) . . . . .34 1/4 faults
1952—Great Britain (D.N. Stewart, W.W. White, H. M. Llewellyn . . . . . . .40.75 faults
1956—Germany (Winkler, Leutke-Westhues, Thiedeman) . . . . .40 faults
1960—Germany (Winkler, Schockemohle, Thiedemann) . . . . .46 1/2 faults
1964—Germany (H. Schridde, K. Jarasinski, H. Winkler) . . . . .68 1/2 faults
1968—Canada (T. Gayford, J. Day, J. Elder) . . . . .102.75 pts.
1972—West Germany (Liggs, Wiltfang, Steenken, Winkler) . . . . 32 faults

Fencing

Individual Foil

1896—E. Gravelotte, France
1900—E. Coste, France
1904—Ramon Fonst, Cuba
1906—Dillon-Cavanagh, France
1912—Nedo Nadi, Italy
1920—Nedo Nadi, Italy
1924—Roger Ducret, France
1928—Ludien Gaudin, France
1932—Gustavo Marzi, Italy
1936—Giulio Gaudini, Italy
1948—Jean Buhan, France
1952—Christian d'Oriola, France
1956—Christian d'Oriola, France
1960—Viktor Zhdanovich, Russia
1964—Egon Franke, Poland
1968—Ian Drimbu, Rumania
1972—Witold Woyda, Poland

Team Foil

1904—Cuba
1920—Italy
1924—France
1928—Italy
1932—France

1936–Italy
1948–France
1952–France
1956–Italy
1960–Russia
1964–Russia
1968–France
1972–Poland

Individual Epee

1896–E. Gravelotte, France
1900–Ramon Fonst, Cuba
1904–Ramon Fonst, Cuba
1906–Comte de la Falaise, France
1908–G. Alibert, France
1912–Paul Anspach, Belgium
1920–A. Massard, France
1924–C. Delporte, Belgium
1928–Lucien Gaudin, France
1932–G. Cornaggia-Medici, Italy
1936–Franco Riccardi, Italy
1948–Luigi Cantone, France
1952–Eduardo Mangiarotti, Italy
1956–Carlo Pavesi, Italy
1960–Giuseppe Delfino, Italy
1964–Grigory Kriss, Russia
1968–Gyozo Kulcsar, Hungary
1972–Csaba Fenyvesi, Hungary

Team Epee

1906–Germany
1908–France
1912–Belgium
1920–Italy
1924–France
1928–Italy
1932–France
1936–Italy
1948–France
1952–Italy
1956–Italy
1960–Italy
1964–Hungary
1968–Hungary
1972–Hungary

Individual Saber

1896–G. Georgiadis, Greece
1900–Comte de la Falaise, France
1904–M. de Diaz, Cuba
1906–G. Georgiadis, Greece
1908–E. Fuchs, Hungary
1912–E. Fuchs, Hungary
1920–Nedo Nadi, Italy
1924–Alexandre Posta, Hungary
1928–E. Tersztyanszky, Hungary
1932–George Piller, Hungary
1936–Endre Kabos, Hungary
1948–Aladar Gerevich, Hungary
1952–G. Kovacs, Hungary
1956–Rudolf Karpati, Hungary
1960–Rudolf Karapati, Hungary
1964–Tibor Pezsa, Hungary
1968–Jerzy Pawlowski, Poland

1972–Victor Sidiak, Russia

Team Saber

1906–Germany
1908–Hungary
1912–Hungary
1920–Italy
1924–Italy
1928–Hungary
1932–Hungary
1936–Hungary
1948–Hungary
1952–Hungary
1956–Hungary
1960–Hungary
1964–Russia
1968–Russia
1972–Italy

Three-Cornered Saber

1906–Gustav Casimir, Germany

Singlestick

1904–A.V.Z. Post, Cuba

Individual Swords

1900–Robert Ayat, France
1904–Ramon Fonst, Cuba

Women–Individual Foil

1904–A.V.Z. Post, Cuba
1924–Mrs. E.O. Osiier, Denmark
1928–Helene Mayer, Germany
1932–Elen Preis, Austria
1936–Ilona Elek, Hungary
1948–Ilona Elik, Hungary
1952–Irene Camber, Italy
1956–Gillian Sheen, Great Britain
1960–Adelheid Schmid, Germany
1964–Ildiko Ujlaki-Rejto, Hungary
1968–Elena Novikova, Russia
1972–Antonnella Lonzo Rango, Italy

Women–Team Foil

1960–Russia
1964–Hungary
1968–Russia
1972–Russia

Field Handball

1936–Germany

Field Hockey

1908–Great Britain
1920–Great Britain
1928–India
1932–India
1936–India
1948–India
1952–India
1956–India
1960–Pakistan
1964–India
1968–Pakistan
1972–West Germany

Golf

1904—George S. Lyon, Canada

Gymnastics—Men

Team

	Points
1904—Germany	....
1906—Denmark and Norway (tie) ..	....
1908—Sweden	438
1912—Italy	265.75
1920—Italy	359.85
1924—Italy	839.056
1928—Switzerland	1718.625
1932—Italy	541.85
1936—Germany	657.43
1948—Finland	1358.3
1952—Russia	574.40
1956—Russia	568.25
1960—Japan	575.20
1964—Japan	577.95
1968—Japan	575.90
1972—Japan	571.25

All-Around Individual

	Points
1900—Sandras, France	320
1904—Anton Heida, United States ..	....
1906—Payssee, France	116
1908—Alberto Braglia, Italy	317
1912—Alberto Braglia, Italy	135
1920—G. Zampori, Italy	88.35
1924—L. Stukely, Yugoslavia	110.34
1928—G. Miez, Switzerland	247.60
1932—Romeo Neri, Italy	140.625
1936—Karl Schwarzmann, Germany .	113.1
1948—V. Huhtanen, Finland	229.7
1952—Victor Tchoukarine, Russia ..	115.70
1956—Victor Tchoukarine, Russia ..	114.25
1960—Boris Shakhlin, Russia	115.95
1964—Yukio Endo, Japan	115.95
1968—Sawao Kato, Japan	115.90
1972—Sawao Kato, Japan	114.650

Long Horse (Vaults)

	Points
1896—Karl Schumann, Germany ...	....
1904—Anton Heida, George Eyser, United States	....
1924—Frank Kriz, United States ...	9.98
1928—E. Mack, Switzerland	9.58
1932—Savino Guglielmetti, Italy ...	18.03
1936—Karl Schwarzmann, Germany .	19.20
1948—P. J. Aaltonen, Finland	39.1
1952—Victor Tchoukarine, Russia ..	19.20
1956—Helmuth Bantz, Germany, and Valentine Mouratov (tie)...	18.85
1960—Boris Shakhlin, Russian, Takashi Ono, Japan (tie)	19.35
1964—Haruhiro Yamashita, Japan ..	19.600
1968—Mikhail Voronin, Russia	19.000
1972—Klaus Koeste, E. Germany ...	18.850

Side Horse

	Points
1896—Zutter, Switzerland	....
1904—Anton Heida, United States ..	42
1924—J. Wilhelm, Switzerland	21.23

1928—H. Hanggi, Switzerland	19.75
1932—Stephen Pelle, Hungary	19.07
1936—Konrad Frey, Germand	19.33
1948—P. J. Aaltonen, Finland	38.7
1952—Victor Tchoukarine, Russia	19.50
1956—Boris Chakhlin, Russia	19.25
1960—Boris Shakhlin, Russia, Eugen Ekman, Finland (tie)	19.375
1964—Miroslav Cerar, Yugoslavia	19.525
1968—Miroslav Cerar, Yugoslavia	19.325
1972—Viktor Klimenko, Russia	19.125

Horizontal Bar

	Points
1896—Herman Weingaertner, Germany	....
1904—Anton Heida, E. A. Hennig, United States (tie)	40
1924—L. Stukely, Yugoslavia	19.73
1928—George Miez, Switzerland	19.17
1932—Dallas Bixler, United States ...	18.33
1936—A. Saarvala, Finland	19.367
1948—Josef Stalder, Switzerland	39.7
1952—Jack Gunthard, Switzerland ..	19.55
1956—Takashi Ono, Japan	19.6
1960—Takashi Ono, Japan	19.60
1964—Boris Shakhlin, Russia	19.625
1968—Mikhail Voronin, Russia	19.550
1972—Mitsuo Tsukahara, Japan	19.725

Parallel Bar

	Points
1896—Alfred Flatow, Germand	....
1904—George Eyser, United States ..	44
1924)A. Guttinger, Switzerland	21.63
1928—L. Vacha, Czechoslovakia	18.83
1932—Romeo Neri, Italy	18.97
1936—Konrad Frey, Germany	19.07
1948—M. Reusch, Switzerland	39.5
1952—Hand Engstar, Switzerland ...	19.65
1956—Victor Tchoukarine, Russia ...	19.2
1960—Boris Shakhlin, Russia	19.40
1964—Yukio Endo, Japan	19.675
1968—Akinori Nakayama, Japan	19.475
1972—Sawao Kato, Japan	19.475

Flying Rings

	Points
1896—Mitropoulos, Greece	....
1904—Herman T. Glass, United States	45
1924—F. Martino, Italy	21.55
1928—L. Stukelj, Yugoslavia	19.25
1932—George Gulack, United States .	18.97
1936—Alois Hudec, Czechoslovakia ..	19.43
1948—K. Frei, Switzerland	39.6
1952—Grant Chaguinian, Russia	19.75
1956—Albert Azarian, Russis	19.35
1960—Albert Azarian, Russia	19.725
1964—Takuji Hayata, Japan	19.475
1968—Akinori Nakayama, Japan	19.450
1972—Akinori Nakayama, Japan	19.350

Free Exercises

	Points
1932—Stephen Pelle, Hungary	....
1936—George Miez, Switzerland	....
1948—V.A. Huhtanen, Finland	229.7
1952—Karl Thoresson, Sweden	19.25

1956—Valentine Mouratov, Russia ... 19.2
1960—Nobuyuki Aihara, Japan 19.45
1964—Franco Menichelli, Italy 19.450
1968—Sawao Kato, Japan 19.475
1972—Nikolai Andrianov, Russia 19.175

Team—Swedish System

	Points
1912—Sweden	937.46
1920—Sweden	1364

Team—Free System

(Exercises, Apparatus)	Points
1912—Norway	114.25
1920—Denmark	....

Team—Special Conditions

1912—Italy
1920—Denmark

Team—Horizontal Bars

1896—Germany ....

Team—Parallel Bars

1896—Germany ....

Rope Climb

	Time
1896—Andriakopoulos, Greece	23.4s.
1904—George Eyser, United States	7s.
1906—G. Aliprantis, Greece	11.4s.
1924—B. Supcik, Czechoslovakia	7.2s.
1932—Raymond Bass, United States	6.7s.

Side Horse (Vaults)

	Points
1924—A. Seguin, France	10
1928—E. Mack, Switzerland	28.75

Tumbling

	Points
1932—Rowland Wolfe, United States	18.9

Indian Club

	Points
1904—E. A. Hennig, United States	13
1932—George Roth, United States	26.9

Gymnastics—Women

Team

	Points
1928—Holland	316.75
1936—Germany	506.50
1948—Czechoslovakia	445.45
1952—Russia	527.03
1956—Russia	444.80
1960—Russia	382.32
1964—Russia	380.890
1968—Russia	382.85
1972—Russia	380.50

All-Around

	Points
1952—Maria Gorokhovakaja, Russia	76.78
1956—Larisa Latynina, Russia	74.931
1960—Larisa Latynina, Russia	77.031
1964—Vera Caslavska, Czechoslovakia	77.564
1968—Vera Caslavskz, Czechoslavakia	78.25
1972—Ludmila Turischeva, Russia	77.025

Beam

	Points
1952—Nina Botcharova, Russia	19.22
1956—Agnes Keleti, Hungary	18.800
1960—Eva Bosakova, Czechoslovakia	19.283

1964—Vera Caslavska, Czechoslovakia 19.499
1968—Natalia Kuchinskaya, Russia ... 19.650
1972—Olga Korbut, Russia 19.400

Floor Exercises

	Points
1952—A. Keleti, Hungary	19.36
1956—Agnes Keleti, Hungary, and Larisa Latynina, Russia (tie)	18.732
1960—Lara Latynina, Russia	19.566
1964—Larisa Latynina, Russia	19.599
1968—Vera Caslavska, Czechoslovakia	19.675
1972—Olga Korbut, Russia	19.575

Side-Horse Vault

	Points
1952—Ekaterina Kalinthouk, Russia	19.20
1956—Larisa Latynina, Russia	18.833
1960—Margarita Nikolaeva, Russia	19.316
1964—Vera Caslavska, Czechoslovakia	19.483
1968—Vera Caslavska, Czechoslovakia	19.775
1972—Karin Janz, E. Germany	19.525

Uneven Bars

	Points
1952—Margit Korondi, Hungary	19.40

Parallel Bars

	Points
1956—Agnes Keleti, Hungary	18.966
1960—Polina Astakhova, Russia	19.616
1964—Polina Astakhova, Russia	19.332
1968—Vera Caslavska, Czechoslovakia	19.650
1972—Karin Janz, E. Germany	19.675

Team Drill

	Points
1952—Sweden	74.20
1956—Hungary	75.2
1960—Russia	77.031

Handball-Team

1972—Yugoslavia

Judo

Lightweight

1964—Takehide Nakatani, Japan
1972—Takao Kawaguchi, Japan

Middleweight

1964—Isao Okano, Japan
1972—Shinobu Sekine, Japan

Welterweight

1972—Toyokazu Nomura, Japan

Light Heavyweight

1972—Shota Chochoshvili, Russia

Heavyweight

1964—Isao Inokuma, Japan
1972—Wim Ruska, Netherlands

Open

1964—Antonius Geesink, Holland
1972—Wim Ruska, Netherlands

Lacrosse

1904—Canada
1908—Canada
1932—United States (demonstration)

Modern Pentathlon
Individual
1912—G. Lilliehook, Sweden
1920—J. Dryssen, Sweden
1924—O. Lindman, Sweden
1928—S. A. Thofelt, Sweden
1932—J. G. Oxenstierna, Sweden
1936—G. Handrick, Germany
1948—Capt. W. Grut, Sweden
1952—Lars Hall, Sweden
1956—Lars Hall, Sweden
1960—Ferenc Nemeth, Hungary
1964—Ferenc Tork, Hungary
1968—Bjorn Ferm, Sweden
1972—Andras Balczo, Hungary

Team
1952—Hungary
1956—Russia
1960—Hungary
1964—Russia
1968—Hungary
1972—Russia

Polo
1908—Great Britain
1920—Great Britain
1924—Argentina
1936—Argentina

Racquets
Men's Singles
1908—E. B. Noel, Great Britain
Men's Doubles
1908—V. H. Pennell, J. J. Astor, Great Britain
Roque
1904—Charles Jacobus, United States

Rowing
Eight-Oared Shell

	Time
1900—United States	6.07.8
1904—United States (demonstration)	....
1908—Great Britain	....
1912—Great Britain	6:15
1920—United States	6:02.6
1924—United States	6:33.4
1928—United States	6:03.2
1932—United States	6:37.4
1936—United States	6:25.4
1948—United States	5:56.7
1952—United States	6:28.9
1956—United States	6:35.2
1960—Germany	5:57.18
1964—United States	6:18.23
1968—West Germany	6:07.00
1972—New Zealand	6:08.94

Single Sculls
1900—Barralet, France 7:35.6
1904—Frank B. Greer, United States . ....
1908—H. T. Blackstaffe, Great Britain ....
1912—W. D. Dinear, Great Britain ... 7:45.6
1920—John B. Kelly, United States .. 7:35
1924—Jack Beresford Jr., Great Britain 7:49.2
1928—Henry Robert Pearce, Australia 7:11
1932—Henry Robert Pearce, Australia 7:44.4
1936—Gustav Schafer, Germany 8:21.5
1948—Mervyn T. Wood, Australia ... 7:24.4
1952—Juri Tjukalov, Russia 8:12.8
1956—Vyacheslav Ivanov, Russia 8:02.5
1960—Vjacheslav Ivanov, Russia 7:13.96
1964—Vjacheslav Ivanov, Russia 7:13.96
1968—Jan Wienese, Netherlands 7:48.80
1972—Yuri Malishev, Russia 7:10.12

Double Sculls
1904—United States
 (demonstration) ....———
1908—J. R. K. Fenning—G. L. Thomson, Great Britain ....———
1920—John B. Kelly—Paul V. Costello, United States
1924—John B. Kelly—Paul V. Costello, United States 6:34
1928—Paul V. Costello—Charles J. McIivaine, United States 6:41.4
1932—Kenneth Myers—W. E. Garrett Gilmore, United States 7:17.4
1936—Jack Beresford—Leslie Southwood, Great Britain 7:20.8
1948—B. H. Bushnell—R. D. Burnell, Great Britain 6:51.3
1952—T. Cappozza—E. Guerrero, Argentina 7:32.2
1956—A. Berkoutov—J. Tjukalov, Russia 7:24
1960—Vaclav Kozak, Pvael Schmidt, Czechoslavakia 6:47.50
1964—Oleg Tiurin, Boris Dubrovsky, Russia 7:10.66
1968—Russia (Anatoly Sass, Alexsandr Timoshinin) 6:51.82
1972—Russia (Aleksandr Timoshinin, Gennadi Korshikov) 7:01.77

Pair-Oared Shell with Coxswain
1900—R. Klein—F. A. Brandt, Holland 7:34.2
1906—Italy (1,600 meters) ....———
1906—Italy (1,000 meters) ....———
1920—M. Olgeni and G. Scatturin, Italy 7:56
1924—M. Candeveau—A. Felber, Switzerland 8:39
1928—H. W. Schochlin—C. F. Schochlin, Switzerland 7:42.6
1932—Joseph A. Schauers—Charles M. Kieffer, United States 8:25.8
1936—Gerhard Gustmann—Herbert Adamski, Germany 8:36.9
1948—F. Pedersen—T. Henriksen, Denmark 8:00.5
1952—R. Salles—G. Mercier, Feance 8:28.6

1956—A. Ayrault—C. Findlay—K.
Seiffert, United States 8:26.1
1960—Bernhard Knubel, Heinz
Renneberg, Klaus Zerta, Germany 7:29.14
1964—Edward Ferry, Conn Findlay,
Kent Mitchell, United States 8:21.33
1968—P. Baran, R. Sambo, B.
Cipolia, Italy 8:04.81
1972—W. Gunkel, J. Lucke, K.
Neubert, East Germany 7:17.25

Pair-Oared Shell without Coxswain

1904—United States 10:57
1908—J. Fenning—G. Thomson,
Great Britain 9:41
1924—W. H. Rosingh—A. C. Beynen,
Holland 8:19.4
1928—K. Moeschter—B. Muller,
Germany 7:06.4
1932—Lewis Clive—H. R. Arthur
Edwards, Great Britain 8:00
1936—Willi Eichhorn—Hugo Strauss,
Germany 8:16.1
1948—J. H. T. Wilson—W. G. R. M.
Laurie, Great Britain 7:21.1
1952—Charles Logg Jr.—Thomas Price,
United States 8:20.7
1956—James Fifer—Duval Hecht,
United States 7:55.4
1960—Valentin Boreiko, Oleg
Golovanov, Russia 7:02.01
1964—George Hungerford, Roger
Jackson, Canada 7:32.94
1968—J. Lucke, H. Bothe,
East Germany 7:26.56
1972—S. Brietzke, W. Mager,
East Germany 6:53.16

Four-Oared Shell with Coxswain

1900—Germany . . . .
1906—Italy . . . .
1912—Germany 6:59.4
1920—Switzerland 6:54
1924—Switzerland 7:18.4
1928—Italy 6:47.8
1932—Germany 7:19.2
1936—Germany 7:6.2
1948—United States 6:50.3
1952—Czechoslovakia 7:33.4
1956—Italy 7:19.4
1960—Germany 6:39.12
1964—Germany 7:00.44
1968—New Zealand 6:45.62
1972—West Germany 6:31.85

Four-Oared Shell without Coxswain

1904—United States . . . .
1908—Great Britain . . . .
1924—Great Britain . . . .
1928—Great Britain 6:36
1932—Great Britain 6:58.2
1936—Germany 7:01.8
1948—Italy 6:39

1952—Yugoslavia 7:16
1956—Canada 7:08.8
1960—United States 6:26.26
1964—Denmark 6:59.30
1968—East Germany 6:39.18
1972—East Germany 6:24.27

Rugby

1900—France
1908—Australia
1920—United States
1924—United States

Shooting

Any Rifle (individual)

1896—G. Orphanidis, Greece
1908—A. Helgerud, Norway
1912—P. R. Colas, France
1920—Sgt. Morris Fisher, United States
1924—Morris Fisher, United States (600 meters)

Free Rifle (50 Meters)

1908— A. A. Carnell, Great Britain
1912—F. S. Hird, United States
1920—L. Nusslein, United States
1924—Charles de Lisle, France
1932—Bertil Ronnmark, Sweden
1936—Willy Rogeberg, Norway
1948—Arthur Cook, United States
1952—Anatoli Bogdanov, Russia

Automatic Pistol or Revolver

1896—Phrangudis, Greece
1900—Larouy, France
1906—LeCoq, France
1908—P. van Asbrock, Belgium
1948—Karoly Takacs, Hungary

1-Man Figure Target with Rings

1912—A. P. Lane, United States
1920—Paraines, Brazil

Figure Shooting (6 Targets)

1924—H. M. Bailey, United States
1932—Renzo Morigi, Italy
1936—Cornelius van Oyen, Germany

Free Pistol

1896—S. Paine, United States
1900—Roedern, Switzerland
1906—G. Orphanidis, Greece
1912—A. P. Lane, United States
1920—Karl Frederick, United States
1936—Torsten Ullman, Sweden
1948—E. Vasquez Cam, Peru
1952—Huelet Benner, United States
1956—Pentti Linnosvuo, Finland
1960—Alexet Gustchin, Russia
1964—Valino Markkanen, Finland
1968—Grigory Kosykh, Russia
1972—Ragnar Skanaker, Sweden

Clay Bird (Trap) Shooting—Individual

1900—R. de Barbarin, France
1906—Gerald Merlin, Great Britain (single shot)
1906—Signey Merlin, Great Britain (double shot)

1908—W. H. Ewing, Canada
1912—James R. Graham, United States
1920—M. Arie, United States
1924—Jules Halasy, Hungary
1952—George Genereux, Canada
1956—Galliano Rossini, Italy
1960—Ion Dumitrescu, Romania
1964—Ennio Mattarelli, Italy
1968—John Braithwaite, Great Britain
1972—Angelo Scalzone, Italy

Clay Bird (Trap) Shooting—Team

1908—Great Britain
1912—United States
1920—United States
1924—United States

Running Deer Shooting

1900—L. Debret, France
1908—O. Swahn, Sweden
1912—Alfred G. A. Swahn, Sweden
1920—O. Olsen, Norway
1924—J. K. Boles, United States
1952—John Larsen Norway
1956—Vitalii Romanenko, Russia

Skeet Shooting—Individual

1968—Yevgeny Petrov, Russia
1972—Konrad Wirnhier, West Germany

Moving Target

1972—Lakov Zhelezniak, Russia

Rapid Fire Pistol

1960—William McMillan, United States
1964—Pentti Linnosvuop, Finland
1968—Jozef Zapedzki, Poland
1972—Jozef Zapedski, Poland

Army Rifle—Individual

1900—Kellemberger, Switzerland
1906—Moreaux, France (200 meters)
  —Richardet, Switzerland (300 meters)
1912—Prokopp, Hungary (300 meters)
  —Colas, France (600 meters)
1920—Olsen, Norway (300 meters, prone)
  —Osburn, United States (300 meters, standing)
  —Johansson, Sweden (600 meters, prone)

Army Rifle—Team

1900—Switzerland
1920—Denmark (300 meters, standing)
  —United States (300 meters, prone)
  —United States (600 meters, prone)

Rifle—Odd Distances

1908—United States (200, 500, 600, 800, 900 and 1,000 yards)
1912—United States (200, 400, 500 and 600 meters)
1920—United States (300 and 600 meters)

Minature Rifle—25 Yards or Meters—Individual

1908—Fleming, Great Britain (moving target)
  —W. E. Styles, Great Britain (disappearing target)

1912—W. Carlberg, Sweden

Rifle—Team

1908—Great Britain (50 and 100 yards)
1912—Sweden (25 meters)
1912—Great Britain (50 meters)
1920—United States (50 meters)

Free Rifle (300 Meters)

1900—Emil Kellenberger, Switzerland
1948—Emil Grunig, Switzerland
1952—Anatoli Bogdanov, Russia
1956—Vassili Borissov, Russia
1960—Hubert Hammerer, Australia
1964—Garry L. Anderson, United States
1968—Gary Anderson, United States
1972—Lones Wigger, United States

Silhouette Pistol

1952—Karoly Takacs, Hungary
1956—Stevan Petrescu, Rumania

Small-Bore Rifle—3 Positions

1952—Erling Kongshaug, Norway
1956—Anatolii Bogdanov, Russia
1960—Viktor Shamburkin, Russia
1964—Lones W. Wigger, United States
1968—Bernd Klingner, W. Germany
1972—John Writer, United States

Small-Bore Rifle—Prone

1952—Yosef Sarbu, Rumania
1956—Gerald Ouellette, Canada
1960—Peter Kohnke, Germany
1964—Laszlo Hammerl, Hungary
1968—Jan Kurka, Czechoslovakia
1972—Ho Jun Li, North Korea

Soccer Football

1900—Great Britain
1904—Great Britain
1906—Denmark
1908—Great Britain
1912—Great Britain
1920—Belgium
1924—Uruguay
1928—Uruguay
1936—Italy
1948—Sweden
1952—Hungary
1956—Russia
1960—Yugoslavia
1964—Hungary
1968—Hungary
1972—Poland

Tennis (Lawn)

Men's Singles

1896—Boland, Great Britain
1900—L. Doherty, Great Britain
1904—Beals C. Wright, United States
1906—Max Decugis, France
1908—M. J. G. Ritchie, Great Britain
1912—C. L. Winslow, South Africa

1920—L. Raymond, South Africa
1924—Vincent Richards, United States

Women's Singles

1900—Miss Cooper, Great Britain
1906—Miss Semyriotou, Greece
1908—Mrs. Lambert Chambers, Great Britain
1912—M. Broquedis, France
1920—Suzanne Lenglen, France
1924—Helen Wills, United States

Men's Doubles

1896—Boland, Great Britain—Traun, Germany
1900—F. and L. Doherty, Great Britain
1904—E.W. Leonard—Beals C. Wright, United States
1906—M. Decugis—M. Germot, France
1908—G.W. Hillyard—F. Doherty, Great Britain
1912—H.A. Kitson—C. Winslow, South Africa
1920—O. Turnbull—M. Woosnam, Great Britain
1924—Vincent Richards—Francis T. Hunter, United States

Women's Doubles

1920—Mrs. J. McNair—K. McKane, Great Britain
1924—Helen Wills—Mrs. George Wightman, United States

Mixed Doubles

1900—F. Doherty—Miss Cooper, Great Britain
1906—Mr. and Mrs. M. Decugis, France
1912—Miss D. Koring—H. Schomburgk, Germany
1920—Max Decugis—Suzanne Lenglen, France
1924—Mrs. George W. Wightman—R. Norris Williams, United States

Tennis (Covered Courts)

Men's Singles

1896—Boland, Great Britain
1908—A. W. Gore, Great Britain
1912—A. H. Gobert, France

Women's Singles

1908—G. Eastlake Smith, Great Britain
1912—Mrs. E. M. Hannam, Great Britain

Men's Doubles

1896—Boland, Great Britain—Fritz Traum, Germany
1908—A.W. Gore—H. Roper Barrett, Great Britain
1912—A.H. Gobert—M. Germot, France

Mixed Doubles

1912—Miss E. M. Hannam—C. P. Dixon, Great Britain

Tennis (English Rules)

Men's Singles

1908—Jay Gould, United States

Tug-of-War

1900—United States
1904—United States
1906—Germany
1908—Great Britain
1912—Sweden

1920—Great Britain

Volleyball

Men

1964—Russia
1968—Russia
1972—Japan

Women

1964—Japan
1968—Russia
1972—Russia

Weight Lifting

Flyweight	Lbs.
1972—Zygmun Smalcerz, Poland	744

Bantamweight

1948—Joe N. De Pietro, United States	677.915
1952—Ivan Ododov, Russia	694.45
1956—Charley Vinci, United States	753.5
1960—Charles Vinci, United States	760
1964—Alexey Vakhonin, Russia	788.14
1968—Mohammad Nassiri, Iran	809.75
1972—Imre Foeldi, Hungary	830.50

Featherweight

1920—L. de Haes, Belgium	485
1924—M. Gabetti, Italy	887.35
1928—F. Andrysek, Austria	633.822
1932—R. Suvigny, France	633.822
1936—Anthony Terlazzo, United States	688.937
1948—M. S. J. Fayad, Egypt	733.02
1952—Rafael Chimishkyan, Russia	744.05
1956—Isaac Berger, United States	776.5
1960—Evgeniy Minaev, Russia	821
1964—Yoshinobu, Russia	876.33
1968—Yoshinobu Miyake, Japan	863.5
1972—Norair Nourikian, Bulgaria	885.5

Lightweight

1920—A. Neyland, Esthonia	567.68
1924—E. Decottignies, France	970.02
1928—K. Helbig, Germany, and H. Hass, Austria (tie)	710.98
1932—Rene Duverger, France	716.495
1936—M. A. Mesbah, Egypt	755.085
1948—I. Shams, Egypt	793.656
1952—Tommy Kono, United States	777.12
1956—Igor Rybak, Russia	837.5
1960—Viktor Bushuev, Russia	876
1964—Waldemar Baszanowski, Poland	953.49
1968—Waldemar Baszanowski, Poland	962.5
1972—Mukharbi Kirzhinov, Russia	1104.11

Middleweight

1920—Gance, France	540.012
1924—P. Galimberti, Italy	1085.725
1928—F. Francois, France	738.54
1932—Rudolf Ismayr, Germany	760.507
1936—Khadr El Touni, Egypt	854.28
1948—F. I. Spellman, United States	859.794
1952—Peter George, United States	881
1956—Fedor Bogdanovskii, Russia	925.75

1960—Alexander Kurynov, Russia 964.25
1964—Hans Zdrazila, Czechoslovakia .. 981.05
1968—Viktor Kurentsov, Russia 1045
1972—Yordan Bikov, Bulgaria 1069

Light Heavyweight

1920—E. Dadine, France 639.334
1924—C. Rigoulot, France 1107.811
1928—E. S. Nosseir, Egypt 782.63
1932—L. Hostin, France 804.679
1936—L. Hostin, France 821.213
1948—Stan Stanczyk, United States ... 920.42
1952—T. Lomakin, Russia 919
1956—Tommy Kono, United States ... 986.25
1960—Iremeusz Polinski, Poland 975.25
1964—Rudolf Plyukfeider, Russia 1047.19
1968—Boris Selitsky, Russia 1067
1972—Leif Jenssen, Norway 1118

Middle Heavyweight

1952—Norbert Schemansky, U.S. 981
1956—Arkadii Vorobiev, Russia 1019.25
1960—Vladimir Golovanov, Russia 1041.25
1964—Vladimir Golovanov, Russia 1074.74
1968—Kaario Kangasniemi, Finland ...1138.50
1972—Andon Nikolov, Bulgaria 1157

Heavyweight

1920—F. Bottini, Italy 595.24
1924—J. Tonani, Italy 1140.879
1928—J. Strassberger, Germany 821.213
1932—J. Skobla, Czechoslovakia 837.748
1936—J. Manger, Germany 903.886
1948—John Davis, United States 997.581
1952—John Davis, United States 1012
1956—Paul Anderson, United States ...1102
1960—Yuriy Vlasov, Russia 1184.25
1964—Leonid Zhabotinsky, Russia 1272.13
1968—Leonid Zhabotinsky, Russia 1261
1972—Yan Talts, Russia 1297

Super Heavyweight

1972—Vassili Alexeev, Russia 1411

One Hand

1896—L. Elliot, Great Britain 156.52
1904—O. C. Osthoff, United States .... 48 pts.
1906—Josef Steinbach, Austria 168.872

Two Hands

1896—V. Jensen, Denmark 245.812
1904—P. Kakousis, Greece 245.799
1906—D. Tofolas, Greece 313.925

Wrestling—Freestyle

Paperweight

1972—Roman Dmitriev, Russia

Flyweight

1904—R. Curry, United States (105 lbs.)
1948—V. L. Vitala, Finland
1952—Hassen Cemici, Turkey
1956—Marian Tsalkalmanidze, Russia
1960—Ahmet Bilek, Turkey
1964—Yoshikatsu Yoshida, Japan

1968—Shigeo Nakata, Japan
1972—Kymoni Kato, Japan

Bantamweight

1904—George N. Mehnert, U.S. (115 lbs.)
1908—George N. Mehnert, U.S. (119 lbs.)
1924—Kustaa Pihalajamaki, Finland
1928—K. Makinen, Finland
1932—Robert Edward Pearce, United States
1936—Odon Zombory, Hungary
1948—Nassuh Akkan, Turkey
1952—Shohachi Ishii, Japan
1956—Mustafa Dagistanli, Turkey
1952—Shohachi Ishii, Japan
1956—Mustafa Dagistanli, Turkey
1960—Terry McCann, United States
1964—Yojiro Uetake, Japan
1968—Yojiro Uetake, Japan
1972— Hideaki Yanagida, Japan

Featherweight

1896—Karl Schumann, Germany
1904—I. Niflot, United States
1908—G. S. Dole, United States
1920—Charles E. Ackerly, United States
1924—Robin Reed, United States
1928—Allie Morrison, United States
1932—Hermann Pihlajamaki, Finland
1936—Kustaa Pihlajamaki, Finland
1948—Gazanfer Bilge, Turkey
1952—Bayram Sit, Turkey
1956—Shoze Sasabara, Japan
1960—Mustafa Daginstanli, Turkey
1964—Osamu Watanabe, Japan
1968—Masaaki Kaneko, Japan
1972—Zagalav Abdulbekov, Russia

Lightweight

1904—B. J. Bradshaw, United States
1908—G. de Relwyskow, Great Britain
1920—Kalle Antilla, Finland
1924—Russell Vis, United States
1928—O. Kapp, Esthonia
1932—Charles Pacome, France
1936—Karoly Karpati, Hungary
1948—Celal Atik, Turkey
1952—Olle Anderberg, Sweden
1956—Emamli Habibi, Iran
1960—Shelby Wilson, United States
1964—Enid Dimov, Bulgaria
1968—Abdollah Movahed, Iran
1972—Dan Gable, United States

Welterweight

1904—O. F. Roehm, United States
1924—Hermann Gehri, Switzerland
1928—A. J. Haavisto, Finland
1932—Jack F. Van Bebber, United States
1936—Frank Lewis, United States
1948—Yasar Dogu, Turkey
1952—William Smith, United States
1956—Mistro Ikeda, Japan
1960—Douglas Blubaugh, United States
1964—Ismail Ogan, Turkey

1968—Mahmud Atalay, Turkey
1972—Wayne Wells, United States

Middleweight

1904—Charles Erickson, United States
1908—S. V. Bacon, Great Britain
1920—E. Leino, Finland
1924—Fritz Haggmann, Switzerland
1928—E. Kyburg, Switzerland
1932—Ivar Johansson, Sweden
1936—Emile Poilve, France
1948—Glenn Brand, United States
1952—David Gimakuridze, Russia
1956—Nikola Nikolov, Bulgaria
1960—Hasan Gungor, Turkey
1964—Prodan Gardjev, Bulgaria
1968—Boris Gurevitch, Russia
1972—Levan Tediashili, Russia

Light Heavyweight

1920—Anders Larsson, Sweden
1924—John Spellman, United States
1928—T. S. Sjostedt, Sweden
1932—Peter Joseph Mehringer, United States
1936—Knut Fridell, Sweden
1948—Henry Wittenberg, United States
1952—Wiking Palm, Sweden
1956—Gholam Takhti, Iran
1960—Ismet Atli, Turkey
1964—Alexander Medved, Russia
1968—Ahmet Ayuk, Turkey
1972—Ben Peterson, United States

Heavyweight

1904—B. Hansen, United States
1908—G. C. O'Kelly, Great Britain
1920—Roth, Switzerland
1924—Harry Steele, United States
1928—Johan C. Richthoff, Sweden
1932—Johan C. Richthoff, Sweden
1936—Kristjan Palusalu, Esthonia
1948—George Bobis, Hungary
1952—Arsen Mekokishvili, Russia
1956—Turkey (Team)
1960—Wilfried Dietrich, Germany
1964—Alexandr Ivanitsky, Russia
1968—Alexandr Medved, Russia
1972—Ivan Yarygin, Russia

Super Heavyweight

1972—Alexandr Medved, Russia

Wrestling (Greco-Roman)

Paperweight

1972—Gheorghe Berceano, Rumania

Flyweight

1948—Pietro Lombardi, Italy
1952—Boris Gourevitch, Russia
1956—Nikolai Soloviev, Russia
1960—Dumitru Pirvulescu, Rumania
1964—Tsutomu Hanahara, Japan
1968—Petar Kirov, Bulgaria
1972—Petar Kirov, Bulgaria

Bantamweight

1924—Edward Putsep, Esthonia
1928—K. Leucht, Germany
1932—Jakob Brendel, Germany
1936—Martin Lorincz, Hungary
1948—K. A. Peterson, Sweden
1952—Imre Hodos, Hungary
1956—Konstantin Vyropaev, Russia
1960—Oleg Laravaev, Russia
1964—Masamitsu Ichiguchi, Japan
1968—Janos Varga, Hungary
1972—Rustem Kazakov, Russia

Featherweight

1912—Kalle Koskelo, Finland
1920—Eriman, Finland
1924—Kalle Antilla, Finland
1928—V. Wali, Esthonia
1932—Giovanni Gozzi, Italy
1936—Yasar Erkan, Turkey
1948—M. Octav, Turkey
1952—Jakov Punkine, Russia
1956—Rauno Makinen, Finland
1960—Muzahir Sille, Turkey
1964—Imre Polyak, Hungary
1968—Roman Rurua, Russia
1972—Gheorghi Markov, Bulgaria

Lightweight

1906—Watzl, Austria
1908—E. Porro, Italy
1912—E. E. Ware, Finland
1920—Vare, Finland
1924—Oskari Friman, Finland
1928—L. Keresztes, Hungary
1932—Erik Malmberg, Sweden
1936—Lauri Koskela, Finland
1948—K. Freij, Sweden
1952—Chasame Safine, Russia
1956—Kyosti Lehtonen, Finland
1960—Avtandil Kordidze, Russia
1964—Kazim Ayvaz, Turkey
1968—Muneji Munemura, Japan
1972—Shamil Khisamutdinov, Russia

Welterweight

1920—Ivar Johansson, Sweden
1932—Ivar Johansson, Sweden
1936—Rodolf Svedberg, Sweden
1948—Gosta Andersson, Sweden
1952—Miklos Szilvasi, Hungary
1956—Mithat Bayrak, Turkey
1960—Mithat Bayrak, Turkey
1964—Anatoly Kolesov, Russia
1968—Rudolf Vesper, E. Germany
1972—Vitezslav Macha, Czechoslovakia

Middleweight

1906—Weckman, Finland
1908—F. M. Martenson, Sweden
1912—C. E. Johansson, Sweden
1920—Westergren, Sweden
1924—Edward Westerlund, Finland
1928—Vaino Kokkinen, Finland

1932–Vaino Kokkinen, Finland
1936–Ivar Johansson, Sweden
1948–R. Gronberg, Sweden
1952–Vuivi Kartozia, Russia
1960–Dimitro Dobrev, Bulgaria
1964–Branislav Simic, Yugoslavia
1968–Lother Metz, E. Germany
1972–Csaba Hegedus, Hungary

Light Heavyweight

1908–W. Weckman, Finland
1912–A. O. Ahlgren, Sweden
1924–Carl Westergren, Sweden
1928–S. Moustafa, Egypt
1932–Rudolph Svensson, Sweden
1936–Axel Cardier, Sweden
1948–Karl Nilsson, Sweden
1952–Kolpo Grondahl, Finland
1956–Valentine Nikolaev, Russia
1960–Tevfik Kis, Turkey
1964–Boyan Alexandrov, Bulgaria
1968–Boyan Radev, Bulgaria
1972–Valery Rezantsev, Russia

Heavyweight

1906–J. Jensen, Denmark
1908–R. Wersz, Hungary
1912–U. Soarela, Finland
1920–Lindfors, Sweden
1924–Henri Deglane, France
1928–J. R. Svensson, Sweden
1932–Carl Westergren, Sweden
1936–Kristjan Palusalu, Estonia
1948–Armet Kirecci, Turkey
1952–Ionganes Kotkas, Russia
1956–Anatolii Parfenov, Russia
1960–Ivan Bogdan, Russia
1964–Istvan Kozma, Hungary
1968–Istvan Kozma, Hungary
1972–Nicolae Martinescu, Rumania

Super Heavyweight

1972–Anatoly Roshin, Russia

Yachting

6-Meter Class

1900–Lerina, Switzerland
1908–Dormy, Great Britain
1912–Mac Miche, France
1920–Jo, Norway
1924–Elisabeth V, Norway
1928–Norna, Norway
1932–Bissbi, Sweden
1936–Lalage, Great Britain
1948–Llanoria, United States
1952–Llanoria, United States

8-Meter Class

1900–Olle, Great Britain
1908–Cobweb, Great Britain
1912–Taifun, Norway
1920–Sildra, Norway
1924–Bera, Norway

1928–L'Aigle, France
1932–Angelita, United States
1936–Italia, Italy

Star Class

1932–Jupiter, United States
1936–Wannsee, Germany
1948–Hilarius, United States
1952–Merope, Italy
1956–Kathleen, United States
1960–Tornado, Russia
1964–Gem, Bahamas
1968–United States
1972–Australia

Firefly Class

1948–Denmark, P. Elvestrom

Monotype Class

1920–Boreas, Holland (2-man dinghy)
1924–L. Huybrechts, Belgium
1928–Thorell, Sweden
1932–Lebrun, France
1936–Kagchelland, Holland

Dragon Class

1948–Pan, Norway
1952–Pan, Norway
1956–Slaghoken II, Sweden
1960–Nirefs, Greece
1964–White Lady, Denmark
1968–United States
1972–Australia

Swallow Class

1948–Swift, Great Britain

2-Ton Boat

1900–de Pourtales, Switzerland

3-Ton Boat

1900–Exshaw, France

30-Meter Class

1920–Kullan, Sweden

40-Meter Class

1920–Sif, Sweden

12-Meter Class

1908–Hera, Great Britain
1912–Magda IV, Norway
1920–Hera, Norway (new)
1920–Atlanta, Norway (old)

10-Meter Class

1912–Kitty, Sweden
1920–Mosk II, Norway (new)
1920–Eleda, Norway (old)

8-, 7-, 6.5-Meter Classes

1908–Heroine, Great Britain (7-m.)
1920–Jerne, Norway (old 8-m.)
1920–Edelweiss, Belgium (old 6-m.)
1920–Oranje, Holland (6.5m.)
1920–Ancora, Great Britain (7-m.)

5.5-Meter Class

1952–Complex II, United States
1956–Rush V, Sweden

1960—Minotaur, United States
1964—Barrabjoey, Australia
1968—Sweden

Finn Class

1952—Denmark
1956—Denmark
1960—Denmark
1964—Germany
1968—Russia
1972—France

Flying Dutchman Class

1960—Sirene, Norway
1964—Pandora, New Zealand
1968—Great Britain
1972—Great Britain

Sharpie Class

1956—Jest, New Zealand

Soling

1972—United States

Tempest

1972—Russia

**WINTER GAMES CHAMPIONS,
1908-1972**

Figure Skating

Men

1908—Ulrich Salchow, Sweden
1920—Gillis Grafstrom, Sweden
1924—Gillis Grafstrom, Sweden
1928—Gillis Grafstrom, Sweden
1932—Karl Schafer, Austria
1936—Karl Schafer, Austria
1948—Richard Button, United States
1952—Richard Button, United States
1956—Hayes Alan Jenkins, United States
1960—David W. Jenkins, United States
1964—Manfred Schnelldorfer, Germany
1968—Wolfgang Schwartz, Austria
1972—Ondrej Nepela, Czechoslovakia

Women

1908—Mrs. Madge Syers, Great Britain
1920—Julin, Sweden
1924—Mrs. Otto von Szabo-Plank, Austria
1928—Sonja Henie, Norway
1932—Sonja Henie, Norway
1936—Sonja Henie, Norway
1948—Barbara Ann Scott, Canada
1952—Jeannette Altwegg, Great Britain
1956—Tenley Albright, United States
1960—Carol Heiss, United States
1964—Sjoukje Dijkstra, Holland
1968—Peggy Fleming, United States
1972—Beatrix Schuba, Austria

Pairs

1908—Miss Hubler—H. Burger, Germany
1920—Mr.—Mrs. Jakobsson, Finland
1924—H. Englemann—A. Berger, Austria
1928—Andree Joly—Pierre Brunet, France
1932—Andree and Pierre Brunet, France
1936—Maxie Herber—Ernst Baier, Germany
1948—Micheline Lannoy—Pierre
          Baugniet, Belgium
1952—Ria and Paul Falk, Germany
1956—Elisabeth Schwarz—Kurt Oppelt, Austria
1960—Barbara Wagner, Robert Paul, Canada
1964—Ludmila Beloussova—Oleg Protopopov,
          Russia
1968—Ludmila Beloussova—Oleg Protopopov,
          Russia
1972—Irina Rodnina—Alexei Ulanov, Russia

Speed Skating

500 Meters

1924—Charles Jewtraw, United States .. 44   s.
1928—Clas Thunberg Finland, and
          Bernt Evensen, Norway (tie) .. 43.4 s.
1932—John A. Shea, United States .... 43.4 s.
1936—Ivar Ballangrud, Norway .... 43.4 s.
1948—Finn Helgesen, Norway .... 43.1 s.
1952—Ken Henry, United States ...... 43.2 s.
1956—Yevgeni Grishin, Russia .... 40.2 s.
1960—Eugeni Grishin, Russia .... 40.2 s.
1964—R. Terrance McDermott, United
          States .... 40.1 s.
1968—Erhard Keller, W. Germany ..... 40.3 s.
1972—Erhard Keller, W. Germany ..... 39.4 s.

1,500 Meters

1924—Clas Thunberg, Finland 2:20.8
1928—Clas Thunberg, Finland 2:21.1
1932—John A. Shea, United States 2:57.5
1936—Charles Mathisen, Norway 2:19.2
1948—Sverre Farstad, Norway 2:17.6
1952—Hjalmar Andersen, Norway 2:20.4
1956—Yevgeni Grishin, Russia, and Yuri
          Mikhailov, Russia (tie) 2:08.6
1960—Roald Edgar Aas, Norway 2:10.4
1964—Ants Anston, Russia 2:10.3
1968—Cornelis Verkerk, Holland 2:03.4
1972—Ard Schenk, Netherlands 2:02.9

5,000 Meters

1924—Clas Thunberg, Finland 8:39
1928—Ivar Ballangrud, Norway 8:50.5
1932—Irving Jaffee, United States 9:40.8
1936—Ivar Ballangrud, Norway 8:19.6
1948—Reidar Liaklev, Norway 8:29.4
1952—Hjalmar Andersen, Norway 8:10.6
1956—Boris Shilkov, Russia 7:48.7
1960—Viktor Kosichkin, Russia 7:51.3
1964—Knut Johannesen, Norway 7:38.4
1968—F. Anton Maier, Norway 7:22.4
1972—Ard Schenk, Netherlands 7:23.6

10,000 Meters

1924—Julien Skutnabb, Finland 18:04.8
1928—Irving Jaffee, United States....*18:36.5
1932—Irving Jaffee, United States.....19:13.6
1936—Ivar Ballangrud, Norway 17:24.3
1948—Ake Seyffarth, Sweden 17:26.3
1952—Hjalmar Andersen, Norway 16:45.8

1956—Sigge Ericsson, Sweden 16:35
1960—Knut Johanneson, Norway 15:46.6
1964—Jonny Nilsson, Sweden 15:50.1
1968—Johnny Hoeglin, Sweden 15:23.6
1972—Ard Schenk, Netherlands 15:01.3

*Thawing of ice caused event to be canceled. Jaffee had best time.

WOMEN'S DIVISION
500 Meters

1960—Helga Haase, Germany 45.9
1964—Lydia Skoblikova, Russia 45.0
1968—Ludmila Titova, Russia 46.1
1972—Anne Henning, United States ... 43.3

1,000 Meters

1960—Klara Guseva, Russia 1:34.1
1964—Lydia Skoblikova, Russia 1:33.2
1968—Carolina Geijssen, Holland 1:32.6
1972—Monika Pflug, W. Germany 1:31.4

1,500 Meters

1960—Lidija Skoblikova, Russia 2:25.2
1964—Lydia Skoblikova, Russia 2:22.6
1968—Kaija Mustonen, Finland 2:22.4
1972—Dianne Holum, United States ... 2:20.8

3,000 Meters

1960—Lidija Skoblikova, Russia 5:14.3
1964—Lydia Skoblikova, Russia 5:14.9
1968—Johanna Schut, Holland 4:56.2
1972—Stien Kaiser Baas, Netherlands .. 4:52.1

Biathlon (Skiing and Shooting)

1960—Klas Lestander, Sweden
1964—Vladimir Melanin, Russia
1968—Magnar Solberg, Norway
1972—Magnar Solberg, Norway

Biathlon Relay

1968—Russia
1972—Russia

Bobsledding
4-Man

1924—Switzerland
1928—United States (5-man)
1932—United States
1936—Switzerland
1948—United States
1952—Germany
1956—Switzerland
1964—Canada
1968—Italy
1972—Switzerland

2-Man

1932—United States
1936—United States
1948—Switzerland
1952—Germany
1956—Italy
1964—Great Britain
1968—Italy

1972—W. Germany

Skeleton

1928—John Heaton, United States
1948—Nino Bibbia, Italy

Luge
Men's Singles

1964—Thomas Kohler, Germany 3:26.77
1968—Manfred Schmid, Austria 2:52.48
1972—Wolfgang Scheidel, E. Germany ..3:27.58

Men's 2 Seater

1964—Josef Fiestmantl and Manfred Stengl, Austria 1:41.62
1968—Klaus Bonsack and Thomas Koehler, East Germany 1:35.85
1972—Paul Hildgartner—Walter Plaikner, Italy and Horst Hornlein—Reinhard Bredow, East Germany (tie) 1:28.35

Women's Singles

1964—Ortrun Enderlein, Germany 3:24.67
1968—Erica Lechner, Italy 2:28.66
1972—Anna M. Muller, E. Germany 2:59.18

Skiing—Men

Nordic (Cross Country)

15 Kilometers (9.3 miles)
(Approx. 18-Kilo course from 1924-1952)

1924—Thorleif Haug, Norway
1928—Johan Grottumsbraaten, Norway
1932—Sven Utterstrom, Sweden
1936—Erik-Aug. Larsson, Sweden
1948—M. Lundstrom, Sweden
1952—Hallgeir Brenden, Norway
1956—Hallgeir Brenden, Norway
1960—Hakon Brusveen, Norway
1964—Eero Mantyranta, Finland
1968—Harald Groenningen, Norway
1972—Sven-Ake Lundback, Sweden

30 Kilometers (18.6 miles)

1956—Veikko Hakulinen, Finland
1960—Sixten Jernberg, Sweden
1964—Eero Mantyranta, Finland
1968—Franco Nones, Italy
1972—Vyacheslav Vedenin, Russia

50 Kilometers (31 miles)

1924—Thorleif Haug, Norway
1928—P. Hedlund, Sweden
1932—Veli Saarinen, Finland
1936—Elis Viklund, Sweden
1948—Nils Karlsson, Sweden
1952—Veikko Hakulinen, Finland
1956—Sixten Jernberg, Sweden
1960—Kalevi Hamalainen, Finland
1964—Sixten Jernberg, Sweden
1968—Ole Ellefsaeter, Norway
1972—Paal Tyldum, Norway

15 Km. Cross-Country & Jumping

1924—Thorleif Haug, Norway

1928—Johan Grottumsbraaten, Norway
1932—Johan Grottumsbraaten, Norway
1936—Oddbjorn Hagen, Norway
1948—Heikki Hasu, Finland
1952—Simon Slattvik, Norway
1956—Sverre Stenersen, Norway
1960—Georg Thoma, Germany
1964—Tormod Knutsen, Norway
1968—Franz Keller, W. Germany
1972—Ulrich Wehling, E. Germany

40-Kilometer Cross-Country Relay

1936—Finland
1948—Sweden
1952—Finland
1956—Russia
1960—Finland
1964—Sweden
1968—Norway
1972—Russia

Ski Jumping (90 Meters)

1924—Jacob T. Thams, Norway
1928—Alfred Andersen, Norway
1932—Birger Ruud, Norway
1936—Birger Ruud, Norway
1948—Petter Hugsted, Norway
1952—Arnfinn Bergmann, Norway
1956—Antti Hyvarinen, Finland
1960—Helmut Recknagel, Germany
1964—Toralf Engan, Norway
1968—Vladimir Beloussov, Russia
1972—Wojiech Fortuna, Poland

Ski Jumping (70 Meters)

1964—Veikko Kankkonen, Finland
1968—Jiri Raska, Czechoslovakia
1972—Yukio Kasaya, Japan

Alpine

Downhill Race

1948—Henri Oreiller, France
1952—Zeno Colo, Italy
1956—Toni Sailer, Austria
1960—Jean Vuarnet, France
1964—Egon Zimmermann, Austria
1968—Jean Claude Killy, France
1972—Bernhard Russi, Switzerland

Slalom

1948—Edi Reinalter, Switzerland
1952—Othmar Schneider, Austria
1956—Toni Sailer, Austria
1960—Ernst Hinterseer, Austria
1964—Josef Stiegler, Austria
1968—Jean Claude Killy, France
1972—Francisco Fernandez Ochoa, Spain

Giant Slalom

1952—Stein Erksen, Norway
1956—Toni Sailer, Austria
1960—Roger Staub, Switzerland
1964—Francois Bonlieu, France
1968—Jean Claude Killy, France
1972—Gustavo Thoeni, Italy

Alpine Combined (Downhill and Slalom)

1936—Franz Pfnur, Germany
1948—Henri Oreiller, France

Skiing—Women

Alpine

Downhill Race

1948—Hedi Schlunegger, Switzerland
1952—Trude Jochum-Beiser, Austria
1956—Madeleine Berthod, Switzerland
1960—Heidi Biebl, Germany
1964—Christl Haas, Austria
1968—Olga Pall, Austria
1972—Marie Therese Nadig, Switzerland

Slalom

1948—Gretchen Fraser, United States
1952—Mrs. Andrea Mead Lawrence, United States
1956—Renee Colliard, Switzerland
1960—Anne Heggtveit, Canada
1964—Christine Goitschel, France
1968—Marielle Goitschel, France
1972—Barbara Cochran, United States

Giant Slalom

1952—Mrs. Andrea Mead Lawrence, United States
1956—Ossi Reichert, Germany
1960—Yvonne Ruegge, Switzerland
1964—Marielle Goitschel, France
1968—Nancy Greene, Canada
1972—Marie Therese Nadig, Switzerland

Alpine Combined (Downhill and Slalom)

1936—Christel Cranz, Germany
1948—Trude Jochum-Beiser, Austria

Nordic (Cross-Country)

5 Kilometers

1964—Claudia Boyarskikh, Russia
1968—Toini Gustafsson, Sweden
1972—Galina Koulacova, Russia

10 Kilometers

1956—Lyubov Kozyreva, Russia
1960—Marija Gusakova, Russia
1964—Claudia Boyarskikh, Russia
1968—Toini Gustafsson, Sweden
1972—Galina Koulacova, Russia

15 Kilometer Relay

1956—Finland
1960—Sweden
1964—Russia
1968—Norway
1972—Russia

Ice Hockey

1920—Canada
1924—Canada
1928—Canada
1932—Canada
1936—Great Britain
1948—Canada
1952—Canada
1956—Russia

1960—United States
1964—Russia
1968—Russia
1972—Russia

Demonstrations

Military Ski Patrol

1924—Switzerland
1928—Norway
1936—Italy
1948—Switzerland

Sled Dog Racing

1932—St. Goddard, Canada

Men's Speed Skating (Four Events)

1924—Clas Thunberg, Finland . . . . 5.5 pts.

Women's Speed Skating (1932)

500 meters—Jean Wilson, Canada 0.58
1,000 meters—Elizabeth Dubois, United
    States 2:04
1,500 meters—Kit Klein, United States 3:06

Curling

1924—Great Britain
1932—Canada (Manitoba)
1936—Austria (Triol)

Winter Pentathlon

1948—Gustav Lindh, Sweden . . . . 14 pts.

PAN-AMERICAN GAMES

Like the Olympic Games, the Pan-American Games are designed to promote good will and understanding among countries. It is believed by the sponsors that more can be accomplished toward this end through sport than through any other endeavor. Whereas the Olympic Games are open to all nations of the world, the Pan-American Games are limited to the countries of the Western Hemisphere.

Originally planned for 1942, the first Pan-American Games were not held until 1951 The reason for the postponement was the outbreak of World War II. The first games were held in February and March, 1951, at Buenos Aires, Argentina. A crowd of 100,000 attended the opening-day ceremonies, which included a parade of the athletes from all competing nations. A Greek athlete, carrying a torch lighted at Mount Olympus, transferred the flame to the Pan-American torch and the Argentine team repeated the Olympic oath on behalf of all the competitors. As President Juan D. Peron pronounced the games open, the Olympic flag was raised.

The Pan-American Games are held every four years.

CHAMPIONS

(Competition only in years shown)

Track and Field—Men

100-Meter Dash

                                   Time

1951—Rafael Fortun, Cuba 0:10.6
1955—J. Rodney Richard, United States 0:10.3
1959—O. Ray Norton, United States . . . 0:10.3
1963—Enrique Figuerola, Cuba 0:10.3
1967—Harry Jerome, Canada 0:10.2
1971—Don Quarrie, Jamaica 0:10.2

200-Meter Dash

1951—Rafael Fortun, Cuba 0:21.3

1955—J. Rodney Richard, United States 0:27.7
1959—O. Ray Norton, United States . . . 0:20.6
1963—Rafael Sandrea, Venezuela 0:21.2
1967—John Carlos, United States 0:20.5
1971—Don Quarrie, Jamaica 0:19.8

400-Meter Run

1951—Malvin Whitfield, United States . 0:47.8
1955—Louis Jones, United States 0:45.4
1959—George Kerr, West Indies 0:46.1
1963—James A. Johnson, United States 0:46.7
1967—Lee Evans, United States 0:44.9
1971—John Smith, United States 0:44.6

800-Meter Run

1951—Mal Whitfield, United States 1:53.2
1955—Arnold Sowell, United States . . . 1:49.7
1959—Thomas Murphy, United States . 1:49.4
1963—Don Bertoia, Canada 1:48.3
1967—Wade Bell, United States 1:49.2
1971—Ken Swenson, United States 1:48.0

1,500-Meter Run

1951—Browning Ross, United States . . . 4:00.4
1955—Juan D. Maranda, Argentina 3:53.2
1959—Dyrol Burleson, United States . . 3:49.1
1963—James E. Grelle, United States . . 3:43.5
1967—Tom Von Ruden, United States . 3:43.4
1971—Marty Liquori, United States . . . 3:42.1

3,000-Meter Steeplechase

1951—Curtis Stone, United States 9:32
1955—Guillermo Sola, Chile 9:46.8
1959—Philip Coleman, United States . . 8:54.4
1963—Jeffrey M. Fishback, United States 9:07.9
1967—Chris McCubbins, United States . 8:38.2
1971—Mike Manley, United States 8:42.2

5,000-Meter Run

1951—Ricardo Bralo, Argentina 14:57.2
1955—Oswaldo Suarez, Argentina 15:30.6
1959—William Dellinger, United States . 14:28.4
1963—Oswaldo Suarez, Argentina 14:25.7

1967—Van Nelson, United States 13:47.4

1971—Steve Prefontaine, United States . 13:52.0

10,000-Meter Run

1951—Curtis Stone, United States 31:08.6

1955—Oswaldo Suarez, Argentina 32:42.6

1959—Oswaldo Suarez, Argentina 30:17.2

1963—Peter J. McArdle, United States . 29:52.1

1967—Van Nelson, United States 29:17.4

1971—Frank Shorter, United States ... 28:50.0

Marathon

1951—Delto Cabrera, Argentina 2:35:00

1955—Doroteo Flores, Buatemala .. 2:59:09.2

1959—John Kelley, United States ... 2:27:54.2

1963—Fidel Negrete Bamboa, Mexico 2:27:56.6

1967—Andy Boychuk, Canada 2:23:02.4

1971—Frank Shorter, United States . 2:22:47.0

110—Meter Hurdles

1951—Dick Attlesey, United States 0:14

1955—Jack Davis, United States 0:14.3

1959—Hayes Jones, United States 0:13.6

1963—H. Blaine Lindgren, United States 0:13.8

1967—Earl McCullouch, United States . 0:13.4

1971—Rodney Milburn, United States . 0:13.4

400—Meter Hurdles

1951—Jaime Aparicio, Columbia 0:53.4

1955—Josh Culbreath, United States ... 0:51.5

1959—Josh Culbreath, United States ... 0:51.2

1963—Juan Pablo Dryska, Argentina ... 0:50.2

1967—Ron Whitney, United States 0:50.7

1971—Ralph Mann, United States 0:49.1

10,000-Meter Walk

1951—Harry Laskau, United States 50:26.8

20,000-Meter Walk

1963—Alex Oakley, Canada 1:42:43.2

1967—Ron Laird, United States 1:33:05.2

1971—Goetz Klopfer, United States . 1:37:37.0

50,000-Meter Walk

1951—Sixto Ibanez, Argentina 5:06:06.8

1955—No competition

1967—Larry Young, United States .. 4:26:20.8

1971—Larry Young, United States .. 4:38:33.0

400-Meter Relay

1951—United States (Donald Campbell,
Richard Attlesey, John Voight,
Arthur Bragg) 0:41

1955—United States (W. Williams, J. D.
Bennett, C. Thomas, R. Richard) 0:40.7

1959—United States (H. Jones, R. Poynter, R. Woodhouse, R. Norton) .. 0:40.4

1963—United States (I. Murchison, B.
Johnson, O. Cassell, E. Young) .. 0:40.4

1967—United States (E. McCullouch, J.
Bright, R. Copeland, W. Turner) . 0:39.0

1971—Jamaica (A. Daley, C. Lawson, L.
Miller, D. Quarrie) 0:39.2

1,600-Meter Relay

1951—United States (Hugo Maiocco,
William Brown, John Voight, Mal

Whitfield) 3:09.9

1955—United States (James Mashburn,
Lonnie Spurrier, James Lea,
Lou Jones) 3:07.2

1959—West Indies (Mal Spence, Mel
Spence, B. Ince, G. Kerr) 3:05.3

1963—United States (R. Edmunds, J.
Johnson, O. Cassell, E. Young) .. 3:09.6

1967—United States (E. Stinson, E.
Taylor, V. Matthews, L. Evans) .. 3:02.0

1971—United States (D. Alexander, F.
Newhouse, T. Turner, J. Smith) . 3:00.6

High Jump

1951—Virgil Severns, United States .6 ft. 4 3/4 in.

1955—Ernie Shelton, United States .6 ft. 7 1/8 in.

1959—Charles Dumas, United States 6 ft. 10 1/2 in.

1963—Gene C. Johnson
United States .... 6 ft. 11 in.

1967—Ed Caruthers, United States 7 ft. 2 1/4 in.

1971—Pat Matzdorf, United States .6 ft. 10 3/4 in.

Broad Jump

1951—Gaylord Bryan, United States . 23 ft. 7 in.

1955—Roselyn Range,
United States .... 26 ft. 4 1/8 in.

1959—Irvin Roberson, United States . 26 ft. 2 in.

1963—Ralph H. Boston,
United States .... 26 ft. 7 1/4 in.

1967—Ralph H. Boston,
United States .... 27 ft. 2 1/2 in.

1971—Arnie Robinson,
United States .... 26 ft. 3 1/4 in.

Triple Jump

1951—Adhemar Ferreira da Silva, Brazil .. 50 ft.

1955—Adhemar Ferreira da Silva,
Brazil .... 54 ft. 4 in.

1959—Adhemar de Silva, Brazil ..... 52 ft. 2 in.

1963—William J. Sharpe,
United States .... 49 ft. 8 1/4 in.

1967—Charlie Craig,
United States .... 54 ft. 3 1/4 in.

1971—Pedro Perez, Cuba .... 57 ft. 1 in.

Shot-Put

1951—James Fuchs,
United States .... 56 ft. 7 1/8 in.

1955—Parry O'Brien,
United States .... 57 ft. 8 1/2 in.

1959—Parry O'Brien,
United States .... 62 ft. 5 1/2 in.

1963—David J. Davis, United States . 60 ft. 9 in.

1967—Randy Matson, United States . 65 ft. 1 in.

1971—Al Feuerbach, United States . 64 ft. 10 in.

Pole Vault

1951—Bob Richards,
United States .... 14 ft. 9 1/2 in.

1955—Bob Richards,
United States .... 14 ft. 9 1/2 in.

1959—Donald Bragg,
United States .... 15 ft. 2 1/2 in.

1963—David E. Tork, United States 16 ft. 3/4 in.

1967—Bob Seagren, United States . . . 16 ft. 1 in.
1971—Jan Johnson, United States 17 ft. 4 3/4 in.

Discus Throw

1951—James Fuchs, United States . 160 ft. 4 in.
1955—Fortune Gordien,
United States . . . . 174 ft. 2 1/2 in.
1959—Alfred Oerter,
United States . . . . 190 ft. 8 1/2 in.
1963—Robert K. Humphreys,
United States . . . . 189 ft. 8 1/2 in.
1967—Gary Carlsen, United States . 188 ft. 8 in.
1971—Dick Drescher, United States 204 ft. 2 in.

Javelin Throw

1951—Ricardo Heber, Argentina 223 ft. 4 2/8 in.
1955—Franklin Held,
United States . . . . 228 ft. 11 in.
1959—Buster Quist,
United States . . . . 231 ft. 3 1/2 in.
1963—Daniel A. Studney,
United States . . . . .248 ft. 1/4 in.
1967—Frank Covelli, United States . 243 ft. 8 in.
1971—Cary Feldman,
United States . . . . 267 ft. 5 in.

Hammer Throw

1951—Emilio Ortiz, Argentina . 157 ft. 7 3/8 in.
1955—Robert Backus,
United States . . . . 180 ft. 1 3/4 in.
1963—Albert W. Hall, United States 205 ft. 10 in.
1967—Tom Gage, United States . . . 214 ft. 4 in.
1971—Al Hall, United States . . . . . . 216 ft. 0 in.

Decathlon

1951—Hernan Figueroa, Chile . . . . . . .6,615 pts.
1955—Rafer Johnson, United States . .6,994 pts.
1959—David Edstrom, United States . .7,254 pts.
1963—John D. Martin, United States .7,445 pts.
1971—Rick Wanamaker,
United States . . . . .7,648 pts.

Track and Field—Women

60-Meter Dash

1951—No competition
1955—Bertha Diaz, Cuba 0:07.5
1959—Isabelle Daniels, United States 0:07.4

100-Meter Dash

1951—Julia Sanchez Deze, Peru 0:12.2
1955—Barbara Jones, United States 0:11.5
1959—Lucinda Williams, United States . . 0:12.1
1963—Edith McGuire, United States 0:11.5
1967—Barbara Ferrell, United States 0:11.5
1971—Iris Davis, United States 0:11.2

200-Meter Run

1951—Jean Patton, United States 0:25.3
1955—No competition
1959—Lucinda Williams, United States . . 0:24.2
1963—Vivian Brown, United States 0:23.9
1967—Wyomia Tyrus, United States 0:23.7
1971—Stephanie Berto, Canada 0:23.5

400-Meter Run

1971—Marilyn Neufville, Jamaica 0:52.3

800-Meter Run

1963—Abigail Hoffman, Canada 2:10.2
1967—Madeline Manning, United States . 2:02.3
1971—Abby Hoffman, Canada 2:05.5

80-Meter Hurdles

1951—Eliana Gaete Lazo, Chile 0:11.9
1955—Eliana Gaete Lazo, Chile 0:11.7
1959—Bertha Diaz, Cuba 0:11.2
1963—JoAnn Terry, United States 0:11.3
1967—Mrs. Cherrie Sherrand,
United States 0:10.8

100-Meter Hurdles

1971—Mrs. Pat Johnson, United States . . 0:13.1

400-Meter Relay

1951—United States (Dolores Dwyer,
Janet Moreau, Nell Jackson, Jean
Patton) 0:48.8
1955—United States (Isabelle Daniels,
Mabel Landry, Mae Faggs, Barbara
Jones) 0:47
1959—United States (Isabelle Daniels,
Wilma Rudolph, Lucinda Williams
Barbara Jones 0:46.4
1963—United States (Willye White,
Marilyn White, Norma Harris, Vivian
Brown) 0:45.6
1967—Cuba (Miguelina Cobian, Violeta
Quezanda Diaz, Aurelia Penton Conde,
Cristina Hechevarria) 0:44.6
1971—United States (O. Brown, P.
Hawkins, M. Render, I. Davis) 0:44.5

1,600-Meter Relay

1971—United States (E. Stroy, M. Laing,
G. Norman, C. Touissant) 3:32.4

Discus Throw

1951—Ingeborg Mello de Preiss,
Argentina . . . . 126 ft. 5 3/4 in.
1955—Ingeborg Pfuller,
Argentina . . . . 141 ft. 8 3/8 in.
1959—Earlene Brown,
United States . . . . 161 ft. 9 1/2 in.
1963—Nancy McCredie, Canada 164 ft. 7 1/2 in.
1967—Carol Moseke, United States . 161 ft. 7 in.
1971—Carmen Romero, Cuba . . . . . 187 ft. 7 in.

Broad Jump

1951—Beatriz Kretchmer, Chile . 17 ft. 9 3/8 in.
1959—Annie Smith, United States 18 ft. 9 3/4 in.
1963—Willye White, United States . 20 ft. 2 in.
1967—Irene Martinez Tartabull, Cuba 20 ft. 9 in.
1971—Brenda Elser, Canada . . . . 21 ft. 1 1/4 in.

Shot-Put

1951—Ingeborg Mello de Preiss,
Argentina . . . . 40 ft. 10 1/8 in.
1955—Earlene Brown (Mrs.),
United States . . . . 48 ft. 2 in.
1963—Nancy McCredie, Canada . . . . 50 ft. 3 in.
1967—Nancy McCredie, Canada . 49 ft. 9 3/4 in.
1971—Lynn Graham, United States . 51 ft. 8 in.

Javelin Throw

1951—Hortensia Lopez Garcia,
Mexico .... 129 ft. 4 1/2 in.
1955—Karen E. Anderson,
United States .... 161 ft. 3 in.
1959—Marlene Ahrens, Chile . . 148 ft. 10 1/2 in.
1963—Marlene Ahrens, Chile . . . 163 ft. 9 3/4 in.
1967—Barbara Friedrich,
United States .... 174 ft. 9 in.
1971—Tomasa Nunez, Cuba ...... 177 ft. 2 in.

High Jump

1951—Jacinta Sandtford, Ecuador 4 ft. 9 1/2 in.
1955—Mildred McDaniel,
United States .... 5 ft. 6 5/16 in.
1959—Ann Flynn, United States ..... 5 ft. 6 in.
1963—Eleanor Montgomery,
United States .... 5 ft. 6 in.
1967—Eleanor Montgomery,
United States .... 5 ft. 10 in.
1971—Debbie Brill, Canada .... 6 ft. 3/4 in.

Pentathlon

1971—Debbie Van Kiekebelt,
Canada .... 4,290 pts.

Swimming—Men

100-Meter Free-Style

1951—Dick Cleveland, United States 0:58.8
1955—Clarke Scholes, United States 0:57.7
1959—Jeffrey Farrell, United States 0:56.3
1963—Stephen E. Clark, United States ....
1967—Don Havens, United States 0:53.79
1971—Frank Heckl, United States 0:52.80

200-Meter Free-Style

1967—Don Schollander, United States . 1:56.01
1971—Frank Heckl, United States 1:56.36

400-Meter Free-Style

1951—Tetsuo Okamoto, Brazil 4:52.4
1955—James McLane, United States 4:51.3
1959—George Breen, United States 4:36.4
1963—Roy A. Saari, United States 4:19.3
1967—Greg Charlton, United States ... 4:10.23
1971—Jim McConica, United States ... 4:08.97

1,500-Meter Free-Style

1951—Tetsuo Okamoto, Brazil 19:23.3
1955—James McLane, United States 20:04
1959—Alan Somers, United States 17:53.2
1963—Roy A. Saari, United States 17:26.2
1967—Mike Burton, United States ... 16:44.40
1971—Pat Miles, United States 16:32.03

100-Meter Backstroke

1951—Allen Stack, United States 1:08
1955—Frank E. McKinney, United States 1:07.1
1959—Frank McKinney, United States .. 1:03.6
1963—Edward C. Bartsch, United States . 1:01.5
1967—Charlie Hickcox, United States .. 1:01.19
1971—Melvin Nash, United States 0:59.84

100-Meter Breaststroke

1967—Jose Fiolo, Brazil 1:07.52
1971—Mark Chatfield, United States ... 1:06.75

100-Meter Butterfly

1967—Mark Spitz, United States 0:56.30
1971—Frank Heckl, United States 0:56.92

200-Meter Backstroke

1967—Ralph Hutton, Canada 2:12.55
1971—Charlie Campbell, United States . 2:07.09

200-Meter Breaststroke

1951—Hector Dominguez Nimo,
Argentina 2:43.8
1955—Hector Dominguez Nimo,
Argentina 2:46.9
1959—William Mulliken, United States .. 2:43.1
1963—Chester A. Jastremski,
United States 2:35.4
1967—Jose Fiolo, Brazil 2:30.42
1971—Rick Colella, United States 2:27.12

200-Meter Butterfly

1951—No competition
1955—Eulalio Rios, Mexico 2:39.8
1959—J. David Gillanders, United States . 2:18.0
1963—Carl J. Robie, United States 2:11.3
1967—Mark Spitz, United States 2:06.42
1971—Jorge Delgado, Ecuador 2:06.41

300-Meter Medley Relay

1951—United States (Allen Stack, Bowen
Stassforth, Richard Cleveland) 3:16.9

400-Meter Medley Relay

1955—United States (Frank McKinney,
Fred Maguire, Leonide Baarcke, Clark
Scholes) 4:29.1
1959—United States (Richard McGeagh,
William Craig, Walter Richardson,
Nicholas Roby) 4:05.6
1967—United States (Dough Russell,
Russ Webb, Mark Spitz, Ken
Walsh) 3:59.31
1971—United States (J. Murphy, B.
Job, J. Heidenreich, F. Heckl) ... 3:56.08

200-Meter Individual Medley

1967—Doug Russell, United States 2:13.22
1971—Steve Furniss, United States 4:42.69

400-Meter Individual Medley

1967—Bill Utley, United States 4:48.12
1971—Steve Furniss, United States 4:42.69

400-Meter Free-Style Relay

1967—United States (Ken Walsh,
Mike Fitzmaurice, Mark Spitz,
Don Schollander) 3:34.08
1971—United States (D. Edgar, S.
Genter, J. Heidenreich, F. Heckl) . 3:32.15

800-Meter Free-Style Relay

1951—United States (Richard Gora,
Burwell Jones, Dick Cleveland,
William Heusner) 9:00.6
1955—United States (Martin P. Smith,
William Yorzyk, Wayne Moore,
James McLane) 9:00

1959—United States (Richard Blick, Peter Sintz, John Rounsavelle, Frank Winters) 8:22.7

1963—United States (Garry Illman, David Lyons, Richard McDonough, Edward Townsend) 8:16.9

1967—United States (Don Schollander, Mark Spitz, Charlie Hickcox, Greg Charlton) 8:00.46

1971—United States (J. Heidenreich, J. McConica, S. Genter, F. Heckl . 7:45.82

3-Meter Springboard Diving

1951—Joaquin Capilla, Mexico
1955—Joaquin Capilla, Mexico
1959—Gary Tobian, United States
1963—Thomas Dinsley, Canada
1967—Bernie Wrightson, United States
1971—Mike Finneran, United States

10-Meter Platform Diving

1951—Joaquin Capilla, Mexico
1955—Joaquin Capilla, Mexico
1959—Alvar Gaxiola, Mexico
1963—Robert D. Webster, United States
1967—Win Young, United States
1971—Rick Early, United States

Swimming—Women

100-Meter Free-Style

1951—Sharon Geary, United States 1:08.4
1955—Helen Stewart, Canada 1:07.7
1959—Christine von Saltza, United States 1:03.8
1963—Terri Stickles, United States 1:02.8
1967—Erika Bricker, United States 1:00.89
1971—Sandy Neilson, United States 1:00.60

200-Meter Free-Style

1951—Ana Maria Schultz, Argentina ... 2:32.4
1955—Wanda Lee Werner, United States 2:32.5
1959—Christine von Saltza, United States 2:18.5
1963—Robyn Johnson, United States... 2:17.5
1967—Pan Kruse, United States 2:11.91
1971—Kim Peyton, United States 2:09.62

400-Meter Free-Style

1951—Ana Maria Schultz, Argentina .. 5:26.7
1955—Beth Whittall, Canada 5:32.4
1959—Christine von Saltza, United States 4:55.9
1963—Sharon Finneran, United States .. 4:52.7
1967—Debbie Meyer, United States 4:32.64
1971—Ann Simmons, United States 4:26.19

800-Meter Free-Style

1967—Debbie Meyer, United States 9:22.86
1971—Cathy Calhoun, United States ... 9:15.19

100-Meter Backstroke

1951—Maureen O'Brien, United States .. 1:18.5
1955—Leonore Fisher, Canada 1:16.7
1959—Carin Cone, United States 1:12.2
1963—Nina Harmar, United States 1:11.5
1967—Elaine Tanner, Canada 1:07.32

1971—Donna Marie Gurr, Canada 1:07.18

100-Meter Breaststroke

1967—Catie Ball, United States 1:14.80
1971—Sylvia Dockerill, Canada 1:18.63

100-Meter Butterfly

1951—No competition
1955—Beth Whittal, Canada 1:16.2
1959—Becky Collins, United States 1:09.5
1963—Kathleen Ellis, United States 2:07.6
1967—Ellie Daniel, United States 2:05.24
1971—Deana Deardurff, United States . 2:50.03

200-Meter Breaststroke

1951—Dorothea Turnbull, Argentina ... 3:08.4
1955—Mary Lou Elsenius, United States 3:08.4
1959—Ann K. Warner, United States ... 2:56.8
1963—Alice Driscoll, United States 2:56.2
1967—Catie Ball, United States 2:42.18
1971—Lynn Colella, United States 2:50.03

200-Meter Backstroke

1967—Elaine Tanner, Canada 2:24.55
1971—Donna Marie Gurr, Canada 2:24.73

200-Meter Butterfly

1967—Claudia Kolb, United States 2:25.49
1971—Lynn Colella, United States 2:23.11

200-Meter Individual Medley

1967—Claudia Kolb, United States 2:26.06
1971—Leslie Cliff, Canada 2:30.03

400-Meter Individual Medley

1967—Claudia Kolb, United States 5:09.68
1971—Leslie Cliff, Canada 5:13.31

300-Meter Relay

1951—United States (Sharon Geary, Carol Pence, Maureen O'Brien) 3:49.3

400-Meter Free-Style Relay

1951—United States (Carol Green, Sharon Geary, Jacqueline Laving, Betty Mullen) 4:37.1

1955—United States (Wanda Werner, Carolyn Green, Gretchen Kluter, Judith T. Roberts) 4:31.8

1959—United States (Molly Botkin, Joan Spillane, Shirley Ann Stobs, Christine von Saltza) 4:17.5

1963—United States (Donna deVarona, Sharon Stouder, Elizabeth Mc-Cleary, Judy Norton) 4:15.7

1967—United States (Wendy Fordyce, Pam Carpinelli, Linda Gustavson, Pam Kruse) 4:04.57

1971—United States (S. Neilson, W. Fordyce, K. McKittrick, L. Skrifans) 4:04.20

400-Meter Medley Relay

1955—United States (Cora O'Connor, Mary Jane Sears, Betty Mullen, Wanda Werner) 5:11.6

1959—United States (Carin Cone, Anne

Bancroft, Becky Collins, Christine
von Saltza) 4:44.6
1963—United States (Virginia Duenkel,
Cynthia Goyette, Sharon Stoud-
er, Donna deVarona) 4:49.1
1967—United States (Kendis Moore, Catie Ball, Ellie Daniel, Wendy For-
dyce) 4:30.0
1971—Canada (D. Gurr, J. Wright, L.
Cliff, A. Coughlan) 4:35.50

3-Meter Springboard Diving

1951—Mary Frances Cunningham, United States
1955—Mrs. Pat K. McCormick, United States
1959—Paula Jean Pope, United States
1963—Barbara McAlister, United States
1967—Sue Cossick, United States
1971—Elizabeth Carruthers, Canada

10-Meter Platform Diving

1951—Mrs. Pat K. McCormick, United States
1955—Mrs. Pat K. McCormick, United States
1959—Paula Jean Pope, United States
1963—Linda Cooper, United States
1967—Lesley Bush, United States
1971—Nancy Robertson, Canada

Sychronized Swimming

Solo

1955—Beulah Bundling, United States
1963—Roberta Armstrong, United States
1971—Heidi O'Rourke, United States

Duet

1955—United States (Connie A. Todoroff-Ellen
G. Richard)
1963—United States (Barbara Burke—Joanne
Schaack)
1971—United States (Heidi O'Rourke—Joan
Lang)

Team

1955—United States
1963—United States
1971—United States

Water Polo

1951—Argentina
1955—Dominican Republic
1959—United States
1963—Brazil
1967—United States
1971—United States

Baseball

1951—Cuba
1955--Dominican Republic
1959—Venezuela
1963—Cuba
1967—United States
1971—Cuba

Basketball

1951—United States
1966—United States
1959—United States
1963—United States
1967—United States
1971—Brazil

Basketball—Women

1951—No competition
1955—United States
1959—United States
1967—Brazil
1971—Brazil

Boxing

Mini-Flyweight

1971—Rafael Carbonell, Cuba

Flyweight

1951—Alberto Barenghi, Argentina
1955—Hilario Correa, Mexico
1959—Miguel A. Botta, Argentina
1963—Floreal Garcia Larrossa, Brazil
1967—Franciso Rodriguez, Venzuela
1971—Franciso Rodriguez, Venezuela

Bantamweight

1951—Ricardo Gonzales, Argentina
1955—Salvador Jesus Enriquez, Venezuela
1959—Waldo Claudiano, Brazil
1963—Abel Almaraz, Argentina
1967—Juvencio Martinez Gonzalez, Mexico
1971—Pedro Flores, Mexico

Featherweight

1951—Francisco Nunez, Argentina
1955—Oswaldo Canete Insfran, Argentina
1959—Carlos Aro, Argentina
1963—Rosemiro dos Santos, Brazil
1967—Miguel Garcia, Argentina
1971—Juan Garcia, Mexico

Lightweight

1951—Oscar Galardo, Argentina
1955—Miguel Angel Pendola, Argentina
1959—Abel Laudonio, Argentina
1963—Roberto Caminero, Cuba
1967—Enrico Blanco, Cuba
1971—Luis Davila, Puerto Rico

Light Welterweight

1951—No competition
1955—J. Carlos Rivero Fernandez, Argentina
1959—Vincent J. Shomo, United States
1963—Adolfo Moreyra, Argentina
1967—James Wallington, United States
1971—Enrique Reguiferos, Cuba

Welterweight

1951—Oscar Pita, Argentina
1955—Joseph Dorando, United States
1959—Alfredo Cornejo, Chile
1963—Misael Vilugron, Chile
1967—Andres Modina Casanola, Cuba
1971—Emilio Correa, Cuba

Light Middleweight

1951—No competition
1955—Paul Wright, United States
1959—Wilbert McClure, United States

1963—Elcio Neves, Brazil
1967—Rolando Garbey, Cuba
1971—Rolando Garbery, Cuba

Middleweight

1951—Ubaldo Pereyra, Argentina
1955—Orville E. Pitts, United States
1959—Abrao de Souza, Brazil
1963—Luiz Cezar, Brazil
1967—Jorge Victor Ahumada, Argentina
1971—Fautino Quinales, Venezuela

Heavyweight

1951—Jorge Vertone, Argentina
1955—Alecsi Pablo Mitef Ochoa
1959—Allen Hudson, United States
1963—Lee W. Carr, United States
1967—Forest Ward, United States
1971—Duane Bobick, United States

Light Heavyweight

1951—Reinaldo Ansaloni, Argentina
1955—Luis Ignacio, Brazil
1959—Amos Johnson, United States
1963—Fred Lewis, United States
1967—Art Redden, United States
1971—Raymond Russell, United States

Cycling

1,000 Meter Sprint, Scratch

1951—A. Gimenez, Argentina
1955—Cenobio Ruiz
1959—Juan Canto, Argentina
1963—Roger Gibbons, Trinidad & Tobago
1967—Roger Gibbons, Trinidad & Tobago
1971—Leslie King, Trinidad

1,000 Meter Time Trials

1955—Antonio DiMicheli, Venezuela
1959—Anezio Argentao, Brazil
1963—Carlos Vasquez, Argentina
1967—Roger Biggon, Trinidad-Tobago
1971—Jocelyn Lovell, Canada

4,000-Meter Individual Pursuit

1951—Jorge Vallmitjana, Argentina
1967—Martin Rodriguez, Columbia
1971—Martin Rodriguez, Columbia

4,000-Meter Team Pursuit

1951—Argentina (Oscar Giacche, Rodolfo Caccavo, Pedro Salas, Alberto Garcia)
1955—Argentina (Clodomiro Cortoni, Richardo Senn, Duilio Biganzoli, Alberti Ferreira)
1959—United States (Richard Cortwright, Charles Hewitt, Robert Pfarr, James Rossi)
1963—Uruguay
1967—Argentina

1,000 Meters Unpaced

1951—Clodomiro Cortoni, Argentina

40-Lap Miss and Out (8-28/100 miles)

1951—Exequiel Ramirez, Chile

10-Mile Scratch Race

1967—Carlos Alvarez, Argentina

100-Meter Team Time Trails

1967—Argentina

Road Race

1951—Oscar Muleiro, Argentina (155.800 kilometers)
1955—Ramon Hoyos, Columbia (105.63 miles)
1959—Ricardo Senn, Argentina
1963—Gregorio Carrizales, Venezuela
1967—Marcel Roy, Canada
1971—John Howard, United States

Road Race—Team

1971—Cuba

150-Lap Point Race

1951—Oscar Giacche, Argentina

Fencing—Men

Individual Foil

1951—Felix Galimi, Argentina
1955—Harold Goldsmith, United States
1959—Harold Goldsmith, United States
1963—Guillermo Saucedo, Argentina
1967—Guillermo Saucedo, Argentina
1971—Eduardo John, Cuba

Individual Saber

1951—Tibor Nyilas, United States
1955—Antonio Haro Oliva, Mexico
1959—Allen Kwartler, United States
1963—Michael A. Dassaro, United States
1967—Anthony (Jack) Keane, United States
1971—Alex Orban, United States

Individual Epee

1951—Villamil, Argentina
1955—Raul Martinez, Argentina
1959—Roland Wommack, United States
1963—Frank D. Anger, United States
1967—Arthur Telles, Brazil
1971—Steve Netburn, United States

Team Foil

1951—United States
1955—Argentina
1959—United States
1963—United States
1967—Argentina
1971—United States

Team Saber

1951—United States
1955—United States
1959—United States
1963—United States
1967—United States
1971—Cuba

Team Epee

1951—Argentina
1955—Argentina
1959—United States
1963—United States
1967—United States
1971—United States

Fencing—Women

Individual Foil

1951—Irigoyen, Argentina
1955—Mrs. Maxine Mitchell, United States
1959—Maria del Pilar Roldan, Mexico
1963—Mireya Rodrigues, Cuba
1967—Pilar Roldan, Mexico
1971—Margarita Rodriguez, Cuba

Team Foil

1963—United States
1967—United States
1971—United States

Field Hockey

1971—Argentina

Gymnastics

Individual All-Around

1951—William Rotzheim, United States
1955—John Beckner, United States
1959—John Beckner, United States
1963—Welhelm Weiler, Canada
1967—Fred Rothlisberger, United States
1971—Jorge Rodriguez, Cuba

Team All-Around

1951—Argentina
1955—United States
1959—United States
1963—United States
1967—United States

Individual Horizontal Bar

1951—William Rotzheim, United States
1955—Abie Grossfeld, United States
1959—Abe Grossfeld, United States
1963—Abe Grossfeld, United States
1967—Fred Rothlisberger, United States
1971—Jorge Rodriguez, Cuba

Team Horizontal Bar

1951—Argentina
1955—United States
1959—United States
1963—United States
1967—United States

Individual Parallel Bars

1951—Pedro Lonchibucco, Argentina
1955—John Beckner, United States
1959—John Beckner, United States
1963—Donald R. Tonry, United States
1967—Fred Rothlisberger—Richard Loyd, United
    States (tie)
1971—John Ellas, United States

Team Parallel Bars

1951—Cuba
1955—United States
1959—United States
1963—United States
1967—United States

Individual Swinging (Flying) Rings

1951—Angel Aguiar, Cuba
1955—Richard Beckner, United States

1959—Jamile Ashmore—Abraham Grossfeld (tie),
1963—Jamile Ashmore, United States

Team Swinging (Flying) Rings

1951—Cuba
1955—United States
1959—United States
1963—United States

Still Rings

1967—Armando Valles, Mexico
1971—John Crosby, United States

Team Still Rings

1967—United States

Individual Pommeled Horse

1951—Rafael Lecuona, Cuba
1955—John Beckner, United States
1959—Gregor Weiss, United States
1963—Garland D. O'Quinn, United States
1967—Mark Cohn, United States
1971—Jorge Rodriguiez, Cuba

Team Pommeled Horse

1951—Argentina
1955—United States
1959—United States
1963—United States
1967—United States

Individual Free Exercise

1951—Juan Caviglia, Argentina
1955—John Beckner, United States
1959—Abe Grossfeld, United States
1963—Wilhelm Weiler, Canada
1967—Hector Ramirez, Cuba
1971—John Crosby, United States

Team Free Exercise

1951—Argentina
1955—United States
1959—United States
1963—United States
1967—United States

Individual Vaulting Horse

1951—Angel Aguiar, Cuba
1955—Joseph Koyts, United States
1959—John Beckner, United States
1963—Wilhelm Weiler, Canada
1967—Jorge Rodriguez, Cuba
1971—Jorge Cuervo, Cuba

Team Vaulting Horse

1951—Cuba
1955—United States
1959—United States
1963—United States
1967—Cuba

Team Side Horse

1955—United States
1959—United States
1963—United States
1967—United States

Individual Rope Climb

1955—Donald Perry, United States
1959—Garvin Smith, United States

Individual Club Swinging

1955—Francisco Jose Alvarez, Mexico
1959—Francisco Alvarez, Mexico

Individual Tumbling

1955—William Roy, United States
1959—Harold Holmes, United States

Individual Trampoline

1955—Donald Harper, United States
1959—Ronald Munn, United States

GYMNASTICS—WOMEN
Individual All-Around

1959—Ernestine Russell, Canada
1963—Doris Fuchs, United States
1967—Linda Metheny, United States
1971—Roxanne Pierce, United States

Team All-Around

1959—United States
1963—United States
1967—United States
1971—United States

Individual Vaulting Horse

1959—Ernestine Russell, Canada
1963—Dale McClements, United States
1967—Linda Metheny, United States
1971—Roxanne Pierce, United States

Individual Balance Beam

1959—Ernestine Russell, Canada
1963—Doris Fuchs, United States
1967—Linda Metheny, United States
1971—Kimberly Chase, United States

Individual Free Exercise

1959—Theresa Montefusco, United States
1963—Avis Tieber, United States
1967—Linda Metheny, United States
1971—Linda Metheny, United States

Individual Uneven Parallel Bars

1959—Ernestine Russell, Canada
1963—Doris Fuchs, United States
1967—Susan McDonnell, Canada
1971—Roxanne Pierce, United States

Pentathlon
Individual

1951—Eric Tinoco Marquez, Brazil
1955—Jose Perez Mier, Mexico
1959—Wenceslau Malta, Brazil
1963—Robert L. Beck, United States

Team

1951—United States
1955—Mexico
1959—United States
1963—United States

Shooting
Individual Service Rifle (3 Positions)

1951—Pablo C. Cagnasso, Argentina
1955—Ramon Hagen, Argentina

Team Service Rifle (3 Positions)

1951—Argentina
1955—Chile

Individual Service Rifle (Standing)

1951—Pablo C. Cagnasso, Argentina

Team Service Rifle (Standing)

1951—Argentina

Individual Free Rifle (300 Meters)

1951—Pablo C. Cagnasso, Argentina

Team Free Rifle (300 Meters)

1951—Argentina

Free-Rifle—3 Position (Aggregate)

1951—Arthur C. Jackson, United States
1955—Pedro Armella, Argentina
1959—Daniel Puckel, United States
1963—Gary L. Anderson, United States

Team Free Rifle (3 Positions)

1951—Argentina
1955—United States
1959—United States
1963—United States

Small Bore Rifle—3 Position (Aggregate)

1955—Arthur Jackson, United States
1959—Daniel Puckel, United States
1963—Gary L. Anderson, United States
1967—Lt. Margaret Thompson, United States
1971—John Writer, United States

Team Small Bore Rifle (3 Positions)

1959—United States
1963—United States
1967—United States
1971—United States

Free Rifle—Prone

1951—Arthur Jackson, United States
1959—Daniel Puckel, United States

Team Free Rifle—Prone

1951—Argentina

Free Rifle—Kneeling

1959—Daniel Puckel, United States

Free Rifle—Standing

1959—Daniel Puckel, United States

Small Bore Rifle—Prone

1959—Gerald Ouellette, Canada
1963—Enrique Forcela, Venezuela
1971—Victor Auer, United States

Team Small Bore Rifle—Prone

1959—Canada
1963—United States
1971—United States

Small Bore Rifle—Kneeling

1959—James Carter, United States

Team Small Bore Rifle—Kneeling
1959—United States

Small Bore Rifle—Standing
1959—James Carter, United States

Small Bore Rifle—(50 Meters)
1955—Arthur Jackson, United States
1967—Alf Mayer, Canada

Team Small Bore Rifle (50 Meters)
1967—United States

Individual Free Pistol
1951—Edwin Vazquez, Peru
1955—Huelet Benner, United States
1959—Nelson Lincoln, United States
1963—Franklin C. Green, United States
1967—S. Sgt. Hershel Anderson, United States
1971—Bertino de Sousa, Brazil

Team Free Pistol
1951—Mexico
1955—United States
1959—United States
1963—United States
1967—United States
1971—United States

Individual Silhouette Pistol
1951—Huelet Benner, United States
1955—Huelet Benner, United States
1959—David Cartes, United States
1963—Cecil L. Wallis, United States

Team Silhouette Pistol
1951—Argentina
1955—United States
1959—United States
1963—United States

Individual Silhouette Pistol (25 meters)
1955—E. S. Valiente, Argentina
1959—Aubrey Smith, United States
1963—Thomas D. Smith, III, United States

Team Silhouette Pistol (25 meters)
1955—United States
1959—United States
1963—United States

Rapid Fire Pistol
1967—Maj. William McMillan, United States
1971—Victor Castellanos, Guatemala

Team Rapid Fire Pistol
1967—United States
1971—Cuba

Center Fire Pistol
1967—Francis Higginson, United States
1971—Francis Higginson, United States

Team Center Fire Pistol
1967—United States
1971—United States

Individual Running Deer (100 meters)
1955—Felipe de Vilmorin Diaz, Mexico

Individual Skeet
1951—Pablo Grossi, Argentina
1955—Kenneth Pendergras, United States
1959—Gilberto Navarro, Chile
1963—Kenneth W. Sedlecky, United States
1967—Lt. Allen Morrison, United States
1971—Robert Schuehle, United States

Team Skeet
1951—Argentina
1959—United States
1963—United States
1967—United States
1971—United States

Weight Lifting
Flyweight
1971—Juan Romero, Colombia 660

Bantamweight
1951—Joe De Pietro, United States 622¼
1955—Charles Vinci, United States 661.39
1959—Charles Vinci, United States 717.0
1963—Dias Martins, British Guiana 693.00
1967—Fernando Baez, Puerto Rico 735½
1971—Rolando Chang, Cuba 753½

Featherweight
1951—Wilkes, Trinidad 716
1955—Carlos Chavez, Panama 733.03
1959—Isaac Berger, United States 782.5
1963—Isaac Berger, United States 797.50
1967—Walter Imahara, United States . . 777
1971—Manuel Mateos, Mexico 770

Lightweight
1951—Joe Pitman, United States 760
1955—Joe Pitman, United States 782.64
1959—Juan Torres, Cuba 766.5
1963—Anthony M. Garcy, United States 836
1967—Pastor Rodriguez, Cuba 848
1971—Pastor Rodriguez, Cuba 863½

Middleweight
1951—Pete George, United States 837¼
1955—Pete George, United States 892.86
1959—Tommy Kono, United States . . . 898.25
1963—Joseph R. Puleo, United States . . 880
1967—Russ Knipp, United States 948
1971—Russ Knipp, United States 990

Light Heavyweight
1951—Stanley Stanczyk, United States . 892½
1955—Tommy Kono, United States . . . 964.51
1959—James George, United States 887
1963—Tommy T. Kono, United States . 957
1967—Joe Puleo, United States 992
1971—Mike Karchut, United States . . . 1,042

Middle Heavyweight
1955—Dave Sheppard, United States . . . 876.33
1959—Clyde Emrich, United States 953 5
1963—William F. March, United States . 1,012
1967—Phil Grippaldi, United States . . . 1,047
1971—Phil Grippaldi, United States . . . 1,089

Heavyweight

1951—John Davis, United States 1,062½
1955—Norbert Schemansky, United
     States 1,041.68
1959—David Ashman, United States . . . 1,047.0
1963—Sidney M. Henry, Jr., United
     States 1,023
1967—Joe Dube, United States 1,162½
1971—Gary Deal, United States 1,171

Super Heavyweight

1971—Ken Patera, United States 1,310

Wrestling

Paperweight

1971—Sergio Gonzalez, United States

Flyweight

1951—Robert H. Peery, United States
1955—Manuel V. Andrade, Venezuela
1959—J. Richard Wilson, United States
1963—Andrew Fitch, United States
1967—Richard Sofman, United States
1971—Miguel Tachin, Cuba

Bantamweight

1951—Richard J. Lemeyre, United States
1955—Jack Blubaugh, United States
1959—David Auble, United States
1963—William G. Riddle, United States
1967—Richard Sanders, United States
1971—Don Behm, United States

Featherweight

1951—Omar Blebel, Argentina
1955—Omar B. Torranzzini, Argentina
1959—Louis Giani, United States
1963—Ronald L. Finley, United States
1967—Mike Young, United States
1971—Dave Pruzansky, United States

Lightweight

1951—Newton E. Copple, United States
1955—Jay T. Evans, United States
1959—James Burke, United States
1963—Gregory K. Ruth, United States
1967—Gerry Bell, United States
1971—Dan Gable, United States

Welterweight

1951—Melvin A. Northrup, United States
1955—Alberto Longarela, Argentina
1959—Douglas Blubaugh, United States
1963—J. Dennis Fitzgerald, United States
1967—Pat Kelly, United States
1971—Francisco Legeaguer, Cuba

Middleweight

1951—Leon Gemuth Hejt, Argentina
1955—Leon Gemuth Hejt, Argentina
1959—James Ferguson, United States
1963—James T. Ferguson, United States
1967—Lt. Wayne Baughman, United States
1971—Lupe Lara, Cuba

Light Heavyweight

1951—Ulises Martorella, Argentina

1955—Alfred E. Paulekas, United States
1959—Frank Rosenmayr, United States
1963—John H. Barden, United States
1967—Harry Houska, United States
1971—Dom Carollo, United States

Heavyweight

1951—Adolfo Ramirez, Argentina
1955—William Kerslake, United States
1959—Dale Lewis, United States
1963—Joe I. James, United States
1967—Larry Kristoff, United States
1971—Russell Hallickson, United States

Super Heavyweight

1971—Jeffrey Smith, United States

Rowing

Single Sculls

1951—Roberto A. Alfieri, Argentina
1955—John B. Kelly Jr., United States
1959—Harry Parker, United States
1963—Seymour L. Cromwell, United States
1967—Alberto Demiddi, Argentina
1971—Albert Demiddi, Argentina

Double Sculls

1951—Guerci—Yedro, Argentina
1955—Walter Goover—James Gardiner,
     United States
1959—John B. Kelly, Jr.—William Knecht,
     United States
1963—Robert C. Lea—William J. Knecht,
     United States
1967—Jim Dietz—Jim Storm, United States
1971—Brazil

Pair-Oared Shell Without Coxswain

1951—Madero—Almiron, Argentina
1955—Jorge and Eduardo Glusman,
     Argentina
1959—Ted Frost—Robert Rogers, United States
1963—Mariano Caulin—Gustavo Perez, Uruguay
1967—Lawrence Hough—Philip Johnson,
     United States
1971—Argentina

Pair-Oared Shell With Coxswain

1951—Mazzolini—Araudo, Argentina
1955—O. Allegretti—R. Bratschi, Argentina
1959—G. Perez—L. Aguiar, Uruguay
1963—E. Ferry—C. Findlay, United States
1967—P. Meek, G. Cadwalader, J. Fuhrman,
     United States
1971—Brazil

4-Oared Shell Without Coxswain

1951—Argentina
1955—Argentina
1959—United States
1963—United States
1967—United States
1971—Brazil

4-Oared Shell With Coxswain

1951—Argentina

1955—Argentina
1959—United States
1963—Argentina
1967—United States
1971—Brazil

8-Oared Shell

1951—Argentina
1955—United States
1959—United States
1963—Canada
1967—United States
1971—Argentina

Soccer

1951—Argentina
1955—Argentina
1959—Argentina
1963—Brazil
1967—Mexico
1971—Argentina

Polo

1951—Argentina

Judo

Lightweight

1963—Toshiyuki Seimo, United States
1967—Takeshi Miura, Brazil

Middleweight

1963—Lhofei Shiozawa, Brazil
1967—Hayward Nishioka, United States

Featherweight

1967—Akira Ono, Brazil

Light-Heavyweight

1967—Michael Johnson, Canada

Heavyweight

1963—George L. Harris, United States
1967—Allen Coage, United States

Open

1963—Ben M. Campbell, United States
1967—Doug Rogers, Canada

Equestrain

Individual Dressage

1951—Jose Larrain Cuevas, Chile
1955—Hector Clavel, Chile
1959—Patricia Galvin, United States
1963—Patricia Galvin, United States
1967—Mrs. Kyra Downton, United States
1971—Christolot Hanson, Canada

Individual 3-Day Event

1951—Julio C. Sagasta, Argentina
1955—Walter Staley, United States
1959—Michael Page, United States
1963—Michael Page, United States
1967—Mike Plumb, United States
1971—Manuel Mendevil, Mexico

Prix des Nations (Jumping)

1955—Lt. Roberto Vinals, Mexico
1963—Mary Mairs, United States

1967—Jim Day, Canada
1971—Eliza de Perez, Mexico

Team 3-Day Event

1951—Argentina
1955—Mexico
1959—Canada
1963—United States
1967—United States
1971—Canada

Team Prix des Nations (Jumping)

1955—Mexico
1959—United States
1963—United States
1967—Brazil
1971—Canada

Grand Prix de Dressage

1959—Chile
1967—Chile
1971—Canada

Tennis

Men's Singles

1951—Enrique Morea, Argentina
1955—Arthur Larsen, United States
1959—Luis Ayala, Chile
1963—Ronald Barnes, Brazil
1967—Thomas Koch, Brazil

Men's Doubles

1951—E. Morea—A. Russell, Argentina
1955—M. Llamas—G. Palafox, Mexico
1959—A. Palafox—G. Palafox, Mexico
1963—R. Barnes—C. Fernandez, Brazil
1967—Thomas Koch—Jose Edson
           Mandarino, Brazil

Women's Singles

1951—Mary T. de Weiss, Argentina
1955—Rosa Maria Reyes, Mexico
1959—Althea Gibson, United States
1963—Maria Bueno, Brazil
1967—Elna Subirats, Mexico

Women's Doubles

1951—M. Weiss—F. de Zappa, Argentina
1955—Rosa Maria and Esther Reyes, Mexico
1959—Y. Ramirez—R. Reyes, Mexico
1963—C. Caldwell—D. Hard, United States
1967—J. Albert—P. Rippy, United States

Mixed Doubles

1951—I. Ramirez—G. Palafox, Mexico
1955—Y. Ramirez—G. Palafox, Mexico
1959—Y. Ramirez—G. Palafox, Mexico
1963—Y. Ramirez—F. Contreras Serrano, Mexico
1967—J. Albert—A. Ashe, United States

Volleyball

Men

1955—United States
1959—United States
1963—Brazil
1967—United States
1971—Cuba

Women

1955—Mexico
1959—Brazil
1963—Brazil
1967—United States
1971—Cuba

Yachting

Snipe Class

1951—Argentina
1959—Brazil
1963—Brazil
1967—Brazil
1971—Brazil

Finn Monotype

1959—Bahama
1963—United States
1967—Brazil
1971—Brazil

Lightning Class

1959—Brazil
1963—United States
1967—United States
1971—Brazil

Star Class

1951—Brazil
1959—Bahama
1963—United States

Flying Dutchman Class

1959—United States
1963—Brazil
1967—United States

Dragon Class

1959—Argentina
1963—Argentina

5.5—Meter Class

1959—United States

POLO

(Courtesy of Mrs. Ruthe Larson, United States Polo Association,
Executive Plaza, 1301 West 22nd St., Oak Brook, Illinois, 60521)

The game of polo perhaps is fewer than 100 years old.

When the statement is made, some persons grow annoyed and aggrieved. They insist that because a historian or two has said so the game dates back a few thousand years, and is one of the oldest that is played.

Such historians belong to a group that places its entire faith on a bit of tapestry, or a work of art, in the British Museum, which shows men riding horses a long time ago. F. Herbert, a British historian, after gazing at the exhibit, stated:

"The British Museum contains many interesting drawings, which leave no doubt that the ancient game of chaugan is identical with the modern game of polo."

Herbert does not say when the tapestry work was completed. He does not say that it actually shows a team of men riding down a ball, with mallet in hand. Nor does anyone else make such a statement. The tapestry, or drawing, shows men riding horseback. The work does not show any goal posts. But various groups insist this bit of art, which may have been put together 500 years ago, or less, is something that was created thousands of years ago and that it is indisputable evidence that the Persians of 4,000 years ago played polo.

Beyond the drawing, there is nothing on earth to support the insistence that polo was a game 4,000 years ago, 1,000 years ago, or earlier than the 1860's. Certainly, if polo had been a game that endured through 40 centuries, somewhere there would be mention of it. But there is none.

It is fact, undeniable fact, that domesticated horses were unknown 4,000 years ago. When found in Libya, horses were very small in size; so small that their only usefulness was in hauling. They could not support a man on their backs until they had been developed, through the process taking about 20 centuries, into animals of size and strength. Even so, it was hundreds of years later before the horse could do more than carry a man of average size over a short route at a slow pace.

Yet historians, looking at a drawing, advise that polo with its demand for wild riding, terrific speed, countless body contacts, was a game that the Persians played 2,500 years *before* the horse was strong enough to do more than jog a short distance with a man on his back.

The situation is further complicated by historians who insist that the Assamese people of India picked up the polo idea from the Persians, 25 or 30 centuries ago, and that the Assamese alone perpetuated the game and kept it their secret until the 1860's.

Just why polo, supposedly so popular with the Persians of about 1500 to 1600 B.C. when horses were little larger than fair-sized dogs of today, was dropped by them and bequeathed only to the Assamese never has been explained.

The true story of polo seems to be the following, which embraces incidents that can be proven and are matter of record—not just some fantastic guesses:

A tribe of horsemen from Manipur in India visited Punjab in 1862 and, for the benefit of

British Army officers, put on an exhibition of wild riding. One called for hitting a ball with a stick while racing up and down field. There were no goal posts, no goal lines. The only reason for the act appeared to be to show the variety of stunts. After the entertainment was over, one of the officers pointing to the odd looking ball, asked, through an interpreter, what it was.

The reply came: "Pulu."

Which is a description of willow root, from which the ball was made.

A few days later, the officers decided to try to imitate some of the fancy riding. Someone provided a willow root ball. The officers made some sticks and began hitting the ball up and down the field, having, as they put it, "a go at this polo." which was what they called the willow root ball, instead of "pulu." But this didn't involve any definite contest. So the next time they rode, they fixed goal lines, chose sides and the game was a crude form of modern polo.

There was no limit as to the size of the teams at first. All who cared to play could, but the sides had to be equal. In time, because there were too many players to be accommodated on the limited field, the size of a team was limited. A number of teams were organized, the rules were constantly changed and the game became a favvorite in and around Punjab.

Polo was confined to India until 1869 when some of the 10th Hussars, returning to England, introduced the game there and the sport swept quickly into favor. Teams were organized throughout England. There came about the inevitable confusion created by a new game—there were no standard rules. This situation was remedied in 1873 by the formation of the Hurlingham Club, which has been the governing body for polo in the British Empire since.

James Gordon Bennett, an American multimillionaire and a great sportsman, saw polo played while on a visit to England in the 1870's. He was greatly impressed. Other Americans of wealth were equally enthusiastic. Bennett arranged for an indoor game to be played at Dickel's Riding Academy in New York, which had a large floor area. The year was 1876, and it was, perhaps, the first indoor game, all those in India and England having been played outdoors. Attendance at the pioneer match was limited mainly to relatives of the players. The game caught their fancy and plans were made for the creation of more teams. An impromptu schedule for 1877 indoor play was arranged.

The American game was indoors until about 1880. Then the outdoor game was tried. In 1885 the Americans weren't sure whether they played the outdoor game as well as the British and decided to make a test. They invited England to send over its crack team—the one that had won the "championship of the British Empire" in the first polo tournament in 1877, or any other combination it might select.

The match, on a best 2-of-3 basis, was played at Newport, R.I., in 1886. The British won the first game, 10 to 4, and apologized for not doing better, claiming to be still wobbly from a rough sea voyage. They proved that this was a truthful alibi by defeating the Americans, 14 to 2, in the second game and taking home the International Polo Challenge Cup.

Occasionally since then, British and American teams have met in outdoor play, and the once mediocre American teams improved so much that the English, despite their wealth of talent recruited from the British Isles, have come off second best.

The record score in major polo was made in 1936 when the United States quartet, in a preliminary, defeated Hurlingham, 20—4. Eric Pedley of the United States scored the single-game total of 12 goals and holds the international match record, with 9, tallied in 1930.

Over a long span, the horses used for polo were of no special type or breed. But as the popularity of the sport spread to all parts of the world and the players came to recognize the importance of the horse in the outcome of the game, there began a concentration on the breeding of mounts especially for polo purposes.

The most courageous animal known to man is the polo horse, formerly referred to as the "polo pony."

Other animals, in moments of savage fury, display insane ferocity and blind courage. Some show an intensity of rage and an immunity to pain exceeding that of a polo horse. But all these are momentary emotions; they come in a flash, endure briefly and subside. The polo horse is different. Life for him, when it is active, demands that he eagerly go into "rideoff" collision with another horse, and, then, having done that, to repeat concussions until his rider calls for another mount. The shocks and fractures suffered sometimes lead to death.

In full pursuit, a polo horse's speed reaches 25 miles an hour. It's a 50-mile an hour impact when two of them meet in a fast "rideoff." But they take what the fates deal out to them, right themselves and go hell-bent again, again and again—with the high courage of martyrs ready to die for a cause.

Pain, cuts, body-racking jolts—these are the lot of a polo horse. The truly great polo horse never reckons the consequences. He knows what is expected of him—and he does it. Never does he purposely halt his momentum in going into a "rideoff." Nor does he dodge contact during any moment in the game.

When the average race horse has done nothing except run six furlongs—time about 1 minute 13 seconds—over an especially prepared track, the task is regarded as so exhausting that he usually gets several days of rest. The polo horse spurts almost as fast as a race horse, absorbs 20 to 50 "body checks" in an afternoon and the next day you find him out on the field practicing for some new adventure.

Polo horses are not of any special breed, nor are they of any definite size now. In the years when the height was limited to 14.2 hands, they were known as "ponies" because of their slight stature and the fact that some of them weighed little more than 600 or 650 pounds. But since thoroughbred horses have been used in polo with considerable success, the animals now are designated officially as "horses," not as "ponies."

In the West, thoroughbreds often are bred to the range mustangs and the result is a polo horse. Range stallions are successfully mated with the 14.2 polo mares. However, odd as it may seem, harness horses cannot be bred to make good polo horses.

The training of a horse for polo is a task that requires endless patience and perhaps four years of unceasing work. The first job of the trainer is to teach the horse to do the things that the ordinary horse never does as a regular thing and to school him to accept philosophically a tremendous number of happenings that would terrorize any other horse.

After a young horse is broken to saddle and has learned to do the ordinary things expected of a saddle horse, he is broken for polo.

Clubs, ropes and mallets are swung around his head, so as to accustom him to a player's action while riding at polo. After that, the horse must learn to come to stop within minimum time, to turn, twist and resume stride with no real loss of momentum. In short, he becomes an equine acrobat.

Then the real test is made. A horse may respond to all other requirements, but if he rebels at collision he is of no use in polo. Many horses learn their lessons perfectly up to that point, and then, lacking the required raw courage, fail in this deciding test.

To enable the young horses to gather confidence, they always are put into the earliest collision with much weaker animals. As they bump off this group, they are given harder tests.

This keeps up until the aspirant has gained some victories over older horses, by which time he is about 5 years of age. Then he is graduated to service in slow and ordinary matches.

The best of this group, after a season or so, are advanced to faster and even faster classes and then—if they are truly great—are used in matches of national and international importance.

At the outset, a young horse is worth little more than his keep. As he advances in knowledge, his value increases. When he has become a star in international contests, he is worth from $1,000 to $10,000—or more—according to how much a poloist may need him. A polo horse is at his peak between the ages of 7 and 12.

The highest price ever paid for a polo horse was in 1928 when Stephen (Laddie) Sanford parted with $22,000 for "Jupiter." This animal was bred in Argentina, brought here for use in a championship match by the Argentines and was sold to Sanford by the invaders. After the sale, Jupiter never amounted to much.

Some years later, John Hay (Jock) Whitney, paid $14,500 for Chingolo, a 7-year-old Argentine pony, and Sanford paid $12,700 for an 8-year-old Argentine named Lucky Strike.

One of the greatest polo horses of all time was Brown Fern, a thoroughbred, owned by Stewart Iglehart of the United States. He wasn't much as a racer while in the stable of Mrs. Isabel Dodge Sloane, but after training became a polo sensation.

Gay Boy was a spectacular polo performer about 25 years ago. Some call him the fastest, bravest and most intelligent of all time. He was bred in Texas. The sire was part or full thoroughbred; the dam was an ordinary range mare used by cowboys. Gay Boy wasn't a brief flash of brilliance. He was "tops" for more than a decade, one of the most enduring animal champions in history.

The cost of training a horse for polo is huge. The danger of crippling or death is great. A star poloist must have many horses. Because of this, polo remains, essentially, a rich man's game.

High-goal polo in this country virtually was blacked out during World War II, but the game returned to prominence with the start of the 1946 season. High-goal polo is a game between two teams in which each team has a total rating or handicap of 20 or more goals. A high-goal player is one with a 5-goal or better rating. All registered players are assigned a rating according to playing ability by the United States Polo Association. Ten goals is the highest rating.

Arena polo has increased in popularity during the postwar years. More and more colleges are adopting it as a part of their athletic programs.

FAMOUS UNITED STATES PLAYERS

Tommy Hitchcock Jr. generally is rated as the greatest player of all time. He first gained international stardom in 1921, was outstanding for almost two decades thereafter and was one of America's most brilliant defenders in the international play against Great Britain for the famed Westchester Cup. Hitchcock was killed during World War II.

Lawrence and J. M. (Monty) Waterbury Jr. were outstanding in their day, as were Foxhall P. Keene, Harry Payne Whitney, Devereux Milburn, Louis E. Stoddard, Malcolm Stevenson, Tommy Hitchcock Sr., John E. Cowdin, R. L. Agassiz, Rene La Montagne, J. Watson Webb and Earl A. S. Hopping. Major Louie A. Beard was headed for top ranking when an injury ended his career.

Among the latter-day American stars are Winston F. C. and Raymond R. Guest, Elmer J. Boeseke Jr., Stewart B. Iglehart, Michael G. Phipps, Elbridge T. Gerry, George K. Oliver, Cecil Smith, H. W. (Rube) Williams, Eric Pedley, William Post 2d, Cyril Harrison, Seymour H. Knox, James P. Mills, J. C. Rathbone, Robert E. Strawbridge Jr., C. V. Whitney, John Hay Whitney, Stephen Sanford, Peter Perkins, F. S. von Stade, R. L. Gerry Jr., G. H. (Pete) Bostwick, Bob Skene, Clarence C. Combs, Alan L. Corey Jr., Al Parsells, Lewis Smith and Harold Barry, Delmar Carroll, Dr. William Linfoot, Philip Iglehart, Roy Barry, Paul (Bill) Barry, Ray Harrington, Jr., John F. Ivory, Jr., William A. Mayer, Northrup R. Knox, Juan Rodriguez, Julio Muller, William T. Ylvisaker, Roy Barry, Jr., Alberto Muller, and Charles William Smith.

The Governors of the USPA agreed in 1972 to accept applications for handicap registration from women players if sponsored by member clubs. So far two ladies have been registered. They are Mrs. Henry Richardson of the Oak Brook Polo Club and Mrs. Sue Sally Hale of the Sleepy Hollow Polo Club.

FOREIGN STARS

F. M. Freake, Lord Wodehouse, L. S. Cheape, Vivian Locket, E. G. Atkinson, Gerald Balding, Capt. C. T. I. Roark, E. H. Tyrrell-Martin, Maj. C. H. Gairdner, Aidan Roark, Capt. H. P. Guinness, H. H. Hughes, all of England; Lewis L. Lacey, Enrique Alberdi, Andres Gazzotti, Manuel Andrada, Jack D. Nelson and Jose C. Reynal, all of Argentina.

Also, Rao Raja Abhey Singh, Rao Raja Hanut Singh, The Maharajah of Jaipur, Maj. A. H. Williams and Eric G. Atkinson of India, and the Australians, Curtis Skene, G. Goulburn, Robert R. Ashton and Irwin Maple-Brown.

ALL-TIME U.S. TEN-GOAL PLAYERS (OUTDOORS)

Fox Hall Keene—1891, 1892, 1894, 1895, 1897, 1898, 1899, 1900, 1901, 1902, 1917, 1918, 1919, 1920.

John E. Cowdin—1894, 1895.

Thomas Hitchcock Sr.—1894, 1900, 1901.

R. L. Agassiz—1894.

Lawrence Waterbury—1900, 1917, 1918, 1919, 1920.

J. M. Waterbury Jr.—1902, 1917, 1918.

Harry Payne Whitney—1917, 1918, 1919, 1920, 1921.

Devereux Milburn—1917, 1918, 1919, 1920, 1921, 1922, 1923, 1924, 1925, 1926, 1927, 1928.

Louis E. Stoddard—1922, 1923.

J. Watson Webb—1922, 1923, 1925.

Thomas Hitchcock Jr.—1922, 1923, 1924, 1925, 1926, 1927, 1928, 1929, 1930, 1931, 1932, 1933, 1934, 1936, 1937, 1938, 1939, 1940.

Malcolm Stevenson—1925, 1928.

Stewart B. Iglehart—1937, 1938, 1939, 1940, 1941, 1942, 1946, 1947, 1948, 1949, 1950, 1952, 1953, 1954, 1955, 1956, 1957, 1958, 1959, 1960, 1961, 1962.

Elmer J. Boeseke Jr.—1934.

Michael G. Phipps—1939, 1946, 1947.

Robert Skene—1951, 1952, 1953, 1954, 1955, 1956, 1957, 1958, 1959, 1960, 1961, 1962, 1963, 1964, 1965.

CHAMPIONS

National Open

1904—WANDERERS (C. Randolph Snowden, John E. Cowdin, J. M. Waterbury Jr., Lawrence Waterbury) 4½; Freebooters 3.

1905—09—No competition

1910—RANELAGH (R. N. Grenfell, F. Grenfell, Earl of Rocksavage, F. A. Gill) 7¾; Point Judith Perroquets 3¾.

1911—No Competition

1912—COOPERSTOWN (F. S. von State, C. C. Rumsey, C. P. Beadleston, Malcolm Stevenson) 9; Bryn Bawr 5¾.

1913—COOPERSTOWN (F. S. von Stade, C. C. Rumsey, C. P. Beadleston, Malcolm Stevenson) 7; Point Judith 2¼.

1914—MEADOW BROOK MAGPIES (N. L. Tilney, J. Watson Webb, W. G. Loew, Howard Phipps) 11; Point Judith-Narragansett 8¾.

1915—No competiton

1916—MEADOW BROOK (Howard Phipps, C. C. Rumsey, W. G. Loew, Devereux Milburn) 8; Coronado 3.

1917—18—No Competition

1919—MEADOW BROOK (F. H. Prince Jr., J. Watson Webb, F. S. von Stade, Devereux Milburn) 5; Cooperstown 4.

1920—MEADOW BROOK (F. S. von Stade, J. Watson Webb, R. E. Strawbridge Jr., Devereux Milburn) 12; Cooperstown 3.

1921—GREAT NECK (L. E. Stoddard, Rodman Wanamaker 2d, J. Watson Webb. R. E. Strawbridge Jr.) 8; Rockaway 6.

1922—ARGENTINE (J. B. Miles, J. D. Nelson, D. B. Miles, L. L. Lacey) 14; Meadow Brook 7.

1923—MEADOW BROOK (Raymond Belmont, Thomas Hitchcock Jr., R. E. Strawbridge Jr., Devereux Milburn) 12; British Army 9.

1924—MIDWICK (E. G. Miller, Eric L. Pedley, A. P. Perkins, Carleton F. Burke) 6; Wanderers 5.

1925—ORANGE COUNTY (W. A. Harriman, J. Watson Webb, Malcolm Stevenson, J. C. Cowdin) 11; Meadow Brook 9.

1926—HURRICANES (Stephen Sanford, Eric L. Pedley, Capt. C. T. I. Roark, R. E. Strawbridge Jr.) 7; Argentine 6.

1927—SANDS POINT (W. A. Harriman, Thomas Hitchcock Jr., J. C. Cowdin, L. E. Stoddard) 11; Army-in-India 7.

1928—MEADOW BROOK (C. V. Whitney, W. F.

C. Guest, J. B. Miles, Malcolm Stevenson) 8; United States Army 5.

1929—HURRICANES (Stephen Sanford, Capt. C. T. I. Roark, J. Watson Webb, R. E. Strawbridge Jr.) 11; Sands Point 7.

1930—HURRICANES (Stephen Sanford, Eric L. Pedley, Capt. C. T. I. Roark, R. E. Strawbridge Jr.) 6; Templeton 5.

1931—SANTA PAULA (Andres Gazzotti, Jose Reynal, Juan Reynal, Manuel Andrada) 11; Hurricanes 8.

1932—TEMPLETON (M. G. Phipps, W. F. C. Guest, S. B. Iglehart, R. R. Guest) 16; Greentree 3.

1933—AURORA (S. H. Knox, J. P. Mills, E. T. Gerry, E. J. Boeseke Jr.) 14; Greentree 11.

1934—TEMPLETON (M. G. Phipps, W. F. C. Guest, S. R. Iglehart, R. R. Guest) 10; Aurora 7.

1935—GREENTREE (G. H. Bostwick, Thomas Hitchcock Jr., Gerald Balding, J. H. Whitney) 7; Aurora 6.

1936—GREENTREE (G. H. Bostwick, Gerald Balding, Thomas Hitchcock Jr., J. H. Whitney) 11; Templeton 10.

1937—OLD WESTBURY (M. G. Phipps, Cecil Smith, S. B. Iglehart, C. V. Whitney) 11; Greentree 6.

1938—OLD WESTBURY (M. G. Phipps, Cecil Smith, S. B. Iglehart, C. V. Whitney) 16; Greentree 7.

1939—BOSTWICK FIELD (G. H. Bostwick, R. L. Gerry Jr., E. T. Gerry, E. H. Tyrrell-Martin) 8; Greentree 7.

1940—AKNUSTI (G. S. Smith, R. L. Gerry Jr., E. T. Gerry, A. L. Corey Jr.) 5; Great Neck 4.

1941—GULF STREAM (J. H. A. Phipps, M. G. Phipps, C. S. von Stade, A. L. Corey Jr.) 10; Aknusti 6.

1942-45—No competition

1946—MEXICO (Gabriel Gracida, Guillermo Gracida, Alejandra Gracida, Jose Gracida) 11; Los Amigos 9.

1947—OLD WESTBURY (Clarence C. Combs Jr., Pedro Silvero, Stewart B. Iglehart, George Oliver) 10; Mexico 7.

1948—HURRICANES (Stephen Sanford, Larry Sheerin, Peter Perkins, Cecil Smith) 7; Great Neck 6.

1949—HURRICANES (Larry Sheerin, Roberto Cavanagh, Cecil Smith, Stephen Sanford) 10; El Trebol 4.

1950—BOSTWICK FIELD (G. H. Bostwick, George K. Oliver, Alan L. Corey Jr., Devereux Milburn Jr.) 7; California 5.

1951—MILWAUKEE (Pedro Silvero, Peter Perkins, George K. Oliver, Robert A. Uihlein Jr.) 6; Meadow Brook 2.

1952—BEVERLY HILLS (Robert Fletcher,

Anthony Veen, Robert Skene, Carlton Beal) 9; San Francisco 6.

1953—MEADOW BROOK (Henry Lewis 3d, Philip Iglehart, Alan Corey Jr., G. H. Bostwick) 7; Chicago 5.

1954—DETROIT CCC—Meadow Brook (A. D. Beveridge, Paul Barry, Alan L. Corey Jr., G. H. Bostwick) 10; Brandywine 5.

1955—DETROIT CCC (A. D. Beveridge, William Linfoot, Paul Barry, Harold Barry) 9; Brandywine 8.

1956—BRANDYWINE (Raworth Williams, Ray Harrington Jr., Clarence C. Combs, William A. Mayer) 11; Aurora 10.

1957—DETROIT CCC (A. D. Beveridge, Robert Beveridge, George Oliver, Harold Barry) 13; Aiken 3.

1958—DALLAS (Dr. Raworth Williams, Dr. William Linfoot, Robert Skene, Luis Ramos) 7; Solocup 5.

1959—CIRCLE F (Delmar Carroll, Ray Harrington, Jr., William A. Mayer, Russel Firestone) 8; Aurora 7.

1960—OAK BROOK CCC (A. D. Beveridge, Wayne Brown, Cecil Smith, Harold Barry) 8; Royal Palm 5.

1961—MILWAUKEE (Robert A. Uihlein Jr., Julio Miller, Guillermo Gracida, George Oliver) 13; Beaver Ridge Farm 9.

1962—SANTA BARBARA (Ronald Tongg, Dr. William Linfoot, Robert Skene, Roy Barry Jr.) 8; Royal Palm 7.

1963—TULSA (John T. Oxley, Ray Harrington, Jr., Harold Barry, Robert D. Beveridge) 7; Crescents 6.

1964—CONCAR OAK BROOK (L. L. Linfoot, Charles Smith, Julio Muller, Jack Murphy) 10; Solo Cup Crescents 9.

1965—OAK BROOK-SANTA BARBARA (Ronald Tongg, Charles W. Smith, Dr. William L. Linfoot, Jack Murphy) 11; Bunntyco 5.

1966—TULSA (John T. Oxley, Ray Harrington, Jr., Harold Barry, Jack Murphy) 10; Fountain Grove 5.

1967—BUNNTYCO—OAK BROOK (Del Carroll, Ray Harrington, Jack Murphy, Dick Bunn) 8; Milwaukee 2.

1968—MIDLAND (George Landreth, Ray Harrington, Jr., Roy Barry, Jr., H. A. (Joe) Barry) 9; Milwaukee 8.

1969—TULSA (James R. Sharp, Thomas Wayman, Ray Harrington, Jr., William G. Atkinson) 11; Milwaukee 10.

1970—TULSA (James R. Sharp, Reuben Evans, Harold Barry; H. A. (Joe) Barry) 9; Oak Brook 5.

1971—OAK BROOK (Hugo Dalmar, Jr., Charles Smith, Allan Scherer, Robert D. Beveridge) 8; Tulso Greenhill 7.

1972—MILWAUKEE (William T. Ylvisaker, Tom Wayman, Benny Gutierrez, Robert A. Uihlein, III) 9; Tulsa 5.

Monty Waterbury Memorial Cup
(Handicap tournament.)

1922–SHELBURNE (L. E. Stoddard, Raymond Belmont, J. Watson Webb, R. E. Strawbridge Jr.) 7; Eastcott 6.

1923–MEADOW BROOK (R. Penn Smith Jr., J. Watson Webb, F. S. von Stade, Devereux Milburn) 14; Hurlingham 10.

1924–ORANGE COUNTY (W. A. Harriman, J. D. Nelson, Malcolm Stevenson, R. E. Strawbridge Jr.) 9; Shelburne 7.

1925–HURRICANES (Stephen Sanford, Capt. C. T. I. Roark, Lord Wodehouse, L. E. Stoddard) 11; Orange County 7.

1926–MEADOW BROOK-ARMY (Capt. C. H. Gerhardt, J. Watson Webb, Capt. P. P. Rodes, Devereux Milburn) 11; Hurricanes 8.

1927–EASTCOTT (A. C. Schwartz, E. A. S. Hopping, E. W. Hopping, J. A. E. Trail) 12; Sands Point 9.

1928–SANDS POINT (E. T. Gerry, W. A. Harriman, S. B. Iglehart, Thomas Hitchcock Jr.) 13; United States Army 11.

1929–GREENTREE (J. H. Whitney, W. F. C. Guest, Eric L. Pedley, E. J. Boeseke Jr.) 18; Old Aiden 8.

1930–ROSLYN (H. E. Talbott Jr., Cecil Smith, H. W. Williams, Gerald Balding) 15; Greentree 6.

1931–TEMPLETON (M. G. Phipps, W. F. C. Guest, R. R. Guest, Devereux Milburn) 11; Greentree 9.

1932–SANDS POINT (Eric L. Pedley, G. H. Bostwick, Thomas Hitchcock Jr., Lindsay Howard) 18; Eastcott 16.

1933–AURORA (S. H. Knox, J. P. Mills, E. T. Gerry, E. J. Boeseke Jr.) 12; Greentree 9.

1934–TEMPLETON (M. G. Phipps, W. F. C. Guest, S. B. Iglehart, R. R. Guest) 9; Aurora 8.

1935–GREENTREE (G. H. Bostwick, Thomas Hitchcock, Jr. Gerald Balding, J. H. Whitney) 14; Templeton 13.

1936–TEMPLETON (M. G. Phipps, J. P. Mills, S. B. Iglehart, W. F. C. Guest, Roberto Cavanagh) 14; Roslyn 13.

1937–OLD WESTBURY (M. G. Phipps, Cecil Smith, S. B. Iglehart, C. V. Whitney) 11; Greentree 10.

1938–AKNUSTI (E. T. Gerry, R. L. Gerry Jr., Capt. C. T. I. Roark, R. R. Guest) 11; Old Westbury 8.

1939–GREENTREE (J. P. Grace Jr., Robert Skene, Thomas Hitchcock Jr., J. H. Whitney) 10; Texas 8.

1940–GREAT NECK (G. H. Mead Jr., J. P. Grace Jr., S. B. Iglehart, R. E. Strawbridge Jr.) 12; Aknusti 5.

1941–GULF STREAM (J. H. A. Phipps, M. G. Phipps, C. S. von Stade, A. L. Corey Jr.) 8; Aknusti 7.

1942-45–No competition

1946–MIRAFLORES (T. Zavaleta, F. Vogelius, E. Brown, O. Tricerri) 12; California 10.

1947–HURRICANES (Pedro Silvera, Clarence C. Combs, A. L. Corey Jr., Larry Sheerin) 9; Westchester 3.

1948–HURRICANES (Larry Sheerin, Peter Perkins, Cecil Smith, Stephen Sanford) 18; Westbury 10.

1949–HURRICANES (Larry Sheerin, Roberto Cavanagh, Cecil Smith, Stephen Sanford) 12; Bostwick Field 8.

1950–CALFORNIA (Robert Fletcher, Clarence C. Combs, Robert Skene, Carlton Beal) 9; Bostwick Field 5.

1951–OAK BROOK TRIPLE C (A. D. Beveridge, William A. Mayer, Peter Perkins, Roy L. Barry) 9; Blind Brook Hurricanes 8.

1952–MILWAUKEE SHAMROCKS (William Ylvisaker, Ray Harrington, Alan Corey Jr., Thomas Cross) 7; Meadow Brook 6.

1953–MILWAUKEE (Pedro Silvero, Ray Harrington Jr., Al Parsells, Robert A. Uihlein Jr.) 8; Meadow Brook 7.

1954–CCC-MEADOW BROOK (A. D. Beveridge, G. H. Bostwick, Alan L. Corey Jr., Harold Barry) 9; Brandywine 8.

1955–No competition.

1956–MEADOW BROOK (Pedro Silvero, Vincent Rizzo, Alan L. Corey Jr., A. G. Pennel) 11; Boca Raton 9.

1957-59–No competition.

1960–TULSA (John Oxley, Jack Oxley, Jules M. Romfh, C. R. Colee) 10; Blind Brook 2.

1961–MILWAUKEE (Guillermo Gracida, Julio Miller, George Oliver, Robert A. Uihlein Jr.) 7; Aiken 6.

1962-1972–No competition.

National Twenty-Goal
(Junior championship from 1900 through 1938.)

1900–PHILADELPHIA 1ST (J. B. Lippincott Jr., M. G. Rosengarten Jr., A. E. Kennedy, J. F. McFadden) 8½; Rockaway 3¼.

1901–ROCKAWAY (W. A. Hazard, R. LaMontagne Jr., R. J. Collier, P. F. Collier) 13; Dedham 7.

1902–ROCKAWAY (A. S. Alexander, R. LaMontagne Jr., F. S. Conover, P. F. Collier) 12½; C. C. Westchester 9.

1903–LAKEWOOD (George J. Gould, Jay Gould, Kingdom Gould, Benjamin Nicoll) 14¾; Bryn Mawr 6¼.

1904–ROCKAWAY 1ST (W. A. Hazard, D. Chauncey Jr., R. LaMontagne Jr., P. F. Collier) 14; Bryn Mawr 2nd 9½.

1905–BRYN MAWR 2ND (Alexander Brown, H. W. Harrison, R. E. Strawbridge, Geo. McFadden) 6½; Squadron A 3¾.

1906–BRYN MAWR FREEBOOTERS (Alexander Brown, W. H. T. Huhn, M. G. Rosengarten Jr., C. Randolph Snowden) 12½; Rockaway 8½.

1907—BRYN MAWR (Alexander Brown, L. L. Downing, W. H. T. Huhn, M. G. Rosengarten Jr.) 10; Onwentsia 5¾.

1908—NEW HAVEN (J. B. Thomas Jr., Hugh Drury, L. E. Stoddard, J. Watson Webb) 15½; Squadron A 4½.

1909—NEW HAVEN (J. B. Thomas Jr., Hugh Drury, L. E. Stoddard, F. S. Butterworth) 7¼; Bryn Mawr 3.

1910—MYOPIA 2ND (Adelbert Ames Jr., Harrison Tweed, Hamilton Hadden, G. G. Amory) 7¼; Bryn Mawr 6½.

1911—BRYN MAWR (Alexander Brown, H. W. Harrison, R. E. Strawbridge, C. R. Snowden) 12; Cooperstown ½.

1912—COOPERSTOWN (F. S. von Stade, C. C. Rumsey, C. P. Beadleston, F. H. Prince, Jr.) 11; Piping Rock 6¾.

1913—COOPERSTOWN (F. S. von Stade, C. C. Rumsey, C. P. Beadleston, Carleton F. Burke) 10¼; Great Neck 7.

1914—MEADOW BROOK MAGPIES (N. L. Tilney, J. Watson Webb, W. G. Loew, Howard Phipps) 11; Aiken Tigers 5½.

1915—BRYN MAWR (Thomas Stokes, E. W. Hopping, R. E. Strawbridge, Alexander Brown) 10½; Point Judith 8½.

1916—MEADOW BROOK 3RD (F. S. von Stade, Raymond Belmont, Thomas Hitchcock Jr., Morgan Belmont) 11½; Point Judith 2¾.

1917-18—No competition.

1919—MEADOW BROOK (J. C. Cooley, Benjamin K. Gatins, G. M. Hecksher, J. G. Milburn Jr.) 4¼; Philadelphia Country Club 3¼.

1920—BRYN MAWR FOXHUNTERS (J. C. Cooley, R. E. Strawbridge Jr., R. E. Strawbridge, C. S. Lee) 9; Philadelphia C. C. 5.

1921—MEADOW BROOK FOXHUNTERS (F. S. von Stade, Rodman Wanamaker 2d, Elliot C. Bacon, R. E. Strawbridge Jr.) 17; Philadelphia Country Club 3.

1922—UNITED STATES ARMY (Maj. A. H. Wilson, Maj. L. A. Beard, Lieut. Col. Lewis Brown Jr., Maj. W. W. Erwin) 8; Meadow Brook 7.

1923—UNITED STATES ARMY (Maj. A. H. Wilson, Maj. L. A. Beard, Lieut. Col. Lewis Brown Jr., Maj. J. K. Herr) 14; Point Judith 6.

1924—MIDWICK (E. G. Miller, Eric L. Pedley, A. P. Perkins, Carleton F. Burke) 16; Rockaway 3.

1925—UNITED STATES ARMY (Maj. A. H. Wilson, Capt. C. H. Gerhardt, Capt. P. P. Rodes, Lieut. J. A. Smith) 12; Bryn Mawr 3.

1926—UNITED STATES ARMY (Lieut. G. C. Benson, Capt. C. H. Gerhardt, Maj. H. D. Chamberlin, Maj. K. C. Greenwald) 16; Bryn Mawr 6.

1927—UNITED STATES ARMY (Capt. C. A. Wilkinson, Capt. C. H. Gerhardt, Capt. J. S. Tate, Capt. G. E. Huthsteiner) 13; Rumson 11.

1928—OLD OAKS (J. C. Cooley, Arthur Borden, Gerald Balding, H. W. Williams) 12; United States Army 8.

1929—OLD AIKEN (E. T. Gerry, J. P. Mills, S. B. Iglehart, J. C. Rathborne) 12; Midwest 5.

1930—UNITED STATES ARMY (Lieut. M. McD. Jones, Capt. C. A. Wilkinson, Capt. P. P. Rodes, Lieut. H. W. Kiefer) 17; Whippany River 7.

1931—ROSLYN (Raymond Firestone, S. H. Knox, H. E. Talbott Jr., William Post 2d) 9; Aiken Knights 6.

1932—UNITED STATES ARMY (Lieut. C. N. McFarland, Maj. C. C. Smith, Lieut. M. McD. Jones, Lieut. G. W. Read Jr.) 11; Bahadurs 8.

1933—AKNUSTI (W. A. Harriman, J. P. Mills, E. T. Gerry, R. L. Gerry Jr.) 11; Aurora 9.

1934—BURNT MILLS (S. P. Farish, Harry East, A. B. Borden, J. T. Mather) 5; United States Army 4.

1935—AIKEN KNIGHTS (G. H. Bostwick, James Curtis, W. F. C. Guest, D. W. Bostwick) 13; Texas 3.

1936—HURRICANES (Stephen Sanford, W. G. Reynolds, T. Q. Preece, Aubrey Floyd) 6; Meadow Brook Ramblers 4.

1937—SANTA BARBARA (Harry East, Alex J. Bullock, E. H. Tyrell-Martin, Charles H. Jackson Jr.) 12; Narragansett 7.

1938—BOSTWICK FIELD (E. H. Gerry, G. H. Bostwick, R. L. Gerry Jr., C. S. von Stade) 8; Aknusti 5.

1939—LEAGUE OF NATIONS (J. K. Secor, Robert Skene, G. K. Oliver, Robert Loewenstein) 15; Hurricanes 9.

1940—GREAT NECK (G. H. Dempsey, J. P. Grace Jr., S. B. Iglehart, E. N. Carpenter) 12; Bostwick Field 7.

1941—BOSTWICK FIELD (Sidney Culver, G. H. Bostwick, C. S. von Stade, A. L. Corey Jr.) 9; Hurricanes 4.

1942-47—No competition.

1948—MEADOW BROOK (Henry Lewis 3d, Martin Christensen, Alan L. Corey Jr., Devereux Milburn Jr.) 7; Hurricanes 6.

1949—MILWAUKEE (Pedro Silvero, Antonio Herreria, W. Gracida, Robert A. Uihlein Jr.) 9; Detroit 8.

1950—MILWAUKEE (Pedro Silvero, Juan Rodriguez, George K. Oliver, Robert A. Uihlein Jr.) 9; Bostwick Field 7.

1951—ARLINGTON FARMS (William Ylvisaker, Tom Cross, Cecil Smith, John F. Hulseman) 8; Sun Team 6.

1952—MEADOW BROOK (Philip Iglehart, Ray Harrington, Alan Corey Jr., Henry Lewis 3d) 12; Milwaukee Shamrocks 1.

1953—AURORA (Robert L. Wickser, Seymour H. Knox 3d, Northrup R. Knox, Lewis Smith) 9; Pittsfield 4.

1954—SAN ANTONIO (A. D. Beveridge, Robert

Beveridge, Paul (Bill) Barry, Harold Barry) 5; Oak Brook 4.

1955—SAN ANTONIO TRIPLE C (Vic Graber, William Wayman, Dr. William Linfoot, Harold Barry, A. D. Beveridge) 6; Milwaukee 4.

1956—SOLO CUP BRANDYWINE (James Kraml Jr., Ray Harrington Jr., William A. Mayer, Stanley Taylor) 12; Boca Raton 8.

1957—SOLO CUP (Vic Graber, Ray Harrington Jr., Dr. William Linfoot, Leo J. Hulseman) 9; Dallas 4.

1958—MEADOW BROOK (David Ellis, Ray Harrington Jr., Alan J. Corey Jr., Alan Jerkins) 9; Aiken 7.

1959—CIRCLE F (Lester Armour, Ray Harrington Jr., William A. Mayer, Russell Firestone) 11; Meadow Brook 5.

1960—ROYAL PALM (Bert Beveridge, Robert Beveridge, Ray Harrington, Benny Guiterez) 6; Circle F 4.

1961—ROYAL PALM (Bert Beveridge, Robert Beveridge, Ray Harrington Jr., Hugo Dalmar) 9; Milwaukee 4.

1962—MILWAUKEE (James Kraml, Jr., Wayne Brown, George Oliver, Robert A. Uihlein Jr.) 8; Santa Barbara 7.

1963—OAK BROOK (James Kraml, Jr., Charles Smith, Cecil Smith, Jack Murphy) 10; Tulsa 7.

1964—OAK BROOK (Hugo Dalmar, Charles Smith, Jack Murphy, William T. Ylvisaker) 8; Tulsa 5.

1965—OAK BROOK-SANTA BARBARA (Ronald Tongg, Charles W. Smith, Jack Murphy, Hugo Dalmar) 7; Milwaukee 2.

1966—SUNNY CLIMES (Thomas Hughes, Ray Harrington, Jr., Roy Barry, Jr., Tim Leonard) 9; Oak Brook 7.

1967—MILWAUKEE (Harold Barry, Benny Gutierrez, Walter Hayden, Bob Uihlein) 11; Blue Ridge Club 7.

1968—OAK BROOK (Thomas Hughes, Charles Smith, Dr. William Linfoot, Richard C. Latham) 12; Keswick-Sunny Clime 9.

1969—OAK BROOK (Thomas Hughes, Jules Romfh, Dr. William Linfoot, H. A. (Joe) Barry) 7; Milwaukee 6.

1970—OAK BROOK (Thomas Hughes, Ronnie Tongg, Dr. William Linfoot, Wm. Cort Linfoot) 9; Tulsa 7.

1971—TULSA GREENHILL (James R. Sharp, Corky Linfoot, Harold Barry, Joe Barry) 8; Milwaukee 6.

1972—RED DOORS FARM (Hugo Dalmar, Jr., William T. Ylvisaker, H. A. (Joe) Barry, Tim Leonard) 10; Sun Ranch 6.

Twelve Goal Intercircuit

1925—FORT BLISS (Capt. D. S. Wood, Maj. H. D. Chamberlin, Capt. L. K. Truscott, Capt. G. E. Huthsteiner) 12; Rockaway 8.

1926—FORT LEAVENWORTH (Capt. C. A. Wilkinson, Capt. C. C. Smith, Maj. I. P. Swift, Maj. I. P. Swift, Maj. J. K. Brown) 13; Rockaway 3.

1927—CHAGRIN VALLEY (J. A. Wigmore, D. S. Ingalls, Capt. W. J. White, T. H. White) 9; Fort Bliss 8.

1928—POINT JUDITH (G. H. Bostwick, William Post 2d, Gerald Dempsey, J. C. Rathborne) 13; Fort Riley 8.

1929—MIDWICK (C. B. Wrightsman, Neil S. McCarthy, J. Howland Paddock, Dr. H. H. Wilson) 10; Oak Brook 9.

1930—(Eastern Division) CHARGRIN VALLEY (Raymond Firestone, Leonard Firestone, Russell Firestone, Cyril Harrison) 13; Fort Bragg 3.

1930—(Western Division) FORT SILL (Lieut. A. R. S. Barden, Lieut. J. W. Clyburn, Maj. H. L. McBride, Maj. J. M. Swing) 9; San Mateo Red Team 4.

1931-32—No competition.

1933—FORT SHERIDAN (Lieut. G. S. Smith, Capt. C. A. Wilkinson, Capt. C. E. Davis, Lieut. L. G. Smith) 8; El Ranchito Polo Club 5.

1934—FAIRFIELD (T. Walsh, C. Stanley, J. Minnick Sr., J. Minnick Jr.) 7; Miami Valley 4.

1935—FORT SHERIDAN (Capt. E. C. Greiner, Maj. C. A. Wilkinson, Lieut. Col. H. D. Chamberlin, Capt. L. G. Smith) —by default.

1936—HOUSTON HUISACHE (Vernon Cook, W. S. Farish Jr., William Dritt, Wynn Humberson, R. D. Farish) 7; Hunting Valley 5.

1937—HOUSTON HUISACHE (R. D. Farish, S. P. Farish, William Dritt, Lieut. A. H. Wilson Jr., Vernon Cook) 10; Field Artillery School 5.

1938—FIELD ARTILLERY SCHOOL (Capt. A. E. Solem, Capt. J. A. Smith Jr., Lieut. D. W. Suddith, Lieut. E. A. Walker) 9; Austin 8.

1939—HOUSTON HUISACHE (R. D. Farish, William Dritt, Harry Evinger, W. S. Farish Jr.) 14; Oak Brook 4.

1940—BLUE HILL FARM (Walter Hayden, Peter Hayden, Hervey Swann, J. M. Romfh) 11; 7-11 Ranch 8.

1941—HOUSTON HUISACHE (R. D. Farish, William Dritt, R. S. Nichoalds, R. Humberson) 15; Ivory Rangers 7.

1942-47—No competition.

1948—DALLAS (Rayworth Williams, Larry Rogers, William Skidmore, M. Samuell) 11; Pittsfield 9.

1949—CON CARS (L. C. Smith, Vic Graber, William Linfoot, Herschel Crites) 10; Pittsfield 6.

1950—WINNETKA (Robert Hulseman, William Ylvisaker, Thomas Cross, Dan Peacock) 9; Valley Ranch 2.

1951—HEALY FARMS (James Healy, Thomas Healy, Jerome Fordan, Michael Healy) 5; Dallas 4.

1952—PITTSFIELD, MASS. (Charles W. Wheeler, A. G. Pennell, Zenas C. Colt, Joseph Poor)

13; Milwaukee Shamrocks 7.

1953—SAN ANTONIO (Bert Beveridge, Robert Beveridge, Harry Evinger, Arthur L. Herman) 8; Central Valley 4.

1954—FAIRFIELD (W. R. Crawford Jr., Zenas C. Colt, Thomas B. Glynn, W. R. Crawford 3d) 10; Dallas 3.

1955—WOODSIDE (Rufus Hayden, L. L. Linfoot, L. R. Linfoot, Robert Bahr) 7; Oak Brook 3.

1956—MIDLAND-LAMESA (Barry Beal, Carlton Beal, Gus White Jr., Carlton Beal Jr.) 9. Tulsa 8.

1957—TULSA (John Oxley, L. L. Linfoot, Clark Hetherington, C. R. Colee) 7; Circle F 5.

1958—OKLAHOMA (John T. Oxley, L. L. Linfoot, Clark Hetherington, C. R. Colee) 9; Menlo Circus 8.

1959—MENLO CIRCUS (William G. Gilmore, David S. Moore, Robert Skene, W. Mackall Jason) 9; Oklahoma 5.

1960—TULSA (John Oxley, Jack Oxley, Jules M. Romfh, C. R. Colee) 9; Aiken 2.

1961—TULSA (John T. Oxley, Loay Wilshire, R. B. Jowell, C. R. Colee) 13; San Antonio 6.

1962—NORMAN BROAD ACRES (A. D. Black, Don Black, Clark Hetherington, Jack F. Dean) 9; Farmington-Columbia 8.

1963—BROOKVILLE (Theodore Shapiro, Frank Rice, Vincent Rizzo, David Rizzo) 9; Farmington-Huisache 8.

1964—TULSA (Thomas E. Oxley, Jack Oxley, Jules M. Romfh, John T. Oxley) 9; Dallas 1.

1965—TULSA (Thomas E. Oxley, Jack Oxley, R. B. Jowell, John T. Oxley) 11; Con-Car 6.

1966—MIDLAND (George Landreth, Harold A. Barry, Robert D. Beveridge, Robert A. Uihlein, Jr.) 6; Barrington 5.

1967—WICHITA, KAN. (Jim Donaldson, Tom Waymen, Bill Waymen, Ted McDermand) 7; Dallas 5.

1968—MIDLAND (George Landreth, Orlando De Hoyos, Robert D. Beveridge, H. A. (Joe) Barry) 10; Tulsa 9.

1969—MENLO PARK (Malcolm MacNaughton, Jr., Wm. Cort Linfoot, Dr. Wm. Linfoot, Thomas Hughes) 10; Tulsa 6.

1970—SPOKANE (Peter Dix, Jr., William George, Pat Dix, Peter Dix, Sr.) 9; Wilson Ranch 4.

1971—BRANDYWINE (Lewis C. Ledyard, III, Richard I. G. Jones, Robert F. Conners, Peter Poor) 9; St. Louis 7.

1972—DALLAS-LONE OAK (Seth Herndon, William H. Hudson, Charles W. Smith, Richard C. Latham) 9; Broad Acres 5.

National Twelve-Goal

1923—PENLLYN (George H. Earle 3d, Albert L. Smith, Barclay McFadden, M. H. Dixon) 8; United States Army 6.

1924—No competition.

1925—FORT BLISS (Capt. D. S. Wood, Maj. H. D. Chamberlin, Capt. L. K. Truscott, Capt. G. E. Huthsteiner) 14; Midwick 5.

1926—FORT LEAVENWORTH (Capt. C. A. Wil-
kinson, Capt. C. C. Smith, Maj. I. P. Swift, Maj. J. K. Brown) 14; Rockaway 1.

1927—FORT BLISS (Lieut. E. F. Thomson, Capt. C. E. Davis, Maj. J. K. Brown, Capt. G. E. Huthsteiner) 11; Cavalry School 7.

1928—FORT RILEY (Capt. V. M. Cannon, Capt. C. Burgess, Capt. L. K. Truscott, Capt. J. C. Short) 10; Point Judith 4.

1929—MIDWICK (C. B. Wrightsman, Neil S. McCarthy, J. Howland Paddock, H. H. Wilson) 11; Fort Leavenworth 7.

1930—(Eastern Division) FORT SAM HOUSTON (Capt. C. P. Chapman, Lieut. Harry Cullins, Capt. W. H. Craig, Capt. John A. Smith Jr.) 10; Rockaway 7.

1930—(Western Division) FORT SILL (Lieut. A. R. S. Barden, Lieut. J. W. Clyburn, Maj. H. L. McBride, Maj. J. M. Swing) 5; San Mateo Blue Team 3.

1931-32—No competition.

1933—FORT SHERIDAN (Lieut. G. S. Smith, Capt. C. A. Wilkinson, Capt. C. E. Davis, Lieut. L. G. Smith) 8; Miami Valley Polo and Hunt Club 6.

1934—MIAMI VALLEY (Britton B. Wood, William B. Wood, H. H. Howard, Stanley Taylor) 3; Iroquois 2.

1935—OAK BROOK (James A. Hannah, George A. Bates, Paul Butler, Herbert J. Lorber) 8; United States Army 3.

1936—FORT MEYER (Lieut. G. R. Gunert, Capt. D. H. Galloway, Capt. J. H. Stadler Jr., Lieut. H. W. Johnson) 7; Houston Huisache 3.

1937—SANTA BARBARA (Oliver Wallop, Hale Marsh, Ray Bell, Charles H. Jackson Jr.) 7; Houston Huisache 6.

1938—No competition.

1939—PEGASUS (Del Carroll, C. C. Combs Jr., C. R. Harrison, Hugo Anson) 12; Houston Huisache 8.

1940—GATES MILLS (J. Knutsen, Alfred House, Courtney Burton, John Hammond) 6; 7—11 Ranch 5.

1941—OAK BROOK (H. O. Owens Jr., Paul Butler, Dan Peacock, Charles Aaberg) 7; Houston Huisache 6.

1942-47—No competition.

1948—PITTSFIELD (Herb Pennell, Thomas Wheeler, Charles Wheeler, Zenas Colt) 11; Dallas 10.

1949—CON CARS (L. C. Smith, Vic Graber, William Linfoot, Herschel Crites) 5; Oak Brook Shamrocks 3.

1950—SUN TEAM (Robert Schless, Paul Butler, Peter Perkins, James Kraml) 7; Winnetka 6.

1951—DALLAS (Raworth Williams, John Ryan, Clarence Starks, Luis Ramos) 4; Healy Farms 3.

1952—BLIND BROOK (Thomas Glynn, Adalbert von Gontard Jr., Cyril R. Harrison, Jack Crawford) 6, Fairfield 5.

1953—EL RANCHITO (A. B. Wharton Jr., William A. Mayer, Jesse Smith, Murray Samuell Jr.) 8; El Paso 4.

1954—FARMINGTON (Barclay Robinson, Zenas C. Colt, Frank Butterworth, Albert Marenholz) 9; Fairfield 6.

1955—WHITE SWAN (Rufus Hayden, L. L. Linfoot, L. R. Linfoot, Hershel Crites) 6; Oak Brook 4.

1956—OAK BROOK-SOLO CUP (Jack Murphy, Hugo Dalmar, Stanley Taylor, Leo Hulseman) 9; Healy Farms 1.

1957—CIRCLE F (R. Firestone, Hugo Dalmar, Paul (Bill) Barry, Jack Murphy) 11; Dallas 4.

1958—OKLAHOMA (John T. Oxley, L. L. Linfoot, Clark Hetherington, C. R. Colee) 11; Crescents 10.

1959—MENLO CIRCUS (Frank A. McNeilly, David S. Moore, Robert Skene, W. Mackall Jason) 13; Solo Cup 7.

1960—TULSA (John Oxley, Jack Oxley, Jules M. Romfh, C. R. Colee) 11; Blind Brook 5.

1961—TULSA (John Oxley, Loay Wilshire, R. B. Jowell, C. R. Colee) 6; Norman 3.

1962—MEMPHIS (Lee Taylor, R. E. L. Wilson III, John B. Armstrong, Arthur L. Herman) 6; Tulsa 4.

1963—MEADOW BROOK (Alan L. Corey, 3rd., Hector Garcia, Alan L. Corey, Jr., Raymond R. Guest, Jr.) 7; Greenwich Patricians 2.

1964—TULSA (Thomas E. Oxley, Jack Oxley, Jules M. Romfh, John T. Oxley) 11; Germantown 2.

1965—TULSA (Thomas E. Oxley, Jack Oxley, R. B. Jowell, John T. Oxley) 10; Broad Acres 9.

1966—TULSA (Joseph Casey, Thomas H. Oxley, Jack Oxley, John T. Oxley) 8; Midland 7.

1967—SAN ANTONIO VAQUEROS (Norman Brink, Luis Ramos, Bob Beveridge, Floyd Heinz) 6; Iran, Texas 5.

1968—MIDLAND (George Landreth, Orlando De Hoyos, Robert D. Beveridge, H. A. (Joe) Barry) 7; Sunny Climes 3.

1969—HI SKY (George Landreth, Wendell Kerley, H.A. (Joe) Barry, Bart Evans) 11; Wilson Ranch 6.

1970—SPOKANE (Peter Dix, Jr., William George, Pat Dix, Peter Dix, Sr.) 9; Midland 8.

1971—WILSON RANCH (William B. Wilson, Corky Linfoot, Bart Evans, Ted McDermand) 7; Norman 5.

1972—RAVENS (William Mulcahy, James J. MacGinley, Robert F. Connors, George Weymouth) 9; Potomac 5.

National Sixteen-Goal

1964—PALM DESERT (C. Heath Manning, L. L. Linfoot, Allan D. Scherer, Tony Veen) 8; Beverly Hills 5.

1965—SANTA BARBARA (Tenney Tongg, Ronald Tongg, Dr. William R. Linfoot, C. Heath Manning) 11; Crescents 10.

1966—SUNNY CLIMES (Thomas Hughes, Ray Harrington, Jr., Roy Barry, Jr., Tim Leonard) 11; Bunntyco 5.

1967—ST LOUIS (Steve Orthwein, Peter Orthwein, Benny Gutierrez, Dolph Orthwein) 9; Milwaukee 8.

1968—MILWAUKEE (James R. Sharp, Thomas Wayman, Harold Barry, Tim Leonard) 11; Midland 8.

1969—TULSA (James R. Sharp, John C. (Jack) Oxley, Benny Gutierrez, John T. Oxley) 10; Meadow Brook 4.

1970—CLOUDY CLIME (Thomas Hughes, William Cort Linfoot, Jack Murphy, Tim Leonard) 9; Milwaukee 4.

1971—MILWAUKEE (Robert A. Uihlein, III, Tom Wayman, Benny Gutierrez, Bill Wayman) 9; Welfare 1.

1972—MEADOW BROOK (Alfred Fortugno, Alan L. Corey, III, Allan D. Scherer, William Russel G. Corey) 7; Midfield 6.

National Fourteen-Goal

1972—Milwaukee (Robert A. Uihlein, III, G. Edward Lutz, Tom Wayman, Robert A. Uihlein, Jr.) 9 Fairfield-Myopia 7.

National Eight-Goal

1972—Tucson (Philip O. Heatley, John W. Donaldson, III, William Sinclair, William C. Dent) 8; New Mexico 7.

Eight Goal Intercircuit

1972—Broad Acres (Robert W. Moore, Mike Carney, Don B. Black, William Clark Hetherington) 7; Dallas-Lone Oak 3.

East-West

1933—Won by WEST (15—11, 8—12, 12—6) at Lake Forest, Ill. WEST: No. 1, Aidan Roark and Eric Pedley; No. 2, E. J. Boeseke Jr.: No. 3, Cecil Smith; Back, H. W. Williams, Neil S. McCarthy and Aidan Roark. EAST: No. 1, Michael Phipps and Winston Guest; No. 2, Thomas Hitchcock Jr. and E. A. S. Hopping; No. 3, Winston Guest and Thomas Hitchcock Jr.; Back, Raymond Guest.

1934—Won by EAST (10—8, 14—13) at Westbury, N.Y. EAST: No. 1, Michael Phipps; No. 2, James P. Mills; No. 3, Winston Guest; Back, William Post 2d. WEST: No. 1, Eric Pedley; No. 2, Elmer J. Boeske Jr. and Cecil Smith; No. 3, Cecil Smith and Aidan Roark; Back, Aidan Roark and Elmer J. Boeseke Jr.

1947—Won by WEST (9—7) at Westbury, N.Y. WEST: No. 1, John Ivory; No. 2, Peter Perkins; No. 3, George Oliver; Back, Tom Guy. EAST: No. 1, G. H. Bostwick; No. 2, J. P. Grace Jr.; No. 3, Stewart B. Iglehart; Back, Alan L. Corey Jr.

1951—Won by WEST (10—2, 4—6, 9—6) at Libertyville, Ill. WEST: No. 1, William Ylvisaker; No. 2, Robert Skene; No. 3, Cecil Smith and Harry Evinger; Back, Stanley Tayler. EAST: No. 1, G. H. Bostwick; No. 2, Albert Parsells; No. 3, Alan L. Corey Jr.; Back, Devereux Milburn Jr.

1951—Won by WEST (9—6, 8—7) at Westbury, N.Y. West: No. 1, William Ylvisaker; No. 2 Robert Skene and Peter Perkins; No. 3 Harry

Evinger and Cecil Smith; Back, Tom Cross. EAST: No. 1, G. H. Bostwick; No. 2, Albert Parsells and Clarence C. Combs Jr.; No. 3, Alan L. Corey Jr.; Back, Devereux Milburn Jr. and Albert Parsells.

(Competition only in years indicated.)

Butler Handicap

1954—CCC-MEADOW BROOK (A. D. Beveridge, G. H. Bostwick, Paul (Bill) Barry, Harold Barry) 12; Oak Brook 6.

1955—MEADOW BROOK (Hugo Dalmar, G. H. Bostwick, Alan L. Corey, Jr., Devereux Milburn, Jr.) 13; Oak Brook 6.

1956—CCC-SELMA (A. D. Beveridge, Robert Beveridge, George Oliver, Harold Barry) 11; Circle F 8.

1957—DETROIT CCC (Bert Beveridge, Robert D. Beveridge, George Oliver, Harold Barry) 8; Solocup-California 5.

1958—OAK BROOK (Hugo Dalmar, Delmar Carroll, Cecil Smith, Jack Murphy) 12: CCC 7.

1959—OAK BROOK-CALIFORNIA (Victor H. Graber, Dr. William R. Linfoot, Cecil Smith, Jack Murphy) 5; CCC 4.

1960—MILWAUKEE (Memo Gracida, Julio Muller, George Oliver, Robert A. Uihlein, Jr.) 13; Circle F 11.

1961— Not Played For.

1962—SANTA BARBARA (Ronald Tongg, Dr. William R. Linfoot, Robert Skene, Roy Barry, Jr.) 8; Royal Palm 4.

1963—COWDRAY PARK (Lord Patrick Beresford, Paul Withers, Sinclair Hill, Major Ronald Ivor Ferguson) 12; Tulsa 10.

1964—1970—No competition

1971—Tulsa Greenhill (James R. Sharp, Allan D. Scherer, Harold Barry, H. A. (Joe Barry) 9; Oak Brook 8.

1972—Oak Brook (Hugo Dalmar, Jr., Charles W. Smith, William G. Atkinson, Bart Evans) 12; Milwaukee 10.

International Matches

Great Britain vs. United States
(Westchester Cup)

1886—Won by GREAT BRITAIN (10—4, 14—2) at Newport, R.I. GREAT BRITAIN: No. 1, Capt. T. Hone; No. 2, Hon. R. Lawley; No. 3, Capt. Malcolm Little; Back, John Watson. UNITED STATES: No. 1, Winthrop K. Thorne; No. 2, R. Belmont; No. 3, Foxhall P. Keene; Back, Thomas Hitchcock.

1902—Won by GREAT BRITAIN (1—2, 6—1, 7—1) at Hurlingham, England. GREAT BRITAIN: No. 1, Cecil P. Nickalls; No. 2, P.W. Nickalls and F. M. Freake; No. 3, Walter Buckmaster and George A. Miller; Back, Charles D. Miller and Walter Buckmaster. UNITED STATES: No. 1, R. L. Agassiz and J. M. Waterbury Jr.; No. 2, J. E. Cowdin and Lawrence Waterbury; No. 3, Foxhall P.

Keene; Back, Lawrence Waterbury and R. L. Agassiz.

1909—Won by UNITED STATES (9—5, 8—2) at Hurlingham. UNITED STATES: No. 1, Lawrence Waterbury; No. 2 J. M. Waterbury Jr.; No. 3, Harry Payne Whitney; Back, Devereux Milburn. GREAT BRITAIN: No. 1, Capt. Herbert H. Wilson and Harry Rich; No. 2 F. M. Freake; No. 3, P. W. Nickalls; Back, Lord Wodehouse and Capt. J. Hardress Lloyd.

1911—Won by UNITED STATES (4½—3, 4½—3½) at Meadow Brook Club, Westbury, N.Y. UNITED STATES: No. 1, Lawrence Waterbury; No. 2, J. M. Waterbury Jr.: No. 3, Harry Payne Whitney; Back, Devereux Milburn. GREAT BRITAIN: No. 1, Capt. Leslie St. G. Cheape; No. 2, A. Noel Edwards; No. 3, Capt. J. Hardress Lloyd; Back, Capt. Herbert H. Wilson.

1913—Won by UNITED STATES (5½—3, 4½—4½) at Meadow Brook. UNITED STATES: No. 1, Lawrence Waterbury and Louis E. Stoddard; No. 2, J. M. Waterbury Jr. and Lawrence Waterbury; No. 3, Harry Payne Whitney; Back, Devereux Milburn. GREAT BRITAIN: No. 1, Capt. Leslie St. G. Cheape; No. 2, Noel Edwards and F. M. Freake; No. 3, Capt. R. G. Ritson; Back, Capt. Vivian N. Lockett.

1914—Won by GREAT BRITAIN (8½—3, 4—2¾) at Meadow Brook. GREAT BRITAIN: No. 1, Capt. H. A. Tomkinson; No. 2, Capt. Leslie St. G. Cheape; No. 3, Maj. F. W. Barrett; Back, Capt. Vivian N. Lockett. UNITED STATES: No. 1, Rene LaMontagne; No. 2 J. M. Waterbury Jr.; No. 3, Devereux Milburn and Lawrence Waterbury; Back, Lawrence Waterbury and Devereux Milburn.

1921—Won by UNITED STATES (11—4, 10—6) at Hurlingham. UNITED STATES: No. 1, Louis E. Stoddard; No. 2, Thomas Hitchcock Jr.; No. 3, Watson Webb; Back, Devereux Milburn. GREAT BRITAIN: No. 1, Lieut. Col. H. A. Tomkinson; No. 2, Maj. F. W. Barrett; No. 3, Lord Wodehouse; Back, Maj. Vivian N. Lockett.

1924—Won by UNITED STATES (16—5, 14—5) at Meadow Brook. UNITED STATES: No. 1, J. Watson Webb; No. 2, Thomas Hitchcock Jr.; No. 3, Malcolm Stevenson and Robert E. Strawbridge Jr.; Back, Devereux Milburn. GREAT BRITAIN: No. 1, Maj. T. W. Kirkwood and Lieut. Col. T. P. Melvill; No. 2, Maj. F. W. Hurndall and Maj. G. H. Phipps-Hornby; No. 3, Maj. E. G. Atkinson; Back, Lewis L. Lacey.

1927—Won by UNITED STATES (13—3, 8—5) at 1, J. Watson Webb; No. 2, Thomas Hitchcock Jr.; No. 3 Malcolm Stevenson; Back, Devereux Milburn. GREAT BRITAIN: No. 1, Capt. Claude E. Pert and Capt. R. George; No. 2, Maj. Austin H. Williams and Capt. J. P.

Dening; No. 3, Capt. C. T. I. Roark, Back, Maj. E. G. Atkinson.

1930—Won by UNITED STATES (10—5, 14—9) at Meadow Brook. UNITED STATES: No. 1, Eric Pedley; No. 2, Earle A. S. Hopping; No. 3, Thomas Hitchcock Jr.; Back, Winston F. C. Guest. GREAT BRITAIN: No. 1, Gerald Balding; No. 2, Lewis L. Lacey; No. 3, Capt. C. T. I. Roark; Back, Humphrey P. Guinness.

1936—Won by UNITED STATES (10—9, 8—6) at Hurlingham. UNITED STATES: No. 1, Eric Pedley; No. 2, Michael G. Phipps; No. 3, Stewart B. Iglehart; Back, Winston F. C. Guest. GREAT BRITAIN: No. 1, Hesketh H. Hughes; No. 2, Gerald Balding; No. 3, Eric H. Tyrrell-Martin; Back, Humphrey P. Guinness.

1939—Won by UNITED STATES (11—7, 9—4) at Meadow Brook. UNITED STATES: No. 1, Michael G. Phipps; No. 2, Thomas Hitchcock Jr.; No. 3, Stewart B. Iglehart; Back, Winston F. C. Guest. GREAT BRITAIN: No. 1, Robert Skene; No. 2, Adian Roark; No. 3, Gerald Balding; Back, Eric H. Tyrrell-Martin.

(Competition only in years indicated.

No competition after 1939).

Argentina vs. United States
(Cup de las Americas)

1928—Won by UNITED STATES (7—6, 7—10, 13—7) at Meadow Brook Club, Westbury, N.Y. UNITED STATES: No. 1, W. A. Harriman; No. 2, Thomas Hitchcock Jr., and E. A. S. Hopping; No. 3, Malcolm Stevenson and Thomas Hitchcock Jr.: Back, Winston F. C. Guest. ARGENTINA: No. 1, Arturo Kenny; No. 2, J. D. Nelson; No. 3, J. B. Miles; Back, Lewis L. Lacey.

1936—Won by ARGENTINA (21—9, 8—4) at Meadow Brook. ARGENTINA: No. 1, Luis Duggan; No. 2, Roberto Cavanagh; No. 3, Andres Gazzotti; Back, Manuel Andrada. UNITED STATES: No. 1, G. H. Bostwick; No. 2 Gerald Balding; No. 3, Thomas Hitchcock Jr.; Back, John Hay Whitney.

1932—Won by UNITED STATES (9—6, 7—8, 12—10) at Buenos Aires. UNITED STATES: No. 1, Michael G. Phipps; No. 2, Elmer J. Boeseke Jr.; No. 3, Winston F. C. Guest; Back, William Post, 2d. ARGENTINA: No. 1, Arturo Kenny; No. 2, J. D. Nelson and Martin Reynal; No. 3, Jose Reynal; Back, Manuel Andrada.

1950—Won by ARGENTINA (14—10, 11—7) at Buenos Aires. ARGENTINA: No. 1, Juan Cavanagh; No. 2, Roberto Cavanagh; No. 3, Enrique Alberdi; Back, Juan C. Alberdi. UNITED STATES: No. 1, Delmar Carroll; No. 2, Peter Perkins; No. 3, George K. Oliver; Back, Lewis Smith.

1966—Won by ARGENTINA (10—6, 14—10) at Buenos Aires. ARGENTINA: No. 1, Gaston Dorignac; No. 2, Horacio Heguy; No. 3, Juan

Carlos Harriott, Capt. Back, Francisco Dorignac. UNITED STATES: No. 1, Northrup R. Knox, Capt. No. 2, Dr. William R. Linfoot; No. 3, Roy Barry, Jr.; Back, Harold Barry.

Mexico vs. United States
(Gen. Manuel Avilla Camacho Cup)

1941—Won by UNITED STATES (6—5, 6—4, 12—4) at Mexico City. UNITED STATES: No. 1, Michael G. Phipps and Henry Lewis; No. 2, Cecil Smith; No. 3, Winston F. C. Guest; Back, Harry Evinger. MEXICO: No. 1, Gabriel Gracida and Eduardo Gallardo; No. 2, Jesus Grijalva and Antonio Nava; No. 3, Ramos Sesma and Juan Gracia; Back, Guillermo Cisneros and Ramos Sesma.

1946—(September) Won by UNITED STATES (10—4, 11—4) at Meadow Brook Club, Westbury, N.Y. UNITED STATES: No. 1, Michael G. Phipps; No. 2, Cecil Smith; No. 3, Stewart B. Iglehart; Back, Peter Perkins. MEXICO: No. 1, Gabriel Gracida; No. 2, Guillermo Gracida; No. 3, Alejandro Gracida; Back, Jose Gracida.

1946—(November) Won by UNITED STATES (7—0, 11—9, 5—4) at San Antonio. UNITED STATES: No. 1, Stephen Sanford; No. 2, Cecil Smith and William Barry; No. 3, Stewart B. Iglehart and Cecil Smith; Back, J. T. Mather. MEXICO: No. 1, Gabriel Gracida and Antonio Hereria; No. 2, Guillermo Gracida; No. 3, Alejandro Gracida; Back, Jose Gracida.

(Competition only in years indicated. No competition after 1946.)

Intercollegiate Championship

1922—Princeton (E. H. Stabler, A. P. Hall, W. T. Fleming)

1923—Yale (H. Baldwin, R. L. Dean, W. K. Muir)

1924—Yale (H. Baldwin, W. K. Muir, S. Hewitt)

1925—Yale (H. Baldwin, A. H. Hunt, W. K. Muir)

1926—Yale (W. R. Barrett, W. F. C. Guest, W. K. Muir)

1927—Not Played For.

1928—Penn. Military College (J. Whitehurst, C. Bower, D. Jones)

1929—Harvard (T. Glynn, E. T. Gerry, Forrester Clark)

1930—Princeton (L. Firestone, J. Lemp, W. Post, II)

1931—Yale (L. A. Baldwin, J. P. Mills, J. C. Rathborne)

1932—Yale (L. A. Baldwin, M. G. Phipps, J. P. Mills)

1933—Harvard (W. C. McGuckin, T. J. Davis, F. S. Nicholas)

1934—Princeton (W. H. Sullivan, M. S. Kemmerer, W. F. Thomas)

1935—United States Military Academy (Cecil Combs, Howell Estes., A. H. Wilson, Jr.)

1936—United States Military Academy (Cecil Combs, Howell Estes, A. H. Wilson, Jr.)

1937—Cornell (S. J. Roberts, C. C. Combs, Jr., Thomas Lawrence.

1938—Yale (A. L. Corey, Jr., Collister Johnson, C. M. Wooley, Jr.)

1938—United States Military Academy (T. J. Christian, W. W. West, F. W. Boye)

1940—Princeton (Paul Miller, Edward C. Rose, Jr., Jules Romfh)

1941—Princeton (Jules Romfh, Edward C. Rose, Jr., Robert Osmun)

1942—Yale (David Wilhelm, John H. Daniels, Robert Johnson)

1943-1946—Not Played For.

1947—United States Military Academy (G. Edwards, N. Ayer, T. Hoffman)

1948—University of Miami (J. R. Evans, J. Mather, R. Knight)

1949—University of Miami (C. Bernard, Jr., J. R. Evans, P. Heise)

1950—University of Miami (C. Bernard, Jr., J. R. Evans, P. Heise)

1951—University of Miami (C. Bernard, Jr., J. R. Evans, P. Heise)

1952—New Mexico Military Institute (W. R. Crawford, III, Rube Evans, Jack Dean)

1953—Yale (Malcolm Wallop, Leverett Miller, James A. Hannah, Jr.)

1954—New Mexico Military Institute (Buzz T. Easterling, Fred Rice, Jack L. Dean)

1955—Cornell (Albert Mitchell, Camilo Saenz, Alberto Santa Maria) 19; Yale 5.

1956—Cornell (Camilo Saenz, H. F. Rice, Jr., Alberto Santa Maria, Mark J. Geronimus) 20; Yale 6.

1957—Yale (George T. Weymouth, Jr., Peter Jackson, Michael Poutiatine) 10; University of Virginia 9.

1958—Cornell (Pablo Toro, Bennet M. Baldwin, Stanley Woolaway) 22; Yale 4.

1959—Cornell (Bennet M. Baldwin, Peter D. Baldwin, Stanley R. Woolaway) 14; Virginia 5.

1960—Yale (Richard Jones, Jarrett H. Vincent, Wilford Welch) 11; Cornell 6.

1961—Cornell (James Morse, Bennet M. Baldwin, Frank Butterworth, III, Patrick Baker) 10; Yale 4.

1962—Cornell (James Morse, Frank S. Butterworth, III, John Walworth, James Reynolds) 14; Yale 5.

1963—Cornell (James R. Morse, Patrick Dix, Paul C. Mountain) 11; Yale 4.

1964—Yale (Thomas Walden, Alan L. Corey, III, Raymond R. Guest, Jr.) 12; Cornell 9.

1965—Yale (Thomas E. Walden, Alan L. Corey, III, Adolph B. Orthwein, Jr.) 12; Cornell 3.

1966—Cornell (Guillermo Santa Maria, James Greenwell, Peter Orthwein) 12; Yale 10.

1967—Yale (Steve Orthwein, Sandy Carden, Paul Whitbeck, Peter Gerard) 12; Cornell 11.

1968—Yale (G. A. Carden, Stephen Orthwein, Peter Gerard) 17; Cornell 13.

1969—Yale (Bill Brown, Alan Harris, Jim Brandi) 17; Cornell 16.

1970—Yale (Bill Brown, Alan Harris, Jim Brandi) 22; Cornell 10.

1971—Yale (Reed Oppenheimer, Al Harris, Peter Ambrus, Jim Vlasic) 12; Yale 11.

1972—University of Connecticut (Duncan Peters, Bill LeRoyer, Rick Voss) 17; University of Virginia 15.

BASIC RULES

Outdoor polo is played by teams of four men: No. 1, No. 2, No. 3 and No. 4, who is generally called the back. The main duty of the No. 1 man is to guard the rival back. The No. 2 man is the offensive man. He is on the receiving end of passes and starts the action toward the opponent's goal. The No. 3 man works on both offense and defense. He is the equivalent of basketball's playmaker. The back in effect is a goal tender. When a rival sends a ball toward the goal, the back's job is to send it back up the field. Arena polo calls for a 3-man team.

A game generally is made up of 6 or 8 chukkers (periods) of play of 7½ minutes each. The field is 300 yards long and 200 wide if unboarded, 300 yeards long and 160 wide if boarded. One point is scored each time the ball is driven between the uprights, which are 24 feet apart and are situated at both ends of the playing field, as in football.

The ball usually is of willow root, 3¼ inches in diameter and 4¼ to 4¾ ounces in weight. Bamboo wood is sometimes used and experiments are being conducted with plastic balls. The players use mallets, similar in shape to those for croquet. They are 50 to 53 inches in length.

(For Olympic champions see section on Olympic Games).

RACQUETS

(Courtesy of Clarence C. Pell, 149 Jericho Turnpike, Old Westbury, N.Y., 11568)

Born of low estate, the game of racquets eventually became a sport of the wealthy, and it still is.

The date of the beginning of racquets has not been determined precisely, but there appears to be no question about the place of its origin—Debtor's Prison in England. This posed a problem for the former jail inmates who became racquets players, for they naturally did not wish to bring to public attention their earlier plight.

Charles Dickens, in "Pickwick Papers," supports the jail house as the possible birth place of the game by presenting a picture of the inmates whiling away their time playing racquets. The prison game was played against a single wall in an open court.

Robert W. Henderson of the Racquet and Tennis Club of New York, in a bulletin sent to the New York Public Library in May, 1936, offered the conclusion that racquets began as a game in the early tennis courts in the 16th Century, when it was played without set rules. He does not dispute the adoption of the game by prisoners.

The first established champion at racquets was Robert Mackey of England, who won the title in 1820 and who made no secret of the fact that he had learned play while confined in the Fleet Street Gaol (jail) in London.

Inmates of the Debtor's Prison, unlike those in many other types of jails in England, where hardened criminals were confined, were permitted outdoor recesses. Seeking some form of diversion, they perhaps first tried handball, but the kind of ball available to them may have been very hard, and stung their hands when they struck with the palms. This caused them to take flat pieces of board, whittle them, forming a handle at one end, while the other, and wider part, was used as the striking surface.

The strange part of this game, with its unfashionable background, is that eventually it was adopted by wealthy aristocrats, became their exclusive property, and was put to play in magnificent indoor courts.

Racquets gained favor as a public sport in England through the latter part of the 18th Century, and was played outdoors with great enthusiasm. Then, for some unknown reason, interest died, and racquets became almost non-existent until revived by pupils at Harrow School, in England, about 1822. This led other schools to take up the game outdoors.

After a time, the pupils, wishing to get in as much play as was possible, but being denied by weather conditions, put a roof over the open courts. This practice continued for a decade, or so, and then the game was taken indoors, and played in what were the gymnasiums of the times.

To make the game more fascinating, the pupils constantly altered the rules, making it more intricate, and such rules required radical changes in the courts. The game began to be played against four walls instead of one, traps were included in play, and the game, as the years went on, practically went out of control of the students, since the rules demanded much more elaborate courts and equipment than the school authorities were willing to build and support.

The first costly court was built at Woolwich, England, in the 1840's. The game attracted a great deal of attention there. This led the Prince's Club, also in England, to devise an even more lavish court in 1853. As time went on, courts of far more magnificent kind, and of greater expense, began to appear in England, Canada and the United States.

The game was introduced into the United States, by way of Canada, and also spread to Bombay, Calcutta, Malta and Buenos Aires. Edward H. LaMontagne came from Canada, about the middle of the 19th Century, to awaken the multitude of New York sportsmen to racquets. He found on his arrival in New York that there was already a court there. It was on Allen Street, off the Bowery. It was a court of mystery. No one to this day has learned when it was built, or who built it, yet there it was, a complete court, in the deserted part of a huge building.

In 1850, the first American court, of whose origin there is a record, was built in the Broadway Racquet Club. Then followed the Gymnasium Club, with a court in 1854. The New York Racquet Court Club, on Twenty-sixth Street, numbering many of the leading sportsmen in its membership, built a court in 1875. The organization grew until it had to move to new quarters, on Forty-third Street, where, in 1891, it opened under the new name of the Racquet and Tennis Club. In 1918 the club took up its present palatial quarters on Park Avenue, which have since been the headquarters for court tennis and racquets devotees.

In 1882, racquets was introduced at St. Paul's School, Concord, N.H. Boston took to the game in 1889 at the Boston A.A., and in 1904 the Tennis and Racquet Club (Boston) was built. The game spread to Philadelphia in 1889, with the building there of the Racquet Club. In 1893 the Chicago A. A. put in courts, the Tuxedo (N.Y.) Club followed in 1902, and in 1906 the Illinois A.C. built a court. In 1909 the University Club of Chicago opened courts in its new quarters, and in 1923 there was built the Racquet Club, with Charles Williams of England in charge. Detroit took up the game in 1903, St. Louis in 1906, and Cleveland and Pittsburgh later.

At the present time, racquets is being actively played in New York, Tuxedo, Boston, and particularly so in Chicago and Detroit. There are far too few courts to handle the play in England.

FAMOUS RACQUETS PLAYERS

Clarence C. Pell is rated as the greatest American racquets player of all time. In his prime, he dominated the amateur field. He won 12 national singles titles, from 1915 to 1933, and, teamed with Stanley G. Mortimer, won the United States doubles title 9 times. Pell won the Tuxedo Gold Racquet for singles play on 14 occasions, won the Canadian singles championship 9 times, teamed in winning the Canadian doubles 6 times, and carried away top honors in the British championship singles in 1925.

Other great American amateurs, in addition to Pell and Mortimer, include: B. Spalding de Garmendia, J. S. Tooker, Clarence H. Mackay, Payne Whitney, Larry Waterbury, Reginald Fincke, Quincy A. Shaw Jr., Huntingdon D. Sheldon, Clarence C. Pell Jr., Dwight Davis, Robert Grant 3d, H. D. Scott, Percy Haughton, Malcolm Kirkbridge, G. H. Brooke, Warren Ingersoll 3d, E. M. Edwards, Harold McCormick, J. Richards Leonard, Joseph Brooks, Dr. Louis F. Bishop, Palmer Dixon, Joseph W. Wear, Stanley W. Pearson, Jr., Peter B. Read, F. F. de Rhain, and E. Fulmann.

The recent United States singles champions at racquets include: Pell Sr., 1931, 1932, 1933; E. M. Edwards, 1934, 1936; Sheldon, 1935; Grant, 1937, 1938, 1939, 1941, 1946, 1948, 1949, 1950, 1951, 1953, with Ingersoll the 1940 winner. No championships were held from 1942 to 1945. Leonard was the 1947 winner and Pearson took the title in 1952.

Lord Aberdare of England was one of the most brilliant players. He starred in singles and also was a winner of important doubles matches, teamed with Dr. H. W. Leatham. Lord Aberdare won many championships in England, and took away with him, in company of J. F. C. Simpson, the United States doubles title in 1928. Two years later he paired with Dr. Leatham to win the U.S. doubles again.

Other fine English players include E. M. Baerlein, Eustace H. Miles, Simpson, Capt. G. N. Scott-Chad, Ian Akers Douglas, David S. Milford, Cosmo S. Crawley, P. Kershaw, P. M. Whitehouse, A. C. Raphael, G. G. Kershaw, R. C. O. Williams, A. Ronald Taylor, R. A. Holt, John H. Pawle, Kenneth A. Wagg, Geoffrey W. T. Atkins and John Thompson. Also, Charles Swallow, Tom Pugh, Richard Bridgman, and Charles Williams.

Among the splendid racquets players in Canada: W. R. Miller, R. E. McDougal, E. Greenshields, F. F. Rolland, H. M. Smith, A. S. Cassils, all of Montreal; Sir John Child of Ottawa, John Rolland and A. C. Pacaud.

Robert Mackey was the first professional champion of the game, winning after liberation from prison and at a time when the sport was an outdoor pastime. Mackey was the titleholder in 1820. Thomas Pittman, John Lamb, J. C. Mitchell and Francis Erwood were succeeding titleholders, as professionals. In 1862, Sir John Hart-Dyke defeated Erwood, and became the first amateur to hold the open championship.

There were six Gray Brothers. Three, Henry, William and Joseph, held the world championship among them from 1863 to 1887, except that H. B. (Punch) Fairs, father of Cecil (Punch) Fairs was champion in 1876 and 1877. Hart-Dyke resigned in 1863 and Henry J. Gray be-

came champion. In 1866 Henry Gray resigned and William Gray succeeded him. He held the title until he died in 1875. H. B. Fairs defeated Joseph Gray in 1876 to become champion. Fairs died in 1878 and Joseph Gray became champion. He held the crown until 1887 when Peter Latham defeated him. In 1888 Walter Gray, another brother, challenged Latham and was beaten. Latham retired in 1902.

There were three Fairs. H. B. Fairs, the racquets champion, and Cecil (Punch) Fairs, the court tennis champion, were father and son (as noted above.) Both were known as Punch. Frank Fairs, brother of Cecil, was a racquets player but not a champion.

In 1903 J. Jamsetji of India and Gilbert Browne of England played to determine Latham's successor. Jamsetji in 1911 and Jock Soutar of Philadelphia took the title from Williams in 1913. Williams regained the championship by defeating Soutar in 1929 and held it until his death in 1935.

In 1937, David S. Milford, English open and amateur champion, defeated Norbert Setzler, open and professional champion of America, for the world open title, and there was no officially decisive action from then until the war halted play.

Milford relinquished the title in 1946. In 1947, James Dear, British professional, and Kenneth Chantler, Montreal professional, met to establish Milford's successor, Chantler having beaten Grant for the American open championship. Dear defeated Chantler to become the new world titleholder. Dear was subsequently defeated by the amateur G. W. T. Atkins of Queens Club, London, and later from the Racquet Club of Chicago, who reigned as world champion until he retired undefeated in 1971 after an unparalled reign.

William Surtees, formerly of Queens Club, London, and now of the Racquet Club in Chicago, became the new world champion in 1972 when he defeated Howard Angus of England in a home-and-home match.

RACQUETS CHAMPIONS

World Open

1820—Robert Mackey, England
1825—Thomas Pittman, England
1834—John Pittman, England
1838—John Lamb, England
1846—J. C. Mitchell, England
1860—Francis Erwood, England
1862—Sir William Hart-Dyke, England
1863-65—H. J. Gray, England
1866-75—William Gray, England
1876-77—H. B. (Punch) Fairs, England
1878-86—Joseph Gray, England
1887—Peter Latham, England
1903—J. Jamsetji, Bombay, India
1911—Charles Williams, England

1913–Jock Soutar, Philadelphia
1929–Charles Williams, Chicago (formerly of England)
1937–David Milford, England
1947–James Dear, England
1951-71–Geoffrey W. T. Atkins, London & Chicago.
1972–William Surtees, Chicago

United States

1890-91–B. Spalding de Garmendia
1892–J. S. Tooker
1893-94–B. Spalding de Garmendia
1895–J. S. Tooker
1896-97–B. Spalding de Garmendia
1898–F. F. Rolland (Canada)
1899–Quincy A. Shaw Jr.
1900–Eustace H. Miles, England
1901–Quincy A. Shaw Jr.
1902–Clarence H. Mackay
1903–Payne Whitney
1904–George H. Brooke
1905–Lawrence Waterbury
1906–Percy D. Haughton
1907–Reginald Fincke
1908–Quincy A. Shaw Jr.
1909–Harold F. McCormick
1910–Quincy A. Shaw Jr.
1911-12–Reginald Fincke
1913-14–Lawrence Waterbury
1915–Clarence C. Pell
1916–Stanley G. Mortimer
1917–Clarence C. Pell
1918-19–No competition
1920-22–Clarence C. Pell
1923–Stanley G. Mortimer
1924-25–Clarence C. Pell
1926–Stanley G. Mortimer
1927-28–Clarence C. Pell
1929–Huntingdon D. Sheldon
1930–Stanley G. Mortimer
1931-33–Clarence C. Pell
1934–E. M. Edwards
1935–Huntingdon D. Sheldon
1936–E. M. Edwards
1937-39–Robert Grant 3d
1940–Warren Ingersoll 3d
1941–Robert Grant 3d
1942-45–No competition
1946–Robert Grant 3d
1947–J. Richards Leonard
1948-51–Robert Grant 3d
1952–Stanley W. Pearson Jr.
1953–Robert Grant 3d.
1954-56–Geoffrey W.T. Atkins, England
1957–Charles Pearson
1958–Clarence C. Pell Jr.
1959-60–Geoffrey W. T. Atkins, England
1961-63–David Norman
1964–P. B. Read
1965–Stephen Cox
1966-67–David Norman

1968–James W. Leonard
1969-70–Geoffrey W. T. Atkins
1971-72–William Surtees

Tuxedo (N.Y.) Gold Racquet Winners

1904–M. S. Barger
1905-07–Clarence H. Mackay
1908–J. G. Douglas
1909–Harold F. McCormick
1910–G. C. Clark
1911-1912–J. G. Douglas
1913–Harold F. McCormick
1914-17–Clarence C. Pell
1918-20–No competition
1921-23–Clarence C. Pell
1924–Stanley G. Mortimer
1925-27–Clarence C. Pell
1928–Stanley G. Mortimer
1929-30–Clarence C. Pell
1931–Stanley G. Mortimer
1932-33–Clarence C. Pell
1934–J. Richards Leonard
1935–Huntingdon B. Sheldon
1936–Clarence C. Pell
1937-39–Robert Grant 3d
1940–J. Richards Leonard
1941–Robert Grant 3d
1942-45–No competition
1946-47–Robert Grant 3d
1948–J. Richards Leonard
1949-50–Robert Grant 3d
1951–R. A. A. Holt, England
1952–Stanley W. Pearson Jr.
1953-56–Geoffrey W. T. Atkins, England
1957–Charles Pearson
1958-60–Geoffrey W. T. Atkins, England
1961–J. C. Bostwick
1962–David Norman
1963-64–Charles J. Swallow
1965–G. H. Bostwick, Jr.
1966–C. M. T. Pugh
1967-69–G. H. Bostwick, Jr.
1970-72–David McClernon, Canada
1973–Howard Angus, England

BASIC RULES OF RACQUETS

The racquets court is an enclosed rectangular space of 60 feet by 30 feet, with front and side playing walls 30 feet high and the backwall extending up 15 feet, above which is the balcony for the gallery. A skylight covers the entire court. The walls and floor are made of cement and are covered with a patented finish.

A service line is painted on the front wall, 9 feet 7½ inches above the floor, and a wooden board is fixed to the bottom of the front wall, extending 27 inches up from the floor. This is known as the "telltale" and the ball must be hit above it to be fair. On the floor, 24 feet from the back wall, is painted a line running the width of the court known as the "short line." The service, in coming off the front wall, must hit in back of this line. Another line runs from the back wall to the center of the short line, forming two service courts, and two service boxes are marked out. In the United States only one service is allowed.

The implements of the game are a racquet and ball. For many years the ball, which measures about 1 inch in diameter, was made of pieces of wool yarn tightly wound around a core, bound with twine and then covered with white kid skin cut into four segments. After the plant was destroyed during World War II, a new method for covering the balls was sought. After much experimentation, a polyethylene ball was developed using adhesive tape as a covering. It used to be that fifty to a hundred balls might be used in a match; now as few as ten to twenty will be used. The racquet is 30 inches long, weighs 8 to 10 ounces and has a circular head with a diameter of 7 or 8 inches.

A point is scored only when the point is won by the server. It is a "hand in" and "hand out" game. Fifteen points constitute game at racquets, except when the score reaches 13-all, or 14-all, when extra points are "set." When championships are involved, play is on the match basis, the basis being best 3 games of 5, or best 4 of 7, as has been decided in advance.

ROLLER SKATING

Competitive artistic roller skating came into prominence in the 1930s after other versions of the sport, mainly racing and marathons, both amateur and professional, had passed through decades of ups and downs.

According to historians, roller skating came into being in the early 1800s when an un-named Hollander attached wooden disks to shoes, supposedly to devise for his countrymen a warm-weather substitute for their favorite sport, ice-skating on the canals.

Since then, skating on wheels has enjoyed a steady growth as a recreation and mild form of exercise as well as a sport that requires a high degree of skill plus years of training and practice.

Today, according to a survey by the Chicago Skate Co. and Roller Skating Foundation of America (R.S.F.A.), there are upwards of 20,000,000 who enjoy roller skating's healthful benefits in North America alone. These participants are of all ages, although youngsters and teen-agers predominate, and are about equally divided between the sexes.

Throughout the United States and Canada, the sport of whirling wheels is enjoyed in its various forms both indoors and outdoors. Covered rinks range from small portable affairs with canvas tops to multi-million dollar palaces with expensive surfaces of top-grade maple that are up to 100 by 200 feet and larger. Wherever there are paved streets and/or sidewalks, street skating is extremely popular, especially among the young. Roller hockey, often played with rare skill, is a favorite among the street skaters.

Latest surveys show that there are between 5,000 and 6,000 rollerdromes in the United States and Canada. In addition, approximately 6,000 churches, elementary schools, high schools and colleges feature roller skating programs as regular athletic and recreational fare for students and guests. Notable collegiate programs include those conducted by the United States Military Academy at West Point and by Purdue University in the midwest.

Another 2,000 programs are sponsored by youth groups, fraternal organizations, business and industrial firms. The Girl Scouts of America allow proficiency badge credits for roller skating skill, the Camp Fire Girls award roller certificates and the Cub Scouts include roller skating in its advancement program as part of the sports elective for arrow point credits.

As a legitimate competitive sport, roller skating may be divided into speed or racing, hockey and artistic. The latter includes figures, freestyle, pair skating, fours, dance and certain novelty events, with judging done by a point system which (except with the standardized dances) is based on "content of program" as well as "manner of performance."

Amateur meets are on the local, state, regional, United States or North American and worldwide level. Each is sanctioned and carefully supervised by one of two rival organizations claiming jurisdiction over the amateur roller skater in North America.

These associations are the United States Amateur Roller Skating Association, 152 W. 42nd St. New York, N.Y. 10036, and the Roller Skating Rink Operators Association, affiliated with the United States of America Roller Skating Confederation. Their address is 7700 "A" Street, Lincoln, Nebraska, 68510.

The R.S.R.O.A., founded and organized in 1937, is the older of the two groups and claims the larger membership. The U.S.A.R.S.A. is a direct member of the Amateur Athletic Union and U.S. Olympic Association and is affiliated with the Amateur Skating Union and other amateur ice groups. It is hoped that roller skating, after years of trying, will soon be an Olympic sport, perhaps as an exhibition in the next Games.

Although competitive skaters normally start serious practice in the early Fall, the season for major competition (State meets and up) begins in the Spring. Meets on a nationwide scope generally are skated in the early Summer, mainly to avoid conflict with school and college schedules of the participants.

Immediately after its 1947 Nationals, the R.S.R.O.A. staged the first World Roller Skating Congress Championships in Oakland, Calif. In December of the same year, the U.S.A.R.S.A. sponsored the first world meet for the Federation Internationale de Patinage a Roulettes in Washington, D.C. Subsequent F.I.P.R. championships with U.S. participation were held in Barcelona, Spain, 1955; Bologna, Italy, 1961; and Miami Beach, Florida, 1962.

U.S. representatives of the R.S.R.O.A. journeyed to New Zealand for a World Congress competition in 1959 and several times to Europe and New Zealand for exhibition tours.

F.I.P.R. World meets, without U.S. representation, were held in Barcelona, Spain, 1949; Torino, Italy, 1951; Dortmund, Germany, 1952; Barcelona, Spain, 1955 and 1956; Bologna, Italy, 1958, and West Berlin, Germany, 1959.

U.S. involvement in world competition has been confined to artistic skating, which originally was copied from the ice. Probably the most spectacular events from a spectator viewpoint are the freestyle and pair-skating contests which involve the kind of jumps, spins, lifts and footwork normally associated with the big professional ice extravaganzas. Dance skating, beautiful to watch but less spectacular, is built around series of intricate steps done to set patterns.

R.S.R.O.A. CHAMPIONS
Senior Speed

Determined on a point basis.

Men

1937—Lloyd Christopher, St. Louis, Mo.
1938—George Moore, Cincinnati, Ohio
1939—No competition
1940—George Moore, Cincinnati, Ohio
1941—William Hay, Chicago, Ill.
1942—Anthony Merrilli, St. Louis, Mo.
1943—Frank Wander, St. Louis, Mo.
1944—Anthony Merrilli, St. Louis, Mo.
1945—No competition
1946-47—Harold Wyant, Dayton, Ohio
1948—Orville Godfrey Jr., Detroit, Mich.
1949—James Hibak, New Westminster, B.C.
1950—Ronald Grina, Portland, Ore.
1951—Harold Slack, Cleveland, Ohio
1952—Earl Knight, Chicago, Ill.
1953-54—Arthur Kerwin, Seattle, Wash.
1955-56—Edgar Watrous, Hartford, Conn.
1957—James Mohler, North Sacramento, Calif.
1958—Richard Edwards, Wichita, Kan.
1959—Gerald Gohs, Detroit
1960—George Grudza, Penndel, Pa.
1961-62—Edward Perales, Gardena, Calif.

1963—Edward Perales, Torrance, Calif.
1964—George Grudza, Riverside, N.J.
1965—Ted Attebury, Long Beach, Calif.
1966—Ted Rendfrey, Riverside, N.J.
1967—John Drewry, Lancaster, Pa.
1968—Malcolm Williamson, Irving, Tex.
1969—Michael Layport, Santa Ana, Calif.
1970-72—Pat Bergin, Irving, Tex.

Women

1938—Vivian Bell, Cincinnati, Ohio
1939—No competition
1940—Verna Picton, Detroit, Mich.
1941—June Prater, Cincinnati, Ohio
1942—Dorothy V. Law, Cleveland, Ohio, and Betty Jane Ross, Detroit, Mich. (tie)
1943—Jeanette Killoren, St. Louis, Mo.
1944—Ruth Jones, Cincinnati, Ohio
1945—No competition
1946—Mary Lou Dauer, Cincinnati, Ohio
1947—Betty Hosek, Seattle, Wash.
1948—Mary Lou Dauer, Cincinnati, Ohio
1949—Rita Conseiller, New Westminster, B.C.
1950—Evalyn Olson, Oakland, Calif.
1951—Betty Jane Hager, Alliance, Ohio
1952—Evalyn Olson, Oakland, Calif.
1953-54—Laurene Anselmy, Pontiac, Mich.
1955-56—Susan Cowan, Greeley, Colo.
1957—Carolyn Sliger, Oklahoma City, Okla.
1958—Suzanne Richardson, Detroit, Mich.
1959-61—Mary Merrell, Fullerton, Calif.
1962—Linda Durbin, Lincoln, Neb.
1963—Mary Lou Kurk, Pontiac, Mich.
1964—Mary Merrell, Santa Ana, Calif.
1965—Janet Ford, Pontiac, Mich.
1966-67—Mary Merrell, Santa Ana, Calif.
1968—Sharon Van Lue, Glendora, Calif.
1969-70—Jan Irwin, Irving, Tex.
1971—Shelley Comella, Portland, Ore.
1972—Jan Irwin, Irving, Tex.

Senior Figure Skating
Men

1939-40—Walter Stokosa, Detroit, Mich.
1941—Robert Ryan, Dayton, Ohio
1942—Kenneth Chase, Dayton, Ohio
1943—Jack Seifert, Dayton, Ohio
1944—Arthur Russell, Oakland, Calif.
1945—No competition
1946—Ted Shufflebarger, Ogden, Utah
1947-48—J. W. Norcross Jr., Greeley, Colo.
1949—Ted Rosdahl, Chicago, Ill.
1950—J. W. Norcross Jr., Greeley, Colo.
1951—Alvin Hurwitz, Brooklyn, N.Y.
1952—Skipper Oakes, San Mateo, Calif.
1953-54—William Pate Jr., Pontiac, Mich.
1955—John Matejec, Pontiac, Mich.
1956-57—Ronald Jellse, Peoria, Ill.
1958—Ricky Mullican, Long Beach, Calif.
1959—Darrell Glenn, Long Beach, Calif.
1960—Thomas Gregory, Pontiac, Mich.
1961-62—Philip Sukel, Oak Lawn, Ill.

1963–John Renz, San Diego, Calif.
1964–John Renz, San Diego, Calif.
1965–Edgar Watrous, New Britain, Conn.
1966–Michael Jacques, Norwood, Mass.
1967-69–Richard Gustafson, New Britain, Conn.
1970–Gary Lintz, Everett, Wash.
1971–Ronald Milton, Norwood, Mass.
1972–William Boyd, Seabrook, Md.

Women

1939–Jane Peace Holcombe, Detroit, Mich.
1940–Margot Allred, Dayton, Ohio
1941-42–Melva Block, Detroit, Mich.
1943–Shirley Snyder, Dayton, Ohio
1944–Dorothy Mae Law, Detroit, Mich.
1945–No competition
1946–Mrs. Margaret Williams McMillan, Cleveland, Ohio
1947–Margaret Wallace, Brooklyn, N.Y.
1948-50–Nancy Lee Parker, Detroit, Mich.
1951-54–Laurence Anselmy, Pontiac, Mich.
1955–Carol Haller, Peoria, Ill.
1956–Joan Brown, St. Louis, Mo.
1957–Lynne Mathewson, Redwood City, Calif.
1958–Carolyn Sliger, Oklahoma City, Okla.
1959–Paulette Stewart, Redwood City, Calif.
1960–Christine Benda, Grandview, Mo.
1961-62–Linda Jo Baker, Atlanta
1963–Sylvia Haffke, Agawam, Mass.
1964-65–Sylvia Haffke, New Britain, Conn.
1966–Linda Hawthorne, Whittier, Calif.
1967-68–Carol Langlois, New Britain, Conn.
1969-70–Margaret Lucas, Riverside, N.J.
1971–Susie Johnson, Ft. Worth, Tex.
1972–Debra Ann Palm, East Meadow, N.Y.

Senior Pairs

1939–Eldora Andrews–William B. Best, Detroit, Mich.
1940–Dorothy Kolb–William Opatrny, Pittsburgh, Pa.
1941–Ann Manion–Walter Stokosa, Detroit, Mich.
1942–Doris Gebreth–Ray Lenty, New York, N.Y.
1943–Margaret Williams–William L. Martin, Detroit, Mich.
1944–Carol Bodden–Thomas Lane, Brooklyn, N.Y.
1945–No competition
1946–Mrs. Marie Rader–Clarence Rader, Cleveland, Ohio
1947–Patricia Ann Carroll–Thomas Lane, Elmhurst, N.Y.
1948–Phyllis Bulleigh–Cecil Davis, Greeley, Colo.
1949–Phyllis Bulleigh–Cecil Davis, Spokane, Wash.
1950–Patricia Ann Carroll–J.W. Norcross Jr., Greeley, Colo.
1951–Phyllis Bulleigh–Cecil Davis, Denver, Colo.
1952-53–Gail Locke–William Pate Jr., Detroit, Mich.
1954–Marilee Olsen–Gary Houck, Middletown, Ohio

1955-56–Patricia Benedict–Warren Colozzo, Brooklyn, N.Y.
1957-58–Ruth Hesseman–Kenneth Trotter, Brooklyn, N.Y.
1959-60–Robert Wollard–Carol Stout, Santa Ana, Calif.
1961–Douglas Eley–Judy Nance, Long Beach, Calif.
1962–Paul Boehm–Pamela Cornwall, Houston, Texas.
1963-65–David Tassinari–Diane Kern, Norwood, Mass.
1966–Michael Jacques–Nancy Lou Johnson, Norwood, Mass.
1967-72–Ron and Gail Robovitsky, Clawson, Mich.

Senior Fours

1942–Sibley, Law, Martin, Moore, Detroit, Mich.
1943–Van Wagner, Carroll, Latin, Smola, Elmhurst, N.Y.
1944–Gallagher, Bodden, Lane, Sokolowski, New York, N.Y.
1945–No competition
1946–Van Wagner, Carroll, Tuohy, Kuester, Elmhurst, N.Y.
1947–No competition
1948–Lane, Carroll, Tuohy, Kuester, Elmhurst, N.Y.
1949–Bauman, McCarthy, Cawley, McSweeney, Brooklyn, N.Y.
1950–Norcross, Carroll, Johnson, Laney, Greeley, Colo.
1951–Gullo, Bury, LaBriola, Grasso, Brooklyn, N.Y.
1952-53–Matejec, Kromis, Pate, Locke, Detroit, Mich.
1954–Clary, Olsen, Houck, Recher, Middletown, Ohio
1955–Glatz, Sakowitz, Pennington, Hess, Long Beach, Calif.
1956–Haller, Jellsey, Anderson, Kock, Peoria, Ill.
1957–Clark, Anderson, Kock, Jellse, Peoria, Ill.
1958–Daniels, Parke, Seabern, Maguire, Santa Ana, Calif.
1959–Kline, Mazo, Trotter, Heesman, Mineola, N.Y.
1960–Parker, Ritchie, Martins, Welch, Pontiac, Mich.
1961–Parker, Ritchie, Schafer, Welch, Pontiac, Mich.
1962–Tassinari, Kern, Welch, Urban, Norwood, Mass.
1963–Souza, Jerue, Toon, Johnson, N. Sacramento, Calif.
1964–Perkins, Fish, Peterka, Montis, Akron, Ohio
1965-66–Tassinari, Kern, Jacques, Johnson, Norwood, Mass.
1967–Melton, Gruber, Williams, Wallis, San Leandro, Calif.
1968–Collier, Marshall, Toon, Jerue, San Leandro, Calif.

1969—Collier, Marshall, Toon, Spangle, San Leandro, Calif.

1970—Spangle, Toon, Jerue, Collier, San Leandro, Calif.

1971—Collier, Marshall, Toon, Jerue, San Leandro, Calif.

1972—Stovall, Hughes, Weber, Hughes, Long Beach, Calif.

Senior Skate Dancing

1939—Virginia Mount—Lloyd G. Young, Detroit, Mich.

1940—Mary Louise Durkin—Gordon B. Finnegan, Mineola, N.Y.

1941—Gladys Koehler—George Werner, Richmond Hill, N.Y.

1942—Mrs. Irene Boyer—Jack Boyer, Columbus, Ohio Page 789-90

1943—Norma Jeanne Wescher—Leo Carsner, Dayton, Ohio

1944—Ruth Crause—James Costigan, Philadelphia, Pa.

1945—No competition

1946—Ruth Crause—James Costigan, Philadelphia, Pa.

1947-49—Bettie Jennings—Cliff Shattenkirk, Seattle, Wash.

1950-53—Joan LaBriola—Robert LaBriola, Brooklyn, N.Y.

1954-56—Marilyn Roberts—Gary Castro, San Francisco, Calif.

1957—Miriam Centaro—Charles Wahlig, Elmont, N.Y.

1958-59—Claire Farrell—Charles Wahlig, Elmont, N.Y.

1960-61—Linda Jo Baker—Jack Greer, Atlanta

1962—Linda Mottice—Adolph Wacker, Canton, Ohio.

1963-68—Linda Mottice—Adolph Wacker, Akron, Ohio

1969—Vicki Freeman—Marc Parker, Pleasanton, Calif.

1970—Sanja Pulitz—Richard Manns, Indianapolis, Ind.

1971—Elayne and Bob Leonard, Santa Ana, Calif.

1972—Marie Spoleti—Joseph Gaudy, Dover, Del.

U.S.A.R.S.A. CHAMPIONS

Senior Speed

Men

1947—Joseph Horvath, Passaic, N.J.

1948—Larry Bissinger, Mount Vernon, N.Y.

1949—James Calder, Alexandria, Va.

1950—William Tourjee, Florham Park, N.J.

1951—Burton Speed, Hackensack, N.J.

1952-53—Edward Horan, Elizabeth, N.J.

1954—Donald DeRoo, Paterson, N.J.

1955—Albert Eckworth, Mount Vernon, N.Y.

1956—Dee Rigg, San Francisco, Calif.

1957—Chester Brosonski, Bayonne, N.J.

1958—James Nolan, Harvey, Ill.

1959—James Richardson

1960—David Babb

1961—David Kieft

1962—Virgil Dooley

1963—Fred Metcalfe, Kokomo, Ind.

1964—Clifford Nazzaro, Hackensack, N.J.

1965—Virgil Dooley, Chicago, Ill.

1966-67—Clifford Nazzaro, Bayonne, N.J.

1968-69—Don Rogers, Pomona, Calif.

1970—M. Leo Mazzulla, Summit, Ill.

1971—Charles Gillette, Livonia, Mich.

1972—No competition

Women

1947—Miriam Hoey, Bayonne, N.J.

1948-49—Doris Dahl, Elizabeth, N.J.

1950—Frances Olsen, Hackensack, N.J.

1951—Marie Grosso, Mount Vernon, N.Y.

1952-54—Ellen Hughes, Bladensburg, Md.

1955-57—Furn Walton, Washington, D.C.

1958—Patricia Lewis, Bladensburg, Md.

1959—Geraldine Gehret

1960-61—Judy Armer

1962-64—Jean Plichta

1965—Ruth Mueller, Reading, Pa.

1966-67—Darlene Mueller, Summit, Ill.

1968—Linda Barber, Grandville, Mich.

1969—Sue Maiberger, Kent, Ohio

1970—Darlene Mueller, Summit, Ill.

1971—Barbara Zawistowski, Elizabeth, N.J.

1972—No competition

Senior Figure Skating

Men

1939-40—Walter Stokosa, Detroit, Mich.

1941—Robert Ryan, Dayton, Ohio

1942—Edward LeMaire, White Plains, N.Y.

1943—William Best, Detroit, Mich.

1944-46—Walter Bickmeyer, Mineola, N.Y.

1947—Donald Mounce, Mineola, N.Y.

1948—Reggie Opie, Mineola, N.Y.

1949-50—Leonard Baggaley, Hackensack, N.J.

1951—Jude Cull, Elizabeth, N.J.

1952—Ronald Rancourt, Mineola, N.Y.

1953—Frank Henrich, Mineola, N.Y.

1954—Jack DeBeve, Washington, D.C.

1955-57—Billy Ferraro, Livonia, Mich.

1958—Paul Zukowski, Elizabeth, N.J.

1959—David Julian, Livonia, Mich.

1960—Paul Zukowski, Elizabeth, N.J.

1961—George Auble, Bayonne, N.J.

1962—Larry Adams, Livonia, Mich.

1963-64—Paul Zukowski, Elizabeth, N.J.

1965—Larry Joe Dorsett, Marion, Ind.

1966-69—Jack Courtney, Marion, Ind.
1970—William Boyd, Marion, Ind.
1971—Randy Dayney, Levittown, N.Y.
1972—No competition

Women

1939—Jane Holcomb, Detroit, Mich.
1940—Margot Allred, Dayton, Ohio
1941—Melva Block, Detroit, Mich.
1942-43—Jean White, Mineola, N.Y.
1944—Theresa Kelsch, Mineola, N.Y.
1945—Irene Maguire, New York
1946-47—June Henrich, Mineola, N.Y.
1948—Charlotte Ludwig, Elizabeth, N.J.
1949-50—June Henrich, Mineola, N.Y.
1951—Mary Louise Leahey, Elizabeth, N.J.
1952—Diane Lanzotti, Elizabeth, N.J.
1953—Ruth Henrich, Mineola, N.Y.
1954-55—Margie Adair, Paterson, N.J.
1956—Doris Dahl, Bayonne, N.J.
1957—Nancy Galbraith, Livonia, Mich.
1958-61—Dawn Brown, Trenton, N.J.
1962-63—Linda Kobane, Levittown, N.Y.
1964—Linda Klein, Levittown, N.Y.
1965—June Goodison, Long Beach, Calif.
1966—Dorothy Cochraine, Levittown, N.Y.
1967—Ingrid McManus, Marion, Ind.
1968—Kathleen Schreiber, Levittown, N.Y.
1969—Dorothy Cochrane, Marion, Ind.
1970—Barbara Francesconi, Levittown, N.Y.
1971—Colleen Giacomo, South Amboy, N.J.
1972—No competition

Senior Mixed Pairs

1939—Eldora Andrews—William Best, Detroit, Mich.
1940—Dorothy Kolb—William Opatrny, Pittsburgh, Pa.
1941—Ann Manion—Walter Stokosa, Detroit, Mich.
1942—Jean White—Chadwick Detrick, Mineola, N.Y.
1943—Dorothy Luginbuhl—Alfred Shady, Mineola, N.Y.
1944—Theresa Kelsch—Edward Blaes, Mineola, N.Y.
1945—No competition
1946—Charlotte Ludwig—Frank Salvage, Elizabeth, N.J.
1947-48—Charlotte Ludwig—Jude Cull, Elizabeth, N.J.
1949—Irma Barnard—Mickey Brown, Plymouth, Mich.
1950-51—Charlotte Ludwig—Jude Cull, Elizabeth, N.J.
1952—Irma Brown—Michael Brown, Ovid, N.Y.
1953—Ruth and Frank Henrich, Mineola, N.Y.

1954-55—Margie Adair—Jack Crichton, Paterson, N.J.
1956-57—Barbara Searles—Billy Ferraro, Livonia, Mich.
1958—Diane Ludwig—Paul Zudowski, Elizabeth, N.J.
1959—David Julian—Linda Kobane, Livonia, Mich.
1960-61—Paul Zukowski—Dianne Ludwig, Elizabeth, N.J.
1962—Raymond and Marlene Steinberg, Livonia, Mich.
1963—John Burton—Linda Klein, Levittown, N.Y.
1964-65—Lyndell Edgington—Charlotte Owings, Marion, Ind.
1966—Burt and Ruth Brinkerhoff, Levittown, N.Y.
1967-69—Jack Courtney—Sheryl Trueman, Marion, Ind.
1970—Tim Abell—Gigi Fox, Harvey, Ill.
1971—William Boyd—Linda Martin, Seabrook, Md.
1972—No competition

Women's Pairs

1943—Jean White—Peggy Prince, Mineola, N.Y.
1944—Yvette Kiefer—Faith Benedict, White Plains, N.Y.
1945-46—Charlotte and Shirley Ludwig, Elizabeth, N.J.
1947—Christine and Genevieve Ross, Pasadena, Calif.
1948-49—Violet Gargano—Mary Louise Leahey, Elizabeth, N.J.
1950-51—Mary Louise Leahey—Charlotte Ludwig, Elizabeth, N.J.
1952—Ruth Henrich—Margaret Meyers, Mineola, N.Y.
1953—Ruth Henrich—Margaret Meyers, Mineola, N.Y.
1954—Margie Adair—Joyce Bonocore, Paterson, N.J.
1955—Margie Adair—Dawn Brown, Paterson, N.J.
1956—Alice Betzler—Elizabeth Cunningham, Bayonne, N.J.
1957-58—Nancy Galbraith—Linda Kobane, Livonia, Mich.
1959—Linda Beaton—Linda Kobane, Livonia, Mich.
1960—Linda Kobane—Marlene Steinberg, Livonia, Mich.
1961—Dawn Brown—Eunice Prokop, Trenton, N.J.
1962-63—Linda Lobane—Linda Klein, Levittown, N.Y.
1964—Trisha Kittle—Charlotte Owings, Marion, Ind.
1965-66—Ruth Brinkerhoff—Barbara Frances-

coni, Levittown, N.Y.

1967—Ingrid McManus—Sheryl Trueman, Marion, Ind.

1968—Kathleen Schreiber—Karen Seekamp, Levittown, N.Y.

1969—Dorothy Cockrane—Sheryl Trueman, Marion, Ind.

1970—Barbara Francesconi—Barbara Kaffka, Levittown, N.Y.

1971—Robin Dayney—June Frees, Levittown, N.Y.

1972—No competition.

Senior Fours

1945—Kelsch, Mounce, Henrich, Bickmeyer, Mineola, N.Y.

1946—Reuter, Reed, Matturo, Luddy, Bayonne, N.J.

1947-48—Gargano, Hoernlein, Leahey, Hackett, Elizabeth, N.J.

1949-51—Ludwig, Cull, Leahey, Callahan, Elizabeth, N.J.

1952—Lanzotti, Haddad, Reed, Thelgen, Elizabeth, N.J.

1953—Dahl, Dahl, Moore, Moore, Bayonne, N.J.

1954—Heisler, Ludwig, Laflin, Schmitt, Elizabeth, N.J.

1954—Heisler, Bonocore, Schmitt, Loeffler, Elizabeth, N.J.

1956—Heisler, Ludwig, Schmidt, Malloy, Elizabeth, N.J.

1957—Kalavatinos, Becker, Godwin, Wheeler, Washington, D.C.

1958-60—Schmid, Jablonski, Zukowski, Ludwig, Elizabeth, N.J.

1961-62—Brown, Speicher, Edginton, Aulberry, Marion, Indiana.

1963-64—Courtney, Kittle, Lambert, Owings, Marion, Ind.

1965—Edgington, Owings, Lambert, Horner, Marion, Ind.

1966—Brinkerhoff, Brinkerhoff, Dayney, Francesconi, Levittown, N.Y.

1967—Trotter, Ramerez, Meisch, Lutz, Elizabeth, N.J.

1968—Neely, Grimes, Spooner, Presson, Blandensburg, Md.

1969-70—Sloan, Klein, Swan, Mueller, Summit, Ill.

1971—Allen, Allen, Austin, Ali, Pasadena & Pomona, Calif.

1972—No competition

Senior Dance

1939—Virginia Mount—Lloyd Young, Detroit, Mich.

1940—Mary Louise Durkin—Gordon Finigan, Mineola, N.Y.

1941-42—Gladys Koehler—George Werner, Richmond Hill, N.Y.

1943—Margaret Mahoney—John Karasony, Mineola, N.Y.

1944-45—Rita Luginbuhl—Fred Ludwig, Mineola, N.Y.

1946—Gladys and George Werner, Mineola, N.Y.

1947—Barbara K. Gallagher—Fred Ludwig, Mineola, N.Y.

1951-52—Ann Feder—Edward O'Donnell, Mineola, N.Y.

1953—Ann Van Lone—Edward O'Donnell, Mineola, N.Y.

1954-55—Barbara McCusker—Edward O'Donnell, Mineola, N.Y.

1956—Jean and Raymond Tiedemann, Mount Vernon, N.Y.

1957—Madelyn Higgins—Earl Roberts, Levittown, N.Y.

1958—Carolyn Elias—William Thelgen, Levittown, N.Y.

1959—Gaile Gilmartin—Marshal Rule, Levittown, N.Y.

1960—Madelyn Higgins—Earl Roberts, Levittown, N.Y.

1961—Janet and Jay Slaughter, Melrose Park, Ill.

1962—Jacqueline Zimmerman—Robert Shaffer, Melrose Park, Ill,

1963-64—John Burton—Linda Klein, Levittown, N.Y.

1965—Warren Dancer—Charlotte Owings, Muncie and Marion, Ind.

1966—Robert Shaffer—Charlotte Owings, Melrose Park, Ill.

1967—Robert Shaffer—Sherry Street Batt, Summit, Ill.

1968-69—Thomas Straker—Bonnie Lambert, Livonia, Mich.

1970-71—Richard Horne—Jane Pankey, Livonia, Mich.

1972—No competition

Relay

1959—Virgil Dooley—Danny Pope, Peru, Indiana.

1960—Frank Ederhardt—Michael Nash, Washington, D.C.

1961—James Pennypacker—James Roth, Reading, Pa.

1962-63—Virgil Dooley—Walter Cooley, Chicago, Ill.

1964—Michael Rogers—Carl Kuzyk, Michigan

1965—Virgil Dooley—Danny Pope, Chicago

1966—Frank Cesarec—Virgil Dooley, Chicago & Milwaukee

1967—Jerry Pallo—Willard Wapp, Milwaukee & Melrose Park, Ill.

1968—Michael Figard—Doug Kraai, Grand Rapids, Mich.

1969—Virgil Dooley—Charles Gillette, Kent, Ohio

1970—Virgil Dooley—Rick Wiers, Livonia, Mich.

1971—Virgil Dooley—Charles Gillette, Livonia, Mich.

1972—No competition

ROQUE AND CROQUET

(Courtesy of Maryalma Yousey, Secretary & Treasurer, The American Roque League, Inc., 4205 Briar Creek Lane, Dallas, Tex., 75214)

Roque is frequently described as outdoor billiards with wickets. The reason is that it has some aspects of billiards and of croquet. It utilizes the basic procedures of croquet and the technique of billiards. The name of roque was arrived at by dropping the C and T of croquet. The name was devised in 1899 by men who believed their game was new and different from croquet, a game that was faster and more scientific.

Croquet has a blurred history. The word is "crochet," in French, and means "crooked stick." The French played it in the 17th Century in a minor way. About then, the English were playing a similar game, known as "pall mall." It is not known whether the English borrowed croquet from France and gave it the "pall mall" name, or vice versa.

The belief exists that croquet was created when lawn bowls was taken indoors, first on floors, later on huge tables. To make lawn bowls intricate, the ball had to be driven through arches, etc., and later into pockets, built into the table. Eventually, the arches were discarded and the balls were shot into pockets—the start of the billiard game. Those who liked that part of the play which required action through wickets took their sport outdoors, made some changes—and the result was croquet (or crochet, as in France.)

But in neither England nor France did the game find many enthusiasts, and it lapsed late in the 17th Century and has no mention through the 18th. One meets it again when John Jacques of France touches on the subject in 1857. This was followed in 1861 by a booklet, "Routlege's Handbook of Croquet," authored by Edmond Routlege of England, probably the first rule book of the game and one which, unto this day, basically governs croquet, and, in a way, its off-shoot—roque.

There was a revival at about the time that Routlege wrote his laws, and the "craze" swept into England and France, moved to Ireland and Scotland and was brought to the United States in the 1870's via Norwich, Conn. The game was taken up by society, first in the New York area and then elsewhere throughout this country. It came into favor about the time lawn tennis was making its earliest bid for fame, and through the 1870's into the 1890's the devotees of croquet outnumbered the tennis enthusiasts by a wide margin.

No estate lawn was considered complete without a croquet set for use by residents and their guests. Public parks, which had not featured any form of sport for play on the grass, began to blossom with croquet sets, put there by civic leaders. The women liked croquet. It was a form of exercise that provided a contest without the speed and continued action called for in tennis. The women, who wore many petticoats in that era, found such apparel a handicap at tennis, but the excess of finery did not handicap them in croquet.

The National Croquet Association was formed in 1882 to supervise the game. Its officials were kept busy well into the 1890's. Then, suddenly, people lost interest in croquet, as tennis made a great leap into favor, and by the arrival of the 20th Century the association found there were no more players to supervise. The sport went into eclipse, almost as precipitately as it had swirled into popularity, and the equipment makers, who had been gathering fortunes, discovered their warehouses to be full of croquet balls and wickets. The collapse of croquet was perhaps the swiftest to occur to any sport that ever had become a national "rage" in the United States.

When the wreckage had been cleared away, it was found that here and there were a few players who felt that the game might be developed into something that would require a high amount of skill. A small group revised the laws, and, at a meeting in Norwich, the name "roque" was adopted, so that the new game might be completely divorced from croquet, in its original pattern.

The Routlege rules for croquet provided for 8 balls of different color, made of sycamore wood and 3¼ inches in diameter; 2 stakes; 10 wire hooks, bridges or arches; and mallets 6 inches long, 7 inches in circumference, with a handle 2½ feet long. The playing area could be from 80 feet to 300 feet in length and 45 feet to 150 feet wide and the game usually was on a lawn.

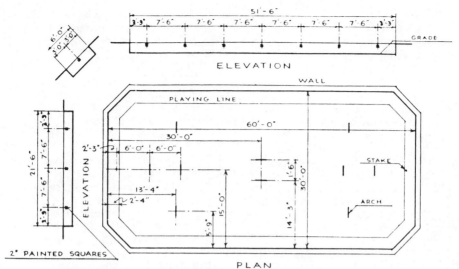

Official Roque Court, Courtesy of The American Roque League, Inc.

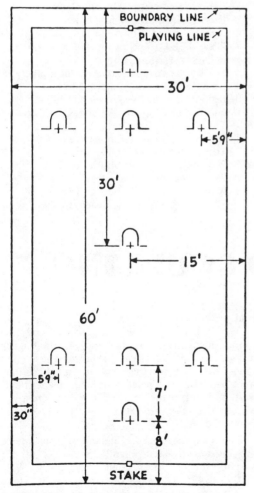

Croquet Playing Area. (Taken from "Sports for Recreation," edited by E. D. Mitchell, A. S. Barnes and Company, New York.)

The roque players, about 1899, transferred from a lawn to a clay court to permit the ball to travel at a higher speed. The playing area was standardized at the shortened size of 60 x 30 feet, and was somewhat octagonal in shape, with concrete borders so that the principle of "English," as used in billiards, might be invoked. Composition balls replaced the wooden ones, the handles of the mallets were shortened and the club ends were of hard rubber, or cement facing instead of wood.

The new game called for 10 arches and 2 stakes. The size of the arches was so decreased that the clearance hole was only a fraction of the inch larger than the ball, requiring a perfect shot to carry through. To assure rigidity the arches were cemented into the ground. Only 4 balls— red, white, blue and black—were employed, and 2 balls were used by each player instead of 1, as in croquet.

The American Roque League was formed in 1916 to govern the game, which gained gradually in favor, and in the 1930's, the Works Progress Administration (W.P.A.) and the National Recreation Association added roque courts to playground equipment. Since that time the army of roque players has increased to thousands. Although the equipment for play, the basic rules and the scoring for roque differ little from croquet, the games are far different in execution.

Croquet is still the game where the player starts off by hitting the stake and then drives through nine arches, hits the other stake and returns to the home stake, the one arriving there first being the winner. The arches in croquet are high and wide, requiring little science to drive through. But in roque, a ball must be hit perfectly to go through the small hoop, and therein lies the outstanding difference in the games.

UNITED STATES CROQUET AND ROQUE CHAMPIONS

1882—A.G. Shipman, New York
1883—G.W. Johnson, Philadelphia, Pa.
1884—George Harland, Norwich, Conn.
1885—Charles Jacobus, Springfield, Conn.
1886—C. Hull Botsford, New York
1887—A. Wambold, Staten Island, N.Y.
1888—Nathan L. Bishop, Norwich, Conn.
1889—G.W. Johnson, Philadelphia, Pa.
1890—George C. Strong, New London, Conn.
1891—Charles G. Smith, Martha's Vineyard, Mass.
1892—G.W. Johnson, Philadelphia, Pa.
1893—William Knecht, Matawan, N.J.
1894—95—George C. Strong, New London, Conn.
1896—Earle C. Butler, Middletown, Conn.
1897—Sackett L. Duryea, Washington
1898—William H. Wahly, Washington
1899—1900—Charles G. Williams, Washington
1901—William H. Wahly, Washington
1902—Sackett L. Duryea, Washington
1903—05—Charles C. Cox, Malden, Mass.
1906—Clifford Howard, Washington
1907—Harold Bosworth, New London, Conn.
1908—Ed Clark, Springfield, Mass.
1909—10—Harold Bosworth, New London, Conn.
1911—12—Ed Clark, Springfield, Mass.
1913—Everett W. Robinson, Mansfield, Mass.
1914—Ed Clark, Springfield, Mass.
1915—16—Harold Bosworth, New London, Conn.
1917—James C. Kirk, Philadelphia, Pa.
1918—Charles G. Williams, Washington
1919—Ed Clark, Springfield, Mass.
1920—F.C. Turner, Pasadena, Calif.
1921—Herbert Sime, Chicago, Ill.
1922—James Keane, Chicago, Ill.
1923—Herbert Sime, Chicago, Ill.
1924—W.W. Wilson, Chicago, Ill.

1925—A.S. Denney, Long Beach, Calif.
1926—A.G. Buffum, Los Angeles, Calif.
1927—O.E. Barnhart, Chicago, Ill.
1928—H.C. Hayden, Cleveland, Ohio
1929—H.L. Smith, Pasadena, Calif.
1930—O.E. Barnhart, Chicago, Ill.
1931—Kenneth Moore, New Paris, Ohio
1932—Ed Clark, Springfield, Mass.
1933—Frank Krause, Pasadena, Calif.
1934—35—O.A. Barnhart, Elgin, Ill.
1936—Phil Wolf, Bellevue, Ohio
1937—George Atkinson, Indianapolis, Ind.
1938 Wallace Martin, Waco, Tex.
1939—W.B. Reed, Fort Worth, Tex.
1940—C.E. Willis, Abilene, Tex.
1941—Pat Winton, Greenville, Tex.
1942—45—No competition
1946—Joe T. Bobbit, Hillsboro, Tex.
1947—49—F.B. Krause, Long Beach, Calif.
1950—E.W. Maddiex, Chicago, Ill.
1951—Bobby Arnold, Glendale, Calif.
1952—Arm G. Kapigian, Glendale, Calif.
1953—Russell Matthews, Winfield, Kan.
1954—Bobby Arnold, Los Angeles, Calif.
1955—(Team)—B.C. McGowan, Dallas, Tex., and Merle Parker, Wichita, Kans.
1956—58—Bobby Arnold, Los Angeles, Calif.
1959—Arm Kapigian, Glendale, Calif.
1960—Bobby Arnold, Los Angeles, Calif.
1961—64—Wayne Stephens, Lubbock, Texas
1965—Tom Puryear, Greenville, Texas
1966—Wayne Stephens, Lubbock, Texas
1967—Tom Puryear, Greenville, Texas
1968—Wayne Stephens, Lubbock, Texas
1969—Robert Arnold, El Monte, Calif.
1970—Wayne Stephens, Lubbock, Texas
1971—72—Jack Green, Long Beach, Calif.

ROWING AND SCULLING

When rowing came into being is hidden in the pages of history. But the art of propelling a boat on water by the use of oars has been in existence a long, long time.

The earliest hand-driven craft were canoes, which date back many centuries. The earliest boats in which oars, or sweeps, played a part, were those pulled by the slaves of the Egyptians, or Roman rulers, before the dawn of the Christian Era.

Whenever the monarchs wanted to go places via water, the boats, then called "barges," were pushed into the lake or river and slaves were put to action at the sweeps. How many were employed depended upon the size of the craft. If it were a huge affair, there might be 50 to 80 oarsmen, two to a seat, each pulling an oar. If the boat were small, the oarsmen were fewer.

Other barges were used in commerce on inland waterways and slaves propelled them, too.

The Romans, no doubt, introduced the English to this form of oarsmanship, but the English refused to call on slaves to power the barges. They hired men for the purpose, and those men were paid. In time, smaller and still smaller boats were built, until they had been reduced to a size where one man, or, at the most, two, could propel a boat.

The Thames River in England became one of the most congested inland waterways of the world during the reign of Henry VIII (1509—1547). The King soon noticed that there were many accidents on the river because of poor oarsmanship. He laid down a rule that none but licensed men could row boats. This meant the serving of an apprenticeship before a man qualified as an oarsman.

Before the death of Henry, there were more than 3,200 licensed oarsmen operating on the Thames, and an even greater number of students. Naturally, with so many watermen in action, there was boasting as to the ability of certain men, and the result was boat racing, usually for side bets.

Thomas Doggett, an actor who died in 1715, provided in his will for a certain fund that was to be paid out in annual installments to the winner of a crew (six men) in a race from London Bridge to Chelsea, a distance of 4½ miles. The race is still staged and is known as Doggett's Coat and Badge race.

Early in the 19th Century, English university students gained the idea that the principle of rowing could be converted into a sport. As a result, there were interclass regattas, followed, finally, by a meeting between Oxford and Cambridge in 1829 in the first of their duels, which have continued since that time in almost unbroken succession: The race has become a "must" in English sport annals.

Regardless of how much one crew might outclass the other in the annual regatta, the shores of the historic Thames River have been lined, through many generations, with crowds that number into the hundreds of thousands. The day of the race is made something of a carnival that no one with a drop of sporting blood is supposed to miss.

The English Henley was first rowed on the Thames on June 14, 1839, and has become the most famous regatta in the world.

The first mention of rowing races in the United States was made in an advertisement that appeared in a New York newspaper in 1811 indicating that the sport had its origin many years earlier and had achieved an importance by 1811 sufficient to warrant promoters to spend money to call attention to a special contest.

The 1811 race was between a boat owned by the Mercantile Advertiser and another whose owner was merely a "Mr. Snyder." There are no data as to the outcome of the duel because there were no sports reporters for the occasion.

Soon afterward there was another rowing contest involving two boats—the "Knickerbocker" of New York and the "Invincible" of Long Island. The course was from Harsimus, N.J., to the flagstaff at the Battery (N.Y.). The race was won by the "Knickerbocker" in a rough sea. The "Knickerbocker" later became the property of Scudder's Museum, which sold it to P.T. Barnum of circus fame. It was destroyed by the fire which consumed his museum.

The "American Star" eventually became recognized as the champion among the rowboats in New York harbor, and when the captain of the British ship "Hussar" was so brash as to hazard the idea that his gig—"Sudden Death"—was a superior skiff, a match race resulted. The side bet was $1,000. The route was from Bedloe's Island, up the Hudson River to Hoboken, N.J., and then to the Battery flagstaff. The race was viewed by "more than 60,000 cheering people," and the "American Star" won by about 400 yards.

The "American Star" later was used to transport General Lafayette of France around New York harbor, and then was presented to him. He sent it to France with the suggestion that French rowboats be patterned after it, "so that France may improve in oarsmanship." As a result, many early French lifeboats were modeled after the "American Star."

The most famous sculling race of the olden days was that between James Lee "of the North River, New York" and William Decker of "the East River, New York." They met in July, 1851, for a side bet of $900, but it was estimated that before the getaway at least $100,000 was at stake on the result, as each man had wagering admirers. The distance was 5 miles, around Bedloe's Island, and Decker won by a fifth of a mile.

As time went on, builders constantly strived for lighter and faster boats and in 1838 there appeared what was called "a whirlwind." This was created by George Speers, who later designed the yacht "America," winner of the first America's Cup race of 1851. Speer's boat, a 4-oared shell with outriggers, was 30 feet long, weighed only 140 pounds, drew only 4 inches of water and could be shot through the water at terrific speed. It was the model that later developed into the present-day racing shell.

The Castle Garden Boat Club was founded in New York in 1834—perhaps the first of its kind. Three years later, the Detroit Boat Club was founded and has maintained a dominant position in U.S. rowing since its origin. This club is acknowledged to be the oldest rowing club in existence.

The Union Boat Club of Boston was founded in 1851. In 1858 the "Schuylkill Navy" was created in Philadelphia by merging into one group the Keystone University, Excelsior, Bachelor and other organizations in the Philadelphia district.

The first actual regatta in the United States is believed to be the one held on the Hudson River, off Peekskill, N.Y., in 1848. All oarsmen were eligible. There was no distinction between amateurs and professionals, but the professionals dominated the scene, since they made sculling a profession.

Not until 1872 was an effort made to separate the professionals from the amateurs, a ruling that was enforced by the Schuylkill Navy for its regatta that year. The law was enacted so that the amateurs, competing among themselves, could gain the trophies that the professionals had monopolized.

COLLEGE ROWING IN THE UNITED STATES

Yale adopted a form of rowing in 1843, the first American college to do so. The original "shell" was a dugout canoe. In 1844 another group of Yale students bought a lapstreak gig and challenged the boys with the canoe, which challenge was immediately accepted.

The canoe defeated the gig by a half-mile. When the gig crew hoisted its boat out of the water, it was discovered that somebody had tied a rope to the keel of the gig, and to the rope was attached a huge slab of stone—a first class anchor.

In 1845 students at Harvard took up oarsmanship, but contests at both Yale and Harvard were interclass until 1852, when the first "regatta" was arranged. W.S. Quigley of the New York *Mail and Express* gave details on early American college rowing and the first Harvard-Yale races in the section on "Aquatics" in "Athletic Sports," published in 1889. He wrote, in part:

"The initial contest between these two colleges [Yale and Harvard] took place in the midsummer of 1852, and from that race the craze for aquatic glory sprang up; a craze that has held a firm root ever since. And in this thirty-seven years of glorious victories and honorable defeats, what grand strides have been made! It is no longer a battle between the rudely constructed boat and its undeveloped rowers, but a fight of the cultured giants in the finest specimen of craft that can be found. . . .

"Although all the big colleges have had voice in the growth of the sport, Yale and Harvard are justly credited with the distinction of having given it its permanent importance. The sport will never die while the blue mingles with the magenta colors. The first race has gone down into the history of the colleges as an intercollegiate affair, but such it really was not. It was not until six years after, or in 1858, that formal arrangements were made for 'an intercollegiate regatta.' It was Harvard which opened the negotiations, and Yale, Trinity, and Brown were not slow in responding.

"All the preliminaries had been attended to and perfected when an unfortunate disaster caused the postponement of the race. This was the drowning of George E. Dunham, the Yale stroke, at Springfield, on July 17 of that year. The accident completely unnerved the men, and the blow was felt for some time after. It was not until the following year that a regular race for the intercollegiate championship took place. The previous contests were of a scrub nature, so much so that they aroused but little interest outside college circles. The initial battle between Harvard and Yale was decided on Aug. 3, 1852. The race came about through a challenge from the blue to the Oneida Club, the Harvard organization.

"Great minds had not considered the power and importance of anything superior to a big, stout barge at that time, and in this style of boat the first race was rowed. Yale owned two or three fairly good boats at that time, but Harvard had only one. This was the Oneida, and she is described as being the finest model of her kind at that time. The craft had originally been built for a race between two Boston clubs, and she was purchased from them in 1845, the year in which the Harvard lads first fell to rowing. The craft was of the lapstreak construction, thirty-seven feet long, and her chief features were a straight stem and no shear. In width she was three and a half feet. Her thole pins were of wood, plain and flat. The boat was floored with wooden strips half way up to the gunwale, and a grating made of hard, unpainted wood decorated each end.

"These gratings were the beauty spots of the craft in the minds of those interested, and the members of the crew used to take turns in polishing them up. For stretchers there were plain bars of wood, the stationary seats were covered with a cushion of red baize, and the tiller-rope was encased in painted canvas. To assist in the navigation of this craft the crew used eight white-ash oars, twelve feet long for the men stationed forward and thirteen feet six inches in length for those amidships. This was the craft used for the first time by Harvard.

"The race was rowed in the Centre Harbor, Lake Winnepeseogee [Winnepesaukee], N.H., at four o'clock in the afternoon, the start being taken from the third blast of a noisy bugle. The course was two miles to windward and straightaway. Not more than a handful of collegians were spectators at this contest, and when the Oneida, of Harvard, defeated the Shawmut or Halcyon, of Yale, a craft thirty-eight feet long, by two full lengths in ten minutes time there was scarcely any excitement. Harvard was much elated over this victory. The men had rowed together a dozen times only before the race, 'for fear of blistering their hands,' as one of them afterwards put it.

"The blue took its defeat with good grace, and before the oars were dry in the boat-house intimated another race. After some wrangling the Connecticut River, Springfield, Mass., was chosen as a course, and the distance was increased to three miles, or one and a half miles down-stream and return. Harvard put two boats in this race, the Iris, an eight-oared barge, and the Y.Y., a four-oared barge. Yale showed up in two six-oared barges, the Nautilus and the Nereid. In this contest, which was rowed on July 21, 1855, outriggers were introduced for the first time, although as early as 1845 they had been used in the Oxford-Cambridge matches abroad. The Y.Y. was of St. John manufacture, outrigged and furnished with spruce oars instead of oak. The eight-oared barge of the college was only slightly outrigged, plain pieces of wood being spiked to the gunwales. The two Yale craft also had wooden outriggers, but bent a trifle and running from the bottom of the craft across the gunwale. . . . The Iris won, with the Y.Y. second, Nereid third and Nautilus last."

Harvard, in a 6-oared shell, won the 1859 regatta, after the 1858 event had been canceled because of the death of the Yale stroke. It was the first in which more than two colleges took part. The event was held on Lake Quinsigamond, near Worcester, Mass.

In 1863 Yale built the first boat house for college crews with the help of faculty donations.

Yale finished in front of Harvard on a circular course in 1870, but Harvard protested, charging Yale with unsportsmanlike conduct. Yale retorted that all this was merely a Harvard excuse for its defeat. The race committee, however, upheld Harvard. Yale was disqualified and the honors went to the Cantabs. Yale, thereupon, vowed never again to row Harvard on a circular course—and never did.

When Yale refused to meet Harvard in 1871, the Crimson joined with Amherst, Brown and Bowdoin to form the first real collegiate boat organization—the Rowing Association of American colleges. Immediately afterward Massachusetts Agricultural became a member and scored a surprise victory.

In 1873, Yale joined the association. The race—a 6-oared event—also included Harvard, Bowdoin, Amherst, Cornell, Columbia, Wesleyan, Trinity, Williams, Dartmouth and Massachusetts Agricultural. Yale won the race. Columbia won the regatta of 1874 and Cornell in 1875, both being on Saratoga Lake, N.Y. The course, since 1872, had been straightaway.

Yale resigned from the association in 1876 and challenged Harvard to a race over a 4-mile route in 8-oared boats, specifying "straight course." Previously races conducted by the association were at 6 oars, over shorter routes. Harvard accepted and the first duel over the standard 4-mile distance, with the present standard equipment, took place in 1876. Yale won in 22 minutes 2 seconds.

Harvard withdrew from the association in 1877 in favor of an annual race with Yale. The regatta consists of three eight-oared races, with varsity, junior varsity and freshman crews participating. The varsities row 4 miles and the junior varsity and freshmen 2 miles.

This series may end in 1974 as Yale is changing to a trimester system with classes ending in May while Harvard ends in mid-June.

HARVARD-YALE VARSITY RACE RECORD

1852 (2 miles)—Harvard (by about 2 lengths)
1853—54—No competition
1855 (3 miles)—Harvard (22:47)
1856—58—No competition
1859 (3 miles)—Harvard (19:18)
1960 (3 miles)—Harvard (18:53)
1861-63—No competition
1864 (3 miles)—Yale (19:01)
1865 (3 miles)—Yale (18:42 1/2)
1866 (3 miles)—Harvard (18:43 1/4)
1867 (3 miles)—Harvard (18:12 3/4)
1868 (3 miles)—Harvard (17:48 1/2)
1869 (3 miles)—Harvard (17:48 1/2)
1870 (3 miles)—Harvard (20:30, Yale disqualified for running into Harvard)
1871—No competition
1872 (3 miles)—Harvard (16:57)
1873 (3 miles)—Yale (16:59)
1874 (3 miles)—Harvard (16:56, Yale collided with Harvard and did not finish)
1875 (3 miles)—Harvard (17:05)
1876 (4 miles)—Yale (22:02)
1877 (4 miles)—Harvard (24:36)
1878 (4 miles)—Harvard (20:44 3/4)
1879 (4 miles)—Harvard (22:15)
1880 (4 miles)—Yale (24:27)
1881 (4 miles)—Yale (22:13)
1882 (4 miles)—Harvard (20:47 1/2)
1883 (4 miles)—Harvard (25:46 1/2)
1884 (4 miles)—Yale (20:31)
1885 (4 miles)—Harvard (25:15 1/2)
1886 (4 miles)—Yale (20:42)
1887 (4 miles)—Yale (22:56)
1888 (4 miles)—Yale (20:10)
1889 (4 miles)—Yale (21:30)
1890 (4 miles)—Yale (21:29)
1891 (4 miles)—Harvard (21:23)
1892 (4 miles)—Yale (20:48)
1893 (4 miles)—Yale (25:01 1/2)
1894 (4 miles)—Yale 34:45 1/2)
1895 (4 miles)—Yale (21:30)
1896—No competition
1897 (4 miles)—Yale (20:44)
1898 (4 miles)—Yale 24:02)
1899 (4 miles)—Harvard (20:52 1/2)
1900 (4 miles)—Yale (21:12 4/5)
1901 (4 miles)—Yale (23:37)
1902 (4 miles)—Yale (20:20)
1903 (4 miles)—Yale (20:19 4/5)
1904 (4 miles)—Yale (21:40 1/2)
1905 (4 miles)—Yale (22:33 1/2)
1906 (4 miles)—Harvard (23:02)
1907 (4 miles)—Yale (21:10)
1908 (4 miles)—Harvard (24:10, Yale stroke taken from shell near three-mile mark)
1909 (4 miles)—Harvard (21:50)
1910 (4 miles)—Harvard (20:46 1/2)
1911 (4 miles)—Harvard (22:44)
1912 (4 miles)—Harvard (21:43 1/2)
1913 (4 miles)—Harvard (21:42)
1914 (4 miles)—Yale (21:16)
1915 (4 miles)—Yale (20:52)
1916 (4 miles)—Harvard (20:02)
1917 No competition
1918 (2 miles)—Harvard (10:58)
1919 4 miles)—Yale 21:42 1/5)

1920 (4 miles)—Harvard (23:11)
1921 (4 miles)—Yale (20:41)
1922 (4 miles)—Yale (21:53)
1923 (4 miles)—Yale (22:10)
1924 (4 miles)—Yale (21:58 3/5)
1925 (4 miles)—Yale (20:26)
1926 (4 miles)—Yale (20:14 2/5)
1927 (4 miles)—Harvard (22:35 1/5)
1928 (4 miles)—Yale (20:21 3/5)
1929 (4 miles)—Yale (21:20)
1930 (4 miles)—Yale (20:09 2/5)
1931 (4 miles)—Harvard (22:21)
1932 (4 miles)—Harvard (21:29)
1933 (4 miles)—Harvard (22:46 3/5)
1934 (4 miles)—Yale (19:51 4/5)
1935 (4 miles)—Yale (20:19)
1936 (4 miles)—Harvard (20:19)
1937 (4 miles)—Harvard (20:02)
1938 (4 miles)—Harvard (20:20)
1939 (4 miles)—Harvard (20:48 2/5)
1940 (4 miles)—Harvard (21:38)
1941 (4 miles)—Harvard (20:40)
1942 (2 miles)—Harvard (10:09 3/5)
1943—45—No competition
1946 (1 3/4 miles)—Harvard (9:18)
1947 (4 miles)—Harvard (20:40)
1948 (4 miles)—Harvard (19:21 2/5, downstream
    and course record)
1949 (4 miles)—Yale (19:21 4/5, both crews
    broke upstream record)
1950 (4 miles)—Harvard (21:36 2/5)
1951 (4 miles)—Harvard (21:26)
1952 (4 miles)—Yale (22:49)
1953 (4 miles)—Harvard (20:09)
1954 (4 miles)—Yale (21:58 2/5)
1955 (4 miles)—Yale (20:05)
1956 (4 miles)—Yale (19:26)
1957 (4 miles)—Yale (20:35)
1958 (4 miles)—Yale (22:39)
1959 (4 miles)—Harvard (19:52)
1960 (4 miles)—Harvard (19:41.2)
1961 (4 miles)—Harvard (22:0)
1962 (4 miles)—Yale (21:26)
1963 (4 miles)—Harvard (19:47)
1964 (4 miles)—Harvard (20:48.2)
1965 (4 miles)—Harvard (19:41.6)
1966 (4 miles)—Harvard (19:44)
1967 (4 miles)—Harvard (22:43.2)
1968 (4 miles)—Harvard (20:21)
1969 (4 miles)—Harvard (19:37.2)
1970 (4 miles)—Harvard (22:02)
1971 (4 miles)—Harvard (20:06)
1972 (4 miles)—Harvard (20:34.8)
1973 (4 miles)—Harvard (19:52.8)

Recapitulation

Harvard 61
Yale. 47

INTERCOLLEGIATE ROWING
ASSOCIATION REGATTA

After Yale and Harvard resigned from the

Rowing Association the organization collapsed. There was no general regatta for colleges other than Yale and Harvard from 1877 to 1895.

In 1895, colleges that featured rowing decided to have some sort of regatta. This led to a general meeting and the formation of a new Rowing Association. Under its auspices, Columbia won in 1895. Cornell won in 1896 and 1897 and Pennsylvania in 1898, 1899.

The success of such regattas influenced the college authorities to reorganize, and, as a consequence, the Intercollegiate Rowing Association was formed in 1899. All colleges with crews were invited to attend the meeting and, later, to participate in the regatta, but Yale and Harvard did not become members.

The I.R.A. decided that it would have, as the outstanding feature of its annual regatta, a 4-mile race for varsity eights, to be rowed on the Hudson River near Poughkeepsie, N.Y. The program additionally included an 8-oared junior varsity race and an 8-oared race contest for freshmen.

The varsity winner of the first Poughkeepsie Regatta was Pennsylvania, doing four miles in 19 minutes 44.4 seconds. The following year the winning Cornell crew cut the time to 18 minutes 53.2 seconds. The record for the course was made by California, in 1939, of 18 minutes 12.6 seconds, shattering the mark of 18 minutes 35.8 seconds made by a California crew in 1928.

Cornell had "powerhouse crews" in the early years and became leader among the varsity race champions. Cornell, a competitor since 1895, has won 18 races.

Cornell, which had something of a monopoly from 1900 to 1930, scored its last varsity victory in 1930 before winning 3 races in a row starting in 1955. From 1930 on Navy, Washington and California have excelled. Washington in 1939 had one of the most remarkable crews in the history of the regatta. But the best it could do was to take second prize, despite the amazing time of 18 minutes 14 seconds, since California had a wonder crew that year, which won in record-smashing time.

Until the 1949 regatta, which drew 12 entries, the record number of crews in the Poughkeepsie event was 11, in 1947 and 1948, and before that 9—in 1930, 1931 and 1941. Since then the number of crews has varied from 10 to 12.

The year 1949 was the last for the I.R.A. Regatta at Poughkeepsie. The stewards shifted the site to Marietta, Ohio, the following year and the townspeople made a gallant effort to keep the classic there, but they had no control over the Ohio River. Flood water ruined the first Marietta Regatta in 1950. The varsity race, won by Washington, was cut to 2 miles.

In 1951, Marietta received another chance,

but again the river was swollen and out of control. The program was held up for 2½ hours and the varsity and junior varsity races were cut from 3 to 2 miles because of the high water and swift current. Wisconsin won the varsity test to become the first eight from the Middle West ever to show the way to the Eastern and Pacific Coast crews in the race.

The I.R.A. stewards settled on Onondaga Lake, Syracuse, N.Y., as the site for the golden jubilee regatta in 1952 and eleven colleges were represented in the feature race. Syracuse has subsequently hosted every I.R.A. regatta since 1952. Led by its varsity, possibly the best in the history of the academy, Navy "swept the river," also winning the junior varsity and freshman races. Navy's varsity, coached by Russell S. Callow, capped an unbeaten season by winning the Olympic championship at Helsinki.

Early in 1947, when plans were being formulated for resumption of the regatta at Poughkeepsie, after a wartime hiatus from 1942 to 1946 it was decided to decrease the varsity distance from 4 to 3 miles. It long has been the contention of many that no more grueling test exists than a 4-mile row. This means sustained action at high speed for an average close to 20 minutes, without time out of any kind for rest or relaxation.

The crews would get away, stroking well beyond 30 to the minute, which meant a great strain on the muscles, the lungs and the heart, and the beat rarely would drop lower. In the last half-mile, or mile, when a final spurt was necessary, the men, under the leadership of the stroke oar, might move the stroking to well beyond 30, meaning that men with tired, aching bodies would be asked to do a herculean feat.

Since the finish of many races found some crew members in a state of collapse, it was felt that shortening the distance by a mile would put less strain upon the oarsmen without detracting from the excitement created by the contests, or making it less a test where watermanship, courage and fine physical condition were important factors in the outcome.

Varsity 8-Oared Shells

1895—At POUGHKEEPSIE (4 Miles)

1, Columbia (time, 21:25); 2, Cornell; 3, Pennsylvania.

1896— At POUGHKEEPSIE (4 Miles)

1, Cornell (19:59); 2, Harvard; 3, Pennsylvania; 4, Columbia.

1897 (June 25)—At POUGHKEEPSIE (4 Miles)

1, Cornell (20:34); 2, Yale; 3, Harvard.

1897 (July 2)— At POUGHKEEPSIE (4 Miles)

1, Cornell (20:47.8); 2, Columbia; 3, Pennsylvania.

1898—At SARATOGA LAKE (3 Miles)

1, Pennsylvania (15:51.5); 2, Cornell; 3, Wisconsin; 4, Columbia.

1899—At POUGHKEEPSIE (4 Miles)

1, Pennsylvania (20:04); 2, Wisconsin; 3, Cornell; 4, Columbia.

1900—At POUGHKEEPSIE (4 Miles)

1, Pennsylvania (19:44.6); 2, Wisconsin; 3, Cornell; 4, Columbia; 5, Georgetown.

1901—At POUGHKEEPSIE (4 Miles)

1, Cornell (18:53.2); 2, Columbia; 3, Wisconsin; 4, Georgetown; 5, Syracuse; 6, Pennsylvania.

1902—At POUGHKEEPSIE (4 Miles)

1, Cornell (19:05.6); 2, Wisconsin; 3, Columbia; 4, Pennsylvania; 5, Syracuse; 6, Georgetown.

1903—At POUGHKEEPSIE (4 Miles)

1, Cornell (18:57); 2, Georgetown; 3, Wisconsin; 4, Pennsylvania; 5, Syracuse; 6, Columbia.

1904—At POUGHKEEPSIE (4 Miles)

1, Syracuse (20:22.6); 2, Cornell; 3, Pennsylvania; 4, Columbia; 5, Georgetown; 6, Wisconsin.

1905—At POUGHKEEPSIE (4 Miles)

1, Cornell (20:29); 2, Syracuse; 3, Georgetown; 4, Columbia; 5, Pennsylvania; 6, Wisconsin.

1906—At POUGHKEEPSIE (4 Miles)

1, Cornell (19:36.8); 2, Pennsylvania; 3, Syracuse; 4, Wisconsin; 5, Columbia, 6, Georgetown.

1907—At POUGHKEEPSIE (4 Miles)

1, Cornell (20:02.4); 2, Columbia; 3, Navy; 4, Pennsylvania; 5, Wisconsin; 6, Georgetown; 7, Syracuse.

1908—At POUGHKEEPSIE (4 Miles)

1, Syracuse (19:24.2); 2, Columbia; 3, Cornell; 4, Pennsylvania; 5, Wisconsin.

1909—At POUGHKEEPSIE (4 Miles)

1, Cornell (20:42.2); 2, Pennsylvania; 3, Columbia; 4, Syracuse; 5, Wisconsin.

1911—At POUGHKEEPSIE (4 Miles)

1, Cornell (20:10.8); 2, Columbia; 3, Pennsylvania; 4, Wisconsin; 5, Syracuse.

1912—At POUGHKEEPSIE (4 Miles)

1, Cornell (19:31.4); 2, Wisconsin; 3, Columbia; 4, Syracuse; 5, Pennsylvania; 6, Stanford.

1913—At POUGHKEEPSIE (4 Miles)

1, Syracuse (19:28.6); 2, Cornell; 3, Washington; 4, Wisconsin; 5, Columbia; 6, Pennsylvania.

1914—At POUGHKEEPSIE (4 Miles)

1, Columbia (19:37.8); 2, Pennsylvania; 3, Cornell; 4, Syracuse; 5, Washington; 6, Wisconsin.

1915—At POUGHKEEPSIE (4 Miles)

1, Cornell (19:36.6); 2, Stanford; 3, Syracuse; 4, Columbia; 5, Pennsylvania.

1916—At POUGHKEEPSIE (4 Miles)

1, Syracuse (20:15.4); 2, Cornell; 3, Columbia; 4, Pennsylvania.

1917–19–NO COMPETITION

1920– At LAKE CAYUGA (2 Miles)

1, Syracuse (11:02.6); 2, Cornell; 3, Columbia; 4, Pennsylvania.

1921–At POUGHKEEPSIE (3 Miles)

1, Navy (14:07); 2, California; 3, Cornell; 4, Pennsylvania; 5, Syracuse; 6, Columbia.

1922–At POUGHKEEPSIE (3 Miles)

1, Navy (13:33.6); 2, Washington; 3, Syracuse; 4, Cornell; 5, Columbia; 6, Pennsylvania.

1923–At POUGHKEEPSIE (3 Miles)

1, Washington (14:03.2); 2, Navy; 3, Columbia; 4, Syracuse; 5, Cornell; 6, Pennsylvania.

1924–At POUGHKEEPSIE (3 Miles)

1, Washington (15:02); 2, Wisconsin; 3, Cornell; 4, Pennsylvania; 5, Syracuse; 6, Columbia.

1925–At POUGHKEEPSIE (4 Miles)

1, Navy (19:24.8); 2, Washington; 3, Wisconsin; 4, Pennsylvania; 5, Cornell; 6, Syracuse; 7, Columbia.

1926–At POUGHKEEPSIE (4 Miles)

1, Washington (19:28.6); 2, Navy; 3, Syracuse; 4, Pennsylvania; 5, Columbia; 6, California; 7, Wisconsin; 8, Cornell.

1927–At POUGHKEEPSIE (4 Miles)

1, Columbia (20:57); 2, Washington; 3, California; 4, Navy; 5, Cornell; 6, Syracuse; 7, Pennsylvania.

1928–At POUGHKEEPSIE (4 Miles)

1, California (18:35.8); 2, Columbia; 3, Washington; 4, Cornell; 5, Navy; 6, Syracuse; 7, Pennsylvania.

1929–At POUGHKEEPSIE (4 Miles)

1, Columbia (22:58); 2, Washington; 3, Pennsylvania; 4, Navy; 5, Wisconsin. M.I.T., Syracuse, California, Cornell swamped in that order.

1930–At POUGHKEEPSIE (4 Miles)

1, Cornell (21:42); 2, Syracuse; 3, M.I.T.; 4, California; 5, Columbia; 6, Washington; 7, Pennsylvania; 8, Wisconsin. Navy swamped.

1931–At POUGHKEEPSIE (4 Miles)

1, Navy (18:54.2); 2, Cornell; 3, Washington; 4, Pennsylvania; 5, Columbia; 6, California; 7, Wisconsin; 8, Cornell.

1932–At POUGHKEEPSIE (4 Miles)

1, California (19:55); 2, Cornell; 3, Washington; 4, Navy; 5, Syracuse; 6, Columbia; 7, Pennsylvania; 8, M.I.T.

1933–NO COMPETITION

1934–At POUGHKEEPSIE (4 Miles)

1, California (19:44); 2, Washington; 3, Navy; 4, Cornell; 5, Pennsylvania; 6, Syracuse; 7, Columbia.

1935–At POUGHKEEPSIE (4 Miles)

1, California (18:52); 2, Cornell; 3, Washington; 4, Navy; 5, Syracuse; 6, Pennsylvania; 7, Columbia.

1936–At POUGHKEEPSIE (4 Miles)

1, Washington (19:09.6); 2, California; 3, Navy; 4, Columbia; 5, Cornell; 6, Pennsylvania; 7, Syracuse.

1937–At POUGHKEEPSIE (4 Miles)

1, Washington (18:33.6); 2, Navy; 3, Cornell; 4, Syracuse; 5, California; 6, Columbia; 7, Wisconsin.

1938–At POUGHKEEPSIE (4 Miles)

1, Navy (18:19); 2, California; 3, Washington; 4, Columbia; 5, Wisconsin; 6, Cornell; 7, Syracuse.

1939–At POUGHKEEPSIE (4 Miles)

1, California (18:12.6); 2, Washington; 3, Navy; 4, Cornell; 5, Syracuse; 6, Wisconsin; 7, Columbia.

1940–At POUGHKEEPSIE (4 Miles)

1, Washington (22:42); 2, Cornell; 3, Syracuse; 4, Navy; 5, California; 6, Columbia; 7, Wisconsin; 8, Princeton.

1941–At POUGHKEEPSIE (4 Miles)

1, Washington (18:53.3); 2, California; 3, Cornell; 4, Syracuse; 5, Princeton; 6, Wisconsin; 7, Rutgers; 8, M.I.T.; 9, Columbia.

1942–46–NO COMPETITION

1947–At POUGHKEEPSIE (3 Miles)

1, Navy (13:59.2); 2, Cornell; 3, Washington; 4, California; 5, Princeton; 6, Pennsylvania; 7, tie among M.I.T., Syracuse, Wisconsin; 10, Rutgers; 11, Columbia.

1948–At POUGHKEEPSIE (3 Miles)

1, Washington (14:06.4); 2, California; 3, Navy; 4, Cornell; 5, M.I.T.; 6, Princeton; 7, Pennsylvania; 8, Wisconsin; 9, Syracuse; 10, Columbia; 11, Rutgers.

1949–At POUGHKEEPSIE (3 Miles)

1, California (14:42.6); 2, Washington; 3, Cornell; 4, Navy; 5, Princeton; 6, Pennsylvania; 7, Wisconsin; 8, Columbia; 9, Syracuse; 10, Stanford; 11, M.I.T.; 12, Rutgers.

1950–At MARIETTA (2 Miles)

1, Washington (8:07.5); 2, California; 3, Wisconsin; 4, Stanford; 5, M.I.T.; 6, Columbia; 7, Cornell; 8, Pennsylvania; 9, Princeton; 10, Syracuse; 11, Rutgers; 12, Navy.

1951–At MARIETTA (2 Miles)

1, Wisconsin (7:50.5); 2, Washington; 3, Princeton; 4, California; 5, Pennsylvania; 6, M.I.T.; 7, Stanford; 8, Syracuse; 9, Cornell; 10, Columbia; 11, Navy; 12, Boston U.

1952–At ONONDAGA LAKE (3 Miles)

1, Navy (15:08.1); 2, Princeton; 3, Cornell; 4, Wisconsin; 5, California; 6, Columbia; 7, Washington; 8, Stanford; 9, Pennsylvania; 10, M.I.T.;

11, Syracuse.

1953—At ONONDAGA LAKE (3 Miles)

1, Navy (15:29.6); 2, Cornell; 3, Washington; 4, Wisconsin; 5, Columbia; 6, California; 7, Pennsylvania; 8, Princeton; 9, Syracuse; 10, M.I.T.; 11, Stanford.

1954—At ONONDAGA LAKE (3 Miles)

1, Navy (16:04:14); 2, Cornell; 3, Washington, 4, Wisconsin; 5, California; 6, Columbia; 7, Pennsylvania; 8, Boston U.; 9, Princeton; 10, M.I.T.; 11, Syracuse. (Navy was disqualified because of ineligible coxswain; no trophies were awarded).

1955—At ONONDAGE LAKE (3 Miles)

1, Cornell (15:49.9); 2, Pennsylvania; 3, Navy; 4, Washington; 5, Stanford, 6, California; 7, Boston U.; 8, Princeton; 9, Wisconsin; 10, M.I.T.; 11, Columbia; 12, Syracuse.

1956—At ONONDAGE LAKE (3 Miles)

1, Cornell (16:22.4); 2, Navy; 3, Wisconsin; 4, Washington; 5, Stanford; 6, Pennsylvania; 7, Princeton; 8, Syracuse; 9, M.I.T.; 10, California; 11, Boston U.; 12, Columbia.

1957—At ONONDAGE LAKE (3 Miles)

1, Cornell (15:26.6); 2, Pennsylvania; 3, Stanford; 4, Princeton; 5, Syracuse; 6, Navy; 7, Dartmouth; 8, M.I.T.; 9, Wisconsin; 10, Columbia.

1958—At ONONDAGE LAKE (3 Miles)

1, Cornell (17:12.1); 2, Navy; 3, Syracuse; 4, Princeton; 5, California; 6, Pennsylvania; 7, Dartmouth; 8, Wisconsin; 9, M.I.T.; 10, Columbia.

1959—At ONONDAGE LAKE (3 Miles)

1, Wisconsin (18:01.7); 2, Syracuse; 3, Navy; 4, California; 5, Washington; 6, Cornell; 7, Dartmouth; 8, Pennsylvania; 9, Princeton; 10, M.I.T.; 11, Columbia.

1960—At ONONDAGE LAKE (3 Miles)

1, California (15:57.0); 2, Navy; 3, Washington; 4, Brown; 5, Cornell. 6, Pennsylvania; 7, Dartmouth; 8, Rutgers; 9, Syracuse; 10, Princeton; 11, Wisconsin; 12, Columbia.

1961—At ONONDAGE LAKE (3 Miles)

1, California (16:49.2); 2, Cornell; 3, M.I.T.; 4, Washington; 5, Pennsylvania; 6, Navy; 7, Brown; 8, Wisconsin; 9, Syracuse; 10, Princeton; 11, Dartmouth. 12, Rutgers; 13, Columbia.

1962—At ONONDAGE LAKE (3 Miles)

1, Cornell (17:02.9); 2, Washington; 3, California; 4, Wisconsin; 5, Pennsylvania; 6, Dartmouth; 7, Brown; 8, Navy; 9, Columbia; 10, Princeton; 11, Syracuse; 12, M.I.T.

1963—At ONONDAGE LAKE (3 Miles)

1, Cornell (17:24); 2, Navy; 3, M.I.T.; 4, California; 5, Wisconsin.

1964—At ONONDAGE LAKE (2000 Meters)

1, California (6:31.1); 2, Washington; 3, Cornell; 4, Princeton; 5, M.I.T.; 6, Navy.

1965—At ONONDAGA LAKE (3 Miles)

1, Navy (16:51.3); 2, Cornell; 3, Washington; 4, Rutgers; 5, Brown; 6, Wisconsin.

1966—At ONONDAGE LAKE (3 Miles)

1, Wisconsin (16:03.4); 2, Navy; 3, Princeton; 4, Brown; 5, Penn.

1967—At ONONDAGE LAKE (3 Miles)

1, Pennsylvania (16:13.9); 2, Wisconsin; 3, Cornell; 4, Princeton; 5, Navy; 6, Brown.

1968—At ONONDAGE LAKE (2000 meters)

1, Pennsylvania (6:15.6); 2, Washington; 3, Princeton; 4, Northeastern; 5, Rutgers; 6, Brown.

1969—At ONONDAGA LAKE (2000 Meters)

1, Pennsylvania (6:30.4); 2, Dartmouth; 3, Washington; 4, Wisconsin; 5, Cornell; 6, Navy.

1970—At ONONDAGE LAKE (2000 Meters)

1, Washington (6:39.3); 2, Wisconsin; 3, Dartmouth; 4, Cornell; 5, Pennsylvania; 6, Brown.

1971—At ONONDAGE LAKE (2000 Meters)

1, Cornell (6:06); 2, Washington; 3, Pennsylvania; 4, Brown; 5, Rutgers; 6, Navy.

1972—At ONONDAGE LAKE (2000 Meters)

1, Pennsylvania (6:22.6); 2, Brown; 3, Wisconsin; 4, Washington; 5, Cornell; 6, Northeastern.

1973—At ONONDAGE LAKE (2000 Meters)

1, Wisconsin (6:21); 2, Brown; 3, Northeastern; 4, Rutgers; 5, Pennsylvania; 6, M.I.T.

Junior Varsity 8-Oared Shells

1914 (2 miles)—Cornell (11:15.6)
1915 (2 miles)—Cornell (10:02)
1916 (2 miles)—Syracuse (11:15.4)
1917—19—No competition
1920 (2 miles)—Cornell (10:45.6)
1921 (2 miles)—Cornell (10:38)
1922 (2 miles)—Cornell (9:08)
1923 (2 miles)—Syracuse (9:50)
1924 (2 miles)—Pennsylvania (10:36.4)
1925 (2 miles)—Washington (10:26)
1926 (3 miles)—Washington (15:40.2)
1927 (3 miles)—Washington (15:12.8)
1928 (3 miles)—Navy (14:18.2)
1929 (3 miles)—Cornell (15:21.2)
1930 (3 miles)—Cornell (16:39)
1931 (3 miles)—Syracuse (14:29.6)
1932 (3 miles)—Syracuse (15:41)
1933—No competition
1934 (3 miles)—Syracuse (15:40.6)
1935 (3 miles)—Washington (14:58.8)
1936 (3 miles)—Washington (14:42.2)
1937 (3 miles)—Washington (13:44)
1938 (3 miles)—Washington (13:49.2)
1939 (3 miles)—Syracuse (13:56.6)
1940 (3 miles)—Washington (no time taken)
1941 (3 miles)—California (14:40)
1942—46—No competition
1947 (3 miles)—California (14:30.3)
1948 (3 miles)—Washington (14:28.6)

1949 (3 miles)—Washington (16:00)
1950 (2 miles)—Washington (8:10.4)
1951 (2 miles)—California (8:05.1)
1952 (3 miles)—Navy (15:37.3)
1953 (3 miles)—Washington (16:30.6)
1954 (3 miles)—Cornell (16:20.6)
1955 (3 miles)—Cornell (16:23.2)
1956 (3 miles)—Washington (17:01.5)
1957 (3 miles)—Cornell (15:46.8)
1958 (3 miles)—Cornell (17:33.5)
1959 (3 miles)—California (17:53.5)
1960 (3 miles)—Cornell (16:12.0)
1961 (3 miles)—Cornell (17:12.7)
1962 (3 miles)—Cornell (16:57.3)
1963 (3 miles)—Navy (17:28.2)
1964 (2000 meters)—Washington (6:14.9)
1965 (3 miles)—Navy (17:07.5)
1966 (3 miles)—Dartmouth (16:25.1)
1967 (3 miles)—Navy (17:28.2)
1968 (2000 meters)—Pennsylvania (6:24.2)
1969 (2000 meters)—Cornell (6:26.6)
1970 (2000 meters)—Pennsylvania (6:58.5)
1971 (2000 meters)—Navy (6:17.2)
1972 (2000 meters)—Washington (6:18.8)
1973 (2000 meters)—Wisconsin (6:28.5)

Freshman 8-Oared Shells

(All races at two miles except in 1950 when the distance was 1 7/8 miles, and in 1964, 1968 through 1973, at 2000 meters.

1896—Cornell (10:18)
1897—Yale (9:19.5)
1897—Cornell (9:21.2)
1898—Cornell (10:57.6)
1899—Cornell (9:55)
1900—Wisconsin (9:45.4)
1901—Pennsylvania (10:20.2)
1902—Cornell (9:39.8)
1903—Cornell (9:18)
1904—Syracuse (10:01)
1905—Cornell (9:39.2)
1906—Syracuse (9:51.6)
1907—Wisconsin (9:58)
1908—Cornell (9:29.6)
1909—Cornell (9:11.6)
1910—Cornell (10:40.2)
1911—Columbia (10:13.2)
1912—Cornell (9:31.4)
1913—Cornell (10:04.8)
1914—Cornell (10:26)
1915—Syracuse (9:29.6)
1916—Cornell (11:05.8)
1917—19—No competition
1920—Cornell (10:45.4)
1921—Cornell (10:32)
1922—Syracuse (9:20.2)
1923—Cornell (9:27.8)
1924—Pennsylvania (10:22.6)
1925—Syracuse (9:59)
1926—Columbia (11:28.6)
1927—Navy (9:45)
1928—Navy (9:42)

1929—Syracuse (10:23.6)
1930—Syracuse (11:18.2)
1931—Washington (9:49.8)
1932—Syracuse (10:59)
1933—No competition
1934—Washington (10:50)
1935—Washington (10:29)
1936—Washington (10:19.6)
1937—Washington (9:15.4)
1938—California (9:30.4)
1939—Washington (9:31)
1940—Cornell (10:55.4)
1941—Cornell (9:57.7)
1942—46—No competition
1947—Washington (9:40.3)
1948—Washington (9:46.9)
1949—Washington (9:40.23)
1950—Washington (7:13.2)
1951—Washington (8:05.4)
1952—Navy (10:16.9)
1953—Washington (10:55.4)
1954—Cornell (10:18.5)
1955—Cornell (10:03.1)
1956—Syracuse (11:12)
1957—Navy (10:25.2)
1958—Cornell (11:23)
1959—Cornell (11:47.5)
1960—Navy (10:45.7)
1961—Washington (10:51.6)
1962—Cornell (11:10.8)
1963—Navy (11:11.0)
1964—(2000 meters)—Wisconsin (6:49.4)
1965—Navy (11:03.4)
1966—Pennsylvania (10:33.5)
1967—Pennsylvania (10:37.4)
1968—(2000 meters)—Pennsylvania (6:18.6)
1969—(2000 meters)—Pennsylvania &
        Washington (tie) (6:27.4)
1970—(2000 meters)—Brown (6:47.2)
1971—(2000 meters)—Pennsylvania (6:16.8)
1972—(2000 meters)—Wisconsin (6:19.8)
1973—(2000 meters)—Wisconsin (6:35.1)

OTHER UNITED STATES COLLEGE REGATTAS

There are a number of regattas in this country in addition to the Harvard-Yale and I.R.A. classics. The Rowe Trophy goes to the chief point-getter in the annual Eastern Association of Rowing Colleges sprint championships, involving varsity, junior varsity and freshman eights. Columbia, Pennsylvania and Princeton meet annually in the Childs Cup Regatta, the oldest trophy race in the United States. The Adams Cup Regatta finds Harvard, Navy and Pennsylvania vying for honors and the Carnegie Cup Regatta brings together Cornell, Princeton and Yale. Princeton, Harvard and M.I.T. row for the Compton Cup. A number of colleges compete for the Dad Vail Trophy, donated by C. Leverich Brett. On the Pacific Coast, California and Washington usually fight it out for the sectional title. For the 150-pounders there are the Wright Cup and the Goldthwait Cup competitions. Also, there are many dual and triangular regattas and other eights are sometimes invited to participate in a cup event. The distances of the races vary from a mile and five-sixteenths to 3 miles.

Childs Cup

Presented in 1879 by the late George W. Childs of Philadelphia for competition among Columbia, Pennsylvania and Princeton. Cornell and Navy on occasion participate by invitation but are not eligible to win the cup. The races were for 4-oared crews through 1887 and 8-oared since 1889. The trophy is the oldest in sprint racing.

1879—Pennsylvania
1880—Columbia
1881—Princeton
1882—84—Pennsylvania
1885—Cornell (Penn won cup)
1886—Pennsylvania (by default)
1887—Cornell (by default, no cup competition)
1888—No competition
1889—Cornell (Columbia won cup)
1890—1911—No competition
1912—Columbia
1913—No competition
1914—Columbia
1915—16—Princeton
1917—No competition
1918—19—Pennsylvania
1920—Navy (Penn won cup)
1921—Columbia
1922—Princeton
1923—Columbia
1924—26—Pennsylvania
1927—Navy (Princeton won cup)
1928—31—Columbia
1932—Pennsylvania
1933—34—Princeton
1935—36—Pennsylvania
1937—Princeton
1938—Pennsylvania
1939—Princeton
1940—Columbia
1941—Princeton
1942—Pennsylvania
1943—Navy (Princeton won cup)
1944—47—No competition
1948—49—Princeton
1950—52—Pennsylvania
1953—Princeton
1954—55—Pennsylvania
1956—57—Princeton
1958—62—Pennsylvania
1963—Columbia
1964—65—Princeton
1966—73—Pennsylvania

Carnegie Cup

Presented for competition among Cornell, Princeton and Yale by Mrs. Andrew Carnegie, whose husband gave Princeton its famous Lake Carnegie. The crews raced from 1911 through 1920 in non-cup regattas.

1911—12—Cornell
1913—Princeton
1914—Cornell
1915—Yale
1916—Cornell
1917—No competition
1918—Princeton
1919—Yale (at Derby)
1919—Cornell (at Ithaca)
1920—Cornell
1921—Princeton
1922—Cornell
1923—25—Yale
1926—No competition
1927—Princeton
1928—30—Yale
1931—Cornell
1932—34—Yale
1935—No competition
1936—Cornell
1937—39—Yale
1940—Cornell
1941—No competition
1942—Princeton
1943—46—No competition
1947—Princeton
1948—Cornell
1949—Princeton
1950—Cornell
1951—Yale
1952—Princeton
1953—55—Cornell
1956—Yale
1957—Cornell
1958—59—Yale
1960—67—Cornell
1968—70—Princeton
1971—72—Cornell

Blackwell Cup

Presented in memory of George Engs Blackwell, Class of 1880, Columbia College, to be competed for by Columbia, Pennsylvania and Yale. The first cup race was held in 1927, although the triangular competition started in 1923. Columbia has not participated for several years.

1923—26—Yale
1927—28—Yale
1929—Columbia
1930—Yale
1931—Columbia
1932—34—Yale
1935—36—Pennsylvania
1937—40—Yale
1941—Columbia
1942—Yale
1943—46—No competition
1947—Yale (cup not at stake)

1948—Yale
1949—50—Pennsylvania
1951—Yale
1952—Pennsylvania
1953—Yale
1954—55—Pennsylvania
1956—59—Yale
1960—Pennsylvania
1961—65—Yale
1966—73—Pennsylvania

Adams Cup

Established in honor of Charles Francis Adams, Secretary of the Navy, 1932, to be competed for annually by Harvard, Navy and Pennsylvania.

1933—Navy
1934—35—Pennsylvania
1936—37—Navy
1938—42—Harvard
1943—47—No competition
1948—51—Harvard
1952—54—Navy
1955—Pennsylvania
1956—58—Harvard
1959—Harvard
1960—Pennsylvania
1961—Navy
1962—63—Pennsylvania
1964—Navy
1965—68—Harvard
1969—70—Pennsylvania
1971—Navy
1972—Harvard

Compton Cup

Dr. Karl T. Compton put up the cup in 1933 for competition among Harvard, M.I.T. and Princeton. The field was broadened in the postwar years and Rutgers now is eligible to win the cup.

1933—36—Princeton
1937—42—Harvard
1943—46—No competition
1947—Harvard (cup not at stake)
1948—50—Harvard
1951—Princeton
1952—Harvard
1953—Princeton
1954—55—Harvard
1956—57—Princeton
1958—61—Harvard
1962—M.I.T.
1963—73—Harvard

Dad Vail

First varsity trophy donated by Russell S. Callow in memory of Harry Emerson (Dad) Vail, former Wisconsin coach. C. Leverich Brett, founder of the regatta, presented the Dad Vail Trophy for the varsity winner in 1939 after Rutgers retired the previous cup.

1934—Marietta

1935—36—Rutgers
1937—No competition
1938—42—Rutgers
1943—46—No competition
1947—50—Boston University
1951—53—La Salle
1954—55—Dartmouth
1956—58—La Salle
1959—61—Brown
1962—Georgetown
1963—Marietta
1964—Georgetown
1965—Northeastern
1966—67—Marietta
1968—69—Georgetown
1970—St. Joseph
1971—Georgetown
1972—Coast Guard
1973—Massachusetts

Goldthwait Cup

Presented in 1925 by Kimball Prince, captain of the 1924 Harvard crew, for competition among the Princeton, Yale and Harvard 150-pound varsities. The cup was awarded retroactively to 1922, the year of the first "Big Three" 150-pound varsity race.

1922—Princeton
1923—Yale
1924—25—Harvard
1926—Princeton
1927—Harvard
1928—Princeton
1929—Harvard
1930—32—Yale
1933—Princeton
1934—Yale
1935—Princeton
1936—37—Yale
1938—42—Harvard
1943—46—No competition
1947—48—Harvard
1949—Princeton
1950—51—Yale
1952—Harvard
1953—57—Princeton
1958—72—Harvard

Pacific Coast Regatta—Western Sprints

(California, Washington and occasionally Stanford. Rowing not recognized as a varsity sport at Stanford and support comes from the students.)

The races were for 4-oared shells from 1903 through 1905 and for 8-oared shells thereafter. In some years two or more races were held.

1903—Washington
1904—California (two races)
1905—California
1905—Washington
1905—California
1906—No competition
1907—Stanford

1907—Washington
1908—California
1908—Washington
1909—10—Stanford
1910—Washington
1911—Stanford
1911—Washington
1912—Stanford
1913—Washington (two races)
1914—Washington (two races)
1915—16—Stanford
1916—Washington (two races)
1917—Washington
1918—No competition
1919—Washington
1920—California
1920—Washington
1921—California
1922—26—Washington
1927—29—California
1930—31—Washington
1932—California
1933—38—Washington
1939—California
1940—42—Washington
1943—California
1944—46—No competition
1947—California
1948—Washington
1949—California
1950—51—Washington
1952—California
1953—59—Washington
1960—California
1961—63—Washington
1964—California
1965—66—Washington
1967—U.C.L.A.
1968—69—Washington
1970—U.C.L.A.
1971—72—Washington

NATIONAL ASSOCIATION OF AMATEUR OARSMEN

Rowing is one of the world's oldest sports and anthropologists have produced evidence which credits the ancient Egyptians as the originators of the sport.

The sport has enjoyed great popularity in the United States for over 125 years with extensive participation by colleges and universities and a large number of Rowing Clubs throughout the country. Collegiate and Club rowing have a tradition and antiquity unequaled by any other athletic activity.

Rowing has undergone a great transition in virtually every aspect of the sport. Stationary seats have been replaced with sliding seats; the eight-oared shell and single sculls have become the traditional prestige boats; professional oarsmen who flourished until 1930 have vanished; and a special weight category for men not more than 150 pounds has been an integral part of U.S. rowing for the past 25 years.

Philadelphia has served as the focal point and headquarters for rowing since its origin in this country and its famous boat house row still numbers many world famous organizations: Vesper Boat Club, Undine Barge Club, Malta Boat Club, Crescent Boat Club, University of Pennsylvania and the Schuylkill Navy, to name a few.

The Schuylkill Navy planned and conducted a major Regatta in 1872 which restricted competition exclusively to amateurs. This concept and the associated Regatta led to the founding of the National Association of Amateur Oarsmen. The N.A.A.O. which was conceived at a convention of all amateur rowing clubs in New York in 1873 has been the ruling body for the sport ever since and has sponsored the National Championship Regatta annually since 1873 except for four war years (1917-18 and 1944-45) when no Regatta was held.

The program calls for seventeen championship events and a high-point team trophy.

Senior (10)—Championship single sculls, senior single sculls, quarter-mile single sculls, double sculls, quadruple sculls, 4-oared shells without coxswain, 4-oared shells with coxswain, 8-oared shells, pair-oared shells without coxswain, pair-oared shells with coxswain.

Intermediate (1)—8-oared shells.

150-pound (6)—Single sculls, quarter-mile single sculls, double sculls, quadruple sculls, 4-oared shells with coxswain, 8-oared shells. (Events limited to oarsmen weighing not more than 145 pounds; weight changed to 150 pounds in 1953.)

Most of the events are at a mile and a quarter.

Collegiate rowing, which is restricted primarily to eight-oared shells, features a dozen or more major Championship Regattas throughout the country each year. In the East, the Intercollegiate Rowing Association, Eastern Sprints and Dad Vail Regattas bring together the best College Eight-Oared Crews. The Western Sprints Regatta provides the major competition for West Coast Crews.

Rowing or crew is separated into two basic categories—sculling and sweeping. In a *sweep boat* each man has one oar and the crew members are alternately staggered so that half row on the starboard side and half row on the port side. In a *sculling event* each man is equipped with two oars which are significantly smaller than a sweep oar. The former category includes pairs, fours and eight-oared shells with and without a coxswain (excluding the eight which always has a coxswain). Sculling competition features singles, doubles and quadruple sculls.

International competition including the Olympics and World Championship Regattas have seven (7) events—Single Sculls, Double Sculls, Pair-Oared Shell with Coxswain, Pair-Oared Shell without Coxswain, Four-Oared Shell with Coxswain, Four-Oared Shell without Coxswain, and Eight-Oared Shell. Traditionally, the United States has been represented by a Collegiate Crew in the Eight-Oared event and Club Oarsmen have manned the other six boats in the Olympic Games.

Championship Singles Sculls

1899—Edward Hanlan Ten Eyck
1900—John Rumohr (rowover)
1901—Edward Hanlan Ten Eyck
1902—C.S. Titus
1903—05—Frank B. Greer
1906—C.S. Titus
1907—Harry S. Bennett
1908—Frank B. Greer
1909—John W. O'Neil
1910—William Mehrhof
1911—12—E.B. Butler (Canada)
1913—15—R. Dibble (Canada)
1916—T.J. Rooney
1917—18—No competition
1919—20—John B. Kelly
1921—Walter M. Hoover
1922—Paul V. Costello
1923—Edward McGuire
1924—W.E. Garrett Gilmore (rowover)
1925—26—Walter M. Hoover
1927—Joseph Wright Jr. (Canada)
1928—G. Chester Turner
1929—Kenneth Myers
1930—33—William G. Miller
1934—Winthrop Rutherfurd Jr.
1935—C.A. Campbell (Canada)
1936—Daniel H. Barrow Jr.
1937—40—Joseph W. Burk (rowover in 1938)
1941—Theodore A. DuBois (Canada)
1942—Joseph Angyal
1943—Arthur Gallagher (rowover)
1944—45—No competition
1946—John B. Kelly Jr.
1947—Theodore A. DuBois (Canada)
1948—John B. Kelly Jr.
1949—Joseph Angyal
1950—John B. Kelly Jr.
1951—Robert Williams (Canada)
1952—56—John B. Kelly Jr.
1957—Thomas McDonough
1958—Paul Ignas
1959—60—Harry Parker
1961—62—Seymour Cromwell
1963—64—Donald Spero
1965—William Maher
1966—Donald Spero
1967—William Maher
1968—Tom McKibbon
1969—William Maher
1970—73—Jim Dietz

Association Single Sculls

(Senior single sculls at 1½ miles, 1873-98.)

1873—Charles Meyers
1874—F.E. Yates
1875—Charles E. Courtney
1876—F.E. Yates
1877—78—George W. Lee
1879—80—F.J. Mumford
1881—82—F.E. Holmes
1883—84—Joseph Laing (Canada)
1885—Daniel J. Murphy
1886—Martin F. Monahan
1887—J.F. Corbett
1888—C.G. Psotta
1889—D. Donahue (Canada)
1890—91—William Caffrey
1892—93—John J. Ryan (Canada)
1894—Ferdinand Koenig
1895—J.J. Whitehead
1896—W.D. McDowell
1897—Joseph Maguire
1898—Edward Hanlan Ten Eyck
1899—John Rumohr (Canada)
1900—Frank B. Greer
1901—C.S. Titus
1902—James B. Juvenal
1903—L.F. Scholes (Canada)
1904—D.B. Duffield
1905—Fred Shepherd
1906—Harry S. Bennett
1907—Durando Miller
1908—John W. O'Neil (Canada)
1909—William Mehrhof
1910—S.F. Gordon
1911—E.B. Butler (Canada)
1912—A.F. Culver (Canada)
1913—R. Dibble (Canada)
1914—John B. Kelly
1915—Waldo Smith
1916—T.J. Rooney
1917—18—No competition
1919—Paul V. Costello
1920—Louis Zoba
1921—Walter M. Hoover
1922—Hilton Belyea (Canada)
1923—Edward McGuire
1924—W.E. Garrett Gilmore
1925—Russell Codman Jr.
1926—Robert H. Agnew
1927—Joseph Wright Jr. (Canada)
1928—G.C. Turner
1929—Kenneth Myers
1930—Leo B. Menne
1931—E.J. McGreal
1932—Wesley E. Bevan
1933—Albert B. Vogt
1934—Winthrop Rutherfurd Jr.
1935—C.A. Campbell (Canada)
1936—Combined with championship singles
1937—Dropped from program
1938—James Russell (Canada)

1939—Frank Silvio
1940—Theodore A. DuBois (Canada)
1941—Joseph Angyal
1942—Howard McCreesh
1943—Arthur Gallagher
1944—45—No competition
1946—John B. Kelly Jr.
1947—Joseph McIntyre
1948—John S. Trinsey
1949—Robert Williams (Canada)
1950—Jack S. Guest Jr. (Canada)
1951—William Knecht
1952—53—Rudy Jezek
1954—Pat Costello
1955—Thomas McDonough
1956—William Reimann
1957—William H. Lang Jr.
1958—Paul Ignas
1959—Harry Parker
1960—Wayne Frye
1961—Seymour Cromwell
1962—Robert Lea III
1963—Donald Spero
1964—David Robinson
1965—William Maher
1966—John Van Bloom
1967—John Nunn
1968—Tom McKibbon
1969—Jim Dietz
1970—Robert Gallagher
1971—Jim Castellan
1972—Jody Trinsey
1973—Dr. Larry Klecatsky

Quarter-Mile Single Sculls

1891—Joseph Bergin
1892—1908—No competition
1909—Fred Fuessel
1910—William Mehrhof
1911—12—E.B. Butler (Canada)
1913—R. Dibble (Canada)
1914—E.B. Butler (Canada)
1915—Walter M. Hoover
1916—T.J. Rooney
1917—18—No competition
1919—20—John B. Kelly
1921—Walter M. Hoover
1922—Louis Zoha
1923—W.E. Garrett Gilmore
1924—25—A.E. Fitzpatrick
1926—Walter M. Hoover
1927—Joseph Wright Jr. (Canada)
1928—W.E. Garrett Gilmore
1929—E.J. McGreal
1930—A.E. Fitzpatrick
1931—E.J. McGreal
1932—W.E. Garrett Gilmore
1933—A.E. Fitzpatrick
1934—Georg von Opel (Germany)
1935—36—Erwin Konrad
1937—Frank Silvio
1938—Joseph Hutton

1939—40—Frank Silvio
1941—Arthur Gallagher
1942—Howard McCreesh
1943—Arthur Gallagher
1944—45—No competition
1946—47—John J. Kieffer
1948—John S. Trinsey
1949—John J. Kieffer
1950—John B. Kelly Jr.
1951—Harold Finigan
1952—53—Larry Kelly
1954—Eugene Loveless
1955—56—William Knecht
1957—Walter Hoover Jr.
1958—Robert Huston
1959—Paul Yeager
1960—William Knecht
1961—64—Seymour Cromwell
1965—Donald Spero
1966—John Sanberg
1967—John Van Bloom
1968—70—Jim Dietz
1971—72—Jon Von Blom
1973—Bill Beldin

Double Sculls

1873—Steele—Witmer
1874—Yates—Curtis
1875—76—Robinson—Courtney
1877—McBeath—Henderson
1878—O'Donnell—Powers
1879—Rathbone—Lyon
1880—Whitaker—Holmes
1881—Appley—Holmes
1882—83—O'Connell—Buckley
1884—Enright—O'Connor (Canada)
1885—Monahan—Monahan (rowover)
1886—Korf—Winand
1887—Regan—Goeffert
1888—Don Amateur R.C. (Canada)
1889—Pilkington—Nagle
1890—Bayside R.C. (Canada)
1891—Mulcahy—M.F. Monahan
1892—Vesper B.C., Philadelphia
1893—Van Vleet—Meegowan
1894—Van Vleet—Baltz
1895—Hawkins—Nagle
1896—Crawford—Howard
1897—Van Vleet—Monaghan
1898—1901—Ten Eyck—Lewis
1902—Vesely—Budric
1903—Scholes—Smith
1904—Mulcahy—Varley
1905—Titus—Steinkamp
1906—Swall—Kirk
1907—Jacob—Bowler (Canada)
1908—Bennett—Warnock
1909—10—Fuessel—Shepherd
1911—Engle—Gordon
1912—Culver—Carruthers (Canada)
1913—Dibble—Lepper (Canada)

1914—Smith—Kelley
1915—16—Osman—Kent
1917—18—No competition
1919—Riverside B.C. Cambridge, Mass.
1920—21—Vesper B.C. (rowover in 1921)
1922—Bachelors Barge Club, Philadelphia
1923—Penn A.C. Rowing Assn., Philadelphia
1924—Undine Barge Club, Philadelphia
1925—Malta B.C., Philadelphia
1926—Undine B.C.
1927—28—Bachelors B.C.
1929—Undine B.C. (rowover)
1930—32—Bachelors B.C.
1933—35—Penn A.C.R.A.
1936—37—Undine B.C.
1938—Bachelors B.C.
1939—Winnipeg (Man.) R.C. (Canada)
1940—Penn A.C.R.A.
1941—Worcester R.C.
1942—Fairmount R.A.
1943—Penn A.C.R.A.
1944—45—No competition
1946—Vesper B.C.
1947—Ottawa R.C. (Canada)
1948—Gallagher—Angyal
1949—Malta B.C.
1950—51—Vesper B.C.
1952—Detroit B.C.
1953—Vesper B.C.
1954—56—Detroit B.C.
1957—Minnesota B.C.
1958—Detroit B.C.
1959—60—Vesper B.C.
1961—Lake Washington R.C.
1962—Vesper B.C.
1963—Riverside B.C.
1964—Vesper B.C.
1965—Fairmount R.A.
1966—Argonaut R.C.
1967—Long Beach R.A.
1968—Vesper B.C.
1969—70—Long Beach R.A.
1971—New York A.C.
1972—Long Beach R.A.
1973—Vesper B.C.

Pair-Oared Shells Without Coxswain

1874—75—Argonauta R.A., Bergen Point, N.J.
1876—Atalanta B.C., New York
1877—Emerald B.C., Detroit
1878—Mutual B.C., Albany N.Y.
1879—Olympic B.C., Albany, N.Y.
1880—Mutual B.C.
1881—Detroit B.C.
1882—84—Mutual B.C. (rowover in 1884)
1885—Ariel B.C., Newark, N.J.
1886—Eureka B.C., Newark, N.J.
1887—Modoc R.C., St. Louis
1888—Seawanhaka B.C., Brooklyn (rowover)
1889—Garfield Beach B.C., Salt Lake City, Utah
1890—Detroit B.C.
1891—92—Atalanta B.C.

1893—Detroit B.C.
1894—Vesper B.C., Philadelphia
1895—Toronto R.C., (Canada)
1896—Pennsylvania B.C., Philadelphia
1897—Argonaut R.C., Toronto (Canada)
1898—99—Pennsylvania B.C.
1900—02—Vesper B.C.
1903—Harlem R.C., New York
1904—05—Seawanhaka B.C.
1906—Metropolitan R.C., New York
1907—Argonaut R.C.
1908—Vesper B.C.
1909—31—No competition
1932—Undine Barge Club, Philadelphia
1933—35—No competition
1936—Penn A.C.R.A., Philadelphia
1937—45—No competition
1946—Fairmount R.A., Philadelphia
1947—West Side R.C., Buffalo, N.Y.
1948—Yale University R.A., New Haven, Conn.
1949—51—Fairmount R.A.
1952—U.S. Naval Academy, Annapolis, Md.
1953—54—Rutgers R.C.
1955—New York A.C.
1956—U.S. Naval Academy
1957—58—Washington A.C., Seattle
1959—60—Lake Washington R.C.
1961—Stanford Crew Assoc.
1962—Lake Washington R.C.
1963—Potomac B.C.
1964—65—Vesper B.C.
1966—Union B.C.
1967—69—Potomac B.C.
1970—71—Union B.C.
1972—Stanford R.A.

Pair-Oared Shells With Coxswain

1932—Pennsylvania Barge Club, Philadelphia
1933—45—No competition
1946—48—Vesper B.C., Philadelphia
1949—50—Fairmount R.A., Philadelphia
1951—New York A.C.
1952—53—Stanford University, Palo Alto, Calif.
1954—55—Fairmount R.A.
1956—Stanford University
1957—Washington A.C., Seattle
1958—Vesper B.C.
1959—Detroit B.C.
1960—Lake Washington R.C.
1961—62—Stanford Crew Assoc.
1963—66—Vesper B.C.
1967—69—Potomac B.C.
1970—Union B.C.
1971—Long Beach A.C.
1972—College B.C.

Quadruple Sculls

1909—10—Nassau B.C., New York
1911—Vesper B.C., Philadelphia
1912—New York A.C., (rowover)
1913—14—Riverside B.C., Cambridge, Mass.
1915—16—Duluth (Minn.) B.C.

1917–18–No competition
1919–New York A.C.
1920–Undine Barge Club, Philadelphia
1921–Duluth B.C.
1922–Vesper B.C.
1923–Duluth B.C.
1924–25–Bachelors Barge Club, Philadelphia
1926–Penn A.C. Rowing Assn., Philadelphia
1927–31–Bachelors Barge Club
1932–33–Penn A.C.R.A.
1934–Ravenswood B.C., Long Island City, N.Y.
1935–Penn A.C.R.A.
1936–Bachelors Barge Club
1937–38–Penn A.C.R.A. (rowover in 1937)
1939–Fairmount R.A., Philadelphia
1940–Bachelors Barge Club
1941–Penn A.C.R.A.
1942–Fairmount R.A.
1943–Penn A.C.R.A.
1944–45–No competition
1946–47–Fairmount R.A.
1948–Vesper B.C.
1949–Fairmount R.A.
1950–51–Vesper B.C.
1952–53–Fairmount R.A.
1954–Detroit B.C.
1955–Vesper B.C.
1956–New York A.C.
1957–Vesper B.C.
1958–59–Detroit B.C.
1960–Undine B.C.
1961–Vesper B.C.
1962–Undine B.C.
1963–64–New York A.C.
1965–67–Fairmount R.A.
1968–Potomac B.C.
1969–Vesper B.C.
1970–New Zealand
1971–Cambridge B.C.
1972–Undine B.C.
1973–Mexico

4-Oared Shells Without Coxswain

1873–Argonauta R.A., Bergen Point, N.J.
1874–Beaverwyck R.C., Albany, N.Y.
1875–76–Atalanta B.C., New York
1877–Emerald B.C., Detroit
1878–Mutual B.C., Albany, N.Y.
1879–81–Hillsdale (Mich.) R.C.
1882–Centennial B.C., Detroit
1883–Eureka B.C., Newark, N.J.
1884–Argonaut R.C., Toronto (Canada)
1885–Nautilus R.C., Hamilton, Ont. (Canada)
1886–Fairmount R.A., Philadelphia
1887–Toronto R.C., (Canada)
1888–Passaic B.C., Newark, N.J.
1889–Winnipeg (Man.) R.C. (Canada)
1890–Bradford B.C., Cambridge, Mass.
1891–Fairmount R.A.
1892–Wyandotte (Mich.), B.C.
1893–Minnesota B.C., St. Paul
1894–Argonaut R.C.

1895–Institute B.C., Newark, N.J.
1896–Winnipeg R.C.
1897–Institute B.C.
1898–Argonaut R.C.
1899–Pennsylvania Barge Club, Philadelphia
1900–Detroit B.C.
1901–Western R.C., St. Louis
1902–03–Winnipeg R.C.
1904–Century B.C., St. Louis
1905–Seawanhaka B.C., Brooklyn
1906–Winnipeg R.C.
1907–Argonaut R.C.
1908–Vesper B.C., Philadelphia
1909–Ottawa R.C. (Canada)
1910–Arundel B.C., Baltimore
1911–Argonaut R.C.
1912–Winnipeg R.C.
1913–Duluth (Minn.) B.C.
1914–University Barge Club, Philadelphia
1915–16–Duluth B.C.
1917–18–No competition
1919–Century B.C.
1920–Pennsylvania Barge Club
1921–Vesper B.C.
1922–Duluth B.C.
1923–Pennsylvania Barge Club
1924–West Philadelphia B.C.
1925–No competition
1926–Bachelors Barge Club
1927–Pennsylvania Barge Club
1928–Bachelors Barge Club
1929–South Side B.C., Quincy, Ill.
1930–31–Bachelors Barge Club
1932–Penn A.C. Rowing Assn., Philadelphia
1933–Bachelors Barge Club
1934–Penn A.C.R.A.
1935–Bachelors Barge Club
1936–39–West Side R.C., Buffalo, N.Y.
1940–Detroit B.C.
1941–43–Fairmount R.A.
1944–45–No competition
1946–Detroit B.C.
1947–Vesper B.C.
1948–Yale University, New Haven, Conn.
1949–50–Vesper B.C.
1951–Fairmount R.A.
1952–53–U.S. Naval Academy, Annapolis, Md.
1954–55–West Side R.C.
1956–Detroit B.C.
1957–Washington A.C., Seattle
1958–West Side R.C.
1959–63–Lake Washington R.C.
1964–St. Catharines R.C.
1965–Vesper B.C.
1966–Stanford Crew Assoc.
1967–72–Vesper B.C.

4-Oared Shells With Coxswain

1919–Century B.C., St. Louis
1920–Pennsylvania Barge Club, Philadelphia
1921–Vesper B.C., Philadelphia
1922–Duluth (Minn.) B.C.

1923–Pennsylvania Barge Club
1924–No record
1925–Pennsylvania Barge Club
1926–Bachelors Barge Club, Philadelphia
1927–Pennsylvania Barge Club
1928–Bachelors Barge Club
1929–Penn A.C. Rowing Assn., Philadelphia
1930–31–Bachelors Barge Club
1932–Penn A.C.R.A.
1933–South End R.C., San Francisco
1934–Penn A.C.R.A. (rowover)
1935–West Side R.C., Buffalo, N.Y.
1936–Riverside B.C., Cambridge, Mass.
1937–38–West Side R.C.
1939–40–Penn A.C.R.A.
1941–West Side R.C.
1942–Fairmount R.A.
1943–Wyandotte (Mich.) B.C.
1944–45–No competition
1946–Detroit B.C.
1947–West Side R.C.
1948–University of Washington, Seattle
1949–51–West Side R.C.
1952–53–University of Washington
1954–Vesper B.C.
1955–56–West Side R.C.
1957–Detroit B.C.
1958–Vesper B.C.
1959–62–Lake Washington R.C.
1963–Riverside B.C.
1964–Harvard University
1965–Vesper B.C.
1966–St. Catharines R.C.
1967–New Zealand
1968–Vesper B.C.
1969–Union B.C.
1970–New Zealand
1971–Vesper B.C.
1972–College B.C.
1973–Vesper B.C.

8-Oared Shells

1880–Dauntless R.C., New York
1881–Narragansett B.C., Providence, R.I.
1882–No competition
1883–84–Metropolitan R.C., New York
1885–Columbia A.C., Washington, D.C.
1886–Fairmount R.A., Philadelphia
1887–Vesper B.C., Philadelphia
1888–Fairmount R.A.
1889–90–Atalanta B.C., New York
1891–92–New York A.C.
1893–Atalanta B.C.
1894–Triton B.C., Newark, N.J.
1895–First Bohemian B.C., New York
1896–Baltimore (Md.) A.C.
1897–99–Pennsylvania Barge Club, Philadelphia
1900–Vesper B.C.
1901–Argonaut R.C., Toronto (Canada)
1902–Vesper B.C.
1903–Winnipeg (Man.) R.C. (Canada)
1904–Vesper B.C.

1905–Argonaut R.C.
1906–Riverside B.C., Cambridge, Mass., and New York A.C. (dead heat)
1907–Argonaut R.C.
1908–09–New York A.C.
1910–Ottawa R.C. (Canada)
1911–Argonaut R.C.
1912–Winnipeg R.C.
1913–16–Duluth (Minn.) B.C.
1917–18–No competition
1919–Duluth B.C.
1920–Navy Athletic Assn., Annapolis, Md.
1921–22–Duluth B.C.
1923–Undine Barge Club, Philadelphia
1924–New York A.C.
1925–Pennsylvania Barge Club
1926–Penn A.C. Rowing Assn., Philadelphia
1927–Wyandotte (Mich.) B.C.
1928–South Side B.C., Quincy, Ill.
1929–Penn A.C.R.A.
1930–Springfield (Mass.) R.A.
1931–34–Penn A.C.R.A.
1935–New York A.C.
1936–University of Washington, Seattle
1937–39–West Side R.C., Buffalo, N.Y.
1940–Penn A.C.R.A.
1941–43–Fairmount R.A.
1944–45–No competition
1946–Detroit B.C.
1947–West Side R.C.
1948–University of California, Berkeley
1949–51–West Side R.C.
1952–53–U.S. Naval Academy, Annapolis, Md.
1954–55–Vesper B.C.
1956–Yale University
1957–West Side R.C.
1958–Vesper B.C.
1959–Lake Washington R.C.
1960–U.S. Naval Academy
1961–Lake Washington R.C.
1962–St. Catherine's (Canada) R.C.
1963–Detroit B.C.
1964–Harvard Univ.–Laconia R.A.
1965–Vesper B.C.
1966–St. Catharines R.C.
1967–New Zealand
1968–St. Catharine's (Canada) R.C.
1969–Union B.C., and Ecorse B.C. (dead heat)
1970–Vesper B.C.
1971–Union B.C.
1972–Vesper B.C.
1973–Cambridge B.C.

Team

(Julius H. Barnes Trophy)

1916–Duluth (Minn.) B.C.
1917–18–No competition
1919–23–Duluth B.C.
1924–Bachelors Barge Club, Philadelphia
1925–Penn A.C. Rowing Assn., Philadelphia
1926–Undine Barge Club, Philadelphia
1927–Argonaut R.C., Toronto (Canada)

1928—Bachelors Barge Club
1929—Undine Barge Club
1930—31—Bachelors Barge Club
1932—34—Penn A.C.R.A.
1935—West Side R.C., Buffalo, N.Y.
1936—Undine Barge Club
1937—39—West Side R.C.
1940—Penn A.C.R.A.
1941—Undine Barge Club
1942—43—Fairmount R.A., Philadelphia
1944—45—No competition
1946—Detroit B.C.
1947—Ecorse (Mich.) B.C.
1948—Vesper B.C., Philadelphia
1949—West Side R.C.
1950—Vesper B.C.
1951—Detroit B.C.
1952—53—New York A.C.
1954—55—Vesper B.C.
1956—59—Detroit B.C.
1960—Vesper B.C.
1961—62—Detroit B.C.
1963—St. Catharines R.C.
1964—65—Vesper B.C.
1966—Union B.C.
1967—68—Vesper B.C.
1969—Potomac B.C.
1970—Vesper B.C.
1971—73—New York A.C.

HENLEY-ON-THAMES ROYAL REGATTA (ENGLAND)

The oldest rowing race, next to Doggett's Coat and Badge, which originated in England in 1715, and the Oxford-Cambridge classic, is the Wingfield Sculls, first held in 1830 on the Thames River, near London. The interest in this singles match soon led to other contests on the same river and, in 1839, the first Henley-on-Thames Royal Regatta was staged. Except for interruptions because of wars, the most famous of all regattas has been an annual event since its inception. The regulation Henley distance is 1 mile 550 yards.

Traditional races at the British Henley follow:
Grand Challenge Cup—8 oars (established 1839)
Stewards' Challenge Cup—4 oars (1841)
Diamond Sculls—Single sculls (1844)
*Silver Goblets and Nickalls' Challenge Cup—Pair oars (1845)
†Wyfold Challenge Cup—4 oars (1855)
Visitors' Challenge Cup—4 oars (1847)
Ladies Challenge Plate—8 oars (1845)
Thames Challenge Cup—8 oars (1868)

*Event called the Silver Wherries until 1850, when it was changed to Silver Goblets. Tom Nickalls donated a Challenge Cup in 1895.
†The Wyfold Cup was given to leading challenger for the Grand Challenge Cup starting in 1847 and continuing for some years.

Diamond Sculls Champions
(Since 1922)
1922—Walter M. Hoover, United States
1923—M.K. Morris, England
1924—26—Jack Beresford Jr., England
1927—R.T. Lee, England
1928—Joseph Wright Jr., Canada
1929—L.H.F. Gunther, Holland
1930—Jack S. Guest, Canada
1931—H. Robert Pearce, Australia
1932—H. Buhtz, Germany
1933—T.G. Askwith, England
1934—H. Buhtz, Germany
1935—36—E. Rufli, Switzerland
1937—J. Hasenohrl, Austria
1938—39—Joseph W. Burk, United States
1940—45—No competition
1946—Jean Sephariades, France
1947—John B. Kelly Jr., United States
1948—Mervyn T. Wood, Australia
1949—John B. Kelly Jr., United States
1950—Anthony Rowe, England
1951—Tony Fox, England
1952—Mervyn T. Wood, Australia
1953—Tony Fox, England
1954—Peter Vlasic, Yugoslavia
1955—56—Teodor Kocerka, Poland
1957—62—Stuart McKenzie, Australia
1963—Don Spero
1964—Seymour Cromwell
1965—Don Spero
1966—Achim Hill
1967—M. Studach
1968—H.A. Wardell—Yerburgh, England
1969—Hans Joachim Bohmer, E. Germany
1970—Jochen Meissner, W. Germany
1971—Alberto Demiddi, Argentina
1972—Alexander Timoschinin, Russia
1973—Sean Drea, Ireland

Other U. S. Winners in British Henley

Grand Challenge Cup—Harvard Athletic Association Boat Club (1914); Harvard University (1939, 1950); University of Pennsylvania (1955); Cornell University (1957).

Thames Challenge Cup—Browne and Nichols School (1929); Kent School (1933, 1938, 1947, 1950); Tabor Academy (1936, 1937, 1939); Princeton University's 150-pound varsity (1948, 1949, 1956, 1957, 1973); Pennsylvania University's 150-pound varsity (1951, 1952); Massachusetts Institute of Technology 150-pound varsity (1954, 1955); Harvard University's 150-pound varsity (1958, 59, 60, 64, 66, 71, 72); Cornell University's 150-pound varsity (1967).

Visitor's Challenge Cup—Columbia College (1878).

America's most prominent entry in the Diamond Sculls at the British Henley in recent years has been John B. Kelly Jr. of Philadelphia, son of a former Olympic champion (1920 and 1924).

The younger Kelly, winner of a number of United States and Canadian titles, made his first appearance in the Diamond Sculls in 1946 at the age of 19, finishing second to Jean Sepphariades of France. Undaunted, young Kelly came back the following year and won the coveted honor. In 1947 he also won the balloting for the James E. Sullivan Memorial Trophy, the outstanding award of the Amateur Athletic Union of the United States. In 1949, Kelly became a two-time winner of the Diamond Sculls and then went to Amsterdam to become the first American to win the European sculling championship.

John B. Kelly Sr. took the American single sculls championship in 1919 and repeated in 1920. He tried to enter the Henley Diamond Sculls in 1920, but was ruled out.

PHILADELPHIA GOLD CHALLENGE CUP

The Philadelphia Gold Challenge Cup, emblematic of the world amateur single sculls championship, was put up by the Schuylkill Navy in 1920 and the first winner was John B. Kelly Sr. at the Olympic Games of that year at Belgium.

Only heavyweight scullers and champions are eligible to compete for the cup. The holder may stipulate that the race be held on his home course, which must be straightaway, not exceed 1½ miles and be not less than 2,000 meters (1 mile 427.25 yards). The winner of the single sculls at the Olympic Games automatically becomes the holder of the cup and his name is inscribed thereon.

ROYAL CANADIAN HENLEY AND FAMOUS CANADIAN OARSMEN

The Royal Canadian Henley Regatta, originated almost 75 years ago, is one of the Dominion's greatest sports events and ranks with the British Henley and the regatta of the N.A.A.O. The Canadian competition takes place on the Welland Canal at St. Catherines, Ont., and brings together the outstanding oarsmen of Canada, the United States and elsewhere, as the races are open to all amateurs. While it is being staged newspapers from all parts of Canada and the United States send reporters and running accounts of the events are broadcast.

The Canadian Henley is the only four-day regatta in North America and is so popular among oarsmen that it draws entries running into the hundreds, including numerous schoolboys. In fact, it is doubtful that there is a rowing regatta in the world that draws as many competitors.

Rowing has enjoyed high favor in Canada for more than 100 years. The great races of an early day were in Halifax harbor, but the scene soon shifted to the Toronto area and races were held in the principal centers in the Dominion.

Canada has produced some of the most skillful oarsmen the world has known. The idol of the 1870's and for years later was the spectacular Edward Hanlan, who knew no peer in artistry with the sculls. Hanlan was perfection in a boat, and to this he added showmanship that made every race in which he competed a superb sports spectacle. He started as an amateur, ran out of competition and, in later years, rowed for huge side bets.

The "Dean of Canadian Rowing," was Joseph Wright Sr., a champion in a shell and an all-round athlete whose feats still are fresh in Canadian memory. He won more rowing titles than any man of his time.

E.A. Thompson was a repeating champion in the 1890's; J.F. Cosgrave was one of the rowing stars of his country. So were E.B. Butler, Robert Dibble, who won the Canadian singles title five times, and Wallace Ross, who succeeded to Hanlan's laurels. Jacob Gill Gaudaur is among the sculling immortals in Canadian history. Joseph Wright Jr., was a durable champion. Jack S. Guest was a great one, too.

Those men are only a few among many who helped make records in the years of their prime and who brought to Canada the honor of developing some of the most remarkable scullers, singles and doubles, as well as crew men, the world has known.

DATA ON SHELLS, OARS, ETC.

C.S. Titus of New York, who won the United States single sculls championship in 1902 and repeated in 1906, stated:

"The modern 8-oared shells weigh about 285 pounds and the propelling sweeps (oars) are about 12 feet in length and weigh about 5 pounds. The 8-oared shell is between 61 feet and 62½ feet in length, 23¾ inches wide, and 9½ inches deep. In the United States they are made of Western cedar. The oars are made of laminated spruce.

"The 4-oared boats weigh about 155 pounds, the oars are practically the same as in 8-oared boats.

"Double scull craft weighs 65 to 70 pounds and single sculls around 27 pounds. Sculling oars are about 9 feet 6 inches long and weigh about 3 pounds 8 ounces.

"In single sculls, the sculler usually strokes about 40 per minute at the getaway, reduces to 35 and, under pressure at the finish, can do 45 or better. At Philadelphia, I was credited with 48 at the finish and chalked up a world record in that race.

"In double sculls, the stroke average is about the same as for singles. But there is a variance in stroke by all oarsmen. Some use a short, fast stroke, which means many per minute. Others use a long stroke, which reduces the number per minute.

"In 4-oared racing, the men using sweeps, instead of sculls, get away at around 40, drop to 30 or 32 and finish at 40—if necessary.

"The 8-oared procedure is a 38 or 40 stroke spurt at the start, then a drop to 32 or so. The boys will shoot up to 38 or 40 for a brief dash, if necessary, at the finish. Occasionally, great champion crews have gone to 42, but they could maintain that pace only for a very brief period."

Scullers use two oars and crew men one.

Calculating Strokes

If 8 strokes in 20 seconds, rate is 24 strokes per minute.

If 8 strokes in 15 seconds, rate is 32 per minute.

If 8 strokes in 12 seconds, rate is 40.

(For Olympic champions see section on Olympic Games.)

RUGBY

Rugby is a British invention. It contains aspects of American-style football, hockey, basketball and soccer. It is considered an ancestor of American football. Though it is popular primarily in the British Isles, it also is played elsewhere, including the United States, on the Eastern and Western coasts. College players, former college football players and many Britons who are now residing here take part in contests in the United States.

The modern game of rugby football originated accidentally. In 1823, William Ellis, a student at Rugby College, England, was involved in an interclass football (soccer) game, play then being at the only rules known—strictly kicking. Ellis, chagrined over his failure to kick the bouncing ball, picked it up and carried it down the field.

His agitated captain made profuse apologies for the Ellis breach of football etiquette. Ellis was subjected to a great deal of criticism because of his act. But the news of his run with the ball got around and certain players felt that the option of kicking or running with the ball might add zest to a contest, and it was adopted forthwith.

In 1839, Arthur Pell, a student at Cambridge and a football player, suggested a "go" at "the game at Rugby." Rugby College, until then, never had deviated from strict soccer, except during the afternoon of Ellis' mental lapse. But when the Ellis play was mentioned, the custom was to refer to it as "that play at Rugby," and eventually it was classified as "Rugby's game."

The Pell plan was adopted as an experiment and it was ruled that a player could run with the ball, if caught on the fly or on first bounce.

Cambridge players, having had their try at it, as suggested by Pell, took an immediate liking to the new form of sport.

In 1841, Rugby College, for the first time, took up play of the game, then generally known as "Rugby's Football." During the next few years, other schools adopted the game and by 1848 it had spread to so many scholastic institutions that team leaders met and standardized rules for "rugby football." At the outset, it was strictly a school game.

Although Oxford students occasionally played at the new game, the college did not adopt it officially until 1869.

The first interscholastic rugby contest did not take place until 1873. All games previously had been interclass. But, in that year, Charterhouse and Westminster met for rugby action, with Westminster the winner.

As early as 1861, the famous Blackheath team, formerly the Black Heathens, whose specialty, of course, was the old-fashioned kicking game, decided, while on a tour, to make some experiments with rugby. The game delighted spectators, and rugby came into national recognition thereafter. But it was some time before it was played throughout the British Isles, even though the game had been imported from England by other countries.

In 1866, Henry Chadwick, a sports writer, then in the United States, by way of England, quoted the rules of rugby in a book on football and cricket, written for Beadle and Company's "Dime Library." While there is nothing to indicate that Americans then took up rugby, the French did adopt the sport, as early as 1870, and students at McGill University, Montreal, were playing it in the early 1870's and introduced it to the United States in 1875.

In 1871 with so many different teams playing rugby under haphazard rules, it was decided there should be a general meeting to revise and modernize the code. The result was a conference, involving 17 clubs, and the creation of the English Rugby Union, a strictly amateur organization. Scotland formed its Rugby Union in 1873 and Ireland organized its Rugby Union in 1874. The original Irish body split up in 1875 and formed Northern and Southern units, but resumed as the Irish Rugby Union in 1881. The Welsh Rugby Union—also an all-amateur body—came into existence in 1881.

Going into the 1890's, it was observed that many rugby players in the British Isles were taking pay for their services. There was a general meeting of the Unions in 1893, and the question of whether the players were—or were not—to be permitted to take pay was brought up. The clique favoring amateurism won by a vote of 282 to 136.

Those who espoused pay for players, to recompense them for "broken time," meaning loss of time from regular occupation while playing the game, organized the Northern Rugby Union in 1895. It was made up of 21 teams from the northern part of England. To avoid confusion with the name used by the amateurs, the professionals renamed themselves Rugby Football League in 1922.

H. Archie Richardson, dealing with the league's operations, said:

"While outright professionalism was barred at the outset, remuneration, not to exceed six shillings a day, was allowed players for 'broken time.' Open professionalism, however, was adopted in 1898, but each player had to follow a legitimate occupation, and severe penalties were provided for failure to comply with that rule.

"According to the present by-laws, players are not paid on an annual basis but by match, and payment is not allowed during the off-season or for time occupied in training. While there is no limit to the amount a club may pay a player, the average is about $20 per match for a victory, about $17 if defeated.

"In 1906 the professional teams were limited to 13 men on a side.

"Two points are scored for a victory, 1 for a tied game in league scoring.

"The annual play-offs among the league divisional winners for the Rugby League Challenge Cup began in 1929. Play in the finals was started at Wembley (London) and continues there."

Rugby games are of 30 or 45-minute halves, with 5 minutes rest between, the basic difference between the Union (amateur) and League (professional) game being that the amateurs use 15 men on a team, while the professional combination is limited to 13. Huddles are not permitted in either game. "Time out" is limited to 3 minutes and is permitted only when a serious injury has happened. If the player cannot continue, he is removed from the game. No substitutions are permitted.

Ellis, the man who started it all, was an almost forgotten figure for many decades. Then the tremendous popularity of the game convinced the authorities at Rugby College that he should be honored. As the result, a small monument was erected on the Rugby campus, bearing this inscription:

THIS STONE
COMMEMORATES THE EXPLOIT OF
WILLIAM WEBB ELLIS
WHO WITH A FINE DISREGARD FOR THE RULES OF
FOOTBALL' AS PLAYED IN HIS TIME'
FIRST TOOK THE BALL IN HIS ARMS AND RAN WITH IT'
THUS ORIGINATING THE DISTINCTIVE FEATURE OF
THE RUGBY GAME
A.D. 1823

Rugby was introduced to the United States in 1875.

While Americans never have taken greatly to rugby, despite its great appeal as a spectator sport, America owns the remarkable distinction of having won the rugby championship of the Olympic Games in 1920 and also 1924, to the astonishment of other players of the world.

The story is one of the epics of sportdom in American annals. In 1905-06, when there was great condemnation of the American game of football, because of many deaths and injuries, various colleges along the Pacific Slope shifted to rugby. Within a decade or so, the American game was reinstated, but rugby had taken hold in California and continued as a popular game at many colleges.

In 1919 a group of American collegians went on a tour of British Columbia, taking on the best teams that could be scheduled. The Americans won so easily, that the boys decided to organize a team for Olympic competition in 1920. There were tryouts, through 1919 and 1920, and the team finally was selected. But the rugby youths learned that no funds had been set aside by the American Olympic Committee to transport a rugby team to Europe—and that the cost of such an excursion was expected to be at least $20,000.

Thereupon, John T. O'Neil, then of Los Angeles and later of San Antonio, Tex.; William F. Humphrey, James Rolph, Sam Goodman and a few other Californians identified with the team, suscribed the needed money, and the little band of Americans, presumed to be hopelessly outclassed, sailed for Europe.

The 1920 players were:

Daniel Carroll, George W. Davis, Charles W. Doe Jr., James P. Fitzpatrick, M. E. Hazeltine, Joseph G. Hunter, Charles T. Meehan, John Muldoon, John T. O'Neil, John C. Patrick, C. E. Righter, Rudolph Scholz, Colby E. Salter, Charles L. Tilden Jr., Harry von Schmidt, Robert (Dink) Templeton, later a famous track and field coach; James Winston and Hector L. Wrenn, all of California, and George W. Fish of New York.

The Americans met the French in the final match and won world honors by 8 to 0. The British Isles were not represented by a team.

In 1924 some of the veterans of the 1920 squad and certain newcomers decided upon another invasion. More than 100 players figured in the tryouts and the following team was selected:

Doe, William Muldoon, Hunter, O'Neil, Scholz, Slater—holdovers from the 1920 squad—and John J. Cashel, Norman Cleveland, Dudley De Groot, later a famous American football player and coach; George Dixon, S. W. Farrish, Charles Grodons, Richard W. Hyland, later a famous American football player and now a celebrated sports writer in Los Angeles; Alan C. Valentine, Phillip Clark, Hugh D. Cunningham, Edward Graff, Caeser Manneli, W. L. Rogers, Edward Turkington and Alan F. Williams, all from California.

A fund of $20,000 was subscribed (most of it by the players) for the trip. The American boys went to Europe, conquered all opposition in the eliminations, and again met France in the final before a crowd of 50,000. The Americans were supposed to be so hopelessly inferior that odds of 20 to 1 were bet against them. France had a team ranked as one of the greatest of all time. In addition to being "outclassed," the Americans were hit by injuries and illnesses, which handicapped them.

At half-time, the United States led, 1 try to 0. The customers assumed the French were "holding back" for the last period of play. Apparently, it was the American squad which was "holding back," since the final score was United States 17, France 3. Therefore, this nation was the winner, twice in succession, of a prized crown in Olympic team competition.

"We won because of some ability and a lot of courage," related Hyland. "I'll cite a sample of the latter. Johnny O'Neil was operated on for appendicitis just before we sailed. He shouldn't have played at all. But he got in there, anyway. He was one of our greatest players. During the game, he was kicked in the stomach, which ripped open the surgical wound. He called for adhesive tape, and did a fast bandaging job. He used up only about two of the three minutes permitted, and then announced he was ready to resume.

"But we wanted Johnny to get off the field. We could not make any substitution for him, but we did not want to risk him to what might be serious harm, if the injury wasn't already serious. But he just tried to laugh off our ideas. One of the boys, trying to talk him out of staying in, hit upon what he thought was a strategic plan to get Johnny out of the danger zone.

"'John,' he said, 'you might as well get back to the bench. In your shape, you won't be of help to us.'

"'Sure, sure,' agreed Johnny O'Neil. 'I know that. Can't kick or run with a ball. But I sure can force those birds to run around me and slow 'em up a bit. Let's get going.'

"With that kind of spirit, how could we lose?"

Rugby in Eastern United States

There have been sporadic attempts through the years to play rugby in the New York area. The most lasting effort got under way in 1929, with the formation of the New York Rugby Football Club by a group of British and Americans who loved the game. The first matches were against the Philadelphia Marines (United States), who had learned the game while stationed in China. Shortly thereafter, the game was introduced at Yale, and later at Princeton and Harvard, through the efforts of the New York club.

Though matches were played against visiting warships and with Montreal, the first important British visitors were the Cambridge University Vandals R.F.C., who played a picked All-East fifteen in September, 1933, and won the closely contested game, 14-9. In 1934 and 1938, Cambridge University teams made tours, handily winning their games. The second tour was under the auspices of the Eastern Rugby Union, which had been formed by the Eastern colleges to observe the rules and laws of the game. By this time there were ten clubs, and active schedules were maintained until the outbreak of war in 1939.

Rugby was continued on a limited basis at Yale, Princeton and Harvard but club rugby was not re-organized until 1952, when the New York Rugby Club was re-formed with the same traditions and, with one exception, the same officers as before.

The game is slowly spreading to other colleges. Rugby is now played both in the spring and autumn at Massachusetts Institute of Technology (M.I.T.), Cornell, Dartmouth, Pennsylvania, Columbia and Wesleyan, in addition to Harvard, Yale and Princeton. These colleges, together with visits from Canadian and Bermuda teams, present a full and lively schedule. Late in 1958 Dartmouth's team toured the British Isles and created quite a stir there by its success.

RUGBY LEAGUE'S MOST FAMOUS KICKER
(Courtesy Rugby Football League of England.)

James Sullivan, born in Cardiff, Wales, on Dec. 2, 1903, kicked 100 or more goals annually for 19 years. During the 1933-34 season he kicked 200. His career was started in a major way when he joined the Wigan (professional) team. His playing career ended after the 1945-46 season.

Sullivan's remarkable record follows:

Season	Goals	Tries	Points
1921-22	108	2	222
1922-23	172	10	374
1923-24	158	1	319
*1924	84	–	168
1924-25	148	3	269
1925-26	148	7	317
1926-27	113	3	235
1927-28	113	3	235
*1928	59	1	121
1928-29	110	3	229
1929-30	114	2	234
1930-31	133	4	278
1931-32	117	5	249
*1932	110	1	223
1932-33	146	5	307
1933-34	200	6	418
1934-35	168	6	354
1935-36	117	4	246
1936-37	120	6	258
1937-38	136	5	287
1938-39	128	4	268

1939-40	78 ...	5	171
1940-41	36 ...	1	75
1941-42	47 ...	1	97
1942-43	63 ...	4	138
1943-44	7 ...	–	14
1944-45	– ...	–	–
1945-46	5 ...	1	13
Totals ..	2,955	94	6,192

*Australian tours.

BASIC RULES

The rugby ball, somewhat like the American football, is oval. However, it is fatter and rounded at the ends and more difficult to throw, easier to dropkick accurately. The American football was shaped like this until the forward pass became popular and its shape was altered.

Forward passing is not allowed in rugby and neither are blocking or interference. No teammate is allowed to be ahead of the man possessing the ball. The rule against interference permits players to wear light equipment of shorts and padless jerseys, similar to soccer uniforms.

The game is unique in that when a player is injured, no one is permitted to substitute for him. The team must play shorthanded if a player is removed. Play is far more fluid and continuous than in American football, being more akin to basketball, hockey and soccer in that respect.

Play is not stopped for downs when the ball-carrier is tackled. When tackled he must immediately release the ball, which is then put in play by the first man who reaches it. He kicks it on the ground. A scrummage, somewhat similar to football's scrimmage, occurs only after certain rule infractions or out-of-bounds plays.

Deliberate kicking of the ball on the ground is permitted and often is considered a good strategic move. There is much more lateral passing in rugby than in American football. The ball usually is passed underhand, often with both hands. The laterals and frequent kicking are the outstanding features of the game, together with its fast pace. American observers call the game a cross between soccer and football.

The "in-goal" area is the area in which the ball must be touched down in order to register a try. If a man crosses into the area without touching the ball down, no try is scored.

The ball is in "touch" when though not in possession of a player it touches or crosses a touch line. If the ball crosses a touch line and is then blown back, it is in touch at the place where it first crossed the line. The ball must be brought into play at the place where it went into touch by being thrown into the field of play so as to touch a player or the ground at least 5 yards from and at right angles to the touch line.

In rugby a try counts 3 points, a conversion after a try 2 additional points, a goal from a free kick or penalty kick 3 points, a dropkicked goal otherwise obtained 3 points. There is a goal on each goal line, equi distant from the sidelines. The posts are 18½ feet apart and connected by a crossbar 10 feet high. Extension of the uprights above the crossbar must be at least 1 foot, but considerably more is desirable to give the kicker a better target, and the officials guidance in determining a score. The field has a width of 75 yards and is a maximum of 110 yards in length. The in-goal area behind the posts must not exceed 25 yards.

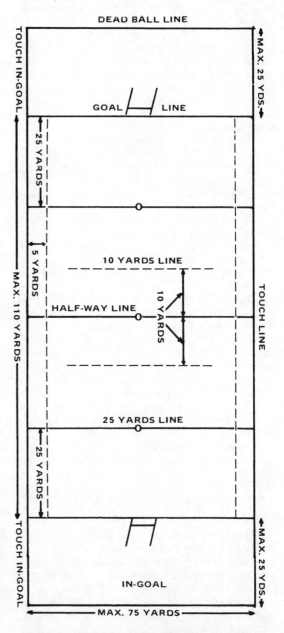

Rugby Field. (Taken from "Rugby Union Football," published by Educational Productions Ltd., London.)

Rugby's Scrummage

The scrummage is awarded to the non-offending team. Technically, it is formed by one or more players from each side closing around the ball when it is on the ground, or by their closing up in readiness to allow the ball to be put on the ground between them. It involves the heavier forward players (corresponding to football linemen). Usually three players (more is illegal) of a team line up together, arms around each other's waists, and three opponents do likewise. These sets of opponents, however, brace themselves against their opponents' shoulders, unlike football where no contact is achieved until the ball is in play.

Back of each trio other forwards line up, usually in a group of two, followed by a group of three. Therefore two 8-man scrummage groups participate, but each group is really a 3–2–3 mass, rather than the single straight line as in football.

A back of the team awarded the scrummage (usually the scrum-half) stands at either end he chooses of the locked scrummage line, and rolls the ball in between the forward trios. He must throw it in midway between the opposing groups—not toward his own trio.

The middle players of each trio then vie to kick the ball back to their scrummage teammates, who in turn attempt to kick it to one of their backs behind the scrummage line. Only kicking—no handling—is permitted in the scrummage line.

Although a player, not an official, throws the ball into the line, there is no actual advantage to either team, since both sides have an equal opportunity to kick it. In this impartiality the scrummage is more akin to hockey's face-off or basketball's jump than to football's scrimmage where the snapper-back starts with actual possession of the ball.

The 3–2–3 formation, cited above, is the most common one, but not mandatory. The rule merely forbids more than three players in the forward line. A variation employs a 2–3–2 line-up with the eighth forward staying outside the scrummage as a sort of "rover" or additional back.

(From Parke Cummings' "The Dictionary of Sports," A.S. Barnes and Company, New York.)

SHOOTING
Rifle

Ever since the invention of firearms, marksmanship, either as a means of acquiring game for sustenance, war or as a sporting diversion, has been a source of delight and pride. As civilization advanced and the need to hunt for food disappeared shooting became a sporting endeavor. Rifles, pistols, revolvers and shotguns are used.

Rifle shooting gained favor as a sport immediately after the Civil War. There was a conviction that what this country needed was high class marksmen, with the long-barreled guns, and, because this was so, most men with such weapons began to practice shooting to a greater degree than ever before.

Prior to the war, the major part of shooting had been in rural communities on Saturday afternoons and Sundays. The shooting matches usually took place in the neighborhood of the country stores. Targets were of various kinds. Many were placards with an "X" to indicate the bullseye. In other instances, some tree or post, similarly marked, was the target.

The men in the pre-war era shot from three positions: standing, on one knee, and flat on the ground with the gun resting on a log or across the top of a small rock. Any shooting method had its merits, so long as accuracy resulted.

When the war was over the city folk, who previously had ignored rifle shooting as a sport, took it up, going to some open space, erecting crude targets and blasting away in the effort to determine who was the best shot. A great assortment of rifles was called into action, each marksman having his favorite. Some clung to the old type, others preferred the new, which had been created for war purposes.

The early guns generally were muzzle loaders, black powder being the propellant. The projectiles were of various kinds, the round ball being the most popular. The loading of such guns, of course, was important, it being done according to the ideas of the individual. If the shooter hit or came close to the bullseye, it meant that his method of loading must be all right. If he missed often, he changed loading methods and, perhaps, the shape of the missile.

In those early years England, like the United States, also felt that expert gunnery was much to be desired. In the 1850's and into the 1860's the Englishmen were encouraged to practice rifle shooting. As early as 1860 targets were erected at Wimbledon and the range became world famous. The English and Irish assembled shooting teams and shot it out to determine which was the superior. While many Americans were gaining rifle practice in actual warfare, the men of Great Britain were having regular shoots of greater and greater importance.

As rifle shooting gained in popularity in the late 1860's in the United States and shooting matches were arranged in many places along the Atlantic Seaboard as well as in the interior as far West as the Mississippi River, there were repeated demands for a governing body.

In 1871 a group of officers in the National Guard felt that the sport had advanced to a point where some executive control must be exercised. This suggestion led to the formation of the National Rifle Association, which ever since has ruled the sport.

The first act of the organization was to standardize the targets, the distances, etc., and to take the sport from chaos to steadiness, and to hold it to such lines, in all the years since.

The association arranged for the first championship matches in 1871, supplanting the impromptu shoots which had been the vogue throughout the country for many years. Its plan brought the greatest rifle shots of the nation into competition with each other, under standardized contest rules, and the matches provided great advances for the sport.

The highlight of the 1871 matches at Creedmoor, Long Island (N.Y.), was brought about by the invasion of a team of rifle shooters from Ireland, representing the Ulster Rifle Club and reputed to be made up of the most accurate shots in the world. The Americans put together a team, but there was no guarantee, at the time, as to its greatness. Men were chosen who, in some other matches, in the old days, had done well. Yet the selection was so good that the United States defeated the invaders, by a margin of 3 points.

So great was the interest in the championships at the national range at Creedmoor in 1872 that over 100,000 persons were spectators. They were taken to the ranges in special trains, or by any form of vehicle that was available. When it is recalled that very few sports events in the 80-odd years since then have attracted greater crowds, the appeal the rifle folks made in so early a time is remarkable.

A new team of Irish rifle shooters in 1872 took rank as the greatest in the British Empire and it hurled a challenge at the men of the United States. The result was the naming of an American team, which journeyed across the Atlantic. The impending match was of great interest to Americans. So keen was the excitement over it that newspapers, which previously had refused to spend as much as a dollar in the cabling of sports news, ordered that the wires buzz with the practice activities of the American team. The match itself was spot news, and there was great exultation in the United States when word was flashed that the Americans had beaten the Irish, and thus gained international supremacy, by a margin of 957 to 921.

The success of the Americans in 1871, against the Irish sharpshooters, was regarded as "one of those things that occasionally happens." The success in 1872 was different. It put the Americans in the forefront in a sport that was international, and the Americans were determined to hold the heights. Therefore, there began intensive search and development of the best type of weapons for high class shooting, and Americans proceeded with experiments, as to different rifles and the way of firing them, designed to keep them champions.

Metallic cartridges had been known before that time, but had not been generally used because they were not regarded as dependable. Little shooting had been done with other than lead for bullets. But the rifle manufacturers began to make better weapons, using a higher grade of steel, and, thus, it was possible for marksmen equipped with such guns to put metal jackets on bullets, which increased velocity. The higher speed flattened the trajectory and lessened the effects of wind, drift and atmospheric conditions.

All this meant to the man who shot both at targets and moving game that absolute accuracy was not so important as it had been and that estimating the distance from gun to target was not required to the ultimate degree as had been the rule in the old days.

When black powder was used as the explosive, the velocity of the bullet was between 1,000 and 1,500 feet per second. As early as 1900, the lighter bullet, plus smokeless powder, had increased the velocity to 2,000 feet per second. Since then, bullet velocity has increased steadily to 4,100 feet, or faster, per second.

A great rifle shooter of the 1870's was as much a public idol, in ratio, as were Babe Ruth, Ty Cobb, Jack Dempsey, John L. Sullivan and other athletes of later eras. He was lionized wherever he went. He was recipient of dinners, of trophies, of huzzahs and wild acclaim. He was regarded as a "magnificent type of American," and no honor was too great to be showered upon him.

When the National Rifle Association came into existence the affiliated clubs were few and the membership was not of great consequence. Amazing progress has been made since its formation. At this time there are thousands of senior and junior clubs identified with the organization and its individual membership numbers hundreds of thousands. A vast number of tournaments are put on annually under its auspices—among senior units, veterans' organizations, colleges, high schools, Y.M.C.A.'s, Boy Scouts and many other groups. The best appear in the national championships, staged each year at various locations throughout the country.

The champions of the pioneer shoots are among the forgotten men of history. Little attention was paid in the records as to who were outstanding. History really begins in 1875, when cup matches became popular. The Leech Cup was great at the time. The first winner was Col. John Bodine. The Marine Corps Cup, inaugurated in 1909, was next in importance, with the Member's Match preceding it, in 1901. In the international field one of the leading current competitions is the Dewar Trophy tournament.

The President's Match also began in 1901. Before this contest there was the Wimbledon Cup, pioneered in 1875 and of international significance. A great many other contests came into existence later. They called for matches at different bores. There were competitions, indoors and outdoors, with pistols gaining recognition, under National Rifle Association auspices, for the first time in 1904.

Many years ago Congress became aware of the importance of the organization and to encourage the sport because of its great value in warfare appropriated funds to continue its existence and to encourage marksmanship.

Both rifle and pistol shooting are organized through the medium of the N.R.A. in this country, as well as the International Shooting Union, for international competition. In addition, the International Olympic Committee has a rifle section and a pistol section and other international events are arranged directly between the N.R.A. and similar national bodies in other countries.

The N.R.A. conducts the annual national championships. Regional affairs, held under the supervision of the governing body, are a step below the title contests. Then come the state championships, district championships and local tournaments, in that order.

The entire competitive program is divided into sections for the smallbore (.22 caliber) rifle, the highpower rifle, and pistols and revolvers. The highpower section of the program is subdivided into events limited to the Army rifle and events open to match rifles with match sights. The pistol section of the program is similarly divided into matches for the .45 service pistol, matches for center-fire revolvers (.32 caliber or larger) and matches for the .22 caliber rim-fire pistols and revolvers.

Service rifle shooters are automatically classified by their Army qualifications. All smallbore rifle shooters and all pistol and revolver shooters are classified on the basis of scores made in registered tournaments. The classifications are Master, Expert, Sharpshooter and Marksman.

The standard ranges for smallbore rifle shooting are 50 feet (indoor and junior), 50 yards, 50 meters, 100 yards and 200 yards. For highpowered rifle shooting the standard ranges are 200 yards, 300, 500, 600, 800, 900 and 1,000. For pistol and revolver shooting, the standard ranges are 50 feet (indoors), 25 and 50 yards (outdoors).

FAMOUS SHOOTERS

Most topflight shooters have gained their fame with specialized rifles, such as those having service and telescopic sights and the smallbore piece, but some were splendid shots with any kind of gun.

Among the outstanding riflemen of all time must be included W.H. Richard of Ohio, Thurman Randle of Texas, John Hessian of Florida, Paul Martin and Sidney Hinds of the United States Army, Morris Fisher and W.J. Whaling of the United States Marine Corps, G.L. Wotkyns of California, and a long list of officers and enlisted men of the United States Marine Corps, Navy and Army who have established record after record in the last half century.

Of the modern-day shooters, Emmett Swanson, Lieut. Remes de la Hunt, United States Marine Corps; Frank Parsons Jr., Washington, D.C.; Arthur Jackson, Brooklyn, N.Y.; William Woodring, New Haven, Conn.; Arthur Cook, Ransford Triggs and William Schweitzer, New Jersey; Robert Perkins, California; Lieut. Col. Walter Walsh, United States Marine Corps; and G. Wayne Moore, Pennsylvania, rank among the best.

NATIONAL CHAMPIONS
Men
Bolt Rifle

1904—George Sayer
1905—James Durward Jr.
1906—T.H. Dillon
1907—W. Lee
1908—A.D. Rothrock
1909—H.O. Roesch
1910—Scott Clark
1911—Charles M. King
1912—No competition
1913—E.W. Sweeting
1914—No competition
1915—J.S. Stewart
1916—W.H. Spencer
1917—No competition
1918—H.J. Mueller
1919—T.B. Crawley
1920—H. Whitaker
1921—Otho Wiggs
1922—Otto Bentz
1923—L.V. Jones
1924—W.W. Ashurst
1925—Charles Hakala
1926—No competition
1927—R.M. Cutts
1928—C.J. Cagle
1929—J.B. Jensen
1930—S. Bartlotti
1931—E.F. Sloan
1932—34—No competition
1935—C.N. Harris
1936—Waldo A. Phinney
1937—James G. Frazer

1938—J.M. Holland
1939—Coats Brown
1940—William J. Coffman
1941—50—No competition
1951—Thomas R. Barnes (NRA match rifle)
1952—Walter R. Walsh (NRA match rifle)
1953—S/Sgt. Don Smith (NRA match rifle)
1954—Clifford Tryon (NRA match rifle)
1955—Lloyd G. Crow Jr. (NRA match rifle)
1956—Lloyd G. Crow Jr. (NRA match rifle)
1957—Ammon E. Bell (NRA match rifle)
1958—Middleton W. Tompkins (NRA match rifle)
1959—Ammon E. Bell
1960—Kenneth C. Erickson
1961—Jay G. Harris
1962—Earl H. Burton
1963—64—M.W. Tompkins
1965—J.A. Clerke
1966—E.J. Shook
1967—68—Middleton W. Tompkins
1969—Theodore R. Fasy
1970—72—Ronald G. Troyer

Service Rifle

1951—Remes de la Hunt
1952—Robert A. Dawson
1953—M/Sgt. Maxim R. Beebe
1954—T.R. Carpenter
1955—John W. Kolb
1956—James E. Hill
1957—Michael Pietrforte
1958—T/Sgt. V.D. Mitchell
1959—Capt. Thomas W. Atwood
1960—Sgt. James T. Lamm
1961—Sgt. Charles D. Davis
1962—Sgt. David A. Luke
1963—Frank Kruk
1964—CPO D.F. Morine Jr.
1965—D.H. Meredith
1966—Capt. M.R. Menlove
1967—Lt. James R. Bowen
1968—S/Sgt. Davis Phelps
1969—S/Sgt. Willie D. Jordan
1970—71—W.O. Robert Goller
1972—SFC Martin D. Edmondson

Smallbore—Prone

1919—G.L. Wotkyns
1920—W.H. Richard
1921—M.D. Snyder
1922—J.F. Hauck
1923—R.H. McGarity
1924—Francis W. Parker
1925—Thomas J. Imler
1926—No competition
1927—R.H. McGarity
1928—V.Z. Canfield
1929—Eric Johnson
1930—Vere F. Hamer
1931—Fred Kuhn
1932—Bradford Wiles
1933—T.P. Samsoe
1934—E.L. Lord

1935—T.P. Samsoe
1936—38—William B. Woodring
1939—Vere Hamer
1940—Dave Carlson
1941—Ransford Triggs
1942—45—No competition
1946—47—G. Wayne Moore
1948—Arthur Cook
1949—Robert McMains
1950—No competition
1951—Mason E. Kline
1952—Robert Perkins
1953—John J. Crowley
1954—Alonzo B. Wood
1955—Viola E. Pollum
1956—J. Kenneth Johnson
1957—John Moschkau
1958—Robert K. Moore
1959—John R. Foster
1960—Alan M. Dapp
1961—62—Tommy G. Pool
1963—Lt. L.W. Wigger Jr.
1964—Capt. P.W. Kendall
1965—66—Capt. L.W. Wigger Jr.
1967—Capt. Bruce A. Meredith
1968—Capt. Donald Adams
1969—S/Sgt. Thomas Whitaker
1970—Capt. David Ross III
1971—John E. Comley
1972—Maj. Presley W. Kendall

Note—When the highpower championships were revived in 1951 after a lapse of 11 years, the course for the national title was changed and the service rifle and sporting rifle competitions were separated. The course of fire prior to 1951 was 1 match. The title has been decided on an aggregate of 4 matches since 1951.

Women
Smallbore—Prone

1941—Susan Cole
1942—45—No competition
1946—47—Adelaide McCord
1948—No competition
1949—Adelaide McCord
1950—No competition
1951—Elinor Bell
1952—Betty Ingleright
1953—Viola E. Pollum
1954—Elinor Bell
1955—56—Viola E. Pollum
1957—Mrs. Bertie Moore
1958—Janet S. Friddell
1959—61—Jilann O. Brunett
1962—Jean Linton
1963—Lenore Lemanski
1964—Jilann O. Brunett
1965—Marianne M. Jensen
1966—67—Inez Sargent
1968—Marianne Jensen
1969—Capt. Margaret T. Murdock
1970—Marianne M. Vitito
1971—Tricia Foster
1972—Capt. Margaret T. Murdock

Pistol

The pistol was invented by Caminello Vitelli about 1540 in the town of Pistoia in the Florentine Province of Italy, where he lived. The weapon derives its name from that of the town.

Vitelli's creation was the answer to the demand for some sort of gun that was not of tremendous weight and could be handled and fired by one man. In an earlier era, the weapons were huge affairs, on the order of cannons. The pistol continued to be the only hand-weapon until some centuries later when Samuel Colt of the United States, improving upon a crude English design, devised the revolver.

The pistol in its original design fired only a single shot, whereas the revolver, having a chamber that turned, could project from 5 to 7 bullets in one loading.

The pistol was not a real success during the lifetime of Vitelli. Those who succeeded him and worked on his principle made the pistol far more effective. Since the pistol was created to succeed the sword in close fighting, it meant that the gun had to function to perfection, else the man, exploding his one shot, left himself to the mercy of his enemy if he missed fire.

The English, more than the Italians, became aware of the value of the pistol and experimented through many generations toward making it a useful weapon for soldiers. The English Army was well equipped with improved pistols in the middle of the 18th Century and placed a great deal of dependence upon the weapon.

Historians generally ignore that "the shot that was heard around the world" was fired from a pistol—not a musket, as is generally supposed. The Revolutionary War actually was started at Lexington, Mass., on April 19, 1775. British Maj. John Pitcairn had ordered the patriots (he called them rebels) to disperse. They ignored him. In rage, Pitcairn whipped out his pistol and fired into the group; the act precipitated the warfare that led to America's independence.

In the early frontier days of the United States, the weapon in use was the pistol. Since it fired only one shot at a time, it meant that men who called it into action had to be deadly in their accuracy. Among the great shots was William F. (Buffalo Bill) Cody, who put on shooting exhibitions in the 1860's, using the pistol, as well as the revolver, which at that time was just coming into general use.

Ira Paine, ranked in his day as the greatest pistol and revolver shot in the world, popularized the pistol as a means of sport and directed attention, especially in Europe, to the value of the revolver, which had not been subjected to much use beyond warfare. The revolver had been useful for soldiers during the Mexican war in the 1840's and was of worth during the Civil War. Paine made Europe aware of its effectiveness as he demonstrated what could be done with a pistol, during exhibitions with both types of guns.

Early in the 1880's, Paine made an exhibition trip into New England, which at the time was interested only in the rifle. Paine's shooting mastery with pistol and revolver influenced the Massachusetts Rifle Association to put targets for both pistols and revolvers on its range and the members thereafter engaged in contests with both weapons.

Yet the interest in those guns was so scant that not until 1900 did riflemen in other states give them recognition by building targets and arranging pistol and revolver programs. Most riflemen opposed the use of the small guns in contests involving marksmanship for the reason that the range of the guns was short, and the assumption was by riflemen, who fired from a greater distance, that it would be the simplest thing in the world to hit a target with a pistol or revolver "from just a couple of steps away."

However, when the rifle shooters were influenced into trying to hit targets with pistols or revolvers, they found that the accomplishment called for marksmanship as great as that needed with rifles. And so pistol and revolver shooting grew in favor, and matches for the United States championship were added to the program of the National Rifle Association of America for the first time at the "shoot" at Sea Girt, N.J., in 1900.

FAMOUS SHOOTERS

Since the turn of the century, when pistol target shooting came into its own as a formalized sport, many outstanding handgun shooters have appeared on the scene. However, in this time the United States has produced two men who are in a class by themselves. They are Master Sergeant Huelet Benner of the United States Army and Lieut. Harry Reeves of the Detroit (Mich.) Police Department. Since World War II these men have dominated the competition and hold practically all the records between them.

Other outstanding shooters of the last 30 years include J. Engbrecht, Los Angeles (Calif.) Police; Charles Askins Jr., United States Army; Lee Echols, United States Border Patrol; Al Hemming, Detroit Police; Emmett Jones, Los Angeles Police; Walter Walsh, United States Marine Corps; P.M. Chapman, United States Border Patrol; Garfield Huddleston, Kansas City (Mo.) Police, and C.A. Brown, Tampa, Fla.

NATIONAL CHAMPIONS

Men

1936—J. Engbrecht
1937—Charles Askins Jr.
1938—Al Hemming

1939—Emmett E. Jones
1940—41—Harry Reeves
1942—45—No competition
1946—Harry Reeves
1947—Huelet Benner
1948—Harry Reeves
1949—Huelet Benner
1950—No competition
1951—Huelet Benner
1952—William T. Toney Jr.
1953—54—Harry Reeves
1955—56—Huelet Benner
1957—William W. McMillan Jr.
1958—James E. Clark
1959—Huelet L. Benner
1960—64—William B. Blankenship
1965—D.L. Hamilton
1966—M. Sgt. R.O. Thompson
1967—M. Sgt. W.B. Blankenship, Jr.
1968—Maj. Franklin Green
1969—P.O. 1 Donald L. Hamilton
1970—W.O. Francis Higginson

1971—S/Sgt. John A. Smith
1972—Sfc. Bonnie D. Harmon
Women
1941—Mildred McCarthy
1942—45—No competition
1946—Alice Mathews
1947—Rosalind Noble
1948—No competition
1949—Alice Mathews
1950—No competition
1951—Gloria Jacobs Norton
1952—Maria Hulseman
1953—Margaret Culbertson
1954—Lucile Chambliss
1955—58—Mrs. Gertrude E. Backstrom
1959—Irma Tesch
1960—61—Lucille Chambliss
1962—Gail N. Liberty
1963—66—Capt. Sallie L.E. Carroll
1967—69—No competition
1970—Maj. Sallie L.E. Carroll
1971—72—S/Sgt. Barbara J. Hile

Trap

English huntsmen in the early part of the 19th Century devised the sport of trapshooting because they had been deprived of the chance to shoot at wild birds.

Throughout the 18th Century there had been greater and greater use of guns for hunting, and, as time went on, the supply of birds grew smaller and smaller. When this situation came about, members of the nobility and aristocracy in England made deals that gave them possession of much of the wide open spaces, which had been favorite public hunting grounds. An old Roman law, which was still in force in England, forbade any private shooting grounds, but the wealthy chose to ignore the law and set up their own game preserves. This ruled out the commoners.

The huntsmen, who were denied their sport, made protests, but it gained them nothing. The wealthy continued to use what previously had been public hunting ground as places where they and their guests alone might shoot, and there the matter ended.

Gunners, thus shut off from their annual hunts, began to experiment in search of a substitute sport. This brought about the formation in 1832 of a shooting club in England known as the "High Hats." It was so called because members placed live birds under their hats and, upon signal, lifted the hats, clamped them back onto their heads and then—and only then—took a shot at the birds, which usually were well on wing.

Soon the supply of birds became exhausted, and the gunners, looking about for a substitute, hit upon a glass ball. This was the first real method of shooting at objects zipped out of a trap.

The balls had a diameter of 2½ inches. They were placed in a cup, which had a spring inside. When the spring was released, the ball flew out. To make things more realistic, the pioneer trapshooters often glued feathers to the ball and when it was hit, they flew in all directions.

Later came the revolving trap, which sent the glass ball in different directions, the shooters not knowing in advance which way the object would fly. This made hitting the target more difficult but it increased skill in handling the gun and resulted in greatly improved marksmanship.

Eventually there was demand for a more difficult target, and this brought about the creation in the 1860's of the first type of clay pigeon. The target was made of regular clay, baked into the shape of a saucer. A tip of cardboard was glued to the edge, perhaps to cause eccentric flight and make shooting more intriguing. It was thrown from a trap, which had a clamp on the end fixed in a sidewise position, so that the target would fly with only the edge exposed.

Such "pigeons," it soon developed, were baked too hard, it being difficult to break them with gunfire. So a cardboard ring, with a rubber balloon about 2 inches in diameter in dead center, was invented. The idea was for the gunner to shatter the red balloon, as the target was sent out of a trap almost identical to that used for clay pigeons. This target was not popular, but by that time trapshooting had firmly established itself as a sport and its enthusiasts experimented vigorously in the hope of perfecting a superior target and trap.

In 1880 a new and lighter type of clay pigeon

was tried. This was easier to smash than the earlier ones. Just when the gunners were about to accept it as standard, an Englishman named McCaskey perfected a target made of a mixture of river silt and pitch—an ideal combination. This became known as the famous "Blue Rock" target. McCaskey later introduced a revolutionary trap, which he named the "Expert," and with this satisfactory target and a well-functioning trap, the sport neared standardization and quickly came into world-wide popularity.

There have been certain improvements on the McCaskey target since then, and many changes of the trap, but McCaskey's creations remain basic. Rotary motion was originated after McCaskey's time, and this solved the last of the trapshooters' many original problems. The big difference between trapshooting and shooting at game birds is this: the clay target has its maximum speed at the start of its flight, whereas the bird starts slowly and increases acceleration.

Trapshooting as a sport was introduced to the United States late in the 1870's. By the early 1880's it had quite a following and this led to the creation of the Interstate Association of Trapshooters, which purchased land on Long Island and conducted both live bird and trapshooting tournaments there under direction of Elmer E. Shaner. It was on these grounds that the Grand American Handicap trapshoot first was conducted. The winner of this annual contest, beginning then and in all the years since, is regarded as the American champion.

In 1900, the Interstate Association was succeeded by the American Trapshooting Association, which became the national governing body. Until 1924, the A.T.A. was controlled by manufacturers of guns and ammunition. In that year it was decided by the trapshooters to divorce it from all "subsidy" and to have the association go on its own as strictly a sports organization. The severance was made and the name changed to its present one of Amateur Trapshooting Association.

The organization now has magnificent quarters at Vandalia, Ohio, and its shooting equipment is without peer in the world. The plant cost over $200,000 and there are about 50 traps. The membership is made up of 48 state trapshooting organizations, with allied membership in Canada.

More than three decades ago, women took up trapshooting and became enthusiasts. The feats of some of them are on a par with the ranking men. They once were limited to competition among their own sex, but the organization now puts on a mixed-team championship match.

The custom is to hold annual state championships in the four outstanding classes. Such state champions, men and women, and others of ranking ability, later go into action in the nationals at Vandalia.

There are championship tests for men, women, juniors, sub-juniors and professionals at Vandalia. The events include the blue-ribbon Grand American Handicap, North American Clay Targets, National Doubles, All-Around, Champion of Champions, High-Over-All and the Preliminary Handicap. In addition, there are class title tests, father-and-son, husband-and-wife, brother-and-brother and others.

In 1900 there were about 3,000 or 4,000 trapshooters in the United States. The total now is well over 100,000. The army greatly increased since the supply of game birds became limited and the gunners took to trapshooting or skeet shooting. The first trapshooting tournament, in 1900, attracted fewer than 100 contestants. Over 3,000 now take part in the tournament annually. During the competition about 2,250,000 shells are exploded. Since shells cost 10 cents and targets 8 cents, it means that about $800,000 is spent during the week for ammunition and targets alone by the marksmen.

The Grand American Handicap calls for shooting at 100 targets from distances between 16 and 25 yards, as the rules may require. The National Doubles contest requires 100 shots; the North American Clay Targets, 200; the High-Over-All is a 1,000-shot affair and 400 shots are taken in the all-around championship.

GRAND AMERICAN HANDICAP WINNERS

Year	Entries		Yds.	Broke
1900	74	R.O. Heikes	22	91
1901	75	E.C. Griffith	19	95
1902	91	C.W. Floyd	18	94
1903	192	M. Diefenderfer	16	94
1904	336	R. Guptil	19	96
1905	352	R.R. Barber	16	99
1906	290	F.E. Rogers	17	94
1907	495	J.J. Blanks	17	96
1908	362	Fred Harlow	16	92
1909	457	Fred Shattuck	18	96
1910	383	R. Thompson	19	100
1911	418	Harvey Dixon	20	99
1912	377	W.E. Phillips	19	96
1913	501	M.S. Hootman	17	97
1914	515	W. Henderson	22	98
1915	884	L.B. Clarke	18	96
1916	683	L.E. Wulf	19	99
1917	808	C.H. Larson	20	98
1918	620	J.D. Henry	16	97
1919	848	G.W. Lorimer	18	98
1920	715	A.L. Ivins	19	99
1921	637	E.F. Haak	21	97
1922	588	J.S. Frink	22	96
1923	513	Mark Arie	23	96
1924	528	H.C. Deck	16	97
1925	710	E.C. Starner	17	98
1926	932	Charles A. Young	23	100
1927	873	Otto Newlin	20	98
1928	891	I. Andrews	20	95
1929	1,100	M. Newman	20	98
1930	966	Alfred Rufus King	16	97

1931	938	Gar. Roebuck 17	96
1932	722	A.E. Sheffield 21	98
1933	597	Walter Beaver 25	98
1934	612	L.G. Dana 17	98
1935	608	J.B. Royall 20	98
1936	704	B.F. Cheek 16	98
1937	932	F.G. Carroll 19	100
1938	814	O.W. West 20	99
1939	757	D.L. Ritchie 20	99
1940	820	E.H. Wolfe 23	98
1941	1,108	Walter Tulburt 18	99
1942	910	J.F. Holderman 20	93
1943	810	Jasper Rogers 18	97
1944	865	L.C. Jepson 19	97
1945	828	Don Englebry 23	99
1946	1,478	Capt. F.J. Bennett 18	98
1947	1,786	H.H. Crossen 22	99
1948	1,678	John W. Schenk 19	99
1949	1,700	Pete Donat 20	100
1950	1,680	Oscar Scheske 19	100
1951	1,695	Mike Wayland 20	99
1952	1,726	Orval Voorhees 18	98
1953	1,949	Raymond A. Williams ...19	98
1954	2,009	Nick Egan 19	99
1955	2,024	Logan Bennett 19	99
1956	2,136	C.W. Brown 20	99
1957	2,142	Carmi Russell Crawford ..22	98
1958	2,202	Emerson Clark 20	99
1959	2,392	Clyde Bailey 21	99
1960	2,429	Roy Foxworthy 20	100
1961	2,353	Steven Foxworthy 20	99
1962	2,414	Milton Young 20	99
1963	2,527	Albert Kees 21	100
1964	2,688	W.E. Duggan 20	99
1965	3,031	Daniel C. Pautler, Jr. 20	99
1966	––	Delbert Grim 23	100
1967	––	Herman Welch 20½	100
1968	––	Denton Childers 21½	100
1969	––	Bernard Bonn, Jr........19	99
1970	––	Charles Harvey 24	98
1971	––	Ralph Davis 20½	98
1972	––	George Mushrush 22	99

Skeet

Skeet shooting is a sport devised by trapshooters and is an American invention, whereas trapshooting originated in England.

The newer sport came into existence in 1910, and, for some time, was known as "Round the Clock Shooting." It was decided the game rated a distinct name, and a contest to find one was instituted by the "National Sportsman" magazine. The winner was Mrs. Gertrude Hurlbutt of Dayton, Mont., who won the $100 prize in a field of 10,000 with the name by which the sport now is known.

Mrs. Hurlbutt chose "skeet" because it is a Scandinavian word meaning "shoot."

Henry E. Ahlin of Boston, one of the pioneers of the sport and for many years secretary of the governing organization, the National Skeet Shooting Association, explaining skeet, stated:

"In skeet shooting, guns are used and fire is directed at targets, the same as in trapshooting. But from there on the technique is radically different, and the sports are not really related.

"Skeet shooting, a purely American and fascinating form of the clay target shooting sport, had a following of 25,000 in the United States before the first World War and many thousands in foreign countries.

"The seed from which the sport of skeet grew was planted on the grounds of the Glen Rock Kennels, Andover, Mass., in 1910. A small group of New England upland game gunners, including the late C.E. Davies, proprietor of the kennels; his son, Henry W. Davies, and William H. Foster, used standard clay targets and clay target throwing traps as a means of obtaining wing shooting practice with their favorite guns.

"There was nothing unusual about this form of practice shooting, since similar attempts to simulate actual shooting conditions with animated targets in one form or another had been tried before. But this form of practice shooting was enjoyed at the Glen Rock field between 1910 and 1915.

"As time went on, a friendly rivalry among members of this group led to the establishment of a more definite program of competitive shooting. This gave each contestant the same series of shots, and, thereby, made competition as equitable as possible.

"This form of shooting, with definite rules governing, was enjoyed between 1915 and 1920. The shooting arrangement at that time was a complete circle of 25 yards radius, with the circle marked off like the face of a clock. The trap, or target-throwing mechanism, was set up at '12 o'clock' and adjusted to throw the clay target directly over '6 o'clock.'

"The program of shots consisted of two from each of the twelve stations. The twenty-fifth shell to complete the round-off then was shot from a position directly in the center of circle, with target representing a direct incomer. This later developed into what is now termed the 'station 8 shot.' It was purposely made a part of the program as excellent training for snap-shooting and fast gun-handling, and now is the most talked about one in the entire shooting course.

" 'Shooting around the clock,' as it was informally referred to in 1920, had many of the elements of the present day skeet program. It soon became popular, and the enthusiastic acceptance of this style of shooting soon indicated that it had possibilities as a new and separate form of sport.

"In 'shooting around the clock' shots were fired to all points of the compass. A farmer, owning land adjoining the shooting field, started a hen farm, to put a stop to shooting in that direction. W.H. Foster, a member of the trio responsible for the invention of skeet, met that problem. He produced a second trap and placed it at the 6 o'clock station marker and adjusted it to throw targets over '12.' This revision produced the same shooting problems as were present in the original clockface set-up.

"Mr. Foster became associate editor of the 'National Sportsman' and the 'Hunting & Fishing' magazines in 1920, and published articles on clock-shooting which appeared in the November, 1920, and November, 1922, issues of 'National Sportsman.'

"Between 1920 and 1926, the same small group, augmented now and then by a few interested visitors, continued to shoot clay targets for wing shooting practice during the closed season on game. Occasional changes in the rules were made to give a closer parallel to game shooting. Important among these changes was the elevation of one of the traps in order to obtain a target more level in flight, and in contrast to the rising target from the other trap.

"Noting the appeal that this form of shooting held for all who had tried their hand at it, Mr. Foster and the publishers of 'National Sportsman' and 'Hunting & Fishing' became convinced that a development of the idea could be made nationally acceptable. With that thought in mind, a few changes were made in shooting rules, including double target shooting at stations 1, 2, 6 and 7. A new set of rules was drawn and the sport was introduced to the shooting public in February, 1936, and they govern the game today."

Jimmy Robinson one of America's leading authorities on both forms of sport, advised:

"Skeet uses the same clay birds that have so long been standard for trapshooting, throwing them in the same way, with the same style of powerful spring catapult, called a trap. The targets—actually molded of filler and pitch and devoid of clay—are saucer shaped and thrown with their convex side up. The trap gives the target a horizontal rotary motion, which causes it to plane. In flight this animated target approximates the swift, steady flight of a quail.

"A standard target is 4½ inches in diameter, weighs about 3¼ ounces and breaks, or pulverizes when struck with bird-shot. Guns used are 12, 20 and 28 gauges and .410 bore. In match shooting there are gauge classes. The standard skeet load for a 12-gauge is 3 drams of powder and 1 1/8 ounces of No. 9 chilled shot.

"Two traps are used, each in a separate small house. The houses face each other 40 yards apart. Each trap throws its target at and over the house of the other trap—always in the same line, at the same elevation. Seventeen out of each 25 are thrown one at a time, the rest in pairs.

"Incidentally, if you are a game shot, your first reaction to skeet pairs is likely to be hostile. You try it for a while. Then you are a skeet shooter.

"Skeet shooting, in comparison with trap-shooting, is comparatively new, but it has had a remarkable growth. Before World War II about 50,000 Americans were devoted to skeet shooting, of whom about 2 per cent were women. But the sport was moving along into remarkable popularity when the war, which had dried up the supply of ammunition and limited the supply of new guns, halted the progress.

"Shells cost skeet shooters 14 cents each, and 50,000,000, or thereabouts, are used per year. Targets cost about 4 cents each, so every time a shooter fires a gun, the cost is 18 cents. A hundred shots a day would make it $18 per day. The shooters must have hunting jackets and, of course, guns, and they spend a lot of money travelling to traps.

"Skeet, only a little more than 20 years old as a standard sport when war broke out, was the one which the Army and Navy decided to draw upon chiefly for instructors in small arms gunnery. Some of the greatest skeet shooters in the United States went into action early and schooled millions of boys in the proper use of a gun. It was a remarkable tribute to skeet that its marksmen were preferred as tutors over those of shooting sports that have been in existence for a great many years.

"Some of the grandest fellows ever identified with skeet shooting were in action during the war. Bob Canfield, one of the best 20-gauge shots in American history, reached the rank of major during the war. He was killed in action. The fate that befell him was the same that was met by so many other famous skeet shooters and, when the war ended, many fine shots of the other years no longer were able to answer the call to action.

FAMOUS SKEET SHOOTERS

Men

Louis Gordon, Texarkana, Ark.; D.W. Conway, Clint, Tex.; Francis Ellis, Jacksonville, Fla.; Mickey Michaelis, Galveston, Tex.; Grant Ilseng, Houston, Tex.; Johnny Garrison, Joplin, Mo.; Tom Sanfilipo, San Francisco; John Dalton Jr., Chevy Chase, Md.; Col. C.T. Edwinson, Austin, Tex.; Frank Dublin, Jacksonville, Tex.; Tommy Spicola, Tampa, Fla., and Ed Calhoun, Salisbury, Md.

Also, Richard Shaughnessy, Boston; Don Sperry, Flint, Mich.; Frank R. Kelly, East Orange, N.J.; Alex Kerr, Beverly Hills, Calif.; Robert Parker, Tulsa, Okla.; H. Lutcher Brown, San Antonio, Tex.; D. Lee Braun, Austin, Tex.;

Gerald Batten, Chicago; Jack Lindsay, Oklahoma City, Okla.; Max Marcum, Louisville, Ky.; Charles Poulton, San Antonio; Henry B. Joy, Detroit; Walter Dinger, Tulsa, Okla.; L.S. Pratt, Indianapolis; Odis Walding, Los Angeles, Dr. LeRoy Childs, Lake Kerr, Fla.; Robert Stack, Los Angeles; S.L. Hutcheson, New York, and William Clayton, Calvin, Okla. Plus, James A. Bellows, Lackland A.F.B., Tex.; Kenneth Sedlecky, Baldwin, Mich.; and Harry Stilwell, Oreland, Pa.

Women

Mrs. Leon Mandel, Chicago; Mrs. Pauline Amburgey, Odessa, Tex.; Nancy Burrus, Dallas, Tex.; Mrs. Fred Alford, Dallas, Tex.; Anne Marasovich, Fabens, Tex.; Mrs. Dorothy Stoner, Los Angeles; Mrs. E.L. Jenkins, Harlingen, Tex.; Mrs. Fay Demand, Scottsdale, Ariz.; Mrs. Alphonso Ragland Jr., Dallas, Tex., and Mrs. Marie Ellis, Jacksonville, Fla.

Others include Abbie Ingalls, Hot Springs, Va.; Elizabeth Small, Detroit, Viola Siedhoff, Wichita, Kan.; Pat Laursen, Akron, Ohio; Mrs. M.L. Smythe, Aurora, Ohio; Mrs. J.A. LaFore, Haverford, Pa.; Mrs. Ann Hecker, Tucson, Ariz., and Carole Simmons, Kansas City, Mo.

Also, Kathless McGinn, Houston, Tex.; Mrs. Katherine Dinning, Ruxton, Md.; Mrs. Max Thomas, Dallas, Tex.; Mrs. Marjorie Annan, Aspen, Colo.; and Mrs. James Coulter, Lake Forest, Ill.

NATIONAL 12 GAUGE CHAMPIONS

(Previously all-bore, all-gauge)

(Courtesy of Mike Henderson, National Skeet Shooting Association)   Score

1935—L.S. Pratt	244 x 250
1936—Richard Shaughnessy	248 x 250
1937—Odis Walding	248 x 250
1938—Henry B. Joy	250 x 250
1939—Walter Dinger	247 x 250
1940—Richard Shaughnessy	249 x 250
1941—Charles Poulton	250 x 250
1942—Dr. LeRoy Childs	250 x 250

1943—45—No competition	
1946—Alex Kerr	250 x 250
1947—Dr. R.F. Westermeier	250 x 250
1948—Sgt. Glenn Van Buren	249 x 250
1949—Sgt. Glenn Van Buren	250 x 250
1950—Francis Ellis	250 x 250
1951—Sgt. Glenn Van Buren	250 x 250
1952—Maj. Harry Trimble	250 x 250
1953—Capt. Charles Bagley	250 x 250
1954—Howard F. Confer	249 x 250
1955—Alex H. Kerr	250 x 250
1956—Jack Horner	250 x 250
1957—M/Sgt. Harold E. Myers	250 x 250
1959—Robert Shuley	250 x 250
1960—Peter Candy	250 x 250
1961—William Hays Rogers	250 x 250
1962—Kenneth D. Gilbert	250 x 250
1963—James A. Bellows	250 x 250
1964—Robert Shuley	250 x 250
1965—James Prall	250 x 250
1966—Vernie Surber	250 x 250
1967—James A. Bellows	250 x 250
1968—Allen F. Buntrock, Thomas J. Heffron Jr. (tie)	250 x 250
1969—Walt Badorck	250 x 250
1970—John Durbin	250 x 250
1971—Dick Bienapfl	250 x 250
1972—Tony Rosetti	250 x 250

CHAMPION OF CHAMPIONS

(4 guns, 25 targets each)

1961—Miner Cliett, Childersburg, Ala.
1962—S/Ldr. B.C. Hartman, Ottawa, Ontario
1963—Kenneth L. Pendergras, Jacksonville, Fla.
1964—George Rasmussen Jr., Palm Beach, Fla.
1965—C.W.O. George Young, Marine Corps
1966—Dr. Eugene Donnelly, Binghamton, N.Y.
1967—Kenny Barnes Jr., Bakersfield, Calif.
1968—James W. Austin, Honolulu, Hawaii
1969—Carl Poston, Sr., Chattanooga, Tenn.
1970—John D'Alessio, Penns Grove, N.J.
1971—Harry Stilwell, Oreland, Pa.
1972—Bruce Kinkner, Phoenix, Ariz.

SHUFFLEBOARD

Since the turn of the century, shuffleboard has been gradually gaining as a participant sport in this country. It owes a great deal for its development to resorts, which feature courts as a means of recreation for guests, both young and old. Shuffleboard is a derivative of lawn bowling but its manner of play is quite similar to curling which is played on ice. The early history of the game is somewhat beclouded.

One historian states it originated in Persia in about 1700 A.D., but several writers fix its beginning in England, about the 13th Century, and quote some regal edicts to authenticate the date.

While the game never was banned in England, various rulers considered it a frivolous occupation and a waste of time and royalty let it be known that play generated its displeasure.

The game, at its peak, in the early centuries in England, never was greatly popular and there is not much mention of it except that play usually was on hard, dirt-packed courts. They had various names for it, depending upon the section where it was played. While "shovel board" was most commonly used, it also was known as "shove groat" and "slide groat."

The Scots, who devised curling on ice, were

fairly enthusiastic about shuffleboard, and it is possible they created the game. In curling, a stone is pushed over the ice toward an object. In shuffleboard, disks are pushed along a smooth surface toward an object.

There is no record when shuffleboard was introduced to the United States. It must have been a sport of some prominence early in the 19th Century, since it was denounced as "a gambler's pastime" in New England in 1845. Public play of the game was prohibited in certain parts of New England.

There is not much history about the game in the United States after its banning, nor is there any reiterated mention of it in England through the middle of the 19th Century. The trail of the game is picked up again in the 1870's, when it became a chief feature of entertainment for passengers on the P & O ocean liners, that sailed between England and Australia.

It became popular as a means of diversion on long voyages and was adopted for ships on other runs. The decks were wide enough and long enough to provide courts and on calm days passengers played the game.

In the late 1890's, shuffleboard was resumed in the United States, but was played chiefly by children. The sport is best when played on a smooth surface, but it can be played on grass, as many children were doing at the turn of the 20th Century.

The present-day (1973) game of shuffleboard, and its current rules and regulations, were started in 1913 by Mr. and Mrs. Robert Ball of Daytona Beach, Fla. They had seen the game played on ships and decided to offer it to the guests of their hotel. Their first court was marked out on the sidewalk in front of the hotel, the Lyndhurst. From that beginning shuffleboard grew to its present popularity.

The game quickly grew in favor among the natives of Florida. The tourists took the idea back home and influenced neighbors to play. As the game increased in popularity and it was observed that it was played according to neighborhood rules, rather than in standardized fashion, a group of enthusiasts got together in 1931, formed the National Shuffleboard Association, rewrote the rules and the game blossomed.

Since at that time many new playgrounds were being created in cities throughout the land, the shuffleboard people influenced the officials to put in shuffleboard courts and supply equipment. As the sport required only moderate exertion, and put a premium on accuracy, it was played by persons of all ages. However, the recreational game, as played by most elderly persons, is not the same as the tournament game played by the younger experts. David Willoughby's book *The Super Athletes* states: "Shuffleboard is probably the least appreciated of all outdoor sports, in its genuine tournament form. Like golf and

bowling, it is non-athletic in the sense of not requiring agility, speed of foot, or unusual strength. However, besides the physical skills involved in the spectacular caroms and angled combinations that the leading players make, the game includes a great deal of hard hitting, which taxes the endurance of a tournament player in singles competition. It is estimated that, in clearing the board, shuffleboard discs travel at more than 60 miles per hour." And unlike golf and bowling, tournament shuffleboard is a game of very complex and intricate strategy.

As early as 1939, before the playground movement had gained its greatest momentum, it was estimated that there were 25,000 shuffleboard players in Florida, and perhaps 200,000 throughout the nation. In 1973, the Florida Shuffleboard Association reported 300 clubs within the state, with 2,913 courts and more than 55,000 members.

In 1951 a survey by the National Recreation Association disclosed the existence of about 5,000 public courts in 455 cities. It was estimated more recently that there were about five million participants. The National Shuffleboard Association reports courts in 39 states, British Columbia, Ontario, and Mexico.

Although much organizational progress has occurred in recent years in California and Arizona, tournament shuffleboard has been for more than forty years primarily a Florida game, and players have come from all over the United States to compete in the Florida winter tournaments. The winter national championships, both singles and doubles, have always been held in Florida. A summer national championship, with a much smaller entry, has been held annually in Michigan, New Hampshire, New Jersey, Ohio, and North Carolina. There are also senior championships for players 60 years of age or older. Open championships have been won at ages from 18 to 60, but the average age of the winners is about 48.

Some years ago, the late Colonel Peter Bullard compiled an All-Time Rating of the leading shufflers, giving points for all Florida statewide expert tournaments and also the summer national championships, from 1928 onward. An updated version of this rating is included herewith.

In 1960, after a seasonal rating was inaugurated, a Masters tournament was sponsored by Joseph Clancy, and later by Harold and Beulah Dunbar, which was restricted to the eight leading men and the eight leading women on the seasonal rating. This is always held at the world's largest shuffleboard club, in St. Petersburg, Florida, at the conclusion of the regular winter season.

(Courtesy of George R. Weaver, 767 21st Ave. North, St. Petersburg, Fla. 33704)

NATIONAL CHAMPIONS
Open Division—Winter Tournament
Men

1931—Carl Bailey
1932—33—Donald Boyle
1934—35—Joseph Norris
1936—Charles Edwards
1937—Wayne Miller
1938—Ray Collins
1939—Wilbert Custer
1940—Charles Edwards
1941—Henry Badum
1942—43—George Johnson
1944—45—No competition
1946—Leslie Vincent
1947—48—Carl Spillman
1949—Carl Breece
1950—Carl Spillman
1951—Henry Badum
1952—Webster Smith
1953—Henry Badum
1954—Larry Schoch
1955—Farrell Bruner
1956—Carl Spillman
1957—Mark Brashares
1958—William Folberth
1959—Farrell Bruner
1960—William Folberth
1961—Mark Brashares
1962—Maurice Krupp
1963—65—William Folberth
1966—Ted Matthews
1967—68—William Folberth
1969—70—Lewis Tansky
1971—Jay Snoddy
1972—Rom Schneider
1973—Lewis Tansky

Women

1933—Katherine Craft
1934—Josephine Matthews
1935—Eva Collins
1936—Augusta McFadden
1937—Josephine Matthews
1938—Martha Martin
1939—Rosalinda Stubbs
1940—Olive McArthur
1941—Bunny Hoover
1942—43—Florence Johnson
1944—45—No competition
1946—Katherine Holm
1947—Carrie Wilcox
1948—Mary Scalise
1949—Florence Johnson
1950—Mary Scalise
1951—52—Carrie Wilcox
1953—Olive McArthur
1954—Mae Hall
1955—57—Miriam McDavid
1958—Mae Hall
1959—Mary Scalise

1960—67—Mae Hall
1968—Clara Hipp
1969—71—Mae Hall
1972—Kate Gruber
1973—Mary Eldridge

Open Division—Summer Tournament
Men

1931—Carl Breece
1932—Alvin Notestine
1933—35—Dwight Hubbard
1936—Charles Edwards
1937—Lew Bensley
1938—40—Dwight Hubbard
1941—Forrest Skiver
1942—46—No competition
1947—Jack Pedersen
1948—Carl Spillman
1949—Leslie Vincent
1950—Frank Henderson
1951—Lyle Broadbent
1952—Henry Andringa
1953—Paul Lennox
1954—Larry Schoch
1955—Alvin Notestine
1956—Jack Gladney
1957—Carl Spillman
1958—59—Maurice Krupp
1960—61—David Karaska
1962—Lyle Wood
1963—Ernest Glenn
1964—Aime Wood
1965—Ernest Glenn
1966—Webster Smith
1967—Ernest Glenn
1968—Jay Snoddy
1969—Lary Faris
1970—Merritt Gordon
1971—Jay Snoddy
1972—Lary Faris

Women

1932—Celia Logan
1933—Gertrude Notestine
1934—Dorothy Edwards
1935—36—Marie Kalember
1937—Augusta McFadden
1938—39—Gertrude Notestine
1940—Bess Geist
1941—Augusta McFadden
1942—46—No competition
1947—Dixie Riddle
1948—Lucille Spillman
1949—Esther Winter
1950—51—Carrie Wilcox
1952—Janet Smith
1953—Esther Winter
1954—Josephine O'Neil
1955—Miriam McDavid
1956—Marion Wheeler
1957—Anna Davis
1958—Mae Hall
1959—Shirley Schneider

1960—Mildred Winans
1961—Elsie Hawkins
1962—Claire Whyte
1963—Josephine Gunn
1964—Ruth Leonard
1965—Mabel Glenn
1966—Mildred Haskin
1967—Mary Shiley
1968—Marie Sutton
1969—Helen Krichbaum
1970—Jean Fisher
1971—Mary Eldridge
1972—Betty Stone

Doubles
Winter
Men

1962—63—Webster Smith—Farrell Bruner
1964—Maynard Page—Hervey Berard
1965—Webster Smith—Farrell Bruner
1966—William Folberth—Henry Andringa
1967—Lew Tansky—Bob Litts
1968—Lyle Cass—Audrey Haley
1969—William Folberth—Henry Andringa
1970—Robert Litts—Jay Snoddy
1971—Harold Burke—Dennis Biroc
1972—73—Robert Litts—Jay Snoddy

Women

1962—Marion Wheeler—Helen Hartnett
1963—Mae Hall—Bess Henderson
1964—Elsie Hawkins—Lucy Magee
1965—Ruth Troeger—Lee Bechtoldt
1966—Ethel Wood—Bethel Smith
1967—Sara Chase—Lucy Magee
1968—69—Mae Hall—Mary Eldridge
1970—Mae Hall—Wilma Krieg
1971—Betty Stone—Jean Fisher
1972—Mae Hall—Lucy Magee
1973—Betty Stone—Audrey Haley

Masters
Men

1960—63—Webster Smith
1964—Lewis Tansky
1965—66—Robert Litts
1967—Jay Snoddy
1968—69—Robert Litts
1970—Jay Snoddy
1971—72—Robert Litts
1973—Jay Snoddy

Women

1960—Mary Luhn
1961—Mary Scalise
1962—68—Mae Hall
1969—Mary Eldridge
1970—71—Mae Hall
1972—Mary Eldridge
1973—Mae Hall

Colonel Bullard's All-Time Rating
1928—1973

Men's Singles	Points
1. Carl Spillman	726
2. Webster Smith	693
3. William Folberth	589
4. Henry Badum	376
5. Lewis Tansky	235
6. Dwight Hubbard	227
7. Farrell Bruner	218
8. Frank Henderson	217
9. Alvin Notestine	213
10. Rexford Farewell	212

Men's Doubles	Points
1. Webster Smith	542
2. Farrell Bruner	365
3. William Folberth	330
4. Robert Litts	303
5. Lyle Cass	301
6. Jay Snoddy	290
7. Lewis Tansky	282
8. Henry Andringa	281
9. Carl Spillman	277
10. Howard Hawkins	168

Women's Singles	Points
1. Mae Hall	1,153
2. Mary Scalise	630
3. Amy Close	385
4. Bess Henderson	362
5. Florence Spink	287
6. Janet Smith	273
7. Esther Kinsella	270
8. Audrey Haley	265
9. Edna Robbins	238
10. Carrie Wilcox	225

Women's Doubles	Points
1. Mae Hall	463
2. Janet Smith	426
3. Mary Scalise	254
4. Audrey Haley	235
5. Elsie Hawkins	202
6. Edna Robbins	199
7. Mary Hinkle	188
8. Bess Henderson	183
9. Wilma Krieg	177
10. Mabel Glenn	149

BASIC RULES

A shuffleboard court is 52 feet long, 6 feet wide, and the surface may be concrete or terrazzo. The composition discs are 1 inch thick, 6 in. diameter, and the weight must be not less than 11½ nor more than 15 ounces. Eight disks make a set—four red, four black. The stick is called a cue. The overall length is 6 feet 3 inches. At the base of the cue is a pushing device, half moon in shape, into which the disks can be fitted and then pushed along the court.

The neutral zone of the court is the 12 feet in dead center, marked by 2 lines. The playing zones thus are 20 feet each. About 3 feet back of each neutral line is the beginning of a triangle, which measures 8 feet from tip to bottom. Each triangle is divided into 6 parts, marked with lines. The player who brings a disk to rest in the top space of the triangle scores 10 points. There are four squares beneath the top of the triangle. Two represent scoring value of 8 points each; the other two 7 points. The sixth and bottom division of the triangle, stretching all the way across the triangle, is the minus square. Any disk or disks ending there penalize a player 10 points for each, which is deducted from his score.

The game can be played singles or doubles. The players alternate in shoving the disks.

The strategy of the game is to knock a rival disk out of scoring position and to replace it with your own, and, of course, try to put the rival disk into the "Minus Ten" department.

Game can be 50, 75 or 100 points.

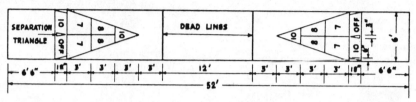

Shuffleboard Court. (Taken from "Sports for Recreation," edited by E. D. Mitchell, A. S. Barnes and Company, New York.)

SKIING

Skiing is both a sport and big business in the United States. From a meager start, it has grown by leaps and bounds in the number of resorts catering to the devotees of the slats. Many wealthy persons were influential in rise of resorts. They invested money in skiing for recreation rather than for income and as a result this country boasts many magnificent skiing areas open to the public.

The sport has many intriguing features that attract enthusiasts, accounting for its growing popularity over the last 25 years. Skiing is challenging to the beginner and expert; it offers beautiful natural settings for recreation; it offers a chance to speed, and it provides pleasant surroundings and opportunities for friendship.

The earliest ski runners presumably were bones from large animals, strapped to the shoes with leather thongs, as were snowshoes. When man sought a faster way of proceeding over frozen wastes, where the land was flat, or progressing over the icy surface of lakes or rivers, he, no doubt, used smaller bones, and those probably, were the pioneer skates, the joints of the bones being smoothed so as to produce a flat surface, which permitted a swift, gliding motion.

There appears to be basis for the conclusion that skis were used in the northern part of Europe and in Asia prior to the Christian Era, but there is little in the way of definite fact to substantiate the date. A pair of skis, pronounced the oldest known to the world, are in the Djugarden Museum at Stockholm, Sweden. Guesses have been made that the skis might be at least 5,000 years old.

The analytical method of determining the ages of ancient ski finds was developed by the Swed-ish scholars, Lennart von Post and Erik Granlund. Through research by famous ethnologists, the ages of many skis found in the bogs of Norway, Sweden and Finland have been determined. A few of those finds and their determined ages establish that the ski found at Hoting in Angermanland is estimated to be between 4,000 and 5,000 years old; the Riihimaki ski found in southern Finland dates back to the Bronze Age; the Arnas ski found in Arnas, Dalarna, Sweden, is estimated to be about 2,500 years old and skis from Kalvtrask in Vasterbotten, Sweden, date back to 2000 B.C., while Evreboe ski pollen is presumed to be about 2,500 years old.

Skada, the giant goddess who in legend was married to Njord, one of the Scandinavian gods, is known as the Goddess of Ski (Odurrdis) in the northern countries of Europe. Uller, the god of winter, always is pictured walking on skis with curved toes, which created the idea that he was so huge that he trod the snow with ships lashed to his feet.

So far as actual history is concerned, skis were first used in warfare in the Battle of Oslo in Norway in 1200 A.D. King Sverre of Sweden equipped his scouts with skis and sent them to reconnoiter the enemy, camped in deep snow, which had marooned him. This makes it appear that skis were not numerous even then, else the entire armies on both sides would have been equipped with them, enabling the troops to navigate through snow and over ice in flat countries.

Apparently the Swedes, after 1200, must have learned a lesson as to the value of skis in warfare. Going into war in 1521 and in later conflicts in 1576, 1590 and 1610 A.D., they equipped all the troops either with skis or snowshoes.

In the 1521 war, the Swedes stretched animal skins between two skis, placed injured comrades on them and, in this fashion, carried them off the fields—the first known stretchers.

The bone-runner ski had no standard size. It was not turned up at the ends, this being impossible. Centuries after the beginning of the Christian Era, wood was substituted. The standard length of the wooden ski was about 7 feet 6 inches. The runners were about 2 inches thick 5 inches wide and about 1 foot of the front end of the ski was turned up, just the way the ski is shown in drawings that deal with legendary gods of the north countries.

Obviously, the drawings were not made until long after wooden skis came into existence, although the gods and goddesses predate them by many centuries. The comparatively modern artists just took the skis which existed in their time, fitted them to the feet of the legendary and paid no heed to the contradiction that their work would bring in the history of the gods and goddesses and the wooden ski with the turned-up toe.

The ski, coming into use when wood was used in their making, sometimes had nothing but a wooden surface. Others had the blade part of the ski covered with strips of thin goat or sheep's skin. Such skis served through the early years and no radical change was made in them until the 16th Century. Then the Swedes, preparing for battle, shortened some of the skis to about 3 feet and made them into a combination of ski and snowshoe, although retaining many of the old style 7-foot 6-inch skis.

Skiing was introduced into Central Europe, via Austria, in 1590, and since then has spread to North America, Japan, Australia, New Zealand, the mountainous regions of South America, the slopes of the snow-capped peaks in Hawaii and parts of India.

Going into the 19th Century, those who used skis for serious purposes also found they could be turned into means for sport. This resulted in impromptu races. Next were some jumping contests, off short hills. There was started in Norway an annual get-together of ski enthusiasts in the 1850's and one and two-day carnivals of sport were conducted.

Along in 1860 the royal family of Norway took cognizance of jumping as a sport. The king donated a trophy to be awarded the champion and appointed a committee to draft rules for annual tournaments, the king designating that it should be in the month of February and that it be at Holmenkollen, near Christiana (now Oslo), where there was a long sloping hill, ideal for a take-off.

Eventually, this tournament became the greatest national sports event in Norway. The "Norwegian Ski Derby" was originated to test the durability of skiers in cross-country racing. Later other forms of ski contests were added to the program.

It is not known who brought the first pair of skis to North America, nor whether the first pair was imported, was created by Indians in Canada or fashioned by settlers from Sweden and Norway. The snowshoe has been known for many generations in Canada, and those who used snowshoes may also have constructed skis for use down steep mountain sides.

For one thing, it is known that during the rush to the Pacific Coast for gold in the 1850's skis were very much in evidence in the snow fastnesses of the Sierra Nevadas.

In Canadian history there is a record of a snow-ice carnival in 1759 and skis, as well as snowshoes, are mentioned as having been put to use. There is nothing written about skis in the United States prior to 1840, when it was stated that "wooden blades, for use on ice and snow, were brought from Norway and were used by the immigrants in the northern part of the Atlantic Seaboard," this perhaps meaning skis, brought by Norwegians to their new homes in upper New England.

One of the most fabulous skiers known to the world was an American—John A. (Snowshoe) Thomson, who carried the United States mail in the high, snow-clad Sierras for about 20 years.

Thomson's route was Placerville, Calif., to Carson City, Nev., and return. The distance was 91 miles and Thomson had to carry a pack of about 100 pounds each way. He began as a mail carrier soon after the California gold rush of 1849, which had attracted him to the West, but brought him no riches.

Thomson was a native of Norway. He learned skiing there, and also the value of snowshoes, as skiing was then called, in traveling over soft, snowbound terrain. His salary was $200 a month and, thanks to Thomson, there was a round-trip regular mail delivery every few days in deepest winter from the East, via Carson City, to California. He usually negotiated the route, up and down high mountains, through appalling drifts of snow, regardless of thermometer reading, within three days, taking about a week for each round trip.

Thomson, after 20 years, felt Congress owed him a debt of $6,000, or so, for underpayment. He filed a claim. Congress sent him a nice letter of thanks—but no check. Citizens, many of whom owed their lives to Thomson's daring rescues, when not on the mail run, subscribed a small sum for him, to show gratitude. Thomson, broken up because of the Congressional rebuff, never recovered from the blow. He died a short time later and is buried in Genoa, Calif.

The first jumpers known to the United States were two young brothers—Torgus and Mikkel Hemmestvedt—who lived in Red Wing, Minn., and gained local fame, which eventually spread throughout the state, by jumping from reasonably high hills, without breaking their necks. That was in 1880. Their playmates soon followed their example and ski jumping became the sport thrill of winter in that part of Minnesota.

The first ski club in the United States was formed by Scandinavians at Berlin, N.H., in January, 1872. It has continued its existence all through the years, but under several different names and now is known as the Nansen Ski Club, in honor of the famous Norwegian explorer. The next came into existence in 1895, and was formed by a group of engineers at Altoona, Pa.

The third ski club was organized late in 1885 at St. Paul, followed almost immediately by the "Den Norske Turn og Skiforening," which was a Minneapolis organization.

On Jan. 19, 1886, twenty-eight Norwegians met at Red Wing, formed the Aurora Ski Club and decided upon a tournament to be held in Red Wing on Feb. 8, 1887. Among the contestants at that first governed tournament were the Hemmestvedt brothers, with Mikkel winning the men's jumping championship.

On Feb. 21, 1904, after the sport of ski jumping had been dormant for about a decade, officials of various ski clubs organized a national body and determined that the contests, scheduled for the next day (Feb. 22), at Ishpeming, Mich., should be conducted as the "National Ski Tournament." Thus, the National Ski Association was founded, with 17 charter members, all from the Middle West.

The name of the organization was changed, in mid-century, to the United States Ski Association, with headquarters at Colorado Springs.

The growth of the organization was healthy going into 1932. There were clubs in most of the states where there was considerable snow and in 1932 a number of interclub and sectional championship tournaments were conducted.

The third Winter Olympics, at Lake Placid, N.Y., in 1932, were attended by many who never before had seen ski exhibitions. The sport caught their fancy. Many returned home determined to take up some form of skiing the following winter—1932-1933—and, as a result, thousands of people who previously had been in the habit of going to the south in the winter, shifted to the northern ares to give skiing a try.

The growth of the sport from that time was remarkable. It picked up devotees by the thousands, then tens of thousands and estimates as to the army of ski enthusiasts now range from 2,000,000 to 3,000,000. Essentially, it is a sport for the young, and the young are in majority among the contestants. But the middle-aged and the elders like the ski sports as spectacles.

The Federation Internationale de Ski (F.I.S.), the first world-wide ruling body for the sport was founded in 1924 with a membership of 26 countries. By 1968, the membership rose to 50 nations. Through the group's direction came competitive competition on a universal scale in downhill, slalom, jumping and cross-country events.

The initial impetus to the formation of the F.I.S. seems to have arisen from constant pressure by prominent European sportsmen for the addition of winter sports to the Olympic program. In 1924, the first Winter Olympic Games were held at Chamonix, France, under the auspices of the International Olympic Committee. Since then the Winter Games have been a regular part of the schedule of the quadrennial competition.

Few sports have gained so greatly in favor in so short a time. The remarkable part is that the growth had to be limited, so far as devotees were concerned, to those areas, generally near the Canadian border, where conditions for skiing were suitable.

Back in the 1920's, the ski enthusiasts numbered no more than 3,500 or 4,000. There were about 75 clubs devoted to the sport, but most were located in the northern part of the Mid West, in upper New England and in the northern sections of New York State.

The Winter Olympics at Lake Placid brought about the first big-time staging of skiing in the United States.

Ski contests are out in the open and as a rule there is no effort to charge admission fees for choice spots near the landing places of jumpers, or the finish line of the races. But the international popularity of the sport is shown by the fact that when the Winter Olympic Games were staged at Garmisch-Partenkirchen in the German Alps in February, 1936, with ski contests featuring the programs, the attendance was 155,000 for the entire show, lasting several days.

An even more emphatic testimonial to the attraction of ski contestants was written during the winter of 1936-1937, when a show at Soldier Field, Chicago, drew 57,000 admissions.

Prior to World War II, indoor ski exhibitions were staged, too, and they lured large crowds, although there was little chance for the jumpers to make leaps from high places, or for the experts in other forms of the sport to demonstrate their skill in real fashion.

Despite the fact that the athlete is warmly clothed and that most of the spectators, who number from 5,000 to 35,000 or 40,000 for important contests, are suitably garbed, the skiers and the onlookers often must take plenty of punishment from the elements to gain their enjoyment. They perhaps have to risk more discomfort than even rugged football players, and the crowds. But they have an enthusiasm that makes them willing to dare anything and to brave anything to gain their fun, either on skis or as watchers of thrilling contests.

Thirty or so years ago there were no more than 15 or 20 places in the United States which provided hills for the jumpers, or suitable terrain for those devoted to other forms of the sport. Few inns kept open to house the ski clan, and after the day of sport was done, the participants were faced with the prospect of traveling many miles for food and shelter.

Today skiing is big business, both from a sport and a recreational standpoint. From the rugged White Mountains of New Hampshire to the lofty peaks of the Sierra Nevadas in California, the country's snowbelt is dotted with resorts, lavish and informal, that make it a billion-dollar industry. Even farms have seen in snow an added source of revenue for the off-season. The owners have hoisted inexpensive rope tows on upper stretches of pasture slopes and chased the cows out of the red barn so that skiers would have a place to drink and talk.

Since ski jumping has been the most publicized phase, the ordinary reader inclines to the idea that the sport begins and ends there. But there are other major forms of skiing and the jumping part, so far as the skier is concerned, is merely the most sensational.

The other phases are:

1. Downhill—most dangerous.
2. Slalom—most graceful.
3. Cross-Country—most grueling.

Jumpers appear to be placing their lives in jeopardy every time they take off into space. But serious accidents are few and fatalities rare because the "flyer" is an accomplished skier and in taking off from lofty inclines is well equipped to do so. The proficient jumper has good balance and knows how to judge flight. Should he fall, he is prepared to do so properly, avoiding serious injury. To the spectator, it appears extremely difficult; to the jumper, it is a pleasant experience.

A jumper is in the air from 3 to 10 seconds, depending upon the steepness of the landing slope. The longer and steeper the slope, naturally, the longer the jump.

In the earliest years of jumping in the United States the record was 82 feet, made by Thomas Walters at Ishpeming, Mich. in 1904. In later years Torger Tokle came from Norway to rank among the greatest leapers ever seen in the United States. While Tokle confined himself to the easy slopes in Eastern America, his jumps were not extremely long. Others, who made their leaps from the high, sharp hills in the West usually outdistanced him. Thus Tokle, with jumps of 150 feet, did not seem to belong in the same class as the experts who were doing 225, 250 or more feet in the West.

In 1941, Tokle made a visit to Leavenworth, Wash., where the slopes are sharp, and hung up a new American mark of 273 feet. Later that year he bettered that with 288, at Hyak, Wash. In 1942 he went to Iron Mountain, Mich., and pushed the American record to 289 feet on the most famous artificial ski-jump site in the world.

Tokle, in his time, was the outstanding performer in the Eastern United States. He answered the call to duty in World War II late in 1942 and was a leader in the ski patrol. The Sportsmanship Brotherhood Trophy was awarded to him posthumously for his outstanding influence in behalf of clean sportsmanship in the United States. Tokle was killed during combat in the mountains of Italy on March 19, 1945.

In his short period of campaigning before he died to "help by adopted land to remain the champion of the small and downtrodden nations of Europe," Sergeant Tokle broke 24 hill records while winning 42 or 48 tournaments.

Since Tokle's record leap, the United States mark has been shattered a dozen times and the current record is 345 feet. Jerry Martin, the North American champion, established that distance in 1971 at Iron Mountain, Mich.

It is interesting to note that records are recognized only for the specific hills they are created on. But since the public dotes on national and world marks, the skiing world resorts to calling long flights such; in reality, they are only records for each specific slide.

Yugoslavia was a favorite place for the famous jumpers in Europe prior to World War II, and at Planica Josef Bradl of Austria made an official world record of 350.96 feet in 1936. Just how much more spectacular has become jumping and just how much sharper are the slopes now used is shown by the fact that the first world record, made by Nils Gjestvang in 1902, was 134 feet—over 216 feet shorter than Bradl's mark.

The end of the war found the jumpers setting their sights on the distance marks. Improved technique and the construction of higher and longer hills helped considerably. Fritz Tschannen of Switzerland soared 393.7 at the old proving ground in Planica in 1948. Two years later a Swede, Dan Netzel, was on hand when Germany's Oberstdorf Hill was tested and he cleared 135 meters (442.7 feet). On March 2, 1951, Tauno Luiro, 19-year-old Finnish electrician, made a sensational leap of 456 feet, the longest flight in ski-jumping history, at Oberstdorf.

In the opinion of many, Alf Engen was, perhaps, the greatest all-around skier the United States has ever known. Engen was in the spotlight in the years preceding the Second World War. When he was a youth, he was beating the veterans. When he was recognized as an old-timer, he beat the youngsters. He won more than a dozen national titles of one kind or another. For a long time he held the jumping record. He was a marvel at cross-country, the spectacular downhill and the slalom.

The United States Ski Association has supervised the expanding army of United States addicts. It has influenced the erection of ski runs in places where none ever was contemplated. It has done much to influence hotels and inn-keepers to remain open throughout the winter. It has divided itself into regional associations, each having jurisdiction over its territory and being responsible to the national body. The officers of the divisional groups elect the national officers.

Some 500 individual clubs with approximately 50,000 members make up the regional associations. It has been the custom of the associations to hold regional championships, and the winners and some of the runners-up usually qualify for the national championships. All such tournaments are strictly amateur. The competitions also include events for women and juniors.

HOW TITLES ARE DECIDED

Jumping

Under U.S.S.A. rules, the winner of a jumping contest is determined on the point system. It is possible for a man to make the longest, as well as the second longest jump, and still fail to win the event. Each contestant is allowed two jumps. These are judged by three officials.

Each official is permitted to cast 40 votes for each jump—or as many of those 40 as he wishes to cast. A jumper could score all the votes—240—for the event, but it is not written any-where that a jumper ever made a perfect score.

Points are voted for four reasons: (1) distance; (2) courage; (3) control while riding the inrun while in flight, while landing and coming to a finish, and (4) form, or gracefulness.

If a man makes the two longest jumps, he automatically gets 60 points for each, or a total of 120. But he still can be defeated if he was out of control during the trip, or if he was awkward in the way he held his arms, or in the sway of his body, or if he became jittery during any part of the trip and failed to show 100 per cent courage. Any of these faults might reduce him to a total of 80 points for those three features, making his grand total only 200 points. In jumping, form counts equally with distance in importance.

Downhill Racing

The purpose of downhill racing is, as the name expresses, leaving a starting point and seeing how fast one can reach the finish, i.e., a race against time. In modern days, the quality of competition has become so keen that in international events as well as major ones in each country, added obstacles are included in the "straight-down" tests. Steep pitches, artificial bumps and ruts, etc., are created so that the skier who takes the biggest risk and is able to maintain his speed through the straightest line will be the winner.

When courses become too hazardous, owing to icy conditions, or some other reason, control and direction flags are used. If the racer does not follow the flags, he is disqualified. In recent years there has been a movement to eliminate downhill races for women, or control them to the extent

of limiting them to a giant slalom. Even in men's races, the inclination is to place more stress on slalom and giant slalom running, since the premium of high speed under hazardous conditions in downhill racing has resulted in numerous accidents.

According to Federation Internationale de Ski rules, no downhill course shall include uphill or level terrain. A trail shall include a fair proportion of steep and difficult terrain. The total vertical drop shall not be less than 2,500 feet for men and 1,500 feet for women in this country.

Slalom

A Slalom course is defined by pairs of flags through which the contestants must ski from start to finish. The purpose of this type of racing is to put a premium on style and speed, to see how fast a racer can negotiate a serpentine course studded with a variety of flag combinations, such as open and close gates, "H's," flushes, corridors, etc. It requires great skill to get the best line approaching the flag combinations and leaving them.

This form of racing on skis has become extremely popular in recent years, especially with women and children. The danger is reduced and the pleasure great. The vertical drop of a national slalom course must be at least 500 feet if the course is to be run twice or at least 1,000 feet if it is to be run once. No gate in the slalom shall be less than 9½ feet wide and the distance from one gate to another shall not be less than 2½ feet. A slalom course for women must not exceed 40 gates. The men's may be more and it is usually between 55 and 60, depending upon the terrain.

Giant Slalom

This type of skiing is similar to slalom running except that the course is much longer and the flags farther apart. The vertical drop of a giant slalom must be at least 1,000 feet and the course is usually prepared the same as for a downhill race except that such parts of the course where control flags are placed must be prepared as for a slalom race. A giant slalom must have at least 20 sets of flags and these must be at least 13 feet apart. The flags must be placed in such a manner that the contestants may clearly and quickly distinguish them even when running at high speed. After a long stretch without flags, the first succeeding set must be marked by control flags.

Cross-Country

This type of racing demands stamina and courage. The races are usually over natural terrain, with one-third of the course uphill, one-third downhill and the other third on the flat or rolling country. The course should provide a test of the competitor's strength, endurance, technique and tactical knowledge. Climbs that are too steep and risky downhill parts, as well as monotonous open spaces, are to be avoided. Artificial obstacles are not allowed. In order to avoid as much undue strain as possible, the first part of the trail should be comparatively easy, the most strenuous part should occur about half-way or in the third quarter of the course. Races are usually at 17, 18 and 50 kilometers, with the 18-kilometer the most popular. The past few years has found cross-country racing a part of the F.I.S. program for women, with distances ranging up to 3 miles.

CHAMPIONS AND RECORDS
F.I.S. and World Championships

Through 1936 these were called Federation Internationale de Ski (F.I.S.) races. Since 1937 they have been designated as world championships.

No competition in the years not listed.

1925

(Johannesbad, Czechoslovakia)
50-km.—Cross-Country—Donth, Czechoslovakia
18-km.—Cross-Country—Nemecky, Czechoslovakia
Jump—Dick, Czechoslovakia
Nordic Combined—Nemecky, Czechoslovakia

1926

(Lahti, Finland)
50-km. Cross-Country—Raivio, Finland
18-km. Cross-Country—J. Grøttumsbraaten, Norway
Jump—Tullin Thams, Norway
Nordic Combined—J. Grøttumsbraaten

1927

(Cortina d'Ampezzo, Italy)
50-km. Cross-Country—John Lindgren, Sweden
18-km. Cross-Country—John Lindgren, Sweden
Jump—Tore Edman, Sweden
Nordic Combined—R. Purkert, Czechoslovakia

1929

(Zakopane Poland)
50-km. Cross-Country—A. Knuttica, Finland
18-km. Cross-Country—Veli Saarinen, Finland
Jump—Sigmund Ruud, Norway
Nordic Combined—Hans Vinjarengen, Norway

1930

(Oslo, Norway)
50-km. Cross-Country—Sven Utterström, Sweden
18-km. Cross-Country—Arne Rudstadstuen, Norway
Jump—Gunnar Adnerson, Norway
Nordic Combined—Hans Vinjarengen, Norway
Military Relay—Norway

1931

(Oberhof, Germany)
10-km. Cross-Country—Ole Stenen, Norway
18-km. Cross-Country—J. Grøttumsbraaten, Norway
Jump—Birger Ruud, Norway

Nordic Combined—Grøttumsbraaten, Norway
(Mürren, Switzerland)
Men's Downhill—Walter Prager, Switzerland
Men's Slalom—David Zogg, Switzerland
Women's Downhill—Miss Mackinnon, England
Women's Slalom—Miss Mackinnon

1932

(No F.I.S. classic or Nordic championships held this year.)
(Cortina d'Ampezzo, Italy)
Men's Downhill—Gustav Lantschner, Austria
Men's Slalom—Dauber, Germany
Men's Combined Downhill-Slalom—Otto Furrer, Switzerland
Women's Downhill—Paula Wiesinger, Italy
Women's Slalom—R. Streiff, Switzerland
Women's Alpine Combined—R. Streiff

1933

(Innsbruck, Austria)
50-km. Cross-Country—Veli Saarinen, Finland
18-km. Cross-Country—Nils Englund, Finland
Jump—M. Reynolds, Switzerland
Nordic Combined—Sven Eriksson, Sweden
Military Relay—Sweden
Men's Downhill—Walter Prager, Switzerland
Special Men's Downhill—Hans Hauser, Austria
Men's Slalom—Anton Seelos, Austria
Men's Alpine Combined Downhill-Slalom—Anton Seelos
Women's Downhill—Inge Wersin-Lantschner, Austria
Women's Slalom—Inge Wersin-Lantschner
Women's Alpine Combined—Inge Wersin-Lantschner

1934

(Sollefteau, Sweden)
50-km. Cross-Country—Elis Viklund, Sweden
18-km. Cross-Country—S. Nurmela, Finland
Jump—K. Johansen, Norway
Nordic Combined—Oddbjørn Hagen, Norway
Military Relay—Finland
(St. Moritz, Switzerland)
Men's Downhill—David Zogg, Switzerland
Men's Slalom—Franz Pfnur, Germany
Men's Alpine Combined—David Zogg, Switzerland
Women's Downhill—A. Ruegg, Switzerland
Women's Slalom—Christel Cranz, Germany
Women's Alpine Combined—Christel Cranz

1935

(Strebski Pleso, Czechoslovakia)
50-km. Cross-Country—Nils Englund, Sweden
18-km. Cross-Country—Klaes Karppinen, Finland
Jump—Birger Ruud, Norway
Nordic Combined—Oddbjørn Hagen, Norway
Military Relay—Finland
(Mürren, Switzerland)
Men's Downhill—F. Zingerle, Austria
Men's Slalom—Anton Seelos, Austria
Men's Alpine Combined—Anton Seelos
Women's Downhill—Christel Cranz, Germany

Women's Slalom—A. Ruegg, Switzerland
Women's Alpine Combined—Christel Cranz

1937

(Chamonix, France)
50-km. Cross-Country—Pekka Niemi, Finland
18-km. Cross-Country—Lars Bergendahl, Norway
Jump—Birger Ruud, Norway
Nordic Combined—Sigurd Roen, Norway
Military Relay—Norway
Men's Downhill—Émile Allais, France
Men's Slalom—Émile Allais
Men's Alpine Combined—Émile Allais
Women's Downhill—Christel Cranz, Germany
Women's Slalom—Christel Cranz
Women's Alpine Combined—Christel Cranz
(World championships in all events held for first time in one place.)

1938

(Lahti, Finland)
50-km. Cross-Country—Kalle Jalkanen, Finland
Jump—Asbjørn Ruud, Norway
Nordic Combined—Olaf Hoffsbakken, Norway
Military Relay—Finland
(Engelberg, Switzerland)
Men's Downhill—James Couttet, France
Men's Slalom—Rudolf Rominger, Switzerland
Men's Alpine Combined—Émile Allais, France
Women's Downhill—Lisa Resch, Germany
Women's Slalom—Christel Cranz, Germany
Women's Alpine Combined—Christel Cranz

1939

(Zakopane, Poland)
50-km. Cross-Country—Lars Bergendahl, Norway
18-km. Cross-Country—Juho Kurikkala, Finland
Jump—Josef Bradl, Austria
Nordic Combined—Hans Beraur, Czechoslovakia
Military Relay—Finland
Men's Downhill—Hellmut Lantschner, Germany
Men's Slalom—Rudolf Rominger, Switzerland
Men's Alpine Combined—Josef Jennewein, Germany
Women's Downhill—Christel Cranz, Germany
Women's Slalom—Christel Cranz
Women's Alpine Combined—Christel Cranz

1940

The F.I.S. championships, scheduled for 1940 in Oslo, Norway, were canceled when that country was invaded by the Germans. The following year, a "world championship" meet was held at Cortina d'Ampezzo, Italy, but the results were not recognized by the F.I.S. at its 1946 Congress in Pau, France. The group ruled that the events were Nazi-controlled and sponsored. No further championships were scheduled by the F.I.S. until 1950, with the United States the scene of the first post-war competition.

(In the years when the Winter Olympics were held, no F.I.S. championships were usually scheduled. Because some of the F.I.S. amateurs were not permitted to participate in the 1936 Winter Games at Garmisch-Partenkirchen, Germany, on account of the interpretation of the word "amateur," a special F.I.S. downhill-slalom competition took place at Innsbruck, Austria. This meet was open to all F.I.S. amateurs. The results, however, were not recognized as championships. It was more or less a protest competition against the International Olympic Committee's ruling on amateurism.)

1950

(Lake Placid, N.Y., and Rumford, Me.)
50-km. Cross-Country—Gunnar Eriksson, Sweden
18-km. Cross-Country—Karl-Erik Aastrom, Sweden
Jump—Hans Bjornstad, Norway
Nordic Combined—Heikki Hasu, Finland
40-km. Relay—Sweden
(*Aspen, Colo.)
Men's Downhill—Zeno Colo, Italy
Men's Slalom—Georges Schneider, Switzerland
Men's Giant Slalom—Zeno Colo
Women's Downhill—Trude Beiser-Jochum, Austria
Women's Slalom—Dagmar Rom, Austria
Women's Giant Slalom—Dagmar Rom
  *F.I.S. dropped Alpine combined championships.

1954

NORDIC
(Falun, Sweden)
Jump—Matti Pietikainen, Finland
Combined—Sverre Stenersen, Norway
15-km. Cross-Country—Veikko Hakulinen, Finland
30-km. Cross-Country—Vladimir Kusin, Russia
50-km. Cross-Country—Vladimir Kusin, Russia
40-km. Relay—Finland
Women's 10-km. Cross-Country—Lyubov Kosyreva, Russia
Women's 15-km. Relay—Russia

ALPINE
(Are, Sweden)
Downhill—Christian Pravda, Austria
Slalom—Stein Eriksen, Norway
Combined—Stein Eriksen
Giant Slalom—Stein Eriksen
Women's Downhill—Ida Schopfer, Switzerland
Women's Slalom—Trude Klecker, Austria
Women's Combined—Ida Schopfer
Women's Giant Slalom—Lucienne Schmith-Couttet, France

1958

NORDIC
(Lahti, Finland)
50-km. Cross-Country—Sixten Jernberg, Sweden
30-km. Cross-Country—Kalevi Haemaelaeinen, Finland
15-km. Cross-Country—Veikko Hakulinen, Finland
Cross-Country Combined—Paavo Korhonen, Finland

Jump—Martii Maatela, Finland
Special Jump—Juhani Karkinen, Finland
40-km. Relay—Sweden
Women's 10-km. Cross-Country—Alevtina Kolchina, Russia
Women's 15-km. Relay—Russia
Nordic Team (unofficial)—Finland

ALPINE
(Bad Gastein, Austria)
Men's Downhill—Toni Sailer, Austria
Men's Slalom—Josl Rieder, Austria
Men's Giant Slalom—Toni Sailer, Austria
Men's Alpine Combined—Toni Sailer, Austria
Men's Alpine Team (unofficial)—Austria
Women's Downhill—Lucile Wheeler, Canada
Women's Slalom—Inger Bjornbakken, Norway
Women's Giant Slalom—Lucile Wheeler, Canada
Women's Alpine Combined—Frieda Danzer,
   Switzerland
Women's Alpine Team (unofficial)—Austria

1962
NORDIC
(Zakopane, Poland)

Men
30-km. Race—Eero Mantyranta, Finland
Combined Jump (60 mm. Hill)—Yosuke Rto,
   Japan
15-km. Race—Alois Kalin, Switzerland
Combined 15-km. Race—Arne Larsen, Norway
Special 15-km. Race—Assar Ronnlund, Sweden
Special Jump (65 mm. Hill)—Toralf Engan, Norway
4 x 10 Relay Race—Sweden
50-km. Race—Sexten Jernberg, Sweden
Special Jump (90 mm. Hill)—Helmut Rechnagel,
   East Germany

Women
10-km. Race—A. Koltjina, Russia
5 x 3 km. Relay Race—Russia

ALPINE
(Chamonix, France)

Men
Special Slalom—Charles Bozon, France
Giant Slalom—Egon Zimmerman, Austria
Downhill—Karl Schranz, Austria
Combined—Karl Schranz, Austria

Women
Giant Slalom—Marianne Jahn, Austria
Special Slalom—Marianne Jahn, Austria
Downhill—Christine Hass, Austria
Combined—Marielle Goitschel, France

1966
NORDIC
(Holmenkollen, Norway)

Men
15-km. Cross-Country—Gjermund Eggen, Norway
30-km. Cross-Country—E. Maentyranta, Finland
50-km. Cross-Country—Gjermund Eggen, Norway

40-km. Relay—Norway
Cross-Country Combined—George Thoma, West
   Germany
Combined Jump—Franz Keller, West Germany
70-meter Jump—Bjoern Wirkola, Norway
90-meter Jump—Bjoern Wirkola, Norway
Women's 10-km. Cross-Country—Claudia Boyarskikh, Russia
Women's 15-km. Relay—Russia

ALPINE
(Portillo, Chile)

Men
Downhill—Jean-Claude Killy, France
Special Slalom—Carlo Senoner, Italy
Giant Slalom—Guy Perillat, France
Alpine Combined—Jean-Claude Killy, France

Women
Downhill—Erika Schinegger, Austria
Special Slalom—Annie Famose, France
Giant Slalom—Marielle Goitschel, France
Alpine Combined—Marielle Goitschel, France

1970
ALPINE
(Val Gardena, Italy)
Men
Downhill—Bernhard Russi, Switzerland
Slalom—Jean-Noel Augert, France
Giant Slalom—Karl Schranz, Austria
Combined—Billy Kidd, United States

Women
Downhill—Anneroesli Zryd, Switzerland
Slalom—Ingrid Lafforgue, France
Giant Slalom—Betsy Clifford, Canada
Combined—Michele Jacot, France

NORDIC
(Strbske Pleso, Czechoslovakia)

Men
70-meter Hill Jump—Gari Napalkov, Russia
90-meter Hill Jump—Gari Napalkov, Russia
15,000-meter Cross-Country—Lars-Goeran Aslund
   Sweden
30,000-meter Cross-Country—Vyacheslav Vedenin
   Russia
50,000-meter Cross-Country—Kalevi Oikarainen,
   Finland
Combined—Ladislav Rygl, Czechoslovakia
40,000-meter Cross-Country Relay—Russia

Women
5,000-meter Cross-Country—Galina Kulakova,
   Russia
10,000-meter Cross-Country—Alevtina Olyunina,
   Russia
15,000-meter Cross-Country Relay—Russia

*(For Olympic champions see section on
Olympic Games.)*

1967 saw a debut of competition for the
World Cup, a new emblem of individual
achievement in international skiing. Skiers earn

points—a maximum of 25 for first place in an event—in nine World Cup meets selected by a special committee. Each racer's three best scores in each of three Alpine events—downhill, slalom and giant slalom—make up his total; a "possible" score for a season is thus 225 points.

World Cup

Men

	Points
1967—Jean-Claude Killy, France	225
1968—Jean-Claude Killy, France	200
1969—Karl Schranz, Austria	182
1970—Karl Schranz, Austria	148
1971—Gustav Thoeni, Italy	155
1972—Gustav Thoeni, Italy	154
1973—Gustav Thoeni, Italy	166

Women

1967—Nance Greene, Canada	176
1968—Nancy Greene, Canada	191
1969—Gertrud Gabl, Austria	131
1970—Michelle Jacot, France	180
1971—Annemarie Proell, Austria	210
1972—Annemarie Proell, Austria	269

National Champions

Early in the history of the United States Ski Association, tournaments were run on a professional basis. The first tournament was held in 1904, but the national medal was not decided upon until 1905, and this tournament was the first national championship officially. The first committee meeting was held at Ishpeming, Mich., in 1904. The winner of the 1904 ski jump has been included in the list of national champions because the tournament was held the day after the inaugural meeting.

The first tournaments consisted only of a professional class. Later an amateur class was instituted. A number of listings show national champions with the amateurs as the official champions, but the professional group was really the better class. The amateurs in those days were considered similar to our present B class.

In December, 1922, it was decided that although all skiers who had been professionals in the past could, in the future, compete for national titles, no skier who competed professionally after that date could take part.

Men's Class A Jumping

1904—Conrad Thompson
1905—Ole Westgaard
1906—Ole Fiering
1907—Olaf Johnnum
1908-09—John Evenson
1910—Anders Haugen
1911—Francis Kempe
1912—Lars Haugen
1913-14—Ragnar Omtvedt
1915—Lars Haugen
1916—Henry Hall
1917—Ragnar Omtvedt
1918—Lars Haugen
1919—No competition
1920—Anders Haugen
1921—Carl Howelson
1922—Lars Haugen
1923—Anders Haugen
1924—Lars Haugen
1925—Alfred Ohrn
1926—Anders Haugen
1927-28—Lars Haugen
1929—Strand Mikkelsen
1930-31—Caspar Oimoen
1932—Anton Lekang
1933—Roy Mikkelsen
1934—Caspar Oimoen
1935—Roy Mikkelsen
1936—George Kotlarek
1937—Sigmund Ruud (Norway)
1938 (Closed)—Sig Ulland
1938 (Open)—Birger Ruud (Norway)
1939—Reidar Andersen (Norway)
1940—Alf Engen
1941—Torger Tokel
1942—Ola Aanjesen (Norway)
1943-45—No competition
1946 (Open)—Alf Engan
1946 (Closed)—Arthur Devlin
1947—Arnholdt Kongsgaard (Norway)
1948—Arne Ulland (Norway)
1949—Petter Hugsted (Norway)
1950—Olavi Kuronen (Finland)
1951—Art Tokle
1952 (Closed)—Clarence Hill
1952 (Open)—Merrill Barber
1953—Art Tokle
1954—Roy Sherwood
1955—Rudi Maki
1956—Keith Zuehlke
1957—Ansten Samuelstuen
1958—Billy Olson
1959—W. P. Erickson
1960—James Brennan
1961-62—Anstan Samuelstuen
1963—Gene Kotlarek
1964—John Balfanz
1965—David Hicks
1966-67—Gene Kotlarek
1968—Jay Martin
1969—Adrian Watt
1970—Bill Bakke
1971—Jerry Martin
1972—Greg Swor

Men's Downhill

1933—Henry Woods
1934—Jonathan Duncan Jr.
1935—Hannes Schroll (Austria)
1936—No competition
1937 (Open-Closed)—Dick Durrance
1938 (Open-Closed)—Ulrich Beutter (Germany)
1939 (Open)—Toni Matt
1939 (Closed)—Dick Durrance

1940 (Open-Closed)—Dick Durrance
1941 (Open)—Toni Matt
1941 (Closed)—William Redlin
1942 (Open)—Martin Fopp
1942 (Closed)—Barney McLean
1943-45—No competition
1946—Steve Knowlton
1947—Karl Molitor (Switzerland)
1948 (Open-Closed)—Jack Reddish
1949 (Closed)—George Macomber
1950 (Open-Closed)—Jim Griffith
1951 (Open)—Ernie McCulloch (Canada)
1951 (Closed)—Jack Nagel
1952 (Open)—Ernie McCulloch
1952 (Closed)—Dick Buek
1953 (Open-Closed)—Ralph Miller
1954—Dick Buek
1955—Chiharu Igaya, Bill Beck (tie)
1956—Billy Woods
1957—Bud Werner
1958—William Smith
1959—Bud Werner
1960—Oddvar Ronnestad
1961—No competition
1962—David Gorsuch
1963—William Marolt
1964—Ni Orsi
1965—Loris Werner
1966—Peter Rohr (Switzerland)
1967—Dennis McCoy
1968—Scott Henderson
1969—Vladimir Sabich
1970—Rod Taylor
1971—Bob Cochran
1972—Steve Lathrop

Men's Slalom

1935—Hannes Schroll (Austria)
1936—No competition
1937 (Open-Closed)—Dick Durrance
1938 (Open-Closed)—Edward Meservey
1939 (Open)—Friedl Pfeifer (Austria)
1939 (Closed)—Dick Durrance
1940 (Open)—Friedl Pfeifer
1940 (Closed)—Dick Durrance
1941 (Open)—Dick Durrance
1941 (Closed)—William Redlin
1942—Sigi Engl
1943 (Closed)—Barney McLean
1944-45—No competition
1946—Dick Movitz
1947—Karl Molitor (Switzerland)
1948 (Open-Closed)—Jack Reddish
1949 (Open-Closed)—George Macomber
1950 (Open)—Ernie McCulloch (Canada) and Jack Reddish (tie)
1950 (Closed)—Jack Reddish
1951 (Open-Closed)—Jack Nagel
1952 (Open-Closed)—Jack Reddish
1953 (Open-Closed)—Chiharu Igaya (Japan)
1954—Chiharu Igaya
1955—Ralph Miller

1956-57—Tom Corcoran
1958—Charles Ferries
1959—Bud Werner
1960—James Heuga
1961—R. Hebron
1962—William Barrier
1963—Charles Ferries
1964—William Marolt
1965—Rod Hebron (Canada)
1966—Guy Perillat (France)
1967—Jim Heuga
1968—Rick Chaffee
1969-70—Bob Cochran
1971—Otto Tschudi (Norway)
1972—Terry Palmer

Men's Cross-Country

(15-Kilometer)
1907—Asario Autio
1908-09—No competition
1910—T. W. Glesne
1911—P. Blege Berg
1912—Julius Blegen
1913—Elinor Lund
1914-15—No competition
1916—Sigurd Overbye
1917-22—No competition
1923—Sigurd Overbye
1924—Robert Reid
1925—Martin Fredboe
1926—Sugurd Overbye
1927—Johan Satre
1928-30—Magnus Satre
1931—No competition
1932—Hjalmar Hvam
1933—Magnus Satre
1934—D. Monson
1935—Ottar Satre
1936—Carl Sunquist
1937—Warren Chivers
1938—Dave Bradley
1939—George Gustavson
1940—Peter Fosseide
1941—George Gustavson
1942—Howard Chivers
1943-46—No competition
1947—Wendell Broomhall
1948—Trygve Nielsen
1949—Hans Holaas
1950—Olavi Alakulpi
1951—Ted Farwell
1952—Silas Dunklee
1953-55—Tauno Pulkkinen
1956—Norman Oakvig
1957—Sven Johansson
1958—Leo Massa (18-k.)
1959-60—Clarence Servold
1961—No competition
1962—Mike Gallagher
1963—Donald MacLeod
1964—Peter Lahdenpera
1965—David Rikert

1966-67—Mike Gallagher
1968—No competition
1969—Clark Matis
1970—Mike Devecka
1971-72—Mike Elliott

Cross-Country
(30 Kilometers)

1958—Leslie Fono
1959—Leo Massa
1960—Richard Taylor
1961—No competition
1962—Raimo Ahti
1963—Ed Williams
1964—Ed Dermers
1965—Bill Spencer
1966—Mike Elliott
1967—Mike Gallagher
1968—No competition
1969—Clark Matis
1970-71—Mike Gallagher
1972—Mike Elliott

Cross-Country
(50 Kilometers)

1971-72—Bob Gray

Cross-Country
(10 Kilometers)

1972—Mike Elliott

40-Kilometer Relay

1963—Canada (Don McLeod, Irvin Servold, Franz Portmann, Clarence Servold)
1964-66—No competition
1967—U.S. Eastern Assoc. (Bob Gray, Terry Morse, Ned Gillette, Mike Gallagher)
1968—No Competition
1969—*U.S. Eastern Assoc. (Peter Davis, Bob Gray, Jon Chaffee)
1970—No Competition
1971—*U.S. Eastern Assoc. (Mike Gallagher, Peter Davis, Bob Gray)
1972—Rocky Mountain Team (Ron Yeager, Mike Elliott, Clark Matis, Larry Martin)
*30-Kilometers

Men's Alpine Combined
(Downhill and slalom.)

1935—Hannes Schroll (Austria)
1936—No competition
1937—(Open-Closed)—Dick Durrance
1938 (Open-Closed)—Ulrich Beutter (Germany)
1939—(Open-Closed)—Dick Durrance
1940—(Open-Closed)—Dick Durrance
1941—(Open)—Toni Matt
1941—(Closed)—William Redlin
1942—(Open)—Alf Engen
1942—(Closed)—Barney McLean
1943-45—No competition
1946—Barney McLean
1947—Karl Molitor (Switzerland)
1948—(Open-Closed)—Jack Reddish
1949—(Open-Closed)—George Macomber
1950—(Open)—Ernie McCulloch, Canada

1950—(Closed)—Jack Reddish
1951—(Open-Closed)—Jack Nagel
1952—(Open-Closed)—Jack Reddish
1953—(Open-Closed)—Ralph Miller
1954-55—Chiharu Igaya
1956—Billy Woods
1957—Tom Corcoran
1958—Frank Brown
1959—Bud Werner
1960—Oddavar Ronnestad
1961—R. Hebron
1962—David Gorsuch
1963—Bud Werner
1964—Gordon Eaton
1965—Peter Duncan (Canada)
1966—Guy Perillat (France)
1967—Dumeng Giovanoli (Switzerland)
1968—Scott Henderson
1969—Malcolm Milne (Australia)
1970—Bill McKay
1971—Bob Cochran
1972—Joe Lamb

Men's Nordic Combined
(Cross-country and jumping.)

1932—Hjalmar Hvam
1933—Magnus Satre
1934-45—No Competition
1937—Warren Chivers
1938—Dave Bradley
1939—Alf Engen
1940—Peter Fosseide
1941—Alf Engen
1942—Howard Chivers
1943-46—No Competition
1947—Ralph Townsend
1948—Robert Wright
1949—Ralph Townsend
1950—Gordon Wren
1951—Ted Farwell
1952—Corey Engen
1953—No Competition
1954—Norman Oakvig
1955—No Competition
1956—Per Staavi
1957—Bill Purcell
1958-60—Alfred Vincellette
1961-62—No Competition
1963—John Bower
1964—Jim Balfanz
1965—David Rikert
1966-67—John Bower
1968—No Competition
1969-70—Jim Miller
1971—Robert Kendall
1972—Jim Miller

Men's Giant Slalom

1949—(Open-Closed)—Dave Lawrence
1950—Hans Senger (Austria)
1951—Ernie McCulloch (Canada)
1952—Gale Spence
1953—(Open-Closed)—Billy Tibbits

1954–Darrel Robison
1955–Ralph Miller
1956–(Open)–Christian Pravda (Austria)
1956–(Closed)–Tom Corcoran
1957–Jan Thortensen
1958–Stanley C. Harwood
1959–Bud Werner
1960–Chiharu Igaya
1961–Gordon Eaton
1962–James Gaddis
1963–Bud Werner
1964–Billy Kidd
1965–William Marolt
1966–Jean-Claude Killy (France)
1967–Dumeng Giovanoli (Switzerland)
1968–Rick Chaffee
1969–Hank Hashiwa
1970–Tyler Palmer
1971–Bob Cochran
1972–Jim Hunter (Canada)

Men's Four-Event All-Around

1939–Dick Durrance
1940–Alf Engen
1941–Alf Engen
1942–Merrill Barber
1943-49–No Competition
1950–Jon Lie (Norway)
No further competition

Women's Downhill

1938–Marian McKean
1939–(Open-Closed)–Elizabeth Woolsey
1940–(Open-Closed)–Grace Carter Lindley
1941–(Open)–Gretchen Fraser
1941–(Closed)–Nancy Reynolds
1942–(Open)–Clarita Heath
1942–(Closed)–Shirley McDonald
1943-45–No Competition
1946–Paula Kann
1947–Rhoda Wurtele (Canada)
1948–(Open-Closed)–Jannette Burr
1949–(Open-Closed)–Andrea Mead
1950–(Open-Closed)–Jannette Burr
1951–Katy Rodolph
1952–Mrs. Andrea Mead Lawrence
1953–(Open)–Sally Neidlinger
1953–(Closed)–Katy Rodolph and Skeeter
    Werner (tie)
1954–Nancy Banks
1955–Mrs. Andrea Mead Lawrence
1956–Katherine Cox
1957–Linda Meyers
1958-59–Beverly Anderson
1960–Nancy Greene
1961–No competition
1962–Sharon Pecjak
1963-64–Jean Saubert
1965–Nancy Greene (Canada)
1966–Madeleine Wuilloud (Switzerland)
1967–Nancy Greene (Canada)
1968-70–Ann Black
1971–Cheryl Bechdolt

1972–Stephane Forrest

Women's Slalom

1938–Grace Carter Lindley
1939–(Open)–Erna Steuri (Switzerland)
1939–(Closed)–Doris Friedrich (Switzerland)
1940–(Open-Closed)–Nancy Reynolds
1941–(Open-Closed)–Marilyn Shaw
1942–(Open-Closed)–Gretchen Fraser
1943-45–No Competition
1946–Rhona Wurtele (Canada)
1947–Olivia Ausoni (Switzerland)
1948–(Open-Closed)–Ann Winn
1949–(Open-Closed)–Andrea Mead
1950–(Open)–Mrs. Georgette Thioliere-Miller
    (France)
1950–(Closed)–Norma Godden
1951–Katy Rodolph
1952–Mrs. Andrea Mead Lawrence
1953–(Open-Closed)–Katy Rodolph
1954–Jill Kinmont
1955–Mrs. Andrea Mead Lawrence
1956-57–Sally Deaver
1958–Beverly Anderson
1959–Linda Meyers
1960–Ann Heggtveit, Nancy Holland (tie)
1961-62–Linda Meyers
1963–Sandra Shellworth
1964–Jean Saubert
1965–Nancy Greene (Canada)
1966–Marielle Goitschel (France)
1967–Penny McCoy
1968–Judy Nagel
1969–Barbara Cochran
1970–Patty Boydston
1971–Barbara Cochran
1972–Marilyn Cochran

Women's Giant Slalom

1949–(Open-Closed)–Katy Rodolph
1950–Resi Hammerer, (Austria)
1951–Mrs. Suzy Harris Rytting
1952–Mrs. Rhona Wurtele Gillis
1953–Mrs. Andrea Mead Lawrence
1954–Dorothy Modenese
1955–Mrs. Jannette Burr Bray
1956–(Open)–Mrs. Rhona Wurtele Gillis
1956–(Closed)–Sally Deaver
1957–Noni Foley
1958-59–Beverly Anderson
1960–Ann Heggtviet
1961–Nancy Holland
1962–Tammy Dix
1963-64–Jean Saubert
1965–Nancy Greene (Canada)
1966–Florence Steurer (France)
1967–Sandra Shellworth
1968–Marilyn Cochran
1969–Barbara Cochran
1970–Susan Corrock
1971–Laurie Kreiner (Canada)
1972–Sandra Poulsen

Women's Alpine Combined

1938—Marian McKean
1939—(Open)—Erna Steuri (Switzerland)
1939—(Closed)—Betty Woolsey
1940—(Open-Closed)—Marilyn Shaw
1941—(Open)—Gretchen Fraser
1941—(Closed)—Nancy Reynolds
1942—(Open)—Clarita Heath
1942—(Closed)—Shirley McDonald
1943-45—No Competition
1946—Rhona Wurtele (Canada)
1947—Rhoda Wurtele
1948—Suzy Harris
1949—(Open-Closed) Andrea Mead
1950—(Open-Closed—Lois Woodworth (Canada)
1951—Katy Rodolph
1952—Mrs. Andrea Mead Lawrence
1953—(Open)—Sally Neidlinger
1953—(Closed)—Katy Rodolph
1954—Nancy Banks
1955—Mrs. Andrea Mead Lawrence
1956—Katherine Cox
1957—Madi Springer-Miller
1958—Beverly Anderson
1959—Linda Meyers
1960—Elizabeth Greene
1961—Nancy Holland
1962—Linda Meyers
1963—Starr Walton
1964—Jean Saubert
1965—Nancy Greene (Canada)
1966—Florence Steurer (France)
1967—Karen Budge
1968—Judy Nagel
1969—No Competition
1970—Rosi Fortna
1971—Judy Crawford (Canada)
1972—No Competition

Women's 5-Kilo Cross Country

1969-70—Martha Rockwell
1971—Sharon Firth (Canada)
1972—Martha Rockwell

Women's 10-Kilo Cross Country

1969—Martha Rockwell (8-Kilo)
1970-72—Martha Rockwell

Women's 15-Kilo Relay

1969—Rocky Mountain Team (Twila Hinkle, Mary Atkins, Kris Zdechlich)
1970—No Competition
1971—Canada, Yukon Div. (Shirley Firth, Anita Allen, Sharon Firth)
1972—U.S. Eastern Team (Ann McKinnon, Liz Chenard, Martha Rockwell)

CANADIAN—AMERICAN TROPHY SERIES

Men's Downhill

1971—Craig Shanholtzer, United States
1972—Rudd Pyles, United States

Men's Slalom

1971—Otto Tschudi, Norway

1972—Steve Lathrop, United States

Men's Giant Slalom

1971—Lance Poulsen, United States
1972—Don Rowles, United States

Men's Jumping

1972—Zdenek Mezi, Canada

Men's 15-Kilo Cross Country

1972—Magne Myrom, Norway

Men's 30-Kilo Cross Country

1972—Audun Nerland, Norway

Men's Overall	Points
1971—Lance Poulsen, United States	105
1972—Don Rowles, Unites States	154

Women's Downhill

1971—Carolyne Oughton, Canada
1972—Stephanie Forrest, United States

Women's Slalom

1971—Karen Budge, United States
1972—Penny Northrup, United States

Women's Giant Slalom

1971—Judy Crawford, Canada
1972—Cheryl Bechdolt, United States

Women's 5-Kilo Cross Country

1972—Martha Rockwell, United States

Women's 10-Kilo Cross Country

1972—Sharon Firth, Canada

Women's Overall	Points
1971—Cheryl Bechdolt, United States	170
1972—Karen Budge, United States	173

National Collegiate Champions

Downhill

1954—Pat Myers, Nevada
1955—Chiharu Igaya, Dartmouth
1956—Walt Taulbee, Washington
1957—Ralph Miller, Dartmouth
1958—Gary Vaughn, Norwich
1959—Marvin Melville, Utah
1960—David Butts, Colorado
1961—Gordon Eaton, Middlebury
1962—Mike Baer, Denver
1963—Dave Gorsuch, Western State, Bill Marolt, Colorado, Buddy Werner, Colo.
1964—John Clough, Middlebury
1965—William Marolt, Colorado
1966—Terje Overland, Denver
1967—Dennis McCoy, Denver
1968—Barney Peet, Fort Lewis
1969—Mike Lafferty, Colorado
1970-72—Otto Tschudi, Denver

Slalom

1954—John L'Orange, Denver
1955-57—Chiharu Igaya, Dartmouth
1958—Robert Gebhardt, Dartmouth
1959—Marvin Melville, Utah
1960—Rudy Ruana, Montana
1961—Buddy Werner, Colorado

1962—James Gaddis, Utah
1963—James Heuga, Colorado
1964—John Clough, Middlebury
1965—Rick Chaffee, Denver
1966—William Marolt, Colorado
1967—Rick Chaffee, Denver
1968—Dennis McCoy, Denver
1969—Paul Rachetto, Denver
1970—Mike Porcarelli, Colorado
1971—Otto Tschudi, Denver
1972—Mike Porcarelli, Colorado

Alpine Combined

1955-56—Chiharu Igaya, Dartmouth
1957—Ralph Miller, Dartmouth
1958—Dave Vorse, Dartmouth
1959—Marvin Melville, Utah
1960—James Gaddis, Utah
1961—Buddy Werner, Colorado
1962—James Gaddis, Utah
1963—Buddy Werner, Colorado
1964—John Clough, Middlebury
1965—Rick Chaffee, Denver
1966—William Marolt, Colorado
1967—Terje Overland, Denver
1968—Dennis McCoy, Denver
1969—Paul Rachetto, Denver
1970—Mike Porcarelli, Colorado
1971—Otto Tschudi, Denver
1972—Mike Porcarelli, Colorado

Cross-Country

1954—Marvin Crawford, Denver
1955—Larry Damon, Vermont
1956—Erik Berggren, Idaho
1957—Mack Miller, Western State
1958-59—Clarence Servold, Denver
1960—John Dendahl, Colorado
1961—Charles Akers, Maine
1962—James Page, Dartmouth
1963—Eddie Demers, Western State
1964—E. Demers, Western State
1965—Mike Elliott, Fort Lewis
1966—Mike Elliott, Fort Lewis
1967—Ned Gillette, Dartmouth
1968-69—Clark Matis, Colorado
1970-71—Ole Hansen, Denver
1972—Stale Engen, Wyoming

Jumping

1954-56—Willis Olson, Denver
1957—Alfred Vincelette, Denver
1958—Oddvar Ronnestad, Denver
1959—David Butts, Colorado
1960—John Dendahl, Colorado
1961—John Bower, Middlebury
1962—Oyvind Floystad, Denver
1963—Tom Nord, Washington
1964—F. Prydz, Utah, Erik Jansen, Denver (tie)
1965—Erik Jansen, Denver
1966—Frithjof Prydz, Utah
1967—Bjorn Loken, Utah
1968—Peter Robes, Wyoming

1969—Odd Hammernes, Denver
1970—Jay Rand, Colorado
1971—Vidar Nilsgard, Colorado
1972—Odd Hammernes, Denver

Nordic Combined

1955-56—Erik Berggren, Idaho
1957—Harold Riiber, Denver
1958—Clarence Servold, Denver
1959—Ted Farwell, Denver
1960—John Dendahl, Colorado
1961—John Bower, Middlebury
1962—Tor Fageraas, Montana State
1963—Aarne Valkama, Denver
1964—Erik Jansen, Denver
1965—Matz Jenssen, Utah
1966—Frithjof Prydz, Utah
1967—Matz Jenssen, Utah
1968—Jim Miller, Fort Lewis
1969—Georg Krog, Denver
1970—Jim Miller, Fort Lewis
1971-72—Bruce Cunningham, New Hampshire

Team

1954-57—Denver
1958—Dartmouth
1959-60—Colorado
1961-67—Denver
1968—Wyoming
1969-71—Denver
1972—Colorado

Skimeister Award

1954—Marvin Crawford, Denver
1955—Les Streeter, Middlebury
1956—John Cross, Denver
1957—Ralph Miller, Dartmouth
1958—Dave Harwood, Dartmouth
1959—Dave Butts, Colorado
1960—John Dendahl, Colorado
1961—Art Bookstrom, Dartmouth
1962-63—James Page, Dartmouth
1964—Jennings Cress, Denver
1965-66—Loris Werner, Western State
1967—Matz Jenssen, Utah
1968—Eric Piene, Wyoming
1969—Ed Damon, Dartmouth
1970-71—John Kendall, New Hampshire
1972—Kim Kendall, Nevada

Jumping Records
American

Year	Distance Feet	Made by	Site
1887	37	Mikkel Hemmestvedt	Red Wing, Minn.
1904	82	Thomas Walters	Ishpeming, Mich.
1905	92½	Julius Kulstadt	Ishpeming, Mich.
1905	106	Gustav Bye	Red Wing, Minn.
1907	112	Ole Feiring	Duluth, Minn.
1907	114	Ole Mangseth	Red Wing, Minn.

Year	Distance feet	Made by	Site
1908	122	John Evenson	Ishpeming, Mich.
1909	130	Ole Larson	Eau Claire, Wis.
1910	138	Oscar Gunderson	Chippewa Falls, Wis.
1910	140	August Nordby	Ishpeming, Mich.
1911	152	Anders Haugen	Ironwood, Mich.
1913	169	Ragnar Omtvedt	Ironwood, Mich.
1913	185	Lars Haugen	Steamboat Springs, Colo.
1916	192	Ragnar Omtvedt	Steamboat Spring, Colo.
1917	203	Henry Hall	Steamboat Spring, Colo.
1919	213	Anders Haugen	Dillon, Colo.
1919	214	Lars Haugen	Steamboat Springs, Colo.
1932	224	Glen Armstrong	Salt Lake City, Utah
1932	235	Hans Beck	Lake Placid, N.Y.
1934	240	John Elvrum	Big Pines, Calif.
1937	242	Alf Engan	Salf Lake City, Utah
1939	251	Alf Engan	Iron Mountain, Mich.
1939	257	Bob Roecker	Iron Mountain, Mich.
1941	267	Alf Engan	Iron Mountain, Mich.
1941	273	Torger Tokle	Leavenworth, Wash.
1941	288	Torger Tokle	Hyak, Wash.
1942	289	Torger Tokle	Iron Mountain, Mich.
1949	290	Sverre Kongsgaard (Norway)	Hyak, Wash.
1949	293	Joe Perrault	Iron Mountain, Mich.
1949	294	Matti Pietikainen (Finland)	Iron Mountain, Mich.
1949	297	Joe Perrault	Iron Mountain, Mich.
1950	297	Gordon Wren	Steamboat Spring, Colo.
1950	297	Billy Olson	Iron Mountain, Mich.
1951	316	Ansten Samuelstuen (Norway)	Steamboat Springs, Colo.
1960	316	James Brennan	Iron Mountain, Mich.
1962	317	John Balfanz	Westby, Wis.
1963	322	Eugene Kotlarek	Steamboat Spring, Colo.
1965	324	Toralf Engan	Leavenworth, Wash.
1965	325	John Balfanz	Iron Mountain, Mich.
1967	335	Bjorn Wirkola	Leavenworth, Wash.
1968	337	Adrian Watt	Iron Mountain, Mich.
1968	338	Bjorn Wirkola	Westby, Wis.
1970	340	Greg Swor	Leavenworth, Wash.
1971	345	Jerry Martin	Iron Mountain, Mich.

European

Year	Distance feet	Made by	Site
1931	265.74	Sigmund Ruud (Norway)	Davos, Switzerland
1933	282.15	Sigmund Ruud (Norway)	Vilars, Switzerland
1934	302	Birger Ruud (Norway)	Planica, Yugoslavia
1935	318	Stanislaus Marusarz (Poland)	Planica, Yugoslavia
1935	325	Fritz Fainersdorfer (Switzerland)	Planica, Yugoslavia
1935	326½	Reidar Andersen (Norway)	Planica, Yugoslavia
1936	351	Josef Bradl (Austria)	Planica, Yugoslavia
1941	387	Rudolph Gehring (Germany)	Planica, Yugoslavia
1948	393.7	Fritz Tschannen (Switzerland)	Planica, Yugoslavia
1950	441	Dan Netzel (Sweden)	Oberstdorf, Germany
1951	451	Tauno Luiro (Finland)	Oberstdorf, Germany
1964	465.11	Dalbar Motejlek (Czechoslovakia)	Oberstdorf, W. Germany

The Federation Internationale de Ski, the world ruling body, considers long jumps as official records only for the specific hill on which the jump was made.

EQUIPMENT

(From "Sports for Recreation," edited by E. D. Mitchell, A. S. Barnes and Company, New York.)

The selection of the proper skis, boots, bindings, poles, waxes and clothing are of the utmost importance.

The ski is a long, narrow, flexible board for traversing snow, one being worn on each foot. The best skis are made from hickory, although laminated hickory skis are popular. Other skis are made from maple, ash, or metals (magnesium), or fiberglass.

A ski should have one groove on the under side which extends from the heel up to the shovel (upturn) but not through the shovel. This insures straight running. Jumping skis are made with two or even three grooves.

The skis have steel edges running the full-length of the bottom side. These give the necessary grip on the snow and also protect the skis and add to their life.

The binding is the device by which the ski is attached to the boot. The bindings have toe irons with either toe clips or leather toe straps to hold the straight boot on the ski. A continuous cable connects a front-throw lever through an adjustable side hitch to a spring cable around the heel of the boot. This cable keeps the boot attached firmly to the ski. There is a metal plate for protection to the ski.

There are a number of different bindings for each type of skiing, that is downhill, touring, cross-country and jumping. All bindings are designed to prevent any lateral movement of the boot. The downhill binding also restricts any rise of the heel from the ski. Touring, cross-country and jumping bindings all permit freedom of the heel to rise.

There are many makes of safety bindings. These are designed to release in a spill, preventing possible injury from falls.

A skier standing in his bindings should be held so solidly in place that he can lean forward as far as a 30-degree angle without losing either his balance or loosening his skis.

Except for skis and bindings, boots are the most important item in the ski wardrobe. The boot, of leather, has a stiff sole, thick and shanked with steel inside; a roomy square toe; a heel with two grooves, one for downhill or rigid binding and one to permit lifting of the heel for cross-country adjustment. By 1969, plastic boots using buckets instead of bootlaces had come into use. The foam-filled boot, for closer fit and lighter weight, became popular in the 70s.

The pole is carried in each hand for pushing, as an aid to balance and for help in climbing, but not for stopping. Poles are made of steel, aluminum and various types of cane or bamboo. Each has a sharp metal tip and a circular ring (snow ring) about 7 inches in diameter, interlaced with thongs, about 5 inches above the tip. At the top of the pole is a leather strap through which the hand is passed so the pole will not be dropped and as an aid in pushing.

Wax is applied to the running surface of the skis to give varying traction and slipperiness as dictated by the condition of the snow (wet or dry, new or old, icy or crusty) and depending on the temperature.

The skier's wardrobe is an important item in the enjoyment of the sport. Under the category of clothing equipment comes underclothing, socks, pants, shirts and sweaters, jackets and windbreakers, mittens, boots and accessories.

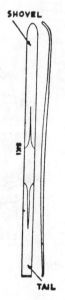

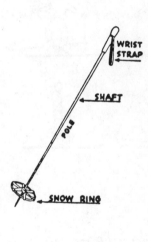

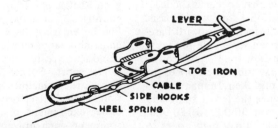

Ski, Pole and Binding. (Taken from "Sports for Recreation," edited by E. D. Mitchell, A. S. Barnes and Company, New York.)

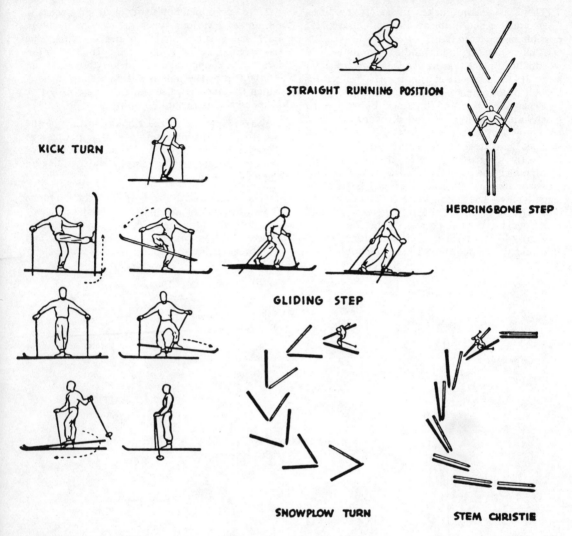

STRAIGHT RUNNING POSITION

KICK TURN

HERRINGBONE STEP

GLIDING STEP

SNOWPLOW TURN

STEM CHRISTIE

Ski Techniques. (Taken from "Sports for Recreation," edited by E. D. Mitchell, A. S. Barnes and Company, New York.)

SOCCER

(Courtesy of United States Soccer Football Association, 350 Fifth Ave., New York, N.Y., 10001)

Few Americans realize that soccer is the leading sport on an international and world basis. The American generally is inclined toward baseball and football (American style). He probably believes that these sports draw the biggest crowds and participating teams pay the highest prices for talent. If he does, he is mistaken. In many countries of the world soccer is the No. 1 sport and top games draw crowds from 50,000 to 150,000. The teams also are willing to pay high prices to acquire the services of ranking stars.

Soccer is played extensively in almost every country in the world under uniform rules. It is a game that is played by over 140 nations. In most countries, particularly those of Europe and South America, it is the predominating sport, enlisting a large number of participants and commanding a greater popular appeal than any other single sport. Soccer furnishes, to the highest degree, the principles of open play, swift action, skill, individual effort, team combination, discipline, excitement and thrills. No game could command such universal appeal, no game could be so widely played, no game could have its beginning, as did soccer, at the time of the Roman occupation of ancient Britain, and live down through the centuries, growing and continuing to grow until it has reached out and touched almost every civilized part of the world, unless it was a game that possessed outstanding merit.

The question often arises: "How old is the game of football?" So obscure is its real origin that one might be forgiven for suggesting that possibly Adam kicked an apple around in the Garden of Eden to the amusement of Eve. However, as early as the days of the Odyssey we learn that Nausicaa and her maidens could be discovered "playing at the caitch." Also that the early Greeks had a game in which a small ball was used and which bore rough resemblance to football. In this game the players of one side had to carry the ball over a line defended by the other, by any means in their power.

The Romans also had a game in which the *follis,* a large inflated ball, was used. The follis, however, was undoubtedly a handball, and the game was probably the same as the "balown ball" of the Middle Ages, in which an inflated ball was knocked into the air and kept there as long as possible. All this, however, may have little concern with football except to show that the follis or "balown ball" was the same that was used in the game of football.

It was at Chester, England, centuries ago, that the people played football on Shrove Tuesday, the contemporary historians stating that the first ball used was the head of a Dane who had been captured and slain, and whose head was kicked about for sport. Derby, England, claims that soccer football was established there, also on a Shrove Tuesday, to celebrate a victory of a troop of British warriors who, in the year 217 A.D., defeated a Roman cohort and drove it out of the ancient gates. It is stated in Glover's "History of Derby," that "the faction fights over the ball between the ecclesiastical districts of Derby are said to have been in vogue from about 217 A.D. until 1846." Fitz-Stephen records, in the year 1175, that the London schoolboys "annually upon Shrove Tuesday go into the fields and play at the well-known game of ball."

In the 14th Century the game appears to have attracted the notice, and drawn the ire, of the authorities. On April 13, 1314, Edward II issued a proclamation forbidding the game as leading to a breach of the peace "forasmuch as there is great noise in the city caused by hustling over large balls from which many evils might arise which God forbid; we commend and forbid, on behalf of the king, on pain of imprisonment, such game to be used in the city in future."

In 1349 football is mentioned in a statute of Edward III, who objected to the game as tending to discourage the practice of archery, upon which the military strength of the country largely depended. Sheriffs were commanded to suppress "such idle practices" as football. The proclamation, apparently, was of little avail,

because 40 years afterward Richard II passed a similar statute (12 Rich. II. c. 6. A.D. 1389) forbidding "all playing at tenise, football and other games" throughout the country.

The same statute was re-enacted by Henry IV in 1401, and later by Henry VIII. Similar measures in Scotland failed to persuade the Scots to give up football and golf. In 1457, James III decreed that "footballe and golfe be utterly cryed down and not to be used," but in 1491 his successor had to prohibit football and golf by a new statute which stated that "in na place of realme ther be used futeball, golfe or other sik unprofitable sportes."

It appears that in Scotland, as in England, the game of football had gained such a foothold as to be strong enough to defy the law. However, in 1497, it is recorded that the high treasurer to James IV paid 2 shillings for "fut balles," from which we are to assume that James IV took a more favorable view of the sport than did his predecessors.

In 1572, Queen Elizabeth issued a proclamation that "no foteballe play be used or suffered within the city of London and the liberties thereof upon pain of imprisonment." For playing football on Sunday, in 1779, one John Wonkell of Durham, England, was sent to prison for one week and ordered to do penance in church.

It is also a matter of record that Oliver Cromwell was a football player; he makes many references to the game in his letters. In one he states that he could well remember the times he had been more afraid of meeting John Wheelright at football than of anything else in the field, as he was infallibly sure of being tripped by him.

In those days games lasted many hours and generally the goals were at the opposite ends of the hamlets or towns. It was lawful to kick an opposing player's shins or trip him; in fact anything went in order to get or keep the ball from an opponent.

The foregoing should be sufficient to indicate the antiquity of the sport. Shakespeare, in his "Comedy of Errors," Act II, had this to say:

"Am I so round with you as you with me
That like a football you do spurn me thus?
You spurn me hence and he will spurn me
    hither;
If I last in this service you must case me in
    leather."

An excerpt from "King Lear," Act I, Scene IV, shows that tripping and "hacking over" were then considered as natural adjuncts to the game.

"Steward—I'll not be strucken, my lord.
Kent—Nor tripped, neither, you base football
    player.
Lear—I thank thee, fellow."

Although it may be true that football, or soccer, in those days found no place in the annals of knight errantry, nevertheless it found a warm spot in the hearts of the common people. Though interdicted by kings and queens, it defied and survived the law; fulminated against by prelates, it flourished against their onslaughts; attacked by the pens of writers, it has outlived them all, for it is now played under the same rules all over the civilized world.

Like billiards, bowling and wrestling, among the oldest sport in the history of mankind, soccer football is believed by many to have had its origin in the Roman Empire. An old volume on "Sports and Their Origin," published in 1618, shows six Romans kicking a round object resembling a ball, and, according to the notation on the page on which this illustration appears is this description: "the above depicts the origin of football." Hence, it would seem that, contrary to the general impression that soccer football is purely a British sport, it had its origin in Rome and was introduced to the ancient Britons by the Roman legions. Soccer football, therefore, has developed down through the ages from a crude to a highly skilled and scientific game. It is now regulated by rules governing both the game and the players, and it is in every way different today from the form in which it was known and practiced even a hundred years ago.

Discovering the real origin of soccer football, however, would be a task beyond the efforts of the greatest historian and would be as impossible of accomplishment as finding the proverbial needle in the proverbial haystack. Its beginning is far too remote and vague, although it was perhaps the first of all games that mankind engaged in, and, possibly, led to other forms of games in which a ball was the objective, such as cricket, croquet, golf, hockey, lacrosse, tennis and similar adaptations.

Soccer football was introduced to the United States gradually, almost timidly in the beginning, and its development has been a slow and gradual process extending over a period of over 80 years. In the 80's and 90's the game was played in haphazard fashion, mostly by scratch teams made up chiefly of Scotch, Irish and English immigrants. Its progress in those early days was spasmodic.

In the beginning, New York, Philadelphia and the West Hudson section of New Jersey led the way, quickly followed by Fall River, Mass., and other New England centers in the East, and by St. Louis, Chicago, Detroit, Cincinnati, Cleveland, Denver and San Francisco in the Middle and Far West.

It was in the late 70's that a number of teams first appeared in the West Hudson section of New Jersey. The early 80's saw an increase in the number of organized teams and interest in the game began to spread, until 1884, when a few men met in Newark, N.J., for the purpose of discussing the advancement of the game of soccer football in the land of their adoption. In whatever part of the world he may find himself, the Briton and the Celt carries his games along with him, and so it came to pass that at the beginning of the 1884–85 season, the American Football Association was instituted and became one of the outstanding pioneer organizations. Prior to this time the game may be said to have been unknown to the American public, there being but a few teams scattered here and there throughout the land and playing on open lots with improvised equipment.

The year 1886 appears to have been a red letter one for soccer football in this country. The first game of soccer ever to be played in Central Park, New York City, was played in 1886, one of the contending teams being known as the "Riversides."

In 1886 the first international game was played when a team selected by the American Football Association from the leading New Jersey teams of that era, invaded Canada, where it met an all-star team in a series of 3 games. The following year the Canadian players came to New Jersey and the same teams engaged in a return 3-game series. The elevens proved to be evenly matched, each finishing with a record, for the combined series, of 2 triumphs, 2 draws and 2 defeats.

The game at this time was taking a firm hold in New England, with Fall River the stronghold, and in 1886 the Bristol County Soccer League was established. The next year the New England Association Football League came into existence. It was also in the middle 1880's that the St. Louis Football Association was founded. As in the East, the sport there was confined chiefly to players of Scotch, Irish and English birth. But the year 1890 marked a new epoch in the game's history in that city. It saw the advent of a real American team composed entirely of natives of St. Louis. This team bore the name of "Kensingtons," and won the pennant that year, and, remarkable to relate, went through the entire season without having a goal scored against it.

About 1890 we first learn of the Churchville Thistles, a team operating in the vicinity of Rochester, N.Y. This team was instrumental, to a great extent, in popularizing soccer in Western New York. It was also in the early 90's that the Pennsylvania Football Union first saw the light of day, but it was not until 1898 that real interest there was manifested in the sport, so much so that in 1901 a reorganization brought about the formation of the Football Association of Eastern Pennsylvania, the forerunner of the present day powerful Football Association of Eastern Pennsylvania and District.

The Denver Association Football Club was founded in 1892 and re-organized in 1898, in which year the famous old "Shamrock" Association Football Club was formed in Cincinnati, Ohio. The season of 1902–03 saw the formation of the California Association Football Union, and on Thanksgiving Day, 1905, soccer had its inception in Cleveland, Ohio. In 1906 the Cleveland Soccer Football League became an accomplished fact.

The visit of the "Pilgrims" to these shores in 1904 did much to place the game on a higher level than it had enjoyed previously. The "Pilgrims" was the first British soccer team to invade this country; it was selected from the leading amateur clubs in England and included several players of international renown, among them the famous Vivian Woodward, that country's crack center forward. Twenty-three games were played, the invaders winning 21 and losing 2.

In those pioneering days all efforts to introduce the game into the universities and colleges met with little success, and it was some time before our institutions of learning could be induced to recognize soccer as a sport. Resistance to its introduction eventually was overcome with the forming of the Intercollegiate Association Football League, whose membership at that time comprised Harvard, Columbia, Pennsylvania, Cornell and Haverford College. Today the sport is in high favor at the colleges with more than 500 featuring it as a varsity sport.

The William H. Maxwell Trophy was first put up for annual competition among the high schools of the city of New York in 1906. This award is competed for under the auspices of the Public Schools Athletic League and was won for the first time by Morris High School.

It was also in 1906 that we were favored with a visit by the Famous Corinthian Football Club of London. As in the case of the Pilgrims' tour, this visit did much toward increasing interest in the game, and though many of the matches played were one-sided, there was no lack of enthusiasm. The visitors played 16 games, of which they won 13, lost 1 and tied 2.

The Pilgrim Soccer Football Club again toured this country in 1909, as did the Corinthians in 1911. Our clubs, however, still were no match for the visitors. Twenty-two games were played by the Pilgrims on their second visit, and they were victorious in 16, tied 4, and suffered defeat twice. The Corinthians on their return engaged in 20 contests. They won 18, lost 1 and tied 1.

The growth of soccer in this country, as compared to other nations, has been slow, chiefly because it was looked upon as a foreign game and because it was erroneously felt that it lacked that combative element that the American public has come to consider as an essential part of sport. However, interest in the game for the game's sake has been increasing rapidly in recent years. It is one sport adapted for international competition. Over 140 nations play soccer, and therein lies its greatest attractiveness—it is the only game played by almost all the nations on the face of the globe. In Scotland and England attendances of 100,000 for Cup finals are not uncommon. In Italy, Austria, Hungary, Germany, France, in practically all European countries crowds ranging from 50,000 and upwards are frequent. The largest stadiums in South America, seating from 50,000 to nearly 200,000, were built solely to stage soccer football games.

With the growth of the sport—from the days when unscheduled and impromptu games were played with pick-up teams to that period in the development and progress of the game when New York, New Jersey, Pennsylvania, Maryland, New England, Michigan, Ohio, Illinois, Missouri, Colorado, Utah and California all had regularly organized leagues with regular schedules of games—came the need for a national organization. It was found to be imperative to gather the loose ends of soccer government throughout the country and to weave them into a national organization of sufficient strength to make rules of qualification and discipline—and to enforce them.

Insofar as the United States is concerned, soccer became a recognized national sport in 1913 with the institution of the United States Football Association, which body was accepted in affiliation with the Federation Internationale de Football Association in 1914. Since that time, while it is true progress has not been meteoric, it has nevertheless been in keeping with the efforts spent upon its development. Approximately 10,000 teams, consisting of 2,000 professionals and 200,000 amateur players, are engaged in playing soccer football in this country and are affiliated with the United States Soccer Football Association through the medium of its 42 subsidiary organizations. Although it is not known accurately, it can be conservatively estimated that a greater number of teams is playing soccer in the playgrounds and the private and public schools and colleges.

While in some quarters the increasing interest in soccer in this country is largely measured by the gate receipts from the more important games, those who do not measure its progress by the monetary returns see the greatest future for the sport in the ever increasing number of schools, colleges and universities that are being won over to the game. There are few institutions of learning that do not have soccer squads; some of them have several teams and many have classed the game as a major letter sport. This increasing development of soccer in the schools throughout the country is a gratifying feature of the game's growth. Not only is the increase in interest in the grammar and grade schools considerable, but in the high and preparatory schools it is almost as great. This is the one phase of the game's advancement that is important to its future welfare—its development through the one medium necessary to its success—the American schoolboy.

Soccer in America is receiving another solid boost as an aftermath of World War II. For one thing, United States military forces stationed in other parts of the world have been devoting more attention to the booting sport, which is the national game in those foreign countries. The Army, Navy, Marines and Air Force have adopted regular soccer programs for their respective groups.

In addition, the easing of immigration regulations has increased the influx of foreigners who, because of their basic interest in the sport, have either initiated or increased interest in the game wherever they have settled.

The National (Open) Challenge Cup competition, emblematic of the United States National soccer championship, was established in 1913 upon the formation of the United States Football Association, while the National Amateur Cup competition came into existence in 1922–23. It was felt, when the United States Football Association was formed, that the institution of a truly national cup competition would bring before the public the fact that soccer was something more than a game played and governed in a haphazard manner; that it was, in fact, a national institution.

The missionary work accomplished through the medium of the National (Open) Cup competition can best be realized by the fact that the entries grew so great that it was found necessary to institute a National Amateur Challenge Cup competition in order to permit the amateur to play in his own sphere and, at the same time, earn national honors of his own, thereby leaving the National Open tournament largely to the professional clubs.

The organization has grown and at this time there are 42 associations in membership, together with a number of associate members, including the Amateur Athletic Union of the United States, the Intercollegiate Soccer Football Association of America, the National Collegiate Athletic Association, the National Federation of State High School Athletic Associations and the National Coaches Association of America.

The United States Soccer Football Association

The birth of the United States Soccer Football Association, which controls the activities of all players, professional and amateur, in the country and represents them in the councils of the Federation Internationale de Football Association, a federation of nations more than 80 strong, was by no means a peaceful incident, but the culmination of a warring period in which different organizations waged a strong rivalry for power.

The chief rivalry existed between the American Football Association, an organization which controlled the professional leagues and clubs in New Jersey, Philadelphia and the New England

States and sponsored the American Cup competition and the more recently organized American Amateur Football Association, which had as its nucleus the New York State Amateur Football Association League.

Both factions staked claims for national recognition at the Internationale Federation Congress at Stockholm in 1912. Thomas W. Cahill of New York, secretary of the A.A.F.A. presented the case for the amateur organization and F.J. Wall, secretary of the English Association, with which the A.F.A. was affiliated, opposed the claims of Cahill on the grounds that his organization did not control the professionals, an essential for a national governing body, and adding that the Congress should not be used as a battle pitch by the rival United States organizations.

Cahill was advised to return home, strive to get both organizations to unite and form a national body from which a claim for recognition would be dealt with in the regular manner. The matter was then referred to the Emergency Committee and was evidently never given further consideration.

Shortly after Cahill's return, both associations appointed committees to iron out the difficulties in the way of an agreement. The A.A.F.A. was represented by Dr. G. Randolph Manning, William A. Campbell a vice president and Nathan Agar, a member of the executive board. The A.F.A. was represented by Joseph Hughes of Paterson, N.J.; John Gundy of Bayonne, N.J.; A.N. Beveridge of Kearny, N.J.; A. Albert Frost of Philadelphia and Andrew M. Brown of New York.

The first meeting took place at the Astor House in New York City on Oct. 12, 1912, and when it appeared that all obstacles to a union had been removed the A.F.A. on Dec. 8 notified the A.A.F.A. that by a vote of 7–6 it had decided to discharge its committee and discontinue the negotiations. The meetings had not been without value, however, for the discussions had made many converts in the ranks of the A.F.A.

The amateurs, seeking additional strength, turned to Philadelphia where the strong and well-governed Allied American F.A. was operating and enlisted the help of Douglas Stewart, president of the Referees' Association of Philadelphia. He, in turn, interested John Farrell and Oliver Hemingway, president and secretary of the Football Association of Philadelphia, and all agreed at a meeting at the Astor House on March 8, 1913, to join with the A.A.F.A. in a drive for a national body.

Invitations to a conference were mailed throughout the country and met with instant response with the result that a meeting was held at the Astor House on April 5, 1913.

Archibald Birse, secretary of the Peel Challenge Cup Commission of Chicago, was elected temporary chairman and Cahill was named temporary secretary.

The new organization was named the United States Football Association and a committee comprising Dr. Manning, Birse, Brown, Farrell, Bagnall, Cowley and Beveridge was named to draft the constitution, rules and bylaws.

A second meeting was held at the Broadway Central Hotel in New York on June 21, 1913, and in the election which ensued, Dr. Manning was named president; Hemingway, vice president; Thomas H. McKnight of Chicago, second vice president; William D. Love of Pawtucket, third vice president; Birse, treasurer, and Cahill, secretary.

An application for recognition was filed with the International Federation by the new organization, while the one from the American Amateur Football Association was withdrawn. Early in August another attempt was made to win the affections of the American Football Association, but the offer was rejected by a vote of 5—4.

At the International Federation Congress at Copenhagen in 1913 the still pending application of the American Football Association was not discussed and on Aug. 15 the United States Football Association was recognized as the national body. Following the receipt of the news, the American Football Association, by a vote of 10—2, decided to rescind its vote of the week previous and join the recognized national organization.

In 1945 the organization decided to insert the word "soccer" in its name. The offices of the United States Soccer Football Association are at 350 Fifth Avenue, New York, New York, 10001.

North American Soccer League

Despite a partial collapse after its second season, 1968, with twelve of the seventeen franchises disillusioned that Professional Soccer would suddenly capture the interest of the American public, the North American Soccer League (NASL) was kept alive by the remaining five franchises. Three years later, in 1971, the NASL had grown back to eight franchises and two divisions. By 1973, with the addition of Philadelphia, the NASL had expanded to nine franchises and three divisions (Montreal, Rochester, and Toronto in the Northern Division; New York, Philadelphia, and Miami in the Eastern Division; and St. Louis, Dallas, and Atlanta in the Southern Division) and further expansion appeared imminent

In 1967 there were two competing leagues, the United Soccer Association (USA), which imported entire foreign teams to represent the twelve franchises for the initial season, and the National Professional Soccer League (NPSL), consisting of 10 teams that recruited domestic and foreign talent. The Los Angeles Wolves represented by Wolverhampton Wanderers of England won the U.S.A. Championship with an incredible 6-5 overtime victory over the Washington Whips, represented by Aberdeen of Scotland. The Oakland Clippers captured the NPSL crown with a two-game, total-goals 4-2 victory over the Baltimore Bays, losing 1-0 in Baltimore before winning 4-1 in Oakland.

In 1968 the two leagues merged into a seventeen team league with the Atlanta Chiefs winning the crown in a playoff with the San Diego Toros. The Kansas City Spurs won the reduced league crown in 1969. Two expansion franchises, the Washington Darts and Rochester Lancers vied for the 1970 NASL Championship with the Lancers winning the first game of the playoff finals 3-0, and held on to win the crown with a 4-3 aggregate as Washington defeated them 3-1 in the second contest.

In 1971 the Dallas Tornado, a perennial cellar dweller, became the NASL's first cinderella team. Finishing second in the Southern Division behind Atlanta, Dallas eliminated defending Champion Rochester, then came from behind winning the final two games against Atlanta, after losing the series opener, to garner their first NASL title.

The 1972 season saw the second-year New York Cosmos capture the NASL crown with a climactic 2-1 victory over the stubborn St. Louis Stars after having eliminated Dallas 1-0 in the Semi-Finals. St. Louis had defeated Rochester 2-0 to reach their first-ever final.

National Challenge Cup

The National Challenge Cup, soccer's most coveted prize in the United States, originally was placed in competition during the 1912—13 season and was offered for amateur play only. Today the competition is open to all professional and amateur teams in this country and the winner is considered the champion of the United States.

In presenting the trophy to the American Amateur Football Association, Sir Thomas R. Dewar, noted British sportsman, addressed the following to Thomas W. Cahill, quoted in the "North American Soccer Guide":

Dewar House, Haymarket, S.W. London,
June 20th, 1912

T.W. Cahill, Esq.;
Representative of American Amateur
Foot Ball Association at Olympic Games,
Anderson Hotel, Fleet St., E.C.

Dear Sir:

In continuation of our conversation this morning with reference to amateur foot ball in America, I am delighted to know that this sport has made such strides in your great republic since the last time I had the privilege of being there.

All my life I have taken a very great interest in association foot ball and with a view to fostering and encouraging such an excellent sport I shall be pleased to offer to the executive board of your association a trophy of $500 value, to be competed for by the clubs of your association. The conditions for the competition I leave to be arranged by your executive in New York.

I hope this will be the means of yet stimulating the interest in the game and may it enthuse the inhabitants from New York to the Pacific Coast and I trust that one day foot ball will be found a formidable rival of that great national game, base ball, a game for which I also have a great respect, having been, in fact, for several years president of the Base Ball Association in England.

Some day I trust you will send a team over here to compete with some of our soccer clubs and so assist to cement those bonds of friendship between our two countries in a manner which can be done through sport more effectively than by any other means, creating through sport that fellow feeling that which all so earnestly desire, that in time it may in truth be said that there is nothing which divides America and the British Isles but the Atlantic Ocean.

With all good wishes for the success of your association.

Yours very truly,
Thomas R. Dewar.

The Yonkers Football Club was the first to win the trophy, defeating the Hollywood Inn F.C. of Yonkers, 3–0, at Lennox Oval in New York City. With the formation of the United States Football Association in 1913, the award, with permission of the donor, became the property of the new organization and was offered in competition as the National Challenge Cup. The first victor was the Brooklyn Field Club in 1914.

Eastern and Western eliminations are held each year, with the winners meeting for the title. The trophy is held by the winning team for one year under $2,000 bond to assure its safe and undamaged return.

National Amateur Challenge Cup

Entries for the National Challenge Cup had increased so rapidly that during the 1922–23 season the United States Football Association decided to organize a tournament so that amateurs could compete annually among themselves for national honors. It was decided to award the National Amateur Challenge Cup to the victor.

In the year of the tournament's inception, inclement weather prevented the event from being carried to a conclusion. The Fleisher Yarn F.C. of Philadelphia and Roxbury (Mass.) F.C. were the divisional finalists in the East, this competition also calling for sectional play-offs. In the West the Jeannette (Pa.) F.C. and the Swedish-American A.A. of Detroit reached the last round.

World Cup

The true world series of sports is soccer's World Cup tournament for the Jules Rimet trophy. National teams of most of the countries of the universe compete in the sectional play-offs to determine the qualifiers who will participate in the final rounds. Usually the field is cut to 16 for the tournament, which is staged every four years midway between the Olympic years.

In a sense, the World Cup might be considered as eclipsing the Olympic play in soccer because it is not restricted to amateurs and therefore really is supposed to be pitting the best players of the world in the competition.

Thus far, none of the North American nations has been able to go far in the competition. The best record of the United States was established in 1950 when the American team stunned the world by defeating England, 1-0, in an early round of the play in Brazil. But it was not enough to carry the Americans into the next round.

Uruguay won the World Cup that year by nosing out Brazil, 2-1. Four years later in Switzerland, West Germany provided a major upset by gaining the Rimet Cup with a 3-2 victory over favored Hungary. In 1958 the tournament was held in Sweden and Brazil finally gained the honors with a 5-2 victory over Sweden in the final.

Brazil became the first nation to repeat as the World Champion in Chile in 1962 with a 3-1 victory over Czechoslovakia in the final. While Brazil faltered in 1966, host England won its first World Cup Championship with a 4-2 triumph over West Germany. Brazil earned outright possession of the coveted Jules Rimet Cup with an unprecedented third title, defeating Italy 4-1 in the 1970 final in Mexico City before a world television audience of over 200 million.

Soccer in the British Isles

Soccer was known in England as football until the latter part of the 19th Century. The circumstances provoking the change follow:

Rugby, devised accidentally at Rugby College in England in 1823, gained tremendously in popularity through the next 40 years and when the word "football" was used, some asked: "Which kind?"

A further form of annoyance manifested itself among the clans devoted strictly to the kicking game, when some advocated the option of carrying the ball, as is permitted in rugby. The result was a meeting in 1863 of the stand-pat group and the formation of the first real governing body of the kicking sport.

The organization called itself the London Football Association and voted to confine play entirely to kicking. Later, to distinguish between the two existing forms of football in England, one was called "rugby" and the other "association." The "association" was reduced to "assoc," and finally abbreviated to its present designation of "soccer."

The Association, at its second meeting, in 1866, made various rule changes and the regulations approved at that time are practically the same as those now recognized throughout the world.

Soccer in the British Isles has contributed some of the greatest names ever to play the game such as Sir Stanley Mathews, Tom Finney, Danny Blanchflower, John Charles, Hughie Gallacher, Frank Swift, Billy Wright, Willie Waddell, Billy Liddell, Alex James, and Ivor Alchurch, and more recently Bobby Charlton, Gordon Banks, Bobby Moore, and George Best. In England the British Isles experienced its greatest hour of glory as the English hosted and won the 1966 World Cup with a dramatic 4-2 victory over West Germany in the final.

That the sport is just as popular in England as baseball or football is in the United States is shown by the fact that it is not unusual for crowds of 100,000 or more to attend the elimination matches and finals in the various competitions. The record attendance for the British Isles was set when 149,547 saw Scotland beat England, 3—1, in the international series at Hampden Park, Glasgow, Scotland, on April 17, 1937. This was a world attendance record for a soccer match until the 1950 World Cup tournament in the new Municipal Stadium at Rio de Janeiro, Brazil, drew crowds of 150,000 and 155,000 in the semi-finals, with a new all-time high of 199,854 attending the final in which Uruguay defeated Brazil, 2—1.

A club match between the Rangers and Hibernians drew 143,570, a record for such a contest, to Hampden Park on March 27, 1948, and the 1923 final between the Bolton Wanderers and West Ham United at Wembley Stadium, London, attracted a record English Cup crowd of 126,047. When a United States team played Scotland at Hampden Park on a mid-week day, April 30, 1952, rain and a 6 P.M. starting time did not stop 107,765 paying fans from seeing the contest.

The United States attendance record is 47,000, set when the Hakoah All-Stars of Austria played at the Polo Grounds, New York, in 1926.

Soccer in Canada

Soccer in Canada in past years has been greatly overshadowed by ice hockey, Canadian football, and more recently baseball. However, with the selection of Montreal as the site for the 1976 Summer Olympics, there is a new sense of urgency to improve the status of the game and to develop Canadian talent. The Canadian government has taken a strong lead by providing essential development funds.

The advent of the North American Soccer League into Montreal and Toronto has created an expanding market for top Canadian talent and has given the game in Canada new impetus. Traditionally most of the players in Canada were immigrants from the British Isles and other European nations.

With the exception of British Columbia, soccer is a summer game since most of the country is covered in snow for most of the winter and early spring. Distances are vast in Canada, the population is scanty, and organization of fixtures still presents difficulties.

The Canadian Soccer Association is the national association. It comprises provincial associations, or where none exist as in the remote provinces, district associations. Each province has a number of district associations to which the leagues are affiliated. The provincial associations vary in importance, with Quebec, Ontario, and British Columbia being well organized. The sparsely populated prairie provinces of Alberta, Manitoba, Saskatchewan, Nova Scotia, and Newfoundland have fewer leagues, but the number of clubs is growing rapidly.

The Dominion Challenge Cup is the national competition. The final is played in August with the venue alternated yearly from West to Mid-West to East.

As in the U.S.A. the future of the sport rests with the young players, who, with the new national emphasis being placed in the game, will benefit from vastly improved development and coaching programs.

U.S. INTERCOLLEGIATE SOCCER

Although soccer football was an intercollegiate sport in a few of the older American colleges and universities prior to 1900, no formal governing body existed until the Intercollegiate Association Football League was organized in the spring of 1905. This group comprised Columbia, Cornell, Harvard, Haverford and Pennsylvania, and in the spring of 1906 engaged in the first league competition, won by Haverford.

In May, 1907, Yale was admitted and the six teams contested for the league championship, playing in both the spring and fall until 1914, when it was decided to eliminate the spring schedule. Since then, with the exception of practice sessions or exhibition matches in March and April, intercollegiate soccer has been generally recognized as a fall sport, although in recent years a number of teams on the Pacific Coast have played virtually all year round.

After completing the league schedule in 1915, Columbia was compelled to withdraw, owing to the loss of playing field facilities, and Pennsylvania, in winning the championship in 1916, defeated Cornell, Harvard, Haverford, Princeton and Yale.

In 1917, owing to the war, Harvard, Princeton and Yale resigned and in 1918 no league matches were staged.

The league was reorganized in 1919, with the

same teams as in 1916, but it was becoming increasingly evident that there was need of an intercollegiate organization of broader scope, to foster adequately the increased interest in the sport, maintain uniform rules and rule interpretations, assist in training competent referees, supervise and promote sectional leagues and, in general, perform the functions of administration necessary to the proper conduct of the game.

Accordingly, in 1925—26 the original league disbanded and the members formed the nucleus of the present organization, the Intercollegiate Soccer Football Association of America. The league Championship Cup was permanently awarded to Pennsylvania as having won the most titles.

The new association received applications from Dartmouth, Lehigh, Penn State, Swarthmore, Syracuse and the United States Naval Academy.

From 1928 until 1931, Temple, Springfield, Brown, Hamilton, Illinois, Ohio State, Massachusetts Institute of Technology, Williams, Amherst, Wesleyan and Western Maryland joined the Association and the scope of intercollegiate competition broadened into generally a series of geographically convenient groups.

By the end of 1952 the ISFA had more than 70 member colleges under its banner. Two decades later in 1972 the ISFA membership had topped the 200 mark, and the total number of colleges with teams sanctioned by the NCAA and NIAA had surpassed 500 member institutions.

The college game had been given a new impetus in 1971 with the advent of a three-year contract with Orange Bowl in Miami to host the NCAA Championship Game, the introduction of a College Senior Bowl in Orlando, Florida in 1972, and the need for a separate NCAA College Division Tournament beginning in 1972.

The North American Soccer League introduced the first College Player draft in 1971, which gave further impetus to the development of better college talent. Many colleges began to give soccer its own showcase, rather than presenting it as a preliminary match to football games, and found that the game can stand on its own merits.

INTERCOLLEGIATE ALL-AMERICAN SELECTIONS

(Selections made by National Soccer Coaches Association of America.)

1945

Goal—Tyree, Army
Right Fullback—Crowley, Army
Left Fullback—Barlow, Temple
Right Halfback—Clayton, Haverford
Center Halfback—Benedict, Army
Left Halfback—Hamilton, Penn State
Outside Right—Matlack, Haverford

Inside Right—Ketchum, Pennsylvania
Center Forward—Salista, Navy
Inside Left—Brice, Yale
Outside Left—Ruggieri, Navy

1946

G—Tyree, Army
RF—Fancher, Dartmouth
LF—Barlow, Temple
RH—Hartman, Penn State
CH—Van Breda Kolff, Princeton
LH—Leaverson, Temple
OR—Molnar, Lehigh
IR—Hamilton, Penn State
CF—Jones, Haverford
IL—McLaughlin, Temple
OL—Blair, Pennsylvania

1947

G—Schaufelberger, Navy
RF—Pederson, Swarthmore
LF—Lambert, Temple
RH—Coulter, Navy
CH—Hogan, Springfield
LH—Peard, Navy
OR—Whatford, Brockport
IR—Hughes, Temple
CF—Jones, Haverford
IL—Valtin, Swarthmore
OL—Rogers, Princeton

1948

G—Theodore Bondi, Brockport
RF—Carmen Moutinho, Springfield
LF—Thomas Lambert, Temple
RH—Robert Brown, Cortland
CH—Ralph Hosterman, Penn State
LH—Andrew Lucine, Haverford
OR—Carlos Fetteroff, Connecticut
IR—Charles Berman, Cornell
CF—Ben Stolzfus, Amherst
IL—James Belt, Maryland
OL—Merritt Baldwin, Connecticut

1949

G—Theodore Bondi, Brockport
RF—James Blozie, Connecticut
LF—Stephan Negoescu, San Francisco
RH—Donald Dunbar, Amherst
CH—Jerome Mahrer, Brooklyn College
LH—Donald Thompson, Brockport
OR—Godfrey Nelson, Trinity
IR—Harry Little, Penn State
CF—Clement Grillo, Brooklyn College
IL—Walter Lownes, Pennsylvania
OL—Louis Dollarton, West Chester

1950

G—Theodore Bondi, Brockport
RF—Richard Mothrope, Brockport
LF—Jackson Hall, Dartmouth
RH—James Hanna, Seton Hall
CH—William Sheppell, Seton Hall
LH—Ralph Stern, West Chester
OR—George Andreadis, Brooklyn College

IR—Harry Little, Penn State
CF—Derl Derr, Cornell
IL—Gustavo Gomez, R.P.I.
OL—Louis Dollarton, West Chester

1951

G—Richard Miller, Oberlin
RF—Thomas Morrell, Indiana U.
LF—Jacques Auguste, R.P.I.
RH—James Hanna, Seton Hall
CH—Robert Palmer, Oberlin
LH—Eugene Orbaker, Brockport
OR—Thomas Kennan, Earlham
IR—George Place, Swarthmore
CF—George Boateng, Cornell
IL—Peter Bellows, Oberlin
OL—Anthony Puglisi, West Chester

1952

G—Will Ferguson, Kenyon
RF—Charles Ufford, Harvard
LF—Jackson Hall, Dartmouth
RH—Joseph Marshall, Springfield
CH—Joseph Moulder, Oberlin
LH—Charles Butt, Springfield
OR—Carl Yoder, Franklin and Marshall
IR—John Dunn, Temple
CF—Joseph Devaney, Pennsylvania
IL—David Strauch, Duke
OL—Anthony Puglisi, West Chester

1953

G—William Cox, San Francisco
RF—Jay Gernand, Springfield
LF—Fred Gahres, East Stroudsburg
RH—Vincent Palmieri, Cortland
CH—Fred James, Duke
LH—Leonard Oliver, Temple
OR—Manuel Ortiz, San Francisco
IR—Henry Ford Jr., Wesleyan
CF—Winfield Carlough, Trinity
IL—Neil Mutschler, Trinity
OL—Gabor Czako, Pennsylvania

1954

G—Bruce Newell, Navy
RF—Robert Siemons, Allegheny
LF—Hector J. Requezes, Duke
RH—Vincent Palmieri, Cortland
CH—Norman Thoms, Oberlin
LH—Leonard Oliver, Temple
OR—Paul Clark, Wheaton
IR—Jack Dunn, Temple
CF—Richard Packer, Penn State
IL—Francis Adams, Army
OL—John Pinezich, Penn State

1955

G—James Davins, Bridgeport
RF—Carlos Ossio, California
LF—Robert Simpson, Temple
RH—Dale Conley, Oberlin
CH—Sergio Rey, West Chester
LH—John Hicks, Indiana
OR—Richard Malinowski, Baltimore

IR—Olher Karawan, Chicago Navy Pier
CF—Richard Packer, Penn State
IL—David Arnold, Wheaton
OL—E.C. Kirk Hall, Amherst

1956

G—Michael Easterling, Wheaton
RF—Paul Coward, Purdue
LF—William Hughes, Brockport State
RH—Thomas Colmey, Duke
CH—Henry Litchfuss, Towson State
LH—Raymond Wilson, West Chester
OR—Kenneth Lindfors, Oberlin
IR—Michael Cooke, Yale
CF—Douglas Raynard, Trinity
IL—Anthony Washofsky, Drexel Tech
OL—Oswald Jethon, Drexel Tech

1957

G—Michael Easterling, Wheaton
RF—John Nelson, Cornell
LF—Paul Coward, Purdue
RH—Daniel Sullivan, Springfield
CH—John Paranos, C.C.N.Y.
LH—Newlin Otto, Earlham
OR—Gerald Husted, Franklin and Marshall
IR—Per Torgerson, Penn State
CF—Telehun Bekele, Purdue
IL—Thomas Fleck, West Chester
OL—Sergei Retivov, Swarthmore

1958

G—Richard Williams, Pennsylvania
RF—John Jennings, Washington College (Md.)
LF—Remo Tabello, U.C.L.A.
RH—Mohamad Gainie, U.C.L.A.
CH—John Meehan, Navy
LF—Newlin Otto, Earlham
OR—Edward Lopresto, U.C.L.A.
IR—Alberto Sarria, Michigan State
CF—Stanley Blugosz, Drexel Tech
IL—Oswald Jethon, Drexel Tech
OL—Theodore Zornow, Rochester

1959

G—John Santos, Fairleigh Dickinson
RB—James Gallo, Temple
LB—Bodhan Huryan, Penn State
RH—Peter Hezekiah, Howard
LH—Joseph Cosgrove, Baltimore
OR—James Taylor, Colgate
IR—W. Chyzowych, Temple
CF—Cecil Heron, Michigan State
IL—Erich Streder, Michigan State
OL—Andam Pintz, Penn State

1960

G—George Politz, Baltimore
RB—Harold Taylor, Haverford
LB—Barry Remley, Westchester
RH—Gyula Kovacsies, Haverford
CH—William Heyen, Brockport
LH—Thomas Scanlon, LaSalle
OR—Chris Sweeney, Cortland
IR—Igor Lissy, Drexel

CF—Walter Schmidt, Rutgers
IL—William Charlton, Temple
OL—James Taylor, Colgate

1961

G—Andre Houtkruyer, C.C.N.Y.
RB—Helmut Poje, Brooklyn
LB—Gerald Li, San Francisco State
RH—Neil Fagan, Navy
CH—Reiner Kemeling, Michigan State
LH—Harry Shirk, East Stroudsberg
OR—Alvord Rutherford, Williams
IR—Magid Kria, Washington
CF—Donald Williams, Westchester
IL—Robert Malone, St. Louis
OL—Kun Choo, California

1962

G—D. Smoyer, Dartmouth
RF—Paul Fardy, Cortland
LF—Louis Buck, Penn
RH—Fritz Kungle, Akron
CH—Reiner Kemeling, Michigan State
LH—Bill Vieth, St. Louis
OR—Gerry Balassi, St. Louis
IR—Karl Kaeser, Navy
CF—Don Williams, West Chester
IL—Rubens Filizola, Michigan State
OL—Keith Van Winkle, Middlebury

1963

G—Roger Curylo, Bridgeport
RF—Thomas Hennessey, St. Louis
LF—Helmut Poje, Brooklyn
RH—Michael Lonergan, Fairleigh Dickinson
CH—Winston Alexis, Howard
LH—Myron Hura, Navy
OR—Christian Ohiri, Harvard
IR—Walter Schmotolocha, Pratt
CF—Anthony Martelli, Hartwick
IL—Al Hershey, Elizabethtown
OL—Keith Van Winkle, Middlebury

1964

G—Tim Tarpley, California
RF—J. Davis Webb, Middlebury
LF—Lee Cook, Trenton (N.J.) State
RH—Don Ceresia, St. Louis
CH—Myron Hura, Navy
LH—Roy Eales, Maryland
OR—Giedris Klivecka, Long Island U.
IR—Payton Fuller, Michigan State
CF—Dan Goldstein, Fairleigh Dickinson
IL—Pat McBride, St. Louis
OL—Albert Korbus, San Jose State

1965

G—Tim Tarpley, California
RF—Peter Prozik, Buffalo State
LF—Lee Cook, Trenton (N.J.) State
RH—John Eastman, Ohio U.
CH—Nick Krat, Michigan State
LH—Steve Varsa, Catholic U.
OR—Carl Gentile, St. Louis
IR—Lewis Frazer, San Jose

CF—Guy Bush, Michigan State
IL—Pat McBride, St. Louis
OL—Janos Benedek, Ithaca

1966

G—John Garrison, Middlebury
RF—Reinhold Jabusch, Long Island U.
LF—Ulick Bourke, Catholic U.
RH—Myron Bakun, Newark
CH—John Boles, Temple
LH—Peter Hens, Michigan State
OR—Jack Kinealy, St. Louis
IR—Donald Prozik, Brockport
CF—Jaffer Kassamali, Amherst
IL—Umit Kesim, Indiana
OL—Victor DeJong, Brown

1967

G—Fred Brunner, Akron
RF—John Marks, Middlebury
LF—Tom Teach, Navy
RH—Ron McEachen, W. Virginia
CH—Patrick Migliore, Brown
LH—Jacob Meehl, Temple
OR—Henry Camacho, San Jose
IR—Sandor Hites, San Francisco
CF—Walter Werner, St. Louis
IL—Kirk Apostolidis, San Francisco
OL—Trevor Harris, Michigan State

1968

G—Ford Bruner, Akron
RF—John Marks, Middlebury
LF—Tom Teach, Navy
RH—Ron McEachen, West Virginia
CH—Patrick Migliore, Brown
LH—Jacob Meehl, Temple
OR—Henry Camacho, San Jose
IR—Sandor Hites, San Francisco
CF—Walter Werner, St. Louis
IL—Kirk Apostolidis, San Francisco
OL—Trevor Harris, Michigan State

1969

G—Bruce Parkhill, LockHaven
RF—Don Fowler, Trenton State
LF—Karim Yassim, Elizabethtown
RH—Len Renery, Columbia
CH—Peter Goosens, San Diego State
LH—Tony Elia, Hartwick
OR—Abdula Jama, N.Y.U.
IR—Alec Popadakis, Hartwick
CF—Bob Durham, Philadelphia Textile
IL—Rasim Tugberk, Maryland
OL—Manuel Hernandez, San Jose State

1970

Goal—William Nutlal, Davis and Elkins
Back—Art Demling, Michigan State
Back—Alan Harte, Quincy
Back—Nick Iwanik, U. of Illinois (Chicago)
Back—Gerardo Pagnani, Eastern Illinois
Back—Aladin Rodrigues, San Jose State
Forward—Al Trost, St. Louis U.
Forward—Stanley Startzell, Pennsylvania

Forward—Alvin Henderson, Howard U.
Forward—Richard Parkinson, Akron
Forward—Randy Smith, Buffalo State

1971

Goal—Cal Kern, Buffalo State
Back—Gerardo Pagnani, Eastern Illinois
Back—Alan Harte, Quincy
Back—William Smyth, Davis and Elkins
Back—Andy Smiles, Ohio U.
Back—John Schneider, Quincy
Forward—Kieth Aqui, Howard
Forward—Alvin Henderson, Howard
Forward—Richard Parkinson, Akron
Forward—John Moore, Brockport State
Forward—Mike Seerey, St. Louis

1972

Goal—Bob Rigby, East Stroudsburg
Back—Alan Harte, Quincy
Back—Gerardo Pagnani, Eastern Illinois
Back—Hans Wango, Davis and Elkins
Back—Gorden Cholmondeley,
    Philadelphia Textile
Back—Christopher Bahr, Penn State
Forward—Ian Bain, Howard
Forward—Andrew Rymarczuk, Penn State
Forward—Chris Papagianis, Harvard
Forward—Eugene Durham, Philadelphia Textile
Forward—Tom Kazemba, Wooster

WORLD CUP CHAMPIONS

(Played every four years)

1930—Uruguay
1934—Italy
1938—Italy
1942 & 46—No competition
1950—Uruguay
1954—West Germany
1958—Brazil
1962—Brazil
1966—England
1970—Brazil

NORTH AMERICAN SOCCER
LEAGUE CHAMPIONS

1967—NPSL—Oakland Clippers; USA—
    Los Angeles Wolves
1968—Atlanta Chiefs
1969—Kansas City Spurs
1970—Rochester Lancers
1971—Dallas Tornado
1972—New York Cosmos

UNITED STATES CHAMPIONS

National Challenge Cup

Competition open to professional and amateur teams in the United States.

1914—Brooklyn (N.Y.) Field Club
1915—16—Bethlehem (Pa.) Steel Co. F.C.
1917—Fall River (Mass.) Rovers
1918—19—Bethlehem Steel Co. F.C.
1920—Benn Miller F.C., St. Louis
1921—Robins Dry Dock F.C., Brooklyn, N.Y.

1922—Scullin Steel F.C., St. Louis
1923—Paterson (N.J.) F.C.
1924—Fall River (Mass.) F.C.
1925—Shawsheen S.C., Andover, Mass.
1926—Bethlehem Steel Co. F.C.
1927—Fall River F.C.
1928—New York Nationals S.C.
1929—Hakoah All-Stars, New York
1930—31—Fall River F.C.
1932—New Bedford (Mass.) F.C.
1933—34—Stix, Baer & Fuller F.C., St. Louis
1935—Central Breweries S.C., St. Louis
1936—First German American S.C., Philadelphia
1937—New York Americans S.C.
1938—Sparta A.B.A., Chicago
1939—St. Mary's Celtic S.C., Brooklyn, N.Y.
1940—No official champion*
1941—Pawtucket (R.I.) F.C.
1942—Gallatin S.C., Pittsburgh
1943—44—Brooklyn (N.Y.) Hispano S.C.
1945—Brookhattan S.C., New York
1946—Vikings, Chicago
1947—Ponta Delgada F.C., Fall River, Mass.
1948—Joe Simpkins S.C., St. Louis
1949—Morgan (Pa.) S.C.
1950—Joe Simpkins S.C.
1951—German-Hungarian S.C., Brooklyn, N.Y.
1952—Harmarville (Pa.) S.C.
1953—Chicago Falcons
1954—New York Americans
1955—Eintracht S.C., Astoria, L.I., N.Y.
1956—Harmarville (Pa.) S.C.
1957—Kutis S.C., St. Louis, Mo.
1958—Los Angeles Kickers
1959—San Pedro Canvasbacks (Calif.)
1960—61—Ukrainian Nationals (Phila.)
1962—New York Hungarians
1963—Philadelphia Ukrainians
1964—Los Angeles Kickers
1965—New York Ukrainians
1966—Philadelphia Ukrainians
1967—69—New York Greek-Americans
1970—Elizabeth (N.J.) S.C.
1971—New York Hota
1972—Elizabeth (N.J.) S.C.

*Baltimore S.C. and the Sparta A.B.A., Chicago, were the finalists.

National Amateur Challenge Cup

1923—No official champion
1924—Fleisher Yarn F.C., Philadelphia
1925—Toledo (Ohio) F.C.
1926—Defenders F.C., New Bedford, Mass.
1927—Heidelberg (Pa.) F.C.
1928—No official champion
1929—Heidelberg F.C.
1930—Raffies F.C., Fall River, Mass.
1931—Goodyear F.C., Akron, Ohio
1932—Shamrock S.C., Cleveland
1933—34—German American S.C., Philadelphia
1935—W.W. Riehl S.C., Castle Shannon, Pa.
1936—First German S.C., Brooklyn, N.Y.
1937—Highlander F.C., Trenton, N.J.

1938—Ponta Delgada F.C., Fall River, Mass.
1939—St. Michael's A.C., Fall River, Mass.
1940—Morgan-Strasser S.C.
1944—45—Eintracht S.C., New York
1946—48—Ponta Delgada F.C.
1949—Elizabeth (N.J.) Sport Club
1950—Ponta Delgada F.C.
1951—German-Hungarian S.C., Brooklyn, N.Y.
1952—St. Louis Raiders
1953—Ponta Delgada F.C., Tiverton, R.I.
1954—Beadling (Pa.) S.C.
1955—Heidelberg (Pa.) Tornadoes
1956—61—Kutis (St. Louis)
1962—Carpathia Kickers (Detroit)
1963—Italian-Americans, Rochester, N.Y.
1964—Schwaben, Chicago
1965—German-Hungarians, Philadelphia
1966—Kickers, Chicago
1967—Italian Americans, Hartford, Conn.
1968—Chicago Kickers
1969—British Lions
1970—Chicago Lions
1971—Kutis (St. Louis)
1972—Busch (St. Louis) S.C.

National Junior Challenge Cup

1935—Reliable Stores F.C., New Bedford, Mass.
1936—37—Hatikvoh F.C., Brooklyn
1938—Lighthouse Boys Club, Philadelphia
1939—40—Avella (Pa.) F.C.
1941—Mercerville S.C., Trenton, N.J.
1942—44—No competition
1945—*Pompei S.C., Baltimore, and Hornets S.C., Chicago (co-champions)
1946—Schumacher S.C., St. Louis
1947—Heidelberg (Pa.) S.C.
1948—49—Lighthouse B.C.
1950—Harrison (N.J.) Boys Club
1951—Seco Boys Club, St. Louis
1952—Killsman S.C., Brooklyn, and Lions S.C., Chicago (co-champions)
1953—Newark S.C. and Hansa, Chicago, co-champions
1954—Hansa, Chicago
1955—Gottschee Blauweiss S.C., Brooklyn, and Schwaben S.C., Chicago (co-champions)
1956—St. Engelbert, St. Louis
1957—Lighthouse Boys Club, Philadelphia
1958—St. Paul, S.C., St. Louis
1959—Ukrainian (New York)
1960—St. Paul (St. Louis)
1961—Hakoah (San Francisco)
1962—Schumachers (St. Louis)
1963—64—Kutis (St. Louis)
1965—I.M. Heart of Mary (St. Louis)
1966—St. William (St. Louis)
1967—Lighthouse Boys (Philadelphia)
1968—69—St. Phillip Neri (St. Louis)
1970—St. Barts (St. Louis)
1971—72—SECO (St. Louis)

*Schumacher S.C. won tournament, but was disqualified for using ineligible players.

NCAA UNIVERSITY DIVISION CHAMPIONS

1959—60—St. Louis University
1961—West Chester State College
1962—63—St. Louis University
1964—Navy
1965—St. Louis University
1966—Univ. of San Francisco
1967—St. Louis U., Michigan State (tie)
1968—Michigan State, Maryland (tie)
1969—70—St. Louis University
1971—Howard University
1972—St. Louis University

CANADIAN CHAMPIONS

1913—14—Norwood Wanders
1915—Winnipeg Scots
1916—18—No competition
1919—Grand Trunk, Que.
1920—Westinghouse, Ont.
1921—Toronto Scots
1922—Calgary Hillhurst
1923—Nanaimo, B.C.
1924—Un. Weston, Winnipeg
1925—Toronto Ulsters
1926—Un. Weston
1927—Nanaimo
1928—Westminster (B.C.) Royals
1929—C.N.R., Montreal
1930—31—Westminster Royals
1932—33—Toronto Scots
1934—Verduns, Montreal
1935—Aldreds, Montreal
1936—Westminster Royals
1937—Johnston Nationals
1938—North Shore, Vancouver
1939—Radials, Vancouver
1940—45—No competition
1946—Toronto Ulsters
1947—St. Andrews, Vancouver
1948—Carsteel, Montreal
1949—North Shore, Vancouver
1950—Vancouver City
1951—Ulster United, Toronto
1952—Steelco, Montreal
1953—Westminster (B.C.) Royals
1954—A.N. and A.F. Scottish, Winnipeg
1955—Westminster (B.C.) Royals
1956—Halecos, Vancouver
1957—Ukrania S.C., Montreal
1958—New Westminster (B.C.) Royals
1959—Alouetts (Montreal)
1960—Westminster Royals (Vancouver)
1961—Concordia (Montreal)
1962—Scottish (Winnepeg)
1963—No competition
1964—Columbus (Vancouver)
1965—66—Firefighters (Vancouver)
1967—Toronto Ballymena
1968—Toronto Royals
1969—Columbus (Vancouver)
1970—Manitoba Selects
1971—Vancouver Eintracht

BRITISH CHAMPIONS
International Series
1883–84–Scotland
1884–85–Scotland
1885–86–England and Scotland (tie)
1886–87–Scotland
1887–88–England
1888–89–Scotland
1889–90–Scotland and England (tie)
1890–91–England
1891–92–England
1892–93–England
1893–94–Scotland
1894–95–England
1895–96–Scotland
1896–97–Scotland
1897–98–England
1898–99–England
1899–1900–Scotland
1900–01–England
1901–02–Scotland
1902–03–England, Ireland and Scotland (tie)
1903–04–England
1904–05–England
1905–06–England and Scotland (tie)
1906–07–Wales
1907–08–Scotland and England (tie)
1908–09–England
1909–10–Scotland
1910–11–England
1911–12–England and Scotland
1912–13–England
1913–14–Ireland
1915–18–No competition
1919–20–Wales
1920–21–Scotland
1921–22–Scotland
1922–23–Scotland
1923–24–Wales
1924–25–Scotland
1925–26–Scotland
1926–27–Scotland and England (tie)
1927–28–Wales
1928–29–Scotland
1929–30–England
1930–31–Scotland and England (tie)
1931–32–England
1932–33–Wales
1933–34–Wales
1934–35–England and Scotland (tie)
1935–36–Scotland
1936–37–Wales
1937–38–England
1938–39–England, Scotland and Wales (tie)
1940–45–No competition
1946–47–England
1947–48–England
1948–49–Scotland
1949–50–England
1950–51–Scotland
1951–52–England and Wales (tie)
1952–53–Scotland and England (tie)

1954–57–England
1957–58–England and Ireland (tie)
1959–England, Northern Ireland (tie)
1960–England, Scotland and Wales (tie)
1961–England
1962–63–Scotland
1964–65–England
1966–Scotland
1967–England
1968–England
1969–England, Scotland and Wales (tie)
1970–England
1971–England and Scotland (tie)
1972–England

English Challenge Cup
(Score of final in parentheses.)
1872–Wanderers beat Royal Engineers (1–0)
1873–Wanderers beat Oxford University (2–0)
1874–Oxford University beat Royal Engineers (2–0)
1875–Royal Engineers beat Old Etonians (2–0)
1876–Wanderers beat Old Etonians (3–0)
1877–Wanderers beat Oxford University (2–0)
1878–Wanderers beat Royal Engineers (3–1)
1879–Old Etonians beat Clapham Rovers (1–0)
1880–Clapham Rovers beat Oxford University (1–0)
1881–Old Carthusians beat Old Etonians (3–0)
1882–Old Etonians beat Blackburn Rovers (1–0)
1883–Blackburn Olympic beat Old Etonians (2–1)
1884–Blackburn Rovers beat Queen's Park of Glasgow (2–1)
1885–Blackburn Rovers beat Queen's Park (2–0)
1886–Blackburn Rovers beat West Bromwich Albion (2–0)
1887–Aston Villa beat West Bromwich Albion (2–0)
1888–West Bromwich Albion beat Preston North End (2–1)
1889–Preston North End beat Wolverhampton Wanderers (3–0)
1890–Blackburn Rovers beat Sheffield Wednesday (6–1)
1891–Blackburn Rovers beat Notts County (3–1)
1892–West Bromwich Albion beat Aston Villa (3–0)
1893–Wolverhampton Wanderers beat Everton (1–0)
1894–Notts County beat Bolton Wanderers (4–1)
1895–Aston Villa beat West Bromwich Albion (1–0)
1896–Sheffield Wednesday beat Wolverhampton Wanderers (2–1)
1897–Aston Villa beat Everton (3–2)
1898–Nottingham Forest beat Derby County (3–1)
1899–Sheffield United beat Derby County (4–1)
1900–Bury beat Southampton (4–0)

1901—Tottenham Hotspur beat Sheffield United
   (3—1)
1902—Sheffield United beat Southampton (2—1)
1903—Bury beat Derby County (6—0)
1904—Manchester City beat Bolton Wanderers
   (1—0)
1905—Aston Villa beat Newcastle United (2—0)
1906—Everton beat Newcastle United (1—0)
1907—Sheffield Wednesday beat Everton (2—1)
1908—Wolverhampton Wanderers beat Newcastle
   United (3—1)
1909—Manchester United beat Bristol City (1—0)
1910—Newcastle United beat Barnsley (2—0)
1911—Bradford City beat Newcastle United
   (1—0)
1912—Barnsley beat West Bromwich Albion
   (1—0)
1913—Aston Villa beat Sunderland (1—0)
1914—Burnley beat Liverpool (1—0)
1915—Sheffield United beat Chelsea (3—0)
1916—19—No competition
1920—Aston Villa beat Huddersfield Town (1—0)
1921—Tottenham Hotspur beat Wolverhampton
   Wanderers (1—0)
1922—Huddersfield Town beat Preston North
   End (1—0)
1923—Bolton Wanderers beat West Ham United
   (2—0)
1924—Newcastle United beat Aston Villa (2—0)
1925—Sheffield United beat Cardiff City (1—0)
1926—Bolton Wanderers beat Manchester City
   (1—0)
1927—Cardiff City beat Arsenal (1—0)
1928—Blackburn Rovers beat Huddersfield Town
   (3—1)
1929—Bolton Wanderers beat Portsmouth (2—0)
1930—Arsenal beat Huddersfield Town (2—0)
1931—West Bromwich Albion beat Birmingham
   (2—1)
1932—Newcastle United beat Arsenal (2—1)
1933—Everton beat Manchester City (3—0.)
1934—Manchester City beat Portsmouth (2—1)
1935—Sheffield Wednesday beat West Bromwich
   Albion (4—2)
1936—Arsenal beat Sheffield United (1—0)
1937—Sunderland beat Preston North End (3—1)
1938—Preston North End beat Huddersfield
   Town (1—0)
1939—Portsmouth beat Wolverhampton
   Wanderers (4—1)
1940—45—No competition
1946—Derby County beat Charlton Athletic
   (4—1)
1947—Charlton Athletic beat Burnley (1—0)
1948—Manchester United beat Blackpool (4—2)
1949—Wolverhampton Wanderers beat Leicester
   City (3—1)
1950—Arsenal beat Liverpool (2—0)
1951—Newcastle United beat Blackpool (2—0)
1952—Newcastle United beat Arsenal (1—0)
1953—Blackpool beat Bolton Wanderers (4—3)
1954—West Bromwich Albion beat Preston North

End (3—2)
1955—Newcastle United beat Manchester City
   (3—1)
1956—Manchester City beat Birmingham City
   (3—1)
1957—Aston Villa beat Manchester United (2—1)
1958—Bolton Wanderers beat Manchester United
   (2—0)
1959—Nottingham Forest beat Luton Town
   (2—1)
1960—Wolverhampton beat Blackburn (3—0)
1961—Tottenham beat Leicester (2—0)
1962—Tottenham beat Burnley (6—1)
1963—Manchester United beat Leicester City
   (3—1)
1964—West Ham United beat Preston N.E. (3—2)
1965—Liverpool beat Leeds United (2—1)
1966—Everton beat Sheffield Wednesday (3—2)
1967—Tottenham United beat Chelsea (2—1)
1968—West Bromwich Albion beat Everton (1—0)
1969—Manchester City beat Leicester City (1—0)
1970—Chelsea beat Leeds United (2—1)
1971—Arsenal beat Liverpool (2—1)
1972—Leeds United beat Arsenal (1—0)

English Amateur Cup

(Score of final in parentheses.)

1894—Old Carthusians beat Casuals (2—1)
1895—Middlesbrough beat Old Carthusians (2—1)
1896—Bishop Auckland beat R.A. Portsmouth
   (1—0)
1897—Old Carthusians beat Stockton (4—1)
1898—Middlesbrough beat Uxbridge (2—1)
1899—Stockton beat Harwich and Parkeston
   (1—0)
1900—Bishop Auckland beat Lowestoft Town
   (5—1)
1901—Crook Town beat King's Lynn (3—0)
1902—Old Malvernians beat Bishop Auckland
   (5—1)
1903—Stockton beat Oxford City (1—0)
1904—Sheffield beat Ealing (3—1)
1905—West Hartlepool beat Clapton (3—2)
1906—Oxford City beat Bishop Auckland (3—0)
1907—Clapton beat Stockton (2—1)
1908—Depot Battalion Royal Engineers beat
   Stockton (2—1)
1909—Clapton beat Eston United (6—0)
1910—R.M.L.I. (Gosport) beat South Bank (2—1)
1911—Bromley beat Bishop Auckland (1—0)
1912—Stockton beat Eston United (1—0)
1913—South Bank beat Oxford City (1—0)
1914—Bishop Auckland beat Northern Nomads
   (1—0)
1915—Clapton beat Bishop Auckland (1—0)
1916—19—No competition
1920—Dulwich Hamlet beat Tufnell Park (1—0)
1921—Bishop Auckland beat Swindon Victoria
   (4—2)
1922—Bishop Auckland beat South Bank (5—2)
1923—London Caledonians beat Evesham Town
   (2—1)

1924—Clapton beat Erith and Belvedere (3—0)
1925—Clapton beat Southall (2—1)
1926—Northern Nomads beat Stockton (7—1)
1927—Leyton beat Barking Town (3—1)
1928—Leyton beat Cockfield (3—2)
1929—Ilford beat Leyton (3—1)
1930—Ilford beat Bournemouth Gasworks Athletic (5—1)
1931—Wycombe Wanderers beat Hayes (1—0)
1932—Dulwich Hamlet beat Marine of Liverpool (7—1)
1933—Kingstonian beat Tockton (4—1)
1934—Dulwich Hamlet beat Leyton (2—1)
1935—Bishop Auckland beat Wimbledon (2—1)
1936—The Casuals beat Ilford (2—0)
1937—Dulwich Hamlet beat Leyton (2—0)
1938—Bromley beat Erith and Belvedere (1—0)
1939—Bishop Auckland beat Willington (3—0)
1940—45—No competition
1946—Barnet beat Bishop Auckland (3—2)
1947—Leytonstone beat Wimbledon (2—1)
1948—Leytonstone beat Barnet (1—0)
1949—Bromley beat Romford (1—0)
1950—Willington beat Bishop Auckland (4—0)
1951—Pegasus beat Bishop Auckland (2—1)
1952—Walthamstow Avenue beat Leyton (2—1)
1953—Pegasus (Oxford and Cambridge universities picked team) beat Harwich Parkeston (6—0)
1954—Crook Town beat Bishop Auckland (1—0, after two 2—2 draws
1955—Bishop Auckland beat Hendon (2—0)
1956—Bishop Auckland beat Corinthian-Casuals (4—1, after 1—1 draw)
1957—Bishop Auckland beat Wycombe Wanderers (3—1)
1958—Woking beat Ilford (3—0)
1959—Crook Town beat Barnet (3—2)
1960—Hendon beat Kingstonian (2—1)
1961—Walthamstow beat W. Auckland Town (2—1)
1962—Crook Town beat Hounslow Town (4—0 after 1—1 draw)
1963—Wimbledon beat Sutton United (4—2)
1964—Crook Town beat Enfield (2—1)
1965—Hendon beat Whitby Town (3—1)
1966—Wealdstone beat Hendon (3—1)
1967—Enfield beat Skelmerdale United (3—0 after 0—0 draw)
1968—Leytonstone beat Chesham United (1—0)
1969—North Shields beat Sutton United (2—1)
1970—Enfield beat Dagenham (5—1)
1971—Skelmersdale United beat Dagenham (4—1)
1972—Hendon beat Enfield (2—0)

Scottish Challenge Cup

(Score of final in parentheses.)

1874—Queen's Park beat Clydesdale (2-0)
1875—Queen's Park beat Renton (3-0)
1876—Queen's Park beat Third Lanark (2-0)
1877—Vale of Leven Beat Rangers (3-2)
1878—Vale of Leven Beat Third Lanark (1-0)

1879—Vale of Leven awarded cup after Rangers failed to appear for play-off after 1-1 draw
1880—Queen's Park beat Thornliebank (3-0)
1881—Queen's Park beat Dumbarton (3-1)
1882—Queen's Park beat Dumbarton (4-1)
1883—Dumbarton beat Vale of Leven (2-1)
1884—Queen's Park awarded cup; Vale of Leven failed to appear
1885—Renton beat Vale of Leven (3—1)
1886—Queen's Park beat Renton (3—1)
1887—Hibernian beat Dumbarton (2—1)
1888—Renton beat Cambuslang (6—1)
1889—Third Lanark beat Celton (2—1)
1890—Queen's Park beat Vale of Leven (2—1)
1891—Hearts beat Dumbarton (1—0)
1892—Celtic beat Queen's Park (5—1)
1893—Queen's Park beat Celtic (2—1)
1894—Rangers beat Celtic (3—1)
1895—St. Bernard's beat Renton (2—1)
1896—Hearts beat Hibernian (3—1)
1897—Rangers beat Dumbarton (5—1)
1898—Rangers beat Kilmarnock (2—0)
1899—Celtic beat Rangers (2—0)
1900—Celtic beat Queen's (4—3)
1901—Hearts beat Celtic (4—3)
1902—Hibernian beat Celtic (1—0)
1903—Rangers beat Hearts (2—0)
1904—Celtic beat Rangers (3—2)
1905—Third Lanark beat Rangers (3—1)
1906—Hearts beat Third Lanark (1—0)
1907—Celtic beat Hearts (3—0)
1908—Celtic beat St. Mirren (5—1)
1909—Because of a riot the cup was withheld after Celtic and Rangers had played two draws
1910—Dundee beat Clyde (2—1)
1911—Celtic beat Hamilton (2—0)
1912—Celtic beat Clyde (2—0)
1913—Falkirk beat Raith Rovers (2—0)
1914—Celtic beat Hibernian (4—1)
1915—19—No competition
1920—Kilmarnock beat Albion Rovers (3—2)
1921—Partick Thistle beat Rangers (1—0)
1922—Morton beat Rangers (1—0)
1923—Celtic beat Hibernian (1—0)
1924—Airdrieonians beat Hibernian (2—0)
1925—Celtic beat Dundee (2—1)
1926—St. Mirren beat Celtic (2—0)
1927—Celtic beat East Fife (3—1)
1928—Rangers beat Celtic (4—0)
1929—Kilmarnock beat Rangers (2—0)
1930—Rangers beat Partick Thistle (2—1)
1931—Celtic beat Motherwell (4—2)
1932—Rangers beat Kilmarnock (3—0)
1933—Celtic beat Motherwell (1—0)
1934—Rangers beat St. Mirren (5—0)
1935—Rangers beat Hamilton (2—1)
1936—Rangers beat Third Lanark (1—0)
1937—Celtic beat Aberdeen (2—1)
1938—East Fife beat Kilmarnock (4—2)
1939—Clyde beat Motherwell (4—0)
1940—46—No competition
1947—Aberdeen beat Hibernian (2—1)

1948—Rangers beat Morton (1—0)
1949—Rangers beat Clyde (4—1)
1950—Rangers beat East Fife (3—0)
1951—Celtic beat Motherwell (1—0)
1952—Motherwell beat Dundee (4—0)
1953—Rangers beat Aberdeen (1—0)
1954—Celtic beat Aberdeen (2—1)
1955—Clyde beat Celtic (1—0)
1956—Hearts beat Celtic (3—1)
1957—Falkirk beat Kilmarnock (2—1)
1958—Clyde beat Hibernian (1—0)
1959—St. Mirren beat Aberdeen (3—1)
1960—Rangers beat Kilmarnock (2—0)
1961—Dunfirmline beat Celtic (2—0)
1962—Rangers beat St. Mirren (2—0)
1963—Rangers beat Celtic (3—0 after 1—1draw)
1964—Rangers beat Dundee (3—1)
1965—Celtic beat Dunfirmline Athletic (3—2)
1966—Rangers beat Celtic (1—0 after 0—0 draw)
1967—Celtic beat Aberdeen (2—0)
1968—Dunfirmline Athletic beat Hearts (3—1)
1969—Celtic beat Rangers (4—0)
1970—Aberdeen beat Celtics (3—1)
1971—Celtic beat Rangers 3—1 after 1—1 draw)
1972—Celtic beat Hibernian (6—1)

English League
(First Division)
1889—90—Preston N.E.
1891—Everton
1892—93—Sunderland
1894—Aston Villa
1895—Sunderland
1896—97—Aston Villa
1898—Sheffield United
1899—1900—Aston Villa
1901—Liverpool
1902—Sunderland
1903—04—Sheffield Wednesday
1905—Newcastle United
1906—Liverpool
1907—Newcastle United
1908—Manchester United
1909—Newcastle United
1910—Aston Villa
1911—Manchester United
1912—Blackburn Rovers
1913—Sunderland
1914—Blackburn Rovers
1915—Everton
1916—19—No competition
1920—West Bromwich Albion
1921—Burnley
1922—23—Liverpool
1924—26—Huddersfield Town
1927—Newcastle United
1928—Everton
1929—30—Sheffield Wednesday
1931—Arsenal
1932—Everton
1933—35—Arsenal

1936—Sunderland
1937—Manchester City
1938—Arsenal
1939—Everton
1940—46—No competition
1947—Liverpool
1948—Arsenal
1949—50—Portsmouth
1951—Tottenham Hotspur
1952—Manchester United
1953—Arsenal (Won on goal average)
1954—Wolverhampton Wanderers
1955—Chelsea
1956—57—Manchester United
1958—59—Wolverhampton Wanderers
1960—Burnley
1961—Tottenham
1962—Ipswich Town
1963—Manchester United
1964—Liverpool
1965—Manchester United
1966—Liverpool
1967—Manchester United
1968—Manchester City
1969—Leeds United
1970—Everton
1971—Arsenal
1972—Derby County

Scottish League
(First Division)
1891—Dumbarton and Rangers (tie)
1892—Dumbarton
1893—94—Celtic
1895—Hearts
1896—Celtic
1897—Hearts
1898—Celtic
1899—1902—Rangers
1903—Hibernian
1904—Third Lanark
1905—10—Celtic
1911—13—Rangers
1914—17—Celtic
1918—Rangers
1919—Celtic
1920—21—Rangers
1922—Celtic
1923—25—Rangers
1926—Celtic
1927—31—Rangers
1932—Motherwell
1933—35—Rangers
1936—Celtic
1937—Rangers
1938—Celtic
1939—Rangers
1940—46—No competition
1947—Rangers
1948—Hibernian
1949—50—Rangers

BASIC RULES

(From "Sports for Recreation," published by A.S. Barnes and Co., New York.)

Soccer is a goal game, the object of which is to advance an inflated round ball toward the opponents' goal and between the goalposts by kicking, dribbling, heading, and, in general, playing it with any part of the body except the arms and hands. One player, however, the goalkeeper, is privileged to use his hands on the ball while he is in his own penalty area.

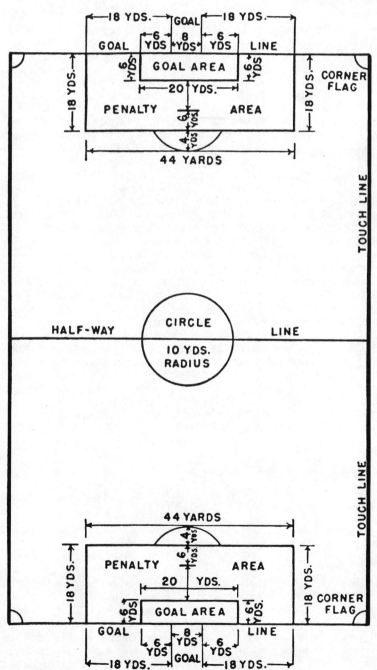

Soccer Field. (Taken from "Sports for Recreation," edited by E. D. Mitchell, A. S. Barnes and Company, New York.)

Each goal consists of two goalposts 8 feet high and placed 8 yards apart, connected by a cross-bar at the top, and with goal nets attached to the rear. The playing area has a maximum length of 120 yards and a minimum length of 100 yards, the width being from 55 to 75 yards. The area is outlined by a white line, and flags are placed in each corner; the sidelines are known as the touch lines, and the end lines as the goal lines.

The halfway line goes from one touch line to the other through the center of the field parallel with the goal lines; midway between the sidelines on this line is a circle in which the ball is centered at the start of the game or after each goal is scored. Rectangular areas are marked out near each goal. The one nearest the goal is the goal area; the other is called the penalty-kick area. Also, at each corner there is marked an area from which the ball must be kicked in case of a corner kick.

The inflated leather- or rubber-covered ball has a circumference of not less than 27 nor more than 28 inches. The weight at the start of the game must be between 14 and 18 ounces; the inflation pressure, not less than 12 nor more than 13 pounds.

Shoes are the most important part of a player's equipment. Regulation shoes are high laced leather ones, cleated with leather or rubber to protect the player against slipping. Shin guards are worn inside knee length socks.

Eleven players make up a soccer team and are named and arranged as follows: one goalkeeper; two fullbacks—right and left; three halfbacks—right, center and left; and five forwards—outside right, inside right, center, inside left and outside left.

The main objective is to put the ball through the opponents' goal and under the crossbar. This is called a goal and scores 1 point. The duration of the game is set by the international rules at forty-five-minute halves with a ten-minute intermission between halves.

Various kinds of kicks are awarded one team because of infringements of rules by the other; free kick, penalty kick, goal kick and corner kick.

Free kicks may be direct or indirect. A direct free kick is awarded to the offended team for the following rules infractions that occur outside the penalty area: illegal charging, goalkeeper carrying the ball, kicking, striking, kneeing, pushing, holding, jumping at an opponent, or a player other than the goalkeeper handling the ball. The kick is taken at the spot of the infraction, and the kicker has the option of passing to a team-mate or trying for a goal.

An indirect free kick is given to the offended team for rules infractions that include illegal substitution and goalkeeper carrying the ball more than four steps when he is in the penalty area. Also, when one team sends the ball out of bounds over the touch line, a member of the other team receives an indirect free kick. This kick is made from the point of the infraction or from the spot where play is stopped and the kicker may not try directly for a goal.

A penalty kick is awarded to the offended team at the penalty-kick mark if a defensive player commits the following acts in his own penalty area: pushing, holding, kneeing, kicking, striking, jumping at an opponent, illegal charging and handling the ball (other than the goalkeeper).

A goal kick is given to the defensive team if the ball goes over the goal line other than between the goalposts and it is last touched by an offensive or attacking player. This kick is made at the spot where the ball crossed the goal line. The goal kick is executed in a manner similar to the kick-off in football.

A corner kick is awarded to the attacking team when the ball passes over the goal line except between the goalposts and it is last touched by a defender. The corner kick is taken from the corner area closest to the spot where the ball passed over the goal line.

(For Olympic champions see section on Olympic Games.)

SOFTBALL

(Courtesy of D. E. Porter, Director, Amateur Softball Association of America,
P. O. Box 11437, Oklahoma City, Oklahoma, 73111)

Softball, many years ago the exclusive recreational sport of the United States, now has a home in almost every country in the world.

The game, originated in the late 1890s, was known in the beginning as mush-ball, kitten-ball, and indoor baseball. In 1926 the game acquired the name it is now known by worldwide, softball.

Softball flourished in the 1930s and early 40s; it became known as the depression sport. People out of work and with little money to spend on high priced entertainment took in softball, either as spectators or participants.

World War II took some steam out of the sport domestically, but the war did help the sport become known in other countries through the thousands of GIs who introduced the sport on atolls in the Pacific, jungles in Asia, and the lowlands of Europe.

After the war the sport gradually created more and more interest as a good recreational sport, and before long hundreds of thousands of teams soon sprang up in every open area where there was room to accommodate the size of a softball diamond.

The beginning of organizing a sport that had been up and down for almost thirty-five years before enough people decided it was time to "get organized" was difficult. Individual promoters and local independent groups wanted no part of an organized sport, especially if it took away their identity, or a fast buck that some of them were making off the sport.

The real beginning and true development of the game as a competitive sport came when the Amateur Softball Association was organized in 1933 and an official playing rules committee IJRCS – International Joint Rules Committee on Softball – was created. Up until that time the sport experienced chaos as an organized sport. Dozens of different playing rules were being used all over the country; there were no set rules of eligibility that applied to every part of the country.

Female participants have been consistently identified with the sport almost since its inception. However, female participation in the game really did not become nationwide until the A.S.A. established and organized national championships in 1933.

From that time on women played an important role in the development and growth of the sport. The list of great teams and players on the feminine side of the ledger equals and at times surpasses the exploits of their male counterparts.

Industry has been a big supporter and sponsor of softball, both in fast and slow pitch. Industrial play became so popular that in 1957 A.S.A. established a separate division of championship play, strictly for industrial teams.

The A.S.A. and the Joint Rules Committee worked closely together in an effort to bring recognition and identity to the game that would in a short time become the largest participation sport in the United States.

Many people ask why softball is so popular, why do over 18 million adults and youngsters play the sport on a competitive basis here in the United States and another five million worldwide? The answer—mainly because competition can be geared to include almost all levels of participation. No other sport has remained so completely an amateur sport.

During the 40s and 50s softball was mainly a fast-pitch game; today the sport is almost 70 percent of the slow-pitch variety in the U.S. Slow pitch started to come forth in the early 60s and steadily made progress while the fast-pitch game diminished because the game sought no relief from allowing the pitchers to completely dominate the game.

In slow-pitch softball, the game has experienced phenomenal growth, so much so that serious problems are developing concerning adequate playing facilities to handle this problem. Recreation departments are overtaxed now with teams who want to play and no place for them to play.

Even though participation is more slanted to slow pitch today, both games enjoy healthy appetites in development and participation.

Fast pitch is making great progress as an international game, so much that there is a good possibility that it will be one of the few new sports added to the Olympic Games. Some forty-seven countries presently have organized fast-pitch competition. It is certain that slow pitch will also develop as an international game and with this the opportunity for more and more people to participate.

Three World Championships of the international variety have been held, with success for both men and women. Softball has played an important role in fostering greater understanding among people, bringing competitors together from every part of the world, in good, spirited sport competition.

FACTS AND FIGURES

There were 128,000 teams and 1,750,000 players registered with the A.S.A. in 1966. In addition, there were about 10,000 leagues, 13,200 closed parks and nearly 16,300 playing areas.

In a recent survey Ohio had paced the nation with 186 lighted parks and New Jersey led in playing areas with over 2,000. Michigan held the record for attendance with 4,756,500. Ohio was first in total games played with 38,415. A single-game attendance record was made when 35,000 saw an area tournament final at Wrigley Field, Los Angeles. The Canadian attendance mark is 17,511, set at a game between the Briggs Manufacturing Company of Detroit and the Hamilton Pee Gees in Toronto in 1941.

A 42-inning game, played at Kenosha, Wis., on Aug. 14, 1942, is the longest on record. The Italian American Club, with its star pitcher, I. A. (Corky) Coraeini, going the distance, won by 1 to 0.

Portland, Oregon and Clearwater, Florida played a 31-inning game in 1963, at Clearwater, Florida, to set a national tournament mark. During the 1949 tourney Herb Dudley of the Clearwater (Fla.) Bombers gained a 21-inning 1–0 victory over the Phillips 66 nine of Okmulgee, Okla., and set a record by striking out 55.

Bertha Ragan, the outstanding woman pitcher of all time, hurled the Orange (Calif.) Lionettes to a 2–1 trimuph in 20 innings over the Fresno (Calif.) Rockets in the national event at Detroit in 1951. Miss Ragan, who had 22 strikeouts, has pitched more than 100 no-hit, no-run games and has 6 perfect games to her credit. She scored 233 shutouts and 4,630 strikeouts.

Her record shows 5 shut-outs, 143 consecutive scoreless innings, 77 strikeouts and an earned-run average of .073 in the 1950 national tournament. In the 1951 national tourney she had 60 strikeouts in 48 innings and allowed 4 runs. In 1952 she raised her strikeout average in the national championship to 68 in 56 innings while permitting 6 runs.

FAMOUS PLAYERS
Men

Arno Lamb, John Spring, George Adams, Dick Dudzik, Albert Gaub, Loren Dinkle, Clarence Miller, Ernest Bertolini, Harvey Sterkel, Whitey Campbell, Herb Dudley, Dave Sayyae, Clyde Dexter, Johnny Overfield, Bob Fesler, Don MacDonald, Al Linde, Ted Czach, John Marsden, Arnold Gilpin, Bill West, Roy Stephenson, Windmill Watson, Ed Bailey, Loon Rosen, Norb Warkem, Shifty Gears, Mack Phillips, John Hunter, King Kong Kelly, Joe Hunt, Jim Ramage, Hugh Johnson, Ed Fiegelski, Leroy Hess, Weldon Haney, and Tom Linson.

Women

Bertha Ragan, Margie Law, Kay Rich, Nelwyn Greer, Jake Duncan, Lu Mahoney, Carolyn Thome, Irene Huber, Elaine Harris, Dot Wilkinson, Terry Hiltz, Bea Sanderson, Freda Savona, Marie Wadlow, Amy Peralta, Betty Grason, Nina Korgan, Toots Nusse, Alma Wilson, Thelma Golden, Dot Underwood, Hazel Gill, Joan Joyce, Lou Albrecht, and Donna LoPiano.

HALL OF FAME

A Hall of Fame honoring softball players was established in 1957 at Oklahoma City. The selections:

Men—Fast Pitch

Harold (Shifty) Gears
Sam (Sambo) Elliott
Al Linde
Bernie Kampschmidt
Clyde (Dizzy) Kirkendall
Jim Ramage
Clarence Miller
John Baker
Warren Gerber
Hugh Johnson
Boll Crain
John Hunter
B. E. "Gene" Martin
Bill West
Tom Castle
Roy Stephenson
Jim Chambers
Robert Forbes
Noland Whitlock
Billy Wojie
Ronald Kronwitter
Le Roy Hess
Bob Sprentall
John Spring
Frankie Williams

John "Buster" Zeigler
Ray "Ned" Wickersham
Don Ropp
Jerry Curtis
Richard Tomlinson

Men—Slow Pitch

Myron Reinhardt

Women—Fast Pitch

Amy Peralta
Marie Wadlow
Betty Grayson
Ruth Sears
Nina Korgan
Kay Rich
Margaret Dobson
Marjorie Law
Carolyn Thome Hart
Jeanne Contel
Mickey Stratton
Dot Wilkinson
Virginia Busick
Bertha Tickey
Estelle "Ricki" Caito
Gloria May

NATIONAL CHAMPIONS—FAST PITCH
(Amateur Softball Association)
Men

1933—J. L. Gills, Chicago
1934—Ke-Nash-A's, Kenosha, Wis.
1935—Crimson Coaches, Toledo, Ohio
1936—Kodak Park, Rochester, N.Y.
1937—Briggs Mfg. Co., Detroit
1938—Pohlers, Cincinnati
1939—Carr's, Covington, Ky.
1940—Kodak Park, Rochester, N.Y.
1941—Bendix Brakes, Sourth Bend, Ind.
1942—Deep Rock Oilers, Tulsa, Okla.
1943-44—Hammer Field, Fresno, Calif.
1945-47—Zollner's Pistons, Fort Wayne, Ind.
1948—Briggs Beautyware, Detroit
1949—Tip Top Clothiers, Toronto, Ont.
1950—Clearwater (Fla.) Bombers
1951—Dow Chemical Co., Midland, Mich.
1952-53—Briggs Beautyware, Detroit
1954—Clearwater (Fla.) Bombers
1955—Raybestos Cardinals, Stratford, Conn.
1956-57—Clearwater (Fla.) Bombers
1958—Raybestos Cardinals, Stratford, Conn.
1959—Aurora, Ill.
1960—Clearwater, Fla.
1961—Aurora, Ill.
1962—Clearwater, Fla.
1963—Clearwater (Fla.) Bombers
1964—Burch Tool, Detroit
1965—Sealmasters, Aurora, Ill.
1966—Clearwater (Fla.) Bombers
1967—Sealmasters, Aurora, Ill.
1968—Clearwater (Fla.) Bombers
1969-70—Raybestos Cardinals, Stratford, Conn.
1971—Welty Way, Cedar Rapids, Iowa

1972–Raybestos Cardinals, Stratford, Conn.

Women

1933–Great Northerns, Chicago
1934–Hart Motors, Chicago
1935–Bloomer Girls, Cleveland
1936-37–National Mfg. Co., Cleveland
1938-39–J. J. Kreig's, Alameda, Calif.
1940–Arizona Ramblers, Phoenix
1941–Higgins Midgets, Tulsa, Okla.
1942-43–Jax Maids, New Orleans
1944–Lind & Pomeroy, Portland, Ore.
1945-47–Jax Maids, New Orleans
1948-49–Arizona Ramblers, Phoenix
1950-52–Orange (Calif.) Lionettes
1953–Betsy Ross Rockets, Fresno, Calif.
1954–Leach Motors Rockets, Fresno, Calif.
1955-56–Orange (Calif.) Lionettes
1957–Fresno (Calif.) Hacienda Rockets
1958–Raybestos Brakettes, Stratford, Conn.
1959-60–Stratford, Conn.
1961–Whittier, Calif.
1962–Orange, Calif.
1963–Raybestos Brakettes, Stratford, Conn.
1964–Erv Lind Florists, Portland, Oregon
1965–Orange Lionettes, Orange, Calif.

1966-68–Raybestos Brakettes, Stratford, Conn.
1969-70–Orange (Calif.) Lionettes
1971-72–Raybestos Brakettes, Stratford, Conn.

WORLD CHAMPIONS

*(Played every two years)

Men

1966–United States at Mexico City
1968–United States at Oklahoma City, Okla.
1972–Canada at Manila, Philippines

Women

1965–Australia at Melbourne, Australia
1970–Japan at Osaka, Japan
*After 1970, Championship held every four years.

BASIC RULES

The playing field is made up of two parts, infield and outfield. The infield is shaped like a baseball "diamond" (square) and is 60 feet square. The distance between bases is 60 feet. Women sometimes use a 45-foot diamond.

The pitching distance is 46 feet for men, 40 for women.

The bat is one piece of wood, not more than

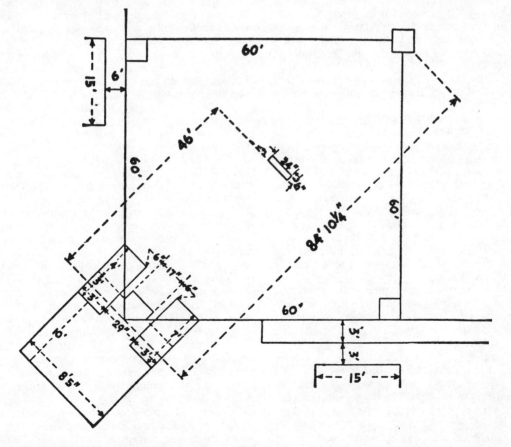

Softball Diamond. (Taken from "Sports for Recreation," edited by E. D. Mitchell, A. S. Barnes and Company, New York.)

34 inches in length, nor 2¼ inches in diameter at the thickest part. The ball is smooth-seam, with leather cover, packed with kapok and tightly wrapped with yarn. The ball shall not weigh less than 6¼ nor more than 7 ounces and shall not be less than 11-7/8 inches nor more than 12-1/8 inches in circumference.

Pitching is underhand.

Only catchers and first basemen are permitted to wear mitts. Others may wear gloves. Men catchers must wear masks, women catchers must wear both mask and chest protectors.

In 1946, teams were reduced from the old number of 10 to 9 players, eliminating the short-fielder. To aid further the offense, which had been left far behind by the defense, the baselines were cut from 60 to 55 feet, but later were returned to 60 feet. Players now occupy the same position as in baseball.

Seven innings make up a game.

In practically all other respects, the rules of play are those which govern baseball.

A recent development in softball has been the slow pitch variety. It is played with a 12-inch ball on a regular-sized diamond and with a 14-inch or 16-inch ball on a 50-foot diamond. It is quite popular in the Chicago area. The growth of teams in numbers has led to the establishment of a national tournament, with two classes of play, Industrial and Open.

SQUASH RACQUETS AND SQUASH TENNIS

(Courtesy of Darwin P. Kingsley, II, Vice President, United States Squash Racquets Association, 211 Ford Road, Bala-Cynwyd, Pa., 19004)

When snow covers the golf courses and tennis courts, Americans frequently turn to the indoor game of squash racquets to keep fit. The game was introduced in the United States in the 1880's but it was not until 50 years later that it took a real hold. The Prince of Wales (the late Duke of Windsor) on a visit here helped put the seal of social approval on it. Then it was discovered that the game also had great merit in physical conditioning.

College clubs, such as Harvard, Yale and Princeton, in New York gave it impetus. Then colleges, country clubs and athletic clubs adopted the sport and the number of persons playing increased from hundreds into the thousands. The game spread from the East to the Middle West and the Pacific Coast and it continues to flourish, as evidenced by the large numbers of entries in the various tournaments. The game has found favor with the women, too, with a rapidly expanding association represented by players all over the country, although mostly on the East Coast.

The game of squash racquets is an offshoot of the racquets sport, and squash tennis is substantially the same as squash racquets, except that the Americans, who devised it, use a tennis ball— thus, squash tennis.

Along in 1850, students at Harrow School in England, which institution had revived the racquets game after it had gone into eclipse, invented squash racquets. The reason was this: the boys wanted to play at racquets, but that game required a huge and costly court. Only two, or four, players could be in action at a time; others had to wait their turn, since there was only one court at Harrow. So the youngsters took the basic principles of racquets, which, in the beginning, had been an outdoor game, and made such changes as would permit play of the new game on a much smaller court than was required for racquets, and which could be played, if the students chose, outdoors.

Play with squash racquets called for a soft ball, instead of the hard ball used in racquets, and there was not the necessity for an elaborate court. It could be played almost anywhere that walls were available, but, naturally, the preference was indoors, where there were square rooms with four walls.

The name of "squash" was given to the game because the soft ball made a "squashy" sound when it hit the wall, instead of a sharp, cracking report, when the racquet ball was batted.

Play at squash provided the youngsters with almost as much action as racquets. For this reason, and because courts were inexpensive, squash became very popular among the schools in England, spreading to the colleges and then to exclusive clubs.

Both the Queen's Club and the Marylebone Cricket Club became leaders in squash late in the 1890's, and into the 20th Century. The late Duke of Windsor, was a squash enthusiast while he was Prince of Wales, and his enthusiasm had much to do with popularizing it. Private clubs throughout England erected squash courts and many famous racquet players deserted that game to play squash.

Squash was introduced into the United States in the 1880's and it is likely that the first organized game was played in 1882 in St. Paul's School, Concord, N.H., following a visit of its master, Rev. James P. Conover, to Montreal, where he had gone to get an idea on how to build a racquets court, as well as one for squash racquets.

The St. Paul boys played the English game at first, but soon began to improvise. They introduced a lawn tennis ball so as to speed up play, substituting it for the less lively squash ball, and this somewhat changed the method of play, enough to make it deviate from the original squash game.

Some time later, Stephen J. Feron of New York, an enthusiast about squash and one of the world's greatest players, tried the tennis ball and tennis bat method. He was satisfied that this speeded play, but he was not able to create the same difficult twists with his rebounds as with the regulation squash ball. Feron finally put some netting around the tennis ball, and this made it possible for him to execute dazzling shots.

So, in a short time, two different games were being played; the regulation with a soft rubber ball, which was inclined to be sluggish, and the other with an inflated ball, smaller than a tennis ball, with tight webbing over the normal cover. To distinguish between the games, the original was officially referred to as "Squash Racquets" and the other as "Squash Tennis." The scoring rules remained the same.

Americans, for a time, played both squash games, but the majority eventually decided upon squash tennis, because the action of the ball was faster. The sport gained favor in New York, Philadelphia, Boston, Chicago and in many cities in the midwest, into the 1920's. But after having enjoyed popularity for about a decade, squash tennis is now virtually a dead game, being played by only a very few individuals in New York City. Squash racquets, which boomed in the 1920s, has undergone an unprecedented growth, with public courts springing up all over the country. In the last five years it has doubled in the number of courts and players alike.

Going into 1930, there was no standardization as to the court of either game. Players seized upon any place with four walls, reasonably high, and with a playing surface of reasonable length and width. As a result, one court might be 40 x 20 feet, for singles play, and another 34 x 22. But when the game became of increasing importance along the Atlantic Seaboard, it was decided, in 1930, that there should be regulations concerning court measurements. (See diagram at end of this section.)

FAMOUS SQUASH PLAYERS
Squash Racquets—Men

John A. Miskey of Philadelphia was the first United States singles champion, winning in 1907, and repeating in 1908 and 1910. William A. Freeland won in 1909, F. S. White in 1911 and M. L. Newhall in 1913. They were Philadelphians.

Constantine Hutchins broke the monopoly by winning for Boston in 1912 and 1914. Stanley W. Pearson, one of the greatest players, was national champion in 1915, 1916, 1917, 1921, 1922 and 1923, there being no tournaments in 1917 and 1918. C. C. Peabody of Boston interrupted the Pearson reign by winning in 1920.

Capt. Gerald Robarts of England won the United States title in 1924.

Other American stars include W. Palmer Dixon, J. Lawrence Pool 2d, Beekman H. Pool, Herbert N. Rawlins Jr., Germain G. Glidden and Calvin MacCracken of New York; J. A. Robinson of Chicago; Mathew Bartlett, Norman Cobot, Charles C. Peabody, M. P. Baker and Henri Salaun, all of Boston; Neil J. Sullivan 2d, Roy R. Coffin, W. H. Tevis Huhn, Donald Strachan, Charles W. Brinton, Stanley W. Pearson Jr., William Slack, Hunter H. Lott Jr., J. M. Walsh and G. Diehl Mateer Jr. of Philadelphia; Edward Hahn of Detroit, and Harry Conlon Jr. of Buffalo.

Coffin and Sullivan stood out as a doubles combination.

The greatest professional squash racquets players were Feron, who pioneered the development of squash tennis; Walter Kinsella, Frank Ward, Lester Cummings, all of New York; Al Ramsay of Cleveland, John Skillman of New Haven, Jim Tully of Pittsburgh, Eddie Reid of Hartford, Jack Summers of Boston, Hashim Khan of Pakistan, Mahmoud Abdel Kerim of Egypt and John Warzycki of Buffalo. Also, Mohibullah Khan, Sharif Khan, John Barnaby, and Victor Niederhoffer.

Squash Racquets—Women

Eleonora Sears of Boston was the first woman champion of the United States, winning in 1928. Mrs. William F. Howe Jr. and Mrs. George (Hazel Hotchkiss) Wightman of Boston, Susan Noel of England and Mrs. Ruth Hall Banks of Philadelphia were champions. Margot Lumb came on from England to take the United States title in 1935. Mrs. Anne Page Homer, Cecile Bowes and Jane Austin, all of Philadelphia, captured singles titles. The Howe family gained additional honors when Elizabeth and Margaret, daughters of Mrs. Howe, won the championships in the 1950s. Mrs. W. Pepper Constable of Princeton, N.J., Mrs. Margaret Varner DuPont of El Paso, Texas, and Mrs. Newton B. Meade of Gulph Mills, Pa., have each won the singles Championship at least three times in recent years. A new family currently dominates the scene, Mrs. F. A. C. Vosters of Wilmington, Del. and her two daughters, Mrs. Halsey Spruance and Mrs. Lealand Moyer. Mrs. Moyer was the National Champion in 1970 and 1972; Mrs. Spruance holds the title for 1973. Mrs. Vosters holds six doubles titles. Collegiate women's squash is expanding. Championships have been held now for nine years, the 1973 champion being Miss Lee Howard of Radcliffe. Collegiate team competition is also being held.

Intercity competition has been held since 1928. This competition was formally named The Howe Cup Competition in 1955 and is held each year with teams participating at the A, B, and C levels and collegiate.

In 1933 the Wolfe-Noel Challenge Cup was put up for international team matches, with the United States and England participating. The trophy was donated by Miss Noel and Mrs. G. Bryans Wolfe, also of England. Interrupted by World War II, the competition was revived in 1949, when Janet Morgan of England became the first foreign player since 1935 to win the United States championship. She repeated the feat in 1955.

The present president of the U.S.W.S.R.A. is Mrs. S.W. Farnsworth, 19 Jackson Rd., Wellesley, Mass., 02181.

Squash Tennis—Men

The first champion was Dr. Alfred Stillman of Boston, winner in 1911, 1912 and 1914. The greatest of all the champions, perhaps, was Harry F. Wolf of the New York Athletic Club, who first took the title in 1930 and was invincible for more than a decade. Other champions were George Whitney, Eric S. Winston, Fillmore Van S. Hyde, John W. Appel Jr., William Rand Jr., all representing the Harvard Club of New York; A. J. Cordier, Thomas R. Coward, F. Barry Ryan Jr., and J. T. P. Sullivan of the Yale Club of New York; R.E. Fink, Crescent Athletic Club, Brooklyn, and Rowland B. Haines of the Columbia University Club, New York.

Also outstanding have been Joseph J. Lordi, New York, A.C.; H. Robert Reeve, Bayside (N.Y.) Tennis Club; Charles M. Bull Jr.; Harold R. Mixsell; Frank A. Sieverman Jr.; Edward R. Larigan; Milton Baron; Walter D. Hoag; Philip T. Moore; Howard J. Rose; C. L. Harrison Jr., University of Cincinnati; George L. Stocking, University of Omaha; Paul H. Goesling, St. Louis University; Henry S. Thorne; Murray Taylor; Barnwell Elliott, Edward G. McLaughlin; Frank Iannicelli; Willard K. Rice; Edmund A. Mays Jr.; Thomas D. Flynn; Frank R. Hanson, and J. Lenox Porter.

The great professional players have included Feron, Frank Ward, Kinsella, William F. Ganley, Tom Iannicelli, Rowland Dufton, James Reid, Frank Lafforgue and John Jacobs.

UNITED STATES SQUASH RACQUETS CHAMPIONS

(Courtesy of United States Squash Racquets Association)

Men's Singles

1907-08—John A. Miskey
1909—William L. Freeland
1910—John A. Miskey

1911—F. S. White
1912—Constantine Hutchins
1913—Mortimer L. Newhall
1914—Constantine Hutchins
1915-17—Stanley W. Pearson
1918-19—No competition
1920—Charles C. Peabody
1921-23—Stanley W. Pearson
1924—Gerald Robarts (England)
1925-26—W. Palmer Dixon
1927—Myles Baker
1928—Herbert N. Rawlins Jr.
1929—J. Lawrence Pool
1930—Herbert N. Rawlins Jr.
1931—J. Lawrence Pool
1932-33—Beekman H. Pool
1934—Neil J. Sullivan 2d
1935—Donald Strachan
1936-38—Germain G. Glidden
1939—Donald Strachan
1940—A. Willing Patterson
1941-42—Charles Brinton
1943-45—No competition
1946—Charles Brinton
1948—Stanley W. Pearson Jr.
1949—Hunter H. Lott, Jr.
1950-51—Edward Hahn, Detroit
1952—Pfc. Harry Conlon Jr.
1953—Ernest Howard (Canada)
1954—G. Diehl Mateer Jr.
1955—Henri Salaun
1956—G. Diehl Mateer Jr.
1957-58—Henri Salaun
1959—Ben Heckscher
1960—G. Diehl Mateer Jr.
1961—Henri R. Salaun
1962—Samuel P. Howe 3rd
1963—Benjamin H. Heckscher
1964—Ralph E. Howe
1965—Stephen T. Vehslage
1966—Victor Niederhoffer
1967—Samuel P. Howe III
1968—Colin Adair
1969-70—Anil Nayar
1971—Colin Adair
1972—Victor Niederhoffer

Men's Doubles

1933-37—Roy R. Coffin—Neil J. Sullivan 2d
1938-42—Hunter H. Lott Jr.—William E. Slack
1943-45—No competion
1946—Charles Brinton—Donald Strachan
1947—Stanely W. Pearson Jr.—David McMullin
1948—Charles Brinton—Stanley W. Pearson Jr.
1949-50—Hunter H. Lott Jr.—G. Diehl Mateer Jr.
1951—G. Diehl Mateer Jr.—Calvin D. MacCracken
1952—Germain G. Glidden—Richard Remsen
1953—Hunter H. Lott Jr.—G. Diehl Mateer Jr.
1954—G. Diehl Mateer Jr.—Richard Squires
1955—Ed and Joe Hahn
1956-57—Carl Badger—James Ethridge 3d
1958-59—G. Diehl Mateer Jr.—John Hentz

1960—James Whitmoyer—Howard Davis
1961-62—G. Diehl Mateer Jr.—John Hentz
1963-64—S. P. Howe III—William Danforth
1965-66—G. Diehl Mateer Jr.—Ralph E. Howe
1967—S. P. Howe III—William Danforth
1968—Victor Neiderhoffer—Victor Elmaleh
1969-71—S. P. Howe III—Ralph E. Howe
1972—Larry Terrell—James Zug

Men's Team

1908-11—Philadelphia
1912—Boston
1913-17—Philadelphia
1918-19—No competition
1920—Boston
1921-22—Philadelphia
1923-24—Boston
1925-27—Harvard University
1928-29—New York
1930—Boston
1931-32—Harvard University
1933—Philadelphia
1934—Cambridge
1935-36—Philadelphia
1937-41—Boston
1942—Detroit
1943-46—No competition
1947—Detroit
1948—Philadelphia
1949-50—Boston
1951—Harvard University
1952-53—Philadelphia
1954—Pacific Coast
1955-56—New York
1957—Pacific Coast
1958—Philadelphia
1959—Yale
1960—Canada
1961—Pacific Coast
1962—Philadelphia
1963—Harvard University
1964—Washington, D.C.
1965-66—New York
1967—Quebec
1968—New York
1969-70—Ontario
1971—Toronto
1972—New York

Men's Professional

1930-32—Jack Summers
1933—John Skillman
1934—Jack Summers
1935—John Skillman
1936—Jim Tully
1937—John Skillman
1938—Al Ramsay
1939—Lester Cummings
1940—Al Ramsay
1941-42—Lester Cummings
1943-45—No competition
1946—Lester Cummings
1947—Eddie Reid

1948—Al Ramsay
1949-50—Eddie Reid
1951—Jim Tully
1952—Eddie Reid
1953-54—John Warzycki
1955—Hashim Khan
1956—Al Chassard
1957-58—Mahmoud Abdel Kerim
1959—Albert E. Chassard
1960—Ramond Widelski
1961-62—Albert E. Chassard
1963-64—Hashim Khan
1965-69—Mohibullah Khan
1970-72—Sharif Khan

Men's Open

1954—Henri Salaun
1955—G. Diehl Mateer Jr.
1956-57—Hashim Khan
1958—Roshan Khan
1959—G. Diehl Mateer Jr.
1960—61—Roshan Khan
1962—Azam Khan
1963—Hashim Khan
1964-65—Mohibullah Khan
1967—Ralph E. Howe
1968—Mohibullah Khan
1969-72—Sharif Khan

Women's Singles

(Courtesy of United States Women's Squash Racquets Association)
1928—Eleonora R. Sears
1929—Mrs. William F. Howe Jr.
1930—Mrs. Hazel Hotchkiss Wightman
1931—Mrs. Ruth Hall Banks
1932—Mrs. William F. Howe Jr.
1933—Susan Noel (England)
1934—Mrs. William F. Howe Jr.
1935—Margot Lumb (England)
1936-37—Anne Page
1938—Cecile Bowes
1939—Anne Page
1940-41—Cecile Bowes
1942-46—No competition
1947—Mrs. Anne Page Homer
1948—Cecile Bowes
1949—Janet Morgan (England)
1950—Elizabeth Howe
1951—Jane Austin
1952-53—Margaret Howe
1954—Lois Dilks
1955—Janet Morgan (England)
1956-59—Mrs. Pepper Constable Jr.
1960-63—Margaret Varner
1964—Mrs. Charles Wetzel
1965—Joyce Davenport
1966-68—Mrs. Newton B. Meade Jr.
1969—Miss Joyce Davenport
1970—Mrs. Leland Moyer
1971—Mrs. T. R. Thesieres
1972—Mrs. Leland Moyer
1973—Mrs. Halsey Spruance

Women's Doubles

1933—Anne Page—Mrs. C. C. Madeira
1934—Mrs. A. J. Lamme Jr.—Margaret Bostwick
1935—Mrs. Ian McKechnie—The Hon. Anne Lytton-Milbanke (England)
1936—Anne Page—Mrs. A. J. Lamme Jr.
1937—Betty Cooke—Mrs. Toby Barrett (England)
1938-39—Mrs. J. E. Bierwith—Mrs. W. H. Adams
1940—No Competition
1941—Elizabeth Pearson—Hope Knowles
1942-47—No Competition
1948—Peggy Scott—Mrs. Dudley Vaill Jr.
1949—Janet Morgan—Mrs. Alice Teague (England)
1950—Jane Austin—Mrs. Hope Knowles Rawls
1951—Mrs. Peggy Scott Carrott—Frances McGurn
1952—Anne Reilly—Mrs. Charles Wetzel
1953-54—Mrs. John E. Newlin—Mrs. Donald Manly-Power
1955—Janet Morgan—Sheila Speight (England)
1956—Mrs. Charles Wetzel—Mrs. H. L. G. Clement
1957-58—Mrs. Donald Manly-Power—Mrs. Carter Simonin
1959—Mrs. Charles Wetzel—Mrs. Carter Simonin
1960—Mrs. Charles Classen—Mrs. H. L. G. Clement
1961—Mrs. John Bottger—Mrs. Nathan Stauffer
1962—Mrs. Charles Classen—Mrs. F. A. C. Vosters Jr.
1963—Mrs. H. G. Macintosh (England)—Mrs. G. E. Marshall (England)
1964—Mrs. Nathan Stauffer—Mrs. Charles Wetzel
1965-67—Mrs. Charles Classen—Mrs. F. A. C. Vosters Jr.
1968—Mrs. Newton B. Meade Jr.—Mrs. F. A. C. Vosters Jr.
1969—Miss Joyce Davenport—Mrs. T. R. Thesieres
1970—Mrs. Nathan P. Stauffer—Mrs. T. R. Thesieres
1971—Mrs. Charles Classen—Mrs. F. A. C. Vosters
1972-73—Mrs. Halsey Spruance—Mrs. F. A. C. Vosters

SQUASH RACQUETS—INTERNATIONAL MATCHES

Lapham Trophy (Men)

(United States vs. Canada)

1922—United States 11, Canada 2, at Boston
1923—United States 9, Canada 2, at Toronto
1924—United States 7-2/3, England 6, Canada 1-1/3, at Philadelphia
1925—United States 10, Canada 5, at Montreal
1926—United States 13, Canada 2, at New York
1927—England 17-1/2, United States 16-1/2, Canada 11, at Toronto
1928—United States 14, Canada 1, at Buffalo
1929—Canada 8, United States 4, at Hamilton, Ont.
1930—United States 8, Canada 1, at Baltimore
1931—Canada 6, United States 5, at Quebec
1932—United States 8, Canada 0, at Hartford, Conn.

1933—Canada 11, United States 4, at Toronto
1934—United States 10, Canada 1, at Cedarhurst, N.Y.
1935—United States 11, Canada 4, at Montreal
1936—United States 10, Canada 2, at Detroit
1937—Canada 8, United States 7, at Montreal
1938—United States 13, Canada 2, at Boston
1939—Canada 11, United States at Toronto
1940—Canada 10, United States 5, at Hartford, Conn.
1941—United States 8, Canada 7, at Toronto
1942—United States 13, Canada 2, at Rochester, N.Y.
1943—Canada 8, United States 4, at Montreal
1944—United States 12, Canada 3, at New York
1945—Canada 12, United States 3, Toronto
1946—United States 13, Canada 2, at Boston
1947—Canada 9, United States 6, at Hamilton, Ont.
1948—United States 10, Canada 5, at Hartford, Conn.
1949—Canada 7, United States 3, at Quebec
1950—United States 7, Canada 6, at Providence
1951—United States 8, Canada 7, at Toronto
1952—Canada 9, United States 6, at Rochester, N.Y.
1953—United States 9, Canada 6, at Montreal
1954—United States 14, Canada 1, at Hartford.
1955—Canada 7, United States 6, at Quebec.
1956—United States 11, Canada 4, at East Providence, R. I.
1957—Canada 11, United States 4, at Hamilton, Ont.
1958—United States 9, Canada 6, at Greenwich, Conn.
1959—Canada 10, United States 5, at Toronto.
1960—Canada 9, United States 6, at Indianapolis, Ind.
1961—United States 8, Canada 7, at Montreal.
1962—United States 11, Canada 4, at Hartford, Conn.
1963—Canada 11, United States 4, at Toronto
1964—United States 9, Canada 6, at Rochester, N.Y.
1965—United States 9, Canada 6, at Montreal
1966—United States 8, Canada 7, at Buffalo
1967—Canada 10, United States 5, at Hamilton, Ont.
1968—United States 9, Canada 6, at Wilmington
1969—United States 13, Canada 2, at Vancouver
1970—United States 11, Canada 4, at Cincinnati
1971—Canada 9, United States 6, at Montreal
1972—United States 11, Canada 4, at Cleveland

Wolfe-Noel Challenge Cup Matches (Women)

(United States vs. Great Britain)

1933—Great Britain 4, United States 1, at the Sleepy Hallow Country Club, Scarborough-on-the-Hudson, N.Y.
1934—Great Britain 5, United States 0, at the

Queen's Club, London, England

1935—United States 3, Great Britain 2, at the Harvard Club, Boston

1936—Great Britain 5, United States 0, at the Lansdowne Club, London

1937—United States 3, Great Britain 2, at the Junior League Club, New York

1938—No Competition

1939—Great Britain 5, United States 0, at the Queen's Club, London

1940-48—No Competition

1949—United States 3, Great Britain 2, at the Merion Cricket Club, Haverford, Pa.

1950—Great Britain 5, United States 0, at the Lansdowne Club, London

1951—No Competition

1952—United States 4, Great Britain 1, at the Harvard Club, Boston

1953—Great Britain 5, United States 0, at the Lansdowne Club, London

1954—No Competition

1955—Great Britain 4, United States, at Merion Cricket Club, Haverford, Pa.

1956—No Competition

1957—Great Britain 5, United States 0, Lansdowne Club, London

1958—No Competition

1959—United States 3, Great Britain 2, at the University of Pennsylvania, Philadelphia

1961—Great Britain 5, United States 0, at Lansdowne Club, London

1962—No Competition

1963—Great Britain 4, United States 1, at Philadelphia Country Club

1964-67—No Competition

1968—Great Britain 5, United States 0, at Lansdowne Club, London

1969-73—No Competition

UNITED STATES SQUASH TENNIS CHAMPIONS

(Men's Singles)

1911-12—Alfred Stillman

1913—George Whitney

1914—Alfred Stillman

1915-17—Eric S. Winston

1918—Fillmore Van S. Hyde

1919—John W. Appel Jr.

1920—Auguste J. Cordier

1921—Fillmore Van S. Hyde

1922—Thomas R. Coward

1923—R. Earl Fink

1924—Fillmore Van S. Hyde

1925—William Rand Jr.

1926—Fillmore Van S. Hyde

1927-29—Rowland B. Haines

1930-40—Harry F. Wolf

1941—Joseph J. Lordi

1942—H. Robert Reeve

1943-45—No Competition

1946—Frank R. Hanson

1947—Frederick B. Ryan Jr.

1948-50—H. Robert Reeve

1951—J. T. P. Sullivan

1952—H. Robert Reeve

1953—Howard J. Rose

1954-56—H. Robert Reeve

1957-59—J. Lenox Porter

1960-62—James Prigoff

1963—John Powers

1964—James Prigoff

1965—No Competition

1966-69—James Prigoff

1970-72—Pedro Bacallao

BASIC RULES OF SQUASH

A regulation singles squash racquets court is 18½ feet wide, 32 feet long and 16 feet high at the frontwall. The sidewalls may be reduced in height toward the back of the court, so that the backwall may be only 9 feet high. The ceiling should be at least 18 feet 6 inches high to allow for lights. Running along the bottom of the frontwall is a telltale made of sheet metal, which is 17 inches high and 1½ inches thick. The telltale is so called because it gives off a metallic ring whenever the ball hits it, thereby informing the players that the shot is not good. On the frontwall is the frontwall service line 6½ feet from the floor. On the floor is the floor service line 10 feet from and parallel to the backwall and extending entirely across the court. A line drawn from the floor service line to the backwall divides the back court into two equal rectangles. Within each rectangle, at the junction of the floor line and the sidewall, is a service box in the form of a quarter segment of a circle with a 4½-foot radius.

For squash racquets doubles there is a larger court, 45 feet long and 25 feet wide with proportional markings. The frontwall is 20 feet high, the frontwall service line 8 feet 2 inches above the floor. The floor service line is 15 feet from the backwall; each service court is 15 by 12½ feet. The backwall is 7 feet high, marked by a backwall line at that point. The telltale and service boxes are the same as for the singles court.

The regulation squash racquets ball is a hollow black rubber ball, slightly larger than a golf ball —1¾ inches in diameter and 1 ounce in weight. The one used in the American singles game has a slow bounce. The ball used for the English singles game and the American doubles game is livelier. The size and slowness of the squash racquets ball make this game different from squash tennis.

The racquet may not be longer than 27 inches—about the length of a badminton racquet. The wooden head is round—the strung surface about 6¾ inches in diamater—and the handle long. The weight varies between 8 and 10 ounces. The racquet resembles a badminton racquet but is built as sturdily as a tennis racquet.

Two players play the singles game, four the doubles. The singles game is by far the better known. In the singles game the server (determined by toss) stands with at least one foot in the right or left arc (his choice) known as the service box and serves the ball to the frontwall above the 6½-foot-high front service line. The ball must land in the opposite service court (unless the opponent volleys it). This service court is a back corner of the court roughly equal to one-sixth of the court's total floor space. Before this served ball has hit the floor again, the opponent must strike it or lose the point. His return must reach the frontwall before it hits the floor. The rally then continues. The ball may hit any number of walls going to or returning from the frontwall, even during service, but a player must make a return stroke before his opponent's shot hits the floor twice. The server serves alternately from the two boxes as long as he continues to win points. Two serves are permitted on each point, and either the serving or receiving side may score a point. If the server fails to serve the second ball properly, he loses the serve and the opponent scores the point. On a fault on the first serve, the ball is not played and the server serves again. It is a fault if the ball falls short of the floor line of the service courts, hits the ceiling, touches the back service line or the screen above it, or in any way fails to make its first bounce in the proper court.

The receiver may take any position he wishes inside of the opposite court and he may use any stroke for the return of the serve. If he volleys (hits the ball before it hits the floor) the serve, he concedes the ball to be good and is responsible for its return. If the ball hits the floor, he must return it on this first bounce. His return ball may hit one or many walls as long as it strikes the frontwall before hitting the floor. The opponent wins a point whenever the ball is not returned properly or whenever the ball rebounds from the frontwall and hits the player before the second bounce.

The play that wins a point and changes the serve is a "hand-in" for the successful player, a "hand-out" for the loser. A hand-out for the server and a hand-in and point for the opponent is declared when the server serves two faults, hits the telltale, misses a ball, or hits the screen above the backwall on a volley.

Since both opponents are in the same court, certain rules about interference are necessary. In general a player may finish his shot without being interfered with, then he must move so as to give his opponent an unimpeded path to the ball. If one player accidentally interferes, this constitutes a hinder and the point is played over. This replay is called a let. If interference is intentional, it constitutes a balk and a point is declared for the player with whom the interference was made. If a let occurs when the server has one fault, the fault is erased and the server is entitled to two more attempts. It is a let when the opponent has been placed in a position where he will be hit by the ball or where he refrains from stroking it for fear of hitting the interfering player.

A game is 15 up, that is, the side that scores 15 points wins the game except in the special situations next described. At 13-all, the side that has first reached the score of 13 points must elect one of the following choices before the next serve: set to 5 points, making the game 18 points; or set to 3 points, making the game 16 points; or no set, in which event the game remains 15. At 14-all, provided the score has not been 13-all, the side that reached the score of 14 first must elect one of the following choices before the next serve: set to 3, making the game 17; or no set, in which event the game remains 15. A match is usually for three of five games or two of three games.

Singles and doubles have the same rules except that in the doubles game two persons are on each side. Each of the two players on a side has a serve. The first partner serves until he loses a point, then the other partner serves until he loses a point. The side has a hand-out when both players have lost a point each; then the opponents serve in the same fashion. The side serving first at the beginning of a game, however, has only one serve. After the order of serving has been established within a side, it may not be changed.

Squash tennis is played in basically the same court as in squash racquets. Very generally the games are similar, but there are important differences as to rules and style of play.

Until 1954 only the server could score a point. At the annual meeting of the National Squash Tennis Association in 1954 this was changed so that every point played is scored for

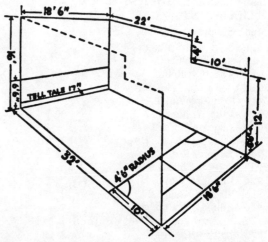

Squash Racquets Court. (Taken from "Sports for Recreation," edited by E. D. Mitchell, A. S. Barnes and Company, New York.)

or against a player, as in squash racquets. The revision, the first basic change is squash tennis since 1890, was designed in the belief that it would result in a fairer comparison of the relative abilities of the players than the old system and thereby facilitate handicapping.

In squash tennis the server stands in what is the service court for squash racquets, not in the arc known as the service box. The serve must be made to land in the opponent's half of the court in front of the floor service line and divided by the extension of the center line going all the way to the frontwall. Therefore the service court in squash tennis is 22' long, bounded by the center line, floor service line, sidewall and frontwall rather than the backwall. The serve may not hit the sidewall in going to the frontwall, but may do so in returning. The backwall line is 4½' high instead of 6½', and a ball going direct from the frontwall over this backwall line loses a point. The serve may never be volleyed. No doubles is played.

Although these rule differences are important, the major differences are in the style of play, and these are caused by the equipment. The green webbed ball, which is 2-3/8 to 2-1/2 inches in diameter and weighs 2 to 2.06 ounces with a pressure not exceeding 34 pounds, is extremely fast. It has double the speed that a lawn tennis ball has over a squash racquets ball. The racquet is necessarily sturdier, and resembles a lawn tennis racquet, being slightly smaller. It does not have a small round head as in squash racquets. This fast ball makes a radically different game. The ball hits many more walls, and angles bewilderingly around the court. Quick reactions and turning and anticipation are essential for skill at the game.

SWIMMING

Man undoubtedly learned to swim as part of his survival pattern. As man developed his ability and technique, swimming competition naturally followed. At first there were endurance contests, then there was a shift to emphasis on speed and today competitive speed swimming is international in scope.

The United States has fared well and is generally rated supreme in swimming competition. But it has not had a monopoly. Japan surpassed this country's swimmers in Olympic competition in the 1930's and then Australian men came to the forefront in the 1950's and 60's. Australian women are currently in the top rank.

The likelihood is that man learned how to swim from watching animals, who usually need no lessons and go into a swimming motion naturally when they hit the water. Man learned because he had seen too many of his fellow-men topple into water and struggle helplessly before drowning.

Just how far back swimming among humans dates is not known. But the ancients were familiar, in a way, with the art. Mosaics unearthed in Pompeii depict men navigating water under their own power. They perhaps used the "doggy" stroke, learned from animals. It meant lots of churning with the hands and arms, but developed little speed. However, it did keep men afloat, and, if the distance were not too far, they made it to the haven of the shore.

The word "swimming" is derived from the old English of "swimmin," and it is established the English were the first people of modern civilization to make a sport of the knack of navigating water with hands and legs. The early English swimmers used the breast stroke, or alternated with the side stroke, and never changed the style until after J. Arthur Trudgen became the teacher of a stroke he had learned during a trip to South America.

The English took to swimming as a means of sport at the turn of the 19th Century and may have been swimmers long before that time.

A book, the "Complete Swimmer," by Guy Larcom and Harold S. Ulen, stated that competitive swimming began about 1837, in London, and, at the time, there were about six pools in that city. The contests were under the auspices of the "National Swimming Society in England." The book also declared that in 1844 some North American Indians swam in London for a silver medal presented by the society and that the winner was Flying Gull, who defeated Tobacco by swimming the length of a 130-foot pool in 30 seconds.

The style of swimming used by the Indians was classified by a London writer as "totally un-European," and he declared that the Indians "thrashed the water violently with their arms, like sails of a windmill, and beat downward with their feet, blowing with force (apparently their breath) and forming grotesque antics."

What the Londoners were looking at was the stroke that in later years came to be known as the crawl and which was used by aborigines, not only in North America, but also in South America, West Africa and the South Pacific islands. The English of that time were not very concerned with high speed over short routes, and, thus, the overhand stroke made little impression upon them, and for another 40 years or so they placed their dependence upon the breast stroke.

A swimming meet was held in what was called the German Gymnasium, at King's Cross, London, on Jan. 7, 1862, under the direction of the Associated Swimming Clubs, proving that in 1862 quite a few swimmers were grouped into enough clubs to cause the creation of an organization to govern the sport.

In the history of early swimming in England, there is no mention as to who built the first tank or where. Since the race of 1844 was in a tank measuring 130 feet, it means that the construction of tanks, even then, was a routine task and that they could be built almost any size the building owner might elect.

In 1869 the old ruling group gave way to a new one called the Amateur Swimming Association of Great Britain. Over 300 clubs became members.

The story of swimming as a sport in England becomes a bit confused between 1869 and the latter part of the 1890's. One learns, without dispute, that Capt. Matthew Webb of England swam the English Channel, using the breast stroke, in August, 1875, being the first to accomplish the difficult trip. But one does not learn much about what was happening in swimming circles in London.

One authority inclines to the idea that Trudgen (sometimes spelled Trudgeon) went to South America in the 1860's and there learned a stroke which was the double overhand; that he became a teacher in England soon thereafter; that he made the stroke so famous it was named after him. But other authorities date his visit in the 1880's, while still another believes it might have been the 1890's.

One historian states that on Nov. 2, 1897, when J.H. Derbyshire, "who had been tutored by Trudgen," swam 100 yards in exactly 60 seconds, he lowered the mark from 76¾ seconds for the route, "which had existed since 1878." All of which was a distinct tribute to Trudgen, his stroke and his teaching, but it appears that the 76¾ mark was not the record.

George D. Baird of Alameda, Calif., lent some old copies of the "Clipper Almanac"—1882, 1887, 1891 and 1897—to H. Archie Richardson, who was tracking down the story on swimming. The Almanac revealed that when Derbyshire, using the "Trudgen stroke," swam 100 yards in 60 seconds he was not establishing a new mark, but was equaling an old one.

The Almanac printed the following records as having been turned in through the years before Derbyshire became acclaimed as something of a super swimmer:

Date	Time	Swimmer	Place
1878	68½ sec.	E.T. Jones	England
Oct. 6, 1879	73¼ sec.	J.S. Moore	England
Sept. 20, 1886	69 sec.	J. Nuttall	England
Sept. 24, 1888	66¼ sec.	J. Nuttall	England
1886	65½ sec.	J. Haggerty	England
Oct. 11, 1894	61 1/5 sec.	J.H. Tyers	England
Dec. 4, 1892	60 sec.	T. Meadham	Sydney

Jones and Haggerty were professionals. Meadham's swim, in Australia, was in a tank requiring 7 turns for 100 yards.

The early records in the United States were no tribute to the prowess of the American water kickers. Prior to the upsurge of J. Scott Leary, the pupil of Syd Cavill, tutor of the "Australian crawl," and the spectacular feats of Charles M. Daniels with the "American crawl," the swimmers in this country obviously were using the breast stroke and turning in mediocre times.

The American records, beginning in 1883 and continuing until Leary's and Daniels' time, are sad spectacles compared with what was being performed in England and Australia. Here are the American marks for 100 yards from 1883 up to and including Leary and Daniels, with their differing crawls (from 1883 to 1887 the meets were sponsored by the New York Athletic Club. The Amateur Athletic Union took over in 1888):

Year	Time	Made by
1883	88¼ s.	A.F. Camacho, Manhattan A.C., New York
1884	81	H.E. Toussaint, New York A.C.
1885	78.4	Herbert Braun, New York
1887	77.2	Herbert Braun, Pastime A.C., New York
1888	76.2	Herbert Braun, Pastime A.C., New York
1894 1896	69.6	A.F. Kenny, Philadelphia
(Sept. 8)	69	George Whittaker, Milwaukee
1897	67.4	D.B. Renear, San Francisco
1900	65.6	E.C. Schaeffer, University of Pennsylvania
1902 1905	64	H. Lemoyne, Boston
(July 18)	60	J. Scott Leary, Olympic Club, San Francisco
1906	57.6	Charles M. Daniels, New York A.C.

Leary made his record at Portland, Ore.

Trudgen, as an amateur in England, used the breast stroke. When he became a teacher, he stressed the double overhand of South America, but apparently failed to observe how the South Americans kicked with their legs. Therefore, Trudgen continued his pupils at the scissor-like movement in the old English stroke. However, Trudgen's success as a tutor was enough to immortalize him by having the overhand stroke called the "Trudgen."

Trudgen deserves all the fame that was his during his lifetime and the glory he since has acquired. But the greatest and the most remarkable revolutions in swimming were wrought by the remarkable Cavill family. They introduced the "Australian crawl," which served Daniels as the model for the present-day "American crawl" stroke.

Frederick Cavill, English-born, was a swimming enthusiast in his youth. Like others of his time, he used the breast stroke. He gained laurels in England for his prowess, and in 1877 followed Captain Webb in trying to swim the English Channel. Cavill came within 50 yards of the English shore in 12 hours 15 minutes, only to fail when watching boatmen refused to send a small craft to guide him the rest of the way through the shallow waters.

In 1878, Cavill went to Australia. There he built and operated the first swimming tanks. He taught swimming. He reared a family, which included six sons—Ernest, Percy, Sydney, Richard, Arthur and Charles. Prior to the dawn of the 20th Century, Cavill took his family on a trip to the South Seas. The Cavills noticed the natives using the double overhand stroke, as had Trudgen, but they went a little further in their observation than Trudgen. They studied the leg action of the islanders and noticed that their "kick" generated extra speed.

The Cavills introduced the new stroke to Australia. The six Cavill boys, who were eager pupils of the father, began to blast records into discard. The Australians called it the "splash stroke." One of the Cavills, asked about it, said it was "like crawling through the water." And so it became known as time went on as the "Australian crawl."

Richard Cavill, presumably the eldest son, went to England in 1902 and, using the "splash" or "crawl," won a championship in a record time of 58.6 seconds, a mark that had been beyond that of any of the pupils of Trudgen, who kicked with less power than the Cavills. Other Cavills were adding to Australia's fame as a land of swimmers and when the Olympic Club of San Francisco decided in 1903 to hire a tutor for its members, it prevailed upon Sydney Cavill to take the job. He remained there for a quarter of a century.

Among Syd's first pupils was J. Scott Leary, an apt student. He broke into the headlines on July 18, 1905, by becoming the first American to swim 100 yards in 60 seconds. Leary, within a short time, won 17 consecutive races and was a sensation in America, where swimming as a sport was just gaining momentum.

Leary's success attracted the attention of Daniels, who, up to the time of Leary's debut as a record smasher, was the best swimmer in the United States. Daniels, who was attached to the New York Athletic Club and had been using the Trudgen stroke, seized the first possible opportunity to see Leary in action. He noticed that Leary, instead of using a scissors-kick, as in the Trudgen, was calling upon something different. Daniels recognized in this the difference between

his speed and that of Leary, who was master of the "Australian crawl."

Daniels, not wishing to ape the Cavill stroke in its entirety, began to experiment with the kick, timing it to the stroking of the arms, and the result is what is known as the "American crawl" of today, which differs very little from the fundamentals of the "Australian crawl" as devised by the pioneering Cavills.

Daniels, a superb swimmer in his prime, perfected the new method of swimming, and then went into action to see what he could do with it. He dived into the 25-yard tank of the New York A.C. on Feb. 22, 1906, swam 100 yards and when he emerged he not only owned the American record, at 57.6 seconds, but also tied the world mark made at Sydney, Australia, Nov. 26, 1904, by Cecil Healy of Australia, using the Australian crawl.

On March 23, 1906 Daniels established a world record of 56 seconds at St. Louis, using his new stroke. Daniels continued to improve, won 33 National A.A.U. championships from 50 yards to the mile, won four Olympic Games titles and reached his peak on April 7, 1910, when he lowered his world record for 100 yards to 54.8 seconds.

Three years later Duke Kahanamoku arrived in San Francisco from Honolulu, and it was noticed he was using the crawl stroke. When asked who had taught him, he said he had known no teacher; that he had learned by watching the older natives; that such a means of swimming had been in use for "many, many generations" in the Hawaiian Islands.

The fact that Cavill's pupils, Daniels with his stroke and the Duke were speed marvels, all at the crawl, finally influenced American teachers to abandon the breast and the side strokes. Most had not been greatly impressed with the "crawl." But since youngsters insisted upon speed to enable them to win championships and prizes, the teachers had to abandon the old routine, and so a decade after Cavill had pioneered the way and nearly as long after Daniels had proven the speed value of the crawl the new stroke was taught as a routine thing, the breast stroke only upon request.

Through the years since Trudgen revolutionized stroking in England, Cavill proceeded with his crawl and Daniels called upon his hybrid stroke, the expression has been created that "swimming records are as fragile as soap bubbles." This is true. Both men and women are swimmers, competing at numerous distances in tanks of many lengths, using various kinds of strokes, so there are countless records under constant attack.

Swimming races for men became part of the first of the modern Olympic Games when they were revived in 1896. The United States gained its first swimming title when Daniels won the

440-yard (now 400 meters) race in 1904.

Within a few Olympiads the Americans came to dominate the men's swimming, but 1932 saw a decline in their superiority. This was not because American swimmers were inferior to those who had flashed before. It simply meant that other nations had gone in for intensive teaching of the sport. Japan, Australia, France and Hungary are among the other nations that have excelled in recent years. In 1948 the United States, on the rise again, made an unprecedented sweep of the men's Olympic swimming events at London.

Contests for women—100 meters free-style and a 400-meter relay—were introduced in the Olympic Games program in 1912. The 100-meter event was captured by Fanny Durack of Australia, one of the great women swimmers of any era.

Through the years there has been much experimentation in distances and courses, and finally it led to the standardization of the distances to be traveled by swimmers. The standard routes in the United States for free-style swimming (metric distances in parenthesis) now are 50 yards, 100 yards (100 meters), 200 yards (200 meters), 500 yards (400 meters), and 1,650 yards (1,500 meters); 100 and 200 yards or meters (backstroke, breaststroke, butterfly); 200 and 400 yards or meters (individual medley); 400 yards or meters (medley relay); 400 meters free-style relay; 800 yards or (for men only) 800 meters (free-style relay).

The Olympic distances for men are 100, 200, 400, and 1,500 meters free-style; 100 and 200 meters for backstroke, breaststroke, and butterfly; 200 and 400 meters for individual medley; 400 meters medley relay; 400 and 800 meters free-style relay; 400 meters free-style relay for women.

Four standard styles are internationally recognized. They are free-style, backstroke, butterfly breast stroke (over-water arm action) and orthodox breast stroke (under-water arm action).

ENGLISH CHANNEL SWIMS

Long ago in England, the endurance record was more eagerly sought than accomplishment against time. The greatest of those distance swimmers was Capt. Matthew Webb, whose exploits caused the dare to be hurled: "Swim the English Channel to prove your greatness."

The Channel is one of the most treacherous small stretches of water, with its tides, swift currents and icy chill.

Captain Webb succeeded on Aug. 24–25, 1875, swimming from Dover, England, to Cape Gris Nez, France, about 20 miles, in 21 hours 45 minutes.

The statement that Webb was the first to swim the channel is disputed by J.W. Forney, in his book "Centennial Commissioner in Europe," which dealt with his work while in France and England. Forney stated that Capt. Paul Boynton, an American, made the swim on April 10, 1875, which was more than four months before Webb's achievement. Forney wrote that Boynton was congratulated by Queen Victoria.

Later-day research, as reported by Sydney Skilton of the "Christian Science Monitor" office in London, indicates that Boynton was aided by a life-saving suit. Boynton, it would appear, buoyed up by the suit, paddled, rather than swam, across the Channel in 23 hours 30 minutes on May 29, 1875. Thus, Webb still rates the credit for being the first to complete the dangerous passage—swimming all the way.

The next successful effort, after Webb, was by Thomas W. Burgess of England on Sept. 5–6, 1911, in 22 hours 35 minutes, just missing Webb's time.

Since Burgess' day, there have been numerous attempts to swim the Channel, and the record shows that the feat has been accomplished numerous times. The generally accepted record for the passage is 10 hours 50 minutes, made by Hassan Abd-el-Rehim of Egypt on Aug. 22, 1950.

Spacek of Bohemia is reported to have crossed in 10 hours 45 minutes in 1927, but this performance does not appear in the "Dover (England) Express," whose list is accepted as official in England.

Edward H. Temme of England was the first to make two crossings. In 1927 he went from France to England in 14 hours 29 minutes and in 1934 made the return trip in 15 hours 54 minutes. Since then a number of men and one woman, Florence Chadwick of San Diego, Calif., have made the crossing both ways.

The first woman to swim the Channel was Gertrude Ederle of the United States. Miss Ederle swam from France to England on Aug. 6, 1926, and her time of 14 hours 31 minutes lowered the existing men's record. The second woman to make the crossing was Mrs. Mille Gade Corson, who accomplished the feat three weeks after Miss Ederle had made the grade.

Miss Chadwick came to the fore among women distance swimmers in the 1950's. In addition to being the only woman to make the Channel crossing both ways, Miss Chadwick, a professional, conquered the 21-mile Catalina Channel in 1952, after having failed in a previous attempt. She covered the distance in 13 hours 47 minutes 32 seconds, breaking the previous record of 15 hours 48 minutes, made by George Young in 1927.

Post-World War II English Channel activity has been featured by mass attempts and races, two of which were very successful. On Aug. 22, 1950, nine succeeded.

Swimming the Channel no longer was a novelty after the 1950 mass performance. A year later, Aug. 16, 1951, a high of eighteen crossings was recorded in another group assault.

The late Frederick Cavill, in 1877, crossed from France to within 50 yards of the English coast in the then incredibly fast time of 12 hours 15 minutes. But, because the hour was 2 A.M. and the French sailors refused to row any farther toward the shore, Cavill had to be taken from the water. When daylight came, it was seen that if he had continued swimming for another 25 yards,

he could have walked ashore.

The record for unsuccessful attempts is 21 by Jabez Wolffe.

The shortest distance between England and France is about 20 miles, but it is estimated that Henry Sullivan of the United States swam 45 miles in 1923, and Webb and Burgess 38 miles each before negotiating the crossing.

Overall Summary, 1875–1972

England to France

Men

First . . . . .Matthew Webb, England, Aug. 25, 1875 .21:45
Fastest . . . . .Lt. Richard Hart Davis, United States, Aug. 21, 1972 . . . . 9:44
Slowest . . . . .Henry Sullivan, United States, Aug. 6, 1923 . . . . .26:50

Women

First . . . .*Florence Chadwick, United States, Sept. 11, 1951 . . . . .16:22
Fastest . . . . .Florence Chadwick, United States, Oct. 12, 1955 . . . . .13:33
Slowest . . . . .Florence Chadwick, United States, Sept. 11, 1951 . . . . .16:22

    *Miss Chadwick has been the only woman to conquer this route. She has done so three times, in 1951, 1953 and 1955.

France to England

Men

First . . . . .Enrico Tiraboschi, Italy, Aug. 12, 1923 .16:33
Fastest . . . . .Barry Watson, England, 1964 . . . .·. 9:35
Slowest . . . . .Philip Mickman, England, Aug. 23, 1949 . . . . .23:48

Women

First . . . . .Gertrude Ederle, United States, Aug. 6, 1926 . . . . .14:31
Fastest . . . . .Linda McGill, Australia, Sept. 29, 1967 . . . . 9:59.57
Slowest . . . . .Ivy Hawke, England, Aug. 19, 1928 . . . . .19:16

Round Trip

First . . . . .Antonio Abertondo, Argentina, 1961 . . . . .43:15
Fastest . . . . .Ted Erikson, United States, 1965 . . . . .30:03

OTHER ENDURANCE SWIMS

The most famous among the long-distance swimming contests for professionals in North America was the Wrigley Swim, first arranged in 1927, for a $25,000 prize. The route was from Catalina to Los Angeles, and the first race was won by George Young of Toronto. Lake Ontario, near Toronto, became the scene for later Wrigley competitions. In 1929 a 10-mile race for women was held in Lake Ontario, with Martha Norelius of New York, who had just turned professional, the winner of the top award of $10,000. The Wrigley swims were abandoned years ago.

Daniel Carpio of Peru became the first to swim the Strait of Gibraltar when he went from continental Spain to Spanish Morocco, a distance of 8 miles, in 9 hours 20 minutes on July 22, 1948.

In 1947, Thomas Blower of Nottingham, England, who made the first of his three conquests of the English Channel in 1937, became the first person to swim the Irish Sea. Blower covered the 25 miles from Donaghadee, Northern Ireland, to a spot 5 miles from Port Patrick, Scotland, in 15 hours 25 minutes.

Another notable long-distance swimmer is India's Mihir Sen. He is the first Indian to swim the English Channel, in Sept. 1958; the first man to swim the Palk Straits, April, 1966; the first Asian to swim the strait of Gibralter, Aug., 1966; the first man to swim the strait of Dardanelles, Sept., 1966; the first Indian to swim the strait of Bosporus, Sept., 1966; and the first non-American and third man to swim the Panama Canal in Oct., 1966.

Endurance Swimmers

The greatest distance swimmer of this, or any other generation, was Pedro A. Candiotti of Argentina, known as the "shark of Quilla Creek." For years he has had the ambition to swim 205 miles down the River Platte from Rosario to Buenos Aires. He has made about 15 unsuccessful attempts. In his try in February, 1943, he was in the water 74 hours and 30 minutes when a rising tide forced him to quit. In February, 1935, he made his longest swim—281 miles—in the Parana River from Santa Fe to Zarate (Argentina) and was in the water for 84 hours.

The world record for long-distance swimming, and also time in the water, is held by John V.

Sigmund of St. Louis. He swam non-stop down the Mississippi River from St. Louis, 292 miles, in 89 hours 42 minutes in July 1940. The distance and time were officially checked.

The next best record is 288 miles, which at the time was the record, made by Clarence Giles, swimming without rest in the Yellowstone River in Montana, between Glendive and Billings, June 30 to July 3, 1939, in 77 hours 31 minutes. Giles' performance, so far as speed is concerned, greatly eclipsed that of Sigmund, who swam four more miles.

The handicap swim record is held by the legless Charlie Zimmy, who, in 1938, swam the Hudson River from Albany to New York, a matter of 147 miles, but without any timing for his feat.

The woman's record for continuous swimming is 87 hours 27 minutes, made by Mrs. Myrtle Huddleston of New York, in 1931. She swam in a tank and broke her earlier mark of 86 hours 16 minutes.

HOW TO SCORE DIVING CONTESTS

Diving contests are determined on the point system. Two factors figure in the tally: (1) the judges' decision on how well the dive was performed and (2) the evaluation of the particular dive executed, which is obtained from the official degree-of-difficulty tables. The average mark of the middle three judges' scores is multiplied by the degree-of-difficulty to give the score for any one dive. These scores are added at the end of the competition to determine the points tallied by each contestant.

In championship competition, each contestant must execute twelve dives. These comprise six optional dives from different groups, the total degree-of-difficulty of which must not exceed 11.0 for the three-meter dives and 10.0 for the one-meter dives, and six optional dives without limit, the sixth being chosen by the competitor from any group.

Five judges mark each dive, with the high score and the low score excluded from the tally. Marking is on this basis:

Completely failed 0   Satisfactory .5 or 6
Unsatisfactory ... 1 or 2   Good ...... 7 to 8.5
Deficient .... 3 or 4   Very Good .. 9 to 10

A typical score for a reasonably well-executed dive would be 6, 7, 7, 7, 8. The 6 and 8 would be excluded, so the diver would receive an official score of 7 or 21 (it is a matter of preference whether the three-judge score is averaged).

This mark of 7 or 21 then would be multiplied by the degree-of-difficulty for the dive in question.

There are 37 approved dives that may be executed from the one-meter board and 49 that may be executed from the three-meter board.

These are arranged in five groups, as follows: (1) the forward dives; (2) the back dives; (3) the gainer dives, in which the diver faces the water but spins backward; (4) the cutaway dives, in which the diver faces the board but spins forward, and (5) the twisting dives, in which the diver's body rotates on his head-to-heels axis. All groups include somersault dives.

Low board degree-of-difficulty ranges from 1.1 for a back jack-knife in the cutaway group to 2.7 for a double twisting forward one-and-one-half somersault. From the high board, the table starts with 1.2 for the back jack-knife and rises to 2.7 for the one-and-one-half twisting one-and-one-half gainer and the back two-and-one-half twisting one-and-one-half somersault.

HELMS ATHLETIC FOUNDATION HONOR ROLL

Swimming

Men

George Breen
Richard Cleveland
Clarence (Buster) Crabbe
Charles Daniels
Jeffrey Farrell
Peter Fick
Ralph Flanagan
Alan Ford
L.B. Goodwin
H. Jamison Handy
Harry Hebner
Chester Jastremski
Duke Kahanamoku
Adolph Kiefer
George Kojac
Ford Kono
Ludy Langer
Michael McDermott
Perry McGillivray
Frank McKinney
James McLane
Jack Medica
Keo Nakama
Yoshi Oyokawa
Wally Ris
Carl Robie
Murray Rose
Norman Ross
Richard Roth
Roy Saari
Carroll Schaeffer
Clark Scholes
Don Schollander
Bill Smith
Walter Spence
Allen Stack
Michael Troy
Joe Verdeur
W.L. Wallen
John Weissmuller
William Woolsey
William Yorzyk

Women

Catherine Ball
Sybil Bauer
Ethelda Bleibtrey
Carin Cone
Ann Curtis
Donna deVarona
Gertrude Ederle
Cathy Ferguson
Carolyn Green
Brenda Helser
Eleanor Holm
Lenore Kight
Claudia Kolb
Helene Madison
Shelley Mann
Nancy Merki
Deborah Meyer
Martha Norelius
Katherine Rawls
Sylvia Ruuska
Sharon Stouder
Chris Von Saltza
Helen Wainwright
Suzanne Zimmerman

Diving

Men

David Browning
Earl Clark
Robert Clotworthy
Richard Degener
Peter Desjardins
George Gaidzik
Bruce Harlan
Sammy Lee
Al Patnik
Clarence Pinkston
Michael Riley
Kenneth Sitzberger
Harold Smith
Gary Tobian
Robert Webster
Albert White
Bernard Wrightson

Women

Leslie Bush
Georgia Coleman
Victoria Draves
Marjorie Gestring
Sue Gossick
Patricia Keller McCormick
Elsie Hanneman McEvoy
Helen Meany
Helen Crlenkovich Morgan
Zoe Ann Olsen
Elizabeth Becker Pinkston
Paula Jean Myers Pope
Dorothy Poynton
Katherine Rawls
Aileen Riggin

Anne Ross
Thelma Payne Sanborn

KIPHUTH'S RECORD

The late Robert J.H. Kiphuth became swimming coach at Yale University in 1918 and coached there through the 1959 season, retiring because of age. In that period his teams won 527 college dual meets and lost 12. By beating Harvard in the closing meeting of the 1959 season, Kiphuth's charges extended their latest winning streak to 182, surpassing the string of 175 set by teams from 1925 to 1937.

Yale had two other outstanding streaks during Kiphuth's reign. From 1918 to 1924, the Elis won 65 in a row and from 1940 to 1945 they took 63 straight.

Kiphuth coached the United States women's Olympic team in 1928 and the men's in 1932, 1936 and 1948. He also was appointed coach of the men's team in 1940, but the Games were not held because of World War II. His 1942 Yale team and his 1949, 1951, 1953, 1954, 1955 and 1957 New Haven Swim Club teams won National Amateur Athletic Union indoor championships and his 1942, 1944, 1951 and 1953 Yale teams annexed National Collegiate Athletic Association crowns.

In addition to coaching hundreds of A.A.U., N.C.A.A. and Eastern League individual titleholders, Kiphuth directed his teams to a remarkable record in the Eastern League. His teams won the Eastern title in 1939, 1940, 1941, 1942, 1943, 1947, 1948, 1949, 1950, 1951, 1952, 1953, 1954, 1955, 1956, 1957, 1958 and 1959.

Kiphuth's Dual-Meet Record

(Excluding alumni meets)

Year	Won	Lost
1918	9	1
1919	7	0
1920	10	0
1921	14	0
1922	14	0
1923	15	0
1924	10	4
1925	14	0
1926	14	0
1927	14	0
1928	14	0
1929	12	0
1930	14	0
1931	14	0
1932	11	0
1933	14	0
1934	14	0
1935	12	0
1936	14	0
1937	14	1
1938	10	3
1939	15	1
1940	15	1
1941	13	0

1942	12	0
1943	11	0
1944	9	0
1945	8	1
1946	7	0
1947	12	0
1948	12	0
1949	13	0
1950	13	0
1951	13	0
1952	13	0
1953	15	0
1954	13	0
1955	14	0
1956	15	0
1957	14	0
1958	13	0
1959	13	0
Totals	527	12

UNITED STATES CHAMPIONS

(Source: Official Amateur Athletic Union Swimming Handbook.)

This list includes the events that are on the current A.A.U. program. Champions of discontinued events may be found in the Official Handbook published by the A.A.U. of the United States, 3400 West 86th St., Indianapolis, Ind., 46862.

The 1972 Olympic trials replaced the A.A.U. outdoor meet.

Outdoor—Men
100-Yard Free-Style—100 Meters

1883—A.F. Camacho .... 1m.28¼s.
1884—H.E. Toussaint .... 1m.21s.
1885—H. Braun .... 1m.18.4s.
1886—H. Braun .... 1m.29.2s.
1887—H. Braun .... 1m.17.2s.
1888—H. Braun .... 1m.16.2s.
1889—W.C. Johnson .... 1m.22.4s.
1890—W.C. Johnson .... 1m.5.2s.
1891—W.C. Johnson .... 1m.10.6s.
1892—A.T. Kenney .... 1m.18.2s.
1893—A.T. Kenney .... 1m.12.4s.
1894—A.T. Kenney .... 1m.9.6s.
1895—No competition
1896—George R. Whittacker .... 1m.13.4s.
1897—D.B. Renear .... 1m.7.4s.
1898—S.P. Avery ....
1899—E.C. Schaeffer .... 1m.8.6s.
1900—E.C. Schaeffer .... 1m.5.6s.
1901—E.C. Schaeffer .... 1m.10s.
1902—E.C. Schaeffer .... 1m.7s.
1903—Fred A. Wenck .... 1m.9.6s.
1904—Zoltan de Holomay .... 1m.2.8s.
1905—Charles M. Daniels .... 1m.3.8s.
1906—Charles M. Daniels .... 1m.
1907—Charles M. Daniels .... 1m.3.4s.
1908—Charles M. Daniels .... 57.3s.
1909—15—No competition

1916—Duke Kahanamoku .... 53.2s.
1917—Duke Kahanamoku .... 54s.
1918—Perry McGillivray .... 56.2s.
1919—Perry McGillivray .... 1m.5.8s.
1920—Duke Kahanamoku .... 55.4s.
1921—P. Kealoha .... 53s.
1922—John Weissmuller .... 52.8s.
1923—John Weissmuller .... 54.6s.
1924—No competition
1925—John Weissmuller .... 52s.
1926—John Weissmuller (100 meters) .... 59.6s.
1927—John Weissmuller (100 meters) ..... 58s.
1928—John Weissmuller (100 meters) .... 57.8s.
1929—Walter Spence (100 meters) .... 1m.2.2s.
1930—George Kojac (100 meters) .... 59.2s.
1931—Manuella Kalili (100 meters) ...... 60.2s.
1932—No competition
1933—James Gilhula (100 meters) .... 1m.1.3s.
1934—Art Highland (100 meters) ..... 1m.1.6s.
1935—Peter Fick (100 meters) .... 59.8s.
1936—Peter Fick (100 meters) .... 58.3s.
1937—Peter Fick (100 meters) .... 59.8s.
1938—Peter Fick (100 meters) .... 1m.00.2s.
1939—Otto Jaretz (100 meters) ...... 1m.00.7s.
1940—Otto Jaretz (110 yards) .... 58.4s.
1941—Takashi Hirose (100 meters) ... 1m.00.1s.
1942—Alan Ford (110 yards) .... 59.4s.
1943—Alan Ford (110 yards) .... 59.5s.
1944—Jerry Kerschner (100 meters) ...... 59s.
1945—Albert Isaacs (100 meters) .... 1m.02.1s.
1946—Bill Smith (100 meters) .... 59s.
1947—Walter Ris (100 meters) .... 58.5s.
1948—Robert Nugent (100 meters) ...... 58.9s.
1949—Robert Gibe (100 meters) .... 58.2s.
1950—Richard Cleveland (110 yards) .... 58.2s.
1951—Richard Cleveland (100 meters) ... 58.0s.
1952—Richard Cleveland (110 yards) .... 58.4s.
1953—Richard Cleveland (100 meters) ... 57.5s.
1954—Richard Cleveland (100 meters) ... 57.5s.
1955—Hendrick Gideonse (100 meters) .. 57.6s.
1956—Dick Hanley (100 meters) .... 56.3s.
1957—Dick Hanley (100 meters) .... 57.3s.
1958—Jon Henricks (100 meters) .... 55.8s.
1959—Jeff Farrell (100 meters) .... 56.9s.
1960—Jeff Farrell (100 meters) .... 54.8s.
1961—Steve Clark (100 meters) .... 54.4s.
1962—Steve Jackman (100 meters) ...... 54.6s.
1963—Steve Clark .... 54.9s.
1964—Don Schollander .... 54s.
1965—Don Roth .... 53.8s.
1966—Don Schollander .... 53.5s.
1967—Don Schollander .... 53.3s.
1968—Mark Spitz (100 meters) .... 53.6s.
1969—Don Havens (100 meters) .... 52.5s.
1970—Frank Heckl (100 meters) .... 52.4s.
1971—Mark Spitz (100 meters) .... 52.4s.
1972—Not held

220-Yard Free-Style—200 Meters

1897—D.M. Reeder .... 2m.57.4s.
1898—H.H. Reeder .... 3m.7.6s.
1899—E.C. Schaeffer .... 2m.53.6s.

1900—E.C. Schaeffer . . . . 3m.7.2s.
1901—E.C. Schaeffer . . . . 2m.50.8s.
1902—E.C. Schaeffer . . . . 2m.58.8s.
1903—Charles Ruberl . . . . 3m.18.4s.
1904—Charles M. Daniels . . . . 2m.44.2s.
1905—Charles M. Daniels . . . . 2m.45s.
1906—Charles M. Daniels . . . . 2m.42.4s.
1907—Charles M. Daniels . . . . 3m.13.8s.
1908—Charles M. Daniels . . . . 2m.36.8s.
1909—No competition
1910—Charles M. Daniels . . . . 2m.33s.
1911-1920—No competition
1921—John Weissmuller . . . . 2m.28s.
1922—John Weissmuller . . . . 2m.22.4s.
1923—Harry Glancy . . . . 2m.36.6s.
1924-33—No competition
1934—James Gilhula . . . . 2m.18.5s.
1935—James Gilhula . . . . 2m.15s.
1936—Tom Haynie . . . . 2m.14.3s.
1937—Irving McCaffrey . . . . 2m.18.8s.
1938—Adolph Kiefer . . . . 2m.18.7s.
1939—Kiyoshi Nakama . . . . 2m.16.3s.
1940—Otto Jaretz . . . . 2m.13.1s.
1941—Bill Smith (200 meters) . . . . . 2m.16.1s.
1942—Bill Smith . . . . 2m.10.7s.
1943—Alan Ford . . . . 2m.19.4s.
1944—Jerry Kerschner (200 meters) . . 2m.12.9s.
1945—Keo Nakama (200 meters) . . . . 2m.18.7s.
1946—Bill Smith (200 meters) . . . . . 2m.14.4s.
1947—Bill Smith (200 meters) . . . . . 2m.12.6s.
1948—Ed Gilbert (200 meters) . . . . . 2m.16.9s.
1949—Yoshiro Hamaguchi
   (200 meters) . . . . 2m.11.0s.
1950—James McLane . . . . 2m.10.5s.
1951—Wayne Moore (200 meters) . . . . 2m.08.4s.
1952—William Woolsey . . . . 2m.13.2s.
1953—Wayne Moore (200 meters) . . . . 2m.09.0s.
1954—Ford Konno (200 meters) . . . . . 2m.10.6s.
1955—William Woolsey (200 meters) . 2m.08.2s.
1956—William Woolsey (200 meters) . 2m.06.5s.
1957—Dick Hanley (200 meters) . . . . . 2m.08.4s.
1958—Jon Henricks (200 meters) . . . . 2m.05.2s.
1959—Jeff Farrell (200 meters) . . . . . 2m.06.9s.
1960—Jeff Farrell (200 meters) . . . . . 2m.03.2s.
1961—Tsuyoshi Yamanaka
   (200 meters) . . . . 2m.00.4s.
1962—Don Schollander (200 meters) . 2m.00.4s.
1963—Don Schollander . . . . 1m.59.0s.
1964—Don Schollander . . . . 1m.57.6s.
1965—Gary Ilman . . . . 1m.59.0s.
1966—Don Schollander . . . . 1m.56.2s.
1967—Don Schollander . . . . 1m.55.7s.
1968—Mark Spitz (200 meters) . . . . . . 1m.57.0s.
1969—Hans Fassnacht (200 meters) . . 1m.56.5s.
1970—Mark Spitz (200 meters) . . . . . . 1m.54.6s.
1971—Mark Spitz (200 meters) . . . . . . 1m.54.7s.
1972—Not held

440-Yard Free-Style—400 Meters

1893—A.T. Kenney . . . . 6m.24.4s.
1894—P.F. Dickey . . . . 7m.24.6s.
1895–1896—No competition

1897—Howard F. Brewer . . . . 7m.8.4s.
1898—Dr. Paul Neumann . . . . 6m.51.4s.
1899—E.C. Schaeffer . . . . 6m.48.6s.
1900—E.C. Schaeffer . . . . 6m.52.8s.
1901—E.C. Schaeffer . . . . 6m.26s.
1902—E.C. Schaeffer . . . . 6m.18.2s.
1903—T.E. Kitching Jr. . . . . 6m.31.6s.
1904—Charles M. Daniels . . . . 6m.16.2s.
1905—L.B. Goodwin . . . . 6m.22s.
1906—Charles M. Daniels . . . . 6m.24s.
1907—Charles M. Daniels . . . . 6m.26.8s.
1908—Charles M. Daniels . . . . 5m.54.2s.
1909—Charles M. Daniels . . . . 5m.57.4s.
1910—Charles M. Daniels . . . . 5m.59.8s.
1911—R.M. Ritter . . . . 5m.52.6s.
1912—R.E. Frizell . . . . 5m.56.8s.
1913—J.C. Wheatley . . . . 6m.4.6s.
1914—H.J. Hebner . . . . 6m.22s.
1915—Ludy Langer . . . . 5m.32.2s.
1916—Ludy Langer . . . . 5m.38.6s.
1917—Norman Ross . . . . 5m.58.6s.
1918—W.L. Wallen . . . . 5m.57.8s.
1919—W.L. Wallen . . . . 5m.45s.
1920—Norman Ross . . . . 5m.40.4s.
1921—Ludy Langer . . . . 5m.45s.
1922—John Weissmuller . . . . 5m.16.4s.
1923—John Weissmuller . . . . 5m.37.4s.
1924—No competition
1925—John Weissmuller . . . . 5m.225.s.
1926—John Weissmuller . . . . 5m.21.8s.
1927—John Weissmuller . . . . 4m.52s.
1928—John Weissmuller . . . . 4m.58.6s.
1929—Clarence Crabbe . . . . 5m.4s.
1930—Maiola Kalili . . . . 4m.56.4s.
1931—Clarence Crabbe . . . . 4m.59.8s.
1932—No competition
1933—Jack Medica 4m.52.8s,
1934—Jack Medica . . . . 4m.50.9s.
1935—John Macionis . . . . 4m.51.6s.
1936—Ralph Flanagan (400 meters) . . 4m.48.6s.
1937—Ralph Flanagan (400 meters) . . . 4m.46s.
1938—Ralph Flanagan . . . . 4m.51.1s.
1939—Ralph Flanagan . . . . 4m.50.2s.
1940—Kiyoshi Nakama . . . . 4m.50.4s.
1941—Bill Smith (400 meters) . . . . . . 4m.47.6s.
1942—Bill Smith . . . . 4m.39.6s.
1943—Eugene Rogers . . . . 5m.04.2s.
1944—Keo Nakama (400 meters) . . . . 4m.53.6s.
1945—Keo Nakama (400 meters) . . . . 5m.05.7s.
1946—James McLane (400 meters) . . . 4m.49.5s.
1947—James McLane (400 meters) . . . 4m.41.9s.
1948—James McLane (400 meters) . . . 4m.53.5s.
1949—Hironoshin Furuhashi
   (400 meters) . . . . 4m.33.3s.
1950—John Marshall . . . . 4m.39.3s.
1951—Wayne Moore (400 meters) . . . . 4m.35.8s.
1952—Ford Konno . . . . 4m.48s.
1953—Ford Konno (400 meters) . . . . . 4m.39.8s.
1954—William Woolsey (400 meters) . 4m.42.3s.
1955—Ford Konno (400 meters) . . . . . 4m.38.7s.
1956—George Breen (400 meters) . . . . 4m.37.6s.
1957—George Breen (400 meters) . . . . 4m.35.1s.

1958—Murray Rose (400 meters) .... 4m.25.5s.
1959—Alan Somers (400 meters) .... 4m.30.6s.
1960—Alan Somers (400 meters) .... 4m.21.9s.
1961—Tsuyoshi Yamanaka
    (400 meters) .... 4m.17.5s.
1962—Murray Rose (400 meters) .... 4m.17.2s.
1963—Don Schollander .... 4m.17.7s.
1964—Don Schollander .... 4m.12.7s.
1965—John Nelson .... 4m.14.1s.
1966—Don Schollander .... 4m.11.6s.
1967—Greg Charlton .... 4m.09.8s.
1968—Ralph Hutton (Canada)
    (400 meters) .... 4m.06.5s.
1969—Hans Fassnacht (400 meters) .. 4m.04.0s.
1970—John Kinsella (400 meters) .... 4m.02.8s.
1971—Tom McBreen (400 meters) ... 4m.02.1s.
1972—Not held

One-Mile Free-Style—1,500 Meters

1877—R. Weissenborn .... 45m.44 1/4s.
1878—H.J. Heath .... 29m.20s.
1879-1882—No competition
1883—R.P. Magee .... 29m.42 1/4s.
1884—R.P. Magee (with tide) ..... 25m.41.5s.
1885—R.P. Magee (with tide) .... 22m.38s.
1886—R.P. Magee (with tide) ...... 29m.02s.
1887—A. Meffert .... 35m.18.2s.
1888—H. Braun .... 26m.57s.
1889—A. Meffert (with tide) ...... 27m.20s.
1890—A. Meffert (with tide) ...... 22m.39.4s.
1891—J.R. Whitmore (with tide) .... 24m.11.6s.
1892—A.T. Kenney (with tide) .... 28m.45.4s.
1893—G. Whittaker (with tide) .... 28m.55.4s.
1894—A.T. Kenney .... 33m.34.4s.
1895—No competition
1896—B.A. Hart .... 30m.27.6s.
1897—Dr. P. Neumann .... 30m.24.4s.
1898—F.A. Wenck .... 29m.51.6s.
1899—F.A. Wenck .... 30m.33.8s.
1900—George W. Van Cleaf ...... 34m.45.6s.
1901—Otto Wahle .... 28m.52.6s.
1902—E. Carroll Schaeffer .... 28m.14.6s.
1903—Charles Ruberl .... 28m.05.6s.
1904—Emil Rausch .... 27m.15.2s.
1905—Charles M. Daniels .... 26m.41.8s.
1906—H.J. Handy .... 28m.43.4s.
1907—H.J. Handy .... 29m.20.8s.
1908—Charles M. Daniels .... 27m.20.6s.
1909—Charles M. Daniels .... 26m.19.6s.
1910—L.B. Goodwin .... 30m.02.4s.
1911—J.H. Reilly .... 25m.40.4s.
1912—L.B. Goodwin .... 25m.25s.
1913—L.B. Goodwin .... 25m.18.4s.
1914—L.B. Goodwin .... 25m.42.2s.
1915—Ludy Langer .... 24m.59.4s.
1916—Ludy Langer .... 23m.22s.
1917—Norman Ross .... 24m.10s.
1918—W.L. Wallen .... 25m.08.6s.
1919—W.L. Wallen .... 25m.37.6s.
1920—Eugene Bolden .... 25m.26.4s.
1921—No competition
1922—Clyde Goldwater .... 25m.02s.

1923—Eugene Bolden .... 25m.06s.
1924—No competition
1925—Harry Glancy .... 24m.27.8s.
1926—Arne Borg .... 21m.46.4s.
1927—Clarence Crabbe .... 22m.52.4s.
1928—Clarence Crabbe .... 21m.35.6s.
1929—Clarence Crabbe .... 22m.09.8s.
1930—Clarence Crabbe .... 21m.27s.
1931—Clarence Crabbe .... 22m.14.8s.
1932—No competition
1933—Ralph Flanagan .... 21m.12.2s.
1934—Jack Medica .... 20m.57.8s.
1935—Ralph Flanagan .... 21m.00.3s.
1936—Ralph Flanagan .... 20m.58.9s.
1937—Ralph Flanagan .... 20m.42.6s.
1938—Ralph Flanagan .... 21m.06.3s.
1939—Ralph Flanagan .... 21m.00.7s.
1940—Bunmei Nakama .... 21m.31.4s.
1941—Kiyoshi Nakama (1,500 meters)19m.55.8s.
1942—Keo Nakama .... 20m.29.0s.
1943—Paul Maloney .... 23m.06.5s.
1944—Keo Nakama (1,500 meters) .. 19m.42.6s.
1945—James McLane (1,500 meters) 19m.49.5s.
1946—James McLane (1,500 meters) 19m.23.1s.
1947—James McLane (1,500 meters) 19m.57.5s.
1948—Jack Taylor (1,500 meters) ... 19m.48.1s.
1949—Hironoshin Furuhashi (1,500
    meters) .... 18m.29.9s.
1950—John Marshall .... 20m.08.6s.
1951—Ford Konno (1,500 meters) .. 18m.46.3s.
1952—Ford Konno (1,500 meters) .. 20m47.1s.
1953—Ford Konno (1,500 meters) .. 19m.20.0s.
1954—Ford Konno (1,500 meters) .. 19m.07.1s.
1955—George Onekea (1,500 meters) 18m.52.3s.
1956—George Breen (1,500 meters) . 18m.27.6s.
1957—George Breen (1,500 meters) . 18m.17.9s.
1958—Murray Rose (1,500 meters) .. 18m.06.4s.
1959—Alan Somers (1,500 meters) .. 17m.51.3s.
1960—George Breen (1,500 meters) . 17m.33.5s.
1961—Roy Saari (1,500 meters) .... 17m.29.8s.
1962—Murray Rose (1,500 meters) .. 17m.16.7s.
1963—Roy Saari .... 17m.34.6s.
1964—Murray Rose (Australia) ..... 17m.01.8s.
1965—Steve Krause .... 16m.58.7s.
1966—Mike Burton .... 16m.41.6s.
1967—Mike Burton .... 16m.34.1s.
1968—Mike Burton (1,500 meters) .. 16m.29.4s.
1969—Mike Burton (1,500 meters) .. 16m.04.5s.
1970—John Kinsella (1,500 meters) . 15m.57.1s.
1971—Mike Burton (1,500 meters) .. 16m.09.6s.
1972—Not held

100-Meter Backstroke—110 Yards

1934—Albert Vande Weghe .... 1m.11s.
1935—Adolph Kiefer .... 1m.07.8s.
1936—Adolph Kiefer .... 1m.06.5s.
1937—Adolph Kiefer .... 1m.06.3s.
1938—Adolph Kiefer .... 1m.07.8s.
1939—Adolph Kiefer .... 1m.06.6s.
1940—Adolph Kiefer (110 yards) .... 1m.05.5s.
1941—Adolph Kiefer .... 1m.06.3s.
1942—Adolph Kiefer .... 1m.6.6s.

1943—Adolph Kiefer . . . . 1m.07s.
1944—Jack Weeden . . . . 1m.12.1s.
1945—Robert E. Cowell . . . . 1m.10.6s.
1946—Harry Holiday . . . . 1m.08s.
1947—Alan Stack . . . . 1m.07.8s.
1948—Allen Stack . . . . 1m.07.7s.
1949—Allen Stack . . . . 1m.07.1s.
1950—Allen Stack (110 yards) . . . . . . 1m.08.2s.
1951—James Thomas . . . . 1m.07.4s.
1952—Yoshinobu Oyakawa (110 yards) 1m.05.7s.
1953—Yoshi Oyakawa . . . . 1m.06.8s.
1954—Albert Wiggins . . . . 1m.07.2s.
1955—Yoshi Oyakawa . . . . 1m.05.3s.
1956—Yoshi Oyakawa . . . . 1m.05.9s.
1957—Frank McKinney . . . . 1m.04.5s.
1958—Frank McKinney . . . . 1m.04.5s.
1959—Frank McKinney . . . . 1m.03.6s.
1960—Tom Stock . . . . 1m.02.9s.
1961—Bob Bennett . . . . 1m.01.3s.
1962—Tom Stock . . . . 1m.01.0s.
1963—Richard McGeagh . . . . 1m.01.7s.
1964—Richard McGeagh . . . . 1m.01.6s.
1965—Thompson Mann . . . . 1m.00.5s.
1966—Charles Hickcox . . . . 1m.01.0s.
1967—Charles Hickcox . . . . 59.7s.
1968—Larry Barbiere . . . . 1m.00.9s.
1969—Mitch Ivey . . . . 1m.00.2s.
1970—Mike Stamm . . . . 58.5s.
1971—Mel Nash . . . . 59.2s.
1972—Not held

200-Meter Backstroke

1963—Tom Stock . . . . 2m.12.4s.
1964—Robert Bennett . . . . 2m.15.7s.
1965—Thompson Mann . . . . 2m.12.4s.
1966—Charles Hickcox . . . . 2m.12.4s.
1967—Charles Hickcox . . . . 2m.12.3s.
1968—Jack Horsley . . . . 2m.12.2s.
1969—Gary Hall . . . . 2m.06.6s.
1970—Mike Stamm . . . . 2m.06.3s.
1971—Charlie Campbell . . . . 2m.07.1s.
1972—Not held

100-Meter Breast Stroke

1951—John Davies . . . . 1m08.4s.
1952—Jerry Holan (110 yards) . . . . . . 1m.09.3s.
1953—John Dudeck . . . . 1m.08.4s.
1954—55—No competition
1956—Robert Hughes . . . . 1m.11.2s.
1957—Robert Hughes . . . . 1m.12.1s.
1958—Manuel Sanguily . . . . 1m.15.9s.
1959—Manuel Sanguilly . . . . 1m.14.6s.
1960—Chet Jastremski . . . . 1m.12.4s.
1961—Chet Jastremski . . . . 1m.07.5s.
1962—Chet Jastremski . . . . 1m.08.2s.
1963—William Craig . . . . 1m.10.2s.
1964—Chet Jastremski . . . . 1m.10.0s.
1965—Tom Tretheway . . . . 1m.08.3s.
1966—Ken Merten . . . . 1m.08.9s.
1967—Ken Merten . . . . 1m.08.7s.
1968—Mike Dirksen . . . . 1m.08.8s.
1969—Jose Fiolo . . . . 1m.06.9s.
1970—Brian Job . . . . 1m.06.4s.

1971—Peder Dahlberg . . . . 1m.06.9s.
1972—Not held

220-Yard Breast Stroke—200 Meters

1906—A.M. Goersling (200 yards) . . . . 3m.01.2s.
1907—H.J. Handy (200 yards) . . . . . . 3m.17.6s.
1908—A.M. Goersling (200 yards) . . . . 2m.46.4s.
1909—A.M. Goersling (200 yards) . . . . . 2m.49s.
1910—20—No competition
1921—M.J. McDermott . . . . 3m.10.4s.
1922—R. Skelton . . . . 3m.22.8s.
1923—R. Skelton . . . . 3m.06.6s.
1924—33—No competition
1934—John Higgins . . . . 2m.55s.
1935—John Higgins . . . . 2m.47.6s.
1936—John Higgins (200 meters) . . . 2m.43.3s.
1937—Ray Kaye . . . . 2m.52.2s.
1938—Jim Werson . . . . 2m.49.2s.
1939—James Skinner . . . . 2m.46.6s.
1940—James Skinner . . . . 2m.48.8s.
1941—Jose Balmores (200 meters) . . . 2m.45.5s.
1942—Jim Counsilman . . . . 2m.45.4s.
1943—Joseph Verdeur . . . . 2m.53.2s.
1944—Joseph Verdeur (200 meters) . . 2m.46.3s.
1945—Dave Seibold (200 meters) . . . . 2m.55.5s.
1946—Joseph Verdeur (200 meters) . . 2m.44.2s.
1947—Joseph Verdeur (200 meters) . . 2m.38.4s.
1948—Joseph Verdeur (200 meters) . . 2m.48.7s.
1949—Joseph Verdeur (200 meters) . . 2m.36.3s.
1950—Robert Brawner . . . . 2m.41.0s.
1951—John Davies (200 meters) . . . . . 2m.35.8s.
1952—Bowen Stassforth . . . . 2m.34.7s.
1953—Dave Hawkins (200 meters) . . . 2m.37.9s.
1954—Dick Fadgen (200 meters) . . . . 2m.49.5s.
1955—Bob Mattson (200 meters) . . . . 2m.46.8s.
1956—Dick Fadgen (200 meters) . . . . 2m.45.8s.
1957—Manuel Sanguily (200 meters) . . 2m.44s.
1958—Norbert Rumpel (200 meters) . 2m.47.8s.
1959—Ronald Clark (200 meters) . . . . 2m.45.6s.
1960—Peter Fogarasy (200 meters) . . . 2m.38.8s.
1961—Chet Jastremski (200 meters) . . 2m.29.6s.
1962—Chet Jastremski (200 meters) . . 2m.30.0s.
1963—Ken Merten . . . . 2m.34.5s.
1964—Chet Jastremski, Bill Craig (tie) 2m.31.8s.
1965—Chet Jastremski . . . . 2m.30.1s.
1966—Ken Merten . . . . 2m.31.2s.
1967—Ken Merten . . . . 2m.30.8s.
1968—Brian Job (200 meters) . . . . 2m.31.2s.
1969—Mike Dirksen (200 meters) . . . . 2m.26.9s.
1970—Brian Job (200 meters) . . . . 2m.24.1s.
1971—Rick Colella (200 meters) . . . . . 2m.25.0s.
1972—Not held

100-Meter Butterfly

1954—Dick Fadgen . . . . 1m.07.4s.
1956—Al Wiggins . . . . 1m.04.2s.
1957—Al Wiggins . . . . 1m.02.8s.
1958—Mike Troy . . . . 1m.02.8s.
1959—Lance Larson . . . . 1m.01.1s.
1960—Lance Larson . . . . 58.7s.
1961—Fred Schmidt . . . . 58.6s.
1962—Ed Spencer . . . . 50.9s.
1963—Walter Richardson . . . . 58.8s.

1964—Walter Richardson ....57.5s.
1965—Luis Nicolao ....57.8s.
1966—Mark Spitz ....58.1s.
1967—Mark Spitz ....56.7s.
1968—Mark Spitz ....57.0s.
1969—Doug Russell ....56.0s.
1970—Mark Spitz ....56.1s.
1971—Mark Spitz ....55.4s.
1972—Not held

200-Meter Butterfly

1955—Bill Yorzyk ....2m.29.1s.
1956—Bill Yorzyk ....2m.24.3s.
1957—Bill Yorzyk .... 2m.22s.
1958—Bill Yorzyk ....2m.22.5s.
1959—Mike Troy ....2m.16.4s.
1960—Mike Troy ....2m.13.4s.
1961—Carl Robie ....2m.12.6s.
1962—Carl Robie ....2m.10.8s.
1963—Carl Robie ....2m.08.8s.
1964—Carl Robie ....2m.09.2s.
1965—Carl Robie ....2m.07.7s.
1966—Phil Houser ....2m.09.9s.
1967—Mark Spitz ....2m.06.4s.
1968—Carl Robie ....2m.08.9s.
1969—Mike Burton ....2m.06.5s.
1970—Gary Hall ....2m.05.0s.
1971—Mark Spitz ....2m.03.8s.
1972—Not held

200-Meter Individual Medley

1963—Dick Roth ....2m.16.0s.
1964—Dick Roth ....2m.15.5s.
1965—Dick Roth ....2m.14.9s.
1966—Greg Buckingham ....2m.12.4s.
1967—Greg Buckingham ....2m.11.3s.
1968—Juan Bello (Peru) ....2m.14.1s.
1969—Gary Hall ....2m.09.6s.
1970—Gary Hall ....2m.09.4s.
1971—Gary Hall ....2m.10.0s.
1972—Not held

400-Meter Individual Medley

1954—Burwell Jones ....5m.29.0s.
1955—George Harrison ....5m.23.3s.
1956—Bill Yorzyk ....5m.19.0s.
1957—Gary Heinrich ....5m.15.6s.
1958—Frank Brunell ....5m.20.6s.
1959—Bill Barton ....5m.14.6s.
1960—Dennis Rounsavelle ....5m.04.5s.
1961—Ted Stickles ....4m.55.6s.
1962—Ted Stickles ....4m.51.5s.
1963—Ted Stickles ....4m.55.0s.
1964—Dick Roth ....4m.48.6s.
1965—Dick Roth ....4m.49.2s.
1966—Dick Roth ....4m.47.9s.
1967—Peter Williams ....4m.50.8s.
1968—Gary Hall ....4m.48.0s.
1969—Gary Hall ....4m.33.9s.
1970—Gary Hall ....4m.31.0s.
1971—Gary Hall ....4m.33.1s.
1972—Not held

400-Meter Medley Relay—440 Yards

1954—North Carolina S.C. (Sonner,
  Fadgen, McIntyre, Mattson) .4m.14.7s.
1955—New Haven S.C. (P. Kennedy, C.
  Hardin, W. Yorzyk, S.
  Gideonse) ....4m.28.6s.
1956—New Haven S.C. (J. Dolbey,
  D. Hardin, W. Yorzyk,
  D. Armstrong) ....4m.26.5s.
1957—Indianapolis A.C. (F. McKinney,
  G. Miki, W. Barton, W. Cass) .4m.21.6s.
1958—Los Angeles A.C. (J. Fellows,
  L. Zechiel, L. Larson,
  J. Henricks) ....4m.24.6s.
1959—Detroit A.C. (J. Smith, R. Clark, C.
  Wooley, D. Gillanders) .....4m.21.9s.
1960—Indianapolis A.C. (F. McKinney,
  Jastremski, M. Tryo, P. Sintz) 4m.09.2s.
1961—Indianapolis A.C. (T. Stock, C. Jastremski, L. Schulhof, P. Sintz) 4m.03.0s.
1962—Indianapolis A.C. (T. Sock, C. Jastremski, F. Schmidt, P. Sintz) 4m.01.6s.
1963—Indianapolis A.C. (Stock, Threthe-
  way, Schmidt, Blick) ....4m.04.9s.
1964—Verdugo Hills S.C. (McGeagh,
  Craig, Spencer, Bates) ......4m.03.8s.
1965—Indianapolis A.C. (Hammer,
  Tretheway, Berry, Windle) ..4m.01.8s.
1966—Los Angeles A.C. (Birnie, Merten,
  Holland, Zorn) ....4m.02.2s.
1967—Santa Clara S.C. (Haywood, Anderson, Spitz, Schollander) .....3m.59.7s.
1968—Santa Clara S.C. (F. Haywood, B. Job,
  M. Spitz, D. Schollander) ...4m.00.3s.
1969—Phillips 66 (C. Campbell, J. Fiolo,
  G. Hall, J. Bello) ....3m.57.5s.
1970—Santa Clara S.C. (M. Ivey, B. Job,
  S. Doyle, M. Pedley) ....3m.55.6s.
1971—Santa Clara S.C.
  (S. Doyle, J. Hencken,
  R. Slevin, E. McCleskey) ....3m.55.2s.
1972—Not held

400-Meter Free-Style Relay

1964—Santa Clara S.C. (Townsend, Jackman, Ilman, Schollander) ...3m.39.4s.
1965—Santa Clara S.C. (Nicolao, Buckingham, Roth, Ilman) ....3m.36.1s.
1966—Santa Clara S.C. (Nicolao, Buckingham, Roth, Schollander) ....3m.35.4s.
1967—Los Angeles A.C. (Kidder, Zorn,
  Havens, Hoag) ....3m.36.4s.
1968—Los Angeles A.C. (B. Johnson, R. Kidder,
  R. Saari, D. Havens) ....3m.35.3s.
1969—Los Angeles A.C. (D. Frawley, H. DeWitt,
  S. Frieken, D. Havens) .....3m.32.8s.
1970—Los Angeles A.C. (D. Havens, M. Weston,
  D. Frawley, F. Heckl) ....3m.28.7s.
1971—Los Angeles A.C. (F. Heckl, S. Tyrell,
  M. Weston, D. Havens) .....3m.32.3s.
1972—Not held

880-Yard Free-Style Relay—800 Meters

1923—Illinois A.C., Chicago (Kruger,
Wallen, McGillivray, Weissmuller) ....10m.05.4s.

1924—Los Angeles A.C. (Smith, Williams, Smith, Kahanamoku) . 10m.34s.

1925—Illinois A.C. .... (No time)

1926—Illinois A.C. .... 9m.43s.

1927—Illinois A.C. (Kimball, Halloran,
Miller, Weissmuller) .... 9m.35s.

1928—Illinois A.C. (Dithmer, O'Connor,
Samson, Weissmuller) ......9m.32.6s.

1929—Hollywood A.C. (Miller, Booth,
Kimball, Clapp) .... 9m.49.2s.

1930—New York A.C. (Zorilla, Fissler,
Ruddy, Kojac) .... 9m.27s.

1931—Hollywood A.C. (Clapp, Manuella
Kalili, Booth, Maiola Kalili) . . 9m.21.8s.

1932—No competition

1933—Los Angeles A.C. (Barthels, Cummings, Kalili, Callaghan) ....9m.40.4s.

1934—Los Angeles A.C. (Wolfe, Callaghan, Boals, Barthels) ......9m.41.9s.

1935—Detroit A.C. (Robertson, Sinkie-
wicz, Haynie, Gilhula) ......9m.21.6s.

1936—Yale University (Hoyt, Breuckel,
Cooke, Macionis) ....9m.22.5s.

1937—Lake Shore A.C., Chicago (McCaffrey, Jaretz, Wilson, Kiefer) ... 9m.20s.

1938—Ohio State Univ. (Quayle, Woodling, Johnson, Neunzig) .....9m.51.4s.

1939—Alexander House C.A., Hawaii
(Neunzig, Hirose, Balmores,
Nakama) .... 9m.21s.

1940—Alexander House C.A. (B. Nakama,
K. Nakama, Balmores, Hirose) 9m.17.3s.

1941—Alexander House C.A. (Hirose, Balmores, Oda, Smith) ....*9m.14.9s.

1942—Ohio State Univ. (J. Ryan, D.
Schnabel, J. Hill, K. Nakama) 9m.13.4s.

1943—Yale University (D. Lyon, D. Morgan, J. Eusden, A. Ford) ....9m.59.3s.

1944—Camp Chikopi, Ann Arbor, Mich.
(N. Adams, T. Coates, J. Gorman, M. Mann) ....10m.04.4s.

1945—Great Lakes N.T.C. (J. Weeden,
T. Gastineau, R. White, C.
Solberg) ....10m.18.6s.

1946—Hawaii University, S.C. (C. Oda,
R. Wright, H. Holiday, W.
Smith) ....9m.25.4s.

1947—Ohio State Univ. (W. Smith, H.
Hirose, R. DeGroot, Jack
Ryan) ....9m.13.8s.

1948—New Haven S.C. (Farnsworth,
Girdes, Gill, McLane) ......9m.21.0s.

1949—Tokyo S.C. (Hamaguchi, Maruyama, Murayama, Furuhashi) 8m.45.4s.

1950—New Haven S.C. (McLane, Scheff,
Moore, Marshall) ....9m.07.0s.

1951—New Haven S.C. (Sheff, Marshall,
McLane, Moore) ....*8m.51.0s.

1952—New Haven S.C. (Marshall, Smith,
McLane, Moore) ....8m.58.8s.

1953—New Haven S.C. (Moore, Marshall,
Phair, Gideonse) ....*9m.07.6s.

1954—New Haven S.C. (Moore, Marshall,
Armstrong, Phair) ....*9m.07.9s.

1955—New Haven S.C. (Phair, Yorzyk,
Armstrong, Smith) ....*8m.54.2s.

1956—New Haven S.C. (D. Armstrong,
R. Anderson, T. Jecko,
W. Yorzyk) ....*8m.53.7s.

1957—New Haven S.C. (R. Anderson,
R. Robinson, R. Aubrey,
T. Jecko) ....*8m.53.7s.

1958—Los Angeles A.C. (P. Fellows,
D. Reddington, J. Henricks,
M. Rose) ....*8m.42.7s.

1959—Indianapolis A.C. (A. Somers, D.
O'Neil, G. Breen, M. Troy) ..8m.35.9s.

1960—Indianapolis A.C. (P. Sintz, G.
Breen, A. Somers, M. Troy) ..8m.17.0s.

1961—Indianapolis A.C. (A. Somers, S.
Allen, M. Troy, P. Sintz) ....8m.17.9s.

1962—Santa Clara S.C. (Wall, Clark,
Townsend, Schollander) ....8m.12.2s.

1963—Santa Clara S.C. (Schollander,
Wall, Clark, Townsend) .....8m.07.6s.

1964—Santa Clara S.C. (Buckingham,
Wall, Ilman, Schollander) .. 8m.09.1s.

1965—Santa Clara S.C. (Wall, Ilman,
Roth, Roth) ....8m.04.6s.

1966—Santa Clara S.C. (Buckingham,
Cummings, Spitz, Schollander)7m.56.9s.

1967—Santa Clara S.C. (Schollander,
Spitz, Wall, Ilman) ....7m.52.1s.

1968—Santa Clara S.C. (Schollander,
B. Berk, G. Buckingham, M.
Spitz) ....7m.55.0s.

1969—Phillips 66 (J. Bello, A. Strenk,
G. Hall, H. Fassnacht) ......7m.52.7s.

1970—Phillips 66 (A. Strenk, G. Hall,
J. Halliday, H. Fassnacht) ...7m.47.6s.

1971—Phillips 66 (A. Strenk, J. Halliday,
W. Furniss, G. Hall) ....7m.48.5s.

1972—Not held

*880—Yards

1-Meter Springboard Diving

1964—66—Bernie Wrightson
1967—70—Jim Henry
1971—Mike Brown
1972—Don Dunfield

10-Foot or 3-Meter Springboard Diving

1921—Arthur W. Hartung
1922—Albert C. White
1923—Clarence Pinkston
1924—Albert C. White
1925—Pete Desjardins
1926—Pete Desjardins
1927—Pete Desjardins
1928—Mickey Riley (Galitzen)

1929—Mickey Riley (Galitzen)
1930—Harold Smith
1931—Harold Smith
1932—No competition
1933—Richard Degener
1934—Richard Degener
1935—Richard Degener
1936—Richard Degener
1937—Al Patnik
1938—Al Patnik
1939—Al Patnik (3 meters)
1940—Al Patnik (3 meters)
1941—Earl Clark (3 meters)
1942—Sammy Lee
1943—Floyd Stauffer
1944—Norman Sper Jr.
1945—Norman Sper Jr.
1946—Bruce Harlan (3 meters)
1947—Bruce Harlan (3 meters)
1948—Bruce Harlan (3 meters)
1949—David Browning (3 meters)
1950—Joe Marino (3 meters)
1951—Robert Clotworthy (3 meters)
1952—David Browning (3 meters)
1953—Robert Clotworthy (3 meters)
1954—Joaquin Capilla (3 meters)
1955—Don Harper
1956—Robert Clotworthy
1957—Ron Smith (3 meters)
1958—Gary Tobian (3 meters)
1959—Don Harper
1960—Sam Hall
1961—John Vogel
1962—Lou Vitucci
1963—Larry Andreasen
1964—65—Bernie Wrightson
1966—Rick Gilbert
1967—Keith Russell
1968—Bernie Wrightson
1969—Jim Henry
1970—Craig Lincoln
1971—Jim Henry
1972—Mike Finneran

Platform Diving

1909—George W. Gaidzik
1910—George W. Gaidzik
1911—George W. Gaidzik
1912—J.F. Dunn
1913—No competition
1914—C. Wolfield
1915—A.E. Downes
1916—A.E. Downes
1917—W. Williams
1918—Clyde Swendson
1919—Fred Spongberg
1920—Clarence Pinkston
1921—Clarence Pinkston
1922—Clarence Pinkston
1923—Clarence Pinkston
1924—Clarence Pinkston
1925—Pete Desjardins

1926—Pete Desjardins
1927—Pete Desjardins
1928—Mickey Riley (Galitzen)
1929—John Riley (Galitzen)
1930—Farid Samaika
1931—Farid Samaika
1932—No competition
1933—Frank Kurtz
1934—Marshall Wayne
1935—Richard Degener
1936—Marshall Wayne
1937—Elbert Root
1938—Elbert Root
1939—Earl Clark
1940—Earl Clark
1941—Earl Clark
1942—Sammy Lee
1943—Miller Anderson
1944—Norman Sper Jr.
1945—No competition
1946—Dr. Sammy Lee
1947—Bruce Harlan
1948—Bruce Harlan
1949—Norman Sper
1950—John McCormack
1951—John McCormack
1952—David Browning
1953—54—Joaquin Capilla
1955—60—Gary Tobian
1961—Don Harper
1962—Robert Webster
1963—Tom Gompf
1964—Bob Webster
1965—Bernie Wrightson
1966—Rick Gilbert
1967—Keith Russell
1968—Win Young
1969—Dick Rydze
1970—Rick Early
1971—Dick Rydze
1972—Rick Early

Indoor—Men

100-Yard Free-Style

1901—E. Carroll Schaeffer . . . . 1m.6.8s.
1902—H. Lemoyne . . . . 1m.4s.
1903—L.B. Goodwin . . . . 1m.9.2s.
1904—05—No competition
1906—Charles M. Daniels . . . . 58s.
1907—08—No competition
1909—Charles M. Daniels . . . . 56.8s.
1910—Charles M. Daniels . . . . 54.8s.
1911—Charles M. Daniels . . . . 56.8s.
1912—Duke Kahanamoku . . . . 57.8s.
1913—H.J. Hebner . . . . 55.4s.
1914—H.J. Hebner . . . . 55.6s.
1915—A.C. Raithel . . . . 54.4s.
1916—Perry McGillivray . . . . 56.2s.
1917—Ted Cann . . . . 55.2s.
1918—Perry McGillivray . . . . 55.4s.
1919—Perry McGillivray . . . . 55.4s.
1920—Ted Cann . . . . 53.6s.

1921—Norman Ross ....58.2s.
1922—John Weissmuller .... 54s.
1923—John Weissmuller ....54.8s.
1924—John Weissmuller ....53.8s.
1925—John Weissmuller ....52.2s.
1926—Walter Laufer ....52.4s.
1927—John Weissmuller ....51.4s.
1928—John Weissmuller ....50.8s.
1929—Walter Laufer ....51.8s.
1930—Walter Laufer ....52.8s.
1931—Albert Schwartz ....53.7s.
1932—Maiola Kalili ....53.8s.
1933—Walter Spence ....53.6s.
1934—Walter Spence ....51.4s.
1935—Peter Fick ....52.6s.
1936—Peter Fick ....51.4s.
1937—Peter Fick ....51.7s.
1938—Peter Fick ....51.6s.
1939—Peter Fick ....52.3s.
1940—Otto Jaretz ....52.3s.
1941—Otto Jaretz ....51.4s.
1942—Bill Prew .... 51s.
1943—Alan Ford ....51.8s.
1944—Bill Smith ....51.6s.
1945—Walter Ris ....51.3s.
1946—Walter Ris ....51.1s.
1947—Walter Ris ....50.9s.
1948—Walter Ris ....50.5s.
1949—Walter Ris ....51.4s.
1950—Clarke Scholes ....51.3s.
1951—Richard Cleveland .... 50s.
1952—Clarke Scholes ....50.2s.
1953—Reid Patterson ....50.6s.
1954—Richard Cleveland ....49.8s.
1955—John Glover ....49.8s.
1956—Rex Aubrey ....49.1s.
1957—Al Wiggins..................50.9s.
1958—Lance Larson ....49.5s.
1959—Lance Larson ....49.2s.
1960—Jeff Farrell ....48.2s.
1961—Steve Clark ....46.8s.
1962—Steve Jackman ....48.3s.
1963—Steven Jackman ....46.5s.
1964—Steve Clark ....47.1s.
1965—Steve Clark ....45.6s.
1966—Steve Rerych ....47.5s.
1967—Donald Havens ....46.0s.
1968—Don Havens ....45.7s.
1969—Don Havens ....45.9s.
1970—David Edgar ....45.2s.
1971—Frank Heckl ....45.5s.
1972—Mark Spitz ....45.1s.

200-Yard Free-Style

1963—Don Schollander ....1m.44.4s.
1964—Don Schollander ....1m.42.6s.
1965—Don Schollander ....1m.41.7s.
1966—Don Schollander ....1m.42.8s.
1967—Don Schollander ....1m.41.2s.
1968—Bill Burrell ....1m.43.5s.
1969—Frank Heckl ....1m.42.3s.
1970—John Kinsella ....1m.40.8s.

1971—Frank Heckl .... 1m.40.5s.
1972—Steve Genter ....1m.39.2s.

500-Yard Free-Style

1963—Roy Saari ....4m.48.2s.
1964—Don Schollander ....4m.44.5s.
1965—Carl Robie ....4m.44.1s.
1966—Greg Buckingham ....4m.41.1s.
1967—Mike Burton ....4m.37.0s.
1968—Trevor Charlton ....4m.37.3s.
1969—Hans Fassnacht ....4m.33.0s.
1970—John Kinsella ....4m.27.1s.
1971—John Kinsella ....4m.28.8s.
1972—John Kinsella ....4m.28.2s.

1,500-Meter Free-Style—1,650 Yards

1932—Clarence Crabbe ....19m.45.6s.
1936—Jack Medica ....19m.06.8s.
1942—Kiyoshi Nakama ....19m.35.4s.
1948—Jack Taylor...............20m.08.2s.
1950—John Marshall ....18m.37.0s.
1951—John Marshall ....18m.10.8s.
1952—Ford Konno ....18m.47.7s.
1953—James McLane ....18m.10.8s.
1954—Ford Konno ....19m.07.8s.
1955—George Breen ....18m.52.4s.
1956—George Breen ....18m.20.2s.
1957—George Breen ....17m.34.0s.
1958—Murray Rose ....18m.28.5s.
1959—Murray Rose ....18m.18.4s.
1960—George Breen ....18m.00.8s.
1961—Murray Rose ....17m.43.7s.
1962—Roy Saari ....16m.54.1s.
1963—Roy Saari ....16m.52.1s.
1964—Roy Saari ....16m.49.3s.
1965—Roy Saari ....16m.49.3s.
1966—Mike Burton ....16m.27.3s.
1967—Mike Burton ....16m.08.0s.
1968—Mike Burton ....16m.04.6s.
1969—Mike Burton ....15m.40.1s.
1970—John Kinsella ....15m.35.9s.
1971—John Kinsella ....15m.42.3s.
1972—John Kinsella ....15m.31.3s.

100-Yard Backstroke

1951—Jack Taylor...............58.5s.
1952—Richard Thoman ....56.9s.
1953—Richard Thoman ....57.5s.
1954—Yoshi Oyakawa ....56.8s.
1955—Yoshi Oyakawa ....57.2s.
1956—Albert Wiggins ....57.0s.
1957—Charles Krepp ....57.8s.
1958—Frank McKinney ....56.5s.
1959—Charles Bittick ....55.5s.
1960—Charles Bittick ....54.4s.
1961—Charles Bittick ....53.4s.
1962—Bob Bennett ....54.1s.
1963—Ens. Charles Bittick ......53.3s.
1964—Bob Bennett ....53.7s.
1965—Thompson Mann ....52.5s.
1966—Rich McGeagh ....53.9s.
1967—Fred Haywood ....52.6s.
1968—Charles Hickcox ....52.5s.

1969—Fred Haywood .... 52.3s.
1970—Mike Stamm .... 51.2s.
1971—Mike Stamm .... 51.5s.
1972—Mike Stamm .... 51.8s.

200-Yard Backstroke

1963—Ens. Charles Bittick .... 1m.55.9s.
1964—Ed Bartsch .... 1m.56.3s.
1965—Thompson Mann .... 1m.56.8s.
1966—Charles Hickcox .... 1m.59.9s.
1967—Mark Mader .... 1m.54.4s.
1968—Charles Hickcox .... 1m.54.9s.
1969—Gary Hall .... 1m.52.0s.
1970—Gary Hall .... 1m.51.4s.
1971—Mike Stamm .... 1m.52.2s.
1972—Mike Stamm .... 1m.51.0s.

100-Yard Butterfly

1954—Dave Hawkins .... 58.8s.
1955—No competition
1956—Albert Wiggins .... 54.5s.
1957—Albert Wiggins .... 55.0s.
1958—Tony Tashnick .... 54.3s.
1959—Frank Legacki .... 53.6s.
1960—Mike Troy .... 53.1s.
1961—Frank Legacki .... 51.9s.
1962—Lary Schulhof .... 52.1s.
1963—Walter Richardson .... 51.5s.
1964—Walter Richardson .... 50.8s.
1965—Luis Nicolao .... 50.9s.
1966—Ross Wales .... 51.3s.
1967—Mark Spitz .... 49.9s.
1968—Mark Spitz .... 49.7s.
1969—Ross Wales .... 50.5s.
1970—Mark Spitz .... 49.1s.
1971—Frank Heckl .... 49.5s.
1972—Mark Spitz .... 48.7s.

220-Yard Butterfly—200 Yards

220 yards from 1955-62

1955—Eulalia Rios .... 2m.30.2s.
1956—Jiro Nagasawa .... 2m.19.4s.
1957—Jack Nelson .... 2m.25.5s.
1958—William Yorzyk .... 2m.18.0s.
1959—Mike Troy .... 2m.18.6s.
1960—Mike Troy .... 2m.12.4s.
1961—Mike Troy .... 2m.10.9s.
1962—Lary Schulhof .... 2m.10.7s.
1963—Fred Schmidt .... 1m.55.2s.
1964—Fred Schmidt .... 1m.53.8s.
1965—Carl Robie .... 1m.52.7s.
1966—Carl Robie .... 1m.54.9s.
1967—Mark Spitz .... 1m.50.6s.
1968—Mark Spitz .... 1m.51.5s.
1969—Mike Burton .... 1m.52.6s.
1970—Gary Hall .... 1m.50.6s.
1971—Gary Hall .... 1m.48.4s.
1972—Mark Spitz .... 1m.49.0s.

100-Yard Breast Stroke

1951—Charles Moss .... 59.3s.
1952—John Davies .... 59.2s.
1953—David Hawkins .... 59.6s.

1954-55—No competition
1956—Donald Kutyna .... 1m.03.0s.
1957—Manuel Sanguily .... 1m.04.0s.
1958—Manuel Sanguily .... 1m.04.2s.
1959—Norbert Rumpel .... 1m.04.9s.
1960—Dick Nelson .... 1m.02.4s.
1961—Chet Jastremski .... 59.6s.
1962—Chet Jastremski .... 59.1s.
1963—Chester Jastremski .... 58.5s.
1964—Bill Craig .... 1m.00.1s.
1965—Paul Scheerer .... 1m.00.4s.
1966—Wayne Anderson .... 1m.01.2s.
1967—Ken Merten .... 58.9s.
1968—Ken Merten .... 58.8s.
1969—Brian Job .... 58.1s.
1970—Brian Job .... 57.2s.
1971—Brian Job .... 57.7s.
1972—Brian Job .... 57.5s.

220-Yard Breast Stroke—200 Yards

200 yards from 1963 on

1906—A. M. Goersling (200 yards) ... 2m.52.6s.
1907-09—No competition
1910—Michael McDermott (200 yards) . 2m.56s.
1911—Michael McDermott (200 years) 2m.43.2s.
1912—Michael McDermott (200 yards) 2m.38.8s.
1913—Michael McDermott (200 yards) 2m.55.4s.
1914—Michael McDermott (200 yards) . 2m.43s.
1915—Michael McDermott (200 yards) . 2m.43s.
1916—Michael McDermott (200 Yards) 2m.43.6s.
1917—Michael McDermott (200 yards) 2m.39.8s.
1918—Michael McDermott (200 yards) 2m.41.4s.
1919—G.H. Taylor (200 yards) ...... 2m.44.4s.
1920—G.H. Taylor (200 yards) ...... 2m.44.8s.
1921—R.D. Skelton .... 3m.2.6s.
1922—Donald McClellan .... 3m.10.4s.
1923—R. Skelton .... 2m.58.6s.
1924—J. Faricy .... 2m.52.4s.
1925—Walter Spence .... 2m.51.8s.
1926—Erich Rademacher .... 2m.46s.
1927—Walter Spence .... 2m.47.6s.
1928—Walter Spence .... 2m.43.6s.
1929—Walter Spence .... 2m.47.6s.
1930—Thomas Blankenburg .... 2m.52.6s.
1931—Leonard Spence .... 2m.44.6s.
1932—Leonard Spence .... 2m.44s.
1933—Leonard Spence .... 2m.45.9s.
1934—Leonard Spence .... 2m.43.5s.
1935—Leonard Spence .... 2m.43.8s.
1936—John H. Higgins .... 2m.39.2s.
1937—John H. Higgins .... 2m.40.5s.
1938—Jack Kasley .... 2m.40s.
1939—Richard R. Hough .... 2m.39.5s.
1940—Richard R. Hough .... 2m.40.8s.
1941—James Skinner .... 2m.41.7s.
1942—James Counsilman .... 2m.39.4s.
1943—Charles Gantner .... 2m.42.4s.
1944—Joseph Verdeur .... 2m.40.3s.
1945—David Seibold .... 2m.47.9s.
1946—Joseph Verdeur .... 2m.35.6s.
1947—Joseph Verdeur .... 2m.35.8s.
1948—Joseph Verdeur .... 2m.30.5s.

1949—Keith Carter . . . . 2m.30.7s.
1950—Robert Brawner . . . . 2m.29.3s.
1951—John Davies . . . . 2m.34.7s.
1952—John Davies . . . . 2m.29.1s.
1953—Jerry Holan . . . . 2m.31s.
1954—Dick Fadgen . . . . 2m.42.9s.
1955—Robert Gawboy . . . . 2m.38.0s.
1956—Dick Fadgen . . . . 2m.37.1s.
1957—Manuel Sanguily . . . . 2m.37.3s.
1958—Fred Munsch . . . . 2m.38.5s.
1959—Norbert Rumpel . . . . 2m.36.1s.
1960—William Mulliken . . . . 2m.34.8s.
1961—Chet Jastremski . . . . 2m.26.8s.
1962—Chet Jastremski . . . . 2m.25.3s.
1963—Chester Jastremski . . . . 2m.09.0s.
1964—Kenjiro Matsumoto (Japan) . . . 2m.09.7s.
1965—Ken Merten . . . . 2m.11.8s.
1966—Ken Merten . . . . 2m.12.5s.
1967—Ken Merten . . . . 2m.10.4s.
1968—Brian Job . . . . 2m.08.0s.
1969—Brian Job . . . . 2m.07.3s.
1970—Brian Job . . . . 2m.04.0s.
1971—Brian Job . . . . 2m.04.4s.
1972—Brian Job . . . . 2m.02.3s.

200-Yard Individual Medley

1959—Joe Hunsaker . . . . 2m.07s.
1960—John McGill . . . . 2m.03.3s.
1961—Ted Stickles . . . . 2m.02.1s.
1962—Chet Jastremski . . . . 1m.59.4s.
1963—Chester Jastremski . . . . 1m.58.5s.
1964—Dick Roth . . . . 1m.58.2s.
1965—Roy Saari . . . . 1m.56.2s.
1966—Bill Utley . . . . 1m.57.8s.
1967—Bill Utley . . . . 1m.55.9s.
1968—Charles Hickcox . . . . 1m.53.3s.
1969—David C. Johnson . . . . 1m.56.2s.
1970—Gary Hall . . . . 1m.54.7s.
1971—Gunnar Larsson . . . . 1m.53.3s.
1972—Gary Hall . . . . 1m.53.1s.

400-Yard Individual Medley

1954—Bert Wardrop . . . . 4m.41.7s.
1955—Jack Wardrop . . . . 4m.36.9s.
1956—Tim Jecko . . . . 4m.46.6s.
1957—Tim Jecko . . . . 4m.39.2s.
1958—George Harrison . . . . 4m.41.3s.
1959—George Harrison . . . . 4m.35.8s.
1960—George Harrison . . . . 4m.28.6s.
1961—Charles Bittick . . . . 4m.23.7s.
1962—Ted Stickles . . . . 4m.18.1s.
1963—Roy Saari . . . . 4m.16.6s.
1964—Dick Roth . . . . 4m.13.2s.
1965—Greg Buckingham . . . . 4m.08.9s.
1966—Dick Roth . . . . 4m.15.5s.
1967—Dick Roth . . . . 4m.09.5s.
1968—Gary Hall . . . . 4m.10.1s.
1969—Gary Hall . . . . 4m.00.9s.
1970—Gary Hall . . . . 3m.59.7s.
1971—Gunnar Larsson . . . . 4m.01.5s.
1972—Gary Hall . . . . 3m.58.0s.

400-Yard Medley Relay

1954—New York A.C. (Auwarter, Pappas,
McDermott, Glover) . . . . 4m.00.9s.
1955—North Carolina A.C. (Mattson,
McIntyre, Fadgen, Sonner) . . 3m.51.5s.
1956—North Carolina A.C. (Sonner,
Fadgen, Nelson, McIntyre) . . 3m.46.0s.
1957—North Carolina A.C. (Krepp,
Fadgen, Nelson, McIntyre) . . 3m.52.2s.
1958—New Haven S.C. (Dolby, Koletsky,
Jecko, Anderson) . . . . 3m.46.6s.
1959—New Haven S.C. (Dolby, Koletsky,
Jecko, Follet) . . . . 3m.47s.
1960—Southern California (C. Bittick,
L. Larson, D. Devine, J. Hen-
ricks) . . . . 3m.42.0s.
1961—North Carolina A.C. (Mann,
Fogarasy, Spencer, Bloom) . . 3m.39.8s.
1962—North Carolina A.C. (Fogarasy,
Mann, McGinty, Spencer) . . . 3m.37.9s.
1963—Indiana University (T. Stock, C.
Jastremski, L. Schulhof, T.
Hayden) . . . . 3m.33.2s.
1964—Yale (R. Goettsche, D. Kiefer, T.
Kennedy, M. Austin) . . . . 3m.33.7s.
1965—Southern California (R. Bennett,
W. Craig, R. McGeagh, R.
Saari) . . . . 3m31.9s.
1966—Southern California (R. Mc-
Geagh, W. Anderson, M. Lam-
bert, R. Saari) . . . . 3m.33.6s.
1967—Santa Clara S.C. (Malley, Mom-
sen, Nicolao, Meyer) . . . . . . 3m.30.4s.
1968—Yale (E. Bettendorf, M. Buckley, R.
Waples, S. Job) . . . . 3m.30.4s.
1969—Yale (E. Bettendorf, P. Long,
P. Katz. S. Job) . . . . 3m.30.4s.
1970—Santa Clara S.C. (M. Ivey, B. Job,
S. Doyle, F. Heath) . . . . 3m.24.1s.
1971—Indiana (M. Stamm, P. Dahlberg,
G. Hall, M. Spitz) . . . . 3m.24.5s.
1972—Indiana (M. Stamm, B. Ladewig,
M. Spitz, G. Conelly) . . . . 3m.24.4s.

400-Yard Free-Style Relay

1910—New York A.C. (Reilly, South,
Nerich, Daniels) . . . . 4m.12s.
1911—New York A.C. (Daniels, Nerich,
O'Sullivan, J.H. Reilly) . . . . . 4m.10.6s.
1912—City A.C. (Frizell, Eddy,
Adae, Ritter) . . . . 3m.59.6s.
1913—Illinois A.C. (P. McGillivray, E.W.
McGillivray, Hebner, Raithel) 3m.46.2s.
1914—Illinois A.C. (Raithel, Vosburgh,
P. McGillivray, Hebner) . . . . . 3m.52.8s.
1915—Illinois A.C. (Raithel, Vosburgh,
P. McGillivray, Hebner) . . . . . 3m.45.6s.
1916—Illinois A.C. (Raithel, Vosburgh,
P. McGillivray, Hebner) . . . . . 3m.42.4s.
1917—Illinois A.C. (P. McGillivray, Hebner, Jones, Raithel) . . . . 3m.42.6s.

1918—Illinois A.C. (Siegel, Jones,
          Raithel, Hebner) . . . . 3m.48.4s.
1919—No competition
1920—Illinois A.C. (McGillivray, Hebner,
          Wallen, Ross) . . . . 3m.47.8s.
1921—Illinois A.C. (P. McGillivray, Heb-
          ner, Wallen, Ross) . . . . 3m.44s.
1922—Illinois A.C. (J. Weissmuller, P. Mc-
          Gillivray, Wallen, Hebner) . . . 3m.43.6s.
1923—Illinois A.C. (J. Weissmuller, P. Mc-
          Gillivray, Ross, Kruger) . . . . . . 3m.42s.
1924—Illinois A.C. (Kruger, Hebner, P.
          McGillivray, J. Weissmuller) . 3m.41.4s.
1925—Illinois A.C. (Kruger, P. McGil-
          livray, Miller, J. Weissmuller) . . 3m.45s.
1926—Cincinnati Central Y.M.C.A.
          (Laufer, Rutledge, Webb,
          Glancy) . . . . 3m.38s.
1927—Chicago A.A. (Greenberg,
          Jones, Howell, Breyer) . . . . . 3m.40.4s.
1928—Illinois A.C. (J. Weissmuller,
          Samson, Hallaran, Miller) . . . 3m.32.6s.
1929—New York A.C. (Harms, Dolges,
          Farley, Fissler) . . . . 3m.43.2s.
1930—Chicago A.A. (Wilcox, Highland,
          Breyer, Corbett) . . . . 3m.39.2s.
1931—New York A.C. (Howland, Dal-
          rymple, Fissler, W. Spence) . . 3m.34.9s.
1932—New York A.C. (Howland, Fissler,
          Kojac, W. Spence) . . . . 3m.31.8s.
1933—New York A.C. (Howland, L.
          Spence, Walter Spence, Fissler)3m.38.1s.
1934—New York A.C. (Fick, Howland,
          L. Spence, Walter Spence) . . . 3m.31.8s.
1935—New York A.C. (Fick, Wallace
          Spence, Leonard Spence, Walter
          Spence) . . . . 3m.34.6s.
1936—New York A.C. (Walter Spence,
          Wallace Spence, Fick, Giesen) 3m.34.2s.
1937—Univ. of Michigan (Tomski, Kirar,
          Haynie, Mowerson) . . . . 3m.31.4s.
1938—Ohio State University (Sabol, John-
          son, Quayle, Neunzig) . . . 3m.31.5s.
1939—New York A.C. (McDermott,
          Reilly, Spence, Fick) . . . . 3m.31.3s.
1940—Univ. of Michigan (Williams,
          Gillis, Barker, Sharemet) . . . . 3m.35.2s.
1941—Chicago Towers Club (Kozlowski,
          Henning, Kirar, Jaretz) . . . . . 3m.29.6s.
1942—Yale University (Lilley, Kelly,
          Pope, Johnson) . . . . 3m.28.6s.
1943—Univ. of Michigan (Church, Holi-
          day, Fries, Patten) . . . . 3m.34.9s.
1944—U.S.N.T.C., Great Lakes (Smith,
          Kerschner, Burton, Ris) . . . . . 3m.29.1s.
1945—Bainbridge, Md. N.T.C. (Hobert,
          Pulakos, Kiefer, Ris) . . . . 3m.38.6s.
1946—Ohio State University (Hill, Coola-
          han, Hobart, Hirose) . . . . 3m.34.6s.
1947—Yale University (Broadbent,
          Morgan, Baribault, Hueber) . . 3m.27.8s.
1948—New Haven S.C. (E. Heuber, F.

Dooley, H. Johnson, A. Ford) 3m.27.3s.
1949—New Haven S.C. (R. Baribault,
          H. Reid, P. Girdes, W.
          Farnsworth) . . . . 3m.28.6s.
1950—New Haven S.C. (J. Blum, W.
          Farnsworth, L. Munson, H.
          Reid) . . . . 3m.26.4s.
1951—New Haven S.C. "A" (Thoman,
          Sheff, Smith, Reid) . . . . 3m.23s.
1952—New Haven S.C. "A" (Thoman,
          Sheff, Donovan, Carroll) . . . . . 3m.23s.
1953—New Haven S.C. "A" (R. Thoman,
          H. Gideonese, K. Donovan,
          D. Sheff) . . . . 3m.23.7s.
1954—New Haven S.C. (Rae, Scheff,
          Gideonse, Donovan) . . . . 3m.25.0s.
1955—New Haven S.C. (Armstrong,
          Gideonse, Aubrey, Donovan) 3m.21.8s.
1956—New Haven S.C. (Cornwell,
          Armstrong, Gideonse, Aubrey)2m.22.2s.
1957—New Haven S.C. (Robinson,
          Cornwell, Armstrong, Jecko) . 3m.27.9s.
1958—Southern California Freshmen
          (Winters, Reddington, Rose,
          Henricks) . . . . 3m.20.4s.
1959—University of Southern California
          (Reddington, Winters, Rose,
          Henricks) . . . . 3m.21.1s.
1960—Southern California (Larson
          Winters, Reddington,
          Henricks) . . . . 3m.16.0s.
1961—New Haven S.C. (Austin, Loofbour-
          row, Tylar, Ball) . . . . 3m.15.9s.
1962—Santa Clara S.C. (S. Clark, E. Town-
          send, N. Schoenman, D.
          Beukers) . . . . 3m.17.4s.
1963—Yale (E. Townsend, D. Lyons, S.
          Clark, M. Austin) . . . . 3m.08.1s.
1964—Yale (S. Clark, T. Garton, D.
          Lyons, M. Austin) . . . . 3m.10.9s.
1965—Southern California (R. Bennett,
          J. McGrath, R. McGeagh, R.
          Saari) . . . . 3m.07.4s.
1966—North Carolina A.C. (J. Her-
          man, E. Schwall, S. Rerych, J.
          Edwards) . . . . 3m.10.9s.
1967—Yale (Waples, Ahern, Kennedy,
          Schollander) . . . . 3m.06.5s.
1968—Phillips 66 (J. MacMillan, K. Hammer,
          R. Grimm, Z. Zorn) . . . . 3m.04.7s.
1969—Southern California (F. Heckl, D.
          Frawley, R. Kidder, D.
          Havens) . . . . 3m05.0s.
1970—Southern California (F. Heckl, R.
          Lyon, D. Frawley, M.
          Mader) . . . . 3m.03.7s.
1971—Southern California (K. Tutt, R.
          Lyon, M. Weston, F.
          Heckl) . . . . 3m.02.8s.
1972—Southern California (E. McClesky,
          K. Tutt, M. Weston, F.
          Heckl) . . . . 3m.03.2s.

800-Yard Free-Style Relay

1966—Yale (R. Schneider, M.
    Ahern, D. Kennedy, D.
    Schollander) .... 7m.04.1s.
1967—Yale (Waples, Schnieder, Ken-
    nedy, Schollander) .... 6m.56.2s.
1968—Indiana A. Team (B. Burrell, B.
    Windle, B. Utley, C.
    Hickcox) .... 6m.55.1s.
1969—Southern California (M. Mader,
    R. Kidder, G. Charlton,
    F. Heckl) .... 6m.53.5s.
1970—Southern California (A. Strenk,
    J. McConica, G. Charleton,
    F. Heckl) .... 6m.47.2s.
1971—Southern California (K. Tutt, A.
    Strenk, J. McConica, F.
    Heckl) .... 6m.42.6s.
1972—Southern California (F. Heckl, K.
    Tutt, E. McClesky, J.
    McConica) .... 6m.42.1s.

Three-Foot or One-Meter Springboard Dive

1923—Leo Fracer
1924—Al White
1925—Al White
1926—Al White
1927—Farid Simaika
1928—Harold D. Smith
1929—Mickey Riley (Galitzen)
1930—Harold Smith
1931—Mickey Riley (Galitzen)
1932—Mickey Riley (Galitzen)
1933—Richard Degener
1934—Richard Degener
1935—Elbert A. Root
1936—Al Greene
1937—Al Patnik
1938—Al Patnik
1939—Al Patnik
1940—Al Patnik
1941—Earl Clark
1942—James Cook
1943—Frank Dempsey
1944—Charles Batterman
1945—Ted Christakos
1946—Miller Anderson
1947—Miller Anderson
1948—Miller Anderson
1949—Bruce Harlan
1950—Bruce Harlan
1951—David Browning
1952—David Browning
1953—Robert Clotworthy
1954—David Browning
1955—Jerry Harrison
1956—Robert Clotworthy
1957—Donald Harper
1958—Gary Tobian
1959—60—Sam Hall
1961—Lou Vitucci
1962—Bob Webster

1963—Richard Gilbert
1964—Ken Sitzberger
1965—Ken Sitzberger
1966—Chuck Knorr
1967—Luis Nino de Rivera
1968—70—Jim Henry
1971—Craig Lincoln
1972—Don Dunfield

Ten-Foot or Three-Meter Springboard Diving

1909—F. Bornaman
1910—George Gaidzik
1911—F. Bornaman
1912—G.W. Gaidzik
1913—Arthur McAleenan
1914—C. Wohlfeld
1915—Arthur McAleenan
1916—Arthur McAleenan
1917—A.E. Downes
1918—A.W. Hartung
1919—Clyde Swendsen
1920—Clyde Swendsen
1921—Clarence Pinkston
1922—Albert C. White
1923—Albert C. White
1924—Albert C. White
1925—Albert C. White
1926—Albert C. White
1927—Pete Desjardins
1928—Pete Desjardins
1929—Mickey Riley (Galitzen)
1930—Mickey Riley (Galitzen)
1931—Mickey Riley (Galitzen)
1932—Richard Degener
1933—Richard Degener
1934—Richard Degener
1935—Richard Degener
1936—Richard Degener
1937—Al Patnik
1938—Al Patnik
1939—Al Patnik
1940—Al Patnik
1941—Earl Clark
1942—Miller Anderson
1943—Frank Dempsey
1944—Charles Batterman
1945—Frank McGuigan
1946—Miller Anderson
1947—Miller Anderson
1948—Miller Anderson
1949—Bruce Harlan
1950—Bruce Harlan
1951—David Browning
1952—David Browning
1953—Jerry Harrison
1954—David Browning
1955—Jerry Harrison
1956—Donald Harper
1957—Glen Whitten
1958—Don Harper
1959—60—Jozsef Gerlach
1961—Ronald O'Brien

1962—Richard Gilbert
1963—Richard Gilbert
1964—Ken Sitzberger
1965—Richard Gilbert
1966—Bernie Wrightson
1967—Keith Russell
1968—69—Win Young
1970—Jim Henry
1971—Michael Finneran
1972—Lt. Phil Boggs

Platform Dive

1964—Lt. Tom Gompf
1965—Chuck Knorr
1966—Chuck Knorr
1967—Keith Russell
1968—Larry Andreason
1969—Dick Rydze
1970—Klaus DiBiasi (Italy)
1971—72—Dick Rydze

Team

1925—Illinois A.C., Chicago (38 points)
1926—Cincinnati Central Y.M.C.A. (48)
1927—Illinois A.C. (42)
1928—Illinois A.C.
1929—New York A.C. (32)
1930—Hollywood A.C. (21); Lake Shore A.C.,
　　　Chicago (21)
1931—Hollywood A.C. (28)
1932—Los Angeles A.C. (45)
1933—New York A.C. (47)
1934—New York A.C. (37)
1935—New York A.C. (33)
1936—Lake Shore A.C. (31)
1937—Lake Shore A.C. (27)
1938—Ohio State University (39)
1939—Ohio State University (28)
1940—University of Michigan (29)
1941—Chicago Towers Club (44)
1942—Yale University (59)
1943—Ohio State University (46)
1944—Great Lakes N.T.S. (54)
1945—Bainbridge N.T.S. (46)
1946—Ohio State University (48)
1947—Ohio State University (64)
1948—Ohio State University (46)
1949—New Haven (Conn.) Swim Club (40)
1950—Yale Freshmen (43)
1951—New Haven S.C. (142)
1952—New Haven S.C. (113)
1953—New Haven S.C. (143)
1954—New Haven S.C. (81)
1955—New Haven S.C. (72)
1956—New Haven S.C. (65)
1957—New Haven S.C. (68)
1958—Southern California Freshmen (55)
1959—University of Southern California
1960—University of Southern California
1961—University of Southern California
1962—University of Southern California
1963—Indiana

1964—Southern California
1965—Southern California
1966—Southern California
1967—Santa Clara S.C.
1968—Indiana
1969—Southern California
1970—Santa Clara S.C.
1971—Indiana
1972—Southern California

Outdoor—Women

100-Yard Free-Style—100 Meters

100 Meter from 1963 on.

1917—Gertrude Artelt . . . . 1m.18.4s.
1918—Charlotte Boyle . . . . 1m.11.6s.
1919—No competition
1920—Ethelda Bleibtrey . . . . 1m.5.2s.
1921—Ethelda Bleibtrey . . . . 1m.3.4s.
1922—Helen Wainwright . . . . 1m.8.4s.
1923—Adelaide Lambert . . . . 1m.13.4s.
1924—Ethel Lackie . . . . 1m.6s.
1925—Doris O'Mara . . . . 1m.7.4s.
1926—Ethel Lackie (100 meters) . . . . 1m.14.4s.
1927—Martha Norelius (100 meters) . . 1m.13.8s.
1928—Eleanor Garratti (100 meters) . . 1m.10.6s.
1929—Eleanor Garratti (100 meters) . . . 1m.9.8s.
1930—Helene Madison (100 meters) . . . 1m.8.2s.
1931—Helene Madison (100 meters) . . . 1m.9.4s.
1932—Jennie Cramer (100 meters) . . . 1m.13.4s.
1933—Lenore Kight (100 meters) . . . . 1m.10.8s.
1934—Olive McKean (100 meters) . . . 1m.11.7s.
1935—Olive McKean (100 meters) . . . 1m.10.2s.
1936—Toni Redfern (100 meters) . . . . 1m.10.1s.
1937—Elizabeth Ryan (100 meters) . . . . 1m.8s.
1938—Virginia Hopkins (100 meters) . 1m.10.5s.
1939—Esther Williams (100 meters) . . . . 1m.9s.
1940—Brenda Helser (110 yards) . . . . 1m.09.6s.
1941—Brenda Helser (100 meters) . . . 1m.09.9s.
1942—Suzanne Zimmerman (100
　　　　meters) . . . . 1m.10.3s.
1943—Brenda Helser (100 meters) . . . 1m.09.3s.
1944—Ann Curtis (100 meters) . . . . . . 1m.09.5s.
1945—Ann Curtis (100 meters) . . . . . . 1m.07.5s.
1946—Brenda Helser (100 meters) . . . 1m.07.2s.
1947—Ann Curtis (100 meters) . . . . 1m.07s.
1948—Ann Curtis (100 meters) . . . . 1m.08s.
1949—Thelma Kalama (110 yards) . . . 1m.10.9s.
1950—Jackie LaVine (100 meters) . . . 1m.10.0s.
1951—Sharon Geary (100 meters) . . . . 1m.07.6s.
1952—No competition
1953—Judy Roberts (110 yards) . . . . . 1m.07.9s.
1954—Jody Alderson (100 meters) . . . 1m.06.1s.
1955—Wanda Werner (100 meters) . . . 1m.06.1s.
1956—Wanda Werner (110 yards) . . . . 1m.06.3s.
1957—Dawn Fraser (110 yards) . . . . . 1m.03.9s.
1958—Chris von Saltza (100 meters) . . 1m.03.5s.
1959—Chris von Saltza (110 yards) . . . 1m.04.8s.
1960—Chris von Saltzá (100 meters) . . 1m.01.6s.
1961—Robyn Johnson (100 meters) . . 1m.03.2s.
1962—Robyn Johnson (100 meters) . . 1m.02.2s.
1963—Robyn Johnson . . . . 1m.01.5s.
1964—Sharon Stouder . . . . 1m.00.7s.

1965–Pokey Watson . . . . 1m.00.7s.
1966–Pokey Watson . . . . 59.9s.
1967–Janie Barkman . . . . 59.8s.
1968–Jane Barkman . . . . 1m.00.1s.
1969–Sue Pedersen . . . . 59.7s.
1970–Cindy Schilling . . . . 1m.00.3s.
1971–Linda Johnson . . . . 1m.00.3s.
1972–Not held

200-Meter Free-Style

1963–Robyn Johnson . . . . 2m.15.6s.
1964–Jeanne Hallock . . . . 2m.13.3s.
1965–Martha Randall . . . . 2m.12.3s.
1966–Pokey Watson . . . . 2m.10.5s.
1967–Pam Kruse . . . . 2m.09.7s.
1968–Eadie Wetzel . . . . 2m.08.8s.
1969–Sue Pedersen . . . . 2m.07.8s.
1970–Ann Simmons . . . . 2m.09.6s.
1971–Linda Johnson . . . . 2m.08.0s.
1972–Not held

440-Yard Free-Style—400 Meters
400 Meters from 1963 on.

1916–Claire Galligan . . . . 7m.43.2s.
1917–Olga Dorfner . . . . 7m.53.4s.
1918–Claire Galligan . . . . 7m.20s.
1919–Ethelda Bleibtrey . . . . 6m.30.2s.
1920–L. Snowgrass . . . . 8m.24s.
1921–Ethelda Bleibtrey . . . . 6m.30s.
1922–Gertrude Ederle . . . . 6m.1.2s.
1923–Gertrude Ederle . . . . 6m.35.4s.
1924–Helen Wainwright . . . . 6m.10.4s.
1925–V. Whitenack . . . . 6m.7s.
1926–Martha Norelius . . . . 6m.6s.
1927–Martha Norelius . . . . 5m.57.2s.
1928–Martha Norelius . . . . 5m.49.6s.
1929–Josephine McKim . . . . 5m.47.4s.
1930–Helene Madison . . . . 5m.39.4s.
1931–Helene Madison . . . . 5m.42.8s.
1932–No competition
1933–Lenore Kight . . . . 5m.33.6s.
1934–Lenore Kight . . . . 5m.40.2s.
1935–Lenore Kight . . . . 5m.32.5s.
1936–Mrs. Lenore Kight Wingard . . . . 5m.37.6s.
1937–Katherine Rawls . . . . 5m.36s.
1938–Katherine Rawls . . . . 5m.34.5s.
1939–Nancy Merki (400 meters) . . . . . 5m.29.6s.
1940–Mary M. Ryan . . . . 5m.30.1s.
1941–Betty Bemis (400 meters) . . . . . 5m.23.7s.
1942–Betty Bemis (400 meters) . . . . . 5m.32.5s.
1943–Ann Curtis (400 meters) . . . . . . 5m.27.8s.
1944–Ann Curtis (400 meters) . . . . . . 5m.32.4s.
1945–Ann Curtis (400 meters) . . . . . . 5m.26.3s.
1946–Ann Curtis (400 meters) . . . . . . 5m.26.7s.
1947–Ann Curtis (400 meters) . . . . . . 5m.21.5s.
1948–Ann Curtis (400 meters) . . . . . . 5m.26.5s.
1949–Thelma Kalama . . . . 5m.41.2s.
1950–Thelma Kalama (400 meters) . . . 5m.30.9s.
1951–Barbara Hobelmann (400
    meters) . . . . 5m.21.6s.
1952–No competition
1953–Delia Meulenkamp . . . . 5m.22.2s.
1954–Carolyn Green (400 meters) . . . 5m.14.7s.

1955–Dougie Gray (400 meters) . . . . . 5m.16.1s.
1956–Marley Shriver . . . . 5m.13.8s.
1957–Lorraine Crapp . . . . 5m.08.5s.
1958–Sylvia Ruuska (400 meters) . . . . 5m.04.1s.
1959–Chris von Saltza (440 yards) . . . 4m.59.6s.
1960–Chris von Saltza (400 meters) . . 4m.46.9s.
1961–Carolyn House (400 meters) . . . 4m.52.5s.
1962–Carolyn House (400 meters) . . . 4m.45.3s.
1963–Robyn Johnson . . . . 4m.46.8s.
1964–Marilyn Ramenofsky . . . . 4m.41.7s.
1965–Martha Randall . . . . 4m.39.5s.
1966–Martha Randall . . . . 4m.38.0s.
1967–Debbie Meyer . . . . 4m.29.0s.
1968–Debbie Meyer . . . . 4m.26.7s.
1969–Debbie Meyer . . . . 4m.26.4s.
1970–Debbie Meyer . . . . 4m.24.3s.
1971–Ann Simmons . . . . 4m.24.8s.
1972–Not held

One-Mile Free-Style—1,500 Meters
1,500 Meters from 1963 on

1916–Claire Galligan . . . . 31m.19.6s.
1917–Claire Galligan . . . . 33m.8s.
1918–Frances Cowells . . . . 33m.3s.
1919–No competition
1920–Ethelda Bleibtrey . . . . 32m.25.2s.
1921–Thelma Darby . . . . 31m.58s.
1922–Helen Wainwright . . . . 26m.44.8s.
1923–Olive Holland . . . . 29m.27.4s.
1924–No competition
1925–Ethel McGary . . . . 26m.27.4s.
1926–Ethel McGary . . . . 26m.33.4s.
1927–Martha Norelius . . . . 24m.19.4s.
1928–Josephine McKim . . . . 24m.49.6s.
1929–Josephine McKim . . . . 25m.10s.
1930–Helene Madison . . . . 24m.32.2s.
1931–Helene Madison . . . . 24m.45s.
1932–No competition
1933–Lenore Kight . . . . 24m.53.8s.
1934–Lenore Kight . . . . 25m.10.5s.
1935–Lenore Kight . . . . 24m.20.4s.
1936–Mrs. Lenore Kight Wingard . . . 24m.07.2s.
1937–Katherine Rawls . . . . 24m.19.6s.
1938–Mrs. Katherine Rawls Thomp-
    son . . . . 23m.47.4s.
1939–Mary M. Ryan . . . . 24m.12.8s.
1940–Mary M. Ryan . . . . 23m.15s.
1941–Nancy Merki (1,500 meters) . . 22m.12.2s.
1942–Nancy Merki (1,500 meters) . . 22m.18.2s.
1943–Florence Schmitt (1,500
    meters) . . . . 22m.25.7s.
1944–Ann Curtis (1,500 meters) . . . . 22m.13.1s.
1945–Marilyn Sahner (1,500 meters) . 21m.59.3s.
1946–Ann Curtis (1,500 meters) . . . . 22m.08.1s.
1947–Marilyn Sahner (1,500 meters) . 22m.23.1s.
1948–Joan Mallory (1,500 meters) . . 22m.58.4s.
1949–Jean Lutyens . . . . 24m.34.5s.
1950–Barbara Hobelmann (1,500
    meters) . . . . 22m.25.7s.
1951–Carolyn Green (1,500 meters) . 21m.48.3s.
1952–No competition
1953–Carolyn Green . . . . 23m.03.4s.

1954—Carolyn Green (1,500 meters) . 21m.08.5s.
1955—Carolyn Green (1,500 meters) . 21m.15.4s.
1956—Carolyn Green (1,650 yards) . . 21m.30.2s.
1957—Carolyn Murray . . . . 22m.13.9s.
1958—Sylvia Ruuska (1,500 meters) . 20m.34.6s.
1959—Sylvia Ruuska (1 mile) . . . . 21m.38.9s.
1960—Carolyn House (1,500 meters) . 19m.45.0s.
1961—Carolyn House (1,500 meters) . 19m.46.3s.
1962—Carolyn House (1,500 meters) . . 18m.44s.
1963—Ginnie Duenkel . . . . 18m.57.9s.
1964—Patty Caretto . . . . 18m.30.5s.
1965—Patty Caretto . . . . 18m.23.7s.
1966—Patty Caretto . . . . 18m.12.9s.
1967—Debbie Meyer . . . . 17m.50.2s.
1968—Debbie Meyer . . . . 17m.38.5s.
1969—Debbie Meyer . . . . 17m.28.4s.
1970—Debbie Meyer . . . . 17m.28.4s.
1971—Cathy Calhoun . . . . 17m.19.2s.
1972—Not held

100-Meter Backstroke—110 Yards

1922—Sybil Bauer . . . . *1m.17.6s.
1923—Sybil Bauer . . . . †2m.4.8s.
1924-1938—No competition
1939—Edith Motridge . . . . 1m.18.9s.
1940—Gloria Callen (110 yards) . . . . . . 1m.18.5s.
1941—Gloria Callen . . . . 1m.17.5s.
1942—Gloria Callen . . . . 1m.18.6s.
1943—Suzanne Zimmerman . . . . 1m.18.3s.
1944—Joan Fogle . . . . 1m.20.2s.
1945—Marion Pontacq . . . . 1m.18.7s.
1946—Suzanne Zimmerman . . . . 1m.18s.
1947—Suzanne Zimmerman . . . . 1m.17.6s.
1948—Suzanne Zimmerman . . . . 1m.16.4s.
1949—Barbara Jensen (110 yards) . . . . 1m.20.3s.
1950—Maureen O'Brien . . . . 1m.17.9s.
1951—Mary Freeman . . . . 1m.18.8s.
1952—No competition
1953—Barbara Stark (110 yards) . . . . . 1m.16.6s.
1954—Shelley Mann . . . . 1m.15.5s.
1955—Carin Cone . . . . 1m.15.6s.
1956—Carin Cone (110 yards) . . . . . . 1m.14.5s.
1957—Carin Cone (110 yards) . . . . . . 1m.13.6s.
1958—Carin Cone . . . . 1m.13.5s.
1959—Carin Cone (110 yards) . . . . . . 1m.13.3s.
1960—Lynn Burke . . . . 1m.10.2s.
1961—Nina Harmer . . . . 1m.11.0s.
1962—Donna de Varona . . . . 1m.10.4s.
1963—Cathy Ferguson . . . . 1m.09.2s.
1964—Cathy Ferguson . . . . 1m.09.2s.
1965—Christine Caron (France) . . . . . . 1m.08.1s.
1966—Ann Fairlie (South Africa) . . . . . 1m.07.9s.
1967—Kendis Moore . . . . 1m.09.2s.
1968—Karen Muir (South Africa) . . . . . 1m.06.9s.
1969—Susie Atwood . . . . 1m.06.0s.
1970—Susie Atwood . . . . 1m.06.2s.
1971—Susie Atwood . . . . 1m.06.7s.
1972—Not held
*100 yards.   †150 yards.

220-Yard Backstroke—200 Meters
200 Meters from 1963 on.
1924—Sybil Bauer . . . . 3m.9.4s.

1925—Sybil Bauer . . . . 3m.11s.
1926—Adelaide Lambert . . . . 3m.15s.
1927—Adelaide Lambert . . . . 3m.11s.
1928—Lisa Lindstrom . . . . 3m.3.4s.
1929—Eleanor Holm . . . . 3m.3.6s.
1930—Eleanor Holm . . . . 3m.5s.
1931—Eleanor Holm . . . . 3m.4.4s.
1932—Eleanor Holm . . . . 2m.57.8s.
1933—Eleanor Holm . . . . 2m.57.2s.
1934—Alice Bridges . . . . 3m.6s.
1935—Elizabeth Kompa . . . . 2m.58.9s.
1936—Eleanor Holm Jarrett . . . . 2m.51.8s.
1937—Erna Kompa . . . . 2m.57.5s.
1938—Jeanne Laupheimer . . . . 3m.2s.
1939-45—No competition
1946—Suzanne Zimmerman (200
     meters) . . . . 2m.48.7s.
1947—Suzanne Zimmerman (200
     meters) . . . . 2m.49s.
1948—Suzanne Zimmerman (200
     meters) . . . . 2m.48.3s.
1949—Barbara Jensen . . . . 2m.54.9s.
1950—Maureen O'Brien (200 meters) . . 2m.51.2s.
1951—Mary Freeman (200 meters) . . . 2m.49.8s.
1952—No competition
1953—Barbara Stark . . . . 2m.45.7s.
1954—Barbara Stark (200 meters) . . . . 2m.47.9s.
1955—Carin Cone (200 meters) . . . . . 2m.45.6s.
1956—Carin Cone . . . . 2m.43.8s.
1957—Chris von Saltza . . . . 2m.40.2s.
1958—Chris von Saltza (200 meters) . . 2m.37.4s.
1959—Carin Cone . . . . 2m.37.9s.
1960—Lynn Burke (200 meters) . . . . . 2m.33.5s.
1961—Nina Harmer (200 meters) . . . . 2m.35.0s.
1962—Virginia Duenkel (200 meters) . . 2m.32.1s.
1963—Ginnie Duenkel . . . . 2m.30.8s.
1964—Cathy Ferguson . . . . 2m.29.2s.
1965—Cathy Ferguson, Judy Humbarger
     (tie) . . . . 2m.28.0s.
1966—Karen Muir (South Africa) . . . . 2m.26.4s.
1967—Kendis Moore . . . . 2m.28.1s.
1968—Karen Muir, (South Africa) . . . . 2m.24.3s.
1969—Susie Atwood . . . . 2m.21.5s.
1970—Susie Atwood . . . . 2m.22.0s.
1971—Susie Atwood . . . . 2m.22.9s.
1972—Not held

100-Yard Breast Stroke—100 Meters
100 meters from 1963 on
1922—Edna O'Connell . . . . 1m.34.2s.
1923-42—No competition
1943—Jane Dillard (100 meters) . . . . . 1m.24.3s.
1944—Jane Dillard Kittleson (100
     meters) . . . . 1m.25.3s.
1945—Jeanne Wilson (100 meters) . . . . 1m.26.2s.
1946—Jeanne Wilson (100 meters) . . . . 1m.26.2s.
1947—Nel Van Vliet (100 meters) . . . . 1m.21.6s.
1948—Jeanne Wilson (100 meters) . . . . 1m.28.9s.
1949—Carol Pence . . . . 1m.25.8s.
1950—Judy Cornell (100 meters) . . . . . 1m.23.1s.
1951—Judy Cornell (100 meters) . . . . . 1m.21.0s.
1952—No competition

1953–Gail Peters (110 yards) . . . . 1m.18.0s.
1954-55–No competition
1956–Mary Jane Sears (110 yards) . . . 1m.22.7s.
1957–Mary Lou Elsenius (100 yards) . 1m.24.9s.
1958–Susan Ordogh (100 meters) . . . . 1m.23.8s.
1959–Marianne Hargreaves (110 yards) 1m.22.4s.
1960–Ann Warner (100 meters) . . . . . 1m.23.4s.
1961–Dale Barnhard (100 meters)   1m.22.6s.
1962–Wiltrud Urselmann (100 meters) 1m.20.6s.
1963–Jean Dellekamp . . . . 1m.20.7s.
1964–Claudia Kolb . . . . 1m.19.0s.
1965–Claudia Kolb . . . . 1m.17.1s.
1966–Catie Ball . . . . 1m.16.4s.
1967–Catie Ball . . . . 1m.14.6s.
1968–Catie Ball . . . . 1m.15.7s.
1969–Kim Brecht . . . . 1m.15.7s.
1970–Linda Kurtz . . . . 1m.16.6s.
1971–Diane Nickloff . . . . 1m.17.1s.
1972–Not Held

100-Meter Butterfly

1954–Shelley Mann . . . . 1m.17.0s.
1955–Betty Mullen . . . . 1m.15.0s.
1956–Shelley Mann (110 yards) . . . . . 1m.11.8s.
1957–Nancy Ramey (110 yards) . . . . 1m.11.3s.
1958–Nancy Ramey . . . . 1m.10.3s.
1959–Becky Collins (110 yards) . . . . . 1m.11.2s.
1960–Becky Collins . . . . 1m.10.8s.
1961–Susan Doerr 1m.08.2.s
1962–Mary Stewart . . . . 1m.07.6s.
1963–Kathy Ellis . . . . 1m.06.2s.
1964–Sharon Stouder . . . . 1m.05.4s.
1965–Sue Pitt . . . . 1m.06.2s.
1966–Sue Pitt . . . . 1m.07.0s.
1967–Ellie Daniel . . . . 1m.05.7s.
1968–Ellie Daniel . . . . 1m.06.9s.
1969–Virginia Durkin . . . . 1m.05.9s.
1970–Alice Jones . . . . 1m.04.1s.
1971–Deena Deardurff . . . . 1m.05.0s.
1972–Not Held

220-Yard Breast Stroke–200 Meters
200 Meters from 1963 on.

1923–Ruth Thomas . . . . 3m.50.6s.
1924–Agnes Geraghty . . . . 3m.35.2s.
1925–Agnes Geraghty . . . . 3m.32.4s.
1926–Agnes Geraghty . . . . 3m.29.4s.
1927–Agnes Geraghty . . . . 3m.28.4s.
1928–Lisa Lindstrom . . . . 3m.19.4s.
1929–Agnes Geraghty . . . . 3m.17s.
1930–Margaret Hoffman . . . . 3m.20s.
1931–Katherine Rawls . . . . 3m.13.6s.
1932–Katherine Rawls . . . . 3m.18.8s.
1933–Margaret Hoffman . . . . 3m.14.6s.
1934–Ann Govednik . . . . 3m.18.3s.
1935–Katherine Rawls . . . . 3m.17.1s.
1936–Iris Cummings . . . . 3m.17.2s.
1937–Iris Cummings . . . . 3m.16.9s.
1938–Iris Cummings . . . . 3m.18.7s.
1939–Fujiko Katsutani (200 meters) . 3m.16.1s.
1940–Fujiko Katsutani . . . . 3m.14.9s.
1941–Patty Aspinall (200 meters) . . . 3m.14.9s.
1942–Patty Aspinall (200 meters) . . . 3m.19.5s.

1943–Patty Aspinall (200 meters) . . . 3m.21.2s.
1944–Nancy Merki (200 meters) . . . . 3m.16.5s.
1945–Clare Lamore (200 meters) . . . . 3m.18.6s.
1946–Nancy Merki (200 meters) . . . . . 3m.15s.
1947–Nel Van Vliet (200 meters) . . . . 2m.58.6s.
1948–Jeanne Wilson (200 meters) . . . 3m.17.7s.
1949–Evelyn Kawamoto . . . . 3m.14.5s.
1950–Marge Hulton (200 meters)
        Evelyn Kawamoto (200 meters) 3m.10.2s.
1951–Carol Pence (200 meters) . . . . . 3m.09.2s.
1952–No competition
1953–Gail Peters . . . . 3m.01.1s.
1954–Mary Jane Sears (200 meters) . . 3m.07.4s.
1955–Mary Jane Sears (200 meters) . . 3m.01.4s.
1956–Mary Jane Sears . . . . 2m.59.0s.
1957–Mary Lou Elsenius . . . . 3m.04.8s.
1958–Susan Ordogh (200 meters) . . . 2m.58.6s.
1959–Ann Warner . . . . 3m.02.4s.
1960–Ann Warner (200 meters) . . . . . 2m.53.3s.
1961–Jean Dellekamp (200 meters) . . 2m.56.7s.
1962–Wiltrud Urselmann (200 meters 2m.53.3s.
1963–Jean Dellekamp . . . . 2m.53.4s.
1964–Claudia Kolb . . . . 2m.49.8s.
1965–Claudia Kolb . . . . 2m.48.6s.
1966–Catie Ball . . . . 2m.44.4s.
1967–Catie Ball . . . . 2m.39.5s.
1968–Catie Ball . . . . 2m.40.9s.
1969–Kim Brecht . . . . 2m.45.4s.
1970–Claudia Clevenger . . . . 2m.44.6s.
1971–Claudia Clevenger . . . . 2m.45.7s.
1972–Not Held

220-Yard Butterfly
200 meters from 1963 on

1956–Shelley Mann . . . . 2m.44.4s.
1957–Jane Wilson . . . . 2m.47.6s.
1958–Sylvia Ruuska (200 meters) . . . 2m.43.6s.
1959–Becky Collins . . . . 2m.37.0s.
1960–Becky Collins (200 meters) . . . . 2m.36.8s.
1961–Becky Collins (200 meters) . . . . 2m.32.8s.
1962–Sharon Finneran (200 meters) . 2m.32.1s.
1963–Sharon Finneran . . . . 2m.31.8s.
1964–Sharon Stouder . . . . 2m.26.4s.
1965–Kendis Moore . . . . 2m.26.3s.
1966–Lee Davis . . . . 2m.27.2s.
1967–Toni Hewitt . . . . 2m.23.6s.
1968–Toni Hewitt . . . . 2m.24.2s.
1969–Lynn Colella . . . . 2m.21.6s.
1970–Alice Jones . . . . 2m.19.3s.
1971–Ellie Daniel . . . . 2m.18.4s.
1972–Not Held

200-Meter Individual Medley

1963–Donna deVarona . . . . 2m.31.8s.
1964–Donna deVarona . . . . 2m.29.9s.
1965–Claudia Kolb . . . . 2m.30.8s.
1966–Claudia Kolb . . . . 2m.27.8s.
1967–Claudia Kolb . . . . 2m.25.0s.
1968–Claudia Kolb . . . . 2m.27.5s.
1969–Lynn Vidali . . . . 2m.26.2s.
1970–Lynn Vidali . . . . 2m.26.0s.
1971–Yoshimi Nishigawa (Japan) . . . . 2m.26.0s.
1972–Not Held

400-Meter Individual Medley

1954—Marie Gillett .... 6m.06.9s.
1955—Marie Gillett .... 6m.01.5s.
1956—Shelley Mann (440 yards) ..... 4m.52.5s.
1957—Sylvia Ruuska (440 yards) .... 5m.49.5s.
1958—Sylvia Ruuska .... 5m.43.7s.
1959—Sylvia Ruuska (440 yards) .... 5m.40.2s.
1960—Donna de Varona .... 5m.36.5s.
1961—Donna de Varona .... 5m.34.5s.
1962—Sharon Finneran .... 5m.24.5s.
1963—Donna deVarona .... 5m.24.5s.
1964—Donna deVarona .... 5m.17.7s.
1965—Mary Ellen Olcese .... 5m.19.6s.
1966—Claudia Kolb .... 5m.08.2s.
1967—Claudia Kolb .... 5m08.2s.
1968—Sue Pedersen .... 5m.10.3s.
1969—Debbie Meyer .... 5m.08.6s.
1970—Susie Atwood .... 5m.07.3s.
1971—Jenny Bartz .... 5m.08.3s.
1972—Not Held

400-Meter Medley Relay

1954—Walter Reed S.C. (Mann, Knapp,
    Sears, Werner) .... 5m.14.0s.
1955—Walter Reed S.C. (Mann, Sears,
    Mullen Werner) .... 5m.07.0s.
1956—Walter Reed S.C. (Mann, Sears,
    Bray, Werner) .... *5m.05.8s.
1957—Santa Clara S.C. (von Saltza,
    Warner, Wilson, Ransom) ..... *5m.06.6s.
1958—Santa Clara S.C. (von Saltza,
    Wilson, Ransom, Warner) .... 5m.00.9s.
1959—Santa Clara S.C. (C. von Saltza,
    A. Warner, K. Simecek, D.
    Ransom) .... 4m.59.9s.
1960—Santa Clara S.C. (L. Burke, A.
    Warner, K. Simecek, C. von Saltza)4m.49.1s.
1961—Vesper Boat Club (N. Harmer, B.
    Chesneau, S. Doerr, L. Hopkins) .4m.50.3s.
1962—Vesper Boat Club (Harmer, Tally,
    Doerr, Randall) .... 4m.47.5s.
1963—Los Angeles A.C. (C. Ferguson,
    C. Ford. M. Templeton, C. House) 4m.44.4s.
1964—Santa Clara S.C. (J. Haroun, C. Kolb,
    D. deVarona, P. Watson) .... 4m.40.3s.
1965—Santa Clara S.C. (C. Kolb, L. Hildreth,
    T. Stickles, P. Watson) .... 4m.38.4s.
1966—Santa Clara S.C. (T. Ogilvie, S. Jones,
    C. Kolb, P. Watson) .... 4m.37.7s.
1967—Santa Clara S.C. (P. Watson, C. Kolb,
    L. Davis, L. Gustavson) .... 4m.34.6s.
1968—Santa Clara S.C., A Team (J. Swagerty,
    J. Henne, C. Kolb, L. Gustavson) . 4m.33.8s.
1969—Lakewood A.C. (S. Atwood, K.
    Brecht, P. Lines, B. Adair) ...... 4m.31.4s.
1970—Lakewood A.C. (S. Atwood, K.
    Brecht, B. Adair, A. Simmons) .. 4m.31.2s.
1971—Phillips 66 (L. Skrifvars, L. Kurtz,
    C. Plaisted, S. Babashoff) ...... 4m.32.0s.
1972—Not Held

*440 Yards

400-Meter Free-Style Relay

1963—Los Angeles A.C. (M. Templeton, S.
    Bakewell, C. House, C. Ferguson) 4m.13.7s.
1964—Santa Clara S.C. (J. Haroun, D.
    deVarona, T. Stickles, P. Watson) 4m.08.5s.
1965—Santa Clara S.C. (T. Stickles, J.
    Haroun, L. Hildreth, P. Watson) .4m.08.6s.
1966—Santa Clara S.C. (L. Gustavson, N.
    Ryan, C. Kolb, P. Watson) ...... 4m.04.5s.
1967—Santa Clara S.C. (L. Gustavson, N.
    Ryan, L. Fritz, P. Watson) ...... 4m.03.5s.
1968—Santa Clara S.C., A. Team (L. Gustavson,
    P. Watson, P. Carpinelli, J. Henne) 4m.02.1s.
1969—Santa Clara S.C. (J. Henne, L. Fritz,
    L. Vidali, L. Gustavson) .... 4m.02.9s.
1970—Santa Clara S.C. (J. Wilk, W. Royden,
    L. Vidali, L. Fritz) .... 4m.06.2s.
1971—Lakewood A.C. (L. Johnson, A.
    Simmons, R. Watt, B. Adair) .... 4m.02.9s.
1972—Not Held

880-Yard Free-Style Relay—800 Meters

800 Meters from 1964 on.

1923—Women's Swimming Association,
    New York (G. Ederle, E. McGary, D.
    O'Mara, A. Riggin) .... 12.15.2s.
1924—Women's S.A. (Wainright, White-
    nack, McGary, Riggin) .... 12m.15.2s.
1925—Women's S.A. (Whitenack,
    O'Mara, McGary, Nilsson) .... 12m.17s.
1926—Women's S.A. .... 11m.45.6s.
1927—Women's S.A. (Whitenack, Lind-
    strom, McGary, Norelius) .... ———
1928—Women's S.A. (Norelius, Lind-
    strom, Holm, McGary) .... ———
1929—Women's S.A. (Holm, Lind-
    strom, McGary, Lambert) .... 11m.22.2s.
1930—Los Angeles A.C. (Cramer,
    Lowe, Hatch, McKim) .... 11m.15.4s.
1931—Los Angeles A.C. (Cramer,
    Forbes, Lowe, McKim) .... 11m.20.4s.
1932—Carnegie Library Club, Home-
    stead, Pa. (J. Gorman, A.M. Gor-
    man, Clark, Kight) .... 11m.17.8s.
1933—Carnegie Library Club, (J. Gor-
    man, A.M. Gorman, Clark, Kight) .. 11m.10s.
1934—Carnegie Library Club (Kight,
    A.M. Gorman, Clark, J. Gorman) .11m.13.3s.
1935—Washington A.C. Seattle (Petty,
    Lea, Buckley, McKean) .... 10m.37.8s.
1936—Washington A.C. (Petty, Lea,
    Buckley, McKean) .... 10m.46.3s.
1937—Washington A.C. (Hughes, Lea,
    Buckley, Mucha) .... 11m.10.4s.
1938—Women's S.A. (Rains, Callen,
    Freeman, Ryan) .... 10m.55.5s.
1939—No competition
1940—Women's S.A. (Holle, Sahner,
    O'Donnell, Rains) .... 10.58.8s.
1941—Riviera Club, Indianapolis,
    Walts, Fogle, Hardin, Bemis) .... *10m.30.7s.
1942—Riviera Club (Walts, Joan

Fogle, Hardin, Bemis) . . . . 11m.09.5s.

1943—Riviera Club "A" (Walts, Joan
Fogle, Hardin, Bemis) . . . . 10m.42.1s.

1944—Riviera Club (Walts, Bemis,
Hardin, Fogle) . . . . 10m.52.2s.

1945—Crystal Plunge, San Fransisco (Sahner, Graham, S. Curtis,
A. Curtis) . . . . 10m.44.5s.

1946—Crystal Plunge (S. Curtis, D.
Maddock, M. Sahner, A. Curtis) . . *11m.10s.

1947—Crystal Plunge (J. Mallory, M.
Hayes, M. Sahner, A. Curtis) . . . . . *11m.10s.

1948—Crystal Plunge (M. Hayes, Mc-
Rae, M. Sahner, A. Curtis) . . . . . *11m.37.4s.

1949—Hawaii "A" (J. Murakami, C.
Kleinschmidt, E. Kawamoto, T.
Kalama) . . . . 10m.42.9s.

1950—Hawaii S.C. (T. Kalama, E. Kaw-
amaoto, C. Kleinschmidt, J. Mura-
kami) . . . . *10m.37.4s.

1951—Lafayette (Ind.) S.C. (K. Clark,
A. Moss, B. Mullen, S. Donahue) . *10m.53.5s.

1952—No competition

1953—Walter Reed S.C. (Gillett,
Freeman, Peters, Mann) . . . . 10m.24.9s.

1954—Ft. Lauderdale S.A. (Aspinall,
Greenlaw, Cahill, Green) . . . . *10m.18.7s.

1955—Walter Reed S.C. (Mann, Gil-
lett, Gray, Werner) . . . . 10m.10.3s.

1956—Walter Reed S.C. (Mann, Gray,
Gillett, Werner) . . . . 10m.9.8s.

1957-63—No competition

1964—Santa Clara S.C. (T. Stickles, S.
Finneran, D. deVarona, P. Watson) . 9m.08.8s.

1965—City of Commerce S.C. (P. Caretto, D. Pfeiffer, M. Campbell,
J. Hallock) . . . . 9m.00.1s.

1966—Santa Clara S.C. (L. Gustavson,
N. Ryan, C. Kolb, P. Watson) . . . . . 8m.55.4s.

1967—Santa Clara S.C. (L. Gustavson,
N. Ryan, P. Watson, C. Kolb) . . . . . 8m.53.0s.

1968—Arden Hills S.C. (D. Meyer, L.
Williams, V. King, S. Pederson) . . . . 8m.46.2s.

1969—Arden Hills S.C. (E. Kossner, V.
King, Meyer, S. Pederson) . . . . 8m.42.3s.

1970—Arden Hills S.C. (N. Spitz, V.
King, E. Kossner, D. Meyer) . . . . . . 8m.49.2s.

1971—Lakewood A.C. (L. Johnson, L.
Kiddy, R. Watt, A. Simmons) . . . . . 8m.35.5s.

1972—Not held

3-Foot or 1-Meter Springboard Diving

1948—Zoe Ann Olsen
1949—Zoe Ann Olsen
1950—Mrs. Patricia Keller McCormick
1951—Mrs. Patricia Keller McCormick
1952—No competition
1953—56—Mrs. Patricia Keller McCormick
1957—58—Paula Jean Myers
1959—Irene MacDonald
1960—63—No competition
1964—Patsy Willard

1965—Joel O'Connell
1966—Joel O'Connell
1967—Micki King
1968—72—Cynthia Potter

10-Foot or 3-Meter Springboard Diving

1921—Helen Meany
1922—Helen Meany
1923—Aileen Riggin
1924—Aileen Riggin
1925—Aileen Riggin
1926—Helen Meany
1927—Helen Meany
1928—Lillian Fergus
1929—Georgia Coleman
1930—Georgia Coleman
1931—Georgia Coleman
1932—Katherine Rawls
1933—Katherine Rawls
1934—Katherine Rawls
1935—Mary Hoerger
1936—Claudia Eckert
1937—Marjorie Gestring
1938—Marjorie Gestring
1939—Helen Crlenkovich
1940—Marjorie Gestring
1941—Helen Crlenkovich (3 meters)
1942—Ann Ross
1943—Ann Ross
1944—Ann Ross
1945—Mrs. Helen Crlenkovich Morgan
1946—Zoe Ann Olsen
1947—Zoe Ann Olsen
1948—Zoe Ann Olsen
1949—Zoe Ann Olsen
1950—Mrs. Patricia Keller McCormick
1951—Mrs. Patricia Keller McCormick
1952—No competition
1953—56—Mrs. Patricia Keller McCormick
1957—58—Paula Jean Myers
1959—Irene MacDonald
1960—Patsy Willard
1961—Joel Lenzi
1962—Barbara McAllister
1963—Jeanne Collier
1964—Mrs. Barbara McAlister Talmage
1965—Micki King
1966—Sue Gossick
1967—Micki King
1968—Jerrie Adair
1969—70—Lt. Micki King
1971—72—Cynthia Potter

Platform Diving

1916—Evelyn Burnett
1917—Aileen Allen
1918—Josephine Bartlett
1919—Betty Grimes
1920—No competition
1921—Helen Meany
1922—Helen Meany
1923—Helen Meany
1924—No competition

1925—Helen Meany
1926—Esther Foley
1927—No competition
1928—Helen Meany
1929—Georgia Coleman
1930—Georgia Coleman
1931—Georgia Coleman
1932—No competition
1933—Dorothy Poynton
1934—Mrs. Dorothy Poynton Hill
1935—Mrs. Dorothy Poynton Hill
1936—Ruth Jump
1937—Ruth Jump
1938—Ruth Jump
1939—Marjorie Gestring
1940—Marjorie Gestring
1941—Helen Crlenkovich
1942—Margaret Reinholdt
1943—Jeanne Kessler
1944—No competition
1945—Mrs. Helen Crlenkovich Morgan
1946—Mrs. Victoria Manalo Draves
1947—Mrs. Victoria Manalo Draves
1948—Mrs. Victoria Manalo Draves
1949—Mrs. Patricia Keller McCormick
1950—Mrs. Patricia Keller McCormick
1951—Mrs. Patricia Keller McCormick
1952—No competition
1953—Paula Jean Myers
1954—Mrs. Patricia Keller McCormick
1955—Juno Irwin
1956—Mrs. Patricia Keller McCormick
1957-58—Paula Jean Myers
1959—Paula Jean Pope
1960—Juno Irwin
1961—Barbara McAllister
1962—Linda Cooper
1963—Barbara Talmage
1964—Patsy Willard
1965—Lesley Bush
1966—Shirley Teeples
1967—Lesley Bush
1968—Ann Peterson
1969—Lt. Micki King
1970-71—Cynthia Potter
1972—Janet Ely

Indoor—Women

100-Yard Free-Style

1916—Olga Dorfner . . . . 1m8.8s.
1917—Olga Dorfner . . . . 1m.7.6s.
1918—Olga Dorfner . . . . 1m.10.6s.
1919—Charlotte Boyle . . . . 1m.8.6s.
1920—Ethelda Bleibtrey . . . . 1m.6.2s.
1921—Charlotte Boyle . . . . 1m.7.2s.
1922—Ethelda Bleibtrey . . . . 1m.7s.
1923—Helen Wainwright . . . . 1m.7.2s.
1924—Helen Wainwright . . . . 1m.7.6s.
1925—Ethel Lackie . . . . 1m.6s.
1926—Ethel Lackie . . . . 1m.3.4s.
1927—Martha Norelius . . . . 1m.4s.
1928—Ethel Lackie . . . . 1m.3.4s.

1929—Albina Osipowich* . . . .
1930—Helene Madison . . . . 1m.6s.
1931—Helene Madison . . . . 1m.3.2s.
1932—Helene Madison . . . . 1m.2.4s.
1933—Lenore Kight . . . . 1m.3.4s.
1934—Olive McKean . . . . 1m.3.8s.
1935—Katherine Rawls . . . . 1m.3s.
1936—Claudia E. Eckert . . . . 1m.2.5s.
1937—Claudia Eckert . . . . 1m.1.8s.
1938—Halina Tomska . . . . 1m.1.3s.
1939—Dorothy Evans . . . . 1m.2s.
1940—Halina Tomska Tullis . . . . 1m.1s.
1941—Patricia McWhorter . . . . 1m.2.8s.
1942—Marilyn Sahner . . . . 1m.01.9s.
1943—Suzanne Zimmerman . . . . 1m.02.2s.
1944—Brenda Helser . . . . 1m.00.9s.
1945—Ann Curtis . . . . 1m.01.9s.
1946—Brenda Helser . . . . 1m.00.4s.
1947—Ann Curtis . . . . 1m.00.3s.
1948—Marie Corridon . . . . 59.9s.
1949—Jakie LaVine . . . . 1m.01.1s.
1950—Marie Corridon . . . . 1m.00.1s.
1951—Jackie LaVine . . . . 60.5s.
1952—Jackie LaVine . . . . 59.1s.
1953—Judy Roberts . . . . 59.2s.
1954—Jody Alderson . . . . 58.5s.
1955—Shelley Mann . . . . 58.7s.
1956—Wanda Werner . . . . 58.6s.
1957—Molly Botkin . . . . 58.3s.
1958—Chris von Saltza . . . . 56.8s.
1959—Shirley Stobs . . . . 57.7s.
1960—Chris von Saltza . . . . 56.3s.
1961—Chris von Saltza . . . . 55.8s.
1962—Robyn Johnson . . . . 55.5s.
1963—Terri Stickles . . . . 55.3s.
1964—Sharon Stouder . . . . 54.2s.
1965—Jeanne Hallock . . . . 54.5s.
1966—Martha Randal . . . . 53.6s.
1967—Erika Bricker . . . . 53.3s.
1968—Jane Barkman . . . . 52.1s.
1969—Wendy Fordyce . . . . 52.8s.
1970—Wendy Fordyce . . . . 52.8s.
1971—Sandy Neilson . . . . 53.2s.
1972—Barbara Shaw . . . . 52.1s.

*Martha Norelius finished first, but was disqualified

200-Yard Free-Style

1965—Penny Estes . . . . 1m.58.2s.
1966—Martha Randall . . . . 1m.56.9s.
1967—Pokey Watson . . . . 1m.54.1s.
1968—Debbie Meyer . . . . 1m.52.1s.
1969—Linda Gustavson . . . . 1m.54.4s.
1970—Wendy Fordyce . . . . 1m.55.5s.
1971—Nancy Spitz . . . . 1m.55.8s.
1972—Kim Peyton . . . . 1m.52.4s.

440-Yard Free-Style

1939—Halina Tomska . . . . 5m.29.5s.
1940—Nancy Merki . . . . 5m.30.3s.
1941—Nancy Merki . . . . 5m.30.1s.
1942—Nancy Merki . . . . 5m.31.6s.
1943—Joan Fogle . . . . 5m.37.4s.

1944—Ann Curtis ....5m.21.7s.
1945—Ann Curtis ....5m.27.7s.
1946—Ann Curtis ....5m.17.1s.
1947—Ann Curtis ....5m.07.9s.
1948—Ann Curtis ....5m.17.9s.
1949—Joan Mallory ....5m.27.1s.
1950—Jackie LaVine ....5m.28.9s.
1951—Ann Moss (400 yards) ....4m.52.3s.
1952—Carolyn Green (400 yards) ....4m.49.6s.
1953—Carolyn Green (500 yards) ....5m.59.1s.
1954—Carol Tait (500 yards) ......6m.00.6s.
1955—Carol Tait (500 yards) ......6m.01.4s.
1956—Dougie Gray (500 yards) ......5m.55.8s.
1957—Sylvia Ruuska (500 yards) ....5m.47.8s.
1958—Sylvia Ruuska (500 yards) ....5m.44.9s.
1959—Sylvia Ruuska (500 yards) ....5m.46.6s.
1960—Chris von Saltza (500 yards) ...5m.37.7s.
1961—Chris von Saltza (500 yards) ...5m.34.5s.
1962—Robyn Johnson (500 yards) ...5m.27.2s.
1963—Sharon Finneran (500 yards) ..5m.23.4s.
1964—Terri Stickles (500 yards) .....5m.19.2s.
1965—Patty Caretto (500 yards) .....5m.15.6s.
1966—Pam Kruse (500 yards) ....5m.15.5s.
1967—Pam Kruse (500 yards) ....5m.06.9s.
1968—Debbie Meyer (500 yards) ....4m.54.1s.
1969—Vicki King (500 yards) ....5m.00.6s.
1970—Debbie Meyer (500 yards) ....5m.00.7s.
1971—Debbie Meyer (500 yards) .....5m.02.8s.
1972—Keena Rothhammer (500 yards) 4m.57.8s.

1,650-Yard Free-Style

1964—Sharon Finneran ....18m.31.5s.
1965—Patty Caretto ....18m.03.6s.
1966—Sharon Finneran ....18m.10.9s.
1967—Debbie Meyer ....17m.38.1s.
1968—Debbie Meyer ....17m.04.4s.
1969—Debbie Meyer ....17m.04.4s.
1970—Debbie Meyer ....16m.54.6s.
1971—Debbie Meyer ....17m.11.8s.
1972—Jo Harshbarger ....16m.59.3s.

100-Yard Backstroke

1920—Ethelda Bleibtrey ....1m.17.4s.
1921—Sybil Bauer ....1m.21s.
1922—Sybil Bauer ....1m.17.6s.
1923—Sybil Bauer ....1m.15.2s.
1924—Sybil Bauer ....1m.14s.
1925—Sybil Bauer ....1m.15s.
1926—Sybil Bauer ....1m.15s.
1927—Corinne Condon ....1m.18.8s.
1928—Corinne Condon ....1m.17.4s.
1929—Joan McSheehy ....1m.15.4s.
1930—Eleanor Holm ....1m.12s.
1931—Eleanor Holm ....1m.14.4s.
1932—Eleanor Holm ....1m.11.6s.
1933—Joan McSheehy ....1m.13.6s.
1934—Eleanor Holm Jarrett ....1m.10.8s.
1935—Eleanor Holm Jarrett.........1m.9.6s.
1936—Eleanor Holm Jarrett ....1m.8.4s.
1937—Dorothy Forbes ....1m.12.1s.
1938—Jeanne Laupheimer ....1m.12.1s.
1939—Helen Perry ....1m.9.2s.
1940—Gloria Callen................1m.9.2s.

1941—Helen Perry ....1m9.7s.
1942—Gloria Callen ....1m.8.5s.
1943—Suzanne Zimmerman ....1m.10.3s.
1944—Suzanne Zimmerman ....1m.11.2s.
1945—Marion Pontacq ....1m.11.4s.
1946—Suzanne Zimmerman ....1m.8.1s.
1947—Suzanne Zimmerman ....1m.8.4s.
1948—Suzanne Zimmerman ....1m.8.2s.
1949—Maureen O'Brien ....1m.8.1s.
1950—Maureen O'Brien ....1m7.4s.
1951—Maureen O'Brien ....1m.8.4s.
1952—Maureen O'Brien ....1m.9s.
1953—Barbara Stark ....1m.8.7s.
1954—Shelley Mann ....1m.06.4s.
1955—Carlie O'Connor ....1m.07.8s.
1956—Carin Cone ....1m.07.2s.
1957—Carin Cone ....1m.03.8s.
1958—Carin Cone ....1m.03.6s.
1959—Carin Cone ....1m.04.3s.
1960—Lynn Burke ....1m.03.0s.
1961—Nina Harmer ....1m.04.2s.
1962—Donna deVarona ....1m.04.0s.
1963—Nina Harmar ....1m.02.6s.
1964—Cathy Ferguson ....1m.01.5s.
1965—Cathy Ferguson ....1m.00.9s.
1966—Elaine Tanner (Canada).......1m.00.7s.
1967—Kay Hall ....1m.01.6s.
1968—Kaye Hall ....59.3s.
1969—Susie Atwood ....58.8s.
1970—Susie Atwood ....58.7s.
1971—Libby Tullis ....1m.01.0s.
1972—Susie Atwood ....58.7s.

200-Yard Backstroke

1948—Suzanne Zimmerman ....2m.29.4s.
1949—Barbara Jensen ....2m.32.6s.
1950—Maureen O'Brien ....2m.29.5s.
1951—Mary Freeman ....2m.32.1s.
1952—Barbara Stark ....2m.27.5s.
1953—Barbara Stark ....2m.27s.
1954—Barbara Stark ....2m.27.5s.
1955—Maureen Murphy ....2m.27.4s.
1956—Carin Cone ....2m.26.4s.
1957—Carin Cone ....2m.25.2s.
1958—Carin Cone ....2m.19.8s.
1959—Carin Cone ....2m.20.2s.
1960—Lynn Burke ....2m.16.7s.
1961—Chris von Saltza ....2m.19.9s.
1962—Donna deVarona ....2m.17.9s.
1963—Ginnie Duenkel ....2m.14.9s.
1964—Cathy Ferguson ....2m.12.8s.
1965—Cathy Ferguson ....2m.13.2s.
1966—Judy Humbarger ....2m.11.8s.
1967—Kendis Moore ....2m.10.2s.
1968—Kaye Hall ....2m.10.8s.
1969—Susie Atwood ....2m.07.5s.
1970—Susie Atwood ....2m.05.8s.
1971—Susie Atwood ....2m.06.0s.
1972—Susie Atwood ....2m.04.0s.

100-Yard Breast Stroke

1920—Eleanor Smith ....1m.25.2s.
1921—Frances Taylor ....1m.31.8s.

1922—Ruth Smith . . . . 1m.23.8s.
1923—25—No competition
1926—Agnes Geraghty . . . . 1m.19.4s.
1927—Agner Geraghty . . . . 1m.22s.
1928—Katherine Mearls . . . . 1m.22.4s.
1929—Jane Fauntz . . . . 1m.21.8s.
1930—Agnes Geraghty . . . . 1m.21.4s.
1931—Margaret Hoffman . . . . 1m.24.4s.
1932—Jane Cadwell . . . . 1m25.6s.
1933—Margaret Hoffman . . . . 1m.21.4s.
1934—Doris Shimman . . . . 1m.20.9s.
1935—Katherine Rawls . . . . 1m20.6s.
1936—Katherine Rawls . . . . 1m.18.6s.
1937—Katherine Rawls . . . . 1m.18.5s.
1938—Katherine Rawls . . . . 1m.18.5s.
1939—42—No competition
1943—Alice Miller . . . . 1m.20.6s.
1944—Patricia Sinclair . . . . 1m.17.5s.
1945—Jeanne Wilson . . . . 1m.15.1s.
1946—Patricia Sinclair . . . . 1m.14.6s.
1947—Clara Lamore . . . . 1m.13.8s.
1948—Carol Pence . . . . 1m.15.2s.
1949—Marge Hulton . . . . 1m.16.5s.
1950—Judy Cornell . . . . 1m.12.6s.
1951—Carol Pence . . . . 1m.12.5s.
1952—Gail Peters . . . . 1m.11.7s.
1953—Gail Peters . . . . 1m.10.6s.
1954—55—No competition
1956—Mary Jane Sears . . . . 1m.12.2s.
1957—Patty Kempner . . . . 1m.15.5s.
1958—Patty Kempner . . . . 1m.13.0s.
1959—Linda Clark . . . . 1m.13.6s.
1960—Susan Rogers . . . . 1m.12.8s.
1961—Jean Ann Dellekamp . . . . 1m.12.9s.
1962—Roby Whipple . . . . 1m.13.3s.
1963—Cynthia Goyette . . . . 1m.11.7s.
1964—Claudia Kolb . . . . 1m.09.3s.
1965—Cynthia Goyette . . . . 1m.09.0s.
1966—Catie Ball . . . . 1m.07.4s.
1967—Catie Ball . . . . 1m.06.6s.
1968—Sharon Wichman . . . . 1m.07.4s.
1969—Sharon Wichman . . . . 1m.07.6s.
1970—Kimla Brecht . . . . 1m.06.5s.
1971—Lynn Colella . . . . 1m.06.7s.
1972—Lynn Vidali . . . . 1m.07.0s.

100-Yard Butterfly

1954—Shelley Mann . . . . 1m.06.5s.
1955—Betty Mullen . . . . 1m.05.4s.
1956—Shelley Mann . . . . 1m.04.1s.
1957—Nancy Ramey . . . . 1m.01.9s.
1958—Nancy Ramey . . . . 1m.02.9s.
1959—Nancy Ramey . . . . 1m.02.0s.
1960—Nancy Ramey . . . . 1m.00.3s.
1961—Katherine Ellis . . . . 1m.01.7s.
1962—Mary Stewart . . . . 59.2s.
1963—Kathy Ellis . . . . 59.2s.
1964—Kathy Ellis . . . . 58.8s.
1965—Sharon Stouder . . . . 58.0s.
1966—Elaine Tanner (Canada) . . . . 58.7s.
1967—Lee Davis . . . . 58.4s.
1968—Ellie Daniel . . . . 58.2s.

1969—Ellie Daniel . . . . 58.3s.
1970—Lynn Colella . . . . 58.0s.
1971—Deena Deardurff . . . . 57.0s.
1972—Deena Deardurff . . . . 57.1s.

200-Yard Butterfly

1956—Shelley Mann . . . . 2m.26.3s.
1957—Shelley Mann . . . . 2m.27.7s.
1958—Nancy Ramey . . . . 2m.19.2s.
1959—Becky Collins . . . . 2m.16.8s.
1960—Beck Collins . . . . 2m.16.9s.
1961—Becky Collins . . . . 2m.18.4s.
1962—Sharon Finneran . . . . 2m.16.2s.
1963—Kim Worley . . . . 2m.15.3s.
1964—Donna deVarona . . . . 2m.10.5s.
1965—Sue Pitt . . . . 2m.09.6s.
1966—Lee Davis . . . . 2m.11.5s.
1967—Lee Davis . . . . 2m.07.9s.
1968—Ellie Daniel . . . . 2m.06.6s.
1969—Ellie Daniel . . . . 2m.06.6s.
1970—Lynn Colella . . . . 2m.03.9s.
1971—Alice Jones . . . . 2m.03.9s.
1972—Karen Moe . . . . 2m.03.3s.

250-Yard Breast Stroke—200 Yards

1917—Mabel Arklie (200 yards) . . . . . 3m.36.8s.
1918—Mabel Arklie (200 yards) . . . . . . 3m.27s.
1919—Eleanor Smith (200 yards) . . . . 3m.10.6s.
1920—22—No competition
1923—Sarah Freeman . . . . 4m.1.2s.
1924—Agnes Geraghty . . . . 3m.40.2s.
1925—Agnes Geraghty . . . . 3m.27.8s.
1926—38—No competition
1939—Helene Rains . . . . 3m.13.3s.
1940—Patty Aspinall . . . . 3m.10.1s.
1941—Patty Aspinall . . . . 3m.7.8s.
1942—Helene Rains . . . . 3m.12s.
1943—June Fogle . . . . 3m.18.8s.
1944—Nancy Merki . . . . 3m.15.5s.
1945—Patricia Sinclair . . . . 3m.13.1s.
1946—Patricia Sinclair . . . . 3m.07.2s.
1947—Nancy Merki . . . . 3m.11.1s.
1948—Clara Lamore . . . . 3m.10.5s.
1949—Nancy M. Lees . . . . 3m.12.2s.
1950—Carol Pence . . . . 3m.01.4s.
1951—Carol Pence (200 yards) . . . . 2m.45s.
1952—Gail Peters (200 yards) . . . . 2m.40.1s.
1953—Gail Peters . . . . 3m.27.4s.
1954—Mary Jane Sears . . . . 3m.29.0s.
1955—Mary Jane Sears . . . . 3m.29.8s.
1956—Mary Jane Sears . . . . 3m.22.1s.
1957—Ivanelle Hoe . . . . 3m.24.3s.
1958—Susan Ordogh . . . . 3m.20.0s.
1959—Susan Ordogh . . . . 3m.24.3s.
1960—Susan Ordogh . . . . 3m.14.6s.
1961—Susan Ordogh . . . . 3m.19.7s.
1962—Andrea Hopkins . . . . 3m.15.2s.
1963—Roby Whipple . . . . 3m.14.7s.
1964—Cynthia Goyette . . . . 3m.09.1s.
1965—Cynthia Goyette (200 yards) . . 2m.26.4s.
1966—Cynthia Goyette (200 yards) . . 2m.25.6s.
1967—Catie Ball (200 yards) . . . . 2m.25.2s.

1968—Sharon Wichman (200 yards) . . 2m.25.2s.
1969—Kim Brecht (200 yards) . . . . . . 2m.24.4s.
1970—Linda Kurtz (200 yards) . . . . . . 2m.23.0s.
1971—Ann Belikow (200 yards) . . . . . 2m.29.6s.
1972—Lynn Colella (200 yards) . . . . . 2m.22.3s.

200-Yard Individual Medley

1963—Donna deVarona . . . . 2m.15.0s.
1964—Donna deVarona . . . . 2m.12.4s.
1965—Jeanne Hallock . . . . 2m.14.2s.
1966—Jane Barkman . . . . 2m.13.8s.
1967—Claudia Kolb . . . . 2m.09.7s.
1968—Claudia Kolb . . . . 2m.08.5s.
1969—Lynn Vidali . . . . 2m.09.2s.
1970—Lynn Vidali . . . . 2m.10.9s.
1971—Susie Atwood . . . . 2m.10.6s.
1972—Jenny Bartz . . . . 2m.08.2s.

400-Yard Individual Medley

1954—Shelley Mann . . . . 5m.18.6s.
1955—Shelley Mann . . . . 5m.19.7s.
1956—Sylvia Ruuska . . . . 5m.14.9s.
1957—Sylvia Ruuska . . . . 5m.08.1s.
1958—Sylvia Ruuska . . . . 5m.03.5s.
1959—Sylvia Ruuska . . . . 4m.58.2s.
1960—Sylvia Ruuska . . . . 4m.57.0s.
1961—Becky Collins . . . . 4m.55.5s.
1962—Sharon Finneran . . . . 4m.52.9s.
1963—Donna deVarona . . . . 4m.47.3s.
1964—Donna deVarona . . . . 4m.42.9s.
1965—Sharon Finneran . . . . 4m.47.4s.
1966—Sharon Finneran . . . . 4m.49.4s.
1967—Sue Pedersen . . . . 4m.37.0s.
1968—Claudia Kolb . . . . 4m.33.2s.
1969—Lynn Vidali . . . . 4m.36.7s.
1970—Debbie Meyer . . . . 4m.34.2s.
1971—Susie Atwood . . . . 4m.34.8s.
1972—Susie Atwood . . . . 4m.28.8s.

400-Yard Medley Relay

1954—Walter Reed S.C. (Mann, Gil-
lett, Sears, Werner) . . . . 4m.37.0s.
1955—Walter Reed S.C. (Mann, Sears,
Mullen, Werner) . . . . 4m.33.5s.
1956—Walter Reed S.C. (Mann, Sears,
Brey, Werner) . . . . 4m.33.5s.
1957—Santa Clara S.C. (von Saltza,
Ransom, Wilson, Mahaney) . . . . 4m.27.4s.
1958—Santa Clara S.C. (von Saltza,
Ransom, Wilson, Honig) . . . . 4m.28.9s.
1959—Berkeley (Calif.) Y.M.C.A. (P.
Russka, Brancroft, Schuler,
S. Ruuska) . . . . 4m.25.4s.
1960—Santa Clara S.C. (Burke, Warner,
Simecek, von Saltza) . . . . 4m.16.2s.
1961—Multnomah A.C. (Gabie, Daniel-
son, Kanaby, Wood) . . . . 4m.20.0s.
1962—Riviera Club, Indianapolis (Gordt,
Brown, McIntire, Marston . . . . 4m.17.9s.
1963—Santa Clara S.C. (D. deVarona,
L. Kurtz, K. Worley, T. Stickles) . . . 4m.09.5s.
1964—Santa Clara S.C. (J. Haroun, C.
Kolb, D. deVarona, T. Stickles) . . . . 4m.07.3s.

1965—City of Commerce S.C. (M. Campbell, S. Nitta, S. Stouder, J.
Hallock) . . . . 4m.06.8s.
1966—Vesper B.C. (N. Thompson, J.
Barkman, L. Davis, M. Randall) . . . . 4m.06.0s.
1967—Santa Clara S.C. (P. Watson, C.
Kolb, L. Hildreth, L. Gustavson) . . . 4m.05.4s.
1968—Santa Clara S.C., A. Team (J.
Swaggerty, J. Henne, C. Kolb, L.
Gustavson) . . . . 4m.02.4s.
1969—Santa Clara S.C. (J. Swaggerty,
J. Henne, L. Vidali, L. Gustavson) . . 4m.00.6s.
1970—Lakewood A.C. (S. Atwood, K.
Brecht, P. Lines, B. Adair) . . . . 4m.01.7s.
1971—Lakewood A.C. (S. Atwood, K.
Brecht, B. Adair, L. Kiddie) . . . . 3m.58.6s.
1972—Lakewood A.C. (S. Atwood, K.
Brecht, D. Schrader, B. Adair) . . . . . 3m.57.4s.

400-Yard Free-Style Relay

1920—Illinois A.C. (first team) (O'Brien,
Ditch, Miller, Bauer) . . . . 4m.43.8s.
1921—Women's Swimming Association,
New York (Boyle, Wainwright,
Ederle, Lord) . . . . 4m.51s.
1922—Women's S.A. (Ederle, Boyle,
Riggin, Wainwright) . . . . 4m.38.6s.
1923—Women's S.A. (Ederle, O'Mara,
Bauer, Riggin) . . . . 4m.49.4s.
1924—No competition
1925—Women's S.A. (Ederle, Riggin,
Lambert, Wainwright) . . . . 4m.43s.
1926—Women's S.A. (440 yards) . . . . . 4m.32.2s.
1927—Women's S.A. (Whitenack, O'Mara,
Lindstrom, Norelius) . . . . 4m.37.4s.
1928—Illinois A.A. (VanMaarth, Shem-
aitis, Quinn, Lackie) . . . . 4m.29.8s.
1929—Illinois W.A.C. . . . .
1930—Women's S.A. (Lindstrom, Ames,
Holm, Lambert) . . . . 4m.19.4s.
1931—Washington A.C. (Schacht, Mc-
Kibben, Gilson, Madison) . . . . 4m.24.8s.
1932—Washington A.C. (Madison, Gil-
son, McKibben, McKean) . . . . 4m.19.2s.
1933—No competition
1934—Carnegie Library Club (Clark,
J. Gorman, A.M. Groman, Kight) . . . . 4m.21s.
1935—Washington A.C. (Buckley, Lea,
McKean, Petty) . . . . 4m.15.3s.
1936—Washington A.C. (Petty, McKean,
Lee, Buckley) . . . . 4m.13.4s.
1937—Washington A.C. (Kilinski, Lea,
Buckley, McKean, Mucha) . . . . 4m.19s.
1938—Washington A.C. (Barker, Schoen-
nauer, Koliski, Lea) . . . . 4m.22s.
1939—Women's S.A. (Fischer, Gallen,
Rains, Ryan) . . . . 4m.18.9s.
1940—Women's S.A. (Fischer, O'Don-
nell, Rains, Ryan) . . . . 4m.14.1s.
1941—Multnomah A.C., Portland, Ore.
(Zimmerman, Merki, Macrae,
Helser) . . . . 4m.12.4s.

1942—Multnomah A.C. (Macrae, Zim-
merman, Merki, Helser) . . . . 4m.12.4s.
1943—Multnomah Club (Hansen, Merki,
Zimmerman, Helser) . . . . 4m.15.5s.
1944—Multnomah Club (Hansen, Zim-
merman, Merki, Helser) . . . . 4m.09.1s.
1945—Crystal Plunge, San Francisco
(S. Curtis, M. Sahner, J. Macrae,
A. Curtis) . . . . 4m.17.3s.
1946—Multnomah A.C. (Hansen, Zim-
merman, Merki, Helser) . . . . 4m.06.5s.
1947—Crystal Plunge (M. Hayes, M.
Sahner, J. Macrae, A. Curtis) . . . . . 4m.08.3s.
1948—Crystal Plunge (M. Hayes, J.
Macrae, M. Sahner, A. Curtis) . . . . 4m.13.5s.
1949—Multnomah Club (Taylor, Ather-
ton, Zimmerman, Lees) . . . . 4m.13.2s.
1950—Town Club, Chicago (O'Brien,
Alderson, Scott, LaVine) . . . . 4m.07.7s.
1951—Lafayette (Ind.) S.C. (S. Dona-
hue, A Hayes, A. Moss, B. Mullen) . . 4m.08.7s.
1952—Town Club "A" (J. LaVine, M.
Kastelyn, J. Alderson, M. Cahill) . . . 4m.05.3s.
1953—Community Builders "A." Chicago
(Shelia Donahue, Jody Alderson,
Jackie LaVine, Marilyn Calderine) . . 4m.04.9s.
1954—Walter Reed S.C. (K. Knapp, W.
Werner, S. Mann, M. Gillett) . . . . . . 3m.59.2s.
1955—Walter Reed S.C. (Mullen, Gillett,
Werner, Mann) . . . . 4m.02.3s.
1956—Lafayette S.C. (Crocker, Love,
Hughes, Rosazza) . . . . 3m.56.8s.
1957—Lafayette S.C. (Love, Hughes,
Whitehall, Rodazza) . . . . 4m.03.8s.
1958—Santa Clara (Calif.) S.C. (Wil-
son, Ransom, Honig, von Saltza) . . . 4m.01.8s.
1959—Berkeley (Calif. Y.M.C.A. (P.
Ruuska, Schuler, Bancroft, S.
Ruusak) . . . . 3m.59.6s.
1960—Multnomah A.C. (Gabie, Matich,
Kanaby, Wood) . . . . 3m.59.5s.
1961—Multnomah A.C. (Matich, Gabie,
Kanaby, Wood) . . . . 3m.51.6s.
1962—Cleveland S.C. (Tucek, Riemen-
schneider, Lloyd, Norton) . . . . 3m.52.2s.
1963—Santa Clara S.C. (T. Stickles, K.
Haines, M. Burbach, D. deVarona) . . 3m.43.9s.
1964—Santa Calra S.C. (T. Stickles, J.
Haroun, P. Watson, D. deVarona) . . 3m.41.2s.
1965—City of Commerce S.C. (S.
Stouder, D. Pfeiffer, M Camp-
bell, J. Hallock) . . . . 3m.40.8s.
1966—Santa Clara S.C. (L. Gustavson, T.
Ogilvie, N. Ryan, P. Watson) . . . . . . 3m.38.5s.
1967—Santa Clara S.C. (L. Gustavson, N.
Ryan, C. Kolb, P. Watson) . . . . 3m.37.1s.
1968—Santa Clara S.C., A. Team (J.
Henne, N. Ryan, P. Watson, L.
Gustavson) . . . . 3m.32.6s.
1969—Santa Clara S.C. (J. Henne, P.
Carpinelli, P. Watson, L. Gustavson) 3m.35.4s.
1970—Jack Nelson S.C. (M. Hays, N.

Fisher, L. Tullis, K. Thomas) . . . . . . 3m.36.1s.
1971—Phillips 66 (L. Skirfunars, C.
Plaisted, K. Hanssen, D. Boone) . . . . 3m.36.6s.
1972—Santa Clara S.C. (M. Brunchurst,
J. Bartz, K. Moe, K. Rothhammer) . . 3m.35.1s.

800-Yard Free-Style Relay

1966—Vesper C.C. (J. Barkman, P.
Hughes, L. Davis, M. Randall) . . . . . 8m.00.4s.
1967—Santa Clara S.C. (L. Gustavson, N.
Ryan, C. Kolb, P. Watson) . . . . 7m.53.7s.
1968—Santa Clara S.C. A. Team (L.
Gustavson, J. Henne, N. Ryan, C.
Kolb) . . . . 7m.42.7s.
1969—Arden Hills S. S. (E. Kossner, V.
King, S. Pederson, D. Meyer) . . . . . . 7m.44.3s.
1970—Arden Hills S.C. (N. Spitz, V.
King, E. Kossner, D. Meyer) . . . . 7m.51.9s.
1971—Arden Hills S.C. (N. Spitz, M.
Shillito, V. King, D. Meyer) . . . . 7m.50.6s.
1972—Santa Clara S.C. (J. Wylie, S.
Berg, J. Bartz, K. Rothhammer) . . . . 7m.36.8s.

Three-Foot or One-Meter Springboard Diving

1923—Aileen Riggin
1924—Elizabeth Becker
1925—Helen Wainwright
1926—Helen Meany
1927—Helen Meany
1928—Helen Meany
1929—Jane Fauntz
1930—Jane Fauntz
1931—Georgia Coleman
1932—Dorothy Poynton
1933—Katherine Rawls
1934—Katherine Rawls
1935—Dorothy Poynton Hill
1936—Marian Mansfield
1937—Arlite Smith
1938—Arlite Smith
1939—Arlite Smith
1940—Mary Patricia Fairbrothe
1941—Anne Ross
1942—Anne Ross
1943—Anne Ross
1944—Anne Ross
1945—Zoe Ann Olsen
1946—Zoe Ann Olsen
1947—Zoe Ann Olsen
1948—Mrs. Victoria Manalo Draves
1949—Zoe Ann Olsen
1950—Sara Wakefield
1951—Mrs. Patricia Keller McCormick
1952—Mrs. Patricia Keller McCormick
1953—Mrs. Patricia Keller McCormick
1954—Mrs. Patricia Keller McCormick
1955—Mrs. Patricia Keller McCormick
1956—Ann Cooper
1957—Paula Jean Myers
1958—Barbara Gilders
1959—Irene MacDonald
1960—Patsy Willard
1961—Joel Dina Lenzi

1962—Patsy Willard
1963—Patsy Willard
1964—Mrs. Barbara McAlister Talmage
1965—Mrs. Joel O'Connell
1966—Mrs. Joel O'Connell
1967—Lesley Bush
1968—Keala O'Sullivan
1969—71—Cynthia Potter
1972—Capt. Micki King

Ten-Foot or Three-Meter Springboard Diving

1916—Aileen Allen
1917—Constance Myers
1918—Thelma Payne
1919—Thelma Payne
1920—Thelma Payne
1921—Helen Wainwright
1922—Elizabeth Becker
1923—Elizabeth Becker
1924—Carol Fletcher
1925—Helen Meany
1926—Betty Pinkston
1927—Helen Meany
1928—Rose Boczek
1929—Georgia Coleman
1930—Georgia Coleman
1931—Georgia Coleman
1932—Georgia Coleman
1933—Dorothy Poynton
1934—Dorothy Poynton
1935—Claudia Eckert
1936—Marjorie Gestring
1937—Marjorie Gestring
1938—Marjorie Gestring
1939—Helen Crlenkovich
1940—Helen Crlenkovich
1941—Helen Crlenkovich
1942—Helen Crlenkovich
1943—Anne Ross
1944—Anne Ross
1945—Zoe Ann Olsen
1946—Patsy-Elsener
1947—Patsy Elsener
1948—Zoe Ann Olsen
1949—Zoe Ann Olsen
1950—Mary Frances Cunningham
1951—Mrs. Patricia Keller McCormick
1952—Mrs. Patricia Keller McCormick
1953—Paula Jean Myers
1954—Mrs. Patricia Keller McCormick
1955—Mrs. Patricia Keller McCormick
1956—Barbara Gilders
1957—Paula Jean Myers
1958—Irene MacDonald
1959—Barbara Gilders
1960—Irene McDonald
1961—Joel Dina Lenzi
1962—Joel Lenzi O'Connell
1963—Barbara McAlister
1964—Mrs. Barbara McAlister Talmage
1965—Mrs. Joel O'Connell
1966—Sue Gossick

1967—Sue Gossick
1968—Lesley Bush
1969—70—Cynthia Potter
1971—Capt. Micki King
1972—Cynthia Potter

Platform Dive

1964—Mrs. Barbara McAlister Talmage
1965—Micki King
1966—Patsy Willard
1967—Patty Simms
1968—Lesley Bush
1969—Beverly Boys
1970—Lani Loken
1971—Capt. Micki King
1972—Ulrika Knape

INTERCOLLEGIATE CHAMPIONS

National Collegiate

For champions in discontinued events, consult NCAA Official Handbook, 1221 Baltimore, Kansas City, Mo., 64105.

Events swum over short course unless otherwise indicated.

50-Yard Free-Style

* 20-yard pool. ** Long course.   Time
1925—Arthur Rule, Navy ....*23.9s.
1926—Harry M. Lewis, Rutgers .... **25s.
1927—William Wright, Columbia ...... **24.9s.
1928—John W. Bryant, Dartmouth ......24.3s.
1929—John W. Bryant, Dartmouth .... 24s.
1930—Albert Schwartz, Northwestern .... 24s.
1931—Edward Scherer, Princeton ....24.6s.
1932—John McKelvey, Stanford .... 24s.
1933—Raymond W. Thompson, Navy ....23.8s.
1934—Charles R. Flachmann, Illinois ....23.8s.
1935—Charles R. Flachmann, Illinois ..... 23s.
1936—Ray Walters, Iowa ....23.2s.
1937—Ed Kirar, Michigan ....23.2s.
1938—Ed Kirar, Michigan ....23.2s.
1939—Charles Barker, Michigan ....23.5s.
1940—Guy Lumsden, Wayne ....23.1s.
1941—Charles Barker, Michigan ....23.0s.
1942—Robert Amundsen, Northwestern ..23.4s.
1943—Henry Kozlowski, Northwestern ...22.1s.
1944—Alan Ford, Yale ....22.2s.
1945—Merton Church, Michigan ....23.2s.
1946—Robert Anderson, Stanford ......23.1s.
1947—Robert Weinberg, Michigan ....23.3s.
1948—Robert Anderson, Stanford ......23.3s.
1949—Robert Weinberg, Michigan ....23.1s.
1950—Edward Garst, Iowa ....23.4s.
1951—Clarke Scholes, Michigan State ....22.9s.
1952—Richard Cleveland, Ohio State ....22.3s.
1953—Don Hill, Michigan ....22.4s.
1954—Dick Cleveland, Ohio State ....22.3s.
1955—Kerry Donovan, Yale ....22.8s.
1956—Rex Aubrey, Yale and Robin
      Moore, Stanford, tie ....22.1s.
1957—Bob Keiter, Amherst ....22.1s.
1958—Gary Morris, Iowa ....22.4s.

1959—Fred Westphal, Wisconsin . . . . 22.3s.
1960—Bruce Hunter, Harvard . . . . 21.9s.
1961—Frank Legacki, Michigan . . . . 21.4s.
1962—Steven Jackman, Minnesota . . . . . 21.1s.
1963—Per Ola Lindberg, Southern
      California . . . . 22.2s.
1964—Mike Austin, Yale . . . . 21.0s.
1965—Steve Clark, Yale . . . . 21.2s.
1966—Sandy Van Kennen, Wesleyan . . . . 21.39s.
1967—Zachary Zorn, U.C.L.A. . . . . 21.12s.
1968—Zac Zorn, U.C.L.A. . . . . 20.99s.
1969—Dan Frawley, So. California . . . . . 21.04s.
1970—David Edgar, Tennessee . . . . 20.93s.
1971—David Edgar, Tennessee . . . . 20.30s.
1972—David Edgar, Tennessee . . . . 20.44s.

100-Yard Free-Style

1925—Ralph Breyer, Northwestern . . . . . . *55s.
1926—Peter H. Wyckoff, Navy . . . . **55.5s.
1927—Carl R. Darnall, Michigan . . . . . . **56.9s.
1928—Carl R. Darnall, Michigan . . . . 55s.
1929—Albert Schwartz, Northwestern . . 53.2s.
1930—Albert Schwartz, Northwestern . . . 55s.
1931—George H. Kojac, Rutgers . . . . 52.6s.
1932—Walter Spence, Rutgers . . . . 53.6s.
1933—Walter Spence, Rutgers . . . . 52.4s.
1934—Walter Spence, Rutgers . . . . 51.6s.
1935—Charles R. Flachmann, Illinois . . . . 52.4s.
1936—Charles Hutter, Harvard . . . . 52.9s.
1937—Ed Kirar, Michigan . . . . 52.3s.
1938—Ed Kirar, Michigan . . . . 52.7s.
1939—   Charles Barker, Michigan . . . . . . 52.9s.
      Paul Wolf, Southern California . . 52.9s.
1940—Gus Sharamet, Michigan . . . . 51.8s.
1941—William A. Prew, Wayne . . . . 52.1s.
1942—Howard Johnson, Yale . . . . 52.4s.
1943—John Patten, Michigan . . . . 52s.
1944—Alan Ford, Yale . . . . 49.7s.
1945—Merton Church, Michigan . . . . 52.3s.
1946—Halo Hirose, Ohio State . . . . 52.1s.
1947—Robert Weinberg, Michigan . . . . . . 52.2s.
1948—Wally Ris, Iowa . . . . 51.5s.
1949—Wally Ris, Iowa . . . . 50.4s.
1950—Clarke Scholes, Michigan State . . . . 50.9s.
1951—Clarke Scholes, Michigan State . . . . . 51s.
1952—Clarke Scholes, Michigan State . . . . 49.9s.
1953—Reid Patterson, Georgia . . . . 50.5s.
1954—Dick Cleveland, Ohio State . . . . 50s.
1955—Rex Aubrey, Yale . . . . 50.7s.
1956—Al Kuhn, Northwestern . . . . 49.3s.
1957—Henry Dyer, Harvard . . . . 49.4s.
1958—Donald Patterson, Michigan State . . 49.5s.
1959—Frank Legacki, Michigan . . . . 49.6s.
1960—Peter Lusk, Yale . . . . 49.4s.
1961—Steven Jackman, Minnesota . . . . . . 48.5s.
1962—Steven Jackman, Minnesota . . . . . . 47.5s.
1963—Per Ola Lindberg, Southern
      California . . . . 47.1s.
1964—Steve Clark, Yale . . . . 46.3s.
1965—Steve Clark, Yale . . . . 46.1s.
1966—Don Roth, Santa Barbara State . . . 46.87s.
1967—Kenneth Walsh, Michigan State . . . . 45.6s.

1968—Zac Zorn, U.C.L.A. . . . . 45.45s.
1969—Francis Heath, U.C.L.A. . . . . 46.24s.
1970—David Edgar, Tennessee . . . . 46.06s.
1971—David Edgar, Tennessee . . . . 44.69s.
1972—David Edgar, Tennessee . . . . 45.00s.

200-Yard Free-Style

1963—Steve Clark, Yale . . . . 1m.46.3s.
1964—Steve Clark, Yale . . . . 1m.44.4s.
1965—Roy Saari, Southern California . 1m.42.9s.
1966—Roy Saari, Southern California 1m.44.66s.
1967—Greg Buckingham, Stanford . . 1m.41.46s.
1968—Don Schollander, Yale . . . . . . 1m.42.04s.
1969—Mark Spitz, Indiana . . . . 1m.39.53s.
1970—Juan Bello, Michigan . . . . 1m.42.70s.
1971—James McConica, So. California 1m.39.75s.
1972—Jerry Heidenreich, SMU . . . . . 1m.38.36s.

500-Yard Free-Style

1963—Jon Konrads, Southern Calif-
      ornia . . . . 4m.50.7s.
1964—Roy Saari, Southern California . 4m.45.8s.
1965—Roy Saari, Southern California . 4m.43.6s.
1966—Roy Saari, Southern California 4m.50.59s.
1967—Greg Buckingham, Stanford . . 4m.37.16s.
1968—Greg Charlton, So. Calif. . . . . . 4m.38.24s.
1969—Mark Spitz, Indiana . . . . 4m.33.48s.
1970—Mike Burton, U.C.L.A. . . . . . . 4m.37.29s.
1971—John Kinsella, Indiana . . . . . . 4m.27.39s.
1972—John Kinsella, Indiana . . . . . . 4m.24.50s.

1,500-Meter Free-Style

(1,650-Yards)

1924—Richard Howell, Northwestern **22m.41s.
1925—31—No competition
1932—Austin Clapp, Stanford . . . . . . 20m.02.2s.
1933—No competition
1934—Jack Medica, Washington . . . . 19m.12.1s.
1935—Jack Medica, Washington . . . 18m.59.3s.
1936—Jack Medica, Washington . . **20m.23.7s.
1937—John Macionis, Yale . . . . 19m.58.5s.
1938—John Macionis, Yale . . . . 20m.15.2s.
1939—Harold Stanhope, Ohio State . 19m.53.8s.
1940—Harold Stanhope, Ohio State**20m.15.8s.
1941—Rene Chouteau, Yale . . . . 19m.43.4s.
1942—Rene Chouteau, Yale . . . . 19m.23.9s.
1943—Keo Nakama, Ohio State . . . . 19m.18.6s.
1944—Keo Nakama, Ohio State . . **20m.02.2s.
1945—Seymour Schlanger, Ohio State 20m.11.4s.
1946—Dave Maclay, Williams . . . . **20m.26.2s.
1947—George Hoogerhyde, Michigan
      State . . . . 19m.44.2s.
1948—Bill Heusner, Northwestern . . . 19m.28.2s.
1949—Bill Heusner, Northwestern . . . 19m.04.8s.
1950—Jack Taylor, Ohio State . . . . . 18m.38.3s.
1951—John Marshall, Yale . . . . 18m.18.8s.
1952—Ford Konno, Ohio State . . . . . . 17m.52s.
1953—Jimmy McLane, Yale . . . . 18m.27.5s.
1954—Ford Konno, Ohio State . . . . . 18m.14.4s.
1955—Ford Konno, Ohio State . . . . . 18m.16.1s.
1956—George Breen, Cortland
      Teachers . . . . 18m.05.9s.
1957—Fritz Myers, Michigan . . . . . . 19m.04.8s.

1958—William Steuart, Michigan State 18m.45.8s.
1959—William Steuart, Michigan State 18m.26.2s.
1960—William Chase, Yale . . . . 17m.48.7s.
1961—Murray Rose, Southern
    California . . . . 17.21.8s.
1962—Murray Rose, Southern
    California . . . . 17m.26.7s.
1963—John Konrads, Southern
    California . . . . 17m.24.0s.
1964—Roy Saari, Southern
    California . . . . 16m.49.5s.
1965—Roy Saari, So. California . . . . . 16m.39.9s.
1966—Roy Saari, So. California . . . . 17m.08.17s.
1967—Michael Burton, U.C.L.A. . . . 16m.17.05s.
1968—Mike Burton, U.C.L.A. . . . . . . 15m.59.4s.
1969—Hans Fassnacht, Long
    Beach State . . . . 15m.54.21s.
1970—Mike Burton, U.C.L.A. . . . . . 16m.10.59s.
1971—John Kinsella, Indiana . . . . . . 15m.26.51s.
1972—John Kinsella, Indiana . . . . . . 15m.33.58s.

100-Yard Backstroke

1950—Bill Sonner, Ohio State . . . . 59.1s.
1951—Richard Thoman, Yale . . . . 57.5s.
1952—Jack Taylor, Ohio State . . . . 57.3s.
1953—Yoshi Oyakawa, Ohio State . . . . . . 56.9s.
1954—Yoshinobu Oyakawa, Ohio State . . . 57s.
1955—Yoshinobu Oyakawa, Ohio State . . . 58s.
1956—Lincoln Hurring, Iowa . . . . 58.1s.
1957—Charles Krepp, North Carolina . . . . 58.1s.
1958—James Dolbey, Yale . . . . 57.8s.
1959—Frank McKinney, Indiana . . . . 56.1s.
1960—Charles Bittick, Southern California 54.4s.
1961—Charles Bittick, Southern California 53.9s.
1962—L.B. Schaefer, Ohio State . . . . 53.9s.
1963—Bob Bennett, Southern California . . 53.8s.
1964—Bob Bennett, Southern California . . 53.1s.
1965—Gary Dilley, Michigan State . . . . . . 52.6s.
1966—Gary Dilley, Michigan State . . . . . 52.30s.
1967—Charles Hickcox, Indiana . . . . 53.17s.
1968—Charles Hickcox, Indiana . . . . 52.20s.
1969—Fred Haywood, Stanford . . . . 52.44s.
1970—Larry Barbiere, Indiana . . . . 51.91s.
1971—Santiago Esteva, Indiana . . . . 51.72s.
1972—Paul Gilbert, Yale . . . . 51.29s.

200-Yard Backstroke

1951—Jack Taylor, Ohio State . . . . . . 2m.07.3s.
1952—Yoshi Oyakawa, Ohio State . . . 2m.07.3s.
1953—Yoshi Oyakawa, Ohio State . . . 2m.05.1s.
1954—Yoshinobu Oyakawa, Ohio State 2m.09.8s.
1955—Yoshinobu Oyakawa, Ohio State 2m.07.7s.
1956—Lincoln Hurring, Iowa . . . . 2m.07.5s.
1957—Charles Krepp, North Carolina . 2m.07.8s.
1958—Dave Pemberton, Northwestern 2m.08.0s.
1959—Frank McKinney, Indiana . . . . . 2m.01.4s.
1960—Charles Bittick, Southern
    California . . . . 2m.00.1s.
1961—Charles Bittick, Southern
    California . . . . 1m.57.1s.
1962—L.B. Schaefer, Ohio State . . . . . 1m.58.7s.
1963—Ed Bartsch, Michigan . . . . 1m.57.8s.
1964—Jed Graef, Princeton . . . . 1m.56.2s.

1965—Gary Dilley, Michigan State . . . 1m.56.2s.
1966—Gary Dilley, Michigan State . . 1m.56.41s.
1967—Charles Hickcox, Indiana . . . . . 1m.55.3s.
1968—Charles Hickcox, Indiana . . . . 1m.54.60s.
1969—Charles Hickcox, Indiana . . . . 1m.53.67s.
1970—Mitch Ivey, Long Beach St. . . . 1m.52.77s.
1971—Gary Hall, Indiana . . . . 1m.50.60s.
1972—Charlie Campbell, Princeton . . 1m.50.55s.

100-Yard Breast Stroke

1957—Julian Dyason, Oklahoma . . . . . . 1m.03s.
1958—Franklin Modine, Michigan State 1m.05.2s.
1959—Gordon Collett, Oklahoma . . . . 1m.03.2s.
1960—Thomas Peterson, Stanford . . . . 1m.03.1s.
1961—Richard Nelson, Michigan . . . . . 1m.02.1s.
1962—Richard Nelson, Michigan . . . . . 1m.01.7s.
1963—Gardiner Green, Princeton—Dick
    Nelson, Michigan (tie) . . . 1m.02.3s.
1964—Bill Craig, Southern California . . . . 59.9s.
1965—Bill Craig, Southern California . 1m.00.3s.
1966—Paul Scheerer, Michigan . . . . . 1m.00.43s.
1967—Kenneth Merten, SMU . . . . 58.54s.
1968—Dick Nesbit, Texas . . . . 59.11s.
1969—Don McKenzie, Indiana . . . . 58.36s.
1970—Brian Job, Stanford . . . . 57.57s.
1971—Brian Job, Stanford . . . . 57.25s.
1972—Tom Bruce, U.C.L.A. . . . . 56.99s.

200-Yard Breast Stroke

1925—John Faricy, Minnesota . . . . . . 2m.40.6s.
1926—H. Charles Allan Jr., Navy . . . **2m.44.7s.
1927—Winston Kratz, Wisconsin . . . **2m.46.3s.
1928—Walter R. Schott, Williams . . . . 2m.39.7s.
1929—Moles, Princeton . . . . 2m.35s.
1930—Moles, Princeton . . . . 2m.36.6s.
1931—John A. Schmieler, Michigan . . 2m.35.6s.
1932—John A. Schmieler, Michigan . . 2m.33.4s.
1933—Donald Horn, Northwestern . . . 2m.29.8s.
1934—Walter Savell Jr., Yale . . . . 2m.30.8s.
1935—Jack Kasley, Michigan . . . . 2m.28.7s.
1936—Jack Kasley, Michigan . . . . 2m.25s.
1937—Jack Kasley, Michigan . . . . 2m.26.6s.
1938—Richard Hough, Princeton . . . . . 2m.23.4s.
1939—Richard Hough, Princeton . . . . . 2m.22s.
1940—John Higgins, Ohio State . . . . . 2m.23.7s.
1941—James Skinner, Michigan . . . . . . 2m.25.9s.
1942—James Skinner, Michigan . . . . . . 2m.23.7s.
1943—Emmet Cashin, Stanford . . . . . . 2m.27.4s.
1944—Carl Paulson, Brown . . . . 2m.28.3s.
1945—Paul Murray, Cornell . . . . 2m.31.2s.
1946—Charles Keating, Cincinnati . . . . 2m.26.2s.
1947—Joe Verdeur, La Salle . . . . 2m.16.8s.
1948—Joe Verdeur, La Salle . . . . 2m.14.7s.
1949—Keith Carter, Purdue . . . . 2m.14.8s.
1950—Robert Brawner, Princeton . . . . 2m.14.3s.
1951—Robert Brawner, Princeton . . . . 2m.18.6s.
1952—John Davies, Michigan . . . . 2m.12.9s.
1953—Gerald Holan, Ohio State . . . . . 2m.14s.
1954—Dave Hawkins, Harvard . . . . 2m.15.4s.
1955—Robert Mattson, North Carolina
    State . . . . 2m.26s.
1956—Richard Fadgen, North Carolina
    State . . . . 2m.23.1s.

1957—Cy Hopkins, Michigan . . . . 2m.20.7s.
1958—Franklin Modine, Michigan State 2m.25.4s.
1959—William Mulliken, Miami (Ohio) 2m.21.3s.
1960—Ronald Clark, Michigan . . . . . . 2m.17.6s.
1961—Ronald Clark, Michigan . . . . . . 2m.13.4s.
1962—Virgil Lukin, Minnesota . . . . . . 2m.16.8s.
1963—Martin Hull, Stanford . . . . 2m.17.0s.
1964—Bill Craig, Southern California . 2m.12.1s.
1965—Tom Trethewey, Indiana . . . . . 2m.10.4s.
1966—Wayne Anderson, Southern
      California . . . . 2m.14.24s.
1967—Kenneth Merten, SMU . . . . 2m.07.9s.
1968—Phil Long, Yale . . . . 2m.11.72s.
1969—Mike Dirksen, Oregon . . . . 2m.08.62s.
1970—Brian Job, Stanford . . . . 2m.05.99s.
1971—Brian Job, Stanford . . . . 2m.03.40s.
1972—Brian Job, Stanford . . . . 2m.02.59s.

100-Yard Butterfly

1950—Robert Brawner, Princeton . . . . 59.9s.
1951—Robert Brawner, Princeton . . . . 1m.01.8s.
1952—John Davies, Michigan . . . . 58.8s.
1953—Robert Clemons, Illinois . . . . . . 1m.00.7s.
1954—David Hawkins, Harvard . . . . 59.4s.
1957—Tim Jecko, Yale . . . . 54.6s.
1958—Tony Tashnick, Michigan . . . . 54.6s.
1959—David Gillanders, Michigan . . . . . . 54.1s.
1960—Mike Troy, Indiana . . . . 53.1s.
1961—David Gillanders, Michigan . . . . . . 52.9s.
1962—Edward Spencer, North Carolina
      State . . . . 52.5s.
1963—Walter Richardson, Minnesota . . . . 51.6s.
1964—Walter Richardson, Minnesota . . . . 50.2s.
1965—Fred Schmidt, Indiana . . . . 51.0s.
1966—Phil Riker, North Carolina . . . . . . 51.19s.
1967—Ross Wales, Princeton . . . . 50.02s.
1968—Doug Russell, Texas . . . . 49.50s.
1969—Mark Spitz, Indiana . . . . 49.69s.
1970—Mark Spitz, Indiana . . . . 49.82s.
1971—Mark Spitz, Indiana . . . . 49.42s.
1972—Mark Spitz, Indiana . . . . 47.98s.

200-Yard Butterfly

1955—Philip Drake, North Carolina . . 2m.13.7s.
1956—Richard Fadgen, North Carolina
      State . . . . 2m.16.3s.
1957—Tim Jecko, Yale . . . . 2m.09.5s.
1958—Tony Tashnick, Michigan . . . . . 2m.04.2s.
1959—David Gillanders, Michigan . . . . 2m.02.5s.
1960—Mike Troy, Indiana . . . . 1m.57.8s.
1961—David Gillanders, Michigan . . . . 1m.58.6s.
1962—Arthur Wolfe, Ohio State . . . . . 1m.58.0s.
1963—Dick McDonough, Villanova . . . 1m.57.3s.
1964—Fred Schmidt, Indiana . . . . 1m.53.5s.
1965—Fred Schmidt, Indiana . . . . 1m.51.4s.
1966—Carl Robie, Michigan . . . . 1m.53.83s.
1967—Carl Robie, Michigan . . . . 1m.52.59s.
1968—Phil Houser, So. California . . . 1m.52.55s.
1969—John Ferris, Stanford . . . . 1m.49.61s.
1970—Mike Burton, U.C.L.A. . . . . . . 1m.51.60s.
1971—Mark Spitz, Indiana . . . . 1m.50.10s.
1972—Mark Spitz, Indiana . . . . 1m.46.89s.

200-Yard Individual Medley

1956—Albert Wiggins, Ohio State . . . . 2m.07.5s.
1957—Tim Jecko, Yale . . . . 2m.09.4s.
1958—Joe Hunsaker, Illinois . . . . 2m.09.6s.
1959—George Harrison, Stanford . . . . 2m.06.7s.
1960—Lance Larson, So. California . . . 2m.03.2s.
1961—John Kelso, Denver . . . . 2m.02.9s.
1962—Marty Mull, Ohio State . . . . . . 2m.02.3s.
1963—Marty Mull, Ohio State . . . . . . 2m.01.6s.
1964—Roy Saari, So. California . . . . . 1m.56.7s.
1965—Bob Hopper, Ohio State . . . . . . 1m.58.1s.
1966—Bill Utley, Indiana . . . . 1m.58.55s.
1967—Richard Roth, Stanford . . . . . 1m.56.09s.
1968—Charles Hickcox, Indiana . . . . 1m.52.56s.
1969—Charles Hickcox, Indiana . . . . 1m.54.43s.
1970—Frank Heckl, So. California . . 1m.55.21s.
1971—Gary Hall, Indiana . . . . 1m.52.20s.
1972—Gary Hall, Indiana . . . . 1m.51.51s.

400-Yard Individual Medley

1963—Ed Townsend, Yale . . . . 4m.22.5s.
1964—Richard McGeagh, Southern
      California . . . . 4m.16.4s.
1965—Carl Robie, Michigan . . . . 4m.16.6s.
1966—Ken Webb, Indiana . . . . 4m.19.81s.
1967—Richard Roth, Stanford . . . . . 4m.12.11s.
1968—Bill Utley, Indiana . . . . 4m.10.85s.
1969—Hans Fassnacht, Long
      Beach St. . . . . 4m.07.77s.
1970—Gary Hall, Indiana . . . . 4m.07.31s.
1971—Gary Hall, Indiana . . . . 3m.58.25s.
1972—Gary Hall, Indiana . . . . 3m.58.71s.

440-Yard Free-Style Relay

1931—Rutgers (George H. Kojac, Nor-
    man M. Kramer, Charles B. Sunder-
    land, John A. Dryfuss) . . . . 3m.39.6s.
1932—Northwestern (Paul Troup, Wilson,
    Arthur Highland, Merton Wilcox) . . 3m.36.6s.
1933—Rutgers (Theodore Brick, Walter
    Ashley, N. M. Krammer, Walter
    Spence) . . . . 3m.39.4s.
1934—Michigan (Julian Robertson,
    Ogden R. Dalrymple, Henry C. Ka-
    menski, Robert J. Renner) . . . . 3m.37.6s.
1935—Michigan (Taylor Drysdale, Robert
    J. Renner, Julian Robertson, Ogden
    R. Dalrymple) . . . . 3m.38.4s.
1936—Iowa (Adolph Jacobsmeyer, Robert
    Christians, Ray Walters, Jack Sieg) . 3m.35.5s.
1937—Michigan (Waldemar Tomski, Tom
    Haynie, Ed Kirar, G. Robert Mow-
    erson) . . . . 3m.32.2s.
1938—Michigan (Waldemar Tomski, Ed-
    ward Hutchens, Tom Haynie, Ed
    Kirar) . . . . 3m.32.7s.
1939—Michigan (Charles L. Barker, Ed-
    ward Hutchens, Tom Haynie, Walde-
    mar Tomski) . . . . 3m.33.5s.
1940—Michigan (Edward Hutchens, John
    C. Gillis, Charles L. Barker, John J.
    Sharamet) . . . . 3m.31s.

1941—Yale (Howard Johnson, Richard
Kelly, Edward Pope, Thomas Britton)3m.31.3s.
1942—Michigan (William D. Burton,
Louis P. Kivi, John R. Patten, John
J. Sharamet) .... 3m.27.8s.
1943—Michigan (Harry Holiday, John
R. Patten, Merton Church, Ace R.
Cory) .... 3m.31.1s.
1944—Michigan (Merton Church,
Charles C. Fries, William E. Kogen,
Gurdon S. H. Pulford) .... 3m.35s.
1945—Michigan (Charles C. Fries, William
Breen, Gurdon S. H. Pulford,
Merton Church) .... 3m.39.8s.
1946—Michigan State (Zigmund Indyke,
John DeMond, James Quigley, Robert
K. Alwardt) .... 3m.37.2s.
1947—Ohio State (William Zemer, Ted
Hobert, Halo Hirose, Bill Smith) ... 3m.30.0s.
1948—Michigan State (Abel O. Gilbert,
George Hoogerhyde, Robert K. All-
wardt, James R. Duke) .... 3m.31s.
1949—Yale (Paul Girds, Bill Farnsworth,
Larry Munson, Ray Reid) .... 3m.27s.
1950—Yale (Bill Farnsworth, Larry Munson, John Blum, Ray Reid) .... 3m.27.9s.
1951—Michigan State (David Hoffman,
James Quigley, Clarke Scholes, George
Hoogergyde) .... 3m.26.7s.
1952—Michigan (Thomas Benner, Burwell
Jones, Donald Hill, Wallace Jeffries) 3m.25.7s.
1953—Michigan (Ron Gora, Burwell
Jones, Thomas Benner, Donald Hill) . 3m.24s.
1954—Michigan (Tom Benner, Ron Gora,
Don Hill, Burwell Jones) .... 3m.26.1s.
1955—Yale (Rex Aubrey, Hendrik Gideonse, Dan Cornwell, Malcolm Aldrich) .... 3m.24.9s.
1956—Yale (Dan Cornwell, Joe Robinson, Dave Armstrong, Hendrik
Gideonse) .... 3m.23.1s.
1957—Yale (Russ Hibbard, Dan Cornwell, Dave Armstrong, Rex Aubrey) 3m.23.8s.
1958—Ohio State (Bob Connell, Charles
Bechtel, Dick Dewey, Joe Van
Horn) .... 3m.23.1s.
1959—Michigan (John McGuire, Carl Woolley,
Dick Hanley, Frank Legacki) ..... 3m.21.6s.
1960—Southern California (Donald Red-
ington, Robert Moulton, Lance
Larson, Jon Henrichs) .... 3m.18.5s.
1961—Harvard (Robert Kaufman, Alan
Engelberg, William Zentgraf,
Bruce Hunter) .... 3m.18.3s.
1962—Michigan State (Jeff Mattson, Doug
Rowe, Bill Wood, Mike Wood) .... 3m.15.8s.
1963—Yale (C. Mussman, E. Townsend,
D. Lyons, M. Austin) .... 3m.13.5s.
1964—Yale (D. Lyons, E. Townsend,
F. Rice, M. Austin) .... 3m.08.7s.
1965—Yale (D. Lyons, D. Kennedy,
R. Townsend, S. Clark .... 3m.07.2s.

1966—Southern California (S. Gilchrist,
J. Lambert, K. Krueger, R. Saari) ... 3m.08.5s.
1967—Stanford (L. Nicolao, W. Meyer,
D. Manning, J. Laney) .... 3m.04.9s.
1968—Yale (S. Job, J. Nelson, R. Waples,
D. Schollander .... 3m.04.10s.
1969—Southern California (D. Frawley, R. Kidder, F. Heckl, D.
Havens) .... 3m.02.77s.
1970—Southern California (G. Charlton,
M. Mader, D. Frawley, R. Lyon) .. 3m.03.91s.
1971—Southern California (K. Tutt, J.
McConica, M. Weston, F. Heckl) .. 3m.02.38s.
1972—Tennessee (K. Knox, T. Lutz,
D. Edgar, J. Trembley) .... 3m.01.11s.

800-Yard Free-Style Relay

1966—Indiana (B. Utley, S. Cordin,
K. Webb, R. Windle) .... 7m.06.64s.
1967—Stanford (R. Roth, P. Siebert,
M. Wall G. Buckingham) .... 6m.54.5s.
1968—Yale (D. Schneider, J. Nelson,
D. Johnson, D. Schollander) ..... 6m.50.77s.
1969—Southern California (G. Watson,
M. Mader, G. Charlton, F. Heckl) .. 6m.49.50s.
1970—Southern California (G. Charlton,
G. Fink, M. Mader, J. McConica) .. 6m.51.77s.
1971—Southern California (J. McConica,
K. Tutt, T. McBreen, F. Heckl) ... 6m.39.04s.
1972—Southern California (E. Mc-
Cleskey, S. Tyrrell, T. McBreen,
J. McConica) .... 6m.38.63s.

400-Yard Medley Relay

1957—Michigan (Don Adamski, Cy Hopkins, Fred Mowrey, Dick Hanley
and Michigan State (Don Nichols,
Paul Reinke, Roger Harmon, Frank
Parish) tie .... 3m.50s.
1958—Yale (James Dolbey, Joe Koletsky,
Tim Jecko, Charles Bronston) ..... 3m.46.8s.
1959—Michigan (John Smith, Ron Clark,
David Gillanders, Dick Hanley) .... 3m.46.1s.
1960—Indiana (Frank McKinney, Gerald
Miki, Mike Troy, Peter Sintz) ...... 3m.40.8s.
1961—Ohio State (L.B. Schaefer, Tom
Kovacs, Arthur Wolfe, John Plain) . 3m.40.3s.
1962—Ohio State (L.B. Shaefer, Tom
Kovacs, Arthur Wolfe, John Plain) . 3m.37.6s.
1963—Minnesota (W. Ericksen, V. Luken,
W. Richardson, S. Jackman) ..... 3m.35.2s.
1964—Southern California (R. Bennett,
W. Craig, J. McGrath, R. Saari) ..... 3m.30.9s.
1965—Indiana (G. Hammer, T. Trethe-
wey, F. Schmidt, R. Williamson) ... 3m.30.7s.
1966—Michigan (R. Kingery, P. Scheerer,
C. Robie, W. Groft) .... 3m.33.36s.
1967—U.C.L.A. (M. Berger, R. Webb,
S. Cole, Z. Zorn) .... 3m.29.5s.
1968—Texas (D. Russell, J. Nesbit, C.
Smith, E. Siefert) .... 3m.31.53s.
1969—Indiana (C. Hickcox, D. Mc-
Kenzie, S. Borowski, B. Bateman). . 3m.25.89s.

1970—Stanford (F. Haywood, B. Job,
J. Ferris, S. Carey) ....3m.24.99s.
1971—Stanford (F. Haywood, B. Job,
J. Ferris, M. Pedley) ....3m.22.51s.
1972—Southern California (B. Kocsis,
D. Mayekawa, F. Heckl, M.
Weston) ....3m.23.11s.

One-Meter Springboard Diving

1924—Robert E. Galbraith, Rutgers ....
1925—Walter Krissell, Columbia ....
1926—William C. O'Brien, Illinois ....
1927—Walter Colbath, Northwestern ....
1928—Walter Colbath, Northwestern ....
1929—Walter Colbath, Northwestern ....
1930—Ed Throndsen, Stanford 109.20
1931—34—No competition
1935—Frank Fehsenfeld, Michigan 105.02
1936—Derland Johnston, Michigan 131.40
1937—Jim Patterson, Ohio State 135.80
1938—Al Patnik, Ohio State 145.14
1939—Al Patnik, Ohio State 131.08
1940—Al Patnik, Ohio State 147.04
1941—Earl Clark, Ohio State 144.90
1942—Frank Dempsey, Ohio State 134.80
1943—Frank Dempsey, Ohio State 141.12
1944—Charles Batterman, Columbia 122.40
1945—Hobart Billingsley, Ohio State ... 121.90
1946—Miller Anderson, Ohio State 101.96
1947—Miller Anderson, Ohio State 151.10
1948—Bruce Harlan, Ohio State 163.87
1949—Bruce Harlan, Ohio State 142.41
1950—Bruce Harlan, Ohio State 145.00
1951—David Browning, Texas 131.43
1952—David Browning, Texas 324.20
1953—Jerry Harrison, Ohio State 485.75
1954—Fletcher Gilders, Ohio State 444.10
1955—Fletcher Gilders, Ohio State 535.05
1956—Frank Fraunfelter, Ohio State ... 514.10
1957—Dick Kimball, Michigan 401.65
1958—Don Harper, Ohio State 481.25
1959—Ron O'Brien, Ohio State 468.95
1960—Sam Hall, Ohio State 510.35
1961—Curtis Genders, Florida State 459.40
1962—Louis Vitucci, Ohio State 470.50
1963—Lou Vitucci, Ohio State 489.70
1964—Richard Gilbert, Indiana 491.70
1965—Ken Sitzberger, Indiana 511.25
1966—Ken Sitzberger, Indiana 488.50
1967—Ken Sitzberger, Indiana 510.25
1968—Jim Henry, Indiana 512.05
1969—Jim Henry, Indiana 531.06
1970—Jim Henry, Indiana 487.56
1971—Mike Finneran, Ohio State 520.98
1972—Todd Smith, Ohio State 508.25

Three-Meter Spring Board Diving

1931—Mickey Riley, Southern Calif..... 134.04
1932—Mickey Riley, Southern Calif..... 146.76
1933—Richard K. Degener, Michigan ... 133.88
1934—Richard K. Degener, Michigan ... 154.64
1935—Frank Fehsenfeld, Michigan 124.40
1936—Frank Fehsenfeld, Michigan 146.22

1937—Ben Grady, Michigan 136.46
1938—Al Patnik, Ohio State 143.92
1939—Al Patnik, Ohio State 161.34
1940—Earl Clark, Ohio State 166.82
1941—Earl Clark, Ohio State 165.40
1942—Frank Dempsey, Ohio State 151.20
1943—Frank Dempsey, Ohio State 155.68
1944—Charles Batterman, Columbia 138.56
1945—Hobart Billingsley, Ohio State ... 132.10
1946—Miller Anderson, Ohio State 118.10
1947—Miller Anderson, Ohio State 172.62
1948—Bruce Harlan, Ohio State ..,..... 174.34
1949—Bruce Harlan, Ohio State 152.37
1950—Bruce Harlan, Ohio State 153.65
1951—David Browning, Texas 144.75
1952—David Browning, Texas 586.40
1953—Robert Clotworthy, Ohio State ... 525.8
1954—Morley Shapiro, Ohio State 530
1955—Gerry Harris, Ohio State 590.25
1956—Don Harper, Ohio State 505.3
1957—Dick Kimball, Michigan 441.35
1958—Don Harper, Ohio State 518.9
1959—Sam Hall, Ohio State 465.10
1960—Sam Hall, Ohio State 503.6
1961—Louis Vitucci, Ohio State 491.65
1962—Louis Vitucci, Ohio State 506.45
1963—Lou Vitucci, Ohio State 496.90
1964—Randall Larson, Ohio State 523.75
1965—Ken Sitzberger, Indiana 565.05
1966—Bernie Wrightson, Arizona St..... 538.90
1967—Ken Sitzberger, Indiana 572.40
1968—Keith Russell, Arizona State 494.55
1969—Jim Henry, Indiana 574.68
1970—Jim Henry, Indiana 550.59
1971—Phil Boggs, Florida State 552.93
1972—Craig Lincoln, Minnesota 545.44

Team

(Only individual competition from 1924 through 1936.)

1937—41—Michigan
1942—Yale
1943—Ohio State
1944—Yale
1945—47—Ohio State
1948—Michigan
1949—52—Ohio State
1953—Yale
1954—56—Ohio State
1957—59—Michigan
1960—Southern California
1961—Michigan
1962—Ohio State
1963—66—Southern California
1967—Stanford
1968—72—Indiana

Eastern Intercollegiate League

1937—38—Harvard
1939—43—Yale
1944—Navy
1945—Army

1946–Navy	1922–Minnesota
1947–60–Yale	1923–25–Northwestern
1961–Navy, Yale (tie)	1926–Minnesota
1962–Harvard	1927–29–Michigan
1963–65–Yale	1930–Northwestern
1966–Army	1931–35–Michigan
1967–70–Yale	1936–Iowa
1971–Pennsylvania	1937–Michigan
1972–Princeton	1938–Ohio State
	1939–42–Michigan
Big Ten	1943–Ohio State
1911–13–Illinois	1944–45–Michigan
1914–15–Northestern	1946–47–Ohio State
1916–Chicago, Northwestern (tie)	1948–Michigan
1917–18–Northwestern	1949–56–Ohio State
1919–Chicago	1957–Michigan State
1920–Northwestern	1958–60–Michigan
1921–Chicago	1961–72–Indiana

World Records

(Accepted by the International Amateur Swimming Federation as of October, 1972)
Note: Effective June 1, 1969, FINA will recognize only records made over a 50-meter course.

MEN

Free-Style

Distance	Time	Holder	Country	Made at	Date
100 mtrs	0:51.22 ...	Mark Spitz	U.S.A.	Munich	Sept. 3, 1972
200 mtrs. ...	1:52.78 ...	Mark Spitz	U.S.A.	Munich	Aug. 29, 1972
400 mtrs. ...	4:00.11 ...	Kurt Krumpholtz	U.S.A.	Chicago	Aug. 4, 1972
800 mtrs. ...	8:23.8	Brad Cooper	Australia	Sydney	Jan. 12, 1972
1,500 mtrs. ...	15:52.58 ...	Mike Burton	U.S.A.	Munich	Sept. 4, 1972

Breast Stroke

100 mtrs.	1:04.94	Nobutaka Taguchi	Japan	Munich	Aug. 30, 1972
200 mtrs.	2:21.55	John Hencken	U.S.A.	Munich	Sept. 2, 1972

Butterfly Stroke

100 mtrs.	0:54.27	Mark Spitz	U.S.A.	Munich	Sept. 1, 1972
200 mtrs.	2:00.70	Mark Spitz	U.S.A.	Munich	Aug. 28, 1972

Back Stroke

100 mtrs.	0:56.58	Roland Matthes	East Germany	Munich	Aug. 29, 1972
200 mtrs.	2:02.82	Roland Matthes	East Germany	Munich	Sept. 2, 1972

Individual Medley

200 mtrs.	2:17.17	Gunnar Larsson	Sweden	Munich	Sept. 3, 1972
400 mtrs.	4:30.81	Gary Hall	U.S.A.	Chicago	Aug. 3, 1972

Medley Relays

400 mtrs.	3:48.16	National Team	U.S.A.	Munich	Sept. 4, 1972

(M. Stamm, T. Bruce, M. Spitz, J. Heidenreich)

Free-Style Relays

400 mtrs.	3:26.42	National Team	U.S.A.	Munich	Aug. 28, 1972

(D. Edgar, J. Murphy, J. Heidenreich, M. Spitz)

800 mtrs.	7:38.78	National Team	U.S.A.	Munich	Aug. 31, 1972

(J. Kinsella, F. Tyler, S. Genter, M. Spitz)

WOMEN

Free-Style

100 mtrs. ...	0:58.5	Shane Gould	Australia	Sydney	Jan. 8, 1972
200 mtrs. ...	2:03.56 ...	Shane Gould	Australia	Munich	Sept. 1, 1972

400 mtrs.	...	4:19.04	...	Shane Gould	....	Australia	...	Munich	....	Aug. 30, 1972
800 mtrs.	...	8:53.68	...	Keena Rothhammer	U.S.A.	.....	Munich	....	Sept. 3, 1972
1,500 mtrs.	...	17:00.6	....	Shane Gould	....	Australia	...	Sydney	....	Dec. 12, 1971

Breast Stroke

| 100 mtrs. | ..... | 1:13.58 | .... | Cathy Carr | ...... | U.S.A. | ..... | Munich | .... | Sept. 2, 1972 |
| 200 mtrs. | ..... | 2:38.5 | .... | Catie Ball | .... | U.S.A. | ..... | Los Angeles | ...... | Aug. 26, 1968 |

Butterfly Stroke

| 100 mtrs. | ..... | 1:03.34 | .... | Mayumi Aoki | .... | Japan | ...... | Munich | .... | Sept. 1, 1972 |
| 200 mtrs. | ..... | 2:15.57 | .... | Karen Moe | ...... | U.S.A. | ..... | Munich | .... | Sept. 4, 1972 |

Back Stroke

| 100 mtrs. | ..... | 1:05.6 | ..... | Karen Muir | ...... | So. Africa | .. | Utrecht | .... | July 6, 1969 |
| 200 mtrs. | ..... | 2:19.19 | .... | Melissa Belote | .... | U.S.A. | ..... | Munich | .... | Sept. 4, 1972 |

Individual Medley

| 200 mtrs. | ..... | 2:23.07 | .... | Shane Gould | .... | Australia | ... | Munich | .... | Aug. 28, 1972 |
| 400 mtrs. | ..... | 5:02.97 | .... | Gail Neall | .... | Australia | ... | Munich | .... | Aug. 31, 1972 |

Medley Relays

| 400 mtrs. | ..... | 4:20.75 | .... | National Team | ... | U.S.A. | ..... | Munich | .... | Sept. 3, 1972 |

(M. Belote, C. Carr, D. Deardurff, S. Neilson)

Free-Style Relays

| 400 mtrs. | ..... | 3:55.19 | .... | National Team | ... | U.S.A. | ..... | Munich | .... | Aug. 30, 1972 |

(S. Neilson, J. Kemp, J. Barkman, S. Babaschoff)

IMPORTANT RULES AND STROKES

(From "Sports for Recreation," published by A. S. Barnes and Co., New York.)

Rules

1. In dual meets, generally two men from each team are allowed in an event.

2. As a general rule, a contestant is not allowed to take part in more than 3 events.

3. Points are usually scored as follows in dual meets: *free-style relay*—first place 8 points, second place 4; *medley relay*—first place 6, second place 3; *all other events*—first place 5, second 3, third 1.

4. At the start the contestants, after lining up behind their starting places, are given the signals: (1) "Take your marks," (2) "Go" or (pistol) shot). Three false starts disqualify a contestant.

5. Disqualification may result if a contestant gets off his course and touches another.

6. A sidestroke movement, if used in the breast stroke, is cause for disqualification.

7. In making a turn while swimming the breast stroke, both hands must touch the end wall of the pool simultaneously. Similarly, at the finish of the breast stroke both hands must touch the pool wall simultaneously.

8. Backstroke swimmers start pushing off from the edge in the water.

9. In making the backstroke turn, contestants are required to let the foremost hand touch the edge of the pool before the turn is made.

Strokes

The common strokes used in swimming are the crawl, the backstroke, the breast stroke, and the side stroke. Variations of these strokes, such as the Trudgen crawl and the single overarm, are valuable for long-distance swimming, recreational swimming and lifesaving. Two breast stroke modifications—the butterfly breast stroke and the fishtail kick—add speed to the breast stroke.

Crawl—The crawl has proved to be, by virtue of the great number of records made with it and by its almost universal usage, the fastest of all swimming strokes. It is used by champions all over the world for both long and short-distance events. The stroke, in addition to offering a maximum of speed with the minimum of waste motion, is graceful without being tiring and is fairly easy to learn.

The stroke is executed with the body prone and flat on the surface of the water; the face is pillowed in the water with the head slightly lifted, water level just above the eyes. The arms operate in alternate pulling motion, with the recovery over the surface of the water—the catch (point at which pull begins) forward, in line with the shoulder. The leg motion (flutter kick) is a series of short alternate up-and-down kicks or beats, with no roll of the hips, working in rhythm with the arms.

Breathing is accomplished by a backward turn and slight raising of the head, exposing the mouth and nose for a brief instance. Inhaling occurs through the mouth at this time. The head is then turned back so that the face is down and the air is completely exhaled through the nose or through the nose and mouth during the time that the face is submerged.

Backstroke—A stroke in which the swimmer is on his back. There are a number of variations to the backstroke, but the comments here concern the racing or alternate-arm stroke. In this, the arms stroke alternately, the recovery being out of water, and do not, as a rule, reach forward quite as directly as in the crawl. The kick is a flutter, with slightly more flexion of the legs, usually six beats to an arm cycle. The backstroke is relatively easy to learn because the actions are similar to the crawl (except that they are performed upside down), and because, with the face upward above the water line, breathing is not a problem. The body is almost straight, with a slight arch from the neck toward the waist, a position easy to attain if the swimmer does not attempt to arch the head too far back in the water. Care must be taken also to refrain from sitting up in the water.

Breast Stroke—The major difference between the crawl and the breast stroke is that the breast stroke requires simultaneous action of both arms of also of both legs, while the crawl requires alternate action. The swimmer is on his breast in the water, and both hands move forward together and draw back simultaneously, the shoulders parallel to the water surface and at right angles to the forward progress. The legs must be drawn up with a distinct bend in the knees, followed by a kicking outward and backward with a separation of the legs laterally. Then the body glides, arms and legs fully extended, toes pointed. The glide is the beginning and end of breast stroking. From the glide position, all three of the breast stroke variations begin—the conventional, the butterfly, and the fishtail.

Sidestroke—A stroke with the body on the side. Arms alternately reach forward under water and, on the pull, sweep to the same side of the swimmer. The kick is the scissors. If one arm recovers out of water, the stroke is called a side overarm. This stroke is not fast and, accordingly, is not used in competition. Both types of sidestroke are excellent for long-distance swimming, where speed is a secondary consideration. It is a restful stroke and can be swum on either side.

By pushing off from shallow water on the edge of the pool, the swimmer comes into a gliding position on the right side, bottom arm extended, and the top arm kept at the thigh. Pull downward with the bottom arm and make a wide sweeping oval. The arm, straight at first, bends as it nears the stomach and then relaxes. While this bottom arm sweep is being made, slide the top arm gradually along past the shoulder and straight out in front, arriving at the extended position just as the bottom arm is being relaxed. Then the top arm makes a similar downward pull. Relax it at about the time the hand reaches the thigh. Meanwhile the bottom arm is recovering by being lifted to the surface of the water and then being straightened out to the starting position.

The kick for the sidestroke is known as the scissors. In the glide position the feet and legs are together. As the bottom arm starts its downward sweep, bring the knees up as though in a running stride position: the bottom leg moves forward and the top leg draws backward, both moving in a plane parallel to the water's surface. Snap the legs together—feet and legs extended—as the bottom arm completes the downward pull.

Inhale through the mouth as the bottom arm is recovering. Exhale through the nose or through the nose and mouth as the downward pull of the bottom arm is being made.

Trudgen Crawl—A double overarm stroke in which the swimmer uses alternate arms, always breathing on the flutter and the scissors kicks. Unlike the crawl, there is a pronounced roll to the side in breathing. Start on the right side, right arm extended, left arm at side of the thigh. The right or bottom arm pulls downward in a long sweep and, as it nears the thigh, the left or top arm starts its recovery. This recovery of the top arm rolls the body from a sideward position to a face downward position. As the top arm catches in the water and starts its downward pull, the bottom arm makes its recovery.

The legs execute a four-beat flutter kick while the bottom arm makes its downward sweep or pull; and then make a scissors kick while the top arm is making its downward pull.

As the downward pull of the top arm is being made, the head is pivoting ready for the inhalation; then, as the top arm recovers, the head has become submerged and exhaling takes place as the bottom arm is making its pull.

Single Overarm—The single overarm stroke is one in which only one of the arms recovers out of the water. By pushing off from shallow water or from the pool's edge, the swimmer comes into a gliding position, lying on the right side, bottom arm extended, top arm held along the side with hand on the thigh. The bottom arm pulls downward. The arm, straight at first, bends as it nears the stomach, then relaxes. While the bottom arm sweep is being made, lift the top arm from its position at the hip out of the water, with elbow high. Bend the elbow as the arm passes the head; then extend the arm so that the hand dips into the water as far over the head as it can reach (recovery.) The fingertips just clear the water. Then make the downward pull of the arm through the water until the arm comes back to its original start position. This lifting of the top arm out of the water during recovery marks the only difference between the sidestroke and the single overarm stroke. The leg movement and the breathing are the same as for the sidestroke.

Butterfly Breast Stroke—A stroke in which the recovery of the arms is out of water, the body lunging to some degree out of water. The pull-through of the arms is longer than in the conventional breast stroke, and the leg propulsion comes as the arms are at the top of their pull. This stroke requires considerable strength and is difficult to do for an appreciable distance.

In short distances, faster times can be made than if the regular breast stroke were used. Pull the arms straight down through the water; do not use the sweeping motion described for the conventional breast stroke. Recover the arms over the surface of the water after they have reached a position slightly below and behind the shoulder.

If the arms are carried farther back, the face and body will be pulled under the water. After the arms have reached the end of the pull, bend the elbows. They lead the arms on the recovery. As the elbows break the surface of the water, the shoulders flip or throw the arms forward over the surface of the water, with the palms of the hands down. As soon as the hands enter the water, start the stroke again. There is no glide in this stroke. The leg movement is the same as for the conventional breast stroke.

Take the breath as the arms reach the midpoint of the downward pull. Lift the face above the surface of the water and inhale and then return it under the water to exhale prior to the recovery of the arms.

Fishtail—In this variation of the breast stroke, the arm stroke is the same as that discussed under the butterfly breast stroke but the kick is entirely different. The legs are kept together and an undulating motion, starting with the hips, passes down the legs. As the motion continues down the legs, the front of the thighs and legs engages the water with the maximum pressure terminating on the lower leg. The pressure developed as a result of the up-and-down thrashing of the legs alternates first on the front of the leg and then on the back of the leg. This kick obtains propulsive force on both the upward and downward thrust of the legs, and eliminates both the resistance of the water on the recovery and the recovery of the legs as in the conventional breast stroke kick.

TABLE TENNIS

(Courtesy of Mrs. Ping Neuberger, Historian, United States Table Tennis Association, 35 West 92nd Street, New York, New York, 10025)

Table tennis is a game played upon a table, usually by two contestants with a small celluloid ball and rackets. The table is 9 ft. long by 5 ft. wide, and its upper surface must be 30 inches from the floor. The table is divided into courts by a white stripe running down its center. These courts are ignored for singles play. Thus, the service can be hit to any part of the playing area. The surface of a standard table is made of three-quarter-inch 5-ply wood, the resiliency of which is such that a standard table tennis ball, when dropped from a height of 12 inches, will rebound to a height of from 8 to 9 inches. Across the center of the table and projecting 6 inches on either side is fixed a net 6 inches high. The celluloid ball is hollow, and from 4½ to 4¾ inches in circumference and between 37 and 39 grains in weight. The rackets may be any shape but usually are oval and made of wood, covered with pimpled rubber or sponge that may be pimpled or inverted, not to exceed 4 mm. on either side.

The essential feature of the game is the stroking of the ball back and forth over the net by the players until one misses the ball, or hits it into the net or off the table; in each of these cases his opponent scores a point. The game is begun by the server, with the hand flat, ball resting in the center of the palm, projecting the ball vertically upward and hit so that it bounces first on his side of the net, then over the net to his opponent's side. The return of service and every shot that follows, is made by stroking the ball back over the net. The ball must be permitted to bounce once before it is returned. The server starts by serving until a total of 5 points have been scored and then his opponent serves for the next 5 points. A game is won by the player first scoring 21 points; however, if the score is tied at 20 points or "deuce," the service changes after each point until one player gains a two-point advantage.

Net and edge balls (shots that hit either the net or table edge) are played exactly as a solid bounce. When a serve touches the net, but is otherwise a good serve, it is played over with no scoring and no penalty. When a ball hits the side edge instead of the top edge of the table, the player who made the shot loses the point. Doubles play differs from singles play in the following instances: 1. Service must be from the right-hand court into the opponent's right-hand court. 2. Each player must hit alternate shots. 3. Each player (except the first server) receives service for 5 points, then serves for 5 points, after which his partner receives and serves.

The true origin of table tennis is unknown, with four or five versions of how it all started. However, most versions agree that the game started about 1890 by the English army officers stationed in India and enjoyed varying degrees of popularity throughout the world. Equipment manufactured around this period for a game called "indoor tennis" marked the beginning of table tennis in the United States. In 1902 the game was called "whiff-waff," "gossimer," and

"Ping Pong"—the latter being a patented trade name. It swept the country as a craze and died out in the fall of the same year. A simultaneous movement started in several parts of the world about 1921 to revive table tennis as a serious sport. As a result, in 1926 a meeting was held in Berlin and with 7 member nations, created the International Table Tennis Federation, a world organization to promote and improve table tennis. The United States Table Tennis Association was founded in 1933 and controls all the tournaments in the U.S., and annually the Nationals are held consisting of matches in men's singles, men's doubles, women's singles, women's doubles, mixed doubles, junior and senior events. The USTTA joined the ITTF in 1933. The International Federation, composed of over 100 member nations, sponsors individual and team play at the World Championships, since 1957, held every two years. The U.S. now holds 12 world titles.

The USA only sent one player to the Worlds in 1934. Sending its first complete team in 1936, the USA won 2 World Titles, Ruth Aarons winning the Women's Singles and Jimmy McClure and Bud Blattner, the Men's Doubles.

The USA was the first country, in 1937, to win both the Swaythling and Corbillon Cups, a record that was not broken until 17 years later by Japan. The Men's Doubles was won again by Jimmy McClure and Bud Blattner. Ruth Aarons was in the finals of the Women's Singles but no winner was declared that year.

The USA was the first to lower the net to 6 inches and to abolish the finger spin serves, and later the ITTF adopted the American expedite rule.

In 1938, the USA won the Men's Doubles title for the 3rd successive year, by Jimmy McClure and Sol Schiff, who replaced Bud Blattner.

Outside of winning the Corbillon Cup in 1949, the only titles won after the war were two Mixed Doubles by the Thall sisters, Thelma partnered by Dick Miles in 1948 and Leah partnered with Erwin Klein in 1956.

TABLE TENNIS CHAMPIONS
World
(Scheduled every two years beginning in 1957)
Men's Singles
(St. Bride Vase)
1927—Roland Jacobi, Hungary
1928—Zolton Mechlovits, Hungary
1929—Frederick J. Perry, England
1930—Viktor Barna, Hungary
1931—Miklos Szabados, Hungary
1932-35—Viktor Barna, Hungary
1936—Standa Kolar, Czechoslovakia
1937—Richard Bergmann, Austria
1938—Bohumil Vana, Czechoslovakia
1939—Richard Bergmann, Austria
1940-46—No Competition

1947—Bohumil Vana, Czechoslovakia
1948—Richard Bergmann, England
1949—John Leach, England
1950—Richard Bergmann, England
1951—John Leach, England
1952—Hiroji Satoh, Japan
1953—Ferenc Sido, Hungary
1954—Ichiro Ogimura, Japan
1955—Toshihaki Tanaka, Japan
1956—Ichiro Ogimura, Japan
1957—Toshihaki Tanaka, Japan
1959—Jung Kuo-tuan, China
1961—Chuang Tse-tung, China
1963—Chuang Tse-tung, China
1965—Chuang Tse-tung, China
1967—Nobuhiko Hasegawa, Japan
1969—Shigeo Itoh, Japan
1971—Stellan Bengtsson, Sweden

Men's Doubles
(Iran Cup)
1927—R. Jacobi—R. Pecsi, Hungary
1928—A. Liebster—R. Tthum, Austria
1929-32—V. Barna—M. Szabados, Hungary
1933—V. Barna—S. Glancz, Hungary
1934-35—V. Barna—M. Szabados, Hungary
1936-37—Robert Blattner—James McClure, United States
1938—James McClure-Sol Schiff, United States
1939—R. Bergmann, Austria—V. Barna, Hungary
1940-46—No Competition
1947—Vana—Slar, Czechoslovakia
1948—Vana—Steipek, Czechoslovakia
1949—F. Tokar—T. Andreadis, Czechoslovakia
1950—F. Sido—F. Soos, Hungary
1951—B. Vana—I. Andreadis, Czechoslovakia
1952—N. Fujiji—T. Hayashi, Japan
1953—F. Sido—J. Koczian, Hungary
1954—Vilim Harangozo—Zarko Dolimar, Yugoslavia
1955—Ivan Andreadis—Ladislav Stipek, Czechoslovakia
1956—Ichiro Ogimura—Yoshio Tomita, Japan
1957—Ivan Andreadis—Ladislav Stipek, Czechoslovakia
1959—Ichiro Ogimura—Teruo Murakami, Japan
1961—Nobuyo Hoshino—Koji Kimura, Japan
1963—C. Shih-lin—W. Chih-liang, China
1965—C. Tse-tung—H. Yin-sheng, China
1967—Hans Alser—Kjell Johansson, Sweden
1969—Hans Alser—Kjell Johansson, Sweden
1971—Istvan Jonyer—Tibor Klampar, Hungary

Women's Singles
(G. Geist Prize)
1927-31—M. Mednyanszky, Hungary
1932-33—A Sipos, Hungary
1934-35—Marie Kettnerova, Czechoslovakia
1936—Ruth Hughes Aarons, United States
1937—Titled declared vacant*
1938—Trudi Pritzi, Austria
1939—Vlasha Depetrisova, Czechoslovakia
1940-46—No competition

1947-49—Giselle Farkas, Hungary
1950-55—Mrs. Angelica Roseanu, Rumania
1956—Tomi Okawa, Japan
1957—Fujie Eguchi, Japan
1959—Kimiyo Matsuzaki, Japan
1961—Chiu Chung-hui, China
1963—Kimiyo Matsuzaki, Japan
1965—Naoko Fukazu, Japan
1967—Sachiko Morisawa, Japan
1969—Toshiko Kowada, Japan
1971—Lin Hui-ching, China
   *Finalists: Ruth Hughes Aarons, United States, and
Trudi Pritzi, Austria.

Women's Doubles
(W. J. Pope Trophy)

1927—M. Mednyanszky, Hungary—F. Flamm, Austria.
1928—E. Metzger—E. Ruester, Germany
1929-34—M. Mednyanszky—A. Sipos, Hungary
1935—M. Kettnerova—M. Smidova, Czechoslovakia
1936-37—V. Depetrisova—V. Votrubcova, Czechoslovakia
1938—Trudi Pritzi—D. Bussnann, Austria
1939-46—No Competition
1947—Trudi Pritzi, Austria—Giselle Farkas, Hungary
1948—Mrs. Vera Thomas—Peggy Franks, England
1949—Helen Elliot, Scotland—Giselle Farkas, Hungary
1950—Dora Boregi, England—Helen Elliot, Scotland
1951—Diana Rowe—Rosalind Rowe, England
1952—Tonnie Nashimura—Shizuka Narahara, Japan
1953—Mrs. Angelica Roseanu, Rumania—Giselle Farkas, Hungary
1954—Diane and Rosalind Rowe, England
1955-56—Mrs. Angelica Roseanu—Ella Zeller, Rumania
1957—L. Mosoczy—A. Simon, Hungary
1959—Taeko Namba—Kazuko Yamaizumi, Japan
1961—Maria Alexandru—Georgeta Pitica, Rumania
1963—K. Matsuzaki—M. Seki, Japan
1965—Lin Hui-ching—Cheng Min-chin, China
1967—Sachiko Morisawa—Saeko Hirota, Japan
1969—Zoya Rudnova—Svetlana Grinberg, Russia
1971—Lin Hui-ching—Cheng Min-chin, China

Mixed Doubles
(Zdenek Heydusek Prize)
(Men listed first)

1927-28—Zolton Mechlovits—M. Mednyanszky, Hungary
1929—I. Kelen—A. Sipos, Hungary
1930-31—M. Szabados—M. Mednyanszky, Hungary
1932—V. Barna—A. Sipos, Hungary
1933—I. Kelen—M. Mednyanszky, Hungary
1934—M. Szabados—M. Mednyanszky, Hungary
1935—V. Barna—A. Sipos, Hungary

1936—M. Hamr—G. Kleinova, Czechoslovakia
1937—B. Vana—V. Votrubcova, Czechoslovakia
1938—Laszlo Bellak, Hungary—W. Woodhead, England
1939—B. Vana—V. Votrubcova, Czechoslovakia
1940-46—No competition
1947—Francois Soos—Giselle Farkas, Hungary
1948—Richard Miles—Thelma Thall, United States
1949-50—Ferenc Sido—Giselle Farkas, Hungary
1951—Bohumil Vana, Czechoslovakia—Angelica Roseanu, Rumania
1952-53—Ferenc Sido, Hungary—Angelica Roseanu, Rumania
1954—Ivan Andreadis, Czechoslovakia—Giselle Farkas, Hungary
1955—Kalman Szepesi—Eva Koczian, Hungary
1956—Erwin Klein—Mrs. Leah Thall Neuberger, United States
1957—Ichiro Ogimura—Fujie Eguchi, Japan
1959—Ichiro Ogimura—Fujie Eguchi, Japan
1961—Ichiro Ogimuro—Kimizo Matsuzaki, Japan
1963—Koji Kimura—Kazuko Ito, Japan
1965—Koji Kimura—Masako Seki, Japan
1967—Nobuhiko Hasegawa—Noriko Yamanaka, Japan
1969—Nobuhiko Hasegawa—Yasuka Konno, Japan
1971—Chang Shih-lin—Lin Hui-ching, China

Men's Team
(Swaythling Cup)

1927-31—Hungary
1932—Czechoslovakia
1933-35—Hungary
1936—Austria
1937—United States
1938—Hungary
1939—Czechoslovakia
1940-46—No Competition
1947-48—Czechoslovakia
1949—Hungary
1950-51—Czechoslovakia
1952—Hungary
1953—England
1954-57—Japan
1959—Japan
1961—China
1963—China
1965—China
1967—Japan
1969—Japan
1971—China

Women's Team
(Marcel Corbillon Cup)

1934—Germany
1935-36—Czechoslovakia
1937—United States
1938—Czechoslovakia
1939—Germany
1940-46—No Competition

1947—Czechoslovakia
1948—England
1949—United States
1950-51—Rumania
1952—Japan
1953—Rumania
1954—Japan
1955-56—Rumania
1957—Japan
1959—Japan
1961—Japan
1963—Japan
1965—China
1967—Japan
1969—Russia
1971—Japan

United States

Men's Singles

1931—Marcus Schussheim
1932—Coleman Clark and Marcus Schussheim*
1933—James M. Jacobson and SidneyHeitner*
1934—James McClure and Sol Schiff*
1935—Abe Berenbaum
1936—(Open)—Viktor Barna (Hungary)
1936—(Closed)—Sol Schiff
1937—(Open)—Laszlo Bellak (Hungary)
1938—Laszlo Bellak
1939—James McClure
1940-42—Louis Pagliaro
1943—William Holzrichter
1944—John Somael
1945-49—Richard Miles
1950—John Leach (England)
1951—Richard Miles
1952—Louis Pagliaro
1953-55—Richard Miles
1956—Erwin Klein
1957—Bernard Bukiet
1958—Martin Reisman
1959—Robert Gusikoff
1960—Martin Reisman
1961—Erwin Klein
1962—Richard Miles
1963—Bernard Bukiet
1964-65—Erwin Klein
1966—Bernard Bukiet
1967—Manji Fukushima
1968-72—Dal Joon Lee
   *Co-champions because there were two national
associations at the time, each with a titleholder.

Men's Doubles

1932—James M. Jacobson—George T. Bacon Jr.
1933—Paul Pearson—Edwin Lewis*
      Ralph Langsam—Lloyd Waterson*
1934—Samuel Silberman—Alan Lobell*
      Sol Schiff—Manny Moskowitz*
1935—A. Berenbaum—Edward Silverglade
1936—(Open)—James McClure—Robert Blattner
1936—(Closed)—James M. Jacobson—Sol Schiff
1937—(Open)—Laszlo Bellak (Hungary)—Standa
      Kolar (Czechoslovakia)

1938—Sol Schiff—James McClure
1939—Laszlo Bellak—Tibor Hazi (Hungary)
1940—Sol Schiff—James McClure
1941-42—Edward Pinner—Cy Sussman
1943—Laszlo Bellak—Tibor Hazi
1944—William Holzrichter—Laszlo Bellak
1945—John Somael—Max Hersh
1946—Edward Pinner—Cy Sussman
1947—Douglas Cartland—Arnold Fetbrod
1948—Tibor Hazi—John Somael
1949—Martin Reisman—Sol Schiff
1950—John Leach—Jack Carrington (England)
1951—Martin Reisman—William Holzrichter
1952—Richard Miles—Sol Schiff
1953—Richard Miles—John Somael
1954—Bernard Bukiet—Tibor Hazi
1955-56—Richard Bergmann—Erwin Klein
1957—Norbert Van Dewalle—William Holzrichter
1958—Richard Miles—Martin Reisman
1959—Sol Schiff—Robert Gusikoff
1960—Daniel Vegh—Emery Lippai
1961—Bernhard Bukiet—Robert Fields
1962—Richard Miles—Norbert van de Walle
1963-65—Bernard Bukiet—Erwin Klein
1966—Jerry Kruskie—Dell Sweeris
1967—Manji Fukushima—Hiroshi Takahasi
1968—Bernard Bukiet—Dell Sweeris
1969-70—Glenn Cowan—Dal Joon Lee
1971-72—Peter Pradit—Dal Joon Lee
   *Co-champions because each association had its own
titleholder.

Women's Singles

1933—Jessie Purves and Mrs. Fanny Pockrose*
1934—Ruth Hughes Aarons and Iris Little*
1935—Ruth Hughes Aarons
1936—(Open)—Ruth Hughes Aarons
1937—(Closed)—Ruth Hughes Aarons
1938-39—Emily Fuller
1940-41—Sally Green
1945—Davida Hawthorn
1946—Bernice Charney
1947—Leah Thall
1948—Peggy McLean
1949—Mrs. Leah Thall Neuberger
1950—Mrs. Reba Kirson Monness
1951-53—Mrs. Leah Thall Neuberger
1954—Mildred Shahian
1955-57—Mrs. Leah Thall Neuberger
1958-59—Susie Hoshi
1960—Sharon Acton
1961—Mrs. Leah Thall Neuberger
1962—Mildred Shahian
1963—Bernice (Charney) Chotras
1964—Valleri Bellini
1965—Patty Martinez
1966—Violetta Nesukaitis
1967—Patty Martinez
1968—Violetta Nesukaitis
1969—Patty Martinez
1970—Violetta Nesukaitis
1971—Connie Sweeris

1972—Wendy Hicks

*Co-champions because each association had its own titleholder.

Women's Doubles

1936—Ruth Hughes Aarons—Ann Digman
1937-38—Emily Fuller—Mrs. Dolores P. Kuenz
1939-40—Sally Green—Mildred Wilkinson
1941—Leah Thall—Mary Baumbach
1942—Mrs. Mae Clouther—Mildred Shahian
1943—Mrs. Mae Clouther—Leah Thall
1944—Leah Thall—Helen Baldwin
1945—Sally Green—Mildred Wilkinson
1946—Mrs. Mae Clouther—Mildred Shahian
1947-48—Leah Thall—Thelma Thall
1949—Mrs. Leah Thall Neuberger—Thelma Thall
1950—Mildred Shahian—Mrs. Magda Rurac
1951-52—Mrs. Leah Thall Neuberger—Mildred Shahian
1953—Mrs. Leah Thall Neuberger—Mrs. Peggy McLean Folke
1954—Mrs. Leah Thall Neuberger—Mildred Shahian
1955—Mrs. Leah Thall Neuberger—Mrs. Peggy McLean Folke
1956—Mrs. Leah Thall Neuberger—Mildred Shahian
1957-58—Sharon Acton—Valerie Smith
1959—Susie Hoshi—Tiny Eller
1960-61—Sharon Acton—Valerie Smith
1962—Barbara Chaimson—Valerie Smith
1963—Barbara Kaminsky—Valerie Smith
1964-65—Donna Chaimson—Connie Stace
1966—Barbara Kaminsky—Violetta Nesukaitis
1967—Patty Martinez—Priscilla Hirschkowitz
1968—Barbara C. Kaminsky—Violetta Nesukaitis
1969-70—Patty Martinez—Wendy Hicks
1971—Wendy Hicks—Connie Sweeris
1972—Mariann Domonko—Violetta Nesukaitis

Mixed Doubles

1935—Sidney Heitner—Ruth Hughes Aarons
1936—Viktor Barna—Ruth Hughes Aarons
1937—Robert Blattner—Ruth Hughes Aarons
1938—John Abrahams—Emily Fuller
1939—Al Nordheim—Mildred Wilkinson
1940—Tibor Hazi—Mrs. Magda Gal Hazi
1941—Laszlo Bellak—Mrs. Reba Kirson Monness
1942-43—William Holzrichter—Leah Thall
1944—Leslie Lowry—Sally Green
1945—Don Lasater—Mrs. Dolores P. Kuenz
1946—Sol Schiff—Peggy McLean
1947—Richard Miles—Betty Blackbourn
1948-49—Sol Schiff—Mrs. Sally Green Prouty
1950—John Leach—Mrs. Sally Green Prouty
1951—Douglas Cartland—Mrs. Leah Thall Neuberger
1952—Sol Schiff—Mrs. Leah Thall Neuberger
1954—Sol Schiff—Mrs. Sally Green Prouty
1955—Richard Miles—Mildred Shahian
1956-58—Sol Schiff—Mrs. Leah Thall Neuberger
1959—Sol Schiff—Tiny Eller
1960-61—Robert Gusikoff—Sharon Acton
1962—Bernard Bukiet—Barbara Chaimson
1963—Bernard Bukiet—Barbara Kaminsky
1964—Robert Fields—Donna Chaimson
1965—Dell Sweeris—Connie Stace
1966—Bernard Bukiet—Barbara Kaminsky
1967—Billie Bergstrand—Patricia Martinez
1968—Dell Sweeris—Connie Stace Sweeris
1969—Dal Joon Lee—Patty Martinez
1970-71—Dell Sweeris—Connie Stace Sweeris
1972—Errol Caetano—Violetta Nesukaitis

In 1934, Ruth Hughes Aarons and Samuel Silberman won the mixed doubles title in the tournament sponsored by the American Ping Pong Association.

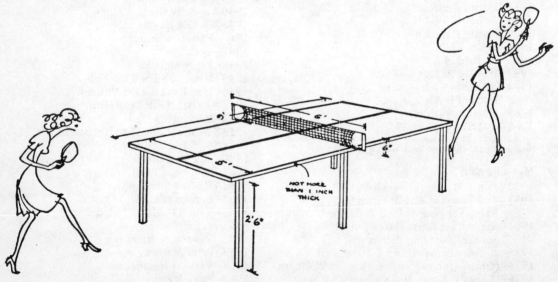

Net and Table used in Table Tennis. (Taken from "Sport for the Fun of It," by John R. Tunis, A. S. Barnes and Company, New York.)

TENNIS

The early history of tennis is obscure. Many contradictory versions of the sport's origin have appeared over the years. Several ancient nations are credited with originating it. We do know that tennis has been played since the 13th Century. The original game is not the one that is commonly know as tennis (lawn tennis). Rather it is court tennis, from which the more popular lawn tennis was developed.

The game of tennis as played by millions in this country was invented in 1873 by Major Walter Clopton Wingfield in Wales in the British Isles. It was adapted from the ancient game of court tennis, described by Allison Danzing, an outstanding authority, as "the ultimate of court games" in his book "The Racquet Game."* In England they call the old game tennis, or real tennis. The new game they term lawn tennis. In America the ancient game is always court tennis and the modern is tennis or lawn tennis.

The origin of court tennis is shrouded in the mists of antiquity. There have been many theories, most of them far-fetched. It has been traced back to a pastime connected with Egyptian-Arabian fertility rites. It has invited association with the games of the Greeks and Romans.

Some writers have connected it with the game of handball that Homer tells us Nausicaa, daughter of King Alcinous of Phaeacia, and her handmaidens played. Several English writers advance the theory that tennis is the offshoot of a game played on horseback, or polo played with racquets. This was a game of the Byzantine Court, termed tzykanion, and French and English Crusaders, we are told, saw it played there and were initiated into it.

Even the origin of the name of the game, tennis, is obscure. The word has passed through many transformations and variations and has baffled etymologists. There is one theory that has gained wide acceptance, though the evidence cited in substantiation is far from satisfying or entirely convincing. It is the theory offered by Jean Jules Jusserand, once ambassador from France to the United States. Mr. Jusserand was a scholar and a student of English literature and devoted much time to the history of sports.

Mr. Jusserand's theory was that tennis came from the French word "tenez," just as the game of tennis, in anything comparable to its form of today, came to England and America by way of France. A famous English etymologist, W. W. Skeet, supported his opinion. Tenez, which originally was spelled "tenetz," meant to "take heed," a directive equivalent to the modern "play."

It is easy, argue these theorists, to see how tenez was adopted as the actual name of the game. But the French had a name for their game—jeu de paume—long before tenez appeared in their literature, as Malcom D. Whitman points out in his "Tennis Origins and Mysteries,"* and the theory falls short of convincing.

Another theory is that the name tennis was derived from an ancient city on the Nile River Delta in Egypt. The city was name Tanis by the Greeks but in the Arabic tongue it was called Tinnis. Late in the 12th Century, according to this theory, French Crusaders brought back from the Arabic speaking countries certain words and forms. One of these was the Arabic word "rahat." It means palm of the hand and, according to scholars, is the origin of the English word racquet. Another Arabic word was hazard, meaning dice and, later, chance. Hazard is a term used today in court tennis.

The city of Tinnis was known for its manufacture of fine linens, and the earliest balls used in tennis were made of light fabric. Quite possibly, according to this theory, the famous "tissus de tennis," or light fabrics of tennis, may have been the source from which the name of the game was derived.

But whatever the origin of the game in its crudest form and of its name may have been, we know definitely that tennis, paume, was played in France in the parks and chateaux in the 13th Century. It was played first with the hand, then with a glove, next with thong bindings, later with the battoir (roughly a paddle) and finally, in the 16th Century, with the racquet. It was played in the open and later indoors when courts were built. Known today in France as "Le Jeu de Paume," or the game of the hand, tennis in those distant days was played in two forms—"Le Jeu de Longue Paume," in the open air, and "Le Jeu de Courte Paume," the indoor game.

The indoor courts in those early years were nothing like the palatial structures of modern times in England and the United States, some of which have cost a quarter of a million dollars, with their sumptuous layouts, appointments and appurtenances. But they had some of the features and outlines of the modern court, with the openings in the walls, the tambour and the grille. The courts were constructed in various types of buildings, cathedrals, monasteries, cloisters, cowsheds, castles and chateaux.

The tambour of the modern court, a jutting out of one of the long walls of the rectangular court, is taken to be a throwback to the flying buttress of the monastery, in which monks were among the earliest players. The galleries or openings in the opposite wall represent the cowsheds. The grille, an opening in one of the end walls, was the buttery hatch of the monastery, and the penthouse, the sloping roof running around three sides of the court, was part of

*Macmillan Company, New York

*Derrydale Press, New York

the cloisters. Such is the generally accepted idea of the evolution of the modern court.

The earliest privately built indoor court of which there is a record was constructed in 1230 by one Peter Garnier in Poitiers. It was not, however, until the 14th Century that the game was taken up in the towns. In the towns there was not the space to play paume in the open and so enclosed courts were set up in whatever edifices were available. They were known as tripots.

The popularity of the game with ecclesiastics in the middle of the 13th Century is shown by the fact that in 1245 the Archbishop of Rouen prohibited priests from playing it. In 1292 thirteen markers of balls for "palm play" were listed in the Role de la Taille of Paris, taken by order of Philippe le Bel.

The sport caught the fancy of royalty and many of the monarchs of France and England became its patrons. In 1308 Philippe le Bel purchased the Hotel de Nesle, in which was built a tennis court, and it was in this chateau that Benvenuto Cellini was to play the game in 1540. Undoubtedly this was one of the very earliest indoor courts constructed in Paris.

Louis X, "Le Hutin," caught a chill in 1316 after playing at paume in the Forest of Vincennes and died shortly after as a result. Charles V had two courts built, one in the palace of the Louvre about 1368 and the other in the Hotel de Beautreillis. Louis XI, Louis XII and Louis XIII also played the game, but not Louis XIV. Billiards was his only sport. Francis I, Henry II and Henry IV were other French kings who were devoted to paume and in England the patrons have included Charles I, Charles II, Edward III, Henry VII, Henry VIII, Edward VII and George V.

Paume became increasingly popular not only with kings but also with the masses in the 14th Century. It became a gambling game, with the public thronging to the courts to make bets and putting the money under the net. It got so bad that Charles V issued an edict against playing the game in Paris in 1369, though he had lost none of his own zest for the sport. The edict did not kill paume, for at the end of the century there was a guild of 1,400 professional masters in Paris.

Restrictive measures were enacted against the playing of tennis in England, also, in 1389. Just when the game was introduced in Britain is not known, but this edict, designed to promote archery, indicates that it was well established there late in the 14th Century. Late in the century, too, appeared the first reference to tennis in English literature–Chaucer's famous phrase in "Troylus and Creysede": "But canstow playen racket to and fro." Ordinances prohibiting tennis play in Holland in 1401 and 1414 show that the game had been introduced into that country before the 15 Century.

Tennis reached the peak of its popularity in both England and France in the 16th and 17th Centuries. The first rules were written by a Frenchman, Forbet, in 1592, to be printed in 1599 and again in 1632 by Hulpeau. Also in the 16th Century or possibly late in the 15th the racquet was introduced. A reference in the "Colloquies" of Erasmus, published in 1527, indicates that the racquet was in use at that time, and there is also mention of the racquet in the first book on court tennis, "Trattato della Palla," by Antonio Scanio de Salo, an Italian, published in 1555.

The Venetian ambassador to France recorded in a letter that there were some 1,800 courts in Paris about 1600. Not only were there courts in every chateau but the game also was becoming a big public spectacle and there was so much gambling and crookedness that tennis fell into disrepute. In England the game had a big vogue during the late Tudor period and the age of the Stuarts. Henry VIII built courts as Whitehall, St. James Palace and Hampton Court Palace. The last named is the oldest in England today and is still in use. Late in the 17th Century the popularity of tennis began to wane in England as well as France, though in 1657 the Dutch ambassador mentioned that there were 114 regular tripots in Paris and the famous court at Versailles was built in 1686. Betting scandals almost killed the game on public courts the middle of the 18th Century.

The French Revolution was a mortal blow to tennis in Paris and there was only one court in use there when the fighting ended. The game made something of a recovery during the time of Napoleon III and interest in the sport was stimulated with the reopening of the Versailles court in 1855, but court tennis has never enjoyed anything like its old popularity in France, though the rise of Pierre Etchebaster to the world championship in 1928 has kept it alive and there has been some activity in Paris, Bordeaux and Pau.

In England the civil war during the reign of Charles I was almost the death knell of tennis and it was not until the Restoration that it was played again to any extent. The upper classes continued to indulge in the sport through the 18th Century but their numbers fell off steadily.

Then early in the 19th Century there was a revival and many private courts were built. Prior to the first World War there were close to a hundred in England. Since then, with England in increasing financial difficulties, taxes mounting and many of the large estates being closed or disposed of in part, most of these courts have been standing idle or dismantled. Today the game is played in a few exclusive clubs such as Queen's and Prince's and at Cambridge University, as well as in a handful of private courts, but, as in France, the number of its votaries is only a handful compared to its followers in the 16th and 17th Centuries.

In 1873, as we have noted, Major Wingfield gave the game of lawn tennis to the world, introducing it as a garden party under the patented name of "Sphairistike." Embodying many of the elements of court tennis, including a bat and ball and net, (all of different specifications), and having much the same scoring system but without the confining walls that are "in play" in the older game, lawn tennis has taken on a far greater vogue in Britain than court tennis ever knew. It has become one of the leading sports there, enjoying royal patronage. From the British Isles the game has spread to almost every civilized country in the world, and the foremost international sporting competition with the exception of the Olympic Games is held annually in lawn tennis for the Davis Cup.

The exact date when court tennis was introduced into the United States has not been established. A court was built by Hollis Hunnewell and Nathaniel Thayer on Buckingham Street, Boston, on the present site of the Back Bay Station, in 1876. This is the first court tennis court of which anything definite is known in America and it was once presumed to have been the first, but evidence has been brought to light indicating that the game was played here much earlier.

In his "Tennis Origins ind Mysteries," to which Robert W. Henderson of the New York Public Library contributed much valuable research work, Malcolm D. Whitman quotes as follows from E. Singleton's "Social New York Under the Georges." "In 1766 James Rivington imported battledores and shuttlecocks, cricket balls, pillets, best racquets for tennis and fives, backgammon tables with men, boxes and dice." Also printed in the Whitman work is an advertisement from the New York Gazette of April 4, 1763, offering at public sale a house which "had a very fine tennis-court, or five-alley."

There is no description of this court, and the Hunnewell-Thayer court in Boston remains the first in America of which anything definite can be said, but it seems fairly certain that the game was known in America at least a hundred years and possibly two hundred years earlier. Convincing evidence of this is found, further, in a document on file in the Stad Huys (City Hall) in Amsterdam, Holland, Quoted by Mr. Whitman, this document, a proclamation by Peter Stuyvesant, Governor of New York, dated Sept. 30, 1659, "interdict and forbid, during divine service on the day aforesaid (Oct. 15, 1659), all exercise and games of tennis, ball-playing, hunting. . . ."

The Boston court of 1876 was opened two years after the game of lawn tennis had been introduced into the United States by way of Bermuda by Mary Outerbridge. As in England and France, lawn tennis (commonly known as tennis in the United States) was to achieve a far greater popularity in America than the older game from which it was derived, but court tennis flourished here until the depression of the 1930's brought about its decline. It has always been a game for men of wealth, played in exclusive clubs and private courts, and never a public spectacle in this country. Jay Gould, Payne Whitney and Clarence Mackay built magnificent courts running into costs of hundreds of thousands of dollars and racquet clubs in New York, Boston, Philadelphia, Tuxedo, N.Y., and Chicago, the Newport, R.I. Casino and several athletic clubs put in courts.

There was never more than a score of courts in the United States and, since the depression and the heavy rise in income tax rates, both private and club courts have shut down until today there are only seven or eight in use. So far as the general public is concerned, court tennis is almost unknown, whereas lawn tennis played by several millions of persons and its championships are among the top sporting events annually, attracting the world's best players and crowds running into the thousands.

By 1973, the interest of the public as participators and spectators, found courts being built all over the U.S. by the thousands.

Court Tennis

(or Royal Tennis)

(Courtesy of Clarence Pell, 149 Jericho Turnpike, Old Westbury, N.Y., 11568)

The first court tennis court built in the United States was opened in October, 1876, in Buckingham Street, Boston, by Hollis Hunnewell and Nathaniel Thayer. A 12-year-old boy who had migrated from England and who was to become world champion, Tom Pettitt, was engaged as assistant to Ted Hunt, English professional in charge of the court. Next, the Newport (R.I.) Casino, opened in 1880, put in a court.

The game in Boston did not thrive until the creation of a court built by the Boston Athletic Association and opened in 1888. The game caught the fancy of many of the members and the popularity of the game became manifest thereafter. In 1891 the game was introduced to New York at the Racquet and Tennis Club. The Chicago A.C. built a court for operation in September, 1893, and the famous court at Tuxedo, N.Y. came into use in 1900.

FAMOUS PLAYERS

The greatest court tennis players ever developed in this country were Pettitt, a professional, and Jay Gould, an amateur, scion of the king of finance. Pettitt was a world champion among the professionals; Gould was an invincible amateur singles champion, and also was the only amateur ever to win the world open championship until Northrup R. Knox, a member of the Racquet & Tennis Club, New York, won the title when he defeated Albert Johnson of England and the United States in 1959.

Pettitt defeated George Lambert at Hampton Court in 1885, 7 sets to 5, for the world championship. In 1890, Pettitt defended the title against Charles Saunders in Dublin and defeated Saunders, 7 sets to 5. Pettitt then resigned. Peter Latham, who had won racquets championship in 1887, challenged Saunders for the tennis crown in 1896 and defeated him. In 1898, Pettitt came out of retirement and challenged Latham. Pettitt was well past his prime and was beaten, 7 sets to 0.

Pettit's feats with a racquet have become legendary. If only half the accomplishments credited to him are fact, he was a miracle man.

Gould, an eager pupil of the world's greatest tutors, many imported from Europe, won his first singles title in 1906, and was defeated only once in a singles match. With W. T. H. Huhn, he won the doubles championship in 1909, 1911, 1912, 1913, 1914, 1915, 1916 and 1917, and then, teamed with Joseph W. Wear, won the doubles honors in 1920, 1921, 1922, 1923, 1924 and 1926. He met his only defeat in 1925 with Wear, losing to the combination of C. S. Cutting and Fulton Cutting.

Gould retired from singles play after 1926, but won the doubles title in 1927, 1928, 1929, 1931 and 1932, teamed with W. C. Wright jr.

The greatest professional of modern times, and perhaps of all time, is Pierre Etchebaster, a native of the Basque country of France. Etchebaster won the world championship in 1928 by defeating G. F. Covey of England, and continued as the champion until he retired in 1954. There was no one in America, in the days of his prime, who remotely approached him, and with the sport practically dead in England, Etchebaser remained secure on his throne.

Making his home in the United States, Pierre successfully defended his crown against Walter Kinsella in 1930, Ogden Phipps in 1937, 1948 and 1949, James Dear of England in 1948 and Alastair B. Martin in 1950 and again in 1952, when he was 58 years old.

Among the other famous professionals of the last 65 years have been: George Lambert, Peter Latham, Cecil (Punch) Fairs, E. Johnston Jr., Covey and Dear, all of England; Ferdinand Garcin of France and Kinsella, Jock Soutar and Jack Johnson of the United States.

The list of great American amateurs, in addition to Gould, includes Richard D. Sears, Fiske Warren, L. M. Stockton, G. R. Fearing Jr., Joshua Crane, G. W. Wightman, F. P. Frazer, E. M. Beals Jr., Richard D. Sears III, all of Boston; B. Spalding de Garmendia, C. E. Sands, C. S. Cutting, Fulton Cutting, Ogden Phipps, J. H. Van Alen, Hewitt Morgan, Martin, Robert L. Gerry, Robert Grant III, G. H. Bostwich Jr., J. F. C. Bostwick, and Eugene Scott of New York and Huhn, Joseph W. Wear, W. C. Wright Jr., William Lingelbach, W. L. Van Alen, E. M. Edwards, G. J. Bijur, James L. Van Alen II, and William J. Clothier, all of Philadelphia.

Martin won the championship in 1941, and after a five-year lapse because of the war, Grant won in 1946 and Beals was the 1947 winner. Phipps, champion from 1934 to 1937, won again in 1948 and 1949, and Martin from 1950 through 1956. Northrup Knox won the U.S. singles from 1957 through 1963 except when J. F. C. Bostwick beat him in 1959. Since 1964 one or the other Bostwick brother had held the championship until 1973 when Howard Angus of England beat both brothers on consecutive days.

CHAMPIONS

World Open

Matches usually are held on a challenge basis.
1885—Thomas Pettitt, Boston
1896—Peter Latham, London
1905—Cecil (Punch) Fairs, London
1907—Peter Latham, London
1908—Cecil (Punch) Fairs, London
1912—G. F. Covey, London
1914—Jay Gould, Philadelphia
1922—G. F. Covey, London
1928-54—Pierre Etchebaster, Paris and New York
1955-56—James Dear
1957—Albert Johnson
1958-69—Northrup Knox
1969-71—G. H. Bostwick Jr.
1972-73—J. F. C. Bostwick

United States

1892—Richard D. Sears
1893—Fiske Warren
1894-95—B. Spalding de Garmendia
1896—Lawrence M. Stockton
1897—George R. Fearing Jr.
1898-99—Lawrence M. Stockton
1900—Eustace H. Miles (England)
1901-04—Joshua Crane
1905—Charles E. Sands
1906-17—Jay Gould
1918-19—No competition
1920-25—Jay Gould
1926—C. Suydam Cutting
1927—George Huband (England and Chicago)
1928-29—Hewitt Morgan
1930—Lord Aberdare (England)
1931-32—William C. Wright
1933—James H. Van Alen

1934-37—Ogden Phipps
1940—James H. Van Alen
1941—Alastair B. Martin
1942-45—No competition
1946—Robert Grant 3d
1947—E. M. Beals
1948-49—Ogden Phipps
1950-56—Alastair B. Martin
1957-58—Northrup Knox
1959—J. C. Bostwick
1960-63—Northrup Knox
1964-65—J. C. Bostwick
1966-69—G. H. Bostwick Jr.
1970—J. F. C. Bostwick
1971—G. H. Bostwick Jr.
1972—J. F. C. Bostwick
1973—Howard Angus (England)

BASIC RULES

Allison Danzig, of The New York Times, an expert on the game, describes court tennis as follows:

"Court tennis is played in a rectangular space measuring 110 feet long by 38 feet wide, enclosed by four cement walls, 30 feet high, with a skylight overhead and cement floor. The net divides the court evenly into service and hazard sides. A roofed shed, known as the penthouse, runs around three sides of the court, and there are netted recesses in the walls under the penthouse known as the dedans, grille and galleries. There is also the tambour, a projection from one of the long walls, traced back to the flying buttress of the monasteries of the Middle Ages.

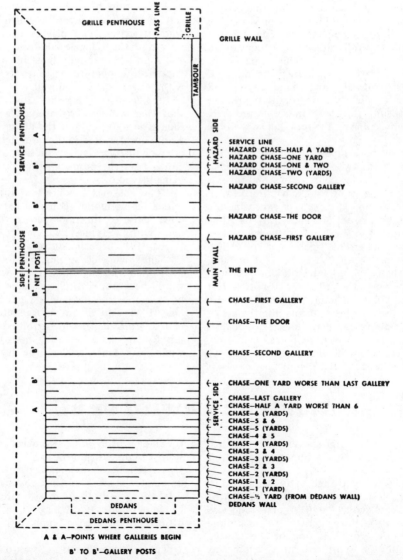

Court Tennis Playing Area. (Taken from "The Lonsdale Book of Sporting Records," Seeley Service and Company, Ltd., London.)

"The players spin a racquet for service and take their sides. The racquet is 27 inches long and 16 ounces in weight. The head, strung with heavy thick gut, has a peculiar inclination on one side to facilitate putting 'cut' on the ball, the stroke being entirely different from that of lawn tennis, though similar to the chop stroke. The ball is made of strips of cloth wound tightly and covered with melton cloth and is a little smaller in diameter than the lawn tennis ball. Approximately fifty are used in a match and they can be used over and over again for practice and then recovered.

"Matches are for the best 2-of-3 (8-game sets) or, in championship play, the best 3-of-5 (6-game sets).

"The general idea of play is to keep the ball going over the net and to put it out of reach of the opponent, as in lawn tennis, but that is only the beginning, for the walls are in play and the penthouse offers a momentary siesta for the players as the ball rolls along its roof and down to the floor. The service, of which there is an almost infinite variety, including the railroad, drop, giraffe, sidewall, underhand twist, and pound, must be delivered on to the penthouse before falling into the court on the hazard side. There is a service line on the roof and two on the floor.

"There are two types of games and the combination of the two. There is the floor game, which is the essence of court tennis, and there is the wall, or forcing, game for the hard hitter with an accurate eye who lacks skill in executing the true court tennis stroke. In a general way, they may be compared to the games of the back-court player with sound ground strokes and the volleyer of lawn tennis.

"If the ball is put into one of the wall openings known as the grille, the dedans and/or the winning gallery, a point is won. Points are also won on the opponent's errors into the net or out of court above the play lines. If the ball is played on the floor, a placement may be scored, as in lawn tennis, but not in every case. Here we come to the heart of the complexity of court tennis, which has been described as a game of moving chess, combining the exactitude of billiards, the coordination of hand and eye of lawn tennis and the generalship, and the quick judgement of polo.

"The floor of the court is marked by lines running parallel to the net. They are known as chase lines and extend at intervals the length of the court, except for a small area at the end of the hazard side. Briefly explained, the case gives player A the opportunity to surpass a stroke by player B which A has been unable to return. For example, B makes a shot that in lawn tennis would go as a placement, A, being unable to reach the ball before it has touched the floor a second time.

"In court tennis, a chase is called at the point where the ball hits the floor the second time. If it strikes within a yard of the end wall on the service side, 'chase a yard' is called by the marker who officiates. The players change sides (the only time they change sides is to play off chases) and A in the next rally must keep the ball going back deep enough to strike on its second bound within a yard of the end wall.

"B keeps returning the ball until A makes a shot that will hit farther than a yard out and then B lets go, winning the point automatically. A, of course, may win the point by putting it out of reach of B inside the yard line, and an error by either loses the point whether or not a chase is being played off.

"The chase is the heart of the game, for it puts a big premium upon skill in cutting the ball down close to the floor and to the ends of the court with the typical court tennis stroke."

A British authority stated:

"The divine chase imposes its fine restraint upon fiery hitting and makes what otherwise would be a stupid display of hard hitting a game of skill and fine judgment," and DeGarsault, in his "L'Art du Paumier—Raquetier et de la Paume," printed in 1767, adopted by the Académie Royale, states: "La Paume is the only game which can take rank in the list of arts and crafts."

Amateur Lawn Tennis

Of all the court games ever devised, lawn tennis has become the most popular throughout the world.

Its devotees in the United States number into the millions, despite the fact that it originated about 100 years ago as "a girl's name" and was subjected, over a long period, to masculine ridicule because "love" is one of the scoring terms used in the sport. No other game was treated with so much indifference and to so many slurs. However, it staggered along under the impact of prejudice for decades until the fine spirit of competition the game provides, the keen sportsmanship it involves and the fair play that dominates it provided the buoyancy which lifted it from obscurity to amazing heights.

Major Walter C. Wingfield, a British Army officer, invented lawn tennis, introducing it at a lawn party in Wales in 1873.

The new game wasn't a "spur of the moment" creation. Wingfield had given thought for some years to originating a form of sport that would be a delight both to players and to onlookers at lawn parties, then so popular among the aristocracy in England. He had been a student of the great indoor game of England—Royal Tennis or Court Tennis in which players batted balls against walls and hit them back on rebounds. It has been contended that Major Wingfield took the basic principles of the indoor court game and adapted them to outdoor play, without walls, such as are used in racquets, but the major always insisted that his game was a modern version of one that had been played in ancient Greece, which he had learned about through research.

"Sphairistike" was the name given to Wingfield's game when he unveiled it in 1873. He claimed it was the same name under which it had been played centuries earlier. However, it developed that "Sphairistike" in Greek was an order "to play," the same as "ten-ez" is an order to play when spoken in French. The major saw commercial possiblities in his game and attempted to patent it, but apparently the gesture gained him nothing.

The original players and the guest spectators referred to the game as "tennis-on-the-lawn" and in time that was changed to the present-day description, "lawn tennis," although few matches now are played on grass, most being staged on skinned courts with hard dirt surfaces and also composition and concrete surfaces.

English youth liked the game because it called for speed, agility and stroking accuracy. The elders liked it because it provided a swift-moving spectacle. But for some time in England it was the exclusive property of the social set in which the major moved.

Usually, any new game lingers long in an experimental state in the land of its origin. But lawn tennis wrote a new chapter into the records. It moved, almost like a comet, to Bermuda, zoomed from there into the United States, and Americans were experimenting with the Wingfield method of outdoor diversion within a year after the major's party of 1873.

One of the major's guest, who participated in the pioneer game, became enthused over it and a fortnight later, when he left for Bermuda, took along a goodly supply of balls and racquets, constructing his own net, not a difficult task, when he reached his station in the West Indies.

The military gentleman had just finished introducing fellow officers to the sport when an American girl—Mary Ewing Outerbridge of Staten Island, New York—arrived in Bermuda for a short vacation. She watched the play, liked it and felt it was one that would intrigue her friends back home.

Miss Outerbridge learned the rules of the game, acquired some tennis balls and a few racquets and sailed for home in March, 1874. When she attempted to clear customs with her paraphernalia, she encountered certain difficulties. The balls and the racquets were taken over by the customs people and kept for a week so that a study could be made as to what taxation—if any—should be levied on the strange looking possessions. The balls and the racquets finally were permitted to clear, duty-free, by a customs official who made mention of the incident, in certain memoirs, when retiring from service years afterward.

The Outerbridge family had membership in the Staten Island Cricket and Baseball Club and Mary received permission to plot out a tennis court on an edge of the cricket field. Apparently, none of her girl friends shared her enthusiasm about the new game, at the outset, and she coaxed into action for the pioneer matches on American soil her brothers, who were fond of athletic contests.

Later, Mary's girl friends took up the game with reluctance, not being sure it was "ladylike" to go racing and leaping in pursuit of a flying or bouncing ball. However, on days when the men played cricket, or baseball, the girls participated in the "holiday" by playing tennis. But the action was slow and consistent with the ideas then concerning womanly dignity.

The Outerbridge boys, however, saw the game as something in which speed and precision could be made into most important factors. They played at tennis and influenced their male friends to join them. Tennis became popular among the Staten Island set, even though many of the men were skittish about indulging in it because a girl had sponsored it and there were a lot of cries about "love," which made it sort of "ladylike." The game, however, weathered the sporadic storms of opposition and was played in New York City, Newport, Boston, Philadelphia and centers where society notables gathered for summer enjoyment.

For years, Nahant, Mass., laid claim to being the first site of the game in the United States. There a court was laid out on the William Appleton estate in 1874 and Dr. James Dwight, "father of American tennis," and F. R. Sears, brother of the first national champion, used it.

According to Gerald C. Young, who became president of the Southern California Tennis Association, his father, William H. Young, after arriving from England in 1879, played tennis on a crude court in Santa Monica, Calif., near where the Municipal Pier now stands. The game, it thus appears, had moved to the Pacific Coast, still without a national governing organization.

However, there was confusion everywhere as to rules, equipment and scoring. Miss Outerbridge had brought to these shores all the knowledge she could gain about the game, but the information from her Bermuda source was vague, since the game at the time was new and not standardized. Through the late 1870's and into 1880, lawn tennis was increasingly played, but met with difficulties because groups had their own rules. A game between players from different sections along the Atlantic Seaboard always was preceded by "mutual agreements," which never were wholly satisfactory.

To end all controversy, E. H. Outerbridge, an older brother of Mary, called a meeting in New York in 1881 of the leaders of all the Eastern clubs where tennis was played. Those pioneers standarized conduct for the game, specified size, weight, etc. of the equipment and organized themselves into the United States Lawn Tennis Association, which, unto this day, has continued the ruling body of the amateur sport in the United States. The new organization devised patterns for play that set a fashion and were adopted throughout the world.

The first National championship was played in 1881, with Richard D. Sears as the winner and W. E. Glyn as the runner-up. The tournament was in August at Newport, R.I. Play for the title continued there until transferred to Forest Hills, N.Y., in 1915. The men's doubles also started in 1881. F. W. Taylor and Clarence M. Clark won the first championship at Newport.

The National women's title matches started in 1887, with Miss Ellen F. Hansell the winner. Play was then at the Philadelphia Cricket Club, where it continued until it was shifted to Forest Hills in 1921. Women's doubles started in Philadelphia in 1890 and the mixed doubles were originated in 1892. The Misses Grace W. and Ellen C. Roosevelt were winners of the first women's doubles. The first mixed doubles crown went to Mabel E. Cahill and Clarence Hobart.

The first men's singles title in California, which may have pioneered state championships, went to William H. Young in 1887.

The growth in the popularity of lawn tennis in the United States was equaled by that in England. The game spread to the British colonies, throughout Europe and finally to all parts of the civilized world.

Lawn tennis received tremendous impetus in the United States and England when Dwight F. Davis of the United States put up a cup in 1900 for play between England and the United States. The competition later became open to teams of all nations. The Davis Cup matches directed world attention to the sport and although, up to the beginning of World War I, the United States, England and Australasia (Australia and New Zealand) had a monopoly on the trophy, other countries developed stars who participated in the elimination matches. Eventually, France, taking enthusiastically to the sport, fashioned teams that became world champions, starting in 1927.

In the beginning of lawn tennis in the United States, and for many years thereafter, the game was almost exclusively the property of the aristocrats. But in time public playgrounds were built and each was equipped with tennis courts, while various neighborhoods throughout the land parcelled off land to serve for tennis. And so the game grew in favor and the sport, which numbered its players by the hundreds in the 1870's and 1880's, the thousands going into the 20th Century, became a pastime for the masses, as well as the classes, and the game, with California eventually becoming the stronghold, has increased its membership into the millions and is played from early youth well into the middle years.

The U.S. Lawn Tennis Association estimates, by 1973, that more than 11 million Americans are now playing tennis, nearly twice the number of ten years ago. A decade ago there were no more than 30 indoor court facilities in the U.S. Today there are more than 1,000, with scores of others now under construction.

The format of competition changed in 1968 when Wimbledon, the London home of what was considered the world championships, let the pros compete. The changes brought about three classes of players—pros, amateurs, and registered players. The registered player (19 years old or over in the U.S.) is technically an amateur who can play for prize money, in addition to expenses, in a tourney. These players are called contract pros and are not eligible for Davis Cup play.

In 1971, a new pro 20-tournament series was organized by Lamar Hunt called the World Championship Tennis (WCT). Players under contract to WCT were banned as of Jan. 1, 1972 from competing in events sanctioned by the International Lawn Tennis Federation (ILTF). An agreement was made between the two allowing the WCT to promote two separate tournament schedules between January and May.

Another important change occured in 1971 involving Davis Cup competition. Since the inception of the matches in 1900, the winning nation did not have to compete, only to defend the trophy in the challenge round at a site of its own choosing. The new ruling abolished the challenge round and required the defending nation to play through from the start.

CHAMPIONS

(Courtesy of the United States Lawn Tennis Association)

Davis Cup Challenge Round Record

Competition is open to men's teams throughout the world. Except for the first year, 1900, the annual challenge round matches have been played in the country of the defending champions. The United States did not participate in 1904, 1912 and 1919.

Year   Result and where played

1900–United States 5, British Isles 0, at Long-
        wood Cricket Club, Boston, Mass.

1901—No competition

1902—United States 3, British Isles 2, at Crescent Athletic Club, Brooklyn, N.Y.

1903—British Isles 4, United States 1, at Longwood Cricket Club, Boston, Mass.

1904—British Isles 5, Belgium 0, at Wimbledon, England.

1905—British Isles 5, United States 0, at Wimbledon.

1906—British Isles 5, United States 0, at Wimbledon.

1907—Australia 3, British Isles 2, at Wimbledon.

1908—Australia 3, United States 2, at Melbourne, Australia.

1909—Australia 5, United States 0, at Sydney, Australia.

1910—No competition

1911—Australia 5, United States 0, at Christchurch, New Zealand.

1912—British Isles 3, Australia 2, at Melbourne.

1913—United States 3, British Isles 2, at Wimbledon.

1914—Australia 3, United States 2, at West Side Tennis Club, Forest Hills, N.Y.

1915-18—No competition

1919—Australia 4, British Isles 1, at Sydney.

1920—United States 5, Australia 0, at Auckland, New Zealand.

1921—United States 5, Japan 0, at Forest Hills.

1922—United States 4, Australasia 1, at Forest Hills.

1923—United States 4, Australasia 1, at Forest Hills.

1924—United States 5, Australasia 0, at Germantown Cricket Club, Philadelphia, Pa.

1925—United States 5, France 0, at Germantown Cricket Club.

1926—United States 4, France 1, at Germantown Cricket Club.

1927—France 3, United States 2, at Germantown Cricket Club.

1928—France 4, United States 1, at Auteuil, Paris, France.

1929—France 3, United States 2, at Auteuil.

1930—France 4, United States 1, at Auteuil.

1931—France 3, Great Britain 2, at Auteuil.

1932—France 3, United States 2, at Auteuil.

1933—Great Britain 3, France 2, at Auteuil.

1934—Great Britain 4, United States 1, at Wimbledon.

1935—Great Britain 5, United States 0, at Wimbledon.

1936—Great Britain 3, Australia 2, at Wimbledon.

1937—United States 4, Great Britain 1, at Wimbledon.

1938—United States 3, Australia 2, at Germantown Cricket Club.

1939—Australia 3, United States 2, at Merion Cricket Club, Haverford, Pa.

1940-45—No competition

1946—United States 5, Australia 0, at Melbourne.

1947—United States 4, Australia 1, at Forest Hills.

1948—United States 5, Australia 0, at Forest Hills.

1949—United States 4, Australia 1, at Forest Hills.

1950—Australia 4, United States 1, at Forest Hills.

1951—Australia 3, United States 2, at Sydney.

1952—Australia 4, United States, 1, at Adelaide, Australia.

1953—Australia 3, United States 2, at Melbourne.

1954—United States 3, Australia 2, at Sydney.

1955—Australia 5, United States 0, at Forest Hills.

1956—Australia 5, United States 0, at Adelaide.

1957—Australia 3, United States 2, at Melbourne.

1958—United States 3, Australia 2, at Brisbane, Australia.

1959—Australia 3, United States 2, at Forest Hills

1960—Australia 4, Italy 1, at Sydney

1961—Australia 5, Italy 0, at Melbourne.

1962—Australia 5, Mexico 0, at Brisbane.

1963—United States 3, Australia 2, at Adelaide, Australia.

1964—Australia 3, United States 2, at Cleveland.

1965—Australia 4, Spain 1, at Sydney

1966—Australia 4, India 1, at Melbourne.

1967—Australia 4, Spain 1, at Brisbane.

1968—United States 4, Australia 1, at Adelaide, Australia.

1969—United States 5, Rumania 0, at Cleveland.

1970—United States 5, W. Germany 0, at Cleveland Heights.

1971—United States 3, Rumania 2, at Charlotte, N.C.

1972—United States 3, Rumania 2, at Bucharest.

Wightman Cup Record

A trophy was donated by Mrs. Hazel Hotchkiss Wightman of the United States for competition among women's teams throughout the world, starting in 1923. Only the United States and England have participated in the matches, with the site alternating between the countries.

1923—United States 7, England 0, at West Side Tennis Club, Forest Hills, N.Y.

1924—England 6, United States 1, at Wimbledon, England.

1925—England 4, United States 3, at Forest Hills.

1926—United States 4, England 3, at Wimbledon.

1927—United States 5, England 2, at Forest Hills.

1928—England 4, United States 3, at Wimbledon.

1929—United States 4, England 3, at Forest Hills.

1930—England 4, United States 3, at Wimbledon.

1931—United States 5, England 2, at Forest
    Hills.
1932—United States 4, England 3, at Wimbledon.
1933—United States 4, England 3, at Forest
    Hills.
1934—United States 5, England 2, at Wimbledon.
1935—United States 4, England 3, at Forest
    Hills.
1936—United States 4, England 3, at Wimbledon.
1937—United States 6, England 1, at Forest
    Hills.
1938—United States 5, England 2, at Wimbledon.
1939—United States 5, England 2, at Forest
    Hills.
1940-45—No competition
1946—United States 7, England 0, at Wimbledon.
1947—United States 7, England 0, at Forest
    Hills.
1948—United States 6, England 1, at Wimbledon.
1949—United States 7, England 0, at Merion
    Cricket Club, Haverford, Pa.
1950—United States 7, England 0, at Wimbledon.
1951—United States 6, England 1, at Longwood
    Cricket Club, Chestnut Hill, Mass.
1952—United States 7, England 0, at Wimbledon.
1953—United States 7, England 0, at Rye, N.Y.
1954—United States 6, England 0, at Wimbledon.
    (One doubles match not played because
    of rain).
1955—United States 6, England 1, at Rye.
1956—United States 5, England 2, at Wimbledon.
1957—United States 6, England 1, at Sewickley,
    Pa.
1958—England 4, United States 3, at Wimbledon.
1959—United States 4, England 3, at Sewickley.
1960—England 4, United States 3, at Wimbledon.
1961—United States 6, England 1, at Chicago.
1962—United States 4, England 3, at Wimbledon.
1963—United States 6, England 1, at Cleveland.
1964—United States 5, England 2, at Wimbledon.
1965—United States 5, England 2, at Cleveland.
1966—United States 4, England 3, at Wimbledon.
1967—United States 6, England 1, at Cleveland.
1968—England 4, United States 3, Wimbledon.
1969—United States 5, England 2, at Cleveland
    Heights.
1970—United States 4, England 3, at Wimbledon.
1971—United States 4, England 3, at Cleveland.
1972—United States 5, England 2, at Wimbledon.

BON BELLE CUP

(Trophy for women's teams in competition
between the U.S. and Australia)
1972—Australia 5, United States 2, at Cleveland

FEDERATION CUP

(Women's team of all nations)
1963—United States 2, Australia 1, at London.
1964—Australia 2, United States 1, at Phila-
    delphia.
1965—Australia 2, United States 1, at Mel-
    bourne, Australia.

1966—United States 3, W. Germany 0, at Turin,
    Italy.
1967—United States 2, England 0, at Berlin,
    Bermany.
1968—Australia 3, Netherlands 0, at Paris,
    France.
1969—United States 2, Australia 1, at Athens,
    Greece.
1970—Australia 3, W. Germany 0, at Freiburg,
    W. Germany.
1971—Australia 3, England 0, at Perth, Australia.
1972—South Africa 2, England 1, at Johannes-
    burg, S. Africa.

Wimbledon Champions

(Starting in 1968 pros admitted).

Although lawn tennis was not started as a
game in England until 1873, the first of the
championships—men's singles—were arranged for
Wimbledon as early as 1877, Spencer W. Gore
being the winner.

How much victory at Wimbledon means to
any player, since its glory is equal to winning the
world championship, was expressed by Mrs.
Helen Wills Moody Roark, often a Wimbledon
victor, in her book, "Tennis,"* published some
years ago and in which she wrote:

"The dream nearest a player's heart is that of
winning a title at historic Wimbledon; to have
one's name inscribed on the shields that carry
those of the winners from the very first, when
tennis was new.

"My feelings as the ball travelled over the net
and I realized that the final match was mine, I
cannot describe. I felt that here was a prize for
all the tennis, all the games I have ever played
since I was a little girl."

*Chas. Scribner's Sons, New York.

Men's Singles

1877—Spencer W. Gore, England
1878—P. Frank Hadow, England
1879-80—J. T. Hartley, England
1881-86—William Renshaw, England
1887—Herbert F. Lawford, England
1888—Ernest Renshaw, England
1889—William Renshaw, England
1890—Willoughby J. Hamilton, England
1891-92—Wilfred Baddeley, England
1893-94—Joshua L. Pim, England
1895—Wilfred Baddeley, England
1896—Harold S. Mahoney, England
1897-1900—Reginald F. Doherty, England
1901—Arthur W. Gore, England
1902-06—Hugh L. Doherty, England
1907—Norman E. Brookes, Australasia
1908-09—Arthur W. Gore, England
1910-13—Anthony F. Wilding, Australasia
1914—Norman E. Brookes, Australasia
1915-18—No competition
1919—Gerald L. Patterson, Australasia
1920-21—William T. Tilden 2d, United States

1922–Gerald L. Patterson, Australasia
1923–William M. Johnston, United States
1924–Jean Borotra, France
1925–Rene Lacoste, France
1926–Jean Borotra, France
1927–Henri Cochet, France
1928–Rene Lacoste, France
1929–Henri Cochet, France
1930–William T. Tilden 2nd, United States
1931–Sidney B. Wood Jr., United States
1932–H. Ellsworth Vines Jr., United States
1933–John H. Crawford, Australia
1934–36–Frederick J. Perry, England
1937–38–J. Donald Budge, United States
1939–Robert L. Riggs, United States
1940–45–No competition
1946–Yvon Petra, France
1947–John A. Kramer, United States
1948–Robert Falkenburg, United States
1949–Frederick R. Schroeder Jr., United States
1950–V. Edward (Budge) Patty, United States
1951–Richard Savitt, United States
1952–Frank Sedgman, Australia
1953–E. Victor Seixas Jr., United States
1954–Jaroslav Drobny, Egypt
1955–Tony Trabert, United States
1956–57–Lewis Hoad, Australia
1958–Ashley Cooper, Australia
1959–Alex Olmedo, United States
1960–Neale Fraser, Australia
1961–62–Rodney Laver, Australia
1963–Chuck McKinley, United States
1964–65–Roy Emerson, Australia
1966–Manuel Santana, Spain
1967–John Newcombe, Australia
1968–69–Rodney Laver, Australia
1970–71–John Newcombe, Australia
1972–Stan Smith, United States
1973–Jan Kodes, Czechoslovakia

Women's Singles

1884-85–Maud Watson, England
1886–Blanche Bingley, England
1887-88–Lottie Dod, England
1889–Mrs. Blanche Bingley Hillyard, England
1890–L. Rice, England
1891-93–Lottie Dod, England
1894–Mrs. Blanche Bingley Hillyard, England
1985-96–Charlotte Cooper, England
1897–Mrs. Blanche Bingley Hillyard, England
1898–Charlotte Cooper, England
1899-1900–Mrs. Blanche Bingley Hillyard, England.
1901–Mrs. Charlotte Cooper Sterry, England.
1902–M. E. Robb, England
1903-04–Dorothy K. Douglass, England
1905–May G. Sutton, United States
1906–Dorothy K. Douglass, England
1907–May G. Sutton, United States
1908–Mrs. Charlotte Cooper Sterry, England
1909–Dorothea Boothby, England

1910-11–Mrs. Dorothy Douglass Chambers, England.
1912–Mr. Ethel W. Larcombe, England
1913-14–Mrs. Dorothy Douglass Chambers, England.
1915-18–No competition
1919-23–Suzanne Lenglen, France
1924–Kathleen McKane, England
1925–Suzanne Lenglen, France
1926–Mrs. Kathleen McKane Godfree, England
1927-29–Helen N. Wills, United States
1930–Mrs. Helen Wills Moody, United States
1931–Cecile Aussem, Germany
1932-33–Mrs. Helen Wills Moody, United States
1934–Dorothy E. Round, England
1935–Mrs. Helen Wills Moody, United States
1936–Helen Hull Jacobs, United States
1937–Dorothy E. Round, England
1938–Mrs. Helen Wills Moody, United States
1939–Alice Marble, United States
1940-45–No competition
1946–Pauline M. Betz, United States
1947–Margaret E. Osborne, United States
1948-50–A. Louise Brough, United States
1951–Doris Hart, United States
1952-54–Maureen Connolly, United States
1955–A. Louise Brough, United States
1956–Shirley J. Fry, United States
1957-58–Althea Gibson, United States
1959-60–Maria Bueno, Brazil
1961–Angela Mortimer, Great Britain
1962–Karen Hantze Susman, United States
1963–Margaret Smith, Australia
1964–Maria Bueno, Brazil
1965–Margaret Smith, Australia
1966-68–Billie Jean King, United States
1969–Ann Hayden Jones, England
1970–Margaret Smith Court, Australia
1971–Evonne Goolagong, Australia
1972-73–Billie Jean King, United States

Men's Doubles

1879–L. R. Erskine–Herbert F. Lawford
1880-81–William Renshaw–Ernest Renshaw
1882–J. T. Hartley–R. T. Richardson
1883–C. W. Grinstead–C. E. Welldon
1884-86–William Renshaw–Ernest Renshaw
1887–P. Bowes-Lyon–H. W. W. Wilberforce
1888-89–William Renshaw–Ernest Renshaw
1890–Joshua L. Pim–F. O. Stoker
1891–Wilfred Baddeley–H. Baddeley
1892–H. S. Barlow–E. W. Lewis
1893–Joshua L. Pim–F. O. Stoker
1894-96–Wilfred Baddeley–H. Baddeley
1897-1901–Reginald F. Doherty–Hugh L. Doherty
1902–Sidney H. Smith–F. L. Riseley
1903-05–Reginald F. Doherty–Hugh L. Doherty
1906–Sidney H. Smith–F. L. Riseley
1907–Norman E. Brooks–Anthony F. Wilding
1908–Anthony F. Wilding–M. J. G. Ritchie
1909–Arthur W. Gore–H. Roper Barrett

1910—Anthony F. Wilding—M. J. G. Ritchie
1911—Max Decugis—Andre H. Gobert
1912-13—H. Roper Barrett—Charles P. Dixon
1914—Norman E. Brooks—Anthony F. Wilding
1915-18—No competition
1919—R. V. Thomas—Patrick O'Hara Wood
1920—R. Norris Williams 2d—Charles S. Garland
1921—Randolph Lycett—M. Woosnam
1922—Randolph Lycett—J. O. Anderson
1923—Randolph Lycett—L. A. Godfree
1924—Vincent Richards—Francis T. Hunter
1925—Jean Borotra—Rene Lacoste
1926—Henri Cochet—Jacques Brugnon
1927—William T. Tilden 2d—Francis T. Hunter
1928—Henri Cochet—Jacques Brugnon
1929-30—Wilmer L. Allison—John Van Ryn
1931—George M. Lott Jr.—John Van Ryn
1932-33—Jean Borotra—Jacques Brugnon
1934—George M. Lott Jr.—Lester R. Stoefen
1935—John H. Crawford—Adrian K. Quist
1936—Charles R. D. Tuckey—George P. Hughes
1937-38—J. Donald Budge—C. Gene Mako
1939—Robert L. Riggs—Elwood T. Cooke
1940—45—No competition
1946—John A. Kramer—Thomas P. Brown Jr.
1947—John A. Kramer—Robert Falkenburg
1948—John E. Bromwich—Frank Sedgman
1949—Frank A. Parker—Richard Gonzales
1950—John E. Bromwich—Adrian K. Quist
1951-52—Frank Sedgman—Kenneth McGregor
1953—Ken Rosewall—Lewis Hoad
1954-55—Rex Hartwig—Mervyn Rose
1956—Lewis Hoad—Ken Rosewall
1957—Gardnar Mulloy—Budge Patty
1958—Sven Davidson—Ulf Schmidt
1959—Neale Fraser—Roy Emerson
1960—Rafael Osuna—Dennis Ralston
1961—Neale Fraser—Roy Emerson
1962—Fred Stolle—Robert Hewitt
1963—Rafael Osuna—Antonio Palafox
1964—Rex Hewitt—Fred Stolle
1965—John Newcombe—Tony Roche
1966—Ken Fletcher—John Newcombe
1967—Bob Hewitt—Frew McMillan
1968-70—John Newcombe—Tony Roche
1971—Rod Laver—Roy Emerson
1972—Bob Hewitt—Frew McMillan
1973—Ilie Nastase—Jim Connors

Women's Doubles

1913—Mrs. McNair—Dorothea Boothby
1914—Elizabeth Ryan—A. M. Morton
1915-18—No competition
1919-23—Suzanne Lenglen—Elizabeth Ryan
1924—Mrs. Hazel Hotchkiss Wightman—Helen
    Wills
1925—Suzanne Lenglen—Elizabeth Ryan
1926—Elizabeth Ryan—Mary K. Browne
1927—Elizabeth Ryan—Helen Wills
1928—Mrs. H. Watson—Peggy Saunders
1929—Mrs. H. Watson—Mrs. Peggy Saunders
    Michell

1930—Elizabeth Ryan—Mrs. Hellen Wills Moody
1931—Mrs. D. C. Shepherd-Barron—Phyllis Mud-
    ford
1932—D. Metaxa—J. Sigart
1933-34—Elizabeth Ryan—Mme. Rene Mathieu
1935-36—Katherine E. Stammers—Freda James
1937—Mme. Rene Mathieu—A. M. Yorke
1938-39—Alice Marble—Mrs. Sarah Palfrey Fab-
    yan
1940-45—No competiton
1946—A. Louise Brough—Margaret E. Osborne
1947—Doris Hart—Mrs. Patricia Canning Todd
1948-50—A. Louise Brough—Mrs. Margaret Os-
    borne du Pont
1951-53—Doris Hart—Shirley J. Fry
1954—A. Louise Brough—Mrs. Margaret Osborne
    du Pont
1955—Angela Mortimer—Anne Shilcock
1956—Angela Buxton—Althea Gibson
1957—Althea Gibson—Darlene Hard
1958—Althea Gibson—Maria Bueno
1959—Jeanne Arth—Darlene Hard
1960—Maria Bueno—Darlene Hard
1961—Karen Hantze—Billie Moffitt
1962—Karen Susman—Billie Moffitt
1963—Maria Bueno—Darlene Hard
1964—Margaret Smith—Lesley Turner
1965—Maria Bueno—Billie Jean Moffitt
1966—Maria Bueno—Nancy Richey
1967-68—Rosemary Casals—Billie Jean King
1969—Margaret Smith Court—Judy Tegart
1970-71—Billie Jean King—Rosemary Casals
1972—Billie Jean King—Betty Stove
1973—Billie Jean King—Rosemary Casals

Mixed Doubles

1913—Mrs. Tuckey—Hope Crisp
1914—Mrs. Larcombe—J. C. Parke
1915-18—No competition
1919—Elizabeth Ryan—Randolph Lycett
1920—Suzanne Lenglen—Gerald L. Patterson
1921—Elizabeth Ryan—Randolph Lycett
1922—Suzanne Lenglen—Patrick O'Hara Wood
1923—Elizabeth Ryan—Randolph Lycett
1924—Kathleen McKane—J. B. Gilbert
1925—Suzanne Lenglen—Jean Borotra
1926—L. A. Godfree—Mrs. Kathleen McKane
    Godfree
1927—Elizabeth Ryan—Francis T. Hunter
1928—Elizabeth Ryan—P. D. B. Spence
1929—Helen Wills—Francis T. Hunter
1930—Elizabeth Ryan—John H. Crawford
1931—Mrs. L. H. Harper—George M. Lott Jr.
1932—Elizabeth Ryan—Enrique Maier
1933—Hilda Krahwinkel—Gottfried von Cramm
1934—Dorothy E. Round—R. Miki
1935-36—Dorothy E. Round—Frederick J. Perry
1937-38—Alice Marble—J. Donald Budge
1939—Alice Marble—Robert L. Riggs
1940-45—No competition
1946—A. Louise Brough—Thomas P. Brown Jr.
1947-48—A. Louise Brough—John E. Bromwich

1949—Mrs. Sheila Summers—Eric Sturgess
1950—A. Louise Brough—Eric Sturgess
1951-52—Doris Hart—Frank Sedgman
1953-55—Doris Hart—E. Victor Seixas Jr.
1956—Shirley J. Fry—E. Victor Seixas Jr.
1957—Darlene Hard—Mervyn Rose
1958—Lorraine Coghlan—Robert Howe
1959—Darlene Hard—Rodney Laver
1960—Darlene Hard—Rodney Laver
1961—Lesley Turner—Fred Stolle
1962—Margaret duPont—Neale Fraser
1963—Margaret Smith—Kenneth Fletcher
1964—Lesley Turner—Fred Stolle
1965—Margaret Smith—Kenneth Fletcher
1966—Margaret Smith—Ken Fletcher
1967—Billie Jean King—Owen Davidson
1968—Margaret Smith Court—Ken Fletcher
1969—Ann Haydon Jones—Fred Stolle
1970—Rosemary Casals—Ilie Nastase
1971—Billie Jean King—Owen Davidson
1972—Rosemary Casals—Ilie Nastase

NATIONAL OUTDOOR CHAMPIONS

The first National lawn tennis tournament was held in 1881 and until 1911 there were seven championships, including the All-Comers singles and All-Comers doubles for men. The All-Comers events were discontinued after 1911. With the inauguration of the open tournament in 1968, the U.S.L.T.A. barred contract professionals in 1968 and 1969.

Men's Singles

1881-87—Richard D. Sears
1888-89—Henry W. Slocum Jr.
1890-92—Oliver S. Campbell
1893-94—Robert D. Wrenn
1895—Fred H. Hovey
1896-97—Robert D. Wrenn
1898-1900—Malcolm D. Whitman
1901-02—William A. Larned
1903—Hugh L. Doherty (England)
1904—Holcombe Ward
1905—Beals C. Wright
1906—William J. Clothier
1907-11—William A. Larned
1912-13—Maurice E. McLoughlin
1914—R. Norris Williams 2d
1915—William M. Johnston
1916—R. Norris Williams 2d
1917-18—R. Lindley Murray*
1919—William M. Johnston
1920-25—William T. Tilden 2d
1926-27—Rene Lacoste (France)
1928—Henri Cochet (France)
1929—William T. Tilden 2d
1930—John H. Doeg
1931-32—H. Ellsworth Vines Jr.
1933-34—Frederick J. Perry (England)
1935—Wilmer L. Allison
1936—Frederick J. Perry (England)
1937-38—J. Donald Budge
1939—Robert L. Riggs

1940—W. Donald McNeill
1941—Robert L. Riggs
1942—Frederick R. Schroeder Jr.
1943—Lt. (j.g.) Joseph R. Hunt
1944-45—Sgt. Frank A. Parker
1946-47—John A. Kramer
1948-49—Richard A. Gonzales
1950—Arthur Larsen
1951-52—Frank Sedgman (Australia)
1953—Tony Trabert
1954—E. Victor Seixas Jr.
1955—Tony Trabert
1956—Kenneth Rosewall (Australia)
1957—Malcolm Anderson (Australia)
1958—Ashley Cooper (Australia)
1959—Neale Fraser (Australia)
1960—Neale Fraser (Australia)
1961—Roy Emerson (Australia)
1962—Rodney Laver (Australia)
1963—Rafael Osuna
1964—Roy Emerson (Australia)
1965—Manuel Santana
1966—Fred Stolle
1967—John Newcombe (Australia)
1968—Arthur Ashe
1969—Stan Smith
1970-72—No competition

*Patriotic tournament in 1917.

Men's Doubles

1881—Clarence M. Clark—F. W. Taylor
1882-84—Richard D. Sears—James Dwight
1885—Richard D. Sears—Joseph S. Clark
1886-87—Richard D. Sears—James Dwight
1888—Oliver S. Campbell—Valentine G. Hall
1889—Henry W. Slocum Jr.—Howard A. Taylor
1890—Valentine G. Hall—Clarence Hobart
1891-92—Oliver S. Campbell—Robert P. Huntington Jr.
1893-94—Clarence Hobart—Fred H. Hovey
1895—Malcolm G. Chace—Robert D. Wrenn
1896—Carr B. Neel—Samuel R. Neel
1897-98—Leonard E. Ware—George P. Sheldon Jr.
1899-1901—Holcombe Ward—Dwight F. Davis
1902-03—Reginald F. Doherty—Hugh L. Doherty (England)
1904-06—Holcombe Ward—Beals C. Wright
1907-10—Harold H. Hackett—Frederick B. Alexander
1911—Raymond D. Little—Gustave F. Touchard
1912-14—Maurice E. McLoughlin—Thomas C. Bundy
1915-16—William M. Johnston—Clarence J. Griffin
1917—Frederick B. Alexander—Harold A. Throckmorton*
1918—William T. Tilden 2d—Vincent Richards
1919—Norman E. Brookes—Gearld L. Patterson (Australasia)
1920—William M. Johnston—Clarence J. Griffin
1921-22—William T. Tilden 2d—Vincent Richards
1923—William T. Tilden 2d—Brian I. C. Norton

1924—Howard O. Kinsey—Robert G. Kinsey
1925-26—Vincent Richards—R. Norris Williams 2d
1927—William T. Tilden Jr.—Francis T. Hunter
1928—George M. Lott Jr.—John F. Hennessey
1929-30—George M. Lott Jr.—John H. Doeg
1931—Wilmer L. Allison—John Van Ryn
1932—H. Ellsworth Vines Jr.—Keith Gledhill
1933-34—George M. Lott Jr.—Lester R. Stoefen
1935—Wilmer L. Allison—John Van Ryn
1936—J. Donald Budge—C. Gene Mako
1937—Gottfried von Cramm—Henner Henkel (Germany)
1938—J. Donald Budge—C. Gene Mako
1939—Adrian K. Quist—John E. Bromwich (Australia)
1940-41—John A. Kramer—Frederick R. Schroeder Jr.
1942—Lt. (j.g.) Gardnar Mulloy—William F. Talbert
1943—John A. Kramer—Cpl. Frank A. Parker
1944—Lt. W. Donald McNeill—a/c Robert Falkenburg
1945—Lt. Gardnar Mulloy—William F. Talbert
1946—Gardnar Mulloy—William F. Talbert
1947—John A. Kramer—Frederick R. Schroeder Jr.
1948—Gardnar Mulloy—William F. Talbert
1949—John E. Bromwich—William Sidwell (Australia)
1950—John E. Bromwich—Frank Sedgman (Australia)
1951—Frank Sedgman—Kenneth McGregor (Australia)
1952—E. Victor Seixas Jr. (U.S.)—Mervyn Rose (Australia)
1953—Rex Hartwig—Mervyn Rose (Australia)
1954—E. Victor Seixas Jr.—Tony Trabert
1955—Kosei Kamo—Atsushi Miyagi (Japan)
1956—Lewis Hoad—Kenneth Rosewall (Australia)
1957—Ashley Cooper—Neale Fraser (Australia)
1958—Hamilton Richardson—Alejandro Olmedo
1959—Neale Fraser—Roy Emerson
1960—Neale Fraser—Roy Emerson
1961—Charles McKinley—Dennis Ralston
1962—Rafael Osuna—Antonio Palafox
1963-64—Chuck McKinley—Dennis Ralston
1965-66—Roy Emerson—Fred Stolle
1967—John Newcombe—Tony Roche (Australia)
1968—Stan Smith—Bob Lutz
1969—Richard Crealy—Allan Stone
1970-72—No competition
*Patriotic tournament.

Women's Singles

1887—Ellen F. Hansell
1888-89—Bertha L. Townsend
1890—Ellen C. Roosevelt
1891-92—Mabel E. Cahill
1893—Aline M. Terry
1894—Helen R. Helwig

1895—Juliette P. Atkinson
1896—Elisabeth H. Moore
1897-98—Juliette P. Atkinson
1899—Marion Jones
1900—Myrtle McAteer
1901—Elisabeth H. Moore
1902—Marion Jones
1903—Elisabeth H. Moore
1904—May G. Sutton
1905—Elisabeth H. Moore
1906—Helen Homans
1907—Evelyn Sears
1908—Mrs. Maud Bargar-Wallach
1909-11—Hazel V. Hotchkiss
1912-14—Mary K. Browne
1915-18—Molla Bjurstedt
1919—Mrs. Hazel Hotchkiss Wightman
1920-22—Mrs. Molla Bjurstedt Mallory
1923-25—Helen N. Wills
1926—Mrs. Molla Bjurstedt Mallory
1927-29—Helen N. Wills
1930—Betty Nuthall (England)
1931—Mrs. Helen Wills Moody
1932-35—Helen Hull Jacobs
1936—Alice Marble
1937—Anita Lizana (Chile)
1938-40—Alice Marble
1941—Mrs. Sarah Palfrey Cooke
1942-44—Pauline M. Betz
1945—Mrs. Sarah Palfrey Cooke
1946—Pauline M. Betz
1947—A. Louise Brough
1948-50—Mrs. Margaret Osborne du Pont
1951-53—Maureen Connolly
1954-55—Doris Hart
1956—Shirley J. Fry
1957-58—Althea Gibson
1959—Maria Bueno
1960-61—Darlene Hard
1962—Margaret Smith
1963-64—Maria Bueno
1965—Margaret Smith
1966—Maria Bueno
1967—Billie Jean King
1968-69—Margaret Smith Court
1970-72—No competition

Women's Doubles

1890—Ellen C. Roosevelt—Grace W. Roosevelt
1891—Mabel E. Cahill—Mrs. W. Fellowes Morgan
1892—Mabel E. Cahill—A. M. McKinley
1893—Aline M. Terry—Hattie Butler
1894-95—Helen R. Helwig—Juliette P. Atkinson
1896—Elisabeth H. Moore—Juliette P. Atkinson
1897-98—Juliette P. Atkinson—Kathleen Atkinson
1899—Jane W. Craven—Myrtle McAteer
1900—Edith Parker—Hallie Champlin
1901—Juliette P. Atkinson—Myrtle McAteer
1902—Juliette P. Atkinson—Marion Jones
1903—Elisabeth H. Moore—Carrie B. Neely

1904–May G. Sutton–Miriam Hall
1905–Helen Homans–Carrie B. Neely
1906–Mrs. L. S. Coe–Mrs. D. S. Platt
1907–Marie Weimer–Carrie B. Neely
1908–Evelyn Sears–Margaret Curtis
1909-10–Hazel V. Hotchkiss–Edith E. Rotch
1911–Hazel V. Hotchkiss–Eleonora Sears
1912–Dorothy Green–Mary K. Browne
1913-14–Mary K. Browne–Mrs. R. H. Williams
1915–Mrs. Hazel Hotchkiss Wightman–Eleonora Sears
1916-17–Molla Bjurstedt–Eleonora Sears
1918-20–Marion Zinderstein–Eleanor Goss
1921–Mary K. Browne–Mrs. R. H. Williams
1922–Mrs. Marion Zinderstein Jessup–Helen N. Wills
1923–Kathleen McKane–Mrs. B. C. Covell (England)
1924–Mrs. Hazel Hotchkiss Wightman–Helen N. Wills
1925–Mary K. Browne–Helen N. Wills
1926–Elizabeth Ryan–Eleanor Goss
1927–Mrs. Kathleen McKane Godfree–Ermyntrude H. Harvey (England)
1928–Mrs. Hazel Hotchkiss Wightman–Helen N. Wills
1929–Mrs. Phoebe Watson–Mrs. Peggy Saunders Michell (England)
1930–Betty Nuthall (England)–Sarah Palfrey
1931–Betty Nuthall–Mrs. Eileen Bennett Whittingstall (England)
1932–Helen Hull Jacobs–Sarah Palfrey
1933–Betty Nuthall–Freda James (England)
1934–Helen Hull Jacobs–Sarah Palfrey
1935–Helen Hull Jacobs–Mrs. Sarah Palfrey Fabyan
1936–Mrs. Marjorie Gladman Van Ryn–Carolin Babcock
1937-39–Mrs. Sarah Palfrey Fabyan–Alice Marble
1940–Sarah Palfrey–Alice Marble
1941–Mrs. Sarah Palfrey Cooke–Margaret E. Osborne
1942-47–A. Louise Brough–Margaret E. Osborne
1948-50–A. Louise Brough–Mrs. Margaret Osborne du Pont
1951-54–Doris Hart–Shirley J. Fry
1955-57–A. Louise Brough–Mrs. Margaret Osborne du Pont
1958-59–Jeanne Arth–Darlene Hard
1960–Maria Bueno–Darlene Hard
1961–Darlene Hard–Lesley Turner
1962–Maria Bueno–Darlene Hard
1963–Robyn Ebbern–Margaret Smith
1964–Billie Jean Moffitt–Mrs. Karen Susman
1965–Carole Graebner–Nancy Richey
1966–Maria Bueno–Nancy Richey
1967–Billie Jean King–Rosemary Casals
1968–Margaret Smith Court–Maria Bueno
1969–Margaret Smith Court–Virginia Wade
1970-72–No competition

Mixed Doubles

1892–Mabel E. Cahill–Clarence Hobart
1893–Ellen C. Roosevelt–Clarence Hobart
1894-96–Juliette P. Atkinson–Edwin P. Fischer
1897–Laura Hensen–D. L. Magruder
1898–Carrie B. Neely–Edwin P. Fischer
1899–Elizabeth J. Rastall–Albert L. Hoskins
1900–Margaret Hunnewell–Alfred Codman
1901–Marion Jones–Raymond D. Little
1902–Elisabeth H. Moore–Wylie C. Grant
1903–Helen Chapman–Harry F. Allen
1904–Elisabeth H. Moore–Wylie C. Grant
1905–Clarence Hobart–Mrs. Clarence Hobart
1906–Sarah Coffin–Edward B. Dewhurst
1907–May Sayres–Wallace F. Johnson
1908–Edith E. Rotch–Nathaniel W. Niles
1909–Hazel V. Hotchkiss–Wallace F. Johnson
1910–Hazel V. Hotchkiss–Joseph R. Carpenter Jr.
1911–Hazel V. Hotchkiss–Wallace F. Johnson
1912–Mary K. Browne–R. Norris Williams 2d
1913-14–Mary K. Browne–William T. Tilden 2d
1915–Mrs. Hazel Hotchkiss Wightman–Harry C. Johnson
1916–Eleonora Sears–Willis E. Davis
1917–Molla Bjurstedt–Irving C. Wright
1918–Mrs. Hazel Hotchkiss Wightman–Irving C. Wright
1919–Marion Zinderstein–Vincent Richards
1920–Mrs. Hazel Hotchkiss Wightman–Wallace F. Johnson
1921–Mary K. Browne–William M. Johnston
1922-23–Mrs. Molla Bjurstedt Mallory–William T. Tilden 2d
1924–Helen N. Wills–Vincent Richards
1925–Kathleen McKane–John B. Hawkes
1926–Elizabeth Ryan–Jean Borotra
1927–Eileen Bennett–Henri Cochet
1928–Helen N. Wills–John B. Hawkes
1929–Betty Nuthall–George M. Lott Jr.
1930–Edith Cross–Wilmer L. Allison
1931–Betty Nuthall–George M. Lott Jr.
1932–Sarah Palfrey–Frederick J. Perry
1933–Elizabeth Ryan–H. Ellsworth Vines Jr.
1934–Helen Hull Jacobs–George M. Lott Jr.
1935–Mrs. Sarah Palfrey Fabyan–Enrique Maier
1936–Alice Marble–C. Gene Mako
1937–Mrs. Sarah Palfrey Fabyan–J. Donald Budge
1938–Alice Marble–J. Donald Budge
1939–Alice Marble–Harry C. Hopman
1940–Alice Marble–Robert L. Riggs
1941–Mrs. Sarah Palfrey Cooke–John A. Kramer
1942–A. Louise Brough–Frederick R. Schroeder Jr.
1943-46–Margaret E. Osborne–William F. Talbert
1947–A. Louise Brough–John E. Bromwich
1948–A. Louise Brough–Thomas P. Brown Jr.
1949–A. Louise Brough–Eric Sturgess
1950–Mrs. Margaret Osborne du Pont–Kenneth McGregor

1951-52—Doris Hart—Frank Sedgman
1953-55—Doris Hart—E. Victor Seixas Jr.
1956—Mrs. Margaret Osborne du Pont—Kenneth Rosewall
1957—Althea Gibson—Kurt Nielsen
1958-60—Mrs. Margaret Osborne du Pont—Neale Fraser
1961—Margaret Smith—Robert Mark
1962—Margaret Smith—Fred Stolle
1963—Margaret Smith—Kenneth Fletcher
1964—Margaret Smith—John Newcombe
1965—Margaret Smith—Fred Stolle
1966—Donna Floyd Fales—Owen Davidson
1967—Billie Jean King—Owen Davidson
1968-72—No competition

United States Open Champions
(At Forest Hills, N.Y.)

Men's Singles

1968—Arthur Ashe, United States
1969—Rod Laver
1970—Ken Rosewall
1971—Stan Smith
1972—Ilia Nastase, Rumania

Women's Singles

1968—Virginia Wade, England
1969-70—Margaret Smith Court, Australia
1971-72—Billie Jean King, United States

Men's Doubles

1968—Stan Smith—Bob Lutz
1969—Fred Stolle—Ken Rosewall
1970—Nikki Pilic—Fred Barthes
1971—John Newcombe—Roger Taylor
1972—Cliff Drysdale—Roger Taylor

Women's Doubles

1968—Maria Bueno—Margaret Smith Court
1969—Darlene Hard—Francoise Durr
1970—Margaret Smith Court—Judy Dalton
1971—Rosemary Casals—Judy Dalton
1972—Francoise Durr—Betty Stove

Mixed Doubles

1968—Mary Ann Eisel—Peter Curtis
1969-70—Margaret Smith Court—Marty Reisson
1971—Billy Jean King—Owen Davidson
1972—Margaret Smith Court—Marty Reisson

National Intercollegiate Champions

(Tournament conducted by United States Lawn Tennis Association prior to 1938; by National Collegiate Athletic Association since 1938.)

Singles and Doubles

1883 (spring)—J. S. Clark, Harvard; J. S. Clark—H. A. Taylor
1883 (fall)—H. A. Taylor, Harvard; H. A. Taylor—P. E. Presby
1884—W. P. Knapp, Yale; W. P. Knapp—W. V. S. Thorne
1885—W. P. Knapp, Yale; W. P. Knapp—A. L. Shipman

1886—G. M. Brinley, Trinity; W. P. Knapp—W. L. Thatcher, Yale
1887—P. S. Sears, Harvard; P. S. Sears—Q. A. Shaw Jr.
1888—P. S. Sears, Harvard; V. G. Hall—O. S. Campbell, Columbia
1889—R. P. Huntington Jr., Yale; O. S. Campbell—A. E. Wright, Columbia
1890—F. H. Hovey, Harvard; Q. A. Shaw Jr.—S. T. Chase, Harvard
1891—F. H. Hovey, Harvard; F. H. Hovey—R. D. Wrenn
1892—W. A. Larned, Cornell; R. D. Wrenn—F. D. Winslow, Harvard
1893—M. G. Chace, Brown; M. G. Chace—C. R. Budlong
1894-95— M. G. Chace, Yale; M. G. Chace—A. E. Foote
1896—M. D. Whitman, Harvard; L. E. Ware—W. M. Scudder, Harvard
1897—S. G. Thomson, Princeton; L. E. Ware—M. D. Whitman, Harvard
1898—L. E. Ware, Harvard; L. E. Ware—M. D. Whitman
1899—D. F. Davis, Harvard; D. F. Davis—Holcombe Ward
1900—R. D. Little, Princeton; R. D. Little—F. B. Alexander
1901—F. B. Alexander, Princeton; H. A. Plummer—S. L. Russell, Yale
1902—W. J. Clothier, Harvard; W. J. Clothier—E. W. Leonard
1903—E. B. Dewhurst, Pennsylvania; B. Colston—E. Clapp, Yale
1904—Robert LeRoy, Columbia; K. H. Behr—G. Bodman, Yale
1905—E. B. Dewhurst, Pennsylvania; E. B. Dewhurst—H. B. Register
1906—Robert LeRoy, Columbia; E. B. Wells—A. Spaulding, Yale
1907—G. P. Gardner Jr., Harvard; N. W. Niles—E. S. Dabney, Harvard
1908—N. W. Niles, Harvard; H. M. Tilden—A. Thayer, Pennsylvania
1909—W. F. Johnson, Pennsylvania; W. F. Johnson—A. Thayer
1910—R. A. Holden Jr., Yale; D. Mathey—B. N. Dell, Princeton
1911—E. H. Whitney, Harvard; D. Mathey—C. T. Butler, Princeton
1912—G. M. Church, Princeton; G. M. Church—W. H. Mace
1913—R. N. Williams 2d, Harvard; W. M. Washburn—J. J. Armstrong, Harvard
1914—G. M. Church, Princeton; R. N. Williams 2d—Richard Harte, Harvard
1915—R. N. Williams 2d, Harvard; R. N. Williams 2d—Richard Harte
1916—G. C. Caner, Harvard; G. C. Caner—Richard Harte
1917-18—No competition
1919—C. S. Garland, Yale; C. S. Garland—K. N. Hawkes

Hawkes

1920—L. M. Banks, Yale; A. Wilder—L. Wiley, Yale

1921—Philip Neer, Stanford; J. B. Fenno Jr.—E. W. Feibleman, Harvard

1922—Lucien E. Williams, Yale; James Davies—Philip Neer, Stanford

1923—Carl H. Fischer, Philadelphia Osteopathy; L. N. White—Louis Thalheimer, Texas

1924—Wallace Scott, Washington; L. N. White-Louis Thalheimer, Texas

1925—E. G. Chandler, California; Gervais Hills—Gerald Stratford, California

1926—E. G. Chandler, California; E. G. Chandler—Tom Stow

1927—Wilmer Allison, Texas; John Van Ryn—Kenneth Appel, Princeton

1928—Julius Seligson, Lehigh; Ralph McElvenny—Alan Herrington, Stanford

1929—Berkeley Bell, Texas; Benjamin Gorchakoff—Arthur Kussman, Occidental

1930—Clifford Sutter, Tulane; Dolf Muehleisen—Robert Muench, California

1931—Keith Gledhill, Stanford; Bruce Barnes—Karl Kamrath, Texas

1932—Clifford Sutter, Tulane; Keith Gledhill—Joseph Coughlin, Stanford

1933—Jack Tidball, U.C.L.A.; Joseph Coughlin—Sam Lee, Stanford

1934—C. Gene Mako, Southern California; C. Gene Mako—G. Philip Castlin

1935—Wilbur Hess, Rice; Paul Newton—Richard Bennett, California

1936—Ernest Sutter, Tulane; W. Bennett Dey—William Seward, Stanford

1937—Ernest Sutter, Tulane; Richard Bennett—Paul Newton, California

1938—Frank D. Guernsey, Rice; Joseph R. Hunt—Lewis Wetherell, Southern California

1939—Frank D. Guernsey, Rice; Douglas Imhoff—Robert Peacock, California

1940—W. Donald McNeill, Kenyon; Laurence A. Dee—James Wade, Stanford

1941—Joseph R. Hunt, U.S. Naval Academy; Charles E. Olewine—Charles T. Mattmann, Southern California

1942—Frederick R. Schroeder Jr., Stanford; Frederick R. Schroeder Jr.—Laurence Dee

1943—Francisco Segura, Miami (Fla.); John Hickman—Walter Driver, Texas

1944—Francisco Segura, Miami; John Hickman—Felix Kelley, Texas

1945—Francisco Segura, Miami; Francisco Segura—Tom Burke

1946—Robert Falkenburg, Southern California; Robert—Tom Falkenburg

1947—Gardner Larned, William and Mary; Sam Match—Bobby Curtis, Rice

1948—Harry Likas, San Francisco; Fred Kovaleski—Bernard Bartzen William and Mary

1949—Jack Tuero, Tulane; Jim Brink—Fred Fisher, Washington (Seattle)

1950—Herbert Flam, U.C.L.A.; Herbert Flam—W. E. Garrett

1951—Tony Trabert, Cincinnati; Earl Cochell—Hugh Stewart, Southern California

1952—Hugh Stewart, Southern California; Hugh Ditzler—Cliff Mayne, Southern California

1953—Hamilton Richardson, Tulane; Lawrence Huebner—Robert Perry, U.C.L.A.

1954—Hamilton Richardson, Tulane; Ronald Livingstone—Robert Perry, U.C.L.A.

1955—Jose Aguero, Tulane; Francisco Contreras—Joaquin Reyes, Southern California

1956—Alejandro Olmedo, Southern California; Francisco Contreras—Alejandro Olmedo, Southern California

1957—Barry MacKay, Michigan; Crawford Henry—Ron Holmberg, Tulane

1958—Alejandro Olmedo, Southern California; Alejandro Olmedo—Edward Atkinson, Southern California

1959—Whitney Reed, San Jose State; Ronald Holmberg—Crawford Henry, Tulane

1960—Larry Nagler, U.C.L.A.; Larry Nagler—Allen Fox, U.C.L.A.

1961—Allen Fox, U.C.L.A. Rafael Osuna—Ramsey Earhart, Southern California

1962—Rafael Osuna, Southern California; Osuna—Ramsey Earhart

1963—Dennis Ralston, Southern California; Ralston—Rafael Osuna, Southern California

1964—Dennis Ralston, Southern California; Ralston—Bill Bond, Southern California

1965—Arthur Ashe, U.C.L.A.; Ashe—Ian Crookenden, U.C.L.A.

1966—Charles Pasarell, U.C.L.A.; Pasarell—Ian Crookenden, U.C.L.A.

1967—Bob Lutz, Southern California; Lutz—Stan Smith, Southern California

1968—Stan Smith, Southern California; Smith—Bob Lutz, Southern California

1969—Joaquin Loyo—Mayo, Southern California; Loyo—Mayo—Marcello Lara, Southern California

1970—Jeff Borowiak, U.C.L.A.; Pat Cramer—Luis Garcia, Miami (Fla.)

1971—Jimmy Connors, U.C.L.A.; Jeff Borowiak—Haroon Rahim, U.C.L.A.

1972—Dick Stockton, Trinty (Tex.); Alex Mayer—Roscoe Tanner, Stanford

1973—Alex Mayer, Stanford; Alex Mayer—Jim Delaney, Stanford

United States Indoor Champions
(Open Tournament Starting 1970)

Men's Singles

1900—J. Appleton Allen
1901—Holcombe Ward
1902—J. Parmly Paret

1903-04—Wylie C. Grant
1905—Edward B. Dewhurst
1906—Wylie C. Grant
1907—Theodore R. Pell
1908—Wylie C. Grant
1990—Theodore R. Pell
1910—Gustave F. Touchard
1911—Theodore R. Pell
1912—Wylie C. Grant
1913-15—Gustave F. Touchard
1916—R. Lindley Murray
1917-18—S. Howard Voshell
1919—Vincent Richards
1920—William T. Tilden 2d
1921—Frank T. Anderson
1922—Francis T. Hunter
1923-24—Vincent Richards
1925—Jean Borotra
1926—Rene Lacoste
1927—Jean Borotra
1928—William Aydelotte
1929—Jean Borotra
1930—Francis T. Hunter
1931—Jean Borotra
1932-33—Gregory S. Mangin
1934—Lester R. Stoefen
1935-36—Gregory S. Mangin
1937—Frank A. Parker
1938—W. Donald McNeill
1939—Wayne Sabin
1940—Robert L. Riggs
1941—Frank L. Kovacs 2d
1942-45—No competition
1946—Francisco Segura
1947—John A. Kramer
1948—William F. Talbert
1949—Richard A. Gonzales
1950—W. Donald McNeill
1951—William F. Talbert
1952—Richard Savitt
1953—Arthur Larsen
1954—Sven Davidson
1955—Tony Trabert
1956—Ulf Schmidt
1957—Kurt Nielsen
1958—Richard Savitt
1959—Alejandro Olmedo
1960—Barry McKay
1961—Richard Savitt
1962—Charles McKinley
1963—Dennis Ralston
1964—Chuck McKinley
1965—Jan-Erik Lundquist
1966-67—Charles Pasarell
1968—Cliff Richey
1969—Stan Smith
1970—Ilie Nastase
1971—Clark Graebner
1972—Stan Smith

Men's Doubles

1900—Calhoun Cragin—J. Parmly Paret

1901—Calhoun Cragin—Oviedo M. Bostwick
1902-04—Wylie C. Grant—Robert LeRoy
1905—Theodore R. Pell—Harry F. Allen
1906-08—Harold H. Hackett—Frederick B. Alexander
1909—Wylie C. Grant—Theodore R. Pell
1910—Gustave F. Touchard—Carlton R. Gardner
1911-12—Frederick B. Alexander—Theodore R. Pell
1913-14—Wylie C. Grant—G. Carleton Shafer
1915—Gustave F. Touchard—Watson M. Washburn
1916—Arthur M. Lovibond—William Rosenbaum
1917—Frederick B. Alexander—William Rosenbaum
1918—G. Carleton Shafer—King Smith
1919-20—William T. Tilden 2d—Vincent Richards
1921—Vincent Richards—S. Howard Voshell
1922—Frank T. Anderson—S. Howard Voshell
1923-24—Vincent Richards—Francis T. Hunter
1925—Jean Borotra—A. W. Asthalter
1926—William T. Tilden 2d—Fred C. Anderson
1927—Jean Borotra—Jacques Brugnon
1928—William Aydelotte—Perrine G. Rockafellow
1929—William T. Tilden 2d—Francis T. Hunter
1930—Perrine G. Rockafellow—Merritt Cutler
1931—Jean Borotra—Christian Boussus
1932—George M. Lott Jr.—John Van Ryn
1933—Clifford Sutter—Eugene McCauliff
1934—George M. Lott Jr.—Lester R. Stoefen
1935—Gregory S. Mangin—Berkeley Bell
1936—Karle Schroder—J. Gilbert Hall
1937—Frank A. Parker—Gregory S. Mangin
1938—Frank J. Bowden—John Pitman
1939—Eugene McCauliff—Clifford Sutter
1940—Robert L. Riggs—Elwood T. Cooke
1941—W. Donald McNeill—Frank D. Guernsey Jr.
1942-45—No competition
1946—W. Donald McNeill—Frank D. Guernsey Jr.
1947—John A. Kramer—Robert Falkenburg
1948—Jean Borotra—Marcel Bernard
1949-51—William F. Talbert—W. Donald McNeill
1952—William F. Talbert—J. Edward (Budge) Patty
1953—Arthur Larsen—Kurt Nielsen
1954—William F. Talbert—Tony Trabert
1955—E. Victor Seixas Jr.—Tony Trabert
1956—Samuel Giammalva—E. Victor Seixas Jr.
1957-58—Grant Golden—Barry MacKay
1959—Alejandro Olmedo—Barry MacKay
1960—Andres Gimeno—Manuel Santana
1961—C. R. Crawford—R. Homlberg
1962—Rodney Laver—Charles McKinley
1963—Dennis Ralston—Chuck McKinley
1964—Manuel Santana—Jose Luis Arilla
1965—Roy Emerson—Fred Stolle
1966—Robert Lutz—Stanley Smith
1967—Charles Pasarell—Arthur Ashe
1968—Thomas Koch—Tom Okker

1969—Stan Smith—Bob Lutz
1970—Arthur Ashe—Stan Smith
1971—Manuel Orantes—Juan Gisbert
1972—Manuel Orantes—Andres Gimeno

Women's Singles

1907—Elisabeth H. Moore
1908-09—Marie Wagner
1910—Mrs. Frederick G. Schmitz
1911—Marie Wagner
1912—No competition
1913-14—Marie Wagner
1915-16—Molla Bjurstedt
1917—Marie Wagner
1918—Molla Bjurstedt
1919—Mrs. Hazel Hotchkiss Wightman
1920—Helene Pollak
1921-22—Mrs. Molla Bjurstedt Mallory
1923—Mrs. Benjamin E. Cole 2d
1924-25—Mrs. Marion Zinderstein Jessup
1926—Elizabeth Ryan
1927—Mrs. Hazel Hotchkiss Wightman
1928—Edith Sigourney
1929—Margaret Blake
1930—Mianne Palfrey
1931—Marjorie Sachs
1932—Marjorie Merrill
1933—Dorrace Chase
1934—Norma Taubele
1935—Jane Sharp
1936—Mrs. Marjorie Gladman Van Ryn
1937—Mme. Sylvia Henrotin
1938—Virginia Hollinger
1939—Pauline M. Betz
1940—Sarah Palfrey
1941—Pauline M. Betz
1942—Mrs. Patricia Canning Todd
1943—Pauline M. Betz
1944—Katharine Winthrop
1945-46—Mrs. Helen Pedersen Rihbany
1947—Pauline M. Betz
1948—Mrs. Patricia Canning Todd
1949—Gertrude A. Moran
1950-51—Nancy Chaffee
1952—Mrs. Nancy Chaffee Kiner
1953—Mrs. Thelma Long
1954—Mrs. Dorothy W. Levine
1955—Katharine Hubbell
1956—Lois Felix
1957—Mrs. Dorothy W. Levine
1958—Nancy O'Connell
1959—Lois Felix
1960—Carole Wright
1961—Janet Hopps
1962—Carole Wright
1963—Carol Hanks
1964—Mary Ann Eisel
1965—Nancy Richey
1966-68—Billie Jean King
1969—Mary Ann Eisel
1970—Mary Ann Eisel Curtis
1971—Billie Jean King

1972—Virginia Wade

Women's Doubles

1908—Mrs. Helen Helwig Pouch—Elisabeth H. Moore
1909—Elisabeth H. Moore—Erna Marcus
1910—Marie Wagner—Clara Kutroff
1911—Elizabeth C. Bunce—Barbara Fleming
1912—No competition
1913—Marie Wagner—Clara Kutroff
1914—Mrs. S.F. Weaver—Clare Cassel
1915—Mrs. Helen Holmans McLean—Mrs. S.F. Weaver
1916—Molla Bjurstedt—Marie Wagner
1917—Marie Wagner—Margaret T. Taylor
1918—Eleanor Goss—Mrs. S.F. Weaver
1919—Mrs. Hazel Hotchkiss Wightman—Marion Zinderstein
1920—Mrs. L. Gouverneur Morris—Helene Pollak
1921—Mrs. Hazel Hotchkiss Wightman—Marion Zinderstein
1922—Mrs. Kathleen McKane Godfree—Mrs. Marion Zinderstein Jessup
1923—Mrs. Benjamin E. Cole 2d—Mrs. Kathleen McKane Godfree
1924—Mrs. Hazel Hotchkiss Wightman—Mrs. Marion Zinderstein Jessup
1925—Mrs. William· Endicott—Mrs. J. Dallas Corbiere
1926—Elizabeth Ryan—Mary K. Browne
1927—Mrs. Hazel Hotchkiss Wightman—Mrs. Marion Zinerstein Jessup
1928-31—Mrs. Hazel Hotchkiss Wightman—Sarah Palfrey
1932—Marjorie Morrill—Mrs. Marjorie Gladman Van Ryn
1933—Mrs. Hazel Hotchkiss Wightman—Sarah Palfrey
1934—Norma Taubele—Jane Sharp
1935-37—Mrs. Dorothy Andrus—Mme. Sylvia Henrotin
1938—Mrs. Virginia R. Johnson—Katharine Winthrop
1939—Norma Taubele—Grace Surber
1940—Gracyn Wheeler—Norma Taubele
1941—Pauline M. Betz—Dorothy M. Bundy
1942—Katharine Winthrop—Mrs. Virginia R. Johnson
1943—Pauline M. Betz—Mrs. Hazel Hotchkiss Wightman
1944-45—Katharine Winthrop—Mrs. Virginia R. Johnson
1946—Mrs. Helen Pedersen Rihbany—Ruth Carter
1947-48—Doris Hart—Barbara Scofield
1949—Gertrude A. Moran—Mrs. Marjorie Gladman Buck
1950-51—Mrs. Marjorie Gladman Buck—Nancy Chaffee
1952—Mrs. Patricia Canning Todd—Mrs. Nancy CHaffee Kiner
1953—Mrs. Thelma Long—Mrs. Barbara Scofield Davidson

1954—Mrs. Dorothy W. Levine—Mrs. Barbara W. Ward
1955—Katharine Hubbell—Ruth Jeffery
1956—Lois Felix—Katharine Hubbell
1957—Mrs. Dorothy W. Levine—Nancy O'Connell
1958—Nancy O'Connell—Carol Hanks
1959—Lois Felix—Kay Hubbell
1960—Mrs. Richard Buck—Ruth Jeffery
1961—Janet Hopps—Katherine Hubbell
1962—Ruth Jeffery—Belmar Gunderson
1963—Carol Hanks—Mary Ann Eisel
1964—Mary Ann Eisel—Katharine Hubbell
1965—Carol Hanks Aucamp—Mary Ann Eisel
1966—Billie Jean King—Rosemary Casals
1967—Carol Hanks Aucamp—Mary Ann Eisel
1968—Billie Jean King—Rosemary Casals
1969—Mary Ann Eisel—Valerie Ziegenfuss
1970—Peaches Bartkowicz—Nancy Richey
1971—Billie Jean King—Rosemary Casals
1972—Rosemary Casals—Virginia Wade

French Outdoor Champions
(Became Open Tournament in 1968)

Men's Singles
1891—Briggs
1892—Schopfer
1893—Riboulet
1894-96—A. Vacherot
1897-1900—P. Ayme
1901—A. Vacherot
1902—M. Vacherot
1903-04—Max Decugis
1905-06—M. Germot
1907-09—Max Decugis
1910—M. Germot
1911—Andre H. Gobert
1912-14—Max Decugis
1915-19—No competition
1920—Andre H. Gobert
1921—J. Samazeuilh
1922—Henri Cochet
1923—P. Blanchy
1924—Jean Borotra
1925—Rene Lacoste
1926—Henri Cochet
1927—Rene Lacoste
1928—Henri Cochet
1929—Rene Lacoste
1930—Henri Cochet
1931—Jean Borotra
1932—Henri Cochet
1933—John H. Crawford
1934—Gottfried von Cramm
1935—Frederick J. Perry
1936—Gottfried von Cramm
1937—Henner Henkel
1938—J. Donald Budge
1939—W. Donald McNeill
1940-45—No competition
1946—Marcel Bernard
1947—Josef Asboth
1948-49—Frank A. Parker

1950—J. Edward (Budge) Patty
1951-52—Jaroslav Drobny
1953—Kenneth Rosewall
1954-55—Tony Trabert
1956—Lewis Hoad
1957—Sven Davidson
1958—Mervyn Rose
1959-60—Nicola Pietrangeli
1961—Manuel Santana
1962—Rodney Laver
1963—Roy Emerson
1964—Manuel Santana
1965—Fred Stolle
1966—Tony Roche
1967—Roy Emerson
1968—Ken Rosewall
1969—Rod Laver
1970-71—Jan Kodes
1972—Andres Gimeno

Women's Singles
1897-99—Mill. Masson
1900—Mlle. Prevost
1901—Mme. P. Girod
1902-03—Mlle. Masson
1904-05—Mlle. K. Gillou
1906—Mme. Fenwick
1907—Mme. de Kermel
1908—Mme. Fenwick
1909-12—J. Mathey
1913-14—Mlle. Broquedis
1915-19—No competition
1920-23—Suzanne Lenglen
1924—Mlle. Vlasto
1925-26—Suzanne Lenglen
1927—K. Bouman
1928-29—Helen N. Wills
1930—Mrs. Helen Wills Moody
1931—Cecile Aussem
1932—Mrs. Helen Wills Modoy
1933-34—Margaret C. Scriven
1935-37—Mrs. Hilda K. Sperling
1938-39—Mme. S. Mathieu
1940-45—No competition
1946—Margaret E. Osborne
1947—Mrs. Patricia Canning Todd
1948—Mme. Nelly Landry
1949—Mrs. Margaret Osborne du Pont
1950—Doris Hart
1951—Shirley J. Fry
1952—Doris Hart
1953—54—Maureen Connolly
1955—Angela Mortimer
1956—Althea Gibson
1957—Shirley Bloomer
1958—Suzy Kormorczi
1959—Christine Truman
1960—Darlene Hard
1961—Anne Haydon
1962—Sandra Reynolds Price
1963—Lesley Turner
1964—Margaret Smith

1965—Lesley Turner
1966—Ann Jones
1967—Francoise Durr
1968—Nancy Richey
1969—70—Margaret Smith Court
1971—Evonne Goolagong
1972—Billie Jean King

Australian Outdoor Champions
(Became Open Tournament in 1969)
Men's Singles

1905—Rodney W. Heath
1906—Anthony F. Wilding
1907—Horace Rice
1908—Frederick B. Alexander
1909—Anthony F. Wilding
1910—Rodney W. Heath
1911—Norman E. Brookes
1912—J. Cecil Parker
1913—E.F. Parker
1914—Patrick O'Hara Wood
1915—F. Gordon Lowe
1916—19—No competition
1920—A.R.F. Kingscote
1921—R.H. Gemmell
1922—James O. Anderson
1923—Patrick O'Hara Wood
1924—25—James O. Anderson
1926—John B. Hawkes
1927—Gerald L. Patterson
1928—Jean Borotra
1929—J. Colin Gregory
1930—E.F. Moon
1931—33—John H. Crawford
1934—Frederick J. Perry
1935—John H. Crawford
1936—Adrian K. Quist
1937—Vivian B. McGrath
1938—J. Donald Budge
1939—John E. Bromwich
1940—Adrian K. Quist
1941—45—No competition
1946—John E. Bromwich
1947—Dinny Pails
1948—Adrian K. Quist
1949—50—Frank Sedgman
1951—Richard Savitt
1952—Kenneth McGregor
1953—Kenneth Rosewall
1954—Mervyn Rose
1955—Kenneth Rosewall
1956—Lewis Hoad
1957—58—Ashley Cooper
1959—Alex Olmedo
1960—Rodney Laver
1961—Roy Emerson
1962—Rodney Laver
1963—67—Roy Emerson
1968—Bill Bowrey
1969—Rod Laver
1970—Arthur Ashe
1971—72—Ken Rosewall

Women's Singles

1922—23—Mrs. Molesworth
1924—Miss Lance
1925—26—Daphne Akhurst
1927—E. Boyd
1928—30—Daphne Akhurst
1931—32—Mrs. Buttsworth
1933—34—Joan Hartigan
1935—Dorothy E. Round
1936—Joan Hartigan
1937—Nancye Wynne
1938—Dorothy M. Bundy
1939—Miss Westacott
1940—Nancye Wynne
1941—45—No competition
1946—48—Mrs. Nancye Wynne Bolton
1949—Doris Hart
1950—A. Louise Brough
1951—Mrs. Nancye Wynne Bolton
1952—Mrs. Thelma Long
1953—Maureen Connolly
1954—Mrs. Thelma Long
1955—Beryl Penrose
1956—Mary Carter
1957—Shirley J. Fry
1958—Angela Mortimer
1959—Mrs. M. Carter Reitano
1960—66—Margaret Smith
1967—Nancy Richey
1968—Billie Jean King
1969—71—Margaret Smith Court
1972—Virginia Wade

Famous Amateurs

Usually, it is difficult to point out a player or two as majestic in their sport. American tennis differs radically from all other sports.

William Tatum Tilden 2d was practically invincible during his prime as an amateur. He was "King of the Nets" in various lands where he appeared, and after he had turned professional and reached an age beyond 50, he still was the man others had to beat to demonstrate supremacy.

Mrs. Helen Wills Moody Roark and Suzanne Lenglen were the outstanding women players. Mrs. Roark had great opposition in her prime. Yet she so dominated all opposition that she must be regarded as the "Queen of the Nets," based on her amazing record.

In the opinion of an overwhelming majority, Tilden was the greatest of the men players and Mrs. Roark the outstanding woman competitor.

Mrs. George W. (Hazel Hotchkiss) Wightman, who has contributed enormously to the game in the United States, also has excelled as a participant.

America hailed a new tennis queen in 1951 when Maureen Connolly of San Diego, Calif., won the National title by beating Shirley J. Fry in the final at Forest Hills. Miss Connolly, only 16 at the time, became the youngest to capture the crown since May G. Sutton won in 1904. In 1952, Miss Connolly won the Wimbledon championship and repeated as U.S. titleholder. In 1953 she made a grand slam of the world's four major titles, Wimbledon, United States, French and Australian. The Californian also took the United States and French crowns in 1954. At the peak of her career she suffered leg injuries in an accident and retired from competition.

William Tatum Tilden 2d's Record

Amateur Championships Won

U.S. Singles—1920, 1921, 1922, 1923, 1924, 1925, 1929.

U.S. Doubles—1918, 1921, 1922, 1923, 1927.

U.S. Mixed Doubles—1913, 1914, 1922, 1923.

U.S. Clay Court Singles—1922, 1923, 1924, 1925, 1926, 1927.

U.S. Indoor Singles—1920.

U.S. Indoor Doubles—1919, 1920, 1926, 1929.

Wimbledon Singles—1920, 1921, 1930.

Wimbledon Doubles—1927.

Austrian Singles, Doubles and Mixed Doubles—1930.

Holland Singles and Doubles—1920, 1930.

Italian Singles—1930.

Record in Davis Cup Singles

	Matches		Sets		Games	
	Won	Lost	Won	Lost	Won	Lost
1920 through 1930	17	5	54	31	459	392

Also shared doubles victories in 1920, 1923, 1924 and 1927.

(Tilden turned professional in 1931.)

Helen Wills' Record

Winner of

U.S. Singles—1923, 1924, 1925, 1927, 1928, 1929, 1931. Lost on default, 1933. (Did not compete 1926, 1930, 1932, 1934, 1935, 1936, 1937, 1938.)

U.S. Doubles—1922, 1924, 1925, 1928.

U.S. Mixed Doubles—1924, 1928.

Wimbledon Singles—1927, 1928, 1929, 1930, 1932, 1933, 1935, 1938. (Did not compete 1931, 1934, 1936, 1937.)

Wimbledon Doubles—1927, 1930.

French Singles—1928, 1929, 1930, 1932.

French Doubles—1932.

U.S. Girls' Singles—1921, 1922.

U.S. Girls' Doubles—1922.

Wightman Cup Singles—Won 18, lost 2 (both in 1924). Won 241 games, lost 130. Sets—won 36, lost 6.

Wightman Cup Doubles—Won 3, lost 7, of which 6 were lost in row—1928, 1929, 1930, 1931, 1932, 1938.

Mrs. Roark (then Mrs. Moody) announced her retirement after defeating Helen Jacobs (U.S.), in 1935 Wimbledon singles. Did not compete in 1936 and 1937. Returned to Wimbledon in 1938, again won title and retired from major tournaments.

On Jan. 7, 1936, in San Francisco, Mrs. Roark (then Mrs. Moody) and Howard Kinsey, a former Davis Cup player, then a professional, volleyed a ball for 78 minutes and the strokes totaled 2,001. The match "contest" ended when Kensey had to quit to give a lesson. Both could have gone on to higher totals, but neither was aware of the "record" until it was pointed out by Henry Roberts Sr., who refereed.

Suzanne Lenglen's Record

Winner of

Wimbledon Singles—1919, 1920, 1921, 1922, 1923, 1925.

Wimbledon Doubles—1919, 1920, 1921, 1922, 1923, 1925.

Wimbledon Mixed Doubles—1920, 1922, 1925.

French Singles—1920, 1921, 1922, 1923, 1925, 1926.

French Doubles—1925, 1926.

French Mixed Doubles—1925, 1926.

(Turned professional in 1926.)

Mrs. George W. Wightman's Record

(Hazel Hotchkiss)

Winner of

U.S. Singles—1909, 1910, 1911, 1919.

U.S. Doubles—1909, 1910, 1911, 1915, 1924, 1928.

U.S. Mixed Doubles—1909, 1910, 1911, 1915, 1918, 1920.

U.S. Singles (Indoors)—1919, 1927.

U.S. Doubles (Indoors)—1919, 1921, 1924, 1927, 1928, 1929, 1930, 1931, 1933, 1943.

U.S. Mixed Doubles (Indoors)—1923, 1924, 1926, 1927, 1928.

Wightman Cup—Played in 4 doubles matches, won 3.

Mrs. Wightman has won about sixty championships in the United States.

World Championship of Tennis

Inaugurated in 1971, pro circuit of 20 tournaments, with prizes totaling over $1 million.

WCT FINALS

1971-72—Ken Rosewall

United States Professional Lawn Tennis

All the gentlemen—and the ladies—who have enriched themselves through play at professional tennis really are indebted to the late promoter, Charles C. (Cash and Carry) Pyle and a lady named Suzanne Lenglen, who lived a spectacular career around the nets of France, England and America and died much too soon.

In 1926, when Pyle was in his heyday as a

promoter and Miss Lenglen was the best known player in tennis, Pyle astonished the racquet world with an offer of $50,000 to Miss Lenglen to tour the United States. The plan seemed fantastic, since tennis crowds up to then were extremely small and the receipts even for the championship matches were minor.

Miss Lenglen, a shrewd woman in the matter of cash, asked Pyle to put up the money in advance. Pyle posted it. He then induced Mary K. Browne, a topnotch American player, to go professional, to furnish competition for the French whirlwind. To add variety to the tour, he influenced four men to join the tour—for pay. They were Vincent Richards, Harvey Snodgrass and Howard O. Kinsey, all of the United States, and Paul Peret of France.

The "crazy excursion" was a magnificent financial success. Miss Lenglen and her co-stars drew crowded houses everywhere. The tour was so successful that Pyle gave Miss Lenglen $25,000 as a bonus, in addition to her $50,000 guarantee. Miss Browne received $25,000. Richards' share was $35,000. Kinsey received $20,000, Snodgrass $12,000, Peret $10,000—and Pyle himself profited $80,000.

Everyone was amazed—except Pyle.

In 1927, the United States Professional Lawn Tennis Association was organized under the leadership of Richards and Kinsey. The plans called for professionalizing any stars who preferred cash to cups. There was much jeering over the plans for the organization at the start. But when, through the years, William T. Tilden 2d, H. Ellsworth Vines Jr., J. Donald Budge, John A. Kramer and many others traded their amateur status for professional roles the jeering ceased and the "pro" game soon enriched many.

Europe at that time had a large group of famous professionals, practically unknown in this country, including Karel Kozeluh, acclaimed as the greatest player, amateur or professional, in the world; Ramon Najuch of Germany; Albert Thomas and Edward Burke of France, and Major Rendall of England.

In 1928, Kozeluh made his first trip to the United States, playing a tour with Richards and competing in the American championship. On the tour, he clearly demonstrated his superiority, but in matches played on grass, where the championship was held and on which Kozeluh had never played previously, Richards' sensational volleying beat the Czech's steadiness, and the American retained his title.

Kozeluh returned in 1929 and, with greater knowledge of the grass surface, defeated Richards in a terrific match.

The biggest forward strides in the new branch of the old game were made in 1931, when Tilden turned professional, together with his old amateur doubles partner, Francis T. Hunter, as well as Robert Seller of California and J. Emmett Pare, former United States clay court champion. Tilden made his pro debut in Madison Square Garden, New York, Feb. 18, 1931, against Kozeluh before a crowd of 13,600, which dropped $36,000 into the till. The group then went on a tour that grossed $238,000. It was evident that the golden days' had dawned for any great player who wanted to turn pro.

After Tilden had pioneered the way, other great players joined the cavalcade: Bruce Barnes, Vines, Budge, George M. Lott Jr., Berkeley Bell and Lester R. Stoefen of the United States; Henri Cochet, the French star; Frederick J. Perry, the great English player, and Hans Nusslein of Germany. As time went on, women joined the delegation: Jane Sharp, Mrs. Ethel Burkhardt Arnold and, later, Alice Marble, Sarah Palfrey, Mrs. Pauline Betz Addie and Gertrude Moran.

Data on the tours, supplied by H. Archie Richardson and other sources, follow:

1931—Tilden versus Kozeluh grossed $238,000.

1932—Tilden versus Richards grossed $86,000.

1933—Tilden versus Nusslein grossed $62,000.

1934—Vines turned pro. Tilden and Vines grossed $243,000,' tour taking in 72 cities. Opening attendance, Madison Square Garden, 14,637; receipts, $30,125. Of tour income, Vines received $52,000; Tilden and William O'Brien, promoter, split balance.

1935—Lott and Stoefen, the world amateur doubles champions, turned pro and went on a national tour with Tilden and Vines. Gross income $188,000.

1936, two tours (sponsored by Tilden and O'Brien). One included Vines, Stofen, Lott and Bell. Others included Tilden, Barnes, Miss Sharp, Mrs. Arnold. Loss on tours about $22,000.

1937—Vines and Perry opened in New York before 17,630, who paid $58,120. Gross was $412,181 for 61 matches. Perry received $91,335; Vines $34,195; Francis T. Hunter and S. Howard Voshell, as promoters, split $56,166. Tilden, appearing a few times, earned $5,200. Vines won 32 matches, Perry 29.

1938—Vines against Perry. Gross income $175,000. Vines and Perry, as co-promoters, divided $34,000. Played 83 matches; Vines won 48, Perry 35.

1939—Vines versus Budge. New York opening, 16,725 attendance, $47,120 receipts. Gross for tour $204,503; attendance, 168,384. Vines received $23,000, Budge $75,000. Budge won 22 matches, Vines 17. Later Budge and Perry made a short tour. Budge was winner of about 75 percent of the matches.

1941—Alice Marble, Mary Hardwick, Budge, Tilden; New York opening drew $25,614; other figures not available.

1942—Budge, Riggs, Perry, Kovacs; receipts for New York opening, $26,404. Played 71 cities; gross attendance, 101,915; receipts not available.

The professionals came back strongly after the war. In December, 1947, Kramer, then the Wimbledon and United States amateur champion, and Riggs launched a tour that attracted receipts of $248,000 for 89 appearances in North America and $135,000 abroad.

In 1949, Richard A. (Pancho) Gonzales left the amateur ranks after he had won his second straight national title and paired with Kramer for a jaunt that reportedly drew $250,000. Late in 1950 Miss Moran, who had astonished staid Wimbledon by wearing a costume that included lace panties, entered the Riggs fold and was joined by Mrs. Pauline Betz Addie, a former Wimbledon and United States champion. Kramer was matched with Francisco (Pancho) Segura in a supporting role that became the feature match and it was estimated the tour drew $175,000.

Kramer, in the role of promoter, signed for another tour a pair of Australians, Frank Sedgman, the world's No. 1 amateur, and Kenneth McGregor, after they had finished the job of beating the United States for the third straight time in the 1952 Davis Cup challenge round matches. This tour, matching Sedgman against Kramer and McGregor against Segura, was a success from the start. It reached Madison Square Garden for a two-day stand on Jan. 10—11, 1953, and, despite bad weather, attracted 20,300 spectators and gross receipts of $62,321. The Australians were guaranteed a minimum of $100,000 ($75,000 to Sedgman and $25,000 to McGregor) as their share of the tour. In the first 50 matches the gross receipts were over $500,000.

On the tours from 1948 to 1953, Kramer demonstrated his invincibility, winning against each opponent. In 1954, Kramer, apparently feeling he had no more worlds to conquer in competition, turned all his talents to promoting world professional tennis tours.

Gonzales, who was shunted to the sidelines after losing to Kramer in 1949, then returned to the limelight. Starting on the comeback trail in 1951, the Californian gradually returned to the top spot in professional tennis, the only man to make such a comeback. In 1954 Pancho defeated Segura and Sedgman in a round-robin jaunt and on the 1955-56 tour, he beat Tony Trabert, who was lured from the amateur ranks with a $75,000 bonus, 74 matches to 27. In 1957, Kenneth Rosewall, a magnificent amateur player from Australia, signed a pro contract for $55,000 and went on tour with Gonzales. Pancho won, 50—26.

Following the Wimbledon tournament of 1957, Lewis Hoad, another Australian and the then reigning amateur player, accepted from Kramer a 25-month contract calling for $125,000, a record guarantee. The signing created

quite a furor in Australia, where hopes had been pinned on Hoad to keep Australia supreme in amateur competition. Hoad had won acclaim early, having been named to the 1952 Australian Davis Cup team at the age of 17. Thereafter he and Rosewall teamed in Australian Davis Cup victories. In 1956, he came within one match of being the first player since Don Budge to win the four major world titles. He captured the Australian, French and Wimbledon singles titles and, hampered by physical handicaps, came within an eyelash of winning the United States crown.

His tour with Gonzales took him around the world, including Australia, and proved highly profitable to Kramer. But Gonzales was not to be denied and Pancho won the tour, 51 to 36.

In 1959 Ashley Cooper and Malcolm Anderson, two more top Australian amateurs, joined Kramer's contingent. Cooper accepted a $100,000 guarantee and Anderson $45,000. The format of the tour was changed to provide round-robin competition, with $90,000 set for distribution during the first 60 matches of the series. In the round-robin competition, a big share of the prize money goes to the featured singles players, and a player must win to remain in that role. The two winners of the previous match play in the next feature game, while the losers play for lesser money.

With the great success of Kramer's professional tours, which he calls world professional championship play, competition among other professionals has dwindled and since 1952 there has been no formal competition for United States professional titles.

The format of professional tennis changed in 1968 with the advent of open competition between amateur and professional players in U.S. and world tournaments. Two new touring groups, the World Championship Tennis and the National Tennis League, were formed to open new fields in prize money.

The United States Professional Tennis Association again resumed competition in 1962.

UNITED STATES PROFESSIONAL CHAMPIONS

Men's Singles

1927-28—Vincent Richards
1929—Karel Kozeluh
1930—Vincent Richards
1931—William T. Tilden 2d
1932—Karel Kozeluh
1933—Vincent Richards
1934—Hans Nusslein
1935—William T. Tilden 2d
1936—Joseph Whalen
1937—Karel Kozeluh
1938—Frederick J. Perry
1939—H. Ellsworth Vines Jr.
1940—J. Donald Budge
1941—Frederick J. Perry

1942—J. Donald Budge
1943—Bruce Barnes
1944—No competition
1945—Welby Van Horn
1946-47—Robert L. Riggs
1948—John A. Kramer
1949—Robert L. Riggs
1950-51—Francisco Segura
1952-61—Not held
1962-63—Tut Bartzen
1964—Sam Giammalva
1965—Mike Davies
1966—Pancho Segura
1967—Sam Giammalva
1968—Not Held
1969—Billy Higgins
1970—Sam Giammalva
1971—Billy Higgins
1972—Ian Crookenden

Men's Doubles

1927-28—No competition
1929—Vincent Richards—Karel Kozeluh
1930-31—Vincent Richards—Howard O. Kinsey
1932—William T. Tilden 2d—Bruce Barnes
1933—Vincent Richards—Charles M. Wood
1934—Bruce Barnes—Emmett Pare
1935—George M. Lott Jr.—Lester R. Stoefen
1936—Charles M. Wood—Harold Blauer
1937—Vincent Richards—George M. Lott Jr.
1938—Vincent Richards—Frederick J. Perry
1939—Bruce Barnes—Keith Gledhill
1940-41—J. Donald Budge—Frederick J. Perry
1942—J. Donald Budge—Robert L. Riggs
1943—Bruce Barnes—C. Gene Mako
1944—No competition
1945—William T. Tilden 2d—Vincent Richards
1946—Frank L. Kovacs 2d—Frederick J. Perry
1947—J. Donald Budge—Robert L. Riggs
1948—John A. Kramer—Francisco Segura
1949—J. Donald Budge—Frank L. Kovacs 2d
1950—Frank L. Kovacs 2d—Welby Van Horn
1951—Francisco Segura—Richard Gonzales
1952-61—Not held
1962—Sam Giammalva—Eugene Garrett
1963-64—Not held
1965—Mike Davies—Allen Quay
1966—Pancho Segura—Mike Davies
1967—Sam Giammalva—Jason Morton
1968—Not held
1969-70—Dick Leach—Robert Potthast
1971—Ramsey Earnhart—Walter Johnson
1972—Dick Leach—Robert Potthast

Tilden's Pro Match Record
(1931 through 1935)

Against	Won	Lost
Kozeluh	79	24
Nusslein	116	47
Richards	32	1
Hunter	10	1
Cochet	1	0
Barnes	22	4

Pare	12	0
Ramon Najuck	28	5
Edward Burke	18	3
Martin Plaa	3	1
Vines	19	61
	340	147

Tilden opened five of his professional tours in New York City, playing before an aggregate attendance of 54,253, who paid $107,625.

Vines' Pro Record

Braven Dyer, in The Los Angeles Times, reported:

"During his pro career, which ran from 1934 through 1939, H. Ellsworth Vines Jr. won 257 and lost 130 matches.

"The only player to win a majority of matches from him was J. Donald Budge, who won 22 of 39 played in 1939. Vines won 61 and lost 19 with Tilden; against Hans Nusslein he won 28 and lost 11; against Lester Stoefen, he won 27 and lost 4; won all 10 against Henri Cochet; against Martin Plaa, won 8 and lost 2; against Robert Ramilion, won 6 and lost 1.

"Vines and Perry played 157 matches of which Vines won 86 and lost 71."

BASIC RULES

The court is 78 feet long and 27 feet wide for singles play and the same length but 36 feet wide for doubles. The net is 3 feet high in the center and 3½ feet high at the net posts. The net posts are located 3 feet outside the sidelines. For doubles a 4½-foot alley is added on either side of the singles court.

On either side of the net parallel to and at a distance of 21 feet from it are the service lines. Another line bisects the net and runs from one service line to the other. This divides the area between the service lines into four service courts, two on either side of the net. The service courts have the same dimensions for both singles and doubles. The area between the service lines and the end lines, called baselines, is called the back court. Courts may be either indoors or outdoors, and are laid out on surfaces such as grass, dirt, clay asphalt, concrete or boards. Most courts are outdoors.

The game is played with a racquet and a ball about 2½ inches in diameter and made of inflated rubber covered with felt. The racquet frame and handle are usually of wood, the head frame usually laminated. The length of the racquet is about 27 inches. The strung striking surface (head) is oval, about 11 inches long and 9 inches wide, including the frame. Strings are usually of split lamb's gut, nylon or heavy silk. Most handles are wound with a leather grip. Handles are flat, square, or oblong and come in different sizes. The most common sizes are 4-1/2, 4-5/8 and 4-3/4 inches. The weight of the racquet for adults varies from about 12 to 14 ounces.

Play is started by a service and each point is started by service. The players spin a racquet or toss a coin for choice of serve. The server must stand behind the baseline between the imaginary plane of the center line and the sideline. He must stroke the ball in the air so as to hit it with the racquet into the opponent's service court diagonally opposite. If the first serve does not go into the opponent's service court, the server gets a second chance to put the ball in play. If he fails again he is charged with a double-fault and loses the point. On the first serve of each game the server serves from the right of the center line into the service court toward his left; thereafter he alternates serving between the right and left courts. The server continues to serve until the first game is completed, after which his opponent serves a game. The service alternates after each game throughout the remainder of the set.

If a player volleys a ball (hits it before it touches the ground), he is responsible for returning it regardless of where he stands. If a ball hits any part of a player's body or clothing he loses the point. The ball must go from the player's racquet directly to the opponent's side of the court (unless the opponent volleys it) except that it may hit the net and dribble over the net. If a ball lands in a player's court and then hits anything save the player's racquet, he loses the point. Players generally serve the ball overhead. Then it is stroked back and forth with ground strokes or drives. Players sometimes arch shots (lob the ball); many advance near the net to volley the ball in the air. The exchange of ball over the net is called a rally. A rally ends when one player (singles) or one team (doubles) fails to make a good return over the net. Either the server or the receiver, by winning a rally, scores a point toward a game.

A game goes to the first player to win 4 points unless deuce (3 points each) is reached. A set goes to the player winning 6 games except for a deuce provision. A match is for 2 of 3 or 3 of 5 sets. Scoring is as follows: the first point won by a player is called 15; the second, 30; the third, 40; and the fourth point is game, except that if the score is tied at 40—40 (deuce), one player or one team needs to win two consecutive points to complete the game. Each player has 0 or "love" at the beginning of each game. If both players get

2 points, it is 30-all. When a player gets 1 point after 40-all, or deuce, the score is called "Advantage." "Advantage in" means the point is won by the server; "advantage out" means the server has lost the point. After advantage in, if the opponent catches up by winning a point, the score returns again to deuce. When calling the score, call the server's score first.

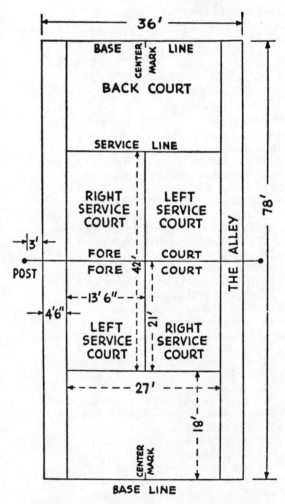

Court for Lawn Tennis. (Taken from "Sports for Recreation," edited by E. D. Mitchell, A. S. Barnes and Company, New York.)

TRACK AND FIELD

Man came by track and field through a natural course of events. In order to survive he had to be able to run, throw and jump, and spent a lot of time developing his talents in these fields. There-

fore, it cannot be said that the events on the modern track and field program are manufactured sporting tests.

In the dawn of civilization, however, man did

not have sports in mind when he perfected himself in running, throwing, wrestling and kindred muscular activities.

The earliest human was not a hunter. He had no equipment. Doubtless he was a vegetarian. But wild animals hunted either man for food or to destroy him. Man, in defense, had to fight back or run from this danger. The fast runner escaped—and lived. The slow of foot were overtaken and killed.

Naturally, parents encouraged their children to run—and to achievement of the highest possible speed. It meant the difference between life and death when chased by animals. Man proceeded to turn on these pursuing animals and pelted them with rocks. If he missed he had to run to safety. Realizing the need of good marksmanship, primitive man practiced for accuracy and that was the start of throwing as a competitive sport.

Earliest man sometimes was trapped into life and death fights against animals, with nothing serving him except his hands and arms. Muscular power was vital to him; that and dexterity of the hands. It is logical to assume that men grappled with each other so as to build strength and develop tricks for subduing animals.

And so wrestling can be presumed to be the third sport of the human race; wrestling of the rough-and-tumble variety, with no holds barred, and use your fists, if you wish.

Obstacles often may have blocked the way of ancient man. They had to be moved by the hands, supported by muscular power. And so this was the origin of weight lifting.

Humans found the weight of obstacles beyond their lifting capacity. They met this problem by leaping over them—and thus was born the jumping art.

These activities came down through the ages into an ancient Greece. That early civilized nation, with its love of the powerful man, began to glorify its athletes—those who could run the fastest, throw the farthest, jump the highest and for the greatest distance; to honor those who were the best wrestlers, the mightiest in lifting weights.

In old Greece, for a reason not clear to moderns, the greatest athlete was the discus throwing champion. Champions in other events were secondary heroes in comparison with the discus artist.

Competitive athletics were as much a part of life in early Greece as they are in America today. When Rome conquered Greece it was in an era when the victors were little concerned about sports, but watching the Greeks gave them the idea they could better the Grecian performances and so the Olympic Games were taken up by the Romans. The Games continued with both Romans and Greeks competing, until they were abolished by order of a Roman monarch in 392 A.D.

There is no record of anything in the way of track and field games from that date until the 12th Century, when the English revived the practice of running, jumping and throwing "for the sport of the thing." The lapse of 8 centuries in sports activities of the kind which had prevailed for so long in Greece constitutes one of the great mysteries of history.

Even discus throwing had ceased, so far as national competition was concerned. There may have been private contests among warriors in the leisure hours, but there was no national, or international rivalry as was the custom for almost 2,000 years. The only evidence which indicates a continuation of some forms of sports after the banning of the Olympic Games is found in the history of horseshoe pitching.

Camp followers took discarded horseshoes, bent them as well as was possible in the rounded form of a discus and tossed them for distance. They must have been aping the soldiers, who continued to be discus throwers to some extent. But there is nothing to show any foot racing, jumping or other activity which came under the heading of sports from the 4th Century until the English of the 12th Century proceeded with their play.

In tracing the important facts in the history of track and field games to get data for a chronology and also the evolutions H. Archie Richardson found among old records a reference to the "Tailtin Games," which were supposed to have been held at Tailiti in County Meath, Ireland, in 1829 B.C. The contests are reported to have included running, jumping, weight events and pole vaulting.

Whether such history is fact or legend is left to the reader to decide. The point is that although the Irish were supposed to have put on such an athletic meet more than 18 centuries before the beginning of the Christian Era and before the Greeks started their games, there is nothing in the history of Ireland to indicate any further games between that challenged date and the 19th Century—a lapse of over 3,700 years.

Search reveals that as early as the 12th Century sports which did not call for important equipment gripped certain English enthusiasts and a field was set apart for their use. Intermittently for the next 675 to 700 years the English indulged in running, jumping and throwing. The sports idea had gained so firm a grip by 1834 that those who were the informal rulers of the games laid down laws specifying the minimum performance that would qualify a man for the privilege of competition in what might be regarded as contests of major significance.

The first college track and field meet took place in 1864 when Oxford competed against Cambridge. This, then, was the real beginning of organized rivalry. Two years later the first national meet was held in London to determine the champions of England. The Canadians picked up the idea of sports competition from England. Americans, taking note of the Oxford-Cambridge competition and of the games under the auspices of the London A.C., created the New York Athletic Club. In 1868 the New York A.C. arranged for the first amateur track and field meet in the history of this nation. It was held indoors.

In 1876 colleges, most of them located along the Atlantic Seaboard, organized what now is known as the Intercollegiate Association of

Amateur Athletes of America—the I.C.A.A.A.A. —and put on this country's pioneer college meet. In the same year there was a contest to determine the champions of the United States, collegians and other amteur athletes being welcome. In 1888 the Amateur Athletic Union of the United States came into existence, outlined the rules for amateur sports, open to all amateurs, collegian or noncollegian, and the real foundation for amateur track and field games was laid, with the I.C.A.A.A.A. sponsoring all strictly collegiate meets and A.A.U. becoming increasingly powerful in the affairs of amateur athletic programs.

Champions and Records

UNITED STATES CHAMPIONS—MEN

(Source: Official Amateur Athletic Union Track and Field Handbook.)

This list includes the events that are on the current A.A.U. program. Champions of long distance running, race walking, and discontinued events may be found in the Official Handbook published by the A.A.U. of the United States, 3400 West 86th Street, Indianapolis, Ind., 46268.

Outdoor

The first amateur championships in this country were conducted by the New York Athletic Club in 1876, 1877 and 1878. From 1879 through 1888, championships were held under the sponsorship of the National Association of Amateur Athletes of America.

Beginning in 1888 and continuing through the present, the Amateur Athletic Union of the United States has conducted annual championships. Two title meets were held in 1888. In the following table of champions the winners at both meets are listed, the A.A.U. (*) and the N.A.A.A.A. (†).

100-Yard Dash—100 Meters

1876-1927, 1929-31, 1953-55, 1957-58, 1961-63, 1965-67, 1969-71: 100 yards. 1928, 1932-52, 1956, 1959-60, 1964, 1968, 1972: 100 meters.

Year and Champion	Time
1876—F. C. Saportas	10 1/2 s.
1877—C. C. McIvor	10 1/2 s.
1878—W. C. Wilmer	10 s.
1879—B. R. Value	10 3/5 s.
1880—L. E. Myers	10 2/5 s.
1881—L. E. Myers	10 1/4 s.
1882—A. Waldron	—
1883—A. Waldron	10 1/4 s.
1884—M. W. Ford	10 4/5 s.
1885—M. W. Ford	10 3/5 s.
1886—M. W. Ford	10 2/5 s.
1887—C. H. Sherrill	10 2/5 s.
1888—*F. Westing	10 3/5 s.
1888—†F. Westing	10 s.
1889—J. Owen Jr.	10 2/5 s.
1890—J. Owen Jr.	9 4/5 s.
1891—L. H. Cary	10 1/5 s.
1892—H. Jewett	10 s.
1893—C. W. Stage	10 1/5 s.
1894—T. I. Lee	10 1/5 s.
1895—Bernard J. Wefers	10 s.
1896—Bernard J. Wefers	10 1/5 s.
1897—Bernard J. Wefers	9 4/5 s.
1898—F. W. Jarvis	10 s.
1899—A. C. Kraenzlein	—
1900—M. W. Long	10 s.
1901—F. M. Sears	9 4/5 s.
1902—P. J. Walsh	10 s.
1903—Archie Hahn	10 1/5 s.
1904—L. Robertson	10 2/5 s.
1905—Charles L. Parsons	9 4/5 s.
1906—Charles J. Seitz	10 1/5 s.
1907—H. J. Huff	10 1/5 s.
1908—W. F. Hamilton	10 1/5 s.
1909—W. Martin	10 1/5 s.
1910—J. M. Rosenberger	10 1/5 s.
1911—Gwin Henry	10 s.
1912—Howard P. Drew	10 s.
1913—Howard P. Drew	10 2/5 s.
1914—J. Loomis	10 1/5 s.
1915—J. Loomis	‡9 4/5 s.
1916—A. E. Ward	10 s.
1917—A. E. Ward	10 1/5 s.
1918—A. H. Henke	10 s.
1919—W. D. Hayes	10 1/5 s.
1920—Loren Murchison	10 s.
1921—Charles W. Paddock	9 3/5 s.
1922—Robert McAllister	10 s.
1923—Loren Murchison	10.1 s.
1924—Charles W. Paddock	9.6 s.
1925—Frank Hussey	9.8 s.
1926—Charles Borah	9 4/5 s.
1927—Chester Bowman	9 3/5 s.
1928—Frank Wykoff	10 3/5 s.
1929—Eddie Tolan	10 s.
1930—Eddie Tolan	9.7 s.
1931—Frank Wykoff	9.5 s.
1932—Ralph Metcalfe	10.6 s.

1933—Ralph Metcalfe	10.5s.	1892—H. Jewett ‡21 4/5s.
1934—Ralph Metcalfe	10.4s.	1893—C. W. Stage 22 1/5s.
1935—Eulace Peacock ‡10.2s.		1894—T. I. Lee 22s.
1936—Jesse Owens	10.4s.	1895—Bernard J. Wefers 21 4/5s.
1937—Perrin Walker	10.7s.	1896—Bernard J. Wefers 23s.
1938—Ben Johnson	10.7s.	1897—Bernard J. Wefers 21 2/5s.
1939—Clyde Jeffrey ‡10.2s.		1898—J. H. Maybury 22 2/5s.
1940—Harold Davis	10.3s.	1899—M. W. Long 22 2/5s.
1941—Barney Ewell	10.3s.	1900—W. S. Edwards 22 3/5s.
1942—Harold Davis	10.5s.	1901—F. M. Sears 22s.
1943—Harold Davis ‡10.3s.		1902—P. J. Walsh 22 4/5s.
1944—Claude Young	10.5s.	1903—Archie Hahn 23 1/5s.
1945—Barney Ewell	10.3s.	1904—William Hogenson 22 4/5s.
1946—Bill Mathis	10.7s.	1905—Archie Hahn 22 1/5s.
1947—Bill Mathis	10.5s.	1906—R. L. Young 22 2/5s.
1948—Barney Ewell	10.6s.	1907—H. J. Huff 22 1/5s.
1949—Andy Stanfield	10.3s.	1908—W. F. Keating 22 2/5s.
1950—Arthur Bragg	10.4s.	1909—W. F. Dawbarn 22 2/5s.
1951—James Golliday	10.3s.	1910—Gwin Henry 22 3/5s.
1952—Dean Smith	10.5s.	1911—J. Nelson 21 4/5s.
1953—Arthur Bragg	9.5s.	1912—A. T. Meyer 21 4/5s.
1954—Arthur Bragg	9.5s.	1913—H. P. Drew 22 4/5s.
1955—Bobby Morrow	9.5s.	1914—I. T. Howe 22 1/5s.
1956—Bobby Morrow	10.3s.	1915—R. F. Morse ‡21 1/5s.
1957—Leamon King	9.7s.	1916—A. E. Ward 21 3/5s.
1958—Bobby Morrow	9.4s.	1917—A. E. Ward 22 1/5s.
1959—Ray Norton	10.5s.	1918—Loren Murhcison 22 2/5s.
1960—Ray Norton	10.5s.	1919—H. Williams 21 4/5s.
1961—Frank Budd	9.2s.	1920—Charles W. Paddock 21 2/5s.
1962—Robert Hayes	9.3s.	1921—Charles W. Paddock 21 4/5s.
1963—Bob Hayes	9.1s.	1922—J. A. Leconey 22.1s.
1964—Bob Hayes	10.3s.	1923—Loren Murchison 22.3s.
1965—George Anderson	9.3s.	1924—Charles W. Paddock 20.8s.
1966—Charlie Greene	9.4s.	1925—Jackson V. Scholz ‡20.8s.
1967—Jim Hines	9.3s.	1926—Tom Sharkey 21 2/5s.
1968—Charlie Greene ‡10.0s.		1927—Charles Borah 21 3/5s.
1969—Ivory Crockett	9.3s.	1928—Charles Borah 21 2/5s.
1970—Ivory Crockett	9.3s.	1929—Eddie Tolan 21.9s.
1971—Dr. Delano Meriwether ‡9.0s.		1930—George Simpson 21.3s.
1972—Robert Taylor	10.2s.	1931—Eddie Tolan 21s.

‡With wind.

220-Yard Dash—200 Meters

1877-1927, 1929-31, 1953-55, 1957-58, 1961-63, 1965-67, 1969-71: 22 20 yards.

1928, 1932-52, 1956, 1959-60, 1964, 1968, 1972: 200 meters.

1877—Edward Merrit	24s.	1932—Ralph Metcalfe 21.5s.
		1933—Ralph Metcalfe 21.1s.
		1934—Ralph Metcalfe 21.3s.
1878—W. C. Wilmer	22 7/8s.	1935—Ralph Metcalfe ‡21s.
1879—L. E. Myers	23 3/5s.	1936—Ralph Metcalfe 21.2s.
1880—L. E. Myers	23 3/5s.	1937—Jack Weiershauser 20.9s.
1881—L. E. Myers	23 1/2s.	1938—Mack Robinson 21.3s.
1882—Henry S. Brooks Jr.	22 3/5s.	1939—Norwood Ewell 21s.
1883—Henry S. Brooks Jr.	22 4/5s.	1940—Harold Davis 20.4s.
1884—L. E. Myers	24 1/5s.	1941—Harold Davis 20.4s.
1885—M. W. Ford	23 4/5s.	1942—Harold Davis 20.9s.
1886—M. W. Ford	23 1/5s.	1943—Harold Davis ‡20.2s.
1887—F. Westing	23 1/5s.	1944—Charles Parker 21.3s.
1888—F. Westing	22 2/5s.	1945—Elmore Harris 21.9s.
1888—*F. Westing	22 2/5s.	1946—Barney Ewell 21.2s.
1889—J. Owen Jr.	23 3/5s.	1947—Barney Ewell 21s.
1890—F. Westing	22 1/5s.	1948—Lloyd LaBeach 21s.
1891—Luther H. Cary	22 4/5s.	1949—Andy Stanfield 20.4s.
		1950—Robert Tyler 21.1s.
		1951—James Ford 20.8s.
		1952—Andy Stanfield 21.1s.
		1953—Andy Stanfield 21.2s.

1954—Arthur Bragg	21.1s.	1911—F. J. Lindberg	49s.
1955—Rod Richards	21s.	1912—T. J. Halpin	49 2/5s.
1956—Thane Baker	20.6s.	1913—C. B. Haff	51 1/5s.
1957—Ollan Cassell	21s.	1914—James E. Meredith	50 1/5s.
1958—Bobby Morrow	20.9s.	1915—James E. Meredith	‡47s.
1959—Ray Norton	20.8s.	1916—T. J. Halpin	49 4/5s.
1960—Ray Norton	20.8s.	1917—F. Shea	49 3/5s.
1961—Paul Drayton	21.0s.	1918—C. C. Shaughnessy	49 2/5s.
1962—Paul Drayton	20.5s.	1919—F. J. Shea	50 1/5s.
1963—Henry Carr, Paul Drayton (tie)	‡20.4s.	1920—F. J. Shea	49s.
1964—Henry Carr	20.6s.	1921—W. E. Stevenson	48 3/5s.
1965—Adolph Plummer	20.6s.	1922—J. W. Driscoll	49.9s.
1966—Jim Hines	20.5s.	1923—H. M. Fitch	50s.
1967—Tommie Smith	20.4s.	1924—James Burgess	49.8s.
1968—Tommie Smith	20.3s.	1925—Cecil G. Cooke	49.2s.
1969—John Carlos	20.2s.	1926—Kenneth Kennedy	48 3/5s.
1970—Ben Vaughan	20.8s.	1927—Herman Phillips	49 3/5s.
1971—Don Quarrie	‡20.2s.	1928—Raymond J. Barbuti	51 2/5s.
1972—Chuck Smith	20.7s.	1929—Reginald F. Bowen	48.4s.

‡ With wind.

440-Yard Run—400 Meters

1876-1927, 1929-31, 1935-55, 1957, 1961-63, 1965-67, 1969-71: 440 yards.

1928, 1932-52, 1956, 1958-60, 1964, 1968, 1972: 400 meters

1876—Edward Merritt	54 1/2s.	1930—Victor Williams	48.8s.
1877—Edward Merritt	55 1/4s.	1931—Victor Williams	48.8s.
1878—F. W. Brown	54 3/8s.	1932—William A. Carr	46.9s.
1879—Lawrence E. Myers	52 2/5s.	1933—Ivan Fuqua	47.7s.
1880—Lawrence E. Myers	52s.	1934—Ivan Fuqua	47.4s.
1881—Lawrence E. Myers	49 2/5s.	1935—Edward O'Brien	47.6s.
1882—Lawrence E. Myers	51 3/5s.	1936—Harold Smallwood	47.3s.
1883—Lawrence E. Myers	52 1/8s.	1937—Ray Malott	47.1s.
1884—Lawrence E. Myers	55 4/5s.	1938—Ray Malott	47.6s.
1885—H. M. Raborg	54 1/5s.	1939—Erwin Miller	48.3s.
1886—J. S. Robertson	52s.	1940—Grover Klemmer	47s.
1887—H. M. Banks	51 4/5s.	1941—Grover Klemmer	46s.
1888—*W. C. Dohm	51s.	1942—Cliff Bourland	46.7s.
1888—†T. J. O'Mahoney	53s.	1943—Cliff Bourland	47.7s.
1889—W. C. Dohm	51 2/5s.	1944—Elmore Harris	48.0s.
1890—W. C. Downs	50s.	1945—Herbert McKenley	48.4s.
1891—W. C. Downs	51s.	1946—Elmore Harris	46.3s.
1892—W. C. Downs	50s.	1947—Herbert McKenley	47.1s.
1893—E. W. Allen	50 2/5s.	1948—Herbert McKenley	46.3s.
1894—T. F. Keane	51s.	1949—George Rhoden	46.4s.
1895—T. E. Burke	49 3/5s.	1950—George Rhoden	46.5s.
1896—T. E. Burke	48 4/5s.	1951—George Rhoden	46.0s.
1897—T. E. Burke	49s.	1952—Mal Whitfield	46.4s.
1898—M. W. Long	52s.	1953—J. W. Mashburn	47.1s.
1899—M. W. Long	50 4/5s.	1954—Jim Lea	46.6s.
1900—M. W. Long	52 3/5s.	1955—Charles Jenkins	46.7s.
1901—H. W. Hayes	52 2/5s.	1956—Tom Courtney	45.8s.
1902—F. R. Moulton	50 4/5s.	1957—Reggie Pearman	46.4s.
1903—H. L. Hillman	52s.	1958—Eddie Southern	45.8s.
1904—D. H. Meyer	51 1/5s.	1959—Eddie Southern	46.1s.
1905—Frank Waller	49 3/5s.	1960—Otis Davis	45.8s.
1906—Frank Waller	50 1/5s.	1961—Otis Davis	46.1s.
1907—J. B. Taylor	51s.	1962—Ulis Williams	45.8s.
1908—Harry Hillman	49 3/5s.	1963—Ulis Williams	45.8s.
1909—E. F. Lindberg	50 2/5s.	1964—Mike Larrabee	46.0s.
1910—W. Hayes	52s.	1965—Ollan Cassell	46.1s.
		1966—Lee Evans	45.9s.
		1967—Lee Evans	45.3s.
		1968—Lee Evans	45.0s.
		1969—Lee Evans	45.6s.
		1970—John Smith	45.7s.

‡ With wind.

1971—John Smith .... 44.5s.
1972—Lee Evans .... 45.0s.

880-Yard Run—800 Meters

1876-1927, 1929-31, 1953-55, 1957-58, 1961-63, 1965-67, 1969-71: 880 yards.
1928, 1932-52, 1956, 1959-70, 1964, 1968, 1972: 800 meters.

1876—H. Lambe .... 2m. 10s.
1877—R. R. Colgate .... 2m. 5 3/4s.
1878—Edward Merritt .... 2m. 5 1/4s.
1879—Lawrence E. Myers .... 2m. 1 2/5s.
1880—Lawrence E. Myers .... 2m. 4 3/5s.
1881—William Smith .... 2m. 4s.
1882—W. H. Goodwin Jr. .... 1m. 56 7/8s.
1883—T. J. Murphy .... 2m. 4 2/5s.
1884—Lawrence E. Myers .... 2m. 9 4/5s.
1885—H. L. Mitchell .... 2m. 2 3/5s.
1886—C. M. Smith .... 2m. 4s.
1887—G. Tracy .... 2m. 1 3/5s.
1888—*G. Tracy .... 2m. 2 1/5s.
1888—†J. W. Moffatt .... 2m. 2 1/5s.
1889—R. A. Ward .... 2m. 6 1/5s.
1890—H. L. Dadman .... 1m. 59 1/5s.
1891—W. C. Dohm .... 2m. 4 1/5s.
1892—T. B. Turner .... 1m. 58 3/5s.
1893—T. B. Turner .... 2m. 1 4/5s.
1894—Charles H. Kilpatrick ...... 1m. 55 4/5s.
1895—Charles H. Kilpatrick ...... 1m. 56 2/5s.
1896—Charles H. Kilpatrick ...... 1m. 57 3/5s.
1897—J. F. Cregan .... 1m. 58 3/5s.
1898—T. E. Burke .... 2m. 2/5s.
1899—H. E. Manvel .... 1m. 58 1/5s.
1900—Alex Grant .... 2m. 4 1/5s.
1901—H. H. Hayes .... 2m. 2 4/5s.
1902—J. H. Wright .... 1m. 59 3/5s.
1903—H. V. Valentine .... 2m. 2 4/5s.
1904—H. V. Valentine .... 2m. 4/5s.
1905—James D. Lightbody .... 2m. 3 3/5s.
1906—M. W. Sheppard .... 1m. 55 2/5s.
1907—M. W. Sheppard .... 1m. 55 1/5s.
1908—M. W. Sheppard .... 1m. 55 3/5s.
1909—C. Edmundson .... 1m. 55 1/5s.
1910—Harry Gissing .... 2m. 1 4/5s.
1911—M. W. Sheppard .... 1m. 54 1/5s.
1912—M. W. Sheppard .... 1m. 57 2/5s.
1913—Homer Baker .... 2m. 1/5s.
1914—Homer Baker .... 1m. 57 3/5s.
1915—L. Campbell .... 2m. 1s.
1916—Don M. Scott .... 1m. 54s.
1917—M. A. Devaney .... 1m. 57s.
1918—T. S. Campbell .... 1m. 56 4/5s.
1919—Joie W. Ray .... 1m. 56s.
1920—Earl Eby .... 1m. 54 1/5s.
1921—A. B. Helffrich .... 1m. 54 4/5s.
1922—A. B. Helffrich .... 1m. 56.3s.
1923—Ray B. Watson .... 1m. 57.2s.
1924—Edward Kirby .... 1m. 58.9s.
1925—A. B. Helffrich .... 1m. 56.6s.
1926—Alva Martin .... 1m. 53 3/5s.
1927—Ray B. Watson .... 1m. 53 3/5s.
1928—Lloyd Hahn .... 1m. 51 2/5s.

1929—Phil Edwards .... 1m. 55.7s.
1930—Edwin Genung .... 1m. 53.4s.
1931—Edwin Genung .... 1m. 52 3/5s.
1932—Edwin Genung .... 1m. 52.6s.
1933—Glenn Cunningham .... 1m. 51.8s.
1934—Ben Eastman .... 1m. 50.8s.
1935—Elroy Robinson .... 1m. 53.1s.
1936—Charles Beetham .... 1m. 50.3s.
1937—John Woodruff .... 1m. 50s.
1938—Howard Borck .... 1m. 51.5s.
1939—Charles Beetham .... 1m. 51.7s.
1940—Charles Beetham .... 1m. 51.1s.
1941—Charles Beetham .... 1m. 50.2s.
1942—John Borican .... 1m. 51.2s.
1943—William Hulse .... 1m. 53.4s.
1944—Robert Kelly .... 1m. 51.8s.
1945—Robert Kelly .... 1m. 54.1s.
1946—John Fulton .... 1m. 52.7s.
1947—Reginald Pearman .... 1m. 50.9s.
1948—Herbert Barten .... 1m. 51.3s.
1949—Mal Whitfield .... 1m. 50.5s.
1950—Mal Whitfield .... 1m. 51.8s.
1951—Mal Whitfield .... 1m. 52.9s.
1952—Reginald Pearman .... 1m. 53.5s.
1953—Mal Whitfield .... 1m. 51.5s.
1954—Mal Whitfield .... 1m. 50.8s.
1955—Arnold Sowell .... 1m. 47.6s.
1956—Arnold Sowell .... 1m. 47.6s.
1957—Tom Courtney .... 1m. 50.1s.
1958—Tom Courtney .... 1m. 49.2s.
1959—Tom Murphy .... 1m. 47.9s.
1960—James Cerveny .... 1m. 48.4s.
1961—James Dupree .... 1m. 48.5s.
1962—Jerry Siebert .... 1m. 47.1s.
1963—Bill Crothers .... 1m. 46.8s.
1964—Jerry Siebert .... 1m. 47.5s.
1965—Morgan Groth .... 1m. 47.7s.
1966—Tom Farrell .... 1m. 47.6s.
1967—Wade Bell .... 1m. 46.1s.
1968—Wade Bell .... 1m. 45.5s.
1969—Byron Dyce .... 1m. 46.6s.
1970—Ken Swenson .... 1m. 47.4s.
1971—Juris Luzins .... 1m. 47.1s.
1972—Dave Wottle .... 1m. 47.3s.

1-Mile Run—1,500 Meters

1876-1927, 1929-31, 1953-55, 1957-58, 1961-63, 1965-67, 1969-71: 1 mile.
1928, 1932-52, 1956, 1959-60, 1964, 1968, 1972: 1,500 meters.

1876—H. Lambe .... 4m. 51 1/5s.
1877—R. Morgan .... 4m. 49 3/4s.
1878—T. H. Smith .... 4m. 51 1/4s.
1879—H. M. Pellatt .... 4m. 42 2/5s.
1880—H. Fredericks .... 4m. 30 3/5s.
1881—H. Fredericks .... 4m. 32 3/5s.
1882—H. Fredericks .... 4m. 36 2/5s.
1883—H. Fredericks .... 4m. 36 4/5s.
1884—P. C. Mederia .... 4m. 36 4/5s.
1885—G. Y. Gilbert .... 4m. 41 1/5s.
1886—E. C. Carter .... 4m. 33 2/5s.
1887—E. C. Carter .... 4m. 30s.

1888—*G. M. Gibbs	4m. 27 1/5s.	1949—John Twomey	3m. 52.6s.
1888—†Thomas P. Conneff	4m. 32 3/5s.	1950—John Twomey	3m. 51.3s.
1889—A. B. George	4m. 36s.	1951—Leonard Truex	3m. 52.0s.
1890—A. B. George	4m. 24 4/5s.	1952—Wes Santee	3m. 49.3s.
1891—Thomas P. Conneff	4m. 30 3/5s.	1953—Wes Santee	4m. 07.6s.
1892—G. W. Orton	4m. 27 4/5s.	1954—Fred Dwyer	4m. 09.5s.
1893—G. W. Orton	4m. 32 4/5s.	1955—Wes Santee	4m. 11.5s.
1894—G. W. Orton	4m. 24 2/5s.	1956—Jerome Walters	3m. 48.4s.
1895—G. W. Orton	4m. 36s.	1957—Mervyn Lincoln	4m. 06.1s.
1896—G. W. Orton	4m. 27s.	1958—Herb Elliott	3m. 57.9s.
1897—J. F. Cregan	4m. 27 3/5s.	1959—Dyrol Burleson	3m. 47.5s.
1898—J. F. Cregan	4m. 47s.	1960—James Grelle	3m. 42.7s.
1899—Alex Grant	4m. 28 1/5s.	1961—Dyrol Burleson	4m. 04.9s.
1900—G. W. Orton	4m. 42 2/5s.	1962—James Beatty	3m. 57.9s.
1901—Alex Grant	4m. 36 2/5s.	1963—Dyrol Burleson	3m. 56.7s.
1902—Alex Grant	4m. 35 4/5s.	1964—Tom O'Hara	3m. 38.1s.
1903—Alex Grant	4m. 52s.	1965—Jim Ryun	3m. 55.3s.
1904—D. C. Munson	4m. 41 1/5s.	1966—Jim Ryun	3m. 58.6s.
1905—James D. Lightbody	4m. 48 4/5s.	1967—Jim Ryun	3m. 51.1s.
1906—F. A. Rodgers	4m. 22 4/5s.	1968—John Mason	3m. 43.1s.
1907—J. P. Sullivan	4m. 29s.	1969—Marty Liquori	3m. 59.5s.
1908—H. L. Trube	4m. 25s.	1970—Howell Michael	4m. 01.8s.
1909—Joe Ballard	4m. 30 1/5s.	1971—Marty Liquori	3m. 56.5s.
1910—J. W. Monument	4m. 31s.	1972—Jerome Howe	3m. 38.2s.
1911—Abel R. Kiviat	4m. 19 3/5s.		
1912—Abel R. Kiviat	4m. 18 3/5s.	**3-Mile Run—5,000 Meters**	
1913—Norman S. Taber	4m. 26 2/5s.	1953-55, 1957-58, 1961-63, 1965-67, 1969-71: 3	
1914—Abel R. Kiviat	4m. 25 1/5s.	mile.	
1915—Joie W. Ray	4m. 23 1/5s.	1932, 1956, 1959-60, 1964, 1968, 1972: 5,000	
1916—I. A. Myer	4m. 22s.	meters.	
1917—Joie W. Ray	4m. 18 2/5s.	1932—Ralph Hill	14m. 55.7s.
1918—Joie W. Ray	4m. 20s.	1933—John Follows	15m. 27s.
1919—Joie W. Ray	4m. 14 2/5s.	1934—Frank Crowley	15m. 18.6s.
1920—Joie W. Ray	4m. 16 1/5s.	1935—Joseph P. McCluskey	15m. 14.1s.
1921—Joie W. Ray	4m. 16 4/5s.	1936—Donald Lash	15m. 4.8s.
1922—Joie W. Ray	4m. 17s.	1937—Joseph P. McCluskey	15m. 4.1s.
1923—Joie W. Ray	4m. 18s.	1938—J. Gregory Rice	15m. 15s.
1924—Ray Buker	4m. 24.8s.	1939—J. Gregory Rice	14m. 50.9s.
1925—Ray Buker	4m. 19.4s.	1940—J. Gregory Rice	14m. 33.4s.
1926—Lloyd Hahn	4m. 16s.	1941—J. Gregory Rice	14m. 45.2s.
1927—Ray Conger	4m. 23 3/5s.	1942—J. Gregory Rice	14m. 39.7s.
1928—Ray Conger	3m. 55s.	1943—Gunder Hagg	14m. 48.5s.
1929—Leo Lermond	4m. 24.6s.	1944—James Rafferty	15m. 22.3s.
1930—Ray Conger	4m. 19.8s.	1945—John Kandl	16m. 14.4s.
1931—Leo Lermond	4m. 15s.	1946—Francis Martin	15m. 50.7s.
1932—Norwood P. Hallowell	3m. 52.7s.	1947—Curtis Stone	15m. 02.7s.
1933—Glenn Cunningham	3m. 52.3s.	1948—Curtis Stone	14m. 49.1s.
1934—William R. Bonthron	3m. 48.8s.	1949—Fred Wilt	14m. 49.3s.
1935—Glenn Cunningham	3m. 52.1s.	1950—Fred Wilt	15m. 19.4s.
1936—Glenn Cunningham	3m. 54.2s.	1951—Fred Wilt	14m. 47.5s.
1937—Glenn Cunningham	3m. 51.8s.	1952—Curtis Stone	15m. 03.3s.
1938—Glenn Cunningham	3m. 52.5s.	1953—Charles Capozzoli	14m. 28.2s.
1939—Blaine Rideout	3m. 51.5s.	1954—Horace Ashenfelter	14m. 18.5s.
1940—Walter Mehl	3m. 47.9s.	1955—Horace Ashenfelter	14m. 45.2s.
1941—Leslie MacMitchell	3m. 53.1s.	1956—Dick Hart	14m. 47.4s.
1942—Gilbert Dodds	3m. 50.2s.	1957—John Macy	13m. 55s.
1943—Gilbert Dodds	3m. 50s.	1958—Alex Henderson	13m. 37.1s.
1944—William Hulse	3m. 54.3s.	1959—William Dellinger	14m. 47.6s.
1945—Roland Sink	3m. 58.4s.	1960—William Dellinger	14m. 26.4s.
1946—Lennart Strand	3m. 54.5s.	1961—Laszlo Tabori	13m. 50.0s.
1947—Gerald Karver	3m. 52.9s.	1962—Murray Halberg	13m. 30.6s.
1948—Gilbert Dodds	3m. 52.1s.	1963—Pat Clohessy	13m. 40.4s.

1964—Bob Schul .... 13m. 56.2s.
1965—Bob Schul .... 13m. 10.4s.
1966—George Young .... 13m. 27.4s.
1967—Gerry Lindgren .... 13m. 10.6s.
1968—Bob Day .... 13m. 50.4s.
1969—Tracy Smith .... 13m. 18.4s.
1970—Frank Shorter .... 13m. 24.2s.
1971—Steve Prefontaine .... 12m. 58.6s.
1972—Mike Keogh .... 13m. 51.7s.

6-Mile Run—10,000 Meters

1925-27, 1929-31, 1953-55, 1957-58, 1961-63, 1965-67, 1969-71: 6 mile.
1928, 1932-52, 1956, 1959-60, 1964, 1968, 1972: 10,000 meters.

1925—George W. Lermond .... 31m. 34.6s.
1926—Philip Osif .... 31m. 31s.
1927—Willie Ritola .... 30m. 43 2/5s.
1928—Joie W. Ray .... 31m. 28 2/5s.
1929—Louis Gregory .... 33m. 47.7s.
1930—Louis Gregory .... 31m. 31.3s.
1931—Louis Gregory .... 31m. 26.4s.
1932—Thomas Ottey .... 32m. 18.2s.
1933—Louis Gregory .... 32m. 39.4s.
1934—Eino Pentti .... 33m. 34.2s.
1935—Thomas Ottey .... 32m. 07.3s.
1936—Donald Lash .... 31m. 06.9s.
1937—Eino Pentti .... 32m. 02s.
1938—Eino Pentti .... 32m. 15.6s.
1939—Louis Gregory .... 33m. 11.5s.
1940—Donald Lash .... 32m. 29.2s.
1941—Louis Gregory .... 33m. 11s.
1942—Joseph P. McCluskey ...... 32m. 28.3s.
1943—Lt. Louis Gregory .... 33m. 22s.
1944—Norman Bright .... 33m. 53s.
1945—Ted Vogel .... 35m. 30.7s.
1946—Edward O'Toole .... 32m. 17.5s.
1947—Edward O'Toole .... 33m. 28.3s.
1948—Edward O'Toole .... 32m. 29.7s.
1949—Fred Wilt .... 31m. 05.7s.
1950—Horace Ashenfelter .... 32m. 44.3s.
1951—Curtis Stone .... 32m. 30.7s.
1952—Curtis Stone .... 30m. 33.4s.
1953—Curtis Stone .... 31m. 18.2s.
1954—Curtis Stone .... 31m. 39.4s.
1955—Dick Hart .... 31m. 58.5s.
1956—Max Truex .... 30m. 52s.
1957—Doug Kyle .... 29m. 22.8s.
1958—John Macy .... 29m. 25.6s.
1959—Max Truex .... 31m. 22.4s.
1960—Al Lawrence .... 30m. 11.4s.
1961—John Gutknecht .... 28m. 52.6s.
1962—Bruce Kidd .... 28m. 23.1s.
1963—Pete McArdle .... 28m. 29.2s.
1964—Pete McArdle .... 30m. 11.0s.
1965—Billy Mills .... 27m. 11.6s.
1966—Tracy Smith .... 28m. 02.0s.
1967—Van Nelson .... 28m. 18.8s.
1968—Tracy Smith .... 28m. 47.0s.
1969—Jack Bacheler .... 28m. 12.2s.
1970—Frank Shorter,
      Jack Bacheler (tie) ......27m. 24.0s.

1971—Frank Shorter .... 27m. 27.2s.
1972—Greg Fredericks .... 28m. 08.8s.

Marathon

1925—Charles L. Mellor ......2h. 33m. 3/5s.
1926—Clarence DeMar ....2h. 45m. 5 1/5s.
1927—Clarence DeMar ....2h. 40m. 22 1/5s.
1928—Clarence DeMar ....2h. 37m. 7 4/5s.
1929—John C. Miles ....2h. 33m. 8 4/5s.
1930—Karl Koski ....2h. 25m. 21 1/5s.
1931—William A. Agee ....2h. 32m. 38s.
1932—Clyde D. Martak ......2h. 58m. 15s.
1933—Dave Komonen ....2h. 53m. 43s.
1934—Dave Komonen ....2h. 43m. 26.6s.
1935—Frank (Pat) Dengis ....2h. 53m. 53s.
1936—Wm. T. McMahon .....2h. 38m. 14 1/5s.
1937—Mel Porter ....2h. 44m. 22s.
1938—Frank (Pat) Dengis ....2h. 39m. 38.2s.
1939—Frank (Pat) Dengis ....2h. 33m. 45.2s.
1940—Gerard Cote ....2h. 34m. 6s.
1941—Joseph Smith ....2h. 36m. 6.8s.
1942—Fred A. McGlone ......2h. 37m. 54s.
1943—Sgt. Gerard Cote ......2h. 38m. 35.3s.
1944—Charles Robbins ......2h. 40m. 48.6s.
1945—Charles Robbins ......2h. 37m. 14s.
1946—Gerard Cote ....2h. 47m. 53.6s.
1947—Ted Vogel ....2h. 40m. 11s.
1948—John A. Kelley ....2h. 48m. 32.3s.
1949—Victor Dyrgall ....2h. 38m. 48.9s.
1950—John A. Kelley ....2h. 45m. 55.3s.
1951—Jesse Van Zant ....2h. 37m. 12.5s.
1952—Victor Dyrgall ....2h. 38m. 24.4s.
1953—Karl Gosta Leandersson .2h. 48m. 12.5s.
1954—Ted Corbitt ....2h. 46m. 13.9s.
1955—Nick Costes ....2h. 31m. 12.4s.
1956—John J. Kelley ....2h. 24m. 52.2s.
1957—John J. Kelley ....2h. 24m. 55.2s.
1958—John J. Kelley ....2h. 21m. 00.4s.
1959—John J. Kelley ....2h. 21m. 54.5s.
1960—John J. Kelley ....2h. 20m. 13.6s.
1961—John J. Kelley ....2h. 26m. 53.4s.
1962—John J. Kelley ....2h. 27m. 39.0s.
1963—John J. Kelley ....2h. 25m. 17.6s.
1964—Leonard Edelen ....2h. 24m. 25.6s.
1965—Gar Williams ....2h. 33m. 50.6s.
1966—Norman Higgins ....2h. 22m. 50.0s.
1967—Ron Daws ....2h. 40m. 07s.
1968—George Young ....2h. 30m. 48s.
1969—Tom Heinonen ....2h. 24m. 43s.
1970—Bob Fitts ....2h. 24m. 10.6s.
1971—Ken Moore ....2h. 16m. 48.6s.
1972—Edmund Norris ....2h. 24m. 42.8s.

120-Yard High Hurdles—110 Meters

1876-1927, 1929-31, 1953-55, 1957-58, 1961-63, 1965-67, 1969-71: 120 yards.
1928, 1932-52, 1956, 1959-60, 1964, 1968, 1972: 110 meters.

1876—George Hitchcock .... 19s.
1877—H. E. Ficken .... 18 1/4s.
1878—H. E. Ficken .... 17 1/4s.
1879—J. E. A. Haigh .... 19s.
1880—H. H. Moritz .... 19 1/5s.

1881—J. T. Tivey	19 1/8s.	1943—Bill Cummins	14.3s.
1882—J. T. Tivey	16 4/5s.	1944—Owen Cassidy	14.9s.
1883—S. A. Safford	19 2/5s.	1945—Charles Morgan	14.9s.
1884—S. A. Safford	18 1/5s.	1946—Harrison Dillard	14.2s.
1885—A. A. Jordan	17 3/5s.	1947—Harrison Dillard	14.0s.
1886—A. A. Jordan	16 1/2s.	1948—William Porter	14.1s.
1887—A. A. Jordan	16 2/5s.	1949—Craig Dixon	13.8s.
1888—*A. A. Jordan	16 1/5s.	1950—Richard Attlesey	13.6s.
1889—G. Schwegler	17s.	1951—Richard Attlesey	13.8s.
1890—F. T. Ducharne	16s.	1952—Harrison Dillard	13.7s.
1891—A. F. Copland	16s.	1953—Jack Davis	13.9s.
1892—F. C. Puffer	‡15 2/5s.	1954—Jack Davis	14s.
1893—F. C. Puffer	16s.	1955—Milt Campbell	13.9s.
1894—S. Chase	15 3/5s.	1956—Lee Calhoun	13.6s.
1895—S. Chase	15 3/4s.	1957—Lee Calhoun	14.2s.
1896—W. B. Rogers	16 1/5s.	1958—Hayes Jones	13.8s.
1897—J. H. Thompson Jr.	16s.	1959—Lee Calhoun	14.0s.
1898—Alvin C. Kraenzlein	15 1/5s.	1960—Hayes Jones	13.6s.
1899—Alvin C. Kraenzlein	15 4/5s.	1961—Hayes Jones	13.6s.
1900—R. F. Hutchison	16 1/5s.	1962—Jerry Tarr	13.4s.
1901—W. T. Fishleigh	16 1/5s.	1963—Hayes Jones	13.4s.
1902—R. H. Hatfield	17 4/5s.	1964—Hayes Jones	13.8s.
1903—F. W. Schule	16 3/5s.	1965—Willie Davenport	13.6s.
1904—F. Castleman	16 1/5s.	1966—Willie Davenport	13.3s.
1905—Hugo Friend	16 1/5s.	1967—Willie Davenport	13.3s.
1906—W. M. Armstrong	16s.	1968—Earl McCullouch	13.5s.
1907—Forrest Smithson	15 3/5s.	1969—Willie Davenport, Leon	
1908—A. B. Shaw	15 1/5s.	Coleman (tie)	13.3s.
1909—Forrest Smithson	15 1/5s.	1970—Thomas Hill	13.3s.
1910—J. Case	15 4/5s.	1971—Rod Milburn	‡13.1s.
1911—A. B. Shaw	15 3/5s.	1972—Rod Milburn	13.4s.
1912—J. P. Nicholson	15 4/5s.	†With wind and five hurdles knocked down.	
1913—F. W. Kelly	16 2/5s.	‡With wind.	
1914—H. Goelitz	16 1/5s.		
1915—F. Murray	‡15s.	**440-Yard Hurdles—400 Meters**	
1916—R. Simpson	14 4/5s.	1914-27, 1929-31, 1953-55, 1957-58, 1961-63,	
1917—H. E. Barron	15s.	1965-67, 1969-71: 440 yards.	
1918—E. J. Thomson	15 1/5s.	1928, 1932-52, 1956, 1959-60, 1964, 1968,	
1919—R. Simpson	15 1/5s.	1972: 400 meters.	
1920—H. E. Barron	15 1/5s.	1914—W. H. Meanix	57 4/5s.
1921—E. J. Thomson	15s.	1915—W. H. Meanix	‡52 3/5s.
1922—E. J. Thomson	15.3s.	1916—W. A. Hummel	54 4/5s.
1923—Karl W. Anderson	15.1s.	1917—Floyd Smart	54 4/5s.
1924—Ivan H. Riley	15.4s.	1918—D. Hause	59s.
1925—George Guthrie	‡14.6s.	1919—Floyd Smart	55 3/5s.
1926—Leighton Dye	14 3/5s.	1920—F. F. Loomis	55s.
1927—C. D. Werner	14 3/5s.	1921—A. Desch	‡53 2/5s.
1928—Stephen E. Anderson	14 4/5s.	1922—Joseph Hall	56.5s.
1929—Stephen E. Anderson	14.9s.	1923—Ivan H. Riley	55.4s.
1930—Stephen E. Anderson	14.4s.	1924—F. Morgan Taylor	54.5s.
1931—Percy Beard	14.2s.	1925—F. Morgan Taylor	‡53.8s
1932—Jack Keller	14.4s.	1926—F. Morgan Taylor	55s.
1933—John Morriss	14.3s.	1927—John A. Gibson	52 3/5s.
1934—Percy Beard	14.6s.	1928—F. Morgan Taylor	52s.
1935—Percy Beard	‡14.2s.	1929—Gordon Allott	54.3s.
1936—Forrest G. Towns	14.2s.	1930—Richard Pomeroy	53.1s.
1937—Allan Tolmich	14.5s.	1931—Victor Burke	54.2s.
1938—Fred Wolcott	14.3s.	1932—Joseph Healy	‖53.5s.
1939—Joe Batiste	14.1s.	1933—Glenn Hardin	52.2s.
1940—Fred Wolcott	13.9s.	1934—Glenn Hardin	51.8s.
1941—Fred Wolcott	13.7s.	1935—Thomas Moore	53.5s.
1942—Bill Cummins	14.1s.	1936—Glenn Hardin	51.6s.

1937–Jack Patterson	52.3s.	1916–M. A. Devaney	10m. 48s.
1938–Jack Patterson	52.8s.	1917-18–No competition	
1939–Roy V. Cochran	51.9s.	1919–M. A. Devaney	10m. 17 2/5s.
1940–Carl McBain	51.6s.	1920–P. Flynn	9m. 58 1/5s.
1941–Arky Erwin	54.5s.	1921–M. A. Devaney	11m. 34s.
1942–J. Walter Smith	52s.	1922–M. A. Devaney	11m. 10 1/5s.
1943–Arky Erwin	53.1s.	1923–Willie Ritola	10m. 45 3/5s.
1944–Arky Erwin	54s.	1924–Marvin Rick	10m. 43.2s.
1945–Dr. Arky Erwin	53.7s.	1925–Russell Payne	10m. 40 4/5s.
1946–Dr. Arky Erwin	55.5s.	1926–Willie Ritola	10m. 34 1/5s.
1947–J. W. Smith	52.3s.	1927–Willie Ritola	10m. 19 2/5s.
1948–Roy Cockran	52.3s.	1928–Wm. O. Spencer	9m. 35 4/5s.
1949–Charles Moore Jr.	51.1s.	1929–David Abbott	10m. 59.1s.
1950–Charles Moore Jr.	53.6s.	1930–Joseph P. McCluskey	10m. 44.2s.
1951–Charles Moore Jr.	51.4s.	1931–Joseph P. McCluskey	10m. 11 3/5s.
1952–Charles Moore Jr.	51.2s.	1932–Joseph P. McCluskey	9m. 14.5s.
1953–Josh Culbreath	52.5s.	1933–Joseph P. McCluskey	9m. 38.5s.
1954–Josh Culbreath	52s.	1934–Harold Manning	9m. 13.1s.
1955–Josh Culbreath	52s.	1935–Joseph P. McCluskey	9m. 30.3s.
1956–Glenn Davis	50.9s.	1936–Harold Manning	9m. 15.1s.
1957–Glenn Davis	50.9s.	1937–Floyd Lochner	9m. 26.6s.
1958–Glenn Davis	49.9s.	1938–Joseph P. McCluskey	9m. 23.3s.
1959–Richard Howard	50.7s.	1939–Joseph P. McCluskey	9m. 23.1s.
1960–Glenn Davis	50.1s.	1940–Joseph P. McCluskey	9m. 16.6s.
1961–Clifton Cushman	50.9s.	1941–Forest Efaw	9m. 13.7s.
1962–Willie Atterberry	50.5s.	1942–George DeGeorge	9m. 16.5s.
1963–Rex Cawley	50.4s.	1943–Lt. Joseph P. McCluskey	9m. 39.7s.
1964–Billy Hardin	50.1s.	1944–Forest Efaw	9m. 39.6s.
1965–Rex Cawley	50.3s.	1945–James Wisner	10m. 00.6s.
1966–Jim Miller	50.1s.	1946–James Rafferty	10m. 01s.
1967–Ron Whitney	50.3s.	1947–Forest Efaw	9m. 32.5s.
1968–Ron Whitney	49.6s.	1948–Forest Efaw	9m. 32.9s.
1969–Ralph Mann	50.1s.	1949–Curt Stone	9m. 31s.
1970–Ralph Mann	49.8s.	1950–Warren Druetzler	9m. 33.6s.
1971–Ralph Mann	49.3s.	1951–Horace Ashenfelter	9m. 24.5s.
1972–Richard Bruggeman	50.0s.	1952–Robert McMullen	9m. 25.3s.

‡ With wind. ‡ One hurdle knocked down. ‖ Glenn Hardin finished first; disqualified for running out of lane.

2-Mile Steeplechase–3,000 Meters

1889-1919, 1921-27, 1929-31, 1953-55, 1957: 2 miles.

1920, 1928, 1932-52, 1956, 1958-72: 3,000 meters.

1889–A. B. George	11m. 17 2/5s.	1953–Horace Ashenfelter	10m. 2.5s.
1890–W. T. Young	10m. 50 2/5s.	1954–William Ashenfelter	10m. 8.2s.
1891–E. W. Hjertberg	11m. 34 3/5s.	1955–Ken Reiser	10m. 20.7s.
1892–E. W. Hjertberg	13m. 10s.	1956–Horace Ashenfelter	9m. 4.1s.
1893–G. W. Orton	12m. 2s.	1957–Charles Jones	9m. 49.6s.
1894–G. W. Orton	12m. 38 4/5s.	1958–Charles Jones	8m. 57.3s.
1895–No competition		1959–Philip Coleman	9m. 19.3s.
1896–G. W. Orton	10m. 58 3/5s.	1960–Philip Coleman	8m. 55.6s.
1897–G. W. Orton	12m. 8 2/5s.	1961–Charles Jones	8m. 48.0s.
1898–G. W. Orton	11m. 41 4/5s.	1962–George Young	8m. 48.2s.
1899–G. W. Orton	11m. 44 3/5s.	1963–Pat Traynor	8m. 51.2s.
1900–A. Grant	12m. 19 2/5s.	1964–Jeff Fishback	8m. 43.6s.
1901–G. W. Orton	11m. 58s.	1965–George Young	8m. 50.6s.
1902–A. L. Newton	12m. 28 4/5s.	1966–Pat Traynor	8m. 40.6s.
1903–No competition		1967–Pat Traynor	8m. 42.0s.
1904–John J. Daly	10m. 51 4/5s.	1968–George Young	8m. 30.6s.
1905–Harvey Cohn	12m. 5 1/5s.	1969–Mike Manley	8m. 36.6s.
1906-15–No competition		1970–Bill Reilly	8m. 34.8s.
		1971–Sid Sink	8m. 26.4s.
		1972–James Dare	8m. 33.7s.

2 Mile Walk–3,000 Meters

1953-55, 1957-59, 1969-71: 2 miles.
1920-52, 1956, 1960-68: 3,000 meters.

1920–William Plant 13m. 8s
1921-34–No competition

1935–Harry Hinkel . . . . 13m. 43.3s.
1936–Harry Hinkel . . . . 13m. 36.8s.
1937–Max Beutel . . . . 14m. 15s.
1938–Henry Cieman . . . . 13m. 39.9s.
1939–Otto Kotraba . . . . 14m. 4.7s.
1940–Otto Kotraba . . . . 13m. 53s.
1941–Joseph Medgyesi . . . . 14m. 37.9s.
1942–John Connolly . . . . 14m. 16.3s.
1943–James Wilson . . . . 14m. 16.9s.
1944–Fred Sharaga . . . . 14m. 8.5s.
1945–Sam Bleifer . . . . 14m. 27.5s.
1946–Ernest Weber . . . . 13m. 51.8s.
1947–Ernest Weber . . . . 14m. 10.1s.
1948–Henry H. Laskau . . . . 13m. 17.9s.
1949–Henry H. Laskau . . . . 13m. 34s.
1950–Henry H. Laskau . . . . 13m. 9.6s.
1951–Henry H. Laskau . . . . 13m. 13.2s.
1952–Henry H. Laskau . . . . 12m. 52.7s.
1953–Henry H. Laskau . . . . 14m. 23.4s.
1954–Henry H. Laskau . . . . 14m. 23.3s.
1955–Henry H. Laskau . . . . 15m. 9.4s.
1956–Henry H. Laskau . . . . 13m. 39s.
1957–Henry H. Laskau . . . . 14m. 28.3s.
1958–John Humcke . . . . 15m. 07.5s.
1959–Elliott Denman . . . . 13m. 52.2s.
1960–Rudy Haluza . . . . 13m. 22.1s.
1961–Ronald Zinn . . . . 14m. 46.8s.
1962–Ronald Zinn . . . . 14m. 35.8s.
1963–Lt. Ron Zinn . . . . 14m. 03.6s.
1964–Ron Zinn . . . . 13m. 48.6s.
1965–Ron Laird . . . . 14m. 04.2s.
1966–Ron Laird . . . . 13m. 52.6s.
1967–Ron Laird . . . . 13m. 41.4s.
1968–Don DeNoon . . . . 12m. 38.0s.
1969–Ron Laird . . . . 13m. 31.6s.
1970–Tom Dooley . . . . 13m. 44.0s.
1971–Larry Young . . . . 13m. 49.5s.
1972–No Competition

3 Mile Walk–5,000 Meters
1972: 5,000 meters
1972–Larry Young . . . . 21m. 39.8s.

440-Yard Relay–400 Meters
1918-31, 1958-72: 440 yards.
1932-57: 400 meters.
1918–Great Lakes Naval Station (Dover,
Erickson, Cass, Loren Murchison) . . . . . 44.4s.
1919–New York A.C. (J. R. Patterson,
Andy Kelly, Fred W. Kelly, Loren Mur-
chison) . . . . 44s.
1920–No competition
1921–New York A.C. (B. J. Wefers Jr., F.
Lovejoy, Ray, Edward Farrell) . . . . 42.4s.
1922–New York A.C. (B. J. Wefers Jr., F.
Lovejoy, J. C. Taylor, Edward Farrell) . . 43.3s.
1923–Newark A.C. (Loren Murchison,
Robert LeGendre, Clarence McKim,
Chester Bowman) . . . . 43.1s.
1924–Newark A.C. (Chester Bowman,
Walter Blauberg, Eldred Andruss, Loren
Murchison) . . . . 43.4s.

1925–New York A.C. (Frank Hussey,
James Todd, J. O. McDonald, Jackson V.
Scholz) . . . . 41.4s.
1926–Newark A.C. (Harwood, Cumming,
Louis A. Clarke, Chester Bowman) . . . . . 41.6s.
1927–Newark A.C. (Chester Bowman, Cur-
rie, Pappas, Cummings) . . . . 41s.
1928–No competition
1929–Los Angeles A.C. (Milton Maurer,
Charles Paddock, Maurice Guyer, Frank
Wykoff) . . . . 41.9s.
1930–Los Angeles A.C. (Bob Maxwell, Vic
Williams, Ray Alf, Hector Dyer) . . . . 42.3s.
1931–Los Angeles A.C. (Henry Taylor, Ken
Robinson, Ray Alf, Frank Wykoff) . . . . 41.6s.
1932–No competition
1933–Newark A.C. (Richard Hardy,
Charles Kelly, Alastair McGaw, Alfred
Maskrey) . . . . 41.6s.
1934–Marquette Univ. (Ned Sengpiel,
Booth, James Jessel, Ralph Metcalfe) . . . 41.4s.
1935–Marquette Univ. Club . . . . 41.2s.
1936–Marquette Club (Ned Sengpiel,
George Dinges, James Jessel, Ralph Met-
calfe) . . . . 41.3s.
1937–Olympic Club (Ray Dean, Al Fitch,
Ray Malott, Jack Weirshauser) . . . . 41.2s.
1938–New York A.C (H. Weast, W. Cook,
R. Rodenkirchen, P. Walker) . . . . 41.9s.
1939–New York A.C. (H. Weast, E. O'Sullivan, K. Clapp, P. Walker) . . . . 41s.
1940–So. Calif. A.A. (B. Willis, M. Anderson, H. Sinclair, E. Morris) . . . . 41.1s.
1941–So. Calif. A.A. (James Reilly, Hubert
Kerns, Clifford Bourland, Peyton Jordan) 42.2s.
1942–New York A.C. (Paul Cowie, Walter
Kruger, Robert Stuart, Chas. Shaw Jr.) . . 43s.
1943–Pioneer Club, N.Y. (Rudolph Nedd,
Ralph Lucia, Clarence Williams, Eddie
Greenidge) . . . . 44.2s.
1944–U.S. Coast Guard (Homer Gillis, Eu-
lace Peacock, Don O'Leary, Herbert
Thompson) . . . . 44.5s.
1945–Pioneer Club, N.Y. (Joseph Payne,
Medford Parker, Rudolph Valentine,
Rudolph Nedd) . . . . 44.4s.
1946–Pioneer Club, N.Y. (Rudolph Nedd,
Rudolph Valentine, Ed Greenidge, Tom
Carey) . . . . 42.7s.
1947–San Antonio A.C. (Bill Martineson,
Perry Samuels, Allen Lawler, Charles
Parker) . . . . 40.9s.
1948–No competition
1949–Long Branch Shore A.C. (Stanfield,
Fox, Slade, McKenley) . . . . 41.5s.
1950–Morgan State College (Sam LaBeacn,
George Rhoden, Arthur Bragg, Robert
Tyler) . . . . 41s.
1951–Morgan State College (Lance Thomp-
son, Byron LaBeach, George Rhoden,
Arthur Bragg) . . . . 41.8s.
1952–Navy Olympics (Scott, Jackson,

Macon, Dennis) .... 42.7s.

1953—Pioneer Club, N.Y. (Brailsford, Conaway, Gathers, Carty) .... 41.1s.

1954—Chicago C. Y. O. (Ira Murchison, Ralph Butler, Al Pritchett, Willie Williams) 40.8s.

1955—Pioneer Club, N. Y. (Arnold Budd, Thomas Beach, James Gathers, Andy Stanfield) .... 41.5s.

1956—East York, Toronto, Track Club (Sam Levenson, Jack Parrington, Bob Harding, Joe Foreman) .... 41.3s.

1957—Pioneer Club, N.Y. (Robert Thomas, Arnold Budd, Tom Beach, Jim Gathers) . 41.4s.

1958—Pioneer Club, N. Y. (Jim Phipps, John Fernandez, Dick Williams, Jim Gathers) .... 42.4s.

1959—Chicago University (Edward Houston, Frank Loomis, Willie May, Ward Miller) .... 42.5s.

1960—Cleveland Striders (Willie Love, Robert Miller, Fred Buckner, Nate Adams) .. 41.4s.

1961—Tarrytown Spike Shoe Club (Les Prinz, Al Washington, Walker Beverly, Mel Blanheim) .... 41.5s.

1962—Pioneer Club, N.Y. (Wilt Jackson, Len Byrd, Hubert Brown, Frank Bowens) 41.8s.

1963—Cleveland Striders (Mel Orr, Bob Bailey, Vic Reed, Willie Love) .... 41.4s.

1964—U.S. Army (Paul Drayton, Mel Pender, Larry Dunn, John Moon) .... 40.3s.

1965—Pioneer Club, N.Y. (Lionel Urgan, Willie Pendergast, Julio Meade, Mel Blenheim) .... 41.9s.

1966—Pioneer Club, N.Y. (Lionel Urgan, Julio Meade, Richard Spooner, John Carlos) .... 41.0s.

1967—Philadelphia Pioneer Club (Tom Randolph, Monty Frazier, Orin Richburg, Erv Hall) .... 40.1s.

1968—New York Pioneer Club .... 42.3s.

1969—No competition

1970—New York Pioneer Club .... 41.5s.

1971—New York Pioneer Club .... 40.9s.

1972—Bohaa, Brooklyn .... 41.3s.

1-Mile Relay—1,600 Meters
1918-31, 1958-72: One mile.
1933-57: 1,600 meters.

1918—Pelham Bay Naval Station (Desch, Feerick, Dernell, O'Brien) 3m. 26s.

1919—Boston A.A. (Driscoll, Meanix, Dudley, Caffrey) .... 3m. 27.2s.

1920—No competition

1921—New York A.C. (B. J. Wefers, Adams, Ray Stevenson) .... 3m. 19.8s.

1922—New York A.C. (B. J. Wefers, J. C. Taylor, Alan B. Helffrich, W. E. Stevenson) .... 3m. 21s.

1923—Univ. of Iowa (H. C. Morrow, G. B. Noll, C. R. Brookins, E. C Wilson) .... 3m. 18.1s.

1924—Boston A.C. (E. S. Dudley, William McKillop, J. J. Sullivan, H. N. Bates) .... 3m. 24.2s.

1925—New York A.C. (Joseph Campbell, John Holden, Joseph Tierney, Alan B. Helffrich) .... 3m. 20.8s.

1926—Illinois A.C. (Stevenson, Taylor, Oestrich, Kennedy) .... 3m. 17.6s.

1927—Illinois A.C. (Oestrich, Taylor, Stevenson, Phillips) .... 3m. 18.4s.

1928—No competition

1929—New York A.C. (Jackson V. Scholz, John Kerr, Victor Burke, Frank J. Cuhel) .... 3m. 17s.

1930—Boston A.A. (George Morin, Charles Sansone, Dana Smith, Donald Fleet) .... 3m. 22s.

1931—Los Angeles A.C. (McKennon, Williamson, Woessner, Williams) .. 3m. 18.4s.

1932—No competition

1933—New Yrok A.C. (Joseph Healey, Howard Jones, Hasket Derby, Karl Warner) .... 3m. 15s.

1934—New York A.C. (Karl Warner, Howard Jones, Joseph Healey, Robert Kane) .... 3m. 18.3s.

1935—New York Curb Exchange (Harold Lamb, Tim Ring, Jim Herbert, Harry Hoffman) .... 3m. 19.1s.

1936—New York A.C. (R. Scallan, E. Brown, J. Hoffstetter, A. Keen) .. 3m. 15.1s.

1937—New York Curb Exchange (Edward O'Sullivan, Edgar Stripling, Glenn Cunningham, James Herbert) 3m. 16s.

1938—New York A.C. (J. Quigley, L. Collado, J. Jackson, E. Rogers) ... 3m. 15.2s.

1939—New York A.C. (E. O'Sullivan, J. Wotters Jr., J. Kelly, J. Quigley) . 3m. 15.4s.

1940—New York A.C. (E. O'Sullivan, D. Wotters, J. Campbell, J. Quigley) 3m. 15s.

1941—So. Calif. A.A. (Vincent Reel, Harold Sinclair, Hubert Kerns, Clifford Bourland) .... 3m. 42.9s.

1942—Wayne University (Linwood Wright, Robert Wingo, Robert Grant, Wayne Hatfield) .... 3m. 18.7s.

1943—Grand St. Boys Assn., N.Y. (Charles Grohsberger, Milton Smith, Frank Cotter, James Herbert) 3m. 23.2s.

1944—N.Y. Pioneer Club (John Taylor, Bill Lubin, Maurice Callender, Warren Bright) .... 3m. 25.5s.

1945—Grand St. Boys Assn., N.Y. (Milton Smith, Eugene Kelly, Gilbert Phillips, James Herbert) ..... 3m. 25.7s.

1946—N.Y. Pioneer Club (Stafford Thompson, Solomon McCants, Warren Bright, Reginald Pearman) 3m. 21.2s.

1947—Los Angeles A.C. (Bill Parker, Will DeLoach, John Wachtler, Cliff Bourland) .... 3m. 15s.

1948—No competition

1949—Long Branch Shore A.C. (Stanfield, Fox, Slade, McKenley) ..... 3m. 08.4s.

1950—Morgan State College (Sam La-
Beach, Bob Tyler, Bill Brown,
George Rhoden) .... 3m. 09.7s.

1951—Grand Street Boys (Morris Curotta, Phil Thigpen, Bob Carter,
Herb McKenley) .... 3m. 12.0s.

1952—Los Angeles A.C. (Nicholson,
Pruitt, Halderman, Lea) .... 3m. 19.9s.

1953—N. Y. Pioneer Club (Brailsford,
Browne, Carty, Pearman) .... 3m. 14.1s.

1954—Pioneer Club, N. Y. (Rudolph
Clarence, Frank Bowens, Reginald
Pearman, William Persichetty) ... 3m. 16.3s.

1955—Pioneer Club, N. Y. (Frank Bowens, Harry Bright, Reginald Pearman, Richard Maiocco) .... 3m. 16s.

1956—Pioneer Club, N. Y. (Frank Bowens, John Tucker, Richard Maiocco, Louis Jones) .... 3m. 13s.

1957—Pioneer Club, N. Y. (Ed Lun-
ford, James Phipps, John Tucker,
Frank Bowens) .... 3m. 14.8s.

1958—East York T. C., Toronto (Al
Smith, Stan Worsford, Ken Vogel-
sang, Ergas Leps) .... 3m. 21.4s.

1959—Pioneer Club, N. Y. (Glen
Shane, James Phipps, James Grant,
Harry Bright) .... 3m. 14.6s.

1960—East York Club (Bud Scott,
Doug Gilbert, Stanley Worsford,
Wilham Crothers) .... 3m. 15.2s.

1961—East York Club (Bud Scott,
Doug Gilbert, George Shepard, William Crothers) .... 3m. 13.8s.

1962—Baltimore Olympic Club (Robert Campbell, Ronald Gill, Jack
Wagner, Walter Johnson) .... 3m. 13.2s.

1963—Pioneer Club, N.Y. (Edgar Lun-
ford, Hamilton McRae, James
Grant, Frank Bowens) .... 3m. 13.1s.

1964—Pioneer Club, N. Y. (Hamilton
McRae, Frank Bowens, James
Grant, Kent Bernard) .... 3m. 11.5s.

1965—Pioneer Club, N.Y. (Vincent
Mathews, John Davis, Carl Richardson, Frank Bowens) .... 3m. 11.9s.

1966—Pioneer Club, N.Y. (Jim
Brown, Glen Shane, Mark Ferrell,
Vince Mathews) .... 3m. 12.2s.

1967—Philadelphia Pioneer Club (Bill
Del Vecchio, Orin Richburg, Tom
Randolph, Jim Burnett) .... 3m. 10.6s.

1968—Philadelphia Pioneer Club .... 3m. 13.1s.

1969—No competition

1970—United A.A., Brooklyn ...... 3m. 14.7s.

1971—United A.A., Brooklyn ...... 3m. 11.5s.

1972—United A.A., Brooklyn ...... 3m. 16.5s.

2 and One-Half Mile Medley Relay

1959—New York A.C. (Thomas Murphy, Brian Condon, Peter Close,

Edward Moran) .... 10m. 00.4s.

1960—New York A.C. (Arthur Evans,
William Lenskold, William
Clancey, Edward Moran) .... 10m. 03.7s.

1961—East York Club (William Crothers, Robert Patterson, James Snider, Bruce Kidd) .... 10m. 03.1s.

1962—East York Club (David Bailey,
James Snider, Al Birtles, Bruce
Kidd) .... 9m. 54.0s.

1963—Toronto Olympic Club (Bob
Taylor, Murray Ruffell, Don
Smith, Jim Irons) .... 9m. 54.4s.

1964—Ridley Township Striders
(Bruce Carter, Ken Reynard, Vic
Zwolak, Pat Traynor) .... 9m. 52.7s.

1965—N.Y. Athletic Club (T. Craclo-
via, David Perry, Rito Cavelti, John
McDonnell) .... 10m. 05.3s.

1966—Shore A.C. (John Kuhi, Bill
Findler, Milt Mathews, Bill Reilly) 10m. 12.8s.

1967—Pasadena A.A. (Phil Potter,
Dennis Woltman, Mike Mukins,
Pete Santos) .... 10m. 13.0s.

1968—New York A.C. .... 9m. 59.4s.

1969—No competition

1970—New York A.C. .... 9m. 59.8s.

1971—New York A.C. .... 9m. 59.8s.

1972—New York A.C. .... 9m. 58.2s.

High Jump

1876—H. E. Ficken .... 5ft. 5in.
1877—H. E. Ficken .... 5ft. 4in.
1878—H. E. Ficken .... 5ft. 5in.
1879—W. Wunder .... 5ft. 7in.
1890—A. L. Carroll .... 5ft. 5in.
1881—C. W. Durand .... 5ft. 8in.
1882—A. L. Carroll .... 5ft. 7in.
1883—M. W. Ford .... 5ft. 8 1/2 in.
1884—J. T. Rindhart .... 5ft. 8in.
1885—W. B. Page .... 5ft. 8 7/8in.
1886—W. B. Page .... 5ft. 9in.
1887—W. B. Page .... 6ft. 1/2in.
1888—*I. D. Wester .... 5ft. 8 1/2in.
1888—+T. M. O'Connor .... 5ft. 9 1/2in.
1889—R. K. Pritchard .... 5ft. 10 1/2in.
1890—H. L. Hallock .... 5ft. 10in.
1891—Alvin Nickerson .... 5ft. 8 1/8in.
1892—Michael F. Sweeney ...... 6ft.
1893—Michael F. Sweeney ...... 5ft. 11in.
1894—Michael F. Sweeney ...... 6ft.
1895—Michael F. Sweeney ...... 6ft.
1896—C. U. Powell .... 5ft. 9 1/2in.
1897—I. K. Baxter .... 6ft. 2 1/4in.
1898—I. K. Baxter .... 6ft.
1899—I. K. Baxter .... 6ft.
1900—I. K. Baxter .... 6ft. 1in.
1901—S. S. Jones .... 6ft. 2in.
1902—I. K. Baxter .... 5ft. 7 1/2in.
1903—S. S. Jones .... 6ft.
1904—S. S. Jones .... 5ft. 9in.
1905—H. W. Kerrigan .... 6ft. 1 1/2in.

1906—J. Neil Patterson	5ft. 11 1/2in.	
1907—Con Leahy	6ft. 1in.	
1908—H. F. Porter	5ft. 11 1/4in.	
1909—Egon Erickson	5ft. 11 3/5in.	
1910—Walter Thomassen	6ft. 2in.	
1911—Henry Grumpelt		
H. F. Porter	6ft. 3in.	
1912—J. O. Johnstone	6ft. 3in.	
1913—A. W. Richards	6ft. 1 3/8in.	
1914—J. Loomis	6ft. 1 7/8in.	
1915—G. Horine	6ft. 3/4in.	
1916—W. Oler Jr.	6ft. 2in.	
1917—Clinton Larsen	6ft. 2 1/2in.	
1918—Carl Rice	6ft. 1 in.	
1919—John Murphy	6ft. 3 3/16in.	
1920—John Murphy	6ft. 4 1/4in.	
1921—D. V. Alberts	6ft. 4in.	
1922—‡D. V. Alberts		
H. M. Osborn	6ft. 5 1/8in.	
1923—LeRoy Brown	6ft. 5 5/8in.	
1924—R. L. Juday	6ft. 4in.	
1925—H. M. Osborn	‡6ft. 7in.	
1926—H. M. Osborn	6ft. 4 1/2in.	
1927—Robert W. King	6ft. 2 5/8in.	
1928—Robert W. King		
Charles E. McGinnis	6ft. 5in.	
1929—Henry Lasallette	6ft. 3 5/8in.	
1930—Anton B. Burg	6ft. 4 7/8in.	
1931—Anton B. Burg	6ft. 5 3/8in.	
1932—Robert Van Osdel		
George Spitz		
Cornelius C. Johnson	6ft. 6 5/8in.	
1933—Cornelius C. Johnson	6ft. 7in.	
1934—Cornelius C. Johnson		
Walter Marty	6ft. 8 5/8in.	
1935—Cornelius C. Johnson	6ft. 7in.	
1936—‡Cornelius C. Johnson		
Melvin Walker		
David Albritton	6ft. 8in.	
1937—David Albritton	6ft. 8 5/8in.	
1938—‡Melvin Walker		
Dave Albritton	6ft. 7in.	
1939—Les Steers	6ft. 8 1/8in.	
1940—Les Steers	6ft. 8 3/4in.	
1941—‡William Stewart		
Les Steers	6ft. 9 3/4in.	
1942—Adam Berry	6ft. 7in.	
1943—Pvt. Peter Watkins	6ft. 7 3/4in.	
1944—Fred Sheffield		
Willard Smith	6ft. 7in.	
1945—David Albritton		
Joshua Williamson		
Richard Schnacke		
Leslie Howe	6ft. 5 3/4in.	
1946—David Albritton	6ft. 6 7/8in.	
1947—Dave Albritton	6ft. 6in.	
1948—Tom Scofield		
William A. Vessie	6ft. 7 5/8in.	
1949—Richard Phillips	6ft. 6 7/8in.	
1950—John Heintzmann		
David Albritton		
Virgil Severns		

Jack Razzeto	6ft. 5 1/2in.
1951—J. Lewis Hall	6ft. 8in.
1952—Walter Davis	6ft. 10 1/2in.
1953—Walter Davis	6ft. 11 1/2in.
1954—Ernie Shelton	6ft. 9 3/4in.
1955—Ernie Shelton	
Charles Dumas	6ft. 10in.
1956—Charles Dumas	6ft. 10in.
1957—Charles Dumas	6ft. 10 1/4in.
1958—Charles Dumas	6ft. 9 3/4in.
1959—Charles Dumas	6ft. 9in.
1960—John Thomas	7ft. 2in.
1961—Robert Avant	7ft. 2in.
1962—John Thomas	6ft. 10in.
1963—Gene Johnson	7ft.
1964—Ed Caruthers	7ft. 1in.
1965—Otis Burrell	7ft.
1966—Otis Burrell	7ft. 2in.
1967—Otis Burrell	7ft. 1/4in.
1968—Ed Hanks	6ft. 11in.
1969—Otis Burrell	7ft. 1in.
1970—Reynaldo Brown	7ft. 1in.
1971—Reynaldo Brown	7ft. 3in.
1972—Barry Schur	7ft. 2in.

‡ Won on jump-off or fewer misses.

Broad Jump

1876—I. Frazier	17ft. 4in.
1877—W. T. Livingston	18ft. 9 1/2in.
1878—W. C. Wilmer	18ft. 9in.
1879—F. J. Kilpatrick	19ft. 6 3/4in.
1880—J. S. Voorhees	21ft. 4in.
1881—J. S. Voorhees	21ft. 4 3/4in.
1882—J. F. Jenkins Jr.	21ft. 5 3/4in.
1883—M. W. Ford	21ft. 7 1/2in.
1884—M. W. Ford	20ft. 1 1/2in.
1885—M. W. Ford	21ft. 6in.
1886—M. W. Ford	22ft. 3/4in.
1887—A. A. Jordan	22ft. 3 1/2in.
1888—*W. Halpin	23ft.
1888—†V. E. Schifferstein	23ft. 1 3/4in.
1889—M. W. Ford	22ft. 7 1/2in.
1890—A. F. Copland	23ft. 3 1/8in.
1891—C. S. Reber	22ft. 4 1/2in.
1892—E. W. Goff	22ft. 6 1/2in.
1893—C. S. Reber	23ft. 4 1/2in.
1894—E. W. Goff	22ft. 5in.
1895—E. B. Bloss	22ft. 2in.
1896—E. B. Bloss	22ft.
1897—E. B. Bloss	21ft. 10 1/2in.
1898—Myer Prinstein	23ft. 7in.
1899—Alvin C. Kraenzlein	23ft. 5in.
1900—H. P. McDonald	22ft.
1901—H. P. McDonald	22ft. 7in.
1902—Myer Prinstein	21ft. 5 1/2in.
1903—P. Molson	22ft. 2 1/2in.
1904—Myer Prinstein	22ft. 4 3/4in.
1905—Hugo Friend	22ft. 10 1/8in.
1906—Myer Prinstein	22ft. 4in.
1907—Dan Kelly	23ft. 11in.
1908—Platt Adams	21ft. 6 1/2in.
1909—Frank Irons	22ft. 5in.

1910—Frank Irons	23ft. 5 1/8in.	1972—Arnie Robinson	26ft. 5 3/4in.
1911—Platt Adams	23ft. 4/10in.	‡ With wind.	
1912—Platt Adams	22.44ft.	**Pole Vault**	
1913—P. Stiles	22ft.	1877—G. McNichol	9ft. 7in.
1914—Platt Adams	23ft. 2in.	1878—A. Ing	9ft. 4in.
1915—H. T. Worthington	23ft. 10in.	1879—W. J. Van Houten	10ft. 4 3/4in.
1916—H. T. Worthington	23ft. 2 1/2in.	1880—W. J. Van Houten	10ft. 11in.
1917—Joseph Irish	22ft. 4 3/4in.	1881—W. J. Van Houten	10ft. 6in.
1918—D. Politzer	22ft. 4in.	1882—B. F. Richardson	10ft.
1919—Floyd Smart	22ft. 7 1/4in.	1883—Hugh H. Baxter	11ft. 1/2in.
1920—Sol Butler	24ft. 8in.	1884—Hugh H. Baxter	10ft. 6in.
1921—E. O. Gourdin	23ft. 7 3/4in.	1885—Hugh H. Baxter	10ft. 3in.
1922—DeHart Hubbard	24ft. 5 1/8in.	1886—Hugh H. Baxter	10ft. 1 1/2in.
1923—DeHart Hubbard	24ft. 7 3/4in.	1887—T. Ray	11ft. 3/4in.
1924—DeHart Hubbard	24ft.	1888—*L. D. Godshall	10ft.
1925—DeHart Hubbard	‡25ft. 4 3/8in.	1888—†G. P. Quin	10ft. 1in.
1926—DeHart Hubbard	25ft. 2 1/2in.	1889—E. L. Stone	10ft.
1927—DeHart Hubbard	25ft. 8 3/4in.	1890—W. S. Rodenbaugh	10ft. 6in.
1928—Edward B. Hamm	25ft. 11 1/8in.	1891—T. Luce	10ft. 6 1/2in.
1929—Edward I. Gordon Jr.	24ft. 4 1/4in.	1892—T. Luce	11 ft.
1930—Alfred H. Bates	24ft. 3 3/4in.	1893—C. T. Buchholz	10ft. 6in.
1931—Alfred H. Bates	24ft. 7in.	1894—C. T. Buchholz	11ft.
1932—Edward Gordon	25ft. 3 3/8in.	1895—H. Thomas	10ft.
1933—Jesse Owens	24ft. 6 3/8in.	1896—F. W. Allis	10ft. 5in.
1934—Jesse Owens	25ft. 7.8in.	1897—J. L. Hurlburt Jr.	11ft. 1in.
1935—Eulace Peacock	26ft. 3in.	1898—R. G. Clapp	10ft. 9in.
1936—Jesse Owens	26ft. 3in.	1899—I. K. Baxter	10ft. 9in.
1937—Kermit King	25ft. 1 1/2in.	1900—Bascom Johnson	11ft. 3in.
1938—William Lacefield	25ft. 3/10in.	1901—C. E. Dvorak	11ft. 3in.
1939—William Lacefield	25ft. 5 1/2in.	1902—A. G. Anderson	10ft. 9in.
1940—William Brown	25ft. 1 1/8in.	1903—Chas. Dvorak	11ft.
1941—William Brown	25ft. 4 1/2in.	1904— ‡H. L. Gardner	
1942—William Brown	24ft. 3 1/2in.	L. G. Williams	10ft. 5 1/4in.
1943—William Christopher	24ft. 4 5/8in.	1905—E. C. Glover	11ft. 6in.
1944—William Lund	23ft. 3 1/2in.	1906—H. L. Moore	
1945—Herbert Douglas	24ft. 1/8in.	‡LeRoy Samse	11ft. 6in.
1946—William Steele	24ft.	1907—E. T. Cooke Jr.	12ft. 3in.
1947—William Steele	24ft. 9 1/4in.	1908—W. Halfpenny	11ft. 9in.
1948—Fred Johnson	25ft. 4 1/2in.	1909—R. Paulding	11ft.
1949—Gay Bryan	25ft. 1 1/2in.	1910—H. S. Babcock	12ft. 1in.
1950—James Holland	25ft. 9in.	1911—E. T. Cooke Jr.	
1951—George Brown	25ft. 8 1/2in.	H. Coyle	
1952—George Brown	25ft. 9in.	S. Bellah	12ft. 6in.
1953—George Brown	25ft. 10 3/4in.	1912—H. S. Babcock	12ft.
1954—John Bennett	24ft. 10 1/4in.	1913—S. B. Wagoner	13ft.
1955—Gregory Bell	26ft. 1/2in.	1914—K. R. Curtis	12ft. 3in.
1956—Ernie Shelby	26ft. 1 1/4in.	1915—S. Bellah	12ft. 9in.
1957—Ernie Shelby	25ft. 2 1/2in.	1916—S. Landers	12ft. 9in.
1958—Ernie Shelby	25ft. 10 1/4in.	1917—Ed Knourek	12ft. 9in.
1959—Gregory Bell	26ft. 1 1/4in.	1918—C. Buck	12ft. 3in.
1960—Hencq Vessier	25ft. 2in.	1919—F. K. Foss	12ft. 9in.
1961—Ralph Boston	26ft. 11 1/4in.	1920— ‡F. K. Foss	
1962—Ralph Boston	26ft. 6in.	E. E. Meyers	13ft. 1in.
1963—Ralph Boston	26ft. 10in.	1921—Ed. Knourek	12ft. 7 1/2in.
1964—Ralph Boston	26ft. 7 1/2in.	1922— ‡Ed. Knourek	
1965—Ralph Boston	26ft. 3 1/2in.	Ralph Spearow	13ft.
1966—Ralph Boston	26ft. 3 1/4in.	1923—E. E. Meyers	13ft. 1in.
1967—Jerry Proctor	26ft. 3/4in.	1924—E. E. Meyers	13ft.
1968—Bob Beamon	27ft. 4in.	1925—Harry Smith	12ft. 11 1/2in.
1969—Bob Beamon	26ft. 11in.	1926— ‡Paul Harrington	
1970—James Moore	26ft. 2 3/4in.	E. E. Meyers	13ft.
1971—Arnie Robinson	26ft. 10 3/4in.	1927—Lee Barnes	13ft.

1928—Lee Barnes	13ft. 9in.		1878—H. E. Buermeyer	37ft. 4in.
1929—Fred Sturdy	13ft. 9 1/4in.		1879—A. W. Adams	36ft. 3 1/8in.
1930—‡Fred Sturdy			1880—A. W. Adams	36ft. 4 7/8in.
Thomas Warne	13ft. 6in.		1881—F. L. Lambrecht	37ft. 5 1/2in.
1931—Jack Wool	13ft. 4 1/2in.		1882—F. L. Lambrecht	39ft. 9 7/8in.
1932—William Graber	14ft. 4 3/8in.		1883—F. L. Lambrecht	43ft.
1933—Matt Gordy			1884—F. L. Lambrecht	39ft. 10 1/2in.
Keith Brown	14ft.		1885—F. L. Lambrecht	42ft. 2 3/8in.
1934—Keith Brown			1886—F. L. Lambrecht	42ft. 1 1/4in.
William Graber			1887—G. R. Gray	42ft. 3in.
Wirt Thompson	13ft. 11 3/8in.		1888—*G. R. Gray	42ft. 10 1/4in.
1935— Earle Meadows			1888—†F. L. Lambrecht	42ft. 4in.
William Sefton	13ft. 10 3/8in.		1889—G. R. Gray	41ft. 4in.
1936—George Varoff	14ft. 6 1/2in.		1890—G. R. Gray	43ft. 9in.
1937—‡William H. Sefton			1891—G. R. Gray	‡46ft. 5 3/4in.
Cornelius Warmerdam			1892—G. R. Gray	43ft. 3 3/4in.
Earle Meadows			1893—G. R. Gray	47ft.
George Varoff	14ft. 7 5/8in.		1894—G. R. Gray	44ft. 8in.
1938—Cornelius Warmerdam	14ft. 5 1/2in.		1895—W. O. Hickok	43ft.
1939—George Varoff	14ft. 4in.		1896—G. R. Gray	44ft. 3 1/8in.
1940—Cornelius Warmerdam	15ft. 1 1/8in.		1897—C. H. Hennemann	42ft. 7 3/4in.
1941—Cornelius Warmerdam	15ft.		1898—Richard Sheldon	43ft. 8 5/8in.
1942—Cornelius Warmerdam	15ft. 2 1/2in.		1899—Richard Sheldon	40ft. 1/2in.
1943—Ens. Cornelius Warmerdam	15ft.		1900—D. Horgan	46ft. 1 1/4in.
1944—Lt. Cornelius Warmerdam	15ft.		1901—F. G. Beck	42ft. 11 1/4in.
1945—Lt. A. Richmond Morcom			1902—G. R. Gray	46ft. 5in.
Robert Phelps	13ft. 6in.		1903—L. E. J. Feuefback	42ft. 11 5/8in.
1946—Irving Moore	14ft. 4 3/4in.		1904—M. J. Sheridan	40ft. 9 1/2in.
1947—A. Richmond Morcom	14ft.		1905—W. W. Coe	49ft. 6in.
1948—Robert Richards			1906—W. W. Coe	46ft. 10 1/2in.
A. Richmond Morcom	14ft. 6in.		1907—Ralph Rose	49ft. 6 1/2in.
1949—Robert Richards	14ft. 4in.		1908—Ralph Rose	49ft. 1/2in.
1950—Robert Richards	14ft. 8in.		1909—Ralph Rose	50.26ft.
1951—Robert Richards	14ft. 4in.		1910—Ralph Rose	49ft. 1in.
1952— Robert Richards			1911—P. J. McDonald	47ft. 9in.
Donald Laz	14ft. 8in.		1912—P. J. McDonald	48.51ft.
1953— Don Laz			1913—L. A. Whitney	46ft. 2 5/8in.
George Mattos	14ft. 1in.		1914—P. J. McDonald	46ft. 3 1/2in.
1954—Robert Richards	15ft. 3 1/2in.		1915—A. W. Mucks	48ft. 11 3/4in.
1955—Robert Richards	15ft.		1916—A. W. Mucks	47ft. 2 1/8in.
1956—Robert Richards	15ft.		1917—A. W. Mucks	45ft. 10 5/8in.
1957—Robert Richards	15ft. 1 1/2in.		1918—Lieut. A. Richards	42ft. 3 3/4in.
1958—Ron Morris	14ft. 9in.		1919—P. J. McDonald	45ft. 8in.
1959—Donald Bragg	15ft. 3in.		1920—P. J. McDonald	47ft. 1/4in.
1960—Aubrey Dooley	15ft. 3/4in.		1921—Clarence Houser	46ft. 11 3/4in.
1961—Ronald Morris	15ft. 8in.		1922—P. J. McDonald	46ft. 11 7/8in.
1962—Ronald Morris	16ft. 1/4in.		1923—O. Wanzer	47ft. 5/8in.
1963—Brian Sternberg	16ft. 4in.		1924—R. G. Hills	46ft. 5 3/4in.
1964—Fred Hansen	17ft.		1925—Clarence Houser	50ft. 1in.
1965—John Pennel	17ft.		1926—Herbert Schwarze	49ft. 10 7/8in.
1966—Bob Seagren	17ft.		1927—John Kuck	48ft. 5in.
1967—Paul Wilson	17ft. 7 3/4in.		1928—Herman Brix	50ft. 11 3/4in.
1968—Dick Railsback	17ft. 1/4in.		1929—Herman Brix	50ft. 2 1/2in.
1969—Bob Seagren	17ft. 6in.		1930—Herman Brix	52ft. 5 3/4in.
1970—Bob Seagren	17ft. 2in.		1931—Herman Brix	50ft. 8 1/4in.
1971—Jan Johnson	17ft. 0in.		1932—Leo J. Sexton	52ft. 8in.
1972—Dave Roberts	18ft. 1/4in.		1933—Jack Torrance	51ft. 4 7/8in.
‡ Won jump-off.			1934—Jack Torrance	55ft. 5in.
			1935—Jack Torrance	51 6 1/4in.

Shot-Put

1876—H. E. Buermeyer	32ft. 5in.		1936—Dimitri Zaitz	50ft. 7 5/8in.
1877—H. E. Buermeyer	37ft. 2in.		1937—James Reynolds	51ft. 7 1/8in.
			1938—Francis Ryan	52ft. 1 1/2in.

1939—Lilburn Williams	53ft. 7in.	
1940—Alfred Blozis	55ft. 3/8in.	
1941—Alfred Blozis	54ft. 5/8in.	
1942—Alfred Blozis	53ft. 8 3/8in.	
1943—Earl Audet	52ft. 11 3/8in.	
1944—Earl Audet	52ft. 8in.	
1945—Wilfred Bangert	52ft. 10in.	
1946—Wilfred Bangert	52ft. 2 1/2in.	
1947—Francis Delaney	52ft. 9 1/2in.	
1948—Francis Delaney	53ft. 8 1/4in.	
1949—James Fuchs	57ft. 2 1/8in.	
1950—James Fuchs	57ft. 2 1/8in.	
1951—Parry O'Brien	55ft. 9 1/4in.	
1952—Parry O'Brien	57ft. 4 3/8in.	
1953—Parry O'Brien	55ft. 10 3/4in.	
1954—Parry O'Brien	58ft. 11 3/4in.	
1955—Parry O'Brien	58ft. 5 3/4in.	
1956—Ken Bantum	59ft. 1 1/2in.	
1957—Bill Neider	61ft. 6 1/2in.	
1958—Parry O'Brien	61ft. 11 1/4in.	
1959—Parry O'Brien	62ft. 2 1/4in.	
1960—Parry O'Brien	62ft. 6 1/4in.	
1961—Dallas Long	62ft. 2in.	
1962—Gary Gubner	63ft. 6 1/2in.	
1963—Dave Davis	62ft. 5 3/4in.	
1964—Randy Matson	64ft. 11in.	
1965—John McGrath	63ft.	
1966—Randy Matson	64ft. 2 1/2in.	
1967—Randy Matson	66ft. 11in.	
1968—Randy Matson	67ft. 5in.	
1969—Neal Steinhauer	67ft. 4in.	
1970—Randy Matson	67ft. 10 1/4in.	
1971—Karl Salb	67ft. 2 3/4in.	
1972—Randy Matson	69ft. 6 1/2in.	

‡ Shot 8 ounces light.

Discus Throw

1897—Charles H. Hennemann	118ft. 9in.
1898—Charles H. Hennemann	108ft. 8 5/8in.
1899—Richard Sheldon	Discus, sh. wt.
1900—Richard Sheldon	114ft.
1901—R. J. Sheridan	111ft. 9 1/2in.
1902—R. J. Sheridan	113ft. 7in.
1903—J. H. Maddock	113ft.
1904—Martin J. Sheridan	119ft. 1 1/2in.
1905—Ralph Rose	117ft. 5in.
1906—Martin J. Sheridan	129ft. 10in.
1907—Martin J. Sheridan	129ft. 5 3/4in.
1908—M. F. Horr	132ft. 9in.
1909—Ralph Rose	131.8ft.
1910—M. H. Giffin	135ft. 6 1/4in.
1911—Martin J. Sheridan	133ft. 9 1/2in.
1912—E. Muller	130.22ft.
1913—E. Muller	132ft. 7 1/8in.
1914—E. Muller	137ft. 1/2in.
1915—A. W. Mucks	146ft. 9 1/4in.
1916—A. W. Mucks	145ft. 4 1/2in.
1917—A. W. Mucks	140ft. 1 1/2in.
1918—E. Muller	136ft.
1919—A. W. Mucks	143ft. 9 3/4in.
1920—A. R. Pope	146ft. 5in.
1921—A. R. Pope	144ft.

1922—A. R. Pope	145ft. 11in.
1923—T. J. Lieb	151ft. 3 3/4in.
1924—T. J. Lieb	144ft. 7 1/4in.
1925—Clarence Houser	156ft. 6in.
1926—Clarence Houser	153ft. 6 1/2in.
1927—Eric C. W. Krenz	146.10ft.
1928—Clarence Houser	153ft. 6 1/4in.
1929—Eric C. W. Krenz	157.2ft.
1930—Paul B. Jessup	169ft. 8 7/8in.
1931—Paul B. Jessup	152ft. 5 1/4in.
1932—John Anderson	165.54ft.
1933—John Anderson	165ft. 1 1/2in.
1934—Robert Jones	155ft. 11in.
1935—Kenneth Carpenter	158ft. 11 1/2in.
1936—Kenneth Carpenter	166ft. 2in.
1937—Phil Levy	163ft. 7 7/8in.
1938—Peter Zagar	167ft. 3 1/4in.
1939—Phil Fox	172ft. 4 1/2in.
1940—Phil Fox	170ft. 4 1/2in.
1941—Archie Harris	167ft. 9 1/2in.
1942—Robert Fitch	166ft. 10in.
1943—Ens. Hugh Cannon	161ft. 2in.
1944—Lt. Hugh Cannon	162ft. 1in.
1945—Jack Donaldson	151ft. 2in.
1946—Robert Fitch	179ft. 1/8in.
1947—Fortune Gordien	174ft. 1 1/2in.
1948—Fortune Gordien	168ft. 5in.
1949—Fortune Gordien	174ft. 5 3/8in.
1950—Fortune Gordien	173ft. 2 1/2in.
1951—Dick Doyle	175ft. 6 1/2in.
1952—Jim Dillion	175ft. 3 5/8in.
1953—Fortune Gordien	183ft. 9 1/2in.
1954—Fortune Gordien	182ft. 2in.
1955—Parry O'Brien	175ft. 7in.
1956—Ron Drummond	180ft. 3in.
1957—Al Oerter	181ft. 6in.
1958—Rink Babka	187ft. 10in.
1959—Al Oerter	186ft. 5in.
1960—Al Oerter	193ft. 9 1/2in.
1961—Jay Silvester	195ft. 8in.
1962—Al Oerter	202ft. 2in.
1963—Jay Silvester	198ft. 11 1/2in.
1964—Al Oerter	201ft. 1 1/2in.
1965—Ludvik Danek (Czech)	205ft. 7in.
1966—Al Oerter	193ft. 9in.
1967—Gary Carlsen	205ft. 10in.
1968—Jay Silvester	203ft. 9in.
1969—Jon Cole	208ft. 10in.
1970—Jay Silvester	205ft. 4in.
1971—Tim Vollmer	208ft. 4in.
1972—Jay Silvester	213ft. 0in.

Javelin Throw

1909—Ralph Rose	141.7ft.
1910—B. Brodd	163ft. 1in.
1911—O. F. Snedigar	165ft. 20/100in.
1912—H. Lott	162.65ft.
1913—B. Brodd	161ft. 3in.
1914—G. A. Bronder Jr.	166ft. 8 1/2in.
1915—G. A. Bronder Jr.	177ft. 7 3/4in.
1916—G. A. Bronder Jr.	190ft. 6in.
1917—G. A. Bronder Jr.	184ft. 1/2in.

1918—G. A. Bronder Jr.	169ft. 10 1/2in.		1881—Frank L. Lambrecht	89ft. 8in.
1919—G. A. Bronder Jr.	176ft. 6in.		1882—Frank L. Lambrecht	93ft. 1/2in.
1920—M. S. Angier	192ft. 10 3/4in.		1883—W. L. Coudon	93ft. 11in.
1921—M. S. Angier	189ft. 3 1/4in.		1884—Frank L. Lambrecht	92ft. 5in.
1922—Flint Hanner	193ft. 2 1/4in.		1885—Frank L. Lambrecht	96ft. 10in.
1923—H. Hoffman	194ft. 7 1/2in.		1886—W. L. Coudon	95ft. 3in.
1924—John Leyden	181ft.		1887—C. A. J. Queckberner	102ft. 7in.
1925—Henry Bonura	213ft. 10 1/2in.		1888—*W. J. M. Barry	127ft. 9in.
1926—John Kuck	199ft. 7in.		1888—†Frank L. Lambrecht	105ft. 1in.
1927—Charles Harlow	193ft. 3 3/4in.		1889—J. S. Mitchel	121ft. 7 1/2in.
1928—Creth B. Hines	202ft. 1 3/4in.		1890—J. S. Mitchel	130ft. 8in.
1929—Jesse P. Mortensen	204.975ft.		1891—J. S. Mitchel	136ft. 1in.
1930—James DeMers	222ft. 6 3/4in.		1892—J. S. Mitchel	140ft. 11in.
1931—James DeMers	216ft. 9.6in.		1893—J. S. Mitchel	134ft. 8in.
1932—Malcolm Metcalf	219.66ft.		1894—J. S. Mitchel	135ft. 9 1/2in.
1933—Lee Bartlett	211ft. 5 1/4in.		1895—J. S. Mitchel	139ft. 2 1/2in.
1934—Ralston Legore	209ft. 6 3/4in.		1896—J. S. Mitchel	134ft. 8 3/4in.
1935—Horace O'Dell	217ft. 1 5/8in.		1897—J. J. Flanagan	148ft. 5in.
1936—John Mottram	214ft. 7 3/8in.		1898—J. J. Flanagan	151ft. 10 1/2in.
1937—William Reitz	224ft. 9 3/8in.		1899—J. J. Flanagan	155ft. 4 1/2in.
1938—Nick Vukmanic	218ft. 7 3/4in.		1900—R. J. Sheridan	138ft. 2in.
1939—Boyd Brown	215ft. 10 3/4in.		1901—J. J. Flanagan	158ft. 10 1/2in.
1940—Boyd Brown	223ft. 1 3/8in.		1902—J. J. Flanagan	151ft. 4in.
1941—Boyd Brown	218ft. 3in.		1903—J. S. Mitchel	140ft. 1in.
1942—Boyd Brown	216ft. 7 1/2in.		1904—A. D. Plaw	162ft.
1943—Martin Biles	202ft. 5in.		1905—A. D. Plaw	163ft. 4in.
1944—Capt. Martin Biles	242ft. 7in.		1906—J. J. Flanagan	166ft. 6 1/2in.
1945—Earl Marshall	215ft. 4in.		1907—J. J. Flanagan	171ft. 3/4in.
1946—Garland Adair	213ft. 7in.		1908—M. J. McGrath	173ft.
1947—Stephen Seymour	248ft. 10in.		1909—Lee Talbott	165.8ft.
1948—Stephen Seymour	230ft. 5in.		1910—M. J. McGrath	168ft. 4 1/2in.
1949—Franklin Held	232ft. 2 1/2in.		1911—Con Walsh	177ft. 6 1/2in.
1950—Dr. Stephen Seymour	228ft. 10 7/8in.		1912—M. J. McGrath	174.67ft.
1951—Franklin Held	241ft. 3/4in.		1913—Patrick J. Ryan	177ft. 7 3/4in.
1952—Bill Miller	236ft. 1in.		1914—Patrick J. Ryan	183ft. 3 3/4in.
1953—Franklin Held	211ft.		1915—Patrick J. Ryan	176ft. 2 3/4in.
1954—Franklin Held	249ft. 8 1/2in.		1916—Patrick J. Ryan	174ft. 8in.
1955—Franklin Held	260ft. 3in.		1917—Patrick J. Ryan	168ft. 7 1/2in.
1956—Cy Young	247ft. 11 1/2in.		1918—M. J. McGrath	173ft. 11 3/4in.
1957—Bob Voiles	251ft. 5 1/2in.		1919—Patrick J. Ryan	175ft. 5 3/4in.
1958—Franklin Held	252ft. 1/2in.		1920—Patrick J. Ryan	169ft. 4in.
1959—Al Cantello	246ft. 9in.		1921—Patrick J. Ryan	170ft. 7 1/2in.
1960—Al Cantello	271ft. 9in.		1922—M. J. McGrath	155ft. 9in.
1961—John Fromm	249ft. 11 1/2in.		1923—Frederick D. Tootell	173ft. 6 5/8in.
1962—Dan Studney	246ft. 6in.		1924—Frederick D. Tootell	173ft. 11 1/2in.
1963—Larry Stuart	255ft. 3in.		1925—M. J. McGrath	172ft. 1/2in.
1964—Frank Covelli	253ft. 7in.		1926—M. J. McGrath	162ft. 10 1/4in.
1965—Bill Floerke	258ft. 7in.		1927—Jack Merchant	170ft. 7 1/2in.
1966—John Tushaus	260ft. 8in.		1928—Edmund Black	166ft. 4 1/4in.
1967—Delmon McNabb	268ft. 3in.		1929—Jack Merchant	170ft. 6in.
1968—Frank Covelli	269ft. 6in.		1930—Norwood G. Wright	163ft. 9 1/4in.
1969—Mark Murro	284ft. 3in.		1931—Edward F. Flanagan	158ft. 8in.
1970—Bill Skinner	276ft. 7in.		1932—Frank Connor	170.90ft.
1971—Bill Skinner	267ft. 2in.		1933—Dr. Patrick O'Callaghan	161ft. 3 3/8in.
1972—Fred Luke	277ft. 5in.		1934—Donald Favor	163ft. 5 3/4in.
			1935—Henry F. Dreyer	168ft. 8 1/2in.

16-lb. Hammer Throw

			1936—William Rowe	175ft. 7in.
1876—William B. Curtis	76ft. 4in.		1937—Irving Folwartshny	173ft. 7 5/8in.
1877—G. D. Parmly	84ft.		1938—Irving Folwartshny	179ft. 3in.
1878—William B. Curtis	80ft. 2in.		1939—Chester Cruikshank	174ft. 1 1/2in.
1879—J. G. McDermott	85ft. 11 1/2in.		1940—Stanley Johnson	182ft. 6 7/16in.
1880—William B. Curtis	87ft. 4 1/4in.		1941—Irving Folwartshny	175ft. 6 1/8in.

1942—Chester Cruikshank	173ft. 8 1/2in.	1906—J. J. Flanagan	35ft. 7in.
1943—Henry F. Dreyer	164ft. 6 3/4in.	1907—J. J. Flanagan	38ft. 8in.
1944—Henry F. Dreyer	166ft. 6 1/2in.	1908—J. J. Flanagan	37ft. 1 1/2in.
1945—Henry F. Dreyer	166ft. 11 1/2in.	1909—Lee Talbott	33.64ft.
1946—Irving Folsworth	169ft. 8in.	1910—Con Walsh	37ft. 1 1/2in.
1947—Robert Bennett	180ft. 11in.	1911—P. J. McDonald	38ft. 9 7/8in.
1948—Robert Bennett	175ft. 7in.	1912—Patrick J. Ryan	37.87ft.
1949—Samuel M. Felton Jr.	176ft. 10in.	1913—M. J. McGrath	38ft. 5 1/2in.
1950—Samuel M. Felton Jr.	187ft. 3 3/4in.	1914—P. J. McDonald	38ft. 5 1/2in.
1951—Samuel M. Felton Jr.	184ft. 2 3/4in.	1915—Lee Talbott	35ft. 9 3/4in.
1952—Thomas Bane	179ft. 11 1/2in.	1916—M. J. McGrath	35ft. 5 1/2in.
1953—Martin Engel	186ft. 9in.	1917—Patrick J. Ryan	33ft. 3in.
1954—Robert Backus	189ft. 3in.	1918—M. J. McGrath	34ft. 9in.
1955—Harold Connolly	199ft. 8in.	1919—P. J. McDonald	37ft. 6in.
1956—Harold Connolly	205ft. 10 1/2in.	1920—P. J. McDonald	37ft. 11 1/4in.
1957—Harold Connolly	216ft. 3in.	1921—P. J. McDonald	37ft. 8in.
1958—Harold Connolly	225ft. 4in.	1922—M. J. McGrath	35ft. 10in.
1959—Harold Connolly	216ft. 10in.	1923—M. J. McGrath	38ft.
1960—Harold Connolly	224ft. 4 1/2in.	1924—M. J. McGrath	35ft. 7in.
1961—Harold Connolly	213ft. 6 1/2in.	1925—M. J. McGrath	36ft. 8 3/8in.
1962—Al Hall	219ft. 3in.	1926—P. J. McDonald	36ft. 6 3/4in.
1963—Al Hall	214ft. 11in.	1927—P. J. McDonald	36ft. 4 1/4in.
1964—Hal Connolly	226ft. 5 1/2in.	1928—P. J. McDonald	33ft. 10 1/4in.
1965—Hal Connolly	232ft. 1in.	1929—P. J. McDonald	35ft. 9in.
1966—Ed Burke	220ft.	1930—Leo J. Sexton	34ft. 6 5/8in.
1967—Ed Burke	235ft. 11in.	1931—Leo J. Sexton	35ft. 1 3/8in.
1968—Ed Burke	217ft.	1932—Leo J. Sexton	35ft. 2in.
1969—Tom Gage	228ft. 5in.	1933—P. J. McDonald	35ft. 5/8in.
1970—George Frenn	230ft.	1934—Clark Haskins	35ft. 1 1/2in.
1971—George Frenn	230ft. 1in.	1935—Clark Haskins	34ft. 6 1/4in.
1972—Al Schoterman	228ft. 1in.	1936—Louis Lepis	35ft. 1 1/8in.

56-Lb. Weight Throw

		1937—Louis Lepis	33ft. 7 1/4in.
		1938—Louis Lepis	35ft. 1/2in.
1878—William B. Curtis	21ft.	1939—Stanley Johnson	34ft. 6 7/8in.
1879—J. McDermott	22ft. 11in.	1940—Henry F. Dreyer	35ft. 6in.
1880—J. McDermott	24ft. 4in.	1941—Frank J. Berst	35ft. 4 7/8in.
1881—J. Britton	24ft.	1942—Frank J. Berst	39ft. 3 1/2in.
1882—H. W. West	24ft. 10 1/2in.	1943—Frank J. Berst	35ft. 2in.
1883—Frank L. Lambrecht	‡25ft. 1 1/4in.	1944—Frank J. Berst	38ft. 4 1/4in.
1884—C. A. J. Queckberner	26ft. 3 1/4in.	1945—Henry F. Dreyer	35ft. 2in.
1885—C. A. J. Queckberner	26ft. 3in.	1946—Frank J. Berst	35ft. 3 1/8in.
1886—C. A. J. Queckberner	25ft. 1in.	1947—Frank J. Berst	46ft. 4 1/2in.
1887—C. A. J. Queckberner	25ft.	1948—Henry F. Dreyer	‡41ft. 2 5/8in.
1888—*W. L. Coudon	27ft. 9in.	1949—Henry F. Dreyer	38ft. 4 3/4in.
1888—†J. S. Mitchel	26ft. 10in.	1950—Frank J. Berst	38ft. 10 1/2in.
1889—W. L. Coudon	27ft. 9 1/2in.	1951—Henry F. Dreyer	41ft. 6 3/4in.
1890—C. A. J. Queckberner	32ft. 10in.	1952—Henry F. Dreyer	40ft. 3 1/8in.
1891—J. S. Mitchel	35ft. 3 1/2in.	1953—Robert Backus	37ft. 2 3/4in.
1892—J. S. Mitchel	34ft. 8 1/4in.	1954—Robert Backus	42ft. 5 1/4in.
1893—J. S. Mitchel	34ft. 5 1/2in.	1955—Robert Backus	43ft. 5in.
1894—J. S. Mitchel	33ft. 7 3/8in.	1956—Robert Backus	43ft.
1895—J. S. Mitchel	32ft. 7 1/2in.	1957—Robert Backus	44ft. 8 1/2in.
1896—J. S. Mitchel	30ft. 7in.	1958—Robert Backus	43ft. 2in.
1897—J. S. Mitchel	32ft. 2in.	1959—Robert Backus	44ft. 3 1/in.
1898—Richard Sheldon	30ft. 11in.	1960-64—No competition	
1899—J. J. Flanagan	33ft. 7 1/4in.	1965—Robert Backus	43ft. 9 1/2in.
1900—J. S. Mitchel	35ft. 5in.	1966-67—No competition	
1901—J. J. Flanagan	30ft. 6in.	1968—George Frenn	47ft. 6 3/4in.
1902—E. Desmarteau	33ft. 6in.	1969—George Frenn	49ft. 7in.
1903—J. S. Mitchel	33ft. 2 3/4in.	1970—No competition	
1904—J. J. Flanagan	35ft. 9in.		
1905—J. S. Mitchel	33ft. 1 1/2in.	‡ Light weight.	

1971—George Frenn .... 49ft. 8 1/2in.
1972—Tom Miller .... 41ft. 6 3/4in.

Hop, Step and Jump

1893—E. B. Bloss .... 48ft. 6in.
1894-1905—No competition
1906—J. F. O'Connell .... 45ft. 3 3/4in.
1907—Platt Adams .... 44ft. 9in.
1908—Platt Adams .... 45ft. 4in.
1909—Frank Irons .... 44.19ft.
1910—D. F. Ahearn .... 48 1/4in.
1911—D. F. Ahearn .... 48.16ft.
1912—Platt Adams .... 45.70ft.
1913—D. F. Ahearn .... 50ft.
1914—D. F. Ahearn .... 48ft. 6 1/8in.
1915—D. F. Ahearn .... 50ft. 11 1/8in.
1916—D. F. Ahearn .... 46ft. 1/2in.
1917—D. F. Ahearn .... 47ft. 8in.
1918—D. F. Ahearn .... 46ft. 3 3/4in.
1919—S. G. Landers .... 47ft. 8 1/2in.
1920—S. G. Landers .... 48ft. 7 9/10in.
1921—K. Geist .... 46ft. 3in.
1922—DeHart Hubbard ..... 48ft. 1 1/2in.
1923—DeHart Hubbard ..... 47ft. 1/2in.
1924—Homer Martin .... 45ft. 8 3/4in.
1925—Homer Martin .... 47ft. 11 1/4in.
1926—Levi Casey .... 49ft. 4 1/4in.
1927—Levi Casey .... 48ft. 4 3/4in.
1928—Levi Casey .... 48ft. 10 1/8in.
1929—Robert Kelley .... 48ft. 6 3/4in.
1930—Levi Casey .... 47ft. 11 5/8in.
1931—Robert Kelley .... 47ft. 7 1/2in.
1932—Sidney Bowman ...... 48ft. 11 1/4in.
1933—Nathan Blair .... 47ft. 3in.
1934—Dudley Wilkins ...... 48ft. 2.25in.
1935—Roland Romero ...... 50ft. 4 7/8in.
1936—William Brown ...... 49ft. 2in.
1937—William Brown ...... 49ft. 7 1/4in.
1938—Herschel Neil .... 48ft. 5.9in.
1939—Herschel Neil .... 47ft. 9 7/8in.
1940—William Brown ...... 50ft. 2 5/8in.
1941—William Brown ...... 50ft. 11 1/2in.
1942—William Brown ...... 48ft. 11 1/2in.
1943—Ens. William Brown .... 45ft. 8in.
1944—Don Barksdale .... 47ft. 2 7/8in.
1945—Burton Cox .... 45ft. 10 3/8in.
1946—Ralph Tate .... 47ft. 11 1/4in.
1947—Bob Beckus .... 45ft. 11 1/4in.
1948—Gaylord Bryan .... 47ft. 11 1/2in.
1949—Gaylord Bryan .... 49ft. 1in.
1950—Gaylord Bryan .... 47ft. 11in.
1951—Gaylord Bryan .... 46ft. 11 1/2in.
1952—Walter Ashbaugh ...... 50ft. 8 3/4in.
1953—George Shaw .... 47ft. 8in.
1954—Claudio Cabrejas ...... 47ft. 3in.
1955—Victor Paredes .... 50ft. 4in.
1956—Willie Hollie .... 49ft. 6in.
1957—Bill Sharpe .... 50ft. 4 1/4in.
1958—Ira Davis .... 50ft. 8 1/4in.
1959—Ira Davis .... 50ft. 6 1/2in.
1960—Ira Davis .... 53ft. 4 1/4in.
1961—William Sharpe .... 52ft. 4 3/4in.

1962—William Sharpe .... 52ft. 1 1/4in.
1963—Kent Floerke .... 51ft. 7 3/4in.
1964—Chris Mousaides ...... 53ft. 1in.
1965—Art Walker .... 53ft. 1in.
1966—Art Walker .... 53ft. 8in.
1967—Charlie Craig .... 53ft. 1 1/2in.
1968—Art Walker .... 53ft. 9 1/4in.
1969—John Craft .... 52ft. 9 1/4in.
1970—Milan Tiff .... 53ft. 0in.
1971—John Craft .... 54ft. 7in.
1972—John Craft .... 54ft. 10in.

Decathlon

	Points
1915—A. Richards	6858.81
1916-19—No competition	
1920—Brutus Hamilton	7022.981
1921—Dan Shea	5849.338
1922—S. H. Thomson	6890.23
1923—Harold M. Osborn	7351.89
1924—Anthony J. Plansky	5901.45
1925—Harold M. Osborn	7706.36
1926—Harold M. Osborn	7187.832
1927—Fait Elkins	7574.42
1928—J. Kenneth Doherty	7600.52
1929—J. Kenneth Doherty	7784.68
1930—Wilson Charles	7313.343
1931—Jess Mortensen	8166.663
1932—James A. Bausch	8103.25
1933—Bernard E. Berlinger	7597.19
1934—Robert Clark	7966.040
1935—Robert Clark	7929.22
1936—Glenn Morris	*7880.0
1937—No competition	
1938—Joseph Scott	6486.0
1939—Joseph Scott	6671
1940—William Watson	7523
1941—John Borican	5666
1942—William Terwilliger	6802
1943—William Watson	5994
1944—Irving Mondschein	5748
1945—Charles Beaudry	5886
1946—Irving Mondschein	6466
1947—Irving Mondschein	6715
1948—Robert Mathias	7224
1949—Robert Mathias	7556
1950—Robert Mathias	8042
1951—Robert Richards	7834
1952—Robert Mathias	7825
1953—Milton Campbell	7235
1954—Robert Richards	6501
1955—Robert Richards	6873
1956—Rafer Johnson	7754
1957—Charles Pratt	7164
1958—Rafer Johnson	7754
1959—Chuang-Kwang Yang	7549
1960—Rafer Johnson	8683
1961—Paul Herman	7142
1962—Chuang-Kwang Yang	8249
1963—Steve Pauly	7852
1964—Chuang-Kwang Yang	8641
1965—Bill Toomey	**7764
1966—Bill Toomey	8234

1967—Bill Toomey	....	7880
1968—Bill Toomey	....	8037
1969—Bill Toomey	....	7818
1970—John Warkentin	....	8026
1971—Rick Wanamaker	....	7989
1972—Jeff Bennett	....	7910

*New scoring system. Current scoring system adopted in 1950.

**New scoring system, 1965.

Pentathlon

	Points
1920—Brutus Hamilton	17
1921—Edward Gourdin	12
1922—Edward Gourdin	10
1923—No competition	
1924—Anthony Woostroff	7
1925—Paul Courtois	11
1926—T. W. Drews	10
1927—Harry Flippen	8
1928—No competition	
1929—Paul Courtois	2900.3836
1930—Bernard E. Berlinger	3462.2
1931—James A. Bausch	3776.585
1932—No competition	
1933—Eulace Peacock	3221.85
1934—Eulace Peacock	3258.40
1935—Clyde Coffman	3084.0
1936—Arkie Trento	*2899.0
1937—Eualce Peacock	3030
1938—John Borican	3304
1939—John Borican	2947
1940—Harry March	2981
1941—John Borican	3244
1942—No competition	
1943—Eulace Peacock	3225
1944—Eulace Peacock	2852
1945—Eulace Peacock	3148
1946—Charles E. Beaudry	2885
1947—John Voight	2972
1948—Russell Thomas	3283
1949—Wilbur Ross	3429
1950—Wilbur Ross	3277
1951—Brayton Norton	3452
1952—Brayton Norton	3129
1953—Brayton Norton	3278
1954—Brayton Norton	3400
1955—Des Koch	3216
1956—Howard Smith	3034
1957—Howard Smith	3362
1958—Howard Smith	3200
1959—Dixon Farmer	3196
1960—Bill Toomey	3010
1961—Bill Toomey	3482
1962—Paul Herman	3389
1963—Bill Toomey	3365
1964—Bill Toomey	3687
1965—Jim Miller	3095
1966—Jeff Bannister	3512
1967—Lynn Baker	3448
1968—Joe Hilbe	3456
1969—Dave Merkowitz	3442
1970—Mike Hill	3316
1971—Rick Wanamaker	3307

1972—Rick Wanamaker	....	3410

* New scoring system.

All-Around

	Points
1884—W. R. Thompson	5304
1885—M. W. Ford	5045
1886—M. W. Ford	5899
1887—A. A. Jordan	5236
1888—M. W. Ford	5161
1889—A. A. Jordan	5520
1890—A. A. Jordan	5358
1891—A. A. Jordan	6189
1892—E. W. Goff	5232
1893—E. W. Goff	4860
1894—E. W. Goff	5748
1895—J. Cosgrove	4406.50
1896—L. P. Sheldon	5380
1897—E. H. Clark	6244.50
1898—E. C. White	5243
1899—J. Fred Powers	6203
1900—H. Gill	6360.50
1901—A. B. Gunn	5739
1902—A. B. Gunn	6260.50
1903—E. H. Clark	6318.25
1904—Thomas Kiely	6086
1905—M. J. Sheridan	6820.50
1906—Thomas Kiely	6274
1907—M. J. Sheridan	7130.50
1908—J. L. Bredemus	5809
1909—M. J. Sheridan	7385
1910—F. C. Thomson	7009
1911—F. C. Thomson	6709
1912—J. L. Bredemus	6303
1913—F. C. Thomson	7411.50
1914—Avery Brundage	6999
1915—No competition	
1916—Avery Brundage	6468.75
1917—H. Goelitz	*5702.166
1918—Avery Brundage	6708.50
1919—S. H. Thomson	6105.25
1920—No competition	
1921—S. H. Thomson	7532.5
1922-41—No competition	
1942—Joshua Williamson	6031
1943-49—No competition	
1950—Dale Keyser	5777
1951—John Voight	5600
1952—Raymond Bussard	5822
1953—Robert Richards	7031
1954—Merwin Carter	5330
1955—Lyman Frasier	6733
1956—Charles Stevenson	7612
1957—Tom Pagani	6741
1958—Tom Pagani	8114.5
1959—Tom Pagani	7874
1960—Charles Stevenson	7555
1961—William Urban	7483
1962—Tom Pagani	8265
1963—Bill Urban	8492
1964—Bill Urban	8177
1965—Bill Urban	7481
1966—Brian Murphy	7541

1967—Bill Urban	8035	
1968—Bill Walsh	7727	
1969—No competition		
1970—Brian Murphy	7564	
1971—Richard Robinson	7279	
1972—Karl Harz	7976	

* New scoring system.

Cross-Country

1890—W. D. Day	47m. 41s.
1891—M. Kennedy	46m. 30 4/5s.
1892—E. C. Carter	43m. 54s.
1893-96—No competition	
1897—G. W. Orton	35m. 58s.
1898—G. W. Orton	35m. 41 2/5s.
1899-1900—No competition	
1901—Jerry Pierce	43m. 27 1/3s.
1902—No competition	
1903—John Joyce	32m. 23 4/5s.
1904—No competition	
1905—W. J. Hail	32m. 59 4/5s.
1906—Frank Nebrich	34m. 29 4/5s.
1907—F. G. Bellars	33m. 12s.
1908—F. G. Bellars	34m. 15 3/5s.
1909—W. J. Kramer	31m. 17 1/5s.
1910—F. G. Bellars	33m. 3s.
1911—W. J. Kramer	37m. 8s.
1912—W. J. Krmaer	34m. 32s.
1913—A. R. Kiviat	33m. 52s.
1914—H. Kolehmainen	33m. 36s.
1915—N. Giannakopoulos	32m. 46 3/5s.
1916—W. Kyronen	32m. 46s.
1917—James Henningan	33m. 58s.
1918—Max Bohland	33m.
1919—Fred Faller	32m. 26 1/5s.
1920—Fred Faller	29m. 1s.
1921—R. E. Johnson	24m. 23 4/5s.
1922—William Ritola	34m. 37s.
1923—William Ritola	31m. 56s.
1924—Fred Wachsmuth	31m. 35s.
1925—William Ritola	29m. 27s.
1926—William Ritola	30m. 3/5s.
1927—William Ritola	29m. 27 1/5s.
1928—Gus Moore	31m. 18s.
1929—Gus Moore	31m. 10s.
1930—William C. Zepp	29m. 43s.
1931—Clark S. Chamberlain	29m. 40 4/5s.
1932—Joseph P. McCluskey	32m. 30s.
1933—R. A. Sears	32m. 51s.
1934—Donald Lash	32m. 17.2s.
1935—Donald Lash	32m. 42.6s.
1936—Donald Lash	32m. 27s.
1937—Donald Lash	32m. 57.4s.
1938—Donald Lash	33m. 33.8s.
1939—Donald Lash	32m. 26s.
1940—Donald Lash	30m. 25.8s.
1941—J. Gregory Rice	29m. 18.7s.
1942—Frank Dixon	31m. 52s.
1943—William Hulse	32m. 41s.
1944—James Rafferty	31m. 38s.
1945—Thomas Quinn	34m. 14s.
1946—Robert Black	32m. 46.4s.

1947—Curtis Stone	32m. 28.7s.
1948—Robert Black	30m. 2s.
1949—Fred Wilt	30m. 31s.
1950—Browning Ross	31m. 24s.
1951—William Ashenfelter	30m. 26s.
1952—Fred Wilt	32m. 31s.
1953—Fred Wilt	31m. 17.6s.
1954—Gordon McKenzie	29m. 27.5s.
1955—Horace Ashenfelter	31m. 39.1s.
1956—Horace Ashenfelter	30m. 8s.
1957—John Macy	31m. 12s.
1958—John Macy	29m. 47.8s.
1959—Al Lawrence	32m. 22.4s.
1960—Al Lawrence	31m. 20.8s.
1961—Bruce Kidd	32m. 02.0s.
1962—Pete McArdle	29m. 53.0s.
1963—Bruce Kidd	30m. 47.2s.
1964—Dave Ellis	30m. 49.5s.
1965—Ron Larrieu	31m. 11.8s.
1966—Ron Larrieu	31m. 23s.
1967—Ken Moore	30m. 08.8s.
1968—John Mason	
1969—Jack Bachelor	
1970-73—Frank Shorter	

Cross-Country Team — Points

	Points
1907—Irish-American A.C.	29
1908—Trinity A.C. (Maloney, Lees, McCarrick, Taylor, Dietas)	78
1909—No record	
1910—New York A.C. (Bellars, McGinn, Smith, Bailey, Fitzgerald)	27
1911—Irish-American A.C. (McNamara, Collins, Huysman, Donnelly, Nelson)	34
1912—Irish-American A.C. (Johannsen, McNamara, Collins, Huysman, Reynolds)	21
1913—Irish-American A.C. (Kiviat, Barden, Eke, Fogel, Dennelly)	32
1914—Irish-American A.C. (Kolehmainen, Fogel, Barden)	16
1915—Irish-American A.C. (Kolehmainen, Barden, Zuna, Weg, Messer)	25
1916—Millrose A.A. (Kyronen, Devaney, Pores, Soukop, Giannakopulus)	30
1917—Dorchester Club (Hennigan, Tuomikoski, Faller, Horne, Linder)	30
1918—Morningside A.C. (Halpin, Touvalides, Lehman, Wiemann, Metzger)	32
1919—Millrose A.A. (Pores, Giannakopulus, Devaney, Voteretsas, deSteffano)	36
1920—Dorchester Club (Faller, Doherty, Ohman, Horne, McAuley)	26
1921—New York A.C. (Leslie, Brennan, Penfield, Cornetta, Sellers)	40
1922—Finnish-American A.C. (Ritola, Prim, Fager, Nilson, Erickson)	42
1923—Meadowbrook A.C. (Studenroth, Miller, Ramsey, Mullan, Worthington)	44
1924—Finnish-American A.C. (Nilson, Prim, Tahkanen, Wilberg, Fager)	31
1925—Finnish-American A.C. (Ritola, Prim, Koski, Fagerlund)	—

1926–Finnish-American A.C. (Ritola, Koski, Fagerlund) .... –
1927–Millrose A.A. (Titterton, Bell, Booth, Ward) 49
1928–Millrose A.A. (Booth, Payne, Ruckel, Totten, Werbin) 40
1929–Dorchester A.C. (Heikkila, Stevens, Zepp, Hennigan, Signor) 33
1930–Millrose A.A. (McArthur, Michelson, McDade, Taylor, Werbin) 46
1931–Indiana University (Brocksmith, Watson, Hornbostel, Kemp, Neese)....... 30
1932–Millrose A.A. (Pentti, Werbin, Titzell, Silverman, Brennan) 19
1933–Millrose A.A. (Gregory, Pentti, McDade, Titzell, Brennan) 31
1934–Millrose A.A. (Pentti, Gregory, P. Mundy, J. Mundy, Titzell) 26
1935–Millrose A.A. (Pentti, Mundy, Gregory, Bertherlot, McDade) 37
1936–Indiana University (Lash, Deckard, Smith, Trutt, Applegate) 15
1937–Millrose A.A. (Gregory, Pentti, Dyrgall, Bertherlot, Federoff) 35
1938–Millrose A.A. (Dyrgall, Federoff, Olexy, Berthelot, Gregory) 29
1939–Millrose A.A. (Federoff, Gregory, Olexy, Bertherlot, Goldberg) 35
1940–New York A.C. (Rafferty, Pentti, Beccali, Venzke, DeGeorge) 23
1941–New York A.C. (Rice, Rafferty, McCluskey, Venzke) 18
1942–Shanahan C.C. (Williams, Karver) 24
1943–U.S. Naval Academy 34
1944–U.S. Navy (Dempsey, Barry, Hall) .... –
1945–New York A.C. (Quinn, O'Toole, Burnham, Borck, George) 19
1946–New York A.C. (Quinn, Thompson, McCluskey, Mannix, Hulse) 34
1947–New York A.C. (Quinn, MacMitchell) . 28
1948–Michigan State College (Druetzler, Mack, Dianetti, Sewell, Irmen) .... –
1949–Syracuse Univ. (Church, Pratt, Perritt) . –
1950–New York A.C. (Schoeffler) 38
1951–New York A.C. (Wilt, Stone, Osterberg, Thompson, Grimm) 29
1952–New York A.C. (Wilt, H. Ashenfelter, W. Ashenfelter, Stone, Trent) 18
1953–New York A.C. (Wilt, Capozzoli, Stone, W. Ashenfelter, H. Ashenfelter) 17
1954–New York A.C. (H. Ashenfelter, Stone, W. Ashenfelter, Schoeffler, Trayford) . 45
1955–New York A.C. (H. Ashenfelter, Wilt, Eckhoff, Dickson, W. Ashenfelter) 28
1956–New York A.C. (H. Ashenfelter, Kopil, King, Dickson, Lubina) 46
1957–New York A.C. (King, McArdle, Stone, Lubina, Dougan) 45
1958–New York A.C. (Mugosa, McArdle, Kopil, Stone, Maxwell) 40
1959–Houston (Lawrence, Macy, Almond, Smartt, Clohessy) .... –

1960–Houston (Lawrence, Macy, Almond, Fleming, Rankin) 33
1961–Houston (Macy, Almond, Clohessy, Elliott, Walker) .... –
1962–New York A.C. (Truex, McGee, Kitt, Sargent, Robertson) .... –
1963–Los Angeles T.C.
1964–Los Angeles T.C.
1965–Toronto Olympic Club
1966–New York A.C.
1967–Toronto Olympic Club
1968–Villanova Univ.
1969-70–Pacific Coast Club
1971-73–Florida Track Club

Indoor

60-Yard Dash
Distance 60 meters in 1933-36, 1938-39, 1942.

Year and champion	Time
1906–C. J. Seitz	6.6s.
1907–J. F. O'Connell	6.6s.
1908–Robert Cloughen	6.6s.
1909–R. W. Gill	6.8s.
1910–Robert Cloughen	6.8s.
1911–A. T. Meyer	6.6s.
1912–15–No competition	
1916–J. G. Loomis	6.4s.
1917–J. G. Loomis	6.4s.
1918–William Ganzemuller	6.8s.
1919–Loren Murchison	6.6s.
1920–Loren Murchison	6.4s.
1921–F. W. Conway	6.6s.
1922–Loren Murchison	6.4s.
1923–Loren Murchison	6.4s.
1924–Loren Murchison	6.6s.
1925–Cecil Coaffee	6.2s.
1926–Chester Bowman	6.2s.
1927–Karl Wildermuth	6.4s.
1928–Karl Wildermuth	6.4s.
1929–James Daley	6.6s.
1930–Chester Bowman	6.4s.
1931–Ira Singer	6.5s.
1932–Emmett Toppino	6.2s.
1933–Ralph Metcalfe	6.7s.
1934–Ralph Metcalfe	6.7s.
1935–Ben Johnson	6.6s.
1936–Ralph Metcalfe	6.7s.
1937–Ben Johnson	6.3s.
1938–Ben Johnson	6.8s.
1939–Herbert Thompson	6.6s.
1940–Mozel Ellerbe	6.2s.
1941–Herbert Thompson	6.2s.
1942–Barney Ewell	6.6s.
1943–Herbert Thompson	6.1s.
1944–Ed Conwell	6.2s.
1945–Corp. Barney Ewell	6.2s.
1946–Thomas A. Carey	6.2s.
1947–Ed Conwell	6.2s.
1948–Ed Conwell	6.3s.
1949–William J. Dwyer	6.1s.
1950–Andrew Stanfield	6.1s.

1951—Edward Conwell	6.2s.		1942—Roy Cochran	1m. 12.4s.
1952—John O'Connell	6.2s.		1943—Lewis Smith	1m. 13s.
1953—John Haines	6.1s.		1944—Robert Ufer	*1m. 11.3s.
1954—John Haines	6.2s.		1945—Elmore T. Harris	1m. 13.2s.
1955—John Haines	6.1s.		1946—Elmore T. Harris	1m. 12.9s.
1956—John Haines	6.2s.		1947—George Guida	1m. 13.7s.
1957—Ira Murchison	6.2s.		1948—Dave Bolen	1m. 11.8s.
1958—Ed Collymore	6.1s.		1949—Dave Bolen	1m. 11.6s.
1959—Paul Winder	6.2s.		1950—Hugo Maiocco	1m. 11.2s.
1960—Paul Winder	6.2s.		1951—Hugo Maiocco	1m. 12.4s.
1961—Frank Budd	6.1s.		1952—Charles Moore	1m. 10.9s.
1962—Frank Budd	6.2s.		1953—Mal Whitfield	1m. 10.4s.
1963—Sam Perry	6.2s.		1954—Reginald Pearman	1m. 11.4s.
1964—Bob Hayes	5.9s.		1955—Charles Jenkins	1m. 11.9s.
1965—Sam Perry	6.0s.		1956—Louis Jones	1m. 11s.
1966—Bill Gaines	6.0s.		1957—Charles Jenkins	1m. 10.4s.
1967—Bill Gaines	6.0s.		1958—Charles Jenkins	1m. 11.3s.
1968—Bill Gaines	6.0s.		1959—Josh Culbreath	1m. 11.1s.
1969—Charlie Greene	6.0s.		1960—Thomas Murphy	1m. 11.7s.
1970—Lt. Charlie Greene	6.0s.		1961—Edward Southern	1m. 11.9s.
1971—Jean-Louis Ravelomanantosa	6.1s.		1962—William Crothers	1m. 10.8s.
1972—Delano Meriwether	6.2s.		1963—Jack Yerman	1m. 09.4s.
1973—Hasley Crawford	6.0s.		1964—Charles Buchta	1m. 12.1s.
			1965—Jack Yerman	1m. 11.3s.

600-Yard Run

Distance 600 meters from 1933 through 1939.

1906—E. B. Parsons	1m. 14.6s.
1907—E. B. Parsons	1m. 14.4s.
1908—Melvin W. Sheppard	1m. 14.8s
1909—Melvin W. Sheppard	1m. 14.6s.
1910—Harry E. Gissing	1m. 14s.
1911—Abel R. Kiviat	1m. 14s.
1912—No competition	
1913—Abel R. Kiviat	1m. 14.2s.
1914—Thomas J. Halpin	1m. 13.4s.
1915—Thomas J. Halpin	1m. 14.8s.
1916—W. J. Bingham	1m. 14.8s.
1917—Earl Eby	1m. 14.2s.
1918—M. Gustavson	1m. 17s.
1919—Jack Sellers	1m. 15.6s.
1920—Earl Eby	1m. 16.8s.
1921—F. L. Murray	1m. 15.6s.
1922—Sid Leslie	1m. 14.8s.
1923—Earl Eby	1m. 14.4s.
1924—Walter Mulvihill	1m. 15.2s.
1925—Vincent Lally	1m. 15.8s.
1926—H. M. Fitch	1m. 14s.
1927—George Leness	1m. 13.2s.
1928—Phil Edwards	1m. 14.2s.
1929—Phil Edwards	1m. 12s.
1930—Phil Edwards	1m. 13.6s.
1931—Phil Edwards	1m. 12.6s.
1932—Alex Wilson	1m. 13s.
1933—Milton Sandler	1m. 21.4s.
1934—Milton Sandler	1m. 22.8s.
1935—Milton Sandler	1m. 21.9s.
1936—Edward T. O'Brien	1m. 21s.
1937—Edward T. O'Brien	1m. 23s.
1938—James Herbert	1m. 20.3s.
1939—Charles Beetham	1m. 21.6s.
1940—Charles Belcher	1m. 11.6s.
1941—James Herbert	1m. 12s.

1966—Theron Lewis	1m. 09.2s.
1967—Jim Kemp	1m. 10.6s.
1968—Martin McGrady	1m. 09.2s.
1969—Martin McGrady	1m. 12.3s.
1970—Martin McGrady	1m. 07.6s.
1971—Andrzej Badenski, Poland	1m. 10.7s.
1972—Lee Evans	1m. 11.3s.
1973—Fred Newhouse	1m. 11.0s.

*Improper start.

1,000-Yard Run

Distance 1,000 meters from 1933 through 1939.

1906—Melvin W. Sheppard	2m. 17.8s.
1907—Melvin W. Sheppard	2m. 25s.
1908—Harry Gissing	2m. 20s.
1909—Harry Gissing	2m. 18.8s.
1910—Harry Gissing	2m. 20s.
1911—Abel R. Kiviat	2m. 16.2s.
1912—No competition	
1913—Abel R. Kiviat	2m. 15.8s.
1914—Abel R. Kiviat	2m. 15.4s.
1915—D.S. Caldwell	2m. 18.8s.
1916—J.W. Overton	2m. 15.4s.
1917—J.W. Overton	2m. 14s.
1918—Joie W. Ray	2m. 14s.
1919—Joie W. Ray	2m. 16.4s.
1920—Joie W. Ray	2m. 15.2s.
1921—Sidney Leslie	2m. 15.4s.
1922—Harold C. Cutbill	2m. 13.4s.
1923—Ray Watson	2m. 15.6s.
1924—George Marsters	2m. 17.6s.
1925—Lloyd Hahn	2m. 13.8s.
1926—Ray E. Dodge	2m. 15.2s.
1927—Lloyd Hahn	2m. 12.8s.
1928—Ray Conger	2m. 15.8s.
1929—Ray Conger	2m. 13.2s.
1930—Dr. Paul Martin	2m. 12.6s.
1931—Ray Conger	2m. 14.1s.

1932—Dale Letts	2m. 13s.	1949—William Slykhuis	4m. 11.2s.
1933—Glen Dawson	2m. 27.4s.	1950—John Joe Barry	4m. 11.5s.
1934—Charles Hornbostel	2m. 28.8s.	1951—Fred Wilt	4m. 9.4s.
1935—Glen Dawson	2m. 30s.	1952—Bill Mack	4m. 11.4s.
1936—Charles Hornbostel	2m. 29s.	1953—Fred Dwyer	4m. 12.4s.
1937—Elroy Robinson	2m. 29.4s.	1954—Josy Barthel	4m. 11.7s.
1938—Francis Slater	2m. 29.3s.	1955—Wes Santee	4m. 07.9s.
1939—John Borican	2m. 28.6s.	1956—Ron Delany	4m. 14.5s.
1940—John Borican	2m. 13s.	1957—Ron Delany	4m. 07s.
1941—John Borican	2m. 11.5s.	1958—Ron Delany	4m. 03.7s.
1942—John Borican	2m. 10.5s.	1959—Ron Delany	4m. 02.5s.
1943—James Rafferty	2m. 12.8s.	1960—Philip Coleman	4m. 09s.
1944—Les Eisenhart	2m. 15s.	1961—James Beatty	4m. 09.3s.
1945—Don L. Burnham	2m. 17.7s.	1962—James Beatty	4m. 00.2s.
1946—Fred Sickinger	2m. 15.8s.	1963—Jim Beatty	3m. 59.0s.
1947—William McGuire	2m. 13.9s.	1964—Ergas Leps (Canada)	4m. 09.6s.
1948—Philip Thigpen	2m. 16.4s.	1965—James Grelle	4m. 07.4s.
1949—Robert Mealey	2m. 13.9s.	1966—James Grelle	4m. 09.5s.
1950—Roscoe L. Browne	2m. 15.6s.	1967—Sam Bair	4m. 03.2s.
1951—Roscoe L. Browne	2m. 14.0s.	1968—Preston Davis	4m. 06.0s.
1952—Don A. Gehrmann	2m. 08.2s.	1969—Henryk Szordykowski (Poland)	4m. 05.0s.
1953—Heinz Ulzheimer	2m. 09.4s.	1970—Martin Liquori	4m. 00.9s.
1954—Mal Whitfield	2m. 11s.	1971—Henryk Szordykowski (Poland)	4m. 06.0s.
1955—Arnold Sowell	2m. 08.2s.	1972—Byron Dyce	4m. 01.8s.
1956—Arnold Sowell	2m. 08.4s.	1973—Martin Liquori	4m. 03.5s.
1957—Arnold Sowell	2m. 12.6s.		
1958—Zbigniew Orywal	2m. 14.1s.		
1959—Zbigniew Orywal	2m. 12.6s.	**2-Mile Run**	
1960—Cary Weisiger	2m. 12.8s.	1899—Alec Grant	10m. 4 4/5s.
1961—Ernest Cunliffe	2m. 08.0s.	1900—Alec Grant	10m. 2 3/5s.
1962—John Reilly	2m. 11.0s.	1901—Alec Grant	9m. 40 4/5s.
1963—William Crothers	2m. 09.8s.	1902—No competition	
1964—Ernie Cunliffe	2m. 14.8s.	1903—Alec Grant	9m. 55 4/5s.
1965—Ted Nelson	2m. 10.5s.	1904—George V. Bonhag	9m. 44s.
1966—Ted Nelson	2m. 07.8s.	1905—George V. Bonhag	9m. 54 4/5s.
1967—Preston Davis	2m. 09.4s.	1906—George V. Bonhag	9m. 47 2/5s.
1968—Tom Von Ruder	2m. 10.7s.	1907—George V. Bonhag	9m. 42 1/5s.
1969—Herb Germann	2m. 08.0s.	1908—M.P. Driscoll	9m. 28 3/5s.
1970—Juris Luzins	2m. 06.2s.	1909—M.P. Driscoll	9m. 39s.
1971—Tom Von Ruden	2m. 07.3s.	1910—J.W. Monument	9m. 36 1/5s.
1972—Josef Plachy (Czech)	2m. 09.8s.	1911—George V. Bonhag	9m. 20 4/5s.
1973—Marcel Phillippe	2m. 08.8s.	1912—No competition	
		1913—W.J. Kramer	9m. 19 1/5s.

1-Mile Run

Distance 1,500 meters from 1933 through 1939.

1932—Gene Venzke	4m. 15s.	1914—H.J. Smith	9m. 18s.
1933—Gene Venzke	3m. 55.4s.	1915—M.A. Devaney	9m. 24 4/5s.
1934—Glenn Cunningham	3m. 52.2s.	1916—Joie W. Ray	9m. 25 4/5s.
1935—Glenn Cunningham	3m. 50.5s.	1917—John Ryan	10m. 4 1/5s.
1936—Gene Venzke	3m. 49.9s.	1918—Edw. J. Garvey Jr.	9m. 40s.
1937—Archie San Romani	3m. 51.2s.	1919—Gordon Nightingale	9m. 28 2/5s.
1938—Glenn Cunningham	3m. 48.4s.	1920—Harry G. Helm	9m. 34 3/5s.
1939—Glenn Cunningham	3m. 54.6s.	1921—Max Bohland	9m. 45 1/5s.
1940—Charles Fenske	4m. 08.8s.	1922—J.W. Romig	9m. 21 1/5s.
1941—Walter Mehl	4m. 10.9s.	1923—Joie W. Ray	9m. 10 2/5s.
1942—Gilbert Dodds	4m. 08.7s.	1924—Joie W. Ray	9m. 32 1/5s.
1943—Frank Dixon	4m. 09.6s.	1925—Paavo Nurmi	9m. 9 3/5s.
1944—Gilbert Dodds	4m. 08.3s.	1926—William Goodwin	9m. 25 2/5s.
1945—James Rafferty	4m. 17.5s.	1927—William Goodwin	9m. 16 1/5s.
1946—Leslie MacMitchell	4m. 18.1s.	1928—Leo Lermond	9m. 16 4/5s.
1947—Gilbert Dodds	4m. 12.7s.	1929—Edvin Wide	9m. 7s.
1948—Thomas Quinn	4m. 13.2s.	1930—Joseph P. McCluskey	9m. 30.3s.
		1931—Leo Lermond	9m. 11.8s.

(Replaced by three-mile run in 1932.)

3-Mile Run

Distance 5,000 meters from 1933 through 1939.

1932—Lt. George Lermond	14m.	26.4s.
1933—Lt. George Lermond	15m.	08.8s.
1934—John Follows	15m.	01.5s.
1935—John Follows	15m.	18.8s.
1936—Norman Bright	15m.	
1937—Norman Bright	14m.	45.8s.
1938—Donald Lash	14m.	.39s.
1939—Donald Lash	14m.	.30.9s.
1940—J. Gregory Rice	13m.	55.9s.
1941—J. Gregory Rice	13m.	51s.
1942—J. Gregory Rice	13m.	45.7s.
1943—J. Gregory Rice	13m.	53.5s.
1944—Oliver Hunter	14m.	22.2s.
1945—Forest C. Efaw	14m.	26.3s.
1946—Forest C. Efaw	14m.	40.1s.
1947—Curtis Stone	14m.	22.6s.
1948—Curtis Stone	14m.	23.6s.
1949—Gaston Reiff	14m.	08.1s.
1950—Curtis Stone	13m.	57.2s.
1951—Curtis Stone	14m.	12.8s.
1952—Horace Ashenfelter	14m.	02.0s.
1953—Horace Ashenfelter	13m.	47.5s.
1954—Horace Ashenfelter	13m.	56.7s.
1955—Horace Ashenfelter	13m.	54s.
1956—Horace Ashenfelter	14m.	09.6s.
1957—John Macy	13m.	57.4s.
1958—Vilisa Mugosa	13m.	54.2s.
1959—William Dellinger	13m.	37s.
1960—Al Lawrence	13m.	26.4s.
1961—Bruce Kidd	13m.	47.0s.
1962—Bruce Kidd	13m.	48.8s.
1963—Marcel Bernard (France)	13m.	38.4s.
1964—Ron Clarke (Australia)	13m.	18.4s.
1965—Billy Mills	13m.	25.4s.
1966—Lajos Mecser (Hungary)	13m.	40.0s.
1967—Terry Smith	13m.	16.2s.
1968—George Young	13m.	17.6s.
1969—George Young	13m.	09.8s.
1970—Arthur Dulong	13m.	19.6s.
1971—Frank Shorter	13m.	10.6s.
1972—Emile Puttemans (Belgium)	13m.	18.4s.
1973—Tracy Smith	13m.	07.2s.

60-Yard High Hurdles

70 yards, 1910—32 and 1940—41.
65 meters, 1933—39.
60 yards, since 1942.

1910—J.L. Hartranft	9.4s.
1911—John J. Eller	9.4s.
1912—No competition	
1913—J.I. Wendell	9.4s.
1914—John J. Eller	9.4s.
1915—D. Trenholm	9.4s.
1916—John J. Eller	9.6s.
1917—E.J. Thompson	9.4s.
1918—Harold Barron	9.6s.
1919—Walker Smith	9.4s.
1920—Walker Smith	9.2s.
1921—Harold Barron	9.4s.
1922—Harold Barron	9.2s.
1923—Karl W. Anderson	8.8s.
1924—Herbert Meyer	9.2s.
1925—Harold M. Osborn	8.6s.
1926—G.P. Guthrie	8.6s.
1927—G.P. Guthrie	9s.
1928—Weem Baskims	9s.
1929—E.M. Wells	8.8s.
1930—Lee Sentman	8.6s.
1931—Percy Beard	8.5s.
1932—Percy Beard	8.7s.
1933—Percy Beard	8.6s.
1934—John Collier	8.7s.
1935—Percy Beard	8.6s.
1936—Sam Allen	8.7s.
1937—Sam Allen	8.8s.
1938—Forrest Towns	8.7s.
1939—Allan Tolmich	8.4s.
1940—Allan Tolmich	8.4s.
1941—Allan Tolmich	8.4s.
1942—Fred Wolcott	7.2s.
1943—Robert E. Wright	7.4s.
1944—Edward Dugger	7.5s.
1945—Edward Dugger	7.5s.
1946—Edward Dugger	7.6s.
1947—Harrison Dillard	7.4s.
1948—Harrison Dillard	7.2s.
1949—Harrison Dillard	7.2s.
1950—Harrison Dillard	7.3s.
1951—Harrison Dillard	7.4s.
1952—Harrison Dillard	7.4s.
1953—Harrison Dillard	7.3s.
1954—Jack Davis	7.3s.
1955—Harrison Dillard	7.3s.
1956—Lee Calhoun	7.2s.
1957—Lee Calhoun	7.2s.
1958—Hayes Jones	7.1s.
1959—Elias Gilbert	7.3s.
1960—Hayes Jones	7.1s.
1961—Hayes Jones	7.0s.
1962—Hayes Jones	7.1s.
1963—Hayes Jones	7.3s.
1964—Hayes Jones	7.0s.
1965—Ralph Boston	7.2s.
1966—Willie Davenport	6.9s.
1967—Willie Davenport	7.0s.
1968—Earl McCullouch	6.9s.
1969—Willie Davenport	7.0s.
1970—Willie Davenport	7.1s.
1971—Willie Davenport	7.0s.
1972—Rod Milburn	7.1s.
1973—Rod Milburn	7.0s.

SPRINT MEDLEY RELAY

Distance 1,000 meters (400—100—200—300) from 1935 through 1939. Distance 1,060 yards (440—100—220—300) from 1940 through 1971. Distance 1,180 yards (440—220—220—300) 1972-1973.

1935—New York Curb Exchange
(Harry Hoffman, John Trachy, Harold Lamb, James Herbert) .... 2m.26.5s.

1936—New York University (Edgar Stripling, W. Eisenberg, E. Krosney, S. Bernstein) .... 2m. 0.4s.

1937—Lenox Hill A.A., N.Y. (Jack Hurley, Albert Glenn, Martin Delaney, Max Jaffe) .... 2m. 0.8s.

1938—New York University (Edgar Stripling, Nat Buschstein, Martin Witte, Curtis Giddings) .... 2m. 0.5s.

1939—New York University (J. Herbert, N. Buschstein, J. McPoland, M. Witte) .... 2m. 0.5s.

1940—New York University (J. Herbert, J. Fangboner, G. Hagans, S. Braun) .... 1m. 54.4s.

1941—New York University (H. Bogrow, J. Fangboner, G. Hagans, Dave Lawyer) .... 1m. 56.2s.

1942—New York University (Stan Braun, Frank Remy, Norman Elson, Dave Lawyer) .... 1m. 57.4s.

1943—Fordham University (Albert Hayden, Frank Keane, Don Leahy, Robert Stuart) .... 1m. 59s.

1944—New York University (Herbert Rubin, David Seltzer, Milford Parker, Ed Conwell) .... 2m. 0.4s.

1945—U.S. Naval Academy (Frederic W. Bouwman, Hugh M. McClellan, John B. VanVelzer, James W. Pettit Jr.) .... 1m. 58.5s.

1946—New York University (Milton Smith, Norman Elson, Homer Gillis, James Gilhooley) .... 1m. 58.3s.

1947—Manhattan College (Al Rogers, Joe Cianciabella, John Gorman, John Quigley) .... 1m. 55.5s.

1948—New York Pioneer Club (Sol McCants, Thomas Carey, Oliver Tucker, Robert Carty) .... 1m. 54.9s.

1949—Villanova (James McKenna, Thomas Irish, Jack Holmes, Joseph McCreary) .... 1m. 55.5s.

1950—Villanova (McKenna, John Furlinger, Holmes, McCreary) .... 1m. 53.6s.

1951—Seton Hall College (Harry Bright, Stanley Bestys, Morris Curotta, Andrew Stanfield) .... 1m. 55.1s.

1952—Manhattan College (Vernon Dixon, John O'Connell, Louis Jones, Robert Carty) .... 1m. 53.1s.

1953—Grand St. Boys' Assn. (H. McKenley, M. Whitfield, G. Rhoden, A. Stanfield). .... 1m. 52s.

1954—New York Pioneer Club (Frank Bowens, James Ryan, James Gathers, Robert Carty) .... 1m. 54.1s.

1955—New York Pioneer Club (Frank Bowens, James Ryan, James Gathers, Andy Stanfield) .... 1m. 53.8s.

1956—Villanova (Charles Jenkins, Gene Maliff, George Sydnor, Al Petersen) .... 1m. 52.9s.

1957—New York Pioneer Club (Frank Bowens, Dick Williams, Tom Beach, James Gathers) .... 1m. 53.5s.

1958—New York A.C. (Steve Bartold, James Warner, Paul Ewing, Grant Scruggs) .... 1m. 55.3s.

1959—Villanova (Ed Collymore, Joe Mannion, James Blackburn, Charles Stead) .... 1m. 53.2s.

1960—Winston-Salem Track Club (Frank Bowens, Robert Manning, Charles Lewis, Francis Washington) 1m. 55.4s.

1961—New York Pioneer Club (Cal Barnes, Ron Basil, Doyle Whittaker, Emil Dufau) .... 1m. 56.1s.

1962—Villanova (Carl Wagner, Alan Jackman, Frank Budd, Paul Drayton) Drayton .... 1m. 53.3s.

1963—Morgan State Frosh (Leonard Moore, Byron Lewis, Spencer Henry, Stephen Wiggins) .... 1m. 55.3s.

1964—North Carolina College (Andrew McCray, Norman Tate, Robert Johnson, Edwin Roberts) .... 1m. 51.3s.

1965—Southern California Striders (Ron Whitney, Larry Dunn, Don Webster, Adolph Plummer) ...... 1m. 54.4s.

1966—Southern University (Theron Lewis, Webster Johnson, Everett Mason, Grundy Harris) .... 1m. 46.5s.

1967—Southern California Striders (Ron Whitney, Larry Dunn, Bob Frey, Bill Toomey) .... 1m. 51.6s.

1968—Santa Clara Valley Youth Village (Tommie Smith, Kirk Clayton, Jerry Williams, John Carlos) ..... 1m. 52.3s.

1969—Grand Street Boys Club, N.Y. (Carl Richardson, John Davis, Russ Rogers, Charlie Mays) .... 1m. 55.7s.

1970—Rutgers (Tom Ulan, John Herma, James Smith, Robert Kerr) ... 1m. 53.4s.

1971—Pacific Coast Club (Jay Elbel, Bob Frey, Terry Musika, Len Van Hofwegen) .... 1m. 53.9s.

1972—Adelphi (Al Salmon, Richard Hardware, William Johnson, Ray Lee) .... 2m. 05.5s.

1973—Essex County College (Alfred Daley, Larry Brown, Kevin Joseph, Ainsley Armstrong) .... 2m. 04.0s.

1-Mile Relay

Distance 1,600 meters from 1933 through 1939.

1933—Univ. of Pennsylvania (John K. Edwards, Howard Jones, Wm. Carr, James Healey) ....3m.21s.

1934—Indiana University (Ivan Fuqa, Wesley Bicking, Marmaduke Hobbs, C. Hornbostel) ....3m.21.4s.

1935—N.Y. Curb Exchange (John Trachy, Harold Lamb, J. Herbert, Harry Hoffman) ....3m.20.7s.

1936—Manhattan College (Matthew Carey, V. Riordan, Edgar Borck, John Wolff) ....3m.19.7s.

1937—N.Y. Curb Exchange (Harold Lamb, Wm. Ray, Harry Hoffman, J. Herbert) .... 3m.19.5s.

1938—New York University (Martin Witte, C. Giddings, Edgar Stripling, J. Herbert) .... 3m.19.4s.

1939—69th Regiment A.A. (H. Borck, R. Squire, L. Burns, C. Beetham) ......3m.17.2s.

1940—New York University (J. Mc-Poland, G. Hagans, H. Bogrow, J. Herbert) .... 3m.20.3s.

1941—Georgetown University (A.J. Rogers, H.P. James, H.J. Short, L.A. Collado) .... 3m.19.5s.

1942—Georgetown University (Jim Fish, Charles Williams, Hugh James, Hugh Short) .... 3m.20.3s.

1943—Seton Hall College (Robert Sovetts, Dan Van Dorpe, Robert Rainier, George Stafurik) ....3m.23.3s.

1944—New York A.C. (John Kelly, Edward Rogers, Alfred Daily, Wesley Wallace) ....3m.26.3s.

1945—New York University (Milford Parker, Stanton Callender, William Lubin, Maurice Callender) ....3m.26s.

1946—New York University (Milford Parker, Robert Hakusaa, William Lubin, Maurice Callender). ....3m.24.7s.

1947—Manhattan College (Al Rogers, Dean Noll, John Gorman, John Quigl Quigley) .... 3m.25.8s.

1948—Seton Hall College (Reginald Marshall, George Stafurick, Philip Palese, Jack Tulp) ....3m.21.9s.

1949—New York University (Hugo Maiocco, Sutton Titus, Reginald Pearman, Jim Gilhooley) ....3m.20.4s.

1950—Morgan State College (Sam La-Beach, Robert Tyler, William Brown, George Rhoden) ....3m.19.9s.

1951—Seton Hall College (David Evans, Edward McArdle, Charles Slade, Robert Carter) ....3m.20.4s.

1952—Fordham University (Joseph Bellantoni, John Albert, William Persichetty, Thomas Murray) ....3m.20.3s.

1953—Manhattan College (Henry Bercuk, R. Lucas, Wallace Pina, Louis Jones) .... 3m.20.8s.

1954—Morgan State (Herman Wade, Otis Johnson, James Rogers, Josh Culbreath) ....3m.18.12s.

1955—Morgan State (Herman Wade, Rudy Solomon, James Rogers, Josh Culbreath) ....3m.18.5s.

1956—New York Pioneer Club (Joe Gold, John Tucker, Richard Maiocco,

Reginald Pearman) ....3m.20.3s.

1957—Villanova (Gene Maliff, John Furlinger, Al Peterson, Ed Collymore) ...3m.20.6s.

1958—Manhattan Freshmen (Tom Greene, Frank Carroll, Art Evans, Kyle Courtney) ....3m.19.6s.

1959—Morgan State (Lou Smith, Tom Anderson, Hosea Smith, Nick Ellis) ..3m.16.6s.

1960—Villanova (Paul Drayton, Robert Coffill, Carl Wagner, Joseph Mannion) 3m.17.7s.

1961—Morgan State (Lou Smith, Thomas Anderson, Lee Martin, Lawson Smart) ....3m.16.3s.

1962—Morgan State (John Bethea, Robert Bagley, Hubert Brown, Lawson Smart) ....3m.18.2s.

1963—Maryland State (Robert Brown, Earl Rogers, Edwin Skinner, Charley Mays) ....3m.16.2s.

1964—Maryland State (Robert Brown, Harley Morris, Edwin Skinner, Earl Rogers) ....3m.16.2s.

1965—Camp Pendleton Marine Corps (Dick Edmunds, Dick Metzgar, Ron Freeman, Jim Heath) ....3m.16.0s.

1966—Southern University (Webster Johnson, Robert Johnson, Everett Mason, Theron Lewis) ....3m.12.6s.

1967—San Jose State (Ken Shackelford, John Bambury, Lee Evans, Tommie Smith) ....3m.14.9s.

1968—U.S. Army, Fort MacArthur (Don Webster, Tom Jones, Bob Tobler, Jim Kemp) ....3m.17.1s.

1969—Sports International Club, Wash. (John Collins, Mark Young, Andy Bell, Ed Roberts) ....3m.18.1s.

1970—Sports International Club, Wash. (John Collins, Martin McGrady, Mark Young, Ed Roberts) ....3m.14.4s.

1971—Villanova (Ken Schappert, Bob Carpenter, Greg Govan, LaMotte Hyman) ....3m.16.9s.

1972—Bohaa, N.Y. (LaMotte Hyman, Greg Dougherty, Larry James, Vincent Matthews) ....3m.14.7s.

1973—Sports International Club, Wash. (Thad Fletcher, Pete Schuder, Bill Barrow, Tommie Turner) ....3m.17.9s.

2-Mile Relay

1942—Seton Hall College (Anthony Luciano, Frank Fletcher, Bob Rainer, Chet Lipski) ....7m.39.8s.

1943—New York University (George Carposi, Ray Zoellner, Frank Dixon, Henry Eckert) ....7m.50s.

1944—Dartmouth College (Wm. Atkinson, Clark Judge, Frank Fox, Don Burnham) ....7m.50.9s.

1945—Mass. Inst. of Tech (Chas. Goebel, Joseph Shea, John Serrie, Royce

Crimmin) . . . . 8m.05s.

1946—Manhattan College (Ignatius Rienzo, Thomas Comerford, Phil V. Connell, Edward Walsh) . . . . 8m.00.5s.

1947—Fordham University (John O'Hare, Joseph Nowicki, Ed Carney, Jerome Connolly) . . . . 7m.50.4s.

1948—Manhattan College (John Moran, James Cavanaugh, Thomas Comerford, Philip O'Connell) . . . . 7m.49.9s.

1949—Univ. of Pennsylvania (Mullen, Uhle, Kirwin, Strasenburgh) . . . . 7m.49.7s.

1950—Georgetown University (O'Brien, David Boland, Smith, Joseph Deady) .7m.44s.

1951—Georgetown University (David Boland, Joseph LaPierre, Carl Joyce, Joseph Deady) . . . . 7m.36.8s.

1952—Georgetown University (Carl Joyce, Joseph LaPierre, David Boland, Richard Saunders) . . . . 7m.41.7s.

1953—Fordham University (Frank Tarsney, William Persichetty, Thomas Keegan, Thomas Courtney) . . . . 7m.44.3s.

1954—Fordham (Terry Foley, Frank Tarsney, Bill Persichetty, Tom Courtney) . . . . 7m.41.1s.

1955—Syracuse (Bob Milner, Les Vielbig, Steve Armstrong, Don Shupe) . . . . . . 7m.39.7s.

1956—Syracuse (Robert Milner, Art Ritchie, Bob Pugsley, Les Vielbig) . . . 7m.37.9s.

1957—Georgetown (John Bisbee, Norm Williams, John Nelson, Bob Carney) .7m.39.6s.

1958—Georgetown (Robert Vinton, John Nelson, Norm Williams, Bob Carney) . . . . 7m.44.6s.

1959—Yale (James Stack, Ned Roach, Ed Slowik, Tom Carroll) . . . . 7m.39.8s.

1960—New York A.C. (Bruce Lockerbie, Pete Levin, Edward McAllister, Mike Caraftis) . . . . 7m.46.2s.

1961—Holy Cross (Jack O'Conner, Jay Bowers, Thomas Noering, Charles Buchta) . . . . 7m.39.7s.

1962—Fordham (Donald O'Connor, Thomas Kenney, Charles Garcia, William Slater) . . . . 7m.40.6s.

1963—Seton Hall (Kevin Hennessey, Edward Wrysch, Tom Tushingham, George Germann) . . . . 7m.33.0s.

1964—Seton Hall (Tom Tushingham, Bruce Andrews, Herb Germann, George Germann) . . . . 7m.36.2s.

1965—Villanova (Jim Orr, Al Adams, Tom Sullivan, Noel Carroll) . . . . 7m.28.2s.

1966—49er T.C. (Dave Kemp, Darryl Taylor, Dave Mellady, Dave Perry) . . . 7m.27.4s.

1967—49er T.C. (Darryl Taylor, John Perry, Tom Von Ruden, Preston Davis) 7m.37.0s.

1968—New York A.C. (Tom Cracovia, George Germann, Frank Tomeo, Herb Germann) . . . . 7m.39.4s.

1969—Chicago Univ. Track Club (Bob

O'Connor, Ken Sparks, John Kenton, Lowell Paul) . . . . 7m.35.0s.

1970—Chicago Univ. Track Club (Bob O'Connor, Ken Sparks, Ralph Schultz, Lowell Paul) . . . . 7m.30.8s.

1971—Chicago Univ. Track Club (Bob O'Connor, Ken Sparks, Ralph Schultz, Lowell Paul) . . . . 7m.28.6s.

1972—Manhattan College (Cliff Bruce, John Lovett, Joe Savage, John Rothrock) . . . . 7m.32.4s.

1973—Chicago Univ. Track Club (Tom Bach, John Marks, Lowell Paul, Ken Sparks) . . . . 7m.29.0s.

1-Mile Walk

1933—39: 1,500 meters.
Not held, 1898—1906; 1910—1919.

1897—Harry Ladd	. . . .	7m. 23s.
1907—Sam Leibgold	. . . .	7m. 41.2s.
1908—Sam Leibgold	. . . .	7m. 19.8s.
1909—Sam Leibgold	. . . .	7m. 13.6s.
1920—J.B. Pearman	. . . .	6m. 39.8s.
1921—R.F. Remer	. . . .	6m. 29s.
1922—William Plant	. . . .	6m. 40.6s.
1923—William Plant	. . . .	6m. 55.8s.
1924—William Plant	. . . .	6m. 43.4s.
1925—Alexander Zeller	. . . .	7m. 04.8s.
1926—Harry Hinkel	. . . .	7m. 3.6s.
1927—William Plant	. . . .	6m. 34.8s.
1928—Harry Hinkel	. . . .	6m. 35.4s.
1929—Harry Hinkel	. . . .	6m. 40.4s.
1930—Michael Pecora	. . . .	6m. 43.4s.
1931—William Carlson	. . . .	6m. 47.8s.
1932—Michael Pecora	. . . .	6m. 27.2s.
1933—William Carlson	. . . .	6m. 15.8s.
1934—Charles Eschenback	. . . .	6m. 14.8s.
1935—Henry Cieman	. . . .	6m. 7.3s.
1936—Charles Eschenback	. . . .	6m. 18.1s.
1937—Nathan Jaeger	. . . .	6m. 20.2s.
1938—Otto Kotraba	. . . .	6m. 21.8s.
1939—Otto Kotraba	. . . .	6m. 23s.
1940—Charles Eschenback	. . . .	6m. 51.7s.
1941—Nathan Jaeger	. . . .	7m. 12.1s.
1942—Albert Cicerone	. . . .	7m. 13.9s.
1943—Sune Carlson	. . . .	7m. 20.4s.
1944—Joseph Megyesy	. . . .	7m. 10.5s.
1945—Joseph Megyesy	. . . .	7m. 13.9s.
1946—Joseph Megyesy	. . . .	7m. 11.4s.
1947—Ernest Weber	. . . .	6m. 44.2s.
1948—Henry H. Laskau	. . . .	6m. 43.8s.
1949—Henry H. Laskau	. . . .	6m. 29.5s.
1950—Henry H. Laskau	. . . .	6m. 43.4s.
1951—Henry H. Laskau	. . . .	6m. 27s.
1952—Henry H. Laskau	. . . .	6m. 28.0s.
1953—Henry H. Laskau	. . . .	6m. 20.6s.
1954—Henry H. Laskau	. . . .	6m. 31.7s.
1955—Henry H. Laskau	. . . .	6m. 30.4s.
1956—Henry H. Laskau	. . . .	6m. 44.5s.
1957—Henry H. Laskau	. . . .	6m. 39.7s.
1958—John Humcke	. . . .	6m. 55.5s.
1959—John Humcke	. . . .	6m. 42.2s.

1960—Frank Sipos	6m. 27.4s.
1961—Ronald Zinn	6m. 38.8s.
1962—Ronald Zinn	6m. 36.0s.
1963—Ronald Zinn	6m. 42.6s.
1964—Ron Laird	6m. 22.7s.
1965—Ronald Zinn	6m. 25.7s.
1966—Ruzy Haluza	6m. 39.2s.
1967—Don DeNoon	6m. 28.0s.
1968—Ron Laird	6m. 16.9s.
1969—Dave Romansky	6m. 21.9s.
1970—Dave Romansky	6m. 14.0s.
1971—Ron Laird	6m. 24.9s.
1972—Dave Romansky	6m. 13.4s.
1973—Ron Daniel	6m. 22.0s.

High Jump

1906—H.A. Gidney	5ft. 10 1/2in.
1907—H.F. Porter	6ft. 1 1/8in.
1908—H.F. Porter	6ft.
1909—H.F. Porter	6ft. 2 1/4in.
1910—J.H. Grumpelt	6ft. 2in.
1911—S.C. Lawrence	6ft. 2 7/8in.
1912—No competition	
1913—J.O. Johnstone	6ft. 1in.
1914—E. Jennings	6ft.
1915—Wesley Oler Jr.	6ft. 2 1/2in.
1916—J.G. Loomis	6ft. 1in.
1917—J.G. Loomis	6ft. 2in.
1918—Egon Erickson	5ft. 10in.
1919—Walter Whalen	6ft.
1920—Walter Whalen	6ft. 3 1/2in.
1921—R.W. Landon	6ft. 1in.
1922—L.T. Brown	6ft.
1923—Harold Osborn	6ft. 4in.
1924—Harold Osborn	6ft. 4in.
1925—Harold Osborn	6ft. 4 1/2in.
1926—Harold Osborn	6ft. 4 3/4in.
1927—C.W. Major	6ft. 4 1/8in.
1928—Anton Burg	6ft. 2 5/8in.
1929—C.W. Major	6ft. 3in.
1930—Anton Burg	6ft. 2in.
1931—Anton Burg	6ft. 6in.
1932—George Spitz	6ft. 7in.
1933—George Spitz	6ft. 8 1/4in.
1934— Walter Marty	
George Spitz	6ft. 7 1/2in.
1935—Cornelius Johnson	6ft. 7in.
1936— *Ed Burke	
Cornelius Johnson	6ft. 8 15/16in.
1937—Ed Burke	6ft. 9 1/4in.
1938— *Lloyd Thompson	
Cornelius Johnson	
Les Steers	
Mel Walker	6ft. 6in.
1939—Mel Walker	6ft. 8in.
1940—Artie Byrnes	6ft. 4 1/2in.
1941—Mel Walker	6ft. 6 1/2in.
1942— Joshua Williamson	
Adam Berry	6ft. 6 1/2in.
1943— William Vessie	
Pvt. Joshua Williamson	6ft. 6in.
1944— William Vessie	

David Albritton	6ft. 6in.
1945— Kenneth G. Wiesner	
Sgt. Joshua Williamson	6ft. 6in.
1946—John Vislocky	6ft. 7in.
1947—John Vislocky	6ft. 7in.
1948—John Vislocky	6ft. 7in.
1949—Dick Phillips	6ft. 7in.
1950—John Vislocky	6ft. 6in.
1951— Jack Razzeto	
John Heintzman	
Joshua Williamson	6ft. 5 1/2in.
1952—J.L. Hall	6ft. 6in.
1953—J.L. Hall	6ft. 8 3/4in.
1954—Herman Wyatt	6ft. 8 1/4in.
1955— J.L. Hall	
Ernie Shelton	6ft. 8 3/4in.
1956—Ernie Shelton	6ft. 9in.
1957—Phil Reavis	6ft. 9 1/2in.
1958—Herman Wyatt	6ft. 7 1/2in.
1959—John Thomas	7ft. 1 1/4in.
1960—John Thomas	7ft. 2in.
1961—Valeri Brumel (USSR)	7ft. 2in.
1962—John Thomas	7ft.
1963—Valeri Brumel (USSR)	7ft. 3 1/2in.
1964—John Thomas	7ft. 1in.
1965—Valeri Brumel (USSR)	7ft. 2in.
1966—John Thomas	7ft.
1967—John Rambo	7ft. 1in.
1968—Valentin Gavrilov (USSR)	7ft. 1in.
1969—John Rambo	6ft. 10in.
1970—Otis Burrell	7ft. 0in.
1971—Reynaldo Brown	7ft. 2in.
1972—Gene White	7ft. 2in.
1973— *Dwight Stones	
Vladimir Abramov (USSR)	7ft. 0in.

*Won on either jump-off or fewer misses.

Broad Jump

1932—Everett Utterback	23ft. 8in.
1933—Theodore Smith	23ft. 1in.
1934—Jesse Owens	25ft. 3 1/4in.
1935—Jesse Owens	25ft. 9in.
1936—Sammy Richardson	24ft. 3in.
1937—Sammy Richardson	24ft. 7 3/8in.
1938—Edward Gordon Jr.	23ft. 4in.
1939—Edward Gordon Jr.	23ft. 10 1/8in.
1940—Anson Perina	23ft. 8 1/8in.
1941—Lockhart B. Rogers	23ft. 8 3/8in.
1942—Jose Bento de Assis	24ft. 7 7/8in.
1943—Pvt. Barney Ewell	23ft. 8in.
1944—Barney Ewell	24ft. 6in.
1945—Corp. Barney Ewell	23ft. 11in.
1946—Samuel Richardson	24ft. 3 3/8in.
1947—Herbert Douglas	24ft. 5 1/8in.
1948—Lorenzo Wright	25ft. 3 3/4in.
1949—Herbert Douglas	24ft. 11 5/8in.
1950—Douglas Fowlkes	24ft. 6 3/4in.
1951—Andrew Stanfield	24ft. 5 1/2in.
1952—Lorenzo Wright	23ft. 9in.
1953—Meredith Gourdine	24ft. 9 1/2in.
1954—Neville Price	24ft. 5 1/2in.
1955—Rosslyn Range	25ft. 1in.

1956—Rosslyn Range . . . . .24ft. 7 1/4in.
1957—George Shaw . . . . .24ft. 9in.
1958—Greg Bell . . . . .25ft. 5 1/4in.
1959—Mike Herman . . . . .25ft. 3/4in.
1960—Irving Roberson . . . . .25ft. 9 1/2in.
1961—Ralph Boston . . . . .26ft. 6 1/4in.
1962—Charles Mays . . . . .24ft. 10 3/4in.
1963—Igor Ter-Ovanesyan (USSR) 26ft. 6 1/2in.
1964—Charlie Mays . . . . .26ft. 1 1/2in.
1965—Igor Ter-Ovenesyan (USSR) 26ft. 2 1/4in.
1966—Norman Tate . . . . .25ft. 1/4in.
1967—Bob Beamon . . . . .26ft. 11 1/2in.
1968—Bob Beamon . . . . .26ft. 11 1/2in.
1969—Norman Tate . . . . .25ft. 8in.
1970—Norman Tate . . . . .26ft. 4 3/4in.
1971—Norman Tate . . . . .26ft. 4 1/4in.
1972—Henry Hines . . . . .25ft. 1 1/4in.
1973—Randy Williams . . . . .26ft. 8 1/4in.

Pole Vault
1906—A.C. Gilbert . . . . .10ft. 9in.
1907—Claude A. Allen . . . . .11ft. 3in.
1908—C. Vezen . . . . .11ft. 2in.
1909—W. Halfpenny . . . . .11ft. 6in.
1910—W. Halfpenny . . . . .11ft. 8in.
1911—Gordon B. Dukes . . . . .11ft. 4in.
1912—24—No competition
1925—Paul W. Jones . . . . .11ft. 2in.
1926—Charles Hoff . . . . .13ft. 6 3/4in.
1927—Sabin W. Carr . . . . .13ft.
1928—Sabin W. Carr . . . . .14ft. 1in.
1929—Fredrick Sturdy . . . . .13ft. 9in.
1930—Fredrick Sturdy . . . . .13ft. 9in.
1931—Fredrick Sturdy . . . . .13ft. 11in.
1932—Fredrick Sturdy . . . . .13ft. 6in.
1933—Keith Brown . . . .
    F.E. Pierce . . . . .13ft. 6in.
1934—William Graber . . . . .13ft. 9in.
1935—Oscar Sutermeister . . . . . .
    Eldon Stutzman . . . .
    Ray Lowry . . . . .13ft. 4in.
1936—*David Hunn . . . .
    Ray Lowry . . . . .13ft. 7in.
1937—Earl Meadows . . . . .14ft. 3in.
1938—*Richard Ganslen . . . .
    George Varoff . . . . .13ft. 6in.
1939—Cornelius Warmerdam . . . .14ft.
1940—Earl Meadows . . . . .14ft. 3 3/8in.
1941—Earl Meadows . . . . .14ft. 4 5/8in.
1942—A. Richmond Morcom . . . .14ft.
1943—Cornelius Warmerdam . . . .15ft. 3 7/8in.
1944—Jack De Field . . . . .14ft.
1945—William Moore . . . . .13ft. 10in.
1946—William Moore . . . . .13ft. 9in.
1947—Guinn Smith . . . . .14ft.
1948—Robert Richards . . . . .14ft. 6in.
1949—A. Richmond Morcom . . . .14ft. 7 7/8in.
1950—Robert Richards . . . . .14ft.
1951—Robert Richards . . . . .15ft.
1952—Robert Richards . . . . .15ft.
1953—Robert Richards . . . . .15ft. 1/2in.
1954—Jerry Welbourne . . . . .14ft. 9in.

1955—Robert Richards . . . . .15ft. 4in.
1956—Don Bragg . . . .
    Robert Richards . . . . .15ft. 1in.
1957—Robert Richards . . . . .15ft. 3in.
1958—Don Bragg . . . .
    Bob Gutowski . . . . .15ft.
1959—Don Bragg . . . . .15ft. 1in.
1960—Don Bragg . . . . .15ft. 5in.
1961—Don Bragg . . . . .15ft. 3in.
1962—Henry Wadsworth . . . . . . .15ft. 4in.
1963—Dave Tork . . . . .15ft. 6in.
1964—John Uelses . . . . .15ft. 6in.
1965—Billy Pemelton . . . . .16ft.
1966—Bob Seagren . . . . .17ft. 1/4in.
1967—Bob Seagren . . . . .17ft. 3/4in.
1968—Dennis Phillips . . . . .17ft. 3/4in.
1969—Peter Chen . . . . .16ft. 6in.
1970—Bob Seagren . . . . .17ft. 0in.
1971—Dick Railsback . . . . .17ft. 6 3/4in.
1972—Kiell Isaksson (Sweden) . . .17ft. 10 1/2in.
1973—Steve Smith . . . . .17ft. 8in.
*Won on either vault-off or fewer misses.

Triple Jump
1966—Art Walker . . . . .54ft. 9 1/2in.
1967—Art Walker . . . . .52ft. 10 1/4in.
1968—Charlie Craig . . . . .54ft. 1 3/4in.
1969—Norman Tate . . . . .53ft. 1in.
1970—Norman Tate . . . . .53ft. 4 1/2in.
1971—Dave Smith . . . . .53ft. 4 3/4in.
1972—John Craft . . . . .54ft. 4 1/4in.
1973—John Craft . . . . .54ft. 8 1/2in.

16-Lb. Shot-Put
1916—P.J. McDonald . . . . .46ft. 7in.
1917—P.J. McDonald . . . . .47ft. 7 1/2in.
1918—D.C. Sinclair . . . . .42ft. 10 3/4in.
1919—P.J. McDonald . . . . .44ft. 7in.
1920—P.J. McDonald . . . . .45ft. 3 1/4in.
1921—P.J. McDonald . . . . .46ft. 3 3/4in.
1922—Ralph Hills . . . . .46ft. 10 3/8in.
1923—Augustus Pope . . . . .43ft. 3 1/2in.
1924—Ralph Hills . . . . .47ft. 11 1/2in.
1925—D.C. Sinclair . . . . .42ft. 3 3/4in.
1926—Herbert H. Schwarze . . . . .50ft. 7 5/8in.
1927—Herbert H. Schwarze . . . . .48ft. 5in.
1928—Herbert H. Schwarze . . . . .49ft. 5in.
1929—Herbert H. Schwarze . . . . .50ft. 3in.
1930—Herman Brix . . . . .51ft. 2 1/2in.
1931—Leo Sexton . . . . .48ft. 11in.
1932—Herman Brix . . . . .51ft. 4 1/2in.
1933—Leo Sexton . . . . .50ft. 8 5/8in.
1934—Thomas Gilbane . . . . .49ft. 7 1/8in.
1935—Jack Torrance . . . . .49ft. 7in.
1936—Dimitri Zaitz . . . . .52ft. 1/2in.
1937—Dimitri Zaitz . . . . .51ft. 4 3/4in.
1938—Francis Ryan . . . . .52ft. 8 1/4in.
1939—Francis Ryan . . . . .50ft. 11in.
1940—Alfred Blozis . . . . .55ft. 8 3/4in.
1941—Alfred Blozis . . . . .55ft. 1/4in.
1942—Alfred Blozis *57ft. 3/4in
1943—Bernard Mayer . . . . .52ft. 4 3/8in.
1944—John Yonaker . . . . .50ft. 8 1/2in.

1945—Wilfred Bangert ....50ft. 5 3/4in.
1946—Bernard Mayer ....52ft. 9 1/8in.
1947—Irving Kintisch ....52ft. 6 1/4in.
1948—Norman Wasser ....53ft. 8 1/2in.
1949—Wilbur Thompson ....54ft. 10 1/8in.
1950—James Fuchs ....56ft. 3 3/8in.
1951—James Fuchs ....57ft. 11 3/8in.
1952—James Fuchs ....56ft. 3 1/8in.
1953—Parry O'Brien ....55ft. 10 3/4in.
1954—Parry O'Brien ....59ft. 4in.
1955—Parry O'Brien ....59ft. 5 1/2in.
1956—Parry O'Brien ....61ft. 5 1/4in.
1957—Parry O'Brien ....59ft. 8in.
1958—Parry O'Brien ....60ft. 1 1/4in.
1959—Parry O'Brien ....62ft. 1 3/4in.
1960—Parry O'Brien ....61ft. 8in.
1961—Parry O'Brien ....61ft. 3in.
1962—Gary Gubner ....62ft. 10in.
1963—Gary Gubner ....62ft. 8 1/4in.
1964—Gary Gubner ....63ft. 2 1/2in.
1965—John McGrath ....62ft. 10 1/4in.
1966—John McGrath ....64ft. 3 1/2in.
1967—George Woods ....63ft. 11 1/4in.
1968—George Woods ....66ft. 3 1/4in.
1969—George Woods ....63ft. 11 1/2in.
1970—Brian Oldfield ....63ft. 10 3/4in.
1971—Al Feuerbach ....66ft. 0in.
1972—Fred DeBernardi ....66ft. 1 1/2in.
1973—George Woods ....69ft. 9 1/2in.
    *Light weight.

35-Lb. Weight Throw

1932—Leo Sexton ....50ft. 9 1/2in.
1933—Mortimer Reznick ....50ft. 10in.
1934—Henry F. Dreyer ....53ft. 8in.
1935—Henry F. Dreyer ....55ft. 3 3/4in.
1936—Irving Folwartshny ......58ft. 1 1/2in.
1937—Irving Folwartshny ......57ft. 4 3/4in.
1938—Irving Folwartshny ......57ft. 2in.
1939—Henry F. Dreyer ....54ft. 5 1/4in.
1940—Niles Perinks ....56ft. 1/4in.
1941—Henry F. Dreyer ....55ft. 8 1/4in.
1942—Henry F. Dreyer ....55ft. 11 1/4in.
1943—Henry F. Dreyer ....55ft. 3 7/8in.
1944—Henry F. Dreyer ....53ft. 1/8in.
1945—Henry F. Dreyer ....55ft. 10 3/8in.
1946—Henry F. Dreyer ....55ft. 1 3/4in.
1947—Henry F. Dreyer ....55ft. 9 3/8in.
1948—Robert Bennett ....56ft. 1in.
1949—Samuel M. Felton Jr. .....57ft. 11 3/4in.
1950—Gilbert J. Borgeson ......57ft. 5 1/4in.
1951—Thomas Bane...........59ft. 4 1/2in.
1952—Gilbert J. Borgeson ......58ft. 10 1/2in.
1953—Stephen Dillon ....58ft. 10 1/4in.
1954—Robert Backus..........63ft. 5in.
1955—Robert Backus..........60ft. 4 1/2in.
1956—Robert Backus..........63ft. 10 1/2in.
1957—Robert Backus..........63ft. 1 1/4in.
1958—Robert Backus..........65ft. 4 1/4in.
1959—Robert Backus..........66ft. 2 3/4in.
1960—Harold Connolly ....71ft. 2 1/2in.
1961—Robert Backus..........66ft. 6in.

1962—Al Hall................64ft. 7 1/4in.
1963—Al Hall................64ft. 7 3/4in.
1964—Al Hall................65ft. 8in.
1965—Hal Connolly ....70ft. 1/2in.
1966—Hal Connolly ....70ft. 11in.
1967—Ed Burke ....69ft. 2in.
1968—Ed Burke ....65ft. 3 1/2in.
1969—Al Hall................70ft. 9in.
1970—George Frenn ....70ft. 5 1/2in.
1971—George Frenn ....71ft. 3 1/2in.
1972—George Frenn ....72ft. 4in.
1973—George Frenn ....69ft. 7 1/4in.

Team
(Points in parentheses.)
Year   Champion
1906—Irish-American AC (89)
1907—New York AC (76)
1908—Irish-American AC (84)
1909—Irish-American AC (69)
1910—New York AC (77)
1911—Irish-American AC (70)
1912—No competition
1913—Irish-American AC (30)
1914—Irish-American AC (46)
1915—Irish-American AC (35)
1916—New York AC (23½)
1917—Chicago AA (37)
1918—Univ. of Pennsylvania (12)
1919—Boston AA (13)
1920—New York AC (29)
1921—New York AC (22)
1922—New York AC (33)
1923—Illinois AC (46)
1924—Illinois AC (21)
1925—ILlinois AC (64)
1926—Illinois AC (46)
1927—New York AC (30)
1928—Illinois AC (28)
1929—Illinois AC (29)
1930—Illinois AC (18)
1931—Illinois AC (16)
1932—New York AC (27½)
1933—New York AC (33)
1934—New York AC (28½)
1935—New York AC (36)
1936—New York AC (27½)
1937—New York AC (12)
1938—New York AC (23)
1939—New York AC (34)
1940—New York AC (86)
1941—New York AC (59.3)
1942—New York AC (20)
1943—New York Univ. (27)
1944—New York AC (21)
1945—New York AC (23)
1946—New York AC (28)
1947—New York Univ. (18½)
1948—New York AC (16)
1949—New York AC (15)
1950—New York AC (17)
1951—New York Pioneer Club (20¼)

1952—New York AC (27)
1953—New York AC (22)
1954—New York AC (32)
1955—N.Y. Pioneer Club (24)
1956—N.Y. Pioneer Club (28)
1957—Villanova (28½)
1958—New York AC (21)
1959—New York AC (21½)
1960—New York AC (24)
1961—New York AC (16)
1962—Villanova (18)
1963—New York A.C. (23)
1964—New York A.C. (18)
1965—Southern California Striders (26)
1966—Southern California Striders (30)
1967—Southern California Striders (32)
1968—Pacific Coast Club (30)
1969—Pacific Coast Club ——
1970—Southern California Striders (26)
(Discontinued team point system)

NATIONAL COLLEGIATE CHAMPIONS
(Source: Official Collegiate Track and Field Handbook.)

100-Yard Dash

1921—Leonard Paulu, Grinnell . . . . .10s.
1922—Leonard Paulu, Grinnell . . . . 9.9s.
1923—Clarke, Johns Hopkins . . . . 9.9s.
1924—No competition
1925—W. DeHart Hubbard, Michigan . . . . . 9.8s.
1926—Roland A. Locke, Nebraska . . . . 9.9s.
1927—Fred Alderman, Michigan State . . . . 9.9s.
1928—Claude A. Bracey, Rice . . . . 9.6s.
1929—George Simpson, Ohio State . . . . . . 9.4s.
1930—Frank Wykoff, So. California . . . . . 9.4s.
1931—Frank Wykoff, So. California . . . . . 9.6s.
1932—Ralph Metcalfe, Marquette . . . . . .*10.2s.
1933—Ralph Metcalfe, Marquette . . . . . . 9.4s.
1934—Ralph Metcalfe, Marquette . . . . . . 9.7s.
1935—Jesse Owens, Ohio State . . . . 9.8s.
1936—Jesse Owens, Ohio State . . . . . .*10.2s.
1937—Sam Stoller, Michigan . . . . 9.7s.
1938—Mozell Ellerbe, Tuskegee . . . . 9.7s.
1939—Mozell Ellerbe, Tuskegee . . . . 9.8s.
1940—Norwood Ewell, Penn State . . . . 9.6s.
1941—Norwood Ewell, Penn State . . . . 9.6s.
1942—Hal Davis, California . . . . 9.6s.
1943—Hal Davis, California . . . .*10s.
1944—Buddy Young, Illinois . . . . 9.7s.
1945—John Van Velzer, Navy . . . . .10.1s.
1946—William Mathis, Illinois . . . . 9.6s.
1947—Mel Patton, So. California . . . . 9.7s.
1948—Mel Patton, So. California . . . .*10.4s.
1949—Mel Patton, So. California . . . . 9.7s.
1950—Bob Boyd, Loyola (Calif.) . . . . 9.8s.
1951—Art Bragg, Morgan State . . . . 9.6s.
1952—Jim Golliday, Northwestern . . . . .*10.4s.
1953—Willie Williams, Illinois . . . . 9.7s.
1954—Willie Williams, Illinois . . . . 9.5s.
1955—Jim Golliday, Northwestern . . . . . . 9.6s.
1956—Bobby Morrow, Abiline Christ . . .*10.4s.
1957—Bobby Morrow, Abilene Christ . . . . 9.4s.

1958—Ira Murchison, Western Michigan . . . 9.5s.
1959—Charles Tidwell, Kansas . . . . 9.3s.
1960—Charles Tidwell, Kansas . . . .*10.2s.
1961—Frank Budd, Villanova . . . . 9.4s.
1962—Frank Budd, Villanova . . . . 9.4s.
1963—Larry Questad, Stanford . . . . 9.7s.
1964—Harry Jerome, Oregon . . . .*10.1s.
1965—Charlie Greene, Nebraska . . . . 9.4s.
1966—Charlie Greene, Nebraska . . . . 9.3s.
1967—Charlie Greene, Nebraska . . . . 9.2s.
1968—Lennox Miller, So. California . . . .*10.1s.
1969—John Carlos, San Jose State . . . . 9.2s.
1970—Eddie Hart, California . . . . 9.4s.
1971—Harrington Jackson, Texas (El Paso) 9.5s.
1972—Warren Edmonson, UCLA . . . .*10.1s.
* 100 meters.

220-Yard Dash

1921—Eric C. Wilson, Iowa . . . . .22.6s.
1922—Leonard Paulu, Grinnell . . . . .21.8s.
1923—Eric C. Wilson, Iowa . . . . .21.9s.
1924—No competition
1925—Glen Gray, Butler . . . . .21.9s.
1926—Roland A. Locke, Nebraska . . . . . . .20.9s.
1927—Fred Alderman, Michigan State . . . .21.1s.
1928—Claude A. Bracey, Rice . . . . .20.9s.
1929—George Simpson, Ohio State . . . . . .20.8s.
1930—George Simpson, Ohio State . . . . . .20.7s.
1931—Eddie Tolan, Michigan . . . . .21.5s.
1932—Ralph Metcalfe, Marquette . . . . . .*20.3s.
1933—Ralph Metcalfe, Marquette . . . . . . .20.4s.
1934—Ralph Metcalfe, Marquette . . . . . . .20.9s.
1935—Jesse Owens, Ohio State . . . . .21.5s.
1936—Jesse Owens, Ohio State . . . .*21.3s.
1937—Ben Johnson, Columbia . . . . .21.3s.
1938—Mack Robinson, Oregon . . . . .21.3s.
1939—Clyde Jeffrey, Stanford . . . . .21.1s.
1940—Norwood Ewell, Penn State . . . . . . .21.1s.
1941—Norwood Ewell, Penn State . . . . . . .21.1s.
1942—Hal Davis, California . . . . .21.2s.
1943—Hal Davis, California . . . . .21.4s.
1944—Buddy Young, Illinois . . . . .21.6s.
1945—Earl Collins, Texas . . . . .22.4s.
1946—Herb McKenley, Illinois . . . . .21.3s.
1947—Herb McKenley, Illinois . . . . .20.7s.
1948—Mel Patton, So. California . . . .*20.7s.
1949—Mel Patton, So. California . . . . . . .20.4s.
1950—Charlie Parker, Texas . . . . .21.5s.
1951—George Rhoden, Morgan State . . . . .20.7s.
1952—Jim Ford, Drake . . . .*21s.
1953—Thane Baker, Kansas State . . . . . . .21.5s.
1954—Charles Thomas, Texas . . . . .20.7s.
1955—Jim Golliday, Northwestern . . . . . .21.1s.
1956—Bobby Morrow, Abilene Christ . . .*20.6s.
1957—Bobby Morrow, Abilene Christ . . . .21.0s.
1958—Ed Collymore, Villanova . . . . .20.7s.
1959—Ray Norton, San Jose State . . . . . . .20.9s.
1960—Charles Tidwell, Kansas . . . .*20.8s.
1961—Frank Budd, Villanova . . . . .20.8s.
1962—Harry Jerome, Oregon . . . . .20.8s.
1963—Henry Carr, Arizona State . . . . .20.5s.
1964—Bob Hayes, Florida A & M . . . . . .*20.4s.

1965—Earl Horner, Villanova . . . . .21.1s.
1966—Tom Jones, U.C.L.A. . . . . .20.9s.
1967—Tommie Smith, San Jose St. . . . . . .20.2s.
1968—Emmett Taylor, Ohio U. . . . .*20.8s.
1969—John Carlos, San Jose State . . . . . .20.2s.
1970—Willie Turner, Oregon State . . . . . . .20.6s.
1971—Larry Black, N. Carolina Central . . .20.5s.
1972—Larry Burton, Purdue . . . .*20.5s.
* 200 meters.

440-Yard Run

1921—Frank J. Shea, Pittsburgh . . . . .49s.
1922—Commodore S. Cochran, Mississippi
    A. & M. . . . . .49.7s.
1923—Commodore S. Cochran, Mississippi
    A. & M. . . . . .49.2s.
1924—No competition
1925—Herman Phillips, Butler . . . . .49.4s.
1926—Herman Phillips, Butler . . . . .48.7s.
1927—Herman Phillips, Butler . . . . .48.5s.
1928—E.L. Spencer, Stanford . . . . .47.7s.
1929—Russ Walter, Northwestern . . . . . . .47.9s.
1930—Reginald Bowen, Pittsburgh . . . . . .48s.
1931—Victor Williams, So. California . . . .48.3s.
1932—Alex Wilson, Notre Dame . . . .*48s.
1933—Glenn Hardin, Louisiana State . . . . .47.1s.
1934—Glenn Hardin, Louisiana State . . . . .47s.
1935—James LuValle, U.C.L.A. . . . . . . .47.7s.
1936—Archie Williams, California . . . . . .*47s.
1937—Loren Benke, Washington State . . . .47.1s.
1938—Ray Mallott, Stanford . . . . .46.8s.
1939—Erwin Miller, So. California . . . . . . .47.5s.
1940—Lee Orr, Washington State . . . . .47.3s.
1941—Hubert Kerns, So. California . . . . . .46.6s.
1942—Cliff Bourland, So. California . . . . .48.2s.
1943—Cliff Bourland, So. California . . . . .48.5s.
1944—Elmore Harris, Morgan State . . . . . .47.9s.
1945—William Kash, Navy . . . . .49.8s.
1946—Herb McKenley, Illinois . . . . .47.5s.
1947—Herb McKenley, Illinois . . . . .46.2s.
1948—Norman Rucks, South Carolina . . .*47.2s.
1949—Charles Moore, Cornell . . . . .47s.
1950—George Rhoden, Morgan State . . . . .47.2s.
1951—George Rhoden, Morgan State . . . . .46.5s.
1952—George Rhoden, Morgan State . . . .*46.3s.
1953—James Lea, So. California . . . . .47s.
1954—Jim Lea, So. California . . . . .46.7s.
1955—J.W. Mashburn, Oklahoma A & M . .46.6s.
1956—J.W. Mashburn, Oklahoma A & M .*46.4s.
1957—Bob McMurray, Morgan State . . . . .46.8s.
1958—Glenn Davis, Ohio State . . . . .45.7s.
1959—Eddie Southern, Texas . . . . .46.4s.
1960—Ted Woods, Colorado . . . .*45.7s.
1961—Adolph Plummer, New Mexico . . . .46.2s.
1962—Hubert Brown, Morgan State . . . . . .46.9s.
1963—Ulis Williams, Arizona State . . . . . .45.8s.
1964—Ulis Williams, Arizona State; Bob
    Tobler, Brigham Young . . . .*45.9s.
1965—Jim Kemp, Kentucky State . . . . . . .46.2s.
1966—Dwight Middleton, Southern
    California .46.3s.
1967—Emmett Taylor, Ohio University . . .45.9s.

1968—Lee Evans, San Jose State . . . .*45.0s.
1969—Curtis Mills, Texas A & M . . . . .44.7s.
1970—Larry James, Villanova . . . . .45.5s.
1971—John Smith, U.C.L.A. . . . . .45.3s.
1972—John Smith, U.C.L.A. . . . .*44.5s.
*400 meters.

880-Yard Run

1921—Earl Eby, Pennsylvania . . . . . . 1m. 57.4s.
1922—Alan Helffrich, Penn State . . . 1m. 58.1s.
1923—Alan Helffrich, Penn State . . . 1m. 56.3s.
1924—No competition
1925—James Charteris, Washington . 1m. 55.4s.
1926—Alvo Martin, Northwestern . .*1m. 51.7s.
1927—John F. Sittig, Illinois . . . . . . 1m. 54.2s.
1928—Virgil Jess Gist, Chicago . . . . 1m. 54.4s.
1929—Edwin B. Genung, Washington 1m. 55s.
1930—Orval J. Martin, Purdue . . . . . 1m. 54.1s.
1931—Dale Letts, Chicago . . . . 1m. 53.5s.
1932—Charles Hornbostel, Indiana . **1m. 52.7s.
1933—Charles Hornbostel, Indiana . . 1m. 50.9s.
1934—Charles Hornbostel, Indiana . . 1m. 51.9s.
1935—Elroy Robinson, Fresno State 1m. 52.9s.
1936—Charles Beetham, Ohio State .**1m. 53s.
1937—John Woodruff, Pittsburgh . . . 1m. 50.3s.
1938—John Woodruff, Pittsburgh . . . 1m. 51.3s.
1939—John Woodruff, Pittsburgh . . . 1m. 51.3s.
1940—Campbell Kane, Indiana . . . . . 1m. 51.5s.
1941—Campbell Kane, Indiana . . . . . 1m. 51.2s.
1942—Bill Lyda, Oklahoma . . . . 1m. 50.8s.
1943—Joe Nowicki, Fordham . . . . . . 1m. 54.2s.
1944—Robert L. Kelley, Illinois . . . . 1m. 55.1s.
1945—Ross Hume, Michigan . . . . 1m. 55.7s.
1946—Smith, Virginia Union . . . . . . 1m. 52.6s.
1947—William Clifford, Ohio State . . 1m. 50.8s.
1948—Mal Whitfield, Ohio State . . .**1m. 51.1s.
1949—Mal Whitfield, Ohio State . . . 1m. 50.3s.
1950—Bill Brown, Morgan State . . . . 1m. 51.2s.
1951—John Barnes, Occidental . . . . . 1m. 50.7s.
1952—John Barnes, Occidental . . . .**1m. 49.6s.
1953—Lang Stanley, San Jose State . 1m. 52.4s.
1954—Arnold Sowell, Pittsburgh . . . 1m. 50.5s.
1955—Tom Courtney, Fordham . . . . 1m. 49.5s.
1956—Arnold Sowell, Pittsburgh . . . 1m. 46.7s.
1957—Don Bowden, California . . . . . 1m. 47.2s.
1958—Ron Delany, Villanova . . . . . . 1m. 48.6s.
1959—George Kerr, Illinois . . . . 1m. 47.8s.
1960—George Kerr, Illinois . . . .**1m. 46.4s.
1961—John Bork, West Michigan . . . 1m. 48.3s.
1962—Jim Dupree, Southern Illinois 1m. 48.2s.
1963—Norm Hoffman, Oregon State 1m. 48.0s.
1964—Tom Farrell, St. John's . . . . . 1m. 48.5s.
1965—Tom Farrell, St. John's . . . . . 1m. 48.1s.
1966—Peter Scott, Nebraska . . . . 1m. 47.9s.
1967—Wade Bell, Oregon . . . . 1m. 47.6s.
1968—Byron Dyce, New York U. . . .**1m. 47.3s.
1969—Byron Dyce, New York U. . . . 1m. 45.9s.
1970—Ken Swenson, Kansas State . . 1m. 46.3s.
1971—Mark Wizenried, Wisconsin . . . 1m. 48.8s.
1972—Willie Thomas, Tennessee . . .**1m. 47.1s.
*Race was 23 feet 3 inches short.
**800 meters.

1-Mile Run

1921—Ray Watson, Kansas State ... 4m. 23.4s.
1922—Larry Shields, Penn State ... 4m. 20.4s.
1923—Schuyler Enck, Penn State ... 4m. 27.4s.
1924—No competition
1925—Jim Reese, Texas .... 4m. 18.8s.
1926—Charles Judge, Notre Dame .. 4m. 22.5s.
1927—Ray Conger, Iowa State ..... 4m. 17.6s.
1928—Rufus Kiser, Washington .... 4m. 17.6s.
1929—Wilbur C. Getz, Alfred ...... 4m. 19.4s.
1930—Joseph Sivak, Butler........ 4m. 19.3s.
1931—Ray Putnam, Iowa State ..... 4m. 18s.
1932—Glenn Cunningham, Kansas ..*3m. 53s.
1933—Glenn Cunningham, Kansas .. 4m. 08.8s.
1934—William Bonthron, Princeton . 4m. 08.9s.
1935—Archie San Romani, Emporia. 4m. 19.1s.
1936—Archie San Romani, Emporia .*3m. 53s.
1937—Charles Fenske, Wisconsin ... 4m. 13.9s.
1938—Louis Zamperini, So. California 4m. 08.3s.
1939—Louis Zamperini, So. California 4m. 13.6s.
1940—John Munski, Missouri ...... 4m. 14.7s.
1941—Leslie MacMitchell, New York
       University .... 4m. 10.4s.
1942—Bob Ginn, Nebraska .... 4m. 11.1s.
1943—Don Burnham, Dartmouth ... 4m. 19.1s.
1944—Robert and Ross Hume,
       Michigan .... 4m. 16.6s.
1945—Ross Hume, Michigan .... 4m. 18.5s.
1946—Robert Rehberg, Illinois ..... 4m. 15.2s.
1947—Gerry Karver, Penn State .... 4m. 17.2s.
1948—Don Gehrmann, Wisconsin ...*3m. 54.3s.
1949—Don Gehrmann, Wisconsin ... 4m. 09.6s.
1950—Don Gehrmann, Wisconsin ... 4m. 12.4s.
1951—Warren Druetzler, Michigan
       State .... 4m. 08.8s.
1952—Bob McMillen, Occidental ...*3m. 50.7s.
1953—Wes Santee, Kansas .... 4m. 03.7s.
1954—Bill Dellinger, Oregon ...... 4m. 13.8s.
1955—Jim Bailey, Oregon .... 4m. 05.6s.
1956—Ron Delany, Villanova ......*3m. 47.3s.
1957—Ron Delany, Villanova ...... 4m. 06.5s.
1958—Ron Delany, Villanova ...... 4m. 03.5s.
1959—Jim Grelle, Oregon .... 4m. 03.9s.
1960—Dyrol Burleson, Oregon .....*3m. 44.2s.
1961—Dyrol Burleson, Oregon ..... 4m. 00.5s.
1962—Dyrol Burleson, Oregon ..... 3m. 59.8s.
1963—Morgan Groth, Oregon State . 4m. 05.3s.
1964—Morgan Groth, Oregon State .*3m. 40.4s.
1965—Bob Day, U.C.L.A. .... 4m. 01.8s.
1966—Dave Patrick, Villanova ..... 4m. 02.1s.
1967—Jim Ryun, Kansas .... 4m. 03.5s.
1968—Dave Patrick, Villanova .....*3m. 39.9s.
1969—Marty Liquori, Villanova .... 3m. 57.7s.
1970—Marty Liquori, Villanova .... 3m. 59.9s.
1971—Marty Liquori, Villanova .... 3m. 57.6s.
1972—Dave Wottle, Bowling Green .*3m. 39.7s.
*1,500 meters.

2-Mile Run

1921—John Romig, Penn State..... 9m. 31s.
1922—Lloyd Rathbun, Iowa State .. 9m. 32.1s.
1923—Booth, Johns Hopkins ...... 9m. 32.2s.

1924—No competition
1925—J. Devine, Washington State .. 9m. 32.8s.
1926—Arnold Gillette, Montana .... 9m. 40.3s.
1927—Melvin Shimek, Marquette ... 9m. 34.4s.
1928—David Abbott, Illinois ...... 9m. 28.8s.
1929—David Abbott, Illinois ...... 9m. 30s.
1930—Harold Manning, Wichita .... 9m. 18.1s.
1931—Clark Chamberlain, Mich. St. . 9m. 23s.
1932—Charles Shugert, Miami (O.) .. 9m. 16.7s.
1933—Michael Pilbrow, Grinnell .... 9m. 22.8s.
1934—Ray Crowley, Manhattan .... 9m. 22.4s.
1935—Floyd Lochner, Oklahoma ... 9m. 26.8s.
1936—Donald Lash, Indiana ......*14m. 58.5s.
1937—Greg Rice, Notre Dame ..... 9m. 14.2s.
1938—Walter Mehl, Wisconsin ..... 9m. 11.1s.
1939—Greg Rice, Notre Dame ..... 9m. 02.6s.
1940—Roy Fehr, Michigan State ... 9m. 18.9s.
1941—Fred Wilt, Indiana .... 9m. 14.4s.
1942—Art Cazares, Fresno State .... 9m. 10s.
1943—Jerry Thompson, Texas ..... 9m. 29.9s.
1944—Francis Martin, Notre Dame .. 9m. 38.4s.
1945—Francis Martin, New York
       University .... 9m. 25.5s.
1946—Francis Martin, New York
       University .... 9m. 38.3s.
1947—Jerry Thompson, Texas ..... 9m. 22.9s.
1948—Jerry Thompson, Texas ....*15m. 4.5s.
1949—Horace Ashenfelter, Penn State 9m. 3.9s.
1950—Don McEwen, Michigan ..... 9m. 1.9s.
1951—Don McEwen, Michigan ..... 9m. 3.2s.
1952—Wes Santee, Kansas ....*14m. 36.3s.
1953—Richard Ferguson, Iowa ..... 9m. 02.7s.
1954—Kikuo Moriya, Wheaton ..... 9m. 22.7s.
1955—Ken Reiser, Oregon .... 9m. 04.5s.
1956—Bill Dellinger, Oregon ....*4m. 48.5s.
1957—Charles Jones, Iowa .... 8m. 57s.
1958—Alex Henderson, Arizona State 8m. 46.3s.
* 5,000 meters

5,000-Meter Run—3-Mile Run

1959—Paul Whiteley, Emporia State .13m. 59.1s.
1960—Al Lawrence, Houston .....*14m. 19.8s.
1961—Pat Clohessy, Houston ......13m. 47.7s.
1962—Pat Clohessy, Houston ......13m. 51.6s.
1963—Julio Marin, Southern Calif. ..14m. 24.9s.
1964—Bill Straub, Army; Jim Murphy,
       Air Force Academy ......*14m. 12.3s.
1965—Doug Brown, Montana ......13m. 40.2s.
1966—Gerry Lindgren, Washington
       State ....13m. 33.7s.
1967—Gerry Lindgren, Washington
       State ....13m. 47.8s.
1968—Gerry Lindgren, Washington
       State ....*13m. 57.2s.
1969—Ole Oleson, So. California ...13m. 41.9s.
1970—Steve Prefontaine, Oregon ...13m. 22.0s.
1971—Steve Prefontaine, Oregon ...13m. 20.0s.
1972—Steve Prefontaine, Oregon ..*13m. 31.4s.
*5,000 meters

10,000-Meter Run—6-Mile Run

1948—Robert Black, Rhode Island
       State ....32m. 13.5s.

1952—Walt Dieke, Wisconsin ...... 32m. 25.1s.
1956—Selwyn Jones, Michigan State 31m. 15.3s.
1963—Julio Martin, So. California .. 30m. 32.9s.
1964—Danny Murphy, San Jose State 29m. 37.8s.
1965—Doug Brown, Montana ...... 27m. 59.2s.
1966—Gerry Lindgren, Washington
State .... 28m. 07.0s.
1967—Gerry Lindgren, Washington
State .... 28m. 44.0s.
1968—Gerry Lindgren, Washington
State .... *29m. 41.0s.
1969—Frank Shorter, Yale .... 29m. 00.2s.
1970—Bob Bertelsen, Ohio U. ..... 27m. 57.5s.
1971—Garry Bjorklund, Minnesota .. 27m. 43.0s.
1972—Johan Halberstadt, Oklahoma
State .... *28m. 50.3s.
* 10,000 meters

120-Yard High Hurdles

1921—Earl J. Thomson, Dartmouth ...... 14.4s.
1922—Harold Barron, Penn State .... 15.4s.
1923—Ivan Riley, Kansas State .... 15.2s.
1924—No competition
1925—Hugo Leistner, Stanford .... 14.6s.
1926—George Guthrie, Ohio State ...... 14.8s.
1927—Weems O. Baskin, Auburn .... 14.9s.
1928—Dwight Kane, Ohio Wesleyan ..... 14.7s.
1929—Richard Rockaway, Ohio State .... 14.7s.
1930—Stephen Anderson, Washington .... 14.4s.
1931—Jack Keller, Ohio State .... 14.6s.
1932—George Saling, Iowa .... *14.2s.
1933—August Meier, Stanford .... 14.2s.
1934—Sam Klopstock, Stanford .... 14.4s.
1935—Sam Allen, Okla. Baptist .... 14.5s.
1936—Forrest Towns, Georgia .... *14.3s.
1937—Forrest Towns, Georgia .... 14.3s.
1938—Fred Wolcott, Rice .... 14.1s.
1939—Fred Wolcott, Rice .... 14.2s.
1940—Ed Dugger, Tufts .... 13.9s.
1941—Robert Wright, Ohio State .... 14s.
1942—Robert Wright, Ohio State .... 14.2s.
1943—William Cummins, Rice .... 14.6s.
1944—David C. Nichols, Illinois .... 15.3s.
1945—George Walker, Illinois .... 14.9s.
1946—Harrison Dillard, Baldwin-
Wallace .... 14.1s.
1947—Harrison Dillard, Baldwin-
Wallace .... 14.1s.
1948—Clyde Scott, Arkansas .... *13.7s.
1949—Craig Dixon, U.C.L.A. .... 13.9s.
1950—Dick Attlesey, So. California ..... 14s.
1951—Jack Davis, So. California .... 13.7s.
1952—Jack Davis, So. California ...... *14s.
1953—Jack Davis, So. California .... 14s.
1954—Willard Thomson, Illinois .... 14.2s.
1955—Milt Campbell, Indiana .... 13.9s.
1956—Lee Calhoun, N. Carolina Coll. ... *13.7s.
1957—Lee Calhoun, N. Carolina Coll. .... 13.6s.
1958—Elias Gilbert, Winston-Salem
Teachers .... 13.9s.
1959—Hayes Jones, Eastern Michigan .... 13.6s.
1960—Jim Johnston, U.C.L.A. .... *14.0s.

1961—Jerry Tarr, Oregon .... 13.9s.
1962—Jerry Tarr, Oregon .... 13.5s.
1963—Robert Green, Southern Illinois ... 14.1s.
1964—Bobby May, Rice .... *13.7s.
1965—Paul Kerry, Southern California ... 13.9s.
1966—Ron Copeland, U.C.L.A. .... 13.6s.
1967—Earl McCullouch, So. California ... 13.4s.
1968—Earl McCullouch, So. California .. *13.4s.
1969—Erv Hall, Villanova .... 13.3s.
1970—Paul Gibson, Texas (El Paso) ...... 13.6s.
1971—Rod Milburn, Southern U. .... 13.6s.
1972—Jerry Wilson, So. California ...... *13.4s.
* 110-meter high hurdles.

220-Yard Low Hurdles

1921—August Desch, Notre Dame .... 24.8s.
1922—Charles Brookins, Iowa .... 24.2s.
1923—Charles Brookins, Iowa .... 23.6s.
1924—No competition
1925—Morgan Taylor, Grinnell .... 24s.
1926—Edward O. Spence, Wayne .... 23.5s.
1927—Edward O. Spence, Wayne .... 23.4s.
1928—Frank J. Cuhel, Iowa .... 23.2s.
1929—Stephen Anderson, Washington .... 23.5s.
1930—Lee Sentman, Illinois .... 23.2s.
1931—Jack Keller, Ohio State .... 23.8s.
1932—Jack Keller, Ohio State .... 22.7s.
1933—Glenn Hardin, Louisiana State ..... 22.9s.
1934—Glenn Hardin, Louisiana State ..... 22.7s.
1935—Jesse Owens, Ohio State .... 23.4s.
1936—Jesse Owens, Ohio State .... 23.1s.
1937—Earl Vickery, So. California .... 23.3s.
1938—Fred Wolcott, Rice .... 23.3s.
1939—Fred Wolcott, Rice .... 23s.
1940—Fred Wolcott, Rice .... 23.1s.
1941—Robert Wright, Ohio State .... 23.4s.
1942—Robert Wright, Ohio State .... 23.7s.
1943—William Cummins, Rice .... 23.9s.
1944—Elmore Harris, Morgan State ...... 23.9s.
1945—George Walker, Illinois .... 24s.
1946—Harrison Dillard, Baldwin-Wallace .. 23s.
1947—Harrison Dillard, Baldwin-Wallace .. 22.3s.
1948—No competition
1949—Craig Dixon, U.C.L.A. .... 22.7s.
1950—Bill Albans, North Carolina .... 23.8s.
1951—Charles Moore, Cornell .... 22.7s.
1952—No competition
1953—Jack Davis, So. California .... 23.3s.
1954—Joe Corley, Illinois .... 22.6s.
1955—Charley Pratt, Manhattan .... 23.1s.
1956—No competition
1957—Ancel Robinson, Fresno State ..... 22.2s.
1958—Charley Tidwell, Kansas .... 22.7s.
1959—Hayes Jones, Eastern Michigan .... 22.5s.
1960—72—No competition

400-Meter Hurdles

1932—Eugene Beatty, Michigan Normal .. 52.9s.
1936—Robert Osgood, Michigan .... 53.4s.
1948—George Walker, Illinois .... 52.4s.
1952—Bob DeVinney, Kansas .... 51.7s.
1956—Aubrey Lewis, Notre Dame .... 51s.
1959—Dick Howard, New Mexico .... 50.6s.

1960—Cliff Cushman, Kansas . . . . 50.8s.
1961—Dixon Farmer, Occidental . . . . 50.8s.
1962—Jerry Tarr, Oregon . . . . 50.3s.
1963—Rex Cawley, Southern California . . 49.6s.
1964—Billy Hardin, Louisiana State . . . . . . 50.2s.
1965—Larry Godfrey, San Diego State . . . 51.5s.
1966—Bob Steele, Michigan State . . . . . . 50.4s.
1967—Bob Steele, Michigan State . . . . . . 50.2s.
1968—Dave Hemery, Boston U. . . . . 49.8s.
1969—Ralph Mann, Brigham Young . . . . 49.6s.
1970—Ralph Mann, Brigham Young . . . . 48.8s.
1971—Ralph Mann, Brigham Young . . . . 49.6s.
1972—Bruce Collins, Penn . . . . 49.1s.

3,000-Meter Steeplechase

1948—Browning Ross, Villanova . . . 9m. 25.7s.
1952—Bob McMullen, San Jose State 9m. 31.2s.
1956—Henry Kennedy, Michigan
         State . . . . 9m. 16.5s.
1959—John Macy, Houston . . . . 9m. 19.1s.
1960—Charles Clark, San Jose State . 9m. 02.1s.
1961—John Lawler, Abilene Christian 9m. 01.1s.
1962—Pat Traynor, Villanova . . . . . . 8m. 48.6s.
1963—Vic Zwolak, Villanova . . . . . . 9m. 10.1s.
1964—Vic Zwolak, Villanova . . . . . . 8m. 42.0s.
1965—Bruce Mortenson, Oregon . . . 9m. 00.8s.
1966—Bob Richards, Brigham Young 8m. 51.6s.
1967—Chris McCubbins, Oklahoma
         State . . . . 8m. 51.4s.
1968—Kerry Pearce, Texas (El Paso) 8m. 50.8s.
1969—Jim Barkley, Oregon State . . . 8m. 44.4s.
1970—Sid Sink, Bowling Green . . . . 8m. 40.9s.
1971—Sid Sink, Bowling Green . . . . 8m. 31.0s.
1972—Joe Lucas, Georgetown . . . . . 8m. 30.1s.

440-Yard Relay

1964—Illinois (Gilwyn Williams, Mel
         Blanheim, Mike Yavorski, Trenton
         Jackson) . . . .   40.1s.
1965—San Jose State (Wayne Herman,
         Lloyd Murad, Maurice Compton,
         Tommie Smith) . . . .   40.5s.
1966—U.C.L.A. (Tom Jones, Bob Frey,
         Ron Copeland, Norm Jackson) . . . .   39.9s.
1967—Southern California (Earl Mc-
         Cullouch, Fred Kuller, O.J. Simpson,
         Lennox Miller) . . . .   38.6s.
1968—Southern California (Earl Mc-
         Cullough, Fred Kuller, O.J. Simpson,
         Lennox Miller) . . . .   39.5s.
1969—San Jose State (Sam Davis, Kirk
         Clayton, Ronnie Ray Smith, John Car-
         los) . . . .   39.1s.
1970—California (Ron Couser, Isaac
         Curtis, Dave Masters, Eddie Hart) . . .   40.3s.
1971—Southern California (Lance Babb,
         Edesel Garrison, Leon Brown, Willie
         Deckard) . . . .   39.5s.
1972—Southern California (Randy Wil-
         liams, Edesel Garrison, Leon Brown,
         Willie Deckard) . . . .   39.6s.

1-Mile Relay

1964—California (Al Courchesne, Dave
         Fishback, Forrest Beaty, Dave Archi-
         bald) . . . . 3m.07.4s.
1965—California (Chuck Glenn, Dave
         Fishback, Forrest Beaty, Dave Archi-
         bald) . . . . 3m.07.5s.
1966—U.C.L.A. (Gene Gall, Don Doman-
         sky, Ron Copeland, Bob Frey) . . . . . 3m.07.5s.
1967—Iowa (Fred Ferree, Carl Frazier,
         Jon Reimer, Mike Mondane) . . . . 3m.06.8s.
1968—Villanova (Hardge Davis, Ken
         Prince, Hal Nichter, Larry James) . . . 3m.08.6s.
1969—U.C.L.A. (John Smith, Len Van
         Hofwegen, Andy Young, Wayne Col-
         lett) . . . . 3m.03.4s.
1970—U.C.L.A. (Bob Langston, John
         Smith, Brad Lyman, Wayne Collett) . 3m.06.1s.
1971—U.C.L.A. (Warren Edmonson,
         Reggie Echols, John Smith, Wayne Col-
         lett) . . . . 3m.04.4s.
1972—U.C.L.A. (Reggie Echols, Ron
         Gaddis, Benny Brown, John Smith) . . 3m.05.3s.

High Jump   Ft.—In.

1921—John Murphy, Notre Dame . . . . . 6—3
1922—John Murphy, Notre Dame; Har-
         old M. Osborn, Illinois . . . . 6—2 5/8
1923—Tom Poor, Kansas . . . . 6—1
1924—No competition
1925—Thomas Branford, Missouri; Jus-
         tin Erving Russell, Chicago; Oather
         Hampton, California . . . . 6—2
1926—Rufus Haggard, Texas . . . . 6—7 1/4
1927—Anton Burg, Chicago; Garland
         Shepherd, Texas . . . . 6—5 1/2
1928—Robert King, Stanford . . . . 6—6 5/8
1929—Parker Shelby, Oklahoma . . . . . . 6—3
1930—James Stewart, So. California . . . 6—3 3/4
1931—Darrell Jones, Ball State . . . . 6—3 3/4
1932—Bert Nelson, Butler . . . . 6—5 3/4
1933—Duncan McNaughton, So. Cali-
         fornia; Vincent Murphy, Notre Dame 6—4
1934—Walter Marty, Fresno State;
         George Spitz, New York University . . 6—6 3/4
1935—Linn Philson, Drake . . . . 6—4 7/8
1936—David Albritton, Ohio State; Mel-
         vin Walker, Ohio State . . . . 6—6 1/8
1937—David Albritton, Ohio State; Gil
         Cruter, Colorado . . . . 6—6 1/4
1938—David Albritton, Ohio State; Gil
         Cruter, Colorado . . . . 6—8 3/4
1939—John Wilson, So. California . . . . . 6—6
1940—John Wilson, So. California; Don
         Canham, Michigan . . . . 6—6 3/8
1941—Lester Steers, Oregon . . . . 6—10 7/8
1942—Adam Berry, Southern . . . . 6—7 3/4
1943—Fred Sheffield, Utah . . . . 6—8
1944—Ken Siesner, Marquette . . . . 6—7 3/16
1945—Fred Sheffield, Utah; Ken Wies-
         ner, Marquette . . . . 6—6 5/8

1946—Ken Wiesner, Marquette 6–8 3/8
1947—Irving Mondschein, N.Y.U. 6–6 13/16
1948—Irving Mondschein, N.Y.U.; Dike
   Eddleman, Illinois 6–7
1949—Dick Phillips, Brown 6–7
1950—Vern McGrew, Rice 6–7
1951—J. Lewis Hall, Florida 6–9
1952—Walt Davis, Texas A.&M.; Emery
   Barnes, Oregon 6–8
1953—Milton Mead, Michigan; J. Lewis
   Hall, Florida; Mark Smith, Wayne ...6–8 1/8
1954—Ernest Shelton, So. California ...6–10 1/4
1955—Ernest Shelton, So. California ...6–11 1/8
1956—Phil Reavis, Villanova; Bob Lang,
   Missouri; Nick Dyer, U.C.L.A. 6–6 1/4
1957—Don Stewart, S.M.U.; Al Urbanc-
   kas, Illinois 6–7 1/2
1958—Don Stewart, S.M.U. 6–9 1/4
1959—Erroll Williams, San Jose State;
   Wayne Moss, Oregon State 6–9 3/4
1960—John Thomas, Boston Univ. 7–0
1961—John Thomas, Boston Univ. 7–2
1962—Roger Olson, California 6–10
1963—Lew Hoyt, Southern California ..6–9 1/4
1964—John Rambo, Long Beach State ..7–1/4
1965—Frank Costello, Maryland 6–11
1966—Otis Burrell, Nevada 7–1
1967—Steve Brown, Idaho 7–1
1968—Dick Fosbury, Oregon State 7–2 1/4
1969—Dick Fosbury, Oregon State 7–2 1/2
1970—Pat Matzdorf, Wisconsin 7–1
1971—Reynaldo Brown, Cal. Poly (San
   Luis Obispo) 7–3
1972—Tom Woods, Oregon State 7–3 1/4

Broad Jump   Ft.–In.
1921—Gaylord Stinchcomb, Ohio State 23–3 3/8
1922—Robert L. LeGendre,
   Georgetown 24–3
1923—W. DeHart Hubbard, Michigan . 25–2
1924—No competition
1925—W. DeHart Hubbard, Michigan . 25–10 7/8
1926—Chere, Illinois Coll. 23–3 1/4
1927—Edward B. Hamm, Georgia Tech 24–1
1928—Edward B. Hamm, Georgia Tech 25–0
1929—Edward Gordon, Iowa 24–8 1/2
1930—Edward Gordon, Iowa 25–0
1931—Edward Gordon, Iowa 24–11 3/8
1932—Charles Lambert Redd, Bradley 25–6 3/8
1933—John William Brooks, Chicago . 24–4 3/4
1934—Al Olson, So. California 25–4 1/4
1935—Jesse Owens, Ohio State 26–1 3/8
1936—Jesse Owens, Ohio State 25–10 7/8
1937—Kermit King, Pittsburgh T.C. .. 25–3 1/4
1938—Bill Lacefield, U.C.L.A. 25–1 1/8
1939—Judson Atchison, Texas 24–9 1/4
1940—Jackie Robinson, U.C.L.A. ... 24–10 1/4
1941—Billy Brown, Louisiana State .. 24–7 3/8
1942—Dallas Dupre, Ohio State 24–2 1/4
1943—William Christopher, Rice 24–7 1/4
1944—Ralph Tyler, Ohio State 23–4 1/2

1945—Henry K. Aihara, Illinois 23–1 5/8
1946—John Robertson, Texas 24–10 1/2
1947—Willie Steele, San Diego State .. 26–6
1948—Willie Steele, San Diego State .. 24–11 1/4
1949—Fred Johnson, Michigan State . 25–2 1/2
1950—Jerome Biffle, Denver 25–4 3/4
1951—George Brown, U.C.L.A. 24–5 3/4
1952—George Brown, U.C.L.A. 25–4 7/8
1953—John Bennett, Marquette 25–3 7/8
1954—John Bennett, Marquette 25–10 3/4
1955—Joel Shankle, Duke 24–3 1/4
1956—Greg Bell, Indiana 25–9 1/4
1957—Greg Bell, Indiana 26–7
1958—Ernie Shelby, Kansas 25–3 1/4
1959—Ernie Shelby, Kansas 25–5
1960—Ralph Boston, Tennessee A & I 25–5 3/4
1961—Don Meyers, Colorado 25–0
1962—Anthony Watson, Oklahoma .. 26–1/2
1963—Clifton Mayfield, Central Ohio
   State 26–7
1964—Gayle Hopkins, Arizona 26–9 1/4
1965—Clarence Robinson, New Mexico 25–10 1/2
1966—Rainer Stenius, Los Angeles
   State 25–1 1/2
1967—Gary Ard, Kansas 25–9
1968—Pertti Pousi, Brigham Young .. 26–3 1/2
1969—Jerry Proctor, Redlands 26–11 3/4
1970—Arnie Robinson, San Diego
   State 25–10 1/2
1971—Bouncy Moore, Oregon 25–9 3/4
1972—Randy Williams, So. California 26–8 1/4
‡ Wind aided

Pole Vault
1921—Longino Welch, Georgia Tech;
   Jenne, Washington State; Lloyd
   Wilder, Wisconsin; Truman P.
   Gardner, Yale 12–0
1922—Allen Norris, California; John
   S. Landowski, Michigan 12–6
1923—Earl McKown, Emporia Teachers; James K. Brooker, Michigan .. 12–11
1924—No competition
1925—Philip M. Northrup, Michigan;
   Kenneth Lancaster, Missouri;
   Frank Potts, Oklahoma; Royal
   Bouscher, Northwestern; Earl
   McKown, Emporia Teachers 12–4
1926—Paul Harrington, Notre Dame . 13–7/8
1927—W. H. Drogemueller, Northwestern 13–0
1928—Ward Edmonds, Stanford 13–6 1/2
1929—Tom Warne, Northwestern;
   Ward Edmonds, Stanford 13–8
1930—Tom Warne, Northwestern ... 13–9 7/8
1931—Tom Warne, Northwestern;
   Verne McDermott, Illinois; William
   Graber, So. California 13–10 5/16
1932—Bryce Beecher, Indiana 13–10
1933—William Graber, So. California;
   Matt Gordy, Louisiana State 13–11 1/16
1934—Jack Rand, San Diego State ... 14–1/2

1935—William Sefton, So. California;
  Earl Meadows, So. California .... 14—1 1/8
1936—William Sefton, So. California;
  Earl Meadows, So. California .... 14—1 3/4
1937—William Sefton, So. California . 14—8 7/8
1938—Loring Day, So. California ... 14—2
1939—Richard V. Ganslen, Columbia 14—5
1940—Kenneth Dills, So. California .. 13—10
1941—Guinn Smith, California; Harold Hunt, Nebraska .... 14—2
1942—Jack DeField, Minnesota ..... 14—1
1943—Jack DeField, Minnesota ..... 14—1
1944—John Schmidt, Ohio State; William Blackwell, Oberlin; Phillip
  Anderson, Notre Dame; Robert
  Phelps, Illinois .... 13—6
1945—Robert Phelps, Illinois ...... 11—6
1946—William Moore, Northwestern . 13—8
1947—Robert Hart, So. California;
  Ray Maggard, U.C.L.A.; William E.
  Moore, Northwestern; George A.
  Rasmussen, Oregon; A. Richmond
  Morcom, New Hampshire; Robert
  Richards, Illinois .... 14—0
1948—Warren Bateman, Colorado;
  George A. Rasmussen, Oregon ... 14—0
1949—Bob Smith, San Diego State .. 14—3
1950—Bob Smith, San Diego State .. 14—2 7/8
1951—Don Laz, Illinois .... 14—9 3/4
1952—Dave Martindale, Idaho; Bill
  Priddy, San Jose State; Gordon
  Riddell, Colorado A.&M.; Dick
  Coleman, Illinois; Lyle Dickey,
  Oregon State .... 13—9
1953—Fred Barnes, Fresno State .... 14—6
1954—Lawrence Anderson, California; Earl Poucher, Florida .... 14—2
1955—Don Bragg, Villanova .... 15—1
1956—Jim Graham, Oklahoma A.&
  M.; Bob Gutowski, Occidental ... 14—8
1957—Bob Gutowski, Occidental ... 15—9 3/4
1958—Jim Johnston, Purdue; Bob Davis, Missouri; Stan Lyons, Ohio
  State; Gene Freudenthal, S. California .... 14—4
1959—Jim Graham, Oklahoma State . 15—2
1960—J.D. Martin, Oklahoma ...... 14—9
1961—George Davies, Oklahoma
  State; Dick Gear, San Jose State;
  Jim Brewer, Southern California .. 15—4
1962—John Belitza, Maryland; Fred
  Hanson, Rice; Don Meyers, Colo- 15—3
  rado, Dexter Elkins, S.M.U. ..... 15—3
1963—Brian Sternberg, Washington .. 16—3 3/4
1964—John Uelses, La Salle 16
1965—William Fosdick, Southern California .... 15—1/2
1966—Chuck Rogers, Colorado 16
1967—Bob Seagren, Southern California .... 17—4
1968—Jon Vaughn, U.C.L.A. ...... 17—1/4

1969—Bob Seagren, So. California ... 17—7 1/2
1970—Jan Johnson, Kansas .... 17—7
1971—Dave Roberts, Rice .... 17—6 1/2
1972—Dave Roberts, Rice .... 17—3

Hop, Step and Jump   Ft.—In.
1932—Charles Lambert Redd, Bradley 48—3 1/4
1936—Herschel Neil, Northwest Missouri .... 48—5 1/8
1948—Loyd Lamois, Minnesota .... 45—10
1952—George Shaw, Columbia ..... 49—1 7/8
1956—Bill Sharpe, West Chester Tea . 50—4 3/4
1959—Jack Smyth, Houston .... 49—7 1/4
1960—Luther Hayes, Southern
  California .... 50—11 1/2
1961—Luther Hayes, Southern
  California .... 51—2 1/4
1962—Kermit Alexander, U.C.L.A. ... 50—11 1/4
1963—Norman Tate, North Carolina
  State .... 51—1/4
1964—Charlie Craig, Fresno State ... 51—8 3/4
1965—Clarence Robinson, New Mexico 50—2
1966—Craig Fergus, San Jose State .. 51—3
1967—Art Baxter, New Mexico ..... 52—4 1/4
1968—Lennox Burgher, Nebraska ... 53—1 3/4
1969—Pertti Pousi, Brigham Young .. 52—1 1/2
1970—Mohinder Gill, Cal. Poly (San
  Luis Obispo) .... 51—9 1/4
1971—Mohinder Gill, Cal. Poly (San
  Luis Obispo) .... 55—1 1/4
1972—James Butte, U.C.L.A. ...... 53—2 1/4

Shot-Put   Ft.—In.
1921—Gus Pope, Washington ...... 45—4 1/2
1922—Jack Merchant, California .... 44—6 1/2
1923—Norman Anderson, Southern
  California .... 46—8
1924—No competition
1925—Glenn Hartranft, Stanford ... 50
1926—John Kuck, Emporia Teachers 50—3/4
1927—Herman Brix, Washington .... 46—7 3/8
1928—Harlow Rothert, Stanford .... 49—10 3/4
1929—Harlow Rothert, Stanford .... 50—3
1930—Harlow Rothert, Stanford .... 51—1 3/4
1931—Robert Hall, So. California ... 49—9
1932—Hugh Rhea, Nebraska .... 50—5 3/4
1933—Jack Torrance, Louisiana State 52—10
1934—Jack Torrance, Louisiana State 54—6 9/16
1935—Elwyn Dees, Kansas .... 51—1 1/8
1936—James Reynolds, Stanford .... 50—5 1/2
1937—Sam Francis, Nebraska ...... 53—6
1938—Elmer Hackney, Kansas State . 51—8 1/2
1939—Elmer Hackney, Kansas State . 55—10 3/8
1940—Alfred Blozis, Georgetown ... 56—1/2
1941—Alfred Blozis, Georgetown ... 54—10 1/2
1942—Alfred Blozis, Georgetown ... 54—9 5/8
1943—Elmer Aussieker, Missouri .... 52—3 3/4
1944—Norman Wasser, N.Y.U. ..... 49—1
1945—Ed Quirk, Missouri .... 53—1/8
1946—Bernard Mayer, N.Y.U. ...... 52—10 1/2
1947—Charles Fonville, Michigan ... 54—7/8

1948—Charles Fonville, Michigan ... 54—7	
1949—Jim Fuchs, Yale .... 56—1 1/2	
1950—Jim Fuchs, Yale .... 56—11 3/16	
1951—Darrow Hooper, Texas A. & M. 53—11	
1952—Parry O'Brien, So. California 57—5/8	
1953—Parry O'Brien, So. California .. 58—7 1/4	
1954—Tom Jones, Miami (Ohio) .... 54—2 7/8	
1955—Bill Nieder, Kansas .... 57—3	
1956—Ken Bantum, Manhattan ..... 60—1/2	
1957—Dave Owen, Michigan .... 59—5 3/4	
1958—Dave Davis, So. California .... 58—6 1/2	
1959—Carl Shine, Pennsylvania ..... 57—11 3/4	
1960—Dallas Long, So. California ... 61—9	
1961—Dallas Long, So. California ... 63—3 1/2	
1962—Dallas Long, So. California ... 64—7	
1963—Gary Gubner, New York U. ... 62—5	
1964—Gary Gubner, New York U. ... 61—8	
1965—Neil Steinhauer, Oregon ..... 62—6	
1966—Randy Matson, Texas A. & M. . 67—1 1/2	
1967—Randy Matson, Texas A. & M. . 67—9 1/4	
1968—Steve Marcus, U.C.L.A. ..... 61—7 3/4	
1969—Karl Salb, Kansas .... 64—9	
1970—Karl Salb, Kansas .... 63—10 1/2	
1971—Karl Salb, Kansas .... 66—11 1/2	
1972—Fred DeBernardi, Texas (El Paso) .... 66—6 1/2	

Discus Throw   Ft.—In.

1921—Gus Pope, Washington ...... 142—2 1/4	
1922—Thomas Lieb, Notre Dame ... 144—2 1/2	
1923—Thomas Lieb, Notre Dame ... 143—4	
1924—No competition	
1925—Clifford Hoffman, Stanford .. 148—4	
1926—Clarence L. Houser, So. California .... 148—11 3/4	
1927—Corson, Coll. of Pacific ...... 144—2 1/2	
1928—Eric Krenz, Stanford .... 149—2	
1929—Peter Rasmus, Ohio State .... 159—1 7/8	
1930—Paul Jessup, Washington ..... 160—9 3/8	
1931—Robert Hall, So. California ... 152—7 1/2	
1932—Frank L. Purma, Illinois ..... 156—4 1/4	
1933—Henry LaBorde, Stanford .... 163—3 3/4	
1934—Gordon Dunn, Stanford ..... 162—7	
1935—Kenneth Carpenter, So. California .... 157—11 1/4	
1936—Kenneth Carpenter, So. California 173	
1937—Pete Zagar, Stanford .... 156—3	
1938—Pete Zagar, Stanford .... 162—3 1/4	
1939—Pete Zagar, Stanford .... 164—1/4	
1940—Archie Harris, Indiana .... 162—4 1/2	
1941—Archie Harris, Indiana .... 174—8 3/4	
1942—Bob Fitch, Minnesota .... 164—8 1/4	
1943—Howard Debus, Nebraska .... 144—4 3/4	
1944—Bill Bangert, Missouri .... 149—5	
1945—Bill Bangert, Missouri .... 151—9 1/8	
1946—Fortune Gordien, Minnesota .. 153—10 3/4	
1947—Fortune Gordien, Minnesota .. 173—3	
1948—Fortune Gordien, Minnesota .. 164—6 1/2	
1949—Victor Frank, Yale .... 168—9 1/2	
1950—Dick Doyle, Montana .... 171—5	
1951—Jim Dillion, Auburn .... 167—5 3/4	

1952—Simeon Iness, So. California .. 173—2 3/8	
1953—Simeon Innes, So. California .. 190—7/8	
1954—Jim Dillion, Auburn .... 176—3	
1955—Des Koch, So. California ..... 176—3/8	
1956—Ron Drummond, U.C.L.A. ... 173—1/2	
1957—Al Oerter, Kansas .... 185—4	
1958—Al Oerter, Kansas; Rink Babka, So. California .... 186—2	
1959—Dick Cochran, Missouri ...... 178—0	
1960—Dick Cochran, Missouri ...... 188—3 1/2	
1961—Glenn Passey, Utah State .... 176—8	
1962—David Weill, Stanford .... 188—1	
1963—David Weill, Stanford .... 181—2 1/2	
1964—Larry Kennedy, New Mexico . 185—2 1/2	
1965—Bob Stoecker, Stanford ..... 183—7 1/2	
1966—Randy Matson, Texas A & M .. 197	
1967—Randy Matson, Texas A & M .. 190—4	
1968—John Van Reenen, Washington State .... 194—10	
1969—John Van Reenen, Washington State .... 200—8	
1970—John Van Reenan, Washington State .... 190—9	
1971—Mike Louisiana, Brigham Young 194—10	
1972—Fred DeBernardi, Texas (El Paso) 186—5	

Javelin Throw   Ft.—In.

1921—Flint Hanner, Stanford ...... 191—2 1/4	
1922—Howard B. Hoffman, Michigan 202—3	
1923—Harry Freida, Chicago .... 191—6	
1924—No competition	
1925—Philip Northrup, Michigan ... 201—11	
1926—Philip Northrup, Michigan ... 200—10	
1927—Doral Pilling, Utah .... 199—8	
1928—Lee N. Barlett, Albion .... 216—7	
1929—Jesse Mortenson, So. California 203—7 3/4	
1930—Kenneth Churchill, California . 204—2	
1931—Kenneth Churchill, California . 215	
1932—George Williams, Hampton ... 215	
1933—Duane Purvis, Purdue .... 216—6 1/4	
1934—Robert Parke, Oregon .... 220—11 5/8	
1935—Charles Gongloff, Pittsburgh .. 221—3 1/8	
1936—Alton Terry, Hardin-Simmons . 226—2 3/4	
1937—Lowell Todd, San Jose State .. 214—9 3/8	
1938—Nick Vukmanic, Penn State .. 215—8 1/8	
1939—Bob Peoples, So. California ... 220—6 1/2	
1940—Martin Biles, California ..... 204—10	
1941—Martin Biles, California ..... 220—1	
1942—Robert Biles, California ..... 213—9 3/4	
1943—George Gast, Iowa State ..... 202—1 1/2	
1944—Bob Ray, Wisconsin .... 174—5/8	
1945—Robert Patton, Navy .... 191—1	
1946—Robert Likens, San Jose State . 198—10 1/2	
1947—Robert Likens, San Jose State . 209—1	
1948—Bud Held, Stanford .... 209—8	
1949—Bud Held, Stanford .... 224—8 1/4	
1950—Bud Held, Stanford .... 216—8 5/8	
1951—Charles Missfeldt, Oregon State 219—4 3/4	
1952—George Roseme, California ... 228—8 3/8	
1953—Dick Genther, So. California .. 216—9 3/4	
1954—Leo Long, Stanford .... 226—8 3/4	
1955—Les Bitner, Kansas .... 246—1	

1956—Phil Conley, Cal. Tech. . . . . . . 239—11
1957—John Fromm, Pac. Lutheran . . 248—1
1958—John Fromm, Pac. Lutheran . . 257—1
1959—Bill Alley, Kansas . . . . 240—5 1/2
1960—Bill Alley, Kansas . . . . 268—9
1961—Chuck Wilkinson, Redlands . . 247—8 1/2
1962—John Sikorsky, So. California . 249—4
1963—Frank Covelli, Arizona State . . 257—8 1/2
1964—Les Tipton, Oregon . . . . 249—10 1/2
1965—John Tushaus, Arizona . . . . . . 250—5 1/2
1966—Jim Stevenson, Penn State . . . 258—5
1967—Delmon McNabb, Louisiana
    State . . . . 263—5
1968—Carl O'Donnell, Washington
    State . . . . 258—11
1969—Mark Murro, Arizona State . . . 265—9
1970—Bill Skinner, Tennessee . . . . . . 270—8
1971—Carl Feldmann, Washington . . 259—0
1972—Rick Dowswell, Ohio . . . . 265—11

Hammer Throw   Ft.—In.
1921—Charles Redmon, Chicago . . . . 133—9 3/4
1922—Jack Merchant, California . . . . 161—4
1923—Frederick D. Tootell, Bowdoin 175—1
1924—No competition
1925—Ray Bunker, Ohio State . . . . . 150—1/2
1926—Harry Hawkins, Michigan . . . . 148—1/4
1927—Donald Gwinn, Pittsburgh . . . 155—9
1928—Wilford H. Ketz, Michigan . . . . 163—8 3/4
1929—Donald Gwinn, Pittsburgh . . . 163—9 3/4
1930—Holley Campbell, Michigan . . . 162—8 1/4
1931—Ivan Dykeman,
    Colorado A. & M. . . . . 162—1 1/2
1932—Grant McDougall, Penn . . . . . . 159—9 3/4
1933—Roderick H. Cox, Michigan . . . 156—3/4
1934—Henry Dreyer, Rhode Island
    State . . . . 169—8 3/8
1935—Anton Kishon, Bates . . . . 168—8 7/8
1936-47—No competition
1948—Samuel M. Felton Jr., Harvard . 170—9 1/4
1949-51—No competition
1952—Gilbert J. Borjeson, Brown . . . 176—4 3/8
1953-55—No competition
1956—Bill McWilliams, Bowdoin . . . . 195—3
1957-58—No competition
1959—John Lawlor, Boston Univ. . . . 207—5
1960—John Lawlor, Boston Univ. . . . 209—2
1961—T. Pagani, California Tech . . . . 194—10 1/2
1962—Edward Bailey, Harvard . . . . . 193—11
1963—George Desnoyers, Boston Col-
    lege . . . . 190—2
1964—Alex Schulten, Bowdoin . . . . . 191—6
1965—John Fiore, Boston College . . . 200—10
1966—John Fiore, Boston College . . . 201—3 1/2
1967—Bob Narcessian, Rhode Island . 197—1/2
1968—Bob Narcessian, Rhode Island . 202—1
1969—Steve DeAutremont, Oregon
    State . . . . 190—5
1970—Steve DeAutremont, Oregon
    State . . . . 203—9
1971—Jacques Accambray, Kent State 227—10
1972—Al Schoterman, Kent State . . . 231—3

Team
1921—Illinois
1922—California
1923—Michigan
1924—No competition
1925—Stanford
1926—Southern California
1927—Illinois
1928—Stanford
1929—Ohio State
1930—31—Southern California
1932—Indiana
1933—Louisiana State
1934—Stanford
1935—43—Southern California
1944—Illinois
1945—Navy
1946—47—Illinois
1948—Minnesota
1949—55—Southern California
1956—U.C.L.A.
1957—Villanova
1958—Southern California
1959—60—Kansas
1961—Southern California
1962—Oregon
1963—Southern California
1964—Oregon
1965—Oregon, Southern California (tie)
1966—U.C.L.A.
1967—68—Southern California
1969—San Jose State
1970—California
1971—72—U.C.L.A.

Cross-Country
1938—Greg Rice, Notre Dame
1939—Walter J. Mehl, Wisconsin
1940—Gil Dodds, Ashland
1941—Fred Wilt, Indiana
1942—Oliver Hunter 3d, Notre Dame
1943—No competition
1944—45—Fred Feiler, Drake
1946—Quentin Brelsford, Ohio Wesleyan
1947—Jack Milne, North Carolina
1948—49—Robert Black, Rhode Island State
1950—51—Herb Semper, Kansas
1952—Charles Capozzoli, Georgetown
1953—Wes Santee, Kansas
1954—Allen Frame, Kansas
1955—Charles Jones, Iowa
1956—Walter McNew, Texas
1957—Max Truex, So. California
1958—Crawford Kennedy, Michigan State
1959—60—Al Lawrence, Houston
1961—Dale Story, Oregon State
1962—Thomas O'Hara, Loyola (Chicago)
1963—Vic Zwolak, Villanova
1964—Elmore Banton, Ohio U.
1965—John Lawson, Kansas
1966—67—Gerry Lindgren, Washington State
1968—Mike Ryan, Air Force

1969—Gerry Lindgren, Washington State
1970—71—Steve Prefontaine, Oregon
1972—Neil Cusack, East Tennessee

Cross-Country—Team

1938—Indiana
1939—Michigan State
1940—Indiana
1941—Rhode Island State
1942—Indiana
1943—No competition
1944—46—Drake
1947—Penn State
1948—49—Michigan State
1950—Penn State
1951—Syracuse
1952—Michigan State
1953—Kansas
1954—Oklahoma A. & M.
1955—56—Michigan State
1957—Notre Dame
1958—59—Michigan State
1960—Houston
1961—Oregon State
1962—63—San Jose State
1964—65—Western Michigan
1966—68—Villanova
1969—Texas (El Paso)
1970—Villanova
1971—Oregon
1972—Tennessee

DECATHLON

1970—Rick Wanamaker, Drake 7,406
1971—Ray Hipp, Ohio State 7,456
1972—Ron Evans, Connecticut 7,571

INDOOR

60-Yard Dash

1965—Charles Greene, Nebraska .... 6.1s.
1966—Charles Greene, Nebraska .... 6.0s.
1967—Charles Greene, Nebraska .... 6.0s.
1968—Jim Green, Kentucky .... 6.0s.
1969—John Carlos, San Jose State .... 6.0s.
1970—Herb Washington, Michigan State ... 5.9s.
1971—Jim Green, Kentucky ... .. 6.0s.
1972—Herb Washington, Michigan State .. 6.1s.
1973—Gerry Tinker, Kent State .... 6.0s.

440-Yard Run

1965—Theron Lewis, Southern U. .... .47 8s.
1966—Don Payne, Kansas State &
   Bill Calhoun, Oklahoma ..... .48 9s
1967—Bill Calhoun, Oklahoma .... .48.9s.
1968—Larry James, Villanova .... .47.0s.
1969—Larry James, Villanova .... .47.3s.
1970—Larry James, Villanova .... .48.3s.
1971—Tom Ulan, Rutgers .... .48.8s.
1972—Larance Jones, Northeast Missouri 48.3s.
1973—Terry Erickson, Southern Ill. ...... .49.0s.

600-Yard Run

1965—Leland Albright, L.S.U. ..... 1m. 10.0s.
1966—Martin McGrady, Central (Ohio)
   State .... 1m. 09.4s.

1967—Steve Carson, Iowa State .... 1m. 10.2s.
1968—Tom Albright, Colgate ...... 1m. 10.6s.
1969—Bill Wehrwein, Michigan
   State .... 1m. 09.8s.
1970—Rick Wohlhuter, Notre Dame . 1m. 09.5s.
1971—Tommie Turner, Murray State 1m. 09.6s.
1972—Dale Gibson, Mississippi State 1m. 11.3s.
1973—Beaufort Brown, Florida .... 1m. 10.0s.

880-Yard Run

1965—Tom Von Ruden, Oklahoma
   State . ... 1m. 51.8s.
1966—Ricardo Urbina, Georgetown . 1m. 51.9s
1967—Dave Patrick, Villanova .... 1m. 48.9s.
1968—Dave Patrick, Villanova ..... 1m. 52.0s.
1969—Frank Murphy, Villanova .... 1m. 51.1s.
1970—Mark Winzenreid, Wisconsin .. 1m. 51.7s.
1971—Mark Winzenreid, Wisconsin .. 1m. 50.9s.
1972—Dave Wottle, Bowling Green . 1m. 51.8s.
1973—Ken Schappert, Villanova .... 1m. 50.4s.

1,000-Yard Run

1965—Robin Lingle, Missouri ...... 2m. 09.9s.
1966—Herb Germann, Seton Hall ... 2m. 12.9s.
1967—Ray Arrington, Wisconsin ... 2m. 07.8s.
1968—Ray Arrington, Wisconsin ... 2m. 09.3s.
1969—Ray Arrington, Wisconsin .. 2m. 08.0s.
1970—Keith Colburn, Harvard ..... 2m. 09. 9s.
1971—Bob Wheeler, Duke .... 2m. 07.4s.
1972—Mike Mosser, West Virginia... 2m. 08 9s.
1973—Tony Waldrop, North Carolina 2m. 10.0s.

1-Mile Run

1965—Chris Johnson,
   Southern California ... 4m. 08.0s.
1966—Conrad Nightingale,
   Kansas State .... 4m. 03.4s.
1967—Jim Ryun, Kansas .... 3m. 58.6s.
1968—Jim Ryun, Kansas .... 4m. 06.8s.
1969—Jim Ryun, Kansas .... 4m. 02.6s.
1970—Howell Michael,
   William & Mary ...... 4m. 03.1s.
1971—Marty Liquori, Villanova .... 4m. 04.7s.
1972—Ken Popeloy, Michigan State . 4m. 02.9s.
1973—Dave Wottle, Bowling Green . 4m. 03.4s.

2-Mile Run

1965—Herald Hadley, Kansas ...... 8m. 56.4s.
1966—Gerry Lindgren, Washington
   State .... 8m. 41.3s.
1967—Gerry Lindgren, Washington
   State .... 8m. 34.7s.
1968—Jim Ryun, Kansas .... 8m. 38.9s.
1969—Ole Oleson, So. Calif. .... 8m. 45.2s.
1970—Jerry Richey, Pittsburgh .... 8m. 39.2s.
1971—Marty Liquori, Villanova .... 8m. 37.1s.
1972—Sid Sink, Bowling Green .... 8m. 36.5s.
1973—Mike Keogh, Manhattan ..... 8m. 39.7s.

60-Yard High Hurdles

1965—Gene Washington, Michigan
   State .... 7.2s.
1966—Jerry Cerulla, Utah State .... 7.2s.
1967—Earl McCullough, So. Calif. .... 7.0s.
1968—Richmond Flowers, Tennessee .... 7.0s.

1969—Erv Hall, Villanova .... 7.0s.
1970—Tom Hill, Arkansas State .... 6.9s.
1971—Marcus Walker, Colorado .... 7.0s.
1972—Tom McMannon, Notre Dame ..... 7.2s.
1973—Rod Milburn, Southern Univ. ..... 6 9s.

1-Mile Relay
1965—Morgan State (Edgehill, Hawthorne, Johnson, Lee) ....3m.15.6s.
1966—Morgan State (R. Pollard, H. Hawthorne, M. Brown, H. Stanback)................3m.16.5s.
1967—Oklahoma (J. Shields, J. Hardwick, T. Melton, B. Calhoun) ....3m.15.5s.
1968—Villanova (Harold Nichter, Hardge Davis, Ken Prince, Larry James) ....3m.14.4s.
1969—Tennessee (Gary Womble, Larry Kelly, Audry Hardy, Hardee McAlhaney) ....3m.14.6s.
1970—Villanova (LaMotte Hyman, Greg Covan, Hardge Davis, Larry James) ....3m.15.3s.
1971—Adelphi (Ray Lee, Keith Davis, Dennis Walker, Clyde McPherson) ....3m.15.5s.
1972—Adelphi (Ray Lee, Keith Davis, Dennis Walker, Clyde McPherson) ....3m.15.8s.
1973—Seton Hall (Mike Tyson, Larry Mustachio, Orlando Greene, Howard Brook) ....3m.17.0s.

2-Mile Relay
1965—Oklahoma State (J. Metcalf, J. Perry, T. Von Ruden, D. Perry)......................7m.27.9s.
1966—Oklahoma State (A. Droke, J. Perry, J. Metcalf, T. Von Ruden)....................7m.30.1s.
1967—Southern California (R. Joyce, D. Buck, D. Carr, C. Trentadue)................7m.30.1s.
1968—Harvard (Trey Burns, Royce Shaw, Jim Baker, Dave McKelvey) ....7m.26.8s.
1969—Kansas State (Dave Peterson, Jerome Howe, Bob Barratti, Ken Swenson) ....7m.32.2s.
1970—Kansas (Dennis Stewart, Jim Neihouse, Roger Kathol, Brian McElroy) ....7m.25 7s.
1971—Texas, El Paso (Peter Romero, Fernando De LaCerda, Rod Hill, Kerry Ellison) ....7m.37.4s.
1972—Illinois (Dave Kaemerer, Ron Phillipps, Lee LaBadie, Rob Mango) ....7m.29.9s.
1973—Fordham (Paul Nowicki, Alex Trammel, John Jurgens, Marcel Philippe) ....7m.31.5s.

Distance Medley Relay
(880, 440, 1,320 yds., 1 mile)
1967—Kansas State (Charles Harper, Terry Holbrook, Wes Dutton, Conrad Nightingale) ....9m.44.6s.
1968—Villanova (Charlie Messenger, Bud Whitehead, Tom Donnelly, Frank Murphy).................9m.49.5s.
1969—Villanova (Andy O'Reilly, Ernie Bradshaw, Chris Mason, Frank Murphy).................9m.45.8s.
1970—Manhattan (John Lovett, Mike Kenney, Al Novell, Tom Donohue)................9m.49.2s.
1971—Pittsburgh (Ken Silay, Doral Watley, Mike Schurko, Jerry Richey) ....9m.45.7s.
1972—Bowling Green (Craig MacDonald, Ted Farver, Sid Sink, Dave Wottle) ....9m.49.5s.
1973—Manhattan (John Lovett, Ray Johnson, Joe Savage, Tony Colon) ....9m.43.8s.

High Jump   Ft.–In.
1965—Frank Costello, Maryland 6–10
1966—Otis Burrell, Nevada 7
1967—Ted Downing, Miami (Ohio) .. 7
1968—Dick Fosbury, Oregon State .. 7–0
1969—Ron Jourdan, Florida 7–3/4
1970—Kenneth Lundmark, Brigham Young 7–0
1971—Pat Matzdorf, Wisconsin 7–2
1972—Chris Dunn, Colgate 7–2 3/4
1973—Chris Dunn, Colgate 7–2

Broad Jump   Ft.–In.
1965—Michael Cole, Maryland 25–1
1966—Rainer Stenius, Los Angeles St. 25–7
1967—Aaron Hopkins, Toledo 24–7 3/4
1968—Bob Beamon, Texas (El Paso). 27–2 3/4
1969—Ron Jessie, Kansas 25–2 1/2
1970—Bill Lightsey, Kentucky 25–2 1/4
1971—Henry Hines, So. Calif. 26–1 1/4
1972—Henry Hines, So. Calif. 25–10
1973—Randy Williams, So. Calif. 26–4 1/4

Pole Vault   Ft.–In.
1965—Robert Yard, Washington St. . 15–8 1/4
1966—Bill Fosdick, So. Calif. 16–1/4
1967—Bob Seagren, So. Calif. 17–1/4
1968—Paul Wilson, So. Calif. 16–8
1969—Lester Smith, Miami (Ohio) .. 16–6
1970—Jim Williamson, Maryland 16–6
1971—Scott Wallick, Miami (Ohio) .. 16–8
1972—Jan Johnson, Alabama 17–1 1/4
1973—Terry Porter, Kansas 17–0

Shot Put   Ft.–In.
1965—Randy Matson, Texas A & M .. 63–2 1/4
1966—George Woods, So. Illinois ... 61–3 1/2
1967—Ken Patera, Brigham Young .. 59–6
1968—John Van Reenen, Washington State 62–1

1969—Karl Salb, Kansas 66–8 3/4
1970—Karl Salb, Kansas 67–2 1/2
1971—Karl Salb, Kansas 65–9
1972—Doug Lane, So. Calif. 64–3 1/2
1973—Hans Hoglund, Texas (El Paso) 64–1 1/4

35-Lb. Weight Throw Ft.–In.
1966—Bob Mead, Manhattan 59–1/2
1967—Andy Yuen, Connecticut 61–9 3/4
1968—Bob Narcessian, Rhode Island . 65–5 3/4
1969—Charles Ajootian, Harvard 61–8 1/2
1970—Ed Nosal, Harvard 63–6 1/4
1971—Al Schoterman, Kent State ... 68–10 1/4
1972-73—No competition

Triple Jump Ft.–In.
1968—Bob Beamon, Texas (El Paso) . 52–3 1/2
1969—Lennox Burgher, Nebraska ... 52–1/2
1970—Milan Tiff, Miami (Ohio) 51–11 1/2
1971—Mohindor Gill, Cal. Poly
    (San Luis Obispo) 52–9 3/4
1972—Barry McClure, Middle
    Tennessee State 52–10 1/4
1973—Barry McClure, Middle
    Tennessee State 54–1 3/4

Team

1965—Missouri
1966—Kansas
1967—Southern California
1968—Villanova
1969-70—Kansas
1971—Villanova
1972—Southern California
1973—Manhattan

I.C.A.A.A.A. CHAMPIONS
(Source: Intercollegiate A.A.A.A. Track and
Field Guide.)

Outdoor

100-Yard Dash
  100 meters, 1933 through 1936.

1876—H. W. Stevens, Williams ....11s.
1877—H. H. Lee, Pennsylvania ....10.2s.
1878—H. H. Lee, Pennsylvania ....10 1/4s.
1879—H. H. Lee, Pennsylvania ....10.8s.
1880—E. J. Wendell, Harvard ....10.8s.
1881—E. J. Wendell, Harvard ....10 1/4s.
1882—H. S. Brooks Jr., Yale ....10.2s.
1883—S. Derickson Jr., Columbia .....10.6s.
1884—H. S. Brooks Jr., Yale ....10.2s.
1885—F. M. Bonine, Michigan ....10.6s.
1886—E. H. Rogers, Harvard ....10.5s.
1887—C. H. Sherrill, Yale ....10.4s.
1888—C. H. Sherrill, Yale ....10.6s.
1889—C. H. Sherrill, Yale ....10.2s.
1890—C. H. Sherrill, Yale ....10.2s.
1891—L.H. Cary, Princeton ....10s.
1892—W. Swayne Jr., Yale ....10.2s.
1893—W.M. Richards, Yale ....10.2s.
1894—E.S. Ramsdell, Pennsylvania ....10s.
1895—J.V. Crum, Iowa ....10s.
1896—B.J. Wefers, Georgetown .... 9.8s.

1897—B.J. Wefers, Georgetown .... 10.4s.
1898—J.W.B. Tewksbury, Pennsylvania . 10s.
1899—J.W.B. Tewksbury, Pennsylvania . 10s.
1900—A.C. Kraenzlein, Pennsylvania .. 10.2s.
1901—M.T. Lightner, Harvard .... * ——
1902—J.S. Westney, Pennsylvania ..... * ——
1903—F.R. Moulton, Yale .... * ——
1904—W.A. Shick Jr., Harvard .... 10s.
1905—W.A. Shick Jr., Harvard .... 10.2s.
1906—N.J. Cartmell, Pennsylvania .... 10.2s.
1907—N.J. Cartmell, Pennsylvania .... 10s.
1908—N.J. Cartmell, Pennsylvania .... 10.6s.
1909—R.C. Foster, Harvard .... 10.2s.
1910—F.L. Ramsdell, Pennsylvania .... 10s.
1911—R.C. Craig, Michigan .... 9.8s.
1912—R.B. Thomas, Princeton .... 10.2s.
1913—J.C. Patterson, Pennsylvania .... 9.8s.
1914—J.E. Bond, Michigan .... 10s.
1915—H.L. Smith, Michigan .... 10s.
1916—H.L. Smith, Michigan .... 10s.
1917—No competition
1918—W.H. Ganzemuller, Penn State .. 10.2s.
1919—W.C. Haymond, Pennsylvania ... 10s.
1920—R.E. Brown, Princeton .... 10.2s.
1921—M.M. Kirksey, Stanford .... 10s.
1922—J.A. LeConey, Lafayette .... 9.7s.
1923—H.B. Lever, Pennsylvania ...... 9.8s.
1924—G.L. Hill, Pennsylvania .... 10s.
1925—Chester Bowman, Syracuse ..... 9.9s.
1926—Henry A. Russell, Cornell ...... 9.7s.
1927—Charles E. Borah, Southern
    California .... 9.8s.
1928—James F. Quinn, Holy Cross .... 9.9s.
1929—Karl H. Wildermuth, Georgetown 10s.
1930—Frank C. Wykoff, Southern
    California .... 9.7s.
1931—Frank C. Wykoff, Southern
    California .... 9.6s.
1932—Frank C. Wykoff, Southern
    California .... 9.9s.
1933—Richard F. Hardy, Cornell ..... 10.8s.
1934—Robert A. Kiesel, California .... 10.6s.
1935—George F. Anderson, California . 10.7s.
1936—Edgar D. Mason, Pittsburgh .... 10.7s.
1937—Benjamin W. Johnson, Columbia 9.8s.
1938—E. Wilbur Greer, Michigan State . 9.9s.
1939—Herbert S. Weast, Columbia .... 9.8s.
1940—Norwood H. Ewell, Penn State .. 9.7s.
1941—Norwood H. Ewell, Penn State .. 9.6s.
1942—Norwood H. Ewell, Penn State .. †9.5s.
1943—Harvey M. Kelsey, Princeton .... 9.7s.
1944—Edward Conwell, New York Univ. 9.8s.
1945—John B. Van Velzer, Navy ...... 10.2s.
1946—Herbert P. Douglas, Pittsburgh .. 9.7s.
1947—Joseph Cianciabella, Manhattan . 9.7s.
1948—Paul F. Cowie, Princeton ...... 9.6s.
1949—Andrew Stanfield, Seton Hall ... 9.8s.
1950—Andrew Stanfield, Seton Hall ... †9.6s.
1951—Andrew Stanfield, Seton Hall ... 9.7s.
1952—John George, California .... 9.9s.
1953—Lindy Remigino, Manhattan .... 10s.
1954—Art Pollard, Penn State .... 9.6s.

1955—John Haines, Pennsylvania	....	9.5s.
1956—Herb Carper, Pittsburgh	....	9.4s.
1957—Ed Collymore, Villanova	....	9.7s.
1958—Ira Davis, LaSalle	....	9.6s.
1959—Robert L. Brown, Penn State	.....	9.9s.
1960—Robert L. Brown, Penn State	.....	9.7s.
1961—Frank Budd, Villanova	....	9.6s.
1962—Frank Budd, Villanova	....	9.6s.
1963—Gerry Ashworth, Dartmouth	.....	9.7s.
1964—Sam Amukun, Colgate	....	9.7s.
1965—Earl Horner, Villanova	....	9.8s.
1966—Sam Perry, Fordham	....	9.6s.
1967—Jim Lee, Maryland	....	9.8s.
1968—Erv Hall, Villanova	....	9.5s.
1969—Don Martin, Yale	....	9.9s.
1970—Bill Krouse, West Chester	....	9.7s.
1971—Donald Schneider, Boston College	..	9.7s.
1972—Jim Scott, Penn State	....	9.7s.
1973—Mike Sands, Penn State	....	9.8s.

* Finished second; name of winner stricken from records.
† With wind.

220-Yard Dash

200 meters, 1933 through 1936.

1877—H.H. Lee, Pennsylvania	....	23.5s.
1878—H.H. Lee, Pennsylvania	....	23.6s.
1879—E.J. Wendell, Harvard	....	24.4s.
1880—E.J. Wendell, Harvard	....	24.4s.
1881—E.J. Wendell, Harvard	....	23.2s.
1882—H.S. Brooks Jr., Yale	....	22 5/8s.
1883—H.S. Brooks Jr., Yale	....	23.2s.
1884—Wendell Baker, Harvard	....	22.4s.
1885—Wendell Baker, Harvard	....	23.6s.
1886—Wendell Baker, Harvard	....	22.8s.
1887—E.H. Rogers, Harvard	....	23s.
1888—C.H. Sherrill, Yale	....	22.6s.
1889—C.H. Sherrill, Yale	....	22.4s.
1890—C.H. Sherrill, Yale	....	22.2s.
1891—L.H. Cary, Princeton	....	21.8s.
1892—W. Swayne Jr., Yale	....	22s.
1893—W.M. Richards, Yale	....	22.6s.
1894—E.S. Ramsdell, Pennsylvania	....	22s.
1895—J.V. Crum, Iowa	....	22s.
1896—B.J. Wefers, Georgetown	......	21.2s.
1897—J.H. Colfelt, Princeton	....	22.6s.
1898—J.W.B. Tewksbury, Pennsylvania	.	21.6s.
1899—J.W.B. Tewksbury, Pennsylvania	.	21.6s.
1900—F.W. Jarvis, Princeton	....	22.2s.
1901—F.M. Sears, Cornell	....	22.6s.
1902—W.T. Lightner, Harvard	....	21.6s.
1903—W.T. Lightner, Harvard	....	22s.
1904—W.A. Shick Jr., Harvard	....	21.4s.
1905—W.A. Shick Jr., Harvard	....	22.2s.
1906—N.J. Cartmell, Pennsylvania	....	23.4s.
1907—N.J. Cartmell, Pennsylvania	....	21.8s.
1908—N.J. Cartmell, Pennsylvania	....	22s.
1909—R.C. Foster, Harvard	....	21.6s.
1910—R.C. Craig, Michigan	....	21.2s.
1911—R.C. Craig, Michigan	....	21.2s.
1912—C.D. Reidpath, Syracuse	....	21.4s.
1913—D.F. Lippincott, Pennsylvania	..	21.2s.

1914—H.H. Seward, Michigan	....	22s.
1915—H.L. Smith, Michigan	....	22s.
1916—W.B. Moore, Princeton	....	21.6s.
1917—No competition		
1918—W.C. Haymond, Pennsylvania	...	21.6s.
1919—W.C. Haymond, Pennsylvania	...	21.6s.
1920—R.E. Brown, Princeton	....	21.8s.
1921—Allen Woodring, Syracuse	......	21.4s.
1922—J.A. LeConey, Lafayette	....	21.3s.
1923—F. Lovejoy Cornell		21.4s.
1924—G.L. Hill, Pennsylvania	....	21.9s.
1925—Henry A. Russell, Cornell	......	21.4s.
1926—Henry A. Russell, Cornell	......	*21s.
1927—Charles E. Borah, So. California	.	20.9s.
1928—Raymond J. Barbuti, Syracuse	..	22.5s.
1929—Richard G. Kent, Colgate	......	21.1s.
1930—Hector M. Dyer, Stanford	......	21.3s.
1931—Eddie Tolan , Michigan	....	21.1s.
1932—Robert A. Kiesel, California	....	21.3s.
1933—Howard M. Jones, Pennsylvania	.	21.3s.
1934—Robert A. Kiesel, California	....	21.1s.
1935—Foy Draper, So. California	.....	*20.8s.
1936—Edgar D. Mason, Pittsburgh	....	21.2s.
1937—Benjamin W. Johnson, Columbia	.	21.2s.
1938—Edgar D. Mason, Pittsburgh	...	22s.
1939—Kenneth D. Clapp, Brown	......	21.2s.
1940—Norwood H. Ewell, Penn State	..	20.9s.
1941—Norwood H. Ewell, Penn State	..	20.7s.
1942—Norwood H. Ewell, Penn State	..	*20.5s.
1943—Harvey M. Kelsey, Princeton	....	21.3s.
1944—James W. Pettit, Navy	....	21.6s.
1945—John B. Van Velzer, Navy	......	22s.
1946—Robert Swain, Marquette	......	22s.
1947—Joseph Cianciabella, Manhattan	.	21.4s.
1948—Paul F. Cowie, Princeton	......	20.8s.
1949—Andrew Stanfield, Seton Hall	...	20.6s.
1950—Robert Carty, Manhattan	......	21.2s.
1951—Andrew Stanfield, Seton Hall	...	20.6s.
1952—Lindy Remigino, Manhattan	....	21.9s.
1953—Lindy Remigino, Manhattan	....	21.7s.
1954—Henry Thresher, Yale	....	20.7s.
1955—Art Pollard, Penn State	....	20.8s.
1956—John Haines, Pennsylvania	.....	20.5s.
1957—Ed Collymore, Villanova	....	21s.
1958—Ed Collymore, Villanova	....	*20.3s.
1959—Ed Collymore, Villanova	....	21.0s.
1960—Robert L. Brown, Penn State	...	20.6s.
1961—Frank Budd, Villanova	....	21.4s.
1962—Frank Budd, Villanova	....	20.6s.
1963—Bob Mattis, Manhattan	....	21.4s.
1964—Earl Horner, Villanova	....	20.9s.
1965—Earl Horner, Villanova	....	21.0s.
1966—Earl Horner, Villanova	....	21.2s.
1967—Rick Owens, Pennsylvania	.....	21.3s.
1968—Roland Merritt, Maryland	......	21.0s.
1969—Raymond Pollard, Morgan State	.	21.6s.
1970—Jim Reed, Amherst	....	21.2s.
1971—Dennis Walker, Adelphi	....	21.0s.
1972—Bruce Collins, Penn	....	21.2s.
1973—Rich Hardware, Adelphi	....	21.3s.

* With wind.

440-Yard Run
400 meters, 1933 through 1936.

1876—H.W. Stevens, Williams .... 56s.
1877—G.M. Hammond, Columbia ..... 54s.
1878—A.I. Burton, Columbia .... 54.2s.
1879—C.H. Cogswell, Dartmouth ..... 54.8s.
1880—E.J. Wendell, Harvard .... 55.2s.
1881—E.A. Ballard, Pennsylvania ..... 53.8s.
1882—W.H. Goodwin Jr., Harvard ..... 53s.
1883—W.H. Goodwin Jr., Harvard ..... 51.2s.
1884—W.H. Goodwin Jr., Harvard ..... 52.6s.
1885—Wendell Baker, Harvard .... 54.4s.
1886—S.G. Wells, Harvard .... 51.8s.
1887—S.G. Wells, Harvard .... 53.6s.
1888—S.G. Wells, Harvard .... 52.6s.
1889—W.C. Dohm, Princeton .... 50s.
1890—W.C. Downs, Harvard .... 50.6s.
1891—G.B. Shattuck, Amherst .... 49.5s.
1892—W.H. Wright, Harvard .... 50.6s.
1893—L. Sayer, Harvard .... 50.8s.
1894—S.M. Merrill, Harvard .... 50.4s.
1895—W.H. Vincent, Harvard .... 50.8s.
1896—T.E. Burke, Boston Univ. ...... 50.4s.
1897—T.E. Burke, Boston Univ. ...... 50.4s.
1898—F.W. Jarvis, Princeton .... 50.8s.
1899—M.W. Long, Columbia .... 49.4s.
1900—D. Boardman, Yale .... 49.6s.
1901—W.J. Holland, Georgetown ..... 51.6s.
1902—W.J. Holland, Georgetown ..... 49.6s.
1903—J.E. Haigh, Harvard .... 50.2s.
1904—J.B. Taylor, Pennsylvania ...... 49.2s.
1905—H.A. Hyman, Pennsylvania ..... 49.4s.
1906—H.M. Rogers, Cornell .... 50.2s.
1907—J.B. Taylor, Pennsylvania ...... 48.8s.
1908—J.B. Taylor, Pennsylvania ...... 52.2s.
1909—T.S. Blumer, Harvard .... 50.6s.
1910—C.D. Reidpath, Syracuse .... 50s.
1911—D.B. Young, Amherst .... 48.8s.
1912—C.D. Reidpath, Syracuse .... 48s.
1913—C.B. Haff, Michigan .... 48.4s.
1914—J.E. Meredith, Pennsylvania .... 48.4s.
1915—J.E. Meredith, Pennsylvania .... 48s.
1916—J.E. Meredith, Pennsylvania .... 48.4s.
1917—No competition
1918—F.J. Shea, Pittsburgh .... 47.6s.
1919—K.A. Mayer, Cornell .... 49.8s.
1920—O.O. Hendrixson, California .... 48.4s.
1921—O.O. Hendrixson, California .... 49s.
1922—J.W. Driscoll, Boston College ... 49.5s.
1923—Allen Woodring, Syracuse ...... 48.2s.
1924—A.B. Helffrich, Penn State ..... 50.1s.
1925—Joseph P. Tierney, Holy Cross .. 47.9s.
1926—Cecil G. Cooke, Syracuse ...... 48.8s.
1927—Frederick P. Alderman, Mich.
       State .... 48.3s.
1928—Raymond J. Barbuti, Syracuse .. 48.8s.
1929—Reginald F. Bowen, Pittsburgh .. 48.4s.
1930—Charles H. Engle, Yale .... 48.2s.
1931—Victor E. Williams, So. California 47.4s.
1932—William A. Carr, Pennsylvania ... 47s.
1933—James E. LuValle, U.C.L.A. .... 46.9s.

1934—Allan F. Blackman, Stanford ... 47.5s.
1935—James E. LuValle, U.C.L.A. .... 47.3s.
1936—Edward T. O'Brien, Syracuse ... 47.1s.
1937—John Y. Woodruff, Pittsburgh ... 47s.
1938—John Y. Woodruff, Pittsburgh ... 47s.
1939—John Y. Woodruff, Pittsburgh ... 47s.
1940—James B. Herbert, New York U. . 48.1s.
1941—John Campbell, Fordham ...... 47.7s.
1942—Hugh Short, Georgetown ...... 47.2s.
1943—John W. Morris, Army .... 48.3s.
1944—James E. McGuire, Colgate .... 48.4s.
1945—William Whittington, Army ..... 49.8s.
1946—William B. Kash, Navy .... 48.6s.
1947—George E. Guida, Villanova .... 47.5s.
1948—Reginald Pearman, New York U. 47.6s.
1949—Frank Fox, Seton Hall .... 48.2s.
1950—Charles Moore, Cornell .... 47.3s.
1951—Richard Maiocco, New York U. . 47.5s.
1952—Richard Maiocco, New York U. . 47.9s.
1953—Morris Curotta, Seton Hall ..... 47.3s.
1954—Louis Jones, Manhattan .... 47.3s.
1955—Charles Jenkins, Villanova ..... 47.2s.
1956—John Haines, Pennsylvania ..... 47.3s.
1957—Charles Jenkins, Villanova ..... 47.4s.
1958—James Norton, Penn State ...... 48.1s.
1959—Basil Ince, Tufts .... 46.9s.
1960—James Weddeburn, New York
       University .... 47.4s.
1961—Richard Edmunds, Princeton ... 48.1s.
1962—Hubert Brown, Morgan State ... 46.7s.
1963—Wendell Mottley, Yale .... 47.3s.
1964—Wendell Mottley, Yale .... 47.0s.
1965—Nick Lee, Morgan State .... 47.4s.
1966—Bill Bruckel, Cornell .... 47.5s.
1967—Mark Young, Yale .... 47.4s.
1968—Larry James, Villanova .... 45.5s.
1969—Larry James, Villanova .... 46.6s.
1970—Larry James, Villanova .... 46.2s.
1971—Clyde McPherson, Adelphi ..... 47.0s.
1972—Mike Black, St. Joseph .... 47.7s.
1973—Ron Zapoticozy, Seton Hall .... 47.5s.

880-Yard Run
800 meters, 1933 through 1936.

1876—R.W. Green, Princeton ....2m. 16.5s.
1877—G.M. Hammond, Columbia ..2m. 20.5s.
1878—A.J. Burton, Columbia ....2m. 8 1/4s.
1879—C.H. Cogswell, Dartmouth ...2m. 12s.
1880—E.A. Ballard, Pennsylvania ...2m. 9.2s.
1881—T.J. Coolidge, Harvard ......2m. 7 3/8s.
1882—W.H. Goodwin Jr., Harvard ..2m. 2.4s.
1883—W.H. Goodwin Jr., Harvard ..2m. 2s.
1884—W.H. Goodwin Jr., Harvard ..2m. 5.5s.
1885—H.L. Mitchell, Yale ....2m. 7.2s.
1886—F.R. Smith, Yale ....2m. 4.2s.
1887—R. Faries, Pennsylvania .....2m. 7s.
1888—H.R. Miles, Harvard ....2m. 2.2s.
1889—W.C. Downs, Harvard ....2m. 2.6s.
1890—W.C. Dohm, Princeton ......1m. 59.2s.
1891—W.B. Wright Jr., Yale ....1m. 59.2s.
1892—T.B. Turner, Princeton ......1m. 59.8s.
1893—J. Corbin, Harvard ....1m. 59.8s.

1894—C.H. Kilpatrick, Union ...... 1m. 59.2s.
1895—E. Hollister, Harvard .... 2m.
1896—E. Hollister, Harvard .... 1m. 56.8s.
1897—E. Hollister, Harvard .... 1m. 58.8s.
1898—J.G. Cregan, Princeton ...... 1m. 58.4s.
1899—T.E. Burke, Harvard .... 1m. 58.8s.
1900—J.M. Perry, Princeton .... 2m. 3.6s.
1901—J.M. Perry, Princeton .... 2m. 3.6s.
1902—H.E. Taylor, Amherst .... 2m. 3/5s.
1903—L.M. Adsit, Princeton .... 2m. 4.4s.
1904—E.B. Parsons, Yale .... 1m. 56.8s.
1905—E.B. Parsons, Yale .... 1m. 56s.
1906—J.C. Carpenter, Cornell ..... 1m. 59.2s.
1907—G. Haskins, Pennsylvania ... 1m. 57.8s.
1908—L.P. Jones, Pennsylvania .... 2m. 2s.
1909—A.F. Beck, Pennsylvania ..... 1m. 56.6s.
1910—G. Whitely, Princeton .... 1m. 57s.
1911—J.P. Jones, Cornell .... 1m. 54.8s.
1912—J.P. Jones, Cornell .... 1m. 53.8s.
1913—G.E. Brown, Yale .... 1m. 55.2s.
1914—D.S. Caldwell, Cornell ...... 1m. 53.4s.
1915—J.E. Meredith, Pennsylvania .. 1m. 54.4s.
1916—J.E. Meredith, Pennsylvania .. 1m. 53s.
1917—No competition
1918—C. Shaw, Columbia .... 1m. 56.8s.
1919—K.A. Mayer, Cornell .... 1m. 56.4s.
1920—Earl W. Eby, Pennsylvania ... 1m. 58s.
1921—Earl W. Eby, Pennsylvania ... 1m. 55.2s.
1922—L.A. Brown, Pennsylvania ... 1m. 55.2s.
1923—A.B. Helffrich, Penn State ... 1m. 55.8s.
1924—John N. Watters, Harvard .... 1m. 55.8s.
1925—George M. Marsters, George-
town .... 1m. 53.5s.
1926—John N. Watters, Harvard ... 1m. 55.8s.
1927—Oliver Proudlock, Syracuse .. 1m. 55s.
1928—Philip A. Edwards, New
York U. .... 1m. 56.8s.
1929—Philip A. Edwards, New
York U. .... 1m. 52.2s.
1930—Russell H. Chapman, Bates ... 1m. 52.4s.
1931—Ben B. Eastman, Stanford ... 1m. 54.4s.
1932—Ben B. Eastman, Stanford .. 1m. 51.9s.
1933—William R. Bonthron,
Princeton .... 1m. 53.5s.
1934—William R. Bonthron,
Princeton .... 1m. 54.8s.
1935—Kenneth D. Black, Maine ... 1m. 54.5s.
1936—Louis P. Burns, Manhattan ... 1m. 54.1s.
1937—John Y. Woodruff, Pittsburgh 1m. 52.1s.
1938—John Y. Woodruff, Pittsburgh 1m. 52.5s.
1939—John Y. Woodruff, Pittsburgh 1m. 51.2s.
1940—Edward Burrowes Jr.,
Princeton 1m. 52.2s
1941—Leslie MacMitchell, New
York U. .... 1m. 53s.
1942—Lynn Radcliffe, Syracuse ... 1m. 53.9s.
1943—Joseph Nowicki, Fordham ... 1m. 55.6s.
1944—Donald L. Burnham,
Dartmouth .... 1m. 54.2s.
1945—John B. Caskey, Navy ...... 2m. 1.8s.
1946—Alvah C. Meeker, Colgate .... 1m. 54.7s.
1947—Reginald Pearman, New

York U. .... 1m. 51.5s.
1948—Jack Dianetti, Michigan State . 1m. 53.2s.
1949—James R. Grosholz, Haverford 1m. 53.3s.
1950—Philip Thigpen, Seton Hall ... 1m. 52.9s.
1951—Robert Mealey, Cornell ..... 1m. 53.2s.
1952—Lon Spurrier, California ..... 1m. 54.3s.
1953—Michael Stanley, Yale ...... 1m. 53.4s.
1954—Arnold Sowell, Pittsburgh ... 1m. 50.3s.
1955—Arnold Sowell, Pittsburgh ... 1m. 49.1s.
1956—Arnold Sowell, Pittsburgh ... 1m. 51.1s.
1957—Ron Delany, Villanova ...... 1m. 49.5s.
1958—Ron Delany, Villanova ...... 1m. 50s.
1959—Edward Moran, Penn State ... 1m. 50.0s.
1960—Thomas Carroll, Yale ...... 1m. 51.9s.
1961—Jon Dante, Villanova ...... 1m. 55.5s.
1962—John Reilly, Georgetown .... 1m. 49.3s.
1963—Noel Carroll, Villanova ...... 1m. 52.4s.
1964—Tom Farrell, St. John's ..... 1m. 49.5s.
1965—Noel Carroll, Villanova ...... 1m. 50.9s.
1966—Rick Urbina, Georgetown ... 1m. 50.7s.
1967—Rick Urbina, Georgetown ... 1m. 50.0s.
1968—Bob Zieminski, Georgetown .. 1m. 48.3s.
1969—Byron Dyce, New York Univ. 1m. 47.4s.
1970—Andy O'Reilly, Villanova .... 1m. 49.7s.
1971—Rick Wohlhuter, Notre Dame . 1m. 49.0s.
1972—Marcelle Phillipe, Fordham .. 1m. 49.7s.
1973—Ken Schappert, Villanova .... 1m. 51.0s.

1-Mile Run

1,500 meters, 1933 through 1936.

1876—E.C. Stimson, Dartmouth ...4m. 58.5s.
1877—W. Bearns, Columbia ......5m. 33s.
1878—M. Paton, Princeton ......5m. 4 3/4s.
1879—C.H. Trask Jr., Columbia ...5m. 24.6s.
1880—Theodore Cuyler, Yale .....4m. 37.6s.
1881—Theodore Cuyler, Yale .....4m. 40 7/8s.
1882—G.B. Morison, Harvard .....4m. 40 7/8s.
1883—G.B. Morison, Harvard .....4m. 38.6s.
1884—R. Faries, Pennsylvania ....4m. 45.2s.
1885—R. Faries, Pennsylvania ....4m. 46.8s.
1886—R. Faries, Pennsylvania ....4m. 38.8s.
1887—W. Harmer, Yale ....4m. 36.8s.
1888—W. Harmer, Yale ....4m. 37.2s.
1889—C.O. Wells, Amherst ......4m. 29.8s.
1890—C.O. Wells, Amherst ......4m. 35.4s.
1891—F.F. Carr, Harvard ....4m. 34.4s.
1892—G. Lowell, Harvard ....4m. 33.4s.
1893—G.O. Jarvis, Wesleyan ......4m. 34.6s.
1894—G.O. Jarvis, Wesleyan ......4m. 26.8s.
1895—G.W. Orton, Pennsylvania ...4m. 23.4s.
1896—G.O. Jarvis, Wesleyan ......4m. 28.8s.
1897—G.W. Orton, Pennsylvania ..4m. 25s.
1898—J.F. Cregan, Princeton .....4m. 23.6s.
1899—J.F. Cregan, Princeton .....4m. 25.2s.
1900—J.F. Cregan, Princeton .....4m. 24.4s.
1901—H.B. Clark, Harvard ....4m. 31.2s.
1902—R.E. Williams, Princeton ....4m. 29.2s.
1903—W.A. Colwell, Harvard .....4m. 30.6s.
1904—D.C. Munson, Cornell ......4m. 25.6s.
1905—D.C. Munson, Cornell ......4m. 25.2s.
1906—G. Haskins, Pennsylvania ...4m. 29.2s.
1907—G. Haskins, Pennsylvania ...4m. 20.6s.

1908—J.P. Halstead, Cornell .... 4m. 30s.
1909—W.C. Paul, Pennsylvania ..... 4m. 17.8s.
1910—P.J. Taylor, Cornell .... 4m. 23.4s.
1911—J.P. Jones, Cornell .... 4m. 15.4s.
1912— J.P. Jones, Cornell .... 4m. 20.6s.
        N.S. Taber, Brown ....
1913—J.P. Jones, Cornell .... 4m. 14.4s.
1914—C.L. Speiden, Cornell .... 4m. 20.2s.
1915—I.D. Mackensie, Princeton .... 4m. 22.8s.
1916—L.V. Windnagle, Cornell ..... 4m. 15s.
1917—No competition
1918—W.G. Kleinspehn, Lafayette .. 4m. 24s.
1919—D.F. O'Connell, Harvard ..... 4m. 23.6s.
1920—M.L. Shields, Penn State ..... 4m. 22.4s.
1921—J.J. Connolly, Georgetown ... 4m. 17.2s.
1922—M.L. Shields, Penn State ..... 4m. 18.4s.
1923—E.B. Kirby, Cornell .... 4m. 17.8s.
1924—S.C. Enck, Penn State .... 4m. 23.8s.
1925—Ellsworth C. Haggerty, Harvard 4m. 25.7s.
1926—Ellsworth C. Haggerty, Harvard 4m. 24s.
1927—William J. Cox, Penn State ... 4m. 21.2s.
1928—Ralph G. Luttman, Harvard .. 4m. 25.4s.
1929—Joseph J. Hickey, New York U 4m. 21.4s.
1930—George Bullwinkle, C.C.N.Y. . 4m. 18.8s.
1931—Norwood P. Hallowell, Harvard 4m. 18s.
1932—Joseph R. Mangan, Cornell ... 4m. 14.8s.
1933—William R. Bonthron,
        Princeton .... 3m. 54s.
1934—William R. Bonthron, Princeton 3m. 56s.
1935—Eugene G. Venzke, Pennsylvania 3m. 57.9s.
1936—Eugene G. Venzke, Pennsylvania 3m. 58.8s.
1937—Louis P. Burns, Manhattan ... 4m. 16.9s.
1938—Edgar H. Borck, Manhattan ... 4m. 13.9s.
1939—Louis S. Zamperini, Southern
        California .... 4m. 11.2s.
1940—Leslie MacMitchell, New York U.4m. 19.4s.
1941—Leslie MacMitchell, New York U.4m. 16s.
1942—Leslie MacMitchell, New York U.4m. 12.2s.
1943—Donald L. Burnham, Dartmouth 4m. 18.2s.
1944—Donald L. Burnham, Dartmouth 4m. 17.8s.
1945—Rudolph Simms, New York U. 4m. 29.4s.
1946—Edward J. Walsh, Manhattan .. 4m. 12.3s.
1947—Gerald T. Karver, Penn State .. 4m. 12.7s.
1948—Gerald T. Karver, Penn State .. 4m. 17.5s.
1949—Neil E. Pratt, Syracuse ...... 4m. 16.4s.
1950—George Wade, Yale .... 4m. 10.3s.
1951—Fred Dwyer, Villanova ...... 4m. 15.4s.
1952—Joseph LaPierre, Georgetown . 4m. 12.4s.
1953—Lewis Olive, Army .... 4m. 11s.
1954—Richard Ollen, Northeastern .. 4m. 15.4s.
1955—Burr Grim, Maryland .... 4m. 09.9s.
1956—Ron Delany, Villanova ...... 4m. 14.4s.
1957—Ron Delany, Villanova ...... 4m. 08.4s.
1958—Ron Delany, Villanova ...... 4m. 07.8s.
1959—Edward Moran, Penn State ... 4m. 09.3s.
1960—Richard Englenbrink, Penn
        State .... 4m. 09.1s.
1961—Steven Paranya, Wesleyan .... 4m. 15.9s.
1962—Mark Mullin, Harvard .... 4m. 06.4s.
1963—Pat Traynor, Villanova ...... 4m. 07.4s.
1964—Dave Farley, Brown .... 4m. 06.6s.
1965—Jim Warner, Army .... 4m. 08.0s.

1966—Dave Patrick, Villanova ...... 4m. 08.6s.
1967—Dave Patrick, Villanova ...... 4m. 04.9s.
1968—Dave Patrick, Villanova ...... 3m. 56.8s.
1969—Martin Liquori, Villanova .... 4m. 03.4s.
1970—Martin Liquori, Villanova .... 3m. 58.5s.
1971—Martin Liquori, Villanova .... 4m. 00.4s.
1972—Mike Keogh, Manhattan ..... 4m. 01.6s.
1973—Tony Colon, Manhattan ..... 4m. 03.4s.

2-Mile Run

3,000 meters, 1933 through 1936.

1899—Alex Grant, Pennsylvania .... 10m. 3.4s.
1900—Alex Grant, Pennsylvania .... 9m. 51.6s.
1901—B.A. Gallagher, Cornell ...... 10m.
1902—A.C. Bowen, Pennsylvania ... 9m. 57s.
1903—W.E. Schutt, Cornell .... 9m. 40s.
1904—W.E. Schutt, Cornell .... 9m. 47.6s.
1905—H.J. Hail, Yale .... 9m. 50.6s.
1906—C.F. Magoffin, Cornell ...... 9m. 56s.
1907—Floyd A. Rowe, Michigan .... 9m. 34.8s.
1908—H.L. Trube, Cornell .... 9m. 56s.
1909—P.J. Taylor, Cornell .... 9m. 27.6s.
1910—T.S. Berna, Cornell .... 9m. 40.6s.
1911—T.S. Berna, Cornell .... 9m. 25.2s.
1912—P.R. Withington, Harvard .... 9m. 24.4s.
1913—W.M. McCurdy, Pennsylvania . 9m. 45.6s.
1914—J.S. Hoffmire, Cornell .... 9m. 23.8s.
1915—D.F. Potter, Cornell .... 9m. 27.2s.
1916—D.F. Potter, Cornell .... 9m. 32.4s.
1917—No competition
1918—I.C. Dresser, Cornell .... 9m. 42.8s.
1919—I.C. Dresser, Cornell .... 9m. 22.4s.
1920—H.H. Brown, Williams ...... 9m. 27.6s.
1921—R.C. Brown, Cornell .... 9m. 32s.
1922—W. Higgins, Columbia ...... 9m. 28.2s.
1923—V.H. Booth, Johns Hopkins .. 9m. 35.8s.
1924—V.H. Booth, Johns Hopkins .. 9m. 36s.
1925—Willard L. Tibbetts, Harvard .. 9m. 26.6s.
1926—Willard L. Tibbetts, Harvard .. 9m. 27.8s.
1927—Charles R. Payne, Pennsylvania 9m. 25.8s.
1928—James L. Reid, Harvard ...... 9m. 42s.
1929—James L. Reid, Harvard ...... 9m. 22s.
1930—Joseph W. Hagen, Columbia .. 9m. 26.8s.
1931—Joseph P. McCluskey, Fordham 9m. 26.6s.
1932—Joseph P. McCluskey, Fordham 9m. 22.2s.
1933—John J. Ryan, Manhattan .... 8m. 36.4s.
1934—Frank A. Crowley, Manhattan . 8m. 39.3s.
1935—Edwin C. Veysey, Colby ..... 8m. 41.5s.
1936—Herbert H. Cornell, Cornell ... 8m. 47.4s.
1937—Howard W. Welch, Cornell ... 9m. 28.4s.
1938—Joseph P. Moclair, Manhattan . 9m. 21.2s.
1939—Albert M. Boulanger, Pittsburgh 9m. 23s.
1940—Andrew E. Neidnig, Manhattan 9m. 18.4s.
1941—Robert Nichols, R.I. State .... 9m. 26.1s.
1942—Robert Nichols, R.I. State .... 9m. 22.9s.
1943—Curtis C. Stone, Penn State ... 9m. 27s.
1944—Clark V. Judge, Dartmouth ... 9m. 39.5s.
1945—John F. Kandl, Cornell ...... 9m. 45.4s.
1946—Frank Martin, New York U. .. 9m. 29.5s.
1947—Curtis C. Stone, Penn State ... 9m. 11.8s.
1948—Horace Ashenfelter, Penn State 9m. 13.2s.
1949—Horace Ashenfelter, Penn State 9m. 9.2s.

1950—Robert Black, Rhode Island
    State . . . . 9m. 16.7s.
1951—John Joe Barry, Villanova . . . . 9m. 24.3s.
1952—Charles Capozzoli, Georgetown 9m. 17.1s.
1953—Charles Capozzoli, Georgetown 9m. 0.2s.
1954—Robert Hollen, Penn State . . . 9m. 22.1s.
1955—George King, N.Y.U. . . . . 9m. 15.7s.
1956—Alex Breckenridge, Villanova . 9m. 20.1s.
1957—Lewis Stieglitz, Connecticut . . 9m. 5.6s.
1958—Crawford Kennedy,
    Michigan State . . . . 9m. 13.5s.
1959—Richard Englebrink, Penn
    State . . . . 9m. 08.9s.

3-Mile Run

1960—Robert Lowe, Brown . . . . 14m. 12.6s.
1961—Robert Lowe, Brown . . . . 14m. 11.8s.
1962—Gerry Norman, Penn State . . . 14m. 20.2s.
1963—Vic Zwolak, Villanova . . . . . . 14m. 05.9s.
1964—Vic Zwolak, Villanova . . . . . . 13m. 53.0s.
1965—Larry Furnell, St. John's . . . . . 13m. 50.6s.
1966—Paul Perry, Georgetown . . . . . 14m. 00.9s.
1967—Steve Stageberg, Georgetown . 13m. 57.2s.
1968—Steve Stageberg, Georgetown . 13m. 32.6s.
1969—Jerry Richey, Pittsburgh . . . . . 13m. 41.4s.
1970—Dick Buerkle, Villanova . . . . . 13m. 34.2s.
1971—Gregory Fredericks, Penn State 13m. 41.2s.
1972—John Hartnett, Villanova . . . . 13m. 42.8s.
1973—Mike Keogh, Manhattan . . . . . 13m. 25.2s.

6-Mile Run

1970—Dick Buerkle, Villanova . . . . . 28m. 34.7s.
1971—Gregory Fredericks, Penn State 28m. 23.8s.
1972—Gregory Fredericks, Penn State 27m. 54.3s.
1973—John Hartnett, Villanova

120-Yard High Hurdles

  100 meters, 1933 through 1936.

1876—W.J. Wakeman, Yale . . . . 18 1/4s.
1877—H. Stevens, Princeton . . . . 18.5s.
1878—J.W. Pryor, Columbia . . . . 21.6s.
1879—J.E. Cowdin, Harvard . . . . 19.2s.
1880—H.B. Strong, Lehigh . . . . 19.5s.
1881—R.T. Morrow, Lehigh . . . . 18 7/8s.
1882—J.F. Jenkins Jr., Columbia . . . . . . 17.6s.
1883—O. Harriman Jr., Princeton . . . . . . 18s.
1884—R. Mulford, Columbia . . . . 17.5s.
1885—W.H. Ludington, Yale . . . . 19.2s.
1886—W.H. Ludington, Yale . . . . 17s.
1887—W.H. Ludington, Yale . . . . 17.4s.
1888—H. Mapes, Columbia . . . . 17.2s.
1889—H. Mapes, Columbia . . . . 16.8s.
1890—H.L. Williams, Yale . . . . 16.2s.
1891—H.L. Williams, Yale . . . . 15.8s.
1892—H.T. Harding, Columbia . . . . 16s.
1893—McL. Van Ingen, Yale . . . . 16.4s.
1894—E.H. Cady, Yale . . . . 16s.
1895—S. Chase, Dartmouth . . . . 15.8s.
1896—E.C. Perkins, Yale . . . . 16.2s.
1897—E.C. Perkins, Yale . . . . 16s.
1898—A.C. Kraenzlein, Pennsylvania . . . 16.6s.
1899—A.C. Kraenzlein, Pennsylvania . . . 15.4s.
1900—A.C. Kraenzlein, Pennsylvania . . . 15.4s.

1901—E.J. Clapp, Yale . . . . 16.2s.
1902—J.H. Converse, Harvard . . . . 15.6s.
1903—E.J. Clapp, Yale . . . . 15.6s.
1904—E.J. Clapp, Yale . . . . 15.8s.
1905—E.S. Amsler, Pennsylvania . . . . . . 15.6s.
1906—J.H. Hubbard, Amherst . . . . 15.8s.
1907—J.C. Garrels, Michigan . . . . 15.2s.
1908—A.B. Shaw, Dartmouth . . . . 15.6s.
1909—L.V. Howe, Yale . . . . 15.4s.
1910—G.A. Chisholm, Yale . . . . 16s.
1911—G.A. Chisholm, Yale . . . . 15.4s.
1912—J.I. Wendell, Wesleyan . . . . 15.6s.
1913—J.I. Wendell, Wesleyan . . . . 15.4s.
1914—G.A. Braun, Dartmouth . . . . 15.6s.
1915—R.B. Ferguson, Pennsylvania . . . . 15.4s.
1916—Fred S. Murray, Stanford . . . . 15s.
1917—No competition
1918—C.R. Erdman, Princeton . . . . 15.4s.
1919—Walker Smith, Cornell . . . . 15.2s.
1920—E.J. Thomson, Dartmouth . . . . . . 14.4s.
1921—E.J. Thomson, Dartmouth . . . . . . 14.8s.
1922—C.R. Hauers, Harvard . . . . 15.3s.
1923—S.H. Thomson, Princeton . . . . . . 15.5s.
1924—C.W. Moore, Penn State . . . . 15.2s.
1925—Leighton W. Dye, Southern Calif. 14.8s.
1926—Leighton W. Dye, Southern Calif. 14.7s.
1927—Eber M. Wells, Dartmouth . . . . . 14.8s.
1928—J. Ross Nichols, Stanford . . . . 15.1s.
1929—John S. Collier, Brown . . . . 14.6s.
1930—Eugene E. Record, Harvard . . . . . 14.8s.
1931—Eugene E. Record, Harvard . . . . . 14.6s.
1932—Eugene E. Record, Harvard . . . . . 15s.
1933—Robert C. Lyon, So. California . 14.8s.
1934—Philip G. Good, Bowdoin . . . . 15.1s.
1935—Philip F. Cope, So. California . . . 14.5s.
1936—John M. Donovan, Dartmouth . . . 14.8s.
1937—John M. Donovan, Dartmouth . . . 14.8s.
1938—Harvey H. Woodstra, Mich. State 14.4s.
1939—James W. Humphrey, So. Calif. . . 14.4s.
1940—Edward Dugger, Tufts . . . . 14.3s.
1941—Edward Dugger, Tufts . . . . 14.1s.
1942—George Gilson, Holy Cross . . . . . . 14.6s.
1943—Thomas H. Todd Jr., Virginia . . . . 14.9s.
1944—Robert H. Banks, Navy . . . . 15.3s.
1945—Clyde L. Scott, Navy . . . . 14.8s.
1946—Joseph F. Conley, Dartmouth . . . 15s.
1947—Sherwood H. Finley, Yale . . . . . . 14.6s.
1948—Paige W. Christiansen, Mich. State 14.9s.
1949—Horace Smith, Michigan State . . . 14.3s.
1950—James Gehrdes, Penn State . . . . . 14.4s.
1951—Walter Ashbaugh, Cornell . . . . . . 14.4s.
1952—Peter McCreary, Dartmouth . . . . 14.5s.
1953—Walter Monahan, Pittsburgh . . . . 14.7s.
1954—Joel Shankle, Duke . . . . 14.3s.
1955—Joel Shankle, Duke . . . . 14.1s.
1956—Rod Perry, Penn State . . . . 14.3s.
1957—Rod Perry, Penn State . . . . 14.2s.
1958—Joel Landau, Harvard . . . . 14.2s.
1959—William Johnson, Maryland . . . . . 14.6s.
1960—Leon Pras, Villanova . . . . 14.1s.
1961—William Johnson, Maryland . . . . . 14.8s.
1962—Leon Pras, Villanova . . . . 14.2s.

1963—Chris Stauffer, Maryland .... 14.4s.
1964—John Bethea, Morgan State ..... 14.3s.
1965—Larry Livers, Villanova .... 14.2s.
1966—David Hemery, Boston U. ...... 14.1s.
1967—Ervin Hall, Villanova .... 14.1s.
1968—Erv Hall, Villanova .... 13.5s.
1969—Erv Hall, Villanova .... 13.9s.
1970—Kwaku Ohene-Frempong, Yale ... 14.0s.
1971—Tom McMannon, Notre Dame ... 13.9s.
1972—Tom McMannon, Notre Dame ... 13.7s.
1973—Charles Dobson, William & Mary . 13.8s.

220-Yard Low Hurdles

200 meters, 1933 through 1936.

1888—C.S. Mandel, Harvard .... 26.8s.
1889—Herbert Mapes, Columbia ...... 26.4s.
1890—J.P. Lee, Harvard .... 25.25s.
1891—H.L. Williams, Yale .... 25.2s.
1892—G.R. Fearing Jr., Harvard ...... 25.4s.
1893—McL. Van Ingen, Yale .... 26.8s.
1894—J.L. Bremer Jr., Harvard .... 25.2s.
1895—J.L. Bremer Jr., Harvard ...... 24.6s.
1896—J.L. Bremer Jr., Harvard ...... 25s.
1897—E.C. Perkins, Yale .... 25.8s.
1898—A.C. Kraenzlein, Pennsylvania ... 23.6s.
1899—A.C. Kraenzlein, Pennsylvania ... 23.8s.
1900—A.C. Kraenzlein, Pennsylvania ... 25.2s.
1901—E.J. Clapp, Yale .... 25.4s.
1902—J.G. Willis, Harvard .... 23.8s.
1903—E.J. Clapp, Yale .... 25.2s.
1904—E.J. Clapp, Yale .... 24.6s.
1905—F.R. Castleman, Colgate .... 24.8s.
1906—F.R. Castleman, Colgate .... 25.2s.
1907—J.C. Garrels, Michigan .... 24s.
1908—L.V. Howe, Yale 24.6s
1909—L.V. Howe, Yale .... 24.4s.
1910—G.P. Gardner, Harvard .... 24.4s.
1911—G.A. Chisholm, Yale .... 24.6s.
1912—J.B. Craig, Michigan .... 24.2s.
1913—J.I. Wendell, Wesleyan .... 23.6s.
1914—R.B. Ferguson, Pennsylvania .... 25.2s.
1915—A.W. Stewart, Princeton .... 24.4s.
1916—Fred S. Murray, Stanford .... 24s.
1917—No competition
1918—C.R. Erdman, Princeton .... 24.4s.
1919—Walker Smith, Cornell .... 24.2s.
1920—W.B. Wells, Stanford .... 23.8s.
1921—E.J. Thomson, Dartmouth ..... 24.4s.
1922—J.C. Taylor, Princeton .... 23.9s.
1923—J.C. Taylor, Princeton .... 23.8s.
1924—R. Haas, Georgetown .... 24.5s.
1925—Kenneth D. Grumbles, So. Calif. 24s.
1926—Kenneth D. Grumbles, So. Calif. *23.4s.
1927—Henry G. Steinbrenner, M.I.T. ... 23.9s.
1928—Sidney B. Kieselhorst, Yale ..... 24.9s.
1929—Sidney B. Kieselhorst, Yale .....*23.3s.
1930—William H. Carls, So. California .. 23.7s.
1931—Ernest A. Payne, Southern Calif. 23.6s.
1932—Harold L. Fates, Yale .... 23.8s.
1933—Alden L. Herbert, Stanford ..... 23.4s.
1934—Samuel C. Klopstock, Stanford .. 23.2s.
1935—James H. Hucker, Cornell ...... 23.3s.

1936—John M. Donovan, Dartmouth ... 23.9s.
1937—James H. Hucker, Cornell ...... 23.2s.
1938—Harvey H. Woodstra, Mich. State 23.8s.
1939—Earl E. Vickery, Southern Calif.. 22.8s.
1940—Edward Dugger, Tufts .... 23.2s.
1941—Harold Stickel, Pittsburgh ...... 23s.
1942—Harold Stickel, Pittsburgh ...... 22.9s.
1943—Warren Halliburton, New York U. 24.1s.
1944—Jerry W. Morrow, Army .... 24.4s.
1945—Jerry W. Morrow, Army .... 23.7s.
1946—Alan A. Snyder, Dartmouth ..... 24.4s.
1947—Fred D. Johnson, Michigan State . 23.7s.
1948—Jeffrey Kirk, Pennsylvania ...... 23.4s.
1949—Horace Smith, Michigan State ... 22.9s.
1950—James Gehrdes, Penn State ..... 23.2s.
1951—Meredith Gourdine, Cornell ..... 23.7s.
1952—Laurence Johnson, Army .... 23.7s.
1953—Charles Pratt, Manhattan ...... 24.1s.
1954—Lester Goble, Alfred .... 23.3s.
1955—Charles Pratt, Manhattan ...... 23s.
1956—Vic Gavin, La Salle .... 23.1s.
1957—Rod Perry, Penn State .... 22.9s.
1958—Joel Landau, Harvard .... 22.9s.
1959—Robert Szeyller, Penn State ..... 23.1s.
* With wind.

440-Yard Hurdles

1960—James Moreland, Brown .... 52.6s.
1961—Jay Luck, Yale .... 53.1s.
1962—Jay Luck, Yale .... 51.7s.
1963—Chris Stauffer, Maryland ...... 51.5s.
1964—Vince McArdle, Manhattan ..... 51.6s.
1965—Tony Lynch, Harvard .... 51.5s.
1966—Richard Johnston, Colgate ..... 51.8s.
1967—Andy Bell, American .... 52.2s.
1968—Dave Hemery, Boston Univ...... 50.4s.
1969—John Hanley, Rutgers .... 51.5s.
1970—Rich Weaver, P.M.C. .... 51.6s.
1971—James Elwell, Temple .... 51.4s.
1972—Bruce Collins, Penn .... 50.9s.
1973—Bruce Collins, Penn .... 51.3s.

440-Yard Relay

1968—Villanova (Dave Fender, Hardage Davis, Erv Hall, Larry James) .... 41.0s.
1969—Yale (Jon Kastendieck, Earl Downing, Melvin Currie, Don Martin)...................... 41.0s.
1970—Maryland (Marv Bush, Marshall Bush, Tyrone Brown, Ralph Jones) 41.2s.
1971—Penn (Marc Newfeld, William Wilson, Fred Samara, Roy Supulski) . 40.9s.
1972—Penn (Bornie Gansle, Bill Wilson, Don Clume, Irv Granum) .... 41.1s.
1973—Adelphi (Kel Siegel, Rich Hardware, Kerry Streets, Dennis Walker) 41.0s.

1-Mile Relay

1939—Southern California (Louis S. Zamperini, Arthur G. Reading, Howard D. Upton, Erwin F. Miller) 3m.19.6s.
1940—N.Y.U. (Stanford Braun,

George Hagans, Harold Bogrow, James B. Herbert) .... 3m. 16s.

1941—N.Y.U. (Stanford Braun, Leslie MacMitchell, George Hagans, Harold Bogrow) .... 3m. 16.4s.

1942—Colgate (John Hall, Thomas Keith, George Tifft, Alfred Diebolt) 3m. 20s.

1943—N.Y.U. (Arthur Herrforth, Walter Welsch, Charles Grohsberger, Frank Cotter) .... 3m. 30.4s.

1944—Army (William E. Whittington, Bernard E. Conor, Robert O. Conrad, George C. Berger) .... 3m. 18.9s.

1945—Navy (Frederic G. Bouwman, Minot Simons, Arthur C. Bigley, William B. Kash) .... 3m. 29.8s.

1946—Navy (Frederic G. Bouwman, James J. Garibaldi, Arthur C. Bigley, William B. Kash) .... 3m. 18.6s.

1947—Army (Michael DeArmond, Charles Nash, James Egger, Jack Hammack) .... 3m. 14s.

1948—Seton Hall (Reginald Marshall, George Stafurick, Philip Thigpen, Frank Fox) .... 3m. 15.1s.

1949—N.Y.U. (John J. Nelson, Hugo V. Maiocco, James F. Gilhooley, Reginald Pearman) .... 3m. 14.4s.

1950—N.Y.U. (Richard Maiocco, Robert Hatch, Hugo V. Maiocco, Reginald Pearman) .... 3m. 13.7s.

1951—Seton Hall (Dale Evans, Charles Slade, Robert Carter, Morris Curotta) ta) .... 3m. 14.5s.

1952—Manhattan (Wallace Pina, Ron Ferraro, Louis Jones, Vernon Dixon) .... 3m. 15.9s.

1953—Columbia (Roy Williams, Stephen Passloff, Rudy Clarence, Fred Schlereth) .... 3m. 15.8s.

1954—Manhattan (Bob English, Ron Lucas, Vern Dixon, Louis Jones) .. 3m. 12.1s.

1955—Villanova (James Moran, Gene Maliff, Al Peterson, Charles Jenkins) 3m. 15.2s.

1956—Villanova (Gene Maliff, Al Peterson, Roland Simpson, Charles Jenkins) .... 3m. 14.9s.

1957—Manhattan (Gerald Ryan, Dennis Burbridge, Ralph Diaz, Dick Simmons) .... 3m. 13.1s.

1958—Manhattan (Thomas Murphy, Ronald Colino, Ralph Diaz, Joseph Soprano) .... 3m. 13.9s.

1959—Manhattan (William Lenskold, Kye Courtney, Ronald Colino, Arthur Evans) .... 3m. 15.0s.

1960—Villanova (Joseph Manion, Carl Wagner, Nicholas DeAngelis, Robert Raemore) .... 3m. 12.0s.

1961—Fordham (Peter Weiss, Thomas Kenney, Douglas Tynan, Frank Tomeo) .... 3m. 18.5s.

1962—Morgan State (John Bethea, Robert Bagley, Hubert Brown, Lawson Smart) .... 3m. 10.6s.

1963—Morgan State (John Bethea, Bob Bagley, Hubert Brown, Nick Lee) .... 3m. 11.7s.

1964—Morgan State (Herman Hawthorn, Bob Bagley, Hubert Brown, Nick Lee) .... 3m. 10.3s.

1965—Morgan State (Dennis Edgehill, Herman Hawthorne, Tim Johnson, Nick Lee) .... 3m. 10.8s.

1966—Morgan State (Herman Hawthorn, Tim Johnson, Mal Brown, Ray Pollard) .... 3m. 13.4s.

1967—(tie)—Yale (Charles Hobbs, Larry Kreider, Steve Bittner, Mark Young) .... 3m. 09.7s.
Villanova (Hal Nichter, Bill Grant, Ken Prince, Bill Heidelberger) ... 3m. 09.7s.

1968—Villanova (Hardage Davis, Hal Nichter, Ken Prince, Larry James) . 3m. 09.1s.

1969—Villanova (Rene Schlag, Lamotte Hyman, Larry James, Hardage Davis) .... 3m. 11.1s.

1970—Villanova (Greg Govan, Martin Liquori, Hardage Davis, Lamotte Hy Hyman) .... 3m. 10.1s.

1971—Adelphi (Ray Lee, Warren Lyons, Keith Davis, Clyde McPherson) 3m. 10.9s.

1972—Navy (Gene Watson, Roger Brueckgauer, John Phelan, Rich Brilla) .... 3m. 11.8s.

3,000 Meter Steeplechase

1960—Robert Lows, Brown .... 9m. 35.0s.
1961—Patrick Traynor, Villanova ... 9m. 25.3s.
1962—Patrick Traynor, Villanova ... 9m. 19.1s.
1963—Pat Traynor, Villanova ...... 9m. 19.7s.
1964—Vic Zwolak, Villanova ...... 9m. 25.7s.
1965—Bill Norris, Boston College ... 9m. 16.3s.
1966—Bill Norris, Boston College ... 9m. 07.7s.
1967—Bill Norris, Boston College ... 9m. 16.5s.
1968—Terry Donnelly, William & Mary .... 8m. 46.2s.
1969—Thomas Donnelly, Villanova .. 8m. 50.9s.
1970—Des McCormack, Villanova ... 8m. 46.1s.
1971—W. Joseph Lucas, Georgetown . 8m. 53.8s.
1972—Bob Childs, Penn .... 8m. 49.0s.
1973—John Hartnett, Villanova .... 8m. 54.2s.

High Jump

1876—J.W. Pryor, Columbia .... 5ft. 4 in.
1877—H.L. Geyelin, Penn .... 4ft. 11 in.
1878—J.P. Conover, Columbia ..... 5ft. 61/2 in.
1879—J.P. Conover, Columbia ..... 5ft. 8 1/4 in.
1880—A.C. Denniston, Harvard .... 5ft. 1 1/4 in.
1881—W. Soren, Harvard .... 5ft. 2 3/4 in.
1882—W. Soren, Harvard .... 5ft. 6 in.
1883—C.H. Atkinson, Harvard ..... 5ft. 8 1/2 in.
1884—C.H. Atkinson, Harvard ..... 5ft. 9 3/4 in.
1885—W.B. Page Jr., Penn. .... 5ft. 11 5/8 in.

1886—W.H. Page Jr., Penn. . . . . 5ft. 11 3/4 in.
1887—W.B. Page Jr., Penn. . . . . 5ft. 7 1/2 in.
1888—I.D. Webster, Penn . . . . 5ft. 11 1/2 in.
1889—I.D. Webster, Penn . . . . 5ft. 6 3/4 in.
1890—G.R. Fearing Jr., Harvard . . . . 5ft. 8 1/4 in.
1891—G.R. Fearing Jr., Harvard . . . . 6ft.
1892—G.R. Fearing Jr., Harvard . . . . . 6ft. 1/2 in.
1893—G.R. Fearing Jr., Harvard . . . 5ft. 10 3/4 in.
1894—C.J. Paine Jr., Harvard . . . . 5ft. 10 1/2 in.
1895—N.T. Leslie, Penn. . . . . 6ft. 1 in.
1896—J.D. Winsor Jr., Penn. . . . . 6ft. 1 in.
1897—J.D. Winsor Jr., Penn. . . . . 6ft. 3 in.
1898—W.G. Morse, Harvard . . . .
    C.U. Powell, Cornell . . . .
    A.N. Rice, Harvard . . . .
    J.D. Winsor Jr., Penn . . . . . . 5ft. 11 1/8 in.
1899—I.K. Baxter, Penn. . . . . 6ft. 2 in.
1900—S.S. Jones, New York Univ. . 5ft. 10 1/2 in.
1901—S.S. Jones, New York Univ. . . 5ft. 9 1/2 in.
1902—W.C. Low, Syracuse . . . . 5ft. 11 in.
1903—R.P. Kernan, Harvard . . . . 6ft. 1 in.
1904—W.C. Lowe, Syracuse . . . . 5ft. 11 in.
1905—J.W. Marshall, Yale . . . . 6ft.
1906—J.W. Marshall, Yale . . . . 5ft. 11 in.
1907—T. Moffit, Penn . . . . 6ft. 3 1/4 in.
1908—R.G. Harwood, Harvard . . . .
    E.R. Palmer, Dartmouth . . . . 5ft. 6 1/2 in.
1909—R.G. Harwood, Harvard . . . .
    R.P. Pope, Harvard . . . .
    S.C. Lawrence, Harvard . . . .
    E.R. Palmer, Dartmouth . . . .
    W. Canfield, Yale . . . . 5ft. 11 1/4 in.
1910—J.W. Burdick, Penn. . . . . 6ft. 1 in.
1911—J.W. Burdick, Penn. . . . .
    G.C. Farrier, Penn. . . . .
    P.W. Dalrymple, M.I.T. . . . . .6ft.
1912—J.W. Burdick, Penn. . . . . 6ft. 3/4 in.
1913—E. Beeson, California . . . .
    J.B. Camp, Harvard . . . . 6ft. 1/8 in.
1914—W.M. Oler Jr., Yale* . . . . 6ft. 2 in.
1915—W.M. Oler Jr., Yale . . . . 6ft. 4 1/2 in.
1916—W.M. Oler Jr., Yale . . . . 6ft. 2 1/4 in.
1917—No competition
1918—M. Firor, Johns Hopkins . . . 5ft. 11 3/8 in.
1919—R.W. Landon, Yale . . . . 6ft. 2 in.
1920—R.W. Landon, Yale . . . . 6ft. 4 in.
1921—H.P. Muller, California . . . .
    R.W. Landon, Yale . . . . 6ft. 3 1/2 in.
1922—Leroy T. Brown, Dartmouth . 6ft. 4 5/8 in.
1923—Leroy T. Brown, Dartmouth . 6ft. 3 3/4 in.
1924—C.T. Flahive, Boston College . 6ft. 2 5/8 in.
1925—Oather L. Hampton, California . . .
    Groverman Blake, Princeton . 6ft. 3 1/8 in.
1926—Robert W. King, Stanford . . . 6ft. 5 3/4 in.
1927—Thomas L. Maynard,
    Dartmouth . . . . 6ft. 4 1/2in.
1928—Robert W. King, Stanford . . . . .6ft.
1929—Benjamin Van D. Hedges,
    Princeton . . . . 6ft. 2 1/2 in.
1930—William B. O'Connor, Columbia . . 6ft. 3in.
1931—William B. O'Connor, Columbia . . 6ft. 5in.
1932—William B. O'Connor, Columbia . .

    Robert L. Van Osdel, So. California 6ft. 4in.
1933—George B. Spitz Jr., N.Y.U. . . 6ft. 6 1/8in.
1934—George B. Spitz Jr., N.Y.U. . . 6ft. 3 1/2in.
1935—Charles R. Scott, Cornell . . . .
    James R. Thomson, M.I.T. . . . . . . 6ft. 3in.
1936—Peter C. Bennett, Pittsburgh . . . . 6ft. 3in.
1937—Edward T. Burke, Marquette . 6ft. 5 1/8in.
1938—Delos P. Thurber,
    So. California . . . . 6ft. 6 5/8in.
1939—Walter A. Arrington, Michigan State
    Clarke Mallery, So. California
    John M. Wilson, So. California . . . 6ft. 4in.
1940—Arthur F. Byrnes, Manhattan . 6ft. 5 1/4in.
1941—Gilbert A. Peters, Colby . . . . 6ft. 4in.
1942—A. Richmond Morcom, New
    Hampshire . . . . 6ft. 4 1/8in.
1943—A. Richmond Morcom, New
    Hampshire . . . . 6ft. 4in.
1944—Benjamin Martin, Navy . . . . 6ft. 1in.
1945—Joseph F. Conley, Dartmouth . . . 6ft. 3in.
1946—Denneth Wiesner, Marquette . 6ft. 6 3/4in.
1947—George E. Heddy, Colgate . . . . . . 6ft. 5in.
1948—Irving Mondschein, N.Y.U. . . 6ft. 6 7/8in.
1949—Irving Mondschein, N.Y.U. . . . . . .
    Richard B. Phillips, Brown . . . 6ft. 7 7/8in.
1950—Robert Jachens, Trinity . . . . . 6ft. 6 3/8in.
1951—Richard Lyster, Temple . . . . 6ft. 5in.
1952—James Webb, La Salle . . . . 6ft. 5 1/2in.
1953—James Herb, Pen State . . . . . . 6ft. 3 1/4in.
1954—Frank Gaffney, Manhattan . . . . .
    John Bennett, Marquette . . . . 6ft. 4 3/4in.
1955—Wilfred Lee, Pennsylvania . . . 6ft. 6 1/2in.
1956—Phil Reavis, Villanova . . . . . . 6ft. 6 1/2in.
1957—Phil Reavis, Villanova . . . . 6ft. 8in.
1958—Phil Reavis, Villanova . . . . 6ft. 10in.
1959—Thomas Tait, Maryland . . . . 6ft. 4in.
1960—John Thomas, Boston Univ. . . 7ft. 1 1/2in.
1961—John Thomas, Boston Univ. . . . . . 6ft. 5in.
1962—John Thomas, Boston Univ. . . 6ft. 9 3/4in.
1963—Sam Streibert, Yale . . . . 6ft. 5in.
1964—John Hartnett, Princeton . . . . 6ft. 6in.
1965—Frank Costello, Maryland . . . . . 6ft. 10in.
1966—Frank Costello, Maryland . . 6ft. 10 1/4in.
1967—Elijah Miller, Rutgers . . . . . . 6ft. 10 1/4in.
1968—Elijah Miller, Rutgers . . . . 7ft. 0in.
1969—Joseph David, Maryland . . . . . . 6ft. 10in.
1970—Joseph David, Maryland . . . . . . 6ft. 10in.
1971—Joseph David, Maryland . . . . 7ft. 0in.
1972—Chris Dunn, Colgate . . . . 7ft. 2in.
1973—Chris Dunn, Colgate . . . . . . 7ft. 1 1/2in.

*Name of competitor tying for 1st place stricken from records.

Broad Jump

1876—H.L. Willoughby, Penn . . . . 18ft. 3 1/2in.
1877—H.H. Lee, Penn . . . . 19ft. 7in.
1878—J.P. Conover, Columbia . . . . 19ft. 2 1/2in.
1879—J.P. Conover, Columbia . . . . 20ft.
1880—G.G. Thayer, Penn . . . . 20ft. 2in.
1881—J.F. Jenkins Jr., Columbia . . 20ft. 9 1/4in.
1882—J.F. Jenkins Jr., Columbia . . . . . . 20ft. 3in.
1883—W. Soren, Harvard . . . . 20ft. 6in.

1884—O. Bodelsen, Columbia .... 21ft. 3 1/2in.
1885—J.D. Bradley, Harvard .... 19ft. 6in.
1886—C.H. Mapes, Columbia ...... 20ft. 11in.
1887—T.G. Shearman Jr., Yale ..... 21ft. 11in.
1888—T.G. Shearman Jr., Yale ...... 20ft. 8in.
1889—T.G. Shearman Jr., Yale ..... 22ft. 6in.
1890—W.C. Dohm, Princeton .... 22ft. 3 1/2in.
1891—V. Mapes, Columbia ..... 22ft. 11 1/4in.
1892—E.B. Bloss, Harvard .... 22ft. 1 1/2in.
1893—E.B. Bloss, Harvard .... 22ft. 9 5/8in.
1894—E.S. Ramsdell, Penn .... 22ft. 1in.
1895—L.P. Sheldon, Yale .... 22ft. 8 1/2in.
1896—L.P. Sheldon, Yale .... 22ft. 3 1/4in.
1897—J.P. Remington, Penn ..... 22ft. 4 7/8in.
1898—M. Prinstein, Syracuse ..... 23ft. 7 3/8in.
1899—A.C. Kraenzlein, Penn ..... 24ft. 4 1/2in.
1900—M. Prinstein, Syracuse .... 23ft. 8in.
1901—C.W. Kennedy, Columbia .. 21ft. 6 3/5in.
1902—A.T. Foster, Amherst .... 21ft. 11in.
1903—W.P. Hubbard, Amherst ... 22ft. 4 5/8in.
1904—R.S. Stangland, Columbia .. 23ft. 6 1/2in.
1905—L.W. Simons, Princeton ... 23ft. 2 1/2in.
1906—W.F. Knox, Yale .... 23ft. 4 1/2in.
1907—W.F. Knox, Yale .... 22ft. 10in.
1908—E.T. Cook, Cornell .... 22ft. 8 1/2in.
1909—E.T. Cook, Cornell .... 22ft. 6 1/4in.
1910—E.M. Roberts, Amherst .... 22ft. 7 1/4in.
1911—R. Holden, Yale .... 22ft. 3 5/8in.
1912—E.L. Mercer, Penn .... 23ft. 10 1/2in.
1913—E.L. Mercer, Penn .... 23ft. 3 7/8in.
1914—P.G. Nordell, Dartmouth .. 22ft. 8 1/2in.
1915—H.T. Worthington, Dart-
         mouth .... 23ft. 9 1/4in.
1916—H.T. Worthington, Dartmouth 24ft. 1/4in.
1917—No competition
1918—R.K. Felter, Cornell .... 22ft. 6in.
1919—C.E. Johnson, Michigan .. 23ft. 10 1/2in.
1920—S.G. Landers, Penn .... 23ft. 8in.
1921—E.O. Gourdin, Harvard ... 23ft. 10 3/4in.
1922—R.L. Legendre, Georgetown 23ft. 7 1/8in.
1923—W.A. Comins, Yale .... 24ft. 4in.
1924—W.A. Comins, Yale .... 24ft. 8in.
1925—Bayes M. Norton, Yale ...... 23ft. 11in.
1926—William A. Dowding, George-
         town .... 23ft. 1 1/2in.
1927—Alfred H. Bates, Penn State . 24ft. 8 1/2in.
1928—Alfred H. Bates, Penn State 24ft. 10 3/8in.
1929—Jesse T. Hill, So. California ...25ft. 7/8in.
1930—Arnold J. West, Stanford ... 24ft. 7 3/8in.
1931—Richard A. Barber, So. Cali-
         fornia .... 25ft. 3 1/2in.
1932—Richard A. Barber, So. Cali-
         fornia .... 25ft. 1 3/4in.
1933—Henry M. Little, William and
         Mary .... 24ft. 4 1/4in.
1934—Robert H. Clark, California . 24ft. 8 1/4in.
1935—Albert R. Olson, So. Califor-
         nia .... 24ft. 10 3/8in.
1936—Milton G. Green, Harvard . 24ft. 9 1/8in.
1937—Benjamin W. Johnson, Col-
         umbia .... 23ft. 6 1/2in.
1938—Anson Perina, Princeton ... 24ft. 6 3/4in.

1939—Anson Perina, Princeton ....24ft. 5 3/4in.
1940—Norwood H. Ewell, Penn
         State ....23ft. 8 1/4in.
1941—Norwood H. Ewell, Penn
         State ....24ft. 2 3/4in.
1942—Norwood H. Ewell, Penn
         State ....24ft. 6 1/4in.
1943—A. Richmond Morcom, New
         Hampshire ....23ft. 10in.
1944—Frederic G. Bouwman, Navy .23ft. 2 1/2in.
1945—Frederic G. Bouwman, Navy .22ft. 5 1/2in.
1946—Herbert P. Douglas, Pitts-
         burgh .... 23ft. 11in.
1947—Fred D. Johnson, Mich. State 24ft. 7 3/8in.
1948—Fred D. Johnson, Mich. State 24ft. 1 5/8in.
1949—Fred D. Johnson, Mich. State . 24ft. 2in.
1950—Edgar Davis, Princeton ....24ft. 7 1/8in.
1951—Meredith Gourdine, Cornell 25ft. 9 3/4in.
1952—F. Morgan Taylor, Princeton 24ft. 3 1/2in.
1953—F. Morgan Taylor, Princeton 23ft. 6 1/2in.
1954—John Bennett, Marquette ..24ft. 7 1/2in.
1955—Joel Shankle, Duke .... 24ft. 8in.
1956—Len Moore, Manhattan ....23ft. 8 1/4in.
1957—Mike Herman, N.Y.U. ....24ft. 3 1/2in.
1958—John Buckley, Villanova .....25ft. 3/4in.
1959—John Buckley, Villanova ... 25ft. 6 1/2in.
1960—Robert Reed, Pennsylvania ...24ft. 1/2in.
1961—Calvin Glass, St. John's ....23ft. 5 1/4in.
1962—Robert Tatnall 23ft. 7 3/4in
1963—Dick Malberger, Holy Cross ... 24ft. 6in.
1964—Michael Cole, Maryland ... 24ft. 4 1/2in.
1965—Michael Cole, Maryland ... 24ft. 5 3/4in.
1966—Thomas Palkie, Navy ....23ft. 11 1/4in.
1967—Del Benjamin, Manhattan ..24ft. 3 1/2in.
1968—Del Benjamin, Manhattan . 24ft. 11 3/4in.
1969—Walter Jones, Cornell .....24ft. 7 1/4in.
1970—Noel Hare, Harvard ....24ft. 3 1/2in.
1971—William Rea, Pittsburgh ...25ft. 9 1/2in.
1972—William Rea, Pittsburgh ...25ft. 1 1/4in.

Pole Vault

1877—J.W. Pryor, Columbia .... 7ft. 4in.
1878—C. Fabrogou, C.C.N.Y. ....9ft.
1879—F.H. Lee, Columbia .... 9ft. 3in.
1880—R.B. Tewksbury, Princeton ..... 9ft. 4in.
1881—F.W. Dalrymple, Lehigh ...... 8ft. 9 in.
1882—W. Soren, Harvard .... 9ft. 6in.
1883—H.P. Toler, Princeton ....10ft.
1884—H.L. Hodge, Princeton ....9ft.
1885—L.D. Godshall, Lafayette .... 9ft. 7 1/4in.
1886—A. Stevens, Columbia ..... 10ft. 3 1/4in.
1887—L.D. Godshall, Lafayette ....10ft.
1888—T.G. Shearman Jr., Yale .... 9ft. 6in.
1889—R.G. Leavitt, Harvard ..... 10ft. 5 1/2in.
1890—E.D. Ryder, Yale ....
         H.F. Welch, Columbia .... 10ft. 7in.
1891—E.D. Ryder, Yale .... 10ft. 9 3/4in.
1892—O.G. Cartwright, Yale ..... 10ft. 5 3/4in.
1893—C.T. Buchholz, Penn...... 10ft. 10 1/2in.
1894—M.H. Kershow, Yale .... 10ft. 9in.
1895—C.T. Buchholz, Penn. ...... 11ft. 3 3/4in.
1896—F.W. Allis, Yale .... 11ft. 1 3/4in.

1897—B. Johnson, Yale .... 11ft. 3 5/8in.
1898—R.G. Clapp, Yale ....
    W.W. Hoyt, Harvard .... 11ft. 4 1/4in.
1899—R.G. Clapp, Yale .... 11ft. 5in.
1900—B. Johnson, Yale .... 11ft. 3 1/4in.
1901—E. Deakin, Penn. ....
    A.W. Coleman, Princeton .....
    C. Dvorak, Michigan ....
    P.A. Moore, Princeton ....
    W. Fishleigh, Michigan ......
    J.H. Ford, Yale .... 10ft. 9in.
1902—D.S. Horton, Princeton .... 11ft. 7in.
1903—H.L. Gardner, Syracuse .... 11ft. 7in.
1904—W. McLanahan, Yale .... 11ft. 83/4in.
1905—W.R. Dray, Yale .... 11ft. 8in.
1906—A.G. Grant, Harvard ....
    T.M. Jackson, Cornell .... 11ft. 10 3/4in.
1907—W.R. Dray, Yale .... 11ft. 11 3/4in.
1908—W.R. Dray, Yale ....
    A.C. Gilbert, Yale ....
    F.T. Nelson, Yale ....
    C.S. Campbell, Yale .... 11ft.
1909—C.S. Campbell, Yale .... 12ft. 3 1/4in.
1910—F.T. Nelson, Yale .... 12ft. 4 3/8in.
1911—H.S. Babcock, Columbia ... 12ft. 8 3/3in.
1912—R.A. Gardner, Yale .... 13ft. 1in.
1913—T. Fiske, Princeton .... 12ft. 8in.
1914—C.E. Buck, Dartmouth ......
    A.L. Milton, Cornell ....
    J.B. Camp, Harvard .... 12ft. 3in.
1915—M.S. Greeley, Harvard .....
    F.K. Foss, Cornell ....
    L. Carter, Yale .... 12ft.
1916—F.K. Foss, Cornell .... 12ft. 8in.
1917—No competition
1918—Roy Easterday, Pittsburgh ....
    J.Z. Jordan, Dartmough .... 12ft. 3in.
1919—E.E. Myers, Dartmouth ...... 12ft. 6in.
1920—E.E. Myers, Dartmouth ...... 12ft. 6in.
1921—A.G. Norris, California ......
    R.N. Harwood, Harvard ......
    G.D. Brown, Yale .... 12ft.
1922—A.G. Norris, California .... 12ft. 9in.
1923—A.G. Norris, California ......
    B.M. Owen, Penn. .... 12ft. 9in.
1924—B.M. Owen, Penn. .... 12ft. 10 1/4in.
1925—Nelson B. Sherrill, Penn. ....13ft.
1926—Sabin W. Carr, Yale .... 13ft. 2in.
1927—Sabin W. Carr, Yale ....14ft.
1928—Sabin W. Carr, Yale .... 13ft. 6in.
1929—Frederic H. Sturdy, Yale .....
    Ward R. Edmonds, Stanford ...
    E. Jack Williams, So. Calif. ..... 13ft. 9in.
1930—Oscar Sutermeister, Harvard ... 13ft. 6in.
1931—William N. Graber, So. Calif. ..14ft. 1/2in.
1932—William N. Garber, So. Calif ...
    William W. Miller, Stanford ...
    Wirt L. Thompson Jr., Yale ... 13ft. 10in.
1933—George G. Jefferson, U.C.L.A.
    William N. Graber, So. Calif. ....
    Bernard W. Deacon, Stanford ..
    Keith S. Brown, Yale .... 13ft. 6in.

1934—Keith S. Brown, Yale ....
    Frank E. Pierce, Yale .... 13ft. 9in.
1935—Keith S. Brown, Yale ...... 14ft. 5 1/8in.
1936—Standish F. Medina, Princeton .. 13ft. 6in.
1937—Standish F. Medina,
    Princeton .... 13ft. 10 1/4in.
1938—Loring T. Day, So. Calif. .....
    Kenneth D. Dills, So. Calif. ....
    William H. Harding, Yale .....
    R. Fuller Patterson, Princeton .. 13ft. 6in.
1939—Loring T. Day, So. Calif. ....
    Richard V. Ganslen, Columbia ......14ft.
1940—O. Guinn Smith, California ....14ft.
1941—Warren Broemel, Columbia .... 13ft. 3in.
1942—Joseph Bakura, Penn. State ...
    A. Richmond Morcom, New
    Hampshire ....
    Theodore Wonch, Michigan State ....13ft.
1943—A. Richmond Morcom, New
    Hampshire ....14ft.
1944—Floyd Sessions, Navy ....
    Philip L. Lansing, Army ....13ft.
1945—Philip L. Lansing, Army ....12ft.
1946—Theodore Wonch, Michigan
    State ....13ft.
1947—Peter G. Harwood, Harvard ....13ft.
1948—John E. Eustis, Yale ....
    Arthur Sherman, R.I. State ....13ft.
1949—Neil J. King, Yale ....
    Arthur Sherman, R.I. State ....13ft.
1950—Arhtur Sherman, R.I. State ...
    George Appel, Yale .... 13ft. 6in.
1951—George Appel, Yale .... 13ft. 4in.
1952—Van Zimmerman, Penn. ......
    Robert Linne, Rhode Island ....13ft.
1953—Van Zimmerman, Penn. ......
    Joseph Perlow, Army .... 13ft. 4in.
1954—James Gulick, Temple ....
    Daniel Lorch, Penn. State .....
    Bruce Hescock, Boston U. ....
    Robert Owen, Pennsylvania .... 13ft. 4in.
1955—Don Bragg, Villanova .... 14ft. 6in.
1956—Don Bragg, Villanova ....15ft.
1957—Don Bragg, Villanova .... 14ft. 4in.
1958—John Gray, Pennsylvania ...... 14ft. 4in.
1959—Bjorn Anderson, Maryland .... 13ft. 9in.
1960—Bjorn Anderson and Bernard
    Berlinger, Pennsylvania and
    Thomas Glass, Maryland and
    Richard Kleinhaus, Michigan
    State .... 14ft. 0in.
1961—John Belitza, Maryland ......
    John Murray, Cornell .... 14ft. 3in.
1962—John Belitza, Maryland ......
    Rolando Cruz, Villanova ...... 15ft. 6in.
1963—Rolando Cruz, Villanova ... 15ft. 7 3/4in.
1964—Rolando Cruz, Villanova ... 16ft. 3 1/2in.
1965—John Uelses, La Salle .... 15ft. 6in.
1966—Vincent Bizzaro, Villanova .... 15ft. 6in.
1967—Peter Chen, American .... 16ft. 0in.
1968—Vincent Bizzaro, Villanova .... 16ft. 4in.
1969—James Williamson, Maryland ... 15ft. 9in.

1970—Tom Blair, Penn. .... 16ft. 0in.
1971—Tom Blair, Penn. .... 16ft. 4in.
1972—Tom Blair, Penn. .... 16ft. 4in.
1973—Jim Kielger, Harvard ...... 16ft. 7 1/4in.

Shot-Put
1876—J.M. Mann, Princeton .....30ft. 11 1/2in.
1877—F. Larkin, Princeton ......33ft.
1878—F. Larkin, Princeton .....32ft. 11 1/2in.
1879—F. Larkin, Princeton .....33ft. 8 1/2in.
1880—A.T. Moore, Stevens ......35ft. 1 1/4in.
1881—A.T. Moore, Stevens ......34ft. 11in.
1882—A.T. Moore, Columbia ....36ft. 3in.
1883—C.H. Kip, Harvard ....35ft. 8in.
1884—D.W. Rickhart, Columbia ..36ft. 3 3/4in.
1885—J.H. Rohrbach, Lafayette* .38ft. 1in.
1886—A.B. Coxe, Yale ....38ft. 9 1/2in.
1887—A.B. Coxe, Yale ....40ft. 9 1/2in.
1888—H. Pennypacker, Harvard ..37ft. 3in.
1889—H.H. Janeway, Princeton ..36ft. 1 1/2in.
1890—H.H. Janeway, Princeton ..39ft. 6 1/2in.
1891—J.R. Finlay, Harvard ......39ft. 6 3/4in.
1892—S.H. Evins, Harvard ....39ft. 9in.
1893—W.O. Hickok, Yale ....41ft. 1/8in.
1894—W.O. Hickok, Yale ....42ft.
1895—W.O. Hickok, Yale ....42ft. 11 1/2in.
1896—R. Sheldon, Yale ....41ft. 11 1/2in.
1897—R. Garrett, Princeton .....41ft. 10 3/4in.
1898—J.C. McCracken, Penn. ....43ft. 8 1/2in.
1899—J.C. McCracken, Penn .....42ft. 1/2in.
1900—F.G. Beck, Yale ....44ft. 3 in.
1901—R. Sheldon, Yale ....43ft. 9 1/4in.
1902—F.G. Beck, Yale ....44ft. 8 1/2in.
1903—F.G. Beck, Yale ....46ft.
1904—F.H. Schoenfuss, Harvard ..44ft. 4in.
1905—F.J. Porter, Cornell ....45ft. 1/2in.
1906—B.T. Stephenson, Harvard ..43ft. 11 1/8in.
1907—W.F. Krueger, Swarthmore .46ft. 5 1/2in.
1908—W.F. Krueger, Swarthmore .44ft.
1909—C.C. Little, Harvard ......46ft. 2in.
1910—J. Horner Jr., Michigan ....46ft. 4 1/2in.
1911—J. Horner Jr., Michigan ....46ft. 7 1/8in.
1912—R.L. Beatty, Columbia ....48ft. 10 3/4in.
1913—L.A. Whitney, Dartmouth ..47ft. 2 5/8in.
1914—R.L. Beatty, Columbia ....48ft. 4in.
1915—L.A. Whitney, Dartmouth ..47ft. 4 7/8in.
1916—Harry B. Liversedge,
        California ....46ft. 2 1/2in.
1917—No competition
1918—W.C. Beers, Dartmouth ....45ft. 1 1/4in.
1919—W.H. Allen, Maine ....44ft. 6 1/4in.
1920—Howard Cann, N.Y.U. .....45ft. 10 1/8in.
1921—J.A. Shelburn, Dartmouth .45ft. 3 1/2in.
1922—Glenn Hartranft, Stanford .48ft. 6 1/8in.
1923—Ralph G. Hills, Princeton ..47ft. 8 3/4in.
1924—Glenn Hartranft, Stanford .49ft. 5 7/8in.
1925—Ralph G. Hills, Princeton ..49ft. 9 5/8in.
1926—Clarence L. Houser,
        So. California ....49ft. 11 3/4in.
1927—Elmer G. Gerkin, California 47ft. 11 3/8in.
1928—Eric C.W. Krenz, Stanford ..50ft. 1in.
1929—Harlow P. Rothert, Stanford 50ft. 3in.

1930—Harlow P. Rothert, Stanford 52ft. 1/4in.
1931—Robert H. Hall,
        So. California ....49ft. 1 7/8in.
1932—Nelson A. Gray, Stanford ..51ft. 11 1/8in.
1933—John C. Lyman, Stanford ..52ft. 8 1/2in.
1934—John C. Lyman, Stanford ..53ft. 2 3/4in.
1935—Anthony Geniawicz,
        Dartmouth ....49ft. 1in.
1936—Anthony Geniawicz,
        Dartmouth ....49ft. 11 1/8in.
1937—Daniel Taylor, Columbia ...50ft. 2 1/2in.
1938—Howard Brill, N.Y.U. .....51ft. 3 1/4in.
1939—Francis J. Ryan, Columbia .52ft. 1 5/8in.
1940—Alfred C. Blozis,
        Georgetown ....53ft. 9 1/4in.
1941—Alfred C. Blozis,
        Georgetown ....54ft. 3in.
1942—Alfred C. Blozis,
        Georgetown ....55ft. 4 7/8in.
1943—George C. Brown, Navy ....50ft. 2 1/4in.
1944—Norman Wasser, N.Y.U. ...47ft. 6 1/8in.
1945—Ralph Davis, Army ....49ft. 3/5in.
1946—Bernard Mayer, N.Y.U. ....52ft. 9in.
1947—Bernard Mayer, N.Y.U. ....52ft. 3 1/2in.
1948—Stanley Lampert, N.Y.U. ..52ft. 5 1/2in.
1949—James E. Fuchs, Yale .....56ft. 3/8in.
1950—James E. Fuchs, Yale .....57ft. 9 1/4in.
1951—John Vishnevsky, Marquette 51ft. 8 1/8in.
1952—Arthur Gardiner, Cornell ..51ft. 2 1/8in.
1953—Albert Thompson,
        Columbia ....51ft. 2in.
1954—Roosevelt Grier, Penn State 53ft. 10 3/4in.
1955—Roosevelt Grier, Penn State 55ft. 11in.
1956—Ken Bantum, Manhattan ...56ft. 8in.
1957—Ken Bantum, Manhattan ...56ft. 5in.
1958—Carl Shine, Pennsylvania ...56ft. 10 1/4in.
1959—Carl Shine, Pennsylvania ...57ft. 7.0in.
1960—Joseph Marchiony,
        Manhattan ....56ft. 3 1/2in.
1961—William Joe, Villanova ....54ft. 1/2in.
1962—Gary Gubner,
        New York Univ. ....62ft. 1 3/4in.
1963—Gary Gubner,
        New York Univ. .... 60ft. 2in.
1964—Gary Gubner,
        New York Univ. ....59ft. 5 1/2in.
1965—Carl Wallin, Northeastern ..56ft. 10 1/2in.
1966—Rod Streart, Duke ....59ft. 11in.
1967—Bob Greenlee, Yale ....55ft. 11 1/4ir..
1968—George Allen, St. John's ..57ft. 1/2in.
1969—John Hanley, Maryland ....59ft. 8 3/4in.
1970—John Hanley, Maryland ....59ft. 7 1/4in.
1971—John Hanley, Maryland ....57ft. 11in.
1972—John Hill, Lehigh ....60ft. 1in.
1973—Scott Haney, Navy ....60ft. 11 1/2in.
* Light weight shot.

Discus Throw
1922—Glenn Hartranft, Stanford 140ft. 1/8in.
1923—William Neufeld, California 138ft. 11 1/2in.
1924—Glenn Hartranft, Stanford 158ft. 1 1/8in.

1925—Clarence L. Houser, So. California ....150ft. 2 1/4in.
1926—Clarence L. Houser, So. California ....151ft. 3 3/8in.
1927—Clifford P. Hoffman, Stanford 150ft. 7in.
1928—Eric C.W. Krenz, Stanford ...154ft. 11in.
1929—Eric C.W. Drenz, Stanford ...153ft. 4in.
1930—Eric C.W. Krenz, Stanford ...163ft. 7 3/8in.
1931—Robert F. Jones, Stanford ...159ft. 2 1/4in.
1932—Robert F. Jones, Stanford ...160ft. 9in.
1933—Henri J. Laborde, Stanford ..162ft. 10 1/2in.
1934—Gordon G. Dunn, Stanford ...158ft. 4in.
1935—Kenneth K. Carpenter, So. California ....159ft. 6in.
1936—Walter D. Wood, Cornell ....158ft. 1 1/2in.
1937—William Rowe, R.I. State ....148ft. 7 1/8in.
1938—John H. Herrick, Harvard ...151ft. 3 1/2in.
1939—Phil C. Gasper, So. California 153ft. 3 1/2in.
1940—Alfred C. Blozis, Georgetown 167ft. 4 5/8in.
1941—Alfred C. Blozis, Georgetown 155ft. 8 3/8in.
1942—Alfred C. Blozis, Georgetown 160ft. 3 7/8in.
1943—Chester J. Lakomski, Holy Cross ....139ft. 1in.
1944—George C. Brown Jr., Navy ..139ft. 5 7/8in.
1945—Gilbert J. Bouley, Cornell ...140ft. 1 1/2in.
1946—Harold M. Barker, Yale .....137ft. 9 1/4in.
1947—Victor H. Frank, Yale ......150ft. 8 5/8in.
1948—Victor H. Frank, Yale ......165ft. 8 7/8in.
1949—Victor H. Frank, Yale ......159ft. 6 1/4in.
1950—Victor H. Frank, Yale ......171ft.
1951—Cumming Clancy, Villanova .158ft. 3/8in.
1952—John Ellis, Lafayette ....154ft. 9in.
1953—John Ellis, Lafayette ....161ft. 3/4in.
1954—Stewart Thomson, Yale ....165ft.
1955—Roosevelt Grier, Penn State .170ft. 6in.
1956—Art Siler, Harvard ....160ft. 5 1/2in.
1957—John Tullar, Penn State .....166ft. 4 1/2in.
1958—Wesley King, Pittsburgh ....160ft. 4in.
1959—Eino Keerd, Boston Univ. ...163ft. 8 1/2in.
1960—Robert Batdorf, Pennsylvania 169ft. 5in.
1961—Edward Kohler, Fordham ... Michael Pyle, Yale ....158ft. 10in.
1962—Gary Gubner, N.Y. Univ. ...168ft. 10 1/2in.
1963—Gary Gubner, N.Y. Univ. ...170ft. 2 1/2in.
1964—John Bakkensen, Harvard ...160ft. 10in.
1965—John Bakkensen, Harvard ...173ft. 8in.
1966—William Belfer, Seton Hall ...178ft. 0in.
1967—William Belfer, Seton Hall ...167ft. 7in.
1968—Charles Drescher, Maryland .170ft. 5in.
1969—Richard Drescher, Maryland .187ft. 2in.
1970—Paul Corrigan, Maryland ....173ft. 8in.
1971—Paul Corrigan, Maryland ....176ft. 3in.
1972—Elio Polselli, Notre Dame ...176ft. 10in.

Javelin Throw

1922—G.E. Bronder, Penn. ....185ft. 8 5/8in.
1923—C.H. Storrs, Yale ....199ft. 1in.
1924—R.W. Gibson, Princeton ....192ft. 1 7/8in.
1925—Edward C. Bench, Yale .....186ft. 4in.
1926—Charles V. Harlow, Stanford .195ft. 3in.
1927—Creth B. Hines, Georgetown .205ft. 7 5/8in.
1928—Creth B. Hines, Georgetown .200ft. 10in.

1929—Leo P. Kibby, Stanford ....204ft. 7in.
1930—Kenneth M. Churchill, California ....212ft. 5in.
1931—Kenneth M. Churchill, California ....220ft. 11 1/4in.
1932—Malcolm W. Metcalf, Dartmouth ....220ft. 10 3/4in.
1933—Horace P. Odell, Manhattan 205ft. 1/2in.
1934—Horace P. Odell, Manhattan 200ft. 4 5/8in.
1935—John D. Mottram, Stanford .213ft. 1in.
1936—Alton L. Bell, Maine ......197ft. 8 1/4in.
1937—Ward L. Cuff, Marquette ...197ft. 5in.
1938—Nick Vukmanic, Penn State 217ft. 6 7/8in.
1939—Robert E. Peoples, So. California ....223ft. 1 1/4in.
1940—Nick Vukmanic, Penn State 212ft. 5 3/4in.
1941—Don Vosberg, Marquette ...200ft. 7in.
1942—Edmund Styrna, New Hampshire ....186ft. 3 3/8in.
1943—William C. Patton, Navy ...193ft. 7 1/2in.
1944—David Murray, Holy Cross ..197ft. 9 1/4in.
1945—William D. Fetzer, Dartmouth   179ft. 11 3/4in.
1946—William E. Chynoweth, Army   210ft. 3 1/4in.
1947—Donald E. Trimble, Harvard 198ft. 5 3/8in.
1948—Richard L. Gelb, Yale .....191ft. 2 1/8in.
1949—Irving G. Bouton, Yale ....197ft. 7 1/2in.
1950—Albert Harnly, Albright ...207ft. 1/4in.
1951—Theodore Roderer, Penn State ....211ft.
1952—Robert Allison, Navy .....225ft. 2 1/4in.
1953—Al Cantello, La Salle ......208ft. 11in.
1954—Al Cantello, La Salle ....205ft. 7 1/2in.
1955—Al Cantello, La Salle ......228ft. 8 1/2in.
1956—Bill Alley, Syracuse ....206ft. 11in.
1957—Don McGorty, Manhattan .209ft. 3 1/2in.
1958—Don McGorty, Manhattan .229ft. 2 1/2in.
1959—Nicholas Kovalakides, Maryland ....222ft. 1/2in.
1960—Nicholas Kovalakides, Maryland ....235ft. 7.0in.
1961—Nicholas Kovalakides, Maryland ....222ft. 4in.
1962—Douglas Kerr, Villanova ...224ft. 10 1/2in.
1963—Dan McDyre, La Salle .....218ft. 1 1/2in.
1964—Ernie Krombolz, Penn State 227ft. 9 1/2in.
1965—Russ White, Maryland .....241ft. 1/2in.
1966—James Stevenson, Penn State 244ft. 5 1/2in.
1967—Wayne Donelon, Maryland .244ft. 4in.
1968—Jim Shillow, Villanova ....234ft. 6in.
1969—John Bacon, Maryland ....249ft. 0in.
1970—Bob Kouvolo, Pittsburgh .251ft. 5in.
1971—Bob Kouvolo, Pittsburgh .249ft. 2in.
1972—Fred DiPalma, Penn ......233ft. 11in.

16-Lb. Hammer Throw

1877—G.D. Parmly, Princeton .....75ft. 10in.
1878—F. Larkin, Princeton ....76ft. 9in.
1879—F. Larkin, Princeton ....87ft. 1in.
1880—J.F. Bush, Columbia ....84ft. 3in.
1881—J.H. Montgomery, Columbia .76ft. 9 1/2in.

1882—D.R. Porter, Columbia ....87ft. 3 1/2in.
1883—C.H. Kip, Harvard ....88ft. 11in.
1884—A.B. Coxe, Yale ....83ft. 6in.
1885—A.B. Coxe, Yale ....88ft. 1/2in.
1886—A.B. Coxe, Yale ....95ft. 11in.
1887—A.B. Coxe, Yale ....98ft. 6in.
1888—A.J. Bowser, Penn .....88ft. 6 1/2in.
1889—A.J. Bowser, Penn ....89ft. 10 1/2in.
1890—B.C. Hinman, Columbia ..94ft. 7in.
1891—J.R. Finlay, Harvard .....107ft. 7 1/2in.
1892—S.H. Evins, Harvard ......104ft. 3/8in.
1893—W.O. Hickok, Yale ......110ft. 4 1/2in.
1894—W.O. Hickok, Yale ......123ft. 9in.
1895—W.O. Hickok, Yale ......135ft. 7 1/2in.
1896—C. Chadwick, Yale ......132ft. 6 1/2in.
1897—W.G. Woodruff, Penn ....136ft. 3in.
1898—J.C. McCracken, Penn ....149ft. 5in.
1899—J.C. McCracken, Penn ....144ft. 1in.
1900—A. Plaw, California ....154ft. 4 1/2in.
1901—J.R. DeWitt, Princeton ....149ft. 4 1/2in.
1902—J.R. DeWitt, Princeton ....164ft. 10in.
1903—J.R. DeWitt, Princeton ....155ft. 8in.
1904—J.R. DeWitt, Princeton ....161ft. 3in.
1905—C. Van Duyne, Syracuse ...149ft. 11in.
1906—M.F. Horr, Syracuse ......147ft. 9 1/2in.
1907—M.F. Horr, Syracuse ......150ft. 1 1/2in.
1908—J.N. Pew, Cornell ....155ft. 2 1/2in.
1909—L.J. Talbott, Cornell ......158ft. 9 1/2in.
1910—C.T. Cooney, Yale ....152ft. 5in.
1911—A.H. Tilley, Dartmouth ...145ft. 11 1/2in.
1912—T. Cable, Harvard ....162ft. 4 1/2in.
1913—T. Cable, Harvard ....156ft.
1914—A.W. Kohler, Michigan ....157ft. 1/2in.
1915—H.P. Bailey, Maine ....165ft. 3/4in.
1916—C.C. Gildersleeve, California 155ft. 1in.
1917—No competition
1918—J.B. Sutherland, Pittsburgh .152ft. 7 1/4in.
1919—L.H. Weld, Dartmouth ....143ft. 2 1/4in.
1920—J.W. Merchant, California ..159ft. 2 3/4in.
1921—G. Dandrow, M.I.T. ......157ft. 4 1/2in.
1922—J.W. Merchant, California ..171ft. 2in.
1923—Frederick D. Tootell,
       Bowdoin ....181ft. 6 1/2in.
1924—G.A. Drew, M.I.T. ....156ft. 1/8in.
1925—Caleb F. Gates, Princeton ..160ft. 10 3/4in.
1926—Carl S. Biggs, Syracuse ....161ft. 9 1/2in.
1927—Marion M. Ide, Penn State ..162ft. 1 1/2in.
1928—Norwood G. Wright, Cornell 167ft. 7 1/2in.
1929—Edmund F. Black, Maine ...163ft.
1930—Frank N. Connor, Yale ....177ft. 10 3/4in.
1931—Frank N. Connor, Yale ....167ft. 2 1/2in.
1932—Peter E. Zaremba, N.Y.U. ..170ft. 6 5/8in.
1933—Peter E. Zaremba, N.Y.U. ..169ft. 4in.
1934—Donald E. Favor, Maine ...170ft. 9in.
1935—Anton Kishon, Bates ......170ft. 11 3/4in.
1936—Irving Folwartshny,
       R.I. State ....172ft. 9 3/8in.
1937—Irving Folwartshny,
       R.I. State ....171ft. 6 3/8in.
1938—Irving Folwartshny,
       R.I. State ....178ft. 9 3/4in.
1939—Robert H. Bennett, Maine .178ft. 11 1/8in.

1940—Robert H. Bennett, Maine .176ft. 8 1/2in.
1941—Mathew J. Flaherty,
       New Hampshire ....173ft. 8 5/8in.
1942—Edmund Styrna, New
       Hampshire ....170ft. 10 3/8in.
1943—William O. Fisher, Harvard .152ft.
1944—Arthur Greenburg,
       R.I. State.............143 11 3/4in.
1945—Leonard Dombrowski,
       Army ....144ft. 11 3/4in.
1946—Frank X. Remaka,
       Holy Cross ....165ft. 7in.
1947—Robert H. Bennett, Brown .174ft. 10 7/8in.
1948—Samuel M. Felton Jr.,
       Harvard ....175ft. 4 1/2in.
1949—Howard S. Reed, Harvard ..160ft. 9 1/4in.
1950—Gilbert J. Borjeson, Brown .169ft. 5in.
1951—Thomas Bane, Tufts ......179ft. 8 3/4in.
1952—Gilbert J. Borjeson, Brown .180ft. 1 5/8in.
1953—Martin Engel, N.Y.U. .....179ft. 3 3/8in.
1954—Martin Engle, N.Y. ....183ft.
1955—Don Seifert, Brown ......186ft. 10in.
1956—Albert Hall, Cornell ......
       Bill McWilliams, Bowdoin .196ft. 2 1/2in.
1957—Peter Harpel, Harvard .....178ft. 8in.
1958—John Lawlor, Boston U. ...198ft. 8in.
1959—John Lawlor, Boston
       University ....208ft. 8 1/2in.
1960—John Lawlor, Boston
       University ....199ft. 7 1/2in.
1961—Arthur Doten, Harvard ....189ft. 10in.
1962—Edward Bailey, Harvard ...192ft. 3in.
1963—George Desnoyers, Boston
       College ....190ft. 4in.
1964—Bill Corsetti, Northeastern .193ft. 6 1/2in.
1965—Tom Gage, Cornell ....197ft. 1 1/2in.
1966—F. Alexis Schulten,
       Bowdoin ....188ft. 1 1/2in.
1967—Bob Narcessian, R.I. ......195ft. 9 1/2in.
1968—Bob Narcessian, R.I. ......201ft. 10in.
1969—Richard Narcessian, R.I. ...194ft. 6in.
1970—Richard Narcessian, R.I. ...195ft. 6in.
1971—William Dineen, Dartmouth 198ft. 3in.
1972—Douglas Greenwood,
       Princeton ....195ft. 3in.

Triple Jump

1963—Chris Ohiri, Harvard ......50ft. 1in.
1964—Chris Ohiri, Harvard ......51ft. 4 3/4in.
1965—Mel Branch, Princeton ....48ft. 7 1/2in.
1966—Edward Marks, Maryland ..49ft. 6 1/2in
1967—Waren Rockwell, Penn State 49ft. 2in.
1968—Ed Marks, Maryland ......50ft. 1in.
1969—Hartley Saunders,
       Morgan State ....48ft. 10 1/4in.
1970—Mike Neff, Maryland ......49ft. 4in.
1971—Glen Faussett, Cornell ....50ft. 7in.
1972—Bill Rea, Pittsburgh ......50ft. 8 1/4in.
1973—Ken McBryde, Manhattan .52ft. 2in.

Team

From 1876 to 1889, only first places were
counted, seconds being counted only in case of a

tie. (Points in parentheses.)

Year and champion
1876—Princeton (4)
1877—Columbia (6)
1878—Columbia (7)
1879—Columbia (6)
1880—Harvard (6)
1881—Harvard (5)
1882—Harvard (6)
1883—Harvard (7)
1884—Harvard (5)
1885—Harvard (4)
1886—Harvard (5)
1887—Yale (6)
1888—Harvard (7)
1889—Yale (4)
1890—Harvard (32)
1891—Harvard (46)
1892—Harvard (48 2/3)
1893—Yale (47 1/3)
1894—Yale (37)
1895—Yale (30)
1896—Yale (41 1/2)
1897—Pennsylvania (34 3/4)
1898—Pennsylvania (50 3/4)
1899—Pennsylvania (57)
1900—Pennsylvania (39)
1901—Harvard (46)
1902—Yale (32 1/2)
1903—Yale (43 1/2)
1904—Yale (33 1/2)
1905—Cornell (30 1/2)
1906—Cornell (38)
1907—Pennsylvania (33)
1908—Cornell (34)
1909—Harvard (39 1/10)
1910—Pennsylvania (27 1/2)
1911—Cornell (30 1/2)
1912—Pennsylvania (28)
1913—Pennsylvania (24)
1914—Cornell (43)
1915—Cornell (45 1/2)
1916—Cornell (45)
1917—No competition
1918—Cornell (47)
1919—Cornell (39 1/2)
1920—Pennsylvania (30 1/2)
1921—California (27 1/2)
1922—California (40 1/2)
1923—California (39 1/2)
1924—Yale (28)
1925—Southern California (33)
1926—Southern California (35 1/2)
1927—Stanford (36)
1928—Stanford (43)
1929—Stanford (45 3/8)
1930—Southern California (44 1/4)
1931—Southern California (46 6/7)
1932—Southern California (62 3/4)
1933—Southern California (47)
1934—Stanford (35 1/4)
1935—Southern California (51)

1936—Cornell (29 1/2)
1937—Pittsburgh (30 1/2)
1938—Southern California (46 1/2)
1939—Southern California (71 1/2)
194)—Pittsburgh (29 1/2)
1941—New York University (31 1/2)
1942—Penn State (25 1/2)
1943—New York University (37)
1944—Navy (81)
1945—Navy (85 3/4)
1946—Navy (36 5/28)
1947—New York University (36)
1948—Yale (35 1/2)
1949—Michigan State (43)
1950—Yale (42)
1951—Cornell (33 1/4)
1952—Manhattan (42)
1953—Manhattan (42)
1954—Penn State (32 1/2)
1955—Manhattan (38)
1956—Manhattan (42 1/2)
1957—Villanova (48)
1958—Villanova (33 5/8)
1959—Penn State
1960—Villanova (38)
1961—Villanova (46)
1962—Villanova (49 1/2)
1963—Villanova (49)
1964—Villanova (45)
1965—Maryland (46)
1966—Maryland (40)
1967—Villanova (37)
1968—Villanova (63)
1969—Maryland (53)
1970—Villanova (60)
1971—Villanova (32)
1972—Pennsylvania (53)
1973—Navy (41)

Cross-Country

1908—H.C. Young, Cornell . . . . 34m. 14s.
1909—Tell S. Berna, Cornell . . . . 33m. 5.5s.
1910—John Paul Jones, Cornell . . . . . 33m. 34s.
1911—John Paul Jones, Cornell . . . . . 34m. 41.6s.
1912—John Paul Jones, Cornell . . . . . 32m. 9.5s.
1913—Robert St. B. Boyd, Harvard . . 34m. 37s.
1914—D.F. Potter, Cornell . . . . 34m. 6/10s.
1915—John W. Overton, Yale . . . . . . 33m. 21.2s.
1916—John W. Overton, Yale . . . . . . 35m. 30.8s.
1917—Ivan C. Dresser, Cornell . . . . . . 33m.
1918—No competition
1919—John Simmons, Syracuse . . . . 32m. 55s.
1920—John L. Romig, Penn State . . . 33m. 1s.
1921—Robert E. Brown, Cornell . . . . 32m. 20.5s.
1922—Walter Higgins, Columbia . . . . 32m. 21.8s.
1923—J. Verne H. Booth, Johns
           Hopkins . . . . 32m. 10s.
1924—Macauley L. Smith, Yale . . . . . 31m. 24s.
1925—Willard L. Tibbetts, Harvard . . 30m. 24s.
1926—William J. Cox, Penn State . . . 30m. 4s.
1927—William J. Cox, Penn State . . . 30m. 36.8s.
1928—James L. Reid, Harvard . . . . . . 30m. 11s.

1929—Francis C. Lindsay, Maine
Harry L. Richardson, Maine . . . 30m. 6s.
1930—Clark S. Chamberlain, Mich.
State . . . . 30m. 19.2s.
1931—Daniel E. Dean, Penn. . . . . 29m. 23s.
1932—George H. Barker, N.Y.U. . . . . 28m. 58.8s.
1933—Thomas C. Ottey, Mich. State . 30m
1934—Thomas C. Ottey, Mich. State . 31m 54.6s.
1935—J. Edward Bechtold,
Michigan State . . . . 26m. 23.6s.
1936—Kenneth Waite, Mich. State . . . 26m. 26.3s.
1937—Howard W. Welch, Cornell . . . 26m. 54s.
1938—William J. SMith, Penn State . . 26m. 33.3s.
1939—Leslie MacMitchell, N.Y.U. . . . 26m. 28.6s.
1940—Leslie MacMitchell, N.Y.U. . . . 26m. 2.8s.
1941—Leslie MacMitchell, N.Y.U. . . . 26m. 40.1s.
1942—Frank Dixon, N.Y.U. . . . . 27m. 8.4s.
1943—Donald Burnham, Dartmouth . 28m. 12.9s.
1944—Vincent W. Barry, Navy . . . . . 27m. 34.1s.
1945—John T. Hanley, Dartmouth . . 28m. 21.3s.
1946—Curtis C. Stone, Penn State . . . 27m. 7.9s.
1947—Robert Black, R.I. State . . . . . 25m. 37.1s.
1948—Robert Black, R.I. State . . . . . 25m. 4/10s.
1949—Richard Shea, Army . . . . 25m. 14.7s.
1950—Richard Shea, Army . . . . 25m. 21.4s.
1951—Richard Shea, Army . . . . 24m. 55.1s.
1952—Charles Capozzoli,
Georgetown . . . . 24m. 30.1s.
1953—Johnny Kelley, Boston U. . . . . 24m. 51.7s.
1954—George Terry, Boston U. . . . . . 24m. 46.4s.
1955—Henry Kennedy, Michigan State 24m.30.3s.
1956—Henry Kennedy, Michigan State 24m.30.3s.
1957—Crawford Kennedy,
Michigan State . . . . 24m.14.8s.
1958—Crawford Kennedy,
Michigan State . . . . 24m.21.4s.
1959—Crawford Kennedy,
Michigan State . . . . 23m.51.8s.
1960—Robert Lowe, Brown . . . . 25m.40.4s.
1961—Stephen Nachooka, Cornell . . 26m.02.9s.
1962—Victor Zwolak, Villanova . . . . 24m.47.3s.
1963—Vic Zwolak, Villanova . . . . . . 24m.46.8s.
1964—Joe Lynch, Georgetown . . . . . 24m.41.8s.
1965—Eamon O'Reilly, Georgetown . 24m.24.2s.
1966—Charles Messenger, Villanova . 24m.15.6s.
1967—Arthur Dulong, Holy Cross . . . 24m.04.4s.
1968—Steve Stageberg, Georgetown
1969—Art Dulong, Holy Cross
1970—Donal Walsh, Villanova
1971—Bob Wheeler, Duke
1972—Mike Keogh, Manhattan

Cross-Country—Team

1908—11—Cornell
1912—Harvard
1913—14—Cornell
1915—Maine
1916—Cornell
1917—Pennsylvania
1918—No competition
1919—Syracuse
1920—21—Cornell

1922—23—Syracuse
1924—Pittsburgh
1925—Syracuse
1926—28—Penn State
1929—Pennsylvania
1930—Penn State
1931—Harvard
1932—Manhattan
1933—37—Michigan State
1938—39—Manhattan
1940—42—Rhode Island State
1943—Dartmouth
1944—Navy
1945—Army
1946—N.Y.U.
1947—Manhattan
1948—Michigan State
1949—Army
1950—51—Penn State
1952—53—Michigan State
1954—Manhattan
1955—Pittsburgh
1956—59—Michigan State
1960—Penn State
1961—Michigan State
1962—Villanova
1963—Notre Dame
1964—65—Georgetown
1966—71—Villanova
1972—Manhattan

Indoor

60-Yard Dash

70-yards, 1922 through 1933; 60 meters, 1934;
50 meters, 1935—36.

1922—J.A. LeConey, Lafayette . . . . 7.3s.
1923—Harold B. Lever, Pennsylvania . . . . . 7.1s.
1924—Chester Bowman, Syracuse . . . . 7.2s.
1925—Alfred H. Miller, Harvard . . . . 7.2s.
1926—Henry A. Russell, Cornell . . . . 7.2s.
1927—Alfred H. Miller, Harvard . . . . 7.2s.
1928—James S. Daley, Holy Cross . . . . 7.2s.
1929—James S. Daley, Holy Cross . . . . 7.3s.
1930—James S. Daley, Holy Cross . . . . 7.3s.
1931—Aloysius J. Kelly, Georgetown . . . . . 7.1s.
1932—George W. Weinstein, New York U. . . 7.2s.
1933—Richard Bell, M.I.T. . . . . 7s.
1934—Samuel W. Maniaci, Columbia . . . . . 6.8s.
1935—Benjamin W. Johnson, Columbia . . . 5.9s.
1936—Arthur L. Thomas, Pittsburgh . . . . . 6s.
1937—Benjamin W. Johnson, Columbia . . . 6.3s.
1938—Benjamin W. Johnson, Columbia . . . 6.3s.
1939—Kenneth D. Clapp, Brown . . . . 6.4s.
1940—Norwood H. Ewell, Penn State . . . . . 6.3s.
1941—Harold Stickel, Pittsburgh . . . . 6.3s.
1942—William Carter, Pittsburgh . . . . 6.2s.
1943—Edward Conwell, New York U. . . . . . 6.3s.
1944—Edward Conwell, New York U. . . . . . 6.3s.
1945—John B. Van Velzer, Navy . . . . 6.3s.
1946—Richard G. Newell, Army . . . . 6.3s.
1947—Joseph Cianciabella, Manhattan . . . . 6.2s.
1948—Joseph Cianciabella, Manhattan . . . . 6.3s.

1949—Andrew Stanfield, Seton Hall ...... 6.2s.
1950—Andrew Stanfield, Seton Hall ...... 6.2s.
1951—Andrew Stanfield, Seton Hall ...... 6.3s.
1952—John O'Connell, Manhattan .... 6.2s.
1953—Robert Keegan, Seton Hall .... 6.2s.
1954—John Haines, Pennsylvania .... 6.3s.
1955—John Haines, Pennsylvania .... 6.3s.
1956—John Haines, Pennsylvania .... 6.1s.
1957—Dave Sime, Duke .... 6.2s.
1958—Ed Collymore, Villanova .... 6.2s.
1959—Ed Collymore, Villanova .... 6.2s.
1960—Frank Budd, Villanova .... 6.2s.
1961—Frank Budd, Villanova .... 6.1s.
1962—Frank Budd, Villanova .... 6.0s.
1963—Bob Mattis, Manhattan .... 6.2s.
1964—Sam Perry, Fordham .... 6.2s.
1965—Sam Perry, Fordham .... 6.3s.
1966—Sam Perry, Fordham .... 6.2s.
1967—James Lee, Maryland .... 6.2s.
1968—Bill Hurd, Notre Dame .... 6.2s.
1969—Bill Hurd, Notre Dame .... 6.2s.
1970—Don Martin, Yale .... 6.2s.
1971—Tony Dedmond, Army .... 6.1s.
1972—Tony Dedmond, Army .... 6.3s.

440-Yard Run

1971—Lamotte Hyman, Villanova .... 48.5s.
1972—Dennis Walker, Adelphi .... 48.7s.

600-Yard Run

600 meters, 1936.

1936—Edward T. O'Brien, Syracuse . 1m. 21.7s.
1937—Edward T. O'Brien, Syracuse . 1m. 13.1s.
1938—Edgar Howard Borck, Manhattan 1m. 12s.
1939—Wesley A. Wallace, Fordham .. 1m. 13.2s.
1940—James B. Herbert, New York U 1m. 11.2s.
1941—John Campbell, Fordham .... 1m. 14.2s.
1942—John Campbell, Fordham .... 1m. 13.4s.
1943—Robert Stuart, Fordham ..... 1m. 14.6s.
1944—John Caskey, Navy .... 1m. 14.8s.
1945—George C. Berger, Army ..... 1m. 14.5s.
1946—Fred R. Sickinger, Manhattan . 1m. 15.8s.
1947—George Guida, Villanova ..... 1m. 14.2s.
1948—Joseph Hall, R.I. State ..... 1m. 13.2s.
1949—Frank Fox, Seton Hall ...... 1m. 15.1s.
1950—Charles Moore, Cornell ...... 1m. 12.2s.
1951—Robert Carter, Seton Hall .... 1m. 12.9s.
1952—Vernon Dixon, Manhattan ... 1m. 11.5s.
1953—Oliver Sax, Penn State .... 1m. 10.4s.
1954—Louis Jones, Manhattan ..... 1m. 11.3s.
1955—Charles Jenkins, Villanova ... 1m. 11.2s.
1956—Charles Jenkins, Villanova ... 1m. 11.9s.
1957—Charles Jenkins, Villanova ... 1m. 12.1s.
1958—Tom Murphy, Manhattan ... 1m. 11s.
1959—James Stack, Yale .... 1m. 12s.
1960—James Stack, Yale .... 1m. 12.5s.
1961—James Stack, Yale .... 1m. 10.6s.
1962—Jay Luck, Yale .... 1m. 11.7s.
1963—Wendell Mottley, Yale ...... 1m. 09.9s.
1964—Wendell Mottley, Yale ...... 1m. 09.3s.
1965—Edward Duchine, Georgetown 1m. 11.6s.
1966—Tom Farrell, St. John's ...... 1m. 11.4s.
1967—Mark Young, Yale .... 1m. 11.5s.

1968—Larry James, Villanova ...... 1m. 10.2s.
1969—Larry James, Villanova ...... 1m. 09.2s.
1970—Larry James, Villanova ...... 1m. 10.4s.
1971—Tom Ulan, Rutgers .... 1m. 08.5s.
1972—Jerald Hassard, Rhode Island.. 1m. 12.4s.

880-Yard Run

1971—John Lovett, Manhattan ..... 1m. 51.5s.
1972—John Lovett, Manhattan ..... 1m. 51.9s.

1,000-Yard Run

1939—Francis G. Slater, Fordham ... 2m. 15.2s.
1940—Edward Burrowes Jr., Princeton 2m. 13.8s.
1941—Walter Cary, Fordham ...... 2m. 15.4s.
1942—Robert E. Williams, Dartmouth 2m. 15s.
1943—Joseph Nowicki, Fordham ... 2m. 14.7s.
1944—Alfred Daily, Manhattan ..... 2m. 16.8s.
1945—Richard N. Hall, Navy .... 2m. 17s.
1946—Stanton Callender, New York U 2m. 17.2s.
1947—William H. Atkinson, Manhattan 2m. 16.3s.
1948—Reginald Pearman, New York U 2m. 16s.
1949—Philip Thigpen, Seton Hall ... 2m. 14.2s.
1950—Phillip Thigpen, Seton Hall ... 2m. 15.2s.
1951—Joseph Deady, Georgetown .. 2m. 11.7s.
1952—Carl Joyce, Georgetown ..... 2m. 13s.
1953—Paul Raudenbush, Pennsylvania 2m. 14.4s.
1954—Thomas Courtney, Fordham .. 2m. 10.9s.
1955—Arnold Sowell, Pittsburgh .... 2m. 14.7s.
1956—Arnold Sowell, Pittsburgh .... 2m. 13.5s.
1957—Ron Delany, Villanova ...... 2m. 14s.
1958—Ron Delany, Villanova ...... 2m. 12.8s.
1959—Ed Moran, Penn State .... 2m. 9.6s.
1960—Thomas Carroll, Yale .... 2m. 12.2s.
1961—Thomas Carroll, Yale .... 2m. 10.7s.
1962—Frank Tomeo, Fordham ..... 2m. 11.5s.
1963—Noel Carroll, Villanova ...... 2m. 11.1s.
1964—Thomas Bauer, St. John's .... 2m. 11.8s.
1965—Noel Carroll, Villanova ...... 2m. 11.5s.
1966—Ricardo Urbina, Georgetown . 2m. 08.8s.
1967—Peter Farrell, Notre Dame .... 2m. 12.5s.
1968—Byron Dyce, New York Univ. . 2m. 10.0s.
1969—Frank Murphy, Villanova .... 2m. 07.1s.
1970—Andy O'Reilly, Villanova .... 2m. 11.7s.
1971—Morgan Mosser, West Virginia . 2m. 07.9s.
1972—Brian McElroy, Villanova .... 2m. 06.9s.

One-Mile Run

1,500 meters, 1934 through 1936.

1922—M. L. Shields, Penn State ..... 4m. 20.8s.
1923—James J. Connolly, Georgetown 4m. 17.8s.
1924—Schuyler C. Enck, Penn State . 4m. 24s.
1925—Leo Larrivee, Holy Cross ..... 4m. 21.1s.
1926—John N. Waters, Harvard ..... 4m. 24.2s.
1927—William J. Cox, Penn State ... 4m. 18.6s.
1928—William J. Cox, Penn State ... 4m. 20s.
1929—Joseph J. Hickey, New York U. 4m. 20s.
1930—William J. McKniff, Penn. .... 4m. 21s.
1931—Carl A. Coan, Pennsylvania ... 4m. 15.2s.
1932—Norwood P. Hallowell .... 4m. 12.4s.
1933—Frank A. Crowley, Manhattan . 4m. 15.6s.
1934—William R. Bonthron, Princeton 3m. 57.4s.
1935—Eugene G. Venzke, Penn. .... 3m. 57.6s.
1936—Louis P. Burns, Manhattan ... 4m. 5s.

1937—Louis P. Burns, Manhattan ... 4m. 20.5s.
1938—Peter B. Bradley, Princeton ... 4m. 19.5s.
1939—Robert P. Hoolahan, Manhattan 4m. 25.2s.
1940—Leslie MacMitchell, New York U.4m. 24.8s.
1941—Leslie MacMitchell, New York U.4m. 12s.
1942—Leslie MacMitchell, New York U.4m. 13.7s.
1943—Donald L. Burnham, Dartmouth 4m. 16.2s.
1944—Donald L. Burnham, Dartmouth 4m. 20.2s.
1945—Vincent W. Barry, Navy ...... 4m. 26.2s.
1946—Edward J. Walsh Jr., Manhattan 4m. 19s.
1947—Gerald T. Karver, Penn State .. 4m. 19.9s.
1948—Gerald T. Karver, Penn State .. 4m. 22.7s.
1949—George Wade, Yale .... 4m. 13.6s.
1950—William Mack, Michigan State . 4m. 11s.
1951—Fred Dwyer, Villanova ...... 4m. 16.2s.
1952—Fred Dwyer, Villanova ...... 4m. 13s.
1953—Fred Dwyer, Villanova ...... 4m. 8.1s.
1954—Richard Ollen, Northeastern .. 4m. 20.1s.
1955—Alex Breckenridge, Villanova . 4m. 19.9s.
1956—Ron Delany, Villanova ...... 4m. 11.4s.
1957—Burr Grim, Maryland .... 4m. 10.1s.
1958—Peter Close, St. John's .... 4m. 10.3s.
1959—Peter Close, St. John's .... 4m. 10.1s.
1960—Ronald Gregory, Notre Dame . 4m. 13.1s.
1961—Steven Paranya, Wesleyan .... 4m. 15.6s.
1962—Victor Zwolak, Villanova .... 4m. 09.3s.
1963—Dave Farley, Brown .... 4m. 13.7s.
1964—Tom Sullivan, Villanova ..... 4m. 11.8s.
1965—Tom Sullivan, Villanova ..... 4m. 09.2s.
1966—Dave Patrick, Villanova ...... 4m. 06.7s.
1967—Dave Patrick, Villanova ...... 4m. 09.4s.
1968—Dave Patrick, Villanova ...... 4m. 06.1s.
1969—Martin Liquori, Villanova .... 4m. 05.3s.
1970—Martin Liquori, Villanova .... 4m. 02.1s.
1971—Martin Liquori, Villanova .... 4m. 06.1s.
1972—Marcel Phillipe, Fordham .... 4m. 04.0s.

Two-Mile Run

3,000 meters, 1934 through 1936.

1922—N. P. Brown, Cornell .... 9m. 45.6s.
1923—Elmer O. McLane, Penn. ..... 9m. 39.3s.
1924—Verne H. Booth, Johns Hopkins 9m. 36s.
1925—Willard L. Tibbetts, Harvard .. 9m. 32.6s.
1926—Willard L. Tibbetts, Harvard .. 9m. 30.8s.
1927—Horace H. Benson, Cornell ... 9m. 37s.
1928—Joseph W. Hagen, Columbia .. 9m. 37.2s.
1929—Joseph W. Hagen, Columbia .. 9m. 31s.
1930—Paul E. Rekers, Penn State ... 9m. 22.8s.
1931—Joseph P. McCluskey, Fordham 9m. 17.8s.
1932—Joseph P. McCluskey, Fordham 9m. 17.6s.
1933—Joseph P. McCluskey, Fordham 9m. 16.2s.
1934—Francis A. McKenna, Manhattan 8m. 54.8s.
1935—Thomas G. Russell, Manhattan 8m. 58.8s.
1936—Wilbur T. Woodland, Yale .... 8m. 55s.
1937—Phillips U. Smith, Rutgers .... 9m. 36.5s.
1938—Robert L. Conkling, Manhattan 9m. 39.2s.
1939—Robert L. Conkling, Manhattan 9m. 37.9s.
1940—William R. Atkinson, Tufts ... 9m. 23.8s.
1941—Michael Prohodsky,
     Northeastern ...(....... 9m. 37.6s.
1942—Leroy Schwarzkopf, Yale .... 9m. 25.7s.
1943—Glenn Masten, Colgate ...... 9m. 25.8s.

1944—John O'Hare, Rochester ..... 9m. 47s.
1945—Armand Osterberg, New York U.9m. 44.7s.
1946—Edward D. O'Toole, Manhattan 9m. 47.2s.
1947—Curtis C. Stone, Penn State ... 9m. 17.6s.
1948—Horace Ashenfelter, Penn State 9m. 14.9s.
1949—Robert Black, Rhode Island
     State .... 9m. 18.1s.
1950—Richard Church, Syracuse .... 9m. 7.2s.
1951—Richard Shea, Army .... 9m. 12.s.
1952—Richard Shea, Army .... 9m. 11s.
1953—Joseph LaPierre, Georgetown . 9m. 8.9s.
1954—Edward Shea, Northeastern .. 9m. 24.5s.
1955—George Terry, Boston U. .... 9m. 16.8s.
1956—George King, N.Y.U. .... 9m. 7s.
1957—Ron Delany, Villanova ...... 9m. 6.6s.
1958—Ron Delany, Villanova ...... 9m. 17.6s.
1959—Richard Engelbrink, Penn State 9m. 13.3s.
1960—Thomas Laris, Dartmouth .... 8m. 59.0s.
1961—Robert Mack, Yale .... 9m. 08.6s.
1962—Robert Mack, Yale .... 8m. 58.3s.
1963—Pat Traynor, Villanova ...... 9m. 02.1s.
1964—Joe Lynch, Georgetown ..... 8m. 59.0s.
1965—William Clark, Notre Dame ... 8m. 52.7s.
1966—Eamon O'Reilly, Georgetown . 8m. 57.8s.
1967—Charles Messinger, Villanova .. 8m. 59.7s.
1968—Sebsibe Mamo, Colby .... 8m. 50.7s.
1969—Art Dulong, Holy Cross ...... 8m. 44.9s.
1970—Dick Buerkle, Villanova ..... 8m. 42.2s.
1971—Jerry Ritchie, Pittsburgh ..... 8m. 42.1s.
1972—Greg Fredericks, Penn State .. 8m. 44.3s.

One-Mile Relay

1,600 meters, 1934-36.

1922—Princeton and Syracuse (dead
     heat) .... 3m. 22.8s.
1923—Syracuse (Allen Woodring,
     Allan Monie, Chester Bowman,
     Ralph Chesley) .... 3m. 23s.
1924—Yale (Bayes M. Norton, Gil-
     bert W. Chapman, Charles S.
     Gage, James O. Geilfuss) .... 3m. 22.9s.
1925—Georgetown (George W. Kin-
     naly, Vernon W. Ascher, Paul F.
     Herlihy, James A. Burgess) ..... 3m. 21.8s.
1926—Holy Cross (Thomas P.
     Roche, Frank A. Burns, Harold J.
     Higgins, Walter J. Mulvihill) .... 3m. 24.4s.
1927—Syracuse (Raymond J. Bar-
     buti, Oliver Proudlock, Ralph R.
     Rubado, Cecil G. Cook) .... 3m. 21.4s.
1928—Syracuse (Harvey A. Andra,
     Kelsey S. Denton, Norman E. St.
     Clair, Raymond J. Barbuti) ..... 3m. 21.2s.
1929—Dartmouth (Malcolm L.
     Pratt, Harris H. Huston, Leon F.
     Andrews, Gerard Swope Jr.) .... 3m. 22s.
1930—Harvard (Francis E. Cum-
     mings, Vernon Munroe, Vincent
     L. Hennessy, Eugene E. Record) . 3m. 20.6s.
1931—Pennsylvania (John K. Ed-
     wards, Horace W. Steel, James C.
     Healey, William A. Carr) .... 3m. 17.8s.

1932—N.Y.U. (Joseph F. Healey, Milton M. Sandler, Sidney B. Schleffar, Harry L. Hoffman) ... 3m. 17.8s.

1933—Pennsylvania (John K. Edwards, Howard Jones, William A. Carr, James C. Healey) .... 3m. 17s.

1934—N.Y.U. (Joseph F. Healey, Harold Lamb, Lester E. Williams, Harry Hoffman) .... 3m. 22.2s.

1935—Manhattan (Matthew T. Carey, William J. Averill, William H. Morrisey, John J. Wolff) ..... 3m. 23.7s.

1936—Manhattan (Matthew T. Carey, Valentine W. Riordan, Richard N. Lundell, John J. Wolff) ... 3m. 22.4s.

1937—Manhattan (Matthew T. Carey, Valentine W. Riordan, Robert J. Reilly, Richard N. Lundell) 3m. 23.1s.

1938—Pittsburgh (Frank Ohl, Albert Ferrara, Allen McKee, John Y. Woodruff) .... 3m.22s.

1939—N.Y.U. (James McPoland, George Hagans, Harold Bogrow, James B. Herbert) .... 3m. 20.3s.

1940—N.Y.U. James McPoland, Stanford Braun, Harold Bogrow, James B. Herbert) .... 3m. 21.6s.

1941—St. John's (Francis Timmes, Carl Fields, Victor Bovino, Albert MacDowell) .... 3m. 21.6s.

1942—Colgate (John B. Hall, George J. Tifft, Thomas W. Keith, Alfred L. Diebolt) .... 3m. 21.4s.

1943—N.Y.U. (Arthur Herrforth, Frank Cotter, Walter Welsch, Charles Grohsberger) .... 3m. 24s.

1944—Tufts (Raymond Southwick, George Kennedy, Edward Palmieri, Harry Drake) .... 3m. 25.4s.

1945—N.Y.U. (Milford Parker, Edmund Wonilowicz, William Lubin, Maurice Callender) .... 3m. 26s.

1946—N.Y.U. (Milford Parker, Robert Hakusa, William Lubin, Maurice Callender) .... 3m. 26.1s.

1947—Seton Hall (Reginald S. Marshall, Frank D. Fox, George B. Stafurik, Philip Palese) .... 3m. 24.2s.

1948—Yale (Edward N. Burdick, Henry F. Stoltman, Scott L. Paradise, Edward F. Sause) .... 3m. 22.4s.

1949—Georgetown (Vincent C. Cino, John P. Lynch, Robert S. Spearman, Edward F. Sause) ... 3m. 21.7s.

1950—Seton Hall (Abe Evans, James Baucom, Charles Slade, Robert Carter) .... 3m.22s.

1951—Seton Hall (Frank Turner, Charles Slade, Morris Curotta, Robert Carter) .... 3m. 19.9s.

1952—Manhattan (Henry Bercuk, Wallace Pina, Ronald Ferraro, Robert Carty) .... 3m. 21.2s.

1953—Manhattan (Henry Bercuk, Ronald Lucas, Wallace Pina, Ronald Ferraro) .... 3m. 21.1s.

1954—Princeton (Thomas Eglin, Richard Yaffa, R. T. Lowry, Joseph Meyers, Jr.) .... 3m. 21.5s.

1955—Pittsburgh (Ed Saunders, Joe Dudas, William Green, Arnold Sowell) .... 3m.19.8s.

1956—Villanova (Gene Maliff, Roland Simpson, Warner Heitmann, Charles Jenkins) .... 3m. 19.6s.

1957—Villanova (Gene Maliff, John Furlinger, Al Peterson, Ed Collymore) .... 3m.20.6s.

1958—Pittsburgh (Zinneford Smith, Vincent Wojnar, Paul Thrash, Mel Barnwell) .... 3m. 20.4s.

1959—Pittsburgh (Zinneford Smith, Jay Moody, Vincent Wojnar, Mel Barnwell) .... 3m.18.6s.

1960—Villanova (Joseph Manion, Carl Wagner, Robert Coffil, Robert Raemore) .... 3m. 18.8s.

1961—Princeton (Forrest Walpole, Whitney Azoy, John Goldner, Richard Edmonds) .... 3m. 20.2s.

1962—N.Y.U. (James Brown, John Stevens, Hamilton McRae, Clifton Bertrand) .... 3m. 19.3s.

1963—Villanova (Ronald Hangey, Larry Livers, Stan Koslowski, Don Webster) .... 2m. 16.3s.

1964—Morgan State (Leonard Moore, Robert Bagley, Hubert Brown, Nick Lee) .... 3m. 16.3s.

1965—Morgan State (Dennis Edgehill, Herman Hawthorne, Tim Johnson, Nick Lee) .... 3m. 18.1s.

1966—American University (Andy Bell, Daniel Frye, Ross Fields, Bob Campbell) .... 3m. 18.9s.

1967—Villanova (Harold Nichter, Bill Grant, Kenneth Prince, Bill Heidelberger) .... 3m.19.2s.

1968—Villanova (Hardage Davis, Harold Nichter, Ken Prince, Larry James) .... 3m. 19.9s.

1969—Villanova (Robert Whitehead, Lamotte Hyman, Hardage Davis, Larry James) .... 3m. 18.7s.

1970—Villanova (Lamotte Hyman, Greg Govan, Hardage Davis, Larry James) .... 3m. 17.4s.

1971—Manhattan (Al Logie, Robert Rampino, Thomas Mauger, Michael Kenny) .... 3m. 17.3s.

1972—Adelphi (Larry Ross, Ray Lee, William Johnson, Dennis Walker) .... 3m.14.9s.

Two-Mile Relay

3,200 meters, 1934 through 1936.

1922—Pennsylvania (G. Meredith, E. McMullen, J. Holden, L. Brown) .. 7m. 55.2s.

1923—Boston College (Thomas F. Cavanaugh, Herbert A. Finnigan, Arthur T. Kirby, Patrick J. Mahoney) 7m. 55.5s.

1924—Georgetown (Edward Brooks, John Holden, George Marsters, Walter Gegan) .... 7m. 56.8s.

1925—Georgetown (Edward J. Swinburne, Edward M. Brooks, John C. Holden, George M. Masters) ..... 7m. 41.6s.

1926—Boston College (Joseph E. Ingoldsby, William T. McKillop, Francis H. McCloskey, Francis J. Daley) .... 7m.51.7s.

1927—Boston College (Joseph E. Ingoldsby, Francis J. Daley, William T. McKillop, Francis H. McCloskey) 7m. 51s.

1928—N.Y.U. (Wm. Phillips, Joseph Mendeloff, Frederick Veit, Philip Edwards) .... 7m. 59.2s.

1929—N.Y.U. (Walter S. Gassner, Wm. Phillips, Frederick Veit, Philip Edwards) .... 7m. 52s.

1930—Bates (Norman Cole, Wallace E. Viles, Rangar G. Lind, Russell H. Chapman) .... 7m. 56.8s.

1931—Boston College (John A. O'Brien, Thomas F. Meagher, Donald A. Fleet, Brendan J. Moynahan) .... 7m. 50.6s.

1932—N.Y.U. (James F. Maloney Jr., Samuel Mothner, Frederick P. Pumphrey, Frank T. Nordell) .... 7m. 48s.

1933—Princeton (Edward O. Hopkins, Walter E. Whitton, George S. Johnston, William R. Bonthron) .. 7m. 46.2s.

1934—Columbia (Carl Jensen, John T. Grady, Kenneth A. Gilmore, William A. Patterson) .... 7m. 46.1s.

1935—Manhattan (Eugene J. Nelley, Paul L. Dee, John A. Thompson, William J. Ray) .... 7m. 58.8s.

1936—Penn State (Duverney C. Book, Merle W. Stitller, Howard A. Downey, Frank R. Baird) .... 7m. 56.1s.

1937—N.Y.U. (Edgar Tait, John J. Perry, Curtis Giddings, Edgar Stripling) , ... 7m. 56.8s.

1938—Fordham (George F. Leary, Joseph R. Fay, Wesley H. Wallace, Francis G. Slater) .... 7m. 55.6s.

1939—N.Y.U. (Martin Witte, David Urbach, Myron Bresnick, Curtis Giddings) .... 7m. 53s.

1940—Fordham (Peter Gallery, Joseph Fay, Edward Shine, Walter Cary) . 7m. 49.9s.

1941—Fordham (Peter Callery, Edward Shine, Walter Cary, Frank Leary) .... 7m. 57.9s.

1942—Fordham (Andrew Lawrence, Edward Shine, Joseph Nowicki, Francis Leary) .... 7m. 52.8s.

1943—Fordham (Andrew Lawrence, John O'Hare, Jerome Connolly, Joseph Nowicki) No. official time

1944—Dartmouth (William Atkinson, Clark Judge, Franklin Fox, Donald L. Burnham) .... 8m. 5.5s.

1945—M.I.T. (Joseph F. Shea, Charles H. Goldie, John A. Serrie Jr., Royce D. Crimmin) .... 8m. 2.3s.

1946—N.Y.U. (Milton Smith, Frank Martin, Henry Eckert, Stanton Callender) .... 8m. 7/10s.

1947—N.Y.U. (Austin Scott, Reginald Pearman, Raymond K. Zoellner, Stanton Callender) .... 7m. 56.6s.

1948—Manhattan (John C. Moran, Arthur J. Sullivan, James A. Cavanaugh, Ignatius J. Rienzo .... 7m. 58s.

1949—Michigan State (Donald L. Makielski, David L. Peppard, William G. Mack, Jack Dianetti) .... 7m. 49.5s.

1950—Georgetown (Patrick O'Brien, David Boland, David Smith, Joseph Deady) .... 7m. 44.9s.

1951—Manhattan (Gerard Vier, Patrick Duffy, Joseph Seebode, Robert McNeill) .... 7m. 48.7s.

1952—Princeton (Richard Driscoll, William Raney, Hugh Campbell, Albin Rauch) .... 7m. 49.2s.

1953—Fordham (Frank Tarsney, William Persichetty, Thomas Keegan, Thomas Courtney) .... 7m. 44.8s.

1954—Syracuse (Jack Hubbard, Les Vielbig, Don Shupe, Steve Armstrong) .... 7m. 42.8s.

1955—Syracuse (Robert Milner, Les Vielbig, Steve Armstrong, Don Shupe) .... 7m. 49.1s.

1956—Pittsburgh (James Moore, Wendall Harford, Perry Jones, Arnold Sowell) .... 7m. 40s.

1957—Georgetown (John Bisbee, Norm Williams, John Nelson, Robert Carney) .... 7m. 48.4s.

1958—Syracuse (Robert McShorley, Larry Twomey, Bryant Wood, Ben Johns) .... 7m. 41.9s.

1959—Manhattan (John Corry, John Harton, Bob McKay, Kye Courtney) 7m. 46.9s.

1960—Villanova (Gerald Hackett, Jon Dante, Nicholas DeAngelis, Patrick Nicastro) .... 7m. 45.8s.

1961—Holy Cross (Charles Buchta, Jon O'Connor, Thomas Noering, Bowers) .... 7m. 43.5s.

1962—Villanova (Gerald Hackett, Patrick Nicastro, Jon Dante, Albert Adams) .... 7m. 45.2s.

1963—Seton Hall (Kevin Hennessey, Ed Wyrsch, Tom Tushingham, George Germann) .... 7m. 39.8s.
1964—Seton Hall (Kevin Hennessey, Herbert Germann, Bruce Andrews, George Germann) .... 7m. 33.4s.
1965—Manhattan (Courtnay Ettricks, Eliasib Acosta, James Sherlock, Joe Kearney) .... 7m. 38.5s.
1966—Fordham (Robert Dyke, James Groark, Brian Hernon, John Fath) 7m. 38.5s.
1967—Manhattan (John Eisner, Otho Van Exel, Brian Kivlin, Joe Kearney) 7m. 35.7s
1968—Villanova (Alan McCafferty, Andy O'Reilly, Craig Nation, Ian Hamilton) .... 7m. 39.2s.
1969—Holy Cross (Arthur Martin, James Walsh, Joe Jamieson, Dan O'Donnell) .... 7m. 40.1s.
1970—Northeastern (Michael Roberts, Michael Scanlon, Ralph Bowman, Francis Kelley) .... 7m. 41.1s.
1971—Villanova (Rick Kell, Karl Kinscherf, Chris Mason, Martin Liquori) .... 7m. 31.6s.
1972—Manhattan (Ray Naudain, Warren Gordon, John Rothrock, Joe Savage) .... 7m. 33.1s.

Distance Medley Relay

1971—Pittsburgh (Ken Silay, Smitty Brown, Mike Schurko, Jerry Richey) .... 9m. 52.5s.
1972—Penn State (Jim Allahand, Karl Tewold, Dan Supulski, Greg Fredericks) .... 9m. 47.8s.

60-Yard High Hurdles
70 yards, 1924-33.
50 meters, 1934-36.

1922—H. E. Barron, Penn State .... 7.8s.
1923—A. B. Treman, Cornell .... 7.9s.
1924—Charles H. Moore, Penn State ...... 9.1s.
1925—Charles H. Moore, Penn State ...... 8.8s.
1926—Raymond G. Hass, Georgetown .... 8.8s.
1927—Eber M. Wells, Dartmouth .... 9s.
1928—John S. Collier, Brown .... 8.7s.
1929—John S. Collier, Brown .... 8.8s.
1930—Solomon Furth, New York Univ. ... 8.8s.
1931—Eugene E. Record, Harvard .... 8.7s.
1932—Eugene E. Record, Harvard .... 8.8s.
1933—George S. Lockwood, Yale .... 8.8s.
1934—Walter S. Merwin, Cornell .... 7s.
1935—Charles O. Pessoni, Manhattan ....
    Philip G. Good, Bowdoin .... 7s.
1936—Milton G. Green, Harvard .... 7s.
1937—John M. Donovan, Dartmouth ..... 7.6s.
1938—Theodore D. Day, Yale .... 7.4s.
1939—Jay M. Shields, Yale .... 7.4s.
1940—Edward Dugger, Tufts .... 7.3s.
1941—Edward Dugger, Tufts .... 7.4s.

1942—Thomas H. Todd Jr., Virginia ...... 7.5s.
1943—Thomas H. Todd Jr., Virginia ...... 7.4s.
1944—Edwin Sparrow, Tufts .... 7.7s.
1945—Jerry W. Morrow, Army .... 7.8s.
1946—Leland D. Christensen, Army ...... 7.6s.
1947—Warren Halliburton, New York Univ. 7.5s.
1948—George Cook, Yale .... 7.5s.
1949—Horace Smith, Michigan State ..... 7.2s.
1950—James Gehrdes, Penn State .... 7.3s.
1951—Meredith Gourdine, Cornell ...... 7.4s.
1952—Peter McCreary, Dartmouth ...... 7.4s.
1953—Jack S. Goldberg, Tufts .... 7.4s.
1954—Warren Lattof, M.I.T. .... 7.5s.
1955—Charles Pratt, Manhattan .... 7.4s.
1956—Rod Perry, Penn State .... 7.3s.
1957—Lou Knight, Manhattan .... 7.2s.
1958—Al Hoddinott, Georgetown .... 7.3s.
1959—Angelo Sinisi, Brown .... 7.3s.
(Number of hurdles increased to 5 in 1960)
1960—William Johnson, Maryland .... 7.4s.
1961—Leon Pras, Villanova .... 7.4s.
1962—Tyrone Pannell, Manhattan ...... 7.4s.
1963—Aggrey Awori, Harvard .... 7.3s.
1964—John Bethea, Morgan State .... 7.4s.
1965—Courtland Gray, Navy .... 7.4s.
1966—Dave Hemery, Boston Univ. ...... 7.2s.
1967—Ervin Hall, Villanova .... 7.4s.
1968—Ervin Hall, Villanova .... 7.2s.
1969—Ervin Hall, Villanova .... 7.2s.
1970—Kwaku Ohene Frepong, Yale ...... 7.3s.
1971—Jeff Howser, Duke .... 7.2s.
1972—Tom McMannon, Notre Dame ..... 7.3s.

High Jump

1922—Leroy Brown, Dartmouth ... 6ft. 4 7/8in.
1923—Leroy Brown, Dartmouth ... 6ft. 2 3/4in.
1924—Clarence T. Flahive, Boston
    College .... 6ft. /8in.
1925—Emerson C. Norton, ...
    Georgetown .... 5ft. 11 1/2in.
1926—Emerson C. Norton, ...
    Georgetown ....
    John H. Moody, ...
    Dartmouth .... 6ft. 1 3/4in.
1927—Thomas L. Maynard, Dartmouth 6ft. 1/2in.
1928—Thomas L. Maynard, Dartmouth ..... 6ft.
1929—Benjamin Van D. Hedges, ...
    Princeton ....
    William M. Pump, Colgate ...... 6ft. 3in.
1930—William B. O'Connor, Columbia .
    George V. Wolf, Yale .... 6ft. 3 1/2in.
1931—John H. Moody, Dartmouth ...
    William B. Newkirk, Penn ......
    William B. O'Connor, Columbia .. 6ft. 3in.
1932—Wm. B. O'Connor, Columbia .... 6ft. 3in.
1933—Robert Pitkin, Columbia ......
    Keith S. Brown, Yale ....
    George B. Spitz Jr., N.Y.U. .... 6ft. 2 3/4in.
1934—George B. Spitz Jr. N.Y.U. .... 6ft. 5 5/8in.
1935—Keith S. Borwn, Yale .... 6ft. 4in.
1936—William H. Eipel, Manhattan .... 6ft. 3in.
1937—James B. Dillingham, Columbia 6ft. 3 3/8in.

1938—Arthur F. Byrnes, Manhattan .... 6ft. 6in.
1939—Arthur F. Byrnes, Manhattan . 6ft. 6 1/4in.
1940—Arthur F. Byrnes, Manhattan.... 6ft. 4in.
1941—Donald F. Blout, Dartmouth . 6ft. 5 5/8in.
1942—A. Richmond Morcom, New ....
    Hampshire .... 6ft. 4in.
1943—William Vessie, Columbia ... 6ft. 7 1/8in.
1944—Bert Atkinson, Navy .... 6ft. 1in.
1945—Paul Robeson Jr., Cornell ....
    Joseph F. Conley, ...
    Dartmouth .... 6ft. 3in.
1946—Paul Robeson Jr., Cornell ...... 6ft. 4in.
1947—Irving Mondschein, N.Y.U. .. 6ft. 7 1/4in.
1948—Irving Mondschein, N.Y.U. ....
    William Vessie, Columbia .... 6ft. 6in.
1949—Richard Phillips, Brown ....
    Richard F. Lyster, Temple ... 6ft. 4 1/2in.
1950—Victor Fritts, Penn State .... 6ft. 4 1/2in.
1951—James Herb, Penn State ..... 6ft. 5 1/2in.
1952—James Webb, La Sal
    Nelson Ehinger, Dartmouth .. 6ft. 5 1/4in.
1953—James Herb, Penn State ..... 6ft. 5 1/8in.
1954—Frank Gaffney, Manhattan ....
    William Antone, M.I.T. ....
    Wilfred Lee, Pennsylvania ... 6ft. 4 3/4in.
1955—Wilfred Lee, Pennsylvania ...... 6ft. 6in.
1956—Phil Reavis, Villanova .... 6ft. 5in.
1957—Phil Reavis, Villanova ....
    Charles Stead, Villanova ..... 6ft. 9 1/2in.
1958—Phil Reavis, Villanova ...... 6ft. 8 3/4in.
1959—Charles Stead, Villanova .... 6ft. 7in.
1960—John Thomas, Boston Univ..... 7ft. 1/2in.
1961—John Thomas, Boston Univ...... 6ft. 6in.
1962—John Thomas, Boston Univ..... 6ft. 11in.
1963—Kevin O'Brien, Holy Cross .... 6ft. 8n.
1964—Christopher Pardee, Harvard .... 6ft. 9in.
1965—Frank Costello, Maryland ....7ft.
1966—Frank Costello, Maryland ..... 6ft. 10in.
1967—Elijah Miller, Rutgers .... 6ft. 9in.
1968—Elijah Miller, Rutgers .... 6ft. 10in.
1969—Lonnie Dalton, West Chester .... 6ft. 9in.
1970—Joseph David, Maryland ...... 6ft. 11in.
1971—Lonnie Dalton, West Chester . 6ft. 11in.
1972—Chris Dunn, Colgate .... 7ft. 0in.

Broad Jump

1922—S. T. Chow, Penn .... 21ft. 10 1/2in.
1923—Albert E. Rose, Penn ...... 22ft. 3 1/2in.
1924—Albert E. Rose, Penn ...... 22ft. 3 1/8in.
1925—William A. Dowding,
    Georgetown .... 23ft. 1 1/8in.
1926—William A. Dowding,
    Georgetown .... 22ft. 7in.
1927—Alfred H. Bates, Penn State .... 23ft. 1in.
1928—Alfred H. BAtes Penn State 22ft. 11 3/4in.
1929—Sol H. Furth, N.Y.U. ...... 22ft. 5 1/4in.
1930—Everett E. Utterback,
    Pitsburgh .... 23ft. 1 1/2in.
1931—Everett E. Utterback,
    Pittsburgh .... 23ft. 9 3/8in.
1932—Charles W. Summerill, Princeton 22ft. 9in.
1933—George B. Spitz Jr., N.Y.U. . 22ft. 4 1/4in.

1934—Henry M. Little, William
    and Mary .... 23ft. 9 1/4in.
1935—Benjamin W. Johnson,
    Columbia .... 23ft. 9 1/4in.
1936—Stanley T. Johnson, M.I.T. .... 23ft. 5in.
1937—Benjamin W. Johnson,
    Columbia .... 24ft. 1/8in.
1938—Anson Perina, Princeton ...... 24ft. 2in.
1939—Anson Perina, Princeton .... 24ft.
1940—Norwood H. Ewell, Penn
    State .... 24ft. 8 1/8in.
1941—Donald F. Blount, Dartmouth 23ft. 9 3/4in.
1942—Norwood H. Ewell, Penn State 25ft. 2 1/2in.
1943—Howard G. Yielding, Army 22ft. 11 3/4in.
1944—Frederic Douwman, Navy . 22ft. 11 1/2in.
1945—Frederic Bouwman, Navy . 23ft. 11 1/2in.
1946—Herbert P. Douglas, Pittsburgh .. 24ft. 2in.
1947—Herbert P. Douglas, Pittsburgh 24ft. 2 7/8in.
1948—Herbert P. Douglas, Pittsburgh . 24ft. 1/4in.
1949—Fred D. Johnson, Mich. State 24ft. 6 1/8in.
1950—Fred D. Johnson, Mich. State 24ft. 8 3/4in.
1951—Andrew Stanfield, Seton Hall 24ft. 5 1/2in.
1952—Meredith Gourdine, Cornell . 24ft. 5 5/8in.
1953—Charles Pratt, Manhattan .. 23ft. 5 1/8in.
1954—Bernard Bruce, Boston U. .. 23ft. 4 3/4in.
1955—Bernard Bruce, Boston U. . 23ft. 10 1/4in.
1956—Len Moore, Manhattan ... 23ft. 5 1/2in.
1957—Mike Herman, N.Y.U. ..... 23ft. 6 1/2in.
1958—Mike Herman, N.Y.U. ..... 24ft. 7 1/2in.
1959—Mike Herman, N.Y.U. .... 25ft. 3/4in.
1960—John Buckley, Villanova ... 23ft. 9 1/4in.
1961—Robert O'Brien, Manhattan .... 24ft. 0in.
1962—Sherman Lewis, Michigan State 23ft. 11in.
1963—Jim Thorell, Navy .... 23ft. 7 1/4in.
1964—Mike Cole, Maryland ..... 24ft. 7in.
1965—Mike Cole, Maryland .... 24ft. 5in.
1966—Ed Marks, Maryland ..... 24ft. 10 3/4in.
1967—Calvin Hill, Yale .... 24ft. 8 3/4in.
1968—Del Benjamin, Manahattan . 24ft. 8 3/4in.
1969—Elliott Garrett, Maryland ...... 24ft. 2in.
1970—Glen Fausett, Cornell ..... 24ft. 1 3/4in.
1971—Fred Samara, Penn .... 24ft. 9 1/2in.
1972—Bill Rea, Pittsburgh ...... 24ft. 10 1/4in.

Triple Jump

1971—Bryant Salter, Pittsburgh ...... 50ft. 1in.
1972—Andris Bilmanis, Maryland . 49ft. 3 1/4in.

Pole Vault

1922—Kenneth P. Libbey, Dartmouth .....12ft.
1923—Nelson B. Sherrill, Penn. ......
    Benjamin M. Penn .... 12ft. 6in.
1924—Benjamin M. Owen, Sylvan ....
    S. Scholpp, Yale Kenneth ......
    P. Libbey, Dartmouth .... 12ft. 6in.
1925—Nelson B. Sherrill, Penn ....13ft.
1926—Stephen R. Bradley, Princeton .. 12ft. 7in.
1927—Stephen R. Bradley, Princeton ..
    Sabin W. Carr, Yale ....13ft.
1928—Sabin W. Carr, Yale .... 13ft. 3 3/4in.
1929—Frederic H. Sturdy, Yale ... 13ft. 7 3/4in.
1930—Bernard E. Berlinger, Penn .....

Everett L. Colyer, Cornell ....
Oscar Sutermeister, Harvard ....13ft.
1931—Bernard E. Berlinger, Penn .....
Everett L. Coyler, Cornell .. 13ft. 8 1/4in.
1932—Theodore H. Lee, Yale .... 13ft. 8 5/8in.
1933—Wirt L. Thompson, Yale ......
Keith S. Brown, Yale ...... 13ft. 9 3/4in.
1934—Keith S. Brown, Yale ....14ft. 7/8in.
1935—Keith S. Brown, Yale .... 14ft. 3 1/4in.
1936—Emil Dubiel, Harvard ....
William H. Harding, Yale ...... 13ft. 3in.
1937—Richard V. Ganslen, Columbia .. 13ft. 9in.
1938—William H. Harding, Yale ...... 13ft. 9in.
1939—Richard V. Ganslen, Columbia .. 13ft. 6in.
1940—Ralph N. Ross, Army ....
Thomas A. Lussen, Yale ....14ft.
1941—Doyle V. Rhoades, Pittsburgh ..
Warren Broemel, Columbia ....
Charles Martin, Manhattan .....
Edward R. Macomber, Yale ....
Frank Cromwell, R.I.State ......13ft.
1942—A. Richmond Morcom, New
Hampshire .... 14ft. 4 1/2in.
1943—A. Richmond Morcom, New ...
Hampshire ....14ft.
1944—Philip L. Lansing, Army ....13ft.
1945—Charles A. Riehl, Navy ....
Augustine Puchrik, Army ....
Kenneth G. Kochel, Army .....
James M. Holcomb, ARmy ....
Philip L. Lansing, Army ....12ft.
1946—John Haughwout, Cornell ..... 12ft. 6in.
1947—A. Richmond Morcom, New
Hampshire .... 13ft. 6in.
1948—Roy Potochnik, Marquette .... 13ft. 4in.
1949—George Appel, Yale ....14ft.
1950—Neil King, Yale ....
Richard Bastar, Army .... 13ft. 6in.
1951—George Appel, Yale ....14ft.
1952—Joseph Perlow, Army .... 13ft. 6in.
1953—Daniel Lorch, Penn State ......
Robert Linne, Rhode Island
State .... 13ft. 4in.
1954—Bruce Hescock, Boston U. ....14ft.
1955—Don Gragg, Villanova .....
Dave Seed, California ....14ft.
1956—Don Bragg, Villanova ...... 15ft. 2in.
1957—Don Bragg, Villanova ....15ft.
1958—Ed Hoyle, Marquette .... 14ft. 8in.
1959—Bjorn Anderson, Maryland
Glen Cividin, Notre Dame ..... 14ft. 3in.
1960—Bjorn Anderson, Maryland ....
Tom Reichert, Notre DAme .... 14ft. 4in.
1961—John Murray, Cornell .... 14ft. 6in.
1962—Rolando Cruz, Villanova ... 15ft. 3 3/4in.
1963—Rolando Cruz, Villanova ...... 16ft. 1in.
1964—John Uelses, La Salle ...... 16ft. 1 1/4in.
1965—John Uelses, La Salle ....16ft.
1966—Thomas Gagner, Maryland ..... 15ft. 4in.
1967—Peter Chen, American .... 15ft. 6in.
1968—Peter Chen, American ..... 16ft. 4 1/4in.
1969—James Williamson, Maryland ... 15ft. 8in.

1970—Thomas Blair, Penn .... 16ft. 4in.
1971—Jerry Klyop, Villanova .... 16ft. 4 1/2in.
1972—Thomas Blair, Penn .... 16ft. 8 1/2in.

Shot-Put

1922—S. Harrison Thomson,
Princeton .... 43ft. 5 1/2in.
1923—Ralph G. Hills, Princeton ... 45ft. 8 1/4in.
1924—Ralph G. Hills, Princeton .....46ft. 3/4in.
1925—Ralph G. Hills, Princeton ... 47ft. 5 3/4in.
1926—Anthony J. Plansky,
Georgetown .... 45ft. 6 1/2in.
1927—Harold Lamberg, Penn ..... 46ft. 4 1/4in.
1928—David Adelman, Georgetown ... 48ft. 8in.
1929—John F. Anderson, Cornell .. 47ft. 7 3/4in.
1930—Leo Sexton, Georgetown ... 48ft. 6 7/8in.
1931—Bernard E. Berlinger, Penn .. 48ft. 6 1/4in.
1932—Otto B. Schoenfeld, Cornell .... 48ft. 6in.
1933—Thomas F. Gilbane, Brown ...47ft. 1/2in.
1934—William H. Niblock, Bowdoin . 49ft. 10in.
1935—Anthony Geniawicz,
Dartmouth .... 48ft. 9in.
1936—Anthony Geniawicz,
Dartmouth .... 49ft. 1 5/8in.
1937—Dimitri N. Zaitz, Boston College
Daniel Taylor, Columbia ... 50ft. 9 5/8in.
1938—Francis J. Ryan, Columbia . 51ft. 10 3/4in.
1939—Francis J. Ryan, Columbia . 50ft. 8 7/8in.
1940—Alfred C. Blozis, Georgetown 55ft. 3 1/4in.
1941—Alfred C. Blozis, Georgetown .. 56ft. 6in.
1942—Alfred C. Blozis, Georgetown 56ft. 3 3/8in.
1943—Bernard Mayer, N.Y.U. .... 52ft. 3 5/8in.
1944—George C. Brown, Navy .... 46ft. 3 3/4in.
1945—Felix A. Blanchard, Army .. 48ft. 3 1/2in.
1946—DeWitt E. Coulter, Army ....53ft. 3/4in.
1947—Bernard Mayer, N.Y.U. .... 50ft. 9in.
1948—James E. Fuchs, Yale ...... 52ft. 9 5/8in.
1949—James E. Fuchs, Yale ...... 55ft. 5 1/4in.
1950—James E. Fuchs, Yale .... 56ft 3/8in.
1951—John Ogle, Manhattan ...... 51ft. 1in.
1952—John S. McCallum, Penn. .... 49ft. 4 1/8in.
1953—Albert Thompson, Columbia 51ft. 9 1/2in.
1954—Albert Thompson Columbia 52ft. 10 3/4in.
1955—Roosevelt Grier, Penn State . 53ft. 4 1/2in.
1956—Ken Bantum, Manhattan ... 55ft. 6 3/4in.
1957—Ken Bantum, Manhattan ... 55ft. 7 1/4in.
1958—Joe Marchiony, Manhattan 54ft. 11 1/4in.
1959—Carl Shine, Pennsylvania .. 54ft. 11 1/2in.
1960—John Marchiony, Manhattan ... 57ft. 0in.
1961—William Joe, Villanova .. 54ft. 6 1/4in.
1962—Gary Gubner, N.Y.U. ...... 64ft. 3 1/2in.
1963—Gary Gubner, New York Univ. . 61ft. 5in.
1964—Gary Gubner, New York
University .... 61ft. 9 3/4in.
1965—Carl Wallin, Northeastern .... 57ft. 11in.
1966—Ernest Hearon, Maryland ... 57ft. 7 1/2in.
1967—George Allen, St. John's ...... 56ft. 9in.
1968—Richard Benka, Harvard ... 57ft. 7 1/4in.
1969—Richard Benka, Harvard ...... 59ft. 1in.
1970—Roger Taylor, Syracuse .... 56ft. 5in.
1971—John Hanley, Maryland ...... 58ft. 10in.
1972—Doug Price, Brown .... 58ft. 8 1/2in.

35-Lb. Weight Throw

1922—J. F. Brown, Harvard . . . . . . .47ft. 11in.
1923—Frederick D. Tootell, Bowdoin 52ft. 9 1/4in.
1924—Caleb F. Gates, Princeton . . . .49ft. 3 3/8in.
1925—Kenneth L. Wentworth, Colby 52ft. 4 5/8in.
1926—Caleb F. Gates, Princeton . . . .47ft. 9 1/2in.
1927—Norwood G. Wright, Cornell . .51ft. 1/2in.
1928—Norwood G. Wright, Cornell . .53ft. 11 1/8in.
1929—Leo Sexton, Georgetown . . . .51ft. 9 3/8in.
1930—Frank J. Weis, Cornell . . . . . .51ft. 9 3/8in.
1931—Fred A. Steiner, Penn. . . . . . .54ft. 9in.
1932—Murdock J. Finlayson, Harvard 50ft. 5 3/8in.
1933—Mortimer M. Reznick, N.Y.U. .53ft. 2 1/4in.
1934—Henry Dreyer, R.I. State . . . . .55ft. 2 1/4in.
1935—Henry Dreyer, R.I. State . . . . .57ft. 9in.
1936—Anton Kishon, Bates . . . . . . .56ft. 8 3/8in.
1937—Irving Folwartshny, R.I. State .57ft. 6 5/8in.
1938—Irving Folwartshny, R.I.State .55ft. 6 3/4in.
1939—William W. McKeever, Cornell .57ft. 3 1/8in.
1940—Robert H. Bennett, Maine . . . .57ft. 4 1/8in.
1941—Norman Wilcox, R.I. State . . .53ft. 9in.
1942—Norman Wilcox, R.I. State . . .56ft. 9in.
1943—William O. Fisher, Harvard . . .50ft. 8 1/2in.
1944—Leon Dombroski, Army . . . . .47ft. 2 1/8in.
1945—Anthony J. Pemico, Penn. . . . .49ft. 11 3/4in.
1946—John W. Fisher, Harvard . . . . .51ft. 11 1/2in.
1947—Robert H. Bennett, Brown . . .54ft. 11 3/4in.
1948—George G. Marsanskis, Maine . . 56ft. 11in.
1949—James Sholtz, Army . . . . .60ft. 7 3/4in.
1950—Gilbert J. Borjeson, Brown . . .56ft. 7 5/8in.
1951—Thomas Bane, Tufts . . . . .60ft. 1/4in.
1952—Gilbert J. Borjeson, Brown . . .58ft. 9 1/4in.
1953—Stephen Dillon, Manhattan . . .58ft. 7 1/2in.
1954—Martin Engel, N.Y.U. . . . . . . .57ft. 6 1/2in.
1955—Stewart Thomson, Yale . . . . .58ft. 11 1/4in.
1956—Albert Hall, Cornell . . . . .62ft. 8 1/2in.
1957—George Bixby, Dartmouth . . .59ft. 5 1/4in.
1958—John Lawlor, Boston U. . . . . .57ft. 6 3/4in.
1959—Eino Keerd, Boston U. . . . . . .60ft. 11 3/4in.
1960—John Lawlor, Boston Univ. . . .63ft. 1/2in.
1961—Henry Sage, Navy . . . . .63ft. 4 1/2in.
1962—Edward Bailey, Harvard . . . . .63ft. 5in.
1963—Dick Ward, Massachusetts . . . .61ft. 9 1/4in.
1964—John Connors, Manhattan . . . .61ft. 5 1/2in.
1965—Alex Schulten, Bowdoin . . . . .61ft. 11 3/4in.
1966—Bob Mead, Manhattan . . . . . . .60ft. 5 1/4in.
1967—John Graham, Army . . . . .60ft. 9 1/2in.
1968—Robert Narcessian, R.I. . . . . .62ft. 10 1/2in.
1969—Edward Nosal, Harvard . . . . .60ft. 9 1/4in.
1970—Thomas Sirvis, Northeastern . .60ft. 9 1/2in.
1971—Thomas Sirvis, Northeastern . .62ft. 8 1/2in.
1972—Frank Bredice, Southern
      Connecticut . . . . .64ft. 9in.

Team

Year and champion
1922—Cornell (35 1/2)
1923—Pennsylvania (29)
1924—Pennsylvania (21 1/3)
1924—Georgetown (37)
1926—Harvard (28)
1927—Harvard (23 3/7)
1928—Cornell (21)
1929—New York University (25)
1930—Cornell (27 1/2)
      Pennsylvania (27 1/2)
1931—Pennsylvania (38 1/10)
1932—New York University (31)
1933—Yale (32)
1934—Manhattan (28 1/2)
1935—Manhattan (26)
1936—Manhattan (26)
1937—Columbia (34 5/14)
1938—Columbia (27)
1939—Manhattan (36)
1940—New York University (27)
1941—Fordham (25 1/4)
1942—Penn State (21 7/10)
1943—New York University (48)
1944—Army (47)
1945—Army (73 1/2)
1946—Army (53 1/2)
1947—New York University (35)
1948—New York University (31 1/2)
1949—Michigan State (35 2/5)
1950—Michigan State (21)
1951—Manhattan (29)
1952—Manhattan (40 1/2)
1953—Manhattan (36)
1954—Yale (19)
1955—Manhattan (27)
1956—Manhattan (36)
1957—Villanova (46)
1958—Villanova (29 1/3)
1959—Penn State (20 17/36)
1960—Villanove (27)
1961—Yale (30)
1962—Villanova (31 1/2)
1963—Villanova (27)
1964—Villanova (22)
1965—Villanova (24)
1966—Maryland (28)
1967—Villanova (36)
1968—Villanova (47)
1969—Villanova (46)
1970—Villanova (41 1/2)
1971—Villanova (42)
1972—Pennsylvania (26)

BOSTON MARATHON WINNERS

1897—J. J. McDermott, New York 2h.55m.10s.
1898—R. J. MacDonald (Canada) . 2h.42m.
1899—L. J. Brignoli, Cambridge,
      Mass. . . . . 2h.54m.38s.
1900—J. J. Caffrey, Hamilton, Ont. 2h.39m.44.4s.
1901—J. J. Caffrey, Hamilton, Ont. 2h.29m.23.6s.
1902—Samuel Mellor,Yonkers, N.Y. 2h.43m.
1903—J. C. Lorden, Cambridge,
      Mass . . . . 2h.41m.29.8s.
1904—Michael Spring, New York . 2h.39m.4.4s.
1905—Fred Lorz, Yonkers, N.Y. . . . 2h.38m.25.4s.
1906—Timothy Ford, Hampshire
      A.A. . . . . 2h.45m.45s.
1907—Thomas Longboat, Toronto 2h.24m.24s.

1908—Thomas Morrissey,
Yonkers, N.Y. .... 2h.25m.43.2s.
1909—Henri Renaud, Nashua,
N.H. .... 2h.53m.36.8s.
1910—Fred L. Cameron, Amherst,
Nova Scotia .... 2h.28m.52.4s.
1911—Clarence DeMar, Melrose,
Mass. .... 2h.21m.39.6s.
1912—Michael J. Ryan, New York 2h.21m.18.2s.
1913—Fritz Carlson, Minneapolis,
Minn. .... 2h.25m.14.8s.
1914—James Duffy, Hamilton, Ont.2h.25m.1.2s.
1915—Edouard Fabre, Montreal,
Que. .... 2h.31m.41.2s.
1916—Arthur Roth, Boston ..... 2h.27m.16.4s.
1917—William Kennedy, New York 2h.28m.37.2s.
1918—No competition
1919—Carl Linder, Quincy, Mass. . 2h.29m.13.4s.
1920—Peter Trivoulides, New York 2h.29m.31s.
1921—Frank Zuna, New York ... 2h.18m.57.6s.
1922—Clarence DeMar, Melrose,
Mass. .... 2h.18m.10s.
1923—Clarence DeMar, Melrose,
Mass. .... 2h.23m.47.4s.
1924—Clarence DeMar, Melrose,
Mass. .... 2h.29m.40.2s.
1925—Charles Mellor, Chicago ... 2h.33m.0.6s.
1926—John Miles, Sydney Mines,
Nova Scotia .... 2h.25m.40.4s.
1927—Clarence DeMar, Melrose,
Mass. .... 2h.40m.22.2s.
1928—Clarence DeMar, Melrose,
Mass. .... 2h.37m.7.8s.
1929—John Miles, Hamilton, Ont. 2h.33m.8.6s.
1930—Clarence DeMar, Melrose,
Mass. .... 2h.34m.48.2s.
1931—James Hennigan, Medford,
Mass. .... 2h.46m.45.8s.
1932—Paul De Bruyn, New York . 2h.33m.36.4s.
1933—Leslie Pawson, Pawtucket,
R.I. .... 2h.31m.1.6s.
1934—Dave Komonen, Sudbury,
Ont. .... 2h.32m.53.8s.
1935—John Kelley, Arlington,
Mass. .... 2h.32m.7.4s.
1936—Ellison Brown, Alton, R.I. . 2h.33m.40.8s.
1937—Walter Young, Verdun, Que. 2h.33m. 20s.
1938—Leslie Pawson, Pawtucket,
R.I. .... 2h.35m.34.8s.
1939—Ellison Brown, Westerly, R.I.2h.28m.51.8s.
1940—Gerard Cote, St. Hyacinthe,
Que. .... 2h.28m.28.6s.
1941—Leslie Pawson, Pawtucket,
R.I. .... 2h.30m.38s.
1942—Joe Smith, Medford, Mass. . 2h.26m.51.2s.
1943—Sgt. Gerard Cote,
Valleyfield, Que. ...... 2h.28m.25.8s.
1944—Gerard Cote, Montreal .... 2h.31m.50.4s.
1945—John Kelley, West Acton,
Mass. .... 2h.30m.40.2s.
1946—Stylianos Kyriakides,
Athens, Greece .... 2h.29m.27s.

1947—Yun Bok Suh, Seoul, Korea 2h.25m.39s.
1948—Gerard Cote, St. Hyacinthe,
Que. .... 2h.31m.2s.
1949—Karl Leandersson, Sweden . 2h.31m.50.8s.
1950—Ham Kee Yong,
Seoul, Korea .... 2h.32m.39s.
1951—Shigeki Tanaka, Hiroshima,
Japan .... 2h.27m.45s.
1952—Doroteo Flores, Guatemala 2h.31m.53s.
1953—Keizo Yamada, Japan ..... 2h.18m.51s.
1954—Veikko Karanen, Finland . 2h.20m.39s.
1955—Hideo Hamamura, Japan .. 2h.18m.22s.
1956—Aniti Viskari, Finland ....2h.14m.14s.
1957—Johnny Kelley, Groton,
Conn. .... 2h.20m.5s.
1958—Franjo Mihalic, Yugoslavia .2h.25m.54s.
1959—Eino Oksanen, Finland .... 2h.22m.42s.
1960—Paavo Kotila, Finland ..... 2h.20m.54s.
1961—Eino Oksanen, Finland .... 2h.23m.29s.
1962—Eino Oksanen, Finland .... 2h.23m.48s.
1963—Aurele Vandendriessche,
Belgium .... 2h.18m.58s.
1964—Aurele Vandendriessche,
Belgium .... 2h.19m.59s.
1965—Morio Shigematsu, Japan .. 2h.16m.33s.
1966—Kenji Kimihara, Japan ....2h.17m.11s.
1967—Dave McKenzie,
New Zealand .... 2h.15m.45s.
1968—Ambrose Burfoot, Wesleyan
Univ. .... 2h.22m.17s.
1969—Yoshiaki Unetani, Japan ..2h.13m.49s.
1970—Ron Hill, England .... 2h.10m.30s.
1971—Alvaro Mejia, Colombia ...2h.18m.45s.
1972—Olavi Suomalainen, Finland 2h.15m.30s.

UNITED STATES CHAMPIONS—WOMEN
(Source: Official Amateur Athletic Union Track
and Field Handbook.)

Outdoor

100-Meter Dash
100 yards: 1923-27, 1929-32, 1955, 1957-58,
1961-63, 1965-66, 1969-70.

1923—Frances Ruppert ....12s.
1924—Frances Ruppert ....12s.
1925—Helen Filkey ....11.4s.
1926—Rosa M. Grosse ....11.8s.
1927—Elta Cartwright ....11.4s.
1928—Elta Cartwright ....12.4s.
1929—Betty Robinson ....11.2s.
1930—Stella Walsh ....11.2s.
1931—Eleanor Egg ....11.4s.
1932—Wilhelmina von Bremen ....12.3s.
1933—Annette Rogers ....12.2s.
1934—No competition
1935—Helen Stephens ....11.6s.
1936—Helen Stephens ....11.7s.
1937—Claire Isicson ....12.8s.
1938—Lula Hymes ....12.4s.
1939—Olive Hasenfus ....12.6s.
1940—Jean Lane ....12s.
1941—Jean Lane ....12.4s.

1942—Alice Coachman	12.1s.
1943—Stella Walsh	11.6s.
1944—Stella Walsh	12.0s.
1945—Alice Coachman	12s.
1946—Alice Coachman	12.3s.
1947—Juanita Watson	13.1s.
1948—Stella Walsh	12.9s.
1949—Jean Patton	12.1s.
1950—Jean Patton	13.3s.
1951—Mary McNabb	12.2s.
1952—Catherine Hardy	12.3s.
1953—Barbara Jones	11.9s.
1954—Barbara Jones	12s.
1955—Mae Faggs	10.8s.
1956—Mae Faggs	11.7s.
1957—Barbara Jones	10.9s.
1958—Margaret Matthews	11.1s.
1959—Wilma Rudolph	12.1s.
1960—Wilma Rudolph	11.5s.
1961—Wilma Rudolph	10.8s.
1962—Wilma Rudolph	10.8s.
1963—Edith McGuire	11.0s.
1964—Wyomia Tyus	11.5s.
1965—Wyomia Tyus	10.5s.
1966—Wyomia Tyus	10.5s.
1967—Barbara Farrell	11.1s.
1968—Margaret Johnson Bailes	11.1s.
1969—Barbara Ferrell	10.7s.
1970—Chi Cheng	10.2s.
1971—Iris Davis	11.2s.
1972—Alice Annum	11.5s.

200-Meter Dash

220 Yards: 1926-32, 1955, 1957-58, 1961-63, 1965-66, 1969-70.

1926—Frances Keddie	28.6s.
1927—Ellen Brough	26.8s.
1928—Florence Wright	27.4s.
1929—Maybelle Gilliland	27.4s.
1930—Stella Walsh	25.4s.
1931—Stella Walsh	26.4s.
1932—Olive Hasenfus	26.5s.
1933—Olive Hasenfus	26.2s.
1934—No competition	
1935—Helen Stephens	24.6s.
1936—Beverly Hobbs	26.6s.
1937—Gertrude Johnson	26s.
1938—Fanny Vitale	26.7s.
1939—Stella Walsh	25.5s.
1940—Stella Walsh	26.1s.
1941—Jean Lane	25.2s.
1942—Stella Walsh	25.4s.
1943—Stella Walsh	26.3s.
1944—Stella Walsh	24.6s.
1945—Stella Walsh	26.6s.
1946—Stella Walsh	26.3s.
1947—Stella Walsh	26.2s.
1948—Stella Walsh	25.5s.
1949—Nell Jackson	24.2s.
1950—Nell Jackson	25s.
1951—Jean Patton	25.4s.
1952—Catherine Hardy	25.5s.

1953—Dolores Dwyer	24.4s.
1954—Mae Faggs	24.5s.
1955—Mae Faggs	25.1s.
1956—Mae Faggs	24.6s.
1957—Isabel Daniels	24.7s.
1058—Lucinda Williams	24.3s.
1959—Isabelle Daniels	24.1s.
1960—Wilma Rudolph	22.9s.
1961—Lacey O'Neill—Vivian Brown	24.1s.
1962—Vivian Brown	24.1s.
1963—Vivian Brown	24.4s.
1964—Edith McGuire	23.6s.
1965—Edith McGuire	23.6s.
1966—Wyomia Tyus	23.8s.
1967—Diana Wilson	23.6s.
1968—Wyomia Tyus	23.5s.
1969—Barbara Ferrell	23.8s.
1970—Chi Cheng	‡22.4s.
1971—Raelene Boyle (Australia)	23.1s.
1972—Alice Annum	23.4s.

‡ Wind aided.

440-Yard Run

400 meters: 1959-60, 1964, 1967-68, 1972

1958—Christine McKenzie	61.6s.
1959—Kimberly Polson	59.0s.
1960—Irene Robertson	59.1s.
1961—Jackie Patterson	59.5s.
1962—Suzanne Knott	58.1s.
1963—Suzanne Knott	57.0s.
1964—Janell Smith	54.7s.
1965—Janell Smith	55.1s.
1966—Charlette Cook	53.4s.
1967—Charlette Cook	52.5s.
1968—Jarvis Scott	52.9s.
1969—Kathy Hammond	54.3s.
1970—Mavis Laing	52.9s.
1971—Mabel Fergerson	53.3s.
1972—Kathy Hammond	52.3s.

880-Yard Run

800 meters: 1959-60, 1964, 1967-68, 1971-72.

1958—Florence McArdle	2m. 26.7s.
1959—Grace Butcher	2m. 21.2s.
1960—Pat Daniels	2m. 17.5s.
1961—Pat Daniels	2m. 19.2s.
1962—Leah Bennett	2m. 12.3s.
1963—Sandra Knott	2m. 12.5s.
1964—Sandra Knott	2m. 10.4s.
1965—Marie Mulder	2m. 11.1s.
1966—Charlette Cook	2m. 05.0s.
1967—Madeline Manning	2m. 03.6s.
1968—Doris Brown	2m. 05.1s.
1969—Madeline Manning	2m. 11.1s.
1970—Cheryl Toussaint	2m. 05.1s.
1971—Cheryl Toussaint	2m. 04.3s.
1972—Carol Hudson; Cheryl Toussaint (tie)	2m. 06.7s.

1,500 Meters Run

1965—Marie Mulder	4m. 36.5s.
1966—Doris Brown	4m. 20.2s.
1967—Natalie Rocha	4m. 29.0s.

1968—Jane Hill . . . . 4m. 46.5s.
1969—Doris Brown . . . . 4m. 27.3s.
1970—Francie Larrieu . . . . 4m. 20.8s.
1971—Kathy Gibbons . . . . 4m. 19.2s.
1972—Francie Larrieu . . . . 4m. 18.4s.

2-Mile Run

3,000 meters: 1972.

1971—Doris Brown . . . . .10m. 07.0s.
1972—Tena Anex . . . . 9m. 46.2s.

Mile Walk

1,500 meters: 1972.

1971—Lynn Olson . . . . 7m. 53.8s.
1972—Jenne Boci . . . . 6m. 59.1s.

Cross Country

1972—Francie Larrieu . . . . 13m. 27.6s.

80-Meter Hurdles

   60 yards, 1923-28.

1923—Hazel Kirk . . . . 9.6s.
1924—Hazel Kirk . . . . 9s.
1925—Helen Filkey . . . . 8.3s.
1926—Helen Filkey . . . . 8.7s.
1927—Helen Filkey . . . . 8.2s.
1928—Helen Filkey . . . . 8.4s.
1929—Helen Filkey . . . . .12.6s.
1930—Evelyn Hall . . . . .13s.
1931—Mildred Didrikson . . . . .12s.
1932—Mildred Didrikson . . . . .12.1s.
1933—Simone Schaller . . . . .12.1s.
1934—No competition
1935—Jean Hiller . . . . .13s.
1936—Anne O'Brien . . . . .12s.
1937—Cora Gaines . . . . .12.8s.
1938—Marie Cotrell . . . . .13s.
1939—Marie Cotrell . . . . .12.5s.
1940—Sybil Cooper . . . . .13.1s.
1941—Leila Perry . . . . .13.2s.
1942—Lillie Purifoy . . . . .12.6s.
1943—Nancy Cowperthwaite . . . . .12.3s.
1944—Lillie Purifoy . . . . .12.8s.
1945—Lillie Purifoy . . . . .12.5s.
1946—Nancy Cowperthwaite . . . . .12.2s.
1947—Nancy Cowperthwaite . . . . .12.6s.
1948—Bernice Robinson . . . . .12.1s.
1949—Bernice Robinson . . . . .11.9s.
1950—Evelyn Lawler . . . . .11.9s.
1951—Nancy C. Phillips . . . . .12.2s.
1952—Constance Darnowski . . . . .12.1s.
1953—Nancy C. Phillips . . . . .12.2s.
1954—Constance Darnowski . . . . .12.2s.
1955—Bertha Diaz . . . . .11.5s.
1956—Bertha Diaz . . . . .11.2s.
1957—Shirley Crowder . . . . .12.4s.
1958—Bertha Diaz . . . . .11.4s.
1959—Shirley Crowder . . . . .11.7s.
1960—Jo Ann Terry . . . . .11.4s.
1961—Cherie Parrish . . . . .11.5s.
1962—Cherie Parrish . . . . .11.3s.
1963—Rosie Bonds . . . . .11.3s.
1964—Rosie Bonds . . . . .10.8s.

1965—No competition
1966—Mrs. Cherrie Sherrard . . . . 10.7s.
1967—Mamie Rallins . . . . 10.9s.
1968—Mamie Rallins . . . . 10.6s.

100-Meter Hurdles

1969—Chi Cheng, Taiwan . . . . 13.7s.
1970—Mamie Rallins . . . . 13.4s.
1971—Pat Van Wolvelaere Johnson . . . . 13.5s.
1972—Mamie Rallins . . . . 13.5s.

200-Meter Hurdles

1963—Sally Griffith . . . . 29.5s.
1964—Sally Griffith . . . . 28.2s.
1965—Jennifer Wingerson (Canada) . . . . . . 27.6s.
1966—Pat Van Wolvelaere . . . . 27.6s.
1967—Pat Van Wolvelaere . . . . 27.8s.
1968—Pat Van Wolvelaere . . . . 27.3s.
1969—Pat Hawkins . . . . .27.4s.
1970—Pat Hawkins . . . . .26.1s.
1971—Pat Hawkins . . . . .26.1s.
1972—Pat Hawkins . . . . .26.3s.

400-Meter Relay

440 yards. 1923-32, 1946, 1955, 1957-58, 1961-63, 1965-66, 1970-71.

1923—Meadowbrook Club (F. Ruppert, D. Bough, G. Rittler, M. Adams) . . . . 52.4s.
1924—Meadowbrook Club (F. Ruppert, G. Rittler, M. Adams, G. Dickson) . . . 57s.
1925—Pasadena A.C. (Nelson, Nichols, Ryden, Doeschlag) . . . . 52.8s.
1926—Toronto Ladies A.C. (Davies, Glover, Bell, Grosse) . . . . 51s.
1927—Pasadena A.C. (Moore, Grassie, Nichols, Vrana) . . . . 52.6s.
1928—No. California A.C. (M. Meyers, R. Stewart, M. Parsons, D. Henders) . 52.2s.
1929—Millrose A.A. (M. Gilliland, J. Cross, C. Jansen, L. McNeil) . . . . 51.2s.
1930—Millrose A.A. (M. Gilliland, J. Cross, C. Jansen, L. McNeil) . . . . 49.4s.
1931—Illinois Women's A.C. (Hall, Todd, Harrington, Rogers) . . . . 51s.
1932—Illinois Women's A.C. (E. Hall, E. Harrington, M. Terwilliger, A. Rogers) .49.4s.
1933—Illinois Women's A.C. (E. Hall, D. Anderson, M.Terwilliger, A.Rogers)49.5s.
1934—No competition
1935—St. Louis A.C. (Bland, Santschi, Webb, Brady) . . . . 51s.
1936—Illinois Catholic W.C. (B. Robinson, E. Harrington, M. Terwilliger, A. Rogers) .48.4s.
1937—Mercury A.C. (I. Wilson, I. Bynoe, E. Dennis, G. Johnson) . . . . 51.2s.
1938—Tuskegee Institute (Birge, Abbott, Brown, Hymes) . . . . 52s.
1939—Tuskegee Institute (Birge, Abbott, Harrison, Hymes) . . . . 49.4s.
1940—Tuskegee Institute (Newell, Abbott, Harrison, Hymes) . . . . 49.3s.

1941—Tuskegee Institute (Newell, Perry, Harrison, Coachman) .... 50s.
1942—Tuskegee Institute (Perry, Coachman, Harris, Purifoy) .... 50.7s.
1943—Toronto Laurel Ladies A.C. .... 50.6s.
1944—Toronto Laurel Ladies A.C. (MacKay, Myers, Wright, Lowe) .... 52.8s.
1945—Toronto Laurel Ladies A.C. (Nancy M. MacKay, Viola Myers, Doris Wright, Jean Lowe) .... 51.4s.
1946—Malvernette A.C., Canada (Nancy MacKay, Ruth Harrigan, Viola Myers, Shirley Eckel) .... 50s.
1947—Tuskegee Institute (M. Walker, J. Watson, M. Griggs, N. Jackson) ... 50.5s.
1948—Tuskegee Institute (M. Walker, J. Watson, T. Manuel, N. Jackson) .. 50.3s.
1949—Tuskegee Institute (N. Jackson, J. Lowe, T. Manuel, E. Hogan) ..... 50s.
1950—Tuskegee Institute .... 50.2s.
1951—Tuskegee Institute (M. McNabb, C. Johnson, E. Lawler, N. Jackson) .. 49.8s.
1952—Police Athletic League (B. Husband, D. Query, C. Robinson, M. Faggs) .52.5s.
1953—Chicago C.Y.O. (Hazel Watkins, Al-Frances, Lyman, Barbara Jones, Mabel Landry) .... 49.7s.
1954—Chicago C.Y.O. (Hazel Watkins, Alfrances Lyman, Mabel Landry, Barbara Jones) .... 49s.
1955—Tennessee State (Martha Hudson, Lucinda Williams, Isabelle Daniels, Mae Faggs) .... 49.1s.
1956—Tennessee State (Martha Hudson, Wilma Rudolph, Isabelle Daniels, Mae Faggs) .... 47.1s.
1957—Tennessee State .... 47s.
1958—Tennessee State A Team (Isabelle Daniels, Lucinda Williams, Barbara Jones, Margaret Matthews) ...... 46.9s.
1959—Tennessee State (Martha Hudson, Isabelle Daniels, Wilma Rudolph, Lucinda Williams) .... 47.5s.
1960—Tennessee State (Martha Hudson, Lucinda Williams, Barbara Jones, Wilma Rudolph) .... 46.1s.
1961—Mayor Daley Team (Willie White, Lacey O'Neal, Doris May, Ernestine Pollards) .... 47.0s.
1962—Tennessee State (Wyomia Tyus, Wilma Rudolph, Edith McGuire, Vivian Brown) .... 46.0s.
1963—Tennessee State (Flossie Wilcher, Wyomia Tyus, Vivian Brown, Edith McGuire) .... 46.7s.
1964—Compton Track Club (No names given) 47.2s.
1965—Tennessee State (Mattiline Render, Calanthia Rollings, Evelyn Harvey, Wyomia Tyus) .(.......... 46.5s.
1966—Tennessee State (Edith McGuire, Isabelle Daniels, Mattiline Render,

Wyomia Tyus) .... 45.7s.
1967—Texas Southern .... 46.3s.
1968—Mayor Daley Y.F., Chicago ...... 45.4s.
1969—Mayor Daley Y.F., Chicago ...... 46.4s.
1970—Tennessee State .... 45.2s.
1971—Tennessee State .... 48.2s.
1972—Sports International .... 45.4s.

880-Yard Medley Relay

800 meters: 1960, 1967-68.

1960—Tennessee State (No names given)1m. 47.3s.
1961—San Mateo, Calif. (Billie Daniels, Jackie Mack, Nancy Duensing, Benetta Johnson) .... 1m. 49.0s.
1962—Chicago Mayor Daley (no names given) .... 1m. 47.1s.
1963—Chicago Mayor Daley (Eddie Robinson, Doris May, Fran Childred, Carol Bush) .... 1m. 46.9s.
1964—Oakettes A.C. (No names given) .1m. 45.5s.
1965—Cleveland Recreation (Gloria Woods, Debbie McDonald, Nathalie Allen, Madeline Manning) 1m. 44.3s.
1966—Cleveland Recreation (Mims, McDonald, Allen, Manning) ... 1m. 44.3s.
1967—Tennessee State .... 1m. 41.7s.
1968—Los Angeles Mercurettes ...... 1m. 41.7s.
1969—Tennessee State .... 1m. 42.4s.
1970—Mayor Daley Y.F., Chicago ... 1m. 43.1s.
1971—Angels Track Club, Seattle .... 1m. 43.5s.
1972—Sports International .... 1m. 40.6s.

1-Mile Relay

1969—Seattle Angel Track Club .... 3m. 47.8s.
1970—Atoms Track Club, Brooklyn . 3m. 41.3s.
1971—Atoms Track Club, Brooklyn . 3m. 38.8s.
1972—Canton (Ohio) Track Club ... 3m. 45.3s.

2-Mile Relay

1972—San Jose (Calif.) .... 9m. 07.3s.

High Jump

1923—Catherine M. Wright .... 4ft. 7 1/2in.
1924—No competition
1925—Elizabeth Stine .... 4ft. 10in.
1926—Catherine Maguire .... 4ft. 11 1/4in.
1927—Catherine Maguire .... 5ft. 1/2in.
1928—Mildred Wiley .... 4ft. 11 3/4in.
1929—Jean Shiley .... 4ft. 9 7/8in.
1930—Jean Shiley .... 5ft. 1in.
1931—Jean Shiley .... 5ft. 2in.
1932—Jean Shiley ....
        Mildred Didrikson .... 5ft. 3 3/16in.
1933—Alice Arden .... 5ft. 3 1/4in.
1934—No competition
1935—Barbara Howe .... 4ft. 11in.
1936—Annette Rogers .... 5ft. 2 1/2in.
1937—Margaret Bergmann .... 4ft. 11 1/2in.
1938—Margaret Bergmann .... 5ft. 2in.
1939—Alice Coachman .... 5ft. 2in.
1940—Alice Coachman .... 4ft. 11in.
1941—Alice Coachman .... 5ft. 2 3/4in.
1942—Alice Coachman .... 4ft. 8in.

1943—Alice Coachman . . . . .5ft.
1944—Alice Coachman . . . . .5ft. 1 5/8in.
1945—Alice Coachman . . . . .5ft.
1946—Alice Coachman . . . . .5ft.
1947—Alice Coachman . . . . .5ft. 1in.
1948—Alice Coachman . . . . .5ft.
1949—Gertrude Orr . . . . .5ft.
1950—Dorothy Chisholm . . . . . . .4ft. 8 1/4in.
1951—Marion Boos . . . . .4ft. 9 3/4in.
1952—Marion Boos . . . . .4ft. 11 5/8in.
1953—Mildred McDaniel . . . . .5ft. 1 1/2in.
1954—Jeanette Cantrell . . . .
      Verneda Thomas . . . . .5ft. 1/4in.
1955—Mildred McDaniel . . . . .5ft. 6 1/2in.
1956—Mildred McDaniel . . . . .5ft. 4in.
1957—Verneda Thomas . . . .
      Neomia Rodgers . . . .
      Hazel Ulmer . . . . .4ft. 10in.
1958—Barbara Brown . . . .
      Rose Robinson . . . . .5ft. 2 1/2in.
1959—Lis Josefsen . . . . .5ft. 4in.
1960—Lis Josefsen . . . . .5ft. 5 1/4in.
1961—Lis Josefsen . . . . .5ft. 1in.
1962—Kinuko Tsutsumi . . . . .5ft. 3in.
1963—Eleanor Montgomery . . . . . .5ft. 8in.
1964—Eleanor Montgomer . . . . . . .5ft. 8in.
1965—Eleanor Montgomery . . . . . .5ft. 7in.
1966—Eleanor Montgomery . . . . . .5ft. 7in.
1967—Eleanor Montgomery . . . . . .5ft. 6 1/4in.
1968—Theresa Thrasher . . . . .5ft. 6in.
1969—Eleanor Montgomery . . . . . .5ft. 11in.
1970—Sally Plihal . . . . .5ft.8in.
1971—Linda Iddings . . . . .5ft. 8in.
1972—Audrey Reid . . . . .6ft. 1/2in.

Broad Jump

1923—Helen Dinnehey . . . . .15ft. 4in.
1924—Dorothy Walsh . . . . .15ft. 3in.
1925—Helen Filkey . . . . .17ft.
1926—Nellie Todd . . . . .16ft. 7 3/8in.
1927—Eleanor Egg . . . . .17ft. 1 3/4in.
1928—Elta Cartwright . . . . .16ft. 10 3/4in.
1929—Nellie Todd . . . . .17ft. 3 1/4in.
1930—Stella Walsh . . . . .18ft. 9 3/8in.
1931—Mildred Didrikson . . . . .17ft. 11 1/2in.
1932—Nellie Todd . . . . .17ft. 6 1/8in.
1933—Genevieve Valvoda . . . . . . .17ft. 2 3/4in.
1934—No competition
1935—Etta Tate . . . . .16ft. 6in.
1936—Mabel Smith . . . . .18ft.
1937—Lula Hymes . . . . .17ft. 8 1/2in.
1938—Lula Hymes . . . . .17ft. 2in.
1939—Stella Walsh . . . . .19ft. 4.8in.
1940—Stella Walsh . . . . .17ft. 7 1/2in.
1941—Stella Walsh . . . . .18ft. 6 3/4in.
1942—Stella Walsh . . . . .17ft. 11in.
1943—Stella Walsh . . . . 9ft. 1in.
1944—Stella Walsh . . . . .17ft. 11 1/8in.
1945—Stella Walsh . . . . .18ft. 3in.
1946—Stella Walsh . . . . .17ft. 3/4in.
1947—Lillie Purifoy . . . . .17ft. 6in.
1948—Stella Walsh . . . . .17ft. 8 1/2in.

1949—Mabel Landry . . . . .17ft. 5in.
1950—Mabel Landry . . . . .17ft. 5 7/8in.
1951—Stella Walsh . . . . .17ft. 3in.
1952—Mabel Landry . . . . .18ft. 1 1/2in.
1953—Mabel Landry . . . . .18ft. 7 1/2in.
1954—Mabel Landry . . . . .17ft. 11in.
1955—Nancy C. Phillips . . . . .17ft. 5 3/4in.
1956—Margaret Matthews . . . . . . .19ft. 4in.
1957—Margaret Matthews . . . . . . .19ft. 5 1/2in.
1958—Margaret Matthews . . . . . . .20ft. 1in.
1959—Margaret Matthews . . . . . . .19ft. 4 1/2in.
1960—Willie White . . . . .19ft. 1 1/2in.
1961—Willie White . . . . .19ft. 11 1/2in.
1962—Willie White . . . . .20ft. 3in.
1963—Edith McGuire . . . . .19ft. 4 3/4in.
1964—Willye White . . . . .21ft. 7in.
1965—Willye White . . . . .20ft. 5 1/2in.
1966—Willye White . . . . .20ft. 7 1/2in.
1967—Pat Winslow . . . . .20ft. 8 1/4in.
1968—Willye White . . . . .20ft. 11 1/4in.
1969—Willye White . . . . .19ft. 8 3/4in.
1970—Willye White . . . . .21ft. 1in.
1971—Kim Attlesey . . . . .20ft. 8 3/4in.
1972—Willye White . . . . .20ft. 6 1/4in.

8-lb. Shot-Put

1923—Bertha Christophel . . . . . . .30ft. 10 1/2in.
1924—Ester Behring . . . . .30ft. 1 1/2in.
1925—Lillian Copeland . . . . . . .32ft. 10 5/8in.
1926—Lillian Copeland . . . . . . .38ft. 3 3/4in.
1927—Lillian Copeland . . . . . . .39ft. 6 1/8in.
1928—Lillian Copeland . . . . . . .40ft. 4 1/4in.
1929—Rena McDonald . . . . .42ft. 3in.
1930—Rena McDonald . . . . .38ft. 11 1/2in.
1931—Lillian Copeland . . . . . . .40ft. 2 3/8in.
1932—Mildred Didrikson . . . . . . .39ft. 6 1/4in.
1933—Catherine Rutherford . . . .38ft. 11 in.
1934—No competition
1935—Rena McDonald . . . . .38ft. 3 7/8in.
1936—Helen Stephens . . . . .41ft. 8 1/2in.
1937—Margaret Bergmann . . . . . .37ft. 6 3/4in.
1938—Catherine Fellmeth . . . . . .38ft. 5 3/4in.
1939—Catherine Fellmeth . . . . . .41ft. 1 3/4in.
1940—Catherine Fellmeth . . . . . .38ft. 3 5/8in.
1941—Catherine Fellmeth . . . . . .37ft. 3/8in.
1942—Ramona Harris . . . . .37ft. 10 1/2in.
1943—Frances Gorn . . . . .37ft. 11in.
1944—Dorothy Dodson . . . . .36ft. 1/4in.
1945—Francis Kaszubski . . . . . . .37ft. 9 7/8in.
1946—Dorothy Dodson . . . . .38ft. 10 3/4in.
1947—Dorothy Dodson . . . . .37ft. 11in.
1948—Frances Kaszubski . . . . . . .40ft. 5 7/8in.
1949—Amelia Bert . . . . .39ft. 8 1/4in.
1950—Frances Kaszubski . . . . . . .39ft. 3 7/8in.
1951—Amelia Bert . . . . .41ft. 3in.
1952—Amelia Bert . . . .
      Janet Dicks . . . . .37ft. 9in.
1953—Amelia Bert . . . . .40ft. 2 1/2in.
1954—Lois Testa . . . . .41ft. 11 3/4in.
1955—Wanda Wejzgrowicz . . . . . .37ft. 4 5/8in.
1956—Earlene Brown . . . . .45ft.
1957—Earlene Brown . . . . .43ft. 1/2in.

1958—Earlene Brown . . . . .47ft. 5 1/2in.
1959—Earlene Brown . . . . .46ft. 4 3/4in.
1960—Earlene Brown . . . . .49ft. 8 1/2in.
1961—Earlene Brown . . . . .47ft. 8 1/2in.
1962—Earlene Brown . . . . .48ft. 10 3/4in.
1963—Sharon Shepherd . . . . . . .48ft. 3 1/2in.
1964—Earlene Brown . . . . .46ft. 11in.
1965—Lynn Graham . . . . .47ft. 7in.
1966—Lynn Graham . . . . .47ft. 11 3/4in.
1967—Maren Seidler . . . . .46ft. 10in.
1968—Maren Seidler 50ft. 3 3/4in
1969—Maren Seidler . . . . .47ft. 10 3/4in.
1970—Lynn Graham . . . . .49ft. 10in.
1971—Lynn Graham . . . . .52ft. 0in.
1972—Maren Seidler . . . . .52ft. 9in.

Discus Throw

1923—Babe M. Wolbert . . . . 71ft. 9 1/2in.
1924—Roberta Ranck . . . . 70ft.
1925—Maybelle Reichardt . . . . . . 87ft. 2 3/4in.
1926—Lillian Copeland . . . . . . .101ft. 1in.
1927—Lillian Copeland . . . . . . .103ft. 8 5/16in.
1928—Maybelle Reichardt . . . . .116ft. 9 1/4in.
1929—Rena McDonald . . . . .113ft. 4in.
1930—Evelyn Farrara . . . . .111ft. 6in.
1931—Evelyn Farrara . . . . .108ft. 10 5/8in.
1932—Ruth Osborn . . . . .133ft. 3/4in.
1933—Ruth Osborn . . . . .123ft. 1/4in.
1934—No competition
1935—Margaret Wright . . . . .113ft. 9 1/2in.
1936—Helen Stephens . . . . .121ft. 6 1/2in.
1937—Elizabeth Lindsey . . . . . .107ft. 11in.
1938—Catherine Fellmeth . . . . . .126ft. 1/4in.
1939—Catherine Fellmeth . . . . . .113ft. 7 1/2in.
1940—Catherine Fellmeth . . . . . .114ft. 11in.
1941—Stella Walsh . . . . .113ft. 10 3/8in.
1942—Stella Walsh . . . . .110ft. 11 3/4in.
1943—Frances Gorn . . . . .109ft. 6 1/4in.
1944—Hattie Turner . . . . .101ft. 7 3/4in.
1945—Frances Kaszubski . . . . . . .103ft. 1/4in.
1946—Dorothy Dodson . . . . .102ft. 6in.
1947—Frances Kaszubski . . . . . . .110ft. 4 3/4in.
1948—Frances Kaszubski . . . . . . .124ft. 3 3/8in.
1949—Frances Kaszubski . . . . . . .123ft. 9in.
1950—Frances Kaszubski . . . . . . .113ft. 4 3/4in.
1951—Frances Kaszubski . . . . . . .121ft. 1/8in.
1952—Janet Dicks . . . . .114ft. 7 1/2in.
1953—Janet Dicks . . . . .123ft. 2in.
1954—Marjorie Larney . . . . .120ft. 11 1/2in.
1955—Alejandra Ilarra . . . . .117ft. 8in.
1956—Pamela Kurrell . . . . .140ft. 11in.
1957—Olga Connolly . . . . .147ft. 8in.
1958—Earlene Brown . . . . .152ft. 5 1/2in.
1959—Earlene Brown . . . . .153ft. 8in.
1960—Olga Connolly . . . . .159ft. 6 1/2in.
1961—Earlene Brown . . . . .149ft. 4 1/2in.
1962—Olga Connolly . . . . .172ft. 2in.
1963—Sharon Shepherd . . . . . . .150ft. 6in.
1964—Mrs. Olga Connolly . . . . .158ft. 4in.
1965—Lynn Graham . . . . .157ft. 9in.
1966—Carol Moeske . . . . .159ft. 8in.
1967—Carol Moeske . . . . .152ft. 5in.

1968—Olga Fikotova Connolly . . .170ft. 10in.
1969—Carol Frost . . . . .167ft. 3in.
1970—Carol Frsot . . . . .172ft. 3in.
1971—Josephine Della Vina . . . . .175ft. 6in.
1972—Josephine Della Vina . . . . .172ft. 0in.

Javelin Throw

1923—Roberta C. Ranck . . . . 59ft. 7 3/4in.
1924—Esther Spargo . . . . 72ft. 5 3/4in.
1925—Aloa Silva . . . . .105ft. 8in.
1926—Lillian Copeland . . . . .112ft. 5 1/2in.
1927—Margaret Jenkins . . . . .127ft. 3 1/2in.
1928—Margaret Jenkins . . . . .112ft. 5 5/8in.
1929—Estelle Hill . . . . .100ft. 5in.
1930—Mildred Didrikson . . . . . . .133ft. 3in.
1931—Lillian Copeland . . . . .116ft. 1 1/2in.
1932—Mildred Didrikson . . . . . . .139ft. 3in.
1933—Nan Gindele . . . . .130ft. 2 1/4in.
1934—No competition
1935—Sylvia Broman . . . . .102ft. 7 5/8in.
1936—Martha Worst . . . . .125ft. 1/4in.
1937—Rose Auerbach . . . . .123ft. 5 1/2in.
1938—Rose Auerbach . . . . .121ft. 6 3/4in.
1939—Dorothy Dodson . . . . .130ft. 9 1/2in.
1940—Dorothy Dodson . . . . .126ft. 1in.
1941—Dorothy Dodson . . . . .128ft. 7 1/8in.
1942—Dorothy Dodson . . . . .122ft. 10 1/2in.
1943—Dorothy Dodson . . . . .111ft. 3in.
1944—Dorothy Dodson . . . . .123ft. 1 1/2in.
1945—Dorothy Dodson . . . . .124ft. 10in.
1946—Dorothy Dodson . . . . .120ft. 2in.
1947—Dorothy Dodson . . . . .122ft. 5in.
1948—Dorothy Dodson . . . . .125ft. 10 3/8in.
1949—Dorothy Dodson . . . . .123ft. 1in.
1950—Amelia Bert . . . . .115ft. 1 3/4in.
1951—Frances Licata . . . . .120ft. 1/2in.
1952—Marjorie Larney . . . . .126ft. 3 7/8in.
1953—Amelia Wershaven . . . . . . .124ft. 7in.
1954—Karen Anderson . . . . .127ft. 1in.
1955—Karen Anderson . . . . .150ft. 1 1/4in.
1956—Karen Anderson . . . . .159ft. 1in.
1957—Marjorie Larney . . . . .187ft. 8in.
1958—Marjorie Larney . . . . .153ft. 7 1/2in.
1959—Marjorie Larney . . . . .152ft. 9 1/2in.
1960—Marjorie Larney . . . . .151ft. 10 1/2in.
1961—Frances Davenport . . . . . . .137ft. 8in.
1962—Kren Mendyka . . . . .158ft. 5in.
1963—Francis Davenport . . . . . . .158ft. 5in.
1964—RaNae Bair . . . . .166ft. 2 1/2in.
1965—RaNae Bair . . . . .175ft. 1/2in.
1966—RaNae Bair . . . . .174ft. 10in.
1967—RaNae Bair . . . . .196ft. 3in.
1968—Barbara Friedrich . . . . . . .178ft. 10in.
1969—Kathy Schmidt . . . . .177ft. 4in.
1970—Sherry Calvert . . . . .184ft. 9in.
1971—Sherry Calvert . . . . .175ft. 7in.
1972—Sherry Calvert . . . . . . : . . .184ft. 0in.

Pentathlon

1959—Ann Roniger
1960—Jo Ann Terry
1961—Billie Pat Daniels

1962—Billie Pat Daniels
1963—64—Pat Daniels
1965—67—Pat Daniels Winslow
1968—Chi Cheng (Taiwan)
1969—Jan Glotzer
1970—71—Pat Daniels Bank
1972—Jennifer Meldrum (Canada)

Team

1959—60—Tennessee State
1961—Mayor Daley Youth Foundation
1962—63—Tennessee State
1964—Compton T.C.
1965—67—Tennessee State
1968—Crown Cities T.C. (Calif.)
1969—Tennessee State
1970—Mayor Daley Y.F.
1971—Atoms T.C. (Brooklyn)
1972—Los Angeles T.C.

Indoor

50-Yard Dash

40 yards, 1927—32; 50 meters, 1933—48; 1957—64.

1927—Rosa M. Grasse . . . . 5.2s.
1928—Katherine Mearle . . . . 5.4s.
1929—Mary L. Carew . . . . 5.6s.
1930—Mary L. Carew . . . . 5.2s.
1931—Mary L. Carew . . . . 5.2s.
1932—Mary L. Carew . . . . 5.6s.
1933—Pearl Young . . . . 6.8s.
1934—Stella Walsh . . . . 7s.
1935—Helen Stephens . . . . 6.6s.
1936—Helen Stephens . . . . 6.4s.
1937—Helen Stephens . . . . 6.5s.
1938—40—No competition
1941—Jean Lane . . . . 6.8s.
1942—44—No competition
1945—Alice Coachman . . . . 6.1s.
1946—Alice Coachman . . . . 6.4s.
1947—No competition
1948—Juanita Watson . . . . 6.5s.
1949—Dolores Dwyer . . . . 6.4s.
1950—Dolores Dwyer . . . . 6.5s.
1951—Catherine Hardy . . . . 6.3s.
1952—Dolores Dwyer . . . . 6.2s.
1953—Mabel Landry . . . . 6.3s.
1954—Mabel Landry . . . . 6.1s.
1955—Isabel Daniels (60 meters) . . . . 7.9s.
1956—Isabel Daniels . . . . 6.2s.
1957—Isabel Daniels . . . . 5.7s.
1958—Isabel Daniels . . . . 5.8s.
1959—Wilma Rudolph . . . . 6.2s.
1960—Wilma Rudolph . . . . 5.9s.
1961—Willie White . . . . 6.0s.
1962—Willie White . . . . 5.9s.
1963—Willie White . . . . 5.9s.
1964—Debbie Thompson . . . . 5.8s.
1965—Wyomia Tyus (60 Yds.) . . . . 6.8s.
1966—Wyomia Tyus (60 Yds.) . . . . 6.5s.
1967—Wyomia Tyus (60 Yds.) . . . . 6.7s.
1968—Barbara Ferrell (60 Yds) . . . . 6.7s.
1969—Barbara Ferrell (60 Yds) . . . . 6.7s.

1970—Chi Cheng (60 Yds) . . . . 6.7s.
1971—Pat Hawkins (60 Yds) . . . . 6.9s.
1972—Iris Davis (60 Yds) . . . . 6.9s.

100-Yard Dash

1950—Jean Patton . . . . 11.8s.
1951—Jean Patton . . . . 11.2s.
1952—Mae Faggs . . . . 11.1s.
1953—Cynthia Robinson . . . . 11.4s.
1954—Barbara Jones . . . . 11.5s.
1955—Barbara Jones . . . . 12.3s.
1956—Isabel Daniels . . . . 11.1s.
1957—Barbara Jones . . . . 11.3s.
1958—Barbara Jones . . . . 11.9s.
1959—Martha Hudson . . . . 11.4s.
1960—Wilma Rudolph . . . . 10.7s.
1961—Wilma Rudolph . . . . 10.8s.
1962—Willie White . . . . 11.2s.
1963—Edith McGuire . . . . 11.8s.
1964—Willie White . . . . 11.8s.
1965—72—No competition

220-Yard Dash

200 meters, 1933—34, 1948.

1928—Irene Moran . . . . 30.8s.
1929—Catherine M. Donovan . . . . 29s.
1930—Stella Walsh . . . . 26.2s.
1931—Stella Walsh . . . . 27.2s.
1932—Catherine Capp . . . . 28.6s.
1933—Annette J. Rogers . . . . 26.8s.
1934—Stella Walsh . . . . 26s.
1935—Stella Walsh . . . . 26.1s.
1936—Annette Rogers . . . . 27.9s.
1937—Helen Stephens . . . . 28.5s.
1938—40—No competition
1941—Jean Lane . . . . 25.1s.
1942—44—No competition
1945—Stella Walsh . . . . 26.3s.
1946—Stella Walsh . . . . 28.6s.
1947—No competition
1948—Audrey Patterson . . . . 26.4s.
1949—Mae Faggs . . . . 25.9s.
1950—Mae Faggs . . . . 27.0s.
1951—Mae Faggs . . . . 26.9s.
1952—Mae Faggs . . . . 26.2s.
1953—Janet Moreau . . . . 26.5s.
1954—Mae Faggs . . . . 26.5s.
1955—Alfrances Lyman . . . . 26.2s.
1956—Mae Faggs . . . . 26.8s.
1957—Lucinda Williams . . . . 26.8s.
1958—Isabel Daniels . . . . 26.2s.
1959—Lucinda Williams . . . . 26.6s.
1960—Wilma Rudolph . . . . 25.7s.
1961—Vivian Brown . . . . 25.2s.
1962—Vivian Brown . . . . 25.5s.
1963—Maralyn White . . . . 24.8s.
1964—Valerie Carter . . . . 26.0s.
1965—Edith McGuire (200 Yds.) . . . . 21.9s.
1966—Edith McGuire . . . . 24.1s.
1967—Una Morris . . . . 25.0s.
1968—Vilma Charlton . . . . 25.1s.
1969—Barbara Ferrell . . . . 27.5s.

1970—Diane Kummer ....24.9s.
1971—Ester Stroy ....24.6s.
1972—Ester Stroy ....24.6s.

440-Yard Dash

1960—Rose Marie Lovelace ....1m.02.1s.
1961—L. Greene ....1m.04.0s.
1962—Sue Knott .... 58.2s.
1963—Suzanne Knott .... 57.0s.
1964—Valerie Carter .... 60.0s.
1965—Janell Smith—Norma Harris (tie) . 56.5s.
1966—Carlette Cook .... 54.2s.
1967—Kathy Hammond .... 55.2s.
1968—Lois Drinkwater .... 56.5s.
1969—Jarvis Scott .... 56.4s.
1970—Kathy Hammond .... 55.2s.
1971—Jarvis Scott .... 55.3s.
1972—Kathy Hammond .... 54.9s.

880-Yard Run

1960—Grace Butcher ....2m.26.8s.
1961—H. Shipley ....2m.21.6s.
1962—Leah Bennett ....2m.17.5s.
1963—Leah Bennett Ferris ....2m.13.6s.
1964—Sandra Knott ....2m.19.7s.
1965—Abby Hoffman ....2m.11.8s.
1966—Mrs. Armus Nagy Szabo
         (Hungary) ....2m.08.6s.
1967—Madeline Manning ....2m.08.4s.
1968—Madeline Manning ....2m.11.8s.
1969—Madeline Manning ....2m.07.9s.
1970—Francie Kraker Johnson ......2m.10.5s.
1971—Abby Hoffman ....2m.08.7s.
1972—Cheryl Toussaint ....2m.08.2s.

1-Mile Run

1968—Doris Brown ....4m.50.1s.
1969—Abby Hoffman (Canada) ......4m.59.3s.
1970—Kathy Gibbons ....4m.58.5s.
1971—Doris Brown ....4m.47.9s.
1972—Doris Brown ....4m.44.0s.

70-Yard Hurdles

1956—Constance Darnowski .... 9.7s.
1959—Jo Ann Terry .... 9.7s.
1960—Jo Ann Terry .... 9.5s.
1961—Jo Ann Terry .... 9.5s.
1962—Jo Ann Terry .... 9.2s.
1963—Jane Smith .... 9.2s.
1964—Jennifer Wingerson .... 9.7s.
1965—Chi Cheng (60 Yd.) .... 7.9s.
1966—Chi Cheng (60 Yd.) .... 7.6s.
1967—Pat Van Wolvelaere (60 Yds.) ...... 7.7s.
1968—Pat Van Wolvelaere (60 Yd.) .... 7.4s.
1969—Mamie Rallins (60 Yd.) .... 7.7s.
1970—Chi Cheng (60 Yd.) .... 7.6s.
1971—Patty Johnson (60 Yd.) .... 7.8s.
1972—Patty Johnson (60 Yd.) .... 7.5s.

640-Yard (4-Lap) Relay

1968—Tennessee State (Wyomia Tyus,
        Marcella Daniel, Karen Dennis,
        Mattilene Render) ....1m.10.8s.
1969—Tennessee State (Matteline Aber,

Iris Davis, Martha Watson, Una
Morris ....1m.12.4s.
1970—Mayor Daley Y.F. (Kathren Jones,
        Willye White, Diane Kummer,
        Mamie Rallins) ....1m.12.3s.
1971—Atoms T.C. (Renee DeSandes,
        Michelle McMillan, Denise
        Hooten, Brenda Merritt) .....1m.14.2s.
1972—Atoms T.C. (Linda Reynolds, Lin-
        da Cordy, Pat Hawkins, Carmen
        Brown) ....1m.10.4s.

1-Mile Relay

1971—Atoms T.C. (Michele McMillan,
        Shelley Marshall, Gail Fitz-
        gerald, Cheryl Toussant) .....3m.54.5s.
1972—New York PAL (Francine Sim-
        uels, Denise Johnson, Valerie
        Carter, Marilyn Bastian) ......3m.51.6s.

Sprint Medley Relay

1968—Los Angeles Mercurettes (Jarvis
        Scott, Pernetta Glenn, Dee De-
        bush, Barbara Ferrell) ....1m.45.1s.
1969—Tennessee State (Madeline Man-
        ning, Matteline Render, Iris
        Davis, Una Morris) ....1m.46.6s.
1970—Atoms T.C. (Gail Fitzgerald, Lin-
        da Reynolds, Linda Cardy, Pat
        Hawkins) ....1m.46.3s.
1971—Atoms T.C. (Gail Fitzgerald, Car-
        men Smith Brown, Denise
        Hooten, Pat Hawkins) ....1m.46.8s.
1972—Los Angeles Mercurettes (Jarvis
        Scott, Barbara Ferrell, Bobby
        Walker, Kathy Smallwood) ...1m.46.2s.

High Jump

1927—Mildred Wiley ....4ft. 9 3/8in.
1928—Mildred Wiley ....4ft. 10 5/8in.
1929—Jean Shiley ....5ft. 3 1/8in.
1930—Jean Shiley ....5ft. 3 1/2in.
1931—Jean Shiley ....5ft. 3in.
1932—Jean Shiley ....5ft. 1 3/4in.
1933—Annette Rogers ....5ft. 1 1/16in.
1934—Alice Arden ....5ft. 1in.
1935—Alice Arden ....4ft. 11 3/4in.
1936—Annette Rogers ....5ft. 1 1/4in.
1937—Loretta Murphy ....4ft. 9in.
1938—40—No competition
1941—Alice Coachman ....5ft. 1in.
1942—44—No competition
1945—Alice Coachman ....4ft. 8in.
1946—Alice Coachman ....4ft. 6 7/8in.
1947—No competition
1948—Emma Reed ....4ft. 11 3/8in.
1949—Nancy Phillips ....4ft. 7in.
1950—Marion Boos ....4ft. 7in.
1951—Marion Boos ....
        Nancy Phillips ....4ft. 10 1/2in.
1952—Marion Boos ....5ft. 3/4in.
1953—Marion Boos ....5ft. 1 1/4in.
1954—Barbara Mueller ....4ft. 10 3/4in.

1955—Mildred McDaniel ....5ft. 2in.
1956—Mildred McDaniel ....5ft. 4in.
1957—Ann Marie Flynn ....5ft. 2in.
1958—Barbara Brown ....
      Ann Marie Flynn ....5ft. 2 1/2in.
1959—Ann Marie Flynn ....5ft. 1/2in.
1960—Darlene Everhart ....5ft. 3 1/2in.
1961—Rose Robinson ....5ft. 4in.
1962—E. Baskerville ....5ft. 2in.
1963—Eleanor Montgomery ......5ft. 5 1/2in.
1964—Eleanor Montgomery ......5ft. 5in.
1965—Iolanda Balas (Rumania) ....5ft. 9in.
1966—Eleanor Montgomery ......5ft. 8in.
1967—Eleanor Montgomary ......5ft. 9in.
1968—Eleanor Montgomery ......5ft. 10 1/2in.
1969—Eleanor Montgomery ......5ft. 10in.
1970—Debbie Brill (Canada) ......5ft. 11in.
1971—Snezana Hrepevnik
      (Yugoslavia) ....6ft. 1/2in.
1972—Debbie Van Kiekebelt
      (Canada) ....5ft. 8in.

Running Long Jump

1962—Willye White ....19ft. 6 1/2in.
1963—Edith McGuire ....19ft. 4in.
1964—No competition
1965—Mary Rand ....20ft. 4in.
1966—Chi Cheng (Taiwan) ......19ft. 9 1/2in.
1967—Martha Watson ....20ft. 6 1/2in.
1968—Tatyana Talisheva (Russia) ..20ft. 4 1/2in.
1969—Irene K. Szewinska (Poland) .20ft. 3 1/4in.
1970—Chi Cheng ....21ft. 3/4in.
1971—Marilyn King ....19ft. 10 3/4in.
1972—Martha Watson ....20ft. 11 3/4in.

8-lb. Shot-Put

1927—Rena McDonald ....32ft. 1 in.
1928—Mabel Travers ....33ft. 3 1/2in.
1929—Rena McDonald ....39ft. 3 5/8in.
1930—Rena McDonald ....38ft. 1 1/4in.
1931—Rena McDonald ....37ft. 6in.
1932—Rena McDonald ....38ft. 6 1/2in.
1933—Rena McDonald ....37ft. 10in.
1934—Rena McDonald ....40ft. 11in.
1935—Helen Stephens ....39ft. 7 1/4in.
1936—Helen Stephens ....41ft. 7in.
1937—Helen Stephens ....44ft. 11 1/2in.
1938—40—No competition
1941—Dorothy Dodson ....35ft. 5/8in.
1942—44—No competition
1945—Dorothy Dodson ....35ft. 1 5/8in.
1946—Dorothy Dodson ....34ft. 6 1/2in.
1947—No competition
1948—Frances Kaszubski ....38ft. 4 3/8in.
1949—Ramona Massey ....38ft. 3in.
1950—Amelia Bert ....38ft. 1/4in.
1951—Frances Kaszubski ....39ft. 1 5/8in.
1952—Amelia Bert ....40ft. 11 5/8in.
1953—Amelia Bert ....40ft. 10 1/2in.
1954—Paula Deubel ....39ft. 11 3/4in.
1955—Lois Testa ....37ft. 6 3/4in.
1956—Adele Tischler ....44ft. 4 1/4in.

1957—Marjorie Larney ....39ft. 1/2in.
1958—Earlene Brown ....49ft. 6in.
1959—Marjorie Larney ....39ft. 7 1/4in.
1960—Sharon Shepherd ....45ft. 3 3/4in.
1961—Cynthia Wyatt ....39ft. 11in.
1962—Sharon Shepherd ....43ft. 9in.
1963—Cynthia Wyatt ....47ft. 1 1/4in.
1964—Sharon Shepherd ....44ft. 9in.
1965—Tamara Press (Russia) .....57ft. 2 1/2in.
1966—Joan Whithead ....40ft. 11 3/4in.
1967—Lynn Graham ....46ft. 4 3/4in.
1968—Maren Seidler ....48ft. 9in.
1969—Maren Seidler ....48ft. 0in.
1970—Mary Jacobsen ....46ft. 9in.
1971—Lynette Matthews ....49ft. 7 3/4in.
1972—Maren Seidler ....50ft. 11 1/2in.

Basketball Throw

1929—Marietta Ceres .... 85ft. 5 3/4in.
1930—Gertrude Meyer .... 82ft. 8 1/4in.
1931—Carolyn Dieckman .... 96ft. 2in.
1932—Carolyn Dieckman .... 87ft. 3/4in.
1933—Nan Gindele .... 101ft. 6 3/4in.
1934—Nan Gindele .... 95ft. 9 1/4in.
1935—Stella Walsh .... 96ft. 5 1/2in.
1936—Nan Gindele .... 94ft. 4 3/4in.
1937—Evelyn Ferrar .... 95ft. 4in.
1938—40—No competition
1941—Marion Twining .... 95ft. 10 1/4in.
1942—44—No competition
1945—Marion Twining .... 89ft. 10 3/4in.
1946—Marion Twining .... 101ft. 4 1/4in.
1947—No competition
1948—Stel Gorka .... 93ft. 7in.
1949—Ottilie Barth .... 94ft. 4 1/2in.
1950—Ottilie Barth .... 101ft. 9 1/2in.
1951—Marion Barone .... 93ft.
1952—Elizabeth Cipolt .... 90ft. 6in.
1953—Ramona Massey .... 95ft. 8in.
1954—Catherine Walsh .... 104ft. 3 1/2in.
1955—Amelia Wershaven .... 98ft. 2in.
1956—Catherine Walsh .... 101ft. 6in.
1957—Amelia Wershaven .... 105ft. 9 1/2in.
1958—Earlene Brown .... 135ft. 2in.
1959—Amelia Wood .... 101 8 1/2in.
1960—Cel Rutledge .... 120ft. 10 1/2in.
1961—J. Hofbauer .... 102ft. 5 1/2in.
1962—Cynthia Wyatt .... 105 7 1/2in.
1963—Linda DeLong .... 103ft. 2in.
1964—Shirley McCondichie ..... 101ft.
1965—Barbara Friedrich .... 107ft. 11in.
1966—Barbara Friedrich .... 134ft. 10in.
1967—Barbara Friedrich .... 131ft. 1 1/2in.
1968—Barbara Friedrich .... 135ft. 0in.
1969—Mary Boron .... 108ft. 7in.
1970—72—No competition

EVOLUTION OF MEN'S WORLD RECORDS

The International Amateur Athletic Federation was officially established at a congress in Berlin in 1913. The first official list of world amateur track and field records was issued by the I.A.A.F. the following June.

Prior to formation of the I.A.A.F., the amateur track and field organizations of each nation approved their own marks and the best in each event were accepted by other amateur bodies as world record.

Although the I.A.A.F. tabulations begin generally with the early years of the 20th Century, earlier records are included in this evolution of world records.

100-Yard Dash

Time	Record-holder and country	Year
10.5s.	B.S. Darbyshire, Great Britain	1864
10s.	J.P. Tennent, Great Britain	1868
10s.	Horace Lee, U.S.	1877
10s.	William Wilmer, U.S.	1878
9.8s.	John Owen Jr., U.S.	1890
9.8s.	W.T. MacPherson, Australia	1891
9.8s.	John Hempton, New Zealand	1892
9.8s.	Charles Stage, U.S.	1893
9.8s.	John Crum, U.S.	1895
9.8s.	C.A. Bradley, Great Britain	1895
9.8s.	Bernard Wefers, U.S.	1895
9.8s.	John Maybury, U.S.	1897
9.8s.	Charles Burroughs, U.S.	1898
9.8s.	John Rush, U.S.	1899
9.8s.	Archie Hahn, U.S.	1901
9.8s.	Edward Merrill, U.S.	1901
9.8s.	William A. Schick, U.S.	1902
9.8s.	Frank M. Sears, U.S.	1903
9.8s.	Charles Blair, U.S.	1903
9.8s.	William Eaton, U.S.	1904
9.8s.	Charles Parsons, U.S.	1905
9.6s.	Daniel Kelly, U.S.	1906
9.6s.	Howard Drew, U.S.	1914
9.6s.	Charles Paddock, U.S.	1921
9.6s.	Charles Paddock, U.S.	1921
9.6s.	Charles Paddock, U.S.	1921
9.6s.	Charles Paddock, U.S.	1921
9.6s.	Cyril Coaffee, Canada	1922
9.6s.	Charles Paddock, U.S.	1924
9.6s.	Charles Paddock, U.S.	1926
9.6s.	DeHart Hubbard, U.S.	1926
9.6s.	Chester Bowman, U.S.	1927
9.5s.	Eddie Tolan, U.S.	1929
9.4s.	Frank Wykoff, U.S.	1930
9.4s.	Daniel Joubert, South Africa	1931
9.4s.	Jesse Owens, U.S.	1935
9.4s.	Jesse Owens, U.S.	1936
9.4s.	Clyde Jeffrey, U.S.	1940
9.4s.	Melvin Patton, U.S.	1947
9.3s.	Melvin Patton, U.S.	1948
9.3s.	H.D. Hogan, Australia	1954
9.3s.	James Golliday, U.S.	1955
9.3s.	Leamon King, U.S.	1956
9.3s.	David Sime, U.S.	1957
9.3s.	Bobby Morrow, U.S.	1957
9.3s.	Ray Norton, U.S.	1958
9.3s.	William Woodhouse, U.S.	1959
9.3s.	Roscoe Cook, U.S.	1959
9.3s.	Ray Norton, U.S.	1960
9.3s.	Frank Budd, U.S.	1961
9.2s.	Frank Budd, U.S.	1961
9.2s.	Henry Jerome, Canada	1962
9.2s.	Henry Jerome, Canada	1962
9.1s.	Robert Hayes, U.S.	1963
9.1s.	Henry Jerome, Canada	1966
9.1s.	Jim Hines, U.S.	1967
9.1s.	Charlie Greene, U.S.	1967
9.1s.	John Carlos, U.S.	1969

220-Yard Dash (Straightaway)

23.5s.	Horace Lee, U.S.	1877
23s.	Fred Saportas, U.S.	1877
22.7/8 s.	William Wilmer, U.S.	1878
22.6s.	Henry Brooks Jr., U.S.	1882
22.4s.	Wendell Baker, U.S.	1884
22s.	Wendell Baker, U.S.	1885
21.8s.	C.G. Wood, Great Britain	1886
21.8s.	Luther Cary, U.S.	1891
21.2s.	Bernard Wefers, U.S.	1896
21.2s.	Ralph Craig, U.S.	1910
21.2s.	Ralph Craig, U.S.	1911
21.2s.	Donald Lippincott, U.S.	1913
21.2s.	Howard Drew, U.S.	1914
21.2s.	Wm. Applegarth, Great Britain	1914
21.2s.	George Parker, U.S.	1914
20.8s.	Charles Paddock, U.S.	1921
20.8s.	Charles Paddock, U.S.	1924
20.6s.	Roland Locke, U.S.	1926
20.3s.	Jesse Owens, U.S.	1935
20.2s.	Melvin Patton, U.S.	1949
20s.	David Sime, U.S.	1956
20s.	Frank Budd, U.S.	1962
19.5s.	Tommie Smith, U.S.	1966

220-Yard Dash (Turn)

20.0s.	Tommie Smith, U.S.	1966

440-Yard Run

56s.	B.S. Darbyshire, Great Britain	1864
55s.	J.H. Ridley, Great Britain	1866
52.75s.	J.H. Ridley, Great Britain	1867
51s.	J.H. Ridley, Great Britain	1868
50.4s.	E.H. Colbeck, Great Britain	1868
49.2s.	Lawrence Myers, U.S.	1879
48.6s.	Lawrence Myers, U.S.	1881
48.2s.	H.C.D. Tindall, Great Britain	1889
47.8s.	Maxwell Long, U.S.	1900
47.4s.	James (Ted) Meredith, U.S.	1916
47.4s.	Ben Eastman, U.S.	1931
47.4s.	Victor Williams, U.S.	1931
46.4s.	Ben Eastman, U.S.	1932
46.4s.	Grover Klemmer, U.S.	1941
46.3s.	H. McKenley, Jamaica, B.W.I.	1947
46s.	H. McKenley, Jamaica, B.W.I.	1948
45.8s.	Jim Lea, U.S.	1956
45.7s.	Glenn Davis, U.S.	1958
44.9s.	Adolph Plummer, U.S.	1963
44.8s.	Tommie Smith, U.S.	1967
44.7s.	Curtis Mills, U.S.	1969
44.5s.	John Smith, U.S.	1971

880-Yard Run

2m. 7.5s. . Richard Webster, Gt. Britain . . .1865
2m. 5s. . . P.M. Thornton, Gt. Britain 1866
2m. . . . . . A.E. Pelham, Great Britain . . .1872
1m. 59s. . Walter Slade, Great Britain . . .1876
1m. 57.5s. F.T. Elborough, Gt. Britain 1876
1m. 56s. . Lawrence Myers, U.S. 1881
1m. 55.4s. Lawrence Myers, U.S. 1884
1m. 54.6s. F.H.K. Cross, Great Britain 1888
1m. 53.4s. Charles Kilpatrick, U.S. 1895
1m. 52.8s. Emilio Lunghi, Italy 1909
1m. 52.5s. James (Ted) Meredith, U.S. . . .1912
1m. 52.2s. James (Ted) Meredith, U.S. . . .1916
1m. 51.6s. Otto Peltzer, Germany 1926
1m. 50.9s. Ben Eastman, U.S. 1932
1m. 49.8s. Ben Eastman, U.S. 1934
1m. 49.6s. Elroy Robinson, U.S. 1937
1m. 49.2s. Sydney Wooderson, Gt. Brit. . . .1938
1m. 49.2s. Malvin Whitfield, U.S. 1950
1m. 48.6s. Mal Whitfield, U.S. 1953
1m. 48.6s. Gunnar Nielsen, Denmark 1954
1m. 47.5s. Lon Spurrier, U.S. 1955
1m. 46.8s. Tom Courtney, U.S. 1957
1m. 45.1s. Peter G. Snell, New Zealand 1962
1m. 44.9s. Jim Ryun, U.S. 1966

1-Mile Run

4m. 56s. . Charles Lawes, Great Britain . . .1864
4m. 36.5s. Richard Webster, Gt. Britain . . .1865
4m. 29s. . Wm. Chinnery, Gt. Britain 1868
4m. 28.8s. W.C. Gibbs, Great Britain 1868
4m. 26s. . Walter Slade, Gt. Britain 1874
4m. 24.5s. Walter Slade, Gt. Britain 1875
4m. 23.2s. Walter George, Gt. Britain 1880
4m. 21.4s. Walter George, Gt. Britain 1882
4m. 19.4s. Walter George, Gt. Britain 1882
4m. 18.4s. Walter George, Gt. Britain 1884
4m. 18.2s. Fred Bacon, Scotland 1894
4m. 17s. . Fred Bacon, Scotland 1895
4m. 15.6s. Thomas Conneff, U.S. 1895
4m. 15.4s. John Paul Jones, U.S. 1911
4m. 14.4s. John Paul Jones, U.S. 1913
4m. 12.6s. Norman Taber, U.S. 1915
4m. 10.4s. Paavo Nurmi, Finland 1923
4m. 9.2s. . Jules Ladoumegue, France 1931
4m. 7.6s. . Jack Lovelock, New Zealand . . .1933
4m. 6.8s. . Glenn Cunningham, U.S. 1934
4m. 6.4s. . Sydney Wooderson, Gt. Brit. . . .1937
4m. 6.2s. . Gunder Hagg, Sweden 1942
4m. 6.2s. . Arne Andersson, Sweden 1942
4m. 4.6s. . Gunder Hagg, Sweden 1942
4m. 2.6s. . Arne Andersson, Sweden 1943
4m. 1.6s. . Arne Andersson, Sweden 1944
4m. 1.4s. . Gunder Hagg, Sweden 1945
3m. 59.4s. Roger Bannister, England 1954
3m. 58s. . John Landy, Australia 1954
3m. 57.2s. Derek Ibbotson, Gt. Britain 1957
3m. 54.5s. Herb Elliott, Australia 1958
3m. 54.4s. Peter G. Snell, New Zealand 1962
3m. 53.6s. Michel Jazy, France 1965
3m. 51.3s. Jim Ryun, U.S. 1966
3m. 51.1s. Jim Ryun, U.S. 1967

2-Mile Run

10m. 5s. . Richard Webster, Gt. Britain . . .1865
9m. 17.4s. Walter George, Gt. Britain 1884
9m. 9.6s. . Alfred Shrubb, Great Britain . . .1904
9m. 1.4s. . Edvin Wide, Sweden 1926
8m. 59.6s. Paavo Nurmi, Finland 1931
8m. 58.4s. Donald Lash, U.S. 1936
8m. 57.4s. Gunnar Hockert, Finland 1936
8m. 56s. . Miklos Szabo, Hungary 1937
8m. 53.2s. Taisto Maki, Finland 1939
8m. 47.8s. Gunder Hagg, Sweden 1942
8m. 46.4s. Gunder Hagg, Sweden 1944
8m. 42.8s. Gunder Hagg, Sweden 1944
8m. 40.4s. Gaston Reiff, Belgium 1952
8m. 33.4s. Sandor Iharos, Hungary 1955
8m. 32s. . A.G. Thomas, Australia 1958
8m. 30s. . Murray Halberg, New Zealand . .1961
8m. 29.8s. James T. Beatty, U.S. 1962
8m. 29.6s. Michel Jazy, France 1963
8m. 22.6s. Michel Jazy, France 1965
8m. 19.8s. Ron Clarke, Australia 1967
8m. 19.6s. Ron Clarke, Australia 1968
8m. 17.8s. Emiel Puttemans, Belgium 1971
8m. 14.0s. Lassee Viren, Finland 1972

3-Mile Run

14m. 17.6s. . . . Alfred Shrubb, Gt. Brit. . .1903
14m. 11.2s. . . . Paavo Nurmi, Finland . . .1923
13m. 50.6s. . . . Lauri Lehtinen, Finland . .1932
13m. 42.4s. . . . Taisto Maki, Finland 1939
13m. 35.4s. . . . Gunder Hagg, Sweden . . .1942
13m. 32.4s. . . . Gunder Hagg, Sweden . . .1942
13m. 32.2s. . . . Fred Green, England 1954
13m. 32.2s. . . . Chris Chataway, England .1954
13m. 26.4s. . . . Vladimir Kuts, U.S.S.R. . .1954
13m. 14.2s. . . . Sandor Iharos, Hungary . .1955
13m. 10.8s. . . . A.G. Thomas, Australia . .1958
13m. 10.0s. . . . Murray Halberg,
                   New Zealand 1961
13m. 04.8s. . . . Michel Jazy, France 1965
12m. 52.4s. . . . Ron Clarke, Australia 1965
12m. 50.4s. . . . Ron Clarke, Australia 1966
12m. 47.8s. . . . Emiel Puttemans, Belgium 1972

6-Mile Run

29m. 59.4s. . . . Alfred Shrubb, Gt. Britain 1904
29m. 36.4s. . . . Paavo Nurmi, Finland . . .1930
29m. 36.4s. . . . Ilmari Salminen, Finland .1937
28m. 55.6s. . . . Taisto Maki, Finland 1939
28m. 38.6s. . . . Viljo Heino, Finland 1944
28m. 30.8s. . . . Viljo Heino, Finland 1949
27m. 59.2s. . . . Emil Zatopck,
                   Czechoslovakia 1954
27m. 43.8s. . . . Sandor Iharos, Hungary . .1956
26m. 47.0s. . . . Ron Clarke, Australia 1965

10-Mile Run

50m. 40.6s. . Alfred Shrubb, Gt. Britain . .1904
50m. 15s. . . Paavo Nurmi, Finland 1928
49m. 41.6s. . Viljo Heino, Finland 1945
49m. 22.2s. . Viljo Heino, Finland 1946
48m. 12s. . . Emil Zatopek, Czechoslo'kia 1951
47m. 47.0s. . B. Heatley, Great Britain 1961

47m. 26.8s. . Mel Batty, Great Britain 1964
47m. 12.8s. . Ron Clarke, Australia 1965
47m. 02.2s. . Ron Hill, Great Britain 1968
46m. 44.0s. . Ron Hill, Great Britain 1968
46m. 37.8s. . Jerome Drayton, Canada ...1970
46m. 04.2s. . Willy Polleunis, Belgium 1972

15-Mile Run

1h. 20m. 4.4s. . F. Appleby, Gt. Britain ..1902
1h. 19m. 48.6s. Erkki Tamila, Finland ...1937
1h. 18m. 48s. . Mikko Hietanen, Finl'd ..1947
1h. 17m. 28.6s. Mikko Hietanen, Finl'd ..1948
1h. 16m. 26.4s. Emil Zatopek, Czecho....1952
1h. 14m. 1s. . . Ron Hill, Great Britain ...1965

1-Hour Run

11mi. 932yds. . Walter George, Gt. Brit. ..1884
11mi. 1,137yds. Alfred Shrubb, Gt. Brit. ..1904
11mi. 1,442yds Jean Bouin, France 1913
11mi. 1,648yds. Paavo Nurmi, Finland ...1928
12mi. 29yds. .. Viljo Heino, Finland 1945
12mi. 269yds. . Emil Zatopek, Czecho ...1951
12mi. 809yds. . Emil Zatopek, Czecho ...1951
12m. 1,006yds. Ron Clarke, Australia 1965
12m. 1,478yds. Gaston Roelants, Belgium 1966
20,784 mt. .... Gaston Roelants, Belgium 1972

100-Meter Dash

12s. ..... Thomas Burke, U.S. 1896
10.8s. ... Frank Jarvis, U.S. 1900
10.6s. ... Donald Lippincott, U.S. 1912
10.6s. ... Jackson Scholz, U.S. 1920
10.4s. ... Charles Paddock, U.S. 1921
10.4s. ... Eddie Tolan, U.S. 1929
10.4s. ... Eddie Tolan, U.S. 1929
10.3s. ... Percy Williams, Canada 1930
10.3s. ... Eddie Tolan, U.S. 1932
10.3s. ... Ralph Metcalfe, U.S. 1933
10.3s. ... Eulace Peacock, U.S. 1934
10.3s. ... Christian Berger, Netherlands ..1934
10.3s. ... Ralph Metcalfe, U.S. 1934
10.3s. ... Ralph Metcalfe, U.S. 1934
10.3s. ... Ryutoku Yoshioka, Japan 1935
10.2s. ... Jesse Owens, U.S. 1936
10.2s. ... Harold Davis, U.S. 1941
10.2s. ... Lloyd LaBeach, Panama 1948
10.2s. ... Norwood Ewell, U.S. 1948
10.2s. ... E. McDonald Bailey, Gt. Britain .1951
10.2s. ... Heinz Futterer, Germany 1954
10.1s. ... Willie Williams, U.S. 1956
10.1s. ... Ira Murchison, U.S. 1956
10s. ..... Armin Hary, West Germany 1960
10s. ..... Henry Jerome, Canada 1960
10s. ..... Horacio Estevez, Venezuela 1964
10s. ..... Robert Hayes, U.S. 1964
10s. ..... Jim Hines, U.S. 1967
10s. ..... Enrique Figuerola, Cuba 1967
9.9s. .... Jim Hines, U.S. 1968
9.9s. .... Charlie Greene, U.S. 1968
9.9s. .... Ronnie Smith, U.S. 1968
9.9s. .... Jim Hines, U.S. 1968
9.9s. .... Eddie Hart, U.S. 1972
9.9s. .... Reynaud Robinson, U.S. 1972

200-Meter Dash (Straightaway)

22.2s. ... Walter Tewksbury, U.S. 1900
21.6s. ... Archie Hahn, U.S. 1904
20.8s. ... Charles Paddock, U.S. 1921
20.8s. ... Charles Paddock, U.S. 1924
20.6s. ... Roland Locke, U.S. 1926
20.6s. ... Ralph Metcalfe, U.S. 1933
20.3s. ... Jesse Owens, U.S. 1935
20.2s. ... Melvin Patton, U.S. 1949
20s. ..... David Sime, U.S. 1956
20s. ..... Frank Budd, U.S. 1962
19.5s. ... Tommie Smith, U.S. 1966

200-Meter Dash (Turn)

19.8s. ... Tommie Smith, U.S. 1968
19.8s. ... Donald Quarrie, Jamaica, B.W.I. 1971

400-Meter Run

54.2s. ... Thomas Burke, U.S. 1896
49.4s. ... Maxwell Long, U.S. 1900
49.2s. ... Harry Hillman, U.S. 1904
48.2s. ... Charles Reidpath, U.S. 1912
47.6s. ... Eric Liddell, Great Britain 1924
47.4s. ... James (Ted) Meredith, U.S. 1916
47s. ..... Emerson Spencer, U.S. 1928
46.2s. ... William Carr, U.S. 1932
46.1s. ... Archie Williams, U.S. 1936
46s. ..... Rudolf Harbig, Germany 1939
46s. ..... Grover Klemmer, U.S. 1941
45.9s. ... Herb McKenley, Jamaica, B.W.I. 1948
45.8s. ... George Rhoden, Jamaica, B.W.I. 1950
45.4s. ... Lou Jones, U.S. 1955
45.2s. ... Lou Jones, U.S. 1956
44.9s. ... Otis Davis, U.S. 1960
44.9s. ... Carl Kauffman, Germany 1960
44.9s. ... Adolph Plummer, U.S. 1963
44.9s. ... Mike Larrabee, U.S. 1964
44.5s. ... Tommie Smith, U.S. 1967
43.8s. ... Lee Evans, U.S. 1968

800-Meter Run

2m. 11s. ... Edwin Flack, Australia 1896
2m. 1.4s. .. Alfred Tysoe, U.S. 1900
1m. 56s. ... James Lightbody, U.S. 1904
1m. 52.8s. . Melvin Sheppard, U.S. 1908
1m. 51.9s. . James (Ted) Meredith, U.S. ...1912
1m. 51.6s. . Otto Peltzer, Germany 1926
1m. 50.6s. . Sera Martin, France 1928
1m. 49.8s. . Thomas Hampson, Gt. Brit. .1932
1m. 49.8s. . Ben Eastman, U.S. 1934
1m. 49.7s. . Glenn Cunningham, U.S. ...1936
1m. 49.6s. . Elroy Robinson, U.S. 1937
1m. 48.4s. . Sydney Wooderson, Gt. Brit. 1938
1m. 46.6s. . Rudolf Harbig, Germany ...1939
1m. 45.7s. . Roger Moens, Belgium 1955
1m. 44.3s. . Peter G. Snell, New Zealand .1962
1m. 44.3s. . Ralph Doubell, Australia ...1968
1m. 44.3s. . David Wottle, U.S. 1972

1,000-Meter Run

2m. 32.3s. . G. Mickler, Germany 1913
2m. 29.1s. . A. Bolin, Sweden 1918
2m. 28.6s. . Sven Lundgren, Sweden 1922

2m. 26.8s. . . Sera Martin, France 1926
2m. 25.8s. . . Otto Peltzer, Germany 1927
2m. 23.6s. . . Jules Ladoumegue, France . .1930
2m. 21.5s. . . Rudolf Harbig, Germany . . .1941
2m. 21.4s. . . Rune Gustafsson, Sweden . . .1946
2m. 21.4s. . . Marcel Hansenne, France . . .1948
2m. 21.3s. . . Olle Aberg, Sweden 1952
2m. 20.4s. . . Audun Boysen, Norway 1953
2m. 19.5s. . . Audun Boysen, Norway 1954
2m. 19s. . . . Audun Boysen, Norway 1955
2m. 19s. . . . Istvan Rozsavolgyi, Hungary .1955
2m. 18.1s. . . Dan Waern, Sweden 1958
2m. 16.7s. . . Siegfried Valentin, Germany .1960
2m. 16.2s. . . Juergen May, East Germany .1965
2m. 16.2s. . . Franz-Josef Kemper,
         West Germany 1966

1,500-Meter Run

4m. 33.2s. . . Edwin Flack, Australia 1896
4m. 6s. . . . . C. Bennett, Great Britain . . .1900
4m. 5.4s. . . James Lightbody, U.S. 1904
4m. 3.4s. . . Melvin Sheppard, U.S. 1908
3m. 56.8s. . . Arnold Jackson, Gt. Britain .1912
3m. 55.8s. . . Abel Kiviat, U.S. 1912
3m. 54.7s. . . J. Zander, Sweden 1917
3m. 52.6s. . . Paavo Nurmi, Finland 1924
3m. 51s. . . . Otto Peltzer, Germany 1926
3m. 49.2s. . . Jules Ladoumegue, France . .1930
3m. 49.2s. . . Luigi Beccali, Italy 1933
3m. 49s. . . . Luigi Beccali, Italy 1933
3m. 48.8s. . . William Bonthron, U.S. 1934
3m. 47.8s. . . Jack Lovelock, New Zealand .1936
3m. 47.6s. . . Gunder Hagg, Sweden 1941
3m. 45.8s. . . Gunder Hagg, Sweden 1942
3m. 45s. . . . Arne Andersson, Sweden . . .1943
3m. 43s. . . . Gunder Hagg, Sweden 1944
3m. 43s. . . . Lennart Strand, Sweden 1947
3m. 41.8s. . . John Landy, Australia 1954
3m. 40.8s. . . Sandor Iharos, Hungary 1955
3m. 40.8s. . . Laszlo Tabori, Hungary 1955
3m. 40.8s. . . Gunnar Nielsen, Denmark . . .1955
3m. 40.6s. . . Istvan Rozsavolgyi, Hungary .1956
3m. 38.1s. . . Stanislav Jungwirth, Czecho. 1957
3m. 36s. . . . Herb Elliott, Australia 1958
3m. 35.6s. . . Herb Elliott, New Zealand . .1960
3m. 33.1s. . . Jim Ryun, U.S. 1967

2,000-Meter Run

5m. 30.4s. . . J. Zander, Sweden 1918
5m. 26.3s. . . Paavo Nurmi, Finland 1922
5m. 26s. . . . Edvin Wide, Sweden 1925
5m. 24.6s. . . Paavo Nurmi, Finland 1927
5m. 23.4s. . . Eino Borg, Finland 1927
5m. 21.8s. . . Jules Ladoumegue, France . .1931
5m. 20.4s. . . Miklos Szabo, Hungary 1936
5m. 18.4s. . . Henry Jonsson, Sweden 1937
5m. 16.8s. . . Archie San Romani, U.S. . . .1937
5m. 16.4s. . . Gunder Hagg, Sweden 1942
5m. 11.8s. . . Gunder Hagg, Sweden 1942
5m. 7s. . . . . Gaston Reiff, Belgium 1948
5m. 2.2s. . . Istvan Rozsavolgyi, Hungary .1955
5m. 1.6s. . . Michel Jazy, France 1962
5m. 1.2s. . . Jozef Odlozil, Czechoslovakia1965

4m. 56.2s. . . Michel Jazy, France 1966

3,000-Meter Run

8m. 36.8s. . . Hannes Kolehmainen, Finl'd .1912
8m. 33.2s. . . J. Zander, Sweden 1918
8m. 28.6s. . . Paavo Nurmi, Finland 1922
8m. 27.6s. . . Edvin Wide, Sweden 1925
8m. 25.4s. . . Paavo Nurmi, Finland 1926
8m. 20.4s. . . Paavo Nurmi, Finland 1926
8m. 18.8s. . . Janusz Kusocinski, Poland . .1932
8m. 18.4s. . . Henry Nielsen, Denmark 1934
8m. 14.8s. . . Gunnar Hockert, Finland . . .1936
8m. 9s. . . . . Henry Kalarne, Sweden 1940
8m. 1.2s. . . Gunder Hagg, Sweden 1942
7m. 58.8s. . . Gaston Reiff, Belgium 1949
7m. 55.6s. . . Sandor Iharos, Hungary 1955
7m. 52.8s. . . Gordon Pirie, Great Britain . .1956
7m. 49.2s. . . Michel Jazy, France 1962
7m. 46.0s. . . S. Hermann, East Germany . .1965
7m. 39.6s. . . Kipchoge Keino, Kenya 1965
7m. 37.6s. . . Emiel Puttemans, Belgium . .1972

5,000-Meter Run

14m. 36.6s. . H. Kolehmainen, Finland . . .1912
14m. 35.4s. . Paavo Nurmi, Finland 1922
14m. 28.2s. . Paavo Nurmi, Finland 1924
14m. 17s. . . Lauri Lehtinen, Finland 1932
14m. 8.8s. . . Taisto Maki, Finland 1939
13m. 58.2s. . Gunder Hagg, Sweden 1942
13m. 57.2s. . Emil Zatopek, Czechoslo'kia 1954
13m. 51.2s. . Vladimir Kuts, U.S.S.R. 1954
13m. 40.6s. . Sandor Iharos, Hungary 1955
13m. 36.8s. . Gordon Pirie, Great Britain . .1956
13m. 35s. . . Vladimir Kuts, U.S.S.R. 1957
13m. 24.2s. . Kipchoge Keino, Kenya 1965
13m. 16.6s. . Ron Clarke, Australia 1966
13m. 13.0s. . Emiel Puttemans, Belgium . .1972

10,000-Meter Run

30m. 58.8s. . Jean Bouin, France 1911
30m. 40.2s. . Paavo Nurmi, Finland 1921
30m. 35.4s. . Willie Ritola, Finland 1924
30m. 23.2s. . Willie Ritola, Finland 1924
30m. 6.2s. . . Paavo Nurmi, Finland 1924
30m. 5.6s. . . Ilmari Salminen, Finland . . .1937
30m. 2s. . . . Taisto Maki, Finland 1938
29m. 52.6s. . Taisto Maki, Finland 1939
29m. 35.4s. . Viljo Heino, Finland 1944
29m. 28.2s. . Emil Zatopek, Czechoslo . . .1949
29m. 27.2s. . Viljo Heino, Finland 1949
29m. 21.2s. . Emil Zatopek, Czechoslo . . .1949
29m. 2.6s. . . Emil Zatopek, Czechoslo . . .1950
28m. 54.2s. . Emil Zatopek, Czechoslo . . .1954
28m. 30.4s. . Vladimir Kuts, U.S.S.R. 1956
28m. 18.8s. . Pyotr Bolotnikov, U.S.S.R. . .1960
28m. 18.2s. . Pyotr Bolotnikov, U.S.S.R. . .1962
28m. 10.6s. . Gaston Roelants, Belgium . . .1965
27m. 39.4s. . Ron Clarke, Australia 1965
27m. 38.4s. . Lasse Viren, Finland 1972

15,000-Meter Run

47m. 18.6s. . Jean Bouin, France 1913
46m. 49.6s. . Paavo Nurmi, Finland 1928
44m. 54.6s. . Emil Zatopek, Czechoslo . . .1951

20,000-Meter Run

1h. 7m. 40.2s.	T. Kolehmainen, Finland	. .1913
1h. 7m. 11.2s.	Albin Stenroos, Finland	. . .1923
1h. 7m. 7.2s.	V. Kyronen, Finland	1924
1h. 6m. 29s.	V. Sipila, Finland	1925
1h. 4m. 38.4s.	Paavo Nurmi, Finland	1930
1h. 4m. 0.2s.	Juan Zabala, Argentina	. . .1936
1h. 3m. 1.2s.	Andras Csaplar, Hungary	. .1941
1h. 2m. 40s.	Viljo Heino, Finland	1949
1h. 1m. 15.8s.	Emil Zatopek, Czechoslo.	.1951
59m. 51.6s.	Emil Zatopek, Czechoslo	. .1951
59m. 22.8s.	Ron Clarke, Australia	1965
58m. 06.2s.	Gaston Roelants, Belgium	. .1966
57m. 44.4s.	Gaston Roelants, Belgium	. .1972

25,000-Meter Run

1h. 26m. 29.6s.	H. Kolehmainen, Finl'd	. .1920
1h. 25m. 19.9s.	H. Kolehmainen, Finl'd	. .1922
1h. 24m. 24s.	Martti Marttelin, Finl'd	. .1928
1h. 23m. 45.8s.	Ernest Harper, Gt. Brit.	. .1929
1h. 22m. 28.8s.	Martti Marttelin, Finl'd	. .1930
1h. 21m. 27s.	Erkki Tamila, Finland	. . .1939
1h. 20m. 14s.	Mikko Hietanen, Finl'd	. .1948
1h. 19m. 11.8s.	Emil Zatopek, Czechoslo.	1952
1h. 17m. 34s.	A. Ivanov, U.S.S.R.	1955
1h. 16m. 36.4s.	Emil Zatopek, Czechoslo.	1955
1h. 15m. 22.6s.	Ron Hill, Great Britain	. . .1965

30,000-Meter Run

1h. 48m. 6.2s.	Albin Stenroos, Finland	. .1915
1h. 47m. 13.4s.	T. Kolehmainen, Finl'd	. .1922
1h. 46m. 11.6s.	Albin Stenroos, Finland	. .1924
1h. 43m. 7.8s.	V. Sipila, Finland	1928
1h. 42m. 30.4s.	Juan Zabala, Argentina	. .1931
1h. 40m. 57.6s.	Jose Ribas, Argentina	1932
1h. 40m. 49.8s.	Mikko Hietanen, Finl'd	. .1947
1h. 40m. 46.4s.	Mikko Hietanen, Finl'd	. .1948
1h. 39m. 14.6s.	F.K. Vanin, U.S.S.R.	1949
1h. 38m. 54s.	J.Z. Maskatchenkov, U.S.S.R.	1951
1h. 35m. 23.8s.	Emil Zatopek, Czechoslo.	1952
1h. 35m. 3.6s.	Antti Viskari, Finland	. . .1956
1h. 35m. 1s.	A. Ivanov, U.S.S.R.	1957
1h. 34m. 41.2s.	A. Vandendriesche, Belgium	1962
1h. 34m. 1.8s.	J. Alder, Great Britain	. . .1964
1h. 32m. 34.6s.	Tim Johnston, Great Britain	1965
1h. 32m. 25.4s.	Jim Hogan, Great Britain	1966

3,000-Meter Steeplechase

8m. 42.2s.	Jouko Kuha, Finland	1968
8m. 22.0s.	Kerry O'Brien, Australia	1970
8m. 20.8s.	Anders Garderud, Sweden	. .1972

120-Yard High Hurdles

17.75s.	A.W.T. Daniel, Great Britain	.1864
16.2s.	S. Palmer, Great Britain	1878
16s.	C.F. Daft, Great Britain	1886
15.8s.	Henry Williams, U.S.	1891
15.75s.	Walter Henry, U.S.	1892
15.6s.	Stephen Chase, U.S.	1894

15.4s.	Stephen Chase, U.S.	1895
15.2s.	Alvin Kraenzlein, U.S.	1898
15s.	Forrest Smithson, U.S.	1908
14.4s.	Earl Thomson, Canada	1920
14.4s.	E. Wennstrom, Sweden	1929
14.4s.	Stephen Anderson, U.S.	1930
14.2s.	Percy Beard, U.S.	1931
14.2s.	Percy Beard, U.S.	1934
14.2s.	Tom Moore, U.S.	1935
14.2s.	Philip Cope, U.S.	1935
14.2s.	Roy Staley, U.S.	1935
14.2s.	Alvin Moreau, U.S.	1935
14.1s.	Forrest Towns, U.S.	1936
14.1s.	Forrest Towns, U.S.	1936
13.7s.	Forrest Towns, U.S.	1936
13.7s.	Fred Wolcott, U.S.	1941
13.6s.	Harrison Dillard, U.S.	1948
13.6s.	Richard Attlesey, U.S.	1950
13.5s.	Richard Attlesey, U.S.	1950
13.5s.	Richard Attlesey, U.S.	1950
13.4s.	Jack Davis, U.S.	1956
13.4s.	Milt Campbell, U.S.	1957
13.2s.	Martin Lauer, Germany	1959
13.2s.	Lee Calhoun, U.S.	1960
13.2s.	Earl McCullouch, U.S.	1967
13.2s.	Erv Hall, U.S.	1969
13.2s.	Willie Davenport, U.S.	1969
13.2s.	Thomas Hill, U.S.	1970
13.0s.	Rod Milburn, U.S.	1971

220-Yard Low Hurdles

27 3/8s.	Charles Wiegand, U.S.	1886
27s.	Alfred Copland, U.S.	1887
26.6s.	Alfred Copland, U.S.	1888
26.4s.	Herbert Mapes, U.S.	1889
25.8s.	Fred Ducharme, U.S.	1890
25.25s.	James Lee, U.S.	1890
24.8s.	James Lee, U.S.	1891
24.6s.	John Bremer, U.S.	1895
23.6s.	Alvin Kraenzlein, U.S.	1898
23.6s.	James Wendell, U.S.	1913
23.6s.	Robert Simpson, U.S.	1916
23.2s.	Charles Brookins, U.S.	1923
23s.	Charles Brookins, U.S.	1924
23s.	Norman Paul, U.S.	1933
22.6s.	Jesse Owens, U.S.	1935
22.5s.	Fred Wolcott, U.S.	1940
22.5s.	Harrison Dillard, U.S.	1946
22.3s.	Harrison Dillard, U.S.	1947
22.2s.	David Sime, U.S.	1956
22.2s.	Jack Davis, U.S.	1956
22.2s.	A. Robinson, U.S.	1957
22.1s.	Elias Gilbert, U.S.	1958
21.9s.	Donald Styron, U.S.	1960

440-Yard Intermediate Hurdles

57.2s.	Godfrey Shaw, Great Britain	. . .1891
56.8s.	George Anderson, Great Britain	.1910
54.2s.	John Norton, U.S.	1920
54.2s.	Lord Burghley, Great Britain	. . .1927
52.6s.	John Gibson, U.S.	1927
52.2s.	Roy Cochran, U.S.	1942

52.2s. ... Richard Ault, U.S. 1949
51.9s. ... Armando Filiput, Italy 1950
51.9s. ... Charles Moore Jr., U.S. 1952
51.6s. ... Charles Moore Jr., U.S. 1952
51.3s. ... Yuri Lituyev, U.S.S.R. 1954
50.7s. ... G.C. Potgieter, South Africa ...1957
49.9s. ... Glenn Davis, U.S. 1958
49.7s. ... Gert Potgieter, South Africa ...1958
49.3s. ... Gert Potgieter, South Africa ...1960
48.8s. ... Ralph Mann, U.S. 1970

110-Meter High Hurdles

15.4s. ..... Alvin Kraenzlein, U.S. 1900
15s. ..... Forrest Smithson, U.S. 1908
14.8s. ..... Earl Thomson, Canada ...1920
14.8s. ..... Sten Pettersson, Sweden 1927
14.6s. ..... G.C. Weightman-Smith,
                South Africa 1928
14.4s. ..... E. Wennstrom, Sweden ...1929
14.4s. ..... Bengt Sjostedt, Finland 1931
14.4s. ..... Percy Beard, U.S. 1932
14.4s. ..... Jack Keller, U.S. 1932
14.4s. ..... George Saling, U.S. 1932
14.4s. ..... John Morriss, U.S. 1933
14.4s. ..... John Morriss, U.S. 1933
14.3s. ..... Percy Beard, U.S. 1934
14.2s. ..... Percy Beard, U.S. 1934
14.2s. ..... Alvin Moreau, U.S. 1935
14.1s. ..... Forrest Towns, U.S. 1936
14.1s. ..... Forrest Towns, U.S. 1936
13.7s. ..... Forrest Towns, U.S. 1936
13.7s. ..... Fred Wolcott, U.S. 1941
13.6s. ..... Richard Attlesey, U.S. 1950
13.5s. ..... Richard Attlesey, U.S. 1950
13.4s. ..... Jack Davis, U.S. 1956
13.2s. ..... Martin Lauer, Germany 1959
13.2s. ..... Lee Calhoun, U.S. 1960
13.2s. ..... Earl McCullouch, U.S. 1967
13.2s. ..... Willie Davenport, U.S. 1969
13.2s. ..... Rodney Milburn, U.S. 1972

200-Meter Low Hurdles

24.6s. ..... Harry Hillman, U.S. 1904
23s. .... Charles Brookins, U.S. 1924
23s. .... Norman Paul, U.S. 1933
22.6s. ..... Jesse Owens, U.S. 1935
22.3s. ..... Fred Wolcott, U.S. 1940
22.3s. ..... Harrison Dillard, U.S. 1947
22.2s. ..... David Sime, U.S. 1956
22.2s. ..... A. Robinson, U.S. 1957
22.1s. ..... Elias Gilbert, U.S. 1958
21.9s. ..... Donald Styron, U.S. 1960

400-Meter Intermediate Hurdles

57.6s. ..... Walter Tewksbury, U.S. 1900
55s. .... Charles Bacon, U.S. 1908
54s. .... Frank Loomis, U.S. 1920
53.8s. ..... Sten Pettersson, Sweden 1925
52s. .... Morgan Taylor, U.S. 1928
52s. .... Glenn Hardin, U.S. 1932
51.8s. ..... Glenn Hardin, U.S. 1934
50.6s. ..... Glenn Hardin, U.S. 1934
50.4s. ..... Yuri Lituyev, U.S.S.R. 1953

49.5s. ..... Glenn Davis, U.S. 1956
49.2s. ..... Glenn Davis, U.S. 1958
49.2s. ..... Salvatore Morale, Italy 1962
49.1s. ..... Rex Cawley, U.S. 1964
48.2s. ..... Dave Hemery, Great Britain .1968
47.8s. ..... John Akii-Bua, Uganda 1972

440-Yard Relay

42.8s. ...United States National Team,
                U.S. (Landers, Davis, W.
                Haymond, Smith) 1919
42.4s. ...New York A.C., U.S. (B. Wefers
                Jr., F. Lovejoy, H. Ray, E.
                Farrell) 1921
42.4s. ...U. of Illinois, U.S. (Sweet,
                Evans, Hughes, Ayres) 1923
42s. .....U. of California, U.S. (Taylor,
                Lee, House, Lloyd) 1925
41s. .....Newark A.C., U.S. (C. Bowman,
                Currie, Pappas, Cumming) .. 1927
40.8s. ...U. of Southern California, U.S.
                (R. Delby, M. Maurer, M.
                Guyer, F. Wykoff) 1931
40.5s. ...U. of Southern California, U.S.
                (L. LaFond, W. Anderson, P.
                Jordan, A. Talley) 1938
40.5s. ...Univ. of Texas, U.S. (F.D.
                Smith, J. Prewitt, A. Frie-
                den, C. Thomas) 1954
40.2s. ...Univ. of Texas, U.S. (F.D.
                Smith, A. Frieden, J. Pre-
                witt, R. Whilden) 1955
39.9s. ...Univ. of Texas, U.S. (W. Wilson,
                E. Southern, H. Gainey, R.
                Whilden) 1957
39.7s. ...Abilene Christian College, U.S.
                (W. Griggs, W. Woodhouse, J.
                Segrest, B. Morrow) 1958
39.6s. ...Univ. of Texas, U.S. (W. Wilson,
                E. Southern, H. Gainey, R.
                Alspaugh) 1959
39.6s. ...Southern Univ., U.S. (H. Nairn,
                G. Harris, W. Johnson, G.
                Anderson) 1966
38.6s. ...Southern California, U.S. (E.
                McCullouch, F. Kuller, O.J.
                Simpson, L. Miller) 1967

880-Yard Relay

1m. 27.8s. United States National Team,
                U.S., (Landers, Davis, W.
                Haymond, Smith) 1919
1m. 27.4s. New York A.C., U.S. (B. Wefers
                Jr., F. Lovejoy, H. Ray, E.
                Farrell) 1921
1m. 25.8s. U. of Southern California, U.S.
                (C. House, H. Smith, C. Bo-
                rah, W. Lewis) 1927
1m. 25s. . Stanford U., U.S. (Kneubuhl,
                Hiserman, R. Malott, J.
                Weiershauser) 1937
1m. 24.4s. U. of Southern California, U.S.
                (M. Patton, R. Frazier, G.

Pasquali, N. Stocks) 1949

1m. 24s. . U. of Southern California, U.S. (M. Patton, R. Frazier, G. Pasquali, N. Stocks) 1949

1m. 23.8s. National Team, U.S. (L. King, A. Stanfield, T. Baker, R. Morrow) 1956

1m. 22.7s. Univ. of Texas, U.S. (W. Wilson, E. Southern, H. Gainey, R. Whilden) 1957

1m. 22.6s. Abilene Christian College, U.S. (W. Woodhouse, J. Segrest, G. Peterson, B. Morrow) ... 1958

1m. 22.1s. San Jose State, U.S. (K. Shackelford, B. Talmadge, L. Evans, T. Smith) 1967

1m. 21.7s. Texas A&M (J.D. Rogers, H. Woods, M. Mills, C. Mills) ... 1970

1-Mile Relay

3m. 18.2s. United States National Team, U.S. (Schaaf, M. Sheppard, H. Gissing, J. Rosenberger) . 1911

3m. 18s. . U. of Pennsylvania, U.S. (Kaufman, Lockwood, D. Lippincott, J. Meredith) 1915

3m. 16.4s. American Legion, Pennsylvania, U.S. (C. Rodgers, E. Eby, L. Brown, R. Maxam) 1921

3m. 13.4s. United States National Team, U.S. (G. Baird, Taylor, R. Barbuti, E. Spencer) 1928

3m. 12.6s. Stanford U., U.S. (M. Shore A. Hables, L. Hables, B. Eastman)1931

3m. 11.6s. U. of California, U.S. (E. Johnson, J. Cassin, H. Smallwood, A. Fitch) 1936

3m. 10.5s. Stanford U., U.S. (E. Clark, C. Shaw, C. Williamson, C. Jeffrey) 1940

3m. 9.4s. U. of California, U.S. (J. Reese, F. Froom, C. Barnes, G. Klemmer) 1941

3m. 8.8s. United States National Team, U.S. (E. Cole, J.W. Mashburn, R. Pearman, M. Whitfield) 1952

3m. 7.3s. U.S. National Team (C. Jenkins, L. Spurrier, T. Courtney, L. Jones) Jones) 1956

3m. 5.6s. U.S. National Team (E. Southern, E. Young, O. Davis, J. Yerman) 1960

3m. 4.5s. Arizona State, U.S. (M. Barrick, H. Carr, R. Freeman, U. Williams) 1963

3m. 4.5s. Southern T.C., U.S. (R. Johnson, A. Gates, E. Mason, T. Lewis) 1965

3m. 2.8s. Trinidad, National Team (L. Yearwood, K. Bernard, E. Roberts, W. Mottley) 1966

2-Mile Relay

7m. 53s. . United States National Team, U.S. (Riley, Bromilow, M. Sheppard, A. Kiviat) 1910

7m. 50.4s. Oxford U. & Cambridge U., Great Britain (Tatham, Stallard, Milligan, B. Rudd) 1920

7m. 49.4s. U. of Pennsylvania, U.S. (J. Meredith, J. Holden, E. McMullen, L. Brown) 1922

7m. 47.6s. Boston College, U.S. (W. McKillop, P. Mahoney, T. Cavanaugh, L. Welch) 1924

7m. 42s. . Georgetown U., U.S. (E. Swinburne, J. Holden, Sullivan, G. Marsters) 1925

7m. 41.4s. Boston A.A., U.S. (S. Martin, C. Sansone, L. Welch, L. Hahn) 1926

7m. 35.8s. United States National Team, U.S. (C. Hornbostel, R. Young, H. Williamson, J. Woodruff) 1936

7m. 34.5s. U. of California, U.S. (J. Reese, G. Klemmer, R. Peter, C. Barnes) 1941

7m. 30.6s. British-Northern Ireland National Team, Gr. B.-N.I. (G. Nankeville, A. Webster, F. Evans, H. Parlett) 1951

7m. 29.2s. United States National Team, U.S. (W. Ashenfelter, R. Pearman, J. Barnes, M. Whitfield) 1952

7m. 27.3s. Fordham Univ., U.S. (T. Foley, T. Tarsney, W. Persichetty, T. Courtney) 1954

7m. 22.9s. U.S. National Team (J. Walter, L. Spurrier, A. Sowell, T. Courtney) 1956

7m. 22.8s. Occidental College, U.S. (T.S. White, D.A. Reisbord, L.G. Wray, T.L. Hadley) 1957

7m. 19.4s. U.S. National Team (E. Cunliffe, T. Murphy, J. Siebert, J. Yerman) 1960

7m. 18.4s. Oklahoma State, U.S. (J. Metcalf, J. Perry, T. Von Ruden, D. Perry) 1965

7m. 16.0s. U.S.S.R. National Team (A. Ustyantsev, R. Mitrofanov, O. Raiko, V. Mikhailov) 1966

7m. 14.6s. West Germany (B. Tummler, W. Adams, H. Norpoth, F. Kemper) 1968

7m. 11.6s. Kenya National Team (N. Bon, H. Nyamau, T. Saisi, R. Ouko) 1970

4-Mile Relay

17m. 51.2s. United States National Team, U.S. (Mahoney, Marceau, Powers, O. Hedlund) 1913

17m. 51.2s. United States National Team,

U.S. (Taylor, Hoffmire, Windnagle, Potter) 1916

17m.45s. . U. of Illinois, U.S. (Yates, Patterson, McGinnis, Wharton) . 1922

17m.21.4s. Illinois A.C., U.S. (E. Krogh, R. Buker, R. Watson, J. Ray) .. 1923

17m.17.2s. United States National Team, U.S. (C. Hornbostel, G. Venzke, A. San Romani, G. Cunningham) 1936

17m.16.2s. Indiana U., U.S. (M. Trutt, J. Smith, T. Deckard, D. Lash) 1937

17m.2.8s. Brandkarens Idrottsklubb, Sweden (A. Jansson, H. Karlen, H. Kalarne, B. Hellstrom) .. 1941

16m.55.8s. Gefle Idrottforening, Sweden (R. Wollgren, I. Bengtsson, O. Aberg, H. Eriksson) 1948

16m.42.8s. Gefle Idrottsforening, Sweden (I. Bengtsson, G. Bergquist, O. Aberg, H. Eriksson) 1949

16m.41s. . British National Team (C. Chataway, G. Nankeville, D. Seaman, R. Bannister) 1953

16m.30.6s. Great Britain and Northern Ireland Team (M. Blagrove, P. Clark, D. Ibbotson, B. Hewson) 1958

16m.25.2s. Hungary National Team (L. Kovacs, B. Szekeres, S. Iharos, I. Rozavolgi) 1959

16m.9s. . . University of Oregon, U.S. (A. San Romani, V. Reeve, K. Forman, D. Burleson) 1962

16m.05.0s. University of Oregon (R. Divine, W. Bell, A. Kvalheim, D. Wilborn) 1968

16m.02.8s. New Zealand National Team (K. Ross, A. Polhill, R. Tayler, R. Quax) 1972

400-Meter Relay

42.3s. ...German National Team, Germany (Halt, Kern, Hermann, Rau) 1912

42.2s. ...United States National Team, U.S. (J. Scholz, L. Murchison, M. Kirksey, C. Paddock) 1920

42s. .....British National Team, Great Britain (H. Abrahams, Rangeley, Royle, Nichol) 1924

42s. .....Dutch National Team, Holland (Boot, Broos, DeVries, Van den Berghe) 1924

41s. .....United States National Team, U.S. (L. Clarke, F. Hussey, J. LeConey, L. Murchison) ... 1924

41s. .....United States National Team, U.S. (L. Clarke, F. Hussey, J. LeConey, L. Murchison) ... 1924

41s. .....Newark A.C., U.S. (C. Bowman, Currie, Pappas, Cumming) .. 1927

41s. .....Sp. C. Eintract, Germany (Geerling, Wichmann, Metzner, Salz) 1928

40.8s. ...German National Team, Germany (Jonath, Korts, Houben, Kornig) 1928

40.8s. ...Sp. C. Charlottenburg, Germany (Kornig, Grosser, Natan, Schloske) 1929

40.8s. ...U. of California, U.S. (R. Delby, M. Maurer, M. Guyer, F. Wykoff) 1931

40s. .....United States National Team, U.S. (R. Kiesel, E. Toppino, H. Dyer, F. Wykoff) 1932

39.8s. ...United States National Team, U.S. (J. Owens, R. Metcalfe, F. Draper, F. Wykoff) 1936

39.5s. ...U.S. National Team (I. Murchison, L. King, T. Baker, B. Morrow) 1956

39.5s. ...German National Team (M. Steinbach, M. Lauer, H. Futterer, M. Germar) 1958

39.5s. ...German National Team (B. Cullmann, A. Hary, W. Mahlendorf, M. Lauer) 1960

39.5s. ...German National Team (B. Cullmann, A. Hary, W. Mahlendorf, M. Lauer) 1960

39.1s. ...U.S. National Team (H. Jones, F. Budd, C. Frazier, P. Drayton) 1961

39s. .....U.S. National Team (P. Drayton, G. Ashworth, D. Stebbins, B. Hayes) 1964

38.2s. ...U.S. National Team (C. Greene, M. Pender, R. Smith, J. Hines) 1968

800-Meter Relay

1m.36s. . A.I.K. Sweden (Ljung, Pettersson, Almqvist, Hakanson) .. 1908

1m.27.8s. U. of Pennsylvania, U.S. (S. Landers, Davis, W. Haymond, Smith) 1919

1m.27.4s. New York A.C., U.S. (B. Wefers Jr., F. Lovejoy, H. Ray, E. Farrell) 1921

1m.25.8s. U. of California, U.S. (C. House, H. Smith, C. Borah, W. Lewis) 1927

1m.25s. Stanford U., U.S. (Kneubuhl, Hiserman, R. Malott, J. Weiershauser) 1937

1m.24.4s. U. of Southern California, U.S. (M. Patton, R. Frazier, G. Pasquali, N. Stocks) 1949

1m.24s. .U. of Southern California, U.S. (M. Patton, R. Frazier, G. Pasquali, N. Stocks) 1949

1m.23.8s. U.S. National Team (L. King, A. Stanfield, T. Baker, B. Morrow) 1956

1m. 22.7s..University of Texas, U.S. (W. Wilson, E. Southern, H. Gainey, R. Whilden) 1957

1m. 22.6s..Abilene Christian College, U.S. (W. Woodhouse, J. Segrest, G. Peterson, B. Morrow) ... 1958

1m. 22.1s..San Jose State (K. Shackleford, B. Talmadge, L. Evans, T. Smith) 1967

1m. 21.7s..Texas A & M (D. Rogers, R. Woods, C. Mills, M. Mills) ... 1970

1m. 21.5s..Italy National Team (F. Ossola, P. Abetti, L. Benedetti, P. Mennea) 1972

1,600-Meter Relay

3m. 18.2s..United States National Team, U.S. (Schaaf, M. Sheppard, H. Gissing, J. Rosenberger) . 1911

3m. 16.6s..United States National Team, U.S. (M. Sheppard, C. Reidpath, J. Meredith, F. Lindberg)1912

3m. 16.4s..American Legion, Pennsylvania, U.S. (C. Rodgers, E. Eby, L. Brown, R. Maxam) 1921

3m. 16s. .United States National Team, U.S. (Cochrane, A. Helffrich, McDonald, Stevenson) 1924

3m. 14.2s..United States National Team, U.S. (G. Baird, F. Alderman, E. Spencer, R. Barbuti) 1928

3m. 13.4s..United States National Team, U.S. (G. Baird, F. Alderman, E. Spencer, R. Barbuti) 1928

3m.12.6s. .Stanford U., U.S. (M. Shore, A. Hables, L. Hables, B. Eastman)1931

3m.8.2s. . United States National Team, U.S. (I. Fuqua, E. Ablowich, K. Warner, W. Carr) 1932

3m. 3.9s. .Jamaican National Team, Jamaica, B.W.I. (A. Wint, L. Laing, H. McKenley, G. Rhoden) 1952

3m. 2.2s. .U.S. National Team (J. Yerman, E. Young, G. Davis, O. Davis) 1960

3m. 1.6s. .Great Britain-Northern Ireland National Team (T. Graham, A. Metcalfe, J. Cooper, R. Brightwell). 1964

3m. 00.7s..U.S. National Team (O. Cassell, M. Larrabee, U. Williams, H. Carr) 1964

2m. 59.6s..U.S. National Team (B. Frey, L. Evans, T. Smith, T. Lewis) .. 1966

2m. 56.1s..U.S. National Team (V. Matthews, R. Freeman, L. James, L. Evans) 1968

3,200-Meter Relay

7m. 41.4s..Boston A.A., U.S. (S. Martin, C. Sansone, L. Welch, L. Hahn) 1926

7m. 35.8s..United States National Team,

U.S. (C. Hornbostel, R. Young, H. Williamson, J. Woodruff) 1936

7m. 30.4s. .German National Team, Germany (Seibert, Grau, Kaindl, R. Harbig) 1941

7m. 29s. . .Swedish National Team, Sweden (T. Sten, O. Linden, S. Lindgard, L. Strand) 1946

7m. 28s. . .Uda, Czechoslovakia (D. Cikel, A. Strzinck, L. Leika, S. Jungwirth) 1953

7m. 15.8s. .Belgian National Team (A. Baillieux, A. Langenus, E. Leva, R. Moens) 1956

7m. 08.6s. .West Germany National Team (M. Kinder, W. Adams, D. Bogatzki, F. Kemper) 1966

6,000-Meter Relay

16m. 40.2s. I. K. Gota, Sweden (Peterson, Lindblom, Falk, Lundgren) . 1919

16m. 37s. .I. F. Linnea, Sweden (Adamsson, Fosselius, Fosselius, E. Wide) 1925

16m. 26.2s. Turun Urheiluliitto, Finland (Koivunalho, Katz, Liewendahl, P. Nurmi) 1926

16m. 11.4s. Turun Urheiluliitto, Finland (Liewendahl, Katz, Koivunalho, P. Nurmi) 1926

15m. 55.6s. English National Team, Great Britain (Harris, Hedges, J. Cornes, Thomas) 1931

15m. 54.8s. Finnish National Team, Finland (Salovaara, Salovaara, Sarkama, Hartikka) 1939

15m. 42s. .Brandkarens Idrottsklubb, Sweden (A. Jansson, H. Karlen, H. Kalarne, B. Hellstrom) .. 1941

15m. 38.6s. Malmo Allm. I.F., Sweden (Jakobson, Stridsberg, L. Strand, G. Hagg) 1945

15m. 34.6s. Gefle Idrottsforening, Sweden (I. Bengtsson, G. Bergquist, O. Aberg, H. Eriksson) 1947

15m. 30.2s. Gefle Idrottsforening, Sweden (O. Aberg, I. Bengtsson, G. Bergquist, H. Eriksson) 1949

15m. 27.2s. British National Team (R. H. Dunkley, D. C. Law, G. Pirie, W. Nankeville) 1953

15m. 21.2s. Budapest Honved, Hungary (L. Tabori, I. Rozsavolgyi, F. Mikes, S. Iharos) 1954

15m. 14.8s. Budapest Honved, Hungary (F. Mikes, L. Tabori, I. Rozsavolgyi, S. Iharos) 1955

15m. 11.4s. East German Team (S. Hermann, K. Richtzenhaim, H. Reinnagel, S. Valentin) 1958

15m. 04.2s. France National Team (J.

Clausse, R. Bogey, M. Jazy,
M. Bernard) 1961

14m. 58s. .Germany National Team (M.
Matuschewski, J. May, S.
Herrmann, S. Valentin) 1963

14m. 49s. .France National Team (P. Ver-
voort, C. Nicolas, M. Jazy, J.
Wadeau) 1965

High Jump

5ft. 6in. . . . . F. H. Gooch, Great Britain . .1864
5ft. 9 in. . . . . T. G. Little, Great Britain . . .1866
5ft. 9in. . . . . J. H. S. Roupel, Great Britain 1866
5ft. 9 1/2in. . R. J. C. Mitchell, Gt. Brit. . . .1871
5ft. 10 in. . . . M. J. Brooks, Great Britain . .1874
6ft. 1/2in. . . . M. J. Brooks, Great Britain . .1876
6ft. 2 1/2in. . M. J. Brooks, Great Britain . .1876
6ft. 2 3/4in. . Patrick Navin, Ireland 1880
6ft. 3 1/2in. . William Page, U.S. 1887
6ft. 4in. . . . . William Page, U.S. 1887
6ft. 4 1/4in. . Michael Sweeney, U.S. 1892
6ft. 4 1/2in. . J. M. Ryan, Ireland 1895
6ft. 5 in. . . . . Michael Sweeney, U.S. 1895
6ft. 5 5/8in. . Michael Sweeney, U.S. 1895
6ft. 5 1/8in. . George Horine, U.S. 1912
6ft. 7in. . . . . George Horine, U.S. 1912
6ft. 7 5/16in. Edward Beeson, U.S. 1914
6ft. 8 1/4in. . Harold Osborn, U.S. 1924
6ft. 8 5/8in. . Walter Marty, U.S. 1933
6ft. 9 1/8in. . Walter Marty, U.S. 1934
6ft. 9 3/4in. . Cornelius Johnson, U.S. 1936
6ft. 9 3/4in. . David Albritton, U.S. 1936
6ft. 10 3/8in. Melvin Walker, U.S. 1937
6ft. 11in. . . . Les Steers, U.S. 1941
6ft. 11 1/2in. Walt Davis, U.S. 1953
7ft. 1/2in. . . Charles Dumas, U.S. 1956
7ft. 1in. . . . . Yuri Stepanov, U.S.S.R. 1957
7ft. 3 3/4in. . John Thomas, U.S. 1960
7ft. 4 1/2in. . Valery Brumel, U.S.S.R. 1961
7ft. 5in. . . . . Valery Brumel, U.S.S.R. 1962
7ft. 5 1/2in. . Valery Brumel, U.S.S.R. 1962
7ft. 5 3/4in. . Valery Brumel, U.S.S.R. 1963
7ft. 6 1/4in. . Pat Matzdorf, U.S. 1971

Broad Jump

18ft. . . . . F.H. Gooch, Great
Britain 1864
22ft. 7in. . . . . . E.J. Davies, Great
Britain 1872
23ft. 1 1/2in. . . J. Lane, Ireland 1874
23ft. 2in. . . . . . Patrick Navin, Ireland . . .1883
23ft. 3in. . . . . . Malcolm Ford, U.S. 1886
23ft. 3 1/8in. . . Alfred Copland, U.S. 1890
23ft. 6 1/2in. . . Charles Reber, U.S. 1891
23ft. 7 1/2in. . . Matthew Rosengrave,
Australia 1896
24ft. 1/2in. . . . W.J.M. Newburn,
Ireland 1898
24ft. 3 1/2in. . . Alvin Kraenzlein, U.S. . . .1899
24ft. 4 1/2in. . . Alvin Kraenzlein, U.S. . . .1899
24ft. 7 1/2in. . . Myer Prinstein, U.S. 1900
25ft. 3in. . . . . . Edward Gourdin, U.S. . . .1921

25ft. 5 3/4in. . . Robert Legendre, U.S. 1924
25ft. 10 7/8in. . DeHard Hubbard, U.S. . . .1925
25ft. 11 1/8in. . Edward Hamm, U.S. 1928
26ft. 1/8in. . . . Silvio Cator, Haiti 1928
26ft. 2 1/8in. . . Chuhei Nambu, Japan . . .1931
26ft. 8 1/4in. . . Jesse Owens, U.S. 1935
26ft. 11 1/4in. . Ralph Boston, U.S.A. . . .1960
27ft. 2in. . . . . . Ralph Boston, U.S.A. . . .1960
27ft. 3 1/2in. . . Igor Ter-Ovanesyan,
U.S.S.R. 1962
27ft. 4 3/4in. . . Ralph Boston, U.S. 1965
27ft. 4 3/4in. . . Igor Ter-Ovanesyan,
U.S.S.R. 1967
29ft. 2 1/4in. . . Bob Beamon, U.S. 1968

Pole Vault

10ft. . . . . J. Wheeler, Great Britain .1866
19ft. 6 1/2in. . . R.J.C. Mitchell, Great
Britain 1868
10ft. 9in. . . . . . H.E. Kayall, Great
Britain 1877
10ft. 11in. . . . . William Van Houten, U.S.1880
11ft. 1/2in. . . . Hugh Baxter, U.S. 1883
11ft. 5in. . . . . . Hugh Baxter, U.S. 1887
11ft. 5 3/8in. . . Walter Rodenbaugh, U.S. .1892
11ft. 10 1/2in. . Raymond Clapp, U.S. . . .1898
12ft. 1 3/10in. . Norman Dole, U.S. 1904
12ft. 2in. . . . . . F. Gouder, France 1905
12ft. 4 7/8in. . . LeRoy Samse, U.S. 1906
12ft. 5 1/2in. . . Walter Dray, U.S. 1907
12ft. 7 1/2in. . . Alfred Gilbert, U.S. 1908
12ft. 9 1/2in. . . Walter Dray, U.S. 1908
12ft. 10 7/8in. . Leland Scott, U.S. 1910
13ft. 1in. . . . . . Robert Gardner, U.S. . . .1912
13ft. 2 1/4in. . . Marc Wright, U.S. 1912
13ft. 5in. . . . . . Frank Foss, U.S. 1920
13ft. 6 1/8in. . . Charles Hoff, Norway . . .1922
13ft. 9 3/4in. . . Charles Hoff, Norway . . .1923
13ft. 10 1/2in. . Charles Hoff, Norway . . .1925
13ft. 11 3/8in. . Charles Hoff, Norway . . .1925
14ft. . . . . Sabin Carr, U.S. 1927
14ft. 1 1/2in. . . Lee Barnes, U.S. 1928
14ft. 4 3/8in. . . William Graber, U.S. 1932
14ft. 5 1/8in. . . Keith Brown, U.S. 1935
14ft. 6 1/2in. . . George Varoff, U.S. 1936
14ft. 11in. . . . . William Sefton, U.S. 1937
14ft. 11in. . . . . Earle Meadows, U.S. 1937
15ft. 1 1/8in. . . Cornelius Warmerdam,
U.S. . . . .·. 1940
15ft. 5 3/4in. . . Cornelius Warmerdam,
U.S. 1941
15ft. 7 3/4in. . . Cornelius Warmerdam,
U.S. 1942
15ft. 8 1/4in. . . R.A. Gutowski, U.S. 1957
15ft. 9 1/4in. . . Donald Bragg, U.S. 1960
15ft. 10 1/4in. . George Davies, U.S. 1961
16ft. 3/4in. . . . John Uelses, U.S. 1962
16ft. 2in. . . . . . David Tork, U.S. 1962
16ft. 2 1/2in. . . Pentti Nikula, Finland . . .1962
16ft. 10 3/4in. . M. Preussger, Germany . .1964
17ft. 4in. . . . . . Fred Hansen, U.S. 1964
17ft. 6 1/4in. . . John Pennel, U.S. 1966

17ft. 7 3/4in.	Paul Wilson, U.S.	1967
17ft. 9in.	Bob Beamon, U.S.	1968
17ft. 10 1/4in.	John Pennel, U.S.	1969
17ft. 10 1/2in.	Wolfgang Norwig, E. Germany	1970
18ft. 1/4in.	Christos Papanicolaou, Greece	1970
18ft. 5 3/4in.	Bob Seagren, U.S.	1972

Shot-Put

30ft. 11 1/2in.	J.M. Mann, U.S.	1876
32ft. 5in.	Henry Buermeyer, U.S.	1876
33ft.	Francis Larkin Jr., U.S.	1877
37ft. 2in.	Henry Buermeyer, U.S.	1877
37ft. 4in.	Henry Buermeyer, U.S.	1878
42ft. 5in.	E.J. Bor, Great Britain	1880
43ft.	Frank Lambrecht, U.S.	1883
43ft. 9in.	J. O'Brien, Great Britain	1885
43ft. 11in.	George Bray, U.S.	1887
44ft. 5in.	George Gray, U.S.	1888
46ft. 2in.	George Gray, U.S.	1890
46ft. 3 1/2in.	George Gray, U.S.	
46ft. 7 3/4in.	George Gray, U.S.	1891
47ft.	George Gray, U.S.	1893
48ft. 2in.	Dennis Horgan, Ireland	1898
48ft. 7in.	Ralph Rose, U.S.	1904
49ft. 6in.	Wesley Coe, U.S.	1905
49ft. 7 1/2in.	Ralph Rose, U.S.	1907
49ft. 10in.	Ralph Rose, U.S.	1908
51ft.	Ralph Rose, U.S.	1909
51ft. 9 5/8in.	Emil Hirschfeld, Germany	1928
52ft. 3/4in.	John Kuck, U.S.	1928
52ft. 7 1/2in.	Emil Hirschfeld, Germany	1928
52ft. 7 1/2in.	Franz Douda, Czechoslovakia	1931
52ft. 7 7/8in.	Zygmunt Heljasz, Poland	1932
53ft. 1/2in.	Leo Sexton, U.S.	1932
53ft. 1 3/4in.	Franz Douda, Czechoslovakia	1932
54ft. 1in.	John Lyman, U.S.	1934
55ft. 1 1/2in.	Jack Torrance, U.S.	1934
55ft. 5in.	Jack Torrance, U.S.	1934
57ft. 1in.	Jack Torrance, U.S.	1934
58ft. 3/8in.	Charles Fonville, U.S.	1948
58ft. 4 3/8in.	James Fuchs, U.S.	1949
58ft. 5 1/2in.	James Fuchs, U.S.	1950
58ft. 8 1/2in.	James Fuchs, U.S.	1950
58ft. 10 1/2in.	James Fuchs, U.S.	1950
59ft. 2 1/4in.	Parry O'Brien, U.S.	1953
60ft. 10in.	Parry O'Brien, U.S.	1954
63ft. 2in.	Parry O'Brien, U.S.	1956
65ft. 7in.	William Nieder, U.S.	1960
65ft. 10in.	William Nieder, U.S.	1960
65ft. 10 1/2in.	Dallas Long, U.S.	1962
70ft. 7 1/4in.	Randy Matson, U.S.	1965
71ft. 5 1/2in.	Randy Matson, U.S.	1967

Discus Throw

95ft. 7 1/2in.	Robert Garrett, U.S.	1896
118ft 9in.	Charles Henneman, U.S.	1897
120ft. 7 3/4in.	Martin Sheridan, U.S.	1901
127ft. 8 3/4in.	Martin Sheridan, U.S.	1902
133ft. 6 1/2in.	Martin Sheridan, U.S.	1904
135ft. 5in.	Martin Sheridan, U.S.	1906
136ft. 10in.	Martin Sheridan, U.S.	1907
139ft. 10 1/2in.	Martin Sheridan, U.S.	1909
141ft. 4 3/8in.	Martin Sheridan, U.S.	1911
145ft. 9 1/2in.	James Duncan, U.S.	1912
156ft. 1 3/8in.	James Duncan, U.S.	1912
156ft. 2 1/2in.	Thomas Lieb, U.S.	1924
157ft. 1 5/8in.	Glenn Hartranft, U.S.	1925
158ft. 1 3/4in.	Clarence Houser, U.S.	1926
163ft. 8 3/4in.	Eric Krenz, U.S.	1929
167ft. 5 3/8in.	Eric Krenz, U.S.	1930
169ft. 8 7/8in.	Paul Jessup, U.S.	1930
171ft. 11 3/4in.	Harald Andersson, Sweden	1934
174ft. 2 1/2in.	Willi Schroeder, Germany	1935
174ft. 8 3/4in.	Archie Harris, U.S.	1941
175ft.	Adolfo Consolini, Italy	1941
177ft. 11in.	Adolfo Consolini, Italy	1946
180ft. 2 3/4in.	Robert Fitch, U.S.	1946
181ft. 6 3/8in.	Adolfo Consolini, Italy	1948
185ft. 2 3/4in.	Fortune Gordien, U.S.	1949
186ft. 11in.	Fortune Gordien, U.S.	1949
194ft. 6in.	Fortune Gordien, U.S.	1953
196ft. 6 1/2in.	Edmund Piatowski, Poland	1959
196ft. 6 1/2in.	Richard Babka, U.S.	1960
199ft. 2 1/2in.	Jay Silvester, U.S.	1961
200ft. 5 1/2in.	Alfred Oerter, U.S.	1962
202ft. 3 3/4in.	Vladimir Trusenev, U.S.S.R.	1962
204ft. 10 1/2in.	Alfred Oerter, U.S.	1962
211ft. 9 1/2in.	Ludvik Danek, Czech.	1964
213ft. 11in.	Ludvik Danek, Czech.	1965
218ft. 4in.	Jay Silvester, U.S.	1968
224ft. 5in.	Jay Silvester, U.S.	1968
224ft. 5 in.	Rickard Bruch, Sweden	1972

Javelin Throw

120ft.	Harald Andersson, Sweden	1904
175ft. 6in.	Eric Lemming, Sweden	1906
188ft.	Eric Lemming, Sweden	1908
191ft. 2 1/8in.	Eric Lemming, Sweden	1911
198ft. 11 3/8in.	Eric Lemming, Sweden	1912
200ft. 1 11/20in.	Julius Saaristo, Finland	1912
204ft. 5 5/8in.	Eric Lemming, Sweden	1912
216ft. 10 3/8in.	Jonni Myyra, Finland	1919
218ft. 6 7/8in.	Gunnar Lindstrom, Sweden	1924
229ft. 3 1/8in.	Eino Penttila, Finland	1927
232ft. 11 5/8in.	E. H. Lundquist, Sweden	1928
234ft. 9 3/4in.	Matti Jarvinen, Finland	1930
235ft. 2 7/8in.	Matti Jarvinen, Finland	1930
235ft. 9 7/8in.	Matti Jarvinen, Finland	1930
239ft. 3 1/4in.	Matti Jarvinen, Finland	1932
242ft. 10 1/4in.	Matti Jarvinen, Finland	1933
243ft. 8 3/8in.	Matti Jarvinen, Finland	1933
244ft. 9 3/8in.	Matti Jarvinen, Finland	1933
249ft. 8 1/8in.	Matti Jarvinen, Finland	1934
251 6 1/8in.	Matti Jarvinen, Finland	1936
255ft. 5 3/4in.	Yrjo Nikkanen, Finland	1938
258ft. 2 3/8in.	Yrjo Nikkanen, Finland	1938

263ft. 10in.	. . . Franklin Held, U.S.	1953
268ft. 2 1/2in.	. Franklin Held, U.S.	1955
281ft. 2in.	. . . . Egil Danielsen, Norway	. .1956
282ft. 3 1/2in.	. Albert Cantello, U.S.	1959
284ft. 7in.	. . . . Carlo Lievore, Italy	1961
300ft. 11in.	. . . Terje Pedersen, Norway	. .1964
307ft. 9in.	. . . . Janis Lusis, U.S.S.R.	1972

Hammer Throw

87ft. 7in.	. . . . . G.R. Thornton, Gt. Brit.	.1866
99ft. 6in.	. . . . . T. Batson, Great Britain	. .1868
101ft. 5in.	. . . . F. Waite, Great Britain	. . .1869
103ft. 11in.	. . . H. Leeke, Great Britain	. .1869
111ft. 7in.	. . . . H. Leeke, Great Britain	. .1872
122ft. 6in.	. . . . S. S. Brown, Great Britain	1873
126ft. 9in.	. . . . G. H. Hales, Great Britain	.1874
130ft.	. . . . William Barry, Ireland	. . .1889
130ft. 8in.	. . . . James Mitchel, U.S.	1890
140ft. 11in.	. . . James Mitchel, U.S.	1892
147ft.	. . . . John Flanagan, U.S.	1896
150ft. 8in.	. . . . John Flanagan, U.S.	1897
151ft. 10 1/2in.	John Flanagan, U.S.	1898
164ft. 6in.	. . . . John Flanagan, U.S.	1899
167ft. 4 1/2in.	. John Flanagan, U.S.	1900
171ft. 9in.	. . . . John Flanagan, U.S.	1901
172ft. 11in.	. . . John Flanagan, U.S.	1904
173ft. 7in.	. . . . Matt McGrath, U.S.	1907
184ft. 8in.	. . . . John Flanagan, U.S.	1909
187ft. 4in.	. . . . Matt McGrath, U.S.	1911
189ft. 6 1/2in.	. Patrick Ryan, U.S.	1913
193ft. 6 7/8in.	. Erwin Blask, Germany	. . .1938
193ft. 7 1/2in.	. Imre Nemeth, Hungary	. .1948
195ft. 5 1/4in.	. Imre Nemeth, Hungary	. .1949
196ft. 5 1/2in.	. Imre Nemeth, Hungary	. .1950
197ft. 11 1/2in.	Jozsef Csermak, Hungary	.1952
200ft. 11in.	. . . Sverre Strandli, Norway	. .1952
204ft. 7in.	. . . . Sverre Strandli, Norway	. .1953
207ft. 9 3/4in.	. M. P. Krivonosov, U.S.S.R.	1954
211ft. 1/2in.	. . M. P. Krivonosov, U.S.S.R.	1955
220ft. 10in.	. . . M. P. Krivonosov, U.S.S.R.	1956
225ft. 4in.	. . . . Harold Connolly, U.S.	. . .1958
230ft. 9in.	. . . . Harold Connolly, U.S.	. . .1960
231ft. 10in.	. . . Harold Connolly, U.S.	. . .1962
241ft. 11in.	. . . Gyula Zsivotzky, Hungary	1965
242ft. 0in.	. . . . Gyula Zsivotzky, Hungary	1968
247ft. 7 1/2in.	. Antoly Bondarchuk, U.S.S.R. 1969
250ft. 8in.	. . . . Walter Schmidt, W. Germany 1971

Triple Jump

(This name has been adopted officially as of Jan. 1, 1963 to replace, "Hop, Step, and Jump")

42ft. 10in.	. . . . John Purcell, Ireland	1884
46ft. 8in.	. . . . . John Purcell, Ireland	1885
46ft. 9in.	. . . . . John Purcell, Ireland	1886
48ft. 3in.	. . . . . John Purcell, Ireland	1887
48ft. 6in.	. . . . . Edward Bloss, U.S.	1893
48ft. 11 1/4in.	. Timothy Ahearne, Ireland	1908
50ft. 11in.	. . . . Daniel Ahearn, U.S.	1909
50ft. 11 1/4in.	. Anthony Winter, Australia 1924

51ft. 1 3/8in.	. . Mikio Oda, Japan	1931
51ft. 7in.	. . . . . Chuhei Nambu, Japan	. . .1932
51ft. 9 3/8in.	. . John Metcalfe, Australia	.1935
52ft. 5 7/8in.	. . Naota Tajima, Japan	1936
52ft. 5 7/8in.	. . Adhemar da Silva, Brazil	.1950
52ft. 6 1/4in.	. . Adhemar da Silva, Brazil	.1951
52ft. 10 1/2in.	. Adhemar da Silva, Brazil	.1952
53ft. 2 1/2in.	. . Adhemar da Silva, Brazil	.1952
53ft. 2 3/4in.	. . L. Scherbakov, U.S.S.R.	.1953
53ft. 3 3/4in.	. . Adhemar da Silva, Brazil	.1955
54ft. 5in.	. . . . . O. Ryakhovsky, U.S.S.R.	1957
54ft. 9 1/2in.	. . Oleg Fedoseyev, U.S.S.R.	1959
55ft. 10 1/4in.	. Josef Schmidt, Poland	. . .1960
57ft. 3/4in.	. . . Viktor Saneyev, U.S.S.R.	1968
57ft. 1in.	. . . . . Pedro Perez Duenas, Cuba 1971
57ft. 2 3/4in.	. . Viktor Saneyev, U.S.S.R.	1972

Decathlon

Current point system adopted in 1950 and used first at Olympic Games in 1952. A previously revised point system was instituted in 1936.

	Points		
Old Table	Revised Table	Current Table	
7,481.69	6,450	——	A. Klumberg, Esthonia 1922
7,710.775	6,877	——	Harold Osborn, U.S. . 1924
7,820.93	6,889	——	Paavo Yrjola, Finland 1926
7,995.19	7,053	——	Paavo Yrjola, Finland 1927
8,053.29	7,071	——	Paavo Yrjola, Finland 1928
8,255.475	7,378	——	Akilles Jarvinen, Finland 1930
8,462.235	7,396	——	James Bausch, U.S. . . 1932
8,467.62	7,432	——	Hans Sievert, Germany 1933
8,790.46	7,824.5	——	Hans Sievert, Germany 1934
	7,900	7,313	Glenn Morris, U.S. 1936
	8,042	7,444	Robert Mathias, U.S. . 1950
		7,887	Robert Mathias, U.S. . 1952
		7,985	Rafer Johnson, U.S. . . . 1955
		8,013	Vasily Kuznetsov, U.S.S.R. 1958
	9,121	8,089	C.K. Yang, Taiwan . . . 1963
		8,230	Russ Hodge, U.S. 1966
		8,319	Kurt Bendlin, W. Germany 1967
		8,417	William Toomey, U.S. 1969
		8,454	Nicolai Avilov, U.S.S.R. 1972

DESCRIPTIONS OF EVENTS

(From E. D. Mitchell's Sports for Recreation," A. S. Barnes and Company, New York.)

The sport of track and field is divided into two types of contests—track events and field events. The track events, consisting of running and hurdling, are usually held on an oval-shaped running track that has a hard level surface topped with cinders and is usually one-fourth of a mile in length and 18 to 32 feet in width. One side of the oval is marked out for short races (dashes). Indoor tracks are much shorter in length (usually 8 to 11 laps to the mile) and have boards, clay or dirt for the running surface. Field events, consisting of jumping, vaulting and weight throwing are usually conducted on the field inside the running track (called the infield). On the infield are pits filled with sawdust, or a mixture of sand and sawdust, for the jumping events, and starting circles and lines for the throwing events. In some cases, the field events are held on a field adjacent to the running track.

The shortest races are ordinarily at distances of 100, 220 and 440 yards (metric equivalents— 90, 180 and 400 meters) outdoors, and 50, 60 or 70 yards indoors. The common middle-distance race (more than ¼ mile in length but less than a mile) is the 880-yard (800 meters) run. The distance races are one mile (1,500 meters) or more and usually include 1- and 2-mile races. There are also relay races in which 4 men make up a team and each individual runs a part of the total distance. In non-medley relays each runner covers an equal distance, while in the medley relays the men run varying distances. The common distances for the non-medley relays are 440 yards (each runner covering 110 yards), 880 yards (220 yards each), 1 mile (¼ mile each), and 2 miles (½ mile each). The medley relays are ordinarily 1 mile and 2½ miles. In the former the runners cover the following distances, respectively: 440, 220, 220 and 880 yards. In the latter the runners cover ¼ mile, ½ mile, ¾ mile and 1 mile respectively.

Hurdling is a running race in which the runner surmounts a series of 10 artificial barriers, called hurdles, that are spaced an equal distance apart on the track. For a high hurdle race the distance is 120 yards. The hurdles are 10 yards apart and are 3½ feet high for college men and adults, 3¼ feet for high school boys and 2 to 2½ feet for girls and women. The low hurdle race for college men and adults is 220 yards in length with the hurdles 20 yards apart and 2½ feet high. In high school competition, this race is at 180 yards with 8 hurdles placed 20 yards apart.

The broad jump is a horizontal jump for distance, usually made with a fast short sprint and a take-off from a wooden slab 8 inches wide and 4 feet long set firmly in the ground and flush with it. The high jump is a vertical jump made from a running start and then over a horizontal bar supported between two upright standards. The pole vault is similar in nature except that the jumper uses a pole about 12 to 16 feet long to assist him in clearing the bar.

The shot is made with a 16-pound metal sphere (12 pounds for high school) and is thrown from a circle 7 feet in diameter. The discus is a wooden disk with a metal rim not less than 8-5/8 inches in over-all circumference and not less than 4 pounds 6.4 ounces (2 kilograms) in total weight. For high school competition, a slightly smaller discus is used. It is thrown from a starting circle 8 feet 2½ inches in diameter. The javelin is a pointed spear-shaped stick not less than 8.53 feet in length and 1.765 pounds in weight.

It is hurled from behind a starting or scratch line.

Cross-country running is a special type of long-distance running. The course is usually laid out over gentle slopes, over grass or ordinary dirt roads and paths which are often cut by uneven ruts, strewn with pebbles and rocks, crossed by ditches or streams, and blocked by gates or fences. Long-distance running events, on the other hand, are held on carefully constructed running tracks and the runner is thereby running over a level, unobstructed course.

Cross-country originated as a sport in England at the time of the modern revival of track and field in the 19th Century. The mild climate of the British Isles coupled with the sporting enthusiasm of the English people has contributed greatly to the popularity of the sport in England. Cross-country was on the Olympic Games program from 1912 to 1924. In the United States it has achieved prominence in recent years, not only as a competitive sport in its own right but also as a conditioner for the regular track season.

High-Jumping Styles

The two accepted high-jumping styles most widely used are the Western roll and the straddle jump. Regardless of the style used, the basic principles of the run and the take-off are the same. The two methods differ, however, in the manner used to clear the body over the bar.

In both styles the take-off is made with the foot closest to the bar. The angle of the body at the take-off is definitely backward with the center of weight directly over the take-off foot. This point is especially important in the straddle jump, where a tendency to bend forward and sideward is often apparent. Lifting the shoulder and arm which are opposite the lead leg aids in preventing this sideward lean.

In clearing the bar, both the straddle- and the Western-style jumpers use what is called a layout, in which the body passes over the bar parallel to it. Regardless of the style, the chief concern in this phase of jumping is getting the hips over the bar. This is done in the Western style by keeping the body fairly erect after the take-off, then lowering the shoulders and head to a minimum clearance, and raising the legs as high as possible. The lead leg is thrust high and is straight as it passes the bar while the jumping leg is tucked underneath it. The body is lifted just high enough to clear the crossbar by turning the hips at the top of the jump. This turn is accomplished by dropping the arm closest to the bar, outward rotation of the toes of the take-off foot, with simultaneous straightening of the same leg and turning the eyes to the left back to the take-off point. This succeeds in lifting the hips over and around the bar. The jumper passes over the bar with his side to the bar. He then lands on the take-off or jumping foot and usually at right angles to the bar.

In the straddle style, the jumper kicks the outside foot high into the air, keeping the upper part of the body erect until this foot (foot farther from the bar) is at bar height. He then starts to turn his body and goes over the crossbar face towards it. The outside arm, head and shoulders clear the bar first. Once these are past the bar, the head and outside shoulder are turned quickly down and in toward the bar so that the eyes look back at the take-off spot. The trailing or take-off leg is relaxed at the knee and is straightened in rhythmical motion or kicked outward suddenly when the jumper is atop the bar. The turn of the hips, which is set in motion by the turning of the shoulders and head, rolls the body over the bar. The landing is on the foot opposite the take-off foot. A good landing is often difficult to make from this jump and consequently the jumper frequently must be prepared to relax and roll on the outside arm or shoulder after hitting on his landing foot.

Walking

Competitive walking—man vs. man or man vs. time—was popularized in England hundreds of years ago. The proximity of cities, the ideal roads for pedestrain traffic and the beautiful countryside were conditions believed to have provided the impetus.

The sport spread to the United States more than a century ago and caught on in professional as well as amateur circles. Although originally the competitions were conducted outdoors, the professionals in the latter part of the 19th Century moved indoors to race on circular or oval tracks.

The latter step was the forerunner of 24-hour "Go-As-You-Please" races, which in turn were succeeded by a 6-day race held in Gilmore's Gardens in New York City. The men walked rapidly as long as they could, then took time out for rests, naps or food. The bicycle replaced the heel-and-toer in 6-day contests and most competitive walking since has been in amateur circles.

Whereas the ordinary pedestrian, going along at a normal pace, will walk a mile in from 12 to 15 minutes, the heel-and-toe speedster—with his powerful stride and piston-like arm action—will negotiate the distance well under 7 minutes. The difference between them lies in the length of the competitive walker's stride, which is some 10 to 16 inches longer then the ordinary stroller's.

LAYOUT

FALL
JUMPER WILL LAND ON LEFT FOOT

TAKE OFF
FROM LEFT FOOT

Western Roll. (Taken from "Sports for Recreation," edited by E. D. Mitchell, A. S. Barnes and Company, New York.)

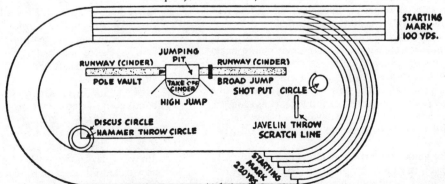

Typical Track Layout. (Taken from "Sports for Recreation," edited by E. D. Mitchell, A. S. Barnes and Company, New York.)

VOLLEYBALL

(Courtesy of Al Monaco, Executive Director, United States Volleyball Association
557 Fourth St., San Francisco, Calif., 94107)

Volleyball is an amateur sport that is adaptable to many situations. It is one of the few truly amateur sports in the world today. No coach, player, manager or official has gotten paid or received remuneration for participation in the game.

The game was invented in 1895 by William G. Morgan, a student at Springfield College and director of the Y.M.C.A. at Holyoke, Mass. It, like basketball, is one of the few "invented" sports that has extended around the world. Morgan named the game Minonette originally but as he experimented with a net and a ball the players "volleyed" the ball back and forth across the net thus he changed the name to volleyball.

Today the game, as played by skilled players, does not consist of simply volleying the ball. The modern game takes as much stamina, speed, agility, skill, conditioning and training as many other sports.

At first, the game was restricted in acceptance to the territory around Holyoke and Springfield. As graduates of Springfield and other Y.M.C.A. personnel observed or participated in the new game they took it to all parts of this country and to some thirty countries abroad.

This team game of six players has altered relatively little in rules from its inception. The rules have been kept simple. The game has remained one of six players except that in the Orient an adaptation was made of a lower net, a larger court and nine players to a team.

It has been established that volleyball today has more participants and spectators than any other team sport in the world except soccer and football. Experts who have made an analysis of this phenomenal growth attribute it to some of the factors that are mentioned in the following paragraphs.

Volleyball can be played with relatively little equipment and, therefore, is ideally suited to the sports program of the "have-not" nations or organizations. A net or rope, a ball and a relatively smooth surface is all that is needed.

Volleyball is adaptable to many levels of participation. It can be played at picnics in the back yard and as a recreation sport with the most unskilled. It is used in many schools, Y.M.C.A.'s and churches. In the top level it is one of the most exacting of sports. Leading coaches seem to think it takes six years to develop a player of top quality capable to compete in national competition.

The game is international in character. In fact, many of the children of other nations have become more adaptable at volleyball than those in our own schools. Some seventy nations are using the game on as many levels.

The armed services have always seen the potential of the sport. During war and peace time it has been one of the favorites on military bases as well on the front lines. During World War II, in the Pacific, as soon as a beachhead was established a few hundred yards deep volleyball nets began to appear on the beaches.

Attention to top level competition has only recently come into volleyball. A look into the annual United States Volleyball Guide will show that some of the best teams and players in the nation are related to the Air Force or the Army.

The exact number of teams and participants in the world is now unknown. Because it is an amateur sport drawing few paid spectators in the country, ways of arriving at accurate figures have not been found.

A reflection of the growth aspect of the game is shown in the fact that it became a part of the Olympic program in Tokyo in 1964. The World Olympic Committee added the sport at a time when it was cutting down on the events.

A synopsis of the historical steps of the game follows:

1896—Morgan's handwritten copy of volleyball rules was turned over to the Y.M.C.A. Physical Director's Conference.

1897—Official volleyball rules were included in Handbook of the Athletic League of Y.M.C.A.'s of North America.

1913—Volleyball was included in the "Far Eastern Games" in Manila, P.I., directed by Elwood S. Brown, International Y.M.C.A. Secretary.

1916—Spalding Blue Cover volleyball rule book published at request of Y.M.C.A. and N.C.A.A. was invited to join with the Y.M.C.A. in promoting the game.

1922—First national Y.M.C.A. volleyball championships held at Brooklyn Central branch, Pittsburgh, Pa., Y.M.C.A. the winner.

1928—United States Volleyball Association was formed: Dr. George J. Fisher President until 1952. (Then Dr. Harold T. Friermood 1952-55, Viggo O. Nelson 1955-59, E. Douglas Boyden 1959-62. Dr. John Brown Jr., first Secretary-Treasurer serving until 1943.)

1928—First U.S.V.B.A. Open Championships conducted in conjunction with 7th National Y.M.C.A. championships: winner Houston, Texas (Y.M.C.A.). First Y.M.C.A. "Veterans" championships conducted (players 35 years of age and over; now called Master's division.)

1933—First book on the game, Volleyball—A Man's Game, written by Robert E. Laveaga, published by A. S. Barnes and Co.

1934—National volleyball referees recognized and approved.

1942—Death of William G. Morgan, volleyball inventor occurred December 27. Publishing of annual volleyball guide shifted from A. G. Spalding & Co., to A. S. Barnes and Co.

1945—"International Volleyball Review," news sheet and magazine began publication. (Dr. David Gordon and Harry S. Wilson, editors.)

1946— National championships resumed following World War II—conducted in Chicago; Pasadena, Calif. (Y.M.C.A.) winner. (M. L. Walters director.)
Avery Brundage invited to advise U.S.V.B.A. on steps required for recognition of volleyball as an Olympic sport. Play Volleyball, two reel, 16mm sound instructional film was produced by Association Films.

1947— International Volleyball Federation was formed in Paris during Volleyball Congress; U.S.V.B.A. a charter member.

1948— U.S.A. volleyball team made a goodwill trip to Europe.

1949— "Time" game was written into rules and approved.
Women's and Collegiate divisions were added to the national U.S.V.B.A. championships held in Los Angeles.
First World's volleyball championships (Men) held in Prague, Czechoslovakia; U.S.S.R. the winner. (Succeeding championships for men and women; 1952-Moscow, 1956-Paris, 1960-Sao Paulo, Brazil, 1962-Moscow.)

1952— Armed Forced division added to U.S.V. B.A. championships in Columbus, O.

1954— U.S.V.B.A. rules were reorganized and coded by Edward P. Lauten.
Volleyball Hall of Fame was established at Helms Athletic Foundation, Los Angeles. Calif.

1955— Volleyball included in Pan American Games at Mexico City. (Also included in Chicago-1959.)

1957— Volleyball designated an official Olympic team sport by the International Olympic Committee at meeting in Sophia, Bulgaria.

1958— Official score sheet was created and a plan for certifying volleyball scorε ς (and timers) was approved.

1961— Volleyball selected for 1964 Olympic Games program in Tokyo. International Volleyball Federation adopted the USA plan of codifying the rules of the game.

1962— International Olympic Committee specified that a women's as well as a men's volleyball division be included in the Tokyo Olympic program.

1963— Pan American Games scheduled in Sao Paulo, Brazil, April 20-May 5; volleyball for men and women.

1964— Olympic Games, Tokyo, Japan, October 10-25; volleyball for men and women.

The governing body of the United States and its territories is the United States Volleyball Association and it has divided the country into seventeen regions with each region having an official representative on the governing board. Many organizations have representatives on the United States Volleyball Association and these are as follows: American Association for Health, Physical Education and Recreation, American Latvian Association, Representatives of United States Volleyball Players, American Turners, Armed Forces, United States Air Force, United States Army, United States Navy, United States Marine Corps, Boy's Clubs of America, National Amateur Athletic Union, National Collegiate Athletic Associations, National Council of Y.M.C.A.'s, National Federation of State High School Athletic Associations, National Jewish Welfare Board, National Recreation Association, Physical Education Society of Y.M.C.A.'s of North America, Society of State Directors of Health, Physical Education and Recreation.

The national competition has been divided into various sections. These include the Collegiate Section, Women's Section, Armed Services Section, Y.M.C.A. Section, Open Section and Senior Open Section (for men over thirty years of age).

The United States Volleyball Association publishes an annual guide and rule book. This may be obtained from United States Volleyball Association printer, Box 109, Berne Indiana.

Since 1946 the United States Volleyball Association has selected several persons each year who have been related to the game twenty years or more and rendered outstanding service to the sport.

The Helms Athletic Foundation has also included in their Athletic Hall of Fame some of the outstanding leaders in volleyball. Selections for leaders in volleyball to date are as follows:

LEADERS IN VOLLEYBALL
(1946-1972 Inclusive)

1961—Albert, Dorothy (Mrs. Ronald)
1951—Anderson, James F. (deceased)
1963—Arnold, David C.
1956—Aujard, M. Henry
1965—Baird, William W.
1966—Bank, Col. Theodore P.
1950—Barber, George F. (deceased)
1946—Batchelor, Harry A.
1961—Booth, Dr. Neville Augustus (deceased)
1957—Boyce, Dorothy C.
1956—Boyden, E. Douglas (deceased)
1954—Breitkrutz, Emil A.
1961—Brown, Dr. John (deceased—posthumous recognition)

1965—Brown, Dr. Robert S.
1966—Brundage, Avery
1962—Bryant, Dr. Rachael Elizabeth
1972—Buckner, Harold
1951—Burke, Prof. Josephine Mary
1949—Burroughs, Dr. W. P.
1958—Burton, Roger G.
1954—Burwinkle, Albert K.
1948—Bush, Wayne L.
1962—Butler, Edward Joseph (deceased)
1961—Caplan, Richard Israel
1959—Carroll, Irwin J.
1969—Chambliss, Gene O.
1958—Chapman, Eric D.
1964—Coleman, Prof. James Eugene
1954—Cotter, Thomas A.
1971—Covello, Leonard
1959—Creswell, George J. Jr.
1947—Cromie, Dr. William J.
1947—Cubbon, Robert C. (deceased)
1950—Danford, Dr. Howard G.
1965—Davies, Glen G.
1950—DeGroot, Lt. Col. E. B.
1969—Edmunson, William C.
1962—Emery, Curtis Roy
1967—Englert, Alice M.
1971—Fields, Sr., Arthur L.
1957—Fish, Alton W.
1946—Fisher, Dr. George J. (deceased)
1948—Foss, Dr. Martin I. (deceased)
1954—Frazer, Alexander C.
1953—Freedman, Stewart S.
1951—Friermood, Dr. Harold T.
　　　　Ghormley, Betty Ann
1960—Gibson, Leonard C.
　　　　Gigone, Otto P.
1958—Giles, H. L.
1957—Gillam, Earnest O. (deceased)
1947—Gordon, Dr. David T. (deceased)
1951—Gray, Dr. J. Henry (deceased)
1955—Grayson, Larry F.
1960—Hagen, Hoadley
1955—Hale, W. T.
1947—Hammersmith, Andrew A.
1952—Harding, Arthur Merl (deceased)
1958—Hartman, Paul C.
1956—Heisler, Edward A.
1949—Hussey, Dr. Marguerite M.
　　　　(Mrs. Laurence Loring)
1946—Idell, A. Provost (deceased)
1961—Igenbergs, Harris
1967—Ignacio, Catalino R.
1952—Jones, Blandford
1953—Kateley, Lawson M.
1967—Kealeha, Harry W.
1963—Kellam, Miss Mary Francis
1968—Keller, Val
1962—Kem, Maj. Shelton D.
1952—Kennedy, Merton H.
1958—Ketchum, John W.
1947—Knabe, Ernest W. (deceased)
1965—Koch, John P.

1964—Koerbel, Frederick G.
1964—Koorhan, Dr. Murray M.
1956—Kunde, Dr. Norman F.
1955—Lauten, Edward P. (deceased)
1947—Laveaga, Robert E. (deceased)
1955—Lehman, Menno I.
1964—Liba, Dr. Marie Rose
1970—Lindsey, Robert L.
1961—Litschauer, Ida (Mrs. Edmund C.)
1952—Lloyd, Frank S. (deceased)
1968—Lowell, John C.
1951—Lu, Dr. Hui-Ching
1966—Lucas, Bertha
1946—Magill, F. G.
1947—Martini, F. C. (deceased)
1972—Mazz, Michael
1947—McCue, Dan
1970—McChesney, Pat A.
1966—McGregor, Judge Calvin C.
1970—Meltzer, Peter S.
1965—Miller, C. L. "Bobb"
1954—Miller, Karl R.
1951—Morgan, William G. (deceased, post-humous recognition of inventor of game of volleyball)
1955—Morrison, Robert
1953—Mundt, Logan C.
1943—Neavles, Claude A.
1952—Nelson, Viggo O. (deceased)
1959—Odeneal, Prof. William T.
1964—Peck, Wilbur Herbert
1961—Peterson, Harold P.
1969—Peterson, Harold W.
1956—Prugh, Harold H.
1957—Renquist, Leslie A.
1946—Robbins, Charles C. (deceased)
1963—Robson, Frances Kay (Mrs. Harold)
1954—Rogers, Dr. James E. (deceased)
1950—Sanders, Dewitt A.
1972—Scates, Allen E.
1959—Scheer, Carl E.
1948—Schwan, Louis A.
1957—Seebolm, William F.
1969—Shanley, Mrs. Lila
1971—Shondell, Donald S.
1950—Smith, Dr. Joseph T.
1962—Smail, Roy E.
1959—Specht, Bernard J.
1965—Specht, Mrs. Bernice B.
1960—Stallcup, Dr. Leonard B.
1949—Stearns, Archie J.
1963—Stevens, Ethel M. (Mrs. Steve)
1946—Stewart, Andrew (deceased, posthumous recognition)
1963—Stubbs, Col. David C.
1950—Taraldsen, Earl N.
1950—Thomas, Royal L.
1972—Thorpe, Joanne
1969—Venable, Sam
1968—Veronee, Marvin Davis
1946—Walker, Albert V.
1948—Walsh, G. Lawrence

1951—Walters, Prof. Marshall L.
1953—Ward, Granville Pearson
1960—Welch, Dr. J. Edmund
1952—Willcox, Judge Herbert A.
1971—Williams, Raymond J.
1947—Wilson, Harry E.
1949—Winston, C. H.
1962—Zimman, Harold Owen

CHAMPIONS
United States Open
1928—Germantown (Pa.) Y.M.C.A.
1929-30—Hyde Park Y.M.C.A., Chicago
1931-32—San Antonio (Tex.) Y.M.C.A.
1933-36—Houston (Tex.) Y.M.C.A.
1937—Duncan Y.M.C.A., Chicago
1938-39—Houston Y.M.C.A.
1940—Los Angeles A.C.
1941-42—North Avenue Larabee Y.M.C.A.,
    Chicago
1943-44—No competition
1945—North Avenue Larrabee Y.M.C.A.
1946—Pasadena (Calif.) Y.M.C.A.
1947—North Avenue Larrabee Y.M.C.A.
1948—Hollywood (Calif.) Y.M.C.A.
1949—Downtown Y.M.C.A., Los Angeles
1950—Long Beach (Calif.) Y.M.C.A.
1951-53—Hollywood Y.M.C.A.
1954-55—Stockton (Calif.) Y.M.C.A.
1956-59—Hollywood Y. M.C.A.
1960—Los Angeles Westside J.C.C.
1961-63—Hollywood Y.M.C.A.
1964—Hollywood Y.M.C.A. Stars
1965—Los Angeles Westside J.C.C.
1966—Santa Monica Sand & Sea Club
1967—Fresno (Calif.) V.C.
1968—Los Angeles Westside Jewish
    Community Center
1969—Los Angeles Y.M.C.A.
1970—Chart House, San Diego
1971—Santa Monica Y.M.C.A.
1972—Chart House, San Diego

National Y.M.C.A.
1922-26—Downtown, Pittsburgh
1927—Hyde Park, Chicago
1928—Germantown, Pa.
1929-30—Hyde Park
1931-32—San Antonio, Tex.
1933-36—Houston, Tex.
1937—Duncan, Chicago
1938-40—Houston
1941—North Avenue Larrabee, Chicago
1942-45—No competition
1946—Pasadena, Calif.
1947—North Avenue Larrabee
1948—Hollywood, Calif.
1949—Downtown, Los Angeles
1950—Long Beach, Calif.
1951-53—Hollywood
1954-55—Stockton, Calif.
1956-63—Hollywood Y.M.C.A.

1964—Hollywood Y.M.C.A. Stars
1965-69—Los Angeles, Downtown, Y.M.C.A.
1970—Santa Barbara Y.M.C.A.
1971-72—Santa Monica Y.M.C.A.

National Masters' Y.M.C.A.
1928—Chattanooga, Tenn.
1929—Springfield, Ohio
1930-31—Lansing, Mich
1932-33—No competition
1934-38—Fort Wayne, Ind.
1939—Pasadena, Calif.
1940—Fort Wayne
1941—Davenport, Iowa
1942—Ann Arbor, Mich.
1943-45—No competition
1946—Houston, Tex.
1947—Greensburg, Ind.
1948—Central, Minneapolis
1949—Embarcadero, San Francisco
1950—Ann Arbor, Mich.
1951-52—Jamaica, N.Y.
1953—Omaha, Neb.
1954—Long Beach, Calif.
1955—Texas Central, Houston
1956—Embarcadero, San Francisco
1957-60—Hollywood Y.M.C.A.
1961-62—Beverly Hills Y.M.C.A.
1963—Houston, Texas Y.M.C.A.
1964—Woonsocket, R.I., Y.M.C.A.
1965—Los Angeles Westside J.C.C.
1966—Long Beach Sand & Sea Club
1967—Los Angeles Westside J.C.C.
1968—Long Beach Y.M.C.A.
1969—Kenneth Allen, Chicago
1970-72—Balboa Bay Club, Calif.

National Intercollegiate
1949-50—Southern California
1951-52—University of Mexico
1953-54—U.C.L.A.
1957-58—Florida State
1959-60—George Williams College
1961-64—Santa Monica City College (Calif.)
1965—U.C.L.A.
1966—Santa Monica City College (Calif.)
1967—U.C.L.A.
1968—San Diego State
1969—University of Calif., Santa Barbara
1970—No competition
1971-72—Santa Monica City College

Women's National
1949—Houston, Tex.
1950—Santa Monica, Calif.
1951—Houston (Tex.) Eagles
1952-53—Voit No. 1, Santa Monica, Calif.
1954—Houston (Tex.) Houstonettes
1955-60—Santa Monica (Calif.) Mariners
1961—Long Beach (Calif.) Breakers
1962-63—Long Beach (Calif.) Aherns
1964—Los Angeles Ahern Shamrocks
1965—Los Angeles Ahern Shamrocks
1966—Los Angeles Renegades

1967-70—Long Beach Shamrocks
1971—Region 13 Stars, Los Angeles
1972—E Pluribus Unum, Texas

National Armed Forces

1952—Los Alamitos (Calif.) Naval Air Station
1954—Hamilton (Calif.) Air Base
1955—Los Alamitos N.A.S.
1956—Hamilton A.F.B.
1957—Ellington A.F.B., Houston
1958—Hickam Field, Honolulu
1959—Los Alamitos N.A.S.
1960-61—Presidio (Calif.) A.D.C.
1962—Alameda (Calif.) N.A.S.
1963—Pacific Command
1965—Pacific Air Forces
1966—Omaha, Nebraska S.A.C.
1967—Strategic Air Command, March A.F.B.
1968—Oakland Army Base, Calif.
1969-72—Pacific Air Force Command

National A.A.U.

Men

1925—San Diego (Calif.) Y.M.C.A.
1926—Central Y.M.C.A., San Francisco
1927-28—Buffalo (N.Y.) A.C.
1929—Rochester (N.Y.) Central Y.M.C.A.
1930—Fort Worth (Tex.) Y.M.C.A.
1931-34—No competition
1935—San Diego Club
1936—Gillam A.C., Fort Worth, Tex.
1937-40—No competition
1941—Long Beach (Calif.) Y.M.C.A.
1942-44—No competition
1945—North Avenue Larrabee Y.M.C.A., Chicago
1946—Pasadena (Calif.) Y.M.C.A.
1949—Camden (N.J.) Y.M.C.A.
1950—North Avenue Larrabee Y.M.C.A., Chicago
1951—Los Angeles A.C.
1952—No competition
1953—Hollywood (Calif.) Y.M.C.A.
1954—No competition
1955—Wilson Avenue Y.M.C.A., Chicago
1956—Houston (Tex.) Y.M.C.A.
1957—No competition
1958—Wilson Avenue Y.M.C.A., Chicago
1963—Los Angeles J.C.C.
1964—Long Beach (Calif.) Centry Club
1965—No competition
1966—Santa Monica (Calif.) Sand & Sea Club
1967-68—Outrigger Canoe Club of Honolulu
1969—U. S. Armed Forces
1970—Chart House, San Diego
1971—Santa Monica Y.M.C.A.
1972—Santa Monica (Calif.) Sand & Sea Club

Women

1953—Voit No. 1, Santa Monica, Calif.
1954-55—No competition
1956—LaRose Houstonettes, Houston, Tex.
1957—No competition
1958—Gage Park, Chicago
1963—Los Angeles Spartans

1964—Long Beach (Calif.) Shamrocks
1965—No competition
1966—Chicago (Ill.) Rebels
1967-68—Los Angeles Renegades
1969—Rebels, Mayor Daley Y.F., Chicago
1970—Los Angeles Renegades, Green
1971—Los Angeles Renegades, Red
1972—Region 13 Seniors, Los Angeles

N.C.A.A.

1970-72—U.C.L.A.

BASIC RULES

Six players make up a team—left, center and right forwards; left, center and right backs. The official court is 60 feet by 30, for both indoor and outdoor play. The same sized court is used for men and women. The net is 32 feet long and 3 feet wide. For the men's game the net is stretched so that the top at center shall be 8 feet

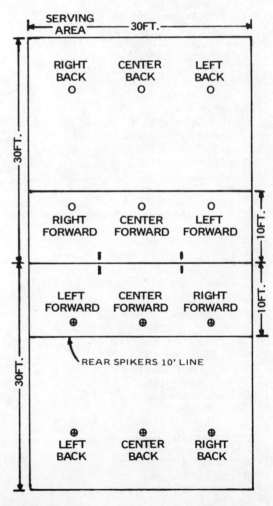

Volleyball Court and Starting Position of Players.

from the ground and the bottom 5 feet. The top height for the women's game is 7 feet 6 inches. The ball is 26 to 27 inches in circumference, weighs 9 to 10 ounces and is inflated to 7 or 8 pounds pressure.

No sticks or bats of any kind are used. Service is made, as in tennis, but the ball is hit with the hand or fist. After that it may be hit with any part of the body, including the feet. Catching or holding the ball is barred.

The object of the game is to hit the ball back and forth across the net, preventing it from touching the floor within the team's own court. The ball may be batted three times by a team before it must be sent across the net. A player may not hit the ball twice in succession, except after a simultaneous touch. The receiver usually relays the ball to a player in a front row who then "sets it up" by hitting it into the air.

Volleying continues back and forth until one of the players makes an error or commits a foul. If the receiving team fails to return the ball, the serving team makes a point and retains the serve. If the serving team fails to make a legal serve or fails to return the ball, it loses the serve and no points are scored for either team.

Fifteen points constitute a game if there is a 2-point lead. If the score reaches 14-14, one team must secure a 2-point advantage to win the game.

A game consists of 8 minutes of playing time. Time is counted only during the period the ball is actually in play. It takes about twenty minutes in all to play a regular game.

WATER POLO

One of the roughest sports in existence is water polo. However, it is not quite so rough now as it used to be. In the days of softball water polo in the United States, the game was really rugged and not for one faint of heart. As a result, games frequently developed into grudge "fights." With the shift to the hard ball, the game, which combines features of basketball, soccer and hockey, has become somewhat more refined. Its main points are fast swimming and skillful ball handling. However, it still is a rough game and its reputation undoubtedly has been detrimental to its growth. Though Europeans generally are credited with playing a more scientific game, the 1956 Olympic game between Hungary and Russia proved that they, too, can indulge in mayhem. In that game, so bitter was the rivalry that several players were well battered.

England was the first civilized country to build indoor swimming tanks and was the first to make swimming a competitive sport.

As a follow-up, one of the inhabitants, whose name is not known, devised the game of water polo, in the 1870's, and those who have played it through the years or have seen the poloists in action, insist it is as rough a game as ever was invented.

Water polo, of course, is governed by rules, and some of those prohibit what might be called unethical tactics. But, in the course of a "good, clean game," the rules are not always observed strictly, and the man who has the ball and wants to advance it toward the enemy goal often is subjected to what might be called a "drowning procedure," if he is reluctant to release such ball.

The game, in addition to calling for some speedy and alert swimming, requires that a player be able to stay under water for a prolonged period—at the muscular "suggestion" of opponents.

The world record for remaining under water without coming up for air is 6 minutes 29 4/5 seconds, made by M. Pauliquen of Paris in 1917. The water polo players are not required to approach the Pauliquen record but during a brisk game a very aggressive player who becomes "target" for enemy action often spends from 30 seconds to about a minute under water, gets a chance to take a breath or two and is forced under again.

Some of the old masters of the game insist that the technique calls for "dunking" a star player frequently and for prolonged periods at the outset of play, this strategy being employed in the effort to "weaken" him by constant loss of breath. What goes on under the surface of the water, beyond the gaze of the officials, is regarded as nobody's business. But victims insist that "it's really rough down there sometimes."

Indoor swimming tanks were unknown in the United States until the 1880's, or perhaps a bit later, and for a while they were used exclusively for swimming purposes. But Americans learned about water polo, which was being played in England under rather haphazard rules, and the Americans adopted the sport and put it to action in the indoor pools of the various athletic clubs.

Since the game had few regulations and there was no exact limit as to roughness, water polo, through its early years in this country, was as rough a game as ever was played. Players grabbed each other where they chose, became locked in wrestling grips, lost interest in the whereabouts of the ball and made it something of the survival of the fittest. In some of the under-water battles, the men let go of one another only when one no longer was able to endure without air and his victim often came to the surface in need of something like a pulmotor.

In 1897, Harold H. Reeder of New York,

sponsor of the sport in the United States, and then a member of the Knickerbocker A.C., put together the first official rules. These were aimed to take the excessive roughness out of play and let victory go to the more scientific and swifter teams, rather than to the ones that were roughest in conduct.

These rules have been altered from time to time to fit into the more modern pattern of play in different sized pools. There was, at the outset, both softball polo, better known as the "American Water Polo" game, and hardball polo, in which Europeans specialize and which is the standard game in Olympic contests. In recent years the softball game has been abandoned in this country in favor of hardball.

A. D. Adamson, for many years swimming coach at Texas Agricultural and Mechanical College advised:

"Although softball polo once was very popular in this country, its very roughness, which put a premium on unethical conduct in the water, sealed its doom, and the hardball polo, much better governed, much faster and more scientific, took its place in the affection of Americans, and now it has become the standard water polo game, approved by the A.A.U., by the Olympic Committees, and by the colleges. Inasmuch as Europe long ago adopted hardball polo, then this form of the sport becomes the standard water polo game throughout the world."

Water polo was an interclub game for quite a few years, with the New York A.C., and the Illinois A.C. having the greatest squads. The Amateur Athletic Union took over control of the sport in 1906 and has conducted the championships since that time.

The New York Athletic Club and the Illinois A.C. have done much to keep the sport alive in this country and for many years monopolized the indoor championship. The New York A.C. won every outdoor hardball title except one from 1906 through 1939. In the 1920's the Chicago A.A. also had powerful squads. In recent years the game has been flourishing on the Pacific Coast.

The sport has produced its surprises, however, and one of them came during the United States Olympic tryouts in 1952 when a team of youngsters representing El Segundo, Calif., a city of about 8,000, won the final and earned a trip to the games at Helsinki, Finland. In 1972, the Olympic trials replaced the AAU National outdoor championship.

Outstanding water poloists include the Ruddy family, Wacker, Farley, Fissler, Coyle, Jenkins, Matalene, Kelly, Ritter, Cattus and Harms of the New York A.C. and Jensen, Vosburgh, Mott, Handy, M. J. and F. O. McDermott, Hebner, McGillivray, Weissmuller, Towne, Howlett, Springer, Budelman, Munson and Rago of the Illinois A.C.

UNITED STATES CHAMPIONS

(Source: The Amateur Athletic Union's Official Swimming Handbook.)

Hardball (Outdoor)

1906-08—New York A.C.
1909—Chicago A.A.
1910-28—No competition
1929-31—New York A.C.
1932—No competition
1933-35—New York A.C.
1936—No competition
1937-39—New York A.C.
1940—No competition
1941—Los Angeles A.C.
1942-46—No competition
1947—Los Angeles A.C.
1948—No competition
1949-50—Whittier (Calif.) S.C.
1951—Illinois A.C., Chicago
1952—Los Alamitos (Calif.) N.A.S.
1953—El Segundo (Calif.) S.C.
1954—New York A.C.
1955—Illinois A.C.
1956—New York A.C.
1957—San Francisco Olympic Club
1958—Illinois A.C.
1959—San Francisco Olympic Club
1960—Toronto W.P.C.
1961—New York A.C.
1962—City of Commerce, Calif.
1963-64—Inland-Nu Pike
1965-66—Foothill A.C., Los Altos, Calif.
1967—Corona del Mar, Calif.
1968—Phillips 66, Long Beach, Calif.
1969-70—DeAnza, Cupertino, Calif.
1971—New York A.C.
1972—Not held

Hardball (Indoor)

1906—Chicago A.A.
1907-09—No competition
1910—Chicago A.A.
1911—Missouri A.C.
1912—Unfinished
1913—No competition
1914-17—Illinois A.C.
1918—Chicago A.A.
1919—Great Lakes N.T.S.
1920—Olympic Club, San Fransisco
1921—Illinois A.C.
1922—New York A.C.
1923-24—Illinois A.C.
1925—Olympic Club
1926—Chicago A.A.
1927—Illinois A.C.
1928—Chicago A.A.
1929—New York A.C.
1930—Illinois A.C.
1931—New York A.C.
1932-34—Illinois A.C.
1935-36—New York A.C.
1937-38—No competition

1939-41—Illinois A.C.
1942-46—No competition
1947—Beilfuss Natatorium, Chicago
1948-51—Illinois A.C.
1952-53—New York A.C.
1954-56—Illinios A.C.
1957—Southern California W.P.C.
1958—New York A.C.
1959-60—Illinois A.C.
1961—Lynwood S.C., Los Angeles
1962—Ann Arbor Swim Club
1963—New York A.C.
1964—Inland-Nu Pike
1965—New York A.C.
1966—City of Commerce S.C.
1967—Mayor Daley Y.F., Chicago
1968—Downey, Calif.
1969—Corona del Mar, Calif.
1970—New York A.C.
1971—DeAnza, Cupertino, Calif.
1972—Concord (Calif.) Dolphins

BASIC RULES

(From "Sports for Recreation," edited by E. D. Mitchell, A. S. Barnes and Company, New York.)

Water polo is a goal game, usually played in a swimming pool, with seven men on a team. One man is the goalie, and he must be so designated before play starts. At the start of the game and following a goal or at the start of a new period, the players of each team are in the water at the end of the pool spread out along their respective goal lines about 1 yard apart. They must be at least 1 yard away from the goalposts. Only two players are permitted to be in the area in front of the open side of the goal before play is actually started. The game begins when the referee blows his whistle and releases or throws the ball into the center of the field of play.

Official rules require no specific dimensions for the field of play, but they do place limitations upon the size of the playing area, which must not exceed 30 nor be less than 19 yards in length. The width of the playing area must not exceed 20 yards, and the water depth must not be less than 3 feet.

The goal is a cagelike structure with wood or metal goalposts 10 feet apart and with a crossbar 3 feet above the surface of the water, provided the water is at least 5 feet deep. Otherwise the crossbar is 8 feet above the bottom of the pool. A net is attached to the goal fixtures to enclose the sides and rear of the cage. It hangs into the water at least 1 foot behind the goal line. The ball is round, leather-covered, fully inflated, 28 inches in circumference and weighs between 14 and 16 ounces.

The object of the game is to throw or place the ball to the opponent's goal. In the process of advancing the ball, the individual having control of it may be attacked or prohibited from advancing it by a defensive player. The methods used to prevent advancing the ball include ducking and holding under the water the player moving the ball; seizing the ball from the player, and knocking the ball from his hands, causing it to float free. If the team is successful in advancing the ball to the the opponent's goal, a goal is

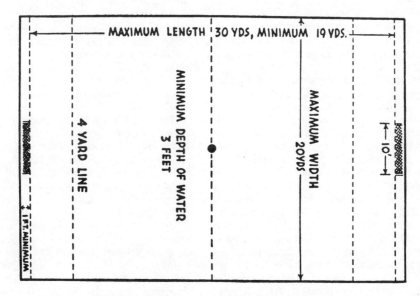

Water Polo Playing Area. (Taken from "Sports for Recreation," edited by E. D. Mitchell, A. S. Barnes and Company, New York.)

scored when the ball passes between the goal-posts and over the goal line. Following a goal, the game is restarted by the referee in the same manner as the game is originally started.

Two 10-minute halves with a 5-minute intermission constitute a game. Time out is called when a goal is scored, for fouls, or when the ball is thrown outside of the field of play. During the 5-minute half-time rest periods the teams change ends of the playing area. Two extra periods of 3-minute duration are played if a game ends in a tie. The extra periods are usually used when a definite result is required, or in a championship match. A 5-minute rest period is provided between the end of the full-time play and the start of any extra-time periods.

Each player, with the exception of the goalkeeper, is allowed to handle the ball with only one hand at a time. Handling the ball simultaneously with both hands results in a violation and allows a member of the opposing team to make a free and unobstructed pass to a team-mate or to dribble the ball himself. This pass is called a free throw. This violation does not permit a free throw at the goal, but rather a free throw or pass to a team-mate. When the referee blows his whistle at the time a player touches the ball with both hands, all players are required to remain in their respective vicinity until the player makes the free throw. Failure to stay in his position is a willful foul and the player is penalized by removal from the game until a goal is scored.

The goalkeeper is required to keep within 4 yards of the goal. He may use both hands in handling the ball. He must not, however, throw the ball more than half the length of the pool.

(For Olympic champions see section on Olympic Games.)

WATER SKIING

(Courtesy of Thomas C. Hardman, Editor & Publisher, *The Water Skier,*
7th St., & Ave. G., S. W., Winter Haven, Fla. 33880

With the improvement and mass production of high-horsepower outboard motors, water skiing has taken an important place in sports. It has been estimated that there are about 10 million devotees. The sport is considered a great deal safer than its snow counterpart.

The first water skis introduced to America in 1922 by Ralph W. Samuelson were eight feet long and nine inches wide with simple leather straps to hold them on. His first attempts were at Lake City, Minn., followed by one-man shows in Michigan and Florida. In 1925, Mr. Samuelson began jumping over five-foot high, lard-greased floats, astounding spectators with jumps up to 60 feet in length.

In 1936 as part of an Aquaplane tournament at Massapequa, New York, the first American competition for water skiers was held and won by Jack Andresen. He demonstrated fundamentals of two and one ski riding and made jumps over a 3½ foot ramp.

Among the spectators was Dan Hains, an aquaplane enthusiast, who quickly became fascinated by waterskiing. So strong was his interest that a few years later, with the help of another ex-aquaplanist, Bruce Parker, he organized the American Water Ski Association. This organization grew rapidly and since 1939 has sanctioned yearly national and regional tournaments. It was for this first tournament in 1939 that Hains conceived the idea of dividing water skiing into the three categories that exist today—Trick Riding, Slalom, and Jumping—with separate titles and prizes for each. In the meantime, Parker toured the East with a professional water ski show, which spread interest in the sport. Water ski shows, begun in the early 1940s at Florida's Cypress Gardens, have been the most influential factor in the burgeoning popularity of the sport.

Following Dan Hains, Chuck Sligh, a noted furniture manufacturer and men's champion in 1941, took over the presidency of the A.W.S.A. Hains then organized what came to be known as the World Water Ski Union for sponsoring international competition.

Significant milestones in the evolution of skiing:

Douglas Fonda's backward one ski starts in 1940 and a year later his back swan, holding the rope with his toe while going backward on one ski. The same year Jack Andresen, from New York, demonstrated turnarounds on short double-ended skis.

In 1946 Willa Worthington of Oregon won the national over-all women's title to start her career as the world's foremost woman water skier of her day. In that same competition, Bud Leach from California demonstrated the large finned, single ski slalom form. He easily won the event and set the style for the slalom technique still in vogue today.

Jumping distance progressed in small, steady increments in competition from about 30 feet in 1939 to present distances of over 160 feet. An innovation to increase distance was started by a group of snow ski jumpers at The Weirs, N.H. They cut diagonally up the ramp away from the boat as they jumped. This not only increases the skier's speed but also permits him to swing around the boat in the air, removing any slack in the rope and making his landing come almost abreast of the boat.

The first national tournament was held in 1939 at Jones Beach State Park, Long Island, N.Y. Except for the war years, tournaments have been held annually since that time.

The governing organization for the organized sport of water skiing in the United States is the American Water Ski Association with headquarters at Seventh Street and Avenue G. Southwest, Winter Haven, Florida. Complete information on the sport, in addition to details on ratings, judges, ski clubs, can be obtained through the Association.

U. S. CHAMPIONS

Men

Over-All
1958—Charles Stearns
1959—Michael Osborn
1960—Charles Stearns
1961—Michael Amsbry
1962—Charles Stearns
1963—Larry Perracho
1964—Joker Osborn
1965—Chuck Stearns
1966—Paul Merrill
1967—Chuck Stearns
1968-72—Mike Suyderhoud

Slalom
1958—Simon Khoury
1959—Joseph Cash
1960—Charles Stearns
1961—James Jackson
1962—Charles Stearns
1963—Chuck Stearns
1964—Joker Osborn
1965—Roland Hillier
1966—Tom Decker
1967—Chuck Stearns
1968—Mike Suyderhoud
1969—Bruce Martin
1970—Mike Suyderhoud
1971-72—Kris LaPoint

Tricks
1958—Charles Stearns
1959—Charles Stearns
1960—Charles Stearns
1961—James Jackson
1962—Al Tyll
1963—Al Tyll
1964—Al Tyll
1965—Al Tyll
1966—Roland Hillier
1967-69—Alan Kempton
1970-71—Ricky McCormick
1972—Robert Kempton

Jumping
1958—Joseph Cash
1959—Michael Osborn, Buster MacCalla

1960—Charles Stearns
1961—Charles Stearns
1962—Larry Penacho
1963—Jimmy Jackson
1964—Jimmy Jackson
1965—Chuck Stearns
1966—Paul Merrill
1967—Chuck Stearns
1968-71—Mike Suyderhoud
1972—Ricky McCormick

Women

Over-All
1958—Nancie Lee Rideout
1959—Nancie Lee Rideout
1960—Norine Bardill
1961—Janelle Kirtley
1962—Jenny Hodges
1963—Barbara Clack
1964—Dicksie Ann Hoyt
1965—Dicksie Ann Hoyt
1966—Barbara Clack
1967—Weslie Walker
1968-70—Liz Allan
1970-72—Liz Allan Shetter

Slalom
1958—Nancie Lee Rideout
1959—Nancie Lee Rideout
1960—Norine Bardill
1961—Jenny Hodges
1962—Jenny Hodges
1963—Janelle Kirtley
1964—Janelle Kirtley
1965—Barbara Clack
1966—Barbara Clack
1967—Stephanie Stephens
1968-70—Liz Allan
1971-72—Christy Lynn Weir

Tricks
1958—Nancie Lee Rideout
1959—Vicki Vance
1960—Norine Bardill
1961—Barbara Cooper
1962—Jenny Hodges
1963—Janelle Kirtley
1964—Dicksie Ann Hoyt
1965—Dicksie Ann Hoyt
1966—Barbara Clack
1967—Weslie Walker
1968-69—Liz Allan
1970—Christy Lynn Weir
1971-72—Liz Allan Shetter

Jumping
1958—Nancie Lee Rideout
1959—Nancie Lee Rideout
1960—Judy Rosch
1961—Janelle Kirtley
1962—Cecele Campbell
1963—Barbara Clack
1964—Barbara Clack
1965—Barbara Clack

1966—Barbara Clack
1967—Barbara Clack
1968-70—Liz Allan
1971—Liz Allan Shetter
1972—Linda Leavengood

BASIC RULES

General

Skis must be at least 3 feet long for juniors, 39 3/8 inches for others, not over 9 27/32 inches wide and may have any type of fixed foot binding and fins. Tow lines are 75 feet long of 1/4 inch braided olefin plastic for jumping and slalom.

Competitions are run in eleven divisions: Junior Boys and Girls (12 years and under), Boys and Girls (13-16 inclusive), Men (17-24 inclusive), Intermediate Men (25-34 inclusive), Women, Senior Men and Women (Men over 35 and Women over 30), and Open Divisions for Men and Women.

Trick Riding

In this event, each contestant may choose his boat, driver, tow line and speed. He is permitted two rides of 20 seconds duration each. A ride starts after the skier enters one end of a 200-yard long course in which he does all the tricks he can. Each trick has been previously assigned a point value corresponding to its difficulty. Repeated tricks do not count. A fall, or stopping before the 20 seconds, ends the run. Judges list the tricks successfully done and add a bonus for riding out the course to determine the total score.

Typical high point tricks include turning around from riding frontward to backward and continuous rotation on two and on a single ski, holding tow line with foot riding forward or backward, turnarounds on the jumping ramp and in the air, and sliding sideways on one ski. Tricks are generally done at 15 to 20 miles per hour.

Slalom

In this event, the skier rides a single ski about 5½ feet long and equipped with a postcard size metal fin to prevent skidding on sharp, fast turns. The slalom course consists of an array of soft, spherical buoys through which a single driver drives the boat for all contestants in a straight course at specified speeds.

The skier follows a sinuous course that takes him from one side of the boat's wake to the other and around the far side of the buoys. A run consists of continuous rides through the course with the skier awarded a point for each buoy passed in the correct path. After each pass the boat speed is increased to certain maximums for various age divisions and then the line is shortened until the contestant misses. There is no judging for form. A fall ends the run.

Although appearing less spectacular than trick riding or jumping, slalom skiing is probably the most strenuous and most difficult to perfect. While boat speeds of up to 36 m.p.h. are specified, the skier goes at speeds of 45 or more while negotiating the curved course.

Jumping

The standard waxed, wooden surfaced jumping ramp is 21 feet long on the slope with a height of 6 feet for men, 5½ feet for intermediate men, and 5 feet for other divisions. The boat drives parallel to one side of the ramp and the skier must cut out of the wake to reach it. Boat speeds are optional up to 35 m.p.h. for men and less for other divisions. There are varied options now.

The distance jumped is surveyed by rifle-like sighting meters from the shore. The tellers on the meter can see within 1 foot where the landing occurred by means of a white circle of bubbles that arises for a second or two from the spot where the center of the ski landed. The best of three jumps determines the score. That the strength and timing of the jumper are important is shown by the fact that with identical boat speeds on the same ramp, distances jumped in the men's division vary from 75 to 160 feet.

Jumping skis are 5½ to 6 feet long and must be extremely durable to last a season. Laminated hickory, ash, and reinforced plastics are used.

Long distance non-stop skiing records are not covered by any official ruling, but are nonetheless of interest. At least one ride of 818 miles on a single ski has been substantiated. Skiing on bare feet has become quite popular, and nonstop barefoot runs of over an hour have been recorded.

Ski racing is also gaining in popularity. Here the endurance of the skier, the speed potential of the tow boat and the skill of the boat driver in recognizing how much speed his skier can take are the ingredients. In most racing a fallen skier may be picked up, but this wastes valuable time. The ability of the team to pick smooth water is another critical factor. Races vary from 5 to 100 miles with speeds of 120 m.p.h.

WEIGHT LIFTING

For a long time when weight lifting was mentioned the mind conjured up a picture of a muscle-bound athlete. Weight lifters have had a long, hard fight trying to erase this erroneous view. Fortunately, in recent years they have been succeeding. Athletes in other sports, such as golf, football, baseball, track and field and tennis, have learned of the benefits of lifting weights and they now include lifting in their training programs to develop regular athletic activity.

Weight lifting did not originate as a sport, nor is it regarded as a form of diversion by persons who must exert the ultimate in muscular power to lift objects out of pathways or hoist some heavy burden to a certain height.

Perhaps the greatest collection of weight lifters the world has had was the group that built the Pyramids.

The Europeans were the first to make a sport of weight lifting. Many centuries ago some villager probably boasted he could lift more than another. A challenge was made, accepted, the contest was under way and the weight lifting sport was launched.

In its early years the sport was popular in Germany, France and the Scandinavian countries. It had its vogue in Egypt and still is a major sport there, as well as in other Near East countries, such as Iran. Early in this century, when standardized weight-lifting competition became popular as an amateur sport throughout the world, the Germans and Egyptians dominated international team contests, including the Olympic Games.

Before amateur regulating bodies standardized the strength tests, however, strong men performed feats for their own enjoyment, the entertainment of friends or performed professionally with carnivals and in vaudeville shows. During the latter part of the 19th Century, Louis Cyr, 300-pound Canadian, Arthur Saxon and Eugene Sandow of Germany, and George Hackenschmidt of Russia did much to popularize weight lifting.

Cyr was a man of great strength. He was approximately 5 feet 10 inches tall and his other measurements included upper arms of more than 20 inches and thighs that were 33 inches around. Massive over-all, he had a 47-inch waist. To demonstrate his strength, Cyr placed his back against the underside of a platform loaded to 4,300 pounds and raised it by exerting the force of his leg and back muscles. He is said to have raised 535 pounds from the floor with one finger, using a ring attached to the weight by a chain. Although his forte was lifting ponderous weights by the strength of his back and legs, Cyr was able to push a 300-pound barbell overhead by the strength of his arms and shoulders.

Saxon was incredibly strong and rugged, although not a huge man at 5' 10" and 210 pounds. Born Arthur Hennig, he assumed the stage name Saxon when he and his brothers Herman and Kurt formed a vaudeville trio. The greatest single strength feat performed by Arthur was his "two hands anyhow" lift of 448 pounds, the most ever lifted overhead by any man before or since without assistance. To make the lift, Saxon shouldered a 336-pound barbell, which he "bent pressed" overhead with his right arm by leaning away from the weight and pushing until his arm was locked. While crouched under the weight, he grasped a 112-pound weight with his free hand, straightened and pushed the smaller weight overhead for a total poundage of 448.

This feat earned Saxon everlasting fame.

Sandow, whose real name was Karl Frederick Mueller, did not compare with Cyr or Saxon for size, being 5ft. 8½ inches, but his feats of strength gained worldwide acclaim. Being able to lift 600 lbs. off the floor with his middle finger, pushing 620 lbs. to arms length while lying on his back, supporting a platform weighing 2,600 lbs. on his chest making a bridge of his body with arms and legs, were only a few of his accomplishments. Even if his prowess did not equal Cyr's or Saxon's, he was undoubtedly known to a greater number of people because of his excellent physique and the showmanship of promoter Florenz Ziegfeld. After gaining success as a strongman and wrestler in Europe, Sandow met Ziegfeld while touring America. Ziegfeld saw the crowd-appeal possibilities of the handsome Sandow and had him emphasize muscular display, posing his powdered-white body like a living statue against a black background. Although the 185-pound Sandow's best bent press of 271 pounds would have been child's play for Saxon, showmanship made Sandow the inspiration of the youth of the day.

Hackenschmidt was one of the first great general sports champions to include weight-lifting exercises in his conditioning routine. In fact, before embarking on the career that was to bring him recognition by many authorities as the greatest professional wrestler of all time, "Hack" won many weight-lifting championships and set a record that has never been exceeded. While supporting his arched body on head and feet in the wrestler's bridge position, Hackenschmidt reached back and pulled a 311-pound barbell to his chest. He then pushed it up to locked arms twice in succession.

Another famed professional wrestler, Henry Steinborn, was the inspiration of many of America's best lifters after World War I. He lifted 300 pounds overhead at innumerable exhibitions.

American amateur lifters first began to challenge the Europeans in the 1930's. Tony Terlazzo was the first American Olympic lifting champion, winning in 1936. One of the most amazing winning streaks in the history of sports was set up by John Davis, when he won the world light-heavyweight title in 1938 at the age of 17 and then moved up to compete as a heavyweight. He remained undefeated until 1953. At his best weight of approximately 225 pounds, Davis became the first amateur to clean and jerk 400 pounds officially. He did it in 1951.

An incredible strength phenomenon came on the weight-lifting scene in the 1950's in the person of Paul Anderson of Toccoa, Ga. He exceeded "world's best on record" marks in his first year of serious weight lifting. A husky youngster who turned down attractive college football scholarship offers to concentrate on being a strongman, Anderson soon packed 300 surprisingly solid pounds on his massive 5-foot-10-inch frame. As an indication of his unusual size, Anderson's wrists measured 9 inches at the age of 21. At the same time had 34-inch thighs and a 23-inch neck. In 1955, with three years of training, he became the first man to score a total of 1,100 pounds on the three standard lifts. He became the first to press 400 pounds. His best official total before he turned professional strongman and wrestler was 1,175 pounds.

Anderson established himself as world champion by competing on standard lifts, but his amazing power is perhaps shown better by some impromptu stunts unmatched by strong men of past or present. His outstanding feat was to take a 900-pound barbell across his shoulders and do three deep knee bends in succession. He was reported to have performed this feat once with 1,000 pounds.

Official modern weight lifting is based on three lifts: the press, the snatch and the clean and jerk.

A press is executed by pulling the barbell to the chest and then pushing it to locked arms overhead while maintaining an erect position and exerting only the strength of the arms and shoulders. In the snatch, the barbell must be pulled from the floor to fully-locked arms overhead without any pause. In this lift, the athlete is permitted to lunge—"split"—under the barbell by springing his legs front and back or to squat under it as it goes up. The clean and jerk is performed by pulling the weight to the chest in one movement, splitting or squatting under it when it cannot be pulled all the way up, and then driving it overhead by a combined leg and arm thrust, again splitting under the weight as it goes up. The winner of a weight-lifting contest is the man who lifts the highest total on the three tests.

Other feats of strength are still practiced informally—such as Anderson's deep knee bends—especially those aid lifters in developing pulling or pushing strength. Among them are the dead lift (from the floor to an erect position with the barbell hanging across the thighs) and bench presses (pushing a barbell to locked arms over the chest while lying on a sturdy bench). Champion heavyweights like Anderson, Davis and Doug Hepburn of Canada were able to dead lift 700 pounds and exercise with 400 pounds or more in the press on bench.

Numerous other exercises are practiced with barbells (and dumbbells) and this if often confused with what is actually a standardized competitive sport. Many of the persons practicing weight *training* exercises are doing so for physical conditioning, to increase strength and thereby improve athletic performance, to improve their physical appearance, or for rehabilitation. In the last-named case, weight training is often prescribed by physicians, in which instance it is usually called "progressive resistance exercise."

UNITED STATES SENIOR CHAMPIONS

112-Pound Class
(Included in 1932; discontinued after 1939)

	Lbs.
1932—Lucian LaPlante	470
1933—Lucian LaPlante	485½
1934—Robert K. Knodle	693
1935—David Rothman	638
1936—John Fritshe	456½
1937—A. Hutchison	515
1938—A. Firpo Lemma	561
1939—A. Firpo Lemma	530

114.5-Pound Class
	Lbs.
1970—Eugene Casasola	605
1971—Dave Moyer	584¼
1972—John Yamauchi	594¾

118-Pound Class
(Included in 1929; discontinued after 1939)

	Lbs.
1929—Robert Knodle	682
1930—Robert Knodle	715
1931—Robert Knodle	715
1932—Joseph Fiorito	485
1933—Joseph Fiorito	496½
1934—Ralph Vieria	731½
1935—Joseph Fiorito	718
1936—Joseph Fiorito	533½
1937—Ed Heffernan	535
1938—B. Leardi	520
1939—B. Leardi	525

123 1/4-Pound Class
(Division at 128 pounds in 1929-1930; 126 pounds, 1930 through 1939; 123 pounds in 1958, 1967; 123 1/2 pounds in 1963 through 1966, 1968; 123.5 pounds in 1969 through 1972.)

	Lbs.
1929—A. Gaukler	665½
1930—J. Arthur Levan	819½
1931—J. Arthur Levan	852½
1932—J. Arthur Levan	540
1933—J. Arthur Levan	568
1934—J. Arthur Levan	830½
1935—J. Arthur Levan	841½
1936—J. Arthur Levan	588½
1937—Mike Mungioli	685
1938—Mike Mungioli	600
1939—Elwood P. Cauffman	560
1940—Joseph Fiorito	550
1941—Wesley Cochrane	616½
1942—Joseph De Pietro	565
1943—Joseph De Pietro	585
1944—Emerick Ishikawa	630
1945—Emerick Ishikawa	635
1946—Joseph De Pietro	646
1947—Joseph De Pietro	615
1948—Joseph De Pietro	675
1949—Joseph De Pietro	620
1950—Joseph De Pietro	635
1951—Joseph De Pietro	640
1952—Richard Tom	628½

1953—Jack Hughes .615
1954—Charles Vinci 690
1955—Charles Vinci 690
1956—Charles Vinci 690
1957—Angel Famiglietti 640
1958—Charles Vinci 715
1959—Charles Vinci 700
1960—Charles Vinci 700
1961—Charles Vinci 740
1962—Dick Krell 670
1963—Shiro Ichinoseka 700
1964—Gary Hanson 700
1965—Gary Hanson 665
1966—Lennell Shepherd 630
1967—Gary Hanson 690
1968—Fernando Baez 740
1969—Fernando Baez 745
1970—Salvador Domingues 650
1971—Salvador Domingues 667
1972—Salvador Domingues 672

132 1/4-Pound Class

(Division at 136 pounds in 1929-1930, changed to 132 and then to 132¼ pounds; 132 pounds in 1958, 1967; 126 pounds in 1969; 132.5 pounds in 1970, 1972)

Lbs.
1929—Richard Bachtell 852½
1930—Richard Bachtell 847
1931—Richard Bachtell 852½
1932—Anthony Terlazzo 570
1933—Michael Fontana 579
1934—Richard Bachtell 896½
1935—Richard Bachtell 935
1936—Anthony Terlazzo 693
1937—Richard Bachtell 635
1938—John Terry 640
1939—John Terry 660
1940—John Terry 665
1941—John Terry 665
1942—Joseph Mills 635
1943—Richard Bachtell 630
1944—Fred Curry 660
1945—Joseph De Pietro 615
1946—Emerick Ishikawa 641
1947—Emerick Ishikawa 670
1948—William Lowrance 675
1949—Richard Tomita 665
1950—Richard Greenawalt 640
1951—George Yoshioka 650
1952—Richard Tomita 661
1953—Mitz O'Shima 680
1954—Yaz Kuzuhara 685
1955—Isaac Berger 705
1956—Isaac Berger 720
1957—Isaac Berger 760
1958—Isaac Berger 800
1959—Isaac Berger 740
1960—Isaac Berger 810
1961—Isaac Berger 790
1962—Walter Imahara 720
1963—Yoshiobu Miyake 800

1964—Isaac Berger 795
1965—Walter Imahara 790
1966—Walter Imahara 765
1967—Walter Imahara 775
1968—Walter Imahara 795
1969—Gary Hanson 770
1970—Fernando Baez 750
1971—No competition
1972—Philip Sanderson 743

148 3/4-Pound Class

(148 pounds in 1958; 148.8 pounds in 1969 through 1972)

Lbs.
1928—Arnie Sundberg 570
1929—Max Rohrer 891
1930—Max Rohrer 935
1931—George Horn 935
1932—Arnie Sundberg 632
1933—Anthony Terlazzo 667
1934—Robert M. Mitchell 990
1935—Anthony Terlazzo 1,006½
1936—John Terpak 737
1937—Anthony Terlazzo 780
1938—Anthony Terlazzo 765
1939—Anthony Terlazzo 805
1940—Anthony Terlazzo 770
1941—Anthony Terlazzo 800
1942—Anthony Terlazzo 760
1943—Anthony Terlazzo 800
1944—Anthony Terlazzo 800
1945—Anthony Terlazzo 760
1946—Peter George 716
1947—Joseph Pitman 705
1948—Joseph Pitman 730
1949—Joseph Pitman 735
1950—Joseph Pitman 765
1951—Joseph Pitman 775
1952—Tommy T. Kono 798
1953—Joseph Pitman 745
1954—Joseph Pitman 755
1955—Joseph Pitman 765
1956—Joseph Pitman 785
1957—Joseph Pitman 770
1958—Kenzie Onuma 795
1959—Paul Goldberg 780
1960—Tony Garcy 780
1961—Paul Goldberg 745
1962—Tony Garcy 800
1963—Tony Garcy 805
1964—James Massai Bu 775
1965—Homer Brannum 820
1966—Larry Mintz 805
1967—Homer Brannum 835
1968—Steve Mansour 820
1969—Steve Mansour 860
1970—James Benjamin 860
1971—James Benjamin 859¾
1972—Dan Cantore 931

165-Pound Class

(165.3 pounds in 1969, 1972)

	Lbs.
1928—B. McDowell	570
1929—A. Faas	902
1930—Arnie Sundberg	968
1931—Arnie Sundberg	940½
1932—Stanley Kratkowski	680
1933—Walter Zagurski	694½
1934—Stanley Kratkowski	1,039½
1935—Stanley Kratkowski	1,095
1936—Stanley Kratkowski	748
1937—John Terpak	805
1938—John Terpak	785
1939—John Terpak	800
1940—*John Terpak	800
1941—*John Terpak	815
1942—John Terpak	800
1943—James Manning	750
1944—John Terpak	800
1945—John Terpak	775
1946—Frank Spellman	831
1947—Stanley Stanczyk	825
1948—Frank Spellman	855
1949—Peter George	830
1950—Peter George	835
1951—Peter George	860
1952—Peter George	860
1953—Tommy T. Kono	915
1954—Bert Elliott	765
1955—Dick Giller	800
1956—*C. Warner	835
1957—Peter George	885
1958—Tommy Kono	890
1959—Tommy Kono	905
1960—Tommy Kono	865
1961—Frank Spellman	800
1962—Joseph Puleo	875
1963—*Hitoshi Ouchi	895
1964—*Joe Puleo	905
1965—*Tony Garcy	880
1966—*Tony Garcy	940
1967—Russell Knipp	955
1968—Russell Knipp	955
1969—Fred Lowe	950
1970—*Fred Lowe	960
1971—*Russell Knipp	1,008½
1972—Fred Lowe	991¾

* 165¼ pounds.

181 1/4-Pound Class

	Lbs.
1928—Al Bevan	605
1929—Albert Manger	957
1930—William L. Good	1,017½
1931—William L. Good	1,056
1932—William L. Good	715
1933—William L. Good	733
1934—Gino Quilici	1,012
1935—S. Weisch	1,023½
1936—John H. Miller	761
1937—William L. Good	800
1938—Stanley Kratkowski	805
1939—John Davis	815
1940—*John Davis	855

	Lbs.
1941—*Frank Kay	850
1942—Frank Kay	860
1943—John Terpak	800
1944—Bill Bush	755
1945—Harold Vinkin	770
1946—Frank Kay	836
1947—John Terpak	840
1948—Stanley Stanczyk	880
1949—Stanley Stanczyk	915
1950—Stanley Stanczyk	910
1951—Stanley Stanczyk	885
1952—Clyde Emrich	864
1953—Stan Stanczyk	915
1954—Tommy T. Kono	930
1955—Tommy T. Kono	940
1956—*Jim George	875
1957—Tommy T. Kono	970
1958—†Jim George	880
1959—Jim George	900
1960—Jim George	915
1961—Tommy Kono	980
1962—Tommy Kono	945
1963—*Tommy Kono	970
1964—*Gary Cleveland	955
1965—*Gary Cleveland	985
1966—*Joe Puleo	935
1967—†Joe Puleo	955
1968—*Joe Puleo	1,025
1969—*Mike Karchut	1,035
1970—*Mike Karchut	1,055
1971—*Mike Karchut	1,008¾
1972—*Mike Karchut	1,041¼

† 181 pounds.
* 181¾ pounds.

198-Pound Class

	Lbs.
1951—Norbert Schemansky	915
1952—Norbert Schemansky	886
1953—Norbert Schemansky	900
1954—Dave Sheppard	975
1955—Dave Sheppard	965
1956—Clyde Emrich	955
1957—Clyde Emrich	910
1958—Fred Schutz	925
1959—Clyde Emrich	945
1960—John Pulskamp	990
1961—Bill March	950
1962—Bill March	975
1963—*Bill March	1,000
1964—*Bill March	1,010
1965—*Bill March	1,020
1966—*B. Bartholomew	985
1967—Phil Grippaldi	1,035
1968—*Philip Grippaldi	1,055
1969—*Frank Capsouras	1,080
1970—*Philip Grippaldi	1,090
1971—*Rick Holbrook	1,097
1972—*Rick Holbrook	1,129¼

* 198¼ pounds.

Heavyweight Class

(242.5 pounds)

	Lbs.
1928—Tom Tyler	760
1929—William Rohrer	1,045
1930—Albert Manger	1,001
1931—William Rohrer	784½
1932—Albert Manger	704
1933—John Mallo	760½
1934—William L. Good	1,210
1935—William L. Good	1,205
1936—John Grimek	786½
1937—David Mayor	835
1938—Steve Stanko	850
1939—Steve Stanko	895
1940—Steve Stanko	950½
1941—John Davis	1,009¾
1942—John Davis	905
1943—John Davis	940
1944—Frank Schofro	850
1945—H.G. Curtis	855
1946—John Davis	918
1947—John Davis	900
1948—John Davis	1,025
1949—Norbert Schemansky	885
1950—John Davis	1,010
1951—John Davis	1,062
1952—John Davis	1,002
1953—John Davis	990
1954—Norbert Schemansky	1,050
1955—Paul Anderson	1,145
1956—Paul Anderson	1,175
1957—Norbert Schemansky	990
1958—David Ashman	1,000
1959—Dave Ashman	1,040
1960—James Bradford	1,085
1961—James Bradford	1,070
1962—Norbert Schemansky	1,140
1963—Sid Henry	1,125
1964—Norbert Schemansky	1,160
1965—Norbert Schemansky	1,155
1966—Gary Gubner	1,170
1967—Bob Bednarski	1,175
1968—Joseph Murray	1,035
1969—Bob Bednarski	1,210
1970—Bob Bednarski	1,185
1971—Gary Deal	1,157¼
1972—Frank Capsouras	1,157

In 1929, 30, 34, 35 there were two extra lifts which increased the total weight lifted.

Super Heavyweight

(over 242.5 pounds)

	Lbs.
1968—Bob Bednarski	1,280
1969—Ken Patera	1,195
1970—Ken Patera	1,285
1971—Ken Patera	1,306¼
1972—Ken Patera	1,339

WORLD RECORDS

Event	Holder	Lbs.	Year

Flyweight—114-Pound Class

Press	A. Gnatov, Russia	265½	1972
Snatch	G. Aung, Burma	231¼	1972
Clean-Jerk	A. Gnatov, Russia	291	1972
Total	S. Holczreiter, Hungary	754¾	1970

Bantam—123-Pound Class

Press	R. Belenkov, Russia	282	1972
Snatch	K. Miki, Japan	250	1968
Clean-Jerk	M. Nassiri, Iran	330½	1968
Total	I. Foldi, Hungary	822	1972

Featherweight—132-Pound Class

Press	I. Foldi, Hungary	303½	1972
Snatch	Y. Miyake, Japan	276½	1969
Clean-Jerk	D. Shanidze, Russia	343¾	1972
Total	D. Shanidze, Russia N. Nourikan, Bulgaria (Tie)	887	1972

Lightweight—148-Pound Class

Press	M. Kuchev, Bulgaria	347	1972
Snatch	W. Baszanowski, Poland	303	1971
Clean-Jerk	M. Kirzhinov, Russia	391¼	1972
Total	M. Kirzhinov, Russia	1,013¾	1972

Middleweight—165-Pound Class

Press	A. Kolodkov, Russia	367	1972
Snatch	M. Trabulsi, Lebanon	321¾	1972
Clean-Jerk	V. Kurentsov, Russia	413¼	1968
Total	Y. Bikov, Bulgaria	1,069	1972

Light-Heavyweight—181-Pound Class

Press	G. Ivanchenko, Russia	393½	1972
Snatch	V. Shariy, Russia	348½	1972
Clean-Jerk	B. Pavlov, Russia	436½	1972
Total	V. Shariy, Russia	1,162½	1972

Middle-Heavyweight—198-Pound Class

Press	D. Rigert, Rusia	436½	1972
Snatch	D. Rigert, Russia	369¼	1972
Clean-Jerk	V. Kolotov, Russia	464	1972
Total	D. Rigert, Russia	1,239¾	1972

Heavyweight—220-Pound Class

Press	Y. Kozin, Russia	470½	1972
Snatch	Y. Talts, Russia	385¾	1972
Clean-Jerk	Y. Talts, Russia	490½	1972
Total	V. Kakubovsky, Russia	1,300¼	1972

Super-Heavyweight—Over 220-Pound Class

Press	V. Alexeev, Russia	521¼	1972
Snatch	V. Alexeev, Russia	396¾	1971
Clean-Jerk	V. Alexeev, Russia	523½	1972
Total	V. Alexeev, Russia	1,421¾	1972

STANDARD TECHNIQUE

In modern weight lifting the three important lifts are:

Two-Hand (or Military) Press—Lift weight from floor, bring to rest on chest, neck or shoulder, then lift to limit of the arms. In this event contestants must toe line and not move away from it. After bringing weight to rest against body, he must hold military position; bending is not allowed.

Clean and Jerk—This can be with either hand, or both hands. Lift weight from floor, rest against chest, lift as high as possible upon call from referee.

Snatch—Can be with either hand, or both. Contestant picks up weight, and in one continuous movement lifts it as high as possible.

There are seven recognized lifts. They are:

1. Two-hand (or military) press.
2. Two-hand snatch.
3. Two-hand clean and jerk.

4. One-hand snatch with right arm.
5. One-hand snatch with left arm.
6. Clean and jerk with right arm.
7. Clean and jerk with left arm.

The athlete must hold the weight for the referee's count of one, two. There are two judges and a referee. If the judges fail to agree, the referee's decision is final under Amateur Athletic Union rules.

WRESTLING

Wrestling can be divided into two categories, professional and amateur. The professional category once had wide appeal but it gradually degenerated until today it is classified as an exhibition, to be viewed much as a farce or comedy. The amateur phase, however, has continued to maintain its prestige and is flourishing in colleges, athletic clubs and high schools.

Wrestling is an instinctive sport, one that seems to come naturally. It brings into play virtually all the muscles of the body. It calls for alertness and skill.

The art of wrestling goes back to antiquity, and was glorious in the years of its prime. It was an old sport when the world was almost new; it was an honored sport. Its devotees in ancient Greece and Rome, and for centuries later, were respected, admired and glorified.

Prehistoric man, realizing that he often might meet wild beasts in close encounter and that the knowledge of effective grips was important, engaged in contests with members of his family, or neighbors, so that each could learn how to grapple effectively with animals.

Wrestling was a sport as far back as civilization can be traced. The oldest actual evidence was uncovered in 1938 by Dr. S. A. Speiser and his party, representing the University of Pennsylvania and the American Schools of Oriental Research, while making excavations in Mesopotamia. They found in the ruins of a temple at Kyafaje, near Bagdad, two slabs. One was of stone, on which in bold relief, were the figures of two pugilists squaring off. The other was a cast bronze figurine showing two wrestlers, each with a hold on the other's hips.

These slabs, created by the Sumerians, an ancient tribe that long since has disappeared, are rated as at least 5,000 years of age.

Wrestling had an important place on all the festival programs of Greece and Rome. It is the one sport that never ceased to exist. All nations, ancient and modern, have had their wrestlers. It was, along with running and jumping, the most natural form of sport because it required no paraphernalia and provided a zestful method of building muscles and developing health.

The Greeks, who regarded a discus thrower as the best type of athlete, placed the wrestler second. Their earliest rules called for wrestling much along the modern catch-as-catch-can, but permitted breaking of fingers, gouging and throttling. Eventually there was demand for bristling action. This brought about the development of the Pancratium, a sort of rough-and-tumble style, no holds barred, grapple, bite, gouge, clinch, strangle, punch, kick—do anything you pleased.

After the Romans had conquered Greece and taken over the supervision of the Olympic Games, they ruled out some of the not-too-refined processes in the Pancratium. They blended their own method of grappling with the earlier form of Grecian wrestling to produce the Greco-Roman style, which endures to this day in Europe—with a few alternations. In Greco-Roman, holds are not permitted below the waist.

Most famous among the Grecian wrestlers of fact and legend was Milo of Croton, six times champion at Olympic and Isthmian Games (early Greek festival contests). Homer's account of the match between Ulysses and Ajax (Iliad 23) is the greatest wrestling story ever written.

Theseus (about 900 B.C.), son of Ageus, King of Athens, is credited with arranging the first standard wrestling rules for the Greeks.

Greek wrestlers oiled their bodies prior to a match and then sprinkled on some "lucky dust," usually brought from one's own neighborhood. At one period it was a rule that a flute must be played all during a match, and this brought about relay flute playing.

The ancient Jews, who rarely figured in sports, were wrestling enthusiasts. Sculptors trace the sport among the Jews to a time very close to the Sumerian Era. Down through the ages thereafter and well along into the Christian Era the Jews produced some mighty wrestlers, and the champion at wrestling was ranked as the most remarkable athlete of the Jewish race.

Wrestling was a sport reserved for royalty and their guests in European countries at the beginning of the Christian Era. Fete days, established by kings, usually found wrestling matches topping the program. Many monarchs, priding themselves first in the possession of a great army, found their next greatest delight in the fact that one of their subjects was a champion at grappling.

International tournaments were frequent through the Middle Ages—and later. France and England had many such contests. For a number of centuries the rulers of those countries always conceded that the nation was superior athletically which, at the moment, housed the winner of a French-English title bout.

During his reign, King Francis I of France (1515–1549) became disgusted with the way his wrestlers were faring against those from England. The easy triumphs of the English gave their ruler, King Henry VIII (1509–1547), a chance to gloat in good natured fashion. King Francis' temper became uncontainable, he jumped to his feet in the royal box, where he was seated with the English King, grabbed King Henry and precipitated a royal wrestling match in public. It didn't go very far because bystanders intervened.

England had almost as many different styles of wrestling as it had towns—one a bit more grueling than the other. The most famous were the Lancashire, Cornish and Devonshire. Annually on St. James' Day in Old London there was an elimination wrestling match, the winner receiving a ram. Those who showed well, although beaten, received a game cock. The style of wrestling at such shows was decided mutually by the contestants and the sponsor.

The Irish had their style of wrestling—slightly more brutal than the English. The Scotch followed the Lancashire style—the roughest in England. The French permitted holds only from the waist up, with tripping prohibited. The Germans, meanwhile, did all their wrestling on the ground.

Since a time preceding the Christian Era, wrestling has been the national sport of Japan, with the gigantic Sumo wrestlers featured at fetes for the Emperor or at any public ceremony of importance. The sons of Sumo wrestlers married the daughters of Sumo wrestlers for more than 20 centuries, the idea being that the mating would result in sons of tremendous bulk and power. It has. The average male Sumo offspring at maturity is 5 feet 8 inches to 5 feet 9 inches in height—exceptional for a native of Nippon—and the weight averages between 300 and 400 pounds. In more modern times the Japanese have been the leading specialists in jujitsu wrestling.

The Indians on the North American continent found sport in wrestling long before Christopher Columbus set sail in 1492. The early Spanish settlers had their wrestling; so did the English, the Dutch and the French in Canada. Every outdoor social gathering found some wrestlers at grips.

The earliest method of organized wrestling in the United States, so far as important contests were concerned, was with Greco-Roman rules prevailing. Ernest Roeber was a wrestler of that type; so were William A. Muldoon and many others of their time, in the late 19th Century. The average neighborhood wrestler not caring much about standard rules, actually introduced the present day catch-as-catch-can style of wrestling, which barred only the strangle-hold.

When Abraham Lincoln was in his prime, there was much wrestling. The performers were permitted to grip wherever the opportunity offered. The method caught public fancy, and Americans, thereafter, abandoned the Greco-Roman method for impromptu bouts and called upon the Americanized catch-as-catch-can style.

Tom Jenkins was the first American professional to advocate such a method, while Roeber, Muldoon and others were concentrating on Greco-Roman. Jenkins' style gained great favor, and the Cleveland (Ohio) rolling-mill worker became the idol of the American fans.

Jenkins was the champion for many years, despite the fact that he was one-eyed. His way of wrestling, gripping anywhere except with the strangle-hold, became more and more in favor. Jenkins side-tracked public interest from the Greco-Roman specialists and became a hero by his long succession of victories. He was, in his generation, the champion of all the wrestlers at the new style, which he helped so much to popularize, and interest in the Greco-Roman contests dwindled, while Americans went into ecstasy over the means Jenkins used to subdue opponents.

While Jenkins, as a professional, was helping to make fame for the new style, which was distinctly American, others of lesser skill became carnival grapplers. They learned the tricks Jenkins employed and then agreed to take on all-comers, offering $25 up to $250, and sometimes $500, to any man whose shoulders they could not pin within a specified time limit.

Jenkins had been at the top for many years when he agreed to take on a newcomer in the person of Frank Gotch, who was a smaller and lighter man. Gotch was regarded as just another victim of the mighty man of Cleveland. But Gotch dethroned Jenkins without difficulty in 1905 and from then, until his retirement in 1913, gained ranking as the greatest catch-as-catch-can wrestler of all time.

Gotch was a man of mighty strength, despite his size. He was master of all the permissible holds; he was daring and brainy. The combination made him superb. During his reign, a great many new-comers arrived in the wrestling ranks, and many Greco-Roman specialists, realizing their own form of sport was in eclipse, switched to catch-as-catch-can, hoping to beat Gotch. Each failed, yet Gotch, once during his remarkable career, lost his title, through accident, but quickly regained it in a return match.

In 1906, Gotch met Freddy Beall. In a wild

scuffle, Gotch was pitched against a ring post and rendered unconscious. While in that condition, Beall pinned him and became the champion. Gotch demanded a return bout, Beall granted it and Gotch toyed with Beall before pinning him in the fall that again made him king.

The great days of wrestling actually began with Gotch, who was recognized as champion and who was a tremendous attraction. He won 154 of 160 matches and would have pinned most modern-day wrestlers within minutes. They wrestled seriously in those days.

Today the professional phase has become strictly show business and exhibitionism to the point where each match must be billed as an exhibition and is confined to the heavyweight class. The public seems to enjoy it, however, and the average wrestler today is good for at least $15,000 a year in earnings. The top ones are in the $100,000 class. They wrestle as many as six times a week, and when the comparison is made to Gotch's 160 matches in a period of eight years, it seems a bit ridiculous.

The debate always will continue as to the identity of the greatest wrestler of all time. Some point to Gotch, but there are many who call George Hackenschmidt, the "Russian Lion," the greatest of all. Hackenschmidt was perhaps the greatest scientific wrestler and was a perfectionist. Tremendously powerful, he scorned rough tactics. He stood 5 feet 10 inches, weighed between 208 and 225 pounds and had a reach of 75 inches. He preceded Gotch in his reign and was virtually through when he wrestled Gotch in Chicago in 1908 and again in 1911. He lost both matches.

After Gotch, wrestling started a trend toward show-boating. The promoters were interested in money more than the art of wrestling and, except for periodic outbreaks toward the legitimate, it never returned to the respectable days of Hackenschmidt and Gotch.

There are great names, however, that will never be forgotten, and even some modern matmen, under the earlier conditions, might have proved capable contenders. The names of Gama the Great, from India, and Youseff Mahmout, the Original Terrible Turk, are sacred to lovers of real wrestling.

In the 1930's, when wrestling was more or less legitimate, there were greats like Strangler Lewis, Stanislaus Zbyszko, Dick Shikat, Jim Londos, Jim Browning, Ray Steele, Rudy Dusek and a host of others. The word "great" in most of these cases is used for the period only.

Currently there are countless claimants for the world heavyweight wrestling championship. Every box-office trick is used to lure the people to the arenas. Television is credited with making millions of professional wrestling fans. The viewers—paying and non-paying—have their heroes and, despite the fact that one can almost always name the winner in advance, they are fanatic in their adulation of their idols. Among their favorites have been Antonino Rocca, the barefooted South American; Primo Carnera, Gene Stanley, Don Eagle, Verne Gagne, Lou Thesz and Frank Sexton. Non-televised shows at Madison Square Garden have been drawing capacity crowds.

Adding to the confusion surrounding professional wrestling in recent years has been the invasion of women in the field. However, contests between women are not permitted in many states. Midget wrestling is also featured and there are tag-team events and free-for-alls.

The men wrestle under colorful names like "Swedish Angel," "Perennial Masked Marvel," "Zebra Kid," "The Great Togo," "Gypsy Joe," and "The Mighty Atlas," to mention a few. "Lords," "barons" and "counts" are common.

Gus Sonnenberg of Dartmouth football fame used the "flying tackle" successfully in the sport in the 1930's and it became almost standard for a professional wrestler to have this as a part of his attacking repertoire. The present-day wrestlers have embellished this with such tactics as biting, gouging, kicking, punching and an item called "dropkicking," which has no connection with football's dropkick, except that the foot is used.

"Dropkicking" in wrestling, as demonstrated by Rocca and the other experts, is an offensive weapon. Instead of hitting an opponent on the chin or side of the head with the hand as in boxing, the foot is used. The blow usually does not help in pinning an opponent, but it is a spectacular maneuver.

Amateur Wrestling

Various tournaments conducted by the Amateur Athletic Union, the colleges, high schools, grammar schools and clubs have kept the sport of amateur wrestling alive in this country. Catch-as-catch-can (free-style) wrestling was the only form used among the amateurs until 1953, when the A.A.U. conducted its first National Greco-Roman championships at Toledo, Ohio. The honor of being America's first Greco-Roman champion went to Bill Kerslake of Cleveland, who won the heavyweight crown after capturing the United States catch-as-catch-can title in the same division the previous night.

An outstanding amateur wrestler in recent years was Henry Wittenberg, a New York policeman. Wittenberg won about 400 matches in succession from 1938 to 1952 before he was beaten by Dale Thomas of East Lansing, Mich., in the 191-pound class at the 1952 Olympic trials at Ames, Iowa.

UNITED STATES AMATEUR CHAMPIONS
(Source: Official A.A.U. Wrestling Guide.)

Catch-as-Catch-Can (Free-Style)

In the early years the weight classes ranged from 105 pounds upward, but until 1913 did not include the 175-pound class. The heavyweight class was instituted in 1904. In 1969, the 105.5-pound class was reinstated and a new class of 220-pounds was added. The weight classes have changed at various times, usually during Olympic years, when they are made to correspond with the metric weights used in the international games. There was no competition in the years not listed.

105 Pounds

1889-90—J. B. Reilly
1891—F. Bertsch
1893—C. Monnypenny
1894—R. Bonnett
1896—H. Cotter
1897—G. W. Owen
1899-1900—G. W. Nelson
1901-02—W. Karl
1903-04—R. Curry
1905—J. Heins
1906—W. Lott
1907—G. Taylor
1908—R. Schwartz
1909-10—G. Taylor
1911—H. Donaldson
1912—G. Taylor
1969—Dale Kestel (105.5 pounds)
1970—Bob Orta (105.5 pounds)
1971—Wayne Holmes (105.5 pounds)
1972—Dale Kestel (105.5 pounds)

108 Pounds

1913—G. Taylor
1914-15—R. Goudie
1916—G. Taylor
1917—C. Benson
1918-19—J. Meagher
1920-21—C. Benson

112 Pounds

1923-24—R. Rowsey
1925—H. DeMarsh
1926—L. Lupton
1927—L. Pfeffer
1928—G. Rosenborg
1929—G. Shoemaker
1930—H. Phillips
1934—R. Johnson
1935—R. Myers
1936—C. E. Ritchie
1937-38—Charles Peterson
1939—H. Farrell
1940—G. Leeman
1941—H. Farrell

115 Pounds

1889-90—F. Mueller
1891—E. Beck
1893—J. Holt
1894—F. Bertsch
1895—M. Kervin
1896-97—R. Bonnett
1899—R. Bonnett

1900—J. Renzlard
1901—G. Owens
1902-04—G. Mehnert
1905-07—G. Bauer
1908—G. Mehnert
1909—G. Bauer
1910—J. Hein
1911—N. Chapman
1912—W. Strohback
1913—J. Hein
1914—J. Vorees
1915—F. Glahe
1916—K. Borsits
1917—L. Servais
1918—V. Vosen
1919—M. Gans
1920—S. Pammow
1921—J. Troyer
1931—J. Sapora
1933—W. Frederick
1942—W. Curtis
1943—F. Preston
1944—C. Parks
1945—Grady Peninger
1946—Arlie Curry
1947—Grady Peninger
1948—Malcolm McDonald
1949—Arnold Plaza
1950—John Harrison
1951—George Creason
1952—Sidney Nodland (114.5 pounds)
1953—Richard Delgado (114.5 pounds)
1953-54—Richard Delgado (114.5 pounds)
1955—Katsutosh Yokoyama, Japan
        114.5 pounds)
1956—Richard Delgado (114.5 pounds)
1957—Takashi Hirata (114.5 pounds)
1958—Tsukuhisa Torikura (114.5 pounds)
1959—Dick Wilson
1960—Gil Sanchez
1961—Dick Wilson
1962—Horyoka Harada
1963—Takashi Hirata
1964—Hiroaki Aoki
1965-66—Ray Sanchez
1967—Noriyuki Suzuki, Japan (114.5 pounds)
1968—Art Chavez (114.5 pounds)
1969—Yasou Katsumura (114.5 pounds)
1970-72—John Morley (114.5 pounds)

118 Pounds

1922—V. Vosen
1923—L. Servais
1925—G. Campbe.
1926—C. Mitchell
1927—L. Lake
1929—T. McCrary
1930—B. Pearce
1932—L. Conti
1934—E. Thom.
1935—R. Perry
1936—J. McDaniels

1937—M. Croft
1938—J. Speicher
1939—T. Imoto
1940—C. Fredericks
1941—J. McDaniels

121 Pounds

1942—R. Barber
1943—P. McDaniel
1944—M. MacDonald
1945—Bill Klein
1946—Dick Hauser
1947—Charles Ridenour
1949—John Harrison
1950—Arnold Plaza
1951—John Lee

123 Pounds

1924—B. Hines
1928—R. Hewill
1932—J. Sapora
1936—R. Flood
1937—W. Duffy
1938—J. McDaniels
1939—E. Collins
1940—Dale Hanson
1941—H. Byrd

125 Pounds

1893—W. Troelsch
1894-95—W. Reilly
1896—E. Harris
1897—A. Meanwell
1899—M. Wiley
1900—A. Kurtzman
1901-04—I. Niflot
1905-06—G. Mehnert
1907-08—Louis Dole
1909—L. Ruggiero
1910—M. Himmelhoch
1911-12—G. Bauer
1913—V. Vosen
1914-15—S. Vorees
1916-17—C. Liljehult
1918—J. Felios
1919—M. Gans
1920—A. Gallas
1921—R. Reed
1922-23—A. Callas
1925—B. Patterson
1926—H. Boyvey
1927—A. Holding
1929—G. Campbell
1930—J. Reed
1931—R. Pearce
1933—M. Andes
1934—J. Gott
1935—R. Flood
1936-41—No competition
1942—S. Marks
1943—C. Ridenour
1944—F. Barkovich
1948—Robert Kitt (125.5 pounds)

1952—Jack Blubaugh (125.5 pounds)
1953—Richard Hauser
1954—Jack Blubaugh (125.5 pounds)
1955—Etsuma Iwano (125.5 pounds)
1956—Bill Carter (125.5 pcunds)
1957-59—Terry McCann
1960—Carmen Molino
1961—Usaki Imaizumi
1962—Dave Auble
1963—Norio Tominaga
1964—Gray Simons
1965—Dick Sanders
1966—Richard Sofman
1967—Rich Sanders
1968—Richard Sofman (125.5 pounds)
1969—Tashio Nakano, Japan (125.5 pounds)
1970—Richard Sanders (125.5 pounds)
1971—Michi Tanaka (125.5 pounds)
1972—John Miller (125.5 pounds)

126 Pounds

1947—Louis Kachiroubas

128 Pounds

1945—Richard Dickerson
1946—Ed Collins
1949—Russell Bush
1950—Richard Hauser
1951—Gene Lybbert

135 Pounds

1889—M. Luttbeg
1891—A. Ullman
1893—C. Clark
1894—A. Lippman
1895—J. McGrew
1896—A. Ullman
1897—H. Wolff
1899-1901—M. Wiley
1902—F. Cook
1903-04—B. Bradshaw
1905—I. Niflot
1906—A. Rubin
1907—B. Bradshaw
1908—G. Dole
1909—S. Fleischer
1910—S. Kennedy
1911—P. Franzke
1912—E. Helikman
1913—A. Anderson
1914—H. Jenkins
1915—O. Runchey
1916—W. Hallas
1917—P. Metropoulos
1918—S. Vorres
1919—B. Johnson
1920—G. Metropoulos
1921—J. Hummerich
1922—R. Reed
1923—J. Voores
1924—R. Reed
1925—L. Brigham
1926-28—A. Morrison

1929–J. Erickson
1930–Z. Letowt
1931–L. Morford
1932–J. Fickel
1933-34–E. Stout
1935–R. Rasor
1936–F. Parkey
1937–G. Hanks
1938–F. Millard
1939–B. Renfo
1940–R. Cheney
1941-42–D. Lee
1943–M. Jennings
1944–V. Cronhardt
1945–Clifford McFarland
1946-47–Lowell Lange
1948–Lee Thomson
1949-50–Lowell Lange
1951–Bill Armstrong (136 pounds)
1952–Josiah Henson (136.5 pounds)
1953–Jim Sinadinos (136 pounds)
1954–Shozo Sasahara (136.5 pounds)
1955–Motoichi Motohashi (136.5 pounds)
1956–Alan Rice (136.5 pounds)
1957–Masashi Kokubo (136.5 pounds)
1958–Naboru Ikeda (136.5 pounds)
1959–S. Nichiwaki
1960–Linn Long
1961–Lee Allen
1962–Osamu Watnabe
1963–Haruo Abe
1964–Mitsuo Hara
1965–Chikara Murane
1966–Mac Motokawa
1967–Bob Buzzard (138.5 pounds)
1968–Masamitsu Ichiguichi (138.5 pounds)
1969–Dan Gabel (136.5 pounds)
1970–Mike Young (136.5 pounds)
1971–Rick Sanders (136.5 pounds)
1972–Tetsu Ikeno (136.5 pounds)

145 Pounds

1897–W. Riggs
1899-1901–M. Wiley
1902–N. Nelson
1903–M. Yokel
1904–O. Roehm
1905–R. Tisney
1906–C. Clapper
1907–Richard Jaeckel
1908–M. Wiley
1909-10–C. Johnson
1911–W. Milchewski
1912–G. Petterson
1913–C. Johnson
1914–H. Jenkins
1915–D. Burns
1916–L. Nelson
1917–H. Jenkins
1918–A. Forst
1919–G. Smith
1920–W. Tikka

1921–R. Vis
1942–D. Arndt
1943–B. Maxwell
1944–L. Cowell
1945–Gale Miklos
1946-47–James Miller
1948–Newton Copple
1949-50–Keith Young
1951–Bob Hoke

147 Pounds

1922-24–R. Vis
1925–K. Truckemuller
1926–R. Myers
1927–R. Prunty
1928–C. Berryman
1929–A. Tomlinson
1930–O. Kapp
1931–A. Tomlinson
1932–B. Bishop
1933–G. Sappington
1934–F. Stout
1935–L. Tomlinson
1936–L. Fegg
1937–E. Bruno
1938–B. Hanson
1939–D. Taylor
1940–E. Viskocil
1941–C. Soukas
1952–Newton Copple (147.5 pounds)
1953–Newton Copple
1954–Tommy Evans (147.5 pounds)
1955–Joe Scandura (147.5 pounds)
1956-57–Tommy Evans (147.5 pounds)
1958-59–Newton Copple (147.5 pounds)
1960–Frank Betucci
1961–Gerald Grenier
1962-68–No competition
1969–Fumiaki Nakamura (149.5 pounds)
1970–Dan Gable (149.5 pounds)
1971–Gene Davis (149.5 pounds)
1972–Mike Young (149.5 pounds)

155 Pounds

1931–O. Kapp
1933–G. Belshaw
1934–E. Kielhorn
1935–F. Lewis
1942–V. Logan
1943–R. Roberts
1944–E. Tomick
1945–Douglas Lee
1946–Robert Roemer
1947–Orville Long
1949-50–Bill Nelson
1951–Keith Young
1963-64–Greg Ruth (154 pounds)
1965–Jim Burke (154 pounds)
1966–Werner Holzer (154 pounds)
1967-68–Bobby Douglas (154 pounds)

158 Pounds

1888–Dr. Shell

1889–M. Lau
1890–G. Haskin
1891–Z. Von Bockman
1893–W. Osgood
1894–F. Ellis
1895–C. Reinicke
1896–A. Ullman
1897–D. Chesterman
1899–A. Mellinger
1900–M. Wiley
1901-02–J. Schmicker
1903–W. Beckman
1904–C. Erikson
1905–W. Schaefer
1906–J. McAfee
1907–F. Marganes
1908–C. Anderson
1909-10–F. Narganes
1911–C. Gesek
1912-13–J. Smith
1914-15–B. Reubin
1916–W. Americus
1917–C. Johnson
1918–Stephensen
1919–G. Tragos
1920–E. Leino
1921–C. Johnson
1932–J. Van Bebber
1936–G. Belshaw
1937-39–W. Jacobs
1940–E. Blake
1941–H. Faucett

160 Pounds

1922–E. Wolf
1923–E. Leino
1924–P. Martter
1925-26–R. Hammonds
1927–F. Collins
1928–L. Appleton
1929–B. Sherman
1930–J. Van Bebber
1948–Leland Merrill (160.5 pounds)
1952–James LaRock (160.5 pounds)
1953–James LaRock
1954–Jay Holt (160.5 pounds)
1955–Dr. Melvin Northrup (160.5 pounds)
1956–Bill Fischer (160.5 pounds)
1957–Doug Blubaugh (160.5 pounds)
1958–Larry Ten Pas (160.5 pounds)
1959–Fritz Fivian (160.5 poudns)
1960–Douglas Blubaugh
1961–Steven Friedman
1962–Kazuo Abe

165 Pounds

1931–J. Van Bebber
1933–B. Hess
1934-35–O. England
1942–J. Scarpello
1943–M. A. Northrup
1944–E. Blake
1945–M. A. Northrup

1946-47–Doug Lee
1949-51–William Smith
1952-68–No competition
1969–Lee Detrick (163 pounds)
1970–Wayne Wells (163 pounds)
1971–Jerry Bell (163 pounds)
1972–Wayne Wells (163 pounds)

174 Pounds

1952–Shuford Swift
1953-54–Dan Hodge
1955–Wenzel Hubel
1956–Dan Hodge
1957–Meb Turner
1958–Wenzel Hubel
1959–Jim Ferguson
1960-62–Jim Ferguson
1963–Dean Lahr (171 pounds)
1964–Len Kauffman (171 pounds)
1965–Russ Camilleri (171 pounds)
1966–Steve Combs (171 pounds)
1967–Pat Kelly (171.5 pounds)
1968–Mike Gallego (171.5 pounds)

175 Pounds

1913–J. Varga
1914-15–E. Caddock
1916–N. Pendleton
1917–D. Verg
1918-20–K. Kunert
1921–F. Myer
1922-23–P. Berlenbach
1924–W. Wright
1925–O. Stuteville
1926–F. Bryan
1927–G Rule
1928–R. Hammonds
1929–K. Krough
1930–G. Stafford
1931–C. Caldwell
1932–J. Schutte
1933–A. Sweet
1934–G. Martin
1935–L. Ricks
1936–R. Voliva
1937-38–A. Crawford
1940-41–H. Wittenberg
1942–G. Inman
1943–D. Thomas
1944–M. A. Northrup
1945–James Dernehl
1946–Frank Bissell
1947-48–Dale Thomas
1949–Shuford Swift
1950–Charles Swift
1951–Louis Holland

180 Pounds

1969–Len Kaufman (180.5 pounds)
1970–Jay Robinson
1971–Russ Camilleri
1972–Jay Robinson (180.5 pounds)

191 Pounds

1922–F. Meyers
1924–Charles Strack
1928–E. Edwards
1932–L. Putrin
1936–L. Ricks
1937–W. Norton
1938–J. Harrell
1939–V. Cavagnaro
1940–Ed Valorz
1941–G. Frei
1942–S. Santo
1943-44–Henry Wittenberg
1945–Robert Wilson
1947-48–Henry Wittenberg
1949–Vern Gagne
1950–David Whinfrey
1951–Harry Lanzi
1952–Henry Wittenberg
1953-54–Dale Thomas
1955–Tim Woodin
1956–Peter Blair
1957–Tim Woodin
1958-60–Frank Rosenmayr
1961–Don Brand
1962–Shunichi Kawano
1963-64–Russ Camilleri
1965–Wayne Baughman
1966–Dean Lahr
1967–Bill Harlow (191.5 pounds)
1968–Russ Camilleri (191.5 pounds)

198 Pounds

1969–Buck Deadrich
1970-72–Wayne Baughman

213 Pounds

1963-64–Dan Brand
1965–Jerry Conine
1966–Ken Johnson
1967-68–Hank Schenk (213.5 pounds)

220 Pounds

1969–Jess Lewis
1970–Larry Kristoff
1971–Dominic Carollo, Hank Schenk (tie)
1972–Buck Deadrich

Heavyweight

1904-05–B. Hansen
1906–M. McAfee
1907-08–J. Gundersen
1909–E. Payne
1910–F. Motis
1911–H. Grim
1912–A. Kaino
1913–J. Gundersen
1914–A. Minkley
1915–E. Caddock
1916–S. Schwartz
1917–D. Very
1918–K. Kunert
1919–S. Czarnecke
1920–N. Pendleton

1921-22–F. Meyers
1923–K. Leppanen
1924–R. Flanders
1925–R. Krouse
1926–Charles Strack
1927–R. Flanders
1928-29–E. George
1930–Earl McCready
1931–R. Jones
1932–L. Hammack
1933–G. Ellison
1934-35–R. Teague
1936–R. Dunn
1937–Richard Vaughn
1938–C. Gustafson
1939–M. Sims
1940–W. Nead
1941–L. Maschi
1942–L. Levy
1943–R. Metzgar
1944-45–Richard Vaughn
1946–Mike DeBiase
1947-48–Ray Gunkel
1949–Robert Maldegan
1950–Fred Stoeker
1951–Carl Abell
1952–Lieut. Richard Clark
1953-60–Bill Kerslake
1961–Dale Lewis
1962–Jiro Seki
1963–Larry Kristoff
1964–Jim Raschke
1965-68–Larry Kristoff
1969–Dale Stearns
1970-72–Greg Wolciechowski

Team

1935-36–Oklahoma A. and M.
1937–Southwestern State T.C.
1938–Oklahoma A. and M.
1939–New York A.C.
1940-41–West Side Y.M.C.A. (New York)
1942–Crescent Club (Tulsa)
1943–West Side Y.M.C.A.
1944–Baltimore Y.M.C.A.
1945–Oklahoma City Y.M.C.A.
1946–New York A.C.
1947–Cornell College (Iowa)
1948–U.S. Naval Academy
1949-51–Iowa State Teachers
1952–Armed Forces
1953–Multnomah A.C., Portland, Ore.
1954–Tulsa Y.M.C.A.
1955–New York A.C.
1956–Sooner A.C.
1957-58–Tulsa Y.M.C.A.
1959–Cowboy A.C., Oklahoma State
1960–New York A.C.
1961-62–San Francisco Olympic Club
1963–Olympic Club of San Francisco
1964–New York A.C.
1965–Multnomah A.C., Portland, Ore.

1966-67—Mayor Daley Y.F., Chicago
1968—San Francisco Olympic Club
1969-72—New York A.C.

UNITED STATES
GRECO-ROMAN CHAMPIONS

105.5 Pounds

1969—Bill Davids
1970—Stanley Opp
1971—Alfredo Olvera, Mexico
1972—Karoly Kanscar

114.5 Pounds

1953—Jerry Davis (114 pounds)
1954—Richard Delgado
1955—Katsutoshi Yokoyama
1956—Ray Osborne
1957—Richard Wilson
1958—Dick Wilson
1959—Richard Wilson
1960—Gilbert Sanchez
1961—Richard Wilson
1962—Skaurama Koji
1963-64—Hiroaki Aoki
1965—Rich Henjyoji
1966—Masashi Ryoba
1967—Dave Hazewinkel
1968—Art Chavez
1969—Yasou Katsumura
1970—Dave Kestel
1971—Enrique Jiminez, Mexico
1972—Mike Thomson

125.5 Pounds

1953—Vern Whitney (125 pounds)
1954—Lee Allen
1955—Shuhei Imada
1956—Jack Blubaugh
1957—Lee Allen
1958—Jerry Wager
1959—Masaaki Hatta
1960—Lynn Griffith
1961—Joseph Gomes
1962—Masamitsu Ichiguicki
1963—Masaki Kiosumi
1964—Takao Ikeuchi
1965—Clem Crow
1966—Jim Hazewinkel
1967—Tomino Michio
1968—Ikeui Yamamoto, Japan
1969—David Hazewinkel
1970—David Hazewinkel, Yasuo Ishii,
      Japan (tie)
1971-72—David Hazewinkel

136.5 Pounds

1953—Jeryl Wilson (136 pounds)
1954—Safi Taha
1955—Todashi Numajiri
1956—Alan Rice
1957—Tom Hall
1958—Naburo Ikeda
1959—Eisuke Kitmara
1960-61—Lee Allen

1962—Nobuyuki Motokawa
1963—Ron Finley (138.5 pounds)
1964—Sam Boone (138.5 pounds)
1965—Chick Murano (138.5 pounds)
1966—Mac Motokawa (138.5 pounds)
1967—Charles Coffee (138.5 pounds)
1968—James Hazewinkel (138.5 pounds)
1969—James Hazewinkel
1970—Masao Hattori
1971—James Hazewinkel
1972—Gary Alexander

147.5 Pounds

1953—Walt Romanowski (147 pounds)
1954—Norman Gill
1955—Newton Copple
1956—Gerald Maurey
1957—Frank Szecsi
1958—Bud Belz
1959—Ben Northrup
1960—Lawrence Wright
1961—Fred Boger
1962—Toshiyoki Sawauchi
1963—Yasuo Horikawa (154 pounds)
1964—Ben Northrup (154 pounds)
1965-66—Robert Douglas (154 pounds)
1967—Ben Northrup (154 pounds)
1968—Fred Lett (154 pounds)
1969—Kenshiro Matsunami (149.5 pounds)
1970-72—Philip Frey (149.5 pounds)

160.5 Pounds

1953—Jack Grubbs (160 pounds)
1954—Jay Holt
1955—Henrik Hansen
1956-57—Khalil Taha
1958—Frank Fejes
1959—Fred Boger
1960—Joseph Vastag
1961—Julius Beno
1962-68—No competition
1969—James Tanniehill (163 pounds)
1970-72—Larry Lyden (163 pounds)

174 Pounds

1953—Ahmet Senol
1954—James Connor
1955—Jim Peckham
1956—Dan Hodge
1957—Barry Billington
1958—Zsolt Csiba
1959—Julius Beno
1960-61—Russell Camilleri
1962—Rudy Williams
1963—Bruce Glenn (171.5 pounds)
1964—Rudy Williams (171.5 pounds)
1965-66—Russ Camilleri (171.5 pounds)
1967—Rudy Williams (171.5 pounds)
1968—Larry Lyden (171.5 pounds)

180.5 Pounds

1969—Rudy Williams
1970—Rudy Williams (180 pounds)
1971—Khosrow Vaziri

1972–Jay Robinson

191 Pounds

1953-54–Dale Thomas
1955–Bob Steckle
1956–Ken Maidlow
1957–Robert Steckle, Canada
1958–Frank Rosenmayr
1959-60–Frank Rosenmayr
1961–Zoltan Pentek
1962–Ronald Lewis
1963–Wayne Baughman
1964–Russ Camilleri
1965–Wayne Baughman
1966–Rudy Williams
1967-68–Wayne Baughman (191.5 pounds)

198 Pounds

1969-72–Wayne Baughman

213.5 Pounds

1963-64–Dan Brand
1965–Art Makinster
1966–Jerry Conine
1967–Gary Stensland
1968–Jess Lewis

220 Pounds

1969–Robert Roop
1970–James Duchen
1971-72–Hank Schenk

Heavyweight

1953-59–Bill Kerslake
1960–Harlow Wilson
1961–Pat Lovell
1962–Harlow Wilson
1963–Garry Stensland
1964–Jim Raschke
1965–Garry Stensland
1966-67–Larry Kristoff
1968–Bob Johnson
1970–Chris Taylor
1971–Jeff Smith
1972–Greg Wojciechowski

NATIONAL COLLEGIATE CHAMPIONS
No competition in years not mentioned.

114.5 Pounds

1948–Arnold Plaza, Purdue

115 Pounds

1928–Harold DeMarsh, Oklahoma A. and M.
1929-30–Joe Sapora, Illinois
1952-54–Hugh Perry, Pittsburgh
1955-57–Terrance McCann, Iowa
1958–Richard Delgado, Oklahoma
1959–Andy Fitch, Yale
1960-62–Elliott Simons, Lock Haven
1963–Arthur Maugham, Moorhead State
1964–Terry Finn, Southern Illinois
1965–Tadaaki Hatta, Oklahoma State
1966-67–Rich Sanders, Portland State
1968–Ken Melchior, Lock Haven
1969–John Miller, Oregon

118 Pounds

1931–John Engel, Lehigh
1933-35–Rex Peery, Oklahoma A. and M.
1937-38–Joe McDaniel, Oklahoma A. and M.
1939-69–No competition
1970-72–Greg Johnson, Michigan State

121 Pounds

1939–Joe McDaniel, Oklahoma A. and M
1940–Robert Antonacci, Indiana
1941-42–Merle Jennings, Michigan State
1946–Cecil Mott, Iowa Teachers
1947–Richard Hauser, Cornell (Iowa)
1949–Arnold Plaza, Purdue
1950–Anthony Gizoni, Waynesburg

123 Pounds

1932–Joseph Puerta, Illinois
1936–Ted Anderson, Central (Okla.)
1951–Anthony Gizoni, Waynesburg
1952–Bill Borders, Oklahoma
1953–Dick Mueller, Minnesota
1954–Richard Govig, Iowa
1955-57–Edwin Peery, Pittsburgh
1958–Paul Powell, Pittsburgh
1959-60–Dave Auble, Cornell
1961–Duwane Miller, Oklahoma
1962–Masaaki Hatta, Oklahoma State
1963–Mike Nissen, Nebraska
1964–Fred Powell, Lock Haven
1965-67–Mike Caruso, Lehigh
1968–Dwayne Keller, Oklahoma State
1969–Wayne Boyd, Temple

125 Pounds

1928–Ralph Lupton, Northwestern
1929-30–Lawrence Mantooth, Oklahoma

125.5 Pounds

1948–George Lewis, Waynesburg

126 Pounds

1931–Robert Pearce, Oklahoma A. and M.
1933-35–Ross Flood, Oklahoma A. and M.
1937–Dale Brand, Cornell (Iowa)
1938–Allen Sapora, Illinois
1970–Dwayne Keller, Oklahoma State
1971–Yoshiro Fujita, Oklahoma State
1972–Pat Milkovich, Michigan State

128 Pounds

1939–Dale Hanson, Minnesota
1940–Harold Byrd, Oklahoma
1941-42–Burl Jennings, Michigan State
1946–Gerald Leeman, Iowa Teachers
1947–Russell Bush, Iowa Teachers
1949–Charles Hetrick, Oklahoma A. and M.
1950–Joe Patacsil, Purdue

130 Pounds

1951–Walter Romanowski, Cornell (Iowa)
1952–Gene Lybbert, Iowa Teachers
1953-54–Norvard Nalan, Michigan
1955-57–Myron Roderick, Oklahoma A. and M.
1958–Les Anderson, Iowa State

1959-60—Stanley Abel, Oklahoma
1961—Larry Lauchle, Pittsburgh
1962-63—Mickey Martin, Oklahoma
1964-66—Yojiro Uetake, Oklahoma State
1967—Harold McGuire, Oklahoma
1968—Dan Gable, Iowa State
1969—David McGuire, Oklahoma

134 Pounds

1932—Edwin Belshaw, Indiana
1936—Wayne Martin, Oklahoma
1937-69—No competition
1970—Darrell Keller, Oklahoma State
1971—Roger Weigel, Oregon State
1972—Gary Barton, Clarion State

135 Pounds

1928—Arthur Holding, Iowa State
1929—George Minot, Illinois
1930—Hugh Linn, Iowa State
1931—Richard Cole, Iowa State
1933—Patrick Devine, Indiana
1934—Wayne Martin, Oklahoma
1935—Vernon Sisney, Oklahoma
1937—Ray Cheney, Iowa Teachers
1938—David Mathews, Oklahoma

136 Pounds

1939—Archie Deutschman, Illinois
1940-41—Al Whitehurst, Oklahoma A. and M.
1942—William Maxwell, Michigan State
1946—David Arndt, Oklahoma A. and M.
1947—Lowell Lange, Cornell (Iowa)
1949-50—Lowell Lange, Cornell (Iowa)

136.5 Pounds

1948—Richard Dickenson, Michigan State

137 Pounds

1951-52—George Layman, Oklahoma A. and M.
1953—Len DeAugustino, Lock Haven
1954—Myron Roderick, Oklahoma A. and M.
1955—Lawrence Fornicola, Penn State
1956-57—Jim Sinadinos, Michigan State
1958—Paul Aubrey, Oklahoma
1959—Larry Hayes, Iowa State
1960—Les Anderson, Iowa State
1961—Norman Young, Michigan State
1962—Bill Carter, Oklahoma
1963—William Dotson, State Col. of Iowa
1964—Michael Sager, Oklahoma
1965—Bill Stuart, Lehigh
1966—Gene Davis, Oklahoma State
1967-68—Dale Anderson, Michigan State
1969—Dan Gable, Iowa State

142 Pounds

1970—Larry Owings, Washington
1971—Darrell Keller, Oklahoma State
1972—Tom Milkovich, Michigan State

145 Pounds

1928—Melvin Clodfelter, Oklahoma A. and M.
1929—George Bancroft, Oklahoma A. and M.
1930—Hardie Lewis, Oklahoma
1931—William Doyle, Kansas State

1932—Hardie Lewis, Oklahoma
1933-34—Allan Kelley, Oklahoma A. and M.
1935—Wayne Martin, Oklahoma
1936—Harley Strong, Oklahoma A. and M.
1937-38—Stanley Henson, Oklahoma A. and M.
1939—Harold Nichols, Michigan
1940—Harold Masem, Lehigh
1941-42—David Arndt, Oklahoma A. and M.
1946-47—William Koll, Iowa Teachers
1949-50—Keith Young, Iowa Teachers
1966—Bill Blacksmith, Lock Haven
1967—Don Henderson, Air Force
1968—Dale Bahr, Iowa State
1969—Mike Grant, Oklahoma

147 Pounds

1951—Keith Young, Iowa Teachers
1952—Tommy Evans, Oklahoma
1953—Frank Bettucci, Cornell (N.Y.)
1954—Tommy Evans, Oklahoma
1955-57—Edward Eichelberger, Lehigh
1958-59—Ron Gray, Iowa State
1960-61—Larry Hayes, Iowa State
1962—Mike Natvig, Army
1963—Mike Natvig, Army
1964—Jerry Stanley, Oklahoma
1965—Veryl Long, Iowa State

147.5 Pounds

1948—William Koll, Iowa Teachers

150 Pounds

1970—Mike Grant, Oklahoma
1971—Stan Dziedzic, Slippery Rock State
1972—Wade Schalles, Clarion State

152 Pounds

1966—Dick Cook, Michigan State
1967—Jim Kamman, Michigan
1968—Wayne Wells, Oklahoma
1969—Gobel Kline, Maryland

155 Pounds

1929—Jack Van Bebber, Oklahoma A. and M.
1930—Otto Kelley, Michigan
1931—Leroy McGuirk, Oklahoma A. and M.
1933—Merrill Frevert, Iowa State
1934—Ben Bishop, Lehigh
1935—Frank Lewis, Oklahoma A. and M.
1937—Bill Keas, Oklahoma
1938—Dale Scrivens, Oklahoma A. and M.
1939—Stanley Henson, Oklahoma A. and M.
1940—Vernon Logan, Oklahoma A. and M.
1941—Earl Van Bebber, Oklahoma A. and M.
1942—Vernon Logan, Oklahoma A. and M.
1946—Bill Courtwright, Michigan
1947—Gail Mikles, Michigan State
1949-50—William Nelson, Iowa Teachers

157 Pounds

1951—Phil Smith, Oklahoma
1952—Bill Weick, Iowa Teachers
1953—James Harmon, Iowa Teachers
1954—Bob Hoke, Michigan State
1955—Bill Weick, Iowa Teachers

1956-57—Larry TenPas, Illinois
1958-59—Dick Beattie, Oklahoma State
1960—Arthur Kraft, Northwestern
1961—Phillip Kinyon, Oklahoma State
1962—Jack Flasche, Colorado State
1963—Kirk Pendleton, Lehigh
1964—Gordon Hossman, Iowa State
1965—Bob Kopnisky, Maryland

158 Pounds

1928—Leslie Beers, Iowa
1932—Carl Dougovito, Michigan
1936—Walter Jacobs, Michigan State
1937-69—No competition
1970—Dave Martin, Iowa State
1971-72—Carl Adams, Iowa State

160.5 Pounds

1948—George St. Clair, Oklahoma A. and M.
1966—Greg Ruth, Oklahoma
1967—Vic Marcucci, Iowa State
1968—Reg Wicks, Iowa State (160 pounds)
1969—Cleo McGlory, Oklahoma (160 pounds)

165 Pounds

1929—Conrad Caldwell, Oklahoma A. and M.
1930-31—Jack Van Bebber, Oklahoma A. and M.
1933—George Martin, Iowa State
1934—Marion Foreman, Oklahoma
1935—Howard Johnston, Penn State
1937—Harvey Base, Oklahoma A. and M.
1938—John Ginay, Illinois
1939—Henry Matthes, Lehigh
1940—Crawford Grenard, Colorado A. and M.
1941-42—Virgil Smith, Oklahoma A. and M.
1946—David Shapiro, Illinois
1947—William Nelson, Iowa Teachers
1949-50—William Smith, Iowa Teachers

167 Pounds

1951—Gene Gibbons, Michigan State
1952—Joe Lemyre, Penn State
1953—Don Dickason, Cornell (N.Y.)
1954—Joe Solomon, Pittsburgh
1955—Fred Davis, Oklahoma A. and M.
1956-57—Edward DeWitt, Pittsburgh
1958—Duane Murty, Oklahoma State
1959—Ed Hamer, Lehigh
1960—Richard Ballinger, Wyoming
1961—Don Conway, Oregon State
1962—Ronald Clinton, Oklahoma State
1963—James Harrison, Pittsburgh
1964—Donald Millard, Southern Illinois
1965—Greg Ruth, Oklahoma
1966—Dave Reinbolt, Ohio State
1967—George Radman, Michigan State
1968—Mike Gallego, Fresno State
1969-70—Jason Smith, Iowa State
1971-72—Andrew Matter, Penn State

174 Pounds

1932—Robert Hess, Iowa State
1936—Harry Broadbent, Oklahoma
1948—Glen Brand, Iowa State

175 Pounds

1928—George Rule, Oklahoma A. and M.
1929—Glenn Stafford, Cornell (N.Y.)
1930-31—Conrad Caldwell, Oklahoma A. and M.
1933—Robert Hess, Iowa State
1934—Richard Voliva, Indiana
1935—Ralph Silverstein, Illinois
1937—John Whitaker, Minnesota
1938—John Harkness, Harvard
1939—Chris Traicoff, Indiana
1940—Don Nichols, Michigan
1941-42—Richard DiBattista, Pennsylvania
1946—George Dorsch, Oklahoma A. and M.
1947—Joe Scarpello, Iowa
1949—James Gregson, Oklahoma A. and M.
1950—Joe Scarpello, Iowa

177 Pounds

1951—Grover Rains, Oklahoma A. and M.
1952—Bentley Lyon, California
1953-54—Ned Blass, Oklahoma A. and M.
1955-57—Dan Hodge, Oklahoma
1958—Gary Kurdelmeier, Iowa
1959—Bill Wright, Minnesota
1960—Roy Conrad, Northern Illinois
1961-62—Robert Johnson, Oklahoma State
1963-64—Dean Lahr, Colorado
1965-66—Tom Peckham, Iowa State
1967—Fred Fozzard, Oklahoma State
1968—Bob Justice, Colorado
1969-70—Chuck Jean, Iowa State
1971—Geoff Baum, Oklahoma State
1972—Bill Murdock, Washington

190 Pounds

1970—Geoff Baum, Oklahoma State
1971-72—Ben Peterson, Iowa State

191 Pounds

1932—Kermit Blosser, Ohio U.
1936—Duke Clemons, Central (Okla.)
1948—Vern Gagne, Minnesota
1952—Harry Lanzi, Toledo
1953—Hudson Samson, Penn State
1954-55—Peter Blair, Navy
1956-57—Kenneth Leuer, Iowa
1958—Kenneth Maidlow, Michigan State
1959—Gordon Trapp, Iowa
1960—George Goodner, Oklahoma
1961—Leonard Lordino, Colorado State
1962—Wayne Baughman, Oklahoma
1963—Jack Barden, Michigan
1964—Harry Houska, Ohio U.
1965—Jack Brisco, Oklahoma State
1966—Bill Harlow, Oklahoma State
1967—Tom Schlendorf, Syracuse
1968—Nick Carollo, Adams State (Colo.)
1969—Tom Kline, Cal. Poly (San Luis Obispo)

Heavyweight

1928-30—Earl McCready, Oklahoma A. and M.
1931-32—Jack Riley, Northwestern
1933-34—Ralph Teague, Southwest Oklahoma
1935—Charles McDaniel, Indiana

1936—Howel Scobey, Lehigh
1937—Lloyd Ricks, Oklahoma A. and M.
1938—Charles McDaniel, Indiana
1939—Johnny Harrell, Oklahoma A. and M.
1940—George Downes, Ohio State
1941—Leonard Levy, Minnesota
1942—Lloyd Arns, Oklahoma A. and M.
1946—George Bollas, Ohio State
1947-48—Dick Hutton, Oklahoma A. and M.
1949—Vern Gagne, Minnesota
1950—Dick Hutton, Oklahoma A. and M.
1951—Bradley Glass, Princeton
1952—Gene Nicks, Oklahoma A. and M.
1953—Dan McNair, Alabama Poly
1954—Gene Nicks, Oklahoma A. and M.
1955—William Oberly, Penn State
1956-57—Gordon Roesler, Oklahoma
1958—Bob Norman, Illinois
1959—Ted Ellis, Oklahoma State
1960-61—Dale Lewis, Oklahoma
1962—Sherwyn Thorson, Iowa
1963—Jim Nance, Syracuse
1964—Joe James, Oklahoma State
1965—Jim Nance, Syracuse
1966—Dave Porter, Michigan
1967—Curly Culp, Arizona State
1968—Dave Porter, Michigan
1969-70—Jess Lewis, Oregon State
1971—Greg Wojciechowski, Toledo
1972—Chris Taylor, Iowa State

Team

1929-31—Oklahoma A. and M.
1932-33—No competition
1934-35—Oklahoma A. and M.
1936—Oklahoma
1937-42—Oklahoma A. and M.
1943-45—No competition
1946—Oklahoma A. and M.
1947—Cornell (Iowa)
1948-49—Oklahoma A. and M.
1950—Iowa Teachers
1951-52—Oklahoma
1953—Penn State
1954-57—Oklahoma A. and M.
1958-59—Oklahoma State
        (formerly Oklahoma A. and M.)
1960—Oklahoma
1961-62—Oklahoma State
1963—Oklahoma
1964—Oklahoma State
1965—Iowa State
1966—Oklahoma State
1967—Michigan State
1968—Oklahoma State
1969-70—Iowa State
1971—Oklahoma State
1972—Iowa State

CONFERENCE TEAM CHAMPIONS

Eastern Intercollegiate Wrestling Assoc.

1923—Cornell
1924-25—Penn State

1926—Cornell
1927—Lehigh and Yale (tie)
1928-29—Lehigh
1930—Cornell
1931-35—Lehigh
1936-37—Penn State
1938-40—Lehigh
1941—Yale and Princeton (tie)
1942—Penn State
1943-46—Navy
1947-48—Lehigh
1949-50—Syracuse
1951-53—Penn State
1954-57—Pittsburgh
1958—Cornell
1959—Lehigh
1960—Pittsburgh and Penn State (tie)
1961—Lehigh
1962—Lehigh
1963—Syracuse
1964—Lehigh
1965—Syracuse
1966-67—Lehigh
1968-70—Navy
1971—Penn State
1972—Navy

Big Ten

1934—Indiana
1935—Illinois
1936—Indiana
1937—Illinois
1938—Michigan
1939-40—Indiana
1941—Minnesota
1942—Purdue
1943—Indiana
1944—Michigan
1945—Purdue
1946-47—Illinois
1948-50—Purdue
1951—Ohio State
1952—Illinois
1953—Michigan
1954—Purdue
1955-56—Michigan
1957—Minnesota
1958—Iowa
1959—Minnesota
1960—Michigan
1961—Michigan State
1962—Iowa
1963-65—Michigan
1966-72—Michigan State

Big Eight
(formerly Big Seven)

1929—Iowa State
1930—Oklahoma
1931—Kansas State
1932—Oklahoma
1933—Iowa State
1934-36—Oklahoma

1937–Iowa State
1938–Oklahoma
1939-40–Kansas State
1941-42–Iowa State
1943-45–No competition
1946-47–Iowa State
1948–Oklahoma
1949–Nebraska
1950-52–Oklahoma
1953-57–Oklahoma
1958–Iowa State
1959–Oklahoma State
1960–Oklahoma
1961-66–Oklahoma State
1967–Oklahoma
1968–Oklahoma State, Oklahoma (tie)
1969–Oklahoma
1970–Iowa
1971-72–Oklahoma State

UNITED SAVINGS
HELMS ATHLETIC FOUNDATION

Hall of Fame

Charles Ackerly
David Arndt
Richard Wayne Baughman
Douglas Blubaugh
Glenn Brand
Conrad Caldwell
Richard Di Batista
George S. Dole
Ross Flood
Vern Gagne
Anthony Gizoni
Larry Hayes
Stanley Henson Jr.
Robert Hess
Don Hodge
Dick Hutton
Burl Jennings
Merle Jennings
Alan D. Kelley
William Kerslake
William H. Koll
Lowell Lange
George Layman
Frank Lewis
Hardie Lewis
Vernon Logan
Terence McCann
Earl McCready
Charles McDaniel
Joseph McDaniel
Lawrence Mantooth
Wayne Martin
George M. Mehnert
Peter Mehringer
Allie Morrison
William J. Nelson
M. A. "Doc" Northup
Edwin Peery
Hugh Peery

Arnold Plaza
Robin Reed
Jack Riley
Joseph Sapora
Joe Scarpello
Elliott Simons
Virgil Smith
William Smith
John Spellman
Harry Steele
Ralph Teague
Jack Van Bebber
Russell Vis
William Weick
Alfred Whitehurst
Shelby Wilson
Henry Wittenberg
Keith Young

AMATEUR RULES

(From E. D. Mitchell's "Sports for Recreation," A. S. Barnes and Company, New York.)

Wrestling is a body-contact sport in which two contestants grapple with each other, each attempting to pin the other's shoulders on a mat, thus obtaining a fall. The sport is conducted on a mat 24 feet square, with a circle 10 feet in diameter painted in the center. In the center of the mat is an arrow 12 inches long indicating the position and the direction the wrestlers are to face in starting a match. Supplementary mats that are 5 feet in width surround the larger mat.

An amateur contest is called a match. Nine minutes constitute a regulation amateur match. If no fall has occurred, the referee awards the bout to the contestant who has accumulated the greater number of points or, in case of a draw, to the wrestler who has shown the greater wrestling ability and aggressiveness. Draws may be awarded only in dual-meet matches. Time advantage starts when one brings his opponent to the mat and continues so long as he retains a position of advantage. First-place matches in tournaments and all dual meet matches are divided into three 3-minute periods. Contestants start the first period in a neutral position on their feet.

The match is terminated if a fall occurs in the first period. If neither contestant obtains a fall in the first period, the referee stops the match and tosses a coin, with the winner of the toss choosing to start the second period behind or underneath in the referee's position on the mat. When the second 3-minute period expires, the referee stops the match and asks the contestant who started behind to take the position underneath at the start of the third 3-minute period, no rest being allowed.

If a contestant obtains a fall in the second 3-minute period, this terminates the period, not the match. The third period starts immediately and terminates either at the elapsed time that ended the second period or when a fall occurs before the elapsed time of the previous period; that is, White secures a fall in 2½ minutes of the second period against Black. The third period ends after 2½ minutes have elapsed. However, if either Black or White obtains a fall in the third period before the elapsed time, he is declared the winner.

The high-school matches are 8 minutes in length and divided into 3 periods of 2 minutes, 3 minutes and 3 minutes, respectively. Matches are controlled in the same manner as above, except that a 1-minute rest is taken between the second and third periods and after a fall occurring in the second period.

Falls must be of the pinning and not the rolling type. Both shoulders must be held in contact with the mat for 2 seconds. The referee counts loud enough so that contestants and spectators can hear, "one thousand and one, one thousand and two."

If one wrestler has a position of advantage as they work themselves off the mat, the referee gives him that advantage at the center of the mat proper, with the referee's position on the mat.

In wrestling, 2 points are awarded for a take down to the mat and maintaining advantage for a reversal of position from defensive position on the mat, and for a near fall, that is, when the defensive wrestler's shoulders are held continuously within approximately 2 inches of the mat or less for 2 full seconds or more. One point is given for an escape from defensive position on the mat and for each full minute of accumulated net time advantage behind, over that of opponent's accumulated time for the 3 periods.

Certain restrictions are placed on the wrestlers as to the holds that they may use. In general, they may employ any holds except hammerlocks, scissors, strangle-holds, headlocks, full nelson, or other punishing holds. Also, wrestlers must wear full-length tights, an outside wrestling supporter or close fitting outside short trunks, and light heelless gymnasium shoes. If shirts are worn, they must be sleeveless.

Referee's Position

In this position, one wrestler is underneath or in the defensive position and the other is on top or in the offensive position (position of advantage). The defensive wrestler is on his hands and knees (shoulder width apart) in the center of the mat. His hands are not less than 12 inches in front of his knees and parallel to his shoulders. The offensive wrestler is on his knees to one side of the defensive man and slightly to the rear. If to the left of the defensive wrestler, he places his right knee alongside the lower left leg of the defender. His right arm is across the lower back and around the abdomen of the defensive man. His left hand grasps the defensive wrestler's left arm at the elbow region.

(For Olympic champions see section on Olympic Games.)

Judo

Judo is a variation of the Japanese sport of jujitsu, a form of wrestling. It calls for skill in the use of blows and in using a rival's strength and weight to his disadvantage. It is primarily a method of self-defense. When it was taught to servicemen during World War II for the purpose of self-preservation, no tactics were barred, of course. It has now become a sport recognized by the Amateur Athletic Union of the United States. Many wrestling holds are used as well as some that are not permitted in wrestling. Under the A.A.U., judo is basically a grappling and throwing contest. The first national championships were held at San Jose, Calif., in 1953.

UNITED STATES CHAMPIONS
130 Pounds and Under

1953—George Hatae
1954—Asao Sakaki
1955—Ben Takahashi
1956—Sumikichi Nozaki
1957—M. Kumamoto
1958-59—Sumikichi Nozaki

139 Pounds and Under

1969—Shiro Oishi
1970—Larry Fukuhara
1971—Rodney Parr
1972—Brian Yakata

140 Pounds and Under

1960—Sumikichi Nozaki
1961—Sumikichi Nozaki
1962—Shintaro Yoshida
1964-68—Yuzo Koga
1969—Shiro Oishi
1970—Larry Fukuhara
1971—Rodney Parr
1972—Brian Yakata

150 Pounds and Under

1953—Charles Nakashima
1954-55—Kenji Yamada
1956—Art Emi
1957—Takao Oishi
1958—Otto Chonko
1963—Toshiyuki Seino
1964—Renzo Shibata
1965—Toshio Seino

160 Pounds and Under

1960—Toshiyuki Seino
1961—Toshio Seino
1962—Kazuo Shinohara
1964—Jim Bregman (165 lbs.)
1965—Hayward Nishioka
1966—Paul Maruyama
1967—Nario Arima
1968-69—Tadashi Hiraoka
1970—Paul Maruyama
1971-72—Patrick Burris

180 Pounds and Under

1953—Moon Kikuchi
1954—Vince Tamura
1955—John Osako
1956—Vince Tamura
1957—Shuzo Kato
1958—John Osako
1959—Vince Tamura
1960-62—Haruo Imamura
1963—Kazuo Shinohara
1964—Harry Kimura
1965—G. Tomada
1966—Hayward Nishioka
1967—Yashuhiko Nagatoshi
1968-69—Masayuki Yamashita
1970—Hayward Nishioka
1971-72—Irwin Cohen

205 Pounds and Under

1964—Kinjiro Emura
1965—Makoto Ombayashi
1966—Motohiko Eguchi
1967—Larry Nelson
1968—Mitsutoshi Watanabe
1969—Toshi Ishinoe
1970—Rodney Haas
1971—Douglas Nelson
1972—Douglas Graham

Over 205 Pounds

1968-70—Allen Coage
1971—Arthur Canario
1972—Douglas Nelson

Heavyweight

1953—Lyle Hunt
1954-55—Gene Lebell
1956—John Osako
1957-58—George Harris
1959—Rudy Williams
1960-61—George Harris
1962—Ben Campbell
1963—Makoto Obayashi

1964—Gotaro Uemura
1966—Allen Coage
1967—Howard Fish
1968—Takenori Itoh
1969—Taizo Noguchi
1970—Kensuke Kobayashi
1971—Roy Sukimoto
1972—Johnny Watts

All-Events

1953—Lyle Hunt
1954-55—Gene Lebell
1956—John Osako
1957-58—George Harris
1959—Rudy Williams
1960—Haruo Imamura
1961—George Harris
1962-63—Kazuo Shinohara
1964—Gotaro Uemura
1965—Hayward Nishioka
1966—Motohiko Eguchi
1967—Yasuhiko Nagatoshi
1968—Mitsutoshi Watanabe
1969—Taizo Noguchi
1970—Allen Coage
1971—Douglas Nelson
1972—No Competition

Team

1953—Hawaii
1954—Seattle
1955-58—Nanka, Los Angeles
1960—Southern Cal.
1961—U.S. Air Force
1962—Southern Pacific
1964—Hokka J.C.
1966-67—Central Coast, San Jose, Calif.
1968—Pacific Association
1969—New York
    (Discontinued)
(Competition not held in every weight class each year. Since 1970, all foreigners must compete in heavyweight or "open" category only.)

YACHTING

Few persons living near any sizable body of water can resist the temptation of yachting, whether in competition or for pleasure. Since World War II, the sport has grown at a rapid rate. One big reason for this has been the drift to suburbia. Former city dwellers tried sailing and liked it. With automobile highways crowded on weekends, they turned to the waterways. Manufacturers began turning out more and more boats and gradually the prices dropped to within reach of thousands and thousands. Many new clubs were formed and municipalities began building marinas. In the field of racing, many new classes have cropped up, and in some places, such as on Long Island Sound, competition goes on year-round, despite wintry weather.

Yachting, broadly speaking, is the use of any privately owned or chartered vessel for pleasure, whether it be racing, coastwise cruising, deep sea voyaging or afternoon sailing. A yacht is any craft so used, whether driven by sail or engines, though small, undecked craft are generally called boats rather than yachts. The old-time connotation of "yachting" as a sport of the wealthy, carried on in large and expensive craft operated by professional crews, no longer applies. Today's average yachtsman is a man of modest means, sailing or operating his own small cruising, racing or day-sailing boat, and it has been estimated that there are 9 million such craft in the United States alone.

With the decline of commercial sailing vessels, of which relatively few remain in service in the world, the sailing yachtsman is the only surviving upholder of the great tradition of sail, which supplied the means of commerce, exploration, travel and naval warfare for many centuries.

The state vessels and pleasure craft of the early Egyptians and Romans may be regarded as the first "yachts," but in a modern sense yachting as a sport seems to have originated in Holland and the word itself stems from the Dutch "jaght" or "jaght schip," probably at first a light, fast naval craft. The sport was introduced in England by King Charles II about 1660, on his return from exile in Holland. The Water Club of Cork Harbor, in Ireland (1720), was the first recorded yacht club, and was followed in England by The Cumberland Fleet (1775), which became the present Royal Thames Yacht Club, and the Yacht Club (1815), now the Royal Yacht Squadron.

The oldest surviving, though it was not the first, yacht club in the United States is the New York Yacht Club, founded in 1844. The Royal Bermuda Y.C. was founded in the same year. However records indicate that even in Colonial times there were privately-owned craft used principally for pleasure in this country. The first sizable vessel built specifically as a yacht in the United States is believed to have been the hermaphrodite brig Cleopatra's Barge, built in 1816 for George Crowninshield, a Salem (Mass.) merchant and shipowner.

International yacht racing began in 1851 when a syndicate of New York Y.C. members built a 101-foot over-all schooner, the America, modeled along lines of the then famous New York pilot schooners. She was sailed to England, where she proved much faster than the British yachts. She won a trophy called the Hundred-Guinea Cup in a race around the Isle of Wight under Royal Yacht Squadron auspices.

Subsequently deeded by the America's owners to the New York Yacht Club and known thenceforth as The America's Cup, this has been the trophy that has given rise to the most famous series of international sailing matches. British and Canadian yachtsmen have striven vainly to wrest it back from the New York Y.C.

After the 1936 race, 21 years passed without a challenge. First the war, then the sky-rocketing cost of building and maintaining yachts of 140 feet overall length like the J Class sloops of the 1930s put racing such boats out of the question. In the later 1950s, therefore, the New York Yacht Club sought and obtained a legal change in the America's Cup Deed of Gift, opening it up to yachts as small as 44 feet waterline length, and permitting the challenger to be shipped across oceans instead of being required to "sail on her own bottom."

This change brought about a British challenge for a race in 1958. This contest proved a rout of the British challenger, Sceptre, in four straight races, by the defender, Columbia, sailed by Briggs Cunningham.

In 1962, a challenge from the Royal Sydney Yacht Squadron resulted in a close-fought series between two evenly matched boats. America's Weatherly, sailed by Emil Mosbacher Jr., won four races to one from the Australian Gretel. The match was by no means as one-sided as the final score would make it appear.

The 1964 series between America and England had Bob Bavier at the helm of Constellation, an Olin Stephens design and owned by a large syndicate, which soundly trounced Peter Scott in Anthony Boyden's Sovereign in four straight races.

In the 1967 series, the second Australian challenge, Bus Mosbacher at the helm of Intreped, another Olin Stephens design, again defeated Jock Sturrock at the helm of the Warwick Hood design, Dame Pattie, in four straight.

The Intreped, with Bill Flicker at the helm, defended her title in 1970 by defeating Australia's Gretel II, 4 races to 1. Disqualification, losing a crewman overboard, fouled sails, and tactical errors, were factors enabling Gretel II, designed by Alan Payne and skippered by Jim Hardy, to win only one race.

The America's Cup races have been held in yachts of the largest classes—up to 145 feet long over-all—but other trophies, competed for in smaller craft have produced more frequent and evenly-matched international competition. Among these are the Seawanhaka Cup, raced for since the 1890's in boats from 15-feet waterline up to Six and Eight-Meter Class sloops; the Sonder Class trophies, which brought various European representatives here in the early 1900's; the British-American, Scandinavian Gold, One Ton and other cups for the Six-Meters, the historic Canada's Cup of the Great Lakes and others.

Ocean racing, the form of yachting competition that attracts the widest popular interest today, started in the winter of 1866 when three schooner yachts raced from New York to England. Trans-Atlantic races have been held intermittently since that time, some of the winners being listed at the end of this article.

Races from the United States to Bermuda were first held in 1906 and have been regular annual or biennial fixtures since 1923, attracting fleets of as many as 135 entries, including many foreign yachts. During the same period the Trans-Pacific or California-Honolulu races have also been growing in interest and keen competition.

In distant parts of the world the Buenos Aires to Rio de Janiero race along the South American coast, and the Sydney-Hobart race from Australia to Tasmania, are comparable events.

The Great Lakes have their Chicago-Mackinac, Bayview (Detroit) and Port Huron—Mackinac and Lake Ontario races, while the Southern Circuit, which includes the Miami-Nassau, St. Petersburg-Fort Lauderdale and other shorter ocean races has grown to prominence. In addition, there are a host of shorter, coastwise open-water races on both coasts of the United States and the Lakes.

Abroad, the Fastnet Rock Race, from the southern coast of England to the Irish coast and back, is outstanding among many deep water races.

In these ocean and long distance coastal races, yachts range in size from approximately 75 down to 35 feet in length, and the races are won and lost on corrected time, each yacht receiving an allowance from the largest or scratch boat in proportion to her size and potential speed.

In class or closed-course racing, the predominating type of yacht today is the one-design racing sloop. Prior to World War I most such racing was in "rating" classes, in which practically every boat was of different design and the speed of the boats themselves was the predominating factor, each owner and designer of a new boat trying to turn out a faster craft than others of her class. The one-design boats of today provide, primarily, a test of skippers and crews, all boats in any one class being, in theory at least, of equal potential speed. The expense of this kind of racing is obviously far less, and that has contributed to the enormous growth of the sport in small craft. Practically all such boats are entirely amateur-manned—in fact the professional racing yacht skipper of other times has virtually ceased to exist.

The first important and still flourishing small one-design class was the Star, a 23-foot over-all fin keel sloop, very fast and sporty. The craft was designed by William Gardner and built by Isaac Smith of Port Washington, N.Y., at the suggestion of the late George A. Corry, who envisioned hundreds of sailors of modest means competing on even terms, whereas at that time, in 1911, there were only dozens. Intended as a poor man's racing boat, the first Stars cost around $250. A Star today costs ten times that much—still a small fraction of the cost of the average ocean racing boat or a rating class boat like a Six-Meter—and many still smaller and less expensive classes exist.

By 1960, the Star class had grown to a world organization with several thousand boats belonging to hundreds of fleets from Sweden to Japan, from Brazil to Australia. It holds annual world, continental and national championships, as well as more localized title affairs.

In the wake of the Stars, hundreds of other one-design classes were designed and built, most of them under 40 feet in length, many under 20. Some have remained purely local classes, with a few, or a few score, boats. Others have surpassed

the Stars in numbers and, while few have quite as widespread a distribution, several of them hold annual or biennial world championships. Some of the most widely known of these classes are the Snipes, Comets, Lightnings, Thistles (all in the 16-to-19-foot length range), and a number of dinghy classes under 12 feet. Of the larger one-design boats the 33-foot International Class is spread from the Baltic to the United States, but most are smaller in numbers and more local in range.

The speed of sailing yachts, an often-argued point, is slow by modern standards. The average speed of the fastest yacht in the 635-mile Newport-to-Bermuda race, for instance, is about 9 knots (nautical miles per hour, a nautical mile being 6,080 feet 2.4 inches). The fastest recorded speed by an America's Cup yacht in a race is a fraction over 13 knots. The fastest type of sailing craft seems to be the American inland lake scow, which under ideal conditions has been clocked at as high as 25 miles per hour.

As great, or even greater speeds have been claimed for sailing craft of multiple-hull design, the two-hulled catamarans and three-hulled trimarans. Like their prehistoric ancestors that sailed the Pacific centuries ago, catamarans have successfully made numerous trans-oceanic passages in recent years. Under their best conditions—fresh-reaching breezes—craft of this type can outsail much larger conventional yachts like 12-meter sloops and ocean racers.

While the competitive side of yachting naturally attracts the most publicity, more yachtsmen go in for the non-competitive side of the sport, cruising.

"Cruising" covers a lot of marine activity, anything from a week-end jaunt with the family aboard a small cabin motor or sailing boat to the sagas of the increasing number of men who shove off alone and sail across oceans, or even around the world in the half-century-old wake of the famous Captain Joshua Slocum.

Yacht racing is peculiar in that it has hundreds of championships but no one over-all champion. All classes have their own champions, but they rarely meet each other since each sails only his kind of boat, and there is no final way of deciding that one skipper or one group of sailors is at the top of the entire sport, even in a limited area, let alone the world.

America's Cup

(Races won in parentheses.)

Dates	Winner and Owner	Loser and Owner
Aug. 22, 1851	America (1), J. C. Stevens, U.S.	*Aurora, J. Le Marchant, England
Aug. 8, 1870	Magic (1), F. Osgood, U.S.	Cambria, J. Ashbury, England
Oct. 16-23, 1871	Columbia (2), F. Osgood, U.S.	Livonia (1), J. Ashbury, England
	Sappho (2), Wm. P. Douglass, U.S.	
Aug. 11-12, 1876	Madeleine (2), J. Dickerson, U. S.	Countess of Dufferin, C. Gifford, Canada
Nov. 9-10, 1881	Mischief (2) J. Busk, U.S.	Atalanta, A. Cuthbert, Canada

Dates	Winner and Owner	Loser and Owner
Sept. 14-16, 1885	*Puritan* (2), J. Forbes, U.S.	*Genesta*, Sir R. Sutton, England
Sept. 9-11, 1886	*Mayflower* (2), Gen. J. Paine, U.S.	*Galatea*, Lt. Henn, R.N., England
Sept. 17-30, 1887	*Volunteer* (2), Gen. J. Paine, U.S.	*Thistle*, J. Bell, England
Oct. 7-13, 1893	*Vigilant* (3), Messrs. Iselin, Morgan, U.S.	*Valkyrie*, Lord Dunraven, England
Sept. 7-12, 1895	*Defender* (3), Messrs. Iselin, Morgan, U.S.	*Valkyrie II*, Lord Dunraven, England
Oct. 16-20, 1899	*Columbia* (3), Messrs. Iselin, Morgan, U.S.	*Shamrock I*, Sir Thomas Lipton, England
Sept 28-Oct. 4, 1901	*Columbia* (3), J. P. Morgan, U.S.	*Shamrock II*, Sir Thomas Lipton, England
Aug. 22-Sept. 3, 1903	*Reliance* (3), Iselin, et al, U.S.	*Shamrock III* Sir Thomas Lipton, England
July 15-27, 1920	*Resolute* (3), R. Emmons, et al, U.S.	*Shamrock IV*, (2), Sir Thomas Lipton, England
Sept. 13-17, 1930	*Enterprise* (4), Aldrich-Vanderbilt, U.S.	*Shamrock V*, Sir Thomas Lipton, England
Sept. 17-25, 1934	*Rainbow* (4), H. S. Vanderbilt, U.S.	*Endeavour* (2), T. O. M. Sopwith, England
July 31-Aug. 5, 1937	*Ranger* (4), H. S. Vanderbilt, U.S.	*Endeavour II*, T. O. M. Sopwith, England
Sept. 20-26, 1958	*Columbia* (4), Henry Sears et al., U.S.	*Sceptre*, Hugh Goodson et al., England
Sept. 15-24, 1962	*Weatherly* (4), Henry Mercer et al, U.S.	*Gretel* (1), Sir Frank Packer, et al, Australia
Sept. 15-21, 1964	*Constellation* (4), W. Gubelmann et al, U.S.	*Sovereign*, Anthony Boyden, England
Sept. 12-18, 1967	*Intrepid* (4), W. Strawbridge et al, U.S.	*Dame Pattie*, Syndicate from Australia
Sept. 15-28, 1970	*Intrepid* (4), N.Y.Y.C. Syndicate, U.S.	*Gretel II* (1), Sydney, Australia Syndicate

*Finished second. First race at 60 miles off Cowes, Isle of Wight, England; from 1870 to 1920 races at 30 miles off New York Bay; from 1930 to 1937 races at 30 miles off Newport, R. I.; 1958 races sailed in 12-meter craft, distance of each race 24 miles.

Schooners—America, Magic, Cambria, Columbia, Sappho, Livonia, Madeleine, Countess of Dufferin. In 1881, Mischief, a sloop, defeated Atalanta, another sloop, and in the races that followed the yachts were sloop rigged.

NOTE: In 1956, the New York Yacht Club gained a court order permitting the revision of the America's Cup race rules and paving the way for resumption of this classic. The order permitted a reduction in size from the large Class J craft and eliminated the requirement that the challenging yachts cross the ocean on their own bottoms. In 1957, the New York Y.C. accepted a challenge from England's Royal Yacht Squadron for an America's Cup match between 12-Meter yachts.

Trans-Atlantic Race

1866—*Henrietta*, James Gordon Bennett, owner (U.S.); schooner, 107 ft. over-all; Sandy Hook to Isle of Wight; 3 starters. Time—13 days 21 hours 45 minutes.

1870—*Cambria*, James Ashbury (England); sch., 108 ft. o.a.; Daunt Rock, Ireland, to Sandy Hook; 2 starters. Time—23 d. 5 hr. 30 m.

1887—*Coronet*, Rufus T. Bush (U.S.); sch., 133 ft. o.a.; Sandy Hook to Cork; 2 starters. Time—14 d. 19 hr. 43 m.

1905—*Atlantic*, Wilson Marshall (U.S.); sch., 185 ft. o.a.; Sandy Hook to the Lizard Light, England; 11 starters. Time—12 d. 4 hr. 1 m. (The Trans-Atlantic sailing record, which still stands)

1928—*Elena*, Wm. B. Bell (U.S.); sch., 136 ft. o.a.; Ambrose Lightship to Santander, Spain; 5 starters. Time—19 d. 29 hr. 36 m. (Class A, winner King of Spain Trophy)

1928—*Nina*, Paul Hammond (U.S.); sch., 59 ft. o.a.; Ambrose Lightship to Santander; 4 starters. Time—23 d. 22 hr. 56 m. (Class B, winner Queen of Spain Trophy)

1931—*Dorade*, Olin J. and Roderick Jr., Stephens (U.S.); yawl, 52 ft. o.a.; Newport, R.I., to

Plymouth, England; 10 starters. Time—17 d. 1 hr. 15 m.

1935—*Stormy Weather*, Phillip Leboutillier (U.S.); yawl, 54 ft. o.a.; Newport to Bergen, Norway; 6 starters. Time—19 d. 5 hr. 32 m.

1936—*Roland von Bremen*, Franz Perlia (Germany); yawl, 59 ft. o.a.; Bermuda to Bremen, Germany; 9 starters. Time—20 d. 37 hr. 49m.

1950—*Cohoe*, K. Adlard Coles (Britain); sloop, 32 ft. o.a.; Bermuda to Plymouth, England; 5 starters. Time—21 d. 9 hr. 14 m.

1951—*Malabar XIII*, Kennon Jewett (U.S.); ketch, 53 ft. o.a.; Havana, Cuba, to San Sebastian, Spain; 4 starters. Time—29 d. 26 m.

1952—*Samuel Pepys*, Royal Naval Sailing Assn. (England); (Lt. Cmdr. Erroll Bruce, master); Bermuda to Plymouth, England; 5 starters. Time—17 d. 5 hr. 4m.

1955—*Carina*, Richard S. Nye (U.S.); new yawl, 53 ft. o.a.; Newport to Marstrand, Sweden, 3,450 miles; 7 starters; Time—20 d. 8 h. 16 m. 28 s.
Mare Nostrum, Enrique Urrutia (Spain), yawl, 72 ft. o.a.; Havana to San Sebastian, Spain, 4,200 miles.

1957—*Carina*, Richard S. Nye (U.S.); yawl, 53 ft. o.a.; Newport to Santander, Spain, 3,000 miles. Time—19 d. 13 h. 28 m. 47.5s. (Corrected time—18d. 2h. 13m. 47.5s.)

1960—*Figaro*, William T. Snaith (U.S.), yawl, 47 ft. 5 in. o.a.; Bermuda to The Skaw lightship, Sweden, 3,370 miles.

1963—*Ondine*, S. A. Long (U.S.); yawl, 57 ft. o.a.; 14 starters; Newport, R.I. to Plymouth, England. Time—18d. 7h. 46m. 29s. (Corrected time—12 d. 13 h. 40 m. 56 s.)

1966—*Ondine*, S. A. Long (U.S.); yawl. 57 ft. o.a.; 42 starters; Bermuda to Denmark. Time—17 d. 7 h. 31 m. 6 s. (Corrected time—14 d. 18 h. 28 m. 56 s.)

1968—*Indigo*, Samuel K. Wellman (U.S.); Class D

yawl; Bermuda to Travemunda, Germany; 32 starters.

1969—*Kialoa II*, John B. Kilroy (U.S.); 73 ft. yawl; Newport, R.I. to Cork, Ireland; 2,750 miles; Elapsed time—13 d. 5 hr. 43 m. (Corrected Time—12 d. 21 hr. 06 m. 35 s.)

1972—*Carina*, Richard Nye (U.S.); 48 ft. sloop; Bermuda to Spain; 2,700 miles; 48 starters; Time—16 d. 7 hr. 52 m. 39 s.

Singlehanded Trans-Atlantic

1960—*Gipsy Moth III*, Francis Chichester (England); sloop, 39 ft. o.a.; England to New York.

1962—*Gipsy Moth III*, Francis Chichester (England); sloop, 39 ft. o.a.; England to New York. Time—33 d. 15 h. 7 m.

1964—*Pen Duick II*, Lt. Eric Tabarly (French Navy); 45 ft. ketch; 14 starters; Plymouth, England to Newport, R.I. Time—27 d. 1 h. 56 m.

1968—*Sir Thomas Lipton*, Geoffrey Williams (England); 57 ft. ketch; Plymouth, England to Newport, R.I.; 35 starters; Time—25 d. 18 hr. 33 m.

1972—*Pen Duick IV*, Alain Colas (France); 67 ft. Aluminum Trimaran; Plymouth, England to Newport, R.I.; 3,000 miles; 54 starters; Time—20 d. 13 hr. 15 m.

Bermuda Race

1906—*Tamerlane*, Frank Maier; yawl; 38 ft. o.a.; 3 starters, from Graesend Bay, N.Y. Best time—126 hr. 9 m.

1907—*Dervish*, H. A. Morss; schooner, 85 ft. o.a.; 12 starters, from Gravesend Bay. Best time—89 hr.

1908—*Venona*, E. J. Bliss; sch., 65 ft. o.a.; 5 starters, from Marblehead, Mass. Best time—100 hr. 19 m. 30 sec.

1909—*Margaret*, Geo. S. Runk; sch., 93 ft. o.a.; 5 starters, from Gravesend. Best time—78 hr. 19 m.

1910—*Vagrant*, H. S. Vanderbilt; sch., 76 ft. o.a.; 2 starters, from Gravesend. Best time—90 hr. 42 m.

1923—*Malabar IV*, John G. Alden; sch., 47 ft. o.a.; 22 starters, from New London, Conn. Best time—112 hr. 18 m. 45 sec.

1924—*Memory*, Robert N. Bavier; yawl, 59 ft. o.a.; 14 starters, from New London. Best time—102 hr. 31 m. 21 sec.

1926—*Malabar VII*, John G. Alden; sch., 54 ft. o.a.; 16 starters, from New London. Best time—118 hr. 6 m. 45 sec.

1928—*Rugosa II*, Russell Grinnell; yawl, 59 ft. o.a.; 25 starters, from New London. Best time—103 hr. 13 m. 43 sec.

1930—*Malay*, R. W. Ferris; sch., 45 ft. o.a.; 42 starters, from New London. Best time—98 hr. 29 m. 39 sec.

1932—*Malabar X*, Alden and Gale; sch., 58 ft. o.a.; 27 starters, from Montauk Pt. Best time—

71 hr. 35 m. 43 sec., by 62-ft. sloop *Highland Light*, Frank C. Paine.

1934—*Edlu*, R. J. Schaefer; sloop, 56 ft. o.a.; 29 starters, from New London. Best time—75 hr. 33 m. 32 sec., by 72-ft. ketch *Vamarie*, V. S. Makaroff. (Fastest time from New London)

1936—*Kirawan*, Robert P. Baruch; sloop, 53 ft. o.a.; 43 starters, from Newport, R.I. Best time—114 hr. 50 m. 13 sec.

1938—*Baruna*, Henry C. Taylor; yawl, 72 ft. o.a.; 38 starters, from Newport. Best time—91 hr. 5 m. 42 sec.

1946—*Gesture*, A. Howard Fuller; sloop, 57 ft. o.a.; 31 starters, from Newport. Best time—119 hr. 3 m. 5 sec.

1948—*Baruna*, H. C. Taylor; 36 starters, from Newport. Best time—87 hr. 9 m. 45 sec.

1950—*Argyll*, Wm. T. Moore; yawl, 57 ft. o.a.; 54 starters, from Newport. Best time—75 hr. 32 m. 9 sec., by 73-ft. yawl *Bolero*, John N. Brown.

1952—*Carina*, Richard S. Nye; yawl, 46 ft. o.a.; 58 starters, from Newport. Best time—97 hr. 16 m. 28 sec.

1954—*Malay*, D. D. Strohmeier; yawl, 39½ ft. o.a.; 77 starters, from Newport. Best corrected time—125 hr. 52 m. 54 sec.

1956—*Finisterre*, Carleton Mitchell; yawl, 38 ft. 8 in. o.a.; 89 starters, from Newport. Best time—70 hr. 11 m. 37 sec. by *Bolero*, Sven Salen (this is the Bermuda course record).

1958—*Finisterre*, Carleton Mitchell; yawl, 39 ft. o.a.; 111 starters, from Newport. Time—3 d. 07 h. 03 m. 38 sec.

1960—*Finisterre*, Carleton Mitchell; yawl, 39 ft. o.a.; 135 starters from Newport. Fastest elapsed time 5:01:13:12 by *Venturer*. (*Finisterre* first yacht to win three times)

1962—*Nina*, DeCoursey Fales; schooner, 59 ft. 132 starters from Newport. Fastest elapsed time 3:08:46:32 by *Northern Light*.

1964—*Burgoo*, Milton Ernstof; Invicta Class Yawl, 37 ft. 8 in. o.a.; 143 starters.

1966—*Thunderbird*, T. Vincent Learson; Cal-40 sloop; 172 starters.

1968—*Robin*, Ted Hood; 52 ft. Class C yawl; 152 starters.

1970—*Carina*, Richard S. Nye; Class C sloop; 149 starters; elapsed time—4 d. 44 m. 135. (Corrected Time—3 d. 7 hr. 42 m. 4 s.)

1972—*Noryema*, owned by Ron Amey, sailed by Ted Hicks; Class C 48 ft. sloop; Time—3 d. 2 hr. 34 m. 58 s.

Note—Distances, from New London, 660 miles; from Montauk, 628 miles; from Newport, 635 miles. Unless indicated best times are by first yacht to finish.

Trans-Pacific Race

Year Winner, owner and course

1906—*Lurline*, H. H. Sinclair (San Pedro, Calif., to

Diamond Head Light, Honolulu)

1908—*Lurline*, H. H. Sinclair (San Pedro-Diamond Head Light)

1910—*Hawaii*, Honolulu Y.C. (San Pedro-Diamond Head Light)

1912—*Lurline*, A. E. Davis (San Pedro-Diamond Head Light)

1923—*Diablo*, A. R. Pedder (Santa Barbara, Claif., to Diamond Head Light)

1925—*Mariner*, L. A. Norris (San Francisco to Papette, Tahiti, 3,687 nautical miles—the longest yacht race ever sailed)

1926—*Invader*, Don M. Lee (San Pedro-Diamond Head Light)

1928—*Teva*, C. W. Stose (Balboa, Calif., to Diamond Head Light)

1930—*Enchantress*, Morgan Adams (San Pedro-Diamond Head Light)

1932—*Fayth*, William S. McNutt (Santa Barbara-Diamond Head Light)

1934—*Manulwa*, Harold Dillingham (San Pedro-Diamond Head Light)

1936—*Dorade*, James Flood (Santa Monica, Calif., to Diamond Head Light)

1939—*Blitzen*, T. J. Reynolds (Treasure Island, San Francisco Bay, to Diamond Head Light, 2,085 nautical miles)

1941—*Escapade*, D. W. Elliott (San Pedro-Diamond Head Light)

1943 and 1945—No races

1947—*Dolphin*, Frank Morgan (San Pedro-Diamond Head Light)

1949—*Kitten*, F. W. Lyon (San Pedro-Diamond Head Light)

1951—*Sea Witch*, A. L. McCormick (San Pedro-Diamond Head Light)

1953—*Staghound*, Ira P. Fulmor (Los Angeles-Diamond Head Light)

1955—*Staghound* Ira P. Fulmor (Los Angeles-Diamond Head Light)

1956—*Jada*, Bill Sturgis (Los Angeles to Tahiti, 3,571 miles)

1957—*Legend*, Charles Ullman (San Francisco-Diamond Head Light)

1959—*Nalu II*, Peter Grant (Los Angeles to Diamond Head Light)

1961—*Nam Sang*, A. B. Robbs Jr. (Los Angeles to Diamond Head)

1963—*Islander*, 40 ft. sloop, Tom Corkett

1965—*Psyche*, Cal-40 sloop, Don Salisbury

1967—*Holiday Too*, Cal-40 sloop, Skip Allan

1968—*Aranji*, Henry Wheeler (Los Angeles to Tahiti)

1968—*Porpoise III*, Bill Killam (Victoria, B.C. to Maui, Hawaii)

1968—*Polynesian Concept*, Buddy Ibsen (San Pedro to Honolulu); Multihull

1969—*Argonaut*, Jon Andron (San Pedro to Honolulu, 2,225 miles); Time—6d. 20 hr. 44 m. 7 s.

1970—*Widgeon*, G. Norman Bacon (San Pedro to Tahiti, 3,571 miles); Time—15 d. 18 hr. 52 m. 42 s.

1970—*Greybeard*, Lol Killam, Canada (Victoria, B.C. to Maui, Hawaii, 2,310 miles); Time—15 d. 15 hr. 45 m. 47 s.

1971—*Windward Passage* Robert Johnson, Hawaii; Class A sloop (Los Angeles to Honolulu, 2,225 miles); Time—9 d. 9 hr. 6 m. 48 s.

1972—*Pen Duick III*, Eric Tabarly, France (Los Angeles to Tahiti, 3,571 miles); Time—18 d. 16 hr. 59 m. 3s.

San Pedro to Honolulu record (2,225 nautical miles)—10 days 10 hours 13 minutes, by 98-foot schooner *Morning Star* in 1949.

Los Angeles to Honolulu record (2,225 miles)—9 days 15 hours 5 minutes 10 seconds, by *Morning Star* in 1955.

Chicago Y.C. to Mackinac Island Race

(R)—Racing (Universal) Division. (C)—Cruising Division.

Year	Winner and Owner
1898—	*Vanenna* (sloop), W. R. Crawford
1904—	*Vencedor* (sloop), Fred Price
1905—	*Mistral* (schooner), D. Lawrence
1906—	*Vanadis* (yawl), G. S. Steere
1907—	*Vencedor* (sloop), G. Tramel
1908-10—	*Valmore* (schooner), W. H. Thompson
1911—	*Mavourneen* (sloop), E. M. Mills
1912—	*Polaris* (yawl), J. O. Heyworth
1913—	*Olympian* (sloop), J. O. Heyworth
1914—	*Olympian* (sloop), Snite and Barcal
1915—	*Leda* (sloop), G. B. Currier
1916—	*Intrepid* (sloop), Snite and Barcal
1917-20—	No races
1921—	*Virginia* (sloop), Carlos Alling
1922—	*Intrepid* (sloop), Prather and Farrell
1923—	*Virginia* (sloop), J. A. Hadwiger
1924—	*Sari* (sloop), B. Carpenter
1925—	*Virginia* (sloop), J. A. Hadwiger
1926—	*Intrepid* (sloop), Prather and Farrell
1927 (R)—	*Siren* (sloop), Karas
1927 (C)—	*Shalomar* (ketch), Herbert
1928 (R)—	*Siren* (sloop), Karas
1928 (C)—	*Comet* (yawl), H. A. Beaumont
1929 (R)—	*Blue Moon* (schooner), H. T. Simmons
1929 (C)—	*Bagheera* (schooner), R. P. Benedict Jr.
1930 (R)—	*Siren* (sloop), Karas Brothers
1930 (C)—	*Cynthia* (yawl), J. L. Williamson
1931 (R)—	*Siren* (sloop), Karas Brothers
1931 (C)—	*Elizabeth* (schooner), Lynn A. Williams
1932 (R)—	*Princess* (sloop), Jedzrykowski-Kallgren
1932 (C)—	*Bagheera* (schooner), R. P. Benedict Jr.
1933 (R)—	*Siren* (sloop), Karas Brothers
1933 (C)—	*Chimon* (schooner), Henry K. Hill
1934 (R)—	*Princess* (sloop), Jedzrykowski-Kallgren
1934 (C)—	*Elizabeth* (schooner), Lynn A. Williams
1935 (R)—	*Princess* (sloop), Jedzrykowski-Kallgren
1935 (C)—	*Elizabeth* (schooner), Lynn A. Williams
1936 (R)—	*Hope* (sloop), Herman E. Karnstedt
1936 (C)—	*Rubaiyat* (cutter), Nathaniel Rubinkam
1937 (R)—	*Revenge* (cutter), Walliser and Griffin

1937 (C)—*Rubaiyat* (cutter), Nathaniel Rubinkam
1938 (R)—*Hope* (sloop), Herman Karnstedt
1938 (C)—*Manitou* (yawl), James R. Lowe
1939 (R)—*Gloriant* (sloop), A. M. Herrmann
1939 (C)—*Bangalore* (cutter), Edward Lumbard
1940 (R)—*Lively Lady* (sloop), Otto Dreher
1940 (C)—*Bangalore* (cutter), Edward Lumbard
1941 (R)—*Lively Lady* (sloop), Otto Dreher
1941 (C)—*Bangalore* (cutter), Edward Lumbard
1942 (R)—*Falcon II* (sloop), Udell and Karas
1942 (C)—*White Cloud* (cutter), Sorenson
1943 (R)—*Gloriat* (sloop), Thomas
1943 (C)—*Lassie* (cutter), Lawrie
1944 (R)—*Falcon II* (sloop), Udell
1944 (C)—*Bangalore Too* (yawl), Lumbard and Kinsey
1945 (R)—*Cara Mia* (sloop), Karas
1945 (C)—*Bangalore Too* (yawl), Lumbard and Kinsey
1946 (R)—*Spindle* (sloop), V. Thomas
1946 (C)—*Blitzen* (cutter), Grates and Knapp
1947 (R)—*Cara Mia* (sloop), L. L. Karas
1947 (C)—*Royona III* (yawl), J. B. Ford Jr.
1948 (R)—*Cara Mia* (yawl), L. L. Karas
1948 (C)—*Taltonah* (ketch), E. B. Talman Jr.
1949 (R)—*Cara Mia* (yawl), L. L. Karas
1949 (C)—*Taltonah* (sloop), E. B. Talman Jr.
1950 (C)—*Fleetwood* (ketch), N. J. Gieb
1951 (C)—*Escapade* (yawl), Wendell Anderson
1952 (Div. I)—*Tahuna* (yawl), P. C. McNulty
1952 (Div. II)—*Fleetwood* (ketch), N. J. Gieb
1953—*Gypsy* (sloop), Joe Schoendorf Jr.
1954—*Taltohna* (cutter), Edgar Tolman
1955—*Revelry* (sloop), Norman Sarns
1956—*Fleetwood* (yawl), Nick Geib
1957—*Meteor III* (sloop), Baker & Clements
1958—*Dyna* (yawl), Clayton Ewing
1959—*Feather II* (yawl), W. G. Peacock
1960—*X-Touche* (sloop), Baker & Clements
1961—*Blue Horizons* (sloop), Richard Kaup
1962—*Flame* (sloop), Jame Doane
1963—*Blitzen*, Tom and Bill Schoendorf
1964—*Talisman*, George Quandee
1965—*Blitzen*, Tom and Bill Schoendorf
1966—*Blitzen*, Tom and Bill Schoendorf
1967—*Diavolo*, Alfred (Pete) Stern
1968—*Comanche*, Tom and Bill Schoendorf
1969—*Norsaga*, Harry Zieman
1970—*Dora*, Lynn Williams
1971—*Endurance*, Roger DeRusha
1972—*Kahili II*, Frank Zurn

Bayview Y.C. to Mackinac Island Race Winners

(R)—Racing. (CA)—Cruising A. (CB)—Cruising B. (CC)—Cruising C. (RC)—Racing-cruising. (RCA—Racing-Cruising A. (RCB)—Racing-Cruising B.

Year and
  class   Yacht and skipper
1925 (A)—*Suez*, H. M. Grant
1925 (B)—*Bernida*, R. J. Pouliot
1926 (A)—*Charlyn*, P. C. Williamson

1926 (B)—*Rascal*, A. F. Jennings
1927 (A)—*Barbette*, T. P. Archer
1927 (B)—*Bernida*, Robert Bryant
1928 (A)—*Viking*, T. B. Farnsworth
1929 (A)—*Barbette*, T. P. Archer
1930 (A)—*Trident*, Sheldon-Booth-Thurber
1931 (A)—*Trident*, Sheldon-Booth-Thurber
1932 (A)—*Melodie*, R. A. Bell
1933 (A)—*Baccarat*, R. A. Alger Jr.
1933 (B)—*Nawanna*, T. B. Farnsworth
1934 (R)—*Margaret F.*, W. P. Fisher (for Clark-DeRoy Inter-City Trophy—won)
1934 (CA)—*Baccarat*, R. A. Alger Jr.
1934 (CB)—*Nawanna*, T. B. Farnsworth
1934 (R)—*Margaret F.*, W. P. Fisher (for Clark-DeRoy Inter-City Trophy—did not win)
1935 (A)—*Baccarat*, R. A. Alger Jr. (Cove Island Buoy course)
1935 (B)—*Alsumar*, Sloss-Petzold (Cove Island Buoy course)
1935 (R)—*Minx*, E. S. Wunsch (Cove Island Buoy course; for Clark-DeRoy Inter-City Trophy—did not win)
1936 (RC)—*Baccarat*, R. A. Alger Jr.
1936 (CA)—*Chantey*, T. B. Farnsworth
1936 (CB)—*Dolphin*, W. L. Rideout
1936 (R)—*Mary K.*, William Koch (for Clark-DeRoy Inter-City Trophy—did not win)
1937 (RC)—*Sonata*, R. R. Williams
1937 (C)—*Royono*, J. B. Ford Jr.
1938 (RC)—*Evening Star*, F. S. Ford
1938 (C)—*Quartermore*, Gordon Mendelssohn
1939 (RC)—*Manitou*, J. R. Lowe (Six Fathom Bank Course)
1939 (C)—*Iolanthe*, E. C. Balch (Six Fathom Bank Course)
1939 (R)—*Miss Decision*, W. F. Shanks (Six Fathom Bank course)
1940 (RCA)—*Manitou*, J. R. Lowe
1940 (RCB)—*Sonata*, R. R. Williams
1940 (CA)—*Rainbow IV*, P. C. Williamson
1940 (CB)—*Duchess*, T. L. Lott
1940 (R)—*Siren*, F M. Temple
1941 (RCA)—*Kittihawk*, Timken Bros.
1941 (RCB)—*Sonata*, R. R. Williams
1941 (CA)—*Chantey*, T. B. Farnsworth
1941 (CB)—*Dutchess*, T. L. Lott
1941 (R)—*Iris*, Harry Fletcher
1942 (RCA)—*Hostess II*, C. W. Beck Jr.
1942 (RCB)—*Apache*, Wilfred Bmeiner
1942 (CA)—*Rainbow IV*, P. C. Williamson
1942 (CB)—*Iolanthe*, E. C. Balch
1942 (R)—*Shamrock*, Ernie Grates
1943 (RCA)—*Estrellita*, George Nauman
1943 (RCB)—*Apache*, Wilfred Gmeiner
1943 (CA)—*Rainbow IV*, P. C. Williamson
1943 (CB)—*Rambler VI*, A. Langhammer
1944 (RCA)—*Blitzen*, Grates-Knapp
1944 (RCB)—*Vitesse II*, Cletus Welling
1944 (CA)—*Kittiwake*, R. Neesley
1944 (CB)—*Metear II*, H. Burkard
1944 (R)—*Bangalore*, E. J. Doyle

1945 (RCA)—*Blitzen*, Grates-Knapp
1945 (RCB)—*Apache*, Wilfred Gmeiner
1945 (R)—*Shamrock*, Kerr-Wunsch (no Cruising Class yachts finished)
1946 (CA)—*Carina*, J. Rider
1946 (CB)—*Stormy Petrel*, Flintermann-Sutter
1946 (CC)—*Hoot Mon*, F. G. Coggin
1946 (R)—*Rangoon*, J. S. Blunt
1947 (CA)—*Spookie*, O. A. Johnson
1947 (CB)—*Kathmar*, D. A. Sloss
1947 (R)—*Nyala*, R. W. Schleman
1948 (CA)—*Blitzen*, Grates-Knapp
1948 (CB)—*Kathmar*, D. A. Sloss
1948 (R)—*Gale*, Harry Nye
1949 (CA)—*Onkahya*, G. Sollitt
1949 (CB)—*Medic III*, Dodenhoff-White
1949 (CC)—*Balquhidder*, Harold McGregor
1949 (R)—*Armida*, Saunders-Hahn
1950—*Escapade*, Wendell Anderson
1951—*Orient*, Paul Smiley
1953—*Escapade*, Wendell Anderson
1954—*Escapade*, Wendell Anderson (From Port Huron)
1955—*Glory Bea II*, Jim Carlin (From Port Huron
1956—*Gypsy*, Joe Schoendorf Jr. (From Port Huron)
1957—*Dyna*, Clayton Ewing (From Port Huron)
1958—*Dyna*, Clayton Ewing (From Port Huron)
1959—*Apache*, Wilfred Gmiener
1960—*Freebooter*, Mac and Bob Pohn
1961—*Sixth Girl*, Joseph Kreuger
1962—*Falcon II*, Clara Jacobs
1963—*Robin*, James Smalley
1964—*Gypsy*, Charles Kotovic
1965—*Gypsy*, Charles Kotovic
1966—*Flying Buffalo*, Maury DeClercq
1967—*Escapade*, Peter Grimm
1968—*Hilaria*, Hugh Schaddelle
1969—*Diavolo*, Peter Stern
1970-71—*Charisma*, Jesse Phillips
1972—*Kahili II*, Frank Zurn
　*Overall winner.

NORTH AMERICAN CHAMPIONSHIPS

(Founded in 1925, award for outstanding sailor in North America.)

Mallory Cup—Men

1954—Eugene Walet III, New Orleans, La.
1955—Bill Buchan, Jr., Seattle, Wash.
1956—Ted Hood, Marblehead, Mass.
1957—George D. O'Day, Marbelhead (Mass.) Frostbite S.C.
1958—Robert A. Mosbacher, Corinthian Y.C., Kemah, Tex.
1959-61—Harry C. Melges, Jr., Wis. Inland Lakes Y.A., Lake Geneva
1962—Jim Payton, Madison, Wis.
1963—James De Witt, Richmond, Calif.
1964—G. S. Freidrichs, Southern Y.C., New Orleans, La.
1965—Cornelius Shields, Jr., Larchmont, N.Y.

1966—William S. Cox, Noroton (Ct.) Y.C.
1967—Clifford Campbell, Toms River (N.J.) Y.C.
1968—James H. Hunt, New Bedford (Mass.) Y.C.
1969—Graham Hall, Larchmont, N.Y.
1970—Dr. John Jennings, St. Petersburg (Fla.) Y.C.
1971—John Kolius, Houston, Tex.
1972—Edwin Sherman, St. Petersburg (Fla.) Y.C.

Adams Cup—Women

1954—Mrs. James M. Mertz, American Y.C., Rye, N.Y.
1955—Toni Monetti, Manhasset Bay (N.Y.) Y.C.
1956—Mrs. Glenn Latimore, Fort Worth, Tex.
1957—Mrs. Robert E. Pegel, Chicago (Ill.) Y.C.
1958—Nancy Meade, American Y.C., Rye, N.Y.
1959—Mrs. James M. Mertz, American Y.C., Rye, N.Y.
1960—Mrs. John Duane, Delray Beach, Fla.
1961—Timothea Schneider, Oyster Bay, N.Y.
1962—Mrs. Sue Sinclair, Noroton (Ct.) Y.C.
1963—Mrs. Allegra Knapp Mertz, American Y.C., Rye, N.Y.
1964—Mrs. Jane Pegel, Lake Geneva (Wis.) Y.C.
1965—Mrs. Timothea Laar, Oyster Bay, N.Y.
1966—Jeri Clark, Corinthian Y.C., Seattle, Wash.
1967—Betty Foulk, Indian Harbor Y.C. Greenwich, Ct.
1968—June Methot, Monmouth B.C., Red Bank, N.J.
1969-70—Mrs. Jan O'Malley, Mantoloking (N.J.) Y.C.
1971—Mrs. Romeyn Everdell, Duxbury, Mass
1972—Sally Lindsay, Dinghy Club, Mass. Bay

Sears Cup—Junior

1954—Harry Jemmett, Kingston (Ont.) Y.C.
1955—Royal Canadian Y.C., Toronto
1956—Alan Holt, Corinthian Y.C., Seattle, Wash.
1957—John Merrifield, Pequot Y.C., Southport, Ct.
1958—Kevin Jaffe, Noroton (Ct.) Y.C.
1959—John Welch, Hudson (Que.) Y.C.
1960—David Miller, Royal Vancouver Y.C.
1961—Steven Wales, Marblehead, Mass.
1962—Henry Sprague III, Newport Harbor (Calif) Y.C.
1963—Meade Batchelor III, Milford, Ct.
1964-65—Robert Doyle, Corinthian Y.C., Marblehead, Mass.
1966—Robert Held, Monmouth B.C., Red Bank N.J.
1967—John Dane, Southern Y.C., New Orleans, La.
1968—John Kolius, Galveston Bay (Tex.) C.A.
1969—Manton D. Scott, Noroton (Ct.) Y.C.
1970—Dan Williams, Houston (Tex.) Y.C.
1971—Charlie Scott, Annapolis, Md.
1972—Clark Thompson, Houston, Tex.

O'Day Trophy—Singlehanded

1962—Peter J. Barrett, Madison, Wis.
1963—Henry Sprague, Jr., Newport Beach, Calif.
1964—Robert Andre, San Diego, Calif.

1965—Colin Park, Vancouver, B.C.
1966—Norman Freeman, Ithaca (N.Y.) Y.C.
1967—Charles Barthop, U.S. Merchant Marine
    Academy

1968-69—Gordon Bowers, Minnetonka Y.C.,
    Wayzata, Mich.
1970-71—Robert E. Doyle, Marblehead, Mass.
1972—Craig Thomas, Seattle Wash.

INDEX